THE ENCYCLOPEDIA OF THE STONE-CAMPBELL MOVEMENT

The
of the

Edited by

With Support from

Encyclopedia Stone-Campbell Movement

Christian Church (Disciples of Christ)
Christian Churches/Churches of Christ
Churches of Christ

Douglas A. Foster, Paul M. Blowers,
Anthony L. Dunnavant & D. Newell Williams

Disciples of Christ Historical Society, *Nashville, Tennessee*
Abilene Christian University, *Abilene, Texas*

William B. Eerdmans Publishing Company
Grand Rapids, Michigan / Cambridge, U.K.

Wm. B. Eerdmans Publishing Co.
255 Jefferson Ave. S.E., Grand Rapids, Michigan 49503 /
P.O. Box 163, Cambridge CB3 9PU U.K.

Printed in the United States of America

09 08 07 06 05 04 7 6 5 4 3 2 1

Library of Congress Cataloging-in-Publication Data

ISBN 0-8028-3898-7

www.eerdmans.com

To the Cause of Christian Unity

". . . that their union may be perfected;
and that the world may know that thou hast sent me,
and that thou lovest them, as thou lovest me."

JOHN 17:23

From Alexander Campbell's *Living Oracles*

Contents

Preface

In 1990 a major religious publishing house brought out a dictionary of American Christianity and announced plans for a series of similar works on specific denominations. Tony Dunnavant of the Christian Church (Disciples of Christ) and Doug Foster of the Churches of Christ independently wrote to the editor of the dictionary suggesting a volume on the Stone-Campbell Movement. Though the publishing house decided that such a volume was outside their normal market, the editor encouraged Dunnavant and Foster to collaborate and pursue other publishing venues, deeming the idea a worthy and important project.

Dunnavant and Foster, who were already friends through Ph.D. work at Vanderbilt and other historical projects, immediately contacted one another and began plans for the volume you now hold. Dunnavant was then professor of church history at Lexington Theological Seminary in Lexington, Kentucky, while Foster was teaching in the History Department of Lipscomb University in Nashville, Tennessee.

The logical place to go for support in this effort was the Disciples of Christ Historical Society in Nashville. The Historical Society had long been the most important repository for materials from the Stone-Campbell Movement and a place that welcomed and served members of all streams of the Movement. President Jim Seale enthusiastically embraced the idea of an encyclopedia of the Movement and began raising funds to ensure that the project would become a reality.

Doug Foster's move to Abilene Christian University in 1991 proved a great advantage to the encyclopedia project as the university became its second major sponsor. Eventually ACU would be responsible for significant funding through provision of office space and personnel that kept the project on course during difficult times.

By 1993 Dunnavant and Foster were convinced that a third General Editor was essential if the book was to reflect adequately the three streams of the Stone-Campbell Movement in America. Dunnavant had recently heard Paul Blowers, member of the Christian Churches/Churches of Christ and professor of church history at Emmanuel School of Religion in Johnson City, Tennessee, present a paper dealing with the significance of Barton W. Stone. Dunnavant suggested that Blowers be invited to fill that third position. When Blowers accepted, the initial team was in place.

The three then turned to the task of assembling a group of scholars from all parts of the Movement to help guide the project. Each General Editor carefully compiled a list of names, then the three proceeded to create two bodies — an editorial board and a senior advisory board. These scholars proved to be essential in formulating policies, finalizing the list of articles, and making dozens of decisions about major articles and authors. They also gave of their expertise to write and edit many of the final entries.

The *Encyclopedia* has been so long in the making that it is already a piece of history in its own right, replete with its own promise and tragedy. The bond that developed among the general editors across the three divided streams of the Stone-Campbell heritage symbolizes the aspiration of this project to be a work of "reconciliation" between alienated siblings. In 1997 when most of the members of the two boards came together at a meeting in Nashville at the Disciples of Christ Historical Society, it marked the single largest gathering of representative scholars and leaders from the three branches of the Stone-Campbell heritage ever to assemble. It was a powerful and symbolic event, one we pray will bear further fruit. As much as an academic work, this *Encyclopedia* is a spiritual "family reunion" after many years of estrangement and mutual ignorance.

The tragedy of the project's history has been no less dramatic, at least to the editors, as it has been interwoven with our personal lives. In 1998 Tony Dunnavant was diagnosed with cancer. One evening later that year, he confessed fears to Blowers and Foster about his possible imminent death, joking about bequeathing the burden of the *Encyclopedia* to them. None of the three took the joke seriously; but in early 2001, after two surgeries and complications from a neurological disease, Dunnavant died. He was a winsome, articulate, funny, sometimes sardonic, but deeply committed Christian scholar who constantly distracted us from the seriousness of our work by witty comments about the idiosyncrasies of our tradition, all the while loving the Stone-Campbell heritage with all his soul. He was a tremendous historian and the reigning expert on the organizational history of the Disciples. He is greatly missed. He is buried, quite appropriately, at the shrine of Cane Ridge, Kentucky, about twenty-five yards from the grave of his hero, Barton W. Stone, and is the first person to be buried at Cane Ridge in recent times.

Newell Williams, already a member of the editorial board, graciously accepted the invitation to serve as Editor from the Disciples stream after Dunnavant's death. Williams's longtime friendship with all the general editors and his accomplishments as a Stone-Campbell historian made him in the view of the two remaining editors and the members of the *Encyclopedia's* boards the ideal person to help them bring the task to completion.

In addition to Dunnavant, eight of our senior consultants for the *Encyclopedia* have passed away in advance of its publication: Enos Dowling (Lincoln Christian College), Robert Fife (Milligan College), Charles Gresham (Kentucky Christian College), Byron Lambert (Fairleigh Dickinson University), Ronald Osborn (Disciples historian and scholar), R. L. Roberts (Abilene Christian University), John Wade (Atlanta Christian College), and Eva Jean Wrather (historian of Alexander Campbell).

This *Encyclopedia,* however, has been a marvelous adventure. The early task of assembling a list of entries comprehending the full historical and theological landscape of our Movement was approached with fear and trembling. The general editors got a head start when Charles Gresham of Kentucky Christian College graciously shared a list of articles he had compiled by going through indexes of histories of the Movement. It took four years simply to finalize that list of entries, and another two years to finish the assigning of articles. We spent months trying to assemble an inventory of periodicals and academic institutions that, at one time or another, had been associated with the Movement. Along the way we had to make major decisions, particularly on biographical articles. Who deserves treatment and who doesn't? Can we possibly hope to be fair to everyone? Will we give even-handed representation and coverage to all three streams of the Movement? How much dirty as well as clean historical laundry do we hang out for the world to see?

The boards decided early that only persons already deceased could have separate biographical entries. This ruling was criticized and questioned by some, yet we knew that including living persons opened the door for even more controversy and criticism. A case could be made for many more individuals who were eligible for inclusion but who were not. The general editors sometimes exercised editorial privilege in these choices, yet the editors and boards insisted that all those included have significant impact on the Movement. A thorough index has been provided to give access to individuals who are not the subject of separate articles.

Significantly, people with very different views, who would at times even be antagonistic toward each other and might never have expected to be included in the same volume, are brought together within the covers of this "family album." The *Encyclopedia,* among other things, will drive home for its readers just how diverse our Movement really is. Archie Word (strident conservative) and Edward Scribner Ames (strident liberal), who in life could never have countenanced each other's views and probably would never have been caught in the same room together, will in death have in these pages to abide a shared, if remotely shared, identity. Our Movement's constituents — like historic North American Protestantism generally — are all over the map, and we general editors and writers have served as the cartographers.

Perhaps the most daunting aspect of this editorial adventure has been the realization that there is so much territory of the Stone-Campbell Movement of which we have been ignorant or unaware. We knew too little about the history of the Stone-Campbell Movement in the British Isles, in Australia and New Zealand, in Korea, in Jamaica, and in other places of the world. We have tried to be international in the scope of this work, yet we must acknowledge that we have of necessity focused more on the Movement in North America. There could be an entire encyclopedia of the Stone-Campbell Movement in Great Britain, or Australia, or New Zealand. Several people have been particularly helpful in broadening the scope of the work. Lyndsay and Lorraine Jacobs, General Secretaries of the World Convention of Churches of Christ, encouraged us from the beginning to make sure we acknowledged the international scope of the Movement. David Thompson (historian of the Movement in Great Britain), Graeme Chapman (historian of the Movement in Australia), and Ronald Fraser, Stewart Lewis, and Claude Cox (historians of the Movement in Canada) provided especially valuable contributions on the long Stone-Campbell traditions in their countries.

The *Encyclopedia* will surely have its critics, from all three branches of the Stone-Campbell tradition, asking why someone or some topic is not included, clamoring that this or that subject has not been handled thoroughly or fairly, and that there are biases of perspective. We determined early that the *Encyclopedia of the Stone-Campbell Movement* would not be simply a historical dictionary, but would strive to be an *interpretive* work reflecting historical consensus among Stone-Campbell scholars. We have worked as hard as is humanly possible to be fair and representative of the wide variety of ideas, experiences, and people who make up the rich heritage that is this Stone-Campbell Movement. We are painfully aware that there are blind spots. Complete comprehension would have been an impossibility, and with that as a goal nothing would have materialized. Our greatest success in this project, God willing, will be to aid conscientious Christians in our often estranged communions and beyond in finding their historical bearings.

History never repeats itself, but it does constantly intrude upon and "haunt" the present and the future. It weighs on us and on our churches in a manner of which we are not always conscious. All of our churches have acquired traditions sometimes mistaken as ordinances of apostolic Christianity. Congregational habits are usually well formed before we become members or assume positions of leadership. But we are part of a Movement of Christian reformation that calls us to continual self-study in the light of the gospel.

We hope that those who read and use *The Encyclopedia of the Stone-Campbell Movement,* both insiders and outsiders, will appreciate it indeed as a "family album" of sorts, but not merely as a source of nostalgic reminiscing on our ancestors in the faith. Nor do we want its readers to use it simply as a denominational factbook, though it will doubtless — and appropriately — serve those ends. It is intended — by its general editors and its more than three hundred authors of seven hundred articles — to be a work of collective reflection on a Movement still in process, a Movement still aspiring to be "the *current* reformation" as its proponents called it in the nineteenth century.

This *Encyclopedia* — added to other enterprises such as the Stone-Campbell Dialogue, the journal *Leaven,* the Restoration Forums, the World Convention of Churches of Christ, and the Disciples of Christ Historical Society — gives us real hope that the lamentable barriers erected in this Movement by the spirit of division are beginning to break down in many places. Numerous voices cry out from the pages of this *Encyclopedia* beckoning us to continue their unfinished work, their pursuit of Christian unity and world mission based on the restoration of the integrity and spirituality of the apostolic church, that the world might believe.

Paul M. Blowers,
Douglas A. Foster,
and
D. Newell Williams

Acknowledgments

A project as complex and as long in the making as this one could never have become reality without the generous help and cooperation of a great host of people and institutions. The general editors gratefully acknowledge their vital contributions.

The Disciples of Christ Historical Society has provided enthusiastic support and sponsorship for the *Encyclopedia* since it was first proposed. Jim Seale, president of the Historical Society at the beginning of the project, believed in the dream and raised initial funding to get the project off the ground. Peter Morgan continued that unwavering support when he became president in 1995 and has seen the project through. Ed Dodds created the initial web page for the society that outlined the *Encyclopedia's* task and the vision behind it for the world to see. Lynne Morgan, Sara Harwell, Elaine Philpott, and Clinton Holloway were immensely helpful in providing answers to research questions from the editors and scores of authors who frequently came to them for help. Lynne and Elaine were key players in searching out and scanning dozens of photos for use in the book. The hospitality of the Historical Society in hosting the two meetings of the senior advisory and editorial boards in crucial stages of the project was indispensable.

Abilene Christian University became a major partner in the task when general editor Doug Foster joined its faculty in 1991. Royce Money, president of the university, and Jack Reese, dean of the College of Biblical Studies, saw the importance of the *Encyclopedia* for both the academy and the church. Through ACU's Center for Restoration Studies, the school provided essential backing in the form of office space and equipment, funding for a project assistant, and access to graduate assistants. Charme Robarts worked as project assistant in the early years of the project's organization, serving as a gracious contact person for authors. Anita Churchill stepped into that role when Charme moved, designing a database to hold the thousands of pieces of information necessary to complete the project. Both Charme and Anita are largely responsible for bringing the *Encyclopedia* to fruition. Erma Jean Loveland, ACU's special collections librarian, and her assistant, Chad Longley, willingly provided assistance in research and scanning of photos. Several graduate assistants have also had a vital hand in the project through the years, including Jeremy Loy, Wesley Mullins, Rob O'Conner, and Brad Sullivan.

Christian Theological Seminary librarian Lorna Shoemaker and assistant librarian for serials and archives Don Haymes provided gracious assistance in locating and copying photos as well as general hospitality when the general editors were working in the CTS collections.

Emmanuel School of Religion also provided hospitality through librarian Thomas E. Stokes, who helped to locate needed photos and material artifacts, as did Rae Augenstein, who took several excellent photos of items in the Emmanuel School of Religion Archives.

One other person was absolutely indispensable in the locating and scanning of photos to illustrate the *Encyclopedia* — Bethany College archivist and coordinator of special collections Jeanne Cobb. Her meticulous search based on the list of articles resulted in dozens of wonderful illustrations that greatly enhance the *Encyclopedia's* usefulness. Her extensive notes on the contents and provenance of each scanned item added important information to the articles and captions.

One of the most encouraging events in the history of the *Encyclopedia* was its acceptance for publication by William B. Eerdmans Publishing Company. A leading publisher of religious books worldwide, Eerdmans quickly recognized the academic integrity as well as the spiritual significance of this project. Charles Van Hof, a senior editor at Eerdmans, shepherded the process along from our first contact. His expertise, support, and kindness have eased the anxieties of the editors at several points in the process of bringing this project to completion.

Senior consultants and editorial board members (listed below) provided essential help and guidance from very early in the process. They assisted in the complex procedure of selecting entries and authors and also wrote a large percentage of the articles themselves. We express special appreciation to board members who went the extra mile by sharing in the editing of articles. These included James O. Duke, W. Clark Gilpin, Debra B. Hull, Peter M. Morgan, R. Edwin Groover, Robert F. Rea, C. Leonard Allen, Carisse Mickey Berryhill, Richard T. Hughes, Kathy J. Pulley, Robert M. Randolph, David E. Harrell, Jr., Lester G. McAllister, William E. Tucker, Robert O. Fife (deceased), Charles Gresham (deceased), James B. North, G. Richard Phillips, Henry E. Webb, Everett Ferguson, Leroy Garrett, Robert E. Hooper, and Thomas H. Olbricht.

In addition, several persons outside the boards contributed valuable time and expertise to edit articles on topics they knew well. These included Wendell Broom (Africa); Loretta Long (Alexander Campbell); Gwyneth Curtis (Europe); Michael Casey (Fundamentalism); Phil Slate (Great Britain); Charles Heaton (Hymnody); Dan Hardin (Korea); Kent Hartman (New Zealand); David Fleer (Preaching); John Mark Hicks (Theology); William Nottingham (Europe); and Ziden Nutt (Africa). We also want to acknowledge the contribution of colleagues who helped with the final proofing of the manuscript: D. Duane Cummins, Terry J. Gardner, Nadia M. Lahutsky, Edward L. McMahon, Peter M. Morgan, and Hans Rollman.

We are deeply grateful to the more than three hundred authors who gave their time and expertise in creating this *Encyclopedia;* and to the hundreds of people across the country, the world, and the streams of the Movement for the encouragement and support they gave to the editors and contributors, often at just the right moment, to keep the project going.

Finally, we acknowledge the contribution of the late Charles Gresham of Kentucky Christian College, who willingly shared a list of articles compiled for a similar book he dreamed of years ago. The result of his careful scrutiny of the indexes of all extant histories of the Movement, his work gave us a tremendous boost as we began our list of articles for the work you now hold.

Editorial Board and Senior Consultants

Contributors

C. Leonard Allen
Siloam Springs, AR

Ronald J. Allen
Christian Theological Seminary

Abel Alvarez
Harvey Drive Church of Christ, McAllen, TX

Carmelo Alvarez
Christian Theological Seminary

Michael C. Armour
Dallas, TX

Lois Artis
Church Finance Council, Christian Church (Disciples of Christ)

D. James Atwood
Texas Christian University

Michael Bain
Atlanta Christian College

William R. Baker
Cincinnati Bible College and Seminary

Blayne A. Banting
Central Christian Church, Charlottetown, PE

William R. Barr
University of Saskatchewan

Robert Bates
Indianapolis, IN

John Bennett
Missouri School of Religion

Carisse Mickey Berryhill
Abilene Christian University

Walter Birney
Copeland, KS

Paul M. Blowers
Emmanuel School of Religion

Michael W. Bollenbaugh
Northwest Christian College

M. Eugene Boring
Brite Divinity School

Larry D. Bouchard
University of Virginia

R. Vernon Boyd
Oakland Church of Christ, Southfield, MI

Kent P. Brantly
Abilene, TX

Edwin L. Broadus
Burlington, Ontario

Peter D. Browning
Drury University

Reuben G. Bullard†
Cincinnati Bible College and Seminary

David Bundy
Fuller Theological Seminary

John Cachiaras
Rochester, MN

Shaun A. Casey
Wesley Theological Seminary

Michael W. Casey
Pepperdine University

Graeme Chapman
Selby, Australia

Carl W. Cheatham
Faulkner University

Richard J. Cherok
Cincinnati Bible College and Seminary

Craig Churchill
Abilene Christian University

Christopher Lee Coble
Lilly Endowment, Inc.

Robert D. Cornwall
First Christian Church, Santa Barbara, CA

Terry Cowan
Bullard, TX

Kirk R. Cowell
Third and Kilgore Church of Christ, Portales, NM

Claude Cox
McMaster Divinity College

Fran Craddock
Indianapolis, IN

Toni Craven
Brite Divinity School

T. Wesley Crawford
Nashville, TN

Paul A. Crow, Jr.
Indianapolis, IN

Jim Cullumber
Christian Church Foundation

D. Duane Cummins
John Hopkins University

Simon J. Dahlman
Milligan College

Ronald Dakin
Ilderton, Ontario

Eleanor A. Daniel
Emmanuel School of Religion

Michael Davison
Christian Church (Disciples of Christ) in Kentucky

Lisa W. Davison
Lexington Theological Seminary

Chris Dewelt
Ozark Christian College

Cindy Dougherty
National Benevolent Association of the Christian Church (Disciples of Christ)

Derrick Doyle
Jonesboro, AR

James O. Duke
Brite Divinity School

C. J. Dull
Central Christian College of the Bible

Prudence Osborn Dyer
Drake University

Kent Ellett
Speedway Church of Christ, Indianapolis, IN

Edgar J. Elliston
Hope International University

David Embree
Christian Campus House

Philip Ewoldsen
W. Terre Haute, IN

Martha Faw
Indianapolis, IN

Everett Ferguson
Abilene Christian University

David A. Fiensy
Kentucky Christian College

Robert O. Fife†
Milligan College

David Filbeck
Christian Mission in the Orient, Chiang Mai, Thailand

David G. Fish
Ozark Christian College

David Fleer
Rochester College

Ronald B. Flowers
Texas Christian University

Robert L. Foster
Dallas, TX

Douglas A. Foster
Abilene Christian University

John R. Foulkes, Sr.
National Convocation of the Christian Church

William K. Fox, Sr.
Raymore, MO

Ronald A. Fraser
Alberta Bible College

Robert L. Friedly
Indianapolis, IN

Vicky Fuqua
Celebration, FL

Steven Tramel Gaines
Abilene, TX

Terry J. Gardner
Indianapolis, IN

H. Lynn Gardner
Ozark Christian College

Contributors

Leroy Garrett
Denton, TX

Daniel Gilbert
Black Mountain, NC

W. Clark Gilpin
University of Chicago

Richard Goode
Lipscomb University

Fran Grace
University of Redlands

Stanley E. Granberg
Cascade College

Gary L. Green
Abilene Christian University

Charles R. Gresham†
Kentucky Christian College

Robert C. Griffin
Bartlett, TN

William A. Griffin
Roanoke Bible College

R. Edwin Groover
Atlanta Christian College

Mark Allen Hahlen
Dallas Christian College

Ricky G. Hale
Crowley's Ridge College

Jess O. Hale
Nashville, TN

Gary H. Hall
Lincoln Christian Seminary

Robert B. Hall
Milligan College

Mark W. Hamilton
Abilene Christian University

Richard L. Hamm
Indianapolis, IN

Alvin D. Hammond
San Jose Christian College

Lowell K. Handy
American Theological Library Association

David Edwin Harrell, Jr.
Auburn University

John P. Harrison
Oklahoma City, OK

Richard L. Harrison, Jr.
Seventh St. Christian Church, Richmond, VA

Wes Harrison
Ohio Valley College

Sara Harwell
Disciples of Christ Historical Society

Don Haymes
Christian Theological Seminary

Harold Hazelip
Lipscomb University

Nancy Heimer
Bloomington, IN

W. Dennis Helsabeck, Jr.
Milligan College

L. Edward Hicks
Faulkner University

John Mark Hicks
Harding Graduate School

Robert Lee Hill
Community Christian Church, Kansas City, MO

Michael W. Hines
First Christian Church, Canton, OH

E. Brooks Holifield
Emory University

Peggy S. Holley
Austin, TX

Gary Holloway
Lipscomb University

Clinton J. Holloway
Disciples of Christ Historical Society

Robert E. Hooper
Lipscomb University

James Huckaba
Philippine College of Ministry

Keith B. Huey
Rochester Hills, MI

Richard T. Hughes
Pepperdine University

Debra B. Hull
Wheeling Jesuit College

John H. Hull
Bethany College

Bill J. Humble
Abilene Christian University

McGarvey Ice
Smyrna, TN

John M. Imbler
Phillips Theological Seminary

Ervin C. Jackson
Heritage Christian University

Lyndsay Jacobs
World Convention of Churches of Christ

Lorraine Jacobs
World Convention of Churches of Christ

Joseph R. Jeter, Jr.
Brite Divinity School

Pablo A. Jimenez
National Hispanic Pastor, Christian Church (Disciples of Christ)

Brian D. Johnson
Lincoln Christian College and Seminary

Melissa Johnson
Abilene Christian University

Billy W. Jones
St. Louis Christian College

L. Wesley Jones
Franklin, TN

Paul H. Jones
Transylvania University

Mark S. Joy
Jamestown College

W. Ray Kelley
Dallas Christian College

C. Wayne Kilpatrick
Heritage Christian University

Michael Kinnamon
Eden Theological Seminary

Lloyd A. Knowles
Great Lakes Christian College

Victor Knowles
Peace on Earth Ministries, Joplin, MO

William E. Kooi, Jr.
Oklahoma Christian University

Naomi D. Kouns
Christian Missionary Fellowship

Kevin R. Kragenbrink
University of California-San Bernadino

Mark Krause
Puget Sound Christian College

Nadia M. Lahutsky
Texas Christian University

R. Scott Lamascus
The Christian Chronicle

Byron C. Lambert†
Fairleigh Dickinson University

Dennis Landon
Higher Education and Leadership Ministries, Christian Church (Disciples of Christ)

Timothy Lee
Brite Divinity School

George R. Lee
Culver-Stockton College

Gary L. Lee
Lawrenceville, GA

Steven S. Lemley
Pepperdine University

Emily Y. Lemley
Pepperdine University

Jack P. Lewis
Harding Graduate School

Stewart J. Lewis
Charlottetown, Prince Edward Island, Canada

Dennis R. Lindsay
Northwest Christian College

David L. Little
Queensland, Australia

James H. Lloyd
Cincinnati Bible College and Seminary

Loretta M. Long
Pepperdine University

Erma Jean Loveland
Abilene Christian University

Hap C. S. Lyda
Southlake, TX

Eric R. Magnusson
Abilene, TX

Mark H. Manassee
Vanderbilt University Medical Center

H. Lee Mason
Cincinnati, OH

Ed Mathews
Abilene Christian University

Lester G. McAllister
Christian Theological Seminary

Contributors

Cynthia Cornwell McCachern
Edmond, OK

Mark McCallon
Abilene Christian University

Curtis D. McClane
Oak Ridge, TN

Jerry D. McCoy
Eureka College, Eureka, IL

David McCracken
Homeland Ministries, Christian Church (Disciples of Christ)

Markus H. McDowell
Pepperdine University

Franklin Reid McGuire
Former Curator, Cane Ridge Meeting House

Phil McIntosh
Salem, OH

James L. McMillan
University of Illinois

Lynn A. McMillon
Oklahoma Christian University

David I. McWhirter
Colorado Springs, CO

Donna J. McWhirter
Colorado Springs, CO

Jason A. Mead
Bluff City, TN

Don L. Meredith
Harding Graduate School of Religion

Terry Miethe
Antioch, TN

George F. Miller
Historic Bethany, Bethany, WV

J. David Miller
Milligan College

Bonnie Miller
Vancouver, WA

William Miller
Raymore, MO

J. Robert Moffett
Houston, TX

Peter M. Morgan
Disciples of Christ Historical Society

William J. Morgan
Dallas Christian College

Phillip Morrison
Franklin, TN

John L. Morrison
Milligan College

Tamsen Murray
Azusa Pacific University

Stafford North
Oklahoma Christian University

James B. North
Cincinnati Bible College and Seminary

William J. Nottingham
Division of Overseas Ministries, Christian Church (Disciples of Christ)

Thomas H. Olbricht
Abilene Christian University

Carroll D. Osburn
Abilene Christian University

Wade E. Osburn
Freed-Hardeman University

Robert J. Owens, Jr.
Lynchburg College

Lester Palmer
Indianapolis, IN

William O. Paulsell
Lexington Theological Seminary

Samuel C. Pearson
Southern Illinois University at Edwardsville

J. Paul Pennington
Cincinnati Bible College and Seminary

Mary Ellen Lantzer Pereira
Northwest Christian College

G. Richard Phillips
Milligan College

David P. Polk
Chalice Press

J. Curtis Pope
Houston, TX

Barry C. Poyner
Truman State University

Doug Priest
CMF International

Samuel F. Pugh
Indianapolis, IN

Kathy J. Pulley
Southwest Missouri State University

Eugene Randall II
Board of Church Extension of Disciples of Christ

Robert Randolph
Massachusetts Institute of Technology

Robert F. Rea
Lincoln Christian College

Daniel D. Redden
Redding, CA

Carson Reed
Westlake Church of Christ, Indianapolis, IN

Stephen L. Regas
Kansas City, MO

William J. Richardson
Emmanuel School of Religion

Robert A. Riester
Allisonville Christian Church, Indianapolis, IN

Edward J. Robinson
Abilene Christian University

Hans Rollman
Memorial University of Newfoundland and Labrador

Parker Rossman
Columbia, MO

J. Cy Rowell
Brite Divinity School

Jerry B. Rushford
Pepperdine University

Charles H. Sanders
Fort Worth, TX

J. Stephen Sandifer
Southwest Central Church of Christ, Houston, TX

Edward H. Sawyer
Culver Stockton College

James M. Seale
Jacksonville, FL

Scott D. Seay
Ashland University

Robert Paul Seesengood
Drew University

James F. Sennett
Lincoln Christian College

Tim Sensing
Abilene Christian University

Harold Shank
Highland Street Church of Christ, Memphis, TN

Robert W. Shaw
Central Christian Church, Coral Gables, FL

Bruce E. Shields
Emmanuel School of Religion

Larry Sivis
Bazetta Christian Church, Cortland, OH

G. Mark Sloneker
Ozark Christian College

L. Thomas Smith, Jr.
Johnson Bible College

Timothy C. Smith
Atlanta, GA

Rondal B. Smith
Pioneer Bible Translators

P. Kent Smith
Abilene Christian University

James C. Smith
Cincinnati Bible College and Seminary

Lee Snyder
University of Nebraska — Kearney

Anthony J. Springer
Dallas Christian University

C. Roy Stauffer
Lindenwood Christian Church, Memphis, TN

Lawrence S. Steinmetz
Office of the General Minister and President, Christian Church (Disciples of Christ)

Thomas E. Stokes
Emmanuel School of Religion

Karen Stroup
Vanderbilt University

Earl R. Stuckenbruck
Milligan College

Larry B. Sullivan
Manhattan Christian College

Phillip Devin Swindle
Pocahontas, AR

William Tabbernee
Phillips Theological Seminary

Myron J. Taylor
Sherman Oaks, CA

Greg Taylor
Nashville, TN

Theodore N. Thomas
Milligan College

Fred P. Thompson
Emmanuel School of Religion

David M. Thompson
University of Cambridge

David Timms
Hope International University

Mark G. Toulouse
Brite Divinity School

William E. Tucker
Texas Christian University

Ann Updegraff Spleth
Indianapolis, IN

Bobby Valentine
Southside Church of Christ, Milwaukee, WI

David A. Vargas
Division of Overseas Ministries, Christian Church (Disciples of Christ)

Lynn Waller
N. Richland Hills, TX

David H. Warren
Jacks Creek, TN

Keith Watkins
Christian Theological Seminary

Harold R. Watkins
Indianapolis, IN

Craig M. Watts
Royal Palm Christian Church, Coral Springs, FL

Joseph Weaks
Bethany Christian Church, Dallas, TX

Henry E. Webb
Milligan College

Gary E. Weedman
Palm Beach Atlantic College

Mark Weedman
Crossroads College

Kevin S. Wells
Brookline, MA

C. Robert Wetzel
Emmanuel School of Religion

James R. Wilburn
Pepperdine University

Paul Allen Williams
University of Nebraska — Omaha

D. Newell Williams
Brite Divinity School

Wendell Willis
Abilene Christian University

Carolyn T. Wilson
Lipscomb University

John F. Wilson
Pepperdine University

John D. Wineland
Kentucky Christian College

James Stephen Wolfgang
University of Kentucky

Candace Wood
Bluefield College of Evangelism

Anthony Wood
Memphis Urban Ministry

Andrew R. Wood
Cincinnati Bible College and Seminary

Charles L. Woodall
Central Christian Church, Memphis, TN

Larry L. Woodard
Boise Bible College

Margo Woodworth
National Evangelistic Association

Herbert Works
Indianapolis, IN

Leonard G. Wymore
Johnson City, TN

Geunhee Yu
Homeland Ministries, Christian Church (Disciples of Christ)

Glenn M. Zuber
Indiana University

Stone-Campbell History Over Three Centuries: A Survey and Analysis

Introduction

The Stone-Campbell Movement came into being as a result of the union in 1832 of two frontier American religious groups: the "Christians," led by Barton W. Stone, and the "Reformers" or "disciples of Christ," led by Alexander Campbell. The united movement was unable to decide on one name, thus in the nineteenth century members of the Stone-Campbell Movement were known variously as Christians and Disciples of Christ, and their churches were identified as Christian Churches or Churches of Christ. By the end of the nineteenth century the united movement had divided into two streams, one taking the name Churches of Christ, the other taking the names Christian Churches and Disciples of Christ. A division in the Disciples of Christ stream was well underway by the 1920s and eventually gave rise to the groups known today as the Christian Church (Disciples of Christ), often referred to as the Disciples, and the Christian Churches/Churches of Christ, sometimes known as independent Christian Churches.

The Challenge of Writing the Movement's History

First-generation leaders of the Stone-Campbell Movement were so consumed by the practical affairs and challenges of their "current reformation" that they had little luxury to reflect at length on the history that had shaped them or the history they were shaping. They did, however, understand themselves as standing in a tradition of reform that had begun at least as early as Luther. Both Stone and Campbell encouraged candidates for ministry to study church history as well as the Bible, and both referred to early Christian literature to defend what they saw as catholic doctrines and practices.

They made some attempts, moreover, to track the progress of their own work in short essays that mixed hopefulness and occasional self-criticism. Barton Stone documented the rise of the "Christian" movement in an 1827 series titled "History of the Christian Church in the West" in the *Christian Messenger.* Alexander Campbell penned several articles detailing the growth of his "disciples of Christ." Some were autobiographical "Notes" from his numerous preaching tours; others were brief excerpts or summaries on the "Progress of Reform"; still others, like his brief essay on "The Crisis" in the 1835 *Millennial Harbinger,* were sober analyses of the Movement's mission and identity. Campbell and others also contributed historical and theological accounts of the Movement to contemporary encyclopedias of religion in the United States, including J. M. Brown's *Encyclopedia of Religious Knowledge* (1836) and John Winebrenner's *History of All Denominations in the United States* (1849).

On rare occasions Campbell pondered the difficulties of writing history with genuine objectivity. One such instance appeared in a short article in the January 1837 *Millennial Harbinger* entitled "Notes of Apostasy — Mixed Motives," originally composed in preparation for his debate with John Baptist Purcell, Roman Catholic Bishop of Cincinnati. Campbell lamented that no authentic history of Christianity had ever been written. "In the most controversial periods of church history," he explained, "there were no disinterested or accomplished neutrals to write a true and faithful history," and in less controversial ages there was no one to expose "the profligacy and corruptions of the reigning party." Certainly, he asserted, everyone could understand "how ill-qualified our opponents would be to write a correct history" of the Stone-Campbell reform. His opponents were like the "orthodox" Christians who had "honored the Novatians, the Donatists, the Paulicians, the Waldenses, the Lollards, and the Protestants with the illustrious titles of errorists, heretics, and schismatics." At the same time he acknowledged that even "amongst our friends there are but few so free from enthusiasm, of so cool and dispassionate a temperament, as to state, without embellishment or addition, the events and incidents of our own history with which they are most intimately acquainted."

Though he was unwilling to deny the theoretical possibility of the existence of a few dispassionate historians who could simply tell it like it was, Campbell recognized that the task of writing history is inevitably done from a particular perspective, a specific context, a viewpoint that cannot help but influence what we include and exclude in our telling of the story, and how we portray the things we do include. Campbell was reminded of Paul's words in 1 Corinthians 13:12 that as long as we are in the flesh we will "see through a mirror dimly."

Early Histories

Campbell, however, at least desired a fair hearing for his movement. One person who aspired to deliver such a history was his scholarly colleague, physician, and close friend Robert Richardson (1806-1876), who, at the request of the Campbell family, produced the *Memoirs of Alexander Campbell.* As the subtitle promises, these two volumes, first published in 1868 and 1870, shortly after Campbell's death, are far more than a biography, embracing "a view of the origin, progress and principles of the religious reformation which [Campbell] advocated." Other important biographies from this era similarly constructed images of their subjects with a view to projecting a grand vision of the work of reform. Examples include Alexander Campbell's portrait of his father, *Memoirs of Elder Thomas Campbell* (1861), John Rogers' *Biography of Elder Barton Warren Stone* (1847), William Baxter's *Life of Walter Scott* (1874), and John Williams's *Life of Elder John Smith* (1870). A. S. Hayden's *Early History of the Disciples in the Western Reserve, Ohio* (1875), though largely a collection of biographies, is the earliest effort to write a history of the Movement in a specific region.

Historiography of the Christian Church (Disciples of Christ)

The first comprehensive history of the Movement, *A History of the Disciples of Christ* (1894) was a brief volume contributed to the "American Church History" series by Disciples pastor B. B. Tyler. It was followed by *The Reformation of the Nineteenth Century* (1901), a series of historical sketches by prominent pastors and missionary leaders compiled by J. H. Garrison (1842-1931), editor of the *Christian-Evangelist.* 1909, the centennial year of the publication of Thomas Campbell's *Declaration and Address,* occasioned two additional comprehensive histories. The shorter of the two, *The Story of a Century,* was the work of J. H. Garrison, who mingled a survey of the Movement's achievements with his own strong challenge to the reformation to adapt itself to changing times and not to lose its nerve. The other, *A Comprehensive History of the Disciples of Christ: Being an Account of a Century's Efforts to Restore Primitive Christianity in Its Faith, Doctrine, and Life,* was the magnum opus of Disciples minister W. T. Moore.

Hayden, Tyler, Garrison and Moore, along with Richardson and the other early biographers, shared the providential, broadly "millennial" view of history common to nineteenth-century Americans. Each situated the Movement in the larger designs of providence. The divine calling of the Movement was to restore Christianity to its original purity and power. Moreover, these writers identified the significant role of American religious liberty in this providential design. The new nation provided the opportunity for throwing off the traditions of state interference and clericalism that had prevented the full reformation of European Christianity. This confidence in the providential vocation of the Stone-Campbell Movement would become a staple of subsequent historiography in all three streams of the tradition.

In the twentieth century professional Disciples historians took up the task of writing comprehensive histories of the Movement in contrast to the earlier efforts of scholarly preachers and editors. The first of the histories by a professional Disciples historian was Errett Gates's *The Disciples of Christ* (1905). Gates interpreted disagreements and controversy within the Movement as the result of conflict between two principles that Thomas Campbell believed should be "cooperative and mutually corrective, the authority of primitive Christianity, and the obligation of Christian unity."

Gates's interpretive stance, that disagreements and controversy within the Movement were the result of conflict between the two principles, or ideals, of restoration and unity, would become a mainstay of Stone-Campbell historiography. None of the twentieth-century professional Disciples historians, however, was more influential than W. E. Garrison (1874-1969), son of J. H. Garrison. Prior to the publication with A. T. DeGroot of his comprehensive *The Disciples of Christ: A History* (1948; rev. ed. 1958), Garrison had published *Religion Follows the Frontier* (1931) and *An American Religious Movement* (1945). Garrison's writings reflect a shift from narratives grounded in an explicit theology of history to those reflecting the historicist assumption that all historical events can be explained by prior historical events. A colleague of church historians Peter Mode and William Warren Sweet at the University of Chicago, Garrison shared their interest in the frontier thesis of historian Frederick Jackson Turner (1861-1932). Turner had argued that expansion into the "free land" of the West created the conditions for the emergence of a distinctively American character and institutions. Following the Turner thesis, Garrison described how pioneer life modified inherited ways and encouraged habits of self-reliance. The pioneer, he averred, was prepared "to believe that even the most fundamental institutions — such as state and church — could be made over if they did not serve his need." Following Sweet, Garrison explained the nineteenth century growth of the Movement in terms of the compatibility between the frontier mind and the Movement's reforming message, which called for a united church free of complex theological doctrines and authoritarian clergy.

Garrison's major interest, however, was not the emergence of the Stone-Campbell Movement in the context of the frontier but in its adaptation to changing social, cultural, and intellectual circumstances. As Garrison well knew, by the 1930s the movement had suffered controversies over organization, the use of instrumental music in worship, and new views of biblical interpretation. In his view, the Movement was passing through a critical phase. The future of the Movement depended upon how individuals responded to the maturing of American society. "The deeper meanings of all the controversies which have disturbed the harmony of the Disciples during the past thirty years," he wrote in 1931, "must be sought in the diversity of attitudes toward what may, to use a somewhat vague term, be called 'liberalism'; and this, in turn, rests upon a diversity of reactions to those social, cultural, and intellectual changes which have accompanied the passing of the frontier."

Another shift in the Movement's historiography, this time regarding the significance of Barton Stone for its formation, occurred between the publication of Garrison's *Religion Follows the Frontier* in 1931 and his *An American Religious Movement* published in 1945. Following Robert Richardson, previous histories of the movement had told the story with a primary focus on Alexander Campbell. In his biography of Campbell, Richardson naturally introduces Stone at the point of Stone's first encounter with Campbell. Most of the material on Stone and his followers comes in a section that includes sketches of the Republican Methodists and the Christian movement of Abner Jones and Elias Smith. Richardson's treatment of the union between the Campbell and Stone movements focuses on followers of Stone who had come under the influence of Campbell. For Richardson, Stone's movement had been a significant tributary that flowed into the stream of Campbellian reform, but rather late in the story. J. H. Garrison's *The Story of a Century* and W. T. Moore's *A Comprehensive History* follow Richardson's basic outline. That both were published in 1909, widely viewed as the centennial of the Movement because it was the centennial year of Thomas Campbell's *Declaration and Address,* is telling. W. E. Garrison's *Religion Follows the Frontier* reflects the same orientation. It begins with an account of the European heritage, discusses Stone briefly in connection with other "prophets among the pioneers" in a part of the volume entitled "backgrounds," and begins the "pioneer period" with the Campbells. In other words, Stone is seen as part of the environment to which the Campbellian reformation adapted.

In contrast, Garrison's *An American Religious Movement* begins with the statement that the Movement "began early in the nineteenth century with the union of two separate movements." The implication of a Campbellite mainstream and Stoneite tributary had been abandoned. This is also evident in the organization of the volume. Chapters on the American scene and on the "Christians" precede the account of "The Coming of the Campbells." This shift in perspective was carried over to Garrison and DeGroot's comprehensive work, *The Disciples of Christ: A History.* After chapters on the general church and its British and American backgrounds, Stone and the Christians are given a chapter preceding the introduction of the Campbells. The same approach concerning the relative significance of Stone and Campbell to the formation of the Movement appears in Lester G. McAllister, Jr. and William E. Tucker's *Journey in Faith,* published in 1975 as the successor to Garrison and DeGroot.

The shift in perception of Stone's role in the formation of the Movement had been anticipated in the brief volume by B. B. Tyler, *A History of the Disciples of Christ,* published in 1894 as part of the "American Church History" series. Tyler began with the American context and sketched the development of the Stone movement before turning to Europe and the Campbells. The change in Garrison's thinking between the publication of *Religion Follows the Frontier* in 1931 and *An American Religious Movement* in 1945 appears to have been a result, however, not of Tyler's work, but the publication of two books highlighting the ministry of Barton Stone and the Christians. A. W. Fortune's *The Disciples in Kentucky* was published in 1932 by the Christian Churches in Kentucky in commemoration of the 1832 union of the followers of Stone and Campbell. Fortune wrote his history with the conviction that historians of the Movement had not given the contribution of Kentucky the "notice which it merits." To rectify this oversight Fortune gave the Stone movement a prominent place in his history.

The same year Bethany Press published *Barton Warren Stone: Pathfinder of Christian Union — A Story of His Life and Times* by Charles Crossfield Ware. In his introduction to Ware's book Elmer Ellsworth Snoddy contended that the Movement had two origins — Campbellite and Stoneite. The Northern (largely Campbellite) root had overshadowed the Southern (Stone's area of strength) in the literature of the Movement, and historians had not felt the need to take Stone and his ideals into account. Such an approach was "wholly unwarranted by historical fact" since "To Stone belongs priority in time, priority in American experience, priority in the ideal of unity, priority in evangelism, priority in the independency of his movement, priority in the complete repudiation of the Calvinistic system of theology, and finally, priority in sacrificial devotion to his cause." Ware's biography contains a wealth of information on Stone's life and ministry intended to substantiate Snoddy's thesis that priority in the history of the Movement belonged to Stone.

The work of Fortune, Snoddy, and Ware in calling attention to Stone's life and contribution was, in turn, a result of the desire of "liberal" Disciples to find a founder with whom they could identify more closely than Alexander Campbell as he was commonly perceived. These Disciples had embraced the "liberalism" noted by Garrison in 1931 as being at the core of the controversies that had disturbed the harmony of the Movement for the past thirty years — a liberalism that Garrison perceived as a response to social, cultural, and intellectual change. These Disciples needed a founder whose views had not been codified into a "Disciples scholasticism," an ecumenical founder whose commitment to Christian unity was not so closely tied to an insistence on restoring the "ancient faith and the ancient order of things." By 1948, it was time for a comprehensive history of the Movement, written by a leading liberal of his day, to include Barton Stone not as precursor but as a founder of the Movement.

Later Disciples studies of Stone included William Garrett West's Yale Ph.D. dissertation, published as *Barton Warren Stone, Early American Advocate of Christian Unity* (1954) and D. Newell Williams, *Barton Stone: A Spiritual Biography* (2000). West explores Stone's unorthodox views of the Trinity and the atonement and his radically sectarian views of civil government. He argues that Christian unity was "the dominant passion" of Stone's life. Williams in no way diminishes Stone's commitment to Christian unity. However, responding to later twentieth-century Disciples concerns for spiritual depth and a distinctively Christian perspective, he contends that no influence was greater in the development of Stone's theology and religious and social practice than his Presbyterian spirituality. Stone, he argues, worshiped the God of love and grace revealed in the gospel of Jesus Christ, maintained a chastened view of human nature, and identified the knowledge, enjoyment, and service of God as the purpose of human life. Further study of Stone was stimulated by the series of bicentennials of events in the history of the Stone movement beginning in 1991 with the 200th anniversary of the construction of the Cane Ridge meeting house. In 1992 the Disciples of Christ Historical Society published *Cane Ridge in Context: Perspectives on Barton W. Stone and the Revival,* edited by Lexington Theological Seminary historian Anthony L. Dunnavant. Dunnavant's particular contribution was to initiate an examination of Stone's place in the historiography of the Movement.

Renewed interest in Stone was accompanied by a renaissance in Campbell studies. Much of the new interest in Campbell emanated from the community of Disciples who studied at Yale Divinity School in the 1940s. Yale dean Luther A. Weigle, though not himself a Stone-Campbell Christian, encouraged study of Campbell. Four Yale dissertations were eventually published. Robert Frederick West in *Alexander Campbell and Natural Religion* (1948) identified Campbell as a champion of biblical revelation against the natural religion of his day. Harold L. Lunger in *The Political Ethics of Alexander Campbell* (1954) showed that Campbell took "a lively interest in the problems of society and accepted a considerable measure of responsibility for political decisions." Granville T. Walker in *Preaching in the Thought of Alexander Campbell* (1954) argued that Campbell's appeal to reason rather than to "emotional frenzy" was for many frontier Americans "the answer to their honest search for the religious life and acceptance with God." D. Ray Lindley in *Apostle of Freedom* (1957) related Campbell's views on the structure and function of the church to "the rethinking of democracy as a way of life" that was occurring in his time. Also published was a Princeton dissertation, Cecil K. Thomas, *Alexander Campbell and His New Version* (1958), which illustrated how Campbell's version of the Bible had anticipated "many of the most striking features of the Revised Standard Version."

Connections between the new studies of Campbell and the Post–World War II United States are evident. Mainstream Protestantism at mid-twentieth century was characterized by a selective embrace of neo-orthodox views of the Bible as revelation, the relationship of the church to social and political democracy, the burgeoning of historical-critical study of the Bible, and a popular quest for the religious life. The Campbell who emerged from the studies of this new generation of graduate-schooled pastors and teachers, though not without his weaknesses and blind spots, was strikingly contemporary with the concerns of post–World War II mainstream American Protestantism.

Bethany College (which Campbell had established on his farm in 1840) and its president, Perry E. Gresham, encouraged further study of Campbell. In 1966 the College published S. Morris Eames, *The Philosophy of Alexander Campbell,* which argued that Campbell had "sought to bring essential religious beliefs and the philosophically novel ideas of his contemporaries into some kind of intellectual harmony." Six years earlier Gresham had compiled a collection of essays titled *The Sage of Bethany: A Pioneer in Broadcloth.* Eva Jean Wrather, whose biography of Campbell remained unpublished at her death in 2001, contributed the final essay. Commenting on the Campbell renaissance of the postwar era, Wrather noted that during the heyday of scientific humanism and with new discoveries in biblical criticism Campbell had gone out of fashion. Yet, she observed, "In the chastened, stricken world of the 1950's, amid the ruins of its fallen idol of man's arrogant self-sufficiency, Alexander Campbell speaks out with sometimes startling relevance."

By 1970 the leadership of the Christian Board of Publication had determined that a new, comprehensive history of the Disciples was in order. Historians Lester G. McAllister, Jr., and William E. Tucker were recruited as writers. Published in 1975, *Journey in Faith: A History of the Christian Church (Disciples of Christ)* became the standard general history of the Disciples. Adopting the basic narrative structure of Garrison and DeGroot's 1948 history, McAllister and Tucker carried the Disciples story through the organizational restructure of 1968 that had resulted in the formation of the Christian Church (Disciples of Christ). The interpretive structure of the new history followed the pattern established by Garrison and DeGroot. Conflict in the Movement had been largely the result of different responses to changing social forces in American life. There was, however, one significant interpretive change. Following the earlier histories, Garrison and DeGroot had asserted that the Movement did not divide over the Civil War. Influenced by the work of David Edwin Harrell, Jr., historian from the Churches of Christ, Tucker and McAllister argued that although technically the Disciples avoided a formal division over the War, "Seeds of discord, sown and cultivated, grew to full bloom with the separation of the Churches of Christ a generation later."

By the time McAllister and Tucker began writing their history a second formal division of the Disciples, resulting in the Christian Churches/Churches of Christ, was an accomplished fact. Possibly for this reason they expressed less hope regarding the immediate prospects of Christian unity than had Garrison and DeGroot. Nevertheless, these Disciples scholars concluded their history of the Movement with a bold declaration: "Until there is unity in the church the Christian Church (Disciples of Christ) will continue its witness to the necessity for a united church based on the scriptures, so that the world may believe."

Historiography of the Churches of Christ

Disciples scholars dominated Stone-Campbell historiography during the first half of the twentieth century. There were historians in Churches of Christ, but the materials they produced largely served as apologies for the distinctive stances taken by Churches of Christ in the division and had little impact on larger historical understandings. Building on the early attitude concerning the Movement's providential role in reforming Christianity, historians in Churches of Christ assumed their stream to be the true and faithful heir of the Movement's ideals, specifically the restoration of the ancient gospel and order. Explicitly or by implication, these first histories portrayed the Disciples as having given up the restoration ideal by adding unauthorized practices to the church's worship and work or pursuing a compromising emphasis on unity. Uncritical acceptance of the notion that the Disciples chose unity and Churches of Christ restoration in the first division is problematic. Nevertheless, early historians of the Movement from Churches of Christ clearly understood their task to include justification of the body's restorationist focus.

John F. Rowe, Cincinnati church leader and publisher, produced the first histories by a writer identified specifically with Churches of Christ. As early as 1877 he wrote *The Disciples of Christ: A Brief History of Their Rise and Progress.* His most important work, however, was written and published in 1884 with at least ten subsequent editions. The book's title explained its thesis: *History of Reformatory Movements: Resulting in a Restoration of the Apostolic Church, With a History of the Nineteen General Church Councils.* Five years later Rowe added an appendix titled *A History of All Innovations from the Third Century Down.* After recounting the basic story of the Protestant Reformation, Rowe portrayed the Stone-Campbell Movement as the culmination of all reform efforts.

Rowe, like other early historians, portrayed the Campbell movement as the chief impetus for restoring apostolic Christianity. It was Alexander Campbell, he said in the Introduction, who had "actually raise[d] up a body of people identical with primitive Christians, both in faith and practice." He relegated Stone to six pages and essentially conflated his theology with that of the Campbells. This tendency to blend Stone's thought into that of the Campbells was the norm for historians from Churches of Christ until much later in the century. At least two factors seem to have contributed to this lack of differentiation: the inaccessibility of primary materials on Stone and embarrassment over Stone's doctrinal stances, especially his beliefs on the Trinity, atonement, and ecstatic revivals.

While Rowe's study had implications for those who might subvert the restoration of the apostolic church, he did not specifically mention the division already underway in the Stone-Campbell Movement. The book provides a picture of the Movement as the church as God intended it, an apostolic body free from the corrupting innovations of previous centuries.

Rowe's history remained the standard among Churches of Christ until 1929. That year F. W. Shepherd, the person who gathered data on Churches of

Christ for the 1906 religious census, wrote *The Church, the Falling Away, and the Restoration.* Published by F. L. Rowe, son of John F. Rowe, the book covered much of the same ground as Rowe's earlier volume, though in briefer form. Beginning with a description of the New Testament church, Shepherd defined the apostasy in terms of the rise of Roman Catholicism. The story of the Stone-Campbell Movement began with Barton Stone's work, though, like Rowe, Shepherd made Stone's thought sound almost identical to Alexander Campbell's. While the book ended abruptly with the story of the union of the Stone and Campbell movements in 1832, the implication again was that the Stone-Campbell Movement had accomplished the task of restoring the New Testament church, now embodied in Churches of Christ. Both Rowe's and Shepherd's books were kept in print well into the second half of the twentieth century.

The other significant early twentieth-century telling of the story of Churches of Christ appeared between 1939 and 1942 in a series of articles published in the *Gospel Advocate.* Written by L. L. Brigance, professor at Freed Hardeman College, and titled "Studies in the Restoration," the articles continued the focus seen in Rowe and Shepherd on restoration of doctrine and practice as the essence of the movement. Even more than Shepherd, Brigance depicted Stone as a precursor to the movement whose theology was essentially identical to Campbell's. Unlike the previous histories, Brigance's spoke openly of the division, decrying the digression by some from the Movement's ideals.

As had already happened among Disciples historians, a shift began to take place in Churches of Christ in the mid-1940s from history written by ministers and editors to history produced by academically trained historians. With this shift began also a move away from the exclusive focus on restoration as the Movement's reason for being and, eventually, an abandonment of the older forms of triumphalism.

A transitional figure in this shift was Homer Hailey, Bible professor at Abilene Christian College and Florida College, who in 1944 earned a Master's degree in church history from Southern Methodist University. The next year he published a revision of his thesis as *Attitudes and Consequences in the Restoration Movement.* Though his work was not intended as a comprehensive history, Hailey gave extensive treatment of what he believed were the Movement's foundational attitudes. His contention was that while the earliest thrust had been the union of Christians, the desire to have New Testament precedent for all they did forced the founding leaders to elevate restoration of the ancient order to primacy. Hailey explained the division as the result of differences over how to regard the silence of Scripture and focused on the questions of the legitimacy of the missionary society and instrumental music in worship. Hailey read widely in the history of the Movement, including W. E. Garrison's 1931 *Religion Follows the Frontier,* which he quotes. This exposure evidently led him to give a more prominent place to the ideal of unity than had been the case with previous histories in Churches of Christ. Nonetheless, Hailey, who would become a leader in the noninstitutional Churches of Christ, insisted that though Campbell believed his platform would lead to unity among Christians, his first commitment was to doctrinal truth rather than "popularity."

In 1949 the first volume of Earl Irvin West's eventual four-volume history appeared titled *The Search for the Ancient Order: A History of the Restoration Movement 1849-1906.* West had earned M.A. and B.D. degrees from the Butler University School of Religion and had just completed a Ph.D. in history at Indiana University the previous year. West's work represented the first truly comprehensive history of the Movement by an academic historian from within Churches of Christ. Yet it continued the interpretative trends seen since John F. Rowe: restoration as the Movement's essence and the triumph of Churches of Christ. When the "ancient order" was eventually restored in Churches of Christ, the body moved through the nineteenth and twentieth centuries fending off all threats to truth and preserving the Movement's authentic heritage relatively unscathed.

In the late 1960s two very different histories appeared from scholars in Churches of Christ that would each make profound contributions to the self-understanding of that stream and the Movement as a whole. The first was the critical social history written by David Edwin Harrell, Jr., a Vanderbilt Ph.D. in church history. Based on work done for his dissertation, Harrell's *Quest for a Christian America: The Disciples of Christ and American Society* (1966) and *The Social Sources of Division in the Disciples of Christ, 1865-1900* (1973) provided overwhelming evidence that the doctrinal positions taken by Churches of Christ in the division were not merely dogged adherence to biblical truths restored by the Stone-Campbell Movement. Rather, they were influenced heavily by the social contexts in which those largely southern and rural churches existed. The Civil War and sectionalism had a major role in shaping their ethos.

Harrell's work revolutionized the historiography of the Movement among emerging scholars, both in Churches of Christ and across the Movement. In a sense, Harrell's work legitimized scholarly historical social inquiry that did not simply replicate earlier consensus interpretations. His personal religious loyalties lay with one of the most conservative subgroups in Churches of Christ, the noninstitutional churches. The focus of his studies reflects in some sense his personal loyalties as he contrasts the ethos of conservatives and liberals. Yet Harrell's work marked the beginning of a shift away from a strictly apologetic or triumphalist interpretation among historians in Churches of Christ. The second "new historian" in Churches of Christ was Bill J. Humble. Humble's 1964 dissertation at the University of Iowa was a history of the nineteenth-century missionary society controversy in which he, like Harrell, acknowledged a major role for the Civil War in sectionalizing the issue and making it divisive. Humble's brief *Story of the Restoration,* published in 1969, was designed as material for adult Sunday School curricula, a very different genre from Harrell's scholarly tomes. Yet because of its accessibility to a wide audience Humble's book had a wide influence in Churches of Christ. Like Harrell, Humble acknowledged the importance of sectional issues in the division and the idea that unity and restoration were antagonistic goals.

What made Humble's interpretation particularly significant was the conclusion to the book. Unlike previous histories from John F. Rowe forward that asserted Churches of Christ to be the restored apostolic church, Humble insisted that the restoration of the church to God's will is a continuing challenge, not a completed task. Robert E. Hooper, history professor at Lipscomb University, took the same approach in his 1993 history *A Distinct People: A History of the Churches of Christ in the 20th Century.*

It was not until a decade later, however, that Leroy Garrett's *The Stone-Campbell Movement* (1981; revised ed. 1994) became the first history by a writer in Churches of Christ to put unity on center stage. The book was published by College Press, operated by members of the Christian Churches/Churches of Christ. Garrett, a Ph.D. in philosophy from Harvard, overtly challenged the assumption that restoration had been the primary theological impulse of the Movement. He insisted that Campbell's emphasis was on the essentials of the ancient faith as the bond of union, not the myriad details that may or may not be relevant to Christian identity. This interpretation, though controversial in Churches of Christ, represented a dramatic reversal of their century-long trend to insist that the Movement's true identity was the quest to restore meticulously the beliefs and practices of the New Testament church. Perhaps as significant, the phrase "Stone-Campbell Movement," coined by Garrett for the book title, has gradually become the standard designation, replacing both "Disciples Movement" and "Restoration Movement" in most scholarly literature.

Richard Hughes's *Reviving the Ancient Faith: The Story of Churches of Christ in America* (1996) represented a major event in the historiography of Churches of Christ and the Movement. Hughes's landmark study asserted that Churches of Christ had as much claim as any stream of the Movement to representing an early authentic mainstream — not merely a divisive offshoot. He asserted that Churches of Christ largely embodied the "apocalyptic sectarianism" of Barton W. Stone — a strain of the Movement that maintained its viability even after the union. This strain eventually separated from the Campbellian "rationalistic sectarianism" of the Disciples but was itself crushed by the same rationalistic tendencies inherited by parts of Churches of Christ.

To say the least, Hughes's work represented an important new set of interpretations. First he elevated the importance of Stone in the Movement, but for very different reasons from those of Disciples historians of the 1930s and 1940s. Stone was not a modern ecumenist but a countercultural radical who counted all things but loss for Christ, and Churches of Christ were Stone's authentic heirs. Yet having made that case, Hughes proceeded to explain the history of Churches of Christ in the twentieth century in a kind of "triumphalism in reverse." The "authentic" sectarian apocalyptic Christianity that defined Churches of Christ in the nineteenth century was lost piece by piece in the controversies of the twentieth — the premillennialism conflict, the anti-institutional fights, and the crisis of the 1960s. Hughes's work in *Reviving the Ancient Faith* continued a trend begun with Harrell's studies that opened the history of the Stone-Campbell Movement and Churches of Christ to a larger world in both academia and religious circles.

The most recent history of the Movement from scholars in Churches of Christ is *Renewing God's People: A Concise History of Churches of Christ* (2001) by Gary Holloway and Douglas A. Foster. Like Hughes, the authors consciously used words in the title that indicated that the task of conforming the church to God's will is a never-ending process. While not rejecting completely the notion of restoration, Holloway and Foster consciously avoided an understanding of restoration that emphasized legalistic replication of doctrine and practice as the chief goal. Rather, the idea of a refugee people, never entirely at home in this world, ever moving toward their true home, became the dominant metaphor.

A century of history writing in Churches of Christ moved from the surety of being the restored apostolic church to a picture of a never-ending effort — one in the larger history of Christ's church — to renew the refugee people who struggle to please God in their specific context. The century was also marked by a significant rise in scholarly production by members of Churches of Christ.

Historiography of the Christian Churches/ Churches of Christ

As Churches of Christ historians have sought to identify a continuing history for that group that is more than the story of a divisive offshoot, historians of the Christian Churches/Churches of Christ have sought to address ideological tensions and institutional schism that transpired within the Disciples of Christ from the 1920s through the 1960s and beyond. Conservatives and moderates alike from among the so-called "independents" rethought the historic plea of the Stone-Campbell Movement not purely as an exercise of historical reflection but with a view to spelling out their own vision of the future mission of the Movement amid the institutional and theological tensions of the twentieth century. Standard Publishing of Cincinnati produced three especially significant histories of the movement by scholars of the Christian Churches/Churches of Christ, each with some distinctive perspectives of its own.

James DeForest Murch's *Christians Only: A History of the Restoration Movement* (1962) was for many years the standard history of the Movement used in colleges and seminaries associated with the Christian Churches/Churches of Christ. Murch, a staunch critic of the perceived liberal drift of the Disciples and first president of the Christian Restoration Association (est. 1925), advances the view that the Stone-Campbell Movement was a culmination of "Free Church" ecclesiology. Taking inspiration from one of the lines of argument pursued by Alexander Campbell in his 1837 debate with the Roman Catholic bishop of Cincinnati, John Baptist Purcell, Murch argues in his introduction to *Christians Only* that the Restoration Movement of Stone and the Campbells stood within a lineage of other such movements in defiance of high-church ecclesiasticism and apostasy. From the Priscillians and Bogomils of antiquity to the Cathari and Waldenses of the pre-Reformation era, and from the Anabaptists to the Scottish restoration inaugurated by the Haldane brothers, God had consistently raised up groups of (often persecuted) witnesses to New Testament Christianity, an "apostolic succession" circumventing Catholicism and Orthodoxy.

From the perspective of Murch's moderate triumphalism, the Stone-Campbell Movement was a culmination in this restorationist succession, but was itself altogether capable of falling short of its true vocation. "Should 'the current reformation' fail in its mission," Murch writes, "God will assuredly raise up another." While asserting that the Great Awakening had providentially prepared the turf for the work of restoration in the American context, it took Thomas Campbell with his *Declaration and Address,* and Alexander Campbell with his *Christian Baptist,* to bring to a head "the greatest religious movement of peculiarly American origin in the history of the Christian church." Their efforts laid the groundwork for a movement that was doctrinally sound, ecclesiologically faithful, and utterly timely. Murch's *Christians Only* deals with Barton Stone only after the Campbells, candidly admitting what he perceived to be Stone's questionable doctrinal positions (especially on the issues of Trinity and Atonement), and insisting that his principal contribution lay in "his irenic spirit, his bent to practical unity, and his deep concern for the saving of lost souls." Murch's sentiments about Stone's limited leadership role in relation to Campbellian restorationism anticipate a larger tendency among Christian Churches/Churches of Christ to downplay Stone's significance in the formation of the movement.

As one of the founders of the National Association of Evangelicals, Murch was intensely interested in the contribution of Stone-Campbell principles to the larger task of Christian unity among conservative evangelicals, particularly in the face of the perceived liberalism of the Christians identified with the modern Ecumenical Movement. In his view, Alexander Campbell's early support for the international Evangelical Alliance had set an important precedent, but so too had his uncompromising adherence to biblical restoration on issues of church organization, baptism, and the like. Murch similarly highlights the leadership of Isaac Errett with his progressive conservatism in the second generation of Disciples of Christ. For Murch, Errett had saved the Disciples from becoming an "isolationist sect" while simultaneously, in his *Our Position* (1870), making an intellectually sophisticated presentation of the restoration plea to the larger Protestant world.

Murch analyzes the early- and mid-twentieth-century woes of the Disciples as the result of a "Great Apostasy" that had led to a "Great Controversy," an all-out ideological battle over the restoration plea with three clear-cut factions: the reactionary "rightist" Churches of Christ that largely segregated themselves from the rest of American Christian culture; the "leftist" liberal Disciples who had introduced a "new gospel" and forsaken the restoration platform entirely; and the "Centrist" faithful who were committed to progressive conservatism. Murch does not directly identify the Centrists with the emerging "independent" Christian Churches, admitting that there were sympathetic fringe groups both on the right and left. Yet in describing the institutional embodiment of the Centrist cause, he lists principally the Bible colleges and missionary enterprises of the rapidly consolidating network of churches that had rallied against the United Christian Missionary Society and against the incipient denominationalization (ecclesiasticism) of the Disciples of Christ.

Murch closes his *Christians Only* with a strong criticism of the compromises he saw in liberal Disciples' involvement in the Ecumenical Movement, with a hopeful statement about the Consultations on Internal Unity that he himself helped lead among interested Centrists from across the Stone-Campbell churches, and with an urgent insistence that the current context of ecumenism was once again an opportune moment for the restoration plea. Murch takes heart in the fact that even within the World Council of Churches there have been elements open to the restoration project: "It would appear that the day may soon come within the counsels of the Ecumenical Movement when sincere advocates of Christian unity will be ready for serious discussion on Scriptural truth."

In 1990, nearly thirty years after the appearance of Murch's *Christians Only,* Standard Publishing released Henry Webb's *In Search of Christian Unity: A History of the Restoration Movement,* justified by the author as a fresh approach that would take into account newer historical perspectives. From the outset, Webb, former professor of church history at Milligan College, departs from Murch's distinctively restorationist reconstruction: "No attempt is made in this work to trace 'the true church' down through the centuries. Since the first century, the church has always numbered within its ranks genuinely devoted saints; and, paradoxically, it has always been in need of reform." Webb thus views the collaborative labor of the early leaders of the Stone-Campbell Movement, despite its unique achievements, as part of the larger work of *reformation* pervasive in church history. Unlike Murch, he is willing to submit the *restoration* ideal itself to closer critical scrutiny, indicating its inherent complexities while insisting still on its viability as a means to an end, the ecclesial reconciliation of Christians.

Also in contrast to Murch, Webb desires to factor sociological and cultural considerations into the interpretation of the movement's formation and history. He is candidly willing, for example, to tie Barton Stone's "Christian movement" in the Old Southwest to the synthetic religious culture of the trans-Appalachian frontier. Moreover, in analyzing the aftermath of the Disciples' struggle over slavery and the Civil War, Webb argues (in agreement with David Edwin Harrell, Jr.) that it was the residual "cultural gap" between the more affluent, urbanized, and industrialized North and the poorer, predominantly rural, and underdeveloped South that precipitated the division between Disciples and Churches of Christ. An issue like instrumental music in worship could thus be understood not exclusively as a hermeneutical conflict, but as an expression of dissent from Southern congregations that were frankly unable to afford amenities like organs or melodeons.

A major contribution of Webb's history is its detailed (and, compared to Murch, less tendentious) treatment of the personal and institutional antagonisms that inaugurated the eventual division between the Christian Church (Disciples of Christ) and the Christian Churches/Churches of Christ. Webb follows Murch's example in highlighting fundamental differences of missiology, ecclesiology, and hermeneutics and the inability of moderates in the Disciples' Commission on Restudy in the 1940s to prevent polarization left and right. Webb claims that moderates were effectively squeezed out as liberals and arch-conservatives brought the Disciples to another open schism. Webb is far more willing than Murch to allow arch-conservatives associated with the *Christian Standard* and the North American Christian Convention to share blame with Disciples liberals for the fracture.

Webb's *In Search of Christian Unity* concludes with an attempt, fair-handedly but critically, to analyze both the strengths of, and the challenges facing, the three enduring branches of the Stone-Campbell tradition. Especially significant is Webb's analysis of the internal dynamics and ecclesiological distinctives of his own fellowship, the Christian Churches/Churches of Christ. Webb carefully considers the commitment of these churches to local congregational autonomy, but seeks to correct the misperception of them as fundamentally "non-cooperative" in view of their abundant parachurch organizations. Webb provides important insights into some of the premier problems facing Christian Churches/Churches of Christ, namely, the incursion of fundamentalism (e.g., the doctrine of biblical inerrancy accepted by some scholars and churches), the debate over women in ministry, and the lamentable lack of theological and sociological diversity among these churches. The upshot of Webb's history, then, is a less triumphalistic rendering of the emergence of the Christian Churches/Churches of Christ as a distinct body, despite the author's clear sympathies at least with moderate representatives of the "independent" resistance to denominationalization.

Standard Publishing released one additional historical survey in the 1990s, *Union in Truth: An Interpretive History of the Restoration Movement* (1994), by James North, professor of church history at Cincinnati Bible College and Seminary. Critical of slightly earlier works like Leroy Garrett's *The Stone-Campbell Movement* for its perceived abandonment of restorationism and Webb's *In Search of Christian Unity* because of its characteristically "middle-of-the-road" perspective, North capitalizes on the long-standing thesis that the movement had suffered a tragic polarization of the principles of unity and restoration. In his revised interpretation, he suggests that the movement stood or fell on its ability to integrate the twin concerns of unity and *biblical authority.* North's conviction clearly is that only through programmatic restoration could the true authority of the Bible be honored as the foundation of Christian unity.

North once again argues that the restoration ideal, while not unique to the Stone-Campbell Movement, had achieved only limited expression in earlier Christian centuries. Like Murch, he insists that the Restoration Movement of the nineteenth century was a culmination — the first time in church history that the principles of unity and biblical authority had been definitively combined. Bolder than Murch, however, North openly asserts that the history of "this [Restoration] movement becomes the history of the Christian Churches and Churches of Christ." North agrees with Webb, however, that the disregard of the intervening history of catholic Christianity between the end of the apostolic age and the appearance of Alexander Campbell was arrogant and presumptuous. Careful to avoid blatant triumphalism, North blasts Murch's reconstruction of a faithful apostolic succession, a "remnant" church thoroughly bypassing Rome and Constantinople. The Campbells did not reinvent apostolic Christianity but, like earlier reformers, had to struggle to discern it and recover it. Thus North combines a sensitivity to the broader historical landscape of reform with a deep conviction about the ultimate expression of restorationism in the Campbell movement and its enduring legacy in the Christian Churches/Churches of Christ.

North agrees with Webb and Murch that the Campbells enjoyed a superior role to Barton Stone in shaping their reformation as a *restoration* movement. Whatever Stone's interest in the spiritual reconciliation of Christians, it took the Campbells to define the movement's commitment to a "union in truth." North in turn traces the development of division in the movement as an ongoing crisis of the authority of Scripture. "Musical instruments, missionary organizations, and located preachers were the symbols that were fought over, but the real issue was the application of biblical authority." With the controversy over instruments, a classic case in point, both sides affirmed the authority of the Bible. The difference lay in the precise application of that authority, namely, how to deal with scriptural silence. Ultimately, in North's view, "non-instrumentalists," by their refusal to entertain the principle of expedience, broke the authority of the Bible from the concern for Christian unity.

In the next phase of division among Disciples, however, it was the liberals who, in their commitment to biblical higher criticism, undermined the integrity and authority of Scripture and again segregated the Bible from the concern for Christian unity. For liberal Disciples ecumenists, the pursuit of unity thus became an end in itself. North's conclusion is blunt: liberals, unlike their nemeses on the opposite extreme, were incapable of any genuine sense of biblical authority and thus embraced ecumenical accommodation instead of unity with conservatives already faithful to the Bible. For all intents and purposes, North declares, the second schism among Disciples, between liberals and "independents," was a fait accompli as early as 1925. In this he departs from the judgment of Murch and Webb that the second division was actualized only after the failure of the Commission on Restudy in the 1940s.

If there is a common thread among the histories of Murch, Webb, and North, it is the burden of determining precisely how the emerging independents, the Christian Churches/Churches of Christ, were legitimate heirs to the unifying "middle" of the Stone-Campbell tradition. With Murch and North, the middle ground lay beneath the feet of conservatives committed to restoration yet leery of the radical separatist mentality of Churches of Christ. For Webb, however, the true moderates have been those independents who have understood the restrictions and complexities of restoration and who, in the spirit of the Commission on Restudy, have looked for a viable consensus to hold together left- and right-leaning extremes for the sake of the integrity and unity of the movement.

Historiography of the Movement in American Religious History

Crucial to the overall historiography of the Stone-Campbell Movement are the observations and analyses of scholars from outside the Movement who have applied their own descriptive models. Whether their portraits are accurate and fair can be debated, but they cannot be ignored since they call attention to issues that "insiders" have not seen and can enrich self-understanding among the churches of the Stone-Campbell tradition.

American religious history as a discipline had its roots in the nineteenth-century attempts both of American historians and American church historians to make sense of the whole "providential" history and destiny of the American nation and its Christian experience. The desire was strong, as Sydney Ahlstrom observes in his *A Religious History of the American People* (1972), for a mainstream "Protestant consensus" interpretation. In the twentieth century, this synthetic urge took on a more critical tone with University of Chicago historian William Warren Sweet, whose work reiterated Frederick Jackson Turner's emphasis on the cultural-historical significance of the "frontier" in the development of American religion. Sweet influenced later "Chicago school" historians like Jerald Brauer, Robert Handy, Winthrop Hudson, Sidney Mead, Martin Marty, and, as noted earlier, the Disciples' own W. E. Garrison.

Many in this distinguished group contributed to the prominent portrait of the Stone-Campbell Movement as a phenomenon par excellence of American frontier religion, with its resistance to ecclesiastical tyranny, distrust of tradition, longing for freedom and democracy, and combination of primitivist and millennialist impulses. These historians furthermore recognized the Movement's basic urge toward Christian unity but played up the sheer irony of its "lapse" into denominationalism. Jerald Brauer's comment in 1953 on the Movement's early constituents is representative: "Their battle cry was, 'Back to the Bible Christianity and unite all the churches of Christ on the basis of that Christianity.' While they sincerely preached and stood for these principles, they became, unfortunately, not a rallying point for unity, but one more denomination competing on the American scene." Winthrop Hudson similarly remarked in 1961, "While winning a significant response among many church members, the 'Christian movement' failed in its objective to unite all Christians, and by the 1830's it had simply become another denomination." And in a sophisticated 1986 work highlighting the ironies in American religion, Martin Marty wrote of the Stone-Campbell Movement: "The most revealing case and one worth dwelling on is that of the Disciples of Christ, which is so rich in ironies and so representative of trends. Nowhere was the power of the denominational mold in an ecumenical age more evident than here."

Consistent with the "Chicago School" approach has been the effort to concentrate on one leitmotif or another as phenomenologically comprehending the Stone-Campbell Movement. The "frontier" thesis was only one such. An ancillary master-theme has been "primitivism" or "restorationism." In an important study in 1976, Samuel Hill set forth a whole typology of restitutionism to characterize religious groups native to American soil. The Churches of Christ, he argued, fell along with the Mormons into the category of "institutional restitutionism," the crusade to reconstruct the true church. Mormons claimed a new and special revelation in doing so; Churches of Christ, by contrast, claimed to do it strictly on the New Testament blueprint. Disciples of Christ, meanwhile, became more resistant to easy labeling. Born in the same cradle of institutional restitutionism, the Disciples ultimately manifested, especially after the division with Churches of Christ, a less patternistic "restitution as relational reconciliation." Ironically along the way, however, they became, institutionally, a denomination, and one that lost its restitutionist impulse.

Another aspect of that irony was played up by Sidney Mead who, as professor in the University of Iowa, helped train a number of historians affiliated with the Stone-Campbell Movement. Mead suggested, as have others, that Alexander Campbell's particular brand of restorationism "put unity and restoration on a collision course." That irony, however, was internal to the Stone-Campbell family. The larger historical irony was that the Campbellites perfectly epitomized a nineteenth-century sect pinning its hopes on the new American republic to guarantee religious pluralism and equalize the various "orthodoxies" of the sects, only to find that an arrangement so sanctioned thoroughly relativized the Disciples' own claim to uniqueness. If, as Mead concurs with Richard Hughes, Campbell ultimately embraced a millennial vision in which world evangelization and the promulgation of American democratic institutions went hand in hand, it was a case of the church conceding to the nation what the church could not do alone. Leaders of the sects scrambled, then, to show how their particular group more decisively contributed to free institutions. The restorationist Campbell did so, says Mead, precisely by constituting "an anti-sectarian sect."

While not ignoring the restorationist impulse, evangelical historians Nathan Hatch and Mark Noll have concentrated on the populist or democratizing ethos of the Stone-Campbell Movement. Hatch, in particular, has developed a kind of "historiography from below," critical of the mainstream "Protestant consensus" interpretations, and hoping to show that the "sectarian fervor" of numerous religious movements on the trans-Appalachian frontier was not simply an obstacle to be overcome by modern "ecumenical respectability" but that it disclosed a genuine spiritual vitality. Campbell's Disciples and Stone's Christians were exquisite models of free-spiritedness, liberation from clerical oppression, and the putting of Christianity back into the hands of simple people who could read the "plain facts" of Scripture for themselves. The leaders and preachers of such populist religious movements on the frontier were, Hatch argues, "phenomenally successful in reaching out to marginal people, in promoting self-education and sheltering participants from indoctrination of elite orthodoxies, in binding people together in supportive communities, and in identifying the aspirations of common people with the will of God." That story, insists Hatch, is worthy in its own right. Though Hatch sees his portrait of the Movement as flattering, his depictions of it as radically populist are clearly overdrawn. In particular, Hatch fails to acknowledge the churchly and traditional aspects of the Christianity of both Stone and Campbell.

Clearly Hatch, like Samuel Hill before him, has relied on "comparative restorationism" in assessing the Stone-Campbell Movement in relation to other frontier groups. Yet another American religious historian, Richard Wentz, an Episcopalian, has subsumed the movement under the category of "restorationist traditions" and the further subcategory of "biblicist and rationalist Christianism." By this he means a rather severe biblical, historical, and theological reductionism. The Movement not only repudiated all prior ecclesiastical tradition, including its own roots in Calvinism, but also prescribed a purely rational faith in Christ, depended on the New Testament as "a self-enclosed rational repository of truth," and, in a "uniquely American spirit," pragmatically focused only on "what works" in faith and practice. In the opening of his book, Wentz confesses his own proclivity for generalizing. That proclivity is certainly in evidence in an account of the Stone-Campbell Movement that lacks nuance and grossly oversimplifies.

A virtue of Wentz's treatment, however, is his attention to the issue of *tradition.* The Stone-Campbell Movement was both impacted by tradition and produced its own traditions. This point is made more forcefully, if briefly, in Sydney Ahlstrom's account of the Movement. Ahlstrom places a caution on the thesis that the "frontier" created its own dynamism (Turner/Sweet) or that democratic restorationism left tradition per se in the dust. "The opposite phenomenon is more striking," he suggests. Whether it was the Westminster Assembly, the English Baptist heritage, the message and methods of John Wesley, or the restorationism of Scotland's Haldane brothers, there were legacies of tradition being carried on and reworked ecclesiologically and theologically. The future was genuinely being created out of the past (or "pasts"), not without the past.

New models for analyzing the Stone-Campbell Movement and other American religious groups are appearing all the time in the field of American religious history, and some will doubtless prove more promising than others. For years historians have rightly paid close attention to the social and ecclesial configuration of frontier religious "movements," how they morphed into "denominations," and how those denominations helped shape the face of American culture. In 1994 a collection appeared from a Lilly Endowment–funded study entitled *Reimagining Denominationalism: Interpretive Essays.* Among other things this project, while not discouraging larger synthetic interpretations of denominationalism, encouraged attention to particularity and to the story of denominations told from within by those who could tell it as sympathetic insiders. Such comes as welcome news for some Stone-Campbell historians, like Leroy Garrett of the Churches of Christ, whose *The Stone-Campbell Movement* marvelously exploits biography and "anecdotal" history as an interpretive model.

The Lilly project also calls attention to a wide array of methodologies that can be applied in fresh reinterpretations of denominational history: congregational studies, anthropology, sociology, history of religions, literary studies, etc. Some of these new lines of inquiry have already gained interest among Stone-Campbell historians. Congregational history was a passion of Anthony Dunnavant, the late Disciples historian who, prior to his death, served as a general editor of the present encyclopedia. As Dunnavant well knew, macro-history cannot be effectively composed without micro-histories. What the "people in the pew" have been doing, and how they interpret their own life in community with one another, has everything to do with how the Stone-Campbell Movement has presented, and will present itself to a wider Christian public.

Summary and Analysis

Several prominent themes and trends link the histories of the Movement. The role of Barton W. Stone in its formation has been a major issue since the beginning. Stone was at first largely minimized as a precursor to the Campbells' reform, which was viewed as the real foundation of the Movement. Alternatively, Stone was often virtually conflated with Alexander Campbell as far as his theological positions. Yet first among Disciples scholars with Fortune and Ware, then later with Richard Hughes and others in Churches of Christ, Stone was made a full-fledged founder, as important as the Campbells and significantly different from them. This resurrection of Stone took vastly different turns. Disciples portrayed Stone as an early ecumenist who provided further justification for the Disciples' entry into the modern Ecumenical Movement. For Hughes, Stone was anything but the liberal ecumenist of the Disciples histories, but embodied an "apocalyptic" worldview that depreciated all human schemes for unity and thus provided a critique of contemporary Churches of Christ. Meanwhile historians from the Christian Churches/Churches of Christ have continued to minimize both Stone's role in the founding of the Movement and his importance for their own identity.

Another common thread throughout the histories of the Movement is triumphalism. Its earliest manifestation, though not always strident, was a portrayal of the Movement as a divine initiative that would restore the church to conformity with God's express will in Scripture. This triumphalism took different forms as the Movement divided. While histories in Disciples of Christ increasingly muted their depiction of the Movement as the answer to Christendom's problems, they asserted that the other streams (first Churches of Christ, then Christian Churches/ Churches of Christ) had missed the true point of the Movement, becoming sidetracked by legalism accompanied by a divisive spirit. Of course, each stream expressed the idea that it was the true heir of the genius of the Movement, and among Churches of Christ and Christian Churches/ Churches of Christ the sense of triumph over all other Christian bodies remained strong. While most recent histories written by members of Churches of Christ express a strong sense of loyalty to that stream of the Movement, they mitigate the triumphalism of earlier generations by discussing both its strengths and weaknesses. They see Churches of Christ as one authentic embodiment of the ethos of the Stone-Campbell Movement and of Christianity as a whole. A similar muting of the earlier triumphalism can be seen in the work of Henry Webb of the Christian Churches/Churches of Christ whose revised *In Search of Christian Unity* was published in 2003 by Churches of Christ–related Abilene Christian University Press.

A third prevalent historiographical trend is the struggle to determine the relationship between unity and restoration. While the term "restoration" is not as common as "reformation" as a designation for the Movement in its early days, the concept of returning to the beliefs and practices of the early church is a major theme from the beginning. By the time the first histories were written, the term itself had become more widely used. The nearly universal assumption was that the earliest leaders saw the restoration of the doctrines and practices clearly taught in the New Testament as the *basis* for Christian unity. The first history to suggest a conflict between the norms of restoration and unity was that of Disciples historian Errett Gates. Gates's analysis became a standard way of describing the differences between Disciples and the other streams of the Movement; in other words, Disciples chose unity while the others chose restoration.

Most early historians in Churches of Christ, while clearly giving priority to the goal of restoring New Testament belief and practice, insisted that only such a restoration could serve as the basis for true unity. They understood this stance to be that of the Movement's founders and did not see themselves as having abandoned the goal of unity. The idea of unity at any cost was regularly excoriated. Yet the goal of unity with all who agreed on what they saw as the simple teaching of Scripture was a common theme. More recently Richard Hughes and Leonard Allen have placed the restorationism of the Stone-Campbell Movement into a larger context of American primitivism to show that the emphasis was a major one in American Christianity.

There has been general agreement in the historiography of the Christian Churches/Churches of Christ that restoration and unity were inseparable in the Movement's original plea, restoration having a certain practical priority since it is the vehicle of unity. For James DeForest Murch restoration was definitive since it not only embodied the Movement's absolute commitment to apostolic precedent but also characterized its historical pedigree in a lineage of providential restoration movements. More recently James North has substituted "biblical authority" for restoration vis-à-vis unity, a terminology perhaps more plausible in the context of larger struggles between Evangelicals and mainline churches in America. Only Henry Webb's history, one of the major ones from this stream of the Movement, qualifies the workability of restoration as a means to unity by pointing out its inherent challenges and difficulties.

Several other trends have also been prominent in the historiography of the Stone-Campbell Movement. The shift from amateurs to professionals, from preachers to academics, as the tellers of the story has made a significant impact on the self-understandings of all three streams, and continues to do so. While academics did often continue to write with an apologetic agenda, the emergence of trained historians in each stream brought a measured, less triumphalistic approach that allowed for new takes on the history of the Movement.

Perhaps one of the most striking occurrences has been the burst of creative historical writing from within Churches of Christ in the last third of the twentieth century. This activity was sparked by the convergence of two factors. First, that stream of the Movement had been moving "across the tracks" for much of the century and began to produce a significant number of doctorates as early as the 1960s, though most were by biblical scholars. Second, at the same time Churches of Christ were seeking to understand their identity in the midst of social and cultural change. The result was new histories that aimed at helping Churches of Christ identify their distinctive heritage and calling. A similar phenomenon had occurred among Disciples in the late nineteenth and early twentieth centuries as they had been challenged with defining themselves in an increasingly urban and pluralistic culture. Errett Gates and W. E. Garrison, among the first Disciples to receive doctorates, sought to do for the Disciples what a later generation of scholars in Churches of Christ would seek to do for their stream of the Movement — reinterpret their past with an eye to the future. Continuing this surge of interest in their heritage, Disciples studying at Yale in the 1940s would produce a study of Barton Stone as a proponent of Christian unity and a renaissance in studies of Alexander Campbell.

The Current and Future State of the Movement's Historiography

Among many, perhaps most, of the active historians of all streams of the Movement today, there is a clear sense that we share a common story. Especially over the past couple of decades conferences and books have brought together scholars from across the spectrum to work jointly on historical studies. *Discipliana,* the journal of the Disciples of Christ Historical Society, has published papers on issues of identity in the three streams of the Movement from the Society's

Forrest Kirkpatrick Historians Seminar. Collaborative volumes on specific historical themes have also appeared, such as *Lectures in Honor of the Alexander Campbell Bicentennial* (1988), *Cane Ridge in Context* (1992), *Founding Vocation and Future Vision* (1999), and *The Quest for Christian Unity, Peace and Purity in Thomas Campbell's Declaration and Address* (2000). The efforts of the Disciples of Christ Historical Society and more recently the Stone-Campbell Dialogue have helped create networks of historians. The internet has also provided a medium for interchange between scholars and amateurs alike from all parts of the Movement who have an interest in its history. From its inception this *Encyclopedia of the Stone-Campbell Movement* has been collaborative at every level, from the General Editors and Boards to the hundreds of authors of the articles it contains.

A comprehensive history of the Movement written jointly by scholars from each of the three major streams may be on the horizon. Points of consensus regarding the telling of the common story are emerging. Moreover, the historians involved in this effort have come to recognize each other as persons of faith, commitment, and insight. In such collaborative endeavors these representatives of the three streams of the Stone-Campbell Movement, which began with a call to manifest the oneness of Christ's church, may yet contribute to the fulfillment of that dream.

BIBLIOGRAPHY Early Histories

William Baxter, *Life of Walter Scott* (1874) • John Thomas Brown, *Churches of Christ* (1904) • Alexander Campbell, "The Disciples of Christ," pp. 462-64 in J. N. Brown, *Encyclopedia of Religious Knowledge* (1836) • Alexander Campbell, *Memoirs of Elder Thomas Campbell* (1861) • A. S. Hayden, *Early History of the Disciples in the Western Reserve, Ohio* (1875, 1972) • James S. Lamar, *Memoirs of Isaac Errett* (1893) • Robert Marshall, *A Brief Historical Account* (1811) • Richard McNemar, *The Kentucky Revival* (1808, 1846) • William Thomas Moore, *A Comprehensive History of the Disciples of Christ: Being an Account of a Century's Efforts to Restore Primitive Christianity in Its Faith, Doctrine and Life* (1909) • Robert Richardson, *Memoirs of Alexander Campbell* (1868-70) • Robert Richardson, "History of the Disciples of Christ," pp. 223-36 in John Winebrenner, ed., *History of All the Denominations in the United States* (1849) • Robert Richardson, *The Principles and Objects of the Religious Reformation* (1853, 1860) • John Rogers, *Biography of Elder Barton Warren Stone* (1847) • Barton Warren Stone, *History of the Christian Church in the West,* in Cane Ridge Reader, ed. Hoke Dickenson (1972) • John Williams, *Life of Elder John Smith* (1870).

BIBLIOGRAPHY Christian Church (Disciples of Christ)

B. A. Abbott, *The Disciples: An Interpretation* (1924, 1926, 1964) • Peter Ainslie, *The Message of the Disciples for the Union of the Church* (1913) • M. Eugene Boring, *Disciples and the Bible: A History of Disciples Biblical Interpretation in North America* (1997) • Edward Louis Cochran, *Captives of the Word* (1969) • M. M. Davis, *How the Disciples Began and Grew* (1915, rev. ed. 1947) • M. M. Davis, *The Restoration Movement of the Nineteenth Century* (1913, repr. ed. 1966) • A. T. DeGroot, *Disciples Thought: A History* (1965) • A. T. DeGroot and W. E. Garrison, *The Disciples of Christ: A History* (1948, 1958) • Stephen J. England, *We Disciples* (1946) • Alonzo W. Fortune, *Origin and Development of the Disciples* (1924, 1944, 1947) • Alonzo W. Fortune, *The Disciples in Kentucky* (1932) • Alonzo W. Fortune, *Adventuring with Disciples Pioneers* (1942) • J. H. Garrison, ed., *The Reformation of the Nineteenth Century* (1901) • J. H. Garrison, *The Story of a Century* (1909) • W. E. Garrison, *Religion Follows the Frontier* (1931) • W. E. Garrison, *An American Religious Movement* (1945, 1946, 1951, 1957, 1966) • W. E. Garrison, *The Disciples of Christ* (1948) • W. E. Garrison, *Whence and Whither Disciples of Christ* (1948) • W. E. Garrison, *Heritage and Destiny* (1961) • Errett Gates, *The Disciples of Christ* (1905) • Cloyd Goodnight, *A Century of Achievement* (1930) • John Louis Hill, *As Others See Us, and As We Are* (1908) • Walter Wilson Jennings, *Origin and Early History of the Disciples of Christ* (1919, repr. ed. 1966) • W. W. Jennings, *A Short History of the Disciples of Christ* (1929) • F. D. Kershner, *The Restoration Handbook* (1918-20, reprint 1960) • F. D. Kershner, *Stars: New History of the Reformation Movement* (1940) • Lester G. McAllister and William E. Tucker, *Journey in Faith: A History of the Christian Church (Disciples of Christ)* (1975) • Vere Hudson Rogers, *The Disciples of Christ: A Study and Discussion Course* (1936, revised ed. 1942) • Kenneth Leroy Teegarden, *We Call Ourselves Disciples* (1975, 1976, 1979, 1983) • Mark G. Toulouse, *Joined in Discipleship: The Shaping of Contempory Disciples Identity* (1992, revised ed. 1997) • B. B. Tyler, *Concerning the Disciples of Christ* (1897) • B. B. Tyler, *History of the Disciples of Christ,* American Church History Series, vol. 12 (1894) • Charles Crossfield Ware, *Barton Warren Stone: Pathfinder of Christian Union. The Story of His Life and Times* (1932) • P. H. Welshimer, *Concerning the Disciples: A Brief Resume of the Movement to Restore the New Testament Church* (1935) • Oliver Read Whitley, *Trumpet Call of Reformation* (1959) • D. Newell Williams, ed., *A Case Study of Mainstream Protestantism: The Disciples Relation to American Culture, 1880-1989* (1991).

BIBLIOGRAPHY Churches of Christ

C. Leonard Allen and Richard T. Hughes, *Discovering Our Roots: The Ancestry of Churches of Christ* (1988) • Michael W. Casey and Douglas A. Foster, eds., *The Stone-Campbell Movement: An International Religious Tradition* (2002) • Leroy Garrett, *The Stone-Campbell Movement: An Anecdotal History of Three Churches* (1981, rev. ed. 1994) • Homer Hailey, *Attitudes and Consequences in the Restoration Movement* (1975) • David Edwin Harrell, Jr., *The Churches of Christ in the Twentieth Century: Homer Hailey's Personal Journey of Faith* (2000) • David Edwin Harrell, Jr., *Quest for a Christian America: The Disciples of Christ and American Soci-*

ety to 1866 (1966) • David Edwin Harrell, Jr., *The Social Sources of Division in the Disciples of Christ, 1865-1900* (1973) • Marvin Hastings, *The Saga of a Movement* (1981) • Monroe Hawley, *Redigging the Wells: Seeking Undenominational Christianity* (1976) • Gary Holloway and Douglas A. Foster, *Renewing God's People: A Concise History of Churches of Christ* (2001) • Robert E. Hooper, *A Distinct People: A History of the Churches of Christ in the 20th Century* (1993) • Richard T. Hughes, *Reviving the Ancient Faith: The Story of Churches of Christ in America* (1996) • Bill J. Humble, *The Story of the Restoration* (1969) • F. W. Mattox, *The Eternal Kingdom: A History of the Church of Christ* (1961) • C. A. Norred, *Seeking the Old Paths* (1933) • Dabney Phillips, *A Medley of the Restoration* (1978) • J. M. Powell, *The Cause We Plead: A Story of the Restoration Movement* (1987) • David Roper, *Voices Crying in the Wilderness: A History of the Lord's Church with Special Emphasis on Australia* (1979) • John F. Rowe, *History of Reformatory Movements: Resulting in a Restoration of the Apostolic Church, with a History of the Nineteen General Church Councils* (1884, 1890, 1892, 1894, numerous reprints) • F. W. Shepherd, *The Church, the Falling Away, and the Restoration* (1929, 1958) • Earl Irvin West, *Search for the Ancient Order: A History of the Restoration Movement*, 4 vols. (1949, 1950, 1979, 1987) • Morris M. Womack, *Thirteen Lessons on Restoration History* (1988).

BIBLIOGRAPHY Christian Churches/Churches of Christ

Enos Dowling, *The Restoration Movement: Study Course for Youth & Adults* (1964) • Harold W. Ford, *A History of the Restoration Plea* (1952) • H. Eugene Johnson, *The Christian Church Plea* (1975) • E. LeRoy Lawson, *The New Testament Church, Then and Now* (1981) • Marshall James Leggett, *Introduction to the Restoration Ideal* (1986) • Dean Mills, *Union on the King's Highway: The Campbell-Stone Heritage of Unity* (1987) • James DeForest Murch, *Christians Only: A History of the Restoration Movement* (1962) • James Brownlee North, *The Church of the New Testament* (1984) • James Brownlee North, *Union in Truth: An Interpretive History of the Restoration Movement* (1994) • John W. Wade, *Pioneers of the Restoration Movement* (1966) • Dean E. Walker, *Adventuring for Christian Unity: A Survey of the History of Churches of Christ (Disciples)* (1935) • Henry E. Webb, *In Search of Christian Unity: A History of the Restoration Movement* (1990).

BIBLIOGRAPHY The Movement in American Religious History

Sydney Ahlstrom, *A Religious History of the American People* (1972); Jerald C. Brauer, *Protestantism in America: A Narrative History* (1953); Nathan O. Hatch, *The Democratization of American Christianity* (1989); Samuel Hill, "A Typology of American Restitutionism," *Journal of the American Academy of Religion* 44 (1976): 65-76; Winthrop Hudson, *American Protestantism* (1961); Martin Marty, *Modern American Religion*, vol. 1: *The Irony of It All, 1893-1919* (1986); Sidney Mead, "The Theology of the Republic and the Orthodox Mind," *Journal of the American Academy of Religion* 44 (1976): 105-13; Robert Bruce Mullin and Russell E. Richey, eds., *Reimagining Denominationalism: Interpretive Essays* (1994); Richard Wentz, *Religion in the New World: The Shaping of Religious Traditions in the United States* (1990).

Paul M. Blowers,
Douglas A. Foster,
and
D. Newell Williams

Chronology

Stone

1772 Barton W. Stone born, Dec. 24

1796 Licensed, Orange Presbytery, Spring

1798 Called: Cane Ridge & Concord, Spring
Ordained by Presbytery of Transylvania, Oct. 4

1801 Great Cane Ridge Revival

1803 Synod of Kentucky: Five withdraw, September 10
Springfield Presbytery organized

1804 *Apology* printed, January
Last Will and Testament, June 28

1824 Stone & Campbell meet

1826 Stone founds the *Christian Messenger*

Campbell

1763 Thomas Campbell born

1788 Alexander Campbell born, Sept. 12

1796 Walter Scott born

1807 Thomas Campbell arrives in Philadelphia, May 13

1809 Alexander Campbell lands in New York, Sept. 29
Declaration & Address published

1811 Brush Run church organized
Campbells immersed, June 12

1813 Brush Run Congregation joins Redstone Baptist Association, Autumn

1823 Alexander Campbell starts the *Christian Baptist*

1824 In Georgetown, Alexander Campbell & Stone meet

1824 (-1829) Alexander Campbell begins series on "A Restoration of the Ancient Order of Things"

1827 Walter Scott becomes evangelist for Mahoning Baptist Association

1829 Campbell-Owen Debate

1830 Mahoning Association dissolves, Dec. 25

1830 Alexander Campbell begins the *Millennial Harbinger*

The United Movement

1831	December joint meeting of Christians and Reformers at Lexington; unite on January 1, 1832
1836	A Church of Christ established by James Wallis in Nottingham, England
	Founding of Bacon College
1837	Campbell-Purcell Debate, Jan. 13-17
1840	Founding of Bethany College
1841	Bethany opened
1843	Campbell-Rice Debate
1844	Stone dies at Hannibal, Missouri, Nov. 9
1849	First national convention at Cincinnati, Ohio; American Christian Missionary Society, Campbell elected president
1851	First missionary, Dr. James T. Barclay, arrives in Jerusalem
1854	Thomas Campbell dies at Bethany
1855	Tolbert Fanning begins publication of the *Gospel Advocate*
1856	Beginning of *American Christian Review*
1863	Beginning of *Gospel Echo* (later *The Christian-Evangelist*)
1866	Alexander Campbell dies at Bethany; beginning of *Christian Standard*
1874	Christian Woman's Board of Missions organized
1875	Foreign Christian Missionary Society organized
1884	Austin McGary begins publication of the *Firm Foundation* in Austin, Texas
1889	Sand Creek "Address and Declaration"
1891	J. M. McCaleb begins long-term mission work in Japan
1891	Nashville Bible School established, later named David Lipscomb University

Christian Churches/Disciples of Christ		Churches of Christ	
		1902	George Phillip Bowser begins the *Christian Echo*
		1906	Acknowledgment of Churches of Christ as separate religious communion in 1906 Religious Census
			Establishment of Childers Classical Institute, later Abilene Christian University
1907	Disciples become charter members of the Federal Council of Churches (later National Council of Churches)		
1909	Centennial Convention in Pittsburgh		
1910	Establishment of Commission on Christian Union (later Council on Christian Unity)		
		1916	R. H. Boll begins editing *Word and Work,* which became the periodical voice for the premillennial Churches of Christ
1917	Organization of International Convention of Disciples of Christ and National Christian Missionary Convention		
1919	Merger of missionary societies to form United Christian Missionary Society		
1920	Beginning of open membership controversy		
1921	Formation of All-Canada Committee		
1925	Establishment of the Christian Restoration Association		
1927	First North American Christian Convention		
1930	World Convention of Churches of Christ organized		
1934	Commission on Restudy of the Disciples of Christ begins; ends 1949		
		1938	Unity meetings organized by James DeForest Murch and Claude F. Witty begin; continue until 1947
1941	Establishment of Disciples of Christ Historical Society	1941	Nashville Christian Institute begins operation
		1943	Olan Hicks begins publication of *Christian Chronicle*

Christian Churches/ Churches of Christ		Christian Church/ Disciples of Christ		Churches of Christ	
				1946	Post–World War II boom in missions begins; sponsoring church plan allows coordination of resources
1947	"Honor Roll of the Faithful" (list of dissident conservative Disciples Churches) begun by the *Christian Standard* (ed. Burris Butler)				
				1949	Roy E. Cogdill begins the *Gospel Guardian,* which will serve the cause of the noninstitutional movement
				1950	Southwestern Christian College opened in Terrell, Texas, for black members of Churches of Christ
				1952	Churches of Christ inaugurate Herald of Truth national radio broadcast
1955	Separate Directory of the Ministry for the (Independent) Christian Churches				
1959	Consultations on Internal Unity begin; continue through 1966	1959	Beginning of Consultations on Internal Unity (through 1966)		
		1960	Authorization of Commission on Brotherhood Restructure	1960	Carl Spain delivers speech condemning segregation in schools operated by Churches of Christ
		1962	Entrance of Disciples into Consultation on Church Unity (COCU)		
		1963	Publication of the Panel of Scholars Reports	1963	First "Exodus" church is planted in West Islip, New York
				1964-65	Churches of Christ exhibit and activities at the New York World's Fair

Christian Churches/ Churches of Christ		Christian Church/ Disciples of Christ		Churches of Christ	
				1967	*Mission* journal begins publication
		1968	Adoption of Provisional Design for the Christian Church (Disciples of Christ)		
1971	Separate listing of "Christian Churches and Churches of Christ" as a religious communion in *Yearbook of American Churches*				
1984	First Restoration Forum held in Joplin, Missouri			1984	Restoration Forums begin as Restoration Summit between Churches of Christ and Christian Churches/Churches of Christ
				1992	*Wineskins* begins publication
		1996	Disciples and the United Church of Christ form the Common Global Ministries Board		
1999	Stone-Campbell Dialogue begun	1999	Stone-Campbell dialogue begun	1999	Stone-Campbell dialogue begun among the three streams

A

Abilene Christian University

School established in 1906 in Abilene, Texas, by members of Churches of Christ. The founder and first president was Tennessee native A. B. Barret (1879-1951), trained under David Lipscomb and James A. Harding at Nashville Bible School. Barrett taught at Southwestern Christian College in Denton, Texas, in 1905, but was convinced a new school was needed in West Texas. The Church of Christ in Abilene along with members of the community offered financial backing to bring the school to the city. Initially named Childers Classical Institute after donor W. H. Childers, the school functioned at first as a preparatory school, providing elementary and high school classes.

The year of the school's opening the U.S. Religious Census documented the division between Churches of Christ and Christian Churches/Disciples. Reflecting those tensions and the fact that most Stone-Campbell educational institutions had identified with the Disciples, the charter stipulated that trustees must be members of a Church of Christ "which takes the New Testament as its only sufficient rule of faith, worship and practice, and rejects from its faith, worship and practice everything not required by either precept or example."

Bible classes were offered tuition free, but were not mandatory. Though in 1909-10 under President R. L. Whiteside (1869-1951) the school offered college-level training, James F. Cox (1878-1968) eliminated those courses in 1911. The school gained considerable financial and educational stability, however, under the presidency of Jesse P. Sewell (1876-1969) between 1912 and 1924. By the end of his first year the school had been granted provisional accreditation as a junior college, and within four years was fully accredited with an "A plus" rating by the Texas Association of Colleges. In the 1919-20 school year Abilene Christian College (the name was officially changed in 1919) became a fully accredited four-year liberal arts college, the first among Churches of Christ. Also beginning that year Bible classes were required of all students.

During World War I, despite pacifist leanings among many leaders in Churches of Christ, Sewell established a unit of the Students' Army Training Corps at the college. Though the unit existed for only six months, the college's cooperation with the war effort, in contrast to schools like Cordell (OK) Christian College, strengthened its image in the community.

One of Sewell's most enduring contributions, though precedents existed from the early days of the school, was the inauguration of the annual Bible Lectures during the last week of February 1918. This Lectureship has grown to become one of the largest annual gatherings of members of Churches of Christ in the world and, along with similar gatherings at other schools, provides networking and formational functions supplied by more formal structures in other religious bodies.

In 1927 under the presidency of Batsell Baxter (1886-1956) the college purchased land northeast of Abilene with plans to relocate because of increased enrollment — around 600 in 1925. By the time of the move in 1929, however, the Great Depression had decimated the school's financial support base,

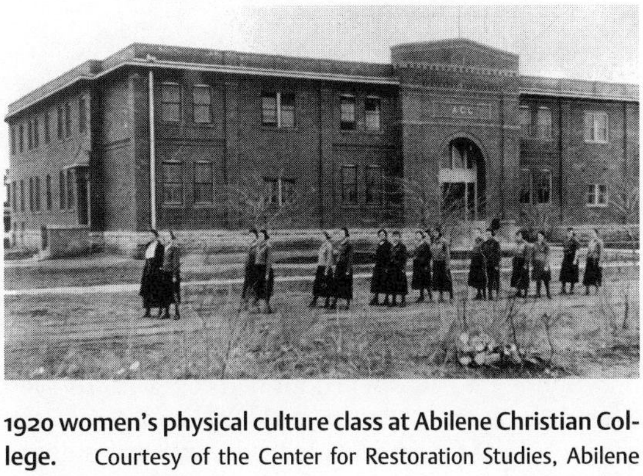

1920 women's physical culture class at Abilene Christian College. Courtesy of the Center for Restoration Studies, Abilene Christian University

threatening the college with bankruptcy. Enrollment declined by 25 percent over the following three years. In 1932 Baxter left to become president of David Lipscomb College in Nashville, Tennessee, and James F. Cox again assumed ACC's presidency. Creditors were moving to force the school into receivership in late 1933 when Baptist philanthropists John and Mary Hardin agreed to provide a loan of $160,000, averting the school's bankruptcy.

As it had in the previous war, the school administration supported U.S. action in World War II. Though the number of male students dropped significantly during the war, at its conclusion ACC experienced rapid increases in student enrollment aided by the GI Bill and increased national prosperity. Between 1945 and 1955 the student body grew from fewer than 500 to over 2,000.

Under the administrations of Don H. Morris from 1940 to 1969 and John C. Stevens from 1969 to 1981, the school expanded academic programs, achieved regional accreditation, undertook major construction projects, and added a graduate school. In 1976 the name was changed to Abilene Christian University. William J. Teague served as President from 1981 to 1991, followed by Royce Money.

Anti-intellectual sentiments in Churches of Christ viewed all efforts at higher education — especially in religion — with suspicion. Nevertheless, Abilene Christian provided the first graduate theological education in Churches of Christ between 1918 and 1924 under President Jesse P. Sewell and the leadership of George A. Klingman (1865-1939) and William Webb Freeman (1887-1954). Strong opposition to seminary-educated ministers by leaders like J. D. Tant and Daniel Sommer led to the demise of the program and the departure of its chief supporters. Charles Roberson, Paul Southern, and J. D. Thomas chaired ACC's Bible Department from the mid-1930s through 1978, an era of increasing emphasis on academic credentialing of faculty. Scholars such as Everett Ferguson, Abraham Malherbe, J. J. M. Roberts, and William Martin were products of the school's instruction in the 1950s.

Graduate studies were reintroduced in the early 1950s. In 1985 the University organized the College of Biblical Studies that houses both undergraduate and graduate theological education, including a Marriage and Family Therapy Program and Graduate School of Theology accredited by the Association of Theological Schools.

Like most Southern schools, ACC was racially segregated during much of its existence. In 1961 it began admitting African Americans to the graduate school, and by 1963 it had opened all its programs. In 1999 President Royce Money publicly confessed the school's sin of racism and pledged its commitment to reconciliation to a large gathering of black members of Churches of Christ at Southwestern Christian College in Terrell, Texas.

In the first decade of the twenty-first century ACU's student body numbered almost 5,000 from all fifty states and scores of nations. Though its constituency is also increasingly religiously diverse, the University administration has publicly committed to maintaining its strong connections to Churches of Christ. A Center for Restoration Studies was established in the mid-1980s as a library and archives for the Stone-Campbell Movement and Churches of Christ. In 2000 ACU Press began publishing "The Heart of the Restoration" series, theological studies designed to address major issues faced by Churches of Christ in the twenty-first century. The school continues to be a major force in Christian liberal arts education and theological training in Churches of Christ and beyond.

See also Cordell Christian College; Harding, James Alexander; Lectureships; Lipscomb, David; Lipscomb University; Sommer, Daniel; Southwestern Christian College; Tant, Jefferson Davis

BIBLIOGRAPHY William Slater Banowsky, *The Mirror of a Movement: Churches of Christ as Seen Through the Abilene Christian College Lectureship* (1965) • Michael W. Casey, "The First Graduate Theological Education in the Churches of Christ, Part 1," *Restoration Quarterly* 44 (Second Quarter 2002): 73-92 • Part 2, *Restoration Quarterly* 44 (Third Quarter 2002): 139-57 • Douglas A. Foster, "An Angry Peace: Race and Religion," *ACU Today* (Spring 2000): 7-20, 39 • Don H. Morris and Max Leach, *Like Stars Shining Brightly: The Personal Story of Abilene Christian University* (1953) • John C. Stevens, *No Ordinary University: The Story of a City Set on a Hill* (1998) • James W. Thompson, "The Formation of an Academic Tradition in Biblical Studies at Abilene Christian University," *Restoration Quarterly* 45 (First and Second Quarter 2003): 15-28 • M. Norvel Young, *A History of Colleges Established and Controlled by Members of the Churches of Christ* (1949).

DOUGLAS A. FOSTER

Abolitionism

The belief that American slavery was inherently evil and therefore must be abolished immediately and unconditionally. Abolitionists opposed the American Colonization Society because of its gradual approach to emancipation of the slaves. Members of the Stone-Campbell Movement held a variety of positions on the issue. Alexander Campbell (1788-1866) urged Henry Clay to submit to Congress in 1832 a proposal that would have used the federal surplus to fund the emancipation and colonization of all slaves. Abolitionists such as Jane C. McKeever, Alexander Campbell's sister, viewed such plans as too slow. John Fee (1816-1901), founder of Berea College, declared that the Colonization plan to settle freed slaves in the new African nation of Liberia was rooted in "unholy prejudice." Barton W. Stone (1772-1844) was a member of the Colonization Society who later endorsed immediate abolition.

A prominent abolitionist in the Stone-Campbell Movement was John Boggs (1810-1897), editor of the antislavery *North-Western Christian Magazine* published in Cincinnati from 1854 to 1858. Boggs was indefatigable in portraying the inhumane face of American slavery.

When the Kansas-Nebraska Act of 1854 adopted the doctrine of "popular sovereignty," Kansas became the scene of a moral struggle between proslavery and abolitionist forces. Evangelist Pardee Butler (1816-1888) determined to enter Kansas as a church planter and abolitionist activist. Despite threats to his personal safety, Butler traveled throughout Kansas establishing churches and campaigning to make the Territory a free State. Once he was "tarred and cottoned" by a pro-slavery mob and later put in a river on a raft to drown. Butler appealed to the American Christian Missionary Society for support but was refused because of his abolitionism. Stung by the rejection, he, Ovid Butler (after whom Butler University was named), and John Boggs led in establishing the openly abolitionist Christian Missionary Society in Indianapolis in 1859.

While at Williams College, future president James A. Garfield (1831-1881) was moved by an abolitionist editor's address to throw his life into the struggle to eradicate slavery. But in the shadow of impending war, Garfield joined other members of the Ohio Legislature in efforts to keep Kentucky in the Union. For this he was deemed a traitor to the abolitionist cause. Garfield, like many others who strongly opposed slavery, had foreseen what he perceived to be an even greater evil: the prospect of a "nation divided against itself."

See also Butler, Ovid; Butler, Pardee; Christian Missionary Society; McKeever, Jane Campbell; *North-Western Christian Magazine*

BIBLIOGRAPHY John Boggs, *Northwestern Christian Magazine* (1854-58) • John Fee, *Anti-Slavery Manual: Or the Wrong of American Slavery Exposed by the Light of the Bible and of Facts; With a Remedy for the Evil* (1848) • Robert Oldham Fife, "Alexander Campbell and the Christian Church in the Slavery Controversy" (Ph.D. dissertation, Indiana University, 1960) • James A. Garfield, *Papers* (Manuscript Division, Library of Congress) • Rosetta B. Hastings, *Personal Recollections of Pardee Butler, With Reminiscences by His Daughter* (1889) • Harold L. Lunger, *The Political Ethics of Alexander Campbell* (1954), pp. 193-232 • D. Newell Williams, "Pursuit of Justice: The Anti-Slavery Pilgrimage of Barton W. Stone," *Encounter* (Winter 2001): 1-23.

ROBERT O. FIFE†

Abortion

Abortion has become an increasingly controversial issue engendering division along social, political, and religious lines. The United States Supreme Court's 1973 landmark legal decision in the case of *Roe v. Wade* escalated the controversy. The court's ruling had the dual effect of expanding abortion rights for women and provoking a reaction, albeit delayed, from conservative Christians across the religious spectrum. The latter phenomenon was reflected most clearly in the growing coalition between the Roman Catholic Church and conservative Protestant groups and in the development of such organizations as the National Right to Life Committee.

Within the Stone-Campbell Movement, divergent views are represented by the Christian Church (Disciples of Christ) official resolution on abortion (1975), with an accent on women's rights and individual conscience, and Churches of Christ and Christian Churches/Churches of Christ that have placed the emphasis on protecting nascent life. The latter groups lack formal bodies to formulate official statements, but the tendencies are nonetheless pronounced and readily discernible from periodical literature, pamphlets, and sermons.

There is a wide diversity of thought within each stream of the Movement, with perhaps the greatest spectrum to be found among Disciples. Among the most vocal Disciples opposing the positions adopted by the General Assembly over the years were members of Disciple Renewal who were also supportive of the group "Disciples for Life."

In the 1980s, opposition to abortion rights by members of Churches of Christ and Christian Churches/Churches of Christ grew. As involvement in the public arena increased, many members became more involved in cooperative efforts with other Christians, especially evangelicals. This type of collaboration has been especially characteristic of Christian Churches/Churches of Christ, but has increasingly typified the activity of many in Churches of Christ as well.

In addition to becoming more vocal in their opposition to abortion, many members — both advocates and opponents of abortion rights — have actively promoted alternatives to abortion including the development of adoption agencies (Christian Homes of Abilene, in Abilene, Texas, for example) and various crisis pregnancy centers. In the midst of divergent views on abortion, many members can unite on the need to broaden concern for fetal life to include an awareness of the need for pastoral care for young women considering abortion as well as enhancing the lives of babies born out of wedlock.

BIBLIOGRAPHY Craig Churchill, "Churches of Christ and Abortion: A Survey of Selected Periodicals," *Restora-*

tion Quarterly 38 (3rd quarter 1996): 129-43 • John P. Marcum, "Family, Birth Control, and Sexuality in the Christian Churches (Disciples of Christ): 1880-1980," *Encounter* 52 (Spring 1991): 105-45 • J. Gordon Melton, *The Churches Speak on Abortion: Official Statements from Religious Bodies and Ecumenical Organizations* (1989) • Elizabeth Phillips, "Abortion and the Ethics of American Christianity" (M.A. thesis, Abilene Christian University, 1999).

CRAIG CHURCHILL

Africa, Missions in

1. Nineteenth-Century Missions
2. Twentieth-Century Missions
   2.1 Christian Church (Disciples of Christ)
   2.2 Churches of Christ
   2.3 Christian Churches/Churches of Christ

1. Nineteenth-Century Missions

Stone-Campbell missions to Africa began in 1853; however, attempts to work in Liberia (1853), Congo (1885), and Nigeria (1895) ended soon after initial efforts. In partnership with African Christians, a later effort to conduct mission work in Congo (1897) became the first successful mission of the Stone-Campbell Movement in Africa.

In 1849, when the American Christian Missionary Society (ACMS) began, the Movement had inspired no mission efforts on the continent of Africa. Yet the appeal of mission to a continent many Westerners viewed as thoroughly exotic in its land and peoples soon registered itself among American Protestants, including constituents of the Stone-Campbell Movement. The first missionary from the Stone-Campbell Movement to Africa was Alexander Cross (c. 1811–1854). Cross was a slave when ACMS Vice President D. S. Burnet (1808-1867) heard him deliver an address on temperance in 1853. Burnet encouraged several churches in Christian County to buy Cross's freedom so that he could go as a missionary to Liberia. After the churches led by the Hopkinsville congregation contributed to his work and made commitments for one year's support, the ACMS sent him to Liberia. Cross reached Monrovia, Liberia, in January 1854. Two months later he fell ill and died, and the ACMS mission to Africa died with him.

In 1885, the Foreign Christian Missionary Society (FCMS) appointed S. M. Jefferson (1849-1914) as a missionary and sent him to London to explore the feasibility of a mission in the Congo Free State. Jefferson consulted with British Baptist missionaries as well as Henry Morton Stanley. At the time, he was advised that it would cost $25,000 in the first year to establish a mission station. As this was prohibitively expensive, he returned to the United States, and the Board of the FCMS decided to postpone the project. Barely two weeks after Archibald McLean (1849-1920) announced the decision, an editorial in the *Christian-Evangelist* (July 23, 1885) indicated disapproval of the plan to send missionaries to Africa. On the other hand, the *Christian Standard* had already published articles supporting missionary endeavors in Congo.

Destined to become the center of the Disciples mission in Congo, the missionary station at Bolenge on the Congo River was purchased by the Foreign Christian Missionary Society (FCMS) from the American Baptist Missionary Union in 1899. The building on the left was the home of pioneer Disciples missionaries Royal John Dye and Eva Nichols Dye. The station supply house is on the right.

Courtesy of the Disciples of Christ Historical Society

After the ill-fated ACMS mission to Liberia and the aborted FCMS mission to Congo, there were some early "independent" mission efforts in Africa. For example, S. M. Cook was in Lagos, Nigeria, in the mid-1890s. There is limited evidence of other independent missionaries and proposals for mission work in Africa. Interest on the part of the Movement's mission societies in sending missionaries to Africa continued, and by the 1890s the *Christian-Evangelist* joined the *Christian Standard* and the *Missionary Intelligencer* in promoting missions to Africa.

With support from the students of Eureka College, the FCMS appointed Ellsworth E. Faris (1874-1953) as a missionary to Congo on July 19, 1895. On January 1, 1897, the FCMS appointed Henry Nicholas Biddle (1872-1898) of Cincinnati, Ohio, as a medical missionary to accompany Faris. Faris and Biddle met in Cincinnati, traveled to Boston, and sailed from Boston on March 5, 1897. After a few weeks in England making arrangements and consulting with more experienced missionaries, the two young men sailed for Congo, landing on May 28, 1897. The FCMS missionaries were eager to establish themselves and begin work, and they located a potential site at Mushie on the Kwamouth River. Due to outspoken Baptist and Presbyterian missionaries outraged about human rights abuses, officials of the Congo Free State were reluctant to have any new Protestant mission stations, and they delayed approving a site for the American Disciples.

By the end of 1897, Faris and Biddle had traveled extensively, including visiting Bolenge, a Baptist station located where the equator crosses the left bank of the Congo River. About the same time the American Baptist Missionary Union (ABMU) decided to sell their station at Bolenge to the Disciples. Biddle became seriously ill, and Faris made arrangements for him to return to the United States and then made his way to Bolenge, arriving on February 1, 1899. On his return voyage to the United States, Biddle died in a hospital in the Canary Islands on October 8, 1898. Biddle's death in missionary service both shocked and inspired Christians in North America.

While studying for mission work in New York, Royal John Dye (1874-1966) and Eva Nichols (1877-1951) heard of Biddle's death. They volunteered to go to Congo, returned home to Ionia, Michigan, where they were married one day and ordained the next, then left soon for Congo. On April 17, 1899, the Dyes arrived at Bolenge with documents authorizing the transfer of the ABMU station to the FCMS missionaries. There they met their colleague Ellsworth Faris.

Four years after Faris was appointed to missionary service and over two years after Faris and Biddle left Boston for central Africa, the FCMS mission had a base on the banks of the Congo River. In addition to the three American Christians, there were three African Christians at Bolenge: Ikoko, a carpenter; Ikoko's wife Bokama; and Josefa, a crippled fisherman of the Lokele tribe. With the support of these Christians, Faris began educational work and itineration; Royal Dye began medical work; and Eva Dye began working with women. Although the Americans had come a long way and were dedicated to their work, Josefa would turn out to be the most important member of the small Christian community at Bolenge.

The evangelistic success of the Disciples in Congo was largely the result of the work of Congolese Christians, including the six Bolenge evangelists pictured in this photograph. Back row, center, is Iso Timothy, one of the earliest Congolese Christian leaders to emerge from the Disciples of Christ Congo Mission. Courtesy of the Disciples of Christ Historical Society

John Sherriff (1864-1935) from Churches of Christ in New Zealand came to South Africa in 1897, working as a stonemason to support himself. He began mission work in Rhodesia (Zimbabwe) in 1898, evangelizing among the Europeans, Coloreds, and Africans in and around Bulawayo. Over the next fifty years nearly twenty missionaries followed him not only from New Zealand but also the United States to open mission work across southern Africa. In 1897, Australian A. M. Ludbrook planted the first congregation of a Cape Town network that would later, with the help of British Disciples, include churches in Johannesburg as well. The Anglo-Boer War (1899-1902) disrupted this ministry expansion.

Thus, at the end of the nineteenth century, missionary work in Congo was firmly established, the work in Liberia was no longer existent, and although there was work in Rhodesia and South Africa, the age of independent or "direct support" missions in Africa had only just begun. PAUL A. WILLIAMS

2. Twentieth-Century Missions

2.1. Christian Church (Disciples of Christ)

Disciples mission work in Africa has especially focused on Congo (from the days of the Congo Free State, 1885-1908, through the era of the Belgian Congo, 1908-1960, and through the various phases of the independent Democratic Republic of Congo, known as the Republic of Zaire from 1971 until 1997). Until the 1960s, the mission in Congo was known as the Disciples of Christ Congo Mission (DCCM). The American Disciples partnership with Congolese Christians produced the largest Disciples church outside of the United States, the Community of Disciples of Christ in Congo (CDCC). In addition to a strong presence in Congo, there has also been much work done in Liberia, South Africa and neighboring nations, and more recently in other African countries.

At the dawn of the twentieth century, FCMS missionaries Ellsworth Faris, Eva Nichols Dye, and Royal John Dye were at work in Bolenge, a mission station located where the equator crosses the left bank of the Congo River. The Congo Free State was in the midst of great turmoil and the missionaries were largely restricted to the area close to Bolenge. From the beginning, the DCCM work was organized in four parts: building, healing, teaching, and preaching. Missionary recruits were assigned to one or more of these tasks, with some missionaries also assuming the critical role of constructing grammars and lesson books and translating the Bible into Lonkundo, an impor-

Mark Njoji, son of a witch doctor and chief, was the first ordained minister of the Stone-Campbell Movement in the Congo. He is pictured while on a 1908 trip to Michigan with medical missionaries Royal and Eva Dye and their children.
Courtesy of the Disciples of Christ Historical Society

tant Bantu language. In addition to the proclamation of the gospel, the DCCM consistently maintained schools (e.g., Congo Christian Institute at Bolenge), hospitals (e.g., the Lockwood-Kinnear Memorial Hospital at Monieka), and industrial work. They also published periodicals, schoolbooks, and Bibles, and engaged in ecumenical relations and projects through the Congo Protestant Council. The DCCM and the Congolese Christians built a foundation on which the CDCC continues to work.

Although facilitated by the missionary community, the success of the DCCM, especially the process of evangelization, was largely the work of Congolese Christians. Three baptized Christians, Ikoko, Bokama, and Josefa, were living in Bolenge when the FCMS missionaries arrived. Soon, other leaders of the small community of Christians and inquirers emerged, most notably Iso Timothy and Mark Njoji. Josefa was largely responsible for the first group of inquirers to be baptized in November 1902, leading to the organization of the Church of Christ at Bolenge on March 5, 1903. After Josefa's death, Mark Njoji emerged as the most important church leader for many decades. One of many local evangelists, Njoji was instrumental in the expansion of the church, becoming the first ordained minister of the Church of Christ at Bolenge on July 4, 1920.

From Bolenge, the Disciples community grew and expanded eastward up a series of tributary rivers establishing stations at Longa (1908), Lotumbe (1910), Monieka (1912), Mondombe (1920), Wema (1925), Bosobele (1945), and Boende (1957). Through the challenges of two World Wars, the Great Depression, and uncounted health problems, the missionary community worked closely with the African Christians to build a self-supporting, self-governing, and self-propagating church. By the end of the colonial period, they had not succeeded in fulfilling that vision, but they continued to make progress.

Congolese Christians had increasing leadership roles through the colonial period; however, national independence in 1960 inspired church leaders to assert greater authority in the work of the church in Congo, with missionaries as their partners. Changes in the relationship between American and Congolese Disciples communities were paralleled by the transition from the Congo Protestant Council to the Church of Christ of Congo, an ecumenical confederation of Protestant church communities. Although the transition from doing mission in a colonial context to a partnership in ministry after independence has not been without difficulties, the American Disciples of Christ continue to work closely with the CDCC, a church with almost one million members.

The establishment of a major institution of higher education in the country, the Protestant University of Congo, was greatly aided by Disciples. When the doors first opened in 1959, J. Richard Dodson, who had previously served as an educational missionary of the Disciples Mission, was chosen dean. The school functioned as a seminary until 1963 when it was given university status by vote of the Congo Protestant Council, thus creating the Protestant University of Congo. Disciple Ben C. Hobgood served as vice president for business affairs and later as recteur (president). At the beginning of the twenty-first century the university has 4,400 students and is led by a Disciple, Dr. B. Ngoy, who became Recteur in 1993.

The story of Disciples missions in Africa also includes Liberia, Zimbabwe, South Africa, and other nations. The unsuccessful mission to Liberia in 1853-54 had not been forgotten. Jacob Kenoly (1876-1911), a graduate of Southern Christian Institute (SCI) in Edwards, Mississippi, went to Liberia in 1905, where he established a mission at Schiefflin. He appealed to Elizabeth "Mother" Ross (1852-1926) and the Christian Woman's Board of Missions (CWBM) for help, and in 1907 the CWBM officially assumed responsibility for the missionary endeavor that was known as the Liberian Christian Institute. After Kenoly's death in 1911,

Affinity with the descendants of former American slaves influenced Jacob Kenoly to go to Liberia in 1905, where he established a mission at Schiefflin. At his request, the Christian Woman's Board of Missions assumed responsibility for the Liberian Christian Institute. Kenoly's school was the second attempt by Disciples to establish a mission in Liberia.
Courtesy of the Disciples of Christ Historical Society

additional CWBM missionaries (including several SCI graduates) joined his wife, Ruth Walker Kenoly, to continue the work. By 1916, the CWBM decided to consolidate its Africa work with the FCMS-supported DCCM and transfer CWBM missionaries to Congo.

The departure of Emory Ross (1887-1973), Ernest Pearson, and other CWBM missionaries to Congo was not the end of the story of the Disciples of Christ connection with Liberia. During his life, Jacob Kenoly had sent three students from Liberia to the SCI in Edwards, Mississippi, one of whom eventually returned to Liberia. After attending SCI, Jerome E. Freeman went to Drake University, where he received his undergraduate degree and studied law. In 1930, the church he attended in Des Moines supported his return to Liberia, where he opened a school in Monrovia called "The Jacob Kenoly Memorial Institute," which continued for at least twenty more years.

In addition to establishing missions in Congo and Liberia, Disciples of Christ worked in other parts of Africa. Missionaries from New Zealand to Southern Rhodesia (now Zimbabwe), John Sherriff and F. L. Hadfield began work near Bulawayo in 1905. Another missionary, R. S. Garfield Todd (1908-2002), became a Member of Parliament and later Prime Minister of Rhodesia. Further south, after an American-trained African began a missionary effort in 1924 in Kimberley, South Africa, the independent Thomas Evangelistic Mission came in 1926 and helped establish several congregations. A Baptist, Basil Holt joined the Disciples and became a general evangelist for the Thomas Mission before moving to the United States in 1930. In the mid-1940s, the United Church Missionary Society (UCMS) sent Holt back to South Africa to help organize and extend the Disciples work there. Relationships with churches in Zimbabwe and South Africa continue to the present. In addition to these historic church relationships, Disciples in North America have developed partnerships and sent personnel to numerous other nations, especially in southern and eastern Africa. These nations include Botswana, Ghana, Kenya, Lesotho, Mozambique, Namibia, Swaziland, Zambia, and others.

For most of the twentieth century, a succession of North American Disciples of Christ institutions oversaw the work in Africa. In the first two decades, the FCMS and CWBM were the principal agencies responsible for the work, combining their forces in Congo in 1916. With the formation of the UCMS in 1919, those societies bequeathed their responsibilities to the Division of Foreign Missions/World Missions of the UCMS. That structural arrangement continued through the next five decades. After the acceptance of the provisional design of the Christian Church (Disciples of Christ) in 1968, the work soon fell under the auspices of the Department of Africa of the Division of World Missions (later named the Division of Overseas Ministries [DOM]).

Increasing cooperation between the United Church Board of World Mission of the United Church of Christ and the DOM of the Christian Church (Disciples of Christ) led to a common ministry in Africa. In 1991, the resignation of the UCBWM Africa executive led to the decision for the DOM Executive Secretary for Africa (Dr. Daniel Hoffman) to oversee the work of both boards in Africa. On January 1, 1996, the DOM, the UCBWM, and their respective denominational structures approved the formation of the Common Global Ministries Board (CGMB). This cooperative mission agency continues its work in Africa at the beginning of the twenty-first century, and for the first time the Executive Secretary for Africa, Rev. Dr. Bonganjalo Goba, is from Africa.

PAUL A. WILLIAMS

2.2. Churches of Christ

At the beginning of the twenty-first century Churches of Christ existed in thirty-three African nations with an estimated 14,000 churches and a membership nearing one million. The largest concentrations were in Nigeria, Malawi, Ghana, Zambia, Zimbabwe, Ethiopia, and Kenya.

There are three distinct eras to this mission work, identifiable by the focus of the work. These are (1) the mission station; (2) the institutional era; and (3) the mission team eras. The first two eras are separated by World War II; the third era is distinguished by a shift in methodology.

The mission station era began in 1896 with the arrival of John Sherriff, who went first to Cape Town, South Africa, then moved to Bulawayo, Southern

Rhodesia, to practice his trade of stone masonry and to preach. Sherriff established a church and a night school to teach his converts to read, especially Scripture. He later built Forest Vale Mission to train national evangelists; the mission station and its educational approach became the hallmark of this era.

Sherriff's evangelism prompted young African Christians such as Peter Masiya and Kambole Mpatamatenga to preach in village initiatives. Sherriff also called for missionaries from both New Zealand and American Churches of Christ. Will (W. N.) (1894-1980) and Delia (1896-1982) Short answered the call, establishing the Sinde Mission. Others followed rapidly: Ray and Zelma Lawyer, John Dow and Alice Merritt, the George M. Scotts, the A. B. Reeses, and the W. L. Browns. New mission stations and schools were opened in Kabanga and Namwianga, Zambia, and Nhowe mission in Zimbabwe. George S. Benson (1898-1991), former missionary to China and longtime President of Harding University, began a lifelong relationship with Namwianga, Zambia, mission in the 1930s through his relationship with Dow Merritt.

Sherriff's work had resulted in congregations in Cape Town and Pretoria. The first preacher of the Churches of Christ in Malawi, Elaton Kundago, became a Christian in Cape Town in 1906. Kundago returned to preach near Blantyre, Nyasaland (Malawi), where he met Joseph Booth, an Australian pastor working with several denominations. Booth, seeking to encourage Kundago's work, wrote Churches of Christ in Britain and Cape Town urging them to send missionaries. George Hills and George Hollis came from Cape Town to Blantyre in 1907 to establish a mission station at Namiwawa. The British church sent Mary Bannister and Henry Philpot to Namiwawa mission in 1912 and 1913. The British churches have maintained involvement in the Malawi mission, centering their work around Gowa Mission. American missionaries established missions at Namikango, Lilongwe, and Lubagha.

World War II marked a new era of expansion in resources and geography. Institutions such as schools and hospitals, rather than mission stations, characterized this era. During this second era Churches of Christ expanded into the majority of the African countries where they now exist.

Eldred Echols's (1920-2003) arrival in Northern Rhodesia in 1944 opened the institutional era. Echols pioneered works in South Africa, Nigeria, Tanzania, and Botswana. In South Africa the Southern Africa Bible School was influential. Two converts from the South African work, Abe Malherbe and Ian Fair, have influenced the American Churches of Christ.

Echols traveled to Nigeria in 1950 and 1951 to investigate reports of a movement led by C. A. O. Essien. Echols found sixty-five churches planted by this man he described as "the Alexander Campbell of Africa." The first American missionaries, Howard Horton (1917-2000) and Jimmy Johnson, arrived in 1952 to strengthen this growing body of believers. Horton began Ukpom Bible College in 1954, which through its post-secondary school, Nigerian Christian Bible College, became the first bachelor's-degree-granting institution of the Churches of Christ in Africa. The board of this college evolved into African Christian Schools Foundation to reflect its broader work in Africa. Another charter institution, Nigerian Christian Hospital, opened in 1965 through the work of Dr. Henry Farrar (b. 1926). African Christian Hospitals was created to oversee this hospital, a task that expanded across Africa, as reflected in its current name: International Health Care Foundation.

Meanwhile, Echols and others moved into the east African nation of Tanganyika (Tanzania) in 1956, establishing Chimala mission. They opened Tanganyika Bible School, a two-year preacher training school. Andrew Connally (b. 1931) continued the Tanzanian work, building Chimala hospital and planting churches in Dar es Salaam, Arusha, and Moshi, Tanzania.

Two other notable expansions in this era were Cameroon and Ghana. In 1956 Wendell Broom (b. 1923) took Nigerian preaching students into Cameroon for an evangelistic campaign and established churches in the English-speaking part of Cameroon. Churches in French-speaking Cameroon began in 1964 when Don Hindsley (b. 1926) and Winfred Wright (b. 1935), American missionaries from France, visited to follow up on French correspondence course students. In 1958 Broom and Sewell Hall (b. 1930) traveled to Ghana to meet a correspondence course student, beginning a work that numbered over 1,400 congregations at the end of the twentieth century. Other West African countries with Churches of Christ include Sierra Leone, Liberia, Togo, Benin, and the Gambia.

Carl Thompson (b. 1933) and Bob Gowen (b. 1931) continued the expansion into Ethiopia in 1960. John Ed Clark, with Ethiopians Behailu Abebe and Demere Chernet, anchored the Ethiopian work that has almost 700 congregations. The sponsorship of a school for the deaf was an integral part of the Ethiopian work.

The shift into the third era of Churches of Christ missions in Africa occurred in the 1970s with the advent of mission teams focusing on specific ethnic groups and their tribal languages. Termed "contextualizing missions," this approach was modeled by the Sotik, Kenya, mission team. The mission teams that followed sought to establish ethnic churches that would be as fully indigenous to their African heritage as possible. These teams are primarily re-

Flags of African nations at Jabulani, a celebration of 100 years of work by Churches of Christ in Africa in August 2002 in North Richland Hills, Texas. Two years earlier the number of African congregations had reached 13,000, equaling numbers in the United States. By the time of the celebration African Churches of Christ outnumbered U.S. congregations.
Courtesy of Center for Restoration Studies

sponsible for mission work in Kenya, Tanzania, Uganda, Benin, Togo, and Botswana.

A fourth era of Church of Christ African missions was anticipated at the 2002 Jabulani Africa — Celebrate Africa — international mission workshop. This event heralded a new partnering relationship between the African and American churches.

STANLEY E. GRANBERG

2.3. Christian Churches/Churches of Christ

The story of the missions of the Christian Churches/Churches of Christ in Africa is one of transition from the pioneering work of underfunded individuals primarily in evangelistic and educational initiatives to multidimensional ministries of increasing missiological and methodological sophistication. It is a story of adaptation amid the dramatic changes from the old colonial order to the political culture of the independent (and often fragile) African nation-states. It is also a story of increasing organization, albeit amid resistance to any form of missionary agency that would preempt the primary role of congregations in missionary support and accountability. Two enduring patterns remain dominant: the older direct-support model, and the model of the structurally minimalist missionary society (sending agency) directly accountable to its network of supporting congregations.

"Independent" mission work in Africa began in earnest in the 1920s, precisely at a time of emerging division between liberal and conservative elements in the Disciples of Christ. The Tabernacle Christian Church in Columbus, Indiana, supported, under the direction of W. H. Book, the mission of a South African native, Thomas Kalane, to his homeland in 1920, a work eventually supervised by O. E. Payne (d. 1925) and C. B. Titus until Titus's return to the United States in 1930. Payne succeeded in rallying a group of antecedent churches into sympathetic affiliation with the Stone-Campbell Movement, while Titus, a vocal critic of the Foreign Christian Missionary Society and advocate of direct-support missions, streamlined the work in South Africa and encouraged the training of indigenous evangelists. Jesse Kellems, a well-educated preacher from the United States, led an evangelistic team to Johannesburg in 1926, conducting extended rallies, boosting the small Christian church already in place in the city, and drawing attention to his ministry in a sensationalized public debate with a local Zionist.

After World War II, Max Ward Randall inaugurated the South African Church of Christ Mission in Cape Town in the early 1950s, leading to construction of a Ministerial Training School. Such schools for educating indigenous evangelists have continued to be a key element in independent missions in Africa. Randall would help pioneer the Central Africa Mission in Zambia beginning in 1962, a country where considerable missionary effort was focused in medical missions and in developing printed materials for locals (tracts, Bible lessons, and a "Bible Correspondence Course").

During the 1950s and 60s, extensive independent missionary initiatives were undertaken in several other African countries as well: Congo, Ghana, Nigeria, and particularly Rhodesia (Zimbabwe). As noted earlier, New Zealand churches had already started mission work in Rhodesia as early as the late 1920s, and the first Americans from Christian Churches/Churches of Christ began arriving in the 1950s, including John Pemberton and physician Dennis Pruett. The Mashoko Bible College began operation in 1958, while Pruett helped spearhead medical missions, including a thriving hospital at Chidamoyo. Schools were also established, and the Zimbabwe Christian College remains a legacy of the work of earlier mission organizers. Archibald C. Watters, a Scotsman and former Disciples missionary in India and professor of missions at the Butler University School of Religion, came to a European congregation in Bulawayo in 1957 under the auspices of the United Christian Missionary Society (UCMS). The church soon cut its ties to the UCMS, enabling Watters and the congregation to work more closely with evangelism to Rhodesian blacks carried on by American and New Zealand missionaries.

From the 1960s on, newer organizations like the Christian Missionary Fellowship (CMF) were working more on a national scale in the United States to rally Christian Churches/Churches of Christ in international missions. CMF inserted a number of mission

Education of indigenous leaders and preachers has played a significant role in Stone-Campbell missions in Africa. Pictured here are Ethiopian evangelists and church leaders in 1995, participating in a training institute in Kiramu (western Ethiopia) operated by Christian Missionary Fellowship, an organization of the Christian Churches/Churches of Christ.
Courtesy of Paul M. Blowers, Emmanuel School of Religion

teams into Ethiopia in the 1960s, a work that was temporarily suspended in 1977 during the period of Marxist rule but revived in 1992 after the downfall of the Marxist government. Here the challenge has been, as in other African countries, to work both in rural and in urban settings to penetrate cultures, Ethiopia being a unique challenge because of the presence of the ancient Ethiopian Orthodox Church, itself resistant to Western missionaries. Medical missions and leadership training for indigenous evangelists have been, and continue to be, significant forms of outreach for CMF in Ethiopia, but also (as of 1978) in Kenya, into which the organization invested considerable resources and personnel in the last quarter of the twentieth century, particularly among the Maasai and Turkana peoples, but now also among the urban poor in Nairobi. CMF also operates missions in Tanzania and the Ivory Coast.

Other significant missionary agencies of the Christian Churches/Churches of Christ working in Africa include the Fellowship of Associates of Medical Evangelism (FAME), which has developed significant medical-clinical work in Ghana and several other African nations, and Pioneer Bible Translators, a group dedicated to producing translations of biblical texts into strategically chosen languages (thus far in Guinea and Tanzania) among the vast array of languages spoken on the African continent. Though not statistically exhaustive, the 2002 *Directory of the Ministry* of the Christian Churches/Churches of Christ listed 167 different missionary initiatives in 17 African nations. Continuing challenges include the expansion of educational opportunities for indigenous leaders, enhancement of communicative media and inland travel, cooperative endeavor with external missionary and relief organizations, and — missiologically speaking — the contextualization of the Stone-Campbell Movement's "plea" within the culture of emerging African churches.

While the three streams of the Stone-Campbell Movement have been largely independent and often critically unaware of each other, in 1985 the first Pan-Africa Conference of missionaries both from the Christian Churches/Churches of Christ and Churches of Christ met to foster mutual awareness and cooperation at Limuru, Kenya. Church of Christ and Christian Churches/Churches of Christ missionaries from Zambia, Zimbabwe, Congo, Nigeria, South Africa, and Malawi participated in this event. This conference has continued on a bi- or tri-annual basis since that time. One recent conference was in Cape Town, South Africa, in 2001. Another cooperative endeavor occurred in Kenya in 1984 when the Churches of Christ and the Christian Churches/Churches of Christ came under the same government registration.

PAUL M. BLOWERS *and* EDGAR J. ELLISTON

See also American Christian Missionary Society; Benson, George Stuart; Christian Missionary Fellowship; Christian Woman's Board of Missions; Direct Support Missions; Dye, Royal John, and Eva Nichols Dye; Foreign Christian Missionary Society, The; Kellems, Jesse Randolph; Missions, Missiology; Pioneer Bible Translators; Sherriff, John; Short, William Newton; Todd, Sir Garfield and Lady Grace; United Christian Missionary Society, The

BIBLIOGRAPHY Bonanga (Eliki Bonanga Lofos'ankoy), "La penetration et l'oeuvre des missionnaires Disciples du Christ a l'Equateur 1897-1964" (M.A. thesis, "Licencié en Théologie," Faculté de Théologie Protestante au Zaire, Kinshasa, 1979) • Louise Browning, *They Went to Africa: Biographies of Missionaries of the Disciples of Christ* (1952) • David Filbeck, *The First Fifty Years: A Brief History of the Direct-Support Missionary Movement* (1980) • Stanley E. Granberg, *100 Years of African Missions: Essays in Honor of Wendell Broom* (2001) • Lora Banks Harrison, *The Church Abroad* (2nd ed. 1969) • Dan C. Hoffman, "Still Caring about South Africa," *The Disciple* (June 1986): 8-12 • Gene E. Johnson, *Congo Centennial: The Second Fifty Years* (1999) • Robert G. Nelson, *Congo Crisis and Christian Mission* (1961) • Ziden Nutt, "History of Missions among Christian Churches/Churches of Christ from 1800-1945." Good News Productions, International (2000) • Doug Priest, *Doing Theology with the Maasai* (1990) • Doug Priest, ed. *Unto the Uttermost: Missions in the Christian Churches/Churches of Christ* (1984) • Max Ward Randall, *We Would Do It Again: A Saga of the Gospel in South Africa* (1958) • Sam Shewmaker, *A Great Light Dawning: Profiles of Christian Faith in Africa* (2002) • Herbert Smith, *Fifty Years in Congo: Disciples of Christ at the Equator* (1949) • *Survey of Ser-*

vice (1928) • Henry E. Webb, "A History of the Independent Mission Movement of the Disciples of Christ" (unpublished D.Theol. thesis, Southern Baptist Theological Seminary, 1954) • Paul A. Williams, "The Disciples of Christ Congo Mission (DCCM), 1897-1932: A Missionary Community in Colonial Central Africa" (unpublished Ph.D. dissertation, University of Chicago, 2000).

African Americans in the Movement

1. Nineteenth Century

1.1. Beginnings to 1861

African Americans were present in the Stone-Campbell Movement soon after its inception. The records of 1820 list African Americans as members of the two earliest congregations at Cane Ridge, Kentucky, and Brush Run, Pennsylvania. In the early 1820s other congregations listing African American members were Pleasant Grove, in Jefferson County, Kentucky; Walnut Spring, near Strasburg, Virginia; and Old Union, in Fayette County, Kentucky.

The earliest African American congregations were the Colored Christian Church, Midway, Kentucky, constituted in 1834; Pickerelltown, in Logan County, Ohio (1838); Lexington, Kentucky (1851); Hancock-Hill Church, Louisville, Kentucky (early 1850s); Free Union Church of Christ, Disciples of Christ, Uniontown/Union Community, North Carolina (1854); Grapevine Christian Church, Nashville, Tennessee (1859); Little Rock Christian Church, in Bourbon County, Kentucky (1861); and other congregations in Washington, Johnson, and Wilkinson Counties in Georgia.

In mixed congregations, offices open to African Americans were those of exhorters (talented persons ordained to preach to African Americans), deacons who served African Americans, and custodians. In separate congregations there also were elders and board members. In free states congregations were usually autonomous; in slave states the mother church supervised the congregation and its officers.

Records of early leaders are sketchy, but these are mentioned: Samuel Buckner and Alexander Campbell at Cane Ridge; Isaac Scott at Raleigh, North Carolina; Abram Williams at Somerset, Kentucky; Thomas Phillips at Lexington; J. D. Smith at Louisville; Henry Newson at Pickerelltown, Ohio; Peter Lowery at Nashville; and Hesiker Hinkel in Washington County, Tennessee.

Founders and early leaders of the Stone-Campbell Movement, notably Thomas and Alexander Campbell, Barton Stone, Walter Scott, and Benjamin Franklin, held classes in religious education for African Americans. The Bible was the textbook, and the "head," or rational, approach to Christianity was fostered, in contrast to "shouting" or "fervent" approaches.

By 1861 the African American membership in mixed congregations numbered about 5,500, and in separate congregations about 1,500. The mixed congregations were in Kansas, Kentucky, Mississippi, Missouri, North Carolina, Ohio, Pennsylvania, Tennessee, Texas, and Virginia. The separate congregations were in Georgia, Kentucky, North Carolina, Ohio, and Tennessee.

1.2. 1861-1876

The freedom granted to African Americans as a result of the Civil War allowed them to initiate the founding of many congregations in this era. Some white-controlled mixed congregations encouraged and assisted African Americans to establish their own congregations rather than granting them fully participating membership in the mixed congregations.

As many as thirty congregations were started in Kentucky. Traveling evangelists such as Buckner, Campbell, George Williams, Leroy Reed, R. Elijah Hathaway, Alpheus Merchant, and Alexander Campbell II spread the tenets of the Stone-Campbell Movement. These men largely supported themselves from their own finances, sometimes receiving meals and lodging from hosts, but seldom more than a dollar or two in love offerings. The congregations known to have been started by these leaders grew to considerable strength: Second Christian Church, North Middletown; and churches in Mt. Sterling, Nicholasville, Danville, Millersburg, and Carlisle.

In North Carolina evangelistic work received considerable support from white district and state conventions. Generally, the Stone-Campbell Movement evangelized only east of the Wilmington-Weldon Railroad, due to a gentlemen's agreement with the O'Kellyites of the Christian Connection. Known African American evangelists and leaders were Alfred (Offie) Pettiford, Joe F. Whitley, R. Esom Green, William Anthony (Bill Ant'ly), Alfred Lovick, Sr., Demus Hargett, Allen Chestnut, and Yancy Porter. Two others who kept detailed records were B. J. Gregory, who received over 3,000 members, and Charles Randolph Davis Whitfield, who baptized 1,857 and gave six sons to the ministry. By 1869 a state convention had been started.

In Georgia at least seven churches were started in this era: Mt. Pisgah and Hopewell at Thomasville; Mt. Olive and Pine Hill in Brooks County; one in Johnson County; one at Mitchell; and the Savannah church in Atlanta. Evangelists and organizers were Joe Corbett; E. L. Whaley, who was financially supported by Mrs. Emily H. Tubman; and George Linder, who was hired by the white Georgia Christian Missionary Convention.

In Tennessee Hesiker Hinkel evangelized in the eastern region. Rufus Conrad evangelized in the central region and perhaps in the western region. Churches begun in this era and named in the records were at Friendship, Trenton, Lynchburg, Pinewood, Fosterville, Little Rock, Capleville, Jamesburg, and Concord. Conrad convened the American Christian Evangelizing and Educational Association in Nashville in May 1867.

In Mississippi, Elder Eleven Woods (Levin Wood) led in the establishment of new churches. He was an effective evangelist and able to enlist significant white support. Woods had come from Warren County. Through his own study of the Bible and through the influence of a white Kentucky businessman, William T. Withers, Woods, who had left the Baptist Church because the Baptists required an "experience" prior to conversion, welcomed the Movement's requirement of a straightforward confession of faith. When Woods evangelized in Grand Gulf, the only church, a Baptist church, accused him of heresy for preaching a "new gospel." Woods was arrested and tried in court, but the judge ruled in his favor, noting that Woods' gospel was scripturally genuine. Woods founded a church in Grand Gulf and several others from Vicksburg to Natchez. He used the legal services of Ovid Butler of Indianapolis in property matters. He enlisted and coached other leaders, among them W. A. Scott, Sr., John Turner, W. A. Parker, John Wormington, George Hall, Ned Patterson, Frank Slater, B. F. Trevillion, Miles Smothers, W. R. Sneed, King R. Brown, and John Lomax. The 1873 Mississippi report to the General Christian Missionary Convention listed twenty congregations, nine preachers, four meetinghouses, and 3,000 members.

In Indianapolis, Indiana, two white members of Christian Chapel Church (now Central Christian), Ovid Butler and D. Orr, began a Sunday School for African Americans in the 1840s. In time they expanded it to include the usual church functions and named it the Christian Mission Chapel. In 1867 the Mission was constituted as a church. Rufus Conrad was called as pastor. In 1869 the church (now Light of the World Christian) changed its name to Second Christian (African). Its Sunday School was transformed in cooperation with the city into Public School #23.

In Texas there were several effective evangelists and leaders. Charles C. Haley organized Clark Street Christian Church in Greenville in 1865 and worked from there to found additional churches in Cason, Daingerfield, and Center Point. He rode his mule in all kinds of weather to preach and lead revivals, usually returning home with very little cash payment, but with offerings of vegetables and meat. After the death of his wife, he married Carie, who became the first president of the Texas Christian Missionary Society for African Americans. His work was continued and expanded by four of his sons who entered the ministry.

In Michigan, Thomas W. Cross emigrated to Wheatland in 1869. In 1870 he organized African Americans, whites, and Indians into the Wheatland Church of Christ. Other ordained Stone-Campbell ministers preached at Wheatland until 1876, when Cross was ordained and called to the pastorate.

By 1876 there were African American congregations in Alabama, Georgia, Indiana, Kansas, Kentucky, Louisiana, Michigan, Mississippi, Missouri, North Carolina, Ohio, South Carolina, Tennessee,

Probably no individual more effectively embodied the tenacious spirit of early African American Disciples of Christ than Preston Taylor (1849-1931), former slave turned preacher and organizer of the National Christian Missionary Convention (1917). Courtesy of the Disciples of Christ Historical Society

Texas, and Virginia. The total membership had increased to approximately 20,000.

1.3. 1876-1899

African American churches in the quarter century after Reconstruction concentrated on evangelism, conventions, and education.

In the South evangelists carried the Stone-Campbell message into Maryland, Florida, and West Virginia. State conventions were organized, although the frequency of meetings varied among the states mainly due to economic factors. The conventions sought to work in harmony with the national structures of the Stone-Campbell Movement. At the state level, usually the main business item was education, held to be a key factor both for general education and for training of additional evangelists and pastors. Educational institutions were opened in Alabama, Kentucky, Mississippi, and Virginia. The National Convention of the Churches of Christ was constituted in 1878, led by Kentuckians H. Malcolm Ayers and Preston Taylor. The Convention met several times throughout the rest of the century, although not always yearly. At the turn of the century the 307 churches in this region claimed 33,145 members, and valued their property at $100,000.

In the Midwest evangelism and conventions were the main concerns. Preston Taylor, hired as National Evangelist by the General Christian Missionary Convention in 1884, worked primarily in this region. Other leaders were A. B. Miller and E. F. Henderson. Illinois was added to the states with churches, and, totaled with Kansas, Ohio, and Missouri, this region counted about 55 churches, 3,000 members, and 35 preachers. The state convention of Missouri met yearly from 1874.

In Texas, Arkansas, and Louisiana, evangelistic efforts brought in many new members. In Texas, strong churches were True Vine in Paris, led by G. W. Crawford; Clay Street in Waco, led by M. T. Brown; and Mt. Vernon, led by Warren Mitchell. In Arkansas, Mancil Bostick and Sarah Lue Bostick evangelized and organized women's missionary societies — Sarah Lue also traveled in a dozen other states on behalf of women's work. Both Texas and Arkansas consolidated their gains with district and state conventions. In Louisiana, various sources reported large numbers of converts, but no organization was developed, and by the end of the century there were no churches of record. Texas and Arkansas claimed approximately 66 churches with 4,000 members by 1899.

In Eastern North Carolina "Disciple Churches" or "Churches of Christ" were formed prolifically. In this region were a variety of Restoration movements, such as O'Kellyites, Free Will Baptists, and Union Baptists. The usual procedure for forming a church was for a preacher to gather adherents, then to apply to a recognized convention for acceptance as a church. The convention was wary of white assistance and so developed churches largely on its own. Some timely assistance was given by John James Harper, later a president of Atlantic Christian College (now Barton College), in matters of finance and ordination. Conventions were of signal importance. Quarterly Conferences, Union Meetings, District Assemblies, and the General Assembly were organized with precise rules of order and exercised disciplinary powers over local churches and preachers. In 1898 the General Assembly began collecting funds for a school for ministerial training. By the end of the century there were an estimated 100 churches with 8,000 members.

The establishment of viable schools and colleges was of great concern to African American churches in this era. Many of their efforts, however, came to naught, inasmuch as monies and personnel were lacking. Plans for schools often never went beyond the talking and hoping stages in the conventions. Several schools were begun, but they lasted for short periods. Some schools of note were Tennessee Manual Labor University (some classes were held as early as 1867) at Murfreesboro, Tennessee, led by Peter Lowery; Louisville Christian Bible School (1873); Southern Christian Institute, Hemingway, Mississippi (1881); Christian Bible College, New Castle, Kentucky (1886), led by J. M. Maimuring and J. August Reed; Louisville Bible School (1892); and Lum Graded School in Alabama (1894), led by H. J. Brayboy. At the end of the century, only Southern Christian Institute (relocated at Edwards, Mississippi), Lum Graded School, and Louisville Bible School were in operation, only the latter offering ministerial training.

Two periodicals are known to have been started: *Assembly Standard* by J. T. Pettiford in 1892, at Plymouth, North Carolina; and *Gospel Plea* by Joel Baer Lehman, the white administrator of Southern Christian Institute, in 1896.

Century-end membership in the United States was approximately 56,300, in 535 churches, in twenty-one states and the federal territory.

HAP C. S. LYDA

2. Twentieth Century

2.1. Christian Church (Disciples of Christ)

Twentieth-century African American Disciples continued the Movement's interest in education. Many believed that education was a way to achieve the Movement's evangelistic potential among African Americans. The Christian Woman's Board of Missions, organized in 1874, shared this vision and sought to further the combined goals of education and evangelism of African Americans. To this end, beginning in 1900 the Board provided administra-

Faculty and students of Southern Christian Institute, Edwards, Mississippi, 1897. Courtesy of the Disciples of Christ Historical Society

tive oversight of fifteen schools founded mainly by black leaders, primarily to prepare African Americans to become teachers or ministers. Despite good intentions, most schools failed after less than a decade of existence.

Southern Christian Institute, Edwards, Mississippi, a mission school headed successively by Joel Baer Lehman (1890-1922) and John Cornelius Long (1925-54), had the longest term of success. In a period when Mississippi spent less than a fifth as much per child on the education of blacks as on whites, SCI educated hundreds of African Americans at the elementary and secondary levels, as well as smaller numbers at the college level. In 1954, when a more adequate system of public education had become available to blacks in Mississippi, the school, which by then had become a junior college, was merged into Toogaloo College.

Jarvis Christian College, founded in 1913 at Hawkins, Texas, was the only black-led and cooperatively initiated mission school that continued into the twenty-first century. It maintained its commitment to provide a high quality Christian-oriented liberal arts college education primarily for African Americans. James Nelson Ervin (1873-1937) was the first president. Sebetha Jenkins, its first woman president, headed the college during the last decade of the twentieth century.

Predominantly African American Disciples of Christ congregations emphasized the primacy of the Bible, baptism by immersion, and the lordship of Jesus Christ. They stressed local autonomy, and sought to practice what they perceived to be the simplicity of the life and order of the New Testament church. They used evangelistic preaching to establish and grow congregations throughout the South. Clergy leadership taught a conservative to moderate theology. "Where the Bible speaks, we speak and where the Bible is silent, we are silent" was a Campbellite principle used extensively by black Disciples in support of baptism by immersion for the remission of sins and weekly to quarterly observance of Holy Communion.

Black Disciples in Eastern North Carolina maintained a distinctive style of Disciples church life. Elders and bishops were linked in an episcopal form of supervision over congregations in districts and assemblies. Also, the foot-washing rite was believed essential in the observance of Holy Communion. This segment of black Disciples of Christ continued to grow east and west of the Tar River, in the Goldsboro-Raleigh and Washington-Norfolk areas. Calling themselves Churches of Christ or Disciples of Christ, they spread northward along the Atlantic seaboard.

Amidst the heated debates over the validity of organized societies versus independent missions and plans for organizing an International Convention, black Disciples planned for the establishment of a national organization. Preston Taylor, by then a highly regarded preacher and respected business entrepreneur in Nashville, Tennessee, issued a call for an African American–led National Christian Missionary Convention (NCMC). Black Disciples Historian Robert L. Jordan stated that the purpose of the Convention, organized August 9, 1917, was "to create a medium of self-expression and cooperative endeavor for development of our churches that our best contribution may be made to our posterity and to the world."

Meeting in Lexington, Kentucky, in 1944, the National Christian Missionary Convention voted to expand their partnership with the United Christian Missionary Society. That action drew many black Disciples into the Movement's heated discussions over the practice of "open membership." Sere Stacy Myers (1898-2000), the presiding president of the NCMC, and Robert Hayes Peoples, a former National field program director, made extensive field trips to sponsor orientation forums among the by then more than 500 predominantly black congregations related to the NCMC. Most congregations maintained affiliation with the NCMC.

A further step toward unity within the Disciples of Christ branch of the Movement came in 1969 when the NCMC voted to abandon annual assemblies and organize the National Convocation of the Christian Church (Disciples of Christ). Its Administrative Secretary and operations were lodged in the Office of the General Minister and President of the Christian Church (Disciples of Christ). The National Convocation became an enabling structure for African American members to receive program services and develop strategies for sharing in the "mainstream" of the denomination.

Many black Disciples had family ties to the nineteenth-century American slave culture and the Civil War. The tension in race relations that confronted Stone-Campbell Movement congregations as they endured slavery and the Civil War in the nineteenth century continued to challenge the Movement in its quest for Christian unity. Black Disciples of Christ sought to enable concerned Disciples to make constructive responses to the challenges of disunity and racial tension.

During the last half of the twentieth century Black Disciples congregations were increasingly influenced by a generation of seminary-educated African American leaders. Their goal was to relate the Disciples tradition to the situation of African Americans in the late twentieth century. During the 1960s a growing number of Disciples ministers followed the thought of African American Disciples seminary professor and historian Kenneth Henry. He urged that it was "important for black Disciples to grasp the soundness of the 'historic Disciple plea,' to update it and relate it to the contemporary situation. . . ." According to Henry, "The idea of the restoration of the New Testament Church, so prominent in the thought of Disciples pioneers, must lead black scholars and lay persons to capture the ideals of Jesus and the early Christians, as free of the distortions of the last 1900 years as possible. . . ." Henry advised, "Liberation is most tangible when it focuses not so much on the limitations from which we seem to be released but also on the ideal that we are free to pursue."

On May 11-13, 1989, seventy black Disciples of Christ leaders of varying backgrounds met as an African American Network in Indianapolis, Indiana, as "an open/voluntary connection . . . interested in and committed to sharing information . . . regarding issues affecting the lives of African Americans within the Christian Church (Disciples of Christ) and the larger community." Participants considered "the wholeness we share within the church, the body of Christ." They concluded that African American Disciples of Christ could enrich the wholeness within the body of Christ by affirming the African American heritage, values and identity, sharing resources, and improving the quality of life for African Americans.

Evidence of the contribution that African American Disciples are making to the whole church is reflected in the fact that some of the more significant contemporary growth among Disciples has occurred within African American congregations. In 2003, there were approximately 435 African American Disciples congregations containing approximately 61,000 participating members. Three of those congregations (Light of the World, Indianapolis; Mississippi Boulevard, Memphis; and Ray of Hope, Decatur, Georgia) were among the largest congregations of the Christian Church (Disciples of Christ), with memberships numbering well over 2,000.

William K. Fox, Sr.

2.2. Churches of Christ

The story of African American Churches of Christ in the twentieth century is a story of courage and conflict, struggle and success, black initiative and white philanthropy. In 1896, a fiery black evangelist, Alexander Campbell (1866-1930), because of what he believed were "unscriptural innovations," severed ties with Preston Taylor and the Lea Avenue Christian Church and began meeting with his family on Hardee Street in Nashville, Tennessee. S. W. Womack (d. 1920) and G. P. Bowser (1874-1950) similarly withdrew from the Gay Street Christian Church to embrace what they saw as the restoration goal of "pure worship." Campbell, Womack, and Bowser in 1900 formed the Jackson Street Church of Christ in Nashville, which became a base for launching Churches of Christ among African Americans in the twentieth century.

Black Churches of Christ in Middle Tennessee made impressive gains in the first half of the twentieth century. In 1928, Bowser wrote of the Churches of Christ among blacks in Middle Tennessee: "From this humble beginning of seven, who were full of zeal and faith, has grown a membership in Nashville around four hundred. A number of preachers and good church workers have developed." Preachers such as Campbell, Womack, and Bowser, based in Nashville, disseminated the gospel throughout the South and to many Northern states, especially Ohio and Indiana.

Bowser was a talented and well-educated minister who had converted from Methodism and "digressivism." In 1909, he established the Silver Point Christian Institute in Silver Point, Tennessee. The school offered Bible classes as well as English, math, and history courses. Even though the school in Silver Point had a short existence, Bowser continued his educational pursuits by establishing the Fort Smith Bowser Christian Institute in Fort Smith, Arkansas, in 1933. This institution lasted thirteen years. The Southern Bible Institute, another Bowser educational project, opened in Fort Worth, Texas, in 1948. A year later, this school evolved into Southwestern Christian College in Terrell, Texas, a school that primarily serves African Americans in Churches of Christ.

More than a gifted preacher and educator, Bowser was also an editor of a religious newspaper, *Christian Echo,* which he founded in 1902 and distributed among black members of Churches of Christ. Bowser remained editor of the journal until his death in 1950. The *Christian Echo* is one of the longest-lived religious journals in the Stone-Campbell Movement and American Christianity.

Another important African American preacher in Churches of Christ in the early twentieth century was Samuel R. Cassius (1853-1931), who preached several years in Oklahoma before planting the first black congregations in Colorado and California. He spent most of his time, however, addressing the race issue and left an important legacy as a racial reformer and racial theologian. In 1920, Cassius published *Third Birth of a Nation,* a stinging indictment of Thomas Dixon's racist novel, *The Clansman* (1905) and D. W. Griffith's movie, *Birth of a Nation* (1915). Cassius's book also challenged American blacks to abandon immorality and religious fanaticism.

Other influential and pioneer evangelists among black Churches of Christ included Levi Kennedy (1899-1971), Thomas H. Busby, John T. Ramsey, Paul D. English (1910-1940), Luke Miller (1904-1962), Alonza Rose (b. 1916), K. K. Mitchell (b. 1928), Thomas O. Jackson (b. 1923), John Henry Clay (b. 1920), Alonzo Jones (1890-1942), S. T. W. Gibbs (b. 1926), O. L. Trone, Sr. (b. 1915), and G. E. Steward (1906-1979). The premier African American preacher in Churches of Christ in the twentieth century, however, was without doubt Marshall Keeble (1878-1968). Born and reared in middle Tennessee, Keeble fell under the religious influence of Womack and Campbell and the social influence of Booker T. Washington. Because of his preaching ability, winsome personality, and accommodating racial posture, Keeble received monetary assistance from A. M. Burton (1879-1966), a devoted Christian and wealthy businessman in Nashville, Tennessee. Generous financial support from Burton and other white philanthropists enabled Keeble to travel throughout North America and reportedly baptize over 30,000 people, while establishing several hundred churches and preaching abroad in Africa, Asia, and Europe. Unlike Bowser who overtly opposed segregationist practices in Churches of Christ, Keeble assumed a public accommodationist stance on racial issues and garnered widespread popularity and support from whites in Churches of Christ.

Keeble's greatest influence, however, was in the American South. In addition to serving as a national and international evangelist, Keeble in 1942 became president of the Nashville Christian Institute, a K-12 school for black students and preachers in Churches of Christ. As president of this institution, he shaped the lives of numerous young preachers such as Jack Evans, Sr. (b. 1937), president of Southwestern Christian College, W. F. Washington, preacher of the Golden Heights Church of Christ in Fort Lauderdale, Florida, and Fred D. Gray (b. 1930), attorney for Rosa Parks and Dr. Martin Luther King, Jr.

During the Civil Rights Era, racial tension engulfed Churches of Christ. Most white colleges barred blacks from admission and attendance. R. N. Hogan (1902-1997), a protégé of Bowser, assumed editorial responsibilities for the *Christian Echo* and used the position to challenge white administrators in Churches of Christ colleges to open their doors to black students. Carl Spain (1917-1990), a Bible professor at Abilene Christian College, joined Hogan and urged his white colleagues to admit African American students. By 1965, most colleges affiliated with Churches of Christ had begun admitting students of African descent.

After the closure of the Nashville Christian Institute in 1967, black leaders in Churches of Christ, feeling they had been slighted when funds from the school went to David Lipscomb College, filed suit against white board members. Fred Gray, a graduate of the Institute, represented the plaintiffs, who eventually lost the case. The Nashville Christian Institute episode created tension between white and black leaders in Churches of Christ. G. P. Holt (1923-2001), a grandson of Bowser and a leader among black Churches of Christ in the second half of the twentieth century, lamented: "We wept because a great brotherhood had been stabbed in the back."

At the beginning of the twenty-first century the numerical strength of black Churches of Christ remained greatest in the South. Five black churches had a membership of over 2,000 each. Two of these congregations were in Texas: Fifth Ward Church of Christ in Houston and Greenville Avenue Church of Christ in Richardson. The other two churches were in Florida: Golden Heights Church of Christ in Fort Lauderdale and Northside Church of Christ in Jacksonville. The Central Church of Christ in Baltimore, Maryland, also claimed a membership of around 2,000. In 1982, twenty-four black Churches of Christ reported baptizing fifty or more people. Thirteen of the twenty-four congregations were in the South.

The last quarter of the twentieth century saw the spread of Churches of Christ among African Americans outside the South. Alonza Rose and Dallas Walker contributed to the growth of black Churches of Christ in Michigan. Levi Kennedy, Jules Hutton, Robert Woods, and Samuel Jordan helped strengthen black Christians in Chicago, Illinois. Eugene Lawton toiled to spread the gospel message in New Jersey, while R. C. Wells and Franklin Florence have worked many years to stabilize black Churches of Christ in New York. G. P. Holt developed one of the largest black churches in Indianapolis, Indiana. Jacob McClinton and Richard Rose have contributed to black church growth in Ohio.

In the West, Samuel R. Cassius and his son Amos L. Cassius (1889-1982) established the first black Church of Christ in California in the 1920s. In 1937, R. N. Hogan (1902-1997) arrived in Los Angeles, California, baptized forty-four people, and founded what is presently known as the Figueroa Church of Christ. A fervent and passionate preacher, Hogan led this congregation to a membership of over 1,000, making it the largest black Church of Christ in the Pacific West. The

Figueroa Church of Christ has been instrumental in founding other churches throughout the United States, and has also demonstrated great interest in foreign missions, particularly in Ethiopia.

Like many of their white counterparts, blacks in Churches of Christ have stressed a cappella singing, weekly communion, baptism for the remission of sins, congregational autonomy, a five-step plan of salvation, and exclusive claims of being the only Christians. In 1979, Floyd Rose, a preacher with great oratorical skill, challenged traditional beliefs and practices among black Churches of Christ and established a Family Baptist Church in Detroit. In his book, *Beyond the Thicket,* Rose delineated what he perceived to be inconsistencies in the doctrines of Churches of Christ. Rose published the book "in the hope that the young men and women in whose hands the future leadership of the Churches of Christ belongs, will help to create an atmosphere of acceptance in which independent minds will feel at home, and ministers are free to preach what they believe and believe what they preach." Dr. Jack Evans, president of Southwestern Christian College and a renowned debater in black Churches of Christ, wrote a reply to Rose. Evans' rejoinder, *Before the Thicket,* argued that Rose deviated from the truth by denying "the one faith of Jesus." The Rose-Evans debates of 1984 represent the tension between progessive and conservative blacks in Churches of Christ. A decade later, Rose published an open letter acknowledging his return to Churches of Christ, though he continues as a progressive voice.

Additionally, twentieth-century blacks in Churches of Christ have had conflict over the authority of evangelists and elders. Unlike their white counterparts who view elders as the leaders of the local church, blacks see the preacher as having equal, if not more, authority than the elders. R. N. Hogan noted that division was widespread in black Churches of Christ because of "rivalry between evangelists and elders." He further stated, "There is not much contention that the evangelist is over the elder, but contention is over the idea that the elder is over the evangelist." Nokomis Yeldell, minister of the Norris Road Church of Christ in Memphis, Tennessee, published a book entitled *The Big Issue: Relationships Between Ministers and Elders,* in which he observed that conflict between preachers and elders was the "most dangerous issue confronting the Lord's Church." He also noted: "I truly believe this is the reason why some preachers (mainly black) do not baptize, train, and appoint men who will in turn restrict their work so they will not be free to do the Lord's work." Other points of contention have centered on rebaptism, worship styles, and marriage, divorce, and remarriage.

Women have also made notable contributions to the growth and development of African American Churches of Christ. Annie C. Tuggle (1890-1976), a black educator and fundraiser for the Silver Point Christian Institute, traveled throughout the South, soliciting funds from white Christians. Tuggle reported that white members of Churches of Christ aided the Silver Point school "both spiritually and financially." Thelma Holt gave great assistance to her father, G. P. Bowser, by promoting his educational endeavors and by publishing his sermons and other writings. Olivia Holt, wife of G. P. Holt, has served as important advisor and nurturer to young females in black Churches of Christ; and she has published several articles in the *Christian Echo* on child rearing and other family-related topics. Sylvia Rose, a former director of the Southwestern Christian College A Cappella Chorus, wrote and produced a number of beautiful and meaningful songs that have given great spiritual edification to African Americans in Churches of Christ. These hymns include "Restore My Soul," "Holy Spirit," and "Mansion, Robe, and Crown."

In the 1990s, Herman E. Wesley III, seeking to offer spiritual rejuvenation to black Churches of Christ, established *The Revivalist.* This newspaper is a complement to the older, more traditional journal, *Christian Echo.* Seeing a need to address economic, social, political, and educational problems in the African American community, Dr. Kenneth Greene, minister of the Metro Church of Christ in Dallas, Texas, created an annual conference, "Strengthening the African-American Family." The purpose of the gathering is to highlight problems of African American families and to examine ways to "liberate African-American families as well as equip them for service, encouragement, and a call for evangelizing other hurting African-American families."

The story of black Churches of Christ in the twentieth century is a story of both self-initiative and white philanthropy. On the one hand, black ministers and members in Churches of Christ conducted their own evangelistic campaigns, published their own newspapers, and built their own churches. On the other hand, liberal financial support from white Christians often made possible the rise of black evangelists, black churches, and black schools. Presently, African American Churches of Christ host their own state and national lectureships, their own state and national youth conferences, and their own bi-annual Crusade for Christ to spread the gospel in large cities throughout the nation. At the end of the twentieth century, black Churches of Christ numbered over 169,000 members in more than 1,200 congregations.

EDWARD J. ROBINSON

2.3. Christian Churches/Churches of Christ

The division between the Disciples of Christ and the Christian Churches/Churches of Christ involved, among other factors, the formation of the North

American Christian Convention (NACC) in 1927. Since the African American constituents had formed the National Christian Missionary Convention of the Disciples of Christ in 1917 as an auxiliary of the new International Convention, the predominantly white leadership of the NACC had little or no contact with African American congregations.

Despite minimal contact, there was growing interest in serving the African American constituents. The *Christian Standard* (the primary periodical of the Christian Churches/Churches of Christ) announced in 1932 the formation of a new column entitled "News of Our Colored Brethren." It carried announcements of conventions, church plantings, and other news items from across the Stone-Campbell churches, including the Disciples.

The *Christian Standard* also published articles by both African American and white authors, calling for stronger evangelistic effort in the African American community and the formation of training institutes for African American ministers. T. R. Everett (1871-1954) from Kentucky was one of the regular contributors from about 1910 into the 1940s. One of his primary themes was a call for assistance from white congregations.

From 1930 to 1945 many African American ministers fellowshiped across the widening cleft between the Christian Churches/Churches of Christ and the Disciples of Christ. Leaders held offices in the state and national conventions within the Disciples organizations but considered themselves independent on the local congregational level.

The defining event came in 1944 when the National Christian Missionary Convention voted to expand their partnership with the United Christian Missionary Society. W. H. "Baltimore" Taylor (1898-1981), President of the Convention, led a small group of individuals to form a new convention, the National Christian Preaching Convention. Working with Taylor were Isaiah Moore (1882-1972), who held numerous offices in Kentucky state conventions and was one of the founders of the College of the Scriptures in Louisville; Robert Lee Peters (1867-1951), who established many churches in North Carolina and Virginia and was co-founder of Winston-Salem Bible College; Dr. George C. Campbell (1872-1949), who was president of Goldsboro Christian Institute (North Carolina) and was Dean of the College of the Scriptures at the time of his death; C. W. Arnold (1907-1999), Ohio minister and founding minister of 92nd Street Church of Christ, Los Angeles, California; J. Salvador Johnson (1876-1961) and Herman Turner, Detroit, Michigan; L. L. Dickerson (1900-1968), Kentucky; Eugene Patterson (1911-1977), minister in North Tazewell, Tennessee; William F. Keys and W. C. Kenard, Brooklyn, New York; and George Moore, Arkansas.

The end of World War II and changes produced by the Civil Rights Movement provided the backdrop for major efforts to work with African Americans by the Christian Churches/Churches of Christ. One of the primary influences of the period was the conflict over integration and segregation within the church. Writers in the *Christian Standard* and other periodicals discussed issues like interracial marriage and black rights, churches in changing communities moving to avoid integration, and claims of historic but token integration.

By the mid-twentieth century, the Christian Churches/Churches of Christ were attempting to make an impact within the African American community in four separate areas.

The first of these was education. During the mid 1940s, two new colleges for training African American ministers were organized. The College of the Scriptures, under the leadership of its first president, Tibbs Maxey (1910-2002), was chartered in Louisville, Kentucky, in June 1945. Leadership of the College was integrated, with Maxey (white) and Dr. George C. Campbell (African American) being Dean and Vice President.

Concurrently, Robert Lee Peters organized the Christian Institute in Winston-Salem, North Carolina. Unable to gain needed financial support, the school closed its doors briefly in 1949. However, through the assistance of a local white minister, Aubrey Payne (1907-1999), it was reorganized in 1950 as Winston-Salem Bible College, with Leland Tyrrell (1912-1985), a white missionary recruit unable to go to South Africa, as president and Peters as academic dean.

Both colleges had an integrated staff, board, and student body (although student bodies were predominately African American). One primary difference between the two institutions was their attitude toward the Disciples of Christ organization and congregations. The College of the Scriptures, located in the Midwest, the heart of Christian Churches/Churches of Christ strength, was more contentious with the Disciples, while Winston-Salem Bible College was more cooperative. This characteristic continued throughout the century and is generally visible in the attitudes of the alumni.

The two colleges worked together as they championed the cause of African American education and evangelism. However, they were in competition as they searched for students, financial support, and public approval. Both colleges had a small full-time student body, the majority being part-time adult learners. Neither college succeeded in maintaining an enrollment of over fifty students for more than a few years. Nevertheless, the two colleges were the primary providers of African American ministerial training for the Christian Churches/Churches of Christ until the end of the twentieth century.

After 1970, many supporters of both colleges suggested that because of improved transportation and communication, limited financial base, and the integration of predominately white Bible Colleges, it might be wise to merge the two colleges. Winston-Salem Bible College made overtures to the College of the Scriptures on two different occasions during the 1980s; however, because of the difference in philosophy regarding cooperation with other organizations and a desire for total independence, a merger was not possible.

A second area in which the Christian Churches/Churches of Christ were attempting to make an impact within the African American community was new church evangelism. Like most Bible Colleges established by the Christian Churches/Churches of Christ, the College of the Scriptures and Winston-Salem Bible College considered new church evangelism a major part of their mission. Their presidents and students traveled extensively to establish new congregations or to provide ministers for those that were struggling.

The *Christian Standard* and the colleges' newsletters carried numerous articles about efforts to start new congregations. Both colleges claimed numerous church plants from 1950 to 1975; however, the majority of their efforts were short-lived because of poor financial support, limited support from local white congregations, and the lack of long-term ministries.

One strategy for evangelism and student recruiting used by both colleges was sponsoring African American Christian Service Camps. Each institution operated a summer youth camp program, utilizing college students and local volunteers to train future students and church leaders. By the end of the century, both camp programs had ended.

From 1975 to 2000 both colleges continued their commitment to evangelism. Although national attitudes toward integration had changed, the need for new congregations in the African American community persisted. Efforts were often directed toward revival of white congregations that found themselves with a dwindling membership in a racially changing community.

Although numerous efforts were made during the last fifty years of the twentieth century to plant new congregations or revive existing ones, success was minimal. In 1950, the Christian Churches/Churches of Christ claimed approximately fifty churches in the African American community, and in 2000 one hundred.

A third area in which the Christian Churches/Churches of Christ were attempting to make an impact within the African American community was conventions. Two primary conventions developed among the African American Christian Churches/Churches of Christ. The roots of the first convention trace back to the Tri-State Christian Convention (North Carolina, Virginia, and West Virginia) that was active in the 1930s; its field secretary was R. L. Peters. As a result of the division with the Disciples, Peters's successors at Winston-Salem Bible College helped organize a new convention, the Tri-State Evangelistic Association, in Tazewell, Virginia, in August 1951. Two of the primary leaders were President Leland Tyrrell and Academic Dean David Cole. The Association has had limited success, but in 2000 member congregations were increasing.

The second convention, the National Christian Preaching Convention, was a direct outgrowth of the division in 1944 with the National Christian Missionary Convention, which was viewed as supporting "open membership." The driving force behind the new convention was W. H. "Baltimore" Taylor, and the first president was C. W. Arnold, a minister from Columbus, Ohio.

Opposition to "open membership" became the primary theme of the new convention and primary point of emphasis from 1944 to 1975. The organizers also founded *The Christian Informer,* edited by Taylor and based in Baltimore, Maryland. Taylor used the *Informer* to regularly attack "open membership," the UCMS, and the Disciples denominational organization. Failure to move away from these issues and dominance by Taylor contributed to the lack of continued support. As Taylor and the founding leaders grew older, the National Christian Preaching Convention eventually closed.

In 1980, a Care and Share Rally was organized under the leadership of Henry Johnson (1918-1995) of Louisville, Kentucky. Most of the original leadership was associated with the College of the Scriptures. The primary mission of the Rally was to provide fellowship for African American ministers and their families.

The Care and Share Rally continued with this mission until 1988 when the mission and name were changed to create the Fellowship of Christians in Urban Services (FOCUS). A new group of young African American ministers committed to urban ministry were now in leadership. Their desire was to encourage urban ministers and to create in both the white and black communities an understanding of the need for such ministries. With the change in direction, some individuals left the convention, but FOCUS attracted both African American and white urban ministers nationally. Although several individuals held the presidency during the first few years, Sam J. Winger (Springfield, Illinois) served as Conference Coordinator from 1988 to 1994.

FOCUS was successful in raising awareness of the need for urban ministry throughout the Christian

Churches/Churches of Christ. However, in August 1994, a controversy over finances and control of the organization resulted in Winger's resignation. In 1995, FOCUS met in Atlanta, Georgia, with a very small attendance and no future conference planned. Winger organized a camp-style meeting in central Indiana that attracted a much smaller and less representative number from the African American community.

Another convention among the African Americans is the Annual Women's Retreat, which was organized in 1980 by the female alumni of the College of the Scriptures. During the next twenty years, under the leadership of Suzie Doswell, the Retreat expanded to include African American women from the entire fellowship of Christian Churches/Churches of Christ.

The fourth area in which the Christian Churches/ Churches of Christ were attempting to make an impact within the African American community was urban ministry. This was a natural outgrowth of African American evangelism, as large numbers of African Americans were migrating to urban areas. The initial vision on urban ministry came from the evangelistic enthusiasm of the College of the Scriptures and Winston-Salem Bible College. These colleges produced alumni who moved into urban areas in the 1960s and right on into the 1990s: Fred Mitchell (Lexington, Kentucky), Richard McCain (Cleveland, Ohio), Sam Winger (Indianapolis, Indiana, and Springfield, Illinois), and William Ellis (Orlando, Florida) from the College of the Scriptures and Robert Woolfolk (Denver, Colorado), Sharon Garvey (Compton, California), Don Dykes (Pittsburgh, Pennsylvania), and Courtney Mitchell (Queens, New York) from Winston-Salem Bible College. Other urban ministers are James Lane (Hartford, Connecticut), Dr. Denzil Holness (Atlanta, Georgia), John Fuller (Indianapolis, Indiana), Don Ellis (Kansas City, Missouri), and Harley Blake (South Bend, Indiana). The majority of these men worked with FOCUS during its history, and were committed to creating a clearer vision of the need for urban ministries in the brotherhood.

As Christian Churches/Churches of Christ were attempting to make an impact within the African American community, American society was having an impact on the churches. While the issue of integration was settled in the public and business arenas, the churches were still attempting to understand and address it. Predominantly white Bible Colleges began integrating in the 1970s, local congregations integrated or moved beginning in the 1960s, and national and state conventions integrated as various state laws permitted.

Major strides were made during the latter part of the century. William Ellis (Orlando, Florida) served as president of the National Missionary Convention in 1986 and spoke for the evening session of the special joint meeting with the North American Christian Convention (Indianapolis, Indiana). John Fuller (Indianapolis, Indiana) served as treasurer for the National Missionary Convention during the 1990s.

Dr. William E. Johnson (b. 1919), vice president/ academic dean at Winston-Salem Bible College, and his wife were acclaimed as "God's Honored Servants" at the North American Christian Convention in St. Louis in 1993. Other African Americans have served on convention programs during the years.

The primary concern of the leaders of the African American churches (listed above under urban ministries), however, was integration of the leadership and a regular presence on the speakers' platform at the North American Christian Convention. Since the leadership changes annually with minimal paid staff, there was no national entity to appeal to for integration.

Beginning in the 1980s, regular efforts were made to reach this goal of recognition and reconciliation. In 1997, under the leadership of James Lane, Hartford, Connecticut, and Dr. W. Ray Kelley, President of Winston-Salem Bible College, a meeting of African American leaders and other interested individuals was scheduled to meet during the North American Christian Convention in Kansas City, Missouri. The President for the 1998 convention, Dennis Slaughter (Dallas, Texas), was also invited. This group met to discuss ways to reach the goal of reconciliation between the NACC and the African American community. A Reconciliation Committee was empowered to meet and create a document to be presented to the Executive Committee of the Convention. The Committee met in September 1997 and scheduled a meeting with the NACC Executive Committee.

Consequently the Executive Committee of the NACC agreed to: (1) create a new permanent position on the Committee to be filled by a minority member; (2) include a minority speaker on the program of every future convention; and (3) address the past history of discrimination and prejudice of the NACC at the 1998 convention. However, at that convention in St. Louis, Missouri, the leadership did not provide the detailed apology that the African Americans had hoped to receive. Their reaction varied; some decided not to attend the convention again, others believed it was a start and should be used as a building block for the future.

As a result of the effort, several letters and articles appeared in the *Christian Standard, Lookout,* and *Horizons* magazines. Kelley published a series on racial reconciliation in *Horizons* during 1998. Dr. Denzil Holness (Atlanta, Georgia) published *The Jonah Syndrome* (1998), which outlined many of the concerns of African American leaders.

As the twenty-first century begins, the number of African Americans within the Christian Churches/

Churches of Christ totals 100 congregations with a combined membership of 500. The number of African Americans in predominantly white congregations is unknown.

The area of greatest potential growth is in the changing communities where local congregations are deciding either to stay in the original community and witness to the coming African American population or to flee to the predominantly white suburbs. The major concern is the lack of trained African American ministers who can serve in these congregations and provide the guidance and leadership necessary to produce strong congregations.

W. RAY KELLEY

See also Bowser, George Philip; Campbell, Alexander (Alex) Cleveland; Cassius, Samuel Robert; *Christian Echo;* College of the Scriptures; *Gospel Advocate, The;* Jarvis Christian College; Keeble, Marshall; National Christian Missionary Convention; National Convocation of the Christian Church (Disciples of Christ); Slavery, The Movement and; Southern Christian Institute; Taylor, Preston; Urban Ministry; Winston-Salem Bible College

BIBLIOGRAPHY *William Joseph Barber, The Disciple Assemblies of Eastern North Carolina* (1966) • Sarah L. Bostick, "A Historical Sketch of the Missionary Work in the State of Arkansas 1897-1947, and a Summary of the National and International Work of Missions" (mimeographed) • Calvin Harrison Bowers, *Realizing the California Dream: The Story of Black Churches of Christ in Los Angeles* (2001) • R. Vernon Boyd, *Undying Dedication: The Story of G. P. Bowser* (1985) • John T. Brown, ed., *Churches of Christ: A Historical, Biographical, and Pictorial History of Churches of Christ in the United States, Australasia, England and Canada* (1904) • Rosa Brown Bracy, *The Negro Disciples of Christ* (ca. 1939) • Brenda M. Cardwell and William K. Fox, Sr., *Journey Toward Wholeness: A History of Black Disciples of Christ in the Mission of the Christian Church* (1990) • J. E. Choate, *Roll Jordan Roll: A Biography of Marshall Keeble* (1974) • Mrs. Effie L. Cunningham, *Work of Disciples of Christ with Negro Americans: A Resume of Church and Evangelistic Work, Educational Enterprise, and Social Service with Negroes in the United States* (ca. 1922) • Pearl Gray Daniels, *The History of the Holt Street Church of Christ* (1997) • Melvin and Sharon B. Fields, *In Other Words* (2001) • Robert O. Fife, "Alexander Campbell and the Christian Church in the Slavery Controversy" (unpublished Ph.D. dissertation, Indiana University, 1960) • Douglas A. Foster, "An Angry Peace: Race and Religion: A Historical Look at Racial Issues in Churches of Christ and Abilene Christian University," *ACU Today* (Spring 2000): 8-20, 39 • William K. Fox et al., *The Untold Story: A Short History of Black Disciples* (1976) • General Christian Missionary Convention, "Work among Negroes in the United States, 1864-1892" (typewritten) • David E. Harrell, *Quest for a Christian America: The Disciples of Christ and American Society to 1866* (1966) • H. Allen Irving, *The Christian Church (Disciples of Christ) PROFILE of the Black Ministers, the Black Church Congregations and Facilities* (1985) • Walter Wilson Jennings, *Origin and Early History of the Disciples of Christ* (1919) • Katherine Johnson, "History of the Midway Colored Christian Church" (typewritten, [1955]) • Robert J. Jordan, *Two Races in One Fellowship* (Detroit: United Christian Church, 1944) • Elmer C. Lewis, "A History of Secondary and Higher Education in Negro Schools Related to the Disciples of Christ" (unpublished Ph.D. dissertation, University of Pittsburgh, 1957) • Alice Liverett, *Biographical Sketches of Leaders of Negro Work of the Disciples of Christ* (1936) • John Cornelius Long, "The Disciples of Christ and Negro Education" (unpublished Ed.D. dissertation, University of Southern California, 1960) • Hap C. S. Lyda, "Black Disciples Roots in Kentucky and Tennessee: 1804-1876," in *Explorations in the Stone-Campbell Traditions: Essays in Honor of Herman A. Norton,* ed. Anthony L. Dunnavant and Richard L. Harrison (1995), pp. 43-53 • Hap C. S. Lyda, "A History of Black Christian Churches (Disciples of Christ) in the United States through 1899" (unpublished Ph.D. dissertation, Vanderbilt University, 1972) • Oma Lou Myers, *Rosa's Song: The Life and Ministry of Rosa Page Welch* (1984) • R. H. Peoples, "Historical Development of Negro Work and Its Relationship to Organized Brotherhood Life" (typewritten) • Clayton Cheyney Smith, *Negro Education and Evangelization* (1909) • Annie C. Tuggle, *Another World Wonder* (c. 1973) • Claude Walker, "Negro Disciples in Kentucky, 1840-1925" (unpublished B.D. thesis, The College of the Bible, 1959).

In addition to the above sources, there are state or area histories of the Stone-Campbell Movement and the Disciples of Christ in which there are relevant chapters or mentions. Many of the sources are in files at the Disciples of Christ Historical Society in Nashville, Tennessee.

Ainslie, Peter (1867-1934)

Ecumenical and social justice leader and pastor.

Peter Ainslie was born June 3, 1867, in Dunnsville, Essex County, Virginia, the son and grandson of Disciples ministers. He enrolled in 1886 at the College of the Bible (now Lexington Theological Seminary) and Transylvania College in Lexington, Kentucky, studying under John W. McGarvey. Because of ill health, Ainslie left college in 1889 without graduating. For two years he supplied the pulpit of a congregation in Newport News, Virginia. In October 1891 he was called as minister of the fifty-member Calhoun Christian Church in Baltimore, Maryland. Under his leadership the congregation grew, relocated, and took the name Christian Temple. During Ainslie's more than forty-year ministry, Christian Temple became a witness to Christian unity, world peace, racial

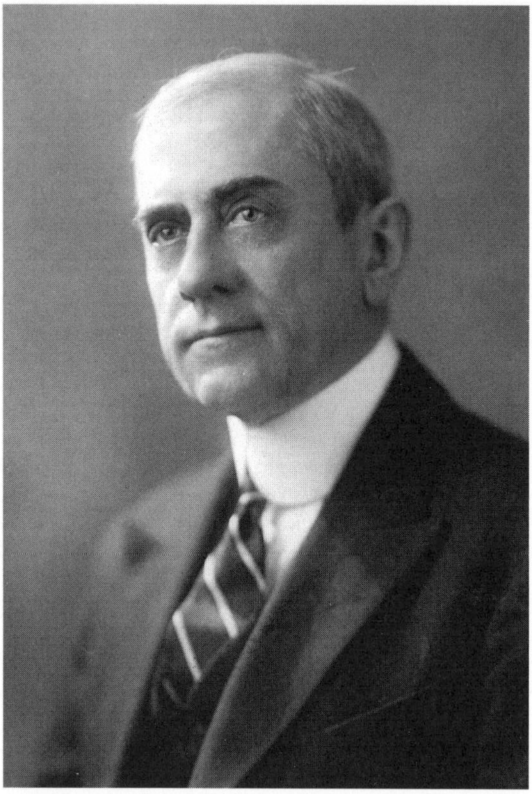

Peter Ainslie (1867-1934) was founding president of the Council on Christian Union, the earliest name of the Council on Christian Unity. Ainslie was active in ecumenical pursuits at both the national and world levels.
Courtesy of the Disciples of Christ Historical Society

inclusiveness, social justice, dialogue between Jews and Christians, and liberal Christianity.

In October 1910 Ainslie served as President of the National Convention of the Disciples of Christ meeting in Topeka, Kansas. He had become convinced that the Disciples were in danger of losing their calling to serve the unity of all Christians. In an address titled "Our Fellowship and the Task," he called on Disciples to reclaim their original ecumenical vocation. Under Ainslie's guidance the Topeka assembly took two far-reaching actions. First, parallel to an action of the Episcopal Church meeting at the same time in Cincinnati, the Disciples called for "a world conference on Christian unity." Second, they established a permanent national ecumenical agency named the Council on Christian Union (CCU) with the mandate of "promoting Christian union at home and throughout the world until the various Christian bodies are knit together in one organic life." Ainslie was elected its first President. In 1911, with $20,000 provided by R. A. Long, Disciples layman and philanthropist, Ainslie and the CCU began *The Christian Union Library* (renamed *The Christian Union Quarterly* in 1913), which became the leading ecumenical journal of the day.

The early Faith and Order Movement saw Ainslie emerge as a central figure. He served on a three-person delegation sent to Great Britain in 1913-14 to secure the participation of the Free Churches in the forthcoming world conference. He was a delegate in the meetings leading to the first World Conference on Faith and Order, including the international preparatory meeting at Geneva, Switzerland, in 1920.

Ainslie represented Disciples in most arenas of the new Ecumenical Movement: the Federal Council of Churches of Christ in America (1908); Andrew Carnegie's Church Peace Union (1914); the World Alliance for Promoting International Friendship Through the Churches, with conferences at Constance, Switzerland (1914), the Hague (1919), and Copenhagen, Denmark (1922); the first conference of the Universal Christian Conference on Life and Work at Stockholm, Sweden (1925); the American Conference on Organic Union (1918-20); and the first World Conference on Faith and Order at Lausanne, Switzerland (1927).

In a time of doctrinal orthodoxy among Disciples, Ainslie pleaded for liberty of opinion. His critique of denominational divisions and sectarianism was severe but loving. Herbert L. Willett observed that Ainslie was "a singular compound of gentleness and inflexibility. In his championship of new and often unpopular causes he was fearless and aggressive." Both because of his personal ecumenical witness and the climate of the times, Ainslie was often "in the eye of a storm of controversy." Many conscientiously opposed the open pulpit, open communion, and open membership. Ainslie affirmed them as signs of the coming unity of all Christians, declaring that the divisive spirit is "the scandal of Christianity." Controversy over such matters often focused on Ainslie, leading him in 1925 to resign from the presidency of the Association for the Promotion of Christian Unity (the new name given the Council on Christian Union in 1913). He attended the Lausanne World Conference on Faith and Order in 1927 not as a delegate but as a member of the Continuation Committee.

After resigning his presidency Ainslie concluded that the divided churches were captive to the powers of denominational idolatry. The ecumenical problem required personal and practical solutions. Unity would be achieved not "from the top" — through high offices in the churches — but "from the bottom" — by the witness and leadership of courageous people in the congregations. So in 1927 Peter Ainslie created the Christian Unity League for Equality and Brotherhood, an association he described as: "A fellowship of adventurous Christians from nearly every communion in America, seeking a practical expression of equality before God in order to raise the standard of Christian brotherhood above every denominational barrier, and to win others into the brotherhood of Jesus Christ."

Ainslie was a prolific writer. His fifteen books focused primarily on Christian unity, world peace, biblical studies and the spiritual life. His titles include: *Religion in Daily Doings* (1903), *The Unfinished Task of the Reformation* (1910), *The Message of the Disciples for the Union of the Church* (Yale Lectures, 1913), *If Not a United Church — What?* (1920), *The Way of Prayer* (1924), and *The Scandal of Christianity* (1929).

Ainslie was given honorary degrees by Drake University (1911), Yale University (1914), and Bethany College (1914). In 1925 he married Mary Elizabeth Weisel, a Christian educator and dean of a Presbyterian girls' seminary in Baltimore. They had two children, Mary Elizabeth and Peter IV. This "flaming apostle of Christian Unity" died of cancer in Baltimore, February 23, 1934. When ecumenical leader John R. Mott addressed the first assembly of the World Council of Churches at Amsterdam in 1948, he included Peter Ainslie III as among the twelve apostles of the modern Ecumenical Movement.

See also Council on Christian Unity; Ecumenical Movement, The

PAUL A. CROW, JR.

BIBLIOGRAPHY Finis S. Idleman, *Peter Ainslie, Ambassador of Good Will* (1941).

Alberta Bible College

Alberta Bible College is a Canadian Bible college associated especially but not exclusively with the Christian Churches/Churches of Christ. Alberta Bible College was founded in 1932 in Lethbridge, Alberta. It was initially a project of the Central Church of Christ and its minister, Charles H. Phillips, who became the College's first principal and instructor. In a special 1932 edition of *The Alberta Christian,* a newsletter of the Alberta Christian Missionary Society, Phillips noted that "There is no question as to the need of such a college in this Northwestern division of our Dominion. We have the young people in our churches. We know of several who would avail themselves of intensive preparation of the various trained ministries of the churches were it possible."

The College was a child of hope for the Stone-Campbell Movement in the context of its growth with the settlement of the Canadian West, and the challenge of developing an indigenous Canadian leadership. Phillips had come originally from London, England, "utterly disgruntled," he once wrote, with the brand of Christianity that perpetuated unbearable inequalities between the clergy and the poor.

Students at first came mostly from Southern Alberta, but within a decade they came from all over Alberta, as well as the rest of Canada. In 1937, the college moved to Calgary, then a growing city of about 85,000, to its original campus on Centre Street. The College was also home for nearly two decades for the Tuxedo Park congregation, later Cambrian Heights Church of Christ and now Bow Valley Christian Church. In 1963 the College moved to a purpose-built facility at 599 Northmount Drive, and in 1997 to its current campus at 635 Northmount Drive. As of 2003, the school enrolled over 160 students from across Canada and several foreign countries. Striving to remain faithful to the Stone-Campbell ecumenical vision, students have represented twenty-seven different Christian traditions.

With the exception of World War II when the entire faculty, in addition to some students, had been called into military service, the College has enjoyed stable leadership. For the most part administration, faculty, and staff have been native Canadians, even though several received degrees from schools in the United States. Exposure to the broader currents of theological debate of the day ensured that the college did not remain an island. Deep tensions emerged, particularly over "open membership," but the institution and its supporting churches were for the most part spared the bitter division experienced by many of its counterparts in the United States. While the school's ideology was far from uniform, particularly in the 1960s, a magnanimous spirit triumphed, together with a feeling on the part of many that the controversies were foreign to Western Canada, if not the mission of the church. Alumni and alumnae have done further studies at Christian Theological Seminary, Cincinnati Bible Seminary, Emmanuel School of Religion, and Lincoln Christian Seminary, among others. The result has been that congregations both of the Christian Church (Disciples of Christ) and the Christian Churches/Churches of Christ in Canada and the United States have drawn, without interruption, graduates from Alberta Bible College. Graduates have also served in thirty-one foreign countries.

From its inception Alberta Bible College has sought to be a catalyst for unity in the Stone-Campbell tradition in Canada. In the 1960s the College hosted an annual, week-long "Minister's Institute" for leadership of all three streams of the Movement, "to promote fellowship and understanding" transcending the Movement's divisions. Conciliatory speakers such as W. Carl Ketcherside were introduced to the Canadian West through this and other special events. A consensus of openness and goodwill has continued to evolve, with the College providing much of the leadership. In 1990, the College initiated the Western Canadian Christian Convention, a convention that includes all three streams of the Stone-Campbell Movement. This, among other factors, has led to a growing interface with the

Churches of Christ. A number from the latter churches have graduated from Alberta Bible College and either serve in or minister to Christian Churches/Churches of Christ or Churches of Christ. The school hired its first instructor from the Churches of Christ in 1997. The College Board now includes people from all three streams of the Movement.

The "classical English Bible curriculum" remains the core of the College's ministerial training program, but as resources have allowed, other majors have been added. A unique emphasis of the academic program has been a heavy concentration on "practical experience." The College has entered an accreditation process with the Accrediting Association of Bible Colleges, and has an articulation agreement with the University of Lethbridge.

The College's sustainability and continuity have depended on the long-standing and sacrificial service of many faculty, staff, and trustees, a number whose service spanned a lifetime: E. E. Breckenridge (1932-1960); W. G. Chapman (1948-1998); James R. Chapman (b. 1949); Aileen Case (1958-1986); and Don Albert (1962-2003).

The College continues to influence the churches in Canada by providing indigenous Canadian leadership. Today its alumni and alumnae account for two-thirds of the leadership in congregations of the Christian Church (Disciples of Christ) and Christian Churches/Churches of Christ in Canada. Many other graduates provide the mainstay of leadership in churches and parachurch ministries both in and beyond the Stone-Campbell tradition. By virtue of this influence, Alberta Bible College serves as a focal point of identity and mission for the Stone-Campbell Movement in Canada.

See also Bible College Movement; Canada, The Movement in; Higher Education, Views of in the Movement

BIBLIOGRAPHY Douglas A. Barrie, *A History of the Christian Church and Christian Church (Disciples of Christ) in Alberta, Canada* (M.A. thesis, Lincoln Christian Seminary, 1975) • Boyd L. Lammiman, *Joy Comes in the Morning* (1992).

RONALD A. FRASER

All Canada Committee

See Canada, The Movement in

American Christian Bible Society

D. S. Burnet, James Challen, and J. J. Moses of Cincinnati published an address in early 1845 calling for the organization of the American Christian Bible Society. Burnet began to dream of a society in 1843 that would circulate the Bible to all parts of the world, with possibly Jerusalem as headquarters. The society was founded on January 27, 1845. The constitution declared that churches and individuals who contributed $100 had the right to appoint one director. This was the first of several Stone-Campbell organizations established before the decade was over, including a national convention, a missionary society, a Sunday School and tract society, and a publications society.

Opposition arose from the beginning from Alexander Campbell and other leaders in Bethany. They argued that it was better to work through the Baptist organization, the American and Foreign Bible Society (est. 1836), which split off from the American Bible Society founded in 1816. The founders of the American Christian Bible Society argued that very little support had been raised among the churches for the Baptist organization, and that Disciples of Christ could raise considerable funds for their own organization because of their attachment to the Bible. It was the hope of Burnet and others to bring out a new translation of the New Testament, perhaps a revision of Alexander Campbell's *The Living Oracles.*

Campbell, though in favor of cooperation, saw the Bible Society and the Publications Society as in competition with Bethany College and his own press efforts. Because of criticism, principally from Bethany, the Society was finally dissolved in 1856. Various Disciples were cooperative with the Baptist Bible Union's effort to bring out a new translation, but when it became clear that Baptist theology would prevail they pulled out. Now, however, the Disciples were without an organization to promote publishing a translation themselves.

See also Bible, Versions and Translations of the

BIBLIOGRAPHY Noel L. Keith, *The Story of D. S. Burnet: Undeserved Obscurity* (1954) • Cecil K. Thomas, *Alexander Campbell and His New Version* (1958).

THOMAS H. OLBRICHT

American Christian Missionary Society

The earliest missionary organization in the Stone-Campbell heritage. The American Christian Missionary Society (ACMS) was a defining work of the Stone-Campbell Movement. It was wrought in the midst of theological differences, fierce opposition, and broad vision. Alexander Campbell had criticized missionary societies in *The Christian Baptist* because they represented denominationalism, confusion, and pretension, and because they distracted people from the church and appeared to preempt the church's own missionary task. He opposed missionary societies not because they were missing from Scripture but because the church is the divinely instituted means of proclaiming the gospel and nothing should take its place.

Campbell wrote in the *Millennial Harbinger* of 1850 that from the very first volume of the *Christian Baptist* he had insisted that the church is the only missionary society. But to consider the missionary society as an instrumentality of the church, for which the church is represented in general convention by elected "messengers," proved to be a different story. The missionary society became a form of the church's presence and outreach, both practically and theologically. It fulfilled this ecclesiological role implicitly for Disciples of Christ until restructure made it explicit a century later.

On October 23, 1849, 156 delegates from eleven states gathered in Cincinnati to form the ACMS. Alexander Campbell was not present but was represented by W. K. Pendleton. The December 1849 edition of the *Millennial Harbinger* contains Campbell's regrets at having been denied the pleasure due to "an unusually severe indisposition" and his hearty endorsement, being "peculiarly gratified." In the *Memoirs of Alexander Campbell,* Robert Richardson says nothing about the organizing of the first convention in Cincinnati and the creation of the ACMS. However, he mentions that a year later, on starting a forty-day trip west with his daughter, Virginia, Campbell stopped in Cincinnati to attend "the anniversary of the Missionary Society." Richardson writes that through the decade until 1863 "he manifested his usual interest in the great subject of missions" and "was accustomed to meet with the ACMS as its president regularly every year, delivering addresses and urging increased liberality."

Alexander Campbell saw the need to give a kind of church structure to the growing movement of preachers and congregations for the "systematic cooperation of the churches for the conversion of the world," as discussed in 1834 in a general meeting called in Wellsburg, (West) Virginia. Meetings were held on a county-wide basis as early as 1829 in Mount Zion, Kentucky, and Barton W. Stone was present and preached for the first statewide meeting in 1839 in Indianapolis, Indiana. State conventions in Kentucky, Virginia, Illinois, and Missouri soon followed. Campbell led the way with a series of essays in the *Millennial Harbinger* of 1842-48 on cooperation and consensual agreement. In 1843, sixty-seven representatives from eight states held a meeting in Lexington to discuss church organization, and later representatives met in Steubenville, Ohio, and elsewhere. David S. Burnet took the lead. He was twenty-years younger than Campbell and had been involved already in the organization of a Bible society largely supported by Ohio Disciples. Burnet became one of the many persons who pushed for decisive discussion leading to the Convention that gave birth to the ACMS, where he served as one of four vice presidents.

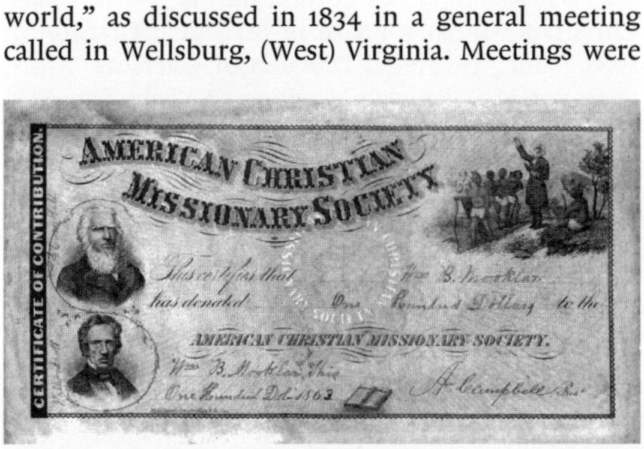

This contribution receipt signed by Alexander Campbell pictures Campbell and Walter Scott on the left and carries a stylized depiction of preaching to heathens in the upper right corner. Courtesy of the Disciples of Christ Historical Society

In Cincinnati, John T. Johnson of Kentucky made the resolution to start a society for world evangelization. Campbell had urged a delegate assembly to be representative of congregations and of the whole body, not just individuals. In addition to the call for world evangelism, the first convention encouraged every congregation to organize Sunday Schools, provide a catalog of books suitable for Sunday School use, encourage the starting of state and district meetings, urge care and examination in ordaining evangelists and ministers upon recommendation of two or more churches, and emphasize the need for the Lord's Day to be kept holy. Life membership was offered at $20 and life directorship at $100, with $10 for churches to have delegate privileges. Twenty vice presidents were named from fifteen states to give geographic breadth to the new movement.

Dr. James T. and Julia Barclay were the first missionaries. In their parlor in Washington, D.C., 1843, the congregation that became the Vermont Avenue Christian Church (and in 1930, the National City Christian Church) was organized. They went to Jerusalem (1851-61) with many supporters, believing that the Jews were to be converted before the return of Christ. The title of Campbell's journal clearly proclaimed the eschatology of the pre–Civil War religious temperament. In the *Millennial Harbinger* of 1841, he explains The Protestant Theory: "The Millennium, so far as the triumphs of Christianity is [sic] concerned, will be a state of greatly enlarged and continuous prosperity, in which the Lord will be exalted and his divine spirit enjoyed in an unprecedented measure. All the conditions of society will be vastly improved; wars shall cease, and peace and good will among men will generally abound. The Jews will be converted, and the fullness of the Gentiles will be brought into the kingdom of the Messiah."

The founding of the ACMS cannot be separated from the millennialist eschatology of the period or from the pragmatism that required a foreign dimension to keep pace with other denominations or to surpass them. D. S. Burnet's book *The Jerusalem Mission* and Dr. Barclay's book *The City of the Great King* illustrate the former, while speeches and articles by various leaders like Isaac Errett emphasize the latter. By the end of the century, eschatology remained strong but essentially in the interest of personal salvation and in the social expression of the coming kingdom of God.

The ACMS also sent J. O. Beardslee to Jamaica in 1858, having offered his services after already serving as a Congregationalist missionary. The society also commissioned Alexander Cross, a freedman, who arrived in Liberia with his family in 1854, only seven years after the founding of the country. Both of these efforts were short-lived, because Cross became ill and died, and funds ran out for Beardslee's support at the time of the Civil War. The Christian Woman's Board of Missions (CWBM) picked up the work later both in Jamaica and Liberia, and the Foreign Christian Missionary Society (FCMS) added other fields of mission in the 1880s.

In 1863, the ACMS renounced its neutrality with respect to the Civil War and supported the Union. This and other controversies, as well as the economic and social effect of the war, brought the organization to the brink of collapse in 1866, the year of Alexander Campbell's death. It recovered slowly under the leadership of W. K. Pendleton, president of Bethany College.

Through the years, the ACMS created standing committees and boards for service to the churches. In 1874, it helped to create the Christian Woman's Board of Missions and a planning committee for the Foreign Christian Missionary Society. In 1883, a Committee on Church Extension was named. A Board of Negro Education and Evangelization was formed in 1890, a Board of Temperance and Social Service in 1907, and a Board of Education in 1894. When the name of the society was chosen, the ACMS explicitly stated that "the missionary cause is one," and there was no distinction of home and foreign enterprise.

Opposition to ACMS actually led to the change of the name in 1869 to General Christian Missionary Convention and back again in 1895. In later years, the ACMS served mainly as a home mission agency helping to start half of the congregations by 1900. Archibald McLean's *Missionary Addresses* tells of the ACMS work among the Cherokees, the evangelization and education of former slaves and their children, aid to churches in Philadelphia, Buffalo, and Chicago, and workers supported in Maine and Canada. He writes of sixty-one cities helped, as well as about organizational work in ten states for expenditure from 1849 to 1894 of over $1 million. By 1895, its Church Extension Fund had helped build 230 churches in thirty-four states and territories, and it continues to exist now as the Board of Church Extension of the Christian Church (Disciples of Christ) in the United States and Canada. This board started a Spanish-speaking congregation in San Antonio, Texas, in 1897 and a Mexican Christian Institute in 1913 that exists today as the Samuel Guy Inman Center.

The ACMS became a founding member of the United Christian Missionary Society (UCMS) with five other boards and societies after the First World War, with ACMS president Frederick W. Burnham named president of the new UCMS. The ACMS and the other missionary societies it helped found (CWBM and FCMS) continued as the United Society from 1920 until 1973. Two units of the Christian Church (Disciples of Christ) have resulted from this institution, namely the Division of Overseas Ministries (DOM) and the Division of Homeland Ministries (DHM). The missionary undertakings of ACMS and the other early societies are everyday concerns of DHM and DOM (through the Common Global Ministries Board founded in 1996 with the United Church of Christ). The legacies of the nineteenth-century ACMS are therefore legion.

A small board of UCMS trustees manages the collective financial legacy of ACMS and the other missionary societies, approximately $40 million, and the Christian Church Foundation, another unit of the church, has been contracted for treasury services since 1993. Every year the ACMS and the other predecessor bodies are called into session, a board and officers elected, minutes recorded, and any business undertaken if necessary at the request of DOM and DHM. The one-hundred-and-fiftieth anniversary of the ACMS was commemorated at the 1999 General Assembly of the Christian Church (Disciples of Christ) in Cincinnati, signaling that its heritage of cooperative mission continues into the twenty-first century.

See also Barclay, James Turner; Burnet, David Staats; Christian Woman's Board of Missions; Division of Homeland Ministries; Division of Overseas Ministries; Foreign Christian Missionary Society, The; Missions, Missiology; United Christian Missionary Society, The

BIBLIOGRAPHY Paul M. Blowers, "'Living in a Land of Prophets': James T. Barclay and an Early Disciples of Christ Mission to Jews in the Holy Land," *Church History* 62 (1992): 494-513, reprinted in *The Stone-Campbell Movement: An International Religious Tradition,* ed. Michael Casey and Douglas A. Foster (2002), pp. 271-91 • D. S. Burnet, *The Jerusalem Mission under the Direction of the American Christian Missionary Society* (1853) • Alexander Campbell, ed., "The Coming of the Lord," *Millennial Harbinger* 5:1 (January 1841): 9 • William J. Nottingham, "Origin and Legacy of the Common Global Ministries Board," *Discipliana* 58 (1998): 80-96.

WILLIAM J. NOTTINGHAM

American Christian Publication Society

See Burnet, David Staats

American Christian Review

The *American Christian Review* was founded in 1856 by Benjamin Franklin (1812-1878), who maintained editorship until his death in 1878. John F. Rowe (1827-1897) continued as editor immediately after Franklin's demise. On the day of his death Franklin was still writing for the *Review.* Begun as a monthly paper, within two years it was published as a weekly and continued as such during his lifetime. The *Review* maintained the strong imprint of Franklin's biblical convictions, and he considered the *Review* his greatest achievement in striving for the apostolic faith against "human innovations" and denominationalism. Soon known as the "Old Reliable," it was the most influential conservative paper in the North during its existence. The masthead accurately reflected Franklin's intent: "Devoted to the Defense, Maintenance and Propagation of Christianity, Religious News and General Intelligence." Various other well-known preachers associated at one time or another with the *Review* included Elijah Goodwin, Moses Lard, C. L. Loos, John Rogers, Daniel Sommer, and, in the beginning years, Isaac Errett.

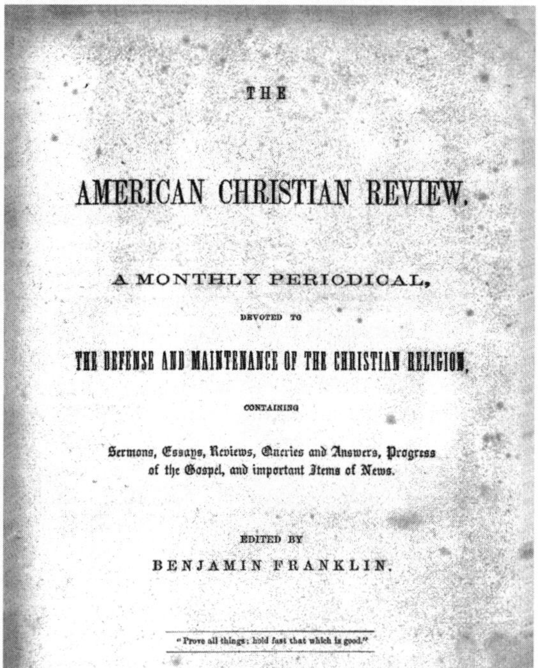
THE

AMERICAN CHRISTIAN REVIEW.

A MONTHLY PERIODICAL,

DEVOTED TO

THE DEFENSE AND MAINTENANCE OF THE CHRISTIAN RELIGION,

CONTAINING

Sermons, Essays, Reviews, Queries and Answers, Progress of the Gospel, and important Items of News.

EDITED BY

BENJAMIN FRANKLIN.

"Prove all things: hold fast that which is good."

CINCINNATI:

PUBLISHED BY BENJAMIN FRANKLIN

No. 60, WEST FOURTH STREET,

1856.

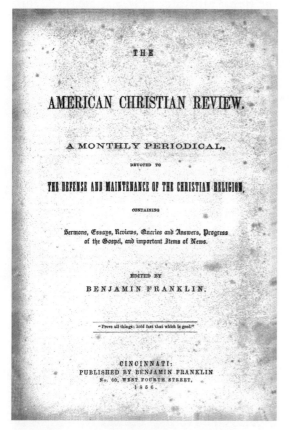

The *American Christian Review* gave Benjamin Franklin a powerful forum for promoting his religious ideas. The paper served as the voice of conservatism in the Northern United States after the Civil War. Courtesy of the Disciples of Christ Historical Society

Published from Cincinnati, Ohio, the *Review* was influential in the South before the Civil War. With a weekly issue of 8,500 copies in 1860, there were up to 1,000 Southern subscribers. The *Review* continued publication during the war, maintaining a constant position of neutrality. The *Review's* neutrality angered many readers on both sides of the conflict, yet earned Franklin a healing influence in the South after the war that other Northern editors did not have. The *American Christian Review* was the only paper to consistently receive favorable press in the pages of the Southern-based *Gospel Advocate.* Nevertheless, after the war the *Review* was primarily a Northern paper.

In content and outlook, the *Review* suited a pioneer rural population growing in appreciation of education and New Testament Christianity. It appealed to those in the Stone-Campbell Movement who considered biblical silence as absolutely prohibitive in determining faith and practice. The *Review* consistently encouraged educational institutions and education in general. While the *Review* initially supported the American Christian Missionary Society, it was firmly against the organization by 1867. It was also against instrumental music in the church assembly and all other "innovations" not directly enjoined by the New Testament. Though Franklin was personally against slavery, the paper took a neutral stance on the subject, arguing that Jesus neither affirmed nor condemned the practice.

A call back to the plain words of the Bible and apostolic Christianity was the raison d'être of the *American Christian Review.* There is a similar polemical tone between the *Review* and Alexander Campbell's *Christian Baptist* of earlier years. The portrayal is unfair as an overgeneralization, however, since there were numerous exceptions, which can be seen by referring to the journal itself. In a growing country where reading material was scarce, the conservative influence of the *American Christian Review* can hardly be overestimated. As time went on, this conservatism received considerable opposition, and in 1866 the *Christian Standard,* with Isaac Errett as editor, was founded as a direct response to counter the perceived lack of engagement with culture and ultra conservatism of the *Review.*

Some of the issues discussed within the pages of the *Review* included open communion, Sunday Schools, Universalism, the Christian's relation to civil government, cooperation between churches, and financial support of preachers, to list only a few.

The *Review* also contained short items of general world news, information on debates, books of interest, and other topics. While the *Review* leaned toward exclusivism and was against working with other religious bodies at that time, it did print favorable news about the work of the American Bible Society and other such efforts.

Although Franklin rarely mentioned the business aspect of running an editorial enterprise, financing a religious paper was a strain on monetary resources. One solution was to accept advertisements from various sources. Back pages abound with patent medicines, cures for opium and morphine addiction, firearms, musical instruments, clothes, tea sets, and many other items for sale. Occasionally bringing about negative responses from readers, this practice was discontinued by Daniel Sommer (1850-1940) after he became editor of the paper, changing its name to the *Octographic Review* in 1887.

After Franklin's death in 1878, Daniel Sommer, who owned and published a religious paper named *The Octograph,* took up the ownership and eventual editorship of the *American Christian Review.* The name was changed to the *Octographic Review* after eliminating all secular advertising. Daniel Sommer and his publication were against pacifism, Bible colleges, and any human addition to what he understood as original Christianity revealed in the New Testament. He understood the local church to be God's redemptive agent in the world and was against any other organization that sought to do either the work of the church or assist in that work. He was considered a conservative among conservatives.

Throughout its history, the *American Christian Review* lived under various names. Benjamin Franklin's original title, *American Christian Review,* endured from 1856 to 1887. Under Daniel Sommer, who regarded the name "American" as too political and unfitting for a paper devoted to another realm, the title was changed to the *Octographic Review* (suggesting eight writers of the New Testament) from 1887 to 1913. Sommer later felt this title was too ungainly and changed it again to the *Apostolic Review* from 1914 to 1939. After Daniel Sommer's death, his heirs published the paper under the original name of the *American Christian Review* from 1940 to 1965. The *Review* ceased publication in 1965 after influencing the more conservative portion of the Stone-Campbell Movement during almost 110 years of continuous publication.

See also *Christian Standard;* Errett, Isaac; Franklin, Benjamin; Goodwin, Elijah; *Gospel Advocate, The;* Lard, Moses E.; Loos, Charles Louis; Rogers, John

BIBLIOGRAPHY Joseph Franklin and J. A. Headington, *The Life and Times of Benjamin Franklin* (1879) • William E. Wallace, *Daniel Sommer, 1850-1940: A Biography* (1969) • Earl Irvin West, *Elder Ben Franklin: Eye of the Storm* (1983).

DAVID L. LITTLE

Ames, Edward Scribner (1870-1958)

Minister of the University Church of the Disciples, professor of philosophy at the University of Chicago, and dean of the Disciples Divinity House.

Ames was the son of a Disciples minister who served churches in Iowa and Illinois. He received degrees from Drake University, Yale University, and the University of Chicago, lecturing in the Department of Philosophy at the latter after receiving his Ph.D. in 1895. In 1897 he became professor of philosophy and education at Butler University.

In 1900 Ames returned to Chicago to begin a forty-year ministry at the Hyde Park (later University) Church across the street from the University of Chicago. The same year he began a thirty-five-year career in the Philosophy Department of the university. He had been particularly influenced in his studies by the works of John Locke (1632-1704), William James (1842-1910), and John Dewey (1859-1952), who was on the Philosophy Department faculty. Ames used the tools of philosophy to refine his Christian faith. In the development of his faith, he employed both higher criticism and the principles of empiricism and pragmatism.

A staunch Disciple, Ames accepted Alexander Campbell's belief that followers of Jesus Christ base their faith on the authority of the Scriptures rather than on the authority of creeds, dogmas, and doctrines. He clarified his personal faith by the new social sciences of the twentieth century. Ames believed that the central doctrine of the New Testament was the Messiahship of Jesus and that the only article of faith was the acceptance of that doctrine with absolute loyalty. Ames's implementation of this "doctrine and article of faith" — which did not require immersion — involved him in the "open membership" controversy in the early 1900s. He also believed that salvation is an ethical life process, fulfilling the natural powers of the soul. He believed that God is still creating and that humanity is an agent of God's creation.

As preacher and pastor, Ames focused on the application of Jesus' teachings to the daily lives of people. He was a strong advocate of the social gospel and of both local and world missions, because he believed it was the duty of all Christians to share their spiritual truth with their neighbors, near and far.

Ames's third vocation was with the Disciples Divinity House of the University of Chicago, established in 1894 and affiliated with the university's Divinity School. In 1900 he became a member of the Board of Trustees, and he was chosen dean in 1927.

Ames retired from his three vocations at five-year

intervals: 1935 from the university, 1940 from the pulpit, and 1945 from the Disciples Divinity House. His books include *The Psychology of Religious Experience* (1910), *The Higher Individualism* (1915), *The New Orthodoxy* (1918), *Religion* (1929), *Letters to God and the Devil* (1933), and his autobiography, *Beyond Theology* (1959).

See also Disciples Divinity House; Liberalism; Open Membership; Theology — Twentieth Century, Disciples of Christ J. ROBERT MOFFETT

BIBLIOGRAPHY Van Meter Ames, ed., *Beyond Theology: The Autobiography of Edward Scribner Ames* (1959).

Andrews, Sarah Shepherd (1893-1961)

Missionary from Churches of Christ to Japan from 1916 until her death September 16, 1961.

The daughter of Will Andrews of Dickson, Tennessee, Andrews was inspired by the work of J. M. McCaleb (1861-1953) to move to Japan. She established at least eight Japanese congregations, including those in Okitsu, Shizuoka, Shemeza, and Numazu. During World War II, despite imprisonment, house arrest, illness, and malnutrition, she continued to care for the poor, sick, and wounded. After the war she opened a home for Japanese widows and encouraged young Japanese men to seek education in the United States, leading to the beginnings of the Japanese Churches of Christ in America. She is buried in Numazu.

See also Asia, Missions in; McCaleb, John Moody

Andrews' grave marker was erected by both Christians and non-Christians. The epitaph in Japanese says in part: "She dedicated her whole life to her beloved Japan and Japanese people. She taught and trained many believers in Jesus Christ and gave all the glory to God. When she knew it was her time to leave, she recited Psalm 103 for hours, which moved those attending her deathbed to tears."
Courtesy of Motoyuki Nomura

BIBLIOGRAPHY Charles W. Doyle, "Sarah Andrews Succumbs to Stroke," *Firm Foundation* 78 (Oct. 3, 1961): 637 • Cindy Novak, "Anxious for Nothing: Sarah Andrews," *20th Century Christian* 45 (June 1983): 29 • Helen Young, "Sarah Andrews: She Dreamed a Dream for Japan," *20th Century Christian* 56 (Nov. 1993): 7-9.

BONNIE MILLER

Anthropology

Christian doctrine of the nature of the human being created by God and placed in a conscious, communicative relationship with God and fellow human beings.

Historically, the scriptural terms "heart, soul, mind, and strength," or "body, soul, and spirit" have been sufficiently vague to allow for diverse interpretations of human nature. Christian anthropology differs from physiology and psychology, however, in its determination to understand human "nature" in the context of the fall of humanity through sin and of human redemption, restoration, and transformation.

In the Stone-Campbell Movement, responses to questions of anthropology have more often been assumed than articulated directly or formally. When addressed, whether directly or indirectly, the views of Barton Stone, Thomas and Alexander Campbell, Walter Scott, and their associates reflected a profound philosophical debt to the British Empiricist John Locke and to Scottish Common Sense Realism. Generally speaking, the early standard-bearers of the Stone-Campbell Movement presupposed the Enlightenment doctrine of the autonomous and self-reflecting transcendental self. In their thinking, the human self might well be influenced by the environmental legacy of sin, but it was hardly "totally depraved" and, once redeemed, could still enjoy the endowments of the tarnished "image of God" (Gen. 1:26).

This view of the self relied on the Cartesian concept of the human being as essentially an *ens cogitans,* a "thinking thing" that can operate independently of the body. It also assumed that the human being is autonomous — that is, an entity independent from not only its own body but also from other "thinking things." As an independent subject, moreover, the self is autonomous from objects in the material world, a remoteness considered to be "objective" since presumably it was removed from the influences of the material world and from the passions and emotions of the physical body. Since the senses are bodily, they are themselves remote from the true self, the *ens cogitans,* and must therefore be reconnected to it so that the self can acquire knowledge. John Locke and his heirs in the Empiricist tradition provided early Stone-Campbell thinkers with sufficient philosophical assurance of the reliability of the senses.

Scottish Common Sense Realism meanwhile was the primary source for their understanding of the precise mental faculties and processes themselves. Accordingly, the human being is initially a virtual *tabula rasa* ("blank slate," Locke's phrase) and shaped by environment and education, but each person has the very same natural powers of reason and judgment to perceive and process truth. This principle proved crucial to Stone-Campbell hermeneutics well into the twentieth century, boosting confidence in the prospect of uniting Christians on a common interpretation of the Bible. Indeed, anthropological and hermeneutical insights developed in tandem in the Movement. Scripture was understood to consist of "facts," atomistic propositions authored by God and perfectly suited to human perception and comprehension.

The makings of a theological anthropology can be found in Alexander Campbell and Walter Scott. Campbell wrote a long series in the *Christian Baptist* (1828-30) on humanity in its primitive state and under the various dispensations; he revisited the issue briefly in *The Christian System* (1835). Scott likewise developed the theme at length in *The Gospel Restored* (1836), distinguishing humanity in the "natural" state, the "preternatural" state, and the state of "respite." In the second generation of the Movement, Robert Milligan resumed the subject in his major work *The Scheme of Redemption* (1868).

"Primitive man" before the fall was established in a regal dignity in the creation, with body, soul, and spirit being a microcosm of the larger earthly, animal, and spiritual realms. This natural state was marked by original innocence, immortality (so long as no sin was committed), righteousness, the pure rule of reason over the passions, and the direct knowledge of God. By contrast, the "preternatural" state of humanity after the fall was characterized by the loss of immortality and attendant guilt, misery, cowardice, shame, estrangement, and the dethroning of reason. Yet humanity retained freedom of the will, despite the abuse of that freedom. In the state of "respite," originating in God's remedial mercy, God introduced an economy of redemption from this subnatural state, in which faith (as opposed to the direct knowledge of God, now lost) became humanity's only means of encountering God under the Patriarchal, Jewish (Mosaic), and Christian dispensations.

Barton Stone and the two Campbells described the effects of sin in severe terms, but skirted the more severe language of high Calvinism. Stone and Thomas Campbell retained the term "depravity," but not *total* depravity, while Alexander Campbell spoke of a "sin of nature," but not *original* sin. Robert Milligan spoke of "total depravity," but only in terms of personal (actual) sin, not an inherited Adamic guilt. Humanity's constitutive capacity for good, the "moral" nature, had undoubtedly been stunted by the fall. Alexander Campbell went so far as to suggest in his debate with Nathan Rice that infants were in need of the same grace of regeneration as adults because the human race was implicated in the sin of its progenitor Adam. Yet Stone, the Campbells, Scott, and others refused to espouse the idea that Adam's posterity actually inherited Adam's own guilt, or that a supernatural *tour de force* of divine grace was necessary over and above the human will to enable it to turn to God and receive redemption and regeneration. Alexander Campbell said that the image of God was "lost" in the fall, but went on to clarify that what was really lost was "the correct idea of God's image" and conformity thereto. Humanity after the fall never lost "the susceptibility of being restored to the image of God."

Revivifying the image of God and overcoming fallenness was, in the divine economy, a matter of engaging human free will and the natural faculties, not of overriding them. Though depraved, Barton Stone argued, fallen human beings were still capacitated moral agents (a view for which Stone was frequently branded a "Pelagian" by his opponents). Alexander Campbell declared in 1838 that "that view is more honorable to the grace of God which relieves me by my own faculties and affections . . . my whole intellectual and moral nature." Robert Milligan, countering the philosophical query of why God had created human beings who could fall from perfection, resorted to the theory, at least as old as Irenaeus of Lyons in the second century, that the human experience of real freedom, despite its consequences, was still ultimately for the *greater good* of humankind.

In time, the Movement drifted from the Reformed language of depravity that the early leaders had used in modified form and began accentuating the grace inherent in human free will. Church of Christ theologian Ronald Highfield has signaled this change in David Walk (1833-1908), a Kentucky pastor who argued as the "apostolic hypothesis," confuting Calvinistic orthodoxy, that humanity only inherited mortality from Adam, not his actual sin and guilt. Each human being, prior to sinning, stood in the same condition morally as Adam before the fall. In this perspective infants did not have the taint of sin whatsoever. Sin itself was existential, realized in actions, not an infection in human nature. Highfield notes that such a view has strongly influenced anthropology in the tradition of Churches of Christ, but in truth, this more humanistic, "quasi-Pelagian" thinking in time took root in all three streams of the Stone-Campbell tradition and still finds wide expression. It suited well the Movement's traditional Common Sense hermeneutic and its epistemological assumptions about the reasonableness of human beings and their universal ability to respond positively to the gospel. It was, moreover, the logical outcome of the Movement's larger rejection of scholastic Calvinism.

Into the late nineteenth and early twentieth centuries, another factor shaping the Movement's anthropology was the interplay of Protestant millennialism and the secular progressivism born of an explosion in the natural and social sciences. Alexander Campbell had openly repudiated what he considered the pseudo-science of phrenology (a movement claiming the ability to measure human intelligence by brain/skull size), with its assertions that human beings were progressively growing ever better and more intelligent, and that the biblical view of the fall and human development was erroneous. "No man that truly (that is, rationally) believes the gospel," Campbell argued in 1852, "fears any thing in the name of science, learning or wisdom, whether called phrenology, pneumatology, psychology or physico-theology." Campbell's generation and conservatives in succeeding generations still considered the Bible the true source of knowledge for the nature and destiny of humankind.

Even moderates like J. H. Garrison, who delivered a paper on "Biblical Anthropology" to the Disciples' World Congress in 1893, insisted that scriptural insight into the divine image in humanity's intellectual, moral, and volitional nature far excelled "material science" with its consideration of the human species as a "splendid animal" and "marvelous organism." By the turn of the twentieth century, however, liberal Disciples were enthusiastically embracing the "hard sciences" of psychology and sociology. Edward Scribner Ames of the University of Chicago composed *The Psychology of Religious Experience* (1910) as a deliberate attempt to analyze the *homo religiosus* from the standpoint of secular anthropology and the history of religions, and with a view to rendering "such topics as inspiration, faith, knowledge, the nature of the soul, personality, religious genius, and the significance of such conceptions as God, free will, the world, evil" transparent to underlying "psychological processes." Ames's work reflected a profound sense of "progress" in civilization and human science, a welcoming of the evolutionary paradigm in the study of human culture and religion, and confidence that all sciences (especially those of psychology and religion) would contribute to the amelioration of society. Liberals often interpreted "sin" more as a social evil than as a personal crime against the holy God, and wholly abandoned the notion of innate depravity as a vestige of outworn orthodoxies.

Conservatives in the Movement continued to have little use for considering anthropological questions for their own sake, dealing with them chiefly as subsidiary to the "plan of salvation." Occasionally they reacted to what they perceived as extravagant science divorced from the biblical witness. David Lipscomb, for example, praised some of the discoveries of evolution, to the extent that they merely demonstrated the orderly unfolding of the wise Creator's plan. Yet Lipscomb and many others in Churches of Christ and conservative Disciples churches repudiated the Darwinist alternative to the biblical account of human origins. Conservatives in the Stone-Campbell churches, like those in fundamentalist and evangelical denominations, grew suspicious in the twentieth century of the "psychologizing" of sin and the reduction of salvation to "self-actualization."

Stone-Campbell conservatives, however, were vulnerable in this regard because their tradition had never viewed human beings as originally sinful or totally depraved. Frederick Kershner, a Disciples scholar in the mid-twentieth century, reflected the dilemma. In his *Religion of Christ* (1911), Kershner, a moderate conservative, manifested the optimistic progressivism of a pre–World War culture, praising the growth of pacifism, greater benevolence, the high moral caliber among political leaders, etc. But by the rise of the Third Reich, Kershner was striking a decidedly different tone, one openly sympathetic to neo-orthodox thinkers like Karl Barth who confronted the specter of a horrific human evil emerging in Europe by calling the church to rediscover the Word of the gracious God standing both in radical judgment of, and partnership with, humankind. Of similar sympathy was Kershner's younger contemporary, the British Disciples theologian William Robinson, who insisted that true humanity, which *is* Jesus Christ, was embodied in the church itself insofar as the church modeled that fellowship of persons, divine and human, that is the "hidden structure of reality."

Since World War II, conservatives as well as liberals in the Movement have left open the door to the anthropological perspectives of the social sciences. Ronald Highfield has observed that Churches of Christ have in recent decades unwittingly absorbed much of personality development theory and "existential psychology." The curriculum of many a Bible college of the Christian Churches/Churches of Christ, moreover, has adopted courses in psychology, sociology, and other social sciences. Pastoral theology and practice in all three streams of the Movement has also revealed the influence of psychology and psychotherapy, particularly in the context of pastoral care and counseling. Disciples pastoral theologians like Charles Kemp (late professor at Brite Divinity School) and Don Browning (University of Chicago) have been pioneers in a theologically critical appropriation of psychological theories in the practice of ministry.

Theological anthropology in the three streams of

the Stone-Campbell Movement has built on the consensus of the Movement's early leadership while adapting to changing contexts. The language of the depravity of human nature is no longer widely used, as sin has been interpreted in existential terms as "falling short" of the glory of God (Rom. 3:23). A strong emphasis on free will, moral responsibility, and cooperation of all the human faculties with divine grace in the realization of salvation has remained characteristic. Ronald Highfield has challenged conservative streams of the Movement to overcome their habitual preoccupation with the immortality of the soul rather than the resurrection of the body, and to understand salvation more in terms of the fullness of "true humanity" modeled in Jesus Christ, a theme also echoed in the work of Disciples theologian Joe R. Jones. Disciples anthropology of late has focused much attention on the social manifestation of human injustice — "sin" as reflected in racism, sexism, classism, etc. — though the challenge here, as Disciples theologians like Clark Williamson and Joe Jones have shown, is to continue to treat these aberrations not simply as social evils but as symptoms of a deeper crisis in the human condition and of an arrogant affront to the gracious God.

See also Creation and Evolution; Hermeneutics; Reason, Place of

BIBLIOGRAPHY Edward Scribner Ames, *The Psychology of Religious Experience* (1910) • Alexander Campbell, "Essays on Man in His Primitive State, and under the Patriarchal, Jewish and Christian Dispensations," nos. 1-16, *Christian Baptist* (1828-30): 463-64, 470-71, 484-85, 494-95, 503-5, 511-12, 521-22, 542-43, 559-60, 574-76, 589-90, 633-34, 637-39, 646-49, 654-56, 656-58 • Alexander Campbell, *The Christian System* (1835) • Alexander Campbell, *Popular Lectures and Addresses* (1886) • Thomas Campbell, "The Disease, the Cure, and the Means of Enjoying It," *Millennial Harbinger* (1847): 661-75 • A. T. DeGroot, *Disciple Thought: A History* (1965), pp. 67-72 • J. H. Garrison, "Biblical Anthropology, the Key to Some Religious Problems," in *Addresses Delivered at the World's Congress* (1893), pp. 81-93 • Ronald Highfield, "Theological Anthropology in the Restoration Movement," *Leaven* 8 (July 1, 2000): 139-43 • Joe R. Jones, "Human Being as Created and Sinful," chap. 6 in *A Grammar of Christian Faith: Systematic Explorations in Christian Life and Doctrine* (2002), vol. 1, pp. 293-364 • David Lipscomb, "Evolution and the Bible," in *Salvation from Sin* (1913), pp. 347-64 • Aylette Raines, "Sin and Its Cure," in *New Testament Christianity*, ed. Z. T. Sweeney (1923), vol. 1, pp. 307-39 • Walter Scott, *The Gospel Restored* (1836) • Barton W Stone et al., *An Abstract of an Apology, for Renouncing the Jurisdiction of the Synod of Kentucky, Being a Compendious View of the Gospel and a Few Remarks on the Confession of Faith* (1804).

PAUL M. BLOWERS *and* WILLIAM KOOI

Armstrong, J. N.

See Harding University

Asia, Missions in

1. Introduction
2. Beginnings
3. Division
4. Another Division
5. Expansion
6. Status Report
   6.1. Churches and Membership
   6.2. Ministries
7. Trends

1. Introduction

Since its beginnings in Asia in 1882, the Stone-Campbell Movement has grown to include thousands of churches and tens of thousands of members from Pakistan and India on the west to Japan and Korea on the east, and from China and Mongolia on the north to Indonesia and the Philippines on the south. This growth resulted from the labors of missionaries sent from Stone-Campbell churches in the United States, Canada, England, Australia, and New Zealand. This growth took place in the midst of controversy that at times threatened to destroy the Movement from within. Indeed, the current divisions in the Stone-Campbell Movement, especially as exemplified in the United States, arose in part due to events that occurred in Asian missions.

2. Beginnings

In 1874 and 1875 the Stone-Campbell Movement in the United States organized respectively the Christian Woman's Board of Missions (CWBM) and the Foreign Christian Missionary Society (FCMS). The purpose of the former was to pursue both home and foreign missions, while the purpose of the latter was to carry the Movement's message to lands outside the United States. Unfortunately, initial forays into foreign mission work by the two organizations were largely unsuccessful.

The tide began to turn, however, when in 1881 both the CWBM and the FCMS focused their attention on Asia, agreeing to send missionaries to India. In 1882, G. L. Wharton (1847-1906) of the FCMS arrived in India. Four single women from the CWBM accompanied him. They were Mary Graybiel (1846-1905), Ada Boyd, Mary Kingsbury, and Laura Kinsey. Eventually they settled in the central part of India, beginning works in Ellichpur, Harda, Mungeli, and Bilaspur. In 1891 Wharton traveled to Australia, where he recruited Mary Thompson to come to India and work in the FCMS mission.

After the beginning in India, missionaries from

Dr. William E. Macklin of Canada (right) went to China as a missionary in 1886. Both a preacher and a physician, he founded the Drum Tower Hospital in Nanking. He is pictured in 1924 with the first convert that he baptized, Shi Kwei-biao. Mr. Shi, who was an opium addict prior to his conversion, was a preacher for more than thirty years.
Courtesy of the Disciples of Christ Historical Society

the FCMS quickly entered other Asian countries. Charles E. (1853-1898) and Laura (1861-1925) Garst and George T. (1843-1920) and Josephine (1850-1885) Smith went to Japan in 1883. They first studied language in Yokohama, then started a work in Akita near the northern tip of the island of Honshu. Josephine Smith became ill in the first months in Japan and died in Akita in 1885, where she and their baby daughter were buried. In 1886, W. E. Macklin, M.D., after spending a short time in Japan, traveled to Shanghai, China. Dr. Macklin then moved to Nanking, where in 1893 he built a hospital. In 1901, W. H. Hanna (1872-1948) and his wife went to the Philippines as Disciples missionaries, beginning their work in Manila. There they gathered an English-speaking congregation while studying Spanish. When Mr. and Mrs. Hermon P. Williams (1872-1958) arrived later that year, they gathered a Spanish-speaking congregation. Since Manila was already receiving considerable attention from other missionaries, the Hannas and the Williams decided to go to northern Luzon, and moved to Laoag.

Also in 1901, W. D. Cunningham (1864-1936) and his wife went to Japan to serve as independent missionaries. He had earlier been rejected for missionary service with the FCMS due to health problems. They acquired the Yotsuya Mission begun by Alice Miller, Lucia Scott, and Carmie Hostetter eleven years earlier and built the mission into one of the most successful of all pre–World War II efforts.

In 1902 the FCMS appointed Susie C. Rijnhart, M.D. (1868-1908), to return to Tibet to resume her mission work in that country. Dr. Rijnhart had already served in Tibet but had returned to North America after her husband had been killed. Two years later, in 1904, Dr. Albert Shelton (1875-1920), famed missionary doctor of the Stone-Campbell Movement, arrived to serve in Tibet until his brutal murder at the hands of robbers in 1920.

Indeed, between 1875 and 1919, over 370 different persons (including husbands and wives) served under the auspices of the FCMS and CWBM in the Asian countries of China, India, Japan, Tibet, and the Philippines.

During this same time, Stone-Campbell churches in other English-speaking nations also sent missionaries to Asia. In 1885 A. F. H. Saw and E. P. Hearndon left England to work with Dr. W. E. Macklin in China. In 1892 John Cook of the British Churches of Christ went to work among the Mon in Burma (Myanmar). Three other men accompanied him: Robert Halliday, Alfred E. Hudson, and William Forrester. Hudson did not stay in Burma but soon crossed over the border into Siam (Thailand) to make contact with the Mon living in Thailand. In 1903 Percy Clark joined Hudson in Thailand in a second mission field of service for the British Churches of Christ.

From the Stone-Campbell Movement in Australia during this time, Robert Middleton went to serve with the China Inland Mission. In 1889, Henry H. Stratton went to India. Two years later, in 1901, Rosa Tonkin went to China to work with the FCMS. In 1909, G. P. Pittman assisted the British Churches of Christ in taking over a Methodist mission in India.

3. Division

The Stone-Campbell Movement came into existence as a unity movement so that the world might believe in Jesus Christ (John 17:21). Ironically, the first crack in the Movement's own unity emerged over missions, specifically over how and how not to support missionaries.

When the American Christian Missionary Society was established in the United States in 1849, there was opposition within the Stone-Campbell Movement to using societies and other parachurch organizations to do the work of evangelism and benevolence. Over the next fifty years this opposition grew, becoming even more intense after the establishment of the Foreign Christian Missionary Society and the Christian Woman's Board of Missions. Four main ob-

Mission volunteers who arrived in Japan April 10, 1892. Left to right: Lucia Scott, Carmie Hostetter, Wilson Kendrick Azbill, Joan McCaleb, and John Moody McCaleb. The team would soon part ways over whether to receive funds from pro-missionary society churches.
Courtesy of the Disciples of Christ Historical Society

jections were raised: (1) such organizations were human innovations; (2) the church and not societies was God's ordained method for evangelism and benevolence; (3) the method that the societies used in raising funds was unscriptural; and (4) since it was the introduction of societies that was causing division, such organizations were heretical and schismatic, dividing the Movement into pro- and anti-society parties.

Those in favor of the societies countered by saying that (1) the church (i.e., the brotherhood of churches) has the freedom to organize and use "expediencies" (e.g., mission societies) in order to obey the Great Commission (Matt. 28:18-20), and (2) the accomplishments of the societies in actually sending out missionaries justified using such parachurch organizations. In short, it was better to use freedom to do something than to object and do nothing.

One result of this controversy was that many churches and prominent individuals in the Stone-Campbell Movement in the United States refused to give money to the societies for foreign mission work.

By the 1890s the situation had deteriorated so badly that Wilson Kendrick Azbill (1848-1929), a former fundraiser for the FCMS, decided that a new approach in supporting missions was needed. Azbill proposed that his new approach begin by sending a team of mission volunteers to Japan. To support this team Azbill announced he would raise funds from churches that were opposed to the missionary societies. These funds would go directly from the churches to the team members and not be channeled first through any parachurch organization. In this way many individuals and churches that found mission societies objectionable could conscientiously support missionaries in proclaiming the gospel around the world.

Initial response to Azbill's proposal was good, many praising it as one around which all parties in the controversy could unite. Azbill was able to raise funds and in February 1892 led a team of six volunteers to Japan to serve independently of any missionary society. In the team were two couples, Mr. and Mrs. J. M. McCaleb and Mr. and Mrs. L. L. Lindsey, and two single women, Lucia Scott and Carmie Hostetter.

Eugenese Snodgrass, missionary with the FCMS, met the Azbill team upon arrival in Japan. Snodgrass informed them that his association with the FCMS was being terminated due to a disagreement over policy. Under the influence of Azbill, however, Snodgrass decided to remain in Japan as an independent missionary. In return Azbill promised to secure funding for Snodgrass from churches in the United States.

Azbill returned to the United States in August 1892 to raise funds for his volunteers. However, he found the task more difficult than he had anticipated. Many churches that opposed the missionary societies were not as willing to support missions as he once supposed. Consequently he turned to pro-society churches as a new source of funding.

When Azbill began to receive funds from pro-society sources, J. M. McCaleb objected and withdrew in 1893 to work independently of Azbill's team of volunteers. Moreover, in 1894 Eugene Snodgrass returned to the United States and assumed the role of mission editor of the *Gospel Advocate,* a Stone-Campbell journal opposed to missionary societies. In his first article in the *Gospel Advocate,* printed in 1895, Snodgrass listed twenty-one missionaries supported by local congregations, many of whom were serving in Japan and China. Wilson Kendrick Azbill and his wife were included in the list.

In 1906 the U.S. Religious Census recognized the division of the Stone-Campbell Movement in its separate listing of two branches, the Disciples of Christ and the Churches of Christ. The division had resulted partly from the intense debate over whether churches could scripturally use missionary societies or should support missionaries directly.

Azbill stayed with the Disciples of Christ after the division, while Snodgrass and McCaleb identified with the Churches of Christ. Eugene Snodgrass died in 1907, but J. M. McCaleb continued serving in Japan for forty-two years.

4. Another Division

The Stone-Campbell Movement was soon torn apart by yet another division. It was a division within the Disciples of Christ and first emerged in missions in Asia. The issue, however, was not the legitimacy of using missionary societies — their legitimacy was already conceded. Rather, the issue was over the proper purpose and goal of the missionary societies.

On one side, many Disciples believed that a chief purpose and goal of the societies was a purpose of the Movement itself, namely, the promotion of unity. But there was one problem. With so many missionary societies plus various other agencies and boards, the Disciples of Christ themselves were not unified. To correct this contradiction many thought that the various societies and boards should be consolidated into one organization with one administrative board. Only in this way could the Disciples of Christ begin to speak with one voice on the subject of unity to a divided Christendom.

On the other side were those who thought that the only proper purpose and goal of the missionary societies was evangelism and the restoration of New Testament Christianity. The fact that there were several societies and boards doing this work was immaterial.

J. H. Garrison first began promoting the unification of the missionary societies in 1892 through the pages of the *Christian-Evangelist,* a Stone-Campbell journal strongly supportive of the societies. Over the next twenty-five years several commissions were established to study how unification could be accomplished. In the meantime, the *Christian Standard,* a journal also in favor of missionary societies, became alarmed over the prospects of unification. The journal's position was that, in addition to being diverted from the primary objectives of evangelism and restoration, unification of the societies would create an organization more powerful than the local congregations.

Despite opposition from the *Christian Standard,* the various missionary societies and boards of the Disciples of Christ were united in 1919 into the United Christian Missionary Society (UCMS). The UCMS assumed administration of 275 missionaries in ten mission fields including the Asian fields of India, the Philippines, China, and Japan.

More crucially, though, the United Christian Missionary Society gave the Disciples of Christ a unified base from which to promote union with other church bodies. Such promotion by the UCMS was not long in coming, for by the early 1920s the UCMS had made agreements to work in federation with several denominational boards in the Orient in order to present a more unified witness in preaching the gospel.

There was one consequence to these agreements, however. Since the denominational boards often did not practice immersion, the agreements meant that the Disciples churches on the mission field would practice *open membership,* that is, accepting the nonimmersed from denominational mission churches as full members (without first being immersed) in Disciples churches. It soon came to light that Disciples of Christ missionaries in China had long been practicing open membership and that the Philippine missionaries had recently approved the practice as well.

Early twentieth-century missionaries to Tibet. Left to right: Dr. Albert L. Shelton, M.D., Dr. Susie C. Rijnhart, M.D., and Mrs. Albert L. (Flora) Shelton. Courtesy of the Disciples of Christ Historical Society

The revelation that open membership was being practiced on the mission fields of the Orient produced a firestorm of controversy among the Disciples of Christ in the United States. Disciples who opposed the practice claimed that it was a denial of all that the Stone-Campbell Movement had struggled for in restoring immersion as the New Testament form of baptism. Disciples in favor defended the practice, saying that the special conditions on the mission field required open membership in order to advance the cause of unity with other church bodies. The Disciples found themselves divided again, this time into conservatives and progressives.

Conservative Disciples failed in their attempts to halt the practice of open membership on the mission fields in Asia. They also failed to convince the leadership of the UCMS to change policy and stop supporting the practice. In 1926 conservative Disciples began to establish their own institutions and mission agencies independent of the UCMS and the International Convention of the Disciples of Christ.

Also at this time conservative Disciple missionaries began to serve as Direct Support missionaries independently of the UCMS. Leslie Wolfe (1876-1945), who had served as a Disciples of Christ missionary for nearly twenty years in the Philippines, was terminated by the UCMS in 1926 for his vigorous opposition to open membership. Wolfe returned to the Philippines in the same year as an independent missionary, however, to serve another twenty years. At the same time Sterling and Dr. Zoena Rothermel, who had been terminated from the UCMS for much the same reason in 1921, returned to resume their mission work in India. In 1927 Harry Shaefer, Sr., resigned from the UCMS, returning to India the following year to continue mission work that he had begun in 1913. In 1929, J. Russell Morse, who had resigned from the UCMS while still in China, returned to that country with plans of entering Tibet with the gospel.

Few realized at the time that another division had taken place. But over the next thirty years it became apparent that this was indeed the case. The Stone-Campbell Movement was now divided into three branches: the Disciples of Christ, the Christian Churches/Churches of Christ, and the Churches of Christ.

5. Expansion

Far from destroying the Stone-Campbell Movement and its missionary outreach, the divisions sketched above in reality set the stage for an even greater expansion of the Movement throughout the world. There is no better illustration of this expansion than what occurred in Asia in the years that followed.

In the early 1920s, Dr. Jeu Hawk, an American-trained physician, returned to his home in Hong Kong and established a Christian church. In 1925 George Benson (1898-1991) arrived from the Churches of Christ and successfully convinced Dr. Hawk and his church to become a part of the Churches of Christ. E. L. Broadus (1896-1942) soon joined Benson, and together they established churches in Hong Kong and the surrounding area.

The Great Depression (1929-41) presented severe economic obstacles in missions. In 1932 the Disciples of Christ closed their mission outpost in Batang, western China, due to lack of funds for rebuilding the outpost after its destruction by Tibetan marauders. On the other hand, by 1932 J. Russell Morse, now affiliated with the Christian Churches/Churches of Christ had redirected his mission work away from Tibet in order to evangelize among the Lisu tribal

Early twentieth-century Disciples missionaries with Chinese Christians. Seated front row, left to right: Frank Garrett, Abram E. Cory, and Charles E. Settlemyer. United Christian Missionary Society policy called for equipping and recognizing national church leaders. Courtesy of the Disciples of Christ Historical Society

people in southwestern China, a new direction that over the following years resulted in thousands of Lisu people becoming Christians. In 1936 John Chase, also of the Christian Churches/Churches of Christ, went to Korea. During the same time Suh Key Dong was converted in the United States and returned to establish several Churches of Christ in northern Korea.

World War II (1941-45) presented even more formidable obstacles in doing mission work. When the Japanese first bombed and then occupied Nanjing in 1937, a small group of foreign nationals established an International Safety Zone to shelter civilians, especially women and children. Four Disciples missionaries helped to save and protect tens of thousands of Chinese: three on the Zone Committee, and reporting to the outside world — James H. McCallum, M. Searle Bates, and Lewis S. C. Smythe; and Minnie Vautrin on the Ginling College grounds (a union Christian school established by Baptists, Methodists, Presbyterians, and Disciples in 1913). All four are recognized today at the Memorial to the Victims of the Nanjing Massacre. When the War began, mission work was suspended in Japan and eastern China, though Sarah Andrews of Churches of Christ remained in the country. In the Philippines the Japanese Army interned Leslie Wolfe, along with many other missionaries and civilians, for the duration of the war. In Thailand Percy Clark and others of the British Churches of Christ were likewise interned. In Korea the Japanese occupation forced many churches to close, and Christians went underground to preserve their faith. In Hong Kong, Ethel Mattley of the Churches of Christ was interned in a concentration camp.

But in India and southwestern China, in areas free from Japanese occupation, mission work continued.

The mission work of the J. Russell Morse family, for example, continued unabated in southwestern China. The story of Dorothy Sterling is particularly worth noting. The U.S. Government had requested J. Russell Morse to assist in searching for and rescuing downed U.S. pilots in his area of China. Morse then interceded with the U.S. Government to give a passport to Dorothy Sterling, who was a single woman and nurse, saying she would be an asset in such search and rescue missions. So in 1944, the U.S. Army Air Force flew Dorothy Sterling to Calcutta, India. She next flew over the Himalayan Mountains in a modified B-26 bomber to Likiang in western China. Then she walked and rode horses for over two weeks to arrive at the mission station of J. Russell Morse.

After the war missionaries returned to Asia to reopen mission stations and churches closed by the war. Others traveled to nations and areas never before entered by missionaries from the Stone-Campbell Movement. Not a few from the United

States had served as soldiers and chaplains in the Armed Services and now wanted to preach the gospel of peace where they once had made war. The Disciples of Christ sent missionaries, some of whom had been in China, to Thailand, and provided much-needed financial help to the mission work of the British Churches of Christ. This effort became part of the Church of Christ in Thailand, a united church. To encourage the Filipino church, the UCMS also supported a Filipino missionary family who worked with the Church of Christ in Thailand.

In 1949 the victory of communism in China, however, quickly put a stop to mission work in that country. Yet many missionaries, upon leaving China, went to surrounding nations to continue their work. C. W. and Lois Callaway of the Christian Churches/Churches of Christ diverted from China to enter Thailand. The family of J. Russell Morse escaped from China into northern Burma. J. Russell himself, however, was captured and imprisoned for eighteen months by the communists. After release from prison he rejoined his family in Burma. In 1951 the Disciples of Christ entered Thailand and provided much-needed financial help to the mission work of Percy Clark of the British Churches of Christ.

The establishment of communism in North Korea wreaked havoc on the churches of the Stone-Campbell Movement there. Many Christians and preachers in the north fled to the south. Those who remained were imprisoned. When North Korea later invaded South Korea in 1950, the communists destroyed church buildings and imprisoned ministers. Many ministers and preachers were taken back to North Korea as the communist forces retreated. Many ministers were murdered. Yet, when the war ended in 1954, the church revived in South Korea under the leadership of national preachers who had remained faithful throughout the war. Missionaries returned to join forces with the national leadership. In 1954 Dale Richeson and Haskell Chesshir (1916-2003) arrived to become the first missionaries of the Churches of Christ in South Korea. One Korean member of the Stone-Campbell Movement who had fled North Korea, fought in the war against North Korea, and later came to the United States was Soon Gook Choi. He was key in beginning Korean American Disciples congregations in the United States. He maintained a vision of bringing together the churches of the Stone-Campbell Movement in Korea, and was active in seeking contact with Christians in North Korea.

The period from 1954 to the end of the twentieth century was a time of unprecedented growth and financing of missions and missionaries from Stone-Campbell churches in the United States. Both Christian Churches/Churches of Christ and Churches of Christ sent out an ever-increasing number of missionaries, even finding new and innovative ways of supporting them with direct funding. War, battles, and economic recession failed to impede this forward march of personnel and money to the work of evangelism, education, and benevolence both in Asia and around the world.

On the other hand, by 1954 the Disciples of Christ had recommended a new policy with regard to missionary outreach. The work of the United Christian Missionary Society was integrated with other mission organizations in order to support a national United Church in each nation in which the UCMS had mission work. As a consequence of this new policy, beginning in the 1960s, this branch of the Stone-Campbell Movement would only "provide missionaries and workers to ecumenical enterprises in which the Disciples of Christ have no expectation of seeing a distinctly Disciple return" (Joseph M. Smith and Vern Rossman 1965). The Disciples of Christ merged their mission work with the national churches of India, Thailand, the Philippines, Japan, and other Pacific Rim nations.

Through the UCMS, missionaries served with the Minahasa Evangelical Church of Indonesia, the church in West Timor, the Presbyterian Church in the Republic of Korea, the Presbyterian Church of Taiwan, the Hong Kong Christian Council, and the Christian Conference of Asia, among others.

After the 1968 restructure which formed the Christian Church (Disciples of Christ), the overseas work of the UCMS became a separately incorporated Division of Overseas Ministries (DOM), reporting to the General Board and the General Assembly. There was no discontinuity with the UCMS context in terms of staff, programs, or relationships.

By the end of the twentieth century there was a Stone-Campbell Movement presence, either through an ecumenical enterprise or more directly through churches and/or missionaries, in twenty-five nations and territories of Asia.

6. Status Report

More revealing of the growth in Asia, however, are the number of churches and Christians reported by missionaries and national evangelists of the Stone Campbell Movement. Accurate statistics are difficult if not impossible to obtain. The Christian Churches/Churches of Christ and Churches of Christ have no central headquarters where such records are collected and maintained. The chief sources of information are individual missionary reports.

6.1. Churches and Membership

Since the beginning of mission work in 1882, India has been a productive field of evangelism for the Stone-Campbell Movement. In the latter part of the twentieth century, for example, missionaries from both the Christian Churches/Churches of Christ and the Churches of Christ reported baptisms into the tens of thousands. While many people have been baptized in India, it is uncertain how many churches were established or how many people remained practicing members of local congregations. Nevertheless, estimates are that there are 2,000 or more churches of the Stone-Campbell Movement in India.

In 1957 Tongkhojang Lunkim initiated a restoration movement among his own Kuki tribe in northeast India. The purpose of the movement was to be Christian only, regardless of ethnic background. The movement soon spread to other tribes and ethnic groups. In 1979 Lunkim affiliated the movement with the Christian Churches/Churches of Christ. In 2001 the movement had grown to more than 50,000 members in over 600 churches.

The DOM continued to serve in various parts of India, helping to educate pastors and teachers, serving in medical institutions, working with a variety of ecumenical efforts, in conjunction with the Church of North India, the Church of South India, and a wide range of Christian institutions — both through missionaries and financially.

The next large concentration of churches and Christians of the Stone-Campbell Movement in Asia resides in the Philippines. One hundred years after the FCMS began mission work there in 1901, Filipino Churches of Christ identified with the Christian Churches/Churches of Christ branch of the Stone-Campbell Movement numbered approximately 1,200 congregations with an estimated membership of more than 150,000 members. In addition, there were over 100 Churches of Christ in the Philippines. The Christian Church (Disciples of Christ) supports the work of the United Church of Christ in the Philippines through DOM.

Another large concentration is found in Myanmar (Burma) and southwestern China. By 2001, from the work of the J. Russell Morse family (since 1929 and now in the third generation of missionaries in Asia), there were an estimated 110,000 Christians of the Lisu and Rawang tribes in Myanmar, plus another 50,000 Lisu Christians in southwestern China. There were additional Lisu Christians located in India and Thailand. Altogether there were upwards of 1,000 congregations among the Lisu and Rawang peoples. These churches, called Churches of Christ, identify with the Christian Churches/Churches of Christ. Evangelists of the Lisu and Rawang churches, moreover, had branched out into surrounding tribes, resulting in more than 15,000 people being baptized.

An interesting by-product stemming from the Stone-Campbell witness of J. Russell Morse occurred after the Cultural Revolution of Mao Tse-Tung had run its course in China (1966-70). Since Morse had earlier used the name Church of Christ in establishing churches among the Lisu, the Chinese government issued a directive that, in keeping with the universality of the name, Lisu congregations of every denominational affiliation should similarly be called Churches of Christ. This directive currently encompasses over 200,000 Lisu believers in southwestern China.

The DOM worked since the early 1970s to develop relationships with the church in China. It has sent a series of teachers of English to teach in Chinese universities, through the Chinese Church's Amity Foundation. Most recently, at the beginning of the twenty-first century it has sent two successive missionaries with Ph.D.s, at the invitation of Nanjing Theological Seminary, to teach there. The church in China is now growing so fast that probably its most critical need is for trained pastors.

The growth of the Stone-Campbell Movement in other Asian countries, while not as spectacular as the above, has nevertheless been significant. Preliminary data from the Christian Churches/Churches of Christ and the Churches of Christ suggest the following combined numbers.

Japan	over 100 churches
Taiwan	8 churches reported
Thailand	approximately 100 churches
Indonesia	approximately 250 churches
Cambodia	80 churches, approximately 10,000 members
South Korea	500 churches
Malaysia	14 churches
Singapore	17 churches
Pakistan	8 churches
Hong Kong	16 churches
Sri Lanka	7 churches

In addition to the above, missionaries from the United States and New Zealand were also working in Mongolia. Non-traditional missionaries (those working in agricultural projects, teaching English, etc.) were similarly serving in China, Laos, and Vietnam.

6.2. Ministries

Another indicator of growth of the Stone-Campbell Movement in Asia is the many types of ministries conducted by missionaries and national workers. For example, the Stone-Campbell Movement has been a movement that emphasizes education. It has been no different for Asia. By the end of the twentieth century, literally scores of Bible institutes for the training of church leaders (elders, deacons, evangelists) dotted the landscape of Asia. Some institutes taught short-term courses, others long-term (two- to four-year curriculum). The Churches of Christ operated two Christian schools in Japan (Japan School of Evangelism and Ibaraki Christian University) and one in South Korea (Korean Christian College).

The Disciples DOM has continued to send missionaries, when requested by nationally autonomous churches, to teach in seminaries and universities. Some of these institutions, such as Northern Christian College in Laoag in the Philippines, or Joshi Sei Gakuin in Japan, were founded by Disciples missionaries many years ago, but have not been controlled from the U.S. for several decades.

Another ministry has been Scripture translation and literature. Stone-Campbell missionaries and national workers translated the Scriptures (Old Testament and New Testament) into several minority languages of India, Myanmar, Thailand, and the Philippines. Literature in the form of hymnbooks, commentaries, workbooks, and correspondence courses were prepared in these languages as well as in the major Asian languages. The Amity Foundation, related to the China Christian Council, has now printed 30 million Bibles since it was built in Nanjing in the 1980s, along with hymnals and Christian education materials. (In fact, they have been exporting Bibles to other countries!)

Missionaries from the Churches of Christ have been especially effective in using Bible correspondence courses in English to make contact with a wide range of people in several Asian nations. Duane Morgan, for example, reported that in 2002 enrollment in the correspondence courses of the World Bible School (WBS) in Indonesia had reached 3,000 students. In Japan at the same time, Masa Monogaki began offering Bible correspondence courses on the internet. Out of these contacts have come many new believers and Churches of Christ in Asia.

Radio broadcasting in Asia has been another ministry conducted by Stone-Campbell missionaries. Using native speakers, programs were broadcast in English and other languages from the Far East Broadcasting Company (FEBC) in the Philippines, Taiwan, Indonesia, and Sri Lanka. These programs were broadcast in both short wave and medium wave, reaching thousands of people throughout Asia. Missionaries have also produced tapes, videos, and filmstrips for distribution and use by evangelists and churches.

In 1981 Alan and Joan Eubanks, Disciples of Christ missionaries, established the Christian Communications Institute (CCI) in Chiang Mai, Thailand. The purpose of the Institute was to train young artists in various art forms (e.g., Thai folk drama, modern dance, etc.) in order to communicate the gospel of Christ in culturally relevant ways and to offer nonviolent alternatives for social change in the areas of drugs, prostitution, AIDS, and corruption. Troupes of young artists from CCI traveled throughout Thailand and to other Asian countries to proclaim the gospel of Christ through drama and dance.

Stone-Campbell missionaries were also engaged in various types of social work in Asia. Orphanages, for example, were operated in India, Taiwan, and South Korea. Medical work, especially leprosy care, was conducted in India and Thailand. As the AIDS epidemic spread, a number of missionaries began to look for ways to minister to both those afflicted and their families.

7. Trends

At the beginning of the twenty-first century, Asia continued to attract many missionaries of the Stone-Campbell Movement from the West, especially the United States. More importantly, though, were several new trends that had also emerged in Stone-Campbell missions in Asia.

The first was that because the work of the Stone-Campbell Movement had grown extensively throughout Asia, the task of evangelism, leadership training, and church oversight was being carried more and more by national leaders. Missionaries found themselves more in the role of administrators and facilitators than in direct evangelism and church planting.

A second trend was the emergence of capable national leaders to assume responsibility over mission work started by Western missionaries in the twentieth century. An example of this development was the work of V. J. Lall in central India. In 1968 Lall objected to merging the mission work of the Disciples of Christ with that of the Church of India. Along with several churches, he withdrew from the Disciples of Christ and affiliated with the Christian Churches/Churches of Christ in order to maintain the Stone-Campbell witness that had begun nearly a century earlier. By 2001 this mission work included fifty-seven churches and forty-seven evangelists plus schools and benevolent work.

A third trend was that congregations in the United States were becoming more willing to entrust through direct support the work of overseeing and expanding the Stone-Campbell Movement throughout Asia to national leaders, thus bypassing traditional oversight by Western missionaries.

No doubt these trends will become the defining mark of the Stone-Campbell Movement in Asia in the twenty-first century, thus assuring the continual growth and expansion of the Movement well into the future.

See also Christian Woman's Board of Missions; Direct Support Missions; Foreign Christian Missionary Society, The; Korea, The Movement in; Missions, Missiology; Open Membership; United Christian Missionary Society, The.

BIBLIOGRAPHY Charles M. Ayuno and Larry P. Arienzano, *History of the Churches of Christ in the Philippines,* "The Church of Christ, Conquering the Challenges of the New Millennium," Program Book of the Centennial Convention of the Churches of Christ in the Philippines (2001), pp. 105-20 • Charles R. Brewer, ed., *A Missionary Pictorial* (1966) • James B. Carr, *The Foreign Missionary Work of the Christian Churches* (1946) • Percy Clark, *Personal History* (Chiang Mai: Church of Christ in Thailand Archives, Payap University [no date]) • *Commission to Japan and the Philippines,* United Christian Missionary Society study book (October 1954) • *A Concise History of the Foreign Christian Missionary Society,* by the missionaries (1910) • *Disciples on the Rim of Asia: A Study Book of the United Christian Missionary Society* (1962) • David Filbeck, *The First Fifty Years: A Brief History of the Direct Support Missionary Movement* (1980) • Ida Withers Harrison, *The Christian Woman's Board of Missions* (1920) • Mark Maxey, *Christians in Japan: 100 Years (1883-1983)* • Archibald McLean, *The Foreign Christian Missionary Society* (1921) • Gertrude Morse, *The Dogs May Bark but the Caravan Moves On* (1998) • E. I. Osgood and Edwin Marx, *The China Christian Mission* (c. 1935) • Joseph M. Smith and Vern Rossman, *Called to Mission and Unity* (1965) • United Christian Missionary Society, *Strategy of World Mission* (1955) • Eric Yip, *History of the Churches of Christ in China and Hong Kong (1925-1997)* • Lynn D. Yocum, ed., *Missionary Pictorial Supplement* (1979) • Yoon Kwon Chae, *A Short History of Korean Christian Churches and Churches of Christ* (no date).

David Filbeck and Robert S. Bates

Asian American Disciples

The Stone-Campbell Movement held its first national convention in Cincinnati, Ohio, in 1849, during the same period that the first Asian people came to the United States. However, the first formal contact between the Movement and Asian Americans was not made until forty-two years later. In 1889 or 1891 (sources differ) the Christian Woman's Board of Missions (CWBM) opened a mission among the Chinese in Portland, Oregon, and it grew so explosively that a Chinese minister (Jeu Hawk) was called to lead the work in 1892. Inspired by their success in Portland, CWBM started (1907) another Chinese mission (Chinese Christian Institute) in San Francisco. Due to anti-Asian hostility reflected in the Chinese Exclusion Acts, the Chinese missions were forced to close in December 1923. Not until sixty-seven years later (1990) was a Disciples Chinese ministry rekindled by a local congregation, First Christian Church in Alhambra, California.

In 1901 a small group of Japanese came into contact with the Christian Missionary Society of Southern California. By 1908 a Japanese Christian Church was organized in Los Angeles with Teizo Kawai as pastor. In 1904 Japanese students began to meet in Berkeley, California, later formalizing as Berkeley Japanese Christian Church in 1914. In 1933 a Filipino Christian Church was founded in Los Angeles, led by Rev. Silvestre Morales. By 1942, nine Japanese Christian churches had been established and each grew rapidly, but all were closed with the internment of Japanese Americans. After their detention, former Japanese Christian Church members founded West Adams Christian Church in Los Angeles in 1948 with Kojiro Unoura as minister. For the next three decades, the Disciples' Asian ministry remained fairly dormant until a great wave of new immigrants from Asia came under the new Immigration Acts of 1965.

In July 1978, through the efforts of Harold Johnson (b. 1921), Executive for Evangelism of the Disciples Division of Homeland Ministries (DHM), the first consultation on Asian ministries was held in Indianapolis. The purpose was threefold: to affirm the unique identity of Asian American Disciples; to raise the consciousness among Disciples of their presence; and to help Disciples attend to the needs of the growing Asian American population. Out of this consultation the Fellowship of Asian American Disciples (FAAD) was organized. The second consultation was held in April 1979, in which FAAD was renamed the American-Asian Disciples (AAD). It was then decided to publish a newsletter with David Kagiwada (1929-1985) and Janet Casey-Allen as the inaugural editors. At the 1979 General Assembly in St. Louis, AAD was formally acknowledged as a constituency. Official recognition of AAD by the General Board of the Christian Church (Disciples of Christ) came in 1984.

The first AAD convocation was held in October 1980 in Indianapolis, with sixteen Asians and three General Office staff participating. David Kagiwada was elected as AAD's first convener. The group decided to hold biennial convocations on even years, alternating with the General Assembly. The second AAD convocation was held in Berkeley, California, in conjunction with the Pacific and Asian Americans Ecumenical Convocation on July 20 through August 1, 1982. Grace Kim was elected as AAD's second Convener.

The third AAD convocation was held in July 1984 in Indianapolis. Soongook Choi (1933-2002) was elected as AAD's third convener. Flor and Orlando Marcelino, both Filipino Canadians, designed the AAD logo and banner. On July 10, 1985, David Kagiwada died, and a scholarship fund was established in his memory at the 1985 General Assembly in Des Moines, Iowa, to be awarded to seminarians of Asian descent. Subsequent conveners/moderators were Wallace Kuroiwa, Soongook Choi, Janet Casey-Allen, Manuel Tamayo, Nobuyoshi Kaneko, Jeri Sias, Timothy Lee, and Kim Tran.

On October 12-14, 1989, DHM called for the third consultation on Asian ministries, which proposed directions for the ministry of the Christian Church (Disciples of Christ) with American Asians. The consultation called for developing ministerial leadership for AAD, establishing AAD member churches, fostering Asian representation on boards of the church, and posting an Asian staff person within DHM for American Asian ministries. The Koreans were to be the initial target among Asians because of the rapid growth of Korean immigrants and the proliferation of Korean Christian ministry within America as well as in Korea. In 1976, Wilshire Korean Christian Church with its pastor Song Cha Kim became the first Korean Disciples congregation.

The 1991 General Assembly (Tulsa, Oklahoma) approved the proposal and directed DHM to create a position exclusively focused on American Asian ministries *(Business Docket No. 9136)*. On February 1, 1992, Geunhee Yu (who held a Ph.D. from Vanderbilt Divinity School) was called to develop and grow Asian ministries. Upon his arrival in 1992, there were eight AAD churches. After ten years the number of AAD churches had exploded to over seventy in 2002, consisting primarily of seven different ethnic and linguistic groups: Chinese, Japanese, Filipino, Korean, Vietnamese, Indonesian, and Samoan.

At the ninth Convocation (Chapman University, 1996), AAD was renamed the North American Pacific/Asian Disciples (NAPAD), to be more inclusive. In 1996, Jaikwan Ahn (b. 1930) was appointed as Director of NAPAD Ministries for the Pacific Southwest region, providing a solid impetus for fast growth within the region. Korean Disciples represent about 75 percent of NAPAD congregations. In January 1995, the Disciples of Christ Korean Ministers Fellowship was organized with Soongook Choi as moderator; it was reorganized as the Korean Disciples Convocation in 2000. Upon Soongook Choi's retirement in March 1997, the Soongook Choi Scholarship Fund was established in honor of his ministry.

In March 2000, the NAPAD Visioning Conference was held in Indianapolis, with representatives from NAPAD, General and Regional Ministries, Higher Education, and local churches. A five-point covenant was created as part of a ten-year action plan for NAPAD ministries. A process to restructure NAPAD ministries was created and authorized, and in 2001 the General Board appointed a Task Force for restructuring. As an integral part of the Christian Church (Disciples of Christ), NAPAD seeks a new identity with self-determination.

BIBLIOGRAPHY Janet Casey-Allen, "Disciples of Asian Origin Vie for Their Place," *The Disciple* 132:5 (May 1994): 8-10 • "History of American Asian Disciples," AAD 1992 Convocation, *Program Book*, pp. 15-17 • Geunhee Yu, "A New Vision for the Church," *Vanguard* (April-June 1993): 12-13 • "Gifts of Asian Disciples," *Vanguard* (July-Sept. 1998): 4 • Timothy Lee, "NAPAD History," *NAPAD Newsletter* (Winter 1998-99): 9 • Guin Stemmler, *A Mini-History: Christian Church (Disciples of Christ)* (1996).

GEUNHEE YU

Association of Disciples Musicians

The national church music fellowship of the Christian Church (Disciples of Christ). Its membership includes both lay and professional ministers of music, clergy, organists, choral directors, handbell directors, liturgical dancers, and vocal/handbell choir members.

The Association of Disciples Musicians (ADM) began with a meeting of nineteen people in Louisville, Kentucky, on October 24, 1960, during the International Convention of the Christian Church. Participants discussed the need for an organization of church musicians and planned a national workshop for the campus of Texas Christian University, August 2-7, 1962. At that time the association would be launched under the guidance of the Department of Church Development of the United Christian Missionary Society. Two hundred twenty-one persons representing twenty-seven states and the Philippines attended the first workshop. This meeting set the precedent for the annual workshop held each year at a different college or university campus.

At the workshop, professional clinicians and ADM members teach seminars and classes in the areas of worship, choral, organ, handbell, and liturgical movement. The experience is further enhanced by daily worship, choral and handbell music reading sessions, music vendors, concerts, and social events. The event concludes with a formal choral, handbell, and instrumental concert presented by workshop participants.

ADM has provided leadership at all levels of the church, supplying choral directors, organists, and combined choirs for General Assemblies of the Christian Church (Disciples of Christ). Regional chapters of ADM have also been chartered to provide opportunities for learning and fellowship in addition to the annual workshop. A major accomplishment for ADM was the sponsorship and publication of the denomination's *Chalice Hymnal* in 1995.

LARRY SIVIS

Association of Disciples for Theological Discussion

One of the most enduring of several study groups created among the Disciples of Christ in the 1950s. Professor Walter Sikes (1896-1966) of Christian Theological Seminary was a major force in organizing the Association, which draws its membership from Disciples college and seminary faculty members who have an interest in exploring contemporary theological issues with specific reference to the tradition of the Disciples of Christ. It was formed at Eureka College in 1957, and subsequent annual meetings have been held in St. Louis or Indianapolis. Meetings characteristically focus on a particular topic; and members present formal papers examining the topic from biblical, historical, theological, and other religious studies fields. The Association was initially supported by the Christian Board of Publication, and has more recently received support from the Division of Higher Education of the Christian Church. Many of the Association's papers have appeared in *Encounter.*

See also Christian Board of Publication; Division of Higher Education; Theology

BIBLIOGRAPHY Samuel C. Pearson, Jr., "The Association of Disciples for Theological Discussion: A Brief Historical Appraisal," *Encounter* 37:3 (Summer 1976): 259-83.

SAMUEL C. PEARSON

Atlanta Christian College

College affiliated with the Christian Churches/Churches of Christ. Atlanta Christian College was founded in 1937 by Judge T. O. Hathcock (1879-1966) following three unsuccessful attempts by Christian churches in Georgia to establish a college earlier in the twentieth century. Judge Hathcock, who from 1914 until 1942 served on the bench in Fulton County, Georgia, was a trustee and benefactor of all three of these earlier ventures — Lamar College (1913-15), Southeastern Christian College (1915-25), and the initial launching of Atlanta Christian College (1928-30). Named in honor of J. S. Lamar, a prominent Georgia preacher who died in 1908, Lamar College in Clarkston was led by Josephus Hopwood. When this college failed after only two years, supporters secured the campus of Perry-Rainey Institute, a Baptist school at Auburn, Georgia, that had also closed. Here Southeastern Christian College operated for ten years under the presidency of John H. Wood and three short-term successors. Inadequate support resulted in this college's closing its doors in 1925. After the first effort to establish Atlanta Christian College on the Hathcocks' property near East Point under the leadership of J. S. Raum in 1928, the coming of the Great Depression forced the suspension of classes at the fledgling institution in 1930.

As a lay leader, Judge Hathcock had worked in 1914 as chairman of the Committee on Information of the General Convention of the Disciples of Christ, meeting that year in Atlanta. In the conflicts among Disciples in the 1920s and following decades, however, Hathcock's sympathies were clearly with those ultimately identified as "independents." He attended the crucial meeting of the International Convention in Memphis in 1926, and he was among those dissidents who left the convention and gathered in the alternative meeting at the nearby Pantages Theater. He often attended the North American Christian Convention in subsequent years. Judge Hathcock was closely associated with Mr. and Mrs. W. D. Cunningham, missionaries to Japan who became for a time the most well known of the "independent" missionaries, and was for a time chairman of the executive committee of the Cunninghams' mission in Japan, the Yotsuya Mission. The Judge was a trustee of Cincinnati Bible Seminary from 1933 until 1937. He was also significantly involved in planting churches and was a pioneer in the Christian service camp movement. From its earliest days, the constituency of Atlanta Christian College has included congregations and individuals identified with the Christian Churches/Churches of Christ.

Throughout its history, Atlanta Christian College has operated on the same campus — now fifty-three acres — in East Point, a suburb of Atlanta. The campus is part of a 300-acre farm inherited by Nora Head Hathcock, who married Judge Hathcock in 1904. With a barn, livestock, and cultivated fields, the campus in its earliest days had a distinctly rural flavor. In fact, when the Hathcock family offered the farm in earlier years as a potential site for Lamar College, Josephus Hopwood declined the offer, observing that the ideal campus would not be so far out in the country and would be located much nearer a railroad line. Such roots provide an interesting contrast with the present suburban setting of the campus.

In 1965 the college was accredited by the American Association of Bible Colleges (AABC), and in 1990 accreditation was granted by the Commission on Colleges of the Southern Association of Colleges and Schools (SACS). The curriculum of the college includes a major or minor in biblical studies for all students as well as majors in humanities, music, early childhood education, human relations, and business.

The charter of Atlanta Christian College, granted in 1928, envisioned an institution that offered instruction in Bible as well as the "arts and sciences." Interestingly, that document does not refer to the school as a Bible college, although the college for a number of decades indisputably regarded itself as a single-purpose institution. That identity was even more apparent when the institution became a member of the AABC in the mid-1960s. In the 1980s, however, the college broadened its curriculum and applied for accreditation by SACS. In 1994, four years after gaining accreditation by SACS, the college voluntarily withdrew from the AABC. The college took this step in conjunction with its decision to require minors (rather than majors) in biblical studies for programs that were not specifically church-related. A Bible college, strictly defined, requires all students to major in biblical studies (or to have double majors, one of which is Bible). Currently, the college is to be found on the spectrum where "Bible college" ends and "Christian liberal arts college" begins or — perhaps more accurately — where those paradigms overlap.

Enrollment in the college declined from the mid-1970s through the mid-1980s. After a decade and a half of growth, in the fall of 1998 the enrollment climbed to 352, eclipsing the previous record enrollment of 331 in 1974. By the fall of 2001, more than 400 students were on campus.

See also Bible College Movement; Higher Education, Views of in the Movement

BIBLIOGRAPHY R. Edwin Groover, "T. O. Hathcock: The Judge and His Work" (unpublished M.Div. thesis, Emmanuel School of Religion, 1972).

R. EDWIN GROOVER

Atlanta Declaration Committee

Group of concerned Disciples of Christ who protested the proposed denominational restructure in the 1960s.

Robert W. Burns (1904-1991), Senior Minister of the Peachtree Christian Church, Atlanta, Georgia, convened the Committee of seventeen members on May 3 and 4, 1967, to draft its *Declaration of Convictions and Concerns,* henceforth known simply as the "Atlanta Declaration." A number in this group were Disciples ministers, but it also included Alfred T. DeGroot, (1903-1992) church historian from Texas Christian University, who wrote a number of essays on ecclesiology reflecting concerns of the Atlanta Declaration Committee.

The Atlanta Declaration targeted the "Provisional Design for Restructure" of the Disciples as violating the authority of Scripture, proposing an "authoritarian, compulsory system" of intercongregational cooperation, and violating individual freedom of conscience. The Committee believed that the Restructure model was inconsistent with the historic Stone-Campbell plea for a free church, and that "institutional and organizational unity" could not substitute for "oneness in faith" as the essence of Christian unity. The appended commentary on the Declaration recommended the retaining of a "voluntary, free-consent cooperative Brotherhood" that would keep the prerogatives of congregations intact.

The Committee continued its efforts through the vote in the final assembly of the International Convention of Christian Churches (Disciples of Christ) but failed in its bid to impede the implementation of Restructure.

See also DeGroot, Alfred T.; Restructure

BIBLIOGRAPHY Atlanta Declaration Committee, *Atlanta Declaration of Convictions and Concerns, with Commentary Authorized by the Atlanta Progress Committee* (May 4, 1967) (pamphlet) • Alfred T. DeGroot, *Extra Ecclesiam Nulla Salus* (and other essays) (1969) • Anthony L. Dunnavant, *Restructure: Four Historical Ideals in the Campbell-Stone Movement and the Development of the Polity of the Christian Church (Disciples of Christ)* (1993).

ROBERT W. SHAW

Atlantic Christian College

See Barton College

Atonement

Doctrine of Christ's work in the remission of human sin, traditionally focusing on the redemptive meaning of Christ's death. The Stone-Campbell Movement's understandings reflect the nineteenth-century theological quarrel between advocates of different theories of atonement.

Three major understandings existed in nineteenth-century America: (1) penal substitution, originally systematized by Anselm of Canterbury and further developed in Protestant theology; (2) the governmental theory, worked out by the seventeenth-century Dutch theologian Hugo Grotius; and (3) the moral influence theory, associated with the medieval theologian Peter Abelard and later with the Socinian movement. Penal substitutionists affirmed that Jesus died vicariously in the place of sinners by suffering the legal penalty of their sins to satisfy God's unbending justice. Governmental theorists believed that Jesus suffered as a warning of God's wrath toward sin as a form of public justice instead of exacting the full penalty of sin according to strict justice. Moral theorists taught that Jesus died as a testimony of God's love to persuade sinners of his grace and denied any association with penal satisfaction or public justice ideas.

Members of the Stone-Campbell Movement debated these three theories throughout the nineteenth century. In the first generation, Barton W. Stone was a moral theorist. The Campbells and Walter Scott sympathized with elements of both the penal substitution and governmental theories. The 1830s and early 1840s witnessed intermittent debate.

Stone rejected penal substitution early in his ministry. His first book was a defense of the moral influence theory (1804), and when Noah Worcester published *The Atoning Sacrifice: A Display of Love — Not of Wrath* (1829), he reviewed it favorably in the *Christian Messenger.* He sanctioned its thesis and recommended his own *Address to the Christian Church* (1821) for further study. Stone believed that the cross of Christ was a significant moral influence on the sinner, but had no moral effect or influence upon God. The purpose of the cross was to lead humanity to repentance; it was not to effect a change in God from wrath to grace. God acted in Christ to effect a change in humanity. Stone's starting point was the theological axiom "God is love," and the function of the cross is to reveal God's love for sinners. Consequently, the cross does not function as a punishment of sin or a sign of wrath, but is God's way of leading sinners to repentance. Stone, therefore, rejected any association of "sin-bearing" with the imputation of sin or forensic justice. There is no barrier to the forgiveness of sins except the impertinence of the sinner.

Stone's theology of atonement was forged in the context of revivalism. As he called sinners to faith in his early years, he was embarrassed by the doctrine of penal substitution, which was said to support either predestination (Christ's death satisfied God's justice for the elect alone) or universal salvation (Christ's death satisfied God's justice for all). Stone opposed both the doctrines of predestination and universal salvation. Out of this embarrassment three convictions were clarified: (1) God loves the world and is willing to save everyone, to which he has given evidence in Jesus Christ; (2) everyone has the capacity to hear and appropriate the transforming gospel of God's gracious love; and (3) universalism must be avoided and urgency of evangelism maintained.

Given the recent union between Christians (Stone) and Reformers (Campbell) in 1832, Alexander Campbell encouraged discussion on the atonement. Thomas Campbell felt that Worcester's theory (thus Stone's) contained "radical mistakes." Both Campbells believed that the moral influence theory did not give sufficient weight to God's justice. Any attempt to explain the cross of Christ as a "mere example, or a display of love, without regard to justice" subverts the "basis of the divine government" and robs "the gospel of all that glorifies the wisdom and power, the justice and mercy of God in putting away sin and in saving the sinner." The justice of God is magnified through the Son's endurance of the "penal effects of sin" or the law's "penalty in behalf of his people." God must be both just and justifier, and this is accomplished through penal substitution where Christ suffers the punishment due humanity. In Christ, God justly put away sin so that the sinner might be saved. Justice, therefore, must be seen as an operative principle in our salvation. The work of Christ is not only a display of love, but is also "as necessary to demonstrating the justice as the goodness of God in forgiving sin."

For Alexander Campbell, Christ was our propitiation and we are justly acquitted from all guilt "because the just desert or wages of [our] sin, viz. sorrows, sufferings, and death, to the full amount of its demerit, has been inflicted upon, and endured by, [our] surety, the Redeemer." For God to acquit the guilty justly, there must be a surety or a substitute who bears the just and "infinite demerit and evil of sin." God's justice must deal with sin as a category rather than merely with the heart of the sinner. Campbell argued that God's immutable holiness necessitates some act of God that vindicates his justice. He rejected any "milder evangelic law" that denies the "real divinity, and legal substitution of Jesus Christ."

In 1834 Walter Scott maintained that the atonement was at least partially a function of justice. God demonstrated his justice in Jesus' "propitiatory sacrifice." Scott rejected both a penal substitution and a moral influence understanding of this justice. On the one hand, the death of Christ was not an "equivalent" or "precise amount of vengeance" rendered to God for sin. This would be a commercial or mercantile sense of justice. If God fully paid the price of sin, there is no room for mercy because the debt would have been discharged. On the other hand, the moral influence view has no role for justice at all. Scott believed that the demonstration of God's justice is political or governmental in character, a position that Alexander Campbell also affirmed. Political justice seeks the "common good" for public safety and respect for law. God as moral governor, "instead of exposing his character for injustice" by ignoring the punishment due to sin, "establishes his character" as a "public functionary." He demonstrates his justice and offers his mercy.

The governmental theory grew in importance in the mid-nineteenth century and was the subject of the longest essay on the atonement in Stone-Campbell history. Under the pseudonym "Clement" in *Lard's Quarterly* (1868), a governmental theorist argued that the necessity of the incarnation is grounded in the necessity of one whose "rank and personal worth" is great enough to call attention to God's administration of his government. The concept of substitution present in the essay does not involve a legal imputation of guilt, but simply a "substitution of his person instead of the offenders; and a substitution of his sufferings instead of their punishment." Christ satisfied the "administrative" justice of God, but not the "commercial" (equivalent payment) or the "retributive" (the full demerit of sin) justice. The death of Christ rendered God propitious in the sense that "it opened a just and honorable way for his grace to be exercised" as the moral governor of the universe. God had a "justifiable reason" to be gracious since proper honor had been displayed to his government and the public good. Other articles followed this lead. The most articulate advocate of the governmental theory was Thomas Munnell.

American theology in general, however, was moving toward the moral influence theory. In the late nineteenth century the Stone-Campbell Movement tended toward moral influence, particularly within the emerging Disciples of Christ. Despite repeated objections from penal and governmental theorists, the moral influence theory grew dominant in some quarters. The major advocate of the moral influence theory in the last quarter of the nineteenth century was J. S. Lamar. He published his views in two major essays, one as an appendix to his 1877 commentary on Luke, and the other as an article in Garrison's 1891 *The Old Faith Restated.* Garrison's *Christian-Evangelist* became a forum for debating the merits of the moral influence theory over against penal and governmental theories, especially in articles by Peter Vogel who engaged Munnell (governmental) and C. S. Pierce (penal) in a vigorous discussion in 1895-96. The moral influence theory generally won the day among the Disciples of Christ.

In the nineteenth century, the general pattern of atonement discussion moved from the penal substitution theory to the governmental theory to the emerging prominence of a moral influence theory. This pattern differs little from the developments within the Reformed and Methodist traditions. However, in the last decade of the nineteenth century and in the first few decades of the twentieth century, the penal substitution theory was renewed in the *Gospel Advocate,* as it had always had a small presence in the *Christian-Evangelist* and a more prominent presence in the *Christian Standard.* The resurgence of the penal understanding might be traced to the influence of James A. Harding, David Lipscomb, and the Nashville Bible School, illustrated by the writings of R. H. Boll. Penal substitution became the dominant understanding of the Churches of Christ, though the governmental theory would sometimes find expression. It was a return to the Campbellian perspective and a rejection of Stone's theory of atonement, made more urgent in the wake of new continental theology and the battle between modernism and fundamentalism.

The discussion of the atonement had by no means dissipated with the deaths of Stone and Campbell. In fact, it was often a centerpiece of discussion. For example, in the first five years of the *Christian Quarterly Review* (April 1882–January 1888), there were six major essays on the doctrine of atonement (two governmental, three moral, and one penal). However, some believed that the discussion was speculative and fruitless.

Three themes were constant in the writings of those who objected to the controversy. First, everyone should speak only in the language of Scripture and eschew all scholastic terms about the atonement. Second, everyone should concentrate on proclaiming the facts of the gospel rather than explaining its philosophy. Third, everyone should resist arguing about theories of atonement since these are unrevealed and therefore divisive. These themes tended to push the understanding of the meaning of the death of Christ into the background while at the same time pushing the human response to the gospel into the foreground. It moved discussion away from what God did to what human beings must do. It moved the discussion from the accomplishment of redemption to its application.

For example, J. W. McGarvey insisted that the discussion of theories was unprofitable and unnecessary. Such theorizing seeks to understand something God did not reveal, and "the human mind can never be sure what his reasoning on the matter is." Instead, McGarvey counseled, "It is enough for us to know and act upon the human side." Several articles by C. W. Sewell in the 1876 *Gospel Advocate* provide the best illustration of this tendency. Sewell asserted that no theory was without defect, and preachers should concentrate only on the facts. We should proclaim the facts, exhort believers to obedience, and avoid all language not found in Scripture.

In Christian Churches/Churches of Christ, the debate over "theories" of atonement was reopened briefly by Jack Cottrell of Cincinnati Bible Seminary in his *What the Bible Says about God the Redeemer* (1987), published in a College Press series that also included *What the Bible Says about Salvation* (1982), by Virgil Warren, formerly of Manhattan Christian College. Cottrell vigorously rejected Warren's "interpersonal" (non-forensic) view of atonement, according to which the notions of genuine substitution and of the "imputation" of punishment to the innocent Christ and of Christ's righteousness to the guilty sinner were displaced by an affirmation that Christ's work was intended principally to overcome alienation and, through forgiveness, bring the reconciliation of divine and human persons. Cottrell attacked Warren's view — which was reminiscent of Barton Stone's understanding of the atonement — by reasserting the principles of substitution and propitiation. Cottrell also dismissed the "governmental" theory, entertained by the Campbells, as biblically groundless.

Such theological debate of atonement has largely subsided, however. Among the more conservative streams of the Stone-Campbell Movement (especially in Churches of Christ and Christian Churches/Churches of Christ) "theological" interpretation has remained primarily a matter of repeating the scriptural language of atonement or undertaking word studies on key biblical terms. In the Christian Church (Disciples of Christ), the older liberalism focused on the imitation of Jesus' sinless and sacrificial life still has its proponents, but some more recent Disciples theologians, and counterparts in the other two streams of the Movement, have encouraged the retention of more classical, historically tested understandings of the work of Christ.

BIBLIOGRAPHY Alexander Campbell and Barton Stone, correspondence on "Atonement," *Millennial Harbinger* (1840-41), also available at http://www.mun.ca/rels/restmov/texts/bstone/mh/ATONE00.HTM •

Thomas Campbell, "Worcester on the Atonement," *Millennial Harbinger* (1833): 256-62 • John Mark Hicks, "What Did Christ's Sacrifice Accomplish? Atonement in Early Stone-Campbell Thought," *Lexington Theological Quarterly* 30 (1995): 145-70 • John Mark Hicks, "Atonement Theology in the Late Nineteenth Century: The Pattern of Discussion within the Stone-Campbell Movement," *Discipliana* 56 (1996): 116-27 • J. S. Lamar, "Appendix to Chapter XXIV: 44-47: The Atonement," in *New Testament Commentary,* vol. 2: *Luke* (1877), pp. 287-300 • David Lipscomb, "The Blood of Christ" and "Vicarious Suffering of Christ," in *Salvation from Sin,* ed. J. W. Shepherd (1913), pp. 158-91 • David Lipscomb, "The Object of Christ's Death," *Gospel Advocate* 25 (1883): 406, 423, 449 • Victor McCracken, "The Unitarian and Orthodox Backgrounds of the Stone-Campbell Atonement Debate," *Discipliana* 58 (1998): 111-25 • Walter Scott, *Hē Nekrōsis, or The Death of Christ, Written for the Recovery of the Church from Sects* (1853) • Barton Stone, *Atonement: The Substance of Two Letters Written to a Friend* (1805) • Barton Stone, *An Address to the Christian Churches* (2nd ed. 1821) • D. Newell Williams, "The Power of Christ's Sacrifice: Barton W. Stone's Doctrine of Atonement," *Discipliana* 54 (Spring 1994): 20-31.

JOHN MARK HICKS

Atwater, Anna Robison (1859-1941)

Anna Robison Atwater (1859-1941) was president of the Christian Woman's Board of Missions in 1919. Convinced that women and men should work together in missions, she became a vice president of the newly formed United Christian Missionary Society in 1920. Courtesy of the Disciples of Christ Historical Society

Leader in the Christian Woman's Board of Missions and the United Christian Missionary Society. Born in Bedford, Ohio, on May 25, 1859, the daughter of Harriet Young and Decker D. Robison, Anna and her siblings raised and educated themselves, following the death of her father when she was four, and her mother when she was twelve. All but one of the five eventually graduated from Hiram College (Anna in 1882). Subsequently, she became a high school principal near Bryan, Ohio, and an organizer for the Christian Woman's Board of Missions (CWBM). Following her marriage to minister/educator John Milton Atwater on June 30, 1892, Anna Atwater became a teacher at Oskaloosa College, Iowa. J. M. Atwater died in 1900, after several years of ill health.

Anna Atwater became president of the Ohio CWBM in 1901, then was elected National CWBM vice president in 1904 and editor of the CWBM periodical, *Missionary Tidings,* in 1905. She succeeded Helen E. Moses (1853-1908) as president of CWBM in 1909, and was unanimously reelected every year until 1920. Anna Atwater served during pivotal CWBM moments — at the Centennial celebration (1909) and during the building of the College of Missions (to educate women and men for mission work) in Indianapolis. Under her leadership, CWBM receipts grew from \$282,000 to \$692,000; total assets grew from \$300,000 to \$1.4 million.

Despite controversy surrounding the dissolution of CWBM as a separate organization and the formation of the United Christian Missionary Society (a unification of several church boards, including CWBM) in 1920, Anna Atwater was convinced that mission work in the United States and abroad could best be accomplished by men and women working together in the same organization. She became second vice president (then first vice president upon the death of Archibald McLean) of the United Christian Missionary Society, and executive secretary for foreign work. She concentrated especially on Latin America until her retirement in 1926. Anna Atwater was revered as a compelling speaker of great power and grace. As the last CWBM president and the first woman vice president of the United Christian Missionary Society, she provided leadership during a time of transition for missionary efforts and women's work in the Christian Church. She died in Grand Rapids, Michigan, on March 23, 1941.

See also Christian Woman's Board of Missions; College of Missions; *Missionary Tidings;* United Christian Missionary Society, The

BIBLIOGRAPHY Lorraine Lollis, *The Shape of Adam's Rib: A Lively History of Women's Work in the Christian Church* (1970).

DEBRA B. HULL

Austin Graduate School of Theology

Theological school associated with Churches of Christ. Austin Graduate School of Theology (formerly the Institute for Christian Studies [ICS]) developed from the Bible Chair program at the University of Texas at Austin. In 1917, the University Avenue Church of Christ established a Bible Chair, offering Bible courses for university credit. Beginning in 1975, under the leadership of Pat E. Harrell, ICS offered a bachelor's degree in biblical studies, initially by arrangement with Abilene Christian University. The Southern Association of Colleges and Schools in 1987 granted the undergraduate program full accreditation. Beginning in 1992, Abilene Christian University offered a master's degree in Bible and religion through courses taught by ICS faculty. In 1995, governance of ICS was placed under an independent Board of Trustees.

In 2001, the school began to offer graduate degrees under the name Austin Graduate School of Theology (AGST), retaining the Institute for Christian Studies name for its research component and continuing an undergraduate program in conjunction with Concordia University, Austin. Distinctive is the diversity of the student body, which includes students from a variety of religious traditions in addition to Churches of Christ. James W. Thompson, David Worley, Carson Stephens, and Stanley G. Reid have served the school as president.

The school's influence is widely felt among Churches of Christ through a number of public-service programs and activities. The annual "Ministers' Sermon Seminar" focuses on expository preaching and attracts over 150 attendees from more than thirty-five states and foreign countries. Publications include the faculty journal *Christian Studies* and an introductory guide to Christian faith written by AGST faculty, *Things That Matter,* which has been translated into eleven languages.

David Worley characterized ICS as "a unique educational center for ministry, in which students are tested to confess their faith within an internationally diverse, multi-confessional University of Texas environment guided by the insights of the Restoration movement." In this context, long-time faculty members Allan J. McNicol and Michael R. Weed have championed a theological orientation sometimes referred to as "neo-conservatism." This approach calls for Churches of Christ to draw upon their own theological tradition in order to engage contemporary culture critically and responsibly.

See also Bible Chair Movement

GARY HOLLOWAY

Australia, The Movement in

1. Beginnings
2. 1860-1875
3. 1875-1910
4. 1910-1939
5. World War II and After
6. Membership

1. Beginnings

The development of Churches of Christ in Australia, in a fragile, inhospitable continent, resulted from individual initiative. While the influence of the American Disciples was not insignificant, the impact of the British Churches predominated. Churches of Christ developed independently in the colonies of New South Wales, Victoria, and South Australia.

There has been considerable debate in recent years concerning the genesis of the Movement in South Australia. It had long been argued that the major initiative was taken by a group of enterprising laymen associated with a small Scotch Baptist Church in Franklyn Street, Adelaide. The dissemination of the writings of Alexander Campbell among the Scotch Baptist membership of the Franklyn Street church resulted in division and the development of a nucleus espousing the views propounded by Campbell. Thomas Magarey, who migrated from Northern Ireland via New Zealand, was the driving force in the young congregation. Relying on this version of events, the beginnings of the movement in South Australia can be traced back to 1846.

The importance of the Franklyn Street congregation in the development of Churches of Christ in South Australia has been challenged by Trevor Lawrie, a descendant of immigrants from Beith and New Mills in Scotland who emigrated to South Australia as a congregation. This group, Lawrie argues, met for worship in Willunga, south of Adelaide, before those from Franklyn Street constituted themselves a Church of Christ. The question of who was first is of little lasting import. It is significant that Churches of Christ in South Australia, the Paradise of Descent, were influenced by Presbyterian traditions filtered through a Scotch Baptist matrix.

By contrast, the pioneering membership of Churches of Christ in New South Wales counted among their number numerous Wesleyan Methodists. Joseph Kingsbury, a veterinarian and former Wesleyan Methodist local preacher, because of his sharp mind and vigorous personality, enjoyed an influence comparable to that of Magarey in South Australia. Progress in New South Wales, in contrast to South Australia, was painfully slow. This was due to

Born in Ireland, Thomas Magarey (1825-1902) immigrated with his family in 1841 to New Zealand, where he was converted by members of the Stone-Campbell Movement in Auckland. He and his brother James moved in 1845 to South Australia, where Magarey became a leader in Churches of Christ for over thirty-five years. He left the Movement in 1880 to join the Plymouth Brethren.
Courtesy of the Disciples of Christ Historical Society

heresy and internal contention, and to the opposition of established denominations that looked with disdain on the comparatively uneducated, lay leadership of Churches of Christ and on their low social and economic status. In South Australia, by contrast, Churches of Christ congregations celebrated the achievements of members who enjoyed wealth and political clout. Whereas relationships between Churches of Christ and other churches in New South Wales were generally acrimonious, those in South Australia were marked by cooperation and mutual respect.

The churches in New South Wales trace their beginnings back to 1852. The following year, a group of immigrants, formerly members of the British Churches of Christ, met in the tent of James Ingram at Prahran, in Melbourne, in the colony of Victoria, to observe the Lord's Supper. The discovery of gold in the early 1850s drew immigrants like a magnet to the newly inaugurated colony. The bulk of the early members of the Victorian Churches of Christ were British immigrants, largely tradesmen and their families, who emigrated to the southern continent in the hope of bettering their condition. Relationships between Churches of Christ and other Christian bodies in Victoria, while less enthusiastic than in South Australia, were far in advance of the situation in New South Wales.

Membership growth was most marked in South Australia and least evident in New South Wales, a fact that correlated with internal harmony/division, socio-economic status, the strength or weakness of other communions in the field, and their attitude toward newcomers.

Churches of Christ were commenced in Tasmania in 1865, in Queensland in 1876, in western Australia in 1891, in Canberra in 1951, and in the Northern Territory in 1978.

It was in this pioneering period that nuances in the theology of Churches of Christ in the different colonies developed. In South Australia attitudes were more open and liberal, whereas in New South Wales suspicious conservatism prevailed. In Victoria, where Robert Service — the father of James Service, Premier of Victoria between 1883 and 1885 — gave a strong lead, enterprise was rewarded. Victoria later took the lead in moving Churches of Christ in Australia toward the ecumenical ideal that had always been part of its plea. Manning Clark, a distinguished Australian historian, argued that the theology of the churches in the three major colonies owed more to the secular philosophies of the founding fathers than to theological factors — the "live and let live" attitude in South Australia, the deep conservatism of the establishment in New South Wales, and the sedate radicalism of the Victorian miners. These influences lived on in the theology of all churches, including Churches of Christ.

In spite of the strength of the British influence on the development of the Australian Churches of Christ in the pioneering era, the Australian movement was no mere imperial outpost. There were differences. The first was the emphasis Australians placed on the celebration of the Supper. Because the Australian churches had few competent "exhorters," the Lord's Supper became the central feature of their services. Second, the Australian Churches, though conservative, exhibited more liberal theological attitudes, particularly during the period of David King's ascendancy in Britain, than did the British churches.

2. 1860-1875

In the early 1860s the lay leadership of the colonies became aware that if the churches were to progress they would need assistance from abroad — experienced if not trained evangelists. An appeal to the British churches proved futile. The American Disciples were also overextended. Eventually, H. S. Earl, a Britisher who had trained at Bethany, Virginia, was approached. He accepted a position in Victoria, where he was spectacularly successful. He was engaged by the Church at Lygon Street in Melbourne but ranged widely, making frequent sorties into the countryside. In the space of a year he added 200 to the total colonial membership of 400. The Australian Churches of Christ were ecstatic. It was hoped that they could secure the services of more Americans. Earl was followed by a trickle of Americans, the first being G. L. Surber and T. J. Gore, who arrived in 1867. The Americans justified the faith placed in them. They were well educated, enterprising, and supplemented the cold, rational logic of Australian Restorationists with an emotional energy. They gave a fillip to the work in Australia.

The advent of the Americans was not universally applauded. Those few Australians who had served the churches as preachers felt pushed into the shade. Furthermore, the success the Americans achieved exacerbated relationships with other churches, which were unhappy with their sheep being stolen. The major point of contention was baptism.

Born in Kentucky and baptized at age 19, Thomas Jefferson Gore (1839-1923) left the United States in 1866 with G. L. Surber and spent the rest of his life ministering among Churches of Christ in South Australia.
Courtesy of Graeme Chapman

Born in England, Henry Samuel Earl (1831-1919) moved to America at age 17 and studied at Bethany College. His evangelistic success on a trip to England from 1861 to 1863 led to an invitation to work in Australia, where he married Anna Jane Magarey in 1867. He labored there and in New Zealand from 1864 to 1873. Courtesy of the Disciples of Christ Historical Society

The influence of the Americans, despite their small number, was considerable. Their preaching was appreciated and produced results. They trained local talent. They were in great demand in suburban and rural churches. They were responsible for developing the first significant journal of the Australian Churches of Christ, the *Australian Christian Pioneer.* They held "protracted meetings," evangelistic crusades. Their influence was further extended as their converts multiplied.

Because of the success they enjoyed, the Americans, in spite of their sensitivity, inadvertently fostered tensions. One question at issue was whether the evangelist should be given greater responsibility for the morning service, which in Australia was seen to be the preserve of the elders. Other issues in debate included the relationship between the evangelist and the elders, the question of whether or not money should be received from the unimmersed, and whether decisions of conferences of churches were binding on congregations.

The American influence was most keenly felt in Victoria and South Australia. Though the New South Wales churches asked for assistance, they were suspicious of the Americans. J. J. Haley, one of the few Americans to minister in New South Wales, on his return to the United States was not slow to point out the difficulties he faced in the Mother Colony, which he argued was more concerned with the preservation of doctrinal purity than with growth. The New South Wales membership was concentrated in the Newtown congregation.

3. 1875-1910

The years 1875 to 1910 witnessed the development of an emerging maturity. This maturity, evidenced in organizational development, growth in confidence, and doctrinal shifts, was paralleled by developments within the nation itself.

Attempts at developing conferences in the earlier period were tentative. As the nineteenth century drew to a close and numbers swelled, it became evident that new organizational structures were imperative. Though it was feared by some that extra-congregational developments could result in the churches being captive to these innovations, the challenges faced by the churches required concerted effort. The majority became convinced that conferences and their agencies were essential to progress. In addition, a printing and publishing company was founded, and evangelistic work was commenced among Australian Chinese and among Kanakas Islanders who had been "blackbirded" or kidnapped to work in Australia. A foreign mission work was also established.

Born in Kentucky, Jesse James Haley (1851-1924) served churches in Australia and New Zealand from 1874 to 1885. After pastorates in San Francisco, Midway, Kentucky, and St. Louis, he served in England under the auspices of the Foreign Christian Missionary Society from 1890 to 1895. His extensive journalistic work included *Makers and Molders of the Reformation Movement* (1914). Courtesy of Graeme Chapman

No longer as defensive or combative as they had been, the Australian Churches of Christ, in the closing decade of the nineteenth century, rediscovered the emphasis on unity that had always been part of their plea. This recovery coincided with an upward social mobility in the membership.

The ecumenical strains that began to be heard once again in their message resulted, not merely from internal developments but also from changes taking place in the wider community. Presbyterian and Methodist Churches, which had splintered, sought to reunite their memberships. Australia-wide unionism exerted an influence, as did the growing interest in the possibility of federating the colonies. Furthermore, Churches of Christ were drawn into association with other Protestants in the bitter sectarian rivalry of the 1890s and through their involvement in the Temperance Movement.

One of the most striking developments to occur during the period 1875-1910 was the liberalizing of the movement's theology. In the early years creeds had been dismissed out of hand as divisive. As the nineteenth century drew to a close, Churches of Christ came to recognize the value of summary statements of belief. The burgeoning membership, second-generation Christians and converts from the "denominations," needed tutoring. The value of theology, at least biblical theology, also came to be appreciated. However, it was the Church's practice and theology of ministry that evidenced the greatest development. Evangelists itinerated less, often settling with local congregations and taking on pastoral responsibilities. Their distinctive role was beginning to be accepted.

While the churches, from the beginning, had argued that local elderships were part of the New Testament pattern, few effective elderships developed. This lack continued to be lamented. It was also beginning to be recognized that the vigorous autonomy that characterized the life of the churches in the early years exacerbated the problem. Members disciplined by one congregation could take up member-

The Cottonville Church of Christ south of Adelaide, South Australia, was opened on Angus Road on July 19, 1896, through the work of M. W. Green, evangelist for the nearby Unley Church. The effort was a mission to "working men" and their families. The Unley, Grote Street, and North Adelaide Churches contributed to the building.
Courtesy of the Disciples of Christ Historical Society

ship with another without being challenged. The suggestion of a united eldership, however, was not taken up. The traditional commitment to local autonomy held up, supported in part by the fiercely egalitarian spirit of Australians.

The period 1875-1910 also witnessed debate over the legitimacy of Sunday Schools, Christian Endeavour Societies, and the use of organs in worship. These issues were eventually decided in the affirmative.

4. 1910-1939

Between 1910 and 1930 Australia was drawn out of its isolation onto the world stage. When Britain declared war on Germany in 1914, Australians, as citizens of the Empire, responded with patriotic fervor.

It was during this twenty-year period that the organizational and theological developments of the previous era were consolidated. The new theological synthesis was expressed with cogency and persuasiveness by A. R. Main, who towered over his peers within Churches of Christ, exerting an extraordinary influence. Main, who had emigrated with his parents from Scotland, enjoyed the rare privilege of being concurrently principal of the National College of the Bible, which had been established in 1906, and editor of the *Australian Christian,* the national journal of Churches of Christ in Australia begun in 1898 by A. B. Maston. Main, who distinguished himself at Melbourne University, encouraged successive generations of students to attempt university work. This process eventually backfired on him, as these students came to challenge his conservatism.

During the Main era, churches worldwide, including Churches of Christ, became increasingly concerned with the question of Christian unity. In 1910 a Congress on Union was called, at which Churches of Christ were represented, Main being one of the representatives. This Congress was to result, in time, in the formation of the Uniting Church, a union involving Presbyterians, Methodists, and Congregationalists.

The 1930s were marked by a worldwide Depression that did not lift until after the outbreak of the Second World War. While the membership of the Churches during the Main era almost doubled, the 1930s witnessed a loss. By 1933 a third of the male population of Australia was out of work. This confronted local churches with enormous difficulties and challenges. During these years state and federal conferences developed Social Service Committees to help relieve the distress.

During the Depression preachers were in a precarious position. Some were discharged by churches

Alexander Russell Main (1876-1945) left Scotland for Australia in 1892 and became one of the chief leaders of the Churches of Christ in that country. He served as lecturer and then principal of the Australian College of the Bible for thirty-two years, then came out of retirement in 1942 to become the first principal of Woolwich Bible College near Sydney. Courtesy of Graeme Chapman

that could no longer afford them. Preachers were forced to compete with each other on the basis of the lowest salary they were willing to accept. The larger Federal Conference departments, particularly the College of the Bible and the Foreign Mission Committee, were the most deeply affected. They survived because their employees were willing to work for pitifully low wages.

5. World War II and After

In September 1939 the world was plunged into another major war. During the First World War debate raged around the question of conscription. Anti-war sentiment was even stronger during the 1939-45 conflict. Churches of Christ offered assistance to conscientious objectors and encouraged members, whatever their attitude to the war, to respect those with different opinions.

When the war concluded, the churches were confronted by new threats, notably Russian Communism and, after 1949, Chinese Communism. As well as needing to confront the issues of the Cold War and the threat of atomic annihilation, the churches were also challenged by an increasing secularism. The presence of these challenges drew denominations together. Unity was becoming a necessity. A new level of ecumenical excitement was evident when the World Council of Churches was formed in Amsterdam in 1948. Unfortunately, within Churches of Christ, this development precipitated a confrontation between enthusiasts and conservatives. Opposition to what was considered a sellout to Liberalism was centered in New South Wales, which established its own college in 1941, ostensibly to enable the Sydney churches to enjoy the benefits of student ministries.

During the late 1950s Churches of Christ became involved in Billy Graham Crusades. Ironically, opposition to the crusades or, rather, a confessed reluctance to be involved in them arose, not among those concerned to preserve Restoration traditions but among the more liberal element in the churches, who argued that Graham's message did not represent a rounded gospel.

Kenmore Christian College, a college for training ministers, was established in Queensland during the 1960s. While the College of the Bible lamented this development, which would further dissipate meager resources, the New South Wales Bible College offered support. James Jauncey, an Australian living in America, was appointed inaugural principal.

The 1960s were a difficult period for all Churches. The West enjoyed unprecedented affluence, while baby boomers, who had known neither depression nor war, flexed their muscles and found their voice. Opposition to the war in Vietnam and agitation for civil rights and changes in university administration reached fever pitch. The churches were losing ground and debilitated by an outmoded theology. Prominent theologians informed members that God was dead. Disillusioned ministers left the ministry.

Change was in the wind in the early 1970s, with the eruption of the Jesus Revolution and the emergence of the Charismatic Movement, which threatened to divide local congregations. Traditionalists and Charismatics eventually came to tolerate each other. Following close on the heels of the Charismatic phenomenon was the Church Growth Movement, introduced to Australia by Churches of Christ. The thinking of Donald McGavran helped raise the spirits and inform the strategizing of Churches of Christ. The churches began thinking big, though there were casualties for the easy optimism the enthusiasm bred. This movement also fostered the development of large churches and a class of senior ministers. Both precipitated debate on the question of leadership. This development coincided, in the wider community, with an era of swashbuckling entrepreneurs, many of whom were to fall from grace when the bubble burst in the late 1980s.

The dismemberment of the Russian empire, the fall of the Berlin wall, the emergence and deflation of the tiger economies in South East Asia, the rise of China to a position of influence, and an increasing focus on the Middle East have altered the demographic, economic, and political balance to such a degree that is difficult to predict the future. A world that is increasingly post-denominational, post-modern, and post-Christian has forced upon the church a new set of missional objectives. These objectives are differently conceived by different groups within Churches of Christ, as within other churches. Church leaders are also aware of the pervasive influence of Pentecostal patterns of ministry and worship, some welcoming and others deprecating them. Furthermore, recognition of the legitimacy of women in ministry is taking hold. Women now hold many senior leadership positions.

Churches of Christ, like other Christian communions, are also having to come to terms with New Age spirituality, and with forms of spirituality informed by Eastern traditions that many in the community feel are more relevant and palatable. It is also being recognized that it is increasingly difficult for any one religious tradition to lay exclusive claim to the truth. This Copernican revolution challenges the Church's historic claim that Jesus represents the only sure route to God. Some among the laity are exercised, if not perplexed, by these issues, particularly the thoughtful. Others recoil in horror and retreat to a defensive conservatism. In between these two groups are those who accept the challenges implicit in these conundra and seek to address their questions with intellectual, moral, and spiritual integrity.

6. Membership

The current membership of the Australian Churches of Christ is 36,500. The number of churches totals 443.

Unlike the Stone-Campbell Movement in the United States, the Australian Churches of Christ were not fractured by open division. Apart from a few individuals who felt disfranchised and gradually withdrew from involvement with "Conference" churches, the Australian movement has been able to accommodate differences. This is reflected in the fact that, while the Australian movement has enjoyed a strong fraternal association with the Christian Church (Disciples of Christ), individual ministers and churches from more conservative enclaves within the movement have fostered association with the Christian Churches/Churches of Christ.

While a number of individuals associated with Australian Churches of Christ welcomed the support and initiative of leaders from the American Churches of Christ, particularly after the advent of J. A. Hudson in 1937, the presence in Australia of "non-instrumental" Churches of Christ resulted largely from American initiative and encouragement. Those Australians drawn to the "non-instrumental" churches, particularly in the early years, were people who were convinced that "conference" churches had departed from the restoration ideal. J. W. Shepherd of Kentucky, later a close associate of David Lipscomb, moved (via New Zealand) to Sydney to become minister of the Elizabeth Street Church of Christ in 1890. While Shepherd returned to the United States in 1862, his conservative positions were passed on to Australian leader J. W. McGregor, who along with A. G. Chaffer and others led a small group of Australians in opposition to instrumental music in worship and extracongregational organization.

In 1937, at the invitation of McGregor, John Allen Hudson of the American Churches of Christ visited the country and reported on the status of the churches. Following Hudson's visit a number of families from the United States came to minister in Australia. One of the first was Charles and Judy Tinius in 1948. Also some conservatives from the Associated Churches of Christ, such as Colin Smith, began ministering in a cappella churches. A peak of forty American missionary familes was reached between 1968 and 1975. In the 1990s approximately 3,000 individuals worshiped in eighty-one a cappella congregations.

See also Great Britain and Ireland, The Movement in; McGavran, Donald A.; New Zealand, The Movement in

BIBLIOGRAPHY Graeme Chapman, *Ballarat Churches of Christ, 1859-1993: A History* (1994) • Graeme Chapman, *No Other Foundation: A Documentary History of Churches of Christ in Australia, 1846-1990*, 3 vols. (1993) • Graeme Chapman, *One Lord, One Faith, One Baptism: A History of Churches of Christ in Australia* (1979) • David Roper, *Voices Crying in the Wilderness: A History of the Lord's Church with Special Emphasis on Australia* (1979).

GRAEME CHAPMAN

Australian Christian

See Australia, The Movement in

B

Babcock, Clara Celestia Hale (1850-1924)

Pioneering woman preacher, one of the first women ordained to ministry in the Stone-Campbell Movement. She baptized 1,502 during thirty-six years of ministry.

She was born May 31, 1850, in Fitchville, Ohio, to Laura and John Hale, Jr., her father a wagon-maker who died before she was a year old. She was influenced by Frederick Paine, a former Methodist Episcopal minister and active prohibitionist, who was her guardian for several years. Clara Hale married Israel R. Babcock on August 9, 1865, and bore six children, but only two survived to adulthood. The Babcocks joined the Stone-Campbell Movement through the influence of revival evangelist George F. Adams at the Sterling (Illinois) Christian Church in 1880. Babcock was active in local civic organizations and became president of the Whiteside County Woman's Christian Temperance Union in 1887. She began to preach regularly at the Erie Christian Church in November 1888 and was ordained there on August 2, 1889, by Andrew Scott of the Sterling Church. She was a popular evangelistic preacher and temperance speaker throughout the region. Babcock held pastorates in Erie, Thomson, Rapid City, and Savanna, Illinois; LeClaire and Dixon, Iowa; Ellendale, North Dakota; and Port Arthur, Ontario. She died on December 12, 1924, in Erie, Illinois.

See also Crank, Sarah Catherine (Sadie) McCoy; Preaching — Nineteenth Century; Temperance; Women in Ministry — Nineteenth Century

BIBLIOGRAPHY Debra B. Hull, *Christian Church Women: Shapers of a Movement* (1994) • Mary Ellen Lantzer, *An Examination of the 1892-1893* Christian Standard *Controversy Concerning Women's Preaching* (1990) • Glenn Zuber, "'The Gospel of Temperance': Early Disciple Women Preachers and the WCTU, 1887-1912," *Discipliana* 53:2 (Summer 1993): 47-60 • Glenn Zuber, "Mainline Women Ministers: Women Missionary and Temperance Organizers Become 'Disciples of Christ' Ministers, 1888-1908," in *The Stone-Campbell Movement: An International Religious Tradition,* ed. Michael Casey and Douglas A. Foster (2002), pp. 292-316.

MARY ELLEN LANTZER PEREIRA

Often regarded as the first woman ordained to the ministry in the Movement, Clara Hale Babcock (1850-1924) served churches in Illinois, Iowa, and North Dakota for over thirty-six years.

Bacon College

Bacon College was the first true institution of higher learning to be founded by members of the Stone-Campbell Movement. The school was opened in 1836 in Georgetown, Kentucky, and chartered by the state legislature in early 1837. Thornton F. Johnson, a professor at Baptist-related Georgetown College, was a member of the united Disciples/Christian church in Georgetown. After a period of conflict with the Baptists, Johnson decided to open a college related to the Stone-Campbell Movement. He asked Walter Scott to lend his name and influence to the establishment of the school. Scott agreed to serve as president for a brief time. After a year Scott relinquished his position and was succeeded by David Staats Burnet.

The college was named Bacon College in honor of Sir Francis Bacon, one of the earliest thinkers of the Enlightenment. This was a way of affirming that the Christian faith is rational and guided by reason. John Locke, another major figure of the Enlightenment, was frequently referred to by Alexander Campbell as "the Christian philosopher." The symbolism of the name "Bacon College" pointed to the grounding of the Stone-Campbell Movement in the rationalism of the Enlightenment.

In 1839, thanks to financial support of Disciples in Harrodsburg, Kentucky, the college relocated to that community. James Shannon became the president. Financial difficulties reduced the college to a preparatory school in the early 1850s. An infusion of money in the mid-1850s and a new charter putting the college in the hands of the Disciples resulted in the reopening of the college as Kentucky University in 1859.

During the Civil War the college was used as a hospital, and soon afterward the main building was destroyed by fire. Meanwhile, Transylvania University in Lexington, Kentucky, had also fallen onto hard times. Transylvania was the oldest institution of higher education west of the Alleghenies. With the Morrill Land Act of 1862 as a stimulus, Bacon College — now Kentucky University — united with Transylvania in Lexington, continuing the Kentucky University name, and in negotiations with the state of Kentucky became a university with a College of the Bible (1865) for the education of ministers, an undergraduate college of arts and sciences, and a state-supported Agricultural and Mechanical College (1866). Thus a church-related university with financial support from the state was established.

The tensions among the various elements and constituencies eventually fragmented the institution, resulting in three separate schools. Two of these, Kentucky University and the College of the Bible, would continue as closely related but separately chartered institutions related to the Disciples stream of the Stone-Campbell Movement. Eventually the Agricultural and Mechanical College would become the University of Kentucky. The liberal arts college descendant of Bacon College/Kentucky University would continue with the name of Kentucky University until 1908, when the name of Transylvania University was reclaimed. The College of the Bible remained on the Transylvania campus until 1949-50. In 1965 it was renamed Lexington Theological Seminary.

See also Lexington Theological Seminary; Transylvania University

BIBLIOGRAPHY D. Duane Cummins, *The Disciples Colleges: A History* (1987) • Dwight E. Stevenson, *The Bacon College Story, 1836-1865* (1962) • Dwight E. Stevenson, *Lexington Theological Seminary, 1865-1965* (1964) • John D. Wright, Jr., *Transylvania: Tutor to the West* (1975).

RICHARD L. HARRISON, JR.

Baconianism

See Common Sense Philosophy

Bader, Jesse Moren (1886-1963)

Disciples of Christ evangelist and leader in the World Convention of Churches of Christ.

Jesse Bader was devoted to evangelism and to the unity of all people under the banner of Christ. Born in Bader, Illinois, he studied at the University of Kansas and graduated from Drake University in 1911. Ordained to the ministry, Bader held pastorates in Kansas and Missouri and served overseas with the Y.M.C.A. during World War I. In 1910 he married Golda Elam, also an ordained minister with her own interests and career in ecumenical affairs, including United Church Women. With the founding of the United Christian Missionary Society in 1920, Bader became the organization's Secretary of Evangelism. His task was to provide effective evangelistic strategies for local churches. Later he was called to head the Department of Evangelism for the Federal Council of Churches. Writing widely in the field of evangelism, his chief text was *Evangelism in a Changing America* (1957). He was also a consultant to Billy Graham. In 1940 he initiated the observance of World Communion Sunday.

His passion for Christian unity led to the organization of the World Convention of Churches of Christ. In 1930 he served as president of the initial convention held in Washington, D.C. Working to bring about fellowship between global manifestations of the Movement and among the divided segments of the church within the United States, Bader served as General Secretary of the World Convention until his death in 1963.

Secretary of Evangelism in the United Christian Missionary Society and later head of the Department of Evangelism of the Federal Council of Churches, Jesse M. Bader (1886-1963) led in the founding of the World Convention of Churches of Christ in 1930. Courtesy of the Disciples of Christ Historical Society

See also Evangelism, Evangelists; World Convention of Churches of Christ, The

BIBLIOGRAPHY Jesse Moren Bader papers, Disciples of Christ Historical Society • Samuel McCrae Cavert, "Jesse Moren Bader: Evangelical and Ecumenical Churchman," in *Herald of the Evangel,* ed. Edwin T. Dahlberg (1965)

CLINTON J. HOLLOWAY

Bales, James David (1915-1995)

Minister, author, and professor at Harding University. James David Bales was born November 5, 1915, at Tacoma, Washington. After the untimely death of his parents, he grew up with grandparents in Fitzgerald, Georgia. He became a Christian at the age of 13 and graduated from Tech High School in Atlanta in 1933. He began preaching in 1934 while a student at Harding College, and during vacations he did evangelistic work in Arkansas and Georgia. After graduating from Harding in 1937, he attended George Peabody College, graduating with an M.A. in 1938.

Bales then moved to Toronto, where he was minister for the Fern Avenue Church of Christ and studied at the University of Toronto. In 1940 he married Mary Smart, and shortly thereafter he moved to San Francisco to preach for the Eighth Avenue congregation. From 1942 to 44, he preached at Whittle Avenue in Oakland. In 1946 Bales received his Ph.D. in philosophy from the University of Southern California. In 1953 he studied at Union Theological Seminary.

Bales served as Professor of Christian Doctrine at Harding University for almost forty-five years and was selected as Distinguished Alumnus in 1976. He was a prolific writer, engaging most controversies in Churches of Christ through his long career. Among his books are *The Holy Spirit and the Christian* (1966), *Modernism: The Trojan Horse in the Church* (1971), *Prophecy and Premillennialism* (1972), *Pentecostalism* (1972), and *Instrumental Music and New Testament Worship* (1973). His controversial stance on divorce and remarriage — that non-Christians were not subject to the Christian laws of marriage and divorce — explained in his book *Not Under Bondage* (1979), made him a subject of controversy in Churches of Christ in his later years.

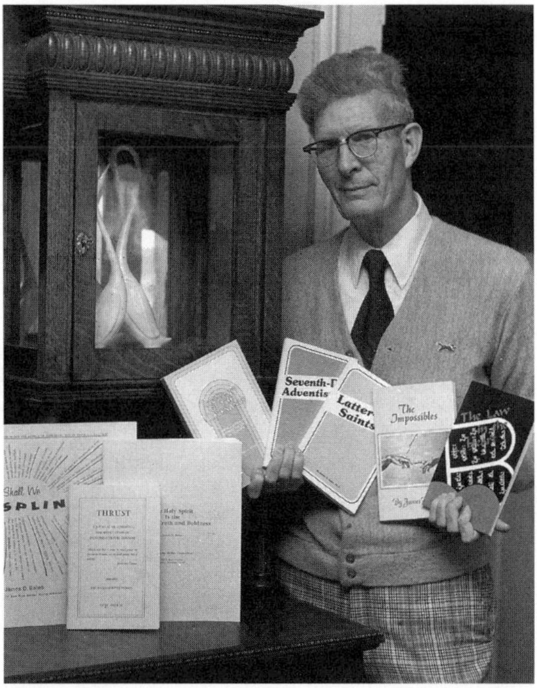

Though primarily known outside Churches of Christ for his anti-communist writings, Bales wrote over thirty books, many dealing with controversial subjects within that body. One of his last publications was a 1992 conservative response to James S. Woodroof's 1990 volume *The Church in Transition* titled *The Church in Transition: To What?* Courtesy of the Center for Restoration Studies, Abilene Christian University

His conservative political views led him to write extensively about freedom and oppression, as well as the relative merits of capitalism versus communism. His book *Communism: Its Faith and Fallacies* (1962) was widely read. Because of his extensive work in this area, his papers were given to the Fullbright collection in the archives of the University of Arkansas at Fayetteville after his death. Although firm in his convictions, Bales was a kind and compassionate man whose gentleness and humor exemplified a genuinely Christian character.

See also Harding University

CARROLL D. OSBURN

Baptism

1. Backgrounds
2. Early Stone-Campbell Movement Leaders on Baptism
   2.1. Alexander Campbell
   2.2. Barton W. Stone
   2.3. Summary
3. Developments in Baptismal Belief in the Stone-Campbell Movement — Nineteenth and Early Twentieth Centuries
   3.1. Churches of Christ
   3.2. Christian Church (Disciples of Christ) and Christian Churches/Churches of Christ
4. More Recent Developments in Baptismal Belief and Practice
   4.1. Christian Church (Disciples of Christ)
   4.2. Christian Churches/Churches of Christ
   4.3. Churches of Christ
5. Conclusion

The churches of the Stone-Campbell Movement have historically held that scriptural baptism consists of the immersion of penitent believers, the culmination of a process of salvation begun with faith in Jesus Christ, repentance of sin, and public confession of faith in Christ, followed by faithful service to Christ as part of a congregation of fellow believers.

1. Backgrounds

The theology of the founding leaders of the Stone-Campbell Movement was influenced by both their Reformation heritage and their experience of nineteenth-century American Christianity. The Lutheran emphasis on baptism as a divinely instituted sign and the promise of the forgiveness of sins was appropriated by Alexander Campbell in his essay on "Remission of Sins," arguably his most important writing on the subject of baptism. Both Stone and Campbell were products of Presbyterianism and the abiding influence of John Calvin. Calvin had defined baptism and the Lord's Supper as outward signs "by which the Lord seals on our consciences the promises of his good will toward us in order to sustain the weakness of our faith; and we in turn attest our piety toward him." Baptism for Calvin was "a testimony of divine grace toward us, confirmed by an outward sign, with mutual attestation of our piety toward him."

The religious context of the American frontier raised two questions for both Stone and Campbell. The first of these questions concerned the mode of baptism. This question was raised by the growing number of Baptists on the frontier who insisted that scriptural baptism was the immersion of believers upon confession of faith. Presbyterians, also numerous on the American frontier, rose to the defense of the practice of infant baptism. Both Stone and Campbell would eventually be convinced that scriptural baptism was immersion of penitent believers.

The second question did not initially concern baptism. This was the question of how a believer could be assured of forgiveness and acceptance with God. Jonathan Edwards, whose views were appropriated by American Presbyterians, argued that the only assurance of forgiveness and acceptance by God was a life of Christian faithfulness, what he called holiness. Edwards understood Christian faithfulness as the result of God's transformation of the heart, a transformation that always accompanied God's acceptance of the sinner. Methodists followed the teaching of John Wesley that one must know that one is forgiven and accepted by God before one can love God and neighbor, that is, before one can be holy. Wesley taught that believers could have a personal assurance of God's love and favor through an immediate witness of the Spirit. This witness or revelation might come as a word spoken by God, as words of Scripture or promise impressed on the mind, or a deep feeling of God's forgiveness and acceptance. Alexander Campbell's understanding of the design or purpose of baptism would be appropriated by the larger Stone-Campbell Movement as its distinctive answer to the question of how a believer could be assured of God's love and favor: baptism was the assurance to a penitent believer of God's forgiveness.

2. Early Stone-Campbell Movement Leaders on Baptism

2.1. Alexander Campbell

Both Thomas and Alexander Campbell were baptized as infants. As early as 1809 the question of the validity of infant baptism had been raised in the Christian Association when its members adopted the slogan, "We speak where the Bible speaks and are silent where the Bible is silent." The issue came to a head for Alexander when his first child was born in 1812. He began a serious study of baptism and concluded that he had not been scripturally baptized.

Baptist pastor Matthias Luce immersed Thomas and Alexander Campbell, along with their wives and three others, on June 12, 1812, on the simple confession that "Jesus is the son of God." In 1826 Luce, then pastor of the Pigeon Creek Baptist Church, was expelled from the Redstone Association along with thirteen other "reforming" churches for refusing to subscribe to the Philadelphia Confession of Faith.
Courtesy of the Disciples of Christ Historical Society

He determined to submit to immersion and persuaded a Baptist minister, Matthias Luce, to perform the act. His wife, parents, a sister, and two others from the Brush Run Church, successor to the Christian Association, were immersed on the same occasion, on a simple profession of faith in Christ.

For Campbell, the issue of who is the proper subject of baptism was related to the nature of the church, its relation to the state, and religious and political freedom. Campbell held that "no one can believe, repent, make confession, or be baptized by proxy, or upon another person's confession." Christianity is "personal," Campbell asserted, "it is neither family nor national." In infant baptism, the baptized had no freedom to say yes or no. Parents confessed their faith, but the infant did not. "It is despotism of the worst kind, to impose upon the conscience," Campbell contended. Reflecting a strong antipathy toward establishment of religion, he feared that religious bodies still established in some of the eastern states as late the first decades of the nineteenth century might move westward and seek to limit religious and political freedom. Campbell, familiar with the role of infant baptism in the state churches of Europe, saw believers' baptism as supporting the church's freedom from interference by the state as well as personal religious freedom.

Moreover, Campbell charged that infant baptism caused the church to compromise its witness and lose its identity. Infant baptism "has carnalized and secularized the church more than any other innovation since the first defection in Christianity." It causes "the discrimination between the world and the church" to be lost. Referring to a period when in the state Church of Scotland the whole nation was baptized, Campbell stated that "all the enormities committed in the realm were committed by members of the church." For Campbell, baptism was for penitent believers ready to subject themselves to the command of the gospel to love God and neighbor. Such a view, he believed, had profound social implications, and he committed his movement to a transformation of society that he understood the gospel to command, including an end to slavery, education for women, and Christian unity.

The Brush Run Church became part of the Redstone Baptist Association in 1815. Alexander Campbell early became a champion for the Baptists on believers' immersion, debating Presbyterians John Walker in 1820 and W. L. Maccalla in 1823. There is, however, a discernible shift in Campbell's understanding of the purpose of baptism during the decade of the 1820s.

In his debate with Walker, Campbell clearly stated that baptism was emblematic of the salvation already received by those who have believed. The renewing of the Holy Spirit preceded and led the believer to baptism as a representation of that completed work of God. Campbell's understanding was essentially that then held by most Baptists.

By the time of the debate with MacCalla, Campbell had begun to make a much more intimate connection between baptism and the remission of sins. He still insisted that forgiveness and salvation come only by the blood of Christ through faith in him. "Real" or "actual" forgiveness comes through faith in Jesus Christ apart from baptism. Yet the "formal" remission of sins comes in the act of baptism.

By the end of the 1820s, however, Campbell had moved beyond this position to merge the points of actual and formal forgiveness. "I do earnestly contend that God, through the blood of Christ, forgives our sins through immersion — through the very act and in the very instant." A person is not clean before he or she is washed, Campbell argued. The clearly visible marker between the state of nature and the state of grace is the act of baptism. No one has any proof of the forgiveness of sins until baptism. No one has ever received pardon of sin by faith only. Water baptism, with faith as the principle of action, is the means through which God by the power of the blood of Christ imparts remission.

Well over one-third of Campbell's theological treatise *The Christian System* is devoted to an exposition of his understanding of baptism and remission of sins. Like Wesley, Campbell argued that the believer's assurance of acceptance by God is the foundation of Christian holiness. Christians are identified by such terms as forgiven, pardoned, justified, sanctified, reconciled, adopted into the family of God, and saved. These terms, Campbell argued, represent a state and not a character, though he insists that "there is a relationship between state and character, or an influence which state has upon character."

> Indeed, the strongest arguments which the apostles used with the Christians to urge them forward in the cultivation and display of all moral and religious excellencies of character are drawn from the meaning and value of the *state* in which they are placed. Because forgiven, they should forgive; because justified, they should live righteously; because sanctified, they should live holy and unblamably; because reconciled to God, they should cultivate peace with all . . . and act benevolently towards all; because adopted they should walk in the dignity and purity of sons of God; because saved, they should abound in thanksgivings, praises, and rejoicings, living soberly, righteously, and godly, looking forward to the blessed hope.

He is explicit in his assertion that baptism is the act by which our state is changed.

> As soon can a person be a citizen before he is born, or have the immunities of an American citizen while an alien, as one enjoy the privileges of a son of God before he is born again. . . . if being born again, or being born of water and the Spirit, is necessary for admission, and if being born of water mean immersion, as clearly proved by all witnesses; then, remission of sins can not, in this life, be constitutionally enjoyed previous to immersion.

Furthermore, Campbell explained that the "washing of regeneration" spoken of in Titus 3:5 was synonymous with immersion. Immersion was not simply a physical act.

> There is no such thing as outward bodily acts in the Christian institution; and less than in all others, in the act of immersion. Then it is that the spirit, soul, and body of man become one with the Lord. Then it is that the power of the Father, Son, and Holy Spirit comes upon us. Then it is that we are enrolled among the children of God, and enter the ark, which will, if we abide in it, transport us to the mount of God.

Campbell's view was a *via media* between the Roman Catholic teaching of *ex opere operato* and Protestant understandings that separated baptism from salvation. Personal faith and repentance were essential for the efficacy of baptism, yet in the baptism of a penitent believer there occurred a real change of state.

The Campbells and their associate Walter Scott, the greatest early evangelist of the Movement, worked as Baptists for almost fifteen years. Yet it became clear to many Baptist leaders that the position Campbell came to hold on baptism was not in keeping with Baptist doctrine. By 1830 many Baptist Associations were divided concerning the "Reformers'" positions. Separation between the "Reformers" and their Baptist colleagues ensued.

Campbell's mature view of baptism appears to be rigid and without exception. Beginning in the 1830s, however, there were three matters about which Campbell would be pressed that had important implications for his teachings on baptism. The first had to do with whether baptism was a work by which one secured pardon. Campbell answered, "We do not place baptism among good works. In baptism we are passive in every thing but in giving our consent." Campbell disagreed with some of his co-workers on the nature of baptism, saying that some had "given to baptism undue eminence — a sort of pardon-procuring, rather than pardon-certifying and enjoying efficacy . . . ; but such has never been my reasonings nor my course." In *The Christian System* he asserts that "to the believing penitent it is the *means* of receiving a formal, distinct, and specific absolution, or release from guilt . . . the full and explicit testimony of God, assuring them of pardon."

The second question had to do with one's knowledge at the time of baptism. Is the immersion of persons who do not understand their sins to be remitted in the act valid? In other words, does ignorance of the full significance of one's immersion invalidate it and require the person to submit to "rebaptism"? Campbell's answer to this question was also clear. If a person had been baptized upon a simple confession of faith in Jesus Christ, he or she was a citizen of God's kingdom. The only thing that could justify someone's rebaptism was if the candidate confessed that he or she did not believe that Jesus was the Messiah, the Son of God, at the time of the first immersion. Campbell certainly believed that it was in baptism that one's sins were forgiven. Yet the knowledge of this at the time of one's baptism was not an essential component of the necessary faith. Trust in a person, not comprehension of a list of facts, was the essential. Perfect knowledge of all that is effected in the act of baptism was not a prerequisite for its validity. Otherwise Paul would have reimmersed the Roman, Galatian, and Corinthian Christians since he had to explain to all of these groups the very meaning of baptism.

Campbell stressed that remission of sins was God's work from first to last. In baptism the penitent believer receives this blessing through faith in Jesus. Baptism does not save because of one's perfect understanding of baptism. It saves because of God's promise. To insist that a person's baptism was invalid because he or she did not know that in baptism their sins were forgiven was to negate Jesus' own statement in Mark 16:16, "The one who believes and is baptized shall be saved."

The third issue concerned whether there are Christians who have not been immersed. That is, are all those who live lives of faith in Christ but who, through ignorance or honest misunderstanding, have never been immersed condemned to eternal damnation? On this matter Campbell made his clearest statement in a series of articles in 1837 in response to a letter from a woman in Lunenburg, Virginia. The incident must be understood in the context of a controversy between Campbell and John Thomas, a British medical doctor who had moved to Virginia and become a leader in the Movement. Thomas had begun a militant advocacy of rebaptism of persons who had been baptized without explicit knowledge of remission of sins. In July 1837 a Thomas supporter wrote Campbell a note expressing surprise that he in an earlier article had written that Christians were to be found in all Protestant parties. "How does one become a Christian?" she asked. "Does the name of Christ or Christian belong to any but those who believe the gospel, repent, and are buried by baptism into the death of Christ?"

Campbell's reply was to the point.

> But who is a Christian? I answer, Every one that believes in his heart that Jesus of Nazareth is the Messiah, the son of God; repents of his sins, and obeys him in all things according to his measure of knowledge of his will. . . . it is possible for Christians to be imperfect in some respects without an absolute forfeiture of the Christian state and character.
>
> I cannot make any one duty the standard of Christian state or character, not even immersion into the name of the Father, of the Son, and of the Holy Spirit, and in my heart regard all that have been sprinkled in infancy without their own knowledge and consent, as aliens from Christ and the well-grounded hope of heaven.
>
> There is no occasion, then, for making immersion, on a profession of the faith, absolutely essential to a Christian — though it may be greatly essential to his sanctification and comfort. My right hand and my right eye are greatly essential to my usefulness and happiness, but not to my life; and as I could not be a perfect man without them, so I cannot be a perfect Christian without a right understanding and a cordial reception of immersion in its true and scriptural meaning and design. But he who thence infers that none are Christians but the immersed, as greatly errs as he who affirms that none are alive but those of full and clear vision.

Campbell's answer caused quite a stir. Some complained that he had effectively neutralized what they had been preaching on the importance of baptism for remission of sins. Campbell answered that he was not speaking of those who obstinately rejected this or any of Christ's ordinances or who willingly neglected to ascertain the will of the Lord. Rather, he spoke of those "who through a simple mistake, involving no perversity of mind, [have] misapprehended the outward baptism." Since baptism was both an inward and an outward act, it was possible for a person to be changed inwardly yet not to be scripturally baptized.

Though Campbell was willing to admit the Christianity of at least some unimmersed believers, his recognition did not extend to accepting them as members of the visible church — the kingdom of God on earth. He disagreed with Barton W. Stone, whose movement generally practiced "open membership." We can only judge by one's visible obedience, Campbell insisted. We cannot set aside a commandment of God and receive persons into the church who have not been immersed into the name of Jesus. God will ultimately judge the hearts of unimmersed believers, but they cannot enjoy the fellowship of God's visible kingdom on earth.

2.2. Barton W. Stone

Though Barton W. Stone preceded the Campbells in his reformatory work, baptism was not as crucial an issue for him and his movement. Stone and several of his Presbyterian associates withdrew from the Synod of Kentucky in 1803 to form their own Springfield Presbytery after charges of heresy were brought against one of their number. As early as 1800 one of Stone's colleagues, Robert Marshall, had become convinced of the truth of believers' immersion. Stone, in trying to dissuade Marshall from this "error" and from uniting with the Baptists, engaged in an exchange of correspondence with him. Stone reported that Marshall's arguments were so convincing that he abandoned the practice of infant baptism.

Stone notes, however, that about the time the "great revival" broke out (1801 in Stone's region of the country) he was distracted from the subject of baptism for several years. When the matter did surface again in his movement around 1807, Stone accepted believers' immersion. However, the matter was left to the individual's conscience. Forbearance was to be the rule, those who chose immersion not despising those who did not and vice versa. Stone also notes that for a time he and others preached baptism for remission of sin, yet admitted that "Into the spirit of the doctrine I was never fully led, until it was revived by Brother Alexander Campbell, some years after."

Stone became increasingly aware of the work of the Campbells during the 1820s. He first met Campbell in 1824. In his autobiography he remarked that the only substantive doctrinal difference he saw between the two of them was Campbell's teaching of baptism for remission of sins. Though Campbell had articulated this teaching in the 1823 debate with Maccalla, the first person in the Movement actually to preach the doctrine of baptism for the remission of sins was B. F. Hall, a minister of the Stone movement. Hall, who had discovered Campbell's teaching in the published version of the Campbell-Maccalla debate, sought to convince a reluctant Stone that this doctrine he had taught earlier in the century but had abandoned was critical to the faithful preaching of the gospel.

Eventually Stone came to hold the same positions as Campbell, except for one. As noted, Campbell denied formal fellowship and communion in the "visible church" to unimmersed persons. In other words, unimmersed persons were not generally allowed to become members of a congregation affiliated with the Campbell reform movement. Stone, while defending the doctrine of immersion for forgiveness of sins, did not exclude the unimmersed from membership in the churches that were part of his movement. "We therefore teach the doctrine, believe, repent and be immersed for the remission of sins; and we endeavor to convince our hearers of its truth; but we exercise patience and forbearance towards such pious persons who cannot be convinced." Stone believed Campbell was wrong in his exclusionary stance.

2.3. *Summary*

The positions outlined above are the most basic beliefs concerning baptism in the Stone-Campbell Movement. The ideas held in common in all parts of the Movement include (1) that scriptural baptism is immersion of believers, and (2) that baptism is the act in which God remits the sins of the penitent believer. Ideas over which there has been controversy in the Movement include (1) whether knowledge of the "design" of baptism (remission of sins) is necessary for its validity, (2) whether the "pious unimmersed" (at least some of them) will be saved, and (3) whether the pious unimmersed may be admitted to membership in the churches (open vs. closed membership). Less discerning teachers who reduced baptism almost to a mechanical action were not representative of the more thoughtful and spiritual leaders.

3. Developments in Baptismal Belief in the Stone-Campbell Movement — Nineteenth and Early Twentieth Centuries

3.1. *Churches of Christ*

Churches of Christ generally embodied the most restrictive stance on baptism from the early Movement, that is, only those who believe and are immersed are Christians. They also held without wavering that it was in the act of baptism that forgiveness of sins took place. Baptism was "completing your obedience," and salvation was not received until obedience was complete.

The most controverted matter in Churches of Christ was that of one's knowledge at the time of baptism. This can be seen most explicitly in the controversy between Austin McGary and David Lipscomb in the 1890s. Lipscomb taught that baptism was the act in which a person's state was completely changed "from one of alienation and rebellion against God to one of acceptance and favor with him." He insisted that God's law required all who would be saved to believe, repent, and be baptized. "If they fail to believe and be baptized, they shall be damned, says the Lord." All a faithful Christian could do was to teach what God had commanded and insist on obeying it. If God had ever told anyone that he or she could be saved without baptism, or by substituting affusion or sprinkling for baptism, Lipscomb stated, he had never been able to find it. It was a great sin and deception against the unimmersed to give them the impression they were safe and in the church of God while they refused to obey God in what Lipscomb once called "his test ordinance." While Christians should kindly bear with and associate with unimmersed believers, he said, they must use every opportunity to urge them to obey the truth, for there was no promise in the Bible for those who refused to perfect their faith by obedience in baptism.

Lipscomb held that if a person believed in Christ, repented of sins, and, desiring to obey God, was immersed, that person was added to the kingdom of God. It made no difference where or by whom the baptism was performed as long as those scriptural components were present. Lipscomb readily admitted that persons in Baptist, Methodist, Presbyterian, and other denominations who had been properly baptized had been added to Christ's church, though he believed they should leave those sectarian organizations to be pleasing to God. Furthermore, he contended that such simple obedience secured all the blessings and privileges promised the Christian regardless of the believer's knowledge of them.

Lipscomb's Campbellian position on the validity of immersion without the knowledge that it was for the forgiveness of sins provoked the ire of a group of rigorists. In 1884 Austin McGary founded a journal titled the *Firm Foundation* to promote the teaching that immersion simply to obey God was not sufficient to make the act valid. Moreover, McGary insisted that since the Church of Christ alone taught baptism for remission of sins, anyone who had been immersed in another religious group must be "rebaptized" in order to be saved and become a member of the Church of Christ.

Lipscomb contended that God would not reject service done in obedience to God's law simply because one did not wait to learn all the blessings and promises connected with the obedience. The "rebaptism" group countered that those baptized into "sect baptism" were not baptized for the right reason; they often believed that their sins were already forgiven and that their baptism was for the purpose of joining a particular denomination. Lipscomb admitted that perhaps that was often true. But "sect baptism" was not restricted to those outside Churches of Christ.

Lipscomb pointed out to the rebaptism forces that it made no sense for a person who had begun a journey and gone a long way on the right road, upon taking a wrong turn, to return to the very beginning. So it was with those who had been scripturally baptized and yet found themselves in sectarian establishments. Such a subsequent wrong turn did not undo their faith, repentance, or baptism. Such persons should keep all that they had that was true and right, and simply get off the wrong road and back on the right one. "We only return to the point at which we erred and there begin aright," he insisted.

The debate between the *Gospel Advocate* and the *Firm Foundation* raged during the 1890s and into the twentieth century. This was the era of the major division between the Churches of Christ and the Disciples of Christ. The intense feelings surrounding that schism and the fear of theological liberalism associated with the Disciples pushed many in Churches of Christ into a reactionary mode. The rigorist position held by McGary became the majority view in Churches of Christ, though the more moderate Lipscomb position never disappeared, especially in Middle Tennessee where Lipscomb's influence was greatest.

Baptism at Wema in Congo. Ministers officiating left to right: Clayton Weeks, A. Dale Fiers (then president of the United Christian Missionary Society), Bonzali Petelo, and Eale Petelo. Courtesy of the Disciples of Christ Historical Society

3.2. Christian Church (Disciples of Christ) and Christian Churches/Churches of Christ

While the most disputed matter in Churches of Christ concerned one's knowledge at the time of baptism, the most controversial issue among the Disciples of Christ and the Christian Churches/Churches of Christ was whether the pious unimmersed may be admitted to membership in the churches. This issue arose for Disciples through their involvement in the modern Ecumenical Movement in the early twentieth century. Two important studies published in the second decade of the century defined the issue. Charles Clayton Morrison, *The Meaning of Baptism* (1914) argued that the pious unimmersed should be admitted to membership in the churches. Though this position was not unlike the one articulated earlier by Stone, it was argued on entirely different grounds. Frederick D. Kershner's *Christian Baptism* (1917) supported admitting to the churches only immersed believers. However, in strains reminiscent of Campbell's Lunenburg correspondence he asserted that "Whoever is realizing Christ in his own life from day to day is a Christian in the vital and fundamental sense, whether in the full formal sense or not."

Morrison and Kershner were both committed to Disciples participation in the Ecumenical Movement. Moreover, their views of baptism were strikingly similar. Three points of agreement may be noted. First, both Morrison and Kershner rejected the tendency of some in the Movement to argue for believers' immersion in ways that failed to acknowledge the genuine Christianity of the pious unimmersed. Second, both Morrison and Kershner described Christianity as essentially the moral or ethical transformation of sinners. Both rejected any form of "legalism" that would reduce baptism to a mechanical action that one must perform in order to be saved. Third, both Morrison and Kershner defined baptism as the initiatory rite of Christianity. Significantly, neither one of them described baptism as providing the penitent sinner with an assurance of the remission of sins. Seemingly the personal religious question that Campbell's view of baptism for remission of sins had answered in the nineteenth century, the matter of how a penitent believer could be assured of acceptance with God, was no longer a live question, at least not in the religious circles of which Morrison and Kershner were a part.

The difference in the positions of Morrison and Kershner concerned the relation of immersion to baptism. Building on Campbell, who had argued that baptism was more than a physical action, Morrison argued that "baptism" is the name for the rite of Christian initiation. It was only by social accident that the early church had appropriated immersion as the sign of that rite. Christ commanded his followers to make disciples and to initiate them into the church. The sign used in the rite of initiation — immersion — was not essential to the rite. Hence, immersed believers should not deny membership in the churches to Christians who had been initiated into the church by some other sign. All disciples of Christ should be regarded as such, regardless of the sign used in their initiation.

Morrison supported the Movement's traditional practice at two points. (1) The churches of the Movement were right not to baptize infants. The church is an "organization in the midst of society, set for the accomplishment of certain moral ends in the lives of its members and in the social order." Consequently, if requirements of membership are conceived as something less than the "self-commitment of one who is spiritually qualified, the spiritual tone and power of the church is bound to be lowered." Infants may be received into the fellowship of the church through a fitting ceremony of dedication, but should not be baptized or initiated into membership until as young persons, capable of self-commitment, they are morally qualified for such membership. Morrison noted that this is the actual practice of pedobaptist churches that do not confer full membership to baptized children until they have been confirmed. (2) The churches of the Movement were right to practice baptism only by immersion. All Christians accepted immersion as baptism, while other modes were in dispute. Hence, practicing immersion alone was a peacemaking measure that promoted the unity of the church. Settling upon one mode of baptism allowed Christians to put aside discussions of the varying modes of baptism and to get on with the work for which baptism sets them apart.

Kershner argued that immersion was essential to the rite of baptism. Sharing Morrison's view that the purpose of Christianity is the moral transformation of both individuals and society, Kershner declared that "The church with its ordinances, its regular appointments for worship, its significant and impressive symbolism, afford the only possible means for the extension and preservation of vital Christianity." It was in this context that the initiatory rite that Christ commanded his followers to observe was to be understood. In contrast to Morrison, who saw the mode of initiation as indifferent, Kershner stated that "while the Founder of the Christian religion might have selected any form of obedience to serve as the overt and initiatory rite admitting men to His church, it is none the less true that the rite which would most impressively symbolize the central fact or facts in His system would be the rite which we should expect Him to choose." Exegeting Romans 6 in connection with 1 Corinthians 15, Kershner concluded that immersion symbolizes (1) the gospel as summarized in the death, burial, and resurrection of Jesus Christ, (2) the experience that every convert must pass through in order to become a Christian, and (3) the Christian hope of the resurrection. Immersion, therefore, was not to be dispensed with in the Christian rite of initiation. At stake in the definition of baptism for Kershner was the power of symbolism — the symbolism of immersion that Christ intended to use for the extension of Christ's reign.

By the 1920s controversy over the admission of the pious unimmersed to membership in the churches was dividing the Disciples into the two communions that would be known by the 1970s as the Christian Church (Disciples of Christ) and the Christian Churches/Churches of Christ. While the Christian Church (Disciples of Christ) would include advocates of what was called open membership (the position advocated by Morrison), the Christian Churches/Churches of Christ uniformly maintained the teaching that while there are Christians among the unimmersed, membership in the churches requires immersion upon a profession of faith.

Through the period of polarization, however, there were some voices of moderation seeking to uphold the immersion of believers as normative while encouraging a more catholic ecclesiological spirit. Three such voices were William Robinson (1888-1963) of the British Churches of Christ, Disciples scholar Stephen England (1895-1987) of Phillips University, and Robert O. Fife (1918-2003), a historian from the Christian Churches/Churches of Christ and former professor at Milligan College.

William Robinson encouraged among Stone-Campbell churches a deeper sensitivity to the *sacramental* character of the church itself and of the "ordinances" of baptism and the Lord's Supper (preferring the term "sacraments" and defending the biblical reasoning for such usage). The unity of the primitive church, he recognized, had been grounded in the sacraments, which were an "extension" of the grace of Christ's incarnation. Baptism as such embodies that grace, enabling the believer to identify with, and co-experience the death, burial, and resurrection of Christ (Rom. 6). Immersion of believers for the remission of sins is the normative demonstration of that reality, simultaneously effecting a "mystical change of being" and an ethical transformation. Recovering the "sacramental principle" of baptism,

Robinson believed, would enable the churches to overcome legalism and individualism about the practice and link it again to the very unity and integrity of the church.

Robinson's sacramentalism in turn had a decisive impact on the thinking of both Stephen England and Robert Fife. England published *The One Baptism* in 1960, when tensions were truly mounting in Disciples ranks in anticipation of a new division. He attempted to accentuate what he saw as the common ground of liberal and conservative Disciples, differences of thinking and practice notwithstanding: that baptism was, strictly speaking, not essential to salvation or even to church membership, but that it pertained to the *bene esse* ("well-being") of Christians, and, what is more, that baptism — the New Testament norm of immersing believers — was indeed essential to Christian unity. England played down "open membership," instead advancing an "inclusive membership" model that, while not absolutely requiring persons transferring to Disciples congregations to be immersed, urged them to do so in the interest of Christian unity. Such could not be interpreted as sectarian triumphalism, for as the immersion of believers was a catholic principle of the New Testament, it belonged to the very integrity of the church. In addition, England, like Robinson before him, believed that fresh exploration of the meaning of New Testament baptism — in particular its character as a "sacramental" embodiment of the death, burial, and resurrection of Christ that remitted sin and gifted the believer with the Holy Spirit — would lend substance to the Disciples' insistence on the practice and display its role in forming the one body of Christ.

In the fourth Consultation on Christian Unity of the Christian Churches in Nashville in 1963, Robert Fife offered a statement on "The Inclusiveness of Church Membership" that he later revised and reissued in 1990. Fife, like England, sought to overcome both excessive accommodation on the one side and legalism on the other. Church "membership" itself needed further study in order to show that in the New Testament it was not mere enrollment but a dynamic and organic incorporation into Christ, union with Christ and with fellow believers in a covenantal relationship. Fife's conclusions paralleled England's at some points, for he too urged congregations not to force baptism on the unimmersed but to encourage and instruct them toward voluntary reception of the sacrament. Such was a matter not only of fidelity to the New Testament but of the integrity of the local church. Meanwhile, those "pious unimmersed" who had not yet received the "right hand of fellowship" could still find in Christian Churches a place to "sustain their membership" precisely by communing at the Lord's Table according to their own conscience. "Unlike the hand of fellowship, which as an *expedient* is linked to the recognition of membership," Fife wrote, "the Lord's Supper has membership significance divinely ordained." Fife's "Eucharistic membership," like England's "inclusive membership," thus sought to lend status to the "pious unimmersed" without waffling on the normativity of believers' immersion and the responsibility of congregations to uphold it.

Discussion of whether the pious unimmersed could be admitted to the church continued through the 1960s. The most radical proposal to emerge in this discussion was Joseph Belcastro, *The Relationship of Baptism to Church Membership* (1963). Belcastro concluded from a fresh study of the New Testament that in the New Testament church baptism was a dramatization of the redemptive experience of the Christian. It was never considered an initiatory rite, or a means of salvation. Rather, it was a vehicle for the expression of and enrichment of the life and witness of persons who, by their faith in Jesus Christ, were already recognized as members of the church. Moving beyond the view that persons who had been initiated by some form other than believers' immersion may be admitted to the churches, Belcastro advanced the conclusion that no form of baptism would be required for membership in a church that rightly interpreted the New Testament teaching of baptism.

4. More Recent Developments in Baptismal Belief and Practice

4.1. Christian Church (Disciples of Christ)

Recent developments in Disciples thought and practice of baptism have been influenced by the continuing participation of the Disciples in the Ecumenical Movement. The 1980s marked a significant era in ecumenical developments with two major publications: *The COCU Consensus: In Quest of a Church of Christ Uniting* by the Consultation on Church Union, and *Baptism, Eucharist and Ministry* by the Faith and Order Commission of the World Council of Churches. In the *COCU Consensus* Disciples, along with the other North American churches in the Consultation on Church Union, declared that baptism is "an act of Christ and a proclamation of the gospel" that "effects, or signifies, the incorporation of the baptized into Christ's death and resurrection, makes them living members of the Church universal, and enables them to confess their faith." The Consultation looked upon the different modes of baptism as highlighting different dimensions of its meaning, with infant baptism laying the stress on God's grace and human need and believers' baptism underlining the personal response to grace and the forgiveness of sin. The *Consensus* concluded that both meanings are important and therefore it is "appropriate that alternative practices be maintained within a Church Uniting."

In their official response to *Baptism, Eucharist and Ministry,* Disciples declared, "We celebrate the theological meaning of baptism articulated in the five aspects developed in BEM in paragraphs 2-7: as liberating participation in Christ's death and resurrection, as conversion of the heart, as a seal of the Holy Spirit, as incorporation into the Body of Christ (not a denomination), and as a sign of the Kingdom of God and the life to come." The response further stated, "While Disciples affirm believers' baptism as the practice of the apostolic Church, we look toward a united church in which — as BEM teaches — both believers' baptism and infant baptism/confirmation can be fully practiced."

The Disciples response to BEM acknowledged that BEM's clearest challenge to Disciples practice comes in paragraph 13: "Baptism is an unrepeatable act. Any practice which might be interpreted as 'rebaptism' must be avoided." Stating that Disciples do not consciously practice "rebaptism," the response noted that a minority of Disciples congregations do require immersion of adults who were baptized in infancy, while other congregations will immerse those who were baptized in infancy but whose conscience now leads them to ask for believers' baptism. While averring that such a service is performed as an act of pastoral care for those persons and as a witness to the New Testament practice, the response admonished that "Clearly Disciples must confront the ecumenical implications of this act which others interpret as 'rebaptism.'"

Growing out of the ecumenical discussion of baptism prompted by the publication of the *COCU Consensus* and *Baptism, Eucharist and Ministry,* the Disciples Council on Christian Unity published Clark M. Williamson, *Baptism: Embodiment of the Gospel: Disciples Baptismal Theology* (1987) as part of its series, The Nature of the Church. Williamson begins his study with a look at both the religious significance of baptism and water in the history of religions and baptism in Judaism. In the critical chapter on baptism in the New Testament Williamson proposes six points for contemporary Disciples to consider. (1) Whereas the New Testament gives us rather little information about the practice of baptism in the early church, it tells us a lot about the various theological interpretations of it in the early churches. (2) There is a variety of such interpretations (Williamson discusses the similarities and differences between baptism in the Gospels, Acts, and Paul). (3) Whereas Disciples have claimed that they could determine the "universal practice" of the early church, the most we can talk about it is "usual" practice (it no longer seems clear that all Christians were baptized, though baptism did become the universal practice; comparisons with proselyte baptism in Judaism suggest that children may have been included in the baptism of households reported in Acts). (4) While Disciples have argued that the Greek verbs meaning "to baptize" had only one meaning, "to immerse," some contemporary scholars disagree. (5) It follows that we must discern a way to be scriptural with regard to baptism without being restorationist with regard to the early church. (6) Williamson argues that "the major *theological* understanding of baptism that Disciples have held — that it is 'one baptism for the remission of sins' — and that it involves a dipolar emphasis on God's grace and the 'amen' ('yes!') of faith, resulting in a morally transformed life of discipleship, is on solid ground in the New Testament." Williamson further concludes:

> Believers' baptism by immersion is the most appropriate and therefore the normative form of Christian baptism. This is the practice which best symbolizes what it means to say 'yes' to the grace of God. It need not be argued, however, that it is the only exclusive form of Christian baptism. But it is that form which makes it clear that the gospel comes to each and all of us as a promise and as a challenge, a promise and challenge that call for a decision from us. We must decide whether to understand ourselves ultimately in terms of and only in terms of God's gracious promise and whether to engage in radical love of the neighbor. So to decide is, by God's grace, to be radically transformed, born anew.

4.2. Christian Churches/Churches of Christ

Christian Churches/Churches of Christ found an early rallying point of their own distinctive identity in their opposition to open membership and their embrace of immersion of believers for the remission of sins as essential to membership in the local church. Such solidarity has not, however, squelched some diversity of interpretation, particularly on the relation between baptism and salvation. Strong restorationists in the ranks of the Christian Churches/Churches of Christ still consider immersion unqualifiedly essential to salvation. Others, probably a majority, would affirm baptism as essential to salvation but retain the caveat that God has the prerogative to save the pious unimmersed. There are different reasonings here. Some churches, tilting toward the mainstream of American Evangelicalism and its "faith only" heritage, and cautious about legalism, have hesitated to make baptism the utterly defining moment in a Christian's salvation. Others, however, like Robert Fife (noted earlier) look to the example of some early leaders of the Stone-Campbell Movement (including Alexander Campbell himself) who refused to make baptism absolutely definitive of a Christian and were careful to safeguard the fact that the pious unimmersed were within the realm of God's graciousness.

There are also some differences on the basic theology of baptism. Strong conservatives have tended to retain the language of baptism as an "ordinance" rather than a "sacrament," and defended immersion on hermeneutical and philological grounds. However, a minority, positively influenced by the legacy of William Robinson, has understood baptism essentially as a sacrament, a unique means by which God communicates his grace through a physical medium, and justified immersion principally as an enactment or embodiment of death, burial, and resurrection with Christ (clearly privileging the text of Romans 6). There is virtual unanimity, however, in the view that true baptism is an act of obedience informed by faith and repentance and vital to the regeneration of believers.

Across the board, Christian Churches/Churches of Christ immerse new believers and strongly encourage those who transfer from non-immersing churches to undergo immersion. Some churches have put considerable emphasis on instructing believers in the importance of immersion. Southeast Christian Church in Louisville, Kentucky, for example, issued in 1996 a personal Bible study on immersion, very much in the tradition of an "inductive" approach to the issue, guiding candidates through scriptural texts and prompting questions aimed at helping them to draw their own positive conclusions.

4.3. Churches of Christ

In the late twentieth century, Churches of Christ were occupied again by the rebaptism controversy, prompted partially by positions taken by the International Church of Christ. Members of that body saw themselves as the only true Christians and insisted on reimmersing all who come into their fellowship, even those previously baptized "for remission of sins" in a Church of Christ. For some in mainstream Churches of Christ this approach forced a reexamination of the subject. Many of the ICOC's harshest critics, however, maintained a similar view and practice. Jimmy Allen, widely respected Bible teacher and evangelist, openly sided with the "Lipscomb" position in his 1991 volume *Re-baptism? What One Must Know to be Born Again.*

Debates between members of Churches of Christ and other religious groups over baptism continued in the twentieth century, though with decreasing frequency. Fundamentalist Baptist Bob Ross of Pasadena, Texas, produced books and pamphlets attacking what he labeled the heresies of "Campbellism," particularly accusing Churches of Christ of teaching baptismal regeneration. Invariably those from Churches of Christ have defended the propositions that baptism is for the remission of sins and is essential for salvation.

The danger in defending such positions in debate is that baptism might come to be regarded as simply a command to be obeyed, a mechanical act to perform. The most constructive statement of the understanding of baptism among Churches of Christ, however, is that it is in the act of baptism, this act of surrender of one's life to God in faith and obedience, that God, by the merits of Christ's blood, cleanses one from sin and truly changes the state of the person from an alien to a citizen of God's kingdom. Baptism is not a human work; it is the place where God does the work that only God can do. This position has been consistently taught in sermons, books, and Sunday School literature through most of the twentieth century. Though Churches of Christ do not use the terms "ordinance" or "sacrament" to describe baptism, their view can rightly be labeled sacramental.

In the late 1980s and following, a perceived lack of teaching on baptism in some circles prompted the publication of a number of studies written to reinforce the importance of baptism and give catechetical instruction to those preparing for it. One trend in the most recent literature is an emphasis on the continuing transformational power of baptism. Baptism's primary importance is not merely as a sign of what happened in the past or a legal requirement. It is the event that places the believer "into Christ" where God does the ongoing work of transformation.

Churches of Christ reflect the same spectrum of beliefs seen above in the Christian Churches/Churches of Christ. This includes a minority that, in rejecting sectarian attitudes that once characterized the body, tends to downplay the Movement's historic teaching on the importance of baptism. Current trends, however, are to reexamine the richness of the biblical teaching of baptism and to reinforce its central and essential place in Christianity.

5. Conclusion

Since the earliest days of the Stone-Campbell Movement baptism has been a priority issue. The Movement is certainly not unique in this. Baptism has since the beginning of the church been at the very core of questions of Christian identity, of salvation, of the church. At no time in the history of the Stone-Campbell Movement has baptism been relegated to a matter of insignificance. Some have accused the Movement of overemphasizing the importance of baptism. Others accuse it of a lack of effort to plumb the profound depth of meaning of baptism and its continuing transformative role in the life of believers. Sentiment across the streams of the Stone-Campbell Movement embraces the words of the World Council of Churches' BEM document: "Baptism is related not only to momentary experience, but to life-long growth into Christ. Those baptized are called upon to reflect the glory of the Lord as they are transformed by the power of the Holy Spirit, into his likeness, with ever-increasing splendor."

See also Baptists; Campbell-Maccalla Debate; Campbell-Rice Debate; Campbell-Walker Debate; *Christian System, The;* International Churches of Christ; Lunenburg Letter, The; McGary, Austin; Open Membership; Regeneration; Salvation

BIBLIOGRAPHY Jimmy Allen, *Rebaptism: What One Must Know to Be Born Again* (1991) • *Baptism, Eucharist and Ministry* (1982) • Joseph Belcastro, *The Relation of Baptism to Church Membership* (1963) • T. W. Brents, *The Gospel Plan of Salvation* (1868) • Alexander Campbell, "The Ancient Gospel — No. VII. Christian Immersion," *Christian Baptist* 5 (July 7, 1828): 277 • Alexander Campbell, *The Christian System* (1839) • Alexander Campbell, *Christian Baptism: With Its Antecedents and Consequents* (1853) • *The COCU Consensus: In Quest of a Church of Christ Uniting* (1984) • Stephen J. England, *The One Baptism* (1960) • Robert O. Fife, "The Inclusiveness of Church Membership," in *Consultation on Internal Unity,* 4th series, ed. Charles R. Gresham (1963), pp. 11-24 • David W. Fletcher, ed., *Baptism and the Remission of Sins* (1990) • John Mark Hicks and Greg Taylor, *Down in the River to Pray: Revisioning Baptism as God's Transforming Work* (2003) • Tommy W. King, "Faith Decisions: Christian Initiation for Children of the Glenwood Church of Christ" (unpublished D.Min. thesis, Abilene Christian University, 1994) • Frederick D. Kershner, *Christian Baptism* (1917) • Allan J. McNicol, *Preparing for Baptism: Becoming Part of the Story of the People of God* (2001) • Robert Milligan, *An Exposition and Defense of the Scheme of Redemption: As It Is Revealed and Taught in the Holy Scriptures* (1868) • Charles Clayton Morrison, *The Meaning of Baptism* (1914) • "No. 8537 Report on Baptism, Eucharist and Ministry," in *Yearbook & Directory 1986 of the Christian Church (Disciples of Christ),* pp. 268-74 • *A Public Debate on Christian Baptism Between the Rev. W. L. McCalla, a Presbyterian Teacher, and Alexander Campbell* (1842) • William Robinson, *Essays on Christian Unity* (1923) • William Robinson, *The Sacraments and Life* (1949) • Bob L. Ross, *Campbellism and Acts 2:38: The Historical Background of the Campbellite Position on Baptismal Remission* (1973) • F. LaGard Smith, *Baptism: The Believer's Wedding Ceremony* (1989) • Clark M. Williamson, *Baptism, Embodiment of the Gospel: Disciples Baptismal Theology* (1987).

DOUGLAS A. FOSTER, PAUL M. BLOWERS, *and* D. NEWELL WILLIAMS

Baptists

The Stone-Campbell Movement's relationship with various Baptist denominational groups.

By the time of the union of the Stone and Campbell movements in the 1830s, both had already established relationships with the major denominations in the west, especially the Baptists. Baptists were diverse in the new republic (hyper-Calvinist Primitive, Calvinist Regular, anti-creedal Separate, Arminian General, and restorationist Landmark, to name a few), and most clergy lacked a basic theological education. Local Baptist associations, not the emerging national missionary organization (Triennial Convention, est. 1814), led Baptists in defining cooperative missions and defending Baptist doctrine based on Baptist confessions of faith (Philadelphia in 1742 and New Hampshire in 1833).

The Great Revival in the West (1797-1805) attracted thousands to its large open-air meetings, with nonsectarian preaching by different denominational preachers, including Baptists. This revival became a catalyst for Barton W. Stone's Christian Movement. The Christian Movement eventually adopted baptism by immersion and experienced sustained growth in Kentucky, Tennessee, and northern Alabama, especially among Separate Baptists, who accepted Stone's anti-confessionalism, expressed in his objections to the Westminster Confession of Faith.

In 1811, the Christian Association of Washington (Pennsylvania) became the Brush Run Church with Thomas Campbell as elder and Alexander Campbell as preacher. The church adopted immersion as its form of baptism on the occasion of the birth of Alexander Campbell's daughter Jane and by his extended Bible study on the subject. The family was immersed by the Baptist preacher Matthias Luce in Buffalo Creek on June 12, 1812. Acceptance of baptism by immersion led the Brush Run church to affiliate with the Redstone Baptist Association in 1815.

This connection between the Campbell movement and the Baptists had several seminal events in its short existence. On September 1, 1816, at the Redstone Baptist Association meeting held at the Cross Creek Baptist Church, Alexander Campbell delivered his famous "Sermon on the Law." Campbell concluded that since an essential difference existed between the Law and the Gospel, the authority of the New Testament superseded that of the Old Testament for Christian thought and practice. Most Baptists on the frontier accepted the equal authority of the testaments.

Next, Alexander Campbell began to represent Baptists in debates with Presbyterians on infant baptism. In the first one (Campbell/Walker in 1820), he debated the mode and subjects of baptism. In the second (Campbell/Maccalla in 1823), he moved to a view on the design of baptism as being for the remission of sins, a view that most Baptists rejected as "baptismal regeneration."

Then, Alexander Campbell turned to the media, publishing his first paper, the *Christian Baptist,* from 1823 to 1830. He was often iconoclastic and irritated many Baptists in a series called "A Restoration of the Ancient Order of Things" that discussed his views on doctrines, clergy, and missions. His attacks against confessionalism attracted some Baptists, especially Separate Baptists, to join the movement. Even before the *Christian Baptist* ceased publication, Campbell had gained a wider Protestant audience and began to publish the *Millennial Harbinger* (1830-70). In this journal, Alexander Campbell continued debating with Baptists such as Andrew Broaddus (1770-1848) of Virginia.

By 1825, the Redstone Association had already excluded churches favoring the Campbell reform, including the Brush Run church. At the same time, the movement made gains among Baptists in the Mahoning Baptist Association of eastern Ohio, which included the church in Wellsburg, (West) Virginia, where Alexander Campbell and his family then worshiped. In this more congenial Baptist association, they became the leading evangelistic influence. With his strongly evangelistic sermons, Walter Scott became the association evangelist in 1827. Yet in 1830, the Campbell reformers dissolved the association and began to move away from the Baptists. Those remaining in the Mahoning Association formed the Beaver Association and released the Beaver Anathema (1829) against the Campbell movement. Many Baptist associations would adopt and even expand on this anathema. By the 1830s, the movement's sojourn with the Baptists was coming to an end.

Many historians have noted major points of conflict between Campbell and the Baptists, some at the beginning, others by the end of the relationship. On religious authority, Campbell's view that authority resided in Scripture alone clashed with the Baptists' use of confessions in defense of their views. On the terms of Christian union, Campbell's free and rational decision of faith and insistence on baptism for the remission of sins collided with the Baptists' more Calvinistic understanding of prevenient grace and election. On the agency of the Holy Spirit in conversion, Campbell's insistence on the work of the Holy Spirit solely in Scripture conflicted with the Baptists' view of the convicting and regenerating power of the Spirit. On missions, Campbell's early anti-cooperative but local church missions stance diverged from the growing Baptist foreign missions efforts. On the Lord's Supper, Campbell's insistence on weekly communion differed from the Baptists' quarterly observance. These issues aided the dissolution of the relationship between Campbell and the Baptists.

As the Disciples, Campbell's preferred name for his movement, moved into Kentucky and began a new relationship with Stone's Christians, Campbell's teachings energized many Baptists such as John T. Johnson and Raccoon John Smith, both of whom affiliated with the Stone-Campbell Movement. In 1832, Johnson and Smith would team with Barton Stone and John Rogers in bringing about a union between Stone's Christians and Campbell's Disciples. In its early history, the Stone-Campbell Movement and the Baptists tried to reconcile differences in 1841 and 1866, but to no avail. John T. Johnson organized a unity meeting at Lexington in 1841 in which many invested great expectations of reconciliation with the Baptists and other groups; Alexander Campbell came and spoke at the event. Yet only one Baptist, Dr. James Fishback of Transylvania University, actually attended.

Meanwhile Baptist leaders such as J. R. Graves (1820-1893), in his *Alexander Campbell and Campbellism Exposed* (1854), and Jeremiah Jeter (1802-1880), in *Campbellism Examined* (1855), were now assessing Campbell's views. Graves, the founder of the Baptist restorationist movement known as the Landmark movement, railed against Campbell and the movement's "alien immersion." While he observed many good things, Jeter noted that the design of baptism was the major impasse between the two groups. Near his death, Alexander Campbell observed the failed attempt between the Disciples and the Baptists as a negative point for the new movement.

Since these early days, through the divisions of the Stone-Campbell Movement, and into the twenty-first century, the Movement has continued to have some relationships with Baptists. The Christian Church (Disciples of Christ) conducted bilateral talks with American Baptists during the first half of the twentieth century, producing a joint hymnal and Sunday School literature in the early 1940s. Following joint conventions in Chicago in 1952, serious union talks between the two groups ended.

In the 1990s, Texas Christian University's Brite Divinity School started a Baptist studies program. In the past, both the Churches of Christ and the Christian Churches/Churches of Christ have engaged Baptists in debates over many issues, but today, many leaders in both groups have attended Baptist seminaries and have had Baptist speakers at their regional and national meetings. During the 1990s a Southern Baptist–Churches of Christ Conversation was sponsored by the Interfaith Witness Department of the Southern Baptist Convention's Home Mission Board, and a Baptist–Churches of Christ Dialogue in Texas was begun in 2002.

See also Baptism; Calvinism; Cane Ridge Revival; *Christian Baptist, The;* Jeter, Jeremiah Bell; Johnson, John T.; Mahoning Baptist Association; Redstone Baptist Association; "Sermon on the Law"

BIBLIOGRAPHY Frank Adkins, *Disciples and Baptists: Their Resemblances and Differences in Belief and Practice* (1896) • Alexander Campbell, "Sermon on the Law," repr. in *Historical Documents Advocating Christian Union,* ed. C. A. Young (1904), pp. 217-82 • J. R. Graves, *Alexander Campbell and Campbellism Exposed* (1854) • Jeremiah Jeter, *Campbellism Examined* (1855) • Leon McBeth, *The Baptist Heritage* (1987) • Franklin Rector, "Baptist-Disciple Conversation Toward Unity," in *Institutionalism and Church Unity,* ed. Nils Ehrenstrom and Walter G. Muelder (1963), pp. 253-74 • James E. Tull, "Alexander Campbell: Advocate of Reformation," in *Shapers of Baptist Thought* (1972), pp. 101-27. ANTHONY J. SPRINGER

Barclay, James Turner (1807-1874)

First international missionary of the Stone-Campbell Movement in the nineteenth century. James Turner Barclay was a native of Scottsville, Albemarle County, Virginia, a graduate of the University of Virginia and of the medical college of the University of Pennsylvania. Barclay ran a medical practice and for a time owned and maintained the Thomas Jefferson estate at Monticello. In 1830 he married Julia Sowers (1813-1908), his partner in future missionary labors, who later became a close confidante of Selina Campbell. The Barclays' younger son John Judson Barclay (1834-1910), destined to a career as a Middle East diplomat, would marry Alexander and Selina Campbell's daughter Decima in 1863.

A Presbyterian layman as well as a physician, James Barclay had initially proposed to undertake missionary work for the Presbyterian Board of Missions but was prevented by family concerns. Having affiliated with the Disciples of Christ in Virginia, he helped in 1843 to organize the congregation in Washington City (D.C.) that is now National City Christian Church. In 1849 Barclay offered himself to the newly formed American Christian Missionary Society (ACMS), zealous to conduct missionary work among Jews in Palestine.

Even before his departure, Barclay emphasized the millennial implications of his mission to the Jews, whom he cast as an indestructible people, bearers of the ancient biblical faith, destined to play an indispensable role in the eschatological consummation of history. The increasing number of Jews relocating in Palestine, the symbolic and prophetic importance of the Holy Land, especially Jerusalem itself, in the final restoration of apostolic Christianity, and the fact that the Protestant "sects" (sure to fall short of accomplishing this restoration) were already locating missions in Palestine, all signaled an opportunity for the Disciples of Christ to seize the prophetic moment. Alexander Campbell, though skeptical of inflated eschatological schemes, nonetheless strongly encouraged Barclay's mission.

The first tenure of Barclay and his family in Jerusalem lasted from the winter of 1851 until the summer of 1854. The mission was heavily frustrated from the outset by strong Jewish resistance to the Christian presence in Palestine, by an oppressive Turkish culture, by friction with other Christian groups (especially Roman Catholics and Eastern Orthodox), and by illness (malaria) within the family. Few Jews were actually converted, the risk of superficial conversion and lapsing was great, and Barclay mused on being more warmly welcomed by Muslims than by Jews. Conversions aside, Barclay was profoundly successful in his medical mission, treating over 2,000 malaria cases in his first year alone. Barclay also became deeply involved in geographical studies and archaeological excavation in Jerusalem, even assisting the eminent American archaeologist Edward Robinson in his investigations. Barclay's own research led him to publish *The City of the Great King* (1858), a crucial source even today for the topography of nineteenth-century Jerusalem.

Commissioned in 1849 to serve as a missionary to Jews in Palestine, James Turner Barclay (1807-1874) and his family worked there from 1851 to 1854 and from 1858 to 1862.
Courtesy of the Disciples of Christ Historical Society

Financial stress on the ACMS caused Barclay and his family to come home to Virginia in 1854, and in 1855, because of his acquired expertise in metallurgy, Barclay was given an appointment at the Philadelphia Mint by President Franklin Pierce. Revitalization in the ACMS enabled the Barclay family to return to Jerusalem in the summer of 1858 — not, however, without controversy. Disciples abolitionists criticized Barclay as a former slave owner at Monticello, and pulled their support in order to form their own "Christian Missionary Society." Even loyal supporters, including the ACMS's own corresponding secretary Isaac Errett, grew skeptical of Barclay's millennial idealism.

In this second term in the Holy Land, Barclay faced even more severe challenges of social and political upheaval, Jewish intransigence, and dubious conversions. Rather than bending to discouragement, however, he now embraced a devout premillennialism and, in articles for the *Millennial Harbinger,* set forth his own grand vision of the approaching return of Christ and the ultimate conversion of the Jews, who would in turn help convert the "fullness of the Gentiles" (Rom. 11:25). He also urged the participation of the American churches in the repatriation of the Jews to expedite the outworking of millennial events. With his work on the brink, the ACMS weakened at home by the Civil War, and many of his former supporters discomfited by his premillennial zeal, Barclay aborted the mission in 1862 and returned to the United States in 1863.

From 1866 to 1868, Barclay served the faculty of Bethany College as a professor of natural sciences, afterward retiring to Alabama until his death. He held out hope for a reinstatement of his Jerusalem mission and continued to publish his views on prophecy and the Jews, though they seemed to fall on deaf ears at a time when missionary societies, let alone millennial speculations, were an increasing object of controversy in the Stone-Campbell Movement. By the turn of the twentieth century, doubtless because of embarrassment over the mission's breakdown and Barclay's controversial eschatology, Disciple leaders largely avoided revisiting or analyzing his work in Palestine, although they continued to honor him as a missionary pioneer and an accomplished researcher in the geography and archaeology of Jerusalem.

See also American Christian Missionary Society; Bethany College; Burnet, David Staats; Campbell, Alexander; Campbell, Selina Huntingdon Bakewell; Christian Missionary Society; Errett, Isaac; Eschatology; Jews and Judaism, Views of in the Movement; Missions, Missiology

BIBLIOGRAPHY James T. Barclay, *The City of the Great King, or Jerusalem As It Was, As It Is, and As It Will Be* (1858) • James T. Barclay, correspondence with Alexander Campbell et al., *Millennial Harbinger* (1850, 1851) • James T. Barclay, "The Welfare of the World Bound Up in the Destiny of Israel" (7 parts), *Millennial Harbinger* (1860): 661-68; (1861): 6-14, 61-9, 121-28, 241-46, 301-7, 361-65 • Paul M. Blowers, "'Living in a Land of Prophets': James T. Barclay and an Early Disciples of Christ Mission to Jews in the Holy Land," *Church History* 62 (1992): 494-513, reprinted in *The Stone-Campbell Movement: An International Religious Tradition,* ed. Douglas A. Foster and Michael W. Casey (2002), pp. 271-91 • D. S. Burnet, *The Jerusalem Mission under the Direction of the American Christian Missionary Society* (1853; repr. 1977) • Jack P. Lewis, "James Turner Barclay: Explorer of Nineteenth-Century Jerusalem," *Biblical Archaeologist* 51 (1988): 163-70.

PAUL M. BLOWERS

Barton College

Related to the Christian Church (Disciples of Christ).

In 1900 Daniel E. Motley, a Johns Hopkins Ph.D., an ordained minister, and the Disciples state evangelist for North Carolina, gazed across the sand and pine of the Carolina coastal plain and spoke with a prophetic flair: "In a vision that shall be more than a vision," he said, "I see yonder in one of our beautiful North Carolina towns, a Christian College with an able Christian faculty." Following two years of spirited effort, his vision became reality. In 1902 the Wilson Education Association offered the former Kinsey Female Seminary and Collegiate Institute along with a gift of $3,036 to the Disciples North Carolina Missionary Convention. From this transaction Atlantic Christian College was incorporated on May 1, 1902. It opened in September of that year with an enrollment of 185, a faculty of nine, and a docket of sixteen fields of study blended into a classical-practical-ministerial curriculum.

In 1955 Atlantic Christian College received its first accreditation by the Southern Association of Colleges and Schools. On September 6, 1990, the institution changed its name to Barton College, its namesake being Barton Warren Stone, one of the principal founders of the Stone-Campbell Movement whose early ministry was in the eastern part of North Carolina and who attended Caldwell Academy in Greensboro.

In 2003 Barton College enrolled 1,300 students, employed seventy-seven faculty, offered six baccalaureate degrees, and held an endowment of $22 million. In addition, the school had developed a "Weekend College" and a lifelong education program to serve nontraditional learners. The official college motto, adopted in 1923, is "They shall have the light of life."

BIBLIOGRAPHY D. Duane Cummins, *The Disciples Colleges: A History* (1987) • Charles C. Ware, *A History of Atlantic Christian College* (1956) • Charles C. Ware, *A History of the Disciples of Christ in North Carolina* (1927).

D. DUANE CUMMINS

Baxter, Batsell Barrett (1916-1982)

Widely known preacher and speaker on the Herald of Truth radio and television ministry sponsored by Churches of Christ.

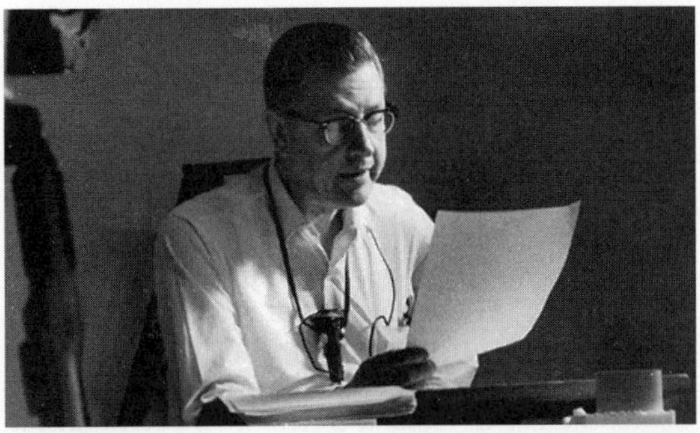

Batsell Barrett Baxter became widely known as host of the Herald of Truth radio and television broadcasts from the 1960s until his death in 1982. Courtesy of the Center for Restoration Studies, Abilene Christian University

Born in Cordell, Oklahoma, the only child of Batsell (1886-1956) and Fay Baxter, he was married to Wanda Roberts of Taft, Texas, for forty-three years. They had three sons, Scott, Alan, and John.

Baxter received the B.S. from Abilene Christian (1938), the M.A. and Ph.D. in Speech Communication from the University of Southern California (1938, 1944), and the B.D. from Vanderbilt (1957).

After teaching Speech Communication at Pepperdine College from 1938 to 1945, Baxter moved to David Lipscomb College to chair the Speech Department from 1945 to 1956. He taught speech communication and homiletics before becoming chair of Lipscomb's Bible Department in 1956, a position he held until just before his death in 1982.

Baxter preached his first sermon at Nashville's Chapel Avenue Church of Christ in 1933. His forty-eight years of ministry with local churches in California and Tennessee included twenty-six years with the Hillsboro congregation in Nashville between 1951 and 1980.

Area-wide preaching services, usually of eight nights' duration, were popular among Churches of Christ in the late 1950s and early 1960s. Baxter preached in three such meetings in San Angelo and Lubbock, Texas, with attendance reaching approximately 10,000 nightly in Lubbock's South Plains Coliseum in 1964. His overseas preaching included series of sermons to the young post–World War II congregations in Frankfurt, Germany (1949); to U.S. military families and their friends in Tokyo, Japan, and Seoul, Korea (1957); a campaign that led to the establishment of the Wembley (London) church (1961); and campaigns in Wembley and Ayleshire, Buckinghamshire, England (1963).

Baxter is perhaps best known for his media ministry through Herald of Truth, a radio and television program that originated in Abilene, Texas, in 1952. He anchored the thirty-minute television program between 1960 and 1982 and was speaker on the thirty-minute radio program for more than a decade, beginning in 1966. At their peaks, the television program was heard on as many as 150 stations and the radio program on approximately 400 stations. Baxter also edited *UpReach* magazine, a full-color, bi-monthly response magazine of the Herald of Truth ministry, from its inception in 1979 until his death in 1982. *UpReach* began circulation with 150,000 copies of each issue.

Although he drew upon a wide range of sources, Baxter's sermons were characterized by originality and by his uniquely personal style. He always spoke in a calm, conversational tone. His gentle spirit influenced an entire generation of preachers in Churches of Christ. His eighteen-year struggle with recurring cancer deepened his empathy with suffering people and heightened their awareness of his genuineness and integrity as a Christian communicator — impressions that traveled through mass media as well.

Baxter authored eleven books, including his posthumously published autobiography, coauthored two books, and coedited an additional seven volumes. His best-known volumes include *The Heart of the Yale Lectures* (1947, repr. 1971), *Speaking for the Master* (1954), *I Believe Because* (1971), and *When Life Tumbles In* (1974).

See also Evangelism, Evangelists; Herald of Truth; Lipscomb University

BIBLIOGRAPHY Batsell Barrett Baxter, *Every Life a Plan of God: The Autobiography of Batsell Barrett Baxter* (1983) • Roland Delevar Roberts, *Batsell Barrett Baxter: The Man and the Message* (1998). HAROLD HAZELIP

Beardslee, J. O.

See American Christian Missionary Society; Jamaica, The Movement in

Beazley, George Grimes, Jr. (1914-1973)

Disciples of Christ pastor and ecumenist.

Born and reared in Danville, Kentucky, he received his B.A. degree (1935) from Centre College in Danville and B.D. (1938) from The College of the Bible (later Lexington Theological Seminary) in Lexington, Kentucky. Ever a pastoral scholar, he engaged in summer graduate studies at the University of Chicago, the University of Missouri, and Union Theological Seminary in New York City. Culver-Stockton College and Centre College awarded him D.D. degrees. Deeply committed to the pastoral ministry, Beazley was the senior minister of the First Christian Church in Richmond, Missouri (1938-47), and the First Christian Church in Bartlesville, Oklahoma (1947-60). In both communities his ministry was marked by dynamic biblical preaching; the engaging of lay people in the study of the Scriptures, theology, and literature; and a commitment to the worldwide church. In 1939 he married Charlotte Strother Holman, a political science major at Transylvania College, with whom he shared a life of devotion and dialogue.

In December 1960 Beazley was called from the pastorate to be the president of the Council on Christian Unity (CCU), the chief ecumenical officer of the Christian Church (Disciples of Christ) in the U.S. and Canada. In this position he followed in the footsteps of Peter Ainslie and brought institutional strength and distinctive leadership to the Disciples' "historic plea" in a new cultural movement. He was a delegate to the New Delhi (1961) and Uppsala (1968) assemblies of the World Council of Churches, and served on its Central Committee (1968-73) and Faith and Order Commission (1961-73). Following a Disciples tradition, he was a member (1961-73) of the Board of the Ecumenical Institute Bossey, outside Geneva, Switzerland. His involvement in conciliar ecumenism in the U.S. included membership on the General Board and other activities of the National Council of Churches of Christ in the U.S.A.

On the eve of Beazley's CCU presidency, the Consultation on Church Union was dramatically born,

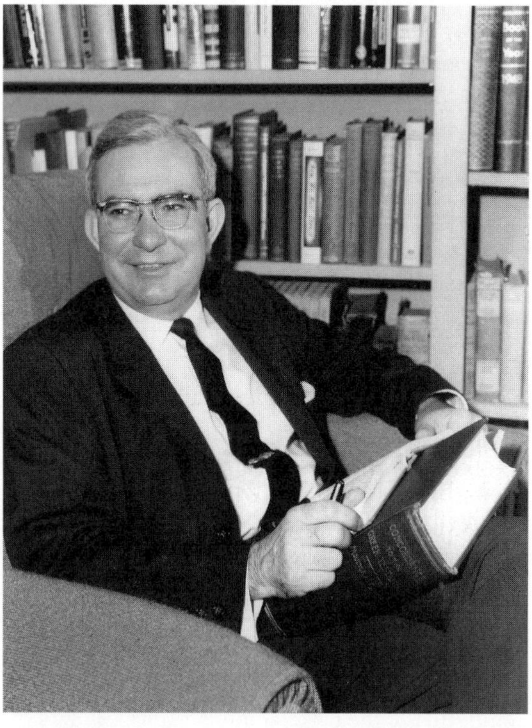

Disciples pastor and second president of the Council on Christian Unity, George G. Beazley (1914-1973) initiated publication of *Mid-Stream* in 1961. He also edited the less formal *News on Christian Unity*, popularly known as "Beazley's Buzz." Courtesy of the Disciples of Christ Historical Society

bringing the Disciples into union conversations with other mainline Protestant and Episcopal churches, including three historic African-American Methodist churches. When the General Assembly of the Christian Church (Disciples of Christ) voted (Los Angeles, 1962) without a dissenting vote to enter this historic venture toward a united church, Beazley became a passionate leader and interpreter of COCU. He served on the Executive Committee (1963-73) and the Plan of Union Commission (1968-70), and was the Consultation's president from 1970 to 1973.

George Beazley was a consummate communicator who sought to bring the vision of Christian unity to Disciples and other traditions. In 1961 he and the CCU established a quarterly ecumenical journal, entitled *Mid-Stream,* that continued until 2002 as a celebrated resource interpreting the many aspects and developments of the Ecumenical Movement. Another popular channel for his occasional reflections was a chatty, honest, and insightful newsletter bearing the title *News on Christian Unity* (1961-73), but widely and affectionately known by its subtitle "Beazley's Buzz." These candid reports — drafted as he traveled across North America and other countries — were read and considered "the inside story" by many church leaders in different parts of the world. His only book was a volume he conceived and edited entitled *The Christian Church (Disciples of Christ): An Interpretative Examination in the Cultural Context* (Bethany Press, 1973). Prepared for a German series on *Churches in the World (Die Kirchen der Welt),* this important but largely overlooked volume sought to define the Disciples' identity and calling in "the present theological, sociological, and cultural confusion of Western man." His love of photography led him to take over 20,000 color slides of countless ecumenical gatherings and his global travels with Charlotte, which compose a visual history of the Ecumenical Movement of his generation.

His journey in the service of unity led George Beazley into dialogue with all Christian traditions — Protestant, Orthodox, and Roman Catholic — and to a devotion to the vision and vocation toward reconciliation in Christ. Symbolic of this ecumenical life was the fact that his death came in Moscow on World Communion Sunday, 1973, while he and Charlotte were on a personal visit to the Russian Orthodox Church.

See also Council on Christian Unity; Ecumenical Movement, The; *Mid-Stream*

BIBLIOGRAPHY Paul A. Crow, Jr., "George G. Beazley, Jr.: One of a Kind Ecumenist," *Mid-Stream: An Ecumenical Journal* 16 (April 1977): 150-56. PAUL A. CROW, JR.

Believer's Church

See Church, Doctrine of the

Bell, R. M.

See Johnson Bible College

Benson, George Stuart (1898-1991)

Missionary for Churches of Christ, Christian college president, and political activist.

After spending eleven years in the Orient developing groundbreaking missionary methodology among Churches of Christ, in 1936 Benson became president of Harding College in Searcy, Arkansas. Harding quickly created the National Education Program (NEP) to promote fiscal conservatism and limited government in America. With financial help from corporate America, the NEP's message reached millions through newspaper columns, educational films, and radio and television programs. Harding's "Freedom Forums" educated thousands of industrial workers and college students. During the ensuing decades, the NEP, while raising millions for Harding, became the standard-bearer for Benson's version of "Americanism." This program was widely regarded as an important intellectual center for the "New Right" movement in American politics that helped foster the conservative resurgence culminating in the election of Ronald Reagan in 1980.

Reagan's election rewarded many grass-roots conservative activists like Benson for their years of hard work behind the scenes. While the NEP gradually lost effectiveness as a conservative political propaganda tool, Harding University, through Benson's leadership, had become one of the nation's strong liberal arts institutions. Today Benson's teachings on traditional American values and free enterprise economics are being carried on through dozens of educational organizations run by his disciples. Before his death, Benson's tireless fund-raising efforts helped secure the financial stability, not only of Harding University, but also of Oklahoma Christian University in Oklahoma City, Oklahoma, and Faulkner University in Montgomery, Alabama.

See also Asia, Missions in; Harding University

BIBLIOGRAPHY Ted Max Altman, "The Contribution of George Benson to Christian Education" (unpublished Ph.D. dissertation, North Texas State University, 1971) • James L. Atteberry, *The Story of Harding College* (1966) • James L. Atteberry, "The Story of Harding College: Spring, 1969," Privately printed by the author (1969) • George S. Benson, *Missionary Experiences*, ed. Phil Watson (1987) • Donald P. Garner, "George S. Benson: Conservative, Anti-Communist, Pro-American Speaker" (unpublished Ph.D. dissertation, Wayne State University, 1963) • L. Edward Hicks, "A Case Study of Conservative Political Education: Dr. George S. Benson and the National Education Program" (unpublished Ph.D. dissertation, Memphis State University, 1990) • L. Edward Hicks, *Sometimes in the Wrong, but Never in Doubt: George S. Benson and the Education of the New Religious Right* (1994) • John C. Stevens, *Before Any Were Willing: The Story of George S. Benson* (1991).

L. EDWARD HICKS

Bentley, Adamson (1785-1864)

Baptist minister and evangelist to the Western Reserve in northeastern Ohio.

Adamson Bentley was born on July 4, 1785, in Allegheny County, Pennsylvania. During his childhood, he moved with his family to Brookfield, Trumbull County, Ohio. The privations of frontier life forbade any extensive educational opportunities for him, although he obtained sufficient education to begin preaching. He became a Christian during his childhood and joined the Baptist Church. He began preaching at the age of 19 and preached for five years as a licentiate. In 1810, he moved to Warren, Ohio, and was formally ordained to the Christian ministry on May 19, 1810. A year later, on May 4, 1811, he was accepted as minister of the Concord Baptist Church, Warren, Ohio. He served as minister of the church for twenty years.

While serving bi-vocationally as the minister of the Concord Baptist Church, he became familiar with the views of Alexander Campbell. In 1821 he had read Campbell's debate with John Walker on baptism. Bentley and his brother-in-law, Sidney Rigdon (1793-1876), visited Alexander Campbell at his home in the summer of 1821 and left convinced of the correctness of Campbell's views. Bentley had further learned of Campbell's teachings when Walter Scott held a revival in Warren, Ohio, in 1828. Bentley and his congregation accepted the views of the Restoration. He had been long bothered by the teaching of strict Calvinism. He was troubled by the idea of the elect and non-elect in regard to the spiritual destinies of his children.

Bentley was a guiding force in encouraging the Baptist ministers in the Western Reserve to meet for annual meetings. These meetings developed into the Mahoning Baptist Association, which was organized in 1820. The Mahoning Baptist Association continued for ten years until its dissolution in August 1830, at Austentown, Ohio, due to the conviction that such organizations were unscriptural. The association continued to meet, but only as a yearly meeting.

In 1829, the Mahoning Association appointed Bentley and Cyrus Bosworth co-evangelists with previously appointed Walter Scott and William Hayden to preach on the Western Reserve — a large tract of land located in northeastern Ohio but claimed by the state of Connecticut. Toward the end of 1831, Bentley moved to Chagrin Falls, where he preached and held revivals. He retired from preaching when he was approaching the age of 80. He died on November 3, 1864, just eight months shy of his eightieth birthday.

See also Evangelism, Evangelists — Early Nineteenth Century; Mahoning Baptist Association; Preaching — Nineteenth Century; Rigdon, Sidney; Scott, Walter

BIBLIOGRAPHY A. S. Hayden, *History of the Disciples on the Western Reserve* (1972) • Thorn Pendleton, *The History of Central Christian Church, Warren, Ohio, 1803-1988* (n.d.).

GARY L. LEE

Bethany College

Related to the Christian Church (Disciples of Christ).

The oldest continuing institution of higher education established by the Stone-Campbell Movement, Bethany College is a highly regarded and well-endowed liberal arts institution located at Bethany, West Virginia, in the Upper Ohio Valley not far from Pittsburgh, Pennsylvania. With approximately 750 students and sixty faculty members, Bethany College is fully accredited by the North Central Association of Colleges and Secondary Schools.

Founded in 1840 by Alexander Campbell (1788-1866), Bethany College throughout the nineteenth and the early part of the twentieth century prepared dedicated lay and ministerial leaders of the Christian Churches and Churches of Christ along with other students who also became community leaders. In more recent years the college has given solid preparation for the general public in such fields as law, medicine, business, science, and communications as well as undergraduate ministerial preparation. The college has hundreds of celebrated graduates at work throughout the United States and the world.

Among the graduates of Bethany college have been several governors and United States senators, a speaker of the House of Representatives, a United States Supreme Court Justice, a number of college and university presidents, distinguished doctors, lawyers, and teachers as well as Christian ministers and missionaries. The College has produced, out of all proportion to its modest enrollment, numerous business leaders, scientists, and artists in various fields. More recently, there has been among Bethany's alumni/ae an award-winning dramatist, a Pulitzer prize–winning poet, a TV news anchor, an Oscar-winning actress, and a judge of the International Court on Inter-American Human Rights.

Bethany College became the chief fruit of Alexander Campbell's intensive study of education. Beginning almost with the first number of his *Millennial Harbinger*, Campbell wrote numerous essays and lectures on the importance of education within the Christian understanding. His ideas were drawn from the best thought of the eighteenth-century Enlightenment, including the economic ideas of Adam Smith, the political and religious principles of John Locke, and the pragmatic understanding of science of Isaac Newton and Francis Bacon.

In the 1830s Campbell increasingly turned his attention to needed reforms in education. Educational reform, in his judgment, had to begin in the colleges where teachers and community leaders were educated. In Campbell's view a new direction was needed for higher education, away from the study of classical literature and the history of Rome and Greece, and toward the philosophy, morals, science, and religion of a new age.

Campbell's experience as a teacher in the earlier Buffalo Seminary (1818-23) led him to believe the current educational system was inadequate for the building of a Christian society within a new nation. Consequently, for over thirty years the broad subject of education and the program of Bethany College received a significant amount of Alexander Campbell's thought and energy.

Bethany College, as well as many other institutions of higher learning in the Stone-Campbell Movement, was conceived and built on Alexander Campbell's educational philosophy developed in the 1830s. A thorough and scholarly study of that philosophy has been made by D. Duane Cummins. According to Cummins, the first principle of Campbell's philosophy was *wholeness of person*, that is, the integration of an individual's physical, mental, and moral powers so that the person may develop a focused personality. His second principle was the *moral formation of character*, believing moral excellence to be the goal of education. He believed that the virtues of benevolence, justice, compassion, and generosity are developed as the moral nature is developed.

The third principle of Campbell's educational philosophy was *study of the Bible*. To develop moral character, systematic instruction in the Bible should be at the center of a college's program. The fourth emphasis of his philosophy was that in the teaching of the young there should be *no sectarian influence*. Colleges should be stripped of their sectarian character and the Bible studied as any other textbook.

The fifth principle of Campbell's educational philosophy was the *perfectibility of individuals*. With proper instruction, individuals could develop a high regard for the moral life. Social reform would come as individual's attained moral judgment. The sixth and final principle was *lifelong learning*. He believed that learning begins in early childhood and continues throughout life. When formal instruction is over, students become responsible for their own increase in knowledge and learning. As Bethany College came into being, Campbell sought to put these principles into practice.

Within the Stone-Campbell Movement Bethany has served literally as a "Mother of Colleges." Among

The Bethany College faculty of 1854-55, pictured in a promotional graphic for the College. Clockwise from the top: Alexander Campbell, W. K. Pendleton, Robert Milligan, P. W. Mosblech, Robert Richardson, and A. F. Ross.
Courtesy of Bethany College

the colleges and universities founded by graduates of Bethany College, established under the influence of Bethany graduates, or whose curriculums were patterned on the Bethany model are Butler University, Indianapolis, Indiana (1850); Columbia College, Columbia, Missouri (1851); Culver-Stockton College, Canton, Missouri (1853); Eureka College, Eureka, Illinois (1855); Drake University, Des Moines, Iowa (1861); Texas Christian University, Fort Worth, Texas (1873); Milligan College, Tennessee (1881); David Lipscomb University, Nashville, Tennessee (1891); Atlantic Christian College (now Barton College), Wilson, North Carolina (1902); and Lynchburg College, Lynchburg, Virginia (1903).

Bethany College, under Alexander Campbell's leadership, began as a unique experiment in Christian higher education and over the last 150 years has continued to be a leader in the field. Early among American colleges to emphasize the sciences, it was one of the first to offer the Bachelor of Science degree. It offered modern languages when many institutions stayed with classical languages. From the beginning a study of the Bible, both the Hebrew and the Christian scriptures, was a part of the student's education. Bethany was among the first colleges offering courses in psychology and sociology. Early in the twentieth century the field of communications came into being, first with courses in journalism, then in radio, and later in television. It was a leader in psychological testing for admission to college along with a student personnel program. It has pioneered in freshman seminars and required study abroad for language majors and senior comprehensive examinations. The college continues to seek to be on the cutting edge of American higher education.

See also Education, Philosophy of; Higher Education, Views of in the Movement

BIBLIOGRAPHY D. Duane Cummins, *The Disciples Colleges: A History* (1987) • Lester G. McAllister, *Bethany: The First 150 Years* (1991). LESTER G. MCALLISTER

Bethany Press

See Chalice Press; Christian Board of Publication

Bible, Authority and Inspiration of the

1. Biblical Authority
2. Controversy over Biblical Inspiration

Protestants usually claim to follow the Bible as the authoritative text for the life of the church, so the Stone-Campbell Movement does not seem to be particularly unique in its attitude toward biblical authority. The Movement's adherents claimed to be a people of the Book. There have been, nonetheless, certain peculiarities and emphases distinctive of the Movement's articulation of biblical inspiration and authority.

1. Biblical Authority

Barton Stone's and Thomas and Alexander Campbell's views of biblical authority were rooted in their Presbyterian heritage. "The whole counsel of God concerning all things necessary," according to the Westminster Confession, "is either expressly set down in Scripture, or by *good and necessary consequence may be deduced* from Scripture." Affirming this Reformed tradition, the issue of biblical authority emerged for Stone first in relation to doctrine. Protesting the proceedings of the 1803 Synod of Kentucky in approving the earlier condemnation of the doctrine of one of their number as "hostile to the interests of all true religion," Stone and four other ministers of the soon-to-be-constituted Springfield Presbytery claimed the privilege of interpreting the Scripture without reference to the Confession, affirming in the very words of the Confession "that the Supreme Judge, by which all controversies of religion are to be determined, and all decrees of councils, opinions of ancient writers, doctrines of men and private spirits, are to be examined, and in whose sentence we are to rest, can be no other than the Holy Spirit speaking in the Scriptures." Noting that for seeking to "obviate" certain "expressions" in the Confession that darkened the doctrines of grace they had been accused of "departing from our Standard," they announced that they were withdrawing from the jurisdiction of the Synod rather than be "prosecuted before a Judge [the Confession], whose authority to decide we cannot in Conscience acknowledge." Less than a year later, observing that "there was neither precept nor example in the New Testament for such confederacies as modern Church Sessions, Presbyteries, Synods, General Assemblies, etc." they had dissolved their Springfield Presbytery, affirming the Bible alone as the standard not only for the doctrine or faith of the church, but also for its order or government.

Drawing on the Confession and John Locke, the Campbells viewed the Bible fundamentally as a constitution for the church to follow. Thomas Campbell narrowed the constitution to the New Testament in the *Declaration and Address:* "[T]he New Testament is as perfect a constitution for the worship, discipline and government of the New Testament Church . . . as the Old Testament was for the . . . Old Testament Church."

Alexander Campbell in 1816 in the *Sermon on the Law* divided history into three dispensations: the Patriarchal, the Mosaic, and the Christian. Christians were to follow the laws found in the Christian age that started with the founding of the church at Pentecost. All scripture, including the gospels that narrated events before Pentecost, that fell into prior dispensations had no authority for Christians — they were to follow only the practices authorized from Acts through Revelation.

Influenced by John Locke, the Campbells viewed the church as a constitutional monarchy ruled by Christ the King. The Bible or the New Testament (specifically Acts through Revelation) had the laws and practices that were to be followed. These laws were to be followed as the commands and the "approved" examples of the apostles and the primitive church found in the New Testament.

Standing in the British empiricist tradition, Thomas and Alexander Campbell used a Baconian methodology of inductively exploring the verses of the Bible as if they were discrete facts waiting to be reassembled into a clear, logical pattern. Alexander stated: "The doctrine of the Bible, on any particular subject of inquiry, can be clearly and satisfactorily ascertained only by a full induction of all that is found in it upon that subject." With the completed induction of the appropriate "facts," Campbell believed, "we can never have any more divine light upon that subject." Campbell believed that knowledge of Christian beliefs derived through this process was scientific and objective.

Alexander Campbell believed that the Scriptures had been interpreted too long through the "colored glasses" of "speculative" systems and creeds instead of directly perceiving the real or true meaning of the text. In excellent Enlightenment fashion, Campbell stove to eliminate all his prejudices before studying Scripture. "I have endeavored to read the Scriptures as though no one had read them before me," he said, "and am as much on my guard against reading them through the medium of my own views yesterday, or a week ago, as I am against being influenced by any foreign name, authority, or system whatever."

Campbell proudly called himself a Baconian, believing that Lord Francis Bacon laid "the foundation for correcting our reasonings" upon human experience. In the Campbell-Owen debate, Campbell proposed that "Any argument, therefore, which we may offer, we wish to be examined by the improved principles of the inductive philosophy, by those very principles which right reason and sound experimental philosophy have sanctioned as their appropriate tests." Accepting Bacon's definition of a "fact" as "something said" or "something done," Campbell believed that the Bible was primarily a book of empirical facts. Showing his belief that the New Testament was a constitution, he thought the most important facts were the New Testament's commands and examples.

Thomas Campbell, like John Locke, believed that the essentials of Christianity could be reduced to a minimum and that all Christians should be united on those essentials. Following Locke and disagreeing with the Westminster Confession, Thomas Campbell in the *Declaration and Address* denied that inferences and deductions from Scripture were authoritative. They are "not formally binding upon the consciences of Christians farther than they perceive the connection. . . . He concluded, "Hence it is evident that no such deductions or inferential truths ought to have a place in the Church's confession." These inferential truths were sustained by deductive logic rather than by the preferred inductive approach. The British empiricist tradition, including Locke and the Common Sense philosophers, attacked deductive patterns claiming deduction revealed no new truths and was subject to sophistry. Through 1830 Alexander Campbell relied almost exclusively on commands and examples, while denying any place for inferences in the constitutional model of constructing authorized practices for Stone-Campbell Movement churches.

Slowly things began to change. Campbell and other leaders realized that many good practices did not have a clear command or example in the New Testament. Campbell began to claim and use "necessary inferences" as a way to find authorized practices hidden within Scripture — things that the first-century church did but were only implied by the biblical text. As his new movement emerged as a separate body, Campbell confronted new practical questions and found "necessary inference" a useful tool to authorize new ideas for his churches.

Meanwhile, in Britain, Richard Whately, an Anglican minister, began to rehabilitate deductive logic in the empiricist tradition. With the publication of *Elements of Logic* (1826) and *Elements of Rhetoric* (1828), Whately argued that Locke and the Common Sense philosophers were wrong about deductive logic and that its place in generating new knowledge was as a supplement to inductive approaches.

When Bethany College was established, Alexander Campbell taught the college course on rhetoric and used Whately's rhetoric book. Robert Richardson assumed the logic and rhetoric courses in 1845, using and recommending both Whately's *Logic* and *Rhetoric*. Several key Stone-Campbell leaders studied logic and rhetoric at Bethany using Whately's texts. Bethany graduates J. W. McGarvey and Moses Lard took the lead in the 1860s formalizing the concept of "necessary inference" as another means to authorize church practices from its constitution, the Bible.

2. Controversy over Biblical Inspiration

Acting often as an unspoken assumption, the leaders of the Stone-Campbell Movement believed that the entire Bible was inspired and infallible. The Bible, God's Word, was divine, and it was through the Scriptures that God's will for the church had been expressed. The church's constitution was pure and error free. Before issues of biblical criticism and Darwinian evolution raised questions about the accuracy of historical accounts, inspiration was rarely discussed.

Alexander Campbell was typical. He believed that the apostles were able "without the possibility of error, to open to mankind the whole will of their Master," and they did this "clearly, accurately, and infallibly." Campbell, however, rejected the "flat" theory of inspiration dominant in the Reformed tradition, the view "that the scriptures claim for every jot and tittle of themselves the same plenary and verbal inspiration." This was "ultraism" and "would greatly impair the reasonings of the most able defenders of the inspiration of the Bible." Only the "ideas and leading terms" of the biblical writers were inspired. Revelation and inspiration went hand in hand. Campbell and others asserted that the truly inspired content of the Scriptures was that which directly communicated the Word of God. The Bible "contained" the Word, but the Word was not evenly distributed across all of the biblical text. Robert Richardson accordingly made a strict distinction between the gospel, the true "standard of orthodoxy" and confessional core of the church, and the Bible as a whole, the broad "circumference" of divine revelation.

These assumptions dominated the second half of the nineteenth century. Robert Milligan (1814-1875) argued that the Bible was inspired and infallible, while his colleague at the College of the Bible in Lexington, Kentucky, J. W. McGarvey (1829-1911), introduced to conservative Disciples the language of "inerrancy."

Meanwhile minority views began to be heard. L. L. Pinkerton (1812-1875) as early as 1849 denied inerrancy. Isaac Errett (1820-1888), editor of the *Christian Standard,* at the 1883 Missouri Christian Lectureship affirmed the inspiration of the Bible and said, "Admitting the fact of inspiration, have we in the inspired Scriptures an *infallible* guide? Are they absolutely free from error? . . . I do not see how we can answer this question affirmatively." Alexander Procter (1825-1900), a classmate of McGarvey at Bethany College, thought modern science proved many of the "facts" of the Bible archaic. Along with the new science, higher criticism of the Bible began to make its way into seminaries and universities and more individuals from the Stone-Campbell Movement began to study at Yale and the University of Chicago, centers of the new critical methods. Slowly the minority view denying inerrancy spread in the Movement.

Edward Scribner Ames (1870-1958) became the leading liberal voice among Disciples as a professor at Butler and the University of Chicago and as the Dean of the Disciples Divinity House. Revelation, for Ames, was accountable to the authority of human experience and reason. The Bible was now to be seen not as an infallible chronicle of supernatural revelation but "a collection of writings reflecting the history of religiously gifted people in their growth and aspirations." Biblical "inspiration" was of a piece with the broader inspiration of enlightened humanity.

Reactions to the new liberal views were fierce. J. W. McGarvey took the lead in the weekly "Biblical Criticism" column in the *Christian Standard* and in his books *The Authorship of the Book of Deuteronomy with Its Bearings on the Higher Criticism of the Pentateuch* (1902) and *Short Essays in Biblical Criticism: Reprinted from the Christian Standard 1893-1904.* He attacked the views of leading biblical scholars in Germany and America and was especially opposed to Disciples scholar Herbert L. Willett (1864-1944). Willett was the first of the Disciples to earn a Ph.D. in biblical studies and the first to study in Germany. Willett became a professor at the University of Chicago and so represented all that McGarvey opposed.

Despite McGarvey's efforts, gradually professors were hired at the College of the Bible who accepted the new critical views. Hall Calhoun (1863-1935), who earned his B.D. degree from Yale and his Ph.D. in

Old Testament under George Foote Moore in 1904, remained loyal to McGarvey's views. In 1917, six years after McGarvey died, Calhoun tried to force the liberal professors out of the College of the Bible but was unsuccessful and resigned his position. While other incidents occurred earlier, the 1917 incident became the catalyst for protracted conflict over issues of fundamentalism and modernism among the Disciples of Christ.

In the 1920s Disciples fundamentalists pressed infallibility and inerrancy as the only understandings of biblical inspiration while liberals permitted a variety of options. In December 1921 a Restoration Congress, called by conservatives, met in Louisville, Kentucky, to press for the "fundamentals of Christianity." E. Lynnwood Crystal, from Louisville, attacked A. W. Fortune (1873-1950), president of the United Christian Missionary Society and W. J. Lhamon (1855-1955), minister from St. Louis, for modernist views of the Bible. Mark Collis, minister from Lexington, Kentucky, likewise blamed "German rationalism," E. S. Ames, and C. C. Morrison (1874-1966), editor of the *Christian Century*, for modernism among the Disciples. The California Bible Congress was held January 1922 at the First Christian Church in Long Beach, California, where leading Disciples fundamentalist George Taubman preached. R. C. Foster spoke on "The Bible and Its Critics." He accused professors in Stone-Campbell Movement schools of teaching students to deceive local congregations in order to introduce modernism. W. F. Richardson, minister in Los Angeles, openly confronted Foster after his speech, accusing him of lies, half-truths, and misrepresentations. Later in April 1922, Hall Calhoun spoke at the Pittsburgh Bible Congress on "Destructive Criticism," attacking biblical higher criticism. The two incompatible views of inspiration festered and eventually contributed to the rupture between the Christian Church (Disciples of Christ) and the Christian Churches/Churches of Christ.

These issues were also significant in the Churches of Christ, even though that body had formed a separate identity before the fundamentalist-modernist controversies of the 1920s. Churches of Christ had uniformly maintained the traditional ideas of inspiration, infallibility, and inerrancy in the nineteenth century. David Lipscomb, for example, in 1890 preferred "any sect" that believed "the Bible as the inspired and infallible word of God, however it might pervert its ordinances" over any other sect that denied "the inspiration of the scriptures" or rejected "the Bible as the infallible word of God, destroying man's faith in it and in Jesus Christ as the Saviour of sinners."

When the fundamentalist-modernist controversies surfaced, attitudes in the Churches of Christ hardened. In 1920 Tennessee preacher Price Billingsley (1877-1959) maintained that inerrancy was the "polestar" of Christianity, the "first of truths to be maintained," or one would be "lost irretrievably." Since "the unerring Spirit was directing" the Bible's authors, the Bible was "beyond our field of criticism." The Churches of Christ, following the controversies in the Disciples of Christ and other religious groups, sided with the emerging fundamentalists on this issue and joined the fray against modernists and higher critics.

In 1922 Churches of Christ had their own controversy over inerrancy and infallibility centered at Abilene Christian College (ACC). William Webb Freeman (1887-1954), on leave of absence from ACC to pursue his Ph.D. in New Testament at Yale, wrote in the *Firm Foundation* that the Bible was infallible in the area of religion but not in science. The response was swift. G. H. P. Showalter (1870-1954), editor of the *Firm Foundation*, thought Freeman had abandoned the fundamentals and was under the influence of German rationalism. He concluded, "Whenever we reach a point where the Bible is looked upon as the word of man rather than the 'word of God,' as it purports to be, we cut loose our moorings from the eternal rock of truth and faith is shipwrecked." Freeman was fired from ACC, and the incident hindered the development of biblical scholarship in Churches of Christ until the 1960s when young scholars began obtaining doctorates and positions in religion at first-tier seminaries and universities.

Christian Churches/Churches of Christ revisited the issue of biblical inerrancy at the 1986 North American Christian Convention, in a debate between conservative scholar Jack Cottrell and moderate minister Myron Taylor on "Inerrancy as a Restoration Principle." Cottrell equated Alexander Campbell's statements about the "infallibility" of God and the sacred writers in communicating revelation with the "total inerrancy" of the Bible. He recommended that "limited inerrancy" — the view of some within the Movement that Scripture is inerrant only with respect to "matters of faith and practice" but "NOT in peripheral areas such as history and science" — ultimately undermined the Movement's stance on the objective authority of the Bible. Myron Taylor responded by dismissing the view that Campbell was an inerrantist and by rejecting the epistemological and other props used by contemporary inerrantists. Inerrantists were claiming more for the Bible than the Bible claims for itself. On the contrary, Taylor argued, the Bible presented no internal theory of a perfect or inerrant text but merely witnessed to the infallible way of salvation.

While almost everyone in the Stone-Campbell tradition has argued that the Bible is authoritative for the church, the meaning and application of that authority ran the theological spectrum from conservative to liberal. Equally fractious were the views of biblical inspiration. The entire tradition, like other Protestant groups in America, was profoundly influenced by the fundamentalist-modernist controversy.

While the Churches of Christ and the Christian Churches/Churches of Christ have continued (until recently) to focus on the Bible as a "constitution," the Disciples of Christ have been characterized by more diverse views with their concentration on the freedom of each individual to interpret Scripture by his or her own conscience. While classical liberalism freed Disciples from fundamentalism and dominated the Disciples until the late 1950s, many Disciples saw liberalism as a dead end and turned to neo-orthodoxy, while at the same time they tried to appropriate elements of the Stone-Campbell heritage congenial to their own critical sensitivities.

Clearly influenced by Karl Barth, Stephen England (1895-1987) of Phillips University rejected liberal humanism and the "left-wing" of the Disciples, arguing instead for a "return to the authority of the New Testament." Reflecting Disciples' diversity, England never articulated a clear theory of biblical authority, believing that the real problem lay with how the Bible was to be interpreted. Echoing the Disciples' dimension of liberty, England saw the New Testament as a set of documents that would free the church in every generation "from every shackle that binds."

For J. Phillip Hyatt (1909-1972), a Disciples biblical scholar at Vanderbilt, the Bible was a place where one encountered the Word of God primarily though the record of the mighty acts of God in history. Christ was the centerpiece of these Acts, holding the entire Bible together. Again for Hyatt, interpretation rather than any fully articulated idea of biblical authority was front and center.

Eugene Boring (b. 1935), Disciples New Testament scholar, notes the same characteristic in the Panel of Scholars project of the late 1950s and early 1960s that "the authority of the Bible is repeatedly both assumed and explicitly affirmed, with the New Testament playing the definitive role." Yet the "nature of biblical authority is rarely spelled out." Influenced by neo-orthodoxy, authority was not seen as propositional, flowing from a constitution, but as "personal encounter with the God who speaks through the Bible."

In recent years Disciples have turned to more dialogic models of biblical authority. In 1995 the Disciples affirmed, "We love the Bible and take it seriously, but we do not demand a uniform approach to Scripture. We believe the Bible bears decisive witness to the gospel of the *living* God." Clark Williamson and others now affirm that the Bible is a "living book" in contrast to a static constitution. The Bible is in dialogue with both its own method of interpretation and the present historical context. The good news that God's love is promised and extended to all people is the centerpiece of the Bible's self-interpretation and criticism.

Many in Churches of Christ and in Christian Churches/Churches of Christ are likewise moving away from the old constitutionalism to a new sensitivity to the character of Scripture as spiritual guide and as a diverse record of the decisive acts of God in salvation history. Narrative theology and hermeneutics have had a positive impact in some quarters, leading many to view the Bible less as a logically ordered body of evidences and propositions than as a multidimensional witness to the God of Jesus Christ.

See also Bible, Interpretation of the; *Declaration and Address;* Fundamentalism; Hermeneutics; *Last Will and Testament of Springfield Presbytery;* Liberalism

BIBLIOGRAPHY Edward Scribner Ames, *The New Orthodoxy* (1918) • *An Apology for Renouncing the Jurisdiction of the Synod of Kentucky* (1804) • Charles Blaisdell, ed., *Conservative/Moderate/Liberal: The Biblical Authority Debate* (1990) • M. Eugene Boring, *Disciples and the Bible: A History of Disciples Biblical Interpretation in North America* (1997) • Alexander Campbell, "Tracts for the People," No. III: "The Bible — Principles of Interpretation," *Millennial Harbinger* (1846): 13-24 • Michael W. Casey, *The Battle Over Hermeneutics in the Stone-Campbell Movement, 1800-1870* (1998) • Michael W. Casey, "The Theory of Logic and Inference in the *Declaration and Address,*" in *The Quest for Christian Unity, Peace, and Purity in Thomas Campbell's Declaration and Address: Text and Studies,* ed. Thomas H. Olbricht and Hans Rollmann (2000), pp. 223-42 • Jack Cottrell and Myron Taylor, "Inerrancy as a Restoration Principle" (unpublished MSS, North American Christian Convention, 1986) • Isaac Errett, "Inspiration," *The Missouri Christian Lectures* (1883) • Homer Hailey, *Inspiration of Scripture* (1971) • *Last Will and Testament of Springfield Presbytery* (1804) • J. W. McGarvey, *Short Essays in Biblical Criticism* (1910) • Robert Richardson, "Inspiration of the Scriptures," *Millennial Harbinger* (1836): 345-49 • Robert Richardson, "Reformation — No. IV," *Millennial Harbinger* (1847): 503-9 • James Stephen Wolfgang, "Fundamentalism and the Churches of Christ, 1910-1930" (unpublished M.A. thesis, Vanderbilt University, 1990).

MICHAEL W. CASEY

Bible, Commentaries on the

1. First-Generation Antipathy to the Commentary Genre
2. Influential Commentaries
3. The Twentieth Century

1. First-Generation Antipathy to the Commentary Genre

From the very beginning the Stone-Campbell Movement was oriented to biblical study and interpretation, but it did not produce full-scale commentaries on the Bible until the second generation. Some reasons for this initial antipathy to the commentary genre are easily understood, for they are endemic to the ethos of the first generation. First, commentaries on the Bible seemed at first to embody "human tradition," considered to be the enemy of authentic understanding of the Bible. Second, the sixteenth-century Reformation principles of the "plain meaning" of Scripture and "the Bible as its own interpreter" seemed to make commentaries unnecessary — despite the fact that Luther and Calvin, admired by Stone and Campbell, wrote extensive commentaries. Third, since the leaders of the first generation were not yet sharply aware that every translation is already an interpretation, they tended to suppose that all that stood in the way of appropriating the "plain meaning" of the text was a good translation, and thus were active in the study of the original languages of Scripture and in the making of modern speech translations.

Two of Alexander Campbell's works, however, are steps in the direction of later commentaries. In *The Living Oracles* (1st ed. 1826), Campbell's adaptation of a British translation of the New Testament by George Campbell, James MacKnight, and Philip Doddridge, Campbell added Prefaces to each book providing historical information necessary for its interpretation. He also added an extensive series of Appendices, including a geographical index, a chronological table, a chronological index of the major events of the Hellenistic era, historical definitions of obscure biblical terms — in short, a miniature historical Bible Dictionary. Campbell's annotated translation of Acts for the American Bible Union was a large, impressive volume somewhat like the International Critical Commentary in format, with much of the page occupied with critical notes not only dealing with textual and linguistic data, but making exegetical comments.

2. Influential Commentaries

From the second generation on, many authors in all branches of the Stone-Campbell Movement published their own commentaries on individual books of the Bible. Though most of these were privately published and idiosyncratic, some became influential within the Movement. Examples are J. L. Martin's commentary on Revelation, *The Voice of the Seven Thunders* (Unity, Ind., 1870), and Henry H. Halley's *Halley's Bible Handbook,* originally privately published in 1924, which went through numerous editions and reprintings and is still available today.

Two commentaries from the late nineteenth century stood out as most influential in that each of them both formed and expressed the hermeneutical mind-set of the second and third generations of the Stone-Campbell Movement (ca. 1866-1929). Both authors studied at Bethany under Alexander Campbell. Both commentaries have been kept in print and are used to this day among some in Churches of Christ and the Christian Churches/Churches of Christ. In addition, one commentary series had considerable influence.

- J. W. McGarvey's two-volume *Commentary on Acts of Apostles* (first ed. 1863; several later editions, then thoroughly revised as *New Commentary on Acts of Apostles,* 1892) was the first full-scale commentary to emerge from the Movement, and it also had the most influence on Stone-Campbell history. It interpreted the text from the perspective of the emerging Disciples agenda: logic and reason as the criteria of truth, restoration of the primitive faith and practice, the "conditions of pardon" as illustrated by the conversion stories in Acts, the identification of the kingdom of God with the church, three different "measures" of the Holy Spirit (baptism, special gifts, general gift), and an emphasis on believers' baptism by immersion for the forgiveness of sins. McGarvey defends the historicity of the details in the Acts narrative against emerging "German rationalism" and harmonizes it with the rest of the New Testament.
- The second most influential commentary in the Stone-Campbell Movement was B. W. Johnson's *The People's New Testament with Notes* (two vols., 1889, 1891), the first Stone-Campbell commentary on the whole New Testament. The volumes presented the text of the 1611 King James Version and the 1881 Revised Version, prefaced each book with a brief historical introduction, and provided annotations, sometimes extensive and substantial, to aid in understanding the text. Less polemical and less narrowly denominational than McGarvey, Johnson nonetheless presents what had become traditional Stone-Campbell perspectives on the biblical text. Uncharacteristic for Stone-Campbell writers, Johnson was very interested in the book of Revelation. His *Notes* on Revelation are disproportionately extensive, interpreting the book as a long-range prophecy of the history of the church from John's time to the end. This interpretation was widely influential among members of the Stone-Campbell Movement of the early twentieth century.
- In 1875 an anonymous group of publishers announced the inauguration of a series of commentaries on the New Testament to include "all the prominent Commentators" in the Movement. The New Testament Commentary series was launched with commentaries on Matthew and Mark by J. W. McGarvey and on Hebrews by Robert Milligan, and shortly incorporated McGarvey's Acts and Moses E. Lard's commentary on

Romans written earlier. All the commentaries in this series were written by and for members of the Movement, were hardly noticed by others, and concentrated on mediating the results of mid-range scholarship to the pastors and laypeople of the Movement. Eleven volumes were projected, embracing the whole New Testament, but only five appeared. This was the only effort of Stone-Campbell Christians to publish a denominational commentary.

3. The Twentieth Century

After the Movement split into three distinguishable groups in the twentieth century, the New Testament Commentary became the Standard Bible Commentary (Standard Publishing Company), narrowing its focus to the McGarvey tradition. This series became the present Standard Bible Studies, written by and for the Christian Churches/Churches of Christ.

Don DeWelt and Seth Wilson of Ozark Bible College initiated another series published by College Press. The Biblical Studies Textbook Series was a forty-four volume set of commentaries on the whole Bible reflecting the spectrum of scholarship of the Christian Churches/Churches of Christ from 1953 to 1988. This series has now been succeeded by The College Press NIV Commentary, several volumes of which have already appeared. This more academically sophisticated series is a cooperative project of scholars from the Christian Churches/Churches of Christ and the Churches of Christ.

Representative of the numerous commentaries written by and for Churches of Christ is The Living Word Commentary (Austin, Tex.: Sweet Publishing Company). This series, edited by John Willis (Old Testament) and Everett Ferguson (New Testament) of Abilene Christian University, originally projected thirty-eight volumes covering the whole Bible, but the Old Testament section has not been completed. The series is based on the Revised Standard Version and is intended to mediate the results of moderate scholarship to pastors and teachers in the congregations.

The Disciples have established no series of commentaries representing their distinctive point of view since the New Testament Commentary, though some Disciples are contributing to the Commentary for Today series currently under way from Chalice Press. A renewal of publishing commentaries in the Disciples tradition is represented by *The People's New Testament with Notes* by M. Eugene Boring and Fred B. Craddock (Chalice Press, 2003), which revives the tradition of B. W. Johnson's one-volume commentary for pastors and laypeople. Several Disciples authors have contributed to established ecumenical series such as The Interpreter's Bible, Interpretation, Harper's Bible Commentary, and The New Interpreter's Bible.

See also Bible, Interpretation of the; College Press; Johnson, Barton Warren; McGarvey, John W.; Milligan, Robert; Standard Publishing Company

BIBLIOGRAPHY M. Eugene Boring, *Disciples and the Bible: The History of Disciples Biblical Interpretation in North America* (1997) • B. W. Johnson, *The People's New Testament with Notes* (1889, 1891) • J. W. McGarvey, *Commentary on Acts of the Apostles* (1863, rev. ed. 1892) • Robert Milligan, *Epistle to the Hebrews* (1875) • Moses Lard, *Commentary on Paul's Letter to Romans* (1875). M. EUGENE BORING

Bible, Interpretation of the

1. 1804-1866: The Formation of an Indigenous Tradition
2. 1866-1892: The Period of "Scholasticism"
3. 1892-1929: The Period of Struggle for the Heritage
4. 1929-1968: The Period of Secularization and Compartmentalization
5. 1968 to the Present

Classic principles and practices for interpreting Scripture in the Stone-Campbell Movement. The heirs of the Movement have come to interpret the Bible using a wide spectrum of methods and conclusions, representing differing responses to a common history. This history can be outlined according to the five generations from the time of Stone and Campbell to the dawn of the twenty-first century.

1. 1804-1866: The Formation of an Indigenous Tradition

This period extends from the *Last Will and Testament of the Springfield Presbytery* to the death of Alexander Campbell. This creative period gave birth to the grand vision of reuniting the church by restoring "New Testament Christianity" and saw the formation of a distinctive hermeneutical tradition corresponding to this vision. All the earliest leaders were intensive biblical students and able teachers and preachers of the Bible, but for three generations the dominant influence on biblical interpretation in the Stone-Campbell Movement was the extended shadow of Alexander Campbell. Campbell's emphases continued to stamp the Movement for decades.

The first of these was the appropriation of biblical content in an accurate translation. Since the first generation regarded the biblical revelation and not the "rubbish of human tradition" as authoritative, the Bible is effective only if its contents are known. The Bible does not fulfill its function in the life of the church merely in a symbolic or iconic manner, but only as its contents are internalized by the membership of the church at large, not only by its designated leaders. A readable translation was thus imperative. While Campbell himself and most of the early leaders and ministers of the Stone-Campbell Movement were fluent in the original languages of the Bible, most readers needed an accurate and readable translation. Campbell perceived that the King James Version of 1611 was already inadequate. He was among the pioneers of "modern speech translations," adapting and publishing his own version of the New Testament translation of three British scholars as *The Living Oracles,* which anticipated several features of later translations such as the Revised Standard Version.

A second Campbellian legacy in the Movement was his populist, public, and rational hermeneutic. Campbell had great confidence that the "ordinary church member" could understand the Bible without authoritative direction from the clergy. The Bible was to be studied in the congregation, where church members would come to an adequate and appropriate understanding of the "plain meaning" of the text if given the proper tools and encouragement. Biblical interpretation was not a secret art to be practiced only by the initiates; rather, it was to be carried on in the open context of preaching, teaching, and discussion within congregational settings. However, Alexander Campbell knew that simply insisting on "the Bible alone" was not enough; he realized that the Bible is of "no value" without "fixed and certain principles of interpretation." He assumed that by following the same rules of interpretation, everyone would arrive at a uniform understanding of the "plain meaning of the text." He rejected both the rationalistic methods of the philosophers and the "allegorical," spiritualizing methods still dominant in the church. Instead he advocated the grammatico-historical method, that is, the "plain meaning" of the text as determined by historical-critical exegesis. His famous seven rules were not original, but were a combination of the generally accepted principles of sound exegesis worked out by Erasmus and the Renaissance humanists and by Campbell's own British rhetorical and philosophical tradition. He outlined these in his *Christianity Restored* (1835) as follows:

> 1. On opening any book in the sacred Scriptures, consider first the historical circumstances of the book. These are the order, the title, the author, the date, the place, and the occasion of it. . . .
>
> 2. In examining the contents of any book, as respects precepts, promises, exhortations, etc., observe who it is that speaks, and under what dispensation he officiates.
>
> 3. To understand the meaning of what is commanded, promised, taught, etc., the same philological principles, deduced from the nature of language, or the same laws of interpretation which are applied to the language of other books, are to be applied to the language of the Bible.
>
> 4. Common usage, which can only be ascertained by testimony, must always decide the meaning of any word which has but one signification; . . .
>
> 5. In all tropical (figurative) language, ascertain the point of resemblance, and judge of the nature of the trope, and its kind, from the point of resemblance.
>
> 6. In the interpretation of symbols, types, allegories, and parables, this rule is supreme: ascertain the point to be illustrated; for comparison is never to be extended beyond that point — to all the attributes, qualities, or circumstances of the symbol, type, allegory, or parable.
>
> 7. For the salutary and sanctifying intelligence of the Oracles of God, the following rule is indispensable: We must come within the understanding distance.
>
> There is a distance which is properly called the speaking distance, or the hearing distance; beyond which the voice reaches not, and the ear hears not. To hear another, we must come within that circle which the voice audibly fills.
>
> Now we may with propriety say, that as it respects God, there is an understanding distance. All beyond that distance cannot understand God; all within it, can easily understand him in all matters of piety and morality. God himself is the center of that circle, and humility is its circumference.

The important point here is that these rules of interpretation represent a public, populist hermeneutic. It was the expression of Campbell's confidence in "common sense" and in the capacity of common people to interpret the Bible responsibly and objectively, if they were given clear instruction on how to do so. Campbell wanted to wrest control of the interpretation of the Bible from the clergy and make it a "public" function open to the common gaze and a process in which all Christians could participate.

Campbell had great confidence in human reason as the guide to authentic interpretation. Having abandoned denominational creeds as the authoritative guide to the meaning of the Bible, and being suspicious of claims that the Holy Spirit illuminated the meaning of the biblical text, Campbell fell back on commonsense reason as the arbiter of biblical truth. At least this was his theory. In practice, he also allowed more room for subjectivity than his theory allowed. In his concluding "Rule 7," for instance, where one would expect to find "reason," what actually appears is "humility" as the prerequisite of coming within the "understanding distance" of the biblical text. Thus also for Campbell, biblical interpretation was not a mechanical application of the rules of grammar and logic, but involved Christian commitment, with humility understood as accepting oneself to be God's creature wanting to do God's will.

Campbell affirmed the Bible as a whole as authoritative for the church, but not in an indiscriminate manner. Combining the covenant theology of the Reformed (Presbyterian) tradition and the common-sense logic prevalent in his British education, he made "dispensational" distinctions within it. One of his rules of interpretation was that to understand any biblical statement, one must consider the dispensation in which it was made, that is, where it appears in the biblical narrative (Rule 2 above). For Campbell, the two great turning points in the biblical story were the giving of the law on Sinai (Exod. 20) and the founding of the church (Acts 2), thus effectively dividing the Bible into the "Patriarchal" (Gen. 1–Exod. 19), "Mosaic" or "Jewish" (Exod. 19–Acts 1) and "Christian" dispensations.

Thus from the very beginning the Stone-Campbell tradition encouraged the making of critical distinctions within the Bible, while affirming that, as a whole, it contained the Word of God. The Old Testament was not directly authoritative for establishing Christian doctrine, but by means of typological interpretation and proof-from-prophecy, Old Testament texts could be used to support Christian doctrine. However, rejecting or ignoring the Old Testament completely is only a "Marcionite" perversion of Campbell's emphasis. The biblical revelation was held together by his emphasis on the series of God's mighty acts in history (which Campbell called "facts") as the unifying narrative of Scripture. While purportedly speaking in terms of a logical system of revelation, Campbell actually found the unity of the Bible to be in the unity of its story of the saving acts of God, not in its systematic coherence. One of the by-products of this "dispensationalism" was to place Jesus in the "Jewish" dispensation and thus theoretically to relativize the importance of Jesus and the Gospels for Christian teaching. Hermeneutical attention was concentrated on Acts and the Epistles. For Campbell himself, Romans, and especially Hebrews, formed the central focus of his "canon-within-the-canon."

Campbell presupposed that the Bible was uniquely inspired by God, but did not have a rigid doctrine of biblical inspiration. He assumed the "rational supernaturalism" typical of other evangelical Protestants of his day. While he could use the language of "infallibility" with reference to the Bible (a usage that predates more recent connotations), he nonetheless understood the biblical texts to be the words and ideas of human authors through which the divine Word came. He acknowledged that these texts could contain human errors, but were infallibly inspired so far as the saving message was concerned. The Bible exercises its authority primarily by "express command" or "approved example" — to which "necessary inference" would later be added in some hermeneutical streams of the Stone-Campbell tradition.

The original emphasis on "common sense" and a "rational approach" to biblical interpretation was directed against an emotional, quasi-"mystical" understanding of the work of the Holy Spirit in the individual's heart, against an arbitrary allegorical interpretation that functioned to harmonize the Bible with "denominational tradition," and against a privileged role for ordained clergy and ecclesiastical officials in determining the meaning of the Bible for the church. To understand the Bible, church members needed neither ecclesiastical tradition nor a special work of the Holy Spirit. An unanticipated problem to plague later generations was that "common sense" and "rational" could come to mean that the Bible could tell the reader nothing that conflicted with "common sense" and "human reason," so that contrary to Campbell's intention, all God's truth would have to be fitted into a human rationalistic system. This could and did happen later in both the conservative and liberal wings of the Movement.

A further problem was the assumption that, once authoritarian tradition and clergy were removed and a common system of "rules of interpretation" was adopted, Christian readers would have no difficulty in agreeing on the "plain meaning" of the text. This in fact tended to open the door to individualistic and divisive interpretations, and to promote division rather than the unity of the church.

2. 1866-1892: The Period of "Scholasticism"

The second generation begins roughly with the death of Alexander Campbell and founding of the *Christian Standard* and extends to the founding of the University of Chicago and the publication of McGarvey's *New Commentary on Acts.* This period saw the solidification of a tradition often known as "The Plea" (for restoration of New Testament Christianity as the basis for a reunited church). While still claiming to reject "human tradition" and abide by "the Bible alone," by the second generation the Stone-Campbell Movement had unintentionally and unconsciously developed a tradition that set the agenda and provided guidelines for interpreting the Bible. The works of Isaac Errett, Robert Milligan, B. W. Johnson, James S. Lamar, and David R. Dungan represent biblical interpretation in the Movement in this period. By the end of this period the distinctive approach to interpretation in the Churches of Christ had become clear, as represented in the work of David Lipscomb.

The first generation of Stone-Campbell leadership had been well educated in non–Stone-Campbell contexts, and had been formed by the churchly ("denominational") traditions in which they had grown up. The second generation was mostly self-taught in the Movement's own educational institutions, and, while still supposing they were free of "human tradition," they were influenced by the inherited tradition of their own Movement that was tending to become dogma. The elements and agenda of this tradition strongly influenced the second generation's approach to the Bible: logic and reason as the criteria of truth; restoration of the primitive faith and practice; the "conditions of pardon" as illustrated by the conversion stories in Acts; the identification of the kingdom of God with the church; three different "measures" of the Holy Spirit (baptism; special gifts; general gift); and an emphasis on believers' baptism by immersion for the forgiveness of sins.

Isaac Errett never wrote a biblical commentary but influenced the developing denomination by his popular, non-academic writings, especially his *Christian Standard* series such as "Evenings with the Bible." He wrote for the "popular mind," the educated layperson in the pew, with a simple, reasonable approach to biblical interpretation that downplayed critical problems without ignoring them. He did not defend a level, homogenized Bible, but advocated the idea of "progressive revelation" in the course of biblical history. On the one hand, this was a development from Campbell's "three dispensation" perspective, but it also provided the foundation for later Disciple liberalism's evolutionary approach to the development of biblical truth.

Robert Milligan hardened the incipient rationalism of the first generation into a rigid rationalistic scheme into which all biblical data were organized. Milligan understood the biblical faith to be logically structured. Human reason could both understand it on its own terms and defend it in logical terms to others who were willing to be honestly reasonable. Errett had concentrated on the "plan of salvation," that is, what human beings must do in order to accept the saving grace of God and make it effective, and made this "plan of salvation" into a grid by which to see and understand biblical issues. Analogously, Milligan made the "scheme of redemption," the outline of God's saving plan for history, the framework of his approach to the Bible. Milligan's *Scheme of Redemption* (1868) became an important resource and guide for understanding the Bible for two generations of ministers in all streams of the Stone-Campbell tradition.

This meant that Milligan perpetuated the agenda formulated by the first generation, with its values and problems. In fact, the larger outline of his book in some measure appropriated that of Walter Scott's earlier work, *The Gospel Restored* (1836).

Among the liabilities of Milligan's approach was his minimizing of the importance of Jesus and the Gospels, so that his discussion of John the Baptist, Jesus, and Christology was only half as long as his discussion of the "Legal Types" of the Old Testament as a witness to the New Testament church. His commentary on the Epistle to the Hebrews is a good example of the careful, thorough biblical interpretation carried on by second-generation scholars. It was the first volume of *The New Testament Commentary,* a multi-volume work that summed up and reflected the biblical work of the Movement in the late nineteenth century.

There are two other "scholastic" works of Stone-Campbell hermeneutics in this second generation worthy of mention. Even before Milligan's books, James S. Lamar, a graduate of Bethany and pastor in Georgia, published in 1860 *The Organon of Scripture: Or the Inductive Method of Biblical Interpretation,* truly a hermeneutical handbook systematizing the Baconian model of "scientific" exegesis from the first generation of the Movement. Lamar treated the Bible as a complex body of facts and evidences that could be collated and rendered thoroughly coherent through disciplined analysis of its language. It suffered from the same glorification of logic at the expense of history found in Milligan, but in other works of actual exegesis Lamar proved much more sensitive to biblical narrative and much less overconfident in the inductive method. D. R. Dungan's much later handbook of *Hermeneutics* (1888), the work of another scholar-pastor, was an additional adjudication of the Baconian/commonsense hermeneutic of Alexander Campbell, and remained in use in many Stone-Campbell colleges for years.

Of a more popular character was B. W. Johnson's *People's New Testament with Notes* (1889-91), which enjoyed wide usage for over a generation. The introductions and annotations to every New Testament book provided clear, nontechnical comments that mediated the mid-range scholarship of the day to the general reading public of the Stone-Campbell Movement. Johnson (like Milligan) was directly influenced by Alexander Campbell (Johnson had studied and taught at Bethany College; Milligan had taught there). Yet Johnson's *People's New Testament* was not an explicit recitation of the key doctrines of the Stone-Campbell tradition. Though he refers often and positively to the standard ("denominational") commentaries of the day, he never cites Campbell or other scholars from the Stone-Campbell tradition. The *People's New Testament* reflects the Stone-Campbell heritage indirectly, for it is with Stone-Campbell eyes focused by the Stone-Campbell agenda and Stone-Campbell perspectives that Johnson sees as the "plain meaning" of the biblical text.

Because he was a towering figure in the emergence of Churches of Christ, David Lipscomb's principles of biblical interpretation demand mention. Lipscomb was committed to the infallibility of the Bible, the validity and necessity of pattern restorationism, and a particular view of eschatology. While the Campbellian stream had tended to play down eschatology and to interpret it in postmillennial "progressive" terms as had Alexander Campbell himself, Lipscomb's eschatology was an extension of Barton W. Stone's apocalyptic sectarianism into the second and third generations. Lipscomb's approach to the Bible manifested little of the positive understanding of historical development and the immanent work of God in history present in Campbell's hermeneutic. Lipscomb was "premillennial" in the sense that he believed the final rule of God on earth would be preceded by the parousia, not in the sense that he believed it would last only a thousand years and then be succeeded by the ultimate rule of God. This issue was to become important in later generations of interpretation in the Churches of Christ, but it bypassed the Disciples.

3. 1892-1929: The Period of Struggle for the Heritage

The period that extends from the founding of the University of Chicago and the publication of J. W. McGarvey's *New Commentary on Acts* to H. L. Willett's retirement from the University of Chicago was marked by the encounter between the developing indigenous ecclesiastical tradition of the Stone-Campbell Movement and the incursion of higher criticism from the academic world. The conflict was embodied in McGarvey and the College of the Bible, on the one hand, and Willett and the Disciples Divinity House of the University of Chicago, on the other. During this period the division between Disciples and the Churches of Christ was largely completed. The end of this period was marked by the tensions that would eventuate in the split between Disciples and the Christian Churches/Churches of Christ.

During this period Disciples scholars such as Willett began to study at interdenominational theological schools and secular universities, and for the first time the Stone-Campbell Movement engaged historical criticism as the primary perspective on biblical interpretation. While Campbell's "Seven Rules" had advocated a kind of historical criticism, traditional conclusions about authorship, date, and the nature of biblical documents had been assumed, so that no one in the first generation had supposed that the consistent application of Campbell's own principles would lead to results that challenged and overturned these conclusions. By the end of the nineteenth century, those who followed the critical method arrived at a new set of conclusions that made the Bible look entirely different. Among these new conclusions: the Pentateuch was not written by Moses but represented a long development within Israel's history; the prophets were not making long-range predictions about Jesus and the church, but spoke to the issues of their own time; the Gospels were not independent "testimonies" that provided "evidence" for the historical facts about Jesus' life and teaching, but were interdependent (Matthew and Luke used Mark and "Q"); also, the Gospels were not written by apostles and contained several layers of reinterpreted traditions.

Most devastating of all for the Disciples paradigm was that, from the critical perspective, the New Testament turned out not to present one consistent picture of "the New Testament church," but a (limited) variety of the faith and practice of earliest Christianity. A choice had to be made, and the battle was fierce. In general, the stream of tradition that became the Christian Church (Disciples of Christ) welcomed biblical criticism and reinterpreted the developing Disciples tradition in the light of the new approach to the Bible, while the elements of the Movement that became the Churches of Christ and the Christian Churches/Churches of Christ held on to the restorationist traditions.

McGarvey's exposition in his *New Commentary on the Acts of the Apostles* (1892) gave a classic summary of traditional Disciples doctrine while resisting the "unbelievers" who were advocating the newer critical approach. Willett's numerous and popular writings interpreted the Bible in the context of the common ground found in mainstream Protestantism that was beginning to adopt the historical-critical approach. A choice now had to be made between the twin pillars that had developed as the foundation of the Stone-Campbell tradition, the restoration of New Testament Christianity and unity of a fragmented church. The first two generations had believed these were not only compatible, but the one was the essential means to the other: unity was the goal, but restoration was the essential means. It now seemed clear to some that the two principles were actually contrary to each other, and those interested in unity with other Christians abandoned the restorationist approach to biblical interpretation, while those who preserved restorationism became less and less ecumenical. Those who adopted historical criticism were able to cooperate with Christians in other denominations who did so, as neither made their denominational tradition the arbiter of hermeneutical truth. Those who held to restorationism as the hermeneutical key found that their appeal to the denominations to return to "the New Testament church" was undercut by historical criticism. While other historical, personal, theological, and sociological factors were involved in the dissolution of the Stone-Campbell Movement into three denominations, whether or not one adopted historical criticism as a valid approach to biblical interpretation was an important issue in the separation of both the Churches of Christ and the Christian Churches/Churches of Christ from the Disciples.

4. 1929-1968: The Period of Secularization and Compartmentalization

This period extended from Willett's retirement from the University of Chicago to the retirement of Stephen J. England from the Graduate Seminary of Phillips University in the same year that saw the emergence of the restructured Christian Church (Disciples of Christ) and the final separation of the Christian Church/Churches of Christ. Near the end of this period the *Panel of Scholars Reports* became a watershed in the history of Disciples approach to the Bible. For most of the first three generations, biblical interpretation as practiced by teachers in the Stone-Campbell Movement was essentially the same in academic and congregational settings. The Bible was interpreted in the classrooms at Bethany, the College of the Bible, and David Lipscomb College in essentially the same way it was interpreted in the pulpits and Sunday School classes of the congregations. A new situation developed in the fourth generation as biblical scholarship moved to the secularized academy. The three branches of the Movement responded to the new situation in biblical studies in distinctive ways.

Disciples' scholars joined the mainstream of academic biblical interpretation. This meant that biblical interpretation in the academy tended to be non-theological, non-churchly. On the secular campus, a "purely historical approach" or "the Bible as literature" dominated the approach to the Bible. Not only were distinctively Disciples perspectives eliminated or minimized, but the Bible as the church's Scripture that functioned as authority for its life and mission was necessarily neglected. The Bible was effectively decanonized not only on the secular campus but also in much of the biblical study done in seminary courses and college and university departments of religion — which tended to become "departments of religious studies." Bible scholars became specialists in one Testament, one author, one book, or one issue, so that they were typically no longer theologians with a churchly orientation, and no longer accepted responsibility for interpreting the Bible as a whole and as canonical Christian Scripture. Much advance was made at the level of academic study of the Bible, and during this period for the first time, several Disciples' scholars received national and international recognition in the academy, among who are Stephen J. England, J. Phillip Hyatt, Leander Keck, and Jack Finegan. Some of this tended to "trickle down" to pastors and congregations in a helpful way, and the denomination as a whole became less rigid and doctrinaire, and more malleable in its approach to the Bible. On the other hand, this development also contributed to the decline of interest and ability in biblical interpretation at the congregational level. While biblical research flourished in the academy, biblical interpretation in the congregations often reverted to pre-critical or ideological understandings, or to repeat the tradition that had become standard interpretation in the nineteenth century.

For the Christian Churches/Churches of Christ during this period, the Bible colleges became the locus of biblical study and interpretation. The major factor in their proliferation was safeguarding the tradition of biblical interpretation that had been developed in the Stone-Campbell Movement from liberalism's historical-critical approach that had taken over the seminaries and universities. During this period, the issue was often framed from the conservative side not as a matter of interpretation but of faith, that is, whether one believes the Bible or not. With some exceptions, the Bible colleges fostered a continuation of the approach to the Bible represented by J. W. McGarvey, emphasized the learning of Bible content seen in terms of the traditional restorationist agenda, and disdained the "unbelieving scholars" of the universities. This style of interpretation is represented by the forty-four volume series of commentaries published by College Press, the Biblical Studies Textbook Series. Near the end of this period, Christian Church/Churches of Christ Bible scholars began to get advanced degrees from recognized universities and to develop a more academically sophisticated approach to the Bible. In cooperation with scholars from the Churches of Christ, some of these have inaugurated The College Press NIV Commentary, a series that has replaced the Biblical Studies Textbook Series and, without totally abandoning the traditional Stone-Campbell agenda, represents an approach to biblical interpretation nearer to "mainline" academic commentaries.

For the most part, the patterns of biblical interpretation in the Churches of Christ during this period followed a different model than either Disciples or Christian Churches/Churches of Christ. Their ministers and Bible teachers were trained almost exclusively in their own schools, but they were liberal arts colleges with a heavy biblical emphasis on the Bethany model, unlike the Bible colleges on the Christian Church/Churches of Christ model. That such schools were not primarily for ministers shows the continuing Stone-Campbell "populist" emphasis, that is, the importance of providing biblical instruction for the church as a whole, not only for its ordained leadership. In the early part of this period such instruction followed the traditional uncritical approach, and there was little gap between Bible instruction in the congregations and what was taught in the colleges and universities. After World War II, especially at the encouragement of scholars like LeMoine Lewis, Abraham Malherbe, and Everett Ferguson, a relatively large number of scholars in the

Churches of Christ received advanced degrees from the biblical departments of leading universities, returned with their new insights to teach in the colleges and universities where leaders (including ministers) were educated, and occasionally moved into teaching positions in denominational and interdenominational seminaries and universities.

5. 1968 to the Present

The current cadre of Bible scholars represents the fifth generation. For the Christian Church (Disciples of Christ), this generation can be designated as the period of "Quest." While there is still a tradition of confessionally oriented biblical scholarship among Disciples, it is difficult to identify, define, and analyze, and Disciples have become ambivalent and uninformed about their own tradition. While a relatively large number of Disciples Bible scholars have attained recognition in academic circles, Bible study in the congregations has languished. Biblical interpretation among the Christian Churches/Churches of Christ has likewise lost many of the traditional emphases of the Stone-Campbell tradition and tended in the direction of conservative evangelicalism in general. While some of their leaders and scholars have attained strong academic credentials in the area of biblical interpretation, this is often not integrated with the theological perspectives that continue to characterize this stream of the Movement. The Churches of Christ have produced a relatively large number of academic Bible scholars, but here the gap between biblical interpretation as carried on in the university and congregational Bible study continues to widen. Each group is confronted with the task of coming to terms in its own way with what it regards as the authentic elements of the tradition of the Stone-Campbell Movement.

See also Bible, Authority and Inspiration of the; Campbell, Alexander; Errett, Isaac; Hermeneutics; Johnson, Barton Warren; Lipscomb, David; McGarvey, John W.; *Scheme of Redemption, The;* Milligan, Robert; Willett, Herbert Lockwood

BIBLIOGRAPHY Anthony Lee Ash, "Old Testament Scholarship and the Restoration Movement," *Restoration Quarterly* 25 (1982): 213-22 • M. Eugene Boring, *Disciples and the Bible: A History of Biblical Interpretation in North America* (1997) • Alexander Campbell, *Christianity Restored* (1835) • Michael W. Casey, *The Battle over Hermeneutics in the Stone-Campbell Movement, 1800-1870* (1998) • David R. Dungan, *Hermeneutics* (1988) • B. W. Johnson, *People's New Testament with Notes* (1889-91) • James S. Lamar, *The Organon of Scripture* (1860) • J. W. McGarvey, *Short Essays in Biblical Criticism* (1910) • J. W. McGarvey, *A Commentary on Acts of the Apostles* (1863) • J. W. McGarvey, *New Commentary on the Acts of the Apostles* (1892) • Robert Milligan, *Reason and Revelation* (1867) • Robert Milligan, *The Scheme of Redemption* (1868) • Thomas H. Olbricht, "Alexander Campbell in the Context of American Biblical Studies (1810-1874)," *Restoration Quarterly* 33 (1991): 13-28 • James Thompson, "New Testament Studies and the Restoration Movement," *Restoration Quarterly* 25 (1982): 223-32 • Herbert L. Willett, *The Bible through the Centuries* (1929).

M. EUGENE BORING

Bible, Versions and Translations of the

At the beginning of the Stone-Campbell Movement there was no viable option on the American scene to the use of the King James Version (KJV). The KJV was completely dominant.

In 1826 Alexander Campbell edited the New Testament that had been issued by George Campbell,

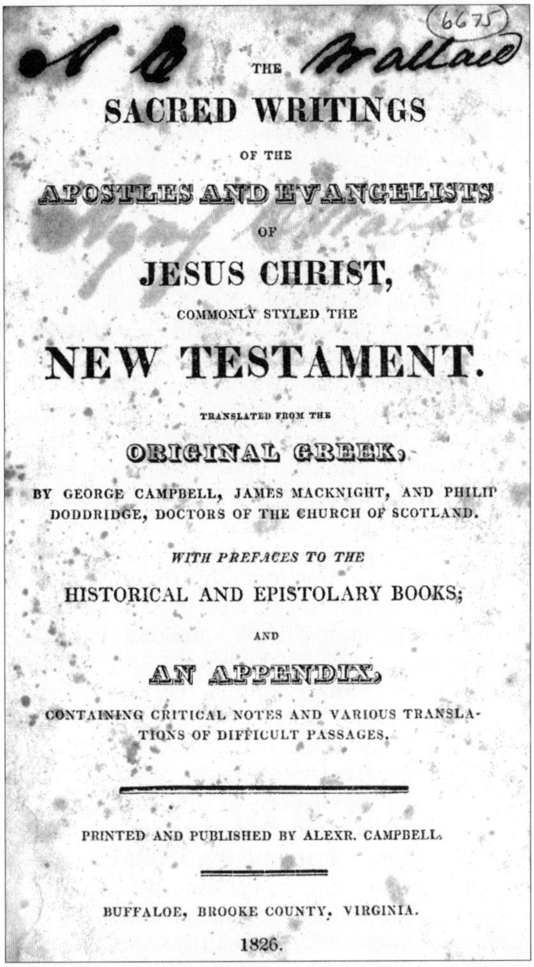
THE
SACRED WRITINGS
OF THE
APOSTLES AND EVANGELISTS
OF
JESUS CHRIST,
COMMONLY STYLED THE
NEW TESTAMENT.
TRANSLATED FROM THE
ORIGINAL GREEK,
BY GEORGE CAMPBELL, JAMES MACKNIGHT, AND PHILIP DODDRIDGE, DOCTORS OF THE CHURCH OF SCOTLAND.
WITH PREFACES TO THE
HISTORICAL AND EPISTOLARY BOOKS;
AND
AN APPENDIX,
CONTAINING CRITICAL NOTES AND VARIOUS TRANSLATIONS OF DIFFICULT PASSAGES.
PRINTED AND PUBLISHED BY ALEXR. CAMPBELL.
BUFFALOE, BROOKE COUNTY, VIRGINIA.
1826.

First edition of Alexander Campbell's version of the New Testament, commonly known as *The Living Oracles.* The work went through several editions and dozens of reprints after its appearance in 1826. Courtesy of the Disciples of Christ Historical Society

James MacKnight, and Philip Doddridge in 1818, adding prefaces, extensive notes, and an appendix, and publishing it under the title *The Living Oracles.* The work, an "immersion version," was extremely popular in the Movement but severely criticized by other church bodies. Though *The Living Oracles* was used primarily by immersionists, Presbyterian P. Marion Simms ranked it as the best New Testament in use at that time. It was a forerunner of modern language translations anticipating readings later used in the American Standard Version (ASV, 1901) and the Revised Standard Version (RSV, 1952), though closer to the RSV. Campbell's use of words like "reform," "immerse," "congregation," "publish" for "preach," "messenger" for "angel," and "reign" for "kingdom," however, were not more widely adopted.

C. K. Thomas argues that the wording of the translations of Rodolphus Dickinson in 1833, of A. C. Kendrick in 1842, of N. N. Whiting in 1849, of S. H. Cone and W. H. Wyckoff in 1851, of Andrews Norton in 1855, and of Robert Young in Edinburgh in 1871 were all influenced by Campbell's publication. Campbell's translation went through numerous editions before his death and was reprinted by the Gospel Advocate Company as late as 2001.

The Stone-Campbell Movement was in the forefront of agitation in the nineteenth century for a revision of the Bible. Campbell insisted that the availability of better text materials, the advance in the knowledge of the Greek language, plus the changes in the English language since 1611 all made revision imperative. Many preachers believed that the translators of the KJV had been unduly influenced by Calvinism and insisted that a better version than the KJV was needed.

The Movement furnished much of the money for the making of the American Bible Union Version. A revision committee was formed in Memphis, Tennessee, in 1852 not to make a translation but to encourage cooperation in the effort. Campbell prepared the preliminary copy of the Book of Acts. Movement leaders, however, were disappointed at the final outcome of the whole New Testament.

Individual translations produced in the nineteenth century by members of the Stone-Campbell Movement include the New Testament issued by H. T. Anderson of Harrodsburg, Kentucky, in 1864 that used "immersion" for baptism. His translation, made after the publication of Tischendorf's text with readings of the manuscript Sinaiticus, was published posthumously in 1918. Benjamin Wilson issued his *Emphatic Diaglott,* an interlinear translation with the Greek text, in 1865. Interestingly, in 1902 this work was endorsed by the Watch Tower Bible and Tract Society. British scholar J. B. Rotherham (1828-1910) published *The Emphasized Bible* in 1878 that eventually went through twelve editions. It was first made from Tregelles's text but was made to conform to the Westcott and Hort text in 1897. The Old Testament conformed to the text of Christian Ginsberg.

Cortes Jackson of Denver, Colorado, translated the New Testament in 1883 using the word "immerse." B. W. Johnson in 1889-91 published *The People's New Testament with Explanatory Notes* that contained both the KJV and English Revised Version texts. This work in many reprints was widely used by members of Stone-Campbell churches for much of the twentieth century.

The English Revised Version (ERV), 1881-85, was considered a great improvement over the KJV. A group of British scholars in consultation with Americans had produced the translation. Isaac Errett is repeatedly listed as a financial contributor to the expenses of the American Revision Committee. Restorationists were disappointed that more attention had not been given to the American suggestions; nevertheless, J. W. McGarvey adopted the ERV for his classes at the College of the Bible and for the revision of his commentary on the Book of Acts. When the American Revised Version was released in 1901, many in the Movement heralded it as the most reliable translation then available.

D. Austen Sommer (1878-1952) issued his *Simplified New Testament,* probably in 1923. E. E. Stringfellow of Des Moines, Iowa, translated the New Testament from the Westcott and Hort text between 1943 and 1945. G. B. Swann published a New Testament in 1947 also from the Westcott and Hort text. While several individuals issued the KJV text with notes in the early twentieth century, there is no evidence in the periodicals of the Movement that anyone was championing the sole use of the KJV until after 1925.

With the issuing of the Revised Standard Version New Testament in 1946, the attitude about versions changed in the more conservative parts of the Movement. R. C. Foster (1888-1970) of the Christian Churches who had dropped off the revision committees, and W. W. Otey (1867-1961) of Churches of Christ produced materials critical of the new version for church members. Foy E. Wallace, Jr. (1896-1979), who could read neither Hebrew nor Greek, became the champion of the use of the KJV and the critic of the use of modern versions in Churches of Christ. After Wallace's death, this mantle was taken up by Robert Taylor, Jr., who also had no formal linguistic training. Several works by those preferring the KJV warned of the dangers of modern versions but were silent about those of the KJV. Some preachers and congregations granted the use of either the KJV or ASV, ignoring the difference in their textual base in the New Testament, while denouncing later versions. A minority of congregations declared that they used only the KJV in the pulpit and in classes.

R. C. Foster, as mentioned, along with H. Leo Boles (1874-1946) of Churches of Christ, had been appointed to committees working on the RSV, though neither was an active participant. Disciples S. A. Weston, Stephen J. England, W. C. Morro, and H. B. Robison were also on the Advisory Committee. Later in the century, Lewis A. Foster (1921-2004) of Christian Churches and Jack P. Lewis (b. 1919) of Churches of Christ had roles in the translation of the New International Version (NIV). Batsell Barrett Baxter (1916-1982) of Churches of Christ was on the North American Overview Committee for the New King James Version. Robert L. Hendren (b. 1930) and Lewis A. Foster worked on its New Testament. Church of Christ scholar J. J. M. Roberts (b. 1939) of Princeton Theological Seminary served as a member of the translation committee that produced the New Revised Standard Version.

In the mid-twentieth century the person in the pew, seeking something more readable and understandable than the KJV, was buying the Revised Standard Version, the New International Version, the New American Standard Version, or the New King James Version. Anecdotal evidence indicates that among Disciples the RSV was popular as a pew Bible, while among Churches of Christ and Christian Churches/Churches of Christ many congregations placed the NIV in pew racks after that complete version became available in 1978.

As was the case in the nineteenth century, various individuals or groups made translations and editions of their own in the late twentieth century. Chester R. Estes of Churches of Christ issued *The Better Version of the New Testament* in 1973 from the text of Griesbach. The World Bible Translation Center of Fort Worth, Texas, sponsored largely by Churches of Christ, issued *The Every Day Bible* in 1982, and the *New Century Version* and the *International Children's Version* in 1986. This Translation Center issued the *Easy-to-Read Version of the Bible* in 1987 and is involved in projects in thirty of the world's languages. Pioneer Bible Translators of Duncanville, Texas, largely supported by Christian Churches/Churches of Christ, has also been active in translating the Bible into languages previously without versions of scripture. Other individual translators from Churches of Christ include Stanley L. Morris, Hugo McCord, George P. Estes, Harold Littrell, and W. E. Paul.

The Stone-Campbell Movement has never had a unified position on Bible versions. For most of the Movement's history the issue of what translation to use has not been a test of fellowship. At the beginning of the twenty-first century the Movement faces the issue of the use of the critical text of the New Testament versus the majority text as the basis of translation. Also, the matter of gender-inclusive language and the formal equivalence versus the dynamic or functional equivalence theories of translation are points of discussion in the larger Christian world that are reflected in the discussion of versions across the streams of the Stone-Campbell Movement.

See also Foster, Rupert Clinton; Rotherham, Joseph Bryant

BIBLIOGRAPHY R. C. Foster, *The Revised Standard Version of the New Testament* (1946) • R. C. Foster, *The Revised Standard Version, A Reply to Dr. Clarence T. Craig* (1947) • Margaret T. Hills, ed., *The English Bible in America* (1961) • Jack P. Lewis, *The English Bible from KJV to NIV* (2nd ed. 1991) • Jack P. Lewis, *Questions You've Asked about Bible Translations* (1991) • David B. McElwain, "A History of Restoration Translations," in *A Handbook on Bible Translations*, ed. T. M. Hightower (1995), pp. 179-99 • W. W. Otey, *Christ or Modernism* (1953) • William E. Paul, "Bible Translations by Members of Disciples of Christ, Churches of Christ, and Christian Churches," *Christian Standard* 131 (March 31, 1996): 257-59 • P. Marion Simms, *The Bible in America* (1936) • Cecil K. Thomas, *Alexander Campbell and His New Version* (1959) • Foy E. Wallace, Jr., *A Review of the New Versions* (1973).

JACK P. LEWIS

Bible Bowl

1. Bible Bowl among the Christian Churches/ Churches of Christ
2. Bible Bowl Programs among the Churches of Christ
3. Contrasts and Comparisons between the Programs

The churches of the Stone-Campbell tradition have historically considered themselves a "people of the Book" who appeal to the Bible alone as their authority in faith and practice. Naturally, then, they have valued programs for teens and pre-teens that foster scriptural literacy. Among these are Bible Bowl quiz programs.

1. Bible Bowl among the Christian Churches/ Churches of Christ

Bible Bowl, the teen Bible quizzing program of the Christian Churches/Churches of Christ, began in 1964 as an adaptation of the then-popular General Electric College Bowl. Dwain Illman and Larry Strange, two Illinois student youth ministers, conducted tournaments at Northwest Christian Church (Decatur, Illinois) and Webber Street Church of Christ (Urbana, Illinois). Illman reported these early competitions in Standard Publishing's teen magazine *Straight* and later called for a national competition. Leonard Wymore, the Director of the North American Christian Convention (NACC) then asked Illman to direct the first National Bible Bowl at the

1965 NACC in Tulsa, Oklahoma. Thirty-one teams from eleven states competed over Mark and 1 Corinthians 15. From that first tournament until 2003, the National Bible Bowl was held annually in conjunction with the NACC. The program has involved as many as 1,000 teams from 750 congregations in thirty-three states, and the national tournament has involved as many as 275 teams. No team is required to participate in any competition prior to the National Bible Bowl Tournament, making it the largest open invitational, double elimination Bible quiz tournament in the world.

The format of the National Bible Bowl was single elimination from 1965 to 1975, but a double elimination format was adopted in 1976. An individual achievement test or "Top Brain" competition was added in 1978. Texts for competition have been whole biblical books or combination texts from various books with the KJV as the official translation text from 1964 until 1987, when the NIV was adopted.

In addition to the national tournament, competition occurs in monthly local "round robins" and on a regional level at tournaments sponsored by Christian church colleges. Nebraska Christian College sponsored the first such tournament in 1973.

In 1999, a Beginner Bowl program was introduced for third through fifth graders. The first National Beginner Bowl tournament was then held in conjunction with the 2000 National Bible Bowl in Louisville, Kentucky.

The organization of Bible Bowl has grown with the program. From 1965 to 1977, a committee of the NACC organized and governed the national tournament, but had a limited role in Bible Bowl at other levels. Beginning in 1977, the NACC responded to Bible Bowl's growth and to a desire for greater uniformity and leadership within all areas of the program. First, the NACC appointed a National Bible Bowl Advisory Committee to make recommendations regarding the national tournament and to standardize the program at all levels. Then, in 2001, the Convention handed over governance and financial responsibility for Bible Bowl to a newly formed independent mission, National Bible Bowl, governed by the National Bible Bowl Board of Directors.

2. Bible Bowl Programs among the Churches of Christ

The high degree of congregational autonomy among the Churches of Christ and their lack of a single unifying agency or publication make it difficult to trace the origins and development of Bible quizzing programs among them. The existence of the Sunset Bible Bowl in Lubbock, Texas, is documented as early as 1969, but earlier quiz competitions among individual congregations in various geographical areas may have occurred.

Participation in Bible Bowls increased in the 1970s and 1980s as individual congregations began to host area, state, and regional Bible Bowl competitions and as Churches of Christ colleges and parachurch events began to conduct Bible quiz events. In 1976, Abilene Christian College (University, hereafter ACU), Harding College (University, hereafter HU), and Oklahoma Christian College (University, hereafter OCU) initiated an annual series of "Big Three Bible Bowl" competitions. Lubbock Christian University (LCU) and Ohio Valley College (OVC) also sponsored annual meets. LCU later partnered with ACU, HU, and OCU and, beginning in 1990, the Big Three Bible Bowl tournaments gave way to a sequence of four annual National Bible Bowl tournaments held on their campuses. Although open to teams from across the United States, these National Bible Bowls primarily have drawn teams from congregations in Midwestern, Southwestern, and Western states. The OVC Bible Bowl, on the other hand, draws primarily from churches in the Ohio River valley, the Southeast, and the Northeast. The Lads to Leaders/Leaderettes and Leadership Training for Christ youth conventions that annually draw thousands of attendees have also contributed to Bible Bowl's popularity as Bible Bowls and Bible quizzes were given significant roles within the convention programs.

Perhaps the most constant figure in the history of Bible Bowl and Bible quizzing among the churches of Christ has been John Kimbrough of Dallas. He began working with Bible Bowls in 1975 while a minister with the Lake Highlands Church of Christ (Dallas, Texas). By 1981, he was organizing several Bible Bowls, including the Big Three Bible Bowls, and preparing study materials for participants as well as writing tournament questions. Although rarely organizing competitions, he continued publishing Bible Bowl and Bible quizzing resources as late as 2003.

3. Contrasts and Comparisons between the Programs

Several contrasts exist between the two Bible Bowl programs. The most obvious difference is in the competition format. The Christian Churches' Bible Bowl uses electronic buzzer systems in an oral game format featuring multiple types of questions and strategies. There is a head-to-head elimination format with two teams pitted against one another in any given round. Written testing of individuals is a separate event from game play. The Churches of Christ Bible Bowl, however, lacks many conventional competition methods. It uses no buzzer systems and rarely uses elimination formats in which two teams are pitted against one another. Instead, competition revolves around a series of tests administered to several teams at once. Team and individual answers are usually presented in non-oral formats.

In Christian Churches Bible Bowl separates teens from pre-teens in two separate events with different rules, Bible Bowl and Beginner Bowl. On the other hand, most Churches of Christ Bible Bowl events allow pre-teens and teens to participate together in the same game under the same rules. This practice among the Churches of Christ facilitates greater participation among smaller congregations. Some Churches of Christ Bible Bowls have adult divisions; no such division exists in Christian Churches Bible Bowl.

In regards to uniformity of rules and practice and level of organization, the two programs reflect the degree of comfort the constituent churches have with extra-congregational organization and authority. In Christian Churches Bible Bowl operates on a truly national level with all competition in a given year culminating in one tournament that crowns a single national champion from among all the teams in the country. A national board of directors selects, provides, and oversees standardized texts, rules for competition, and study materials. Bible Bowl events among the Churches of Christ, on the other hand, have more variety in rules and procedures. No single tournament among them results in a true "national champion." Instead, their "big events" are tournaments of a more regional character.

The greater number of churches within the Churches of Christ, the inclusion of more pre-teens within the program, and the greater flexibility of Bible Bowl among the Churches of Christ have led to a greater number of participating teams and young people than is found in the Christian Churches program. Moreover, the two programs reflect the geographical strengths of the two groups. While the greater number of teams in Churches of Christ Bible Bowl are from the South and Southwest, these areas, with the exception of Florida, have fewer participants in the Christian Churches Bible Bowl. Conversely, the two most represented states in Christian Church Bible Bowl, Ohio and Indiana, are less represented in Churches of Christ Bible Bowl.

More significant than the differences between the programs are the similarities in the programs' goals and outcomes. Both have assisted participants to expand their view of the church by providing opportunities to fellowship with young people from many different congregations. Church-related colleges among both groups have used Bible Bowl events to recruit students. Most importantly, the programs both have used competition to encourage knowledge of the biblical text, to develop leaders within the church, and to promote spiritual growth, team spirit, and Christian fellowship.

See also Abilene Christian University; Harding University; Louisville Bible College; Lubbock Christian University; Nebraska Christian College; North American Christian Convention; Oklahoma Christian University

BIBLIOGRAPHY Gary E. Coleman, "Bible Bowl," in *North American Gold: The Story of 50 North American Christian Conventions,* ed. Edwin V. Hayden (1989), pp. 149-59 • "Dallas: Bible Bowl Scheduled," *Christian Chronicle* 41.11 (1 November 1984): 5 • "Durango Wins National Bible Bowl," *Rocky Mountain Christian* 23.2 (January 1995): 5 • Mark Allen Hahlen, "More Than Winning," *Christian Standard* (22 July 1979): 15-16 • Dwain C. Illman, "Silver Anniversary Bible Bowl," *Christian Standard* (17 September 1989): 8-9 • Scott Lamascus, "Bible Bowls," *Christian Chronicle* 44.4 (April 1987): 10-12 • David S. Phillips, "The Growth of Bible Bowl," *Christian Standard* (26 February 1978): 19 • Bret Talley, "The Changing Face of Bible Bowl," *Christian Standard* (17 February 2002): 11.

MARK ALLEN HAHLEN

Bible Chair Movement

Promoted by the Christian Woman's Board of Missions (CWBM), the Bible Chair Movement was conceived in the late nineteenth century to respond to two developments: (1) separation of church and state prohibited teaching religion in public education, and (2) state universities were drawing increasing numbers of students away from church-related colleges. Bible Chairs provided instruction in religion at state universities, but under the auspices and financial support of religious groups rather than the state.

The idea apparently originated in 1892 with Charles A. Young, pastor of the Disciples church in Ann Arbor, Michigan. The first chair opened at the University of Michigan in 1893. It stimulated such interest among Disciples that Young resigned his pastorate to become a CWBM worker to raise money for Bible Chairs. On a trip to Virginia, he interested people in the work. A chair opened at the University of Virginia, first as a lecture series in 1897 through 1899 and then as a full program of instruction in the 1899-1900 academic year. Young was the first teacher. (At the end of the 1900-1901 year Young resigned to join the staff of a Disciples' paper, the *Christian Oracle,* later called *The Christian Century,* and never worked with Bible Chairs again.)

With chairs established at two prestigious universities, the idea gained momentum. Chairs were created at other schools in rapid succession, the principal ones being the universities of Georgia (1897), Kansas (1901), and Texas (1905), all under CWBM auspices, and at the universities of Missouri (1896) and Indiana (1910), sponsored by state Disciples organizations.

Bible Chairs were distinguished from other campus ministry programs. Although chair personnel ministered to students' needs in the traditional, pas-

After beginning classes in the Disciples Church building in Ann Arbor in 1893 with faculty Herbert L. Willett and Clinton Lockhart, the Bible Chair at the University of Michigan purchased Newberry Hall with money raised by the Christian Woman's Board of Missions. Courtesy of the Disciples of Christ Historical Society

toral way, the academic study of religion became the chairs' hallmark. Young's successor, William M. Forrest, who taught at the University of Virginia 1903-39, knew that students would be more interested in the courses if they could get credit toward their degrees. Forrest persuaded the administration; Virginia granted credit for religion courses beginning in 1905-6, the first state university to do so. Most of the other schools at which the Disciples had Bible Chairs eventually granted credit: Missouri, 1906-7; Texas, 1910-11; Kansas, 1921-22; Indiana, 1953-54. In most cases this was initially an experiment, with a small number of courses receiving credit. Later, in some schools, the number increased until students could major in religion. But only at Virginia was the Bible Chair absorbed into the University to become a department, in 1909.

The Churches of Christ began Bible Chair work in 1918. In that year Jesse P. Sewell, President of Abilene Christian College, wrote an article suggesting that "a Christian chapter house" be established at the University of Texas or some other major state university, so the graduates of Church of Christ junior colleges could go there to complete their work in a theologically sound program. The Bible Chair opened in the fall semester, 1918, at the University of Texas. Its teachers were G. H. P. Showalter, editor of *Firm Foundation,* and Charles H. Roberson. In 1920-21 the University allowed up to two credits in Bible toward the B.A. degree. The Chair was continually in precarious financial condition. In spite of frequent contributions from Showalter's personal funds and his frequent appeals in *Firm Foundation,* the Chair closed in 1928 from lack of funds. However, other chairs opened, most notable of which were Oklahoma, 1928; Texas A&M, 1935; Oklahoma A&M, either 1929 or 1939 (the records are not clear); Texas Tech, 1947; and perhaps most important of all, Eastern New Mexico, 1947, with its long-time director and mentor to other Church of Christ Bible Chair directors, Stephen Eckstein. The chair at the University of Texas resumed in 1951.

On June 7, 1955, *Firm Foundation* ran a Bible Chair issue. It listed fifteen Bible Chairs, including nine never mentioned before in Churches of Christ literature. The issue stimulated interest in the movement, and twelve more chairs were initiated from 1955 to 1957. Since then, Churches of Christ have invested enormous energy in Bible Chairs, both domestically and abroad. Many programs gave academic credit, sometimes a major in Bible. However, over time the emphasis changed away from academic teaching and toward traditional, pastoral, campus ministry. The *Bible Chair Journal* (1958), later *Campus Journal* (after 1969), reported on and stimulated the campus ministry movement, as did the Bible Chair Lectures (1957), later called the National Campus Ministers' Seminar. The shift away from academic work to evangelistic ministry, for both Disciples and Churches of Christ, was accelerated by Supreme Court decisions (1962, 1963) allowing the teaching of religion in state universities.

See also Austin Graduate School of Theology; Christian Woman's Board of Missions

BIBLIOGRAPHY Ronald B. Flowers, *The Bible Chair Movement in the Disciples of Christ Tradition: Attempts to Teach Religion in State Universities* (1967) • Thomas R. McCormick, *Campus Ministry in the Coming Age* (1987) • Rick Rowland, *Campus Ministries: A Historical Study of Churches of Christ Campus Ministries and Selected College Ministries from 1706 to 1990* (1991).

RONALD B. FLOWERS

Bible College Movement

A development within late-nineteenth-century and early-twentieth-century American religious and educational history that saw new institutions of higher learning created specifically to train vocational workers for the churches.

In the recent history of religious education, a tension has developed between training in the liberal arts from an openly Christian perspective, and vocational training for ministry. At the time when religious higher education began to proliferate in America in the nineteenth century, most denominations were comfortable with the former. Ministerial students received their baccalaureate degree from a private, church-sponsored college. Preparation for ministry entailed study of the liberal arts in conjunction with practical mentoring by a veteran minister. When the demands for ministerial education became more intense, seminaries emerged to provide specific ministerial preparation beyond undergraduate education in a public or private college — a model typical of most mainline denominations in the United States.

This system, however, went through a significant transition in the late nineteenth century as theological liberalism took root across denominational lines, and many faculty at church-sponsored schools were teaching from the new perspective. Numerous conservative evangelicals claimed in response that such institutions had betrayed their trust. The result was a host of new Bible institutes, Bible schools, and Bible colleges. Among the first of these were Nyack Missionary College (1882) in New York and Moody Bible Institute (1886) in Chicago. Several hundred had emerged by the mid-twentieth century. With many supporters themselves fearing that these schools were inferior academically, the Accrediting Association of Bible Colleges (AABC) formed in 1947 to establish and monitor accreditation. The AABC now accredits about one hundred Bible colleges.

Much the same pattern is observable in the history of higher education in the Stone-Campbell Movement. The Movement developed dozens of schools in the nineteenth century, the flagship institution being Bethany College, started by Alexander Campbell. One of the primary purposes for these schools was ministerial preparation, although they were actually liberal arts colleges. Bethany itself turned out numerous ministers and missionaries.

By the beginning of the twentieth century, however, many of these same schools had embraced liberal theology and biblical higher criticism. Conservative churches no longer trusted many of these schools, and so educational alternatives emerged. It is significant that the Bible colleges that developed were almost entirely aligned with the conservative Disciples churches, that is, the emerging Christian Churches/Churches of Christ, rather than the other two major streams of the Stone-Campbell Movement. In time all liberal arts colleges except Milligan College in Tennessee retained affiliation with the Christian Church (Disciples of Christ). There are no Bible colleges today in the Disciples denomination, though Northwest Christian College in Oregon maintains relationships both with the Christian Church (Disciples of Christ) and the Christian Churches/Churches of Christ. The Churches of Christ have continued Alexander Campbell's model and now operate several Christian liberal arts colleges. Although the Churches of Christ have a number of "preaching schools," normally hosted by a local congregation and a respected preacher, there are almost no Bible colleges as such among their number.

Some of the earliest of the Bible Colleges among the Christian Churches/Churches of Christ came into being before the polarization over liberalism. Johnson Bible College (1893) began as the School of the Evangelists, specifically to train ministers. Northwest Christian College (1895) was established to provide a general biblical education. Minnesota Bible College (1913) began for the express purpose of training leaders to become missionaries. Kentucky Christian College (1919) began as the Christian Normal Institute to train public school teachers.

However, the next generation of Bible colleges reflected the anti-liberal attitudes of the conservative Disciples churches of the time. Some of these colleges posed themselves as replacements for specific schools perceived to have been "taken over" by liberalism. Cincinnati Bible Seminary (1924) was begun in "response to infidelity," and was meant to be a replacement for the College of the Bible (now Lexington Theological Seminary) in Lexington, Kentucky. Pacific Christian College (1928) was begun as the "CBS of the west" to replace Chapman College in Los Angeles. Ozark Christian College (1942) in Missouri was begun to "train a faithful ministry." Nebraska Christian College (1944) was started to train preachers who were "true to Christ and the Bible." Lincoln Christian College (1944) began to "fill the depleted ranks of Gospel preachers and teachers," replacing Eureka College in Illinois. Roanoke Bible College (1948) in eastern North Carolina was started under the claim of being "wholly loyal" and out of a concern for the liberal drift of Atlantic Christian College.

In the next generation, however, a different philosophy, conceiving the Bible college as a matrix of evangelism, generated numerous additional schools. The idea was that pulling together the resources for a faculty also meant concentrating a number of capable preachers and teachers in a given locale. These individuals then radiated out from the school conducting meetings, reviving moribund churches, and starting new ones. In addition, the students at the school could also commute to weekend preaching ministries and carry on the same kinds of evangelistic activity. With Bible colleges often becoming catalysts for evangelism in a given area, hundreds of new church plants followed on the heels of educational development.

Central to the idea of a Bible college is biblical teaching. The AABC requires that all its schools have degree programs in which Bible/theology is the primary major. Degree concentrations in ministry, Christian education, missions, or similar areas are actually a secondary curriculum focus. There are also required courses in general education. Bible colleges focus on this tripartite approach to education: Bible/theology, general education, and professional study for ministry.

Maintaining academic standards in the Bible colleges has always been a controversial topic in their history. In their early years many of the schools were regarded as intellectual lightweights at best. In the last couple of decades, however, most of these schools have chosen to come under the scrutiny of established accrediting agencies so that their programs and graduates can be accepted in the larger educational world. Of the approximately thirty-five Bible colleges of the Christian Churches/Churches of Christ 60 percent have accreditation in the AABC, 30 percent have regional accreditation, and 15 percent have both. Many of these schools are heavily staffed with faculty who hold earned doctorates, and rising standards of faculty credentials are uniform for these schools. But there are still a few small schools that have no accreditation, marginal faculty credentials, and questionable academic programs.

The approximately thirty schools that hold accreditation employ over 400 full-time professors, have over 8,000 full-time students, and grant a total of about 1,400 four-year degrees each spring. Several of them have libraries well in excess of 100,000 volumes.

The Bible colleges play a leading role in the life and labors of the Christian Churches/Churches of Christ. Previous generations were largely influenced by "editor-bishops" and journals; the current generation is greatly influenced by the leadership of the Bible colleges. A large percentage of ministers and missionaries in Christian Churches/Churches of Christ are alumni or alumnae of these schools. These schools radiate influence in their respective regions and have often left an indelible stamp on the theology and practices of the churches of those regions.

See also Christian Churches/Churches of Christ; Fundamentalism; Higher Education, Views of in the Movement

BIBLIOGRAPHY Alfred T. DeGroot, *New Possibilities for Disciples and Independents* (1963) • W. C. Ringenberg, "Bible Institutes and Colleges," in *Dictionary of Christianity in America,* ed. Daniel G. Reid (1990) • Gerald Tiffin, "The Interaction of the Bible College Movement and the Independent Disciples of Christ Denomination" (unpublished Ph.D. dissertation, Stanford University, 1968) • S. A. Witmer, *The Bible College Story: Education with Dimension* (1962).

JAMES B. NORTH

Bishops

See Elders, Eldership

Blakemore, William Barnett, Jr. (1912-1975)

Disciples minister, theologian, and Dean of the Disciples Divinity House of the University of Chicago from 1945 to 1975, who was a prominent influence among the Disciples of Christ during the post–World War II era.

Blakemore was born in Perth, Western Australia, where his father, a Transylvania College graduate, was pastor of a Christian Church. After moving to a Melbourne parish in 1918, the family returned to St. Louis in 1925. There Blakemore received a B.S. degree in chemical engineering from Washington University in 1933. However, the Christian ministry beckoned him, and in 1935 Blakemore enrolled in the Divinity School of the University of Chicago. He earned A.M., B.D., and Ph.D. degrees at Chicago, the latter in 1941.

Following graduation, Blakemore was appointed to Chicago's Divinity School faculty. At the time of his death, he was Professor of Ecumenical Christianity in the Divinity School. He was named Assistant Dean of Disciples Divinity House in 1944, Acting Dean and then Dean in 1945. He held this post for the remainder of his life. In 1942 he and Josephine Gilstrap were married.

Blakemore is most commonly remembered for his long tenure as Dean of Disciples Divinity House. However, he was also a much appreciated pastor and preacher and was Dean of the University's Rockefeller Memorial Chapel from 1959 to 1965. He was a member of the Panel of Scholars of the Christian Church from its inception in 1956 until its dissolution in 1962, served as chair after 1958, and was general editor of the Panel's three-volume report, *The Renewal of Church: The Panel of Scholars Reports,* as well as editor of the third volume in this series. He was a longtime member of the American Youth Foundation's Board of Trustees, presided over the Church Federation of Greater Chicago in 1967-68, and was a Protestant Observer to the Second Vatican Council in 1964 and 1965. At the time of his death, Blakemore was president of the World Convention of Churches of Christ.

See also Disciples Divinity House; Panel of Scholars

BIBLIOGRAPHY W. B. Blakemore, *Encountering God* (1965) • W. B. Blakemore, *Quest for Intelligence in Ministry: The Story of the First Seventy-Five Years of the Disciples Divinity House of the University of Chicago* (1970) • W. B. Blakemore, ed., *The Renewal of Church: The Panel of Scholars Reports,* 3 vols. (1963) • See also Blakemore's papers, indexed and archived in the library of the University of Chicago • Samuel C. Pearson, "Barnett Blakemore and Disciples Divinity House of the University of Chicago, 1945-1975," *Encounter* 62:2 (Spring 2001): 111-25.

SAMUEL C. PEARSON

Bluefield College of Evangelism

Bible college associated with the Christian Churches/Churches of Christ.

With its first classes convening in the fall of 1971, Bluefield College of Evangelism was established by David E. Branholm in Bluefield, West Virginia. As a traveling evangelist, Branholm observed, while conducting revivals in the coal fields of West Virginia, Kentucky, and Virginia, that the region of Appalachia and its churches were in need of a college rooted in the tradition of the Bible college movement of the Christian Churches/Churches of Christ, and an institution devoted to the eclectic venture of theory and praxis. As inherent in the college's title, it was to be dedicated to academic excellence coupled with what Branholm referred to as "Preparation in personal evangelism."

Branholm desired to establish a college in the Appalachian region, not only because of the region's appeal but also because of his fear that many of the Bible colleges were moving toward a liberal arts form of educational philosophy, which, to him, would eventuate in a shortage of qualified ministers for the churches.

The college continues to the present under the same educational philosophy, although several presidents have succeeded Branholm since his death in 1975. BILLY W. JONES

Board of Church Extension

A general administrative unit of the Christian Church (Disciples of Christ).

Also known as Church Extension, the Board was organized at the 1883 General Christian Missionary Convention (GCMC) in Cincinnati to help house new congregations. First Christian Church, Atchison, Kansas, received the first loan ($500) in 1884. F. M. Rains became the first executive secretary in 1887, and in October 1888, at the Springfield, Illinois, GCMC, Church Extension became an incorporated entity within the American Christian Missionary Society (ACMS). George Muckley was executive secretary 1890-1926, increasing funds to $2 million during the greatest membership growth of the Disciples of Christ.

Church Extension became the Department of Church Erection of the United Christian Missionary Society in 1920 and continued as a department of UCMS until January 1934, when it became a separate corporation. During the 1930s the Board forgave over $1 million to congregational borrowers and provided salary support to over 100 ministers. Congregations opened savings accounts in the 1930s. To meet the postwar church building loan demands, individual investment opportunities became available during the 1940s. Interest-free loans were created to serve new, minority, and overseas congregations.

In 1969 the Board made critical decisions with regard to the finalizing of the division of the Christian Church (Disciples of Christ) and the Christian Churches/Churches of Christ that occurred with the restructuring of the Disciples agencies. While priority was to be given to congregations of the Christian Church (Disciples of Christ), it was decided to continue serving, on a case-by-case basis, congregations of all branches of the Stone-Campbell Movement. Moving into the current millennium, the Board has introduced low interest accessibility loans, renewed emphasis on establishing new churches, and provided easier access to services via the Internet.

Total assets of Church Extension have grown from less than $3,500 in 1883 to $130.7 million at the beginning of the twenty-first century, with net assets at $21.8 million. HAROLD R. WATKINS

Board of Higher Education

See Division of Higher Education

Board of Temperance

See Temperance

Boise Bible College

Bible college associated with the Christian Churches/Churches of Christ.

Boise Bible College (BBC) was founded in 1945 by Orin Hardenbrook, a graduate of San Jose Bible College. Hardenbrook suggested the need for a Bible college in the Intermountain West to provide trained leaders for Christian Churches/Churches of Christ in what at the time was the least populated region in the continental United States. The college originally operated in a local congregation. Classes opened in September 1945 in the basement of Boise's First Church of Christ, where Hardenbrook was senior minister.

The enrollment grew slowly during these early years from ten to fifteen students to around fifty students in 1975. Under the presidency of Richard Ewing (1975-90), the college was incorporated into a separate entity from the mother church and moved into an adjacent sixteen-acre campus. A new board of directors was elected to replace the elders of First Church of Christ, in the first steps toward accreditation. In the late 1980s, the college acquired the library holdings of the closed Intermountain Bible College in Colorado, and received accreditation from the Accrediting Association of Bible Colleges in 1989. Enrollment grew to the eighties and new professors formerly of Cincinnati Bible Seminary were added to the faculty. In the 1990s, the college saw its enrollment surpass 100 and its campus expanded.

BBC offers Associate and Bachelor's degrees in Bible and Christian Ministries. Areas of concentrated study in ministry include Christian education, youth ministry, women's ministry, church growth, church music, and missions.

BBC graduates serve in all three streams of the Stone-Campbell Movement, with the majority in Christian Churches/Churches of Christ. Many serve in worship, youth, and preaching ministries in churches throughout the Pacific Northwest, others in Christian schools and institutions of Christian higher education, and still others on the mission field in Europe, Africa, and Asia.

LARRY L. WOODARD

Boles, H. Leo

See Gospel Advocate, The

Boll, Robert Henry (1875-1956)

Preacher, author, and educator in Churches of Christ.

Born into a Roman Catholic family at Badenweiler, Baden, Germany, Boll left high school prematurely after the remarriage of his mother, and immigrated with relatives to America in 1890. After transitional employment in Ohio, he found work as a farmhand in Tennessee. Here he came under the influence of a state legislator and a teacher in a private school who were members of Churches of Christ. He was baptized on April 14, 1895, by Samuel Harris at Rock Spring Church of Christ near LaVergne, Tennessee. From 1895 to 1900 he attended Nashville Bible School and also taught German and French there. From 1901 to the end of 1903, Boll traveled as a preacher establishing churches, notably in Texas. In 1904 he succeeded George Klingman in the pulpit at Portland Avenue Church of Christ in Louisville, Kentucky, where, with the exception of one year of teaching at a Christian school in Lawrenceburg, Tennessee, he remained until his death in 1956.

As a prolific religious writer, Boll contributed to a variety of journals, notably *Gospel Advocate, The Way, The Gospel Review, The Leader and the Way,* and *Word and Work.* He wrote mainly on spiritual, exegetical, and apologetic topics and in 1909 became the front-page editor of the *Gospel Advocate,* a position he was forced to relinquish in 1915 when controversy developed about his views on eschatology and the importance of prophetic literature for Bible study. The dispute with the owners and fellow editors of the journal was also affected by editorial rivalries and generational conflicts. In the painful and gradual process of overcoming belief in the magisterial authority of the Roman Catholic Church prior to his conversion, Boll came to insist on a "simple Christianity" unfettered by any magisterial judgments and editorial theological consensuses. In 1916 he became editor of the New Orleans–based *Word and Work,* moving it to Louisville, where it became the periodical voice of premillennial Churches of Christ.

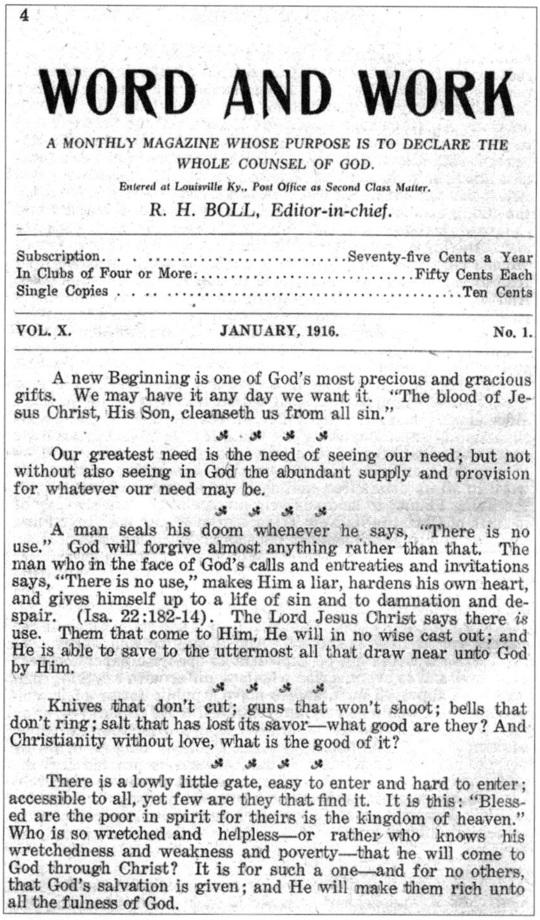

4

WORD AND WORK

A MONTHLY MAGAZINE WHOSE PURPOSE IS TO DECLARE THE WHOLE COUNSEL OF GOD.

Entered at Louisville Ky., Post Office as Second Class Matter.

R. H. BOLL, Editor-in-chief.

Subscription . . . . Seventy-five Cents a Year
In Clubs of Four or More . . . . Fifty Cents Each
Single Copies . . . . Ten Cents

VOL. X. JANUARY, 1916. No. 1.

A new Beginning is one of God's most precious and gracious gifts. We may have it any day we want it. "The blood of Jesus Christ, His Son, cleanseth us from all sin."

Our greatest need is the need of seeing our need; but not without also seeing in God the abundant supply and provision for whatever our need may be.

A man seals his doom whenever he says, "There is no use." God will forgive almost anything rather than that. The man who in the face of God's calls and entreaties and invitations says, "There is no use," makes Him a liar, hardens his own heart, and gives himself up to a life of sin and to damnation and despair. (Isa. 22:182-14). The Lord Jesus Christ says there *is* use. Them that come to Him, He will in no wise cast out; and He is able to save to the uttermost all that draw near unto God by Him.

Knives that don't cut; guns that won't shoot; bells that don't ring; salt that has lost its savor—what good are they? And Christianity without love, what is the good of it?

There is a lowly little gate, easy to enter and hard to enter; accessible to all, yet few are they that find it. It is this: "Blessed are the poor in spirit for theirs is the kingdom of heaven." Who is so wretched and helpless—or rather who knows his wretchedness and weakness and poverty—that he will come to God through Christ? It is for such a one—and for no others, that God's salvation is given; and He will make them rich unto all the fulness of God.

When Boll was finally relieved of his front-page column in the *Gospel Advocate,* he acquired the journal *Word and Work.* The paper became and continues to serve as the voice of the premillennial Churches of Christ. The "whole counsel of God" mentioned in the masthead refers to the prophetic elements of Scripture the other papers had excluded.
Courtesy Center for Restoration Studies, Abilene Christian University

Theologically and ecclesiologically, Boll stood in the countercultural tradition of James A. Harding (1848-1922) and the Nashville Bible School, developing its thought along fundamentalist lines. In his teaching Boll emphasized a premillennialism similar to that of Cyrus I. Scofield and William E. Blackstone, joining to it at the center of his thought a pronounced doctrine of grace and the personal indwelling of the Holy Spirit. Boll's interest in eschatology was guided by his effort to restore to the church this vital dimension of early Christian life and thought and maintaining it as motivation for Christian spirituality and foreign missions. His focus on eschatology clashed, however, with the church-centered religiosity of many contemporary leaders among Churches of Christ, who in reaction to Boll's premillennialism began to espouse a decisive amillennialism in eschatology, as found, for example, in H. Leo Boles's (1874-1946) written debate with Boll and in the writings and debates of Foy E. Wallace, Jr. (1896-1979).

A pacific individual, Boll poured his ministerial energies into preaching, teaching, and writing. His interest in training ministers gave rise to a Bible School that eventually developed into Southeastern Christian College. His pedagogical and anti-modernist concerns resulted also in the founding of a Christian school, which remained attached to Portland Avenue Church of Christ in Louisville at the beginning of the twenty-first century. In the 1930s and 1940s, the fellowship of premillennial Churches of Christ experienced much opposition from their amillennial opponents and began to foster relations with other constituencies, such as Christian Churches/Churches of Christ. By the end of the twentieth century the schism between premillennial and amillennial Churches of Christ was gradually disappearing. With the 2000 edition of Mac Lynn's directory, *Churches of Christ in the United States,* premillennial congregations were no longer distinguished from others.

See also Eschatology; Harding, James Alexander; Wallace, Foy E., Jr.; *Word and Work*

BIBLIOGRAPHY R. H. Boll, ed., *Word and Work* (1916-56) • R. H. Boll, *Truth and Grace* (1917) • R. H. Boll, *The Book of Revelation: A Brief and Simple Exposition of the Last Book of the Bible* (1923) • R. H. Boll, *The Kingdom of God: A Survey-study of the Bible's Principal Theme* (1924) • R. H. Boll, *The Second Coming of Our Lord Jesus Christ: Three Sermons and a Question Box* (1924) • Robert H. Boll and H. Leo Boles, *Unfulfilled Prophecy: A Discussion on Prophetic Themes* (1928) • Thomas G. Bradshaw, *R. H. Boll: Controversy and Accomplishment Among Churches of Christ* (1998) • Hans Rollmann, "'Our Steadfastness and Perseverance Depends on Perpetual Expectation of Our Lord': The Development of Robert Henry Boll's Premillennialism (1895-1915)," *Discipliana* 59 (Winter 1999): 113-26.

HANS ROLLMANN

Boston Church of Christ

See International Churches of Christ

Bowser, George Philip (1874-1950)

Twentieth-century leader in black Churches of Christ. Although he and the noted evangelist Marshall Keeble were friends, their careers took opposite paths in response to racial prejudice. Keeble was an accommodationist, while Bowser overtly opposed the system of segregation and discrimination characteristic of both society and church.

Bowser was raised a Methodist and received an excellent education at a Methodist school for blacks in Nashville. He studied Greek, Hebrew, French, German, and Latin. He suffered the loss of one arm when injured by a train. At 18 he was licensed to exhort in the African Methodist Episcopal Church, but quit preaching due to lack of support. An elderly minister in Nashville led him into the Stone-Campbell Movement, and he was baptized in the Gay Street Christian Church in 1897.

Bowser soon joined other black leaders who began an a cappella Church of Christ in Nashville. Bowser founded *The Christian Echo* in 1902, one of the longest-running religious papers in the Movement. In 1907 he established his first school in the Jackson Street Church of Christ in Nashville, then in 1909 he established the Silver Point Christian Institute in Silver Point, Tennessee, which he operated until 1918.

In 1920 wealthy Christian insurance man A. M. Burton purchased a building in Nashville to establish a school for blacks, with Bowser teaching the Bible. The school was named the Southern Practical Institute, and a white Christian, C. E. W. Dorris, was appointed superintendent, with Bowser serving as principal. The school failed, however, when Bowser refused to accept Dorris's insistence that black students enter by the back door.

Bowser began the Bowser Christian Institute in 1938 in Fort Smith, Arkansas, and operated it until 1946. He operated other schools in Detroit, Michigan, and Fort Worth, Texas. This last effort led to the establishment of Southwestern Christian College in Terrell, Texas, in the fall of 1950. He is known as the father of Christian education among blacks in Churches of Christ.

See also African Americans in the Movement; Southwestern Christian College

BIBLIOGRAPHY R. Vernon Boyd, *Undying Dedication: The Story of G. P. Bowser* (1985) • George Phillip Bowser, *Bowser's Sermons: Sayings, Questions, Outlines, Lectures and Editorials,* ed. Thelma M. Holt (1964) • J. S. Winston, "George Phillip Bowser: An Outstanding Pioneer, Educator, Preacher," *Christian Echo* 84 (November 1992): 2.

R. VERNON BOYD

Breakenridge, Melvin

See Canada, The Movement in

Brewer, Grover Cleveland (1884-1956)

Leader among Churches of Christ in the first half of the twentieth century. He especially influenced attitudes toward congregational development, Fundamentalism, and political assessment. Brewer was born in Lawrenceburg, Tennessee, to a Baptist family. Shortly after his baptism by J. J. Castleberry in 1900, he began preaching and debating. He studied for a year at Ashley S. Johnson's Bible school at Kimberlin Heights, Tennessee, but then moved to Nashville Bible School (now Lipscomb University), graduating in 1911. He also took correspondence courses from Moody Bible Institute. He preached for large churches in Tennessee, Los Angeles, and Texas, including Broadway Church of Christ in Lubbock.

Brewer was an early proponent of "located" preachers and large congregations. He promoted church bulletins, membership lists and directories, church budgets, pledging, and multiple cups for communion. He favored large mission programs with congregational cooperation and church support of Christian colleges. He published these views often, in books, tracts, and religious journals.

In the 1920s, Brewer began speaking and debating in Fundamentalist circles as well as in Churches of Christ on evolution, prohibition, communism, and Catholicism. In 1953 he began *Voice of Freedom,* which explored these topics. He claimed to maintain the Lipscomb perspective on nonparticipation in war, but encouraged Christians to vote.

Brewer was a consummate orator at his best, with a sonorous but sometimes gruff voice. He was noted for rigor of argument and the marshaling of biblical texts and contemporary data. His preaching heralded salvation by grace and the nondenominational character of Christianity. He insisted that the sign where he last preached in Memphis, Tennessee, simply declare, "Jackson Avenue Church." Though he participated at first in unity talks organized by Claude Witty and James DeForest Murch, he later refused to support the effort. He challenged Foy E. Wallace, Jr.'s crusade against premillennialism, but declared himself an amillennialist.

See also Creation and Evolution; Fundamentalism; Johnson Bible College; Lipscomb University; Ministry; Missions, Missiology; Unity, Christian; *Voice of Freedom, The;* Wallace, Foy E., Jr.

BIBLIOGRAPHY G. C. Brewer, *Forty Years on the Firing Line* (1948) • G. C. Brewer, *A Story of Toil and Tears, of Love and Laughter: Being the Autobiography of G. C. Brewer* (1957) • Warren Jones, "G. C. Brewer: Debater, Lecturer, and Preacher" (unpublished Ph.D. dissertation, Wayne State University, 1958) • Norman Parks, "G. C. Brewer, Controversialist," *Discipliana* 44 (1984): 56.

THOMAS H. OLBRICHT

Brite Divinity School

Related to the Christian Church (Disciples of Christ).

Brite had its origin as the Bible department of Texas Christian University. The university, originally AddRan Male and Female College, was founded in Thorp Spring, Texas, in 1873 by two Disciples preachers, Addison and Randolph Clark. As the university moved, first to Waco and then, in 1910, to Fort Worth, the Bible department grew under the leadership of such teacher-administrators as Ely V. Zollars, Frank H. Marshall, Clinton Lockhart, and the primary benefactor of the department, West Texas rancher Lucas Charles Brite. Supporters decided to incorporate the department in 1914 to give it legal standing. They named the institution Brite College of the Bible in recognition of the Brite family's support. A building was erected and a new era in ministerial education began with four faculty members and a few dozen students.

The central figure in Brite's first half-century was Colby D. Hall. He was named dean of Brite after its incorporation and served in that post for an astonishing thirty-three years. During the first quarter-century of its life, Brite was a solid, conservative, and unspectacular school. Brite achieved full accreditation from the American Association of Theological Schools in 1941 and, after that a new generation of faculty and students arrived to ignite an explosion of theological education, producing one of the golden ages of the school. Students from the classes of 1947 to 1949 formed a significant portion of the pastoral, academic, and denominational leadership of the Christian Church (Disciples of Christ) during the last half of the twentieth century.

In 1947 D. Ray Lindley assumed the deanship. He was followed by Amarillo pastor Roy Snodgrass in 1950 and Houston pastor Elmer Henson in 1955. During this period the faculty doubled in size to meet the growing student body which now topped 100, the new Religion Center was built at Texas Christian University with a wing for Brite, and the school was racially integrated. In 1963, as Brite approached its golden anniversary, the school was rechartered as Brite Divinity School, the regnant title for university-related theological schools at that time. The B.D. degree, first awarded in 1907, was changed to the M.Div. in 1967, and a Pastoral Care Center was established in 1968.

William E. Tucker, later chancellor of Texas Christian University, became dean of Brite in 1971. Under his leadership, academic standards were raised and tenure standards tightened. The D.Min. degree was inaugurated in 1971. The faculty became widely recognized not only by the church but also within their respective disciplines. However, it became clear that a long-term problem required addressing: Brite had little endowment of its own and consistently ran a deficit.

Tucker was succeeded by M. Jack Suggs in 1977. A financial campaign, the first to be held by a single unit related to the University, added $8 million to the endowment. The endowment grew to $18 million by 1990 and by 2000 stood at $70 million. The third wave of Brite faculty was added during Suggs's tenure as dean, expanding the faculty to sixteen members.

Upon Suggs's retirement in 1989, Leo Perdue was elected dean. A number of significant changes took place during his administration. Alongside the historic Disciples relationship, Brite developed programs in Methodist and Baptist studies, and work continues toward a Presbyterian studies program. Rapid expansion in the area of global and interfaith studies led to the establishment of programs in Jewish studies, Korean studies, and Latina/o studies. Brite's first Ph.D. programs were established in 1997 in two areas, Biblical Interpretation and Pastoral Theology and Pastoral Counseling. Total enrollment in the various master's programs and doctoral programs climbed toward 300. Brite's first student housing was built in the 1940s. New housing was erected as Leibrock Village was completed in 2001. Additional students and programs have left the school seriously short of academic space, and, in 2003, plans were under way for a new academic building.

Of primary importance during this period has been the 1999 clarification of the relationship between Brite and Texas Christian University. Brite has always been legally autonomous, but for most of its existence was unable to function in that way. The new intercorporate agreement recognizes that Brite is no longer a constituent but an affiliate school of the university. The relationship between the two institutions remains strong. Some titles and roles have changed. Dean Perdue, who was chief operating officer of Brite, became president and chief executive officer. Mark Toulouse, who was associate dean, became executive vice president and dean. In 2003 D. Newell Williams was elected to follow Perdue as Brite's second president. Brite Divinity School will soon be one hundred years old and plans to serve the church and academy for many years to come.

See also Hall, Colby; Suggs, Marion Jack; Texas Christian University

BIBLIOGRAPHY Brite Divinity School, *Self-Study Report, 2000* • Joseph R. Jeter, Jr., *Brite Divinity School: An Historical Sketch* (1989).

JOSEPH R. JETER, JR.

British Millennial Harbinger

Principal journal among British Churches of Christ between 1848 and 1865.

The *British Millennial Harbinger (BMH)* was part of a continuous series with varying titles beginning in 1837 and continuing to 1889. In March 1837 James Wallis of Nottingham published the first issue of the *Christian Messenger and Reformer,* following the discontinuance of William Jones's *Millennial Harbinger* in 1836. The intention of the journal was to publish more of Alexander Campbell's writings, which Wallis expected to achieve in four volumes. The supplementary running head for the first issue was "A Voice from America." The third issue included extracts from Campbell's *Christianity Restored* (1835).

By the end of the first volume Wallis was reprinting not only his correspondence with Campbell, but also his correspondence with other churches in Britain and editors in the United States who had become aware of him through Campbell's publication of his letters. The subtitle of the fourth volume omitted reference to "the publication of the writings of A. Campbell and others" and simply referred to "the dissemination of Primitive Christianity." Although sales had not matched expenditure, Wallis decided in February 1841 to continue with a fifth volume. The exchange of correspondence in the *Messenger* led to the decision to hold the first Cooperative Meeting in Edinburgh in August 1842. Monthly circulation was reckoned to be about 600 copies in April 1845. A new series, enlarged to demy-octavo, and entitled *The Christian Messenger and Family Magazine, Devoted to the Dissemination of Primitive Christianity,* began in May 1845. It was divided into distinct sections: Essays, Dialogues, etc.; Original Communications, etc.; Queries and Replies; and Items of News, Statistics, etc. At the Cooperation Meeting in 1847 Wallis spoke of the financial loss sustained in producing the *Messenger,* but he was urged to continue and was given £100 as a subsidy.

From January 1848 the third series began, entitled *The British Millennial Harbinger and Family Magazine Devoted to the Spread of Primitive Christianity.* The change of name was to avoid confusion with an Episcopalian magazine with the earlier name; the term "Millennial" was said to have a biblical meaning only, and Campbell's magazine was not mentioned. More space was given to news and comment from within the British Isles, though items of foreign news appeared regularly, especially from Australia where emigration was increasing. From 1850 Wallis aimed to use about half of the space for material by Campbell and his American colleagues. The *BMH* is the main source for reports, including the resolutions, of the Annual Meeting before the *Year Book* began in 1886. In December 1861 Wallis handed the *BMH* over to David King. King, who had contributed eight pages a month since 1857, particularly on news of other British Churches, reduced the number of pages and the price. The final phrase in the title became "'the spread of Christianity as it was at the first and the defence and promotion of Biblical Truth."

Unlike Wallis, King was less inclined to publish material he disagreed with, except to make hostile comments. The general mix of articles continued as before, but King's combative debating style became more prominent. He was uncomfortable with the word *Millennial* and dropped it from the title in 1866. The deaths of Campbell in 1866 and of Wallis in 1867 coincided with deteriorating relations with the American churches over the terms of admission to communion. Hence King's sympathy for Franklin's *American Christian Review* and Fanning and Lipscomb's *Gospel Advocate* presaged his criticism of Robert Richardson when the latter's biography of Campbell was published.

In 1871 the title changed again, to *The Ecclesiastical Observer,* with more space given to the reporting of current events, including the disestablishment movement and even political comment. Between 1876 and 1883 the magazine was published fortnightly, and the price was reduced to twopence. Much space was taken up in 1878 with the publication of the Letters to the Churches in America authorized by the Annual Meeting of 1877 and responses to them; there was also strong criticism of the new Foreign Christian Missionary Society initiatives in Southampton and Chester. The size of the magazine diminished in the 1880s; the monthly publication after 1884 was no larger than the previous fortnightly one, and by the late 1880s the size was sixteen pages.

The *Christian Advocate,* edited by T. H. Milner of Edinburgh from 1857 until his death in 1865, was a monthly magazine commended by the Annual Meeting of the Scottish Churches of Christ. In 1873 it was revived with a wider coverage of news and articles. The editor was John Aitken, Secretary of the Scottish Evangelist Committee. He gave it up in 1877, ostensibly because of lack of time and assistance; but he clearly disliked the developing theological controversies in British Churches of Christ. A year later the Scottish Annual Meeting appointed a committee to revive it and invited G. Y. Tickle, whom Aitken had asked to help him, to edit it, which he did from 1879 to 1888. One of the first articles to appear was Isaac Errett's "Our Position" (1873), with an editorial note that they did not approve of every part of the statement. The *Christian Advocate* was more open: for example, Tickle published a sympathetic series of articles by J. B. Rotherham on Richardson's book on *The Holy Spirit* in 1879 that King had criticized. It did not refer to the American controversy until the formation of the Christian Association in 1881, when there was a clear rebuke about the break in fellowship.

In 1889 the Annual Meeting agreed to establish a new magazine, combining the *Ecclesiastical Observer* and the *Christian Advocate,* which began in 1890. Its title was the *Bible Advocate,* and King was editor in chief. Lancelot Oliver, who edited the *Christian Advocate* after Tickle, was one of the assistants and took over after King's death in 1894. The name of the magazine changed to *Christian Advocate* in 1921 and continued until the dissolution of the Association in 1979.

See also Foreign Christian Missionary Society, The; Great Britain and Ireland, Churches of Christ in; Tickle, Gilbert Young; Wallis, James

BIBLIOGRAPHY David Michael Thompson, *Let Sects and Parties Fall: A Short History of the Association of Churches of Christ in Great Britain and Ireland* (1980).

DAVID M. THOMPSON

Broaddus, Andrew

See Baptists

Broadus, David Thompson (1852-1924)

Minister and editor in Churches of Christ. Though Broadus was a native of Garrard County, Kentucky, he did his major work in Kansas, where he lived thirty-four of his last forty years. After teaching school ten years, he began preaching at his home congregation, Scotts Fork Christian Church, in 1880. In 1884 he moved to southern Kansas and preached at various locations before moving in 1892 to Belle Plaine, Kansas, where he preached for the Church of Christ during twelve of his fifteen years there. Meanwhile he did evangelistic work in Kansas, Missouri, and Indian territory. Early in his career he identified with conservatives in controversies separating Disciples of Christ and Churches of Christ.

After leaving Kansas to preach six years near Moriarty, New Mexico, and in Canadian, Texas, Broadus moved to Wichita, Kansas, in 1912 as minister for the Church of Christ and front-page editor for R. N. Gardner's *Christian Companion.* When the paper moved to Odessa, Missouri, in 1915, Broadus and Homer E. Moore (1868-1941) began the *Christian Worker,* which Broadus edited until he died. His work in Wichita as editor and as minister of a growing church meeting in two locations (later Central Church of Christ and West Douglas Church of Christ) expanded his influence. During his twelve-year ministry there, the church adapted to its urban challenge and increased from 150 members to about 400. Broadus exercised a moderating influence in the controversies that arose in Churches of Christ in the twentieth century. His work as preacher and editor helped keep most Churches of Christ in Kansas in the fellowship's mainstream.

BIBLIOGRAPHY *Christian Worker* (Wichita, Kansas), February 1915–October 30, 1924.

EDWIN L. BROADUS

Brush Run Church

First church of the Campbell movement. The Christian Association of Washington was formed under the direction of Thomas Campbell at Buffaloe, Penn-

Before the Brush Run church (pictured here in reconstructed form) was even built, Alexander Campbell delivered a dedicatory sermon on the site in September 1810, using the text of Job 8:7, "Though thy beginning was small, thy latter end should greatly increase." Courtesy of Bethany College

sylvania, on August 17, 1809. The organization specifically stated that it was not a church; it was merely a group of voluntary advocates for church reform who were to meet twice a year, principally to collect money to support ministers who shared their vision of "promoting simple evangelical christianity, free from all mixture of human opinions and inventions of men."

The Christian Association initially tried to form an ecclesiastical union with the Presbyterian Synod of Pittsburgh, but it encountered hostility and rejection. On May 4, 1811, the members of the Association met at Brush Run, appointed Thomas Campbell elder, licensed Alexander Campbell to preach, and chose four deacons. The next day, Sunday, the church held its first communion service. The congregation was made up of about thirty regular members. A meetinghouse was erected in the valley of Brush Run, about two miles above its junction with Buffalo Creek.

Alexander Campbell was ordained on January 1, 1812, and on the certificate registering his ordination at the Brooke County courthouse, Thomas Campbell identifies himself as "Senior minister of the First Church of the Christian Association of Washington, meeting at Cross-roads and Brush Run, Washington County, Pennsylvania."

The congregation was aware of the seeming contradiction between its existence as an independent religious body and its belief that "the church of Christ upon earth is essentially, intentionally, and constitutionally one," so in the fall of 1815 it welcomed the opportunity to unite with an association of Baptist churches in western Pennsylvania, the Redstone Association, on condition that the Brush Run church "should be allowed to teach and preach whatever we learned from the Holy Scriptures, regardless of any creed or formula in Christendom."

A minority of clergy in the Redstone Association opposed the influence of Alexander Campbell and organized a campaign to bring him to trial for heresy. To circumvent this movement, in 1823 Campbell and about thirty other members of the Brush Run church were issued letters of dismission in order to establish a new congregation in Wellsburg. The Wellsburg church then united with the Mahoning Association of Ohio, which was more sympathetic to the views of the Campbells. By early in the year 1824 most of the Brush Run congregation had transferred membership to the Wellsburg church, but services continued to be held in the Brush Run Meeting House for another few years.

In 1842 the building was sold, moved to West Middletown, and put to various secular uses. In later years what remained of it was removed to the grounds of the Campbell Homestead in Bethany, where it deteriorated until the last of the debris was cleared away in 1990.

See also *Declaration and Address*

BIBLIOGRAPHY Alexander Campbell, "Anecdotes, Incidents & Facts," *Millennial Harbinger* (1848): 279, 344, 522, 552, 701 • Robert Richardson, *Memoirs of Alexander Campbell,* 2 vols. (1868, 1870). GEORGE F. MILLER

Buckner, George Walker (1893-1981)

Distinguished editor, ecumenist, and statesman among the Disciples of Christ.

Buckner was born in Pike County, Missouri, on October 1, 1893. After his high school years in Missouri, he studied at the University School in Southport, England (1912-13), and the Gymnasium Schule at Langenburg, Germany (1913). His college studies took him to Culver-Stockton College (B.A, 1914, and M.A., 1915) and Central Wesleyan College (M.A., 1916). Among the honorary degrees awarded him were the D.D., Hastings (Nebraska) College, 1925; L.L.D. Culver-Stockton College, 1940; and D.Litt., Atlantic Christian College (now Barton College), 1953. He married Winifred Magee, August 24, 1915, with whom he had three children.

Buckner was ordained into the ministry by the Disciples of Christ in 1915. His pastorates included small congregations in Mokane, La Monte, and Lee's Summit, Missouri (1916-21); First Christian Church (Disciples of Christ), Hastings, Nebraska (1921-27); and Central Christian Church, Grand Rapids, Michigan (1927-35).

From 1935 to 1961 Buckner was the editor of *World Call,* the international magazine of the Disciples of Christ, leading it to a position of distinction in American religious journalism. From 1941 to 1961 he also served as the executive director of the Association for the Promotion of Christian Unity (renamed the Council on Christian Unity in 1961). His travels took him on editorial missions to the Middle East, Asia, and the Holy Land. During his tenure in this dual leadership role he was a member of the Provisional Committee for the World Council of Churches (WCC) "in process of formation" (1944-48), and the WCC's first Central Committee (1948-61); a delegate to the WCC's first assembly (1948) at Amsterdam, the Netherlands, and the second assembly (1954) at Evanston, Illinois. He was the first of the Disciples to serve on the founding board of the WCC's Ecumenical Institute Bossey at Celigny, Switzerland (1946-61), a legacy continued by George G. Beazley, Jr., Paul A. Crow, Jr., and Robert K. Welsh — all presidents of the Council on Christian Unity. In other ecumenical arenas Buckner served on the boards of the Federal Council of Churches of Christ in America (1940-50) and the National Council of the Churches of Christ in the U.S.A. (1950-60). He had the distinction of being one of the few ecumenists who attended all three of the historic ecumenical conferences in the late 1930s: the World Conference on Church, Community and State (Life and Work), at Oxford, England (July 1937); the Second World Conference on Faith and Order, at Edinburgh, Scotland (July 1937); and the meeting of the International Missionary Council at Tambaram/Madras, India (December 1938). This Disciples ecumenist retired in 1961, when the Association was reshaped to become the Council on Christian Unity under the presidency of George G. Beazley, Jr.

Buckner was the author of two ecumenical books: *Concerns of a World Church* (1943) and *The Winds of God* (1947). In a major gift to Christian unity he was instrumental in encouraging the WCC to begin research and in securing the funds among Disciples of Christ for the publication of *The History of the Ecumenical Movement, Volume 1* (1954). Enjoying twenty years of retirement, he died in 1981, at the age of 88. In his generation few Disciples were more articulate as advocates and spokespersons for the Church's mission and unity.

BIBLIOGRAPHY George Walker Buckner, *Concerns of a World Church* (1943) • George Walker Buckner, *The Winds of God: Christian Unity, Cooperation and World Fellowship* (1947).

PAUL A. CROW, JR.

Bullard, Chester A. (1809-1893)

Evangelist and reformer in Virginia. Chester A. Bullard came to the Stone-Campbell Movement independently, after carefully considering its appeal for a restoration of the New Testament church. A native of Massachusetts, Bullard had moved as a child with his sister Nancy to Staunton, Virginia, where he came in contact with the Methodists and began attending their services. In 1818 the Christian church movement had penetrated southern Virginia through the work of Joseph Thomas. Thomas was influential in the New Rich Baptist Association, one of whose leaders, Landon Duncan, was willing to drop the Baptist name in favor of the simple name "Christian."

Sometime in the 1820s Bullard moved farther west to Christiansburg, Virginia. Here, at age 17, Bullard began to seek the assurance of salvation. Knowing only Methodist and Baptist doctrine and practices, he linked this "assurance" with some kind of religious experience. After further biblical study he connected assurance of pardon with baptism itself, though he was aided in this direction by neither Baptists nor Methodists. At this same time Bullard was studying medicine and in a journey home came across Landon Duncan, who was by this time affiliated with Barton W. Stone.

At the age of 21 Bullard preached his first sermon, and he continued to preach for the remainder of his career. Not only did he begin a miniature "restoration movement" in southwest Virginia, establishing and ministering to Christian churches in that region, but in the 1830s Bullard became acquainted with Alexander Campbell and the Disciples of Christ. He began to correspond with the churches in the Campbell movement and sent reports to the *Millennial Harbinger,* such that by the late 1840s Bullard's network of churches had effectively amalgamated with the larger Movement through congregational and evangelistic cooperation. Bullard died in 1893.

See also Evangelism, Evangelists — Early Nineteenth Century

BIBLIOGRAPHY Chester A. Bullard, "Autobiography," *Christian Standard* 29 (1893): 210, 247-48, 307-8 • H. Jackson Darst, *Ante-Bellum Virginia Disciples* (1959) • Frederick A. Hodge, *The Plea and the Pioneers in Virginia* (1905) • Mary A. Kearns, "A Merging of Two Restoration Movements: Contributions of Dr. Chester A. Bullard to the Stone-Campbell Movement" (unpublished M.Div. thesis, Emmanuel School of Religion, 1996) • John Z. Tyler, *The Disciples of Christ in Virginia* (1879).

CHARLES R. GRESHAM

Burnet, David Staats (1808-1867)

Society organizer and mission advocate of the Stone-Campbell Movement in the mid-nineteenth century.

David Staats Burnet was born in Ohio and raised as a Presbyterian in a prominent political family. As a teenager he became a follower of Alexander Campbell. Burnet moved early into leadership in the

Campbell movement, became a highly effective pastor and evangelist and a prolific writer and editor, and served as president of Bacon College (1837-39). In 1835 he published a revised edition of Campbell's first journal, the *Christian Baptist,* which included some of Campbell's own corrections and Burnet's stylistic improvements. In 1845 Burnet led in the organization of the American Christian Bible Society, the first national institution of the Stone-Campbell Movement. This was followed quickly by the Sunday School and Tract Society (variously named). Both were located in Cincinnati.

Neither of these Societies received broad support, and Alexander Campbell himself saw them as mimicking work already begun by other denominations and as financial competition for the Movement's fledgling colleges. Burnet countered Campbell's criticisms point for point and forged ahead, winning his approval. In 1849 Burnet played the key role in organizing the first general convention of the Disciples of Christ in October 1849, which inaugurated the American Christian Missionary Society, the first widely accepted — though still controversial — national organization of the Movement. After the convention, Alexander Campbell removed his former objections and wrote, "These Societies we cannot but hail as greatly contributing to the advancement of the cause we have been so long pleading before God and the people."

See also American Christian Bible Society; American Christian Missionary Society; Missionary Societies, Controversy over; Missions, Missiology; Societies

BIBLIOGRAPHY D. S. Burnet (with Alexander Campbell's remarks), "American Christian Bible Society," *Millennial Harbinger* (1845): 366-73, 452-60 • D. S. Burnet, "Bible Societies," *Millennial Harbinger* (1849): 451-53 • D. S. Burnet, *The Jerusalem Mission under the Direction of the American Christian Missionary Society* (1853; repr. 1977) • Noel L. Keith, *The Story of D. S. Burnet: Undeserved Obscurity* (1954) • W. K. Pendleton (with Alexander Campbell's remarks), "The Convention of Christian Churches," *Millennial Harbinger* (1849): 689-96.

RICHARD L. HARRISON, JR.

Burnett, Thomas Raines (1842-1916)

Preacher, author, poet, and controversialist born near Nickajack Lake, Tennessee.

Burnett's family moved from Tennessee to Texas when he was 8 years old, and he was educated for six years in local Texas schools. He served in the 34th Texas Cavalry and Polignac's brigade during the Civil War, seeing action at least seven times.

Burnett described his family religion as "Wesleyan," and he grew up as a Methodist. Following the war, Burnett taught school and edited several small Texas newspapers. Immersed by Professor Charles Carlton in 1874, Burnett established the *Christian Messenger* at Bonham, Texas, in 1875, appointing Carlton its first editor.

Through the *Messenger,* Burnett resisted the introduction of instrumental music into Texas churches, fought the idea of the "hired preacher," and attacked Austin McGary's demand for rebaptism of converts already immersed. In 1894 Burnett sold the *Messenger* to the *Gospel Advocate,* joining the *Advocate* staff with a page called "Burnett's Budget."

David Lipscomb generally agreed with Burnett's doctrinal positions, but found disagreeable Burnett's penchant for controversy, including "cuts and innuendoes." In 1899 Lipscomb terminated Burnett's editorial connection with the *Advocate.* By 1901 Burnett had turned *Burnett's Budget* into a four-page monthly periodical, and through its pages he continued to articulate his views with wit, humorous rhyme, sarcasm, and vitriol until his death in 1916.

Burnett produced eighteen popular books and tracts, including *Center Shots* (1912), *Hezekiah Jones* (1895), *Valid Baptism: A Discussion Between A. McGary and T. R. Burnett* (1898), and three volumes of *Doctrinal Poetry* (1905, 1910, and 1913).

See also Baptism; *Gospel Advocate, The;* Lipscomb, David; McGary, Austin

BIBLIOGRAPHY Terry J. Gardner, "T. R. Burnett — Master of Repartee," *Faith and Facts* 23 (April 1995): 121-39 • Charles R. Nichol, *Gospel Preachers Who Blazed the Trail* (1911, 1955) • John T. Oakley, *J. N. Hall's Campbellite Catechism with Conflicting Answers of Two Distinguished Campbellites, A. McGary and T. R. Burnett* (1898).

TERRY J. GARDNER

Butler, Burris (1909-1982)

Editor of *Christian Standard* from 1944 to 1957, vice president and publisher at Standard Publishing when he retired in 1971.

Butler urged conservative readers to get on with the business of restoring "New Testament Christianity" and pursuing the "unity of all believers on the basis of the authority of the Bible." Eventually Butler called for those opposed to liberalism and denominationalism to consolidate their protest. Beginning in 1947, he inaugurated in the *Christian Standard* a listing of dissenting churches, the "Stand Up and Be Counted"/"Roll Call of the Faithful" campaign. Some praised this "call" as unifying while others in the Stone-Campbell Movement criticized it as divisive. From all perspectives, however, Butler was a key figure in further accelerating the departure of the Christian Churches/Churches of Christ from the Christian Church (Disciples of Christ).

See also *Christian Standard;* Committee of 1000

BIBLIOGRAPHY G. Mark Sloneker, *"You Can't Do That!" The Life and Labors of Burris Butler* (1995).

G. MARK SLONEKER

Butler, Ovid (1801-1881)

Early Disciples of Christ abolitionist and founding president of Butler University.

Born in 1801, Ovid Butler spent much of his youth in Rush County, Indiana. His parents came under the influence of the Campbell movement in the 1830s. As a young man, Butler finally acquiesced to his father's request and examined some of Alexander Campbell's writing. That resulted in Butler's baptism and alignment with the Campbell movement. Trained in law, Ovid Butler moved in 1835 to Indianapolis, where he had a successful law practice until his retirement in 1847.

During the annual meetings of delegates from churches throughout Indiana, interest emerged in starting a school that would provide education for the youth within the state and region. Butler, along with James Mathes and Elijah Goodwin, took an early lead in such discussions. Funds were raised, and in 1852 the school was organized.

On July 27, 1852, Ovid Butler was elected president of the newly formed North Western Christian University in Indianapolis. In the fall of that year, the board accepted Butler's offer of a twenty-five-acre property on the near north side of Indianapolis. The university became a major training center for the Stone-Campbell Movement in the Midwest. His leadership was formally recognized in 1877 when the school's name was changed to Butler University. He died in 1881.

Ideologically, Butler was a strong abolitionist. Butler and others in Indiana were critical of Alexander Campbell's neutral stance and Southern connections in the 1850s. Campbell's reluctant support for the dreams of a school in Indiana only added to the tension. This gave rise to a controversy in 1855 when several students were expelled by Bethany College over issues revolving around slavery and subsequently enrolled at North Western Christian University.

In 1859 Butler led in the organization of the Christian Missionary Society to support abolitionist missionary Pardee Butler (no relation) and to give expression to anti-slavery sentiment in the Movement.

See also Abolitionism; Butler, Pardee; Butler University; Christian Missionary Society

BIBLIOGRAPHY Hilton U. Brown, *A Book of Memories* (1951) • Frederick I. Murphy, "North Western Christian University and the Education of the Ministry" (unpublished M.A. thesis, Butler University, 1960) • Henry K. Shaw, *Hoosier Disciples* (1966).

CARSON REED

Butler, Pardee (1816-1888)

Influential evangelist and radical social activist.

Born in New York and reared in Ohio, Butler moved to the Kansas Territory in 1855 after the passage of the Kansas-Nebraska Acts. By 1858 he had organized seven churches and helped organize the first state convention. Denied funding from the American Christian Missionary Society because he refused to ignore the slavery issue, in 1859 he received support as a Kansas evangelist from the abolitionist Christian Missionary Society. By 1860 Butler had established twenty churches with nearly 1,000 total members. Best remembered for uncompromising social activism, he was rafted out of Atchison, Kansas, for his "free soiler" position. When he returned, he narrowly escaped hanging but was tarred and cottoned. After the Civil War Butler worked for prohibition, helping Kansas to become the first state to prohibit alcohol in 1888. At his death he was hailed as one of the great pioneers of Kansas. Butler wrote many articles for Stone-Campbell Movement periodicals.

See also Abolitionism; Christian Missionary Society

BIBLIOGRAPHY Pardee Butler, *Personal Recollections of Pardee Butler with Reminiscences by His Daughter, Mrs. Rosetta B. Hastings . . .* (1889) • Daniel Thomas Johnson, "Pardee Butler: Kansas Abolitionist" (unpublished M.A. thesis, Kansas State University, 1962).

ROBERT F. REA

Butler School of Religion

See Christian Theological Seminary

Butler University

Formerly related to the Disciples of Christ.

Butler University was chartered January 15, 1850 as North Western Christian University. As early as 1847, efforts had begun to establish a Disciples college in Indiana. In 1848 the Indiana State Convention of Disciples meeting at Little Flat Rock voted to raise funds for a college intended to provide a "free soil" alternative to Bethany College in western Virginia. The chartering of Butler brought Bethany President Alexander Campbell to Indiana in November 1850 for a visit with attorney and abolitionist leader Ovid Butler about the impending competition with Bethany. Butler and his colleagues insisted on the development of the college, but agreed to fund the "Indiana Chair of Ancient Languages" at Bethany as the price of peace with Campbell. Under the leadership of John O'Kane ways were found to successfully fund the design and construction of a university building, but funds for the Indiana Chair at Bethany did not materialize. The students and faculty moved into the thoughtfully designed building located in Indianapolis at the corner of 13th Street and College Avenue, on April 9, 1855.

By 1870, the school was a victim of its own success. It had outgrown its downtown facilities. In addition, it had provided generous financial assistance to impoverished students and was in dire financial straits. This led to administrative changes and a move to the newly designed suburb of Irvington, a location that allowed the necessary space for the development of a modern campus. Ovid Butler (who owned 51 percent of the corporation stock) funded much of the transition. The new quarters were completed in time to host graduation in 1876. On February 28, 1877, the university was renamed Butler University in honor of its patron.

Throughout the next decades the faculty of the university included numerous nationally known figures. After World War I, space for development of the university again became a concern. Through gifts of the Rockefellers and the Irwin-Sweeney families of Columbus, Indiana, a large 246-acre campus was secured in the Indianapolis suburb of Fairview. Building began in 1926 with Arthur Jordan Memorial Hall and athletic facilities. Classes began at the present campus in 1928-29 with 3,047 students.

The College of Religion was founded on Butler University land in 1924-25 under the leadership of Frederick D. Kershner. It remained associated with the university until 1958 when it was renamed Christian Theological Seminary and eventually moved to an adjacent property. The Trustees broke the connection with the Christian Churches, and Butler University became a secular private liberal arts university. In 1978 the university requested of the Division of Higher Education of the Christian Church (Disciples of Christ) that Butler no longer be listed in any Disciples publication as having a historical relationship with the denomination.

Today Butler is a nationally recognized residential, liberal arts–oriented university containing five colleges, 4,326 students, 60 majors, and 256 faculty.

BIBLIOGRAPHY Hilton U. Brown, *A Book of Memories* (1951) • Lee Burns, "The Beginnings of Butler College," Butler *Alumni Quarterly* 15:1 (April 1926) • W. Cauble, *Disciples of Christ in Indiana* (1930) • D. Duane Cummins, *The Disciples Colleges: A History* (1987) • Henry K. Shaw, *Hoosier Disciples* (1966) • Henry K. Shaw, "The Founding of Butler University, 1847-1855," *Indiana Magazine of History* 58:3 (Sept. 1962).

DAVID BUNDY

C

Calhoun, Hall Laurie (1863-1935)

Evangelist, scholar, and educator among Disciples of Christ and Churches of Christ. Born on a farm near Conyersville, Tennessee.

As a youth Calhoun attended high schools in Mayfield, Kentucky, and Union City, Tennessee, and qualified for an appointment to the United States Military Academy at West Point. His passion for knowledge of the Bible, however, impelled him in 1888 toward the College of the Bible in Lexington, Kentucky. There scholar and teacher J. W. McGarvey (1829-1911) would become Calhoun's mentor and the decisive influence in all of his life and work.

Calhoun completed both the Bachelor of Arts at Kentucky University and the Classical Diploma of the College of the Bible in 1892, compressing a seven-year course into four years. In 1890 he married Mary Ettah Stacey, and five children eventually blessed their marriage. By 1893, after a year of teaching in a Lexington preparatory school, Calhoun returned to Conyersville, teaching school and preaching by appointment. In 1895 he conducted 17 "protracted meetings" and preached 507 sermons resulting in 425 conversions. By November 1895 Calhoun was the minister of the Tenth Street Christian Church in Paducah, Kentucky.

While the College of the Bible had shaped Calhoun as a preacher, McGarvey's example had also infused the young evangelist with a desire to teach. He wanted nothing more than to return to Lexington as a professor. In April 1897 David Lipscomb and James A. Harding invited Calhoun to an interview in Nashville, Tennessee, hoping to employ him as a teacher in their Nashville Bible School. Calhoun recounted this meeting in detail as part of a sworn deposition given in the Newbern, Tennessee, church-property lawsuit in 1904. Harding insisted that Calhoun cease to preach for congregations using musical instruments in worship; Calhoun had refused. That pronouncement ended any possibility of a teaching appointment for Calhoun in Nashville. In private and public dialogue with Lipscomb and with Louisville evangelist Marshall Clement Kurfees (1856-1931), Calhoun continued to seek a "golden mean" between the arrogance of the innovators and the obstinacy of the resisters.

Calhoun's attempt to bridge the widening breach failed, even as his opportunities for teaching and advanced study multiplied. By 1900 Arvey Glenn Freed (1863-1931) had appointed Calhoun principal of the Bible Department in Georgie Robertson Christian College in Henderson, Tennessee, but Calhoun was already engaged in conversations with McGarvey and his colleagues that would realize his ambition to return to Lexington. In offering Calhoun a teaching appointment, the College of the Bible also agreed to assist him in pursuing graduate theological education. Calhoun received his Bachelor of Divinity degree from Yale in June 1902. From there he and his family moved to Cambridge, Massachusetts, where he pursued a doctorate in Old Testament studies at Harvard Divinity School under the guidance of George Foote Moore, recently arrived from Andover Seminary.

At both Yale and Harvard, Calhoun was immersed in the study of the so-called "higher criticism" of biblical texts. Gifted with immense powers of concentration and recall, boundless energy, rigid discipline, and infinite attention to detail, Calhoun learned his lessons well, passing examinations with honors. However, except for studies of what was then called "elocution" with some of the leading professors of public address, he intended to oppose rather than to use what he learned. His dissertation, more than 700 pages handwritten in ledgers, exhausted the minutia of the Old Latin text of Leviticus. It was an archetype of evasion, carefully constructed to conceal its author's loathing for the discipline he had undertaken to understand, narrowly focused to avoid any suggestion of critical relevance to any matter of faith, even while displaying his mastery of languages and discrete details. Having satisfied his teachers, Calhoun moved his family to Lexington and spoke at the bac-

Though educated at Yale and Harvard in higher critical studies, Hall L. Calhoun (1863-1935) strongly opposed critical methods of biblical study, as did his mentor, J. W. McGarvey. In 1917 as dean of the College of the Bible he was involved in accusing the president, R. H. Crossfield, and several teachers of teaching "destructive criticism." Courtesy of the Center for Restoration Studies, Abilene Christian University

calaureate service of the College of the Bible in June 1904, leaving Harvard to deliver his diploma in the mail.

On returning to Lexington, Calhoun found the aging McGarvey in decline; other members of the faculty he had known soon died or retired. Calhoun functioned as McGarvey's second and assistant and was appointed dean in August 1911, expecting that he would become president upon McGarvey's death, which occurred in October. However, Kentucky University had become, once more, Transylvania University; Richard Henry Crossfield (1868-1951), president of Transylvania, was appointed by the board of the College of the Bible to succeed McGarvey, and became president of both institutions.

Crossfield soon began in hiring, curriculum, and policy a transition from Bible college to mainstream theological seminary. Calhoun, despite his education at Yale and Harvard, was not prepared to make that journey. Yet Calhoun had no taste whatsoever for public controversy and conflict. He might express vehement criticism of certain ideas or persons in private or in the classroom, offering alternative opinions, but in public he was inclined to be a conciliator and peacemaker.

Tensions within the College of the Bible finally exploded into open conflict in March 1917, when a student letter charging Crossfield and several faculty members with professing "destructive criticism" and evolution was published in the *Christian Standard,* along with a lengthy rebuttal from Crossfield. Calhoun first came to the defense of the protesting students in an agonizingly indirect statement: "In response to certain inquiries which have come to me, I feel that candor compels me to state that for more than a year, I have been fully convinced that destructive criticism was being taught in the College of the Bible." The board of the College of the Bible assembled to conduct a hearing of the charges for eight days in May 1917. Calhoun, the dean, now called to present charges against his own faculty, soon found himself on trial. He resigned his office in the evening of the fourth day, and soon left Lexington. The detailed charges he had been unable to present to the board now appeared week after week in the *Christian Standard,* widening and intensifying a schism already under way among Disciples. Calhoun's failed prosecution became a watershed for academic freedom among Disciples of Christ and a call to arms among "Independents" and Churches of Christ.

Thomas Ellsworth Cramblet brought Calhoun to Bethany College with the promise to develop a graduate program in religion, but Cramblett died in 1919, and his successors had neither the money nor the will to continue the experiment. Calhoun continued to teach at Bethany until 1925, growing more restive as he perceived Bethany and the Disciples drifting in the direction that the College of the Bible had taken. In 1924 he began negotiating with Nicholas Brodie Hardeman (1874-1965), whom he had known at Georgie Robertson Christian College at the turn of the century, to join in the administration of its successor, Freed-Hardeman College. After many letters and conversations, which involved not only Hardeman but also M. C. Kurfees and Fletcher Walten Smith (1858-1930), Calhoun agreed to do essentially what Harding and Lipscomb had demanded almost twenty-seven years earlier. He severed all formal connections with Disciples institutions and declared the use of both instrumental music and extra-congregational "societies" to be no longer "expedient" but "sinful." In years to come he would be forced to repeat this recantation again and again.

Calhoun was appointed associate president and head of the Department of Classical Languages and Bible at Freed-Hardeman College. Students responded positively to Calhoun's preaching in the local church and to the content of his Bible teaching, but chafed under his demanding discipline in the dormitories and in his classrooms. By the end of the year Calhoun sank into a severe depression, resigned his position, and moved his family to Nashville.

Calhoun spent a month in a sanitarium. In the depths of that crisis in the summer of 1926, it appeared that he might never preach or teach again. George Bethurum, an elder of the Belmont Church of Christ in Nashville, took in the Calhoun family and saw to their needs. With the daily encouragement of his eldest son, John, Calhoun gradually regained his health, and by autumn he was preaching for the Belmont congregation. Calhoun came to the attention of Nashville businessman Andrew Mizell Burton (1879-1966), a pioneer of urban ministry in Nashville's Central Church of Christ and a conscientious promoter of mass evangelism. By the summer of 1927 Calhoun was preaching daily on Burton's radio station, WLAC, building an audience estimated in the hundreds of thousands at the height of radio's novelty and becoming one of the first effective electronic evangelists of any religious group.

With Burton's support, Calhoun now taught part-time at David Lipscomb College, the heir to Nashville Bible School, where he had once been turned away. There he ignited the scholarly ambitions of future leaders like Frank Pack (1916-1998). At the same time he continued to seek common ground with the people in the Christian Churches with whom he had fought the battle in Lexington. Now firmly opposed to the symbols of "digression" that he had once tolerated in the interest of a broader unity, Calhoun still wanted the fellowship of people he had felt forced to leave behind.

Calhoun's last radio sermon, in September 1935, focused on the words of 2 Timothy 4:6-8: "I have fought the good fight, I have finished the course, I have kept the faith." He died the next day. The ideals of Christian scholarship, Christian education, and Christian unity for which he had lived had eluded him. Calhoun remains a symbol of a troubled generation. Yet he was not without honor in his own time and place. His funeral was moved to the War Memorial Building in Nashville, for no other sanctuary in that city could then hold the thousands who sought to mourn his passing.

See also Bible, Interpretation of the; Freed-Hardeman University; Harding, James Alexander; Lexington Theological Seminary; McGarvey, John W.; Transylvania University

BIBLIOGRAPHY Scott C. Billingsley, "The Newbern Trial: A Study of Restorationism and Primitivism in American Religion" (unpublished M.A. thesis, Middle Tennessee State University, 1996) • H. Leo Boles, "The Newbern Trial: April, 1903 to January, 1905 Dyersburg, Tennessee" (1905) • Adron Doran and Julian E. Choate, *The Christian Scholar: A Biography of Hall Laurie Calhoun* (1985) • Edward Ormand Hale, "A Man in Controversy: Hall Laurie Calhoun" (unpublished M.Div. thesis, Lexington Theological Seminary, 1978) • Don Haymes, "Hall Calhoun and His 'Nashville Brethren,' 1897-1935," *Restoration Quarterly* 27 (First Quarter 1984): 37-48.

DON HAYMES

Calvinism

1. The Rise and Development of Calvinism
2. Calvinism and the Stone-Campbell Movement

Strictly speaking, the term *Calvinism* refers to the theology of John Calvin (1509-1564), French-born leader of the Protestant Reformation in Geneva, Switzerland. The term is used more often as a label for churches and theologies representative of the direct or continuing influence of Calvin's teachings. Hence the word is a common, though inexact, synonym for the "Reformed church heritage" as distinct from the Lutheran, Anglican, and Anabaptist or "free church" traditions of the Reformation.

1. The Rise and Development of Calvinism

During his university studies Calvin moved from Catholicism to Christian humanism and then "evangelical" (gospel-centered) convictions. Fleeing persecution in France, he emerged as a Reformation leader first in Geneva (1536-39), then in Strassburg, with Martin Bucer and others committed to a "reformed church" (1539-41), and thereafter again in Geneva. As head of Geneva's company of pastors, he sought to formulate a wholly biblical theology, transform the city into a model of Christian faithfulness, encourage Swiss and other reformers to join in common cause, and promote the growth of churches "reformed" by their conformity to the doctrine, church order, practices, and ethics of the Word of God as set forth in Scripture.

Calvin's theology was that of a second-generation reformer, both a synthesis and a rethinking of themes prominent in emergent Protestantism. These included the preeminent authority of the Scriptures over church traditions and human wisdom; the universality and depth of human sin; the sovereignty of God, and of God's saving mercy in Jesus Christ; justification by grace through faith rather than works righteousness; and the joint roles of Scripture and the Spirit's power for conversion and faithfulness. Among the distinguishing marks of Calvinist reform were emphasis on the continuities between the Old Testament and New Testament; the identification of baptism and the eucharist as sacramental means and "signs and seals" of grace ordained by Christ, and the "spiritual presence" of Christ in the eucharist; the use of biblical moral commands as guidelines for sanctification following justification; the necessity of individual and church discipline for holiness; and shared governance of the church by councils of ministers and laity.

Institutes of the Christian Religion was Calvin's magnum opus and the single most influential text for Calvinism's ongoing development, although the impact of Calvin's writings on Reformed theology generally led to variations and offshoots of Calvinism independent of Calvin scholarship per se. The spread of Reformed Protestantism and the many generations of Calvin interpreters in diverse contexts have made "Calvinism" a moving target of historical study. The late sixteenth and seventeenth centuries saw the rise of scholastic systems of Calvinist orthodoxy, sometimes linked and sometimes at odds with grassroots movements of devotional and moral fervor, for example, precisionism in the Netherlands and Puritanism in Great Britain. Elaborations and reapplications of Calvin's views during this era in effect gave "Calvinism" new definition. Emphasis on covenantal relations between God and God's people became one signature theme. Predestination was yet another. Indeed, based on the canons of the Reformed Synod of Dort (1618) and similar, although modified, teachings in the Westminster Assembly's Confession and Catechisms (1640s), predestinarianism gained widespread recognition as the touchstone of Calvinist orthodoxy. In the battle against Arminianism, the shorthand for high Calvinism in the seventeenth century became the "five points" of the famous TULIP acrostic: (1) total depravity; (2) unconditional election; (3) limited atonement; (4) irresistible grace; and (5) the perseverance of the saints.

Eighteenth-century Calvinism was roiled by disputes over Pietism, the Enlightenment, and church-state relations. Whether to tighten or relax now "traditional" standards of doctrine and order — and how to enforce such changes — were controversial, frequently church-dividing issues in an age when revivalism, "conversion experiences," and disciplinary rigor competed with rational religion, freedom of inquiry and conscience, and staid moralism. With the nineteenth century came forceful reformulations of Calvinist orthodoxy by Abraham Kuyper and Herman Bavinck in the Netherlands, Auguste Lecerf in France, and "the Princeton school" theologians in the United States (Charles Hodge et al.). Neoconfessionalists of the day, however, faced ever-growing challenge from those who wished to free Reformed theology, including Calvinism, from its scholastic-era forms, recover its biblical and historic essentials, and revamp its message and mission in light of the advances and urgent needs of modern culture. Diverse moderate, mediating, and liberal theologians were revisionist Calvinists of this sort, for example, Friedrich Schleiermacher and Ernst Troeltsch in Germany, John McLeod Campbell in Scotland, and in America the Mercersburg theologians John W. Nevin and Philip Schaff, the Congregationalist Horace Bushnell, and advocates of progressive orthodoxy. New cross-currents of Calvinist-Reformed theology emerged with twentieth-century neo-orthodoxy and a "renaissance" of Calvin study, and came to expression in the writings of Karl Barth, Emil Brunner, and the American brothers Reinhold and H. Richard Niebuhr.

2. Calvinism and the Stone-Campbell Movement

The earliest leaders of the Stone-Campbell Movement were former Presbyterians (mainly Seceder Presbyterians) thoroughly familiar with the principal tenets of Calvinist theology as enshrined in the Westminster Confession and conveyed through the various Presbyterian and Puritan traditions in Britain and America. Their reaction to this theological heritage has occasionally been stereotyped as categorically negative (see Hatch 1989). In truth their response to Calvinism was multileveled and multifaceted. Reformed hermeneutical and theological insights, after all, were basic to their intellectual formation. Thomas Campbell's thinking on inferential reasoning in the interpretation of Scripture, for example, owed much to the legacy of the Westminster Divines. Barton Stone read Calvinist sources in his formal preparation for Presbyterian ministry, albeit through an increasingly critical lens. Alexander Campbell and others saw value in the covenant theology of the Dutch Reformed scholar Johannes Cocceius as an attempt to mitigate the doctrine of divine election and to establish a more dynamic understanding of the economy of redemption. Early Stone-Campbell theology is replete with language borrowed from the Reformed heritage, including the description of salvation as "enjoyment" of the benefits of divine grace.

Historically, however, the Stone-Campbell Movement's posture toward Calvinism took shape not in dispassionate academic discussion but in the highly charged competitive and polemical atmosphere in which the Movement forged itself. On occasion the Movement's early leaders targeted the "high" Calvinism of scholastic Puritanism and Presbyterianism, but the Calvinism they engaged most frequently was the more moderate version of the frontier. This hybrid Calvinism had two important influences. One was the Common Sense philosophy that had deeply affected Presbyterians, Congregationalists, and Baptists alike with its emphasis on free will and the prerogatives of rational human judgment. The other was the fluid religious culture of frontier revivalism in which, amid the prevailing preoccupation with the conversion experience, the preaching of divine sovereignty and human incapacity had begun to be tempered by new emphases on proactive means of grace and on the believer's responsibility to cooperate in the working out of salvation.

This moderating trend did not go unnoticed. Alexander Campbell wrote in 1830 that "the standard of orthodoxy [among Presbyterians] is lowering; and . . . a more liberal and rational system of theology is prevailing among them; and we are confident that it must continue to prevail." Recognizing that Calvinism was being increasingly "arminianized," he quipped in 1836, "we have 'moderate calvinism' as the sediment of the old *opus operatum* of John Wesley, and the absolute fate of John [Calvin] of Geneva." An anonymous writer observed in Stone's *Christian Messenger* in 1828 that the new Calvinism consisted precisely in keeping the "peculiar [five] points" hidden in order to avoid controversy.

Stone-Campbell leaders regularly joined in the lampooning of the old system of "TULIP" Calvinism, which they caricatured as just another bankrupt "ism," a pedantry unbecoming of the gospel. Barton Stone told in his autobiography of having abandoned the "labyrinth of Calvinism" to enter the "rich pastures of gospel liberty." Alexander Campbell, too, reproved the Calvinism he had learned as a youth, explaining in 1830 that "the good effects of memorizing the New Testament were neutralized by the trash which the 'Westminster Divines' had obliged me to interlard with it." He also conveniently stereotyped Calvinism in its "antinomian" extreme, amplifying its emphasis on predestination in order to show how it undermined Christian evangelism and ethics alike. Such rhetoric, as Nathan Hatch has shown, was not uncommon in frontier religious culture where the parodying of outworn theological systems thrived.

Yet the criticism ran deeper. Historically Calvinism's alleged theological sophistication had, in Alexander Campbell's judgment, been bought at the price of fomenting division. He blamed it in *The Christian System* for producing ten different sects within the Presbyterian tradition alone. What is more, the Calvinism of the frontier, the Calvinism Campbell confronted both in his association with Baptists and in his early debates with Presbyterians John Walker, William Maccalla, and Nathan Rice, was flawed in its whole understanding of the *ordo salutis,* the orderly process of salvation. Not only had Presbyterian Calvinism tried in vain to justify infant baptism on a faulty alignment of old and new covenants, specifically a faulty typology of circumcision, but it had confounded the whole process of conversion and regeneration by dissociating the operations of the Spirit from the converting Word, and by relegating the *regenerative* work of the Holy Spirit to the dramatic bestowal of saving faith rather than to the baptism of the conscious believer, the "bath of regeneration" (Tit. 3:5). In the Rice debate, probably the most extensive exposition of his criticism of Calvinism, Campbell summarized his grievance: "I, therefore, *ex animo,* repudiate their whole theory of mystic influence, and metaphysical regeneration, as a vision of visions, a dream of dreams, at war with philosophy, with the philosophy of mind, with the Bible, with reason, with common sense, and with all Christian experience."

Alexander Campbell and his associates continually insisted that their Movement had risen above the fray of current theological conflicts. Campbell wrote in the 1834 *Millennial Harbinger:* "We have no wish or inclination to prove Calvinism or Arminianism to be true. We only say that neither of them is the gospel which Peter preached. . . . The effects of [our] preaching differ from the effects of Calvinist and Arminian preaching as much as these systems differ from the Apostles." Yet as the internal theological differences between Campbell's Disciples and Stone's Christians began to sink in, and as the maturing Movement confronted the need for a more constructive engagement with the theological systems of the day in order to establish its own identity, the tone changed somewhat. As early as 1835, in an article on "The Crisis" of identity in the *Millennial Harbinger,* Campbell expressed his concern that the Movement was being stereotyped simply as one of militant anti-Calvinism or anti-Trinitarianism. In a much more irenic tone, he mused that "Calvinism, as a system of religious philosophy, taken as a whole, in the moderated tone of the present century, is, perhaps, as good a system of religious philosophy as arminianism. At all events, if I could dissect my own speculations, I opine there would be more of John Calvin than of James Arminius in my moral philosophy; and I think it is so with the great majority of all our public advocates so far as I am intimately acquainted with their opinions." Campbell went on again to state that the battles between Calvinism and Arminianism need not be revisited in his Movement, since its purpose was "contending for Bibleism against all other *isms* ancient and modern"; yet he had conceded a certain dependence on the broad Reformed heritage with its unmistakable commitment to God's justifying and transforming grace and its interest in the material, covenantal manifestation of the kingdom of God on earth. Elsewhere, however, it was clear that, consciously or unconsciously, the teaching of Barton Stone and the Campbells — especially on the role of free will in cooperating with divine grace — tilted more toward Arminianism. Alexander Campbell's own views on the atonement owed much to the Dutch Arminian theologian Hugo Grotius.

Thomas Campbell was more explicit than his son

in acknowledging a debt to the Reformed theological tradition. His reverence for the Westminster Confession as a catechetical tool, if not a test of fellowship, was obvious in the *Declaration and Address* (1809). When he entered the debate over the atonement with Barton Stone and with various outsiders to the Stone-Campbell Movement, he vigorously defended the doctrine of substitution much maligned by the rationalists but cherished in classical Calvinist soteriology. When describing human sinfulness, Thomas Campbell used the language of human nature's "guilt," "depravity," and "perishing condition." And as Robert Richardson reports in his *Memoirs of Alexander Campbell,* during the exoneration of Aylett Raines, an evangelist who held Universalist convictions, the elder Campbell betrayed his own loyalty to Reformed teaching on the final judgment: "[Mr. Raines] is philosophically a Restorationist [Universalist] and I am a Calvinist, but notwithstanding this difference of opinion between us, I would put my right hand into the fire and have it burnt off before I would hold up my hands against him."

If some of the Stone-Campbell Movement's early leaders could be claimed as critical insiders to the Reformed heritage, subsequent generations in the Movement saw themselves as definite outsiders. Disciples conservatives and forbears of the Churches of Christ, in particular, continued the early leaders' polemic against Calvinist doctrines of election, conversion, and regeneration, with little new being added to the Campbellian arsenal. Benjamin Franklin publicly debated the issue of predestination with Presbyterian minister James Matthews in Cincinnati in 1852, arguing, among other things, that the "elect" ("us") mentioned by Paul in Ephesians 1:4-12 were none other than the prophets and apostles, on whom God conferred the true mystery of predestination, that is, his plan for *all* humanity to hear and receive the gospel. T. W. Brents offered a full critique of Calvinist soteriology in his influential work, *The Gospel Plan of Salvation* (1889). In the twentieth century as well, internal controversies arose in Churches of Christ over the incursion of allegedly "Neo-Calvinist" notions of grace and justification. K. C. Moser, a minister and writer in Churches of Christ in Texas and Oklahoma, was stereotyped a "Calvinist" by critics for teaching that the righteousness of Christ was not simply transferred to the believer for fulfilling the outlined conditions of the "plan of salvation" but "imputed" to the one who puts simple personal trust in the crucified Christ.

Although conservative Disciples at the turn of the twentieth century broadly shared with Old School Presbyterians a commitment to the Common Sense hermeneutic (with its emphasis on the static character of revelation as opposed to new "evolutionary" paradigms), and some, like J. W. McGarvey, sympathized with the doctrine of the plenary verbal inspiration (and inerrancy) of the Bible upheld by Reformed fundamentalists, they fiercely maintained that their restoration of apostolic Christianity precluded mingling with "human" systems like Calvinism. From a quite different perspective, Disciples liberals saw the old Calvinism as passé because, in the dawning ecumenical age, all creedal systems were happily collapsing.

Later in the twentieth century, a handful of Disciples theologians sought constructively to engage Reformed neo-orthodoxy in representative figures like Karl Barth and Emil Brunner. Frederick Kershner, William Robinson, and others looked favorably on Barth's understanding of the *personal* communication of the Word of God "enacted" and not simply spoken in the biblical revelation. They suggested that such had been anticipated already in the thought of Thomas and Alexander Campbell with their emphasis on God's person manifested through Mighty Acts, the "gospel facts" as the Campbells termed them.

Of late, Christian Churches/Churches of Christ and Churches of Christ have had the most consistent interaction with the mainstream of American Evangelicalism, with its strong roots in the Reformed theological tradition. On occasion congregations have found common cause with Baptists, conservative Presbyterians, Evangelical Free Churches, and other "Calvinist" denominations in everything from the sharing of Sunday School curricula to involvements in the Pro-Life movement. With few exceptions, however, such interaction has not been accompanied by serious theological engagement, other than occasional exchanges on issues like biblical authority and inerrancy.

See also Anthropology; Atonement; Baptists; Campbell-Rice Debate; Conversion; Covenant (Federal) Theology; Presbyterians, Presbyterianism; Regeneration; Theology — Nineteenth Century

BIBLIOGRAPHY Paul M. Blowers, "Neither Calvinists nor Arminians, but Simply Christians: The Stone-Campbell Movement as a Theological Resistance Movement," *Lexington Theological Quarterly* 35 (2000): 133-54 • T. W. Brents, *The Gospel Plan of Salvation* (1889) • Alexander Campbell and Nathan L. Rice, *A Debate Between Rev. A. Campbell and Rev. N. L. Rice on the Action, Subject, Design and Administrator of Christian Baptism* (1844) • James O. Duke, "The Nineteenth Century Reformation in Historical-Theological Perspective: The First One Hundred Years," in *Christian Faith Seeking Historical Understanding: Essays in Honor of H. Jack Forstman,* ed. James O. Duke and Anthony L. Dunnavant (1997), pp. 159-86 • Benjamin Franklin and James Matthews, *Predestination, and the Foreknowledge of God: A Discussion* (1852) • Nathan O. Hatch, *The Democratization of American Christianity* (1989) • John T.

McNeill, *The History and Character of Calvinism* (1954) • William J. Richardson, *The Role of Grace in the Thought of Alexander Campbell* (1991) • Tom Roberts, *Neo-Calvinism in the Church of Christ* (1980) • Barton W. Stone, with John Rogers, *A Biography of Elder Barton Warren Stone* • D. Newell Williams, *Barton Stone: A Spiritual Autobiography* (2000).

PAUL M. BLOWERS *and* JAMES O. DUKE

Campbell, Alexander (1788-1866)

Founder in 1809 with his father Thomas Campbell of a movement to unite Christians on the basis of the restoration of primitive Christianity. In 1832 this movement united with the Barton W. Stone movement to form the Stone-Campbell Movement.

1. Introduction: "The Greatest Promoter of This Reformation"

When Alexander Campbell died in Bethany, West Virginia, in 1866, he had long been acknowledged as the "greatest promoter of this reformation." He was one of its founders and had been its recognized leader for more than half a century. It was by then a respectable community that numbered upwards of half a million, and it enjoyed considerable international outreach. He was its representative speaker and debater. His journals and books reflected its ideals and mission. It could be said that the Movement was his alter ego.

Campbell was as well known as any religious figure of the mid-frontier between 1830 and 1860. He traveled widely and attracted large crowds. More imposing than handsome, he stood almost six feet tall and bore the mien of a cultured European. He was urbane, intellectual, and eloquent. Those who heard him described him as "the master of assemblies."

1.1. Speaker and Preacher

In keeping with his times, it was not unusual for him to speak for two or three hours — and without notes. Well read in the classics as well as history, literature, philosophy, and religion, he ranged widely over various areas of knowledge in his discourses, whatever the subject. He lectured nearly as easily on moral philosophy, the Anglo-Saxon language, the amelioration of society, phrenology, scientific farming, and the American republic as upon the Scriptures. He addressed skeptics as well as believers, and politicians as well as educators. His consuming themes, by both voice and pen, had to do with what he called "the new reformation" and "the ancient order of things."

While given to redundancy as a speaker as well as a writer, he was seldom, if ever, boring. While always serious, he was pleasant and affable. He was never given to levity in the pulpit. He was not a storyteller in the usual sense, and he did not talk about himself. He was always informative, usually interesting, and occasionally scintillating.

A Presbyterian minister — who heard him out of curiosity and with a critical ear — conceded that Campbell's discourse on Psalm 24, which was in exaltation of the risen Christ, was the most impressive

Portrait of Alexander Campbell by William Cogswell c. 1840.
Courtesy of Bethany College

display of divine eloquence he had ever heard. James Madison, former U.S. president — who often heard Campbell while they served together at the 1829 Virginia Constitutional Convention — revealed that he considered Alexander Campbell the best expositor of the Scriptures he had ever heard.

A common response from his auditors was that they were unconscious of time, however long he spoke, and they were impressed that he was as poised in the pulpit as if he were in his own parlor. Those who expected eloquent oratory were surprised to find him conversational in tone and quiet in demeanor. Despite his erudition, he was disarmingly plain and simple. Once positioned before an audience, he never moved from that position — not even during a two- or three-hour discourse. In his latter years he would lean slightly on a cane that he took with him to the pulpit. His gestures were few, but he did sometimes emphasize a point with a sharp rap of his cane against the floor. He would also on occasion, in urging a point, bring his hand down lightly on his closed Bible on the lectern before him.

He trusted the common person to comprehend his most seminal and profound concepts. He did not save his groundbreaking ideas for educators or the clergy, but freely shared them with the rank and file. He did not have one message for the elite and another for the ordinary folk. He wrote and spoke as if he would be understood by all. He was a man for all seasons and for all people. Whether in a mansion in New Orleans or a coal miner's shack in Kentucky, his manner was the same.

While we have few of his sermons — perhaps because he put few in print — his numerous travel letters, published in his journals, reveal some things about his preaching. One of his favorite sermons was "The Sun of Righteousness," based on Malachi 4:2, in which he treated God's revelation as a progressive unveiling of light. There was first the starlight age (Patriarchal), then the moonlight age (Mosaic), then the twilight age (John the Baptist), and at last the sunlight age (Christian) that brought the Messiah as the sun of righteousness.

This was vintage Campbell. He preferred wide-ranging discourses that sought to integrate the various tributaries of God's disclosure of God's purposes. Another frequent topic was "The Philanthropy of God," which, while based on John 3:16, was a broad sweep of Scripture in reference to what God has done for humanity. This was the sermon he gave before statesmen from both houses of Congress and their families in the House chamber in 1850. This has incorrectly been described as a sermon delivered before a called joint-session of Congress.

1.2. Reaction and Opposition

Campbell had such a reputation by this time that a former president of Amherst College wrote of him in 1850: "Mr. Campbell has for more than twenty years wielded a power over men's minds, on the subject of religion, which has no parallel in the Protestant history of this country, nor of the Romish either." He went on to say that no one else had ever made such inroads into other denominations. He explained that this was due, as he saw it, to Campbell's rare combination of talents, which he listed as: a great knowledge of human nature, a superior education, smooth and captivating eloquence as a preacher, a skilled debater, an untiring industry of his pen and press, and his vast personal acquaintance in his wide circuits.

But he had his antagonists. J. B. Jeter, a prominent Virginia Baptist, wrote disparagingly of him in 1855 in *Campbellism Examined,* a widely acclaimed exposure of the errors of "the current reformation." A few years later — following a visit with Campbell in Richmond — Jeter gave his opinion of the reformer in a Baptist journal. He allowed that Campbell was a good man and that the principles he advocated were right in the main, but that he was visionary, erratic, and unpredictable. Moreover, he so often and so glaringly contradicted himself that he could only conclude that there was "a screw loose in his mental machinery." This became more evident as Campbell grew older, Jeter insisted, until it terminated in "downright monomania." Employing the derogatory tag of "Campbellism," one Baptist journal remarked that the Movement was "spreading like a mighty contagion through the Western states, wasting Zion in its progress." It complained that "one-half of the Baptist churches in Ohio have embraced its sentiments," and added, "In Kentucky its desolations are even greater than in Ohio."

Campbell usually responded to his critics. Concerning the term Campbellism, he rejoined, "Men fond of nicknaming are usually weak in reason, argument, and proof." As for Jeter, the response in part was, "Our brother Jeter — *Brother,* did I say? Yes, and I will not erase it, our brother Jeter. . . ." He did not pass up a chance to show that he could disagree with persons and still accept them as brothers or sisters — a basic principle of his plea for reformation.

1.3. Diverse Interests

His interests were vast and diverse. He served as postmaster of the village of Bethany. With the accompanying franking rights he sent out free of charge over several decades nearly a million copies of his journals, books, Bibles, and hymnals.

While at first reluctant, he entered politics long enough to serve as a delegate to the 1829 Virginia Constitutional Convention. He was also reluctant to debate, but eventually concluded that in some ways a week of debating was more effective than a year of preaching. He had five public debates that were published in book form and several written discussions.

Considering that his father was an educator before him, it is not surprising that he was committed to education. Not only did he operate a boys' school in his home as early as 1818, but he founded a college on his own farm in 1840. He not only served the college as professor, treasurer, and president for a quarter of a century, but helped fund it in its early years with his own money. Along the way, he worked out an impressive philosophy of education that became the source of numerous lectures across the country.

It was hardly predictable that he would be an entrepreneur, something his father was not. Starting with 140 acres of land that his father-in-law had given to him and his wife to keep them from migrating to Ohio, he eventually owned 1,500 acres. He bought land as far west as Indiana. Part of the campus of Indiana University was once owned by Alexander Campbell, and most of the campus of Bethany College was once part of the Campbell farm.

On those fertile acres he raised merino sheep imported from his native Ireland, which proved profitable. He was active in the American Wool Growers Association. He corresponded with John Brown, the abolitionist, who was also a wool grower. They had a common interest in defending the rights of the wool growers, which they believed were threatened by the wool buyers. But Campbell did not share Brown's abolitionist views, even though he was anti-slavery and freed his own slaves.

Members of the Campbell family, including Alexander and Selina, pictured here in the front yard of their Bethany home. Courtesy of Bethany College

He also farmed those acres, doing some of the work himself, especially in his earlier years. Virtually all the food served at the family table, which included many guests, was raised on the farm. The food was prepared by hired help, and, until they were freed, slaves.

He became known not only for his journals and debates, but also as a translator of the New Testament. His *Living Oracles* — the name it assumed, but actually published as "The Sacred Writings of the Apostles and Evangelists of Jesus Christ, Commonly Called the New Testament, Translated from the Original Greek" — was actually a revision of an earlier English translation. He later translated in full the book of Acts for the American Bible Union's version of the New Testament.

He was even a hymnologist, though he could hardly carry a tune. He published *Psalms, Hymns, and Spiritual Songs, Original and Selected,* with 511 entries — lyrics only — four of which he composed. It too went through several editions, and, like most of his publications, was financially profitable.

1.4. Wealth and Grief

He became quite wealthy. His estate was valued at nearly $200,000, which would be several millions by today's count. His will favored the heirs of his "second family," leading to its being challenged in court and reflecting alienation in Campbell's own family, surely a source of grief to Campbell in his later years.

But Campbell was no stranger to grief. He lost his first wife when he was but thirty-eight, and eventually buried ten of his fourteen children — "six of them daughters, all young mothers," he lamented. The bitterest loss of all, however, was the drowning death of his highly promising, 10-year-old son Wickliffe in 1847 when the reformer was in Britain. It afflicted the family with "superlative severity," as Campbell described it.

The Civil War compounded his sorrows. It not only divided his adopted country — which he had envisioned as the sanctuary of "the millennial church" — but it threatened the welfare of his reformation, especially in the South. It was a sad day when he could no longer send mail to his vast constituency in the Southern states. And once the war was over, he had to witness the trial of his son, Alexander Campbell, Jr., in nearby Wellsburg, who was accused of treason against the United States after serving as an officer in the Confederate Army. Although the son was pardoned by the president, it further intensified the pain of his aging father.

His response to these losses was reflective of his piety and spirituality. As for the loss of Wickliffe, known for his "precocious piety," Campbell admitted that he had never been afraid of evil tidings, but "in this case God thought good to take to himself the choicest lamb from my flock, and has not revealed to me the reason why." But God is too wise to err and too kind to afflict his children without cause, he concluded. While God's ways cannot be traced, he ventured that Wickliffe was "drafted" due to his unique character to serve elsewhere in God's vast universe.

1.5. Personal Piety: A Principle of Reformation

He dealt with the mystery of the premature death of exemplary Christians in pietistic terms. "We must not think it strange," he wrote following Wickliffe's death, "if God will make all saints after death ministers of mercy or of public utility in some of the grand departments of this stupendous universe." He went on to suggest that God needs noble souls to minister elsewhere in the universe as much as he needs angels to serve on planet earth. He was enough of a Calvinist to acknowledge God's complete sovereignty over all his creation. God never acts without purpose in the life of his children.

He included piety in his "essential attributes of the proposed reformation." Reformation was not merely doctrinal but personal, and he insisted that "We all need reformation." When he listed his "principal articles," he included: "More piety and devotion — more power and praise — more private meditation and communion with God, than appears to obtain amongst the great mass of those called Christians." He also called for self-denial and strict self-government.

He appears to have been as pious as he was intellectual, which was part of his endowment from his deeply spiritual father and his Calvinistic upbringing. There were morning and evening devotionals in his home. His children memorized and quoted Scripture in the family circle. They sang and prayed together, and he talked to them of eternal verities in the simplest terms, drawing illustrations from things they understood. One visitor to the family circle tells how Campbell on one occasion stretched out his hand before the children, referred to it as an example of God's majestic handiwork, and proceeded to point out amazing facts about the mechanism of the hand. Regarding the advantages of private prayer, he once wrote that prayer implies more than we express, even more than we are able to express. It implies that God hears what is to human ears inaudible whispers, and "he reads what we ourselves cannot read — the language of our agonies and unutterable sighs and emotions."

While he preferred kneeling in both private and public prayer, he granted that standing was "Divinely sanctioned" for both prayer and praise — including lifting up holy hands. It was when he saw congregations *sitting* in prayer that he was indignant — "a heart-chilling and soul-paralyzing spectacle." "Sitting worshipers are lazy-bodies," he complained, noting that if angels cast their crowns before the Lamb of God, we should be willing to submit our bodies in his presence. He applied this to giving thanks at the table at home. To "sit and address God is most indecorous and disorderly," except for physical disability. "Shall a man arise to speak to a respectable friend, and sit down to thank God for his daily repasts?" he asked.

1.6. The Jovial "Bishop"

He was not as solemn and austere as he is sometimes depicted. Around Bethany he was seen as the jovial and friendly "Bishop." He was sometimes seen in public in old farm clothes and a beat-up white hat, and he was known to wear jeans in the pulpit. He had a hearty appetite and slept soundly for seven hours each night, but was usually up by 4 AM in order to get in sixteen hours of work and study. He worked in the fields and repaired fences like any other farmer. He talked with his fellow farmers about their mutual problems. And on an 1858 visit to Washington he was the dinner guest of President James Buchanan in the White House, where he was equally at home.

When he was 71 he anticipated travel as if he were half that age, and with the spirit of a poet: "We promise ourselves, the Lord willing, a visit to Iowa when the birds are singing, and the Prairie flowers are blooming in all their loveliness and beauty." In the same travel letter he wrote of "those grand Christian excellencies" which prepare and purify the heart, and make it suitable for "the pure and Holy Spirit that condescends to become a guest in the Christian's bosom." It may have been this concern to make his body a temple of the Spirit that led him to give up tobacco.

He had a sense of humor. While a house guest in Scotland, he bounded down the stairs on one occasion singing, "The Campbells are coming, Aha, Aha!" When a skeptic challenged him with, "Would you have me trust in the bare, bare, naked truth?" he retorted with, "Yes, as naked as two bares can make it!" When asked about what he thought of growing old, he said, "Well, considering the alternative. . . ." In defense of a crying baby, he granted that wailing was not his favorite music, but that the baby should be listened to, for it was claiming its rights: "There are rights for men, rights for women, and baby rights!"

One gets an on-the-scene view of his good humor amidst difficulty when he was speaking in Martinsville, Indiana, in 1851, and was disturbed by crying babies. There were "some fifteen parts rending the air," and he was so overwhelmed that, "Cried down, I sat down." He called on John O'Kane — who was traveling with him and who had a powerful voice — to speak in his place. As O'Kane spoke, the babies were "allured into a speculative silence." With the babies quiet, O'Kane motioned for Campbell to resume his subject. But he no more than began when the babies resumed their wailing, all in concert! With the mothers at their wit's end, and with no one willing to give way, "I confessed myself wholly vanquished, drew to a close, and dismissed the assembly."

Campbell's joy of living was rooted in his profound expectations of what God was about to do in and through America. That he named his journal *The Millennial Harbinger* is evidence of this. Especially in his earlier years Campbell actually believed that a millennial reign of peace and righteousness was in the offing, including a united church with America at its center. He saw his Movement as a harbinger to that end. He often gave expression to a favorite motto: "Expect great things, attempt great things, and great things will follow."

2. The Formative Years: Born of Calvinist Piety (1788-1807)

2.1. Family Background

Alexander Campbell was born to Thomas and Jane Corneigle Campbell on September 12, 1788, near Ballymena in the parish of Broughshane, County Antrim, Ireland. Thomas was by lineage an Argyle Scot, and Jane descended from the French Huguenots. Thomas was of medium stature and handsome, while Jane was tall, erect, and "remarkably retiring in her disposition and manners." In a memoir to his mother in his old age, Alexander described her as "the beau ideal of the Christian mother," and regardless of all the hardships she had to bear he never heard her complain.

He esteemed his father not only the best teacher he ever knew, but the most pious as well. He was devoted to and never neglected the spiritual disciplines. When the father was widowed, aged, and blind, he lived with his son in Bethany. Alexander was sometimes in his father's presence when he was unaware that anyone was around. He would often be whispering a psalm or quietly singing a hymn, interspersed with cries of "Glory be to God." He saw his father as constantly in the presence of God.

Alexander and his six younger siblings grew up in a home with "a family altar." Morning and evening there were prayers, singing, and recitation of memorized Scripture. Later in life he credited both of his parents with urging him to memorize large portions of the Bible. Once he had a family of his own, he carried on the "family altar" tradition, long a part of strict Calvinist piety.

2.2. Early Education

Except for brief periods in a grammar school and an academy conducted by his uncles, Alexander was "home schooled" by his father. While as a young man he was more interested in sports than study, he eventually cultivated an insatiable appetite for books and ideas. He developed a remarkably retentive memory, which might explain how he could discourse for hours without notes. He memorized not only large portions of Scripture, but hymns and choice selections from world literature, especially the British poets. He also studied Latin, French, Greek, and moral philosophy, especially John Locke, whose ideas on civil and religious liberty substantially influenced his thinking. He also began a lifelong interest in John Milton.

His father grew up an Anglican but eventually became an ordained minister in the Seceder Presbyterian Church. To supplement his meager income, he conducted private schools in his own home or in the homes of others, there being no public schools. When in 1804 he started a school in Rich Hill near Armagh in northern Ireland, Alexander, then 16, was academically prepared to serve as his assistant. Some of his siblings were among his students. He soon gained a reputation as an excellent teacher, and was largely responsible for the school's growing enrollment.

In 1798 his father had become pastor of the Ahorey Presbyterian Church a few miles from Rich Hill. It was a church destined to play a significant role in Campbell history. It now has a tower that honors Thomas Campbell and a stained-glass window that memorializes Alexander Campbell.

2.3. Earliest Religious Experiences

Becoming a teacher was a turning point in young Campbell's life. While he was still taking advanced studies from his father, he was coming into his own. In his late teens he began to take both life and religion more seriously. While his father was urging him to consider the ministry, he was struggling with his religious faith. Unsure of his own salvation, he walked in secluded places and prayed for some assurance of pardon.

From the time he first began to read the Bible he believed in Jesus as the Christ, but he did not have the feeling of his salvation that he supposed he should have. This caused him great distress of soul, and he had "the awakenings of a guilty conscience." Recalling this in later life, he wrote, "Finally, after many strugglings, I was able to put my trust in the Saviour, and to feel my reliance on him as the only Saviour of sinners." This gave him the peace he sought. He remembered that it never entered his head to investigate the subject of baptism, which, after a few more years, would demand much of his attention.

Once he was received as a member of the Ahorey Presbyterian Church, he began to take more seriously his father's desire that he devote himself to the ministry. He entered an extensive study of theology and church history. At the outset he was disturbed by things in the religious world that were to challenge him for the rest of his life — ignorance, superstition, priest-ridden oppression, and particularly divisions among Christians.

His father had borne such concerns for years. He had sought to restore peace among the factions in his own Seceder church to no avail. He was also grieved that church doctrines were related more to creeds than to the Bible. And he was so concerned to instill spiritual discipline and to nurture people in the Scriptures that his church at Ahorey became known as the best educated in the presbytery. But his efforts — particularly his attempt to unite the warring Seceder factions — not only were unappreciated but brought painful opposition. His son was later to explain that his father's failure was the result of having attempted the impossible, a reformation within the Seceder sects.

2.4. Thomas's Migration to America

Besides such discouragement, Thomas Campbell's health grew delicate. His doctor advised a lengthy sea voyage. He decided to sail to America — not only for health's sake, but to search out what might possibly be a new home for his family in the New World. If it worked out, the family would join him. Alexander, almost 19, would administer the school, continue his private studies, and help his mother care for the children.

Thomas Campbell embarked at Londonderry, Ireland, on the ship *Brutus* for Philadelphia on April 8, 1807. It was another turning point in the Campbell story. Thomas would soon have experiences on the American frontier that would lay the groundwork for the movement that he and his son would lead. At Rich Hill, with a covey of children at his feet, Alexander could hardly have imagined what was destined for him — some of it soon.

3. Called to Be a Reformer (1807-23)

3.1. Experiences in Scotland

Thomas Campbell was in America for fifteen months before he finally decided that there was a future for him and his family in the New World. He had problems with leaders of the Seceder church in America similar to those he had back home, and he had difficulty locating an appropriate situation for the family. But he had met new friends, some of whom encouraged him in his efforts to effect change in the church, and he saw exciting challenges on a new frontier.

He sent word for the family to join him in time for them to board the *Hibernia* at Londonderry for Philadelphia on October 1, 1808. Alexander had turned 20 the month before. After two days at sea the ship went aground in a storm near an island of the Hebrides. While probably no one was in any real danger, it seemed so at the time. They made it to shore safely, and Alexander was able to save his father's books. More significantly, the trauma of the near-tragedy at sea settled the question of his life's calling. He resolved that stormy night that he would follow in the steps of his father and devote himself to the service of the church as a minister of the gospel.

Since they were not able to book passage on another ship until the following summer, the family took lodgings in Glasgow. This enabled Alexander to attend Glasgow University, which was then at the zenith of its fame. It was, moreover, the university his father had attended. He took courses with two professors who had taught his father twenty-five years earlier.

The 300 days he spent in Glasgow appear providential, for he had experiences both in the university and in the area churches that were to influence his life's work substantially. His studies at the university included Greek, literature, French, and philosophy. The latter course exposed him to the Common Sense philosophy that pervaded the Scottish universities at the time and that was to help shape his interpretation of Scripture.

In the area churches he was exposed to various reformation efforts that were going on within the

Church of Scotland, the state church. These included Independents affiliated with John Glas and Robert Sandeman and a movement led by James and Robert Haldane. These movements had separated from the state church mainly over the independence of each congregation and the freedom of private interpretation of Scripture. They had in view the restoration of primitive Christianity.

Alexander especially identified with Greville Ewing, pastor of a large independent church in Glasgow that was reflective of the changes taking place. It was in small gatherings in Ewing's home where lively issues were freely discussed that he began to take the issues of reformation seriously.

The changes that Ewing called for included weekly Communion, the Bible to the exclusion of human creeds, congregational autonomy, plurality of elders in each church, the rights of lay ministers, the rejection of clerical privilege, and the practice of mutual ministry. Ewing also held the view that faith is based on testimony rather than being supernaturally induced.

These views were to serve as foundation stones for Campbell's efforts in America. But they did not include baptism by immersion. When the Haldanes finally adopted this view, Ewing disagreed, insisting that infant sprinkling was scriptural. Campbell's high regard for Ewing may help explain his reluctance to adopt baptism by immersion.

Nor did the Scottish reformers include unity as part of their reformation. This was the unique feature of what became the Campbell plea. While the Scots called for a restoration of primitive Christianity as if it were the end in view, the Campbells made it a means to an end — the end being the unity of all believers in Christ.

The Scottish influence also helped to turn young Campbell away from a sectarian view of the church. In later years he recalled that he first "imbibed disgust at the popular schemes, chiefly while a student at Glasgow." This "disgust," a common trait of reformers, included his distaste for the sectarian bickering and factionalism that he experienced in his own Seceder church. He was exposed to a more loving and conciliatory spirit in the person of Greville Ewing. He knew that as a faithful Seceder he could not accept Ewing and the other reformers who were not Seceders as equals in the church. Even an exemplary Christian like Greville Ewing would not be allowed to break bread in the Seceder church.

This is what was bothering him when it came time for his church's semi-annual Communion service. He dutifully went before the elders to be examined as to his worthiness to take part. He obtained the usual leaden token that would allow him a place at the Communion table. On that fateful Lord's Day in the spring of 1809, he waited in line to enter the Communion room, nursing his doubts about it all. He kept dropping back in line, trying to decide what to do. When he was at last seated at the table, he placed his token in the plate, but let the elements pass before him without partaking.

This was a private expression of his repudiation of sectarianism. It was a defining moment in his life, a quiet but resolute turn in a new direction. He made no defiant speech; he did not walk out in protest. It might not even have been noticed by those near him that he had refused Communion. But he knew in his heart that it meant he would no longer be a sectarian. He was now a free person in Christ. It could be said that in that Communion service the movement he would soon launch in America was born. It was his call to be a reformer.

It says something for his maturity that at only 20 he decided for the time being to be a quiet rebel. He did not reveal his feelings to the church authorities. He thought it best to arrive in America with his proper credentials as a member of the Seceder church in good standing.

3.2. Migration to America

The family sailed from Greenoch, Scotland, on August 3, 1809, aboard the *Latonia,* and arrived in New York on September 29. By stagecoach and wagon they made their way to Philadelphia. There they hired a wagoner to bear them across hundreds of miles of wilderness toward Washington, Pennsylvania, where their new home awaited them. They made some thirty miles a day, sometimes walking, sometimes riding in the wagon. Alexander marveled over the vast reaches of the frontier so different from his native Ireland. Thomas Campbell met the family with extra horses some three days from their new home, and the family was at last reunited after a separation of two years.

Since father and son had both undergone substantial change in their thinking, they were at first hesitant to unburden themselves to each other. They soon believed, however, that providence had brought them to one mind in regard to the reformation of the church. Even before they reached their destination they talked of the need of a plea for Christian unity based on the Bible alone.

Thomas's reformation efforts had led to the creation of a society known as the Christian Association of Washington. It was a society — not a church — with a mission to work within the churches for peace and unity. As a manifesto for the society, Thomas had just written the *Declaration and Address,* which Alexander read while it was still in proof sheets soon after his arrival.

These entities proved to be rich resources for their upcoming reformation. The society, consisting of thirty members, eventually became their first church contrary to its original intention. The church, which was simply called Brush Run church, was organized May 4, 1811. The *Declaration and Address* became their charter for Christian unity in setting forth what both Thomas and Alexander saw as irrefutable principles for the oneness of all believers in Christ.

3.3. *Ordination and Marriage*

Alexander spent his first two years in America continuing his studies, preaching his first sermon, being ordained to the ministry, getting married, and submitting to baptism by immersion, somewhat in that order. Now that he was committed to the Christian ministry, he placed himself under a rigid regimen of studies. He preached his first sermon on July 10, 1810, on Matthew 7:24-27, and went on to give 100 sermons over the next year. He was ordained to the ministry by the Brush Run Church with his father officiating on January 1, 1812.

Since he had resolved to preach without pay, his father predicted that he would wear many a tattered coat. Instead, he married into a family of some means. John Brown, a farmer and carpenter who owned considerable acreage around what is now Bethany, had an 18-year-old daughter named Margaret, also born of Presbyterian piety. When Alexander came to their home to deliver some books Mr. Brown had borrowed from Thomas, he and Margaret met and fell in love. They were married on March 12, 1811. This was the beginning of Campbell's fifty-five-year residency in Bethany. Mr. Brown deeded the home and farm to the young couple as an incentive to remain in Bethany when there was talk of their migrating to Ohio.

3.4. *Baptism by Immersion*

His first theological crisis came with the birth of his first child. He had to decide if she should be baptized as he and all good Presbyterians had been in their infancy. He not only searched the Greek New Testament for an answer, but also consulted those scholars who wrote in defense of infant baptism. His study led to more than he was expecting. He not only decided against baptism for his infant daughter, but also resolved that he himself should be baptized by immersion, which he now had concluded was the only valid baptism. Margaret joined him in his resolution.

He asked Baptist minister Matthias Luce to immerse him simply on his confession that Jesus is the Christ. Luce was at first hesitant, saying it was contrary to Baptist practice, but he agreed to do so because he saw it as consistent with the New Testament.

He and his father had discussed and questioned the validity of infant baptism on occasion, but passed it off as a matter of opinion. Concerning the question of the possible immersion of believers who had already been baptized as infants, Thomas observed that it would hardly be appropriate to go out of the church in order to come back in again. He expressed concern that rebaptism would tend to "dechristianize the whole Christian world."

When Alexander revealed his intentions to his father, he was told that he had to do what he saw to be his duty. He assumed that his father would, at best, be tolerant toward his decision. But when it came time for the baptism, Thomas Campbell and his wife not only came along, but brought a change of clothing with them. It was June 12, 1812. On that day seven persons were immersed in Buffalo Creek, which winds its way through Bethany. Thirteen more were immersed at the next meeting of the Brush Run Church. Alexander would later suggest that it may have been the first time in the new Republic that people were immersed simply upon their profession of faith in Christ.

It was clearly a turning point in the Campbell story when father and son repudiated infant baptism by publicly being immersed. It was a defining moment in that it both separated them from their Presbyterian heritage once and for all and identified them with the Baptists, where they were "uneasily bosomed," as Walter Scott put it, for the next two decades. It also catapulted Alexander into the leadership of the emerging reformation. Henceforth the son was the principal leader of the movement, though only 23.

Alexander rejected his father's fear that by being immersed after being sprinkled as an infant he had "dechristianized" himself or others. He had always been a Christian, he believed, but now that he had found more truth, he had obeyed it. He was himself an example of the definition of a Christian he was later to give: "A Christian is one who believes that Jesus is the Christ, repents of his sins, and obeys him in all things according to his understanding."

3.5. *Among the Baptists*

For the next few years he tended his farm, watched over a growing family, conducted a school in his home, and itinerated among the Baptists. Since his repudiation of infant baptism and submission to baptism by immersion, he was increasingly accepted by the Baptists. Once he began to champion baptism by immersion in public debates, many Baptists deemed him a hero.

While he never in any official way personally became a Baptist, he had become for all practical purposes a Baptist. The first two Campbell churches, Brush Run and Wellsburg, belonged to Baptist associations, and his people were first known as "Reformed Baptists." His first journal was named the *Christian Baptist.* And he resolved early on that he would work among the Baptists as long as he could be free in Christ.

This continued until well into the 1820s when his followers began to be "forced out" by Baptist Associations. Until his dying day he regretted that his people and the Baptists ever had to separate. And yet when Baptists in Kentucky were generously embracing him, he cautioned them, "I have almost as much against you as I do the pedobaptists." And when the Brush Run church joined the Redstone Baptist Association, it prepared a document that set forth the conditions under which it would be a member, including the freedom to interpret the Scriptures as it understood them, apart from any creed.

3.6. "Sermon on the Law"

His reputation among the Baptists nevertheless grew steadily until 1816 when the Redstone Association had its annual meeting at the Cross Creek Baptist church only ten miles from his home. It was expected that he would be the keynote speaker. But the pastor of the church, who nursed prejudices against Campbell, blocked the move and put in his own man. But when that man became ill — which Campbell later described as "providential" — even the pastor agreed that Campbell should speak.

This presentation, which became known as the "Sermon on the Law," was another turning point in the Campbell story. Some historians have named this occasion the beginning of the Movement, and Campbell himself said thirty years later that had it not been for that sermon and the opposition it generated he might never have launched his reformation.

"The Sermon on the Law" articulated a critical hermeneutical principle. Taking his text from Romans 8:3, he argued that the Old Testament and the New Testament reflect different systems and different covenants, and that the Christian is "not under law but under grace." God has dealt with humanity through a series of covenants, he claimed, and when the law of Moses fulfilled its purpose as a covenant, it gave way to the new covenant of Christ. The Christian dispensation is not merely a continuation of the Mosaic law as was commonly taught in Calvinist theology, but a new system of grace.

This was too much for some of the "law preachers," as Campbell dubbed those who in his view wanted to bind Christians to the demands of the old Mosaic system. The pastor of the Cross Creek church quickly rallied opposition and moved against Campbell, insisting that "This is not Baptist doctrine," and that it should be exposed as heresy. Since wiser heads prevailed, Campbell was spared public repudiation at the time. It was nonetheless, as he afterwards put it, the beginning of a "seven year's war" with the Baptists.

3.7. Buffalo Seminary

In 1818 he started a school in his own home called Buffalo Seminary. He used the main floor for classrooms and the upstairs for a dormitory. This forced his growing family into the basement, a move he was later to regret, for he feared the dampness of the basement may have hastened the premature death from tuberculosis of his wife Margaret. This is unlikely, however, since all five of her daughters were also to succumb to the same disease at about her same age.

Even though the school soon had more pupils than he could accept, he found himself serving as a caretaker for young students who did not share his spiritual interests. The school held little prospect of producing co-workers for his budding reformation, so after four years he closed it. Even so, some of his students became doctors and lawyers and were grateful for what he had done for them.

3.8. First Two Debates

While still conducting his school, Campbell launched a new dimension to his ministry: debating. It was not uncommon for Presbyterians to challenge Baptists to debate their differences on baptism. Since Presbyterians generally had a better-educated clergy, the challenges usually went unheeded. While the "Sermon on the Law" had established Campbell as controversial and as a different kind of Baptist, he was nonetheless

Portrait of Alexander Campbell c. 1827 or 1835 by Washington Bogart Cooper. Courtesy of Bethany College

deemed sound on baptism and singularly capable of defending the Baptists against the pedobaptists.

In 1820 he debated John Walker, a Seceder Presbyterian minister, in Mt. Pleasant, Ohio, and three years later he debated W. L. Maccalla, also a Presbyterian, in Washington, Kentucky. He was reluctant to engage in the first debate, but it proved to be such an effective venue for the promulgation of his ideas that he was the challenger in the second debate. While both debates were on the mode of baptism, they allowed him not only to defend the Baptist position on immersion but also to venture more deeply into the design of baptism.

In the first debate he introduced Acts 2:38 — destined to be a pivotal passage in his reformation — but only in reference to his argument against infant baptism. At that time he did not see even his own immersion in reference to the remission of sins. It was in the second debate that he postulated for the first time that the purpose of baptism was to give the believer an assurance of the remission of sins. He distinguished between real and formal remission of sins, explaining that individuals are "really" saved when they believe, "formally" saved when they are immersed. "The water of baptism, then, formally washes away our sins. The blood of Christ really washes away our sins," he said in the Maccalla debate. Seventeen years later, in response to some who were giving "an undue eminence" to baptism, he appealed to the Maccalla debate as correctly representing his position that baptism is "pardon-certifying" rather than "pardon-procuring."

These first two debates proved so effective in promoting his reformation that he went on record saying, "We are fully persuaded that a week's debating is worth a year's preaching." Both debates were published, and thousands of copies were sold. This all served to popularize the name of Alexander Campbell and the cause of reformation that he represented.

4. The Aggressive Years (1823-30)

4.1. Campbell the Editor

In 1823 he became an editor, the forte of his ministry for the rest of his life. If it was as a debater that he launched his reformation, it was as an editor that he solidified it. While some may have thought of Campbell as young and brash when editor of the *Christian Baptist,* he was in fact almost 35 when he began the journal and 41 when he concluded it — the mid-years of one's career in his time. Nor was he brash or reckless, considering the maturity and sophistication of his writings during those seven years. But he was bold, aggressive, and sometimes offensive — or, as he put it, "tart and severe," especially to the clergy.

From the outset he more than hinted that the new journal would be a hard-hitting publication. In the prospectus to the *Christian Baptist* he announced that the "sole object" was not only "the eviction of truth" but "the exposing of error in doctrine and practice." In the preface to the first issue he admitted that it was rare for an editor to do what he had in mind — to oppose the errors of those with whom he was identified and looked to for support. If such a one appears in any party, he ventured, he would be met with frowns, and would either have to lay his hand upon his mouth or be shown the door. He made it clear that he intended neither to keep his mouth shut nor to walk out the door.

He suspected that his efforts might "be blasted by the poisonous breath of sectarian zeal and of an aspiring priesthood." He was persuaded that the church had seriously departed from the apostolic faith and was in deep apostasy and that the clergy was largely responsible. He explained in later years that he sometimes spoke with "asperity" of the clergy, which he considered contrary to his nature, because he thought it took that to get their attention as to the seriousness of their transgressions.

He sometimes wrote with the anger of an Old Testament prophet: "My very soul is stirred within me when I think of what a world of mischief the popular clergy have done. They have shut up everybody's mouth but their own; and theirs they will not open unless they are paid for it." He not only called them "hirelings" and "stall-fed clergy," but even "antichrist." He ventured that if he could not prove that the clergy "as a body collective" were not antichrist, then he could prove no proposition at all.

The clergy, he suggested, "hanker after titles," the D.D. degree in particular. When a Baptist clergy friend of his turned down the honor, Campbell commented: "When the degree was conferred on him, he, like a Christian, declined it." In his "Third Epistle of Peter," published in the *Christian Baptist* in 1824, he excoriated the clergy to the point of appearing to be deliberately offensive. He charged not only that the clergy "fleece the flock" for money, but also that they feigned to make the people think they cared for their souls while they did it. They also "make the people blind in the midst of light."

Some of his readers, including some of his supporters, saw this as unnecessarily offensive. Students in a New York seminary cancelled their subscriptions, charging that he was on "a confirmed course of ridicule and sarcasm." A Baptist minister whom Campbell respected and often quoted urged that he be "not so strong and extreme," observing that he had two personalities — gracious in the social circle, but otherwise when writing. Another respected correspondent wrote to him that "it is thought that your feelings are not of the most peaceful nature" and accused him of forgetting such Christian virtues as gentleness and kindness. His severest critics called up such adjectives as "mischievous," "incendiary," and "dangerous to our children." His journal "sowed seeds of discord among brethren."

But Campbell did not retract or apologize, and he showed little interest in defending himself. He pointed out that there are instances in which a reformer may have to use severe language as did John the Baptist and even Jesus himself in order to alert the church to "the moral malady" that consumes its spiritual life. He did in time tone down his rhetoric, however, and became more conciliatory toward the clergy.

The *Christian Baptist* was far more than the editor's occasional anticlerical diatribes. It was concerned with the reformation of both the church and society — "the art of living well" as the editor expressed it. The source of such well-being is found in "the ancient gospel." Campbell thus wrote series on "The Ancient Gospel" and "A Restoration of the Ancient Order of Things" in which he sought to correct the deficiencies of the modern church by way of a restoration of primitive Christianity. A restoration of "ordinances" — baptism, the Lord's Supper, the Lord's day, the Bible — received special attention. Restoration was a basic motif, such as restoration of pure speech, proper church discipline, church offices, the spirit of the primitive Christians, and even love feasts.

The editor appears to have gone out of his way to be fair and open. He invited his readers to write to him their objections to anything in the paper. He promised to respond. Much of the journal is made up of letters from readers and his responses. He allowed "the other side" to be heard, including scathing criticism of himself. He was cooperative and conciliatory toward other religious papers, even when they were critical. He quoted from seventy-nine different journals during those seven years, often commending what they had to say. He was an editor sensitive to the church at large, one who had an ecumenical outlook. But he was always a reformer and an agent for change.

4.2. Sectarianism Is "The Offspring of Hell"

While he was sometimes caustic in the *Christian Baptist,* he was never sectarian in the sense that he saw his movement as exclusively the body of Christ and his people as the only true Christians. In 1825, in response to a reader, he made it clear that he had put that kind of thinking behind him: "I was once so straight that like the Indian's tree I leaned a little the other way. . . . I was so strict a Separatist that I would neither pray nor sing praises with any one who was not as perfect as I supposed myself." He went on to brand such exclusiveness as "Protestant monkery" and sectarianism as "the offspring of hell."

Throughout the seven volumes of *The Christian Baptist* he was eminently ecumenical in his plea for the unity of all believers. To a reader with whom he did not agree on a number of issues, he wrote: "I will esteem you and love you, as I do every man, of whatever name, who believes sincerely that Jesus is the Messiah, and hopes in his salvation." To another correspondent he said: "I declare non-fellowship with no man who owns the Lord in word and deed. Such is a Christian. He that denies the Lord in word and deed is not a Christian."

Again in 1825, while yet with the Baptists, he explained: "I have no idea of adding to the catalogue of new sects. This game has been played too long. I labor to see sectarianism abolished, and all Christians of every name united upon the one foundation on which the apostolic church was founded." He was confident that the church would one day be united again as it was in apostolic times, but only through a restoration of the ancient order of things. The reformed church would be a united church, and the united church would be "the millennial church."

When Campbell brought the *Christian Baptist* to a close in July 1830, he had already begun a new journal with a significant name change, the *Millennial Harbinger.* The journal would anticipate and help to usher in the coming millennium by pleading for the unity of all Christians through the restoration of primitive Christianity. The new journal would take up where the old one left off. He closed down the *Christian Baptist* partly to avoid the danger of the name compromising his nonsectarian plea: "Hating sects and sectarian names, I resolved to keep the name of the *Christian Baptist* from being fixed on us."

4.3. The Living Oracles: *Translation of the New Testament*

In 1826 Campbell published a translation of the New Testament popularly known as *The Living Oracles.* It was based on a translation by Scottish scholars and included extensive critical notes. He made some daring changes, some of which did not go well with his own followers. One was the omission of Acts 8:37, a favorite Baptist proof text. The use of "immerse" for "baptize" might have pleased the Baptists, but "John, the Immerser" removed their name from the Bible. He used "congregation" for "church," eliminated "thy," "thou," and "thine," and changed "repent" to "reform" and "preach" to "proclaim," making his translation too different from earlier ones for most people.

While the new version went through several editions and revisions, even after his death it enjoyed only modest acceptance. Yet it further established Alexander Campbell as a reformer and strengthened both his reputation and his movement. It was, however, an achievement that on one occasion was turned against him. Three years later, when he served as a delegate to the Virginia Constitutional Convention, a fellow delegate opposed Campbell with: "Mr. Chairman, even the God of heaven cannot please this man, for he has a Bible all his own."

4.4. Virginia Constitutional Convention

Campbell's participation as a delegate to the 1829 Virginia Constitutional Convention, his only formal venture into politics, placed him in the company of two former presidents, James Madison and James Monroe, as well as Chief Justice John Marshall and Virginia Governor William B. Giles. While the experience had little bearing on his role as a reformer, it gave him the unique opportunity to preach in various churches while in Richmond those several months and to be heard by the great and the near great.

James Madison was one who heard him, and while he spoke highly of Campbell's role in the Convention, he added, "But it is as a theologian that Mr. Campbell must be known. It was my pleasure to hear him very often as a preacher of the gospel, and I regard him as the ablest and most original expounder of the Scriptures I have ever heard."

4.5. Campbell-Owen Debate

It was also in 1829 that he had his third debate. This time his opponent was an eminent Scottish socialist named Robert Owen who was known for his denunciation of religion and Christianity in particular. As Campbell saw it, the debate was as much about hope as anything, for he held that however successful Owen's socialist enterprises might be, one cannot be happy in this world without the hope of immortality beyond the grave.

Observers were impressed that two men as radically different in their views as Campbell and Owen could be as gracious toward each other as they were. The debate gave prestige and visibility to the new church that was emerging, especially since Campbell was defending the entire Christian community against Owen's charge that religion was opposed to the social good.

4.6. Barton W. Stone

Alexander Campbell first met Barton W. Stone in 1824 during the second of Campbell's many visits to Kentucky. It was the beginning of a long and fruitful relationship. Together they forged a unity movement unique to American church history. Stone had priority in time in that his efforts had begun as early as the Cane Ridge Revival in 1801. Campbell had priority in leadership because of the strength of his public persona and because he exercised leadership for twenty years beyond Stone's death.

Stone recognized Campbell's unique qualifications early in their work together: "I am constrained, and willingly constrained, to acknowledge him as the greatest promoter of this reformation of any man living." Campbell, in turn, referred to Stone as "the honored instrument of bringing many out of the ranks of human tradition and putting into their hands the Book of Books as their only confession of faith and rule of life."

Stone esteemed Campbell as having fewer faults than any man he knew, while Campbell referred to him as "the venerable Barton W. Stone." While they were not side-by-side co-laborers, they were both editors who led parallel movements that eventually united. They corresponded, publishing their exchanges in each other's papers, and they sometimes disagreed. When an opponent in a debate with Campbell took advantage of his differences with Stone, the reformer replied, referring to his relationship with Stone: "Our bond of union is not opinion, nor unity of opinion. It is one Lord, one faith, one baptism." He went on to say that their relationship to each other and to their entire movement was "so sacred" and "so perfectly catholic" that anyone who loves Christ could unite with them.

This was the genius of the plea advocated by both of them: Christians may differ on opinions and marginal issues and be united on the essentials. They exemplified this in their own rather uneven relationship. In spite of vigorous differences, they found oneness in their common devotion to Jesus Christ and in their mutual passion for the unity of all God's people. It was because of this kind of example and leadership that the Stone and Campbell movements became one unity movement in 1832.

5. Realization and Revision (1830-55)

5.1. Harbinger of the Millennium

While Campbell's passion for a coming millennium expressed itself even in the name of his new journal, his position was quite different from the popular millennial views of his day. "Millerism" was the most spectacular, mainly because it dared to name 1843 as the year that the Lord would come and bring the world to an end. Campbell responded to this popular theory in a series on "The Coming of the Lord" that ran through twenty-six installments. It began in 1841 and ran through the year that the Lord was due to come. He referred to its promoter, New York Baptist minister William Miller, as a good and sincere man, though mistaken.

Campbell pointed out that all the theories agreed that there would be a millennium and that the Lord would come. It was a question of whether he came before or after the millennium. Miller claimed the Lord would come before the millennium, which today is known as premillennialism. Campbell held that Jesus would come after the millennium, now referred to as postmillennialism. But he concluded his

Campbell pictured here c. 1848 with three of his children (by his second wife Selina), Virginia, Decima, and William.
Courtesy of Bethany College

series with a surprising turn: the Lord will come "in a way which perchance but few of us either expect or are at all prepared for."

Campbell expected "great changes in the world" that would bring about the "amelioration" of society as well as the church. In a series on "Millennium" beginning in the first issue of his new journal (January 1830), he identified the changes he anticipated. It included the triumph of Christianity over the world, the end of sectarianism, and the union of Christians. It would be a time of extended prosperity around the world, and not necessarily limited to a literal 1,000 years. Wars would cease, and peace and goodwill would generally prevail. The Jews would turn to Jesus Christ as their Messiah. The weather would be mild. Crimes and punishment would cease. Health would be more vigorous, labor less arduous, lands more fertile. The knowledge of the Lord would cover the earth as the waters cover the sea. America, his adopted country, would be its epicenter.

These were his expectations when at age 41 he began the *Millennial Harbinger.* Not only was a millennium on the horizon, but his journal was its harbinger. He was not only announcing its coming, but was an agent to effect its arrival. Yet it would be gradual in its unfolding. In the "Prospectus" to the new journal he detailed some things he hoped to accomplish. This included disquisitions on the treatment of African slaves as "preparatory to their emancipation, and exaltation from their present degraded condition." There could not, of course, be slavery during the millennium, and yet freedom would come gradually.

His chief concern as a harbinger of the millennium was the elimination of sectarianism. The gospel cannot triumph until Christians "bury the tomahawk of party conflicts." He insisted that "No sect can be the basis of the Millennial Church." He cried out like a prophet against sectarian establishments: "All the platforms, all the foundations of the sects are, therefore, too narrow and too weak to sustain the Millennial Church; and therefore must be pulled down."

He began his series on "Millennium" by asking, "Will sects ever cease?" His position was that sects have to end before there can be a millennium. And they will end only when religious parties cease making opinions a test of communion, and unite upon the simple facts of the gospel. When told that people cannot give up their opinions, his response was: "We do not ask them to give up their opinions — We ask them not to impose them upon others. Let them hold their opinions; but let them hold them as private property."

5.2. Essentials of Reformation

For over three decades his plea as editor of the *Millennial Harbinger* was that the essentials of the gospel — the facts of what God has said or done through Christ — are clearly identifiable. Upon these all Christians can unite. Opinions were to be held as private property and are not to be imposed on others. Believers may be wrong in their understanding and still be accepted: "I never did at anytime exclude a man from the kingdom of God for mere imbecility of intellect; or, in other words, because he could not assent to my opinions."

Sure of his stand against sectarianism, he boldly asserted: "I will now show how they cannot make a sect of us. We will acknowledge all as Christians who acknowledge the gospel facts, and obey Jesus Christ." He looked for no new sun or no new revelation of the Spirit, but only the ancient gospel, which must be "disinterred from the rubbish of the dark ages, and made to assume its former simplicity, sublimity, and majesty."

In the 1836 *Harbinger* he spelled out what he referred to as "the central attributes of the proposed reformation for which we contend." They reveal a balance between doctrine and ethics:

1. a more intimate acquaintance with the holy oracles of both Testaments;
2. a weekly meeting on the Lord's Day in honor of the risen Lord, with the Lord's Supper the most cardinal and essential part;
3. a stricter discipline in the church, and greater attention to good order and behavior;
4. a more Christian morality in keeping promises, doing justly, and loving mercy;
5. more gravity, temperance, moderation, more self-denial, and strict self-government;
6. more piety and devotion, more prayer and praise, more communion with God;
7. more cooperation among all churches in the work of converting the world.

A year later he drew up "a synopsis of the grand items of the reformation for which we have contended and still contend." While it included most of the same items as before, this time he listed his "essentials" under four chapter headings: (1) For the Healing of Divisions among Christians; (2) Principles and Objects of Church Reform; (3) Principles to the Proper Dispensation of the Gospel; (4) Personal and Family Reformation.

Under the first heading he added as essential to unity: "The restoration of a pure speech, or the calling of Bible things by Bible names." Under the second he identified the church as composed of those who confess Jesus to be the Messiah, the Son of God, and put him on in baptism. Under the third heading he was careful to identify the gospel not as theory or doctrine but "the proclamation in the name of God of remission of sins and eternal life through the sacrifice and mediation of Jesus Christ to everyone who obeys him in the instituted way." In the fourth chapter he called for a personal reformation that included intelligence, purity, and happiness. He added: "We want and must have a radical and thorough reformation in family religion and family education."

He had reason in the 1830s to hold these as realistic goals. The preaching of the ancient gospel and the restoration of the ancient order of things he saw taking place would unite the Christians in all the sects in the millennial church and ameliorate all society.

5.3. Rude Awakening

Time was not on Alexander Campbell's side. His vision of a triumphant future in a glorious new world of plenty gradually gave way to a rude awakening. Conditions in America were deteriorating, not improving. There were financial depressions. Slavery was not dissipating but growing worse. Sects continued to multiply. They were not burying the tomahawk of party conflicts. While his movement enjoyed impressive growth, it was not measuring up to his millennial expectation. Besides, it had problems of its own, which took much of his time and effort. In the years leading up to the Civil War he wrote less about a coming millennium. They were years of realization and revision. There was no millennium on the horizon, no millennial church, and no church uniting. If Campbell's millennial views were correct, things would be improving. It was time for a midcourse correction.

A telltale sign of a change in his thinking is when he began to refer to what had been "a movement" as a denomination. Such language as "our denomination" and "other denominations" in the *Millennial Harbinger* would not have appeared in *The Christian Baptist.* We have seen that he had no intention of starting another denomination. He had launched a "new reformation," as he liked to call it, in the church. It was neither a sect nor a denomination. Yet in time he realized with regret that it had been necessary to add another denomination to American society.

Though he and others in the movement continued to refer to their efforts as a reformation, and it was still a unity movement, it was now "a denomination" in the church. While accepting denominational status, Campbell was adamant about not being a sect. "Denomination" meant that they were a distinct religious body with clearly defined marks of identification, such as a particular name or names. A sect claims to be within itself the entirety of the body of Christ, to the exclusion of all other Christians. He therefore clearly distinguished between a sect and a denomination. But he was now issuing the denial in broader terms: "You'll never make a sect of us, because we are catholic, very catholic." In these years of revision *catholic* became a self-identifying term for Campbell.

By 1849 Campbell's new church had its own missionary organization, known as the American Christian Missionary Society, and he served as its first president. In *Christian Baptist* days not only was there no such organization, but he was critical of such innovations.

Since a denomination by definition has a name, Campbell and Stone debated what name they should wear. Using Acts 11:26 as a proof text, Stone argued that they should call themselves "Christians" since it was a divinely given name, and that their congregations should be called Christian Churches or Churches of Christ. Campbell disputed Stone's claim that the name "Christian" had been divinely appointed. He stated that he had "no objection to the name Christian if we only deserve it." He preferred simply "disciples of Christ" because of its greater antiquity and modesty. The problem was resolved, by happenstance rather than by decree, by wearing all three names — Christian Churches, Churches of Christ, Disciples of Christ.

5.4. Church Organization

In his earlier years there was little or no cooperation among the congregations. The polity was a radical congregationalism, with each church going its own way. By 1841 there were nearly 2,000 congregations representing almost every state in the union and several foreign countries. They could no longer function as a loose network of radically independent churches. Campbell began a series of essays on church cooperation that signaled a dramatic change from his *Christian Baptist* days. "Our organization and discipline are greatly defective, and essentially inadequate to the present condition and wants of society," he wrote. He may have surprised his readers when he went on to say, "A book is not sufficient to govern the church."

He pointed out that one cannot simply hand a Bible to a congregation and leave it to its own devices. Laws are not self-enforcing but are executed through duly ordained agents. That is why God placed apostles, prophets, evangelists, and pastors in the church. Likewise, if congregations are to act in concert if they are to cooperate at all, it must be through some agency. Campbell identified five things that they could not effectively accomplish without "a more ample, extensive church organization": the distribution of the Bible abroad, missionary work, improving Christian ministry, checking and removing impostors in the ministry, and church-wide cooperation.

When some of his people questioned the creation of agencies, seeing it as contrary to their plea for "a restoration of the ancient order," Campbell complained that "There is too much squeamishness about the manner of co-operation." One is not to look to the New Testament for a "model" for every detail of the church's work such as Moses' specifications for the building of the tabernacle. It would be impossible for the New Testament to provide details for every aspect of the church's mission, he insisted. One may as well ask for a precept for translating the Bible from Greek to English or for the building of a meetinghouse. He lamented that some of his people would rather do nothing, even withholding the gospel from the masses, for fear that they might do something the wrong way.

Many of his followers had no problem in forming agencies and learning to cooperate. Not only did they have a missionary society by 1849, but by the 1840s they had numerous local, area, and state agencies. By 1845 there was the American Christian Bible Society and a Sunday School and Tract Society. By 1849 there was a national convention. And by 1845 there were three colleges, counting Campbell's own Bethany College.

He also softened his anticlerical rhetoric. He had always allowed for a special class of preachers sent out and supported financially by the congregations. They were to be evangelists, preaching to the lost and organizing churches. Likewise he had held that local elders, supported financially by the congregation, and deacons were to care for established churches, insisting that it was a "satire" on a church to hire someone from outside the congregation to preach for it. He had always been concerned about "wandering stars," preachers who were unsent and unwanted, and sometimes ill-prepared or morally irresponsible. While he had earlier been critical of seminaries, he now looked to the colleges, including his own, as an answer to an uneducated ministry.

5.5. *Mid-Course Correction*

Equally significant was his mid-course correction in reference to his plea for unity. By the 1840s he was referring less to a unity based on "a restoration of the ancient order" or a restoration of primitive Christianity. In an 1839 essay, he stated that while unity had been his "darling theme" all along, "it was some time before we could see clearly the ground on which all true Christians could form one visible and harmonious union."

In an ecumenical gathering in Lexington, Kentucky, in 1841, he set forth what that ground was: "the catholic rule of union." It read: "Whatever in faith, in piety, and morality is catholic, or universally admitted by all parties, shall be adopted as the basis of union." He submitted this as a resolution before the large audience, which gave its approval by an overwhelming standing vote. It recognized that while people will differ to the point of disunity on what constitutes a restoration of primitive Christianity, they can unite on the basics of the faith that they hold in common.

While Campbell advocated this revised catholic approach to unity for the rest of his life, he is remembered for his earlier emphasis on unity through restoration. He often expressed the catholic rule for unity in terms of "the seven facts" of Ephesians 4:4-6, which he sometimes reduced to three, "one Lord, one faith, one baptism." We unite on the facts themselves, not theories or opinions about the facts. He also sometimes expressed the catholic rule in terms of uniting upon the universal principles of the faith centered in Jesus Christ while allowing for differences in particulars. He cultivated a fondness for the term "catholic." "We are catholics," he liked to say — not Greek or Roman Catholic — just catholic. They had a catholic rule of faith and practice, the Bible; they wore a catholic name or names; they practiced a catholic baptism; they served a catholic table; they had a catholic plea for unity.

5.6. *More Debates*

He continued to debate during this period of his life. His 1837 debate in Cincinnati with Roman Catholic Bishop John Baptist Purcell established him as a representative and defender of Protestantism, perhaps even as a religious statesman. Not only were the disputants charitable toward each other, even brotherly, they became lasting friends. And yet one proposition that Campbell affirmed was that the Roman church was "the 'Babylon' of John, the 'Man of Sin' of Paul, and the Empire of the 'Youngest Horn' of Daniel's Sea Monster." It was a charge made by Protestants since Luther.

Campbell esteemed Purcell as the fairest man he had debated, while Purcell described Campbell as "a most lovable character who treated me in every way and on all occasions like a brother." He thought history would be kind to Campbell, giving him a place alongside Luther, Calvin, and Wesley.

In 1843 he debated yet another Presbyterian, Nathan L. Rice of Paris, Kentucky. Three issues were discussed: baptism, the Holy Spirit, and creeds. In published form it ran 912 pages, with more than half of these given to baptism. The disputants went after each other four hours a day for sixteen days, and it got personal. When Campbell referred to the clergy as "venal," Rice fired back that there was not a single Presbyterian minister that had one-tenth the wealth Campbell had. And when Campbell suggested that the position he had taken was an unpopular cause, Rice assured him that he had gained much more popularity than if he had remained a Presbyterian. Henry Clay, one of the most widely known statesmen of the day, served as moderator of the debate at the Main Street Christian Church in Lexington, Kentucky. This debate, like the previous ones, was well attended, and, once in book form, widely read. It opened still more doors for Alexander Campbell.

Besides his five major debates, all of which were published, there were lesser skirmishes that also played a role in defining his ministry. It was his practice when lecturing to invite local clergy to respond to his presentation. A respondent might talk for an hour while he listened. He would then give a rejoinder, all in good grace. Such sessions would begin at candlelighting or around 4 PM and continue for three hours or more. There were often also morning sessions. Conversation, often with the same disputants, would continue on into the evening at a "repast" in a home. Some observers saw Campbell most "in his element" as a conversationalist, and he was always as gracious as he was informed.

One such disputant was Obadiah Jennings, Nashville lawyer and Presbyterian minister. Their 1830 confrontation in that city evolved into a full-blown debate, with moderators and all. Not long after the debate, Jennings died. Campbell wrote a conciliatory obituary in his journal. Jennings's nephew, editor of a religious journal unfriendly to Campbell, published what he claimed to be an account of the debate, titled *Debate on Campbellism,* which he sold for 75 cents. In a review that ran for three installments, Campbell charged that it was a fraud in that it did not even discuss the debate in Nashville, and was written by one who was not even present. He thought it should be titled *Seventy-five cents worth of slander against Alexander Campbell.*

This was typical of some of Campbell's opposition in those days. There were numerous tracts, pamphlets, and books either examining or exposing "Campbellism." Campbell considered them studied efforts to misrepresent his position. The most notable was *Campbellism Examined* by J. B. Jeter, an influential Baptist minister, in 1855. Campbell took it seriously enough to ask Moses E. Lard, one of his brighter students at Bethany and a gifted scholar, to respond to it in a volume titled *A Review of Campbellism Examined.*

Some of his debates were not oral or public, but appeared only in written form in his own journal and in some journal representing the other side. One such debate was on Universalism with Dolphus Skinner, a minister of the Universalist Church. Beginning in 1837 after the Purcell debate, it ran for three years and there were forty exchanges. They did not mince words. Campbell told Skinner that his doctrine "makes Satan a metaphor, hell a fable, and punishment after death a mere bugbear." Skinner told Campbell that in previous debates he had had the advantage in that he was on the side of truth. In this debate, however, he had espoused "the cause of endless malevolence, sin, and misery," and that he would therefore provide him every advantage.

They had agreed that one of them would publish the debate in book form. Campbell deferred to Skinner, hoping it might circulate well among Universalists. Since only 1,500 copies were issued, it soon became a collector's item. The Universalists claimed victory, accusing Campbell of not wanting it published. Thirty years later, a year after Campbell's death, the Universalists were still claiming victory. W. K. Pendleton, Campbell's successor as editor of the *Harbinger,* felt it necessary to set the record straight by republishing the agreement that Campbell and Skinner had made in 1837. He explained that anyone who knew Alexander Campbell would know he was never reluctant either to defend his opinions or to publish his defense.

5.7. Extensive Traveler

Campbell was one of the most traveled people of his day. For forty years he traversed virtually every nook and corner of the new republic, especially its heartland. He grew with his adopted country, traveling first by horseback, gig, and stagecoach; then by steamboat and railway. He claimed to have traveled on the first railroad built in this country. He was impressed that "the cars" could move along on steel rails at forty miles an hour. His travel letters tell of accidents on rivers and rails alike. He took a sleigh ride through the streets of Chicago when it was but a village.

Except when the river was too shallow, he would take a steamer at Wellsburg, six miles from Bethany, for his frequent visits to the South, first on the Ohio River, then on the Mississippi, all the way to New Orleans. The river was too shallow for travel when he was to be in Ohio for the Maccalla debate. He made the 300-mile journey on horseback in company with future Mormon Sidney Rigdon. It took them ten days. Carriages and stagecoaches were not all that much faster, and hardly less arduous. But there was comfort, sometimes even luxury, on the rails and especially the steamers. He did much of his writing on board a steamer and sometimes preached upon request.

As his five daughters, the children of his first wife, grew older, he would take them, one at a time, on some of his appointments, usually in the South. It was not unusual for an enterprising young man to ask the father for the daughter's hand in marriage without ever approaching the young lady.

His journeys were frequently incredibly extended and demanding, taking him away from home for months at a time, and on a schedule that would overwhelm most people. In 1836 he wrote concerning a trip to the Northeast: "After an absence from home of 94 days, in which I delivered 93 discourses, averaging one hour and twenty minutes, and traveled about 2000 miles, I arrived safely at home." He added that some seventy people were immersed into Christ. On such trips there would be in addition to his public discourses hundreds of hours of conversation in homes, which were actually further discourses, only less formal. Those present may have had questions to ask, but they wanted *him* to do the talking.

He sometimes found himself in a place where he had no appointment and where no one knew he was in town. One such place was Zanesville, Ohio, in 1830. After checking in at the local hotel and getting permission from the sheriff to use the courthouse, he hired a boy to go to the homes in town and announce that Alexander Campbell would speak at the courthouse at candlelighting. That is all it took to have a full house for preaching. He often spoke in buildings of other churches.

From his travel letters we learn something of what he talked about. He chose the expository method over what he criticized as "textuary preaching," exploiting a verse of Scripture to support a topical sermon. Preferring to preach on entire chapters, he had his favorite portions of the Bible, such as 1 Samuel 15, Acts 2, 1 Corinthians 13, Ephesians 1, Hebrews 1, and Revelation 20. One young man who heard him discourse on Hebrews 1 in reference to the glory of Christ wrote of it decades later after he had become a distinguished physician: "I never had heard anything that approached the power of that discourse, nor have I ever heard it equaled since. That speech on Hebrews lifted me into a world of thought of which I had previously known nothing. It has been 45 years since I heard that public discourse, and it is as vivid to my memory, I think, as when I first heard it."

5.8. Jailed in Scotland

In 1847 he made a trip to England, Scotland, and Ireland, his only visit abroad except for occasional excursions into Canada. He took funds with him raised by some of his churches for famine-stricken Ireland. He bore a letter from Henry Clay introducing him to British dignitaries, which he used for visits to both the House of Commons and the House of Lords. He spoke in large halls all across England. In Liverpool 2,500 heard him speak on the Holy Spirit. He gave several addresses in a Baptist church in Banbury. He had audiences of 3,000 in such places as Manchester, Wigan, and Halifax. He was the honored guest at the annual convention of the British Churches of Christ, then made up of twenty-seven congregations.

In London he gave fifteen lectures in quick succession, and was afterwards so exhausted that he stole away to Paris for a few days of rest. He returned to London to address a society of skeptics at the "Hall of Debate" on *Has God Ever Spoken to Man?* The address set off such a stormy and prolonged debate among the skeptics that Campbell finally gave up on them and quietly excused himself. By midnight the skeptics had settled down to the extent that they passed a resolution thanking Mr. Campbell for his visit.

All went well for him until he got to Scotland, the country from which he had left for the New World thirty-eight years before. While he was engaged in speaking to large crowds in various cities, including an enthusiastic assembly at a Church of Scotland, the Anti-Slavery Society of Scotland posted notices derogatory of Campbell wherever he spoke. The notices read, "Beware! The Rev. Alexander Campbell of Virginia, United States of America, has been a slaveholder himself and is still a defender of manstealers."

Members of the society had interviewed him on the subject of slavery, and were not satisfied with the distinction he drew between being anti-slavery, which he was, and being an abolitionist, which he was not. Even though he had freed his slaves, it was indictment enough that he had ever been a slaveholder. They not only launched an attack on him but challenged him to debate their champion James Robertson on the subject. He informed the public through an Edinburgh newspaper that he would be pleased to accept the challenge so long as this Robertson was not the one who was excluded from a Baptist Church for "violating the Fifth Commandment in reference to his mother." Robertson sued for libel. Campbell in turn labeled the attacks as both false and calumnious.

The affair so excited the public that Campbell had even larger audiences wherever he spoke. Not being one to walk away from a fight, he devoted one lecture to the subject of slavery, fully explaining his position. It aroused considerable interest and became a bit stormy, considering the disturbances caused by his enemies. But he continued his lectures throughout Scotland until a warrant was issued for his arrest in Lanark. He was returned to Glasgow and incarcerated in the renowned Bridewell Prison.

Portrait of Alexander Campbell by James Bogle, c. 1850-52.
Courtesy of Bethany College

His friends offered to make bond for his release, but he refused, explaining, "I thought it might be of great value to the cause of my Master if I should give myself into the hands of my persecutors." He was convinced that the slavery charge was but a ruse, and that the real reason for the persecution was his plea for reformation.

His ten days in prison were not all that bad, though he did contract a cold that limited his speaking schedule after his release. Sisters in the church were allowed to wait on him and to spruce up his cell. And the jailer placed no limitation on the number of visitors, with as many as eleven in his cell at a time when the law allowed but two. It turned out that in Scotland he lectured not only to full halls and full churches, but even to a full prison cell.

The judge at last ruled that the warrant against him was illegal, and the perpetrator fled the country, forfeiting his bond. The money was given to Campbell, who passed it along to Scottish charities.

However grievous all this may have been to him, it did not compare with the devastation he was to experience once he returned home. It was during this time that his son Wickliffe drowned.

5.9. Bethany College

When he founded Bethany College on his own farm in 1840, he intended it to be part of his reformation, even if it was late in coming. After a decade as the college's president he wrote of it: "It was in its conception, is now in its existence, and will ever be in its fortunes, identified with the cause of the Reformation, and essential to its prosperity." He lived to see the college produce some of the Movement's most eminent leaders, including J. W. McGarvey and Moses E. Lard, and such political figures as Champ Clark (Speaker of the House) and Joseph L. Clark (US Supreme Court). Future President James A. Garfield served as a trustee of the college.

He believed that education must touch the heart as well as the head and that it is "the art of living," not simply a preparation for living. Its disciplines are literature, science, music, and religion. The college may have reflected that philosophy, but it was a constant problem to him. By the time he was in his sixties, then serving as professor and treasurer as well as president, he complained that the college had been "a perpetual incubus and trouble." Since "incubus" means nightmare, it must have been a heavy burden in his old age — and that was before the college burned and had to be rebuilt and before a student uprising over slavery.

5.10. Publications

During these two and a half decades he was a prodigious publisher. With his *Millennial Harbinger's* monthly forty-eight pages of small type, plus reams of "Extras" and other publications, he turned out what was virtually a book a month.

Christianity Restored (408 pages, 1835) bore a title that he did not choose (perhaps a mistake of the publisher) and that embarrassed him, for he did not claim that Christianity began only with his reformation. While it was a compilation of principal "Extras" from the *Harbinger,* he added a revealing preface about his work. He went on record to say that he agreed with some others that he had best expressed his principles of reformation in the *Christian Baptist* — the very venue that some criticized as expressive of his immaturity. He also expressed a desire for "rectifying some extremes" of some of his followers, including what he referred to as "ultraist" views on baptism.

In that preface he also spelled out what he called the "capital principle" of his plea for unity drawn from twenty-five years of controversy. He said the principle was "inscribed upon our banners when we withdrew from the ranks of the sects." It read: "Making faith in Jesus as the true Messiah and obedience to him as our Lawgiver and King, the only test of Christian character, and the only bond of Christian union, communion, and cooperation, irrespective of all creeds, opinions, commandments, and traditions of men."

He sometimes published his own books and even

printed them on his presses in Bethany. This was the case with *The Christian System in Reference to the Union of Christians and a Restoration of Primitive Christianity* (313 pages, 1839). This volume, popularly known as *The Christian System,* was a revision of the earlier *Christianity Restored* and had a telling influence on the theology of his people for generations, remaining in print through the twentieth century. He wrote at length on such themes as the kingdom of God and the remission of sins.

His 1827 version of the New Testament, popularly known as *The Living Oracles,* continued in print through the 1850s and beyond. A fifth edition appeared in 1872 in a large-print, artistically embossed volume of 452 pages of text and 111 pages of helps.

His *Psalms, Hymns, and Spiritual Songs, Original and Selected,* originally published about 1835, continued to be used by many churches. He issued a fifth edition with a gilded, designed cover in 1856. Three of his co-laborers — Walter Scott, Barton W. Stone, and John T. Johnson — joined him as editors, all four described as "Elders of the Christian Church." This handsome volume with the simple title *Christian Hymn Book* in gold lettering was also printed on his presses, as were all forty-seven volumes of his two journals.

Alexander Campbell pictured here at Bethany in 1858, with the original caption "Bishop in His Study." Future U.S. President James A. Garfield, upon visiting Campbell in this study in 1853, wrote of him, "He is a living wonder . . . a new man every time you meet him, for his mind seems to be taking a sweep through the universe and is enlightening new objects at every inch of its orbit." Courtesy of Bethany College

His presses also produced *Christian Baptism: With Its Antecedents and Consequences* in 1851. All five of his published major debates stayed in print during most of these years.

These publishing ventures not only furthered his cause, but they were financially profitable. As noted earlier, his franking privileges as postmaster of the village of Bethany allowed him to mail all these items free of charge. At least some of the profit went to his favorite charities, one being the American Christian Missionary Society.

He continued to write and publish into his sunset years.

6. The Sunset Years (1855-66)

6.1. A Book Dedicated to His Wife

In 1861, at age 73, Campbell authored an impressive volume of 647 pages titled *Popular Lectures and Addresses,* issued by a Philadelphia publisher. While the essays were selected from those he had already published, primarily in the *Millennial Harbinger,* the book is witness to a continuing demand for his writings even in his declining years. In the preface the publisher refers to the author as "one of the most original minds and profound thinkers of the age," and as one who "throws new light upon whatever he touches." He went on to say that Alexander Campbell had "entered the great harvest fields of truth and observation and has brought home the riches of his herculean labors."

The essays selected bear witness not only to the wide range of Campbell's interests and areas of competence but to his trust in ordinary people to apply their minds to weightier matters. The subjects included moral philosophy, capital punishment, war, demonology, phrenology, life and death, and philosophy of memory, as well as more common subjects like public schools, colleges, woman and her mission, and a Fourth-of-July oration.

He dedicated the book to "Selina Huntington Campbell, My Dutiful and Affectionate Wife, Who Has Greatly Assisted Me In My Labors In The Gospel, At Home and Abroad." This makes for an interesting footnote to Campbell history in that some historians have seen the second wife as overshadowed by the first.

Campbell married his first wife, Margaret, in 1811, only to lose her sixteen years later. She left five young daughters for someone else to care for. Selina was Margaret's younger friend, who helped care for her and the children during her prolonged illness. Margaret deemed it appropriate to suggest to her husband, in case he chose to marry again, that he consider Selina. He considered it. Less than a year later, in 1828, he and Selina were married. He therefore dedicated the book to his wife of forty-three years. In 1882 Selina would write a book about her husband, *Home Life and Reminiscences of Alexander Campbell by His Wife.*

6.2. Memoirs of Thomas Campbell

Another volume he published in these later years was *Memoirs of Elder Thomas Campbell* (1861), in which he revealed some intimate scenes from the life of his father, who spent his last years in the son's home. Now blind, "Father Campbell," as they called him, would sit alone and quote psalms and other favorite scriptures for hours. He would ask visitors and family members to check him for accuracy as he quoted the Bible. J. W. McGarvey, then a student at Bethany, was one of the visitors who afterwards recalled that "Father Campbell" quoted lengthy portions of Scripture without missing a single word.

Campbell used this book to put his father's *Declaration and Address,* first published in 1809, back in print, and he used the occasion to comment on that founding document. It was "the embryo" of the principles that forged their reformation, he asserted, and he claimed that he had never read or heard the first objection "plausible in the least degree" to any position set forth in the document. He believed that it took the only plausible ground for the realization of the unity for which Christ prayed. He also used the book to tell of how when he had decided to be "evangelically baptized" in 1812, his father joined him. It was a watershed event in their lives together.

6.3. Translation of Acts

Through the years writing was apparently easy for Campbell. Usually he would have written enough before breakfast to keep his typesetters busy all day. This was not the case with his translation of the book of Acts, published in 1858. He worked so long and so arduously on this assignment that it substantially impaired both his mental and physical health. He complained in a letter to a family member: "I have been more oppressed and broken down with hard labor this year past than at any period of my life." He not only had the task of translating the Greek into English that corrected perceived errors of the Authorized Version (KJV), but he had to supply copious critical notes.

He gave up his farming duties for the time, depriving himself of his usual exercise, and limited his work at the college and other duties. This went on for "many months" until his friends began to notice a change in his behavior. In his public speeches he faltered for words and appeared to forget. In private conversation he was confused about events of the past, and at the college and the *Harbinger* office he had difficulty performing as usual.

While improvement came with his return to travel, which he always found to be a respite from pressures at home, it was the beginning of what some historians have referred to as his years of senility, particularly in the early 1860s. But his senility may not have been as prominent or permanent as supposed. In spite of some episodes of mental fatigue, he did some of his most meaningful travel and some of his most effective writing in this last decade of his life.

Even while he was working on Acts, he stole away long enough in 1855 for a trip to Nashville with his wife. But it was not exactly a vacation. His mission was not unlike that of a "bishop" caring for an erring parish. Jesse B. Ferguson, popular young minister of the Christian Church in Nashville, was teaching universalism, unitarianism, and spiritualism, and Campbell hoped to save both him and the church by open discussion. Yet Ferguson claimed to have received a message from the late W. E. Channing, noted Boston Unitarian, telling him to have nothing to do with Alexander Campbell.

In spite of being unable to confront Ferguson personally — "thwarted by a ghost," Campbell quipped — the aging reformer succeeded in convincing much of the congregation to repudiate Ferguson's leadership. The crisis affected all of Nashville, making it appropriate for Campbell to address a huge crowd at the Methodist Church as well as to minister to his own people at the Christian Church. Writing about this crisis afterwards in the *Harbinger,* he penned one of his most sublime essays about the sufficiency of the Christian faith. He asked how anyone "believingly immersed into Jesus Christ" could turn from the great Teacher sent from God, the Light of the world, and consult with spirits of the dead on the pretense of more light.

6.4. Travel in Old Age

Until the outbreak of the Civil War in 1861, Campbell traveled extensively in spite of his advancing age. In 1855 he was in Canada, eastern Virginia, Baltimore, and Washington, D.C. In 1856 he visited churches in Kentucky for forty-eight days, then went to Ohio for annual meetings of the churches, and from there to New York City for the annual meeting of the American Bible Union, which had commissioned his translation of Acts. He hurriedly filled an appointment in Danbury, Connecticut, and then traveled to Cincinnati to address a literary society and attend meetings of the American Christian Missionary Society.

In 1857 he traveled widely in the South as far as New Orleans and returned home by way of Richmond and Washington, D.C., a total of 6,000 miles. He said the trip had two purposes: to plead the cause of original Christianity and to promote the interests of Bethany College. Later that year he traveled to Cincinnati again, then to Illinois and Iowa. In all these places he addressed churches filled to capacity, those of other denominations as well as his own.

Near the end of 1857 the main building of Bethany College was destroyed by fire. Though classes continued uninterrupted, he was forced to travel even more to raise funds for the erection of an even better edifice. By now he admitted that he was tired and would rather stay home, but "I cannot rest from my labors till I am called also to rest with my fathers." He called on W. K. Pendleton, vice president of the college and his son-in-law, to go with him.

For the next several months they traveled far and wide among the churches, both preaching and raising money for the college. In a letter to his wife from Kentucky in 1858, he revealed something of their method: "He preaches for the college, and I for the church." That must have meant that the vice president made the pitch for funds, while he preached the gospel. They succeeded in their mission, and in 1859 the cornerstone was laid for one of the most impressive college edifices in the nation at that time. Old Main, as it is now called, is registered as a national historic site.

While they were in Louisville, the editor of the *Louisville Journal* wrote an editorial titled "Alexander Campbell." He described him as "venerable and distinguished," and as "unquestionably one of the most extraordinary men of our times." He went on to say that "His personal excellence is certainly without stain or a shadow," and that "No poet's soul is more crowded with imagery than is his with the ripest forms of thought." He concluded, "In his essential character, he belongs to no sect or party, but to the world."

With Selina at his side, he continued his extensive visits among the churches from the spring of 1859 until the spring of 1861, when the outbreak of the Civil War brought his travels to a virtual standstill. In 1859 he was in the South again, Tennessee, Alabama, Mississippi, and Louisiana, and in Kentucky he again addressed the American Christian Missionary Society for which he still served as president. They went on to Missouri and even as far as Kansas. He was always in demand and always had full houses, those of other churches as well as his own.

In 1860-61 Isaac Errett accompanied Campbell and Selina on a demanding schedule in Indiana. It lasted for eight weeks, and Campbell averaged more than one address each day. He was now 72. This long, arduous journey of 2,000 miles seemed to improve his health and vigor.

6.5. Impact of Civil War

Isaac Errett was again with the two of them in the spring of 1861 on a trip to eastern Virginia, a journey cut short by the outbreak of war. When Campbell heard on April 12 that Fort Sumter had been fired on, he cancelled all further appointments and returned to Bethany. On his way back to western Virginia he was grieved to see ample preparations for the bloody conflict. He was by conviction a pacifist and had long opposed his nation going to war. But he was not surprised. As early as 1840 he had predicted that it was inevitable. "The South will never surrender the institution of slavery without bloodshed," he had told a friend.

The war was devastating to Alexander Campbell. It did far more than curtail his travel, which was the heart of his ministry. Since much of his patronage was in the South, it decimated his outreach. There was no longer postal service to the South, greatly reducing his mailing list for the *Harbinger,* though it continued to be published. The enrollment at the college, also heavily dependent on Southern patronage, was reduced to a shadow of what it had been. Both college and journal were in fact threatened with extinction. And, as noted above, he had a son involved in the conflict.

Moreover, his church was threatened by division into North and South, as were other churches. And what was to become of his dream of "the millennial church" in this new republic, his adopted country, called of God to usher in a new age of unity and peace in society and church alike?

6.6. In Spite of Old Age

He persevered through four years of war. He continued to travel, though now nearer home. He continued his morning lectures at the college, at least for a while longer, and he continued as president, at least in name, until death. He continued to do his part of the preaching at the Bethany church. And he continued to write for the *Harbinger,* and served as its editor until 1864.

He still had a commanding and venerable appearance. His abundant hair and ample beard were now of silvery whiteness. He was still tall and erect, but by his mid-70s he began to appear tremulous and enfeebled. He became increasingly forgetful. He would start to leave for the college for his morning lecture, only to be reminded that he no longer had to do that. Once in the pulpit at the Bethany church he was so confused that W. K. Pendleton urged him to step down and give place to Dr. Robert Richardson. But still he sat and listened to his physician friend with rapt attention. When his daughter Decima Barclay recounted her experiences in Cyprus and the Holy Land, he responded as if he himself had been there. He would occasionally sit up in bed during the night and utter prayers and sermons as if he were in a public service.

Even in his last year he wrote letters and pub-

Photograph of Alexander Campbell c. 1859-61 in Matthew Brady's National Portrait Gallery.
Courtesy of Bethany College

lished essays in the *Harbinger.* He made a trip to Louisville where he addressed two churches with such vigor and presence of mind as to surprise his friends. And when he gave what proved to be his last sermon, at the Bethany church only a few months before his death, his mind seemed "unusually alert and vigorous." His sermon, drawn from Ephesians 1, was on one of his favorite themes — the eternal purpose of God as fulfilled in Jesus Christ. It was described as "one of the most interesting and animated discourses of his life."

His *Harbinger* articles during this time also indicated that he was still focused on his life's mission. An 1862 essay on "Union, Union, Union" once more issued an urgent call for the unity of all Christians, and he once more appealed to "the seven superlative facts" of Ephesians 4:4-6 as the grounds for that unity. These seven facts are not opinions, theories, or speculations, he insisted, but they are "the die and cornice of the house of God" and the foundation of Christ's church. Unity on this foundation is practicable, he urged, but on any other foundation it is impracticable. Yet these seven facts unite only in an atmosphere of forbearance and longsuffering. He drew an illustration from the dreadful war that was raging between the states. Just as a nation cannot find peace without these virtues, so a church cannot preserve unity.

He had a penchant for writing prefaces, and they were often autobiographical, even self-searching. In the 1864 *Harbinger,* two years before his demise, he wrote his last preface, and it was introspective. "For forty years we have not been an unfaithful nor an unwatchful sentinel upon the walls of Zion," he mused. He had cherished the hope of ending his service beneath peaceful and hopeful skies, but how could he expect his "wily foe" to ever sleep in his work of evil and mischief? "The times are full of corruption," he wrote, "and the church is contaminated with the times." We must remember that we, as the people of God, are not of this world, he urged.

"Shall we see our long labors go down in the storm of an hour, and give ourselves and our charge, without an effort or struggle, up to the devouring elements?" he asked his readers. He had his answer. While he and his followers were in a perpetual war to the end, they would not give up. He issued a challenge: "Who are the faithful ones, that stand ready to help us in this work?" While a weary veteran, he wrote as if he had just begun to fight.

6.7. Last Essay

He wrote his last article in November 1865, four months prior to his death. Simply titled "The Gospel," Campbell reiterated "the seven Facts that constitute the whole gospel." These are the birth, life, death, burial, resurrection, ascension, and coronation of Christ. These had always been the identifiable core of the New Testament for Campbell, "the Apostles' testimony," and the basis for Christian unity. In an interesting way Campbell's insight anticipated some twentieth-century scholarship, particularly the work of C. H. Dodd, who outlined the apostolic kerygma from diverse texts across the New Testament.

Campbell's plea for unity since *Christian Baptist* days had been related to the distinction he made between preaching the gospel and teaching the apostle's doctrine. The gospel consists of facts that we accept or reject, while doctrine involves theological opinion over which we can and will differ. Campbell never understood believing facts to be simple intellectual assent to information but a transforming appropriation of the reality to which the facts point. In the case of the gospel the facts point to the proposition that God is love. Campbell had long maintained that this proposition alone had the power to unite believers to God and one another. Believing and obeying the gospel unites us in Christ and is the basis of our unity and fellowship. The apostles' teaching is the curriculum we study once we are enrolled in Christ's school. In that school we are in different grades and we can and will differ in understanding.

This distinction was so vital to Campbell that he presumed one could not have a proper understanding of the New Testament without recognizing it. It is not surprising, then, that he made it part of his last essay.

6.8. New Heavens and a New Earth

In the last paragraph of his last essay he briefly details his view of the eternal state. The present material universe will be wholly regenerated. Of this we can be sure, he said, for he who sits upon the throne has promised, "Behold, I make all things new." Consequently, there will be new heavens and a new earth. This means, as he saw it, "new tenantries, new employment, new pleasures, new joys, new ecstacies." Then in his final line he recognized a limitation that included himself: "There is a fullness of joy, a fullness of glory, and a fullness of blessedness, of which no living man, however enlightened, however enlarged, however gifted, ever formed or entertained one adequate conception."

Hope was a constant theme in his essays and discourses all through the years. He often reminded his audiences that the "one hope" of the world was the seven facts of the gospel, and that it is faith, hope, and love that endure forever. It was an assurance that served him till the end.

His longtime friend and physician, Robert Richardson, called on him shortly before his death. He told him that the Reformers — meaning their people — and the Baptists were meeting in hopes of effecting a union between the two groups. "There was never any sufficient reason for a separation between us and the Baptists," Campbell responded. He went on to say, "We ought to have remained one people, and to have labored together to restore the primitive faith and practice." Another visitor during this time, Joseph King, a fellow minister, reported that when he talked to Campbell about the unity meeting with the Baptists, Campbell openly wept with joy over the prospects of such a union.

It seemed appropriate that even at death's door Alexander Campbell would be praying and talking — even weeping — about the unity of God's people.

BIBLIOGRAPHY Selina Campbell, *Home Life and Reminiscences of Alexander Campbell* (1882) • Louis Cochran and Leroy Garrett, *Alexander Campbell: The Man and His Mission* (1965) • Alger M. Fitch, *Alexander Campbell: Preacher of Reform and Reformer of Preaching* (1988) • Winfred E. Garrison, *Alexander Campbell's Theology, Its Sources and Historical Setting* (1900) • Perry E. Gresham, ed., *The Sage of Bethany: A Pioneer in Broadcloth* (1988) • Richard T. Hughes, "From Primitive Church to Civil Religion: The Millennial Odyssey of Alexander Campbell," *Journal of the American Academy of Religion* 44 (1976): 87-103 • Jesse Kellems, *Alexander Campbell and the Disciples* (1930) • D. Ray Lindley, *Apostle of Freedom* (1957) • Harold L. Lunger, *The Political Ethics of Alexander Campbell* (1954) • Thomas H. Olbricht, "The Relevance of Alexander Campbell for Today," *Restoration Quarterly* 30 (1988): 159-68 • Robert Richardson, *Memoirs of Alexander Campbell*, 2 vols. (1868) • James L. Seale, ed., *Lectures in Honor of Alexander Campbell Bicentennial, 1788-1988* (1988) • Mark G. Toulouse, "Campbellism and Postmillennialism," *Discipliana* 60 (2000): 78-96.

LEROY GARRETT

Campbell, Alexander (Alex) Cleveland (1866-1930)

African American preacher in the Stone-Campbell Movement in Tennessee.

Campbell was a fiery preacher, baptized in Wartrace, Tennessee, by D. M. Keeble, uncle of Marshall Keeble (1878-1968). He was the first African American known to have withdrawn from a church over the issues dividing the Movement at the end of the nineteenth century. He was a member of the Lea Avenue Church in Nashville, Tennessee. While a guest speaker was preaching in the absence of regular minister Preston Taylor, Campbell stood to challenge the innovations, including instrumental music in worship, being promoted by that speaker. Campbell's challenge was answered when the organist was told to drown him out with music. Campbell was unsuccessful in persuading the people of the Lea Avenue congregation to agree with his positions, so he began a church in his home. S. W. Womack (d. 1920) and other Christians who disagreed with the innovations soon joined Campbell. Many of the African American Churches of Christ in the middle Tennessee area had their origin in his ministry.

See also African Americans in the Movement; Keeble, Marshall; Taylor, Preston

BIBLIOGRAPHY J. E. Choate, *Roll Jordan Roll* (1968).

ERVIN C. JACKSON

Campbell, Selina Huntington Bakewell (1802-1897)

Second wife of Alexander Campbell. Born November 12, 1802, at Lichfield, England, the only daughter of Samuel and Ann Maria Bean Bakewell's six children. She was named for the eighteenth-century Methodist philanthropist and activist Lady Selina, Countess of Huntington.

Selina Bakewell arrived with her family at Wellsburg, (West) Virginia, in the upper Ohio Valley in

Portrait of Selina Campbell by James Bogle, c. 1851-52.
Courtesy of Bethany College

1804. There she attended Old Brick Academy, her only formal education. She then managed the household for her brothers and mother after her father Samuel left the family, taking his fourth son Theron with him, to escape debtors' prison in 1816. Horatio, the second son, struggled to support the family with a small glassmaking factory.

In 1821, at the age of 19, Selina Bakewell was baptized by her future husband, Alexander Campbell, after several years of attending Wellsburg Church of Christ, the second church founded by Campbell. Ann Maria Bean Bakewell's family had been Baptists for several generations — her maternal grandfather, George Bean, serving as a deacon at the Baptist Church in Shrewsbury, England. The Wellsburg Church had been formed through the merging of the Wellsburg Baptist Church with some members of the first Campbell church at Brush Run in Pennsylvania. After joining the Wellsburg church, Selina formed such a close relationship with Campbell and his family, especially his wife Margaret Brown Campbell, that as Margaret lay dying of tuberculosis in late 1827, she secured her husband's promise that he would consider the young Miss Bakewell for the role of stepmother to their five daughters.

On July 31, 1828, 26-year-old Selina married her former mentor, Alexander Campbell, at the home of her brother, Horatio. Selina then moved to her husband's estate in Bethany on Buffalo Creek several miles south of Wellsburg. She would spend most of the rest of her life on the farm her husband received from his first wife's family. Alexander was already two decades into his preaching and publishing career. Marriage to such a prominent man brought a number of challenges for the new Mrs. Campbell. Unlike her predecessor, she had been raised in town, which left her unprepared for many aspects of life on her husband's farm. Fortunately, she learned very quickly.

The most pressing challenge presented itself immediately. Only a year after their marriage, Alexander left Bethany for Richmond to participate in the Virginia Constitutional Convention of 1829-30. Alexander's correspondence to her during the time he was away testifies to the close, affectionate nature of their relationship regardless of the origins of their marriage. His letters contain passionate expressions of his deep love and affection for his bride and his appreciation for her work in maintaining their household. In her husband's absence, Selina managed a several-hundred-acre farm, cared for four of her stepdaughters, and hosted dozens of houseguests. She also gave birth to a child of her own in June 1829, just a few weeks before her husband's departure. The daughter was given the name Margaret Brown Campbell after her father's first wife. The list of tasks necessary to run such a household and raise her family was enormous, but it was a role Selina apparently embraced as her contribution to her husband's life and ministry.

Selina's support of her husband's ministry came in several forms. For instance, during his absence while at the Virginia Constitutional Convention, Selina managed her husband's many business activities from their home. With the help of his secretary, Selina often oversaw shipments from his printing press, planned the production of crops on the farm, and maintained his correspondence with contacts around the country.

Often, however, her most important role was mother to her five stepdaughters and later to her own six children. Both Alexander and Selina valued motherhood highly. In common with many others of the day, they considered it a holy vocation and important part of forming the character of children. This was a role assigned to women by God manifest in their more gentle nature and domestic abilities. It was also a very time-consuming role for Selina Campbell. Following Margaret's birth, Selina had three sons, Wickliffe, Alexander Jr., and William, and two more daughters, Virginia and Decima.

Of her children, Selina developed the closest relationship with Wickliffe. The two were constantly in each other's company. Young Wickliffe seemed the most likely of Campbell's fourteen children to follow in his father's footsteps. His serious nature and love for memorizing Scripture caused all around him to expect a brilliant future for him. His tragic drowning at age 10 sent shockwaves through the Campbell family and their friends. The tragedy probably affected Selina most profoundly. She immediately fell into a deep depression. At times Alexander would find her crying at their son's gravesite or swimming in the creek where he drowned. Her recovery from this devastating loss did not come until another great tragedy. In the fall of 1847, only a few months after Wickliffe's death, Selina's eldest daughter, Margaret Brown Campbell Ewing, died from tuberculosis, a disease that had already claimed all of Alexander's children from his first marriage. Margaret's newborn son, Selina's first grandchild, died soon after. In the wake of the two deaths, guests of the Campbells witnessed Selina's sudden return to her responsibilities. She later described her depression over Wickliffe's death as a reminder from God that she had given too much of her attention to the child. It was a lesson she remembered the rest of her life. Somehow the death of Margaret and her child brought Selina back to a realization of her duties and reconciled her to God's sovereign power over her family.

In addition to motherhood, Selina also acted as hostess of the Campbell Mansion. As her husband's fame as a preacher, teacher, and writer grew, so did the number of people journeying to his home to visit him. The Campbell dining room table sat thirty, and it was often full. Selina took pride in her ability to care for the bodies of her guests while her husband fed their minds. This task required vast amounts of labor. From her brother Theron, who operated a general store in southern Virginia, she obtained many of the items she needed to run the household. These items included dozens of yards of black fabric from which she fashioned mourning clothes for the family, as well as dozens of dishes and various food items. With the help of several servants, who were often slaves the Campbells would educate and then free after a few years of service, Selina managed to feed, house, and often clothe the hundreds of visitors to the Campbell Mansion at Bethany. The house was so well known that it eventually acquired the name of "the Mecca of Campbellism." Both Alexander and Selina took pride in their willingness to house any who came to their door.

The Campbells also combined their energies in several projects that significantly impacted the Movement. Perhaps the most important of these was the founding of Bethany College in 1847. The college was an extension of both Selina and Alexander's support for the beneficial effects of education on the mind and the importance of instruction in both

Selina and Alexander Campbell photographed at the time of their visit to Cincinnati for the convention of the American Christian Missionary Society, 1860. Twenty-four years younger than her husband, Selina outlived him by thirty-one years. Courtesy of Bethany College

moral and intellectual endeavors. While her husband raised funds for the college, Selina directed preparations for the living quarters of the students, and upon their arrival she often hosted them in the Campbell home for evenings of dining and singing. Though the school's main building tragically burned in 1857, the Campbells were successful in rebuilding it on an even grander scale after several years of fundraising.

By 1860 Alexander Campbell had mostly retired from his life of preaching and teaching. His health failed and his mind wandered, but he was at last restored to his wife. The last years of their marriage were perhaps the happiest as the couple spent more time together than at any other time. By 1866, however, Campbell was near death. Selina remained steadfast at her husband's side and could hardly be persuaded to leave him even to eat or rest. His death on March 4, 1866, sent her into a deep mourning from which she never completely emerged, though she lived another thirty-one years. Ironically, the death of her husband provided an opportunity for his followers to express their respect and affection for his widow, whom they recognized as his faithful companion and an invaluable participant in her husband's life and ministry.

After her husband's death, Selina's activities changed significantly, becoming more public. In particular, she found time to write more than a hundred articles that appeared in various religious publications. As a more than competent author and thinker, Selina Campbell often commented on issues that captured her attention — some cultural, others political or philosophical. They included articles opposing dancing, supporting the importance of simple worship, and demonstrating the importance of reading Christian biographies. Several newspaper editors commented on her skills as a writer as they published her articles. Many of her writings demonstrated the importance of her faith in a personal, active, and righteous God. Her favorite author was John Newton, best known as the composer of the hymn "Amazing Grace." She admired the deep Christian commitment that had brought him out of a life as a slave trader and into a life of service and ministry in England. Selina read the Bible daily and was familiar with its contents. She constantly offered Scripture to her children as a guide to making decisions and living righteously. This faith provided the lens through which she interpreted the society she observed.

Like many Christians of her era, Selina Campbell distrusted the social scene she associated with town living. Issues of dancing, parties, and fancy dress struck deep chords within her conscience. She worried that these activities distracted Christians from their relationship with God and left them no time for sober reflection and meditation on scriptural principles and the love of God. But Selina's proscriptions regarding worldly entertainment did not prevent Christians from fellowshiping with each other through singing, sharing meals, and celebrating birthdays. These were common activities at the Campbell Mansion throughout her lifetime.

It was in the often delicate arena of gender relations that the wife of Alexander Campbell showed some of her most brilliant abilities and her strong belief in the vast potential of women's active role in society and church life. Occasionally frustrated with those who placed arbitrary limits on women's potential and God-given aptitude, she strongly promoted expanded roles for women in church and society that would, however, not undermine their traditional domestic role.

One of Selina's most enduring interests was the development of missions efforts in both the United States and abroad. She especially emphasized the importance of women in this effort and used her skills as an author to expand their contribution. As with many other nineteenth-century American women, Selina Campbell's life had been fundamentally altered by reading the best-selling autobiography of one of the first American missionaries overseas, Ann Judson. Mrs. Judson and her husband, Adoniram, served as Baptist missionaries in Burma in the early nineteenth century. Judson's death in a foreign land while serving her God inspired Selina and drew her interest to missions activities. In 1856, she began a new movement among women in the Stone-Campbell Movement when she published the first female call for support for missions. The article appeared in her husband's journal, *Millennial Harbinger,* and was titled "To My Christian Sisters in Common Faith." Though short and simple in its appeal for funds for Mary Williams (then the Movement's only missionary), it nonetheless represented the first public notice by a woman attempting to raise funds in support of foreign missions in the Stone-Campbell Movement. Selina had resorted to this action because of her disappointment with the ineffectiveness of the American Christian Missionary Society, which had been founded in 1849. Later, in 1874, she would welcome the organization of the Christian Woman's Board of Missions. She served as president of the organization's second chapter, the West Virginia chapter.

Alexander Campbell's widow also believed strongly in the importance of personal evangelism, especially for women. Not only were they responsible for the religious instruction of their children, but their interaction with other women as they pursued their domestic activities provided opportunities to share their faith with a number of people. Thus, women's evangelism did not require public preaching, which could threaten their family life, but instead was based on the traditional domestic role women already fulfilled. In this way, every woman served the cause of Christ without violating what she saw as God's prescribed role for women in the home.

While at Bethany Mansion in the 1880s, Selina completed one of her most beloved writing projects, *Home Life and Reminiscences of Alexander Campbell.* Nearly two decades previously, Dr. Robert Richardson, a close friend and physician to the Campbell family, had presented Selina with his two-volume biography of her husband's life. She had provided him with much of the material in the form of her husband's papers, none of which she ever allowed to be destroyed. She had eagerly accepted it and praised his rendition of her husband's contributions to American religion and to his family. But she also felt the half had never been told, and she claimed that her family and friends beseeched her with requests to provide further insight into the life of Alexander Campbell. *Home Life* was the product of a woman in her eighties who deeply appreciated the teachings of her husband and presented them in the context of their family life

Selina Campbell with her daughter Virginia (Campbell) Thompson and her grandchildren Virginia and William, c. 1880. Courtesy of Bethany College

and mutual affection. It remains a valuable source for understanding the domestic life of the Campbell family, which in turn sheds light on Alexander Campbell's public life as a preacher and teacher.

The last years of Selina's life were spent mainly with her children and grandchildren. She rarely attended public gatherings. But as she grew older, she found the mansion hard to maintain on her own, so she often lived for months at a time with one or the other of her daughters. Extended absences from her home did not prevent her from longing to spend her last days on earth surrounded by the source of all her memories. Throughout the 1880s and 1890s, she increasingly spent her time at the mansion. She and her closest friend, Julia Barclay, became a familiar sight to the residents of Bethany as they sat in their rocking chairs on the porch of Bethany Mansion. Mrs. Barclay was the widow of the first Disciples overseas missionary, James Barclay (1807-1874). One of her sons had married Selina's daughter, and the other son married Selina's niece, forging an even stronger bond between the two friends. Selina remained grateful for the younger woman's companionship until the end of her life.

Mid-1897 brought articles in newspapers throughout West Virginia about the 95-year-old Widow Campbell's attack of influenza. Though her family and friends hoped she would recover and live to see a full century, Selina's illness worsened until she passed away on June 28, 1897. Newspapers throughout West Virginia and Kentucky carried obituaries of the "Mother in Israel." Her funeral attracted hundreds of mourners to Bethany Mansion, a testament to her leadership and the affection they held for the gentle sister in Christ.

BIBLIOGRAPHY Selina Campbell, *Home Life and Reminiscences of Alexander Campbell* (1882) • Loretta M. Long, *The Life of Selina Campbell: A Fellow Soldier in the Cause of Reformation* (2001). LORETTA M. LONG

Campbell, Thomas (1763-1854)

Founder in 1809 with his son Alexander of a movement for the union of Christians by a restoration of the New Testament church. The union of this movement in 1832 with followers of Barton W. Stone formed the Stone-Campbell Movement.

Thomas Campbell was born February 1, 1763, near Newry in County Down, Ireland, and died in Bethany, West Virginia, January 4, 1854, a month short of his ninety-first birthday.

From the late 1790s to 1807 he labored unsuccessfully in Northern Ireland and Scotland to bring about unity among disparate Presbyterian groups. Settling on the American frontier on his arrival from Ireland, Campbell became aware of the sectarian spirit brought by the settlers to their new home, yet at the same time was sensitive to the possibilities for a fresh start that a new and free country offered. He devoted himself to advocating the primacy of Scripture in the church, believing this could become a means of Christian unity.

Thomas Campbell's son Alexander, who became the leader of the movement and gave it his own interpretation, built on ideas and foundations initiated by his father. Thomas passionately believed that there ought to be no sectarian divisions in the church and that such divisions stemmed from the imposition of "human opinions" on pure apostolic Christianity as revealed in the New Testament. Therefore, by eliminating all doctrines and practices that were not as old as the New Testament, unity would prevail. In most writings concerning the Stone-Campbell Movement, Thomas all but disappears historically after the publication in 1809 of his important statement on Christian unity, the *Declaration and Address.* Through the succeeding years, however, he remained a wise counselor and guide for his son and others in the movement. The father and son complemented each other in personality and intellect.

Portrait of Thomas Campbell by Thomas Sully. His son Alexander testified, "Growth in grace and the union of Christians on an evangelical basis, were the cherished themes of his preachings, teachings, and exhortations during the last twenty years of his life." Courtesy of Bethany College

Thomas Campbell's ancestral family was not Presbyterian. His father Archibald was born Roman Catholic but at the time of his marriage became an Anglican, worshiping God, he was fond of saying, "according to act of Parliament." Thomas was the oldest of eight children. He was educated in a military regimental school where the students received an English classical education. This consisted of studies in English grammar and reading, Latin and Greek, writing and arithmetic.

Campbell was of a deeply religious nature. Finding the formality of the Anglican tradition forbidding, he sought fellowship with the Seceder Presbyterians, those who had insisted on the right to select their own ministers when the Church of Scotland sought to limit selection. Thomas found the life and order of the Seceders more congenial to his nature. After attending their meetings a short while, he put himself under their religious guidance and, ultimately, took membership in the Seceder congregation at Newry. Shortly thereafter he determined to devote his life to the preaching of the gospel.

Thomas's first vocation was teaching school. Through the influence of a fellow Seceder, a full-time position was obtained for him at a school at Sheepbridge, a village about two miles from Newry. John Kinley, a man of means, was so impressed with his ability and promise that Kinley offered to finance Thomas's further education if he would carry out his original intention of entering the ministry. In 1783, shortly after his twentieth birthday, he entered the University of Glasgow.

Young Campbell was probably enrolled in the regular course in the Faculty of Arts. There he came under the influence of the empiricism of John Locke and the rationalistic philosophy of David Hume. The "common sense" philosophy of Thomas Reid, which gave full support to orthodox Christian faith, undoubtedly had a great influence on the development of his deepest convictions.

Thomas Campbell completed his course with honors about 1786, and in 1787 he entered the theological school maintained by the Anti-Burgher branch of the Seceder church. Anti-Burghers were those Seceders who differed over the question as to whether the mayors of Scottish cities should swear to support the established church. The school was under the direction of Rev. Archibald Bruce, a leading minister of the Anti-Burghers. The course of study, leading to licensing and ultimately to ordination, consisted of attendance at yearly sessions of eight weeks each over a five-year period.

The school week consisted of a general lecture on Monday, sermons by students on Tuesday, a lecture in Latin on systematic theology on Wednesday, an examination on the theology lecture on Thursday, more student sermons on Friday, and, on Saturday, a lecture on the Confession of Faith. He finished his course in 1791.

It was probably while teaching school at Ballymena in County Antrim between sessions at the theological school that Thomas met his future wife, Jane Corneigle (1764-1835), a descendant of French Huguenots. The exact date is not known, but probably Jane and Thomas were married sometime in June 1787. Their first child, a son, Alexander, was born September 12, 1788.

Shortly after Thomas Campbell completed his work at the theological school, he and his family returned to the Sheepbridge area, where Thomas continued to teach school and to preach occasionally for Seceder congregations of the area. While living in the town of Market Hill two daughters were born: Dorothea, born July 27, 1793, and Nancy, born September 18, 1795.

About 1798, Campbell was ordained at the time that he accepted a call to become the pastor of a Seceder congregation recently established at Ahorey, in the open country near the village of Rich Hill not far from Armagh. The family moved to a small farm near Rich Hill.

Thomas Campbell's ministry at Ahorey coincided with troublesome years of religious conflict. Organizations of Roman Catholics and of Protestants were formed for the purpose of driving the other out. These conflicts culminated in the rebellions of 1798 and 1803. Peace was partially restored by a new agreement between the parties, but many Irishmen were still discontent.

The family grew larger with the addition of a third daughter, Jane, born June 25, 1800; a second son, Thomas, born May 1, 1802; another son, Archibald, born April 4, 1804; and finally another daughter, Alicia, born April 1806. With seven children in the family Campbell found his expenses greatly increased. Unable to manage on a preacher's small salary, Campbell began to look for some means to add to his income.

Considerably occupied in teaching his own family, he decided it might be profitable to establish an academy that would be available to the public. When a house suitable for use both as a home and a school was found in nearby Rich Hill, the family moved there from the farm, and an academy was opened.

Even though he was a member of the Anti-Burgher Seceders, Campbell always displayed a surprising independence of mind. After he moved to Rich Hill, several influences began to work on Thomas, bringing him to a less rigid Calvinism: (1) the Independents (Congregationalists) he met in the village, (2) the "evangelical" revival going on about him evidenced by such men as James A. Handane (1768-1851), and (3) his increasing concern over the sectarian spirit of the Seceders.

Rebuffed in attempts to reunite the several Presbyterian groups and discouraged by renewed violence between Protestants and Catholics, Campbell decided to leave Ireland. He migrated to the United States in 1807, leaving the family in the charge of 19-year-old Alexander.

Upon arrival in Philadelphia he found the Associate Synod of North America (the organization of the Seceders in the United States) in session. Many persons known to him in Ireland had earlier settled in Pennsylvania. At his request, he was assigned by the synod to the Chartiers Presbytery in the western part of the state and moved immediately to the town of Washington.

Probably one of the best-educated clergy on the frontier, Campbell was soon in conflict with several of the native-born and less educated Presbyterian leaders. Censured by the Presbytery for his failure to follow orthodox practice in offering the Lord's Supper only to Seceders and having failed in his appeal to the Associate Synod in its next meeting, Campbell resigned from his ministry in that organization.

Under the influence of a fresh environment and with the hope that the religious quarrels of Ireland could be prevented in the new land, Thomas Campbell next began to preach for and to cooperate with all Christians, of whatever persuasion. This led in 1809 to the formation of "The Christian Association of Washington."

Before long the leaders of the new organization asked him to draw up a statement of their purposes and objectives. This resulted in a document called the *Declaration and Address,* read and approved at a special meeting of the association on September 7, 1809. It was published sometime during the last two weeks of that year.

The full title of the document is the *Declaration and Address of the Christian Association of Washington County, Washington, Pennsylvania.* It reveals more fully than anything else the spirit and genius of Thomas Campbell and is his major literary work. Rouse and Neil, in their definitive history of the ecumenical movement, call the report "one of the most important documents on the ecumenical movement to come out of North America." An unpretentious document, it has as a major presupposition that the church of Christ is one but has been divided into different parties by doctrines and practices not authorized by the New Testament.

The document reflects the philosophical studies of Thomas Campbell at the University of Glasgow, chiefly the views of John Locke (1632-1704). Prominent in the document are ideas taken almost directly from Locke's *Essay Concerning Human Understanding* and his *Letter Concerning Toleration.* Campbell reflects Locke's ideas on the purpose of the church, Locke's concept of a voluntary association of those interested in unity, as well as Locke's assumption that individuals have the right to organize a church to worship God as they think proper.

The *Declaration and Address* is important as the founding document of the Campbell movement and was so recognized at the centennial celebration of 1909. Hardly noticed by the religious leaders of the day, the document has had great significance in the development of the Stone-Campbell Movement. Thomas Campbell believed he had discovered an infallible formula for Christian union and only incidentally considered the possibility of its potential problems.

In the midst of these labors, about the first week in October 1809, Thomas received word that his family had arrived safely in New York, had proceeded by stagecoach to Philadelphia, and soon would be on their way to join him. About ten days later the family was reunited, having been separated for over two years. After meeting somewhere in the Allegheny Mountains on the road from Philadelphia, Thomas Campbell accompanied his family to a home he had prepared for them in Washington.

By the spring of 1810 little progress had been made in the cause of Christian union proposed by

Thomas. The proposals of the *Declaration and Address* had been little discussed, and no other groups had sought to form an organization similar to the Christian Association of Washington. Campbell was joined in his labors at this time by the recently arrived Alexander, who preached his first sermon in July 1810 at a meeting of the Association, which was rapidly taking on the characteristics of a church.

Thomas was greatly concerned over this development. In the *Declaration and Address* he had been careful to state that the Christian Association was not to be considered a church. He was distressed at the idea that he should be instrumental in the creation of yet another sect, further dividing the church of Christ. To avoid this possibility Campbell was encouraged to believe the Christian Association would be accepted into the fellowship of the Pittsburgh Synod of the Presbyterian Church in the United States of America. Though the PCUSA was more inclusive than the Seceder Synod, it was not to be. At a meeting of the Synod at Washington in October 1810 the request for recognition of the Christian Association was denied. Out of this disappointment in the spring of 1811 the Association constituted itself a church and built a meeting house in the valley of Brush Run.

The Brush Run church accepted the congregational form of government. They also early adopted immersion as the scriptural form of baptism. For these two actions their Presbyterian neighbors bitterly attacked Thomas Campbell and his followers, calling them "reformers."

Young Alexander, licensed to preach by the Brush Run church, was ordained January 1, 1812. Within a short while he assumed leadership of the movement, and Thomas moved into the background. For the next forty-five years the father became an able and willing assistant to the son.

With the adoption of immersion, Thomas and Alexander Campbell were brought into fellowship with the Baptists. Between 1812 and 1814 increasingly friendly relations with the Baptists led the Campbells to apply for admission to the Redstone Baptist Association. Before doing so the members of the Brush Run church discussed the matter thoroughly and presented their views to the Association in a written statement. They made known their opposition to written creeds and expressed their willingness to join the Association provided they should be allowed to teach and preach only what they derived from the Bible. After much debate the majority of the Association voted to admit the Brush Run congregation to membership in September 1815.

Sometime earlier Thomas Campbell had become convinced that his ministry would have wider influence in another section of the country and decided to move ninety miles west to a farm about two miles from Cambridge, Ohio. Before leaving for Ohio, Thomas announced his decision to follow his son's lead and preach without compensation. To support his family, in addition to farming, Campbell opened a school in Cambridge.

By late fall of 1815, having heard of an opportunity for a school in Pittsburgh, Campbell moved his family there. His main motivation in moving, however, was the opportunity to organize a congregation on New Testament principles. By the fall of 1817 Campbell, anxious to minister to the needs of a newer frontier, moved his family to Boone County, Kentucky, just opposite Cincinnati, and established a school, a base from which he could travel about the countryside and preach. Between 1817 and 1819 Campbell made several visits and preaching tours into Indiana. Campbell and his family were settled comfortably into their new home in northern Kentucky until a disturbing experience in the summer of 1819. On a Sunday afternoon Thomas preached to a group of slaves and on the next day was told that what he had done was illegal. Refusing to live where he could not freely preach the gospel, Thomas immediately made plans to return to western Pennsylvania. By the fall of 1819 the family had settled near the village of West Middletown, about seven miles from Bethany. From here he could assist Alexander in teaching at Buffalo Seminary, which had been opened in 1818, and also minister to the Brush Run church.

After it began publication in 1823, Thomas Campbell wrote for, and occasionally edited, the *Christian Baptist.* He did the same after 1830 when Alexander began publication of the *Millennial Harbinger.* In 1828, at the request of Alexander, Thomas made a trip to the Western Reserve to observe Walter Scott's ministry and report on his phenomenal success to a somewhat dubious younger Campbell. Thomas's affirmative report was enough to quell Alexander's anxieties. About 1830 Thomas took an important and extensive preaching trip to eastern Virginia and North Carolina that resulted in the organization of a number of congregations. After the death of his wife in 1835 he made his home with his son at Bethany. From 1843, about the time of his eightieth birthday, until his last days, he stayed in retirement at Bethany.

Thomas remained in fair health until just a few weeks before his death. About the middle of December 1853, he was stricken with digestive difficulties. Patient and calm during three weeks of illness, he passed away on January 4, 1854. Surrounded by his children and grandchildren, he quietly slipped away and was laid to rest in the Campbell cemetery beside his wife, Jane.

In the 1830s, and later in the 1840s, Campbell was frustrated in his attempts to call the movement away from bitterness and controversy, and to return it to the fundamental principle and objective of the "Declaration and Address," that of Christian unity based on New Testament teaching. Thomas Campbell recognized that a sectarian spirit had developed in the movement to "restore the purity of the early church."

Nevertheless, Thomas Campbell made significant and permanent contributions to the Movement's identity. It must never be forgotten that the father was chief teacher of his son. He guided much of Alexander's elementary training in Ireland, and it was he who prepared him for the university. It was the father who continued the son's instruction when Alexander arrived in the United States.

Not the least of Thomas Campbell's contributions was the steadying influence he had on the newly formed movement. He was much less iconoclastic than Alexander. He recognized the debt the Movement owed to the Reformed tradition and was a witness to the historic Christian faith as affirmed in evangelical Christianity. While the father and son did not always agree on the advisability of certain actions, they did agree on the "gospel facts" that bind all Christians in fellowship. Of equal importance, Thomas served as a check against the son's excesses. The father gave crucial assistance to Alexander in keeping the movement from utter confusion in those early days when ministers from diverse backgrounds were being assimilated into the movement, a number of new congregations were being formed, and many new members were being added.

When Thomas Campbell's life is viewed as a whole, it is clear that he sought to base his life and his preaching on the Scriptures. It was a lifelong habit for him to memorize a portion of the Bible every day. An educated, humble minister, he opened his mind and heart to receive God's truth as it was revealed to him. In his *Memoirs of Elder Thomas Campbell* his son Alexander eulogized his father: "I knew no man that so uniformly, so undeviatingly, practiced what he taught."

BIBLIOGRAPHY Alexander Campbell, *Memoirs of Elder Thomas Campbell: Together with a Brief Memoir of Mrs. Jane Campbell* (1861; repr. 1954) • William Herbert Hanna, *Thomas Campbell: Seceder and Christian Union Advocate* (1935; repr. 1986) • Lester G. McAllister, *Thomas Campbell — Man of the Book* (1954) • Thomas H. Olbricht and Hans Rollmann, *The Quest for Christian Unity, Peace, and Purity in Thomas Campbell's 'Declaration and Address'* (2000) • Robert Richardson, *Memoirs of A. Campbell*, 2 vols. (1868, 1870).

LESTER G. MCALLISTER

Campbell Institute

Organization founded by a group of young Disciples who had studied in graduate schools and were concerned to reconcile academic and religious values and loyalties.

Established at the 1896 National Convention of the Disciples of Christ, the Institute was closely associated for its entire history with the Disciples Divinity House of the University of Chicago. Edward Scribner Ames was a dominant influence on the Institute. He served as its first president and edited its journal *The Scroll* from 1903 to 1908 and again from 1925 to 1951. Institute meetings were normally held at Disciples Divinity House after 1928. "Aftersessions," late evening meetings for discussion of issues affecting the churches, were held in connection with meetings of the National or International Convention. Through its meetings and its journal, the Institute expressed support for the social gospel, biblical criticism, and Christian unity.

Conservative Disciples criticized the Institute along with other evidences of liberalism within the denomination. Nonetheless, many moderate as well as liberal Disciples found the Institute a welcome forum for free and frank discussion of issues affecting the life of the Movement, and it prospered for more than fifty years as it continued to consider issues of practical church life, social issues, denominational history and thought, and contemporary religious currents.

After graduate education for ministry became the accepted standard among Disciples, the need for the Institute as a support group declined. Furthermore, many of the positions espoused by the Institute became widely accepted among the Disciples. Consequently interest in the Institute began to decline in the 1950s, and Institute ties to Disciples Divinity House were significantly reduced after 1958. A membership meeting voted to dissolve the Institute in 1975, and it ceased operations with publication of a final, historical issue of *The Scroll* in 1978.

BIBLIOGRAPHY Samuel C. Pearson, "The Campbell Institute: Herald of the Transformation of an American Religious Tradition," *The Scroll* LXII (Spring 1978): 3-63 •Herbert L. Willett, Orvis F. Jordan, and Charles M. Sharpe, eds., *PROGRESS: Anniversary Volume of the Campbell Institute on the Completion of Twenty Years of History (1917).*

SAMUEL C. PEARSON

Campbell-Maccalla Debate

Debate between Alexander Campbell and Presbyterian minister William L. Maccalla in Washington, Kentucky, beginning October 15, 1823.

The debate, Campbell's second public debate, focused on the subjects and action of baptism. Maccalla argued that the Old Testament church and New Testament church were identical and that each had its distinctive seal — circumcision in the Old Testament and infant baptism in the New Testament. Though Maccalla was in the negative, he persisted in reading a lengthy manuscript he had prepared before the debate and ignored Campbell's arguments. This continued through eight days.

Campbell argued that in the New Testament baptism was always for believers, never infants. He affirmed that immersion was the only valid baptism and argued from the meaning of the Greek *baptizein,* the doctrinal import of baptism as a burial, and the testimony of certain early church fathers. Campbell also presented a new and significant view of the *design* of baptism, namely that it is for the remission of sins and essential to "formal" forgiveness and admission to Christ's kingdom. Campbell had hinted at these views in debate with John Walker (1820), and now this was a publicly proclaimed conviction he shared with Walter Scott.

This was Campbell's first trip to Kentucky, and it opened the door for him to spread his reform views among Kentucky Baptists. But for them, the debate was a mixed blessing. They thought he had bested Maccalla but were disturbed at his non-Baptist views on the two covenants and the purpose of baptism. Campbell distributed copies of the *Christian Baptist,* and within a year he had 1,000 subscribers in Kentucky. He made a preaching tour of Kentucky in 1824, visited Georgetown, and met Barton W. Stone, and eight years later the Stone and Campbell movements in Kentucky came together.

See also Baptism; Campbell-Rice Debate; Campbell-Walker Debate; Debates, Debating; Presbyterians, Presbyterianism

BIBLIOGRAPHY Alexander Campbell and William Maccalla, *A Public Debate on Christian Baptism Between the Rev. W. L. Maccalla, a Presbyterian Teacher, and Alexander Campbell, to Which Is Added an Essay on the Christian Religion, by A. Campbell* (1842) • John Mark Hicks, "The Recovery of the Ancient Gospel: Alexander Campbell and the Design of Baptism," in *Baptism and the Remission of Sins,* ed. David Fletcher (1990), pp. 111-70 • Bill J. Humble, *Campbell and Controversy: The Story of Alexander Campbell's Great Debates with Skepticism, Catholicism, and Presbyterianism* (1952; repr. 1986).

BILL J. HUMBLE

Campbell-Owen Debate

Public debate in 1829 between Alexander Campbell and Robert Owen, socialist and religious skeptic.

Scottish industrialist and social philosopher Robert Owen (1771-1858) came to the United States in 1825 with the hope of establishing a utopian community that would effect worldwide social reform. Influenced by radical Enlightenment rationalism, Owen opposed revealed religion and espoused a conviction that human character is, without exception, formed by one's environment. Thus, to reform society, people had only to create a controlled environment that would expose children from their earliest infancy to rational thought and good habits, while protecting them from religious superstition and vice. This was the objective of his community at New Harmony, Indiana, and he was certain its success would gain universal acceptance until a secular state of millennial bliss engulfed all of society.

Though Owen's experiment at New Harmony failed in 1827, he remained undaunted about the correctness of his philosophy. In 1828, while traveling the country promoting his ideas, Owen challenged the clergy of New Orleans to defend their religious beliefs in a public discussion. In a separate incident at roughly the same time, Alexander Campbell rejected an invitation to debate one of Owen's disciples, claiming he would rather engage the leader of the Owenite movement in a discussion of his system's moral and religious philosophy. As the prospective disputants became aware of the challenges, they began making plans for a formal debate to be held the following year in Cincinnati, Ohio.

Beginning on April 13, 1829, and lasting eight days (exclusive of Sunday), Alexander Campbell and Robert Owen squared off before crowds in excess of 1,200 people for what Cincinnati editor Timothy Flint referred to as a "combat, unparalleled in the annals of disputation." In the contest's preliminary discussions the debaters agreed that they would speak alternately for half an hour, with Owen leading off. The propositions to be discussed were the five issues of Owen's challenge to the clergy of New Orleans:

1. That all the religions of the world have been founded on human ignorance.
2. That they are directly opposed to the never-changing laws of our nature.
3. That they have been, and are, the real sources of vice, disunion, and misery of every description.
4. That they are now the only real bar to the formation of a society of virtue, intelligence, sincerity, and benevolence.
5. That they can no longer be maintained except through the ignorance of the mass of people and the tyranny of the few over the mass.

From early in the debate, Owen made it clear that his intention was not to contend with Campbell in a verbal exchange over the propositions. Rather, he used the debate as an opportunity to impart to the audience twelve "fundamental laws of human nature" consonant with his doctrine of environmental determinism. Throughout the disputation, Owen failed to address the issues raised by Campbell, but used his time to repeat and explain his twelve fundamental laws. These laws, which were repeated no fewer than twelve times throughout the contest, were the basis of Owen's argument.

Amid numerous unsuccessful attempts to force Owen to deal with the debating points, Campbell employed a modified form of the ontological argument for God's existence to counter his antagonist's anti-religious inclinations. Relying on John Locke's epistemology and on the British metaphysical philosophers who greatly influenced both disputants, Campbell argued that all original ideas are a result of sensation and reflection upon objects that have been revealed to the senses. Where, he asked, did the archetypal concepts of a creator God and spiritual things derive? Aside from a divine revelation of these ideas, Campbell maintained, they cannot find their origin in the human experience.

Unable to respond to Campbell's assertions and having nothing new to add to the repetition of his fundamental laws, Owen proposed that his opponent be permitted to conclude his argument without interruption. What followed was a twelve-hour oration (delivered in two-hour segments) in which Campbell examined the historic and prophetic evidences of Christianity, the genius of the Christian religion, and the inadequacies of Owen's social system. The debate was ultimately brought to a conclusion when Campbell requested that the members of the audience who believed in the truth of the Christian religion stand up. The response was nearly universal. He then asked for any onlookers who were doubtful of Christianity's truth to arise, but only three people responded.

As a result of his widely heralded victory and the debate's subsequent publication, Campbell's reputation advanced beyond the regional boundaries that had limited his influence. This enabled his plea for Christian reform to gain a more extensive hearing, while making him an esteemed figure in American Christianity. Furthermore, his opposition to Owen's unbelief brought additional challenges from skepticism that established Campbell as one of the leading defenders of the Christian faith in antebellum America.

See also Anthropology; Debates, Debating; Reason, Place of

BIBLIOGRAPHY Alexander Campbell and Robert Owen, *The Evidences of Christianity* (1829) • Robert O. Fife, "In the Spirit of the Prophets: Alexander Campbell as a Social Thinker," in *Lectures in Honor of the Alexander Campbell Bicentennial, 1788-1988* (1988), pp. 19-45 • J. J. Haley, *Debates That Made History* (1920) • Bill J. Humble, *Campbell and Controversy* (1952) • Earl I. West, "Early Cincinnati's 'Unprecedented Spectacle,'" reprinted in *The Stone-Campbell Movement: An International Religious Tradition,* ed. Michael W. Casey and Douglas A. Foster (2002), pp. 189-203.

RICHARD J. CHEROK

Campbell-Purcell Debate

Alexander Campbell's debate with the Archbishop of Cincinnati, John Baptist Purcell (1800-1883), was his fourth major public debate and established Campbell's national reputation as a defender of Protestantism. This debate was in many ways a meeting of mirror images. Like Campbell, Purcell was Irish by birth, deeply interested in education, and had a notable reputation as an apologist for his religious heritage. The two met in 1836 at an education conference in Cincinnati, and after a brief interchange Campbell agreed to return the following year for a more substantive discussion. The debate itself took place January 13-21, 1837, in Cincinnati with significant public and media attention. The transcript was published in book form that same year.

Campbell had first formulated his anti-Catholic theology in response to the 1833 Hughes-Breckenridge debate, and again in a series of *Millennial Harbinger* articles preparing for the Purcell debate. Building on this groundwork, he pressed two basic themes against Purcell. First, Campbell insisted on the absolute priority of Scripture and rejected Purcell's claim that ecclesiastical tradition stood alongside the Bible. For Campbell the biblical "facts" contained the true faith, so that only the Bible could sufficiently guide the church's faith and practice.

Purcell admitted that faith begins with the Scriptures, but he also held that the true faith is embodied in the faith and tradition of the Roman Catholic Church. To counter Purcell's "tradition" argument, Campbell asserted that the true Church descended, not through the Roman Catholic Church, but through an "apostolic" lineage of schismatic groups such as the Novatians and the Waldenses — any group that provided the church with a "reforming impulse."

Second, both Campbell and Purcell took pains to show how their own traditions were consistent with the ideals of American society. Campbell contended that Roman Catholic allegiance to the Pope kept Catholics from giving full allegiance to the United States, and he warned of a Jesuit invasion intent on subjugating Americans to Rome. Purcell responded by asserting that the Pope's authority was spiritual and in no way interfered with the demands of citizenship; the Pope's authority was essentially conservative and reconcilable with any form of government. Campbell's concern here reflects his growing conviction that the civil liberty and "Christian principles" on which America was founded would make possible the oncoming millennium.

Although Campbell gained tremendous notoriety from his encounter with Purcell, he curtailed his anti-Catholic activity sharply after this debate. On several occasions, including a letter published in

Purcell's journal, *The Catholic Telegraph,* Campbell explicitly distanced himself from the anti-Catholic Nativist movement, condemning its "fierce denunciatory and vindictive spirit." Likewise, Campbell and Purcell maintained an amiable personal relationship, and the two continued to profess admiration for each other even after the debate was over.

See also Roman Catholicism — Nineteenth Century

BIBLIOGRAPHY Alexander Campbell and John Purcell, *A Debate on the Roman Catholic Religion* (1837) • Carroll Ellis, "The Backgrounds of the Campbell-Purcell Debate of 1837," *Southern Speech Journal* 11 (1945): 32-41 • Mark Weedman, "History as Authority in Alexander Campbell's 1837 Debate with Bishop Purcell," *Fides et Historia* 28 (1996): 17-34 • Eva Jean Wrather, "A Nineteenth-Century Disciples-Catholic Dialogue: The Campbell-Purcell Debate of 1837," *Mid-Stream* 25 (1986): 368-74.

MARK WEEDMAN

Campbell-Rice Debate

Alexander Campbell's debate (1843) with Presbyterian minister and theologian Nathan L. Rice focused on the function and practice of Christian baptism, the role of the Holy Spirit in conversion, and the place and effect of creeds in the life of the church. It was Campbell's fifth, longest, and last major debate, taking place more than twenty years after his first debate.

The Kentucky Presbyterians had lost significant numbers to the Stone-Campbell Movement, and by 1842 the "Christians" outnumbered them five to one. John H. Brown, a representative of the Presbyterian Synod of Kentucky, approached Campbell about engaging in debate with one of their number. After a lengthy and somewhat contentious correspondence over Campbell's opponent and the propositions for debate, Nathan L. Rice of Paris, Kentucky, was selected as the unofficial representative of the Presbyterian synod. Rice proved to be an astute, though combative, adversary.

A committee composed of representatives from each side made final preparations. Henry Clay, the famed Kentucky statesman from Lexington, was chosen to serve as moderator. Each side hired a stenographer to take notes of the debate that would be published along with the preliminary correspondence. This resulted in the 1844 publication of a 912-page small print volume.

Main Street Christian Church, Lexington, Kentucky (a building no longer extant), was the site for the debate, chosen because of its large seating capacity. The debate began on Wednesday, November 15, 1843, with daily sessions, except Sunday, from 10:00 AM to 2:00 PM and some evenings, and concluded on Saturday, December 2. It was a lively and entertaining, though divisive, event. Rice was thoroughly acquainted with Campbell's written work and frequently referred to it in an effort to show that his ideas had changed over time and were self-contradictory. An important example was Rice's attempt to show, using Campbell's own statements, that he had contradicted himself on the issue of "open communion" with the unimmersed.

The topics of debate began with Campbell affirming that "immersion in water of a proper subject, into the name of the Father, the Son, and the Holy Spirit, is the one, only apostolic or Christian baptism." Campbell tried to show that "to dip, plunge, immerse" is the primary meaning of the Greek verb *baptizō,* by citing lexical, classical, and biblical sources. This, coupled with the scriptural affirmation that there is "one Lord, one faith, one baptism," led him to conclude that immersion is the one and only apostolic or Christian form of baptism.

In traditional debating fashion, Rice noted that if he could cite an exception to the meaning and usage of *baptō* and *baptizō,* he would defeat Campbell's affirmation since it is stated as a universal. Ranging over the same categories of lexical, classical, and biblical (mainly Greek Old Testament instances of *baptizō*) sources, Rice cited cases where the word means "wash" or "dye" and does not indicate "dip" or "immerse." He contended that these are central meanings of the word, whereas Campbell insisted that they are extended meanings.

Rice then affirmed that "the infant of a believing parent is a scriptural subject of baptism." He pointed to the fact that much of Christendom had for centuries considered sprinkling of infants to be Christian baptism. He argued that baptism is analogous to circumcision and that circumcision was administered to infants. He also cited general references to the administration of baptism in the New Testament that can be understood to include children and infants.

Campbell noted that simply because many, or even a majority of persons, believe something does not necessarily mean that it is true. He pointed, as he had in earlier public debates with Presbyterians John Walker and William Maccalla, to the dissimilarities between circumcision and baptism and contended that the New Testament supports believers' baptism.

Campbell next affirmed that "Christian baptism is for the remission of past sins." Campbell introduced scriptures that connect forgiveness and salvation to baptism, particularly the words of Peter (Acts 2:38) and the words of Jesus (Mark 16:16). Rice countered by citing scriptures that link faith to salvation without mentioning baptism, particularly John 3:16, 18. Campbell acknowledged that baptism was linked with faith and repentance, but stressed that baptism should be considered a crucial element in faithful response because it was the express command of the

Master. There might be times when baptism is humanly impossible, but this does not negate its general place in the plan of conversion and salvation.

In the next proposition Rice affirmed that baptism is to be administered only by a bishop or ordained presbyter. He supported his position by noting the importance of baptism for entrance into the family of Christ and, hence, the importance of controlling that entry through the administration by duly qualified and certified individuals. To open the administration of baptism to any and all laypersons is to open the church to the grave possibility of harm by impious individuals. In addition, Scripture assigns baptism to the eleven apostles (Matt. 28:16-20). It is the general human practice to pass on duties and privileges to those who are ordained by original officeholders. It makes sense that the church would follow a similar practice.

Campbell responded by noting that Rice had offered no "Thus saith the Lord" for his position and that apostolic succession has no basis in Scripture. He also argued that the book of Acts and the letters of Paul paint a picture of early Christianity in which all believers are commissioned to share the gospel and where many, if not all, kinds of Christians baptize those who respond to their witness. Campbell stressed that he was for good order in the church and that in most cases baptism should be done by those specially designated by the church, but that there is no need or scriptural basis to restrict the administration of baptism to bishops and ordained presbyters.

Campbell then affirmed that in conversion and sanctification the Spirit of God operates on persons only through the Word of truth. Contrary to some teaching, Campbell held that conversion, regeneration, and sanctification are not three separate changes but reflect different dimensions of one and the same change. It is a moral, spiritual change, not a legal or physical change. Campbell held that a moral change comes through motives, through arguments, and arguments involve language. Therefore Campbell concluded that the Holy Spirit effects conversion/sanctification through the Word of truth. In addition, Campbell asserted, history reveals that there has been no Christian conversion without the word of the gospel, the words of the Bible.

Rice held a doctrine of special divine influence. The Spirit usually works through the Word, but not always. The doctrine of total depravity implies that there must be a change of the human heart before one can even rightly hear and respond to the Word; hence the Spirit must sometimes work apart from the Word. And if infants and idiots, who cannot respond to language and argument, are to be saved from damnation, the Spirit must graciously do its work apart from the Word.

Campbell claimed that it was irrelevant to talk of infants and conversion. Where there is no understanding, there can be no disposition at all. And where there is no disposition, there can be no change of heart. Furthermore, Campbell stressed that he did not deny that the Spirit *might* work in the world apart from the Word. He simply argued that regarding Christian conversion and sanctification — the focus of the proposition under debate — there was no basis to conclude from Scripture or from life experience that the Spirit ever works apart from the Word.

Finally, Campbell affirmed that human creeds, as bonds of union and communion, were necessarily heretical and schismatic. Campbell argued that creeds are fallible because they are human productions, reflecting the character of their age. There is no "Thus saith the Lord" for the formulation and use of creeds. The Bible, rather than creeds, is the appropriate basis of faith because it reflects the divine lawgiver and is a simpler and yet richer basis for reflection than creeds. Creeds function as the basis of churches and as such reflect and produce party differences. History demonstrates the divisiveness of creeds.

Rice noted Campbell's assertion that there is no scriptural mandate for creeds, but he asked, Is everything unlawful that is not scripturally commanded? Creeds are not created for division but to publish the understandings of a denomination, providing a means to assess a group, to correct misunderstandings, to ascertain the qualification of ministers, and to guide instruction of the faithful. Creedal assent is not required for membership. In addition, Rice claimed that there was more unity among and between denominations with creeds than there was among Campbell's churches.

Both debaters closed with a call for greater Christian unity, though they continued to differ on the appropriate means for achieving that unity.

After the debate both sides claimed victory. In many ways Rice and Campbell were evenly matched. With the passage of time and the effect of the published volume, some evidence suggests that Campbell had gotten the better of the contest. The Christians (Reformers) continued to expand. There are testimonials to the influence of Campbell's printed arguments. Presbyterian John Brown, early eager to circulate the printed record of the debate, later sold his copyright to a "Christian" in Jacksonville, Illinois.

Though the debate did not settle the issues and achieve unity, it provides a good example of Campbell's thinking on several important issues at a defining point in the early development of the Stone-Campbell Movement.

See also Baptism; Campbell-Maccalla Debate; Campbell-Walker Debate; Conversion; Creeds and Confessions; Holy Spirit, Doctrine of the; Presbyterians, Presbyterianism; Regeneration; Sanctification, Doctrine of

BIBLIOGRAPHY Alexander Campbell and Nathan L. Rice, *A Debate Between Rev. A. Campbell and Rev. N. L. Rice on the Action, Subject, Design and Administrator of Christian Baptism* (1844) • J. J. Haley, *Debates That Made History: The Story of Alexander Campbell's Debates* (1920) • John Mark Hicks, "Alexander Campbell on Christians Among the Sects," in *Baptism and the Remission of Sins,* ed. David Fletcher (1990), pp. 171-202 • Bill J. Humble, *Campbell and Controversy* (1952).

EDWARD H. SAWYER

Campbell-Skinner Debate

Written debate on Universalism between Alexander Campbell and Dolphus Skinner (1800-1869) published between March 1837 and August 1839 in the *Millennial Harbinger* and the *Evangelical Magazine and Gospel Advocate* of Utica, New York.

The debate was the continuation of a written discussion begun in 1835 between Campbell and another Restorationist Universalist minister, G. W. Montgomery, over the issue of the limited or eternal nature of future punishment. The discussion with Skinner was delayed because of Campbell's debate with Roman Catholic Bishop John B. Purcell in Cincinnati, January 1837.

Propositions centered on whether biblical words like *Sheol, Hades,* and *Gehenna* signified a place of endless misery, whether *'ôlām* and *aiōn* meant duration without end, and whether endless holiness and happiness would be the ultimate destiny of all humanity. The articles were marred by constant bickering and accusations of misrepresentation, leading Campbell to express regret at having agreed to participate. Campbell gave Skinner rights to publish the debate, which he did in 1840.

See also Campbell-Purcell Debate; Universalism

BIBLIOGRAPHY Alexander Campbell and Dolphus Skinner, *A Discussion of the Doctrines of Endless Misery and Universal Salvation: In an Epistolary Correspondence Between Alexander Campbell and Dolphus Skinner* (1840; repr. ed. 1966) • W. K. Pendleton, "Universalism: Query About the Discussion with Mr. Skinner," *Millennial Harbinger* 38 (April 1867): 166-69.

DOUGLAS A. FOSTER

Campbell-Walker Debate

Debate between Alexander Campbell and John Walker, a Presbyterian minister, at Mount Pleasant, Ohio, June 19-20, 1820.

When the Baptists asked Campbell to debate Walker, he "hesitated for a little," in deference to his father's aversion to public controversy, but later agreed. The debate, Campbell's first, focused on infant baptism. Walker argued that the Old and New Covenants were essentially one and that infant baptism was the seal of the New Covenant as circumcision was for the Old. Campbell argued that the New Testament was essentially different and "better" than the Old Testament, a theological position found earlier in the *Declaration and Address* (1809) and the "Sermon on the Law" (1816). In the New Testament, the gift of the Holy Spirit took the place of circumcision as the seal of the covenant.

Walker was ill prepared to debate Campbell, and on the second day, just as they were to begin discussing the action of baptism, he proposed that the debate end with one more speech by each party. Campbell was surprised but agreed to conclude with two more speeches each and used his two to argue that baptism must be by immersion.

Campbell and his father edited and published the debate as taken from Alexander's notes. The sale of the first edition of 1,000 copies was quickly followed by the second edition of 3,000 copies.

The debate had several results. As Campbell discovered his natural abilities in polemics, he would welcome future opportunities for debates. He sensed the power of the printed page when he saw how widely the printed debate was read and discussed, and he was soon planning his first periodical, the *Christian Baptist.* Later generations of Stone-Campbell preachers, following Campbell's lead, would hold hundreds of public debates, and the popularity of these forums continued well into the twentieth century.

See also Baptism; Campbell-Maccalla Debate; Campbell-Rice Debate; Debates, Debating; Presbyterians, Presbyterianism

BIBLIOGRAPHY Alexander Campbell and John Walker, *A Debate on Christian Baptism, Between Mr. John Walker, a Minister of the Secession, and Alexander Campbell . . .* (1822) • John Mark Hicks, "The Recovery of the Ancient Gospel: Alexander Campbell and the Design of Baptism," in *Baptism and the Remission of Sins,* ed. David Fletcher (1990), pp. 111-70 • Bill J. Humble, *Campbell and Controversy* (1952).

BILL J. HUMBLE

Camps

1. Christian Churches (Disciples of Christ)
2. Christian Churches/Churches of Christ
3. Churches of Christ

1. Christian Churches (Disciples of Christ)

Befitting a movement born from "camp meetings," individual congregations offered "camp" experiences for young people either on their own or in partnership with other congregations in their geographical area early, though there is no clear indication when this began. Cynthia Pearl Maus (1880-

1970) of the United Christian Missionary Society began the young people's summer conference movement which focused on leadership education with senior high age youth. Success led to a program designed for junior high age youth in 1939.

Every region of the Christian Church (Disciples of Christ) offers some form of camping or outdoor ministry program during the summer months of each year. Christmount Christian Assembly [http://www.christmount.com] in North Carolina, the Rickman Center [http://www.midamericadisciples.org/rickmancenter.htm] in Missouri, and the Christian Conference Center [http://www.uppermidwestcc.org/ministries_ccc.html] in Iowa are examples of quality programs operating on modern year-round sites. Many regions have outdoor ministry websites that tell the stories of their individual histories of camping. Links to many of these sites can be found at the Division of Home Missions website, http://discipesyouth.com/links/content.html.

Summer camp experiences continue to be one of the most important ministerial vocation recruitment paths that the Christian Church (Disciples of Christ) has as part of its past and its present. The community experienced around the campfire continues to shape the lay leaders and clergy of the Christian Church (Disciples of Christ).

2. Christian Churches/Churches of Christ

"Camps" are facilities for extended spiritual retreat and renewal, usually in remote rural or wilderness areas. The Christian (Service) Camp movement was designed to provide a novel environment and opportunities for learning, fellowship, spiritual renewal, and recreation beyond the physical restrictions of the local congregation. The movement had its beginnings among conservative Disciples of Christ churches in the 1920s. By 1927 five such camps were under way.

Among early persons holding interest in this new activity were Mildred Welshimer Phillips (1902-1983) and Fred Gielow (1893-1941), who gave impetus to the establishment of a camp at Erie Side, Willowby, Ohio, in the northeastern part of the state in 1929. Lake James Christian Assembly acquired its lakefront property in northeastern Indiana in 1927 and began operation by 1929. A formal committee was set up in Cincinnati during December of the same year to consider this expanding camp movement. It included James DeForest Murch (1892-1973), Robert Tuck (1898-1989), J. Merrill Appelgate (1903-1988), and Guy P. Leavett (1899-1971). These individuals determined that the camps would be of service to, and not exercise authority over, the supporting churches. In other words, the camps would not become formal intercongregational structures or impose on the prerogatives of congregational independence.

Especially after World War II, camps and camping programs grew geographically across the United States, usually under the guidance of trustees from local supporting congregations. "Deans" were selected to arrange personnel and curricula for camp programs, concentrated often in weeklong sessions during summers. Rustic settings provided special and favorable conditions for Bible study, spiritual growth, and renewed interest in the natural creation. Increasingly, there were conversions and baptisms, and some more mature campers committed themselves to full-time Christian service.

The camp movement continued to expand such that by 1970 an annual National Camp Leaders Conference was organized, which in turn began to give an award recognizing an outstanding camp director of the year among camps of the Christian Churches/Churches of Christ. A variation from the norm appeared in 1999, when Southeast Christian Church in Louisville, Kentucky, the single largest congregation of the Christian Churches/Churches of Christ, established its own service camp, Country Lake, in southern Indiana.

A number of camps have equipped their facilities with lodges and conference centers for year-round functions such as adult retreats and leadership conferences. In a new venture, three camp directors and their staffs (among twenty-one others) applied for and received an Eli Lilly Endowment grant of $600,000 in 1999 for the improvement of their respective facilities: the Lake James, Allendale, and Rainbow Camps in Indiana.

The Lookout, a popular journal of Christian Churches/Churches of Christ, featured camp enrollment activity and camper dedications each year from 1935 to 1995. Feature articles on Christian camps have also regularly appeared in the *Christian Standard.* The 2002 *Directory of the Ministry* for Christian Churches/Churches of Christ listed 110 camps in 34 states including Ontario, Canada.

REUBEN G. BULLARD

3. Churches of Christ

There is no uniform rule for camp organization or structure among Churches of Christ. For much of the body's history, many congregations have supported the idea of Christian camping or church camps. Some of the earliest camps among Churches of Christ were begun in the 1930s and the 1940s in locations ranging from Ontario, Canada (Camp Omagh), to the state of Texas (Pecos River Family Encampment). These early camps originated as gospel meetings, summer Bible schools, and vacations to the country for city dwellers, but they later grew into regular camp sessions for families and young people. This transition took place predominately after the Second World War.

Today numerous church camps in North America are run by members of Churches of Christ. A number of universities affiliated with Churches of Christ direct summer camps for youth. Other camps are under the leadership of independent boards of directors. Many camps function solely on a volunteer basis. However, some camps hire a director or groundskeeper to manage the facilities, along with a staff of volunteers.

Since 1967 there have been annual meetings of the National Christian Camping Workshop at various campsites across North America. This workshop, as well as the National Association of Christian Camps (founded in 1998), serves as a medium through which members of Churches of Christ from the United States and Canada are able to share ideas concerning the ministry of Christian Camping.

KENT P. BRANTLY

See also Educational Ministry; Maus, Cynthia Pearl; Youth Groups, Youth Ministry

BIBLIOGRAPHY Robert Dale Bell, "The Development of Camp Curriculum for Northward Christian Assembly" (unpublished M.A. thesis, Cincinnati Bible Seminary, 1987) • George Gurganus, *Christian Camps* (1958) • National Association of Christian Camps, http://www.naccamps.org (2002) • Richard Virgil Smith, "The Curriculum of the Christian Service Camp" (unpublished B.Th. thesis, Cincinnati Bible Seminary, 1960) • Glenn P. Willeford, *A History of the Pecos River Family Encampment, 1940-1996* (1996).

Campus Advance

See Campus Ministry

Campus Evangelism Movement

See Campus Ministry

Campus Ministry

1. Christian Church (Disciples of Christ)
2. Churches of Christ
3. Christian Churches/Churches of Christ

1. Christian Church (Disciples of Christ)

Concern for campus ministry began as early as the 1890s in the Stone-Campbell Movement. The earliest form of campus ministry took the form of Bible Chairs attached to state colleges or universities in which Bible and religion classes were taught. The idea of a Bible Chair as a means by which the church could minister to students at state-funded schools was suggested as early as 1882 by Congregational minister Leonard W. Bacon. In 1893 the Christian Woman's Board of Missions (CWBM) founded the first Bible Chair at the University of Michigan at the urging of Charles A. Young (1881-1927), minister of the Disciples church in Ann Arbor. This placed the Movement in the role of trailblazer in campus ministry in the United States.

Having established themselves as a body concerned with higher education, the CWBM developed the concept of creating teaching positions in secular institutions that were endowed and chosen by the church. This allowed university students to take religion courses and the Disciples to minister to the spiritual lives of their young people attending state schools. Economically, this program was less expensive than establishing new colleges.

Implementation of this idea, however, met with significant resistance from sources outside the church, who saw such a program as a violation of the principle of separation of church and state. Disciples countered these accusations by explaining that the Bible Chair program would not use government funds to teach religious education; in fact, students often did not receive college credit for their course work in religion. To further establish the validity of these faculty positions, it was required that teaching be non-dogmatic and reflect scholarly methodology and interpretations. Some state institutions were convinced while others did not allow Bible Chairs on their campuses. The University of Virginia was the first school to give academic credit to students who took classes offered by a Bible Chair faculty member. Programs were also established at the University of Georgia and the University of Kansas at the turn of the century and at the University of Texas in 1905.

In addition to teaching responsibilities, persons serving as Bible Chair faculty on state university campuses provided needed pastoral care for students, both for Disciples and those of other denominations. By the 1920s other groups had established successful Bible Chair programs, some moving ahead of older Disciples programs. During the Depression era, Disciples were not able to fund the faculty appointments adequately and some had to be discontinued. The first Bible Chair, at the University of Michigan, was closed in 1932. However, the commitment to ministry among college students did not lessen among Disciples. Ms. Lura Aspinwald became the Director of Student Work in 1935. She visited different schools and instituted the Student Work Bulletin. Gradually, many state schools began to accept the ministers on campus and came to see them as valuable chaplains.

The post–World War II era saw an incredible increase in college attendance, due in part to the GI Bill of Rights. Despite a slight decline in the 1950s, enrollment grew to the point that more campus ministers were needed. In 1956 the Student Work Office joined efforts with the Board of Higher Education officially to recognize the title "Campus Minister." In 1957 the Disciples Youth Fellowship, which had split from the Christian Youth Fellowship in 1946 to minister specifically to college students, joined with the United Campus Christian Fellowship (which then included the campus ministries of the Evangelical United Brethren Church, the United Church of Christ, and the United Presbyterian Church) to work together in meeting the needs of the large number of students.

The 1960s saw continuing growth in the populations of college campuses. In order to meet the increasing needs and respond to losses in funding, Disciples continued to form new partnerships with other denominations. One was the National Campus Ministers Association organized in 1964. In 1968 the Board of Higher Education of the Christian Church (Disciples of Christ) created the Commission on Ministries in Higher Education, which eventually did much of its work in conjunction with the United Ministries of Higher Education, the successor to the United Campus Christian Fellowship. This organization allowed for the sharing of ideas, staff, funds, and programs among the member denominations.

The social revolutions of the 1970s (e.g., civil rights movement, peace movement, feminist movement) resulted in a "counter-culture" atmosphere on many college and university campuses. The response of Disciples congregations who supported the Commission on Ministries in Higher Education was one of resistance and withdrawal of funding. The late twentieth century was marked by the closing of some campus ministries on state campuses, while Disciples-related colleges and universities maintained chaplains (i.e., campus ministers, deans of the chapel) on their campuses. Disciples continue to participate in the Council for Ecumenical Student Christian Ministries (CESCM) as well as the Higher Education Ministries Arena (HEMA), which is a resource center for Protestant denominations working in partnership to minister to students on college and university campuses. Oversight for campus ministry is housed under the umbrella of the Division of Higher Education. LISA W. DAVISON

2. Churches of Christ

The first campus ministry for Churches of Christ began when a Bible Chair was established in 1918 at the University of Texas. G. H. P. Showalter (1870-1954), editor of the *Firm Foundation,* and Charles H. Roberson (1879-1953) were the first instructors. The University of Texas Bible Chair failed in 1928, but reopened in 1951 and continued operation into the 1980s. It set the stage for other pioneering efforts from the 1920s to the 1950s from Florida to California. In the 1950s and early 1960s many new Bible Chairs were established by Churches of Christ. The first Bible Chair Lectureship (later called the National Campus Ministers Seminar and now the National Campus Ministries Seminar) was held in Lubbock, Texas, in 1957.

The Bible Chairs offered Bible courses for credit, yet a chief purpose was to provide a place of spiritual development for college-age youth of Churches of Christ who were attending state universities. Both nurturing and evangelistic efforts outside of the classroom were priorities. In the 1960s there was an increase in the number of students from Churches of Christ seeking graduate degrees in religion. The number began to exceed available academic posts in colleges and universities affiliated with Churches of Christ. Many of those with graduate degrees sought teaching positions at Bible Chairs, increasing the academic thoroughness of the Bible courses.

About the same time, in 1967 a parachurch organization modeled after Bill Bright's Campus Crusade and named Campus Evangelism emerged. Campus Evangelism emphasized active evangelism over other purposes and launched a renewed interest in campus ministries that did not offer courses for university credit. The organization came under attack, however, for its increasingly nontraditional ideas on such matters as the operation of the Holy Spirit and fellowship with members of other churches. After the organization folded in 1970, Chuck Lucas (b. 1938) and the Crossroads Church of Christ in Gainesville, Florida, began to advocate aggressive evangelistic tactics for all campuses. Lucas and the Crossroads movement attempted to take over the National Campus Ministers' Seminar, laid the groundwork for Kip McKean's leadership of the International Churches of Christ, and caused many churches to end their campus ministries in the 1980s. In 1978, however, Churches of Christ still sponsored 166 campus ministries on the campuses of colleges and universities across the United States.

Campus ministries have recovered slowly from the controversies of the 1980s. At the beginning of the twenty-first century all three of the earlier models exist, some maintaining the nurturing Bible Chair, others with a strong academic emphasis, while a few maintain an evangelistic thrust. *Campus Crosswalk* (first called *Bible Chair Journal* when it began in 1958) is the publication of Campus Ministries in Churches of Christ, keeping the various ministries connected and informed with newspaper and worldwide web formats. MICHAEL W. CASEY

3. Christian Churches/Churches of Christ

Conservative Disciples churches, later known as Christian Churches/Churches of Christ, planted Bible colleges sometimes in close proximity to secular universities. At least four such schools were established adjacent to state university campuses in order to provide mutual benefits for both Bible college and university students. A number of Bible colleges still offer joint degree programs with local state universities.

Following World War II, churches began to address the spiritual needs of their members' children in the state university environment and initiated some local, congregationally-based outreach ministries. Richard Carpenter began full-time work at the University of Kentucky and Gerald Gibson started such a ministry at the University of Minnesota in 1958. Dr. Stanley Smith pioneered such a ministry at the University of Illinois in 1963. By the end of the 1960s, the Christian Churches/Churches of Christ claimed over thirty such campus ministries.

The National Association of Christian Student Foundations (now the National Association of Christian Campus Ministries) was formed in 1963 as a voluntary association of campus ministers' retreats and student leadership conferences.

By 2000 there were 101 campus ministries in the United States associated with the Christian Churches/Churches of Christ, primarily (but not exclusively) distributed in the Midwest and Southeast. They go by a variety of names, the most common being "Christian Student Fellowship" and "Christian Campus House." Most are overseen by regional boards, made of representatives from supporting congregations. Financial support for these ministries comes voluntarily from churches, alumni, and other interested individuals. In many cases the campus ministry includes residential facilities to house students and enhance their involvement in the ministry.

The campus ministries of the Christian Churches/Churches of Christ are transdenominational in student involvement. Programming normally includes large group Bible studies, worship services, small fellowship groups, and opportunities for ministerial service in the local community. Mission trips are an important part of most campus ministries, and hundreds of alumni are now serving as full-time missionaries.

In the last years of the twentieth century, campus ministries have teamed with mission organizations (especially Christian Missionary Fellowship) to plant campus ministries outside the United States. Currently there are campus ministries affiliated with the Christian Churches/Churches of Christ operating in Europe, Asia, Brazil, Chile, and Mexico.

DAVID EMBREE

See also Bible Chair Movement; Christian Woman's Board of Missions; Division of Higher Education; Higher Education, Views of in the Movement; International Churches of Christ

BIBLIOGRAPHY D. Duane Cummins, *The Disciples Colleges: A History* (1987) • Doug Dickey, *Campus Ministry* (1994) • Ronald B. Flowers, "The Bible Chair Movement in the Disciples of Christ Tradition: Attempts to Teach Religion in State Universities" (Ph.D. dissertation, University of Iowa, 1967) • Ronald B. Flowers, "The Bible Chair Movement, 1918-1964," *Mission* (June 1980): 3-7 • Charles Garrison, *Forgotten Christians* (1967) • Thomas R. McCormick, *Campus Ministry in the Coming Age* (1987) • Rick Rowland, *Campus Ministries: A Historical Study of Churches of Christ Campus Ministries and Selected College Ministries from 1706 to 1990* (1991) • Greg Swinney, ed., *Taking Education Higher* (1993) • Roger Thomas, ed., *The Gospel Goes to College* (1975) • John F. Wilson, "Campus Ministry in the Past Twenty Years: Some Personal Reflections," *Mission* (June 1980): 8-12.

Canada, The Movement in

The Stone-Campbell Movement began in Canada through the migration of Baptists from Scotland to the Maritime Provinces and Ontario in the early nineteenth century. While the writings of Alexander Campbell and Barton W. Stone ultimately had profound impact on the Movement in Canada, as did migrations and educational influence from the Movement in the United States, the story of the Canadian Movement is not complete without the conjoining story of westward migration of early Scottish and Scotch Baptist settlers and ideas. A lingering creative tension between the Stone-Campbell Movement's historic motifs — "restoration," "unity," and "mission" — characterizes the ethos of the Movement in Canada as it continues to define itself at the dawn of the twenty-first century.

Founded July 1, 1867, Canada is a federal union of ten provinces and three territories. The latter include the Yukon, the Northwest Territories, and Nunavut. The only Stone-Campbell congregation in these territories meets at Yellowknife, Northwest Territories. The province of Quebec, populous but French-speaking and predominantly Roman Catholic, has known a small Stone-Campbell presence since the early twentieth century, at least in Montreal. Three Churches of Christ meet in Montreal; one in Quebec City; one in Plessisville. Newfoundland and Labrador had United States military congregations in the 1950s and 1960s, at St. John's, Argentia, Stephenville, and Goose Bay. Newfoundland has one congregation in Harbour Grace established in 1996. Hence the story of the Stone-Campbell Movement in Canada unfolds principally in the eight provinces that compose the Maritimes, Ontario, the Prairies, and British Columbia.

1. The Canadian Maritimes

The Maritime Provinces of Canada — New Brunswick, Nova Scotia, and Prince Edward Island — witnessed the beginning of the Stone-Campbell Movement as early as 1810. The first advocates of this thinking were of Scottish background. Four key leaders came to the Maritimes with beliefs and practices that eventually led to the development of the Christian Churches/Churches of Christ, Churches of Christ, and Christian Church (Disciples of Christ).

These four influential individuals were John R. Stewart, Alexander Crawford, James Murray, and John Stevenson. John R. Stewart came to Prince Edward Island, settling in the Crossroads area near Charlottetown in 1809. Stewart had been deeply influenced by the Scotch Baptists of his homeland. Although he had not been immersed, he started a congregation in Crossroads/Keppoch where the Lord's Supper was administered weekly. This was the first restorationist congregation in Canada, just a year after Thomas and Alexander Campbell formed the Brush Run church in the United States.

Alexander Crawford, born 1786 in Argyllshire, Scotland, came to the Yarmouth area of Nova Scotia from the Island of Arran in November 1810. Crawford had come under the influence of the Haldane brothers of Scotland and had seen the remarkable revival of evangelical religion in Scotland as a result of their "non-denominational, lay" effort. Crawford had been a student at the Haldane Seminary in Edinburgh prior to coming to Canada, and had been present during the controversial acceptance of baptism by immersion by Robert and James Haldane. It is obvious from Crawford's teaching that some of his thinking bore the influence of the Scotch Baptists more than that of the Haldanes. He believed in and advocated mutual ministry, and rejected all creeds, paid ministry, and emotionalism, preferring the "rational" faith of the Scottish Enlightenment. In 1811 he visited Prince Edward Island and baptized several, including John Stewart. Crawford became the first person to administer baptism by immersion in Prince Edward Island. Eventually he moved to the Island and became the most important early leader of the Movement there.

James Murray was immersed in 1809 and became a member of the Scotch Baptist church in Fogglyloan, Scotland. Arriving in Nova Scotia in May 1811, he became the driving force behind what became known as the Congregation of Disciples of Christ at River John. This name was used at the time of their incorporation in November 1855, but the congregation had been meeting weekly since June 18, 1815.

Although raised in a Presbyterian minister's home, John Stevenson eventually became a Scotch Baptist in his hometown of Paisley, Scotland. He made his way to Prince Edward Island in 1820, where he put down roots in New Glasgow. By the early 1820s he was leading a congregation in his barn that weekly remembered the Lord's Supper and preached "New Testament Christianity."

In addition to the efforts of these four men, a significant work started in Halifax in the mid-1820s. It became increasingly important as a conduit for early influence from the United States on the previously started congregations. One key figure in Halifax was Richard Creed of England. The Halifax work was an outgrowth of St. Paul's Anglican Church and was first referred to as a "Baptist church." In 1825 Alexander Crawford heard of this work while attending the Baptist Association meeting in Nova Scotia, and he began communicating with the congregation.

Around this time, William W. Ashley introduced Alexander Campbell's writings to the Halifax group. Ashley was born in North Carolina and came to Nova Scotia in the 1820s after marrying a woman from Milton, Nova Scotia. According to the 1832 *Millennial Harbinger,* Ashley had come into contact with Campbell's writings through a certain "FEW." This was apparently Francis W. Emmons of Lisbon, Ohio, where famed preacher Walter Scott began his evangelistic efforts. This is especially noteworthy since Scott himself had Scotch Baptist connections through his onetime friend George Forrester of Pittsburgh, Pennsylvania. Such "restoration" influences as Scott on Ashley would probably have enabled a more sympathetic hearing in the Maritimes for Campbell's views than for other early American church reformers. Ashley traveled much of the Maritimes on behalf of the Temperance Movement, and carried Campbell's *Christian Baptist* with him.

In 1833 the Halifax congregation published the first journal of the Stone-Campbell Movement in the Maritimes. Entitled *The Christian Gleaner,* it was primarily a reprint of the *Christian Baptist.* It was in Halifax that the Canadian Movement and the Movement begun in the United States began to converge. At the same time, some of the aforementioned restoration pioneers encountered difficulties with the Associated Baptists of Nova Scotia and New Brunswick. Most of the churches had joined the association, but they were not happy with several aspects of their involvement. At a lengthy meeting on September 30, 1833, at Crossroads, Prince Edward Island, this controversy came to a head. The Prince Edward Island archives contain information on this meeting under the heading "a last ditch stand by Nova Scotia Associated Baptist Missionaries." The main controversy concerned those marrying outside the Scotch Baptist umbrella, with the more conservative Island churches believing that those who did so should be excommunicated. There was also disagreement over creeds and clergy. The Association required that all participating churches would have to swear acceptance of the Articles of Faith and Practice and that they would be led by ordained "clergy."

New Glasgow, an Island church, was one of the congregations that refused to accept these requirements. This congregation established contact with Halifax, inquiring of the Nova Scotia congregation how New Glasgow could be set up as a "church" without accepting creeds or confessions of faith. In October 1836 Halifax replied with a letter informing them of how such a church could be constituted published in the December *The Christian Gleaner.* In February, 1837, as a companion to the earlier correspondence, *The Gleaner* published a document written by a London Baptist Church titled "Christian Principles &c. of a Church of Christ in Halifax, N.S.," as a statement of belief.

The impact of the Movement in the United States spread further under the influence of William Wentworth Eaton, originally of Cornwallis, Nova Scotia, but now working in Saint John, New Brunswick. He had Primitive Methodist roots, but had become familiar with the restoration principles from Ashley's visits. Eventually Eaton started *The Christian,* a magazine devoted to "the Faith and Practice of Primitive Christianity." Eaton eventually taught at Bethany College, the college started by Alexander Campbell in western Virginia, and became a strong voice for the Stone-Campbell Movement.

Connections with the Movement in the United States influenced the Maritime churches in three important ways. First, some of the Baptists from the Nova Scotia and the New Brunswick Association had always had problems with these "Scotch Baptists." The relationship with the Movement from the States allowed them to label these people "Campbellites" and remove from them the Baptist name and connection. Second, there was much more talk about baptism and its design being for the remission of sins. Third, a stronger desire and emphasis on the unity of believers and a call for the restoration of New Testament Christianity as its basis became the focus in the Maritimes.

Eventually these new congregations began to organize themselves. On Prince Edward Island, some association was in place by the 1850s. A work entitled "Minute Book PEI Christian Book 2: 1869-1925" has been preserved. The fact that it is Book 2 indicates an earlier record book. By 1855 churches in the Maritimes were gathering for what they called "the Annual." This continued each year until this event became known as the Maritime Christian Missionary Society in 1902, which continues today among Canadian Disciples.

The issue of the legitimacy of instrumental music in worship was never as contentious an issue as other ones in the Movement in the Maritimes. While the visit of the restorationist hardliner Benjamin Franklin to the area in 1869 drew large crowds and contributed to the conservatism of Maritime churches, his firm belief that preachers had to trust the Lord and the people for support helped foster a major dilemma. The "paid clergy" issue seems to have been more controversial and divisive than the use of musical instruments. The one exception was in West Gore, Nova Scotia, where instruments became truly divisive, apparently as a result of the move of the Talman brothers to West Gore from Ontario in the early twentieth century. While in West Gore, the Talmans started the Maritime Bible and Literary College, and this became a hub of anti-instrumental influence for the churches. Other than in West Gore, the use of an organ did not divide the churches until the 1950s when several missionaries from the United States came to the area. The a cappella constituency remains small in the region, with only six congregations in the Maritimes, and none on Prince Edward Island at present.

In 1922 most congregations of the Churches of Christ, conservative Christian Churches, and Christian Churches (Disciples of Christ) became a part of the All Canada Program. "All Canada" was an attempt to synergize the efforts of provincial missions agencies through a centralization of organization and stewardship initiatives and a standardization of Canadian literature and curriculum for boys and girls. The governing body of the All Canada Program, called the All Canada Committee, was largely dominated by leaders who were theologically more liberal, several of whom where advocates of "open membership." The organization of the Canadian churches followed much the same course as in the United States, and effected the same divergent outcomes. Mounting tensions over the place of "agencies," emerging hierarchies, the nature of the church, and open membership continued for the next three decades. Finally, in August 1948, at the Prince Edward Island session of the Maritime Convention in New Glasgow, nine Island leaders presented a declaration marking their withdrawal from All Canada due to modernism and open membership. This sparked a heated debate that went on for many years, resulting in time in the withdrawal of most of the Disciple congregations from the main fold. At present only four congregations remain with the Christian Church (Disciples of Christ), and all of these are located in Nova Scotia.

The largest branch of the Stone-Campbell heritage in the Maritimes, therefore, is what many call the "independents," Christian Churches/Churches of Christ. Of a total of forty-four churches of the Stone-Campbell heritage, thirty-four are independent. Total membership is about 2,900, with about 2,300 of these being independent. Since the division of the 1950s, these churches have rallied around Maritime Christian College (est. 1960) and Partners in Atlantic Canada Evangelism (PACE) along with other efforts to spread the restoration plea.

Efforts have been made to initiate fellowship between the three branches of the Movement. Often speakers have been used from different wings for lectures or gatherings such as the Maritime Christian Fellowship. The Church of Christ Development Company, of Disciples origin, has assisted several of the "independent" building projects.

2. The Movement in Ontario

The beginnings of the Movement in Ontario lie with the immigration of Baptists from Scotland in the early nineteenth century. In Ontario those traditions interacted with the Christian Connection and the influence of Alexander Campbell. As these Baptist churches became a part of the Disciples of Christ they increasingly merged with the larger American Stone-Campbell Movement so that since the end of the nineteenth century the shape of the tradition has been determined largely by events in the United States, though it has continued to have its own character because of the uniquely Canadian context.

2.1. Beginnings: The Haldanes

Scotch Baptists immersed James Haldane in April 1808, six months before Alexander Campbell arrived in Glasgow to await departure for America. Already by 1805 the evangelistic movement that James and his brother Robert underwrote had led to the establishment of several Baptist churches of the English order in Scotland, including at Bellanoch in the West Highlands. County Argyll, where Bellanoch is located, is particularly important for the unfolding of the story. This county hosted an interconnected group of Haldane agents, and others influenced by the Haldanes, who would later emigrate to Canada West (i.e., Ontario). These individuals include James Black, born in Kilmartin parish, near Bellanoch, baptized by Dugald Sinclair in 1817, who came to southwestern Ontario, to Aldborough Township, in 1820; Donald McVicar, Haldane agent and ordained Baptist preacher, who also came to Aldborough in 1818; Dugald Sinclair, ordained Baptist, who followed McVicar as pastor at Bellanoch in 1815, moved the church to Lochgilphead, and emigrated to Lobo Township in 1831; and John McKellar, from Argyll, who came to Lobo Township around 1818, but whose group had communion only when McVicar, ordained, was present. Other leaders who emigrated from Scotland include Alex Anderson, from Perthshire, who came in 1832; John Menzies, a Scotch Baptist, also from Perthshire, c. 1821; and Alexander Stewart. Another early preacher was Edmund Sheppard, who came from Nottingham in 1843 as a Disciple. Geoffrey Ellis points out that "no individuals of American descent took a leading role in the establishment of the Disciples of Christ in Canada West."

2.2. Scottish and Scotch Baptists

By 1834 Scottish Baptists of the English order and Scotch Baptists had separated, and their distinctions were brought to the Canadian frontier. The latter, who opposed an "ordained," supported ministry and accepted only "mutual ministry," were by far the smaller group. In Ontario their point of view was championed by David Oliphant, Sr., a Scotch Baptist who moved to Eramosa Township from Dundas (Hamilton) in 1832. This view of ministry was later promoted vigorously and rancorously by James Beaty, Sr. through the *Bible Index* (1872?-1893), with a lasting, divisive effect. Beaty, from County Caven, Ireland, came to Toronto in 1818 by way of New York City and became a prominent politician.

2.3. Contacts with Campbell and Stone

In the 1820s the Christian Connection established itself on the north shore of Lake Ontario. Its association, however, was not primarily with the movement of Barton Stone, whose "Christian" churches had loosely affiliated with the Christian Connection as early as 1810, but with the Connection as it came from the American Northeast by way of New York State. In 1825 a Conference was organized, and by 1834 it could report that there were about twenty churches. Three of these, at Keswick, Ringwood, and Stouffville, continue to this day as part of the Conference of Congregationalist Christian Churches, a group that has swelled from five churches to dozens across Canada thanks to a small exodus from the United Church at the end of the twentieth century. Joseph Ash, while a member of the Christian Connection, was reading both Alexander Campbell's *Millennial Harbinger* and Barton Stone's *Christian Messenger.* Stone's death in 1844 left only the powerful influence of Campbell. At a meeting of its Conference in 1834 at Whitby — two years after the Stone and Campbell groups joined in the United States — the Christian Connection delegates had a vote on whether to join the Disciples. The proposal was defeated by the tie-breaking vote of the chair. Ash left, and historian Reuben Butchart credits him with establishing the first Disciples church in Ontario without Scottish Baptist or Scotch Baptist roots, at Cobourg in 1836.

The ties with Campbell became increasingly strong, beginning in the 1830s. James Black read the *Harbinger* in 1833, introduced to it by David Oliphant, Sr.; Daniel Wiers, who, with others, started the Disciples church in Beamsville, read the *Christian Baptist* in the 1830s. In a report to the *Millennial Harbinger* in August 1843 a group of sixteen Ontario churches is enumerated; the study by Geoffrey Ellis adds eight to these for a total of twenty-four and a combined membership of over 500. Relations with Campbell were deepened when students like David Oliphant, Jr. (graduated 1844), and Edmund Sheppard studied at Bethany College (c. 1846-49). The exposure to Campbell's thought brought with it the two poles of his ecclesiology: (1) the unity of all believers; and (2) restoration. The tension between the two would later fracture the entire North American movement, in Canada as in the United States.

Campbell's visit to Ontario in 1855 was particularly important for cementing relations. James Black had suggested a visit in a letter published in the March 1842 *Millennial Harbinger,* but by the time Campbell arrived he was sixty-six and suffering from rheumatism. Nevertheless, he traveled through the Niagara Peninsula, to Toronto and east of Toronto, to the old churches in Esquesing and Everton, and by way of London to Detroit. Early in his trip he stayed overnight with James Black, who had also been a Presbyterian; in Toronto he visited with prominent church leaders and preached in a large Baptist meetinghouse; in London he preached in the Methodist Episcopal Church, and in Detroit at the Lutheran meetinghouse. Such invitations indicate his ecumenical bearing and the esteem in which he was held by the larger Christian community.

David Oliphant, Jr. (1821-1885), whose father had been one of the pioneers of the Movement in Canada, studied under Alexander Campbell at Bethany College. He edited a number of journals and wrote one of the earliest histories of the Stone-Campbell Movement published serially beginning in 1880. From Reuben Butchart's *The Disciples of Christ in Canada Since 1830*

2.4. The Editors

The direction of the Movement in Ontario, as in the United States, was profoundly affected by those who edited church papers. Joseph Ash edited the first of these, the *Christian Vindicator,* which appeared in June 1837. The most prolific and influential editor in the mid-nineteenth century was David Oliphant, Jr., who edited the first of several papers, *Witness of Truth,* from Picton in 1845. His papers continued until 1865, and Disciples on the north and south shores of Lake Ontario generally aligned themselves with the conservatism that he had received from his Scotch Baptist father. Along with his own editorial work, in earlier issues he reprinted articles from the *Christian Baptist* and *Millennial Harbinger.*

Oliphant's conservatism paled alongside the combatively anticlerical views of James Beaty, Sr., whose views shaped the *Bible Index,* edited for the most part by nephews James Beaty, Jr., and Robert Beaty. The *Christian Worker,* edited by H. B. Sherman, appeared as a counterpoint to the *Index.* It was published in Owen Sound, then Meaford, from 1881 to 1886. George Munro and T. L. Fowler edited *The Ontario Evangelist* (later *The Canadian Evangelist,* then *The Disciple of Christ and Canadian Evangelist*) from 1886 to 1896.

In the twentieth century the most important papers have been *The Canadian Disciple,* published in its early years in Toronto and Owen Sound, and edited for the first seven years by Reuben Butchart; and *The Gospel Herald,* begun in Radville, Saskatchewan, in 1936 but published from 1953 in Beamsville, Ontario; its editors included Robert Sinclair, J. C. Bailey, and from 1953 Roy C. Merritt and Eugene Perry. The "independent" Christian Churches/Churches of Christ started *The Canadian Christian Harbinger* in Toronto in 1962, and it continued there until its relocation to British Columbia in 1976/77; it ceased publication in 1989.

2.5. *Tensions and Divisions*

Toward the end of the nineteenth century, issues that were present from the beginning in Ontario became points of division. Those issues related especially to methods of evangelism and to questions of ministry in the local church. At the start evangelism was largely a matter of "lay" preachers, who were farmers or in business, gathering groups around themselves — made easier by a common emigration, with the preaching sometimes in Gaelic — and making preaching trips to visit churches and start new ones. These churches were for the most part rural. But society was advancing, people were moving to the cities, travel was easier; prominent American preachers like Benjamin Franklin or Isaac Errett could make trips into Ontario to preach and debate. Bright young people went to the United States to study, to Lexington or Nashville; some returned, but many did not, a problem that continues in the twenty-first century.

By 1900 there were about eighty churches in Ontario, but they had already been drawn into the American orbit and were dividing along the lines of division there. "A controversial spirit within," as Geoffrey Ellis calls it, sapped energies and played havoc with the plea for Christian unity.

James Black proposed the establishment in Canada of a branch of the Highland Baptists Missionary Society, an organization similar to the successful Haldane initiative. In 1846 the first formally organized "cooperation" began at Norval; Black was the primary figure in its emergence. The idea was to form an overseeing group that would hire evangelists to work with churches to spread the gospel and begin new churches. In 1870 the Grey County Cooperation was formed at Meaford; seven churches pledged support and resolved to hire an evangelist. The most important of these local efforts was the one Black started, and in the 1870s cooperation was centered mainly in Wellington County. In 1883 it gave way to the "Ontario Cooperation of Disciples of Christ" (which continues to the present), and in 1921 it gave impetus to the formation of the All-Canada Committee of the Disciples. The increasing size of such organizations seems to have concretized opposition: small local efforts were one thing, a national organization another. David Oliphant, Jr., was a major critic, and it was his ongoing arguments with Benjamin Franklin of the *American Christian Review* that changed Franklin's position.

The idea of located ministers made advances in the 1870s, which naturally led to the question of their education. The College of the Disciples opened at St. Thomas in 1895 and had a positive impact on the growth of churches in southwestern Ontario. It continued until about 1910. Then Disciples sought out relations with the University of Toronto and McMaster University for the training of ministers. This continued until 1958 when the College of Churches of Christ in Canada began funding ministerial candidates at accredited universities and seminaries. For a period early in the twentieth century, a cappella churches operated Beamsville Bible School (1903-16); later, in 1952, Great Lakes Christian College began in the same town; a provincial charter (1987) enabled its sister institution, Great Lakes Bible College, to confer degrees. The Bible College operates now in Waterloo, out of the facilities of the Waterloo Church of Christ. For their part the Christian Churches/Churches of Christ opened Ontario Bible College (1939-43), Toronto Christian Seminary (1958-64), then Ontario Christian Seminary (1972-98). Arrangements exist with McMaster Divinity College in Hamilton whereby adherents of the Movement can substitute historical and polity courses for those required of Baptists seeking degrees. Educational efforts have always struggled against the relatively small size of their constituency.

A final source of division involved worship, in particular the use of organs in worship. Their introduction in the 1880s was not a matter of fellowship for some; for others it was, and certainly it became increasingly such. When the American census in 1906 for the first time recorded Churches of Christ separately, the same division existed in Ontario. Division in Ontario at the end of the nineteenth century indicated a 60/40 ratio of Disciples to Churches of Christ.

2.6. *The Twentieth Century and Beyond*

Trajectories begun in the nineteenth century continued through the twentieth. At the end of the twentieth century there were about 95 congregations of the Stone-Campbell tradition in Ontario. Some 72 of these are Churches of Christ; about a dozen each are Christian Church (Disciples of Christ) or else Christian Churches/Churches of Christ. Their combined membership is probably about 6,000. The significant events of the twentieth century are the emergence of the Christian Churches/Churches of Christ amidst the restructuring of the Disciples; union conversations, from 1969 to 1986, between Disciples and the United Church of Canada and the Anglican Church; the development of church camping programs at Selkirk (Disciples), Omagh (Churches of Christ), Primrose (Christian Churches/Churches of Christ), and other locations; in 1968 Grove Park Home for Senior Citizens opened in Barrie, a ministry of Churches of Christ; in 2001 an Archives was established at McMaster Divinity College.

3. Western Canada

3.1. *The Prairies*

While most of the other regions of Canada by 1870 had taken on substantially the religious, social, and political character they have today, the Canadian prairies remained virtually unsettled. New settlement was spurred with the National Policy of 1875, instituted under the leadership of Canada's first Prime Minister, Sir John A. MacDonald. Articulating and acting on sentiments long held in central Canada, MacDonald launched a process of settlement and protection of the Canadian West: "If we don't settle it, the Yankees will!"

The North-West Mounted Police were created in 1873, and within two years had established outposts across the prairies. By 1885 the transcontinental railway reached the west coast of British Columbia, opening the vast economic opportunities of prairie lands and resources. The same year the North West Rebellion led by Louis Riel was put down in Saskatchewan. The consequent historiographical controversy aside, the imposition of a British (vs. French) land survey system made possible "law and order" in the West, as well as one of the promises of the National Policy, 160 acres of "free" homestead land for any male age 21 or older. By the late nineteenth and early twentieth centuries the trickle of immigration so induced became a flood of "homesteaders" from Eastern Canada, the British Isles, the United States, and central Europe. Heirs of the Stone-Campbell Movement were among them. They took their place in farming and in the permanent communities of the emerging "prairie" provinces of Canada: Manitoba, Saskatchewan, and Alberta.

3.2. Manitoba

The first Church of Christ on the Canadian Prairies met November 10, 1881, at a Red River settlement called Portage la Prairie, Manitoba. It represented the convergence of the aspirations of some Ontario women who sent Andrew Scott, an Ontario man, and the presence of a group of families who had migrated from Ridgeway, Ontario, in 1871. The Thomas Sissons, William Kitson, Mrs. J. Conner, A. Yuill, Peter Campbell, and F. Ogletree families had kept their faith through communion and worship in their homes through the intervening years. In 1882 a meeting hall was erected, followed in 1903 with a substantial stone building that became a Manitoba Heritage site, ultimately sold to another Christian group in 1995.

Through the impetus of M. P. Hayden of Ontario and the evangelistic ministry of J. A. Romig of the American Christian Missionary Society, the First Church of Christ (Kate Street, Winnipeg; later Home Street Christian, and now Broadway Disciples United) was established in 1902. This was the first collaboration of American and Canadian organizations in the West and led to the Western Canada Christian Missionary Association, which proved to be too far reaching for lasting effect. George H. Stewart from Everton, Ontario, also played a key role in the Kate Street endeavor, which later became Home Street Christian Church. In the 1970s there was a split at Home Street over the proposal to "pair" with the United Church of Canada. The Spruce Street Church of Christ emerged for about ten years before being subsumed by charismatic interests. In the late 1990s Home Street became Broadway Disciples United, the oldest Disciples congregation in the West, now largely Filipino in membership.

The oldest Church of Christ was established in 1888 when a large number from the congregation at Meaford, Ontario, moved to Carman, Manitoba. Folk from Carmen as well as the British Isles began to meet in a new assembly in Winnipeg in 1901.

With help from the Portage and Home Street churches, together with continued funding from Ontario, St. James Church of Christ (Disciples) was established in 1906. There had been earlier attempts at Minnedosa, Rat Portage (now Kenora), Swan River, Riding Mountain, and Norwood. Fluctuations in population brought about by the vagaries of prairie farming — including weather patterns and produce prices, urbanization, and a lack of leadership — all militated against deep roots for most of these works. The diaries of M. P. Hayden, an early Stone-Campbell evangelist from Ontario, provide primary insight into the "life situation" of early church work in Manitoba. At its peak prior to World War II, there were fifteen Stone-Campbell Movement congregations. Today there is one congregation of the Christian Church (Disciples of Christ) and two of the Christian Churches/Churches of Christ, all in Winnipeg and all second-generation Canadian-Filipino. There are also seven Churches of Christ in Manitoba, predominantly rural, with a total membership of about 800.

3.3. Saskatchewan

From 1905, when Saskatchewan joined the Confederation of Canada, until 1915 ten churches were planted in Saskatchewan. With the exception of two (Saskatoon and Regina) all were rural. The first Saskatchewan church was the result of the western migration of the E. C. Jones family from Wiarton, Ontario, in 1890. For a number of years they opened their home to neighbors on Sundays for worship and communion. In 1906 the Joneses moved to Milestone, on the "Sioux Line" (railway) south of Regina, and invited J. A. Romig for evangelistic meetings. A congregation was organized and a building erected the same year.

The Yellow Grass congregation arose out of the work of the John M. Ford family, arriving from Bowmanville, Ontario, in 1904. Historian Reuben Butchart calls Ford "the founder of the Saskatchewan [independent and Disciples] churches." With the assistance of the Milestone church and the evangelistic efforts of Romig, the church was established in 1907. The presence of the railway to the United States, together with the organization of the church, made Yellow Grass an attractive place for immigrants from the midwestern United States. The church became a blending of Eastern Canadian and American church cultures, a pattern that would become firmly established in the Canadian West. Yellow Grass became distinctive in its prolific contribution to Christian leadership. To Butchart's record of 14 may be added 21, for a total of 35 who have entered ministry over the last five decades. While most from the early years made contributions to the Movement in the United States, among whom are Harold Hockley (former minister of the influential Westwood Cheviot Christian Church in Cincinnati) and Floyd Clark (Academic Dean, Johnson Bible College), others have remained to work in Canada.

In 1910 the first Church of Christ congregation at Wawota, Saskatchewan, emerged, again through the gathering of immigrants from Ontario and Great Britain. Mary Muirhead observes that it was not until the 1950s that American churches began to send "missionaries" north. A pattern emerged in the development of the early Saskatchewan Churches of Christ whereby the one-room "schoolhouse," allowed for and built in every township under the National Policy, became the center of religious life as well. A number of young women were teachers, notably Ellen Black (La Rose), Elsie Black (Cutting), Mary Curtis (Schroeder), Clarice Hurlburt (Mooney), Lavine Jelsing (Bailey), Signe Jelsing (MacLeod), Pearl Perry (Orr), and Lillian Torkelson. These women used their schools for community goodwill, church planting, and "protracted meetings" held by itinerant evangelists. One at Brooking lasted for forty-seven days under the preaching of H. A. Rogers. There were very few "located" preachers in the early days, a result of economic necessity more than religious practice. Consequently most of the teachers and preachers were "tentmakers" who supported themselves with other vocations. H. A. Rogers was a farmer and beekeeper; W. Orr was a carpenter; D. A. Sinclair farmed; and H. E. Forman worked on the railway and preached in Regina.

A building for the Regina Church of Christ (later Regina Avenue Christian Church [Disciples of Christ]) was purchased in 1919 by R. J. Westaway, president of the Missionary Society of the Church of Christ in Saskatchewan. John H. Wells of St. Louis, Missouri, arrived in 1920 to establish the church. In 2000 the building was sold.

All streams of the Stone-Campbell Movement utilized regular extra-congregational gatherings for instruction and encouragement. For the establishment and growth of the Churches of Christ these were especially important. The first Saskatchewan summer "Bible schools" were held at Minton (1931), Radville (1932), Perryville (1933), and Horse Creek (Bengough) (1936). It was during the winter school at Radville in 1945-46 that plans came together for a Christian high school, Radville Christian College. Land was donated and a building constructed by W. Orr. Lillian Torkelson was the first principal. This school later moved to Weyburn, where it became Western Christian College. In 2003 it moved to Regina after a number of years in Dauphin, Manitoba. Macrorie Camp (1957-95) was also influential in helping to overcome sectarian tendencies in the West. It was established to advance fellowship between Churches of Christ and "independent" Christian Churches/Churches of Christ. Carl Ketcherside was a frequent speaker, and the camp contributed much to encouraging a more irenic approach to the restoration program.

3.4. Alberta

Douglas Barrie, in his thesis on the Movement in Alberta, attests that "The early leaders of the Restoration Movement in [Alberta] were pioneers in the finest sense of that word." Many had come to farm or ranch, but at the same time had a real vision for putting in place the Christian roots for nation building. They farmed to pay expenses, and had a desire to establish strong churches in the new land. Others came: businessmen, teachers, tradespeople, civil servants, and so forth. M. B. Ryan commented that they possessed the "shepherd heart."

The first organized work in Alberta was the Broadway Church of Christ (now Nanton), established in 1904. The Montgomery, Carmack, and Mrs. Samuel McMaster families were newly arrived from Missouri by way of Washington state and were instrumental in the establishment of the church. It began, like so many churches, as a Sunday School in the home. The first building was built on McMaster family land and served as both a school and a church. The first leaders, both Ontario natives, served as evangelists and schoolteachers. The surrounding communities of Champion, Reid Hill, Barons, and Vulcan were evangelized.

Within a decade, there were seventeen congregations prospering in Alberta: Great Bend, Erskine, Ponoka, Lethbridge, Calgary Central, Edmonton First, Edmonton Church of Christ (a cappella), Calgary Church of Christ (a cappella), Wrentham, Lake DeMay, Vermillion, Innisfree, Alix, Champion, Clyde, Stony Plain, and Black Diamond.

The pattern worked well. Immigrants would arrive with their faith, and gather for Sunday School and the Lord's Supper, sometimes for several years. R. H. Simpson, an Ontario merchant, conducted a Sunday School above his store at Great Bend. Hanna began a joint work of immigrants from Ontario, including a cappella folk, as a Sunday School in the home of Mrs. O. E. Payne. Shortly thereafter, the "scattered would be gathered." M. B. Ryan, the Superintendent of the Alberta Christian Missionary Society and originally of Scotch Baptist parentage in Nova Scotia, figured prominently in this "gathering" of Christians into churches. He reported of the establishment of First Christian Church, Edmonton: "It is a cosmopolitan group, with members from Nova Scotia, Old Ontario, New Ontario, Michigan, Missouri, Nebraska, Iowa, Illinois, and Washington, but they were all Disciples of Christ to the core." Evangelistic teams would often be invited to conduct meetings. Prominent among these were R. J. Westaway, J. W. Jenkins, J. A. Romig, and the Cave Sisters, the latter being an evangelistic team sponsored by the American Christian Missionary Society.

Some realized their interest in the social dimensions of the gospel. Among them George F. Root and Gus Carl Bergman hosted the Alberta Cattleman's Association in Erskine, Alberta, in 1905 and 1906. They were Disciples from Iowa, where they had been friends and partners. G. C. Bergman was later instrumental in the formation of the first church in Edmonton. Henry Wise Wood, one of the most politically influential Albertans of his day, moved to Carstairs, Alberta, from Hannibal, Missouri, in 1905. His social egalitarianism was firmly planted in his American Disciples roots, where he had been part of the Farmers Equity Movement. When he came north, he joined the Canadian Society of Equity and was a charter member of the United Farmers of Alberta (UFA), serving as president of this provincial body from 1916 to 1931. He was also chairperson of the Alberta Wheat Pool Board from 1923 to 1937. He declined several leading political appointments. *MacLean's* magazine called him the "Moses" of Alberta for his firm belief in agricultural cooperation. His opponents called him "the would-be Lenin of Canada." For his service to agriculture in the Canadian West, King George V awarded him the "Commander of the Order of St. Michael and St. George."

With the establishment of Alberta Bible College in 1932 in Lethbridge, indigenous resources for church leadership and planting began to emerge. Staff, graduates, and students led established congregations, and dependence on American or Eastern leadership began to wane, a process that has continued to the present day. Toward mid-century, liberal theology increased, and it was especially strident in the All Canada Committee. In spite of the consequent fading influence of agencies, thirteen churches were either formed or revived in the period 1945-60 in Alberta through the work of both Disciples and Christian Churches/Churches of Christ. In 1991 the Alberta Church Planting Association was formed, which has been a catalyst for three church plants in Alberta in the 1990s.

Archibald McLean (1849-1920), president of the Foreign Christian Missionary Society and a native of Prince Edward Island, took great interest in the Alberta work and made trips to Alberta prior to his death in 1920. He was a passionate advocate of missions and was among those who planted the seed that has yielded effort and interest in missions that continues to the present. In the 1940s there was a surge of missionary support from Western Canada, mostly Alberta: Tom and Leota Rash, Frank and Marie Remple, David and Lois Rees, and Edna Hunt went to India; Bill and Melba Rees went to South Africa. In the 1960s J. C. Bailey of the Churches of Christ became a one-man advocate and catalyst for work in India. Throughout the 1990s there has been strong Western Canadian interest in sending foreign workers, whether these be Canadians (three career, eleven short-term missionaries) or internationals (seven in all) who received training at Alberta Bible College or Western Christian College and returned to their respective countries.

At the end of the twentieth century there were thirty-two churches in Alberta (seventeen Christian Churches/Churches of Christ, ten Churches of Christ, four Christian Church [Disciples of Christ], and one "bridge" congregation).

3.5. British Columbia

Members of the Churches of Christ first settled in Victoria, British Columbia, during the first decade of the twentieth century. The Percy Bailey, Jaffray, and McMurchie families came from England and Ontario. In 1910 six other families banded together to purchase a small building in Vancouver. In turn, they amalgamated with a church started on Lulu Island (Richmond) and became the Oakridge Church. In the 1920s a church was begun in Creston.

Similarly, in 1905 Central Christian Church (Disciples of Christ) began in Vancouver as a gathering of folk who had settled from Ontario and the Maritimes. Considerable funding for this effort came from the American Christian Missionary Society and from Ontario. In 1911 the work divided into First Christian and Central. The two reunited in 1918 as Shelton Memorial Church.

As the economy fluctuated in a predominantly resources-based economy, congregations gained or lost members. By 1949 there was only one Church of Christ and one Disciples of Christ church, both in Vancouver. There were no Christian Churches/Churches of Christ in British Columbia.

Between the 1950s and the early 1980s there was a surge of migration from eastern, central, and prairie provinces and the United States to the Vancouver area, as well as the interior. There were ten Christian Churches/Churches of Christ planted in these two decades: Nanaimo, Lumby, Westsyde (Kamloops), Blackpool, Vavenby, Clearwater, Armstrong, Coldstream (Vernon), Fort Fraser, and Wynndel. There were also three Bible Camps: Mt. Benson Christian Camp (Vancouver Island), Double V-M Bible Camp (Okanagan), and Dunn Lake Bible Camp (North Thompson). The key catalysts for this work were Don and Carolyn Albert, graduates of Minnesota Bible College who had come to Canada in 1958. Others have played key sustaining roles, most of them either on mission support or working at other jobs to support their ministry.

In the same period Churches of Christ were started in Nanaimo, Salmon Arm, Vernon, Kelowna, Kamloops, Prince George, Abbotsford, Burnaby, Coquitlam, Surrey, Delta, Cranbrook, Prince Rupert, Revelstoke, and Port Alberni. A private Christian school has also been sponsored at Salmon Arm. Much of this activity was fueled by an influx of preachers into British Columbia who were supported fully by churches in the United States or eastern Canada.

During the last two decades of the twentieth century the Stone-Campbell Movement in British Columbia has gone through a time of consolidation, redefinition, and struggle. Some of the works started during rapid expansion have proven to be unsustainable. There have been great challenges in developing indigenous support for the work. At the same time important progress has been made toward fellowship and cooperation between Christian Churches/Churches of Christ and Churches of Christ.

3.6. Scattered Disciples — Lasting Effects

Where many scattered Disciples in the early years of Western Canadian history were often assimilated into other churches, in at least two instances we find isolated families conducting Sunday Schools with the dream of establishing a church. The T. L. Rash family was one such family at Taber, Alberta, where Sunday School work beginning in 1918, sporadic evangelistic meetings over many years, and the continued influence of nearby ministers such as J. R. Chapman of Lethbridge finally resulted in an established church in 1954. A similar situation emerged in Grande Prairie, where the F. A. Johnston family had moved from Lacombe to Grande Prairie in 1910. M. B. Ryan and others made contact with them and encouraged them, but no resources were put into the establishment of a church. Sunday School was carried on, and it was reported in the 1922 yearbook that the group had a church membership of twenty. It took the collaboration of other dedicated individuals, including some from the Vulcan church, to help formally found the church in Grand Prairie in 1946.

Many prairie churches, however, did not last. Factors such as the lack of leadership and the transient settlement patterns, as folk moved to the most productive land or to cities, militated against deep roots. The church at Zealandia did not last because the soil was poor and homesteading was not viable. Through the witness of that church C. H. Phillips came to Christ in "full obedience." He would later found Alberta Bible College, Ontario Bible College, and, in the United States, Puget Sound Christian College.

3.7. Unity, Tensions, and Divisions

Many of the tensions and divisions of immigrant homelands were perpetuated in Western Canada. Divisions over hermeneutics and instrumental music were planted early in the West. This was the case despite the fact that there had been early "bridging" attempts, notably Hanna, Yellow Grass, and Central Church in Calgary, which had been reasonably successful. In a context of sectarianism that frowned on association between Church of Christ constituents and others, the light of unity glowed, however dimly. This is evidenced in two noble church planting experiments. In 1955 folk from both Churches of Christ and Christian Churches/Churches of Christ at Outlook, Saskatchewan, began to meet, and continue to do so. In 1973 folk from all three streams of the Stone-Campbell tradition at Westlock, Alberta, met for about a decade, before constituents of the Churches of Christ and the Christian Churches/Churches of Christ separated from Disciples.

Alberta Bible College has played a significant role in promoting unity through the involvement of conciliatory speakers such as the late Carl Ketcherside at college events, the hosting of a Minister's Institute in the 1960s and 1970s designed for leaders to study and fellowship, and the initiation of the Western Canadian Christian Convention in 1989 for all three streams. The College has also educated leaders for all three streams in Canada. Evidence that stronger bridges are already being put in place are found in the presence of board members of Alberta Bible College (1932-) and Camp Christian (1935-) from all three streams, a joint Western Canadian Ministers and Spouses Retreat (2000-), the sharing of camping and retreat programs and leadership in Alberta and British Columbia, and the continued flow of graduates from both Western Christian College and Alberta Bible College into all three streams of the Stone-Campbell Movement.

In the case of Christian Churches/Churches of Christ ("independents") and Disciples of Christ ("cooperatives") in Western Canada, division has been muted from the beginning. The battle lines drawn in the Maritimes, Ontario, and the United States were never fully reproduced in Western Canada, at least as full-blown fractures, even to the present day. There were tensions, particularly over "open membership," in the 1960s. Some of these are recorded in the minutes of the Board of Alberta Bible College. However, the view that most of these battles were "foreign" to their experience allowed a freer, more irenic spirit to prevail and even flourish in the West.

Several factors have contributed to this. First was the cosmopolitan character of the life of the early Stone-Campbell churches in Canada. People from many different backgrounds came together voluntarily or there was no church. On an ideological level, this cosmopolitan balance established creative tensions that moderated extreme positions. Western Disciples have consequently had a tendency to be more conservative than many of their counterparts elsewhere, while Christian Churches/Churches of Christ in the West have had a tendency to be less sectarian than their counterparts elsewhere. Leading Disciples, such as John and Meredith Bergman, were deeply evangelistic and rejected "open membership." Leaders from Christian Churches/Churches of Christ such as Ed Benoit and E. G. Hansell were preachers as well as provincial and federal politicians, and they generated deep and abiding interests in the social implications of the gospel. Moderates like Melvin Breakenridge, Owen Still, Boyd Lammiman, and George Chapman did not appreciate "labels." They advocated and practiced the principle that the "restoration project" included the New Testament "spirit" and "fruits," especially "speaking the truth in love," whether to believers or non-believers.

A second reason for the muting of division was the cooperative pragmatism of evangelistic efforts. The impetus for pragmatic evangelism that dominated the first seventy and the last thirty years of the Stone-Campbell Movement in Western Canada actually created fellowship. Whether sponsored by local initiatives or by provincial, national, or international agencies, evangelism has been a shared project, regardless of method. In his musing about why the Movement in Canada had not grown as fast as her American counterpart, Reuben Butchart suggests that in America "the Reformation and the Plea for New Testament Christianity was turned into a hard and fast legality, about the methods of the work, rather than the work itself." For most of her history, the Movement in Western Canada has been spared this tendency.

Third, the experience of nonsectarian fellowship among young people mitigated potential tensions. Camps, retreats, and conferences have been a forum for this experience. Of particular note is the unique Prairie Young People's Association, established in 1928 as a concurrent conference of the Alberta Christian Missionary Society. It provided for rich, nonsectarian fellowship, developed by young people, for young people. Recent semi-annual conferences have hosted 500 youth traveling vast distances across the West. Similarly, Youth Alive in Christ provides summer ministry opportunities for teams of four or five young adults to serve churches and camps in Western Canada, Ontario, and Montana, where local resources are limited. This was initiated in 1972 by Gordon Fraser and Rick Rehn and is now managed by Alberta Bible College.

Fourth, the Church of Christ Development Corporation has played a conciliatory role. Established in 1958 by John Bergman in Edmonton, it is a financial arm of the Christian Church (Disciples of Christ) in Canada, providing friendly terms and competitive rates for the purchase and development of church property. Millions of dollars have been available for any qualifying Canadian project in any stream of the Movement, and this has made possible significant church and parachurch development.

3.8. Editors and Other Directional Influence in the West

In other times and places, the "editor-bishops," as historian W. T. Moore called them, played a dominant role in determining the direction of the Stone-Campbell Movement. Early in the development of the churches in Western Canada this was the case as well. M. B. Ryan was a regular contributor to the *Christian Standard,* the *Christian-Evangelist,* and the *Canadian Disciple,* serving as a contributing editor of the latter. The first periodical to be published in the Canadian West was *The Alberta Christian* in 1931, by C. H. Phillips. In 1936 *The Gospel Herald* began publication in Radville, Saskatchewan, by Robert Sinclair, and later, J. C. Bailey. From 1953 to the present it has been circulated from Beamsville, Ontario, with Eugene Perry being the dominant voice. In 1941 Phillips merged the *Alberta Christian* with the *Christian Chronicle* under the name of the latter, designed to serve both the interests of Alberta Bible College and the churches. This periodical ceased publication in 1949. In 1950 Melvin Breakenridge, Principal of Alberta Bible College, commenced publication of the *Evangel.* It has continued to the present under E. G. Hansell, James Chapman, Boyd Lammiman, and Ronald Fraser. James Chapman of Vulcan, Alberta, published *The Christian Harbinger* from 1949 to 1955. In Saskatchewan Alvin Jennings published the *Saskatoon Star,* and Clinton Brazle published *Living Stones* from Weyburn. Ed and Mary Benoit began *The Christian Compass* while serving in Yellowgrass, Saskatchewan, in 1948. It was subsumed in 1967 when Don Lewis of Vernon, British Columbia, published the *Western Christian,* which in 1976 merged with the *Canadian Christian Harbinger,* which had been published in Toronto for several years. It ceased publication in 1989, when Lewis returned to Joplin, Missouri. Since 1980 Church of Christ women have published *Sister Triangle.*

Voices other than those of local editors have also been influential in Western Canada. The *Christian Standard* and *The Disciple* have circulated widely, as did the *Mission Messenger,* edited by W. Carl Ketcherside and Leroy Garrett of the Churches of Christ. (The ecumenical spirit of the latter found fertile ground in Western Canada, in all three streams of the Movement.) From 1976 until 1996, the weekly *To You with Love* television broadcast, first aired locally in Calgary, and then nationally, was a directional voice for at least the constituents of Christian Churches/Churches of

Christ in the West, bringing focus and energy to the task of evangelism. Its host was R. Allan Dunbar, minister of the Cambrian Heights Church of Christ. Dunbar also pioneered an unapologetic participation in the broader Christian community, working within and outside the Movement to draw Christians together in the evangelistic task. His involvement with the Billy Graham School of Evangelism, nomination as one of the three most influential Calgarians of the twentieth century, and his current role as Executive Director of the North American Christian Convention underscore his broad reception and influence.

3.9. The Twentieth Century and Beyond

At the end of the twentieth century there were eighty-four churches (fifty-one Churches of Christ, six Disciples of Christ, and twenty-seven Christian Churches/Churches of Christ) in Western Canada, with a combined membership of about 6,400, of which 3,036 were in Churches of Christ. Perhaps the most significant trends have been the following. First is the emergence of urban congregations of all three streams of the Movement, including twelve larger (200-plus), multiple-staffed churches. A second trend is the continuing struggle for identity. Among Christian Churches/Churches of Christ and some Churches of Christ it has been a struggle of identity within mainstream evangelicalism. Among some Churches of Christ, the struggle has been within the broader Stone-Campbell fellowship. The identity crisis has been felt as well among "paired" Disciples with the United Church of Canada. Among all streams of the Movement the struggle for identity goes on as interrelationships are renegotiated in the context of decreasing sectarianism and increasing evangelistic opportunity. A third trend is the decline of the Disciples of Christ. A fourth is the developing indigenous character facilitated both by Western Canadian Christian higher education in developing leaders and a growing loss of connection to eastern and American roots. A fifth trend is a decreasing leadership drain to the United States, as churches become self-supporting. A sixth and final trend is the increased partnering in ministry opportunities, including church planting. The hosting of the World Convention of the Churches of Christ in Calgary in 1996 was both boosted by, and a boost to, such cooperative venture.

4. The Movement in Canada at the Beginning of the Twenty-First Century

At the beginning of the twenty-first century there are 222 congregations, with a combined membership of about 15,300 people, in the Stone-Campbell Movement in Canada. The history of the Movement has unfolded with unique influences and diverse trajectories. The dominant, early, and lingering influence has been that of the Scotch Baptists, with the influence of Stone and Campbell as mediated by Americans coming later. There is a continuing search for identity in all three streams, and there are unfolding relationships, typical of a "movement" resisting denominational consolidation. There is much hope across Canada that the kingdom has much to gain by embracing the mission that unites the churches of the Stone-Campbell heritage.

See also Alberta Bible College; Christian Connection; Haldane, Robert, and James Alexander Haldane; Maritime Christian College; McLean, Archibald; Western Christian College

BIBLIOGRAPHY (1) The Canadian Maritimes: Reuben Butchart, *The Disciples of Christ in Canada since 1830* (1948) • W. H. Harding, *Beginnings of Churches of Christ in the Maritimes* (1939) • Stewart Lewis, "The Scotch Baptist Influence on the Christian Churches of the Maritimes" (unpublished M.A. thesis, Cincinnati Bible Seminary, 1984) • Shirley L. Muir, *Disciples in Canada* (1966) • Robert E. Shaw, *Historical Sketch, 1831-1956: Disciples of Christ North Street Christian Church, Halifax* (c. 1956) • Harley Walker, *Milton Church of Christ (Disciples of Christ) 1934-1900* (1986).

(2) Ontario: Joseph Ash, *Reminiscences: History of the Rise and Progress of Our Cause in Canada* (1998) • Reuben Butchart, *The Disciples of Christ in Canada since 1830* (1949) • Claude E. Cox, ed., *The Campbell-Stone Movement in Ontario* (1995) • Geoffrey H. Ellis, "An Inquiry into the Growth of the Disciples of Christ in 19th Century Ontario" (unpublished M.T.S. thesis, Waterloo Lutheran Seminary, 1993) • Eugene C. Perry, "A History of Religious Periodicals in the Restoration Movement in Canada" (unpublished M.A. thesis, Pepperdine University, 1971).

(3) Western Canada: Don Albert, "Church Planting Theory in British Columbia" (unpublished paper, Alberta Bible College Archives, 2003) • Doug Barrie, "A History of the Christian Church and Christian Church (Disciples of Christ) in Alberta" (unpublished M.A. thesis, Lincoln Christian Seminary, 1975) • Melvin Breakenridge, "The Story of Alberta Bible College: 50th Anniversary Presentation" (Alberta Bible College Archives, 1982) • Reuben Butchart, *A Flame of the Lord's Kindling* (1933) • Reuben Butchart, *History of the Disciples of Christ in Canada Since 1830* (1949) • *Canadian Christian Harbinger* (periodical) • *The Canadian Disciple* (periodical) • *The Christian Compass* (periodical, Alberta Bible College Archives) • *Gospel Herald* (periodical) • Jim Hawkins, "The Churches of Christ in British Columbia" (unpublished paper, Alberta Bible College Archives, 2002) • M. P. Hayden, "Diaries" (unpublished, Alberta Bible College Archives) • Boyd L. Lammiman, "Joy Comes in the Morning: Alberta Bible College 60th Anniversary Publication" (Alberta Bible College Library, 1992) • Minutes of the Alberta Christian Missionary Society (Alberta Bible College Archives) • Mary Muirhead, "*A Cappella* Churches on the Prairies" (unpublished paper, Alberta Bible College Archives, 2003) • Bob Parker, "Breaking Down Barriers: Presenta-

tion to the Western Canadian Christian Convention" (unpublished paper, Alberta Bible College Archives, 1999). RONALD A. FRASER, STEWART J. LEWIS, *and* CLAUDE COX

Cane Ridge Meetinghouse

Earliest historic site of the Stone-Campbell Movement, located in Bourbon County, Kentucky.

Barton W. Stone began his ministry with the Cane Ridge Presbyterian Church in 1796 and was ordained here on October 4, 1798. Here occurred the great revival of August 1801 and the signing of the *Last Will and Testament of the Springfield Presbytery* on June 28, 1804. It was an integrated and anti-slavery congregation in the early 1800s and was the first church of the movement to baptize by immersion, using Stoner Creek in nearby Paris, Kentucky.

The Meeting House was built in 1791 of blue ash logs. Its dimensions are approximately fifty feet by thirty feet, with an eight-by-two-foot alcove or "pen" on each long wall. A raised boxed pulpit was set in the north alcove. The structure contains logs as long as thirty-six feet and sixteen inches square. Every log is shaped, some with ornamentation. A three-sided gallery is supported by eighteen posts. Here, at first, African American members of the congregation sat; no stairs were included originally, and these members climbed a ladder to enter through an upper window. Main access to the Meeting House was by a doorway at either end. No floor was laid for some years; later puncheon logs provided flooring. The high-pitched roof of whip-sawed sheathing was covered with shakes or shingles held by wooden pins.

The congregation renovated the Meeting House twice. In 1829, the gallery was removed and taken to a member's barn, where it was used as a hayloft for 129 years. A ceiling was added to hide the beams, and chandeliers were installed. Plaster was put over the logs, and a tongue-and-groove floor was installed on top of the puncheon logs. Seats with backs replaced earlier puncheon log benches. Outside, white frame siding covered the walls.

In 1882 a center aisle was created. The boxed pulpit was removed and the eastern door closed. A poplar plank floor was laid, and a free-standing pulpit was placed on a platform in the center of the east wall. A communion table and elders' chairs were at the front. New pews were built. A pot-bellied stove provided the first-ever heat for the room. A reed organ and kerosene lamps completed the renovation. The Meeting House continued to be used in this form until the congregation ceased to meet in 1921.

In 1932 the Cane Ridge Preservation Project came into existence to oversee restoration. The outside siding and inside ceiling and plaster were removed. The east door was reopened, and the gallery was retrieved

The original meetinghouse was typical of the log construction used on the American frontier and included a large elevated "box" pulpit. Courtesy Center for Restoration Studies, Abilene Christian University

from the barn and reinstalled to an almost perfect fit as the building had never shifted. Stairs for the gallery were built. The 1882 floor and pews were retained. Seats were arranged in a "U" configuration around the boxed pulpit and centered communion table and elders' chairs. A superstructure to protect the log church was built with native limestone and dedicated as a shrine to Christian unity in 1957.

Throughout its existence, the congregational cemetery received the faithful of the past. The graves of Stone and his first wife, Elizabeth Campbell, several early leaders of the Stone-Campbell Movement, two veterans of the American War of Independence, and members of the congregation both black and white are found within its grounds. With the closing of the church in 1921 burials ceased for over eighty years until the interment of Stone-Campbell scholar Anthony L. Dunnavant in February 2001.

A museum was built on the grounds in 1975 to house a growing collection of historical materials. It was expanded in 1989 to provide more exhibit space, and a sheltered picnic pavilion was added. The trustees of the Project, who represent nearby Disciples congregations and Kentucky Disciples schools, continue to care for Cane Ridge and offer programs such as the annual Cane Ridge Day. In August 2001 thousands of Stone-Campbell Christians from all three streams of the Movement gathered for over a week of commemoration and worship in recognition of the 200th anniversary of the Cane Ridge Revival.

See also Cane Ridge Revival; Stone, Barton Warren

BIBLIOGRAPHY James R. Rogers, *The Cane Ridge Meeting House* (1910) • Rhodes Thompson, *Voices from Cane Ridge* (1954) . FRANKLIN REID MCGUIRE

The "rediscovery" of Stone by Disciples in the 1930s led to the organization of the Cane Ridge Preservation Project to restore and protect the meetinghouse. After the U.S. Department of the Interior recognized it as a building of national significance in 1934, the Preservation Project began raising money for a limestone superstucture to protect the meetinghouse. The structure, shown here, was completed and dedicated in 1957. Courtesy of the Center for Restoration Studies, Abilene Christian University

Cane Ridge Revival

Most famous camp meeting or sacrament of the Great Revival in the West (1797-1805); hosted by the Presbyterian Church at Cane Ridge, Kentucky, and its pastor, Barton W. Stone, August 6-12, 1801.

Little is known of the arrangements made in preparation for this meeting. Four-day celebrations of communion, with two days of preparation beginning on Friday, followed by the reenactment of the Supper on Sunday and a thanksgiving sermon on Monday, were a well-established Presbyterian practice with roots in the Church of Scotland. Word of the upcoming sacrament at Cane Ridge was spread through a network of religious activities that Stone made sure included Methodists as well as Presbyterians. Accounts of the meeting refer to the "tent" — a covered lecture platform or stage made of wood located 100 yards to the southwest of the meetinghouse. Based on attendance reports in the thousands for Presbyterian sacraments in central Kentucky earlier in the summer, such structures were necessary since the log meetinghouse had a maximum capacity of 400.

People began arriving at Cane Ridge during the day on Friday, August 6. The first scheduled service was in the evening, with Presbyterian minister Matthew Houston preaching. The service was in the packed meetinghouse, where some lingered all night. Rain may have curtailed the numbers. Presbyterian minister John Lyle and others worshiped that evening in the home of Cane Ridge elder Andrew Irvine. No doubt worship was also conducted in the homes of other members of the congregation who, like Irvine, provided hospitality to visitors who had come some distance to participate in the sacrament.

Saturday a growing crowd filled the grounds of the meeting house and spread into the adjoining grove owned by a Methodist, Ilai Nunn. The number of wagons camped on the grounds, at least over Saturday and Sunday, was estimated at between 125 and 148, covering, as one observer reported, an area the equivalent of four city blocks. In addition, thousands of participants arrived for the day, including not only those who lived within horseback riding distance but also people who found accommodations in neighboring communities.

Estimates of the number of people on the grounds Saturday and Sunday ranged from 10,000 to 20,000 and beyond. Since most daily visitors had to come by horse or wagon, logistical considerations, including space to accommodate animals, suggest that no more than 10,000 persons could have been on the grounds at any one time. It is possible that 20,000 different people (nearly 10 percent of the recorded population of Kentucky in 1800) were at Cane Ridge at some time during the week.

The first sermon Saturday morning was delivered in the meetinghouse. In the afternoon, preaching was continuous both in the meetinghouse and from the tent. Before dark the grounds echoed with penitent cries and shouts. People crowded into the meetinghouse to hear Stone and others preach. People began falling, a phenomenon that had marked the revival since Methodists had been included in the leadership of the Presbyterian sacraments, beginning in Logan County, Kentucky, in the summer of 1800.

In his autobiography, Stone described the phenomenon as he first observed it early in the spring of 1801. "Many, very many fell down, as men slain in battle, and continued for hours together in an apparently breathless and motionless state — sometimes for a few moments reviving, and exhibiting symptoms of life by a deep groan, or piercing shriek, or by a prayer for mercy most fervently uttered." Gradually they would obtain release; the "gloomy cloud, which had covered their faces" giving way first to smiles of hope and then of joy, they would finally rise "shouting deliverance" and would address the surrounding crowd "in language truly eloquent and impressive." "With astonishment," Stone exclaimed, "did I hear men, women and children declaring the wonderful works of God, and the glorious mysteries of the gospel." He reported that their appeals to others were "solemn, heart-penetrating, bold and free." Noting that he was amazed at "the knowledge of gospel truth displayed" in their addresses, he observed that, hearing their appeals, others would fall

Associated with the Great Revival in the West (1797-1805), the Cane Ridge Meeting, August 6-12, 1801, was the culmination of a wave of religious excitement that spread across northern Kentucky during the spring and summer of 1801. Beginning with the regularly scheduled four-day Presbyterian sacramental meeting at Fleming Creek, northeast of Lexington, the first weekend in May, attendance and the remarkable phenomena of "falling" increased at the regularly scheduled Presbyterian sacramental meetings that followed at Cabin Creek, Concord, Salem, Point Pleasant, Lexington, Indian Creek, and Paris. Methodists and Baptists joined in many of the meetings. Courtesy of the Disciples of Christ Historical Society

down "into the same state from which the speakers had just been delivered."

At Cane Ridge, some of the persons who fell were removed to some place where a smaller group could offer prayer on their behalf and engage in singing hymns. Others were allowed to remain where they fell. On Saturday evening, the sweltering heat inside the meetinghouse, along with the growing emotional pitch, drove Presbyterian preacher Lyle outdoors, where he and two other Presbyterian preachers, Richard McNemar and Matthew Houston, preached from the stand.

Sunday, the day reserved for the celebration of the sacrament, was marked by a steady, pouring rain. In the morning, exhorting and sermons were offered in the meetinghouse. Presbyterian minister Robert Marshall gave the traditional action sermon from the stand, identifying the character of persons invited to the Table. The Supper itself was served in the meetinghouse. Once inside, communicants were seated at long tables set up in the aisles, heard the scriptural words of institution joined with prayer, and received the elements of bread and wine. Estimates of the number of communicants ranged from 800 to 1,100. Since no more than 100 could be seated in the meetinghouse at one time, at least eight table sittings, with Presbyterian ministers administering the Supper on a rotating basis, succeeded one another as the service continued late into the afternoon.

Stone, along with local Methodist preacher William Burke, had promoted the meeting as a "united sacrament." Not all Presbyterians, however, were as enthusiastic as Stone about uniting in communion with the Methodists. Early Sunday morning, in response to their concerns, Stone asked Burke to make a statement from the stand regarding "how the Methodists held certain doctrines" before final arrangements were made regarding the administration of the sacrament. Taking Stone's request as an insult, Burke challenged him to do likewise for the Presbyterians, and Stone quickly withdrew the request. Without further conversation, Burke mounted the trunk of a fallen tree that had lodged against another tree about a hundred feet east of the meetinghouse and began to pray, sing, and preach. Another Methodist held "an umbrella affixed to a long pole" over Burke's head. A large crowd quickly gathered, and many fell.

Stone reported that during the course of the meeting "Four or five preachers were frequently speaking at the same time, in different parts of the encampment, without confusion." With persons falling throughout the camp added to the simultaneous preaching, one participant remarked, "The noise was like the roar of Niagara." Sunday, in addition to preaching from the tent and from Burke's fallen tree, there was also preaching by an unidentified African American preacher to a group comprised largely of African Americans probably about 150 yards southeast of the meetinghouse. One participant counted "seven ministers, all preaching at one time" in different parts of the camp, some using stumps and wagons as makeshift platforms.

By Sunday evening the rain had ended, and praying, preaching, exhorting, and falling continued throughout the camp. After the thanksgiving sermon on Monday, the normal communion schedule had been fulfilled. What followed was directed by the demand of the people for more singing, praying, and preaching and the willingness of preachers to minister to them. Many participants had to leave, but the meeting continued. New arrivals kept coming until Wednesday or even, by some reports, Thursday, when organized activity came to an end. Stone indicated that the meeting would have continued even longer had provisions in the neighborhood not been exhausted. Throughout the meeting, but especially after Sunday, persons who fell addressed the crowds. Lyle reported that "Their orations consist of the plain and essential truths of the gospel that they themselves have been powerfully convinced of, but they speak them with all the feeling and pathos that human nature affected with the most important objects is capable of." He further noted, "They speak much of the fullness [of] Christ, his willingness to save etc."

As many as eighteen Presbyterian ministers participated in the meeting. Most were from Bourbon County or adjoining counties, though a few came from a distance of from thirty to fifty miles. John Rankin traveled nearly 300 miles from Logan County. In most cases, church members had accompanied their ministers, thus helping to account for the 800 to 1,100 who received the sacrament. Methodist preachers included William Burke, Benjamin Lakin, Benjamin Northcott, and Samuel Hitt. Methodists also received the sacrament, though given the total number who communed and the large number of Presbyterian congregations represented, probably no more than 200 of them.

Stone reported in his autobiography that both "Methodist and Baptist preachers aided in the work." Other accounts of the meeting refer occasionally to the presence of Baptists and Baptist preachers, though none is recorded as preaching in the meetinghouse or from the tent. Cane Ridge coincided with the annual meeting of the Elkhorn Baptist Association, which convened at Higby's meetinghouse approximately six miles from Lexington. Baptist worship there attracted an estimated 8,000 to 10,000 people, including, no doubt, a large number of the Baptist preachers in central Kentucky. Also, since Baptists viewed Presbyterians and Methodists as improperly baptized and would not join them in communion, Baptist preachers may have had reservations about participating in a "united" sacramental meeting. Some Baptist ministers may have served as exhorters. However, one did not have to be a preacher to exhort. Literally hundreds of persons exhorted at Cane Ridge, including men, women, and children.

The number who fell may have reached 1,000 — estimates ranged from 300 to 3,000. Given the size of the meeting and the high level of confusion, it was difficult to judge the number of converts. In an account of the revival published in 1827, Stone acknowledged that the number of converts could never be ascertained, but he added that it was thought to have been between 500 and 1,000. In his autobiography, he eschewed offering even an estimate of the number of converts, declaring instead that "The number converted will be known only in eternity."

BIBLIOGRAPHY Paul Conkin, *Cane Ridge: America's Pentecost* (1990) • Leigh Eric Schmidt, *Holy Fairs: Scottish Communions and American Revivals in the Early Modern Period* (1989) • D. Newell Williams, *Barton Stone: A Spiritual Biography* (2000).

D. Newell Williams

Cascade College

Four-year Christian college in Portland, Oregon, affiliated with the Churches of Christ and operating as a branch campus of Oklahoma Christian University. The school offers degrees in biblical studies, business, teacher education, liberal studies, English, and psychology.

The thirteen-acre Portland campus was originally the site of Columbia Christian College, which operated as an independent institution from 1956 to 1993. L. D. Webb (b. 1915) served as first president of Columbia Bible School, which was organized by Portland area members of Churches of Christ in 1947 in a local church building. That school was forerunner to the Columbia Christian Schools (K-12), out of which grew Columbia Christian College.

J. P. Sanders (1906-2002) served as president of the college during its formative years in the 1970s. Other important figures were E. W. McMillan (1889-1991), who taught several years at Columbia, and Bob Rowland, who served several years as president. Columbia was a junior college from 1956 until 1975, when it was accredited as a four-year college by the Northwest Association of Schools and Colleges. Accreditation was eventually revoked, however, largely because of financial instability.

When financial difficulties forced the closing of the college in 1993, its facilities and administration were offered to Oklahoma Christian University, which then established Cascade College as a branch college to the university. Cascade was consequently accredited by the North Central Association of Colleges and Schools as a part of Oklahoma Christian and shares international study programs, distance learning options, and administrative functions with its sponsoring institution. Since its opening for classes in 1994, Cascade had grown in enrollment to over 300 students by 2002. The majority of Cascade's students are from Oregon, Washington, and California, most in the 18- to 25-year-old age group. Approximately 60 percent are members of Churches of Christ. Alumni of Columbia Christian and Cascade have played a significant role in providing leaders for congregations of the Churches of Christ in the Northwest, where the number of congregations grew from about 70 in the 1940s to nearly 400 by the beginning of the twenty-first century. Kevin Jacobs served as executive vice president from 1993 to 1995, and Dennis Lynn became president in 1996.

See also Columbia Christian College; McMillan, Edward Washington; Oklahoma Christian University

John F. Wilson

Cassius, Samuel Robert (1853-1931)

African American preacher and racial reformer.

Cassius began preaching in Sigourney, Iowa, in 1880. Eleven years later Cassius moved to Oklahoma Territory to preach, believing it was a place where blacks and native Americans could be free of racial prejudice and discrimination because of the low white population. In the spring of 1892 he began preaching for the first black congregation in Oklahoma Territory in Springvale Township, and in 1900 he moved to Tohee where he operated the Tohee Industrial School. In 1902 Cassius became the first African American preacher from the Stone-Campbell Movement to preach in the Los Angeles area. Later, in 1924, he and his son A. L. Cassius would establish the first black Church of Christ in southern California.

Cassius began annual meetings for black Christians in Oklahoma in 1899, and he established the Missionary Executive Board of the Colored Disciples in Oklahoma in 1909, serving as the body's first president. He became disillusioned with the organization, however, and moved in 1915 to Austin, Texas, to preach for a time. In addition to his later work in California, in 1927 Cassius established a church in Denver, Colorado, beginning with twenty-six Christians.

Cassius published frequent reports and articles in the *Christian Leader* and the *Gospel Advocate*. J. E. Choate recorded that Cassius was known for "chastising white brethren for their lack of interest in the Negro." He argued for racial separation because of the white Christians' lack of interest in and antagonism toward blacks. In 1920 he published *Third Birth of a Nation,* a strong attack against American racism.

See also African Americans in the Movement

BIBLIOGRAPHY Calvin H. Bowers, *Realizing the California Dream: The Story of the Black Churches of Christ in Los Angeles* (2001) • S. R. Cassius, *The Third Birth of a Nation* (1920; rev. ed. 1925) • J. E. Choate, *Roll Jordan Roll: A Biography of Marshall Keeble* (1968). ERVIN C. JACKSON

Centennial Convention, The

The October 11-19, 1909, General Convention that celebrated the one hundredth anniversary of the publication of the *Declaration and Address,* then generally considered the earliest expression of principles advocated by the Stone-Campbell Movement.

The convention was held in Pittsburgh, Pennsylvania, the nearest city to Washington, Pennsylvania, where the *Declaration and Address* was first printed. Careful preparations were made by a committee from the various agencies represented in the General Convention. The theme for the Convention expressed the aim of the Movement: "The Union of All Believers, on a Basis of Holy Scriptures, to the end that the World may be Evangelized."

Logistics of the Convention exceeded anything hitherto attempted. Chartered trains were organized in several areas of the nation. Hotel facilities were inadequate, and residents shared their homes with participants. Since no auditorium could accommodate

On Saturday, October 16, the Convention had a special service to honor "veterans," men and women over 70 years old who had given their lives in service to the Movement. Among those seated in the front row are J. W. McGarvey (2nd from left), C. L. Loos (3rd from left), and Helen Moses (lower right corner). Courtesy of the Disciples of Christ Historical Society

the 25,000 in attendance, it was necessary to hold simultaneous sessions in the largest churches in the city. On the Sunday of the Convention, 250 churches welcomed Disciple preachers into their pulpits. That afternoon a huge communion service, possibly the largest ever observed in America, was held in Forbes Field, home of the Pittsburgh Pirates baseball team. The magnitude of the Convention and the dynamic of its witness caused the religious world to take note.

Significant consequences may be traced to this Convention. Agency cooperation led to unification in 1919. Energy was generated for the Men and Millions Movement, which was launched in 1913 to raise $6,300,000 and enlist 1,000 men for ministry abroad or at home.

BIBLIOGRAPHY *Centennial Convention Report* (1909).
HENRY E. WEBB

Center for Restoration Studies

Repository for collecting, arranging, and preserving books and archival collections related to the Stone-Campbell Movement, especially Churches of Christ.

Opening in 1986 in Brown Library of Abilene Christian University, the Center for Restoration Studies is dedicated to acquiring and preserving materials important for the self-understanding of the heritage of Churches of Christ, serving the interests of historians, ministers, and students. The Center houses personal paper collections of a number of twentieth-century leaders in Churches of Christ. Museum holdings include the pulpit Thomas Campbell preached

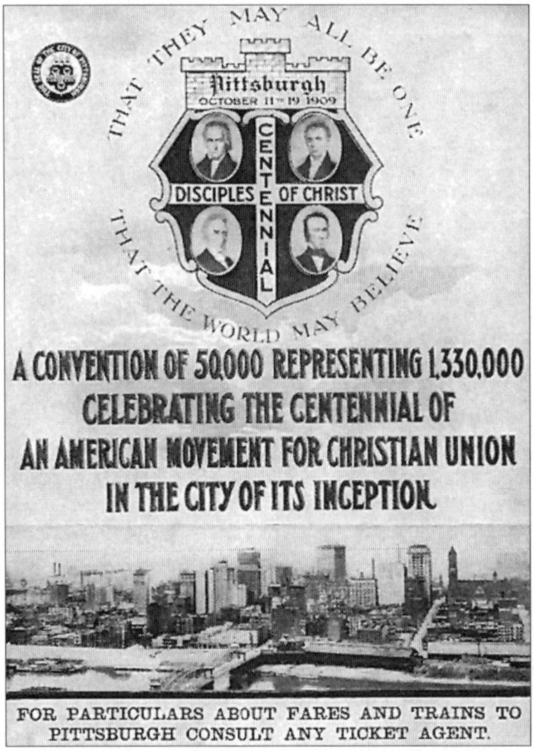
THAT THEY MAY ALL BE ONE
THAT THE WORLD MAY BELIEVE
Pittsburgh
OCTOBER 11-19 1909
CENTENNIAL
DISCIPLES OF CHRIST
A CONVENTION OF 50,000 REPRESENTING 1,330,000
CELEBRATING THE CENTENNIAL OF
AN AMERICAN MOVEMENT FOR CHRISTIAN UNION
IN THE CITY OF ITS INCEPTION.
FOR PARTICULARS ABOUT FARES AND TRAINS TO
PITTSBURGH CONSULT ANY TICKET AGENT.

Poster used to advertise the Centennial Convention in 1909.

from at the Ahorey Church in Northern Ireland, an oil painting of Alexander Campbell, and handwritten letters from Campbell and Barton W. Stone.

In the mid-1990s the Center began a long-term project of scanning and making available on-line a variety of documents unique to its collection. These images, as well as the Center's book and archival holdings, may be searched on-line through the library link at Abilene Christian University's web site.

Dr. Bill J. Humble and Dr. Douglas A. Foster have served as Center Director, with R. L. Roberts (1925-1998) and Erma Jean Loveland as archivist.

BIBLIOGRAPHY "Historical Center Begun," *Christian Chronicle* 41 (1 March 1984) • Bill J. Humble, "Remembering Our Roots," *Image* 1 (July 1985): 24.

ERMA JEAN LOVELAND

Central Christian College of the Bible

Bible college in Moberly, Missouri, affiliated with the Christian Churches/Churches of Christ.

Central Christian College of the Bible (CCCB) was founded in 1957, although it grew out of an earlier effort, Chillicothe Bible College, founded in Chillicothe, Missouri, in 1952 and closed in 1956. Individuals from churches in the area who wished to see a Bible college continue in north-central Missouri convened a steering committee in 1957, resulting in the formation of Central Christian College of the Bible.

Classes opened in the fall of 1957 in a building that once housed a parochial school. The first semester saw an enrollment of only fourteen full-time students, but over a hundred part-time students attended evening classes. There were five full-time faculty members in the beginning, two of whom, Gareth Reese and Lloyd M. Pelfrey, are still serving the college over forty years later.

In 1968 the college moved to its present location on a forty-acre campus on the southern edge of Moberly. CCCB received accreditation from the Accrediting Association of Bible Colleges in 1982. Since it is a Bible college, all degree programs entail heavy concentrations in biblical studies. Degree programs provide majors or minors in Preaching Ministry, Christian Education, Youth and Family Ministry, Counseling, Cross-Cultural Ministry, Deaf Ministry, Music Ministry, and General Ministry.

The affairs of the college are overseen by a seventeen-person Board of Directors drawn from a variety of vocational fields, including businessmen, educators, and ministers. CCCB has played a significant role in supplying ministers for, and strengthening the work of, Christian Churches/Churches of Christ in northern Missouri and in neighboring states. The school's rural location gives students ample opportunities to gain ministry experience in area churches. Recent enrollments have ranged between 125 and 150 students, with a current full-time faculty of seven.

See also Bible College Movement; Higher Education, Views of in the Movement MARK S. JOY

Chalice Press

An imprint of Christian Board of Publication (CBP), established in 1991 by editor-in-chief David P. Polk as a successor to The Bethany Press (1954-83) and CBP Press (1984-90).

Chalice Press expanded rapidly into a wide range of "books for the thinking, caring church" that attempted to address the person in the pew with serious but accessible Christian scholarship. Although primarily serving the Christian Church (Disciples of Christ), of which CBP is a general administrative unit, the press from the outset reached out to other moderate to liberal church constituencies, and more recently has also been publishing authors from the Churches of Christ and the Christian Churches/Churches of Christ. In 1995 it brought out the highly acclaimed and widely used *Chalice Hymnal,* following up with a collection of contemporary church music called *Chalice Praise* in 2003. Chalice Press expanded its activities in 1997 with the addition of an academic line in the areas of Bible, theology, homiletics, pastoral care, Christian education, and multicultural studies, with Jon L. Berquist serving as academic editor.

See also Christian Board of Publication

DAVID P. POLK

Chaplaincy

Chaplains are ministers who usually minister in positions other than those of the located church ministry. Chaplains often serve in conjunction with federal, state, and local governments, or else in a variety of institutional settings. As representatives of their faith group, chaplains conduct religious services according to the customs and traditions of their heritage and provide various types of pastoral care. Chaplains normally require ecclesiastical endorsement or certification as a condition of their employment.

Federal chaplaincies are the most common in governmental service, operating in the context of: (1) the military services' active and reserve components, for example, the Army, Navy, and Air Force, as well as the Army and Air National Guards and the Civil Air Patrol; (2) the Veterans Administration, which includes its domiciliaries and its general and psychiatric hospitals; and (3) the Federal Prison Service, which includes ministries in correctional facilities, penitentiaries, youth centers, and camps.

Institutional chaplaincies and counseling ministries among others include those positions with alcohol and drug centers, correctional schools and centers, juvenile courts, counseling and pastoral care centers, Clinical Pastoral Education (CPE) training programs, mental health centers, hospitals, nursing care facilities, police and fire departments, and prisons (city, county, and state).

Ministers and chaplains of the Stone-Campbell Movement seek endorsement according to their respective affiliation within the tradition. The Chaplaincy and Specialized Ministries program of the Division of Homeland Ministries of the Christian Church (Disciples of Christ) oversees the support and certification of Disciples chaplains. Formal endorsement comes from the denomination's Committee on Chaplaincy Endorsement and Services. In keeping with standards of local congregational authority, Churches of Christ rely on the elders of the Fairfax Church of Christ (Fairfax, Virginia) to endorse chaplains from their stream of the Movement. Those desiring endorsement by the Christian Churches/Churches of Christ seek endorsement by the Chaplaincy Endorsement Commission of the Christian Churches/Churches of Christ. Ministers of the Disciple Heritage Fellowship seek endorsement from the National Association of Evangelicals.

THOMAS E. STOKES

Chapman University

Related to the Christian Church (Disciples of Christ).

Chapman University traces its roots to Hesperian College, founded in 1861. The university claims that Hesperian College was opened at the very hour of Abraham Lincoln's inauguration as the sixteenth president of the United States. Later Hesperian and several other institutions came together to form California Christian College in Los Angeles. In 1934 the college was renamed for C. C. Chapman, a real estate investor, rancher, and pioneer Orange County church leader. The college moved to Orange, California, in 1954 and changed its name to Chapman University in 1991.

The school has a strong commitment to international education and innovative undergraduate and graduate programs. Its mission statement commits the university to providing personalized education of distinction that leads to inquiring, ethical, and productive lives as global citizens. The university is made up of the Wilkinson College of Letters and Sciences, School of Business and Economics, School of Communication Arts, School of Education, School of Film and Television, School of Law, School of Music, Graduate Studies, and the College of Lifelong Learning.

Chapman has twenty-one endowed academic chairs, ten endowed professorships, and five endowed research and educational centers; it has a full-time faculty of 263 and an enrollment (full-time equivalent) of 2,851 undergraduate and 1,024 graduate students on its Orange campus and 2,812 in its academic centers. Among its distinctions, the university lists that it is Orange County's most comprehensive independent university; offers forty fields of undergraduate study and twenty graduate programs; has the most sustained increase in grade point average and average SAT scores of any comprehensive U.S. college or university between 1991 and 2001; has a $200 million campaign supporting facilities, endowment, scholarships, and programs; the law school received provisional American Bar Association approval in its third year; the size of the campus nearly doubled during the 1990s; twenty intercollegiate athletic teams competed in NCAA Division III and club sports, with many student-athletes receiving academic All-American awards.

The university has a historic covenant with the Christian Church (Disciples of Christ), which the university reports lives on through its focus on the development of the ethical, spiritual, physical, and intellectual facets of the individual. The university offers, but does not require, a variety of religious courses and activities and employs a dean of the chapel who oversees an active ecumenical program designed to meet the spiritual needs of a student body that is religiously very diverse. It also has a full-time director of church relations to strengthen the university's covenant with the Christian Church (Disciples of Christ) as well as providing programs for the broader ecumenical community.

Chapman University's most popular degrees are in the fields of Business, Film and Television, Movement and Exercise Science, Communications, Theatre and Dance, Music, Liberal Studies, Psychology, and English. TERRY MIETHE

Charismatics

The term "charismatic" has been used in the broad sense to identify persons who claim a supernatural manifestation of the Holy Spirit in Christian experience. Charismatics have not typically been prominent in any of the streams of the Stone-Campbell Movement, though the work of the Holy Spirit has been a major concern and source of controversy.

The Stone wing of the Stone-Campbell Movement grew out of the Great Western Revival in which bodily "exercises" such as falling, jerking, dancing, barking, laughing, running, and singing were prominent. Stone himself did not resist these exercises because he thought they resulted in new spiritual awareness, but he also recognized abuses in these behaviors and did not regularly promote them. Alexander Campbell censured all such behavior as "enthusiasm," arguing that it distracted people from hearing the gospel and experiencing its true spiritual delight. Walter Scott argued that the Holy Spirit worked only through Scripture in the preaching of the gospel to bring about conversion, and entered the Christian only as an indwelling presence upon immersion in water. After the efforts at union, beginning in 1832, the views of Campbell and Scott prevailed over those of Stone. Many in the New England, Virginia, and Kentucky/Ohio Christian Churches retained strong support of the bodily exercises and refused to unite with Campbell. These churches united after the Civil War with the Christian Connexion.

A nineteenth-century challenge to the Campbell/Scott consensus concerning the work of the Holy Spirit can be seen in the controversy involving W. S. Russell. Russell was a minister and educator from Jacksonville, Illinois, who had graduated from Bethany College, and who shared his teacher Robert Richardson's dismay over an entrenched rationalism and lack of spirituality in the Stone-Campbell Movement. Russell began to place ever-greater emphasis on the vitality of the Holy Spirit in Christian experience. Russell criticized as constrictive Alexander Campbell's principle that the Spirit works only through the written Word, and he pressed the view that the Spirit wrote directly and indelibly on the convicted sinner's heart to drive home the power of the Word. For this, Russell, having gained a following in Illinois, was accused by Campbell and others of creating schism. Even his former teacher Robert Richardson censured him.

In the twentieth century, discussion of the work of the Holy Spirit has been driven by the rise and expansion of the Pentecostal movement. Originating at the beginning of the twentieth century in Kansas and California, Pentecostal theology emphasized individual gifts of tongue speaking, faith healing, and prophesying. Conservative Stone-Campbell preachers challenged Pentecostals to debate. Pentecostal claims were ridiculed in newspaper ads offering rewards of up to $1,000 for evidence of miraculous healing. Conservative leaders in the Movement reasserted their understanding of Campbellian rationalism to combat the threat of losses to Pentecostalism. Leaders in the more moderate and liberal parts of the Movement rejected Pentecostal claims on the ground of scientific rationalism and historical-critical approaches to Scripture that challenged the reality of the miraculous in Christian history overall. Speaking in terms that conservatives and liberals alike could affirm, J. H. Garrison wrote in 1905 in *The Holy Spirit* that the gifts were a condition of the infant church, and in its now more mature stage "such infantile helps would no longer be necessary."

In the 1960s charismatic phenomena appeared in mainstream Protestant churches, beginning with Dennis Bennett, an Episcopalian in Van Nuys, California. The special focus was tongue speaking and the leading of God in life's activities. These interests spread like wildfire across the mainstream churches and into the Roman Catholic Church, soon totaling upwards of 25,000 persons. These groups attracted younger persons in the Churches of Christ and Christian Churches/Churches of Christ at the end of the 1960s. The older rationalism had broken down with the rise of existentialism and later deconstructionism, paving the way for openness to less constrained and more emotive experiences. In addition, the anti-institutionalism born of the counterculture and anti–Vietnam War protests impacted youth across the streams of the Movement. Juan Carlos Ortiz's *Discipleship* and David Wilkerson's *The Cross and the Switchblade* influenced many conservative Stone-Campbell Christians.

By the middle of the 1960s, groups of younger members of Churches of Christ had claimed the gift of speaking in tongues in Nashville, Houston, and Los Angeles, at Abilene Christian College, York College in Nebraska, Harding College in Searcy, Arkansas, and elsewhere. By the early 1970s, Pat Boone of Churches of Christ took up charismatic interests, as did various persons at the Belmont Church of Christ in Nashville, for which Don Finto preached. These developments, though involving less than 5 percent of the members, were widely criticized by leading preachers and college administrators, and most of the persons involved departed for newly emerging charismatic churches. Some of the more academic ended up at Oral Roberts University or Regent University. Some persons had charismatic interests but were quiet about them and stayed in Churches of Christ.

The interest in the charismatic movement has been similar in Christian Churches/Churches of Christ. A small number of students has been involved in charismatic interests at Lincoln Christian College and Seminary, at Milligan College, and at San Jose Christian College. The leadership by and large resisted these trends. A few professors in the colleges of this stream have dropped older cessationist views that the special gifts ended at the close of the first century.

In the late 1980s a new denomination called Christ's Church Fellowship was launched, drawing members from across the streams of the Movement, especially Christian Churches/Churches of Christ and the Christian Church (Disciples of Christ). Headquartered in Cincinnati and led by Tom Smith, who had attended Lincoln Christian Seminary, the group emphasized healing and other charismatic gifts and published its own journal, *Paraclete.* It has reported almost 100 congregations in the United States and internationally, most of which are new church plants. Charismatic practices have appeared in Dallas, Atlanta, and elsewhere among members of Churches of Christ influenced by the writings of Jack Deere. The main charismatic thrust among Disciples has been among Puerto Rican Disciples and the African-American Assembly Disciples churches in North Carolina and Virginia.

Charismatic hymnody and physical postures of prayer and praise have influenced many churches, including those of the Stone-Campbell Movement. The charismatic movement has encouraged openness to the direct guidance of the Spirit in daily life and to the ministry of angels. The International Church of Christ, formerly the Boston Movement, rejected speaking in tongues and healing, yet the pyramid style of discipling with prayer partners and hierarchical leadership was borrowed from charismatics.

See also Cane Ridge Revival; Christ's Church Fellowship; Great Awakenings; Heresy, Heretics; Holy Spirit, Doctrine of the; Russell, Walter Scott

BIBLIOGRAPHY Amy Artman, "The Encounter of North American Stone-Campbell Christians with the Pentecostal/Charismatic Movement," *Discipliana* 62 (2002): 81-93 • James D. Bales, *Pat Boone and the Gift of Tongues* (1970) • Simon J. Dahlman, "Christ's Church Fellowship: New Denomination Formed," *Christian Standard* 124 (1989): 278-79 • John Deere, *Surprised by the Voice of God: How God Speaks Today Through Prophecies, Dreams, and Visions* (1996) • J. H. Garrison, *The Holy Spirit* (1905); W. J. Hollenweger, *The Pentecostals* (1972) • Charles H. Kraft, *Christianity with Power: Your Worldview and Your Experiences of the Supernatural* (1989) • Richard Quebedeaux, *The New Charismatics II* (1983) • Ken Waters, "Charismatics: The View from Within," *Mission* 9 (1976): 221-24 • Ken Waters, *The Acts of the Holy Spirit in the Church of Christ Today* (1971).

THOMAS H. OLBRICHT

Chi Rho Fellowship

See Youth Groups, Youth Ministry

Children's Homes and Orphanages

1. Christian Church (Disciples of Christ)
2. Churches of Christ
3. Christian Churches/Churches of Christ

1. Christian Church (Disciples of Christ)

The first benevolent institution of the Stone-Campbell Movement was the Kentucky Female Orphans School (now Midway College), established in 1849 in Midway, Kentucky. Begun by James W. Parrish and John J. Johnson following the vision of L. L. Pinkerton, the school was among the earliest such institutions in the United States. Walter Scott had attempted to start a similar school for boys, but it was never begun.

The aftermath of the Civil War created an increased need to care for and educate orphaned children. Furthermore, the change and growth then taking place in agricultural America created a demand for children in that labor force. By the 1870s, orphanages and schools for orphans were sprouting up all over the country. Churches of the Movement established an orphan school at Camden Point, Missouri, and later Add-Ran College (now Texas Christian University) included an orphan's department.

In Louisville, Kentucky, in the early 1880s William Broadhurst, who had spent his formative years at the Kentucky Female Orphan's School where his father was principal, began taking in orphans. Broadhurst's commitment to orphaned children led to the establishment of the Christian Church Widow's and Orphan's Home, now the Christian Church Homes of Kentucky, where several hundred children and their families continue to be served each year.

In the late 1880s, Mattie Hart Younkin (d. 1908) and six other women met at First Christian Church in St. Louis to pray for those in need. Their idea of a nationally coordinated ministry to widows and orphans took several years to gain acceptance, but it resulted in 1887 in the establishment of the National Benevolent Association (NBA), which is the social service agency of the Christian Church (Disciples of Christ) and, at the beginning of the twenty-first century, the third-largest not-for-profit organization in the United States.

The focus of the NBA in the earliest days was providing primary education and custodial care for orphans. The NBA's operations have grown through the years to include community-based family services, day treatment, residential treatment, subacute care, emergency shelters, adoption services, early intervention services, family preservation, therapeutic foster care, adventure and wilderness camping, special education, and professional and family training. Several thousand children and their families are served each year in multiple locations and facilities in numerous states across the country.

Daniel Gilbert

2. Churches of Christ

In the year 2000, approximately sixty children's homes affiliated with Churches of Christ were operated in the United States. Such homes rely on the financial support of congregations and individuals to provide residential assistance to orphaned children. In the 1920s, however, an issue arose concerning whether congregations should financially support the work of children's homes. Churches were in agreement that benevolence to those in need was a vital part of Christian living but differed on the methods by which it would be practiced. It was difficult for many churches to see a pattern in the New Testament for the support of extra-congregational institutions such as children's homes, which typically existed apart from a congregation and without the direct guidance of the church's elders. Some opposed Christian colleges and missionary societies for the same reasons. In Churches of Christ, cooperation among congregations was also a disputed matter that some believed was not supported by Scripture. In the eyes of many, the New Testament described local congregations and individual Christians caring for those in need. As a result, some viewed children's homes as inappropriate since they were financially supported by several different congregations.

Periodical literature, college lectureships, and formal debates regularly addressed the children's home controversy from the 1930s to the 1960s. Congregations that opposed church-supported children's homes became known as "non-institutional" Churches of Christ. In spite of opposition by non-institutional segments of the church, children's homes associated with Churches of Christ, such as the Tipton Orphan Home (1924, Tipton, Oklahoma) and the Boles Orphan Home (1924, Quinlin, Texas), survived and slowly grew in number throughout the middle to late twentieth century.

Wade E. Osburn

3. Christian Churches/Churches of Christ

Even as the second division of the Movement was taking shape, many members of Christian Churches/Churches of Christ continued to support the home founded by the National Benevolent Association (NBA) in St. Louis in 1889. Yet these churches also looked to establish new benevolent projects. Early local ventures in Cincinnati (1864) and Louisville (1884) set the tone for these later works. In 1921 Sam Hurley and churches around Grundy, Virginia, established the Mountain Mission School, supported by churches in many states with money, work projects, food, and clothing.

More than two dozen children's homes now employ a variety of methods as they endeavor to provide for the physical, spiritual, emotional, and social needs of the children they serve. The Grundy School continues to maintain an institutional orphanage structure, while more recent efforts have built houses where houseparents live with small groups of children. Some are homes in the suburbs, while others are on ranches or farms. Many include Christian schools in order to teach spiritual values, but some allow children to attend public schools.

Certain homes reach beyond orphaned and abandoned children and minister to those who are abused, have special physical or emotional needs, or come from dysfunctional homes. Some provide foster care, adoption services, pregnancy support, family counseling, and services that help children return to or stay with their own families. Sometimes staffs include licensed therapists, social workers, case managers, and psychiatrists. Though administrators strive to meet state guidelines, they typically refuse government funds, fearing obligations that might jeopardize the homes' Christian mission.

Orphanages, sometimes accompanied by schools and hospitals, have also been established cross culturally and internationally with the help of supporting churches or parachurch organizations.

James H. Lloyd

See also Noninstitutional Movement

BIBLIOGRAPHY Hiram J. Lester and Marjorie Lee Lester, *Inasmuch . . . , The Saga of NBA* (1987) • James M. Seale, *A Century of Faith and Caring: A Comprehensive History of the Christian Church Homes of Kentucky, Inc.* (1984) • Thomas B. Warren, *Lectures on Church Cooperation and Orphan Homes* (1958) • Henry E. Webb, "A History of the Independent Mission Movement of the Disciples of Christ" (unpublished D.Theol. Thesis, Southern Baptist Theological Seminary, 1954) • Herbert E. Winkler, *Congregational Cooperation of Churches of Christ,* 2nd ed. (1961).

Christadelphians

See Thomas, John

Christian, The (1870-1882, 1960-1973)

Influential journal of the Disciples of Christ.

The name "Christian" is at least part of the title of 339 different periodicals of the Stone-Campbell Movement, according to historian Winfred E. Garrison, son of the editor of one of those periodicals. Fourteen of them were called simply *The Christian.*

When J. H. Garrison merged a former Kansas City

publication called *The Christian* with his *Gospel Echo* in Macomb, Illinois, in 1872, he carried both names for a short while, then moved the journal to St. Louis as *The Christian,* renaming it *The Christian-Evangelist* in 1882 after another merger.

But in 1960 the highly respected *Christian-Evangelist* became *The Christian* again under the editorship of former Lexington Theological Seminary church history professor Howard E. Short. Short edited the magazine as a thirty-two-page weekly for thirteen years before his retirement and the merger of the magazine in 1974 with the mission journal *World Call* to form *The Disciple.*

Short was a Disciples denominational figure with a stature as an editor unlike any since Garrison. He continued as editor a task he began while at the seminary, interpreting the Sunday School lessons on the magazine's pages, offering that service for more than a quarter century. The magazine carried the brunt of the Disciples promotion of a Restructure approved in 1968 to acknowledge the Disciples' growing acceptance of a church organization that recognized three interrelated "manifestations" of church: congregational, regional, and general. Short had chaired the Panel of Scholars that produced the theological underpinning for Restructure from June 1956 to September 1958.

The magazine varied little in its format over the thirteen years. It included editorials by Short, a section of news, a brief piece of fiction, a couple of two-page articles — one aimed at the laity, the other at ministers — and a page of answers to questions posed by readers. When Wilbur Cramblett, president of Christian Board of Publication, first hired Short as editor, Short was given to understand that it was "your paper," and he undertook to edit it with the same independence that Garrison had half a century earlier. The acerbic Short, maintaining his theological freedom, did not hesitate to argue with those who wrote letters to the editor, printing what he termed his own "sarcastic" comments after letters with which he disagreed.

See also Journalism; Restructure

ROBERT L. FRIEDLY

Christian, The Name

See Names of the Movement

Christian Association of Washington

The Christian Association of Washington was an organization conceived by Thomas Campbell and a group of supporters for the purpose of promoting Christian unity through a focus on the evangelical Christianity his readers held in common.

After Campbell's withdrawal from the Chartiers Presbytery and the Associate Synod of North America, he did not cease his ministerial labors. Between 1809 and 1810 he continued to meet groups of friends and acquaintances in religious services, regularly preaching and administering the Lord's Supper in the vicinity of Washington, Pennsylvania. Those who attended Campbell's unauthorized services came from the various Presbyterian groups in the community and other denominations, though some had never belonged to any church but were in agreement with Campbell's ideas. It soon became apparent that something should be done to make a more permanent arrangement.

Early in the summer of 1809, a number of interested persons gathered at the home of Abraham Altars on the road between Washington and Mt. Pleasant to discuss next moves. After an opening prayer Thomas Campbell reminded the group of his dissatisfaction with division in the church. Petty controversies over minor opinions should be set aside. He proposed the Bible as the only basis for belief and practice, which would become the means of reuniting the church. Campbell closed his presentation by suggesting a "rule" on which he believed the group could act: "Where the Scriptures speak, we speak; and where the Scriptures are silent, we are silent." Before adjourning, those assembled adopted this statement as a guide for all their actions.

While in Ireland, Campbell had been interested in and joined an evangelical society while minister at Ahorey. In Rich Hill he often heard the Haldanes and other visiting speakers in the Independent (Congregational) meetinghouse. Undoubtedly these experiences led Thomas to the idea of forming a Christian organization that would not be a church, but an agency to which individuals could belong. There was no suggestion of forming a new religious movement.

A second meeting was held on August 17, 1809. Those attending were in general agreement and chose as the name of their organization the Christian Association of Washington (after the Pennsylvania county in which they lived). A committee of twenty-one members was appointed to consider procedure. Their first action was to agree that there should be a published statement of the purposes and objectives of the organization. Their second action was to ask Thomas Campbell to write such a document.

By September 7, 1809, the document was completed and read at a special meeting of the leaders of the association held at the home of Jacob Donaldson. It was approved unanimously, and plans were made for its publication. Sometime in the last two weeks of 1809 the *Declaration and Address of the Christian Association of Washington* came from the press. It has since become one of the basic documents of the Stone-Campbell Movement.

Upon its publication Thomas Campbell saw that copies were given to ministers of every denomination in the area, asking them to give serious consideration to the proposals in the document. To Campbell's and the group's great disappointment, the *Declaration and Address* received little attention by anyone.

As the months passed Thomas Campbell came to believe that the Christian Association must become an independent church in order to carry out the functions of a Christian group. Therefore, at the last meeting of the association, May 4, 1811, the Christian Association of Washington constituted itself a church with a congregational form of church government and thereafter was known as Brush Run church.

See also Brush Run Church; Campbell, Thomas; *Declaration and Address;* Presbyterians, Presbyterianism

BIBLIOGRAPHY Lester G. McAllister, *Thomas Campbell — Man of the Book* (1954). LESTER G. MCALLISTER

Christian Baptist, The

Twenty-four-page monthly edited by Alexander Campbell from 1823 to 1830. It was the first magazine in the Stone-Campbell Movement.

Although Thomas Campbell proposed publishing a monthly in 1809, his project never materialized. In 1823, however, his son Alexander was surprised by the large readership of his debate with Presbyterian W. L. Maccalla. Recognizing that an audience existed for what he had to say, he built a print shop on his land in Brooke County, Virginia, conferred with his father and with Walter Scott, then issued a prospectus for *The Christian Baptist.* Both Alexander Campbell and Scott later took credit for originating the name. In either case, the title created identification between Campbell and the Baptist denomination with which he and his reformers then identified. To honor his adopted country, Campbell wrote the first page on July 4, 1823.

His prospectus revealed the orientation of his monthly: "The 'Christian Baptist' shall espouse the cause of no religious sect, excepting that ancient sect called 'Christians first at Antioch.' Its sole object shall be the eviction of truth, and the exposure of error in doctrine and practice." He planned to use its pages, according to his biographer, to "startle the entire religious community," for "he conceived the people to be so completely under the dominion of the clergy at this time that nothing but bold and decisive measures could arouse them to proper inquiry." Consequently, he adopted a lively, sarcastic style. Though he was unsparing in his assaults on what he saw as error, he offered equal space in his pages to anyone who wished to write against him.

During the next seven years, he dealt with a variety of matters both ephemeral and lasting, along with Thomas Campbell (writing under the initials

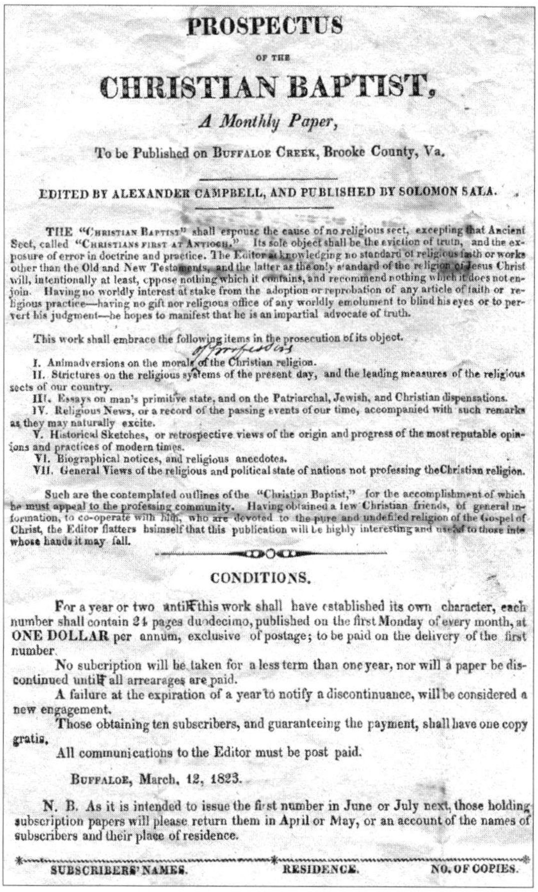

PROSPECTUS

OF THE

CHRISTIAN BAPTIST,

A Monthly Paper,

To be Published on BUFFALOE CREEK, Brooke County, Va.

EDITED BY ALEXANDER CAMPBELL, AND PUBLISHED BY SOLOMON SALA.

THE "CHRISTIAN BAPTIST" shall espouse the cause of no religious sect, excepting that Ancient Sect, called "CHRISTIANS FIRST AT ANTIOCH." Its sole object shall be the eviction of truth, and the exposure of error in doctrine and practice. The Editor acknowledging no standard of religious faith or works other than the Old and New Testaments, and the latter as the only standard of the religion of Jesus Christ will, intentionally at least, oppose nothing which it contains, and recommend nothing which it does not enjoin. Having no worldly interest at stake from the adoption or reprobation of any article of faith or religious practice—having no gift nor religious office of any worldly emolument to blind his eyes or to pervert his judgment—he hopes to manifest that he is an impartial advocate of truth.

This work shall embrace the following items in the prosecution of its object.

I. Animadversions on the morals of the Christian religion.
II. Strictures on the religious systems of the present day, and the leading measures of the religious sects of our country.
III. Essays on man's primitive state, and on the Patriarchal, Jewish, and Christian dispensations.
IV. Religious News, or a record of the passing events of our time, accompanied with such remarks as they may naturally excite.
V. Historical Sketches, or retrospective views of the origin and progress of the most reputable opinions and practices of modern times.
VI. Biographical notices, and religious anecdotes.
VII. General Views of the religious and political state of nations not professing theChristian religion.

Such are the contemplated outlines of the "Christian Baptist," for the accomplishment of which he must appeal to the professing community. Having obtained a few Christian friends, of general information, to co-operate with him, who are devoted to the pure and undefiled religion of the Gospel of Christ, the Editor flatters hsimself that this publication will be highly interesting and useful to those into whose hands it may fall.

CONDITIONS.

For a year or two until this work shall have established its own character, each number shall contain 24 pages duodecimo, published on the first Monday of every month, at ONE DOLLAR per annum, exclusive of postage; to be paid on the delivery of the first number.

No subcription will be taken for a less term than one year, nor will a paper be discontinued until all arrearages are paid.

A failure at the expiration of a year to notify a discontinuance, will be considered a new engagement.

Those obtaining ten subscribers, and guaranteeing the payment, shall have one copy gratis.

All communications to the Editor must be post paid.

BUFFALOE, March, 12, 1823.

N. B. As it is intended to issue the first number in June or July next, those holding subscription papers will please return them in April or May, or an account of the names of subscribers and their place of residence.

SUBSCRIBERS' NAMES.	RESIDENCE.	NO. OF COPIES.

"Prospectus" of the *Christian Baptist,* Alexander Campbell's first editorial venture. The journal included his long and influential series on "A Restoration of the Ancient Order of Things" (1825-1829). Courtesy of Bethany College

"T.W.") and Walter Scott ("Philip"). Among Campbell's most influential articles were "The Parable of the Iron Bedstead," "The Third Epistle of Peter," his series on "A Restoration of the Ancient Order of Things," and "Essays on Man in His Primitive State and under the Patriarchal, Jewish and Christian Dispensations," in which he set forth his view of God's successive economies.

As postmaster of Buffaloe, Virginia, he was able to mail the *Christian Baptist* for free, a fortunate perquisite since its circulation increased literally daily. The effects of Campbell's periodical were remarkable. His writing demanded attention for its iconoclastic content and pungent style. By March 1824, some Baptist ministers began to see a threat in the monthly journal and began to preach against it and forbid their congregations to read it.

Campbell's pen was directed against missionary societies, creeds, the "hireling" clergy, "text preaching," church hierarchies, revival meetings, and Calvinistic notions of conversion. In contrast, he wrote constructively about understanding the Bible, the simplicity of primitive Christianity, the work of the Holy Spirit, the history of Protestantism, the nature of Christ, the content of the ancient gospel, and the scriptural mode of baptism.

Though its effects were felt as far away as Europe, the *Christian Baptist*'s immediate impact was in Virginia. Frederick Hodge wrote in his 1905 history of the movement in Virginia that it "first demonstrated to religious professors and teachers in Eastern Virginia the need of a thorough restitution of the primitive Apostolic Christianity."

Numerous correspondents testified to the effectiveness of the journal in converting unbelievers and enlisting new reformers. F. W. Emmons, Thomas Henley, and Raccoon John Smith all became members of the reformation after reading it. Samuel Rogers said that Barton W. Stone gave him the Bible but Campbell taught him how to read it.

The *Christian Baptist* came to an end after seven years for several reasons. First, Campbell feared that his reformers were becoming known as "Christian Baptists." In addition, the Baptists, after enduring his criticisms for years, began to evict the reformers during 1828-30, so the title of the journal increasingly no longer reflected his church affiliation or that of his enlarged readership. In January 1830 he started a new journal with a milder tone — the *Millennial Harbinger.* He continued to publish *The Christian Baptist* through July to complete the full seven volumes.

In 1835 there remained enough demand for Campbell's classic essays that D. S. Burnet reprinted the *Christian Baptist* in a one-volume edition "with Mr. Campbell's last corrections." Gary Lee's 1981 Lincoln Seminary thesis "Analysis and Index" describes the differences among various editions of the periodical.

While many readers of the *Christian Baptist* found liberation in its pages, to its editor it became constricting after it was concluded. The Stone-Campbell Movement was then experiencing explosive growth and needed to construct its own identity. Campbell adapted well to new rhetorical opportunities, but some readers criticized him for abandoning the principles of the *Christian Baptist.* He was charged with leaving his positions on a number of matters, including the impropriety of conventions and missionary societies and the need for professional clergy in the Movement. However, Campbell wrote, in 1855, "We never preached nor taught any thing as a portion of our *faith,* since the day of the Christian Baptist, which we have retracted."

In a recent second wave of criticism, some scholars agree that he did abandon his early positions in the *Christian Baptist.* Rhetorician Michael Casey asserts that Campbell employed a different hermeneutic after the *Christian Baptist,* for he was later willing to argue from inference as well as from command and example. Richard Hughes claims that, while the earlier Campbell advocated simple Christianity as a common religion for all, he later recognized that the United States already had a primordial Protestantism as a national religion. Hughes further argues that the Disciples of Christ are the heirs of the Protestant Campbell, but the Churches of Christ are the heirs of the *Christian Baptist* Campbell, for the journal "decisively shaped the Churches of Christ" with a sectarian vision of "restoring and maintaining the true church."

In contrast, other scholars like David Edwin Harrell, Jr., Peter Verkruyse, Lee Snyder, and Richard Tristano find Campbell to be consistent; the changes in his public emphases were due to the changing exigencies of his rhetorical situations.

See also Baptists; Burnet, David Staats; Campbell, Alexander; Campbell-Maccalla Debate; *Millennial Harbinger, The;* Rogers, Samuel; Scott, Walter; Smith, "Raccoon" John

BIBLIOGRAPHY D. S. Burnet, "In Memoriam: President Alexander Campbell," *Millennial Harbinger* (July 1866): 301-21 • Alexander Campbell, "The Disciples of Christ of the 19th Century," *Millennial Harbinger* (April 1855): 206-11 • Michael W. Casey, *The Battle over Hermeneutics in the Stone-Campbell Movement, 1800-1870* (1998) • A. S. Hayden, *Early History of the Disciples in the Western Reserve, Ohio; With Biographical Sketches of the Principal Agents in Their Religious Movement* (1875) • Frederick Arthur Hodge, *The Plea and the Pioneers in Virginia* (1905) • Gary Holloway, "Alexander Campbell as a Publisher," *Restoration Quarterly* 37 (January 1995): 28-35 • Richard T. Hughes, "From Primitive Church to Civil Religion: The Millennial Odyssey of Alexander Campbell," *Journal of the American Academy of Religion* 44 (March 1976): 87-103 • Nick Kassebaum, "Alexander Campbell and The Christian Baptist on Church and State," *Restoration Quarterly* 12 (April and July 1969): 91-104 • Gary L. Lee, "Analysis and Index of *The Christian Baptist,* 1823-1830" (unpublished M.A. thesis, Lincoln Christian Seminary, 1981) • Gary L. Lee, "Background of The Christian Baptist," in *The Christian Baptist,* ed. D. S. Burnet (repr. 1983), pp. 1-36 • Lewis Leroy Snyder, "Alexander Campbell as a Change-Agent within the Stone-Campbell Movement from 1830-1840" (unpublished Ph.D. dissertation, 1987).

LEE SNYDER

Christian Board of Publication

General administrative unit of the Christian Church (Disciples of Christ) located in St. Louis, Missouri.

In 1910 Robert A. Long bought Christian Publishing Company from James H. Garrison, longtime editor of *The Christian-Evangelist,* and gave it to the denomination as a non-profit "brotherhood publishing house," with a 1911 charter and a self-perpetuating board of directors. Long served as president of the board throughout the rest of his life, and Garrison continued to edit the magazine for a number of years. Christian Board of Publication (CBP) eventually added books and church school curriculum publication as well as a merchandise division to its scope of activities. The first Bethany Bookstore was established in 1941 in St. Louis and served the community for over half a century. In 1952 the company moved administrative and editorial operations into a new building at Pine and Beaumont, adjacent to facilities subsequently utilized for production and offset printing. A book imprint was established in 1954 and has continued under a succession of names (The Bethany Press, CBP Press, Chalice Press). In 1986, after years of declining revenues, the printing operation was closed, buildings were sold, and remaining activities were moved into leased facilities. Continuing declines in income and a quarter century of annual negative balances brought about the termination of the merchandise division in 1999 and the cessation of *The Disciple* magazine in 2001. Curriculum editing ceased the following year.

See also Chalice Press; *Christian-Evangelist, The; Disciple, The* — David P. Polk

Christian Board of Publication (CBP) Press

See Chalice Press

Christian Century, The

Influential ecumenical journal historically related to the Disciples of Christ.

The Christian Century started as a local denominational publication speaking for Disciples of Christ in Des Moines, Iowa, and surrounding regions. In 1884 the journal's first editor, D. R. Lucas, chose the name *Christian Oracle* and adopted the motto "Speak as the Oracles of God." In the midst of financial difficulty, the periodical moved to Chicago in 1891 and found support from Herbert L. Willett, Edward Scribner Ames, and other Disciples leaders associated with the University of Chicago. Near the end of the century, Charles Clayton Morrison, a young Disciples minister, arrived in Chicago to serve a small West Side church. He quickly became connected with the small group of university-related Disciples supporting the magazine.

These Chicago Disciples sought new ways to relate science to religion and adapted their own Christian presuppositions in light of their findings. Willett, one of the journal's part-time editors, began to use the pages of the *Christian Oracle* to educate lay people about new scientific and historical developments in biblical scholarship. Like many Christians of their time, these Disciples believed America stood poised to play a significant role in the Christianization and elevation of the world. This viewpoint led to a change of name. Beginning with the first issue of 1900, the journal took the name *The Christian Century.* The new moniker arose from editorial confidence that "the coming century" was "to witness greater triumphs in Christianity than any previous century has ever witnessed." Events early in the twentieth century challenged that optimism to the breaking point, but the name remained.

In 1908 Morrison bought the magazine, and he became its editor for the next forty years. In 1917, after realizing that many new subscribers were not Disciples, Morrison added a new subtitle, "An Undenominational Journal of Religion." Ever since, the *Century* has represented ecumenical Christianity in its struggle with the changing religious and cultural scene. As an independent weekly, the *Century* has consistently provided its readership with conscientious discussion of controversial issues. Its nondenominational status, ecumenical concern, and international focus have helped to maintain the loyalty of its readers.

See also Disciples Divinity House; Morrison, Charles Clayton; Willett, Herbert Lockwood

BIBLIOGRAPHY L. Delloff, M. Marty, D. Peerman, J. Wall, *A Century of the* CENTURY (1987) • Mark G. Toulouse, "CHRISTIAN CENTURY: History Front Pew," *Media History Digest* (Spring-Summer 1989): 13-21.

Mark G. Toulouse

Christian Chronicle, The

Newspaper for Churches of Christ begun in 1943 and published since 1981 as a service to the church by Oklahoma Christian University, Oklahoma City. Principal publishers or editors of the *Chronicle* and their dates of service include Olan L. Hicks (1943-54); James Walter Nichols (1954-67); Ralph B. Sweet (1967-72); Haskell Chesshir (1972-76); John Beckloff (1976-80); Howard W. Norton (1981-96); and Bailey B. McBride (1996-present).

Encouraged by a National Council and inspired by long-time Abilene Christian University journalism professor Charlie Marler, who designed the reborn newspaper in 1981, the *Chronicle* of the Oklahoma Christian era has been characterized by its mission to "inform, inspire, and unite" the Churches of Christ through "journalistic excellence." Managing editors Lane Cubstead (1959-66) and Joy McMillon (1983-89) established benchmarks of excellence in reporting.

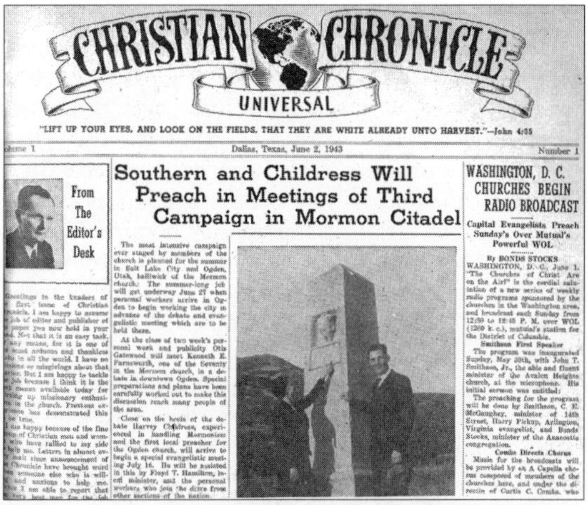
CHRISTIAN CHRONICLE
UNIVERSAL
"LIFT UP YOUR EYES, AND LOOK ON THE FIELDS, THAT THEY ARE WHITE ALREADY UNTO HARVEST."—John 4:35
Volume 1 | Dallas, Texas, June 2, 1943 | Number 1

From The Editor's Desk

Southern and Childress Will Preach in Meetings of Third Campaign in Mormon Citadel

The most intensive campaign ever staged by members of the church is planned for the summer in Salt Lake City and Ogden, Utah, balliwick of the Mormon church. The summer-long job will get underway June 27 when personal workers arrive in Ogden to begin working the city in advance of the debate and evangelistic meeting which are to be held there.

WASHINGTON, D. C. CHURCHES BEGIN RADIO BROADCAST

Capital Evangelists Preach Sunday's Over Mutual's Powerful WOL

By BONDS STOCKS

WASHINGTON, D. C., June 1. "The Churches of Christ Are on the Air!" is the cordial salutation of a new series of weekly radio programs sponsored by the churches in the Washington area, and broadcast each Sunday from 12:30 to 12:45 P. M. over WOL (1260 k. c.), mutual's station for the District of Columbia.

Smithson First Speaker

The first issue of the *Christian Chronicle* focused on mission efforts carried on by Churches of Christ in both the United States and abroad. The *Chronicle* is one of the most important sources of primary historical information on worldwide missions carried out by Churches of Christ.

Courtesy of the Center for Restoration Studies, Abilene Christian University

The commitment to "news not views" stands in contrast to the tradition of so-called editor bishops.

Throughout the Oklahoma Christian era, the newspaper has maintained a journalistic stance embodied in characteristics such as the organization of content into opinion and news sections; the use of scope, impact, prominence, and timeliness as gatekeeping news values; and the effort to avoid partisanship or a divisive spirit. The newspaper also fulfills a function as the community's unofficial journal of record by publishing obituaries, ministerial moves, and a calendar of events. The "Doors" column is a community service that allows financial needs to be publicized.

The *Chronicle* is not circulated in bundles but is sent to individual addresses and is financed by a one-time enrollment fee, advertising revenues, and donations. Currently circulated to more than 100,000 homes in fifty states, the newspaper has both reflected and shaped its readers in the last half of the twentieth century. During the Hicks era, for example, a part of the newspaper's mission was to "stir up missionary zeal and activity." Hicks and his writers, such as Otis Gatewood (1911-1999) and Hugo McCord (1911-2004), worked to set this agenda among churches. The newspaper's influence on missions was documented in a 1995 Abilene Christian University M.A. thesis. The *Chronicle* published a special supplement about a 1968 meeting between black and white leaders in Churches of Christ attempting to end racial segregation in congregations. In the 1980s and 1990s, the newspaper sought to promote integrity through reporting and cohesion among congregations through its editorials and policies during periods of anxiety regarding matters such as a nationally visible lawsuit regarding church governance and the discipling movement of the controversial Boston Church of Christ.

In a survey of ministers in Churches of Christ in the early 1990s, 68 percent of respondents read the *Chronicle* and 88 percent of those said they agreed with its format and content. Survey editors wrote, "This comes as no surprise given the widespread distribution of the newspaper, and its reputation for balanced coverage of news of interest to members of the Churches of Christ."

In 1999 a random survey asked *Chronicle* readers about their attitudes, perceptions, and uses of the newspaper. Ninety-two percent reported that they were "very satisfied" or "satisfied" with the paper. Over 60 percent of households reported that more than one individual read each issue of the *Chronicle* received by that household, and 75 percent said they read all or most of each issue. The *Christian Chronicle* is by far the most-read paper in Churches of Christ and exercises an influence for cohesiveness in this part of the Stone-Campbell Movement.

See also Oklahoma Christian University

BIBLIOGRAPHY James Bost, "*The Christian Chronicle* Research Report: Executive Summary" (Nov. 29, 1999) • Douglas A. Foster, Mel E. Hailey, and Thomas L. Winter, *Ministers at the Millennium: A Survey of Preachers in Churches of Christ* (2000) • Roger Massey, "A Historical Study of *The Christian Chronicle*'s Coverage and Promotion of Foreign Missions Among the Churches of Christ" (unpublished M.A. Thesis, Abilene Christian University, 1995) • Bailey B. McBride, "The Chronicle Legacy: Documenting Fifty Years," *The Christian Chronicle* 50 (April 1993): 11-18 • Bailey McBride, "60 Years of Service: An Historical Overview," *Christian Chronicle* 60 (June 2003): 17-20.

R. SCOTT LAMASCUS

Christian Church (Disciples of Christ)

One of three religious bodies that trace their origin to the Stone-Campbell Movement of the nineteenth century.

The Christian Church (Disciples of Christ) is the only one of the three that willingly accepts a denominational label. Contemporary congregations are generally known as "Christian Churches," as in First Christian Church or University Christian Church, while members refer to themselves as "Disciples." In 1968 Disciples adopted their current name, the Christian Church (Disciples of Christ). Kenneth Teegarden, a former general minister and president for Disciples, once offered a defining summary of the name: "The generic first part, *Christian Church,* points to our objective of unity; the distinguishing second part, *Disciples of Christ,* reminds us that we have not arrived."

Disciples historically have been deeply influenced by their American context. This influence surfaces especially in their commitment to support the right of all people to think through the claims of religion for themselves. The American cultural commitment to personal liberty in matters of religion has also surfaced among Disciples as a deep commitment to both the importance of lay participation in congregational life and the ability of congregations to own their property, select their pastoral leadership, and govern their affairs. Offering further testimony to the connections between Disciples and American cultural values is the fact that three U.S. presidents (James A. Garfield, Lyndon Baines Johnson, and Ronald Reagan) possessed religious roots nurtured within Disciples congregations.

To understand the developments that led to the emergence of contemporary Disciples of Christ, one must look first to the crucial half-century period from about 1870 to 1920. During these years, Disciples made adjustments within their intellectual and institutional life that created the kinds of trajectories that eventually brought them to their current identity and location within American Protestantism.

From their beginnings, Disciples have asserted the authority of the Bible for Christian faith and life. The founding Disciples' consideration of the Bible as canon, as authoritative source, also included an understanding that the Bible contained propositional truth that could be stated in clear and unmistakable terms, such as "God is love" and "Christ died for all." They also believed it contained a clear roadmap that could be followed in establishing all matters of practice and structure for the church. In essence, early Disciples understood the Bible, especially the New Testament, as the source of the Christian's faith and as a "constitution" for the church.

Founders among Disciples, including Thomas and Alexander Campbell, Barton Stone, and Walter Scott, guarded jealously the right of all Christians to approach the Bible and read it for themselves. Higher church authorities and the creeds and confessions of the churches were not needed to dictate the proper meaning. Early Disciples believed that the meaning of the Bible, at least where it counted, was always clear. Their hopes for Christian unity rested on this assumption. When reasonable people read the Bible, these early Disciples asserted, they would reach conclusions with which other reasonable people would find agreement.

Early Disciples did, however, also recognize that scriptural declarations — even those passages of the Bible connected to a "Thus saith the Lord" — often led to secondary inferences. Inferences were not as clear as declarations. For this reason, the declarations were binding on Christians for faith and practice while most inferences were not. Some inferences, those that seemed "necessary," were treated differently. When "approved examples" (or "approved precedents") found in the Bible pointed clearly to practices of early congregations and Christians, they became binding as well. The dismissal of denominational traditions and dependence upon either the propositional word or approved examples of the Bible led to particular emphases within Disciples church life: baptism by immersion for believers, the practice of the Lord's Supper on the first day of the week, a stress on the unity of all who proclaim Jesus as the Christ, confidence that history would culminate in the eschatological triumph of God's redemption, and a leading role for lay people within congregational life.

The fact that Alexander Campbell and other early-nineteenth-century Disciples took a propositional approach to the Bible does not imply necessarily that they took an uncritical approach to it. Campbell developed a careful and scholarly hermeneutic. He affirmed the fact that biblical authors often made their own observations and utilized their own experience in communicating ideas found in the Bible. As M. Eugene Boring has pointed out, this allowed Campbell to be discriminating in his reading of the Bible. Not all the words of the Bible were seen to be synonymous with divine revelation. Campbell set forth hermeneutical principles to help readers to make the proper kinds of distinctions between the human character of the book and the divine revelation it contained.

After the Civil War, Disciples slowly modified their approach to Scripture. Leaders among Disciples, from the 1880s forward, became familiar with a new methodology of biblical interpretation developed in Germany. This new method, known as higher criticism or historical criticism, went beyond the textual criticism so ably practiced by Alexander Campbell. Higher critics addressed larger questions of background, date, authorship, sources, literary characteristics, and other such considerations. Those who utilized higher critical investigation began to challenge traditional assumptions about the Bible. They openly questioned, among other things, the apostolic authorship and historical reliability of the four Gospels. They also emphasized the degree to which culture and the needs of biblical times had colored the expressions and content of the Bible itself. In short, propositions and practices found in the Bible simply were not as authoritative once higher criticism did its work.

It took a while for Disciples to warm up to the work of the higher critics, but by the 1920s many of them had. Herbert L. Willett, by the time he wrote regularly for the *Christian-Evangelist* (after 1896), had begun to question Mosaic authorship of the Pentateuch and had accepted a new, much later date for the writing of the book of Daniel. Yet Willett's views of the New Testament were not all that different from those of John W. McGarvey, the chief Disciples opponent of the work of the higher critics. By 1920, however, Willett openly challenged Pauline authorship of the Pastoral Epistles and, over the next decade, moved more solidly toward ratifying the conclusions of the higher critics on other important New Testament interpretations as well.

Near the opening of the twentieth century, therefore, Disciples leaders revealed their willingness to embrace the developing "liberal" vision of American Protestantism. During these years, Protestants became more interested in examining human experience as a framework for theology. Many shifted their search for the knowledge of God away from propositions and doctrinal systems to their experience of God, both personally and in the world around them. Developments in science contributed to these endeavors. The work of Charles Darwin led Protestants to think differently about both history and revelation. They were more interested in tracing human evolution through history than they were in depending upon a creation story that emphasized human tendencies toward sin.

Protestant theologians spoke of how Christian witness shifted and changed through time. They stressed a dynamic Christianity. Sterile forms of theological orthodoxy, for these Protestants, quickly lost their relevancy. Instead, they studied religion using a variety of tools, including those provided by the developing fields of sociology and psychology. The comparative study of religion emerged as a field, and some Protestants entertained the possibility that God might be as active in other world religions as in Christianity.

During this fifty-year period (1870-1920), American Protestantism became interested in the social application of Christian theology. By 1920 the Social Gospel movement, growing out of the Christocentric liberalism that flourished among Protestants, had reached full bloom. Disciples joined the movement late, but joined it nonetheless. Disciples translated the movement primarily into efforts to build the kingdom of God on earth. From their beginnings, Disciples possessed a theological vision that gave wide significance to eschatology. Generally, with some exceptions, Disciples held to a postmillennial kind of optimism that history was moving toward the kingdom of God. With Alexander Campbell, the initiative for that move always remained with God. By the 1920s Disciples had shifted more of the initiative into human hands.

Interestingly, Disciples embraced Christocentric liberalism to its fullest extent just as the movement began to give way, among other Protestants, to the neo-orthodoxy found in the theologies of Karl Barth and Reinhold Niebuhr. From the 1920s through the 1940s, Disciples mission leadership stressed human goodness over sin and shared an optimistic belief that Christian actions could overcome human need and contribute to the establishment of the kingdom of God on earth. Above all, these thinkers featured Christ as the center of their theology by lifting up the relevance of his life both as model and source for the ethical and religious life of all humanity. For them, Christ-centered beliefs about reality were verified by the practical results of Christian experience. The holocaust, World War II, and the dropping of atomic bombs on Nagasaki and Hiroshima eventually burst this bubble of optimistic postmillennialism among Disciples and served to chasten other aspects of their liberalism.

Disciples did not share all the assumptions of emergent Protestant liberalism at the beginning of the twentieth century. Many Disciples did not share any of them. But the social context of these shifts in American religious experience provided the background for the controversies that flowed in Disciples life through much of the century. Regardless of the potential for controversy, some Disciples leaders affirmed the conclusions of the higher critics and abandoned a propositional approach to the Bible. As Boring's research has shown, over time a chasm developed between the views of Disciples biblical scholars and common understandings of how the Bible works and functions within the life of the church itself. Today's Disciples continue to struggle with how to affirm both the authority of the Bible and the conclusions of the higher critics. Lay people among Disciples are especially unclear about what scholarly biblical interpretation really means for the life of the church.

The context of "modern" movements within American Protestantism at the end of the nineteenth century challenged Disciples on several other fronts. Armed with a new appreciation for the diversity of the gospel message in different times and circumstances, some late-nineteenth-century Disciples expressed a more open appraisal of the work of other denominations. For many Disciples, openness to denominational cooperation emerged from pragmatic circumstances more than from theological reflection. There was so much to accomplish in world mission. Exposure to missionary leaders from other denominations led Archibald McLean, president of the Foreign Christian Missionary Society, to an understanding that these were well-meaning Christian people. Perhaps together, through cooperation, they could get the job done more quickly. For a few other Disciples, a conscientious and historical approach to both theology and biblical interpretation led them to doubt that any group of Christians, even the ancient Christians, could truly capture the divine message in its entirety. The Disciples' energetic commitment to restore early Christian faith and practice began to wane while their desire for ecumenical cooperation increased.

As the nineteenth century gave way to the twentieth century, Disciples understood that their own work in missions was, perhaps, not all that different from the work of others. This attitude affected Disciples mission work both at home and abroad. By the early 1900s, leadership of both the Christian Woman's Board of Missions and the Foreign Christian Missionary Society worked cooperatively with other denominations on the mission field. Comity agreements dividing the mission territory among the denominations became common. While Disciples leadership viewed such cooperation as essential in the daunting task of world mission, conservative Disciples interpreted such actions as an abandonment of Disciples commitments and responsibilities.

These trends on the mission field were accompanied by a commitment among Disciples leaders, whether for pragmatic or theological reasons, to participate in the "federation" of American churches and international churches. Even though Disciples had no formal structure or ability to recognize their own status as a "denomination," they managed to join other founding denominations in the establishment of the Federal Council of Churches of Christ (FCC) by 1908. Again, more conservative Disciples viewed such activities as an abandonment of the historic plea of Disciples to call Christians out of denominations and back to the simple gospel. With the formation of the United Christian Missionary Society in 1919, these ecumenical trends among Disciples continued despite setbacks caused by divisive internal battles, marked especially by the lengthy controversy over open membership, the practice of admitting into the membership of the churches Christians who had not received believers' immersion.

Disciples were present at the creation of both the World Council of Churches (1948) and the National Council of Churches of Christ (1950). Many Disciples (including Edgar DeWitt Jones, Roy G. Ross, J. Irwin Miller, and Joan Brown Campbell) have served the National Council of Churches in leadership capacities. Disciples joined the Consultation on Church Union (COCU) near its beginnings in 1960, and have seen it through to its current manifestation as Churches Uniting in Christ (CUIC). Paul Crow (COCU) and Michael Kinnamon (CUIC) have provided executive leadership for these organizations. Participation in ecumenical circles marked Disciples life throughout the twentieth century.

New methods of biblical interpretation and increasing ecumenical involvement did not stand alone as controversial elements in Disciples life near the end of the nineteenth century. D. Newell Williams's study (1985) of the evolution of Disciples ministry outlines other tensions that had emerged. After 1870 congregations began to shift the practice of ministry away from the leadership of local elders, often uncompensated, toward a model of settled ministry, where ordained ministers who were college-educated were called to congregational leadership from outside the local community. This transition in Disciples church life led to serious tensions both within individual congregations and within the Movement itself. By the 1920s the work of elders had been further reduced by the development of the "functional plan" of ministry. The goal of the plan was to reduce the power a small group of elders held in many congregations by creating committees that spread the work of the church throughout the membership. By the mid-1940s, elders had assumed a self-conscious identity as "lay" leadership and the office of "ordained minister" had fully emerged.

During the first half of the twentieth century, regional oversight of congregational ministry became more prominent. Most areas of Disciples work employed evangelists during this period. Cooperative efforts among the area's congregations financed their work. The work of these evangelists slowly began to include oversight of ministers within the area. By 1939 the annual Disciples convention recommended that each region of Disciples life develop an ordination council that would meet whenever congregations recommended ordination for a ministerial candidate. Even though a majority of congregations initially ignored this recommendation, Disciples slowly shifted authority for ordination from the congregational to the regional level of the church's life. Churchwide policies for ordination were developed by 1971 and have served Disciples, allowing for various amendments, since that time.

As the role of "minister" developed, an accompanying expectation for ministerial education appeared. A study of Disciples ministry conducted by Mark Chaves showed that, by 1909, 95 percent of the ministers of Disciples largest congregations had earned a college degree from a Disciples institution, but only 5 percent possessed a seminary degree. By 1985, 81 percent had degrees from Disciples colleges and 97 percent possessed seminary degrees.

A second study, conducted by Edwin Becker in the late 1980s, revealed that, by 1920, 105 Disciples ministers had received the seminary degree from the divinity school at Yale University, and 48 more had received the degree from the University of Chicago Divinity School. By 1940, 183 more Disciples had received degrees from Yale, while 25 more had graduated from Chicago. In addition, 48 Disciples had earned Ph.D. degrees from the divinity schools at Yale (12) and Chicago (36) by 1940. Graduates from these ecumenical programs contributed to shaping notions of ministry among Disciples in more inclusive directions. Though women were ordained among Disciples as early as the late 1880s, they have struggled to achieve equality in ministry. Today, women ministers serve approximately 25 percent of all recognized congregations among Disciples and serve in key leadership roles throughout the denomination.

D. Duane Cummins has shown the priority Disciples have placed on education. Between 1870 and 1899 alone, Disciples founded 83 institutions of higher learning. Part of this enthusiasm, no doubt, can be attributed to emerging theological differences among Disciples and the attempt to "school" the future properly. But it is also true that ministers believed in the importance of education for the future of the church. Aided by financial backing provided by their local communities, Disciples founded colleges wherever they could, 209 colleges and universities in the 150 years between 1836 and 1986.

Today, Disciples claim affiliation with seventeen colleges and universities, fourteen of them related through an explicit covenant with the denomination. These schools are diverse, with vast numbers of students coming from religious affiliations other than Disciples. Four theological seminaries (Brite Divinity School, Christian Theological Seminary, Lexington Theological Seminary, and Phillips Theological Seminary) are associated with Disciples. Similarly, each of these schools is ecumenical in orientation, possessing very diverse communities of students, faculty, and board members. In addition, Disciples maintain support for three "foundation houses" located at the University of Chicago, at Vanderbilt University, and in Claremont, California. These houses support Disciples students attending to master's or doctoral work in non-Disciples institutions.

During the late 1950s and early 1960s, largely as a result of their ecumenical commitments and emerging theological awareness, Disciples engaged in organized studies of both their theological and organizational lives. On the theological side of their self-examination, the United Christian Missionary Society (UCMS) and the Council on Christian Unity co-sponsored a Commission on the Theology of Mission that met from 1958 to 1962. In addition, Willard Wickizer (UCMS) and Harlie L. Smith (Board of Higher Education) gathered a group of Disciples pastors and scholars and charged them with the task of reexamining the beliefs and doctrines of the Disciples. The essays from this latter group were published in 1963 as a three-volume series under the title *The Panel of Scholars Reports.*

On the organizational side, a committee chaired by Wickizer recommended in 1960 that the International Convention appoint a commission charged with preparing a proposal for the restructure of the church's organization. The next year, the Los Angeles International Convention elected 125 members to serve three-year terms on a new Commission on Brotherhood Restructure. In 1968, at the conclusion of the process, Disciples reorganized their polity and, for the first time, officially recognized their status as one of the denominations in America. They adopted a theology of covenant to govern the relations of congregational, regional, and general "manifestations" of the church, abandoning, at least theologically, the pattern of completely autonomous congregations and agencies.

With the conclusion of this process, known generally as "Restructure," the Disciples adopted their current name, the Christian Church (Disciples of Christ). The name change, which changed the plural "Christian Churches" to the singular "Christian Church," resulted from a growing theological commitment to a broader notion of the church and its work. When understood in the context of the denomination, the word "church" signifies the recognition that congregations and regional and general units have covenanted together with one another to form one church body, complete with an acceptance of responsibilities implied by such a relationship. When understood in the context of the universal church, the parenthetical phrase "Disciples of Christ" is meant to signify the recognition that Disciples of Christ do not constitute the whole church. Rather, they understand themselves to be but one partial and fragmentary expression of the church, a group longing for the time when all Christians might find more tangible ways to express the theological reality of the church's unity.

Ironically, the Disciples' move toward Restructure actually led to the second formal division suffered by Disciples in their brief history. Though Disciples have stressed Christian unity from their origins, they have suffered two significant schisms. During the second and third generations of Disciples life, the Movement's rapid growth led to unforeseen polity considerations, especially those associated with organization, authority, and order. Differences in how to handle these considerations rapidly surfaced. Various factions espoused different aspects of the Disciples' plea: some lifted up the need to restore early church practice, while others proclaimed unity as the prime objective of the Movement. Those known today as Disciples defended the latter, while more conservative members of the Movement held out for the former.

In 1906, in a split caused by both theological and, as David Edwin Harrell has so clearly shown, sociological developments after the Civil War, Disciples lost around 160,000 members as the Churches of Christ claimed a separate identity. This split did not resolve the differences among Disciples. Disagreements about baptism, biblical interpretation, and the structure of missionary societies continued to heat up. The open membership controversy, surfacing shortly after the establishment of the United Christian Missionary Society in 1919, kept the temperature at the boiling point for well over a decade. Finally, nearly half a century later, in response to Disciples Restructure, approximately 750,000 Christians in about 3,500 congregations withdrew from Disciples life and formed the Christian Churches/ Churches of Christ.

As of 2001, Disciples of Christ reported just over 807,000 total members. These members were dispersed in approximately 3,743 congregations. The states of Texas, Indiana, Kentucky, Missouri, and Ohio contain about one-third of all Disciples. Since the 1960s, the membership of Disciples, like other moderate Protestant denominations, has suffered a considerable decline. An important study funded by the Lilly Endowment (published in 1991 and edited by D. Newell Williams) examined the relation of Disciples to American culture between 1880 and 1989. Essays in this study indicated that the numerical decline of Disciples has been due, in large part, to their failure to keep and to attract younger adults, particularly those born near the end of the "baby boom" generation.

Not all Disciples congregations have declined in membership. Many ethnic congregations have experienced rapid growth. Haitian Disciples in New York, Korean Disciples in California, and Hispanic Disciples in the Southern portions of the country have all seen strong growth. Three of the five largest congregations among Disciples at the front end of the twenty-first century are predominantly African American, and these congregations continue rapid growth. Though Hispanic and Asian Disciples are considerably fewer in number than African American Disciples, their growth in the last few decades has also been impressive.

Hispanic Disciples formed a National Hispanic and Bilingual Fellowship in 1981. In 2003 Hispanic Disciples could boast of approximately 123 congregations, about 50 of which had been developed within the last two years (about 6,000 participating Hispanic Disciples members). Central Florida saw the largest concentration of growth. In 1975 there were no Hispanic congregations in Florida; by 2003 there were six congregations in central Florida alone attracting over 1,500 people every Sunday. A full one-third of all Disciples in Florida in 2003 were Hispanics.

Asian Disciples began organizing in the late 1970s with the development of the Fellowship of Asian American Disciples. By 1996 the organization became known as the North American Pacific Asian Disciples (NAPAD) and had assumed a prominent place in the life of the denomination. There were approximately 80 NAPAD congregations in 2003, 58 of them Korean (about 3,500 members). The remaining congregations consist mostly of Filipino, Chinese, Vietnamese, Japanese, Indonesian, Laotian, and Samoan churches (another approximately 1,000 members). In addition, there are a number of Asian and Pacific Islanders who are members of Disciples congregations not directly affiliated with NAPAD.

African American Disciples possess a history of association that goes all the way back to the beginning of Disciples life. Their separate organizational life began in 1917 when Preston Taylor led black Disciples in founding the National Christian Missionary Convention. They found it necessary to organize the separate, but cooperating, convention because they knew there were no possibilities of whites sharing leadership in their near future. Until 1960 African American Disciples had separate agencies and programs in most areas of church life. By 1969 Disciples merged the National Christian Missionary Convention and the newly established Christian Church (Disciples of Christ). In 1970 black Disciples formed the National Convocation of the Christian Church, which has, since that time, met every other year to discuss their special concerns. Some of the more significant growth among contemporary Disciples has occurred within African American congregations. In 2003 there were approximately 435 African American Disciples congregations containing approximately 61,000 participating members.

The denominational study edited by Williams suggested that contemporary Disciples have been

Walter D. Bingham (b. 1921) was elected moderator of the Christian Church (Disciples of Christ) by the General Assembly meeting in Louisville in 1971, the first black Disciple to serve in that capacity. Courtesy of the Disciples of Christ Historical Society

plagued by a gap between the theological and moral views of Disciples ministers and those of the active members of their congregations. Ministers tend to be more liberal in their approach to theology than is true of the active members of Disciples congregations. Williams suggested that this gap has been sustained through the Disciples' inability "to engage in serious and sustained dialogue regarding the issues that divide [them]." Disciples, through the twentieth century, like many other moderately inclined denominational traditions, have had a difficult time communicating a clear identity, one that articulates a distinctively Christian norm for judging theological statements and moral action.

A shift in the relationship between so-called "mainstream" Protestantism and American culture has also contributed to a loss of membership in these denominational traditions. American culture has become significantly more pluralistic. By the end of the 1960s, the fragmentation of Protestantism and the increased diversity of America's religions have led to a popular concern that public life in America find expression free of Protestant or even Christian associations. Protestant traditions no longer benefit from close connections between values traditionally associated with them and American culture. In addition, American religious culture has moved into a period of "post-denominationalism," where denominational identification is often eschewed by large numbers of Americans. Disciples have been slow to adjust to these realities and, like other mainstream groups, have continued to lose membership.

In spite of declining membership, Disciples have sought to maintain a significant ministerial presence in the United States and beyond. At the dawn of the twenty-first century, the National Benevolent Association (NBA) for Disciples operated 87 facilities in 22 states, with at least 17 more under development or construction. The NBA served nearly 30,000 people in the year 2000 through its residential and community-based social programs.

Disciples have also participated meaningfully in theological dialogues that have accompanied their responsibilities in various ecumenical organizations. The General Assembly of Disciples affirmed both the *Baptism, Eucharist and Ministry* document published by the Faith and Order Commission of the World Council of Churches in 1982 and the *COCU Consensus* document published in 1984. These theological documents worked toward theological consensus and led Disciples, throughout the 1980s, to produce documents of their own related to authority, baptism, ministry, and the Lord's Supper, among other topics. In 1987, for example, the General Assembly affirmed a "Word to the Church on Baptism," produced by the Disciples Commission on Theology (related to the Disciples Council on Christian Unity). This document recognized formally that infant baptism is a legitimate form of baptism and also endorsed the ecumenical view that baptism is to be administered only once.

Perhaps the most important ecumenical development in recent years for Disciples has been their "ecumenical partnership" with the United Church of Christ (UCC). After years of investigating full union between the two churches, they entered a partnership in 1985 that reached "full communion" by 1989. Both churches maintain their separate existence as denominations, but share in ministry and mission together, with full recognition of one another's members and ministers. This partnership helped to shape Churches Uniting in Christ (CUIC), the proposal that brought nine denominations, Disciples and the United Church of Christ among them, into partnership in Christian mission with one another in January of 2002.

The clearest example of the joint efforts in ministry Disciples and the United Church of Christ have undertaken together is the creation of the Common Global Ministries Board (CGMB) that began functioning in 1996. The CGMB is composed of twenty members named by each of the two denominations and six other members named from partner churches around the world. The board has responsibility for oversight of all mission activities for both Disciples and the United Church of Christ. The board supports the work of ministry among the 2.7 million indigenous Christians who call themselves Disciples across the world. In addition, the board continues to work closely with the united churches (all of which have historical connections to Disciples or UCC mission work over the past 100-plus years) located in Japan, Hong Kong, Thailand, Philippines, Northern India, Jamaica, Britain, South Africa, China, and other parts of the world.

Under the leadership of former General Minister and President Richard Hamm, Disciples created a "2020 vision" for the denomination, referring to goals they want to accomplish by the year 2020. The core values of this vision identify three marks for the faithful church: true community, a deep Christian spirituality, and a passion for justice. In order to move toward this vision, Disciples have implemented several initiatives.

They have entered a "process of discernment" to address the place of gay and lesbian persons in the life of the church and other important issues they face as a community. Disciples have also set goals for leadership development, the revitalization of existing congregations, and the establishment of new congregations. In addition, Disciples are working to increase the significance of their work among Hispanics, African Americans, and Asians to bring percentages of their ethnic membership more closely into line with percentages in the general population. In these ways, Disciples hope to stem the tide of decline, give way to growth, and live out the mission of "a faithful church" as they approach the year 2020.

BIBLIOGRAPHY M. Eugene Boring, *Disciples and the Bible: A History of Disciples Biblical Interpretation in North America* (1997) • D. Duane Cummins, *The Disciples Colleges: A History* (1987) • Anthony L. Dunnavant, *Restructure: Four Historical Ideals in the Campbell-Stone Movement and the Development of the Polity of the Christian Church (Disciples of Christ)* (1993) • Robert L. Friedly and D. Duane Cummins, *The Search for Identity: Disciples of Christ — The Restructure Years* (1987) • Richard L. Hamm, *2020 Vision for the Christian Church (Disciples of Christ)* (2001) • David E. Harrell, *The Social Sources of Division in the Disciples of Christ, 1865-1900* (1973; repr. ed. 2003) • Kenneth Lawrence, ed., *Classic Themes of Disciples Theology: Rethinking the Traditional Affirmations of the Christian Church (Disciples of Christ)* (1986) • *The Renewal of Church: The Panel of Scholars Reports,* 3 vols. (1963) • Kenneth L. Teegarden, *We Call Ourselves Disciples* (1975) • Mark G. Toulouse, *Joined in Discipleship: The Shaping of Contemporary Disciples Identity* (1997) • D. Newell Williams, *Ministry Among Disciples: Past, Present, and Future* (1985) • D. Newell Williams, ed., *A Case Study of Mainstream Protestantism: The Disciples' Relation to American Culture, 1880-1989* (1991).

MARK G. TOULOUSE

Christian Church Foundation

Founded in 1961 to undergird the mission of the Christian Church (Disciples of Christ) in its various manifestations through permanent funds. It was the brainchild of Spencer P. Austin and the Unified Promotion board.

The Foundation received its first bequest — $7,242.93 — from the estate of Ethel Boyers of California, and by 1964 had hired James R. Reed as its first staff person. Distributions to church causes in 1965 totaled a mere $729 to seventy-two entities.

With the consulting services of Marvin G. Osborn, and the influence of such Disciples as Harry T. Ice, Theodore P. Beasley, and A. Dale Fiers, trust in the Foundation grew, along with its assets. Upon the deaths of Fiers's sister and brother-in-law, Othel and DeWitt Brown, the Foundation received 92 percent of the Brown estate, totaling about $8 million. The Foundation established the Fiers-Brown Society to honor those persons who use the Foundation in planned giving.

In 1975, assets of the Oreon E. Scott Foundation — totaling $1.2 million — were added to the Foundation.

When Reed retired as president in 1991, the Foundation had assets of $48 million and was distributing $2.1 million a year.

James P. Johnson was named president in the fall of 1991. Under his leadership, the Foundation broadened its ministry to include serving as an investment manager for money owned by congregations, regions, general units, and other institutions of the Christian Church (Disciples of Christ). By 2002 nearly half of the Foundation's $250.2 million in assets consisted of these invested funds. Distributions totaled $13.4 million.

The Foundation also played a key part in the largest bequest made to the Christian Church (Disciples of Christ). When Allan and Marie Brady of Arizona died in the late 1990s, the bulk of their estate — roughly $10.8 million — went to various Disciples causes.

Gary Kidwell was named Senior Vice President of Development in 2001 and became the Foundation's president upon the retirement of Johnson in 2003.

See also Unified Promotion

JIM CULLUMBER

Christian Church Homes of Kentucky

The Christian Church Widows' and Orphans' Home of Kentucky, chartered by the state and opened in 1884, was the beginning of organized benevolent work within the Stone-Campbell Movement. In 1929 more than 200 boys, girls, and women were cared for in the Homes.

When divisions occurred in the Stone-Campbell Movement, the Homes adapted. Support came from congregations of the Christian Churches/Churches of Christ and the Christian Church (Disciples of Christ). They continue to work together to support and guide this ministry. The Homes are a recognized organization of the Christian Church (Disciples of Christ).

A change of name from the Widows' and Orphans' Home to the Christian Church Homes of Kentucky came in 1960, heralding internal changes taking place. Orphan care became a residential program primarily for emotionally disturbed children. Care for the aging diversified to include men and women living in various settings from apartments to skilled nursing, displacing the earlier model of an "old folks" home.

Continuing to be leaders in the field of care for young and old, the Homes were one of the first benevolent groups to move to a "campus" concept, providing for individual homes, apartments, assisted living, and intermediate and skilled nursing care within a common area. These campuses are now located across the state of Kentucky. As the twentieth century came to a close, the Homes had also become involved in community programs for developmentally disabled youth and adults and in psychiatric residential treatment centers for children. All of these programs, serving over 2,500 persons, are under the supervision of a board of directors made up of representatives of both the Christian Church (Disciples of Christ) and the Christian Churches/Churches of Christ. Total assets of the Homes approach $100 million.

See also Children's Homes and Orphanages; Homes and Services for the Aged

JAMES M. SEALE

BIBLIOGRAPHY James M. Seale, *A Century of Faith and Caring* (1984).

Christian Churches/Churches of Christ

Christian Churches/Churches of Christ is one of three religious bodies that trace their origin to the Stone-Campbell Movement of the nineteenth century. The cumbersome name derives from the fact that both titles have been used from the very beginning of the Movement to designate individual congregations, and both titles were taken by various individual congregations that broke from the Christian Church (Disciples of Christ).

Christian Churches/Churches of Christ became a distinct and identifiable religious body through a long process of separation from the denomination known currently as the Christian Church (Disciples of Christ). The division developed out of three major controversies during the first two decades of the twentieth century that served as polarizing factors within the larger fellowship. One controversy was the theological development of modernism and liberalism, a factor that proved to be divisive in many other Protestant bodies. A second was the origin of the ecumenical movement, which led to the organization of the Federal Council of Churches in 1908. This issue precipitated a controversy over whether Disciples membership and involvement in the Federal Council was a step toward realization of the Stone-Campbell Movement's ideal of unity or a denial of the Movement's aims by recognizing the legitimacy of denominations and embracing denominational status for Disciples. The third issue was open membership, the practice of admitting into full membership of the churches persons who had not been baptized by immersion, usually persons who had been sprinkled as infants. Generally those who held a favorable view of one of these issues tended to favor the others as well. In a congregationally governed body issues such as the above could become divisive only as they affected extra-congregational activities and agencies.

Modernism became a divisive issue when retirements brought faculty changes in the major ministerial training institution, the College of the Bible in Lexington, Kentucky. The new professors were charged with teachings that ran counter to biblical views held by the older faculty and many alumni. Intense conflict followed, and the trustees conducted an investigation in 1917 that exonerated the accused but did not satisfy the dissidents. Frustrated in their attempt to recover the College of the Bible, those who believed that the future of the Disciples was threatened responded by establishing "faithful" Bible colleges as a means of providing ministers for churches that resisted the new theological trends.

Conflict arose over interchurch relations when the Disciples participated in plans to form the Federal Council of Churches in 1905. Since they were historically opposed to denominations, the response among Disciples was ambivalent. Some (in the spirit of J. H. Garrison) viewed this limited degree of cooperation as a step toward eventual curtailment of denominational significance and hence as a step toward the unity that the Movement advocated. Others saw the entry of Disciples into an interdenominational body as tacit approval of the denominational system and a repudiation of the historic plea. The controversy was so sharp at the General Convention in Norfolk, Virginia, in 1907 and the prospect for approval so bleak that the move to join the Federal Council of Churches was not placed on the agenda of the business session of the Convention but was approved at a special "mass meeting" held separately. Thus, by an unusual stratagem, Disciples of Christ were a founding denomination of the Council, but the significant opposition within prevented Disciples from meeting their portion of the Council's budget for many years.

Open membership became a serious issue in 1920 when the missionaries in China sought permission of the Executive Committee of the United Christian Missionary Society to initiate this practice. The Committee wavered, and a serious conflict followed when the matter was publicized in the *Christian Standard,* one of the major journals of conservative Disciples churches. Those opposed to this innovation demanded the recall of the missionaries involved (1925, Oklahoma City Convention), but the Society's officials did not comply. Further efforts to secure the recall of the pro–open membership missionaries were blocked at the 1926 Memphis Convention, and the resulting frustration created a widely held conviction that central, monolithic organizations were dangerous because they were beyond the control of the constituency that sustained them. Many congregations withdrew support from the United Christian Missionary Society (UCMS), the official missionary agency of the Disciples of Christ. Seeking a viable mission alternative, these congregations found that a few missionaries were already working independently of the UCMS, so support was diverted to them. Some missionaries resigned from the UCMS and began to work independently, hence the name "Independent," which characterized this network of churches for decades.

Generally overlooked has been a sociological factor, an urban/rural polarity, underlying the doctrinal issues at stake and helping to drive the separation. Over much of the twentieth century, two religio-cultural mentalities were emerging, with rural-based conservatives and urban-based liberals viewing such matters as organizational efficiency and centralization of authority from very different perspectives.

Eventually a new convention was organized. The North American Christian Convention held its first sessions in 1927 in Indianapolis, Indiana. With the passage of years, this Convention would become the umbrella organization providing identity for all the congregations and agencies of Christian Churches/Churches of Christ.

A significant influence in developing cohesiveness among churches abandoning the older agencies was the *Christian Standard,* a journal published in Cincinnati, Ohio, and widely circulated since its founding in 1866. It was the most influential journal among the more conservative churches that opposed the policies of the UCMS. Its fidelity to the historic aims of the Movement and its strong editorial voice provided needed leadership and cohesion at a critical juncture. The publisher, Standard Publishing Company, provided a full range of Sunday School literature, youth materials, and books for the emerging group of dissenting congregations. Although privately owned by the Errett family of Cincinnati, its generous support of the new direction taken by the conservative leadership after 1926 continued unabated.

Associated with the *Christian Standard* in forging new directions for the emerging Movement was *The Restoration Herald,* published by the Christian Restoration Association, also based in Cincinnati. Even more conservative than the *Christian Standard,* it was recognized for its outspoken policy of hostility toward the old Disciple leadership and the agencies associated with the UCMS.

Churches disillusioned with trends within the International Convention of Disciples of Christ found their rallying center in the North American Christian Convention, which met sporadically until 1950. It was conceived as a gathering where all Disciples could find fellowship free from the conflicts that had marked the International Convention of Disciples of Christ. Primarily an assembly for preaching on themes dear to the Stone-Campbell tradition, no business was to be conducted and no organizational matters were to be considered, thus avoiding the conflicts that had troubled the older International Convention. However, it soon became evident that two conventions were impractical and that each one was becoming the center of gravity for positions that were increasingly irreconcilable.

An effort to avoid schism was initiated at the 1934 International Convention in Des Moines, Iowa, when a Commission on Restudy of the Disciples of Christ was appointed and charged with examining the heritage of the Stone-Campbell Movement and recommending measures to avert impending division. The Commission met thrice annually until 1948 and carefully defined the points at issue. When it recommended that the two Conventions meet back-to-back in the same city, serious opposition arose from the more militant wings of both factions, effectively frustrating the conciliatory aims of the Commission. A "Stand Up and Be Counted" campaign was sponsored by the *Christian Standard,* which, in response, only intensified efforts to promote open member-

"Honor Roll" Grows With Every Mail

Churches Pass Resolutions; Ministers, Elders, and Other Christians Affirm Stand for Undenominational Christianity and New Testament Order

Meanwhile Church at Harrisonburg, Va., Faces Court Battle to Keep Possession of Church Building; Committee of 1,000 Raises Defense Fund

WE present on this page a portion of the names received in response to our call to stand up and be counted. We intend to print every name received, but we must ask you to be patient with us, as our space limitations will permit us to present only a comparatively small group each week.

May we urge the importance of this record. You may need it at some future time to prove that a corporation outside your local congregation has no legal authority over your congregation. This list may prove helpful in stopping the misrepresentations of the "International" Convention and its affiliated organizations.

Let neither pride nor modesty stand in the way. Send in the names!

HONOR ROLL OF THE FAITHFUL

Churches

Central Church of Christ, Streator, Ill.
Church of Christ, Berryville, Ark.
Christian Church, Arcadia, Tex.
Madisonville Christian Church, Cincinnati, O.
Christian Church, Germantown, Ky.
Christian Church, La Monte, Mo.
First Christian Church, Lake Wales, Fla.
Christian Church, Mena, Ark.
Christian Church, Phillipsburg, Mo.
First Christian Church, West Frankfort, Ill.
First Christian Church, Lexington, Ky.
Southwood Church of Christ, Columbus, O.
Christian Church, Carterville, Ill.
Christian Church, River View, Ala.
Christian Church, Memphis, Mo.
Maple Avenue Christian Church, Terre Haute, Ind.
Central Christian Church, Tampa, Fla.
Elkhorn City Church of Christ, Praise, Ky.
Church of Christ, Bagley, Ia.
First Christian Church, Devine, Tex.
Christian Church, Inavale, Neb.
First Christian Church, Jennings, La.
Christian Church, Mound Valley, Kan.
First Christian Church, Willow Springs, Mo.
Church of Christ, Corona, Calif.
Pilgrim Christian Tabernacle, Buffalo, N. Y.
Berkeley Christian Church, Denver, Col.
Church of Christ, Montezuma, O.
First Christian Church, Snyder, Tex.
Church of Christ, Sebring, O.
Frank Pierce Church of Christ, Kalona, Ia.
Church of Christ, Protection, Kan.
First Christian Church, Batesville, Ark.
Church of Christ, Kokomo, Ind.
Fairmount Avenue Church of Christ, Richmond, Va.
First Christian Church, New Salem, Pa.
First Christian Church, Piggott, Ark.
Dean Avenue Christian Church, Terre Haute, Ind.

Ministers

W. C. Burris, West Frankfort, Ill.
Cecil M. Platt, Lexington, Ky.
J. E. Bronson, Columbus, O.
Stafford E. Davis, Williamstown, Ky.
Paul C. Keeling, Carterville, Ill.
Carroll Langston, Mt. Pulaski, Ill.
N. S. Carpenter, Arapahoe, Neb.
Robert F. Puckett, River View, Ala.
G. Lolin Eaton, Memphis, Mo.
A. L. Althaus, Terre Haute, Ind.

HELP DEFEND THIS LOCAL CHURCH!

by Contributing to the Harrisonburg Defense Fund, Care of Committee of One Thousand, Box 748, Jefferson City, Mo.

The church of Christ, Harrisonburg, Va., is engaged in a struggle for its life as it faces a court battle to keep possession of its property. The Committee of One Thousand reported in our June 14 issue that this battle has been forced upon this local church only after the "State Secretary" had been frustrated in an effort to force a surprise congregational election at a prayer meeting.

The opposition forces are being financed from the outside, presumably by the office of the V. C. M. S. As the Harrisonburg congregation faces this crucial test it needs the help of loyal friends.

To show our good faith in endorsing and urging support for the defense of Harrisonburg in their hour of trial, the "Christian Standard" is forwarding a check for $100 to the Harrisonburg Defense Fund, care of Committee of One Thousand, Box 748, Jefferson City, Mo.

Donald R. Hurley, Portage la Prairie, Man., Can.
Oren H. Whitton, Tampa, Fla.
H. J. Farmer, Praise, Ky.
Carl Holdsworth, Bagley, Ia.
Ray T. Anderson, Devine, Tex.
Jesse A. Mason, Texarkana, Ark.
Everett Keifer, Inavale, Neb.
Harold Maffitt, Jennings, La.
Roy F. Horton, Thayer, Kan.
W. R. Zimmerman, Willow Springs, Mo.
Ivan Williams, Corona, Calif.
R. G. D. Gerkin, Shoals, Ind.
Ernest Hunter Wray, Buffalo, N. Y.
Francis Henry Gibson, Lorain, O.
C. F. Lee, Denver, Col.
Roy B. Shaw, San Jose, Calif.
Robert Lee Powell, Montezuma, O.
Dale J. Benjamin, Snyder, Tex.
Paul D. Magnuson, Sebring, O.
Mark F. Harris, Protection, Kan.
Raymond Phillips, Batesville, Ark.
Rolland A. Steever, Kokomo, Ind.
Orville Hodge, Buffalo, Mo.
William W. Wilson, Richmond, Va.
G. C. Clark, New Salem, Pa.
C. W. Johnstone, Piggott, Ark.
Ira M. Adams, Terre Haute, Ind.
A. D. McMurray, Plainfield, Ind.
S. O. Redacre, Phoenix, Ariz.
Waldo E. Brown, Worthington, Minn.
L. A. Dunham, Chadron, Neb.
W. C. Harris, Columbia, Mo.
Jean M. Shelley, Meridian, Ida.
Joe Ben Rhodes, Orlando, Fla.
J. E. Nichols, Plainville, Ind.
D. F. Tyndall, San Antonio, Tex.

RESOLUTIONS PASSED BY CHURCHES

TELEGRAMS

St. James, Mo., June 7.—We want the world to know that Christ is our master. It is time for His people to take a stand.—St. James Christian Church, Fred R. Barber, Minister; Dr. W. H. Breuer, Chairman of Board; A. O. Byrd, Bible-school Superintendent.

Tampa, Fla., June 15.—Congregation passed by unanimous vote resolution declaring itself to be free from the dictates, wishes, and desires of any ecclesiastical body, missionary organization, or federal council.—Oren H. Whitton, Minister, Central Christian Church.

Berryville, Ark.
June 16, 1947.

At a board meeting of the Berryville (Ark.) Christian Church, on June 13, the following recommendations and resolutions were presented by the minister, Burl H. Candler:

"Understanding the policy and polity of the United Christian Missionary Society, and such other agencies with which they are affiliated; whose policy is a denial of the Scriptures and the authority of Christ, I refuse to accept a call to the ministry of any congregation which will not sever all connections with such agencies. Therefore, I ask the church board of the Berryville Christian Church to accept the following resolutions, and the ratification by the congregation of these resolutions on the first Lord's Day following this meeting:

"Whereas the United Christian Missionary Society and the Christian Board of Publication, and other associated agencies are not in accord with the Scriptures; practice and endorse open membership; and agree to comity agreements. Be it resolved that the Berryville Christian Church board and congregation withdraw all support, financial and otherwise, from the United Christian Missionary Society; the Christian Board of Publication; Laymen's League; Federal Council of the Churches of Christ in America; and all other such agencies which are not in harmony with Christ and the Scriptures.

"Be it further resolved, that no minister, evangelist, or any other worker shall be called to serve this congregation in any phase who is not in full accord with these resolutions.

"(Signed) BURL H. CANDLER,
"Minister of the gospel of Christ."

The above was acted upon at once, and without a dissenting vote of all members of the board present, passed, and was signed by the following members: E. O. Carr, chairman; A. L. Hanna, W. T. Hutchinson, F. L. Vawter, J. P. Hanna, A. J. Clark, Roy B. Leach, and D. C. West.

The foregoing was presented to the congregation by the chairman of the church board, E. O. Carr, after the Sunday morning service, Sunday, June 15. The resolutions were adopted by the congregation without a dissenting vote.

[Other similar resolutions are on hand in our office and will be published in early issues.—Ed.]

FOR JUNE 28, 1947 (451) Page Three

As editor of the *Christian Standard,* Burris Butler (1909-1982) began publishing the "Honor Roll of the Faithful" in 1947 as a register of local churches opposing the perceived organizational hegemony of the United Christian Missionary Society and the liberal tendencies of mainline Disciples of Christ. The Honor Roll thus anticipated a separate *Directory of the Ministry* of "independent" Christian Churches/Churches of Christ. Page appearing in the *Christian Standard,* June 28, 1947

ship within the International Convention body. Later movement toward total denominationalization and "Restructure" of the Disciples of Christ completed the process of division. However, some of the older agencies of the Christian Church (Disciples of Christ) — the official designation of the restructured denomination — have continued to make their services available to Christian Churches/Churches of Christ. Notable in this respect are the Pension Fund, the Board of Church Extension, and the Disciples of Christ Historical Society.

In 1950 the North American Christian Convention abandoned its irregularity and became a permanent institution. In 1963 an office was established in Cincinnati, and a full-time convention director was engaged. Prior to this time, most conventions were held in Ohio and Indiana, but since becoming a permanent organization the convention has moved nationwide and once even held its sessions in Canada. It has evolved into a family gathering with a variety of workshops, meetings, and activities that appeal to all ages. Attendance often exceeds 25,000. The convention continues to eschew any official status and avoids any kind of formal policy-making action or endorsement. It remains the largest national gathering of the Christian Churches/Churches of Christ. Most of the many agencies that derive their support from the churches are represented in exhibits at this convention.

A second meeting of national scope among Christian Churches/Churches of Christ is the National Missionary Convention. Inasmuch as missionary strategy and policy were a major cause of the disaffection leading to the origin of the North American Christian Convention, it was natural that missions would be given a significant place in the sessions of the convention. As the international mission enterprise proliferated following World War II, it was difficult to provide missionaries with what many of them deemed to be an adequate place on the programs. Accordingly, missionaries called a meeting at the 1951 convention in Springfield, Illinois, and organized the National Missionary Convention for more satisfactory promotion of their cause. This convention is not an annual gathering but has developed a large constituency. It is managed by missionaries, and occasionally its sessions are held in conjunction with the North American Christian Convention.

Disillusionment with their seeming inability to influence the policies and actions of the central agencies of the Disciples of Christ accounts for the fact that the North American Christian Convention disavows any suggestion that it officially represents the churches or that it seeks in any way to direct policies affecting the work of the local church. Similarly, Christian Churches/Churches of Christ have opted for a polity fiercely protective of congregational autonomy. This is evident from the total absence of any organizational tie uniting the fellowship of some 5,500 congregations and hundreds of agencies. There is powerful resistance to any effort that might be seen as compromising in any way the complete and total autonomy of each congregation. Thus all extra-congregational efforts and agencies (and there are many) rise *ad hoc* from private initiative and are sustained by continuing endorsement from supporting congregations and individuals. Some of the larger congregations assume total responsibility for a missionary family or team. Most opt for partial support and send periodic offerings to the missionary's forwarding committee. This would appear to constitute an unstable base of support for missionary enterprises, but in practice it has proven to be as stable and effective as those methods utilized by more highly organized denominations. Missionaries must be self-motivated, and because their work depends on the participation of interested individuals and congregations, personal contacts with congregations are of vital importance. Friendships and loyalties are established that prove to be functional and enduring. Most independent missionaries form oversight committees that are usually incorporated in their home state and hold title to real properties purchased for use by the mission. Thereby the work of the mission is carried forth should a particular missionary retire or otherwise be unable to continue service.

Leonard Wymore (b. 1921) served as Executive Director of the North American Christian Convention from 1961 to 1986, from which position he played an important role in promoting interest in Christian unity and world evangelization among the Christian Churches/Churches of Christ.

Photo appearing in Edwin Hayden, *North American Gold*, 1989

Few would deny that the independent/direct support method of doing missions employed by Christian Churches/Churches of Christ involves some problems. Few of the religious communions that are more highly structured, however, can rival Christian Churches/Churches of Christ in the number of missionaries that are sustained on the fields. Missions continue to be a focus of major interest among most of the churches, claiming a considerable portion of each congregation's budget.

True to the Stone-Campbell heritage, Christian Churches/Churches of Christ practice immersion of believers as the only valid baptism because they understand this to be the only method of baptism found in the New Testament and practiced by the early church. They insist that baptism finds its meaning as it relates to forgiveness of sin; but they emphatically reject any form of water regeneration, a charge that is sometimes wrongfully made because of the emphasis placed on this ordinance.

The other ordinance/sacrament (the latter term is seldom heard) found in Christian Churches/Churches of Christ is the Lord's Supper, which is observed every Sunday in every congregation. This, too, is believed to have been the practice of the early church, and thus it holds a central place in the churches' effort to "restore" early Christian faith and practice. Emphasis is generally focused on the memorial nature of the Supper. Elders usually preside at the table, although this is not mandated. The Supper is made available to all believers ("open communion").

Other than the "Petrine confession" of Christ's divinity found in Matthew 16:18 there is no creedal formula that unites Christian Churches/Churches of Christ. The historic slogan "No Creed but Christ" is taken very seriously. Theological definitions are viewed as barriers to Christian unity and hence rejected as a basis of fellowship. There is little question that this rejection of theological formulation has sometimes resulted inadvertently in a degree of theological shallowness and simplistic biblicism, but it is an important component of the heritage of the Stone-Campbell Movement and a basic conviction endorsed by the whole fellowship.

The philosophical roots of the Stone-Campbell Movement lie in the Enlightenment. The empiricism of John Locke, modified by the Common Sense realism of Thomas Reid, provided the basic thought patterns for all three of the branches of this Movement. Emphasis on free inquiry tended to discourage "fundamentalism" per se among the Movement's heirs. In spite of certain similarities of emphasis, such as common rejection of certain findings of biblical higher criticism and an occasional advocacy of biblical inerrancy in some quarters, classic Protestant fundamentalism (of the Reformed/Calvinist type) has held little appeal for Christian Churches/Churches of Christ.

Christian Churches/Churches of Christ adamantly refused to regard any institution or organization other than the local congregation as in any sense "church." They insist that the church as such inheres primarily in the local congregation, itself understood as a microcosm of the church universal. Each congregation elects elders and deacons, who have sole responsibility to direct the affairs of the local church.

Christian Churches/Churches of Christ ordain their ministers and invest sole authority to do so in the local congregation. The strong emphasis on the priesthood of every believer, however, leaves little room for much distinction between clergy and laity. Thus, laypersons may conduct baptisms, and lay elders may preside at communion services. There is no system of ministerial placement among the churches. Each congregation seeks and employs its own minister(s). There is no uniform plan for pension or care for retired ministers. Several pension programs are available, and each minister plans for his or her own future needs. Churches often contribute to the minister's pension arrangement, but there is no uniformity in this matter.

Women's role in leadership is limited. Rarely are women engaged as preachers or senior pastors or elected to the eldership; however, women are regularly accepted for missionary service, and many serve as teachers in Bible colleges. Women often hold senior staff positions in local churches in education, children's ministries, and youth ministries; and in many congregations, women are admitted to the ministry of deacons. The ministry role of women in the life of these churches has slowly increased in recent decades.

Evangelism is a continuing emphasis among Christian Churches/Churches of Christ. The methods have changed from the revival meetings of bygone years to newer forms suggested by the church growth movement; but the impulses have not abated. Many "mega-churches" with attendance averages in excess of 1,000 can be identified. As of 2004, the largest of these is the Southeast Christian Church in Louisville, Kentucky.

Reliable statistics on the status and growth of Christian Churches/Churches of Christ are difficult to obtain prior to 1955, when an annual *Directory of the Ministry* was first published. Many congregations of this fellowship continued to be listed in the *Yearbook of Disciples of Christ* until the Restructure of the Disciples in 1968. At the beginning of the twenty-first century, the *Directory of the Ministry of the Christian Churches/Churches of Christ* reports 1,333,000 members in 5,554 congregations in the United States and Canada. The body is served by a large number of agencies and institutions. Youth work in the churches is augmented by some 100 summer camps, many of which have well-developed facilities providing year-round programs for conferences, etc. The churches sponsor 118 homes for children or retired persons, 85 elementary-level Christian schools, and 75 campus ministries.

The crisis in ministerial education, previously noted in conjunction with the controversy over the advance of modernist theology, and the fact that most of the older colleges and universities of the Disciples were associated with the Division of Higher Education of the Disciples of Christ, forced the emerging Christian Churches/Disciples of Christ to create Bible colleges. Thirty-two Bible colleges are affiliated with Christian Churches/Churches of Christ. Originally directed primarily toward ministerial education, many of these institutions are no longer called "Bible Colleges." They have broadened the scope of their curricular offerings in the liberal arts and sciences and have in many cases gained regional accreditation.

Three fully accredited graduate seminaries (Emmanuel School of Religion, Cincinnati Bible Seminary, and Lincoln Christian Seminary) and one liberal arts college (Milligan College) furnish additional educational opportunities.

Nationwide, 100 evangelistic associations engaging in the work of establishing new churches are listed in the *Directory.* Publications needed to support the programs of the churches are supplied by two agencies: Standard Publishing Company (Cincinnati) and College Press (Joplin, Missouri).

The strong missionary heritage of Christian Churches/Churches of Christ is reflected in the more than 1,000 persons currently serving in some capacity in the mission activities sustained by the churches. Outside the United States, twenty-seven Bible Colleges endeavor to provide education for indigenous ministry. Many missions operate primary schools, and some provide homes for needy or abandoned children. At least one hospital and a number of clinics are maintained by missionaries from these churches. Missiologists in the fellowship claim that there are now more members of Christian Churches/Churches of Christ in the Third World than can currently be found in the United States.

Recognition of some of the problems inherent in the independent/direct support method of doing missions led to establishment in 1948 of the Christian Missionary Fellowship. This organization screens missionary candidates, provides limited supervision of fieldwork, and otherwise utilizes many of the procedures of organized mission activity; but it makes no claim to be the sole mission agency through which Christian Churches/Churches of Christ must do mission work. Based in Indianapolis, its outreach is multinational. Churches preferring a more structured mission program have found this agency to be useful.

Christian Churches/Churches of Christ are not formally involved in any aspect of the ecumenical movement. This is due not only to the paucity of mechanisms enabling these churches to join a council but also to the continuing conviction that such official recognition of denominational status would be a repudiation of the Stone-Campbell heritage. Nonetheless, ministers from these congregations have no hesitation about participating in local ministerial associations, and they generally support community efforts in association with other Christian bodies. In 1983 a cluster of concerned individuals from the Christian Churches/Churches of Christ helped initiate an "Open Forum" for constructive dialogue with representatives from the Church of God (Anderson, Indiana). Finally, missionaries often engage in cooperative activity with missionaries from other Christian bodies as they seek to make an impact on non-Christian cultures.

At the turn of the twenty-first century, when the memories and much of the animosity of the conflicts of earlier years have faded and new leadership has emerged, there is discernible longing for closer ties between the disparate bodies of the Stone-Campbell Movement. Serious questions are being raised about the long-term significance of some of the issues that seemed to hold critical importance in years past. A growing awareness of this is apparent in all branches of the Stone-Campbell Movement and manifested among Christian Churches/Churches of Christ both in the Restoration Forums with Churches of Christ and in the recent gatherings of the Stone-Campbell Dialogue.

See also Bible College Movement; Christian Church (Disciples of Christ); Christian Missionary Fellowship; *Christian Standard;* Churches of Christ; College Press; Evangelical; Fundamentalism; Missions, Missiology; National Missionary Convention; North American Christian Convention; Standard Publishing Company; Theology — Christian Churches/Churches of Christ

BIBLIOGRAPHY C. J. Dull, "Intellectual Factions and Groupings in the Independent Christian Churches," *The [Cincinnati Bible] Seminary Review* 31 (1985): 91-118 • David Filbeck, *The First Fifty Years: A Brief History of the Independent Mission Movement* (1980) • Byron Lambert, "From Rural Churches to an Urban World: Shifting Frontiers and the Invisible Hand," *Discipliana* 55 (1995): 67-80 • Zella McLean, ed., *Directory of the Ministry: A Yearbook of Christian Churches and Churches of Christ* (published annually) • James DeForest Murch, *Christians Only* (1962) • James North, *Unity in Truth: An Interpretive History of the Restoration Movement* (1994) • G. Richard Phillips, "From Modern Theology to a Post-Modern World: Christian

Churches and Churches of Christ," *Discipliana* 54 (1994): 83-95 • Rondal Smith, "The Independent Christian Churches Face a Multicultural Twenty-First Century," *Discipliana* 57 (1997): 35-46 • Henry E. Webb, *In Search of Christian Unity: A History of the Restoration Movement,* 2nd ed. (2003) • C. Robert Wetzel, "Christian Churches/ Churches of Christ at 2001: In Search of a Theological Center," *Stone-Campbell Journal* 4 (2001): 3-12 • Flavil Yeakley, "Recent Patterns of Growth and Decline among Heirs of the Restoration Movement," *Restoration Quarterly* 37 (1995): 45-50. HENRY E. WEBB

Christian Connection

Designation for movement founded by Abner Jones and Elias Smith in New England, but later the amalgamation of non–Stone-Campbell "Christians." By 1808 Smith had heard of the James O'Kelly Christians (1794) in Virginia and the Barton W. Stone Christians (1804) in Kentucky. By 1810 these groups all declared themselves one, with 20,000 adherents. But it was not until after the Civil War that conferences were held that included an appropriate number of believers from all three groups. The preferred name was "The Christian Church."

Abner Jones founded churches in Lyndon, Vermont (1801), and in Hanover and Piedmont, New Hampshire (1802), and in 1803 Jones encouraged Elias Smith to found another in Portsmouth, New Hampshire. Both Jones and Smith were Baptists and emulated the approaches to evangelism and conversion characterized by the Second Great Awakening in New England. They rejected election and predestination and sometimes preached at Freewill Baptist congregations, but maintained their independence. In 1807 Daniel Hix of Dartmouth, Massachusetts, came into the movement along with his congregation of about 300. In 1808 Smith founded the *Herald of Gospel Liberty,* in which he declared that just as the United States achieved freedom from England, so Christians should seek liberty from European denominations by embracing the New Testament alone.

Elias Smith departed for the Universalists in 1817, resulting in instability in the movement. Renewed energy was exerted to strengthen the Conferences so as to forestall other defections. By 1823 Robert Foster reported 181 ministers, most of them in western New York (46), Vermont (40), and eastern New York (31). The Christians rapidly moved west, and in Ohio, Indiana, Michigan, and Illinois associated with persons from the O'Kelly and Stone movements. Second-generation preachers from New York now moved to the forefront, including David Millard (1794-1873), Joseph Badger (1792-1852), and Simon Clough (1793-1844) of Boston, all of whom battled Trinitarianism. Because of their views on the Trinity they had contacts with the Unitarians and were declared partners

Abner Jones (1772-1841) founded the first three congregations of the New England Christian Connection. For most of his life he also served as a physician in Vermont, New Hampshire, Massachusetts, and New York.

Courtesy of the Disciples of Christ Historical Society

in the operation of Meadville Theological Seminary, but their contribution was negligible. They also founded new journals, the *Gospel Luminary* (1825-32) and the *Christian Palladium* (1832-60).

In 1832 the Stone Christians commenced uniting with the Campbell-Scott Christians in the Ohio Valley. The Christians from the O'Kelly and Jones-Smith movements were not involved, except for those who had entered into relations with the Stone Christians west of the Appalachians. These eastern Christians highlighted the conversion experience, quarterly celebration of the Lord's Supper, and anti-Trinitarianism, thereby conflicting with Campbell-Scott commitments. In like manner, about half of the Stone Christians did not enter the Campbell merger. A major critic of the amalgamation was Matthew Gardner (1790-1873) of Ohio.

In the 1840s the Jones-Smith Christians lost several members to the William Miller (1782-1849) followers, who in turn founded the Christian Advent Church. Joshua V. Himes (1805-1895), a Boston Christian Connection minister, became William Miller's chief publicist and preached Miller's funeral.

After the Civil War the Christian Connection (or Connexion) became more centralized, with offices in Dayton, Ohio. In 1931 the Christian Connection merged with the Congregational Church to form the Congregational Christian Church. In 1957 the Congregational Christian Church merged with the Evangelical and Reformed Church to become the United Church of Christ.

See also Democratization; Jones, Abner; O'Kelly, James; Republican Methodists; Smith, Elias; Unitarians; Universalism

BIBLIOGRAPHY Nathan O. Hatch, *The Democratization of American Christianity* (1989) • Michael G. Kenny, *The Perfect Law of Liberty: Elias Smith and the Providential History of America* (1994) • Milo True Morrill, *A History of the Christian Denomination in America* (1911) • Thomas H. Olbricht, "Christian Connexion and Unitarian Relationships, 1800-1844," *Restoration Quarterly* 9 (1966): 160-86.

THOMAS H. OLBRICHT

Christian Echo

Founded in 1902 by G. P. Bowser (1874-1950), the *Christian Echo* is the oldest periodical in circulation among African American Churches of Christ. Beginning publication with a small hand press in his home, Bowser saw the venture as an important means of encouraging and instructing Christians in the black community, of dealing with racial issues generally ignored in other journals, and of providing a means of communication between black Churches of Christ. For its first half-century the *Christian Echo* was closely associated with several of Bowser's educational ventures, most notably Silver Point Christian Institute in Silver Point, Tennessee, and Bowser Christian Institute in Fort Smith, Arkansas. At both of these schools, Bowser operated a printing business, which improved the quality of the magazine and provided work for needy students.

In 1949, one year before his death, Bowser turned over editorial and publishing responsibilities to one of those students who had worked with him in printing the *Christian Echo,* R. N. Hogan (1902-1997). During Hogan's nearly fifty years as editor, he used the journal as a mouthpiece to raise civil rights awareness among members of white Churches of Christ. Decrying the exclusion of black Christians from all Southern colleges operated by members of Churches of Christ, Hogan asserted that the New Testament was a pattern not only for church membership and organization but also for racial relations, and that any compromise on the biblical ideal was equivalent to toleration of doctrinal error. Hogan served as editor of the *Christian Echo* until his death, at which time his coworker, Bethel Smith, continued its publication through 2000. At that point its archives and editorial responsibilities were turned over to Southwestern Christian College in Terrell, Texas. Since that time the magazine continued to be published as a bimonthly journal, with president Jack Evans (b. 1937) serving as publisher and vice president James Maxwell (b. 1938) as editor.

Preach The Word — The Christian Echo — Holding The Truth in Love

VOLUME 37. FORT SMITH, ARK., AUG. 20, 1942 NUMBER 16.

The Use Of Water In Material and Spiritual Things

Fred D. Cowan

If people could realize the value and the essentiality of water in spiritual things as they do in material things it would put out of business all of those who preach faith alone, getting religion and all such doctrines which originated in the hearts of uninspired men.

In the first three verses of the Bible there are three very important things mentioned in connection with the creation of the heavens and the earth. They are water, spirit and light. Each of these are essential to every living thing under the sun. Just imagine our trying to get along without water or without spirit or without light. No water, no spirit; no spirit, no life; no life, no light. For the life is the light of man. (John 1:4) The water and the spirit were together in the beginning and we find no place in the Bible where God ever separated them. They function as do the male and female, and are referred to as such in the word of the Lord. The Holy Spirit is referred to as he. (John 15:26; 16:13-15) The water is referred to as she. (John 1:15) With these facts understood we can understand Christ's expression in John 3:5: "Except ye be born of water (the female factor) and of the Spirit (the male factor) ye cannot enter the kingdom of God." In the physical birth there must be both the male and female factors. There must also be the male and female in the spiritual birth.

The seed of the kingdom is the word of God. (Luke 8:11) The word of God is the Spirit of God. (John 6: 63) The word of God is the gospel of Christ. Paul said we are begotten by the gospel. (1 Cor. 4:15) James said: "Of his own will begot he us by the word of truth." (James 1:18) Let's see how the water and the Spirit worked together in the new births recorded in the Acts of the Apostles. When the church was established on the day of Pentecost, Peter preached the first gospel sermon in fact, after the promised spirit came with power. (Joel 2:28; Acts 2:14-17) And after hearing this sermon about three thousand of the Jews there assembled believed it, and said unto Peter and to the rest of the apostles, "Men and brethren, what shall we do?" Then Peter said unto them, "Repent, and be baptized everyone of you in the name of Jesus Christ for the remission of sins, and ye shall receive the gift of the Holy Ghost." These were the first to obey the words of Christ, to be born of water and of the Spirit.

Some claim that the baptism that Peter commanded was the baptism of the Holy Ghost. It could not have been, for they were to receive the promise of the Holy Ghost after they had complied with the command to be baptized. This promise of the Holy Ghost was to the Gentiles as well as to the Jews, for Peter said so in the 39th verse; that it was to all that are afar off even as many as the Lord our God shall call. And God said: "Look ye unto me all ye ends of the earth and be ye saved." (Isa. 45:22; 53)

If any one will open his eyes and look at the many examples recorded in the book of Acts he will see what is required of him in order to be saved. The eunuch who was returning from Jerusalem was reading the 53rd chapter of Isaiah. He was looking for salvation, and the Lord opened his eyes of understanding through Philip's preaching. And he also said, See here is water what doth hinder me to be baptized. And the preacher said, Thou mayest if thou believeth. And he said I believe that Jesus Christ is the Son of God. And he commanded the chariot to stand still; and they went down both into the water, both Philip and the eunuch and he baptized him. And when they were come up out of the water, the Spirit of the Lord caught away Philip that the eunuch saw him no more, and he went on his way rejoicing. (Acts 8:32-40)

Saul was looking for salvation and the Lord sent unto him Ananias, the preacher, who said: "Why tarriest thou, arise and be baptized and wash away thy sins, calling on the name of the Lord." (Acts 22:16) Some one will say, I know the Bible says all that; but water cannot wash away sins for it says in Rev. 1:5 that Christ washed us from our sins in his own blood. True he washes us from our sins in his own blood; but you cannot reach the blood short of the water.

Paul said in Rom. 6:3, that so many of us as were baptized into Jesus Christ were baptized in his death. Christ shed his blood in his death and when we are baptized in water we contact the blood. For blood and water came forth out of his side when he was pierced by one of the soldiers when he was crucified. Therefore the blood and the water are still together. Faith in the gospel of Christ, repentance of all our sins and the confession that Jesus is the Son of God, are the veins through which the blood flows in the act of obedience which leads us to the water. And there is where the cleansing takes place and there is where we become as a little child in complete humility and obedience to him who died to save us. Remember his words to Peter, "If I wash thee not thou hast no part with me." (John 13:8)

The journalistic voice of Black Churches of Christ, the *Christian Echo* consistently attacked and called for an end to the widespread racism in the body. Theologically the paper reflected the most conservative positions held by Churches of Christ generally in the twentieth century.

Courtesy of the Disciples of Christ Historical Society

Unfortunately for historians, in 1946 archival materials on the early issues of the *Christian Echo* were destroyed in an automobile accident as G. P. Bowser was moving to Detroit. Therefore, early issues have been difficult to locate, complicating research. Southwestern Christian College, however, is organizing materials from its publication archives and other sources, in hopes that near complete records can be available in the future.

See also African Americans in the Movement; Bowser, George Philip; Hogan, Richard Nathaniel; Southwestern Christian College

JESSE CURTIS POPE

Christian Endeavor

See Young People's Society of Christian Endeavor

Christian-Evangelist, The

Journal circulating in the Stone-Campbell Movement in the late nineteenth through the mid-twentieth centuries, known for its moderate ideological position.

The Christian-Evangelist commenced in 1882, as a combination of predecessors. J. H. Garrison served as the first editor until resigning in 1912 and continued writing a regular column until his retirement in 1928. The journal continued under this title until being merged with *Front Rank* and renamed *The Christian* in 1960; then in 1974 *The Christian* merged with *World Call* (founded in 1918) and was renamed *The Disciple.* Publication of *The Disciple* was suspended in 2002. *The Christian-Evangelist* and its successors were a weekly publication after 1882. Conservatives saw the journal as representing left-of-center perspectives, and its editorial position dissatisfied fervent liberals. Radicals on the left and strong traditionalists on the right often criticized *The Christian-Evangelist's* essays and editorials.

The first predecessor of *The Christian-Evangelist* was *The Gospel Echo,* a monthly, founded in 1863 in Carrollton, Illinois, by Elijah L. Craig. In 1868 John C. Reynolds bought the paper, moved to Macomb, Illinois, and invited J. H. Garrison to join him as associate pastor of the Macomb Christian Church and co-editor of the journal. While the *Echo* advocated basically conservative causes, the editors sided with the *Christian Standard,* then the leading "left wing" journal. In 1871 the name of the *Echo* was changed to *The Christian Missionary* and it became a weekly publication. In the meantime a publication called *The Christian,* edited by Alexander Proctor, George W. Longan, and others, commenced in 1870 and was suspended in 1872. Garrison took over the paper, merged it with his paper as *The Christian* in 1873, and moved to Quincy, Illinois, then again to St. Louis, Missouri, in 1874. In 1882 Garrison merged *The Christian* with *The Evangelist,* published in Oskaloosa, Iowa, and edited by B. W. Johnson and Francis M. Call. *The Evangelist* (not to be confused with Walter Scott's earlier journal of the same name) was founded as *The Western Evangelist* by Daniel Bates at Mt. Pleasant, Iowa, in 1850. Having merged their journalistic enterprises, Garrison and Johnson served as co-editors until Johnson's death in 1894. By 1884 *The Christian-Evangelist* had 25,000 subscribers. In 1911 *The Christian-Evangelist* became an official publication under the auspices of the Christian Board of Publication. Garrison stepped down as editor-in-chief February 2, 1912. Editors following Garrison were Frederick D. Kershner (1915-17), B. D. Abbott (1917-34), Willard E. Shelton (1934-38), George A. Campbell (1938-40), Raphael H. Miller (1941-48), Lin D. Cartwright (1948-58), and Howard E. Short (1959).

Through the years Garrison commented on the major activities of the Stone-Campbell Movement and the various controversies that arose. He presented positions on subjects discussed in the churches and commended openness to views he himself rejected, for example, membership without immersion. His voice was therefore perceived, especially by those on the right, as leading the Movement into liberalism. He was open to biblical criticism, but opposed radical versions of it, as well as of evolution. He retained the basic consensus views of earlier leaders of the Stone-Campbell Movement. In the journal he pushed for the Disciples' entry into the Federal Council of Churches, mergers with the Baptists, and cooperation with other mainstream Protestant churches. Garrison's successor, Frederick Kershner, also pursued a *via media,* remaining conservative on issues like open membership but resisting legalism and exclusivism in the Movement. Kershner reflected at length on controversial issues in his "As I Think on These Things" column.

The Christian and *The Disciple* sought to remain with these moderating positions as official journals for the Disciples of Christ and therefore reflected mainstream outlooks.

See also *Christian, The; Disciple, The;* Garrison, James Harvey; Journalism; Kershner, Frederick D.

BIBLIOGRAPHY *The Christian-Evangelist Index, 1863-1958,* 3 vols. (1958) • *Disciples World* • William E. Tucker, *J. H. Garrison and Disciples of Christ* (1964).

THOMAS H. OLBRICHT

Christian Foundation, The

A charitable trust incorporated in the State of Indiana in 1922 to give financial support to institutions and causes promoting restoration of New Testament Christianity.

William G. Irwin and Marshall Reeves, wealthy business leaders of Columbus, Indiana, led in the creation of The Christian Foundation. Both were closely associated with Frederick D. Kershner, whose aim was to establish a conservative to moderate graduate theological school in Indianapolis in cooperation with Butler University. Following consultations with Disciples leaders from across the nation, a corporation was formed, and nine men were named directors, four from Danville, Indiana, and five from Columbus. The first benefactions made by the Foundation were to Butler University Foundation (designated for the School of Religion), and Cincinnati Bible Seminary (of special interest to the Reeves family).

The Foundation gave financial support to a number of enterprises that were not linked with the "Co-operative" efforts of the Disciples of Christ, as the latter were believed to have abandoned the goal of restoring New Testament Christianity. It underwrote the salary of Ralph Records, president of Cincinnati Bible Seminary. It supported the annual Lake James School of Mission, and it published a new hymnal. But the main focus of interest was Butler University School of Religion. The Foundation's support of this seminary made it possible for students to pursue graduate studies without tuition costs. In 1942 the Foundation was the major source of providing the school a magnificent new building on the university campus. A similar building was contemplated for Cincinnati Bible Seminary, but internal difficulties at the Seminary aborted it.

A major shift of interest and direction for the Christian Foundation occurred abruptly in 1944. Irwin died suddenly on December 14, 1943, as did Edwin R. Errett, editor of the *Christian Standard,* little more than a month later. Irwin and Errett, though conservative, had always been committed to maintaining the unity of the Disciples of Christ. Directors of the Foundation were aware of an *ad hoc* "committee on Action" that was bringing pressure to bear within Standard Publishing Company to force a militant policy against the "Cooperative" wing of the Disciples of Christ, a policy that Errett had opposed. The tendency was to blame this anti-Disciples group for Errett's death. Financial support for all activities not Disciples-related was soon terminated.

Will Irwin was a bachelor, and his nephew, J. Irwin Miller, succeeded him as head of the family's extensive business interests. He was a committed Disciple whose interests were wholly ecumenical and not at all in sympathy with the earlier policies of the Foundation (in 1960, Miller became the first lay person to serve as president of the National Council of Churches). Within the Foundation, he augmented efforts to make the School of Religion (since 1959, Christian Theological Seminary) a leading ecumenical seminary. In 1964 the assets of The Christian Foundation, totaling almost $6 million, were turned over to Christian Theological Seminary, and The Christian Foundation was dissolved.

HENRY E. WEBB

Christian Leader

Journal established in late 1886 by John F. Rowe (1827-1897). Earlier that year Rowe had been forced out as editor of the *American Christian Review,* one of the leading conservative journals in the North, after a failed attempt to buy the paper at less than its market value.

After Rowe's death in 1897, James S. Bell (1838-1910) became editor and Fred L. Rowe (1866-1947), John's son, became general manager and owner. In 1904 James A. Harding (1848-1922) merged his journal *The Way* with the *Christian Leader.* Harding became co-editor with Bell, and the journal was published as *Christian Leader and The Way* until 1912 when Harding resigned. Also in 1904, the *Leader* absorbed the *Gospel Review,* and its editor, Joe Warlick (1866-1941) of Dallas, Texas, also became a co-editor. With these mergers and with J. N. Armstrong, R. C. Bell, Jesse P. Sewell, and R. H. Boll as staff writers, the *Leader* became a national journal rivaling the *Gospel Advocate, Firm Foundation,* and *American Christian Review,* the better-known journals of the Churches of Christ.

After Harding, Joseph Cain, Ira C. Moore, J. W. Shepherd, and T. Q. Martin served as the editors. From 1904 until 1939, many writers who had been shut out of the other major journals in Churches of Christ because of theological positions were allowed to write in the *Leader.*

Under Fred Rowe's management the *Leader* also became a leading publisher of books, debates, and sermons for Churches of Christ. For many years Rowe published the Abilene Christian College Bible Lectures.

During the Depression negative journalism in the Churches of Christ increased. A group of leaders, especially those supportive of the colleges of the Churches of Christ, wanted to establish a national journal that was positive in tone and used the best design possible. Clinton Davidson (1888-1967), who had earned a fortune during the Depression as an insurance salesman and estate planner based in New York City, spearheaded the effort. Davidson assembled an impressive editorial board of leading preachers and businessmen and selected E. W. McMillan (1889-1991), one of the leading young preachers of the time, as editor. Davidson bought the *Christian Leader* from Fred Rowe, who wanted to retire from the publishing business.

From 1939 to 1941, the design quality of the *Leader* was unmatched by any journal in the Churches of Christ. The more open tone of the journal, however, was not always well received by the other journals. Foy E. Wallace, Jr. (1896-1979), editor of the *Bible Banner,* led the attacks. By 1941 Davidson was losing money and sold the *Leader* to G. H. P. Showalter.

The *Leader* never recovered. It was sold repeatedly and went through a series of editors. The readership was confined mainly to the North, and the quality declined. The *Leader* had a brief revival in the early 1950s when Burton Coffman (b. 1905) edited it, serving at the same time as preacher of the Manhattan Church of Christ in New York City. Later, Doward Anguish of Dresden, Ohio, was editor and publisher. The *Leader* was last published in 1960, its important journalistic role mostly forgotten among Churches of Christ.

See also *American Christian Review;* Boll, Robert Henry; *Firm Foundation; Gospel Advocate, The;* Harding, James

Alexander; McMillan, Edward Washington; Shepherd, James Walton; Wallace, Foy Esco, Jr.

BIBLIOGRAPHY Don Haymes, "Lectureships (Churches of Christ)," in *Encyclopedia of Religion in the South* (1984) • John Mark Hicks, "The Gracious Separatist: Moral and Positive Law in the Theology of James A. Harding," *Restoration Quarterly* 42 (3rd quarter 2000): 129-47.

MICHAEL W. CASEY

Christian Men's Fellowship

Name of Disciples Men's organizations.

The creation of a Department of Men's Work in the United Christian Missionary Society was the result of a growing insistence on the part of various groups of laymen over a period of years. Long before any program or department was developed at the general level, groups of Disciples laymen had formed and begun holding meetings. The 1944 Columbus International Convention approved a resolution recommending "that a department of laymen's organization be created with a full time executive secretary in The United Christian Missionary Society." In response, the trustees of the United Christian Missionary Society in 1945 established a department of laymen's work to be known temporarily as "Department of Lay Activities." Later it became the Department of Men's Work.

The first national laymen's retreat was held at the Cane Ridge Meeting House near Paris, Kentucky, August 11-14, 1949. A second national retreat for men was held at Bethany, West Virginia, in August 1951. Several thousand men from throughout the United States and Canada attended. The same year the general men's program and organizations in Disciples congregations were given the name Christian Men's Fellowship (CMF). The goal of CMF was to foster fellowship, study, and service among the men of a congregation. Opportunities for wider fellowship have been provided in area and general gatherings.

In 1968 the departments of Christian Women's Fellowship and Men's Work became part of the Division of Church Life and Work of the United Christian Missionary Society. It remained there when the Division was renamed the Division of Homeland Ministries in 1971 and when it was incorporated as a separate entity in 1973. In 1975 the department was renamed the Department of Church Men. In 1984 the name changed to Office of Men's Ministries. In 1992 it became the General Conference of Disciples Men.

DAVID MCCRACKEN

Christian Messenger

Monthly journal edited by Barton Warren Stone (1772-1844) and published from November 1826 to April 1845 (fourteen volumes), with publication suspended January 1837 through August 1840, and for a few months in each of the years 1841-44.

Volumes 1-8 (Nov. 1826–Dec. 1834) were published from Georgetown, Kentucky. John T. Johnson co-edited volumes 6-8. Volumes 9-14 (Jan. 1835–April 1845) were published from Jacksonville, Illinois. Jacob Creath, Jr., and T. M. Allen assisted with volume 11. D. P. Henderson co-edited volumes 13 and 14 and continued the publication for a few months after Stone's death. The *Messenger* was merged in 1847 with *The Bible Advocate*. It was a twenty-four-page publication in pamphlet form and originally printed by *The American Sentinel* in Georgetown at the annual subscription price of one dollar.

The paper struggled constantly for survival. Stone frequently apologized for the quality of paper and type and regularly pleaded with agents to collect and with subscribers to pay. Suspensions of publication were primarily duc to finances. After three years Stone complained that the *Messenger* had gone to 2,000 subscribers but receipts had little more than paid the printer and paper maker. Evidently few copies were bound.

The *Messenger* was an invaluable means of expression and communication for Stone's followers. In the absence of any general organization among the churches, it became the chief instrument of their unity. It also served to establish stronger ties with the New England Christians (followers of Abner Jones and Elias Smith) and the O'Kelly Christians in the East. Stone's early series, "History of the Christian Church in the West," was likely directed to those audiences. Publication of an advertisement for the *Signs of the Times* in the early 1840s at the "special request" of Joshua V. Himes, editor and Christian minister in Boston, illustrates this communication through the *Messenger*.

The first issue announced that the journal's purpose was to investigate honestly the "declension" of religion and to "point the way of reformation." A later restatement said: "To destroy sectarianism, and sectarian props, creeds and names . . . to promote love, peace and unity among Christians . . . to free the Bible from the rubbish of human tradition . . . these shall be the polar star to which our attention and exertion shall be chiefly directed." In an 1835 issue Stone avowed, "For thirty-two years of my ministry I have kept in view the unity of Christians as my polar star."

The *Christian Messenger* was characterized by several theological emphases. A pervasive theme was liberty, the freedom to read and interpret Scripture for oneself without mediation of clergy or creed. Stone referred to the break with Presbyterianism as "the declaration of our independence."

Closely related was the persistent theme of Christian unity. Unlike the modern ecumenical movement, Stone viewed all denominational structures as equally wrong and constituting "Babylon" and "a wilderness of confusion." He regularly called for people to abandon "Babylon" and to unite on the New Testament alone. By reading the Scriptures for oneself and acting independently on personal conviction of truth, "all would flow together in one body." Unity was not mere doctrinal conformity. "The Scriptures will never keep together in union and fellowship members not in the spirit of the Scriptures, which is love, peace, unity, forbearance, and cheerful obedience. This is the spirit of the great Head of the body."

The *Messenger* was a significant tool in the promulgation of the union of Stone and Campbell followers in 1831-32 through the joint editorship of Stone and John T. Johnson (from the Campbell side) from 1832 to 1834. The co-editors promoted the union with glowing reports of the "progress and triumph of truth."

In the *Messenger*'s pages Stone repeatedly defended his unorthodox doctrines of the Trinity and the atonement. He argued against the orthodox doctrine of the Trinity upon rational grounds, but his final appeal was to Scripture. "It is not revealed, and therefore not necessary for us to know." He believed an Arian-like doctrine that Jesus was the firstborn of God, created before time and the world, and that he had all the fullness of the godhead in himself. The Holy Spirit was the "power and energy of God, and never a third person in deity."

Substitutionary atonement was contrary to reason, Scripture, and civil law. Christ did not "purchase" mankind's salvation; he died to open the way to salvation. His death was an expression of the depth of God's love for sinners and a lesson in the type of obedience and holiness required of Christians. Stone corresponded with Alexander Campbell on the Trinity in 1827 in the *Christian Baptist* and *Christian Messenger,* with Thomas Campbell on the atonement in the *Messenger* in 1833, and with Alexander Campbell on the atonement in the *Messenger* and *Millennial Harbinger* during 1840-41.

A frequent topic was the appeal to Christians to manumit their slaves and deliver them to the American Colonization Society. A probable reason for Stone's move to Jacksonville, Illinois, in 1834 was his strong desire to emancipate the seven slaves bequeathed to his wife and her children forever by her mother. Since he could not emancipate them, he would emancipate himself and his family from them by moving to a free state.

Another frequent theme of the *Messenger* was Stone's radical notion of separation from the world and its values — the consciousness that Christians have no abiding place here but "are as strangers and pilgrims seeking a better country." Sometimes this consciousness accompanied an explicitly premillennial belief. "Jesus Christ will shortly put them [human governments] all down, and reign with his Saints on earth a thousand years. . . . Then shall all man made laws and governments be burnt up forever." Toward the end of his life he admonished his readers to have nothing to do with politics or civil government aside from paying taxes and obeying civil laws that were not in conflict with the law of Christ.

See also *Christian Baptist, The;* Creath, Jacob, Jr.; Johnson, John T.; *Millennial Harbinger, The;* Stone, Barton Warren

BIBLIOGRAPHY Ruth E. Browning, *Name Index to the Christian Messenger,* http//www.mun.ca/rels/restmov/texts/resources/index.html • Barry A. Jones and Charles C. Dorsey, eds., *An Index to the Christian Messenger* (1984) • R. L. Roberts, *Subject Index to the Christian Messenger* (1978) (in Vol. 14 of the Star Bible Publications 1978 reprint edition) • Charles Crossfield Ware, *Barton Warren Stone: Pathfinder of Christian Union* (1932) • William G. West, *Barton Warren Stone: Early American Advocate of Christian Unity* (1954) • D. Newell Williams, *Barton Stone: A Spiritual Biography* (2000).

CARL W. CHEATHAM

Christian Missionary Fellowship

Missionary organization affiliated with the Christians Churches/Churches of Christ.

Christian Missionary Fellowship (CMF) was born in the minds of a small group of theological centrists who saw it as an alternative to both the United Christian Missionary Society's (UCMS) institutionalized approach to missions and the independent, direct support model that developed in opposition to the UCMS among conservative Disciples churches. Two key CMF founders were O. D. Johnson, a minister and former missionary to India, and Dean E. Walker, a scholar and academic administrator.

CMF was incorporated on February 28, 1949, in Junction City, Kansas, "to evangelize the non-Christian people of the world in the order, manner, and fashion of a missionary society and toward this purpose to recruit and send forth missionaries." The organization's by-laws identify "members" of CMF as contributors to the Fellowship and missionary recruits of the Fellowship. Members of the board of directors are elected by this aggregate membership to serve a three-year term. They manage the Fellowship and employ a general director who oversees and coordinates the activities of CMF. The CMF headquarters are located in Indianapolis, Indiana.

From its early years, CMF has sought cooperation and support from churches while preserving the churches' freedom in selecting a missionary or mis-

Effie and Ray Giles (seated left and center) were among the earliest missionaries of Christian Missionary Fellowship in Ethiopia in the 1960s and again in the 1990s after the fall of Ethiopia's Marxist regime. Intermittently in the 1980s, the couple ministered in famine relief efforts in that same country. Courtesy of the Christian Missionary Fellowship

sion strategy. CMF missionaries are closely linked and responsive to their senders, maintaining relationships with their supporting churches. On the field they work in semi-autonomous teams that are accountable to the mission. The active involvement of the board of directors, the personal investment of the missionaries, administrative effectiveness in the home office in Indianapolis, and mission education in supporting congregations have all been vital to CMF's continuing international ministry.

CMF missionaries entered India and Japan in the early years and remain at work in Brazil, Ethiopia, Indonesia, Kenya, Mexico, Tanzania, England, Thailand, Vietnam, Ivory Coast, China, and Chile. Influenced by missiologist Donald McGavran's thinking, CMF has sought to establish church planting movements and train indigenous leaders. It has also devoted itself to careful study of the challenges of crosscultural communication and ministry.

In recent years, CMF has undertaken bivocational work in locations traditionally closed to missions, and has begun campus ministries overseas, intercultural ministries in the United States, work among the urban poor, and focused church planting.

See also Africa, Missions in — Christian Churches/Churches of Christ; Asia, Missions in; Latin America and Caribbean, Missions in; McGavran, Donald A.; Missions, Missiology NAOMI D. KOUNS

Christian Missionary Society

Abolitionist missionary society established in Indianapolis in 1859 to protest the American Christian Missionary Society's (ACMS) perceived neutral position toward slavery.

The result of long-standing tensions between pro- and anti-slavery groups in the Stone-Campbell Movement, the society's formation was sparked by the ACMS's 1858 denial of a request for support as a missionary in Kansas by militant abolitionist preacher Pardee Butler (1816-1888). Though himself antislavery, ACMS President Isaac Errett (1820-1888) informed Butler that the society would not fund his work if he preached abolitionism. Butler denounced the ACMS for siding "with the rich and powerful against the poor and oppressed."

John Boggs (1810-1897), editor of the abolitionist *Gospel Luminary* (formerly *Northwestern Christian Magazine*), along with Indianapolis lawyer Ovid Butler (1801-1881) called for a Northwestern Christian Convention of antislavery advocates in September 1859. The meeting took place November 1 at the Central Christian Church in Indianapolis. The convention chartered the "North Western" Christian Missionary Society (CMS) for all who could no longer support the ACMS for ignoring "the question of American slavery in its moral character and aspects."

The society modestly funded Pardee Butler and sponsored a mission in Minnesota in 1860-61. When the Civil War broke out, leaders of the Christian Missionary Society expected the ACMS to declare itself to be clearly anti-slavery. The unofficial 1861 resolution by which members of the ACMS declared their loyalty to the Union was not sufficient for the CMS. However, when the older body passed a strong formal resolution denouncing Southerners as armed traitors in its 1863 meeting, the Christian Missionary Society voted to disband and work through the ACMS.

Though able to do relatively little in its four-year history, the CMS reflected the Stone-Campbell Movement's deep sectional divisions, divisions that existed in every American religious body as a result of national sectionalization and Civil War.

See also American Christian Missionary Society; Butler, Ovid; Butler, Pardee; Errett, Isaac

BIBLIOGRAPHY Mrs. Rosetta Butler Hastings, *Personal Recollections of Pardee Butler, With Reminiscences* (1889) • Eileen Gordon Vandergrift, "The Christian Missionary Society: A Study in the Influence of Slavery on the Disciples of Christ" (M.A. thesis, Butler University, 1945).

DOUGLAS A. FOSTER

Christian Restoration Association

Conservative evangelistic organization influential during the early division between Christian Churches/Churches of Christ and the Christian Church (Disciples of Christ).

The Christian Restoration Association (CRA) began with the bequest of Sidney Clarke, a Cincinnati businessman, effective upon his wife's death (1919), that his estate be used to establish new churches. With the Richmond Street Christian Church of Cincinnati administering the estate, thirty congregations were started and about 200 others strengthened by 1921. To permit contributions, the Clarke Fund was separately incorporated in 1922, with a new periodical, *Facts.* The Fund became the Christian Restoration Association (1925) and its periodical *The Restoration Herald.* James DeForest Murch became its first editor and took the title of president of the CRA. Sixteen independent agencies were already identified with it.

Cincinnati Bible Seminary's founding (1924) was an outgrowth; the CRA's head was *ex officio* the school's president until the two entities had become fully separate in 1928. Harvey Bream, Jr., later led both organizations at different times. Murch's presidency (1925-33) brought an emphasis on foreign missions, with the CRA becoming a clearinghouse to coordinate support for "independent" missionaries — Leslie Wolfe, J. Russell Morse, Enrique Westrup — who had separated from the United Christian Missionary Society. Afterward, the "president" of the CRA became "executive director," and domestic concerns began to predominate. Relations with Disciples of Christ agencies (especially the United Christian Missionary Society) in the mid-twentieth century continued to deteriorate, and the CRA intervened to help congregations that desired to distance themselves from what conservatives saw as an institutional leviathan. Robert Elmore (editor of *The Restoration Herald,* 1938-60) was sued unsuccessfully (1952-53) for libel. Attorney Luther Burrus coordinated responses for congregations under suit from Disciples agencies. Overall, the CRA postured itself as a defender of the "restoration" principle against liberalism and denominationalism, and strongly supported the ultimate separation of the "independent" Christian Churches/Churches of Christ from the (restructured) Christian Church (Disciples of Christ).

Continuing CRA operations include support of evangelists, publishing (tracts, booklets, and *The Restoration Herald*), a correspondence school (Christian Bible Institute), leadership training, lending to congregations ("Recycled Riches"), camps, and promotion of missions.

See also Committee of 1000; Elmore, Robert Emmett; Fundamentalism; Murch, James DeForest; *Restoration Herald, The; Touchstone, The*

BIBLIOGRAPHY Stephen J. Corey, *Fifty Years of Attack and Controversy: The Consequences Among Disciples of Christ* (1953) • Robert H. Craycraft, Jr., "*The Restoration Herald:* An Historical Analysis" (unpublished M.Div. thesis, Cincinnati Bible Seminary, 1984) • David Filbeck, *The First Fifty Years: A Brief History of the Direct-Support Missionary Movement* (1980)• H. Lee Mason, *A Brief History of the Christian Restoration Association* (1995). C. J. DULL

Christian Service Camp Movement

See Camps

Christian Standard

The *Christian Standard,* a weekly journal that played a major role in the history of Disciples of Christ and Christian Churches, was launched in 1866. At the time of its inaugural, the devastating Civil War had recently ended and Alexander Campbell, editor of the influential *Millennial Harbinger,* lay on his deathbed. A new era was dawning for the nation, and also for the Stone-Campbell Movement. New opportunities called for a new kind of journalism, a weekly publication that had appeal to a wider readership. Five men met in December 1865 in the home of T. W. Phillips, Sr., in Newcastle, Pennsylvania, to launch a journal that would carry news from the churches and articles of interest in a broader range of subjects than had been the case hitherto. Incorporators of the new company were W. S. Streator, W. J. Ford, J. P. Robinson, T. W. Phillips, C. M. Phillips, G. W. M. Yost, James A. Garfield, and Isaac Errett. Errett was named editor of the new journal, which was called *Christian Standard.*

The journal was first published in Cleveland, Ohio. Within two years, it amassed such indebtedness that the incorporators were happy to turn the assets over to Isaac Errett, if he would be willing to assume the debt. To survive, Errett accepted the position of president of Alliance College in Ohio, which he held until 1869. He then accepted the offer of R. W. Carroll to underwrite the publication of the journal if Errett would move it to Cincinnati. Soon, circulation improved to the point that Errett could liquidate the debt, and he became the sole owner of the new Standard Publishing Company. Errett continued as editor of *Christian Standard* until his death in 1888. The *Christian Standard* quickly became a vigorous champion of the missionary cause among Disciples, and Errett himself served as the first president of the Foreign Christian Missionary Society, organized in 1875.

The *Christian Standard* was launched during a troublesome period in the saga of the Stone-Campbell Movement. North-South postwar tensions were at their peak, and Isaac Errett had been chairman of a session of the Missionary Society in 1863 when a pro-North resolution was adopted. Consequently, he was disliked in the South, an attitude that was augmented by Errett's toleration of the introduction of musical instruments in some of the churches in the North, an innovation condemned in the South. Thus, many congregations regarded the *Christian Standard*

S. S. Lappin (left) served as editor of the *Christian Standard* from 1909 to 1917. He and P. H. Welshimer, minister of First Christian Church, Canton, Ohio, from 1902 to 1957, provided leadership for conservatives who increasingly resisted theological liberalism in the International Convention.
Courtesy of Johnson Bible College Photo Archive

as a Northern journal and opted to read the *Gospel Advocate,* a rival journal published in Nashville, Tennessee. This journalistic polarization thus developed hand in hand with ideological tensions.

The beginning of the twentieth century saw a growing trend toward liberalism and modernism among the Disciples of Christ, of increasing concern to conservative churches. The *Christian Standard* devoted its resources to combating liberalism, signaled by the inclusion of a regular column on "Biblical Criticism" by the conservative scholar J. W. McGarvey from 1893 to 1904. While never opting for the fundamentalist alternative, the successive editors consistently maintained a conservative posture. After Errett's death, his son Russell inherited the publishing company. Fiercely loyal to his father's convictions, Russell Errett became troubled over developments within the board of managers of the United Christian Missionary Society (UCMS) in 1920, particularly over policies adopted with reference to open membership.

During the 1920s, the *Christian Standard* became the major voice of opposition to the UCMS, and it provided leadership to those churches that coalesced after 1927 in the North American Christian Convention. The editor at this time was Edwin Errett, a grandnephew of Isaac Errett. Edwin Errett's policy was to support all of the Disciple agencies except the missionary society. The *Christian Standard* became an early advocate of independent missions but not a proponent of schism within the ranks of the Movement. Errett staunchly maintained that the fellowship of the Disciples of Christ was one, but he insisted that congregations should have freedom within that unity to choose which mission method they preferred. Thus, under Errett's editorship, reports and promotion of all of the agencies associated with the organized activity of Disciples appeared in the pages of *Christian Standard,* except for the UCMS.

Eventually there arose a growing sentiment among some of the younger leaders of conservative Disciples churches to disavow all agencies and associations related to Disciples of Christ in Indianapolis. This gained expression in the formation of a Committee on Action in 1943, which aimed to turn the *Christian Standard* toward a more strident policy. The chairman of the committee was Burris Butler, who succeeded as editor of the journal following the sudden death of Edwin Errett in 1944. Willard H. Mohorter, secretary of Standard Publishing Company, announced the policy change on December 4, 1943. *Christian Standard* issued a Call for Enlistment and followed with an aggressive program called "Stand Up and Be Counted," which urged ministers and congregations to register opposition to all agencies associated with the International Convention of Disciples of Christ. The journal began publishing an "Honor Roll of the Faithful" in 1947. Thus erupted a period of hostility that, along with other developments within the Disciples of Christ, resulted in outright schism within a decade.

In the latter half of the twentieth century, the *Christian Standard* confined its interest to the Christian Churches/Churches of Christ. It remains the major journal of this fellowship, providing communication and guidance to the more than 5,000 congregations that have no organizational connection other than the (non-delegate) North American Christian Convention. The *Christian Standard* thus fills a definite need for cohesion and networking among Christian Churches/Churches of Christ.

The leadership role of editors and journals has been very prominent in the Stone-Campbell Movement. In recent decades this leadership has suffered relative decline, due largely to the rise of other media resources and the increasing secularization of the culture. Still, the *Christian Standard* has no journalistic rival among Christian Churches/Churches of Christ.

See also Butler, Burris; Christian Churches/Churches of Christ; Errett, Isaac; Errett, Edwin Reeder; Journalism; *Lookout, The; Restoration Herald, The;* Standard Publishing Company; *Touchstone, The*

BIBLIOGRAPHY Brian P. Clark, "An Analysis of the Organizing Functions of the *Christian Standard* in the Restoration Movement Christian Churches/Churches of Christ" (unpublished M.A. thesis, Wheaton College, 1998) • Richard Hughes, Howard Short, and Henry E. Webb, *The Power of the Press: Studies of the "Gospel Advocate," the "Christian Standard," and the "Christian-Evangelist"* (1987) • G. Mark Sloneker, *"You Can't Do That!" The Life and Labors of Burris Butler: An Account of a Ministry at "Christian Standard" and with Standard Publishing Company* (1995).

HENRY E. WEBB

Christian System, The

Book authored by Alexander Campbell, the full title of which is *The Christian System, in Reference to the Union of Christians, and a Restoration of Primitive Christianity, as Plead in the Current Reformation.*

The volume was published in 1839 by Forrester & Campbell of Pittsburgh. *The Christian System* was actually the second edition of an 1835 work that appeared with the words *Christianity Restored* on the spine, a title supplied by the publisher, not Campbell, and published with the full name *A Connected View of the Principles and Rules by Which the Living Oracles May Be Intelligibly and Certainly Interpreted.* The book contained original essays as well as pieces reprinted from extras in the *Millennial Harbinger.*

Christianity Restored outlined hermeneutical principles that would enable Christians to unite on some of the basic constitutive elements of primitive Christianity. The book was divided into three sections: (1) Principles of Interpretation; (2) Foundations of Christian Union; and (3) Elements of Original Christianity, including essays titled "Kingdom of Heaven," "Remission of Sins," "Breaking the Loaf," "Dialogue on the Holy Spirit," and "Concluding Address to the Citizens of the Kingdom." It also contained two essays that were omitted from the 1839 *Christian System.* "Principles and Rules" explained the historical-critical method for interpreting Scripture. *The Christian System* of 1839 replaced the hermeneutical essay with a new one titled "The Christian System." The "Dialogue on the Holy Spirit," which originally appeared as a series in the *Millennial Harbinger,* was excluded because Thomas Campbell disapproved of its speculative language. In its place Campbell added several essays on "Church Order."

Christianity Restored and *The Christian System* served as the first systematic theology of the young movement, intended to deflect misrepresentations and misconceptions by opponents. The second, which was widely reprinted and is available in dozens of editions, was foundational to the theology of the Stone-Campbell Movement. It grounded and shaped the theological thought of many of the Movement's ministers and teachers.

See also Campbell, Alexander; *Millennial Harbinger, The*

JOHN MARK HICKS

Christian Theological Seminary

Related to the Christian Church (Disciples of Christ).

This graduate theological school was founded in Indianapolis, Indiana, in 1925 as the College of Religion of Butler University through the close cooperation of Frederick D. Kershner, a widely known educator; William G. Irwin, a prominent businessperson and leader of the Christian Churches in Indiana; and Hilton U. Brown, president of Butler University. Kershner's intention was that this institution would be the "central training school for the Disciples of Christ," and he proposed that a national endowment — the Christian Foundation — be established to fund the program. Under Kershner's leadership, a strong, conservative faculty was called, including Dean E. Walker and T. W. Nakarai. An interdenominational student body was enlisted, the theological journal *Shane Quarterly* was established, and a building was erected on the Butler campus. The seminary's special collection of books and periodicals related to the Restoration Movement was begun.

Shortly before Irwin died, he and three other trustees of the College of Religion (Hugh T. Miller, Nettie Miller, and Edwin Errett) nominated Orman Leroy Shelton, a pastor in Kansas City, to succeed Kershner as dean. During Shelton's administration (1944-59), the institution came to be known as the School of Religion, Butler University, and it moved into the center of the "cooperative" life and work of the Disciples of Christ. William Robinson, longtime leader of British Churches of Christ, succeeded Kershner as professor of Christian doctrine. Following World War II, the seminary and Butler University faced the need to expand their campuses. With the leadership of trustee J. Irwin Miller, the seminary became a separate corporation in 1958, taking the name Christian Theological Seminary, and relocated to a site a short distance from Butler University. The two institutions established a pattern of academic cooperation.

During the presidency of Beauford A. Norris (1959-74), he and Dean Ronald E. Osborn led the reconstituted seminary as it revised its academic program in response to the significant changes in American life and religion. It developed a distinctive campus, designed by architect Edward Larrabee Barnes, and began its collection of art by major contemporary artists. During these years, Christian Theological Seminary became a prominent mainstream Protestant seminary. Among its special emphases during the 1960s and the 1970s were religious broadcasting, drama, pastoral care and counseling, ecumenism, and process theology. The seminary's journal was renamed *Encounter,* and, under the long-term editorship of Osborn and later of Clark M. Williamson, the scope of the journal was broadened.

During the presidencies of Thomas J. Liggett (1974-86) and Richard D. N. Dickinson, Jr. (1986-97), and with academic leadership by deans Joe R. Jones and D. Newell Williams, Christian Theological Seminary continued to develop along the lines already established. Significant new financial resources were developed, the campus was completed, and the academic program was expanded. Among the new developments in its academic program were studies in Jewish and Christian relationships, the contributions of theologians from the Third World, and Christianity and the arts. The completion of Sweeney Chapel in 1987, through gifts from Clementine Miller Tangeman and others, enlarged the possibilities for the seminary's offerings in church music and worship. The presidency of Edward L. Wheeler began in 1997. Clark M. Williamson was appointed dean in 1998, followed by Carolyn Higginbotham in 2002.

The most important degree program throughout the seminary's history has been the three-year program that most churches recommend as standard preparation for ordination. Until the mid-twentieth century, this degree was titled Bachelor of Divinity (B.D.), but later came to be called the Master of Divinity (M.Div.). The Seminary has also offered a more specialized graduate degree, which has been called the Master of Theology (M.Th.) or the Master of Sacred Theology (S.T.M.). Since the mid-1970s, the seminary has offered a professional doctorate, the Doctor of Ministry (D.Min.). It has also offered degrees in Christian education, communications, pastoral counseling, and church music.

In the words of President Emeritus Thomas J. Liggett, this seminary "has understood its mission to be the preparation of leaders for service in the church and the world. Education for ministry has been understood not as an 'end in itself,' but as a means to the greater end of a more faithful church and a world of increasing justice and peace."

BIBLIOGRAPHY Keith Watkins, *Christian Theological Seminary, Indianapolis: A History of Education for Ministry* (2001).

KEITH WATKINS

Christian Unity

See Unity, Christian

Christian Woman's Benevolent Association

The Christian Woman's Benevolent Association (CWBA) was begun in 1911 as the result of a disagreement about the administration of the National Benevolent Association (NBA). The leader of this group was a woman named Fannie Shedd Ayars. She had been a prominent leader in the beginnings of the NBA and was known for her tireless efforts on behalf of the poor and defenseless. Ayars was raised in a staunch Presbyterian home and had been the only one in her family to join the Stone-Campbell Movement. One explanation for the split was that the NBA had adopted a policy that would essentially eliminate women from management positions of the various benevolent institutions.

The CWBA was based in St. Louis and received most of its funding from more conservative Disciples of Christ, even gaining workers from the Cincinnati Bible Seminary. The CWBA maintained oversight of three institutions: Mothers' and Babes' Home (organized in 1899), Christian Old People's Home (organized in 1911), and Christian Hospital (organized in 1903). When Ayars died in 1936, many believed that the CWBA would not survive, but it did. Letha B. Shepherd followed her as president, and the boards of the three institutions were reorganized to work better in unison. In 1952 the CWBA was incorporated to handle better the legal and financial affairs of the three institutions. It continues to be a vital arm of the Christian Churches/Churches of Christ.

See also Christian Churches/Churches of Christ; National Benevolent Association of the Christian Church (Disciples of Christ)

BIBLIOGRAPHY *Christian Standard* various issues (esp. May 1912; Aug. 1936; May 1938; Feb. 1950; Feb. 1952).

LISA W. DAVISON

Christian Woman's Board of Missions

The Christian Woman's Board of Missions (CWBM) was founded October 21, 1874, during a meeting of the American Christian Missionary Society (ACMS) at Richmond Street Christian Church in Cincinnati. Its purpose was to share the gospel message and improve the lives of women and children in the United States and abroad. Although CWBM was one of thirty-three denominational missionary societies established during a thirty-year period beginning in 1860, it was the first to serve both foreign and domestic missions, to employ both men and women, and to be managed entirely by women.

CWBM was a grassroots organization, made up of a large number of local church societies, supported with many small contributions, and committed to educating women and children about mission concerns. Many CWBM members were also active in other nineteenth-century reform efforts, principally suffrage and temperance, but CWBM was the "grand passion" in the lives of many nineteenth- and twentieth-century Christian Church women who devoted their spiritual, intellectual, and financial resources to its work.

CWBM's founder, Carolyn Neville Pearre (1831-1910), became aware of mission needs at home and abroad and saw an untapped potential for response in Christian Church women. She asked Thomas Munnell (1823-1898), then secretary of the ACMS, to allow women from local missionary societies to meet together and discuss formation of a churchwide board. Munnell replied, "This is a flame of the Lord's kindling and no man can extinguish it." Isaac Errett, editor of the *Christian Standard,* J. H. Garrison, editor of *The Christian-Evangelist,* and Mrs. M. M. B. Goodwin (d. 1885), editor of *The Christian Monitor,* offered vital editorial support and publicity during the organization's early years. CWBM's first officers were Maria Butler Jameson (d. 1911), president; Nannie Ledgerwood Burgess (1836-1902), treasurer; Sarah Wallace, recording secretary; and Caroline Neville Pearre, corresponding secretary.

In 1876 CWBM established its first mission post in Jamaica and sent out its first missionaries, Dr. and Mrs. W. H. Williams. Jennie Laughlin, the first single woman missionary, followed in 1878. CWBM's major efforts, however, were in India, beginning in 1881, and included establishing schools, orphanages, hospitals, churches, and evangelizing in *zenanas* (the small part of the household to which women and children were restricted). Maria Graybiel, Ada Boyd, Mary Kingsbury, and Laura Kinsey were the first missionaries to India. CWBM also supported work in Mexico, Puerto Rico, Argentina, and Japan.

In the United States, CWBM served the mountain schools of Appalachia, established Bible Chairs in five universities, developed outreach programs for Asians living in California, built educational opportunities for African Americans, and did settlement work among the urban poor. In both the United States and abroad, CWBM missionaries were particularly effective working with women and children in areas where it would be awkward or impossible for men to go.

At the end of the nineteenth century, many women still had little access to educational opportunities. *Missionary Tidings,* published by CWBM beginning in 1883, contained letters from missionaries, financial appeals, and news of the organization and provided women with home and church study materials. The College of Missions, established by CWBM in 1910 in Indianapolis, gave women missionaries needed theological and practical training. Women whose opportunities were limited in the United States studied there, then responded to their call to preach, evangelize, teach, or become physicians through missionary service.

Involving children in mission work was an important CWBM goal. Nancy Burns Atkinson established the first children's missionary society in Wabash, Indiana, in 1874, and Charlotte McGrew King was the first secretary of the CWBM Young People's Department. Pennies collected from children helped establish a church in Japan and orphanages in India. CWBM also published mission magazines for children — *Little Builders at Work, Junior Builders,* and *King's Builders.* In the last year of CWBM's existence, 30,000 child members in more than 120 children's societies had raised $500,000 for mission work.

Fundraising was vital to the ongoing work of CWBM. Elmira Dickinson, a faculty member at Eureka College and its first woman trustee, was motivated in her effective CWBM fundraising by her own unrealized desire to become a missionary. Rosetta Butler Hastings raised mission money from poor rural farm wives and mothers in the West. Her initial request was for 15¢ per month per member.

Although there were separate black and white CWBM organizations, they did work cooperatively. Sarah Lue Bostick (1868-1948) organized CWBM chapters among African American churches, the first in Pea Ridge, Arkansas, in 1896. Other prominent African American CWBM leaders were Rosa Brown Bracy, Rosa V. Brown, Mary L. Mead, Eliza Graves, and Mrs. J. B. Parsons. Contributions from African American auxiliaries supported such efforts as the endowment of the Bible Chair at the University of Michigan and the work of Jacob Kenoly (1876-1911), an African American missionary in Liberia. CWBM also took over the management of the Southern Christian Institute in 1900 and established Jarvis Christian Institute (later Jarvis Christian College). By the turn of the century, African Americans were holding a separate convention, the National CWBM, which later evolved into the National Christian Missionary Convention.

There were also CWBM societies in Canada, the first organized by Carrie Angle in Wainfleet, Ontario, in 1884. One of many notable missionaries was Dr. Susie Carson Rijnhart-Moyes, the first Canadian woman to earn first-class honors in medicine, who served with her husband in Tibet. In 1913 the Canadian CWBM and the United States CWBM merged.

On October 20, 1919, after five years of study, CWBM joined with several other groups to form the

United Christian Missionary Society. CWBM brought the bulk of the financial resources and membership into the new organization and insisted that the new organization have equal numbers of men and women on its committees.

During its forty-five years, CWBM established local mission societies in 43 states, enrolled over 100,000 members, contributed over $7 million to mission work, and supported mission fields in 10 countries, with 974 missionaries serving 68 churches, 284 schools, and 9 hospitals.

See also American Christian Missionary Society; College of Missions; Jarvis Christian College; *Missionary Tidings;* Munnell, Thomas; National Christian Missionary Convention; Pearre, Caroline Neville; Southern Christian Institute; United Christian Missionary Society

BIBLIOGRAPHY *Christian Woman's Board of Missions: United Christian Missionary Society Golden Jubilee, 1874-1924* (1924) • Elmira J. Dickenson, *Historical Sketch of the Christian Woman's Board of Missions* (c. 1911) • Douglas A. Foster, "Feminism vs. Feminization: The Case of the Christian Woman's Board of Missions," *Discipliana* 64:1 (2004): 17-30 • Ida Withers Harrison, *History of the Christian Woman's Board of Missions* (1920) • Ian McCrae, Paul Diebold, and Julia Fangmeier, *Mission Accomplished: The Missions Building, Its History and Its People* (1995).

DEBRA B. HULL

Christian Women's Fellowship

Women's organization of the Christian Church (Disciples of Christ). Since 1949, Disciples of Christ women have organized and maintained congregational, regional, and world groups called Christian Women's Fellowship, commonly referred to as CWF.

Earlier, organized women's work among Disciples of Christ had its roots in the Christian Woman's Board of Missions (CWBM), formed in 1874. The CWBM was unique in that it was organized and managed entirely by women, devised its own methods of raising funds, and developed a network of communication and support among state auxiliaries, while creating and maintaining areas of missionary work around the world, employing both women and men.

In 1949, as a result of a ten-day consultation held at Turkey Run State Park, Indiana, the CWF was created with this purpose: "To develop all women in Christian living and Christian service." In 1973 an expanded purpose statement was adopted: "To provide opportunities for spiritual growth, enrichment, education and creative ministries to enable women to develop a sense of personal responsibility for the whole mission of the church of Jesus Christ."

Women from Canada and the United States came together at the International Convention in 1953, where they launched the International Christian Women's Fellowship (ICWF). Officers were elected and a Commission was formed that included state representatives and a new ICWF Advisory Council; it planned programs and organizational materials for local CWFs. In 1955 women from twenty countries met in Toronto, Canada, to finalize and approve plans for the World CWF. On the first day of the Jubilee Assembly of the World Convention of Churches of Christ, 1,475 women heard about "a channel by which all . . . may be joined in fellowship and through which by prayer, study, and service they may make a contribution to the extension of the kingdom of God." A session for women is held at each World Convention.

Little more than a decade later, in 1968, when there were 4,070 local CWFs with 214,912 members and annual giving of $2,342,148, a Consultation for Disciples Women was held. The Consultation set future directions for Disciples women and the CWF that reflected the current women's movement in society. In 1973 the Department of Christian Women's Fellowship became the Department of Church Women. In response to an ICWF resolution adopted by the 1973 General Assembly, the number of women on general, regional, and local church and agency boards increased. Many congregations established elderships and diaconates with women and men serving together.

Beginning in 1975, the ICWF broadened its programs to include special seminars that brought together all Disciples women, including the growing number of women ministers. Among these seminars were assertiveness training with a biblical foundation, money management workshops, clergywomen-laywomen conversations, and cross-cultural events. Multicultural leadership became more visible: the ICWF elected an African American woman as president and later an Asian woman as vice president; Hispanic women established a CWF network. Internationally focused, the "Woman to Woman Worldwide" program began in 1987 to send CWF leaders to countries of current mission study to make one-to-one connections with the women there, also bringing women from other countries to visit locally in the United States.

In response to an Action Research Project report, the ICWF Cabinet and ICWF Executive Committee were established in 1983 to provide wider representation in decision making and to clarify responsibilities for and within the CWF.

While the CWF continued to be a major contributor to Basic Mission Finance of the Christian Church (Disciples of Christ), a steady decline in financial giving alarmed CWF leaders. At the 1986 Quadrennial, CWFs pledged to increase their giving annually for five years, which in 1989 reached $3,225,360.

When the restructure of the Division of Homeland Ministries threatened to end a cohesive staff for women, CWF women across North America wrote letters of protest negotiating for an Office of Disciples Women.

In 1999 a CWF Survey indicated that flexibility was of paramount importance and that the actions of churchwomen needed to be incorporated and recognized within the CWF. In response to this finding, in 2002 a logo was introduced that identifies the CWF as the organization for Disciples women within the wider term "Women's Ministries–Disciples of Christ."

BIBLIOGRAPHY Fran Craddock, Martha Faw, and Nancy Heimer, *In the Fullness of Time: A History of Women in the Christian Church (Disciples of Christ)* (1999) • Caroline Pearre, "Our Beginning," *Missionary Tidings* (August 1899).

FRAN CRADDOCK, MARTHA FAW, *and* NANCY HEIMER

Christian Youth Fellowship

Name for high-school-age youth groups in the Christian Church (Disciples of Christ).

The Christian Youth Fellowship (CYF) developed out of the work of the Division of Christian Education in ministering to Disciples young people and the programming known as the Young People's Society of Christian Endeavor (or simply "Christian Endeavor"), which began in 1881. Beginning in 1926 in Memphis, Tennessee, the United Christian Missionary Society (UCMS) held youth conventions in conjunction with the International Convention of the Disciples of Christ as a result of the work of Cynthia Pearl Maus. At the 1938 International Convention, the Christian Youth Fellowship was proposed and adopted as the new, more far-reaching youth program. Under the leadership of Myron T. Hopper (1903-1960), CYF was developed to provide leadership training for Disciples young people.

The International CYF Commission, organized at Lakeside, Ohio, in 1944, was attended by youth and adults representing Disciples churches throughout the United States and Canada. It was a racially inclusive event that took place annually to plan the events and themes of youth ministry for Disciples youth programming. Its popularity was immediate, and by 1960 there were thirty-five state/regional CYF commissions active throughout the United States and Canada. One of the primary modes of youth ministry was the summer camp and conference system. Many of the persons serving in ministry at present received their call to ordained church service through these events. Overall, the church has benefited from the formative role of CYF in raising up leaders for ministry.

Among conservative Disciples churches that eventually became Christian Churches/Churches of Christ, some congregations' teenage youth groups retained the "CYF" title, though increasingly the disaffiliation from the Christian Church (Disciples of Christ) led most of those churches to discontinue identification with the historic organization.

See also Camps — Christian Church (Disciples of Christ); Young People's Society of Christian Endeavor; Youth Groups, Youth Ministry

LISA W. DAVISON

Christmount Christian Assembly

National conference center for the Christian Church (Disciples of Christ).

Founded in 1948, Christmount is one of several denominational conference centers located near the Blue Ridge Mountains in western North Carolina. First known as Southeastern Christian Assembly, the 1947 North Carolina Christian Missionary Convention meeting in Asheville, North Carolina, authorized the purchase of the 543-acre Spanish Castle Estate, formerly owned by noted architect Rafael Guastavino (1842-1908). The 1949 Centennial Convention of the Christian Churches held in Cincinnati, Ohio, accepted the Assembly as an agency of the International Convention of Christian Churches.

The name was changed to Christmount Christian Assembly in 1953 in a "$1,000 Lot for New Name" contest led by Dr. Gaines M. Cook, executive secretary of the 1953 International Convention of Disciples of Christ held in Portland, Oregon. Cook also served as executive director of the Assembly from 1968 to 1976.

The guest house, dining hall, cabins, campsites, trails, playgrounds, gardens, and worship areas provide areas for respite as well as for educational and outdoor ministries. Visitors enjoy the moderate climate, clear spring water, and extravaganza of native flowering trees and wildflowers, such as mountain laurel, rhododendrons, spring trillium, and rare "lady slippers," as well as stunning fall color and winter snow. Disciples clergy originally built many of the private homes on the Christmount grounds. Eight acres of the original Guastavino property were placed on the National Register of Historic Places in 1989.

Christmount Christian Assembly reports to the General Assembly of the Christian Church (Disciples of Christ) through Homeland Ministries as a recognized organization.

Executive directors include Dr. Howard S. Hilley (1949-59), the Rev. Charles L. Strong (1959-60), Dr. Gaines M. Cook (1968-76), the Rev. Melba Banks (1977-94), the Rev. Jerald E. Fuqua (1996-97), and Michael Murphy (1998-present).

BIBLIOGRAPHY Vicky Fuqua, ed., *For Days That Count* (1997).

VICKY FUQUA

Christology

Christology seeks to answer two classic questions: Who is Jesus Christ? and How are his life and work salvific for humanity? The Stone-Campbell Movement has from the beginning sought to base its theology on Scripture and has been averse to making postbiblical creedal statements normative tests of fellowship. Believing that the New Testament is sufficiently clear on this matter, the Movement has had a strong Christocentric focus, exemplified in the slogan "no creed but Christ." Following the lead of Alexander Campbell, Stone-Campbell churches have required for membership the simple confession of Peter: "Jesus is the Christ, the Son of the living God" (Matt. 16:16). Allowing considerable breadth of opinion as to the nature of Christ, this affirmation allowed for union between theological voices as diverse as Alexander Campbell and Barton Stone, and has led to significant christological diversity among the theological descendants of these two founding figures.

Though reluctant to use the term "Trinity" for God, Thomas and Alexander Campbell were Trinitarians. For Alexander Campbell, though the Godhead is "essentially and necessarily singular, it is certainly plural in its personal manifestations. Hence we have the Father, Son, and Holy Spirit equally divine, though personally distinct from each other." Campbell disputed the Nicene language of the Son being "eternally begotten" of the Father, but affirmed an eternal "uncreated" relation between God and his Word, thus guaranteeing the full divinity of the Son. With this foundation, both Thomas and Alexander Campbell taught that Jesus Christ was the incarnation of the eternal Word of God, his assumption of our human nature in its degraded condition. Turning to the Reformed doctrine of Christ's threefold office of prophet, priest, and king, Campbell conceived of Christ fulfilling the priestly role by offering himself as an atoning sacrifice, not to gain God's mercy, but to satisfy God's "law and justice"; the prophetic role by speaking the oracles of God and God's will for humanity; and the kingly role by inaugurating the kingdom of heaven and serving as lawgiver and judge of this kingdom. The "kingdom" motif was essential for Campbell in connecting the various phases of christological affirmation: the preexistence, incarnation, passion, exaltation, and enthronement (postexistence) of Christ. It bespoke Christ's authority in heaven and on earth, an authority that had to be demonstrated through the subjugation of the world to Christ, the "hereditary Monarch of the universe." The biblical revelation was about the appointment of Christ to bring God's rule on earth to completion, to save the creation from its "preternatural" state.

Barton Stone shared the Campbells' reluctance to use nonbiblical language, but he went beyond them in jettisoning the classical doctrine of the Trinity. Seeking a simpler Christology that would make sense of the biblical testimony concerning the person of Christ and Christ's relationship to God, Stone denied that Christ had existed from eternity or was coequal with God the Father. Instead, Christ was the first begotten of God the Father, by whom and through whom God created all things. Neither a created being nor merely human, Christ derived his being from God the Father and therefore shared God's essence or substance. Following Isaac Watts, Stone taught that God created the human soul of Jesus and joined that soul with the divine essence prior to the incarnation. Thus, Stone was comfortable with a view that subordinated Christ to God, but saw Christ as the true image of God in whom the "fullness of the God dwelt bodily." As to the atonement, Stone differed significantly from Campbell, denying the ideas of both substitution and satisfaction. Instead, Christ was the mediator between humanity and God, seeking to make them one, showing forth God's love for humanity and therefore leading humanity to reconciliation with God.

Walter Scott contributed, particularly in his book on *The Messiahship* (1859), an extensive analysis of the hermeneutical conditions of christological affirmation. Scott was not innovative in the substance of Christology, but sought to decipher from the Bible a logical scheme of evidences (especially those of prophecy and miracles) for Christ's messianic identity. This evidentiary model of christological construction went hand in hand with Scott's whole development of a program of evangelism aimed at bringing the believer into a faith-relation with the person of Jesus Christ. Scott represented very well the Movement's dogged adherence to scriptural rather than scholastic or creedal language to identify Jesus Christ, and thus his Christology was focused largely on images or titles of Christ and the messianic *mission* as the basis for a practical soteriology.

Alexander Campbell and Walter Scott largely inspired the Christology of the second generation of the Movement, a leading voice of which was Robert Milligan in his great systematic work *The Scheme of Redemption* (1868). Like Campbell, Milligan used the inductive method to reason from Scripture to a doctrine of the person of Christ. Affirming Christ's true humanity, Milligan also recognized Christ's unity with God, insisting that Christ shared fully with the Father and the Holy Spirit in the work of creation and redemption. Though he sought to avoid theological speculation, he insisted that the incarnate Word of God was truly God. Milligan therefore provided the Movement with a thoroughly orthodox voice, a voice that remains strong within the more conservative branches of the Movement. Another second-generation voice was W. K. Pendleton, who, in the last volume of the *Millennial Harbinger,* reviewed the history of Christology and revealed a heightened appreciation for the Chalcedonian Definition of Christ as "one person in two (divine and human) natures." Pendleton concluded that "this formula gradually settled in the minds of the greatest representative minds of the church and has become the generally accepted expression of orthodoxy on the whole subject." While the Christology of Campbell and Scott had often departed from the ecumenical christological tradition more linguistically than materially, Pendleton reflected a new appreciation, rather than dismissal, of classical formulations. Not all in subsequent generations, however, would follow Pendleton's lead, due to an engrained aversion to "opinions" confuting the "plain truth" of Scripture concerning Christ.

At the beginning of the twentieth century, new, more liberal voices exerted themselves. A key voice among liberal Disciples was Edward Scribner Ames, who sought to reconcile the Christian faith with philosophical idealism and psychology. Ames conceived of Christ as the supreme moral and spiritual example of a life lived in faithfulness to God. Taking a track between Milligan and Ames were more moderate voices, including Frederick Kershner and William Robinson. These theologians sought to balance an openness to modern theological trends with remaining orthodox. Kershner focused on the moral and ethical aspects of Christology, while Robinson interacted with neo-orthodoxy and remained orthodox on questions of the divinity of Christ and the Trinity. Robinson insisted that, while Stone-Campbell churches emphasized Christ's work of redemption, they did not make specific theories part of the faith.

Since the middle of the twentieth century the Movement's christological reflections have followed these three trajectories, with the more conservative and evangelical branches following, in the main, the views of Milligan. Allan McNicol, a theologian from the Churches of Christ, has of late called attention to the problem of a domesticated Christology among the conservative segments of the Movement. Christology (often more presupposed than given to continued critical construction) was for Churches of Christ the crucial grounding of ecclesiology; but in subsequent efforts to personalize Christ's rule over Christian life there arose an individualistic piety that had the effect of reducing Christ as the Lord of the church to a "friend" of Christians, catering to individuals' spiritual needs. McNicol has therefore called Churches of Christ to a renewed sense of the regal Christ as cosmic mediator of divine grace. Douglas Foster has nonetheless also revealed an opposite trend among some Church of Christ thinkers in the twentieth century, a tendency to elevate Christ to a quasi-Apollinarian extreme that undermines his true humanity.

The more liberal trajectory of the Stone-Campbell tradition, though sharing some of the conservative streams' resistance to abstract Christology not grounded in lived Christianity, has taken several different tracks fed by the crucial input of both reason and experience. Process theologian David Griffin makes use of the philosophy of Alfred North Whitehead and conceives of Christ as the incarnation of the Logos or "primordial nature of God," with Jesus being the "decisive revelation" of the divine reality that opens humanity to "being creatively transformed." Clark Williamson works with Process categories, but pays special attention to the effect of the Holocaust on Christian theology. In light of that event, he maintains, one must recognize that in encountering Jesus one encounters the God of Israel. Thus, in Jesus the Gentiles are called into relationship with the God of Israel. Feminist theologian Rita Nakashima Brock can speak of the risen Christ being experienced, even dispersed in the community, so that Christ is the *erōs* (love) that binds the community of faith together. A third path is exemplified in the work of Joe R. Jones, who, like Robinson, has developed a thoroughly trinitarian Christology in keeping with the Councils of Nicea and Chalcedon. In doing so, Jones has also challenged the classical definitions of God's impassibility and immutability.

Douglas Foster has observed of the overall shape of Christology in the Stone-Campbell tradition that, in the nineteenth century, it was often more reactionary than constructive, directed to Calvinist, Roman Catholic, or even Mormon aberrations, and that it was framed largely through the lenses of ecclesiology and soteriology. Indeed, christological issues were most often raised in the context of immediate questions of the scheme of conversion and regeneration authorized by Christ and of how Christ's authority was expressed institutionally in the church's organization and practices.

See also Atonement; Creeds and Confessions; God, Doctrine of; Justification, Doctrine of; Salvation

BIBLIOGRAPHY Edward Scribner Ames, *The Divinity of Christ* (1911) • James D. Bales, *The Biblical Doctrine of Christ* (1966) • William R. Barr, "Christology in Disciples Tradition: An Assessment and Proposal," in *Classic Themes of Disciples Theology,* ed. Kenneth Lawrence (1986), pp. 9-28 • Rita Nakashima Brock, *Journeys by Heart: A Christology of Erotic Power* (1988) • Alexander Campbell, *The Christian System* (1835) • Douglas A. Foster, "Christology in the Stone-Campbell Movement: An Exploratory Survey" (unpublished paper for the Restoration Theological Research Fellowship, 1999) • David Ray Griffin, *A Process Christology* (1973) • Joe R. Jones, *A Grammar of Christian*

Faith, 2 vols. (2002) • Donn Leach, *What the Bible Says about Jesus* (1989) • David Lipscomb, "Jesus Christ — Who and What Is He?" in *Salvation from Sin* (1913), pp. 52-75 • Allan McNicol, "Jesus: Savior of the Isolated Individual, or the Body?" *Leaven* 8 (2000): 124-28 • Robert Milligan, *The Scheme of Redemption* (1868) • W. K. Pendleton, "The History of the Doctrine of Christology: A Lecture," *Millennial Harbinger* (1870): 86-98 • William Robinson, *What Churches of Christ Stand For* (1946) • Walter Scott, *The Messiahship* (1859) • Stephen V. Sprinkle, *Disciples and Theology: Understanding the Faith of a People in Covenant* (1999) • Barton W. Stone, *Address to the Churches* (2nd ed. 1841), in *Works of Elder B. W. Stone,* ed. James Mathes (1859), pp. 46-163 • D. Newell Williams, *Barton Stone: A Spiritual Biography* (2000) • Clark M. Williamson, *Way of Blessing, Way of Life* (1999). ROBERT D. CORNWALL

Christ's Church Fellowship

Denomination founded in 1988 in Cincinnati, Ohio, drawing most of its original members from congregations and individuals of the Stone-Campbell heritage.

Early leaders of Christ's Church Fellowship (CCF) claimed the Cane Ridge Revival as the defining event in the Stone-Campbell Movement's formative history. While affirming most of the beliefs and practices associated with that Movement, including the baptism of believers by immersion (which was nevertheless not considered "essential" for salvation) and the weekly celebration of the Lord's Supper, from its beginning CCF distinguished itself as part of the so-called Third Wave of the Holy Spirit, placing an emphasis on spiritual gifts and apostolic authority. For a time CCF published a journal, *Paraclete,* in hopes of expanding its congregational network and fostering connections with the larger charismatic renewal movement in the United States.

CCF churches teach that all the gifts described in the New Testament, including so-called miraculous gifts (e.g., glossalalia, prophecy), are operative in the present day. The churches also maintain that the five "offices" listed in Ephesians 4:11 — apostles, prophets, evangelists, pastors, and teachers — should be recognized and operative in the modern-day church.

The CCF is governed through a leadership presbytery selected by the General Presbytery, the biannual gathering of congregational representatives. The leadership presbytery is composed of apostles, pastors, prophets, and elders. In CCF polity, apostles are recognized as spiritual leaders who oversee groups of congregations in particular geographical areas. Administratively, a president is elected from the leadership presbytery to oversee the administration and communication of the denomination.

See also Holy Spirit, Doctrine of the

BIBLIOGRAPHY Simon J. Dahlman, "Christ's Church Fellowship: New Denomination Formed," *Christian Standard* 124 (1989): 278-79. SIMON J. DAHLMAN

Church, Doctrine of the

Doctrine of the people of God in Christ and its expression in the gathered community(ies) of believers.

Ecclesiology (the doctrine of the church) has been a central concern of the Stone-Campbell Movement because it arose in a context of Protestant disunity that raised questions related to practical aspects of church life. The goal of conversion of the world to Christ required the union of Christians, and the means of attaining this union was the restoration of New Testament Christianity in essentials and liberty in other matters. Dealing with division between Protestant churches separated by creeds and different polities, the Campbells, Stone, and others focused on the common Christianity that all groups shared. Disavowing creeds and theologies as the basis of fellowship, they advocated unity on the practices authorized by the apostles for the New Testament churches. This put an emphasis on questions of organization and worship in the effort to seek a common ground on which to unite. Those concerns were part of a much broader consensus on theological matters of God, Christ, and soteriology. These doctrines were often simply assumed and in time neglected. Hence, concerns over polity, assembly activities, and church membership, when divorced from the original context of the Movement and especially from the larger theological framework in which they were articulated, have seemed for some latter-day adherents to be external and unjustified. Not only has the church been a central concern of the Stone-Campbell Movement, but ecclesiological issues enter prominently into its divisions.

The principal branches of the Stone-Campbell Movement have developed different ecclesiologies: (1) the Disciples have restructured their organizations to assume features of a mainline Protestant denomination; (2) Christian Churches/Churches of Christ practice a modified connectionalism with self-governing congregations and a voluntary North American Christian Convention that serves as an umbrella with annual mass meetings of individuals for fellowship, information, and edification; (3) Churches of Christ adhere to a strict congregationalism that cooperates in various projects overseen by one congregation or organized as parachurch enterprises, but many congregations hold themselves apart from such cooperative projects.

Already in 1811, David Purviance, an associate of Barton W. Stone, wrote a pamphlet in which he affirmed that the holy Scriptures are sufficient for the faith, discipline, and unity of Christians. After setting forth a church order drawn from the Scriptures, he declared: "I think it dishonoring to the king and head of the church, to suppose that the laws he has given are insufficient for the government of his kingdom." For the followers of Stone, the Bible was all that was needed for the organization of the church, and all arrangements were to be tested by the Bible; for the followers of Campbell, adhering to the biblical pattern would bring renewal and blessing to the church.

Alexander Campbell was the creative genius behind the ecclesiology of the Stone-Campbell Movement. In his series on the "Ancient Order of Things" in the *Christian Baptist,* Campbell advocated a radical primitivism. In later writings collected in *The Christian System* and in articles in the *Millennial Harbinger,* he elaborated a mature, thought-out ecclesiology for those who responded to his call for a restoration of the ancient order. He insisted on the visible church as a social institution and had no patience with the concept of an invisible church. The nature of this church is defined by its relation to the kingdom of God. Although the kingdom of God is broader than the church, in the Christian age they are almost interchangeable terms, with the church constituting the subjects of the kingdom. Campbell believed in separation of church and state. The church is a divine creation, taking its beginning from the descent of the Holy Spirit on the first Pentecost after the resurrection of Christ (Acts 2). Its membership is those penitent believers who trust in the blood of Jesus for remission of sins and who confess the Lord by being immersed into the Father, Son, and Holy Spirit. The unity of the church is achieved by making the terms of fellowship equivalent to conditions of citizenship in the kingdom of God and Christ.

Alexander Campbell understood the organization of the church to be divinely given. The church is a "Christocracy" in which the rulers or bishops make no laws but only see that Christ's laws are known and obeyed. Each congregation as a miniature or individual representation of the whole body of Christ is independent. This congregational independence included antisociety sentiments in articles in the *Christian Baptist* but was modified, or developed (according to one's perspective), in the later Campbell's advocacy of representative delegate conventions in his articles on cooperation in the *Millennial Harbinger.* Campbell was against all priestcraft or sacerdotalism, and he insisted that the church has no clergy class. The priesthood of all believers, however, is not the priesthood of every believer but the priesthood of the whole community. The ministry of the church includes extraordinary ministers — apostles and prophets, who continue to exercise their ministries through the Scriptures — and ordinary ministers — evangelists, bishops, and deacons, who are chosen and set apart through prayer and the laying on of hands by the local congregation. The functions of the church are represented by these ministers. The evangelists (or messengers) preach, baptize, instruct, and plant and set in order new churches. Elders (bishops) teach, preside, and govern under the law of Christ. Deacons (and in certain situations deaconesses) set three tables: the Lord's table, the bishop's table, and the poor's table. The church meets on the Lord's Day for reading, teaching, exhortation, prayer, praise, and the Lord's Supper. Discipline is a congregational responsibility under the leadership of its elders.

Since Campbell's views were broadly influential, other representatives of Stone-Campbell ecclesiology may be treated more briefly. Barton W. Stone agreed with the emphasis on the local church but gave less attention to details of church order; for him the indwelling of the Holy Spirit was the central element of ecclesiology. The elimination of structures would allow spiritual union to emerge. Walter Scott, if anything, gave more emphasis to restoration of the ancient order than did Campbell, but he too changed his views to an advocacy of societies as the means of Christian cooperation.

Robert Milligan gave the classic systematic statement of Restoration ecclesiology. He set the doctrine of the church in the total biblical context of human redemption. Beginning with the doctrines of God, creation, human nature, and the fall, his treatment of the development of the divine plan of salvation includes Old Testament history and its types of Christian institutions. The discussion of New Testament texts begins with Christology and the work of the Holy Spirit as the basis for extensive consideration of the ministry, ordinances, members, organization, congregational cooperation, and discipline of the church before ending with the fortunes and destiny of the church.

The dissolutions of the Springfield Presbytery by Stone and his associates and of the Mahoning Association by Campbell's followers expressed the view that extra-local organizations were unscriptural and promoted an ecclesiasticism that inhibited Christian unity and freedom of conscience by giving authority to a body outside the local congregation. These actions signaled that the reformers respectively were no longer Presbyterians or Baptists but did not mark a shift to radical independency. The *Last Will and Testament of Springfield Presbytery* expressed a spiritual rather than an organizational unity among churches. Alexander Campbell himself was not fully sympathetic with the dissolution of the Mahoning Association, and he began to seek an adequate extra-congregational structure for his followers.

Efforts to find ways in which independent congregations could cooperate brought not only strains on the unity of the Movement but also reflection on aspects of the organization of the church. Campbell argued that cooperation was necessary in order to achieve the purposes of the church and that the manner of cooperation was not dictated by Scripture. He called for meetings of messengers of the churches on district, state, and national levels. What emerged from early district and state cooperative meetings was an organization of individuals instead of Campbell's plan for delegated messengers from churches. David S. Burnet was the most important individual in this development, and he played a key role in the formation of the American Christian Missionary Society (ACMS — October 1849), the most important of several societies that were formed. Advocates were looking for ways in which the churches could cooperate more efficiently to spread the gospel while preserving their independence, but opponents were fearful of creating the kind of ecclesiasticism that they had abandoned in leaving other religious bodies. Those who were cautious about the Society saw features like permanent officers, membership based on a subscription fee, and the passing of resolutions as creating a human organization separate from the churches to do the work of the churches. Resolutions favoring the Union during and after the Civil War not only alienated Southern Christians but also were a factor in raising doubts among some in the North (such as Benjamin Franklin) about how scriptural the organization was. The ACMS raised an important issue for thinking about the church: Does one begin with the church in its universal sense (for which one seeks organizational manifestations) or with its local manifestations as the primary instrument of work?

When the ACMS faltered from lack of support after the Civil War, the Louisville Plan of 1869 briefly changed the approach from a society of contributing individuals to a delegate convention of representatives from local congregations and state conventions. This latter approach, too, was an unacceptable means of coöperation to conservatives, for whom any entity that was more than a mass meeting for edification and exchange of information set up an ecclesiastical body between the churches and the work to be done. The missionary societies were a major factor in the division between the Disciples of Christ and the Churches of Christ. J. H. Garrison and Isaac Errett were champions of the missionary society as a means to cooperate in evangelism with no legislative or judicial function in regard to faith and practice. David Lipscomb was a leader of Southern Christians who opposed any cooperation that created an organization apart from local churches to do the work assigned by Scripture to the churches. In the controversies after the Civil War, J. W. McGarvey represented a middle ground that did not survive: opposition to instrumental music but support of the missionary society.

The last quarter of the nineteenth century and early years of the twentieth century saw the organization of many cooperative enterprises among Disciples. The convention in 1917 sought to bring these agencies under one umbrella with a combination of a mass assembly of all who attended and a delegate body composed of members elected by state conventions (the Committee on Recommendations). In 1919 the convention created the United Christian Missionary Society (UCMS) out of the ACMS, the Christian Woman's Board of Missions (1874), and the Foreign Christian Missionary Society (1875).

Against these cooperative trends some Disciples, disturbed by theological liberalism and the acceptance of higher criticism at Disciples' schools and by leaders of the convention as well as by the centralization of authority in the UCMS, formed the North American Christian Convention (NACC). The NACC, which held its first meeting in 1927, was a beginning organizational wedge between Disciples and the Christian Churches/Churches of Christ. Debate on "open membership" (acceptance of unimmersed believers into fellowship) exposed the different ecclesiologies of those who thought in terms of the church universal against those who emphasized the restoration of the primitive church. Independents continued the ecclesiology represented by the conservative Disciple T. W. Phillips. Echoing Alexander Campbell's blend of Scripture and reason, he restated the classic form of the Restoration Plea and concluded from his study of the cases of conversion in Acts that no one was baptized before having faith or after being pardoned, and no unbaptized person was ever addressed as a Christian.

William Robinson, a British Disciple, was active in the ecumenical movement, even offering the (British) Churches of Christ as a "bridge church." With reference to issues of ecumenicity, he analyzed the doctrine of the church in the various parts of the New Testament, following critical conclusions on their date and authorship. Disciples were charter members of the Federal Council of Churches in the United States and supported the National and World Councils.

Although the Commission on Restudy of the Disciples of Christ issued a report in 1946 that basically reaffirmed the restorationism of the Stone-Campbell Movement, many leading Disciples were looking to the ecumenical movement instead of restorationism as the means to achieve Christian unity. The repudiation of the restoration plea came in *The Renewal of Church: The Panel of Scholars Reports* published in 1963. Mission and unity were considered the primary goals, and since restoration was now considered to be based on assumptions about the early church and the New Testament that historical study seemed to render untenable and moreover to be a hindrance to these goals, it was to be abandoned. W. B. Blakemore, one of the editors of the reports, identified a type of "congregationalism" in which all levels of associations or conventions participate in and are manifestations of the church universal that is prior to the local congregation.

Disciples replaced the restoration model of church organization with a functional model and began the formal process of assuming denominational status. In 1958 the Committee on Brotherhood Structure began the work that culminated in the adoption of "A Provisional Design for the Christian Church (Disciples of Christ)" at Kansas City in 1968. Kenneth L. Teegarden was the "architect" of Restructure; Ronald Osborn played a key role in its development. There was considerable continuity in the constituent organizations, but the language changed to that of a denomination. The various organizations were consolidated into a single entity containing "manifestations" of the church. The General Assembly was a proportionately representative body with voting delegates and was promoted as corresponding to the model of a general organization favored by Campbell. The resultant denomination was in its theory a church rather than a collection of churches, but not the whole church. The changes in name from International Convention of Disciples of Christ (1917) to International Convention of Christian Churches (Disciples of Christ) in 1957 to General Assembly of the Christian Church (Disciples of Christ) in 1968 mark the changes in the perception of the convention from an association of persons to an association of churches (plural) to a manifestation of the church (singular), or denomination.

Whereas the leadership of the Disciples abandoned the idea of restoration and accepted denominational status, Christian Churches/Churches of Christ have maintained the restoration plea, have been reluctant to admit denominational language for themselves, and have continued the society method of church cooperation, in effect denying (in contrast to the Disciples) the churchly character of all structures beyond the local congregation.

Members of Churches of Christ have written many books maintaining the restoration plea for an undenominational New Testament church, but some take a distinctive approach. Representative of those stressing the New Testament pattern is G. C. Brewer, who concentrates on the practical implementation of matters of polity. Although the title of the work by Rubel Shelley and Randall Harris might seem to claim otherwise, their text says that the church is not perfectly restored but is a pilgrim people bearing witness to the kingdom of God. Everett Ferguson restates a restoration doctrine of the church within the framework of biblical theology and incorporates insights from twentieth-century scholarship. Leonard Allen moves the discussion from polity to lifestyle. Two opposite tendencies in ecclesiology emerged from within Churches of Christ in the second half of the twentieth century. The noninstitutional churches of Christ have opposed projects both by parachurch organizations and by one congregation that require support from many congregations and individuals. The International Church of Christ has broken ties with Churches of Christ and has followed a hierarchical structure.

Despite their divisions, ecclesiology remains an area in which the Stone-Campbell churches have something not only distinctive but also constructive to offer to the larger Christian world. These contributions to ecclesiology include the following points, adhered to with varying degrees of emphasis by all the branches: (1) a strong or "high" doctrine of the importance of the church, balancing the Movement's emphasis on individual liberty; (2) the emphasis on a visible unity of the church and the local congregation as the center of the Christian life; (3) the clarification of the relation of salvation to church membership — what saves also makes one a member of the church; (4) the approach of uniting on what nearly every Christian agrees is right and proper instead of maintaining division over what may be contended for as acceptable but may not be generally accepted.

BIBLIOGRAPHY Leonard C. Allen, *The Cruciform Church* (1990) • W. B. Blakemore, *The Discovery of the Church: A History of Disciple Ecclesiology* (1966) • G. C. Brewer, *The Model Church* (1919; repr. 1957) • Anthony L. Dunnavant, *Restructure: Four Historical Ideals in the Campbell-Stone Movement and the Development of the Polity of the Christian Church (Disciples of Christ)* (1993) • Everett Ferguson, "The Doctrine of the Church in the Writings of Alexander Campbell," *Restoration Quarterly* 2 (1958): 228-44 • Everett Ferguson, *The Church of Christ: A Biblical Ecclesiology for Today* (1996) • D. Ray Lindley, *The Apostle of Freedom* (1957) • Robert Milligan, *The Scheme of Redemption* (1868) • Thomas H. Olbricht and Hans Rollmann, eds., *The Quest for Christian Unity, Peace, and Purity in Thomas Campbell's Declaration and Address,* ATLA Monograph Series 46 (2000) (articles by Straughn, Blowers, Foster, and Dull are relevant to the doctrine of the church) • Ronald E. Osborn, Ralph G. Wilburn, and William Barnett Blakemore, eds., *Renewal of the Church: The Panel of Scholars Reports,* 3 vols. (1963) • Thomas W. Phillips, *The Church of Christ* (1905) • David Purviance, "Observations on the Constitution, Unity, and Discipline of the Church of Christ" (1811; microfilm, University of Kentucky, 24 pp.) • William Robinson, *The Biblical Doctrine of the Church* (1948; rev. ed. 1955) • Rubel Shelley and Randall J. Harris, *The Second Incarnation: A Theology for the 21st Century Church* (1992) • Eva Jean Wrather, *Creative Freedom in Action: Alexander Campbell on the Structure of the Church* (1968).

EVERETT FERGUSON

Church Finance Council

General administrative unit of the Christian Church (Disciples of Christ), it implements a churchwide system of mission funding, promotes faithful Christian stewardship, and provides treasury services. The Church Finance Council replaced Unified Promotion on July 1, 1974. According to Spencer Austin, "Church Finance Council is an agency of the whole church and is a shared responsibility of the general units, institutions of higher education, regions, and congregations, working cooperatively to finance the mission of the whole church."

The Church Finance Council promotes and interprets the three annual mission funds — the common mission fund for whole church mission, Reconciliation, and Week of Compassion — of the Christian Church (Disciples of Christ). The General Board of the Christian Church (Disciples of Christ) changed the name of the common mission fund in 1974 from Unified Promotion to Basic Mission Finance. The General Board changed the name of the common mission fund again in 2002 to the Disciples Mission Fund, which became effective in 2003.

In its role as church treasury, the Church Finance Council functions as a central receiving and disbursing agency for the mission funds of the whole church. The common mission fund (currently called the Disciples Mission Fund) is distributed to seventy-three mission partners who receive the funds and implement outreach mission locally, regionally, and globally on behalf of the entire communion. The Reconciliation Fund, established in 1968 to promote racial justice, currently focuses on the elimination of systemic racism within the structures of the Christian Church (Disciples of Christ). The Week of Compassion Fund was established in response to the devastation in Europe following World War II and has evolved into the church's disaster relief/emergency response and economic development fund. The Church Finance Council distributes Week of Compassion funds based upon allocation or grant-making decisions of groups authorized by the General Board of the Christian Church (Disciples of Christ) to make disaster response decisions.

The Church Finance Council develops resources, enables short-term mission trips, and provides training that encourages and inspires Disciples to make faithful Christian stewardship responses to God's grace.

See also Unified Promotion

BIBLIOGRAPHY Spencer Austin, "Unified Devotion: A Fifty Year Struggle," *Discipliana* 45:1 (1985): 3-6, 13.

LOIS ARTIS

Church Growth Movement

Movement in the last half of the twentieth century devoted to research and methodology of church growth among constituents of various evangelical Protestant denominations, and pioneered by Stone-Campbell missiologist Donald McGavran.

While the expectation that the church would grow has been present since the writing of the Acts of the Apostles, the "science" of church growth is a relatively recent phenomenon. Further, although the principles of the church growth movement are now applied to "domestic" churches (i.e., those reaching out to and serving people of their own culture), those principles were originally developed and applied only within a missionary or cross-cultural context.

Most would trace the beginnings of the church growth movement to Donald Anderson McGavran. McGavran was born in India of missionary parents in December 1897, so it was not surprising that he and his wife Mary embarked for India in 1923 as missionaries with a missionary society of what is now the Christian Church (Disciples of Christ). In the next two decades, McGavran became increasingly concerned about the methodology accepted without question by other missionaries, which seemed to produce very little fruit. He saw every site in which a missionary was laboring as a "sown field" where a harvest should be expected. These insights were strengthened when, as part of a survey team in South India, he saw great "people movements" to Christ occurring, largely a result of the adoption of an effective strategy.

McGavran continued to seek to identify the key elements of a fruitful missionary approach; these later became the fundamental principles within the church growth movement in missions: (1) in-depth analysis; (2) balance in the functions of missions (e.g., education, evangelism, benevolence); (3) concentration on responsive populations of the world; (4) use of social sciences to enhance church growth, particularly cultural anthropology and sociology; (5) widespread distribution of church growth information; (6) pragmatism (methods adopted) coupled with absolutism (biblical truth); and (7) a nondenominational approach to church growth studies.

McGavran left his India missionary service in 1954. From the United States, he began to refine his ideas to test their applicability in countries and cultures other than India and to promote this innovative approach to missions. He traveled to a variety of countries to observe and discuss with missionaries their concerns and his insights. He longed for a "Church Growth Association" or an "Institute of Church Growth," a vehicle that would serve as a clearinghouse for information about "people movements," where peoples were turning to Christ in large numbers rather than one-by-one. Such an association or institute would publish new information and could equip missionaries to apply "church growth thinking" to their fields.

That dream, the Institute of Church Growth, opened formally in January 1961 on the campus of Northwest Christian College in Eugene, Oregon. The response was positive and enthusiastic. In 1965, in order to enable more people to study church growth, McGavran accepted an invitation from Fuller Theological Seminary in Pasadena, California, to the seminary's new School of World Mission, on the condition that its name would include "Institute of Church Growth."

One way to visualize the development of church growth thinking is with an hourglass-shaped diagram. During his India years, others — contemporaries of McGavran but not always aware of his thinking or in contact with him — were struggling with similar issues in missions. In the 1950s and 1960s, however, it was McGavran alone who came to embody the basic elements of church growth thinking. By the early 1970s, colleagues of McGavran in the Institute of Church Growth and School of World Mission at Fuller were further developing his principles and widely expanding their application. In particular, C. Peter Wagner saw the relevance of McGavran's ideas to the desire of churches to reach people in their own neighborhoods and within their own cultures.

The principles of the church growth approach have not been without their critics, but the basic ideas have found support in many denominations. Courses in church growth are now offered in numerous Christian colleges and seminaries both within and beyond the Stone-Campbell Movement. Advocates have refined the original principles and applied them in new ways. It is not an exaggeration to describe the church growth movement as making a highly significant impact on the development of mission and local church methodologies in the last half of the twentieth century. The multiculturalism in many Western societies today and the impact of postmodernism have opened the door for applying church growth approaches in First World settings. While the impact of the church growth movement today is not in any way limited to the Stone-Campbell Movement in which it had its roots, it is accurate to say that within this Movement the idea was born, was nurtured, and became available to the church as a whole.

See also Evangelists, Evangelism — Twentieth Century; McGavran, Donald A.; Missions, Missiology

BIBLIOGRAPHY Donald A. McGavran, *Understanding Church Growth* (1970; rev. ed. 1990) • Donald A. McGavran, ed., *Church Growth and Christian Mission* (1965) • Donald McGavran and George G. Hunter III, *Church Growth: Strategies That Work* (1980) • Donald McGavran and Wayne Weld, *Principles of Church Growth* (2nd ed. 1974) • James C. Smith, "Without Crossing Barriers: The Homogeneous Unit Concept in the Writings of Donald Anderson McGavran" (unpublished D.Miss. dissertation, Fuller Theological Seminary, 1976).

HERBERT WORKS

Church Planting Associations

Parachurch organizations that raise funds, train and recruit leaders, and promote vision among churches to plant new churches in the United States and around the world. Often these groups focus on specific regions as indicated by their names, like Northern California Evangelistic Association (NCEA) or Chicago District Evangelizing Association (CDEA). However, many look to reach into regions beyond their immediate vicinity. For example, NCEA also has church plants in Washington, Nevada, and Texas. Christian Churches/Churches of Christ have more than forty such associations.

The Churches of Christ do not have any church planting associations but have depended historically on the individual or concerted efforts of local congregations. The Christian Church (Disciples of Christ) plants churches through its regional organizations, with assistance from the Disciples' Board of Church Extension.

Most associations started in the latter half of the twentieth century, though the Virginia Evangelizing Fellowship, founded in 1939, serves as a notable exception. Early on, most associations funded a single minister and his family to plant a church in a city or town. However, these churches developed slowly and often remained small after twenty or thirty years. In more recent years many associations moved toward a team approach, which proved more effective. Thus churches planted in the first forty years of Go Ye Chapel Mission in New York City numbered 1,100 total members; between 1992 and 2002, on the other hand, churches planted totaled over 3,500 members.

The mission of many associations today is to plant self-supporting, self-sustaining churches that will in turn plant other churches. To achieve this goal the associations utilize several strategies. First, most use a general profile to gauge the potential success of individuals interested in church planting. Second, groups like NCEA and CDEA are developing models of church planting that others can reproduce in different contexts. Additionally, some employ coaches or mentors to help teams effectively plant a church. Team Expansion, based in Louisville, Kentucky, uses veteran church planters to consult with new teams to develop strategies and skills for outreach in their respective locales. Finally, some groups try to aid the process by planting churches near a "hub" church, promoting shared use of resources. In 2003 NCEA became a nationwide church planting ministry named Stadia.

See also Evangelism, Evangelists — Christian Churches/Churches of Christ

BIBLIOGRAPHY Brett Andrews, "Church Planting: One Story," *Christian Standard* 137 (2002): 326-27 • Marcus Bigelow and Roger Gibson, "Should I Plant a Church?" *Christian Standard* 137 (2002): 238-39 • Joe Boyd, "Missionary Church Planting," *Christian Standard* 137 (2002): 134-35 • Stadia: New Church Stratigies, www.stadia.cc.

Robert L. Foster

Church Women United

An inclusive, interdenominational, American organization of Christian women, Church Women United (CWU) was first named United Council of Church Women. In the forefront of interchurch cooperation, ecumenism, racial integration, church social action, and local involvement, CWU supports state and city units in social projects, women's rights, memorial days, and church programs. Three major observations are central events: World Day of Prayer, continuing a tradition begun in 1887; May Friendship Day, to strengthen communities; and World Community Day, emphasizing peace and justice. Taking pride in helping differing denominations find unity in the Body of Christ, the organization is made up of Protestant, Roman Catholic, Orthodox, and other Christian members. CWU publishes *The Churchwoman.*

Disciples leader Daisy June Trout was instrumental in arranging the foundational meeting in Atlantic City, December 11-13, 1941, with representatives from the National Council of Church Women, the Council of Women for Home Missions, and the Committee on Women's Work of the Foreign Missions Conference. The organization's official position of Christian pacifism was adopted at the first meeting in the wake of the Pearl Harbor attack.

In 1945 the organization urged the United States to join the United Nations (UN); CWU continues to have consultative status with the UN. In 1950 the organization's name became United Church Women as one of the founding ecumenical movements of the National Council of Churches of Christ in the U.S.A., but changed to Church Women United in 1966 when its relationship to the NCC was dissolved. National headquarters are maintained in New York City and Washington, D.C., to coordinate programs and lobby Congress.

Christian Women's Fellowship is a denominational supporting organization to CWU, and the Disciples of Christ have a permanent representative on the Common Council. Disciples of Christ have provided CWU leadership at all levels, including three CWU presidents. Mossie Allman Wyker (1950-55) emphasized New Testament study and equality in Christ, leading to official policies supporting women's ordination and racial equality. Concern for international pacifism expanded under Mary Louise Rowand (1977-80), with human rights emphasized in relations with Christian women's groups of other nations. Susan Shank Mix (1996-2000) oversaw the "Women Leading in Community" program created to support leadership in all aspects of society.

See also Christian Women's Fellowship

BIBLIOGRAPHY *Church Women United Handbook and Directory, September 2001–August 2002* • Glades Milky, *Follow Those Women: Church Women in the Ecumenical Movement: A History of the Development of United Work among Women of the Protestant Churches of the United States* (1961) • Margaret Shannon, *Just Because: The Story of the National Movement of Church Women United in the U.S.A. 1941 through 1975* (1977) • *60th Anniversary Memory Book: Anthology of Church Women United's History, 1941-2001.*

Lowell K. Handy

Churches of Christ

1. Current Data
2. Organizational Structure
3. In the Context of the Stone-Campbell Movement
4. History
5. Sources of Church Growth
6. Missions
7. Black Churches
8. Education and Scholarship
9. Controversies
10. The Genius of the Churches of Christ

1. Current Data

Churches of Christ emerged in the first major division of the Stone-Campbell Movement at the end of the nineteenth century as those who maintained a strict understanding of the directives and silences of the Bible. By 1906 the United States Bureau of the Census in a special religious census had distinguished Churches of Christ as a separate entity from Disciples of Christ. Advocacy of missionary organizations (societies), both home and foreign, and the use of instrumental music in worship — "innovations" that leaders of Churches of Christ vehemently opposed — furnished the immediate causes of separation. Churches of Christ count approximately 1,300,000 members in the United States, more than 1,000,000 in Africa, an estimated 1,000,000 in India, and perhaps 50,000 in Central and South America. Total membership in the world exceeds 3,000,000.

In the United States the majority of members are located in the mid-section of the country from Pittsburgh to El Paso, with the northern border extending from Pittsburgh through Indianapolis, St. Louis, Wichita, and Albuquerque, and the southern through Atlanta, Montgomery, Baton Rouge, Houston, and San Antonio. More than 28 percent of members of Churches of Christ live in Texas (293,000) and Tennessee (170,000). Tennessee claims the highest percentage of members of Churches of Christ in relation to population. About 5,000 members reside in New England, about 20,000 in the Middle Atlantic states, 160,000 in the South Atlantic states, 170,000 in the upper Midwest, 46,000 in the Rocky Mountain states, and 86,000 on the Pacific rim.

The total number of congregations of Churches of Christ in the United States and territories exceeds 13,000. These congregations average approximately 100 members. There are 60 congregations with more than 1,000 members, and 250 with between 500 and 1,000 members.

Mainstream Churches of Christ account for about 75 percent of the congregations and 87 percent of the membership. The remaining churches comprise four major groupings. For the most part these groups depart from the consensus in practices rather than in theological perspectives. The largest group had separated by 1960, with 2,055 churches identifying themselves as noninstitutional. They oppose parachurch organizations of all kinds and eschew special ministries and related facilities. About 1,100 congregations oppose the use of church classes, arguing that the assembly should not be divided even for children. About 550 congregations oppose use of multiple communion cups, some of these also opposing classes. Another group of about 130 congregations emphasize mutual edification by various leaders in the churches and oppose one person doing most of the preaching. Congregations in these four groupings are smaller in size, and many do not recognize the validity of the other groups.

About 1,240 congregations of Churches of Christ have predominantly African American membership, with about 172,000 members. The number of independent Spanish-speaking congregations in the United States is 240 with about 10,000 members, most in Texas, Puerto Rico, and California. Korean, Chinese, Haitian, Filipino, and Japanese congregations exist in smaller numbers. Many congregations, especially in heavily populated regions, have a rich diversity of membership from varied racial, ethnic, educational, professional, non-professional, and socioeconomic backgrounds.

Into the early 1990s the churches influenced by the Crossroads congregation in Gainesville, Florida, and the Boston Church of Christ in Boston, Massachusetts, were counted as congregations of the Churches of Christ. Since that time they have designated themselves an independent group — the International Church of Christ (ICOC). Until the end of 2002 Kip McKean led the ICOC. After an internal struggle, Al Baird and Bob Gempel of the Los Angeles Church of Christ emerged at the top of a more complex leadership structure. More prerogative is being given to the local congregations, though the ICOC maintains a hierarchical and structured ecclesiology emphasizing evangelism and one-on-one discipling. Leaders in mainstream Churches of Christ dispute their polity and methods. The ICOC claims 430 congregations located mostly in major cities throughout the world, with about 135,000 members.

2. Organizational Structure

Churches of Christ from the beginning have maintained no formal organizational structures larger than the local congregations and no official journals or vehicles declaring sanctioned positions. Church leaders and preachers are highly entrepreneurial. Consensus views do, however, often emerge through the influence of opinion leaders who express themselves in journals, at lectureships, or at area preacher meetings and other gatherings. Until the 1980s, editors, especially of the *Gospel Advocate* (1855-) and the *Firm Foundation* (1884-), were significant molders of consensus views. Journal editors promoted standard commitments and criticized views and proposals that deviated from normative positions. Since the 1980s lectureship speakers and leaders at Christian universities have been more influential than editors. B. C. Goodpasture (1895-1977), editor of the *Gospel Advocate* in the mid-twentieth century, characterized the methods through which consensus and deviations in the churches are achieved as "a wild democracy." Those who lose in consensus battles develop new constituencies and communication channels.

3. In the Context of the Stone-Campbell Movement

Perspectives of early leaders among Churches of Christ represented trajectories in the Stone-Campbell Movement that were already present in the beginning. Some of these trajectories could be traced to Alexander Campbell, Walter Scott, and Barton W. Stone, while others were minority views of secondary leaders. In preserving certain beliefs and practices of Campbell, Scott, and Stone, these early leaders of Churches of Christ could in part justify their claim that they were the true heirs of the Movement while Disciples had departed from the "old paths" by encouraging innovation.

Although they may have read few writings of the pioneers, early leaders in Churches of Christ emphasized foundational principles of Stone, Campbell, and Scott, including unity grounded in New Testament precepts, evangelism, baptism as immersion for the remission of sins, millennialism, opposition to credalism and theological constructs, anticlericalism, literalistic grammatico-historical hermeneutics, congregational independence, leadership by elders and deacons rather than settled ministers, membership initiative, unadorned buildings, simple worship services, straightforward preaching, pure life, and weekly observation of the Lord's Supper. Most trajectories in the Stone-Campbell Movement have emphasized the ancient order of Alexander Campbell and the ancient gospel of Walter Scott — ecclesiology and soteriology.

Thought shapers in Churches of Christ did not, however, follow Stone, Campbell, and Scott in seeking unity with other groups and in opening toward denominational cooperation or some semblance of inclusivism. Likewise they became much more suspicious of congregational cooperation than the major early leaders. They restricted the work of the Holy Spirit to a role in the inspiration of Scripture and tended to be more suspicious of advanced education. In these tendencies they took up certain teachings of Arthur Crihfield, John R. Howard, and Matthias Winans — criticized from the beginning by Stone, Campbell, and Scott — including a bare-bones presentation of the plan of salvation, mechanistic Bible interpretation, a word-alone view of the work of the Holy Spirit, a radical anticlericalism, an extreme understanding of congregational independence, radical exclusivism, and constant intramural and extramural debating.

Churches of Christ, therefore, did not simply replicate early trajectories. In addition, disparate outlooks anticipated future conflicts among those identified as Churches of Christ in 1906.

4. History

The 1906 Federal Census provided the Churches of Christ with a decisive, self-conscious acceptance of separation from the Christian Church (or Disciples of Christ). "Church of Christ" had been employed as a self-designation by restorationist churches from the beginning, but from the latter part of the nineteenth century became increasingly the appellation of those congregations opposed to mission societies and instruments in worship. Signs of stresses and strains accelerated in the Stone-Campbell Movement after the Civil War. Churches troubled by innovations began seeking fellowship of likeminded congregations, as is clear in the *Gospel Advocate,* edited by David Lipscomb, and the *Firm Foundation,* edited by Austin McGary. The *Christian Standard,* edited by Isaac Errett in Cincinnati, became the journal for more "progressive" churches. In Indianapolis, Benjamin Franklin (1812-1878), editor of *American Christian Review* from 1856 until his death, at first actively promoted mission societies, but by the 1870s saw that various leaders had conceived new visions for ministry and church life that he was not prepared to accept. Daniel Sommer, his successor, agitated for a break with the progressives, especially in his "Sand Creek Address and Declaration" of 1889. By 1901 David Sylvester Ligon in his "Portraiture of Gospel Preachers" had printed pictures of 260 preachers he considered faithful leaders and promoters of the movement, including significant beginning fathers, such as Stone, the Campbells, Scott, Smith, and others.

R. L. Roberts and Richard T. Hughes have argued that a significant majority of the preachers who eventually ministered in Churches of Christ grew up among those who were either from the Stone movement or influenced by them. This may have been the case in Tennessee and Alabama, but less so in Kentucky and even decreasingly so north of the Ohio River and into Arkansas and Texas. In 1836 Tolbert Fanning spent several months traveling to the northeast with Alexander Campbell and was especially influenced by him. In turn Fanning decisively influenced David Lipscomb, who had come from a Baptist background through contact with restorationists in the Stone orbit. Many early preachers who influenced later leaders of Churches of Christ had been Baptists and embraced restorationism through Campbell's writing in the *Christian Baptist* and later the *Millennial Harbinger.* One such influential regional leader was John M. Barnes of Alabama, a graduate of Bethany College.

Hughes is correct to identify predispositions from Stone that continue in Churches of Christ through Lipscomb and others, though many of these traits may be found in the same region among preachers influenced by "Raccoon" John Smith and other Baptists who, like him, became allied with Alexander Campbell. Stone was particularly interested in a plain style of life that avoided ostentation and government involvement. He also embraced pacifism and millennialism, more specifically a form of historical premillennialism. This complex of commitments Hughes labels "apocalyptic." Lipscomb appears to fit the apocalyptic mold, yet many commitments of Campbell may also be found in Lipscomb and others, especially his emphasis on literalistic adherence to the ancient order, the role of baptism in remission of sins, and a more empirically rationalistic hermeneutic. Stone was much more a child of the Second Great Awakening with its emotional aspects than Alexander Campbell or Lipscomb.

David Edwin Harrell, Jr., clearly established the "sectional" and social origins of Churches of Christ. In 1906, 159,658 members were assigned to Churches of Christ out of 1,142,359 in the larger Stone-Campbell Movement. Most of these 159,658 lived in Tennessee, northern Alabama and Mississippi, Arkansas, and Texas. North of the Ohio River only Indiana could count more than 5,000. Furthermore, whereas the whole movement in 1906 was predominantly rural, Churches of Christ were even more so. The leadership continued to support minimally organized church life and worship, and simplicity in church buildings, sermonizing, and teaching. In the manner of the "holiness" prohibitions of the second awakening they opposed drinking alcohol, dancing, card playing, frivolous activities on Sunday, theater attendance, extravagant clothing, and cosmetics. They emphasized abstaining from the ways of denominations or sectarians, as well as from "the world." They often denounced societal improvement like that promoted by the social gospel, emphasizing rather what they perceived to be practical, individualistic biblical morality.

Leaders among Churches of Christ at the beginning of the twentieth century shared many concerns with rising fundamentalism. They argued for the full inspiration of the Bible, its literal interpretation, and use of Bible commentaries that adhered to these views. Prominent preachers resisted evolution, higher criticism, the social gospel, and "worldly" morality. In contrast to a majority of fundamentalists, Churches of Christ remained adamantly anti-Calvinistic in soteriology. Sermons were more rationally structured, depicting salvation as obedience to the proclaimed facts of the gospel rather than as the result of an emotional, Spirit-initiated conversion. Churches of Christ claimed to replicate the church of the New Testament and to realize the kingdom of God through the advance of the earthly church. Leaders were rapidly moving away from ideas of a radical premillennial inbreaking of God through the reign of his Son on the earth. In these ways they differed from both fundamentalism and evangelicalism as defined at the end of the twentieth century.

From the perspective of Churches of Christ, the 1906 division preserved preaching focused on the New Testament church and the gospel plan of salvation. In respect to the church, they emphasized the external features regarding congregational independence, rule by elders and deacons, simplicity in worship, and lessons on concrete contrasts with the church polity and procedures of other religious groups. The initiatives for church growth lay with the local church officers and members as well as with the preachers. Lessons on the gospel plan of salvation emphasized the human actions of hearing, believing, repenting, confessing, and being baptized. Evangelistic preaching was cogently organized and didactically presented as contrasted with the approaches to salvation of the American Protestant churches, especially those in the rural sectors. Leaders in Churches of Christ argued against modern pastor systems, ornamentation in both buildings and worship, ministerial alliances, parachurch organizations, higher criticism of the Bible, evolution, dispensational premillennialism, public involvement of women in church leadership and worship, worldly morals, and member support of private help organizations such as the Red Cross.

In the early 1900s many preachers were without a college education. Yet they were well schooled in the English Bible and in various religious journals. A small number, however, did earn college degrees, and the percentage increased after World War II. At the beginning of the twenty-first century more than 90 percent had either college degrees or certificates from schools of preaching. Individual congregations of Churches of Christ determine who shall minister in their churches. Larger congregations tend to demand more experience and education than smaller ones. No formal ordination ceremony of preachers occurs, though some are legally ordained by the attestation of the elders of the congregation to fulfill state requirements in regard to performing marriages. Prior to World War II congregations employed only a preaching minister, if any at all. Since the 1950s larger congregations added, in order of frequency, ministers for youth, education, involvement, family, college students, and counseling. In some cases ministers have a dual role, for example, family and involvement minister.

Preachers from the beginning encouraged a deep commitment to the life of the congregation and a developed personal spiritual life, to be cultivated through regular attendance at assemblies of the churches on Sunday mornings and nights. Midweek gatherings became increasingly popular in the 1940s and consisted of teaching sessions for all ages. Daily reading of the Scriptures, family devotionals, dedicated giving, a personal prayer life, and a concern for those less fortunate were also encouraged. While some early preachers in Churches of Christ could be characterized as wranglers, many of them were deeply religious persons who encouraged others to develop a Christ-like life.

Membership in Churches of Christ grew rapidly. Twenty years after the 1906 census the numbers almost doubled to 317,937. By 1936 they had almost tripled from the earliest count to 433,714. Most of the growth occurred in rural areas and in the region running from Knoxville, Tennessee, to El Paso, Texas. Centers of concentration of membership developed around Nashville, Huntsville, Louisville, Shreveport, Memphis, Jonesboro, Little Rock, Tulsa, Oklahoma City, Dallas, Fort Worth, Houston, Austin, Abilene, Lubbock, and Los Angeles.

5. Sources of Church Growth

For much of the twentieth century the main avenue for growth was the gospel meeting. Patterned after the revivals of the awakenings and the later protracted meetings, these meetings were characterized by reasoned teaching rather than emotionalism, Churches of Christ usually avoiding the term "revival." Almost every preacher held gospel meetings, an indication of the continued understanding of the minister as evangelist. Pay was never a primary concern, so that every church regardless of how large or small had a gospel meeting at least annually. Most new churches were planted by first holding a gospel meeting. Preachers who became especially known in the early and mid-twentieth century for holding such meetings include Theophilus Brown Larimore, David Lipscomb, James A. Harding, Thomas Wesley Brents, Jefferson Davis Tant, Robertson Lafayette Whiteside, Charles Ready Nichol, Nicholas Brodie Hardeman, Gus Nichols, Grover Cleveland Brewer, Marshall Keeble, Foy E. Wallace, Jr., Horace Wooton Busby, Sr., and Homer Hailey.

By the 1930s gospel meetings tended to last two weeks through three Sundays. Meetings typically began with a focus on the church: its name, its identity, its officers, and its worship. Other common themes included undenominational Christianity and the "Restoration Plea." In the second week sermons shifted to a focus on the gospel plan of salvation — usually one night each on hearing, believing, repenting, confessing, and being baptized. The final sermons detailed the contrasting joys of heaven and tortures of hell. At the close of the sermon an invitation song was sung and people were exhorted either to be baptized or to commit themselves to faithful church involvement anew ("being restored").

These gospel meetings were highly successful in raising the level of awareness of spiritual matters in the churches and the communities in which they were held. These were special times for spiritual formation of youth, encouragement to active church involvement and leadership among the adults, and decisions to preach the gospel among young men. While gospel meetings still persist in some circles, they have become less common because of competition with movies, television, organized public school and professional sports activities, and the wide-ranging social opportunities that increasing affluence and the automobile made possible in the south-central United States.

In the 1960s, perhaps recognizing the success of major campaigns like those of Billy Graham, churches in larger cities held citywide campaigns in major auditoriums and sports stadiums. Favorite speakers were Jimmy Allen, professor of Bible at Harding College, and Batsell Barrett Baxter, chair of the Bible department at David Lipscomb College. These efforts declined in the 1980s. Campaigns also flourished in areas in which Churches of Christ were few and small, mostly in the northern tier of states from coast to coast. Campaigners went from door to door, teaching when possible, with preaching at night in a church building or other public facility. Campaigners were often college students. Andy T. Ritchie, who taught Bible at Harding, pioneered in these campaigns, and Owen D. Olbricht has continued them since 1964. Most colleges affiliated with Churches of Christ in the late twentieth century began sponsoring annual "Spring Break" and summer campaigns to involve students in national and international evangelism.

Religious debates provided another means of getting the attention of persons, especially in small cities and rural communities. Debating became popular in regions where Churches of Christ were strong, and more than 12,000 have been documented. Joe S. Warlick (1866-1941) alone claimed more than 400. Debates continued through World War II, but declined after that. Most preachers in Churches of Christ in the first half of the twentieth century had engaged in one or more debates. Though gospel meetings were not designed specifically as evangelistic efforts, often preachers held them immediately after the debate, resulting in conversions. Some preachers, notably Warlick and Jefferson Davis Tant (1861-1941), did see debates as a primary means to evangelize.

Radio programs became a means of evangelism since the early days of the medium. Hall Calhoun (1863-1935) in the 1930s preached daily on radio station WLAC in Nashville. After World War II, with the proliferation of stations, programs sponsored by Churches of Christ could be heard in many small towns in regions where they were strong. Generally an individual congregation arranged for the programs, though they sometimes received funds from other churches. No funds were solicited from listeners. Some of these programs later were broadcast on television or television cable stations. These programs were perceived as opportunities for teaching and usually had a didactic quality.

In the early 1950s James Walter Nichols (1927-1973) and James D. Willeford (1916-1992) proposed a national network radio program. Because of the antipathy toward parachurch organizations in Churches of Christ, however, it was not clear how this might be achieved. The Fifth and Highland Church of Christ in Abilene, Texas, took full charge of the program The Herald of Truth, and requested that other congregations assist. The program began with the greeting, "The Churches of Christ salute you." Persons were employed to raise funds among the churches. After a time Batsell Barrett Baxter of Nashville became the featured speaker. Baxter employed a direct, conversational style and approached topics more as teaching than exhortation. The Herald of Truth later entered television broadcasting and other forms of media. Other congregations began additional regional and national programs, including "Amazing Grace," sponsored by the Madison, Tennessee, Church of

Christ, and "The International Gospel Hour," first sponsored by the Walnut Street Church of Christ in Texarkana, Texas, and later by the Church of Christ in West Fayetteville, Tennessee.

6. Missions

Churches were planted abroad in much the same manner as in the United States, that is, by entrepreneurial effort. Persons wishing to evangelize in a foreign land proceeded to solicit support from churches and individuals. At first, these funds were often sent directly to the missionary. By the 1950s it became standard practice for a missionary to seek out a sponsoring congregation. All funds solicited were then sent to that church; the church in turn sent them to the missionary. In this way the missionary was much more likely to receive funds regularly. Some missionaries still operate without a sponsoring congregation, and some receive funds directly as well as through a sponsoring congregation.

John Moody McCaleb (1861-1953) began work in Japan in 1892 and continued until 1941, becoming the best-known early missionary in Churches of Christ. In the division between Churches of Christ and Disciples of Christ, McCaleb cast his lot with Churches of Christ and became a prototype for later missionaries through reports he published in journals and books. Missions in Japan received much attention between the World Wars and afterward. Though a core of congregations and educational efforts resulted, numbers remain small with about 4,000 members.

Don Carlos Janes (1877-1944) of Louisville, Kentucky, though not a missionary himself, became the leading promoter of missions in the first four decades of the twentieth century. Traveling constantly, visiting churches, and writing letters, Janes recruited missionaries and found support for them. His articles appeared in most of the prominent journals as well as in his *Boosters' Bulletin* and *Missionary Messenger,* encouraging churches to plant congregations in foreign countries and support missionaries. Janes collected and disbursed money for missionaries and arranged their travel to and from mission points. Various teachers in the colleges, especially David Lipscomb College, also encouraged mission efforts.

By the turn of the twentieth century missionary efforts began in Africa through the work of John Sherriff (1864-1935) from New Zealand. William Newton Short and J. D. Merritt followed in the 1920s. After World War II several different persons entered Africa, sometimes as mission teams. George Stuart Benson (1898-1991) and family arrived in China in 1925, followed by Emmett Lackey Broadus (1896-1942) in 1927.

After World War II missions outside the United States accelerated exponentially. Military personnel and civilians involved in the war had become both promoters of missions and missionaries. Japan, Europe, and Korea received the first attention, but soon missionaries were flocking to Africa, Central and South America, Australia, and Southeast Asia. With more than 500 missionaries in foreign fields, interest in mission education grew. George P. Gurganus (1916-1992) established mission programs at Freed-Hardeman, Harding Graduate School, and Abilene Christian, promoting indigenous missions as envisioned by Donald McGavran. He also encouraged mission teams, one of the first of which entered São Paulo, Brazil, in 1967. Leaders among the indigenous peoples in India, Africa, and South America have proceeded to promote training of preachers, planting of churches, and teaching of Bible correspondence courses. Numerous teams of preachers from the United States have spent a month or more in India, evangelizing periodically. Among those who have organized these efforts for almost three decades are Don Browning, Ron Clayton, Charles Scott, and Jerris Bullard. Indigenous Indian preachers have done the majority of the evangelistic work in that country as in Africa, so that there are now more members of Churches of Christ elsewhere than in the United States.

7. Black Churches

Americans of African descent, both slave and free, were present in congregations of the Stone-Campbell Movement almost from its inception. In the hardening of attitudes that followed the Civil War, black Christians who had previously been part of white congregations, even though they were seated apart, were now systematically excluded or encouraged to form separate, segregated congregations. David Lipscomb protested this practice, advocating full fellowship for all races, to no avail.

At the beginning of the twentieth century, three prominent black evangelists were writing reports and articles regularly for journals of the Churches of Christ. S. W. Womack (d. 1920) and Alexander Cleveland Campbell (1866-1930) worked in Tennessee and wrote for the "colored page" of the *Gospel Advocate.* Samuel Robert Cassius (1853-1931) ranged through the Northern, Midwestern, and Western states from his base in the Oklahoma Territory, writing for the *Christian Leader* as well as the *Gospel Advocate* and several other publications. Cassius tried to found an "industrial school" at Tohee, Oklahoma, blending Christian instruction with the model of vocational education pioneered by Booker T. Washington at Tuskegee.

In Tennessee two younger men, both also influenced by Washington, were beginning careers of profound and lasting significance. George Philip Bowser (1874-1950), a preacher and journeyman printer,

Former slave and tireless evangelist, Samuel R. Cassius (1853-1931) attacked racism in the churches in numerous articles and a book *Third Birth of a Nation* (c. 1920), though he argued for separation of the races because of his experience of white antagonism toward blacks. He refused to recognize the division in the Movement, publishing in the *Christian-Evangelist, Christian Standard,* and *Gospel Advocate.*
Courtesy of the Disciples of Christ Historical Society

opened a school in Nashville in 1907 along lines that Cassius had earlier proposed, the first of several academies in which he aimed to educate preachers and church workers who would be self-supporting. Already Bowser had begun publishing the *Christian Echo,* the first avenue of communication among black churches that whites did not control. Although black members participated in integrated Churches of Christ outside the South and some in pockets even in the South, most black members of Churches of Christ gathered in black churches. By 1927 Bowser could list twenty-six independent black congregations with 1,165 members. Marshall Keeble (1878-1968), a son-in-law of Womack who had begun preaching in Nashville in 1897, was traveling as an itinerant evangelist by 1914. After 1920, with full financial support from wealthy whites, Keeble traveled throughout the South and beyond, becoming the most successful evangelist among Churches of Christ. In 1931 alone, Keeble preached in fourteen campaigns, planting six new churches and baptizing 1,071 persons. After 1942 Keeble presided over Nashville Christian Institute, established by his white supporters to train black preachers and church workers. Now he traveled with several young "preacher boys" in tow, extending and amplifying his appeal and raising money for the school as he made converts. From 1939 to 1950 Keeble was also listed as editor of *Christian Counselor,* published by the Gospel Advocate Company.

Both Keeble and Bowser baptized converts who became preachers and trained others to preach. In 1945 Annie Clay Tuggle displayed the portraits and biographies of 103 black preachers in her directory, *Our Ministers and Song Leaders of the Church of Christ.* A 1974 directory listed 151 *Black Preachers of Today,* only a sample of the potential total. Bowser's protégé, Richard Nathaniel Hogan (1902-1997), flourished as an evangelist in the 1930s and after 1939 as minister of the Figueroa Street church in Los Angeles, for many years the largest black congregation in Churches of Christ. After Bowser's death in 1950, Hogan extended his influence as editor of the *Christian Echo.*

Since 1945 black Churches of Christ have expanded in inner cities, especially in Newark, Detroit, Chicago, Los Angeles, Atlanta, Dallas, and Houston. All schools affiliated with Churches of Christ now admit black students, but many black preachers have attended Southwestern Christian College (SWCC) in Terrell, Texas, founded in 1950 to educate black preachers and church leaders in a segregated environment. At that time only Pepperdine College admitted black students. SWCC remains a predominantly black college. Black Churches of Christ sponsor an annual national lectureship and youth conference and a biannual evangelistic crusade.

8. Education and Scholarship

When division became "official" in 1906, several colleges were clearly associated with Churches of Christ. Tolbert Fanning (1810-1874), who founded Franklin College (1845-1866) near Nashville, Tennessee, set the pattern with a curriculum modeled after that of Bethany College, founded by Alexander Campbell in 1840. Colleges existing in 1906 include Burritt College (Spencer, Tennessee, 1849-1939), Georgie Robertson Christian College (1897-1907, the immediate predecessor of Freed-Hardeman), Nashville Bible School (1891- , now Lipscomb University), Potter Bible School (1901), Thorpe Spring (1873-1931), Western Bible and Literary College (1905-1916, a forerunner of Harding), and Abilene Christian (1906-). Some suspicion of formal education persisted among the churches, but a clear majority favored an educated constituency and ministry. These institutions were not dedicated solely to training preachers, but from the beginning they were designed as liberal arts colleges. Campbell argued that education was important to understanding the Scriptures, a conviction that continues.

Nashville Bible School, founded by David Lipscomb and James A. Harding, had trained many leading preachers by 1906, and especially future educators. Colleges and universities founded more recently, including Pepperdine (1937-), Harding (1922-), Faulkner (1942- , formerly Alabama Christian), Florida College (1946-), Oklahoma Christian (1949-), Ohio Valley (1956-), York (1956-), Lubbock Christian (1957-), and Rochester (1959-). Graduate programs, especially offering degrees in Bible, were launched beginning with Pepperdine in 1944, then Abilene Christian (1953) and Harding Graduate School (1954). Several of the other schools now offer graduate programs. In the 1960s, in part because of a preacher shortage but also because of government assistance available to veterans, unaccredited preaching schools were established, including Sunset School of Preaching (Lubbock, Texas, 1961), Brown Trail School of Preaching (Hurst, Texas, 1963), and White's Ferry Road School of Preaching (West Monroe, Louisiana, 1964). Sunset has now become Sunset International Bible Institute. These schools, after the pattern of the Herald of Truth, are under the control of a single congregation that in turn receives contributions from other congregations. The number of students in these schools has steadily declined in recent years so that several no longer exist, including White's Ferry Road.

9. Controversies

Churches of Christ have been faced with numerous controversies from the beginning. Along with objection to mission organizations and instrumental music was also an objection to located preachers, that is, preachers who work full time for one congregation. The polemic against located ministers was especially strong in the writing of Austin McGary (1846-1928) of Texas in the 1880s. David Lipscomb shared McGary's view. Not until the early decades of the twentieth century did some churches appoint ministers to do most of the preaching, and many churches did not employ preachers until after World War II. Some leaders, especially Daniel Sommer (1850-1940) and, later, Carl Ketcherside (1908-1989), asserted that all capable men of the congregation should share in preaching and teaching or, as they called it, mutual ministry.

Premillennialism emerged as a major point of controversy after 1910. Prior to that time many leaders in Churches of Christ were moderate historical premillennialists, though not advocating any specific interpretations. As dispensational premillennialism emphasizing the rapture, the national restoration of the Jewish people, the future of the church, and the battle of Armageddon developed among fundamentalists, leaders in Churches of Christ generally retreated from millenarian ideas. Preachers such as Foy E. Wallace, Jr. (1896-1979), in effect pushed premillennial advocates such as Robert Henry Boll into a separate fellowship. In the late twentieth century premillennial Churches of Christ have asked not to be distinguished from mainstream Churches of Christ in Mac Lynn's directory, *Churches of Christ in the United States.*

In the 1950s a significant group opposed the creation of extra-congregational institutions that they believed were unscriptural and undermined the prerogatives and responsibilities of local churches and individual Christians. They opposed the rapid increase in such church-sponsored programs and services as children's homes, homes for the elderly, campus ministries, gymnasiums, kitchen facilities, parachurch organizations such as the Herald of Truth, and community service centers designed to care for the needy. These continuing controversies resulted in a group of churches usually designated noninstitutional, with Florida College as a center for training preachers.

Another controversy has to do with an emphasis on God's grace as promoted by such persons as Kenney Carl Moser (1893-1976), Grover Cleveland Brewer (1884-1956), and others in the 1930s. Only since the 1980s have their views been widely accepted. In the 1980s a heated discussion focused on hermeneutics. Drawing on Thomas Campbell, Churches of Christ historically determined "essentials" in Scripture by seeking commands, examples, and, later, necessary inferences. Some argued that this hermeneutic tended toward legalism, and that it is better to understand Scripture primarily through the lens of the character of God, Christ, and the Holy Spirit for determining church and personal life. Traditionalists labeled this approach a "new hermeneutic" and urged rejection of it and the change agents advocating it.

Discussion of the role of women in the life of the church in the 1990s has resulted in women playing larger roles in teaching youth, coordinating youth programs, and serving as college ministers. Not many churches have yet, however, involved women in public worship leadership. More congregations permit praying and teaching in adult classes by both males and females.

Worship also became a major focus in the 1990s. Traditionally a song leader has selected songs with another designated person, often an elder or a preacher, selecting persons to pray, read Scriptures, or serve at the Lord's Table. In larger congregations names may be printed in a church bulletin or order of worship. A recent development is the worship team, in which a worship leader selects hymns and Scripture readings, then along with several persons with microphones leads the congregation in worship. A majority of churches, however, are indifferent to these arrangements or insist that the practice is not authorized in the New Testament.

As was common among several religious groups at the end of the twentieth century, a small number of Churches of Christ attempted to reinvent the congregation as a community church, identifying as Churches of Christ only secondarily. Those taking this approach point to the success of community evangelical and charismatic churches. For Churches of Christ results have been mixed. Much earlier, leading ministers such as G. C. Brewer had insisted that in order to be undenominational a congregation should simply be identified as "the church" at such and such a location. Some churches, mostly larger ones, have become less exclusive and more cooperative with other religious groups. Other leaders have, predictably, opposed any move toward inclusivism.

10. The Genius of the Churches of Christ

Churches of Christ have affirmed the centrality of Scripture. They have demanded commitment to church life and the responsibility of all members for the church. They have emphasized church planting and evangelism. They have engaged in a genuine struggle with biblical precedents. They have encouraged personal commitment to the Lord in devotional life and in a biblical ethics and morality with concern for the needy. They have sought strong bonds and networks of community, with knowledge of other members nationally and internationally. Some areas that have caused friction in the body at the beginning of the twenty-first century include a residual legalism, a growing disposition toward evangelicalism in some quarters, and a continuing exclusivism that is coming increasingly under fire.

BIBLIOGRAPHY William S. Banowsky, *Mirror of a Movement* (1965) • Leroy Garrett, *The Stone-Campbell Movement: An Anecdotal History of Three Churches* (1981, rev. 1994) • David Edwin Harrell, Jr., *Quest for a Christian America: The Disciples of Christ and American Society to 1866* (1966; repr. ed. 2003) • David Edwin Harrell, Jr., *The Social Sources of Division in the Disciples of Christ, 1865-1900* (1973; repr. ed. 2003) • David Edwin Harrell, Jr., *The Churches of Christ in the Twentieth Century: Homer Hailey's Personal Journey of Faith* (2000) • Gary Holloway and Douglas A. Foster, *Renewing God's People: A Concise History of Churches of Christ* (2001) • Robert E. Hooper, *A Distinct People: A History of Churches of Christ in the Twentieth Century* (1993) • Richard T. Hughes, *Reviving the Ancient Faith: The Story of Churches of Christ in America* (1996) • Richard T. Hughes and R. L. Roberts, *The Churches of Christ* (2001) • Mac Lynn, *Churches of Christ in the United States 2003* (2003) • Mac Lynn, *Churches of Christ around the World* (2003) • Thomas H. Olbricht, *Hearing God's Voice: My Life with Scripture in the Churches of Christ* (1996) • Richard M. Tristano, *The Origins of the Restoration Movement: An Intellectual History* (1988) • Earl West, *Search for the Ancient Order*, 4 vols. (1949, 1950, 1979, 1988) • M. Norvel Young, *A History of Colleges Established and Controlled by Members of the Churches of Christ* (1949). THOMAS H. OLBRICHT

Church of Christ, The, by a Layman

See Phillips, Thomas W.

Church of Christ Development Company

See Canada, The Movement in

Church of God (Anderson, Indiana)

See Open Forum

Churches of Christ Theological College (Mulgrave)

See Australia, The Movement in

Churches of Christ Theological College in New South Wales

See Australia, The Movement in

Cincinnati Bible College and Seminary

Bible college and seminary affiliated with the Christian Churches/Churches of Christ.

Early in the twentieth century, conservative Disciples of Christ churches struggled in a variety of contexts with the impact of liberalism and modernism. Many young graduate students from these churches had been exposed to liberalism in higher education, some even bringing liberal ideas to bear on the church ministries and agencies they eventually served. Heated controversies developed over such issues as open membership, comity agreements in the domains of international mission work, and higher criticism of the Bible in church-related schools.

The College of the Bible (now Lexington Theological Seminary) in Lexington, Kentucky, under the presidency of J. W. McGarvey, had long been a bastion of conservative thinking on these issues, but McGarvey died in 1911. A new president and new faculty reflected a more liberal perspective, and by 1917 the school was clearly in sympathy with liberal ideas.

Many individuals and churches in Kentucky and Ohio fought hard to reverse the liberal tide, particularly Standard Publishing of Cincinnati. Since such efforts were unavailing, however, conservatives compensated by establishing "replacement" schools to train young men for the ministry. In 1923 McGarvey Bible College was begun in Louisville, Kentucky. That same year Cincinnati Bible Institute was started in Cincinnati by the Clarke Fund, which in 1925 be-

Dubbed the "Old Guard" at Cincinnati Bible Seminary, Ralph Records (1883-1965), Rupert C. Foster (1888-1970), and Ira Boswell (1866-1950) fiercely resisted the incursions of liberalism and modernism in the Stone-Campbell Movement and defended the "Bible College" as the preferred model of Christian higher education. Photo appearing in the *Christian Standard*, March 23, 1940

came the Christian Restoration Association. Within a year, the leaders of both schools came to believe that there was no need for two schools only a hundred miles apart doing much the same thing. The two therefore merged in 1924 to form Cincinnati Bible Seminary (CBS), which continued to operate under the Clarke Fund/Christian Restoration Association umbrella until it received its own charter in 1928. Classes began in September 1924.

Because the school was begun as a reaction to theological liberalism, its curriculum clearly reflected its conservative orientation. President Ralph Records led the school for its first twenty-four years. Rupert C. Foster was one of the founding faculty members and continued to teach until his death in 1970. George Mark Elliott joined the faculty in 1937 and taught until 1972. This trio was emphatic in its resistance to the new liberalism and earned a reputation, for themselves and their college, of being feisty and pugnacious defenders of the faith. Throughout the decades of the 1940s, '50s, and '60s, graduates of CBS continued to reflect the aggressive antagonism they had learned in the classroom under Foster and Elliott.

The school therefore became well known for defending the conservative viewpoint with respect both to biblical hermeneutics and local church practices. Because of its strong emphasis on "Preaching the Word," the school turned out hundreds of ministers, evangelists, and missionaries who mounted aggressive evangelistic campaigns. At one point the school claimed that one-third of all missionaries from the Christian Churches/Churches of Christ were CBS alumni.

The school has long had as its slogan "Scholarship in an Atmosphere of Faith." These twin goals indicate the school's desire to blend academic competency with a conservative faith perspective. By the 1950s the school was adding new faculty with significant academic credentials. Increasingly it was approaching national higher education standards. In 1966 Cincinnati Bible College was accepted into the Accrediting Association of Bible Colleges. In 1989 both college and graduate school were granted regional accreditation by the North Central Association of Colleges and Schools.

Although the school offered graduate instruction from its very beginning, the graduate school was given a separate administration and recognition in 1956 with Lewis A. Foster (Ph.D., Harvard; son of Rupert C. Foster) serving as dean. The graduate school has continued to grow, and currently it constitutes approximately one-third of full-time faculty as well as of total student matriculation. Because the word "Seminary" normally connotes graduate-level education for ministry, this often created confusion in understanding the work of the College. In order to clarify this, the school changed its name in 1987 to Cincinnati Bible College and Seminary.

While maintaining its identity as a Bible college and minister-training institution, the school has also included academic programs in Christian education, church music, and teacher education. Most of the classes in the seminary focus on practical ministry, but there are also academic programs in Bible, theology, church history, and a clinical counseling degree that leads to state licensure.

In the first seventy-five years of its existence, the school has seen about 10,000 students pass through its halls and has granted about 3,000 degrees. In recent years about 80-100 bachelor's degrees and 60-70 graduate degrees have been awarded each spring. The school estimates that currently about 20 percent of all ministers serving Christian Churches/Churches of Christ have received all or part of their education at Cincinnati Bible College and Seminary. The same applies for about 20 percent of all missionaries.

See also Bible College Movement; Christian Restoration Association; Foster, Rupert Clinton; Fundamentalism; Higher Education, Views of in the Movement

JAMES B. NORTH

Civil Government

See Lipscomb, David

Civil War, The

Members of the Stone-Campbell Movement in both the North and the South probably answered the call to arms during the Civil War in the same proportions as members of other religious groups. Large numbers of young men enlisted and fought in the armies of both the Union and the Confederacy. The Movement's colleges were virtually deserted because students, often accompanied by their teachers, volunteered for battle. Eureka College in Illinois graduated only three male students during the war years. Among the more notable and visible military leaders from the Movement were General James A. Garfield in the Union army and Barton W. Stone, Jr., son of one of the Movement's revered founders, who rose to the rank of colonel in the Confederate army.

A number of prominent Stone-Campbell Movement preachers served as chaplains during the Civil War, and many others preached to the troops from time to time. Benjamin F. Hall, a prominent Texas preacher, was chaplain in the Sixth Texas Cavalry, a unit composed mostly of members of the Christian Church of Grayson County, Texas. Before being appointed director of hospital facilities for the Confederate Army of the West, Thomas W. Caskey, probably the most prominent preacher of the Movement in Mississippi before the Civil War, served as chaplain of the Eighteenth Mississippi Regiment.

Former preacher and college president, James A. Garfield eagerly accepted command of the Forty-second Ohio and rose rapidly to the rank of major general. He recruited hundreds of Disciples into his regiment. Courtesy of the Disciples of Christ Historical Society

While members of the Stone-Campbell Movement in both North and South were prominent supporters of the war, a strain of sectarian disdain for the affairs of the world colored the thought of many of the Movement's early leaders, including Alexander Campbell, making them unwilling to endorse either side in the conflict. In addition, a large percentage of the Movement's membership in 1860 was concentrated in the border region stretching from western Virginia to Missouri, an area where anti-war sentiment was strong throughout the war. As a result, many important leaders in the Stone-Campbell Movement were either neutral or outspoken pacifists during the struggle. The aging Campbell, whose postmillennial hopes for the nation were dashed by the Civil War, was deeply distressed by the bellicose pronouncements of some church leaders. Campbell and his son-in-law, William K. Pendleton, who was largely responsible for editing the *Millennial Harbinger* during the war, maintained a neutral stance in the Movement's most important magazine. Most other Movement journals published during the war years followed the example of the *Harbinger.*

Early in the war a number of respected border state preachers aggressively tried to quell the war spirit. In September 1861, the *Christian Pioneer,* a Missouri paper, published the names of twenty-three prominent preachers that its editors believed to be neutral. Included were Campbell and Pendleton of Bethany, West Virginia; Cincinnati preachers Benjamin Franklin and David S. Burnet; Tolbert Fanning and Philip Fall from Tennessee; and eleven Missouri and Kentucky preachers. The list was overly optimistic; some of those listed soon became outspoken advocates of the Union cause.

Among the churches of the Stone-Campbell Movement, the most consistently pacifist region throughout the Civil War was Tennessee. Not a single notable church leader in that state supported the war effort. While some Tennessee preachers opposed the war because of the same ambivalence and divided loyalty characteristic of many border state Christians, an important group in the state embraced traditional pacifist beliefs building on a persistent though ill-defined pacifist tradition in the Movement during the antebellum period.

In hindsight, from the viewpoint of the Stone-Campbell Movement, the most auspicious events during the war years transpired during the meetings of the American Christian Missionary Society in 1861 and 1863. In 1861 the society was the Movement's only semblance of national organization, and its actions were critically important symbolically. The 1861 meeting in Cincinnati attracted a large crowd, including the venerable Alexander Campbell and the dashing figure of Colonel James A. Garfield, a former preacher and college president. The delegates were almost evenly divided between a group of avid Northern war supporters and another group of border state moderates. No Southerners attended the meeting. Supporters of the Union cause attempted to introduce a resolution supporting the Union. The society had scrupulously avoided addressing controversial social issues in the past, including slavery, and moderate delegates won a vote to declare the resolution out of order. The convention adjourned after the vote, and war enthusiasts convened a ten-minute rump session. In that session the resolution was passed with only one dissenting vote. The 1861 convention thus ended in an impasse. While pleased that the resolution had not been passed in a formal session of the convention, border state moderates were concerned that the growing war hysteria would ultimately estrange Southern churches. Despite the unofficial passage of resolutions in the rump session, disgruntled Union supporters left the convention more resolved than ever to persuade their church to make a clear statement in opposition to rebellion.

The 1862 meeting of the society passed without controversy, but by 1863 war enthusiasts had lost patience with the moderates in their midst. Resolutions were introduced assuring the society's "allegiance" to the government, tendering "our sympathies to our brave and noble soldiers in the fields, who are defending us from the attempts of armed traitors to overthrow our government," and promising to pray for the nation's legitimate rulers in accord with the biblical injunction to "obey magistrates." Kentuckian James W. McGarvey led a fight to keep the resolutions from a vote, but the strategy that had succeeded two years earlier was easily defeated and the resolutions were overwhelmingly passed. McGarvey and other moderates were disconsolate. Following the convention, he wrote in the *American Christian Quarterly Review,* "I have judged the American Christian Missionary Society, and have decided for myself, that it should now cease to exist."

In 1866 respected Missouri preacher and editor Moses E. Lard asked the question in his journal, *Lard's Quarterly,* "Can we divide?" In the tense months following the collapse of the Confederacy, Lard noted, he had frequently encountered church members who predicted that the Movement would divide along sectional lines. He believed, as did most of those who chronicled the Movement's history in subsequent years, that it would not, indeed could not, divide. He insisted that it had survived the national tensions created by slavery and Civil War as a united church. Historian Winfred Earnest Garrison later surmised in *Religion Follows the Frontier* that the Civil War was "not divisive at all," as have most other historians of the Movement.

Son of evangelist John Allen Gano, Richard M. Gano (1830-1913) helped organize the Grapevine Volunteers of Tarrant County, Texas, in June 1861. He rose quickly in the Confederate Army, and by the end of 1863 had attained the rank of Brigadier General. After the war he was ordained and spent the rest of his life as a minister. Courtesy of the Center for Restoration Studies, Abilene Christian University

In some respects it is accurate to say that the Stone-Campbell Movement did not divide during the sectional crisis over slavery and the Civil War — as had the Methodist, Baptist, and Presbyterian churches. Aside from the American Christian Missionary Society, the Movement had no national denominational structure; consequently, no authoritative body had the power to affirm either unity or division. In this loose organizational environment, Christians in both North and South continued to regard one another as brothers and sisters before, during, and after the Civil War. On the other hand, the foray of the American Christian Missionary Society into politics with the passage of loyalty resolutions had considerable symbolic and real significance. In the South, distrust and hatred of the society lingered after the war and surfaced in a variety of ways in the last three decades of the nineteenth century.

Hope for a cordial restoration of fellowship after the war was dampened by the appearance in early 1866 of two sectionally oriented weekly church periodicals. The *Gospel Advocate* and *Christian Standard* became respectively the Movement's most influential Southern and Northern journals throughout the remainder of the century. By 1866 many Northern church leaders were openly critical of the neutral stance taken by the *Millennial Harbinger* and the *American Christian Review* during the war. Plans to establish a new journal came to fruition in April 1866 with the founding of the *Christian Standard.* Edited by Isaac Errett, one of the most respected churchmen in the North, and supported by Representative James A. Garfield of Ohio and the wealthy Thomas W. Phillips of Pennsylvania, the *Standard* reflected the confidence and mood of self-importance of the growing churches of the North. The editor of the *Standard* madc it clear that the paper was established to give voice to those who had been loyal to the government during the war.

More portentous in pointing toward an impending sectional division in the Movement was the post-war course of the *Gospel Advocate,* which resumed publication in January 1866 after an interruption of four years. David Lipscomb and Tolbert Fanning, the editors of the magazine, immediately denounced those who had supported the war in both North and South. Isaac Errett charged that the *Advocate* began in 1866 with "an appeal to men of southern blood"; in the decades that followed, the paper rarely missed a chance to remind its largely Southern clientele that the leaders of the churches of the North had been "strong Union men."

The sectional animosities so obvious in the wake of the Civil War mingled easily with diverging theological views in the last third of the nineteenth century. In the North members largely embraced the triumphant and optimistic national mood of the late nineteenth century, evolving into a successful and influential denomination by 1900. On the other hand, many in the Southern churches embraced a separationist theology that rejected Christian participation in civil government. David Lipscomb became the chief spokesperson for a theology that condemned all political activities on the part of Christians, frequently pointing to the damage that partisanship had done to the cause of Christ during and after the Civil War. Lipscomb's views, published in the *Gospel Advocate* and collected in a small book published in 1889 titled *Civil Government: Its Origin, Mission and Destiny, and the Christian's Relation to It,* included a radical pacifism and a broader rejection of Christian participation in voting and holding public office. Many Southerners, deeply chagrined by Northern support for the Union cause, and particularly by the actions of the American Christian Missionary Society, found Lipscomb's arguments persuasive.

The sectional nature of the division in the Stone-Campbell Movement that separated the Disciples of Christ and Churches of Christ in the late nineteenth and early twentieth century is well documented. In the 1906 survey of religious bodies conducted by the United States Census Bureau, which formally recognized the two groups as distinct religious bodies, 101,734 of the reported 159,658 members of Churches of Christ lived in the eleven former states of the Confederacy. Another 30,206 lived in the four border states of Kentucky, West Virginia, Missouri, and Oklahoma. The only state north of the Ohio River reporting more than 5,000 members of Churches of Christ was Indiana. On the other hand, less than 15 percent of the nearly one million members of the Disciples of Christ lived in the eleven Southern states. In short, in the wake of the Civil War, the conservative Churches of Christ were extraordinarily successful in rallying support in the South.

A number of sociological and theological factors contributed to the sectional division in the movement at the end of the nineteenth century. Church members in the South were more rural and poorer than their counterparts in the North. And while the churches of the North embraced the triumphant, progressive spirit of the age, the economic and cultural backwardness of the South proved to be a seedbed for a sectarian religious enthusiasm. Feelings of alienation flourished in the deprivation of the post–Civil War South.

Though the division between the Disciples of Christ and Churches of Christ at the turn of the twentieth century bears no simple or singular explanation, the Civil War nonetheless stands as a watershed in the history of the Stone-Campbell Movement, as it does in the history of the nation. In the long run, it was unlikely that people who had been unwilling to remain a part of the same country would dwell in peace in the same church.

BIBLIOGRAPHY Earl Eugene Eminhizer, "The Abolitionists Among the Disciples of Christ" (Th.D. thesis, Southern California School of Theology, 1968) • Robert Oldham Fife, "Alexander Campbell and the Christian Church in the Slavery Controversy" (Ph.D. thesis, Indiana University, 1960) • David Edwin Harrell, Jr., *Quest for a Christian America* (1966; repr. ed. 2003) • David Edwin Harrell, Jr., "The Sectional Origins of the Churches of Christ," *Journal of Southern History* 30 (August 1964): 261-77 • David Edwin Harrell, Jr., "Disciples of Christ Pacifism in Nineteenth-Century Tennessee," *Tennessee Historical Quarterly* 21 (September 1962): 263-74 • Delbert Dayton Keesee, "The Churches of Christ During the War Between the States" (M.A. thesis, Division of Graduate Instruction, Butler University, 1954) • Moses Lard, "Can

We Divide?" *Lard's Quarterly* 3 (April 1866): 330-36 • Steven Smith Lemley, "Political and Social Division Among Disciples of Christ" (M.A. thesis, Pepperdine College, 1970) • *Report of Proceedings of the Fifteenth Anniversary Meeting of the American Christian Missionary Society, Held in Cincinnati, October 20, 21, 22, 1863* (1863) • Eileen Gordon Vandergrift, "The Christian Missionary Society: A Study of the Influence of Slavery on the Disciples of Christ" (M.A. thesis, Butler School of Religion, 1945) • Earl Irvin West, *The Trials of the Ancient Order: 1844-1865* (1993).

DAVID EDWIN HARRELL, JR.

Close Communion

See Lord's Supper, The

Cochrane, Louis

See Literature

Cogdill, Roy E. (1907-1985)

Attorney, evangelist, debater, and publisher among noninstitutional Churches of Christ. Born April 24, 1907, in Hobart, Oklahoma.

Cogdill attended the high school division of Western Oklahoma Christian College at Cordell and Abilene Christian College, where he became class president and an outstanding debater. He returned to Oklahoma to preach at Frederick in 1925 and married Lorraine Burke.

Cogdill moved to Dallas in 1926, spending the next eighteen years preaching in that part of Texas. In 1931 throat surgery forced a short hiatus from preaching, during which time he edited the "Texas Department" for the *Firm Foundation*. He also became a subscription agent for the rival *Gospel Advocate*, then edited by Foy E. Wallace, Jr., who served as a mentor to Cogdill.

In 1937 Cogdill graduated from Jefferson Law School in Dallas, embarking upon a profitable law practice while continuing his preaching. In 1938 Cogdill published *The New Testament Church*, which over his lifetime was translated into a half-dozen languages, selling hundreds of thousands of copies. He was also involved in extensive preaching in gospel meetings.

By 1943 Cogdill left his law practice, returning to "full time" preaching at the South National Church of Christ in Springfield, Missouri. Moving to Houston in 1944, Cogdill worked in a two-preacher arrangement with Luther Blackmon at the Norhill congregation. Cogdill formed a publishing company that produced books of sermons preached in the Houston Music Hall in 1945 and 1946 by Foy E. Wallace, Jr.: *God's Prophetic Word*, an attack on premillennial doctrines, and *Bulwarks of the Faith*, which challenged Roman Catholic and Protestant theologies. Cogdill's printing firm formed a religious division to print Wallace's periodical, the *Bible Banner*.

During this period Cogdill formed a friendship with Fanning Yater Tant (1908-1997). The two collaborated with J. P. Sanders (1906-2002) and C. A. Norred (1888-1969) to produce *Preaching in the Twentieth Century*, which launched John Allen Hudson's Old Path Book Club. Tant later became the managing editor of the *Gospel Guardian*, renewing Foy E. Wallace, Jr.'s paper first published in the 1930s. A rift with Wallace did not deter Cogdill or Tant from pursuing a strict noninstitutional approach, challenging the increasing funding by churches of colleges, orphanages, hospitals, homes for the aged, "sponsoring church" radio and TV ministries, and other parachurch organizations.

In the early 1950s, the Cogdill family moved to Jordan, Ontario, where the congregation sponsored summer mission works in the province, buying radio airtime and renting public halls where Cogdill preached nightly. Cogdill also returned to the United States frequently to conduct gospel meeting work. A serious automobile accident near Gallup, New Mexico, while returning from a California meeting prompted his return to Texas, where Cogdill preached at San Antonio's West Avenue Church of Christ from 1954 to 1956.

By this time, debates and journal articles over "institutionalism" were in full bloom, and Cogdill moved to Lufkin, Texas, to oversee his publishing ventures. In 1957 Cogdill published *Walking by Faith*, dealing specifically with the "institutional" issues. In November 1957 Cogdill and Guy N. Woods (1908-1993) met in Birmingham, Alabama, for what many considered the definitive debate on these questions.

His wife's health problems caused Cogdill to settle in Nacogdoches, Texas, in 1958, where she died June 23, 1960. Cogdill plunged into a hectic series of cross-country meetings, including a second debate with Guy N. Woods at Newbern, Tennessee, in 1961. After marrying Venita Faulkner of Oklahoma City, Cogdill preached for congregations there, in California, and in Florida. Renewed publishing ventures involved merging the Gospel Guardian Foundation with *Truth Magazine* to produce the weekly *Guardian of Truth* and two Bible class literature series: *Truth in Life* and a reprint of Sweet Publishing's *Journeys through the Bible*, renamed *Walking with God*.

Cogdill was a leading participant in, and later published the speeches from, the 1968 Arlington (Texas) Meeting that brought together leaders from both sides of the institutional issues. In 1971 Cogdill returned to Texas, where he spent most of the rest of his life working with the Spring Branch, Conroe, and Katy Churches of Christ. He died May 15, 1985, and is buried at Hobart, Oklahoma.

See also Florida College; Noninstitutional Movement; Sweet Publishing Company; Wallace, Foy Esco, Jr.; Woods, Guy Napoleon

JAMES STEPHEN WOLFGANG

Colegio Bíblico

Bible college affiliated with the Christian/Churches of Christ.

Located in Eagle Pass, Texas, the college was founded in 1945 by Harland and Frances Cary, and offers training for Christian ministry to Spanish-speaking people from throughout Latin America. Since 1996 the school has also offered classes across the Rio Grande River in Piedras Negras, Mexico, under the name Seminario Bíblico.

See also Bible College Movement; Hispanics in the Movement; Latin America and Caribbean, Missions in

MARK S. JOY

College of Churches of Christ in Canada

Founded in 1927 to facilitate the education of ministerial leadership for Disciples of Christ in Canada.

Small numbers, great distances, and the appeal of "greener pastures" south of the Canadian/United States border have always complicated the training of Disciples ministers in Canada. Although successful Bible colleges were established in a number of Canadian locations, the quest for a stronger program of higher education remained. As early as 1892 the Ontario Cooperation undertook a lectureship series in Toronto, and about 1895 it shifted attention to a college being established in St. Thomas, Ontario. It started off well with a moderate endowment, a new building, and about nineteen students, but eventually dissension about doctrine and loss of leadership proved to be too much. Sometime after 1909 "Sinclair College" (as it had become known) was no longer able to continue.

Ongoing interest by the Ontario Cooperation in reestablishing a college in Toronto led to affiliating with a Toronto university. In 1925 the Ontario Cooperation approved a model that envisaged affiliation with a secular institution for a general B.A. degree and cooperation with an existing theological college for ministerial instruction. In conjunction with those studies, Disciples students would attend a series of lectures from an instructor acceptable to the Cooperation on subjects important to the Disciples of Christ. It was anticipated that these lectures eventually would be approved as valid toward the degree programs. That model was put into operation in 1926 in cooperation with McMaster University. A residence was secured for students, and in October of 1927 the "College, Churches of Christ in Canada, Inc." received its incorporation. Eventually the Sinclair Endowment, originally designated for the St. Thomas College, was transferred. Additional gifts and endowments were added over the years. When McMaster University moved to Hamilton in 1930, the College was able to affiliate with the University of Toronto. In addition to the students in residence, extension courses were offered across Canada.

While the principles adopted in 1925 are still at the essence of the College of Churches of Christ in Canada, there is no longer a residence and there is no longer a formal affiliation with any one university. Students who have been approved as Candidates for Ministry by the All Canada Committee are encouraged to attend their baccalaureate studies at an accredited university in their area and to obtain their graduate ministerial studies from an approved seminary, supplementing their education with extension courses of particular interest to Disciples of Christ in Canada. Financial assistance is provided at 50 percent tuition for undergraduate studies and 100 percent tuition for M.Div. or similar ministerial degrees. Continuing education for Disciples ministers is approved and assisted on a case-by-case basis, as funds are available. Lay ministry education is currently being explored. Lectureships are offered at the All Canada Convention and on other occasions as opportunities and funds allow.

The College is managed by an elected membership from churches across Canada with a board of managers elected from that membership.

RONALD DAKIN

College of Missions

Graduate-level institution for training missionaries of the Disciples of Christ and other Protestant groups, located in Indianapolis, Indiana, from 1910 to 1927.

Although the idea had been around since 1884, the Christian Woman's Board of Missions (CWBM) began to consider seriously the possibility of an advanced missionary training school in 1906. During the Centennial Convention of 1909, Mrs. Helen E. Moses was unable to travel to the convention for health reasons, and as she contemplated the work of the CWBM she decided to promote the idea of a Missionary Training School funded by centennial offerings. Major gifts were received to purchase property, to build a building, and to fund a school. On August 18, 1910, the Sarah Davis Deterding Memorial Building, better known as the Missions Building, was dedicated in Indianapolis. In addition to offices for the school and the CWBM, the building contained classrooms, dormitories, a kitchen, and other facilities. In May 1910, Professor Charles T. Paul accepted an offer to become the principal of the school, and the first courses were offered in September 1910. Two years later, it became the College of Missions, and Professor Paul its president.

From the beginning, the CWBM organized a curriculum and hired a faculty around the intellectual and practical needs of missionary candidates. Based on the recommendations of the Edinburgh Missionary Conference of 1910 and the needs of the missionaries of the Disciples of Christ, the curriculum included courses in biblical studies, the history of Christianity, the theory and practice of Christian missions, the history of the Disciples of Christ, as well as specialized courses in the areas of Disciples foreign missions. In addition to literature and linguistics, the latter included courses in various foreign languages: Chinese, French, Hindi, Japanese, Lonkundo, Portuguese, Spanish, Tibetan, and Urdu. Other academic courses included Colonial Government and International Law, Medicine and Hygiene, Pedagogy, Philosophy and Ethics, the Religions of the World, and Sociology. Finally, there were courses in bookkeeping and photography. In order to support such an ambitious curriculum, the faculty of the College of Missions included distinguished scholars from a variety of disciplines, including missionaries John G. McGavran (India) and Andrew F. Hensey (Congo).

Although predominantly Disciples of Christ, students of the College included members of a variety of Christian communions, including Reformed, Friends, Mennonites, and others. These students contributed to the life of the church through service in home and foreign missions, and their theses are a continuing legacy and contribution to scholarship. Many of the theses may be found in the Disciples of Christ Historical Society (Nashville, Tennessee).

In 1927 the College of Missions began a partnership with the Kennedy School of Missions in Hartford, Connecticut. Its faculty, students, and material resources went to Connecticut to strengthen the interdenominational training center. Disciples missionary candidates continued to go to Hartford in subsequent decades for graduate training in fields related to their work. For a few years after the partnership with the Kennedy School began, Professor Paul offered extension courses in Indianapolis; later, the College of Missions sponsored summer orientation programs at Crystal Lake, Michigan. The original Missions Building in Indianapolis served as the physical headquarters of the United Christian Missionary Society and, later, the Christian Church (Disciples of Christ) until the General Units moved to the Disciples Center in 1994.

BIBLIOGRAPHY Ida Withers Harrison, *History of the Christian Woman's Board of Missions* (1920) (see esp. chap. 13, "College of Missions," pp. 143-53) • *Survey of Service* (1928) (see esp. chap. 30, "College of Missions," pp. 521-33).

PAUL ALLEN WILLIAMS

College of the Bible

See Lexington Theological Seminary

College of the Scriptures

Institution developed for college and seminary studies for African Americans in Louisville, Kentucky, affiliated with the Christian Churches/Churches of Christ.

The College of the Scriptures was formed in Louisville, Kentucky, on May 18, 1945, and was intended not only as a residential school but also as a source of correspondence course work for African American women and men who could not attend the school full time. The college had its opening convocation on September 14, 1945, and classes began four days later with just two students. Its founder and first president was Robert Tibbs Maxey, Jr. (1910-2002), the son of a preacher, the brother of three ministers of the Christian Churches/Churches of Christ, and an evangelist himself. Maxey's life's work was to use his influence as a Caucasian male to bridge the divide between the races in the church and the larger society.

Although of small beginnings, the College of the Scriptures filled a great need among the African American Christian Churches/Churches of Christ in Kentucky and beyond. The city of Louisville was chosen as the location for the college due to the positive response the idea of the school had received from the black churches in Kentucky. In addition, this location was considered not too far North and not too far away from its primary constituents, would-be preachers for African American congregations. The college still maintains this original vision and mission.

See also African Americans in the Movement — Christian Churches/Churches of Christ; Bible College Movement; Higher Education, Views of in the Movement; Winston-Salem Bible College

BIBLIOGRAPHY Robert Tibbs Maxey, Jr., *One Wide River* (1960).

LISA W. DAVISON

College Press

Publishing house associated with the Christian Churches/Churches of Christ.

Don DeWelt (1919-1990) began College Press Publishing Company in Joplin, Missouri, in May of 1959. As a professor with Ozark Bible College (now Ozark Christian College), DeWelt began publishing materials for his classes. Using the slogan "Every Christian a Bible student," DeWelt sought to call all Christians to a more serious attitude regarding their spiritual development.

College Press has since grown from an entrepreneurial effort to a small corporation of over forty employees dedicated to publishing Christian books, Sunday School curricula, and related Bible study materials in both print and electronic formats. While primarily serving churches of the Stone-Campbell Movement, the company also caters to the larger Christian bookstore marketplace. College Press publishes biblical commentaries written by authors from both the Christian Churches/Churches of Christ and Churches of Christ. Chris DeWelt, son of the press's founder, has served as president since 1988.

College Press has also reprinted abundant resources from Stone-Campbell history, including the full *Millennial Harbinger* in 1976 and again in 1987, as well as the *Biography of Elder Barton Warren Stone* and Walter Scott's *The Gospel Restored.* In 1998 a new scholarly journal was launched, *The Stone-Campbell Journal,* under the editorship of William Baker. Studies in academic areas as well as practical books on themes such as family issues and ministry concerns have been characteristic of College Press publications.

See also DeWelt, Don; Standard Publishing Company; *Stone-Campbell Journal* CHRIS DEWELT

Collis, Mark (1851-1955)

Minister and educator known as one of the leading figures in the division of the Disciples and the Christian Churches/Churches of Christ.

He was born in London, England, and spent his early life in Adelaide, Australia. He came to America in 1874 to study in Lexington and eventually earned degrees from the College of the Bible and Kentucky University (now Transylvania University). In 1881 he married Mary Gibney. His ministerial career was spent wholly within the state of Kentucky. His most notable pastorate was with the historic Broadway Church in Lexington from 1892 to 1930 and as minister emeritus until his death. During his time at Broadway more than 6,300 people were added to the membership. In addition, Collis taught at the College of the Bible and served on the board, beginning in 1886. Elevated to chairman in 1897, he resigned that position in 1918 in opposition to the school's acceptance of modernism. He also served on the board and as chairman of the Kentucky Female Orphan School in Midway for more than six decades. As a member of the Committee on Future Action, Collis was one of the original founders and visionaries of the North American Christian Convention.

BIBLIOGRAPHY Mark Collis papers, Disciples of Christ Historical Society. CLINTON J. HOLLOWAY

Columbia Christian College

Columbia Christian College grew out of Columbia Bible School, an elementary and secondary school founded in Portland, Oregon, in 1946. Opening with eight grades on September 8, 1947, the school met originally at the Central Church of Christ, then located at 7th and Hassalo. Six years later the school moved to 90th and Glisan, building on land donated by the county and a local utility company. The new facility was constructed entirely by volunteer labor, with one salaried builder serving as a coordinator.

Columbia started its first high school classes in 1951 and began a junior college in 1956. The college attained four-year status in 1971, and received its accreditation in 1975 under J. P. Sanders, the college's fifth president.

At its highest level of enrollment the college had approximately 350 undergraduates and offered degrees in Bible, business, education, and music. Major financial difficulties in the 1980s cost the school its accreditation in the early 1990s. The college closed its doors in 1993 and offered its facilities to Oklahoma Christian University as a branch campus, which opened for classes as Cascade College in 1994. The elementary and high school divisions have continued to operate under a separate board as Columbia Christian Academy.

During its 37-year existence, Columbia Christian College was served by eight presidents: L. D. Webb (1956-58), Truman Ethridge (1958-59), Robert Rowland (1959-68), Rex Johnston (1969-74), J. P. Sanders (1974-81), Michael Armour (1983-86), Gary Elliott (1986-91), and Don Gardner (1992-93).

See also Cascade College; Oklahoma Christian University MICHAEL C. ARMOUR

Commission on Brotherhood Restructure

See Restructure

Commission on Restudy of the Disciples of Christ

Created in 1934 by the International Convention of Disciples of Christ "to restudy of the origin, history, slogans, successes, failures of the movement . . . with the purpose of a more effective and more united program and closer Christian fellowship among us."

Previous decades had seen the rise of serious tensions among Disciples of Christ over methods and policies of various agencies involved in missionary, benevolent, and educational programs, the relation of these organizations to the church, and the viability of the plea for restoration and unity in the face of more recent biblical scholarship. There was the possibility that yet another division in the Movement would be added to the one that had created Churches of Christ.

The commission was to comprise members proportionately representative of "the various phases and schools of thought in the institutional life among us." Over the years, through filling vacancies and additions, the commission numbered thirty-seven participants. The list of their names was a "who's who" of notables in Disciples of Christ. The commission was chaired in succession by F. D. Kershner (1875-1953), R. H. Miller (1874-1963), and O. L. Shelton (1895-1959). It met three times each year — once to conduct business, twice for discussion of issues. Despite the tensions inherent in the questions at issue, in time the commissioners were able to develop a rapport that fostered free exchange of views in an atmosphere of goodwill. Over the twelve years of its tenure, the group heard over seventy papers related to questions being considered.

Overtures were made to Churches of Christ to participate in the commission. Claude F. Witty (1877-1952), Church of Christ minister in Detroit, Michigan, having participated in a similar project in the Detroit area, expressed interest in the project and, although not a commissioner, contributed a paper, "The Restudy of Christian Unity," published in *Shane Quarterly* (1941). However, Churches of Christ were indisposed to accept the invitation to participate in the commission.

In 1946 a definitive analysis of the present status of the Movement compared to its past was prepared by C. C. Morrison (1874-1966) and Dean E. Walker (1898-1988) at the request of the commission and with minor modification adopted as representing its views. It treated such matters as the following: (1) the Disciples, "denomination or movement"; (2) the New Testament as normative for church order; (3) the relation of the church local and the church catholic: (4) the role of associations, conventions; (5) the historic plea of the Disciples; and (6) matters of faith and practice. In each instance the analysis stated points of agreement concerning the early stance of the Movement, then identified current attitudes favoring either the retention of earlier practices and views, their refinement, or, in some instances, their abandonment.

Notwithstanding the variant views described in the commission's 1946 report, its 1947 report identified "significant points of agreement" among Disciples. Briefly, they were as follows: (1) the confession of Jesus Christ as Lord and Savior as the basis of Christian fellowship; (2) the New Testament as our "primary source" for knowing the "will of God and the revelation of God in Christ"; (3) the local church as self-governing and free in its utilization of vehicles, whether organizational or directly supported, for service and fellowship; (4) the proclamation of the gospel of Christ as the message of salvation and the source of "our largest unity"; (5) Christian unity, with Christ at its center, by restoration of New Testament Christianity as necessary "to the realization of God's program for redemption"; (6) the Disciples' "practical insight into the New Testament fellowship" as their contribution to the whole divided body of Christ.

On the basis of common ground it found in the above affirmations, the commission proposed (1) that persons in "positions of trust in both congregations and general work . . . examine their work in the light of the above unifying center," (2) that diversity in methods not be considered a barrier to fellowship of believers, (3) that Disciples embrace the principles expressed in the maxim, "In faith unity, in opinions liberty, in all things love," in facing the challenges addressed by the commission, and (4) that there be a "continuous study of the New Testament church — its origin and nature, its structure and function, its mission and hope."

In its final report (1948) the commission declared that despite past failures there remained a basis of the Movement to "write a better history." But there were "immediate problems" requiring attention — (1) to distinguish the "nature of our agreements and differences"; (2) to "discover, maintain and enjoy fellowship"; and (3) to "educate our people . . . of the nature of our movement." It then issued a call to Disciples to abandon divisive particularisms, grant freedom of opinion, and recover the sense of mission that requires the unity of Christ's believers for its achievement.

The commission concluded its work by citing its own experience as evidence of the good resulting from "serious and constructive discussion of the tensions and problems that are among us," and urged that groups be formed in every sector of the Disciples of Christ to study the matters dealt with by the commission, confident that it would elicit responses similar to its own. However, this hope was not realized. Elements at either end of the theological spectrum preferred outright division and were unwilling to act upon the commission's recommendations. Neither of the major journals would print the report; nor were any steps taken by International Convention leadership to facilitate discussion of the report. Some historians, especially in the Christian Churches/Churches of Christ, have seen this failure to act on the report as a major step toward division between the Disciples and Christian Churches/Churches of Christ.

Despite the lack of success in achieving its intended goal, the commission produced a document representing one of the most significant exercises in consensus in the Movement's history. The continuing witness of the commission to unity within the Stone-Campbell Movement can be seen in organizations that commissioners supported and helped to shape: the Disciples of Christ Historical Society, the European Evangelistic Society, and the World Convention of Churches of Christ.

See also *Consensus Fidelium;* Consultation on the Internal Unity of Christian Churches; Kershner, Frederick D.; Unity, Christian

BIBLIOGRAPHY *The Report of the Commission on Restudy of the Disciples of Christ,* International Convention of the Disciples of Christ (1948) • D. Newell Williams, "Overcoming a Liberal-Conservative Divide: The Commission on Restudy of the Disciples of Christ," in *Christian Faith Seeking Historical Understanding: Essays in Honor of H. Jack Forstman,* ed. James O. Duke and Anthony L. Dunnavant (1997): 246-76.

WILLIAM J. RICHARDSON

Committee of 1000

The Committee of 1000, a group of conservative Disciples from Missouri, formed at Rolla in April 1946 during the Christian Restoration Association's Restoration Congress. Based in Jefferson City, attorney Willis Meredith and lay leader Heber Nations led this group, though the committee did not submit the names of their membership. They aimed to expose Disciples leaders and agencies who attacked the authenticity of the Bible, to inform church members of these views, and to support "all of our missionary and evangelistic enterprises which are true to the Bible."

One early treatise ("Attacks on the Holy Bible by Christian Board of Publication and United Christian Missionary Society Leaders and Literature," 1946) condemned Disciples leaders C. E. Lemmon and Robert M. Hopkins concerning their critical views on the accuracy and miracles of the Bible. The Committee of 1000 defined these men as "infidels." At the end of this treatise, the Committee drafted a petition for its readers to enlist in its cause.

The Committee of 1000 disparaged the Disciples leadership during the 1946 International Convention of the Disciples of Christ in Columbus, Ohio. They bought a full-page ad in the August 7, 1946, *Ohio State Journal* to attack Disciples institutions, including the International Convention. This ad brought new charges of financial mismanagement. When given an opportunity by the newspaper, the International Convention chose to ignore the ad, brushing it off as another long-standing attempt to persuade the Disciples into debate.

The *Christian Standard* and its editor Burris Butler always endorsed the Committee of 1000 and reprinted its news, treatise, and ad with approving editorial comment. The *Christian Standard* even reported donating $100 to the Committee in late August 1946. By late 1949, the *Restoration Herald* reported that the Committee of 1000 had disbanded upon the death of Heber and the resignation of Meredith.

See also Butler, Burris; Christian Restoration Association; *Christian Standard; Restoration Herald, The*

BIBLIOGRAPHY *Christian Standard* 84 (1949): 521-26, 561-63, 595-96 • Committee of 1000, "Attacks on the Holy Bible by Christian Board of Publication and United Christian Missionary Society Leaders and Literature" (1946) • Stephen Corey, *Fifty Years of Attack and Controversy: The Consequences Among Disciples of Christ* (1953).

ANTHONY J. SPRINGER

Common Sense Philosophy

A philosophical movement of the eighteenth century rooted in Scotland.

Scottish philosopher Thomas Reid (1710-1796) developed a response to the skepticism of David Hume (1711-1776) and of French enlightenment philosophers as they responded to the epistemological crisis resulting from the thinking of John Locke (1632-1704). By *communis sensus,* or "common sense," Reid meant that people universally accept the data provided by the senses they share with all humans as reliable signs of external reality.

The Scottish philosophy was a broad attempt in philosophy, theology, science, and the humanities to show the Christian faith to be reasonable in a world where empirical methods of knowing reigned. The intended means of doing so was "natural philosophy," that is, describing human processes of cognition, reasoning, aesthetics, motivation, communication, and interaction by empirical methods. Scottish universities adapted the empirical methods of Bacon to new subject areas, founding the social sciences of economics, sociology, and psychology in the process.

One important motive of the Scottish philosophers was to defend Christianity against skepticism by exonerating belief from the charge of superstition. In conversation with Reid and his Wise Club colleagues at Aberdeen, George Campbell (1719-1796) in *The Philosophy of Rhetoric* (1776) developed Reid's philosophical work into a doctrine of testimony, hailed as the definitive answer to Hume's attack on the credibility of miracles. This innovative effort to assert the reasonableness of belief in a modern scientific age was accomplished by laying down the criteria by which testimony to any event could be considered reliable, thereby removing accounts of miraculous events from criticism concerning their inherent probability and instead asking whether the witnesses to the event could be considered credible.

The Scottish philosophy heavily influenced the American educational scene, especially through Princeton University. Scottish approaches to curriculum and communication persisted, even when Scottish philosophical discourse was eclipsed in American universities by the popularity of Immanuel Kant (1724-1804).

George Jardine (1742-1827), Professor of Logic and Belles-Lettres at Glasgow University, was a curriculum reformer and a disciple of Reid. Jardine taught Baconian methods of reasoning to Thomas and Alexander Campbell when each was his student. Alexander Campbell (1788-1866) was eager to point out the advantages of Baconian reasoning and consistently relied throughout his career on inductive argumentation from observation and testimony. He designed the curriculum of Bethany College along Scottish lines. He treated the Scripture as ancient literature amenable to empirical methods of grammatical and historical analysis, and as reliable testimony to ancient events and practices.

Common Sense reasoning appealed to the independent attitudes of the American frontier because it maintained that readers could approach and understand Scripture directly. This doctrine of the perspicuity (clarity and accessibility) of Scripture suited the temper of Jacksonian democracy. The heritage of these attitudes toward Scripture in Stone-Campbell Movement congregations was the expectation that everyone could and should know the Bible and was individually responsible to understand it and to live according to its teachings. When combined with a rejection of Calvinist soteriology, the Common Sense hermeneutic offered the Movement an evangelistic methodology very appealing to a population that appreciated individual judgment and personal freedom.

See also Anthropology; Bethany College; Hermeneutics; Locke, John; Rationalism; Reason, Place of

BIBLIOGRAPHY Clarence R. Athearn, *The Religious Education of Alexander Campbell* (1928) • Carisse Mickey Berryhill, "Scottish Rhetoric and the *Declaration and Address*," in *The Quest for Christian Unity, Peace, and Purity in Thomas Campbell's Declaration and Address* (2000) • Carisse Mickey Berryhill, "Sense, Expression, and Purpose: Alexander Campbell's Natural Philosophy of Rhetoric," *Restoration Quarterly* 30 (1988): 111-24 • George Campbell, *Philosophy of Rhetoric* (1776) • William L. Davidson, "Scottish Philosophy," in *Encyclopaedia of Religion and Ethics,* ed. James Hastings (1955), 11:261-71 • George Jardine, *Outlines of Philosophical Education, Illustrated by the Method of Teaching the Logic Class in the University of Glasgow,* 2nd ed. (1825) • Thomas Reid, *Inquiry into the Human Mind on the Principles of Common Sense* (1764) • Robert F. West, *Alexander Campbell and Natural Religion* (1948).

CARISSE MICKEY BERRYHILL

Congregational Life

1. Christian Churches/Churches of Christ
2. Christian Church (Disciples of Christ)
3. Churches of Christ

1. Christian Churches/Churches of Christ

These churches normally focus their weekly activities on three principal meeting times: Sunday morning, Sunday evening, and Wednesday evening. Sunday mornings include worship services and Sunday School classes usually focused on Bible study. Sunday evening worship sometimes abbreviates the morning service, or else provides special programming to enhance congregational ministries or spiritual life. Wednesday night activities frequently include prayer services, Bible study, a combination of both, or programs on select topics.

Monthly meetings can typically include gatherings of congregational leadership groups, area women's or men's social gatherings, and representative participation in the board meetings of local benevolent institutions or evangelistic organizations. The churches vary on the frequency of internal board meetings and congregational business meetings. Yearly activities often include stewardship emphases, international mission emphases, some form of election of congregational leaders (elders and deacons), retreats, and participation in the North American Christian Convention. There are some annual statewide conventions.

Youth and children frequently meet for activities in the same time periods as adults but with activities geared toward their concerns. Some congregations host "children's church," a youth-oriented service. During the summer children often attend Vacation Bible School and camps, while junior high and teens participate in Christian service camps, retreats, annual teen conventions, and short-term mission trips.

Many congregations regularly provide benevolence services (e.g., food pantries, clothing ministries) and pastoral care for church members and the local community. Larger churches frequently offer counseling services, recovery groups, and family ministries. Some larger congregations have "family life centers" for spiritual and recreational activities. Small group ministries are becoming increasingly important, especially in larger churches.

"Contemporary" worship — favoring choruses (not hymns), open expression of emotions, narrative preaching, and versatility in the order of worship — is steadily increasing. Numerous churches host "seeker services" on Saturday or Sunday to evangelize their community, despite the criticism that they accommodate to popular culture, "dumb down" the gospel, and displace the centrality of the Lord's Supper for fear of alienating the "unchurched."

Christian Churches/Churches of Christ have in recent years internally debated not only worship "styles" but also the role of women in ministry and other issues. Most congregations, however, have found a strong rallying point in their commitment to evangelistic mission at home and abroad, and many concentrate significant congregational resources — and activities — to this end.

ROBERT L. FOSTER

2. Christian Church (Disciples of Christ)

The mid-twentieth-century development of the "functional department" structure for congregational planning among Disciples broadened and diversified the leadership base of congregations and enriched and enlivened church life in the post-war period when people were looking for a more programmatic church structure. Monthly meetings of congregational leaders for planning and oversight of the church program continue in most congregations. Sometimes the meetings of committees and departments became ends in themselves, and opportunities for fellowship and pastoral care became as important as the intended ministry and mission.

More recently, Christian Education, fellowship events, and, in particular, service projects have reclaimed a more central role in congregational life. In some congregations, Christian Education retains the traditional Sunday School structure, though usually with a broadened variety of curriculum. Elsewhere, weekday Bible study and home groups for learning, fellowship, and mutual support have become predominant. Yearly activities include mission education opportunities, sometimes related to annual mission offerings. Some congregations participate in study tours to learn of needs and the work of the church in other parts of the world. Many congregations organize a summer Vacation Church School for children, while youth participate in camps and conferences organized by the regional church.

Fellowship events may be the traditional congregational potluck dinner, but more often interpersonal connections take place in smaller face-to-face groupings. Christian Women's Fellowship groups continue in many congregations, often combining education, worship, and service with fellowship opportunities. Some congregations have some form of men's organization, though such fellowship groups are less common. Youth also have fellowship groups that engage in various activities, including recreation, spiritual retreats, study, and service. Congregational representatives attend biennial regional and general assemblies of the Christian Church (Disciples of Christ).

Service projects may be as simple as serving a meal in a homeless shelter or delivering Christmas baskets to the needy. Alternatively, this ministry may be as involved as an overseas mission project or building a Habitat for Humanity home. In some rare cases, deeply committed congregations and their leadership may also work for systemic change in the society.

Through the changes in church life in the nineteenth and twentieth centuries, and into the twenty-first, worship has remained the central focus of Disciples congregations. Rare indeed is a congregation where other aspects of church life involve more people or demand more central focus than Sunday morning worship. Almost universally, this has been a relatively formal, free-church worship, involving a congregationally determined order of hymnody, prayers, Scripture, preaching, and weekly Lord's Supper, led by clergy and laity together. In recent years some congregations have added a special program for engaging children in worship through stories from the Bible called "Children, Wonder and Worship." Congregations have experimented with "contemporary" worship (replacing hymns with choruses, using multimedia and dramatic presentations) on Sunday mornings or at another time, usually as a means of evangelism. Responses to contemporary worship, especially when it has replaced the congregation's traditional Sunday morning service, have been mixed.

ROBERT A. RIESTER

3. Churches of Christ

When Churches of Christ emerged as a separate entity at the beginning of the twentieth century, most congregations were located in rural areas or small towns. The rhythm of congregational life revolved around Sunday and mid-week worship services. In the summer, congregations held annual gospel meetings. A feature of these meetings was a Sunday dinner on the church grounds or in a town park. These were the singular large social gatherings for most congregations.

After World War II, fellowship spaces in church buildings became popular in larger congregations, with meals and other activities often held before or after services. Later many congregations constructed large family life centers, allowing for a variety of social and recreational activities at any time of the week, including sports teams, teacher and staff appreciation banquets, and programs for area youth groups.

In the 1970s care groups became popular in larger congregations, with group leaders normally hosting members at their homes. Gatherings could be held any night of the week or rotated on Sunday nights. Some congregations focused on the shepherding function of the elders and designated their gatherings as shepherding groups, assigning every member of the congregation to a group.

Many churches offer a wide variety of congregational activities geared toward specific constituencies. While summer Vacation Bible Schools and church camps were common from at least the 1950s, full-blown youth and children's programs became the norm in many churches as youth directors and educational ministers were hired or members volunteered for such service. A growing trend in the late twentieth century was ministry to older adult members. Women's Bible classes one morning each week have also become a staple of many congregations. A variety of congregational ministries involving members has developed, including evangelistic outreach, neighborhood child care and nursery school programs, and service to the needy. Some churches sponsor Homes for the Aged, Children's Homes, and primary and secondary schools on their property.

As is the case with the other streams of the Movement, the most important part of congregational life for Churches of Christ is the church's corporate worship on Sunday. Churches of Christ have not escaped the controversies concerning styles of worship. While the a cappella tradition continues almost universally, disputes over music style, order of worship, and worship leadership — especially focused on the use of "praise teams" made of men and women to lead singing — have caused problems in some congregations. While a few churches adopted a "seeker service" format in the late twentieth century, most congregations continue to see the service as primarily a time for Christian worship and edification, though never devoid of an evangelistic component.

THOMAS H. OLBRICHT

See also Camps; Christian Church (Disciples of Christ); Christian Churches/Churches of Christ; Churches of Christ; Educational Ministry; Evangelism, Evangelists; Ministry; Pastoral Care; Worship; Youth Groups, Youth Ministry

Congress of Disciples

Annual conference held from 1899 through 1928 to provide an open forum for Disciples clergy and scholars to discuss current trends in biblical criticism, philosophy, ecumenism, and doctrinal as well as practical theology. Originally envisioned by James H. Garrison as a unifying element within the Stone-Campbell Movement, in practice it irrevocably divided the churches along conservative, progressive, and liberal lines.

Behind the formation of the Congress of Disciples was the use of German "higher criticism" in the biblical scholarship of H. C. Garvin and H. L. Willett. J. W. McGarvey, through his column "Biblical Criticism" in the *Christian Standard,* called for the rejection of such approaches in favor of established church usage, while J. J. Haley and J. H. Garrison, with *The Christian-Evangelist,* appealed to "Christian liberty" and Thomas Campbell's *Declaration and Address* for freedom of thought and expression in the church. In 1890 J. H. Garrison proposed a meeting of clergy for the purpose of considering changes in church doctrine and practice. It was thought best to keep such debates away from the "unlearned" laity, who, it was assumed, could not understand them, though the popular church presses were pursuing a running battle over Bible study that was avidly followed in the pews.

The first meeting was held in St. Louis, April 25, 1899. Five major discussion papers were presented, formally responded to, and debated, including proposals on biblical studies, theology, church polity, and Disciples worship. Though the presenters were progressive and liberal clergy, the conference was well attended by conservative ministers. The success of the first meeting led to a plan to hold a similar gathering every year at a different city in Midwestern America. A proposal at the first meeting to make the Congress of Disciples a major event at the 1903 St. Louis World's Fair did not impress the fair planners, and in 1903 the Congress was held in Cincinnati.

Beginning in 1902 J. H. Garrison became involved in the creation of the Federal Council of Churches, an American ecumenical organization favored by progressive and liberal Disciples but rejected by conservative congregations; the Congress of Disciples was used as a platform for urging membership in the "federation." In pursuit of interdenominational unity, non-Disciples speakers were invited to the Congress beginning in 1906. Until 1907 the majority of Congress attendees defined themselves as conservative, but that year a progressive-liberal coalition pushed through a resolution favoring federation membership, and from then on the Congress essentially consisted of progressive and liberal factions.

Throughout the later meetings the Congress increasingly viewed the church through the lenses of sociological and political structures. Progressives envisioned a slow evolution of the church and theology, and through them of society, while liberals opted for immediate social action and a cessation of outmoded church doctrine. Agreeing on unification of church agencies and Christian social obligations, both sides continued dialogue. A schism widened as progressive members continued to press for Christian union, communion with as many other denominations as possible, and concern for rural congregations, while liberals insisted on acting on truth as reason dictated, breaking relations with theologically and socially conservative churches, and an emphasis on urban ministry. At the 1928 Indianapolis Congress the papers of both factions reflected an optimistic vision of the future. The 1929 economic crash appears to have brought the Congress of Disciples, and its optimism, to a close.

BIBLIOGRAPHY James H. Garrison, *Our First Congress* (1900) • Errett Gates, *The Disciples of Christ* (1905), pp. 312-24.

LOWELL K. HANDY

Consensus Fidelium

Notion of the historic "consensus of the faithful," the collective reasoning of Christian believers through the centuries who validate the church's interpretation of biblical truth.

The tendency of the Common Sense/Baconian model of biblical interpretation in the early Stone-Campbell Movement was to collapse the temporal and cultural distance between the biblical revelation and its ever-contemporary audience of respondents. Through appropriate critical interpretation, the biblical text was understood to communicate the same thing, normally by the common usage *(usus loquendi)* of words, to every generation and context. Every generation of Christians, as it were, confirms and applies in its own contexts the one *original* meaning.

While Alexander Campbell and other early leaders occasionally acknowledge historical interpretations of biblical texts for instructive purposes (e.g., citation of specific patristic authorities in support of believers' immersion), they showed little concern for the issue of historical *development* in Christian understanding. They would certainly have rejected the Roman Catholic doctrine of the "fuller sense" *(sensus plenior)* of biblical texts, the possibility of the church discerning deeper meaning as it plumbs the whole of Scripture and develops over time its own interpretive tradition. Instead, they assumed that there was a consistent hermeneutical rationality of the Christian faithful for all time, not coerced by ecclesiastical authority but freely exercised, as Thomas Campbell put it in his *Declaration and Address* (1809), by all Christians applying "right reason" to the demonstrable truths of Scripture. Such judgment could not, says Campbell, be decreed by General Council, by an ecclesiastical elite. Moreover, "it is not the voice of the multitude [or 'majority vote'], but the voice of truth, that has power with the conscience; that can produce rational conviction and acceptable obedience."

In the twentieth century, with the maturing of the ecumenical movement, certain Disciples thinkers picked up on this notion for their own purposes and connected it with the historic concept, articulated especially in the Anglican heritage but ultimately also in Roman Catholicism (cf. Vatican II, *Lumen Gentium,* ch. 12), of the *consensus fidelium.* Some, like W. E. Garrison, A. T. DeGroot, and Frederick Kershner, in arguing that the Stone-Campbell Movement stood for the liberation of the universal conscience and "common mind" of the Christian faithful, emphasized this consensus as a quasi-democratic principle of free and critical inquiry — but so too as a truly ecumenical principle basic to the catholic unity of the church.

In *The Christian Union Overture* (1923), a commentary on the *Declaration and Address,* Kershner interpreted Thomas Campbell to mean that "the common mind, the universal reason, is not always incarnate in the prejudiced and turbulent mass of humanity. It is, however, always present in the thoughtful consensus of the majority of intelligent, candid, and honest seekers after truth." Kershner concluded that the early leaders of the Stone-Campbell Movement "had immense faith in democracy, in the rationality of the average mind and they believed that progress is made best by the slower movement which is involved in the consensus of many minds, than by the flashlight program of individual genius." Nevertheless, Kershner argued that for both Thomas and Alexander Campbell, as for his own generation, this consensus would find its clearest expression through thoughtful, critical scholarship speaking on behalf of all the Christian faithful. The consensus was not, then, reducible to sheer populism, despite Alexander Campbell's affinity for the expression *vox populi, vox Dei.*

William Robinson of the British Churches of Christ agreed that truth was to be discerned not by allegedly infallible ecclesiastical decrees but by an educated and prayerful consensus of all Christians. In 1955 he wrote: "There can be such a thing as a *consensus fidelium,* and it need not be a *managed consensus.* Such a consensus must be the voice of the church, and if so it must represent the whole church, clergy and laity. Even in Protestantism there is too much reliance on the clergy. But the laity must be included. Further it must be a decision in the spirit of prayer and communion — in worship. It is then that the earthly and the heavenly planes intermingle."

A. T. DeGroot argued in his *Disciple Thought: A History* (1965) that for the Disciples, as "Free Church Catholics," the *consensus fidelium* could not function simply as an individualistic prerogative — despite the emphasis of early leaders of the Stone-Campbell Movement on the right of private judgment — but as a *heuristic* principle for Christians everywhere within their congregational (and inter-congregational) contexts.

The Stone-Campbell churches, like other denominational traditions, have had difficulty in effectively exercising the *consensus fidelium* within their fold, but there have occasionally been some significant attempts. One was the Commission on Restudy of the Disciples of Christ in the 1940s, an extended and concerted effort to achieve consensus among liberals, moderates, and conservatives for the sake of maintaining unity in the Movement. Another of late has been the "Process of Discernment" within the Christian Church (Disciples of Christ), an endeavor to integrate congregations into finding consensus on issues like biblical authority and social justice.

See also *Declaration and Address;* DeGroot, Alfred T.; Fathers of the Church, Appeal to the; Kershner, Frederick D.; Robinson, William

BIBLIOGRAPHY A. T. DeGroot, *Disciple Thought: A History* (1965) • Frederick D. Kershner, *The Christian Union Overture* (1923) • Frederick W. Norris, "Apostolic, Catholic, and Sensible: The *Consensus Fidelium*," in *Essays on New Testament Christianity*, ed. C. Robert Wetzel (1978), pp. 15-29 • William Robinson, *Completing the Reformation: The Doctrine of the Priesthood of All Believers* (1955).

PAUL M. BLOWERS

Consultation on Church Union

The nine-church Consultation on Church Union (COCU) came into being in response to a sermon by Eugene Carson Blake on December 4, 1960, at Grace Cathedral (Episcopal) in San Francisco. Entitled "A Proposal Toward the Reunion of Christ's Church," this sermon captured the imagination and hope of the churches and media (Dr. Blake's picture was on the cover of *Time* magazine) and initiated the journey toward a united church "truly catholic, truly evangelical, and truly reformed." Eventually nine different and diverse churches joined this journey toward reconciliation: the African Methodist Episcopal Church, the African American Episcopal Zion Church, the Christian Methodist Episcopal Church, the Christian Church (Disciples of Christ), the Episcopal Church, the International Council of Community Churches, the Presbyterian Church (USA), the United Church of Christ, and the United Methodist Church. The Christian Church (Disciples of Christ) became a member church by the action of the 1962 International Convention at Los Angeles, with its delegation being seated at the third (1963) plenary at Princeton, New Jersey.

The Consultation's first plenary met at Washington, D.C., in April 1962. Its early plenaries — substantially led by a commission of prominent theologians and church leaders — focused on historic church-dividing issues such as Scripture and tradition, baptism, the Lord's Supper (Eucharist), and the ministry. In time their labors brought new openness to each other and eventually an emerging consensus. Their agreements reflected the notable work of the Faith and Order Commission of the World Council of Churches that eventually produced the historic *Baptism, Eucharist and Ministry* (1982). This work led to approval of *Principles of Church Union* (1966), which offered a theological consensus that would be the foundation for future steps and stages.

In 1970 a major step came when *A Plan of Union for the Church of Christ Uniting* was approved by the plenary at Dallas and sent to the churches for "study and response," not decision. Reflecting the dimensions of a reconciled church, it had chapters on the nature of the church; marks of church membership; the apostolic faith as expressed in Scripture and tradition; worship and the sacraments of baptism and the Lord's Supper; the ministry of the whole people of God — laity and ordained, including the ministry of deacons, presbyters (pastors), and bishops; and church structures. *A Plan* also proposed that the provisional name be the Church of Christ Uniting (the "ing" suggesting a dynamic, ongoing process). Time would reveal that the highest anxiety by the churches was focused on structure. In the responses received, the concept of the "parish" was resisted and seen as a threat to the nature of congregations. The proposed parish was a cluster of congregations from different traditions and hopefully black and white constituencies functioning under a parish council. The parish would be the primary place of identity and mission; worship would be in the congregations. The responses to the theological sections of *A Plan* were, in balance, affirmative.

A part of the creativity of the COCU process was in developing liturgical texts. In 1969 the Commission on Worship — one of its most gifted and productive working groups — produced the first COCU liturgy, *An Order of Worship for the Proclamation of the Word of God and the Celebration of the Lord's Supper*. For decades this liturgy was celebrated in countless local and national ecumenical services across the country. It became a proleptic experience of the anticipated unity. In later years the commission produced an *Order for the Celebration of Holy Baptism with Commentary* (1973), an *Affirmation on Mutual Recognition of Members in One Baptism* (1974), a *Lectionary* (1974), and *Word, Bread, Cup* (1978). All were liturgical signs of the unity already given and still to be realized by these churches.

In the early 1970s signs of a changing cultural and ecumenical situation came in the United States and around the world that foretold the need of the churches to rethink the approach to church unity and its forms. For COCU it meant that reconciliation of the churches would need to be pursued within the context of cultural upheaval and conflict. These new conflicts in society led COCU to confess that "new church-dividing issues" are sources of alienation and distrust among the churches and have to be addressed if the Church of Christ Uniting was truly to be an event of reconciliation and renewal. Three such divisions — racism, sexism, and handicapism — were placed centrally on COCU's agenda.

At the 1971 plenary in Denver COCU began to focus on "living our way to union" through local models of unity. Two experimental models were developed. Interim Eucharistic Fellowships brought congregations together to study and pray for the unity of the church and to celebrate the Lord's Supper together. Generating Communities were a cluster of congregations from different COCU traditions that covenanted to build a sense of community around regular celebrations of the Eucharist and to work for justice, inclusiveness, and unity.

By 1985 the theological sections of *A Plan of Union,* revised and informed by reflections on the new church-dividing issues, were sent to the churches in the document *The COCU Consensus: In Quest of a Church of Christ Uniting.* In essence this document was the theological basis for the future. A second new document, *Churches in Covenant Communion: The Church of Christ Uniting,* offered a new form of church union, variously called "covenanting" or "covenant communion" (1988). Covenant communion was spoken of as a kind of unity that is organic and visible, but not organizational. The polities and practices of the covenanting churches would remain intact "for the foreseeable future." The churches would be drawn together by eight elements: claiming unity in faith; seeking unity with wholeness (racial and gender justice); mutual recognition of members in one baptism; mutual recognition of each other as churches; mutual recognition and reconciliation of ordained ministries; celebrating the Eucharist together; engaging together in Christ's mission; and the formation of covenanting councils. Compared to other models of church union, covenant communion represents the visible unity of the church without merging structures and would hold together all the diversities among Christian churches in one koinonia. This new model brought a sense of exuberance from the member churches. The negativism of the response to earlier proposals seemed to be in the past.

When the churches gathered at St. Louis, in January 1999, for the eighteenth COCU plenary, it was discovered that two of the churches were not ready to enter into covenant communion. The Episcopal Church felt it could not yet act affirmatively on the reconciliation of ministries because of uncertainty about the sincerity of the other churches toward the threefold ministry and bishops in historic succession. Equally hesitant — on the other side of the issue — was the Presbyterian Church, which when voting by presbyteries on the acceptance of *Churches in Covenant Communion* failed to get a majority approval of the office of bishop. In the midst of this crisis the churches in COCU did not walk away from each other but decided to pray together, negotiate, and find a way through. Careful, late night negotiations led to the plenary's decision to remove in the proposed text any requirement for the mutual *reconciliation* of these ministries, and to invite all nine churches to approve the other seven elements of covenant communion. Under a new name, Churches Uniting in Christ (CUIC), this new ecumenical life was celebrated at a Eucharistic service during the Week of Prayer for Christian Unity in 2002. Centrally related to CUIC is a commitment by all the churches to engage in the struggle for racial justice as "a central sign of our life together." The 1999 plenary also left a promissory note that a theological group would soon begin work toward clarifying any misunderstandings and developing a confident consensus on the mutual recognition and reconciliation of ministries. If that commitment were to be pursued soon and effectively, a service of reconciliation of the ordained ministries of these nine churches would be held by the year 2007.

Since their entrance into the Consultation in 1963, members and ministers of the Christian Church (Disciples of Christ) have offered substantial leadership to this emerging church "truly catholic, truly evangelical, truly reformed." This participation, they affirmed, was a fulfillment of the prayer of their Lord (John 17) and of the reconciling witness of their forebears. Included were George G. Beazley, Jr., and William Jackson Jarman, the first Disciples representatives in 1963 on COCU's executive committee, who laid the foundations for the Disciples' full commitment. Dr. Beazley was president of COCU from 1970 to 1973. Paul A. Crow, Jr., was elected the first general secretary (1968-74) and afterwards served for twenty-five years on the executive committee and various commissions. Keith Watkins was a major voice on the Commission on Worship. Albert M. Pennybacker served many years on the executive committee, including task forces on racism, as did Mildred Slack and Suzanne Webb. In 1999 Robert K. Welsh became the treasurer and member of the executive committee. In the same year Michael Kinnamon became COCU's part-time general secretary. Other Disciples who exercised particular leadership across the years were Walter D. Bingham, Ronald E. Osborn, Dolores Highbaugh, Vance Martin, Fran Craddock, Kenneth L. Teegarden, Paul S. Stauffer, Robert L. Friedly, Colbert Cartwright, and Nancy E. Fowler.

BIBLIOGRAPHY *Churches in Covenant Communion* (1989, 1995) • *The COCU Consensus: In Quest of a Church of Christ Uniting* (1985, 1991) • Paul A. Crow, Jr., and William Jerry Boney, eds., *Church Union at Midpoint* (1972) • Various issues of *Mid-Stream: An Ecumenical Journal,* esp. 34:3-4 (July/October 1995) on "The Promise of COCU"; 37:3-4 (July/October 1998) on "Preparatory Papers on COCU's 18th Plenary, St. Louis, 1999"; 39:1-2 (January/April 2000), "The Digest of the 18th (1999) Plenary of the Consultation on Church Union."

PAUL A. CROW, JR.

Consultation on the Internal Unity of Christian Churches

Series of meetings of concerned individuals to explore the unity and diversity of Disciples of Christ churches with a hope of keeping conservatives ("independents") and progressives ("cooperatives") together.

The first such consultation was held June 2-3, 1959, on the campus of Friends University, Wichita, Kansas. At that time, in the region of Kansas and Oklahoma, lines of emerging division within Christian Churches were not carefully drawn. Subsequent meetings were held at the Broadway Christian Church, Wichita, Kansas, February 9-10, 1960; Wheeling Avenue Christian Church, Tulsa, Oklahoma, February 27–March 1, 1962; the Disciples of Christ Historical Society, Nashville, Tennessee, April 11-13, 1963; the Christian Board of Publication, St. Louis, Missouri, February 1964; and the Overland Park Christian Church, Kansas City, Missouri, March 1-2, 1965. The seventh and final consultation convened at Phillips University in Enid, Oklahoma, February 28–March 2, 1966.

Professor Jim Carr of Manhattan Bible College was the first chairman of the Consultation's continuation committee. Ting Champie, a minister from Enid, Oklahoma, succeeded Carr; and Champie's successor was Charles Gresham, who presided at the final four meetings and edited seven reports containing the papers of the various consultations. The conference participants produced important essays on unity and ecclesiology. For example, James DeForest Murch of the emerging Christian Churches/Churches of Christ offered an elaborate study of "The Restoration Plea in an Ecumenical Era" at the second consultation, while Disciples historian Ronald Osborn tendered a substantive critique of the restoration principle at the fifth consultation.

The meetings were helpful, but little was accomplished relative to the overall goal, as the majority of the "cooperative" Disciples were moving toward embracing denominational restructure while conservative "independents" continued their strong resistance to denominational agencies and their defense of local church autonomy. As Stephen England lamented in the last consultation, its work was compromised by the fact that the participants actually represented only themselves and not their larger groups and because the positive work of the meetings did not translate into institutional change.

BIBLIOGRAPHY Charles R. Gresham, ed., *The Consultations on the Internal Unity of Christian Churches* (series of five booklets, 1960-66) • Charles R. Gresham, *A History and Evaluation of the Consultations on Internal Unity, 1959-1966* (unpublished manuscript, Kentucky Christian College, 1980).

CHARLES R. GRESHAM

Conventions

Voluntary or official (delegate) gatherings for organizational, missionary, and evangelistic interests.

Heirs of the Stone-Campbell Movement, with its strong and early emphasis on congregational independence, struggled historically over the biblical legitimacy and organizational workability of conventions, despite Alexander Campbell's strong encouragement of congregations to cooperate in the work of Christian unity and evangelism.

Perhaps the first extra-congregational gathering in Stone-Campbell history took place when Stone's "Christians" and Campbell's "Disciples" agreed to join forces in Lexington, Kentucky, in 1832, though only a few representatives of the two movements forged the agreement. Also in the 1830s, the first statewide gatherings emerged in Kentucky, Missouri, Iowa, and Indiana. Others appeared later on, and have had considerable importance, such as the ongoing annual Oregon Christian Convention in Turner, Oregon, which convenes in a large tabernacle-style meetinghouse and still celebrates its frontier roots.

Fear of, and open opposition to, extracongregational organization (whether "conventions" or formal "societies") emerged on the grounds that such was not explicitly authorized or modeled in the writings of the New Testament. Walter Scott, for instance, questioned whether there existed a New Testament precedent for fundraising by any body outside of the local fellowship. Initially, Alexander Campbell agreed. By the 1840s, however, Campbell had been convinced of the merits of at least *some* form of cooperation. In 1845 Campbell actually recommended gatherings of "deputies, messengers, or representatives" from local congregations and acknowledged the potential of such gatherings so long as they remained *voluntary.*

The formation of the American Christian Bible Society marked the first attempt at *national-scale* cooperation. Launched in 1845 by D. S. Burnet, the Society was headquartered in Cincinnati. Its constitution provided for paid individual membership and called for an annual meeting. Campbell was leery of the organization on the grounds that it had not been sanctioned by the whole of the Movement; nevertheless, he supported it. Characteristic of the Society was its constituency; it existed as an organization of individuals, not of congregations.

Not until 1849 did the first national convention come together in Cincinnati. In attendance were 156 delegates, from one hundred churches and eleven states. Because Campbell was ill, he did not attend (though there is evidence that his absence was a signal of strong initial protest). His ultimate support for the gathering, however, was manifest in his agreement to serve as the annual convention's first president. At this convention, resolutions were passed to promote the organization of state meetings. From this, the American Christian Missionary

Society was formed, absorbing the Bible Society as well as a recently created tract society.

The 1869 convention in Louisville was marked by the adoption of the Louisville Plan. The plan emphasized missions and aimed "to promote the harmonious cooperation of all the State and District Boards and Conventions." Under the plan, a General Christian Missionary Convention (GCMC) was created to oversee missionary activity, indicating the close connection between "conventions" and "societies" in Disciples thinking. Participation was based upon paid congregational membership (as opposed to individual membership). The plan presupposed the existence of state conventions and called for two delegates from each state, plus one per 5,000 Disciples residing in that state. This move toward "convention" as an actual collective organization of congregations, if not incongruent with the ethos of the Stone-Campbell Movement, was premature. By 1873 the Louisville Plan and the idea of congregational membership had been practically abandoned; the GCMC began to solicit financial contributions from individuals directly. Membership based upon individual support was reinstated in 1881, and the Louisville Plan was formally laid to rest in 1895.

Frederick D. Kershner, while editor of the *Christian-Evangelist,* proposed in 1916 a system of twin conventions modeled after the bicameral legislature of the United States. Z. T. Sweeney wrote much of the constitution of the newly proposed convention, whose "legislation" would be primarily *advisory* rather than policy-making, strictly speaking. Coupled with a mass meeting of registered individual participants would be a Committee on Recommendations, comprised of one delegate from each state convention, plus one per 25,000 Disciples residing in that state. Despite protests from the *Christian Standard,* the International Convention of the Disciples of Christ was formed in Kansas City in 1917 on the basis of this type of organization. Along with the formation of the United Christian Missionary Society (UCMS) in 1920, it signaled a growing urge toward centralization among Disciples. Soon the International Convention expanded its own internal structure, inaugurating a Committee on Budgets and Promotional Relationships which, like the UCMS itself, would help address funding issues among the "societies" of the Disciples of Christ and alleviate competition among them.

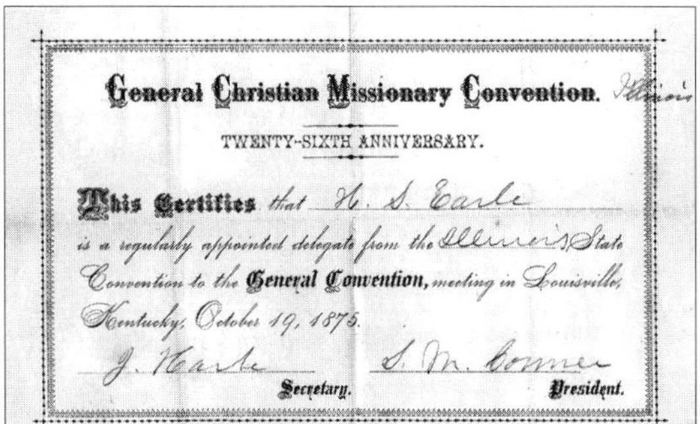
General Christian Missionary Convention.

TWENTY-SIXTH ANNIVERSARY.

This Certifies that H. S. Earle is a regularly appointed delegate from the Illinois State Convention to the General Convention, meeting in Louisville, Kentucky, October 19, 1875.

Secretary. President.

The General Christian Missionary Convention was created by the 1869 Louisville Plan that set up a convention consisting of delegates chosen from state conventions. This certificate authorizes Henry S. Earl, former evangelist in England, Australia and New Zealand, as a delegate to the General Convention from the Illinois State Convention. By 1881 the delegate structure had proven unworkable and individual memberships again became the norm. Courtesy of the Disciples of Christ Historical Society

In this same period, African American Disciples had formed their own convention, the National Convention of Churches of Christ, later changed to the National Christian Missionary Convention (NCMC), seeking to represent and cultivate the life and work of African American congregations. White Disciples leaders attempted, unsuccessfully, to convince leaders of the new Convention to merge their assembly into the International Convention; it did not do so, but did accept the status of an "auxiliary" of the new International Convention. A further step toward unity within the Disciples of Christ stream of the Movement came in 1969 when the NCMC, meeting in Lexington, Kentucky, voted to merge the Convention into the General Assembly of the newly forming Christian Church (Disciples of Christ) and to organize a National Convocation to address the distinctive concerns of African Americans in the denomination.

In 1889, as the missionary societies were beginning to flourish, the forbears of the Churches of Christ sought to distinguish themselves at an annual encampment at Sand Creek, Illinois. Congregations withdrew from the larger fellowship based on their observation that missionary societies (and thus conventions) were not explicitly prescribed in the New Testament. Such dissent anticipated the later wariness of Churches of Christ toward large regular gatherings that would in any way hint of formal conventions representing churches. Over the course of the twentieth century, however, Churches of Christ did develop venues for mutual edification. Annual Bible Lectureships have continued for decades in five Church of Christ colleges (Abilene Christian University, Pepperdine University, Harding University, Freed-Hardeman University, and David Lipscomb University). As Douglas Foster writes, "While our lectureships have no official status or legislative powers, they certainly provide a forum for noted preachers to assert their conclusions on theological topics, from the routine to the controversial. With audi-

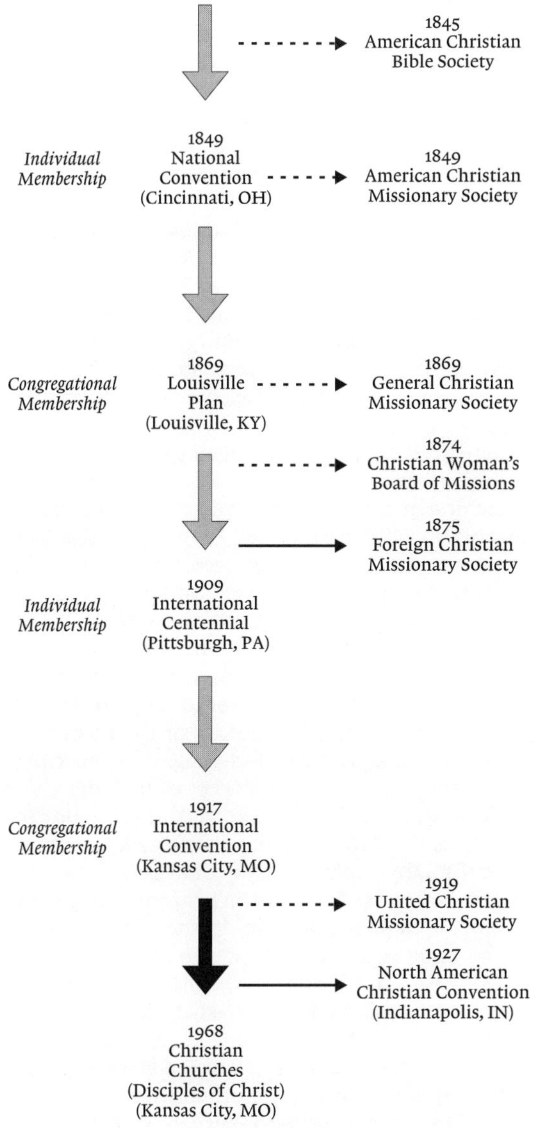

ences from all parts of the country, the powerfully presented positions are often carried back to local congregations and preached to many thousands more."

When the *Christian Standard* reported that the International Convention of the Disciples in Memphis in 1926, which had addressed charges of the practice of "open membership" by missionaries of the UCMS, was a "convention of bad faith," a concurrent "protest convention" was born. The North American Christian Convention (NACC) first assembled in Indianapolis in 1927. At least some of its organizers and early supporters were reacting to what they perceived as leanings toward centralization among Disciples. Other supporters, however, such as Frederick Kershner, continued to insist that the NACC was not intended to preempt the International Convention but to serve an ulterior need of edification for Disciples churches, the need for a "preaching convention." One can scarcely deny, however, the NACC's original role in consolidating conservative Disciples in opposition to the perceived liberal and denominationalist drift of the Disciples' International Convention and the UCMS. Nonetheless, its role as a rallying point for the ministries of the Christian Churches/Churches of Christ has remained limited to edification (preaching, worship, workshops) and to the promotion of various missions and ministries. Having no policy-making powers, the NACC does have an executive committee that chooses speakers and focuses the themes or issues to be addressed in each assembly, themes considered significant for individual congregations. Influential speakers and workshop leaders themselves have in the NACC a significant venue for conveying their perspectives and theological dispositions.

At the 1960 International Convention of the Disciples in Louisville, advocates of streamlining and centralization made their intentions of forming a denomination clear. A "Provisional Design" was set forth in Dallas in 1966, and the Christian Churches (Disciples of Christ) became official in Kansas City in 1968. The functions of the International Convention of the Disciples of Christ — as of 1957 titled the International Convention of the Christian Churches (Disciples of Christ) — were transitioned into the new General Assembly of the Christian Church (Disciples of Christ), which began its biennial conventions in Seattle in 1969. As Anthony Dunnavant has pointed out, there was significant new language with the advent of the General Assembly. No longer would the Disciples' Convention be a convention of "churches" but of "a church" with its own representative body, receiving recommendations from the newly formed General Board. The new General Assembly has sought to represent the agencies and congregations of the Christian Church (Disciples of Christ) without infringing on the rights of the local churches. The Assembly regularly discusses and acts on a variety of resolutions (both "Operational Business Items" and consensus "Sense of the Assembly" statements).

One enduring assembly that has managed, through years of internal strife within the Movement, to work toward reconciliation and common witness among churches of all three streams of the Stone-Campbell tradition is the World Convention of Churches of Christ, pioneered by Jesse Bader (1886-1963), formally established in 1930, and continuing to meet on a quadrennial basis. The World Convention is not a policy-making convention but a forum for fellowship, edification, and mutual encouragement among Stone-Campbell churches internationally.

See also American Christian Bible Society; American Christian Missionary Society; Burnet, David Staats; International Convention of the Disciples of Christ; Lectureships; Louisville Plan, The; Missionary Societies, Controversy over; National Christian Missionary Convention; North American Christian Convention; Societies; United Christian Missionary Society, The; World Convention of the Churches of Christ, The

BIBLIOGRAPHY A. T. DeGroot, *The Convention Among the Disciples of Christ* (1958) • James DeForest Murch, "Where We Have Been, Where We Are, Where We Are Going Organizationally: Conventions" (Address to the North American Christian Convention, Cincinnati, Ohio, July 8, 1971) • Anthony L. Dunnavant, *Restructure: Four Historical Ideals in the Campbell-Stone Movement and the Development of the Polity of the Christian Church (Disciples of Christ)* (1993) • Douglas A. Foster, "Lectureships: Our National 'Conventions,'" in *Will the Cycle Be Unbroken? Churches of Christ Face the 21st Century* (1994), pp. 73-77 • W. K. Pendleton (with Alexander Campbell's remarks), "The Convention of Christian Churches," *Millennial Harbinger* (1849): 689-96 • W. A. Schullenberger, "The International Convention of the Disciples of Christ," *Shane Quarterly* 3 (1942): 59-64 • Dean E. Walker, "The North American Christian Convention," *Shane Quarterly* 3 (1942): 65-72.

TIMOTHY C. SMITH

Conversion

Traditionally, the initial turning to faith by the Christian. The term is also sometimes used to describe the process of Christian growth over a lifetime.

The Stone movement began in the context of the Great Western Revival (1797-1805), in which Presbyterian, Methodist, and Baptist revivalists alike asserted that human beings are sinners. The common revival technique, aimed at producing conviction of sin, included preaching the law and denouncing sin. Hearers struggled to overcome sin and were advised by the preachers to pray for an infusion of grace (the Holy Spirit), assuring salvation. The revival was accompanied by the falling exercise as early as 1800 and later by other physical responses identified as "the jerks" and the "laughing" and "dancing" exercises.

While Barton W. Stone was an enthusiastic supporter of the revival and led his Presbyterian congregations at Cane Ridge and Concord to participate in the revival, his Presbyterian colleagues soon noticed that his preaching did not include the typical emphasis on the law as a means to produce conviction of sin. Instead, he urged sinners to believe the gospel of God's love revealed in Jesus Christ. As for conviction of sin, Stone wrote in 1804, "The sinner's fears may be awakened by the thunders of Mount Sinai [a reference to the law]; but it is only a view of the holiness, goodness, love, — and the free unmerited grace and mercy of God, which produces true conviction and true repentance, and which humbles the soul, slays the enmity of the heart, and makes him willing to depart from all iniquity." The Presbyterians also noted that, like the Methodists, Stone had rejected the doctrine of predestination. This led to controversy among the Presbyterians and to Stone's withdrawal from the Synod of Kentucky in September 1803.

Early on, Alexander Campbell challenged several revivalist assumptions, especially the notion that the preaching of the law produced conviction of sin. A conclusion he drew in "The Sermon on the Law" (1816) was that "there is no necessity for preaching the Law to prepare men for receiving the Gospel." He cited Peter's sermon on Pentecost as fulfilling the Savior's promise (John 16) that the Spirit would convict people of sin "because they do not believe in me." He asserted that in none of the eight or ten conversions in Acts did the apostles or their associates invoke the law as part of their gospel preaching. Moreover, he rejected the concept of total depravity. If persons were totally depraved, their condition would be no different from that of Satan himself. Also, if totally depraved, how could persons become "worse and worse," as stated in Scripture? Like Stone, Campbell emphasized belief in the love of God revealed in Jesus Christ as the key to conversion. "It is in the person and mission of the Incarnate Word that we learn that *God* is *Love*... That God gave his Son for us, and yet gives his Spirit to us — and thus gives us himself — are the mysterious and transcendent proofs of the most august proposition in the universe." In the debate with Nathan Rice, Campbell identified five steps in the process of conversion. "1. The word spoken [Gospel]; 2. hearing; 3. believing; 4. feeling; 5. doing."

Concerning conversion as a lifelong process, Campbell dismissed both the "word alone" and "spirit alone" explanations. Separating them had the effect of regarding the Spirit and the Word as "two independent and wholly distinct powers or influences," whereas both the Spirit and the Word are involved. In the Rice debate Campbell insisted that the Spirit is the agent that "quickens"; the Living Word, as the instrument, is the "incorruptible seed which, when planted in the heart . . . fructifies into eternal life." He identified "Living Word" with the proposition "Jesus is the Messiah, the Son of God, and Savior of the world."

Campbell's colleague Walter Scott employed a "Five Finger Exercise" to summarize the process of conversion: faith, repentance, baptism, remission of sins, gift of the Holy Spirit. These steps presupposed the gospel and offered an alternative to the more common early nineteenth-century revival practice of praying at the altar or mourner's bench for an infusion of grace (the Holy Spirit) to assure salvation while struggling to overcome sin. Scott's preaching proved to be very effective.

Neither Stone, Campbell, nor Scott believed that conversion required the creation of new capacities in the one to be converted as had been commonly taught by Presbyterian revivalists. For believers in Jesus as crucified and risen Lord, the response of faith did not differ from their response to any meaningful fact of existence brought to their mind by testimony. Appropriate feeling and action followed. Nor was it necessary that converts be aware of obeying "steps." Persons were not born again by having a correct understanding of regeneration. Analyses of the process of conversion were not intended for the prospective convert but for the understanding and use of persons engaged in the ministry of regeneration. Later some constituents of the Movement presented Scott's "steps" as the substance of the gospel and obeying them as the means of achieving acceptance — a practice open to the charge of legalism.

The success of Finney and Moody in bringing revival to the cities encouraged evangelists of the Stone-Campbell Movement in the latter half of the nineteenth century to employ similar means of attracting large numbers of people. In contrast to Moody's "faith only" preaching, they presented the "terms of salvation" derived from the book of Acts — with impressive results.

A change of attitude toward conversion came with the liberal movement in the period between the two World Wars. Liberals decried emphasis upon fulfilling "conditions of salvation" because it conveyed the notion of a transcendent God who required obedience to secure certain benefits. Instead, God was "Creative Intelligence," immanent in nature and human experience. Conversion consisted in surrendering oneself to the whole of reality, known through experience, and developing a mystical life like that of Jesus. On the other end of the spectrum, controversy erupted in Churches of Christ beginning in the 1930s over "legalistic" applications of the "plan of salvation" cherished in Stone-Campbell evangelism. K. C. Moser, a Church of Christ minister, led the way toward understanding grace, justification, and conversion more in terms of personal relationship with Christ than in terms of the sheer fulfillment of ordinances.

The number and types of programs of evangelism in congregations of the Movement at the beginning of the twenty-first century vary significantly. The "five steps" formula, as such, is not always utilized. However, for persons coming initially into Christian discipleship, common practice still emphasizes faith, decision (commitment to Christ), an affirmation of faith (the "good confession"), and baptism.

See also Evangelism, Evangelists; Five Finger Exercise; Holy Spirit, Doctrine of the; Justification, Doctrine of; Regeneration; Salvation; Sanctification, Doctrine of; "Sermon on the Law"

BIBLIOGRAPHY C. M. Chilton, "Mystical Conversion and the Disciples," *Shane Quarterly* (1941): 185-88 • A. I. Hobbs, "Conversion — What Is It and How Produced?" in *The Gospel Preacher*, ed. A. B. Maston (1894), pp. 207-27 • William Robinson, *What Churches of Christ Stand For* (1926) • Howard E. Short, *Doctrine and Thought of the Disciples of Christ* (1951) • Dwight E. Stevenson, *Walter Scott: Voice of the Golden Oracle* (1946) • D. Newell Williams, *Barton Stone: A Spiritual Biography* (2000) • D. Newell Williams, "The Gospel as the Power of God to Salvation: Alexander Campbell and Experimental Religion," in *Lectures in Honor of the Alexander Campbell Bicentennial, 1788-1988* (1988), pp. 127-48 • D. Newell Williams, "Bringing a Vision to Life: Walter Scott and the Restored Church," in *Walter Scott: A Nineteenth-Century Evangelical*, ed. Mark G. Toulouse (1999), pp. 123-33 • E. V. Zollars, *The Commission Executed, or a Study of the New Testament Conversions and Other Evangelistic Topics* (1912).

WILLIAM J. RICHARDSON

Coop, Timothy (1817-1887)

Leader of a division among British Churches of Christ.

Coop was born on May 28, 1817, in the parish of West Houghton, Lancashire. His father, a Wesleyan Methodist and Sunday School superintendent, was a weaver. After leaving school Timothy was apprenticed to a cloth dealer in Wigan and eventually took over the firm. In 1841 William Haigh, a commercial traveler from Huddersfield, persuaded him of the scriptural necessity of believers' baptism. This aroused the hostility of his Wesleyan colleagues, so Coop met with three others to break bread every week and preached regularly in the marketplace. In 1845 he met James Wallis, and from 1847 the Wigan church was listed as a Church of Christ. Coop was Chairman of the Annual Meeting in 1854 and 1863.

From 1861 to 1878 Coop was treasurer of the General Evangelist Committee and supported a vigorous program of evangelism, using American methods to form a new church in Southport when he moved there in 1863. He sympathized with open communion and was impressed by Henry Earl's success in Southampton from 1875. In 1878 he offered the Foreign Christian Missionary Society £1,000 for every

£2,000 the Society would contribute toward supporting evangelists in Britain. On his return from a world tour in 1881, he led in the formation of the Christian Association, to the dismay of his former colleagues in the General Evangelist Committee. He also provided the financial support for a new weekly paper, *The Christian Commonwealth*, edited by W. T. Moore. On his last visit to America in 1886 he stayed in Wichita, Kansas, to help the new Garfield University, and died there on May 15, 1887. The university collapsed in 1890.

Coop's enthusiasm for evangelism, coupled with his wealth and generosity, enabled him to sponsor a rival Disciples' movement in Britain, causing a division that lasted until 1917. Moore portrayed the division as a dispute with David King; but other British leaders, both friends and relatives, disagreed with Coop's actions, despite their personal friendship.

See also *British Millennial Harbinger;* King, David; Moore, William Thomas

BIBLIOGRAPHY W. T. Moore, *The Life of Timothy Coop* (1889) • Review of Moore, *The Life of Timothy Coop*, by Lancelot Oliver, *Christian Advocate* (1889): 244-47, 278-88.

DAVID M. THOMPSON

Cordell Christian College

College affiliated with Churches of Christ founded in 1907 by three local businessmen in Cordell, Oklahoma.

Cordell Christian College grew to be the largest college for Churches of Christ until it was closed in 1918 under the pressures of wartime hysteria. The school was reestablished as Western Oklahoma Christian College in 1921, renamed Oklahoma Christian College in 1925, and remained open until legal and financial problems forced school closure in 1931 during the Great Depression.

J. N. Armstrong (1870-1944) became president of Cordell Christian in 1908 after the first president, J. H. Lawson (1867-1935), resigned. Armstrong was a graduate of Nashville Bible School and the son-in-law of James A. Harding (1848-1922), one of the founders of the Nashville school. Armstrong accepted the pacifist and apolitical position of his father-in-law and David Lipscomb.

The United States entered World War I in April 1917 and passed a conscription act on May 18, with all draft-age men registering on June 5. During the Civil War David Lipscomb and the Churches of Christ in Tennessee opposed Christians serving in any capacity in the military. World War I tested these beliefs as patriotism ran high and most Americans came to favor the war. Armstrong tried to avoid the extreme antagonism against pacifists and conscientious objectors by advocating that his male students take the legal noncombatant option provided by the Selective Service Act. By August 1917, fifty Cordell students and three teachers were in the military. Most took noncombatant work, but eighteen volunteered.

Faculty member S. A. Bell wrote an article in the *Gospel Herald*, edited by Armstrong, arguing that Christians should not accept noncombatant status. Three students refused noncombatant work, were court-martialed, and were sent to the disciplinary barracks of Fort Leavenworth. The local postmaster decided that Bell's article violated the Espionage and Sedition Act that made it illegal to publish materials that discouraged men from obeying the draft laws. This prompted the Bureau of Investigation (now the Federal Bureau of Investigation) to place Armstrong and the college under surveillance.

The pacifist sentiment aroused the opposition of the local county council of defense toward Armstrong and Cordell. Through a hearing, and threats of violence, the council ordered Cordell closed. Cordell's board of regents appealed to the Oklahoma State Council of Defense, who sent Oklahoma Supreme Court Judge Thomas Owens to conduct his own hearing. Owens announced that Armstrong and the college had done nothing wrong, but he counseled Armstrong and the regents to close the school voluntarily because of widespread local opposition. Armstrong left, and in 1919 he became the president of Harper College in Harper, Kansas.

See also Harding, James Alexander; Harding University; Lipscomb, David; Pacifism

BIBLIOGRAPHY Michael W. Casey, "The Closing of Cordell Christian College: A Microcosm of American Intolerance During World War I," *The Chronicles of Oklahoma* 76 (Spring 1998): 20-37 • Michael W. Casey and Michael A. Jordan, "Free Speech in Time of War: Government Surveillance of the Churches of Christ in World War I," *Free Speech Yearbook* 34 (1996): 102-11 • Norman L. Parks, *Cordell's Christian College* (1994) • M. Norvel Young, *A History of Colleges Established and Controlled by Members of Churches of Christ* (1949).

MICHAEL W. CASEY

Corey, Stephen Jared (1873-1962)

Born in Rolla, Missouri, Corey studied at the School of Mines, Rolla, Missouri, and at the University of Nebraska. In Lincoln, he came into contact with Christian Endeavor and the Disciples of Christ. He began preaching in Nebraska and served as student pastor at Waterloo, Nebraska (1897-98). He was ordained in 1898. Corey studied theology at Rochester (New York) Theological Seminary (1898-1901) while serving as pastor in Rochester (1898-1903). While in

Rochester he married Edith C. Webster in October 1901.

In 1903 Corey became secretary of the New York Christian Missionary Society. His work was noticed by F. M. Rains, who invited him to apply to work at the national office of the Foreign Christian Missionary Society (FCMS). He served as foreign secretary of that organization from 1905 to 1919 and then of the successor organization, the United Christian Missionary Society (UCMS), from 1919 to 1929. Additionally he served as vice president of the UCMS from 1919 to 1930 and then as president from 1930 to 1939.

During the years as secretary he promoted mission and mission education in local congregations and traveled to visit UCMS mission efforts around the world. This produced a number of books that establish him as an important observer and theorist of mission. The evolution of his mission theory is exemplary of mainline Protestant North American mission thought in all its stages. His first books, *Ten Lessons in World Conquest* (1911) and *Missions in the Modern Sunday School* (1911), are in the conversionist traditions of such influential figures as John R. Mott and Robert Speer, pioneers of the explosion of missionary and ecumenical activity in the early twentieth century. Visiting mission work in the Congo (cf. *Among Central African Tribes,* 1912) and Asia (cf. *Report of the Commission to the Far East of the Foreign Christian Missionary Society,* 1914; *Among Asia's Needy Millions,* 1915) convinced Corey of the importance of missionary educational work as the basis for the establishment of Disciples churches, but also of the importance of *indigenous* evangelism. To this was added the importance of social ministry, reflected in his *Among South American Friends* (1925). He encouraged preachers to proclaim this mission theory in *The Preacher and His Missionary Message* (1935). His passionate *Beyond Statistics: The Wider Range of World Missions* (1937), within the theological framework of the "Kingdom of God," devoted chapters to "uplift," "better living," "health," "goodwill," literature translation, "penetration" (success of mission), and ecumenical cooperation. He closed with a lament about the declining interest in mission in the North American churches.

Two crises dominated his years as secretary and president of the FCMS/UCMS. The first was the Depression, which made it impossible to continue the missionary program as before. Over 150 missionaries were recalled because of lack of funds, and the staff of the UCMS was decreased. More debilitating was the debate within the Disciples of Christ about cooperative ministries. The editors of the *Christian Standard,* published in Cincinnati, attacked him on mission theory and organizational issues and called into question his personal integrity. The details of this debate are summarized with extensive quotes and documentation in Corey's *Fifty Years of Heresy Hunting: The Aftermath* (n.d.), revised and published as *Fifty Years of Attack and Controversy: The Consequences Among Disciples of Christ* (1953). This work brought swift reaction from conservatives, with Robert Elmore of the Christian Restoration Association publishing a long incremental response to the "Corey manuscript" in *The Restoration Herald* (1956-60).

In 1939 Corey was elected president of the College of the Bible, Lexington, Kentucky. He was instrumental in moving the institution from its cramped quarters at Transylvania University to its present site adjacent to the University of Kentucky. He taught missions at the College of the Bible and served as chaplain to drug addicts at the U.S. Public Health Hospital in Lexington. After retirement in 1945, he continued his work as chaplain, did evangelistic work in the region, and wrote Sunday School lessons for the Disciples' *First Rank.* In 1951 the Coreys retired to Santa Monica, California, and then to Sacramento, California. He died in 1962.

See also Elmore, Robert Emmett; Foreign Christian Missionary Society, The; Lexington Theological Seminary; Missions, Missiology; United Christian Missionary Society, The

BIBLIOGRAPHY Stephen J. Corey, *Among Asia's Needy Millions* (1915) • Stephen J. Corey, *Among Central African Tribes* (1912) • Stephen J. Corey, *Among South American Friends* (1925) • Stephen J. Corey, *Beyond Statistics: The Wider Range of World Missions* (1937) • Stephen J. Corey, *Fifty Years of Attack and Controversy: The Consequences Among Disciples of Christ* (1953) • Robert E. Elmore, incremental reprint with critical comments of Stephen Corey's *Fifty Years of Attack and Controversy* in *The Restoration Herald* 29-35 (1956-60) • Mark G. Toulouse, "Practical Concern and Theological Neglect: The UCMS and the Open Membership Controversy," in *A Case Study of Mainstream Protestantism: The Disciples' Relation to American Culture, 1880-1989,* ed. D. Newell Williams (1991), pp. 194-235.

MARK G. TOULOUSE

Cory, Abram Edward (1873-1952)

Disciples of Christ minister, missionary, denominational executive, and ecumenist.

Born August 13, 1873, in Osceola, Iowa, Cory studied at Eureka College (B.A., L.L.D.), Drake University (M.A., D.D.), and did graduate work at Columbia University and Union Theological Seminary, New York.

He began his career as a pastor serving churches in Tingley, Boone, and Oskaloosa, Iowa. Cory then became a missionary to China (1897-1912). He was summoned home to raise money for missions in a project that became the Men and Millions Movement, which under the leadership of Cory and Raphael H. Miller raised $6 million in five years.

During World War I, he served as chaplain with the First Infantry in the Philippines and worked with the YMCA. After the war, he worked in the short-lived Inter-Church World Movement. He returned to the pastorate and served eight years at Gordon Street Christian Church in Kinston, North Carolina. During this time, he served as president of the International Convention of Disciples of Christ, 1923-24.

Cory served as the founding director of the Disciples Pension Fund (1930-40), a program for which he tirelessly traveled the country. From 1941 to 1950 he taught at the Butler School of Religion as professor of mission. An ardent ecumenist, he also served on the executive committee of the Federal Council of Churches and as vice president of the International Christian Endeavor Society.

Cory died March 20, 1952, in Indianapolis and was buried in Crown Hill Cemetery. A colleague at Butler School of Religion memorialized him:

> Cory was one of the great crusaders of all time. He was a sort of reincarnation of Peter the Hermit and was incomparably the foremost gospel promoter that the Disciples have thus far produced. . . . It is an infinite pity that he could not have been given leadership of that crusade for peace about which he dreamed thirty years ago.

BIBLIOGRAPHY "Abram E. Cory, Disciple Minister, Missionary, Educator and Administrator, Dies at Age of 78," *Christian-Evangelist* 90 (April 9, 1952): 356, 362 • Abram Edward Cory, *Shall the Citizens of Hawaii Tolerate Iwilei?* (1901?) • Abram Edward Cory, *A Discourse Delivered by Abram E. Cory at the Honolulu Christian Church, Feb. 24, 1901, Revised and Enlarged Since First Publication* (1901) • Abram Edward Cory, *Out Where the World Begins: A Story of a Far Country* (1921) • Abram Edward Cory, *The Trail to the Hearts of Men: A Story of East and West* (1916) • Abram Edward Cory, *Voices of the Sanctuary: Interpretations by Ministers of Disciples of Christ* (1930) • "Fallen Asleep," *Christian Standard* 88 (April 5, 1952): 217 • Frederick D. Kershner, "Abe Cory," *Christian-Evangelist* 90 (April 16, 1952): 377 • W. A. Shullenberger, "A. E. Cory: The Man and His Times," *Christian-Evangelist* 90 (April 23, 1952): 407.

DAVID BUNDY

Cotner College

Disciples of Christ educational enterprise in Nebraska.

In 1887 members of the Movement in Nebraska accepted land donated by business leaders in Lincoln to build what was originally called Nebraska Christian University (NCU). On a high spot in a plain northeast of Lincoln, NCU occupied a picturesque four-story structure that was considered the finest building in the state. The location, "Bethany Heights," was named in honor of Alexander Campbell's college. A town was laid out with streets named after other Disciples schools, such as Drake and Butler. In 1889 the university opened with thirty students.

When philanthropist Samuel Cotner donated fifty-five acres of land to the university a year later, it was renamed Cotner University. Its first (acting) president was Prince William Aylsworth, a Bethany College graduate. He was succeeded by David R. Dungan, a prominent evangelist.

Cotner's aspirations were always frustrated by a lack of money. For short periods, it operated an academy, medical and dental schools (later part of the University of Nebraska), and a summer program in Colorado. In 1919 the school eliminated its professional degrees and became Cotner College. Chronic financial problems were due partly to low student enrollments (250 in 1925-26). In spite of such hardships, the school attained national reputations in football, basketball, competitive debate, and eloquence.

Cotner graduated a remarkable number of leaders. By 1924 the school's alumni included six college presidents, thirty-eight professors, fifty-three missionaries, and three hundred ministers, including half of the Disciples ministers in the state.

Buffeted by the Great Depression, Cotner closed in 1933. Thirteen years later, it reopened as the Cotner School of Religion. Its new mission was to offer courses in religion to students at the University of Nebraska. Later, when the School of Religion was no longer viable, Cotner again transformed its ministry by endowing a Chair of Religious Studies at the University of Nebraska. The first occupant of this chair was John D. Turner.

The Cotner College Commission on Continuing Education provides lectures and scholarships to serve religious leaders in Nebraska.

See also Dungan, David R.; Higher Education, Views of in the Movement

BIBLIOGRAPHY Perry Epler Gresham, *Campbell and the Colleges* (1973) • Leon A. Moomaw, *History of Cotner University, Including the Early Religious and Educational Movement of the Christian Church in Nebraska* (1916) • Floyd W. Reeves and John Dale Russell, *College Organization and Administration: A Report Based upon a Series of Surveys of Church Colleges* (1929).

Repositories of material on Cotner College are held at the Nebraska State Historical Society in Lincoln, Nebraska; the Disciples of Christ Historical Society in Nashville; and the Cotner College Commission, housed at the Christian Church (Disciples of Christ) office in Lincoln.

LEE SNYDER

Council of Agencies

Disciples council for program coordination and planning, established by the 1949 International Convention.

The Council of Agencies was envisioned "as a clearinghouse among the agencies for clearance of impingements or overlapping of work and long-range planning." Membership included general organizations, such as the Board of Church Extension, the Pension Fund, and the National Benevolent Association, as well as state societies and Board of Higher Education–related institutions. Although participation was initially voluntary, a 1952 change in the by-laws of the Intentional Convention required all member agencies of the convention to belong to the council. In addition to the general agencies, regional societies, and educational institutions, five representatives selected annually by the convention were members of the council.

At the Council of Agencies meeting for the 1954-56 biennium, a Committee on Future Work was appointed under the leadership of A. Dale Fiers. When this committee reported to the Council of Agencies in 1956, one of its recommendations was the formation of a permanent subcommittee on Brotherhood Organization and Inter-Agency Relationships. During 1958 the council sponsored a series of Listening Conferences, a summary of the findings of which was presented at the 1958 meeting of the council. At the same meeting Willard M. Wickizer, executive secretary of the Division of Home Missions of the United Christian Missionary Society, presented a paper titled "Ideas for Brotherhood Restructure."

As a result of Wickizer's suggestions and the redirected work of the Council, a Committee on Brotherhood Structure was appointed on October 15, 1958. Two basic decisions made by this committee were that the "leadership in any program of restructure" ought to be "centered in the International Convention itself as the voice of all the churches" and that "thorough cooperation between the churches and the agencies" would be necessary "to create a total program for the church."

In 1959 the board of directors of the International Convention reported to the convention their intention of recommending the creation of a Commission on Brotherhood Structure. Whether intentionally or not, the planning emphasis of the Council of Agencies led directly to the restructure of the Disciples that was approved by the convention in 1968.

See also Restructure; United Christian Missionary Society, The; Wickizer, Willard Morgan

BIBLIOGRAPHY Spencer P. Austin, "Our Channels of Service," in *Primer for New Disciples: A Guide Book for New Members of the Christian Churches (Disciples of Christ)*, ed. Samuel F. Pugh (1963) • Anthony L. Dunnavant, *Restructure: Four Historical Ideals in the Campbell-Stone Movement and the Development of the Polity of the Disciples of Christ* (1993) • Loren E. Lair, *The Christian Churches and Their Work* (1963) • *Yearbook and Directory of the Christian Church (Disciples of Christ)* (1949-68).

JOHN M. IMBLER

Council on Christian Unity

1. Ecumenical Literature and Interpretation
2. Ecumenical Leadership Formation
3. Local and Regional Ecumenism
4. Conciliar Ecumenism
5. Church Union and Ecumenical Partnerships
6. International Dialogues
7. Disciples Ecumenical Consultative Council

General Administrative unit of the Christian Church (Disciples of Christ) in the United States and Canada entrusted with the responsibility to give leadership toward the fulfillment of Jesus Christ's prayer "that they all may be one . . . so that the world may believe" (John 17).

Its specific mandate, as articulated in 1979, is "to enable and empower the Christian Church (Disciples of Christ) to affirm the biblical calling to the unity of the one Church of Jesus Christ and to manifest visibly God's word of love, reconciliation and peace in its life and mission." As the coordinating center for the Disciples ecumenical witness, the Council on Christian Unity (CCU) works in partnership with congregations, regions, the General Assembly, theological seminaries, other general units, partner churches, and varied ecumenical agencies.

The CCU was founded in October 1910 — the year the modern ecumenical movement was born — when the Disciples national convention, gathered at Topeka, Kansas, voted to establish the Council on Christian Union. In 1916 its name was changed to the Association for the Promotion of Christian Unity, and in 1954 to the Council on Christian Unity. The Council's original mandate was "to promote Christian union at home and throughout the world until the various Christian bodies are knit together in one organic life." Its enabling functions were "to watch for every indication of Christian unity and to hasten the time by intercessory prayer, friendly conferences and the distribution of irenic literature, 'til we all attain unto the unity of the faith." With this action the Disciples of Christ became the first church in North America, and arguably the world, to establish a permanent instrumentality with such a representative ecumenical mandate.

Throughout its history of almost a century the CCU has been led by only five presidents or executive officers: Peter Ainslie III (1910-34), George Walker Buckner (1941-61) George G. Beazley, Jr. (1961-73),

Paul A. Crow, Jr. (1974-98), and Robert K. Welsh (1999-).

1. Ecumenical Literature and Interpretation

In one of his initial actions Peter Ainslie founded and edited *The Christian Union Quarterly* (1911-1935), which was for twenty-five years the most significant international journal devoted to Christian unity. In 1961 George Beazley renewed this lineage with the quarterly publication named *Mid-Stream: An Ecumenical Journal*. Across its history *Mid-Stream* had three editors: Beazley (1961-73), Paul Crow (1974-98), and Robert Welsh (1999-2002) — all three presidents of the CCU.

Ecumenical books published under the sponsorship of the CCU have included Howard E. Short, *Christian Unity Is Our Business* (1953); George Walker Buckner, Jr., *Concerns of the World Church* (1943) and *The Winds of God: Christian Unity, Cooperation and World Fellowship* (1947); Winfred E. Garrison, *Christian Unity and the Disciples of Christ* (1955); George G. Beazley, Jr., ed., *The Christian Church (Disciples of Christ): An Interpretative Examination in the Cultural Context* (1973); and Paul A. Crow, Jr., and James O. Duke, eds., *The Church for Disciples of Christ* (1998). Special issues of *Mid-Stream* offered interpretative resources related to World Council of Churches (WCC) assemblies and programs, conferences on Faith and Order, Mission and Evangelism, Interchurch Aid, Refugee and World Service, plenaries of the Consultation on Church Union, sessions of the Disciples of Christ–Roman Catholic International Dialogue, and other ecumenical developments.

2. Ecumenical Leadership Formation

The CCU has been committed in each generation to identifying and equipping Disciples ministers, lay people, and younger theologians to give leadership — locally, nationally, and internationally — to the ecumenical movement. This priority led the CCU to be significantly involved in the WCC's Ecumenical Institute Bossey, especially in offering scholarships and sending Disciples to its Graduate School for Ecumenical Studies and seminars. Four presidents of the CCU — Buckner, Beazley, Crow, and Welsh — have served on Bossey's Board, the latter two serving as moderator. Howard E. Short and Clark Williamson were sent as tutors to the Graduate School.

Disciples give leadership at the annual National Workshop on Christian Unity that gathers Protestant, Roman Catholic, and Orthodox ecumenists from across the United States and Canada for lectures, seminars, and fellowship. The CCU staff makes teaching visits to theological seminaries in order to convey the call to Christian unity and the significance of the ecumenical movement to future pastors and teachers.

3. Local and Regional Ecumenism

Particular emphasis is given by the CCU to nurturing the vision of Christian unity among Disciples congregations and regions. In 1997 the CCU published a booklet entitled "Ecumenical Guidelines for Congregations." The CCU staff leads "ecumenical saturation weekends" in congregations, involving preaching and teaching about the biblical vision of unity and informing them of the ecumenical commitments and decisions that lie before the churches. A partnership exists between the CCU and regional ecumenical commissions. (In 1987 twenty-four of the thirty-five Disciples regions had such commissions, but by 2002 only a handful continue to function because of declining finances and a lessening of commitment to Christian unity.) Disciples have given extraordinary leadership among state and metropolitan ecumenical bodies in the United States The staff of these councils — many of whom are Disciples — are brought together under the National Association of Ecumenical Staff (NAES).

In 1982 the CCU inaugurated the annual Peter Ainslie Lecture on Christian Unity, with the first being held at the Christian Temple, the congregation in Baltimore, Maryland, founded by and served for decades by Peter Ainslie. Annually this endowed lecture brings a distinguished ecumenical leader to a local community in the United States (a Disciples congregation, educational institution, or church assembly) to reflect in the context of worship on the calling to Christian unity. The array of international Ainslie lecturers has included Cardinal Johannes Willebrands, Lesslie Newbigin, Albert C. Outler, Archbishop of Canterbury Robert C. Runcie, Fred B. Craddock, Emilio Castro, and Mary Tanner. While based in Dallas, Texas, the Joe A. and Nancy Vaughn Stalcup Lecture on Christian Unity makes a similar witness to unity. Stalcup lecturers have included Leander Keck, Rita Nakashima Brock, and Ambassador Andrew Young.

4. Conciliar Ecumenism

Disciples were formative members of the Federal Council of Churches in America (1908), the National Council of Churches of Christ in the U.S.A. (NCCC, 1950), the Canadian Council of Churches (1944), and the World Council of Churches (1948). The CCU plays an enabling role in linking Disciples to these instruments of cooperation in unity, mission, justice, and peace. Two Disciples have served as the general secretary of the NCCC: Roy G. Ross and Joan Brown Campbell.

Disciples believe the WCC is "a privileged instrument" of the worldwide movement of unity and mission. Representatives to its Central Committee have included three CCU presidents — Buckner, Beazley, and Crow — as well as J. Irwin Miller, Raymond Cuthbert, Jean Woolfolk, and more recently General Minister and President Richard L. Hamm. Throughout the WCC's life, Disciples — frequently through the CCU — have seconded staff members to their Geneva staff, including Robert Tobias (Interchurch Aid), Lucy Griffith (World Youth Projects), Rosemary Roberts (Scholarships), Donald Newby (Youth Department), William J. Nottingham (Youth), John Fulton (Communications), and a succession of four staff to the Faith and Order Commission — Robert Welsh, Stephen V. Cranford, Michael Kinnamon, and Thomas F. Best.

5. Church Union and Ecumenical Partnerships

Among the earliest unity conversations initiated by the CCU were a series (1911-18) with the Episcopal, Presbyterian, Congregational, and Northern Baptist churches. Later attempts at church union included the Conference on Organic Union (1918-20), which produced the unsuccessful Philadelphia Plan. From 1947 to 1952 Disciples and American Baptists pursued union conversations, but discovered that the common practice of believers' baptism by immersion was not a sufficient basis to unite these two traditions. The Conference on Church Union (1946-58) explored the possibility of church union among nine churches, which "already accord one another mutual recognition of ministries and sacraments." The Disciples editor and theologian Charles Clayton Morrison drafted its plan of union, colloquially named the Greenwich Plan because of the Connecticut city where all its meetings were held. In later decades the CCU gave central leadership to two other highly visible, and more successful, unity ventures in the U.S. In 1962 the Christian Church (Disciples of Christ) and the United Church of Christ (a 1957 union of the Congregational Christian Church and the Evangelical and Reformed Church) initiated church union conversations, which were temporarily suspended in 1966. Resumed in 1977, this bilateral process eventuated in a "Declaration of Ecumenical Partnership" (1985) and finally (1989) in a decision to declare that these two churches are in "full communion."

In one of the most dramatic ecumenical actions in the twentieth century, the Consultation on Church Union (COCU) was launched in 1960, drawing nine mainline Protestant churches into a common search for a united church "truly catholic, truly evangelical, and truly reformed." At Los Angeles in 1962 the International Convention voted to become a full member church of this history-making venture. Throughout its history the Disciples have been fully committed to COCU's vision and hard decisions. George G. Beazley, Jr., served a three-year term (1970-73) as president, and Paul A. Crow, Jr., was for six years (1968-74) the first general secretary. Other Disciples served COCU in strategic roles. After decades of ups and downs, the Consultation reached its fruition in January 2002 when these nine churches, by votes of their highest assemblies, became Churches Uniting in Christ (CUIC). These churches committed themselves to a shared life in faith, sacraments, mission, and combating racism. They promised to work together toward the reconciliation of their ordained ministries, the thorny issue yet to be agreed upon.

On the international scene the CCU has been related to union negotiations and united churches that involve Disciples, for example, in the Congo (Zaire), Great Britain, North India, Southern Africa, Jamaica, Australia, New Zealand, and Canada.

6. International Dialogues

Between 1967 and 1973 a bilateral dialogue was pursued in the U.S. between the Christian Church (Disciples of Christ) and the U.S. Catholic Bishops' Commission for Ecumenical Dialogue. This venture was inspired by George G. Beazley, Jr., and Archbishop (later Cardinal) William Baum of Washington. Its first and final report was entitled *An Adventure in Understanding* (1973).

At the initiative of Paul Crow and Cardinal Johannes Willebrands, the International Disciples of Christ–Roman Catholic Dialogue was begun in 1977. The official sponsors were the Council on Christian Unity and the newly formed (1975) international Disciples Ecumenical Consultative Council (DECC) and the Vatican's Pontifical Council for Promoting Christian Unity. The International Commission for Dialogue, composed of theologians and pastors, women and men from both traditions, has completed three multiyear periods. The first round (1977-82) produced an "agreed account" bearing the title *Apostolicity and Catholicity;* the second agreed account (1983-92) was entitled *The Church as Communion in Christ;* and the third round (1993-2002) offered *Receiving and Handing on the Faith: The Mission and Responsibility of the Church.* This dialogue's fourth round will begin in 2004.

Disciples and the Reformed/Presbyterian churches have long been close partners in the ecumenical movement, especially in the WCC, the NCCC, and COCU. Both belong to united churches in North India, Japan, Southern Africa, Thailand, Congo, the United Kingdom, and Jamaica. In March 1987 the DECC and the World Alliance of Reformed Churches (WARC) convened an international dialogue in Birmingham, England, which explored four themes: common doctrinal roots, the sacraments of baptism and the Lord's Supper, the ministry, and models of Christian unity. The dialogue's report concluded that there are "no theological obstacles" between these two traditions, and declared, "The Disciples of Christ and the Reformed Churches recognize and accept each other as visible expressions of the one Church of Christ." A second consultation in January 2002 recommended that the WARC and the DECC should develop a "comprehensive partnership in pursuit of the vision of the two [Christian World Communions] becoming one."

During the Cold War the NCCC built bridges of Christian friendship between churches in the Soviet Union and the U.S. by planning exchange visits of Christians from both countries. The first American delegation to visit the USSR in the 1960s was led by J. Irwin Miller, a prominent Disciples lay leader, industrialist, and president of the NCCC. In 1973, while on a visit with his wife to the Orthodox Church in Moscow, George Beazley died of a heart attack. The enormous pastoral care given to Mrs. Beazley led the 1973 General Assembly to vote a resolution of gratitude to the Russian Orthodox Church. In the mid-1980s over 200 Disciples shared in ecumenical visits to Russia coordinated by the NCCC. In April 1987 an official Disciples of Christ–Russian Orthodox dialogue began under the aegis of the CCU. A delegation of ten Disciples, including General Minister and President John O. Humbert, traveled to the USSR for the first session of the dialogue at the Department of External Relations at the St. Danilov Monastery in Moscow and with the theological faculties at Zagorsk, Leningrad, and Odessa. The themes addressed were "Baptism, Eucharist and Ministry" and "Peacemaking in a Nuclear Age." In 1990 — as the transition from rigid Marxism to *perestroika* was happening — the second dialogue took place at Orthodox theological communities in St. Petersburg (formerly Leningrad) and Moscow. The themes were "The Renewal of Parish Life" and "The Church's Diaconal Ministry in Society."

In 1996 an international dialogue with the Evangelical Lutheran Church in Finland had its first encounter in Indianapolis under the auspices of the CCU. Disciples and the Finnish delegation, led by Presiding Archbishop John Vikstrom, engaged in theological reflections and learned of congregational life in the U.S. In 1998 a Disciples delegation traveled to Finland to explore theological understandings of ecumenism and the nature of the church and to understand the realities of church life in that Scandinavian country.

In June and November of 1999 the Stone-Campbell Dialogue began among individuals of the Christian Church (Disciples of Christ), the Churches of Christ, and the Christian Churches/Churches of Christ, all of whom have common roots in the nineteenth-century Stone-Campbell Movement. In addition, inspired by the 2001 celebration of the 200th anniversary of the famous Cane Ridge Revival in Bourbon County, Kentucky, some local worship services in different parts of the U.S. have brought congregations of these three divided traditions into fellowship.

7. Disciples Ecumenical Consultative Council

The CCU gave leadership in the formation of the DECC, first constituted in 1975 during the Fifth Assembly of the World Council of Churches at Nairobi, Kenya. Members of this Christian World Communion are Disciples churches from different parts of the world and united churches that contain former Disciples in their membership. The DECC's primary purposes are (1) to deepen the international fellowship (*koinōnia*) among these churches and to encourage their participation in the movement toward the visible unity God wills for all the churches; (2) to encourage participation in the ecumenical movement through joint theological study, church unity conversations and international dialogues, and programs of joint action and witness; (3) to gather, share, and evaluate information about Disciples' ecumenical activities in local, national, and regional situations around the world; and (4) to appoint representatives of the DECC to ecumenical bodies and activities such as the World Council of Churches, Christian World Communions, and the Roman Catholic Church.

In its unique history and myriad witnesses the Council on Christian Unity has given immeasurable leadership toward keeping the Disciples of Christ informed and committed to the vision of visible unity among all Christian churches.

See also Ainslie, Peter; Consultation on Church Union; Ecumenical Movement; *Mid-Stream;* Unity, Christian

BIBLIOGRAPHY Peter Ainslie, *Towards Christian Unity* (1918) • "Association for the Promotion of Christian Unity," in *Survey of Service: Organizations Represented in the International Convention of the Disciples of Christ* (1928), pp. 664-71 • CCU Annual Reports to the General Assembly (International Convention), published in the *Yearbook of the Christian Church (Disciples of Christ)* (1910-present) • Paul A. Crow, Jr., "The Christian Church (Disciples of Christ) in the Ecumenical Movement," in *The Christian Church (Disciples of Christ): An Interpretative Examination in Cultural Context,* ed. George G. Beazley, Jr. (1973), pp. 252-94 • W. E. Garrison, "The Council on Christian Unity," in his *Christian Unity and Disciples of Christ* (1955), pp. 159-76 • Ronald E. Osborn, "Disciples of Christ and Union Among Denominations," *The Shane Quarterly* 16:2 (April 1955): 253-94.

PAUL A. CROW, JR.

Covenant (Federal) Theology

Extensive theological movement, born of the Reformed heritage, to which early Stone-Campbell leaders reacted both positively and negatively.

Covenant or "federal" theology developed in the sixteenth and seventeenth centuries particularly in the Netherlands and Great Britain, largely as an effort to mitigate the impact of the rigid doctrine of predestination articulated in Reformed scholasticism in the era following John Calvin. Where Calvin had treated divine election as a topic for consideration under the doctrinal category of sin and salvation, Reformed scholastic dogma placed it under the heading of the doctrine of the being and purpose of God, making it the keystone of its system. Covenant theology, in response, injected the element of contingency into humanity's relation to God by viewing God's relation to Adam as operating like a type of contractual or bilateral arrangement. Covenant theologians posited two such arrangements in the biblical revelation: (1) a covenant of works (law) given to Adam and, through him, to the whole human race; and (2) the covenant of grace, made with Adam and Eve after their fall. The Bible, beginning at Genesis 3:15, conveyed the outworking of the covenant of grace comprehending both Old Testament and New Testament.

The Decalogue was fundamental to the whole system. Edward Fisher explained in the *Marrow of Modern Divinity* (1645) how Adam violated all Ten Commandments when he ate the forbidden fruit. Fisher stated three facts about the Decalogue: (1) all Adam's progeny are bound by the law but, after the fall, cannot attain life by it; (2) the substance of the law is contained in the gospel because Christ placed himself under it and fulfilled it on our behalf; and (3) it now serves as the law of Christ — the rule of life for believers. The above conceptions of the role of the law have led some analysts to observe that the covenant of grace is in reality "the covenant of works in disguise." The covenant of works is the basic covenant.

Covenant theology also served the cause of political philosophers in the sixteenth and seventeenth centuries who found in the concept of a natural moral law the basis for emphasizing human duty and responsibility.

Federal theology became the organizing principle of an entire theological system. It was formalized in the Westminster Confession (1647), and hence became a cardinal doctrinal element in the Church of Scotland, among English and American Puritans, and among adherents of the Baptist Philadelphia Confession in America.

The distinctions described above mark the difference between Campbell and his Presbyterian, Puritan, and Baptist contemporaries. While thoroughly committed to the role of progressive covenants in God's dealing with mankind, he held that grace underlies them all. He rejected the idea that Adam was under a covenant of works. He could identify nine covenants in the Old Testament. All were "covenants of promise" in the history of salvation, with grace their operative principle. He found differences with the covenant theology of Johannes Cocceius (1603-1669), despite his indebtedness to the Dutch theologian as a model of careful exegesis of Scripture. Campbell would not make a covenant of works the foundation of his system. Overtones of his views on covenant theology were present as early as 1816 in his "Sermon on the Law," in which he depicted the New Covenant in Jesus Christ as transcending everything before it. This view was further enhanced in subsequent exegesis of Hebrews, a favored text in the Stone-Campbell Movement, with its dialectic of Old and New Covenants. This dialectic proved especially important to Campbell (and others) in confuting Presbyterians who argued a correlation between circumcision and infant baptism under the one covenant of grace. Campbell in fact developed much of his covenant theology precisely in his public debates on baptism, as well as in his writing on other soteriological issues.

Campbell's views on covenant theology endured throughout the Stone-Campbell Movement in the twentieth century. Two exemplary works bearing this influence were Ashley Johnson's *Sermons on the Two Covenants* (1949) and Mont Smith's *What the Bible Says about Covenant* (1981), both from the tradition of the Christian Churches/Churches of Christ. In the Christian Church (Disciples of Christ), the tendency has been to move from the strictly soteriological to the *ecclesiological* dimension of covenant theology, a trend that began with the denominational Restructure in the 1960s.

See also Baptism; Grace, Doctrine of; Hermeneutics; Presbyterians, Presbyterianism; Salvation; "Sermon on the Law"

BIBLIOGRAPHY Alexander Campbell, "Sermon on the Law," reprinted in *Historical Documents Advocating Christian Union,* ed. C. A. Young (1904), pp. 211-82 • Alexander Campbell, "Tracts for the People — No. VI: Covenants of Promise," *Millennial Harbinger* (1846): 253-64 (reprinted in his *Christian Baptism* [1851], pp. 89-102) • Ashley Johnson, *Sermons on the Two Covenants* (1949) • Charles S. McCoy, "The Covenant Theology of Johannes Cocceius" (unpublished Ph.D. dissertation, Yale University, 1957) • William J. Richardson, *The Role of Grace in the Thought of Alexander Campbell* (1991) • Mont Smith, *What the Bible Says About Covenant* (1981) • John Von Rohr, *The Covenant of Grace in Puritan Thought* (1987).

WILLIAM J. RICHARDSON

Crank, Sarah Catherine (Sadie) McCoy (1863-1948)

Evangelist and one of the first women ordained in the Stone-Campbell Movement.

Sarah Catherine (Sadie) McCoy was born near Breckenridge, Illinois, on August 15, 1863, and baptized in Bear Creek, May 1887. She became an evangelist and was hired by James Rawser Crank from the Illinois State Sunday School Society to lead teaching services and revival meetings. At one meeting, worshipers came forward to confess Jesus as Lord. Despite being torn between denying those confessions and recognizing a woman's authority to receive them, church authorities ordained Sadie McCoy in Marceline, Illinois, on March 17, 1892; a year later she married J. R. Crank.

During her ministry she baptized between five and seven thousand people, officiated at 361 weddings and more than 1,000 funerals, organized or reorganized 50 rural churches, and was an active member of the Christian Woman's Board of Missions and the Woman's Christian Temperance Union. Sadie Crank died on September 20, 1948, in Greenfield, Illinois.

DEBRA B. HULL

See also Temperance; Women in Ministry — Nineteenth Century

Creath, Jacob, Jr. (1799-1886)

Ex-Baptist preacher who became a defender of strict restorationism in the Stone-Campbell Movement.

The son of a Baptist minister, Jacob Creath was one of sixteen children. He was born in Mecklenburg County, Virginia, on January 17, 1799. As the second of nine sons, five of whom became ministers, Creath was the product of a deeply religious home in which Scripture reading, the recitation of hymns, and the practice of prayer were common. Having grown up on a farm, hard work was also a staple of life for Creath and remained so until his later years.

Creath was baptized at a Baptist church meeting in May of 1817 and preached his first sermon shortly thereafter. He was licensed to preach in February of 1818 and received most of his ministerial training under Abner W. Clopton at the University of North Carolina at Chapel Hill, and at Columbia College in Washington, D.C., under William Staughton.

Creath traveled and preached in various states and was no stranger to controversy, having been burned in effigy early on at Natchez, Mississippi. Alexander Campbell's *Christian Baptist* struck a responsive chord with Creath, and he grew increasingly at odds with many of his Baptist brethren both in his "denial of the direct operation of the Spirit of God upon the sinner's heart, previous to the exercise of faith upon his part," and for adopting the "Bible alone" apart from creeds as the infallible guide for faith. Creath, along with his uncle, Jacob Creath, Sr., and "Raccoon" John Smith, was expelled from Baptist fellowship in Kentucky in 1830.

Just as controversy marked Creath's relationships with many Baptists, so too was he quickly at odds with many within the Stone-Campbell Movement.

Creath was once called "the John Knox of the restoration" by John F. Rowe because of his stern and unrelenting opposition to what he saw as innovations in the Movement.
Courtesy of the Disciples of Christ Historical Society

Creath preferred the "Old Paths" represented by Barton W. Stone and the Alexander Campbell of the *Christian Baptist* and early *Millennial Harbinger* period, and he vigorously opposed what he viewed as illegitimate innovations, like missionary and Bible societies and instrumental music in worship. As Creath himself later put it, "I have withstood papists and sects more than fifty years and now I have to withstand our own people, just before I leave the world."

Creath's virtues and vices were often two sides of the same coin: he was a serious man of passionate conviction and fiery temper; devout and rigid; candid and combative. Creath contributed to the spread of the Stone-Campbell Movement in several states, especially in Missouri where he spent the bulk of his years. His first wife, Susan Bedford, died July 16, 1841, of consumption; he married Prudence Rogers in March of 1842.

Creath was a preacher, a farmer, an author and editor, and an agent of the Bible Revision Association. His efforts earned him the nickname "Iron Duke of the Restoration." When he died on January 9, 1886, he was buried, without a funeral service, in a plain coffin with his New Testament and a copy of Campbell's *Living Oracles* as a pillow.

See also Baptists; Evangelism, Evangelists — Nineteenth Century

BIBLIOGRAPHY "Bible Alone Rejected by the Conventionists," *Gospel Advocate* 19 (1877): 724 • Jacob Creath, *Biographical Sketches of Elder Wm. Creath* (1866) • Philip Donan, *Memoir of Jacob Creath, Jr.* (1872) • T. P. Haley, *Historical and Biographical Sketches of the Early Churches and Pioneer Preachers of the Christian Church in Missouri* (1888), pp. 427-55 • "Old and New Things Contrasted," *Gospel Advocate* 19 (1877): 756.

CRAIG CHURCHILL

Creation and Evolution

Though the emergence of modern science raised concern in some quarters with respect to the compatibility of scientific and biblical conceptions of the physical universe, it was not until Charles Darwin's (1809-1882) publication of *Origin of Species* in 1859 and *Descent of Man* in 1871 that the potential for open conflict was fully realized. Prior to the nineteenth century, Calvin's distinction between the religious ideas of the Bible, which carried the weight of divine authority, and scientific ideas, which reflected the prevailing scientific worldview of the authors, seemed satisfactory to most Protestants. However, Darwinian evolutionary theory, offering a dramatic alternative to the biblical narrative of a creation ex nihilo, challenged both the argument from design as proof of the existence of God, a notion that undergirded much eighteenth-century English theology, and the assumption of the unique creation of the human species in the image of God.

A clerical attack on Darwinian ideas was launched in 1860 in Britain and a bit later in the United States. Charles Hodge (1797-1878) of Princeton Seminary offered a serious critique of Darwinian thought, but few theologians followed this course. While many continued to reject evolutionary ideas, criticism steadily declined among the liberal clergy and in the universities as the century neared its close. Some resolved the conflict by separating the two worlds of religion and science, while many others joined Lyman Abbott (1835-1922) in affirming that "evolution is God's way of doing things." The Stone-Campbell Movement remained relatively isolated from this discussion until the twentieth century.

One critical voice early on, however, was David Lipscomb, who published articles on evolution and on new findings in the field of geology. Lipscomb welcomed the notion of "evolution" both as the unfolding or development of a living thing from its embryonic beginnings and as the development of higher and more perfect forms of being from lower and lesser ones. In the latter case, he said, "education and evolution mean much the same thing. To educate is to draw out or awake to a higher degree the faculties — mental, moral, and fleshly — involved or dormant and rudimentary in persons, beasts, or plants." These forms of "evolution" were innocuous because they simply indicated the Creator's orderly plan and were consonant with facts already revealed in the Bible. Darwinism was another thing altogether. Lipscomb categorically rejected the hypothesis that human life had evolved from an inferior original, the same primal source shared by all other forms of life. Ultimately he insisted that the Bible alone contained the true science and the touchstone of all human theories and conjectures, whether concerning biological evolution or geology.

The Scopes "Monkey" trial in Dayton, Tennessee, in 1925 heightened American awareness of the issue but served largely to identify creationist or anti-evolutionary thought with Protestant fundamentalism. Among conservative Disciples, who did not identify fully with the fundamentalist crusade, there was open sympathy for the creationist position, as evidenced in the *Christian Standard*'s reprinting of a discourse against scientific materialism by William Jennings Bryan. E. A. Elam (1855-1929), a preacher and writer from the Churches of Christ in Tennessee, countered the new theories of evolution with a book on the subject in 1925.

There the matter rested until the 1960s. Biologists continued to make significant advances working with evolutionary assumptions, though few high school biology teachers were prepared to risk criticism by openly teaching ideas of evolution in the classroom. Public controversy was infrequent. Strongest opposition to evolutionary ideas was located in the Southwest and California, and there group attitudes on this issue closely paralleled attitudes on other religious and social issues. A survey of church members in northern California in 1963 revealed that more than a quarter of them opposed evolutionary ideas, but far more startling were the differences among church groups. Only 11 percent of liberal Protestants, including Disciples of Christ, publicly opposed evolutionary ideas, whereas the percentage figure for Churches of Christ was 78.

Thereafter, as federal court decisions made it clear that any effort to teach creationism as a biblically based religious idea in the schools would be found unconstitutional, efforts were mounted to present creationist ideas as scientifically grounded. This effort found some support among the Churches of Christ, a number of whose scientists joined the Creation Research Society, which was founded in 1963 "to provide authoritative, well documented materials and textbooks to support the scientific evidences of Biblical Creation." The Society, as the leading institutional advocate of what came to be termed scientific creationism, engages in the preparation and distribution of a wide range of creationist literature through which it exposes gaps in evolutionary theory and disagreements among evolutionists, on the one hand, and offers creationism as a more satisfactory explanation, on the other. Its greatest successes have been in the area of shaping school curricula and textbooks; its impact on the scientific and academic community has been negligible. Other such organizations have also emerged, advancing creation science. At least one such group has represented its work at the North American Christian Convention as recently as 1995, and not a few Christian Churches/Churches of Christ have hosted seminars from creationist organizations.

The Creation Research Society has insisted that its members affirm belief in Jesus Christ as Savior and has shown little interest in creationist theories other than those found in the Bible. Thus, while scientific creationists insist that they advocate science rather than religion, this claim has been difficult to sustain. An Arkansas law of 1981 framed by creation science advocates and declaring that "public schools within this State shall give balanced treatment to creation-science and to evolution science" led to a dramatic hearing in federal court in which both parties to the suit presented theologians and scientists as expert witnesses in support of their positions. Publicity accorded this case significantly increased the level of public awareness of the issues involved. Although the Arkansas statute was found unconstitutional and the court declared that "the *only* real effect of Act 590 is the advancement of religion," many states have subsequently attempted to craft legislation designed to achieve similar aims without raising the constitutional problems of Act 590, and state and local school boards frequently permit equal time policies. The sharp differences noted in 1963 among groups within the Stone-Campbell Movement with respect to belief in evolution or creationism undoubtedly continue today, but the real focus of the conflict is in the schools rather than the churches.

One of the few recent thinkers from the Stone-Campbell heritage to deal substantively with the nature of creation has been Disciples theologian Joe R. Jones, who has largely rejected the creationist agenda as an attempt to "set up an alternative 'science' against evolution" and justify it alone as biblical. Jones has called for a constructive engagement of scientific hypotheses about the actual physical origins of the world, but with due attention to the critical limitations and liabilities of human science and with appropriate recognition of theology's primary interests in the Creator's providence, love, and teleological relationship with the creation.

See also Anthropology; God, Doctrine of

BIBLIOGRAPHY Michael W. Casey, "The Interpretation of Genesis One in the Churches of Christ: The Origins of Fundamentalist Reactions to Evolution and Biblical Criticism in the 1920s" (unpublished M.A. thesis, Abilene Christian University, 1989) • Jack Cottrell, *What the Bible Says About God the Creator* (1983) • E. A. Elam, ed., *The Bible Versus Theories of Evolution* (1925) • Joe R. Jones, *A Grammar of Christian Faith* (2000), vol. 1, pp. 233-92 • David Lipscomb, "Evolution and the Bible," in *Salvation from Sin* (1913), pp. 347-64 • David Lipscomb, "Geology and the Bible," in *Salvation from Sin* (1913), pp. 365-74.

SAMUEL C. PEARSON

Creeds and Confessions

Summaries of Christian belief — historically used in baptism, liturgy, instruction, or as tests of orthodoxy or terms of communion in the church — that have frequently come under intense criticism in the Stone-Campbell Movement.

Ironically, the Stone-Campbell Movement emerged from the broad matrix of the Reformed (Calvinist) heritage, the Protestant tradition most prolific in the production of creeds and catechisms. During the Great Western Revival, the frontier phase of the Second Great Awakening, old orthodoxies were continually being called into question. Not only Calvinist theology itself but also its Anglo-American benchmark, the Westminster Confession, drew fire from "Christian" movements, Baptists, Methodists, and eventually Disciples of Christ. These dissenters cherished the commonsense ability of individual Christians to understand the "plain facts" of Scripture for themselves, without the imposition of "human" authorities (i.e., popes, councils, clerics, theologians).

Few embodied this critical ethos more potently than Barton W. Stone, who, with grave reservations about the Westminster Confession, passed the ordination test of the Presbytery of Transylvania (Kentucky) merely by conceding that he adopted the creed "as far as I see it consistent with the word of God." Stone's disenchantment with Calvinism developed hand in hand with his disgust at creeds as "nuisances of religious society, and the very bane of Christian unity." His sentiments were detailed in the *Apology of the Springfield Presbytery* (1804). Creeds were, categorically, instruments of ecclesiastical tyranny, enslaving the free consciences of Christians and spawning sectarianism. Creeds detracted from the simpler and plainer truth of the Bible itself, the "catholic" foundation of Christian union. Creeds, the *Apology* further argued, might have begun as means to summarize or explain biblical truth but inevitably took on a life of their own, engendering artificial unity at best, open schism at worst. Stone (and his fellow writers of the *Apology*) targeted the Westminster Confession in particular because its doctrine of election undermined the core gospel of God's gracious love for all sinners.

Much of the early criticism from Thomas and Alexander Campbell centered on the historic tendency of creeds to supplant the primary authority of Scripture. In Proposition Six of the *Declaration and Address* (1809), Thomas Campbell asserted that although "inferences and deductions" from Scripture, when "fairly inferred," could legitimately be considered biblical doctrine, they could not be forced upon the consciences of believers beyond their ability to comprehend them; hence, "no such deductions or inferential truths ought to have any place in the church's confession." By "confession" here, he meant the basic test of faith for receiving persons into fellowship. Elsewhere in the *Declaration and Address,* the elder Campbell conceded the value of historic confessions of faith (primarily the Westminster Confession) for *catechetical* purposes. That allowance was qualified, however, by his insistence on the sufficiency — *and perspicuity* — of Scripture itself. There would be no need to decipher the "essentials" from the nonessentials in the Bible (a classic justification for creeds) because the scriptural directives binding on all Christians, and instrumental to Christian unity, were already "self-evident."

Early in his *Christian Baptist* series on "A Restoration of the Ancient Order of Things" (1825-29), Alexander Campbell bluntly argued that human creeds, because they were absent from the New Testament, should be summarily discarded. Echoing Barton Stone's concern, he attacked the traditional rationale that creeds were intended to clarify what was obscure in Scripture. He cited language from the Westminster Confession to claim that the opposite was true. Phrases like the Son being "eternally begotten" of the Father (originally from the Nicene Creed) and the prolix expressions detailing God's predestination and foreknowledge rendered complex what was simple in the scriptural language of the Holy Spirit. Campbell resorted to a *reductio ad absurdum* by qualifying all human creeds as "inferences of the human understanding speculating upon the revelation of God" and as invariably divisive. "Their being held as a nominal bond of union, gives rise to hypocrisy, prevarication, lying, and, in many instances, to the basest injustice." Thus, Campbell declared, "he that advocates the necessity of creeds of human contrivance to the unity of the church unconsciously impeaches the wisdom of God, arraigns the benevolence of the Saviour, and censures the revelation of the Spirit."

Alexander Campbell further articulated this diatribe in a long exchange on creeds in his 1843 debate with Nathan Rice, though his point remained that — *as bonds of union or terms of communion* — creeds were "necessarily heretical and schismatical." He described, at the outset, a historical process of degeneration. The apostolic church had the original testimony it termed simply "the faith," "the form of sound words," the "gospel"; the second- and third-century church had numerous "symbols" of faith serving to mark the believer at baptism; afterward came the ancient ecumenical creeds (the Nicene, Apostles', and Athanasian), which had "fewer aberrations" than the much later Protestant creeds; these latter, proliferating since the sixteenth century, were the most alien from Scripture and most divisive of all. Campbell went on in the debate with Rice to argue thirteen reasons for banning creeds as terms of communion: (1) their human fallibility; (2) their tendency to evict conscientious souls; (3) their intrinsic intolerance; (4) their affront to Christ's supreme authority; (5) the New Testament's prohibition of creeds — especially Paul's admonishing Timothy to "hold fast the form of sound words" (2 Tim. 3:5); (6) the fact that in the first two centuries of its history the church was happy without them; (7) their transmutation into "constitutions" for new denominations; (8) their discouragement of deeper inquiry into scriptural truth; (9) their frustration of spirituality; (10) their illusion of providing greater clarity than the Bible itself; (11) their hostility to reformation and great reformers; (12) their tendency to be "superfluous and redundant"; and (13) their summary inhibition of Christian unity.

An able opponent, Nathan Rice countered Campbell with serious rejoinders about the utility of creeds. He actually agreed with Campbell that Scripture's own language was simpler and clearer than the creeds, but reminded him that human interpretation is fallible, and that many a theological deviant, claiming a pure conscience and recourse to the Bible, had confounded the plain meaning. The united church inevitably needed parameters of tolerable diversity that only creeds, as digests of *scriptural* truth, could provide. Citing Campbell's own forceful treatment of the schismatic Dr. John Thomas, Rice charged that Campbell and the Disciples had themselves set strict standards for acceptable interpretation. Campbell responded by reiterating the clarity of Scripture and his confidence in the triumph of reasonable minds. True schismatics were always self-evidently in the wrong and thus indicted themselves. "We *know* whom to exclude."

Elsewhere, moreover, Rice concurred with Campbell that creeds could never substitute for the Bible itself and were not to be, strictly speaking, a condition for church membership. They were definitely tests for ministry candidates, but for all others, as "pupils," they provided the basic doctrinal groundwork, or information, that members should be able to identify with and that they would come to learn more fully in the context of the church. Campbell himself, Rice asserted, was providing precisely these kinds of guidelines in writings like *The Christian Sys-*

tem. No Christian community, indeed no Christian unity, could be viable without standards of scriptural interpretation. Rice was saying that Stone-Campbell churches, like all others, had to be *realistic* about the decisive role of theology in the life of the church.

Two challenges for the Stone-Campbell Movement, separate but interrelated, came into sharp focus in the Campbell-Rice debate: the need for a confession of faith properly basic to church membership and instrumental to Christian unity; and the need for a "rule of faith" drawn from Scripture itself, an instructional guide or syllabus for faithful appropriation of the biblical truth that, over time, would nurture the church's unity and preempt schism.

Already in 1825, Campbell had written, "Human creeds may be reformed and re-reformed, and be erroneous still, like their authors; but the inspired creed needs no reformation, being, like its author, infallible." But what was this "inspired" and "infallible" creed? Barton Stone called "the Bible" creed. In the Rice debate, Campbell called the New Testament creed. Yet these appeared too general. Walter Scott answered with what he called the "golden oracle." *The* Christian creed, the proposition around which the whole faith rotated, was the Petrine Confession: Jesus is the Christ (Matt. 16:16). On this confession alone was a person baptized and admitted into the church body; on it alone was Christian unity anchored. Robert Richardson and others further explained that this confession was not just assent to a fact but *trust* in (and commitment to) the *person* of Christ. It was immortalized in the slogan "No creed but Christ," destined to be recalled again and again in the later history of the Stone-Campbell Movement.

Substantiating or fleshing out the "Christ" creed, however, was crucial for a Movement that, from the 1830s through the 1850s, was rapidly gaining adherents, needing to represent itself doctrinally, and experiencing for itself the internal challenges of heresy and schism. Walter Scott did not intend his "Five Finger Exercise" to be creedal as such, but it was inseparable from the "Christ" creed, serving as an outline of the "plan of salvation" and an eventual staple for educating new converts in Stone-Campbell churches. In *The Christian System,* Alexander Campbell summed up the apostolic faith in certain "gospel facts" or "moral facts," principally the story of Christ's incarnation, death, resurrection, and ascension for our sake. Indeed, as early as 1832, transcending some of his former iconoclasm, Campbell went so far as to endorse the historic Apostles' Creed as a faithful rendition of the "gospel facts." Thomas Campbell proposed his own alternative summary of five "gospel facts" in a synopsis published in the 1844 *Millennial Harbinger:* (1) the incarnation; (2) the coming of the Holy Spirit on Christ's human nature; (3) Christ's suffering and death; (4) his resurrection and exaltation; and (5) the descent of the Holy Spirit at Pentecost.

Later generations of Stone-Campbell leaders regularly reasserted the founders' disavowal of humanly contrived creeds as tests of communion. Stalwart restorationists (Moses Lard, J. W. McGarvey, David Lipscomb, et al.) considered it a watchword of the Movement in their ongoing crusade to distinguish "the Bible" from "theology," "truth" from "opinion." Moderates like Isaac Errett, however, still saw the need for some kind of representative confessional statement. In 1863 he issued a "Synopsis of the Faith" cataloging some distinctive Stone-Campbell beliefs: the authority of Old Testament and New Testament; the "tri-unity of God" stated in New Testament terms; the divinity of Christ; the "mighty facts" of Christ's death and resurrection, being the true "*essentials* of the Christian religion"; faith and repentance as prerequisites to baptism; baptism for the remission of sins; baptism by immersion, etc. Errett insisted that this synopsis was not a creed but a "declaration of our faith and aims" in the service of "vital religion." That did not stop Moses Lard from vilifying the synopsis as a creed indeed, "a genuine snake in the grass, wearing a honeyed name."

Many moderates in the second and third generation simply chose to extol the Stone-Campbell Movement's achievement in restoring the Petrine Confession to its rightful primacy. James S. Lamar noted some virtues of the Apostles' Creed, but it too, he claimed, contained fatally flawed language, like its affirmation that Christ "descended into hell" (a phrase Alexander Campbell simply considered synonymous with burial in a grave) or its extolling of the "Holy Catholic Church." The Petrine Confession, on the other hand, had no deficiency, redundancy, or ambiguity. It simply expressed fact, "notwithstanding the mysteries that may inhere in the subject matter." It was comprehensive, catholic, divine. "It expresses the one only essential confessional truth, and leaves it alone," wrote Lamar. W. T. Moore likewise conducted a detailed survey of the historic creeds, only to conclude that the Petrine Confession alone affirmed the *person* of Christ himself, not doctrine *about* Christ.

Liberal Disciples in the early twentieth century had their own reasons for repudiating creeds. They could identify with Alexander Campbell's statement in the Rice debate that creeds had proliferated in "less favored ages than the present." In their own age of "progress," "social Christianity," and ecumenical reconciliation, there simply was no room for theologically and metaphysically weighted confessions that rendered Christianity doctrinaire and irrelevant. Liberals, however, could still identify with "no creed but Christ" interpreted as simple commitment to Jesus of Nazareth and emptied of abstractions about his divinity and atoning work.

A voice of moderation in the mid-twentieth century was William Robinson, theologian and ecumenical activist from the British Churches of Christ, who took up the issue of creeds in his *Essays on Christian Unity* (1923) and other later writings. Robinson identified four approaches to creeds: (1) no creeds; (2) "No Creed but the Bible"; (3) no creed save the Nicene or Apostles'; and (4) the Petrine Confession as a sufficient basis of Christian fellowship and ecclesial unity. Robinson rejected the first as naively divorcing doctrine and ethics, and the second as inviting an unrealistic and unhistorical biblicism. He strongly asserted the fourth position, which he saw as a positive contribution of the Stone-Campbell tradition to the modern ecumenical movement. Yet Robinson also expressed deep sympathy both for the Nicene and Apostles' Creeds as time-tested statements of the historic Christian faith. Both of these ancient ecumenical confessions, in his judgment, had liturgical or doxological value and evoked the fullness of the catholic faith toward which baptized Christians should be educated over time.

Attitudes toward creeds in the three streams of the Stone-Campbell Movement in more recent decades can largely be summarized by looking at how each has appropriated "No creed but Christ." Churches of Christ and Christian Churches/Churches of Christ have generally taken this slogan as a *restoration* principle. To confess Christ as Lord is, for conservatives in both streams, tantamount to submitting to the full authority of the New Testament. Intrinsically it carries with it the obligation of immersion for the remission of sins, and allegiance to the apostolic pattern of faith and practice within the context of the local church. Some moderates, subtly distinguishing between the superior authority of the *person* of Christ and the authority of the apostolic order as such, have instead suggested that the "Christ" creed is primarily a test of loyalty to Christ himself, and that the believer, as a follower of Christ, commits to Christ's own will as conveyed through the New Testament. In the Christian Church (Disciples of Christ) this latter sense of the "Christ" creed has been more prevalent. Dwight Stevenson, of the Panel of Scholars in the 1960s, insisted that "No Creed but Christ" and "No Creed but the Bible" were very different proposals, as different as allegiance to Christ and allegiance to the strict letter of the scriptural text.

Few from any of the three streams of the Movement have clamored to reclaim the use of the theologically motivated creeds from Protestant history. The ancient ecumenical confessions have fared a little better in some quarters, as having liturgical value or as aiding ecumenical relationships. Frederick Norris of the Christian Churches/Churches of Christ has published an interpretive work on the Nicene Creed in the interest of Protestant–Roman Catholic reconciliation; but his perspective is by no means typical. The Christian Church (Disciples of Christ) favorably received the Faith and Order Commission's statement on "The Apostolic Faith," published in 1987 in the form of an ecumenical commentary on the Nicene Creed; but very few Disciples ecumenists were involved in the actual formation of the document. There has been renewed interest in, and use of, the Apostles' Creed, especially in the Christian Church (Disciples of Christ) and a small number of Christian Churches/Churches of Christ — facilitated perhaps by Alexander Campbell's own endorsement of this confession.

Of late M. Eugene Boring, a Disciples New Testament scholar, has offered, in his history of Stone-Campbell biblical interpretation, an appraisal of anti-creedalism in the Movement's heritage and called for fresh reappropriation of "No Creed but Christ." Drawing on the acquired sensitivities of the Stone-Campbell Movement and reflecting critically on the function of creeds in the church, Boring has proposed a "rule of faith" for Disciples and other sympathizers among the Stone-Campbell churches that frames the "Christ" creed within the dramatic fullness of the biblical revelation: (1) Creation; (2) Covenant; (3) Christ; (4) Church; and (5) Consummation. Boring recommends this rule of faith, not as a new test of fellowship, but for liturgical, catechetical, and hermeneutical usage.

See also Bible, Authority and Inspiration of the; Bible, Interpretation of the; Calvinism; Campbell-Rice Debate; *Declaration and Address;* Faith; Five Finger Exercise; God, Doctrine of; Heresy, Heretics; Robinson, William; "Synopsis of the Faith"; Theology — Nineteenth Century

BIBLIOGRAPHY M. Eugene Boring, *Disciples and the Bible: A History of Disciples Biblical Interpretation in North America* (1997) • Alexander Campbell, "A Restoration of the Ancient Order of Things," nos. 1-2, 17, *Christian Baptist* (1825, 1827): 126-28, 133-36, 312-14 • Alexander Campbell, "Reply to Barnabas" (on the Apostles' Creed), *Millennial Harbinger* (1832): 602-4 • Alexander Campbell and Nathan L. Rice, *A Debate . . . on the Action, Subject, Design and Administrator of Christian Baptism* (1844), pp. 759-912 • Thomas Campbell, *Declaration and Address* (1809) • Thomas Campbell, "A Synopsis of Christianity," *Millennial Harbinger* (1844): 481-91 • Isaac Errett, "A Synopsis of the Faith and Practice of the Church of Christ," *Lards Quarterly* 1 (1863): 95-100 (with "Remarks" by Moses Lard, 100-107) • James S. Lamar, "The Basis of Christian Union," *Christian Quarterly* 5 (1873): 182-91 • Moses Lard, "Human Creeds as Tests of Truth Make Void the Word of God," *Lard's Quarterly* (1863): 60-84 • W. T. Moore, "The Creed Question," *Christian Quarterly* 2 (1870): 1-34 • Frederick W. Norris, *The Apostolic Faith: Protestants and Roman Catholics* (1992) • Ronald E. Osborn, "Confession and Catholicity: The Rightful Function of Creeds in the Life of the Church," *Mid-Stream* 16 (1977): 198-205 • John Rogers, *The Biography of Elder Barton Warren Stone* (1847) • Dwight E. Stevenson, "Faith versus Theology in the Thought of the Disciple Fathers," in *The Renewal of Church: The Panel Reports,* vol. 2: *The Reformation of Tradition* (1963), pp. 33-60 • Walter Scott, *To Themelion: The Union of Christians on Christian Principles* (1852).

PAUL M. BLOWERS

Crihfield, Arthur (1802-1852)

Founder, editor, and publisher of the *Heretic Detector,* which he operated from 1837 to 1842.

In defense of the journal's title, Crihfield asserted that detecting heretics was "a necessary act of the church." His articles were directed toward not only members of the Stone-Campbell Movement but also other Christian groups. Crihfield believed and articulated the view that only members of the Churches of Christ could be saved.

Crihfield praised Alexander Campbell for having "restored the gospel," and the two men enjoyed a friendship early in Crihfield's career. However, Campbell's optimism, ecumenism, and attendance at national meetings soon became too much for Crihfield to tolerate. Crihfield, like many others in the years leading to the Civil War, became increasingly pessimistic about humanity and came to oppose Campbell's optimistic postmillennial views. He adopted a strong premillennial view of Christ's second coming, believing that only the second advent of Christ would end human evil.

When Crihfield ceased publication of the *Heretic Detector,* he edited the *Christian Family Library* in 1842, then the *Orthodox Preacher* from 1843 to 1846. The latter publication advocated Millerite views of an imminent end of the world. In an 1843 article in the *Millennial Harbinger,* Campbell criticized Crihfield's millennial position, cautioning his readers against becoming excited about predictions of the end of the world in 1843.

Strongly alienated from Campbell and the direction he saw the Stone-Campbell Movement going, Crihfield left in 1847 and joined the Episcopal Church. Before his death on October 14, 1852, however, he returned to the Stone-Campbell Movement.

See also Campbell, Alexander; Eschatology

BIBLIOGRAPHY Alexander Campbell, "The Orthodox Preacher," *Millennial Harbinger* 7 (February 1843): 93-94 • Arthur Crihfield, "The Heretic Detector and Reformer," *The Christian* 1 (July 1837): 146-48 • Arthur Crihfield, *An Address to the Disciples Church, Sometimes Called The Reformation; Containing Reasons for Withdrawing from That Body* (1849) • Editor, "Obituary," *Christian Record* 3 (January 1853): 224 • Walter Scott, "Editorial Correspondence," *The Protestant Unionist* 3 (March 31, 1847): 66 • Earl Irvin West, "Elder Ben Franklin: The Eye of the Storm," *Gospel Advocate* 124 (March 18, 1982): 173-75.

T. WESLEY CRAWFORD

Cross, Alexander

See Africa, Missions in; American Christian Missionary Society

Crossroads College

Bible college affiliated with the Christian Churches/Churches of Christ.

Crossroads College, formerly Minnesota Bible College, was founded in 1913 as International Christian Missionary Bible College in Minneapolis, Minnesota, and is among the oldest Bible colleges of the Stone-Campbell heritage. The founders hoped to establish an institution for evangelizing and educating among the forty million immigrants flooding the upper Midwest in the early decades of the twentieth century. The college remained in Minneapolis, adjacent to the campus of the University of Minnesota, for fifty-eight years. In 1971 the college was moved to a new campus in Rochester, Minnesota.

The college's roots in the Stone-Campbell Movement are traced to its founders, David E. Olson (1878-1943) and Julius Stone (1852-1936), both of Lutheran backgrounds, who had embraced ideals of unity and simple apostolic Christianity before they came in contact with each other or with the Stone-Campbell Movement. Olson was a graduate of Eugene Bible University (now Northwest Christian College) and an enduring friend of its founding president, Eugene C. Sanderson, who deepened Olson's Stone-Campbell roots. By 1909, Julius Stone was preaching among the Scandinavians in Minneapolis with the assistance of the Disciples' American Christian Missionary Society. That same year Olson returned to Minneapolis, where he and Stone collaborated to evangelize Scandinavians and envisioned a Bible college to serve this purpose.

Olson saw the college location across from the University of Minnesota to be ideally suited to its cause. Its stated mission was "to receive, care for and properly train Christian leaders among these millions who shall be able to help us make of these world representatives true American citizens; through them to evangelize the world." Olson, Stone, and the faculty of the new school translated this statement into a curricular program: "a liberal education, a thorough Biblical education, and an adequate practical training in the preaching of the Gospel." The faculty and departments reflected the international outreach of the college; for example, Julius Stone led the Scandinavian Department, W. D.

David the Syrian Department, and G. H. Cachiaras the Departments of Greek, New Testament, and Americanization.

In the middle 1930s, Minnesota Bible College drew many students by a dual emphasis on biblical studies and music education. In 1948 it achieved charter membership in the American Association of Bible Colleges (now the Accrediting Association of Bible Colleges). In the late 1960s the college developed its lower- and upper-division curricula for generalized and specialized educational ministry for the whole church; other curricular adjustments took place in the 1970s to 1990s. In 1999 Minnesota Bible College and Puget Sound Bible College (Edmonds, Washington) were invited by Hope International University (Fullerton, California) to become part of a multi-campus Christian University; the merger, however, was put on indefinite hold.

The Minneapolis campus in its first phase consisted of three buildings. The college building that rose near the University of Minnesota was a one-hundred-foot-square, domed, three-level structure of neo-classical design, complete with marbled interior and white floor tile of mosaic design for the hallways, stairs, and lobby areas. The college was moved to Rochester, Minnesota, in 1971 after fifty-eight years in Minneapolis. Its new campus includes the Academic Building (with classroom space, chapel, and offices), the G. H. Cachiaras Memorial Library, and student housing.

The college's name changed to Minnesota Bible College from 1924 to 1932, when Eugene C. Sanderson became the second president and the school was affiliated with the International Bible Mission headquartered at Eugene Bible University. During this period it became one of several institutions identified collectively as Christian Temples University. In 1932 the college name was changed to Minnesota Bible University. In 1942 it was incorporated once again as Minnesota Bible College. In 2002 the college completely changed its name to Crossroads College.

The new name of Crossroads College was intended in part to reflect the school's broadened curriculum. The academic program currently offers three degrees. The two-year Associate of Arts degree focuses on Bible, liberal arts, and Christian service. The Bachelor of Arts and Bachelor of Science degrees have a mandatory Bible/Theology major with optional "Ministry" and "Professional" tracks, the latter of which is intended to provide more diverse career opportunities beyond traditional ministries. All degree programs include an important "spiritual formation" component. JOHN CACHIARAS

See also Bible College Movement; Sanderson, Eugene C.

Crossroads Movement

See International Churches of Christ

Crowley's Ridge College

Two-year liberal arts institution of higher learning affiliated with Churches of Christ.

At the beginning of the twenty-first century it was the only junior college associated with that stream of the Movement. The school confers Associate of Arts degrees in both General Studies and Bible and is accredited by the North Central Association of Colleges and Schools. The campus is located on 115 acres atop Crowley's Ridge in Paragould, Arkansas.

The founder and first president of Crowley's Ridge College was Emmett F. Smith, Jr. (1920-1997). Smith was inspired by previous attempts at Christian education in Northeast Arkansas — namely, MONEA Christian College in Rector, and Croft College in rural Greene County, both of which had ceased to exist by the 1930s — to establish Crowley's Ridge Academy, a K-12 Christian academy, in 1953. On January 1, 1960, he led an organizational meeting to plan the establishment of a college. Groundbreaking ceremonies were held on January 28, 1964, and classes began in July of that year with eighty students enrolled. Crowley's Ridge College and Crowley's Ridge Academy operated under the same governing board from 1964 until 1975, when financial concerns forced the legal separation of the two.

In the beginning, Crowley's Ridge College was heralded as an "accelerated institution of higher education." Operating under the motto "Education Without Waste," the college divided its academic year into two sessions. The sessions were divided into two twelve-week semesters, each comprised of two six-week terms. Under this system a student could earn sixty-four semester hours in forty-eight weeks of residence, thus completing the A.A. degree in one calendar year. This accelerated program was neither as popular among students nor as accepted among senior institutions as had been hoped. The accelerated program was discontinued in 1974 in favor of a four-semester system. The academic year remained forty-eight weeks, consisting of four twelve-week semesters. In 1980 the standard two-semester system was adopted.

Five presidents have served the school: Emmett F. Smith, Jr. (1964-73), Albert Lemmons (1973-75), Joe K. Alley (1975-82), Larry M. Bills (1987-2001), and Arvil E. Hill (2001-present). From 1982 to 1985, and from 1986 to 1987, Crowley's Ridge College operated directly under the board's fiscal oversight, with Phillip Wilkerson, Vice President for Operations, supervising day-to-day operations.

PHILLIP DEVIN SWINDLE

Culver-Stockton College

Related to the Christian Church (Disciples of Christ).

Founded by members of the Movement in Missouri as Christian University in 1853, it was the first college west of the Mississippi River chartered to educate both males and females. Its early leaders, D. Pat Henderson and Dr. James Shannon, chose Canton, Missouri, because of its location on the Mississippi River and the enthusiasm of Lewis County Disciples for higher education. An imposing structure was ready for occupancy in 1856. During the Civil War, federal troops occupying the campus vandalized the building.

After the war, the college reopened under President Ben Smith's leadership, but made little sustained progress until Dr. Carl Johann became president in 1902. During Johann's administration the college was greatly aided financially by Robert Stockton and Mary Culver. In 1917 the school's name was changed to Culver-Stockton College. In 1924 the college was accredited by the North Central Association.

The college struggled from 1930 to 1945 but experienced a brief boom period after World War II. Postwar building projects required spending much of the endowment, and the college was financially troubled in 1956. New president Dr. Fred Helsabeck quickly restored confidence, and the college rapidly grew in students, faculty, facilities, and endowment. After a lull in the mid-1970s, Dr. Robert Brown became president in 1977, and another growth spurt occurred. For the first time in college history, enrollment exceeded 1,000 students. Campus buildings were renovated or improved, and a new gymnasium was built.

Dr. Ed Strong became president in 1992. Improvements in campus beautification, computerization, sports facilities, and buildings continued. Enrollment in 2001 was 821, and the college endowment in June 2002 was approximately $21 million. A new science center was completed in 2002. President Strong was succeeded in 2003 by William L. Fox.

BIBLIOGRAPHY George R. Lee, *Culver-Stockton College: The First 130 Years* (1983) • George Peters, *Dreams Come True* (1941).

GEORGE R. LEE

D

Dallas Christian College

Bible college associated with the Christian Churches/Churches of Christ, founded in 1950 and located in Dallas, Texas.

On May 10, 1949, former missionary and college planter Vernon Newland met with forty individuals from conservative Disciples of Christ churches. They discussed establishing a Bible college in Texas to train leaders for Christian ministry. Dallas Christian College (DCC) thus opened for classes on September 12, 1950, to educate Christian leaders in Texas and the Southwest.

DCC's founding leadership envisioned three main purposes for the school: (1) to be an evangelistic catalyst, aiding in the planting or reopening of local churches; (2) to oppose the perceived growing liberalism and secularism in America, especially as they observed in liberal Disciples of Christ churches that would later become the Christian Church (Disciples of Christ); (3) to send out preachers and Christian leaders "into every field with a training as scholarly as attainable, scriptural in its maintenance of the New Testament position, and with the greatest passion ever felt for lost souls; guided by the lessons of the ages which have been proven fruitful in reaching the hearer and winning the sinner to Christ."

DCC started with a college campus in Dallas's Cole Park neighborhood and with a faculty of four, including founder Vernon Newland. Courses centered on biblical studies and preaching. Students and faculty served the churches that the college started or reopened. In the spring of 1957 the college moved into a new facility at the corner of Carroll and San Jacinto in Dallas.

From its early decades, DCC saw periods of growth and decline related to administrative stability and campus needs. In the fall of 1967, the college moved from its second Dallas location to its third location, the present campus on twenty-two acres in the north Dallas suburb of Farmers Branch. Since 1967, the college has developed this campus into a five-building complex with classrooms, offices, dormitories, food services, and athletic venues. Also in 1967, philosopher and writer C. C. Crawford joined the faculty and gave it added credibility. With its new campus and exposure, the college experienced growth and received accreditation from the Accrediting Association of Bible Colleges in 1978.

While DCC has remained committed to biblical studies as its curricular core, it has also diversified its degree programs. Currently DCC offers a degree with a double major in Bible and in professional fields of study such as ministry, education, business, and counseling. Students combine the double major with general studies courses and core courses in ministry. In the spring of 1995, the "Quest" adult degree-completion program began and presently offers degrees in ministry and business. DCC students participate in an active program of Christian service and chapel attendance.

The sustained campus, integrated degrees, and administrative stability led the college to record growth in the late 1990s. With over 2,000 students in the college's history, graduates serve in various ministries throughout the world. The school is seeking to meet the educational needs of an increasingly diverse student body and to encourage leadership of churches and Christian organizations in Texas, the Southwest, and around the globe.

See also Bible College Movement; Higher Education, Views of in the Movement; Newland, Vernon M.

BIBLIOGRAPHY Gary M. Newland, "If You Are Ever Going to Do Something for God, Do it Now! The Pioneering Work of Vernon M. Newland" (unpublished M.Div. thesis, Emmanuel School of Religion, 1989).

ANTHONY J. SPRINGER

Dampier, Joseph H. (1908-1984)

Pastor, academic administrator, and professor affiliated with the Christian Churches/Churches of Christ.

A native of Ontario, Canada, Dampier was a graduate of Cincinnati Bible Seminary and the University of Pittsburgh, later receiving honorary doctorates from Atlanta Christian College and Johnson Bible College. Dampier served pastoral ministries in Indiana, Pennsylvania, and Tennessee. He was a member of the Commission on Restudy of the Disciples of Christ in the 1940s, the Continuation Committee of the North American Christian Convention (of which convention he was president in 1951), and the Publishing Committee of Standard Publishing Company. Dampier was named provost at Milligan College in 1958 and in 1965 dean of Emmanuel School of Religion in Johnson City, Tennessee, where he finished his career as a professor of Christian ministries. Theologically Dampier was a moderate conservative (or "free church catholic") who hoped to avert division between the Christian Churches/Churches of Christ and the emerging Christian Church (Disciples of Christ). Along with his close academic colleague, Dean E. Walker, he placed great emphasis on the education of local pastors to be ecclesiologically astute and committed to Christian unity. Dampier authored *A Workbook on Christian Doctrine* (1943), used in many local churches.

See also Commission on Restudy of the Disciples of Christ; Emmanuel School of Religion; Milligan College; Walker, Dean Everest HENRY E. WEBB

Dasher, Christian Herman (1786?-1866)

Christian Herman Dasher was born in the Salzburger Lutheran settlement of Ebenezer, founded in the 1730s in Effingham County, near Savannah, Georgia. Apparently, prior to his acquaintance with the *Christian Baptist* and *Millennial Harbinger,* Dasher had reached conclusions alien to his Lutheran heritage, concluding that baptism was immersion. Frustrated in his attempts to find someone willing to immerse him, he chanced to meet a Mrs. Threadcraft of Savannah who told him of S. C. Dunning, a former Baptist with convictions like his own. Dasher went to Savannah, studied with Dunning, and the two baptized one another according to their understanding of the Scriptures. Returning home, Dasher baptized his wife, his wife's sister, and her husband. This group began holding services in the Dasher home as early as 1819. Dasher's original congregation continued into the twenty-first century as the Old Oak Grove Church of Christ.

In 1832, when Indian lands opened up in southern Georgia, Dasher led a group, including a number from the church in Ebenezer, to Lowndes County near present-day Valdosta. Dasher continued his teaching, and his followers met in homes and called themselves "Disciples of Christ." Many Stone-Campbell churches in South Georgia trace their origins to the work of Dasher.

Though raised a Lutheran, Christian Herman Dasher came to hold believers' immersion for the remission of sins. He and former Baptist minister S. C. Dunning immersed one another in 1819, yet each underwent several other immersions over the years as they learned more about the rite and considered their former baptisms invalid.

BIBLIOGRAPHY J. Edward Moseley, *Disciples of Christ in Georgia* (1954) • James A. Harding, "The Church of God at Valdosta, Ga.," *Gospel Advocate* (February 15, 1883) • W. Ralph Wharton, *The Salzburgers, Georgia and Christian Herman Dasher* (n.d.). CARL W. CHEATHAM

Deacons, Diaconate

Ministers or servants of the church. Although the Greek word is used thirty times in the New Testament, only three occurrences are generally accepted as a distinct church ministry: Philemon 1:1; and 1 Timothy 3:8-13 (twice).

The early leadership of the Stone-Campbell Movement came from a Presbyterian background, but the membership largely had roots in the Baptist tradition. The Campbells' background in Scottish Presbyterianism included the diaconal understanding of John Knox. The Baptists also considered deacons to be essential to church life.

Thomas Campbell organized the Brush Run church on Saturday, May 4, 1811, with one elder (Thomas Campbell), four deacons, and Alexander Campbell, who was ordained to preach the gospel. Alexander Campbell described the deacon as "the steward, the treasurer, the almoner of the church, . . . Conversant with the sick and the poor, intimate with the rich and more affluent brethren, familiar with all, and devoted to the Lord in all their services." They therefore led in the benevolent work of the church.

Alexander saw the need for two "distinct offices" in the church community, "the office of presiding, i.e. instructing and directing; and the office of ministering, i.e. of executing all the wishes of the community." These are the offices of "bishops and deacons, or overseers and ministers." Campbell taught the need for a plurality of each, but also left room for special circumstances and admitted that the Scriptures did not address the question directly.

Campbell's views were mirrored in the writings of the other early standard-bearers of the Movement, including his son-in-law and co-editor, W. K. Pendleton, who insisted that every church had to have a plurality of deacons, after the analogy of the Jewish synagogue, whose duties would be to collect and appropriate the church's offering, care for the sick, serve in worship services, minister at the Lord's Table, and attend to the secular interests essential to the life of the congregation. Pendleton also strongly emphasized the role of deaconesses, who were to attend to those more delicate aspects of the diaconate to which deacons could not normally attend.

Details of diaconal service were frequently debated in the Movement. The word "office" and the authority of the deacon were widely discussed. Robert Milligan attached a special place to preaching and stated that a deacon must not teach "as an officer of the church." Tolbert Fanning, on the other hand, rejected the use of the term "office" by anyone in the church, stating that the words "shepherds," "deacons," and "ministers" were incidental and descriptive but never official designations. He held that "instead of the deacons being merely committee-men, hand laborers, and inferiors, we can discover no work too high or too spiritual for them, and no position too elevated for them to occupy."

Some churches had annual diaconal elections; others had periodic reviews; still others gave permanent appointment to deacons. Some writers felt that only elders could receive money for the church, giving the example of the Jerusalem church; others felt that deacons were to oversee all aspects of finance. Some taught that deacons should never receive any financial compensation for their labor, while others advocated paid deacons. Others debated whether or not the seven in Acts 6 were deacons in an official sense and therefore could be used as a paradigm for the diaconate. Some demanded a plurality of deacons, while others defended as few as one deacon for a small church.

The debates over the qualifications given in 1 Timothy 3 also produced many writings, though most of the articles were directed toward bishops/elders, with deacons mentioned peripherally. The usual discussions concerned marriage, children, and the use of alcohol. Champions of nearly every position can be found.

Virtually all Stone-Campbell writers of the nineteenth century advocated female deacons in the churches, though most were clear to distinguish deaconesses' ministry from that of deacons. The consensus was that women who served as deaconesses were not to be teachers of men or have authority over men. Their sphere of work was with women and children. Early documents demonstrate the service of deaconesses in many churches, primarily in the Northern areas of the Movement. J. W. McGarvey, in the significant year 1906, wrote strongly against female deacons and cited women who were ambitious for offices and who usurped the powers of deacons. With the division of the Churches of Christ and the Disciples, the Northern culture often retained deaconesses while the South denied such recognition.

Disciples moved during the middle years of the twentieth century to adopt a "functional" plan of congregational organization, that tended to blur distinctions between elders and deacons. Elders and deacons, alike, served as members of functional departments such as worship, evangelism, and outreach. Likewise, the distinction between deacons and deaconesses was dropped in favor of the concept of the "one diaconate."

During the first half of the twentieth century, the military model became predominant for elders and deacons in Christian Churches/Churches of Christ and Disciples of Christ — elders being officers and deacons the enlisted men. Financial control over building programs, staff, and outreach remained a strong matter of contention between them. The second half of the century was marked by an organizational shift in churches to team ministries. Many churches have struggled with the transition from the more traditional diaconate to a participatory leadership style, resulting in deacons who are managers of groups of church members serving in specialized areas. This has also resurrected the discussion of female deacons in Churches of Christ, resulting in a great diversity of practice.

See also Educational Ministry; Elders, Eldership; Local Autonomy; Ministry; Pastoral Care

BIBLIOGRAPHY Alexander Campbell, "A Restoration of the Ancient Order of Things," No. 19: "The Deacon's Office," *Christian Baptist* 4 (1826): 335-36 • Robert Milligan, "The Permanent Orders of the Christian Ministry," *Millennial Harbinger* (1855): 623-35, 685-702 • *One Diaconate: Women and Men Building a Community of Ministry and Service* (1977) • W. K. Pendleton, "Discipline — No. VII," *Millennial Harbinger* (1858): 289-95 • J. S. Sandifer, *Deacons: Male and Female* (1989) • D. Newell Williams, *Ministry Among Disciples: Past, Present, and Future* (1985).

J. STEPHEN SANDIFER

Debates, Debating

Public oral debates, with specified questions and set rules of procedure, designated moderators, and in some cases official judges.

Public debates became an important strategy in the Stone-Campbell Movement after Alexander Campbell debated the Associate Reformed Presbyterian minister John Walker in Mt. Pleasant, Ohio (June 19-20, 1820), on the right of infants to baptism. Initially reluctant to engage in such events, Campbell later agreed to participate in four other debates, which helped to spread the news of his reform movement. Barton W. Stone had reservations about such public debates, and Thomas Campbell also disliked them, but Alexander Campbell's success as a debater initiated a practice among Stone-Campbell constituents that continued into the twentieth century.

The practice continued an ancient Christian tradition. The book of Acts pictured the apostle Paul debating with Athenians, second-century apologists conducted public debates, medieval universities employed public disputations for pedagogical purposes, and the sixteenth-century Reformation made debate an instrument of reform. In America, Catholic missionaries, Puritan ministers, and Baptist and Quaker dissenters conducted public debates in the seventeenth century, but after the American Revolution, debating assumed unprecedented popularity, partly as a means of serious theological engagement, partly as a vehicle of denominational competition, and partly as an agency of popular entertainment.

Campbell's five debates included topics that became popular among American religious debaters. On October 15-21, 1823, he debated the Presbyterian William L. Maccalla in Washington, Kentucky, on the meaning and proper subjects of baptism. On April 13-21, 1829, he battled the skeptic and social reformer Robert Owen in Cincinnati, Ohio, on the evidences of Christianity. On January 13-21, 1837, he debated the Catholic bishop of Cincinnati, John Purcell, on the church, the apostolic succession, infallibility, Catholic doctrine, and religious authority. On November 15-30, 1843, Campbell and the Presbyterian minister N. L. Rice debated on baptism, the activity of the Spirit in conversion and sanctification, and the authority of creeds. Each debate resulted in a book based on the transcript, and the events sometimes marked important turning points in Campbell's own theology. His debate with Maccalla gave him the occasion to defend publicly his emerging convictions about the linkage between baptism and the remission of sins, and his contest with Purcell led him to identify his movement more closely with broader Protestant ideals.

Such debates became popular cultural events, and secular newspapers both advertised and reported on them. Papers from Cincinnati to New York City carried reports of Campbell's debate with Owen, which attracted an audience of more than 1,200 people for eight days. Ministers from multiple denominations took up the practice, and some became specialists on designated topics, champions who traveled from state to state at the invitation of local groups to defend the doctrines and practices of their traditions. While some debates descended into sarcasm and theatrics, others attained a remarkable level of popular scholarly interchange.

When the Disciples of Christ minister Lawrence Bramblett Wilkes of Lexington, Kentucky, for example, debated the Methodist Jacob Ditzler of Louisville in Louisville's Weisiger Hall for ten days in 1870 on the subject of baptism, the two men engaged in close readings of the biblical texts, drawing on German and American biblical criticism, the Babylonian Mishnah and the Gemara, the manuscript collections Vaticanus, Sinaiticus, and Alexandrinus, the Greek, Hebrew, Syriac, Coptic, and Latin manuscripts of the Bible, and the authors of the early church. They bolstered their cases with citations from lexicographers, translators, and modern critics. They debated the meaning of words in Greek, Hebrew, Syriac, Peshito-Syriac, Chaldaic, and Latin. They cited both English and German textual critics. They debated four hours a day, two in the morning and two in the afternoon, and guests from out of town stayed in local homes in order to attend the event. The Louisville *Courier-Journal* reported that the hall remained "well-filled" despite extremely cold weather. The event resulted in the publication of a 708-page book entitled *The Louisville Debate* (1871).

Debates also inevitably played a decisive role in the theological definition of the Stone-Campbell Movement, a movement that had spurned scholastic theology and authoritative councils of learned clergy. Campbell's debates on baptism inevitably contested numerous aspects of Reformed theology and established positions on issues like covenant theology and the role of the Holy Spirit in conversion and regeneration. Benjamin Franklin's 1852 debate in Cincinnati with Presbyterian James Matthews was a sophisticated response to Calvinist notions of election and predestination, lingering points of tension between Disciples and Presbyterians.

Debating remained popular among restorationists in the twentieth century. The forensic superstars included such regional celebrities as J. D. Tant of

Texas, who held more than 350 such contests between 1885 and 1941. In a 1959 survey of 2,706 ministers in the Churches of Christ, the rhetorician James Swinney discovered 215 preachers who said that they engaged in public debating, and he calculated that they had held roughly 4,400 debates, each lasting from one to fourteen days, mainly in the rural areas and small towns of the South and lower Midwest. Another student of the Stone-Campbell Movement has compiled an online list of 9,000 such debates, around 500 in the nineteenth century and more than 8,500 in the twentieth. By the late-nineteenth century, the debates ceased to have the cultural prominence they once had when newspapers sent reporters and large crowds gathered. In a more ecumenical era, debating struck many as outmoded, yet the practice has continued to flourish in parts of American Protestantism, and the Stone-Campbell tradition has continued to sponsor such events.

See also Campbell-Maccalla Debate; Campbell-Owen Debate; Campbell-Purcell Debate; Campbell-Rice Debate; Campbell-Skinner Debate; Campbell-Walker Debate

BIBLIOGRAPHY Alexander Campbell and William Maccalla, *A Public Debate on Christian Baptism between the Rev. W. L. Maccalla, a Presbyterian Teacher, and Alexander Campbell, to Which Is Added an Essay on the Christian Religion, by A. Campbell* (1842) • Alexander Campbell and Robert Owen, *The Evidences of Christianity* (1829) • Alexander Campbell and John Purcell, *A Debate on the Roman Catholic Religion* (1837) • Alexander Campbell and Nathan L. Rice, *A Debate between Rev. A. Campbell and Rev. N. L. Rice on the Action, Subject, Design and Administrator of Christian Baptism* (1844) • Alexander Campbell and John Walker, *A Debate on Christian Baptism, Between Mr. John Walker, a Minister of the Secession, and Alexander Campbell . . .* (1822) • Jacob Ditzler and L. B. Wilkes, *The Louisville Debate* (1871) • Benjamin Franklin and James Matthews, *Predestination, and the Foreknowledge of God: A Discussion* (1852) • E. Brooks Holifield, "Theology as Entertainment: Oral Debate in American Religion," *Church History* 67 (1998): 499-520 • L. B. Sullivan, "Tant, J(efferson) D(avis)," in *Dictionary of Christianity in America,* ed. Daniel G. Reid et al. (1990), p. 1158 • James P. Swinney, "A Survey of Religious Debate Attitudes Among Ministers of the Churches of Christ," *Restoration Quarterly* 6 (1962): 85-91; 9 (1966): 91-95 • Thomas Thrasher, "The Encyclopedia of Religious Debates" (on-line: http://www.ptc.dcs.edu/teacherpages/tthrasher/listings/LISTINGS.HTM)

E. BROOKS HOLIFIELD

Declaration and Address

Appeal for Christian unity based on a common core of evangelical commitments written by Thomas Campbell (1763-1854) and published in 1809 to explain the form and purpose of the Christian Association of Washington; ultimately considered, along with the *Last Will and Testament of the Springfield Presbytery,* a "charter document" of the Stone-Campbell Movement.

As a young minister in Northern Ireland, Thomas Campbell had sought to foster an "ecumenical" spirit among Protestant churches through his participation in the Evangelical Society of Ulster. Relocated in western Pennsylvania, he became deeply concerned over the divisions among Christian bodies, especially the harshness of the schism within his own Seceder Presbyterian church, which undermined effective ministry on the sparsely populated frontier. After separating from the Associate Reformed Synod, Campbell and a group of supporters organized the Christian Association of Washington to promote "simple evangelical Christianity." Campbell composed the *Declaration and Address* with a strong sense that America was a uniquely graced land of opportunity and freedom in which, through collective reasoning and self-discipline, the divided churches could come together solely under the apostolic rule of the New Testament for the effective evangelization of the frontier and the whole world. Early in the document, Campbell strikes a millennial tone, suggesting that recent political and religious events (both revolutions and ecclesiastical controversy) in Europe and America signaled a new age in which the cause of "Zion," the campaign for Christian unity and evangelical mission, would be embraced by churches universally.

The *Declaration and Address* has three principal parts. The "Declaration" authorizes the formation of the Christian Association of Washington. The "Address" universalizes the purpose of the Association and expounds at length on the imperative of Christian unity. The long "Appendix" defends the motivation and modality of the Association and responds to anticipated objections to the proposals made in the document.

In setting forth the plan of the Christian Association, the Declaration thoroughly intertwines the themes of Christian reconciliation and human salvation. The Association will work for Christian unity, and the *modus operandi* will be, not a new church, but a collaboration of "voluntary advocates of church reformation" in the cause of "promoting a pure evangelical reformation, by the simple preaching of the everlasting gospel, and the administration of its ordinances in an exact conformity to the Divine Standard." Already in the Address, the "restoration" principle is explicit. The Christian Association is to be a particular, localized embodiment of a much larger task of the whole church to "practice that simple original form of Christianity, expressly exhibited on the sacred page."

Throughout the subsequent Address, therefore, the unity and the evangelistic mission of the church are one and the same project. Christian unity is not an end in itself but a means to a greater end, the "grand design" of the Christian religion "to reconcile and unite men to God, and to each other, in truth and love, to the glory of God, and their own present and eternal good." Campbell discourses on ecclesial schism as outright sin, an affront to God, and presupposes that the urgent summons to Christian unity is not his own but belongs to the whole church. "The cause that we advocate is not our own peculiar, nor the cause of any party, considered as such; it is a common cause, the cause of Christ and our brethren of all denominations."

The heart of the Address is the thirteen Propositions, a platform for unity that Campbell submits for consideration by all sympathetic Christians. The thirteen can effectively be reduced to five basic principles:

1. The church of Christ on earth is "essentially, intentionally, and constitutionally one," in which case schism is a "horrid evil" destructive of the visible body of Christ. Local congregations ("societies") of Christians are the expression of this one universal church and, as such, should not be divided from one another but exercise the same mind.
2. Only the authority of Jesus Christ and his apostles, as enjoined upon the New Testament church "either in express terms, or by approved precedent," is binding upon Christians and sets the "terms of communion" in the church. That authority is conveyed preeminently through the New Testament, which, though "inseparably connected" with the Old Testament, is the sole "constitution" of the church. Thus no human authority can presume to supplement the silence of Scripture or impose new commands or ordinances so as to redefine the terms of communion in the church.
3. Theological inferences from Scripture, when "fairly inferred," may be considered biblical doctrine, but are not binding on Christians' consciences farther than their ability to comprehend them, and cannot become terms of communion. (Theology, in other words, has a relative, catechetical value, but cannot define the basis of Christian fellowship.)
4. Only a consciousness of sin, profession of faith in Jesus Christ, and manifest obedience to him are the terms for admission to the church. Since division in the church has always been, and is now, spurred by Christians' imposing "human inventions," it is incumbent on all to respect the divinely authorized terms of communion.
5. Matters of "expedience" in the execution of the divine ordinances must be identified as such and acted on without becoming objects of contention.

Campbell's commitment to *restoration,* the recovery

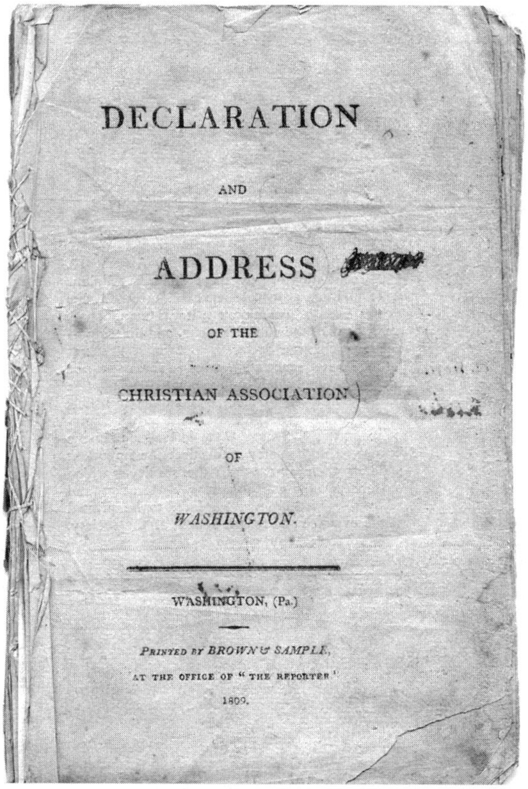

In the pages of his *Declaration and Address* (1809), Thomas Campbell held up the cause of Christian unity not as his private concern but as self-evidently "a common cause, the cause of Christ and our brethren of all denominations."
Courtesy of Bethany College

of the example and life of the apostolic church, is evident in his very language for the authority of the New Testament. Throughout the *Declaration and Address* he speaks of the New Testament as a "constitution" and "directory" for the church, and as containing the "law" binding on all Christian consciences. Christians need no longer dwell on the "trite indefinite distinction between essentials, and non-essentials, in matters of revealed truth and duty." Scripture has set out orderly standards of faith and practice, such that the goal should be "a permanent scriptural unity amongst the churches, upon the solid basis of universally acknowledged, and self-evident truths."

Deeply influenced by Common Sense philosophy and epistemology, Campbell exudes confidence that the "intelligent and consecrated minds" of Christians can arrive at a viable consensus on the interpretation and application of the New Testament. He is not altogether naive to the difficulties past and present of such an undertaking. Indeed, he acknowledges that all Christians, himself included, have their biases of perspective. Thus the work of restoring the rightful authority of the New Testament in order to reunite the church will require both the practice of forbearance (a quality of Christian character) and shared hermeneutical self-discipline. Still, Christians universally can lean on the prior integrity and coherence of the apostolic model of the church revealed in the New Testament.

In the Appendix to the *Declaration and Address,* Campbell fends off the potential charges of factiousness, on the one hand, and latitudinarianism, on the other. Anticipating the former, he returns to what he believes to be a thoroughly catholic principle in his appeal for unity: the hermeneutical distinction between the express rule of Scripture and human inferences. Given this distinction, no Christian should be excluded from the fellowship of the church for refusing anything for which there is not a "thus saith the Lord." Freedom of conscience in matters of "private opinion" is vital. "This we see was actually the case in the apostolic churches, without any breach of Christian unity." Thereupon anticipating the charge of latitudinarianism, Campbell happily embraces the label if it means an allowance for gracious and charitable diversity accompanying conformity to the express rule of Scripture. Holding utterly identical views on divinely revealed truths, let alone achieving unanimity in matters of opinion, would be not only "morally impossible" but undesirable, since such would "render useless some of those gracious, self-denying, and compassionate precepts of mutual sympathy and forbearance, which the word of God enjoins upon his people."

Campbell in his Appendix furthermore contrasts the "cheap and easy orthodoxy" propped up by creeds and confessions with the portrait of a community of disciples committed to "searching the Scriptures, with reliance upon [the] Holy Spirit." Christian unity, in his view, hinges not on an ecclesiastically engineered orthodoxy but on a universal *consensus fidelium:* "the common sense . . . of christians, exercised upon the plainest and most obvious facts, divinely recorded for their instruction." This does not excuse the church from its *teaching* discipline. On the contrary, the Westminster Confession and Catechisms, and other such "excellent performances," are useful for catechetical purposes, but only in conjunction with the direct study of Scripture. Campbell recommends, in good Reformed fashion, the interpretation of Scripture with Scripture: "to understand one part of it by the assistance of another." Only the Bible itself will ultimately satisfy a faith seeking understanding, keep Christians appropriately focused on the express word of Scripture, and thereby secure the unity and integrity of the church.

Subsequent interpreters of the *Declaration and Address* in the history of the Stone-Campbell Movement have debated whether "restoration" or "unity" was the preeminent agenda of the document. Conservatives have sometimes claimed that Thomas Campbell was promoting a literal restoration of the lost apostolic church, wherein Christian unity was wholly a matter of reinstating the New Testament "ordinances." Beginning in the early twentieth century, liberals played down Campbell's restorationist language and insisted that the true ideal of the *Declaration and Address* was a unity focused on the lowest common denominator of Christian faith and genuinely accommodating theological (so also denominational) diversity. Both the conservative and liberal readings, however, betray biases not internal to the document itself.

In more recent years an increasing number of thinkers from across the streams of the Stone-Campbell Movement affirm that *both* restoration and unity were thoroughly integrated in Campbell's program and should be so today, notwithstanding the tensions involved in such an enterprise. Campbell's model of restoration required more than a strictly "legal" adherence to the New Testament pattern of the church; but so too his unity ideal invested more credence in the express rule of Scripture than in any human ability to reconcile differences and set the tolerable limits of diversity in the church.

The *Declaration and Address* has been described, even by outsiders to the Stone-Campbell Movement, as a seminal document in American ecumenism. An even more favorable assessment is that it anticipated themes taken up in the early sessions of the World Conference on Faith and Order. Those who work their way through Thomas Campbell's complex writing style, typical of his time, will find a perspective rightly characterized as "free church catholic." Throughout the work, appropriate to context, he used terms such as "catholic," "holy," "essentially one" and, most frequently, "apostolic," not as formulaic, but as representations of the given nature of the church. The *Declaration and Address* was an appeal to the one, holy, catholic, and apostolic church grounded in the apostolic tradition embodied in New Testament Scripture.

See also Bible, Authority and Inspiration of the; Campbell, Thomas; Church, Doctrine of the; *Consensus Fidelium;* Essentials vs. Adiaphora; *Last Will and Testament of Springfield Presbytery;* "Restoration," Meanings of within the Movement; Unity, Christian

BIBLIOGRAPHY Alexander Campbell, *Memoirs of Elder Thomas Campbell* (1861) • Thomas Campbell, *Declaration and Address of the Christian Association of Washington* (1809) • Frederick D. Kershner, *The Christian Union Overture: An Interpretation of the Declaration and Address of Thomas Campbell* (1923); Thomas H. Olbricht and Hans Rollmann, eds., *The Quest for Christian Unity, Peace, and Purity in Thomas Campbell's Declaration and Address: Texts and Studies* (2000); David Thompson, "The Irish Background to

Thomas Campbell's *Declaration and Address,*" *Discipliana* 46 (1986): 23-27.

PAUL M. BLOWERS *and* WILLIAM J. RICHARDSON

DeGroot, Alfred T. (1903-1992)

Disciples pastor, educator, historian, and ecumenist.

Having held teaching positions at Butler University and Drake University, Alfred DeGroot served as Dean of the Graduate School of Arts and Sciences at Texas Christian University (1949-56) and was Distinguished Professor of Church History there as well. For a time he also served as Archivist for the Faith and Order Movement of the National Council of Churches.

DeGroot is perhaps best known for co-authoring, with Winfred Garrison, *The Disciples of Christ: A History* (1st ed. 1948), one of the most influential histories of the Stone-Campbell Movement during the mid- and late-twentieth century. He also composed perhaps the only comprehensive study of formative Stone-Campbell theology, *Disciple Thought: A History* (1965).

DeGroot was one of a cluster of moderately conservative Disciple intellectuals seeking to negotiate a nineteenth-century movement through the storm and stress of fundamentalism and liberalism into the uncharted territory of the ecumenical age. His passion was ecclesiology, and much of his writing dealt with questions of authority, polity, and the viability of the "restoration" model of ecclesial reform. For DeGroot, the Disciples of Christ were "Free Church Catholics" who spurned episcopal and magisterial authoritarianism (both of the Roman Catholic *and* Protestant types) and pursued the restoration of apostolic Christianity in terms of a universal consensus on divine truth. Restoration was accordingly an ongoing, dynamic, heuristic enterprise engaging "all serious and sober students of the Christian faith." Echoing the epistemological confidence in "Common Sense" of the Stone-Campbell Movement's early generations, DeGroot argued that the Disciples of Christ uniquely contributed to the broader ecumenical search for Christian unity a virtually "scientific" discipline in exercising the Church's consensual "common mind." Such meant not that revealed truth was simply to be submitted to a democratic vote, but that essential truths would be discerned by testing and processing them in the actual communal life of churches, under the guide of a competent and intellectually qualified leadership, and in the spirit of fellowship. "Continued fellowship in search of agreement," DeGroot wrote in 1963, "is the only way of achieving a *consensus fidelium.*"

In the *practical* pursuit of unity, DeGroot recommended in his collection of essays entitled *The Nature of the Church* (1961) that the Disciples of Christ adhere to the strengths of the Movement's original plea, including the "pristine concern for mutual dependence of local churches and individual Christians, the internal phase of ecumenicity." DeGroot was impatient, however, with parochial restorationism, and vigorously criticized the emergence of a separate body of "independent" Christian Churches, deemed by him "Church of Christ Number Two" — a group he still sought constructively to engage even after the Restructure of the Disciples of Christ. DeGroot shared with conservatives the "norm theory" of the Church, but insisted in *The Restoration Principle* (1960) that what was to be "restored" from the apostolic model was less a strict apostolic pattern of ordinances than the objectives, vision, freedom, and spirituality of the primitive Christians.

On the other side, DeGroot also censured Disciple progressives for abandoning restoration altogether and putting far too much confidence in institutional reconfigurations. In the 1960s, while remaining committed to the Ecumenical Movement, DeGroot vigorously criticized the Disciples' involvement in the Consultation on Church Union (COCU), and subsequently the Restructure design itself, which for him represented misguided attempts to engineer Christian unity through *denominational* assimilation to the American Protestant mainline. In 1967 he helped draft the "Atlanta Declaration," which protested the Restructure for attempting to override the freedom of local congregations with an "authoritarian, connectional system" and denominational hierarchy. DeGroot also penned essays critical of the prospective episcopacy and ministerial "succession" discernible in the Restructure plan.

DeGroot made it clear that "Free Church Catholicism" was not invented by the Stone-Campbell Movement, any more than was the campaign for Christian unity. But it was indeed the movement's true identity and vocation, challenging the Disciples to pursue the *via media* through, and beyond, the dual illusions of patternistic restorationism and mainline Protestant ecclesiasticism.

See also Atlanta Declaration Committee; *Consensus Fidelium;* Restructure; "Restoration," Meanings of within the Movement; Texas Christian University

BIBLIOGRAPHY Alfred T. DeGroot, *Church of Christ Number Two* (1958) • Alfred T. DeGroot, *The Convention Among Disciples of Christ* (1958) • Alfred T. DeGroot, *Disciple Thought: A History* (1965) • Alfred T. DeGroot, *Extra Ecclesiam Nulla Salus* (and other essays) (1969) • Alfred T. DeGroot, *The Nature of the Church* (1961) • Alfred T. DeGroot, *New Possibilities for Disciples and Independents* (1963) • Alfred T. DeGroot, *The Restoration Principle* (1960) • Alfred T. DeGroot, with W. E. Garrison, *The Disciples of Christ: A History* (1948; rev. ed. 1958)

PAUL M. BLOWERS

Democratization

American historians and American religious historians, some of them positively influenced by the French statesman Alexis de Tocqueville's early observations in his *Democracy in America* (1835), have for quite some time traced the influence of democratic philosophy and idealism in various forms of American culture beyond the strictly political sphere. Tocqueville's comments on the democratic spirit expressing itself in American religion were highly illuminating. Also instructive and influential was the thesis of historian Frederick Jackson Turner (1861-1932), who theorized that the "frontier," the ideal of a free land with unlimited opportunity, helped shape values of popular sovereignty and self-reliance in the ever-expanding American West, notably in frontier religion. Turner's perspective was echoed in the work of University of Chicago historian William Warren Sweet, who carefully tracked the development of various Protestant groups on the American frontier. Trained at Chicago, Disciples of Christ historian W. E. Garrison (1874-1969) adapted Turner's frontier theory to the study of the Stone-Campbell Movement in his *Religion Follows the Frontier* (1931) and *An American Religious Movement* (1945). Garrison's work was the first attempt of an "insider" critically to articulate the importance of the culture of the frontier to the development of the Stone-Campbell Movement.

Unquestionably the most significant and influential attempt of an "outsider" to interpret the role of the frontier and of democratic idealism in the shaping of the Stone-Campbell Movement was the publication of *The Democratization of American Christianity* (1989), by Nathan O. Hatch of the University of Notre Dame. In the era of the early American Republic, Hatch argues, a number of religious groups on the trans-Appalachian frontier — including, among others, Elias Smith's New England Christians, James O'Kelly's Republican Methodists, Barton Stone's Christian Movement, and Alexander Campbell's Disciples of Christ — conducted a veritable revolution in American Protestantism, truly declaring independence from older ecclesiastical establishments still tied to the Old World. "Democratization" in these groups manifested itself in various ways: militant anticlericalism, resistance to older theological systems, redefinition of ecclesiastical authority from the ground up, development of a populist religious culture (journalism et al.), and the general articulation of a "theology of the people." Hatch focuses on Barton Stone, among others, as a model of this culture of religious protest and urge toward popular sovereignty in the church. Accordingly, Stone represented very well the reaction to clericalism, theological scholasticism (especially Calvinism), and a fervent "Back to the Bible" crusade to liberate individual Christians to interpret the Bible for themselves. Alexander Campbell, Hatch argues, represented a brand of restorationism in its own way deeply democratic.

Reception of Hatch's "democratization" thesis among historians from within the Stone-Campbell Movement has been mixed. Some have been appreciative of his descriptive model, insofar as it helps explain the Movement's early polemic against the theological and ecclesiastical powers of the time, and because it provides a coherent cultural context for the early Movement's restoration program. Others have criticized Hatch's thesis for oversimplifying issues of authority in the Movement, exaggerating its "leveling" mentality, and not taking into account, amid the democratizing impulses, the counterbalances of *de facto* "episcopacy" exercised by powerful leaders and editors. The caricature of a "back to the Bible" movement, moreover, can fail to account for the fact that certain of the Stone-Campbell Movement's early leadership inevitably both recognized and dealt with the consequences of an exaggerated emphasis on the perspicuity of Scripture and the rights of individuals to interpret the Bible for themselves.

Ultimately the democratization thesis has struck deep chords among the heirs of the Stone-Campbell Movement. Some believe that this populist interpretation has gone far enough and desire to play up the connections of the Movement to the denominational mainstream in America. Others affirm democratization as bespeaking the deep commitment of the early Movement to a form of Christianity not enslaved to denominational institutions and fiercely protective of the prerogatives of the churches to govern themselves.

See also Liberty; Local Autonomy; O'Kelly, James; Republican Methodists; Smith, Elias

BIBLIOGRAPHY David E. Harrell, "The Agrarian Myth and the Disciples of Christ in the Nineteenth Century," in *The Stone-Campbell Movement: An International Religious Tradition,* ed. Michael W. Casey and Douglas A. Foster (2002), pp. 147-59 • Nathan O. Hatch, *The Democratization of American Christianity* (1989) • Nathan O. Hatch, "The Christian Movement and the Demand for a Theology of the People," reprinted in *The Stone-Campbell Movement: An International Religious Tradition,* ed. Michael W. Casey and Douglas A. Foster (2002), pp. 121-46 • Ronald E. Osborn, *Experiment in Liberty: The Ideal of Freedom in the Experience of the Disciples of Christ* (1978) • D. Newell Williams, *Barton Stone: A Spiritual Biography* (2000).

PAUL M. BLOWERS

Denominationalism

System in which congregations that share theological beliefs, religious experiences, and religious practices identify themselves by name and organization as a separate part of Christianity. They may also share a common ethnic, cultural, class, national, or geographical heritage.

In the early twentieth century Ernst Troeltsch in his *Social Teachings of the Christian Church* identified denominations as older established bodies who were at home in their culture. Sects, on the other hand, were newer groups with an exclusivist self-understanding who saw themselves arrayed against the prevailing culture.

In the nineteenth century such distinctions were not as carefully made. In the literature of the Stone-Campbell Movement the terms "denominationalism" and "sectarianism" were generally used interchangeably. From its beginnings the leaders of the Movement rejected denominationalism as a system because it legitimated and perpetuated division among Christians. While admitting that the Movement itself constituted a denomination, Alexander Campbell and other early leaders consistently urged Christians to abandon loyalty to denominational structures and creeds and come together to work and worship simply as Christians or disciples of Christ.

Barton Stone and his colleagues in the *Last Will and Testament of Springfield Presbytery* willed the demise of their denominational body and its sinking into union "with the body of Christ at large." Though they did not advocate radical congregationalism and did not reject what they viewed as legitimate extra-congregational ministerial functions, they denied that presbyteries, synods, and General Assemblies were scriptural and vowed never to delegate authority to such organizations again.

Thomas Campbell in his *Declaration and Address* likewise attacked the system of denominationalism that characterized Protestantism. Identification with one party inherently precluded the scriptural purity of communion between Christians, which in turn affected the "comfort, glory, and usefulness" of Christ's church. As in the *Last Will and Testament,* Campbell called on his "dear brethren of all denominations" to work for the end of the denominational system that kept believers apart and thus debilitated the church of Christ.

The seeds for the later insistence by some that the churches of the Movement did not constitute a denomination were also found in the "Declaration and Address." Campbell insisted in the Appendix that those who maintained Scripture alone as their standard did not constitute a party. He insisted, however, that only those clear statements of Scripture universally agreed on could be made terms of fellowship in contrast to the inferential statements made in most denominational confessions.

Benjamin Lyon Smith, editor of the *Millennial Harbinger Abridged* of 1902, took issue with a December 1840 article in which Alexander Campbell used the term "denomination" for the Movement. Smith asserted that the use of the word for the Movement was offensive, and that the majority of the members of the Movement had not followed Campbell in using it. We prefer, he continued, to be considered a movement in the church, pleading for the union of Christians through a return to the teaching and practice of the New Testament church. "The Disciples of Christ can not consent to become a denomination until we consent to degenerate into a sect."

Some version of this sentiment was the majority position in the Movement at the time of its first division. Churches of Christ insisted that they were not a denomination. Their literature often contrasted "the church" with "the denominations" and accused Christian Churches of leaving simple New Testament truth to become another denomination. Though many in Churches of Christ continued to see themselves as a movement in the church, others took the bolder stance that Churches of Christ constituted the universal church. Any move away from the traditional teachings and practices constituted for them a move toward apostasy and denominationalism.

Conservatives in Christian Churches and Disciples also rejected the tag of denomination. Part of the tension resulting in the separation between Christian Churches/Churches of Christ and the Christian Church (Disciples of Christ) was the move toward official recognition of the denominational status of the churches and creation of a more efficient structure. For several years after their separation from the Disciples, independent Christian Churches were identified in the National Council of Churches' *Yearbook of American and Canadian Churches* as the "Undenominational Fellowship of Christian Churches and Churches of Christ." Though many in Disciples leadership had long understood themselves as working for unity as one church among many, the restructure of the Christian Church (Disciples of Christ) in 1968 marked overt recognition of the body's denominational status.

How to balance opposition to denominationalism with the reality of existence as a separate body (or bodies) has posed a dilemma for the churches of the Stone-Campbell Movement from its beginning. The stance that denies legitimacy to all other Christian bodies upholds unity at the expense of self-criticism and legitimate diversity. The stance that concedes its denominational status does so at the risk of losing a strong witness against the church's divisions. Though the three streams of the Stone-Campbell Movement have generally chosen different approaches, each continues to struggle with this dilemma.

BIBLIOGRAPHY S. C. Bailey, *Denominationalism — Church of Christ — Which?* (1900) • H. Leo Boles, "The Sin of Denominationalism," *Gospel Advocate* 84 (1942): 820 • Murry Mark Campbell, *Why Denominationalism?* (1985) • Samuel G. Dawson, *The Way of Christ Without Denominationalism* (1988) • Anthony L. Dunnavant, "Disciples Leaders' Changing Posture Regarding the United States and 'Denominationalism,' 1880-1980," in *A Case Study of Mainstream Protestantism: The Disciples Relation to American Culture, 1880-1989*, ed. D. Newell Williams (1991), pp. 171-93 • Charles Clayton Morrison, *The Unfinished Reformation* (1953) • William J. Nottingham, "Mission as Ecclesiology: Christian Identity and the Burden of Denominationalism," in *The Vision of Christian Unity*, ed. Thomas F. Best (1997), pp. 133-47 • Ronald E. Osborn, "A Theology of Denominations and Principles for Brotherhood Restructure," in *The Revival of the Churches*, ed. William Barnett Blakemore, Jr., vol. 1 of *The Renewal of Church: The Panel of Scholars Reports* (1963), pp. 82-111.

DOUGLAS A. FOSTER

Devotional Literature

Writings focused on the themes of spiritual devotion and personal piety in the Stone-Campbell tradition.

If the Bible is the devotional book of Protestants, it was the sole devotional literature of the early Stone-Campbell Movement. The four key founders — Thomas Campbell, Alexander Campbell, Walter Scott, and Barton W. Stone — all shared elements of the piety of their Puritan and Presbyterian background as shaped by the Enlightenment emphasis on reason. For example, on the one hand Alexander Campbell could praise the Bible as a book of "facts," but in his personal and family devotions he also rhapsodized on the Bible as a treasury of worship and prayer.

Since the Bible was *the* book of devotion, none of the four founders wrote other "spiritual" works, and they used other devotional literature only sparingly. However, the articles Barton W. Stone wrote in the *Christian Messenger* during the last ten years of his life come close to devotional literature. In them, he displays a warm piety concerned with the direct presence of the Holy Spirit in the life of the Christian.

If not Stone, then the first early leader to produce devotional writings was Robert Richardson. His communion and worship meditations published first in the *Millennial Harbinger* were later collected in book form as *Communings in the Sanctuary* (1872), the first genuine devotional classic in the Stone-Campbell Movement. Although he speaks of contemplating the mystery of God, a theme common in mystical theology, Richardson does not reveal the sources of his thought, whether he was influenced by earlier Christian devotional works or by Scripture alone. Richardson had been raised an Anglican, and it is not unlikely that in his past he had been exposed to the great classics of Anglican spirituality. Moreover, traces of themes from Anglican and Reformed sacramental spirituality appear in *Communings in the Sanctuary*, such as the "spiritual presence" of Christ in the Eucharist.

More typical of second-generation leaders is another series of articles written for the *Millennial Harbinger*, later published as *Treatise on Prayer* by Robert Milligan. Milligan relies on Scripture as his only source of meditation on prayer. The bibliocentrism is further reflected in Isaac Errett's *Walks About Jerusalem* (1871) and his three volumes of *Evenings with the Bible* (1884-89). One sees it in a series of sermons on prayer in book form, *The Life of Trust* by Ashley S. Johnson, and in Benjamin Franklin's sermon on prayer in volume 2 of *The Gospel Preacher*. Published sermons have in fact been a key "devotional" genre in Stone-Campbell literature, at least those of biblical exposition for purposes of edifying the saints. An example is W. T. Moore's anthology of sermons of influential Disciples, *The Living Pulpit of the Christian Church* (1869). Hymnody, too, has been a very important genre of devotional literature, with some of the most substantial religious poetry of the Movement being put to song.

Perhaps the first writer in the Movement who explicitly uses devotional literature from earlier sources is James H. Garrison (1842-1931) in his book *Alone with God* (1891). In that work, he quotes or adapts the writings of Thomas à Kempis (1380-1471), the Anglican *Book of Common Prayer*, and his contemporaries Lyman Abbott (1835-1922), Austin Phelps (1820-1890), William Landels (1823-1899), and Elizabeth Sewell (1815-1906). Scripture and hymns are his favorite sources.

About the time of the division between Disciples and Churches of Christ, Disciples writers began to reflect their liberal theology in their approach to devotional writing. W. E. Garrison (1874-1969) and Edward Scribner Ames (1870-1958) agree that Christianity is based on experience, but not on a mystical experience that brings knowledge of God. They have a pragmatic spirituality, not a mystical one. The same holds true of the work of Herbert L. Willett and C. C. Morrison, *The Daily Altar* (1918), widely read even beyond the Disciples of Christ. By contrast, Peter Ainslie, in his book *God and Me*, quotes from the early Christian bishop Ambrose of Milan, the medieval monastics Bernard of Clairvaux and Francis of Assisi, and the seventeenth-century Anglican writer Lancelot Andrewes to make the case for Bible study that leads to a deeper experience of fellowship with the Divine. Frederick Kershner, in a series of articles in the *Christian-Evangelist*, goes farther by saying that it is the neglect of mysticism that has been the greatest weakness in the Disciples' theology and practice. He calls for a direct consciousness of the reality of the spiritual world.

During the twentieth century, most devotional writing among the Disciples was published in the *Christian-Evangelist,* which later became *The Christian* and then *The Disciple.* Daily devotion guides such as *The Secret Place* and recent publications like *Partners in Prayer* and *Fellowship of Prayer* from the Christian Board of Publication find use among the Disciples.

Among Churches of Christ, there were no book-length devotional works published in the first half of the twentieth century, although there were articles on prayer and family devotions in the *Gospel Advocate* and in the *Firm Foundation.* From 1950 to 1990, there were a few devotional books such as *The Minister's Spiritual Life,* by E. W. McMillan (1959), *Prayer and Fasting,* by Albert Lemmons (1978), along with a series of books from Leroy Brownlow, whose publishing company (founded in 1959) has been the most prolific source of devotional material in Churches of Christ.

As with the Disciples, most devotional material among Churches of Christ has appeared in periodicals such as *Twentieth-Century Christian (Twenty-First Century Christian* since 1990), *Christian Woman, Christian Bible Teacher, Image,* and *Wineskins* (*New Wineskins* since 2001). Of particular importance is the daily devotional guide, *Power for Today,* published since 1955 with almost 47,000 subscribers by 2002. Until recently, Church of Christ devotional material used the Bible as its only source and reflected the early Disciples' rejection of mystical theology. On a more scholarly level, C. Leonard Allen has given much thought to the historic problem of rationalism in Churches of Christ, and in a recent work with Danny Gray Swick, *Participating in God's Life* (2001), Allen has urgently appealed for a deeper, more spiritually enriching trinitarian spirituality.

Among Christian Churches/Churches of Christ the story is similar. There are a few book-length volumes on prayer and a few books of collected Communion meditations, but most devotional writing is published in periodicals, particularly the *Christian Standard* and *The Lookout.* On the scholarly level, Frederick Kershner's one-time student, Byron C. Lambert, former professor at Fairleigh Dickinson University and a retired minister of the Christian Churches/Churches of Christ, was one of the original founders of the International C. S. Lewis Society and has both written and lectured on the work of Lewis, J. R. R. Tolkien, Paul Elmer More, and others.

Why has so little devotional literature been published by the Movement? The primary answer lies in the historic theological rationalism that caused the Stone-Campbell Movement to judge the larger Christian spiritual tradition solely by its excesses. The liberalism and pragmatism of the Disciples fed that prejudice against mysticism. The rationalistic, bibliocentric conservatism among Churches of Christ and Christian Churches/Churches of Christ led them to do the same. Ironically, what all three branches have in common is a willingness to use devotional literature from contemporary Christians outside the Movement. The ecumenical impulse led Disciples to those sources. Among Churches of Christ, it has been common to accept "denominational" devotional literature as valuable, since it does not contain "doctrine."

All three branches of the Movement now are more aware of the importance of spiritual formation and open to the rich resources available in the devotional writings of Christians throughout the ages. Those writings as well as a continued emphasis on the devotional power of the Bible serve as the foundation of recent works by Disciples such as William O. Paulsell and Bonnie Bowman Thurston (Thurston being a specialist on the spirituality of the late Trappist monk and spiritual author Thomas Merton). By contrast, the best-selling works of Church of Christ minister Max Lucado, with a readership extending well beyond the Stone-Campbell churches, are almost exclusively reflections on Scripture.

See also Holy Spirit, Doctrine of the; Hymnody; Literature; Preaching — Nineteenth Century; Sanctification, Doctrine of

BIBLIOGRAPHY C. Leonard Allen and Danny Gray Swick, *Participating in God's Life: Two Crossroads for Churches of Christ* (2001) • Pat Brooks, "Robert Richardson: Nineteenth Century Advocate of Spirituality," *Restoration Quarterly* 21 (1978): 135-49 • J. H. Garrison, *Alone with God* (1891) • E. W. McMillan, *The Minister's Spiritual Life* (1959) • Ronald E. Osborn, "Hidden Heritage: Spirituality in the Disciples Tradition," *Mid-Stream* 36 (1997): 239-71 • William O. Paulsell, *Disciples at Prayer* (1995) • Robert Richardson, *Communings in the Sanctuary* (1872; repr., ed. C. Leonard Allen, 2000).

GARY HOLLOWAY

DeWelt, Don (1919-1990)

Evangelist, teacher, publisher, and unity advocate from the Christian Churches/Churches of Christ.

During his career DeWelt taught at San Jose Bible College (1943-56) and Ozark Bible College (1957-84). In 1959 he and his wife Elsie founded College Press Publishing Company in Joplin, Missouri, which, among other publishing projects, undertook to reprint primary resources from the early history of the Stone-Campbell Movement, including Alexander Campbell's *Millennial Harbinger.* In 1984 DeWelt helped organize the Restoration Forum, an annual gathering promoting mutual understanding and reconciliation between Christian Churches/Churches of Christ and Churches of Christ. In 1984 DeWelt began publishing *One Body,* also to call attention to the imperative of unity. DeWelt was known for his irenic spirit and emphasis on the Holy Spirit and personal worship, as well as on Christian unity.

BIBLIOGRAPHY Don DeWelt, *Happy on My Way to Heaven* (1989). VICTOR KNOWLES

Direct Support Missions

One method of supporting missionaries financially used by the Christian Churches/Churches of Christ.

On this model, a missionary seeks funds from congregations and individuals (as opposed to a denominational missionary agency) and then serves in faith that funds will be sent, normally on a monthly basis, during his or her missionary tenure.

W. K. Azbill (1892) and W. C. Cunningham (1901) pioneered this method in the Stone-Campbell Movement while raising funds to serve as independent missionaries in Japan. The method was not seriously considered, however, until the breach deepened between conservative and liberal Disciples of Christ in the 1920s. Conservative Disciples of Christ were alarmed at the tendency toward a more liberal interpretation of the Scriptures and toward interdenominational cooperation that they observed in the United Christian Missionary Society (UCMS). Consequently James DeForest Murch of the Christian Restoration Association, the *Christian Standard,* and others urged churches to direct financial support to conservative missionaries so they could serve independently of the United Christian Missionary Society.

In the twentieth century direct support missions grew in popularity and played a major role in the emergence of the Christian Churches/Churches of Christ as a separate fellowship from the Christian Church (Disciples of Christ). By 1999 direct support missionaries numbered more than 1,200 personnel serving in over seventy nations. In addition, numerous home missions, parachurch organizations, and educational institutions throughout the United States received direct support in the same manner.

BIBLIOGRAPHY David Filbeck, *The First Fifty Years: A Brief History of the Direct Support Missionary Movement* (1980) • Henry E. Webb, "A History of the Independent Mission Movement of the Disciples of Christ" (unpublished Th.D. thesis, Southern Baptist Theological Seminary, 1954). DAVID FILBECK

One of the pioneering "independent" (direct-support) missionaries of the Disciples of Christ was Leslie Wolfe (1876-1945) in the Philippines, who had resigned his twenty-year commission with the United Christian Missionary Society over the issue of open membership. Wolfe was among missionaries interned by the Japanese in the Philippines during World War II. Photo appearing in the *Christian Standard,* December 14, 1940

Directory of the Ministry

The *Directory of the Ministry* is an annual listing of 5,600 congregations and personnel choosing to be identified with the fellowship known as Christian Churches/Churches of Christ. Congregations listed in this publication therefore do not have standing with the Christian Churches (Disciples of Christ), though some originated within the Disciples fold prior to the denominational restructure in the late 1960s. These churches are also separately identified from the Churches of Christ.

Until 1955, an unofficial loose-leaf notebook was used to document the Christian Churches/Churches of Christ in the United States. Starting in 1955, Ralph and Zella McLean took on the task of publishing an annual listing of "independent" Christian Churches. After some initial financial troubles precluding annual publication, the Directory of the Ministry has appeared consistently each year since 1963. The Directory is currently edited and published by the McLeans' daughter, Judy Noll, in Springfield, Illinois. It remains an "unofficial" directory, in no way claiming to identify or represent a "denomination" as such.

Annually, about 5,000 copies are sold nationwide and to overseas missionaries as the primary listing of Christian Churches/Churches of Christ for (1) statewide membership; (2) Bible college listings and statistics; (3) church listings of membership and current addresses; (4) military and hospital chaplains; (5) conventions; (6) radio and TV ministries; (7) benevolent agencies; (8) new churches; and (9) missionaries by country and their respective forwarding agents.

The stated purpose as summarized in the 2001 edition is "to provide in one handy, ready-reference volume, the names, addresses, and work of a large number of ministers, missionaries, and other Christian workers who with good will share to a large degree a common work and fellowship in the ministry of the gospel and the restoration of undenominational New Testament Christianity."

See also Christian Churches/Churches of Christ

LARRY L. WOODARD

Disciple, The

Disciples of Christ journal.

The Disciple was the fruit of a merger between the news and opinion journal *The Christian* and the mission magazine *World Call* in 1974. The magazine started out as a bi-weekly, then became a monthly early in its life. It was published for twenty-eight years before suspension by the Christian Board of Publication in a financial crunch early in 2002. The magazine suffered from a decline in denominational membership and loss of a Sunday School audience, falling an average of nearly 5 percent in circulation each year of its life. The final circulation was 19,000.

James L. Merrell, the last editor of *World Call,* was the founding editor, serving fifteen years before his return to the pastoral ministry in 1989. Under Merrell, the magazine added color to its covers and brought technological innovations into the production. Robert L. Friedly succeeded Merrell in 1990, the magazine's editorial offices moving from St. Louis to Indianapolis to be closer to the center of denominational activity. Friedly edited the journal for more than eight years, extending the use of color inside and, with associate editor Patricia R. Case, developing imaginative approaches to content. Case followed Friedly in the editor's chair in 1998. She arranged for a redesign, expanded the magazine to full color, and increased its promotion and design innovations. The magazine won numerous awards from its peers in Associated Church Press. Case resigned in late 2001 when it became evident that the magazine was going to close; her associate, Dan Gangler, edited the magazine's final issue.

See also *Christian, The; Christian-Evangelist; Disciples-World*

ROBERT L. FRIEDLY

Disciple Heritage Fellowship

An organization of theologically conservative congregations.

The roots of the Disciple Heritage Fellowship can be traced through Disciple Renewal — a renewal movement that began in the Christian Church (Disciples of Christ) — to the now defunct Christian Mission Awareness (CMA). Although CMA was initiated to question how the Disciples of Christ were spending some of their mission money, Disciple Renewal (DR) came into being in 1985 to provide a voice for conservative Disciples congregations and individuals. Key in the foundation of the fellowship were Richard Bowman, Douglas Harvey, and Kevin and Linda Ray.

By 1983 a small but growing number of Disciples had demonstrated concern over what they believed to be a liberalizing trend among the Disciples of Christ over such issues as the unique lordship of Jesus Christ, the authority of the Bible, and the practice of homosexuality among Christians. They believed that the Disciples of Christ no longer held to the basic tenets of the Stone-Campbell Movement. Following the rejection of a resolution regarding the inspiration of Scripture before the General Assembly of the Christian Church (Disciples of Christ) in 1985, DR began making plans to address those and other issues through the forum of a journal also entitled *Disciple Renewal.* Their expressed goal was renewal from within.

By 1987 the Disciple Renewal movement had named an Executive and Advisory Board and incorporated in the State of Illinois. Their activities included continued participation in the General Board and the General Assembly of the Disciples as well as the continued publication of the DR journal and the beginning of Disciple Renewal Conferences. The year 1989 saw the publication of *Lifting Up Jesus,* a compendium of traditional Disciple beliefs on key issues by twelve authors.

The Disciple Heritage Fellowship (DHF) was born in 1995 as a fellowship of autonomous churches. About half are formally associated with the Disciples of Christ; half are not. These congregations did not unite with the Christian Churches/Churches of Christ because many DHF congregations practice open membership and the ordination of female clergy. In 2002 the DHF officially included sixty congregations as well as 100 supporting churches.

JAMES HUCKABA

Disciple Renewal

See Disciple Heritage Fellowship

Disciples Divinity House

An institution providing housing, financial aid, and denominational instruction for students preparing for ministry in the Christian Church (Disciples of Christ).

Two such Houses are currently in operation: one at the University of Chicago Divinity School, and the other at the Divinity School of Vanderbilt University. Although not degree-granting institutions, the Houses enjoy a formal relationship with their respective divinity schools regarding Disciple admissions, faculty resources, and some curricular matters. Currently both Houses also enjoy a formal relationship with the Division of Higher Education of the Christian Church (Disciples of Christ).

The idea of the Disciples Divinity House emerged in the late nineteenth and early twentieth centuries as Disciples leaders developed a new model of ministerial preparation to meet the challenges of the modern era. This innovative model emphasized (1) instruction beyond the bachelor's degree; (2) scientific and historical studies of religion in the context of a research university; (3) application of Christian theological reasoning to the problems of modern society; and (4) cultivating a self-consciously Disciples community in academically high-level ecumenical theological institutions. Though no longer "new" in the chronological sense, this developmental and contextual model of ministerial preparation remains innovative and continues to shape the educational philosophy and mission of both Disciples Divinity Houses.

Chartered in 1894, the Disciples Divinity House of the University of Chicago Divinity School resulted from the pioneering efforts of Herbert Lockwood Willett, who was the organization's first dean and served until 1921. Initially only providing financial assistance and cultivating denominational identity for Disciples students at the Divinity School, the House built its first residence in 1928 and added a chapel in 1930. These facilities, which still serve the House at the beginning of the twenty-first century, reflect the model of a college at Oxford. Disciples lay leader Gertrude Sutcliffe — already largely responsible for underwriting these building projects — labored alongside Dean E. S. Ames throughout the 1930s in an aggressive campaign to increase the House's endowment. By 1940 the endowment easily provided sufficient income to underwrite fully the theological education of its constituency. William Barnett Blakemore, dean of the House from 1945 to 1975, established many of the programs and policies that continue to define the House. Perhaps most significantly, Dean Blakemore formalized a scholarship program for Ph. D. students, insisting that the House prepare scholars and teachers for the church as well as pastors. Under the steady deanships of Don Browning and Clark Gilpin, the House weathered well the anti-institutional era of the late 1970s and 1980s by finding creative ways of articulating the House's mission in very difficult times for the church. Dean Kristine Culp, perhaps the first Disciples woman to hold a major administrative post in theological education, began leading the house in 1991. Not only did Dean Culp lead the House in a joyous celebration of its centennial, but she also organized a highly successful capital campaign to renovate its physical plant and enlarge its endowment.

George N. Mayhew, a graduate of the University of Chicago Divinity School, was instrumental in founding the Disciples Foundation at the Vanderbilt University School of Religion in 1927. In its early years, the principal focus was providing financial assistance and cultivating denominational identity for Disciples students at the School of Religion. By 1942 the Vanderbilt Disciple House purchased its first residence, which served also as the headquarters of the Tennessee Christian Missionary Society (TCMS). Because of this new partnership, TCMS state secretary W. P. Harmon assumed leadership of the Foundation, and the name was officially changed to the Disciples Divinity House. By 1950, however, in the midst of financial difficulties and contests over leadership with Harmon's successor, the partnership between the House and TCMS was formally dissolved. The House maintained ownership of the property and was rechartered.

Newly appointed Vanderbilt church history professor and Disciples minister Herman A. Norton assumed the deanship of the House in 1951, a position that he held until 1986. Under Norton's leadership, the House experienced tremendous growth: a new two-story residential facility was dedicated in 1959, with a third story being added by 1967; Disciples enrollment at Vanderbilt Divinity School hovered in the high fifties throughout his tenure; and the endowment grew steadily. Under the deanship of Norton's successor, Richard Harrison, increases in tuition costs along with declining enrollment proved to be difficult challenges for Vanderbilt's Disciples Divinity House in the 1980s and early 1990s. Following his appointment in 1995, Dean Mark Miller-McLemore generated a renewed vigor among the House leadership, undertook aggressive recruitment efforts, and stimulated promising financial commitments to the organization from the denomination, from alumni/ae, and from friends of the House.

Without question, the principal legacy of the Disciples Divinity Houses has been the impressive list of their alumni/ae: faithful congregational ministers, visionary denominational leaders and ecumenists, dedicated domestic and foreign missionaries, innovative leaders in social justice ministries, and leading scholars in all fields of theological education.

BIBLIOGRAPHY William Barnett Blakemore, *Quest for Intelligence in Ministry: The Story of the First Seventy-Five Years of the Disciples Divinity House of the University of Chicago* (1970) • Anthony L. Dunnavant, "Educating Disciples," in *Vanderbilt Divinity School: Education, Contest, and Change,* ed. Dale A. Johnson (2001), pp. 311-26.

SCOTT D. SEAY

Disciples Ecumenical Consultative Council

The international Christian World Communion that joins together Disciples of Christ churches and united churches linked to the Disciples tradition; it is the forum through which these churches make common witness to the visible unity of the one Church of Jesus Christ.

The primary purposes of the Disciples Ecumenical Consultative Council (DECC) are (1) to deepen the fellowship *(koinōnia)* among these Disciples and united churches and to encourage their participation, locally and globally, in the movement committed to the visible unity that God wills for all Christians; (2) to coordinate common theological and ecumenical studies, especially related to bilateral dialogues and multilateral ecumenical conversations; (3) to gather, share, and evaluate information about Disciples ecumenical activities in local, national, and regional settings; and (4) to appoint official representatives of the DECC to international bilateral dialogues and to international ecumenical bodies such as the Central Committee, commissions, and assemblies of the World Council of Churches. Through the DECC Disciples have engaged in international dialogues with the Roman Catholic Church, the World Alliance of Reformed Churches, the Russian Orthodox Church, and the Evangelical Lutheran Church in Finland.

The DECC's founding meeting was in November/December 1975, at Nairobi, Kenya, during the 5th Assembly of the World Council of Churches (WCC). At this time the purposes of the DECC were defined, an executive committee was appointed, and the president of the U.S. Council on Christian Unity was elected to serve as the DECC's general secretary.

The first International Conference took place at Kingston, Jamaica, October 6-12, 1979. The theme was "Your Kingdom Come: Mission and Unity in a Global Perspective," a theme chosen in concert with the WCC's 1980 World Conference on Mission and Evangelism, which met at Melbourne, Australia, under the theme "Your Kingdom Come." Over 100 delegates and observer-consultants from twelve countries came to Jamaica. Members of the DECC at that time included Disciples and united churches in Argentina, Australia, Canada, Congo, Cuba, Great Britain, Jamaica, Mexico, New Hebrides, New Zealand, Paraguay, Puerto Rico, and the USA. United Church members were the United Reformed Church in the United Kingdom and the Eglise du Christ au Congo.

Special papers related to the conference theme were presented by leaders from the global Christian community: "Disciples of Christ Amid the Universal Church's Search for Wholeness" (Paul A. Crow, Jr., USA); "The Mission and Unity of the Church in a Global Context (Emilio Castro, Uruguay, WCC); "Thy Kingdom Come: An African Response" (Efefe Elonda, Zaire); "Thy Kingdom Come: An American Response" (Albert M. Pennybacker, USA); "The Mission of the Church in the 1980s" (Jeanne Hendrickse, Southern Africa); "Sharing the Cup of Suffering and the Church's Mission" (Koson Srisong, Thailand); "Evangelism as Redemption, Liberation and Community" (Ron M. O'Grady, New Zealand); "The Shape of the Unity We Seek" (Philip Morgan, British Council of Churches, London); "The Unity of Women and Men in the Struggle for Justice and Liberation" (Sylvia Talbot, USA/Caribbean Council of Churches). Biblical lectures were given by Beatriz Couch, professor of biblical studies at Union Theological Seminary in Buenos Aires, Argentina. The Honorable Michael Manley, the Prime Minister of Jamaica, addressed the assembly about the critical struggles of Third World nations.

The DECC's second International Conference took place at Des Moines, Iowa, July 27-31, 1985, just prior to the General Assembly of the Christian Church (Disciples of Christ) in the USA and Canada. The theme was "Disciples Identity in an Ecumenical Age." By this time the member churches had increased to twenty, with the additional participation of churches from Indonesia, India, Taiwan, Japan, South Africa, Lesoto, Brazil, Costa Rica, and Switzerland. The predominant focus was upon *Baptism, Eucharist and Ministry* (*BEM*), the historic Lima text developed over a fifty-year process by the WCC's Commission on Faith and Order and sent in 1982 to the member churches for their study and official response. At the Des Moines conference Disciples from many countries responded positively to *BEM*'s ecumenical vision.

The working agenda at Des Moines was punctuated with papers by Disciples theologians from differing theological and cultural contexts: "A Cry for Peace" (Carmelo E. Álvarez, Puerto Rico); "The Challenge of *Baptism, Eucharist and Ministry* to the Disciples" (Thomas F. Best, WCC Faith and Order Commission, Geneva, Switzerland); "Disciples Readiness for the Reception of BEM" (William Tabbernee, Australia, later USA); "Episcope and Oversight Among Disciples" (David M. Thompson, England); "Episcope and Oversight: An African Perspective" (Efefe Elonda, Zaire); "Women in the Struggle for True Community: A Caribbean Perspective" (Hazel G. Byfield, Jamaica); "Asian Women's Role in Church and Society" (Sun Ai Park, Singapore); "Global Mission: Issues and Imperatives Facing Disciples" (William J. Nottingham, USA); "Disciples Identity in an Ecumenical Age" (Paul A. Crow, Jr., USA). These theological papers, the conference message, and the reports from the participating churches made the Des Moines conference — as one delegate evaluated — "one of the most notable assemblies in Disciples history." A third international conference is being planned for the summer of 2004 in Brighton, England.

The DECC continues to give worldwide Disciples of Christ a timely and official voice in the ecumenical movement, a sense of *koinōnia* and common witness amid the diversity this tradition reflects, and an arena where the theological issues that confront Christ's Church can be addressed in the context of the twenty-first century.

See also Disciples of Christ–Roman Catholic International Dialogue

BIBLIOGRAPHY "Addresses and Reports of the First International Conference of the Disciples Ecumenical Consultative Conference," *Mid-Stream* 19:2 (April 1980) • "Addresses and Reports of the Second International Conference of the DECC," *Mid-Stream* 25:1 (January 1986) • Paul A. Crow, Jr., "Disciples of Christ Amid the Churches' Search for Global Witness," *Mid-Stream* 19:2 (April 1980): 132-41 • Paul A. Crow, Jr., "Disciples of Christ — Russian Orthodox Dialogue," *DEM*, p. 334 • "Papers and Addresses from the International Dialogue of the DECC and the World Alliance of Reformed Churches, Birmingham, England, March 9-11, 1987," *Mid-Stream* 27:2 (April 1988) • Alan P. Sell, ed., *Reformed and Disciples of Christ Dialogue* (1985) • David M. Thompson, "Disciples-Reformed Dialogue," in *Dictionary of the Ecumenical Movement,* ed. Nicholas Lossky et al., 2nd ed. (2002), pp. 332-33 • *Towards Church Fellowship: Report of the Dialogue between Reformed and Disciples* (1988).

PAUL A. CROW, JR.

Disciples Hymnbook

See Hymnody

Disciples of Christ Historical Society

Historical archives and research center for studies in the history of the Stone-Campbell Movement, located in Nashville, Tennessee.

Almost a decade before the founding of the Disciples of Christ Historical Society, Claude Spencer (1898-1979), librarian at Culver-Stockton College in Missouri, not only wrote down ideas for a historical collection for the Stone-Campbell Movement but actually started the collection. It was founded for the purposes of gathering, preserving, and making available the large trove of documentary and material sources pertaining to the Movement. By action of the Disciples' International Convention, the Disciples of Christ Historical Society was created on May 5, 1941. Membership on the Board was drawn from across the life of the Stone-Campbell churches at that time.

When the collection outgrew the space given it at Culver-Stockton College, a new home was sought. From numerous cities considered, a location near Vanderbilt University in Nashville, Tennessee, was chosen to be the home of the Society. The primary reasons were Vanderbilt's offer of free space for the collection for five years, the work of community and church leaders to raise the money to move the collection there, and the fact that Vanderbilt was a neutral location not connected with any other institution.

Office space was rented near the Vanderbilt campus, and Claude Spencer continued to serve as the first curator. The Society moved into its permanent home, the Thomas W. Phillips Memorial Building, in 1958. It was designed in the great tradition of Gothic architecture and art, employing stone sculpture and stained glass to depict divine revelation and religious history. This building, costing more than a million dollars, was a gift of the Phillips family in

The Library and Archives of the Disciples of Christ Historical Society are housed in the Thomas W. Phillips Memorial in Nashville, Tennessee. The Phillips Memorial also includes a lecture hall, named in 2003 in honor of A. Dale Fiers, and a museum. Completed in 1958 at a cost of more than a million dollars, the building was a gift to the Society from the Phillips family in memory of their father, a well-known lay leader of the Movement. Courtesy of the Disciples of Christ Historical Society

memory of T. W. Phillips, Sr., of Butler, Pennsylvania, who had been an outstanding layman in the Stone-Campbell Movement.

Besides its beauty and sophistication, the building had a climate-controlled archives and library space to assure the best preservation possible for the collection. A trained librarian oversees the proper care and cataloguing of the books and archives. A museum provides display space for historical artifacts.

From its beginning the collection of books, papers, memorabilia, and records came from the broad sweep of the Stone-Campbell Movement. Members of all three branches of the Movement still serve on the Society's Board of Trustees. Editors and authors of books published by the Society and speakers for its regular lectureships and seminars are drawn from all three branches of the Movement. The library and archives are open to researchers who come from around the world and from many denominational backgrounds. Students and writers have used the study carrels at the Society to write numerous doctoral dissertations and books.

The basic funding for the Society comes from the Disciples fund-raising procedure, Disciples Mission Fund, formerly Basic Mission Finance, through which congregations and individuals give funds to help support the educational, benevolent, missions, regional, and general ministries of the church. About one-third of the funding for the Society comes from earnings of an endowment program that has been developed to undergird the future of the library and archives, with contributions coming from across the Movement. The Society also receives income from memberships and for services rendered.

The Society is one of the few free-standing religious libraries and archives in the nation. Its collection of Stone-Campbell material is the largest to be found anywhere, and it is one of the largest Protestant libraries and archives in the United States. The library contains more than 37,000 volumes written about the Movement or by persons in the Movement. There are more than 35,000 biographical files and personal paper collections, 23,000 congregational files, and several thousand audio-visual tapes, films, and computer files. In 1985 the Society entered the On-Line Center for Library Cataloguing (OCLC) so that its records and material would be available on the worldwide computer network. This on-line computer connection makes interlibrary loan of books possible and provides for a web site and e-mail communication. It is the official library and archives for the Christian Church (Disciples of Christ), while "unofficially" housing very large collections of resources on the other two streams of the Stone-Campbell tradition.

With age the Society has moved confidently into a strong program of cultivating historical knowledge through lectures, publication of books, indexes, monographs, and the Society's quarterly journal, *Discipliana*. Conferences for congregational historians and for church historians are sponsored by the Society. Endowed lectureships are presented in various sites around the country.

An outstanding seminary student's historical paper is recognized through an annual competition, and assistance is available to encourage young history scholars to attend lectures presented by the Society where they can meet and form mentoring relationships with scholars already established in the field of Stone-Campbell history. These are just a few of the ways the Historical Society is working to uncover history, share history, and indeed "make" history as the church moves from century to century.

The Society boasts the fact that it is one of the very few organized or institutional bodies bringing together leaders and laypersons from all three streams of the Stone-Campbell heritage. The present *Encyclopedia of the Stone-Campbell Movement*, published under the auspices of the Society in partnership with the Center for Restoration Studies at Abilene Christian University, and bringing together writers from across the Movement, is clear evidence of collaborative work supported by the Society.

See also Spencer, Claude E.

BIBLIOGRAPHY James M. Seale, *Forward from the Past: The First Fifty Years of the Disciples of Christ Historical Society* (1991).

JAMES M. SEALE

Disciples of Christ–Roman Catholic International Dialogue

One of the fruits of the Second Vatican Council was the launching of international dialogues between the Roman Catholic Church and other major Christian world communions, such as the Orthodox, Lutherans, Anglicans, Methodists, Reformed, Baptists, and the Disciples of Christ. These theological dialogues constitute a new dimension to the search for visible unity.

The first official expression of the Disciples of Christ–Roman Catholic dialogue took place in the United States and was sponsored by the U.S. Committee for Ecumenical and Interreligious Affairs of the National Conference of Catholic Bishops, and the Council on Christian Unity (CCU) of the Christian Church (Disciples of Christ) in the United States and Canada. This dialogue was inspired by George G. Beazley, Jr., president of the CCU, and Monsignor (later Cardinal Archbishop of Washington) William Baum. During its six years (1967-73) this dialogue met ten times and addressed such themes as the nature of the unity we seek, the Eucharist (Lord's Supper) as a symbol and agent of unity, a responsible theology for intercommunion or eucharistic sharing, Christian marriage and the pastoral concern for mixed marriages, the ordained ministry, the theology and practice of baptism, and the concept of "the parish" in *A Plan of Union for the Church of Christ Uniting* (1970) developed by the Consultation on Church Union. In 1973 the theological and pastoral insights of this dialogue were published in the report *An Adventure in Understanding.*

After Beazley's death from a heart attack while in Moscow in October 1973, the national dialogue was succeeded by an international one. This wider dialogue resulted from two years of preparatory conversations (1975-77) between Paul A. Crow, Jr., the new president of the CCU and general secretary of the newly formed (1975) international Disciples Ecumenical Consultative Council (DECC), and Cardinal Johannes Willebrands, president of the Vatican's Pontifical Council for Promoting Christian Unity.

From the beginning this dialogue's goal was distinctly more than a "spiritual" unity, or cooperation in biblical scholarship or social action, or common fellowship and mission through councils of churches. The ultimate goal is full visible unity in faith, sacraments, ministry, and witness in the world. In other words, the journey is toward the full manifestation of the unity given by Christ. This particular dialogue began with several defining marks when compared to other dialogues of the Catholic Church. For the first time among all such dialogues the Disciples of Christ–Roman Catholic International Commission included women theologians. Equally innovative was the full participation of theologians from Zaire (Congo), Puerto Rico, Jamaica, and Kenya. Further, in contrast to other dialogues, no formal division ever occurred nor were any anathemas ever pronounced between these two traditions.

Across its twenty-five-year history the comoderators have been — from the Roman Catholic side — Bishop Stanley J. Ott, Auxiliary Bishop of New Orleans (1977-82); Archbishop Samuel Carter, SJ, of Kingston, Jamaica (1983-94); and Archbishop Daniel Buechlein, OSB, of Indianapolis (1995-), and from the Disciples tradition Paul A. Crow, Jr. (1977-2002).

The first round of meetings of the International Commission for Dialogue lasted from 1977 to 1982. Symbolically, the first session met in Indianapolis, headquarters of the Disciples Council on Christian Unity. As would be the case in every session of the dialogue's history, biblical studies taught by leading scholars — one Roman Catholic and one Disciples — were central to the agenda. These biblical scholars have included professors John Meier, M. Jack Suggs, and M. Eugene Boring. Another mark of this dialogue has been the practice of worshiping each time with a local congregation, Disciples or Roman Catholic, wherever the two delegations meet. In the first round, four themes constituted the agenda: (1) the nature of the church and elements of its unity; (2) baptism as gift and call in the search for unity; (3) faith and Tradition in the life of the church; and (4) the dynamics of unity and division. Each theme represented a theological encounter, revealing both consensus and difficult tensions — inevitable marks of any authentic ecumenical dialogue. In 1982 the first report to the churches was published under the title *Apostolicity and Catholicity in the Visible Unity of the Church.* Partial yet fundamental agreements were reached on spiritual ecumenism, baptism, and the relation between faith and Tradition.

The second phase of the dialogue (1983-92) brought the commission together seven times in the United States and at such other places as Venice, Italy; Mandeville, Jamaica; Cambridge, England; Toronto, Canada; and Rome. The themes addressed during this decade were the New Testament concept of *koinōnia* (communion) and the nature of the church, the church as a sacramental community and a community of faith, the Lord's Supper (Eucharist) and the visible unity of the church, and the apostolic tradition and the church's ministry. The second agreed account (1992) bore the title *The Church as Communion in Christ,* which reported that while this dialogue reveals historic differences conditioned by a Catholic ethos and a Protestant ethos, it also foretells that Disciples and Roman Catholics share "a convergence of vision" about the church. This convergence includes such things as a conviction that the full visible unity of the church is essential; a conviction that the faith of each individual Christian is inseparable from the faith of the community; the mutual recognition of each other's baptism; and the belief that the common profession of the gospel is one sign of our visible unity. Other key issues addressed were the church as new creation and communion; the visibility of the church's *koinōnia* as revealed in the Eucharist (Lord's Supper); the life and witness of the church in continuity with the apostolic Tradition; and the role of the ordained ministry in maintaining the faith of the apostles. With critical insight the document speaks of the unity of the church being a sign of God's gift to and intention for the whole world. "We are able to affirm gladly the traditional conviction that the Church is at one and the same time an epiphany of the destiny which God wills for all humanity and a means to achieve that unity. . . . By drawing people out of isolation and into communion (*koinōnia*) God makes a new creation — a new humanity now established as children of God."

The dialogue's third phase (1993-2002) focused on the theme, especially critical between Disciples and Roman Catholics, of "the Individual and the Church." For a decade the annual subthemes included "Faith: The Individual and the Church" (Indianapolis, 1994); "The Gospel and the Church" (Monastery of Bose, Magnano, Italy, 1995); "The Content and Authority of the Early Ecumenical Councils" (Bethany College, 1996); "The Canon and the Authority of Scripture" (Venice, Italy, 1997); "The Teaching Office of the Church" (Aibonito, Puerto Rico, 1998); "Conscience and Community: Formation and Practice" (St. Meinrad Archabbey, Indiana, 1999); and "Evangelization: The Goal of the Church's Teaching" (Halifax, Nova Scotia, Canada, 2000).

The eventual third agreed account bears the title *Receiving and Handing on the Faith: The Mission and Responsibility of the Church* (2002). By far the most mature document to come from this dialogue, it reveals "many unexpected agreements." These include a common understanding on the following: the Word of God, proclaimed and received, defines the church as a missionary community called to invite persons to become part of the community of believers; the church is mandated to hold on to the memory of the apostolic community of what God has done in Christ; the canon of the Scriptures, the theological definitions of the first seven ecumenical councils ("where more agreement about these was discovered than we previously recognized"), and the historic declarations (creeds) of the apostolic faith are instruments of handing on the faith; the discernment of the gospel requires both the individual's freedom of conscience and the church's role in helping members to make informed decisions; the discernment of the authentic meaning of God's revealed Word involves the gifts of ordained ministers; and all baptized Christians are called to the work of evangelization. In conclusion, the commission affirms that the unity of the church and the evangelization of the world are deeply intertwined. This theological insight expresses a consensus between Vatican II's *Decree on Ecumenism* and the teachings of Thomas Campbell, Alexander Campbell, Barton Warren Stone, and the continuous tradition of the Disciples of Christ.

At its beginning some ecumenical observers did not see great promise in this dialogue, especially because of the differences of size, power, history, and ecclesiology. Yet the ensuing decades have given ample evidence of ecumenical progress of historic proportions. This international dialogue remains a providential and central part of the future and the faithfulness of the Disciples of Christ.

PAUL A. CROW, JR.

See also Disciples Ecumenical Consultative Council; Roman Catholicism — Twentieth Century

BIBLIOGRAPHY All official papers and reports of this dialogue appear continuously in *Mid-Stream: An Ecumenical Journal,* from 18:4 (October 1979) to 41:4 (October 2002)

Nadia M. Lahutsky, "Christian Faith and the Oneness of the Church: The Disciples of Christ and Roman Catholic Dialogue," in *Christian Faith Seeking Understanding: Essays in Honor of H. Jack Forstman,* ed. James O. Duke and Anthony L. Dunnavant (1997), pp. 291-304 • Thomas P. Looney, "The Concept of Koinonia in the Disciples of Christ–Roman Catholic International Dialogue Commission," vols. 1 and 2 (unpublished dissertation, Catholic University of America, 1997) • David M. Thompson, "The Disciples of Christ–Roman Catholic International Dialogue, 1977-1997: Historical Perspectives," in *The Vision of Christian Unity: Essays in Honor of Paul A. Crow, Jr.,* ed. Thomas F. Best and Theodore J. Nottingham (1997), pp. 163-77 • Jean-Marie Roger Tillard, "The Contribution of the Disciples of Christ–Roman Catholic Dialogue for the Ecclesiology of the Ecumenical Movement," *Mid-Stream* 31:1 (January 1992): 14-25 • Jean-Marie Roger Tillard, "Disciples–Roman Catholic Dialogue," in *Dictionary of the Ecumenical Movement,* 2nd ed. (2002), p. 333 • Cardinal Johannes Willebrands, "The Significance of the Roman Catholic–Disciples of Christ International Dialogue," *Mid-Stream* 22:1 (1983).

Disciples Peace Fellowship

Peace organization of the Christian Church (Disciples of Christ).

Founded in 1935 during the International Convention of the Disciples of Christ in San Antonio, Texas, the Disciples Peace Fellowship (DPF) is one of the oldest organizations associated with the Fellowship of Reconciliation's Interfaith Peace Fellowship alliance. Given the pacifist commitment of many early Stone-Campbell leaders, it is not surprising that after World War I Disciples created an organization in support of wider social and political movements to abolish war (e.g., Kellogg-Briand Pact, Oxford Pledge Movement, and the War Resisters League).

In conjunction with editorials in *The Christian Evangelist* and *World Call,* members of the Department of Social Education and Social Action prepared the ground for the eventual founding of the DPF on October 18, 1935. The seventy-five individuals participating in the inaugural meeting elected Joseph B. Hunter as the first president, with Willard Shelton, Mary Roberts Crowley, and James Crain serving as vice president, secretary-treasurer, and executive secretary, respectively. This October 18 gathering also ratified a "Covenant," which denounced war as "pagan, futile and destructive of spiritual values for which the Church of Christ stands," and pledged to work against "military preparations." One year later the DPF had grown to a membership of 700. A 1936

DPF survey found that although pacifism remained a deeply held conviction among many Disciples, disagreements over absolutist and conditional forms of pacifism would challenge the Fellowship's work. During World War II, for example, the DPF debated whether and how to support the few conscientious objectors (COs) from Disciples churches. Lacking denominational support, the DPF worked through Mennonite, Friends, and Church of the Brethren agencies. During the Cold War and Vietnam eras, the DPF utilized the services of individuals like Bill Herod and Michael Stainton to increase the number of Disciples COs, and shepherded a resolution through to ratification whereby the denomination would support conscientious objection to selected wars and military actions (i.e., conditional pacifism). During this time the DPF also expanded its understanding of "peace" to include broader social and economic concerns (e.g., poverty and hunger).

Since 1979 the DPF has reported to the General Assembly of the Christian Church (Disciples of Christ) through the Division of Homeland Ministries, and today it focuses its work on four initiatives: demilitarization and the reduction of the nuclear threat; abolition of the death penalty; economic justice for labor; and ethical accountability in investments by churches and individuals. Toward these ends the DPF sends "peace interns" to address youth at church camps and conventions and drafts resolutions for the General Assemblies, and publishes its quarterly newsletter *News Notes*. The DPF also maintains affiliation with the Fellowship of Reconciliation, the National Coalition to Abolish the Death Penalty, the Center on Conscience and War, and the Interfaith Center on Corporate Responsibility.

See also Pacifism; Page, Kirby

BIBLIOGRAPHY Mark May, "Disciples Peace Fellowship: Historical Formation and the First Twenty Years, 1935-1955," *Discipliana* (1980): 19-26 • Ian McCrae, "The Disciples Peace Fellowship: Celebrating a Golden Anniversary," *Discipliana* (1985): 24-27.

RICHARD GOODE

Disciples Seminary Foundation

Related to the Christian Church (Disciples of Christ).

The Disciples Seminary Foundation was incorporated on October 20, 1960, to provide seminary education for Disciples of Christ students in Southern California. In 1957 the Southern California Convention of the Christian Churches (Disciples of Christ) established a seminary committee that recommended that the Convention accept an invitation to link with the established and accredited Methodist-related Southern California School of Theology at Claremont. After approval from the convention, a board was elected. The board began a search for an executive director, calling Donald Reisinger, then assistant executive secretary of the Disciples Board of Higher Education.

Reisinger began his tenure at the Foundation on May 1, 1962, offering counsel to Disciples students at the seminary, teaching courses in Disciples history and polity, and raising funds to support the programs of the Foundation and to provide for permanent buildings. A new office building and thirty-unit apartment complex on the School of Theology campus was dedicated on October 24, 1965.

In 1973 Reisinger helped bring Dr. Ronald Osborn, then dean of Christian Theological Seminary in Indianapolis, to the School of Theology as Disciples Professor of American Church History. Also during the 1970s the Seminary Foundation established comity agreements with other Disciples regional judicatories in the West.

In 1987 the Seminary Foundation established a relationship with the Pacific School of Religion in Berkeley, opening an office there in January 1988. Also in 1987, the Foundation sold its buildings to the School of Theology, leasing office space back until other suitable facilities could be found. The Foundation was able to expand its ministries further when it received the property of Central Christian Church in San Diego. This led to the establishment of the Disciples Center for Education, Ecumenism, and Ministry on November 20, 1993.

In January 1994 the Foundation moved to leased offices at Indian Hill and Foothill Boulevard in Claremont, staying there until a new facility was constructed in May 1999 at Yale and Foothill. During the 1990s the Foundation expanded its offerings in continuing education for both laity and clergy, culminating in the establishment and administration of the Institute for Continuing Ministry Studies in the fall of 1997. The Seminary Foundation administers this program for the Claremont Theological Cluster, a consortium of five area institutions of theological education. The need to provide education for the growing number of Korean Disciples students led in 1995 to the establishment of a relationship with San Francisco Theological Seminary in Southern California for a dual language MATS program. As the new millennium began, certificate programs for lay ministries were inaugurated.

Having served in variously titled capacities since 1962, President Reisinger retired on July 1, 2000. He was succeeded by Mary Anne Parrott, who had first joined the Foundation staff in 1973, also serving in a variety of capacities. Today the Disciples Seminary Foundation provides support for Disciples and United Church of Christ seminarians and graduate students in religion at Claremont and San Francisco

Bay area schools. It also offers continuing education courses and resources for laity and clergy.

BIBLIOGRAPHY *Disciples Seminary Foundation: 20th Anniversary* (1980) • Rod Parrott, "History and Retrospective — A Biographical Essay," *Impact* (2000): 1-10.

ROBERT D. CORNWALL

Disciples Student Fellowship

Organization of Disciples students.

The Disciples Student Fellowship (DSF) was formed at the first national student conference of Christian Church students, held at Drake University during Christmas vacation in 1949. It was created as a "movement" of students themselves. College student groups had long gathered at nearby congregations, with varied names; for example, the "Christian Student Congregation" at First Christian Church in Columbia, Missouri, had celebrated its fiftieth anniversary in 1945. Disciples students from eight campuses in Oklahoma had met on their own initiative in 1940 to form the Oklahoma State "Student Christian Youth Fellowship." When John McCaw, later dean of Drake University Divinity School, became National Director of Student Work in 1945, he called meetings of student leaders from which grew the national DSF.

From its beginning the DSF had a strong ecumenical emphasis because of Disciples' commitment to church unity. It supported campus ecumenical councils, the national United Student Christian Council, and the World Student Christian Federation (WSCF), a fellowship of student Christian movements on five continents. DSF also raised money from students to help build a chapel for Protestant students at the University of the Philippines.

DSF succeeded in recruiting significant church leadership and recruits for the ministry from non-church colleges and universities. National DSF presidents took a year out of school to visit universities. Several of them later became seminary professors.

The annual August conferences of the DSF grew from 300 to 600 students. Speakers included distinguished scholars, such as missions historian Kenneth Scott Latourette. They featured Bible study, lectures on ecumenical issues, and many workshops for the exchange of practical and program ideas for local student groups — for example, a ministry to teenagers in reformatories and study of the Christian vocation of students and faculty to help universities serve the needs of humanity. One year the conference program was on "the future of the Disciples," with speakers and workshops exploring various options for achieving church unity. That led to conversations with denominational and interdenominational student movements about merging into a united student Christian movement in the United States. The DSF sent representatives to every national conference where such ideas were being discussed. The DSF expressed the hope that a merger of student groups might lead to merger of those denominations in later decades, just as the WSCF had nurtured leaders for the creation of the World Council of Churches. At the Estes Park DSF conference, August 26, 1960, the DSF voted to merge into the United Student Christian Fellowship, which had announced its intention to find and experiment with the most organic union possible, in contrast to councils of churches. Nationally, the DSF ended with this merger, but many local groups continued.

In 1991 Disciples of Christ and United Church of Christ students began meeting to form a "student ecumenical partnership," which at the turn of the century was making plans for a new kind of student movement.

PARKER ROSSMAN

DisciplesWorld

DisciplesWorld is a Disciples monthly magazine initiated by a group of volunteers led by James C. Suggs, retired president of Christian Board of Publication, after the demise of *The Disciple* magazine in 2002. It was rushed into print forty-four days after incorporation as a new entity seeking "recognized organization" status in the Christian Church (Disciples of Christ). The speed was prompted by the desire of the incorporators to avoid a single month among the Disciples without a general circulation journal.

See also *Disciple, The*

ROBERT L. FRIEDLY

Discipliana

See Disciples of Christ Historical Society

Discipline, Church

Church discipline refers to actions taken by the church with the purpose of keeping members on the path to spiritual maturity. Often, however, church discipline is used specifically to mean correcting members who are erring doctrinally or morally in order to keep the member and the church body from suffering more serious consequences. While church discipline is often used almost synonymously with its most serious form, "disfellowshipping," it more broadly refers to any activities that have the desired effect of correcting or reproving incorrect belief or improper behavior. In a very long series on discipline in the *Millennial Harbinger* (1847-50), doubtless reflecting the increasing challenges faced by the growing Stone-Campbell Movement, W. K. Pendleton identified no fewer than four biblically inspired meanings of "discipline" for the church: (1) instruction in right doctrine; (2) the preservation of order and the regulation of the "social or congregational exercises of the body"; (3) exhortation and reproof addressed to the spiritual integrity of the faithful; and finally (4) the "cutting off" of obstinate or incorrigible offenders from the church body. Pendleton recognized that discipline also entailed consideration of the larger, "official" structure of the church's ministry as purposed for the training of the saints.

In another way, church discipline can be thought of in the two general categories of preventative discipline and restorative discipline. Preventative discipline would include teaching, counseling, accountability, or any other practice of the church that would prevent a member from falling into error. Restorative discipline would take over once a fellow Christian was perceived to be engaged in an incorrect teaching or practice.

From the beginning, the devotion of the Stone-Campbell Movement to restoring "New Testament Christianity" included an attempt to restore those practices of discipline found regularly in the pages of the New Testament. Historically, however, there have been flourishes of particular attention paid to these practices. As one surveys the writings throughout the history of the Movement, these times of high attention have often been the result of particular issues or behaviors that were noted as ones to which the church needed to respond. Alexander Campbell's teaching on church discipline appears early, in his series on "A Restoration of the Ancient Order of Things" in the *Christian Baptist.* In these articles, Campbell includes two lengthy sections, one on slander and the other on breaking promises to incur debts. Campbell notes that there were, even at that time, other behaviors that the church tended to discipline more often, but he cited these as worthy of special attention. While sexual sin seems to be consistently mentioned as worthy of discipline, other issues arise at various historical points — for example, members' non-attendance at church meetings and issues surrounding divorce and remarriage. While behavioral issues seem to be far more often cited as appropriate reasons for employing church discipline, doctrinal issues are also understood as being appropriately treated by church discipline.

Because of the Stone-Campbell Movement's historic commitment to the autonomy of the local congregation, church discipline refers for the most part to the action of the local church toward one of its own members, although it has been the basis for calls of one group of congregations to break fellowship with other congregations. Alexander Campbell and other early leaders were deeply concerned with cases of church discipline, especially regarding lapsed evangelists or elders. In his discussion of discipline in *The Christian System* (1839), Campbell focused responsibility for discipline on a church's eldership and decried the chaos of too much "democracy," allowing everyone in the church a voice in disciplinary matters. In 1844 Campbell reprinted the statement on church order of an Ohio elder (C. Bosworth), endorsing his view that in certain instances it was better for a congregation to refer a case to the more neutral judgment of other congregations, as cases of discipline could easily wreak havoc in a vulnerable church.

In keeping with the teachings of the New Testament, church discipline is practiced within the churches of the Stone-Campbell Movement for three reasons: (1) in order to restore the believer who is sinning (1 Cor. 5:5); (2) to maintain the holiness of the congregation; (3) to insure that the church continues to provide a positive example to unbelievers.

Matthew 18:15-20 gives the framework for the way church discipline should be practiced within the church. The practice of church discipline varies somewhat within the churches of the Stone-Campbell Movement, but the following would be generally descriptive of the process. First, discipline is to be done in a context of prayer (James 5:15-16; 1 John 5:16). Second, as mentioned previously, it is motivated by love and concern for the member being disciplined (Gal. 6:1). Third, Matthew 18:15 teaches that the person should be approached personally and privately. It should be noted that a textual variant in this verse has caused some to question whether this teaching applies to all sin or only to an offense committed against the person enjoined to go to the one at fault. Alexander Campbell's comments on this subject indicate that he understood the latter. Fourth, if going in person is not successful, then two or three witnesses are to be taken in accordance with Deuteronomy 19:15. Because of this reference to the Old Testament juridical system, it appears that the purpose of this step is to insure the reliability of the witnessed offense in addition to the primary purpose of attempting to convince the Christian of his or her error. Fifth, if this step is unsuccessful, the church is to be told. There is some discussion over whether this indicates that the entire matter is to be made known to the church or that there is an unresolved issue in need of correction. There seems to be a general agreement that no more than is expressly necessary to be made known should be made known. Sixth, if the person at fault still does not turn from his or her error, the final disciplinary step is that the person is to be put out of the fellowship. This is also called withdrawing fellowship, excommunication, or "disfellowshipping." In 1 Corinthians 5:5 Paul calls this handing the person "over to Satan." It should be noted that even this most serious step is done for the purpose of trying to convince the offender of his or her error, and with the expectation that if so convinced that person will resume fellowship with the church (2 Cor. 2:5-8).

Normally in the Christian Church (Disciples of Christ), matters of ministerial discipline can be referred to a particular region's Commission on Ministry, whereas in the Christian Churches/Churches of Christ and Churches of Christ, discipline of leaders is still the responsibility of the local congregation itself, under the guidance of its eldership. With cases of unruly or deviant laypersons, the local church's own leadership has the prerogative of discipline in all three branches of the Movement.

In 1981 a former member brought suit against the Collinsville (Oklahoma) Church of Christ for invasion of privacy. Though it is far from the only case involving the practice of church discipline, it was widely reported in secular news and Christian publications and thus sparked a reexamination of this issue, which is reflected by the number of articles appearing in many Stone-Campbell Movement publications. In this case, the member won and was initially awarded damages in the sum of $390,000. The case was then appealed to the Oklahoma Supreme Court where the justices, after keeping it under advisement for a lengthy period of time, reversed the decision and remanded the case.

See also Local Autonomy; Ministry

BIBLIOGRAPHY C. Bosworth, "Church Order," *Millennial Harbinger* (1844): 67-70 • Alexander Campbell, "A Restoration of the Ancient Order of Things," Nos. 23-31: "Discipline," *Christian Baptist* 5-6 (1828-29): 440-42, 467-8, 471-72, 485-86, 500-501, 509-10, 530-31, 549-51 • Alexander Campbell, *The Christian System* (1839), ch. 26: "The Christian Discipline" • William L. Hayden, *Church Polity* (1894) • Ronald B. Flowers, "Can Churches Discipline Members and Win in Court?" *Journal of Church and State* 27 (1985): 483-98 • W. K. Pendleton, "Discipline" (21 parts), *Millennial Harbinger* (1847-50).

BRIAN D. JOHNSON

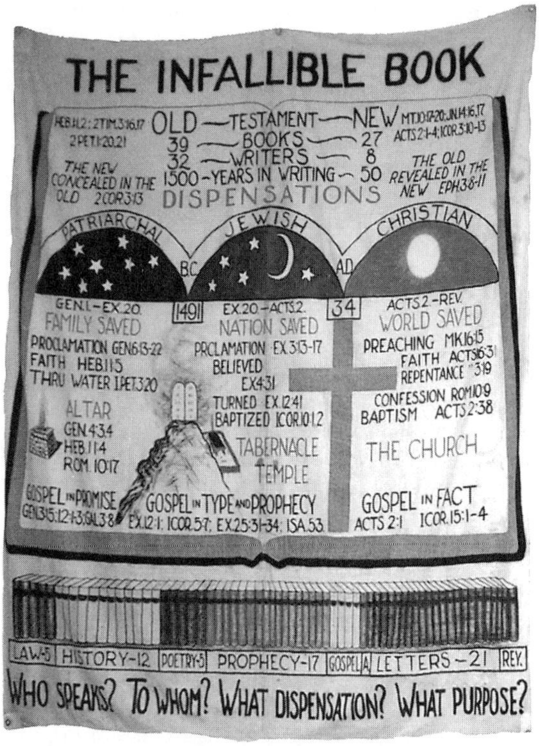

Graphic preaching charts like the one pictured here from Oregon in 1933 were regularly used by Stone-Campbell evangelists in the nineteenth and early twentieth centuries to illustrate the scheme of the Three Dispensations and other biblical themes. Courtesy of Emmanuel School of Religion Archives

Dispensations

Doctrine of the progressive unfolding of divinely purposed revelatory phases or orders.

The early Stone-Campbell-Scott perspective on dispensationalism was indebted to the federal or covenantal theology of Dutch scholars, especially Hugo Grotius (1583-1645) and Johannes Cocceius (1603-1669). Cocceius held that, as the result of the failure of the covenant of works with Adam, God instituted the covenant of grace in three dispensations: the patriarchal, the Mosaic, and the Christian. Dispensationalism not only established a groundwork for what is authoritative in each dispensation; it also provided a means of relating the dispensations. In effect, it became a biblical theology, featuring promise and fulfillment, with each succeeding dispensation canceling out or fulfilling the preceding one. This threefold dispensationalism was widely accepted in nineteenth-century American Protestant circles, especially among groups with Reformed roots. At the turn of the twentieth century, Disciples trained at Yale and Chicago applauded the benefits of dispensationalism, which they argued provided a precursor for progressive or developmental views of God's relationship with humanity.

A mainstay of nineteenth-century evangelism, the three dispensations are still widely taught in more conservative circles across the spectrum of the Stone-Campbell Movement, especially through video materials produced by Jule Miller of Houston, Texas. After World War II, scholars in the Movement became less enamored with claims of accommodative or progressive revelation, which held that the later the revelation is, the more enlightened it is. Likewise scholars, especially those trained in Old

Testament, came to the conclusion that a rigid threefold dispensationalism could not, in fact, be supported by the Scriptures. In certain conservative Protestant churches in the late nineteenth and early twentieth centuries, other visions of dispensationalism — particularly the multifold dispensations as outlined by John Nelson Darby (1800-1882) and C. I. Scofield (1843-1921) — achieved acceptance, and premillennial dispensationalism became a major factor in the rise of fundamentalism.

See also Bible, Authority and Inspiration of the; Bible, Interpretation of the; Covenant (Federal) Theology; Eschatology; Hermeneutics; Revelation

BIBLIOGRAPHY M. Eugene Boring, *Disciples and the Bible: A History of Disciples Biblical Interpretation in North America* (1997) • D. S. Burnet, "Preface to the Stereotype Edition," *Christian Baptist* (rev. ed. 1835), pp. iii-vi • Winfred Ernest Garrison, *Alexander Campbell's Theology* (1900) • J. J. Haley, "The Progress of Revelation, or the Three Dispensations, Their Limits and Characteristics," in *The Old Faith Restated,* ed. J. H. Garrison (1891), pp. 120-48 • Thomas H. Olbricht, *Hearing God's Voice: My Life with Scripture in the Churches of Christ* (1996).

THOMAS H. OLBRICHT

Division of Higher Education

General administrative unit of the Christian Church (Disciples of Christ) responsible for relations between the church and its affiliated colleges, universities, theological institutions, and student ministries.

The Division of Higher Education (DHE) began as the education board of the American Christian Missionary Society in 1894, with the goals of strengthening the credibility of the Movement's colleges and schools and stimulating concern for their futures. The Association of Colleges of the Disciples of Christ succeeded the board in 1910. In 1914 a new Board of Education of Disciples of Christ was formed to raise and distribute funds through the Men and Millions program. From 1934 to 1938 the Board became the Department of Higher Education of the United Christian Missionary Society (UCMS), and student work was added to its responsibilities. At the same time a separate College Association of Disciples of Christ was created to become an academic consultation service to educational institutions. In 1938 the College Association became the Board of Higher Education, separate from UCMS, and the functions of the Department of Higher Education were returned to it. The board became an administrative unit of the Christian Church (Disciples of Christ) following the 1968 restructure and was renamed Division of Higher Education in 1977.

Functioning through most of the twentieth century as an advocate for the Movement's colleges, the board helped schools raise capital, recruit students, heighten standards, and increase administrative efficiency; made territorial assignments; and represented the institutions' interests to the churches. After 1945 the board also helped to develop theological institutions. Following the 1968 creation of the Christian Church (Disciples of Christ), and acknowledging the increasing stability and independence of the educational institutions, the board has increasingly taken responsibility for recruiting Disciples students, providing scholarship aid, nurturing leaders for the church, and representing the church's mission to the institutions. Sixteen directors plus the chairs of three affiliated councils (Colleges and Universities, Theological Education, Student Ministries) govern the division, which also reports to the General Board and General Assembly of the Christian Church (Disciples of Christ). On August 1, 2004, the name became Higher Education and Leadership Ministries.

BIBLIOGRAPHY D. Duane Cummins, *The Disciples Colleges: A History* (1987) • Griffith A. Hamlin, *The Origin and Development of the Board of Higher Education of the Christian Church (Disciples of Christ) 1894-1968* (1968) • Howard E. Short, "Celebrating Lifelong Learning: A Centennial History of the Division of Higher Education," *Disciples Theological Digest* 9:1 (1994).

DENNIS LANDON

Division of Homeland Ministries

A general administrative unit of the Christian Church (Disciples of Christ) in the United States and Canada, Homeland Ministries is an enabling and coordinating division of the Disciples that works in partnership with regions, congregations, other general units, and various constituency groups in the area of congregational program, leadership development, and mission in North America. It functions under the authority of, and reports regularly to, the General Assembly of the Christian Church (Disciples of Christ).

The Division of Homeland Ministries was created by the General Assembly in 1968, as a part of the (then Provisional) Design of the Christian Church (Disciples of Christ). Prior to that time, Homeland Ministries and Overseas Ministries were two divisions within the United Christian Missionary Society. The United Christian Missionary Society itself was created by the 1920 International Convention, combining the Foreign Christian Missionary Society, the American Christian Missionary Society, and the Christian Woman's Board of Mission into one organization. Therefore Homeland Ministries' traditions go back well beyond the formation of the division in 1968.

The Division works closely with a number of recognized and program partner organizations within the Christian Church (Disciples of Christ). These include, but are not limited to,

- the Disciples Peace Fellowship
- the Disciples Chaplains Association
- the National Convocation
- the National Evangelistic Association
- International Christian Women's Fellowship
- Disciples Men
- the Association of Disciple Musicians
- the North American Pacific Asian Disciples
- Disciples Young Adult Network
- Disciples Youth
- New Church Development (with the Board of Church Extension).

In addition, the Division has oversight of the historic mission centers of the Christian Church (Disciples of Christ): All Peoples Christian Center in Los Angeles, California; Inman Christian Center in San Antonio, Texas; Kentucky Appalachian Ministry (in partnership with the region of Kentucky); and Yakima Christian Center in Yakima, Washington.

With such diversity of connections and assignments, the Division has a distinguished history of providing resources, training leaders, and offering direction to the Disciples. Since its formation in 1968, the Division has emphasized different approaches to this task. In its first years it worked with the regions to define the relationships with their staff and programs following the division into units of the former United Christian Missionary Society (UCMS). Under UCMS, program staff working in the state societies were on the staff of UCMS. Following the 1968 Restructuring, these persons became the staff of the regions. It took some time for the various responsibilities and accountabilities to be ironed out. Relations between the regions and the Division have continued to require attention as the regions and the Division share responsibility for extending the ministry of Christ in mission, witness, and service among the people and social structures of North America and nurturing and equipping congregations in their ministry.

In the 1970s the Division had a strong emphasis on training leaders for the church and on social justice and peace concerns. Through the 1980s and 1990s the emphasis was on congregational establishment and vitality. In the twenty-first century, as the Christian Church (Disciples of Christ) continues to change and evolve, all of these areas have renewed importance. Of particular concern is the reenvisioning of relationships with constituency groups and program partners to work together to strengthen congregational life and mission.

The Division of Homeland Ministries has had four presidents. The first, Kenneth Kuntz (1970-82), emphasized organizational development in the transition from UCMS to the Division. The second, John R. Compton (1983-89), was the first African American to serve as a general unit president for the Christian Church (Disciples of Christ). His tenure emphasized creating a more effective and professional staff and changing the operations of the Board of Directors from a program-management style to a policy-making style. The third president, Ann Updegraff Spleth (1990-2000), was the Division's first female president and, at the time of her election, the youngest person to be elected to a general unit presidency. Her tenure involved a restructuring of the division into three flexible and interactive centers of ministry to serve congregations more effectively.

Arnold C. Nelson, Jr., the Division's fourth president, was elected in 2002. Since 2002 the Division of Homeland Ministries has done business as Disciples Home Missions. Its focus has been on congregational transformation, leader development, and clergy care.

See also American Christian Missionary Society; Christian Church (Disciples of Christ); Christian Woman's Board of Mission; Christian Women's Fellowship; Division of Overseas Ministries; Foreign Christian Missionary Society, The; United Christian Missionary Society, The

Ann Updegraff Spleth

Division of Overseas Ministries

Disciples program and administrative unit for ecumenical participation in world mission and evangelism; relates to partner churches in sending and receiving missionaries and sharing life in Christ, as well as concern for human rights, witness for peace with justice for all peoples, protection of the environment, and interreligious dialogue and cooperation. Since the 1960s there have been joint executive offices for geographical regions with the United Church Board for World Ministries (UCBWM), later Wider Church Ministries of the United Church of Christ, and full cooperation of the two churches in the Common Global Ministries Board since April 1996. In 2004, approximately 200 missionaries, short-term volunteers, and interns were serving at the invitation of churches, councils of churches, and mission institutions in ninety countries.

The Division of Overseas Ministries (DOM) was created by the restructure of the Disciples in April 1970, when the 120-member board of managers of the United Christian Missionary Society (UCMS) was dissolved and the board of trustees reorganized into separate boards of DOM and the Division of Homeland Ministries (DHM). Upon election by the General Assembly in Cincinnati, October 27, 1973, the DOM board of directors met for the first time November 20, 1973, under the presidency of Robert A. Thomas and chairperson Owen D. Hungerford. To a great extent, the board continued the ministries of the Division of World Mission of the UCMS and related offices dating from 1920 and the founding missionary societies American Christian Missionary Society, Christian Woman's Board of Missions, and Foreign Christian Missionary Society of the nineteenth century.

The first area executives were Robert G. Nelson (Africa), Joseph M. Smith (East Asia), Robert A. Thomas (Europe and the Middle East), Telfer Mook (India and Nepal), William J. Nottingham (Latin America and Caribbean), and Garland Farmer (Finance and Personnel). Mook and Nottingham were joint appointments with UCBWM from the start. Robert Thomas came to the presidency from being senior minister at University Christian Church in Seattle, Washington, bringing to the position the perspective of a local pastor deeply committed to the ecumenical movement and to the process of uniting congregations and regions into a covenantal church. The purpose of restructure and the creation of DOM and DHM was to make global mission a commitment of the whole church and not the voluntary or congregational support of a missionary society. T. J. Liggett, predecessor of Dr. Thomas and successor of Mae Yoho Ward in the Division of World Mission and of A. Dale Fiers and Virgil Sly in the UCMS presidency, made the transition possible, showing the close relation between the practice of mission and the ecclesiology of restructure.

Emphasis on gender equality, diversity, and antiracism has been prominent in the history of DOM, both in the appointment of mission personnel and in the election of officers. Christine Rouse was vice president in 1984, when Alice Langford became treasurer, and Julia Brown Karimu vice president in 1985 and again in 2004. Ann Douglas became Latin America/Caribbean executive in 1977, and Luz Bacerra executive of Southeast Asia for both the Presbyterians and the Disciples in 1984. Faithful to the earlier commitment of UCMS, the board of directors has been 50 percent men and women, and so is the forty-six-member Common Global Ministries Board. There has been constant sharing with the Week of Compassion in the support of fraternal workers, later called global mission interns, since the transfer of the program to DOM in 1971 from DHM volunteer services.

Significant in the years since the founding of DOM has been the struggle against dictatorship in Latin America and East Asia; Disciples or partners were taken prisoner in Argentina, Paraguay, El Salvador, the Philippines, and South Korea in the 1970s and 1980s. The opening of relationships with Pentecostal churches occurred in Cuba, Chile, Nicaragua, along with the older partnership in Venezuela through Juan Marcos and Flor Rivera and Dean and Grace Rogers, later Charles and Ruth Wallace. The Church of North India was formed in 1972 after many years of planning and internal conflict, and part of the Church of Christ in Britain joined with the United Reformed Church of the United Kingdom.

After thirty years of silence, the emergence of the post-denominational church in the People's Republic of China brought the first Christian visitors to Indianapolis in 1979, and in 2000 a Disciple of Chinese origin, Zhu Xiaoling, became executive for East Asia and the Pacific. Consultations with the Disciples of Christ Community of the Church of Christ in Zaire were held in 1980 and 1992, under the leadership of Daniel C. Hoffman, to face the mounting problems of ministry and support, followed by another in 2004 when the country was again Congo and Bonganjalo Goba was executive. The struggle against apartheid in South Africa required the controversial support of the board in 1986 for a grant to the Programme to Combat Racism of the World Council of Churches, under the presidency of Maureen Osuga.

The ecumenical nature of missionary assignments came with the appointment of David Blackburn to work with Dom Helder Camara, Roman Catholic archbishop of Recife, Brazil, and Itoko Maeda with the mission program of the Japanese Kyodan in Bolivia. The first People to People delegation visited Vietnam under the leadership of Barbara Fuller and the presidencies of Jean Tucker and Chris Hobgood in 1983. In the 1990s the Disciples of Jamaica formed with others the United Church in Jamaica and the Cayman Islands, and DOM pursued the complex process of constituting the Common Global Ministries Board with the United Church of Christ. Peace and the creation of a Palestinian state was a priority for justice with ecumenical partners in the Middle East, and the HIV/AIDS crisis became a focus of healing and preventive ministries, especially with churches in Africa.

In the new century, "critical presence" has become DOM/Global Ministries' strategic approach in all phases of its mission. This means to be timely and appropriately meeting God's people and creation at the point of deepest need — spiritually, physically, emotionally, and/or economically. Under this new approach, priority is given to ministries of *acompañamiento* to and with people in critical situations (being there in various forms and modes of presence). This may include pastoral ministries related to fear and hopelessness where people are desperate for meaning; ministries in dangerous or life-threatening situations related to social, economic, or political realities; partners living in countries where the Christian faith is a minority faith; inter-faith relations and conflict resolution; and areas where DOM/Global Ministries can offer a distinctive presence.

Robert A. Thomas was president 1969-83, William J. Nottingham 1984-93, Patricia M. Tucker 1994-2002, and David A. Vargas 2003 to present. They have taken turns with the presidents of DHM to preside over the continuing board of trustees of the UCMS, in cooperation with the Christian Church Foundation. There have been close relations with other units of the church in the General Minister and President's cabinet and on the boards of some units, in cooperation with regional ministers and the General Board of the Church. Since 1996, the DOM president has also been co-executive of the Common Global Ministries Board.

See also American Christian Missionary Society; Christian Woman's Board of Missions; Division of Homeland Ministries; Foreign Christian Missionary Society, The; Restructure; United Christian Missionary Society, The

WILLIAM J. NOTTINGHAM AND DAVID A. VARGAS

Dowling, Enos (1905-1997)

Indiana preacher, librarian at Butler School of Religion (1939-51), founding dean of Lincoln Christian Seminary, and professor there (1953-74).

Dowling taught church history at Lincoln, especially Stone-Campbell history, publishing *The Restoration Movement* (1964) and numerous articles, poems, lessons, lectures, and songs. He undertook significant research in the hymnody of the Movement and compiled the largest collection of Stone-Campbell hymnals (over 180 volumes). In addition, Dowling produced a widely used *Restoration Documents* packet, a compilation of primary sources from the history of the Stone-Campbell Movement. He also restored, compiled, and reprinted more than thirty volumes of early Stone-Campbell documents on subjects such as biblical inspiration and interpretation, atonement, Trinity, Christology, and the name "Christian."

See also Hymnody; Lincoln Christian College and Seminary

BIBLIOGRAPHY Enos Dowling, *The Restoration Movement* (1964) • Enos Dowling, ed., *Hymn and Gospel Song Books of the Restoration Movement: A Preliminary Bibliography* (1975) • Enos Dowling, ed., *Restoration Documents* (1979).

ROBERT F. REA

Drake University

Historically related to the Christian Church (Disciples of Christ).

Drake University was founded as Oskaloosa College, the first Christian college in Iowa. Because of declining economic conditions, the Disciples of Christ in Iowa were forced to move the college. In 1881 a group led by George Thomas Carpenter went to Des Moines and found support there for the move. In March 1881, with a $20,000 pledge from General Francis Marion Drake of Centerville, Iowa, a Civil War general, former Iowa Governor, banker, railroad builder, and attorney, the school was renamed in his honor.

The school's founders wanted an institution that was broad-based and nonsectarian. To establish such an educational climate for the school, they issued the following statement: "This University has been designed upon a broad and modern basis. The articles of incorporation provide that all its departments shall be open to all without distinction of sex, religion or race. In its management and influence, it will aim at being Christian, without being sectarian." The university continues to be guided by this statement of nondiscrimination and the progressive vision of its founders.

Drake has more than 120 acres within ten minutes of downtown Des Moines. It offers more than 75 undergraduate majors and many graduate programs. The university is made up of six colleges and schools: the College of Business and Public Administration, Pharmacy and Health Sciences, and Arts and Sciences (including Fine Arts), and the Schools of Law, Education, and Journalism and Mass Communication. The enrollment is 3,295 undergraduate full-time students and over 1,500 full- and part-time graduate students. The university participates in NCAA Division I athletic events. The Campaign for Drake raised more than $130 million for the university from 1989 to 1994. Drake's second national study commission, Campaign Drake, set a goal of raising $190 million by May 2002.

TERRY MIETHE

Dungan, David R. (1837-1921)

Biblical and hermeneutical scholar of the third generation of the Stone-Campbell Movement.

David Roberts Dungan was born in Noble County, Indiana. In 1852 his family moved to Harrison County, Iowa. Dungan was baptized at 21 and commenced preaching. He married Mary Ann Kinnis in 1861 and had two daughters and eight sons.

He attended Kentucky University (now Transylvania University) and in 1883 received his Master's degree from Drake University. The University of Nebraska conferred the degree of L.L.D. on him in 1891; he served the university as a regent for six years.

In 1860 Dungan preached for a mission cooperative in Iowa and Nebraska. He later served the Nebraska General Missionary Board for six years with R. G. Barrow, planting 137 congregations. He engaged in 37 debates with Mormons, Methodists, Adventists, Baptists, atheists, and Quakers. He was an ardent prohibitionist and wrote in favor of women preaching. He preached in Iowa after 1874, and from 1883 to 1890 taught Bible at Drake University, where he also served as vice president and acting president.

In 1890 he served as president of Cotner College, Lincoln, Nebraska, then as president and dean of the Bible Department of Christian University (now Culver-Stockton College), Canton, Missouri.

Dungan published six books and authored a number of articles, lectures, booklets, and tracts. He also composed an apologetic work on the Movement, *Our Plea and Our Mission* (1876), and a novel entitled *On the Rock* (1872) that likewise commended the Movement's ideals. He contributed a substantial analysis of the Lord's Supper to J. H. Garrison's classic collection of studies on Stone-Campbell thought and practice, *The Old Faith Restated* (1889).

His most significant and enduring book was *Hermeneutics: A Textbook* (1888; 400 pages), reprinted repeatedly since then. Dungan drew upon the hermeneutical principles of Johann August Ernesti (1707-1781), Moses Stuart (1780-1852), and Milton Terry (1846-1914). The thesis of the book is that a sound, inductive hermeneutic will go a long way toward healing the divisions of the church.

See also Bible, Interpretation of the; Cotner College; Culver-Stockton College; Hermeneutics; Literature; Lord's Supper, The; Temperance

BIBLIOGRAPHY M. Eugene Boring, *Disciples and the Bible: A History of Disciples Biblical Interpretation in North America* (1997) • David R. Dungan, *Hermeneutics* (1888) • David R. Dungan, "The Lord's Supper," in *The Old Faith Restated,* ed. J. H. Garrison (1891), pp. 231-53 • David R. Dungan, *On the Rock* (1872) • David R. Dungan, *Our Plea and Our Mission* (1876). THOMAS H. OLBRICHT

Dunlavy, John (1769-1826)

Founder with Barton W. Stone and three other Presbyterian ministers of the Springfield Presbytery in September 1803 and, nine months later, of the Christian Church in the West, prior to uniting with the Shakers.

Dunlavy was born in western Pennsylvania. He received his classical education from Princeton-educated Robert Finley, who had preceded Stone as pastor of the Cane Ridge congregation.

On September 10, 1803, Dunlavy, who was pastor of the Presbyterian Church at Eagle Creek, joined his brother-in-law Richard McNemar (who had also studied with Finley), John Thompson (another graduate of Finley's academy), Robert Marshall, and Barton Stone in withdrawing from the jurisdiction of the Synod of Kentucky. Earlier that week the Synod, meeting in Lexington, had approved the proceedings of Washington Presbytery's October 1802 theological examination of Richard McNemar that had condemned McNemar's views as "dangerous to the souls of men, and hostile to the interests of all true religion." In the same action the Synod had censured the Washington Presbytery for appointing McNemar to preach after having condemned his doctrine and also for rejecting a later petition calling for an examination of John Thompson and a second examination of McNemar in April 1803. Two days later, on September 12, 1803, the five ministers constituted themselves as a presbytery, taking the name Springfield for the town in southern Ohio where the Washington Presbytery had met when it rejected the petition to examine McNemar and Thompson.

Stone reported that following their withdrawal from the jurisdiction of the Synod the growing popularity of the Springfield Presbytery was a concern to its leaders, as they were committed to Christian unity and did not desire to become another denomination or "party." At a meeting of the Presbytery at Cane Ridge in June of 1804 McNemar proposed a solution to the problem of their becoming another "party" or denomination with a document that he had drafted, entitled *Last Will and Testament of Springfield Presbytery.* In signing this document Dunlavy and the other members of the newly formed presbytery willed that their presbytery "die, be dissolved, and sink into union with the Body of Christ at large." At the same meeting they determined to take "no other name than *Christians.*"

Early in the spring of 1805 Shaker missionaries appeared in the West, having been commissioned by the Shaker leadership in New Lebanon, New York, to present their testimony to the Christians. McNemar granted the missionaries permission to address his congregation at Turtle Creek in southern Ohio on Sunday, March 23. The missionaries remained at Turtle Creek for several days, lodging at the home of Malcolm Worley. Worley had been a Presbyterian elder at Turtle Creek and later a licentiate of the Springfield Presbytery. On March 27 he became the first Shaker convert in the West. Within less than a month, McNemar followed suit, along with several other families from the Turtle Creek congregation. On July 29 Dunlavy and several families from the Eagle Creek church also united with the Shakers.

Dunlavy has not been noted for any distinctive contribution to the Springfield Presbytery or the Christian Church. He did, however, make a distinctive contribution to the development of the Shakers. His *The Manifesto, or a Declaration of the Doctrines and Practices of the Church of Christ* (1818) was the first systematic theology of the Shakers. Dunlavy rejected Calvinist ideas of election and reprobation (as had the Springfield Presbytery), as well as the imputation of original sin and the substitutionary interpretation of the atonement (as had the Christians). He underscored the freedom and responsibility of sinners to accept the gospel, Christ as an example for believers, the role of obedience in justification, and the goal of a sinless life. He provided a context for understanding distinctive Shaker practices such as celibacy. He also explicated the Shaker view of the resurrection, which he equated with spiritual regeneration. Historians date the beginnings of Shaker theology from publication of Dunlavy's *Manifesto* and an earlier work by David Darrow, Joseph Meacham, and Benjamin Seth Youngs titled the *Testimony,* which employed a history of salvation genre in contrast to Dunlavy's systematic approach.

See also Springfield Presbytery; *Last Will and Testament of Springfield Presbytery;* McNemar, Richard

BIBLIOGRAPHY Douglas A. Foster, "The Last Will and Testament of Springfield Presbytery: Its Presbyterian Context and Signers," *Stone-Campbell Journal* • Stephen J. Stein, *The Shaker Experience in America: A History of the United Society of Believers* (1992).

D. NEWELL WILLIAMS

Eva Nichols Dye (1877-1951) converted Bolenge into a written language. She wrote the first grammar, a dictionary, school textbooks, and a hymnal and translated much of the Bible into the native tongue, with the help of her husband, missionary doctor Royal John Dye (1874-1966), and others. She is pictured with students of one of her first schools.
Courtesy of the Disciples of Christ Historical Society

Dye, Royal John (1874-1966), and Eva Nichols Dye (1877-1951)

Pioneer medical missionaries to the Congo in Africa who later served as field representatives for the missionary societies, inspiring mission work in subsequent generations.

Born in Iona, Michigan, the Dyes received their medical training in New York; Royal became a doctor and Eva a nurse. The two were ordained on January 16, 1899, married the next day, and sailed for Africa two days later. Together with E. E. Faris, who preceded them, they began the work in Bolenge within that same year. In addition to their medical and evangelistic work, Eva was primarily responsible for converting Bolenge into a written language. She wrote the first grammar, a dictionary, school textbooks, and a hymnal and translated much of the Scriptures into the native tongue, with the help of her husband and others. For much of their African ministry Dr. Dye was the only medical doctor within 1,000 miles of the Congo River. During a furlough, the couple were instrumental in raising the funds for the mission steamer *Oregon,* dedicated in 1909 and used on the river for several decades. Returning to America in 1911, Royal Dye became a field worker for the Foreign Christian Missionary Society and later was field secretary for the United Christian Missionary Society until 1942.

See also Africa, Missions in

BIBLIOGRAPHY Polly Caroline Dye, *In His Glad Service: The Story of Royal J. and Eva Dye* (1975) • Royal J. and Eva N. Dye papers, Disciples of Christ Historical Society.

CLINTON J. HOLLOWAY

E

Eastern Christian College

See Lincoln Christian College and Seminary

Ecclesiastic Reformer

Published in Kentucky from 1848 to 1852, a journal promoting various organizational efforts during a period of intense growth of the Stone-Campbell Movement.

The *Ecclesiastic Reformer* billed itself as a periodical "devoted to practical piety." The editors were also keen supporters of the cooperation movement and devoted many pages to recording in great detail the development of national and statewide cooperative societies.

The *Ecclesiastic Reformer* was begun in Harrodsburg, Kentucky, under the leadership of Carroll Kendrick (1815-1891). Kendrick had been approached in late 1847 by "the leading brothers of this part of Kentucky," who made a written request that he begin publishing a religious paper for the Kentucky area and pledged to cover any losses he might incur in the first year. Given freedom to decide the character of the paper, Kendrick settled upon *Ecclesiastic Reformer* as the title. "We determined," he wrote, "to bend our energies to the *practical reformation of the church*." In his eyes, the church of his era was guilty of being better at theory than at practice. "The disparity between what we *understand* and what we *do* is on the increase." Each issue began with the words of Matthew 7:21, "Not every one who saith unto me Lord, Lord, shall enter into the kingdom of Heaven, but he that doeth the will of my Father, which is in heaven."

Kendrick made every effort to trim costs, and prided himself on the affordability of the periodical. It was largely due to cost concerns that the offices of the paper were moved from Harrodsburg to Frankfort in late 1849. In another cost-cutting effort, the paper changed formats. Originally a weekly periodical, in its later years the *Reformer* was issued in a larger, biweekly edition.

In 1850 the *Ecclesiastic Reformer* began taking special interest in the cooperation effort. "The burden of this paper will be to improve the churches. Subservient to this end, we shall notice, particularly, the general proceedings of the recent [missionary] convention in Cincinnati, and especially the societies there formed and recommended to the brethren."

In 1851 Kendrick moved to Texas to serve as a missionary, and the duties of chief editor were divided among L. L. Pinkerton, J. Jackson, and J. Henshall. They continued to track efforts toward state organization. Among other benefits, they hoped that organization would help promote better pay for ministers. To expect young men to be drawn to the ministry under conditions then current, they believed, would be to "expect a miracle." The paper continued two years under their editorship, before ceasing publication.

Over the course of its five-year run, the *Ecclesiastic Reformer* merged with at least two other papers, the *Christian Mirror* in 1849 and the *Christian Messenger and Bible Advocate* in 1850.

See also Journalism; Pinkerton, Lewis Letig

BIBLIOGRAPHY Carroll Kendrick, "Introduction," *The Ecclesiastic Reformer* 2 (February 24, 1849): 1-2 • Carroll Kendrick, "An Important Change," *The Ecclesiastic Reformer* 2 (December 15, 1849): 645-47 • L. L. Pinkerton, "Introduction," *The Ecclesiastic Reformer* 4 (January 1, 1851): 3-5.

KIRK R. COWELL

Ecclesiology

See Church, Doctrine of the

Ecumenical Movement, The

Twentieth-century movement among numerous Christian bodies to effect the visible unity of the church.

The adjective "ecumenical" is derived from the Greek word *oikoumenē,* which is used in the New Testament to mean "the whole inhabited earth." Gradually, the word came to refer to the whole church, as opposed to that which is divisive, or to the whole faith of the church, as opposed to that which is partial. Any effort aimed at promoting the wholeness of the church — its faith, life, and witness — can properly be called ecumenical.

The term "ecumenical movement," however, has a more particular meaning. Churches are generally said to be participants in the ecumenical movement if they are members of, or work in cooperation with, the World Council of Churches (WCC) or the various national-level councils. Other recognizable expressions of the ecumenical movement include theological dialogues aimed at achieving visible communion and regular, shared celebrations such as the Week of Prayer for Christian Unity.

Unity has always been a prominent theme in discussion of the church, and over the centuries sporadic efforts have been made to heal its evident divisions. In the nineteenth century, individual Christians began to work together, beyond the boundaries of their churches, through such organizations as the YMCA and YWCA, the Student Christian Movement, the World Sunday School Convention, and numerous mission and Bible societies.

The beginning of the ecumenical movement, however, is often identified with a world mission conference held in Edinburgh, Scotland, in 1910. That conference inspired three streams of ecumenical activity that reflect the movement's continuing priorities: (1) "Faith and Order" is that part of the movement concerned with overcoming doctrinal barriers to visible unity of the church (e.g., disagreements over sacraments, ministry, and church authority). (2) "Life and Work" is that part of the movement concerned with fostering common Christian response to such things as war, poverty, oppression, and natural calamity. (3) The International Missionary Council had as its goal the promotion of a more cooperative approach to evangelism and to the support of new churches around the world.

These three streams of modern ecumenism held separate world conferences during the 1920s and 1930s, but by 1937 the leaders of Faith and Order and Life and Work had determined that their efforts should be integrated, a decision that led to the formation of the WCC following World War II. The International Missionary Council joined the WCC in 1961. Creation of the WCC brought unity, service, and mission onto the same agenda; and it also signaled that ecumenism was now a movement of the churches and not only of committed individual Christians.

The ecumenical movement was almost entirely an intra-Protestant affair until 1920, when the Patriarchate of Constantinople, spiritual center of Eastern Orthodox Christianity, issued an encyclical calling for better relations among Christians and for the establishment of a "league between the churches." Several Orthodox churches were founding members of the WCC in 1948, and the remainder of Eastern and Oriental Orthodox churches joined the World Council in the early 1960s.

Until the 1950s the official position of the Roman Catholic Church was that unity could happen only when non-Catholics "returned to the one true church"; thus it forbade its members to participate in ecumenical dialogues or conferences. This changed dramatically, however, when in 1962 Pope John XXIII convened the Second Vatican Council (Vatican II). This gathering of Roman Catholic bishops issued, among other documents, the *Decree on Ecumenism (Unitatis Redintegratio),* which spoke of all baptized Christians as sisters and brothers, deplored the sins against unity committed over the centuries by Catholics and Protestants alike, and called on "the Catholic faithful to take an active and intelligent part in the work of ecumenism." While not a member of the WCC, the Roman Catholic Church works closely with the World Council on numerous projects and sends official participants to its major conferences and assemblies.

Proponents of the ecumenical movement regard the following as among its most notable achievements:

1. Councils of Churches — through which churches engage together in such things as public policy advocacy, emergency relief, worship, and theological discussion — are now present in most U.S. cities and states, as well as in ninety countries.
2. Official church-to-church conversations aimed at overcoming historical divisions have mushroomed since Vatican II, and many of them have reached substantial levels of theological agreement. A good example is the international Lutheran–Roman Catholic dialogue, which led in 1999 to an agreed statement on "justification by faith," the doctrine that was at the heart of Reformation-era controversies.
3. Probably the most influential theological text of the ecumenical movement is *Baptism, Eucharist and Ministry (BEM),* produced by the WCC's Faith and Order Commission and sent to the churches for official response in 1982. *BEM* has been translated into more than forty languages, been used as an official teaching document in many churches, and served as a resource for other ecumenical dialogues.
4. United churches, which result from the structural union of churches from two or more confessional families, have been formed since World War II in countries around the world, including the United

States (e.g., the United Church of Christ). Over the past generation, churches have been less inclined toward structural union and more inclined toward the development of covenants that include the sharing of sacraments and mission. A major example of this trend is the 2002 inauguration of Churches Uniting in Christ, which involves nine U.S. denominations, three of which are predominantly African American.

5. For much of the nineteenth and twentieth centuries, mission was a matter of churches in traditionally Christian countries sending missionaries and resources to other parts of the world. Contact brought about by the ecumenical movement, however, has helped churches, in many cases, move from patterns of dependency to reciprocal, partner relationships.
6. Proselytism, the use of coercion or improper persuasion in order to convince other Christians to join "our church," has been repeatedly rejected by churches involved in the ecumenical movement.
7. Churches involved in the movement have frequently come to one another's assistance since World War II through such organizations as Church World Service, which, until recently, was a department of the National Council of the Churches of Christ in the U.S.A. (NCCC). Ecumenical dialogue has also forged a broad commitment to condemn racism as incompatible with Christian faith; and concerted ecumenical action contributed to the collapse of apartheid in South Africa.
8. Local ecumenical initiatives — including social justice networks, yoked ministries, interdenominational chaplaincies, and community-wide worship on special occasions — have so proliferated that it is impossible to keep track of them.

All parts of the Stone-Campbell Movement are committed to the unity of the church, but only the Disciples of Christ have participated fully in the ecumenical movement described above. The Christian Church (Disciples of Christ) in the U.S. and Canada was a founding member of the WCC and of the NCCC. The Disciples of Christ was one of the nine member churches of the Consultation on Church Union (COCU), which led to the formation of Churches Uniting in Christ and has entered into a full communion relationship with the United Church of Christ. Energy and direction for this work have come from the Disciples Council on Christian Unity, the first agency of its kind created by a denomination to promote the unity of the church.

Through what is known as the Disciples Ecumenical Consultative Council, Disciples around the world have been in dialogue with the Roman Catholic Church since 1977. International dialogues have also been undertaken with the Russian Orthodox Church and the World Alliance of Reformed Churches. Disciples communities in Japan, the Philippines, Thailand, southern Africa, north India, the Congo, and the United Kingdom have become part of united churches in those countries.

Disciples ministers such as Peter Ainslie and Charles Clayton Morrison were present at early conferences of Life and Work and Faith and Order; and over the past half century Disciples have given prominent leadership to ecumenical organizations. Roy Ross and Joan Campbell have served as general secretaries of the U.S. National Council of Churches, Paul Crow and Michael Kinnamon as general secretaries of the Consultation on Church Union. Disciples have also directed numerous state and local councils.

Perhaps the phrase that best expresses the motivation for such involvement in the ecumenical movement is "Christians only but not the only Christians." Disciples leaders argue that other denominations — despite different baptismal practices, different patterns of decision making, and use of creeds — are parts of the one body of Christ. Disciples continue to witness to their historic understanding of church, but they do so through cooperation and dialogue. The "sharing of gifts" that comes through ecumenical relations is, Disciples contend, an appropriate way to pursue the "polar star" of unity.

Individual members of Churches of Christ and Christian Churches/Churches of Christ do, in some places, participate in ministerial associations or take part in local ecumenical events. Individual scholars from both of these streams have been members of the NCCC's Faith and Order Commission. Generally speaking, however, the congregations and members of the Churches of Christ and Christian Churches/Churches of Christ have avoided involvement in the organizations and activities of the ecumenical movement for at least three reasons.

First, they have argued, along with other evangelical churches, that the ecumenical movement pursues unity at the expense of truth. Some members maintain that their community *is* the one church, founded at Pentecost, and thus that unity can occur only when believers join in local congregations on the basis of the pure teachings of Scripture set forth in the Stone-Campbell Movement. Others, while acknowledging members of other churches as Christians, still contend that agreement on key restoration principles must precede cooperation or union.

Second, prominent ecumenical bodies such as the WCC have been frequently identified with what are often perceived as left-wing causes: for example, economic justice for the poor and support for groups engaged in sometimes violent struggles against oppression. Most councils of churches have not taken stands on such issues as abortion and homosexuality, but they include churches with "liberal" positions on these subjects.

Third, even if they are inclined toward ecumenical participation, leaders of the Churches of Christ and Christian Churches/Churches of Christ find it difficult to know how to connect with the movement. Membership in a council of churches, for example, is generally by denomination or regional judicatory. This does not fit the organizational pattern of either group.

At the turn of the twenty-first century, leaders of both the world and national councils were expressing a desire to reach out to a wider range of churches — which means taking account of criticisms leveled at the movement by churches not previously involved. These efforts may be complicated, however, by other likely developments, including greater attention to interfaith dialogue.

See also Ainslie, Peter; Consultation on Church Union; Council on Christian Unity; Disciples Ecumenical Consultative Council; Disciples of Christ–Roman Catholic International Dialogue; Morrison, Charles Clayton; Unity, Christian

BIBLIOGRAPHY Jeffrey Gros, Eamon McManus, and Ann Riggs, *Introduction to Ecumenism* (1998) • Michael Kinnamon and Brian E. Cope, eds., *The Ecumenical Movement: An Anthology of Key Texts and Voices* (1997) • Nicholas Lossky, ed., *Dictionary of the Ecumenical Movement* (1991) • Ruth Rouse, Stephen Neill, and Harold Edward Fey, *A History of the Ecumenical Movement, 1517-1948,* 4th ed. (1993).

MICHAEL KINNAMON

Education

See Education, Philosophy of; Higher Education, Views of in the Movement

Education, Philosophy of

Philosophical and biblical-hermeneutical framework for the education of human beings both in religious and secular (public school) contexts.

The Stone-Campbell Movement's mid-nineteenth-century educational philosophy revolved around one central frontier educator: Alexander Campbell (1788-1866). With the social and cultural development of the American frontier, his educational philosophy underwent numerous challenges and diverse interpretations well beyond his death.

Campbell believed that the immediate goal of education should be the religious and moral endowment of the individual person. Intellectual cultivation facilitated that end. God's revelation to humankind in the Bible contained the basis of all morality. Espousing an epistemology informed by Baconian science, Lockean empiricism, and Scottish Common Sense philosophy, Campbell viewed the human mind as a blank slate *(tabula rasa)* on which could be impressed the moral precepts of divine revelation. These were learned and imbued through experience; they were not innate to the person, to be coaxed out by instruction, a method often employed in the prevailing Idealist (Platonic-Augustinian-Calvinist) tradition.

Campbell's educational epistemology developed in tandem with his biblical hermeneutics. Wrong interpretation equaled wrong morality. Campbell's hermeneutics, shared by the early leaders of the Movement, needed neither the Roman Catholic Church's official interpretation of Scripture nor Calvinism's "mystical" illumination via the Holy Spirit to come to grips with the Bible's moral directives. Any person schooled in the proper hermeneutical tools could experience proper moral direction through disciplined, rational biblical study.

Development of proper moral conduct necessitated an appropriate and ongoing educational experience, one that clearly presupposed the freedom of the will. Campbell rejected, as did his followers, the Calvinistic notion that God's grace descended irresistibly on God's elect, enabling them to understand the Bible. Divine illumination played no part in Campbell's educational philosophy. Exercising the rational will alone enabled the human to appropriate the Bible's moral message.

Campbell further believed that the Bible, more than any other book, should be studied in the "common school" (tax-supported public school) because it promoted a common morality. Biblical moral principles, again, were directly available to any rational reader/interpreter, regardless of background or gender, and, with the right instructional discipline, all persons could appropriate those principles in a way that would serve the amelioration of society. Ideally for Campbell, the educational experience, from parental instruction in infancy, through the early years of common school, and on through the college, should actualize the student's moral potential and equip that student to be useful in society, and, as a consequence, to enjoy happiness. Felicity was a natural outgrowth of proper moral conduct in society. Therefore, personal morality was not an end in itself; it was a means to an end: the good society.

For Campbell, knowledge of any kind, human or divine, came via sense experience. Moral ideas, ultimately originating with God and revealed through the Bible, penetrated the domain of human experience and could be written on the mind. Thus it was imperative to strengthen the powers of reason in order more properly to entertain those moral ideas when presented in the biblical-educational experience. For Campbell, reason and revelation went hand in hand. Not unlike St. Thomas Aquinas long before him, Campbell saw God reaching down to humankind with revelation, and earthlings reaching up to God through reason, experience being the common meeting ground for both. In this experience the human exercised four powers: instinct, the five senses, reason, and faith. Human instinct at best was feeble. The five senses were shared with the animal world. Reason, however, distinguished the human from the animal since it allowed one to order the world logically. But faith, the most ennobling of all the human powers, enabled one to accept the testimony of others, past and present, and particularly the testimony of divine revelation.

Since the Bible, according to Campbell, could be taught and understood in a rational, nonmystical manner, its common moral-religious principles could escape sectarian manipulation. Horace Mann (1796-1859), renowned Massachusetts educator and contemporary of Campbell, fought diligently to rid the state's schools of frequent sectarian control of education. Mann, affiliated with the Christian movement in New England and himself a Sunday School teacher, advocated biblical, nonsectarian teaching, similar to Campbell's, in the public schools. Not surprisingly, both incurred the wrath of religious establishments. Charged with advocating a godless classroom, Campbell and Mann alike countered that the Bible was a universal moral textbook sufficient (alone sufficient) to support a common morality.

Ideally Campbell felt that the common school should develop a student's ability to employ the "seven arts" of thinking, speaking, reading, singing, writing, calculating, and bookkeeping. These "seven arts" constituted a pragmatic and teleological discipline, stressing process as much as content, skills more than simple memorization, long a staple of Western education.

These arts meshed the moral and intellectual, and prepared the student for the collegiate experience. Campbell thoroughly dismissed rank rationalism, however, declaring it a dangerous enemy of moral training, resulting, he feared, in morally rudderless individuals. True morality and community derived from divine revelation, not from human reason or ingenuity — a position Campbell had hammered out in his 1829 debate with socialist philosopher Robert Owen.

In 1840 Alexander Campbell established Bethany College, where he hoped to put into practice what he had so long advocated. He deemphasized, but did not eliminate, the traditional classical studies derived from the trivium (grammar, logic, and rhetoric) and the quadrivium (arithmetic, music, geometry, and astronomy), instead encouraging a more Enlightenment-oriented and pragmatic curriculum. Bethany's areas of learning included (1) ancient languages and history; (2) algebra and general mathematics; (3) chemistry; (4) natural philosophy and other natural sciences; (5) mental philosophy, evidences of Christianity, morals, and political economy; and (6) grammar, logic, rhetoric, and criticism. Clearly science and historical topics enjoyed a heightened presence, undergirded by the Bible as the basis of all the arts and sciences.

Early twentieth-century photograph of Bethany College. Like many in his day, Alexander Campbell had believed that schools should be established far from the distracting influences of urban life. Courtesy of the Disciples of Christ Historical Society

Campbell himself lectured daily on various religious, biblical, and moral topics, but he wanted Bethany to be neither a seminary nor a theological school, for which he had contempt; both alternatives he saw as sectarian. Nevertheless, to graduate from Bethany required a diploma that certified the student's intellectual and moral preparedness.

Though Campbell promoted primarily his own beloved Bethany, he supported other educational efforts such as Bacon College in Harrodsburg, Kentucky (named after Francis Bacon, the founder of the inductive scientific method), and Franklin College in Nashville, Tennessee. Campbell had encouraged education of slaves in the antebellum period and was a strong proponent of women's education, endorsing a number of female academies that he held to the same philosophical standard as all other schools.

From the inception of Bethany (1840) through the twentieth century, the relative presence or absence of the Bible within the Stone-Campbell tradition of higher education — diversely manifested in liberal arts colleges and universities, seminaries and divinity schools, Bible chairs in secular colleges, and the Bible colleges themselves — has sparked controversy. When biblical higher criticism came into its own at the turn of the twentieth century, a major controversy arose between conservatives and liberals over the relative importance of the secular sciences in understanding and interpreting the Bible. Campbell established the theme of biblically centered holistic education; others produced a broad range of variations on that theme. Through the twentieth century, Stone-Campbell liberal arts colleges and universities were inevitably challenged to find a golden mean between biblical and secular learning, with the result that not a few liberal arts schools — like many in other American Protestant denominations — underwent increasing secularization and saw a departmentalization (critics would say compartmentalization) of biblical instruction. Bible colleges, on the other hand, originally fiercely protective of a biblically focused curriculum, were challenged to accommodate more and more of the liberal arts in an effort to be holistic, and to afford their graduates vocational opportunities within secular society.

Alexander Campbell emphasized, however, that whatever the balance, educational philosophy should lead to uniting "the pair so long disjoin'd, knowledge and vital piety." Short of that goal and its social embodiments, education would utterly fail in its moral obligations.

See also Anthropology; Bethany College; Campbell, Alexander; Campbell-Owen Debate; Common Sense Philosophy; Educational Ministry; Higher Education, Views of in the Movement; Locke, John; Reason, Place of

BIBLIOGRAPHY Alexander Campbell, "Address: Is Moral Philosophy an Inductive Science?" *Popular Lectures and Addresses* (1866), pp. 95-124 • "Address on Colleges," *Popular Lectures and Addresses* (1866), pp. 291-310 • Alexander Campbell, "Address on Common Schools," *Popular Lectures and Addresses* (1866), pp. 247-71 • Alexander Campbell, "Address on Education," *Popular Lectures and Addresses* (1866), pp. 230-46 • Alexander Campbell, "Address on the Importance of Uniting the Moral with the Intellectual Culture of the Mind," *Popular Lectures and Addresses* (1866), pp. 453-84 • Duane D. Cummins, "Educational Philosophy of Alexander Campbell," *Discipliana* 59 (1999): 5-15 • Morris A. Eames, *The Philosophy of Alexander Campbell* (1966) • Perry E. Gresham, *Campbell and the Colleges* (1973) • John L. Morrison, *Alexander Campbell: Educating the Moral Person* (1991) • Thomas H. Olbricht, "Alexander Campbell as an Educator," in *Lectures in Honor of the Alexander Campbell Bicentennial* (1988), pp. 79-100 • William B. Sharratt, "The Theory of Religious Education of Alexander Campbell and Its Influence upon the Educational Attitudes of the Disciples of Christ" (Ph.D. dissertation, New York University, 1930) • L. Thomas Smith, Jr., "The Amelioration of Society: Alexander Campbell and Educational Reform in Antebellum America" (Ph.D. dissertation, University of Tennessee, 1990) • Gerald C. Tiffin, "Disciples and Higher Education: Nineteenth Century Roots and Twenty-First Century Concerns," *Discipliana* 59 (1999): 17-24.

JOHN L. MORRISON

Educational Ministry

1. Christian Church (Disciples of Christ)
2. Christian Churches/Churches of Christ
3. Churches of Christ
4. Summary

Within five years of the beginning of the first Sunday School in England, the United States began to see the development of this phenomenon on their own shores. The movement was led by the American Sunday School Union, established in 1824. The aim of this union was to teach the Bible in local congregations. Neither Alexander Campbell nor Barton Stone supported the Sunday School movement, as they saw the union as trying to teach and enforce creeds and doctrines of sectarian religious establishments. Stone, however, saw great value in Sunday Schools that taught the poor to read. Only over time did the founders recognize the need for such educational endeavors as Sunday Schools, in addition to the important educational roles of schools and the family.

1. Christian Church (Disciples of Christ)

In the 1840s Stone-Campbell Movement churches formed a Sunday School Society, holding a national convention in 1849. However, it was not until the National Bible School Association became part of the American Christian Missionary Society that a successful effort in educational ministry began. Between 1860 and 1903 churches in Ohio, Indiana, Illinois, Kentucky, Missouri, Michigan, Kansas, Oregon, Iowa, and southern California began state Sunday School organizations. Leaders in this effort were Isaac Errett, J. W. McGarvey, A. C. Hopkins, and others.

In the larger history of Protestant Christian education in America the period from 1860 to 1910 has been called the era of the "Sunday School Movement." During this period, emphasis was placed on the training of teachers and the development of uniform lessons. Initially, Disciples produced their own curriculum, a series of question books based on various biblical books. In the late 1800s they began to embrace the International Lessons for educational resources. The Bible, however, remained the primary focus of curriculum.

A series of developments between 1910 and 1960 were significant for the development of educational ministry in the Disciples of Christ. In 1910 the Disciples acquired a publishing house, the Christian Board of Publication. Then the United Christian Missionary Society was created in 1920, which brought the American Christian Missionary Society and other Disciples organizations under one administration. Through a series of transitions, the Sunday School Council of Evangelical Denominations and the International Sunday School Association became the International Council of Religious Education in 1922, which later emerged as the Division of Christian Education of the National Council of Churches in the U.S.A. in 1950. In 1914 Disciples educational leader Walter Scott Athearn had introduced and lobbied for the Church School concept, which promoted the incorporation of education into all components of congregational life. As for curriculum, a new pedagogical approach had begun in 1910, when Protestant denominations started using curricula designed for specific age groups. Though struggles emerged and subsided over curriculum content, the majority of Disciples saw the Church School approach as a way to incorporate into congregational life many of their primary beliefs: freedom, ecumenism, historical study of the Bible, an emphasis on education for all, and the accessibility of God's word to all persons.

Another important reform of religious education, in which the Disciples took an energetic lead, was the development of religious education as a profession. In 1906 Eureka College offered the first religious education courses at a Disciples college. The first undergraduate professorship in religious education was established at Drake University in 1910, and a similar step was taken by Bethany College in 1914. Soon, all Disciples four-year undergraduate institutions had chairs or departments in religious education. Likewise, the educational endeavors of the American Christian Missionary Society were expanded to include more than just Sunday School classes on Sunday mornings. Strides were made in missionary education, church camp curriculum, and other methods to incorporate education into the mission of the church.

Disciples have maintained a commitment to the Church School approach of Athearn. Some congregations find that their children's and youth programs prosper but adult education falters, while others have experienced the opposite. Feeling the effects of cultural developments, Church School has struggled along with other programs offered by Disciples congregations. Educational ministry, though, continues to branch out into new arenas such as small groups, spiritual development, and lay theological education. With declining membership and the financial struggles of the publishing house, Disciples (like all moderate to liberal mainstream Protestant denominations) will continue to face important decisions about the role of education in their future.

LISA W. DAVISON

2. Christian Churches/Churches of Christ

Christian education, as it is called among the Christian Churches/Churches of Christ, in contrast to the term "religious education" used by many in mainstream denominations, includes Sunday Schools, youth groups, children's church, Vacation Bible School, small groups, and sometimes camping experiences.

Many early Stone-Campbell leaders were wary of the Sunday School movement because they feared it would become a center for creedal teaching. However, the commitment of the early leaders to an informed, educated membership, along with the rapid growth and apparent success of the Sunday School in the United States, soon eased some of their concerns. Sunday Schools became a part of Stone-Campbell churches from an early date. Other Christian education programs such as youth groups and Vacation Bible School found their way into Stone-Campbell churches as these programs were developed.

Much of the history of Christian education in local churches in the Christian Churches/Churches of Christ is interwoven with the history of Standard Publishing Company in Cincinnati, Ohio. From its earliest days, the *Christian Standard,* under the leadership of Isaac Errett, each week featured a treatment of the International Sunday School lesson, a practice that continued into the twenty-first century.

In the last quarter of the nineteenth century Standard Publishing Company launched *The Lookout* to be a voice for Christian education in the local church. *The Lookout* became a strong influence, especially for Sunday School, in the early part of the twentieth century when Herbert Moninger (1876-1911) was called from a highly successful pastorate in Zanesville, Ohio, to be the editor of the magazine. Moninger used the pages of this journal to promote Sunday School development in local churches. One of the most aggressive campaigns was the Loyal Movement in which *The Lookout* promoted the establishment of Loyal classes in every church of its readership. Classes were begun — Loyal Men, Loyal Women, Loyal Daughters, Loyal Sons — all designed to expand Sunday Schools and engage people in Bible study. The success of the movement can be identified even today: many churches with a long history still have a Loyal Women's class or a Loyal class of some kind.

Moninger knew that if the Loyal Movement were to work, it would require aggressive teacher training in local churches. He developed a program he called Training for Service, a nearly year-long program designed to acquaint would-be teachers with the Bible and how to teach it. He himself taught it in many churches in the Cincinnati area. The Training for Service materials have remained for a century, revised first by C. J. Sharp, then by Orin Root, then by Eleanor Daniel, and are still available in a twenty-six week course called "Training for Service: A Survey of the Bible." Moninger's life was cut short at age 35, but his influence remained. Adult Bible classes were a strong and enduring part of Christian Churches/Churches of Christ, some of these classes being very large.

Standard Publishing also led in efforts to develop childhood education in the local church. Near the end of the second decade of the twentieth century, they hired Lily Faris, a professor at Ohio University, to develop their early childhood curriculum. Miss Lily, as she was fondly known, developed what were then innovative teaching methods for children. Her most enduring methodological contribution was flannelgraph, which became a staple for teaching children. She was also a masterful storyteller and provided many stories for teaching children. Like Moninger, she engaged in training local church teachers for effective work.

The third major Standard Publishing contribution was Vacation Bible School (VBS) curriculum. The VBS had been introduced before the turn of the century, but it was Standard that first provided a VBS curriculum that could be used by the local churches. They have produced VBS curriculum annually since toward the end of the second decade of the nineteenth century.

By the 1920s, Christian education in local churches was well established. From that time, however, some among the Disciples of Christ and Christian Churches began to pursue divergent routes. Many of the larger churches were influenced by educators such as William Clayton Bower (1878-1982), who was trained in biblical higher criticism and engaged in the progressive education movement as the two became articulated as a philosophy by the Religious Education Association. Christian Churches/Churches of Christ continued their emphasis on basic Bible literacy and generally used curricula obtained from Standard Publishing Company. Increasingly, Disciples of Christ turned to the Christian Board of Publication for resources.

On the whole, Christian Churches/Churches of Christ continued their Christian education ministries with lay leadership while Disciples of Christ were more likely to have professional educators on their staff. This situation remained much the same until the 1960s. During the 1960s and 1970s, many Christian Churches/Churches of Christ began to add staff persons whose function was to work with lay leaders on existing Christian education programs and to develop new programs. By the 1990s, professional Christian education leadership in local churches was a norm among Christian Churches/Churches of Christ, even in relatively small congregations.

The current state of Christian education in the local church among Christian Churches/Churches of Christ is mixed. Many have thriving programs with a wide variety of teaching activities and resources for all age levels. Others continue to have traditional programs, but with little engagement from the average church member and little enthusiasm for the programs they do have. Some churches have opted to eliminate adult Sunday School, moving instead to small groups. But others use small groups as a supplement to their adult Sunday School classes that serve as strong teaching and shepherding groups. Curricula are as varied as programming. Some churches continue to use the curriculum from Standard Publishing; others seek curricula from a wide variety of sources. ELEANOR A. DANIEL

3. Churches of Christ

At the beginning of the twentieth century Churches of Christ experienced sharp disagreements over the legitimacy of Sunday Schools, reflecting attitudes from the Movement's earliest leaders. Many congregations began to incorporate classes based on age into their programs. The most conservative restorationists in Churches of Christ objected to the Sunday School because it was not authorized by Scripture. Others opposed it because, as conducted by other religious bodies, it was an extracongregational organization with its own officers and governance. The fact that women often taught the classes was another point of contention for some. Several hundred non-Bible-class congregations had separated from mainstream Churches of Christ by the 1920s. These churches emphasize the responsibility of parents to teach their children and the corporate nature of instruction in the church. The majority of Churches of Christ, however, accepted the Sunday School as an integral part of their educational ministry.

The Gospel Advocate and Firm Foundation publishing houses were producing Sunday School and Bible study materials for all ages by the early twentieth century. For many years the biblical texts for the curricula followed the Uniform Lessons used by most Protestant denominations. Two other major publishers of Christian education material among Churches of Christ in the twentieth century were Twentieth Century Christian (founded 1938) and Sweet Publishing Company (founded c. 1946), the latter publishing a widely used series of literature titled *Journeys Through the Bible.*

Training of Sunday School teachers became an important early focus in Churches of Christ. Among the earliest educators who developed teacher training materials were Jesse P. Sewell (1876-1969) and Henry Eli Speck (1885-1966), who coauthored *The Church and Her Ideal Educational Situation* in 1933 and conducted hundreds of "Training for Service" schools across the country. Henry E. Speck, Jr., also a leader in Christian education, revised his father's book in 1963 and taught Christian education for many years in the Bible department of Abilene Christian College. In the 1980s Sweet Publishing Company adapted a curriculum from Gospel Light Publications based on cognitive discovery concepts, developing an extensive teacher training program known as NTI (National Training Institute). Sweet sent Christian educators to churches across the United States to conduct workshops for teachers in this new approach.

Local churches began to hire full-time staff devoted to Christian education in the mid-1950s. One of the first was Fred G. Allen, Jr. (1918-2000), who in 1956 was hired by the Jackson Park Church of Christ in Nashville, Tennessee. In 1960 the first meeting of what would become the Christian Education Conference drew twenty full-time education directors in Churches of Christ. Duties of these education directors included selecting and training teachers, organizing Vacation Bible Schools and the overall Bible School curriculum, purchasing literature, and making recommendations on equipment needed and building needs for the most effective teaching.

Several colleges affiliated with Churches of Christ added departments of Christian education to train education ministers in the mid-twentieth century. At the end of the century, however, traditional emphases on Christian education in colleges and churches gave way to specialization in areas such as youth, children's, and family ministry.

In 1955 Abilene Christian University began a special annual summer gathering for Bible school teachers known as the Bible Teachers Workshop. The following year educators in Churches of Christ began a monthly journal titled *Christian Bible Teacher*. Designed to give Bible School teachers of all age groups continuing training and materials, the magazine continues to be published into the twenty-first century. Christian Education Conferences, conducted under the auspices of the Christian Education Association, have met continuously since 1960 (except 1962). DOUGLAS A. FOSTER

4. Summary

On the whole, it seems that no common philosophy of education would characterize churches of the Stone-Campbell Movement in the earliest days of the twenty-first century. But the growing churches have strong, active, professionally led Christian education programs with a high level of volunteer involvement.

See also Camps; Christian Board of Publication; Errett, Isaac; *Lookout, The;* McGarvey, John W.; Standard Publishing Company; Sweet Publishing Company; Twenty-first Century Christian; Youth Groups, Youth Ministry

BIBLIOGRAPHY Christian Education Association, http://www.christianeducator.org/history.html • Eleanor A. Daniel and John W. Wade, eds., *Foundations for Christian Education* (1999) • James DeForest Murch, *Christian Education in the Local Church* (1943) • Bill Patterson, "Educational Ministry Home Page," http://cconline.faithsite.com/default.asp?FP=1354 • J. Cy Rowell and Jack L. Seymour, "Identity and Unity: Disciples of Christ Education," in *A Case Study of Mainstream Protestantism: The Disciples' Relation to American Culture, 1880-1989,* ed. D. Newell Williams (1991) • Joseph Enloe Sanders, "Major Theological Beliefs of Churches of Christ and Their Implications for Christian Education" (Ph.D. dissertation, Boston University, 1957) • John Ralph Scudder, Jr., "A History of Disciple Theories of Religious Education," *The College of the Bible Quarterly* 40 (April 1963): 7-80 • Henry E. Speck, Jr., *The Church's Educational Program* (1963) • David Wray, "Patterns of Classroom Instruction Since 1970," in *Christian Scholars Conference 1985 Papers* (1985).

Elders, Eldership

Office of supervisory ministry in the local congregation historically understood in the Stone-Campbell Movement, through comparative interpretation of Acts and the Pauline epistles, to be one and the same office as that of "bishop."

A distinctive history has shaped the ministry of eldership in the churches of the Stone-Campbell Movement. Alexander Campbell sought to reform and unite the Protestant churches in his adopted America. One of the obstacles to overcome was a system of ministry dependent upon leadership of the clergy. He saw a clergy system that produced individuals who could all too easily be caricatured as self-interested, sectarian, and authoritarian. He believed that this system discouraged ministry of the whole body of Christ. Campbell's reformation, including its leadership, was defined, and given direction and energy, by close study of the New Testament. He had also learned much from the Scottish reformers Robert and James Haldane on social worship and William Ballantine on eldership. As stated in his chapter on ministry in the *Christian System,* Campbell sought to restore the "immutable ministry of the Christian community . . . composed of bishops, deacons, and evangelists." Christ's own ministry was lodged in a royal priesthood, the community of believers; but that did not mean that all persons of the church were suited and equipped to do all things or to serve in positions of ministerial leadership.

Evangelists did not serve the congregations directly but, as in the primitive church, as itinerants sent out by the congregations for the proclamation of the gospel, making converts, and planting churches. Deacons, like elders, focused their ministries within a given congregation. They were called by and accountable to the congregation. They served the functions of treasurers, almoners, stewards, doorkeepers, and messengers.

Elders *(presbyteroi),* also called bishops or overseers *(episkopoi)* in the New Testament, were authorized by the congregation "to preside over, to instruct, and to edify the community — to feed the church of the Lord with knowledge and understanding — and to watch for their souls as those that must give account to the Lord at his appearing." Each congregation was to have or to equip local persons qualified by biblical standards to serve as elder. The combined gifts of teaching, shepherding, overseeing, and presiding were beyond the qualifications of any one individual. The congregations needed to be led by a local group of bishops, a "plurality" of elders. According to Campbell, these officers were to be ordained and compensated. On the latter score, however, congregations typically fell short of Campbell's teaching.

Alexander Campbell's view of the office of elder was further articulated in the second generation by Robert Milligan, who studied in some detail the New Testament evidence of a "permanent" ministry and reiterated the identification of elders and bishops. Milligan also warned against any confusion of the separate offices of elder and evangelist. Elders were to attend principally to the spiritual interests and pastoral needs of the congregation. "This is the limit of their office. This is their proper sphere of labor. To preach the gospel to the heathen, they have no commission."

Yet the early appropriation of Campbell's views did not endure without some rethinking and adjustment as new issues began to emerge. One such issue was the official ministerial status of "settled" preachers in local congregations. As early as the 1840s some congregations began to invite young college graduates to settle in their communities. In contrast to the pattern that had developed with the earlier elders, these individuals were to be compensated for performing ministerial duties. By 1865 a specialized "College of the Bible" in Lexington, Kentucky, was graduating leaders to minister to the congregations. The arrival of a located, compensated, professional ministry produced fundamental changes in the Movement's "system" of ministry.

Two opposing views developed simultaneously on adjusting the established system of ministry to accommodate the new professional ministry. The discussion was lengthy and heated during the 1890s. J. W. McGarvey and L. B. Wilkes championed the view that the minister was principally a hired evangelist. Ministers, according to this view, were "settled" evangelists who served at the call of the elders and under their strict supervision. The professional minister was clearly subject to the oversight and rule of the elders.

The opposite view, held by influential journalists such as Isaac Errett and J. H. Garrison, was that the minister was himself an elder. In fact, the minister was the leading elder, a first among equals. Elders would advise, serve at the Lord's Table, and shepherd. The minister, as elder, would carry primary responsibility for teaching and preaching.

The twentieth century saw the Stone-Campbell Movement divide into three separate fellowships. The Churches of Christ have primarily followed and developed the position of J. W. McGarvey, whereby the minister is subject to the local elders. These congregations have also placed a high value on having elders whose knowledge of Scripture is mature enough to qualify them in oversight and teaching as well as in governance.

Congregations of the Christian Churches/Churches of Christ adopted one or the other of these traditional models and sometimes experienced tension in the congregation over which model was preferable. In addition, the Christian Churches/Churches of Christ in the late twentieth century saw changes in eldership with the development of so-called megachurches. In those cases the minister often assumed a role paralleling that of a corporate chief executive officer. Elders in such large congregations are called together for advice and consent. In cases of extreme conflict they may hold veto power over the proposals of the pastor.

Only a very few Christian Churches/Churches of Christ ordain women to eldership in local congregations, and there is no discernible widespread trend in that direction either in those churches or in Churches of Christ.

For years the Christian Church (Disciples of Christ) largely disempowered the eldership as a ruling office with the introduction of functional committees and term-limited boards. Elders became "honorary" figures who were by-and-large respected as informal shepherds and valued for their iconic presence as they shared ministry with their pastor(s) at the Lord's Table. Historian Ronald Osborn explained the "mystique" of Disciples elders, deriving especially from their service at the Lord's Supper, with the spiritual witness of the prayers at the Table of persons who made a living in vocations very different from church ministry.

The Disciples of Christ in the late twentieth century have seen a revitalization of elders in some congregations. Women began to serve as elders after serious discussion, often taking several years. Their knowledge, often their passion for mission, their deep spirituality, and their sense of vocation contributed to the renewal of the ministry of eldership. Also, the Disciples Seminary Foundation and the Division of Homeland Ministries did extensive work in reempowering elders as teachers, shepherds, and "wisdom figures" in congregational governance.

The Stone-Campbell eldership, often perceived as an anomaly in churches outside that tradition, has survived and often prospered, demonstrating flexibility while staying deeply rooted in the ministerial system recommended by Alexander Campbell.

See also Deacons, Diaconate; Evangelism, Evangelists; Ministry

BIBLIOGRAPHY H. Leo Boles, *The Eldership of the Churches of Christ* (n.d.) • Alexander Campbell, *The Christian System* (1839) • Albert Lewis Deveny, *The Church and Its Elders: A Study in Spiritual Mechanics* (1941); Robert Milligan, "The Permanent Christian Ministry," no. 2: "Of Elders," *Millennial Harbinger* (1855): 685-93 • J. W. McGarvey, *A Treatise on the Eldership: A Series of Editorial Articles Originally Published in the "Apostolic Times"* (1870) • Peter M. Morgan, *Disciples Eldership: A Quest for Identity and Ministry* (1986) • Ronald E. Osborn, "The Eldership Among Disciples of Christ," *Mid-Stream* 6 (1967): 74-112 • W. R. Walker, *A Functioning Eldership* (1942) • D. Newell Williams, *Ministry Among Disciples: Past, Present, and Future* (1985) • Flavil R. Yeakley, Jr., *Church Leadership and Organization: A Doctrinal and Practical Study of the Leadership Role of Elders* (1986). PETER M. MORGAN

Elmore, Robert Emmett (1878-1968)

Conservative activist and editor in the early- and mid-twentieth-century opposition to perceived denominationalism among the Disciples of Christ.

As secretary on the Executive Committee of the Foreign Christian Missionary Society, Elmore in 1920 first came into public prominence by calling attention to the practice of "open membership" among Disciples missionaries in China, which helped bring about the eruption of a long and widespread controversy over the issue.

Elmore, along with James DeForest Murch, was an instrumental leader of the Cincinnati-based Christian Restoration Association (CRA), which sought to hold the Disciples to strict "restoration" standards of unity, ecclesiology, and mission. Elmore served as editor of the conservative journal *The Touchstone* (formerly *The Spotlight*) from 1925 to 1927, and later of *The Restoration Herald*, voice of the CRA, from 1938 until 1960. In this capacity Elmore heavily criticized what he viewed as the agents of ecclesiasticism, especially the United Christian Missionary Society (UCMS).

Distinctive of Elmore's defiance was his identification of the UCMS, open membership, ecumenism, and liberal theology as merely facets of one and the same modernism or "rationalism" threatening to undermine the Stone-Campbell Movement. The Disciples of Christ, in his view, were at a cultural crossroads to decide whether they would remain faithful to the work of restoring New Testament Christianity or align themselves with the trappings of "progressive" culture ("Social Christianity," the religion of psychology, German historical-critical scholarship, etc.). Elmore himself came under fierce criticism from Disciples "cooperatives" such as Stephen Corey, whose book documenting conservative ("independent") attacks on Disciples agencies was reprinted incrementally with Elmore's rejoinders in *The Restoration Herald* from 1954 to 1960.

See also Christian Restoration Association; Fundamentalism; Murch, James DeForest; Open Membership; *Restoration Herald, The; Touchstone, The*

BIBLIOGRAPHY Stephen J. Corey, *Fifty Years of Attack and Controversy: The Consequences Among the Disciples of Christ* (1953) • Robert E. Elmore, "Christianity and Rationalism," in *The Watchword of the Restoration Vindicated* (1939), pp. 73-91 • Kevin R. Kragenbrink, "Dividing the Disciples: Social, Cultural, and Intellectual Sources of Division in the Disciples of Christ, 1919-1945" (unpublished Ph.D. dissertation, Auburn University, 1996).

PAUL M. BLOWERS

Emmanuel School of Religion

Graduate seminary related to the Christian Churches/Churches of Christ.

Emmanuel School of Religion was founded in Johnson City, Tennessee, by a constituency — mainly ministers and laypersons identified with the Christian Churches/Churches of Christ and with the Christian Church (Disciples of Christ) — who were concerned, on the one hand, with the liberal drift of Disciples seminaries and, on the other, with the restorationist fundamentalism reflected in some institutions of the Christian Churches/Churches of Christ. Dean E. Walker (1898-1988), former professor at Butler University School of Religion, president of Milligan College, and founding president of Emmanuel, significantly shaped the vision of the school. A conservative Disciple and "free church catholic" by disposition, yet ultimately nonparticipant in the denominational Restructure of the Disciples of Christ, Walker had been positively influenced by Frederick Kershner and by his experience in the Disciples' Commission on Restudy in the 1940s. Walker was committed to the classical Stone-Campbell understanding of theology essentially as biblical interpretation and was open to higher-critical scholarship so long as it was tempered by respect for the divine authority of the Word.

Emmanuel was chartered by the state of Tennessee in 1961 and began admitting students in 1965, with an initial enrollment of thirty-five. Prior to this date Milligan College had offered a few graduate-level courses in anticipation of the opening of a new seminary. Library resources, facilities for administrative offices, and classrooms were provided by Milligan College on a rental basis. The B. D. Phillips

Charitable Trust of Butler, Pennsylvania, provided the financial resources from which most of the land was purchased for Emmanuel's relocation on a bluff overlooking the Milligan College campus. The new building was completed and began operations in 1973. Emmanuel and Milligan enjoy mutuality at various levels, academic and cultural, but remain separate institutions. Emmanuel received accreditation from the Association of Theological Schools in the United States and Canada in 1981 and from the Southern Association of Colleges and Schools in 1986.

The seminary operates under the authority and oversight of two official bodies: Trustees, and Associates in Christian Education. Trustees are legally responsible for the fiscal and institutional affairs of the school. Associates in Christian Education are representatives of the local churches that established the school and maintain it by their financial support. Associates function in an advisory capacity.

The Emmanuel Library houses over 130,000 volumes, along with a substantial collection of microfilm and microfiche materials. Holdings include the extensive private collection of Paul Schubert, late professor of New Testament at Yale, the Beauford H. Bryant New Testament Seminar Library, as well as the Restoration (Stone-Campbell) Archives.

Emmanuel offers three degrees: the Master of Divinity, Master of Arts in Religion, and Doctor of Ministry. Five "areas" (as opposed to "departments," strictly speaking) comprise the Emmanuel curriculum: Hebrew Bible/Old Testament, New Testament, church history and historical theology, Christian doctrine (theological studies), and ministries (pastoral ministry, worship and preaching, missions, and Christian education). Because of its integration of critical models for biblical study, and because the school has no formal statement requiring commitment to the doctrine of biblical inerrancy, Emmanuel has occasionally received intense criticism from some constituents of the Christian Churches/Churches of Christ. In keeping with its understanding of the Stone-Campbell Movement, the school officially subscribes to no theological creeds or statements of faith, insisting only on the general principles of (1) faith in Jesus of Nazareth as Son of God, Christ, and Lord, and (2) reception of Holy Scripture as inspired witness to the Word of God.

While the student body of Emmanuel consists primarily of men and women preparing for ministry and mission work among Christian Churches/Churches of Christ, the seminary draws students from all three streams of the Stone-Campbell Movement, officially states its service to all three streams, and has had faculty from all three streams. Admission is open to students of other denominational affiliations as well, and enrollment of students from other denominations has increased over the last twenty years.

See also Higher Education, Views of in the Movement; Dampier, Joseph; Milligan College; Phillips, Benjamin Dwight; Walker, Dean Everest

PAUL M. BLOWERS *and* FRED P. THOMPSON

England, Stephen J. (1895-1987)

Academician, minister, and biblical scholar of the Christian Church (Disciples of Christ). Concurrently serving as a seminary dean and local church minister, Stephen Jackson England embodied the ministry of a "scholar-pastor" throughout his career.

Born in Salida, Colorado, on October 1, 1895, England grew up in the Christian Church there. Studies at Colorado College (1913-15) enabled him to teach school near Great Bend, Kansas (1915-18), where he was ordained (December 23, 1917). After military service (1918-19), he pastored the Mackville, Kansas, church (1919-21) until enrolling at Phillips University (A.B., 1924; A.M., 1925; B.D., 1926). He taught New Testament at Phillips from 1926, simultaneously earning a Th.M. at Princeton (1928) and a Ph.D. at Yale (1940).

In 1942 England became the second dean of Phillips University's College of the Bible, and in 1951 he became the founding dean of the Graduate Seminary of Phillips University (now Phillips Theological Seminary). He wrote six books on traditional Stone-Campbell themes but engaging European theological scholarship. He also served on the advisory council for the publication of the Revised Standard Version of the Bible and was a major contributor to the groundbreaking *Panel of Scholars Reports* in the 1960s. England attended the Third World Conference on Faith and Order (Lund, 1952) and a number of gatherings of the World Conventions of Churches of Christ.

England was a mediating figure in an era that saw polarization of conservative and liberal Disciples. In his book *The One Baptism* (1960) and elsewhere, he rejected open membership and argued that those sprinkled as infants should be immersed for the sake of Christian unity. He advocated a reappropriation of the restoration principle conditioned by attention to critical New Testament scholarship, and he looked for a revitalized understanding of the role of the Holy Spirit in the life of the church. His theological disposition has been described by Eugene Boring as "a combination of 'old liberal' and 'new orthodox,' aspiring to transcend the liberal-fundamentalist dichotomy that had seized much of American Protestantism in his time."

As president of the final International Convention of the Disciples of Christ (1966) and moderator

Dean of the Graduate Theological Seminary and professor of New Testament at Phillips, Stephen J. England (1895-1987) was president of the final International Convention of the Disciples of Christ (1966) and moderator of the inaugural General Assembly of the Christian Church (Disciples of Christ).
Courtesy of the Disciples of Christ Historical Society

of the inaugural General Assembly of the Christian Church (Disciples of Christ), he was also one of the Stone-Campbell Movement's preeminent twentieth-century churchmen.

England retired as dean of the Phillips Seminary in 1962 but continued to teach until 1970. He died on March 8, 1987.

See also Baptism; Open Membership; Panel of Scholars; Phillips Theological Seminary; Phillips University

BIBLIOGRAPHY M. Eugene Boring, *Disciples and the Bible: A History of Disciples Biblical Interpretation in North America* (1997) • George England, *In a Tall Shadow* (1990) • Stephen J. England, *The Apostolic Church: Some Aspects of Its Faith and Life* (1947) • Stephen J. England, "The Holy Spirit," in *The Renewal of Church: The Panel of Scholars Reports*, vol. 3: *The Reformation of Tradition* (1963), pp. 111-34 • Stephen J. England, *Oklahoma Christians* (1975) • Stephen J. England, *The One Baptism: Baptism and Christian Unity, with Special Reference to Disciples of Christ* (1960).

WILLIAM TABBERNEE

Errett, Edwin Reeder (1891-1944)

Grandnephew of the early Disciple leader Isaac Errett, editor of the *Christian Standard* (1929-44), and broadly respected champion of Christian unity.

Edwin Errett was the voice of conservative moderation in a difficult era. He manifested concern for the unity of the church catholic as a delegate to the Faith and Order conference in Edinburgh, 1937. He also encouraged Disciple participation in discussions toward the founding of the World Council of Churches. Within the Movement his irenic spirit coexisted with the firm conviction that denominational agencies should not define Disciples. Errett supported some cooperative efforts (Pension Fund, National Benevolent Association) but not all (United Christian Missionary Society). A member of the Commission on Restudy of the Disciples during the early 1940s, he editorialized in the *Christian Standard* that "the peril we always face is not merely the continued existence of 'a United Society denomination,' but the creation of an anti-United Society denomination, if you please." Some leaders (both "cooperative" and "independent") disagreed with Errett's views. During a time of change in editorial policy at the *Christian Standard* in late 1943 and early 1944 he died suddenly, the moderate "martyr to a lost cause" of internal unity for Disciples.

BIBLIOGRAPHY Edwin R. Errett, editorials in the *Christian Standard* (1929-44) • Edwin R. Errett, "The Faith of the Church in God," in *International Convention: Disciples of Christ, Columbus, Ohio, October 26-31, 1937* (1938), pp. 63-73 • Henry Webb, "Edwin R. Errett: Martyr to a Lost Cause," *Leaven* 7 (1999): 48-51.

W. DENNIS HELSABECK, JR.

Errett, Isaac (1820-1888)

Preacher, missionary society leader, and editor of the *Christian Standard* from its beginning in 1866 until his death.

Errett's father, Henry (d. 1825), immigrated from Ireland, where he was a member of a Scotch Baptist congregation, a restorationist group that followed the ideas of John Glas and Robert Sandeman but adopted the practice of immersion. Henry became a leader in a New York Scotch Baptist congregation and authored a tract on the purpose and effect of baptism that greatly influenced Walter Scott.

After Henry's death, the family moved first to New Jersey and then in 1832 to frontier Pittsburgh, where they attended an independent church similar to the one in New York. In 1832 Isaac and his brother Russell were immersed, and in 1839 Isaac became the congregation's regular minister. In 1844 he accepted the ministry of the church at New Lisbon, Ohio, formerly a Baptist church in the Mahoning Association that had come into the Stone-Campbell Movement in 1827 through the efforts of Walter Scott. Later Errett preached for the North Bloomfield and Warren, Ohio, churches.

From 1857 to 1860 Errett served as corresponding secretary of the American Christian Missionary Society. In 1861 and 1862 he was a coeditor of the *Millennial Harbinger* as well as a fundraiser for Campbell's Bethany College. In October 1861, just after the outbreak of the Civil War, Errett was chosen to preside

Despite the charge of trying to impose a creed, second-generation leader Isaac Errett (1820-1888) intended his "Synopsis of the Faith" to be a positive public articulation of the Movement's positions on various points of Christian doctrine. Courtesy of Bethany College

in place of the aged Alexander Campbell at the meeting of the American Christian Missionary Society in Cincinnati. Because of the war, members from Southern states were unable to attend. Rumors of the Missionary Society's lack of loyalty to the United States government prompted the introduction of a resolution calling on the churches "to do all in their power to sustain the proper and constituted authorities of the Union." The resolution was seconded, but David S. Burnet, founder of the American Christian Bible Society, raised a point of order, insisting that the topic was not germane to the business of the convention. Errett ruled that the resolution was in order, but on appeal the group overturned his ruling. In an odd turn of events, the "official" session was recessed for ten minutes, and the group passed the resolution as a "mass meeting" of individual Christians rather than as the American Christian Missionary Society. Two years later, as the War raged on, Errett was presiding again when a much stronger resolution was introduced denouncing "the attempts of armed traitors to overthrow our government." When Errett this time declared the resolution out of order, remembering the events of 1861, he was surprised to find his action reversed again. This time the resolution was passed as an official act of the Society. Members of the Southern churches and pacifists among Northern Christians never forgot Errett's apparent approval of the so-called war resolutions.

In late 1862 Errett became minister for the Jefferson Avenue and Beaubien Street Church in Detroit. Two incidents there focused the ire of conservatives in the Movement on him. First, in 1863 he published a tract titled "A Synopsis of the Faith and Practice of the Church of Christ," designed as a brief statement of the Stone-Campbell Movement's beliefs for interested outsiders. Editors like Benjamin Franklin and Moses Lard, however, attacked the "Synopsis" as a creed. The other event involved the gift of a silver doorplate with the inscription "Rev. I. Errett." The news spread that Errett was calling himself Reverend, and several editors denounced him as an example of shameful conformity to the "priest-ridden sects." Errett, however, largely ignored the criticism. He proved to be an effective minister during his ten years in Michigan, helping to establish as many as six congregations and adding 2,000 members. He served for one year as minister in Chicago, his ministry there terminating with the great fire of 1873.

In 1865 Errett accepted a position at the Western Reserve Eclectic Institute (later Hiram College) as principal and professor. While there the most significant event of his life occurred — his appointment as editor of the newly founded *Christian Standard.* The motivation for this new publishing venture included a mixture of financial, political, and religious factors. According to Errett's biographer, J. S. Lamar, several influential leaders became convinced that the Movement needed a popular-level weekly paper that would promote a more progressive spirit than the two major papers then published, the *American Christian Review* and the *Gospel Advocate.* On December 22, 1865, an organizational meeting was held at the home of oil millionaire Thomas W. Phillips. Four days later, at a second meeting, capital stock for the Christian Standard Company was fixed at $100,000, and Isaac Errett was unanimously elected editor of the paper. The stockholders of the company, including future president James A. Garfield, believed the venture was a sound financial investment and anticipated making a substantial profit.

Political motivation was involved as well. Several years after Errett's death, David Lipscomb wrote of a conversation he had with Errett in 1867 when Lipscomb was in Cleveland for medical treatment. Lipscomb explained that the editor of the *American Christian Review,* Benjamin Franklin, like many church leaders, had tried to remain neutral during the Civil War and had refused to allow articles in his paper that would stir up sectional hatred. Errett told

Lipscomb in 1867 that the *Standard* had been started because Franklin would not allow the pro-Union people to publish their views on the duty of Christians to support the government in time of war.

The paper began in April 1866, but when the paper failed to make a profit for the stockholders they dissolved the association in January 1868 and gave the company to Errett. He was to continue publishing the *Standard* and pay off the company's debts. After taking ownership of the company, Errett developed a more moderate national image. He attempted to smooth over rough feelings with Southern Christians in 1867 and 1868, particularly David Lipscomb, and even advised preachers to avoid entanglements in political affairs, a position that Lipscomb and his mentor Tolbert Fanning held. Errett had reached a position of great influence in the Movement. Some clearly viewed him as Alexander Campbell's successor.

In 1874 Errett gave his influence and support to the formation of the Christian Woman's Board of Missions in a famous article titled "Help These Women." The following year he helped to organize the Foreign Christian Missionary Society and was elected its first president, a position he held until his death. Largely because of Errett's efforts through the *Christian Standard* and personal solicitation, funding for the various missionary societies increased from between $5,000 and $10,000 a year to almost $60,000 a year by 1888.

Errett played a key role in trying to diffuse the internal tensions threatening the Stone-Campbell Movement in the late 1800s. He saw two groups posing a danger to unity. The first he identified as those who introduced false tests of fellowship, allowing differences of opinion and matters of inference or expediency to become points of division. The second were those who, through a worldly desire to introduce things not necessarily wrong in themselves, but by a "reckless abuse of their Christian liberty, or by persistence in a needless course," became an offense to others and thereby disturbed the peace of the church. Both positions, he insisted, were sins against the integrity of the body of Christ.

Early in 1887 ill health forced Errett to suspend his work and take an extended vacation. Friends raised money to send him on a tour through Europe, Egypt, and Palestine that lasted several months. That October he attended the annual meeting of the Foreign Christian Missionary Society for the last time. He died December 19, 1888, at his home in Terrace Park, Ohio.

Errett's work is found chiefly in his editorials in the *Christian Standard.* Collections of his articles and lectures appeared in volumes titled *Walks about Jerusalem* (1871), *Talks to Bereans* (1872), *Letters to a Young Christian* (1877), *Evenings with the Bible* (1884-89, 3 vols.), and *Linsey-Woolsey* (1893). His pamphlet "Our Position," similar to his earlier "Synopsis of the Faith," was widely distributed for many years as a concise statement of the Movement's beliefs and principles.

Interpretations of Isaac Errett range from praising him for having saved the Movement from becoming a legalistic sect to blaming him for leading a large portion of it into digression from truth. He exercised tremendous influence as editor of the *Christian Standard,* and his views on a wide variety of issues gained wide circulation and approval.

See also American Christian Missionary Society; Baptists; *Christian Standard;* Christian Woman's Board of Missions; Foreign Christian Missionary Society, The; Glas, John; Hiram College; Lipscomb, David; "Synopsis of the Faith"; Unity, Christian

BIBLIOGRAPHY Isaac Errett, *Our Position: A Brief Statement of the Distinctive Features of the Plea for Reformation Urged by the People Known as Disciples of Christ* (c. 1870) • Isaac Errett, *The True Basis of Christian Union: A Sermon Preached in the Central Christian Church, Cincinnati, March 5, 1871* (1871) • Isaac Errett, "The Grounds of Christian Fellowship," in *The Missouri Christian Lectures* (1888) • Douglas A. Foster, "Isaac Errett: Unity and Expediency," *Restoration Quarterly* 36 (1994): 139-51 • J. S. Lamar, *Memoirs of Isaac Errett with Selections from His Writings,* 2 vols. (1893).

DOUGLAS A. FOSTER

Errett, Russell (1845-1931)

Son of Isaac Errett, first editor of the *Christian Standard,* and owner of Standard Publishing of Cincinnati, Ohio.

When his father died in 1888, Russell assumed the management of the company. He wrote an occasional editorial and article, but his gifts were in the management of the company, which he developed into a leading religious publisher. Standard Publishing was a pioneer in developing literature and periodicals for Sunday Schools, was the first publisher of lesson quarterlies graded for the various age levels, and was the first to provide full-color offset printing of Bible School literature.

Russell Errett was passionately devoted to the faith and the policies of his father, and he was determined that Standard Publishing Company be dedicated to promoting the aims of the Stone-Campbell Movement. When he perceived that these aims were threatened, he became involved in conflicts with those whom he believed were seriously modifying the aims of the Movement as he understood them.

Russell Errett was survived by a son and two daughters. His elder son, in whom he had placed high hopes, drowned while a student at Bethany College. Errett's younger son was incapable of managing the company, so Errett provided in his will that ownership of Standard Publishing revert to his children, but the management would be placed in the hands of four prominent Stone-Campbell leaders, thus insuring perpetuation of the purpose of the company. He provided that a non-profit holding company be organized that would indemnify the heirs and operate the company for the purpose he held dear.

Six months after his death, his children filed suit, broke the will on a technicality, and assumed control of the company. Management fell to a son-in-law, Harry Baird, who had little interest in the Stone-Campbell Movement. His assistant manager, Willard Mohorter, operated the company and attempted to perpetuate the purposes for which the company had been founded.

See also *Christian Standard;* Errett, Isaac; Standard Publishing Company HENRY E. WEBB

Eschatology

Theological term that denotes the final end of humankind and the world; the doctrine of last things. Although the term itself does not appear in Stone-Campbell literature until relatively recently, it reflects the apocalyptic expectations of the Movement's revivalistic roots and millennial thought and action in the nineteenth and twentieth centuries.

The Stoneites and "Newlight" Christians that emerged from the Cane Ridge Revival shared a common eschatological horizon with Thomas Campbell and the Christian Association of Washington, rooted religiously and theologically in the Second Great Awakening. The piety of the Cane Ridge revival contained an apocalyptic element that linked evangelization, conversion, and Christian unity with an expectation of imminent divine intervention in human affairs. It found expression in the program of the Christians reflected in *The Last Will and Testament of Springfield Presbytery* (1804). The document urged preachers and people to exhibit a spirit of unity "while they behold the signs of the times, look up and confidently expect that redemption draweth nigh." The eschatology of Thomas Campbell's *Declaration and Address* (1809) combines a critical, apocalyptic judgment of European state churches and their hierarchies with an eschatological action program for America, calling for unimpeded and united evangelism as well as a return to normative Christian beginnings. All of this was in preparation for Christ's return, which would follow the conversion of the Jews and the fullness of the Gentiles. Elias Smith, one of the founders of the Christian Connexion, opposed the New England clergy and their politically sanctioned religion with his radical restitutionist program of biblical Christianity. For Smith, such religion represented the apocalyptic forces of Anti-Christ. He held specific historical premillennial views of the impending reign of Christ with his saints, followed, however, not by the punishment of the wicked but by their final annihilation.

According to his former Newlight associate John Dunlavy, Barton W. Stone interpreted prophetic texts such as Zechariah 10:1 in a proleptic or even realized way during the Cane Ridge Revival. Stone saw Christ's judgment as taking place through gospel proclamation and Christian living. Though Stone came to espouse a historical premillennialism, like some of the postmillennialists he considered the nearness of the end an incentive and summons to accomplish Christian unity and abolish slavery. Yet his separatist and pacifist convictions as well as his dualistic estimate of God's kingdom and the world are, according to D. Newell Williams, not an outcome of his premillennialism but a consequence of his disillusionment with party politics.

As the unpublished Australian manuscripts of Alexander Campbell show, he exhibited an early interest in millennial thought. In the first issue of the *Millennial Harbinger* in 1830 he expressed his postmillennialism by defining "The Millennium" as "the consummation of that ultimate amelioration of society proposed in the Christian Scriptures." Following the optimistic tradition of his father's *Declaration and Address,* Campbell's "millennial church" was based on a recovery of the "Ancient Order of Things," or the ordinances, practices, and faith of early Christianity. He anchored Christian unity not in creeds but in a strict adherence to "gospel facts." For Campbell, the millennial church, while otherwise otherworldly, would labor in the earthly arena where God's saving activity through Christ takes place and depends on human cooperation. Despite a tension between unity and restoration in Campbell's vision of the church, Mark G. Toulouse draws attention to a consistent and enduring element in Campbell's eschatology that preserves God's transcendence and the distinction between the kingdom of Christ and the kingdom of God. The final, everlasting kingdom of God cannot be equated with the kingdom of Christ, which for Campbell was nearly identical with the millennial church, nor was there a vital role for Protestant America in ushering in the kingdom of God. That role was reserved for the church. As the reign of God's sovereignty and grace, the final kingdom would remain ultimately inaccessible to human control and instrumentation.

Three eschatologically oriented American movements influenced the Stone-Campbell Movement in the nineteenth century: Shakers, Mormons, and William Miller's premillennialism. Shaker missionaries from New York visited churches in Kentucky and Ohio in the early 1800s, converting several promi-

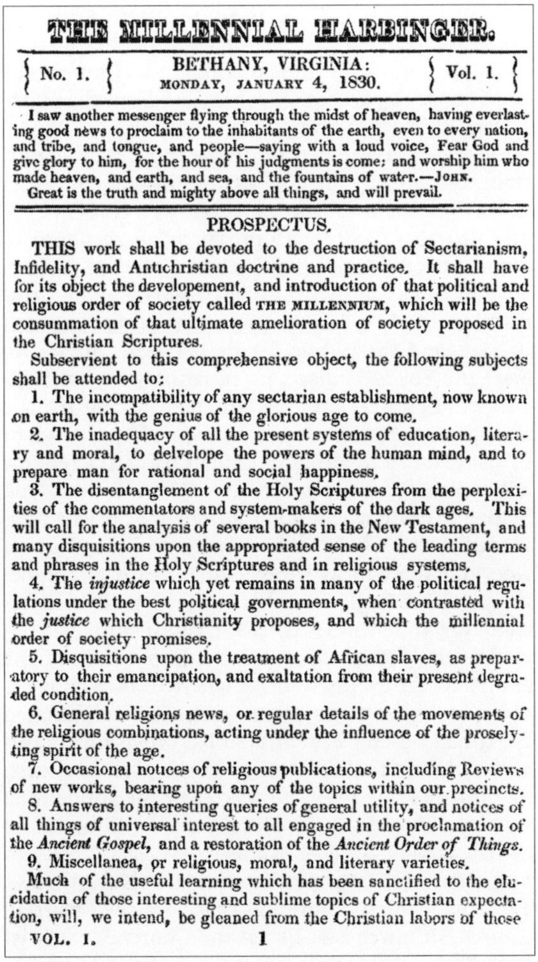

THE MILLENNIAL HARBINGER.

No. 1. | BETHANY, VIRGINIA: MONDAY, JANUARY 4, 1830. | Vol. 1.

I saw another messenger flying through the midst of heaven, having everlasting good news to proclaim to the inhabitants of the earth, even to every nation, and tribe, and tongue, and people—saying with a loud voice, Fear God and give glory to him, for the hour of his judgments is come: and worship him who made heaven, and earth, and sea, and the fountains of water.—JOHN.

Great is the truth and mighty above all things, and will prevail.

PROSPECTUS.

THIS work shall be devoted to the destruction of Sectarianism, Infidelity, and Antichristian doctrine and practice. It shall have for its object the developement, and introduction of that political and religious order of society called THE MILLENNIUM, which will be the consummation of that ultimate amelioration of society proposed in the Christian Scriptures.

Subservient to this comprehensive object, the following subjects shall be attended to:

1. The incompatibility of any sectarian establishment, now known on earth, with the genius of the glorious age to come.

2. The inadequacy of all the present systems of education, literary and moral, to delvelope the powers of the human mind, and to prepare man for rational and social happiness.

3. The disentanglement of the Holy Scriptures from the perplexities of the commentators and system-makers of the dark ages. This will call for the analysis of several books in the New Testament, and many disquisitions upon the appropriated sense of the leading terms and phrases in the Holy Scriptures and in religious systems.

4. The *injustice* which yet remains in many of the political regulations under the best political governments, when contrasted with the *justice* which Christianity proposes, and which the millennial order of society promises.

5. Disquisitions upon the treatment of African slaves, as preparatory to their emancipation, and exaltation from their present degraded condition.

6. General religions news, or regular details of the movements of the religious combinations, acting under the influence of the proselyting spirit of the age.

7. Occasional notices of religious publications, including Reviews of new works, bearing upon any of the topics within our precincts.

8. Answers to interesting queries of general utility, and notices of all things of universal interest to all engaged in the proclamation of the *Ancient Gospel*, and a restoration of the *Ancient Order of Things*.

9. Miscellanea, or religious, moral, and literary varieties.

Much of the useful learning which has been sanctified to the elucidation of those interesting and sublime topics of Christian expectation, will, we intend, be gleaned from the Christian labors of those

VOL. I. 1

Alexander Campbell's optimism about the American republic and the growing success of his religious reform led him to name his second journal begun in January 1830 the *Millennial Harbinger.* The "Prospectus" outlines areas for chief attention to bring in the millennium, including the move toward the end of slavery. Courtesy of Emmanuel School of Religion Archives

nent Newlight leaders to their millennial church, notably Richard McNemar and John Dunlavy. They in turn became articulate Shaker apologists and theologians. The Shakers built on the millennial expectations and experiential needs of those affected by the revival and interpreted their own ethical rigorism and realized eschatology as continuing and completing the work begun by the revival.

Two prominent members of the Stone-Campbell Movement took significant leadership roles in the emerging Latter-Day Saints: Sidney Rigdon, the main advisor to Joseph Smith and a future contender in the succession struggle, and Parley Parker Pratt, who became the chief Mormon apologist and theologian of the early period. Mormons shared with the early Stone-Campbell Movement a restitutionist and millennial agenda. Yet in contrast to arguments by Campbell and Scott that spiritual gifts had ceased, Latter-Day Saints based their "restitution of all things" on a recovery of early Christian charismata, including prophecy and revelation, which they considered an authoritative endowment for the endtime. As Rigdon observed in a critique of Walter Scott, "It is the gift of the Holy Ghost as administered by the apostles, by the laying on of hands, which makes the difference, and it is this alone, and the society which has this power are the people of God and those who have not are not." Rigdon's communitarian interests, once rebuffed by Alexander Campbell, helped to shape and maintain the vision of an imminent Mormon Zion in America prior to the premillennial return of Christ. David Edwin Harrell has argued that Shaker and Mormon defections from the Christians and Disciples "drained off the most radical fringes in both of the movements."

The premillennialism and apocalyptic date-setting of William Miller quickened the eschatological pulse of the Movement during the 1830s and 1840s, notably in its journals. The discussion helped Alexander Campbell to develop and publicize his postmillennial alternative as the "Protestant view" in the *Millennial Harbinger.* His early associate Walter Scott, however, while reluctant to set an ultimate date for the return of Christ, supported the Millerite movement in his journal *The Evangelist,* as did some other editors in America and Britain.

In the wake of the Millerites' "great disappointment" after the failed premillennial predictions of Christ's return in 1843 and 1844, Walter Scott returned to the postmillennialism he had once espoused in the *Christian Baptist.* In his new journal, *The Protestant Unionist,* he preached anti-Catholicism and Protestant solidarity. Subsequently, many in the Movement came to view kingdom-building as a task that would transform the social order. At the same time, however, they retained exegetically an interpretation of Revelation that was historical and apocalyptic and expected Christ's literal return at the end of the millennium. In the twentieth century, faith in the transcendence of God and the distinction between the kingdom of God and the kingdom of Christ gave way to an immanent liberalism stressing human activity over divine initiative. In addition, many came to focus on individual "soul-winning," while ministers and missionaries advanced American cultural ideals at home and on the mission field. Only after World War II did a culture-critical attitude prevail, redefining mission as witness and reestablishing the kingdom of God as a gift as well as a goal and challenge for the church. It is not surprising that

Disciples exegetical literature did not seriously engage the book of Revelation in the twentieth century until the scholarly commentary by M. Eugene Boring, published in 1989. Never prominent among Disciples, premillennialism asserted itself only among some conservatives, notably the leader of Christian Action, C. G. Kindred (1866-1954).

World conditions and a more modest premillennialism that renounced date-setting in the late nineteenth century made premillennialism an attractive option for many in the part of the Movement that would become Churches of Christ. Editors and educators such as Moses E. Lard, Tolbert Fanning, and James A. Harding entertained premillennial views, while the events of the Turko-Russian War stimulated apocalyptic thinking. Premillennialism as articulated in the papers of the Prophetic Conference of 1878 was well received in the Movement's journals. In the Nashville Bible School and other educational institutions with which he was associated, James A. Harding exposed a generation of students to premillennial thinking. Whether, as Richard T. Hughes suggested, a wider Southern theological tradition linked the Nashville Bible School and its teachers and students, such as David Lipscomb, James A. Harding, and Robert Henry Boll, with the apocalyptic thought world of Barton W. Stone and the Newlight Christians remains a matter of scholarly discussion.

At the beginning of the twentieth century an entirely new theological element entered the eschatological discussion among Churches of Christ, building on existing historical premillennialism. Fundamentalism, with its dispensational, futuristic premillennialism that divided history into periods of human failure and reserved the bulk of prophetic predictions for the immediate future, attracted a group of young preachers around Robert Henry Boll and the journal *Word and Work,* especially as world conditions worsened prior to World War I. Otherworldliness and pacifism among Churches of Christ came together with a selective ecumenism with other conservative Protestants resisting modernity. Opposition to modern biblical criticism closely accompanied a biblical literalism needed for interpretation of "prophecy." Premillennialists also stood in the vanguard of promoting foreign missions in anticipation of the end, but they understood mission as a witness to the nations rather than as a process of national conversion or global improvement. Don Carlos Janes and his Louisville-based journals *Encouragement Magazine, Boosters' Bulletin,* and *Missionary Messenger* promoted missionary work to Japan, China, Africa, and the Philippines. Premillennialists contributed significantly to the musical culture of Churches of Christ through publication of the hymnal *Great Songs of the Church,* edited by Elmer Leon Jorgenson. Separate educational facilities, such as Southeastern Christian College at Winchester, Kentucky, provided institutional continuity for these premillennial Churches of Christ once the process of separation from the mainstream had been accomplished.

Two debates helped to define the eschatological stance adopted by the majority of Churches of Christ in the 1930s and following, partly as a consequence of cultural accommodation, partly in response to dispensational premillennialism: H. Leo Boles's written discussion with Robert Henry Boll on "Unfulfilled Prophecy" in the pages of the *Gospel Advocate* in 1927, and the public debate between Charles M. Neal and Foy E. Wallace, Jr., in January 1933 at Winchester, Kentucky. In the nineteenth century the amillennial position that expected no literal reign of Christ prior to the final judgment had attracted few adherents. Twentieth-century debates, however, helped to entrench among Churches of Christ a total identification of the church with the kingdom of God and the end as the personal death of the believer, with a final judgment at the general resurrection in an indefinite future. Such amillennialist convictions helped to safeguard the importance of the church as the exclusive place where God's saving activity in Christ takes place. Such views eliminated the threat posed by premillennial, provisional views of the church that subordinated the present church to a future kingdom. The success of the amillennial view continues into the present among Churches of Christ, as Max Lucado's *When Christ Comes: The Beginning of the Very Best* (1999) demonstrates. Nevertheless, anecdotal evidence indicates that both the Christian Churches/Churches of Christ and Churches of Christ have been increasingly affected by the popular appeal of evangelical dispensationalism.

Strict Preterism, or "Transmillennialism," is a twentieth-century minority position among Churches of Christ espoused by Max King, his son Tim, and a small number of Churches of Christ in Ohio. This view holds "that AD 30 to 70 represented the millennial reign of Christ, and that this Last Days period transformed all things and ushered in the new covenantal kingdom." Tim King is the central figure of a "Presence Movement" among today's preterist churches. In his publications, seminars, and webcasts he seeks to draw theological consequences from preterist eschatology and proposes a transformative, holistic solution to human fears and needs on the basis of God's abiding love and presence.

An enduring "apocalyptic" countercultural spirit among Southern Christians is, according to Richard T. Hughes, a factor in the eventual separation of Churches of Christ from Disciples. This much-discussed historiographical issue has also contributed to a theological reevaluation of Barton W. Stone's significance. In the book *The Worldly Church: A*

Call for Biblical Renewal, C. Leonard Allen, Richard T. Hughes, and Michael R. Weed do not mention specifically the apocalyptic millennial element. Yet in the book's suggested reversal of cultural accommodation that Churches of Christ are said to have undergone, the authors attempt to recover some of the same countercultural values identified by Hughes and Allen as constituting the "apocalyptic Spirit" of Stone and the Southern Christians, such as care for the underprivileged and a spirit of holiness as consequences of a life lived under the exclusive rule of God.

Notably among Disciples, Mark G. Toulouse identifies "the eschatological principle" of the Stone-Campbell Movement as an enduring theological identity marker retaining significance for the present. While Toulouse rejects as dated many specifics of Campbell's millennialism, the central role accorded to Christ in the history of salvation and the "fundamental understanding of a God who seeks our redemption and calls us into the future with hope" remain of lasting importance. The late Disciples historian and theologian Anthony L. Dunnavant considered as "highly relevant" the "Disciples tradition's evangelistic zeal and its grounding in Christian hope."

See also Boll, Robert Henry; Dunlavy, John; Harding, James Alexander; Janes, Don Carlos; McNemar, Richard; *Protestant Unionist, The;* Rigdon, Sidney

BIBLIOGRAPHY H. Leo Boles and R. H. Boll, *Unfulfilled Prophecy: A Discussion on Prophetic Themes* (1928) • Eugene Boring, "Disciples Interpretation of Revelation at the Turn of the Century," *Discipliana* 59:3 (Fall 1999): 67-81 • Anthony L. Dunnavant, "Evangelization and Eschatology: Lost Link in the Disciples Tradition," *Lexington Theological Quarterly* (Spring 1993): 47-51 • Timothy Earl Fulop, "Elias Smith and the Quest for Gospel Liberty: Popular Religion and Democratic Radicalism in Early Nineteenth-Century New England" (Ph.D. dissertation, Princeton University, 1992) • David Edwin Harrell, Jr., "Walter Scott and the Nineteenth-Century Evangelical Spirit," in *Walter Scott: A Nineteenth-Century Evangelical,* ed. Mark G. Toulouse (1999), pp. 23-35 • Richard T. Hughes, "From Primitive Church to Protestant Nation: The Millennial Odyssey of Alexander Campbell," in Richard T. Hughes and C. Leonard Allen, *Illusions of Innocence: Protestant Primitivism in America, 1630-1875* (1988), pp. 170-87 • Michael G. Kenny, *The Perfect Law of Liberty: Elias Smith and the Providential History of America* (1994) • Max Lucado, *When Christ Comes: The Beginning of the Very Best* (1999) • Charles M. Neal and Foy E. Wallace, *Neal-Wallace Discussion on the Thousand Years Reign of Christ* (1933) • Philip [Walter Scott], "On the Millennium," *Christian Baptist* 3 (July 1826): 250-51; 4 (September 1826): 265-66 • "Prospectus," *Millennial Harbinger* 1:1 (January 4, 1830): 1-3 • Sidney Rigdon, "For the Messenger and Advocate," *Latter Day Saints' Messenger and Advocate* 2:4 (January 1836): 241-45 • Hans Rollmann, "The Eschatology of the *Declaration and Address,*" in *The Quest for Christian Unity, Peace, and Purity in Thomas Campbell's Declaration and Address: Texts and Studies,* ed. Thomas H. Olbricht and Hans Rollmann (2000), pp. 341-63 • Hans Rollmann, "'Our Steadfastness and Perseverance Depends on Perpetual Expectation of Our Lord': The Development of Robert Henry Boll's Premillennialism (1895-1915)," *Discipliana* 59:4 (Winter 1999): 113-26 • Mark G. Toulouse, "The Kingdom of God and Disciples of Christ," *Discipliana* 62:1 (Spring 2002): 3-24 • Richard S. Van Wagoner, *Sidney Rigdon: A Portrait of Religious Excess* (1994) • D. Newell Williams, "From Trusting Congress to Renouncing Human Governments: The Millennial Odyssey of Barton W. Stone," *Discipliana* 61:3 (Fall 2001): 67-81 • James Stephen Wolfgang, "Millennial Themes in the Restoration Movement: Civil War to 1900," *Discipliana* 62:4 (Winter 2002): 99-115.

HANS ROLLMANN

Essentials vs. Adiaphora

Adiaphora is a word of Greek origin meaning things morally indifferent, that is, neither good nor bad in themselves.

In Christianity and the Stone-Campbell Movement the idea of adiaphora has focused primarily on whether beliefs and practices not specifically commanded or endorsed by Scripture can be considered legitimate.

The question of how to regard the Bible's silence was raised early in Christian history. In the third century Christians raised the question of the propriety of attending the pagan spectacles and wearing the laurel leaf. Some said that, since these things were not specifically prohibited in Scripture, they were permitted, allowing for a range of adiaphora or indifferent matters. Tertullian, on the other hand, strongly insisted that whatever was not clearly commanded or permitted in Scripture was forbidden; in other words, there are no indifferent things.

In his study of Anglican adiaphorism Bernard Verkamp points out three distinguishable positions. The first reflects Tertullian's biblical reductionism that rejects anything not explicitly commanded or permitted in Scripture as sinful. The second says that things "not repugnant" to Scripture are to be permitted, even though not mentioned in the Bible. Not all such things should be allowed regardless of circumstances, however. Because they were inherently neutral, their retention or rejection could be determined only by extrinsic factors. They might be used or not used according to the dictates of faith and love in each situation. The third stance Verkamp identifies as that of the early "puritans." They defined adiaphora not simply as those things that were "not repugnant," but as those things that were in "positive accord" with the general direction of Scripture for the glory of God and the edification of God's people. The end result of this position is often the same as the biblical reductionist approach, allowing for only a very strict understanding of adiaphora.

All these categories can be seen in the Stone-Campbell Movement. In the *Declaration and Address* Thomas Campbell insisted that things neither expressly commanded nor prohibited in Scripture, matters of "private opinion and human invention," were responsible for dividing Christians. In Proposition 3 of the document Campbell contended that only things expressly taught in Scripture could be required as terms of communion. Yet in the Appendix he indicated that nonessentials, particularly as embodied in the creeds and confessions of the churches, were not themselves evil, but became so when they divided Christians. Later Campbell endorsed the Westminster Confession of Faith as "eminently useful" for understanding the truths of Scripture. Clearly he saw a restricted realm of allowed nonessentials that would have to be relinquished if they proved divisive in any way.

David Lipscomb clearly fit the category of biblical reductionism. He believed that Christians were required to reject from God's service everything not required by Scripture. For Lipscomb the category of "indifferent" matters did not exist. On the other hand, Isaac Errett, in his famous pamphlet "Our Position," listed matters of inference, expediency, and opinion as areas of belief or practice in which there was to be the largest liberty. However, Errett restricted the liberty with which these indifferent things could be used. The prejudices and welfare of all, directed by the "law of love" stated in 1 Corinthians 8:13, would be determinative, he said. He saw instrumental music in worship and the missionary society to be indifferent matters — neither their use nor non-use was essentially connected to salvation. He emphasized repeatedly that such things that did not involve explicit biblical commands, prohibitions, or permissions were of themselves indifferent. No one could legitimately divide Christians over them. They were things which of themselves were neither right nor wrong, but permissible when they could be made to glorify God and edify Christians. Errett saw indifferent matters becoming a problem when they were elevated to the status of essentials by some.

J. H. Garrison took the larger view of adiaphora, stating that the only essential for one to be a Christian was personal faith in and loyalty to Jesus. With this view he allowed for a larger area of adiaphora than did Errett, and by the end of his life had even yielded on baptism. He aggressively attacked the biblical reductionist position, denying that the Bible was a book of prescriptions. He believed that the strict position would, in fact, destroy the Movement's plea for unity. It is not difficult to see why such friction developed between Lipscomb and Garrison. For Garrison, anything not overtly disloyal to Christ might be used to glorify God and strengthen Christians.

In the twentieth century members of Churches of Christ tended to take a strict stand toward adiaphora, refusing to allow for the legitimacy of any belief or practice not specified by Scripture. This stance was not always consistent, however, as evidenced by controversies over issues such as located preachers and Sunday Schools. The other parts of the Movement allowed for such nonessentials as instrumental music in worship and missionary societies. Yet as the second division took shape, Disciples generally allowed for a wide area of permissible beliefs and practices, while Christian Churches/Churches of Christ were more restrictive in their view of legitimate nonessentials.

See also *Declaration and Address;* Errett, Isaac; Expedients; Garrison, James Harvey; Lipscomb, David; "Synopsis of the Faith"

BIBLIOGRAPHY Douglas A. Foster, "The Struggle for Unity During the Period of Division of the Restoration Movement, 1875-1900" (unpublished Ph.D. dissertation, Vanderbilt University, 1987) • Bernard J. Verkamp, *The Indifferent Mean: Adiaphorism in the English Reformation to 1554* (1977).

DOUGLAS A. FOSTER

Ethics

See Abolitionism; Abortion; Pacifism; Race Relations

Eureka College

Related to the Christian Church (Disciples of Christ).

Eureka College was founded by abolitionist members of the Stone-Campbell Movement who had moved from Kentucky to the area in Illinois then known as Walnut Hill. The college was preceded by the short-lived Walnut Grove Academy, which operated from 1848 through 1854. During the lifetime of the academy many local leaders had begun to urge the establishment of a college. At an 1851 Convention of the Christian Church of Illinois, proponents of the college declared their desire "to establish an institution of learning where the young people of both sexes might receive the advantages of a liberal education under the care and influence of Christian teachers entirely free from all sectarian prejudices." The Illinois General Assembly granted a charter in the name of "The Trustees of Eureka College" on February 6, 1855.

The new college opened in September 1855 with Elder William M. Brown as president of a faculty of seven. In its first year the college enrolled 131 men and 82 women. It was the first college in Illinois and only the third in the nation to admit men and women on an equal basis.

Two founders of the college gave approximately twenty acres as a site for the college. By the beginning of the twenty-first century the campus had grown to 112 acres. In 1858 the first permanent building was completed and named Recitation Hall. The second permanent building, the Chapel, was completed in 1869. Both buildings remain in use and are now listed on the National Register of Historic Sites.

In succeeding years the college frequently struggled with financial and other crises. Many students and some faculty lost their lives or were seriously wounded as members of Company G, 17th Illinois Infantry. The Great Depression contributed to the college's losing its regional accreditation from 1936 to 1962. In the 1940s the college was also caught in the middle of the dispute between Disciples who supported the International Convention of the Disciples of Christ and members of the Movement who did not.

Eureka has remained committed to providing a nonsectarian, liberal arts education. Its curriculum includes twenty-nine majors, with most students pursuing majors in business administration, elementary education, or secondary education. In 2003 the college had an enrollment of approximately 510 full-time students and forty-seven full-time faculty. George A. Hearne is president of the college.

Many ministers and missionaries of the Disciples of Christ received their undergraduate education at Eureka. Other alumni include forty-two college presidents, half a dozen governors and members of Congress, as well as a President of the United States, Ronald W. Reagan, class of 1932.

BIBLIOGRAPHY Harold Adams, *The History of Eureka College, 1855-1982* (1982) • Elmira Dickinson, ed., *A History of Eureka College* (1894). JERRY D. MCCOY

Europe, Missions in

1. Introduction

Churches of the Stone-Campbell Movement have engaged in a wide range of mission activities in Europe that began in the 1870s and continue into the twenty-first century. These concerns include benevolent and relief work, evangelistic and church-planting efforts, fraternal support of like-minded groups and individuals, higher education and ministerial training, publication of literature, and the general propagation of principles of the Stone-Campbell Movement.

American missionary involvement in Europe evolved in relation to the changing political landscape of the Continent and was particularly affected by wars fought on European soil during the twentieth century. The Russian Revolution and the two World Wars made their impact during the first half of the century, while the latter half was dominated by the Cold War. Thus it is useful to discuss European missions in terms of the pre– and post–World War II eras.

2. Missions in Europe Prior to World War II

2.1. England, Denmark, France, and Scandinavia

The earliest missionary enterprises in Europe included initiatives in England, France, Denmark, and Scandinavia. The Disciples' Foreign Christian Missionary Society (FCMS), established in 1875 to carry on mission work in "non-Christian lands," actually began its work in Europe. American Disciple Henry Earl had evangelized in Britain several years prior to the establishment of the FCMS and by 1875 had secured sufficient funds for further work. Earl intended, with or without the FCMS, to return to Britain and establish new churches. Being unable to persuade Earl to select another field more in keeping with their primary aim, the FCMS commissioned him as their first missionary.

Within a couple of years of its founding, the FCMS had commissioned additional evangelists to England, as well as missionaries to Scandinavia and to Paris, France. Europe was thus established as the primary foreign mission field. Disciples Yearbooks from the early 1900s list as many as fifteen missionaries active in Great Britain and around ten workers in Scandinavia.

By the end of World War I the work in Britain had not satisfied the hopes of the Americans who had invested time and money there. Nonetheless, with the financial aid of American Disciples, the British churches in 1920 established Overdale College in Birmingham, a step that very likely insured the survival of the Fellowship of Churches of Christ in the decades to follow. These churches reached the peak of their strength in the 1920s with approximately 400 congregations in the British Isles and a total membership of over 16,000.

By contrast, the work in Scandinavia could boast only "two churches and a mission in Denmark and some ten or twelve churches in Norway." American involvement in Scandinavia was minimal by the middle of the twentieth century. The mission in Paris died a much earlier death when the FCMS suspended its work there in 1886 — less than ten years after it had been begun.

2.2. Western Europe

The earliest aim of Stone-Campbell missions in Western Europe was primarily the establishment of new congregations around principles of the Stone-Campbell Movement. The state churches of Western Europe were often viewed as antagonists to Christian unity, and the witness of dissenting groups was held up as exemplary. One American visitor to Germany in 1900, John G. M. Luttenberger, lamented the opposition posed by the Lutheran Church and noted: "It will be very difficult to establish our plea in Germany."

Beginning in the 1890s, missionary activities in Churches of Christ were stimulated through a raised awareness among the students of Nashville Bible School and the sister colleges formed by teachers and students of this institution. Joseph Baumann, a former Nashville Bible School student, evangelized and sought to encourage missionary work in his native Germany in the first decade of the twentieth century, but without lasting success.

Some thirty years later this interest in Germany was given new life when an outspoken German theologian from Berlin named Dr. Ludwig von Gerdtell captured attention in America. Von Gerdtell's rhetoric about Christian unity based on the teachings of the New Testament inspired a group of Americans to establish the European Evangelistic Society (EES). While Von Gerdtell himself fled to America during the Third Reich, some of the congregations he had established survived through the end of the twentieth century. These groups, however, tended to be so sectarian that Americans who took up von Gerdtell's agenda were unable to gain their partnership.

A nonconformist attitude toward missions in Western Europe was an embarrassment to the FCMS, but there were sufficient independent missionaries who were prepared to engage in European missions with or without the Society's support. In addition to the established missions in England, France, and Scandinavia, numerous issues of *Christian Standard* around the turn of the twentieth century report work in Albania, Belgium, Bohemia, Bulgaria, Germany, Holland, Hungary, Portugal, Romania, and Serbia. However, political and social unrest on the Continent were not conducive to sustained efforts in these areas, and direct involvement by American missionaries had all but ceased by the end of World War II.

2.3. Russia, Poland, and Eastern Europe

American involvement in Russia began in the early 1900s largely as a cooperative effort with an indigenous reform movement in that country. Partly through contacts in Scandinavia and Poland, and partly through contacts with Russian immigrants in New York City's East Side, American Disciples became aware of a "Restoration Movement in the Russian Empire," as Z. T. Sweeney reported. This movement, known variously as "Gospel Christians," "Bible Christians," and "The Evangelical Christian Union," stemmed from the 1850s. It was started by a General Pashkoff, later dubbed by Americans "the Alexander Campbell of Russia." At a 1912 convention of these churches in St. Petersburg their total membership was estimated at 100,000. In the aftermath of the Russian Revolution, these reformers and American Disciples saw a great opportunity for evangelism, which had not been possible under the Czars. Initially, American involvement with the Russian Christians had to do with the raising of funds to establish a Bible College in St. Petersburg.

Later, in the wake of World War I, Americans increasingly engaged in relief efforts among the destitute Russian people. The mid-1920s brought renewed hope for evangelism, and American supporters launched a campaign to raise $100,000 for the advancement of the cause in Russia. By the end of World War II this fellowship of Christians in Russia numbered two million members.

Meanwhile in Poland another indigenous missionary movement was under way under the leadership of a Polish Christian named Konstantin Jaroszewicz. An emigrant to the United States in the early 1900s, Jaroszewicz studied at Johnson Bible College and served a term as a missionary of the American Christian Missionary Society (ACMS). In 1921 he returned to his homeland and began a vigorous program of evangelism, church planting, and humanitarian relief. In less than twenty years this Polish "restoration movement" had grown to include 78 organized congregations, 400 mission points, and a nationwide membership of 40,000. Fifteen hundred delegates from the Union of Churches of Christ in Poland gathered for a convention at Wladimir Walynsk in August 1939. The mood of the conference was optimistic, in spite of rumors of war. Plans were laid for a Polish Bible College. These plans, along with the strong momentum of this indigenous movement, were shattered when Hitler's armies invaded Poland the next month. Nonetheless, by the time Soviet rule descended on Poland there were more than 250,000 members of this church movement.

3. Missions in Europe After World War II

The years of reconstruction after World War II witnessed an explosion of new American missionary initiatives in Europe. Stone-Campbell missionaries increasingly demonstrated the distinctive interests of the three American branches of the Movement. The Disciples of Christ preferred to channel their efforts through newly developing ecumenical bodies in Europe. Their fraternal workers served within established structures of Europe's historical churches. Disciples military chaplains also cultivated relationships with traditional churches in areas where they were stationed. The Christian Churches/Churches of Christ and Churches of Christ, on the other hand, envisioned greater opportunities for evangelism apart from the state churches. One attempt to combine the missionary concerns of all three branches of the movement was that of the European Evangelistic Society (EES) based in Tübingen, Germany. Due to internal tensions among the three American branches of the Movement, however, some in each branch viewed the activities of the EES with suspicion.

3.1. Germany and Western Europe

Immediately following World War II, West Germany emerged as a new focus for mission. The stationing of American occupation troops afforded an inroad into German society that had not existed previously. This, coupled with the mammoth needs for postwar reconstruction and humanitarian aid, allowed new mission works to take roots quickly. Churches of Christ were swift to seize this opportunity. Pioneer missionaries Otis Gatewood and Richard Walker prepared themselves as early as 1942 for postwar initiatives by studying German at the University of Utah. A prominent minister at Broadway Church of Christ in Lubbock, Texas, G. C. Brewer, was called in 1943 to "Evangelizing the World in the Post-War Period," while a premier mission publication, *The Harvest Field,* challenged its readers in 1942 with specific reference to Germany: "Let us love our enemies by proclaiming to them the gospel of peace." After a planning meeting for prospective missionaries to Germany at George Pepperdine College in 1944 and a survey trip by Otis Gatewood and businessman Paul Sherrod shortly after the war, the Broadway Church of Christ held a special lectureship in August 1946 to discuss cooperation for evangelism and benevolence in Europe and Asia. Churches of Christ had been reluctant to create structures for such cooperation since the missionary controversy in the 1800s. Nevertheless, a system of "sponsoring churches" developed that allowed the elders of a local congregation to coordinate fund-raising and exercising oversight in specific mission points. Broadway became a "sponsoring church" for the work in Germany, while Crescent Hill in Brownsfield, Texas, served that role for Italy. A national newspaper for members of Churches of Christ, *The Christian Chronicle,* was established in 1943 by Olan Hicks to promote missions. Much of the history of post–World War II missions by Churches of Christ is recorded in the paper.

In February 1947 Churches of Christ received from Lucius D. Clay, the Deputy Military Governor for Germany, the first permit of any American religious group to send missionaries to Germany. They established two centers for their work in the American-occupied zone, Frankfurt and Munich, and spread from there through an active program of church plantings throughout German-speaking Europe. Under the direction of Otis Gatewood and Roy Palmer, Frankfurt became a central point of benevolence and education. A Boy's Home sought to alleviate the homelessness of youth while thousands of care packages sent by members of American churches of Christ relieved some of the starvation and poverty among the population. A large building complex housing a church and a theological college was erected near the campus of the University of Frankfurt; it served to train the early leadership among the German churches. From 1970 to 1982, a Bible school at Heidelberg, affiliated with Pepperdine University, provided theological and pastoral education. Beginning in the 1960s, mission work in Germany was strengthened through summer campaigns by students from Christian colleges and universities. While German-speaking churches remained dependent upon American support and personnel for many years, the picture has changed in the last decades. Some of the literature of Churches of Christ sought to address German religious needs in German terms, notably through the journal *Der Christ im zwanzigsten Jahrhundert* (*Twentieth-Century Christian*), edited by Dieter Alten, Hans Godwin Grimm, and Reiner Kallus, as well as a German publishing house, Verlag Lebendiges Wort, in Augsburg and Berlin. The communal identity of the German churches has been strengthened by annual retreats and lectureships for men, women, families, and children. A retreat center in Gemünden provides the location for many such gatherings. A radio program, directed by Gottfried Reichel and aired over Radio Luxembourg, extended the influence of Churches of Christ beyond the local congregations. Today there are over 40 established, albeit small, "Gemeinden Christ" (Churches of Christ) in Germany, Austria, and Switzerland, including six in the former East Germany.

Missionaries from the Christian Churches/Churches of Christ also utilized American military communities as bases for mission in Germany, but they were unable to match the success of the Churches of Christ. Italy proved a more fertile field for the Christian Churches/Churches of Christ. As a result of the pioneering work of Guy and Thelma Mayfield from 1945 onward, congregations were planted in Bari and other cities of Italy, and a Bible Seminary was established to train Italian leaders. Eventually, missionaries of the Christian Churches/ Churches of Christ in Western Europe established a network and set up semi-annual retreats for fellowship and mutual support. From the 1980s onward, Team Expansion and Christian Missionary Fellowship also adopted Western Europe as a field for new church planting. By the mid-1990s the *Directory of the Ministry* listed missionaries of the Christian Churches/Churches of Christ working in Belarus, Belgium, England, France, Germany, Hungary, Ireland, Italy, Portugal, Russia, Scotland, Spain, and the Ukraine.

The Christian Church (Disciples of Christ) chose to work in partnership with Europe's historical churches through ecumenical bodies that emerged following the war. The first fraternal workers from Disciples were sent to France to help with refugees, youth programs, and pastoral work, numbering twenty-nine from 1945 to 2003. Young volunteers were sent to Oldenburg, Germany, Ionnina, Greece, and many ecumenical work camps. Over the years, out of a total of 130, twenty fraternal workers were sent to churches and social ministries in Berlin alone, when it was the center between East and West and offered the opportunity to meet Christians living under Communism. Cooperation with the World Council of Churches (WCC), inaugurated in 1948 in Amsterdam and headquartered in Geneva, resulted in the Disciples' seconding personnel to fill staff positions, including Thomas F. Best, who served as executive secretary for Faith and Order from 1983 for over twenty years. Scholarships and other support were provided to the Bossey Ecumenical Institute, and Robert A. Thomas, president of the Disciples' Division of Overseas Ministries 1969-83, was executive for Europe and served on the WCC Commission on World Mission and Evangelism, successor to the International Missionary Council.

Beginning in 1987, the Disciples Council on Christian Unity engaged in a formal dialogue with the Russian Orthodox Church. Since the 1990s, the Christian Church (Disciples of Christ) and its Common Global Ministries Board, in covenant with the United Church of Christ, has focused much of its energy on ecumenical partnership in the common struggle for international peace and justice, humanitarian relief in the name of Christ, environmental concerns, and dialogue with non-Christian faiths. The Board established a "Joint Office" for Europe in 1994 and has entered into partnerships with the Evangelical Church of the Union in Germany, a church of some nine million members joining Reformed and Lutheran traditions, and the Reformed Church of France, consisting of 380 local churches and 300,000 members.

3.2. Great Britain

Following World War II, the Churches of Christ in Great Britain were facing steady decline and an uncertain future. American Disciples sent sixteen couples to pastor congregations of the British Churches of Christ. In the 1970s British leaders and most of the congregations voted to disband the Association, close Overdale College, and join forces with the United Reformed Church in Great Britain. Disciples have continued to send fraternal workers to Britain, who now serve the United Reformed Church in the United Kingdom.

British congregations opposed to joining the United Reformed Church appealed to American churches for help. As a result, a number of missionaries, pastors, and evangelists mainly from the Christian Churches/Churches of Christ raised financial support to go to Britain and work with existing congregations. In 1980 the British-American Fellowship Committee, a cooperative effort from both sides of the Atlantic, founded Springdale College in Birmingham to provide ministerial training for a newly organized Fellowship of Churches of Christ in Great Britain. At the beginning of the third millennium, nationwide membership of the Fellowship numbered around 1,000.

A number of conservative Churches of Christ were referred to pejoratively by the Association churches as "Old Paths" churches. The decisive break between the two groups came in the early 1940s as a result of dissent that had begun in the 1920s. The issues involved objections to higher criticism mediated through Overdale College, affiliation with the "Student Christian Union" and closer ties with Protestant churches, admission of the unimmersed to the Lord's Supper, the use of instrumental music in worhip, expanded roles for women, and matters of church organization. Few full-time evangelists were left, and some churches languished. Beginning in the 1950s ties were strengthened between North American a cappella churches and the conservative British churches. Some financial and personnel help came from the United States and Canada. Older churches were strengthened, while new congregations were formed in England, Scotland, and Northern Ireland. The Northern Ireland Bible School flourished in Belfast for several years. Because of civil unrest in Ireland the school was moved to Corby, Northamptonshire, and renamed British Bible Schol. The "Open Bible School," an advanced correspondence study program, continues to operate from Scotland. In spite of a controversy in the 1960s and '70s about the Lord's Supper, specifically about the use of "individual cups," the churches have remained in fellowship and, as a whole, have grown. By 2004 over forty evangelists were working among at least eighty congregations in the United Kingdom. A current directory may be accessed at www.christian-worker.org.uk.

3.3. Central and Eastern Europe

Soviet rule effectively cut off Eastern Europe from direct American missionary involvement during the Cold War era. Apart from brief visits to encourage local Christians and to bring humanitarian aid, Western Christians were unable to establish mission points in the East. With the dawn of *perestroika* and the subsequent fall of the Iron Curtain, the situation changed overnight. Central and Eastern Europe suddenly presented a mission field potentially ripe for the harvest, and missionaries from all over the West — including members of the Stone-Campbell Movement — scrambled to answer the call. Evangelism, church planting, and humanitarian assistance for the poverty-stricken peoples of Eastern Europe were the main foci of these efforts.

One prominent effort of the Stone-Campbell churches was the mission of TCM International. Originally established in 1957 as Toronto Christian Mission, within just a few years TCM expanded its mission to Eastern Europe. With an operating base near Vienna, Austria, TCM provided Bibles, food, clothing, medicines, and leadership training resources to Christians in the East — including the Russians and Poles who had earlier links with American Disciples. American backing enabled the Polish Churches of Christ to realize one of their dreams with the establishment of the Christian Bible Institute in Warsaw in 1986. At its base in Vienna, TCM (now renamed Training Christians for Ministry) also established the Institute of Biblical Studies as a cooperative effort with Churches in the East and financially backed by American churches. By 2002 TCM was providing Certificate, M.A., and M.Div. programs for 430 students from fourteen countries in Central and Eastern Europe, assisted by faculty drawn mainly for short-term teaching from Bible colleges and seminaries of the Christian Churches/Churches of Christ.

Churches of Christ began a concerted effort to print and distribute Bibles and Bible study literature to people behind the iron curtain with the establishment of Eastern European Mission and Bible Foundation (EEM) in 1961. That year seven families moved to Vienna, Austria, to establish a base for missions to Eastern Europe. Because of restrictions imposed by Eastern European governments during the Cold War, the group focused on finding ways to deliver printed materials into the communist-controlled countries. In 1974 EEM began its own printing and distribution center in Vienna, which continues to operate. In 1978 the Bammel Road Church of Christ in Houston, Texas, assumed oversight of the work of EEM. The ministry translates and prints in twenty languages; in its first four decades it distributed over eight million Bibles and related materials in Eastern Europe and Russia.

The Global Ministries Board of the Christian Church (Disciples of Christ) and the United Church of Christ has focused its concern for Eastern Europe on helping the revitalization of the Reformed Church in Hungary, especially in its educational endeavors with four theological schools and a network of church-related secondary schools. It has also engaged faculty to work in Lithuania Christian College, founded in 1991 and seeking to enhance Christian ministry in the post-Soviet era.

See also American Christian Missionary Society; European Evangelistic Society; Foreign Christian Missionary Society, The; Gatewood, Otis; Great Britain and Ireland, Churches of Christ in; Missions, Missiology; Russia, Gospel Christians in; Springdale College

BIBLIOGRAPHY Christian Worker Directory of Churches of Christ in the United Kingdom (a cappella), on-line at http://www.Christian-worker.org.uk • Lynn Elkins and Archibald McLean, *The History of the Foreign Christian Missionary Society* (1919) • Phillip Wayne Elkins, *Church Sponsored Missions: An Evaluation of Churches of Christ* (1974) • Otis Gatewood, *Preaching in the Footsteps of Hitler* (1960) • Robert M. Hopkins, "Our Brethren in Europe," *The World Call* (September 1927): 24-25 • L. Wesley Jones, *The Real Russians* (1995) • *Lubbock Lectures on Mission Work* (1946) • John G. M. Luttenberger, "A Word from Germany," *Christian-Evangelist* (1900): 1171 • Mac Lynn, *Churches of Christ Around the World* (2003); • Z. T. Sweeney, "Restoration Movement in the Russian Empire," *The Christian-Evangelist* (1913): 890-91 • Gailyn Van Rheenen and Bob Waldron, *The Status of Missions in Churches of Christ* (2002); • Albert Wardin, "The Disciples of Christ and Ties with Russia," *Discipliana* 52 (Fall 1992): 33, 35-41 • Henry Webb, "History of Churches of Christ in Poland," *Discipliana* 52 (1992); 33, 42-43.

DENNIS R. LINDSAY

European Evangelistic Society

Organization supported principally by the Christian Churches/Churches of Christ and Christian Church (Disciples of Christ), which sponsors evangelistic activity and Christian scholarship in Tübingen, Germany.

The European Evangelistic Society (EES), incorporated in the State of Indiana on July 16, 1946, was a sequel to the German Evangelical Association, formed in September 1930 to endorse the evangelistic work of German scholar Ludwig von Gerdtell, so that he could proceed under the aegis of a recognized body of churches whose object was to conform faith and practice to the New Testament interpreted in the context of the Bible as a whole. That legacy, which included reports to the International Convention of Disciples of Christ, continues with reports to the General Assembly of the Christian Church (Disciples of Christ).

After Tübingen, Germany, was chosen as the university city in which to locate the mission of EES, entry was undertaken in late summer of 1949. Property was acquired in February 1962 at Wilhelmstrasse 100. The building, a sturdy structure of four levels, stands only a short distance from the library of the Karl Eberhard University. In this building are housed both the Christliche Gemeinde (Christian Church) and the Institut zur Erforschung des Urchristentums (Institute for the Study of Christian Origins). Holdings of the library are also catalogued in the university library.

A college adjacent to a university was envisioned at first, but by the time the building was obtained, institutes had emerged in association with the University of Tübingen's Evangelische Fakultät (Protestant Faculty) to specialize in supportive research. The Institute for the Study of Christian Origins enabled personnel of the EES to carry on scholarly work and to serve alongside other university institutes. The arrangement did not involve a formal relationship to those institutes, but it did guarantee acceptance of the EES work to the extent of its assistance and contributions to the larger academic life of the university.

Scholars in the Institute for the Study of Christian Origins research aspects of the gospel and the life of the church in the light of ancient cultural contexts. EES urges the participation of scholars locally and globally and encourages the infusion of that scholarship with concern for evangelism, worship, and Christian unity. To that end the Institute and "Gemeinde" are deliberately conjoined in the endeavor of the EES.

EES remains one of the few organizations receiving support from, participation of, or endorsement by individuals, churches, and conventions of all three branches of the Stone-Campbell tradition.

See also Europe, Missions in

EARL R. STUCKENBRUCK

Evangelical

Term used to identify conservative Protestants who distinguished themselves from fundamentalism in the mid-twentieth century.

Since the Reformation, Protestant churches have laid claim to the term "evangelical," rooted in the Greek *euangelion,* "good news," in the interest of identifying their teaching as based on the gospel. In the nineteenth century the term referred to all Protestant denominations, often to make the distinction from Catholics and new movements like the Mormons and Seventh Day Adventists. Thomas Campbell identified his movement as part of "Evangelical Christianity" in the *Declaration and Address.* The fundamentalist-modernist controversy of the twentieth century significantly altered the theological makeup of American Protestantism. By mid-century some conservatives claimed the term "Evangelical" to distinguish themselves from both modernists and fundamentalists, while still affirming the plenary verbal inspiration and sole authority of Scripture and placing a pietistic emphasis on a personal saving relationship with God through Jesus Christ.

Although Churches of Christ and Christian Churches/Churches of Christ have had much in common with this evangelical ethos, they have generally remained aloof from the broader evangelical movement. Sharing the generic evangelical affirmation of biblical authority, conservative churches of the Stone-Campbell Movement have distinguished themselves from evangelicalism by their anti-creedalism, concern for proper church order, and insistence that salvation results from a rational acceptance of the facts of the gospel, accompanied by baptism for the remission of sins. Most members of the more liberal Christian Church (Disciples of Christ) differ from both evangelicals and conservative restorationists over definitions of biblical authority.

In spite of this aloofness, each branch of the Movement has evangelical connections. A controversial book by K. C. Moser of the Churches of Christ titled *The Way of Salvation* (1932) was perceived as taking an evangelical turn in its definition of faith as personal relationship with and trust in Christ for salvation, not rational obedience to commands. Heavily criticized, Moser opened the door for a larger emphasis on grace in Churches of Christ. Jack Lewis, longtime professor at Harding Graduate School of Religion, did translation work for the New International Version (NIV), sponsored by the Evangelical Theological Society. In the 1990s the writings of Max Lucado, Texas minister and author also from Churches of Christ, have gained broad popularity and a substantial readership among American evangelicals.

The Christian Churches/Churches of Christ have been more open to the evangelical movement, with James DeForest Murch being the most significant example. Murch served as editor from 1945 to 1959 of the National Association of Evangelicals' magazine *United Evangelical Action* and as managing editor of *Christianity Today.* Lewis Foster of Cincinnati Bible Seminary worked on the NIV and New King James

Version, translations sponsored by evangelicals. Christian Church Bible colleges represent the largest contingent of schools accredited by the American Association of Bible Colleges.

Missiologist Donald McGavran, a prominent Disciples "evangelical," was the recognized pioneer of the church growth movement and founding dean of Fuller Theological Seminary's School of World Mission. Disciple Renewal, founded in 1985, is a conservative evangelical Disciples organization advocating biblical infallibility and salvation in Christ alone. Disciple Renewal also created Disciples Heritage Fellowship as an alternate structure for disenchanted Disciples evangelicals.

See also Moser, Kenneth Carl; Murch, James DeForest

BIBLIOGRAPHY William Baker, ed., *Evangelicalism and the Stone-Campbell Movement* (2002) • Grant Edwards, "Disciples of Christ," in *Evangelical Renewal in the Mainline Churches,* ed. Ronald H. Nash (1987) • Richard T. Hughes, "Are Restorationists Evangelicals?" in *The Variety of American Evangelicalism,* ed. Donald W. Dayton and Robert K. Johnston (1991) • James DeForest Murch, *Adventuring for Christ in Changing Times* (1973)

ROBERT D. CORNWALL

Evangelical Alliance

An early ecumenical organization.

The Evangelical Alliance was inaugurated in Liverpool, England, in August 1845. Formal organization occurred the next year, 1846, in London, England, with the first session held at the Free Mason's Hall on Great Queen Street. Celebrated American church leaders such as Lyman Beecher, L. M. Dewitt, and William Patton were in attendance, as well as Belgian, French, English, Scottish, and Prussian representatives from predominantly Reformed (Calvinist) backgrounds. Those present soon adopted a platform of nine affirmations: (1) the authority and inspiration of Scripture; (2) the triune God; (3) humanity's total depravity; (4) the incarnation of the Son of God; (5) justification by faith alone; (6) the work of the Holy Spirit in conversion and sanctification; (7) the right of private judgment in interpreting Scripture; (8) the threefold institutions of the evangelical ministry, baptism, and the Lord's Supper; and (9) the eschatological realities of immortality, bodily resurrection, and divine judgment.

Alexander Campbell commented that, "stript of their metaphysical terminology," these propositions would be acceptable to him, and eventually he offered his own commentary on, and reworking of, the alliance's dogmatic principles. Initially, however, he criticized what appeared to him to be an "alliance of sects." "The central truth of the Evangelical Alliance is the maintenance of Protestantism. The central truth of Christian Union is the sanctification of the faithful and the conversion of all nations to Christ." Were it truly an "evangelical" alliance and not a Protestant coalition, argued Campbell, the Lord Jesus Christ would be the center. Thus the Evangelical Alliance could only hope to unite some denominations on a few particulars, make them feel more tolerant of each other, and lend them some resolve against "popery"; but it was destined to fall short of restoring primitive Christianity as the basis of Christian unity.

Despite his suspicions, Campbell declared his openness to all attempts to promote the "Union of Christians, on Christian grounds and for Christian objects." Though British Churches of Christ urged Campbell to attend the inaugural meeting, W. K. Pendleton represented the Movement in Campbell's place. Shortly thereafter, perhaps owing to Pendleton's enthusiasm, Campbell spoke far more favorably of the Evangelical Alliance, at least as a preliminary step toward a "more rational and scriptural" plan of union. He even compared it favorably to his father's Christian Association of Washington insofar as both organizations spurned status as a new "church." Campbell pledged to "cordially sympathize" with the Alliance, and "to the utmost of my power, to cooperate with them just as far and as long as they please to permit me."

Following the Civil War the Evangelical Alliance established a formal organizational presence in the United States. At its 1893 meeting in Chicago Philip Schaff, the renowned American church historian and ecumenist, declared that the Alliance offered the best hope for the reunion of Christendom of any organization that he knew about. In the late 1890s theological liberals began to withdraw from the Alliance, and its influence diminished.

See also Ecumenical Movement, The; Pendleton, William Kimbrough; Unity, Christian

BIBLIOGRAPHY Alexander Campbell, "Christian Union," nos. 6-10 (Evangelical Alliance), *Millennial Harbinger* (1847): 31-35, 78-83, 165-70, 217-21, 253-55 • Alexander Campbell and W. K. Pendleton, "The Evangelical Alliance," *Millennial Harbinger* (1846): 382-88, 445-48, 624-31, 673-83 • J. D. Murch, *Cooperation Without Compromise: A History of the National Association of Evangelicals* (1956).

CHARLES R. GRESHAM

Evangelical Society of Ulster

Organization promoting evangelism and reconciliation in Northern Ireland in the late eighteenth century.

George Hamilton, minister of Armagh's Burgher congregation, along with several other ministers and laymen, including Thomas Campbell, established the Evangelical Society of Ulster (ESU) on October 10, 1798, in Armagh, Ireland. The society's purpose was ecumenical and evangelistic in nature. It urged ministers, regardless of denominational affiliation, to unite in a common cause to preach the gospel to the lost.

Modeling itself after the London Missionary Society, the ESU collected dues to help fund the publication and distribution of religious tracts among the poor as well as fund itinerant preachers to evangelize Irish villages that did not have ministers. By doing so, the ESU became one of the first evangelical organizations to be an interdenominational basis for evangelism. At its inception, Thomas Campbell became one of the society's elected officers and paid the first year's dues.

Within the first three months, the society grew from its original thirteen ministers to thirty-three ministers, collectively representing four denominations. One of the first major steps taken by the society was to make a formal request to the London Missionary Society that they send two itinerant preachers to Ireland. By the spring of 1799, the society had 115 members and a promise from the London Missionary Society for the two preachers. The preachers came to Ireland in May and stayed until early October of the same year, preaching at times as a team and at other times on separate circuits.

In the summer of 1799, the Antiburgher synod, to which Campbell belonged, met and concluded that the ESU's principles were too ecclesiastically permissive and would destroy the gospel and undermine Christ's Kingdom. It then began to put pressure on Thomas Campbell (the only Antiburgher minister in the society) to leave it. By the summer of the next year, Campbell conformed to the decision of the Antiburgher synod and left the society. Though he was forced out, the direction and principles of this society were formative for Campbell. Once he arrived in America, he continued to seek to experience a nonsectarian community that would unify behind the spreading of the gospel. It is clear, moreover, that the society provided something of a model for Campbell's new initiative in Pennsylvania, the Christian Association of Washington.

See also Campbell, Thomas; Christian Association of Washington

BIBLIOGRAPHY Hiram Lester, "Alexander Campbell's Early Baptism in Ecumenicity and Sectarianism," *Restoration Quarterly* 30 (1988): 85-101 • Hiram Lester, "An Irish Precursor for Thomas Campbell's *Declaration and Address*," *Encounter* 50:3 (1989): 247-67 • A. R. Scott, "Thomas Campbell's Ministry at Ahorey," *Restoration Quarterly* 29 (1987): 229-34.

JOHN P. HARRISON

Evangelism, Evangelists

Evangelism is the promulgation of the gospel through media and methods suitable to a given historical and cultural context. The consensus plea of the Stone-Campbell Movement in its formative years was the pursuit of Christian unity for the purpose of effective world evangelization. The Movement committed itself early on to recovering the ideals and offices of the evangelism of the apostolic churches as evidenced in the New Testament, though the Movement has had to accommodate its evangelistic endeavors to its own changing cultural and geographical frontiers. The role of the "evangelist" has likewise seen considerable adaptation.

1. Nineteenth Century

The fact that Alexander Campbell did not see himself as an evangelist served to define the work of evangelism for the early Movement. He was an editor, he explained in the 1830 *Millennial Harbinger,* "and when I make a tour, it is more to disseminate the general principles of reformation, than to proclaim the ancient gospel for the purpose of converting sinners to God." Campbell defined an evangelist as an itinerant who preaches the gospel, converts sinners, plants churches, and assists in ordaining elders and setting churches in order. Such a person would then leave the new church in the care of its pastors (elders) and move on.

As with Methodists and other groups on the trans-Appalachian frontier, this view of evangelism principally in terms of itinerancy more or less prevailed throughout the nineteenth century, albeit not always with the effect Alexander Campbell envisioned. The most serious problem was that the evangelist "moved on" too soon, leaving the infant congregation ill-equipped to carry on. A further problem was the inadequate financial support of the evangelists, with some of them destitute and unable to continue their work.

Those who did this work are mostly lost to history, unsung and unknown. Numbered in the hundreds, they took the gospel to the far reaches of the frontier. They were farmers, teachers, merchants, lawyers, even doctors and dentists, who left their means of livelihood, at least part of the year, to preach "the ancient gospel" and to build churches after "the ancient order." They were known for uncommon devotion and sacrifice, especially in the earlier generations. Their families back home, who were left to mind the store or run the farm, also sacrificed.

They preached in homes, barns, brush arbors, schoolhouses, courthouses, railway stations, outofdoors, as well as in churches. Meetings ran from a few days to several weeks. Advanced advertising was unnecessary. News of the evangelist's arrival, often with no advance notice, spread quickly. It was a social event well attended, and was for some the only recreation and contact with the outside world.

Methods varied. Evangelists associated with the Stone movement continued to use the "mourner's bench" for some time. There were testimonials and exchanges with the audience. Long sermons were common, punctuated with lively stories and illustrations. Some evangelists sang as well as preached. Knowles Shaw (1834-1878), for example, took his melodeon along with him in the meetings he held in Ohio, Indiana, Michigan, and other states. Audiences came to hear him sing and remained to hear him preach. Even though he died at age 44, he had garnered some 20,000 converts.

As for what they preached, the theme was set early on by Walter Scott (1796-1861), who is arguably the most important evangelist in the history of the Stone-Campbell Movement. J. J. Haley began the tradition of naming Walter Scott among "the big four of the current reformation," the others being Barton Stone and Thomas and Alexander Campbell. Haley claimed for Scott that the Campbell movement would not have survived except for his phenomenal evangelistic successes.

Sent out in 1827 by the Mahoning Association of Ohio, made up of "Reformed" Baptist churches sympathetic to the Campbell movement, Scott gained more than 2,000 additions during the first two years evangelizing the Western Reserve. His labors in the ensuing years were so effective that his work positioned the Campbell movement, by then some 12,000 strong, to unite with the Stone movement in 1832.

Scott's unique methodology influenced other evangelists for generations to come. His famous "Five Finger Exercise" provided a simple plan of how to become a Christian. When the sinner believes that Jesus is the Christ, repents of his or her sins, and is baptized, God grants the remission of sins and the gift of the Holy Spirit. These were not presented as arbitrary steps, but as part of a dynamic presentation of Jesus Christ as the crucified and risen Lord. It was in fact difficult for a sinner to remain in his or her seat in the face of Scott's fervent preaching. Scott influenced the character of evangelism, not only in methodology and content but in effectiveness as well. Throughout the nineteenth century it was common for evangelists to report hundreds of baptisms annually. Even a revival of only a few days might result in twenty to thirty additions.

Scott provided not only concrete evangelistic methods but also the biblical-hermeneutical foundation for those methods. In works like his *The Gospel Restored* (1836) and *The Messiahship* (1849), he developed a model for understanding the progressive revelation of Scripture in terms of a grand body of evidences for the central proposition of Christian faith and evangelism, the declaration that Jesus is the Christ. The Five Finger Exercise was in effect shorthand for the broader plan of salvation spread across Scripture and concentrated in the New Testament, and the new believer was called in simple and abbreviated terms to affirm the very same truth at which the scholar arrived through assiduous exegesis.

The caption on the back of this photo reads: "The residence at Lisbon, Ohio, where Walter Scott first declared the Gospel Plan of Salvation in full." The account of Scott's November 18, 1827, sermon appears in William Baxter's *Life of Elder Walter Scott.* Courtesy of the Disciples of Christ Historical Society

Besides Scott, other prominent early Stone-Campbell evangelists include John T. Johnson (1788-1856) and "Raccoon" John Smith (1784-1868), who were so successful in Kentucky that the Movement in that state numbered 50,000 by the 1850s. Elijah Goodwin (1807-1879) and James M. Mathes (1808-1892) baptized thousands in Indiana, a state that enjoyed some of the greatest numerical growth of the Movement in its early history.

Benjamin F. Hall (1803-1873), a dentist ordained to preach by Barton W. Stone, was an evangelist-at-large in that he roamed the frontier with abandon, baptizing thousands and forming scores of churches. His prize convert was Tolbert Fanning (1810-1874), who evangelized extensively in Tennessee and Alabama. T. M. Allen (1797-1871), who sent in hundreds of reports from the field to Campbell's and Stone's journals, worked especially in Missouri. He organized eighteen churches and baptized 3,570. Isaac Errett (1820-1888), heir to Campbell's mantle, evangelized in Michigan before founding the *Christian Standard.* Pardee Butler (1816-1888) achieved impressive results in Kansas, while A. L. Todd was a circuit-riding evangelist in Oregon as early as the 1850s.

There were also women evangelists. Elias Smith and James O'Kelly had "female preachers" in the eastern Christian Movement as early as the 1790s. The most noted were Abigail Roberts (1791-1841) and Nancy Crum (1776-1815), who converted hundreds and started a number of churches. Some of their male converts became preachers. Debra B. Hull in her study of women preachers in the Christian Church found numerous female evangelists in the western wing of the Movement as early as the 1830s, although they became fewer in succeeding decades. The "Three Marys" of Somerset, Pennsylvania, started the church in that town and built it to 400 members by the 1840s.

Clara Hale Babcock (1850-1924) and Sadie McCoy Crank (1863-1948), the first women to be ordained in the Movement, evangelized in the Midwest with impressive results. Babcock had 1,400 conversions in twenty-eight revivals, while Crank baptized upwards of 7,000 and organized fifty churches.

In 1887 Thomas Munnell, minister and missionary organizer from Ohio, published a short but substantial study of *Evangelists and Their Work in the Churches,* assessing the role of evangelists in the New Testament and the viability of the office among the churches of the Stone-Campbell Movement. Munnell concluded that the office of evangelist was crucial for the churches and was not intended to inhibit the ministry of elders and deacons. Evangelists were needed to continue itinerant ministry and church planting, to serve as proxy bishops until congregations could raise up their own leaders, and to do cross-congregational pastoral care where needed. Munnell decried the disorganization reigning in some areas: "Every one goes his own way, duplicating many times protracted-meetings, in good churches, but leaving the mountains of Kentucky and similar places to their chances of inexperienced elders and preachers, and sometimes unauthorized evangelists." Evangelists were crucial bearers of the *apostolic* ministry, a ministry that demanded organization and support, lest "we can never unite the energies of the churches in any general enterprise."

LEROY GARRETT

2. Twentieth Century

2.1. Christian Church (Disciples of Christ)

The Disciples of Christ entered the twentieth century committed to evangelism. Quickly, however, many churches developed a growing interest in social issues facing society. Some Disciples came to believe that the chief role of the church was to redeem society, while others believed that the only business of the church was to convert individuals who could then change the social order. Thus began a division of opinion among Disciples that continued throughout the twentieth century.

Disciples began to put more focus on organization and structure for programming, especially missionary efforts in the early twentieth century. Nevertheless their evangelistic efforts in North America continued strong. In 1904 a Board of Evangelism was formed as a part of the American Christian Missionary Society. At the same time, a group of professional evangelists organized the National Evangelistic Association (NEA). This association promoted and encouraged a spirit of evangelism among Disciples preachers, musicians, and churches.

Some of the best-known Disciples evangelists of the early twentieth century were James H. O. Smith (1857-1935), James V. Coombs (1849-1920), and George F. Hall (b. 1864). They traveled with musicians from one place to another holding revival campaigns to "win souls for Christ." Their converts numbered in the thousands.

By far the most celebrated and successful Disciples evangelist of the time was Charles Reign Scoville (1869-1937). Scoville served as president of the NEA from 1920 to 1926, not only traveling throughout the United States but also leading an evangelistic team on a mission around the world. It was not unusual for Scoville to gain as many as 1,500 converts during an extended meeting.

Another Disciples evangelist who became widely recognized after World War I was Jesse M. Bader (1886-1963). Using the slogan "Each one win one" and promoting visitation evangelism, Bader became prominent not only among Disciples but among other American denominations as well. According to Bader in his annual report to the NEA for 1929, "Nothing less than the evangelization of the whole world is the purpose and passion of Jesus. We are partners with him in this superhuman task, [for] the accomplishment of which, he has promised superhuman power."

Jesse Bader became the first superintendent of evangelism for the United Christian Missionary Society in 1920, and then in 1932 he became head of the Department of Evangelism for the Federal Council of Churches, a national ecumenical organization. He retired in 1953, only to become the first general secretary of the World Convention of Churches of Christ, an organization he had founded in 1930. He served in that position until his death in 1963. Encouraging both ministers and lay people in the work of evangelism, he said, "What our Lord made primary, we have no right to make secondary."

During the Depression years and World War II, Disciples' growth slowed, as it did with other churches. But following the war, enthusiasm was renewed. In 1946 the International Convention enthusiastically approved "A Crusade for a Christian World." From 1947 to 1950 Disciples set a goal of organizing 200 new congregations. The NEA also added the goal of 900,000 new members to the Christian Church. While not entirely successful in its goals, the "Crusade" brought new life to the Disciples and their local congregations.

The 1950s marked the last decade of the twentieth century when churches and religion in general were celebrated by the larger American culture. Not only was membership at an all-time high in the 1950s, but many new congregations were established and existing ones expanded. It was a boom time in church building. Many congregations began to move from downtown locations into the suburbs to better reach people for Christ. The Korean War of 1951-53 slowed but did not stop the growth and expansion. New and large church buildings allowed for expanded programs that attracted more members. By 1955 the Disciples had reached their peak membership of nearly two million.

The events of the turbulent 1960s began to change the landscape for Disciples as they did for most American institutions. Not only did American culture see strong currents of anti-institutionalism (including anti-organized religion), but Disciples began a process of organizational Restructure culminating in 1968. With the growing social and political agenda of the 1960s, especially civil rights and the war in Vietnam, the focus of attention began to shift away from evangelism and "soul saving" to social action. Still, evangelism was not totally abandoned. Plans were laid for a "Decade of Decision" program for 1960-70 with emphasis on education, evangelism, and stewardship.

In the 1970s and 1980s the NEA clearly took the lead in Disciples evangelism. Deeply concerned about declining membership, the NEA set its goals: "Every Disciple Pastor a Functioning Evangelist, Every Disciple Member a Witnessing Christian, Every Disciple Congregation a Growing Congregation." The NEA wanted to reverse the numerical decline that began in the mid-1960s and return Disciples membership to its 1960 level. Feeling that their pattern of meeting prior to the biennial General Assembly was not enough, the NEA established an every-other-year National Evangelism Workshop (NEW) for the years the General Assembly did not meet. This began to attract thousands of Disciples ministers and lay persons. The key leader of the NEA, Herb Miller, also began to write popular books on practical ways to do evangelism. Then a monthly publication called *Net Results* was begun, with Miller as editor.

In addition to the work of the NEA, Disciples established a "Growth for Witness" program in 1981; began to hold evangelism "festivals" across the country; focused on reaching youth and young adults as well as African Americans, Hispanics, and Asians; and began to train "Pastor/Developers" to start new congregations. Disciples also used the media of radio and television, and later the Internet, to do the work of evangelism. Disciples leadership hoped this would stem the tide of declining membership.

By the 1990s some Disciples were beginning to acknowledge dramatic changes taking place in the church. New styles of worship began to appear in Disciples congregations. A new focus on the importance of small groups and the witness of laity began to emerge. As the twentieth century ended, these changes were becoming more common among Disciples congregations. Under the leadership of General Minister and President Richard L. Hamm, Disciples set goals for leadership development, the revitalization of existing congregations, and the establishment of new congregations.

C. Roy Stauffer

2.2. Churches of Christ

The term "evangelist" has generally been used among members of Churches of Christ as a designation for anyone devoted to public proclamation of the Scriptures. Therefore, in common parlance the term has been considered synonymous with "minister" or "preacher" (but never with "pastor," which would apply only to someone serving as an elder), the only distinction between the terms being the focus on the message rather than on the service or act of proclamation. While these terms have usually been considered interchangeable biblical designations, the role of the evangelist has at times proved quite controversial within Churches of Christ. In the early days of the Movement, Alexander Campbell and others spoke out vehemently against what they called the "clergy" or the "pastor" system. In Campbell's view the denominations had fostered a clergy-laity distinction with no basis in Scripture and had developed an unhealthy dependence on a "hireling priesthood" that stifled true evangelism. These abuses, and his own determination to take no remuneration for his preaching, led him to oppose fixed salaries for preachers and to discourage one evangelist doing all the preaching in a congregation lest the clergy system be resurrected.

After Campbell's death in 1866, however, a growing number of leaders in the Movement began to suggest that Campbell had gone too far in his opposition to local evangelists, and by the century's end many churches in the Movement were employing located ministers with fixed salaries. Among Churches of Christ, however, the trend toward located evangelists continued to receive opposition. At the turn of the twentieth century, John E. Dunn wrote several articles in the *Gospel Advocate* opposing located preachers as an unscriptural innovation that had contributed to the Disciples' digression from the New Testament pattern. Charging that evangelists "love ease" and that churches loved to be entertained by polished speakers, Dunn encouraged churches to develop their own teachers and let evangelists preach in "protracted meetings" wherever possible, saving souls and establishing churches. David Lipscomb and others on the *Gospel Advocate* staff concurred with Dunn's sentiments but did not press the issue as forcefully as Dunn.

Citing examples of evangelists who had worked successfully for local congregations, M. C. Kurfees, a minister in Louisville, Kentucky, countered Dunn's and Lipscomb's arguments, pointing out that while a clergy system might emerge if evangelists stifled the work by doing everything for a congregation and not developing local talent, such a result was not necessary.

Earl I. West argues that the acceptance of evangelists in local congregations finally won the day because those congregations that had them were more effective in reaching converts. Located preachers who generally had more time for study were also more effective in edifying the congregation in their teaching and preaching.

By mid-century, most opposition to evangelists working regularly with congregations had disappeared in mainstream Churches of Christ. Though most saw a local supported evangelist as the ideal for church growth, tenures were often short, and many small churches failed to adequately supply the evangelist's needs.

Outside mainstream Churches of Christ, opposition to located evangelists continued beyond mid-century. In the Midwest, Daniel Sommer continued to address this issue among his conservative followers, and his spiritual heirs, W. Carl Ketcherside and Leroy Garrett, writing in the *Mission Messenger,* occasionally brought the issue to attention. Four debates in the 1950s — the G. K. Wallace–W. Carl Ketcherside Debate (Paragould, Arkansas, 1952), the Flavil L. Colley–W. Carl Ketcherside Debate (Dallas, 1953), the Bill J. Humble–Leroy Garrett Debate (Kansas City, 1954), and the George W. DeHoff–Leroy Garrett Debate (Nashville, 1954) — provided the most articulate expressions of continued opposition to local, salaried evangelists and the biblical arguments for and against such an arrangement. While some leaders like Homer Hailey issued occasional warnings about the development of nonbiblical patterns of ministry, by the 1950s most vocal opposition to full-time evangelists was rare.

While full-time evangelists or preachers working with one congregation became the norm in Churches of Christ, for much of the twentieth century even these "located" evangelists continued to travel elsewhere for one or more weeks during the year to hold evangelistic "Gospel Meetings." Preachers routinely sent reports of their meetings to papers like the *Gospel Advocate* and *Firm Foundation,* giving the number of baptisms and restorations. Yet, as in the earliest days of the Movement, much of the evangelism that took place in the first half of the century was done by nonprofessionals who established churches in towns and cities across the country as they moved into new locations for work or financial opportunities. Also, evangelists like E. C. Fuqua (b. 1876), J. C. Estes (1866-1940), and J. D. Burleson (b. 1856) preached and established hundreds of churches in the early 1900s without promise of financial support. Often use was made of tents where church buildings were not available.

Another method of evangelism used during the twentieth century was large evangelistic meetings involving the cooperation of multiple congregations. One of the most famous of these efforts was the Hardeman Tabernacle Meetings in Nashville, Tennessee. Educator and preacher N. B. Hardeman (1874-1965) was invited to preach in the Ryman Tabernacle in a series that lasted from March 28 to April 16, 1922. The meetings proved so successful that a second series was conducted the following year that resulted in over a hundred baptisms. Eventually Hardeman returned to Nashville three more times, in 1928, 1938, and 1942. Later in the century the crusade model was used by Churches of Christ in several large cities. Willard Collins (b. 1915) of Lipscomb University preached and Mack Wayne Craig (b. 1925) led singing in another major Nashville gathering in October 1962. The person most identified with this method in recent times is Jimmy Allen (b. 1930), who preached in numerous evangelistic campaigns between 1964 and 1982, baptizing more than 7,000 persons.

Several significant parachurch organizations designed to aid the churches in their evangelism were established after World War II, including Herald of Truth International, World Radio, and World Bible School. Dozens of such non-local efforts, usually overseen by the elders of a specific congregation but supported by churches and individuals across the world, use a variety of electronic and print media to spread the gospel. Speakers for these institutions, like Batsell Barrett Baxter (1916-1982) of the Herald of Truth, have often become among the most widely known and respected evangelists in Churches of Christ.

At the beginning of the twenty-first century, Churches of Christ see the work of evangelists as an almost essential part of a congregation's life and work. In local congregations of mainstream Churches of Christ, the work of evangelists has come to involve more edification than "first principles" instruction, as well as a more differentiated and specialized focus, with many churches employing youth ministers, pulpit ministers, ministers of involvement, etc., to meet diverse needs. Education and preparation for ministry have also become more important to mainstream churches, and the trend seems likely to continue.

J. CURTIS POPE

2.3. Christian Churches/Churches of Christ

For Christian Churches/Churches of Christ during the twentieth century, evangelism has involved innovation in methodology, proliferation in the establishment of organizations for evangelistic promotion, endeavors to recruit persons for evangelistic enterprises, and commitment to numerical growth of local congregations.

One important early factor was the establishment of Bible colleges. Although these institutions were committed to higher education, they were also utilized as tools for evangelism and discipleship. Some examples from across the century would include the School of the Evangelists (now Johnson Bible College, est. 1893) in Tennessee; Cincinnati Bible College (est. 1924); Lincoln Christian College (est. 1944) in Illinois; St. Louis Christian College (est. 1956); and Bluefield College of Evangelism (est. 1971) in West Virginia. These and other Bible colleges founded in the twentieth century not only contributed to the establishment, ministry personnel, and growth of numerous congregations in the United States but also played a major role in rallying churches' support for international missions.

Local evangelistic revivals — often hosted by congregations, usually for a week at a time — were prevalent in the twentieth century. Crusade evangelism was conducted both by professional itinerants and evangelistic organizations. The former can be exemplified in the work of such individual evangelists as Tommy Oakes (b. 1947), Johnny Hall (1914-1991), David E. Branholm (1940-1975), and O. George Stansberry (b. 1925), and the latter in the work of such individuals and their organizations as Victor Knowles, Jr. (b. 1945), with his Peace on Earth Ministries, George Melton (b. 1937) of The Melton Family Singers, and Larry Wiseman (b. 1942) with Person to Person Evangelism. "Music evangelism" has been integral to both the local-revival and crusade methods. The mid-twentieth century saw a proliferation of ministries of "song evangelists" (e.g., Lowell "Shorty" Mason) and of gospel music teams, like J. D. and Gladys Smith, the Payne Sisters, the Vernon Brothers, and the Gospel Lads, who traveled across the country performing in small and large venues alike.

With the dawning of radio and television technology, the Christian Churches/Churches of Christ utilized these media prolifically for evangelistic purposes. Ed Bousman (b. 1918) established the "God Is Just a Prayer Away" radio ministry. In 1943 Ard Hoven and others began "The Christian's Hour" radio broadcast based at Cincinnati Bible Seminary. In 1952 Walter and Mainie Coble of Garrett, Indiana, started the Gospel Broadcasting Mission (later moved to Wisconsin) to transmit evangelistic programming overseas. In 1956 the four Vernon Brothers established one of the first television ministries among Christian Churches/Churches of Christ, the Christian TV Mission, based in Springfield, Missouri. Cecil Todd (b. 1931) of Joplin, Missouri, was a pioneer "televangelist" in the 1960s and 1970s with his program "Revival Fires."

The single most crucial spearhead for evangelism in the twentieth century, however, was individual congregations with high-profile preachers. P. H. Welshimer (1873-1957) ministered to the First Christian Church, Canton, Ohio, which grew to over 5,000 members and remained for many years the largest congregation among Christian Churches/Churches of Christ. Welshimer exemplified for a whole generation the critical importance of evangelistic ministry as a congregationally based initiative. His legacy may be found in a number of so-called "mega-churches" that have grown to 3,000 or more members in the fellowship of Christian Churches/Churches of Christ, largely through influential preachers and specialized evangelistic ministries. Some examples would be the Southeast Christian Church in Louisville, Kentucky (with a membership of over 15,000); Southland Christian Church in Lexington, Kentucky; East 91st St. Christian Church in Indianapolis; Central Christian Church in Mesa, Arizona; and Central Christian Church in Las Vegas, Nevada.

Throughout the twentieth century individuals and organizations were intentionally committed to the establishment of new congregations. Methods included individuals planting congregations on their own, congregations committing a portion of their membership to the establishment of new churches in the same locale, and specialized organizations that approached church planting on a more scientific basis (i.e., through demographics, site location studies, mass mailings, etc.). For instance, Virgil Felton (b. 1916) founded New Churches of Christ Evangelism in Michigan, an organization that for over forty years planted congregations in Florida, Indiana, Michigan, and Ohio. A number of ministers from across the country came together to found Double Vision in 1986, a church-planting ministry operative nationwide. Besides specialized church-planting organizations, numerous congregations within given regions have united financial and personnel resources in "evangelizing associations" dedicated to establishing new churches. Examples would include the Chicago District Evangelizing Association, Empire State Evangelizing Association (New York), Go

Ye Chapel Mission (New York City), Southern California Evangelizing Association, and the Virginia Evangelizing Fellowship.

Christian Churches/Churches of Christ have made a considerable investment not only in church planting but also in church growth. Donald McGavran (1897-1990), a missiologist and church growth expert whose ministry extended to all branches of the Stone-Campbell tradition, has been an inspirational figure in helping leaders to understand evangelistic outreach and local congregational growth. The National Church Growth Research Center, founded in 1972 and spearheaded by Paul Benjamin, has also played an important role in the study and encouragement of evangelism and church growth among the Christian Churches/Churches of Christ. BILLY W. JONES

See also Babcock, Claria Celestia Hale; Baxter, Batsell Barrett; Bible College Movement; Butler, Pardee; Church Growth Movement; Church Planting Associations; Congregational Life; Crank, Sarah Catherine (Sadie) McCoy; Errett, Isaac; Five Finger Exercise; Goodwin, Elijah; Hall, Benjamin Franklin; Hardeman, Nicholas Brodie; Herald of Truth; Johnson, John T.; Mahoning Baptist Association; McGavran, Donald A.; Ministry; National Church Growth Research Center; Preaching; Radio and Television; Scott, Walter; Shaw, Knowles; Smith, "Raccoon" John; Welshimer, Pearl Howard; Worship

BIBLIOGRAPHY Jesse M. Bader, *Evangelism in a Changing America* (1957) • William Baxter, *Life of Elder Walter Scott* (1874) • William Baxter, *The Life of Knowles Shaw, the Singing Evangelist* (1879) • Paul Benjamin, *The Equipping Ministry* (1978) • H. Leo Boles, *Biographical Sketches of Gospel Preachers* (1932) • Lin D. Cartwright, *Evangelism for Today* (1934) • Mark Collis, "The Restoration Movement and the Spirit of Evangelism," *Christian Standard* 68 (1933): 73-74 • Joe S. Ellis, *The Church on Purpose* (1982) • J. J. Haley, *Makers and Molders of the Reformation* (1914) • Richard L. Hamm, *2020 Vision for the Christian Church (Disciples of Christ)* (2001) • N. B. Hardeman, *Hardeman's Tabernacle Sermons*, 5 vols. (1922, 1923, 1928, 1938, 1943) • David Edwin Harrell, Jr., *The Churches of Christ in the Twentieth Century: Homer Hailey's Personal Journey of Faith* (2000) • Traverce Harrison and Cecil J. Sharp, *Evangelism: The Man, the Message, the Method* (1924) • A. S. Hayden, *Early History of the Disciples in the Western Reserve, Ohio* (1875) • Alvin Jennings, *T. M. Allen* (1977) • Debra B. Hull, *Christian Church Women* (1994) • Donald McGavran, *Understanding Church Growth* (1970) • Herb Miller, "Contemporary Disciples Evangelism: The Erosion of Biblical Christianity," *Mid-Stream* 26 (1987): 351-70 • Thomas Munnell, *Evangelists and Their Work in the Churches* (1887) • Walter Scott, "On Teaching Christianity," *Christian Baptist* 1 (1823): 10-11, 23-25, 36-38, 46-48 • Charles Reign Scoville, *Every Christian an Evangelist* (pamphlet, 1906) • C. Roy Stauffer, *A History of the National Evangelistic Association of the Christian Church (Disciples of Christ)* (1983) • Dwight E. Stevenson, *Walter Scott: Voice of the Golden Oracle* (1946) • Mark G. Toulouse, ed., *Walter Scott: A Nineteenth-Century Evangelical* (1999) • P. H. Welshimer, *New Testament Evangelism* (pamphlet, n.d.) • Earl I. West, *The Search for the Ancient Order*, vol. 3 (1979) • D. Newell Williams, "The History of Disciples Evangelism: 'If I Or An Angel Should Preach Another Gospel . . . ,'" *Mid-Stream* 26 (1987): 339-50 • John Augustus Williams, *Life of Elder John Smith* (1870) • E. V. Zollars, *The Commission Executed, or a Study of the New Testament Conversions and Other Evangelistic Topics* (1912).

Elmer Kile (1910-1968), founder of the Go Ye Chapel Mission (est. 1948) of the Christian Churches/Churches of Christ, pulled a "chapel on wheels" around metropolitan New York City to draw attention to his evangelistic and church-planting ministry. Courtesy of Disciples of Christ Historical Society

Evangelist, The

Periodical published by Walter Scott from 1832 until 1844.

From 1827 to 1830, Walter Scott was itinerant evangelist for the Mahoning Baptist Association in Ohio. During this time he was the first evangelist of the Stone-Campbell Movement systematically to preach faith, repentance, and baptism for the remission of sins. The Campbells and others had been writing and debating in favor of such a position, but Scott turned this into a popular appeal, and during these three years he baptized more than 3,000.

Following this period of almost constant travel on

horseback and being away from family, Scott was exhausted both physically and mentally. He moved to Cincinnati to preach but lacked the fire he once had shown, and he determined he could best serve the cause through writing.

Thus on January 2, 1832, Scott launched a new periodical called *The Evangelist.* In this first issue, he wrote:

> Brethren, I have as you are aware, been engaged in the late endeavors to restore ancient christianity, from the beginning; know much of all that has been doing; have witnessed the blessed effects of administering the gospel according to the apostolic plan, and have watched over its progress through the land, with intense interest. The cause is still advancing and I am persuaded that nothing but more zeal in our labors . . . [is] necessary to make it triumph among men. [B]eing anxious to disseminate the principles and advance the science of eternal life, I have resolved, with the help of the Lord, to avail myself of the advantages afforded by the press.

Scott offered the monthly publication of twenty-four pages for one dollar a year, paid in advance, and a dollar and half paid at the end of the year. The first issue shows the range of topics typically covered: "God Created Man in His Own Likeness," "Christianity," "Swearing," "Messiah," "Sacred Colloquy on the Ancient Gospel" (an imaginary conversation), "Three Divine Institutions," "The Reformation," and "The Philosophy of Religion."

At the end of 1835, Scott ceased publication of *The Evangelist* to give attention to writing a 576-page book called *The Gospel Restored.* Publication of the paper resumed in January 1838, published bi-monthly in a forty-eight-page format. From the end of 1838 to 1844, when Scott ceased publication of *The Evangelist,* there was an occasional running feud between Scott and Alexander Campbell over some of the details of who deserved credit for first preaching baptism for the remission of sins and similar matters. Dwight Stephenson, biographer of Scott, states, "Although Walter Scott had been literally correct as to the facts in dispute, he came away from the encounter with a diminished prestige." Likely, this conflict contributed to the demise of *The Evangelist.*

William Baxter, in his *Life of Elder Walter Scott* (1874), indicates that many of the essays that appeared in *The Evangelist* "were republished, not only in this country, but also in the old world; and few writers have had the satisfaction of seeing their views so widely spread and so generally adopted as did he."

See also Journalism; Scott, Walter

BIBLIOGRAPHY William Baxter, *Life of Elder Walter Scott* (1874) • Dwight E. Stevenson, *Walter Scott: Voice of the Golden Oracle* (1946).

STAFFORD NORTH

Ewing, Greville (1767-1841)

Scottish Independent church reformer credited with influencing Alexander Campbell's developing views on the congregational structure of the church and the weekly celebration of the Lord's Supper. Ewing is considered by many to be the founder of modern Scottish congregationalism.

Son of Alexander Ewing, an Edinburgh math teacher, Ewing studied at the University of Edinburgh. He began his career as an assistant pastor at Lady Glenorchy's Chapel, an independent chapel of the Church of Scotland in Edinburgh. Ewing became a popular preacher who focused his attention on missions. In 1794 he was writing reports to *Evangelical Magazine* and was an associate of David Bogue and William Innes. In 1796 Ewing and Charles Stuart began the Edinburgh Missionary Society and *The Mis-*

Greville Ewing represented to Alexander Campbell a form of Scottish restorationism that championed the integrity of the local congregation as the basic political structure of the church. Ewing greatly influenced the younger Campbell during 1808-9 while the family waited opportunity to join Thomas in America. The baptism controversy between Ewing and the Haldanes forced Campbell to examine the issue of believers' immersion for the first time.

Courtesy of Bethany College

sionary Magazine (now *The Scottish Congregationalist*). These endeavors prepared for the future association with Robert and James Haldane.

Ewing left the Church of Scotland in 1798, and with the Haldanes and Innes began the Tabernacle Church in Edinburgh in January 1799. Ewing primarily composed the founding principles of that church, outlining New Testament authority, the plurality of elders, deacons to administer the weekly collection to the poor, and weekly Lord's Supper. That same year in which Ewing began the Glasgow Tabernacle, Innes started the Dundee Tabernacle and Ewing became head of Robert Haldane's seminary in Edinburgh. Ewing and Robert Haldane parted company in 1808 (Ewing opposing believers' immersion), and in 1811 Ewing helped to form the Glasgow Theological Academy. He led in creating Scottish Congregationalism and did much to promote the study of the Bible in the original languages, publishing both a Greek grammar and a Greek lexicon in 1801.

During Alexander Campbell's short-term relocation in Scotland following his shipwreck in 1808, Greville Ewing assisted him in getting situated for studies at the University of Glasgow. Ewing also became something of a mentor to Campbell, occasionally hosting him in his home. Ewing and Campbell came to agree on congregational polity and regular celebration of the Lord's Supper but ultimately differed over the immersion of believers.

BIBLIOGRAPHY Harry Escott, *A History of Scottish Congregationalism* (1960) • Greville Ewing, *An Essay on Baptism* (1823) • Greville Ewing, *Facts and Documents Respecting the Connections Which Have Subsisted between Robert Haldane, Esq. and Greville Ewing* (1809) • Alexander Haldane, *Lives of Robert and James Alexander Haldane*, 4th ed. (1885) • Robert Richardson, *Memoirs of Alexander Campbell* (1868), vol. 1, pp. 128-93.

LYNN A. MCMILLON

Exodus Movement of the 1960s

Domestic missions effort in Churches of Christ that involved moving a fully formed congregation into a growing area in the northern United States.

Launched in 1963, the initial project in New York attracted widespread attention among Churches of Christ and in the popular media. The ensuing movement resulted in a number of new congregations and has had a lasting influence on mission strategy in the Churches of Christ.

The decade following World War II saw a dramatic increase in worldwide mission work by Churches of Christ. By the late 1950s, however, mission-sponsoring churches were beginning to understand more about the challenges of such work. Culture shock, fatigue, and loneliness often led to short missionary tenures. To face some of those challenges, both foreign and domestic workers began to speak of the need for missionary teams.

After three years of work in Maine, minister Dwain Evans (b. 1933) returned to Texas with his young family convinced of the great missionary opportunity in the northeastern states and also of the need of a mission team. In 1961 Evans began enlisting families to join him in a new kind of domestic mission work.

Evans's idea was to import a fully formed congregation into a major northern city, complete with elders, deacons, and full-time ministers. The group would also include members who would seek employment in the community, providing workers and financial support for the new church.

With the help of public relations executive Walter Burch (b. 1927), the forming team began a major planning and publicity campaign. After extensive research, West Islip, New York, was selected as the location, and the new work was named Exodus Bay Shore. The North Richland Hills Church of Christ in Fort Worth, Texas, agreed to sponsor the new ministry.

In the time leading up to the team's arrival on Long Island in 1963, Evans and others traveled widely among Churches of Christ making the case

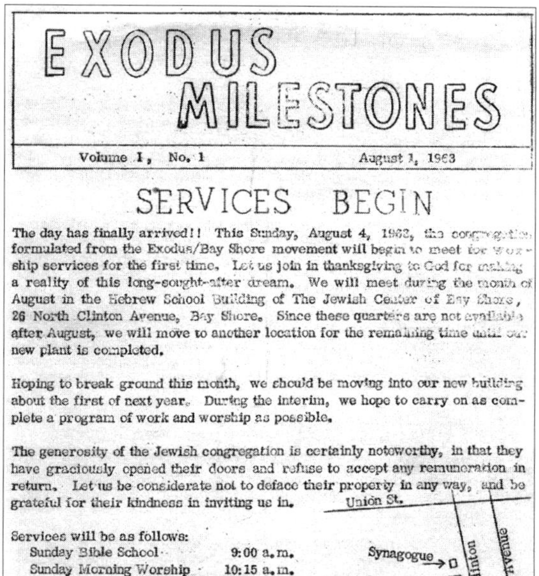

EXODUS MILESTONES

Volume I, No. 1 August 1, 1963

SERVICES BEGIN

The day has finally arrived!! This Sunday, August 4, 1963, the congregation formulated from the Exodus/Bay Shore movement will begin to meet for worship services for the first time. Let us join in thanksgiving to God for making a reality of this long-sought-after dream. We will meet during the month of August in the Hebrew School Building of The Jewish Center of Bay Shore, 26 North Clinton Avenue, Bay Shore. Since these quarters are not available after August, we will move to another location for the remaining time until our new plant is completed.

Hoping to break ground this month, we should be moving into our new building about the first of next year. During the interim, we hope to carry on as complete a program of work and worship as possible.

The generosity of the Jewish congregation is certainly noteworthy, in that they have graciously opened their doors and refuse to accept any remuneration in return. Let us be considerate not to deface their property in any way, and be grateful for their kindness in inviting us in.

Services will be as follows:

Sunday Bible School	9:00 a.m.
Sunday Morning Worship	10:15 a.m.
Sunday Evening Worship	6:00 p.m.
Wednesday Evening Worship	7:30 p.m.

A Men's Business Meeting is scheduled for 5:00 p.m. each Sunday in August.

Bulletin announcing the first meeting of the new Exodus Bay Shore church. Early meetings were held in the Jewish Center of Bay Shore. Courtesy of the Center for Restoration Studies, Abilene Christian University

for their work and soliciting involvement. Exodus Bay Shore became widely known through publicity at lectureships and in periodicals. As many as 1,500 families indicated that they were considering the move to New York. In the end 215 individuals representing eighty-five families arrived the first year.

The Exodus Movement captured attention outside the Churches of Christ as well. In addition to an article in *Time* titled "The Campbellites Are Coming," pieces appeared in *The Wall Street Journal, Newsweek,* and large local papers. Evans was asked to present the Exodus story at the U.S. conference of the World Council of Churches.

Enormous effort characterized the early work at West Islip: 75,000 homes were visited by church members in the first three years, and 200 Long Islanders were baptized and became members of the congregation.

In the meantime, other Exodus church plants, sponsored by other Southern congregations, were being planned and sent out. Additional Exodus churches were established in Connecticut, Delaware, Massachusetts, New Hampshire, New Jersey, New York, and Canada.

The early goals and promise of this approach, however, were not to be realized. Merging people of different backgrounds and subcultures into a new church proved more difficult than expected. Stresses often led to relationship breakdown in the teams, and the surrounding communities were sometimes less than enthusiastic about Southerners and their ideas of church. The combination of internal and external stress was often overwhelming for the teams. In West Islip, by 1965 only twenty-five of the original eighty-five families remained. By 1975, about thirty of the original 215 individuals were left.

Despite the difficulties encountered by the Exodus Movement, a number of the congregations that were begun have survived and thrived. Several of the supporting congregations learned from their experiences and become leaders in team church planting. The wide publicity the Exodus Movement received and the influence of its sponsoring congregations contributed to the strong emphasis on team-based missions found among Churches of Christ at the beginning of the twenty-first century.

See also Missions, Missiology

BIBLIOGRAPHY "Ecumenical Conference Requests Information on Exodus Churches," *Christian Chronicle* 25 (November 25, 1968): 1 • *Exodus Bay Shore Master Plan of Action* (1964) • Don Haymes, "From Exodus Bay Shore to the Church in West Islip: Historical Notes on a Movement Still Moving" (unpublished paper, 1998) • David Young, "Challenge of the Exodus Movements," in *Harding University Lectures* (1966), pp. 24ff.

P. KENT SMITH

Expedients

Procedures or practices that, while not explicitly enjoined by the biblical text, are nonetheless not explicitly prohibited and thus are considered permissible because they are instrumental (or "expedient") to the execution of some other clear biblical command.

Alexander Campbell defined "expedients" as the "circumstantials of the gospel and of the church of Christ, [wherein] the people of God are left to their own discretion to the facilities and exigencies of society." The principle of expediency, treated explicitly by Paul in the New Testament (1 Cor. 6:12; 10:23), has at times instigated key differences in Stone-Campbell biblical interpretation, worship, and congregational practice.

In general, traditional Stone-Campbell thinking asserted that the Bible alone is the authoritative basis for all matters of Christian faith and practice. Many argued that churches were not free to adopt practices that depart from ancient Christian practice and example as presented in the New Testament; anything not explicitly commanded, shown by example, or unambiguously inferable was forbidden. This general policy, however, became problematic when considering issues like professional ministers, church publications, congregational ownership of property, intercongregational cooperation in mission or relief work, and musical accompaniment to congregational singing. Is, for example, the employment of a professionally trained, full-time minister "expedient" to biblical commands regarding teaching, maintaining sound doctrine, and evangelism, or is it an "innovation" and departure from apostolic precedent? Recognizing this dilemma, Alexander Campbell dealt with expedients in an entire chapter of his *Christian System* (1839).

Alexander Campbell argued that expedients should be determined "by the wisdom and good sense of individuals and communities." Absolute unanimity on such issues, however, was impossible, and so it was necessary to decide them in "the spirit of concession, subordination, bearing, forbearing, submitting to one another," but the final say lay with the majority perspective to the extent it cumulatively reflected age, wisdom, and knowledge. Later leaders such as Isaac Errett insisted during the time of the Stone-Campbell Movement's first developing division that there could be great variety among the churches over matters of expediency. No such choice should ever be made a test of fellowship or a cause of division.

However, the precise identification of what is, and what is not, "expedient" was then and remains a point of contention among many Stone-Campbell congregations, particularly with regard to instrumental music in worship, the support of parachurch institutions (such as private colleges and orphanages), a central disciplinary and organizational body, and missionary societies.

See also Bible, Interpretation of the; Essentials vs. Adiaphora; Hermeneutics; Instrumental Music; Worship

BIBLIOGRAPHY Alexander Campbell, *The Christian System*, ch. 27, "Expediency" (1839) • Douglas A. Foster, "Isaac Errett: Unity and Expediency," *Restoration Quarterly* 36 (1994): 139-51 • A. S. Hayden, "Expediency and Progress," *Millennial Harbinger* (1868): 135-44 • J. W. McGarvey, "Bro. Hayden on Expediency and Progress," *Millennial Harbinger* 39 (1868): 213-19 • J. D. Thomas, *We Be Brethren: A Study in Biblical Interpretation* (1958).

ROBERT PAUL SEESENGOOD

F

Faith

Belief in the gospel, which in the Stone-Campbell heritage has been understood both as conviction about the scriptural testimony to the work of God in Jesus Christ and trust in the person of Christ.

Early leaders of the Stone-Campbell Movement, as the result of influence by the British Enlightenment and in an effort to combat Calvinist views of faith, tended to identify faith as simple belief in biblical "facts." Stone identified faith as "admitting the truth [of the gospel] into the heart." Faith did not depend on a prior holy disposition, as his Calvinist critics argued, but "on the strength of the testimony" of the gospel, that is, the credibility of the biblical witness. Stone acknowledged that faith had been defined as "coming to Christ" or "trusting in Him" but insisted that this was "not faith, but manifestly its fruits," as no one "will come to him or trust in him, till they believe in him, as able and willing to save them."

Following in the tradition of the American Presbyterian Samuel Davies, Stone asserted, "There is sufficient evidence in the word [of the gospel] to produce faith." Therefore, sinners who heard the gospel but did not believe were without excuse. Stone illustrated his point with an analogy: "If a man be in a dungeon, and light be emitted, he must see, if he does not shut his eyes against the light." Stone argued that in like manner, "when the gospel is preached in the spirit, the light beams upon sinners in darkness, and were they not to resist the light, or shut their eyes against it, they would see, and believe without a previous mechanical operation, to enable them to believe." Stone defined the difference between his views of faith and those of his Calvinist critics as follows. "They say the mind must be enlightened by the spirit, in some secret, mysterious way, to see and *approve* the truth, before the sinner can believe it. We say, the truth which the spirit speaks, is that which enlightens the mind; and which cannot produce this effect until it is believed."

Stone, like Alexander Campbell later, did not preach the law to convict sinners of their sin as a preparation for their believing the gospel. Rather, he declared that the gospel or testimony that God "has given of himself in his Word" is the "discerner of the thoughts and intents of the heart." "The testimony of God being now admitted as true," he argued, "the sinner discovers how unlike he is to God; the more he sees of God, the more he abhors himself." "The sinner's fears," he asserted, "may be awakened by the thunders of Mount Sinai [a reference to the Ten Commandments]; but it is only a view of the holiness, goodness, love, — and the free, unmerited grace and mercy of God, which produces true conviction and true repentance, and which humbles the soul, slays the enmity of the heart, and makes him willing to depart from all iniquity." The sinner who receives God's word, Stone continued, "adores the riches of divine grace, which is extended to such a poor polluted worm of the dust. He hates sin, and laments over it, because he sees it is committed against a God of infinite holiness, condescension and love." For Stone, as also for Campbell, it was through God's self-disclosure in the gospel, and not the law, that the Spirit of God convicted sinners of their sin and made them willing to "come to Christ" for salvation from both the power and the penalty of sin.

Alexander Campbell, like Stone, defined faith as belief in testimony, or more specifically "conviction of the truth of testimony, whether that testimony be human or divine." Faith carries with it a *confidence* in the source of the testimony. Faith in human testimony is important because it allows us to commune with the living and the dead, to appropriate the witnesses of those in the past. Belief in the testimony of divine revelation, on the other hand, gives us a vision of creation and of eternity.

Walter Scott presented views similar to those of Campbell and Stone. "Faith, then, human or divine, is trust or confidence in the testimony or experience of another. . . . What is the *Christian faith? Ans.* It is confidence in the testimony of the apostles concerning Jesus Christ, that he did rise from the dead, that he was recognized at Jordan by the Father as His Son." Scott declared that faith does not arise from an operation of the Holy Spirit, for then it would be by inspiration and not by the testimony of the apostles.

Alexander Campbell made much of the sequence in which faith occurs: fact, testimony, faith, and feeling. The facts and testimony upon which faith is based are found in the Bible. "The Bible is a book of facts, not of opinions, theories, abstract generalities, nor of verbal definitions. It is a book of awful facts, grand and sublime beyond description." Campbell further believed that the fact to which the Bible gives testimony is that Jesus is the Son of God. Faith is therefore ultimately located *in him.* "Any belief, then, that does not terminate in our personal confidence in Jesus as the Christ, and to induce trustful submission to him, is not faith unfeigned; but a dead faith, and can not save the soul."

Some opponents of Campbell accused him of holding views similar to those of the Scottish reformers John Glas and Robert Sandeman, who were accused of teaching that faith was mere assent to facts regarding Christ. Campbell, however, considered their views "frigid and defective." Campbell's colleague Robert Richardson reiterated the notion of faith preeminently as trust in the person of Christ. He saw this implied in the New Testament phrase "faith into *(eis)* Christ" (e.g., Acts 24:24; Gal. 2:16; Col. 2:5), a phrase Jesus himself used in asking the blind man, "Do you believe in *(eis)* the Son of Man?" (John 9:35). Such was not logical reliance on a cold hard fact, but a commitment to the person of Christ. Only this kind of faith, said Richardson, was capable of increasing or maturing.

Richardson developed this view of faith in a lengthy and heated exchange with Tolbert Fanning, whom he accused of abandoning this New Testament understanding of faith for the "sensualistic" philosophy (epistemology) of John Locke, which terminated faith wholly in objective facts. Richardson showed profound concern that the Stone-Campbell Movement, with its Lockean–Common Sense philosophical bent, could easily become bogged down in "theories" of faith at the expense of faith itself. Such was part of a larger concern to encourage the spiritual sensitivities of the Movement's constituents to the grand mysteries of the Christian faith that went beyond the bald "letter" of the scriptural text.

The Campbell-Scott-Richardson understanding of the nature of faith prevailed in much of the Stone-Campbell Movement well into the twentieth century. Some conservatives dissented, however, from placing more emphasis on its personal or subjective character than its objective grounds. Moses Lard, for example, took issue with Alexander Campbell's translation of the definition of faith in Hebrews 11:1, "the confidence *(hypostasis)* of things hoped for, and the conviction of things not seen." Lard argued that *hypostasis* was better translated "ground" or "basis," and that the phrase itself was better rendered "faith is the basis of the hope in things," that is, belief in the proposition that Jesus is the Christ as the grounds for hoping for eternal things. Lard reaffirmed Campbell's translation "*conviction* of things unseen" since conviction implied "the highest mental assurance that a thing is true." Yet in further suggesting that such conviction (as virtual certainty) could not be intensified, Lard seemed to been returning to precisely the kind of "terminal" faith that Robert Richardson had decried in Tolbert Fanning.

Robert Sandeman (1718-1771), son-in-law of John Glas, wrote in his *Letters on Theron and Aspasio* that "justification comes from bare faith," that is, simply believing that the testimony of God in Scripture is true. Courtesy Lynn McMillon, Oklahoma Christian University

In subsequent generations of the Movement, the two definitions of faith as belief in revealed facts and trust in the person of Christ have stood in a healthy tension. Conservatives in the tradition of J. W. McGarvey put great emphasis on biblical apologetics and on the order and coherence of the "faith once delivered." Other exponents continued to stress the aspect of personal encounter and *faithfulness* to Christ. Some in the Christian Church (Disciples of Christ) in the twentieth century, in focusing on a Christ-centered personal faith, argued that overemphasis upon the facts of the Bible could distort the biblical vision. Dwight E. Stevenson of the Panel of Scholars wrote in 1963:

> While the [Stone-Campbell Movement's] fathers were right in insisting upon the Christian faith as a personal commitment to Christ, they did not adhere consistently to this single standard but added to it a belief in the letter of the Bible, selectively interpreted. Thus, to state the anomaly as boldly as possible, the movement is at one and the same time Christocentric and bibliocentric. This dualism appears in the statement of the first two principles of the movement. When the distinction between faith and opinion was made, opinion was identified with speculative theology, faith with the Bible. Thus faith, in this setting, is not a different kind of believing from creedal dogma but merely the same kind of believing focused upon the Bible as its object.

Treating faith as the consequence of the accumulating of discrete facts — in the tradition of Tolbert Fanning, et al. — has also come in for criticism in Churches of Christ in the last decades of the twentieth century. According to historian and theologian C. Leonard Allen, who seeks to recover the legacy of Robert Richardson, faith should be perceived as a commitment to the mystery of the cross.

> The traditional approach elevated inorganic, impersonal, and mechanistic models of the Bible, the church, and the Christian life. In this it simply reflected the Enlightened spirit of the age. . . . The Bible became an inert object, a compendium of separate facts and commands rather than a unified, personal story of God's acts and character. . . . Thus the gospel, in one of the most common traditional formulations, consisted of "facts to be believed" (which satisfies the human intellect), "commands to be obeyed" (which challenges human willpower), and "promises to be enjoyed" (which appeal to human emotion).

Allen and others have also decried the persistence, in Churches of Christ, of a "faith *in* the Bible" rather than the "faith *of* the Bible," and have called for renewal of the latter as the kind of growing and vital faith that is nurtured by the scriptural narratives and deeply connected to Christian worship.

See also Conversion; Fanning, Tolbert; Five Finger Exercise; Rationalism; Reason, Place of; Richardson, Robert

BIBLIOGRAPHY C. Leonard Allen, *The Cruciform Church: Becoming a Cross-Shaped People in a Secular World* (1990) • C. Leonard Allen and Danny Gray Swick, *Participating in God's Life: Two Crossroads for Churches of Christ* (2001) • Alexander Campbell, *The Christian System* (1839) • Alexander Campbell, "Tracts for the People — No. IV: Faith," *Millennial Harbinger* (1846): 73-84 • Moses Lard, "Faith — Its Definition," *Lard's Quarterly* 4 (1867): 225-39 • Robert Richardson, "Faith versus Philosophy — No. 5," *Millennial Harbinger* (1857): 395-406 • Robert Richardson, "Principles and Purposes of the Reformation" (4 parts), *Millennial Harbinger* (1852): 577-87, 601-17, 686-90, 696-707 • Walter Scott, *The Gospel Restored* (1836) • Dwight E. Stevenson, "Faith versus Theology in the Thought of the Disciple Fathers," in *The Renewal of Church: The Panel Reports,* vol. 1: *The Reformation of Tradition* (1963), pp. 33-60 • D. Newell Williams, *Barton Stone: A Spiritual Biography* (2000).

PAUL M. BLOWERS *and* THOMAS H. OLBRICHT

Fall, Philip Slater (1798-1890)

Organizer and leader in the Stone-Campbell Movement in Kentucky and Tennessee. Born in 1798, at the age of 20 Fall was baptized by immersion, and two years later was ordained. In 1821 he made several preaching tours of Kentucky and Tennessee, married Anne Apperson Bacon, and became pastor of the First Baptist Church in Frankfort. In less than two years he had moved to the First Baptist Church in Louisville and led the congregation to accept the principles of the Stone-Campbell Movement.

Strongly influenced by Alexander Campbell's "Sermon on the Law" (1816), Fall taught that "the Scriptures of the Old and New Testaments are the only and all-sufficient rule of faith and manners." In 1825 Fall concluded his Louisville ministry and moved to Nashville. Early in his tenure at the Baptist Church there the congregation adopted principles of the Stone-Campbell reformation. (This congregation is now the Vine Street Christian Church.)

In 1830 Fall returned to Louisville, where he served the church for almost thirty years. He moved back to Nashville in 1858, and after guiding the congregation through the trying years of the Civil War and Reconstruction, he returned to his wife's home in Poplar Hill, Kentucky, for his remaining years.

Fall directed and taught at several academies that attracted young women from all over the United States, including the daughters of Walter Scott and Alexander Campbell. He and Campbell shared an interest in free, universal public education. In the 1830s and 1840s both men served as vice president of the Western Literary Institute and College of Professional

Teachers. In 1837 Fall was elected trustee of Bacon College in Kentucky, and in 1843 he became a trustee of Bethany College, a position he held for forty-three years.

See also Bacon College; Baptists; Bethany College

BIBLIOGRAPHY James Arthur Cox, *Incidents in the Life of Philip Slater Fall* (1951) • Herman Norton, *Fall of Vine Street: The Life Story of Philip Slater Fall* (1951) • Herman Norton, *Tennessee Christians* (1971).

SARA HARWELL

Family, The

Conflict over what a family should and should not be was quite apparent in nineteenth- as well as twentieth-century America.

The late French scholar Philippe Aries (1914-1984) was largely responsible for making historians aware that the family has a history — in other words, that the institution has changed over time. While granting that the term "family" may sometimes be used too loosely — that merely calling some novel domestic arrangement a "family" does not make it one — historians of the family are as a rule reluctant to speak of "the traditional family" as a static reality.

Alexander Campbell and other prominent leaders of the Stone-Campbell Movement promoted a view of the family that paid homage to certain biblical concepts, especially to the convictions that God's will was for one husband and one wife to live together until one or the other died and that the nurture of children is a matter of profound significance. Campbell and other leaders of the Movement held convictions about the family that were widely shared in nineteenth-century America.

Pioneers of the Movement were active during the era that saw the emergence of "the modern American family," to use the words of Carl N. Degler (b. 1921). As a result of the Industrial Revolution, fathers in cities and small towns were quite frequently at work, and away from home, for many hours each week. With fathers more likely than in earlier years to be absent from home, mothers were especially extolled as the primary caregivers to children. John Demos (b. 1937) sees the early nineteenth century in America as a period of decline in the status of women, increased concern about the discipline of children, a renewal of more restrictive sexual mores, and the emergence of a movement to give to the family itself greater significance than ever. The domestic manual, a new literary genre, gained popularity.

Especially in the nineteenth century, periodicals of the Stone-Campbell Movement often promoted a view of the patriarchal family that held sway in that time in America. Some have designated this mainline perspective as the "cult of domesticity." This point of view stressed two very well-defined spheres — one for husbands and the other for wives. Men were expected to focus their energies on the public world. They were to have preeminence in the workplace, in politics, in every realm beyond the home. Women, on the other hand, were to devote themselves almost entirely to their families. Promoters of domesticity regarded the nurture of children as an especially feminine virtue.

In an era before psychologists and medical professionals came to prominence, nineteenth-century Americans turned largely to religious spokesmen and to women who shared the prevailing sentiments for advice on such topics as motherhood and childrearing. Alexander Campbell and other "editor bishops" of the Stone-Campbell Movement in its first century dispensed much domestic advice that at the moment undoubtedly was regarded as timeless. As one reads materials produced by Campbell and his associates, the nineteenth-century American flavor of many pronouncements about the family is readily apparent.

See also Campbell, Alexander

BIBLIOGRAPHY Philippe Aries, *Centuries of Childhood: A Social History of Family Life* (1962) • Carl N. Degler, *At Odds: Women and the Family in America from the Revolution to the Present* (1980) • John Demos, *A Little Commonwealth: Family Life in Plymouth Colony* (1970) • R. Edwin Groover, *The Well-Ordered Home: Alexander Campbell and the Family* (1988).

R. EDWIN GROOVER

Fanning, Charlotte Fall (1809-1896)

School organizer and teacher, along with her husband Tolbert Fanning, in the antebellum and postbellum South. Born near London, England, on April 10, 1809, Charlotte Fall moved to the United States as a child. She taught for a while at Nashville Female Academy, and in 1837 married widower Tolbert Fanning. After running a series of schools and completing an evangelism tour in the southern United States, the couple opened Franklin College and an associated "girls' school," run by Charlotte, in 1845. The two schools were technically separate, although women and men taking the same class often participated in common recitation sessions. The schools closed during the Civil War, reopening in the fall of 1865.

A few months later, a fire destroyed several college buildings, and the couple opened Hope Institute, a "school for girls and young ladies," the following fall. Together they ran the Institute until 1874, when Tolbert died. Ten years later, Charlotte opened Fanning Orphan School on the grounds of the former Hope Institute. Although she was a staunch Southerner and supporter of the Confeder-

Daughter of Phillip Fall and wife of Tolbert Fanning, Charlotte Fall Fanning (1809-1896) operated a girls' school associated with Franklin College from 1845 until the Civil War. She and her husband opened Hope Institute in 1866, also a girls' school. In 1884, ten years after her husband's death, she closed Hope and opened Fanning Orphan School on the site of the former Institute.
Courtesy of the Disciples of Christ Historical Society

acy, through the Fanning Orphan School Charlotte provided educational opportunities for poor and rich, black and white. She led the School, and conducted classes there, until shortly before her death on August 15, 1896.

See also Children's Homes and Orphanages; Education, Philosophy of; Fanning, Tolbert

JOHN H. HULL

BIBLIOGRAPHY Emma Page, *The Life Work of Mrs. Charlotte Fanning* (1907).

Fanning, Tolbert (1810-1874)

One of the most influential church leaders in the South before the Civil War.

Born in Cannon County, Tennessee, Fanning and his family moved to Lauderdale County, Alabama, around 1818. Fanning was converted in 1827 by the preaching of B. F. Hall (1803-1873) and baptized by James E. Matthews, associates of Barton Stone. In 1831 he entered the University of Nashville, from which he graduated in 1835. During his years of college Fanning preached off and on for the Nashville church as well as other area congregations. In 1835 and 1836 he traveled with Alexander Campbell on extensive preaching tours. He operated two female academies near Nashville between 1837 and 1842 before founding Franklin College in 1845. Among scores of influential graduates was David Lipscomb (1831-1917), whose work and teachings closely mirrored Fanning's.

In addition to his educational endeavors, Fanning was also an innovative farmer. He co-edited the *Agriculturist* magazine from 1840 to 1845, and the *Naturalist* from 1846 to 1850.

It was through his journalistic efforts that he had his greatest influence on the Stone-Campbell Movement. He began *The Christian Review* in 1844 but turned it over to Jesse B. Ferguson in 1847, who renamed it the *Christian Magazine*. The *Gospel Advocate*, launched in 1855, became one of the most influential papers among Churches of Christ for over a century. He published the *Religious Historian* from 1872 until his death in 1874.

Editor and educator Tolbert Fanning (1810-1874) played a major role in the early shaping of Churches of Christ as a separate body. He became a strong opponent of the American Christian Missionary Society and dedicated himself "to restore the service of God to the order God gave in the New Testament."

Fanning encouraged cooperation meetings between churches from the early 1840s, helping to found the Nashville Committee for Evangelism and the Tennessee State Cooperation, later known as the Christian Evangelizing Society of Tennessee. However, in the early 1850s he began to question their constitutions and doctrinal resolutions. When the national American Christian Missionary Society passed resolutions against the South in 1861 and 1863, Fanning declared that no Christian should support it until it had repented of the evil of calling for the blood of fellow Christians.

During the Civil War Franklin College was forced to close by the departure of the majority of students, and the buildings were occupied by federal troops as barracks. Fanning's efforts to revive the school after the War met with only moderate success until his death in 1874.

A major rift between Fanning and Alexander Campbell was precipitated by a series of articles written in 1856 by Robert Richardson (1806-1876) in which he attacked the view that the Bible was as a blueprint for the church or a book of facts rather than a conduit for spiritual transformation. Richardson asserted that many in the Movement had unwittingly imposed Lockean philosophy on the Bible, effectively quenching the power of the word. In a response in the *Gospel Advocate* Fanning accused Richardson of abandoning correct thinking for speculative philosophy, contending that John Locke had revealed the way to correct thinking. Campbell seemed to side with Fanning at first, but in 1858 reversed his stance and attacked Fanning on behalf of Richardson.

The incident reflects developing ideological differences between Churches of Christ and Disciples of Christ, with the powerful assumptions of Lockean philosophy continuing to dominate among Churches of Christ well into the twentieth century. Fanning's monumental influence helped define much of what Churches of Christ became in comparison to the Disciples.

Fanning died in 1874, the result of injuries sustained from being gored by a bull. He was buried at his farm, Elm Crag, but later reinterred in Nashville's Mount Olivet Cemetery when the Nashville airport acquired that land.

See also American Christian Missionary Society; Franklin College; *Gospel Advocate, The;* Hall, Benjamin Franklin; Lipscomb, David; Richardson, Robert

JAMES R. WILBURN

BIBLIOGRAPHY Robert E. Hooper, *A Call to Remember: Chapters in Nashville Restoration History* (1977) • Darren Ross Johnson, "Tolbert Fanning vs. Robert Richardson: Battling for the Birthrights of the 'People of the Book'" (unpublished M.Div. thesis, Emmanuel School of Religion, 1999) • James E. Scobey, *Franklin College and Its Influences* (1906) • James R. Wilburn, *The Hazard of the Die: Tolbert Fanning and the Restoration Movement* (1969).

Fathers of the Church, Appeal to the

The Eastern Orthodox and Roman Catholic Churches alike have for centuries grounded their canonical teachings and practices both in the decrees of the ecumenical councils and in the *consensus patrum,* the combined witness of the ancient "Fathers of the Church." But Protestant churches followed suit. Influenced by the reawakening of patristic scholarship in the late Renaissance period, Luther, Melanchthon, Calvin, Bucer, and other reformers regularly made use of patristic authorities (especially, but not exclusively Augustine) exegetically, theologically, and polemically — albeit in subservience to the primary authority of Scripture. Anglican divines in the seventeenth century cherished the *consensus patrum,* while Puritans used the fathers only selectively, appealing principally to those who, in their judgment, upheld the strict letter of apostolic Christianity, not lapsing into speculation and heresy.

Barton Stone, the Campbells, and other early leaders of the Stone-Campbell movement were thoroughly aware of these patterns of appeal. Alexander Campbell, in particular, cited patristic authorities (usually secondhand) in arguing his case against infant baptism, and appealed in the *Christian System* to Tertullian's famous critique of the practice (*De baptismo,* ch. 18) and to one of Origen's homilies on Luke. In his *Christian Baptism* (1851) he further used patristic references to evidence the endurance of immersion in the early church. Later writers in the Movement, including Robert Milligan in his *The Scheme of Redemption* (1868), followed Campbell's lead in citing the ancients concerning baptismal practice.

More interesting, perhaps, is Campbell's use of the Fathers in justifying the practice of weekly communion in his 1825 *Christian Baptist* series on "A Restoration of the Ancient Order of Things." Knowing full well that there was no explicit scriptural dictate on the frequency of the Lord's Supper, Campbell found an "approved precedent" for weekly observance from certain New Testament texts. In support, moreover, he also cited ancient authorities, beginning with Justin Martyr, claiming *historical* rather than criteriological motives: "We lay no stress upon what is no better than the traditions of the church, or upon the testimony of those called the *primitive* fathers, in settling any part of christian worship or christian obedience." Such citations, he says, served merely as a "corroborating influence in authentic history" and held no "divine authority." Such was the closest thing, however, to a Campbellian argument from tradition.

In other polemical contexts, too, Campbell relied on patristic sources. In the 1843 *Millennial Harbinger*, for example, he used them to confute an Episcopalian's claim that monarchical diocesan episcopacy had evolved naturally from apostolic precedent. Furthermore, in his debate with Bishop John Baptist Purcell of Cincinnati in 1837, he employed them to refute the argument that there had always been a consistent means of electing popes in the Roman Church. Later on, amid the maturing of scientific skepticism and biblical higher criticism, J. W. McGarvey culled substantial patristic material to establish the genuineness of canonical New Testament books in his 1886 work on *The Evidences of Christianity*.

There is little indication in the Stone-Campbell Movement's early literature of reading the fathers for edification or theological enrichment. A rare example is Robert Richardson's sympathetic recall, in his *The Office of the Holy Spirit* (1872), of Augustine's conversion story as evidence of God's providence preparing persons through diverse circumstances for the decisive change wrought by the Word of God.

More recently among the Stone-Campbell churches, whether compensating for the historic bias against pre-Protestant traditions or as a sign of greater ecumenical openness, there has been an increased interest in the study of patristic sources for historical-theological purposes, as seen, for example, in A. T. DeGroot's pioneering study of the patristic background to *The Restoration Principle* (1960). Interestingly, representatives from all three branches of the Stone-Campbell tradition have been deeply involved in the formation and continuing development of the North American Patristics Society. Three have in fact served as past presidents of the society: Everett Ferguson (Churches of Christ); Frederick Norris (Christian Churches/Churches of Christ), and William Tabbernee (Christian Church [Disciples of Christ]).

BIBLIOGRAPHY A. T. DeGroot, *The Restoration Principle* (1960), chs. 2-4 • Ronald Heine, "Alexander Campbell and the Church Fathers," *Christian Standard* 124 (1989): 909-10 • Robert Thompson, "An Examination of Alexander Campbell's Use of Patristic Literature" (unpublished M.Div. thesis, Emmanuel School of Religion, 1983).

PAUL M. BLOWERS

Faulkner University

University affiliated with Churches of Christ, chartered in 1942 as Montgomery Bible School in Montgomery, Alabama.

The school's purpose statements reflect the educational tradition inherited from Alexander Campbell, emphasizing liberal arts education with Bible instruction for every student. The original statement explained that the school was founded "for the purpose of teaching the Bible, for teaching men and women to expound the Bible, to promote education so that they may more efficiently preach the gospel as prescribed by the Holy Spirit." In 1953 its name was changed to Alabama Christian College and the purpose statement revised, "to maintain an educational institution where each student is taught the Bible daily in conjunction with his study of the academic arts and sciences and the vocations." In 1965 the college moved to its present seventy-four-acre site on the Atlanta Highway in northeast Montgomery.

In 1973 the Alabama Christian School of Religion became a separate entity. Rex A. Turner, Sr. (1913-2001), co-founder (with Joe B. Greer and Leonard Johnson) and longtime president of Alabama Christian College, became president of the new institution, called Southern Christian University.

Alabama Christian College purchased the Jones School of Law (founded in 1928) in 1983, and two years later the college was renamed Faulkner University in honor of Dr. James H. Faulkner, Sr., longtime chairman of the board and a major benefactor of the college. Located in the heart of the Confederacy and in a city associated with significant racial strife during the civil rights movement, the institution integrated in the early 1960s and has been characterized as "a beacon in the community for harmonious racial relationships." At the beginning of the twenty-first century, the school consisted of a liberal arts college, a college of business, a school of biblical studies, and the Jones School of Law, with branch campuses in Birmingham, Huntsville, and Mobile, Alabama. The Southern Association of Colleges and Schools accredits its bachelor's and master's degrees. Total enrollment in 2001 reached 2,600.

See also Education, Philosophy of

JOHN F. WILSON

Federation

Creation of structures allowing denominations to cooperate while maintaining their separate identities. Begun in the United States in 1901 with the National Federation of Churches and Church Workers.

The 1902 Disciples General Convention at Omaha approved the principle of federation with the passage of a much debated resolution introduced by James H. Garrison (1842-1931). Objectors insisted that participation would concede the legitimacy of denominationalism, make the Movement a denomination, and substitute a lesser goal for the Movement's plea for unity. The issues of baptism and open membership were also tied to the discussion.

Though Garrison worked with American church leaders to formulate plans for a Federal Council of Churches of Christ in 1905, the issue was tabled in the Disciples General Convention because of its potential for division and the informality of the Movement's organization. A mass meeting held in conjunction with the 1907 General Convention in Norfolk, Virginia, however, committed Disciples to membership in the Federal Council.

Editor of the *Christian Standard* J. A. Lord (1849-1922) led the opposition to federation, while leaders like Peter Ainslie (1867-1934) and Jesse M. Bader (1886-1963) were enthusiastic supporters. Federation and participation in the Ecumenical Movement became a key issue in the division between Disciples and Christian Churches/Churches of Christ.

See also Ainslie, Peter; Bader, Jesse Moren; *Christian Standard;* Ecumenical Movement, The; Garrison, James Harvey; Unity, Christian

BIBLIOGRAPHY Winfred E. Garrison, *Christian Unity and Disciples of Christ* (1955). DOUGLAS A. FOSTER

Fellowship of Professors

Annual meeting of teachers of Bible and related disciplines who serve in colleges, seminaries, and universities primarily of the Christian Churches/Churches of Christ.

Ed Nelson and Bill Gwaltney of Milligan College, David Fiensy of Kentucky Christian College, and Gerald Mattingly of Johnson Bible College planned a meeting for mutual support and fellowship among colleagues in higher Christian education. Johnson Bible College, Knoxville, Tennessee, has hosted each annual meeting since the Fellowship's first gathering in the fall of 1981. Ninety-one persons from eighteen educational institutions have participated in programs consisting of scholarly papers, panel discussions, devotions, and addresses. Each meeting has a theme such as a particular book of the Bible, Christ and culture, worship, or issues facing the Stone-Campbell Movement. A younger Fellowship of Professors has met annually since 1989 at St. Louis Christian College, Florissant, Missouri.

MICHAEL BAIN

Ferguson, Jesse Babcock (1819-1870)

Nashville preacher often considered one of the early "heretics" of the Stone-Campbell Movement.

Jesse Babcock Ferguson was famous in his day as one of the most eloquent orators in the South. He is remembered today for his unconventional beliefs on the possibility of Christ evangelizing souls after their deaths, followed by his full conversion to universalist and spiritualist beliefs.

Though sickly in his youth, Ferguson as a young adult became a Stone-Campbell preacher and, within four years, enjoyed a national reputation for his eloquence. He began writing for *The Heretic Detector,* where he rose to joint editor, and contributed to Tolbert Fanning's *Christian Review,* which he later edited under the name *Christian Magazine.* In May of 1842, Ferguson was invited to Nashville to hold meetings. Members of the Church of Christ in Nashville pursued him for four years to become their full-time minister. He served from 1846 to 1852, and the congregation grew quickly during his tenure.

In the April 1852 issue of *Christian Magazine,* Ferguson published his essay "The Spirits in Prison," which contended, on the basis of 1 Peter 3:18–4:6, that Christ had preached to the souls of the dead during the period between his death and resurrection. Soon after, Alexander Campbell reprinted Ferguson's essay in the *Millennial Harbinger* along with a fourteen-page condemnation of it. Some have seen Campbell's reaction as unfair since, although Ferguson clearly indicated that only those dead who had never in life had the first chance to hear the gospel would be evangelized in the underworld, Campbell stereotyped him as a virtual universalist preaching a "second chance" gospel.

As the controversy with Campbell intensified, Ferguson's views became increasingly unorthodox until, ultimately, he fully embraced universalism. In mid-1853 he admitted to being a spiritualist, regularly seeking to communicate with the dead. His congregation had continued to support him, but the latest revelations caused a rift among the members. Campbell came to Nashville to denounce Ferguson's spiritualism, and Ferguson resigned from the congregation in 1856.

During and after the Civil War, Ferguson traveled extensively, lecturing and preaching. He returned to Tennessee in the 1860s, where his real estate investments had made him a wealthy man. Ferguson was making plans to begin a utopian spiritualist settlement in the Tennessee countryside when he died in September 1870.

See also Fanning, Tolbert; Heresy, Heretics; Universalism

BIBLIOGRAPHY H. Leo Boles, *Biographical Sketches of Gospel Preachers* (1932), pp. 186-91 • Alexander Campbell, "The Attack of the *Millennial Harbinger* on the *Christian Magazine,*" *Millennial Harbinger* (1852): 497-505 • Alexander Campbell, "The *Christian Magazine,*" *Millennial Harbinger* (1852): 390-98, 628-34 • Alexander Campbell, "A New Discovery," *Millennial Harbinger* (1852): 487-97 • Alexander Campbell, "The Spirits in Prison," *Millennial Harbinger* (1852): 487-97 • J. Brooks Major, "The Campbell-Ferguson Controversy," in *Explorations in the Stone-Campbell Traditions: Essays in Honor of Herman A. Norton,* ed. Anthony L. Dunnavant and Richard L. Harrison, Jr. (1995), pp. 55-70 • Johnny Ray Tucker, *Like a Meteor Across the Horizon: The Jesse B. Ferguson Story* (1978) •

James R. Wilburn, *The Hazard of the Die: Tolbert Fanning and the Restoration Movement* (1980).

SARA HARWELL

Fey, Harold Edward (1898-1990)

Disciples journalist, educator, and missionary. Born October 10, 1898, Elwood, Indiana; died January 30, 1990, Claremont, California. Married Golda Esper Conwell, July 20, 1922, at Oneida, Kansas. Children: Russell Conwell, Constance Ann, and Gordon, who died in early adulthood. Mother: Eva Gant, 1872-1972. Father: Edward Fey, 1875-1959. He had four sisters and one brother.

He attended grade school at Elwood, Indiana. In 1910 the family moved to Nebraska, where he finished high school at Red Cloud in 1917. He received the Bachelor of Arts degree from Cotner College, Lincoln, Nebraska, in 1922 and the Bachelor of Divinity degree from Yale Divinity School in 1927. He was ordained into the ministry of the Disciples of Christ in 1923.

Fey held several student pastorates and between 1927 and 1929 was minister of the First Christian Church, Hastings, Nebraska. Harold and Golda Fey were missionaries in the Philippines from July 1929 to December 1931, teaching at Union Theological Seminary, Manila. They returned to the United States during the Depression.

Fey edited *World Call,* the missionary magazine of the Disciples, between 1932 and 1934. In 1935 he became the Executive Secretary of the Fellowship of Reconciliation. He was active in the formation of the World Council of Churches. In 1940 he was called to the staff of the *Christian Century* magazine (becoming editor in 1956), serving until 1964. From 1964 until his retirement in 1975 he was Professor of Christian Ethics at Christian Theological Seminary, Indianapolis. In 1976 the Feys moved to Pilgrim Place, Claremont, California, a retirement community for Christian workers.

Among his published writings are *A Pacifist Handbook* (1939), *The Lord's Supper — Seven Meanings* (1946), *Indians and Other Americans* (1959) (co-authored with D'Arcy McNickle), and *The Ecumenical Advance* (vol. 2 of the *The History of the Ecumenical Movement*) (1970).

Fey was honored with a membership in Sigma Chi Delta, a journalistic fraternity (1948). He also received two honorary degrees: Doctor of Divinity, Chicago Theological Seminary, 1948; Humanities, Culver-Stockton College, 1963.

LESTER G. MCALLISTER

Fiers, A. Dale (1906-2003)

Disciples of Christ pastor, missionary executive, and first General Minister and President of the Christian Church (Disciples of Christ).

Born December 17, 1906, in the rural, county seat town of Kankakee, Illinois, Fiers began his formal education in Kankakee's Von Steuben School (1912). Following an exploratory train trip to Florida, Dale's father, George, decided to sell his construction business and move the family from Illinois to West Palm Beach. The Fiers arrived in 1913. George gave oversight to the construction of a new Christian Church while his wife, Leah, gave pastoral leadership. Leah, one of the first women ordained as a Disciples minister, was the predominant influence on young Dale's life. An extraordinary high school athlete, Dale was named to both the all-state football and baseball teams. Although his friends and coaches urged him to attend one of the Florida colleges, he chose instead to attend Bethany College, where he enrolled in 1925, having decided on ministry as his life's work.

Fiers served student pastorates at McKinleyville, West Virginia; Allison, Pennsylvania; and Smithfield, Ohio. He also found time to be active in campus life and to excel in three sports, and he was repeatedly

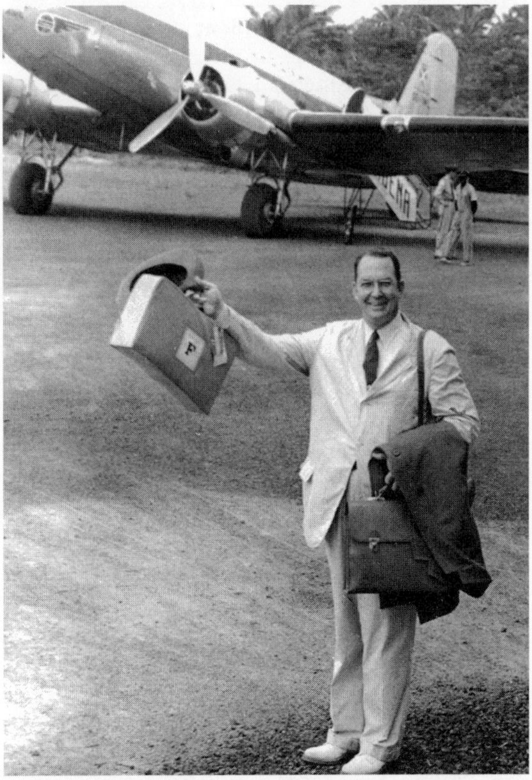

As president of the United Christian Missionary Society, A. Dale Fiers (1906-2003) visited mission stations around the world, advocating the transfer of leadership of all aspects of mission activity from North American missionaries to local church leaders. Courtesy of the Disciples of Christ Historical Society

lauded by all the regional sports writers. Following graduation and ordination (June 1929) he accepted his first full-time pastorate at the 200-member Christian Church in Shadyside, Ohio. Here he met Betty Chute Kuntz, to whom he was married July 14, 1931, and with whom he shared life for sixty-seven years. Two children, Barbara (1936) and Alan (1939), were born to their union.

In September 1931 Fiers enrolled at Yale Divinity School to enrich his preparation for ministry. Among other professors he studied with H. Richard Niebuhr, graduating in 1935. He accepted a call to High Street Christian Church in Hamilton, Ohio, where he remained until 1939. From 1939 to 1945 he served as minister of Central Christian Church in Newark, Ohio. And from 1945 until 1951, he was senior minister at the 1,800-member Euclid Avenue Christian Church in Cleveland, Ohio. During these years he served on numerous major boards of the Christian Church, including the Board of Higher Education, the Church Finance Council, and the Council on Christian Unity. He was also a trustee at Butler University, Bethany College, and Jarvis Christian College. He was elected president of the Cleveland Church Federation, and his personal leadership extended to all of American Protestantism with his election to the General Board and Executive Committee of the National Council of Churches of Christ. He was also an official delegate to the General Assemblies of the World Council of Churches in New Delhi, India, and Uppsala, Sweden.

In September 1951 Fiers was elected president of the United Christian Missionary Society, which he led for thirteen years. During the final two years he was simultaneously executive secretary of the Commission on Brotherhood Restructure. In 1964 he was elected executive secretary of the International Convention of Christian Churches, a position he filled until the Kansas City Convention in 1968, when the new Provisional Design was adopted; he was named the first general minister and president of the 1.3 million-member denomination. He served in that capacity until his retirement (1973). Fiers is widely recognized as having been a key architect of the restructured Christian Church (Disciples of Christ).

Fiers remained active during his retirement years, ministering in interim pastorates at First Christian Church, Naples, Florida (1974); North Dade Christian Church, Miami, Florida (1975); First Christian Church, Miami, Florida (1976); Park Avenue Christian Church, New York (1977); Parkway Christian Church, Plantation, Florida (1982); and Seventh Street Christian Church, Richmond, Virginia (1983). From 1974 through 1984 he served as president of the National City Christian Church Corporation

Included among his published works are *This Is Missions* (1953); *The Christian World Mission* (1966); *Prayer and the Great Decisions of Life* (1961); and *Lord, Teach Us to Pray* (1960). He was inducted into numerous halls of fame, recognized nationally and internationally by many ecumenical and church bodies for his contributions to the life of the universal church, and revered as the single most important leader of the Christian Church (Disciples of Christ) in the twentieth century. Until his death in 2003 at the age of 96, Fiers's long and generous ministry continued with sermons, public addresses, and leadership roles in both the local and regional church.

BIBLIOGRAPHY D. Duane Cummins, *Dale Fiers: Twentieth Century Disciple* (2003) • Robert L. Friedly, "A. Dale Fiers: Our First General Minister and President," *Four Faces of Christian Ministry* (1973), pp. 9-17 • H. B. McCormick, "The Work Is in Good Hands," *World Call* (July 1951): 13.

D. DUANE CUMMINS

Fife, Robert Oldham (1918-2003)

Historian and unity activist from the Christian Churches/Churches of Christ.

A graduate of Johnson Bible College, Butler University School of Religion, and Indiana University (Ph.D. in history, 1960), Fife served as an Army chaplain in World War II and was in the first wave of infantrymen to liberate the Nazi death camp at Dachau, Poland. He later served a number of church ministries and taught history at Milligan College and Emmanuel School of Religion. In the 1980s he helped to establish the Westwood Christian Foundation, a joint venture in graduate theological education, drawing together the resources of Emmanuel School of Religion, Pepperdine University, Fuller Theological Seminary, and University of California–Los Angeles (UCLA). In 1990 the foundation's educational program was dissolved in order to inaugurate a professorship in early Christian studies at UCLA.

Fife was a moderating and irenic activist for unity in the period of division between the Christian Church (Disciples of Christ) and the Christian Churches/Churches of Christ. He actively participated in the Consultations on Internal Unity in the early 1960s, was a leading voice in the North American Christian Convention, lectured widely even beyond the Christian Churches/Churches of Christ, and retained close personal friendships across all three streams of the Stone-Campbell Movement.

Consistently interested in racial reconciliation and social justice, Fife focused much of his writing on ecclesiology and the critical appropriation of the Stone-Campbell "restoration" plea. Deeply influenced by the likes of Frederick Kershner, William Robinson, Alfred T. DeGroot, and Dean E. Walker, Fife articulated what he termed a "classical Disciple" or "free church catholic" understanding of the church's organization and mission. He stressed Alexander Campbell's vision of a balance of universality and particularity as intrinsic to the nature of the church, and he defined Christian unity both as a gift (grace) and as an imperative that necessitated an ongoing process of ecclesial reformation. In interpreting the "restoration" principle, Fife resisted denominational restructure on the one hand, and a rigid congregationalist patternism on the other. True restoration, he asserted, was registered less in conformity to a scriptural blueprint of the church than in the depth of Christian fellowship under the primary authority of Christ. He reasserted that the New Testament ordinances were crucial, but only within the context of gracious accommodation and a humble spirit of discipleship.

See also Consultation on the Internal Unity of Christian Churches; Westwood Christian Foundation

BIBLIOGRAPHY P. Dwayne Curry, "Robert Oldham Fife: A 'Classical Disciple' in the Stone-Campbell Movement" (unpublished M.Div. thesis, Emmanuel School of Religion, 2000) • Robert O. Fife, "Alexander Campbell and the Christian Church in the Slavery Controversy" (unpublished Ph.D. dissertation, Indiana University, 1960) • Robert O. Fife, *Celebration of Heritage* (1992) • Robert O. Fife, *Conveying the Incarnation* (1993) • Robert O. Fife, *Horizons of Reformation* (1999) • Robert O. Fife, *Teeth on Edge* (1971).

PAUL M. BLOWERS

Firm Foundation

One of two major papers serving Churches of Christ between the 1880s and the 1980s (the other being the *Gospel Advocate*).

The *Firm Foundation* was established in Austin, Texas, by Austin McGary (1846-1928) in 1884 especially to combat David Lipscomb's position regarding rebaptism. As the second oldest publication among Churches of Christ, the *Firm Foundation* provides a window into the minds of numerous past and present leaders of the Movement regarding a wide spectrum of issues such as baptism, church polity, and racism.

McGary's father played a pivotal role in the war for Texas's independence, and Austin followed in his father's footsteps as a Confederate soldier in the Civil War (though his father did not support the Confederate cause). Following McGary's conversion in 1881, he carried his soldier mentality into the church. Only three years after he became a Christian, he established the *Firm Foundation* in order to fight another battle — this time against David Lipscomb.

David Lipscomb (1831-1917) and his fellow Middle Tennesseeans regularly accepted Baptists who sought membership into Churches of Christ without requiring their rebaptism. In the mind of McGary, however, baptism in the Baptist Church did not constitute legitimate baptism because it was not "for the remission of sins." Consequently, McGary required Baptists to submit to rebaptism before entering Churches of Christ. The first fifteen years of the *Firm Foundation* record McGary's position in an on-going debate with David Lipscomb and the *Gospel Advocate.* McGary's position became the majority position in Churches of Christ for much of the twentieth century.

The subsequent editors of the *Firm Foundation* continued its strident voice. In 1902 G. W. Savage (1860-1923) took the reins from McGary, and in 1906 a group of editors operated the publication until G. H. P. Showalter (1870-1954) assumed control in 1908. From 1908 until 1983, only two men occupied the editorship of *Firm Foundation:* Showalter and Reuel Lemmons (1912-1989). During these years, these two men steered the *Firm Foundation* along the path of mainstream Churches of Christ, and the rivalry with the *Gospel Advocate* was muted. Many church leaders wrote for and supported both journals.

After Showalter's death in 1954, his family decided to maintain ownership of the publication but to select a new editor. At no other time in its history has the *Firm Foundation* had a greater impact on Churches of Christ than when under the editorship of Reuel Lemmons. Though criticized by some for being able to speak equally well on all sides of any issue, Lemmons provided a voice of moderation between progressives and conservatives, often criticizing both. He reflected the majority voice in mainstream Churches of Christ on such issues as the American civil rights movement and the role of the Holy Spirit, though he published the views of many with differing stances.

In August 1983 the Showalter family sold the Firm Foundation Publishing House to H. A. (Buster) Dobbs and Bill Cline, resulting in a noticeable change. In Lemmons' final editorial, he wrote disapprovingly of the change of policy and direction of the paper under the new owners. The front-page headline of the first issue under the new ownership read "The Only Christians." While Lemmons had tried to balance the *Firm Foundation* in a position between progressives and conservatives in Churches of Christ, the new leadership elected to articulate only the voice of a strongly conservative constituency. At the beginning of the twenty-first century, the *Firm Foundation* understood its role to be primarily one of targeting progressives and "change agents," especially in educational institutions and highly visible congregations of Churches of Christ. It continued to express the views of ultraconservative members of Churches of Christ on a monthly basis under the ownership and editorship of Dobbs.

See also Baptism; Journalism; Lemmons, Reuel Gordon; Lipscomb, David; McGary, Austin

BIBLIOGRAPHY Lane Cubstead, "The Firm Foundation, 1884-1957: The History of a Pioneer Religious Journal and Its Editors" (unpublished M.J. thesis, University of Texas, 1957) • *Firm Foundation,* available from http://www.bible-infonet.org/ff/ • Reuel Lemmons, "Finis," *Firm Foundation* 100 (23 August 1983): 2 • Thomas B. Warren, "The Only Christians," *Firm Foundation* 100 (30 August 1983): 1.

T. WESLEY CRAWFORD

First Century Christian

Periodical serving Churches of Christ, founded by Roy Hearn (1911-2000) and Franklin Camp (1915-1991) in 1967 and published in Memphis, Tennessee.

Its stated purpose was "to expose and stand against radicalism, liberalism, modernism, and any other 'ism' that threatens the peace, unity, and purity of the church." Hearn and Camp were leaders among conservative Churches of Christ in an era of great change. *First Century Christian* was one of a number of publications appearing at that time that proposed to defend traditional restorationist viewpoints, especially against new publications like *Mission* that challenged traditional thinking. Between 1974 and 1977 Max R. Miller (b. 1925) joined Hearn and Camp as co-editor. Publication was suspended between May 1977 and December 1988, but was resumed by Hearn the following year. At the beginning of the twenty-first century the paper was published bi-monthly.

See also Journalism; *Mission*

WES HARRISON

Fishback, James

See Baptists

Five Finger Exercise

Mnemonic developed by Walter Scott (1796-1861) and used throughout churches of the Movement in subsequent generations.

During his term as an evangelist for the Mahoning Baptist Association (1827-30) in Ohio, Scott developed the Five Finger Exercise as a summary of the plan of salvation used for preaching and teaching purposes.

Typically Scott would ride into a village and find a group of children. He would have them hold up their left hands and, beginning with the thumb, point to each finger and repeat the words "faith, repentance, baptism, remission of sins, gift of the Holy Spirit." He often paired "and eternal life" with the Holy Spirit, on the little finger. The children would repeat the game until they had mastered the "faith in their fingers." He would then send them to their homes to tell their parents that a man would preach that same gospel that night at the schoolhouse. They were not to forget to tell their parents the faith of their hands.

This sketch, published in *A Mini-History: The Christian Church (Disciples of Christ)* in 1974, depicts Walter Scott teaching a group of children his innovative evangelistic method. Scott emphasized the ability of all to accept the simple gospel facts and submit to God's will in baptism.
Courtesy of the Disciples of Christ Historical Society

Scott's Five Finger Exercise was more profound than a mere child's game. This mnemonic represented a distinctive sequence of conversion and regeneration to be contrasted with the *ordo salutis* in Reformed (Calvinist) soteriology. Faith, belief in God's offer of salvation through Jesus Christ, was *the* first step. Opinion of the day, by contrast, held that a dramatic working of the Holy Spirit was the initial step in bringing one to discover whether he or she was among God's elect.

In Scott's view, Scripture presented Jesus Christ as the "golden oracle," God's way of entering into covenant relationship. The convert was simply to believe the facts of the gospel, repent, and be baptized. Baptism was the pivotal step. In baptism, the believer obeyed, in love, the Christ who first loved the believer. Baptism was also the initial part of God's covenant action. It was the means by which God provided assurance of the remission of sin. God continued to act by bestowing on the believer the gifts of forgiveness of sin, the Holy Spirit, and eternal life.

Walter Scott's Five Finger Exercise communicated effectively. It expressed serious thought with simplicity. It combined innovative evangelistic technique with a critically sharpened soteriology. Serious theology was expressed in a way that enabled even children to be witnesses to the gospel.

See also Evangelism, Evangelists — Early Nineteenth Century; Scott, Walter

BIBLIOGRAPHY James O. Duke, "Walter Scott: Theologian," in *Walter Scott: A Nineteenth-Century Evangelical,* ed. Mark G. Toulouse (1999), pp. 61-78 • Dwight E. Stevenson, *Walter Scott: Voice of the Golden Oracle* (1946)

PETER M. MORGAN

Florida Christian College

Bible college associated with the Christian Churches/Churches of Christ.

Located in Kissimmee, Florida Christian College (FCC) first offered classes in 1976 at the First Christian Church in Orlando under the name of Central Florida Bible College. In 1985, during the tenure of the college's second president, Marion Henderson, the school moved to its present campus in Kissimmee and changed its name.

FCC's educational philosophy recognizes the full and final authority — and inerrancy — of the Bible. As a Bible college, FCC affirms several points of doctrine held in common with evangelical Protestantism, such as the inspiration of the Bible as the infallible Word of God for both faith and practice, the virgin birth of Jesus, his bodily resurrection, his promised return to earth, and the affirmation that the church constitutes God's people on earth. In addition to these doctrinal beliefs, the influence of the Stone-Campbell Movement is evident in the school's firm commitment to (1) a rational-moral conversion empowered by the Word of God; (2) salvation by faith, rather than by experience; (3) baptism (immersion) into Christ for the remission of sins and the gift of the Holy Spirit; and (4) obedience to the teachings of Scripture in regard to such matters as oversight of the church and the celebration of the Lord's Supper.

FCC's curriculum and four- and two-year degree programs focus on biblical studies and Christian ministries and are designed to train undergraduates both for church ministries (pastoral ministry, music ministry, Christian education, youth ministry, etc.) and missionary work abroad.

DANIEL D. REDDEN

Florida College

College affiliated with non-institutional Churches of Christ, chartered in 1944 at Temple Terrace, Florida, by a group of Florida businessmen and church leaders. The original name was Florida Christian College. The school opened in the fall of 1946 with approximately 100 students at both high school and college levels. Veteran preacher and educator L. R. Wilson (1896-1968) was the first president, serving from 1946 to 1949. In 1963 the institution's name was changed to Florida College.

James R. Cope (1917-1999) became the school's second president in 1949. Cope, a respected preacher and protégé of N. B. Hardeman (1874-1965), served as president of the school until 1982, leaving a deep imprint on the college. Cope sought to enhance the college's prestige among Churches of Christ by building a strong Bible Department and recruiting a number of nationally known evangelists to teach at the young school. By the mid-1950s Cope had put together an administrative team that guided the school's development for two decades, including vice president and head of the Bible Department Homer Hailey (1903-2000) and academic dean Clinton Hamilton (1924-1999).

Throughout most of its history, Florida College remained a small school serving mostly its own region. In 1954 the school was accredited by the Southern Association of Colleges and Schools as a liberal arts junior college. In 1996 the college received accreditation to award a Bachelor of Arts degree in Biblical Studies and subsequently developed four-year programs in Elementary Education and Liberal Studies.

Florida College was founded at a time when Churches of Christ were engaged in a factious debate about the proper relationship between the churches and colleges and other institutions. A majority of the school's original board, including its first chairman, C. Ed Owings, and its most important financial booster, Lee Warren Boswell, opposed church contributions to colleges. By the time he became president, James R. Cope had also come to be associated with the "anti-institutional" position. Florida [Christian] College was one of a number of newly established colleges after World War II that refused donations from churches, but as the debate over a nexus of issues called "institutionalism" became more and more heated and divisive in the 1950s, only Florida [Christian] College clearly sided with those opposed to church donations. The college made an effort to find a middle ground; its 1954 lectureship featured speakers on both sides, including the most articulate spokesman for sponsoring church arrangements in the conduct of missions, Otis Gatewood (1911-1999). By the end of the 1950s the *Gospel Advocate* had targeted the college as a haven for radicals and marked its teachers and students as "antis."

Florida College grew slowly through the years, drawing support largely from the small non-institutional churches that were more or less isolated from the mainstream of Churches of Christ by the early 1960s. The school continued to refuse contributions from churches but was sustained by a national core of individual supporters.

Bob Owen, a former dean of students and business manager at the college, succeeded Cope as president of Florida College in 1982, serving until 1991. A respected civic leader in the Temple Terrace community and a widely known preacher, Owen enhanced the reputation of Florida College as a Bible school.

Owen was succeeded in 1991 by C. G. "Colly" Caldwell (b. 1943), a former student, teacher, and dean of students at the college. Caldwell had earned a doctorate at Vanderbilt University in 1980, and in 1981 President Cope had appointed him academic dean. Caldwell guided the expansion of the school into a four-year college. In the 1990s Florida College markedly upgraded its faculty and its facilities. The percentage of the faculty holding Ph.D. degrees increased to around 25 percent by the end of the century, and the campus added new dormitory, classroom, and library facilities. Enrollments began to climb after the addition of four-year programs, and in the 2001 academic year the school had a full-time equivalency enrollment of 554.

The continued growth and vitality of Florida College were to some degree a measure of the growth of noninstitutional Churches of Christ in the 1980s and 1990s. The Florida College Bible Lectureship, held each year in February, remained the most important national gathering for members of non-institutional Churches of Christ, usually attracting more than 2,000 people.

See also Gatewood, Otis; Hailey, Homer; Hardeman, Nicholas Brodie; Noninstitutional Movement

BIBLIOGRAPHY Margie H. Garrett, *Making a Difference: Florida College, the First Fifty Years* (1996) • John A. Smith, *Index to the Florida College Annual Lectures, 1974-1986* (1986).

DAVID EDWIN HARRELL, JR.

Foreign Christian Missionary Society, The

Missionary organization formed by the Disciples of Christ in the late nineteenth century, and later dissolved into the United Christian Missionary Society.

The Foreign Christian Missionary Society (FCMS) was conceived at the same General Convention of the Disciples as the Christian Woman's Board of Missions (CWBM) in Cincinnati in 1874, by the appointment of a committee to prepare definite organizational plans for the following year, because, as Archibald McLean wrote in 1904, the Convention had not had sufficient time to initiate it. W. T. Moore, pastor of Central Christian Church in Cincinnati, convened a group of men to discuss how the Disciples of Christ as a "brotherhood" of individuals and congregations could become active in foreign missions again, as they had been in Jerusalem and Jamaica before the Civil War.

It was not meant to be a "men's movement" but a movement of the whole church in the manner of the American Christian Missionary Society. McLean commented on "Women and the Society" in his *History of the FCMS,* saying, "The sex line was never drawn by the Society," and he paid tribute to eleven women by name who were "all friends of the CWBM, but their hearts were large enough to take in both [societies]." This approach had ecclesiological implications. Along with the commitment to cooperation for world mission practiced by the women's organization, the FCMS theology of mission would help shape the United Christian Missionary Society and the much later restructure of the Christian Church (Disciples of Christ).

The committee met in Indianapolis that summer and drafted a tentative constitution specifically for foreign missions. During the General Convention at Louisville on October 22, 1875, the plans were adopted after a moving address by Isaac Errett, who was elected president. McLean said: "There was a sense of the Divine presence, a conviction that what was being done was in harmony with the purpose of God in the ages."

The first missionaries were sent not to so-called non-Christian lands but to England, Denmark, Norway, Sweden, France, as well as to Orthodox Constantinople and Anatolia. All of these endeavors were promoted by people who had been in these countries before as members of some other denomination. Only in Britain has there been a continuing relationship with Churches of Christ based on the first FCMS initiatives, though most of those British congregations merged into the United Reformed Church in 1982.

In March 1882 the Foreign Society voted to send two couples to India "as soon as sufficient funds were in hand." On September 16, 1882, the Whartons, the Nortons, and four young women appointed by the

The East India home and mission station of the G. L. Wharton family about 1890. Wharton was sent to India by the Foreign Christian Missionary Society in 1882.
Courtesy of the Disciples of Christ Historical Society

CWBM left the United States for the first permanent church planting of the new era.

The Garsts and the Smiths were the first missionaries sent to Japan in 1883. They were joined the following year by a medical doctor, W. E. Macklin of Ontario, Canada, who determined that Japanese physicians made his ministry there unnecessary, so he went on to China in 1885. That same year, there were conversations with Henry M. Stanley and others in Britain about beginning work in Africa, which proved to be a false start. The number of missionaries in the field was 108 in 1899, the year the "station" at Bolenge in the Belgian Congo was purchased from the American Baptists to begin what is today the Disciples of Christ Community of l'Eglise du Christ au Congo, formerly Zaire. Ellsworth Faris, later professor of sociology at the University of Chicago, and Dr. and Mrs. Royal J. Dye brought fame and enthusiasm among Disciples for the work in Africa. The Hannas and the Williamses went to the Philippines in 1901.

Laura and Dorothy Delany of a Detroit pastor's family, granddaughters of pioneer evangelist Jonas Hartzell, became the first Disciple missionaries in the historically important missions of Japan and China, along with their husbands Garst and Macklin. Native Canadians Archibald McLean and William Macklin are a reminder of the contribution of Canada to organized Disciples missionary work. The FCMS was an international organization from the start, with support and personnel coming not only from Canada but also from England and Australia.

From this point forward, one man largely assured the momentum: Archibald McLean. A graduate of Bethany College and president there 1889-91, he was pastor at Mt. Healthy Church in Cincinnati when called to be part-time and then full-time secretary of the FCMS. No one identified so fully with the enterprise as he or represented more exactly what it would become in the twentieth century. He attended the first ecumenical conference on foreign missions in London June 9-19, 1888, rejoicing in "the unity and cooperation among the many missionary societies and the many churches represented," attending another in New York in 1900. He was head of a delegation of twenty-three Disciples at the Edinburgh World Missionary Conference June 14-24, 1910, where 160 missionary organizations met together.

Conspicuously absent from McLean's leadership was the millennialism of the earlier Stone-Campbell Movement and its missionary objectives. Strong was the concentration on social ministries and personal evangelism. Methods employed by the FCMS included "evangelistic, educational, medical, literary, industrial, orphanage, and leper relief," according to the *Concise History by the Missionaries* of 1910 and the glowing anniversary report called "Forty Years of Service for the King," delivered by McLean in Los Angeles on July 20, 1915. By that time 315 missionaries had been sent out, and the year's income was over $6 million.

Archibald McLean (right) served as secretary of the FCMS from 1882 until it became part of the United Christian Missionary Society in 1919. He is pictured with Dr. and Mrs. Ashley S. Johnson in 1909 when McLean was commencement speaker at Johnson Bible College.
Courtesy of Johnson Bible College Photo Archive

The year after the Foreign Society was organized, the General Convention unanimously adopted this resolution: "That we most cordially invite these organizations [CWBM and FCMS] to a close alliance with the American Christian Missionary Society in every practical way; and still we look forward hopefully to the time when such a general cooperation of our churches shall be secured as may enable us to resolve these organizations into one, efficient for domestic and foreign work." This vision culminated in the creation of the United Christian Missionary Society in 1920. The missionary work and ecumenical spirit of the FCMS continue as part of the Common Global Ministries Board, constituted by the Christian Church (Disciples of Christ) and the United Church of Christ in 1996.

See also American Christian Missionary Society; Africa, Missions in; Asia, Missions in; Christian Woman's Board of Missions; Europe, Missions in; McLean, Archibald; Missions, Missiology; United Christian Missionary Society, The; Women in Ministry

BIBLIOGRAPHY *A Concise History of the Foreign Christian Missionary Society by the Missionaries* (1910) • Archibald McLean, *History of the Foreign Christian Missionary Society* (1919) • William R. Warren, *The Life and Labors of Archibald McLean* (1923).

WILLIAM J. NOTTINGHAM

Fortune, Alonzo Willard (1873-1950)

Disciples pastor, professor, and writer of the early twentieth century.

He earned a B.A. and M.A. from Hiram College (1898, 1900), a B.D. and Ph.D. from the University of Chicago with a thesis on Paul's concept of authority (1905, 1915), and was awarded an honorary L.L.D. degree from Transylvania University in 1930. He served pastorates in the Christian Church in Chagrin Falls, Ohio, 1899-1901, the First Christian Church in Rochester, New York, 1901-4, and the Walnut Hills Christian Church in Cincinnati, 1907-12. He then moved to Lexington to become the new Professor of Doctrine at the College of the Bible, teaching there until 1922 as well as serving as the dean from 1917. He left the College to become the pastor of Central Christian Church in Lexington, where he served until his failing eyesight forced his retirement in 1944. The author of numerous books, he was also a member of the Commission on Restudy of the Disciples of Christ, begun in 1934, and was the president of the International Convention of the Disciples of Christ in 1936-37.

See also Commission on Restudy of the Disciples of Christ; International Convention of the Disciples of Christ; Lexington Theological Seminary; Transylvania University

BIBLIOGRAPHY A. W. Fortune, *The Conception of Authority in Pauline Writings* (1915) • A. W. Fortune, *The Origin and Development of the Disciples* (1924) • A. W. Fortune, *The Church of the Future* (1930) • A. W. Fortune, *The Disciples in Kentucky* (1932) • A. W. Fortune, *Thinking Things Through with E. E. Snoddy* (1940) • A. W. Fortune, *Adventuring with Disciples Pioneers* (1942). JASON A. MEAD

Foster, Rupert Clinton (1888-1970)

Minister and educator from the Christian Churches/Churches of Christ.

Educated at Transylvania College, the College of the Bible, and Yale, Foster did three years of doctoral study at Harvard Divinity School until forced out of school by ill health. Foster ministered to churches in Massachusetts, Kentucky, and Ohio (1912-31). He taught New Testament at McGarvey Bible College in Louisville (1923-24) and Cincinnati Bible Seminary (1924-70).

Revered by his students for his Bible teaching, Foster was also a bellicose defender of the faith, which he saw being undermined by modernism and theological liberalism. He sought to shape the vision and the curriculum of Cincinnati Bible Seminary accordingly. His most significant book was his 1,426-page *Studies in the Life of Christ,* written from 1938 to 1962.

See also Cincinnati Bible College and Seminary; Fundamentalism JAMES B. NORTH

Franklin, Benjamin (1812-1878)

Influential evangelist, editor, and debater in the Stone-Campbell Movement, ultimately a leading opponent of missionary societies and other nineteenth-century parachurch agencies.

Born on February 1, 1812, in Belmont County, Ohio, Franklin was named for his great-uncle, the famed Philadelphia inventor and statesman.

Franklin moved to Henry County, Indiana, near Middletown, in 1832. The following year, having purchased an eighty-acre farm, cleared the land, and built a cabin, he married Mary Personnet; eventually they would have eleven children. Raised a Methodist, Franklin heard the preaching of Samuel Rogers, who had been converted by Barton W. Stone in Kentucky. Samuel Rogers baptized Franklin, Franklin's brother Daniel, and Rogers's son, John I. Rogers, in December 1834, whereupon Franklin turned from an occasionally rowdy frontier lifestyle to serious study of the Bible.

Young Franklin began preaching wherever opportunity existed. His direct, unsophisticated style was well received by many of the "common people" to whom he appealed, and Franklin was instrumental in beginning many new congregations. In the 1840s Franklin moved to various locations in eastern Indiana to work successively with congregations at New Lisbon, Bethel, Centerville, and Milton.

Perceiving that editing a religious periodical was an effective way to expand his opportunities to proclaim the gospel and strengthen Christians, Franklin began editing a series of journals, beginning in 1845 with the *Reformer* (later renamed the *Western Reformer*). By 1850 Franklin entered an agreement with David S. Burnet to edit the *Christian Age,* which Burnet had merged with Walter Scott's *Protestant Unionist.* Franklin moved to Burnet's home at Hygeia, Ohio (near Cincinnati), to work with Burnet.

Much has been made of the social and economic disparities of this relationship. Burnet's family was wealthy and respectable; his father had been mayor of Cincinnati, and an uncle served as U.S. senator from Ohio. Burnet had married the daughter of General John S. Gano, of an equally prominent family in Kentucky and, later, Texas. Franklin's family lived in a barn converted to living quarters near Burnet's spacious house; they walked to church while Burnet's family rode in a fine carriage. Still, Franklin and Burnet were able to make common cause in the preaching of the gospel. While living in the Cincinnati area, Franklin preached for the Clinton Street church and the church in Covington, Kentucky, just across the Ohio River.

At first supportive of the American Christian Missionary Society, Franklin later became an outspoken opponent of such parachurch agencies. Although self-conscious about his lack of formal education throughout his life, Franklin supported the foundation of Northwestern Christian University (later Butler University) in Indianapolis. Largely self-educated and possessing native writing and speaking abilities, Franklin consciously appealed to the "common man" among converts to a restored Christianity.

In 1856 Franklin began a new monthly paper, the *American Christian Review,* which was successful enough that it became a weekly by 1858. Franklin continued as editor until his death in 1878. Moses E. Lard, John Rogers, Elijah Goodwin, Charles L. Loos, and Isaac Errett were among the announced regular contributors.

The growing popularity of the *Review* and Franklin's increased visibility in the Stone-Campbell Movement made him, by some accounts, the most influential preacher and editor among the Disciples of Christ following the death of Alexander Campbell. But Franklin was not universally popular. An advocate of pacifism at least as early as the Mexican War of 1846-47, Franklin found it difficult to maintain a pacifist position during the Civil War. Viewed with suspicion by many Southerners because of his birth and residence in the North, he was suspected by some Northerners of harboring secessionist sympathies, and was accused of treason, cowardice, and other vices both in the secular press and by some Christians. Franklin continued to preach wherever he had an audience, whether North or South. In August 1862 he was engaged in evangelistic meetings with the church at Richmond, Kentucky, during the battle that was fought there when Confederate forces under Braxton Bragg and William Kirby Smith moved into Kentucky.

In 1864 Franklin moved his family from Cincinnati to Anderson, Indiana, where his son Joseph was preaching. As controversies over the missionary society and other agencies became heated, the *American Christian Review,* called "Old Faithful" by its supporters, became increasingly vocal in opposition to various parachurch agencies.

Franklin conducted approximately twenty-five formal religious debates with members of various denominations during his lifetime, five of which were published. His preaching took him to many places in the United States and Canada, and estimates of the number of people he baptized exceeded 10,000. Franklin published sermons in *The Gospel Preacher* (2 vols.), which sold well and was often reprinted, as was a widely circulated tract, *Sincerity Seeking the Way to Heaven.*

Benjamin Franklin died October 22, 1878, and is buried at Anderson, Indiana. His son Joseph, coauthor of a biography of Benjamin Franklin, preached and taught school for many years at Anderson and Bedford, Indiana. Benjamin Franklin's daughters, Stella and Josepha, served as missionaries in India. Franklin also had significant influence on the young preacher Daniel Sommer, who became the long-tenured editor of the *American Christian Review* in 1886.

See also *American Christian Review;* Civil War, The; Missionary Societies, Controversy over; Pacifism; Sommer, Daniel

BIBLIOGRAPHY Ottis Castleberry, *They Heard Him Gladly* (1963) • Benjamin Franklin, "The Church — Its Identity," in *The Living Pulpit of the Christian Church,* ed. W. T. Moore (1868), pp. 341-56 • Benjamin Franklin, *The Gospel Preacher,* 2 vols. (1869, 1877) • Joseph Franklin and Joel A. Headington, *The Life and Times of Elder Benjamin Franklin* (1879) • Earl I. West, *Elder Ben Franklin: Eye of the Storm* (1983).

JAMES STEPHEN WOLFGANG

Franklin College

First Stone-Campbell college founded in Tennessee.

Established in 1845 by evangelist, editor, and educator Tolbert Fanning on his farm Elm Crag near Nashville, it was named for Benjamin Franklin, the Founding Father and practical philosopher.

The college charter did not mention religion, as Fanning did not want the school to be denominational in character. However, most members of the faculty were members of the Stone-Campbell Movement, and all subjects were taught in harmony with Fanning's understanding of Christian principles. In addition, the college congregation, located on campus, played an important part in each student's life.

Franklin was one of the earliest colleges to combine a classical and liberal arts education with the study of agriculture and mechanical crafts. In addition, Fanning encouraged students to engage in some form of manual labor to help pay their tuition and board. Students worked as blacksmiths, coach makers, saddlers, cobblers, tailors, and cabinet makers.

Each student was required to join one of two literary societies: the Appollonean or the Euphonean. Each society had its own meeting hall and library of 1,000 volumes. The societies held their debates on Saturdays, discussing an issue from two points of view: logical and sentimental. They discussed such timely issues as the merits of abolition (the affirmative won) and the morality of the war with Mexico.

In 1861 the college had undergone a recent reorganization and had a student body of almost 100 and an impressive physical plant. By June most of the young men had left to join the Confederate army, and the college suspended operations. Three weeks after Fanning reopened Franklin College in October 1865, the main building was destroyed by fire, along with most of the books and laboratory equipment. Fanning understood that citizens of the impoverished South could not contribute to a rebuilding program, so the college was not resurrected. Tolbert Fanning's brother, A. J. (Jack) Fanning, operated a school at the same location. In addition, a female school, Minerva College, founded in 1849 as a companion school to Franklin, was renamed Hope Institute and was operated by Fanning until his accidental death in 1874. Franklin College's influence continued to be felt long after its demise through the leadership of graduates such as William and David Lipscomb.

See also Education, Philosophy of; Fanning, Tolbert; Lipscomb, David

BIBLIOGRAPHY James Edward Scobey, ed., *Franklin College and Its Influences* (1906) • James R. Wilburn, *The Hazard of the Die: Tolbert Fanning and the Restoration Movement* (1969, 1980), chap. 6, "Greater Than Storming a Castle: Franklin College" • M. Norvel Young, *A History of Colleges Established and Controlled by Members of the Churches of Christ* (1949), "Franklin College, Nashville, Tennessee, 1845-1866," pp. 34-52. SARA HARWELL

Freed, A. G.

See Freed-Hardeman University

Freed-Hardeman University

A liberal arts college associated with Churches of Christ.

A. G. Freed (1863-1931) and his former student N. B. Hardeman (1874-1965) founded the university as the for-profit National Teachers' Normal and Business College (NTNBC) in 1908 in Henderson, Tennessee. Earlier institutions in Henderson associated with the Stone-Campbell Movement included West Tennessee Christian College (founded 1885) and Georgie Robertson Christian College (1897-1907). Freed was president of both predecessor institutions, the latter until forced to resign for failing to support the Tennessee Christian Missionary Society. A board of trustees purchased the school from the founders in 1919 and renamed it Freed-Hardeman College. It became a university in 1990.

Like other early-twentieth-century schools begun by the emerging Churches of Christ, NTNBC offered instruction on both the collegiate and secondary levels. Bible courses were popular but not required at first. Also like other such institutions, the school struggled financially for several decades. Major gifts by Paul Gray (1867-1929) in 1928 and J. W. Brooks in 1931 allowed the school to pay its debts by 1937.

For decades, the school bore the stamp of Hardeman, a popular preacher known for numerous gospel meetings and the famed "Tabernacle Sermons," which marked Churches of Christ as a religious group to be reckoned with. A friend of many Southern politicians and a regular on the Tennessee walking horse circuit, Hardeman used his powerful connections to strengthen the college bearing his name. His tenure ended in controversy in 1950 after he severely criticized a student for bringing a complaint against one of the women faculty members. Half the student body went on strike, triggering an investigation by the Board and the election of H. A. Dixon as president. Before he left, however, Hardeman had placed the school on a sound financial footing.

The long tenures of its leaders have brought remarkable stability to the university. Presidents and co-presidents with their terms of service include: A. G. Freed (1908-22), N. B. Hardeman (1919-23, 1925-50), C. P. Roland and W. C. Hall (1923-25), Hall Calhoun (1925-26), H. A. Dixon (1950-69), E. Claude Gardner (1969-90), and Milton Sewell (1990-). These presidents have insured that the university consistently represented the most conservative positions of Churches of Christ.

Another institution important to conservative Churches of Christ has been the Freed-Hardeman Bible Lectureship, held each February since 1937. For decades the daily "Open Forum" led by Guy N. Woods (1908-1993) of the *Gospel Advocate* (succeeded in the 1980s by Alan E. Highers) encouraged adherence to traditional positions and resistance to religious innovation of any sort.

For many years Freed-Hardeman was one of the most important educational centers for training preachers and other leaders for Churches of Christ. At the beginning of the twenty-first century it continued to provide ministers and leaders especially for conservative Churches of Christ, as well as to prepare professionals in many fields. The student body consistently exceeded 1,500 in this period.

See also Calhoun, Hall Laurie; Education, Philosophy of; Hardeman, Nicholas Brodie

BIBLIOGRAPHY *Leadership, Service and Philanthropy* (1999, 2000, 2001, 2002) • Morris Lynn McCauley, *Freed-Hardeman College Lectures: 1969-1970: Rhetoric of Reaction* (unpublished M.A. thesis, LSU, 1972) • J. Marvin Powell and Mary Nelle Hardeman Powers, *N.B.H.: A Biography of Nicholas Brodie Hardeman* (1964) • Special issue *Jackson (Tennessee) Sun*, November 24, 1957 (devoted entirely to the history of Freed-Hardeman College) • M. Norvel Young, *A History of Colleges Established and Controlled by Members of Churches of Christ* (1949).

MARK W. HAMILTON

Freedmen's Missionary Society

Pioneer effort of the Disciples during the Reconstruction period to improve the situation of the freedmen of the Southern states.

In 1865 the Board of Trustees of the Western Reserve Ecclectic Institute, now Hiram College, proposed to add to the curriculum a "course of Biblical Lectures" designed to aid candidates for ministry who had neither the means nor opportunity for theological training. The principal instructors for the course, which lasted only for the summers of 1866 and 1867, included Robert Milligan, Isaac Errett, D. S. Burnet, A. S. Hayden, Charles L. Loos, and others.

Near the close of the second course of 1867, George Washington Neely, a Southerner by birth, delivered an address to the class in which he powerfully described the need for evangelization and education among the recently enslaved people of the Southern states. (At least one source attributes the address to Loos.) The result was so stunning that the class organized themselves into a society for the purpose of sending missionaries into this fertile territory. Together the students pledged over $1,700 to support the work.

Orrin Gates and Mary Atwater, selected as the Society's first recruits, set up their work in Lowndes County, Alabama, in the fall of 1867. They were soon joined by Neely. By the following spring, Gates, fearing for his personal safety, had abandoned the work, citing among the difficulties "fierce and bitter opposition," presumably from the white population. The work, however, continued as Neely preached, established churches, and trained workers, and as Atwater conducted primary education and established schools. Neely early advocated that the work could best be carried out by educating men of color to preach the gospel. Perpetually plagued by a lack of funds, only about one-third of the initial pledges were ever paid, and the work was declared dead in January of 1870.

Neely and Atwater eventually married and carried on the work among the poor of the South, establishing a number of churches and schools over the next three decades. In 1892 an article appeared in the *Christian Standard* calling for the work of the Freedmen's Missionary Society to be renewed. As far as can be determined, the call fell on deaf ears.

See also Hiram College; Missions, Missiology; Slavery, The Movement and CLINTON J. HOLLOWAY

Freedom

See Liberty

Fundamentalism

Conservative response to Protestant theological liberalism.

The term "fundamentalist" was coined in 1920 by Baptist Curtis Lee Laws, editor of the *Watchman-Examiner,* of those ready "to do battle royal for the Fundamentals." As primarily a doctrinal reaction to liberalism, fundamentalism reflects a deeper "culture war" on the American social and intellectual landscape. The branches of the Stone-Campbell Movement in the 1920s, the Disciples of Christ and Churches of Christ, were both significantly involved in the culture war. To the extent that certain Disciples embraced liberalism, the Disciples were drawn more deeply into the conflict than Churches of Christ.

Particularly significant was the struggle over scriptural authority. Strongly conservative Disciples, as well as many members of Churches of Christ, felt only an inerrant or infallible — interpreted as "incapable of error" — Bible could preserve the church of the New Testament. Nevertheless, the most conservative in both groups expressed opposition to the term "fundamentalism," since its principal advocates, many of whom were Calvinists, represented positions contrary to the Stone-Campbell heritage, especially on baptism.

Another battleground was the doctrine of creation. Like many conservative Presbyterians still tied to the tradition of Baconian science and Common Sense philosophy, with its strong emphasis on God's direct work of creation and institution of fixed laws of nature, conservatives within the Stone-Campbell Movement similarly refuted the theory of evolution. As the *Christian Standard* and *Gospel Advocate* attest, numerous conservatives in the Movement openly sympathized with William Jennings Bryan's creationist position in the famed Scopes "Monkey" Trial in Dayton, Tennessee, in 1925.

Among Disciples, the struggle and often the terminology of fundamentalism paralleled doctrinal and institutional controversies within mainline denominations. The most contentious issue was missions. In response to open-membership practices of the United Christian Missionary Society, the Christian Restoration Association (CRA, est. 1925) became a clearinghouse for independent missions and other organizations; later it deferred to the growing direct-support method and concentrated its energies domestically. It was instrumental in the founding and early support of Cincinnati Bible Seminary, the flagship fundamentalist school, with R. C. Foster its leading scholar. During this struggle James DeForest Murch emerged as the strong leader of the CRA, subsequently becoming an editor for Standard Publishing, editor of *United Evangelical Action,* managing editor of *Christianity Today,* president of National Religious Broadcasters, and writer of the authorized history of the National Association of Evangelicals (NAE). A personal experience caused Murch to found Christian Action in 1933, an organization devoted to spiritual renewal among conservative Disciples, which included George Knepper, who had been influenced by the English holiness Keswick Movement. While some (e.g., R. E. Elmore, R. C. Foster) called early on for separation from liberal Disciples, Murch's initiatives — from rapprochement with the International Convention (1929), to unity meetings with Churches of Christ, to building the NAE — represented a more moderate fundamentalism or emerging "neo-evangelicalism."

Mass revivalism, certainly a hallmark of broader fundamentalism in American culture in the early and mid-twentieth century, flourished among conservative Disciples (many evangelists imitating Billy Sunday). Premillennialism, while not strong among Disciples fundamentalists, did have a distinguished advocate in the figure of C. G. Kindred, a Christian Action leader. A. B. McReynolds of the Kiamichi Mission in Oklahoma represented anti-communist political activism, as did his protégé, Billy James Hargis, who attended Ozark Bible College.

Disciples conservatives increasingly embraced much of the language and culture of fundamentalism. The term "Bible Institute," popularized by Chicago's Moody Bible Institute, was adopted (e.g., Lincoln Bible Institute) and, while there were not "Bible" Churches, "Bible Congresses" met and "New Testament" was used to describe "Christianity" and congregations. Standard Publishing printed editions of Tabernacle Hymns, a fundamentalist staple. In a 1923 book, Presbyterian fundamentalist J. Gresham Machen contrasted true Christianity and liberalism, a theme echoed in a *Christian Standard* article by W. R. Walker the following year. The adjective "independent" — often used of those leaving liberal denominations (e.g., Independent Fundamental Churches of America, Independent Board of Presbyterian Foreign Missions) was increasingly attached to dissident Disciple churches. Similarly, fundamentalist anti-denominationalism found resonance within conservative Disciples ranks.

Among Churches of Christ, since there were few liberals to purge, the prevailing connection to broader American fundamentalism was opposition to evolution, and even the firing of W. W. Freeman from Abilene Christian College in 1922, though primarily over biblical inspiration and the use of higher criticism, involved his views of science. L. D. Hill, Speaker of the Tennessee Senate, was instrumental in passing the state's anti-evolution bill. J. W. Henley, J. H. Lawson, and M. S. Mason, all from Churches of Christ, advocated similar laws in Oklahoma and Arkansas, while A. B. Barret and G. C. Brewer emerged as popular anti-evolution speakers. W. W. Otey's book *Creation or Evolution* was reissued by Eerdmans (1938). *Firm Foundation* and *Gospel Advocate* praised and reprinted William Jennings Bryan, and occasionally other fundamentalists. Revivalism generally was important, and the best example, Hardeman's Tabernacle Sermons, drew inspiration from revival meetings held by Sam Jones and Gypsy Smith at Nashville's Ryman Auditorium; indeed, at least one sermon was based on Bryan's own remarks. While an inner holiness emphasis was absent, the social reform agenda (e.g., prohibition) was virtually identical. The appeal reached at least some immigrants, most notably R. H. Boll, editor of *Word and Work,* the most prominent premillennial publication of premillennial Churches of Christ, and George Klingman, evangelist and educator.

Following John Scopes's conviction in Tennessee and the quiet removal of evolution from biology texts, the need for fundamentalist cooperation dimmed. The attack of Foy E. Wallace, Jr., and others on Church of Christ premillennialists (Boll, et al.) was extended to fundamentalists. Wallace debated J. Frank Norris, the noted Baptist fundamentalist, who earlier had worked with G. C. Brewer in anti-evolution efforts.

By the mid-twentieth century, some conservatives began to reject the anti-intellectualism and resistance to social action associated with fundamentalism, eventually identifying themselves as evangelicals. Among them was James DeForest Murch, who profoundly influenced Christian Churches/Churches of Christ from the 1940s through the 1960s.

See also Bible, Authority and Inspiration of the; Bible College Movement; Boll, Robert Henry; Brewer, Grover Cleveland; Christian Restoration Association; Cincinnati Bible College and Seminary; Common Sense Philosophy; Creation and Evolution; Elmore, Robert Emmott; Evangelical; Foster, Rupert Clinton; Liberalism; McReynolds, Albert Badger; Murch, James DeForest; Temperance; Wallace, Foy Esco, Jr.

BIBLIOGRAPHY Michael W. Casey, "The Interpretation of Genesis One in the Churches of Christ: The Origins of Fundamentalist Reactions to Evolution and Biblical Criticism in the 1920s" (unpublished M.A. thesis, Abilene Christian University, 1989) • Kevin R. Kragenbrink, "Dividing the Disciples: Social, Cultural, and Intellectual Sources of Division in the Disciples of Christ" (unpublished Ph.D. dissertation, Auburn University, 1996) • James DeForest Murch, *Adventuring for Christ in Changing Times* (1973) • James B. North, "The Fundamentalist Controversy Among the Disciples of Christ, 1890-1930" (unpublished Ph.D. dissertation, University of Illinois, 1973) • James Stephen Wolfgang, "Fundamentalism and the Churches of Christ, 1910-1930" (unpublished M.A. thesis, Vanderbilt University, 1990).

C. J. DULL

G

Gano, John Allen (1805-1887)

Kentucky preacher and the longest living link to the Stone movement of the early nineteenth century.

As a young man Gano was schooled at Georgetown, Kentucky, under Barton Stone and even lived in Stone's home. He was immersed by evangelist Thomas M. Allen in July 1827 and began preaching almost immediately.

Through marriage in 1827 he inherited a large Georgian residence ("Bellevue") set in a 500-acre bluegrass farm in Centerville, Kentucky. He lived and farmed there for sixty years and devoted his ministerial labors to the four nearby Christian churches at Leesburg, Old Union, Newtown, and Antioch. As a stockman and landowner he accumulated a considerable estate, and therefore he never accepted any financial remuneration for his preaching.

His *Christian Messenger* article in 1831 in support of a weekly celebration of the Lord's Supper was endorsed by Stone and was influential in leading the Stone movement churches to adopt the practice. This helped pave the way for the union with the Campbell movement in 1832, with Gano playing a prominent role in the unity meetings. Following the merger he became a co-laborer with John T. Johnson, a preacher from the Campbell movement, and they evangelized together in central Kentucky for more than twenty years.

In the years 1830-60, John Allen Gano established numerous congregations and was one of the most successful evangelists in Kentucky. A powerful and eloquent exhorter, and celebrated for his melodious voice, he came to be known affectionately as "The Apollos of the West." His labors were principally in central Kentucky, but extended occasionally into adjoining states, and he made one tour into Louisiana and established a church in Baton Rouge. He baptized more than 10,000 persons during his sixty-year ministry. His last article on "The Organ in Worship," written shortly before his death, was a solemn protest against the use of musical instruments in public worship that was threatening to divide the church.

See also Evangelism, Evangelists — Early Nineteenth Century; Johnson, John T.; Lord's Supper, The

BIBLIOGRAPHY Mark Collis, "The Restoration Movement and the Spirit of Evangelism," *Christian Standard* 68 (1933): 73-74 • J. A. Gano, "The Lord's Supper," *Christian Messenger* (1831): 30-34. JERRY B. RUSHFORD

For his eloquence in the pulpit, John Allen Gano was dubbed the "Apollos of the West" in the Stone-Campbell Movement.
Courtesy of Bethany College

Gano, Richard Montgomery (1830-1913)

One-time Confederate army officer, later prolific evangelist of the Stone-Campbell Movement in Texas.

The son of evangelist John Allen Gano, Richard Gano was born in Centerville, Kentucky, June 18, 1830, and was baptized by his father in 1840 in the North Elkhorn River near the Old Union meetinghouse in Bourbon County, Kentucky. He received his college training at Bacon and Bethany Colleges and at Louisville Medical University. He married Mattie Welch, a descendant of Barton W. Stone, in 1853, and they moved to Grapevine Prairie in Tarrant County, Texas, in 1856.

Richard Gano was elected to the Texas State Legislature in 1860. Although he opposed secession, when the Civil War began he supported the Confederate cause. Gano recruited 180 men in 1862 and headed for Tennessee as captain of "Gano's Battalion." He served with General John Hunt Morgan for fifteen months of continuous fighting in Tennessee and Kentucky and was elevated in rank to major and then colonel. Later he was sent to the Trans-Mississippi Department and served in Arkansas and Indian Territory. Altogether he fought in seventy-two battles and was victorious in sixty-eight of them. Gano was officially promoted to Brigadier General by Jefferson Davis in March 1865. Following the war he moved his family back to Kentucky.

R. L. Roberts said of Richard Gano: "During the war he led his men, doctored them when they were wounded and preached to them on Sunday." However, he was not formally set apart for the ministry until July 8, 1866, when he was ordained by his father and Dr. W. H. Hopson at the Old Union meetinghouse in Bourbon County, Kentucky. Gano wrote of this decision: "After the close of the Civil War I laid down my sword of steel and took up the word of God as the weapon of my warfare." He was soon preaching to large crowds in Kentucky and Tennessee. As David Lipscomb observed: "His reputation as a soldier commended him to the mass of the people in this country."

In the fall of 1872, Richard Gano preached at a successful meeting in Dallas, Texas, and baptized thirty-two people into Christ. The following year he moved his family from Kentucky to Dallas, and this city became his home for the last forty years of his life. The church in Dallas was divided in August 1877 when one group adopted the use of musical instruments and formed the Commerce Street Christian Church. Gano remained with the original congregation and served as an elder of the Pearl and Bryan Church of Christ in Dallas for more than thirty years until his death in 1913. This congregation is now the Highland Oaks Church of Christ.

Richard and Mattie Gano had twelve children, nine of whom lived to maturity. Richard baptized all nine of his children into Christ. Three of his sons became lawyers, and the law firm of Gano, Gano, and Gano was one of the most prestigious in Dallas. His oldest son, William B. Gano, was chairman of the board of Southwestern Christian College in Denton, Texas, and assisted in writing the legal charter for Gunter Bible College and for Childers Classical Institute, which eventually became Abilene Christian University.

In addition to his long ministry in Dallas, Richard Gano preached in numerous gospel meetings in Kentucky, Tennessee, and Texas. Toward the end of his life he wrote that he had baptized more than 6,800 people. He died in Dallas on March 27, 1913, and was buried next to his wife in Oakland Cemetery. Gano Street in Dallas is named for him, and in the 1970s the Gano Log House on Grapevine Prairie was renovated and moved to a prominent location in Old City Park in Dallas.

Richard Gano's father had immersed more than 10,000 converts in a ministry that spanned sixty years, and the son immersed nearly 7,000 converts in a ministry of more than forty-five years. It is unlikely that any father-son team in the history of the Stone-Campbell Movement baptized more people into Christ.

See also Gano, John Allen

BIBLIOGRAPHY Jerry B. Rushford, "The Apollos of the West: The Life of John Allen Gano" (unpublished M.A. thesis, Abilene Christian University, 1972) • Jerry B. Rushford, "General Richard M. Gano (1830-1913)" (unpublished typescript, Center for Restoration Studies, Abilene Christian University).

JERRY B. RUSHFORD

Garfield, James Abram (1831-1881)

Disciples preacher and educator, and the twentieth president of the United States, also the second president to be assassinated while in office.

Garfield, the only preacher ever to occupy the White House, was deeply influenced by the social, intellectual, and religious ferment of the early decades of the nineteenth century that helped to shape the Stone-Campbell Movement. Garfield's life fell precisely within the fifty-year period of the growth and expansion of the Movement following the historic merger of the Stone and Campbell movements on January 1, 1832.

Garfield was reared on Ohio's Western Reserve, a major geographical theater of the Stone-Campbell Movement, and at the age of 18 (1850) was baptized by a Disciples preacher. While a student at the Western Reserve Eclectic Institute (1851-54), an academy

James A. Garfield
Courtesy of Bethany College

of the Disciples of Christ at Hiram, Ohio (later to become Hiram College), he cultivated an inner circle of friends and developed the ability to preach. Two years at Williams College (1854-56) enlarged his intellectual horizons and convinced him that the ministry was "an unpromising field" for him. By the time Garfield returned to teach at Hiram, he was already formulating plans for entering "the field of statesmanship" through the "educational portal."

In the first three years after his return to Hiram (1856-59), Garfield was made president of the Eclectic, married into a strong Stone-Campbell family in Hiram, and became "a favorite preacher" among Western Reserve Disciples. At the same time he was laying the groundwork for a political career with the Eclectic as a base and his beloved "Hiram circle" of Stone-Campbell colleagues as associates and supporters. In 1859, with the support of several influential Disciples, Garfield won election to the Ohio Senate and "gained a step in the direction of my purpose." At the yearly meeting of Disciples of Christ he argued that there was a greater need of "manly men in politics" than there was of preachers.

At the outbreak of the Civil War, Garfield saw his course clearly. Governor Dennison of Ohio assured him that successful military leaders would rule the nation for twenty years after the war, and he eagerly accepted command of the Forty-Second Ohio. With evangelistic fervor he recruited hundreds of Disciples into his regiment. His passionate speech at the 1861 convention of the American Christian Missionary Society led that organization to adopt a resolution of loyalty to the Union. During Garfield's military years (1861-63) he won rapid promotion to the rank of major general, and through the diligent work of his Disciples associates back home he won election to Congress. His congressional career began in December 1863 and continued until the autumn of 1880, when he was elected to the Presidency.

As a member of the Hiram College board, Garfield initiated a theological department at the school in 1866. In that same year he was the catalyst behind the establishment of a significant new periodical called the *Christian Standard.* He conceived of merging the school and the paper in hopes of encouraging moderation in the Stone-Campbell Movement, but in this he failed. However, he continued to support the "new and better movement" he saw emerging in the ministries of progressive Disciples like Lewis Pinkerton and Burke Hinsdale. Throughout his career as a congressman, Garfield was always faithful in his attendance at the Vermont Avenue Christian Church. He took the lead in helping the congregation raise money to purchase a larger church building in 1869, and he occasionally taught in the Sunday School program.

Ohio Disciples helped Garfield build a political base (he won ten consecutive elections in the Western Reserve), and in turn shared in the prestige and influence of his expanding career. Disciples of Christ in many states were active in Garfield's presidential campaign, and through his victory they enjoyed the fruits of worldwide publicity for their young religious movement. After Garfield's assassination, Disciples were prominently involved in his funerals. Frederick D. Power, minister of the Vermont Avenue Christian Church, delivered the memorial address before President Chester A. Arthur and other dignitaries in the rotunda of the Capitol in Washington, D.C., and Isaac Errett, editor of the *Christian Standard,* preached the eulogy before what was "the largest funeral gathering in the history of the nation" at Lakeview Cemetery in Cleveland, Ohio.

Among the many tributes to the slain President was one by Dr. Noah Porter, president of Yale College, who wrote: "In my judgment, there is no more interesting feature of his character than his loyal allegiance to the body of Christians in which he was trained, and the fervent sympathy with which he shared in their Christian communion. . . . President Garfield adhered to the church of his mother, the church in which he was trained, and which he had served as a pillar and an evangelist." Following the assassination and funerals, the Disciples sought to perpetuate Garfield's memory in such projects as the construction of a new church building for the Vermont Avenue Christian Church (which the press called the Garfield Memorial Church) and in the founding of Garfield University in Wichita, Kansas.

See also Hiram College

BIBLIOGRAPHY William R. Balch, *The Life of James Abram Garfield* (1881) • Harry Brown and Frederick Williams, eds., *Diary of James Garfield* • Burke A. Hinsdale, ed., *Works of James Abram Garfield* (repr. ed. 1982) • Allan Peskin, *Garfield: A Biography* (1978) • William C. Ringenberg, "The Religious Thought and Practice of James A. Garfield," in *The Stone-Campbell Movement: An International Religious Tradition,* ed. Michael W. Casey and Douglas A. Foster (2002), pp. 219-33 • Jerry B. Rushford, "Political Disciple: The Relationship Between James A. Garfield and the Disciples of Christ" (Ph.D. dissertation, University of California, Santa Barbara, 1977) • Howard E. Short, "President Garfield's Religious Heritage and What He Did with It," *Hayes Historical Society* 4 (1983): 5-20 • Theodore Clarke Smith, ed., *The Life and Letters of James Abram Garfield* (1925; repr. 1968) • W. W. Wasson, *James A. Garfield: His Religion and Education* (1952).

JERRY B. RUSHFORD

Garrison, James Harvey (1842-1931)

Disciples minister, editor, and publisher, and unity activist.

J. H. Garrison was born near the village of Ozark (about fourteen miles from Springfield), Missouri. A decade earlier his Baptist parents, James and Diana Kyle Garrison, had moved to southwest Missouri from Hawkins County in east Tennessee. The twelfth of their thirteen children (nine boys and four girls), he grew up on a farm and attended several schools in the vicinity.

When the Civil War turned parts of southwest Missouri into battlefields, Garrison joined the Home Guards in Springfield. Then he became a Union soldier, enlisting in Company F of the Twenty-Fourth Missouri Infantry. Wounded (a shattered leg) in the Battle of Pea Ridge, Arkansas, he recuperated at his parents' home and spent the final three years of the war as captain in command of Company G of the Eighth Missouri Cavalry Volunteers. With the war behind him, a 23-year-old Garrison entered Abingdon College (absorbed by Eureka College in 1884) and completed the four-year classical course in three years. There, a Baptist like his parents, he became a member of the Disciples and met his future wife, also a student at Abingdon. Garrison married Judith Elizabeth Garrett a week after both of them received college degrees. They had two sons: Arthur, an itinerant musician, and the multitalented Winfred Ernest,

As founder and editor of the *Christian-Evangelist* for thirty years, J. H. Garrison (1842-1931) built the journal into one of the most influential among "progressives" in the Movement.

who became an eminent church historian at the University of Chicago.

Garrison began his ministry as associate at the First Christian Church in Macomb, Illinois. The pastor, John C. Reynolds, also taught Greek and Latin at Abingdon and edited a monthly, *The Gospel Echo.* In the concluding number of 1868, he announced that "Bro. J. H. Garrison" had agreed to share the responsibility of the periodical with him. Out of college only a few months, Garrison launched a career in religious journalism that would continue without interruption for the remainder of his life. Over the next three years Reynolds relied increasingly upon his younger colleague to edit and publish the paper. Having decided to convert the monthly into a weekly, Garrison moved it to Quincy, Illinois, in early 1872. Thereafter he became sole editor and assumed the full financial burden of the modest enterprise. To expand the paper, he renamed it *The Christian,* moved the headquarters to St. Louis, and brought about a merger with *The Evangelist,* published by Barton W. Johnson. The first issue of *The Christian-Evangelist* appeared on October 5, 1882. Until Johnson's death about twelve years later (in May 1894), he served as co-editor, but Garrison was the dominant partner and determined editorial tone and direction. While the subscription list expanded from 16,000 to 25,000 in their time together, the growing influence of *The Christian-Evangelist* outdistanced the increase in circulation. Indeed, it came to be the preeminent journal in shaping religious opinion among Disciples. Advancing in age and needing to get his finances in order, Garrison sold his company in late 1909 to Robert A. Long, who gifted it to the Disciples for the establishment of a denominational publishing house (the Christian Board of Publication). Garrison remained editor-in-chief of *The Christian-Evangelist* until retiring on February 2, 1912, his seventieth birthday.

Throughout his editorial career, Garrison gave full and forceful expression to the Stone-Campbell emphasis on uniting a divided church by restoring New Testament Christianity. He was not, however, strict in interpreting Christian primitivism, as his endorsement of musical instruments in worship and support of missionary societies attest. Because of his place in the Movement, he became embroiled in controversy. He resolutely opposed the opening of membership in congregations to the "pious unimmersed" (believers who had been baptized but not immersed). In the debate over the nature of the Bible, he opted for a dynamic rather than a mechanical theory of biblical inspiration. Defending and encouraging the critical study of the Scriptures, he nevertheless took exception to many conclusions of the biblical critics.

The defining theme of his editorial witness was his unwavering advocacy of Christian unity. Concerned for the viability of the Stone-Campbell Movement, Garrison edited two sets of articles by various authors on the Movement's achievements, one doctrinal, *The Old Faith Restated* (1891), another historical, *The Reformation of the Nineteenth Century* (1901). In 1909, the year of the Disciples of Christ Centennial, he published *The Story of a Century,* his own challenge to the Disciples not to lose nerve and invoking them to adapt the Movement's plea to changing times and contexts. Garrison played the decisive role in enabling Disciples to become an official participant in the Federal (later National) Council of Churches, convinced that the Stone-Campbell Movement had a viable program for unity to bring before the larger church. His book on *Christian Union* (1906), a historical analysis of the theme, conveyed his passion for reconciliation among Christians. A theological moderate, he was a man of deep piety. Several of his books, including *Alone with God,* were devotional in focus.

In retirement, Garrison and his wife moved to California to be near their son, Ernest. In addition to completing his autobiography, *Memories and Experiences,* he continued for many years to write his weekly article entitled "The Easy Chair" for *The Christian-Evangelist.* Revered late in his career as a leading thinker in the Movement, he died less than three weeks before his eighty-ninth birthday in Los Angeles.

See also *Christian-Evangelist, The;* Garrison, Winfred Ernest; Unity, Christian

BIBLIOGRAPHY Douglas A. Foster, "The Struggle for Unity during the Period of Division of the Restoration Movement" (unpublished Ph.D. dissertation, Vanderbilt University, 1987) • J. H. Garrison, *Alone with God* (1891) • J. H. Garrison, *Christian Union: A Historical Study* (1906) • J. H. Garrison, *Memories and Experiences: A Brief Story of a Long Life* (1926), J. H. Garrison, ed., *The Old Faith Restated* (1891) • J. H. Garrison, ed., *The Reformation of the Nineteenth Century* (1909) • J. H. Garrison, *The Story of a Century* (1909) • William E. Tucker, *J. H. Garrison and Disciples of Christ* (1964). WILLIAM E. TUCKER

Garrison, Winfred Ernest (1874-1969)

The most prominent twentieth-century historian of the Disciples of Christ, Winfred E. Garrison pursued a varied and distinguished career as an educator, journalist, literary critic, sculptor, and ecumenical leader. A son of the noted Disciples of Christ religious journalist James Harvey Garrison (1842-1931), Winfred E. Garrison was reared in St. Louis. He earned bachelor's degrees at both Eureka College (1892) and Yale (1894), and received his Ph.D. in 1897 from the University of Chicago, where he wrote a dissertation on the historical sources and context of Alexander Campbell's theology.

Garrison's teaching career began in 1898 at Butler University in Indianapolis, where he married Annie Dye in 1900. He served as Butler's president from 1904 to 1906, but tuberculosis forced him to resign at age 32, and he moved to New Mexico to regain his health. There he not only recovered physically but resumed his educational career, serving as the president of New Mexico Agricultural and Mechanical College (today New Mexico State University) from 1908 to 1913. Moving to California in 1913, Garrison became the founder and headmaster of the Claremont School for Boys.

While a graduate student, Garrison had figured prominently in the founding in 1894 of the Disciples Divinity House of the University of Chicago. On April 1, 1921, he succeeded his friend Herbert Lockwood Willett as the dean of Disciples House, with appointment as associate professor of church history at the university. The years of Garrison's deanship (1921-27) proved pivotal for Disciples House. He worked with its board of trustees to raise money for a building and,

Winfred Ernest Garrison (1874-1969) was the most significant twentieth-century Disciples historian of the Stone-Campbell Movement.

in the process, shifted the architectural design away from classrooms and offices to make it a residential center, like a college at Oxford University, with common rooms, chapel, and library. The architectural changes confirmed the identity of Disciples House as a religious and intellectual center for Disciples of Christ students, whose coursework and degrees would be fully pursued at the University of Chicago.

The conclusion of his term as dean of Disciples House brought to a close more than twenty years of educational administration and freed Garrison for three extraordinarily productive decades of writing. He had become literary editor of the *Christian Century* in 1923 and continued in that post until 1955, gaining particular distinction as book review editor for this ecumenical journal. Meanwhile, he returned to the historical scholarship that had begun with his doctoral dissertation on Alexander Campbell and produced a series of interpretive histories of the Disciples of Christ: *Religion Follows the Frontier* (1931), *An American Religious Movement* (1945), and, with Alfred T. DeGroot, *The Disciples of Christ: A History* (1948; rev. ed. 1958). In 1975 Lester G. McAllister and William E. Tucker rewrote and extended Garrison and DeGroot's history but retained its basic historical structure, under the title *Journey in Faith: A History of the Christian Church (Disciples of Christ)*. Thus, for much of the twentieth century, Garrison's interpretive paradigm dominated Disciples of Christ historiography.

In addition to his studies of the Disciples of Christ, Garrison also wrote more widely on the modern, especially American, history of Christianity. He was elected president of the American Society of Church History for 1927-28, and his book *The March of Faith* (1933) was among the earliest efforts to provide a historical account of the American churches in the period following the Civil War. Although Garrison retired from his faculty position at the University of Chicago in 1943, this did not conclude his academic career, which he resumed in 1951, at age 77, in the Department of Philosophy and Religion at the University of Houston.

Garrison had long demonstrated a commitment to Christian unity, writing on the topic for his father's journal, the *Christian-Evangelist,* in the first decade of the twentieth century. After he completed his term as dean of Disciples House, this ecumenical interest found particular expression in international developments leading toward the World Council of Churches. Garrison was a delegate to the World Conferences on Faith and Order at Edinburgh in 1937 and at Lund in 1952. He had incisive perspectives on the cultural and social factors that had influenced the history of Christian unity, and he expressed these views in such books as *Christian Unity and Disciples of Christ* (1955) and *The Quest and Character of a United Church* (1957).

Garrison's cosmopolitan interests extended beyond religion and historical scholarship to active engagement in the fine arts. He was a hymnodist and poet, a violinist and pianist. He made perhaps his most distinctive and enduring contribution as a sculptor, after a period of study with the Czech sculptor Albin Polacek at the Art Institute of Chicago. His most notable works, displayed internationally in Disciples of Christ churches and educational institutions, were bas-relief portraits and busts of figures ranging from the founders of the Disciples of Christ to Cyrano de Bergerac.

Winfred E. Garrison was a founding member in 1941 of the Disciples of Christ Historical Society and served as its president from 1947 to 1950 (as well as an honorary presidency in 1953). His contributions to the historiography of the Disciples of Christ are honored by a medallion in the stained glass windows of the Historical Society's headquarters in Nashville, Tennessee. Garrison died in Houston, Texas, on February 6, 1969, at age 94.

See also *Christian Century, The;* DeGroot, Alfred T.; Disciples of Christ Historical Society; Disciples Divinity House; Garrison, James Harvey; Historiography, Stone-Campbell Movement; Willett, Herbert Lockwood

BIBLIOGRAPHY Garrison Memorial Issue, *Discipliana* 29 (Summer 1969) • W. E. Garrison, *Alexander Campbell's Theology* (1900) • W. E. Garrison, *Christian Unity and the Disciples of Christ* (1955) • W. E. Garrison, *Religion Follows the Frontier: A History of the Disciples of Christ* (1931) • W. E. Garrison and A. T. DeGroot, *The Disciples of Christ: A History* (1948; 2nd ed. 1958) • W. Clark Gilpin, "Faith on the Frontier: Historical Interpretations of the Disciples of Christ," in *A Case Study of Mainstream Protestantism: The Disciples' Relation to American Culture, 1880-1989*, ed. D. Newell Williams (1991). W. CLARK GILPIN

Gates, Errett (1870-1951)

Author of one of the first histories to be written about the Stone-Campbell Movement by an academic historian.

Gates became associated with Herbert Lockwood Willett at the University of Chicago and the growing Disciples presence there, serving as the pastor of the Hyde Park Church after Willett and before Edward Ames. After earning a Ph.D. from Chicago in 1902 (with a thesis on Baptist-Disciple relations), he continued to serve as an instructor in history with the Disciples Divinity House from 1902 to 1917, as well as an associate editor for the *Christian Century.*

He was apparently the first to propose a formal Disciples Historical Society in 1901, but was basically ignored. In a letter to *Discipliana* in 1943, he reminisced about his service at the Divinity House. Besides teaching, he was also asked to devote much time to fundraising, and he felt torn between three desires: to fulfill his obligations in raising money for the House, to create a better-educated ministry within the ranks of the Disciples, and to preserve the papers and writings of Disciples leaders. He felt that he did not succeed with either of the first two, but he was pleased that the Historical Society was eventually founded and was carrying on this work.

See also Ames, Edward Scribner; *Christian Century, The;* Disciples Divinity House; Disciples of Christ Historical Society; Willett, Herbert Lockwood

BIBLIOGRAPHY Errett Gates, *The Early Relation and Separation of Baptists and Disciples* (1902) • Errett Gates, *The Disciples of Christ* (1905) • Errett Gates, "Development of Modern Christianity," in *Guide to the Study of the Christian Religion* (1916) • Errett Gates, "Letter from Errett Gates," *Discipliana* (January 1943): 36. JASON A. MEAD

Gatewood, Otis (1911-1999)

Pioneer and visionary during the twentieth-century expansion of missionary efforts in Churches of Christ.

Otis Gatewood was born in Meridian, Texas, and educated at Texas Tech University, Abilene Christian University, Pepperdine University, and the University of Utah at Salt Lake City. He began his church-planting work in Eunice and Las Vegas, New Mexico, in 1937. In 1939 Gatewood moved to Salt Lake City to begin a work that targeted Mormons.

Gatewood was a champion of the "sponsoring church" model of cooperative mission work. In 1937 he became the first full-time missionary of the Broadway Church of Christ in Lubbock, Texas, to which churches from across the country sent funds to support his early mission efforts. Following the fall of the Nazi government, Gatewood moved to Germany in 1947 and established a base in Frankfurt for coordinating missions to West Germany. He was granted the Distinguished Service Cross from the nation of Germany for his efforts in coordinating humanitarian aid for the nation in the wake of World War II.

Gatewood was a great proponent of Christian higher education, especially to prepare missionaries. He founded European Christian College (now International University) in Vienna, Austria, and utilized it as a launching pad for sending students behind the Iron Curtain and to every region of Europe. He also served as the first president of Michigan Christian College (now Rochester College) in Rochester, Michigan; as chancellor of Columbia Christian College; as director of East European School of Evangelism; as chairman of the advisory and development council for Harding University's MISSION/PREPARE program; and as professor of missions at Harding University Graduate School of Religion. Of his many publications, his most important work was *Contact,* a magazine designed to keep Christian military and mission points in contact with each other and their constituencies back home.

See also Columbia Christian College; Europe, Missions in — Churches of Christ; Noninstitutional Movement

BIBLIOGRAPHY Otis Gatewood, *Preaching in the Footsteps of Hitler* (1960) • Otis Gatewood, *Three Debates with Four of the Best Mormon Scholars* (2000) • Bailey McBride and Glover Shipp, "The Legacy of Otis Gatewood," *The Christian Chronicle* 56 (November 1999): 18-19 • Bailey McBride, "Church Growth: Gatewood Affects Mission Climate," *The Christian Chronicle* 41 (April 1984): 24.
ERIC R. MAGNUSSON

Gay and Lesbian Rights

The belief that gay and lesbian persons should be granted the rights of freedom and equality under the law. These rights may include nondiscrimination in employment, housing, citizenship, property ownership, health and insurance benefits, child custody, and estate law. The freedom to engage in mutually consenting homosexual relations without legal prosecution is also included. For some, such rights entail the liberty to establish a legally recognized "domestic partnership" or gay marriage. Within the church, "gay and lesbian rights" call for equal participation in church fellowship and leadership, including ordination. The appeal to such rights may also involve the request for liturgical recognition through same-sex covenant ceremonies or weddings.

From the 1970s through the beginning of the twenty-first century, hundreds of articles on this subject were published within journals, newspapers, and magazines associated with churches of the Stone-Campbell Movement. Church assembly statements were forthcoming, in particular, from the Christian Church (Disciples of Christ).

In 1977 a Disciples of Christ General Assembly "Resolution Concerning Civil Liberties of Homosexual Persons" was approved that supported rights for gays and lesbians and rejected "sodomy laws." "[W]hile neither approving of nor condemning homosexuality," it "urge[d] the passage of legislation on local, state and national levels which will end the denial of civil rights and the violation of civil liberties for reasons of sexual orientation" (*1978 Year Book and Directory*, p. 234). At that same assembly, a "Study Document on Homosexuality and the Church" was approved (pp. 236-46). The document included biblical, cultural, biological, and psychological aspects of homosexuality and raised questions for further study. Much of its contents suggested that the traditional condemnation of homosexuality within church and society might need rethinking. However, the 1979 General Assembly adopted a resolution that did not support the ordination of "persons who engage in homosexual practices" (*1980 Year Book and Directory*, p. 297).

In 1993 the Disciples of Christ General Assembly adopted a "Resolution Concerning Civil Rights" that reaffirmed its 1977 stance. It contended that "various campaigns across the country conducted in the name of 'no special rights for gay, lesbian and bisexual persons' misrepresent legitimate claims for persons who seek equal application of the law" (*1994 Year Book and Directory*, p. 332). In 1998 the Office of General Minister and President approved a process for discerning the role of gays and lesbians in the life of the church.

As of 2003 over fifty "Open and Affirming" Disciples ministries are recognized by the Gay and Lesbian Affirming Disciples (GLAD) Alliance. All support gay and lesbian rights in church and society. However, the Region of Northern California–Nevada is the sole Disciples region that officially welcomes sexually active gay and lesbian Christians as candidates for the ordained ministry.

Most literature written within the Churches of Christ and the Christian Churches/Churches of Christ, as well as the more conservative part of the Disciples of Christ, rejects the concept of gay and lesbian rights as inconsistent with the Stone-Campbell Movement. Magazines such as *Firm Foundation, Gospel Advocate,* and *Disciple Renewal* have given extensive attention to this topic. The primary concern focuses on the judged inconsistency of gay and lesbian sexual activity with the Bible. Special attention is given to Leviticus 18:22 and 20:13; 1 Corinthians 6:9; Romans 1:26-32; and 1 Timothy 1:10. A corollary criticism is lodged against contemporary biblical scholars who are alleged to reinterpret or simply reject biblical verses that appear to condemn same-sex relations. Attention is also given to social-scientific evidence that concludes that the gay and lesbian population is smaller than some supporters of gay rights claim. Moreover, there is concern expressed about the possible negative effects on families if gay rights laws are passed. In the midst of the condemnation, much anti-gay rights restorationist writing encourages congregations to love gay and lesbian people, to welcome them into the church after repentance, and to be nurturing of their parents and family members. Strategies for counseling are also mentioned.

Attitudes of the laity within the Stone-Campbell Movement vary but tend toward a negative judgment. According to a 1987 study by Wade Clark Roof and William McKinney, only 18 percent of Disciples laity and 8 percent of Churches of Christ members would agree that "homosexuality is not always wrong." In a 1991 published poll by James L. Guth and Helen Lee Turner, 79 percent of Disciples pastors favored gay rights, but according to Bruce A. Greer only 34 percent of frequently attending Disciples laity would permit a gay or lesbian person to teach in a college or university. D. Newell Williams contends that issues of geography (e.g., North/South, urban/rural), educational level, and class strongly shape attitudes. Within church discussions, debates about the authority of Scripture and its proper interpretation also continue to play a central role in this discussion.

See also GLAD (Gay, Lesbian, and Affirming Disciples) Alliance, Inc.

BIBLIOGRAPHY George F. Beals, "Homosexuality," *Firm Foundation* 109:11 (1994): 19-21 • Richard M. Bowman, "Indiana Regional Assembly: One Region's Struggle with the Homosexuality Issue," *Disciple Renewal* 13:3 (2000): 1, 3, 8 • Steven B. Campbell, "Divine Right Vs. Gay Rights," *Gospel Advocate* 129:29 (1987): 754, 756 • Joan Dennehy et al., *Celebrating the Journey: 20 GLAD Years & Counting* (1999) • Bruce A. Greer, "Active and Inactive Disciples, Presbyterians, and Southern Baptists: A Comparative Socioeconomic, Religious, and Political Profile," in *A Case Study in Mainstream Protestantism: The Disciples' Relation to American Culture, 1880-1989*, ed. D. Newell Williams (1991) • James L. Guth and Helen Lee Turner,

"Pastoral Politics in the 1988 Election: Disciples as Compared to Presbyterians and Southern Baptists," in *A Case Study in Mainstream Protestantism: The Disciples' Relation to American Culture, 1880-1989,* ed. D. Newell Williams (1991) • F. Furman Kearley, "Homosexuality: Correcting the Politically Correct," *Gospel Advocate* 140:12 (1998): 35-36 • "Resolution Concerning Civil Liberties of Homosexual Persons, No. 7747," *1978 Year Book and Directory: Christian Church (Disciples of Christ)* • "Resolution Concerning Civil Rights, No. 9334," *1994 Year Book and Directory: Christian Church (Disciples of Christ)* • Wade Clark Roof and William McKinney, *American Mainline Religion: Its Changing Shape and Future* (1987) • "A Study Document on Homosexuality and the Church, No. 7750," *1978 Year Book and Directory: Christian Church (Disciples of Christ)* • L. Kevin Vick, "Accept Alternative Lifestyle?" *Firm Foundation* 109:3 (1994): 19-21 • D. Newell Williams, "Disciples and the Liberal Conservative Debate," *Disciples Theological Digest* 7:2 (1992): 5-25 • Clark M. Williamson, ed., "Disciple Theology: Ordination and Homosexuality," *Encounter* 40:3 (1979): 197-272. PETER D. BROWNING

GLAD (Gay, Lesbian, and Affirming Disciples) Alliance, Inc.

Organization of gay, lesbian, and affirming Disciples of Christ.

In 1979 the General Assembly of the Christian Church (Disciples of Christ) passed a resolution supporting the rights of homosexuals. At that same assembly GLAD was formed.

GLAD sees itself as identifying with marginalized people much as Jesus' ministry did. GLAD proclaims the authority of Jesus Christ and seeks to be a visible presence faithfully calling the church into a new and inclusive future.

GLAD has a yearly national conference, state and local groups, committees, and a newsletter. GLAD sponsors the Open and Affirming Ministries Program to empower congregations toward full inclusivity.

See also Gay and Lesbian Rights

PHILLIP EWOLDSEN

Glas, John (1695-1773)

Scottish reformer and forebear of American restorationists.

Born to Thomas and Agnes Glas of Fife County, Scotland, Glas held an M.A. from St. Andrews (1713) and did further study at the University of Edinburgh. He was a minister in the Church of Scotland, licensed in 1718, ordained in 1719 at Tealing, and finally deposed in 1730. Glas's 1725 sermonic challenge of the National Covenant and Solemn League and Covenant of the Church of Scotland led to the formation of The Tealing "Society" July 13, 1725, with ten members. In *The Testimony of the King of Martyrs Concerning His Kingdom* (1727) Glas stressed separation of church and state and denied the national covenants. The resultant controversy led to Glas's censure in 1728. Glas's daughter Katharine married Robert Sandeman in 1737. Approximately two dozen congregations comprised this fellowship in Scotland, which called itself the "Church of Christ" but has been dubbed "Glasites" by historians.

This oil portrait of John Glas was painted in 1767 by William Millar and hung for many years in the Glasite meetinghouse in Edinburgh. Courtesy of Lynn McMillon, Oklahoma Christian University

Scripture alone was authoritative, especially the New Testament. Glas followed the Anabaptist call for the restitution of the first-century church, and he taught local congregational autonomy under elders and served by deacons, separation of church and state, baptism as a symbolic remission of sins in the blood of Christ, and weekly celebration of the Lord's Supper. Other practices included weekly offerings, called the "fellowship," and the agape feast, a common fellowship meal in homes. Worship centered on the reading of Scripture, sermon, prayer, and a cappella singing of psalms only. Strict church discipline necessitated small congregations so that harmony of members was maintained in order for the Lord's Supper to be observed.

Glas's impact on the early Stone-Campbell Movement was only indirect. His brand of restorationism, keen on the reinstating of the primitive order of the church, was a clear precursor of the "restoration of the ancient order of things" advanced by Alexander Campbell and his associates a century later in the United States.

See also Ewing, Greville; Haldane, Robert, and James Alexander Haldane; Sandeman, Robert

BIBLIOGRAPHY John Glas, *The Marrow of Ancient Divinity* (1803) • John Glas, *Memoirs of Mr. John Glas* (1828) • John Glas, *A Narrative of the Rise and Progress of the Controversy about the National Covenants* (2nd ed. 1828) • John Glas, *A Plea for Pure and Undefiled Religion* (1887) • John Glas, *The Works of Mr. John Glas,* 5 vols. (1782) • Lynn A. McMillon, "The Quest for the Apostolic Church: A Study of Scottish Origins of American Restorationism" (Ph.D. dissertation, Baylor University, 1972; reissued as *Restoration Roots,* 1982).

LYNN A. MCMILLON

Glen Leith College of the Bible

See New Zealand, The Movement in

Go Ye Chapels

See Urban Ministry

God, Doctrine of

Theological reflection on the nature, attributes, and actions of God.

The Stone-Campbell Movement emerged at a time when classic Christian doctrines like that of the Trinity were coming under intense criticism not only from Deists and Unitarians but also from evangelicals who assumed that the Scriptures were far simpler and clearer on the nature of God than any humanly contrived dogmatic system. Barton Stone, for example, describes in his autobiography how, in his assigned reading as a candidate for the Presbyterian ministry, he was put off by the obscurity with which the Dutch theologian Herman Witsius had defended the tri-unity of God. He was positively drawn, however, to Isaac Watts, the celebrated British evangelical scholar, whose own large book on the Trinity attempted to demystify the doctrine.

In time the Trinity proved to be an extraordinary test case in the Movement's commitment to Proposition Six of Thomas Campbell's *Declaration and Address,* whereby "fairly inferred" deductions from Scripture could legitimately be called "the doctrine of God's holy word" but not imposed upon the free consciences of Christians beyond their ability to comprehend them. Repartee over the Trinity began very early between Barton Stone and Alexander Campbell. In 1827 Stone openly criticized Campbell for trying to defend the trinitarian "system" and so buckling under to the same Calvinist dogmatists that Campbell had otherwise vehemently opposed: "I would advise my dear brother not to soar too high on fancy's wings above the humble grounds of the gospel, lest others adventuring may be precipitated to ruin." Stone continued to publish his criticism of classic Trinitarianism, voicing his distrust of theological paradoxes and balking at the confusion created for simple believers by the historic attempts to uphold the "threeness" of the one God. Affirmations of three substantial "Persons," he believed, led inevitably to tri-theism. Moreover, Stone was less willing than Campbell to concede the mysteriousness of God's nature, since such had historically been used to dupe the Christian masses. "Mystery is one of the names of the whore of Babylon, written in large letters on her forehead."

Pressured to counter accusations of Unitarianism and Arianism, Stone had tried to clarify his views, particularly on the relation of the Father and the Son, in his "Address to the Churches" (2nd ed. 1821). Taking John 10:30 and 14:28 at face value, he concluded that their "oneness" was not constituted of metaphysical substance but of "spirit, purpose, and mind." On the divinity per se of the Son, Stone was fully aware of the soteriological importance of elevating Christ, but struggled to define his preexistence within the Godhead. The historic notion of "eternal generation" he deemed an aberration, yet a "created" Son was likewise problematic. For a while Stone found Isaac Watts's views helpful on the *soul* of Christ as preexisting his incarnation. Ultimately, claiming a scriptural solution to the problem, he proposed his own *via media:* "My own views of the Son of God are that he did not begin to exist 1820 years ago, nor did he exist from eternity; but was the first begotten of the Father before time or creation began — that he was sent by the Father 1820 years ago into the world, and united with a body, prepared for him; and that in him dwelt all the fullness of Godhead bodily (cf. Col. 2:9)."

Stone's clear desire was to keep the discussion at the level of Christology — the agency of Christ the Redeemer as definitive of his relation to the Father — and thereby avoid altogether the conundrums of the "immanent Trinity" (the internal nature of God). Stone nonetheless remained suspect among many of Campbell's followers for his views on this very subject. Stone and his followers continued to fend off the charge of Unitarianism, as basic trinitarian loyalty had inevitably become a point of tension in the union of the Stone and Campbell movements in 1832.

Alexander Campbell had his own bone to pick with classical Trinitarianism, but mainly, as he argued in his series on "A Restoration of the Ancient Order of Things" in the *Christian Baptist,* for its often convoluted and unbiblical *language* in describing the divine interrelations. He strongly attacked, as had Stone, the Nicene terminology of an "eternal generation" of the Son from the Father. But early on Campbell also showed his aversion to Unitarianism and, in the article on "The Trinitarian System" that provoked Barton Stone's wrath, positively affirmed an "uncreated and unoriginated relation" between the Father and his Logos, based on the prologue to John's Gospel. In a broader historical perspective, then, Campbell grounded his own Trinitarianism in the notion of the Logos (Word) as God's preexistent mediator to the world, who became incarnate in Jesus of Nazareth — a view congenial with early, pre-Nicene theologians like Justin Martyr. As Campbell clarifies in the *Christian System,* "While, then, the phrase 'Son of God' denotes a temporal relation, the phrase 'the word of God' denotes an eternal, unoriginated relation. There was a *word of God* from eternity, but the Son of God began to be in the days of Augustus Caesar. 'Thou art my Son, this day have I begotten thee.' He was by his resurrection from the dead declared to be the Son of God with a power and evidence extraordinary and divine."

Like Stone's, Campbell's Trinitarianism was dictated largely by his Christology, not vice versa; indeed, much of his discourse appears superficially more "Binitarian," since he did not elaborate upon the ontological relation between the Father and the Spirit and felt no need to provide his own alternative to the historic language of the "procession" of the Spirit enshrined in the Nicene Creed.

While Campbell shared Stone's aversion to the traditional Niceno-Constantinopolitan language of the one divine *essence (ousia)* in three co-eternal "Persons" *(hypostaseis)* who share the same perfections of uncreated being, he still was more willing than Stone to speak of a genuine plurality of Persons in the *nature* of God. "For the divine nature," Campbell writes in the *Christian System,* "may be communicated or imparted in some sense; and indeed while it is essentially and necessarily singular, it is certainly plural in its personal manifestations. Hence we have the Father, Son, and Holy Spirit equally divine, though personally distinct from each other. We have in fact, but one God, one Lord, one Holy Spirit; yet these are equally possessed of one and of the same divine nature." In the 1846 *Millennial Harbinger* he added, "They are in nature one, but in personal and official relation three."

Consistently Alexander Campbell emphasized the reality of the three divine Persons principally at the level of the "economic" rather than the "immanent" Trinity (though he did not use those terms). What was vital to Christian understanding was not their mysterious internal relations but their self-revelation *to us.* In 1839 in the *Christian System,* Campbell wrote: "Anciently, or before time, it *was* God, the Word of God, and the Spirit of God. But now, in the development of the Christian scheme, *it is* 'the Father, the Son, and the Holy Spirit' — one God, one Lord, one Spirit." Seven years later in the *Millennial Harbinger,* he declared, "We speculate not upon God, nor upon divinity, nor upon *unity, plurality,* or *trinity* or tri-unity. But we have a manifestation of God out of humanity in the Father, of God in humanity in the Son, and of God with humanity in the Holy Spirit." As Thomas Campbell had reiterated in the *Christian Baptist,* "Thus we worship the Father, through the Son, by the Spirit."

Alexander Campbell likewise insisted that overly speculative trinitarian theology failed to recognize the constraints on human conceptualization of the Godhead. He wrote in 1833: "Language fails and thought cannot reach the relation in which the Father and the Son have existed, now exist, and shall forever exist. But that there is, and was, and evermore will be, society in God himself, a plurality as well as unity in the Divine nature, are inferences which do obtrude themselves on my mind in reflecting upon the divine communications to our race." Responding to Stone's criticism, and betraying his own suspicion of Stone's Unitarian penchant, Campbell insisted that he found the trinitarian position altogether reasonable in relation to Unitarianism, but disclaimed absolute loyalty to either position.

Despite such assertions of neutrality, Campbell did take Unitarianism to task in 1846 when confronted with the overtures of eastern Unitarians for Christian union on a nondogmatic basis. Unitarians, he argued, viewed God strictly as one "Person" in the image of a human person, lacking any sense of a divine *nature* given to a plurality of Persons. Though still disclaiming dependence on "scholastic" Trinitarianism, as he called it, Campbell admitted that "Trinitarianism . . . is, to my mind, incomparably more rational and intelligible than [Unitarianism's] 'one personal being' without a habitation or a name known to mortals." Worse still, Unitarians misconstrued the preexistence, incarnation, and atoning sacrifice of Christ, reducing him to a mere creature and his death to that of a martyr. Campbell ultimately could not countenance reconciliation with Unitarians merely on the affirmation of Jesus as Messiah and Lord since their confession of this truth lacked solid doctrinal grounding.

Alexander Campbell bequeathed on the Movement's subsequent generations an enduring conviction that they were pursuing only a truly biblical Trinitarianism that circumvented the scholastic theological systems of earlier centuries. Among second-generation leaders, Isaac Errett, in his *Our Position* (1873), argued this as a distinctive of the Stone-Campbell Movement in contrast to other evangelical traditions: "While accepting fully and unequivocally the Scripture statements concerning what is usually called the trinity of persons in the Godhead, we repudiate alike the philosophical and theological speculations of Trinitarians and Unitarians, and all unauthorized forms of speech on a question which transcends human reason, and on which it becomes us to speak 'in words which the Holy Spirit teaches.'" Others, like conservative pioneer Moses Lard, refuted the trinitarian affiliation altogether. Having read an earlier tract by Errett entitled "A Synopsis of the Faith" that eschewed metaphysical Trinitarianism but stated that "we recognize the tri-unity of the Godhead in the teachings of the New Testament," Lard lampooned the declaration in 1863 as "contradictory and ridiculous," "an humble petition to Orthodoxy to be permitted to return to her embrace."

From Alexander Campbell as well, the Movement generally learned to treat theology per se less as a science of intimate knowledge of the Trinity than as exegetically warranted inferential reasoning about God's attributes and actions in the context of the whole system of revelation (both natural and supernatural) and redemption. W. E. Garrison was quite right that "Campbell's God was a king, a lawgiver and a system-maker." The principal early leaders of the Stone-Campbell Movement were less directly indebted to the patristic and ecumenical-conciliar tradition than to the covenant theology of the Reformed heritage, with its endeavor to map the many aspects of the bilateral relationship between God and fallen humanity mediated by Christ. Major works like Campbell's own *The Christian System* (1839), Walter Scott's *The Gospel Restored* (1836) and *The Messiahship* (1859), and Robert Milligan's *The Scheme of Redemption* (1868) aspired mainly to relate the character of God as Creator, Provider, and Redeemer. Milligan, for example, sets out in merely five pages the unity, plurality, and transcendent attributes of God, while spending the rest of his massive tome outlining the economy of salvation. Scott, for his part, spent much of his "systematic" labor on dispensational concerns and the biblical evidences for the Messiahship of Jesus.

In the twentieth century, the three branches of the Stone-Campbell tradition appropriated this legacy in their own respective ways. Attaching themselves to the ideal of a *nondogmatic* theology, early liberals among the Disciples of Christ like Edward Scribner Ames, author of *The New Orthodoxy* (1918), urged that the only approach to God was through a critically responsible fidelity to the simple ethical gospel of Jesus of Nazareth, embodying the great truth that God *is* first and foremost "love." In such a perspective, classical Trinitarianism was an unfortunate, irrelevant vestige of the patristic and medieval past. On the other end of the spectrum, conservatives of both Churches of Christ and later the Christian Churches/Churches of Christ held fast to the primacy of Christology and soteriology and perpetuated the resistance to all speculative theologies that, in their view, drifted from the clarity of scriptural language concerning God's nature and thus distracted Christians from the central gospel message. Yet an "innocent" Trinitarianism persisted. No less a figure than David Lipscomb, while committing to "Bible only" language for God, nonetheless waxed eloquent on the triune God: "There are three distinct persons represented as God, yet in nature one and divine, one in purpose and aim, one in all the works of God. Yet in that oneness each had his own specific, distinct office to fulfill or work to perform in all that was done by God, and the others did not interfere with his work." More recently some conservatives have begun openly to defend a classical understanding of the Trinity (see Highfield; Turner and Myers; Lanier, all from Churches of Christ) or to sanction metaphysical language of God as consistent with Scripture (e.g., Cottrell, from Christian Churches/Churches of Christ), though most conservatives have remained skeptical of creedal Trinitarianism.

A few theological moderates among Disciples of Christ in the twentieth century sought more of a constructive engagement both with classical Trinitarianism and with modern systematic theologians like Karl Barth and Emil Brunner. British Disciple William Robinson, in his *Whither Theology?* (1947), made few actual references to his own heritage but did propose that Alexander Campbell "anticipated" the Barthian notion of the *Word-in-person* as humanity's principal access to God. Robinson sought to rehabilitate Campbell's basic intuition that the Bible communicates more the character and *Person* of God than sheer abstractions about divinity. The Trinity had to be understood accordingly: "God is Love. This involves the notion of fellowship in the Godhead. We say that God is personal: in a sense we ought to say that God is supra-personal. Supra-personality is fellowship. In the Christian experience, this develops into the knowledge of God as Father, Son, and Holy Spirit — the Doctrine of the Trinity." Elsewhere Robinson expressed qualified sympathy with the Nicene Creed and its affirmation of the triune God.

In more recent decades there has been a renewed interest in Robinson's theological legacy among some scholars and leaders in the Christian Churches/Churches of Christ and the Christian Church (Disciples of Christ) who are appreciative of his attempt to construct a bridge between the Stone-Campbell heritage and classical Christian theology. Other representatives from Churches of Christ and from Christian Churches/Churches of Christ, however, have found common cause with Evangelical theologies (see Baker) and with "apologetics," the defense of theism against philosophical skepticism (see Miethe and Habermas). On the whole, however, conservatives have continued to work out their "doctrine of God" through exegetical studies and biblical commentaries, not systematic theologies or engagement with contemporary theological trends.

Some more ecumenically disposed theologians of the Christian Church (Disciples of Christ), emboldened by the efforts of the Panel of Scholars (1963) to rehabilitate theology in Disciples circles, have reworked the Campbellian emphasis on covenantal theology (e.g., Osborn, Sprinkle), though mainly for ecclesiological purposes. Perhaps the most serious attempt at rehabilitating Trinitarianism in the Stone-Campbell tradition of late has been the work of Joe R. Jones, whose *A Grammar of Christian Faith* (2002) is keen on carefully nuanced language of being and person in God, while (true to the Disciples ethos) privileging the "economic" Trinity of the scriptural witness. Other Disciples theologians have interacted with a variety of initiatives challenging traditional categories for conceiving and speaking of God, such as process (see Cobb and Griffin), post-Holocaust (see Williamson), and feminist (see Serene Jones) theologies. The controversy over gender-inclusive theological language (or indifference to the issue in many conservative churches) is just one significant gauge of the wide breadth of perspective among the heirs of a nineteenth-century Movement that cherished freedom of opinion and decried the tyranny of dogmatic systems.

See also *Christian System, The;* Christology; Faith; Grace, Doctrine of; *Gospel Restored, The;* Holy Spirit, Doctrine of the; Salvation; *Scheme of Redemption, The;* "Synopsis of the Faith"; Theology; Unitarians

BIBLIOGRAPHY William Baker, ed., *Evangelicalism and the Stone-Campbell Movement* (2002) • W. B. Blakemore, Ronald Osborn, and Ralph Wilburn, eds., *The Renewal of Church: The Panel of Scholars Reports,* 3 vols. (1963) • M. Eugene Boring, *Disciples and the Bible: A History of Disciples Biblical Interpretation in North America* (1997) • Alexander Campbell, "To the *Christian Messenger,*" *Christian Messenger* (1827): 6-10 • Alexander Campbell, *The Christian System,* chs. 3-5 (2nd ed. 1839) • Alexander Campbell, "Theology — Natural and Revealed," *Millennial Harbinger* (1853): 285-92 • Alexander Campbell, "The Trinitarian System," *Christian Baptist* (1827): 333-35 • Alexander Campbell, "Unitarianism, or Remarks on Christian Union," *Millennial Harbinger* (1846): 216-25, 388-94, 450-54, 634-38, 686-95 • John B. Cobb and David Ray Griffin, *Process Theology: An Introductory Exposition* (1976) • Jack Cottrell, *What the Bible Says About God the Creator* (1983) • A. T. DeGroot, *Disciple Thought: A History,* ch. 3 (1965) • W. E. Garrison, "The Idea of God," in *Variations on a Theme: "God Saw That It Was Good"* (1964), pp. 58-89 • John Mark Hicks, "The Doctrine of God," *Leaven* 8 (2000): 118-23 • Ronald Highfield, "Does the Doctrine of the Trinity Make a Difference?" in *Theology Matters: Answers for the Church Today,* ed. Gary Holloway et al. (1998), pp. 15-26 • Joe R. Jones, *A Grammar of Christian Faith,* 2 vols. (2002) • Serene Jones, *Feminist Theory and Christian Theology* (2000) • Roy Lanier, *The Timeless Trinity for the Ceaseless Centuries* (1974) • David Lipscomb, "God — Who and What Is He?" in *Salvation from Sin* (1913), pp. 26-51 • Terry Miethe and Gary Habermas, *Why Believe? God Exists: Rethinking the Case for God and Christianity* (1993) • Robert Milligan, *The Scheme of Redemption* (1868) • Ronald Osborn, *The Faith We Affirm: Basic Beliefs of Disciples of Christ* (1979) • William Robinson, *Whither Theology? Some Essential Biblical Patterns* (1947) • Stephen Sprinkle, *Disciples and Theology: Understanding the Faith of a People in Covenant* (1999) • Barton W. Stone, "Address to the Churches," 2nd ed. in *Works of Elder B. W. Stone,* ed. James Mathes (2nd ed. 1859), pp. 50-84 • Barton W. Stone, "To the *Christian Baptist,*" *Christian Messenger* (1827): 204-9 • J. J. Turner and Edward Myers, *Doctrine of the Godhead: A Study of the Father, Son, and Holy Spirit* (1973) • D. Newell Williams, *Barton Stone: A Spiritual Biography* (2000) • Clark Williamson, *A Guest in the House of Israel: Post-Holocaust Church Theology* (1993) • Clark Williamson, *Way of Blessing, Way of Life* (1999).

PAUL M. BLOWERS

Goodpasture, Benton Cordell (1894-1977)

According to many observers, the most powerful person in Churches of Christ from the late 1940s until his death in 1977.

Born at Rocky Mound, Tennessee, Goodpasture attended Nashville Bible School, where he studied under H. Leo Boles (1874-1946), posting an outstanding record as a student. In 1918 he married Emily Cleveland Cliett. From that year until 1939, he preached in Shelbyville, Tennessee; Florence, Alabama; and Atlanta, Georgia. In 1939 Leon McQuiddy (1887-1950) selected Goodpasture to be the editor of the *Gospel Advocate.* The paper had moved West for its two previous editors, Foy E. Wallace, Jr. (1896-1979), and John T. Hinds (1867-1938). Goodpasture lived east of the Mississippi River and was a graduate of Nashville Bible School (today Lipscomb University).

Goodpasture's reputation in 1939 was not as wide in Churches of Christ as that of the two previous editors. He brought two important recommendations with him, however — those of H. Leo Boles and Leon McQuiddy, the paper's publisher. Under his guidance the *Gospel Advocate* dealt with a number of critical issues facing Churches of Christ during the mid-twentieth century, including the premillennial controversy, the Murch-Witty "unity" meetings, issues

Powerful editor of the *Gospel Advocate* from 1939 until his death in 1977, Benton Cordell Goodpasture was a key figure in opposing the noninstitutional movement in Churches of Christ.

surrounding World War II, and the institutional conflicts of the 1950s. Goodpasture's editorials were a major factor in the separation of the noninstitutional churches from the mainstream.

During Goodpasture's tenure as editor, the *Gospel Advocate*'s circulation continued to climb. By the early 1950s, the number grew to 20,000. During the centennial drive of 1955, the subscription list reached an all-time peak of 100,000. It finally leveled off at about 30,000 near the time of Goodpasture's death.

See also *Gospel Advocate, The;* Lipscomb University; Murch, James DeForest; Noninstitutional Movement

BIBLIOGRAPHY J. E. Choate, *The Anchor That Holds: A Biography of Benton Cordell Goodpasture* (1971) • Willard Collins and J. Cliett Goodpasture, *Sermons and Lectures of B. C. Goodpasture* (1964) • David Edwin Harrell, Jr., "B. C. Goodpasture: Leader of Institutional Thought," in *They Being Dead Yet Speak,* ed. Melvin D. Curry (1981).

ROBERT E. HOOPER

Goodwin, Elijah (1807-1879)

Evangelist in the Stone-Campbell Movement in Indiana in the nineteenth century.

An Ohio native, Elijah Goodwin overcame a sickly childhood, poverty, and almost no formal education to become a leading evangelist in Indiana and later an editor of the *Christian Record.* He had been taught to read, and on his own he advanced his knowledge by having better-educated friends teach him how to use Greek in his studies of Scripture.

Goodwin moved beyond his own Methodist rearing by the appeal to his intellect and good heart of "New Lights" or "Stoneite" Christians. He was drawn by the teaching of God's love, a hallmark of Stoneite preaching. He labored sacrificially to share the gospel that had transformed his own life.

In 1827 Goodwin agreed to preach around a 600-mile circuit of Posey, Crawford, Monroe, and Vigo Counties in southwestern Indiana, plus two counties in Illinois. He made that circuit every eight weeks. In a year he typically traveled 3,500 miles on foot and sometimes by horse. He preached about 380 sermons. His supporters commissioned him to "Go preach and we will see that you do not suffer." Under such a contract he was rarely paid. He went on to become pastor of congregations at Bloomington and Madison, and Central Christian Church and Third Christian Church in Indianapolis.

Like many nineteenth-century evangelists, Elijah Goodwin was underpaid and overworked but carried on a substantial itinerant ministry on the Indiana frontier.
Courtesy of the Disciples of Christ Historical Society

He was a persuasive debater, particularly in the cause of believers' baptism, and there were mass baptisms after some of his debates. On one occasion he immersed the wife of one of the debate moderators. His preaching ministry was later balanced by his editorship of the *Christian Record.* He was also a significant influence in the establishment of Northwestern Christian University (now Butler University).

Goodwin was fervently committed to the restoration principle, and he wrote on the nature of the church. He pointed out the various features of the apostolic order of the church and argued that, while Catholic and Protestant groups had fallen short of the ancient "sect" of Christians in its original integrity, anyone — no matter their name or background — who conformed to this model could rightly claim to be the true church of Jesus Christ. He lamented regarding the Stone-Campbell Movement itself that it had not sufficiently manifested the oneness of Christ's body: "We have said more on this subject than any other people during the last quarter of a century, and yet we do not exhibit to the world any more of that union than we ought."

This pioneer evangelist died at the age of 72. His contemporaries eulogized him by reporting that he had lived a disciplined, sacrificial life.

See also Evangelism, Evangelists — Nineteenth Century; Goodwin, Marcia Melissa Bassett

BIBLIOGRAPHY Elijah Goodwin, "The Church the Body of Christ," reprinted in Z. T. Sweeney, *New Testament Christianity* (1923), vol. 1, pp. 170-97 • Elijah Goodwin, "The Sect Everywhere Spoken Against," reprinted in Z. T. Sweeney, *New Testament Christianity* (1923), vol. 1, pp. 29-59 • L. C. Rudolph, *Hoosier Faiths* (1994) • Henry K. Shaw, *Hoosier Disciples* (1966).

PETER M. MORGAN

Goodwin, Marcia Melissa Bassett (?-1885)

Marcia Melissa Bassett Goodwin was probably the first Disciples of Christ churchwoman to serve as an editor of both secular and religious publications. With her husband, Elijah Goodwin, whom she married in 1864, she co-authored and edited *The American Housewife* from 1869 until they sold the magazine in 1872. From 1863 to 1888 she edited and published the *Christian Companion,* which featured news of women's mission work. Goodwin also wrote specifically for Disciples women, editing and publishing *The Christian Monitor,* known as the pioneer magazine devoted to the sisterhood of the reformation. This magazine, begun in 1866, represented a merger of two of her previous publications, *Mother's Monitor* and *Ladies' Christian Monitor.* Always one to encourage women's initiatives in the church, Goodwin wrote in that magazine, "Failure is a word that has never been written upon the banner of the sisters of the Church of Christ."

Editor and missionary leader Marcia M. B. Goodwin (d. 1885) edited and published *Christian Companion* and *The Christian Monitor,* the latter a magazine devoted specifically to the women of the Stone-Campbell Movement.

Courtesy of the Disciples of Christ Historical Society

Marcia Goodwin was a member of the committee that drafted the constitution for the Christian Woman's Board of Missions (CWBM) and subsequently edited the official CWBM periodical, *Missionary Tidings.* The first issue was published in May 1883, a four-page, monthly newsletter that cost 25 cents per year. Due to ill health, Goodwin continued as editor just five months. She died in 1885 and was eulogized by the women's missionary society of Third Christian Church in Indianapolis on April 26, 1885.

See also Christian Woman's Board of Missions; Goodwin, Elijah; Women in Ministry — Nineteenth Century

DEBRA B. HULL

Gospel Advocate

Journal founded in 1855 by Tolbert Fanning (1810-1874) in Nashville, Tennessee.

William Lipscomb (1829-1908) served as co-editor of the paper until 1861 when the Civil War forced suspension of publication. The postwar *Advocate* began in 1866 with Fanning as editor and David Lipscomb (1831-1917) as co-editor, though Lipscomb soon became editor, a position he held for almost fifty years. Weekly publication began in 1866 and continued until 1978. Publication was bi-monthly from 1978 to 1987, after which the journal became a monthly. For much of the twentieth century the Tennessee-based *Gospel Advocate* was the premier platform of influence within Churches of Christ. It had 112 years as a continuous weekly religious paper, and it is the oldest continuing journal in that part of the Movement.

Fanning's purpose for beginning the *Gospel Advocate* was to create a forum for discussion on the subject of church cooperation and human organizations in the church, among other concerns. The paper was for open discussion of biblical issues and against clerical hierarchy. Fanning also hoped that the *Gospel Advocate* would undo some of the controversy caused by his previous paper, the *Christian Review*, started in 1844. This paper, renamed the *Christian Magazine* under the editorship of Jesse B. Ferguson, divided Churches of Christ around Nashville by espousing spiritualism and universalism. Fanning regretted the part he played in giving Ferguson an opportunity to appear before a wider audience through the pages of the paper. This incident provided a major impetus for the founding of the *Gospel Advocate.*

The *Advocate* sought, in the words of Thomas Campbell, to "speak where the Bible speaks and be silent where the Bible is silent." Fanning viewed biblical silence as strictly prohibitive. The *Advocate's* pages contained news from the churches, Bible lessons, questions and answers, correspondence from readers, book reviews, and other information that the editors thought spiritually helpful. It also contained farming observations and news helpful for a rural population.

For fifty years after the Civil War, David Lipscomb's voice was effectively heard through the pages of the *Advocate* on a weekly basis, making him by far the most influential spokesperson for Churches of Christ in the South. The *Gospel Advocate* was the only paper that many Christians in the South felt they could rely on, particularly after the war. Most Northern journals were pro-Union in their sentiments, if not their statements, effectively alienating Southern church members. The *Advocate* spoke out against missionary societies, musical instruments in the worship assembly, and human agencies to do work assigned to the church. Lipscomb's position was that any work assigned to the church should be done only through the local congregation. The *Advocate* under Lipscomb also strongly advocated pacifism and Christian nonparticipation in government. Under the later editorship of J. C. McQuiddy (1858-1924) and with strong pressure from the U.S. government in 1917, this general direction was reversed. Arguably, this event with others in 1917 marked a shift in perspective of the *Advocate's* outlook from countercultural to seeing the Bible as the originator and supporter of Western civilization.

Henry Leo Boles (1874-1946) became a key figure in the leadership of the *Gospel Advocate* in the twentieth century, serving as editor from 1920 to 1923 and a prolific staff writer until his death. Boles had earned the confidence of David Lipscomb when he came as a student to Nashville Bible School in 1903. After Boles joined the faculty, Lipscomb recommended him for the presidency of the school in 1913, a post he held from 1913 to 1920, and again from 1923 to 1932. Boles combined his writing and editorial talents with his work as an educator, administrator, and preacher to become one of the most widely known leaders in Churches of Christ. Among his contributions were commentaries on Matthew (1936), Luke (1940), and Acts (1941), as well as books on the eldership (1900) and the Holy Spirit (1942), all published by the Gospel Advocate Company. In 1928 he represented the *Gospel Advocate*'s position on premillennialism in a written debate with R. H. Boll published in serial form in the journal, then later as a book titled *Unfulfilled Prophecy.*

Always conservative and Bible-based, the tone and direction of the *Advocate* varied depending on the editor at the helm. Under David Lipscomb, the journal rejected everything not explicitly permitted by Scripture. Unity was obtained by following exactly the words of Scripture without addition or subtraction. The rejection of missionary societies and instruments in the assembly on the basis of biblical silence are only two examples. Under Foy E. Wallace, Jr., the *Advocate* continued the fight relentlessly against premillennialism, a fight that had begun under J. C. McQuiddy in 1916. During his thirty-eight years from 1939 to 1977 as the second longest serving *Advocate* editor, B. C. Goodpasture (1894-1977) became one of the most influential leaders in mainstream Churches of Christ. During the 1950s he used the paper to isolate the noninstitutional churches from the mainstream. Noninstitutional churches usually agreed with their opponents on the mission of the church; the difference was over how this mission should be accomplished.

Through sixteen editors, from Fanning in 1855 to the beginning of the twenty-first century with Neil Anderson (b. 1938), the intended aim of the *Gospel Advocate* has been to promote Christianity that reflects New Testament precedence based on positive biblical commands, examples, and necessary inferences. A look through the pages of the *Advocate* provides a picture of the concerns of Churches of Christ throughout their existence. While no journal in Churches of Christ in the late twentieth century commanded a large readership or reflected a mainstream consensus, the *Advocate* continued to identify and address matters of importance, provide biblical studies, and supply news of interest to many in mainstream Churches of Christ.

See also Fanning, Tolbert; Ferguson, Jesse Babcock; Goodpasture, Benton Cordell; Lipscomb, David; Noninstitutional Movement; Pacifism; Wallace, Foy E., Jr.

BIBLIOGRAPHY Thomas L. Campbell, "The Contributions of David Lipscomb and the *Gospel Advocate* to Religious Education in the Churches of Christ" (unpublished D.R.E. dissertation, Southern Baptist Theological Seminary, 1968) • John Allen Chalk, "History of the *Gospel Advocate,* 1855-1868: Its Social and Political Conscience" (unpublished M.A. thesis, Tennessee Technological University, 1967) • *The Gospel Advocate Celebrates Its 100th Anniversary, 1855-1955* (1955) • John C. Hardin, "B. C. Goodpasture, the *Gospel Advocate,* and Churches of Christ, 1939-1959" (unpublished M.A. thesis, Auburn University, 2002) • Richard T. Hughes, Henry E. Webb, and Howard E. Short, *The Power of the Press: Studies of the Gospel Advocate, the Christian Standard, and the Christian-Evangelist* (1987).

DAVID L. LITTLE

Gospel Echo

Disciples of Christ journal; predecessor of *The Christian-Evangelist.*

Established at Carrollton, Illinois, in January 1863 as a monthly periodical, *The Gospel Echo* grew through mergers and acquisitions into *The Christian-Evangelist* (renamed *The Christian* and then *The Disciple*). Founder Elijah L. Craig sold the publication and turned over management to John C. Reynolds in 1868. Reynolds moved the paper to Macomb, Illinois, where he served as pastor of the Christian Church in addition to teaching ancient languages at Abingdon College.

In early 1869 Reynolds attracted one of his former Abingdon students, James H. Garrison, to join him as co-editor of *The Gospel Echo.* Working together for the next three years, the two men advocated "the primitive order of things" but supported cooperative causes at home and abroad. Soon Reynolds began to take on additional responsibilities in the life of Disciples, including corresponding secretary of the Illinois State Missionary Society, while Garrison focused his attention on managing their venture in journalism.

Under Garrison's leadership, *The Gospel Echo* absorbed two other struggling periodicals, became a weekly at the urging of subscribers, and moved to Quincy, Illinois. Thereafter the fate of the enterprise fell solely on his shoulders; he became publisher as well as editor. Determined to expand circulation, in 1873 he renamed his paper *The Christian,* moved it to St. Louis, and negotiated a merger with *The Evangelist* in 1882 to form *The Christian-Evangelist.* Over the next quarter-century or so, Garrison and his colleagues grew the journal into a powerful medium of expression among Disciples across the nation and beyond.

BIBLIOGRAPHY J. Edward Moseley, "The Christian-Evangelist: A Genealogical Chart," *The Christian-Evangelist* (Jan. 6, 1938): 26-27 • William E. Tucker, *J. H. Garrison and Disciples of Christ* (1964), pp. 38-60.

WILLIAM E. TUCKER

Gospel Restored, The

Voluminous work (576 pages) published by Walter Scott (1796-1861) in 1836, expounding a "uniform authoritative plan of preaching" the "ancient gospel."

While others had successfully rejected human creeds and made pleas for the restoration of the church's "ancient order," Scott believed his "ancient gospel" was the culminating recovery among the early Reformers, which led him to expect the imminent arrival of the millennium.

Scott insisted that the central message of Scripture is the "divine oracle" uttered by the Father at Christ's baptism: "Behold my Son, the Beloved in whom I delight" (Matt. 3:17). The restoration of the gospel was about preaching this, the Bible's only creed, in its "pristine singleness." While Scott acknowledged a wider doctrinal system, his vision of apostolic preaching required only that Jesus be proclaimed as the Christ and that people be exhorted to receive Jesus in faith and in the manner God directs. This six-item presentation of the gospel (often reduced to a "five-finger exercise") was intended to be an alternative to scholastic Calvinism. In Scott's presentation the ancient gospel had two parts, each with three elements: duties that humans undertake (faith, repentance, and baptism), and privileges that God supplies (remission of sins, the gift of the Holy Spirit, and eternal life).

Indebted to Scottish Common Sense Philosophy, Scott believed that religious knowledge was obtained through the senses. Faith was not the result of an unmediated experience of the Holy Spirit. It was a rational decision to be reached upon the evaluation of scriptural testimony. Faith thus preceded the gift of the Holy Spirit, who was given not to make persons believe but in order to sanctify those who did. Thus, Scott's rearrangement of the *ordo salutis* hinged on his rationalistic anthropology. The six-part gospel was the corresponding remedy for the six-part structure of human sinfulness that included "the love of sin, the practice of it, the state of it, its guilt, its power and its punishment."

The doctrine of baptism for the remission of sin was met with charges of works-righteousness. Yet

Scott believed that he maintained the divine initiative. The Holy Spirit, by authoring Scripture, had employed "moral and verbal means" with which to draw people into relationship with God. Faith was an other-regarding trust in Christ. Scott writes, "We are forgiven, then, not because we are baptized, but because we need forgiveness, and are by faith prepared to receive it through the merits of Christ alone."

Scott's claim to have personally "restored the gospel" was a matter of some controversy. Yet his successful preaching put the distinctive emphases contained in *The Gospel Restored* to practical evangelistic use. His book was a fully fleshed out presentation of the "Ancient Gospel." He wrote almost two hundred pages on the Old Testament backdrop for salvation and averaged almost seventy pages on each of the six items. He complained even before the book was published that many others were using a bare-bones version of the plan. The book anticipated Robert Milligan's *The Scheme of Redemption* (1868), which became the standard text of this variety in subsequent generations. Scott's "Five Finger Exercise" inspired later understanding of the New Testament, though subsequent versions of the five-point plan focused more exclusively on human response to the gospel (hearing, believing, repenting, confessing, and being baptized).

The Gospel Restored has ongoing significance for the Stone-Campbell Movement in terms of its insistence on the centrality of Scripture as God's means of communicating love, the centrality of Jesus Christ in that communication, and the centrality of baptism as a means of conveying Christian assurance.

See also Evangelism, Evangelists — Early Nineteenth Century; Faith; Five Finger Exercise; *Messiahship, The; Scheme of Redemption, The;* Scott, Walter

BIBLIOGRAPHY William Baxter, *Life of Elder Walter Scott* (1874) • James O. Duke, "Walter Scott: Theologian," in *Walter Scott: A Nineteenth-Century Evangelical,* ed. Mark G. Toulouse (1999), pp. 61-78 • Dwight E. Stevenson, *Walter Scott: Voice of the Golden Oracle* (1946).

KENT ELLETT

Grace, Doctrine of

Charis (grace) is the Greek rendering of the Hebrew *chen* (favor), although the term *chesed* (covenant love) more closely approximates its uses in the New Testament. In the New Testament *charis* is used to denote the goodwill, lovingkindness, or favor of God. Luther declared that grace is "God acting out of his deepest being," and Barth that it is "an inner mode of being in God Himself." Grace is indicative of the utter freedom of God in relation to his creation, his sheer prerogative to save, and more specifically his willingness to forgive sinners (Rom. 3:24) and restore them to fellowship. Grace also refers to the goodness of God operative in the transformation of human life ("this grace in which we stand," Rom. 5:2, RSV) and to the ecclesial fruit of God's mercy as the church responds in thankfulness and in concern for fellow believers (2 Cor. 8:1-5). God's lovingkindness became incarnate in Jesus Christ (John 1:14, 16-17), who embodied the full revelation of the gracious plan of God that was nascent in God's covenantal interactions with Israel.

Barton Stone and Thomas and Alexander Campbell concurred with the judgment of Western theological tradition since Augustine that divine grace was the font from which flowed all aspects of the Christian system. They presupposed this fact and saw no need to belabor the definition of grace, although they clearly had differences with some of their Protestant forbears on the precise outworking of God's salvific plan. In "A Compendious View of the Gospel," Barton Stone wrote: "It is only a view of the holiness, goodness, love, — and the free, unmerited grace and *mercy* of God, which produces true conviction and true repentance, and which humbles the soul, slays the enmity of the heart, and makes [the sinner] willing to depart from all iniquity. He adores the riches of divine grace, which is extended to such a poor polluted worm of the dust." Stone continued to identify grace primarily with the love of God, God's compassion toward sinners demonstrated through the sacrificial life and death of Jesus Christ.

Alexander Campbell insisted that grace was the basic "moving cause" in salvation, the "effects" of which were regeneration, justification, sanctification, reconciliation, and adoption. Grace established the whole objective scheme, not only of conversion and regeneration, but also the orderly arrangement of the new life in Christ. "In the Kingdom of Heaven," Campbell wrote in *The Christian System,* "the antecedent blessings are the constitution of grace, the king, and all that he did, suffered, and sustained for our redemption. These were finished before we came upon the stage of action. This is all favor, pure favor, sovereign favor: for there can be no favor that is not free and sovereign."

In an extended statement Campbell indicated how grace is communicated through the media of revealed ordinances:

> All the wisdom, power, love, mercy, compassion, or *grace of God* is in the ordinances of the Kingdom of heaven; and if all grace be in them it can only be enjoyed through them. What, then, under the present administration of the Kingdom of heaven, are the ordinances which contain the grace of God? They are preaching the gospel — immersion in the name of Jesus into the name of the Father, and of the Son, and of the Holy Spirit — the reading and teaching

the Living Oracles — the Lord's day — the Lord's supper — fasting — prayer — confession of sins — and praise. To these may be added other appointments of God, such as exhortation, admonition, discipline, etc.; for these also are ordinances of God; and, indeed, all statutes and commandments are ordinances: but we speak not at present of those ordinances which concern the good order of the kingdom, but of those which are primary means of enjoyment. These primary and sacred ordinances of the Kingdom of Heaven are the means of our individual enjoyment of the present salvation of God.

Early thinkers of the Stone-Campbell tradition took issue with a number of elements in the Reformed doctrine of grace that they encountered in scholastic Presbyterian theology and in some revivalist preaching. They dissented sharply, for example, from the close connection of grace with a doctrine of election and with the notion of eternal divine decrees of predestination and reprobation. They rejected the view that the "covenant of grace" comprehended both Old Testament and New Testament, and the concomitant principle that the law was necessary even for Christians in the convicting of sin. Finally, they also repudiated the notion of grace as the "irresistible" activity of the Holy Spirit in regenerating persons prior to, and as necessary for, their coming to faith.

J. W. McGarvey represented this strongly anti-Calvinist view of grace in the Movement's second and third generation, assailing what he alleged was an artificial nomenclature of "sovereign grace," "saving grace," "almighty grace," "free grace," "special grace," "state of grace," "covenant of grace," "saving graces" (even though Alexander Campbell and others had still used some of these phrases). McGarvey especially attacked what he alleged to be an obscure notion of "infused" grace. Seeking to demystify the concept, McGarvey identified the simple scriptural meaning of *grace* as God's disposition of *favor* toward humanity and humanity's reciprocal disposition of *gratitude*. More specifically, grace denoted the embodiment of God's favor in kindnesses to humanity, such as the offering of the gospel to the Gentiles.

Thomas Munnell, a minister and leader of the Disciples of Christ in Ohio in the mid-nineteenth century, took issue with McGarvey's objectivism and argued that the purpose of divine grace was precisely the *infusion* of grace into human hearts, "an internal, *subjective* blessing, and not only an objective something to be contemplated at a distance." "Spiritual strength, then, is the highest definition of grace. Not Christ's strength in heaven, or on earth objectively considered, but his *strength in Paul,* to enable him to bear the thorn." McGarvey's view, though the dominant one in the Movement, appeared rationalistic and mechanical to Munnell. McGarvey countered by stating that "Bro. Munnell seems somewhat fond of religious mist, and to think that it adds richness to our religion." But Munnell responded by defending the scriptural warrants for the idea of infusion (e.g., Rom. 5:5, the "shedding abroad" of the love of God in human hearts).

At the turn of the twentieth century, liberals yearned to dispense with the supernaturalism associated with traditional Protestant teaching on grace. Edward Scribner Ames best epitomized this trend in the Stone-Campbell Movement. For Ames, it was enough to claim that "God is love," but dogmatic understandings of grace as mediated through the atoning "work" of Christ and as setting in motion a multidimensional scheme of salvation were untenable. Ames claimed that "God is as good and as gracious as Jesus Christ" but also that Christ is "a kind of pledge and promise of what other human beings may accomplish." Disciples liberals thus shared the perspective of other Protestant liberals in seeing grace as a divine attribute that had its highest example or manifestation in the self-giving ethics of Jesus; but it was not exclusively accessible through him. Indeed, much emphasis was placed on the general manifestation of grace in the world, in keeping with the view that God was not a transcendent judge but a spirit immanent in human religious and cultural progress.

Most constituents of the Movement, however, to the extent that they relied on the thinking of the early leadership and affirmed the supernatural character and christocentric focus of divine grace, struggled with the relation between this grace and the imperatives of the gospel. Is the gospel a *quid pro quo* transaction in which one's obedience is viewed as achieving acceptability and effecting a change of mind in God? Or does the fact that grace is extended without regard to merit in human beings mean that it is to be understood as *unconditional,* so as to render human response superfluous? The distinction between the so-called "obligations of grace" and the "conditions of grace," while real, has not been easily drawn. The perennial challenge to the Stone-Campbell Movement, with its historic urge to answer the Philippian jailer's question in Acts 16:30 ("What must I do to be saved?"), has been to remain ever mindful that God's favor, unconditioned, is prior to, and the basis for, the responses human beings are called to make to that grace.

Churches of Christ in the twentieth century experienced an extended controversy (1930s-1960s) on the character of divine grace, revolving largely around the figure of minister-scholar K. C. Moser (1893-1976). Moser expressed deep concern that the "plan of salvation" being preached from many a pulpit and upheld in Church of Christ publications was quickly becoming an object of devotion in and of itself, dangerously bordering on a new legalism wherein the constitutive actions of conversion and regeneration, especially baptism itself, would become works meriting justification before God. Moser reasserted the contrast between grace and law, faith and works, and divine and human righteousness, and insisted on the principle of salvation (and justification) by grace through faith — a faith that informs repentance, confession, and baptism. Moser's premier critics, R. L. Whiteside, Foy E. Wallace, Jr., and Guy N. Woods, keen to defend the "plan" as constitutive of the gospel, dismissed Moser's views on grace and faith as a reversion to Calvinism. Moser persisted with not only a substantial book (*The Way of Salvation,* 1932) but also an influential pamphlet ("Christ Versus a 'Plan,'" 1952) that sought to refocus attention on the person and work of Jesus Christ as embodying God's grace toward sinners. "The conditions of salvation," wrote Moser, "are not merely responses to a king possessing 'all authority,' but responses to Christ as a sin-offering." Moser's theology of grace was a broadside against not only soteriological legalism but also the rationalistic hermeneutic that had interpreted the gospel merely as a programmatic guidebook for salvation. Moser's work ultimately had significant impact on other leaders and thinkers in twentieth-century Churches of Christ, such as G. C. Brewer, R. C. Bell, and J. D. Thomas.

Accusations of "Neo-Calvinism" did not die out with K. C. Moser among Churches of Christ. Tom Roberts, a minister in Texas, similarly criticized Carl Ketcherside and Leroy Garrett, leaders who encouraged a more conciliatory spirit toward paedobaptist denominations, for separating the "gospel" of grace from right doctrine and obeying the commands of Christ. Ketcherside and Garrett taught that the gospel of grace was communicated principally in terms of the core facts of Christ's redemptive work, that this alone truly commanded personal faith and could serve as the basis of Christian unity. They shared Moser's concern with legalism. Roberts and like-minded critics, however, insisted that the gospel was inseparable from the full gamut of "doctrine" setting forth the conditions of justification and salvation. "Legalism" was in their view an unfair label pinned on those who took seriously the New Testament emphasis on obedience and on "working out your salvation" as objectively outlined in Scripture.

Historically in the three streams of the Stone-Campbell Movement, the theme of divine grace has been explored principally through exegesis, especially in numerous published commentaries on Romans. Few are the "systematic" expositions of the theme, save in larger works on biblical soteriology (e.g., A. Campbell's *The Christian System,* 1839; R. Milligan's *The Scheme of Redemption,* 1868). From the Christian Churches/Churches of Christ, one such systematic work is that of conservative theologian Jack Cottrell, whose *What the Bible Says About God the Redeemer* (1987) reasserts, for a Stone-Campbell audience, classic Protestant emphases on the sheer freedom, gratuity, depth, and sovereignty of God's grace. Cottrell relies heavily on Karl Barth and on a number of contemporary evangelical theologians (J. I. Packer, et al.), with very little recourse to early Stone-Campbell sources.

In the Christian Church (Disciples of Christ) the theme of grace has often emerged in conversation with more recent theological movements. For example, Serene Jones, a Disciples feminist theologian and author of *Feminist Theory and Christian Theology: Cartographies of Grace* (2000), has called for a reworking of Protestant notions of grace, justification, and sanctification in the light of feminist concerns. Jones argues that justification and sanctification are to be "reversed" in the context of God's graciousness toward marginalized women, who need first and foremost "to inhabit a space where God's grace nurtures and forms persons," making them holy and whole before they face the justifying (crucifying) grace that forgives the sins of old "constructions" of personal identity in which women have been caught. Expressing a different concern, Clark Williamson, a Disciples systematic theologian, has explored in depth the ramifications of the Holocaust and historic Christian anti-Judaism for a theology of grace, one that takes serious account of the relationship between Jews and Gentiles in God's gracious eschatological plan. Most of these new emphases by Disciples theologians, however, draw little if any substance from the insights of earlier generations of Stone-Campbell thinkers.

See also Atonement; Calvinism; Conversion; Covenant (Federal) Theology; Faith; Justification, Doctrine of; Ketcherside, W. Carl; Moser, Kenneth Carl; Regeneration; Salvation; Sanctification, Doctrine of

BIBLIOGRAPHY Edward Scribner Ames, *The Divinity of Christ* (1911) • Alexander Campbell, *The Christian System* (1835) • Jack Cottrell, *What the Bible Says About God the Redeemer* (1987) • John Mark Hicks, "K. C. Moser and Churches of Christ: A Historical Perspective," *Restoration Quarterly* 37 (1995): 139-57 • J. W. McGarvey, "Grace, Graces, States of Grace," *Millennial Harbinger* (1864): 58-62 • J. W. McGarvey, "A New Definition of Grace," *Millennial Harbinger* (1864): 227-30 • K. C. Moser, "Christ Versus a 'Plan'" (pamphlet, 1952) • K. C. Moser, *The Way of Salvation, Being an Exposition of God's Method of Justification through Christ* (1932) • Thomas Munnell, "Grace and Infusion," *Millennial Harbinger* (1864): 263-66 • Thomas Munnell, "Review of J. W. McGarvey on Grace," *Millennial Harbinger* (1864): 158-62 • William J. Richardson, *The Role of Grace in the Thought of Alexander Campbell* (1991) • Tom Roberts, *Neo-Calvinism in the Church of Christ* (1980) •

Barton W. Stone, "A Compendious View of the Gospel," in John Rogers and Barton Stone, *The Biography of Elder Barton Warren Stone* (1847), pp. 191-221 • J. D. Thomas, *The Biblical Doctrine of Grace* (1977) • Clark Williamson, *A Guest in the House of Israel* (1993).

PAUL M. BLOWERS *and* WILLIAM J. RICHARDSON

Graham, Robert (1822-1901)

Educator of ministers in the Stone-Campbell Movement in the late nineteenth century.

Graham was born in Liverpool, England, in 1822. His mother was of a Methodist background and his father a sea captain. When a boy, he was exposed occasionally to the adventures of the high sea on his father's sailing ship. Later the family moved to America and settled in Pittsburgh, where Graham became an apprentice carpenter. While working his trade he was hired by Alexander Campbell to be carpenter of Bethany College. Campbell recognized Graham's talent for ministry and saw to his education. Graham described that occurrence as "the turning point in my life." Later Campbell described his former student as "the greatest discovery I ever made."

When Graham left Bethany he ventured into an area then considered the very border of civilization by European Americans, the wilderness village of Fayetteville, Arkansas. He represented Campbell as an agent of the *Millennial Harbinger* and Bethany College. In that wilderness, Graham preached into life a congregation. His commitment to a learned faith led him to found Arkansas College, the first institution of higher learning in the state. When the Civil War came, his Union sympathies were too out of line for him to be effective, so he left the area. When the war ended, the congregation turned its building from a war hospital to a thriving center for establishing churches. His college was resurrected and stands today as the University of Arkansas.

His teaching career in Kentucky began with a one-year term on the faculty of Kentucky University in 1859. He returned in 1866 to become presiding officer of that university's liberal arts college. In 1869 he became president of Hocker Female College (later called Hamilton). At the death of President Robert Milligan, Graham became president of the College of the Bible (now Lexington Theological Seminary) in Kentucky. He served as president from 1875 to 1895, longer than any who have held that office to date. In addition to his administrative and fund-raising duties, he taught English literature and homiletics and later added mental and moral philosophy. In the exceptional faculty of his era it is said that J. W. McGarvey was admired, Isaiah Grubbs was loved, and Graham was revered. In 1889 Kentucky University recognized his accomplishments as an educator by awarding him the L.L.D. degree.

See also Education, Philosophy of; Lexington Theological Seminary; McGarvey, John W.

BIBLIOGRAPHY Robert Graham, "Early Trials and Triumphs," *Christian Standard* 32 (March 21, 1896): 359; 32 (March 28, 1896): 391 • Frederick D. Kershner, "Comets and Constellations," *Christian Standard* 77 (March 7, 1942): 223-24, 240 • N. M. Ragland, "A History of First Christian Church, Fayetteville, Arkansas" (unpublished manuscript, Disciples of Christ Historical Society, c. 1925) • Dwight E. Stevenson, *Lexington Theological Seminary: 1865-1965* (1964).

PETER M. MORGAN

Great Awakenings

Historic periods in which American Protestants perceived intensive and diverse manifestations of the Spirit of God in revitalizing Christian faith, experience, and service.

Religious awakenings among Protestants in America have done much to define American religion over the past 250 years. They have fostered large interdenominational assemblies, increased interest in missions, heightened spiritual awareness and passion, employed direct exhortation, used modern communication technologies, engendered societies for social reform and for spiritual and moral improvement, and encouraged establishment of institutions of higher education. Awakenings have especially captivated evangelical and conservative groups. Among the more celebrated American Protestant awakenings are the (First) Great Awakening (1720-40), the Second Great Awakening (1790-1840), the Prayer Meeting Revival (1857-59), and Post–World War II Revivalism (1950-60).

The first signs of the Great Awakening resulted from the preaching of Theodorus Jacobus Frelinghuysen (1691-1747) in the Raritan Valley of New Jersey. Frelinghuysen, who immigrated from the Netherlands in 1720, was influenced by the continental Pietists. He made a considerable impression on William Tennant (1673-1746) and Gilbert Tennant (1703-1764), as well as Jonathan Edwards. William Tennant, a Presbyterian, took up the revivalist challenge and opened a school for young men, including his four sons, which later was named the Log College. His son Gilbert was one of the significant revivalists in the Great Awakening and was sought out by the British evangelist George Whitefield (1715-1770) in 1739. He emphasized extempore preaching and especially the use of personal pronouns. Jonathan Edwards (1703-1758), a Yale graduate, followed the course of the awakening, and his preaching sparked a major revival in his Northampton, Massachusetts, congregation in the years 1734-35. In 1737 Edwards published *A Faithful Narrative of the Surprising Work of God in the Conversion of Many Hundred Souls in Northampton,* which served as a handbook for the revivals that swept the colonies from North to South.

The effects of the Great Awakening still lingered as the new groups that later fed the Stone-Campbell Movement emerged, especially on two fronts: in the middle colonies (specifically Virginia and North Carolina) among the followers of James O'Kelly, who led a schism of "Republican Methodists" from the Methodist Episcopal Church; and in New England, with the "Christian Connection" begun by Abner Jones and Elias Smith. Jones and Smith followed awakening-style evangelism, eliciting experiential conversion and engaging in regional itinerancy, where an evangelist preached two or three times in a locale and then moved on, accompanied by young apprentices who served as exhorters.

The Second Great Awakening was fueled by the camp meetings, which picked up intensity in Logan County, Kentucky, in 1800. A new arrival in the state, Barton W. Stone (1772-1844) traveled westward to witness the excitement stirred up by James McGready (c. 1758-1817), whom he had heard preach in North Carolina. Stone returned to his Cane Ridge congregation in Bourbon County, Kentucky, and sent invitations to the great 1801 camp meeting that became the benchmark for all later ones. People traveled to the camp meetings from long distances, and the preachers proclaimed day and night at improvised pulpits in the woods. The invitation to enter a designated area or pen, in order to come to terms with one's salvation, developed in the camp meeting setting. The invitation was later designated an altar call to the mourner's bench when extended in church buildings.

The Second Great Awakening greatly influenced evangelization in the Stone-Campbell Movement. The Awakening's southern phase, the "Great Western Revival," of which the Cane Ridge Revival was the centerpiece, was an important matrix of Barton Stone's reform movement. Although Thomas and Alexander Campbell and their followers resisted the influence of the camp meetings because of their alleged spiritual manipulation, Walter Scott, the preeminent Disciples evangelist in the Ohio Valley, sought a method of evangelism that still had mass appeal, albeit through the preaching of the gospel in terms of a rational and coherent plan of salvation. Scott adapted the invitation by calling convicted sinners to be baptized rather than to struggle on the mourner's bench. Thomas and Alexander Campbell, though unaccustomed to eliciting conversions in this manner, soon emulated these approaches.

The Second Great Awakening has been called an "organizing process" because it not only led to mass evangelism of the trans-Appalachian frontier but also helped to spur Christians in newly founded communities to create a religious and educational infrastructure that heretofore had not existed. The Stone-Campbell Movement, like the Presbyterians, Baptists, Methodists, and other religious groups on the frontier, created social networks and helped to erect a culture significantly dependent on the mass communication provided by religious journalism and on the church-related colleges that would train not only pastors but other needed professionals.

The prayer meeting revival of 1857-59 commenced in New York City with noon prayer meetings arranged by Jeremiah Lanphier of the Dutch Reformed Church. It spread to Chicago, then many other cities, the British Isles, and around the world. It brought to prominence a number of noted evangelists such as Dwight L. Moody, William Booth, and Charles Spurgeon. Constituents of the Stone-Campbell Movement were not prominent in the cities at this time, but even they were influenced by the resulting midweek prayer services that became standard in mainstream Protestant churches.

After World War II certain young evangelists came to the forefront, especially the fundamentalist Billy Graham and the Pentecostal Oral Roberts. As the awakening accelerated, they spoke in large auditoriums and stadiums and soon developed interdenominational evangelistic organizations. They utilized national radio networks, and as television came to the forefront they launched popular programs. Evangelistically oriented persons in Churches of Christ and conservative Disciples churches were caught up in this new wave. At first the new religious excitement increased the emphasis on standardized gospel meetings. Soon, however, large auditorium and stadium gatherings became popular and network radio and television programs were launched.

See also Cane Ridge Revival; Charismatics; Evangelism, Evangelists — Nineteenth Century; New Light Presbyterians

BIBLIOGRAPHY John Boles, *The Great Revival: Beginnings of the Bible Belt* (1996) • Anthony L. Dunnavant, ed., *Cane Ridge in Context* (1992) • Nathan O. Hatch, *The Democratization of American Christianity* (1989) • Donald Mathews, "The Second Great Awakening as an Organizing Process: A Hypothesis," *American Quarterly* 20 (1969): 23-43 • William G. McLoughlin, Jr., *Modern Revivalism: Charles Grandison Finney to Billy Graham* (1959) • Thomas H. Olbricht, "The Invitation: A Historical Survey," *Restoration Quarterly* 5 (1961): 6-16 • Max Ward Randall, *The Great Awakenings and the Restoration Movement* (1983).

THOMAS H. OLBRICHT

Great Britain and Ireland, Churches of Christ in

1. Origins to 1842

Although Thomas Campbell was a Seceder Presbyterian Minister in Ireland before emigrating to the United States, that Presbyterian background probably influenced only one congregation in Britain or Ireland, that in Dungannon, County Tyrone, formed by Robert Tener in 1810. The thought of Thomas's son, Alexander Campbell (rather than Barton Stone), was most influential in shaping the British movement. Campbell first became known in England through *The Millennial Harbinger and Voluntary Church Advocate,* a monthly magazine published by the Scotch Baptist elder William Jones in 1835-36. The Scotch Baptists (like the former Church of Scotland minister John Glas, by whom they were influenced) emphasized the restoration of New Testament Christianity; Jones was particularly attracted by Campbell's *Christian Baptist.* However, Jones criticized Campbell for denying total depravity and the influence of the Holy Spirit in conversion, and for believing that baptism effected the remission of sins.

James Wallis and others withdrew from the Scotch Baptist church in Nottingham in December 1836 to form a Church of Christ. Other congregations both within and outside the Scotch Baptists were discovering Campbell at the same time. In March 1837 Wallis began a new magazine, the *British Millennial Harbinger.* In 1839 George C. Reid, pastor of an independent congregation in Dundee, was converted to believers' baptism and made two long evangelistic tours of Scotland and England. His suggestion in November 1841 of "a correct and co-operative plan" for evangelization led to the first Cooperative Meeting of Churches of Christ in Great Britain in Edinburgh in August 1842. Some fifty churches were listed, with a total membership of around 1,600. Their unanimous resolution "that this meeting deem it binding upon them, as disciples of Jesus Christ, to cooperate for the maintenance of evangelists to proclaim the gospel" became the primary purpose of the subsequent association. A committee of three members was formed to collect contributions. The name "Churches of Christ" was formally commended in a resolution of the Annual Meeting of 1870.

2. 1842-1917

The 1840s were a troubled time in Britain, economically and politically. By 1845 the system of cooperative evangelism collapsed because of lack of funds. There were signs of division in various congregations involving new Adventist ideas (associated with William Miller). In 1847 Alexander Campbell visited Britain for a four-month tour and presided at the second Cooperative Meeting of the British Churches at Chester in October. The number of churches had risen to eighty and the membership to 2,300. After 1847 meetings were held annually, except for 1940. District associations to support evangelists were formed in the north of Scotland, Fife, London, Newcastle, and Lancashire.

In 1854 the General Evangelist Committee decided to plant a church in Manchester and invited four evangelists, including J. B. Rotherham and David King, to do this in 1855. In 1858 Rotherham and King were invited to establish a church in Birmingham. King took over the *British Millennial Harbinger* in 1862 and became the leading spokesman for the Movement in Britain. Other prominent leaders were G. Y. Tickle of Liverpool, John Crook of Southport, and Timothy Coop of Wigan, who were chairman, secretary, and treasurer of the General Evangelist Committee. The number of evangelists gradually increased, and from 1866 their training was supervised by David King. The Annual Meeting appointed a Training Committee, which became permanent from 1883, and established a Publications Committee in 1885, which reprinted American publications and published tracts by British authors. Sunday School conferences began in the 1860s; in 1876 a national Sunday School Committee was appointed, which was transferred to the superintendence of the Annual Meeting in 1887. From 1880 there were annual Sisters' Meetings and Temperance Meetings, but their committees did not become part of the Annual Meeting until after the First World War. Although Sydney Black spoke positively of the role of women in the church in a Conference paper of 1889, the discussion showed that many still took a conservative position. Temperance work was controversial, not because of any doubt about total abstinence but because it might involve a nonbiblical test of fellowship and cooperation with non-church members. By 1892 the number of churches had nearly doubled and the membership increased more than threefold. Its distribution also changed: growth was more rapid in England than in Scotland or Wales; and half the members lived in the midlands and north of England. Growth took place in mining areas and in textile towns, with shoemaking also important in the midlands.

From 1890 younger men were pressing for a Forward Movement, reflected in the aggressive evangelism of Sydney Black, who had founded churches in Leominster, Ross on Wye, and York in the 1880s. He visited Australia, New Zealand, and the United States in 1891 to raise money for his London mission, Twynholm Hall, established at Fulham Cross in 1894 with a range of weeknight social activities comparable to other metropolitan churches and quite unlike other British Churches of Christ. By 1900 it was the largest church in the Association, with a membership of over 400. Black died in 1903 at age 43. Nevertheless the rate of growth of the churches was slowing: in the twenty-five years after 1892 membership increased by 50 percent compared with 150 percent in the same period before 1892. However, unlike the major British Free Churches, whose membership peaked around 1906, Churches of Christ membership continued to grow until 1930. New churches were opened in the Potteries and South Wales. Financial support from the churches did not match the enthusiasm of the leaders; a Finance Committee was appointed in 1904 to stimulate systematic giving. The appointment of a paid secretary to the General Evangelist Committee, James Flisher of Manchester, indicated willingness to develop national organization. In 1912 the first Home Missions Sister, Mrs. Ethel B. Cranfield, a trained nurse, was appointed to work with the churches in Glasgow, and two more were appointed in the following year. A central book depot was opened in Birmingham in 1903, combining the work of the Publishing, Magazine, and Sunday School Committees. The first official hymnbook, *Hymns for Churches of Christ,* was published in 1908 with 1,036 hymns; this replaced the hymnbooks published by Wallis in 1841 and twice enlarged, and that edited by King and Tickle in 1888.

The South African War of 1899-1902 exposed differences of view in the churches about imperial policy in general and the war in particular. Hitherto Churches of Christ, like the other Free Churches, would have been assumed to be generally anti-imperialist and anti-militarist. This may always have been too simple, but greater size, broadening social composition, and wider changes in British public opinion made the position more complex by 1900. The First World War stretched the tension between these differences of view to breaking point. Many young men volunteered to fight and were killed on the Western Front. Lloyd George, the prime minister who introduced conscription in 1916, came from a Churches of Christ family. After conscription some local church leaders sat on the tribunals that heard the cases of pacifist church members with conscientious objections to military service. This was particularly divisive in a small community, and it had a polarizing effect similar to that of the Civil War in the American Churches.

2.1. The Christian Association

Differences between the Churches on each side of the Atlantic resulted in the establishment of a separate group of Churches of Christ, known as the Christian Association, in 1881. This began with a difference over whether unbaptized believers might be admitted to communion, but other issues were also involved. The British Churches generally limited communion to those baptized as believers, and they regularly criticized Baptist churches in England and Wales, which moved toward "open communion" in the nineteenth century. Campbell's remarks on this in the Campbell-Rice debate of 1844 aroused some unfavorable comment in Britain, and he was questioned about his views during his visit to Britain in 1847. In 1859 the Annual Meeting asked its chairman, G. Y. Tickle, to write to Campbell to ascertain whether the American churches admitted the unbaptized to communion; Campbell replied that they neither invited nor debarred them. Henry Earl, an English graduate of Bethany College, returned to England in 1861 and offered his services as an evangelist. After some questioning about communion, Earl's offer was accepted, and he worked effectively for three years before leaving for Australia in 1864. In 1866 the Annual Meeting resolved (by a majority) not to cooperate with anyone, from America or elsewhere, "who knowingly communes with unbaptized persons, or who, in any way, advocates such communion." After Alexander Campbell's death in the same year, the differences within the Movement in America that had already been exposed by the Civil War became more apparent. The sympathies of the British Churches generally lay with the more conservative Americans; and the increase of college-trained preachers in America in contrast to the British practice of mutual edification by several elders at the Lord's Supper was as significant in the developing suspicion of American practice as open communion. G. Y. Tickle made this point in a Conference paper at the 1872 Annual Meeting, which also declined to accept an offer of evangelistic help from the United States.

In 1875 the newly formed Foreign Christian Missionary Society appointed Henry Earl (with some hesitation) as a missionary to England, and after a series of mass meetings involving a large choir he formed a church in Southampton and baptized thirty members. Some of the British church leaders, especially Timothy Coop of Wigan, were impressed by Earl's success; but others, led by King and Tickle, were more critical. In January 1878 the second Foreign Christian Missionary Society (FCMS) missionary, Marion D. Todd, came to work in Chester along similar lines; the church there, which had dwindled in size, identified itself with the new work and left the Association in 1883. Coop visited the United States and offered £1,000 for every £2,000 the FCMS put up for missionary work in Britain. W. T. Moore, minister of the large Central Christian Church in Cincinnati, offered to return with Coop and became minister of the church at Mornington Road, Southport; the members returned to their former chapel in Sussex Road, which was given to them by

Coop, who resigned from the General Evangelist Committee. The churches in Chester and Southport were in direct competition with existing Churches of Christ, unlike that in Southampton, which was not near any existing congregation. The formation of the Christian Association in 1881 institutionalized the separation. Moore, who was on the liberal side of the American churches, moved to London in 1881 and became minister of the West London Tabernacle, previously an independent congregation, where he founded a weekly magazine, the *Christian Commonwealth*, with Coop's financial support.

In 1901 the Christian Association passed a resolution in favor of closer cooperation with the older body of churches, and a series of meetings was held between 1902 and 1905. The differences that were identified were the admission of the unbaptized to communion, pastors assigned to single congregations, readiness to accept offerings from nonchurch members, and the use of instrumental music. Another committee was set up in 1910, but it was discharged without achieving anything in 1913. In 1916 George W. Buckner, president of the Christian Association Conference, proposed a new initiative for union with the older Association; and in 1917 both Conferences accepted proposals that provided a basis for the Christian Association churches to join the old Association. Fifteen churches did so, with a total membership of around 1,300; two did not, including the original church at Southampton, which has remained an independent evangelical congregation ever since. However, further discussion over baptism, communion, and Christian unity led to the withdrawal of four other churches in the 1920s.

2.2. Non-Instrumental Churches

In 1906 the American Religious Census distinguished between non-instrumental churches and others in the Stone-Campbell Movement for the first time, describing the former as "Churches of Christ" and the latter as "Disciples of Christ" or "Christian Churches." This distinction of name has never been used in the British Isles, or the British Commonwealth generally, where "Church of Christ" was the generic name. Instrumental music as such did not cause division in Britain before the First World War; and, as in other churches where the issue arose, the use of an organ was initially a sign of increasing affluence and social aspiration rather than a matter of theological principle.

Pacifism and conscientious objection to military service were more divisive because they led to the organization of a national conference of those opposed to the war in June 1916. Subsequent conferences were held in Leicester in 1917, and in Leicester and Birmingham during 1918. The leaders of this pacifist movement were often also active Trade Unionists and supporters of the infant Labour Party. Although some were later leaders in "Old Paths" churches, there is no simple correlation between the various issues. For example, Walter Crosthwaite and T. S. Entwistle were the only evangelists to join the non-instrumental churches when they withdrew from the Association; but R. K. Francis, who was also a pacifist, remained with the Association, and one of the most influential spokesmen for pacifism in the British Churches after 1918 was William Robinson, principal of Overdale College, who had been awarded a Military Cross for bravery in the First World War and changed his views on war because of his wartime experiences.

In 1908 Ivie Campbell of Glasgow founded a monthly magazine, *The Interpreter*, which opposed instrumental music and Conference committees, and later supported the opponents of the war and closer relations with the Christian Association. In 1916 the title changed to *The Apostolic Messenger*, and W. M. Kempster became editor; it became the *Bible Advocate* after the official magazine changed its name to *Christian Advocate* in 1921; and in 1934 it became the *Scripture Standard*, with Walter Crosthwaite as editor. This magazine was the focus of all criticism of the leadership of the Annual Conference. In the early 1920s it criticized the theological college at Overdale and its affiliation with the Student Christian Movement, and later the policy of British missionaries in Nyasaland on communion.

The first conference of "Old Paths" churches — so called because of Jeremiah 6:16, a favorite text of David King, which Crosthwaite used regularly — was held in 1924, and these were later held twice a year. Formal separation took a little longer. The communion question was discussed again in the late 1920s because some felt that the agreement reached with the Christian Association in 1917 was too liberal. In 1930 nine conservative churches gave notice of withdrawal, although only two did withdraw in 1931, followed by two more in 1934: these were in the mining area around Slamannan between Edinburgh and Glasgow, where Crosthwaite was the local evangelist. Ecumenical developments were opposed: affiliation to the World Council of Churches (1938), the Free Church Federal Council (1940), and the British Council of Churches (1942) was regarded as compromising traditional principles. At root there was a difference in attitude to Scripture: the critical approach taught at Overdale College was rejected, and several churches claimed that the Association no longer regarded the Bible as "an all-sufficient rule of faith and practice." A discussion between representatives appointed by each side in 1943 achieved nothing; between 1943 and 1947 nineteen more churches withdrew from the Association, and further withdrawals took place subsequently.

At first the seceding churches maintained a similar framework for corporate activity to that of the Association. They supported the churches in Nyasaland, led by Frederick Nkhonde, head teacher at Mlanje, which separated from those led by the British missionaries. However, under the influence of American Churches of Christ ministers, often present in the United Kingdom as chaplains to the American Army and Air Force, the "Conference" structures were abandoned. Despite initial British hostility, the American practice of placing ministers with particular congregations was introduced, and even individual cups at communion. These innovations were accepted by some but resisted by others, particularly in Scotland and Lancashire. The *Scripture Standard* continues as the magazine of the more conservative congregations in Scotland and the north of England; from the 1960s a new magazine, *The Christian Worker,* was established, which circulates among congregations in England. With increasing help from the United States, the number of congregations by the end of the century was around sixty, with about 2,000 members.

3. 1917-1981

The accession of the Christian Association churches stimulated ecumenical activity among the older churches. The Christian Association leaders had been active ecumenically since 1910; although the Conference declined to join the new Federal Council of Free Churches in 1919, it did take part in the Preparatory Conference on Faith and Order at Geneva in 1920. In 1917 the Conference approved a scheme to establish a theological college with a minimum course of three years, which had been under discussion since 1912; a house named Overdale in Birmingham was purchased in 1919, and William Robinson was appointed as principal. John M'Cartney, who had been responsible for correspondence classes since 1896, became a lecturer at the college. In 1923 Joseph Smith was appointed as lecturer in Old and New Testament. As a young man Smith was one of the first public exponents of a critical approach to Scripture in 1892. Criticism of Smith led to a demand for his resignation in 1926, but his scholarly integrity was vindicated. In 1931 he died suddenly, to be replaced by James Gray. Overdale moved to Selly Oak, Birmingham, to become one of the Selly Oak Colleges, where it remained until its closure in 1977.

The previously unofficial Temperance Committee reported directly to the Conference from 1920, and an organizing secretary (R. H. Parker) was appointed. The Young Men's Convention was first held in 1924, and a similar event for young women from 1927; this led to the formation of the Fellowship of Youth in 1929, with local youth groups in districts and churches. The Conference set up a Central Council (of the Chairmen of all Standing Committees) in 1930 to coordinate committee proposals requiring significant expenditure. The appointment of a financial and organizing secretary was recommended, and the first full-time salaried general secretary (Leslie Colver) was appointed in 1948.

In the twenty-five years after 1930 the membership declined by 50 percent, and by a similar proportion in the next twenty years. The withdrawal of some congregations was one reason but not the decisive one. Nor was the Second World War, though bombing and the need to relocate in new housing areas, which was increasingly difficult with declining financial resources, affected some churches. In the 1950s and 1960s, Disciples of Christ in the United States gave some ministerial assistance. Ministers spent longer periods with local churches, as the old system of itinerant evangelists was abandoned.

Christian unity issues became more important. Discussions with the Baptist Union about closer cooperation (1942-51) foundered because of open communion. In 1956 the Conference recommended that local churches offer communion to occasional visitors from other churches who were not baptized as believers, and this was gradually adopted. In 1964 a Faith and Order Conference organized by the British Council of Churches gave a fresh impulse to the search for church union. After discussions with both the Baptists and the Congregational-Presbyterian Joint Committee, a majority of the churches supported conversations for union with the United Reformed Church (the Congregational-Presbyterian union of 1972). Proposals for union were published in 1976, but although a majority of Churches of Christ voted in favor, the legally required majorities of two-thirds of the congregations representing three-quarters of the membership were not obtained. In 1979 the churches voted to dissolve the Association on March 31, 1980, to allow each congregation to act as it wished. A new association of forty churches that wished to unite with the United Reformed Church was set up, and this union took place in 1981. Twenty-four churches (with one new church) formed the Fellowship of Churches of Christ, which admitted four new churches in 1980-81; nine churches initially joined neither association, although two later joined the Fellowship. In the early 1980s the Fellowship began developing relations with Christian Churches/Churches of Christ in the United States in hopes of seeking a common vision of the Stone-Campbell Movement's mission. A British-American Fellowship Committee of interested individuals and churches was formed in the late 1970s, leading to the reorganization of Overdale College under the new name of Springdale College. The Christian Missionary Fellowship, a missionary agency of the Christian Churches/Churches of

Christ, has also continued a work of church renewal and church-planting in Great Britain.

Work in the UK by North American Churches of Christ began in the 1940s. It consisted of both assisting national evangelists in the post–World War II period and sending workers to start new churches. In the 1940s American churches furnished assistance to Albert Winstanley and Frank Worgan after they refused support by the "Evangelistic Committee." Not until the late 1950s did the first American workers take up residence in the UK. Clyde Findley moved to Edinburgh, and soon afterward Dale Buckley and Jerry Porter moved to Glasgow. In 1961, at the request of Leonard Channing, the Hillsboro Church of Christ of Nashville, Tennessee, sent the E. P. Lake family (from Canada) and the Philip Slates (USA) to Wembley in suburban London to plant a new church. That work began with a campaign, the first of several in that decade. New churches were started in both older cities and the New Towns through the work of both national evangelists and North American workers. Because of past experiences with workers from the American Disciples of Christ and differing views of Christians participating in carnal warfare, the conservative British Christians were suspicious of the new evangelists. But over time, through joint work and favorable associations, fellowship was realized. Schools begun by Americans were eventually operated exclusively by British workers. British Christians edited the papers and operated correspondence courses. Currently as many as forty evangelists, only a few from the United States, work among no fewer than eighty congregations in England, Northern Ireland, Scotland and Wales. A few Americans have been sent to Southern Ireland to plant new churches.

4. Overseas Missions

The British Churches were slow to engage in overseas missions, although emigrants helped to establish Churches of Christ in Australia and New Zealand in the 1840s. John Crook urged that the churches should begin overseas mission work in a series of articles in the *Christian Advocate* for 1886 and read a Conference paper on the subject in 1891. The Annual Meeting appointed a Foreign Missionary Committee in 1892; three missionaries sailed for Burma in October, and work was begun among the Talaing people. It expanded across the border into Siam (now Thailand) in 1903, and in 1912 efforts were concentrated at Nakom Pathom when the Burma mission was transferred to the American Baptists. In 1903 work was begun with Australian Churches of Christ to assist the churches in South Africa; this extended as far north as Bulawayo (in modern Zimbabwe), where responsibility was handed over to the New Zealand Churches in 1906. In 1908 a mission was established at Namiwawa in Nyasaland (now Malawi). Finally in 1909 a mission was taken over in Daltonganj in Palamau, India, and another at Dudhi in 1914, taken over from the London Missionary Society.

In 1915 the Chilembwe Rising in Nyasaland led to a government ban on missionary work by Churches of Christ, because of their alleged links with Chilembwe, which was not lifted until 1927. In 1928 the Baptist Industrial Mission at Gowa was taken over. The requirement (later dropped) that the mission should join the Federated Missions, which would have involved willingness to receive one another's members, was used by some conservatives to criticize the Foreign Missionary Committee. Work continued in Siam, but India was the main area of expansion, with new work begun at Latehar in 1917 and Bhandaria in the 1930s.

By 1940 the Missionary Committee was running short of money and missionaries. The missionaries in Siam were interned after the Japanese invasion, and after 1945 the work was transferred to the United Christian Missionary Society (UCMS) in the United States. It became part of the united Church of Christ in Thailand in 1962. The expansion of work in India to Surguja in Madhya Pradesh led to legal harassment by local Hindus, which caused much anxiety in the early 1950s. In 1969 the Indian churches voted to become part of the new Church of North India, formed in 1971. When Malawi achieved independence in 1964, the mission became officially the Churches of Christ in Malawi. In 1978 they became members of the Council for World Mission, the successor to the London Missionary Society.

5. Theological Emphases

Their Scotch Baptist roots led the British Churches of Christ to emphasize the restoration of New Testament Christianity rather than the pursuit of Christian unity, in the belief that the former was the only way to the latter. Alexander Campbell's writings were admired and reprinted in Britain, but they were never regarded as beyond challenge, as the discussion over admission to communion in the 1860s demonstrated. After Campbell's death no subsequent American leader's works were so widely reprinted. David King, like Campbell, debated with secularist speakers and with ministers of other churches. The style of discussion was more like eighteenth-century rationalism than evangelicalism; and there was a tendency to concentrate on persuading members of other churches that their view of the church, baptism, or the Lord's Supper was wrong rather than preaching the gospel to the unchurched. The leaders of the Forward Movement of the 1890s lamented King's failure to engage with developments in New Testament scholarship that were vital for a plausible contemporary presentation of New

Testament Christianity. Sydney Black, and later William Robinson, spent time at Mansfield College, Oxford; and Joseph Smith attended W. H. Moulton's lectures on the New Testament while working as a marine engineer in Newcastle.

Awareness of wider theological developments brought a more open attitude to other church communions. Thus the staff of Overdale College was intimately involved in ecumenical work, and the Conference's Union Committee, which became a standing committee in 1926, acted as a theological advisory group for the churches. William Robinson's theological work was focused on topics that had direct ecumenical implications, especially the nature of the church and the sacraments. There were special Commissions on Ordination (1936-41), the main recommendations of which were adopted in 1942, and on the Ministry (1947-53). Much of the Union Committee's work in the 1960s was concerned with Faith and Order matters and church union schemes abroad. The fact that Overdale College was their only college meant that British Churches of Christ ministers tended to be ecumenical in their theological approach; conservative evangelicals were unusual. By 1980 strict restorationism was confined to the a cappella churches.

See also *British Millennial Harbinger;* Coop, Timothy; Europe, Missions in; King, David; "Old Path, The"; Robinson, William; Rotherham, Joseph Bryant; Springdale College; Tickle, Gilbert Young; Wallis, James

BIBLIOGRAPHY T. J. Ainsworth, *Sydney Black* (1911) • Louis Billington, "The Churches of Christ in Britain: A Study in Nineteenth-Century Sectarianism," in *The Stone-Campbell Movement: An International Religious Tradition,* ed. Michael W. Casey and Douglas A. Foster (2002), pp. 367-97 • William Robinson, *What Churches of Christ Stand For* (1926) • David M. Thompson, *Let Sects and Parties Fall* (1980) • A. C. Watters, *History of the British Churches of Christ* (1948). DAVID M. THOMPSON

Great Lakes Christian College

Bible college affiliated with the Christian Churches/Churches of Christ.

Great Lakes Christian College was founded as Great Lakes Bible College in 1949 at Rock Lake Christian Assembly in Vestaburg, Michigan. It was established out of concern for the feeble condition of the thirty-five to forty Christian Churches/Churches of Christ in Michigan, many without preachers. Ministerial students who left the state to attend Bible college were not returning.

Eight students began classes under some area ministers in the log cabin of Ralph Woodard, the school's first president (1949-57). Enrollment increased to thirty-one in 1950, so the college purchased the nearby eighty-acre Rosema family farm. The farmhouse was converted into a chapel, classrooms, offices, cafeteria, and dormitory, while the old chicken coop was remodeled to house twenty-four men.

Woodard resigned in 1957, believing his own academic limitations would hamper the college's future development. Desiring better student employment opportunities and a more centrally located campus, the college purchased the seven-acre Dodge Estate in Lansing, the state capital. Sixty-one students enrolled in 1958. The Dodge Mansion was refurbished as a multipurpose building, library and chapel buildings were constructed, and houses were purchased for dormitories.

In the 1960s the college recommitted itself to the training of ministers for Great Lakes congregations. A close relationship was developed with Virgil Felton, head of New Churches of Christ Evangelism, a church-planting organization for the broader Great Lakes region. Expanded enrollments induced the college to relocate again in 1972, to the forty-acre Huxtable farm west of Lansing in Delta Township. A large administration building and dormitory were completed, and the Michigan State Board of Education granted the college official recognition. In 1977 the college received accreditation from the American Association of Bible Colleges. Enrollment grew in the 1970s but declined in the 1980s; yet the college was able to establish cooperative academic relationships with Michigan State University and other colleges for Christian students desiring non-ministry vocations. In the 1990s the school secured financial stability and changed its name from Great Lakes Bible College to Great Lakes Christian College in 1992. Its principal purpose remains the education of men and women for church ministries and international mission work, with special focus on service to approximately 125 affiliated Christian Churches/Churches of Christ in the Great Lakes area.

See also Bible College Movement; Higher Education, Views of in the Movement LLOYD KNOWLES

Great Western Revival

See Cane Ridge Revival; Great Awakenings

Gresham, Perry Epler (1907-1994)

Disciples pastor, educator, author, and poet.

Perry Gresham, youngest of four children, was born in Covina, California, December 19, 1907, the son of George E. and Mary Epler Gresham. Perry's grandfather, Daniel Epler, migrated to Elbert, Colorado, from the Midwest by wagon train at the end of

Pastor and author Perry E. Gresham (1907-1994), president of Bethany College from 1952 to 1971, walks beside Bethany's historic Old Main. Courtesy of the Disciples of Christ Historical Society

the Civil War. The Gresham family arrived during the 1890s. George and Mary were wed in Elbert (1898), and after an eight-year stay in California, where Perry was born, they returned to the Colorado ranchland (1912).

Young Perry grew up on the family ranch in the days before school buses. He rode his saddle horse four miles to Elbert High School but soon dropped out, opting to work on highway construction, hauling sand with a team and wagon. By age 19, he owned a small herd of cattle and a Buick convertible.

Persistently recruited by the president of Colorado Bible College, Perry left the ranch and highway construction to attend that Denver institution. Simultaneously, he attended Denver Junior College and within one year received his high school diploma. On December 6, 1926, he was married to Elsie Enez Stambrough, soprano in the choir at Central Christian Church, which housed the Bible College Perry was attending. For the next three years the newlyweds shared in building and pastoring the new University Place Christian Church in Denver.

In September 1929, the Greshams moved to Fort Worth, Texas, where Perry entered Texas Christian University (TCU) to study for the ministry. He graduated in two years (1931) with a B.A. degree, Summa Cum Laude, while at the same time teaching as a graduate instructor in Greek and philosophy. On December 1, 1931, a son, Glen Edward, was born to them. By 1933 Perry had completed the B.D. degree at Brite College of the Bible. During the following decade (1932-43), he was minister of University Christian Church in Fort Worth and a professor of philosophy at TCU. Granted a leave of absence in 1939-40, Perry pursued postgraduate work as a Margaret Hoe Scholar at Columbia University. He had earlier taken postgraduate work at the University of Chicago and later added postdoctoral work at Union Theological Seminary and the University of Edinburgh.

Beginning in 1943, he was senior minister for four years at University Christian Church in Seattle, Washington, and taught at the University of Washington. He then served a six-year pastorate with Central Woodward Christian Church in Detroit, Michigan, and also taught at the Detroit branch of the University of Michigan. While there, his wife Elsie died suddenly in March 1948 of a heart attack.

In December 1952, Perry Gresham was elected president of Bethany College, where he would serve with distinction for nineteen years. He was married to accomplished musician Aleece Fickling Cowan, May 6, 1953. Perry, Aleece, and her teenage daughter, Nancy, moved to Bethany College, and Perry officially assumed the duties of the presidency in September.

Perry Gresham was president of the International Convention of Christian Churches (1960-61), a member of the twenty-five-person Commission on Faith and Order of the World Council of Churches, and a member of numerous boards of the Christian Church (Disciples of Christ), including the Board of Higher Education. He was a renowned speaker for church gatherings in the United States and around the world, having addressed the International Convention nineteen times, being regularly featured on CBS Church of the Air, and for several years serving as summer minister at Old Renfield Church in Glasgow, Scotland. In a 1952 poll of Disciples ministers, he was named the outstanding preacher among Disciples by *The Christian Century Pulpit* magazine.

He was the author of numerous books, including *Incipient Gnosticism in the New Testament* (1933), *Disciples of the High Calling* (1953), *Sage of Bethany* (1959), *Campbell and the Colleges* (1972), *With Wings of Eagles* (1980), *Toasts — Plain, Spicy and Wry* (1985), *Growing Up in the Ranchland* (1993), and *The Sign of the Golden Grasshopper: A Biography of Sir Thomas Gresham* (1994). Among his many honors were four Freedom Foundation Awards, sixteen honorary degrees, honorary citizenship in six states, and numerous citations in a wide range of Who's Who publications. He was a Life Fellow of the International Institute of Arts and Fellows, chairman of the North Central Association of Colleges and Universities, chairman of the Foundation for Economic Education, and a member of the Author's Club of London, in addition to numerous local and regional leadership positions in educational agencies. In addition, he was a director of several corporations, including Cooper Tire and Rubber Company and the John A. Hartford Foundation.

During the last decade of his life, Gresham was involved with senior citizens' issues and continued his work as an author, poet, and lecturer. He died September 10, 1994, at his home in North Carolina and was buried in the Campbell Cemetery in Bethany, West Virginia.

BIBLIOGRAPHY *The Blue Book* • James W. Carty, Jr., *The Gresham Years* (1970) • "Educator Elected Convention President," *The Christian* 32:5 (October 26, 1960): 1 • "Perry E. Gresham, Educator and Churchman, Chosen Bethany Head," *Bethany College Bulletin* 46:3 (April 1953): 3 • *Sunday News Register* (Wheeling, West Virginia) (September 11, 1994): 1 • *Who's Who in America* • *Who's Who in the World* • *Who's Who in American Education.*

D. DUANE CUMMINS

H

Haggard, Rice (1769-1819)

Reformer and pamphleteer associated with the Republican Methodists of Virginia.

Rice Haggard is credited with influencing two frontier reform movements to adopt the name "Christian": James O'Kelly's Republican Methodists (in Haggard's native Virginia) and Barton W. Stone and his associates (in Kentucky). Ordained by Methodists in 1791, Haggard joined the "O'Kelly Secession" and suggested the "Christian" nomenclature in 1794. These Christian churches joined the New England movement of Elias Smith and Abner Jones in the Christian Connection, ultimately destined to be a part of the United Church of Christ.

In June of 1804, now ministering in Kentucky and undoubtedly familiar with Stone's activities, Haggard was present — "having lately united with us," in Stone's words — for the disbanding of the Springfield Presbytery. His treatise of that year, *On the Sacred Import of the Christian Name,* later lost but ρεφοςερεδ by John Neth of Milligan College in 1953, accompanied Haggard's call for the exclusive use of the name "Christian" for all followers of Christ. Barton Stone appreciatively cited the contribution of "Elder Rice Haggard" in his autobiography. It was these events in 1804, Stone said, that signaled "the commencement of that reformation."

The themes of Haggard's pamphlet contain remarkable affinities with, if not a direct influence on, the emphases of Stone's "Christian churches" in Kentucky. Citing the scriptural precedent for the use of the name "Christian," Haggard gives a rehearsal of church history, the evolution of other names, and the "partyism" that accompanies such a variety of denominations (names). He then proposes a plan for healing and restoring such a divided church: the recognition of one God, one Savior, one source of confession (the Bible), one form of discipline (the New Testament), in essence one church under one name.

Colby Hall and John Neth, while strongly suggesting that Haggard's contribution to the Move-

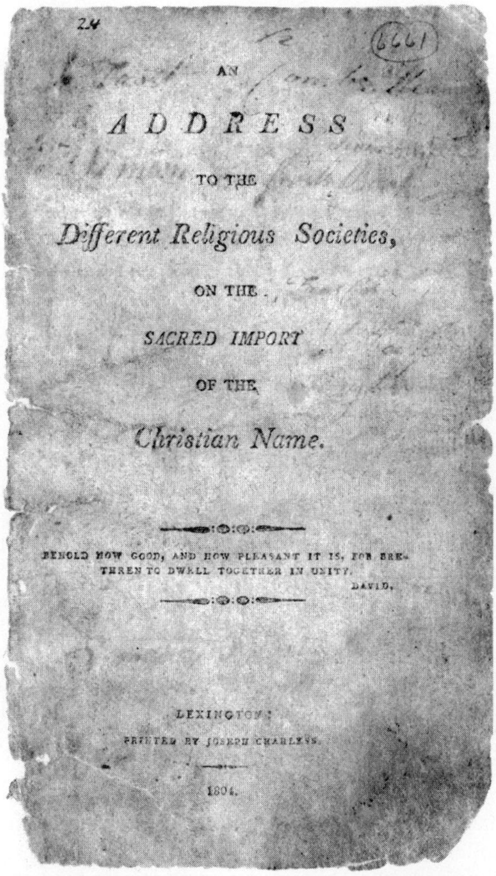
AN
ADDRESS
TO THE
Different Religious Societies,
ON THE
SACRED IMPORT
OF THE
Christian Name.

BEHOLD HOW GOOD, AND HOW PLEASANT IT IS, FOR BRETHREN TO DWELL TOGETHER IN UNITY.
DAVID.

LEXINGTON:
PRINTED BY JOSEPH CHARLESS.
1804.

Haggard published his treatise on "the Christian Name" anonymously, referring to himself as one who "feels himself united to that *one body* of which *Christ is the head,* and all his people fellow members." Though it was lost, John W. Neth, Jr., discovered a copy of the material in Elias Smith's *Herald of Gospel Liberty* in 1953. Later that year the Disciples of Christ Historical Society obtained the copy pictured here from the Cincinnati public library. The Historical Society published a facsimile edition the following year.

Courtesy of the Disciples of Christ Historical Society

ment warrants significantly greater attention than it receives, note that his early demise in 1819 ultimately served to deprive Rice Haggard of his standing alongside the Campbells, Stone, and Scott in the Movement's early leadership.

See also Christian Connection; Jones, Abner; Names of the Movement; O'Kelly, James; Smith, Elias

BIBLIOGRAPHY Rice Haggard, *An Address to the Different Religious Societies on the Sacred Import of the Christian Name* (1804; reissued with a preface by John Neth, Jr., 1954) • Colby D. Hall, *Rice Haggard: The American Frontier Evangelist Who Revived the Name Christian* (1957).

W. DENNIS HELSABECK, JR.

Hailey, Homer (1903-2000)

Evangelist, educator, and author in twentieth-century Churches of Christ, and a central participant in the division over "institutionalism" in that body.

Born on a ranch northeast of Marshall, Texas, Hailey migrated westward with his family through several locations in Texas and ultimately settled in Arizona, in the Sulphur Springs Valley near Willcox, about 1910. Family members read and were influenced by the *Firm Foundation,* but worshiped with instrumental Christian Churches when no non-instrumental congregation existed where they lived. An evangelist from the Arizona Christian Missionary Society had established a Christian Church at Willcox, and Hailey was baptized there in 1922, abandoning a typical frontier lifestyle that included drinking and occasional fisticuffs. Studying the Bible ever more seriously over the next several years, Hailey determined to attend college, and in 1926 he visited Texas Christian University (TCU) at the suggestion of one of the members of the Willcox Christian Church. Feeling socially out of place at TCU, Hailey was encouraged by his grandmother Collins, an avid *Firm Foundation* reader, to attend Abilene Christian College (ACC), and Hailey enrolled there in the fall of 1926 at age 23.

After studying the instrumental music question, Hailey began worshiping with the non-instrumental College Church of Christ. He had visited the Christian Church in Abilene, but again felt he did not fit in well with the more socially prominent congregation. Returning to Willcox to preach during the summer of 1928, he requested that the singing be a capella. The church agreed, asking Haley to lead the singing. He later commented that his song leading was probably "the best argument for the use of instrumental music."

Graduating from Abilene Christian College in 1930, Hailey married Lois Manly, the adopted daughter of a prominent Abilene-area ranching family. After serving one year as principal at the ACC Academy, he returned to Arizona to work with a congregation in Tempe. In 1932 the Haileys returned to Abilene, beginning a productive eleven-year ministry with the Fifth & Highland Church of Christ. In 1934 he began teaching Bible at ACC, where his straightforward, Bible-centered teaching made him popular with students. Hailey, a boxer, avid weight lifter, and bodybuilder, also formed a strong relationship with many of the student-athletes at ACC with whom he worked out.

By the mid-1940s, as Abilene Christian College aspired to higher academic standards, Hailey joined other faculty who sought graduate degrees in their disciplines. Enrolling at Southern Methodist University in Dallas, he completed an M.A. in church history in 1944. His thesis, a history of controversial issues in the history of Churches of Christ and Christian Churches, was published in 1945 by the Old Paths Book Club as *Attitudes and Consequences in the Restoration Movement.* However, Hailey's plans to return to ACC were vetoed by the head of the Bible department, Charles H. Roberson (1879-1953), whom Hailey had offended by his support of Foy E. Wallace, Jr.'s campaign against premillennialism. Furthermore, Hailey was diagnosed with cancer in 1944 and began a treatment regimen at a Houston clinic. While there in early 1945, Hailey was able to hear Wallace's sermons in the Houston Music Hall on premillennialism (later published as *God's Prophetic Word*).

Unable to return to ACC, Hailey accepted an invitation to preach for the Central Church of Christ in Los Angeles. After a year, Central supported Hailey as he moved to Honolulu, where he started the Honolulu Bible School and helped the multiracial Waipahu congregation grow in the post–World War II environment. Hailey's success in local congregational evangelism and preaching in gospel meetings resulted in the book *Let's Go Fishing for Men,* published in 1951 by the *Christian Chronicle.*

Because the GI bill had created an explosion in college enrollments, ACC had created a new Christian Education department. Hailey's growing evangelistic success and his graduate degree made him an attractive candidate, and so the Hailey family returned to Abilene in 1948. However, as other faculty returned to Abilene after World War II with even more advanced degrees, Hailey sensed a change in the climate of his alma mater. When James R. Cope, president of Florida Christian College (a new school located in the Tampa suburb of Temple Terrace), asked Hailey to head the Bible department there, Hailey found the prospect attractive. A protégé of N. B. Hardeman, Cope had accepted the challenge of building a new school, assembling a talented faculty that included Bill J. Humble (b. 1926), Pat

Hardeman (b. 1925), G. K. Wallace (1903-1988), Aaron W. Dicus (1888-1978), Clinton Hamilton (1924-1999), and others. Wooing Hailey away from ACC was a coup for the new school and its young president, and Hailey helped attract other faculty as well as students.

Hailey spent the next twenty-two years as vice president and chair of the Bible Department at Florida College (as the school became known), continuing a heavy schedule of preaching in gospel meetings during the summer months. During that period, the controversy over whether congregations should support colleges, orphanages, homes for the elderly, and other parachurch institutions, including radio and television ministries "sponsored" by large congregations, boiled over in a full-fledged division. Though he was not prominently involved in the argumentation and discussion, Hailey's very association with the "antis" at FCC was enough to make him persona non grata in many places that welcomed him in prior years. Hailey also exerted a profound influence, particularly in the study of the Old Testament, on many noninstitutional preachers, many of whom, including most of the current Florida College Bible faculty, were his students.

In 1954 Lois Hailey, who had experienced bouts of unexplained poor health for years, died. An autopsy revealed that she had suffered from a type of brain tumor that had likely gotten progressively worse since childhood. The following year Homer wed Widna Kirby, a widow whom he had met during one of his meetings in Abilene.

During his years at Florida, Hailey continued to write and began publishing Bible commentaries on the Minor Prophets (1972), the Gospel of John (1973), Revelation (1979), and Isaiah (1985). Unlike his earlier works, Hailey's commentaries were published by the evangelical publisher Baker Book House of Grand Rapids, Michigan, giving Hailey's work a wider market outside Churches of Christ.

Hailey retired from teaching in 1973, at age 70, and left Florida to return to Arizona. Continuing to write and hold gospel meetings well into the 1990s, Hailey became involved in a controversy over his teaching on divorce and remarriage, leading him to publish his views in a booklet, "Divorced and Remarried Who Would Come to Christ." Friends convinced him to produce a two-volume set of *Hailey's Comments.* He also published a commentary on Job, and a work on eternal punishment was published after his death at age 97 in November 2000.

See also Abilene Christian University; *Firm Foundation;* Florida College; Noninstitutional Movement

BIBLIOGRAPHY David Edwin Harrell, Jr., *Churches of Christ in the Twentieth Century: Homer Haley's Personal Journey of Faith* (2000). JAMES STEPHEN WOLFGANG

Haldane, Robert (1764-1842), and James Alexander Haldane (1768-1851)

Leaders of a Scottish evangelical reform movement that influenced Thomas and Alexander Campbell.

Robert Haldane (1764-1842) and James Alexander Haldane (1768-1851), formerly of the Church of Scotland, led a congregationalist movement "from which," in Robert Richardson's words, "[Alexander] Campbell received his first impulse as a religious reformer, and which may be justly regarded, indeed, as the *first phase* of that religious reformation which he subsequently carried out so successfully to its legitimate issues." The Haldanes' primary concern was evangelism, bolstered by an efficient system of lay preaching and itinerancy. James Haldane had founded the Society for Propagating the Gospel at Home in 1798; shortly thereafter, the Haldane brothers, William Innes, and Greville Ewing formed the Tabernacle church in Edinburgh, committed to an apostolic model of congregational government and worship; such "tabernacles" were formed in other cities as well. In 1799 Robert began a seminary and appointed Greville Ewing as head. The seminary also trained Glasite ministers and required students to read the works of John Glas and Robert Sandeman. Alexander Campbell visited the tabernacle in Edinburgh when he traveled in Britain in 1847.

The Haldanes fervently believed in the authority of the New Testament to provide a pattern of faith and practice for the church. They remained committed to congregational autonomy and the twofold office of elders and deacons. The Lord's Supper was to be celebrated weekly, but as a memorial rather than a sacrament. The Haldanes were paedobaptists until 1808, when they embraced believers' immersion.

Alexander Campbell formed connections with the Haldane movement principally through Greville Ewing, with whom he was closely associated during his brief stint of university studies at Glasgow in 1808-9. Robert Richardson reports that Campbell was positively influenced by the Haldanes in three basic areas: their understanding of faith as not only rational belief of testimony but personal trust in Christ; their advancement of a congregational church polity; and their ultimate commitment to the immersion of believers.

The Haldane connection spread to Pennsylvania and included George Forrester, a Scottish minister in Pittsburgh who mentored Walter Scott and immersed the prolific early Disciple evangelist in 1819.

See also Ewing, Greville; Glas, John; Sandeman, Robert

BIBLIOGRAPHY Camille Dean, "Evangelicals or Restorationists? The Careers of Robert and James Haldane in Cultural and Political Context" (Ph.D. dissertation, Texas Christian University, 1999) • Alexander Haldane, *Memoirs of the Lives of Robert Haldane of Airthrey, and of his Brother, James Alexander Haldane* (1853) • James Alexander Haldane, *A View of the Social Worship and Ordinances by the First Christians* (1805) • Lynn A. McMillon, "The Quest for the Apostolic Church: A Study of Scottish Origins of American Restorationism" (Ph.D. dissertation, Baylor University, 1972), rewritten as *Restoration Roots* (1982). LYNN A. MCMILLON

Hall, Benjamin Franklin (1803-1873)

B. F. Hall, born in Nicholas County, Kentucky, in 1803, was the archetype of the itinerant evangelist in the first generation of the Stone-Campbell Movement. He was a dentist, physician, lawyer, teacher, farmer, real estate broker, and developer. He also served as an editor, a state evangelist, author of a hymnal, and military chaplain. He was ordained in 1825 by Barton W. Stone; went on a preaching tour in 1833 of Virginia, New York, and Baltimore with Alexander Campbell; converted Tolbert Fanning (1810-1874); and baptized John A. Gano (1805-1887) in 1826. He preached widely, especially in the South, though he preached as far away as Philadelphia in 1848. He moved to Texas in 1856 but continued his frequent preaching trips. Hall was a fanatical supporter of the Confederacy during the Civil War and served for nine months as chaplain in the Sixth Texas Cavalry commanded by Barton W. Stone, Jr. He died in 1873 in Grayson County, Texas.

See also Evangelism, Evangelists — Nineteenth Century; Fanning, Tolbert; Gano, John Allen

BIBLIOGRAPHY B. F. Hall, *The Proud Preacher: The Autobiography of B. F. Hall* (1869) • R. L. Roberts, Jr., "B. F. Hall: Pioneer Evangelist and Herald of Hope," *Restoration Quarterly* 8 (4th Quarter 1965): 248-59 • R. L. Roberts, Jr., "Benjamin Franklin Hall, 1803-1873," *Restoration Quarterly* 20 (3rd Quarter 1977): 156-68 • D. Newell Williams, "The Autobiography of B. F. Hall," *Discipliana* 50 (Spring 1990): 10. CHARLES L. WOODALL

Hall, Colby D. (1875-1963)

Disciples educator, historian, pastor, and author, Colby D. Hall was born in Kentucky in 1875. The family moved to Windom, Kansas, in 1882, and then on to Waco, Texas, in 1890. Colby Hall was a direct descendant of Caleb Hall, Sr., who was a member of the Cane Ridge, Kentucky, congregation. Hall completed his undergraduate theological studies at Add-Ran University (now Texas Christian University, TCU), under the tutelage of Addison Clark and J. B. Sweeney (a pupil of J. W. McGarvey). He then entered Transylvania College in Lexington as a junior and graduated with a B.A. in 1902. After a year of teaching and preaching, he entered Columbia University in New York, receiving the next year a Master of Arts in Sociology, minoring in psychology and economics.

Hall began his career at TCU in 1912, teaching Bible and social service. He then served as dean of AddRan College as well as dean of Brite College of the Bible. He was dean of TCU from 1920 until 1943 and dean of Brite College from 1915 until 1947. He was a professor of history of religion until retiring in 1950, at the age of 75.

He was deeply troubled by the divisions within the Stone-Campbell Movement. He was a pleasant, irenic person, always interested in teaching well the Christian faith and serving others. His published works include *History of Texas Christian University* (1947), *Texas Disciples* (1953), *Rice Haggard: The American Frontier Evangelist Who Revived the Name Christian* (1957), and *Gay Nineties* (1961). ROBERT B. HALL

Hardeman, Nicholas Brodie (1874-1965)

Nicholas Brodie Hardeman (always "Brodie" to family and friends) was one of the most important evangelists and educators for Churches of Christ during the first half of the twentieth century. Together with G. C. Brewer (1884-1956) and Foy E. Wallace, Jr. (1896-1979), he is responsible for setting the course Churches of

Evangelist and educator Nicholas Brodie Hardeman (1874-1965).

Christ followed in the second half of the century. Historian Leroy Garrett described the three as "a triumvirate of leadership." He was educated at West Tennessee Christian College, receiving the B.A. in 1895 and the M.A. in 1899 (by then the school was renamed Georgie Robertson Christian College). Here he came under the influence of A. G. Freed (1863-1931). In 1897 Hardeman joined Freed in teaching at the same institution.

Hardeman was a consummate orator. Often called "the Prince of Preachers," he held the largest revival meetings for his time among Churches of Christ, the so-called "Tabernacle Sermons." Delivered in Nashville on five separate occasions between the years 1922 and 1942, these revivals drew crowds of up to 8,000 people, with 2,000 or more turned away. Thousands more read the sermons daily in the local newspapers, and, starting with the third series, untold numbers heard them over the radio. Eventually collected into five volumes, these sermons were often memorized word-for-word and delivered by aspiring young preachers eager to emulate the "Hardeman" style.

Though distinguished in appearance and bearing, Hardeman was a practitioner of what some have termed the "hard, fighting" style of preaching. In his biography his daughter perhaps best captured this militant posture when she entitled the chapter on her father's debating career as "Give 'em Hell . . . in a Christian Spirit." Of his seventeen public debates, the last two were his most significant. In 1923 he met Ira M. Boswell of the Christian Churches in a Nashville debate over the use of instrumental music in worship. The result was a great deal of publicity for Hardeman and Churches of Christ in that area. In 1938 he met the Baptist debater Ben M. Bogard (1868-1951) in a public debate held in Little Rock, Arkansas, covering the work of the Holy Spirit and the necessity of baptism, among other issues.

Hardeman's most important contribution was the school that he and A. G. Freed founded in 1908 at Henderson, Tennessee, where they emulated the Campbellian ideal of preparing preachers in the context of a liberal arts education. At first called the National Teachers' Normal and Business College, the school was renamed Freed-Hardeman College in 1919 in their honor. From 1925 to 1950 Hardeman served as its president. Through the thousands of preachers that he trained, he exerted a powerful influence on Churches of Christ throughout the twentieth century. In grateful appreciation, on his 85th birthday more than 750 people and several dignitaries gathered at the Peabody Hotel in Memphis in 1959 for a dinner in his honor.

See also Brewer, Grover Cleveland; Evangelism, Evangelists; Freed-Hardeman University; Wallace, Foy Esco, Jr.

BIBLIOGRAPHY L. L. Brigance, "Sketch of the Author's Life," in *Hardeman's Tabernacle Sermons,* vol. 2 (1923; repr. 1991), pp. 9-25 • Richard T. Hughes and R. L. Roberts, *The Churches of Christ* (2001) • James Marvin Powell and Mary Nelle Hardeman Powers, *N.B.H.: A Biography of Nicholas Brodie Hardeman* (1964).

DAVID H. WARREN

Harding, James Alexander (1848-1922)

Evangelist and educator in Churches of Christ.

Harding's parents were strong members of the Christian Church in Winchester, Kentucky, where Harding was born, until the introduction of musical instruments in 1897. James A. Harding married Carrie Knight in 1871 (d. 1876), and Pattie Cobb in 1878. Harding graduated from Bethany College in 1869, then served as a schoolteacher in Hopkinsville. For the next seventeen years he was occupied in full-time itinerant evangelism, holding approximately 300 gospel meetings of from two to ten weeks each. He was also a debater, conducting fifty debates, including four published ones: in 1884 with Methodist J. M. Wilkinson on the mode and subjects of baptism; in 1888 with Methodist John H. Nichols on the

In addition to his evangelistic, educational, and journalistic work, Harding held more than fifty debates during his career, most focusing on baptism. Courtesy of the Center for Restoration Studies, Abilene Christian University

necessity of immersion; in 1889 with Baptist J. B. Moody on baptism and the work of the Holy Spirit; and again with Nichols in 1890.

Harding was cofounder and president of Nashville Bible School in Nashville, Tennessee, from 1891 to 1901, when he moved to Bowling Green, Kentucky, to become founder and president of Potter Bible School, where he served from 1901 to 1912. He spent his last years again as an itinerant evangelist. In addition to his teaching and evangelism, he was a contributing and associate editor for the *Gospel Advocate* from 1882 to 1890, editor of *The Way* from 1899 to 1903, co-editor of *The Christian Leader and the Way* from 1904 to 1912, and co-editor of the *Gospel Herald* from 1912 to 1915. Harding's final years were marred by frequent blackouts and senility due to poor circulation.

Harding was the father and theological mentor of the Bible School movement among Churches of Christ. Emphasizing grace, a dynamic understanding of special divine providence, and the personal indwelling and enabling work of the Spirit, his theology had an eschatological (historic premillennialist) and pietistic (Bible reading, prayer, attendance at the Lord's Table, and tithing as "means of grace") impulse. The kingdom of God, he believed, was advanced through evangelism rather than through political and military action. Ecclesiologically, he was a separatist who regarded immersion, instrumental music, and missionary societies as decisive terms of communion.

See also Debates, Debating; *Gospel Advocate, The;* Lipscomb, David; Lipscomb University; Potter Bible College

BIBLIOGRAPHY James A. Harding texts, available online at http://www.mun.ca/rels/restmov/people/jharding.html • John Mark Hicks, "The Gracious Separatist: Moral and Positive Law in the Theology of James A. Harding," *Restoration Quarterly* 42 (3rd Quarter 2000): 129-47 • L. C. Sears, *The Eyes of Jehovah* (1970).

JOHN MARK HICKS

Harding University

University located in Searcy, Arkansas, and affiliated with Churches of Christ.

Harding began as a senior college in 1924, when two junior colleges, Arkansas Christian College (chartered in 1919) and Harper (Kansas) College (founded in 1915) merged facilities and assets and adopted the name Harding College. The new school was located on the campus of Arkansas Christian College in Morrilton, Arkansas.

With the merger, J. N. Armstrong (1870-1944), who had served five years as Harper's president, became president of Harding College, and A. S. Croom (1892-1985), president of Arkansas Christian for two years, became vice president for business affairs. The college was renamed for James A. Harding, cofounder and first president of Nashville Bible School (now Lipscomb University). Harding was Armstrong's father-in-law, and along with David Lipscomb was a formative influence in his life. From these mentors Armstrong inherited a strong sense of the value of Christian higher education and a great reliance on divine providence, as well as commitment to pacifism and tolerance for a range of millennial views. The college was criticized in some quarters at the time for reflecting these beliefs of its leader, particularly for failing to denounce premillennial teachers like R. H. Boll.

In 1934 Harding was moved to its present site in Searcy, Arkansas, to the campus of a former Methodist women's institution, Galloway College. One of Harding's first graduates, George S. Benson (1898-1991), returned from mission work in China in 1936 to assume the presidency of his alma mater. This vigorous leader quickly rescued the college from its deep indebtedness and launched it on a journey toward financial stability and national visibility. As a former missionary, Benson encouraged a continued emphasis on missions, and Harding became a source of a large percentage of the overseas missionaries of Churches of Christ. He also initiated programs that were strongly anti-communist, founding the National Education Program and soliciting support from wealthy business leaders outside of the Churches of Christ who were willing to help support a college whose slogan was, "Where Christian and American ideas go hand in hand." Benson's tenure lasted twenty-nine years (to 1965). His legacy was a multimillion-dollar campus, regional accreditation, growing enrollments, significant alumni involvement and leadership in Churches of Christ worldwide, and a nationally known identification with conservative political ideology.

The Harding University Graduate School of Religion was an outgrowth of graduate studies in religion that began on the Searcy campus in 1952. An extension program offering graduate courses in Memphis, Tennessee, started in 1955, and in 1958 the Harding University Graduate School of Religion became a permanent Memphis branch of Harding University and a major center for the training of ministers for Churches of Christ. Dr. W. B. West (1907-1994) was the founding dean.

Dr. Clifton L. Ganus, Jr. (b. 1922), a 1943 graduate, served as president from 1965 to 1987. During his administration, enrollment increased from 1,472 to 2,767, significant facilities expansion occurred, and in 1979 the institution was renamed Harding University. The nursing program, the social work program, the "Mission Prepare" program, the School of

Biblical Studies, and the Harding University in Florence (Italy) program were developed during his administration. The Graduate School of Religion in Memphis experienced significant growth, received accreditation by the Southern Association of Colleges and Schools, and added the Doctor of Ministry degree to its program. Upon his retirement, Dr. Ganus became Harding's first chancellor.

Dr. David B. Burkes became Harding's fourth president in May 1987. A 1965 graduate, he had previously served as dean of the School of Business. In 2001 the university's enrollment reached 5,013 students, and the campus in Searcy consisted of forty-three buildings on 200 acres and a 219-member faculty, 70 percent of whom held terminal degrees.

See also Benson, George Stuart; Boll, Robert Henry; Harding, James Alexander

BIBLIOGRAPHY David B. Burkes, *Against the Grain: The Mission of Harding University* (1998) • Bill Flatt, *Harding University Graduate School of Religion: 25 Years in Memphis* (1983) • Eloise Muncy and John Williams, *Making History: Ray Muncy in His Time* (2002) • James Don Nichols, "A History of Harding College, 1924-1984" (unpublished Ed.D. thesis, University of Arkansas, 1985) • M. Norvel Young, *A History of Colleges Established and Controlled by Members of the Churches of Christ* (1949).

JOHN F. WILSON

Harper, William Rainey

See Disciples Divinity House

Hathcock, T. O.

See Atlanta Christian College

Hayden, Amos Sutton (1813-1880)

Evangelist, minister, college administrator, and early historian of the Stone-Campbell Movement in Ohio.

Hayden was born September 17, 1813, in Youngstown, Ohio, the youngest of eight children of a musical family. His older brother William was a convert of Walter Scott's evangelistic campaign and became Scott's singer and exhorter. Hayden grew up on a farm but was able to receive a simple classical education. On May 31, 1837, he married Sarah M. Ely, who remained important to his career and religious life from that time on. In 1828, under Walter Scott's influence, Hayden affiliated with the Stone-Campbell Movement, and about 1832 he became one of its evangelists. By 1840 he had become the local minister of the congregation in Collamer, Cuyahoga County, Ohio. He remained with that church for some ten years, and returned to that church and area after a stint as a college principal.

Hayden was one of the founders of the Western Reserve Eclectic Institute (later Hiram College) in 1850. He served the new institute as principal or president from its founding until 1857, at which point he was succeeded by James A. Garfield. In the years 1858-59 he became principal of the McNeely Normal School at Hopeville, Ohio. Following this one-year stint, he returned to the Collamer church to preach and lived in that area until his death on September 10, 1880.

During his final ministry he authored *The Christian Hymnal and Tune Book* (1870) and *Early History of the Disciples in the Western Reserve, Ohio* (1875). The latter is the primary history of the evangelizing and reforming enterprises of Walter Scott and other Disciple preachers of the Mahoning Association in Ohio, and it chronicles the Association's eventual dissolution. Hayden provides a bird's-eye view of the dynamics of frontier evangelism in a geographic area of prolific growth among the Disciples of Christ in the mid-nineteenth century and gives evidence of the Movement's struggle to negotiate its way between formal structural association and loose-knit congregationalism.

BIBLIOGRAPHY A. S. Hayden, *Early History of the Disciples in the Western Reserve, Ohio* (1875) • W. T. Moore, ed., *The Living Pulpit of the Christian Church* (1869), pp. 495-96.

CHARLES R. GRESHAM

Herald of Truth

A religious broadcasting ministry of Churches of Christ, the first program sponsored by this body to be heard nationally on network radio and television. The visibility of the Herald of Truth brought credibility to a Movement whose social identity was changing. It also became a model for mass media evangelism for other religious programs.

Herald of Truth emerged from the visionary work of James Walter Nichols (1927-1973) and James D. Willeford (1916-1992). Both Nichols and Willeford broadcast local radio shows in Iowa and Wisconsin but dreamed of a national program. The Highland Church of Christ in Abilene, Texas, assumed oversight of the project in 1951. Nichols presented the first Herald of Truth program, entitled "Churches of Christ Salute You," from Abilene's city auditorium, airing on the ABC Radio Network February 10, 1952. Thirty-one ABC stations broadcast the first show. That number grew to 85 ABC stations by the summer of 1952, and to 250 by January 1953. At its peak, 578 stations carried the broadcast.

Various elders of the Highland Church of Christ signed personal bank notes to keep the program on the air, evidence of Highland's commitment through the years. To date, Herald of Truth has never solicited funds from its listeners. When Highland launched the program, it took the stance that if God were behind the effort other churches would support it. Although computer records go back only to 1965, about 5,000 different churches and 150,000 individuals have supported Herald of Truth through the years. In the beginning, the elders previewed every script and every tape. The inclusion of the "plan of salvation" that included baptism was required of every broadcast.

Noninstitutional Churches of Christ registered strong opposition to the prospect of a single congregation controlling both the finances and the content of a project that represented Churches of Christ worldwide. The "sponsoring church" concept developed into a major divisive issue during the 1950s and 1960s. The noninstitutional paper *Guardian of Truth* retrospectively reported in January 1993, "This enterprise [Herald of Truth] was to become a part of the 'centerpiece' that would produce a major division in Churches of Christ."

With the emergence of television's popularity and the changing listening habits of the culture, Herald of Truth expanded its ministry to television in 1954. By 1959 the Mutual Broadcasting System picked up the program on radio. In 1963 it became part of the Armed Forces Radio and Television System around the world. By 1968 NBC carried the TV broadcast coast to coast. Hosts included George Bailey (b. 1922), Batsell Barrett Baxter (1916-1982), John Allen Chalk (b. 1937), Harold Hazelip (b. 1930), Joe Barnett (b. 1933), Ken Durham, and Randy Becton.

In 1971 the 30-minute radio format changed to "Heartbeat," short daily radio spots hosted by Landon Saunders. In 1984 Glenn Owen (1936-2001) began the "Let's Talk" daily radio program that presented the gospel through 1999 in a more conversational style. In 1979 Herald of Truth launched a new publication called *UpReach,* a magazine for better living. *UpReach* has been sent to homes across the United States and distributed to doctors' offices, hospitals, and prisons.

In the 1970s some conservatives in Churches of Christ began to question the nontraditional approach taken by the new "Heartbeat" broadcast, especially the fact that the "plan of salvation" was no longer presented in each show. They were also alarmed at reports of inroads of charismatic teaching into the Fifth and Highland Church of Christ. A meeting to confront leaders of the Highland Church took place September 10, 1973, in Memphis, Tennessee. A conservative campaign to discourage churches from supporting the ministry had already begun before the meeting but increased afterward. E. R. Harper (1897-1986), former elder at 5th and Highland who had defended the practice of the sponsoring congregation against noninstitutional opponents, now led the opposition to continued support of the program. Herald of Truth continued to operate, though a number of congregations did stop their aid. The controversy continued for several years and marked one of the points of demarcation in a late-twentieth-century rift between conservatives and progressives in Churches of Christ.

Crosscultural outreach has been a primary focus of the ministry since 1966. Select broadcasts have aired over the entire former Soviet Union. Juan Monroy, Pedro Rivas, and Lou Seckler have spearheaded efforts to Spanish-speaking people. For example, 44 of 450 congregations of Churches of Christ in Mexico are able to trace their origins to Herald of Truth ministries.

When cable television became a widely used media, Herald of Truth again adapted to the times. "Hope for Life's Journey," hosted by Randy Becton, became a focal point of the ministry. A more diverse audience and greater response rates to reruns give the show a longer and more effective life than possible on commercial television. "His Word for His World," a new radio program emphasizing the reading of Scripture on the air, debuted at the beginning of the twenty-first century.

See also Baxter, Batsell Barrett; Noninstitutional Movement; Radio and Television

BIBLIOGRAPHY John Marion Barton, "The Preaching on Herald of Truth Radio, 1952-1969" (Ph.D. dissertation, Pennsylvania State University, 1975) • Robert Wayne Dockery, "'Three American Revolutions': A Study of Social Change in the Churches of Christ As Evidenced in the 'Herald of Truth' Radio Series" (M.A. thesis, Louisiana State University, 1973) • E. R. Harper and Fanning Yater Tant, *Harper Tant Debate, Abilene, Texas, November 27-30, 1955* (1956) • "The Herald of Truth History Time Line," available on-line at http://www.heraldoftruth.org/about/ • *Memphis Meeting with the Representatives of Herald of Truth* (1973) • Deby K. Samuels, "The Herald of Truth: An Impossible Dream," *Firm Foundation* 94 (February 1977): 8-9 (special 25th anniversary of Herald of Truth edition).

TIM SENSING

Heresy, Heretics

From Greek *hairesis,* meaning choice or opinion; came historically to signify both doctrinal error and schism.

When W. K. Pendleton (1817-1899), one of Alexander Campbell's co-editors, quoted Augustine as saying "I may err, but I will not be a heretic," he gave the essence of the Movement's early understanding of heresy. It had more to do with bad behavior than with wrong doctrine. Pendleton went on to quote one of Campbell's favorite scholars, George Campbell of Aberdeen, Scotland, that "error alone, however gross" was not considered sufficient to warrant the charge of heresy during the first five centuries of the church. Pendleton agreed that "malignity or perverseness of disposition was held essential to this crime."

When Alexander Campbell was reminded that people are not likely to give up their opinions even for the sake of unity, he replied, "We do not ask them to give up their opinions. We ask them only not to impose them upon others." Opinions may be held as "private property," but they cannot be made the measure of all Christians. This is heresy, imposing opinions upon others as tests of communion.

Campbell distinguished between errors of the mind, which might be caused by "imbecility of intellect," and errors of the heart, which bred the sectarian spirit. He was critical of those in the history of the church who excluded others who were simply mistaken in doctrine. He went on to say that he had never rejected a person simply because he disagreed with that person. As early as 1830 Campbell insisted that he and his followers could never be accused of being sectarian or heretical because "We will acknowledge all as Christians who acknowledge the gospel facts, and obey Jesus Christ."

But in fact there were some whom Campbell would reject, and here he pinpointed the meaning of heresy: "If he will dogmatize and become a factionist, we reject him — not because of his opinions, but because of his attempting to make a faction, or to lord it over God's heritage." It is in this context that Campbell told the story of Aylett Raines (1788-1881), a universalist preacher who was immersed and affiliated with the Campbell movement. Some sought to declare "non-fellowship" with him, as Campbell put it, because he still held some of his universalist views. Raines stated that he would hold his views as his own opinions; he would not press them, and would express them only when asked. That was good enough for both Thomas and Alexander Campbell, who spoke up in Raines's defense, noting that one's private opinions did not keep one from faithfully preaching the ancient gospel. This case defined the Movement's early view of heresy: a heretic is not one who simply holds an erroneous position, but one who seeks to create a faction.

While Barton W. Stone's views were similar, he went even further than Campbell in that he made even baptism by immersion a matter of opinion. People could not be blamed for having diverse opinions, he granted, but they were culpable when they attached such importance to them as to reject those who did not agree with those opinions. To Stone this was heresy. In 1831 Stone wrote, "My opinion is that immersion only is baptism. . . . But shall I make my opinion a term of Christian fellowship?" Radically narrowing the category of those often deemed "heretics," he urged: "Let us still acknowledge all to be our brethren, who believe in the Lord Jesus, and humbly and honestly obey him, as far as they know his will, and their duty." Three years earlier Stone had given this definition: "A heretic is one who factiously draws away a party or sect after him from the body or church of Christ, and forms a distinct denomination." Drawing on Galatians 5:20, he names heresy as a work of the flesh. Anyone who has that love that unites and suffers long cannot be a heretic. He stated that those who perpetuate divisions are as guilty as those who create them.

The ensuing history of the Movement provides numerous instances in which this earlier position on heresy was tested. The earliest case was the defection of Sidney Rigdon (1793-1876), a co-laborer with Alexander Campbell, to the Mormons in 1830, including the rebaptism of a number of Disciples into the new Mormon church. While Rigdon was never formally excluded by any congregation, he was quickly and summarily recognized as a heretic. This was far more than simply a private opinion. Rigdon had "renounced the ancient gospel," as Campbell put it, and "fallen into the snare of the Devil in joining the Mormonites." As for the comparatively few that he lost to the Mormons, Campbell did not mince words: "Every person who receives the book of Mormon is an apostate from all that we ever professed."

John Thomas, a physician and an editor as early as 1834, presented a different kind of problem. He exaggerated the Movement's position on baptism by insisting that a believer must understand that baptism is for the remission of sins at the time of his or her immersion — "an intelligent faith," as he described it. This led to a vigorous campaign to reimmerse all the Baptists he could persuade that had come into the Movement without being rebaptized. As Baptists they had only been "baptized into Antichrist" according to Thomas.

To Campbell this was a deplorable departure from what had been practiced from the outset, and it "paganized all immersed persons." He held that reimmersion was never in order unless the person was "destitute of faith in Christ" at the time of his or her baptism. Thomas was an "infallible dogmatist" out to create his own party. The controversy brewed for fifteen years, resulting in Thomas creating his own church, the Christadelphians.

There was a place in the Movement for one as opinionated as John Thomas so long as he tempered his attitude and behavior. Or as David King (1819-1894) of England put it when commenting on Thomas's proposed visit to the British churches: they would be pleased to have him "if he would proclaim

Father of the Christadelphians, John Thomas (1805-1871) taught that for baptism to be valid the baptized must understand that the act is for the remission of sins at the time of their immersion. He also advocated a form of annihilationism, denying the resurrection of any but the righteous.
Courtesy of the Disciples of Christ Historical Society

the gospel, and not more than incidentally introduce his favorite topic."

Two young ministers in the 1850s, Walter Scott Russell, president of Berean College in Jacksonville, Illinois, and I. N. Carmen, minister of the Christian Church in Ashland, Ohio, taught that the Holy Spirit operated over and beyond the written Word in converting and sanctifying sinners. Russell divided his church over the issue, and Carmen held separate gatherings to promote his views.

Campbell, who had earlier praised Russell, a graduate of Bethany, now ruled in 1860, not unlike a bishop, that Russell was "a schismatic, and, as such, cannot be esteemed and regarded as a brother in communion with us." Carmen's case led to the first "heresy trial" in the history of the Movement, with leading evangelists serving as judges. When they found him guilty, his congregation publicly announced that "Carmen had voluntarily withdrawn from the church and was no longer a member of our brotherhood."

These two cases led Robert Richardson (1806-1876) to comment upon the nature of heresy. The views of Russell and Carmen were not all that different from those of other leaders of the Movement, he allowed. They were heretics, not because of their opinions, but because they imposed them upon others to the point of division.

Perhaps the most notable nineteenth-century heretic was Jesse B. Ferguson, popular minister of the 500-member Church of Christ in Nashville and a widely read editor and writer. At the center of the furor was Ferguson's controversial exegesis of 1 Peter 3:18-20 and 4:1-6. Campbell and others charged him with propagating "a post-mortem gospel" that allowed for "a second chance" after death, although a close reading of Ferguson indicates that he was arguing that Christ, in evangelizing the "spirits in prison," was merely offering the gospel for the first time to those dead who had never had access to it in this life. Campbell, however, successfully urged the condemnation of Ferguson for undermining the integrity of the gospel.

Ferguson at last divided the church over spiritualism, which included conducting séances and communicating with the dead. He sought to change the Church of Christ in Nashville into "a humanitarian Church," and the elders were forced to go to court to reclaim the building, only to see it mysteriously burned to the ground. Ferguson preached in a Nashville theater for a time, traveled, dabbled in politics, and farmed in Tennessee and Arkansas. At his passing in 1870 David Lipscomb (1831-1917) described him as at one time "the most popular preacher in the South," one that Campbell, however, felt confident in describing as "an infidel at heart."

These instances of heresy helped the Movement to define itself theologically. While it allowed for differences for the sake of unity, it saw that the line for unity in diversity had to be drawn somewhere.

After the Civil War the churches of the Movement seem to have reverted to a more popular view of heresy and heretics, defining them in terms of false doctrine or unscriptural methods. "Innovations," as some called them, caused stress in the Movement. Missionary and benevolent societies, organization of churches (local, state, national), instrumental music in worship, Sunday Schools, resident ministers, choirs, and stained glass were deemed heretical by those who saw them as departures from "the ancient order."

The influence of modern biblical criticism brought still more charges of heresy. As ministers and college professors became better educated — some of them took doctorates from Chicago and Yale — "liberalism" or "modernism" emerged as a new heresy in churches and colleges alike. The 1917 heresy trial at the College of the Bible (later Lexington

Theological Seminary), in which four liberal professors were exonerated of the charge of having departed from "the fundamental conceptions and convictions" of the Movement, has been seen as a defining moment in that institution's history. At the same time the "Bible college" movement began in the 1920s in protest to the "modernism" of the old liberal arts colleges. In Churches of Christ, William Webb Freeman, Bible professor at Abilene Christian College, was dismissed in 1922 over issues of biblical inspiration and interpretation.

The impact of church federation and the ecumenical movement brought still more accusations of heresy, along with still more division. The suspicion of heresy in foreign missions where missionaries entered into comity agreements with "denominational" missionaries and were accused of practicing open membership contributed to the separation of Christian Churches/Churches of Christ from the Disciples of Christ. To cooperate with the denominations in any way or enter into fellowship with them was deemed to be heresy by many in the more conservative streams of the Stone-Campbell Movement.

Ultimately the Movement came to understand heresy in terms of both error in practice (whether in reference to worship, organization, or missions) and error in doctrine. The early identification of heresy as a divisive spirit gave way to a broader delineation of heresy as theological deviance. In time the Movement discovered the need to mark out the tolerable limits of diversity.

See also Ferguson, Jesse Babcock; Liberty; Raines, Aylett; Rigdon, Sidney; Russell, Walter Scott; Thomas, John; Universalism

BIBLIOGRAPHY Alexander Campbell, "Delusions," *Millennial Harbinger* (1831): 85-96 • Alexander Campbell, "Sidney Rigdon," *Millennial Harbinger* (1831): 100-101 • Alexander Campbell, "Re-Immersion," *Millennial Harbinger* (1835): 418-20 • Alexander Campbell, "Heresy," ch. 28 in *The Christian System* (2nd ed. 1839), pp. 99-108 • Alexander Campbell, "Dr. Thomas," *Millennial Harbinger* (1844): 203-15 • Alexander Campbell, "A New Discovery," *Millennial Harbinger* (1852): 313-29 • Alexander Campbell, *"The Christian Magazine," Millennial Harbinger* (1852): 390-98, 628-34 • Alexander Campbell, "Spirits in Prison," *Millennial Harbinger* (1852): 487-97 • Alexander Campbell, "Philosophy, Dogmatism, Schism," *Millennial Harbinger* (1860): 13-20 • Robert Richardson, "Doubtful Disputations," *Millennial Harbinger* (1860): 21-28 • Barton Stone, "Opinions," *Christian Messenger* 5 (1831): 19-21 • Barton Stone, "Heresy," *Christian Messenger* 3 (1828): 195-98 • Barton Stone, "Schism," "Heresy," and "Shakerism," in *An Address to the Churches* (2nd ed. 1821), in *Works of Elder Barton Warren Stone*, pp. 98-102

LEROY GARRETT

Hermeneutics

1. The Tripartite Formula
2. The Dispensations
3. The Grammatico-Historical Method

The science of interpreting the Scriptures, and a critically important component in the reforming principles of the Stone-Campbell Movement. The early hermeneutics of the Movement had roots both in the Reformed tradition and in the British Enlightenment. Three formative components of Stone-Campbell hermeneutics should be noted: (1) the tripartite formula: "express terms," "approved precedence," and "inference"; (2) the doctrine of dispensations; and (3) grammatico-historical criticism. In the twentieth century, as the Movement fissured, differing approaches to biblical interpretation emerged.

1. The Tripartite Formula

Thomas Campbell in the *Declaration and Address* (1809) wrote of the authority for Christians of "express terms" and "approved precedents" in the New Testament. He affirmed the value of inferences, but declared that conclusions from inferences should not be bound on other believers as terms of communion. The earliest recorded instance of this tripartite formula may be that of Edward Dering (1540-1576), an early English Puritan, who wrote of deductions, commands, and examples. In the view of Thomas Campbell, except where Scripture is explicit in express terms and approved precedents, freedom obtains. The fifth proposition of his *Declaration and Address,* reflecting Locke's *Letters on Toleration,* reads: "That with respect to the commands and ordinances of our Lord Jesus Christ, where the Scriptures are silent, as to the express time or manner of performance, if any such there be; no human authority has power to interfere, in order to supply the supposed deficiency, by making laws for the Church."

Thomas Campbell contended that he was neither too limiting nor too permissive. He recognized that opinions persist, but opinions are never mandates for the church. Nothing within Scripture can be a matter of opinion. Though Alexander Campbell and most other leaders of the Movement in the nineteenth century embraced the views of Thomas Campbell, as the century wore on the inference became important in setting out positions and methods, as Michael W. Casey has established.

In the twentieth century the Christian Church (Disciples of Christ) largely abandoned the tripartite formula for the larger theological sense of the Scriptures obtained through historical-critical interpretation. Eugene Boring has argued that the Disciples now need to recover their own "rule of faith," which centers in "No creed but Christ; no book but the Bible." He believes the creed should be fleshed out additionally by a biblical theology focusing on the five salvific realities of creation, covenant, Christ, church, and consummation.

In the first half of the twentieth century in Churches of Christ the tripartite formula remained sacrosanct, but under the thesis that an express declaration eliminates alternatives. For example, the command to sing and make melody in the heart excludes the playing of an instrument. The Christian Churches/Churches of Christ have also maintained the older hermeneutic, but they assert that unless a practice is expressly forbidden, freedom exists. For example, since the playing of instruments is not expressly forbidden, their use is optional. As long as restoring the New Testament church was the driving motive, the tripartite formula was useful. More recently, with a focus on "spiritual" issues like discipleship, servanthood, family, and praise, use of the formula has declined in Churches of Christ and in the Christian Churches/Churches of Christ. Critics of deviations from the older hermeneutic have charged that a "new hermeneutic" has come to the fore.

2. The Dispensations

Thomas Campbell initiated a major hermeneutical move in specifying the New Testament alone as the basis for Christian belief and practice, upon which his son Alexander later elaborated in the well-known "Sermon on the Law," delivered in 1816. In the fourth Proposition of his *Declaration and Address,* Campbell declared that although Old Testament and New Testament were inseparably related, only the New Testament could be the "constitution" of the church for the worship, discipline, and government of the Old Testament church, and the particular duties of its members.

This relegation of the Old Testament to a non-authoritative status for Christian worship, discipline, and government ran counter to the Reformed positions of Calvin, Zwingli, Knox, and the Puritans. Calvinists saw another use for the Old Testament in convicting sinners of their need for repentance. Alexander Campbell rejected this use of the law as well, commenting pointedly in his "Sermon on the Law" (1816): "There is no necessity for preaching the law in order to prepare men for receiving the gospel."

The early Stone-Campbell perspective on the three dispensations was largely indebted to the covenant (federal) theology of the Dutch scholars Hugo Grotius (1583-1645) and Johannes Cocceius (1603-1669). Cocceius held that as the result of the failure of the covenant of works with Adam, God instituted the covenant of grace in three dispensations: the Patriarchal, the Mosaic, and the Christian. This scheme both established a groundwork for what was authoritative in each dispensation and provided a means of relating the dispensations to each other. In effect, it became a biblical theology, featuring promise and fulfillment. An example of a "biblical theology" so organized in the nineteenth-century Stone-Campbell Movement was Robert Milligan's often-reprinted *An Exposition and Defense of the Scheme of Redemption* (1868). By the end of the nineteenth century, J. J. Haley showcased once again the doctrine of dispensations in an extensive essay on progressive revelation in the influential volume *The Old Faith Restated* (1891).

There were American dispensational counterparts in various other quarters, for example, in the lectures of David Tappan (1752-1803), a moderate Calvinist and Hollis Professor at Harvard. Furthermore, the Campbells were influenced by John Locke and his heirs, who had chiefly sought to root Christianity in the Gospels, and secondarily in the letters of Paul. The Campbells, for their part, focused on their own "canon within the canon," privileging Acts and the epistles, especially Hebrews, rather than the Gospels.

With the coming of the social gospel in the progressive Disciples stream of the Stone-Campbell Movement and its attendant interest in the Old Testament prophets, the distinctive threefold dispensationalism began to erode. An early scholar to highlight the prophets was Herbert L. Willett (1864-1944) of the University of Chicago, followed somewhat later by Phillip Hyatt (1909-1972) of Vanderbilt, along with several noted ministers. Sensitized to the importance of the study of the Old Testament in its own right rather than merely as antecedent to study of the New Testament, Disciples scholars Walter Harrelson (b. 1919) and Leo G. Perdue (b. 1947) have further eroded the dispensational approach to biblical scholarship.

At the level of local churches as well, there has been some response to the tendency of the older dispensational approach to relativize the Old Testament and thus undermine its importance. In the past thirty years Old Testament studies have increased in adult classes in Churches of Christ and their colleges through the influence of Jack P. Lewis (b. 1919) of Harding Graduate School, John T. Willis (b. 1933) of Abilene Christian University, Rick Marrs (b. 1952) of Pepperdine University, Thomas H. Olbricht (b. 1929), formerly of Abilene Christian and Pepperdine, and J. J. M. Roberts (b. 1940) of Princeton Theological Seminary. Several of these scholars have argued that while the Old Testament is not authoritative for Christians in its institutions it is authoritative in its theology. Renewed interest in the Old Testament may be found in Christian Churches/Churches of Christ colleges and churches, but not to the extent it is found in the other two major streams of the Movement.

3. The Grammatico-Historical Method

Alexander Campbell addressed the principles of interpretation in *Millennial Harbinger* "Extras" in the early 1830s and published them together in a book titled *Christianity Restored* in 1835. His declared purpose was to identify "the principles by which the Christian institution may be certainly and satisfactorily ascertained."

Campbell believed that the "scientific" — that is, systematic — interpretation of Scripture should proceed according to the same rules for understanding any other document. In that regard, though his "Principles" were sketchy, they were abreast of the best hermeneutical and exegetical principles of the time, especially of the tradition of the German scholar Johann Ernesti as mediated through Moses Stuart of Andover Seminary, the foremost American biblical scholar of the era. This tradition was followed by David R. Dungan and to a lesser extent by J. S. Lamar, who emphasized "inductive" or Baconian interpretation. This tradition was also heavily informed by classical rhetoric. Campbell acquainted himself with the most advanced grammatico-historical-literary scholarship in the early nineteenth century, especially British-American approaches, but also the German works that had been translated.

Drawing on the principles of German Lutheran theologian Johan Ernesti, David R. Dungan (1837-1921) published his 400-page *Hermeneutics* in 1888.
Courtesy of the Disciples of Christ Historical Society

It is noteworthy that Alexander Campbell never carefully coordinated these 1835 "Principles" with either dispensationalism or the tripartite formula. The latter does not appear at all in the "Principles of Interpretation," though the dispensational aspect receives passing mention. The same obtains in later books on hermeneutics in the Stone-Campbell Movement, namely those of Lamar, Dungan, and J. D. Thomas.

After Campbell's time, the grammatico-historical interpretation of Scripture developed dramatically in Germany, then in Great Britain and the United States. Identified as "higher" criticism, it became a major controversy in the United States at the turn of the twentieth century. Since a number of Disciples, both professors and ministers, were trained at Yale, Chicago, and Vanderbilt, these perspectives gained currency in that stream of the Movement. It was in part because of their rejection of the more radical biblical criticism that the Christian Churches/Churches of Christ went their own way in the period from the 1920s through the 1960s, even though there were some within their ranks who embraced (and still do) aspects of the higher-critical methodologies. Institutions such as Milligan College and Emmanuel School of Religion have been particularly open to these methods, though under the discipline of a conservative theology. Many of the Bible colleges and seminaries of the Christian Churches/Churches of Christ, however, still hold suspect the current scholarly consensus in biblical-critical studies. That suspicion is observable, for example, in many of the biblical commentaries produced by College Press and Standard Publishing.

Numerous scholars in Churches of Christ at the end of the twentieth century had more freely embraced the methods of the biblical critics, but not so much their antisupernaturalistic views. Biblical theology — focusing on the mighty acts of God in salvation history rather the command-example-inference hermeneutic — had also made headway in Churches of Christ. However, in the Stone-Campbell Movement classical grammatico-historical-literary methodologies prevail, and that has been the foundation of openness in some quarters to other contemporary alternative approaches such as sociological, rhetorical, reader-response, or narrative criticism.

See also Bible, Authority and Inspiration of the; Bible, Commentaries on the; Bible, Interpretation of the; Common Sense Philosophy; Covenant (Federal) Theology; Dispensations; Dungan, David R.; Lamar, James S.; Milligan, Robert; Rationalism; Reason, Place of; Revelation

BIBLIOGRAPHY M. Eugene Boring, *Disciples and the Bible: A History of Disciples Biblical Interpretation in North America* (1997) • Alexander Campbell, "Principles of Interpretation," in *Christianity Restored* (1835) • Michael W. Casey, *The Battle over Hermeneutics in the Stone-Campbell Movement, 1808-1870* (1998) • David R. Dungan, *Hermeneutics: A Textbook* (1888) • J. A. Ernesti, *Elements of Interpretation,* trans. Moses Stuart (1822) • J. J. Halley, "The Progress of Revelation, or, the Three Dispensations — Their Limits and Their Characteristics," in *The Old Faith Restated,* ed. J. H. Garrison (1891), vol. 1, pp. 120-48 • Hal Hougey, *The Quest for Understandable Hermeneutics* (1997) • J. S. Lamar, *The Organon of Scripture* (1860) • Robert Milligan, *Reason and Revelation* (1867) • Thomas H. Olbricht, *Hearing God's Voice: My Life with Scripture in the Churches of Christ* (1996) • J. D. Thomas, *We Be Brethren* (1958) • J. D. Thomas, *Harmonizing Hermeneutics* (1991).

THOMAS H. OLBRICHT

Higher Education and Leadership Ministries of the Christian Church (Disciples of Christ)

See Division of Higher Education

Higher Education, Views of in the Movement

1. Factors Influencing the Founding of Private Colleges in the Early Nineteenth Century
2. Early Stone-Campbell Colleges
3. Alexander Campbell on College Education
4. Stone-Campbell Colleges, 1840 to 1866
5. Stone-Campbell Colleges, 1866 to 1900
6. Stone-Campbell Colleges, 1900 to 2000

Education at the undergraduate and graduate levels has long been affiliated with the churches of the Stone-Campbell Movement. In 1836 Bacon College was founded in Georgetown, Kentucky, as the first higher education institution in the Stone-Campbell Movement. Sustaining the life of that college became the earliest form of cooperative mission. From that beginning, an educational ministry was launched that eventually brought the founding of 215 known colleges and universities along with 207 academies and institutes. Across seventeen decades, more than one million persons have been educated in these schools and untold millions of dollars have been contributed to them. It is both the oldest and largest mission outreach of the Stone-Campbell Movement.

1. Factors Influencing the Founding of Private Colleges in the Early Nineteenth Century

Early nineteenth-century Americans debated whether education would be a function of the church or of the state. A significant factor contributing to the early dominance of denominational colleges was the landmark 1819 Supreme Court decision, *Dartmouth College v. Woodward.* The dispute was over institutional control. Was Dartmouth a public institution subject to the state legislature or a private institution subject to its own board of trustees? The court ruled Dartmouth a private corporation, a product of private philanthropy subject to its own board of trustees and safeguarded from interference by a state legislature. This decision checked the development of state universities until the post–Civil War period. It also cleared the way for the separate development of state and private colleges, gave classic expression to an American concept of community control, and unleashed an era of denominational college-founding.

The sociocultural rhythms of Jacksonian America, calling for "useful" knowledge and espousing egalitarian patterns of thought, helped to shape the development of these colleges. The Jacksonian order was marked by an enormous belief in the worth, capacity, and perfectibility of the individual. There was a lack of confidence in older, elite American institutions. Protestant churches, newly energized by revivalism, were engaged in intense denominational rivalry. The American frontier witnessed the rapid creation of a cultural infrastructure. Both the Jacksonian cultural ethos and the church factored into the development of the new educational institutions of the Stone-Campbell Movement.

2. Early Stone-Campbell Colleges

During the decade of the 1830s, the push for colleges among the frontier churches and communities gained full momentum. The contagion of college-building was especially strong between 1830 and 1860, known as the "Golden Age" for founding small, rural denominational colleges, typically with six to twelve professors and 100 to 300 students. In this highly competitive atmosphere, Baptists declared that every state would have its own Baptist college, and soon thereafter Methodists voted to place a college in every annual conference.

Fourteen educational institutions are known to have been founded in the Stone-Campbell Movement prior to 1840. Eleven of those were established during the 1830s. Four were founded in Indiana and seven in Kentucky, with others in Ohio, Pennsylvania, and Virginia. Not one of the fourteen institutions survived beyond the Civil War. Only two of the institutions were colleges. The others were academies, institutes, or seminaries, all forerunners of the modern primary, middle, and senior high schools. Financed on a modest scale, they regularly solicited congregations as well as individual members for contributions and only subsequently called for church endorsement.

These institutions were privately organized, owned, and maintained by influential personalities within the Stone-Campbell Movement. Individual organizers were not agents of any ecclesiastical authority, but the congregations often played a significant role in supporting and sustaining the institutions, which were always nevertheless regarded as part of the Movement. These early schools produced more than a proportionate share of national leaders. Wayne County Seminary in Centerville, Indiana, for example, during its short history counted among its students future governors and generals Oliver P. Morton, Lew Wallace, and Ambrose Burnside. Teachers, lawyers, doctors, and ministers educated in the Movement's schools could be numbered by the score.

Stone-Campbell schools were pioneers in extending education to females and in developing coeducational institutions. Poplar Hill Academy, founded in 1831 by Philip S. Fall in Kentucky, was one of the earliest female schools in the nation, preceding by five years the founding of Mt. Holyoke Female Seminary for girls in Massachusetts, generally considered a landmark in the history of education for women. Virtually every institution founded by the Stone-Campbell Movement was either coeducational or female. Perhaps in no other area did the Movement so clearly mark itself as part of the egalitarian West. This demonstrates that the mission of founding colleges within the Movement was infused with social purpose as well as a commitment to learning.

Although Alexander Campbell had founded Buffalo Seminary in his home as early as 1818, he soon discontinued the operation and, judging from his writings in the *Millennial Harbinger,* had been reluctant to support the founding of colleges since that time. Until 1840 most were founded without his full support; nevertheless he was busy developing an educational philosophy that would shape the founding of educational institutions within the Movement for the remainder of the century and beyond.

3. Alexander Campbell on College Education

Campbell's educational philosophy was developed through the study of the orthodox sources of his day with little attention to those who were considered the leaders of early nineteenth-century educational reform. He studied carefully the writings of Francis Bacon, the Swiss educator De Fellenberg, and especially the essays of Thomas Smith Grimke, a Carolina barrister and member, along with Campbell, of Cincinnati's Western Literary Institute and College of Professional Teachers. Most influential was John Locke and his treatise entitled *Thoughts on Education.* From these sources, Campbell developed what would have been considered in his time a conservative, conventional, or classical view of education.

Missing from his sources are the innovative work of Francis Wayland at Brown University; the forward-looking dual track curriculum of President Nott at Union College; the innovations of President Henry Tappan in building the University of Michigan; the reforms of Henry Dwight and others. Missing, too, is the Yale Report of 1828, considered a landmark in the history of higher education. Although Campbell nearly mirrored its content as well as the Yale curriculum in the founding of Bethany College twelve years later, there is no reference to it in any of his published works. The Yale Report is viewed today as a product of the humanist, liberal arts tradition, a conventional, classical educational philosophy quite contrary to the buoyant, optimistic expansiveness of the Jacksonian Age.

The predominant feature of Campbell's educational philosophy was the moral formation of character. He believed that moral excellence was the chief end of education, that the spirit was the radiating center of the whole human system. The moral nature of persons, he argued, is superior to their intellectual and physical nature because it is in the moral nature of persons that the virtues of benevolence, justice, compassion, and generosity are developed and that human excellence is achieved. Moral excellence appeared repeatedly in Campbell's writings and invariably referred to what he believed the most important characteristic of an educated person. "The formation of moral character, the culture of the heart," he wrote in 1840, "is the supreme end of education. . . . with me education and the formation of moral character are identical expressions."

What Campbell achieved at Bethany College, founded on his farm in 1840, was a philosophical blend of Christian and Enlightenment ideals. He

Bethany College became for many nineteenth-century members of the Stone-Campbell Movement the premier institution of higher education.

fashioned a collegiate education that served the intellectual, moral, vocational, and religious development of students, an education that served the wholeness of a person, an education illuminated by the polar star of moral coherence.

4. Stone-Campbell Colleges, 1840 to 1866

Individual constituents founded 115 educational institutions in the Movement in the period between 1840 and 1866, the year of Alexander Campbell's death. Of that number, eighty-three constituted an uncoordinated, localized, and disparate network of private high schools, variously called academies, institutes, or seminaries. Life for most was of short duration. As predecessors of the public high school, they represented an ephemeral and transitional stage in American education. No charters, no catalogues, and few records remain to testify that they existed; but their contributions to the literacy of the Movement and of the society are incalculable. The academies, institutes, and seminaries made their contributions over a short historical period, quickly becoming obsolete, and were soon crowded out of existence by the rapidly expanding public school system. The strongest among them made a gradual transition to two- or four-year colleges.

Of the Movement's 115 institutions, thirty-two were colleges, rooted in the settled ways of rural communities where they attempted to insulate themselves from what they thought to be the evils of urban America. Stone-Campbell colleges sprouted all over the western landscape where the proliferation of industry, railroads, canals, roads, mining, and agriculture created a heavy demand for technicians and managers. In spite of their rural isolation, colleges within the Movement were continually faced with the dilemma of whether their primary obligation was to serve the community or to serve learning. They tried to serve both.

Entrepreneurial ministers or professional educators who were church members founded most colleges within the Movement in that era. These colleges mirrored the educational model offered at Bethany College and were among the earliest schools to pioneer the concept of coeducation and female education. Curriculum was characterized by an emphasis upon biblical literacy, classical languages and literature, moral character, and natural sciences. Graduates were attracted most strongly to public service — education and ministry — with law a close third. Unfortunately, the mortality rate among these new schools was 80 percent, a rate that would last throughout the century.

5. Stone-Campbell Colleges, 1866 to 1900

The Civil War was a watershed in the history of American higher education, separating the era of the small, sectarian college from the era of the large, secular university. The post–Civil War industrial boom spawned the rise of the university, a response to demands for vocational and specialized education in a capital-driven economy. Founded by wealthy industrialists rather than clergy, and administered by professional academics instead of ministers, new secular universities appeared.

But the Stone-Campbell Movement was not idle. Between 1867 and 1899 the Movement established seventy-nine colleges and seventy-four academies and institutes. The border states of Kentucky and Missouri accounted for twenty and eighteen colleges respectively, while the South, heartland of the future Churches of Christ, established a total of twenty-five colleges, fifteen of those in Tennessee and eight in Texas. Twelve colleges were founded north of the Mason-Dixon Line, of which eight were in Ohio. The remaining colleges were established in the trans-Missouri West, primarily in California and Oregon. In addition, the Movement originated the campus ministry movement along with creating Bible chairs, divinity houses, and schools of religion within the growing university system as a means of serving those members who elected to attend tax-supported state universities.

Of the seventy-four academies and institutes, thirty-seven were founded in the eleven former Confederate states, sixteen in the border states, twelve in the North, and nine in the West. Public high schools were scarce outside the cities until the 1890s; and the Movement with its rural orientation continued to establish a sizeable number of these institutions, but at a declining rate and predominately in the South, where there was no compulsory school attendance law until the 1890s. Impoverished by the war and missing a generation of college-age youth who had died in battle, the South was unable to respond to postwar educational reforms. Colleges in Southern states held closely to the classical curriculum and were less inclined than colleges in other sections to incorporate the new elective system or other developments of the period.

There were fifteen attempts between 1868 and 1950 to found a college for African American constituents of the Movement. Most failed before they actually began or at best lasted on average for two to seven years. Among the more successful efforts were Southern Christian Institute, which functioned from 1872 to 1954, and Jarvis Christian College, Hawkins, Texas, founded in 1913, which continues in covenant with the Christian Church (Disciples of Christ).

Late in the nineteenth century, ideological tensions in the Movement impacted the life of the colleges. Debate occurred regularly among alumni, church leaders, and trustees on the character of the colleges as either too secularized or too sectarian. Theological disagreement within the Movement set school against school and created bitter internal factions on many campuses. The story of college founding in Texas provides a devastating example of the effect of theological division upon resources and loyalties. Twenty-three colleges were founded in Texas between 1865 and 1929, twelve by the Churches of Christ and eleven by the Disciples of Christ. The Churches of Christ colleges averaged ten years of life while the Disciples colleges averaged twenty-two years. Only three of these early institutions exist today: Abilene Christian University, related to the Churches of Christ; and Texas Christian University and Jarvis Christian College, in covenant with the Christian Church (Disciples of Christ). The excessive number of schools spawned out of theological rivalry spread the resources of the Movement much too thin and must be recognized as a major factor contributing to their failure.

The Campbellian principle of "non-sectarianism" weakened in the years following the Civil War. Competition with the new state universities led to the idea that educating ministers should occur in the undergraduate colleges in the Movement. The effect was to increase the role of the colleges as servants to the Movement. Controversy over the theological orthodoxy of college presidents and curricula suggested that faith was beginning to supersede knowledge. The Stone-Campbell colleges were significantly more sectarian during the late nineteenth century than they had been during the early years of founding prior to the Civil War.

6. Stone-Campbell Colleges, 1900 to 2000

The third and last significant period of college founding within the Movement lasted from 1900 to 1920, when fifty-four institutions took root. Twenty-nine of those institutions were established in former Confederate states and were largely affiliated with Churches of Christ; nine were founded in border states; ten were founded in the North; and six were founded in the Far West.

These institutions were still under the influence of Campbellian educational philosophy, but with a stronger sectarian tone. In fact, most of them were best characterized as Bible colleges with large numbers of their students preparing to enter some form of ministry. The average enrollment per institution during the first two decades of the century was just over 300 students. The presidents were, almost to a person, ordained ministers, recipients of undergraduate degrees from other Stone-Campbell–related colleges, recipients of advanced degrees in theology, and recipients of their first administrative experience at still another college within the Movement. The Stone-Campbell network tended to produce its own

"College men" at a conference at Winona Lake, Indiana, August 1910. *Front:* T. E. Cramblet, E. V. Zollars (Oklahoma Christian University, later Phillips University), Jones Johnson, Chancellor, Oesonger; *Back:* Ashley S. Johnson (Johnson Bible College), Thompson, Gray, Professor Taylor, M. L. Bates, Josephus Hopwood (Milligan College).

Courtesy of Johnson Bible College Photo Archive

leadership, which often isolated it from the main currents of educational reform.

College founding within the Movement between 1920 and the late 1960s produced sixty colleges, along with an assorted list of twenty-nine Bible colleges, schools, academies, and seminaries. The overwhelming number of twentieth-century colleges were founded by Churches of Christ and Christian Churches/Churches of Christ. The Disciples decelerated their efforts to establish new institutions and concentrated their energy on developing cooperation, a covenantal relationship, among the existing institutions through a general service agency first called the Board of Education (1894) and then in 1978 renamed the Division of Higher Education of the Christian Church (Disciples of Christ). Disciples have not established a new four-year college since the appearance of Jarvis Christian College in 1913. The last higher education institution of any kind to be established by Disciples as of 2004 was the Disciples Seminary Foundation at Claremont, California, in 1960.

Across the 166 years from the founding of Bacon College to the present, the Stone-Campbell Movement made four distinct and unique contributions to American higher education: (1) the significant place given to the study of the Bible in the undergraduate curriculum; (2) the pioneering of coeducation and female education; (3) the establishment of Bible chairs, divinity houses, and schools of religion at tax-supported colleges and universities — considered by many as the most original contribution; and (4) development and advancement of the concept of campus ministry on state-owned campuses. It is a legacy that speaks forcefully for the role of the church in the educational enterprise.

See also Bethany College; Bible Chair Movement; Bible College Movement; Campus Ministry; Division of Higher Education; Education, Philosophy of

BIBLIOGRAPHY Rolla J. Bennett, "History of the Founding of Educational Institutions by the Disciples in Virginia and West Virginia" (unpublished Ph.D. dissertation, University of Pittsburgh, 1932) • G. T. Carpenter, "Our Colleges," *Christian Quarterly Review* 4 (1885) • D. Duane Cummins, *The Disciples Colleges: A History* (1987) • D. Duane Cummins, "Educational Philosophy of Alexander Campbell," *Discipliana* 59 (1999): 5-15 • Gustave Ferre, "A Concept of Higher Education and Its Relation to the Christian Faith as Evidenced in the Writings of Alexander Campbell" (unpublished Ph.D. dissertation, Vanderbilt University, 1958) • Albertina A. Forrest, "Status of Education Among Disciples," *The New Christian Quarterly* 5 (1896) • Perry E. Gresham, *Campbell and the Colleges* (1973) • John L. Morrison, *Alexander Campbell: Educating the Moral Person* (1991) • William B. Sharratt, "The Theory of Religious Education of Alexander Campbell and Its Influence upon the Educational Attitudes of the Disciples of Christ" (unpublished Ph.D. dissertation, New York University, 1930) • Donald Tewksbury, *The Founding of American Colleges and Universities Before the Civil War* (1932) • Gerald C. Tiffin, "Disciples and Higher Education: Nineteenth-Century Roots and Twenty-First Century Concerns," *Discipliana* 59 (1999): 17-24.

D. DUANE CUMMINS

Hiram College

Related to the Christian Church (Disciples of Christ).

The Western Reserve Eclectic Institute, Hiram, Ohio, was one of the earliest educational institutions established by the Disciples of Christ. Its principals and presidents include some of the most distinguished names in the Stone-Campbell Movement, such as A. S. Hayden, James Garfield, and E. V. Zollars.

The genesis of the Western Reserve Eclectic Institute occurred in 1849 during a yearly meeting of the Disciples of Christ in Russell, Ohio. Mr. A. L. Soule invited any interested individuals to meet at his house to discuss the dream of starting a school. This meeting was the culmination of William Hayden's efforts, who had previously worked to maintain interest in the idea. The meeting resulted in the formation of an investigating committee to explore the concept. Mr. Latin Soule chaired the meeting, and Amos Sutton Hayden (brother to William Hayden) was chosen as secretary. Following several meetings, concrete steps toward the establishment of the school were taken at Ravenna, Ohio, on October 3, 1849. It was there that a discussion took place about the type of institution to be established — college or high school. The decision was made to begin a high school–level institution.

The location committee was chosen, and they visited the seven townships that wanted the school. During the November 7, 1849, meeting, in Aurora, Ohio, the site of the school was chosen by ballot. Hiram was selected after twelve ballots. The town was perceived to have many advantages: it was at a distance from large towns, the environment of the region was considered healthy and beneficial, there was an active Disciples of Christ church, and the town had pledged $4,000 in subscriptions to help establish the school.

When the school was established in 1850, the name Western Reserve Eclectic Institute was suggested by Isaac Errett, minister to the Disciples of Christ Church in North Bloomfield, Ohio. The coeducational institution began its first term of instruction on November 27, 1850, with Amos Sutton Hayden serving as principal and teacher. The faculty was completed with the inclusion of Thomas Munnell, teaching ancient languages and history, and Mrs. Phoebe M. Drake, who was principal of the primary department. The school was an immediate success, achieving a record enrollment in 1852-53 of some 529 students. This record would stand unchallenged until after World War II.

The name of the school was changed on February 20, 1867, to Hiram College, to reflect the higher academic status and goals of the college. The last commencement of the Western Reserve Eclectic Institute was held on June 13, 1867. Hiram College began its first classes on August 13, 1867. Hiram College continued the coeducational status of the institute. Dr. Silas E. Shephard was the first president of the college. The college was not a Bible college or theological school, although a biblical department was established for the training of ministers. The college was given the authority to grant degrees, a privilege the institute had never enjoyed. The North Central Association of Schools and Colleges accredited Hiram College in 1914. Accreditation by the Association of American Universities followed in 1928.

In the 1930s Hiram developed the "Hiram Study Plan," which substituted intensive nine-week courses for the multiple courses typically pursued by college students. This program identified Hiram as an innovator in the field of undergraduate higher education. In 1977 Hiram introduced its Weekend College to make Hiram courses available to nontraditional students. Total Hiram enrollment in spring 2003 was 941 full-time and 258 part-time students, coming from twenty-seven states and territories and nineteen countries.

See also Garfield, James Abram; Hayden, Amos Sutton; Munnell, Thomas; Zollars, Ely Vaughan

BIBLIOGRAPHY F. Green, *History of Hiram College* (1901) • A. Hayden, *A History of the Disciples on the Western Reserve* • M. Treudley, *Prelude to the Future — The First Hundred Years of Hiram College* (1950).

GARY L. LEE

Hiram House

A settlement house organized in a blighted, immigrant neighborhood of Cleveland, Ohio, in 1896 by George A. Bellamy (1873-1960), a graduate of Disciples of Christ–related Hiram College.

Settlement houses were a social experiment designed to alleviate the rapidly growing social problems of urban America. From a religious perspective, such efforts were part of the Social Gospel, in which the church moved from addressing primarily the salvation of the individual soul to the socioeconomic and educational improvement of society at large. Using his alma mater as a namesake, Bellamy's Hiram House became the first settlement house in Ohio, and one of the first in the entire country. It was designed to provide a safe, clean, healthy, and intellectually stimulating haven within which originally economically deprived immigrants could socialize and learn to become good American citizens. Innovative and energetic, Bellamy also established an effective kindergarten and children's clubs that both took care of young children, allowing mothers time to work, and kept older children occupied during after-school hours with constructive activities. Recognizing the healthy stimulation of outdoor recreation, he established the first lighted playground in the United States and became a sought-after consultant for such recreational projects throughout the nation.

Hiram House was closed in 1947, but its camping and recreational dimension maintains a vibrant existence as Hiram House Camp, located at Chagrin Falls near Cleveland.

BIBLIOGRAPHY "George A. Bellamy," in *American Settlement Houses and Progressive Social Reform: An Encyclopedia of the American Settlement Movement* (1999).

WES HARRISON

Hispanics in the Movement

1. Introduction

Although the Stone-Campbell Movement reached Texas by 1824 — when it was still a Mexican territory — no concerted effort was made to reach Hispanics until the end of the nineteenth century. There were two reasons for such inaction. First, the Stone-Campbell Movement was an American frontier phenomenon that shared many of the ideological presuppositions of its time. It was shaped, thus, by the manifest destiny ideology, the myth that the frontier land was a "wilderness" to be conquered and civilized, and "paradigms of difference in which the indigenous people were identified as inferior because of their race, religion, and culture." Second, Hispanics were largely considered foreigners; they were not considered real "Americans." This presupposition allowed members of the Stone-Campbell Movement to overlook even the people of Mexican ancestry who had lived for several generations in Texas, Oklahoma, New Mexico, Arizona, and California.

To some extent, these ideas still determine the role of Hispanics in the Stone-Campbell Movement. The churches of the Stone-Campbell Movement have been mainly "American" churches that serve primarily people of Anglo-European descent and whose outreach to Hispanics is one among many efforts to diversify their racial, ethnic, and cultural base. In many ways, Hispanics are still seen as "foreigners."

One figure from the early nineteenth century deserves mention. In 1823 José María Jesús Carvajal (1810-1874) from San Antonio (then part of Mexico) moved to Kentucky at the invitation of Littleberry Hawkins, a traveling merchant. In Kentucky he was baptized in 1826 at the Reformed Baptist Church in Lexington and heard Alexander Campbell preach. The next year, at age 17, he moved to Bethany, where he studied and lived with the Campbells until 1830. Upon returning to San Antonio, his training in Stone-Campbell principles led him to distribute Spanish-language Bibles and preach in his home region. His political ideals, however, also learned during his sojourn in Kentucky and Virginia, led him to devote most of his energies to revolution and political freedom for the northern states of Mexico. His religious work resulted in no lasting presence of the Stone-Campbell Movement in Texas or Mexico.

2. Missionary Foci: Texas and Puerto Rico

The end of the nineteenth century saw the beginnings of missionary work with Spanish-speaking people in the continental United States and in the Caribbean. In both cases, the line between overseas and domestic missions was somewhat blurred. In both cases, these missionary efforts led to the creation of congregations in foreign countries and in the United States.

The Movement began to reach out to Hispanics in the borderlands of the continental United States by the end of the nineteenth century. Spanish-speaking congregations were established in northern Mexico and in south and central Texas. In both cases, the church planters were mainly American missionaries who were fluent in Spanish or who spoke through interpreters. North of the border, some ministers began to reach out to Hispanics, using bilingual "Tejanos" to translate their sermons.

As early as 1871 some interest in evangelizing Hispanics was seen when J. R. Wilmeth made a survey trip to Mexico and urged readers of the *Gospel Advocate* to consider moving to the country to establish a Christian colony as a base for evangelization. Early in 1898 Wilmeth's brother, C. M. Wilmeth, did lead a group of Texas members of Churches of Christ to establish a colony near Bryan City, not far from Tampico. His death in October crippled the effort, but the colonization idea continued to be viable especially in Churches of Christ until the Mexican Revolution and political unrest that began in 1910. Focus then shifted to work among Hispanics in the southwestern United States.

Congregations were established in several cities, the first being Mexican Christian Church in San Antonio, which was organized by pastor Y. Quintero in 1899. By 1916 Hispanic Disciples created the "State Mexican S. S. Convention," whose records mention seven congregations: two in Mexico, two in San Antonio, one in Sabinas, one in Lockhart, and another in Robstown. However, the situation of these congregations was fluid. Some of them closed for several years before being restarted. Others closed permanently years later. In still other cases, the establishment or closing of Hispanic congregations depended on the comings and goings of Anglo-European ministers interested in reaching Hispanics, bilingual preachers, and Hispanic pastors.

A factor that still hinders Hispanic ministries in the Southwest is that little or no efforts were made to train Mexican Christians for ministry. Many of the ministers who established the first congregations came from Mexico, products of the missionary efforts in that country.

A second focus of the Movement's missionary efforts among Hispanics was Puerto Rico, which became a territory of the United States in 1898, ceded by Spain after losing the Spanish-American War. Missionaries sent by the American Christian Missionary Society and the Christian Woman's Board of Missions reached the island by 1899.

Puerto Rican Disciples have played a prominent role in the development of Hispanic ministries in the Christian Church (Disciples of Christ) in the United States and Canada. Puerto Rican ministers, serving mainly Puerto Rican immigrants, established the first Hispanic Disciples congregations in the Northeast. As in Texas, Disciples in the Northeast made little or no efforts to train Hispanic ministers. Instead, they imported Puerto Rican ministers who were usually graduates from the Evangelical Seminary of Puerto Rico and ordained by the Disciples on that island.

La Hermosa Christian Church was the first Hispanic Disciples congregation established in New York. The origins of this congregation point to another trend in Hispanic ministries among Disciples. La Hermosa was established in 1939 by an independent group of Puerto Rican immigrants. At the very beginning, the congregation was not related to the Disciples. However, through contacts with the Disciples in Puerto Rico, the congregation became a Disciples congregation in 1943 after securing the services of Pablo Cotto, who came originally from Dajaos Christian Church, the second oldest Disciples congregation in Puerto Rico.

La Hermosa Christian Church helped to establish several Hispanic congregations in the greater New York area. It also ushered some independent congregations into the Disciples fold. For decades, it functioned as the "mother church" of most Hispanic Disciples congregations in the region. Later on, other Hispanic congregations in other parts of the country followed the model established by La Hermosa.

At the beginning of the twenty-first century, the Southwest and the Northeast continue to be the two foci of Hispanic ministries among Disciples. The patterns established from the very beginning have been difficult to change. It is still the case that many Hispanic ministers have little or no formal theological education. Many immigrated to the United States after completing their theological education and obtaining their ordination elsewhere; many Hispanic ministers — including key leaders of the Hispanic Disciples — still come from Puerto Rico.

3. Christian Church (Disciples of Christ)

3.1. Changing Policies and Leadership

A critical aspect of this history is the changing missionary, ministerial, and evangelistic policies followed by the Disciples in their dealings with Hispanics. As demonstrated by Daisy L. Machado, by 1919 the presence of Mexicans in Texas was referred to as the "Mexican problem" in the Disciples newspapers. This reaction was no doubt due to the increased migration of Mexicans who, fleeing the revolution, had moved into the southwest borderlands of the United States. The issue is, How can a church minister effectively to a population that is considered foreign, inferior, and transitory?

In part, Disciples responded by establishing a missionary model that tried to assist the community. The goal was to create institutions that would offer social services in conjunction with the established congregations. The congregation would serve the "spiritual needs" and the civic institution the social ones. The creation of the Mexican Christian Institute in 1913 — later to be known as the Inman Christian Center — alongside Mexican Christian Church in San Antonio was an expression of this missionary model. This model was largely ineffective, particularly because it could not be replicated in other parts of the country. Even in San Antonio, the center became larger and more influential than the congregations. Machado asserts that the center provided "Texas Disciples a way to assume the role of benevolent giant as opposed to that of humble servant. Given the many layers of manifest destiny ideology so prevalent during this time, the important task of 'civilizing and Christianizing' inferior 'strangers' was a role the Disciples understood."

Another perceived problem was the way in which second-generation Hispanics — particularly Puerto Ricans in the Northeast — clung to their roots, their language, and their customs. Byron Spice, in his book *Discípulos Americanos (Spanish American Disciples): Sixty-five Years of Ministry to Spanish-Speaking Persons* (1964) argues: "The second generation English-speaking Puerto Rican is in many ways a 'lost' generation. He still feels too Puerto Rican to be completely at home among 'Americanos' and too 'Americano' to be comfortable with the 'old folks.'" Spice, who served as Director of Homeland Ministries of the United Missionary Society, expected Hispanics to fully integrate themselves to the American "melting pot": "Complete acculturation would probably be experienced when Spanish-speaking people completely accept our Anglo culture (including language, food habits, mannerisms) and are completely accepted by Anglos. Acculturation is certainly taking place but it varies in degree from city to city." He saw Hispanic congregations as bridges, needed only for first-generation immigrants whose children would surely become members of Anglo-European congregations: "The Spanish-language churches provide a training ground where Spanish-speaking persons can prepare themselves to take their places as members and possible leaders in English-speaking churches. . . . Perhaps the goal of our work is to bring about such a degree of acculturation that eventually all will worship in English-speaking churches." Therefore, Spice believed that Hispanic and bilingual congregations were a temporary phenomenon, needed only for a relatively short time. This is clear in the following assertion: "There are indications that the Spanish language will be used in certain areas of the United States for at least another twenty-five or thirty years."

Even though many of Spice's ideas have been proven wrong by time, his leadership was key in the development of Disciples Hispanic ministries. First, his book correctly interpreted many aspects of Hispanic life, asserting that Hispanics were bicultural people. Second, it provided good advice on how non-Hispanics could relate to Hispanics. Third, Spice organized a Consultation on Hispanic Ministry, held in Indianapolis May 9-13, 1966. The meeting included Hispanic-American leaders as well as representatives from Disciples-related churches in Mexico and Puerto Rico. Although he repeated there his mistaken idea that Hispanic congregations were to be bridges that would solely facilitate the integration of Spanish-speaking people to Anglo-European congregations, the meeting gave Hispanic leaders an opportunity to network in ways never done before. Finally, in 1969 Spice called Domingo Rodríguez (b. 1918) to serve as director of the Office of Programs and Services for Hispanic and Bilingual Congregations of the Division of Homeland Ministries of the United Missionary Society. Rodríguez was the first Hispanic to serve in such a capacity. Born, raised, educated, and ordained in Puerto Rico, he had also served as pastor of La Hermosa Christian Church (1953-55). More importantly, Rodríguez had also served as the first executive secretary of the Christian Church (Disciples of Christ) in Puerto Rico (1958-62).

When Domingo Rodríguez came to his new position he found that, after seventy years of ministry, there were only eighteen Hispanic and bilingual Disciples congregations in the United States. In his brief tenure (1969-72), Domingo made significant changes. He established an aggressive church revitalization and church planting policy. For example, he reopened Emmanuel Christian Church in San Benito, Texas, and recruited the couple who founded Fuente de Vida Christian Church in Gardena, California. Rodríguez also organized the first Conference on Hispanic American Ministries, held in Indianapolis April 6-10, 1970. A total of thirty-eight ministers, representing eleven states, participated in the conference. This meeting provided opportunities for networking, for reaching common agreements, and for planning for the future, establishing a Committee on Guidelines for Strategy and Action.

Placing Hispanic ministries under the care of an experienced and visionary Hispanic minister changed the face of the Christian Church (Disciples of Christ) in the United States and Canada. First, it furthered tremendous church growth among Hispanic Disciples. Second, it caused important structural changes in the denomination.

3.2. Congregational Growth

Hispanic Disciples grew tremendously during the last four decades of the twentieth century. As stated, after the first seventy years of Disciples Hispanic ministries only eighteen congregations survived. At the beginning of the twenty-first century, there were over 120 Hispanic and Bilingual congregations and missions in the Christian Church (Disciples of Christ) in the United States and Canada.

This rapid growth is the result of several factors. The first is the continuous growth of the Hispanic population in the United States. In 1964 the Census estimated that 6 million Hispanics lived in the United States. By 2002, according to the Census, the Hispanic population was over 38 million people.

A second factor, related to the first, is changing patterns of migration. For example, in the late 1970s Puerto Ricans began to migrate to Florida in large numbers. At the time there were no Hispanic Disciples congregations in the State. Today there are twenty-two Hispanic and Bilingual congregations, most led by Puerto Rican ministers. By the same token, the increased migration of Central Americans and Mexican Americans to the Southwest explains the new crop of congregations in Texas and California.

A third factor is the new missionary policies promoted by Hispanic Disciples leaders. The aggressive church revitalization and planting policy begun by Rodríguez was followed by his immediate successors, Lucas Torres (b. 1933), David Vargas (b. 1944), and Luis Ferrer (b. 1944). In particular, Vargas's ministry was determinant in this process, given his excellent administrative, planning, and organizational skills.

Finally, the organization of the National Hispanic and Bilingual Fellowship and of several Hispanic Conventions in different parts of the country gave Hispanic Disciples the opportunity to better organize, to decide their own future, and to develop effective tools and policies for ministry.

3.3. Structural Changes

After the 1970 Conference on Hispanic Ministries, Hispanic leaders continued meeting regularly at General Assemblies and special meetings. The Committee on Guidelines for Strategy and Action reorganized itself in October 1971 as a board, creating the Conference of Hispanic American Ministers. In October 1973, the group called on Lucas Torres to organize a strategic planning event. The National Strategy Conference on Hispanic Ministries took place in New York during the summer of 1975. Its main achievement was the creation of a Committee on Hispanic Ministries. The Hispanic Caucus was born out of this body. The importance of the caucus cannot be minimized. This body developed the plans that led to the creation of the National Hispanic and Bilingual Fellowship of the Christian Church (Disciples of Christ) in the United States and Canada and the celebration of the First National Hispanic and Bilingual Assembly.

Torres's leadership was also characterized by educational efforts, which included publishing among other resources "Dignidad," a book on Hispanic ministries and culture. He also organized the first "Encuentro Hispano," a biennial meeting that takes place at every General Assembly.

David Vargas succeeded Torres in 1978. Like Rodríguez and Torres, he was born, raised, educated, and ordained by the Disciples in Puerto Rico. Vargas shepherded Hispanic Disciples through a treacherous political process. First, he strengthened the existing Hispanic conventions. Besides the Southwest Convention, Hispanics had organized the Northeast Convention (1958) and the Midwest Convention (1978). Later on Hispanics organized the Southeast (1990) and the Pacific Southwest (1990) Conventions. These structures not only provided opportunities for networking but also promoted leadership development and the establishment of new congregations. Second, Vargas led the Hispanic Caucus in the process of establishing the Hispanic and Bilingual Fellowship in 1980 and organizing its first Assembly on June 24-26, 1981.

Luis Ferrer succeeded Vargas in 1983, when Vargas became executive secretary for Latin America and the Caribbean of the Division of Overseas Ministries. Like his predecessors, Ferrer is an ethnic Puerto Rican. In contrast to his predecessors, Ferrer grew up and was educated and ordained in the States. Under Ferrer's tenure the Hispanic Caucus embarked on its most ambitious project: changing the structure of the Christian Church (Disciples of Christ) in the United States and Canada.

Until the early 1990s, Hispanic ministries among Disciples had been coordinated from an office in the Department of Evangelism of the Division of Homeland Ministries. The growth and increased agency of Hispanic Disciples created serious tensions between Hispanic leaders and the Division. After exploring different alternatives — which included the creation of a non-geographic region — the group promoted the idea of creating an office that would respond directly to the General Board of the Church. This gave the office great flexibility and independence. Furthermore, this gave Hispanics the opportunity to elect their own leaders, leaders that would be primarily accountable to them.

The new general ministry, established in 1991, was called the Central Pastoral Office for Hispanic Ministries. Its manager is the National Pastor for Hispanic Ministries. The word "national" refers to the fact that Hispanics constitute a "nation" within the United States. The Central Pastoral Office for Hispanic Ministries has the following objectives: to develop programs and to offer pastoral care to Hispanic ministers, lay leaders, and congregations; to advise and counsel the different regional and general bodies of the Christian Church (Disciples of Christ) on Hispanic ministry; and to be an advocate for Hispanic Disciples. The Pastoral Commission for Hispanic Ministries is the governing board of the Central Pastoral Office for Hispanic Ministries. This is composed of the Hispanic Caucus, plus a representative of General Ministries, a representative from Regional Ministries, two members of the General Board, and the general minister and president.

The first National Pastor for Hispanic Ministries was David A. Vargas, whose leadership had been determinant in this process. Vargas served on a part-time basis until 1993. Lucas Torres served in this position until his retirement in 1999. Torres's tenure was marked by several achievements, such as holding a second Strategic Conference, developing a hymnal in Spanish, and publishing several worship resources for Hispanic congregations. Since 2000, Pablo A. Jiménez (b. 1960) has served as National Pastor. Jiménez has developed several educational resources in Spanish, such as the Christian Video Library and "Camino al Discipulado," a curriculum resource for the formation of new believers.

PABLO A. JIMÉNEZ

4. Churches of Christ (Iglesias de Cristo)

Though some work was done by members of Churches of Christ among the Hispanic community of El Paso, Texas, by E. N. Glenn and a Mexican preacher named J. M. Martínez as early as 1911, the story of Iglesias de Cristo begins in 1919. That year Howard Schug (1881-1969), a language professor at Abilene Christian University, began going door to door and reading Bible stories to children in the Mexican neighborhoods of Abilene. This eventually led to the baptism of some adults and the beginning of Hispanic ministry in the United States by Churches of Christ. In 1924 several congregations, led by the University Church of Christ in Abilene, built a building at North 2nd and Cottonwood Streets for Spanish-speaking members. Early preachers and missionaries in the effort to evangelize the Spanish speaking were John F. Wolfe (1901-1987) in El Paso; Hilario Zamorano in Dallas, Los Angeles, and Austin; Mack Kercheville and Caledonio Zúñiga in El Paso; and J. W. Treat (1907-1998) in Abilene. Some not only did local work but also helped encourage the work in other places both in the United States and in Mexico.

In 1928 there were about eighty known members of Iglesias de Cristo with their numbers clustered in and around west Texas. By 1930 the number had grown to around 250 members with the addition of works in the Rio Grande Valley of South Texas. In 1958 the numbers had grown to fifty congregations with 2,000 members.

While the movement to evangelize the Spanish-speaking population was led by Anglos like Schug, Treat, Wolfe, and Haven Miller, a key element in the early success of their efforts was the training of indigenous converts to take the lead in local works. Almost exclusively the early work among the Spanish speaking in Churches of Christ was among Mexicans in Texas. William N. (Bill) Stivers in California and Carl James in Florida helped the work to spread outside of Texas. The Sunset School of Preaching in Lubbock, Texas, trained many of the preachers that have worked with Iglesias de Cristo. Preaching schools in Torreon and Monterrey, Mexico, have also provided a large number of Spanish-speaking preachers for Iglesias de Cristo.

In 1995 there were an estimated 215 congregations of Iglesias de Cristo in the United States, 141 of them in Texas. California followed with forty-three, then Florida with seven. Estimates of nationwide membership were around 10,000. In 1930 Howard Schug was motivated by the fact that there were about half a million Mexicans on the northern side of the Rio Grande. Today there are about 40 million Hispanics in the United States, and all signs point to continuing explosive growth among this section of the population.

After enjoying significant success in Hispanic outreach during the period between 1950 and the early 1970s, numerical growth ceased. While the desire to evangelize the Hispanic community continued strong in Churches of Christ, ignorance of sociological factors severely limited effectiveness. While Hispanics (especially among the Mexican community) were once a monolingual people that lived in secluded enclaves and had little to do with the mainstream culture, that is no longer the case. Because the majority of congregations of Iglesias de Cristo are located in Texas, recent strategies have focused on understanding and influencing the Texas churches in order to change the national picture. In south Texas society, for example, most professional roles are filled by Hispanics. Teachers, lawyers, and doctors increasingly come from the Hispanic community. While there are still many who are content to live in "little Mexico," younger generations are being educated in and mainstreaming into the dominant culture. At the same time, the dominant church model in Iglesias de Cristo continues to require people either to live in the "barrio" or return to the barrio in order to participate in church life. In order to continue to reach the Hispanic population of Texas and the rest of the United States, leaders in Iglesias de Cristo are creating new models of "doing church" that resonate with Hispanic culture and experience.

A second factor that has limited effectiveness in recent decades is the lack of theological education among Hispanic ministers. As Hispanics achieve higher educational levels, the need for church leaders to keep pace and lead the way is increasingly crucial. The growing gap between the education of Hispanics in general and most ministers in Iglesias de Cristo has led to many preachers being seen as ignorant or irrelevant. Often the Spanish-speaking congregations serve more as a cultural preservation society than as a colony or outpost of the kingdom of God. One area that Hispanic leaders see as a hopeful sign is the interest colleges and universities affiliated with Churches of Christ have taken in the success of Hispanic ministries in recent years. Efforts to provide culturally relevant theological training will be an increasing priority in these schools in the twenty-first century. ABEL ALVAREZ

5. Christian Churches/Churches of Christ

Involvement of Christian Churches/Churches of Christ in ministry to and with Hispanics has its early roots in independent missionary and evangelistic initiatives in Mexico. In more recent years these churches have cultivated new initiatives to Hispanic American communities, principally (but not exclusively) in larger cities, based not only on renewed awareness of the need for "homeland" missions but on sensitivity to a lack of ethnic diversity among the Christian Churches/Churches of Christ.

Independent missions in Mexico were boosted in 1945 by the establishment of a Spanish-speaking college, Colegio Biblico. The school was strategically located in Eagle Pass, Texas, just across the Mexican border, and while its primary purpose was (and is) to educate ministers and leaders for Mexican churches, the college has also had graduates serving ministries in the United States. The Mexican-American border in time came to be an area of concentrated outreach to Hispanics among Christian Churches/Churches of Christ. The work of Spanish American Evangelism (now Spanish American Evangelistic Ministries [SAEM]), established in 1964 by Freeman Bump, reflects the pattern of independent missions inevitably moving toward greater organizational sophistication. What began largely as a church-planting mission has come to include multifaceted ministries of publication (tracts and Bibles), broadcasting, and benevolence. SAEM's original ministry was to Hispanics of El Paso and Cuidad Juárez, but the organization has increasingly envisioned itself as advocating for missions of the Christian Churches/Churches of Christ to Spanish-speaking peoples throughout the world. SAEM now produces a *Spanish Directory of the Ministry* listing missionary and ministerial endeavors of these churches among Hispanics in North America and worldwide.

Other missionary organizations of the Christian Churches/Churches of Christ have also launched work among Hispanic communities within the United States. Since 1998, the Indianapolis-based Christian Missionary Fellowship has planted "intercultural" ministries to Hispanics in the greater Los Angeles area and in Indianapolis. The model is one of creating strong local churches with Spanish-speaking ministers and worship, and with ministries specifically targeting the needs of urban-dwelling Hispanics (e.g., Spanish-speaking Sunday Schools and Bible studies; sponsorship of courses in English as a second language; Vacation Bible School programs; mothers' clubs; and children's clubs).

Team Expansion, a Louisville-based missionary organization, has likewise made commitments to church planting, evangelism, and the training of ethnic Hispanic ministers and leaders principally in the greater Miami area and in the Pacific Northwest.

The same pattern of missionary strategy has been undertaken among Portuguese-speaking immigrant communities in the Northeast under the auspices of Hisportic Christian Mission, founded in 1984 and headquartered in East Providence, Rhode Island. Since its inception the mission has been focused and, as of 2003, had seventeen congregations in its registry — all served by native Portuguese-speaking (Brazilian) ministers — spread from Massachusetts to New Jersey.

Over and beyond missions to Hispanics maintained by missionary organizations, most of which primarily build networks of support and facilitate the ministries of direct-support missionaries, individual congregations of the Christian Churches/Churches of Christ have also undertaken their own Hispanic ministries. The pattern of an Anglo congregation "hosting" a Spanish-speaking congregation or worship services, or partnering with Hispanic Christians in a given locale, has gradually increased in various parts of the United States.

PAUL M. BLOWERS

6. Hopes and Challenges

The future of Hispanic ministries in the Stone-Campbell Movement seems positive. The creation among Disciples of the Central Pastoral Office for Hispanic Ministries has opened many possibilities for change. The rapid establishment of new Hispanic and bilingual congregations in all three streams of the Movement promises to transform the face of the churches. In Disciples organizations a clear evidence of this is the election of Paul D. Rivera as moderator of the Church (1999-2001) and of David A. Vargas as president of the Division of Overseas Ministries in 2003.

However, Hispanics also face several challenges. Leadership development continues to be problematic. Access to contextual theological education is still poor. The presence of Hispanic scholars in the Movement's theological schools is minimal, a fact that explains in part the absence of Hispanic seminarians. Disciples Hispanic ministries are also still overly dependent on immigrant pastors, a situation highlighted by the fact that since Rodríguez, all top Hispanic executives have been ethnic Puerto Ricans, most of whom have been trained and ordained by the Disciples in Puerto Rico.

The hegemony of Puerto Ricans among Hispanic Disciples churches also presents a difficult challenge. The leadership dilemma is worsened by the rapid growth of congregations that now serve Central Americans and Mexican Americans. Puerto Ricans are already the minority in most congregations outside the Eastern seaboard. Disciples must develop more leaders from the diverse ethnic backgrounds that comprise the Hispanic community.

Financing is another serious challenge across the board. Hispanics — particularly Mexican Americans — have lower incomes than the population at large. On average, a Hispanic congregation needs two or three times the number of members of an Anglo-European congregation in order to sustain a full-time minister. This challenge is compounded by a paternalistic mentality that still permeates certain sectors of the churches of the Movement, where people volunteer to share "their" funds with Hispanics, as if Hispanics were outsiders.

Finally, Hispanic ministry is one of the growing edges in the churches of the Stone-Campbell Movement. How the churches of this heritage will be able to nurture this expanding movement is a most serious challenge for the future.

See also Christian Missionary Fellowship; Colegio Biblico; Direct Support Missions; Inman Christian Center; Latin America and Caribbean, Missions in

BIBLIOGRAPHY Abel Alvarez, "History of Iglesias de Cristo to the Present," Abilene Christian University Bible Lectures, 2000 • Harland Cary, "The Ministry of Colegio Biblico," *Christian Standard* 82 (1946): 817-18 • Marilyn Custer, ed., *Directorio del Ministerio de las Iglesias Cristianas y Iglesias de Cristo de Habla Hispana,* published annually, available at http://www.spanam.org/Directorio.pdf • E. N. Glenn, "Why Not a Mission Among the Mexicans?" *Firm Foundation* 37 (December 14, 1920): 2 • Robert L. Johnston, J. W. Treat, and Howard Schug, *The Harvest Field* (1958) • Daisy L. Machado, *Of Borders and Margins: Hispanic Disciples in Texas, 1888-1945* (2003) • Santiago Piñon, "An Ecclesiology for the People: The Church and Iglesias de Cristo" (M.A. thesis, Abilene Christian University, 2003) • Domingo Rodríguez, *Vivencias y Memorias de un Pastor* (1999) • Howard Schug and Jesse P. Sewell, *The Harvest Field* (1947) • Glover Shipp, "Hispanic Ministries," *Christian Chronicle* 52 (August 1995): center spread • Fernando Soto, *La Reforma Presente: Historia del Movimiento de Restauracion de Stone y Campbell* (1997) • Byron Spice, *Discipulos Americanos (Spanish American Disciples): Sixty-five Years of Ministry to Spanish-Speaking Persons* (1964) • David A. Vargas, *Somos Uno: Trasfondo Histórico de la Confraternidad Hispana y Bilingüe.*

Historiography, Stone-Campbell Movement

The writing of history or histories of the Stone-Campbell Movement, or the study and analysis of those written histories. Most histories of the Movement have been written from the perspective of persons from the Christian Church (Disciples of Christ), Churches of Christ, or Christian Churches/Churches of Christ. See "Stone-Campbell History Over Three Centuries: A Survey and Analysis," pp. xxi-xxxv.

Hogan, Richard Nathaniel (1902-1997)

An influential leader of African American Churches of Christ in the twentieth century.

He was born in Monroe County, Arkansas, in 1902. Although reared by his grandparents, Hogan was deeply influenced by G. P. Bowser (1874-1950), a gifted preacher, educator, and editor for black Churches of Christ. Hogan received ministerial training from Bowser at the Silver Point Christian Institute in Silver Point, Tennessee.

This early picture of Hogan exudes his confidence and fearlessness in preaching a "hard gospel" that attacked both denominationalism and the Christian schools that refused to enroll black students. In a June 1959 article "The Sin of Being a Respecter of Persons" in the *Christian Echo,* Hogan blasted segregated schools. Courtesy of the Center for Restoration Studies, Abilene Christian University

In 1920 Hogan and his wife, Maggie Bullock, moved to Detroit, Michigan, where, in addition to preaching, he worked as a plumber and in the automobile industry. A decade later they moved to Chicago, where he helped found a church on the South Side. Between 1933 and 1936, Hogan crisscrossed the country preaching, baptizing, and establishing churches.

In 1937 Hogan went to Los Angeles and established the 110th and Wilmington Church of Christ with forty-four members. Presently known as the Figueroa Church of Christ, this church increased to over 1,000 members through the efforts of Hogan, making it the largest Church of Christ west of the Rocky Mountains. More than a well-known evangelist in the state of California, Hogan became a national leader of black Churches of Christ in 1951, when he assumed the editorship of the *Christian Echo,* a religious journal founded by Bowser in 1902. A staunch supporter of Christian education, Hogan helped to stabilize Southwestern Christian College in Terrell, Texas, and to save the school from closing its doors. Hogan was also a fierce opponent of segregation and racism, calling on white leaders of Christian colleges to open their doors to African American students in the 1960s.

See also African Americans in the Movement; Bowser, George Philip; *Christian Echo;* Southwestern Christian College

BIBLIOGRAPHY Calvin H. Bowers, *Realizing the California Dream: The Story of Black Churches of Christ in Los Angeles* (2001) • R. N. Hogan, *Sermons by Hogan* (1940) • Billie Silvey, "R. N. Hogan: From Nashville 'Boy Preacher' to Spiritual Reference Source for Christians," *Christian Chronicle* (August 1993): 7. EDWARD J. ROBINSON

Holman, Silena Moore (1850-1915)

Temperance leader and vocal advocate for women's equality in the church.

Silena was born July 9, 1850, in Moore County, Tennessee. When her father was killed in the Civil War, Silena, the oldest of five children, took responsibility for the family finances by teaching school. She was only fourteen at the time. She married T. P. Holman, a doctor, in January of 1875. As a mother of eight children, she managed to serve the public for over thirty-five years. During her fifteen-year tenure as president of the Tennessee Woman's Christian Temperance Union (WCTU), the organization grew to over 4,000 members.

In the Stone-Campbell Movement, her recognition came from published articles and letters in response to those in the church who wanted to keep women from positions of leadership. Holman's campaign for women's rights began in 1888, when she responded to an article by David Lipscomb, editor of the *Gospel Advocate,* which stated that women should not have authority over men nor should they teach mixed groups. Holman's response, entitled "Let Your Women Keep Silent," challenged traditional biblical interpretations in the Movement and their applications to the church. Her article sparked lively debate between her and Lipscomb, among others, over the issue of women's role in the church.

Holman maintained the traditional view that the husband was the head of the family and that a woman's primary obligation is to her family. However, in her writings she lifted up biblical women who were placed in positions of power, not by humans but by God. She argued that there was no reason to believe that women's brains were inferior to men's and that any knowledgeable woman was free to teach women and men about the Bible and faith.

In the 1890s Holman was among the voices arguing for a "new woman" as a model for the church. Proponents of the "new woman" supported women's suffrage, involvement in reform organizations (e.g., WCTU), better education for women, and more leadership positions held by women in the churches. Holman herself was a living example of the "new woman." She not only engaged in the debate about women's leadership, but also, out of her work with the WCTU, again faced off with Lipscomb about the use of wine for communion. A dedicated wife, mother, church woman, and capable debater, Silena Holman was also an articulate writer, with over 100 published articles. Two years before she died, Holman wrote "The Woman Question" (1913), published in the *Gospel Advocate,* in which she continued her support for women's ability to teach male and female audiences.

When she died on September 18, 1915, over 1,000 people attended her funeral. The well-known evangelist T. B. Larimore (1843-1929) conducted her funeral. She had asked Larimore to do the funeral because she said, "I want no man to apologize for my work, and I know he [Larimore] will never do that." In 1917 a portrait of Silena M. Holman was hung in the Tennessee state capitol, an honor given to only one other woman.

See also *Gospel Advocate, The;* Larimore, Theophilus Brown; Lipscomb, David; Temperance; Women in Ministry

BIBLIOGRAPHY C. Leonard Allen, "Silena Moore Holman (1850-1915), Voice of the 'New Woman' among Churches of Christ," *Discipliana* 56 (Spring 1996): 3-11 • Mary B. Bang, "A Marvelous Leader — A Comrade Beloved," *Union Signal* (September 1915) • Silena M. Holman, "Let Your Women Keep Silent," *Gospel Advocate* 30 (August 1888): 8. LISA W. DAVISON

Holy Spirit, Doctrine of the

Teaching on the Spirit as the Third Person of the divine Trinity and on the Spirit's operation in the economy of salvation.

Except for polemical purposes, leaders of the Stone-Campbell Movement have devoted little time to the doctrine of the Holy Spirit. There are several reasons. One is the Movement's historic aversion to speculative theology and its uneasiness in appropriating classical Trinitarianism. The precise relation of the Holy Spirit to the Father (as source of divinity) within the "immanent" Trinity — understood in the tradition of the Nicene Creed as a relation of eternal "procession" — was never a subject of substantial reflection in the Movement's history. Stephen England, in a study of Stone-Campbell views of the Holy Spirit among Disciples of Christ in the mid-twentieth century, concluded that many constituents were, functionally speaking, "Monarchians" (or "Sabellians") of the early Christian type who viewed the Spirit as a pure manifestation of the one God but struggled to see the Spirit as a distinct divine Person within the Trinity.

Doubtless another important reason for the Movement's historic lack of concentration on the Holy Spirit is the early leaders' experience with frontier revivalism. While Barton W. Stone got his inspiration for Christian unity at the Cane Ridge Revival of 1801 and believed the "exercises" occurring at the meeting were productive of good, he never encouraged them in the newly formed Christian Churches. On their side, Thomas and Alexander Campbell and their co-laborers were appalled by the "exercises." In their minds such perceived special interventions of the Holy Spirit were unjustified in Scripture and threatened the basis of Christian unity as the goal to which they were committed.

The ascription of theological "rationalism" to leaders in the Stone-Campbell Movement has come largely from their negative reaction to such varieties of spirituality, not out of their more affirmative convictions regarding spiritual experience. Stone-Campbell Movement adherents have held throughout their history, with some exceptions (e.g., B. W. Stone) and after much debate, to a three-personal God, where the Holy Spirit is an equal member of the Godhead; to the church as a creation of the Holy Spirit; to the Scriptures, New and Old, as both inspired by, and brought together through, the agency of the Holy Spirit; and to the work of the Holy Spirit as that of converting the world to Christ and residing in the lives of Christians for their spiritual fulfillment. Among the more liberal leaders and thinkers of the twentieth century, the Holy Spirit was seen as working institutionally to bring about social change in the interests of human justice. Nevertheless many partisans of the Stone-Campbell Movement have been unapologetically supernaturalistic in outlook, while carrying certain Enlightenment convictions into their work, including trust in human reason, contempt for theological niceties, and commitment to the practically achievable.

Stone-Campbell Movement leaders historically spent most of their energies defending a rationalistic view of the Holy Spirit's work in conversion. Their understandings were never uniform, however, and fall into four discernible categories. The first may be called the *verbal-restrictive* (or verbal-intensive) position, which holds that the work of the Holy Spirit is wholly immanent in the Word of Scripture — that is, that the Holy Spirit operates on the human heart *mediately* through fact and argumentation drawn from the Bible. There is no way of knowing what proportion of the Movement's adherents have worked from this perspective, but it has represented the purest reaction against the idea of special intervention by the Holy Spirit and has been expressed most often among thinkers in the more conservative streams of the Movement.

Perhaps the classic statement of the idea that the Spirit operates only through the written Word came from the pen of longtime preacher Zachary Taylor Sweeney. His book, titled *The Spirit and the Word: A Treatise on the Holy Spirit in the Light of a Rational Interpretation of the Word of God,* was first published in 1919 by the Christian Standard Company and was later reprinted by the Gospel Advocate Company. Sweeney examined every scripture used by advocates of a literal personal indwelling of the Holy Spirit, concluding that in every case the Spirit accomplished its work through the Bible. "It is not claimed that a direct indwelling of the Spirit makes any new revelations, adds any new reasons or offers any new motives than are found in the word of God. Of what use, then, would a direct indwelling Spirit be?" Sweeney's argument is in essence a restatement of Alexander Campbell's most rationalistic statements on the subject.

Another view could be termed the *verbal-augmentative* position, according to which the Holy Spirit invests the written and spoken Word with special powers beyond the text itself, a power especially suited to reach the human soul. Alexander Campbell was the verbal-augmentativist par excellence. In his *The Christian System* (1839) Campbell had appeared to argue the verbal-restrictivist position when he wrote, "Whatever the word does, the Spirit does; and whatsoever the Spirit does in the work of converting men, the word does." But when his debating partner N. L. Rice quoted these and other statements in *The Christian System* in his debate with Campbell in 1843, Campbell argued vehemently that he was not a pure "verbalist" and that he was as supernaturalistic as

Rice, believing that "Every word of God *has life* in it." He argued that there is a vitality in the Word, needing only proper soil in which to grow, so that when the Word "is planted in the moral constitution of man it will . . . fructify unto eternal life."

In his *Christian Baptism* (1844) Campbell developed this theme even further. Rejecting the Word-alone, Spirit-alone, and Spirit first–Word second operations, he stated his own position as one where the Holy Spirit "clothes Himself" with gospel words and arguments and "quickens" what is sown in the heart. He supported his view with fourteen separate arguments, but he nowhere explained just how the Holy Spirit "livens" Scripture. He admitted that behind the Word the Holy Spirit can in unknown ways touch the soul "by fixing attention upon [the Word], or removing, providentially, obstructions," but whether the Spirit actually does so he neither affirmed nor denied. His views can be seen reflected in the name given to his New Testament translation, *The Living Oracles,* but he never developed his doctrine in such a way as to make clear whether he was using "living" metaphorically or in the causative-relational sense.

Walter Scott, the greatest evangelist in the Campbell wing of the movement, in his *Discourse on the Holy Spirit* (1831), tried to check the excessive rationalism of some of those who, misunderstanding Campbell, were preaching a "Word-alone" theory of conversion. He endeavored to show that the indwelling of the Holy Spirit could come only through obedience to the Word, and that once in the believer's heart the Spirit did produce manifold fruit. Scott did not say in so many words that the Word had augmentative potencies, as Campbell did, but he did oppose the reductive rationalism of many in the Movement.

A third discernible position in the Movement is the *verbal-coefficient.* In this view the Holy Spirit *accompanies* the preaching of the written Word, the Spirit and the Word working independently of each other but *in harmony.* This view both saves the real presence of the Holy Spirit as a Person distinct from any fallible verbal presentation of the truth and prevents a conception of the written Word from being some kind of fourth presentation of the Godhead, a divine power-in-itself. Most Stone-Campbell Movement leaders appear to have taken this softer approach to the relation between the Spirit and the Word because it allows the believer both immediate access to the presence of the Spirit in accordance with the promise of Acts 2:38, a thematic text in the life of the Stone-Campbell Movement, and freedom to study the Word historically and critically as the authoritative text in the life of the church. In the latter half of the nineteenth century, Robert Milligan's *The Scheme of Redemption* (1868) helped to elaborate this view. Milligan agreed with Campbell and Scott that in the conversion of sinners the Holy Spirit acts on them through the announcement of the good news (Rom. 1:16; 1 Cor. 4:14-15), but that this view must not be carried to extremes. He argued that no one can set limits on what the Spirit can do and that the Spirit "may exert many influences of which we know nothing" through sickness and death in a family, calamity in a community, a sense in the sinner's heart of life's emptiness, fright in the case of the Philippian jailer, and prayer and piety in the heart of a Cornelius. He pointed out that there would be no renewing power in these providences apart from the meaning they come to have through the gospel, but the Spirit is not entirely confined to the written Word.

In 1872 Alexander Campbell's associate and biographer, Robert Richardson, published *A Scriptural View of the Office of the Holy Spirit,* which supports the verbal-coefficient view of the work of the Spirit, not just in conversion but in sanctification. Richardson, who had deep concerns about the attrition of spirituality in the Stone-Campbell Movement, deplored

Robert Richardson, colleague of Alexander Campbell at Bethany College, championed the doctrine of the personal indwelling of the Holy Spirit in baptized Christians, having perceived an incipient rationalism in the worship and piety of Stone-Campbell churches. Courtesy of Bethany College

both the view that the Holy Spirit is a mere "influence" as held by Socinians and Pelagians and the idea of "the ardent sensuist" who has to *feel* the Spirit's presence before he turns to Christ. He argued that in apostolic times such theories were unknown; the approach was simply to preach the gospel and leave the results to the Holy Spirit. God might grant repentance to such hearers, but *how* this happened was not speculated on. It was sufficient to know that the Holy Spirit accompanied the Word and brought the fruits. Richardson's book is more devotional than theological in approach, but it gives an indication of where the Movement was going after Campbell.

Another important study of the Holy Spirit came at the turn of the twentieth century with J. H. Garrison's *The Holy Spirit: His Personality, Mission, and Modes of Activity* (1905). Garrison, historian and prolific writer, was then editor of the *Christian-Evangelist.* Garrison was known for taking moderately liberal positions in the internal controversies of the day, desiring to keep the unity of the Movement intact by way of generosity of spirit to all sides. With respect to conversion Garrison concurred with Milligan and Richardson that although the Spirit's mission is to convict the world of sin, the Spirit never does so independently of a knowledge of the gospel. At the same time Garrison censured those who think that God's Spirit operates only through the words of the Bible. He stated that a preacher, by his intonations, gestures, kindness in deed, and potency of spiritual example, brings the Holy Spirit to bear on the listeners' lives. "We have not learned all the ways of the Spirit," he said, and argued that we should recognize all believers whose lives show their kinship to the Holy Spirit, the assumption being that all sincere Christians, whatever their theories of conversion and sanctification, obey Christ to the limit of their understanding. It is clear that Garrison gave further enhancement to the verbal-coefficient (or verbal-accompaniment) approach to the work of the Holy Spirit.

A fourth position, largely a development of the early to mid-twentieth century, is the *verbal-transcendent* (or Spirit-intensive) view. There are varying ways in which this view is developed, but the general notion is that the Holy Spirit can and sometimes does act apart from the Word and immediately on the heart of the unbeliever who, while he or she believes the gospel, cannot will to change his or her life without a special spiritual impulsion. This was the position of a minority of charismatics, some of whom separated from the Christian Churches/Churches of Christ in the late twentieth century to form Christ's Church Fellowship.

The verbal-transcendent view has come about primarily, however, in connection with attempts to promote the deeper Christian life. One of the first promoters of the emphasis was James DeForest Murch, for a short while editor of the *Christian Standard,* then founder and editor of *United Evangelical Action,* official organ of the National Association of Evangelicals, then managing editor of the newly founded *Christianity Today.* Murch, who with Claude Witty and Carl Ketcherside of the Churches of Christ was trying to promote unity between the divided churches of the Stone-Campbell Movement, believed that what had been sorely lacking, and was now necessary to bring reconciliation, was to emphasize the work of the Holy Spirit in the church. Along with leading preachers like George Knepper, J. B. Hunley, C. G. Kindred, J. M. Appelgate, and others, Murch helped to launch the Christian Action and Quiet Time movements to encourage Christian spirituality among the churches. Ketcherside, editor of the Church of Christ journal *Mission Messenger,* resolving to put sectarianism aside, called for "the dynamic of love" as the secret of healing a divided Movement and spoke at any "brotherhood" gathering that would invite him. One of his purposes was to bring the Holy Spirit into the lives of his co-believers. Ketcherside and historian Leroy Garrett held a forum on the Holy Spirit, later published as *The Holy Spirit in Our Lives Today* (1966).

The *verbal-restrictive* or "word only" theory was widely held in Churches of Christ in the twentieth century, though a variety of understandings could be seen, including the nonmiraculous personal indwelling of the Spirit in the Christian. In the mid-1960s a controversy flared between "word only" advocates and those who taught a literal indwelling. J. D. Thomas of Abilene Christian College penned a series of articles championing the literal indwelling position, later published in 1966 as *The Spirit and Spirituality.* Proponents of the "word only" theory included Foy E. Wallace, Jr., who also wrote a series of articles in the *Firm Foundation* published in 1967 as *The Mission and the Medium of the Holy Spirit.*

This incident reflected the growing tensions aggravated by stories of "conversions" of leaders, including several elders and preachers in Churches of Christ, to charismatic belief and practice. In a publication of the Full Gospel Business Men's Fellowship International titled *The Acts of the Holy Spirit in the Church of Christ Today,* fourteen former ministers and leaders in Churches of Christ gave their testimony of charismatic conversion. In 1969 Pat Boone, popular actor, entertainer, and member of Churches of Christ, announced he had experienced a baptism of the Holy Spirit. His 1970 book, *A New Song,* was greeted by even stronger assertions from the word-only proponents that any other understanding of the work of the Holy Spirit would inevitably lead to what they characterized as the kind of beliefs and behavior seen in Boone. Another leader in Churches of

Christ who advocated charismatic views of the work of the Spirit is Jim Bevis, who worked through his annual Conference on Spiritual Renewal to introduce ministers in Churches of Christ to charismatic or third wave understandings of the role of the Spirit in the church. For a while the Conference published *Paraclete Journal* as a renewal magazine for all three streams of the Stone-Campbell Movement.

Some recent examinations of the work of the Holy Spirit among people of the Stone-Campbell Movement include, on the side of Christian Churches/Churches of Christ, Don DeWelt's four-volume *The Power of the Holy Spirit* (1989); Knofel Staton's *Don't Divorce the Holy Spirit* (1974); and the Emmanuel School of Religion's series, *Lectures on the Holy Spirit,* by the faculty of that school, delivered November-December 1971. On the side of the Churches of Christ there are C. Leonard Allen and Danny Swick's *Participating in God's Life* (2001); Garth Black's *The Holy Spirit* (1984); and a second edition of J. D. Thomas's *The Spirit and Spirituality* (1981). From the Christian Church (Disciples of Christ) are Clark Williamson's *Way of Blessing, Way of Life: A Theology* (1999) and a brief work by Disciples Heritage Fellowship leader Richard M. Bowman, *The Holy Spirit in Today's Church* (1996). All of these efforts represent the work of Stone-Campbell thinkers to revise the stark rationalism and formality that they believe have too often characterized the Movement's doctrine of the Holy Spirit.

See also Charismatics; Conversion; Five Finger Exercise; God, Doctrine of; Regeneration; Russell, Walter Scott; Sanctification, Doctrine of

BIBLIOGRAPHY C. Leonard Allen, *The Cruciform Church: Becoming a Cross-Shaped People in a Secular World* (1990) • C. Leonard Allen and Danny Swick, *Participating in God's Life* (2001) • Garth Black, *The Holy Spirit* (1984) • Richard M. Bowman, *The Holy Spirit in Today's Church* (1996) • Alexander Campbell, *The Christian System* (1839) • Alexander Campbell, *A Debate Between Rev. A. Campbell and Rev. N. L. Rice, on the Action, Subject, Design, and Administrator of Christian Baptism* (1844) • Don DeWelt, *The Power of the Holy Spirit,* 4 vols. (1989) • Stephen England, "The Holy Spirit in the Thought and Life of the Disciples of Christ," in *The Renewal of the Church: The Panel Reports,* vol. 1: *The Reformation of Tradition* (1963), pp. 111-34 • Douglas A. Foster, "Waves of the Spirit Against a Rational Rock: The Impact of the Pentecostal, Charismatic, and Third Wave Movements on American Churches of Christ," *Restoration Quarterly* 45 (1st and 2nd quarter 2003): 95-105 • J. H. Garrison, *The Holy Spirit: His Personality, Mission, and Modes of Activity* (1905) • J. B. Hunley, *Pentecost and the Holy Spirit* (1928) • A. B. Jones, *The Spiritual Side of Our Plea* (1901) • W. Carl Ketcherside, ed., *The Holy Spirit in Our Lives Today* (1966) • Robert Milligan, *An Exposition and Defense of the Scheme of Redemption, As It Is Revealed and Taught in the Holy Scriptures* (rev. ed. 1869) • James DeForest Murch, ed., *Christian Action Addresses,* Bks. I and II (1934-35) • Robert Richardson, *A Scriptural View of the Office of the Holy Spirit* (1872) • Walter Scott, *A Discourse on the Holy Spirit* (2nd ed. 1831) • Knofel Staton, *Don't Divorce the Holy Spirit* (1974) • Z. T. Sweeney, *The Spirit and the Word* (1919) • J. D. Thomas, *The Spirit and Spirituality* (1981) • Clark Williamson, *Way of Blessing, Way of Life: A Theology* (1999).

BYRON C. LAMBERT

Home and State Missions Planning Council

Disciples program-coordinating council established by the 1938 International Convention.

For many years it was recognized that the programs of the Division of Home Missions of the United Christian Missionary Society (UCMS), which employed program staff in Christian education, youth, women's work, and evangelism in the states and provinces, and the programs of the state and provincial missionary societies had many interests in common. The impetus for a coordinating council came from Willard M. Wickizer, chair of the UCMS Division of Home Missions. Wickizer called for greater coordination of the work of the Division and the state and provincial societies at the 1936 annual meeting of the secretaries of the state and provincial missionary societies. The following year a meeting of state and provincial secretaries and board members devised a plan for cooperative program planning that became the Home and State Missions Planning Council.

The Council was made up of representatives of the Home Missions Department of the UCMS whose program staff worked in the states and provinces, the executives of the participating state and provincial societies, and thirty persons elected at large. The work of the Council was divided among nine standing committees: Local Church Life, Evangelism, Effective Ministry, Town and Country Church, Christian Service, Missionary Policy and Strategy, World Outreach, Urban Work, and Stewardship. While each society was free to determine what program plans and materials were to be used, the Council provided a vehicle for cooperative strategic planning and the generation and distribution of program resources. Among its achievements was the publication of Orman L. Shelton's *The Church Functioning Effectively* (1946), which outlined an inclusive model of local church organization that was adopted by many Disciples congregations, and G. Edwin Osborn's *Christian Worship: A Service Book,* a comprehensive worship resource that standardized a form of worship in hundreds of Disciples congregations.

The Council served effectively until 1972, giving

innovative and coordinated leadership to the home mission program of the Disciples. Following the restructure of the Disciples approved in 1968, funding for program staff in regions was allocated to the regions (which replaced the earlier state and provincial societies) rather than the newly formed Division of Homeland Ministries. Program planning and coordination was lodged with the General Board of the Christian Church (Disciples of Christ).

BIBLIOGRAPHY Anthony L. Dunnavant, *Restructure: Four Historical Ideals in the Campbell-Stone Movement and the Development of the Polity of the Christian Church (Disciples of Christ)* (1993). D. NEWELL WILLIAMS

Homes and Services for the Aged

1. Christian Church (Disciples of Christ)
2. Christian Churches/Churches of Christ
3. Churches of Christ

1. Christian Church (Disciples of Christ)

From its earliest days, Disciples of Christ, like society at large, considered the care of the needy, both young and old, to be a family and local matter. It was not until the late nineteenth century that the first parachurch organizations were established to provide care, in a structured way, for aging persons. With life expectancy at only about forty years into the early part of the twentieth century, the numbers of aging persons in need was relatively small.

Pioneers of care for the elderly among Disciples were Matilda (Mattie) Hart Younkin (d. 1908) of St. Louis and Rev. William Broadhurst of Louisville. In February 1886 Younkin gathered with six other women at First Christian Church in St. Louis to pray for those in need. From this small beginning emerged the ministry of the National Benevolent Association (NBA) of the Christian Church (Disciples of Christ), incorporated in Missouri the following year. In 2003 the NBA served almost 20,000 older adults, with a full range of services, including skilled nursing care, assisted living, and independent living, in over ninety facilities across the country, and was listed as the third largest not-for-profit organization in the United States by the American Senior Housing Association.

Like other outreach groups founded in the late nineteenth century, the NBA initially served orphans in their first Home in St. Louis in February 1891. The first permanent facility for older adults was opened in Jacksonville, Illinois, in March 1901, due to the generosity and commitment of members of Central Christian Church in that city. The next two locations for older adults were in New York and Oregon, fulfilling part of Mattie Younkin's dream that the NBA would be a national organization.

In 1872 Rev. William Broadhurst, minister of Floyd and Chestnut Christian Church in Louisville, Kentucky, obtained a charter for the Christian Church Widow's and Orphan's Home, which became The Christian Church Homes of Kentucky in 1960. The first facility, housing two young girls, opened in 1884 in Louisville. The first older woman was admitted in 1912; the first man came with his wife in 1957.

The Christian Church Homes of Kentucky has maintained a positive working relationship with many congregations of the Christian Churches/Churches of Christ in Kentucky. In 2003 they served over 1,800 older persons from diverse backgrounds with programs and facilities in eight Kentucky communities. DANIEL GILBERT

2. Christian Churches/Churches of Christ

Early benevolent work with the aged grew out of concern for widows and poverty-stricken ministers. Since Christians often cared for their own aged family members, retirement homes were late to develop. The Christian Woman's Benevolent Association established a facility in St. Louis in 1911. A Louisville home opened its doors to fifteen widows in 1912. Both operations continue, the latter one (now Christian Church Homes of Kentucky) having expanded to five complexes, aided by both Christian Churches/Churches of Christ and by congregations of the Christian Church (Disciples of Christ).

As churches supported these early works, they founded other projects such as Turner Retirement Homes (1933) in Oregon, designed to care for retired church workers. The number of homes for the aged rose slowly and then increased sharply after 1975. In 2003 over forty were in operation nationwide.

Food, shelter, and nursing care were once considered adequate, but now homes for the aged provide specialized services, including independent and assisted living, short-term and Alzheimer's care facilities, and in-home services. Some care centers have also opened up apartment- and condominium-style living with gift shops, solariums, patios, and recreational facilities. Specialized activities, recreation, and group trips are scheduled. As a result some persons arrange to enter these homes while still relatively young. Area churches frequently provide personnel for leading worship services and for pastoral visitation, and many homes have their own chaplains.

Licensure, government regulations, participation in Medicaid and Medicare, and the rise in health care costs make operations increasingly complex. These homes still depend mostly upon congregational support and auxiliaries that contribute money from fundraising events. Some missionaries are also establishing senior care facilities in other countries.

JAMES H. LLOYD

3. Churches of Christ

Many of the earliest homes for the aged in Churches of Christ were rather informal arrangements designed to take care of elderly ministers and widows. Of the facilities still in existence today, the Church of Christ Home for the Aged, organized in 1924 by the Chapel Avenue Church of Christ in Nashville, Tennessee, is the oldest. Since the Social Security Act was not passed until 1935, the home (called Eastland Christian Haven from 2001) began solely through the donations of area Christians, and it continues to be supported by Churches of Christ. Along with orphanages, homes for the aged were at the center of the institutional controversy of the 1950s. In the Woods-Cogdill debate in 1957, "the homes for the aged among us" are mentioned several times.

From 1930 to 1960 the elderly population in the United States more than doubled. The growth of Churches of Christ after World War II, along with government programs such as the Kerr-Mills Bill (1960), Medicare and Medicaid (1965), led to the establishment of dozens of assisted-living facilities. In 2001, the Pruett Gerontology Center at Abilene Christian University listed 106 housing facilities for older adults in nineteen states and Canada associated with Churches of Christ, ranging from assisted living to complete nursing care. The Pruett Gerontology Center has hosted an annual National Elder Housing Conference for professionals and individuals affiliated with Churches of Christ since 1988 and issues the Ira Mackie Housing Excellence Award to individuals who have promoted excellence within the elder housing ministry. KEVIN S. WELLS

See also Christian Church Homes of Kentucky; National Benevolent Association of the Christian Church (Disciples of Christ); Noninstitutional Movement

BIBLIOGRAPHY Hiram J. Lester and Marjorie Lee Lester, *Inasmuch . . . The Saga of NBA* (1987) • James M. Seale, *A Century of Faith and Caring* (1984) • *Yearbook of the Benevolent, Educational and Evangelistic Activities of Churches of Christ and Interested Individuals* (1967-).

Hope International University

Christian college affiliated with the Christian Churches/Churches of Christ.

Hope International University began on October 9, 1928, as Pacific Bible Seminary, founded at a time of increasing polarization between conservative and liberal Disciples of Christ. James DeForest Murch, who had been pivotal in the founding of the Cincinnati Bible Institute and Seminary just four years earlier, was also instrumental in advocating the establishment of a college on the Pacific coast to address the needs of conservative Disciples churches.

The college first opened classes at the Alvarado Church of Christ in Los Angeles on January 3, 1929. In 1930 the institution moved to Long Beach, California, meeting at First Christian Church until the earthquake of 1933 forced the students and faculty to meet in a small house. In 1936 property was purchased in Long Beach and developed for use in 1940. The college relocated from Long Beach to an eleven-acre Fullerton campus (a former shopping center) in 1973; this campus was expanded in 1995 to the fifteen acres currently in use.

In 1962, after thirty-four years in existence, Pacific Bible Seminary underwent a name change and became Pacific Christian College. It used this name exclusively for thirty-five years, until 1997, when it became Hope International University. This latter change reflected the broadening of the school's educational agenda and graduate programs.

The university currently consists of three main schools. The undergraduate school, retaining the name Pacific Christian College, offers associate and bachelor degrees in biblical studies and Christian ministry and has expanded its majors to include various fields in the arts and sciences. The School of Graduate Studies offers master-level degrees in religious studies, church music, education, counseling, business, and management. The School of Professional Studies offers associate and bachelor degree programs for adult and nontraditional students. There is also an Institute of International Studies that provides English-language training for international students.

The student body from 1928 to 1940 rarely exceeded forty. Between 1940 and 1952 this figure rose to nearly seventy. Enrollment growth has continued steadily since. In 2001 the total student body for the university reached over 1,000. In the first twenty-two years of its history there were just eighty-six graduates; in 2001 alone there were over 200.

The university motto "Preparing Servant Leaders" was adopted in the 1970s and continues to express the twin emphases of the institution today: servant leadership and the priesthood of all believers. It continues a tradition of training men and women for Christian service in a variety of fields, including professional ministry, psychology and counseling, management, and education — all with a strong mission emphasis.

See also Bible College Movement; Higher Education, Views of in the Movement

BIBLIOGRAPHY G. C. Tiffin, K. Stranlund, and M. Warner, eds., "Framing the Future: The First Twenty-Five Years of Pacific Christian College, 1928-1953" (unpublished MS, 1979) • G. C. Tiffin, "The Interaction of the Bible College Movement and the Independent Disciples of Christ Denomination" (unpublished Ph.D. dissertation, Stanford University, 1968).

DAVID TIMMS

Hopwood, Josephus (1843-1935)

Preacher and educator known for founding educational institutions in the Stone-Campbell Movement.

Born in Kentucky, he was educated at Abingdon and The College of the Bible. Together with his wife, Sarah LaRue, in 1875 Hopwood took over the Buffalo Institute in Tennessee. In 1881 the school was enlarged and renamed Milligan College. They founded Virginia Christian College (now Lynchburg) in 1903 and Lamar College in 1913; and they helped establish the Mountain Mission School of Grundy, Virginia, in 1921. Their motto was "Christan Education — The Hope of the World."

See also Lynchburg College; Milligan College

BIBLIOGRAPHY Josephus Hopwood, *A Journey Through the Years: An Autobiography* (1932).

CLINTON J. HOLLOWAY

Josephus Hopwood, assisted by his wife Sarah, founded Milligan College in northeast Tennessee and Lynchburg College in Virginia. Hopwood wrote, "The Christian college must unite and utilize both the science of nature and the light of the Book, bring forth a growing and perfecting life in the church and thereby leaven all society."
Courtesy of Milligan College Archives

Hostetler, Joseph (1797-1866)

Early Dunker convert to the Stone-Campbell Movement and organizer of churches.

Hostetler spread the Movement in Indiana, Illinois, Kentucky, Ohio, and Wisconsin. Born in Kentucky, to Dunker parents, he was ordained in 1821 into a Brethren community stressing no creeds, pietism, love feasts, and pacifism. Upon reading an issue of the *Christian Baptist,* he wrote a letter, published in December 1825, inquiring about aspects of Alexander Campbell's beliefs; the following year he preached on "primitive Christianity," which led to his break with the Dunkers. Hostetler evangelized, formally debated, and wrote in support of the Movement. With James M. Mathes in 1842 he composed *Calumnies Refuted,* a tract defending "Campbellism." He co-founded Liberty Church, Indiana (1819, aligned with the Movement by 1839), and Church of Christ, Decatur, Illinois (1833). In 1861 he retired to Lovington, Illinois.

BIBLIOGRAPHY David B. Eller, "Hoosier Brethren and the Origins of the Restoration Movement," *Indiana Magazine of History* 7 (March 1980): 1-20 • Madison Evans, *Biographical Sketches of the Pioneer Preachers of Indiana* (1862), pp. 57-74.

LOWELL K. HANDY

Hymnody

Traditions of hymn composition and usage in the Movement.

The hymnody of the Stone-Campbell Movement arose as singing evangelists, poets, musicians, teachers, and publishers built on a Protestant musical foundation. The Movement has enjoyed modest influence on evangelical musical literature while remaining stylistically indistinct from the larger culture of Protestant music. Singing became a tool for articulating doctrine, encouraging faithfulness, and building congregational spirit. Issues surrounding music were both the cause and symptom of one of the Movement's major schisms.

In 1828 Alexander Campbell published *Psalms, Hymns and Spiritual Songs.* The next year Barton Stone and Thomas Adams published *The Christian Hymn Book.* Stone and Campbell combined their material and, with the cooperation of John T. Johnson and Walter Scott, republished *Psalms, Hymns and Spiritual Songs* in an enlarged form in 1834. Subsequent editions of this 370-page hymnal appeared in 1843, 1853, 1864, and 1882 (the last edition under the title *Christian Hymnal*).

This influential 1834 publication was not the first musical offering from restorationists. Abner Jones, Elias Smith, James O'Kelly, the "White Pilgrim" Joseph Thomas, Rice Haggard, Stone's Springfield Presbytery associates David Purviance and John Thompson, and others had all brought out hymnals previously. The early books contained lyrics without musical notation, the inclusion of which, opined Campbell, would have been a distraction from the truth and power of the words. Other than texts from Isaac Watts and John and Charles Wesley, most of the entries in these first hymnals are rarely sung today.

Campbell favored the Movement's having but one unifying hymnal, but musical taste and market forces dictated otherwise. Silas White Leonard and Augustus Damon Fillmore brought out *The Christian Psalmist* in 1847. This first hymnal within the Movement to feature musical notation sold over half a million copies in eighteen editions. Amos Sutton Hayden published *The Sacred Melodeon* in shape notes the next year.

Being enthusiastic singers, Christians in the Stone-Campbell tradition naturally generated their own songs. James Henry Fillmore (1849-1936; "I Am Resolved"), Walter Stillman Martin (1842-1935; "God Will Take Care of You"), Jessie Hunter Brown Pounds (1861-1921; "Beautiful Isle of Somewhere"), J. H. Rosecrans (1844-1926; "There Is a Habitation"), Knowles Shaw (1834-1878; "Bringing in the Sheaves"), and A. J. Showalter (1858-1924; "Leaning on the Everlasting Arms") are among the nineteenth-century Stone-Campbell lyricists who enjoyed publication outside the Movement.

Stone-Campbell congregations across the board sing a wide variety of music, but the Movement's composers have worked mostly in two styles: gospel song and Southern gospel. Gospel song has its roots in the work of American composer William Bradbury (1816-1868), whose musical style Phillip P. Bliss used prolifically to support the popular evangelistic campaigns of Dwight L. Moody. The lyrics of gospel song are less grave than those of hymns, usually addressing the saved and unsaved in evangelistic gatherings rather than being expressions of adoration, prayer, or praise addressed to God. Easy to learn, in part because of typical reassertive refrains following each stanza, gospel song is hortatory, encouraging, and rhetorical. Major keys prevail in four-part harmony.

Southern gospel music is a development of the early twentieth century. It is rhythmically and emotionally upbeat, frequently using a call-and-response motif. Also generally written in a major key for four voices, Southern gospel melody makes a statement that the harmonic voices repeat. Both of these song forms lend themselves to congregational singing. For the sincere but musically unsophisticated, gospel song and Southern gospel provided musical media in which all could easily participate. Indeed, Southern gospel, with its call-and-response style, obviated the need for congregational hymnals.

By far the most serious musical issue to face the Movement was the adoption of instrumental accompaniment in worship. For the pioneer generation this was not an issue, as most early nineteenth-century American churches sang unaccompanied. With growing prosperity, improved schooling, and increasing cultural sophistication came the idea of introducing instrumentation. This controversial practice, allegedly first introduced in 1859 in Midway, Kentucky, by Lewis L. Pinkerton (1812-1875), gradually split the Movement into "instrumental" and "a cappella" factions, with each side quoting Scripture to support its position. Crucial to the a cappella churches was the absence of a direct New Testament command to use instruments. They cited Ephesians 5:19 and Colossians 3:16, which commend "singing" without mention of "playing." Instrumentalists found no scriptural condemnation of instruments and pointed to Psalm 150 and Revelation 5:8 and 8:7. The controversy had deeper roots in hermeneutical presuppositions and sectionalism. The instrumental controversy was both a symptom and a cause of the division that split the Stone-Campbell Movement in the last third of the nineteenth century.

Stone-Campbell hymnists continued to write and sing (and play) into the new century. In popular singing schools Christians learned new hymns and acquired skills in part-singing and sight-reading, frequently through the use of the shape-note system. The singing schools, frequently promoted by publishing firms, became venues for introducing new music and lyrics, training musical lay leadership, and hawking new hymnals.

Ambitious publishing houses encouraged the emergence of new music. Among prominent twentieth-century lyricists were Virgil P. Brock (1887-1978; "Beyond the Sunset"), Albert E. Brumley (1905-1977; "I'll Fly Away"), L. O. Sanderson (1901-1992; "Be With Me, Lord"), Austin Taylor (1881-1973; "Closer to Thee"), and Tillit S. Teddlie (1885-1987; "Worthy Art Thou"). Similarly, trained musicians provided new music for the growing number of lyricists. Among the composers were Brock, Brumley, and Sanderson.

The publishers also contributed to the proliferation of hymnals. The descendant of the original Stone-Campbell collaboration, *Christian Hymnal, Revised* (1882), predominated within the instrumental congregations, but because the American Christian Missionary Society (ACMS) held the copyright, non-instrumental congregations disregarded it. (Most a cappella churches opposed working through supra-congregational institutions such as missionary societies.) The Fillmore Music House (Cincinnati) had produced its *New Christian Hymn and Tune Book* in 1882, which vied within instrumental churches with the ACMS book. The Firm Foundation published numerous inexpensive collections of hymns primarily for use within Churches of Christ.

Robert Henry Boll (1875-1956), editor of *Word and Work*, provided yet another alternative to the ACMS hymnal when he called Elmer Leon Jorgenson (1886-1968) to edit *Great Songs of the Church* in 1921. Boll held to premillennialism, a position that was becoming increasingly controversial just as the hymnal appeared. The strength of *Great Songs of the Church* became evident when churches chose to use it in spite of its connection to "Bollism." Jorgenson produced a physically durable hymnal with a broad musical selection arranged in alphabetical order. It elevated the level of singing within the entire Stone-Campbell Movement. *Great Songs of the Church Number Two* followed in 1937, a collection of six hundred hymns.

Responding to the reluctance of some churches to adopt a premillennial hymnal, the Gospel Advocate Company of Nashville, Tennessee, contracted with L. O. Sanderson to edit *Christian Hymns* in 1933, followed by *Christian Hymns Number Two* in 1948. *Christian Hymns* was a less ambitious work than *Great Songs,* but it had the virtue of disseminating a number of its editor's finer hymns. *Great Songs of the Church* proved popular in both instrumental and a cappella congregations for fifty years. Among Disciples of Christ, the *Chalice Hymnal* (Chalice Press) predominated during the latter part of the twentieth century. Howard Publishing Company's *Songs of Faith and Praise* was used by many a cappella churches in the last decade of the century.

Toward the end of the twentieth century Stone-Campbell churches found themselves in the midst of a multiplication of Christian music accompanied by market evangelicalism. New hymnals proliferated, and individual lyricists, composers, and recording artists whose roots were in Stone-Campbell churches found popular acclaim. Rich Mullins (1955-1984), a former student at Cincinnati Bible College, brought "Awesome God" to the top of the charts and between the covers of a broad array of hymnals. Singer Debby Boone went gold on the popular music charts with "You Light Up My Life," as did Amy Grant on the Christian charts with "El Shaddai." Both had roots in Churches of Christ. The development of richly orchestrated, complexly produced, fashionably marketed music with a Christian message resulted in a controversy within the instrumental churches when worshipers wanted to bring the modern praise choruses and modern instrumentation into the house of the Lord. In many congregations a battle over worship style ensued.

Indeed, by 2000, churches in all the streams of the Stone-Campbell Movement were challenging their musical traditions. Within Churches of Christ, random congregations began to admit instruments on special occasions, and, more frequently, "praise teams" replaced the traditional song leaders. Instrumental churches adjusted — or refused to adjust — to electric guitars, electronic keyboards, and percussion sets. Hymnals in some churches became passé as computer-generated texts and graphics projected on overhead screens replaced them.

The Stone-Campbell Movement has participated lustily and reverently in musical worship. Its musicians have expanded the repertoire, occasionally providing both lyrics and music that the broader evangelical world has adopted. Stylistically, Stone-Campbell hymnody has been derivative rather than formative, with the Movement reflecting rather than illuminating the musical milieu that the congregations inhabit.

An important historical resource for study of Stone-Campbell hymnology is the "Hymnals of the Stone-Campbell Movement: Enos E. Dowling Hymnal Collection," accumulated by the late historian Enos Dowling (1905-1997) and housed in the library of Lincoln Christian College and Seminary (online: http://www.lccs.edu/library/hymnals).

See also Boll, Robert Henry; Devotional Literature; Dowling, Enos; Instrumental Music; Pounds, Jessie Brown; Shaw, Knowles; Worship

BIBLIOGRAPHY George Brandon, "The Hymnody of the Disciples of Christ in the U.S.A.," *Hymn* 15 (1964): 15-22 • William Rees Bryant, "The Contributions of Churches of Christ to Evangelical Hymnody" (unpublished M.A. thesis, California State University, 1992) • Enos E. Dowling, ed., *Hymn and Gospel Song Books of the Restoration Movement: A Bibliography,* 2nd ed. (1988) • Dan Dozier, *Come Let Us Adore Him: Dealing with Struggle over Style of Worship in Christian Churches and Churches of Christ* (1994) • Gene C. Finley, ed., *Our Garden of Song* (1980) • Kenneth C. Hanson, "The Hymnology and Hymnals of the Restoration Movement" (unpublished B.D. Thesis, Butler University School of Religion, 1951) • Charles Heaton, "The Disciples of Christ and Sacred Music" (unpublished Ph.D. dissertation, Union Theological Seminary, 1956) • Harold Holland, "The Hymnody of the Churches of Christ," *Hymn* 30 (1979): 263-68 • "Hymnals of the Stone-Campbell Movement: Enos E. Dowling Hymnal Collection" (on-line: http://www.lccs.edu/library/hymnals) • Forrest McCann, "A History of *Great Songs of the Church,*" *Restoration Quarterly* 38 (1996): 219-28 • Forrest McCann, *Hymns and History* (1997) • Peter Morgan, "Disciples Hymnbooks: A Continuing Quest for Harmony," *Discipliana* 55 (1995): 46-63.

THEODORE N. THOMAS

I

Ibaraki Christian University

University with roots beginning in 1948 founded by American and Japanese members of Churches of Christ with input from other Japanese Christian groups.

Soon after World War II several missionary families from American Churches of Christ entered Japan, where a beachhead had been established in the 1890s. O. D. Bixler (1896-1968) and Logan Fox, Sr., who were in Japan prior to the war, spearheaded efforts to start a school and raised a considerable sum of money from members of Churches of Christ in America. E. W. McMillan (1889-1991) made a survey trip in 1947 and was appointed the first president. As a result, thirty-five acres were purchased and a senior high school was founded in 1948, with a junior college following in 1950. Early leaders among the Americans included McMillan, Logan Fox, Harry Robert Fox, Jr., Joe Cannon, Virgil Lawyer, Charles Doyle, R. C. Cannon, and Joe Betts. Japanese leaders were Shoichi Oka, Sakari Nagano, and Ryohachi Shigekuni. Ibaraki Christian College was founded in 1967.

The university is located in Hitachi City, Ibaraki Prefecture, Japan, eighty-five miles northeast of Tokyo. In the 1970s the influence of Churches of Christ began to wane, resulting in few remaining connections. In April 2000, the name Ibaraki Christian College was changed to Ibaraki Christian University. The university consists of three undergraduate colleges (College of Literature, College of Life Sciences, and a Junior College that was being phased out early in the twenty-first century), a College of Nursing, and a graduate school that was begun in 1995. In 2003 the total number of faculty was ninety and total enrollment about 2,200. Primary and secondary schools are also located on the campus and enroll more students than the university. Kindergarten programs are maintained at three different Churches of Christ in the Ibaraki area as well.

The Japanese Ministry of Education supplies funds. A new chapel has been constructed, and the chaplain in 2003, Yoshiya Noguchi, was a member of Churches of Christ whose salary was paid from university funds. The chairman of the board at that time, Akira Hirose, was an elder at the Mito Church of Christ. About 1 percent of the students profess Christianity.

See also McMillan, Edward Washington

BIBLIOGRAPHY Charles R. Brewer, ed., *A Missionary Pictorial* (1966) • Ibaraki Christian University Web Page: http://www.icc.ac.jp. THOMAS H. OLBRICHT

Iglesias de Cristo

See Hispanics in the Movement

Ijams, E. H. (1886-1982)

Preacher and educator in Churches of Christ.

Born in Florence, Alabama, Ijams received degrees from George Peabody College (B.S., 1918; M.A. 1927) and Harding College (L.L.D., 1934). He served as minister for several Churches of Christ, including Central in Nashville from 1925 to 1928, Central in Los Angeles from 1928 to 1932, Belmont in Nashville from 1943 to 1951, Union Avenue in Memphis from 1953 to 1958, and Highland Street in Memphis from 1958 until his death in 1982. He also served at David Lipscomb College as professor (1923-27), dean (1932-34), and president (1934-43). Other educational endeavors included consultation work on the founding of Pepperdine College (1928-32); serving as president of Georgia Christian School (1951-53); and teaching on the faculty of Harding Graduate School (1956-59). He authored three books and wrote the Crusader series of adult Sunday School curricula published by 20th Century Christian.

Ijams emerged as a leader in Churches of Christ in the last two-thirds of the twentieth century, seeking to move churches away from a sole focus on orthodoxy to an emphasis on the practice of Christian living. In the church prospectus for founding the Central Church of Christ in Nashville, he wrote, "Practical Christianity? What is it? It is worshiping God and serving man." He led that congregation to significant ministry to the poor in the 1920s and 30s, including free medical and dental care, daily meals, and dormitories for young men and women seeking work in the city.

In church controversies, he was described as a "gentle spirit." Severely criticized by some for refusing to condemn those who held premillennial beliefs, he was forced from the presidency of David Lipscomb College in the controversy. He was a strong advocate for Christian education from Sunday School to college, leading Lipscomb through difficult financial times. Ijams was a sought-after workshop speaker known for presentations on the Christian family; he officiated at 2,000 weddings and mentored many church leaders. In all his ministry Christian ethics was central: "Quicken your conscience to the holiness of God. Purge your imagination with the beauty of God. Open your heart to the love of God."

BIBLIOGRAPHY Paul Brown, "E. H. Ijams and a Dream for a City (Central Church, Nashville)," *Gospel Advocate* 134 (January 1992): 24 • Landon B. Saunders, "E. H. Ijams — A Vessel of Honor," *21st Century Christian* 56 (November 1993): 10 • Harold Shank, "Nashville's Central Church of Christ: The First Fifty Years," *Restoration Quarterly* 41 (1st Quarter 1999): 11.

HAROLD SHANK

Illinois Disciples Foundation

Disciples of Christ campus ministry at the University of Illinois at Urbana-Champaign (UIUC).

Chartered in 1916 by the Illinois Christian Missionary Society, the foundation grew out of the ministry to university students of Stephen E. Fisher, pastor of University Place Christian Church of Champaign. Organizers saw the foundation as an institutional response to the growth of state universities that were not related to any religious tradition. Illinois Disciples Foundation (IDF) was the first campus ministry of the Disciples and the second foundation for campus ministry in the United States, preceded only by the Wesley Methodist Foundation also at UIUC, initiated through the efforts of a Methodist friend and Champaign ministerial colleague of Fisher's. By 1923 the Foundation was serving over 800 Disciples students and had a full-time staff of five: two assistant pastors to Fisher, who continued as pastor of University Place Christian Church, a chaperon of Bethany House (a residence for Disciples women students), an instructor in religious education, and a promotional secretary. William Jackson Jarman served as campus minister from 1948 to 1963, playing a pivotal role in the construction of the extensive IDF facilities. During the late 1950s IDF became involved in the civil rights movement. Jim Holiman, campus minister from 1963 to 2000, led IDF to take an increasingly prominent role in social justice issues and to identify itself as a "peace with justice" campus ministry.

See also Campus Ministry — Christian Church (Disciples of Christ)

BIBLIOGRAPHY *The Voice,* periodical of the Illinois Disciples Foundation.

D. NEWELL WILLIAMS

Independents

See Christian Churches/Churches of Christ

Inman Christian Center

The Inman Christian Center was created in San Antonio, Texas, in 1913 as the Mexican Christian Institute. The mission of the organization was to offer a comprehensive program of social work that would provide greater contact with the Spanish-speaking community. The center provided a free medical clinic, a day nursery, a kindergarten, and a variety of course offerings. Initially, the Center was linked with Mexican Christian Church, established in 1899. The congregation met at the Center until 1925, when it built a separate building. This tandem arrangement was seen as a missionary model to be followed in other cities, organizing a congregation that would provide for the spiritual needs and a civic center that would tend to the social problems of the Hispanic community. The model could not be replicated successfully in other places and was abandoned.

In 1953, on its fortieth anniversary, the Institute was renamed the Inman Christian Center in honor of Samuel Guy Inman (1877-1965), Disciples missionary to Mexico and executive secretary from 1916 to 1939 of the Protestant Committee on Cooperation in Latin America. The Center is recognized as an organization related to the Christian Church (Disciples of Christ) in the United States and Canada, through the Division of Homeland Ministries. The Center, which is headed by a twenty-one-person governing board, offers day care services, develops children and youth programs, runs a residential treatment center for inhalant abusers, and manages six apartment complexes for the elderly, the disabled, and the mentally retarded, among other services.

PABLO A. JIMÉNEZ

See also Hispanics in the Movement — Christian Church (Disciples of Christ)

Institut zur Erforschung des Urchristentums

See European Evangelistic Society

Institute for Christian Studies

See Austin Graduate School of Theology

Instrumental Music

In keeping with their Reformed background, the churches of the Stone, Campbell, and related movements did not use musical instruments for worship in their early years. Many religious bodies experienced controversy over the introduction of musical instruments into worship during the eighteenth to twentieth centuries; this was especially so for Reformed and Anabaptist churches, but Jewish synagogues were also affected. The Stone-Campbell Movement shared this experience, except that, unlike in most other groups, the issue became a focal point of division.

Discussion of the propriety of using instruments of music in worship appears in the Movement's journals as early as 1849. Questions about their use or articles in their favor, as in the *Christian Record* and the *Ecclesiastical Reformer,* met with largely unfavorable responses from leaders in the Movement. Alexander Campbell was dismissive of the arguments for instruments, declaring in 1851 that "those who have no real devotion or spirituality in them" might find them desirable or necessary, "But I presume, to all spiritually-minded Christians such aids would be as a cow bell in a concert." Nevertheless, some churches began employing instruments. Examples include the Sixth Street Church in Cincinnati, where D. S. Burnet (1808-1867) preached, which began using musical instruments by 1855, and the Midway, Kentucky, church, under the leadership of L. L. Pinkerton (1812-1875), which was using instruments by 1860.

Growing discussion of instrumental music, especially the use of the organ, matched growing acceptance of it in the decade after the Civil War. The first main discussion occurred in the pages of the *Millennial Harbinger* in 1864-65 between J. W. McGarvey (1829-1911) and A. S. Hayden. McGarvey characterized the early years of the "present Reformation" as declaring the instrument "unscriptural, inharmonious with the Christian institution, and a source of corruption." Hayden, in agreement with the paper's editor W. K. Pendleton (1817-1899), rejected McGarvey's argument that the silence of Scripture was prohibitive in regard to worship and claimed that the use of an instrument was a matter of expediency. Moses E. Lard (1818-1880) denied that instrumental music belonged in the realm of expediency and in a March

The melodeon introduced into the Midway, Kentucky, Christian Church around 1859 by L. L. Pinkerton. Midway was one of the first congregations of the Movement to use instruments in worship. The melodeon is on display in the library at Midway College.

1864 article in his journal *Lard's Quarterly* anticipated the future division in calling on opponents of the instrument to separate from churches using it. The *Apostolic Times* tried to maintain a middle ground in the controversies of the period, supporting missionary societies but opposing instrumental music. Later the *Christian Evangelist,* edited by J. H. Garrison (1842-1931), sided with those who favored liberty for the use of instruments.

Although the opponents of instrumental music argued from the lack of explicit New Testament authorization and its supporters appealed to liberty and expediency, other factors were involved in the controversy. J. S. Lamar considered the use of an organ as "an inevitable consequence of growth and culture." Larger and wealthier churches required the things associated with their position in society. Conversely, poorer and rural Christians associated the organ with other things they considered an accommodation to the ways of the world — expensive buildings, padded pews, stained glass, pastors as clergymen. Another factor adding animosity to the conflict was sectional prejudice in the defeated South against the victorious North. The use of musical instruments initially spread mainly in urban areas of the North; the Southern churches overwhelmingly were without instruments, so there was initially not much discussion. Opposition to instrumental music in the South was solidified under the influence of the *Gospel Advocate* and David Lipscomb, who among other things reasoned that the non-use of an instrument was "safe" ground. The a cappella practice in turn became part of the identity of the largely Southern Churches of Christ.

The *Christian Standard* under Isaac Errett (1820-1888) tried to plot a middle road through the instrument controversy to maintain unity. After publishing articles pro (e.g., A. B. Chamberlain) and con (notably by Robert Richardson), Errett gave his views in a series of editorials in 1870. He recognized the evolution in taste that demanded better music and placed instruments in worship in the area of expediency as an aid to improve the often deplorable singing in the churches; but he advised that the law of love and the law of liberty prohibited the introduction of an instrument where even a small minority of members opposed it. In a May 1870 editorial he stated, "We shall advise our brethren everywhere, for the sake of peace, . . . to discard the use of instruments in the Churches. At the same time, we set ourselves most decidedly against all attempts to create division in the Churches on the ground of difference in regard to an expedient." He further offered the judgment that "Cheerful and hearty congregational singing . . . will be found to be as attractive as the organ, and far more comforting and edifying."

This approach was not sufficient for Benjamin Franklin (1812-1878), editor of the *American Christian Review,* who had written against instrumental music in worship in 1860 and became more strident in response to Errett. For him the instrument was not a matter of opinion or expediency but the violation of an important principle. He declared a policy of separation without division from those who used the instrument in their services, advising those who withdrew to go quietly, to declare non-fellowship with no one, and leave the door open for reconciliation. Errett's policy resulted in increasing acceptance of instrumental music, and Franklin's opposition had limited success; indeed, Errett observed that use of instruments increased with the bitterness of the denunciations. By the end of the 1880s the majority of the Stone-Campbell churches in the North favored instruments.

Whatever part economic and cultural factors played in the controversy over the presence of instruments in worship, many participants soon observed that an important factor producing division was different approaches to scriptural authority and interpretation. Opponents saw the silence of Scripture as prohibitive, whereas supporters saw it as allowing liberty. As often happens in doctrinal controversy, people on both sides began to see values in their practice they had not previously recognized. Those engaged in a cappella singing came to a greater appreciation of the power and effectiveness of vocal music, and advocates of instrumental music solidified their views about the dangers of legalism and the contribution made to unity by broader principles of interpretation.

In the North, the Sand Creek "Address and Declaration" in Shelby County, Illinois, August 18, 1889, under the influence of Daniel Sommer (1850-1940), denounced instruments of music among many other items with which conservative churches found themselves at odds with the progressive majority. The document's declaration of non-fellowship with many with whom there had been unity was representative of increasing strains in the Stone-Campbell Movement in the last third of the nineteenth century. Division between the instrumental Christian Churches and non-instrumental Churches of Christ (the distinction in names was never clear-cut) was a long and complex process. Instrumental music took a prominent place in the controversy and was more divisive than other differences because it was highly visible and something in which those conscientiously opposed could not participate, forcing them to meet separately. The religious census of 1906 that listed Churches of Christ separately from Christian Churches was a recognition of a division that had been developing over decades rather than the date of the division, and congregations continued to divide after this date.

During the twentieth century both sides refined their arguments. Advocates of instrumental music in worship, in addition to making the plea for liberty and expediency in using instruments to improve singing, have called attention to the favorable notices of instrumental music in worship in the Old Testament, the absence of a condemnation of instruments in the New Testament in contrast to the explicit words about circumcision and animal sacrifice, and the presence of instruments in heaven according to Revelation. Opponents of instrumental music have responded by pointing to the connection of instruments with the abrogated temple ritual, the figurative nature of language in Revelation, and historical evidence for the absence of instruments in the Jewish synagogue and the early church. Their central concern, however, has been absence of explicit authorization for instruments, supported by examples from Scripture of God's judgment on unauthorized worship. Churches of Christ also contended that instruments do not accord with or aid the spiritual purposes of vocal music in Christian worship. The contemporary discussion centers on hermeneutical questions — the nature of Scripture, the significance of history, the theology of worship. Supporters of instruments accuse opponents of legalism, and non-instrumentalists accuse those who favor them of adhering to a system of interpretation that would allow many items unacceptable even to them into the worship. Neither side has been wholly consistent in the application of its principles. Both sides have accused the other of causing the division.

A central issue in regard to the question of New Testament authorization or silence about instrumental music concerns the meaning of the Greek words *psallō* and *psalmos.* M. C. Kurfees (1856-1931) argued that despite their etymology these terms were used in the New Testament only for vocal music sung with the heart. O. E. Payne responded with the claim that an instrument inhered in the Greek words. Kurfees responded with an extensive review. Everett Ferguson (b. 1933) added to the argument against instrumental music with a comprehensive survey of these words in patristic literature; he further sought a theological basis for the New Testament and historical evidence.

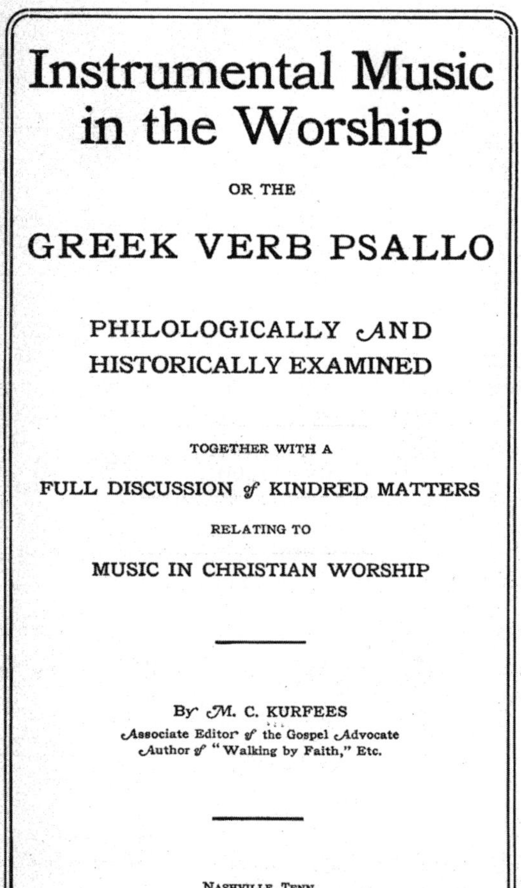

Instrumental Music in the Worship

OR THE

GREEK VERB PSALLO

PHILOLOGICALLY AND HISTORICALLY EXAMINED

TOGETHER WITH A

FULL DISCUSSION of KINDRED MATTERS

RELATING TO

MUSIC IN CHRISTIAN WORSHIP

By M. C. KURFEES

Associate Editor of the Gospel Advocate

Author of "Walking by Faith," Etc.

NASHVILLE, TENN.

McQUIDDY PRINTING COMPANY

1911

The arguments made against instrumental music in worship by M. C. Kurfees (1856-1931) in his 1911 study of the Greek word *psallō* became a key part of the opposition to instruments by Churches of Christ in the twentieth century.

Courtesy of the Center for Restoration Studies, Abilene Christian University

The twentieth century produced numerous debates on the subject of instrumental music in worship. Two that are representative and influential bracket the era of debate on the subject. The debate between W. W. Otey (1867-1961) and J. B. Briney (1839-1927) was held in Louisville, Kentucky, September 14-18, 1908. Otey affirmed that instrumental music in worship is sinful, making the arguments that (1) it comes from humans, not God; (2) it violates the law of expediency; and (3) it violates the law of liberty. Briney, who earlier in life had written in opposition to instruments, contended that what is commanded in the Old Testament, if not forbidden in the New Testament, is allowable. He affirmed that the instrument is a matter of permission, not command, and that his opponent's arguments depended on inferences. Rubel Shelly (b. 1945) and Dwaine Dunning met in debate March 15-18, 1976, in Mason City, Iowa. Shelly covered most of the ground traditionally argued by opponents of the instrument but centered his attention on the authority principle and the proper use of human reason in interpreting Scripture. Dunning, while insisting that music was a "low priority" item, claimed that no biblical verse states that singing is authorized "worship," words must be defined as they are used elsewhere in Scripture, instruments belong in the realm of liberty, and the system of interpretation advocated by Shelly had produced multiple divisions among Churches of Christ.

A century of debates (oral and written), church splits, and occasional lawsuits over possession of property left a trail of bitterness and alienation. Positions in regard to instrumental music, along with positions on other differences, have become institutionalized in the major segments of the Stone-Campbell Movement, but friendly discussions between representatives of its different branches continue to take place over these and other matters, and changes by individuals and occasionally congregations from one viewpoint to the other occurs.

The interpretations of the instrumental music controversy by modern historians reflect their own attitudes on the issue. Earl Irvin West of Churches of Christ collected many quotations, especially from the anti-instrument camp, for his *Search for the Ancient Order* series. W. E. Garrison and A. T. DeGroot, in *Disciples of Christ: A History,* omitted the negative comment of Alexander Campbell on instruments in worship, saw the controversy largely in social and cultural terms, and observed that the anti-organ argument had as its premise "we cannot know what acts of worship are acceptable to God except by express statements of revelation." James DeForest Murch in his *Christians Only* regarded the opposition to instruments as representing a legalistic spirit that made a law out of the silence of Scripture. Lester G. McAllister and William E. Tucker in *Journey in Faith* understood the "organ" controversy as illustrative of different approaches to culture and the church. Leroy Garrett explained in *The Stone-Campbell Movement* that the problem was not different approaches to Scripture as such, but allowing different interpretations to divide believers. Henry E. Webb took the position that the issue was "to become the harshest and most divisive in the period following the Civil War" in his *In Search of Christian Unity.* James B. North in *Unity in Truth* treated the controversy as one example of the "real issue," "the application of biblical authority." Richard T. Hughes in *Reviving the Ancient Faith* said instrumental music and the missionary society became divisive only after it became apparent that the Stone-Campbell Movement contained two irreconcilable traditions, "one defined by ecumenical progressivism and the other by sectarian primitivism."

A development among Churches of Christ in the late twentieth century was the formation of "a cappella bands," in which instrumental sounds are imitated by the voice, but these seldom appear in the assemblies and have met with disapproval among conservatives. The issue has lessened in importance in progressive Churches of Christ, and a few began to use instruments in at least some of their worship services. As in the larger Christian world, Christian Churches/Churches of Christ and the Christian Church (Disciples of Christ) have seen increasing acceptance of guitars and instrumental ensembles into their services in addition to traditional pianos and organs.

See also *American Christian Review;* Bible, Interpretation of the; Burnet, David Staats; Campbell, Alexander; *Christian-Evangelist, The; Christian Standard; Ecclesiastical Reformer;* Errett, Isaac; Franklin, Benjamin; Garrison, James Harvey; *Gospel Advocate, The;* Hayden, Amos Sutton; Hermeneutics; Lamar, James S.; Lard, Moses E.; *Lard's Quarterly;* Lipscomb, David; McGarvey, John W.; Missionary Societies, Controversy over; Murch, James DeForest; Pinkerton, Lewis Letig; Richardson, Robert; Sand Creek "Address and Declaration"; Sommer, Daniel; Worship

BIBLIOGRAPHY Tom Burgess, *Documents on Instrumental Music* (1966) • J. E. Choate and William Woodson, *Sounding Brass and Clanging Cymbals: The History and Significance of Instrumental Music in the Restoration Movement (1827-1968)* (1990) • Everett Ferguson, *A Cappella Music in the Public Worship of the Church* (1972; 3rd ed. 1999) • M. C. Kurfees, review of O. E. Payne's Book on *Psallō* (1922) • M. C. Kurfees, *Instrumental Music in the Worship* (1911; repr. 1950) • David M. Music, *Instruments in Church: A Collection of Source Documents* (1998); • W. W. Otey and J. B. Briney, *Otey-Briney Debate* (1908), pp. 11-159 • O. E. Payne, *Instrumental Music Is Scriptural* (1920) • Rubel Shelly and Dwaine Dunning, *Shelly-Dunning Debate* (1977).

EVERETT FERGUSON

Integrity

Journal operated by progressive members of Churches of Christ, begun at Flint, Michigan, in June 1969 and continuing publication until May 2002.

During its thirty-three-year ministry the journal sought to be a forum open to discussing the current issues troubling and plaguing the unity of Stone-Campbell churches.

The original editorial by Hoy Ledbetter (b. 1932) set the direction and tone of this publication for the next three decades. Emphasizing the two foundational principles of all Protestantism (the supreme authority of the Bible and the right of individual interpretation), Ledbetter indicated that the greatest need of the present hour was genuine honesty.

The original editorial board (Hoy Ledbetter, David Elkins, Frank Rester, and Dean Thoroman) and a corporation composed of Michigan residents from area Churches of Christ were drawn together by a common vision that deplored sectarianism and a party spirit. This spirit of unity was contained in the dictum, "We fellowship people, not ideas."

The tone of the journal set an irenic atmosphere in which the "sacred cows" of the Stone-Campbell Movement could be questioned, challenged, and either rejected or accepted. The spirit of inquiry, intellectual honesty, and the joy of fellowship proved to be the hallmarks of this journal. It was recognized as one of the few papers in the Stone-Campbell Movement that reflected a more "progressive attitude toward issues that were dividing congregations."

This progressive attitude was perceived by some as threatening to the mainline churches, and the *Gospel Advocate* and *Firm Foundation* basically ignored the existence of the journal. Editors and writers were willing to tackle the philosophical and practical implications of the Restoration ideal. Over its thirty-three-year history four issues, more than any others, seemed to dominate the emotional energy and drive dedicated to this journal: the unity of all believers, the authoritarianism of local elderships, women's role in the church, and the work of the Holy Spirit in conversion and sanctification.

A collective angst among Stone-Campbell churches seemed to surface around the polarities of restorationism and holiness, conviction and compassion, and grace and law. At the core of this anxiety lay a struggle for a more biblically responsible hermeneutic that took seriously the cultural, historical, linguistic, and theological centers of biblical faith.

Over the course of thirty-three years five individuals served as editors-in-chief: Hoy Ledbetter, Joseph Jones, Diane G. H. Kilmer, J. Bruce Kilmer, and Curtis D. McClane. Through their leadership the journal existed solely on donations from the readership, which made this a unique publication in the history of the Stone-Campbell Movement.

BIBLIOGRAPHY Hoy Ledbetter et al., eds., *Integrity* (1969-2002). CURTIS D. MCCLANE

Intermountain Bible College

Bible college affiliated with the Christian Churches/Churches of Christ.

Intermountain Bible College (IBC) operated in Grand Junction, Colorado, from 1946 to 1985 in order to provide leadership for churches of the Stone-Campbell tradition in the Intermountain West. IBC and its leaders established twenty-seven churches in the region, often beginning as Sunday Schools.

Area churches incorporated IBC in March 1946 and purchased property near Mesa College, the local junior college. Classes began in September with eleven full-time students. Erskine Scates, Sr., Earl Heald, and John Ball, each a graduate of Phillips University in Oklahoma, were the founders and first teachers. Students could enroll at both IBC and Mesa, an arrangement that allowed IBC coursework to be granted credit at Mesa (now Mesa State College), in spite of IBC's unaccredited status. Enrollment peaked at 121 in January 1975.

The college purchased twenty-two acres in December 1974. Fund-raising for construction projects began, simultaneous with leadership transition. President Scates retired January 1, 1978, and died in July 1979. Construction proceeded, as did efforts to secure accreditation with the Accrediting Association of Bible Colleges, which extended Applicant Status in October 1979. Classes moved to the new campus in January 1980.

Enrollment totaled a little over 100 in 1980-81, but dropped to 65 by 1983-84. In 1982 the regional economy went into sharp decline, weakening the college's financial condition. In October 1984, the Accrediting Association of Bible Colleges removed IBC from the accreditation process due to its declining enrollments and financial struggles. In February the Board of Trustees voted to cease academic operations on June 30, 1985.

The Trustees established the IBC Founders Fund, using net proceeds from property sales, mineral rights, annuities, and bequests to fund scholarships for area students enrolling at other Christian colleges. Hope International University in Fullerton, California, agreed to serve as custodian of academic records. Historical documents are now stored both at Hope International and at Clifton (Colorado) Christian Church. TAMSEN MURRAY

International Churches of Christ

Discipling movement that separated from mainline Churches of Christ in 1993.

The International Churches of Christ (ICOC) began among Churches of Christ during the 1970s through the campus ministry of Chuck Lucas (b. 1938) at the Crossroads Church of Christ in Gainesville, Florida. Commonly known in the 1980s as the "Boston movement" because national leadership was centered in the Boston Church of Christ, the group broke with mainline Churches of Christ formally in 1993 when it organized under the name of International Churches of Christ with world headquarters in Los Angeles, California. In 2002 the ICOC claimed over 130,000 members in 430 congregations in more than 170 countries.

Converted through discipling methods as a college student by Lucas, Kip McKean moved in 1979 to Lexington, Massachusetts, where he called thirty "would-be disciples" in the Lexington Church of Christ (later renamed the Boston Church of Christ) to redefine their commitment to Christ. Through the use of "discipling partners," the congregation rapidly grew, exceeding 3,000 in attendance by 1982. In the ICOC, each member has a discipling partner who oversees his or her spiritual development.

Although the growth of the Boston Church of Christ drew the attention of other congregations throughout the United States, many became concerned about certain practices of the group. In 1988 a sociologist from Harding University, Flavil Yeakley (b. 1934), interviewed hundreds of members, and concluded in his book *Discipling Dilemma* that unhealthy changes in personality were commonly taking place among the members of the movement. Area universities began to accuse the Boston Church of Christ of cultic practices and banned representatives from campuses because of the group's aggressive recruiting methods. Local and national media also reported alleged abuses within the authoritarian structure of the church, because members were required to obey their disciplers in all matters. Church of Christ periodicals decried the developing hierarchal structure, but younger members in many parts of the country were attracted by the prophetic vision and rapid success in Boston.

When the Boston Church of Christ began to plant daughter congregations in other parts of the United States, it became clear that they did not consider members of mainline Churches of Christ to be Christians. Through a process called "restructuring," members from the Boston group would move to a city, join a Church of Christ, and influence leaders within the congregation to move to Boston for retraining. Many leaders of existing congregations did go for training, which included re-baptism, in the 1980s, but the effort to exert authority over whole congregations met with very limited success. As with many pietist movements in Christian history, many first-generation leaders became disillusioned and left the movement by the early 1990s. The Crossroads Church in Gainesville repudiated the movement in 1990 and sought to restore ties to mainline Churches of Christ in a letter written to the *Christian Chronicle.*

In a 1992 issue of his periodical *Upside Down,* Kip McKean's apology for the movement, "Revolution Through Restoration," described the problem of "unbelieving seminaries and dying denominations with systems of doctrines that have been compromised and crystallized short of the Word of God." Although some of the restorationist language in the article is very similar to that of the early days of Alexander Campbell's *Christian Baptist,* the moral authority which McKean claimed for himself, and the pyramidal structure that he advocated, envisioned a polity very different from the congregational autonomy cherished by the Stone-Campbell Movement.

The ICOC is divided into nine world sectors. At the beginning of 2003, changes in the way authority was exercised within this system were taking place. While the previous structure consisted of nine "World Sector Leaders" under McKean as "World Mission Evangelist," following the resignation of McKean in November 2002, new efforts were being made to include more leaders in the guidance of each sector. In February 2004 tentative efforts by some ICOC leaders at reconciliation with mainline Churches of Christ were begun in conjunction with the Abilene Christian University Lectureship.

The ICOC continues as a religious sect, but its international humanitarian ministry, HOPE Worldwide, is an officially recognized nongovernmental organization that has established relationships with many foreign governments unavailable to Churches of Christ. The fact that ICOC congregations are typically multicultural has also gained the positive attention of national media in recent years. A considerable ministry of women to other women, as well as the involvement of instrumental music in worship, further distinguish the ICOC from mainline Churches of Christ.

See also Campus Ministry

BIBLIOGRAPHY Lindy Adams, "ICOC and Mainline Forum: A Meeting of the Minds," *Christian Chronicle* 61 (April 2004): 17-19 • Carol Giambalvo, *The Boston Movement: Critical Perspectives on the International Churches of Christ* (1996) • Jerry Jones, *What Does the Boston Movement Teach?* 3 vols. (1990) • Martin Edward Wooten, "The Boston Movement as a Revitalization Movement" (D.Min. thesis, Harding Graduate School of Theology, 1990) • Flavil Yeakley, *Discipling Dilemma: A Study of the Discipling Movement in Churches of Christ* (1988).

KEVIN S. WELLS

International Convention of the Disciples of Christ

Major gathering of the Disciples of Christ in the early- and mid-twentieth century, predecessor of the General Assembly of the Christian Church (Disciples of Christ).

While the centennial celebration of the Stone-Campbell Movement in Pittsburgh in 1909 was referred to as the "International Centennial and Convention of the Disciples of Christ," it actually predated the first *structured* International Convention by eight years. Yet the Movement was already beginning to exhibit gravitation toward a convention of the centralized and mainstream variety.

In 1912, for example, a constitution for the General Convention of Churches of Christ — "a general convention of churches" constructed on a "delegate basis" — was presented in Louisville and approved. (The first General Convention actually took place in Topeka in 1913.) Support for the measure was nearly unanimous. However, the General Convention scarcely enjoyed popular support thereafter. The Sweeney Resolution, passed in 1916, called upon a committee of five delegates to infuse the weakening 1912 agreement with somewhat more of a business orientation.

Such was the context for the November 2, 1916, edition of the *Christian-Evangelist,* in which editor Frederick D. Kershner proposed a system of twin conventions modeled after the bicameral legislature of the United States. The *Christian Standard* expressed contempt for such a structure. Nevertheless, those who were anxious for a more unified organization called the first meeting of the International Convention of the Disciples of Christ in Kansas City in 1917.

Z. T. Sweeney (1849-1926) was largely responsible for drafting the new Convention's constitution, as well as for much of its American bureaucratic character. A Committee on Recommendations, comprised of one delegate from each state convention, plus an additional delegate for each 25,000 Disciples residing in that state, was designed to augment the mass meeting of registered individual participants. Significantly, all "legislation" was to remain merely "advisory" in nature. Formally, the International Convention of the Disciples of Christ was founded (according to its Articles of Incorporation) "to promote cooperation, economy and efficiency among the various general agencies," to "be the advisory to the missionary, educational and philanthropic interests" of the Movement, and "to promote a closer fellowship" among the Movement's congregations. The International Convention, then, replaced the General Convention. Graham Frank was its first secretary and served until 1946 — the same year that a headquarters was established for the Convention and an executive staff called together in Indianapolis.

The inclination for consolidation led, in 1919, to the creation of the United Christian Missionary Society (UCMS) — an umbrella under which six separate agencies were synthesized. It combined the work of, among others, the American Christian Missionary Society, the Christian Woman's Board of Missions, and the Foreign Christian Missionary Society.

A "protest convention" was thereupon orchestrated in 1926 as the *Christian Standard* reported that the International Convention in Memphis had devolved into a "convention of bad faith." Disgruntled with the shift toward centralization, as well as with reports of open membership on the mission field, dissenters moved in 1927 to establish their own North American Christian Convention. It has been asserted that the protest was more a reaction against the UCMS than against the International Convention itself. In fact, the UCMS more or less eclipsed the International Convention as a vehicle for consolidation before 1934.

In 1934 a Commission of Restudy of the Disciples of Christ was created at the meeting of the International Convention in Des Moines to recover some of what had initially made unity possible among participants in the Stone-Campbell Movement. The Commission reported to the Convention in 1946 and sought to establish study groups among congregations on the subject. The commission was dissolved in 1949 and its Report to the International Convention was largely ignored.

Also in 1949, a "Council of Agencies" was recommended to coordinate the work of the different agencies of the Disciples of Christ and to conduct an ongoing study of the denomination's long-range planning and organization. Eventually, participation in the Council became obligatory for any agency that reported to the International Convention.

The name of the International Convention of the Disciples of Christ was changed to the "International Convention of Christian Churches (Disciples of Christ)" in Des Moines in 1956. The consolidation necessary for the creation of a denomination was set in motion shortly thereafter. At a Conference on Unification in 1958, leaders proposed strategies for the unification of state boards. At the International Convention in Denver in 1959, "Restructure of the Brotherhood" became a priority. Those involved in the push for centralization finally made their intentions of forming a denomination clear in Louisville in 1960. Then, in 1961, a Commission on Brotherhood Structure was established. In 1966 a "Provisional Design" for the Disciples of Christ was set forth in Dallas. Finally, in 1968, the new denomination became official at the meeting of the International Convention in Kansas City. The International Convention would be superseded by the General Assembly of the Christian Church (Disciples of Christ), though the actual structure and relation of Disciples agencies and congregations had changed little.

See also American Christian Missionary Society; Commission on Restudy of the Disciples of Christ; Conventions; Kershner, Frederick D.; North American Christian Convention; Restructure; Sweeney, Zachary Taylor; United Christian Missionary Society, The

BIBLIOGRAPHY A. T. DeGroot, *The Convention Among the Disciples of Christ* (1958) • Anthony L. Dunnavant, *Four Historical Ideals in the Campbell-Stone Movement and the Development of the Polity of the Christian Church (Disciples of Christ)* (1993) TIMOTHY C. SMITH

Internet Resources on the Stone-Campbell Movement

The Internet contains a wealth of electronic information related to the Stone-Campbell Movement. The most comprehensive site is Hans Rollmann's "The Restoration Movement" (http://www.mun.ca/rels/restmov/restmov.html), based at the Memorial University of Newfoundland. Resources available include electronic versions of texts by Stone-Campbell personalities, biographical sketches, portraits, texts from periodicals, and thematic studies. The content of the site is inclusive of the three major segments of the Movement. Information is also available about religious movements related to the Stone-Campbell Movement, including such groups as the Christadelphians, International Church of Christ, and the Christian Denomination. There are links to other significant Stone-Campbell web sites such as educational institutions, organizations affiliated with the three main branches of the Movement, periodicals, denominational offices, on-line publications, and reference sources such as bibliographies, searchable databases, and indexes of periodicals.

Most Stone-Campbell Movement colleges, seminaries, and universities have web sites, and many make their on-line catalogs available via the Internet using a web browser. A number of Stone-Campbell publishers have web sites that allow online browsing and purchasing of books.

For the hymnology of the Stone-Campbell Movement one can access the on-line version of Enos Dowling's hymnbook collection at http://www.lccs.edu/library/hymnals.

The official site of the Christian Church (Disciples of Christ) is http://www.disciples.org/, providing links to the principal institutional arms of the denomination. The undenominational character of the Christian Churches/Churches of Christ and of the Churches of Christ means that no "official" web site exists for these segments of the Movement. There are, however, unofficially representative ones in operation. Especially important for Christian Churches/Churches of Christ is the web site of the North American Christian Convention (http://www.naccthe connectingplace.org). An important informational resource for Churches of Christ may be found at http://church-of-christ.org. Many local congregations also have their own web sites.

Other useful sites are an index to names appearing in obituaries in the *Gospel Advocate* from 1844 to 1994 (http://academic.lipscomb.edu/gaobit) and the Restoration Serials Index, which includes author and keyword searching of articles from over seventy Stone-Campbell Movement journals (http://www.bible.acu.edu/rsi).

Sites related to historical societies and archival materials are the Disciples of Christ Historical Society (http://www.dishistsoc.org) and the Center for Restoration Studies (http://www.bible.acu.edu/crs).

Electronic mailing lists include Stone-Campbell for the discussion of historical issues and DOCDISC for the discussion of issues related to the Christian Church (Disciples of Christ). Information on subscribing to these discussion groups may be found at http://www.mun.ca/rels/restmov/subs/resource.html.

JAMES L. MCMILLAN

J

Jackson, Thomas

See New Zealand, The Movement in

Jamaica, The Movement in

Early missionary initiative of the Stone-Campbell Movement in the Caribbean.

Located about a hundred miles south of Cuba in the tropical climate of the Caribbean, the island of Jamaica has been a concentration for Stone-Campbell missions from all three streams of the Movement for over 150 years. The Jamaican government does not support churches or religion, but it does not discourage religious practices. Religious instruction is very common in the elementary grades, with a set curriculum agreed upon by the Catholic and Protestant churches. According to the *CIA World Factbook,* 61.3 percent of Jamaica's population is Protestant. Roman Catholics make up 4 percent, while other religious groups and cults make up 34.7 percent. Self-governing congregations from different denominations, such as Baptists, Methodists, and Anglicans, were established as early as 1842.

The Disciples of Christ started recording their mission work in 1838, when Julius Oliver Beardslee visited Jamaica after graduating from Oberlin Collegiate Institute in Ohio. He noticed the potential for mission work there and preached in several congregations, including some in the British West Indies. He returned to Jamaica with financial backing by the American Christian Missionary Society (ACMS) in 1857 to start a congregation in Kingston. The Oberlin Congregational Church, which was started fifteen miles from Kingston in 1858, later transferred to the Disciples of Christ in 1861. In the 1859 *Millennial Harbinger,* Alexander Campbell published an article that included a letter from Beardslee reporting the work that was being done in Jamaica. Almost one year later, in December 1859, another letter in the *Millennial Harbinger* from Beardslee appeared indicating a net increase of 19 members from the original 18 founding members to reach a total of 37 members. In June of 1860, the *Millennial Harbinger* reported an increase to 50 members. Various reports on the efforts of this congregation continued until Beardslee left Jamaica in 1864. The Christian Woman's Board of Missions (CWBM) started another missionary effort in Jamaica to continue his work when the organization was formed in 1874. Its work in Jamaica was then transferred to the United Christian Missionary Society in 1922, the legacy of which remains today among the Disciples congregations still operating in the country, which are now part of the United Church in Jamaica and the Cayman Islands.

The first spearhead of "independent" missions of the Stone-Campbell Movement, the Jamaica Christian Mission, formally dates from the arrival of Luke Douglas Elliot in 1939, who helped start a congregation in the St. Catherine parish. But before Elliot, C. Vincent Hall, a former officer in the British army, who had Congregationalist and Baptist connections but eventually affiliated with the Churches of Christ, had already worked since 1935 to plant churches in Jamaica. On a successful fund-raising tour in the United States in 1938, Elliot responded to Hall's appeal for the establishment of a Bible college in Jamaica. Elliot began a college, and in the early 1950s he was succeeded by Woodrow Phillips and Donald Fream (connected with the Christian Churches/Churches of Christ), who continued evangelistic efforts and maintained the Jamaica Bible Seminary until its closure in 1959. Throughout the 1950s, the Christian Churches/Churches of Christ continued church planting and inaugurated the Jamaica Christian Boys' Home.

A number of other independent missions have been undertaken by individuals from the Christian Churches/Churches of Christ since the 1950s. In 1994 the Jamaica Christian College and Bible Seminary was reopened with help from churches in Florida and continues with a full academic program and a faculty of native Jamaicans and numerous visiting professors from the United States.

When Clifford Edwards disassociated from the Disciples of Christ in 1958, he called upon the Churches of Christ to join him in Jamaica. In 1966 the Pearl Street Church of Christ in Denton, Texas, and the North Davis Church of Christ in Arlington, Texas, organized several survey trips to Jamaica. By 1967 three survey trips had been made that convinced the elders of the congregations to support missionaries to Jamaica. A team thereupon moved to Kingston and established the Mona congregation in 1967.

The Jamaica School of Preaching and Biblical Studies began in 1970 after the purchase of the Mona theater building. This building also serves as the meeting place for the Mona Church of Christ. Guy V. Caskey was the first director of the school. The original purpose of the school and the facilities was threefold: to train young men to be preachers, to provide offices to house a Bible chair for the University of the West Indies, and to produce books, tracts, and other literature. The school has had approximately 20 to 26 students enrolled per year since it began in 1970, and since its inception has graduated about 70 men from the program. The purpose of the Jamaica School of Preaching is to prepare men to preach the gospel throughout the Caribbean, including Haiti, the Dominican Republic, Puerto Rico, and Cuba. The opening of such a school in the capital of Jamaica has been a moving force in the planting of churches of Christ in Jamaica and throughout countries in the Caribbean.

Other efforts in the 1960s included the radio program Christ for Jamaica, led by Marvin Crowson, Milo Hadwin, and Jerry Thompson; distribution of tracts; enrollment in correspondence courses; and the 1960 Jamaican Group made up of students from Harding College who planned to move to Jamaica in the summer of 1964.

A growing number of Churches of Christ have been involved in missionary work in Jamaica, with a major surge of congregations starting in the late 1960s and early 1970s with the help of established congregations in the United States. Many congregations have either dissolved or merged with other congregations since the 1970s due to lack of funds, lack of members, or both. Another surge of congregations began in the early 1980s, mostly through the efforts of the East Tallassee Church of Christ in Alabama, which is still involved in mission efforts to Jamaica today. Documentation of missionary efforts of the Churches of Christ can be traced back as far as 1958; however, the *World Christian Encyclopedia* indicates that missionaries affiliated with the Stone-Campbell Movement came to Jamaica in 1885, before the 1906 distinction of Churches of Christ as a separate religious body. The Churches of Christ are still conducting missionary efforts and campaigns to Jamaica and the Caribbean; however, the Pentecostal revival of the 1990s in Jamaica may have hindered efforts, especially in urban areas. A Caribbean Mission Workshop was held in 1999 in Morton, Mississippi, and another workshop was held in May of 2000 in Florence, Alabama, sponsored by the East Tallassee congregation.

In December of 1992, congregations of the Christian Church (Disciples of Christ) in Jamaica formally united with the United Churches of Christ (UCC) there to form the United Church in Jamaica and the Cayman Islands. In its joint Global Ministries initiative with the United Church of Christ, the Christian Church (Disciples of Christ) has focused attention primarily on the UCC's preexisting involvements in reconciliation and redressing of social and economic injustice in Jamaica, amid significant social and political unrest in the country in recent years.

The "Organized churches and denominations in Jamaica" table from the *World Christian Encyclopedia* has listed the Christian Churches/Churches of Christ as having 39 congregations in Jamaica. The Churches of Christ have 16 congregations, and the Disciples of Christ have 70 congregations listed. According to *Churches of Christ Around the World,* there are 48 congregations in 13 parishes of Jamaica, which would seem to be more accurate since this work gives specific attention only to Churches of Christ rather than to the other streams of the Stone-Campbell tradition.

See also American Christian Missionary Society; Direct Support Missions; Latin America and Caribbean, Missions in

BIBLIOGRAPHY Mac Lynn, ed., *Churches of Christ Around the World: Exclusive of the United States and Her Territories* (1990, 2003) • Bailey B. McBride, "Jamaica: Caribbean Island Churches Continue to Grow," *Christian Chronicle* 44 (1987): 24 • Donald McGavran, *Church Growth in Jamaica: A Preview of Things to Come in Many Lands* (1962) • Robert G. Nelson, *Disciples of Christ in Jamaica, 1858-1958* (1958)

MELISSA JOHNSON

Janes, Don Carlos (1877-1944)

Evangelist, author, editor, missionary entrepreneur, and premillennial propagandist among Churches of Christ.

Baptized by W. O. Thompson in 1892, he preached his first sermon in January 1897 to the Church of Christ at Malta, Ohio, where he was ordained as an evangelist on February 3, 1898. By 1899 he was traveling throughout the Midwest preaching and contributing articles to Daniel Sommer's *Octographic Review* and William F. Parmiter's *Primitive Christian.*

Janes entered Potter Bible College (Bowling

Green, Kentucky) in 1901. When missionary William J. Bishop (1872-1913) lectured at Potter in 1902, Janes awakened to the call of world missions. While still a student in 1904 he sailed to Europe, Asia Minor, Egypt, Syria, and the Holy Land, sending reports to religious journals and Ohio newspapers, and collecting facts, impressions, and reflections that he would publish in his first two books, *A Trip Abroad* (1905) and *The Cedric Papers* (1906). One week after his return, on December 22, 1904, Janes married Myrtie Leola Porter (1881-1941) and returned to his studies at Potter. When their teacher John Nelson Armstrong (1870-1944) organized Western Bible and Literary College (Odessa, Missouri) in 1905, the Janeses were among the first students to enroll.

As Janes completed work at Western he established lifelong friendships with music teacher Elmer Leon Jorgenson (1886-1968) and Robert Henry Boll (1875-1956), who visited the campus as preacher and lecturer. Accompanied by Jorgenson, Janes spent the summer of 1907 in an intensive evangelistic campaign in Iowa, speaking 156 times in 114 days. By then he also had begun another lifelong passion, the study of "prophecy."

Janes's education and travel had endowed him with a world consciousness and convinced him that the challenge of worldwide Christian mission was paramount. In the vacuum produced by controversy over missionary societies, consciousness of world missions and missionaries was almost nonexistent in Churches of Christ. Janes's world consciousness, fired by anticipation of an imminent, premillennial *eschaton,* led him to fill that void. He began to develop a network of missionaries, potential missionaries, prospective supporters, and useful resources and services that would form the core of his life's work.

For two years after leaving Potter, Janes preached for a church in Cincinnati, then he and his wife moved to Louisville, Kentucky, in 1910 and became members of the Highland Church of Christ where E. L. Jorgenson was preacher. From there Janes continued his work for missions, beginning in 1911 *Encouragement Magazine,* the first of his monthly periodicals designed to recruit and encourage missionaries and their supporters. By 1915 R. H. Boll was arranging to acquire the monthly *Word and Work* and move it to Louisville. Janes ended *Encouragement* and at the beginning of 1916 began a regular column in *Word and Work* that would continue for the rest of his life.

Already Janes was soliciting financial contributions for missionaries and distributing them at his own expense. With J. M. McCaleb, missionary to Japan, he established a revolving fund to provide housing for missionaries on the field; missionaries could borrow money to purchase property and build or renovate, repaying the loan at enough interest to maintain the fund and make future loans possible. World War I delayed the Janeses' plans for a trip around the world to visit missionaries and scout new fields. They finally departed on October 7, 1920, and visited Japan, China, Singapore, Burma, India, Egypt, Palestine, and Europe. Returning to Louisville in May 1922, after 590 days and more than 36,000 miles, Janes digested the journey in *Our World Tour* (1924), which conveyed the urgency and the immensity of the challenge he saw for Christian missions in the 1920s.

In January 1924 Janes began publishing his monthly *Boosters' Bulletin,* which became *Missionary Messenger* in 1929. The Janeses had sold Bibles, books, office equipment, and supplies to support themselves and their work. In 1929, as Myrtie Janes was becoming seriously ill, Janes expanded his "printing office" into a printing business. By 1943 he claimed to have printed and distributed four million tracts, most of them evangelistic, some discussing the means and support of missions and a few others teaching premillennial topics. Janes identified and recruited missionaries and missionary supporters; solicited, collected, and disbursed missionary funds; arranged, scheduled, and paid for missionary travel; and managed the operations of the missionary housing fund.

When the Highland church in 1918 divided over Jorgenson's premillennial teaching, Jorgenson and Janes emerged tainted by the conflict. Critics inevitably called Janes "a one-man missionary society." The ad hoc, voluntary nature of his missions enterprise was at once its greatest weakness as well as its greatest strength. Mounting opposition to premillennial teaching among Churches of Christ made Janes a figure of controversy. Charges that he supported only premillennial believers on the mission field, however, would not stick; J. M. McCaleb, unimpeachably amillennial, was his partner of longest duration. Questions about his handling of money would never go away, although the Janeses lived sacrificially. As opposition became bitterly divisive, Janes sought contact with sympathetic Disciples, corresponding with Frederick Doyle Kershner (1875-1953) and others, and eagerly participating in the Murch-Witty unity gatherings of the late 1930s and early 1940s. His press published the *Christian Unity Quarterly* that grew from those meetings.

Janes was a pacifist and opposed Christian participation in warfare. In 1939 he wrote a forty-five page essay on "the Christian's proper attitude toward carnal warfare," sending it to libraries of all schools among Churches of Christ and Disciples, as well as the Library of Congress.

Myrtie Janes died in August 1941. Janes immersed himself in his work until a few weeks before he died on January 20, 1944. He stipulated in his will that missionary funds were to be kept in trust and distributed to the missionaries whom his work had supported. The bulk of his personal estate went to support publications documenting the history and tenets of premillennialism. Janes had worked for years on this project, amassing a large library and traveling to others to do research. Janes's will and Jorgenson's execution of it sealed the exclusion of premillennial believers from the fellowship of mainstream Churches of Christ for decades to come. Yet Janes left a legacy that continued to bear fruit on mission fields. The number of missionaries from Churches of Christ had increased from 8 in 1892, to 32 by 1926, to 60 by 1932, and in 1942, as the world plunged into war once more, 37 remained in place and another 24 were "home on account of war, education and surgery." Janes had opened the eyes of countless congregations and individuals to the challenges and possibilities of world missions, and after the war, in a time of new, global consciousness and unprecedented prosperity, they would open their hearts and pocketbooks as well. Missions flowered and multiplied beyond anything that even Janes could have imagined in his years of struggle and sacrifice.

See also Boll, Robert Henry; Eschatology; McCaleb, John Moody; Missions, Missiology; Murch, James DeForest; *Word and Work*

BIBLIOGRAPHY Don Carlos Janes, ed., *Encouragement Magazine* (1911-15) • Don Carlos Janes, ed., *Boosters' Bulletin* (1924-28) • Don Carlos Janes, ed., *Missionary Messenger* (1929-44) • Don Carlos Janes, *A Trip Abroad: An Account of a Journey to the Earthly Canaan and the Land of the Ancient Pharaohs* (1905) • Don Carlos Janes, *The Cedric Papers: A Collection of Sketches on Miscellaneous Subjects Written Mainly While on a Voyage from Liverpool to New York on the Steamship Cedric* (1906) • Don Carlos Janes, *Our World Tour: Personal Observations and Experiences on a Trip Around the World, 1920-1922* (1924) • *Faith of Our Fathers: A Compendium of Scripture Teaching on Prophecy and Unity, Extracts, Clear and Rare, from the "Fathers" and the Reformers, Precious Reprints from the Men of the "Restoration Movement" with Special Articles by the Editor and Others on the Fellowship Problems of Our Day*, ed. E. L. Jorgenson [from material provided by Don Carlos Janes and published serially in *Word and Work* from 1945 to 1952 according to the provisions of Janes's will] (1953) • Don Carlos Janes's personal papers, Archives of Christian Theological Seminary, Indianapolis, Indiana.

DON HAYMES

Japan, Missions in

See Asia, Missions in

Jardine, George

See Common Sense Philosophy

Jarvis Christian College

Related to the Christian Church (Disciples of Christ).

Disciples established Jarvis Christian College to educate black Americans. Strongly committed to the Disciples heritage, Jarvis serves African Americans from all denominations. Financial gifts from Major J. J. Jarvis, Ida Van Zandt, and the Negro Woman's Society of the Disciples made it possible for Jarvis Christian College to open its doors in 1912 in Hawkins, Texas. Dr. J. N. Ervin, a Booker T. Washington–like figure, became the first president of Jarvis Christian College in 1912, holding that post until 1938.

Beginning as a high school, Jarvis Christian College became a junior college in 1928 before becoming a four-year college in 1950. In 1964 the college became affiliated with Texas Christian University; this affiliation ceased twelve years later. In 1967 the school gained full membership and accreditation into the Southern Association of Colleges and Schools, and in 1968 it obtained full membership in the Association of Texas Colleges and Universities. Under its tenth president, Dr. Sebetha Jenkins, Jarvis Christian College remains committed to preparing youth to be Christian leaders, offering Bachelor of Arts, Bachelor of Science, and Bachelor in Business Administration degrees and boasting an enrollment of over 500 students.

BIBLIOGRAPHY E. B. Bynum, *These Carry the Torch* (1946) • Clifford H. Taylor, Jr., "Jarvis Christian College" (B.A. Thesis, Texas Christian University, 1946).

EDWARD J. ROBINSON

First named Jarvis Christian Institute following the model of Southern Christian Institute in Mississippi, Jarvis Christian College began classes in 1913 on 456 acres deeded to the Christian Woman's Board of Missions by J. J. and Ida Van Zandt Jarvis for a school for black youth. The men standing at the far left and far right are likely T. A. Frost and C. A. Berry respectively. The building was Forest Hall, named after Thomas Buchanan Forest. Courtesy of the Disciples of Christ Historical Society

Jenkins, Burris

See Lexington Theological Seminary

Jesus Christ

See Christology

Jeter, Jeremiah Bell (1802-1880)

Baptist critic of the Stone-Campbell Movement.

Jeremiah Bell Jeter was the oldest son of seven children, born to Pleasant and Jane Eke (Hatcher) Jeter in Bedford County, Virginia, on July 18, 1802. Although Bedford County was predominantly Baptist, Jeter was relatively uneducated in the Christian faith. He nonetheless read the Bible frequently, and in the summer of 1821 attended a revival in Bedford. He then began to study the Scriptures and eventually accepted Christ as his Savior and was baptized in December of the same year. He became a Baptist minister in 1824 and preached mostly in the vicinity of Richmond, Virginia.

Virginia Baptist leader Jeremiah Bell Jeter (1802-1880), author of *Campbellism Examined* and *Campbell Re-Examined*, was part of an April 1866 meeting in Richmond between leaders in the Stone-Campbell Movement and the Southern Baptist Convention. He concluded that though reunion talks were premature, by continued discussion and "reasonable concessions . . . gradual assimilation could occur."

Jeter first came into contact with Alexander Campbell and the term "restoration" in 1825 and had numerous conversations with people who supported Campbell and the Movement. In response to concerns and a petition of fellow prominent Baptists, Jeter wrote the book *Campbellism Examined* (1855), whose purpose was "to promote the cause of truth and piety" and "to furnish a faithful delineation of the system — its principles, spirit and influence — to censure the evil, and commend the good." In the work, Jeter attacked Campbell's errant views of conversion, particularly his confinement of the role of the Holy Spirit merely to that of persuasion with respect to the arguments and meaning of the scriptural Word. Campbell's review of Jeter's book appeared in the 1855 volume of the *Millennial Harbinger* as an "Introduction" to a book he planned to write but never published. Moses E. Lard wrote a nearly 300-page response in 1857 that was endorsed by Campbell. Jeter wrote the pamphlet "Campbellism Re-examined" in 1856 as a response to Campbell's review of the first book. Jeter's last confrontation with Campbell, during a meeting of the Baptists and Reformers in Richmond, involved discussion of baptism and regeneration and ended politely but not amiably.

See also Baptists; Conversion; Outsiders' Views of the Movement; Lard, Moses E.

BIBLIOGRAPHY Alexander Campbell, "'Campbellism Examined,' by Jeremiah Jeter" (book review), *Millennial Harbinger* (1855): 61-75, 140-45, 181-90, 257-65, 305-11, 366-72, 438-46, 448-57, 547-54 • William Eldridge Hatcher, *Life of J. B. Jeter* (1887) • Jeremiah Bell Jeter, *Campbellism Examined* (1855) • Moses E. Lard, *A Review of Rev. J. B. Jeter's book entitled "Campbellism Examined"* (1857).

MELISSA JOHNSON

Jews and Judaism, Views of in the Movement

American Protestants in the nineteenth century were deeply interested in the global migrations of Jews and with the gradual increase of Jewish relocation in Palestine preceding the rise of modern Zionism. Protestant eschatology was a strong motivator. Both postmillennialists, who summoned the churches to work under divine providence gradually to usher in the millennial order, and premillennialists, who expected God's dramatic intervention to impose Christ's millennial reign, were convinced that the converted Jewish people would be a key agent in the glorious outcome of history. The scientific study of biblical prophecy and popular Christian fascination with the "signs of the times" generated continuing speculation about the Jews' imminent involvement in the evangelization and transformation of the world.

First-generation leaders of the Stone-Campbell Movement were well aware that the London Jews Society and other organizations were already evangelizing Jews. By 1819 the American Board of Commissioners for Foreign Missions had dispatched its first two missionaries to Jews in Palestine. Other American Protestant missionary societies followed suit. Early Stone-Campbell periodicals — Barton Stone's *Christian Messenger,* Walter Scott's *The Evangelist,* and Alexander Campbell's *Millennial Harbinger* — included abundant excerpts from outside literature documenting Jewish migrations and conversions. Stone, Scott, Campbell, and others candidly expressed their hopes for the successful evangelization of the Jewish people, despite Campbell's early skepticism about Jews committing to Christ. Walter Scott, though by no means a conscious Christian Zionist, deduced in the name of scientific exegesis that the repatriation and political restoration of the Jews were destined to be part of the millennial timetable. While later disavowing this premillennial enthusiasm in favor of a more spiritualized millennialism, others would take up the prophetic mantle, including Robert Milligan at Bethany College (1854-59), whose substantial studies of prophecy — and of the Jews' role in the millennium — were published by Alexander Campbell in the *Millennial Harbinger.*

A turning point came in 1849, when the Stone-Campbell Movement made its first *practical* commitment to missionary work among Jews. The newly formed American Christian Missionary Society commissioned its first international missionary, Dr. James Barclay of Virginia, to evangelize Jews in Palestine. Hopes were running high that Barclay's mission would help effect the restoration of New Testament Christianity (concurrently the inauguration of the millennial order) in the Holy Land itself, the cradle of world Christianity. At this point Alexander Campbell remained guardedly approving of prophecy science but discouraged extravagant speculations. Barclay's first term of service (1851-54) was largely a failure, with few Jews converted. His second term (1858-62) was likewise dismal, compelling Barclay not to spurn the Jewish mission but to embrace a strident premillennialism and to refocus his energies on the repatriation of the Jews as antecedent to their mass conversion. Still in the Holy Land, he formed in 1860 a pan-denominational "Abrahamic League for the Restoration of Israel." After his return to the United States he continued to publish his premillennial views in the *Millennial Harbinger,* though by this time Alexander Campbell, Isaac Errett, and other leaders had wearied of Barclay's quixotic zeal and of inflated prophetic expectations of the Jews' precise role in the millennium.

Over and beyond eschatological expectations and missionary commitments, a truly consistent element in nineteenth-century attitudes toward the Jews and Judaism in the Stone-Campbell Movement was a doctrine of revelation that situated Judaism within an outline of progressive dispensations, Patriarchal, Mosaic, and Christian. This scheme, combined with the Campbellian principle of the superior authority of New Testament to Old Testament and of Gospel to Law (see Alexander Campbell's 1816 *Sermon on the Law*), thoroughly relativized Judaism vis-à-vis Christianity. As a result, Stone-Campbell Christians tended to be intrigued by Judaism as a relic of the biblical past bearing the dignity of Abraham, while simultaneously they disparaged it as a religion laboring under a covenant now thoroughly superseded in Christ.

A vivid example of such attitudes is Alexander Campbell's own 1830 "Dialogue with a Jew," a recorded conversation with the "Ruler of a synagogue" in Richmond, Virginia, who had been impressed by Campbell's defense of revealed religion against Robert Owen. Campbell insisted, "I can never reproach a Jew. We Gentiles are debtors to the seed of Abraham for all that gives us elevation of character." Yet in what followed, Campbell reintroduced the longstanding Christian argument that the Jews had historically suffered so severely precisely because they crucified the Christ, and he further engaged the elderly teacher in an extended debate on messianic prophecy in obvious hopes of undermining his defense of the Jewish interpretation.

Similarly in 1864, J. W. McGarvey visited a synagogue service in Louisville, confessing his deep interest in Judaism but concluding that "I never realized how completely Israel was bereft, when stripped of her temple, her altar, her priesthood and victims. All that is left of her ancient heritage is the Synagogue, where the reading of the Law but mocks their inability to observe its requirements. . . . Will the vail [sic] ever be taken away? Will the captive daughter of Zion ever return to her native honor? Let the student of prophecy answer."

By the late nineteenth and early twentieth centuries, most constituents of the Stone-Campbell Movement had little memory of the missionary labors of James Barclay, and yet, while the wave of prophetic enthusiasm had subsided, there was some lingering interest both in missions to the Jews and in the political restoration of Israel. Advocates were few, but no less a figure than J. W. McGarvey, by this time a leading conservative Disciples biblical scholar, still affirmed in the 1903 *Christian Standard* that the repatriation of already converted Jews would figure into the millennium, but that now the Jews' own Zionist movement, rather than Protestant Christian activism, would likely be God's instrument in bringing this about. Conservative Disciples continued to support small-scale Jewish evangelism like the "Christian Witness to Israel" mission in New York City in the 1920s and 1930s.

Among Churches of Christ, occasional articles concerning the punishment, conversion, and salvation of the Jews by David Lipscomb, E. G. Sewell, H. Leo Boles, and others appeared in the pages of the *Gospel Advocate* from the 1880s well into the 1930s. Ultimately, however, the journal adopted the general position that the Jews' historic survival of toils and persecution was evidence that God was holding out hope for them, though the Jews were subject to exactly the same gospel and the same conditions of faith as Gentiles. Evangelism among Jews was occasionally but not systematically endorsed. Churches of Christ succeeded, nevertheless, in sending out some Jewish Christian evangelists to make inroads among potential Jewish converts. One such was Stephen D. Eckstein, who carried on Jewish evangelism in Dallas in the 1920s and in Kansas City in the 1940s. Like McGarvey before him, Eckstein held hope for Jewish Zionism as an instrument toward the repatriation and conversion of the world's Jews. Reporting the progress of his mission in the journal *Word and Work,* Eckstein insisted that Jews needed to be led beyond legal religiosity to the Christian gospel that "offers salvation to all alike, and on the same terms."

Meanwhile biblical scholars of the Stone-Campbell heritage remained interested in Jewish history and institutions primarily as background for the study of the New Testament. Disciples liberals, however, espoused a new openness to, and tolerance of, the Jewish people and Jewish faith in keeping with their minimally dogmatic Christianity. In his *The Jew Through the Centuries* (1932), Herbert L. Willett of the University of Chicago acknowledged the historic barriers to Christian-Jewish relations. "As long as [Jesus] was interpreted under a trinitarian formula, the strict monotheism of the Jews was shocked and repelled. With the passing of that conception of deity, a new door opens to Jewish and Christian fellowship, and to a recognition of Jesus as the chief contribution of Jewish life to the world." Jews as Jews and Christians as Christians, Willett suggested, could now contribute side by side to humanitarian culture worldwide in accordance with "the wide circle of Jesus' life and ideals."

Such goodwill at home nevertheless failed to induce sufficient sympathy from the Stone-Campbell churches to prompt any substantial outcry against Nazi mistreatment of the Jews in Europe during World War II — a failure shared by other American Protestant churches. Some did note this tragic silence, including Disciples theologian Frederick Kershner in the *Christian-Evangelist.* Bemoaning the "indifference of English and American Christians to the extinction of the Jews," he wrote prophetically in 1943, "Hitler's treatment of this persecuted people will be one of the dark spots in contemporary history, but the indifference of democratic nations to the whole problem will also make uncomfortable reading for decent people in years to come." There were some calls after the war for reparations for the Jewish people. *Christian-Evangelist* editor R. H. Miller announced in 1945 his support for "the creation of a Jewish commonwealth in Palestine [as] as a concern of Christians who cannot separate themselves from this people who share with them The Bible, the great moral and social ideals of the Jewish prophets and the history-making characters of the Old Testament."

At the other extreme, during the 1940s and 1950s there is evidence of participation by some staunch conservatives from the Stone-Campbell churches in right-wing groups such as the Ku Klux Klan, whose anti-Semitic activism was hardly a secret. The most sensational case was Louisiana Disciples minister Gerald L. K. Smith, who founded the Christian Nationalist Crusade in 1942 and published the strongly anti-Semitic monthly *The Cross and the Flag* in hopes of rallying evangelicals to protect Protestant America from ethnic and religious rivals. His special target was, in his own words, the "highly organized campaign to substitute Jewish tradition for Christian tradition."

In more recent decades, attitudes within Christian Churches/Churches of Christ and Churches of Christ parallel those of the nineteenth century in many respects, for one finds, broadly speaking, a reverence for the legacy of the Jews as a covenant people combined with the acknowledgment of their providential survival, their contemporary spiritual poverty, and their consequent need for the gospel. It has not been uncommon in some local congregations of the Christian Churches/Churches of Christ and Churches of Christ to find sympathy for, or even financial support of, evangelistic missions to the Jews, including groups like the American Board of Missions to the Jews (now Chosen People Ministries) and "Jews for Jesus." One influential spokesman was W. Carl Ketcherside of the Churches of Christ, whose *Talks to Jews and Non-Jews* (1977) urged respect for the Jewish heritage and people but claimed that contemporary Judaism, infiltrated (like liberal Christianity) with rationalism and humanism, could not, with its ideals of social justice, transform the world or deliver a gospel of forgiveness. Ketcherside encouraged Jews to accept Jesus as the *personal* Messiah proclaimed by the prophets, and so also to retain their identity as "Messianic Jews" or "Jews for Jesus."

Some small-scale, localized missionary initiatives

have emerged within the Christian Churches/Churches of Christ from time to time. "Emeth," in the greater Chicago area, for example, was begun in the 1980s by a Jewish Christian graduate of Lincoln Christian College as an endeavor not only to convert Jews but to enlist greater support for "Messianic" congregations serving both Gentile and Jewish converts.

Interest in biblical prophecy, including support for Israel and its role in the millennial timetable, has once again been heavily promoted by the Texas-based Lamb and Lion Ministries, founded in 1980 by David Reagan, who has sought an audience both from Churches of Christ and Christian Churches/Churches of Christ. Calling the Jewish people "God's prophetic time clock," Reagan has constructed, on the basis of Old Testament prophecies and Romans 11:1-6, 25-29, a vision of the Jews undergoing an unparalleled future tribulation, followed by the salvation of the "remnant" and the ultimate repatriation of all converted Jews in Israel, thereupon to be established as "the prime nation of the world during the Millennial Reign of Jesus."

The General Assembly of the Christian Church (Disciples of Christ) has instead promoted the renewal of interfaith dialogue, and passed resolutions (Nos. 7732, 8132, 8946) to this effect. In 1993 the General Assembly accepted a report (No. 9313) from the Disciples' Commission on Theology that encouraged broad congregational involvement in restudying the church's relation to Jews on biblical, historical, and theological grounds but stopped short of condemning evangelization of Jews altogether. The document asserted that the apostle Paul himself saw the continuing existence of Jews who did not confess the lordship of Jesus precisely as a "mystery and witness to the church" within God's inscrutable plan (Rom. 11:33).

A few Disciples scholars have thus encouraged Christian-Jewish reconciliation as an ethical and theological priority. Clark Williamson, exponent of a "Post-Holocaust theology," argued in his *A Guest in the House of Israel* (1993) that "the mission of the church is one that it shares *with* the people Israel, not one that it is to take *to* the people Israel." Williamson and Walter Harrelson, a Disciples biblical scholar, have been members of the Christian Scholars Group on Christian-Jewish Relations, and helped draft its 2002 statement "A Sacred Obligation: Rethinking Christian Faith in Relation to Judaism and the Jewish People." Among other things, this document rejected Christian missions to convert Jews and affirmed that Jews still dwell in an efficacious and *saving* covenant with God. The document has gained sympathy in the Christian Church (Disciples of Christ), but conservatives from the other two branches of the Stone-Campbell Movement largely

Among the most committed activists for interfaith dialogue between the Disciples of Christ and the Jewish community in the post-Holocaust era has been Clark Williamson, professor emeritus of theology at Christian Theological Seminary in Indianapolis. Courtesy of Christian Theological Seminary

resist notions of Jewish exceptionalism and discourage anything implying universalism.

To summarize, perspectives on the Jews and Judaism in the streams of the Stone-Campbell Movement mirror the full spectrum of attitudes in American Protestant history. One would be hard pressed to find a broad or persistent racial anti-Semitism (as distinct from theological anti-Judaism). Members of Stone-Campbell churches in the nineteenth century were largely isolated, socially and culturally, from Jewish communities. Judaism was for them part of both the biblical past and the prophetic future, and the challenge was to discern how world Jewry *here and now* would make the connecting links between that past and future. Most presumed, in a naively philo-Semitic spirit, that the Jews would need help from the church, and thus supported — if at times tentatively — missions to the Jews, with or without millennial expectations. The twentieth century brought more liberal attitudes in some quarters, an appreciation of Judaism in partnership with Christianity for humane and benevolent purposes. But even these more tolerant attitudes varied. Many early liberals still tended to see Judaism as a religion struggling to overcome its historic legalism, leaving behind its cultural ghetto and emerging into modernity. More recently some liberals, even a few sympathetic conservatives, have committed to *theological* affirmations of Judaism's own unique witness and its importance in revising the Christian worldview. Neither Barton Stone nor Alexander Campbell could ever have conceded this, but neither could they have imagined the mutual engagement of the two religions on a level playing field.

See also Barclay, James Turner; Bible, Interpretation of the; Dispensations; Hermeneutics; Race Relations; Smith, Gerald L. K.

BIBLIOGRAPHY James T. Barclay, "The Welfare of the World Bound Up in the Destiny of Israel" (7 parts), *Millennial Harbinger* (1860): 661-68; (1861): 6-14, 61-69, 121-28, 241-46, 301-7, 361-65 • Paul M. Blowers, "'Living in a Land of Prophets': James T. Barclay and an Early Disciples of Christ Mission to Jews in the Holy Land," *Church History* 62 (1992): 494-513, reprinted in *The Stone-Campbell Movement: An International Religious Tradition,* ed. Michael W. Casey and Douglas A. Foster (2002), pp. 271-91 • Alexander Campbell, "Dialogue with a Jew," *Millennial Harbinger* (1830): 561-67 • Commission on Theology of the Christian Church (Disciples of Christ), *The Church and the Jewish People: A Study Guide for the Christian Church (Disciples of Christ)* (1993) • Stephen D. Eckstein, *From Sinai to Calvary: An Autobiography* (1959) • W. Carl Ketcherside, *Talks to Jews and Non-Jews* (1977) • J. W. McGarvey, "Visit to a Synagogue," *Millennial Harbinger* (1864): 337-41 • Robert Milligan, "Prophecy," nos. 10-14, *Millennial Harbinger* (1856): 556-76, 601-7, 661-67; (1857): 19-24, 61-67 • David Reagan, *The Master Plan: Making Sense of the Controversies Surrounding Biblical Prophecy Today* (1993) • Barton W. Stone, "The Future Restoration of Israel," *Christian Messenger* (1844): 84-87 • Herbert L. Willett, *The Jew Through the Centuries* (1932) • Clark Williamson, *A Guest in the House of Israel: Post-Holocaust Church Theology* (1993).

PAUL M. BLOWERS

Johnson, Ashley S. (1857-1925)

Founder and first president of Johnson Bible College, Kimberlin Heights, Tennessee.

Born in Knox County, Tennessee, Johnson entered the ministry shortly after his conversion at age 20, embarking on a career as evangelist, author, and educator. While working as the State Evangelist for the South Carolina Missionary Cooperation in 1883, Johnson conceived his Correspondence Bible College, a four-year course of Bible study "by mail" that enrolled more than 3,000 students from 1886 to 1912. Out of his concern for training preachers, especially for the impoverished South, Johnson established the School of the Evangelists in 1893 (renamed Johnson Bible College in 1909). He served as president until his death in 1925 and was succeeded by his wife, Emma E. Strawn Johnson. Johnson edited several journals and authored seventeen books, including *The Great Controversy,* which went through eleven editions and over 150,000 copies in print. His *Condensed Bible Cyclopedia* functioned as the companion volume to the Correspondence Bible College lessons.

Ashley S. Johnson (1857-1925), along with his wife Emma E. Johnson, began the School of the Evangelists in 1894 (renamed Johnson Bible College in 1909) to train ministers. They also started an academy and work program to allow the poor to complete high school.

Courtesy of the Disciples of Christ Historical Society

See also Johnson Bible College

BIBLIOGRAPHY Robert E. Black, *The Story of Johnson Bible College* (1951) • Alva Ross Brown, *Faith, Prayer, Work: Being the Story of Johnson Bible College with Choice Quotations from Ashley S. Johnson* (n.d.) • L. Thomas Smith, Jr., *Above Every Other Desire: A Centennial History of Johnson Bible College, 1893-1993* (1993).

L. THOMAS SMITH, JR.

Johnson, Barton Warren (1833-1894)

Biblical scholar and journal editor of the Stone-Campbell Movement in the nineteenth century.

An Illinois native and 1856 graduate of Bethany College, Johnson embarked on a teaching career that included posts at Eureka College (Illinois), his alma mater Bethany, and Oskaloosa College (Iowa), where he became president in 1868. While at Eureka, Johnson was corresponding secretary for the American Christian Missionary Society in 1863. His influence spread among churches as a pastor, through Sunday School material he produced with the Christian Publishing Company, and through the commentaries he wrote on the Gospel of John and the Apocalypse. His *People's New Testament with Notes* (1889-91) was a widely popular annotated Bible that continued to be used through the twentieth century.

However, his greatest impact was through the more than twenty years he served as an editor of *The Evangelist* (1870-82) and *The Christian-Evangelist* (1883-94). Johnson stands in the tradition of the Stone-Campbell Movement in which the editors of the primary journals within the fellowship were the functional "bishops" of the church. His debut article in *The Evangelist* in 1870 encouraged readers to hunger for theological integrity. Throughout his years of writing, he continued to stress the need for clarity, combating the theological indifference concerning issues such as baptism, communion, and world mission that threatened the identity of the Disciples of Christ. A true restorationist, Johnson settled biblical and ecclesiastical questions by appealing to apostolic precedent.

See also Bible, Commentaries on the; Bible, Interpretation of the; *Christian-Evangelist, The*

BIBLIOGRAPHY M. Eugene Boring, *Disciples and the Bible: A History of Disciples Biblical Interpretation in North America* (1997) • Barton W. Johnson, ed., *The Christian International Lesson Commentary* (1885-86, 1888-94) • Barton W. Johnson, *John: A Commentary for the Peoples Based on Both Versions* (1886) • Barton W. Johnson, *The People's New Testament: The Common and Revised Versions with References and Colored Maps, with Explanatory Notes,* 2 vols. (1889-1891) • Barton W. Johnson, *Vision of the Ages: or, Lectures on the Apocalypse, A Complete View on the Book of Revelation* (1881) • Barton W. Johnson, *Young Folks in Bible Lands, Including Travels in Asia Minor, Excursions to Tarsus, Antioch, and Damascus and the Tour of Palestine, with Historical Explanation* (1892).

JOSEPH A. WEAKS

Johnson, John T. (1788-1756)

Evangelist and unity activist, a pivotal figure in the merger of the Stone and Campbell reform movements in 1832.

Johnson was born at Great Crossings, Kentucky, and from that community served in the military (War of 1812) and then in the Kentucky state legislature, followed by two terms in the United States Congress. His brother, Richard M. Johnson, was Vice President of the United States during the Van Buren administration. In response to the urging of Alexander Campbell, Johnson became a minister. Because of his affiliation with Campbell, the Great Crossings Baptist Church would not admit him to his home church pulpit, so he established a new congregation. At this time he lived in Georgetown, Kentucky, where he became acquainted with Barton Stone and the Christian churches. The two worked together to plan the meetings in late 1831 (Georgetown and Lexington, Kentucky) that resulted in the union of the Stone and Campbell movements there. Johnson was committed to the ideals of the unity of Christians and to the shaping of a distinctive model of Christian reformation. He was a leader in early efforts at cooperation within the Stone-Campbell Movement and in conversations with other Christian groups. Johnson also served as one of the vice presidents of the American Christian Missionary Society.

Helping to negotiate the union of the Stone and Campbell movements, J. T. Johnson insisted that viable Christian unity and discipleship depended on the reformation of character — "in heart, word, and deed." Courtesy of the Disciples of Christ Historical Society

He served as a co-editor on a number of magazines and other writing projects, including Barton Stone's *Christian Messenger.*

See also American Christian Missionary Society; *Christian Messenger;* Evangelism, Evangelists — Nineteenth Century; Stone, Barton Warren; Unity, Christian

BIBLIOGRAPHY John T. Johnson, "Reformation," *Christian Messenger* 7 (1833): 233-36, 289-92 • John T. Johnson, "Union of Christians," *Christian Messenger* 6 (1832): 40-42 • John Rogers, *Biography of Elder J. T. Johnson* (1861; repr. 1956). RICHARD L. HARRISON, JR.

Johnson Bible College

Bible college associated with the Christian Churches/Churches of Christ.

Johnson Bible College (JBC) is a single-purpose educational institution offering a Bible major and specialty programs for students seeking church-related vocations. It was founded as The School of the Evangelists in 1893 by Ashley S. Johnson at Kimberlin Heights, Tennessee, approximately twelve miles southeast of Knoxville. Johnson, an evangelist, author, and educator, transformed his Correspondence Bible College (est. 1886) into an institution designed to provide an education for "the poor young man who desires, above every other desire, to preach the Gospel." The name of the institution was changed to Johnson Bible College in 1909 to honor its founder. It is the second oldest continuing Bible college in the United States, accredited by the American Association of Bible Colleges, and was one of the first two Bible colleges to be accredited by the Commission on Colleges of the Southern Association of Colleges and Schools.

Ashley S. Johnson (president, 1893-1925) and his wife, Emma E. Johnson (president, 1925-27), built the college to provide not only a Bible-centered curriculum to train ministers but also an academy for those who had not completed high school, along with a work program whereby students could pay for their education. The School of the Evangelists began classes in February 1894 with about forty students and a curriculum reflecting the early program at Bethany College. In spite of difficulties such as the destruction of the main building by fire in 1904 (the new main building opened approximately one year later), the college made steady progress in the number of students, graduates, college facilities, and financial base (enrolling nearly 4,000 and graduating over 200 students during Ashley Johnson's tenure). The renaming of the "School" to Johnson Bible College in 1909 reflected not only the students' respect for the founders but also the development of a higher level of academic respectability.

The difficult years of the Depression severely strained the college's resources and the efforts of President Alva Ross Brown (1927-41), but the college experienced modest growth in spite of the financial difficulties, and its alumni made significant contributions not only as preachers but in academics, missions, and military chaplaincy as well. Brown was succeeded by Robert M. Bell (1941-68), preacher and economics professor at the University of Tennessee, who returned the college to a solid financial base and widened the college's influence. Even though there were a small number of females enrolled at the college throughout its existence, it officially became coeducational in 1948. The college attempted to remain unaffected by the divisive issues within the Stone-Campbell Movement of the mid-twentieth century, but during Bell's tenure it drew most of its students and support from Christian Churches/Churches of Christ.

The college has seen increased growth during the administration of David L. Eubanks (1969-). Even though the curriculum has been expanded to include teacher education and counseling departments, and a broadened definition of ministry including specialties in youth, children's, missions, worship, and telecommunications ministry, JBC retains its emphasis on the preaching ministry. The current academic programs include Associate-, Bachelor-, and Master-level degrees. The campus has been expanded, and the college has achieved record enrollments (a 79 percent increase from 1996 to 2002). In 2002 the college had enrolled 824 students and was near completion of a $22 million building campaign for dormitories and classroom facilities.

See also Bible College Movement; Higher Education, Views of in the Movement; Johnson, Ashley S.

BIBLIOGRAPHY Robert E. Black, *The Story of Johnson Bible College* (1951) • Alva Ross Brown, *Faith, Prayer, Work: Being the Story of Johnson Bible College with Choice Quotations from Ashley S. Johnson* (n.d.) • Ashley S. Johnson, *The Story of a Check for $100* (1900) • L. Thomas Smith, Jr., *Above Every Other Desire: A Centennial History of Johnson Bible College, 1893-1993* (1993). L. THOMAS SMITH, JR.

Jones, Abner (1772-1841)

Church reformer and restoration advocate in New England.

Abner Jones founded the first three congregations (the first at Lyndon, Vermont) of the so-called New England "Christian Connection," and remained a respected leader until his death. He was born in Royalston, Massachusetts, but in 1780 the family, who were Baptists, moved to Bridgewater, Vermont. At 19 he experienced a conversion, commenced to preach but rejected Calvinistic election and predestination, and therefore sought ordination from the Freewill Baptists. He declared himself, however, an unencumbered Christian, dedicated to the teaching of the Scriptures alone. Most of his life he also served as a physician in Vermont, New Hampshire, Massachusetts, and New York. He was more irenic than Elias Smith, who joined Jones in 1803, but who became a Universalist in 1817. After 1817 second-generation leadership in the Christian Connection eclipsed Jones.

See also Christian Connection; New England "Christians"; Smith, Elias; Universalism

BIBLIOGRAPHY Nathan O. Hatch, *The Democratization of American Christianity* (1989) • Abner Jones, *Memoirs of the Life and Experience, Travels and Preaching of Abner Jones* (1807) • A. D. Jones, *Memoirs of Elder Abner Jones* (1842) • Thomas H. Olbricht, "Christian Connexion and Unitarian Relationships 1800-1844," *Restoration Quarterly* 9 (1966): 160-86.

THOMAS H. OLBRICHT

Jones, Edgar DeWitt (1876-1956)

Disciples of Christ minister and ecumenist.

Jones was one of America's premier pulpit orators of the twentieth century. Born in Hearne, Texas, he first studied for a career in law but later made the transition to ministry. Jones graduated from Transylvania University, where Roger Nooe had been his roommate. The two remained lifelong friends, sharing their passions for preaching and unity. Ordained in 1901, the following year Jones married Frances Rumble. He held pastorates in Kentucky, Ohio, Illinois, and, most notably, at the Central Woodward Church in Detroit, Michigan, beginning in 1920. He was associated with Central Woodward as minister until 1940 and held the position of minister emeritus until his death. His preaching claimed a wide audience from both the pulpit and the printed page. Many of his sermons were published, including several book-length collections and anthologies.

He took seriously the Movement's historic plea for unity and gave leadership to a number of ecumenical ventures, including serving as president of the Federal Council of Churches and as president of the Association for the Promotion of Christian Unity, later the Council on Christian Unity. He was also a president of the International Convention. His frequent writings and speaking also included a biography of Abraham Lincoln, of whom he was a noted scholar and memorabilia collector.

See also Council on Christian Unity; Ecumenical Movement, The

BIBLIOGRAPHY Edgar DeWitt Jones papers, Disciples of Christ Historical Society.

CLINTON J. HOLLOWAY

Jones, Jim (1931-1978)

Pastor of Peoples Temple, a congregation of the Christian Church (Disciples of Christ), in which 918 members committed mass suicide in Guyana.

Jones pastored racially integrated congregations in Indianapolis and outside San Francisco, as well as in Guyana. Peoples Temple, 7,500 strong, was hailed as a leading congregation in social justice ministries. Fearing reprisals after killing members of an American congressional and media delegation investigating "Jonestown," Jones led congregation members in drinking a cyanide-laced beverage.

Jones's credentials as a minister in the Christian Church (Disciples of Christ) were a factor in the body's reexamination of its process of ordination.

BIBLIOGRAPHY David Chidester, *Salvation and Suicide: An Interpretation of Jim Jones, the Peoples Temple, and Jonestown* (1988) • Tim Reiterman, with John Jacobs, *Raven: The Untold Story of The Rev. Jim Jones and His People* (1982) • Steve Rose, *Jesus and Jim Jones* (1979).

KAREN STROUP

In response to ordained Disciples minister Jim Jones's role in the Jonestown tragedy of 1978, the General Assembly of the Christian Church (Disciples of Christ) amended its Policies and Criteria to specify that in order to maintain standing a minister must continue to meet the personal qualifications required for admission to the order of ministry.

Courtesy of the Disciples of Christ Historical Society

Jorgenson, E. L.

See Hymnody

Journalism

The religious press and its periodical literature has played a major role in the history of the Stone-Campbell Movement. W. T. Moore's celebrated dictum that the Movement did not have bishops, it had editors, is only partly a jest; it contains much truth. In the absence of an ecclesiastical hierarchy, the Stone-Campbell Movement's theology, identity, and character were shaped by editors on the pages of dozens of free journals. Historian and editor Moore wrote in 1909, "From the beginning of the movement to the present time (a full century), the chief authority in regard to all important questions has been the Disciple press." The Movement's vitality came in no small measure from the interchanges in the journals. The editors shared their deepest spiritual insights, their opinions, and their prejudices with each other and with the world. Founders Alexander Campbell and Barton W. Stone even quarreled in their respective publications over what to call their followers, Campbell preferring "Disciples," Stone "Christians."

Through their writings, Stone, Campbell, and the other editors excited a frontier American population eager to hear of a Christian group willing to put aside the trappings of denominationalism in the interest of simple "New Testament Christianity." The journals played no small part in the growth of the Movement. They helped promote a general organization. They helped launch overseas missionary involvement through information, editorial prodding, and fund-raising. They engaged the debate on such things as the necessity of immersion, the means to missionary endeavor, and biblical interpretation. Likewise, the differences that eventually split the Movement into three parts were fueled and magnified by the acidity and stubbornness of some of the "editor-bishops." Historian Leroy Garrett, himself a former editor of *Restoration Review,* has blamed the divisions on "ambitious editors" when irenic spirits in the Movement might have permitted diversity to exist.

As many as 400 journals related to the Stone-Campbell Movement were founded, 100 of them in the four decades prior to the Civil War. Most were the private enterprises of lone but enthusiastic preachers, lasting but a year or two and disappearing for lack of funds or a market. Some were weeklies, some monthlies, some quarterlies. Many were small, newsletter-type publications. Alexander Campbell complained that there "is an editorial mania abroad in the land," expressing his wish for fewer editors and fewer periodicals — perhaps to ease competition with his own.

Campbell's *Christian Baptist* (1823) was the first journal directly related to the Movement. Campbell was 35 years old and just eleven years past his first sermon. Barton Stone initiated his own journalistic enterprise with the *Christian Messenger* (1826), as did Walter Scott with *The Evangelist* (1832). Campbell initiated his journal when he saw how readily people clamored for copies of the text of one of his debates. The *Christian Baptist* lasted until the Movement broke its informal ties with the Baptists, the *Millennial Harbinger* (1830) replacing it and becoming the journal more widely associated with Campbell. The *Harbinger* continued for forty years, outlasting Campbell himself by four but remaining the authoritative compendium of Campbellian thought.

Campbell described the *Christian Baptist* as "an impartial advocate of truth." He also outlined a prospective sevenfold content that would not be far different from a list compiled by church journals in the twenty-first century: critiques on morals, observations about religious systems, essays on the faith, religious news and comment, historical and biographical information, religious anecdotes, and evaluation of mission work abroad. He observed: "The editor flatters himself that this publication will be highly interesting and useful to those into whose hands it may fall."

While Campbell's journalistic venture may have been first among the Christians and Disciples, who later joined forces, the New England "Christians" were actually first. Elias Smith (1769-1846) founded the *Herald of Gospel Liberty* (1808), devoted to the principles of restoring apostolic Christianity and championing individual freedom of religious conscience. The journal is often touted as the first American religious newspaper. The early journals in the Stone-Campbell Movement had fascinating names. One was the *Northern Reformer, Heretic Detector and Evangelical Review* (1837), published by Arthur Crihfield, a preacher in Middleburgh, Ohio — the centerpiece of the title surely throwing a scare into anyone bent on going astray. While Disciples were, and are, scarce in Canada, there were journals in Nova Scotia, Ontario, and New Brunswick before 1840, evidence of the early impact of the Stone-Campbell Movement above the border. The *Canadian Disciple,* the first All-Canada publication, which still exists, was founded in 1923 in Toronto.

Tolbert Fanning (1810-1874) began the *Gospel Advocate* in Nashville, Tennessee, in 1855. This was Fanning's second journalistic effort. He had founded the *Christian Review* in 1844, which was renamed the *Christian Magazine* in 1847 by its new editor, Jesse B. Ferguson. The controversy over Ferguson's ideas of universalism and spiritualism in 1852

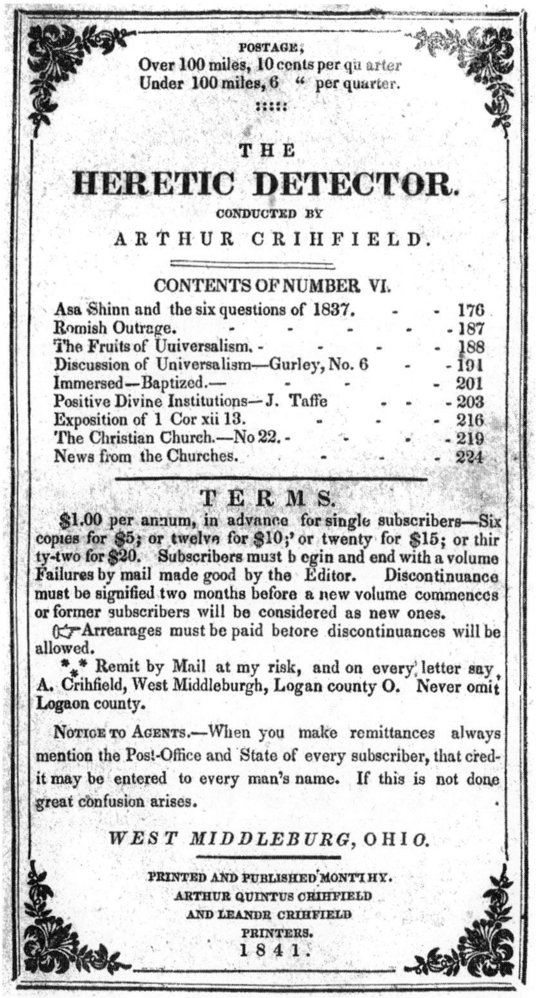
POSTAGE,
Over 100 miles, 10 cents per quarter
Under 100 miles, 6 " per quarter.

THE
HERETIC DETECTOR.
CONDUCTED BY
ARTHUR CRIHFIELD.

CONTENTS OF NUMBER VI.

TERMS.

$1.00 per annum, in advance for single subscribers—Six copies for $5; or twelve for $10;' or twenty for $15; or thirty-two for $20. Subscribers must b egin and end with a volume Failures by mail made good by the Editor. Discontinuance must be signified two months before a new volume commences or former subscribers will be considered as new ones.

☞Arrearages must be paid before discontinuances will be allowed.

*** Remit by Mail at my risk, and on every letter say, A. Crihfield, West Middleburgh, Logan county O. Never omit Logaon county.

NOTICE TO AGENTS.—When you make remittances always mention the Post-Office and State of every subscriber, that credit may be entered to every man's name. If this is not done great confusion arises.

WEST MIDDLEBURG, OHIO.

PRINTED AND PUBLISHED MONTHLY.
ARTHUR QUINTUS CRIHFIELD
AND LEANDR CRIHFIELD
PRINTERS.
1841.

Arthur Crihfield's *The Heretic Detector* (1837-1842) was one of scores of journals founded by individuals related to the Movement in the four decades prior to the Civil War.
Courtesy of the Disciples of Christ Historical Society

led to the paper's demise the following year. Fanning established the *Gospel Advocate* in a sense to take the place of the former paper, to be a forum for free discussion of religious matters, particularly the issue of cooperation through mission societies and other extra-congregational organizations.

Fanning and his successor, David Lipscomb (1831-1917), who edited the journal for forty-six years, were extremely influential leaders in Churches of Christ. They clearly fit the role of editor bishop. Fanning was a pacifist and grieved over what he saw as the politicizing of the Northern church, evidenced by the American Christian Missionary Society's resolutions in favor of the Union in the Civil War. When Fanning and Lipscomb resumed publishing the paper in 1866, it had a decidedly Southern character despite its denial of being a sectional paper. Though an admirer of Alexander Campbell, Fanning became engrossed in a heated editorial exchange with Campbell and Robert Richardson in 1857, with Fanning accusing Campbell of lapsing into senility and virtually atheistic teachings. Fanning's successor Lipscomb had a more welcoming spirit and a strong social conscience. He deplored racial separation in the church, and, in the dark days of reconstruction, advocated through his journal that Southerners send aid to Chicago after the great fire. Lipscomb gradually shifted into an uncompromising position against biblical criticism, missionary societies, and musical instruments in worship.

The *Gospel Advocate* became one of the most powerful thought-shaping institutions of the Movement among those Southern congregations that became Churches of Christ. Though the paper closed briefly during the Civil War, it has otherwise been published continuously by members of Churches of Christ, holding the record for journalistic longevity in the Movement.

The other journal that has exercised a major influence on Churches of Christ through the late nineteenth and twentieth centuries is the *Firm Foundation,* established in Austin, Texas, in September 1884 by Austin McGary. He determined to start the paper after attending the Texas State Meeting that year and being dismayed by what he saw as a rapid move toward unscriptural innovations. McGary also opposed the practice of David Lipscomb and others who did not require persons immersed in Baptist or other churches to be "rebaptized" to become part of Churches of Christ. The early tone of the paper was often acerbic and critical. In 1908, after a period of relative instability, G. H. P. Showalter (1870-1954) bought the paper and became editor. While some rivalry existed early between the *Gospel Advocate* and *Firm Foundation,* for most of the twentieth century the two papers reflected mainstream views in Churches of Christ.

The *American Christian Review* (est. 1856) may have been the most influential journal of the period immediately after Campbell's decline. Its editor was Benjamin Franklin (1812-1878), a distant relative of the historic figure of the same name. Franklin opposed musical instruments in worship and took other conservative positions, though he counseled against dividing over such issues or making them tests of fellowship. Nevertheless, the popularity of the *Review* and its strongly conservative positions made it the target for the establishment of a rival journal of a more moderate nature. Campbell's associate Isaac Errett (1820-1888) collaborated with the Phillips family of New Castle, Pennsylvania, and with the former Disciples college president, soon-to-be President of the United States, James A. Garfield (1831-1881), to found a journal in Cleveland called *The Christian Standard* (est. 1866). The *Standard's* first issue carried the notice of Campbell's death and marked the beginning of a struggle for the mantle of the Movement. Errett believed strongly in freedom of opinion but had some opinions that drew the wrath of other editors. For instance, he refused to support biblical inerrancy. He favored relationships with Christians from other church traditions and supported open communion. Errett is credited by some with keeping the Movement from being captured by legalism or exclusivism. He moved his publication to Cincinnati and included in it poetry, essays, correspondence, foreign religious news, Bible studies, family and missionary items, and features in politics, commerce, and science. The aim of Disciples, he wrote, is union upon Christ, not upon their own interpretation of the Bible or on a specific theory of the ancient order of things.

When the Christian Woman's Board of Missions organized in 1874 to make up for perceived mission failures, the new society was encouraged by both Errett's *Christian Standard* and J. H. Garrison's (1842-1931) *Christian-Evangelist* (1869), published in St. Louis. Early on, the woman's board linked up with the *Christian Monitor,* published monthly by Marcia Goodwin of Indianapolis. Nine years later, when the women decided they wanted their own journal, Goodwin was engaged to edit *Missionary Tidings,* a name she coined as the first issue was about to go to press. The magazine grew quickly to forty pages, and when it merged in 1918 with four other mission publications its circulation had reached 54,000 subscribers. The merger came with the founding of the United Christian Missionary Society. The other four journals had 36,000 subscribers combined. The merger resulted in *World Call.* Effie L. Cunningham was the editor of *Missionary Tidings* during its last nine years. She became associate editor of *World Call.* Bess White Cochran was the only female editor-in-chief of *World Call* in its more than a half century of existence, serving from 1929 to 1932.

Errett died in 1888, and editor Garrison of the *Christian-Evangelist* became the dominant figure among Disciples. With Errett gone, the *Christian Standard* began a move to the right, taking positions such as opposition to higher biblical criticism, while the *Christian-Evangelist* represented the more liberal view. The *Standard* continued as the journal of the Christian Churches/Churches of Christ from the 1920s through the 1960s as conservative congregations pulled away from the more liberal Disciples and became the third stream of the Stone-Campbell Movement. The *Standard,* under the umbrella of Standard Publishing Company, has continued into the twenty-first century, 16-24 pages weekly, carrying Bible School lessons, feature stories, church news, ministry themes, and other types of articles.

J. H. Garrison gained prominence as a denominational figure as well as editor, truly an "editor bishop." While he had some personally conservative views, he was the champion of the ecumenically oriented wing of the Movement. He advocated interchurch cooperation, and he gave the name to the first national ecumenical body: The Federal Council of Churches. Through the pages of the *Christian-Evangelist* he supported the women's foreign missions initiative. He began the special day offerings among Disciples in support of missions. He chaired the planning for the 1909 Centennial Convention in Pittsburgh, the largest gathering of Disciples up to that time. Garrison spoke for the liberal position in a controversy over biblical criticism and the social gospel, engaging liberal writers like Herbert L. Willett as

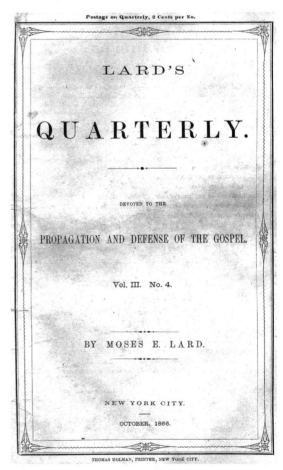

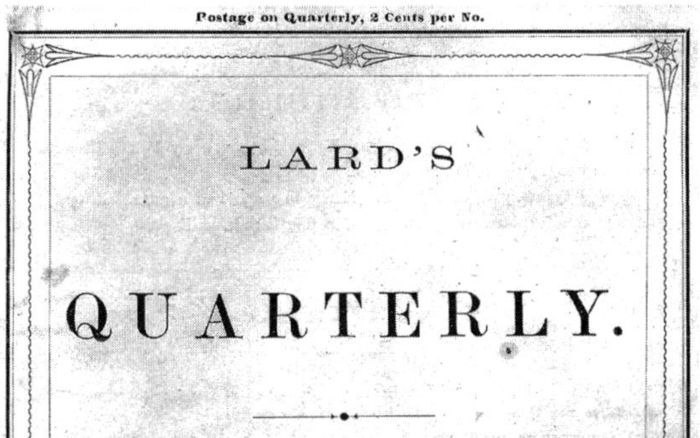

Postage on Quarterly, 2 Cents per No.

LARD'S

QUARTERLY.

DEVOTED TO THE

PROPAGATION AND DEFENSE OF THE GOSPEL.

Vol. III. No. 4.

BY MOSES E. LARD.

NEW YORK CITY.

OCTOBER, 1866.

THOMAS HOLMAN, PRINTER, NEW YORK CITY.

Lard's Quarterly, **published by Moses E. Lard from 1863 to 1868, aimed to promote serious discussion and to sharpen the theological focus of the Movement.**

Courtesy of the Disciples of Christ Historical Society

columnists. In a financial bind, he sold the magazine to lumberman Robert A. Long in 1909, who promptly gave it to the Disciples as the basis of the Christian Board of Publication. What once was only a magazine became a non-profit business that developed Christian books, education materials, and other church resources. Garrison continued to identify with the magazine as a columnist long after his editorship, the ties extending for a total of about sixty years.

The Disciples of Christ also contributed significantly to ecumenical journalism. A Disciples publication that began in Des Moines in 1884 under another name moved to Chicago in 1888 and in 1900 became the *Christian Century.* Chicago Disciples pastor Charles Clayton Morrison purchased it in 1908 and gradually converted it to a nondenominational journal over the next decade, feeding off the energy of the early ecumenical stirrings in America. It remains the leading ecumenical journal in the United States. Disciple Harold Fey was one of its mid-twentieth-century editors.

After Garrison, the *Christian-Evangelist* continued under eight editors until 1959, when it was merged with *Front Rank,* a Sunday School publication, and became simply *The Christian* the following year during the editorship of Howard E. Short. Short himself was an episcopal-like figure among Disciples, having taught church history at Lexington Theological Seminary and chaired the Panel of Scholars, which compiled a body of Disciples theology in the 1950s and 1960s. He also served as the denominational Sunday School lesson interpreter for more than a quarter of a century. After Short's retirement and the earlier retirement of Samuel F. Pugh, editor of *World Call,* the Christian Board of Publication merged the two magazines into a single semi-monthly publication called *The Disciple* in 1974. James E. Merrell was the last editor of *World Call* and the first of the new magazine. He shaped *The Disciple* as its editor for fifteen years, adding graphic changes and venturesome content before returning to the pastorate in 1989 after nearly thirty-five years of service to Disciples journalism. Robert L. Friedly and Patricia Case followed Merrell as editor of *The Disciple.*

In 1990 James C. Suggs, a trained journalist (Texas Christian University), who had only recently become president of Christian Board of Publication, issued a remarkable statement that underscored the depth of the tradition of free journalism among the followers of Stone and Campbell. For the Disciples it reminded a relatively new "denomination" that the press would not be at the beck and call of authority figures. Suggs wrote in his only editorial as head of the publishing house that the church's General Board, its general minister and president, and its publisher would not make editorial decisions. Only the editor would make them. The editor would be free to "warn, prod, criticize, differ or blow the whistle" if necessary with respect to the church establishment. Then Suggs launched into a classic free journalism rationale: "In a free church as in a free society, people need access to information other than that to which 'spin' has been added. A journal that earns credibility through objectivity assumes that people can be trusted to discern the truth, recognize sham, make choices, interpret scriptures, think theologically, respond conscientiously and otherwise engage in communication that does not end with telling or hearing. It is to work for faithfulness and vitality in the Christian Church that *The Disciple* will retain editorial freedom — and exercise it." During his nine years as president of the publishing house he refrained even from speaking to the editor about magazine content, and in the general cabinet of the Disciples of Christ he defended the editor's right to edit free from the cabinet's, and the publisher's, control or pressure.

Four years after Suggs retired in 1997, Christian Board of Publication suspended *The Disciple* during a financial crisis. The magazine was the last of the general circulation news and information magazines of the Disciples stream of the Movement, and Suggs, bolstered by a $100,000 gift from a couple in Dallas and with the help of retired denominational volunteers, initiated a new magazine called *DisciplesWorld,* with which he maintained the same editorial hands-off policy, confining himself to business decisions. In 2003 Disciples pastor Verity Jones was named publisher and editor of the new magazine.

For Christian Churches/Churches of Christ, the *Christian Standard* remains the single most influential journal, and, while concentrating its attention mainly on non-controversial features, occasionally publishes articles expressing different points of view on debatable issues (e.g., styles of worship and music, and the role of women in ministry). The *Standard* also produces one issue per year devoted to the colleges and seminaries of the Christian Churches/Churches of Christ, giving enrollment and faculty statistics and describing significant developments in the life of each school.

Though the *Gospel Advocate* and *Firm Foundation* continued to be published in Churches of Christ at the beginning of the twenty-first century, neither exercised the kind of wide influence that had once characterized those journals and their editorial policies. Under the editorship of Reuel Lemmons (1912-1989) from 1955 to 1983, the *Firm Foundation* pursued a moderate course that allowed for free discussion of issues. In 1983, however, the Showalter family, who had owned the paper since 1908, sold it to H. A. Dobbs and Bill Cline, who immediately moved it in a decidedly more conservative and strident direction. Former readers unhappy with that paper's new direction founded a new journal in 1985 titled *Image* with Lemmons as editor. In 1992 a bolder journalistic effort to promote reform in Churches of Christ was launched by ministers Rubel Shelly, Mike Cope, and Phillip Morrison in Nashville, Tennessee. Named *Wineskins,* the paper represents a progressive movement that rejects exclusivist attitudes and positions often characteristic of this body. In 1997 *Image* ceased publication and merged its subscription list with that of *Wineskins. Wineskins* became a completely electronic magazine in 2004. At the beginning of the twenty-first century the numerous journals in Churches of Christ represent a spectrum of theological positions from traditional to progressive, with no one publication dominant.

See also *American Christian Review; Christian, The; Christian Baptist, The; Christian-Evangelist, The; Christian Messenger; Christian Standard; Disciple, The; Evangelist, The; Firm Foundation; Gospel Advocate, The; Millennial Harbinger, The; Missionary Tidings; Wineskins* Magazine; *World Call*

BIBLIOGRAPHY Brian P. Clark, "An Analysis of the Organizing Functions of the *Christian Standard* in the Restoration Movement Christian Churches/Churches of Christ" (unpublished M.A. thesis, Wheaton College, 1998) • Douglas A. Foster, *Will the Cycle Be Unbroken: Churches of Christ Face the Twenty-First Century* (1994); Nathan O. Hatch, *The Democratization of American Christianity* (1989) • Gary Holloway, "Alexander Campbell as a Publisher," *Restoration Quarterly* 37 (1995): 28-35 • Richard Hughes, Howard Short, and Henry Webb, *The Power of the Press: Studies of the "Gospel Advocate," the "Christian Standard," and the "Christian-Evangelist"* (1987) • James Brooks Major, "The Role of Periodicals in the Development of the Disciples of Christ, 1850-1910 (unpublished Ph.D. dissertation, Vanderbilt University, 1966).

ROBERT L. FRIEDLY

Justification, Doctrine of

1. Justification in Context
2. Justification by Faith Alone?
3. The "Righteousness" of Faith

Doctrine explaining how sinners are forgiven through divine grace and how they appropriate the righteousness of God through faith.

The term *dikaiosunē* ("righteousness") and its cognates are used in the Septuagint and the New Testament to translate the Hebrew *tsedāqah,* the notion of standing in a right relationship with God and of the obligations deriving from that relationship. Justification, as a significant theme especially in the writings of Paul, was understood by the Greek Church Fathers (beginning with Origen) largely in terms of the gracious moral and spiritual transformation of the believer and the appropriation of a real virtue of righteousness. With the Vulgate's translation of *tsedāqah* as *justitia,* the Latin Church Fathers introduced legal and forensic categories into the interpretation of justification in the Bible. In Western medieval thought justification was the culmination of a process in which divinely "infused" grace produced in the believer qualities that merited acceptance. Sixteenth-century Reformers, on the other hand, viewed justification in forensic terms as God's declaring the believer righteous through the "imputation" of the merits of Christ. This view strictly separated justification and sanctification, the latter describing a subsequent state in the life of the believer.

The Stone-Campbell Movement accepted some aspects of classical Protestant teaching on justification but departed from others. Alexander Campbell, for example, said that he could agree with Martin Luther that the doctrine of justification was the test on which the church stood or fell, but he hardly embraced every aspect of Luther's teaching on it. The Movement's early leaders determined to reassess the issue through close study of the New Testament language of justification, while conscious of the fact that the Protestant churches had laid an enormous stake in this doctrine and were acutely opposed to any implication of works-righteousness. The development of the Movement's own teaching revolved around (1) the definition of justification in larger soteriological context and as indicating the remission of sins; (2) the question of whether justification is by faith alone; and (3) the nature of the righteousness bestowed on the believer.

1. Justification in Context

Most Stone-Campbell theologians in the nineteenth century concurred with Alexander Campbell that justification was not a climactic moment in which the sinner is "declared" righteous through faith, or a fixed point within a rigidly defined *ordo salutis,* but one among other gracious *effects* of the whole economy of conversion and regeneration. In his book *Christian Baptism* (1851), Campbell specifically claimed that a purely forensic or legal justification was *not* justification by grace because it was utterly impossible for sinful humanity. Justification was rather a "profound . . . [but] revealed mystery" wherein God himself was "justified" (i.e., propitiated) by the death of his Son, enabling *forgiven* sinners to enjoy the "favour and friendship" of the Lord.

Barton Stone named justification as one of the designs of the sacrifice of Christ, along with purgation from sin, reconciliation, propitiation, redemption, and forgiveness. Campbell similarly argued that in the scheme of regeneration, with baptism as the culminating event granting formal remission of sins, the penitent believer was translated to a multifaceted new state. In his long essay on "The Remission of Sins" in *The Christian System,* Campbell concluded that new converts were addressed in the New Testament as "pardoned, justified, sanctified, reconciled, adopted, and saved." All of these indicated both a change of *state* in relation to God and a dynamic *process* of transformation. In the 1859 *Millennial Harbinger,* he further clarified that there cannot be "degrees" in justification, sanctification, adoption, or regeneration, but there can indeed be degrees in the "enjoyment" thereof and in concomitant Christian character.

Borrowing Campbell's language of justification as indicating a "change of state," A. B. Jones, a leader and editor in Missouri, similarly concluded in 1901 that Christ is "the means, the medium, and the mediator, by which and by whom we are transformed and transferred — not transformed nor transferred in our *nature,* but transformed in our moral *character,* and transferred in our moral *state.*" Justification, as remission of sin, was crucial because it signaled the dramatic cleansing of conscience necessary to new life in Christ.

Many Stone-Campbell theologians rejected Protestant theories of justification as sheer "imputation." Indeed, Barton Stone's rejection of imputation in its classic Reformed version incurred the fierce criticism of his former colleagues in the Springfield Presbytery, Robert Marshall and John Thompson. Years later, nevertheless, A. B. Jones called imputation a theological counterfeit, as if by some sovereign act or "spiritual legerdemain" God assigned the undeserving sinner the deserved (and superabundant) righteousness of Christ. Campbell had been satisfied with defining justification as pardon, but later writers saw the need for further nuancing. In the 1885 Missouri Christian Lectures, for example, C. A. Hedrick argued that pardon in a purely legal or forensic sense was insufficient since it did not penetrate the cause of the crime or remove the desire to sin, when what the sinner most needs is to be thoroughly changed and turned toward God. Hedrick distinguished forensic "pardon" from the biblical notion of "forgiveness," which entailed both the compassion of the one wronged and the exacting of a remedial cost from the wrongdoer. Justification, like salvation as a whole, was a *gift* of divine grace still requiring the engagement of the cooperating human will.

Jesse Kellems, a scholar-pastor of the Disciples of Christ in the first half of the twentieth century, acknowledged in his *Studies in the Forgiveness of Sins* (1926) that Paul employed forensic language to describe justification, but noted that he used it mainly for contextual purposes and thoroughly qualified it with his "biological terminology" of dying to sin and rising with Christ (Rom. 6), putting on Christ (Gal. 3:27), being "in Christ" as a "new creature" (2 Cor. 5:17).

2. Justification by Faith Alone?

Given this holistic definition of justification as forgiveness and attendant transformation, it follows that Stone-Campbell thinkers largely rejected a strict doctrine of justification by faith alone. In *The Christian System,* Alexander Campbell identified no fewer than seven different "causes" of justification, the first three of which left no mistake about the *divine* initiative: (1) grace as the "moving cause" (Rom. 3:24; Titus 3:7); (2) Jesus Christ as the "efficient cause" (Gal. 2:16); (3) his blood as the "procuring cause" (Rom. 5:9); (4) knowledge as the "disposing cause" (Isa. 43:11); (5) the name of Christ as the "immediate cause" (1 Cor. 6:11); (6) faith as the "formal cause" (Rom. 5:1; Gal. 2:16; 3:24); and (7) works as the "concurring cause" (James 2:21, 24, 26). "Why pick one as definitive?" asked Campbell, since "every one in its own place is essentially necessary."

J. W. McGarvey, the renowned biblical scholar of the Movement's third generation, took up the apparent tension between justification by faith in the writings of Paul and justification by works in James. Acknowledging that this had induced Luther's antipathy toward James, and critical of various Protestant theories to reconcile Paul and James, McGarvey offered his own explanation. Paul rejected justification by "works of law" in the sense of deeds of any *moral* law (Jewish and Gentile), in which case "pardon" would be impossible because only the morally perfect could be justified, as something "owed" them. Sinful humanity, however, needed pardon as a sheer act of gracious favor, available to the penitent believer. James's justification "by works" had to do with works of obedience to Christ, which were a response to "positive law" (divine command) grounded in faith. The first of such works, then, must be baptism: "Faith . . . whatever else may accompany it, remains a dead faith, ineffective for justification, until it leads the believer into the water; then it is no longer without works, and the sinner is justified by faith not without works." Faith was still primary, but what was "reckoned righteous" (Rom. 4:5) was the faith fulfilled in baptism and leading to the godly Christian life.

Neither McGarvey nor any other major Stone-Campbell theologian affirmed baptism, let alone faith, as a meritorious work, earning righteousness. Faith, repentance, and baptism were, in Campbell's words, "means of enjoyment" of the sheer graciousness of God, exhibiting the magnificent economy of regeneration. In the mid-twentieth century, a controversy erupted in the Churches of Christ based on concerns that the Movement's "plan of salvation" (especially baptism) had created a new sort of legalism disconnected from an adequate theology of grace. Prominent writers like R. L. Whiteside, Foy E. Wallace, Jr., Guy N. Woods, and others were so deeply concerned with strict obedience of the revealed steps of conversion and regeneration that they seemed to some to be proclaiming a works-righteousness inconsistent with the gospel. K. C. Moser (1893-1976), a minister-scholar who served Churches of Christ in Texas and Oklahoma, responded by restating the vital relation between faith and baptism and focusing on the *person* of the crucified Christ. Christ, argued Moser, did not set forth an "arbitrary" group of salvific actions but invited faith as trust *in him* and the embodiment of that faith in baptism. Moser also reintroduced the notion of "imputed" righteousness in qualified form. Christ alone merited righteousness and communicated that righteousness to the penitent and baptized believer, not as a feigned declaration of innocence but as the basis for identifying with his death and resurrection and for sharing new life "in Christ." Moser's views were echoed by Roy Key, another Church of Christ thinker who further insisted on the principle that God's righteousness is a gift granted to the one who puts trust in Christ.

3. The "Righteousness" of Faith

Though critical of much Protestant theology of "imputed" righteousness, Stone-Campbell thinkers developed their own understanding of the righteousness "reckoned" to penitent believers. A. B. Jones's 1901 study of "Righteousness and Law" provides a good summary. Righteousness, he suggested, was a *relational* term bespeaking the total surrender to Christ, through a faith in the righteousness of Christ, a confidence "in the righteousness of trusting in the righteousness of God." Such made "imputed" righteousness real, not fictitious. The believer did not simply borrow the clothing of Christ's righteousness but, having been forgiven and changed, was truly clothed in his righteousness, "a personal righteousness of life and character." As Jesse Kellems argued, justification flowed into sanctification in a process of growth and maturation in Christ.

On the heels of the controversy surrounding K. C. Moser, the notion of imputation continued to be heavily debated among some within Churches of Christ well into the 1980s. Those who used the language of Christ's righteousness being conferred on the undeserving sinner were alleged by some critics of teaching a purely "extrinsic" or "umbrella-theory" of justification that undermined the necessity of full obedience to the saving commands of Christ. Tom Roberts, a Church of Christ minister, published a substantial volume outlining the errors of "Neo-Calvinists" who embraced such views simply in order to avoid the accusation of legalism. Much of this controversy focused on meticulous exegesis of the language of faith, righteousness, and justification in Romans.

Generally, however, the Movement has followed Stone, Campbell, McGarvey, Jones, Kellems, and others in regarding justification as directed toward a right personal relationship with God and the behavioral obligations deriving from that relationship. "Justification by faith in Christ," Campbell summarized, "is . . . the imbodiment [sic] of views in perfect harmony with truth, with our condition, with the whole revealed character of God, and, necessarily, tends to humility, gratitude, piety, and humanity." Concomitant with this understanding of justification and righteousness has been a view of human sinfulness as grounded less in "infraction" than in personal rebellion and alienation, rendering purely legal or forensic analogies of little effect in conveying the remedial plan of God. The apostolic declaration that in Christ God was seeking to reconcile humanity to himself (Rom. 5:10; 2 Cor. 5:18-19; Col. 1:20) has historically suggested to Stone-Campbell Christians that God's primary concern is to overcome alienation through a multifaceted economy wherein justification (forgiveness of sins) goes hand in hand with the other "enjoyed" graces of sanctification, adoption, salvation.

See also Baptism; Faith; Grace, Doctrine of; Moser, Kenneth Carl; Regeneration; Salvation; Sanctification, Doctrine of

BIBLIOGRAPHY Alexander Campbell, *Christian Baptism* (1851) • Alexander Campbell, *The Christian System* (1839) • Alexander Campbell, "Justification," *Millennial Harbinger* (1851): 318-25; Alexander Campbell, "Review of Archippus," no. III, *Millennial Harbinger* (1831): 266-71 • I. B. Grubbs, "The Doctrine of Justification by Faith," in *The Old Faith Restated,* ed. J. H. Garrison (1891), pp. 149-67 • C. A. Hedrick, "The Philosophy of the Remission of Sins," *The Missouri Christian Lectures, 1884-1885* (1886), pp. 247-67 • John Mark Hicks, "K. C. Moser and Churches of Christ: A Historical Perspective," *Restoration Quarterly* 37 (1995): 139-57 • A. B. Jones, "Righteousness and Law," in *The Spiritual Side of Our Plea* (1901), pp. 363-94 • Jesse Kellems, *Studies in the Forgiveness of Sins* (1926) • Roy Key, "The Righteousness of God," *Gospel Advocate* 88 (1946): 74-75, 78-79 • J. W. McGarvey, "Justification by Faith," *Lard's Quarterly* 3 (1866): 113-29 • Alister E. McGrath, *Iustitia Dei: A History of the Christian Doctrine of Justification,* 2 vols. (2nd ed. 1998) • K. C. Moser, "Christ Versus a 'Plan'" (pamphlet, 1952) • K. C. Moser, *The Way of Salvation, Being an Exposition of God's Method of Justification Through Christ* (1932) • Tom Roberts, *Neo-Calvinism in the Church of Christ* (1980) • Barton Stone, "Justification," *Christian Messenger* (1843): 9-12 • Barton Stone, "Sacrificial Blood," no. II, *Christian Messenger* (1836): 161-65, 181.

PAUL M. BLOWERS *and* WILLIAM J. RICHARDSON

K

Kagawada, David

See Asian American Disciples

Keeble, Marshall (1878-1968)

Evangelist among black Churches of Christ.

Born to former slaves near Murfreesboro, Tennessee, Keeble became in time the most successful evangelist among Churches of Christ, baptizing as many as 30,000. As a youth with a seventh-grade education, Keeble labored in a soap factory until he married Minnie Womack, a daughter of minister S. W. Womack (d. 1920). The newly married couple opened a grocery store in Nashville. Under the tutelage of his wife and his father-in-law, Keeble began preaching in Nashville churches by 1897, and by 1914 was traveling on his own as an itinerant evangelist while his wife minded the store.

In 1918 Keeble planted a church at Oak Grove, near Henderson, Tennessee, baptizing eighty-four persons and coming to the attention of N. B. Hardeman (1874-1965), influential president of nearby Freed-Hardeman College. From 1920 until his death, Keeble traveled throughout the American South and, ultimately, worldwide at the expense of Nashville millionaire A. M. Burton (1879-1966). In 1931 Keeble brought 1,071 blacks and an untold number of whites to decisions that resulted in baptism. That year Keeble preached in fourteen campaigns, establishing six new churches. In Bradenton, Florida, Keeble and his helpers baptized 115 persons in one day and a total of 286 during that campaign. Keeble's 1931 sermons in Valdosta, Georgia — where 166 were baptized — were recorded by stenographers, and the transcripts became the basis of a small volume edited by another influential patron, Benton Cordell Goodpasture (1895-1977).

After 1942 Keeble was nominally president of Nashville Christian Institute (NCI), a private academy designed to educate young blacks for ministry and evangelism. He traveled extensively in the company of young "preacher boys," evangelizing and raising money for the school. His fees for preaching were paid directly to NCI, since A. M. Burton provided Keeble's salary and expenses. From 1939 to 1950 Keeble was also the nominal editor of *Christian Counselor,* a monthly journal for blacks published by

Marshall Keeble was the most widely known black evangelist in twentieth-century Churches of Christ. Though some accused Keeble of accommodating to white racist policies of segregation and discrimination, his efforts helped produce a generation of leaders who provided crucial guidance to the body in the late twentieth century. Courtesy of the Center for Restoration Studies, Abilene Christian University

the Gospel Advocate Company. Both the school and the journal were projected, at least in part, by the Nashville white establishment to offset the independent efforts of George Philip Bowser (1874-1950), who, unlike Keeble, spoke out against racial segregation in the churches. The journal failed in its mission, but did not cease publication until Bowser's death. NCI continued until desegregation and the civil rights movement had made it an anachronism; it closed in 1967, less than a year before Keeble's death.

From the beginning of his career Keeble proved a master of the English Bible and human psychology, by his own account finding in Booker T. Washington a primary role model. Keeble's relations with his white patrons, who plainly sought to use him as an instrument of social control, were inevitably laden with ambiguity. He did not simply tell whites what they wanted to hear. Keeble was, rather, the first evangelist among Churches of Christ to transcend the "color line," and very nearly the last. He spoke often in homespun parables that communicated to blacks quite differently than to whites, but ultimately Keeble communicated "good news" to blacks and whites alike.

White contemporaries often eulogized Keeble's "humility," but few have understood it for what it was. Keeble's humility was genuine, but was founded on the bravado of Brer Rabbit, who in countless slave tales outwits the Fox and the Bear by pitting his weakness against their strength. No one in his time and place possessed more formidable psychological and rhetorical weapons than Keeble or wielded them more effectively.

Keeble enjoyed the patronage of the powerful and radiated joy in his life and work, but he did not escape the suffering imposed on every American of African descent in his time and place. He was often threatened and physically assaulted by white supremacists in towns where he preached to mixed audiences.

His doctrine reflected the prevailing conservative understandings of white Churches of Christ concerning the boundaries of the church and baptism. As one white contemporary remarked, "Keeble preached it *hard*." Keeble never missed an opportunity to champion the value of immersion over what he called "dry cleaning." "The devil wants you dry," he told his audiences, "so you'll burn better." Keeble believed fervently and proved repeatedly that there was no argument that he and the Bible could not win. "The Bible is right!" he declared, and he left no room for doubt that he was on the Bible's side. Yet Keeble delivered his hard, uncompromising message with elegant wit and unalloyed love; his parables, carefully couched in the images and idioms of his audiences, conveyed his practical guidance for everyday life and his truly evangelical call to share in the hope of heaven.

Keeble's life had been hard in many ways. His first wife and all five of his children preceded him in death. He suffered indignity, insult, and injury from racists in and out of the church. Such assaults did not deter him, but neither did he resist them directly. When Keeble died two weeks after the assassination of Martin Luther King, Jr., many of his white eulogists offered invidious comparisons between Keeble and King. Yet one of his "preacher boys," Fred D. Gray (b. 1930), inspired by Keeble's preaching and example, had by then become the attorney who helped overturn *de jure* segregation and discrimination in the American South, representing Rosa Parks, King, the Southern Christian Leadership Conference, and many other activists and causes in the civil rights struggle.

See also African Americans in the Movement; Bowser, George Philip; Goodpasture, Benton Cordell; Hardeman, Nicholas Brodie; Nashville Christian Institute

BIBLIOGRAPHY Willie T. Cato, *His Hand and Heart: The Wit and Wisdom of Marshall Keeble* (1990) • Julian E. Choate, *Roll Jordan Roll: A Biography of Marshall Keeble* (1968) • B. C. Goodpasture, ed., *Biography and Sermons of Marshall Keeble* (1931) • Marshal Keeble, *From Mule Back to Super Jet with the Gospel* (1962) • Paul D. Phillips, "The Interracial Impact of Marshall Keeble, Black Evangelist, 1878-1968," in *The Stone-Campbell Movement: An International Religious Tradition,* ed. Michael W. Casey and Douglas A. Foster (2002), pp. 317-28 • Forrest Neil Rhodes, "A Study of the Sources of Marshall Keeble's Effectiveness as a Preacher" (unpublished Ph.D. dissertation, Southern Illinois University, 1970).

DON HAYMES

Kellems, Jesse Randolph (1892-1980)

Minister and scholar of the Disciples of Christ in the mid-twentieth century.

Jesse Randolph Kellems (1892-1980) was a minister, evangelist, legislator, and founding minister of Westwood Hills Christian Church in Los Angeles.

Both Kellems' father and mother were ministers and professors. Kellem was educated in the University of Oregon, Eugene Divinity School (now Northwest Christian College), Temple University School of Theology, and the University of Edinburgh. For twenty-five years an evangelist, Kellems conducted some 300 campaigns in the United States, Canada, Australia, New Zealand, Great Britain, and South Africa. He preached more than 14,000 sermons to approximately 5,375,000 people. His evangelistic campaigns lasted from three to fifteen weeks with nearly 100,000 converts. Some of the great campaigns included: Pittsburgh, Kansas (709 additions); University Church, Seattle (440), and Akron, Ohio (979). The South African Campaign lasted two years and established seven congregations with 2,500 members.

Kellems authored seven books, including a respected volume on Campbellian theology, *Alexander Campbell and the Disciples,* which was remarkable in its reconciling of the basic principles of the Stone-Campbell Movement with the generally accepted scholarship of its time. Beyond his service to the church, Kellems spent six years as a representative to the state legislature of California.

See also Africa, Missions in; Justification, Doctrine of

BIBLIOGRAPHY Jesse Kellems, *Alexander Campbell and the Disciples* (1930).

MYRON J. TAYLOR

Kemp, Charles Frederick (1912-1994)

Disciples of Christ pastor, counselor, scholar, and author.

Kemp earned Bachelor's and Master's degrees from Drake University, the Bachelor of Divinity degree from Colgate-Rochester Divinity School, and the Doctor of Philosophy degree from University of Nebraska.

Kemp believed that the training of ministers relied too heavily upon the work of secular psychology. During his doctoral studies he examined the history of pastors who were effective counselors. The results of that research were published in 1947 as *Physicians of the Soul.* This work established Kemp as one of the pioneers of the pastoral counseling movement. He authored seventeen books and numerous articles in the pastoral counseling field.

After serving pastorates at Wellsville, N.Y., Red Oak, Iowa, and Lincoln, Nebraska, Kemp became Distinguished Professor of Pastoral Care and Pastoral Psychology at Brite Divinity School, Texas Christian University, in 1957. In 1968 he founded the Pastoral Care and Training Center at Brite. Following his retirement from Brite in 1979, Kemp joined the staff of University Christian Church in Fort Worth, Texas, as Pastoral Consultant.

An avid golfer, Kemp also became interested in the mental/spiritual approach to the game of golf. That interest led to the publication of three books, the last entitled *They Played with a Quiet Mind* (1991). These publications caught the interest of professional golfers in the United States. Several professional golfers, both women and men, sought his counsel to improve the mental approach to their games.

BIBLIOGRAPHY Oren H. Baker, "Charles Frederick Kemp: Man of the Month," *Pastoral Psychology* 13 (January 1963): 4.

CHARLES H. SANDERS

Leading Disciples educator and author in pastoral care, Charles Kemp (1912-1994) attracted the attention of professional golfers with his publication of three books on the mental/spiritual approach to the game.
Courtesy of the Disciples of Christ Historical Society

Kenmore Bible College

See Australia, The Movement in

Kentucky Christian College

Bible college affiliated with the Christian Churches/Churches of Christ. Kentucky Christian College (or Christian Normal Institute, as it was called at its founding) came into existence in 1919. Though classes began in the fall of 1919, the articles of incorporation were not signed until December of that year. It was (and is) located in Grayson, Kentucky, in the eastern part of the state, a region that experienced significant social and economic need at the time of the college's establishment.

Kentucky Christian College had three principal founders, John William Lusby, Robert Burns Neal, and John O'Kane Snodgrass. Lusby, a former lawyer and school administrator, and founder of a high school, established the precursory Normal (teacher-training) school in Grayson, and served as its first president. Lusby was an active member of the First Christian Church in Grayson and had deep concerns for ministry needs in eastern Kentucky.

Robert Burns Neal had been in the area a number of years before J. W. Lusby arrived. As the premier evangelist for Christian churches in eastern Kentucky, he had encouraged church planting and evangelistic initiatives, and located ministries in all of the eastern counties. In his last years (he died in 1925) he resided at Grayson, continuing his itinerant evangelism and his writing ministry. He had long been a supporter of Morehead Academy, in Morehead, Kentucky, forty miles to the west of Grayson. Morehead had been organized by the Disciples of Christ in Kentucky in the 1880s and had been turned over to the Christian Woman's Board of Missions (Indianapolis) in 1900. After 1910, as CWBM institutions were perceived to be drifting in a more liberal direction, Neal began to agitate for a college more deeply committed to the Stone-Campbell "restoration plea." This agitation resulted in the formation of Christian Normal Institute out of the Normal academy that J. W. Lusby had already begun.

J. O. Snodgrass, named after the famed Stone-Campbell evangelist John O'Kane, held degrees from Drake University and, together with his wife Rosella, a graduate of Oskaloosa College, was hired by Lusby and Neal as the core faculty of Christian Normal Institute. The two had embraced the opportunity to transfer their teaching ministry to needy students in the eastern Kentucky region. They were joined in their teaching duties by other faculty from the local community.

At the outset, Christian Normal Institute comprised a grade school program, a high school, and a Normal school. By the mid-1930s, the school consisted of an academy (high school curriculum), a junior college, and a senior college. By the 1940s, the Kentucky State Board of Education had bought the Morehead Academy (with its well-established Normal program) from the Christian Woman's Board of Missions and had created a State Normal school on that campus (now Morehead State University). The Normal school at Grayson was deemed less and less important and, as it was clearly evolving into a Bible college for educating ministers for the churches, changed its name in 1944 to Kentucky Christian College.

Over the past several decades, the college's faculty has been expanded and the curriculum has been consistently updated. Most current faculty members have earned doctorates in their teaching fields. New programs in Teacher Education (1984), Psychology (1987), Social Work (1988), Business (1988), History (1998), Intercultural Studies (1998), and Pre-Law (1998) have been inaugurated. The college is accredited by the Southern Association of Schools and Colleges, and has an expanded 110-acre campus in Grayson.

See also Bible College Movement; Higher Education, Views of in the Movement

BIBLIOGRAPHY Max Earl Brandon, "The Views and Principles of J. W. Lusby in the Founding of Kentucky Christian College, Grayson, Kentucky, 1901-1937" (unpublished M.A. thesis, Northeast Missouri State Teacher's College, 1961) • Alva D. Snodgrass, "The History of Christian Normal Institute" (unpublished B.D. thesis, School of Religion, Butler University, 1944) • James R. Wright, "A History of Kentucky Christian College, 1945-1970" (unpublished M.R.E. thesis, Emmanuel School of Religion, 1971).

CHARLES R. GRESHAM

Kershner, Frederick D. (1875-1953)

Academician, theologian, editor, and preacher of the Disciples of Christ in the first half of the twentieth century.

Educated at Kentucky University and Princeton, Kershner served as president of Milligan College (1908-11) and of Texas Christian University (1911-15). He edited the *Christian-Evangelist* (1915-17) and was book editor for the *Christian Standard* (1918-20). During 1919-20 he helped establish the Christian Foundation, which led to the formation of the Butler University School of Religion (now Christian Theological Seminary) in Indianapolis, of which institution he was dean from 1924 to 1944. From 1920 to 1924 he was professor of Christian Doctrine at Drake University, Des Moines, Iowa. When he took up his duties at the Butler University School of Religion he also headed the department of Christian Doctrine until his retirement. He remained Dean Emeritus and Professor of Christian Doctrine there until 1951, two years before his death.

Kershner consciously sought to be a mediator in the mounting polarization between liberal and conservative Disciples in the early twentieth century. He took a middle position between the theological liberalism of figures like Edward Scribner Ames of the University of Chicago and the restorationist conservatism of figures like Robert E. Elmore, editor of the *Restoration Herald* in Cincinnati. He was open to the possibilities of serious Disciples participation in the Ecumenical Movement and himself served on the Disciples' Council on Christian Unity spearheaded by Peter Ainslie. Yet Kershner opposed "open membership" for compromising the Stone-Campbell Movement's historic position on the immersion of believers as basic to incorporation in the Body of Christ.

Founding dean of the College of Religion at Butler University (later Christian Theological Seminary), Frederick D. Kershner (1875-1953) served from 1935 to 1943 as chair of the Commission on Restudy of the Disciples of Christ. The Commission brought together conservative, moderate, and liberal Disciples in a final effort to prevent a second division in the Movement. Courtesy of the Disciples of Christ Historical Society

Kershner embraced the "restoration" principle but sought to qualify it. He believed that Thomas Campbell had probably been overconfident of the church's ability to arrive at agreement on the "self-evident" truths of the New Testament order of things. The restoration enterprise demanded that the church be a community of ongoing discipleship, as exemplified in the earliest church, constituted of believers "enrolled in the school where the gospel of Jesus was taught." Mechanical restorationism was no substitute for the gradual process of critical inquiry and spiritual growth necessary to the building of consensus on biblical truth.

Kershner has rightly been called a "free church catholic," and in his *The Christian Union Overture* (1923), a commentary on the *Declaration and Address*, he clearly interpreted Thomas Campbell in the same mold. He believed that Campbell had developed a "high" doctrine of the church, and took it on himself to encourage the Disciples of Christ, on the brink of another division, to dedicate themselves yet again to the "one, holy, catholic and apostolic church." Kershner also believed that the Campbells invested great faith in the collective reasoning, the "common mind" of Christians across history and culture. He shared the vision of a universal *consensus fidelium:* the whole of the Christian faithful, under the guide of the best biblical scholarship, achieving consecrated agreement on the New Testament's normative standards for the church's faith and practice. This alone, not creeds or theological systems, could secure the unity of the church. Thus Kershner was a strong advocate of the Disciples conventions. He was president of the International Convention in Columbus, Ohio, in 1938, but was equally supportive of the North American Christian Convention, appearing on its very first program in 1927. Probably his greatest achievement as a mediator was his service as chairman of the Commission on Restudy of the Disciples of Christ (1934-46), which brought together liberal, moderate, and conservative leaders in hopes of preserving unity.

Kershner was a prolific writer. His column "As I Think on These Things" was carried for over thirty years in the moderate *Christian-Evangelist,* yet he wrote some of his best work in the more conservative *Christian Standard,* like the "Stars" and "Comets and Constellations" biographical and historical series (1940-43). Among his more influential books were *The Religion of Christ* (1911, rev. 1917), a work in Christian ethics; *The Restoration Handbook* (1918-20), a four-volume set of historical-doctrinal studies for congregational use; *The Christian Union Overture* (1923); and *Pioneers of Christian Thought* (1930), a survey of theological thought from the apostle Paul to Albrecht Ritschl.

Kershner's irenic spirit infused all of his work. He maintained personal friendships with both the ultra-conservative Church of Christ leader Daniel Sommer and the liberal Peter Ainslie. His summation of the Christian virtue of *agapē* as "intelligent good will" became a popular watchword among his students and those who shared his desire to avert further disunity in the Stone-Campbell Movement.

See also *Christian-Evangelist, The;* Christian Theological Seminary; Commission on Restudy of the Disciples of Christ; *Consensus Fidelium;* "Restoration," Meanings of within the Movement

BIBLIOGRAPHY Paul M. Blowers, "Restoring the One, Holy, Catholic, and Apostolic Church: The *Declaration and Address* as Interpreted by William Robinson and Frederick Doyle Kershner," in *The Quest for Christian Unity, Peace, and Purity: Texts and Studies,* ed. Thomas H. Olbricht and Hans Rollmann (2000), pp. 365-88 • Frederick D. Kershner, *The Religion of Christ* (1911, rev. 1917) • Frederick D. Kershner, *The Restoration Handbook,* 4 vols. (1918-20) • Frederick D. Kershner, *The Christian Union Overture: An Interpretation of the Declaration and Address of*

Thomas Campbell (1923) • Frederick D. Kershner, "One Holy, Catholic, and Apostolic Church," *Christian Standard* 73 (1938): 1029-32 • Frederick D. Kershner, *Pioneers of Christian Thought* (1930) • Byron C. Lambert, "'The Middle Way' of Frederick D. Kershner" (essay privately published by Emmanuel School of Religion, Johnson City, Tennessee, 1998) • D. Newell Williams, "Overcoming a Liberal-Conservative Divide: The Commission on Restudy of the Disciples of Christ," in *Christian Faith Seeking Historical Understanding: Essays in Honor of H. Jack Forstman,* ed. James Duke and Anthony L. Dunnavant (1997), pp. 246-76. BYRON C. LAMBERT

Ketcherside, W. Carl (1908-1989)

Evangelist, debater, and editor of *Mission Messenger* journal.

Born in Cantwell, Missouri, in 1908, Carl Ketcherside was the son of an uneducated miner-preacher. Though he had only a limited formal education, he became impressively literate through years of wide and careful reading. He was regarded as a prodigy by some as he became "the boy preacher" when barely 12.

His sixty-nine years as a preacher began in the "Sommerite" Churches of Christ, among whom, at an early age, he became widely influential as an evangelist, debater, and editor. While in his twenties, he received personal assurance from Daniel Sommer that, just as Benjamin Franklin's mantle had fallen on Sommer, Sommer's mantle would fall upon him.

Ketcherside did not take Sommer's charge lightly. While still comparatively young, he debated the Sommerite issues (anti-college, anti-pastor system) with eminent leaders in the mainline Churches of Christ, including Rue Porter, G. C. Brewer, and G. K. Wallace.

In 1940 he began publishing the *Mission Messenger,* which continued for thirty-six years. For almost two decades this journal championed the Sommerite cause, as did the editor's extensive preaching and debating. By 1957, however, a dramatic change occurred. Ketcherside confessed that he had been sectarian in his earlier ministry and resolved that he would henceforth work for peace and unity among all heirs of the Restoration heritage.

From this time until his death in 1989, he insisted that mutual love is the only answer to "problems in long division." He widely proclaimed that, "Wherever God has a child, I have a brother or sister." Resolved no longer to debate his brothers and sisters, he rather called them together in unity meetings across the country.

During these years Ketcherside spoke on virtually every college campus among all three streams of the Stone-Campbell Movement, as well as at hundreds of congregations of all persuasions. His message was compelling, reflecting his own transformation: "It is time for a new day to dawn. We have led in dividing, now let us lead in uniting."

Historian Richard Hughes named him as one of the founders of the "progressive movement" that emerged among Churches of Christ in the 1960s. His influence upon Christian Churches/Churches of Christ and Disciples of Christ was also evident.

In his retiring years he gave most of his time to a ministry in the St. Louis inner city called Cornerstone. The ministry provided teaching, feeding, and clothing for the poor and the marginalized.

See also *Mission Messenger;* Sommer, Daniel

BIBLIOGRAPHY W. Carl Ketcherside, *Pilgrimage of Joy: An Autobiography of Carl Ketcherside* (1991) • W. Carl Ketcherside, "The Authority Totem," in *Christian Commandos* (1969), p. 126 • *The Works of W. Carl Ketcherside,* 30 books in 12 vols. (1991). LEROY GARRETT

Kiamichi Mission

Evangelistic mission in Oklahoma associated with the Christian Churches/Churches of Christ.

In the Talihina, Oklahoma, area, A. B. ("Brother Mac") McReynolds started the Kiamichi Mountains Christian Mission to evangelize Native Americans, start churches, and bring worship services to southeast Oklahoma. McReynolds held a two-week revival in August 1940 where many were baptized and requested regularly scheduled Sunday Schools and preaching in the surrounding communities. With its first church service in October 1941, the mission eventually had twenty-two preaching points with ten remaining churches. McReynolds purchased a campground, "Christ's 40 Acres," near Honobia, Oklahoma, in 1946. In 1949 he launched a men's retreat, the Kiamichi Clinic, receiving national notoriety for its pro-Restoration preaching and pro-American praying against the threat of a growing global communism. Many preachers in the Christian Churches/Churches of Christ have spoken at the patriotic and evangelistic gathering, as well as personalities from outside the Stone-Campbell tradition like radio commentator Paul Harvey.

See also Evangelism, Evangelists — Christian Churches/Churches of Christ; McReynolds, Albert Badger

BIBLIOGRAPHY *Kiamichi Mountain Christian Mission News* (newsletter) • *Sessions of the Kiamichi Clinic* (sermons of the Kiamichi Clinic) (1949-).

ANTHONY J. SPRINGER

King, David (1819-1894)

Evangelist, publisher, writer, and pioneering leader of the Stone-Campbell Movement in Great Britain in the mid- and late-nineteenth century.

David King was born in London on February 28, 1819. After leaving school at the age of 12 to help his widowed mother, he was introduced by a friend to the local Wesleyan Methodist chapel, where he was converted and became a member. In 1840 he came across a copy of the *Christian Messenger* and obtained the address of John Black, pastor of the Church of Christ in Camden Town. Black baptized him in 1842 along with his wife, Louisa, whom he had married in 1839. From 1848 the London churches supported him as an evangelist. He was asked by the General Evangelist Committee in 1855 to help plant a church in Manchester, and again in 1858 to help plant a church in Birmingham. He moved there permanently three years later. In 1866 he began the work of training evangelists, which he continued until 1879. King followed Campbell's tradition of public debates with persons of opposing views, the most famous being that with the atheist Charles Bradlaugh in 1870. He also debated over baptism, Christadelphianism, and spiritualism.

King's first magazine was the *Bible Advocate,* a penny monthly that ran from 1847 to 1849, followed by *Quo Warranto.* He also edited *The Old Paths* (continued by his widow), *The Sunbeam* (a Sunday School paper), and the *British Millennial Harbinger* and its successors from 1861. His other writings were mainly pamphlets. He revised James Wallis's hymnbook in 1868, and edited a further book with G. Y. Tickle in 1888. King was Chairman of the Annual Meeting of Stone-Campbell churches in 1870, 1874, and 1878, and was one of the chief spokespersons for British opposition to the American churches' practice of open communion. He died on June 26, 1894, leaving a public reputation as an indomitable battler for truth, while those who knew him privately testified to his personal kindness and gentleness.

See also *British Millennial Harbinger;* Great Britain and Ireland, Churches of Christ in; Rotherham, Joseph Bryant; Wallis, James

BIBLIOGRAPHY Louis Billington, "The Churches of Christ in Britain: A Study in Nineteenth-Century Sectarianism," in *The Stone-Campbell Movement: An International Religious Tradition,* ed. Michael W. Casey and Douglas A. Foster (2002), pp. 367-97 • Louisa King, ed., *Memoir of David King with Various Papers and Addresses* (1897)

DAVID M. THOMPSON

Korea, The Movement in

The earliest record of the Stone-Campbell Movement in Korea dates to 1907, when William D. Cunningham, a Disciples missionary to Japan, briefly visited the country. As a result of this visit, two Koreans were trained by Cunningham's Yotsuya Mission in Tokyo and sent to Korea as missionaries. Li Wan Kyun is credited with establishing the first Stone-Campbell churches in Korea. His work and the work of other early native missionaries yielded over half a dozen congregations, but by the early 1940s the congregations were either dissolved or subsumed under other denominations, partly due to the Japanese colonial government's harsh policies.

A key figure early on was John T. Chase, an American who had spent the years 1927 to 1934 in the Yotsuya Mission and moved to Korea as an independent missionary in 1936, inaugurating the Korean Christian Mission. Chase hired a Korean tutor, Y. H. Kim, whom he later converted, and Kim in turn planted the Shin Dang Chung Christian Church, which quickly outgrew its first building. Chase also established a Bible Institute to educate native Korean evangelists. Among his early students was a former Methodist, Sang Hyun Chae, who planted the To Nam Dong Christian Church in Seoul and later assumed responsibility for the Bible Institute. Chae became an influential church leader in the Korean Christian Churches at a time of severe governmental suspicion and repression.

Also significant was the work of Sung Nak-so, an erstwhile Salvation Army cadet, who had independently developed sympathy with "restoration" principles. By 1930 Sung and William Cunningham met, and at the latter's request Sung ministered to a community of Koreans in Japan. In September 1931 Sung returned to Korea as supervisor of the Yotsuya Mission's Korean initiative, but he soon fell out with Cunningham and pursued his own course, establishing six churches by the end of the decade, some of which still thrive.

Korean Churches of Christ also began in the early 1930s. Dong Suk-kee and Kang Myung-suk were pioneers in this effort, both converts to the Stone-Campbell Movement from Methodism, having made the transition while studying at Stone-Campbell schools in the United States — Dong at Cincinnati Bible Seminary in the late 1920s, Kang at Freed-Hardeman College in the mid-1930s. By the end of the 1930s, they had founded over a dozen congregations in Korea, with support from American churches.

Almost all Stone-Campbell Movement missionaries to Korea were Americans. Christian Church missionary J. Michael Shelley led the way, arriving with his family in 1935, but leaving within a year due in part to illness. The work of John Chase, beginning in 1936, has already been noted. The next significant American missionary was John J. Hill, a graduate of Johnson Bible College and Butler University School of Religion, who arrived in 1939 and stayed until his retirement in 1972, excepting the years when he was on furloughs or forced to leave by various exigencies. Hill, his Korean colleagues, and later arriving missionaries founded new congregations and orphanages and built up the Bible college that later became Seoul Christian University. American Dale Richeson arrived in 1954 as the first Western Church of Christ missionary to Korea, shortly followed by Haskell Chesshir and Bill Ramsey. They built on the foundation laid by Kang and Dong; Chesshir, in particular, was noteworthy for purchasing a large tract of land where he began a model dairy farm and a Bible college that eventually became Korean Christian University.

During the first half of the twentieth century, Koreans were subjected to harsh Japanese colonial rule (1910-45) and a devastating civil war (1950-53). The Stone-Campbell Movement, along with other Christian communities, suffered. Churches were shut down, their leaders persecuted. For a time, beginning in 1945, all Christian churches in Korea were ordered to give up their denominational names and be identified simply as the "Korean Japanese Christian Church." Among the indigenous Stone-Campbell leaders to be persecuted was Choi Sang-hyun, a Christian Church minister and noted intellectual who was abducted by the communists in 1950 and presumed killed. Yet the churches persisted and grew. Near the end of Japanese rule, only 13 or so Stone-Campbell churches remained; by 1955, the number grew to at least 65; by 1980, to 200; and to 400 by the end of the twentieth century, 100 of which are affiliated with Churches of Christ, the rest with the Christian Churches/Churches of Christ. There is no Christian Church (Disciples of Christ) congregation in Korea because Disciples did not plant churches in Korea.

BIBLIOGRAPHY Christian J. Chae, *Chasing the Truth: The Patches of the One Hundred Patches Preacher* (unpublished M.A.R. thesis, Emmanuel School of Religion, 1996) • Yoon Hwan Chae, *My Dear American Friends: Excerpts from the Letters of Brother Chae, 1975-1981* (1982) • John T. Chase, "The Korean Mission in Retrospect," *The Korean Messenger* (May 1946): 2-3 • John T. Chase, "Missions in Korea," *Christian Standard* 73 (1938): 334, 336.

TIMOTHY LEE

Krutsinger, William Henry (1838-1916)

Indiana preacher, debater, writer, and educator.

Born in Orange County, he grew up in rural Indiana, plowing, planting, hoeing, and mowing. Krutsinger was educated in the common schools and at Salem, Indiana, by James G. May.

Early in his career Krutsinger was a frequent companion of Indiana evangelist and apocalyptic visionary Joseph Lemuel Martin. By 1874 Krutsinger was Professor of Languages and English Literature in James M. Mathes's Male and Female College at Bedford, Indiana, earning regional recognition as a leading teacher of languages, especially Greek.

In the early 1880s Krutsinger established a "Bible Training School" in his home at Ellettsville, Indiana. In his school Krutsinger educated from six to twelve young men to be preachers. Among those who studied in this school were Arvy Glenn Freed, Frederick Louis Rowe, Homer Howard Adamson, William Morten Davis, and David Sylvester Ligon.

Krutsinger contributed occasional articles to the *Christian Record, Gospel Advocate,* and *Gospel Echo.* In 1906 and 1907 Krutsinger helped to edit the first lists of "The Preachers of Churches of Christ." He died in 1916 at Bloomington, Indiana.

BIBLIOGRAPHY Terry J. Gardner, *Faith and Facts* 30 (January 2002).

TERRY J. GARDNER

L

Ladies' Aid Society

An organization for supporting the work of the church in many Disciples of Christ congregations during the last quarter of the nineteenth century and the first quarter of the twentieth century. Society members usually paid dues, participated in a process of initiation, and were added to an official membership list.

The work of the Aid Society was mostly financial support of the congregation. The Society would hold bake sales, community dinners, or bazaars in order to fund the congregation's work or pay for new building projects. The purpose of the Aid Society was not, however, purely financial. Many Aid Societies were also involved in benevolence, visitation, and evangelism.

Organizational development mirrored that of missionary societies in the Movement, and in the early twentieth century Ladies' Aid Societies began to unite in larger endeavors. The Ladies' Aid Societies of Southern California united their efforts to help the Christian Missionary Society of Southern California establish new churches and erect new buildings.

See also Women in Ministry

BIBLIOGRAPHY Mrs. R. L. Brown, "Southern California Ladies' Aid Societies Organized," *Christian-Evangelist* 54 (1916): 1205 • Mrs. E. E. Mack, "What Can an Aid Society Do?" *Christian-Evangelist* 54 (1916): 874 • C. J. Sharp, "Church Efficiency (is the ladies' aid a spiritual asset or liability?)," *Christian Standard* 53 (1918): 896.

DERRICK DOYLE

Lamar, James Sanford (1829-1908)

Preacher, editor, and scholar of biblical hermeneutics in the second generation of the Stone-Campbell Movement.

J. S. Lamar was born in Gwinnett County, Georgia, May 18, 1829, the second son of Philip and Margaret Anthony Lamar. He studied at the LaHatt academy and was admitted to the bar in Columbus, Georgia, in 1850. John Tillery, who had studied at Franklin College, studied with Lamar concerning the Movement's restorationist principles. Later John Reeves, a Freewill Baptist minister, baptized Lamar.

After his conversion, Lamar enrolled at Campbell's Bethany college in 1853 and graduated in July 1854 as valedictorian of a class of seventeen. Alexander Campbell, Isaac Errett, D. S. Burnet, W. K. Pendleton, and Robert Richardson ordained him at Bethany. The same year he began to preach for the

James S. Lamar (1829-1908) authored *The Organon of Scripture* (1860), which became a virtual handbook of "inductive" biblical hermeneutics in the Stone-Campbell Movement.
Courtesy of Bethany College

First Christian Church in Augusta, Georgia. Before long, with A. G. Thomas, he began publishing a paper called the *Christian Union* that was critical of *The American Christian Review* and the *Gospel Advocate.*

Lamar received the M.A. degree from Bethany College in 1859 and was chosen a trustee of Bethany the same year. Also in 1859, Lamar was elected one of the vice presidents of the American Christian Missionary Society at its annual meeting in Cincinnati. In 1866 he was influential in the beginning of the *Christian Standard,* with Isaac Errett as the first editor. By 1869 he became the associate editor of the paper. Lamar later became the biographer of Isaac Errett.

In 1860 Lamar published *The Organon of Scripture,* a handbook of biblical interpretation that enhanced his reputation throughout the Stone-Campbell Movement. Aspiring to break through the prevailing "mystic" and "dogmatic" traditions of interpretation, Lamar invoked "Lord [Francis] Bacon" as the author of his theological method, by which he expected to establish pure facts of Scripture as "objects of precise and certain knowledge." He argued that when Christians gave up theories and creeds and accepted "Scriptural facts," the Bible's impeccable internal logic, then unity among Christians would occur and the church would be restored to its primitive purity. Lamar's *Organon* effectively systematized the grammatical-critical model of interpretation advanced by first-generation leaders like Alexander Campbell and Walter Scott. It exuded enthusiasm that at last the Bible would be liberated from the ecclesiastical and theological powers that had inhibited its authority in and for the church.

In later years, however, in his own preaching and exegetical labors, Lamar backed away from some of the rationalism of his earlier work and became more of a realist about the difficulties of interpreting Scripture and the role of theology. He moved increasingly from a "No Creed but the Bible" to a "No Creed but Christ" position, arguing that the simple confession of Jesus as Christ and Lord was the only true foundation for Christian unity.

Lamar married Mary Rucker, with whom he had three children. Two children died of tuberculosis. The oldest child, Joseph Rucker Lamar, became an associate justice of the United States Supreme Court in 1910. Lamar ministered to Christian Churches in Georgia throughout his life.

See also Bible, Interpretation of the; *Christian Standard, The;* Errett, Isaac; Hermeneutics

BIBLIOGRAPHY C. Leonard Allen, "Freedom from Dogma: James S. Lamar and the Disciples of Christ," in *Illusions of Innocence: Protestant Primitivism in America, 1630-1875* (1988), pp. 153-69 • M. Eugene Boring, *Disciples and the Bible: A History of Disciples Biblical Interpretation in North America* (1997) • Stephen Broyles, "James Sanford Lamar and the Substructure of Biblical Interpretation in the Restoration Movement," *Restoration Quarterly* 29 (1987): 143-51 • James S. Lamar, "The Basis of Christian Union," *Christian Quarterly* 5 (1873): 182-91 • James S. Lamar, "The History of Redemption Reproduced in the Redeemed," in *The Living Pulpit of the Christian Church,* ed. W. T. Moore (1868), pp. 401-10 • James S. Lamar, *Memoirs of Isaac Errett,* 2 vols. (1893) • James S. Lamar, *The Organon of Scripture: Or, the Inductive Method of Biblical Interpretation* (1860) • Edward J. Mosely, *Disciples of Christ in Georgia* (1954) • Tim Sensing, "Baconian Method and Preaching in the Stone-Campbell Movement," *Stone-Campbell Journal* 4 (2001): 163-87.

TIM SENSING

Lappin, Samuel Strahl (1870-1960)

Preacher, professor, author, and editor in Christian Churches/Churches of Christ.

Samuel Strahl Lappin was born on September 20, 1870, in Wayne County, Illinois; he died December 29, 1960, at Bedford, Indiana. Lappin had studied at Eureka College in Illinois, and went on to serve churches at Toluca, Washburn, Paxton, Atlanta, and Stanford, Illinois; Erlanger, Kentucky; Bethany, West Virginia; and Bedford, Indiana. Lappin joined the editorial staff of the *Christian Standard* in 1909 and served as the editor from 1909 to 1917. He was a professor at Bethany College in West Virginia, 1918-19. He wrote five books: *Where the Long Trail Begins, Wren's Nest, The Training of the Church, Lappin's Sermon Outlines,* and *Run, Sammy, Run.* Two of his four siblings were also minister-scholars in the Stone-Campbell tradition: John, a professor at Phillips University, in Enid, Oklahoma; and William, professor and dean at Johnson Bible College.

GARY E. WEEDMAN

Lappin, William Otis (1877-1966)

Preacher, college professor, college president, and dean.

William Otis Lappin was born on July 20, 1877; he died April 21, 1966. Lappin had studied at Eureka College in Illinois and received an M.A. degree in 1918 from the University of Chicago. He had a twin brother, John, who was also a preacher and professor, and three other siblings, one of whom, Samuel, was a preacher, professor, and editor. Lappin began preaching in country churches in Southern Illinois in May 1898. He served as professor at Atlantic Christian College in Wilson, North Carolina, from 1913 to 1918; president of Morehead Normal School from 1918 to 1923; professor at Milligan College from 1923 to 1928; and professor and dean at Johnson Bible College from 1928 to 1959. He served as acting president of Johnson Bible College for several months following the death of President Alva Ross Brown in March 1941.

GARY E. WEEDMAN

Lard, Moses E. (1818-1880)

Evangelist and editor in Missouri and Kentucky.

Lard was born in Shelbyville, Tennessee, October 10, 1818, and died in Lexington, Kentucky, June 17, 1880. When Lard was 11, his family moved to Ray County, Missouri, where numerous persons from the Stone-Campbell Movement lived, many of whom had also migrated from Kentucky. Upon being convinced of the validity of the Movement's plea he was baptized in 1841, and he immediately secured preaching appointments.

In 1845, now married with two children, Lard, upon the encouragement of General Alexander W. Doniphan, enrolled at Bethany College, founded by Alexander Campbell in 1840. He graduated as valedictorian in 1849. He returned to Missouri and served churches until the Civil War, at which time he moved to Kentucky and then Canada as the result of his pacifist views. He left Missouri because he refused to take a Missouri-legislated oath requiring ministers to declare their loyalty to the Union. Upon returning from Canada he lived in Lexington, Kentucky, where he preached, wrote, and edited journals.

He was selected by Alexander Campbell to respond to Jeremiah B. Jeter, the Baptist controversialist, who in 1855 published a popular refutation of Alexander Campbell's views. Lard's book was titled, *A Review of Rev. J. B. Jeter's Book Entitled "Campbellism Examined"* (1857). He founded and published *Lard's Quarterly* from 1863 to 1868, thereafter writing for or editing the *Apostolic Times.*

One of his most important legacies to the Movement was his 1875 commentary on Romans, often reprinted in both America and Great Britain, titled *Commentary on Paul's Letter to Romans: with a Revised Greek Text, Compiled from the Best Recent Authors, and A New Translation.* He provided a summary of the meaning of the sections in Romans, notes on each verse, and the new translation, which was his own. Despite reading several other commentaries, he rarely cited them. The commentary has been regarded as a competent scholarly treatment both for then and now.

In 1866 Lard wrote a much quoted article, "Can We Divide?" After noting divisions in major American Protestant denominations brought about by the Civil War, Lard argued that the Stone-Campbell Movement would never divide over opinion. He called for every Christian in both North and South to "show himself a master in efforts to heal whatever of alienation may yet remain. Let not a word be said in any pulpit, not a remark be dropped in the social circle, not a paragraph or sentence be written in any paper, that can chafe or wound. And if heretofore we have known it let us never more know any North or South in our ranks."

Lard was principally a preacher, author, and editor. He described his activities at the height of his career in 1864: "From April, 1863, to April, 1864, I preached about three hundred and seventy discourses. These averaged one hour and fifteen minutes each in length; that is, I stood in the pulpit four hundred and sixty-two hours in the year. The result of this labor was about three hundred and fifty confessions. . . . To this is to be added writing for the *Quarterly,* correcting proof, traveling, and heavy domestic duties." Much of his preaching was in "protracted meetings," and he argued that the sermons should be equally proportioned toward outsiders and church members.

In his crucial 1863 article titled "The Reformation for which We Are Pleading — What Is It?" Lard declared that the reformation (1) must rest in the expressed will of Christ, (2) be both doctrinal and practical, and (3) constitute a complete return to primitive Christianity in doctrine, practice, and spirit. Among restorationists, Lard occupied moderate positions, approving mission societies but opposing creeds, open communion, instrumental music, and a settled ministry. He was a pacifist, but while he thought Christians should refrain from unethical political involvement, he held it appropriate both to hold office and to vote. Late in life he argued against everlasting punishment. As a writer and speaker he was clear, vital, and eloquent, though sometimes also disputatious.

See also Civil War, The; Instrumental Music; Pacifism; Universalism

BIBLIOGRAPHY Kenneth van Deusen, *Moses Lard That Prince of Preachers* (1987) • David L. Little, "Moses E. Lard and Romans: Lessons Learned from the Making of a Restoration Commentary," *Restoration Quarterly* 41 (3rd Quarter 1999): 129ff. • Works of Moses E. Lard, available on-line at http://www.mun.ca/rels/restmov/people/mlard.html.

THOMAS H. OLBRICHT

Lard's Quarterly

Religious journal published by Moses E. Lard from 1863 to 1868.

On April 5, 1859, Lard had announced in the *American Christian Review* a new publication to be titled the *Christian Quarterly.* The 2,000 subscribers he anticipated, however, were not forthcoming due largely to the national unrest preceding the Civil War. In September 1863 he became the first in the Movement to launch a quarterly, then titled *Lard's Quarterly,* from Georgetown, Kentucky, with the succeeding four volumes printed in Lexington.

Lard argued that a quarterly provided a greater opportunity to set out the aims of primitive Christianity, give adequate space for discussing the cause of truth, and provide a suitable vehicle for new writers. Opposing views were to be permitted, including articles from "Baptists and Pedo-baptists." The journal was also to include biographies of earlier religious leaders, news of congregational events, victories of faith, and book reviews. The war and its aftermath resulted in declining numbers of subscribers. Because of his moderate views, Lard antagonized the more militant on both sides. Finally, in the fifth year, April 1868, Lard announced the demise of the journal.

Lard himself produced most of the articles (almost 200). Other frequent contributors were Thomas Munnell (10 essays), J. W. McGarvey (8), and Ira B. Grubbs (7). Lard published articles by a number of progressive authors, including Robert Graham, C. L. Loos, G. W. Longan, and Alexander Proctor. While a wide variety of topics was discussed, those frequently appearing were immersion, the work of the Holy Spirit, pacifism and war, restorationism, creeds, preachers, ministerial training, instrumental music, millennialism, and mission societies.

The Old Paths Book Club reprinted the five volumes of *Lard's Quarterly* in 1949-50. An index to the journal, compiled by Ernie Stefanik, is available at http://www.mun.ca/rels/restmov/texts/mlard/lq/LQ-INDEX.HTM.

See also Lard, Moses E. — THOMAS H. OLBRICHT

Larimore, Emma Page (1855-1943)

Teacher, stenographer, writer, editor, and second wife of T. B. Larimore.

Born on a plantation near Donelson, Tennessee, she was educated by Charlotte Fanning (1809-1896) at Hope Institute and the Tennessee Normal School in Nashville, Tennessee.

In 1884 Emma Page rejoined Charlotte Fanning as a teacher in the Fanning Orphan School, on the grounds of the former Hope Institute, where she taught the girls "literary subjects." She also edited a column in the *Gospel Advocate,* where her "Children's Corner" ran for several years. In the column Page dispensed wisdom and encouragement to young children, often addressing those who were bereft of parents or siblings due to death.

Emma Page recorded, edited, and published the sermons of Theophilus Brown Larimore (1843-1929), her most enduring work. Although Fletcher Douglas Srygley (1856-1900) was credited with editing the first volume of Larimore's letters and sermons, much of the editorial work fell to Page because of Srygley's ill health, and she completed the second and third volumes alone.

T. B. Larimore's first wife, the former Julia Esther Gresham, died in 1907, and on January 1, 1911, Emma Page married her famous subject. In 1911 the Larimores traveled extensively across North America doing evangelistic work, and Emma chronicled those travels in yet another Larimore book entitled *Our Corner Book: From Maine to Mexico, From Canada to Cuba.* In 1931, following Larimore's death, she completed a final book titled *Life, Letters and Sermons of T. B. Larimore.* In 1943 Emma Page Larimore died in Santa Ana, California, and was buried next to her husband in Fair Haven Cemetery.

See also Fanning, Charlotte Fall; *Gospel Advocate, The;* Larimore, Theophilus Brown

BIBLIOGRAPHY Emma Page, *The Life and Work of Mrs. Charlotte Fanning* (1907) • Emma Page, ed., *Letters and Sermons of T. B. Larimore,* vol. II (1904) • Emma Page, ed., *Letters and Sermons of T. B. Larimore,* vol. III (1910) • Emma Page Larimore, *Life, Letters and Sermons of T. B. Larimore* (1931) • Emma Page Larimore, *Our Corner Book: From Maine to Mexico, From Canada to Cuba* (1912) • Fletcher Douglas Srygley, ed., *Letters and Sermons of T. B. Larimore* (1900). — TERRY J. GARDNER

Larimore, Theophilus Brown (1843-1929)

Evangelist and educator who maintained fellowship across lines of division in the Stone-Campbell Movement.

Born in Jefferson County, Tennessee, he moved with his mother and siblings to Sequatchie County in 1852. In 1859-61 he attended Mossy Creek Baptist College (today Carson-Newman) in Jefferson City,

T. B. Larimore and his second wife, writer and educator Emma Page Larimore. Larimore was one of the most widely known and loved evangelists in the Stone-Campbell Movement in the late 1800s and early 1900s. While personally conservative, he refused to take sides in the growing division, setting an example of dogged commitment to unity. Courtesy of the Center for Restoration Studies, Abilene Christian University/The Disciples of Christ Historical Society

Tennessee. While serving as a scout for the Confederate Army in fall 1863 he was captured by federal troops but released after taking the noncombatant oath. He and his family then moved to Hopkinsville, Kentucky, where a Christian Church elder, Enos Campbell, taught and baptized him.

To train for ministry he studied at Franklin College, operated by Tolbert and A. J. Fanning near Nashville, Tennessee, graduating in 1867. He preached and taught school in northern Alabama and middle Tennessee, marrying Esther Gresham of Florence in 1868. In 1871 he opened Mars Hill Academy on land inherited from his wife near Florence, Alabama. In 1875 and 1876 Larimore edited an irenic and short-lived paper titled the *Little Angel.* Though he spent several months each year in evangelistic work while running Mars Hill Academy, he finally closed the school in 1887 to be able to devote full time to evangelism.

Larimore developed the practice of remaining at a place as long as he and the host congregation believed he was doing good. His longest evangelistic meeting lasted from January 4 to June 7, 1894, in Sherman, Texas. He preached twice every day and three times on Sunday, with 254 additions to the church.

In 1897 former Mars Hill pupil and Alabama state evangelist Oscar Pendleton Spiegel (1866-1947) in an "Open Letter" challenged Larimore to declare his position on matters dividing the movement, including instruments in worship, missionary societies, and salaried preachers. In his reply Larimore refused to take sides, insisting that he would never renounce those who did not understand the issues as he did.

After Esther's death in 1907, he married Emma Page of Nashville in 1911 and continued a heavy schedule of travel and preaching. He was involved in an unsuccessful attempt to establish a Christian school and community in Gainesville, Florida, in 1912-13, publishing the paper *Our Florida Friend* to gain publicity for the effort.

After short stints in Henderson, Tennessee (1914-15), Berkeley, California (1918-22), and Washington, D.C. (1922-25), the Larimores moved back to California, first to Berkeley, then to Santa Ana. He wrote frequently for the *Gospel Advocate* in the 1920s and continued to preach widely until the last move to Berkeley. He died at Santa Ana on March 18, 1929, from complications of a hip fracture. Tributes to Larimore appeared in the journals of all parts of the Stone-Campbell Movement, a testimony to his efforts to maintain unity in the midst of division.

See also Fanning, Tolbert; Larimore, Emma Page; Mars Hill Bible School

BIBLIOGRAPHY Douglas A. Foster, *As Good as the Best: A Sketch of the Life of Theophilus Brown Larimore* (1984) • Emma Page Larimore, *Life, Letters and Sermons of T. B. Larimore* (1931) • J. M. Powell, *The Man from Mars Hill: The Life and Times of T. B. Larimore* (2002) • F. D. Srygley, *Smiles and Tears or Larimore and His Boys* (1889) • F. D. Srygley and Emma Page, *Letters and Sermons of T. B. Larimore,* 3 vols. (1900, 1904, 1910).

DOUGLAS A. FOSTER

Last Will and Testament of Springfield Presbytery

Founding document of the Christian Church movement associated with Barton W. Stone, signed June 28, 1804.

The Springfield Presbytery, which issued the document, had been organized on September 12, 1803. Two days earlier Barton W. Stone, Robert Marshall, John Dunlavy, Richard McNemar, and John Thompson had withdrawn from the jurisdiction of the Presbyterian Synod of Kentucky rather than suffer censure for having departed from the doctrines of the Westminster Confession.

The *Last Will and Testament* was written by Richard McNemar, who brought a draft of the document with him to the June 1804 meeting of the presbytery at Cane Ridge. By signing the document, the members of the presbytery concluded their less-than-ten-month history as the Springfield Presbytery, declaring, "We *will,* that this body die, be dissolved, and sink into union with the Body of Christ at large." Stone reported that, in addition to signing the *Last Will and Testament,* he and his colleagues determined at the June 1804 meeting to take "no other name than *christians,*" noting that "Christians" was "the name first given by divine authority to the disciples of Christ."

Appended to the *Last Will and Testament,* which the members of the presbytery signed as "witnesses," was "The Witnesses' Address," which stated their reason for dissolving their presbytery. They noted that they had viewed with deep concern "the divisions, and party spirit among professing Christians, principally owing to the adoption of human creeds and forms of government." Though they had "endeavored to cultivate a spirit of love and unity with all Christians," they had found it "extremely difficult to suppress the idea that they themselves were a party separate from others." This difficulty, they confessed, had "increased in proportion to their success in the ministry." Moreover, jealousies had been "excited in the minds of other denominations; and a temptation was laid before those who were connected with the various parties, to view them in the same light." At their final meeting as a presbytery they had begun to prepare for publication an address titled "Observations on Church Government" in which the world would see "the beautiful simplicity of Christian church government, stript of human inventions and lordly traditions." As they had proceeded in their investigation of that subject, they had "soon found that there was neither precept nor example in the New Testament for such confederacies as modern Church Sessions, Presbyteries, Synods, General Assemblies, etc." They had realized that "However just . . . their views of church government might have been, they would have gone out under the name and sanction of a self-constituted body." Therefore, "from a principle of love to Christians of every name, the precious cause of Jesus, and dying sinners who are kept from the Lord by the existence of sects and parties in the church," they had "cheerfully consented to retire from the din and fury of conflicting parties — sink out of the view of fleshly minds, and die the death."

By retiring from "the din and fury of conflicting parties" and sinking out of the view of "fleshly minds," they did not, however, intend to retire from public view. Writing of themselves in the third person, they declared that, though dead as a presbytery and "stript of their mortal frame," they "yet live and speak in the land of gospel liberty . . . blow the trumpet of jubilee, and willingly devote themselves to the help of the Lord against the mighty." Moreover, they published the *Last Will and Testament* as a *tract,* along with an announcement of a mass meeting for those embracing like sentiments at Marshall's Bethel Church over the weekend of October 14, 1804. Far from seeking to disappear from public view, they noted that Bethel, seven miles northwest of Lexington, was a central location for attendance from Kentucky, Ohio, and Tennessee.

Marshall and Thompson observed that the presbytery was encouraged to adopt the *Last Will and Testament* by their belief that the millennium, the one-thousand year rule of Christ that many Christians believed was prophesied in Revelation 20:1-6, was near. This millennial expectation was rooted in the signers' experience of the Great Revival in the West (1797-1805). Four- to six-day sacramental meetings with attendance in the thousands, in which Presbyterians and Methodists communed together and large numbers of all ages professed faith, characterized the revival. The revival was also characterized by a growing sentiment against slavery and a concomitant increase in the manumission of slaves.

The association of church growth and the increasing social influence of Christianity with the coming of the millennium can be traced through English Puritanism as far back as the sixteenth century. In the eighteenth century, Jonathan Edwards had referred to the worldwide evangelism and social transformation that he taught would usher in the millennium as "the glorious work of God," speculating that it would require 250 years for God to complete this work, which Edwards hoped had begun in his life. The signers declared, "We *will,* that preachers and people, cultivate a spirit of mutual forbearance; pray more and dispute less; and while they *behold the signs of the times,* look up, and *confidently expect that redemption draweth nigh.*" In their "Witnesses' Address," they called on all Christians to join them "in crying to God day and night, to remove the obstacles which stand in the way of his work, and give him no rest *till he make Jerusalem a praise in the earth.*" In conclusion, they announced, "We heartily unite with our Christian brethren of every name, in thanksgiving to God for the display of his goodness in *the glorious work* he is carrying on in our Western country, which we *hope* will terminate in the *universal* spread of the gospel, and the *unity* of the church" (italics added). In dissolving their presbytery, the signers of the *Last Will and Testament,* encouraged by the evangelistic and social impact of the Great Revival, sought to hasten the coming of Christ's earthly rule.

The *Last Will and Testament* has sometimes been viewed as a declaration of radical congregationalism. However, the signers did not give up the ministerial authority traditionally granted to Presbyterian ministers. The extent of the Presbyterian ministerial prerogatives that they *willed* to give up can be measured by examining the four "items" of the *Last Will and Testament* that bear directly on the calling and authority of ministers.

1. "We *will,* that our power of making laws for the government of the church, and executing them by delegated authority, forever cease." The *Form of Government* of the Presbyterian Church stated that "all church power . . . is only ministerial and declarative; *that is to say* that the Holy Scriptures are the only rule of faith and manners; that no church judicatory ought to pretend to make laws, to bind the conscience in virtue of their own authority; and that all their decisions should be founded upon the revealed will of God." Rule in the Presbyterian tradition was explicitly defined as "the right of judgment upon laws already made," while the business of "making laws" for the church was explicitly forbidden. Thus, for the presbytery to renounce their power of making laws for the church was to affirm what Presbyterians officially taught. It did not mean that they were giving up their responsibility to rule on the meaning of the Scriptures. Rather, they were charging Presbyterians with violating their own standards by what they saw as their "making laws" for the church.

2. "We *will,* that candidates for the gospel ministry henceforth study the Holy Scriptures with fervent prayer, and obtain license from God to preach the simple Gospel, *with the Holy Ghost sent down from heaven,* without any mixture of philosophy, vain deceit, traditions of men, or the rudiments of the world." The subject of this item was not the licensing

of candidates for the ministry, but their studies. The signers willed that candidates for the ministry study the Scriptures with fervent prayer, rather than the Presbyterian Confession, in order to preach the simple gospel with the unction of the Holy Spirit. The Presbyterian Confession was, in their view, a "mixture of philosophy, vain deceit, traditions of men, and rudiments of the world."

3. "We *will,* that the Church of Christ resume her native right of internal government — try her candidates for the ministry, as to their soundness in faith, acquaintance with experimental religion, gravity, and aptness to teach; and to admit no other proof of their authority, but Christ speaking in them." The concern, again, was the Confession of Faith. Rather than trying ministerial candidates by their adherence to the Confession, the church should try ministerial candidates according to its own judgment of "Christ speaking" in them.

4. "We *will,* that each particular church as a body, actuated by the same spirit, choose her own preacher . . . and never henceforth delegate her right of government to any man or set of men, whatever." Presbyterians taught that congregations were to elect their own officers, but that ordination was the work of the ministry. In the final section of the *Last Will and Testament,* the signers indicated that, though dead as the Springfield Presbytery, they would still "assist in ordaining elders, or pastors." Even many years later Stone affirmed, "Without the commendation of the church, the elders [or pastors] should ordain no man; without the satisfaction of the elders [or pastors], the church should not urge it to be done." The members of the former presbytery did not reject the role of ministers in the oversight of the ministry but what they considered synodical interference in the tasks of congregations and ministers (presbyteries) in the calling and oversight of ministers.

This *"item"* also called for congregations to support their preacher "by a free will offering, without a written *call* or *subscription.*" Ministers were not to be bound by a written call and subscription to support the doctrines of a particular party, as Stone had believed that he had been prior to releasing his congregations from their salary obligations to him and literally tearing up their subscription papers in their presence after withdrawing from the jurisdiction of the synod. The signers of the *Last Will and Testament* opposed financial arrangements that would bind the doctrinal freedom of the minister, but they did not oppose financial support of the ministry.

See also Ministry; Springfield Presbytery; Stone, Barton Warren

BIBLIOGRAPHY "Last Will and Testament of Springfield Presbytery," in Barton W. Stone, *The Biography of Eld. Barton Warren Stone, Written by Himself, with Additions and Reflections by Eld. John Rogers* (1847), reprinted in *The Cane Ridge Reader,* ed. Hoke S. Dickinson (1972) • Robert Marshall and John Thompson, *A Brief Historical Account of Sundry Things in the Doctrines and State of the Christian, or as It Is Commonly Called, The New Light Church, Containing Their Testimony Against Several Doctrines Held in That Church, and Its Disorganized State; Together with Some Reasons Why Those Two Brethren Purpose to Seek for a More Pure and Orderly Connection* (1811) • D. Newell Williams, *Barton Stone: A Spiritual Biography* (2000).

D. NEWELL WILLIAMS

Latin America and Caribbean, Missions in

1. Christian Church (Disciples of Christ)
2. Christian Churches/Churches of Christ
3. Churches of Christ

1. Christian Church (Disciples of Christ)

The first missionary sent by the Stone-Campbell Movement to Mexico was M. L. Hoblit, sponsored by the Christian Woman's Board of Missions (CWBM) to begin a work in 1895. Hoblit began in Ciudad Juárez, then moved to Monterrey in 1897. There he established a school for boys and began plans for a print shop to provide Christian literature.

Eventually others answered the call to work in Mexico, including Mr. and Mrs. A. G. Alderman. Hoblit resigned from the work and left Monterrey in 1899, and Mr. Alderman took over the leadership. By now the work included schools taught in English and Spanish, worship services, visitation, a reading room, and a print shop. Alderman led in the formal organization of the Christian Church in Monterrey, September 14, 1901.

When Alderman died of yellow fever in 1903, Thomas M. Westrup assumed the leadership in Monterrey. Westrup had lived in Mexico since the age of 15. He had come into the Stone-Campbell Movement in 1901 and served the mission as editor of Spanish publications, translator, song writer, and preacher. So well were his hymns received by churches throughout the country that Westrup became known as the "Father of Mexican Hymnology." When Westrup died in 1909, his son Enrique T. Westrup carried on the work, and under his leadership it continued to grow and expand into the surrounding area.

The organized work of the Disciples of Christ, meanwhile, had sent Samuel Guy Inman to Monterrey in 1905; Inman later established the People's Institute at Piedras Negras, across the border from Eagle Pass, Texas. In 1913 Inman founded the Mexican Christian Institute in San Antonio, Texas, for victims of the Mexican Revolution (1910-17). The revolution changed the nature of missionary work; the new constitution officially prohibited it and denied the right of Mexican or foreign churches to own property, a restriction that continued until the papal visit to Mexico of John Paul II in 1979. These restrictions resulted in dissimulation and official corruption that has never been adequately recorded by U.S. mission bodies.

Latin America was not included in the 1910 Edinburgh World Missionary Conference at the insistence of the Germans, who considered the region to be part of Christendom. North American mission organizations responded in 1916 by holding in Panama the First Latin American Congress on Christian Work. Inman was elected executive secretary of the newly formed Committee on Cooperation in Latin America (CCLA), representing thirty Protestant mission organizations of the United States and Canada, a position he held until retirement in 1940. He was frequently called upon as advisor to President Franklin Roosevelt and attended the San Francisco Conference to organize the United Nations in 1945 as a consultant for the U.S. Department of State. The policy of the Disciples to take political questions seriously as an aspect of mission is seen in his article in *The Atlantic Monthly* of July 1924, entitled "Imperialistic America," describing U.S. military and economic dominance of Central American and Caribbean neighbors.

The CWBM accepted a comity agreement with others working in Mexico at a meeting in Cincinnati in 1919 to move their concentration to Central Mexico. E. T. Westrup strongly opposed this decision, pulling out of the CWBM and appealing through the *Christian Standard* for direct support from the churches. Under the comity agreement, the Disciples of Christ worked mainly in the central Mexican states of Aguascalientes, Jalisco, and San Luis Potosí. In the city of Aguascalientes, they established the Morelos Center, which they took over from the Methodists. Presbyterians in Zacatecas refused to obey the U.S. board to give their churches to the Disciples and became the only mainline denomination to be self-supporting for the next half-century. Mountain of Light Farm and Hope Hospital and social centers in Aguascalientes and San Luis Potosí resulted in ministries that expanded to Reynosa and Ciudad Juárez on the U.S. border. Three generations of the Huegel family served as missionaries in Mexico. Leila Callender, Courtney and Lois Swander, and Lloyd and Janice Tatlock served full missionary careers. In cooperation with United Church of Christ Hispanic Ministries, the Alberto Rembao Ecumenical Center for U.S.-Mexican research, reflection, and leadership development was established in Guadalajara in 1992, staffed by Global Ministries missionaries Justino Pérez and Zaida Rivera of Puerto Rico.

MISSIONARY TIDINGS

"BEHOLD, I BRING YOU GOOD TIDINGS OF GREAT JOY." LUKE 2:10.

Vol. XXI. INDIANAPOLIS, IND., SEPTEMBER, 1903. No. 5.

OUR MISSIONARIES TO THE BOYS' ORPHANAGE, PORTO RICO.
Wenona. Marjorie. Mrs. Rose B. Wilkinson.
Ruth. Mr. H. G. Wilkinson. Erma.

A SOLITARY WAY.

There is a mystery in human hearts,
And though we be encircled by a host
Of those who love us well, and are beloved,
To every one of us, from time to time,
There comes a sense of utter loneliness.
Our dearest friend is stranger to our joy,
And can not realize our bitterness.
"There is not one who really understands,
Not one to enter into all I feel;"
Such is the cry of each of us in turn;
We wander in a solitary way.
No matter what or where our lot may be;
Each heart, mysterious even to itself,
Must live its inner life in solitude.

And would you know the reason why this is?
It is because the Lord desires our love.
In every heart He wishes to be first.
He therefore keeps the secret key Himself,
To open all its chambers, and to bless,
With perfect sympathy and holy peace,
Each solitary soul which comes to Him.
So when we feel this loneliness it is
The voice of Jesus saying, "Come unto Me!"
And every time we are "not understood,"
It is a call to us to come again;
For Christ alone can satisfy the soul,
And those who walk with Him from day to day
Can never have a solitary way.

And when beneath some heavy cross you faint,
And say, "I can not bear this load alone."
You say the truth. Christ made it purposely
So heavy that you must return to Him.
The bitter grief, which "no one understands,"
Conveys a secret message from the King,
Entreating you to come to Him again.
The Man of Sorrows understands it well;
In all points tempted He can feel with you.
You can not come too often, or too near—
The Son of God is infinite in grace.
His presence satisfies the longing soul,
And those who walk with Him from day to day
Can never have a solitary way.

—Selected.

"A sculptor raised a work sublime
Before the people's rapturous gaze;
He heard the murmur of the throng
While friends pressed round with words of praise.
He bowed his head before them all;
He looked at what his hands had done.
'Not mine the glory be,' he said,
'The thought revealed was Love's alone.' "

Missionary Tidings, **the journal of the Christian Woman's Board of Missions, featured a missionary family in Puerto Rico.** Courtesy of the Disciples of Christ Historical Society

One of the converts in San Luis Potosi was Antonio Medina, the son of a multimillionaire, who had studied to be a Roman Catholic priest before the Mexican Revolution closed all seminaries in 1916. Medina served with the Mexican delegation to the League of Nations in France and studied at the University of Paris. He bought a New Testament and, returning home, visited a Disciples of Christ congregation in San Luis Potosí. He was baptized in 1927 and began preaching and establishing independent congregations, including a large one in Estancia, Zacatecas. In 1932 he married Victoria Infante, and together the Medinas established a Christian hospital.

Elsewhere in Latin America and the Caribbean, missionaries from the Stone-Campbell Movement were working in several countries. The mission of J. O. Beardslee in Jamaica, which had been interrupted by the U.S. Civil War, was reopened in 1876 by Mr. and Mrs. W. H. Williams and W. K. Azbill. The church became autonomous following national independence from Britain in the 1960s, and in 1992 joined with others to form the United Church in Jamaica and the Cayman Islands. Richmond Nelson, principal of Oberlin High School, became known internationally through his presidency of the World Convention of Churches of Christ. Bevis and Hazel Byfield, Derek and Yvonne Davidson, and Alice and Stotrell Lowe earned graduate degrees in the United States. The United Theological College of the West Indies, dating back to 1841, counts 900 graduates for church leadership since its dedication in 1966 by ten denominations of the English-speaking Caribbean and the Theological Education Fund of the World Council of Churches. Missionary Alan Hunter assisted Horace Russell, a Jamaican Baptist, in building and inaugurating the new seminary.

Following the Spanish American War, the CWBM also saw an opportunity to work in Puerto Rico, where it established an orphanage for girls in 1900 and the first church in 1901. Missionaries included Vera and Mayme Carpenter from 1906 to 1944 and C. Manly and Selah Morton, 1923-43, after having served in Argentina and Paraguay for five years. Joaquín Vargas wrote the history of Disciples of Puerto Rico in 1988, recording the growth to 20,000 members, 82 ordained pastors, 21 lay pastors, and 33 ministerial candidates as of that date. The history of the Revival of the 1930s and conflicts with the United Christian Missionary Society (UCMS) and Disciples Overseas Ministries are documented as well as reconciliation in later years. The Evangelical Seminary of Puerto Rico in Río Piedras was founded in 1919 by six denominations. T. J. Liggett, who served with his wife Virginia as UCMS missionaries in Argentina from 1946, was president 1957 to 1965. The seminary flourished after the Cuban Revolution (1959), when relations with the seminary in Matanzas became practically impossible.

The World Convention of Churches of Christ met in San Juan in 1965, under the leadership of Florentino Santana. Puerto Rican Disciples were missionaries in Latin America: notably Juan Marcos and Flor Rivera, Felix and Maria Ortiz, Carmelo Alvarez, Raquel Rodríguez, Luis and Genoveva del Pilar, and Jorge Bardéguez. Eunice Santana Velez was one of the eight presidents of the World Council of Churches, 1991-98. About thirty others served congregations in the United States, from Florida to California, beginning with Pablo and Epifania Cotto, who founded La Hermosa on 110th Street in New York City in 1938. Domingo Rodríguez was the first Hispanic to serve in the office for Hispanic and Bilingual Ministries of Disciples Homeland Ministries in 1968, and Lucas Torres became the first national Hispanic pastor for the denomination from 1993 to 1999, succeeded by Pablo A. Jiménez. David A. Vargas, following twenty years as executive for Latin America and the Caribbean, became president of the Division of Overseas Ministries and co-executive of Global Ministries in 2003.

The Foreign Christian Missionary Society sent Mr. and Mrs. McPherson and Mr. and Mrs. Melvin Menges to Cuba in 1899. These two couples worked in Havana, Matanzas, and Cidra. A comity agreement led to an exchange with the Presbyterians for the area of Bayamón in Puerto Rico in 1919. The first Cuban moderator of the Reformed Church of Cuba was Julio A. Fuentes of the former Disciples community. The Cuban Revolution of 1959 resulted in churches continuing without missionaries for many years. The Division of Overseas Ministries became partners with the Christian Pentecostal Church of Cuba in 1975, when Francisco Martínez attended the World Council of Churches General Assembly in Nairobi, sponsored as an observer by Disciples. Relations were maintained across political and ideological lines by visits and scholarship projects, in spite of the trade embargo by the United States, to ensure Christian unity and mutual support.

John B. Ie Rouet worked in British Guiana intermittently from 1889 until 1906. Under the sponsorship of the Christian Woman's Board of Missions, the Burners opened a mission in the Argentine Republic in 1905. J. D. Montgomery, missionary with his wife Ruth for many years in Jamaica, first served in Argentina and wrote the history *Disciples of Christ in Argentina, 1906-1956*. Ecumenical relations included Colegio Ward, Aurora publishing house, ISEDET graduate theological school, the United Board of Missions (JUM) work with the Toba Indians, and councils of churches. Felipe Adolf of the partner Evangelical Congregational Church was the first general secretary of the Latin American Council of Churches (CLAI), 1984 to 1998, with offices in Quito, Ecuador. Ángel Peiro was Latin America secretary for the World Council of Churches in Geneva for many years. Luis and Magdalena Parrilla directed a school in Villa Mitre, where a family planning program received recognition from the United Nations. Esther Iglesias, Oswaldo Guiducci, and Pedro Manoukian were prominent leaders. Norberto Sarli went to Paraguay as director of Colegio Internacional, and Inez Petersen de Sarli, M.D., served as director of Friendship Mission in Asunción. During the military regimes following the death of Juan Perón in 1974, 30,000 people disappeared, and friends of the Division of Overseas Missionaries were jailed or killed. Since that time the impunity of officers who committed human rights violations was a subject of Christian protest and witness.

As a result of the missionary conference in Panama in 1916, C. Manly and Selah Morton went to Paraguay in 1918 to continue the work begun by Methodists in 1886. They started Colegio Internacional in 1920. George and Joyce Wiley were among many missionaries in Latin America who served 25 to 35 years. Hortensia Ferreira, pastor, was the first Paraguayan director of the prestigious school more than a half-century later. Ray and Betty Mills, who wished to give social awareness to the students of the upper-middle-class school, founded Friendship Mission in 1953, which maintained its independence throughout the dictatorship of General Alfredo Stroessner for thirty-five years. Missionary director Victor Vaca and educator Frisco Gilchrist were jailed in 1976, along with Paraguayan coworkers, on charges of leftist subversion and were unjustly expelled from the country. General Stroessner was driven from the country in 1989.

Two World Wars and the Depression slowed foreign missionary efforts. However, following World War II there was a surge in the growth of independent missions and the number of missionary recruits. A number of them turned their eyes toward Latin America and the Caribbean.

By this time the divisions separating the three streams of the Stone-Campbell Movement had been clearly defined. The Disciples of Christ continued moving more toward ecumenical cooperation with the World Council of Churches (founded in 1948), CLAI, and the Caribbean Council of Churches. The Pentecostal Union of Venezuela initiated contacts with the United Christian Missionary Society after sharing preaching missions with Disciples of Puerto Rico and entered into cooperation with longtime Latin America executive (1941-65) Mae Yoho Ward. Juan Marcos and Flor Rivera initiated the fraternal ministry with Exeario Sosa, who was proud of the fact that ties with the Disciples did not preclude relating to whatever other churches the Union chose. Grace and Dean Rogers were among missionaries who served with them after many years in Paraguay and Argentina, as did R. Q. and Annamae Adams and Charles and Ruth Chavez Wallace. The Commission of Evangelical Pentecostals of Latin America (CEPAL) was assigned a staff person beginning in 2002.

As human rights violations spread across South America in the 1960s and 1970s and in Central America in the 1980s, partnerships were developed with churches that did not have a Disciples missionary history. Close ties were formed with the Pentecostal Church of Chile after the coup d'état of General Augusto Pinochet and the death of the elected president Salvador Allende in 1973. An association with the Evangelical Lutheran Church of El Salvador was formed in the midst of the war to help protect Bishop Medardo Gómez and pastors of the Emmanuel Baptist Church through Wayne Steinert, who was later missionary in Swaziland and was murdered in South Africa. The Salvadoran Lutheran University faculty included an environmental scientist concerned with health issues of air, water, and municipal garbage dumps and a sociologist focusing on family relations and the rights of women, evidence of the wide range of Disciples missionary concerns.

The Christian mission of Nicaragua developed close relations after 1986. Through Global Ministries with the Wider Church Ministries of the United Church of Christ, Disciples became partners with the Evangelical and Reformed Church of Honduras, the Christian Congregational Church of Mexico, the Ecumenical Foundation for Integral Development Training and Education (FEDICE) of Ecuador, the Evangelical Congregational Churches in Brazil and Argentina of immigrant German origin, and the United Evangelical Church of Puerto Rico. Missionaries have served indiscriminately among them, and they have contributed in many ways to the churches of the North. Haiti has had a place of special regard since staff was provided to the National Spiritual Council of Churches (CONASPEH), a grouping of 4,000 congregations and mission centers, since 1989. Personnel have been sent elsewhere on occasion, such as Brazil, Ecuador, Guatemala, and the Dominican Republic. The priorities of Global Ministries include solidarity with the poorest, protection of the environment, social justice, and Christian unity.

T. J. Liggett became the last president of the UCMS (1968-73), which was restructured in the formation of the Christian Church (Disciples of Christ) in the United States and Canada. William J. Nottingham succeeded him as executive for Latin America and the Caribbean, jointly with the United Church Board for World Ministries (1968-76), and was president of the Division of Overseas Ministries from 1984 to 1994.

The emergence of liberation theology at the Roman Catholic Bishops Conference (CELAM) at Medellín, Colombia, in 1968, and other effects of the Second Vatican Council in Rome (1962-65), brought profound changes in the life of Latin American churches and the ecumenical missionary movement. Disciples were active in periodic ecumenical conferences in Buenos Aires (1949), Lima (1961), and later, leading to the formation of the Latin American Council of Churches (CLAI) in 1984. Ecumenical publishing houses and union bookstores produced a constant flow of high quality theological books over many years.

The Christian Church (Disciples of Christ) has experienced a decline in the number of missionaries in recent years, due partly to a lack of funds but also to the policy to recognize national autonomous churches and their leadership and to support mission projects together. The 2001 *Year Book & Directory* classifies "regular missionaries" as those appointed and supported by the Division of Overseas Missionaries (DOM) or by the Common Global Ministries Board (CGMB), a cooperative ministry with the United Church of Christ.

Others working in missionary endeavors are classified as global mission interns, international associates, long-term or short-term volunteers, and overseas associates. According to the Year Book, all missionary personnel number 292, serving in fifty countries. However, only 112 are "regular missionaries," and 25 of the 292 workers are in Latin America or the Caribbean. Much of their ministry is ecumenical and involves a variety of services from "pastoral work" to "human rights" and "ecology."

Countries in which the DOM/CGMB claim work at the beginning of the twenty-first century are Argentina, Brazil, Chile, the Dominican Republic, Ecuador, Guatemala, Haiti, Honduras, Nicaragua, Mexico, Jamaica, and Puerto Rico.

William J. Nottingham *and* William J. Morgan

2. Christian Churches/Churches of Christ

Early in the history of "independent" or "direct support" missions among conservative Christian Churches opposed to large-scale missionary societies, Latin America became an important mission field. In Mexico and in Central and South America, as elsewhere, individual families supported by a single congregation or a small network of churches often launched such initiatives. Moreover, in these regions, as elsewhere, independent missions normally began as evangelistic enterprises that would often expand to include schools, Bible institutes, publication ministries, and benevolent operations. Ideologically, these missions were strongly motivated by the ideal of "restoring New Testament Christianity" in regions largely dominated either by Roman Catholicism or native religions. Much independent missionary literature thus projected the goal of establishing "New Testament churches" in Latin America.

Mexico was the first spearhead of independent missions in Latin America, not only because it bordered the United States but also because of the controversy that had already erupted between progressives and conservatives over the Christian Woman's Board of Missions' 1919 comity agreement that ceded the Disciples' mission in Monterrey to the Methodists. Enrique T. Westrup protested by forming an independent Mexican Society for Christian Missions, thus pioneering a new kind of missionary "agency" that would help pool financial and spiritual support from local churches without functioning as a governing body over missionary activities on the field. Westrup remained active in evangelistic ministry in Monterrey until his death in 1967.

A boon for independent missions in Mexico was the establishment of Colegio Bíblico in Eagle Pass, Texas (on the Rio Grande River), by Harland Cary in 1945. The college has remained a major influence in recruiting and educating Mexican nationals for ministry in their own country. The training of indigenous leaders was a priority, and independent missionaries created more than one Bible institute within Mexico itself. Numerous direct support missionary families from the United States relocated in Mexico during the 1950s and 1960s, undertaking a wide array of evangelistic, benevolent, and educational initiatives with names like the Western Mexico Christian Mission and the Calexico-Mexicali Mission.

Further south in Latin America, a similar pattern took shape early on. The Brazil Christian Mission began through a fund raised in 1943 by the fiftieth-anniversary graduating class of Johnson Bible College (Tennessee) to support Lloyd Sanders, whose family went to Brazil in 1948 and headquartered in the city of Goiania. Brazil Christian Mission was essentially an evangelistic and church-planting initiative that in the 1950s developed Christian day schools, a leadership training school (the Instituto Cristão de Goiania), and a publication venture. Its work expanded in the late 1950s and 1960s to the new capital of Brazilia and Rio de Janeiro, while also attempting to penetrate rural areas in Brazil. The Amazon Valley Christian Mission (est. 1949), also staffed by Anglo families from the United States, likewise purposed itself as evangelizing and extending "New Testament Christianity" among Brazilian Indians in the interior of the country; in time it formed a home for indigent and orphaned children, a publication house (the Amazon Valley Christian Literature Service), and the Belem Bible Seminary (later Para Bible Institute).

In Chile, the same pattern obtained. Bertrand Smith, a former Wesleyan Methodist newly zealous for the "plea" of the Stone-Campbell Movement, desired in his own words to "break into that priest-laden land" of South America in order to establish "New Testament" churches. Smith and his family moved to Valparaiso, Chile, in 1949. An early challenge was government registration for new church bodies. Smith worked to establish an autonomous Christian congregation that sought such licensing and determined that any newly planted church would do the same for itself, so that the government would not identify the churches collectively as a denomination. Smith's work inaugurated radio, publication, and educational ministries. In the city of Concepción in 1955, Smith, though ardent in his insistence on preaching the gospel and plea of the Stone-Campbell Movement (including immersion of believers), actually preached in Presbyterian and Pentecostal Methodist churches, seeking to find common cause with other evangelical Protestants in a predominantly Roman Catholic country. Smith's work would lead to the location of other independent missionary families in Chile in the 1960s and

1970s. One independent missionary, Ed Holt, based in the capital city of Santiago, sought to extend evangelistic efforts by designing a Bible correspondence course specifically adapted to Chileans, challenging conservative (Roman Catholic) and leftist (Marxist) perspectives alike. Supporters justified such literary and instructional campaigns as necessary instruments for contextualizing the Stone-Campbell message in new cultural settings.

Other independent missions began in the 1940s through 1960s throughout Latin America and the Caribbean, including the countries of Colombia, Argentina, El Salvador, Barbados, and the Bahamas. The pattern was consistent: individual families ventured out with direct financial support from either a single congregation or a cluster of congregations.

In the 1960s, Christian Missionary Fellowship (CMF), a growing missions agency of the Christian Churches/Churches of Christ, began its own initiatives in Latin America. Though labeled by its conservative critics a compromising *via media* between the pure direct support missions model and the more highly organized agencies of the Disciples of Christ, CMF attempted to enhance the networks of support, cross-cultural sophistication, and accountability of missionaries. The organization first planted missionaries in Brazil beginning in 1957, in Mexico beginning in 1980, and in Chile beginning in 1988. The Brazilian work proved an important testing ground for indigenization, as in the 1980s leadership in the Brazilian congregations planted by CMF transitioned to native Brazilians, and the agency began outreach to middle-class as well as working-class persons. In more recent years CMF has inaugurated a "Globalscope" mission aimed at developing campus ministries in university settings overseas. Two such initiatives have begun in Mexico City and Santiago, Chile; another has begun in Campinas, in Brazil.

In 1997 one of CMF's missionaries in Hispanic congregational ministry in Southern California, Fernando Soto, a native Chilean, published Spanish translations of Thomas Campbell's *Declaration and Address,* the *Last Will and Testament of the Springfield Presbytery,* and other charter documents of the Stone-Campbell Movement, along with a history of the Movement in Spanish — all to be used by Spanish-speaking congregations in the United States and in Latin America.

Recent statistics and surveys, including those provided by the *Directorio del Ministerio de las Iglesias Cristianas e Iglesias de Cristo de Habla Hispana,* indicate the presence of missionaries and congregations of the Christian Churches/Churches of Christ in Mexico and in the Central American countries of Belize, Costa Rica, El Salvador, Guatemala, and Panama; in the South American countries of Argentina, Brazil, Chile, Colombia, Ecuador, Guyana, and Venezuela; and in the Caribbean countries of Bahamas, Barbados, the Dominican Republic, Grand Cayman, Grenada, Haiti, Jamaica, Puerto Rico, St. Vincent, Trinidad, and the West Indies.

William J. Morgan *and* Paul M. Blowers

3. Churches of Christ

The strongly congregational approach to missions taken by Churches of Christ meant that initiatives were numerous throughout the twentieth century in Latin America as elsewhere. The first work by the group among a Latin American population occurred in 1921 in Abilene, Texas, when Howard Schug (1881-1969) took a Spanish version of the New Testament to the Hispanic portion of town and went door to door asking people to read specific Scriptures. Schug's efforts resulted in a small church meeting on Cottonwood Street, later moving to Graham Street, where the work is still active today.

Schug's efforts also influenced a 1928 Abilene Christian College graduate named J. W. Treat (1907-1998). Though Treat never worked full time for the ministry, he began multiple Hispanic works in northern Mexico and southwest Texas, including congregations in San Angelo, Colorado City, and Sweetwater, Texas. Treat's most important work, however, was the translation of hundreds of songs into Spanish and the publication of a Spanish hymnal that is still widely used by Churches of Christ throughout Latin America.

In 1952 the first missionary of the Churches of Christ to establish a lasting work in South America, D. H. Hadwin (1906-1996), arrived in Montevideo, Uruguay. After two years and the baptism of six persons, Hadwin moved to Europe. Among those six converts was Pablo Lazaga, who has continued as an active leader into the twenty-first century.

In 1961 Chilean Atilio Pinto arrived to assist. The work in Uruguay received another major reinforcement in 1976 when Jack Walker, Foree Grove, and Mike Strawn arrived from the Sunset International Bible Institute. Other workers would arrive in the early 1990s, including the families of Ronnie Rama, Dan Coker, Bryan Elliot, Greg Sparks, and Warren Roane. In 2003 only the Warren Roane family continued work in Montevideo, serving as adjunct faculty for the Abilene Christian University study abroad academic program there.

In nearby Argentina, the first convert in Churches of Christ came on April 14, 1957, when F. M. Perry of New York met Silverio Ojeda of Buenos Aires, an ex-priest who had been corresponding with H. R. Zamorano in Fort Worth, Texas. Perry baptized Ojeda but had little time for continued study due to the nature of his business. Later that year Harlan Overton (b. 1932) traveled to Buenos Aires, where he visited with Ojeda for two weeks, baptized another individual, and arranged for Ojeda to be supported as a full-time minister by the Church of Christ in Saginaw, Texas. In 1958 Ronald Davis and Lionel Cortez of Abilene Christian University moved to Buenos Aires to assist Ojeda. Upon returning to the States, Cortez devoted himself to the translation of Spanish literature with the Western Christian Foundation in Wichita Falls, Texas. In 1960 the Robert Tipton family joined the work in Buenos Aires, and two small independent congregations were established. After the departure of the three missionary families, the local churches maintained themselves until the arrival of the Dick Treat, Ted Presley, Reece Mitchell, Jake Vincent, and George Roggendorff families, along with Joel Banks, in 1972-73. Later, in 1980, the team of the Glen Henton, Craig Webb, and Stephen Teel families joined with Jay and Cathy Ables to work in the suburbs. Missionary activity among the Churches of Christ in Buenos Aires received little reinforcement from the U.S. churches until the arrival of a five-family team in 2000 who focused on the establishment of a congregation in the central portion of town. Team members include the Mike Dotson, Eric Henton, and Chris Kelly families and Steve Atkins. Glen and Kathy Henton of the 1980 team later returned to the field to assist with this work.

In Cordova, a major campaign effort in 1985 resulted in fifty-nine baptisms and the establishment of a new congregation. The families of Jerry Hill, Norman Huff, Bill Richardson, Roland Bowen, and Ken Terrell were involved in the initial effort. The Richardsons returned to Cordova in 1989 accompanied by team members Jim Gregory, Mark Edge, and Allen Nickson and their families. By the year 2001, the work was left in the hands of the Argentine Christians. Similarly, Fernando "Butch" and Patricia Sandoval began a work in 1993 in Mendoza that was left in the care of the Argentine Christians in 1998.

Chile received its first activity from the Churches of Christ in the late 1950s when Evert Pickartz preached a campaign in Santiago, Chile. The effort resulted in the baptism of Atilio Pinto, who traveled to Montevideo as a missionary in 1962. In 1961 Vernon Hawkins and Phil Morgan established congregations in Talca and Roberto. With the assistance of Jack Speer and Gary Lutes, by 1970 the work in Santiago had grown to include two small congregations and a third congregation of approximately 150 members. After visiting the States on furlough in 1970, Lutes returned to Santiago to find that the Speers had led most of the members into Pentecostalism. After the arrival of a three-family team from the Bear Valley School of Preaching (including the John Matins and Ron Roberts families) in 1985 and the arrival of Roland Bowen, Lutes left Chile. At that time, approximately seven congregations of the Churches of Christ existed in the capital city. In 1981 the Tom Hook and Don Henson families moved to Santiago; the Hooks would later move to Viña del Mar to begin a new work. Two missionary families who had previously served in Argentina also joined the Chilean work in the 1990s (Butch Sandoval, 1991, moved to Viña del Mar to work with the Hooks; Bill Richardson, 1992, to Santiago).

At the time of writing the Sandoval and Hook families continue in Viña del Mar, focusing efforts on conducting a Bible school with open enrollment. Hook also helps to coordinate a study abroad program for Harding University. Harry Hamilton arrived in the early 1990s and works throughout the country encouraging small congregations and studying with students generated by World Bible School correspondence courses or television programs produced by Con La Biblia Abierta. In Santiago, a seven-unit team composed of the Scott Emery family, Mark Dean family, Keith Kilmer family, Zane Perkins family, Kelly Grant family, Jill del Rio, and Elizabeth Villalon work with a new congregation planted in the middle-class area of La Providencia.

Churches of Christ entered Paraguay through short-term efforts of the Southern Hills Church of Christ of Abilene, Texas (1968, no baptisms), and the Northside Church of Christ of Austin, Texas. Northside assisted Luis Ramírez of Montevideo, who moved to Paraguay in 1976. Only one North American missionary family (Forrest McDonald family, 1981-84) worked in Paraguay for the Churches of Christ until the arrival of a team from Freed-Hardeman University arrived in 2003 through the Continent of Great Cities ministry. The team was composed of Chris and Vickie Fry, Ethan and Ashley Hardin, Vanessa Heady, and Enoch Rinks, and it located in Asunción.

In 1968 and 1971, World Radio, sponsored by White's Ferry Road Church of Christ in West Monroe, Louisiana, was broadcasting in La Paz, Bolivia. In 1973 Glen Kramar (missionary to Lima) and Dick Treat (missionary to Buenos Aires) made separate trips to Santa Cruz to visit and baptize correspondence course students. Later that year Jerry and Ann Hill moved to Santa Cruz, Bolivia, from Guatemala to work with the church for three months. In 1983 a team of four families from Oklahoma University moved to La Paz. The Ken Hynes family worked in and out of the country from 1983 till 2002 assisting churches in La Paz and Santa Cruz.

In 1963 the Glen and Janice Kramar family began a five-year work in Lima, Peru. This effort was greatly enhanced by the work of the Bert Perry family, Hans Dederscheck family, and Jacobo Chalco family in the early 1970s. Dederscheck focused heavily on the publication of evangelistic literature in Spanish. By 1990 the effects of the Shining Path terrorist group had forced all missionaries to leave Lima. A small team composed of Paul and Amy Dowell and Kevin Wright arrived in Lima from the Sunset International Bible Institute in 2002.

The work in Ecuador began when a U.S. AID worker named M. A. Stinson arrived in 1965, working for a short time with Dan Dever in Quito. Two years later N. E. Sewell arrived and worked in Ecuador for ten years. Sewell's dedication to placing locals in full evangelism, hosting continuous campaign activity, and establishing a long-term presence resulted in hundreds of baptisms every year through the early 1970s. In 1972 the Bobby Orr, Ike Hamilton, and Daniel Knight families joined Sewell's work. However, in 1973 persecution broke out that resulted in many houses being burned and people being abused. In 1978 the missionary workforce consisted of three North Americans: Ed Sewell and Luis McBride in Cuenca and Dave Hartshorn in Quito. A new effort from the Sunset International Bible Institute arrived in Quito in 1989, but after only a short period of time only the Kent Marcum family continued. The Marcums focused on leadership and preacher training by establishing a satellite of the Sunset International Bible Institute. In Cuenca, the Ron McClung, John Cannon, John Harris, and Deryk Pritchard families arrived in 1999 with the goal of establishing a congregation among the middle class.

The first missionaries from North American Churches of Christ, Jaime Solar and Dr. Charles F. Krull, arrived in Colombia in 1965. In 1967 the work was augmented by the arrival of B. K. Morgan and Richard Treat; V. T. Smith arrived in 1968. Morgan and Smith were vocational missionaries working with an American petroleum company. These men invited Dan Coker to visit the country and hold a campaign. Coker responded and for several years visited three to four times per year to help solidify the church in Bogotá. Richard Treat subsequently moved to Bogotá as a single man (prior to moving to Buenos Aires in 1972) and was later joined by Pedro Villa of Texas and John Jacobo of Fresno, California. During these years local authorities often harassed the work; this was the case in 1969 when Carl James moved from Guatemala to Medellín. He was joined for four years by James Holland and several apprentices from York College. One of those student missionaries, Harland Rall, returned with his wife Katherine and joined the team in Medellín. Later the Bobby Morgan family (ten-year workers) and a group of fifteen Adventures in Missions (AIM) workers from Sunset International Bible Institute (two-year workers) arrived. Work also extended to other major cities in the late 1960s in the north and central regions through evangelistic campaigns held by several U.S. evangelists and in the south where Ed Sewell led campaigns that established seven congregations.

In 1982 a team arrived in Bucaramanga from the Sunset International Bible Institute that included Johnny and Zoe Perkins, Tommy Nuckels, Raye Kramar, and David Turner. The Perkins family was evacuated in 1987 when the local police intercepted reports of a planned attack against the family by local drug dealers. With the continued escalation of violence in the country, all missionaries from Churches of Christ eventually left. National evangelists who continued to plant churches include Rafael Serrano, Jairo Badillo, Joaquín Suárez, Blas Negrete, Daniel Jaramillo, and others. Since the mid-1980s two hundred congregations have been planted through the impact of the World Radio broadcast. A new effort to evangelize Bogotá was undertaken through the combined efforts of the Continent of Great Cities organization in Abilene, Texas, and the Baxter Institute in Tegucigalpa, Honduras. These agencies partnered to send a nine-person Latin American team from Honduras to Bogotá in May 2003.

The activity of the Churches of Christ in Venezuela began through the efforts of a Venezuelan, Carlos Huerta, who was converted in California in 1953 and then returned to Venezuela. In 1957-58 N. A. Merritt, Sonny Edwards, Armando Ávila, and Joe Earl Morris met in Caracas. None were full-time missionaries, but they worked together to obtain recognition from the government as a legal entity. The first full-time workers arrived in 1961 when Clifford Tucker moved to Caracas with his family. An accident in 1963 claimed the life of his daughter, and the Tuckers returned to the States. Similarly, Frank Traylor worked in the area from 1962 to 1964, especially using the radio for evangelization, but was forced to leave because of his wife's ill health.

In 1977 the Bob Brown family moved from Trinidad and Tobago to begin working in Caracas. Brown focused heavily on placing young locals in full-time ministry and partnering with Harding University summer campaigns to establish new congregations. In the 1980s Brown was joined by the Jon Steffins, Albert Acosta, Geoff Guiseman, and Larry Moran families, along with many mature Venezuelan preachers who all worked in the central valley in or near Caracas. Following the departure of the other North Americans, Brown was joined by Ron Cox in 1994, who labored in Caracas for nine years. Brown returned to the States in 1995. The combined efforts of these missionaries and local workers resulted in fifty church plants in twenty years both inside and outside of the capital. Outside of Caracas, the Gary Green family worked to plant a church in the interior city of Puerto Ordaz from 1993 until late 2000. Green focused on ministry to the local colleges and young couples. Michelle Goff arrived in 2002 and was serving as the only U.S. missionary in Venezuela at the time of writing, though almost thirty Venezuelans now serve as preachers around the country.

The work in Brazil began around 1927 when two families, the Virgil Smith family and the O. S. Boyer family, moved to Pernambuco in northeastern Brazil. Two years later they were joined by the George Johnson family. By 1935 they reported the establishment of twenty congregations in that state and the adjoining states of Ceara and Alagoas. Within a short time, however, these congregations distanced themselves from the Stone-Campbell Movement, most moving into Pentecostalism.

Work in the São Paulo area began in 1957 with the arrival of Arlie and Alma Smith. Yet it was a subsequent wave of missionaries who came three years later that had the greatest impact on São Paulo. The team was birthed on the Abilene Christian University campus when students Howard and Jane Norton began to meet and pray with Don and Carol Vinzant. Interest in their plans grew, and within a few weeks fifteen families had committed themselves to the effort. On June 1, 1961, the vanguard of the effort sailed from Houston to Santos, Brazil, and then made its way to São Paulo; they would be joined within a year by the remainder of the workers. The families of Jerry Campbell, Allen Dutton, Jarrell Edwards, Jack Hill, Lynn Huff, Robert Humphries, Walter Kreidel, Ellis Long, Glenn Looper, David Mickey, Howard Norton, Glenn Owen, John Pennisi, Ted Stewart, Leon Tester, and Don Vinzant composed the team. The team quickly divided into committees and subcommittees such as finances, benevolence, Bible school, correspondence courses, English lectures, fellowship, hospital and sick, journalism, mission textbook, parliamentarian, personal work, Portuguese preaching, public relations, secretary, treasurer, visual aids, and worship. After ten years several of the initial team returned to the States but were replaced by a "second wave" of missionaries, including the families of Allen Huff, Ron Prater, Roger Dickson, John Curtis, and Bryan Bost. After twenty years of work they established seventeen churches with 712 members.

Churches of Christ continue to plant churches throughout Brazil, with works in Fortaleza, Campinas, Recife, Salvador, Brasília, Natal, Belo Horizonte, Curitiba, Campo Grande, Porto Alegre, Vitória, and other cities. Many of these works were started by teams of four to eight families. Bible camp work, publications, correspondence course programs, radio-television ministries, and a nationwide training school have played significant roles in the development of the church in Brazil. Brazilian churches such as the Belo Horizonte congregation are now actively sending mission teams to unreached areas of their country.

The work in Guyana begun by the Jerry Browning and Delbert Bradley families came to a halt in 1968-69 when the missionaries were denied the renewal of their visas. In 1980 the Church of Christ in Spanish Fort, Alabama, targeted Guyana with correspondence courses. Subsequent campaigns from 1982 to 1985 led by Don Starks, Bennie Mullins, and others and working with correspondence course students resulted in the establishment of a stable congregation in Georgetown. Mullins took early retirement and moved to Georgetown to found and direct the Guyana International Bible Institute. The institute was directed at the time of writing by Jerry and Mary Cantrell with the assistance of Kyle and Tiffany Cantrell and Steve and Monica Foster. Partners in Progress, a medical missionary organization based in Little Rock, Arkansas, conducts multiple medical missions to Guyana every summer. Doug and Dawn Winder and Mike and Sandy Roberts work with local churches, while missionaries Kenneth and Samantha Finlayson direct the One Hope Children's Home.

The small country of Surinam received attention from Jim Lanier, a vocational missionary from 1971 to 1975, who established a small congregation in Paramaribo. The work continued after Lanier's departure in the hands of the local members.

The work of the Churches of Christ in Central America has been even more concentrated than efforts in South America.

In Guatemala mission work began in 1959 with the arrival of the Jerry Hill, Carl James, Hignacio Huerta, and Floyd Hill families, who established five churches in their first year. Dan and Elise Coker joined the team in July 1963. The workers used correspondence courses and campaigns as the primary tools for evangelistic growth. This work was the "beachhead" of later works, and the first mission work conducted by Churches of Christ located between Mexico and Colombia. Hill and Coker would assist many teams and new church plants all over Latin America.

Later in Guatemala, a four-family team composed of Ralph and Susie McCluggage, Richard and Karen Reinhold, Roger and Mary Beth McCown, and Pat and Carol Hile arrived in the central highlands to work among the Quiche people in 1970. The team learned both Spanish and Quiche, helped translate the New Testament into Quiche, planted churches, and assisted in community health care. Simultaneous efforts by missionaries Joe and Jana Lee established a work in remote La Florida in January 1971. Early converts Luciano Ramos and Efraín Pérez with other local preachers went on to convert thousands and establish twenty-five congregations in the rugged Guatemalan highlands. In the urban area, Bob and Gina Waldron and coworker Tom Martin began a work on October 3, 1976, centered on urban teens that flourishes into the twenty-first century.

Jerry Hill of the Guatemala work drove to El Salvador to baptize contacts from correspondence courses and put them in touch with Senior Master Sergeant Jack Petrie and his wife Norma, who were in San Salvador with U.S. AID. The Petries began to meet with the new Christians, and a church was established in 1963. Jerry Hill frequented the work until the arrival of Bill and Jerry Wilson, the first full-time missionaries of the Churches of Christ in El Salvador, in 1965. The Wilsons had to return to the United States about 1970 for health reasons. At that time Armando Mejía, a Salvadoran converted in the United States and a graduate of the Sunset International Bible Institute who had been preaching in Nicaragua, moved back to El Salvador. In August 1971 the Rudy and Glenda Wray family and Larry and Judy White family moved to San Salvador, where they discovered ten churches with 170 in attendance. The Wrays were replaced in 1974 by the Don Hatch family. The missionaries coordinated a school of preaching for a few years but opted to focus on more evangelistic activities such as correspondence courses, radio evangelism, and tent meetings as well as leadership training through night classes and national seminars conducted every three months. When the last of the missionaries departed in 1979, the work remained in the hands of local evangelists, who guided the church during the difficult period of civil war. After the war, the churches reported growth to nearly 100 churches with 10,000 members.

The first Church of Christ in Honduras was formed in Tegucigalpa when Dan Coker arrived in 1969 from Guatemala and was given a job with the Honduran Ministry of Education. An evangelistic campaign in the El Pedregal barrio resulted in eighteen baptisms and a new church that would later begin nineteen congregations in the capital city. Relief work and humanitarian aid have been a major component of evangelism in Honduras. Such was the case in 1974 when Israel Flores, a young Mexican, arrived on the north coast of Honduras with the relief brigades who came to help the victims of Hurricane Fifi. Preaching among the wreckage of La Ceiba, Flores and others baptized thirty-eight people and began a church that would later generate six other congregations. Evangelist Medardo Gómez became a Christian while visiting La Ceiba and later established multiple congregations on the Nicaraguan border. Following the devastation of Hurricane Mitch in 1998, relief efforts led to the establishment of a thriving congregation led by Jarrod Brown in Barrio Julio Midence in Choluteca. This work continues to rebuild the spiritual and physical life of the community through evangelistic campaigns, construction projects, a medical clinic, and a kindergarten. Today in Honduras there are over 200 congregations with membership near 7,000, four Bible training schools, two elementary schools, several orphanages, prison ministries, a drug and alcohol treatment facility that draws from all over Central America, and many other programs of social service and ministry.

Military personnel were responsible for the earliest efforts of Churches of Christ in Panama. Earliest reports mention a soldier conducting worship in 1940. Later, in 1942, Gerald and Frances Fruzia began a work in Cristobal. The Canal Zone would later be the site of the first permanent building when Dean Rhodes moved there in 1945; Fruzia became the preacher for the congregation. Other early works include the efforts of John Wright in 1958 and Burl Brockman, his replacement, who established the church in Chilibri. Brockman used whatever means available to engage people in religious conversations, including sharing newspapers or offering haircuts on the street. In 1965 Carl James left his work in Guatemala to establish a school of preaching in Panama that continued in operation in the twenty-first century.

The work of Churches of Christ in Nicaragua is almost totally attributable to the efforts of Nicaraguans. In 1968 Armando Mejía organized an exodus of Christian families from El Salvador to Managua. Upon arriving in Managua, January 11, 1969, Mejía joined Juan Mendoza Donaire, who had been baptized earlier in Costa Rica. Early Salvadoran converts Pedro Batres, Julio Mejía, and Otoniel Rosales, among others, became some of the first preachers in Nicaragua. Three congregations in the Managua area now number over 300 in attendance.

The first assembly of Churches of Christ in Costa Rica occurred when N. C. Fine and John Kling, workers with U.S. AID, began to offer free Bible correspondence courses. Among the early converts was Efraín Valverde, who later played a prominent role in radio and television ministries and authored several books. Ray and Liz Bynum and the Norman Fox family were the first full-time workers in Costa Rica; the Bynums worked in Costa Rica from 1967 till 2003. After establishing thirty-nine congregations through locally trained evangelists, Bynum focused on initiating a cell church model prior to his departure. Today over 2,000 members of Churches of Christ assemble in Costa Rica.

Belize received its first efforts from Churches of Christ through short-term workers. Luther Savage worked full time in the country for one year, baptizing many and leaving a fledgling church. One of the first converts in this group was Hugh Frazier, who remained faithful to the work and gave it stability for many years. Ralph Jones later arrived to reinforce the work. Belize has received a large number of short-term workers and campaigners over the years.

Just prior to 1900, several members of Churches of Christ established small communities in the states of Tamaulipas and San Luis Potosí in northern Mexico. Many died from infectious diseases, and the survivors later fled the country due to the Mexican Revolution. No evidence of their communities exists today.

The modern work of the Churches of Christ in Mexico began with the conversion of Pedro Rivas, who had fled to Los Fresnos, Texas, to escape the Mexican Revolution. Supported financially and spiritually by local farmers, Rivas attended Freed-Hardeman University, graduating in May 1932. Rivas returned to Torreon, Coahuila, in north-central Mexico, where he worked as a vocational missionary and successfully established a congregation in 1941. Later Rivas entered the ministry full time with support from Christians in Brownsville, Texas. Rivas established the Torreon School of Preaching, from which many young workers were dispersed across northern Mexico, planting churches. Leonard Haven Miller of Abilene, Texas, was instrumental in traveling to Mexico multiple times each year to teach in these fledgling works as well as to expose potential U.S. supporters to the local preachers so that funding could be secured for salaries. Miller continued working throughout Mexico as an itinerate preacher and teacher for more than three decades. In 1959 reports counted forty congregations of the Churches of Christ in Mexico.

In 1987 the Sunset Church of Christ in Lubbock, Texas, sent a seven-family team to Mexico City to plant churches. Since that time teams have been sent to Toluca, Cuernavaca, and Guadalajara. In 2003 another team was being trained at the Sunset International Bible Institute for León, Mexico. Also in 2003 a four-family team began a new work in the southern section of Mexico City, while a team from the Richland Hills Church of Christ began a work in Morelia. The Church of Christ in Toluca ordained elders in November 2001 and began evangelizing the region by sending out teams from the local congregation.

In 1937 J. R. Jiménez, a Cuban living in Key West, Florida, was baptized. He later returned to Havana, Cuba, and in 1940 reported over 100 Christians in a newly formed congregation. Similarly, Ernesto Estedes of Tampa became a Christian in 1939 and returned to Pinar del Río and Matanzas in 1941, where he established three congregations in Pinar and seven in Matanzas. Following the takeover of communism in 1959, the work in Cuba was greatly curtailed. However, policies changed at the beginning of the twenty-first century, producing an open yet cautious atmosphere in which local churches can interact. In 2000 leaders from Churches of Christ from all over Cuba gathered in the national rotunda for a national conference. Annual gatherings have continued in order to maintain fellowship among the congregations. In addition, leadership training has been conducted in Havana twice a year through the efforts of Christians from the southern United States. Just over 100 congregations of the Churches of Christ exist on the island.

Baptism in Mexico Courtesy of the Disciples of Christ Historical Society

The work in Puerto Rico began in the early 1950s with the arrival of a soldier named Burl Buckman. After arrival, Buckman petitioned friends in the States to send him tracts in Spanish that he could distribute to the public. He converted a group and formed them into a church. At the same time, a commercial pilot named Clark Hannah was flying routinely from New York City to Puerto Rico and began to offer correspondence courses in the local papers of San Juan. The great response resulted in a short trip by John Young and Joe McKissick in April 1953; McKissick baptized Gregorio Rodríguez. McKissick's home congregation, the Dalhart, Texas, Church of Christ, then supported Winston Atkinson as a missionary to San Juan. Due to his involvement in a fatal car accident, Atkinson was forced to leave the island. Dwayne Davenport followed as a long-term worker, while others such as Jack Fogerty led short campaigns to San Juan. In 1957 Harlan Overton moved to Puerto Rico. Later still, José Cuéllar, a retired postal worker from New York, joined the work in Puerto Rico.

The islands of the Lesser Antilles, especially Antigua, Martinique, Trinidad, and Tobago, were evangelized through the efforts of men such as Roger Dixon and Bob Brown who used radio messages to teach tens of thousands of people.

Many mission activities in the Churches of Christ have grown out of or developed into mission organizations. For example, the Pan American Lectureship is an annual event that brings together missionaries, supporters, and others interested in Latin America for a week of lectures, reports, and fellowship. The lectures began in 1963 when Reuel Lemmons, then editor of the *Firm Foundation,* approached others interested in Latin America about joining him for a unique lecture series in Guatemala City. The November 1963 conference was a success, and Lemmons soon convened an ad hoc committee to aid him in planning an annual lectureship. The forty-first annual lecture series planned by Jim Frazier of Minden, Louisiana; Howard Norton of Searcy, Arkansas; and Dan Coker of Toluca, Mexico, was held in Vitoria, Brazil, November 2003.

One of the long-range effects generated by the 1961 São Paulo effort came in 1968 when the missionaries planned a larger evangelistic thrust into the other major urban centers of Brazil and called it Brazil Breakthrough. Over time the vision grew to include an organization that would recruit, train, and facilitate church plants in all capital cities of South America. The name was changed in 1979 to Continent of Great Cities. Since 1976 this effort has been conducted under the oversight of the Central Church of Christ in Amarillo, Texas. Since 1998, Continent of Great Cities has met its self-imposed goal of sending at least one team to the field per year: for example, in 1998 four families to Rio de Janeiro, Brazil; in 1999 seven families to Santiago, Chile; in 2001 five families to Buenos Aires, Argentina; in 2002 a team of five families to Porto Alegre, Brazil; and in 2003 four families to Asunción, Paraguay. At the time of writing the Continent of Great Cities ministry has trained and sent 214 missionaries representing 21 teams to major Latin American cities.

Members of those teams received their missions and theological training from various institutions among Churches of Christ, including Abilene Christian University, Lubbock Christian University, Oklahoma Christian University, Harding University, Freed-Hardeman University, Pepperdine University, Lipscomb University, Austin Graduate School of Theology, York College, and the Sunset International Bible Institute (SIBI). SIBI also has branch training institutes in Miami, Florida; Toluca, Mexico; and Quito, Ecuador. SIBI, Abilene Christian University, Harding University, and Continent of Great Cities have united with local workers in Miami to formulate a twenty-year strategy for joint evangelization of the Latin American population of Miami. Plans are for the first of twelve church plant teams in the "Latin American Mission Project — Miami" to arrive in 2005.

Several universities also have been instrumental in promoting short-term missions among students. York College (Mission Apprentice Program — MAP; now defunct), SIBI (Adventures in Missions program — AIM; over 30 years and growing) and Abilene Christian University (previous MARK program; current Worldwide Witness program) have sent many students to Latin America as six-month to two-year interns, many of whom have become long-term missionaries.

In 1952 Pedro Rivas established the Torreon School of Preaching, which has now trained hundreds of ministers and greatly accelerated the rate of church plantings in northern Mexico. Another major force in church planting in Latin America among the Churches of Christ has been the Baxter Institute of Biblical and Cultural Studies, which was established by Harris Goodwin in 1964 in Mexico City. In 1978 the institute was moved to Tegucigalpa, Honduras, where in 1996 it came under the direction of Calvin Henry. With students from fifteen countries of Latin America studying in a four-year program leading to a university degree of Licenciatura en Teología, Baxter is the largest ministerial training program of the Churches of Christ in Latin America. Over 300 graduates of this school have established churches in most of the countries of Latin America.

An effort designed to equip all Christians for ministry is the Instituto Latinamericano de Estudios Bíblicos (ILEB), currently based at Toluca, Mexico, and directed by Dr. Dan Coker. Plans have been made to move the institute to the Dallas–Fort Worth area in order to ease long-distance travel and to facilitate the dissemination of literature.

Another important work is the Herald of Truth ministries sponsored by the Highland Church of Christ in Abilene, Texas. On January 1, 1971, Herald of Truth began broadcasting five-minute messages by former São Paulo missionary Glenn Owen to Mexico. Then two local evangelists delivered radio messages until the hiring of Lou Seckler in April 1973. The next year Seckler became director of the Mexican work. Under his leadership the ministry began to air television programs to much of Mexico in December 1978. Follow-up campaigns by various U.S. churches often generated new congregations, and missionaries moved to sites of new responses to begin congregations: Liberto Ovalle to Tapachula in 1975, Aroher and Betty Lopez to Acapulco in 1979, Alfonso Pastrana to Guadalajara in 1983, and Daniel Martínez to Tampico in 1989. The ministry has also continued to nurture church growth in Mexico by providing annual training seminars for ministers.

A more recent media work capitalizing on new technologies aired a pilot program in 1989 in Miami. The program, called Con La Biblia Abierta, was shown locally in 1990 before being syndicated in mid-decade. Today it is seen on 4,962 channels in twenty countries and forty-nine U.S. states. At least seventeen churches have been planted as a direct result of the program, which is filmed in Miami at the

Hialeah Church of Christ under the direction of Rex Morgan. Through the program, speakers Efraín Valverde and Luis Estrada address topics such as family issues, the church, and knowing Christ.

Print ministry has also been important in the work in Latin America. Three of the primary efforts are the La Voz Eterna magazine and tract ministry based in Houston, Texas (c. 1963), and the ministries of Worldwide Spanish Literature Ministry–Western Christian Foundation based in Wichita Falls, Texas, and La Espada del Espíritu based in Baymon, Puerto Rico.

Relief efforts have long been an area of focus for the Churches of Christ. Organizations that have worked throughout Latin America at different times and that continue to provide for the physical as well as spiritual needs of the population include Health Talents International (founded in 1973 in Birmingham, Alabama, concentrating on work in Guatemala and Honduras) and Healing Hands International (which grew out of a student-led project at Lipscomb University in 1991 and was formed into a non-profit organization in 1994). Bridges to the World promotes holistic ministry in Latin American third-world countries, including church planting, leadership development, education, medicine and dentistry, business, and agriculture. Established as a separate entity in 2001, Bridges grew out of Global Campaigns, an effort supported for over twenty years by Bridge's director Jack Walker's sponsoring congregation, Southern Hills Church of Christ in Abilene, Texas. PREDISAN is one of the few humanitarian efforts of its size to be conducted year round in Latin America. Based in Catacamas, Honduras, and overseen by Northlake Church of Christ in Tucker, Georgia, PREDISAN ("predicar" = preach; "sanar" = heal) began in August 1986 when the Dr. Robert Clark family, Wayne and Rosemary Gaines, and Don Walton moved to the area to teach graduates of the Honduras Bible School how to implement holistic healthcare in their ministries.

GARY L. GREEN

See also American Christian Missionary Society; Christian Missionary Fellowship; Christian Woman's Board of Missions; Colegio Biblico; Direct Support Missions; Foreign Christian Missionary Society, The; Hispanics in the Movement; Inman Christian Center; Jamaica, The Movement in; Missions, Missiology; Puerto Rico, The Movement in; United Christian Missionary Society, The

BIBLIOGRAPHY *Anukan Directory of Christian Churches and Churches of Christ* (2000) • Stephen J. Corey, *Among South American Friends: The Journal of a Visit to South America* (1925) • *Directorio del Ministerio de las Iglesias Cristianas e Iglesias de Cristo de Habla Hispana* (2002) (online: http://www.spanam.org/Directorio.pdf) • David Filbeck, *The First Fifty Years: A Brief History of the Direct Support Missionary Movement* (1980) • Phillip Wayne Elkins, *Church-Sponsored Missions: An Evaluation of Churches of Christ* (1974) • Teston Gilpatrick, *Lessons in Missions from Twenty Years in São Paulo* (1982) • William D. Hall, *Missions Follow New Frontiers* (1958) • Harding University Center for World Missions, "First Steps in Foreign Evangelism in Restoration History," available at http://www.harding.edu/cwm/Resources/Generalarticles/restorationhistory.htm • Lora Banks Harrison, *The Church Abroad* (rev. ed., 1969) • Samuel Guy Inman, *Christian Cooperation in Latin America* (1917) • *Journal of Applied Missiology,* Institute for Missions and Evangelism of Abilene Christian University, Abilene, Texas • Archibald McLean, *The History of the Foreign Christian Missionary Society* (1919) • *Mission Services Association Missionary Directory* (2002) • William J. Nottingham, "Beyond All Borders," *The Indiana Christian* (December 2002/January 2003): 5 • São Paulo Brazil Mission Team, *Steps into the Mission Field: From First Concepts to First Converts* (1978) • Bertrand Smith, *400 Years after Valdivia* (1957) • Gary Joe Sorrells, "The Continent of Great Cities Ministry: A Goal and a Strategy for Church Establishment in Urban South America (unpublished D.Min. thesis, Abilene Christian University, 1994) • Fernando Soto, *La Reforma Presente: Historia del Movimiento de Restauración de Stone y Campbell* (1997) • E. T. Westrup, "A Son's Tribute," *Missionary Tidings* 27 (1910): 399.

La Voz Eterna

Spanish-language journal published by members of Churches of Christ.

The journal was founded by Harris Goodwin in 1963 as a monthly. In the same year he founded the Leta Baxter Bible Training School in Mexico City, later named Baxter Institute and moved to Tegucigalpa, Honduras. It was a general religious journal for Spanish-speaking leaders and members in Churches of Christ especially in Mexico and in Central and South America. In 1966 the paper's format consisted of twenty-four 8½ by 11 pages with a multi-colored cover — similar to the format of the *Firm Foundation* but without the extensive news items found in that paper. Many of the articles in the early years were translations of materials that had appeared first in English-language journals like *Twentieth Century Christian.* Soon persons from Central America emerged as major writers, especially Arnoldo Mejía of Tegucigalpa, Honduras. In 1992 Goodwin was listed as director and Mejía as subdirector. From 1963 until 1970 *La Voz Eterna* was published in Mexico City, and after that in Houston, Texas.

See also Journalism; Latin America and Caribbean, Missions in

THOMAS H. OLBRICHT

Leaven, A Journal of Ministry

Quarterly journal of ministry for churches of the Stone-Campbell Movement.

The genesis of *Leaven* came out of the demise of *Mission* when Mark Love and three *Mission* board members (Wayne Dockery, Michael W. Casey, and Paul Watson) met in 1988 to discuss beginning a journal that would bring theological reflection to ministry for Churches of Christ. The journal was to be for church leaders and ministers, but grounded in scholarly interpretation and research. The issues would be thematic, with a guest editor for each issue.

After incorporating in Texas, *Leaven* published its first issue in 1990 on worship. For the first few years, Mark Love oversaw the technical and editorial responsibilities of the journal in Texas and then Oregon. This burden proved difficult for one person. Though Love and the board found it easier than expected to obtain financial support, it was difficult to meet publication deadlines. This prompted a change in 1994. That year D'Esta and Stuart Love (Mark Love's parents) assumed general editorship of the journal from their location at Pepperdine University. The support of the Pepperdine community and the Loves' dedication brought stability and further growth to *Leaven*.

The next stage of *Leaven's* growth came in 1997 through an alliance with educational leaders in Christian Churches/Churches of Christ David Matson, Robert Wetzel, Leonard Wymore, and others at Emmanuel School of Religion and Milligan College. In 2001 *Leaven* became an official publication of the Religion Division at Pepperdine University.

See also Emmanuel School of Religion; Milligan College; *Mission;* Pepperdine University

MARKUS H. MCDOWELL

Lectureships

Bible lectureships in the Stone-Campbell Movement developed primarily in connection with institutions affiliated with Churches of Christ and, most prominently, in college and university settings. As Churches of Christ rejected General Conventions and missionary societies, the less formal lectureships provided many of the same functions — fellowship, networking, and examination of doctrinal issues. Though there were nineteenth-century precursors such as the Missouri Christian Lectureship, lectureships were born in the soil of the early twentieth century and continued to flourish at the beginning of the twenty-first.

In these typically annual forums, many of the most capable preachers and teachers in Churches of Christ give sermons and lessons on select themes or biblical texts. Thus, presentations are not only important instructional aids and avenues for spiritual formation; they also provide helpful windows for viewing developments within the larger body. The following are representative of the types of themes treated over the years: the value of Christian education; the inspiration and authority of Scripture; the relationship between the Bible and science — including the issue of evolution; the nature of God; the divinity of Christ and Christ's redemptive work for humankind; baptism for remission of sins; Christian living; the family; and a host of issues relating to the doctrine and work of the church.

As in Churches of Christ generally, social issues have not been emphasized. One notable exception was Carl Spain's (1917-1990) remarkable presentation, "Modern Challenges to Christian Morals," at the Abilene Christian College Lectureship of 1960. Heralded by William Banowsky (b. 1936) as "the most spectacular speech ever delivered in Abilene," Spain's lecture issued a challenge to Churches of Christ to correct the racial inequities associated with segregation. Spain specifically targeted the exclusionary admission practices in private Christian schools, and his comments engendered considerable discussion while contributing, to some extent, to change.

Among the most influential annual lectureships today — with beginning dates for lectureships given in parentheses — are those that meet at Abilene Christian University (lectures formally initiated in 1918), Freed-Hardeman University (1937), Harding University (1924), Lipscomb University (1947), Lubbock Christian University (1957), Oklahoma Christian University (1950), and Pepperdine University (1943). The Tulsa Soul-Winning Workshop (1976), sponsored by the Garnett Road Church of Christ, has been the premier evangelistic lectureship. The Nashville Jubilee (1989-2000), sponsored by several middle Tennessee congregations, represented progressive ideas in Churches of Christ and attracted large crowds during its existence.

Some churches have become disaffected with the direction and stances reflected in the university-sponsored lectures; leaders from these churches have started new lectureships with decidedly different stances to correct what they believe to be departures from orthodoxy. Representative of this latter group are the Denton Lectures (in Denton, Texas), the Florida School of Preaching Lectures, and the Memphis School of Preaching Lectures.

As gathering places for literally thousands of church members from all over the world, lectureships serve important social functions. Ancillary activities or events include meetings, exhibits, displays, and promotional features for various organizations. The advertising opportunities for sponsoring groups, and the economic benefits for host communities, provide additional commercial benefits.

While Churches of Christ have been characterized, in part, by a lack of formal organization at the national level, lectureships have served as important mechanisms for providing informal structure and control. In its early years, lectureships served as unifying events for Churches of Christ in the aftermath of the Movement's division; more recently, they have illustrated the divisions within the fellowship.

It is difficult to understand Churches of Christ in the twentieth century without taking into consideration lectureships, both for their ability to reflect what was going on in the larger Movement and culture and for the powerful ways in which they have shaped the thought of leaders and churches. William Banowsky's comments on the Abilene Lectures are apt and apply more broadly to lectureships in general: "The Lectureship has been the most vital pulpit of a pulpit-sparked movement."

See also Missouri Christian Lectureship; North American Christian Convention

BIBLIOGRAPHY William S. Banowsky, *The Mirror of a Movement* (1965) • Douglas A. Foster, *Will the Cycle Be Unbroken* (1994), pp. 73-77 • Don Haymes, "Lectureships (Churches of Christ)," in *Encyclopedia of Religion in the South,* ed. Samuel S. Hill (1984), pp. 401-2.

CRAIG S. CHURCHILL

Lemmons, Reuel Gordon (1912-1989)

Influential preacher and, from 1955 to 1983, editor of the *Firm Foundation,* second oldest publication among Churches of Christ. During his tenure as editor, his articles tended to reflect a middle ground between conservatives and progressives in Churches of Christ, both poles receiving his criticism on occasion. He has often been characterized as an "editor-bishop" because of the influence his words had on the mainstream of this part of the Movement.

Lemmons served as editor of *Firm Foundation* during the American civil rights movement. True to form, he articulated the most commonly held beliefs among members of Churches of Christ during this period. He minimized racism in Churches of Christ, stating, "We believe that racial prejudice is gross in an infinitesimally small part of the body of Christ." This statement invited sharp criticism from African American Churches of Christ. Nevertheless, Lemmons most often received accolades from his peers because he was not afraid to voice many of the concerns of the body. Among issues addressed in his editorials were the role of the Holy Spirit, religious legalism, the social gospel, gambling, the sale of liquor, the theory of evolution in textbooks, and the Vietnam War. Critics sometimes charged Lemmons, however, with speaking well on every side of the issues.

Lemmons ended his tenure as editor of *Firm Foundation* in 1983 when the publication was sold to H. A. (Buster) Dobbs and Bill Cline. In 1985 he began editing the newly established *Image* magazine, and he served in this capacity until his death in 1989. A strong advocate for World Bible School, he also edited *Action,* a periodical dedicated to this cause. Following his death, friends described him as a man of courage who loved the church and worked tirelessly for world evangelism.

See also African Americans in the Movement; *Firm Foundation;* World Bible School

BIBLIOGRAPHY Denny Boultinghouse, ed., Special Issue: "Reuel Gordon Lemmons: July 8, 1912–January 25, 1989," *Image* 5 (March 1989): 4 • Reuel Lemmons and Denny Boultinghouse, *A Decade of Reflection: Image Editorials, 1985-1995* (1995).

T. WESLEY CRAWFORD

Lester, Hiram Jefferson (1933-1998)

Preacher, educator, and historian of the Christian Church (Disciples of Christ) in the twentieth century.

A native of Roanoke, Alabama, Lester earned B.A. degrees from Johnson Bible College in 1955 and Phillips University in 1960, a B.D. from Phillips University in 1959, and an M.A. and Ph.D., both in New Testament, from Yale University, in 1962 and 1974, respectively.

He began preaching for congregations of the Disciples of Christ in the Blue Ridge Mountains of North Carolina while still a student at Johnson Bible College, then served many congregations, most on an interim basis, during the course of a long ministry, culminating with a nine-year term as the pastor of the First Christian Church in Pasadena, California, 1989-98.

From 1965 to 1988, Lester served as a professor of religious studies at Alexander Campbell's Bethany College. He devoted much of his time and energy during the Bethany years to understanding and interpreting both Campbell and the religious tradition he helped to establish. Especially notable were his efforts to restore, preserve, and interpret some of the more significant Campbell sites for the hundreds of people who visited Bethany College every year. Lester was also an expert on the Irish roots of Thomas and Alexander Campbell.

Lester wrote numerous articles on the two Campbells, culminating in a seminal article entitled "The Form and Function of the *Declaration and Address*" that appeared (posthumously) in *The Quest for Christian Unity, Peace, and Purity in Thomas Campbell's* Declaration and Address (2000). Lester died while deeply involved in the on-line exchange of papers on the *Declaration and Address* that formed the basis of the *Quest* volume. In the years leading up to his death in

1998, he had been working on a biography of Alexander Campbell.

Although Lester spent his life principally in the context of the Christian Church (Disciples of Christ), he built bridges to Churches of Christ and Christian Churches/Churches of Christ throughout his career and was known as a strong encourager of younger scholars in Stone-Campbell studies.

See also Bethany College; *Declaration and Address*

BIBLIOGRAPHY Hiram J. Lester, "Alexander Campbell's Early Baptism in Ecumenicity and Sectarianism," *Restoration Quarterly* 30 (1988): 85-101 • Hiram J. Lester, "The Form and Function of the *Declaration and Address,*" in *The Quest for Christian Unity, Peace, and Purity in Thomas Campbell's* Declaration and Address, ed. Thomas H. Olbricht and Hans Rollmann (2000), pp. 173-92.

RICHARD T. HUGHES

Lexington Theological Seminary

Graduate theological seminary affiliated with the Christian Church (Disciples of Christ).

Lexington Theological Seminary, located in Lexington, Kentucky, is the oldest theological seminary of the Stone-Campbell Movement. The school was founded in 1865 as the College of the Bible. In 1965 the name was changed to Lexington Theological Seminary so as to reflect changes in the nature of ministerial education. It is formally related to the Disciples through the Division of Higher Education of the Christian Church (Disciples of Christ).

The College of the Bible was part of a reorganization of two institutions suffering from the impact of the Civil War, along with the opportunities made available to the states by the Morrill Land Act of 1862. In Harrodsburg, Kentucky, Bacon College, the first college established by the Stone-Campbell Movement, then under the name of Kentucky University, needed a campus and financial support. Transylvania University in Lexington had a modest campus, but was desperately short of funds. Meanwhile, the state of Kentucky wanted to make use of the offers of federal support through the Morrill Land Act and establish an agricultural and mechanical college.

A carefully crafted coalition of church-related and state institutions was put together under the name of Kentucky University. Robert Milligan (1814-1875) was named the first president of the College of the Bible. A "University Regent" had administrative oversight responsibility for each of the elements of the university. There were inherent tensions within an institution that included two church-related elements (the College of the Bible [COB] and the College of Arts and Sciences) and two state-supported elements (the Agricultural and Mechanical College [A & M] and the College of Law).

(left to right) I. B. Grubbs, C. L. Loos, and J. W. McGarvey represented conservative scholarship at the College of the Bible. After McGarvey's death in 1911 and the retirement of the other two, more liberal professors were hired to take their positions. Courtesy of the Johnson Bible College Photo Archive

Meanwhile, across Kentucky there was an outcry from non-Disciples distressed about the state working hand-in-glove with a denominational institution. The amount of time given to the establishment of the A & M College on the part of Regent Bowman, personal conflict between Bowman and COB Professor J. W. McGarvey (1829-1911), and the financial panic of 1873 all contributed to the collapse of the joint church-state school.

In 1877 an independent College of the Bible was created. The state legislature pulled the A & M College out of the university and established what would ultimately become the University of Kentucky. What was left was essentially a college of arts and sciences, still under the name of Kentucky University and clearly affiliated with the Disciples of Christ in Kentucky. In 1908 the school would reclaim the older name of Transylvania College.

The College of the Bible had been supported throughout the conflict by the Kentucky Christian Education Society, an agency of the Disciples in Kentucky. The creation of an independent College of the Bible had come out of a meeting sponsored by the Kentucky Christian Education Society. Once the state-supported A & M College had withdrawn, the College of the Bible was invited by Kentucky University to return to campus with full use of classrooms and free living space for students. The two institutions also agreed that their students could take courses from both institutions at no additional cost to the students. In 1895 a College of the Bible building was opened on the campus of Kentucky University.

The initial leadership of the new College of the

Bible included Robert Graham as president and John W. McGarvey as professor of Bible. At first, most of the courses taken by students in the College of the Bible were undergraduate-level classes since most of the students lacked an undergraduate degree. At the end of their studies they would receive an "English Diploma." Those who already had a bachelor's degree took more advanced courses and earned a Classical Diploma, representing graduate-level work. The Classical Diploma students were required to study the biblical languages of Hebrew and Greek.

In 1895 McGarvey became president of the College of the Bible, and served until his death in 1911. He also taught throughout this period. McGarvey was conservative in his approach to theological issues and the interpretation of the Bible. Nevertheless, he did finally relent and allowed women to take courses in the College of the Bible.

McGarvey led the College of the Bible to be a leader in the preparation of those who would focus on educational ministry in the churches. The school established a department of "Bible School Pedagogy," and with the support of the Kentucky Bible School Association raised funds for the first endowed professorial chair in religious education in the United States.

Under McGarvey, education was controlled carefully by the faculty. In Bible, the only textbooks were the Bible, McGarvey's own books, and books dealing with biblical languages. Few professors gave assignments that required independent study in the library. Most courses were graded on how well the student could repeat the professors' lectures and recite memorized materials.

Nevertheless, the education was rigorous. This was particularly true for those in the Classical Diploma track. That degree expanded from a two-year to a three-year curriculum by the year 1900. In addition to Bible, students studied church history, theology, preaching, philosophy, and English literature.

From 1865 to 1900, virtually every professor teaching in the seminary was educated at Bethany and/or the College of the Bible. After 1900, that began to change. Upon McGarvey's death in 1911, a new generation of faculty brought new ideas about education. In 1914 the Classical Diploma was replaced by the then standard graduate professional degree of Bachelor of Divinity. The English Diploma was gradually eliminated, and by 1938 only graduate degrees were available. Students were required henceforth to have an undergraduate degree before entering the College of the Bible. This was the trend in theological education across the United States at the time. The College of the Bible was one of the charter members of the American Association of Theological Schools (now the Association of Theological Schools), which became the primary accrediting agency for seminaries.

The move to a graduate program meant that the relationship between the College of the Bible and Transylvania had to change. So long as both institutions had undergraduate students, it was easy for students in one school to take courses in the other. This process of change was complicated by the fact that from McGarvey's death until 1938, the two institutions shared the same president.

The first of these shared presidents was Richard H. Crossfield, who served the College of the Bible from 1912 to 1921. Under Crossfield's leadership the College of the Bible became the center of one of the major battles in the division between the more conservative and the more liberal Disciples churches. In the early years of this conflict McGarvey had kept the College of the Bible firmly in the more conservative, Restorationist camp. He wrote regularly for the *Christian Standard*. McGarvey had brought his former student, Hall Laurie Calhoun, to the faculty. Calhoun was faithful to McGarvey's conservative perspective. Shortly before his death, McGarvey appointed Calhoun as dean of the College of the Bible. When McGarvey died, Calhoun was made acting president, but he did not receive the permanent appointment. That went to R. H. Crossfield, who was already president of Transylvania College. Crossfield and Calhoun had been at odds for several years, often over issues that broke down along conservative-liberal lines.

Meanwhile, from 1911 to 1914, every professor who had taught with McGarvey retired, died, or departed for another position, with the one exception of Calhoun. Crossfield replaced the McGarvey faculty with persons who were moderately liberal, including Alonzo Willard Fortune and William Clayton Bower. Questions about the orthodoxy of the faculty began to appear in the *Christian Standard*.

The issue came to a head in 1917. A student at the College of the Bible wrote a letter to the *Christian Standard* accusing Crossfield and most of the faculty of "destructive criticism" of the Bible. The trustees of the College of the Bible investigated and exonerated the faculty, proclaiming in the process that Disciples do not hold heresy trials. The *Christian Standard* treated the questions about the faculty as a matter of profound importance, and a national debate on biblical interpretation and theological perspective was fully engaged. As the conflict continued, other issues and other institutions became the center of focus. Eventually this would lead to a second schism in the Stone-Campbell Movement. Clearly the early major engagement leading to division was the struggle over the faculty at the College of the Bible. One result was that the more conservative leaders in the Movement realized that they needed to have their own institutions for the education of ministers.

The new College of the Bible faculty included several who had earned the Ph.D. degree from some of the leading institutions of that day, including Harvard, Yale, and Chicago. They brought to the classroom an orientation toward library research and broad reading for students. Lecture courses with recitations of memorized material gave way to formal lectures on a variety of subjects and seminars where students presented their research findings and engaged in the critique of their classmates' ideas. Elective courses were introduced in 1915. From the 1920s forward courses in all areas, including Bible, became more specialized. Students were allowed to develop a major area of emphasis based on their own interests. Courses on the Bible were openly modernist in perspective.

The study of theology has been a concern for the Stone-Campbell Movement since the first generation struggled with theology as a field of apologetics that was seen as undergirding sectarianism. Theology in the earliest days of the College of the Bible was offered primarily through courses on the content of the Bible. By the late nineteenth century the word "theology" began to appear in the seminary catalog, but under the heading of "doctrine" and with the proviso that it was based on the interpretation of Scripture and would avoid "philosophical speculation." The text for the course was Robert Milligan's *The Scheme of Redemption,* essentially a recapitulation of Alexander Campbell's thought.

With the change of the faculty after 1911, theology came to be more and more central to the education of ministers. From the 1920s to the mid 1960s, the number of courses in theology doubled. The field name of "doctrine" would continue until 1965, when the curriculum dropped the phrase "Doctrinal Field" in favor of "Area of Theological Studies." However, throughout the period after the death of McGarvey, the major theological themes and thinkers that have dominated mainstream Christianity have been a regular part of the curriculum at the College of the Bible/Lexington Theological Seminary. This is further evidence that the College of the Bible made a clear and distinct move into a more liberal theological position after McGarvey's death.

Courses in practical theology expanded beyond the earlier emphasis on preaching. The influence of the Social Gospel can be seen in course descriptions. Religious education offerings made use of the rapid growth of the field of psychology. Far more attention was being given to the study and practice of worship as an area of concern for ministers.

Throughout, there was a growing commitment to the integration of theory and practice. Prior to 1900 student preaching was discouraged, largely because the students came to the College of the Bible with only modest educational preparation. By 1920 service to small churches in the region around Lexington was seen as a kind of laboratory for ministerial education, and it had the additional benefit of providing income to financially strapped students. George V. Moore came to the faculty in 1927 and spent thirty-five years developing field education as an integral part of the overall degree program. In all of these curricular changes and developments, the issues that were debated during the 1917 conflict over the teaching of the Bible reveal starkly how thoroughly the moderately liberal perspective carried the day at the College of the Bible.

By the late 1930s it was becoming increasingly apparent that the facilities available to the College of the Bible on the campus of Transylvania College were no longer adequate, and Transylvania was feeling the need for more space for its own programs. As funds were raised for a new and separate campus, representatives from the University of Kentucky encouraged the relocation of the seminary on a hill overlooking the university. Since the seminary had become a graduate educational institution, the university saw the advantage of having access to an institution of learning in the field of religion. In return, the university offered a wide range of graduate programs that could be useful to supplement and augment the seminary curriculum. Philosophy, psychology, history, and literature were among the most obvious areas of interest to the College of the Bible. Also, to have easy access to the university library would allow the seminary to focus its own library on the field of religion and ministry.

The university and the seminary have cooperated on a number of degree programs. Early in their relationship they put together a double competency program by which students could earn the Master of Divinity or Master of Arts degree from the seminary and a Master of Social Work from the university in significantly less time than if the two degrees were taken consecutively. In recent years seminary students have been able to earn a certificate in gerontology from the university as a part of their seminary curriculum. Most recently the two institutions have put together a joint degree program leading to a degree in church music.

Under the leadership of President Kenneth B. Bowen a new seminary campus began to take shape. President Riley B. Montgomery led the formal move to the new campus in 1950. At the heart of the new campus was a library that came to be one of the greatest assets of the College of the Bible.

As the school approached its centennial celebration, Montgomery guided the institution through a change of name to Lexington Theological Seminary (LTS). In the public mind a college was an undergraduate institution. And in the middle of the twentieth century, a school with the name "Bible" seemed to convey a sectarian meaning — another indication of the perspective that had emerged at the College of the Bible since the death of McGarvey. Further, in the almost a hundred years of independence from Transylvania College, many people had continued to link the two institutions together. Trustees were certain that financial support for ministerial education would increase when the seminary could be seen as physically separate from Transylvania. During the 1960s LTS followed the trend of most other theological seminaries by replacing the nomenclature of the Bachelor of Divinity degree with the Master of Divinity designation. Soon after, the seminary added the Doctor of Ministry degree to its offerings.

The College of the Bible/Lexington Theological Seminary had weathered many a financial storm over its first century. But none was more dire than the one that wracked the school in the 1960s. A chain of virtually unavoidable financial circumstances severely threatened the school's survival. W. A. Welsh came as president in 1965, and within a year he led the school back to balanced budgets. During the presidency of Wayne H. Bell, 1974-86, LTS saw its endowment begin to grow and provide fiscal stability for the seminary.

Under the leadership of William O. Paulsell, president from 1987 to 1992, the seminary cooperated with the Roman Catholic Diocese of Lexington by developing two master's degree programs to prepare laypersons and lay religious persons for service within the Roman Catholic Church.

These degrees reflect the ecumenical commitment of the seminary that can be traced to the changes in philosophy in the seminary in the years since the 1910s. The College of the Bible/Lexington Theological Seminary adopted and advanced the Disciples participation in the ecumenical movement. In 1938 the College of the Bible pioneered ecumenical studies by offering the first course in a seminary on the ecumenical church. For most of a century the student body has been ecumenically diverse, and for many decades the faculty and staff have included persons from many different traditions, both Christian and occasionally from non-Christian faith communities. Over the last few decades, the student body has included about twenty different denominations. The non-Disciples generally represent about half of the student population. In the 1960s LTS was a leader in forming the Theological Educational Association of Mid-America, an ecumenical consortium of five seminaries from the Baptist, Methodist, Presbyterian, Roman Catholic, and Disciples traditions. In the 1990s the seminary with the support of the Lexington Jewish community established the Moosnick lecture, then the Moosnick Professorship in Judaic Studies.

See also Bacon College; Calhoun, Hall Laurie; Fortune, Alonzo Willard; Higher Education, Views of in the Movement; McGarvey, John W.; Milligan, Robert; Transylvania University

BIBLIOGRAPHY Richard L. Harrison, Jr., "Disciples Theological Formation: From a College of the Bible to a Theological Seminary," in *A Case Study of Mainstream Protestantism: The Disciples' Relation to American Culture, 1880-1989*, ed. D. Newell Williams (1991), pp. 281-98 • Dwight E. Stevenson, *Lexington Theological Seminary, 1865-1965: The College of the Bible Century* (1964).

RICHARD L. HARRISON, JR.

Liberalism

Alignment in the Disciples of Christ in the late nineteenth and twentieth centuries, composed both of ideological and pragmatist proponents, that repudiated the older restorationism and embraced a more progressive and "modernist" worldview in the name of the Stone-Campbell "plea."

"Liberalism" so commonly refers to "openness or willingness to change" that further specifications of its meaning are invariably both context-situated and fluid. The term is affixed to a wide variety of standpoints or movements in Christian history, and "liberal" as a label of group self-identity or the identity of others is typically a value-charged term of approval or reproach. Its primary import for studies of the Stone-Campbell Movement relates to developments in "modern Protestant liberalism."

Liberalism emerged as an identifiable movement around 1800, first in Western Europe and then in North America. It rose to ascendancy, by fitful steps, in many Protestant churches by 1900. Its influence peaked in Europe at the outbreak of World War I and in the United States after World War II. The dominance of German thinkers, reconstructing theology after Pietism and the Enlightenment and pursuing post-Kantian, Romantic lines of thought, is registered by shorthand references to "Protestant liberalism from Schleiermacher to Ritschl." Most countries, however, have similar lists of famous names and schools: England, for example, designates Coleridge, Maurice, the Broad Church, and Social Christianity, while the United States refers to Emerson and Transcendentalism, Bushnell, the Andover liberals, the Chicago school, and the Social Gospel.

Theological liberalism was well advanced in Europe, especially Germany, before crossing to America in the 1830s and 1840s. It circulated widely among America's evangelical Protestants before reaching Stone-Campbell churches. But the word "liberal" had a prehistory worth noting. Post-Enlightenment

Unitarianism was called "liberal religion." Its criticisms and "corrections" of cardinal tenets of its own Puritan-Calvinist heritage put "liberal" into use among orthodox-minded Calvinists as a term of reproach for similar deviations from confessional norms. Stone-Campbell churches disavowed liberalism along with conservatism and every other nonbiblical party label and sectarian name. Yet defenders of orthodoxies were troubled that apart from and despite stressing the Bible, confessing Jesus Christ, baptism, and the Lord's Supper, the new Movement neither established nor enforced any doctrinal standards. It extolled liberty and rights — free inquiry, rights of conscience and judgment, congregational independence — on the matters and with rhetoric associated with "liberality." It declared itself "beyond" Calvinism, Arminianism, and all "isms," but its "plan of salvation" seemed to reduce conversion to freewill human believing. From the standpoint of historic Evangelical Protestantism, antitraditionalism made thc Stone-Campbell Movement "liberal," not "conservative."

Within the Movement the word "liberal" gained wider currency after the Civil War. Trans-Atlantic liberalism then on the march exhibited continuities with earlier versions: Age of Reason ideals of liberties, rights, toleration, and cultivation of learning carried over. In other respects it was distinctly post-Enlightenment. Religion, it maintained, was at its heart neither metaphysics nor morality but an inward spiritual sensing of divine infinite spirit in the universe, forming and transforming nature, history, and human lives. Protestant liberals were fervently concerned to resensitize Christianity itself to the presence and power of God, made manifest as infinite love in the finite person Jesus Christ and ever thereafter through his spirit in the life of the church. Liberals expressed this concern in diverse ways, and necessarily so, they avowed, since matters of infinite spirit and vital faith defied imprisonment in human language or any finite forms. They evoked a multiplicity of expressions, symbolic rather than literal, which must change with changing times.

Amid America's changing times liberals sought to free their churches from bondage to teachings found false or outmoded in light of advances of learning, and to mobilize them for a "higher" moral service to the world. As Christ's was a ministry of selfless love on behalf of others, and responsive to their needs, so Christianity's calling was to express God's compassion, promote the moral and material improvement of societies as well as individuals, and extend the benefits of Protestant faith and modern Christian civilization around the globe. The faithful thereby advanced the progress, the "building," of the kingdom of God on earth.

Such views gathered power between 1875 and 1900. They gained visibility in Disciples circles in the 1890s. With the founding of the Disciples Divinity House at the University of Chicago in 1894 and the Campbell Institute in 1896, they gained their first institutional bases. Liberal attitudes and interests were already spreading by then, reinforced by increasing relations between Disciples and Protestantism's liberals in colleges and seminaries, in ministers' meetings and civic groups, and in evangelistic, educational, benevolent, and moral crusades, including home and foreign missions. Concerns of "Brotherhood" enterprises (Social Gospel, ecumenics, etc.) are better leading indicators of Disciples liberalization than are scattered instances of ministers and laity endorsing liberal scholarship, biblical higher criticism, or Darwinian science. The ideals, spirit, and causes of liberalism, conveyed mainly by "middle class" sociocultural trends, attracted Disciples before, and more than, its avant-garde intellectualism did.

Early twentieth-century Disciples modernist Edward Scribner Ames (1870-1958) taught philosophy at the University of Chicago, was minister of the Hyde Park (later University) Christian Church in Chicago, and dean of the Disciples Divinity House of the University of Chicago.
Courtesy of the Disciples of Christ Historical Society

The Disciples "Brotherhood" underwent institutional liberalization between 1910 and 1930 and acquired sociological status as a "mainline denomination." Liberal victory in the College of the Bible "heresy trial" paralleled similar conflicts in Protestantism's schools, as did disagreements over international organization, open membership, and ecumenism. Identification with "mainline" — "liberal" — churches persisted thereafter, despite the wide diversity of Disciples' opinion (much of it antiliberal) and long after signature themes of classical liberal theology had yielded to in-coming theological movements. The liberal label remained apt mainly, perhaps only, because such features and changes were characteristic of churches whose histories included passage through "the liberal era."

The era of Disciples *theological* liberalism extends roughly from 1910 to 1950. All of the leading types of liberal thinking found their Disciples representatives, from progressive Christianity, personalism, the Social Gospel, and pragmatism to empirical, naturalist, and process theologies. The most popular, influential forms were evangelical (Christocentric) liberalism and modernistic liberalism, often conflated as modernist (versus fundamentalist), but not altogether identical. The former sought from biblical studies, and particularly studies of "the historical Jesus," the basic beliefs and values of the Christian faith demanding expression in up-to-date terms and actions. The latter examined Christianity, like other religions, for examples of and resources for contributions to humanity's growth in understanding and devotion to civilized ideals. Both liberalisms coexisted among Disciples at Chicago, where Herbert L. Willett was a classic evangelical liberal and Edward Scribner Ames, author of the liberal manifesto *The New Orthodoxy* (1918), was a no-nonsense exponent of modernism.

Most Disciples liberals were "mixed types." Peter Ainslie, for example, had little interest in reformulating church doctrine; his causes were Christian unity and world peace. Many other famed tall-steeple preachers — Edgar DeWitt Jones, to cite just one — were intentionally eclectic and practically minded. Social concern advocates were many; leaders included Alva W. Taylor, Joseph B. Hunter, Walter Sikes, James A. Crain, and Harold Fey. William Clayton Bower urged coming generations to employ current pedagogy in Christian (preferably religious) education. Psychology, especially psychology of religion, influenced studies of worship and stimulated the pastoral care and counseling movement. Historical and comparative studies of world religions entered into missionary training. In terms of "history as biography," the career of Charles Clayton Morrison is a window on Protestant liberalism at large and among Disciples. His life experiences, writings, and editorial oversight of the *Christian Century* record the vast range, variations, twists, and turns of liberalism. Morrison also identified early on, in the phrase "the liberalism of neo-orthodoxy," the thrust and tenor of theological thinking that many Disciples after World War II adopted in place of then "old" liberal views. Frederick Kershner, a moderate Disciples editor, theologian, and academician, went even further than Morrison. Though sympathetic to aspects of the Social Gospel and a declared pacifist, Kershner wearied of ideological liberalism in relation to the original plea of the Stone-Campbell Movement and became increasingly sympathetic to certain features of Neo-Orthodoxy (especially Barth's theology of the Word), particularly after the rise of Hitler's Third Reich.

Liberals were not invariably fond of the word "theology" or inclined to revisit historic debates over doctrine. To many, the word was a relic of bygone days, and immoderate concern for doctrinal tradition was an obstacle to fulfilling the church's mission. Liberals specialized in exploring the human side of faith and faithfulness. Theology and philosophy figured in these studies, but historical, social scientific, and ethical inquiries were deemed more illumining and productive — and needed to keep philosophy and theology close to actual experience and biblical, "practical" Christianity. Hence liberals typically interpreted the Scriptures and church traditions *in terms of* their origins and forms within human history, their roles in and effects on believers' lives, and their social implications.

This was the approach taken by the foremost historians of Stone-Campbell Disciples history. Liberals undertook to write the first genuinely critical histories of the Movement and founded a long-lasting liberal historiographical tradition. The dominant, though not lone, historian was Winfred E. Garrison, who deployed the full arsenal of "Chicago School" learning, including "the frontier thesis" concerning American Christianity made famous by Frederick Jackson Turner. The liberal historians had unusually significant influence in shaping Disciples' self-identity in the "creedless," free-church Brotherhood. Liberal historiography told of a people who abandoned the old world of dogmatism and ecclesiasticism, made a fresh start in Christian living, and by relying on the Bible's original, simple teachings, their intelligence and adaptability, and much hard work for Christ's cause, progressed, as did their nation, to greatness. Despite liberal historiography's manifold merits, its minimization of theological content and its accentuation of Americanism in the Stone-Campbell heritage left Disciples scrambling for resources and clear direction in face of the changes and challenges of the last half of the twentieth century.

See also Ainslie, Peter; Ames, Edward Scribner; Bible, Interpretation of the; *Christian Century, The;* Creation and Evolution; Disciples Divinity House; Fey, Harold

Edward; Fundamentalism; Garrison, Winfred Ernest; Historiography, Stone-Campbell Movement; Jones, Edgar De Witt; Kershner, Frederick D.; Morrison, Charles Clayton; Pinkerton, Lewis Letig; "Plea," The; Willett, Herbert Lockwood

BIBLIOGRAPHY Edward Scribner Ames, *The New Orthodoxy* (1918; 2nd ed. 1925) • George G. Beazley, Jr., ed., *The Christian Church (Disciples of Christ): An Interpretative Examination in the Cultural Context* (1973) • M. Eugene Boring, *Disciples and the Bible: A History of Disciples Biblical Interpretation in North America* (1997) • Gary Dorrien, *The Making of American Liberal Theology,* vol. 1 (2003) • William R. Hutchison, *The Modernist Impulse in American Protestantism* (1992) • Charles Clayton Morrison, *What Is Christianity?* (1940) • Mark G. Toulouse, *Joined in Discipleship: The Shaping of a Contemporary Disciples Identity* (2nd ed. 1997) • H. L. Willett et al., eds., *Progress: Anniversary Volume of the Campbell Institute on the Completion of Twenty Years of History* (1917) • D. Newell Williams, ed., *A Case Study of Mainstream Protestantism: The Disciples' Relation to American Culture, 1880-1989* (1991). JAMES O. DUKE

Liberty

Principle of ecclesiastical freedom embraced by the Stone-Campbell Movement, sometimes in concert with the idealization of American political freedom.

The Stone-Campbell Movement was birthed within the era of the early American Republic, when the young nation was still processing, both politically and culturally, the idealized right to life, liberty, and the pursuit of happiness, and when it was still coming to grips with the constitutional separation of church and state. American religious culture in the time of Barton Stone and the Campbells, moreover, was deeply influenced by the so-called Didactic Enlightenment (viz., Lockean epistemology, Baconian science, and Scottish Common Sense philosophy), by Jeffersonian democratic idealism, and by principles of religious toleration inherited from John Locke and other prophetic figures.

Many in the early Stone-Campbell Movement believed that the American Republic signaled a *novus ordo seclorum* ("new order of the ages") that would thoroughly transcend the constraints of the political and ecclesiastical systems of the Old World — the vestiges of which these leaders saw in the theological intolerance and clericalism of their own Presbyterian tradition. The "restoration of New Testament Christianity" would intrinsically entail a liberation of individual consciences, the only restraining principle being a common agreement on, and submission to, what Thomas Campbell, in his *Declaration and Address* (1809), called the "self-evident" truths of apostolic Scripture.

Yet the Campbells and other early leaders were keen students of the New Testament's own ideal of liberty, and in analyzing it they typically did not distinguish between freedom as a soteriological notion (cf. Gal. 5:1; John 8:32) and freedom as an ecclesiological principle. The freedom to which Christ liberated sinners was to be exercised not as sheer individual fiat but in community with other believers. Freedom was to be nurtured as a crucial, if fragile, ecclesial virtue.

Liberty was a key theme in the *Declaration and Address,* as Thomas Campbell urged fellow Christians to "resume that precious, that dear bought liberty, wherewith Christ has made his people free; a liberty from subjection to any authority but his own, in matters of religion." Campbell envisioned his reformation in one sense as a mutual exercise in this very liberty, an honoring of genuine freedom of opinion in matters of theological inference that would nonetheless demand the most astute discipline and cultivation.

If Thomas Campbell represented the irenic side of this appeal for freedom, its polemical edge was manifested in Barton Stone, who described his own spiritual pilgrimage as one of transition from the "labyrinth of Calvinism" into the "rich pastures of Gospel liberty." Scholastic Reformed theology, in his judgment, was a "clog on Christianity," a bondage of free consciences, obscuring believers' access to the simple and reasonable testimony of the gospel. Liberation not only from speculative theologies but also from ecclesiastical hierarchy was imperative. When Stone and the other founders of the Springfield Presbytery took issue with the Synod of Kentucky for their ill-treatment of Richard McNemar, Stone describes how he and his colleagues drew up their own "declaration of independence," a formal protest asserting that they no longer acknowledged the Synod's jurisdiction.

The Springfield Presbytery that embodied this protest, however, proved a short-lived venture since its ultimate demonstration of liberation was precisely to disband. The *Last Will and Testament of the Springfield Presbytery* (1804) resounds the liberty theme. Legislative bodies are to end in order to grant "the people" a "free course to the Bible." Congregations are to resume their "native right of internal government." They are to support their ministers by a "free will offering." Stone thus envisioned the unified church as a free association of Christians consolidated solely through mutual obedience to the commands of the gospel.

Alexander Campbell, in what Anthony Dunnavant and others have identified as his "providential worldview," championed the cause of ecclesiastical liberation in tandem with growing confidence in the new political system of the American republic. The global triumph of "New Testament Christianity" in the millennium would be paralleled by the global advance of American democratic institutions. In 1830 Campbell asserted in an *Oration in Honor of the Fourth of July* that the American Revolution was but "the precursor of a revolution of infinitely more importance for mankind . . . the emancipation of the human mind from the shackles of superstition, and the introduction of human beings into the full fruition of the reign of heaven." By 1852, in his address *On the Destiny of Our Country,* he hardly restrained his enthusiasm for the unique millennial mission of Britain and America as standard bearers of true Protestantism: "To Protestant America and Protestant England, young gentlemen, the world must look for its emancipation from the most heartless spiritual despotism that ever disfranchised, enslaved and degraded human kind. This is our special mission into the world as a nation and a people; and for this purpose the Ruler of nations has raised us up and made us the wonder and the admiration of the world."

An important test case in realizing this "liberating" millennial hope was the internal controversy over slavery and the Civil War. Disciples abolitionists believed it a matter of biblical and moral principle that the liberating gospel of Jesus Christ could never abide the social reality of human slavery. Gradualists like Campbell, however, cautioned against raising the civil liberties of slaves above the liberty (of social, political, and theological convictions) practiced and protected in the church. For Campbell and others of the same mind, it simply was not an option to seek the liberation of slaves precisely through an ecclesiastical *coercion* of Christian slaveholders.

Second- and third-generation Disciples, sobered by the tragedy of the Civil War, reacted differently to Campbell's millennial vision of liberating the church, and, through the church partnered with the nation, liberating the world. Harvey Everest (1831-1900), one-time president of Butler University, appropriated Campbell's vision and saw the Disciples' role as one of progressive kingdom-building. "The Germanic tribes," he wrote, "stood for individual liberty and social equality, while it seems to be the work of the Anglo-Saxon race to bring the whole world under the sway of Christian civilization." David Lipscomb, strong voice of the Churches of Christ, articulated a dissenting view in his book on *Civil Government* (1910), which distanced commitment to the restoration of New Testament Christianity from any collusion with earthly governments, even that of the United States. Freedom in Christ could never be compared or confused with the freedoms allegedly guaranteed by self-interested human regimes.

Meanwhile numerous standard bearers of the Movement concentrated simply on reclaiming Thomas Campbell's ecumenical appeal for the unity of Christians on essential truths amid respectful freedom of opinion in all other matters. Isaac Errett, in his influential statement *Our Position* (1873), indicated faith in the person of Christ as divine Savior, and obedience to his explicit commands, as the bottom line of unity. "In judgments merely inferential," Errett added, "we reach conclusions as nearly unanimous as we can; and where we fail, exercise forbearance, in the confidence that God will lead us into final agreement. In matters of expediency, where we are left free to follow our own best judgment, we allow the majority to rule. In matters of opinion that is, matters touching which the Bible is either silent or so obscure in its revelations as not to admit of definite conclusions we allow the largest liberty, so long as none judges his brother, or insists on forcing his own opinion on others, or on making them an occasion of strife."

Errett, like other Disciples before him, echoed Peter Meiderlin's famous dictum, "In essentials unity, in non-essentials liberty, in all things charity." The continuing challenge for the Stone-Campbell Movement was to discern the reasonable limits of freedom in Christ. At the Centennial Convention in Pittsburgh in 1909, W. E. Crabtree (1868-1930), a San Diego minister, admonished the Disciples not to allow their strong appeal for freedom of individual conscience to give way to an unhealthy individualism such as had already fostered the proliferation of denominations in America.

Not surprisingly, liberty was a central theme amid the two historic divisions in the Stone-Campbell Movement. At the time of the division between Disciples and Churches of Christ, David Lipscomb, in his book *Christian Unity* (1910), interpreted the dilemma in terms of the Disciples having *exaggerated* liberty to the point of compromising the churches' ability to unite on the self-evident truths and commands of Scripture. Church history, argued Lipscomb, admitted of two basic groups, the (restorationist) faithful who sought to determine and apply what the Bible demands for the sake of genuine unity, and those more liberally disposed, who, in their own self-interest, pressed the frontiers of what the Bible would allow. Churches of Christ thus represented the former, Disciples the latter.

By contrast, forebears of the Christian Churches/Churches of Christ in the early twentieth century often pled their case in terms of a *violation* of the liberty of individual consciences on the part of "denominational" agencies and executives of the Disciples. They protested what they perceived as an emerging ecclesiasticism that would effectively preempt the rights and prerogatives of local congregations. In response, when the Disciples reorganized in the 1960s and 1970s under the Restructure design, theorists of the new plan (e.g., Ronald E. Osborn) insisted that Restructure's intention was simply the exercise of a more responsible freedom. The general, regional, congregational, and individual components of the new polity were to be held together in "free and voluntary relationships" by "a covenant of mutual consent." As Osborn insisted, the design "empowers the church through its General Assembly to develop policies and procedures for the whole, which will be interpreted and administered by the regions, at the same time granting the right of any member or congregation to dissent 'in love' from an action taken by the larger body."

Churches of Christ, Christian Churches/Churches of Christ, and the Christian Church (Disciples of Christ) all therefore have claimed in their respective ways to manifest the ideal of liberty of the founding generation of the Stone-Campbell Movement.

See also *Consensus Fidelium; Declaration and Address;* Democratization; Expedients; *Last Will and Testament of Springfield Presbytery;* Local Autonomy; Slavery, The Movement and; Slogans

BIBLIOGRAPHY Alexander Campbell, "Oration in Honor of the Fourth of July, 1830," *Popular Lectures and Addresses* (1866), pp. 367-78 • Alexander Campbell, "The Destiny of Our Country," *Popular Lectures and Addresses* (1866), pp. 163-85 • Thomas Campbell, *Declaration and Address* (1809) • W. E. Crabtree, "Liberty — Union — Charity," in *Centennial Convention Report,* ed. W. R. Warren (1909), pp. 497-500 • Isaac Errett, *Our Position* (1873), reprinted in *Documents Advocating Christian Union,* ed. C. H. Young (1904), pp. 289-314 • Nathan O. Hatch, "The Christian Movement and the Demand for a Theology of the People," *Journal of American History* 67 (1980): 545-67 • Nathan O. Hatch, *The Democratization of American Christianity* (1989) • Richard T. Hughes and C. Leonard Allen, *Illusions of Innocence: Protestant Primitivism in America, 1630-1875* (1988) • Richard T. Hughes, Anthony L. Dunnavant, and Paul M. Blowers, *Founding Vocation and Future Vision: The Self-Understanding of Disciples of Christ and Churches of Christ* (1999) • David Lipscomb, *Christian Unity: How Promoted, How Destroyed* (1910) • William Moorhouse, "The Restoration Movement: The Rhetoric of Jacksonian Restorationism in a Frontier Religion" (unpublished Ph.D. dissertation, Indiana University, 1968) • Ronald E. Osborn, *Experiment in Liberty: The Ideal of Freedom in the Experience of the Disciples of Christ* (1978) • John Rogers, with Barton Stone, *The Biography of Elder Barton Warren Stone* (1847).

PAUL M. BLOWERS

Ligon, David Sylvester (1866-1956)

Preacher and pioneer in the graphic arts in the Stone-Campbell Movement.

Ligon was born in Hopkins County, Kentucky, and reared in Arkansas. Ligon's extensive education included William Henry Krutsinger's Bible Training School, Georgie Robertson Christian College, and graduate degrees from the Christian College of Oskaloosa, Iowa.

As an itinerant evangelist, Ligon by his own account "never served as a local evangelist," although he "preached at a few places for a period of a year or more." He engaged in several debates and often lectured on evolution. In that interest he published *The Baylor Reptile* and *Dr. Dart's Origin of Man and Scientific Problems Exposed.*

Best known for graphic art and photography, Ligon first issued "Ligon's Portraiture of Gospel Preachers" in 1899, featuring likenesses of 196 preachers. In 1901 he added sixty-four portraits, and in this form the 36-by-26-inch print sold for $2.00 postpaid. In 1906 Ligon published *The Divine Library,* a Bible chart printed on good cloth, 60 by 36 inches, selling for $1.75. By 1907 he offered a 20-by-21-inch chromograph, "Two Ways of Life," a visual aid for sermons. Ligon produced temperance postcards, poems, and pictures with Bible themes until his death in 1956.

See also Evangelism, Evangelists — The Nineteenth Century

BIBLIOGRAPHY Charles Ready Nichol, *Gospel Preachers Who Blazed The Trail* (1911; repr. 1955).

TERRY J. GARDNER

Lincoln Christian College and Seminary

Christian Churches/Churches of Christ college in Lincoln, Illinois, providing undergraduate and graduate education.

Perceiving the widespread need in the Midwest and nationwide for ministerial leadership, Earl C. Hargrove, minister of Lincoln Christian Church from 1937 to 1950, led a number of concerned individuals in conceiving a school in Lincoln, Illinois, for training preachers and church workers. On February 24, 1944, at a statewide evangelistic rally at Lincoln Christian Church, Hargrove announced, "The preachers are coming." After recruiting funds, faculty, and students, Lincoln Bible Institute (LBI) began in the fall of 1944.

Meeting the first year in rented quarters of nearby Lincoln College, LBI soon purchased a downtown Lincoln building that served the school from 1945 until 1951. In 1950 ground was broken for a new campus east of Lincoln. By 1961 dormitories and other facilities were dedicated. In 1966 Restoration Hall was dedicated to house the graduate seminary. The next decade saw the construction of a chapel and additional housing.

Lincoln Bible Institute adjoined a seminary in 1951 with Enos Dowling (1905-1997), a scholar of Stone-Campbell history, as its first dean. In 1961 LBI became Lincoln Christian College (LCC), and its graduate school became Lincoln Christian Seminary (LCS). In 1984 the two officially adopted the combined name of Lincoln Christian College and Seminary (LCCS).

Today the Lincoln campus of LCCS consists of fourteen major buildings on over 200 acres. The Library and Media Center have about 125,000 volumes, as well as access privileges to other libraries in Illinois. LCCS offers programs at the Chicago Center for Urban Mission, LCC East (Bel Air, Maryland), and Restoration House (Manchester, New Hampshire).

LCC offers A.A., B.S., and B.A. degrees. Bachelor degree students have a Bible/theology major, with second majors offered in several areas of ministry: preaching, evangelism/church planting, youth ministry, cross-cultural ministry (missions or bivocational missions), Christian education, small groups, family life, children, early childhood, music, and Christian business administration. LCS offers five degrees: Master of Divinity, Master of Arts, Master of Arts in Counseling Ministry, Master of Arts in Urban Mission, and Master of Arts in Ministry to Muslims. The Master of Arts offers four majors, with several areas of concentration in each: Bible (general Bible, Old Testament, New Testament, biblical languages); Christian theology (church history/historical theology, contemporary Christian theology and philosophy, Christian apologetics); leadership ministry (preaching, Christian education, pastoral care and counseling, general ministry); world mission/church growth (missions, church growth, new church planting, Bible translation).

LCCS is accredited by the North Central Association of Colleges and Schools. In addition, the Association of Theological Schools in the United States and Canada accredits the seminary and the Accrediting Association of Bible Colleges accredits the college.

LCCS alumni have served in nearly every state and in over fifty-seven countries around the world. Graduates have served or are serving in pastoral and other associate ministries in Christian Churches/Churches of Christ, in institutional chaplaincies, and in international mission work. Numerous graduates also serve on the faculties of colleges and seminaries supported by Christian Churches/Churches of Christ.

See also Bible College Movement; Dowling, Enos; Higher Education, Views of in the Movement

BIBLIOGRAPHY Alan W. Kline, "A Vision and Its Fulfillment: Earl C. Hargrove and Lincoln Christian College, 1944-1972" (unpublished M.A. thesis, Lincoln Christian Seminary, 1973) • Gene R. Shepherd, *Born to Preach: The Life and Ministry of Earl C. Hargrove* (1993).

ROBERT F. REA

Lindsay, Vachel (1879-1931)

Disciples of Christ poet.

Nicholas Vachel Lindsay was born in Springfield, Illinois, November 10, 1879, and died December 5, 1931. His father was a physician, and his mother was quite artistic and an ardent member of the Movement of Kentucky heritage.

Vachel Lindsay (as he was commonly known) finished high school in 1897, attended Hiram College in Ohio with the thought of entering the ministry, and then studied art at the Chicago Art Institute from 1900 to 1908. While at Chicago he worked in Marshall Field's wholesale department. In 1905 he began lecturing for the YMCA, and this led to his famous walking tours of America, reciting, often chanting, his own verses and poetry and selling his drawings and poems for food and travel.

His first book of poetry, *General William Booth Enters Into Heaven and Other Poems,* attracted little attention when it was published in 1913, but his 1914 successor, *The Camp and Other Poems,* met with popular acclaim. He became one of the best-known American

Possibly best known for his widely published "Abraham Lincoln Walks at Midnight," Vachel Lindsay (1890-1931) also wrote poems reflective of his Stone-Campbell heritage, including "Alexander Campbell" and "A Rhymed Address to All Renegade Campbellites Exhorting Them to Return."
Courtesy of the Disciples of Christ Historical Society

poets, and his *Abraham Lincoln Walks at Midnight* is found in a number of American anthologies.

On May 18, 1928, he was married to Elizabeth Connor of Spokane, Washington. Their union produced two children, a son and a daughter.

Lindsay remained a staunch member of the Movement throughout his years. His famous poem "The Congo" was dedicated to Roy Eldred and was written (some have said) after hearing a mission program on the Congo work of the Foreign Christian Missionary Society of the Disciples of Christ. His poems "Alexander Campbell" and "A Rhymed Address to All Renegade Campbellites Exhorting Them to Return" were directed toward those who would deny their Campbellian heritage. His sister, Olive Wakefield, was a Disciples of Christ missionary and contributed a sketch of her relationship with her brother to the *Shane Quarterly*. An outstanding American poet, Lindsay was also a stout "Campbellite."

BIBLIOGRAPHY Perry E. Gresham, *The Bronco That Could Not Be Broken* (1986) • Nicholas V. Lindsay, *Collected Poems* (1925) • *The Shane Quarterly* Nos. 2 and 3 (April-July 1944), Vachel Lindsay Number, article by his sister, Olive Lindsay Wakefield, and others.

CHARLES R. GRESHAM

Lipscomb, David (1831-1917)

Tennessee preacher, educator, and editor of the *Gospel Advocate* for forty-six years.

David Lipscomb was the son of Granville and Ann Lipscomb of Franklin County, Tennessee. His parents left the Baptist church to follow the reformation ideas of Alexander Campbell near the time of David's birth. Convinced that the Bible condemned slavery, the Lipscombs moved with their slaves to Illinois in 1834 to set them free. The impact of this event helped to form David's adult understanding that Christianity does not allow racial division of the church. The next year, while still in Illinois, Ann Lipscomb and three of her children died of fever following a flood of the prairie east of Springfield. After the family returned to Tennessee, in 1846 his father sent him to Franklin College near Nashville to study under Tolbert Fanning. Lipscomb graduated in 1849. By his own admission, he was not a good speaker. However, he decided to preach as long as he could do some good. He often crossed battle lines during the Civil War to minister to churches that otherwise would not have any instruction.

The events of the Civil War greatly changed David Lipscomb. Prior to the conflict, he had been a confirmed advocate of American democracy, even calling it "the first fruits of Christianity." However, four years of viewing the war up close caused him to change his entire emphasis on the Christian religion. During the war he had begun a study of the relationship of the Christian and government. In fact, he was often considered a traitor, especially to the South, because he preached against Christians' participation in war. The immediate outcome of his changed emphasis was the acceptance of a Mennonite-like position toward the Christian and government. Although he had voted in the national elections of 1856 and 1860, he no longer believed that Christians should go to war or participate in government. He based his views on the idea of two kingdoms — the kingdom of God and the kingdom of the world. This idea caused him to reassess his views of the church, education, and all relationships in the world. He included his views on government in a series of articles that appeared in the *Gospel Advocate* following the Civil War, later published as a book titled *Civil Government*. His critics believed that he was bitter because the South had lost the war. Southerners, who became confirmed Democrats after the Civil War, accused him of being a "black Republican." However, he believed his newly discovered positions were basic to his understanding of Christianity.

The Civil War years were not all negative for Lipscomb. In 1862 he married Margaret Zellner of Maury County, Tennessee. Living first in Lawrence County, they moved to Bell's Bend (Davidson County) in 1863 so their child could be born in their own home. Margaret gave birth to Zellner on September 25, 1863. Nine months later, on June 25, 1864, Zellner died. Constructing a box for a coffin, the grieving young couple crossed Federal and Confederate lines to bury Zellner in her family cemetery in Maury County. Unable to have other children, the Lipscombs opened their home to numerous children, especially those of their brothers and sisters.

Lipscomb was influenced by a number of leaders. As a mature adult, he believed that he had read everything written by Alexander Campbell. His most immediate influence was his teacher, Tolbert Fanning, whom Lipscomb joined after the Civil War to reissue the *Gospel Advocate*. Fanning began publishing the *Advocate* in 1855 to advocate the "true" gospel and to oppose the intrusion of the newly formed American Christian Missionary Society (ACMS) into the nineteenth-century Reformation Movement. Following the bitter strife of the Civil War, the two men believed that Southern members of the Movement needed a voice. Although Fanning participated in the reissue of the *Advocate*, David and Margaret Lipscomb published, edited, and distributed the paper in a region without the financial means to support a religious paper. Although he never formally committed to publishing the *Advocate*, Lipscomb nevertheless continued as publisher and editor for forty-six years.

Although Lipscomb emerged from the Civil War with a Southern bias, he was never as bitter as his mentor Fanning. In fact, he believed that if the war had done nothing more than free the slaves, it had served a good purpose. However, Lipscomb did not allow Northern members to escape without a challenge. Because the American Christian Missionary Society had supported the North in the war, he refused to sell Campbell's hymnal, now owned by the ACMS, through the *Gospel Advocate,* calling it "bloodstained." Lipscomb had visited among the churches in Kentucky looking for an editor for the paper, even approaching John W. McGarvey. But Lipscomb was finally told that if the *Advocate* did not support the Society, the Kentucky-society Disciples would not support the *Advocate.*

Besides his opposition to the missionary society, Lipscomb opposed the use of instruments in worship. Conscious that he was tone deaf, he was not quick to make a decision on instruments. His earliest statement on the issue suggested a very conservative view of Scripture: Why accept something that is doubtful when it is possible to do something known to be acceptable to God? His final position on the instrument was enunciated in 1878, advocating a strong a cappella position.

Although the missionary society and the use of instruments were important issues for Lipscomb, his most significant disagreement with the Disciples had to do with German liberal theology, which he believed had invaded the Disciples through the pages of the *Christian-Evangelist* and the Disciples House at the University of Chicago. He held James H. Garrison, editor of the *Christian-Evangelist,* Alexander Proctor, George W. Longan, and Herbert L. Willett responsible for leading the Disciples in a new direction, far removed from the positions of Thomas and Alexander Campbell. Although Lipscomb read only part of German theology (it put him to sleep), he strongly endorsed John W. McGarvey's writings against higher criticism. Though he gave ample space to the call for the celebration of the fiftieth anniversary of the founding of the American Christian Missionary Society in 1899, he could not participate. In 1909, the hundredth anniversary of Thomas Campbell's *Declaration and Address,* Lipscomb noted in the *Advocate* the internal conflicts in the Christian Churches. He was not surprised at the conflict caused by Garrison and Willett on one side and the editors and writers of the *Christian Standard* on the other.

Lipscomb's Christianity had a very practical dimension as well as a controversial one. Besides dealing with the issues that dominated the late nineteenth century, Lipscomb reached out to those in need. The South was destitute following the Civil War, especially across northern Georgia and northern Alabama. Through the pages of the *Gospel Advocate,* he, along with Philip Fall and V. M. Metcalf, raised large sums of money from Christians across the United States and received wagonloads of corn and other grains. Churches in Kentucky and Tennessee sent barrels of bacon to the destitute. Years later he looked back on the years 1866-68 as his best work. In 1873 a cholera epidemic struck the city of Nashville. Lipscomb, never a healthy person, chose to remain in the city to care for those who could not escape. Aided by young men from the Christian Church, he did most of his work among the black community unable to flee the city. He and his assistants went into the houses, where they cared for the dying and fed the living. Lipscomb shared his buggy with Catholic sisters who had also remained to help the poor.

As conservative sentiments grew throughout the Midwest and South, Lipscomb became the voice of moderation. Austin McGary, editor of the *Firm Foundation,* called him a liberal. They differed on their understanding of baptism. Daniel Sommer became a critic of Lipscomb. Even though Lipscomb agreed

Editor of the *Gospel Advocate* for forty-six years, and co-founder in 1891 of Nashville Bible School (today Lipscomb University), David Lipscomb exercised tremendous influence on the minds and hearts of Southern members of the Movement after the Civil War. Courtesy of the Center for Restoration Studies, Abilene Christian University

with many of Sommer's conclusions in the *Address and Declaration* of 1889, he could not share the attitude Sommer had toward those with whom he disagreed. Lipscomb, although conservative, was more inclusive than either McGary or Sommer. It is this moderation that he passed on to many conservatives who became known as Churches of Christ, particularly in middle Tennessee. Thus, in 1906, when the director of the U.S. religious census wanted to know if the Disciples of Christ were divided, it was Lipscomb who answered for the conservatives. In his response to Director S. N. D. North, he stated: "There is a distinct people taking the word of God as their only sufficient rule of faith, calling their churches 'churches of Christ' or 'churches of God,' distinct and separate in name, work, or rule of faith, from all other bodies or peoples." Beginning with the first U.S. religious census, Churches of Christ were listed separately from the Disciples of Christ.

From the time Lipscomb attended Franklin College he remained interested in education. He attempted to establish a network of Christian schools in middle Tennessee before the Civil War. After the war, he attempted to rebuild Franklin College. Both efforts failed. However, he supported education, especially where the Bible was taught, through editorials in the *Advocate.* Therefore it was only natural that he, along with his friend James A. Harding, should propose the founding of a new school in Nashville. On October 5, 1891, the two men and William Lipscomb, David's older brother, welcomed nine students to a rented building at 180 Filmore Street. This was the beginning of the Nashville Bible School. Today it continues as Lipscomb University.

Although Lipscomb preached throughout middle Tennessee and southern Kentucky, his greatest contributions came through the Nashville Bible School, the *Gospel Advocate,* and his other writings. His first book-length publication was *Civil Government* (1889). He said at its publication: "It is a question of great importance to the church and Christians. . . . We believe that nothing we ever wrote so nearly affects the vital interests of the church of Christ and of the salvation of the world as this little book." He issued a pamphlet in 1890 titled *Christian Unity: How Promoted, How Destroyed.* Beginning in 1893, Lipscomb authored the *Advocate's* teacher's comments on the International Sunday School lessons. When in 1897 the book of Acts was a theme of the series, instead of simply writing the comments, he authored a commentary on Acts. His other publications, including commentaries on New Testament books, were edited works. Among the most important edited volumes were *Queries and Answers,* edited by J. W. Shepherd. M. C. Kurfees edited a volume titled *Questions and Answers by Lipscomb and (E. G.) Sewell.* Sewell served as coeditor of the *Advocate* after 1870. The best source for understanding Lipscomb's theology is an edited volume by Shepherd, *Salvation from Sin.*

David Lipscomb died on Sunday, November 11, 1917, at the age of 86 in his home, Avalon, on the campus of the Nashville Bible School. E. G. Sewell, who shared the editor's chair with Lipscomb for forty-six years, stated at his funeral: "He has lived a faithful, Christian life, and his life work will live on. That will not die, that will not pass out now as he passes, that will not go down to the grave as he goes to the grave. His life work will go on and on for years to come." His influence continues into the twenty-first century.

See also American Christian Missionary Society; Campbell, Alexander; Fanning, Tolbert; Franklin College; *Gospel Advocate, The;* Lipscomb University; McGarvey, John W.; McGary, Austin; Procter, Alexander; Sewell, Elisha Granville; Shepherd, James Walton; Sommer, Daniel; Willett, Herbert Lockwood

BIBLIOGRAPHY Robert E. Hooper, *Crying in the Wilderness: A Biography of David Lipscomb* (1979) • David Lipscomb, *Civil Government: Its Origin, Mission and Destiny, and the Christian's Relation to It* (1889, 1913) • David Lipscomb, *Salvation from Sin* (1913) • Earl I. West, *The Life and Times of David Lipscomb* (1954).

ROBERT E. HOOPER

Lipscomb University

School affiliated with Churches of Christ begun as Nashville Bible School in 1891 in Nashville, Tennessee.

The school started with nine students and three faculty: James A. Harding (1848-1922), and brothers David (1831-1917) and William Lipscomb (1829-1908). All three teachers were products of schools within the Stone-Campbell Movement, Harding having graduated from Bethany College and both Lipscombs from Franklin College.

The genesis of the school was in 1889 when James A. Harding came to Nashville for a number of preaching engagements. Lipscomb discussed with Harding his idea for a school where the Bible would be at the heart of the curriculum. Lipscomb's vision was very much like that implemented earlier by Alexander Campbell in his Bethany College. Bible would be part of the course of studies for every student regardless of their vocational choice. Harding liked the idea, but he could not come to Nashville permanently for two years. The school opened October 5, 1891, in a rented building at 180 Filmore Street.

In its third session in 1893 Nashville Bible School moved to a more permanent home on Olympic Street in south Nashville. J. N. Armstrong (1870-1944), later founder of what is now Harding University, questioned the quality of facilities and faculty when he

After studying for three years at Nashville Bible School, Henry Leo Boles (1874-1946) was hired as a faculty member in 1906 to teach philosophy and math. In 1913 the Board named Boles president of the school, a position he held until 1920, then again from 1923 to 1932. He was also an editor and staff writer for the *Gospel Advocate* for many years, and engaged R. H. Boll in a written debate on premillennialism.

first arrived on campus as a student in 1893. After one year, he changed his mind. Following his graduation, he stayed as a member of the faculty and also married the superintendent's daughter, Woodson Harding. When James A. Harding left Nashville in 1901 to establish the Potter Bible College in Bowling Green, Kentucky, Armstrong followed.

The growth of the school prompted David and Margaret Lipscomb to give a large portion of their farm on Granny White Pike to the school in the fall of 1903. Although the buildings were not finished, students arrived in greater numbers than ever before. During the next ten years, William Anderson (1848-1905), Dr. J. S. Ward, and E. A. Elam (1855-1929) gave direction to the school. Lipscomb remained as chairman of the board of trustees until his death.

Following Lipscomb's death in 1917, "Aunt Mag" Lipscomb gave permission to H. Leo Boles (1874-1946), the first graduate of the school to become its president, and the board of trustees to change the name of the school to David Lipscomb College in 1918. The school continued to grow, but the Great Depression and the loss of both men's and women's residence halls by fire placed a burden of debt on the school. Major financial help came from A. M. Burton, founder and president of Nashville's Life and Casualty Insurance Company, Helena Johnson, and a group of Nashville businessmen. The administration of E. H. Ijams raised $325,000 during the 1930s — a tremendous amount considering the difficult times in the American South.

World War II was both bad news and good news for the school. Large numbers of students went into the military, leaving the school with a greatly decreased enrollment. In addition, in 1943 the college faced a trying change of administrations. Batsell Baxter, who had served as president during the early Depression years, again accepted the presidency after the resignation of E. H. Ijams, who had been accused of having premillennial sympathies. Yet this was also a time of planning for the return of military personnel who would seek higher education under the G. I. Bill. A. M. Burton and the newly elected president in 1946, Athens Clay Pullias (1910-1985), made plans to construct new buildings and prepare Lipscomb to become a senior college. The school undertook significant building projects between 1946 and 1953 and received accreditation as a senior college from the Southern Association of Colleges and Schools in December 1954.

Campus facilities were not sufficient to enlarge the student body beyond 1,200 or 1,300 students. Therefore, plans evolved to construct a much needed science building, a dining center, a large high-rise residence hall for men, and an additional residence hall for women. These efforts were completed between 1960 and 1968, increasing the student capacity to over 2,000 and resulting in a significant advance in enrollment.

In 1977 Willard Collins (b. 1915), who had attended the school in the 1930s and served as its vice president since 1944, became president of David Lipscomb College. He succeeded Athens Clay Pullias, who had served as president longer than anyone in the school's history. Pullias had lost his ability to raise funds for the school and had lost the confidence of Churches of Christ in middle Tennessee. The school was in financial difficulty, owing several million dollars to local banks. Collins quickly began mending fences with Lipscomb's patrons and the churches of the area by, among other things, constructing a long-promised high-school gymnasium and other needed facilities. Collins was soon able to pay off the school's debt. The most important academic change at Lipscomb under Collins's administration was the addition of an M.A. degree in Bible that received full accreditation in 1987. This was Lipscomb's first step in graduate studies.

Dr. Harold Hazelip (b. 1930), dean of Harding Graduate School of Religion in Memphis, Tennessee, and a Lipscomb graduate, became president of the school in 1986. Hazelip led in changing the status of the school from college to university in 1988. Because of the M.A. in Bible and the prospect of additional graduate work, the change seemed to be in line with the direction of the school. Under Hazelip's administration the university added graduate programs in education.

During the 1990s the campus expanded dramatically with a new student activities center and university library, as well as buildings for the elementary and secondary schools, and new baseball, softball, and tennis facilities. Lipscomb was among the first colleges to install a campus-wide fiber-optic system for computers.

In 1997 Dr. Hazelip retired as president of the university, succeeded by Dr. Steve Flatt, a 1973 graduate of Lipscomb. In the first two years of Flatt's administration, the university was divided into schools with their own deans. Plans have been implemented to greatly expand the campus. As a part of the School of Business, the university added several M.A. programs in the fall of 1999. In April 2000 the Lipscomb board of directors initiated a $150,000,000 five-year "Lighting the Way" campaign.

From a small beginning in 1891, David Lipscomb's idea of an educational institution to benefit young people has grown into a large enterprise, with 1,500 students in kindergarten through the twelfth grade and more than 2,500 students in the university at the beginning of the twenty-first century. Each student is in a Bible class and chapel service every school day.

See also Bethany College; Fanning, Tolbert; Franklin College; *Gospel Advocate, The;* Harding, James Alexander; Harding University; Ijams, E. H.; Lipscomb, David; Potter Bible College

BIBLIOGRAPHY Robert E. Hooper, *Crying in the Wilderness: A Biography of David Lipscomb* (1979) • Robert E. Hooper and G. David England, *A Century of Memories: Centennial Celebration, David Lipscomb University, 1891-1991* (1992) • Robert E. Hooper and Jim Turner, *G. Willard Collins: The People Person* (1986).

ROBERT E. HOOPER

Literature

Many poets, novelists, and playwrights have been associated with the Movement in varying degrees. Some have enjoyed writing as a hobby, while others have written as part of their life's work. Many have just "dabbled" in writing, sometimes publishing a one-time novel or book of poetry, but more often collecting their manuscripts for their own enjoyment and that of their friends and family. The contributors include both ministers and lay people. Out of all these poets and novelists many have become widely read, and others have had limited readership.

The Disciples of Christ Historical Society has in its catalog more than 250 novels, 550 publications of poems, and 200 plays written by constituents of the Movement. Claude Spencer, in the 1940s, published a list of poets and novelists that contains over 125 names of poets and over 100 names of novelists. If additions had been made over the subsequent years, Spencer's list would at least have doubled by the year 2000. Although this is by no means a complete list of published authors, it is an indication that members of the Movement have made very significant contributions to American literature.

Many of the novels and collections of poetry and some of the plays are meditative in nature. They were meant to reinforce a reader's dedication to Christ and move him or her toward leading a more Christian life. Several of the poems and plays were written specifically to be used in Church School exercises and entertainments.

Harold Bell Wright (1872-1944) wrote novels about Kentucky life, as did James Lane Allen (1849-1925) and John Uri Lloyd (1849-1936). Interestingly, these novels tended to be very moralistic. For example, in 1901 Allen published his novel *Warick of the Knobs,* in which the main character denies any possible redemption for those who do not follow the same narrow, judgmental, and vindictive God he did. On the other hand, Wright's 1919 novel *The Re-creation of Brian Kent* was a story of redemption made possible through human love and trust.

General Lew Wallace (1827-1905) of Crawfordsville, Indiana, wrote about early Christian times in his best-selling *Ben Hur,* twice produced as a motion picture. Fannie Caldwell Macauley (1863-1941) wrote "romantic" novels. MacKinley Kantor (1904-1977) and Peter Clark McFarlane (1871-1924) wrote historical novels. Wayne D. Overholser wrote novels about the West. Louis Cochran (1899-1974) composed novels concerning the history of the Stone-Campbell Movement itself, including one about the history of the Disciples, *Captives of the Word* (1969), another about the life of Alexander Campbell, *The Fool of God* (1958), and still another entitled *Raccoon John Smith* (1963).

Writers such as Adalaid Gail Frost (1868-1928) wrote novels centered on the mission fields of the Disciples of Christ, and Lulu Linton wrote short novels that highlighted the work of the Christian Woman's Board of Missions. Jessie Brown Pounds (1861-1921) wrote "inspirational" novels as well as many poems. A common theme for Mrs. Pounds was Alexander Campbell and his desire to return to the faith and practices of the New Testament. This was especially true in her final novel, *Rachel Sylvestrie,* published in 1904.

Children's literature is another outstanding genre for writers of the Campbell Stone Movement. Alice Caldwell Hegan Rice (1870-1942) wrote *Mrs. Wiggs of the Cabbage Patch* and other children's stories that were quite popular in their day. More recently, Mary Blair Immel and Diane Himmelheber have written novels for young people. Bob Hartman (b. 1955), a minister and writer of the Christian Churches/Churches of Christ, has been an accomplished writer of children's books, including *The Wolf Who Cried Boy* (2002), *The Lion Storyteller Bedtime Book* (2003), *Grumblebunny* (2003), *Easter Angels* (1999), *Early Saints of God* (1998), and *Angels, Angels All Around* (1993).

Several well-known missionaries, ministers, and leaders in the Movement wrote novels. David Roberts Dungan (1837-1920) wrote *On the Rock,* a very popular novel that went through many printings. James Challen (1802-1878), Samuel Harden Church (1858-1943), Abram E. Cory (1873-1952), Charles Dietze (1919-1996), Marion Duncan (1896-1977), Jack Finegan (b. 1908), Burris Jenkins (1869-1945), and Ashley Johnson (1857-1925) were also among these novelists. Frederick Kershner (1875-1953), former dean and professor at the Butler University School of Religion and chair of the Commission on Restudy in the 1940s, was an accomplished literary critic. Marti Steussy, a Disciples professor of biblical interpretation at Christian Theological Seminary in Indianapolis, has published two science fiction novels, *Forest in the Night* (1987) and *Dreams of Dawn* (1988).

There have been uncountable poets within the Stone-Campbell Movement. Most of these were often privately published and had a very limited audience. Some of the better-known poets wrote for religious publications. This poetry was often published later in book form. The topics were not of necessity overtly religious in nature.

Thomas Curtis Clark (1877-1953) wrote poems for the *Christian Century.* Helen Louise Welshimer (1901-1954) wrote for publications associated with the Christian Churches/Churches of Christ as well as for *Good Housekeeping* and the *Chicago Tribune.* Samuel Frank Pugh (b. 1904) wrote for *World Call* and the *Christian-Evangelist* and then had them published privately. Patrick Overton (fl. 1970s to present), a Missouri minister, wrote a book of poems and has written critiques of literature. William Thomas Moore (1832-1926) and Mayme Garner Miller are among those who contributed regularly to periodical publications of the Movement.

Among the poets who were better known by those outside the Movement are Marshall Wingfield (1893-1961), who later became an Episcopalian, Chauncey Roscoe Piety (1885-1972), Charles Edwin Markham (1852-1940), Nicholas Vachel Lindsay (1879-1931), and Winfred Ernest Garrison (1874-1969). A well-known minister whose poems were often set to music, many times his own compositions, is Carlton Buck (b. 1901).

Many of the plays by Stone-Campbell Movement playwrights were written as Church School exercises or youth projects. Eleanor Bang Stock, Beulah Gertrude Squires, Maude Taylor Sarvis, Grace Winifred McGavran (b. 1896), Mabel Anna Niedermeyer McCaw (b. 1899), Harold Franklin Humbert (1893-1980), Hazel Florence Harker (1887-1964), Ellean Lemon Hale (b. 1914), Lois Anna Ely (1888-1972), Lucy King DeMoss, Mary Beckwith Butchart (1890-1981), Elizabeth C. Blosser (d. 1952), and Elma Newell Atkins (1882-1970) contributed to this useful collection. In more recent times Gayle Schoepf and Marjorie Lee Reinstedt Lester have written plays dealing with Stone-Campbell history. By the beginning of the twenty-first century Max Lucado of Churches of Christ had become a widely read author. His contributions included several children's books as well as adult devotional literature.

DAVID I. MCWHIRTER *and*
DONNA J. MCWHIRTER

Living Oracles

See Bible, Versions and Translations of the

Local Autonomy

The principle of the integrity and self-government of the local congregation in the broader body of the church.

In the post-Revolutionary era, amid the growing momentum of populism and democratization in a variety of cultural expressions, leaders of the Stone-Campbell Movement and other "restoration" movements pursued sweeping reforms aimed at undermining hierarchical ecclesiastical government and returning to what they believed was an apostolic principle of the rights of the local church to conduct its own affairs. An important example had already been set in Scotland in the eighteenth and early nineteenth century by a cluster of Scottish restorationists (John Glas, Robert Sandeman, and later the Haldane brothers and Greville Ewing) who considered local congregational independence a priority in the recovery of apostolic Christianity.

In America in 1792, James O'Kelly (1735-1826), along with several other Methodist ministers, formed the Republican Methodist Church over the question of the right of ministers to determine their own preaching itinerary. In 1794 they adopted the name "Christian Church" and declared complete equality among preachers. Though conferences continued to be held, their role was purely advisory. In a separate movement, Elias Smith (1769-1846) and Abner Jones (1772-1841) left the New England Baptists so as to establish independent congregations. Jones was ordained by a Freewill Baptist Association, but as a "Christian Minister." Both Jones and Smith declared that association meetings were too directive and therefore discouraged such gatherings. These "Christian Connexion" churches did, however, ordain through the laying on of hands of an aggregation of ministerial peers. The second generation of Christian Connection preachers gave much more emphasis to conferences, but they, like the O'Kelly Christians, understood their capacity as advisory.

In the aftermath of multi-denominational evangelism at Cane Ridge, Barton W. Stone and several other Presbyterian ministers in Kentucky and Ohio broke away to form the Springfield Presbytery. By June 28, 1804, the Springfield Presbytery dissolved and published the reasons in *The Last Will and Testament of Springfield Presbytery,* proposing to "sink into union with the body of Christ at large." Governance thereafter was left up to individual congregations, though periodic gatherings continued for the purpose of mutual encouragement and the ordination of candidates for ministry.

Thomas and Alexander Campbell were both born in Northern Ireland and trained as Presbyterian ministers, but upon immigrating soon found themselves as independents in southwestern Pennsylvania. After 1815 they cast their lot with the Redstone Baptist Association. In his years as editor of the *Christian Baptist,* Alexander Campbell argued against hierarchical ecclesiastical structures but did not attack associations as such. As the relationship with the Redstone Association became tenuous, the Campbells joined the Mahoning Baptist Association of northeastern Ohio in 1825. In 1830 this association decided to dissolve, but to continue periodic meetings for the purposes of worship and hearing reports from the evangelists and churches. Alexander Campbell expressed some dismay over the dissolution of the association, an indication that while he strongly upheld the integrity and freedom of the local church, he was also concerned about mutual cooperation and accountability.

In his chapter on "The Body of Christ" in *The Christian System* (1839), Campbell argued that the local congregation was a microcosm of the larger global "congregation," that the particularity and universality of the church were intrinsically inseparable. This perspective qualified his ideas of local autonomy. In his considerable writings on church organization in the *Millennial Harbinger* in the 1840s and 1850s, Campbell did not see the congregation as an end in itself, and he decried the pattern of Puritan congregational*ism* that enabled the local church to become a miniature kingdom unto itself. In one essay in the British journal *Christian Messenger and Reformer,* he described the ideal scenario of mutual accountability among congregations, in what amounted to a modified Presbyterianism that still allowed for *ad hoc* consultations of the elders of the churches in a matter such as the screening of acceptable elders. In disciplinary matters, such as compromised moral behavior on the part of an evangelist, Campbell approved the feasibility in some instances of congregations appealing cases to other (neutral) congregations for their judgment.

After the union of the Stone and Campbell movements, regional and state associations began to spring up in the 1840s for evangelization, and in 1849 the national American Christian Missionary Society was founded. After the Civil War active resistance to these societies increased, especially among those who rallied around David Lipscomb, Benjamin Franklin, and Daniel Sommer. The common objection was that local autonomy prevailed in the New Testament churches. The separate census report in 1906 for Churches of Christ included most of those churches who opposed the societies and who held to a stricter form of congregational independence.

The battles continue to rage in Churches of Christ over ways of creating ministries that are too large for a single congregation, such as network media programs, missions in a Third World country, and large-scale area campaigns. The Herald of Truth radio broadcast established a model whereby Highland Church of Christ (Abilene, Texas) made all the decisions regarding the program but received money from other congregations throughout the world. Other churches undertook large-scale media programs or mission efforts employing the same pattern. Those who objected congealed into churches that identify themselves as "noninstitutional." Noninstitutional leaders argue that there is no scriptural warrant for a congregation receiving funds from another congregation.

During the mid-twentieth century, among conservative Disciples churches (forerunners of the separate Christian Churches/Churches of Christ), strong opposition arose to the theology and policies of large societies, especially the United Christian Missionary Society. Many churches thus began funding "direct support" missionaries, independent of any sending agency. The fear of an emerging denominational superstructure lording over the freedom of local congregations became a major rallying point in the eventual departure of the "independent" Christian Churches/Churches of Christ from the Disciples of Christ fold. To date, Christian Churches/Churches of Christ across the board remain committed to congregational autonomy. Struggles concerning congregational networking for supporting educational and missionary ventures have occasionally arisen (e.g., resistance to organized agencies like the Christian Missionary Fellowship), but not to the extent found in Churches of Christ.

Despite differing views of ways in which churches can work together, and despite the Disciples' creating regional and national ministries, all spectra of the Stone-Campbell Movement still affirm congregational independence. The Christian Church (Disciples of Christ), by its official denominational organization, asserts that the actions of its General Assembly cannot violate the freedom or the conscience of its constituent local churches.

See also Church, Doctrine of the; Democratization; Direct Support Missions; Discipline, Church; *Last Will and Testament of Springfield Presbytery;* Liberty; Missionary Societies, Controversy over

BIBLIOGRAPHY Alexander Campbell, *The Christian System* (1839) • Alexander Campbell, "Church Organization," No. II, *Millennial Harbinger* (1849): 220-24 • David Edwin Harrell, Jr., *The Churches of Christ in the Twentieth Century: Homer Hailey's Personal Journey of Faith* (2000) • William Robinson, "Did Alexander Campbell Believe in Congregationalism?" *Shane Quarterly* 15 (1954): 5-12 • Fred P. Thompson, "Local Autonomy as a Problem of Brotherhood Unity," in *The Second Consultation on Internal Unity,* ed. Charles Gresham (1960), pp. 92-100.

THOMAS H. OLBRICHT

Locke, John (1632-1704)

British philosopher and proponent of religious toleration.

Dubbed "the Christian philosopher" by Thomas and Alexander Campbell, Locke's philosophy, especially his epistemology, deeply influenced the Stone-Campbell Movement both directly through his writings and indirectly through Scottish Common Sense Realism. The British empiricist philosopher defined the Enlightenment for American theology in the eighteenth and early nineteenth centuries. Three of Locke's books were particularly significant for the Campbells' philosophical and theological development. His *Essay Concerning Human Understanding* (1689) shaped their epistemology, his *A Letter Concerning Toleration* (1690) partly formed their understanding of unity and the virtue of tolerance, and his *The Reasonableness of Christianity* (1695) forged the theological method whereby they eschewed speculative theories and concentrated on the "facts" of the gospel system. Apologetically, Alexander Campbell was a practitioner of the "Christian Evidence" movement, which was rooted in Locke and implemented by William Paley (1743-1805). Theologically, Campbell intended to root his thought in the simple confession that Jesus is the Christ and the minimal "facts" of the Christian story. The confession of these facts and a concomitant moral and religious life provided the foundation of unity for both Locke and Campbell.

See also Common Sense Philosophy; Hermeneutics; Rationalism; Reason, Place of; Theology — Nineteenth Century

BIBLIOGRAPHY Billy D. Bowen, "Knowledge, the Existence of God, and Faith: John Locke's Influence on Alexander Campbell's Theology" (Ph.D. dissertation, Michigan State University, 1978) • Michael W. Casey, "The Origins of the Hermeneutics of the Churches of Christ, Part Two: The Philosophical Background," *Restoration Quarterly* 31 (1989): 193-206 • Leslie L. Kingsbury, "The Philosophical Influences Bearing on Alexander Campbell and the Beginnings of the Disciples of Christ Movement" (Ph.D. dissertation, Edinburgh University, 1954) • Samuel Pearson, "Faith and Reason in Disciples Theology," in *Classic Themes of Disciples Theology,* ed. Kenneth Lawrence (1986), pp. 101-29.

JOHN MARK HICKS

Long, Robert Alexander (1850-1933)

Noted Kansas City Disciple, lumber magnate, and philanthropist. Long used his wealth and fundraising skills to benefit Disciples causes. Known for his purchase and gift of the Christian Board of Publication, he was also a major force behind the Men and Millions Movement and the establishment of the National City Christian Church.

See also Christian Board of Publication; Men and Millions Movement, The

BIBLIOGRAPHY Lenoire K. Bradley, *Robert Alexander Long: A Lumberman of the Gilded Age* (1988).

STEPHEN L. REGAS

Lookout, The

Second major periodical of the Standard Publishing Company, serving a readership primarily from the Christian Churches/Churches of Christ.

Standard Publishing's premier journal was, and is, the *Christian Standard,* which was established in 1866. The *Young People's Standard* (now *The Lookout*) was first published in 1899. Jessie H. Brown was the first editor, from March 10, 1894, to December 26, 1896. Brown married John E. Pounds in 1896. Her career included not only the editorship of *The Young People's Standard* but also the writing of poetry. Many of her poems were set to music and released as hymns. "I Know That My Redeemer Liveth," "The Touch of His Hand on Mine," and "Beautiful Isle of Somewhere" are a few of her hymns. It was under the leadership of Jessie Brown that the name of the periodical was changed from the *Young People's Standard* to *The Lookout,* a change signaling a shift in emphasis from a magazine for adolescents to a publication for older teens and adults. The name was taken from a committee name, the Lookout Committee, an arm of the Christian Endeavor organization charged with promoting the Christian Endeavor movement. *The Lookout* had a broader scope in Christian education, aiming to advance and strengthen Sunday Schools.

Beginning with the January 2, 1897, issue, Mattie M. Boteler and Phillip Y. Pendleton were co-editors. Boteler became sole editor with the January 11, 1902, issue. She held the position until February 20, 1910, and during her tenure started the inclusion of Sunday School attendance figures, a feature in *The Lookout* that continued until 1968.

Herbert Moninger became the third editor of *The Lookout.* He had been a minister in Steubenville, Ohio, and a staff member of Standard Publishing prior to his new post. He wrote the Christian education teacher training book entitled *Training for Service. The Lookout* carried the attendance figures and news of country-wide teacher training classes. After some brief editorships, James DeForest Murch became co-editor from 1917 through 1919, then sole editor until 1925, when he went on to new work with the Christian Restoration Association in Cincinnati.

Guy P. Leavitt succeeded Murch as editor and served until 1956. His support of Christian education through *The Lookout* earned him the title "Mr. Sunday School." During Leavitt's tenure, *The Lookout* missed only one week of publication, due to a flood in Cincinnati, Ohio, that kept the magazine from being shipped from the office. Leonard Wymore, eventual director of the North American Christian Convention, served as editor from October 1956 until December 1957. His successor, Jay Sheffield, had a long editorial tenure from 1958 to 1975.

Orrin Root, a respected minister and regular contributor to *The Lookout* and *The Christian Standard,* served as editor pro tempore for thirteen months during 1975-76 and was succeeded in 1976 by Mark Taylor, who held the post until 1990. During Taylor's term, *The Lookout* celebrated the bicentennial of the Sunday School with a special edition of the magazine, October 5, 1980. *The Lookout* also broadened its focus by addressing such social and moral concerns as pornography and obscenity. Simon J. Dahlman continued expanding that horizon in his editorship from 1990 to 1996. David Faust, a pastor and professor at Cincinnati Bible College (president since 2002), assumed the position of editor on July 14, 1996. He remained in the position until March 1, 2001, when Shawn McMullen became editor and Faust the executive editor of *The Lookout.*

See also *Christian Standard;* Murch, James DeForest; Pounds, Jessie Brown; Standard Publishing Company

BIBLIOGRAPHY Leonard Wymore, "5200 Issues — And Still Counting!" *The Lookout* (1994). GARY L. LEE

Loos, Charles Louis (1823-1912)

Disciples of Christ educator.

Charles Loos was born in the Alsace region of France to a French father and a German mother. His family settled in Ohio in 1834. He was raised Lutheran, but joined a Campbell-related congregation when he was 14. He graduated from Bethany College in 1846. Over the next several years he taught, preached, was an author, and co-edited the *Millennial Harbinger.* In 1857 he became president of Eureka College. A year and a half later he joined the faculty of Bethany College as professor of ancient and modern languages. This was followed by seventeen years as president of Kentucky University (1880-1897), during which time he also taught ancient Greek. After retirement he continued to teach Greek. He influenced several generations of ministers through his rigorous teaching of Greek and Hebrew and the general breadth of his intellectual interests. He served as president of the Foreign Christian Missionary Society from 1888 to 1900.

BIBLIOGRAPHY Lester G. McAllister, *Bethany: The First 150 Years* (1991) • J. D. Wright, Jr., *Transylvania: Tutor to the West* (1975). RICHARD L. HARRISON, JR.

Lord's Day, The

Christian practice, originating in the apostolic period and given official endorsement by the Emperor Constantine in the fourth century, of setting aside Sunday, the day of the resurrection, as the normative day of Christian worship.

The term "Lord's Day" is actually found only once in the New Testament (Rev. 1:10). An editorial in the *Christian Standard* of 1893 listed four questions people commonly were asking about the Lord's Day. Is the law of the seventh-day Sabbath still binding? If the day has been changed to the first day of the week, is the first day to be held binding under the fourth commandment (Exod. 20:8-11)? If the day is not to be considered under the fourth commandment, may we go about our regular avocations on the first day? Was there a Sabbath before Moses?

These questions had been asked since the early days of the Stone-Campbell Movement, and the same issues had arisen in earlier Protestant (and broader Christian) tradition. The numerous articles about the Lord's Day and Sabbath in the *Millennial Harbinger* and *Christian Standard* in the nineteenth century demonstrate the controversy. It appears, however, that the early disagreement was over calling Sunday the Sabbath and making the fourth commandment apply to Sunday. Later on the controversy focused more on the appropriateness of designating the first day over the seventh day as the proper day of Christian worship.

Alexander Campbell in the *Christian Baptist* of 1823 addressed the earlier issue. Some Baptists had claimed that a Sabbath had been observed in the garden of Eden on the first day of the week and was maintained by the Patriarchs. Now, in the Christian era, they maintained, we should restore the Sabbath to its proper day. Campbell — in keeping with the strict law/gospel dialectic he set forth in his 1816 "Sermon on the Law" — replied that the Old Testament Sabbath was strictly for the Jews, that it was only a shadow or type, and that, at any rate, Christ himself had set aside the Old Testament law.

The later controversy was taken up by Robert Milligan in his *Scheme of Redemption* (1868), and his response may be taken as representative. He argued that Sunday is the Lord's Day, not the seventh day, on the basis of seven facts: (1) Christ arose on the first day; (2) he first met with his disciples on the first day (John 20:19-29); (3) the Holy Spirit came on the first day (since Pentecost begins on the first day of the week, Acts 2:1-4); (4) the church began on the first day (Acts 11:15); (5) the early Christians met on the first day (Acts 20:6-7; 1 Cor 16:1-2; also numerous patristic authorities); (6) John called this day the Lord's Day (Rev. 1:10); and (7) Ezekiel prophesied about this day (Ezek 46:1). Indeed, Milligan maintained, the Sabbath mentioned in the last nine chapters of Ezekiel is not the Jewish Sabbath but the Lord's Day.

In 1886 D. R. Dungan, then president of Drake University, engaged D. M. Canright, a Seventh-Day Adventist apologist, in a public debate on the subject of Sabbath and Lord's Day. A year later Canright renounced Adventism and in 1915 published a major work defending Sunday as the true Lord's Day for Christians — a work read by many Stone-Campbell constituents and later reprinted in the Restoration Reprint Library (1966).

Strikingly, many in the Movement, including Robert Milligan himself, while disavowing the Sabbath discipline in principle, demanded in practice that Sunday be observed as a day of rest. "Thus," wrote Milligan, "much of the traveling, visiting, reading, conversations and other exercises of this day are an abomination in the sight of God." The above-mentioned editorial from the *Christian Standard* in 1893 initially observed that the early Christians probably did not abstain from their employment on the first day. Yet the editor went on to condemn a preacher/dentist for accepting patients on Sunday. For nineteenth- and early-twentieth-century American Protestants, still deeply impacted by the legacy of Puritanism and its Christian social disciplines, there were clearly strong cultural inducements for observing Sunday as a sabbatical day consecrated to the Lord.

See also Lord's Supper, The; Worship — Nineteenth Century

BIBLIOGRAPHY Alexander Campbell, "Address to the Readers of the *Christian Baptist*," no. 3, *Christian Baptist* (1823): 43-46 • Alexander Campbell et al., "The Lord's Day," in *The Millennial Harbinger Abridged*, ed. B. L. Smith (1902), pp. 151-62 • D. M. Canright, *The Lord's Day From Neither Catholics Nor Pagans: An Answer to Seventh-Day Adventism on This Subject* (1915) • D. R. Dungan, *Sabbath or Lord's Day? Which?* (n.d.) • Editorial, "The Lord's Day" *Christian Standard* 29 (1893): 426 • Robert Milligan, *The Scheme of Redemption* (1868). DAVID A. FIENSY

Lord's Supper, The

Regular observance of the communion meal instituted by Christ at the Last Supper.

One of the most distinctive practices that early leaders of the Stone-Campbell Movement established as a mark of their return to apostolic Christianity was that of weekly communion. When Thomas and Alexander Campbell and their associates formed the Brush Run church, Washington County, Pennsylvania, in May 1811, their first act of worship was the observance of the Lord's Supper, which they resolved to celebrate weekly thereafter.

1. Frequency and Practice

In his long *Christian Baptist* series on "A Restoration of the Ancient Order of Things," Alexander Campbell included an apology for weekly observance of the Supper, examining in detail what the New Testament says about the practice of the primitive church and concluding with supportive testimony of leading Protestant reformers (including John Calvin) on the subject. Though recognizing that there was not a "thus saith the Lord" for weekly celebration in the New Testament, this was a clear case of "approved precedent." "Apostolic example," wrote Campbell on this point, "is justly esteemed of equal authority with an apostolic precept." The very meaning of the Supper, as well as the brief descriptions of regular observance in the New Testament churches (Acts 2:42; 20:7), was sufficient to commend celebration *at least* on every Lord's Day. Barton Stone drew the same conclusion, albeit more concisely, in his *Christian*

Messenger in 1829. Though he cautioned against letting the issue become divisive, in 1831 Stone heartily endorsed J. A. Gano's defense of weekly communion, reflecting the fact that Stone's churches had committed to the practice only slightly later than Campbell's.

Campbell presented his definitive exposition of the celebration of the Supper in *The Christian System* (1835), an exposition that has molded the thinking and practice of congregations in all branches of the Stone-Campbell Movement ever since. Here Campbell suggests that the Supper is commemorative in character and belongs to the whole community of believers. He unfolds his argument in seven statements:

- there is a house on earth called the house of God;
- in the house of God there is the table of the Lord;
- on that table there is of necessity but one loaf;
- since all Christians are priests, they all may partake of that loaf;
- the one loaf must be visibly broken before the saints feed on it (and after giving thanks for it);
- the breaking of the loaf and the drinking of the cup commemorate the Lord's death; and
- the Supper is an instituted part of the worship of all Christian assemblies in all their stated meetings (i.e., times of formal worship).

Campbell ultimately devoted most space to supporting the last proposition (the issue of frequency).

Campbell called attention to the spiritual uplift that weekly observance of the Supper gave the believer, since it centered on the joy to be found in the new covenant and corrected the solemn gloom that pervaded the quarterly and semi-annual communions of the established denominations. Because the feast was primarily memorial in character, he argued, it promoted the unity of the church by making believers one in a shared memory. He closed his essay in the *Christian System* with a narrative account of a simple worship service that he believed exhibited the ideal celebration. In this service a senior member of the congregation, not necessarily an ordained elder or teacher (often there was no one qualified for that capacity in some of the churches) takes the loaf, gives thanks for it, breaks it, and hands it to the disciples on each side of him, who pass the broken loaf from one to another, until all have eaten of it. In the same way the leader then takes the cup, returns thanks for it, hands it to one of the disciples sitting beside him, who drinks from it and passes it on, each communicant repeating the action until all have partaken. Following this, an offering is received for the poor. Campbell added that the table was set before the service, that prayers, hymns, and Scripture readings all appropriate to setting the mood for the Supper were used, and that only afterwards were those present invited to share passages of Scripture with comments or lessons for the edification of others present. It is clear from this scenario that Campbell considered the Lord's Supper absolutely central to Christian worship.

Communion chalice given to Alexander Campbell during the trip in which he was interned briefly in Glasgow, Scotland, in 1847. The chalice was later used by the Campbell family in their home in Bethany, Virginia.

Courtesy of Emmanuel School of Religion Archives

Historically the worship of congregations in the Stone-Campbell tradition moved away from Campbell's idealization. As the Movement expanded and many churches increased in size, it became customary to employ evangelists or preachers, with the result that the Protestant tendency to give preaching special prominence in Sunday worship grew up alongside the observance of the Lord's Supper, the result being the shared centrality of preaching and communing. The growing practice of having a plurality of ordained elders in each congregation also changed the way the Supper was served. Usually two such officers presided at the table, one to give thanks for the loaf, the other for the cup, and servers or deacons then acted to help pass the emblems among the believers. Because of the size of many congregations, two chalices and two patens would be used in the distribution, with a flagon on the table used to refill the cups, if needed, and a white linen cloth kept over the tableware both before and after the observance. In most early church buildings, along the wall facing the congregation was a slightly raised platform with a pulpit at its front and center, with the Lord's Table immediately below it on the floor and at the head of the center aisle, as a symbol of the level community of all believers.

A number of social developments also began to change the face of the Supper, at least among American churches. The Temperance movement in the nineteenth century forced the churches to reexamine the use of fermented wine as presenting a temptation to believers susceptible to alcohol addiction, so the use of unfermented grape juice gradually became customary among the churches. D. R. Dungan, a respected Stone-Campbell scholar-pastor in Iowa, argued in 1889 that Jesus could not possibly have instituted the use of wine because the symbolically potent "fruit of the vine" vanishes if left to ferment into alcohol. "And for a church of Christ to be celebrating the Lord's death with drugged liquors, made of alcohol and poisons, is a shame, and should be discontinued at once." The vast majority of churches across all three streams of the Stone-Campbell tradition — excepting a very small segment of Churches of Christ that retain wine only — still celebrate the Supper with grape juice.

Another development in the nineteenth century, the alarming spread of tuberculosis, induced churches to replace the use of the single cup with small individual cups distributed in trays to the congregants (in time coupled with trays of pre-fractured bread morsels). This "hygienic" practice, while typical of the majority of Stone-Campbell churches up to the present, was not accepted without some controversy. In the 1920s a group of Church of Christ leaders already opposed to Sunday Schools also consolidated resistance to multiple communion cups, which they considered a departure from the apostolic practice. Thus a small segment of "One Cup" Churches of Christ, concentrated mainly in Texas, have strictly upheld single cup observance of the Lord's Supper. British Churches of Christ as well retained the one cup for many years, a custom championed by William Robinson not only because it was the ancient usage but because of its profound symbolism. Of late, a number of congregations both of the Christian Church (Disciples of Christ) and the Christian Churches/Churches of Christ have returned to using one cup through intinction, a practice familiar from the Methodist tradition in which worshipers dip their portions of bread in the common cup.

One of the difficulties of describing observance of the Lord's Supper in churches of the three branches of the Stone-Campbell Movement is that their respective growth into millions of congregants, combined with a persistent individualism and spirit of independence, have generated a variety of communal practices among them. While there has been open division over the issue (as seen with the One Cup Churches of Christ), often there is nothing more than inconvenience involved in learning what is expected when visiting from one congregation to another. In some churches only the elders may preside at the table, while in others any adult may preside.

Some churches offer the communion only at the Sunday morning services, while others offer it at Sunday evening services, during the week (e.g., Maundy Thursday), at private home gatherings, at concluding summer service camp meetings, and at annual conventions (fully consonant with Alexander Campbell's claim that the church is free to observe the Supper in multiple settings). Some hold that a believer should take the communion only once on a Sunday if there is more than one service, others that a believer can freely partake as many times as he or she wishes. Most congregations now send communion out on Sundays to shut-in members and even to those temporarily ill or in the hospital.

The use of brief meditations just before the action at the table, read by the minister, one of the elders, or a layperson invited to do so, has also become a widespread practice. While some churches position the Supper prior to the sermon in the worship service, others situate it after the sermon, such that the concluding hymns of invitation are a sign of the climactic importance of the Supper, demonstrating its superiority to preaching as the evangelical center of worship ("proclaiming the Lord's death until he comes"). As a sign of the equality of male and female in the church, congregations of the Christian Church (Disciples of Christ) elect women to the eldership, and a woman and a man often stand together at the Lord's Table to give thanks for the bread and cup. The election of women to the eldership has happened only in rare instances among Christian Churches/Churches of Christ and is almost wholly proscribed among Churches of Christ.

The architectural dimension of the celebration is not without significance. In recent years churches both of the Christian Church (Disciples of Christ) and the Christian Churches/Churches of Christ have adopted the "divided chancel" as a setting for the Supper, with the table at the center-rear of the chancel and the pulpit and lectern positioned equidistant at its front. The arrangement gives a better view of what takes place at the table, makes it physically more prominent, and usually aligns it with the baptistery above and behind it, placing the two rites in visual relationship with each other.

Disciples scholar and liturgist Keith Watkins has proposed an adaptation of the Western Rite for use in the churches that would suit the divided chancel, and while some congregations have been open to a more liturgically disciplined service, others are resistant. Going in just the opposite direction, a small minority of Christian Churches/Churches of Christ, following the "seeker sensitive" model, have removed the table either to a side room or to the rear of the sanctuary and conduct the Supper inconspicuously, reasoning that overt Christian symbolism in a service might prove a stumbling block to unbelievers who find traditional Christianity offensive.

2. "Open" versus "Close" Communion

The issue of "open" and "close" communion (i.e., whether or not to admit the "pious unimmersed" to the Lord's Supper) came up in the churches of the Stone and Campbell movements alike. As early as 1829 in his *Christian Messenger,* Barton Stone answered criticism for holding simultaneously that the pious unimmersed are not "lawfully members of the body of Christ" yet that they "honestly err" and are sufficiently "Christian," and that there simply is no scriptural reason for barring them from the Lord's table. "Why cannot I enjoy fellowship with him in the supper, if I cannot in his baptism?" "If I err, let it be on the side of charity."

By the time of the union of the Stone and Campbell movements in 1832, however, there was pressure from Campbell's churches on Stone's not to invite systematically the pious unimmersed to the table such as would compromise the Movement's hard line on immersion. Raccoon John Smith, in a conciliatory sermon aimed at securing the Disciples' trust of Stone's churches, reported that he never saw any of those churches, despite their forbearing spirit, proactively inviting (or forbidding) the unimmersed to commune. A certain "Juvenis," writing pseudonymously in the 1843 *Christian Messenger,* spoke for what had become the normative practice in Stone's churches, declaring that it was the prerogative of individual Christians to examine themselves (1 Cor. 11:28) to decide whether they were worthy to partake of the Supper.

Alexander Campbell, for his part, struggled over this issue, fearing in the 1829 *Christian Baptist* that open communion not only lacked scriptural warrant but threatened to undermine the apostolic injunction of immersion. For the next three decades he seemed to go back and forth on the issue, desiring to express a generous Christian spirit while still adhering closely to the "ancient order." He decried the "sectarians" who fenced each other from the table for doctrinal or political reasons, yet in the mid-1830s he repudiated open communion as "making void" the precedent of the apostolic church, and in one 1859 statement he asserted that Scripture explicitly licensed the invitation only of *immersed* persons to the Lord's Supper. Nevertheless, Campbell also on occasion indicated his willingness to break bread with the pious unimmersed among the denominations. In the debate with Presbyterian theologian Nathan Rice in 1843, the well-read Rice actually accused Campbell of contradicting himself on this issue, forcing him to clarify the semantics of "open" communion. Campbell in turn distinguished between communing in good conscience with the pious unimmersed, which he and many of his associates did, and proactively *inviting* the unimmersed to the table, which he denied as a regular practice among Disciples of Christ congregations.

Second-generation leaders in the Movement give evidence that the issue of open versus close communion continued to arise from time to time. Isaac Errett and Robert Richardson confirmed what, by the 1860s, they saw as the settled position of the Disciples of Christ. Errett urged that whatever their error on baptism, there were indeed Christians among the "sects," and that "our practice, therefore, is *neither to invite nor reject* particular classes of persons, but to spread the table in the name of the Lord, for the Lord's people, and allow all to come who will, each on his own responsibility." Robert Richardson confirmed this and censured those who, while upholding this practice in principle, still presumed that "*no* unimmersed persons are Christians [and that] all immersed persons are Christians." In 1863 Moses Lard sharply dissented, arguing that the pious unimmersed only "seemed" to commune; their lack of immersion bespoke an inadequate faith, which thus "vitiated" their genuine participation in the Supper.

Despite some resistance and some divergent theological accents, a consensus emerged among the heirs of Stone and Campbell. "Open communion" as free access to the table for the conscientious — enshrined in the oft repeated phrase "we neither invite, nor debar" — became the predominant usage in all streams of the Stone-Campbell Movement. Not all constituents, however, have interpreted this "openness" the same way. For some, the Movement's passive form of the practice, though it hardly recruits the pious unimmersed to the table, has been tantamount to an ecumenical overture, a positive gesture to the denominations of their shared status in the kingdom. For others it has remained simply the *via media* by which to be simultaneously gracious toward the pious unimmersed and adamant on immersion. For still others, disinclined toward any overtures to the "sects," it has been a matter of strictly interpreting

1 Corinthians 11:28 in terms of individual freedom of religious conscience before a table that belongs to the Lord alone. This last position, for those who advance it, ultimately implies restriction; paradoxically, they could in their own way sympathize with the Roman Catholic watchword that communion is a "sign" of Christian unity, not a "means" to it.

3. The Meaning of the Supper

Historically, churches of the Stone-Campbell tradition, in their understanding of the meaning of the Lord's Supper, have ranged between seeing it primarily as an ordinance of commemoration (a position usually identified with the Protestant reformer Huldrych Zwingli) and viewing it in broadly sacramental terms (a legacy of the Reformed heritage and of Anglicanism, emphasizing Christ's *spiritual presence* and the faithful's "spiritual feeding" on his body). The former, the memorialistic perspective, was predominant in the early Movement and still prevails in many quarters today. Alexander Campbell's own preference for it, noted earlier, is forcefully reiterated in his 1846 response to a query from "Disciplus" (Robert Richardson) asking whether the Supper was more than a mere memorial. "Does it not stand in the same place with regard to remission of sins to the *Christian,* that baptism does to the *alien,* or believing penitent?" Was it not effectively a sacrament (though Richardson did not use this term) of assurance of the remission of postbaptismal sin? Campbell answered unambiguously in the negative, restating that the Supper was "emblematic," "commemorative," a "weekly memento" that believers' sins were already expiated by Christ's blood. In short, "it is not an ordinance for receiving new blessings, but for commemorating those already received."

Later apologists in the Movement argued that Campbell and other early leaders never had in mind a "bare memorial," but a rich recall, a demonstration and rehearsal "proclaiming the Lord's death until he comes." W. B. Blakemore, reporting to the Disciples' Panel of Scholars in the early 1960s, saw the Movement recovering the biblical interplay of God's "remembrance" of the faithful and their reciprocal remembrance of his salvific acts. In the Supper, he suggested, "the role of remembrance is not that it brings the Lord into our presence, but that remembrance opens our eyes to him into whose presence we have already been brought by faith." W. R. Walker, of the Christian Churches/Churches of Christ, insisted that the memorial entailed a deeper "solemn vow" of covenant renewal, while his son Dean E. Walker similarly invoked the image of personal "oath," the original meaning of *sacramentum.*

Shifts toward acknowledging Christ's *eucharistic presence,* however, began to appear as early as the mid-nineteenth century amid discussion of the peculiar subjective benefits of the Lord's Supper for Christians beyond the more objective benefits suggested by Alexander Campbell. The one-time Anglican Robert Richardson (1806-1876), who sometimes candidly criticized Campbell's positions, upheld the deeper *mystical* meaning of the Supper in the context of his larger campaign to reform worship and spirituality in the Movement. In his series "Communings in the Sanctuary," published in the *Millennial Harbinger* and later in book form (1872), Richardson thoroughly and poetically intermingled commemorative and sacramental language: "It is here [in the Supper] that we may revive the recollections of the past, and bid the burial-places of memory give up their dead that we may go with them even into the Holy City. . . . And it is here, above all, that the films of error may be taken from our eyes that we may recognize the spiritual presence of our Savior, and that he may be made known to us in the breaking of the bread (cf. Luke 24:30-31)." Richardson was insistent on recovering the New Testament's own "realist" language for communing with Christ.

Robert Milligan (1814-1875) expressed similar sensitivities. In his highly influential book *The Scheme of Redemption* (1868), Milligan held that the great enemy of worship was "formalism," going through the motions of worship without reflection. He thus urged Christians to prepare for communion through fasting, prayer, and decent attire and to avoid unseemly worldly activities on the Lord's Day. It was only through preparation to commune that the disciple could truly discern the body of the Lord, dine spiritually on his flesh and blood, and receive a foretaste of the marriage supper of the Lamb. Like Richardson, Milligan was receptive to the mystical dimension of the Lord's Supper. He stated that the Supper is "more than the mere recollection of a feast. *It is intended also to be the medium of furnishing spiritual nourishment to the hungry and thirsty soul.*" The bread and the wine were not turned into flesh and blood, but what is symbolized by them is *spiritually* eaten and digested, if taken properly, and the soul of the believer is truly nourished and built up.

While a rich literature about the Supper accrued among Stone-Campbell churches between the Civil War and the first quarter of the twentieth century, most of it was inspirational and edificatory rather than theological in character (e.g., G. L. Brokaw, ed., *The Lord's Supper,* 1903), and it did not move the thinking of major leaders of the Stone-Campbell Movement much beyond the entrenched memorialism of earlier generations devoted to restoring the communion ordinance. In the *Christian Standard* in 1915, Disciples scholar Frederick Kershner recalled three classic understandings of the Supper: (1) Roman Catholic transubstantiation; (2) Zwinglian memorialism, which largely ignored the issue of Christ's presence and which was prevalent in Stone-Campbell churches; and (3) the Lutheran doctrine of "consubstantiation" that allowed for the presence of Christ without violating the physical elements of bread and wine. Kershner claimed his preference for the Lutheran view, clearly cutting against the grain of the traditional mainstream yet signaling a renewed sensitivity to the mystical dimension of the Supper.

Only between the two World Wars, however, was a doctrine of eucharistic presence developed more fully in the Stone-Campbell tradition through the work of Principal William Robinson of Overdale College, Birmingham, England, and those in the United States who were influenced by him, like Dean E. Walker (1898-1988) and Robinson's students at Butler University School of Religion (now Christian Theological Seminary) after he arrived there in 1950. Robinson claimed that his insights were not revisionist, but simply a development of thoughts already present in nineteenth-century reformers like Walter Scott in America and David King in England. Indeed, the Stone-Campbell churches in Britain had already developed a rich communion piety celebrating the presence of Christ. Robinson echoed themes not only from his predecessor David King but also from the evocative eucharistic hymns of G. Y. Tickle (1819-88), an elder of the Church of Christ in Liverpool.

Robinson developed his views in a number of books and communion guides, chief among them *Essays on Christian Unity* (1922) and *A Companion to the Communion Service* (1942). He was very influential in Great Britain through his long editorship of the *Christian Advocate* and his participation in the emerging Faith and Order movement. Robinson objected to any view of the Lord's Supper that reduced it to a purely prescriptive and memorialistic rite. He insisted on applying the term "sacrament" to baptism and the Lord's Supper, thereby breaking with the linguistic usage of the Stone-Campbell Movement. *Sacrament,* he argued, while neither scriptural nor free from certain objectionable theological connotations, was still preferable to *ordinance* (also nonscriptural) for bringing to light neglected aspects of the Supper found in passages like 1 Corinthians 10:3-4, 16-17; 11:29-34. Baptism and the Eucharist were not merely aids to the imagination or occasions for spiritual autosuggestion, as a purely commemorative observance would recommend, but planes of spiritual interaction with God.

Robinson, while upholding the mystery of the Supper, defended against any implication of a magical or mechanical mode of its efficacy. Yet a sacrament was decidedly bodily specific. In the absolute, God is everywhere at once; but in time and space where human beings live, he must be present concretely and actually. This holds true for the incarnation itself, and for all those divinely appointed means of being present, where those means are humanly identifiable and performable. The Lord's Supper is one of those divinely established, bodily specific means by which we meet Christ and feed on his presence. Salvation begins on earth when Christ enables believers to share in his indwelling grace and power; but this is achieved principally in the corporate life of the church where believers are inseminated with the Holy Spirit, being "supernaturalized" and made into channels of grace themselves. Striking a contrast with earlier doctrines of the Real Presence, Robinson articulated a notion of the "Real Action" of Christ, which, while upholding the objective and mystical reality, required voluntary, ethical, and corporate participation.

On Sunday, October 17, the last day of the 1909 Centennial Convention, over 25,000 attendees gathered to take communion at Pittsburgh's Forbes Field. A hundred elders presided and 500 deacons served during the one-hour service, described by the *Christian Standard* as "the crowning feature" of the Convention. Courtesy of the Disciples of Christ Historical Society

Robinson explained that, unlike the Roman Catholic doctrine where Christ's presence is actualized through the transubstantiated bread and wine, the true reality of Christ comes to worshipers in the *act* of eating and drinking, in the dynamic of spiritual participation. Robinson held that Christ's gift of his body and blood is structurally tied to reality in the eschatological sense. Christ's sacrifice in its "once-for-all-ness" covers the whole of time at every point, from the foundation of the world (Rom. 13:8) to the very last moment when the Lord returns (1 Cor. 11:26). Eschatologically, when the sacrament is celebrated, the crucified Lord becomes our contemporary; Jesus is not re-crucified at every Lord's Supper in history when it is celebrated, as the medieval mind misunderstood, but he is re-called, as it were, to the *present* moment in solidarity with his church. Like Robert Richardson long before him, and W. B. Blakemore after him, Robinson sought not to undermine the commemorative dimension, cherished in the Stone-Campbell heritage, but to exploit its deeper reality. He therefore plumbed the New Testament usage of *anamnēsis* in its sense of rehearsal and profound ritual remembrance bringing the past action of God to bear immediately on the present.

Another major historical and theological study of the Lord's Supper from within the Stone-Campbell tradition was published by Robinson's younger contemporary, Harold Fey, former editor of *World Call* and editor of *The Christian Century* (1955-64). Fey's *The Lord's Supper: Seven Meanings* (1948) highlighted, in particular, the *ecclesial* dimension of the Lord's Supper, which he understood to be a feast par excellence of reconciliation and solidarity with the church and with Christ. Fey did not finally settle the issue of "ordinance" versus "sacrament" but clearly tilted toward the latter, quoting the Swedish theologian Yngve Brilioth's claim that Christ is the "true celebrant" at the table, "personally feeding his own with the sacred gifts, and imparting his own great gift, the forgiveness of sins and communion with God through him."

4. A Tradition in Three Streams

None of the three streams of the Movement is absolutely univocal in its testimony to the antecedent traditions of Stone-Campbell communion theology and practice. Each, however, has adjusted that legacy to its own peculiar context. Each, moreover, has striven in its own ways to safeguard the primacy and centrality of the Lord's Supper in the worship of the church.

The Christian Church (Disciples of Christ) has in recent decades upheld both memorialistic and sacramental accents in its eucharistic teaching, and furthermore has articulated that teaching in the light of denominational restructure and an ever deepening involvement in the ecumenical movement. Eucharistic thought and practice — in a fellowship that chose the chalice as its denominational logo — have focused on themes like covenant, ecclesial wholeness, empowerment for service, inclusiveness, and unity-in-diversity. The Disciples reacted quite favorably to the Faith and Order Commission's *Baptism, Eucharist and Ministry* document (1982) with its affirmation of a latitude of meanings and practices in the pursuit of Christian unity.

Churches of Christ have continued a heritage of recommitment to the apostolic norm of communion faith and practice, guided by the example of the Movement's first-generation leaders. Differences persist, as noted with regard to the One-Cup (and wine-only) groups, but there is a consensus among Churches of Christ that the Supper is primarily a commemorative celebration and should be the soul of Christian worship. Some more recent Church of Christ theologians, like John Mark Hicks, have aspired to educate congregations in the deeper biblical and ecclesial dimensions of the communion meal and to overcome the individualistic pietism that has often characterized observance of the Supper.

Generally speaking, Christian Churches/Churches of Christ have also adhered closely to the memorialistic legacy of Stone-Campbell communion theology and practice, as can be seen in a published literature of "communion meditations" and in occasional instructional essays in periodicals like the *Christian Standard.* Nevertheless, renewed interest in the "sacramental tradition" of the likes of Richardson, Milligan, Kershner, and Robinson has increased in some quarters, centered particularly at Milligan College and Emmanuel School of Religion. A volume of reprinted essays of William Robinson, Harold Fey, and others, edited by Charles Gresham and Tom Lawson under the title *The Lord's Supper: Historical Writings on Its Meaning to the Body of Christ* (1993), is evidence that this minority perspective has gained sympathizers. Included in this collection is a study by Byron C. Lambert outlining ten meanings of the Supper for Christian Churches/Churches of Christ, but which effectively reflect its significance in the broader Stone-Campbell heritage. The Supper, Lambert concludes, has been (1) an act of obedience; (2) an act of remembrance; (3) an act of thanksgiving; (4) a proclamation ("of the Lord's death . . ."); (5) a prophecy (". . . until he comes"); (6) the sign of the New Covenant; (7) a service at an altar, honoring the "bread of the Presence;" (8) an act of self-examination; (9) a communion with Christ and fellow believers; and (10) an act of spiritual feeding on Christ.

See also Baptism; Fey, Harold Edward; Gano, John Allen; Milligan, Robert; Ordinance; Repentance; Richardson, Robert; Robinson, William; Sacrament; Temperance; Worship

BIBLIOGRAPHY W. B. Blakemore, "Worship and the Lord's Supper," in *The Renewal of Church: The Panel Reports,* vol. 3: *The Revival of the Churches* (1963), pp. 227-50 • John L. Brandt, ed., *The Lord's Supper* (1889) • G. L. Brokaw, ed., *The Lord's Supper* (1903) • Alexander Campbell, *The Christian System* (2nd ed. 1839) • Alexander Campbell, "A Restoration of the Ancient Order of Things," nos. 6-9, *Christian Baptist* (1825): 174-76, 180-82, 188-89, 194-95 • Alexander Campbell, "What Is the Real Design of the Lord's Supper?" *Millennial Harbinger* (1846): 396 • James G. Clague, "The Place of Jesus Christ in the Lord's Supper," in *The Renewal of Church: The Panel Reports,* vol. 2: *The Reconstruction of Theology* (1963), pp. 287-301 • James O. Duke, "The Disciples and the Lord's Supper: A Historical Perspective," *Encounter* 50 (1989): 1-28 • James O. Duke and Richard L. Harrison, *The Lord's Supper* (1993) • David R. Dungan, "The Lord's Supper," in *The Old Faith Restated,* ed. J. H. Garrison (1891), pp. 231-53 •

Isaac Errett, Robert Richardson, and W. K. Pendleton, "Communion with the 'Sects,'" *Millennial Harbinger* (1861): 710-14 • Harold Fey, *The Lord's Supper: Seven Meanings* (1948) • J. A. Gano, "The Lord's Supper," *Christian Messenger* (1831): 30-34 • Charles Gresham and Tom Lawson, eds., *The Lord's Supper: Historical Writings on Its Meaning to the Body of Christ* (1993) • Richard L. Harrison, "Early Disciples Sacramental Theology: Catholic, Reformed, and Free," in *Classic Themes in Disciples Theology*, ed. Kenneth Lawrence (1986), pp. 49-100 • John Mark Hicks, *Come to the Table: Revisioning the Lord's Supper* (2002) • Frederick D. Kershner, "This Is My Body," *Christian Standard* 50 (1915): 1016-17 • Nadia Lahutsky et al., "Setting the Table: Meanings of Communion," in *Setting the Table: Women in Theological Conversation*, ed. R. N. Brock et al. (1995), pp. 249-68 • Byron C. Lambert, *The Restoration of the Lord's Supper and the Sacramental Principle: With Special Reference to the Thought of William Robinson* (1992) • Moses Lard, "Do the Unimmersed Commune?" *Lard's Quarterly* 1 (1863): 41-53 • Johnny Melton, "The Lord's Supper in the Life of the Churches of Christ: Form, Function and Meaning — A Theological Investigation" (unpublished D.Min. thesis, Erskine Theological Seminary, 1995) • Robert Milligan, "The Lord's Supper: Its Design," nos. 1-2, *Millennial Harbinger* (1859): 601-5, 679-84 • Robert Milligan, *The Scheme of Redemption* (1868) • Andrew Paris, *What the Bible Says About the Lord's Supper* (1986) • Robert Richardson, *Communings in the Sanctuary* (1872) • William Robinson, *The Administration of the Lord's Supper* (1947) • William Robinson, *A Companion to the Communion Service* (1942) • William Robinson, *Essays on Christian Unity* (1923) • William Robinson, "The Meaning of *Anamnēsis*," *Shane Quarterly* 14 (1953): 20-24 • William Robinson, *The Sacraments and Life* (1949) • Barton W. Stone, "The Lord's Supper," *Christian Messenger* (1834): 176-77 • David M. Thompson, "A Disciples View of the Lord's Supper and the Unity of the Church," *Mid-Stream* 27 (1986): 357-72 • Ronny F. Wade, *The Sun Will Shine Again, Someday: A History of the Non-Class, One Cup Churches of Christ* (1986) • Keith Watkins, "Naïve Sacramentalism: Barton W. Stone's Sacramental Theology," *Encounter* 49 (1988): 37-51 • Keith Watkins, *The Communion Service: A Model for Christian Churches* (1983) • Keith Watkins, "Shifting Left/Shifting Right: Changing Eucharistic Practices in Churches of the Stone-Campbell Tradition," *Discipliana* 56 (1996): 35-48.

PAUL M. BLOWERS *and* BYRON C. LAMBERT

Louisville Bible College

Bible college affiliated with the Christian Churches/ Churches of Christ.

Louisville, Kentucky, was the location of an earlier Bible college, McGarvey Bible College (est. 1923), named for the renowned conservative biblical scholar J. W. McGarvey. In 1924 that school merged with the Cincinnati Bible Institute (est. 1923) to become Cincinnati Bible Seminary. In 1948 some leaders at Cincinnati Bible Seminary returned to Louisville, Kentucky, to organize a new college, Louisville Bible College, which held its first classes in 1949 at its main building near the University of Louisville campus. These leaders from Cincinnati included Frank W. Buck, Ira M. Boswell, Henry G. Davis, Robert Charles Buck, and Ralph L. Records.

From its earliest mission statement, Louisville Bible College desired "to train young men for the ministry of the Gospel of Jesus Christ and young women for Christian service." All officials and faculty must believe in a statement of faith that includes the deity of Jesus Christ, the inspiration and inerrancy of the Bible, and the Church of Christ as revealed in the New Testament. The college's curriculum has traditionally centered on biblical studies, with related courses in church history, speech, English, and apologetics for the training of Christian workers.

From 1950 to 1990, the college saw periods of growth and decline in the shadow of larger Bible colleges in the Ohio Valley region. The college made its appeal to educate ministers and churches in rural Kentucky and southern Indiana. In the 1990s, while the number of full-time students remained low, Louisville Bible College experienced substantial growth in the number of total students attending the college.

In the fall of 1990, the college moved from its original location to its current nine-and-one-half-acre campus in southeastern Jefferson County. The college also diversified its degree programs to include a certificate, associate degrees, bachelor degrees, and master's degrees with special emphasis on biblical counseling and biblical preaching. The college does not, however, have accreditation of the Accrediting Association of Bible Colleges. It utilizes an entirely part-time faculty who combine ministry experience with academic credentials. Louisville Bible College has also developed non-traditional forms of education that encourage short-term and off-campus learning. While the college has concentrated its influence in the Louisville vicinity, recent developments have enabled Louisville Bible College to foster its relationship with the rural churches of Kentucky and southern Indiana.

See also Bible College Movement; Higher Education, Views of in the Movement

BIBLIOGRAPHY Thomas R. Edwards, *A History of Louisville Bible College* (1999). ANTHONY J. SPRINGER

Louisville Plan, The

A plan for organizing missions in the Stone-Campbell Movement, adopted in 1869 at the meeting of the General Convention in Louisville, Kentucky.

The Louisville Plan arose from a perceived need to reorganize the American Christian Missionary Society (ACMS) in a way that would be acceptable to more members of the Movement. Contingents within the Stone-Campbell Movement, however, continued to regard extra-congregational organizations in any form as problematic.

Established in 1849, the ACMS did not meet with the expected success, especially in the foreign mission field. Attempts to redesign the society to make it more acceptable to its detractors and more effective in terms of its missionary enterprise were not sufficient, many believed, to salvage the ACMS in its then present form. Increased hostility toward the ACMS because of its "war resolutions" further weakened the body. A group of twenty prominent persons representing both supporters and critics was appointed to devise a system that would correct the deficiencies of the ACMS and find reception among the churches. Notable members of the committee chaired by W. T. Moore were Isaac Errett, C. L. Loos, James S. Lamar, Moses E. Lard, Alexander Procter, William K. Pendleton, and Benjamin Franklin.

At the 1869 Convention in Louisville, Kentucky, a plan drafted by the committee during the previous year was approved. This was the first time the convention had convened in assembly outside of Cincinnati, Ohio. The selection of Louisville was perceived as a means of reconciliation by inviting Northern and Southern churches together on neutral ground. Organizers hoped a new meeting site could provide an amicable environment in which to promote a new organizational design.

The Louisville Plan had the effect of more tightly structuring a loose confederation of churches whose members participated in conventions through district and state organizations. It sought to capitalize on those existing conventions through layers of boards comprised of delegates. Each board was to be managed by an employed corresponding secretary and presided over by a president.

There were four essential points to the Louisville Plan. Messengers or delegates from local churches were elected to district meetings. From district meetings delegates were elected to state meetings. The general missionary conventions were to have a predetermined number of delegates elected from the states. Each state was allotted two delegates plus one for every 5,000 additional members. The change was significant in more than just name, for the general convention was no longer a mass meeting as the ACMS had been but a delegate assembly of some 150 selected individuals.

The financial design had a pyramidal shape similar to that of the delegate selection. At the base of the pyramid, local churches were to designate pledges intended to serve all three levels of the structure. Money from the churches was sent directly to the district, which then kept one-half of the contributions for its mission work and internal administration. The other half was sent by the district to the state society for its mission work and internal administration. The state society forwarded half of its amount on to the general board of the missionary convention.

The Louisville Plan was received with enthusiasm at the adopting convention with only two dissenting votes. Even before it was fully tested, though, it broke down, primarily because of resistance from local church people. The money pledged by the congregations, probably reluctantly, was not faithfully sent. Not enough was received to fund adequately the secretary's salary at the general board level, much less to finance any missionary efforts.

The Plan also failed for a variety of theological and ecclesiological reasons. Throughout the churches there was fear of too much authority being lodged with the general board. The leadership at all levels was not prepared to administer such an intricate structure and was unsure how to manage it. Even with the selection of Louisville as a reconciling maneuver in the immediate postwar period, regionalism survived, thereby stalling cooperative efforts. The Plan itself had a divisive effect. Despite the overwhelmingly affirmative vote, it still was regarded by neither the pro nor the anti factions as a completely suitable system. Expectedly, some continued to argue that such a plan was not authorized by Scripture and therefore was unscriptural. No structure larger than the local church was appropriate. Finally, there were those who saw participation in such organizations as a test of fellowship. Under the ACMS system, membership was voluntary, as were the financial contributions, and the conventions were viewed as associations of individuals rather than delegate gatherings or church assemblies.

While not officially dissolved until 1895 when the name of the General Missionary Convention was changed back to the American Christian Missionary Society, the Louisville Plan was essentially defunct in 1872. The ACMS was resurrected with individuals rather than churches requested to undergird and sustain the work.

See also American Christian Missionary Society; Errett, Isaac; Foreign Christian Missionary Society, The; Franklin, Benjamin; Lamar, James Sanford; Lard, Moses E.; Loos, Charles Louis; Milligan, Robert; Moore, William Thomas; Munnell, Thomas; Pendleton, William Kimbrough; Proctor, Alexander; United Christian Missionary Society, The

BIBLIOGRAPHY William E. Tucker, *J. H. Garrison and Disciples of Christ* (1964).

JOHN M. IMBLER

Lubbock Christian University

Liberal arts institution, awarding bachelor's and master's degrees and related to Churches of Christ.

The university was launched as a two-year (junior) college in 1957, following three years of operation of Lubbock Christian School (a K-12 school still on the university campus). Opening with only 120 students and a faculty of seventeen, by 1999 the college was a university with enrollment nearing 1,400 and with a full-time faculty of sixty-five. The years of greatest movement began in 1968 when the board of trustees made the decision to expand to a four-year college.

With many sources of leadership and major funding, two stand out: J. E. "Gene" Hancock and his wife, Eileen, began their involvement in 1964 with a gift to build the Betty Hancock Student Center, named in honor of their deceased daughter, and the J. E. and L. E. Mabee Foundation whose gifts have funded the construction of seven buildings and the renovation of several others.

In addition to other important gifts in support of the school, J. E. Hancock's 1976 gift of 4,000 acres of farmland to serve as the site of a massive environmental study led to a farming operation utilizing the application of treated effluent and, twenty years later, to the sale of the land to the city of Lubbock for $6 million, which was added to the university endowment in 1999. In recognition of their work with the school, the university's College of Liberal Arts was named in honor of J. E. and Eileen Hancock in 1989.

Important points in the history of the institution include the appointment of F. W. Mattox (1909-2001) as founding president (1956), accreditation as a junior college (1959), the summer program "Encounter" for high school students (began 1970), accreditation as a senior college (1973), establishment of the Institute of Water Research and the effluent land-application water project (1979), designation as a university (1987), accreditation of the social work program by the Council on Social Work Education (1988), the establishment of a graduate program in ministry (1988), the founding of the nursing program (1991), the acquisition of Pine Springs Christian Camp near Cloudcroft, New Mexico (1995), the establishment of the environmental science program (1995), the accreditation of the nursing program by the National League of Nursing (1995), the founding of the College of Education and the Center for Character Education (1996), the establishment of a graduate program in education (1997), many years of recognition from the Templeton Foundation for free enterprise education and for character education, several national championships in the Students in Free Enterprise competition, and national athletic titles in rodeo, baseball, and cross country.

Following F. W. Mattox, who retired in 1974, presidents who have led the school are W. Joe Hacker (1974-76), Harvie M. Pruitt (1976-82), Steven S. Lemley (1982-93), and L. Ken Jones (inaugurated in 1993). Chairing the board of trustees since the founding of Lubbock Christian School in 1954 have been J. B. McCorkle, Paul Sherrod, Lennis Baker, J. E. Hancock, and Jerry Harris (beginning in 1997).

STEVEN S. LEMLEY

Lunenburg Letter, The

Controversial letter appealing to Alexander Campbell to address the status of unimmersed believers.

The significance of the Lunenburg Letter (1837) is not so much the letter itself, but Alexander Campbell's reply to it. The letter was written by "a conscientious sister," as Campbell described her, in Lunenburg, Virginia, who had been struck by some things Campbell had been saying in the *Millennial Harbinger,* such as his statement that "we find in all Protestant parties Christians as exemplary as ourselves."

She saw this as a contradiction to what he had taught about baptism by immersion as prerequisite to being a Christian. "Will you be so good as to let me know how anyone becomes a Christian?" she asked, and went on to inquire, "Does the name of Christ or Christian belong to any but those who believe the gospel, repent, and are buried by baptism into the death of Christ?"

Campbell's reply was direct: "But who is a Christian? I answer, Every one that believes in his heart that Jesus of Nazareth is the Messiah, the Son of God; repents of his sins, and obeys him in all things according to his measure of knowledge of his will." He went on to say that one may be imperfect in some respects and still be a Christian: "A perfect man in Christ or a perfect Christian is one thing; and a 'babe in Christ,' a stripling in the faith, or an imperfect Christian, is another. The New Testament recognizes both the perfect man and the imperfect man in Christ."

Campbell stated unequivocally: "I cannot, therefore, make any one duty the standard of Christian state or character, not even immersion." He said he was unwilling to regard those who had been sprinkled in infancy without their own knowledge and consent as aliens from Christ and without hope of heaven.

He pressed the point further: "Should I find a Pedobaptist more intelligent in the Christian Scriptures, more spiritually-minded and more devoted to the Lord than a Baptist, or one immersed on a profession of the ancient faith, I could not hesitate a moment in giving the preference of my heart to him that loveth much. Did I act otherwise I would be a pure sectarian, a Pharisee among Christians."

As for those who may be mistaken about baptism, he allowed: "Ignorance is always a crime when it is voluntary; and innocent when it is involuntary." Since he could not prove that those who neglect baptism by immersion are voluntarily ignorant, he could only conclude: "There is no occasion, then, for making immersion, on a profession of the faith, absolutely essential to a Christian — though it may be greatly essential to his sanctification and comfort."

When this exchange appeared in his *Millennial Harbinger,* Campbell was so taken by the negative response that he quipped that it proved that "there are but few 'Campbellites' in the country." He conceded it had caused the Movement's constituents pain and had given pleasure to his sectarian friends. He was accused of inconsistency and of surrendering his original position. This led to two more essays on "Christians Among the Sects" in which he defended himself against these charges.

Campbell may not have helped matters when, in his rejoinder, he agreed with the sister in Lunenburg that the term "Christian" was first given to immersed believers and to none else, but then added, "We do not believe it was given to them because they were immersed, but because they had put on Christ." He insisted that since his *Christian Baptist* days over a decade earlier, and in his debate with Robert Owen in 1829, he had repeatedly taken the position that there were Christians in all the denominations. Moreover, he observed, "what could mean all that we have written upon the union of Christians on apostolic grounds, had we taught that all Christians in the world were already united in our own community."

This episode becomes more understandable when one realizes that at this time Campbell was coping with one of the Movement's first heresies, one having to do with extreme views on baptism. John Thomas, a physician who became an editor of some influence, insisted that for baptism to be valid one must understand that it is for the remission of sins. He caused a furor when he made it his mission to reimmerse those he persuaded to his position. Campbell saw this as sectarian and vigorously opposed Thomas's efforts, even declaring that he could no longer be recognized as a brother. W. K. Pendleton revealed twenty-five years later that the sister in Lunenburg was "conspicuous in her zeal for 'Thomasism.'" Some thus theorize that Thomas himself actually wrote the Lunenburg Letter pseudonymously, seeking to trap Campbell in a compromised position toward immersion. Campbell may have implied this in the correspondence, though he never mentions Thomas's name. But it helps to explain his relentless pursuit of the woman's questions, and his zeal to spare the Movement from a legalistic view of baptism and to preserve a more open view of who is a Christian.

As for defining a Christian, the correspondence allowed Campbell to state his "favorite and oft-repeated definition," one different from that first given in the Lunenburg response: "A Christian is one that habitually believes all that Christ says, and habitually does all that he bids him."

Later interpretation of the Lunenburg Letter controversy, which extended well into 1840 in the *Millennial Harbinger,* followed the emerging polarities in the Stone-Campbell Movement. Some conservative restorationists viewed Campbell's response to the Lunenburg Letter as a temporary lapse in his otherwise rigorous position on immersion as basic to Christian identity; moderates and liberals, by contrast, construed his response as proof of an emerging conciliatory and ecumenical spirit on Campbell's part.

See also Baptism; Thomas, John; Unity, Christian

BIBLIOGRAPHY Alexander Campbell, "Any Christians Among Protestant Parties," *Millennial Harbinger* (1837): 41-44 • Alexander Campbell, "Christians Among the Sects," *Millennial Harbinger* (1837): 506-8 • Alexander Campbell, "Any Christians Among the Sects?" *Millennial Harbinger* (1837): 561-67 (all this correspondence compiled on-line at: http://www.bible.acu.edu/stone-campbell/Etexts/lun16.html) • John Mark Hicks, "Alexander Campbell on Christians Among the Sects," in *Baptism and the Remission of Sins: An Historical Perspective,* ed. David W. Fletcher (1990), pp. 171-202.

LEROY GARRETT

Lynchburg College

Liberal arts college associated with the Christian Church (Disciples of Christ). Founded in 1903 by Josephus Hopwood on the rolling hills of the Piedmont region of Virginia, Lynchburg College has been associated with the Stone-Campbell Movement since its beginning. The school was originally named Virginia Christian College. A group of ministers and business leaders sought out Hopwood, who was serving as president of Milligan College in Tennessee, to help them establish a Christian school in Virginia. The college, from its inception, was a liberal arts and coeducational institution. This latter characteristic was uncommon during the early twentieth century, but Hopwood and his wife, Sarah LaRue Hopwood, were strong proponents for this pedagogical approach. Lynchburg College is the second oldest coeducational undergraduate school in the state of Virginia.

When the college opened, it had only one building, Westover Hall, a resort house purchased by the supporters of the school and Hopwood. The faculty consisted of eleven members, and there were only fifty-five students. The school changed its name from Virginia Christian College to Lynchburg College in 1919 due to the possibility of confusing the college with another school with the initials VCC. The new name also reflected the fact that Lynchburg College had grown in reputation and recruitment outside of the Virginia state borders.

The campus was expanded to include three more buildings in 1909, including Hopwood Hall and Carnegie Hall. Among those who funded this expansion was Andrew Carnegie. In the following decades, more facilities were built, but the original facility, Westover Hall, became no longer usable and had to be torn down.

Lynchburg College continues its original commitment to a solid liberal arts education in a coeducational environment. Its curriculum has expanded to include a variety of majors/minors and graduate studies in business and education.

See also Higher Education, Views of in the Movement; Hopwood, Josephus

BIBLIOGRAPHY D. Duane Cummins, *The Disciples Colleges: A History* (1987) • Orville Wake, "A History of Lynchburg College 1903-1953" (doctoral dissertation, University of Virginia, 1957).

LISA W. DAVISON

Lynn, Benjamin (1750-1814)

Independent restorationist leader born in Chester County, Pennsylvania. At age 17 he went into the Ohio woods and lived for seven years among the native Americans. During the American Revolutionary War he aided American forces and settlers withstand the siege of Fort Harrodsburg, Kentucky, through his knowledge of the native Americans. During that six-month siege of 1777 he was converted to the Baptist Church and after the war began to preach. One author called him the "Daniel Boone of the Kentucky Baptists." In 1805 he became disillusioned with Baptist doctrine and made a thorough study of the Scriptures. He then began an effort to restore the New Testament church as he saw it. In 1805 he heard of Barton W. Stone and traveled the eighty miles from Bardstown, Kentucky, where he was living, to Cane Ridge, where Stone immersed him. In 1810 he moved to Huntsville, Alabama, where he died in 1814. Before his death he had established an independent Church of Christ in that city.

Benjamin Lynn's legacy lives on through the Chisholms, D'Spains, and Clarks. His grandson, Lynn D'Spain, was an early pioneer preacher who with Mansil Matthews (1806-1891) led a caravan of members of the Movement to Texas in 1836. His great-grandsons were Addison and Randolph Clark, sons of Joseph Clark (1815-1901) who founded Add-Ran College, forerunner of Texas Christian University. Benjamin Lynn's name lives on in churches in Alabama and Texas and in place names in Kentucky like Lynn Creek and Nolin Lake. Lynn should be ranked with John Mulkey and Rice Haggard as leaders who began independent restoration movements in the early American frontier.

See also Haggard, Rice; Matthews Family; Mulkey, John; Texas Christian University

BIBLIOGRAPHY Joseph Lynn Clark, *Thank God We Made It! A Family Affair With Education* (1969).

C. WAYNE KILPATRICK

M

Maccalla, William

See Campbell-Maccalla Debate

Magarey, Thomas

See Australia, The Movement in

Magic Valley Christian College

Liberal arts college affiliated with Churches of Christ that operated from 1958 to 1969 in Albion, Idaho. The school's first president, Tennessee minister and publisher George W. DeHoff (1913-1993), opened the school in 1958 for 102 students from sixteen states.

The Idaho State Legislature had established the campus in 1893 as Albion State Normal School, later renamed Southern Idaho College of Education. In a 1951 economy drive, the state closed the school, and in 1957 Idaho Governor Robert Smylie turned the property over to Boise lumberman Dallas Harris, president of the Magic Valley Christian College (MVCC) board, on a 99-year lease with a payment of $100 per year. The charter authorized MVCC to operate an educational facility offering two years of high school and two years of college.

The $5 million campus consisted of 41 acres and 22 buildings, and was located on the edge of the fertile Magic Valley in the Sawtooth Mountains. The fewer than 3,000 members of the Churches of Christ in Idaho and surrounding states soon found the maintenance and support of the school to be difficult.

In 1964 Donald R. Neilson (b. 1929), Utah minister and the second president of MVCC, trimmed course offerings in an effort to cut costs. Finally in March 1969, MVCC accepted a proposal to close the Albion campus and relocate to Baker, Oregon. The school reopened as Baker College in fall 1969 but closed the following year. Records are located at Cascade College in Portland, Oregon.

See also Cascade College

BIBLIOGRAPHY *Magic Valley Christian College Bulletin* (1958) • "Senate Vote Okays Bill to Allow Lease of SICE for School," *Times News* (January 30, 1957).

ERMA JEAN LOVELAND

Mahoning Baptist Association

Baptist association in the Mahoning Valley of Ohio closely associated with the reform movement of Thomas and Alexander Campbell affiliated in its early years.

From its formation in 1820, the Mahoning Baptist Association was filled with ideas of religious reformation. A. S. Hayden reports in his early history of the Disciples of Christ in Ohio that the Mahoning Association founded itself on the Philadelphia Confession of Faith as its "organic law," but that it tolerated doctrinal diversity and valued open discussion. Alexander Campbell's relationship with members of the Mahoning Association began as early as 1821. His published debates with Presbyterians John Walker and William Maccalla, and his new journal, the *Christian Baptist,* were very well received by participating ministers, men who were equally impressed by Campbell's compelling critique of Calvinism and his preaching of the simple gospel. In 1824 the association heartily adopted the very same ecumenical, reforming views that nearly led to Alexander Campbell's excommunication from the Redstone Baptist Association.

In 1827 the Mahoning Association chose Walter Scott to serve as its evangelist. Scott brought clarity and power to the reforming thoughts of the day. He won thousands of converts during his three-year evangelistic ministry. In August of 1830, the association disbanded. Alexander Campbell reflected favorably on the Baptist associational model as a form of intercongregational evangelistic cooperation. He saw them — and the Mahoning Association in particular — as "congenial with our age and country, and adaptable to the wants of the people" because they were consensual, covenantal, and flexible. Campbell

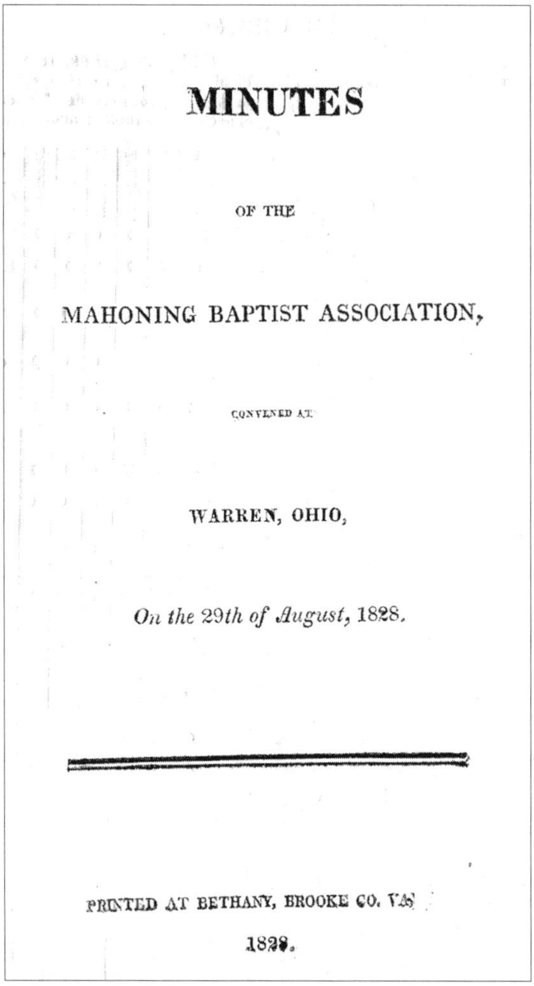
MINUTES

OF THE

MAHONING BAPTIST ASSOCIATION,

CONVENED AT

WARREN, OHIO,

On the 29th of August, 1828.

PRINTED AT BETHANY, BROOKE CO. VA.

1828.

Minutes of the Mahoning Baptist Association, 1828. The Association, with its minimalist structure and commitment to evangelistic cooperation, was a good organizational fit for the Campbells and their followers in the early years of their reform movement. Courtesy of Bethany College

lamented the dissolution of the Mahoning Association and considered it premature. After its disbanding, he even purportedly made a speech declaring in favor of an evangelistic system patterned after the Methodist model of circuit preaching.

A number of historians of the Stone-Campbell Movement have dated the beginning of the Disciples of Christ from the dissolution of the Mahoning Baptist Association, since it truly marked their independent existence.

See also Baptists; Bentley, Adamson; Evangelism, Evangelists — Nineteenth Century; Hayden, Amos Sutton; Redstone Baptist Association; Rigdon, Sidney; Scott, Walter

BIBLIOGRAPHY William Baxter, *Life of Elder Walter Scott* (1874) • Alexander Campbell, "Anecdotes, Incidents, and Facts Connected with the History of the Current Reformation, Never Before Published — No. VI," *Millennial Harbinger* (1849): 46-49 • Alexander Campbell, "Church Organization — nos. III-IV," *Millennial Harbinger* (1849): 269-73 • A. S. Hayden, *Early History of the Disciples in the Western Reserve, Ohio* (1875) • Robert Richardson, *Memoirs of Alexander Campbell,* vol. 2 (1869).

PHIL MCINTOSH

Manhattan Christian College

Bible college in Manhattan, Kansas, associated with the Christian Churches/Churches of Christ.

The school was founded in 1927 as Kansas Bible College by Eugene C. Sanderson, partially embodying his dream of a Bible college adjacent to every state college or university. In its early days the college was a branch of the International Bible Mission and Eugene Bible University (now Northwest Christian College), Eugene, Oregon. Financial difficulties made it necessary to reorganize every year for the first three years. The college eventually took the name of Christian Workers University, and then Manhattan Bible College. This name, adopted in 1930, lasted until 1971, when the name was changed to Manhattan Christian College to reflect a broadening of curricular opportunities.

Many of the college's early financial problems were due to Sanderson's simultaneous involvement in several other Christian enterprises. These were all linked together under one organization (The International Bible Mission), and all were in debt. One early criticism of the college was that all the important decisions were being made for it in Oregon by trustees who had no ties to Kansas. This made churches and individuals in Kansas reluctant to support the school. Sanderson was eventually asked to resign, and the college was chartered as Manhattan Bible College with a local board of trustees.

Even with a new name, new charter, and new trustees the college had a huge debt. Most of this had been incurred erecting a main building directly across the street from Kansas State University. The Great Depression and the dust bowl conditions in Kansas further exacerbated the school's financial woes. As a result the main building was lost to foreclosure in 1937. The college continued to function in rented facilities. In 1943 the college regained its building.

T. H. Johnson served as president until his death in 1952. After two brief presidencies Wilford F. Lown became president in 1955, and the college began further campus expansion and academic innovation and enjoyed increased enrollment. The campus grew in size from a mere quarter of a city block to four square blocks. New buildings were built and acquired, including a library, a dining facility, and a residence hall.

In 1968 cooperative programs were begun with Kansas State University. This arrangement allowed students to attend both schools and receive a degree from both. This was an innovative concept among Bible colleges and was widely criticized at the time as compromising their purpose. The success of this program, however, caused other colleges to inaugurate similar relationships with state universities. Better facilities and greater academic opportunities led to a substantial increase in enrollment.

The 1980s and 1990s saw financial problems and regrouping. Fund-raising campaigns made possible additional campus expansion in 1986 and 1993. The early years of Kenneth Cable's current presidency were devoted to achieving financial stability. Most of the campus had been built by borrowing money, which created considerable debt. Academic development continued with the inauguration in 1994 of a degree completion program for adults. In 2000 regional accreditation was achieved. In 2002 the enrollment approached 400. The college is accredited by the Accrediting Association of Bible Colleges (1949) and the North Central Association of Colleges and Schools (2000).

In its early years Manhattan tried to be a bridge between Disciples of Christ "cooperatives" and "independents." It was often characterized as a "middle of the road college." In the 1960s, with the denominational restructure of the Christian Church (Disciples of Christ), the college's administration and trustees chose identification with the Christian Churches/Churches of Christ. The college has nonetheless remained open to fellowship with all the heirs of the Stone-Campbell Movement and with those outside the Movement as well.

The college has remained committed to the priesthood of all believers and the principle that Christians are called to ministry in whatever their vocation. This is the rationale behind the dual degree and degree completion programs. Manhattan graduates now serve in a variety of church ministries, missionary work, and even secular vocations.

See also Bible College Movement; Higher Education, Views of in the Movement; Sanderson, Eugene C.

LARRY B. SULLIVAN

Maritime Christian College

Bible college serving the Christian Churches/Churches of Christ in the Canadian Atlantic (Maritime) provinces.

In the mid-twentieth century, the churches of the region experienced the continued loss of ministerial students to schools in western Canada and the United States as well as growing suspicions of theological liberalism associated with the College of Churches of Christ in Toronto, Ontario. In response, the elders and minister of Central Christian Church in Charlottetown, Prince Edward Island, along with other area ministers, met in 1959 to discuss the possibility of a local Bible college. Maritime Christian College was established the next year using the facilities of Central Christian Church, with its minister, Charles P. Herndon, serving as founding president. Shortly thereafter, Kenneth T. Norris was given the responsibility of guiding the young institution through its first two decades. The majority of the college board members in the early years were elders at Central Christian Church, but in 1972 the board was restructured to incorporate broader representation from other congregations in the region. Successive presidents were Stewart Lewis (1980-95), Merle Zimmerman (1996-2000), and Fred Osborne (2000-).

The college continues to offer undergraduate degrees and programs to prepare students for various church ministries both domestic and cross-cultural. Extension courses were offered intermittently in Antigua, West Indies, from 1977 to 1990.

In 1993 the college relocated to its present campus directly across from the University of Prince Edward Island. Maritime Christian College sponsors the annual K. T. Norris Lectureship, first established in 1962. The quarterly newsletter *The Maritime Messenger* was first published in 1962.

See also Bible College Movement; Canada, The Movement in; Higher Education, Views of in the Movement

BIBLIOGRAPHY Reuben Butchart, *The Disciples of Christ in Canada Since 1830* (1949) • Reuben Butchart, *The Central Christian Church: Its Origins and Growth* (1975) • Reuben Butchart, *Maritime Christian College Decade Books* (1970, 1980, 1990, 2000).

BLAYNE A. BANTING

Mars Hill Bible School

Christian elementary and secondary school near Florence, Alabama, operated by members of Churches of Christ. Established in 1947 on the site of T. B. Larimore's Mars Hill Academy (1871-87).

Partly in response to the devastating moral implications of World War II, members of Churches of Christ in the Shoals area of northwest Alabama proposed the construction of a Christian school similar to one begun in 1943 in Athens, Alabama. A local physician, W. W. Alexander, purchased property from the son of T. B. Larimore, Virgil, who still lived on the family property near Florence where Larimore had operated his nineteenth-century Academy. Businessmen M. S. Killen and Charlie G. Morris provided

T. B. Larimore's home near Florence, Alabama. From 1871 to 1887 it housed Larimore's Mars Hill Academy. In 1947 members of Churches of Christ purchased the site for Mars Hill Bible School. The home is on the National Register of Historic Places. Courtesy of the Disciples of Christ Historical Society

equipment and buses. Irven Lee served as the first president.

At its opening in September 1947, almost 400 students were enrolled. The original Larimore home built in 1870 served as the main classroom building. New classroom buildings were erected in 1958, 1964, and 1988. The school was accredited by the Alabama State Department of Education from the beginning and received regional accreditation from the Southern Association of Colleges and Schools in 1972. Both the high school and elementary received Excellence in Education Awards from the U.S. Department of Education in 1987, and the school has continued to be a leader in academics in the region. In the 1970s enrollment climbed to over 800; since then it has continued to hold steady at around 1,000 students.

Larimore's Mars Hill Academy trained ministers and lay leaders who established hundreds of Churches of Christ, especially in north Alabama and middle Tennessee. Mars Hill Bible School and its predecessor have been a major factor in the continuing strength of Churches of Christ in that area of the country.

See also Larimore, Theophilus Brown

BIBLIOGRAPHY Nan Ray Alexander, *It Was Their Spirit That Made It Go: The Athens Bible School Story in Its Early Days, 1943-1955* (1997) • Mars Hill Bible School, *Something Special* (1977) • Mars Hill Bible School, *Reaching for the Gold: 1871-1997* (1997). DOUGLAS A. FOSTER

Matthews Family

Members of the Matthews family were among the earliest followers of Barton Stone. Joseph Matthews (1766-1855) formed friendships with Kentucky preachers Benjamin Lynn (1750-1814) and John Mulkey (1806-1882) by 1805. His 1807 relocation to northern Alabama established the Movement on that frontier. Matthews accompanied the 1835 "church on wheels" to Texas with son Mansil Walter Matthews (1806-1891), who noted in 1855 that his father had been a "member of the Church of Christ — 60 years." In a *Christian Messenger* obituary, James Evans Matthews (1799-1867) observed that his father Robert Matthews (1772-1833) had been a member of the Christian Church from 1803. These early dates suggest possible links to the O'Kelly Christians.

By 1825 James Matthews was emerging as a leading evangelist in Alabama, Tennessee, and Mississippi. He was born March 19, 1799, in Laurens County, South Carolina, and moved with his family to Madison County, Alabama, in 1811. Benjamin Lynn exposed him to the Stone-Campbell Movement, and he began preaching in 1826. Later that year he moved to Florence, Alabama, and in August he baptized Tolbert Fanning after B. F. Hall preached on "Baptism for Remission of Sins." Matthews's three articles published in 1829 in the *Christian Messenger,* titled "Gospel Plan for Saving Sinners," outlined the concept of baptism for the remission of sins for many in the Stone Movement. By 1832 Campbell's "Reformers" had joined Stoneite preachers in promoting this doctrine in northern Alabama. Matthews expressed alarm over their "censorious spirit" and use of the doctrine as a test of communion, urging instead a "reformation in spirit and practice." Matthews moved from Florence, Alabama, to Tate County, Mississippi, in 1837 and in 1842 was elected state auditor of public accounts. He served as representative from 1856 until the end of 1857, and he continued to preach until his death on June 29, 1867.

In 1836 Mansil W. Matthews became the first evangelist from the Stone Movement in Texas, and he remained an influential preacher there for fifty-five years. John Mulkey baptized Matthews in 1823, following which his father Joseph C. Matthews apprenticed him to Benjamin F. Hall. Matthews began preaching by 1825, attending area conferences and holding protracted meetings among the Stone congregations of northern Alabama and central Tennessee. In late 1835, Mansil Matthews, assisted by Benjamin Lynn D'Spain, led a caravan of Texas-bound Christians from Tennessee and Alabama, the group becoming known as the "church on wheels." Matthews was one of the most active Texas preachers during the antebellum years, laboring throughout northeast and central Texas. As early as 1842, his home congregation of White Oak numbered 150 members. Matthews also practiced law and medicine, dabbled in politics, farmed, and speculated in land. His varied interests and nomadic nature engendered criticism from some preachers and editors who believed that he should be fully devoted to preaching.

Though a wealthy slaveholder, Mansil Matthews remained a Union man and opposed secession. Rebel authorities convicted him of treason, but the intervention of an influential Masonic brother saved his life. Though his influence diminished in postwar Texas, Matthews could still attract crowds of 2,000 listeners. As divisions widened within the Movement, Matthews remained in the conservative camp, expressing support for those positions taken by the *Gospel Advocate.* Matthews preached at Paradise, Texas, only days before his death, capping a sixty-six-year preaching career.

Other noted members of the Matthews family who were active in evangelism include Governor Joseph Warren Matthews (1807-1862) of Mississippi who promoted the work in that state and in Tennessee, and noted writer and speaker William J. Barbee (1816-1892), who worked throughout the upper South, Midwest, and Texas. Texas evangelists included Abner Hill (1788-1861), John Clinton Matthews (1825-1901), and Samuel Mathis Crisp (1814-1892). Allie Barbee Lewis (1855-1892) was a popular contributor to religious periodicals.

See also Fanning, Tolbert; Hall, Benjamin Franklin; Lynn, Benjamin; Mulkey, John; Stone, Barton Warren

BIBLIOGRAPHY Original Documents of the Matthews Papers, Mary Counts Burnett Library, Texas Christian University, Fort Worth, Texas • B. F. Hall, *The Proud Preacher: The Autobiography of B. F. Hall* (1869) • James E. Matthews, "The Gospel Plan for Saving Sinners," *Christian Messenger* 3 (April/May/July 1829): 125-29, 150-54, 211-13 • Matthews Collection, Bancroft Library, University of California at Berkeley, Berkeley, California • W. C. Rogers, *Recollection of Men of Faith* (1889), pp. 132-34.

TERRY COWAN *and* C. WAYNE KILPATRICK

Maus, Cynthia Pearl (1880-1970)

Disciples of Christ Christian educator, youth minister, and author.

Born on a farm near Clyde, Iowa, and educated at the State Normal School in Emporia, Kansas, and at Northwestern University, Maus served in the department of church school literature for the Christian Board of Publication beginning in 1910. There she helped create the "graded lessons" for the religious education of children. In 1914 she became National Young People's Superintendent in the American Christian Missionary Society, and she helped establish vacation Bible school, weekday Bible school, summer camps and conferences (the first being in 1919), and International Youth Conventions (the first in Memphis in 1926). In addition, she authored books on issues in religious education and a number of volumes on religion and the fine arts, which include anthologies of prose, poetry, music, and paintings organized around such themes as Christ, Mary, and the Old Testament. An often-cited quotation illustrates her devotion to religious education and the arts: "You may have tangible wealth untold, caskets of jewels and coffers of gold. Richer than I you could never be; I know someone who told stories to me." She was honored by the children of Bolenge, Belgian Congo, in 1956, and granted an honorary degree from Chapman College in 1958.

See also American Christian Missionary Society; Christian Board of Publication DEBRA B. HULL

McCaleb, John Moody (1861-1953)

Preacher, teacher, author, and pioneer missionary for Churches of Christ.

A young and vigorous J. M. McCaleb left for mission work in Japan in 1892. He refused to accept money from any missionary society, instead soliciting funds from Churches of Christ in America, teaching English, and operating a farm. In 1907 McCaleb had materials shipped from America to build a Tennessee-style house, now a cultural monument and museum to McCaleb and Christian missions in Japan.
Courtesy of the Center for Restoration Studies, Abilene Christian University

Born in Tennessee and educated at the College of the Bible in Lexington, Kentucky, McCaleb and his wife, Della, left for Japan with a group of workers headed by W. K. Azbill (1848-1929) in March 1892. Though Azbill did not philosophically oppose missionary societies, he had pledged to accept funds only from individuals and churches that did not work through the society. When in 1893 Azbill accepted funds from a Young People's Christian Endeavor Society at a church in Ohio, McCaleb withdrew from the group and worked independently. Because funds were meager, he supplemented his income by teaching English in Tokyo.

The work was difficult and discouraging, with many converts "leaving the faith." However, by 1909, McCaleb counted 650 baptisms in seven churches. Co-workers came and left. McCaleb was frequently embroiled in controversy over paying local preachers "whose faith was not much deeper then their pockets." Because Della had frequent health problems, she returned with the children to America. McCaleb was separated from his family for most of the remaining thirty-five years he labored on the mission field. He did make several trips back to America to report and raise funds. Because he was partially supported by premillennial congregations in Louisville, Kentucky, he was sometimes accused of holding premillennial beliefs himself, making fund-raising more difficult. Because of the war, he was forced to leave Japan in 1941. He taught at Pepperdine College until a heart attack in 1945 left him bedridden. He died eight years later.

McCaleb engaged in the less spectacular work of seed sowing and foundation laying. He advocated indigenous church principles (though he himself refused to eat Japanese food and live in Japanese housing). He opposed buying insurance because "it demonstrated a distrust in God."

McCaleb had a keen sense of humor, was humble, strong in faith, fervent in prayer, and industrious. He wrote eleven books, authored more than a dozen tracts, and composed 1,400 poems, almost all of which had a religious theme. McCaleb proved the possibility and respectability of foreign missions for Churches of Christ. He was a spokesperson for missions, a recruiter of missionaries, and an example of self-sacrifice for the cause of world evangelism.

See also Asia, Missions in; Eschatology

BIBLIOGRAPHY David Filbeck, *The First Fifty Years: A Brief History of the Direct Support Missionary Movement* (1980) • J. M. McCaleb, *From Idols to God: Or, My Religious Experience* (1907) • J. M. McCaleb, *On the Trail of the Missionaries* (1930) • Gary Turner, *Pioneer to Japan: A Biography of J. M. McCaleb* (M.A. thesis, Abilene Christian University, 1972).

ED MATHEWS

McGarvey, John W. (1829-1911)

Conservative biblical scholar and Christian apologist of the Disciples of Christ in the late nineteenth and early twentieth centuries.

McGarvey was born March 1, 1829, in Hopkinsville, Kentucky, and grew up in Tremont, Illinois. At age 18 he entered Bethany College (April 1847), where he was baptized, and decided immediately to become a minister. At Bethany he became well acquainted with the Campbells and was often a guest in their home, where he frequently read the Bible to the blind and aged Thomas Campbell. McGarvey excelled at Bethany, graduated in three and a half years, and on July 4, 1850, received the bachelor's degree and delivered the Greek oration.

After a brief period of teaching school in Missouri, in 1862 he was called to be pastor of the Main Street Christian Church in Lexington, Kentucky. Shortly thereafter he became the first professor of sacred history in the newly founded College of the Bible (now Lexington Theological Seminary), where, except for a brief period of expulsion, he would remain until his death in 1911.

Although McGarvey did not become president of the College of the Bible until 1895, he immediately became the dominant personality and most influential professor. By his disciplined classroom teaching, concentrating on biblical content, and by his prolific writings, he influenced two generations of Disciples of Christ ministers. Among his most important books, two must be mentioned.

His *Commentary on Acts* (1863, 1892) is unquestionably one of the most influential biblical commentaries in the Stone-Campbell tradition, both expressing and shaping the Movement's approach to Scripture. It set forth the "plan of salvation," the "pattern" of "the New Testament church," and what had become the traditional Disciples understanding of the Holy Spirit. It also showcased the Stone-Campbell Movement's profound proclivity for the book of Acts as a virtual "canon within the canon."

Lands of the Bible (1880): in the time when academic study of biblical geography was just beginning and before scientific archaeology had begun, McGarvey's observations on his trip to Israel, Palestine, Turkey, Greece, and Italy resulted in a large and thorough work that became one of the first scholarly products of the Stone-Campbell tradition to be used outside Disciples of Christ circles.

Throughout his career, McGarvey resisted what he regarded as the unbelief (and secularism) inherent in the critical methods of biblical interpretation being adopted by some Disciples pastors and teachers. He wrote several apologetic works defending the traditional positions (e.g., *Evidences of Christianity* [1886] and *The Authorship of the Book of Deuteronomy and Its*

Bearings on the Higher Criticism of the Pentateuch [1902]), as well as a weekly column, "Biblical Criticism," in the *Christian Standard* (1893-1904; later published as a book, 1910), in which he attacked new higher critical theories (e.g., the Documentary Hypothesis and comparative Near Eastern creation "myths").

McGarvey embodied the "old paths" hermeneutics in the so-called "progressive era." He adhered fervently to a doctrine of revelation understood in positivistic, static, and factual terms, thereby continuing to feed the restorationist mind-set. McGarvey blasted the effort of the higher critics to admit evolutionary development, change, and variation as intrinsic to the biblical revelation, a revelation that needed to be interpreted strictly in terms of a consistent logical pattern of divine disclosure addressed to human beings whose reasoning powers remained the same throughout history. Even the "dispensations," as highlighted by earlier Stone-Campbell interpreters, admitted of no internal development, since they followed a revelatory plan that was fixed by God from the very beginning.

With this conservative hermeneutics and articulated response to liberalism, McGarvey became a heroic figure both in the Churches of Christ and in the Bible college movement of the Christian Churches/Churches of Christ later in the twentieth century. His commentaries and other works were standard reading in many colleges and seminaries for years.

See also Bethany College; Bible, Authority and Inspiration of the; Bible, Interpretation of the; Lexington Theological Seminary

BIBLIOGRAPHY M. Eugene Boring, *Disciples and the Bible: A History of Disciples Biblical Interpretation in North America* (1997) • J. W. McGarvey, *A Commentary on the Acts of the Apostles* (1863; new ed. 1892) • J. W. McGarvey, *Evidences of Christianity* (1886) • J. W. McGarvey, *Lands of the Bible* (1880) • J. W. McGarvey, *Short Essays in Biblical Criticism* (1910) • W. C. Morro, *"Brother McGarvey": The Life of President J. W. McGarvey of the College of the Bible, Lexington, Kentucky* (1940) • Dwight E. Stevenson and De Loris Stevenson, eds., "The Autobiography of J. W. McGarvey (1829-1911)," Special Edition, *The College of the Bible Quarterly* 37 (1960).

M. EUGENE BORING

McGary, Austin (1846-1928)

Texas sheriff, preacher, debater, editor, and businessman, born in Huntsville, son of a soldier in the Texas Revolution.

McGary grew up in a rough, frontier environment. When the Civil War began, he enlisted in the Huntsville Grays but did not see battle action.

McGary described his youth and early manhood as "wayward." In 1869, involved in what he later called "a serious difficulty with two men in Midway, Texas," McGary killed one of them and seriously wounded the other. Charged with murder, McGary pled self-defense and was acquitted. In 1877, as sheriff of Madison County, Texas, McGary shot and killed a suspect who "made a desperate effort to draw his pistol." Later he took a job transporting convicts across the open plains to the state penitentiary.

In 1881, a "skeptic" at age 35, McGary determined to study the evidences for Christianity, beginning by reading the Campbell-Owen debate. He heard Harry Hamilton in a series of sermons, and on December 24, 1881, Hamilton baptized McGary. Soon McGary began to preach. By early 1884 he was discussing the design and administration of baptism with David Lipscomb (1831-1917) in the *Gospel Advocate* and Thomas Raines Burnett (1842-1916) in the *Christian Messenger.*

In September 1884 McGary founded the *Firm Foundation* to counter the influence of the *Advocate* and *Messenger* on the issue of baptism. McGary affirmed that "belief that baptism is for remission of sins is essential to its validity" against all challengers, including Burnett in written debate (1899). According to McGary, "only those who are baptized with an understanding that it is for remission of sins, have obeyed the law of Christ."

Lipscomb and Burnett opposed McGary's view of baptism, arguing that any persons baptized to obey God, even if they were ignorant of the design of forgiveness of sins, were still acceptable to God. Lipscomb and Burnett sometimes accepted those who had been immersed in Baptist churches without requiring that they be reimmersed. McGary called this practice "shaking in the Baptists." On other fronts he attacked the use of musical instruments in worship and excoriated missionary societies. Over time most Churches of Christ embraced McGary's rejection of Baptist baptism and Disciples "digressions."

In 1902 McGary was forced to resign as editor of the *Firm Foundation* due to his "rough" style of writing. Although McGary had no financial interest in the paper at the time of his dismissal, his forced surrender of editorial control left him bitter toward the paper's owners.

After losing control of the *Firm Foundation,* McGary founded *The Gospel Outlook* (1903-5), in which the always outspoken editor bitterly attacked the management of the *Firm Foundation* and the "insincere, dissembling, double-dealing, Janus-faced" David Lipscomb. "Charity demands," McGary wrote, "that I shall brand him as a willful perverter of the truth he pretends to love, and a religious reprobate of the most hypocritical cast." By 1923 McGary regretted his harsh judgment and offered friends of Lipscomb an apology in the *Gospel Advocate.*

McGary merged the *Gospel Outlook* with the *Eye-*

Opener when a patent-medicine remedy called the "Burlington Treatment," sold through the religious press, turned out to be tar water and "Dr. Burlington" turned out to be McGary. This scandal damaged McGary's reputation and ended the *Outlook,* but did not diminish his devotion to his causes.

McGary's last religious journal, *Open Arena* (1914-16), championed his view of baptism. Near the end of his life McGary wrote for the *Gospel Advocate,* which he had so long opposed. He died in 1928 at Houston, Texas.

See also Baptism; Burnett, Thomas Raines; *Firm Foundation; Gospel Advocate, The;* Lipscomb, David

BIBLIOGRAPHY Thomas Raines Burnett, *Doctrinal Poetry, First Volume* (c. 1907) • Jerry Gross, "The Rebaptism Controversy Among Churches of Christ," in *Baptism and the Remission of Sins: An Historical Perspective,* ed. David W. Fletcher (1990), pp. 297-332 • John T. Oakley, *J. N. Hall's Campbellite Catechism with Conflicting Answers of Two Distinguished Campbellites A. McGary and T. R. Burnett* (1898) • Fletcher Douglas Srygley, *Biographies and Sermons* (1898).

TERRY J. GARDNER

McGavran, Donald A. (1897-1990)

"Apostle of church growth" and the foremost evangelical missiologist of his time, also considered the founder of the contemporary church growth movement.

Born to missionary parents in India, McGavran was educated at Butler University (B.A.), Yale Divinity School (M.Div.), the College of Missions (M.A.), and Columbia University (Ph.D.). He returned to India after seminary and served from 1923 through 1954 with the United Christian Missionary Society. McGavran founded the Institute of Church Growth at Northwest Christian College, Eugene, Oregon, in 1961, which in 1965 became the School of World Mission at Fuller Theological Seminary, Pasadena, California, of which he was the founding dean. He founded and edited the *Church Growth Bulletin* and authored, co-authored, and edited nearly thirty books. *Bridges of God* redefined missions mid-century, and *Understanding Church Growth* became a widely used textbook.

He married Mary Howard and had four children. At the time of his death, the McGavrans held membership in the South Pasadena Christian Church (Disciples), the Duarte Christian Church (Christian Church/Churches of Christ), and the Arcadia Church of Christ (Churches of Christ), reflective of his commitment to the wholeness of the Stone-Campbell tradition.

See also Butler University; College of Missions; Missions, Missiology; Northwest Christian College; United Christian Missionary Society, The

BIBLIOGRAPHY Donald McGavran, *Understanding Church Growth* (1970) • Vernon J. Middleton, *The Development of a Missiologist: The Life and Thought of Donald Anderson McGavran, 1897 to 1965* (1990) • James C. Smith, "Without Crossing Barriers: The Homogeneous Unit Concept in the Writings of Donald Anderson McGavran" (D.Miss. thesis, Fuller Theological Seminary, 1976) • Herbert M. Works, *The Church Growth Movement to 1965: An Historical Perspective* (1974).

JAMES C. SMITH

McKeever, Jane Campbell (1800-1871)

The fourth of Thomas and Jane Corneigle Campbell's seven children.

Jane Campbell McKeever was born in Ahorey, Ireland, on June 25, 1800. Thomas emigrated to the United States in 1807, followed by Jane and the rest of the family in 1809. After living in several locations in Pennsylvania, Ohio, and Kentucky, in 1819 the family settled in West Middletown, Pennsylvania, within ten miles of her brother Alexander Campbell in Bethany, (West) Virginia. There Jane married Matthew McKeever; they eventually had nine children, and adopted at least a dozen others.

By 1830 Jane had opened a home school, Pleasant Hill Seminary, which educated boys and girls. In 1842, two years after Alexander Campbell founded Bethany College, Jane's school became Pleasant Hill Female Seminary, with Jane as its principal for most of the next quarter century. Many of the courses in its three-year curriculum were identical to those of Bethany College. Several of the seminary's graduates became influential in the Restoration Movement during the late nineteenth and early twentieth centuries.

Unlike her brother Alexander, Jane was a firm abolitionist. The McKeevers ran a station of the Underground Railroad on their farm, and Jane made clear her antislavery sentiments in a letter to the *North-Western Christian Magazine.*

As her health declined in the 1860s, Jane relinquished control of the seminary and moved to Harrisville, Ohio, to live with her daughter, Lorinda McKeever Wilkin. She continued a spirited correspondence with family members until shortly before her death on December 10, 1871.

See also Abolitionism; McKeever Family; Pleasant Hill Female Seminary

BIBLIOGRAPHY Jane Reader Errett, "Pleasant Hill Seminary," *Christian Standard* 46 (1910): 1396-1400 • John H. Hull, "Jane Campbell McKeever," *Discipliana* 52:1 (1992): 7-12 • Phoebe A. Murdock, "Pleasant Hill Seminary" (unpublished manuscript, no date, Pleasant Hill Seminary Collection of Mrs. Jane Fulcher, West Middletown, Pennslyvania).

JOHN H. HULL

McKeever Family

Early influential family in the reform movement of Thomas and Alexander Campbell.

In 1792 William (1758?-1838) and Mary McFadden McKeever (1767?-1840) moved from Ireland to the United States, eventually settling in West Middletown, Pennsylvania, in 1794. Originally Methodists, the McKeevers and their descendants played important roles in the first half-century of the Stone-Campbell Movement. Although not members of the original Brush Run church, the McKeevers joined the Disciples congregation that formed in the late 1820s after the Brush Run church disbanded. The newly formed congregation met in a building owned by Matthew McKeever, son of William and Mary, until a church was built in 1837.

William was the first in a long line of McKeever abolitionists and ran a station on the Underground Railroad, as did his sons Thomas and Matthew (husband of Alexander Campbell's sister Jane). More than once escaped slaves were recaptured on Matthew's farm, only to be released to freedom by order of a local Justice of the Peace — in one case, Thomas McKeever himself. Even Matthew and Jane's teenage son, Thomas Campbell McKeever, helped smuggle slaves to freedom while he was a student at Bethany College.

The McKeevers also were active in early Disciples educational efforts. Jane Campbell, then her son Thomas Campbell McKeever, ran Pleasant Hill Female Seminary for about twenty-five years, starting in 1842. After Thomas's death in 1866, his wife, Martha McAyle McKeever, became superintendent until Pleasant Hill closed in the early 1870s. Matthew and Jane's daughter, Mary Jane Campbell McKeever, conducted schools in Kentucky, Missouri, and Oregon, while another daughter, Lorinda McKeever Wilkin, and a granddaughter, Ella McKeever, taught at Pleasant Hill.

See also Abolitionism; McKeever, Jane Campbell; Pleasant Hill Female Seminary

BIBLIOGRAPHY Bernice Bartley Bushfield, *The McKeevers and Allied Families of West Middletown, Washington County, Pennsylvania* (1959) • Boyd Crumrine, ed., *History of Washington County, Pennsylvania* (1882) • Matthew McKeever, "The Underground Railroad" (unpublished manuscript, 1880, Bethany College Archives).

JOHN H. HULL

McLean, Archibald (1849-1920)

For more than thirty-eight years, Archibald McLean devoted himself to the cause of Christian missions. He was born near Summerside in Prince Edward Island, Canada. During five years working as an apprentice in carriage building, McLean came under the influence of a minister associated with Disciples who baptized him in 1867 and encouraged him to become involved in the ministry. McLean made his way to Bethany College, graduating in 1874. He became pastor of the Mt. Healthy Christian Church, located in a little village about ten miles from Cincinnati.

In 1874, the year of his ordination, McLean met in the basement of the Richmond Street Christian Church in Cincinnati with other Disciples to discuss foreign missions. A year later, the Foreign Christian Missionary Society was born and established its headquarters in Cincinnati. When the first secretary of the society resigned in 1882, the executive committee chose McLean as his successor. Though he continued in his pastorate for the next three years, McLean traveled and spoke tirelessly on behalf of foreign missions. In addition, his great propensity to write and publish brought great benefit to the missionary enterprise among Disciples. McLean authored seven books and published numerous tracts dealing with missions. He served the Foreign Christian Missionary Society as its president until it merged with the United Christian Missionary Society in 1920. He served the latter as vice president to the end of his life.

During a time when congregational pressures among Disciples pushed in the direction of isolationism, McLean sought and maintained ecumenical relationships with other Protestant groups and leaders in missions. He served as a delegate to most of the major ecumenical missionary conferences held during his lifetime. In these ways, he began to shift Disciples' focus for mission from restoration of an ancient plea to federation (ecumenical partnerships) supported for the sake of preaching the gospel most effectively in foreign lands.

See also Foreign Christian Missionary Society, The; Missions, Missiology; United Christian Missionary Society, The

BIBLIOGRAPHY Archibald McLean, *Missionary Addresses* (1895) • Archibald McLean, *A Circuit of the Globe* (1897) • Archibald McLean, *The History of the Foreign Christian Missionary Society* (1919) • W. R. Warren, *The Life and Labors of Archibald McLean* (1923).

MARK G. TOULOUSE

McMillan, Edward Washington (1889-1991)

Educator and minister in twentieth-century Churches of Christ.

Born in New Baden, Texas, on September 27, 1889, McMillan died on February 15, 1991. Nurtured in the non-Sunday School Churches of Christ, he attended Gunter Bible College and Austin College, and received his master's degree in 1921 from Baylor University. He completed coursework for his doctorate at

Southwestern Baptist Theological Seminary in Fort Worth, Texas. McMillan served on the faculties of Abilene Christian College, where he chaired the Bible department from 1928 to 1935, Lubbock Christian College, and Columbia Christian College in Portland, Oregon. He was founder and president of Ibaraki Christian College in Japan and was the first president of Southwestern Christian College in Terrell, Texas.

McMillan served congregations in Texas, Tennessee, and California. His evangelistic work took him to China, Japan, India, and Korea. He edited *The Christian Leader* from 1938 to 1941 and authored hundreds of articles for religious publications. Among his other publications are *Class Notes on Sacred History,* volumes 1 and 2 (College Press, 1932), *The Church and the Adult* (Gospel Advocate, 1937), *Worldliness in the Church* (Gospel Press, 1951), and *The Minister's Spiritual Life* (Firm Foundation, 1958).

See also Columbia Christian College; Ibaraki Christian University; Southwestern Christian College

BIBLIOGRAPHY Dan Anders, "People Heart," *Image* 7 (May 1991): 6 • Jimmie Moore Mankin, "E. W. McMillan Still Made an Impact at 100 Years of Age," *Christian Chronicle* 50 (August 1993): 11. SHAUN A. CASEY

McNeely, Cyrus (1809-1890)

Educator, reformer, and antislavery activist of the early Stone-Campbell Movement.

Cyrus McNeely was born in Cadiz, Ohio, in 1809 and was raised in a Presbyterian family. As a young man he was influenced by Alexander Campbell's writings and became convinced of the importance of believers' baptism, weekly observance of the Lord's Supper, and the ability of those not ordained to perform baptisms. Consequently, he remained affiliated with the Disciples of Christ as a layperson throughout the rest of his life.

In 1841 McNeely was listed as an "overseer" (coauthor) of *Address to Disciples: The Sin of Slavery.* He continued his antislavery writings until the Civil War, ran a station on the Underground Railroad, and was instrumental in inducing Thomas and Alexander Campbell to clarify their positions on slavery and, eventually, on the Fugitive Slave Act. However, when the Civil War began, McNeely remained a pacifist.

McNeely married Jane Donaldson of Cincinnati in 1837. Like her husband, she was an active abolitionist and was interested in education. In the early 1850s, probably at Jane's suggestion, McNeely founded a school for young women in Hopedale, Ohio. By 1856, in cooperation with the Ohio State Teachers' Association, it was reorganized as coeducational McNeely Normal School, educating prospective teachers. Again reorganized in 1879 as Hopedale Normal College, the institution continued to educate teachers and added B.A. and B.S. degree tracks. The institution educated thousands of students before closing in 1895, five years after Cyrus McNeely's death.

See also Abolitionism; Civil War, The; Slavery, The Movement and

BIBLIOGRAPHY *Commemorative Biographical Record of the Counties of Harrison and Carroll, Ohio* (1891), pp. 105-6 • R. H. Eckelberry, "The McNeely Normal School and Hopedale Normal College," *Ohio Archaeological and Historical Quarterly* 40 (1931): 86-136 • *McNeely Normal School of Ohio Catalogue and Circular* (1857) • Henry K. Shaw, *Buckeye Disciples* (1952). JOHN H. HULL

McNemar, Richard (1770-1839)

Founder with Barton W. Stone and three other Presbyterian ministers of the Springfield Presbytery in September 1803 and, nine months later, of the Christian Church in the West, prior to uniting with the Shakers; author of the *Last Will and Testament of Springfield Presbytery.*

Raised in a Presbyterian community in western Pennsylvania, McNemar accompanied the Presbyterian minister Robert Finley to Kentucky and settled with him in the Cane Ridge community in 1789. He gained a classical education in a nearby academy conducted by the Princeton-educated Finley and early became an elder in the Cane Ridge church. He was licensed to preach at Cane Ridge in 1797 and was subsequently ordained at Cabin Creek.

During the winter of 1801, three elders of the Cabin Creek congregation noted that McNemar had begun to "deviate" in his preaching from the doctrines of the Confession of Faith. Individually and as a session — the official governing body of the congregation — they conversed with him regarding their concerns, but with no effect other than "to make him more zealous in propagating those sentiments" that they opposed, sentiments that he appears to have learned from Barton Stone, who had followed Finley as pastor of the Cane Ridge church. In the fall, just months after the great Cane Ridge Meeting in which McNemar had played a prominent role, the Cabin Creek elders sent a statement of charges against McNemar's doctrine to the meeting of the Washington Presbytery in Springfield, Ohio. After reviewing the charges, the presbytery concluded that it would be "irregular to take any further notice of them," as no one at the meeting proposed to substantiate them. In the spring of 1802, McNemar accepted a call through the Washington Presbytery to the Turtle Creek congregation in southern Ohio.

In the fall of 1802, charges were brought against McNemar at the meeting of the Washington Presbytery in Cincinnati. An elder from the Cincinnati congregation stated that he had heard that McNemar was a propagator of false doctrine and requested that the presbytery investigate the matter. McNemar opposed the Cincinnati elder's request for an investigation of his doctrine, stating that charges could regularly come before presbytery only in writing. Nevertheless, the presbytery proceeded to examine McNemar on the doctrines of particular election, human depravity, the atonement, the application of the atonement to sinners, the necessity of a divine agency in the application of the atonement to sinners, and the nature of faith. The presbytery concluded that McNemar's views were "strictly Arminian, though clothed in such expressions, and handed out in such manner, as to keep the body of the people in the dark, and lead them insensibly into Arminian principles; which are dangerous to the souls of men and hostile to the interests of all true religion." Jacob Arminius (1560-1609) was a Dutch theologian who had opposed the doctrine of predestination. Surprisingly, the presbytery also reappointed McNemar for one half of his time to the Turtle Creek congregation and for the other half to Orangedale, Clear Creek, Beulah, and Forks of Mad River.

Six months later, the Washington Presbytery meeting at Springfield received a petition from fourteen persons from the congregations of Beulah, Turtle Creek, Clear Creek, Bethany, Hopewell, Duck Creek, and Cincinnati requesting a reexamination of McNemar on his "free will or Arminian doctrines" and also a like examination of John Thompson, minister of the Springfield church. The presbytery ruled that to engage in an examination of McNemar and Thompson in response to the petition would be "out of order," presumably because it contained neither charges nor names of witnesses. At the same meeting, McNemar received a call through the presbytery to spend the whole of his time at Turtle Creek.

McNemar's opponents appealed the conflicting actions of the Washington Presbytery to the Lexington, Kentucky, meeting of the Synod of Kentucky in September 1803. The Synod approved the examination of McNemar by the Washington Presbytery in the fall of 1802 that had been conducted without written charges or witnesses and had condemned McNemar's views; it also censured the Washington Presbytery for rejecting a petition calling for examinations of McNemar and Thompson in April 1803. Perceiving the direction of the Synod's actions, McNemar, Thompson, Stone, and two other ministers who shared their theological views, Robert Marshall and John Dunlavy, met during a short recess of the Synod on Saturday, September 10, and determined to withdraw from the jurisdiction of the Synod, though not from communion with its members. Two days later the five ministers constituted themselves as a presbytery, taking the name Springfield for the town in southern Ohio where the Washington Presbytery had rejected petitions to examine McNemar and Thompson.

As with events leading to the withdrawal of the Springfield Presbytery from the Synod of Kentucky, McNemar played a leading role in the emergence of the Christian Church in the West. Stone reported that following their withdrawal from the jurisdiction of the Synod the growing popularity of the Springfield Presbytery was a concern to its leaders, as they were committed to Christian unity and did not desire to become another denomination or "party." At a meeting of the presbytery at Cane Ridge in June of 1804 McNemar proposed a solution to the problem of their becoming another "party" or denomination with a document that he had drafted, titled *Last Will and Testament of Springfield Presbytery.* In signing this document the members of the newly formed presbytery willed that their presbytery "die, be dissolved, and sink into union with the Body of Christ at large." At the same meeting they determined to take "no other name than *Christians.*"

McNemar's ideas also played a leading role in the development of what became known as Stone's doctrine of the atonement. During the winter of 1804 the Springfield Presbytery became troubled by implications of the commonly held substitutionary interpretation of the doctrine. At a meeting of the presbytery at Springfield in March of 1804, McNemar outlined the leading principles of an alternative interpretation. Though Stone was initially unconvinced, by the June meeting of the presbytery Stone's further study of the doctrine had led him, along with the other members of the presbytery, to accept McNemar's principles. During the winter of 1805 Stone addressed two letters rehearsing his study of the doctrine to Presbyterian minister Matthew Houston, the substance of which he published in the spring of 1805 as *Atonement: The Substance of Two Letters Written to a Friend.*

Shortly after Stone's publication of *Atonement,* Shaker missionaries appeared in the West, having been commissioned by the Shaker leadership in New Lebanon, New York, to present their testimony to the Christians. In contrast to Stone, Thompson, and Marshall, who soon emerged as opponents of the Shaker gospel, McNemar granted the missionaries permission to address his congregation. Thus on Sunday, March 23, the Shaker missionaries made their first public presentation in the West to the Turtle Creek church.

McNemar reported that the message the missionaries delivered at Turtle Creek could have been "summed up" in the following saying of Jesus: "If any man come after me, let him deny himself and take up his cross, and follow me. For whosoever will save his life shall lose it; and whosoever will lose his life for my sake shall find it." McNemar related that after expressing on behalf of themselves and the church that had sent them "great union with the work of God that had been for years past among the people," they testified that "the time was now come for them to enter into actual possession of that salvation, of which they had received the promise — [and] That the way to attain it was by self denial, taking up a full cross against the world, the flesh and all evil in our knowledge, and following Christ, walking as he walked, and being in all things conformed to him, as our pattern and head." McNemar stated that the missionaries taught that the first step in the saving work "was to confess all our sins, and when we had confessed them, forsake them forever." The missionaries promised, McNemar continued, that in so doing they would "receive that measure of the holy spirit, which would be an overcoming power," not only sufficient to keep them "out of all actual sin and defilement, but to cleanse and purify both soul and body from the very nature of evil." They also announced that "Christ had now made his second and last appearance, for a final settlement with every soul of man." In private conversation with the missionaries McNemar learned that the forsaking of sin of which the Shakers spoke included marital relations, and that the Shakers counted it "their distinguishing privilege to preserve their bodies in sanctification and honor," believing that the "lust of the flesh" was the source of every branch of evil, including pride, covetousness, anger, and hatred.

The missionaries remained at Turtle Creek for several days, lodging at the home of Malcolm Worley. Worley had been a Presbyterian elder at Turtle Creek and later a licentiate of the Springfield Presbytery. On March 27, he became the first Shaker convert in the West. Within less than a month, McNemar followed suit, reporting that his conversion had been accompanied by a vision of a guiding hand and a miraculous healing. By the end of April, thirty members of the Turtle Creek congregation had united with the Shakers. John Dunlavy, McNemar's brother-in-law and another founding member of the Springfield Presbytery, also became a Shaker. Stone accounted for the success of the Shakers among the Christians by observing that, as many of the Christians "were breathing after perfect holiness, they were disposed to listen to any proposition by which they might advance to that desirable state." Surely, as the Shaker missionaries themselves noted, the millennialism of the Christians, their belief that God's work in the Great Revival was evidence that the millennium, the much-hoped-for thousand-year reign of Christ on earth, was near, also contributed to their receptivity to the Shaker message.

McNemar's leadership was embraced by the Shakers, as it had been earlier by the Springfield Presbytery and the Christians. He soon emerged as a prominent spokesman for the Shakers, playing a critical role in their expansion in the Ohio Valley. In 1808 he published *The Kentucky Revival, or A Short History of the Late Extraordinary Out-pouring of the Spirit of God, in the Western States of America, Agreeably to Scripture-Promises, and Prophecies Concerning the Latter Day: With A Brief Account of the Entrance and Progress of What the World Call Shakerism, Among the Subjects of the Late Revival in Ohio and Kentucky. Presented to the True Zion-Traveller, As a Memorial of the Wilderness Journey.* Although historians have viewed this work as an unbiased account of the Great Revival, it is better understood as an apology for the Shakers. In the last years of his life McNemar found himself on the losing side of a battle in the West that involved a fresh wave of spiritualism among younger members of the movement. However, the story that Stone repeated in his autobiography, that McNemar was "excluded by the Shakers from their society, in a miserable, penniless condition" is an exaggeration. In fact, McNemar was vindicated by the Shaker leadership in the East, and, though still something of an outsider in the Western Shaker community he had helped to build, he was formally reconciled with his chief opponent.

Stone believed that the success of the Shaker missionaries had a lasting impact on the Christians — an impact for the good. That good respected the doctrinal temperament of the Christians. "By it we are taught," he wrote in 1827, "to check our minds from indulging too freely in vain speculations, and to examine well by the Bible, every doctrine presented for our acceptance." Moreover, the success of the Shaker mission had provided a practical lesson in Christian humility: "We are also taught," he observed, "our entire dependence upon the great Head of the Church for all good, and that he only can keep us from falling."

See also Dunlavy, John; *Last Will and Testament of Springfield Presbytery;* Springfield Presbytery

BIBLIOGRAPHY *An Apology for Renouncing the Jurisdiction of the Synod of Kentucky. To which is added a Compendious View of the Gospel, and a few remarks on the Confession of Faith* (1801) • Robert Marshall and John Thompson, *A Brief Historical Account of Sundry Things in the Doctrines and State of the Christian, or as it is Commonly Called, the Newlight Church, Containing their Testimony Against Several Doctrines Held in that Church, and its Disorganized State; Together with Some Reasons Why Those Two Brethren Purpose to Seek for a More Pure and Orderly Connection* (1803) • Stephen J. Stein, *The Shaker Experience in America: A History of the United Society of Believers* (1992) • D. Newell Williams, *Barton Stone: A Spiritual Biography* (2000).

D. NEWELL WILLIAMS

McQuiddy, J. C.

See *Gospel Advocate, The*

McReynolds, Albert Badger (1897-1980)

Evangelist, home mission organizer, and writer associated with the Christian Churches/Churches of Christ in Oklahoma and Missouri.

A graduate of Texas Christian University, Albert Badger McReynolds spent his early years in ministry as an evangelist, first with Texas Christian University's Brite School of the Bible (now Brite Divinity School), then as a nationally recognized revival speaker. Known to many as "Brother Mac," McReynolds was induced by health concerns to move in 1940 to the Talihina, Oklahoma, area, where he founded the Kiamichi Mountains Christian Mission to evangelize Native Americans and start churches in southeast Oklahoma. In 1949, on property called "Christ's 40 Acres" near Honobia, Oklahoma, he launched a men's retreat, the Kiamichi Clinic, receiving national notoriety for its pro–"Restoration Movement" preaching and pro-American prayer amid the looming threat of a growing global communism. Many preachers in the Christian Churches/Churches of Christ, as well as famous personalities like radio commentator Paul Harvey, spoke at the Kiamichi Clinic. As the director of the mission and retreat, McReynolds influenced many young people in the region who attended Bible college, many of whom became revivalists and staunch anticommunists — among them Billy James Hargis, Cecil Todd, and Riley Donica.

During his lifetime, McReynolds wrote many articles for the *Christian Standard* and had many sermons transcribed and collected. The most frequently published collection was *Soul Winning and Stewardship Sermons.*

See also Kiamichi Mission

BIBLIOGRAPHY A. B. McReynolds, *Soul Winning and Stewardship Sermons* (3rd ed. 1963) • *Sessions of the Kiamichi Clinic* (1949-).

ANTHONY J. SPRINGER

Memoirs of Alexander Campbell

The first complete account of the life, character, and work of Alexander Campbell and to date still the most extensive.

Its author, Robert Richardson, began work on the book after Campbell's death in 1866. J. B. Lippincott of Philadelphia published volume 1 (560 pages) in 1868 and volume 2 (688 pages) in 1870. An 1871 printing, "complete, two volumes in one," followed. Reprinted on occasion, the *Memoirs* is now also available in electronic format on the Internet.

Richardson had been from his youth a close friend and coworker of Alexander Campbell, Thomas Campbell, and Walter Scott. He reported that he had long been interested in writing such a book and collected reminiscences and documents for that purpose. He wrote at the request and with the permission of the Campbell family and was aided by their family papers and recollections. These multiple insider connections distinguish the *Memoirs* from every other biographical work on Alexander Campbell. No later researcher can fully replicate Richardson's sources or grant an equally firsthand perspective on all the events he covers.

The title "memoirs" was a genre decision on Richardson's part. The book is an "authorized biography." Yet it includes large amounts of autobiographical materials of Campbell, and it often explicitly adopts a Campbell-eye viewpoint on things. At the same time, its aim and scope are expansive, embracing, as its subtitle indicates, "a view of the origin, progress, and principles of the religious reformation." By design and in effect the *Memoirs* is not only the first comprehensive Campbell biography but also the first general history of the Stone-Campbell Movement. Interpretively, it bears an important relationship to an earlier work of Richardson, *The Principles and Objects of Religious Reformation Urged by A. Campbell and Others* (1853).

The weaving of these interpretive elements displays Richardson's cultural contemporaneity and his skills as a "literary" historian. Events and considerations before, distant from, and outside Campbell's direct purview are artfully incorporated into the biographical-chronological sequencing of the book's chapters. The portrait of Campbell, frankly commemorative and at times adulatory, is painted in Romantic era "hero in history" fashion. Likewise Romantic are its many descriptions of historical settings and natural surroundings and its polished, rather florid expository prose. Current canons of critical history, however, are observed and observable, for example, in Richardson's reliance on and treatment of documentary sources and honest admissions of uncertainties and divergent or disputed judgments.

The *Memoirs* has been immensely influential. It set a long-enduring pattern for both the interpretation of Campbell and the historiography of the Movement's early years, with Campbell in the starring role. Later histories, critical and uncritical alike, have relied on it. It is a treasure-trove of lore about "the founders" and "the time of origins" that countless Disciples have passed down over the years without always citing, if they even knew, their source of information. It will remain an indispensable resource for studies of the early Stone-Campbell Movement.

See also Campbell, Alexander; Historiography, Stone-Campbell Movement; Richardson, Robert; Scott, Walter

BIBLIOGRAPHY Robert Richardson, *Memoirs of Alexander Campbell, Embracing a View of the Origin, Progress and Principles of the Religious Reformation Which He Advocated*, 2 vols. (1868, 1870); available on-line: http://www.mun.ca/rels/restmov/texts/rrichardson/mac/MAC100A.HTM.

JAMES O. DUKE

Men and Millions Movement, The

A campaign inaugurated in 1913 designed to secure, within five years, $6.3 million and 100 new workers for Disciples missionary, benevolent, and educational agencies.

The campaign was an outgrowth of optimism and unity generated by the Disciples Centennial celebration, which concluded in 1909 with a large, enthusiastic convention in Pittsburgh. The Brotherhood of the Disciples (1908), an organization dedicated to recruiting business leaders for service in the church, and the Million Dollar Campaign for foreign missions (1911) also helped to bring about the Men and Millions Movement.

Incorporated under Ohio state laws, the movement was directed by an executive committee composed of agency leaders. To meet the financial goal, the campaign first focused on individuals thought capable of larger donations ($500 and up). Later, through the Every Member Canvass, the cause was presented directly to Disciples congregations across America.

The progress of the campaign and the work of Disciples agencies were significantly disrupted by the outbreak of war in Europe. The Foreign Christian Missionary Society was particularly affected, but all Disciples agencies were threatened by declining receipts, inflation, rising indebtedness, problems in travel and communication, and the loss of staff members to wartime service.

The War Emergency Drive of 1918 proved successful in addressing many of the needs of the agencies and in revitalizing the Men and Millions Movement. By 1919, $7.1 million in contributions and pledges had been received, and over 8,000 Disciples of high school and college age had pledged to consider missionary service or some other church vocation.

See also American Christian Missionary Society; Board of Church Extension; Christian Woman's Board of Missions; Foreign Christian Missionary Society, The; McLean, Archibald; National Benevolent Association of the Christian Church (Disciples of Christ); United Christian Missionary Society, The

BIBLIOGRAPHY D. James Atwood, "The Impact of World War I on the Agencies of the Disciples of Christ" (Ph.D. dissertation, Vanderbilt University, 1978) • Archibald McLean, chairman, *Report of the Executive Committee of The Men and Millions Movement: History and Report* (1919).

D. JAMES ATWOOD

Messiahship, The

Significant work of Christology and biblical interpretation produced by Walter Scott in 1859.

The Messiahship was published after decades of reflection, just one year before the author's death. Its purpose was twofold: to show that the Old Testament proves its divine authority by proving its author is God, and that the New Testament proves its divine authority by proving that Jesus Christ is the Messiah, the Son of God. The proof that the author of the Old Testament is God is its numerous types and prophecies of the Messiah. The New Testament substantiates this proof by showing that Jesus Christ meets all the conditions of the Old Testament Messiah.

The book is divided into four parts. The first part lays out the argument from Old Testament types and prophecy. The main types are Adam, the flood, Melchizedek, Moses, and Aaron. The argument from prophecy is based on Daniel 2, 7–9, and 11. The accuracy of these prophecies is illustrated by describing their application to the ancient nations of Assyria, Persia, Greece, and Rome. This historical progression culminates in the coming of the kingdom of God. This first part also contains a section trying to show that the pope and the Catholic Church are the eleventh horn of the fourth beast in Daniel 7:8 and the beast in Revelation 13. Part Two of the book briefly summarizes the results of the lengthy exposition in Part One.

Part Three is a demonstration that Jesus fulfilled the types and prophecies of the Old Testament. It contains many lengthy quotations from Scripture.

Part Four addresses "Political Christianity." Having already written heavily on millennial themes in his earlier career, Scott attempts to show that the improvement of government through the centuries, culminating in Great Britain and the United States, proves that the prophecy of Isaiah 65:17 is coming to pass. The "new heavens and new earth" mean a new government and new people. America is the first of messianic nations.

The book concludes with a description of Christian character, which is essential to life in the new heaven and new earth.

See also Bible, Interpretation of the; Christology; Eschatology; *Gospel Restored, The;* Scott, Walter

BIBLIOGRAPHY Walter Scott, *The Messiahship, or Great Demonstration, Written for the Union of Christians, or Christian Principles, as Pled for in the Current Reformation* (1859).

GARY H. HALL

Mexico, Missions in

See Latin America and Caribbean, Missions in

Midland College

Two-year college, operating from 1910 until 1921, in Midland, Texas, and affiliated with the Disciples of Christ.

The declared purpose of the school was "above all else . . . to send out into the world men and women of true worth." To that end, the college offered a broad range of courses, including required Bible classes, along with such diverse subjects as botany and psychology. Extracurricular activities included an orchestra, choral club, and men and women's literary societies. The school also operated numerous athletic programs for male and female students. The college published a weekly newspaper, *The Coyote,* and an annual, *The Sandstorm.*

Twenty-seven students were enrolled when classes began in September 1910; but by the end of October, approximately sixty-five students were attending. Enrollment for the college peaked at approximately 250 students in 1917. As growth leveled off, the college experienced increasing financial difficulty, exacerbated by the inability of students to pay their bills. Eventually the school was forced to close its doors, ceasing operation in 1921. It relocated to Cisco, Texas, in 1922, where it operated for a time as Cisco Christian College and now exists as the state-supported Cisco Junior College. The current Midland College has no connection to the defunct institution.

KIRK R. COWELL

Mid-South Christian College

Bible college affiliated with the Christian Churches/Churches of Christ, established in Memphis, Tennessee, in 1959.

Under the leadership of Vernon M. Newland, then the academic dean of St. Louis Christian College, a group of forty people from the mid-South region gathered in early 1959 to discuss the establishment of a new college. As a result of their efforts, Memphis Christian College, the predecessor to Mid-South Christian College, began holding classes at a local church in September 1959.

With Newland as the college's first president, a piece of property in southeast Memphis was purchased in 1960 as the site of the college's new campus. The institution experienced modest growth throughout the 1960s and early 1970s before relocating in 1973 to a rural campus of 160 acres in northwest Mississippi, some fifty miles south of Memphis. In conjunction with this move, the institution changed its name to Mid-South Christian College.

When enrollment growth failed to match facility improvements at the isolated Mississippi campus, trustees called for a return to Memphis in 1987. By selling their Mississippi property and purchasing a facility on Elvis Presley Boulevard, the college's administration believed they could erase the school's debt and continue operations. The failure to sell the Mississippi campus, however, resulted in accrued debts that forced the college to file a Chapter 11 Reorganization petition with the United States Bankruptcy Court in 1989. The college returned to its original Memphis campus in 1990, leasing the facility from the Memphis Christian Academy Trust.

From this location the college continues to operate as an institution for the education of Christian ministers and workers.

See also Bible College Movement; Higher Education, Views of in the Movement; Newland, Vernon M.

RICHARD J. CHEROK

Mid-Stream

Theological and ecumenical journal published quarterly by the Disciples' Council on Christian Unity (CCU) from 1961 to 2002.

Its purpose was to nurture and communicate the biblical and theological understanding of the unity for which Christ prayed and to share ideas and developments emerging in the modern ecumenical movement. It informed ministers, lay people, theologians, and key leaders of the churches of the prospects of Christian unity.

Mid-Stream, published in Indianapolis, was launched and given its name by George G. Beazley, Jr., as he assumed the presidency of the CCU. It stands in continuity with two earlier ecumenical journals published by the Disciples of Christ: *The Christian Union Quarterly* (1911-35), edited by Peter Ainslie and published in Baltimore, Maryland, and its renamed successor *Christendom* (1935-48), edited by Charles Clayton Morrison and published in Chicago.

In its history *Mid-Stream* had only three editors, all presidents of the Council on Christian Unity: George G. Beazley, Jr. (1961-74), Paul A. Crow, Jr. (1975-99), and Robert K. Welsh (1999-2002).

Mid-Stream is a depository of papers and actions of most of the unity initiatives from 1961 to 2002, particularly those that involve the Disciples. The unity conversations between the Disciples and the United Church of Christ were resumed in 1961 and developed through several stages, reaching "full communion" in 1993. The papers interpreting this ecumenical quest between these two traditions, including its various commissions and official actions by the general assembly and synod, were published in *Mid-Stream.*

The minutes, reports, and documents of the Consultation on Church Union (COCU; 1962-2002) were printed in special issues, called *Digests.* In addition to the documents that tell the administrative history of COCU, *Mid-Stream* includes papers on baptism, the Lord's Supper (Eucharist), ministry, structure, cultural issues faced by these churches, and reports of the many COCU commissions that served the cause of church union. The foundational documents include *Principles of Church Union* (1967), *A Plan of Union for the Church of Christ Uniting* (1970), *The COCU Consensus* (1984), and *The National Act of Worship Celebrating the Inauguration of Churches Uniting in Christ (CUIC)* in 2002.

In the international context *Mid-Stream* published papers, reports, and reflections from consultations of united and uniting churches held at the Ecumenical Institute in Bossey, Switzerland (1967); Limuru, Kenya (1970); Toronto, Canada (1975); Colombia, Sri Lanka (1981); Potsdam, German Democratic Republic (1985); Ocho Rios, Jamaica (1995); and Dreibergen, the Netherlands (2002).

Mid-Stream concentrated in a major way on the life and witness of the World Council of Churches (WCC). Special issues focused on its assemblies at New Delhi, India (1961); Uppsala, Sweden (1968); Nairobi, Kenya (1975); Vancouver, Canada (1982); Canberra, Australia (1991); and Harare, Zimbabwe (1998). Other issues interpreted the World Missionary Conferences at Melbourne, Australia (1980), and San Antonio, Texas (1989). A miscellany of documents and reports also appeared interpreting WCC consultations on such themes as "Justice, Service and Interchurch Aid," "Social Ethics," "Black Ecumenism," "The Unity of the Church and Renewal of Human Community," "Concepts of Unity and Models of Union," "Ecumenism and Spirituality," "Baptism, Eucharist and Ministry," "The Ordination of Women," and "The Witness of the Orthodox Church."

The labors of the Faith and Order Commissions of the WCC and the National Council of Churches of Christ in the U.S.A. (NCCC) received frequent focus in *Mid-Stream.* Special issues were published on the World Conferences on Faith and Order at Montreal, Canada (1960), and Santiago de Compostela, Spain (1993). Reports and interpretations appeared related to meetings of the Faith and Order Commission in Bangalore, India (1978); Budapest, Hungary (1989); Dublin, Ireland (1992); and Moshi, Tanzania (1996).

Studies and consultations of the NCCC also received attention under such themes as "The Meaning of Salvation," "Evangelism and Pluralism," "The Church and the Poor," "The Black Church's Witness to the Apostolic Faith," and "Local and Regional Ecumenism." In addition, reports on the meetings of the NCCC's general assembly and general board can be found in *Mid-Stream.*

Mid-Stream published reflections, reports, and interpretative articles about many of the international dialogues that emerged after Vatican II. Some dialogues that received little space in other ecumenical journals were the Disciples of Christ–Roman Catholic, Disciples of Christ–Russian Orthodox, Disciples of Christ–United Church of Canada, and Disciples of Christ–Reformed. Other articles tell of the dialogues of the Roman Catholic Church with the Orthodox, Lutherans, Anglicans, and Pentecostals. Appearing every three to four years were accounts of the Forum on Bilateral Dialogues, which drew together representatives of all international dialogues.

One of the goals of *Mid-Stream* was to share the ecumenical vision and leadership of the Disciples of Christ with other churches throughout the world. In fulfillment of this goal the theological work, Bible studies, and agreed accounts of the Disciples of Christ–Roman Catholic International Dialogue were published. Particularly important are the three agreed accounts that chart the progress toward unity between these two communions: *Apostolicity and Catholicity* (1982), *The Church as Communion in Christ* (1993), and *Receiving and Handing On the Faith: The Mission and Responsibility of the Church* (2002).

A goldmine of ecumenical thought appears in the annual Peter Ainslie Lecture on Christian Unity (1981-2002), held in different congregations or theological seminaries throughout the United States. Among the nineteen Ainslie lectures published are the reflections of noted ecumenists such as Johannes Cardinal Willebrands, Bishop Lesslie Newbigin, Albert C. Outler, Kosuke Koyama, Archbishop Iakovos, Archbishop of Canterbury Robert A. K. Runcie, Fred B. Craddock, Mary Tanner, Emilio Castro, and Geoffrey Wainwright.

Among the authors of articles that appeared annually in *Mid-Stream* were the names of a virtual Who's Who among ecumenical theologians of the world: W. A. Visser 't Hooft, Lukas Vischer, Nikos Nissiotis, Ronald E. Osborn, Oliver Tomkins, Jean-Marie Tillard, O.P., James H. Cone, Wolfhart Pannenberg, José Míguez-Bonino, H. Jackson Forstman, William D. Watley, Mary Tanner, Gabriel Fackre, Clark M. Williamson, Jaroslav Pelikan, Peggy Way, Thomas Hoyt, Joseph Sittler, Gunther Gassmann, Letty Russell, John Deschner, Paul Abrecht, Thomas F. Best, Phillip Potter, and Konrad Raiser.

Mid-Stream was one of the major contributions of the Disciples of Christ to the whole ecumenical movement. For pastors, lay people, and scholars who desire to understand the significance of the ecumenical movement for the churches and the world, especially from 1961 to 2002, it is an essential tool. In spring 2003 the CCU began publication of *Call to Unity,* a resource for congregations to promote local ecumenism.

BIBLIOGRAPHY All numbers of *Mid-Stream,* from November 1961 to 2002 • Paul A. Crow, Jr., "A New Beginning: Mid-Stream," *Mid-Stream* 14:1 (January 1975): iii-vi.

PAUL A. CROW, JR.

Midway College

Liberal arts college associated with the Christian Church (Disciples of Christ).

Midway College began as the Kentucky Female Orphan School in 1847, an institution for financially disadvantaged young women to prepare for a teaching career. Lewis L. Pinkerton, a physician and minister of the Disciples of Christ, was the visionary for this unprecedented educational venture. James Ware Parrish, an elder in Pinkerton's congregation, raised the funds needed to begin the school. The two men joined with other like-minded people to provide a formal education for women in the antebellum state of Kentucky. At this time, girls were taught to read only so that they could read to their children when they became mothers. Female orphans were not recipients of this basic knowledge and were usually destined for a life as a maid or laborer. As a solution to this situation, Pinkerton proposed a plan to educate these women in the liberal arts and to graduate teachers. His dreams reaped more than he expected when Midway-educated teachers were influential in the education of rural Kentuckians and others in the region.

When Kentucky Female Orphan School opened its door on October 3, 1847, there were fourteen students ranging in age from 3 to 15. The school had already received publicity through the *Millennial Harbinger,* and Alexander Campbell had praised Pinkerton and the motivation behind the school.

Today, Midway College maintains its connection to the Christian Church (Disciples of Christ) and is the only women's college in the state of Kentucky.

See also Education, Philosophy of; Higher Education, Views of in the Movement; Pinkerton, Lewis Letig.

BIBLIOGRAPHY Harry Giovannoli, *Kentucky Female Orphan School* (1930) • Lucy Peterson, *Miss Lucy's Story* (1960).

LISA W. DAVISON

Midwest Christian College

See Ozark Christian College

Midwestern School of Evangelism

See Ottumwa Brethren

Millennial Harbinger, The

Journal begun in January 1830 by Alexander Campbell to promote his ideas of religious reform.

The previous year Campbell had decided that his first journal, the iconoclastic *Christian Baptist,* had served its purpose. He feared that the paper's title was becoming a denominational name for the followers of his reform and was convinced that his readers were ready for something more constructive. Since he was still completing his "Search for the Ancient Order" series in the *Christian Baptist,* however, Campbell continued that journal through July 1830, publishing both it and the *Millennial Harbinger* for seven months.

The *Millennial Harbinger* became the most important forum for shaping the thought and practice of the Stone-Campbell Movement before the Civil War. In the prospectus Campbell explained that the paper would have two purposes: to destroy sectarianism, infidelity, and anti-Christian doctrine and practice; and to introduce "that political and religious order of society called THE MILLENNIUM, which will be the consummation of that ultimate amelioration of society proposed in the Christian Scriptures." Campbell, along with many other Americans, believed that in America, with God's help, Christians would eradicate earthly problems and usher in the millennial age. In Campbell's view this would be the result of a restoration of the primitive church, which would in turn effect Christian unity and the conversion of the world. He saw the *Millennial Harbinger* as key to the dissemination of ideas that would usher in the millennial reign of God.

Like the *Christian Baptist,* the *Millennial Harbinger* included correspondence from friends and critics, reprinted articles from other journals, and carried news items concerning the advance of the reform. Yet its substantial discussions of matters of theology and polity were extremely important for giving a discernible shape and direction to the fledgling Movement.

In the early 1830s the journal actively reported on the progress and difficulties of the union with the churches of Barton W. Stone's Christian movement. Campbell used the *Harbinger* to deal with internal opponents like John Thomas, later founder of the Christadelphians, whose insistence on rebaptism of Christians from other immersionist groups provoked a controversy in 1837. In 1853 Campbell used the pages of the *Harbinger* to attack the ideas of Jesse B. Ferguson, popular preacher and editor in Nashville, Tennessee, who had embraced unitarianism, universalism, and spiritualism. Written debates with Dolphus Skinner in 1837-39 on the doctrines of universalism and with Barton W. Stone in 1840-41 on the nature of the atonement showed Campbell's "orthodoxy" on key Christian doctrines.

Extremely important in the Movement's development was Campbell's series published between 1842 and 1849 advocating increased cooperation between the churches and a more extensive organization. In August 1849 Campbell called for a national meeting of delegates selected by the churches of the Movement. The first national convention was convened in October 1849 in Cincinnati, Ohio. It was not, however, a body of elected delegates but a mass meeting open to all. The convention approved the creation of the American Christian Missionary Society with Campbell as its president. The constitution of the ACMS and a full report of the meeting appeared in the *Harbinger,* and its pages reported on subsequent conventions throughout its publication history.

The *Millennial Harbinger* was also important in the efforts to avoid fragmentation in the Movement over slavery. Though Campbell opposed slavery and severely chastised slave traders in his earlier writing, his materials in the *Harbinger* were geared toward averting polarization over the issue. When the Methodist and Baptist denominations divided over slavery in 1844 and 1845, Campbell wrote an eight-article series titled "Our Position to American Slavery." He concluded that, though he regarded slavery as out of harmony with the spirit and genius of the age, "the relation of master and slave is no where condemned in the Holy Scriptures as morally wrong." Furthermore, he contended, "no Christian community can religiously make the simple relation of master and slave a subject of discipline or a term of communion." He refused to allow inflammatory articles from either side in the *Harbinger.*

One of Campbell's eccentricities is reflected in the way he numbered the volumes of his journals. In keeping with the biblical significance of seven as perfection or completeness, he began a new series after every seven volumes. This started with the completion of the seven volumes of the *Christian Baptist* and continued through five series of the *Millennial Harbinger.* Only after he relinquished the journal to his son-in-law, W. K. Pendleton (1817-1899), in 1864 did this practice stop.

Campbell's active participation in the *Harbinger* gradually diminished in the 1850s, with Pendleton taking on increasingly more of the editorial work. Pendleton used a considerable amount of material from Isaac Errett, who became editor of the *Christian Standard* at its beginning in 1866, and brought in Charles L. Loos as coeditor in 1864. When Campbell died in 1866, supporters persuaded Pendleton to continue the paper because it was the "powerful directing journalistic organ of our Reformation."

Yet the days of the *Harbinger's* prominence were past. Even before Campbell's death his position on slavery had affected circulation, especially as sectional tensions increased in the 1850s. When the outbreak of the Civil War disrupted mail service and virtually eliminated the *Harbinger's* Southern subscription base, the editors were forced to reduce the number of pages per issue from sixty to forty-eight between 1862 and 1866 to cut expenses. Though the journal returned to sixty pages in 1867, the editors could never restore it to its previous prominence. Pendleton was simply not as dynamic and interesting an editor as Campbell. Competition from several weekly religious papers like the *Christian Standard* that carried material of a more popular nature had begun to cut into the strongly theological monthly's support before the war. Pendleton decided to cease publication at the end of 1870.

The success of the *Millennial Harbinger* depended greatly upon and reflected the skill of Alexander Campbell as a religious controversialist and reformer. When Campbell died in 1866, the *Harbinger's* influence and support was already waning. Yet it and its predecessor had been essential vehicles in the formation and development of the Stone-Campbell Movement.

See also American Christian Missionary Society; *Christian Baptist, The;* Eschatology; Pendleton, William Kimbrough; Slavery, The Movement and

BIBLIOGRAPHY A reprint of the full forty-one volumes of the *Millennial Harbinger* was done in the 1950s and 1960s by the Old Paths Book Club of Rosemead, California. Also in 1976 and again in 1987 College Press of Joplin, Missouri, produced reprint editions. *The Millennial Harbinger Abridged* (2 vols.), published in 1902 by Standard Publishing Company of Cincinnati, was itself reprinted in 1965 by the Old Paths Book Club. Each volume of the journal contains an index based on article titles. *An Index to the Millennial Harbinger* by David McWhirter was published by College Press in 1981. In addition, a fifty-page "Index to the Forty Volumes of the Millennial Harbinger" is included in volume two of *The Millennial Harbinger Abridged* (1902) and in the final (1870) volume of the College Press reprints of the entire set.

DOUGLAS A. FOSTER

Milligan, Robert (1814-1875)

Prominent second-generation scholar and educator in the Stone-Campbell Movement.

Robert Milligan's life as teacher, thinker, and author was associated both with Kentucky (Cane Ridge and Lexington) and with Bethany. In both geographical centers he consciously carried on the work of the first generation of reformers, and his own influence carried well beyond his death in 1875.

Milligan was born in 1814 in County Tyrone, in Northern Ireland, and moved to Ohio with his parents in 1818. During his boyhood on the farm he had an accident that resulted in internal injuries and induced Milligan to pursue a career free from physical labor. From 1831 to 1837 he studied at academies in Pennsylvania, among them a four-year classical liberal arts course taught by John Gamble, graduate of the University of Edinburgh. The son of a ruling elder in the Associate Reformed (Seceder) Presbyterian Church, Robert became a full communicant of that denomination in 1835.

Seeking a milder climate, Milligan moved in 1837 to Bourbon County, Kentucky, to establish a classical school at Flat Rock, near Cane Ridge. Questions from his Greek students about Scripture passages, as well as his own curiosity, led to a growing desire to reexamine his own understandings. In March 1838 he was immersed by Elder John Irvine of the church at Cane Ridge. Though not directly in the company of Barton Stone (who had moved to Illinois in 1834), Milligan was henceforth linked to the Stone-Campbell Movement.

Determined now to attend college, Milligan left for Yale in 1839 but was persuaded by friends to attend Washington College in Washington, Pennsylvania (near Bethany). He was granted the A.B. in 1840 and asked to assume Washington's Chair of English Literature, also teaching Greek and Latin. The M.A. followed in 1843. In 1850 he was transferred to the Chair for Chemistry and Natural History. Milligan was set apart for ministry in 1842, and among those laying hands on him was the venerable Thomas Campbell.

A brief tenure followed at Indiana University (1852-54), teaching mathematics, chemistry, and astronomy. Alexander Campbell, knowing Milligan during his years at Washington, called him to Bethany's Chair of Mathematics in 1854. As professor, elder of the Bethany church, and for three years coeditor of the *Millennial Harbinger* — alongside Campbell, Robert Richardson, and W. K. Pendleton — Milligan was a polymath widely held in high esteem.

In 1859 Milligan accepted the presidency of Kentucky University (predecessor of Transylvania University), then in Harrodsburg. He taught sacred history and related subjects as well. Upon the university's move to Lexington in 1866, he confined his leadership and teaching to its College of the Bible. Despite illness and serious physical limitations, he continued to teach until his death.

It was during these years that he authored works of enduring influence among Disciples. *Reason and Revelation* (1867), written both for his students and for serious biblical learners in the churches, is a systematic introduction to the nature, design, inspiration, content, and interpretation of the Bible. It stands as one of the two or three most important works on hermeneutics in the nineteenth-century Movement. Milligan's *Scheme of Redemption* (1868) continued his view that history and Scripture holistically unfold God's plan of salvation. Taken together, the influence of these two books is considered by some to be an "unofficial theology" for

Robert Milligan, seated here with his wife and children in 1858, while still serving as a professor at Bethany College.
Courtesy of Bethany College

succeeding generations within segments of the Movement. While appreciative of Milligan, some modern scholars find his rationalistic approach to be less critical than that of first-generation Disciples like Alexander Campbell. One certainly finds in his work the echoes of a Walter Scott–type reduction of the scheme of biblical revelation to a grand complex of evidences and logical propositions centered on the Messiahship of Jesus and the means to salvation. As provincial writings that articulate to insiders the group understandings of an emerging fellowship, Milligan's works are seen to be lagging behind the developments both in Europe and in leading American universities. His deep involvement in the "science" of biblical prophecy and his speculations about the timetable of millennial events also raise suspicions for more recent readers. At the same time, however, many find parts of his *Scheme of Redemption* to be classic Stone-Campbell articulations still helpful to this day, particularly in practical areas like church leadership, as in his section on the "Ministry of the Church." All would agree, however, that his influence was great in the decades to follow.

Over and beyond his two great tomes noted above, Milligan published a significant commentary, *Epistle to the Hebrews* (1875), and articles on a broad variety of topics in the *Millennial Harbinger.*

A mere half-decade after Milligan's death, a student from his Lexington days, Josephus Hopwood, honored Milligan in the naming of a new liberal arts college in Tennessee. Though he never taught at Milligan College, the name was a fitting tribute to Milligan's enduring influence, irenic spirit, breadth of scholarship, and academic commitments in the Stone-Campbell heritage.

See also Bethany College; Bible, Interpretation of the; Hermeneutics; Lexington Theological Seminary; Reason, Place of; Revelation; Theology — Nineteenth Century; Transylvania University

BIBLIOGRAPHY M. Eugene Boring, *Disciples and the Bible: A History of Disciples Biblical Interpretation in North America* (1997) • Robert Milligan, *Epistle to the Hebrews* (1875) • Robert Milligan, *An Exposition and Defense of the Scheme of Redemption as It Is Revealed and Taught in Holy Scriptures* (1868) • Robert Milligan, *Reason and Revelation, or The Province of Reason in Matters Pertaining to Divine Revelation Defined and Illustrated and the Paramount Authority of the Holy Scriptures Vindicated* (1867) • Thomas H. Olbricht, "Robert Milligan: Teacher, Theologian, Minister," *Leaven* 8 (2000): 153-57.

W. DENNIS HELSABECK, JR.

Milligan College

Christian liberal arts college affiliated with the Christian Churches/Churches of Christ. The college is located just east of Johnson City, Tennessee, in the mountainous northeastern corner of the state.

The origins of the college date back to the Buffalo Creek Christian Church (today Hopwood Memorial Christian Church), which hosted a "field school" meeting in its building as early as 1840. Students continued to meet in the church building until after the Civil War, when the school moved to its own building and expanded its focus to educate students from primary to post-secondary levels. On December 10, 1866, the school was incorporated by the Tennessee State Legislature as Buffalo Male and Female Institute. Its early commitment to educating both young men and young women made it one of the earliest coeducational institutions in the country.

Wilson Gilvan Barker served as Buffalo Institute's first president beginning in 1866. The school did not become firmly established, however, until 1875 with the arrival of Civil War veteran Josephus Hopwood and his wife, Sarah Eleanor LaRue Hopwood. The Hopwoods' vision that Christian education was "the hope of the world" led them to the war-torn South, which they saw in desperate need of transformation. Taking on the school's leadership as a missionary endeavor, the Hopwoods began recruiting door-to-door on horseback, taking enrollment from 85 to almost 170 in the first four years. In 1881 the cornerstone was laid for a new classroom building, and the school was renamed Milligan College in honor of Hopwood's teacher Robert Milligan, the highly respected scholar of biblical theology who taught at the College of the Bible in Lexington, Kentucky, and previously at Alexander Campbell's Bethany College. Milligan College was granted a new charter by the state of Tennessee in 1882, allowing it to confer academic degrees.

Milligan had a number of short-term presidencies in the early twentieth century, including that of Frederick Doyle Kershner (1908-11), destined to be a major Disciples of Christ theologian and churchman at mid-century. Henry J. and Perlea Derthick arrived at the school in 1917 and led Milligan College into a new era. During their thirty-three-year stay (1917-40), Milligan's campus added a new classroom building, dormitory, and gym. Henry Derthick devoted himself to fund-raising, and his wife oversaw the affairs of campus life. In the mid-1920s the school began working toward accreditation with the Southern College Association. In 1928 the college charter was again changed, making it an undenominational Christian institution and breaking its formal ties with the Disciples of Christ.

Charles E. Burns (1940-44) succeeded Derthick as president. Very soon the student pool and cash donations decreased, due in part to the war effort. By 1943 the entire school was turned over to the United States Navy for use as a base in the Navy V-12 program. Milligan was the only college in the nation to undergo a complete forfeiture of its program and facilities for the war effort. Returning the college to civilian status was the task of President Virgil Elliott (1944-48). He developed strong athletic and music programs on the campus and recruited new faculty, including Mildred Welshimer (daughter of the influential preacher P. H. Welshimer of Canton, Ohio), to help reestablish the school's ties with the Disciples of

Hosting the Navy V-12 program in the 1940s, Milligan College was the only college in the United States to be taken completely over by the military for officer training during World War II. Photo appearing in the *Christian Standard*, October 21, 1944

Christ. The college ultimately identified with the more moderately conservative Disciples churches that were resistant to the prospects of denominational reorganization but leery of another division in the Movement.

That posture was championed by Dean E. Walker, who was called from Butler University School of Religion to the Milligan presidency in 1950 (-1968), in hopes of resolving fiscal and enrollment problems and the dilemma of an outdated campus. With the help of faculty, staff, and supporters, a slow rebuilding process began. Over the next two decades new dormitories, the P. H. Welshimer Memorial Library, a student union, and the Seeger Memorial Chapel were built. Strengthening of faculty and curriculum led to full accreditation by the Southern Association of Colleges and Schools in 1960. Enrollment peaked at more than 850 students in the late 1960s, as the baby boomers came of age. During this time, Emmanuel School of Religion was founded and initially convened classes on the Milligan campus.

Under the presidency of Jess W. Johnson (1968-81) campus growth continued with the addition of a science building, the Steve Lacy Fieldhouse, and a new president's home. Further academic advances were also made despite growing obstacles. Debt from the Walker-era chapel, social and political upheaval in the Vietnam war era, economic recession, and financial management problems created significant institutional challenges.

The college's next president, Marshall J. Leggett (1982-97), again began the rebuilding process. Large amounts of debt were eliminated and economic stability returned as Leggett canvassed the churches and individuals in the first of many financial campaigns. Building renovations, a new student union, and new dormitories strengthened the campus. Additional majors were developed and a master's degree in education was instituted. Enrollment continued to grow during this period.

Continued growth and new curricular emphases characterize Milligan under the presidency of Donald R. Jeanes (1997-). At present the college enjoys an expanding and uniquely integrated curriculum in biblical studies and the arts and sciences, offering more than two dozen majors in eight academic areas: biblical learning; humane learning; performing, visual, and communicative arts; business; education; nursing; scientific learning; and social learning. In addition, the college has an evening degree-completion program for working adults, a master of education, a master of science in occupational therapy, and a master in business administration program. The college maintains close relations with Emmanuel School of Religion, a graduate seminary of the Christian Churches/Churches of Christ located immediately across the street from the Milligan campus.

Milligan College is the only Christian liberal arts college associated with the Christian Churches/Churches of Christ. Its academic philosophy centers on the education of Christian servant-leaders for all vocations, in addition to preparation for the formal church-related ministry. Of late, the college has drawn students from thirty-six states and nine nations. More than 900 students enroll in undergraduate and graduate programs each year.

See also Emmanuel School of Religion; Higher Education, Views of in the Movement; Hopwood, Josephus; Kershner, Frederick D.; Walker, Dean Everest

BIBLIOGRAPHY Cynthia Ann Cornwell, *Beside the Waters of the Buffalo: A History of Milligan College to 1941* (1989) • Clinton J. Holloway, "*Age Deo Fide et Amore*: A History of Milligan College, 1940-1968" (M.A.R. thesis, Emmanuel School of Religion, 1998) • Josephus Hopwood, *A Journey Through the Years: An Autobiography* (1932) • Dean E. Walker, "The Mission of a Christian College," in *Adventuring for Christian Unity and Other Essays* (1992), pp. 235-53.

CYNTHIA CORNWELL MCCACHERN
and CLINTON J. HOLLOWAY

Ministerial Training

See Education, Philosophy of; Higher Education, Views of in the Movement

Ministry

1. Nineteenth-Century Views of Ministry
   - 1.1. Stone's Views
   - 1.2. Campbell's Views
   - 1.3. The "Minister" System
   - 1.4. Secretaries, Superintendents, and State Evangelists
2. Twentieth-Century Developments
   - 2.1. Christian Church (Disciples of Christ)
     - 2.1.1. Authority to Ordain
     - 2.1.2. Ordained and Licensed Ministers
     - 2.1.3. Regional and General Offices
     - 2.1.4. Ministerial Standing
     - 2.1.5. Elders and Deacons
     - 2.1.6. Women Ministers
   - 2.2. Churches of Christ
     - 2.2.1. Elders and Deacons
     - 2.2.2. Evangelists or Preachers
     - 2.2.3. Women Leaders
   - 2.3. Christian Churches/Churches of Christ
3. Conclusion

Ministry in the Stone-Campbell Movement has been understood as *leadership* in the teaching, service, and oversight or care of the church. Though there were significant differences in the views of ministry taught by Stone and Campbell, both were influenced by the Reformed tradition. The different understandings and practices of ministry that have developed in the three streams of the Movement are all rooted in the Reformed tradition.

1. Nineteenth-Century Views of Ministry

1.1. Stone's Views

Barton Stone's background was Presbyterian. In keeping with Presbyterian tradition, he taught that the "pastoral" office included persons identified as "bishops, elders, pastors, and evangelists." The work of this office was to preach and teach the gospel, administer the ordinances of baptism and the Lord's Supper, and exercise church discipline (moral oversight of the congregation). For Stone, as for Presbyterians, the terms "bishop," "elder," and "pastor" referred to located ministers who served established congregations, while the term "evangelist" referred to traveling ministers whose special work was the organization of new congregations. In keeping with Presbyterian practice, Stone taught that congregations were normally to have one bishop, elder, or pastor.

Stone differed from Presbyterians in regard to the second office of Presbyterian polity, the office of "ruling elder." According to Presbyterian polity, the ruling elder is a "representative of the people" who shares with the ministers in exercising government and discipline in the church, but not in preaching and teaching the gospel or administering baptism and the Lord's Supper. During most of his ministry, Stone argued that there was no authorization in Scripture for an elder who did not teach. In this regard, Stone's view of ministry was more clerical than that of the Presbyterians. While the Presbyterians would allow an officer designated as "representative of the people" to share with the pastor in the government of the congregation, Stone would allow the pastor, alone, to have rule of the church. Toward the end of his life, in response to his growing concern for moral oversight in the church, Stone reversed his thoughts on the office of ruling elder, allowing that some older men may act as rulers in the church, even though they are not qualified to teach, preach, or administer the sacraments.

Stone's followers had deacons as well as ruling elders and pastors. Stone shared the Presbyterian understanding that the work of deacons was to care for the poor and manage the temporal affairs of the church.

Stone taught that the power of ordination to the offices of the church rested in the pastoral office. Like the Presbyterians, he believed that congregations were to elect their own officers but that ordination was the work of the elders or pastors. For Stone, pastoral authority was further reflected in his view of the appropriate procedures for the discipline of pastors. Although a pastor could be tried for disorderly conduct by the congregation, a pastor could be tried for "teaching false doctrine" only by a conference of pastors.

The *Last Will and Testament of Springfield Presbytery*, the document by which Stone and his colleagues announced their rejection of Presbyterianism, has sometimes been read as an assault on the Presbyterian understanding of the pastoral office and ordination. Careful scrutiny of four of the "items" of the *Last Will and Testament* that bear directly on the ministry shows that Stone and his followers did not reject the Presbyterian understanding of ministry. Stone's views on ministry were little other than Presbyterianism, minus those aspects of Presbyterian judicial practice that he believed were not warranted from Scripture and stood in the way of Christian unity. The pastors or elders of Stone's churches were ordained to preach the gospel, administer the ordinances, and exercise rule in the congregation. They alone had the power to discipline a fellow pastor charged with teaching false doctrine and to ordain others to the offices of the church.

1.2. Campbell's Views

Alexander Campbell's views on ministry eclipsed Stone's views following the union of the forces of Stone and Campbell. As with Stone, Campbell's background was Presbyterian. However, his views on ministry were also influenced by the views of Scottish Baptists and Independents. During the 1820s Campbell waged war against the "clergy" through the pages of the *Christian Baptist*, the monthly journal he began in 1823. For Campbell, the term "clergy" referred to persons who practiced the ministry out of love of self, rather than love of God and neighbor. Campbell's opposition to the clergy, however, was not confined to individuals. Rather, like the Scottish Baptists and Independents, he opposed the whole clerical system.

According to Campbell, two props supported the clerical system. The first of these props was the "alleged special call of God to what is commonly called the work of the ministry." Campbell argued that clergy misused the idea of a call to ministry to enhance the authority of their ministrations and person. The second prop of the clerical system was "the necessity of a consociation of those called ones" for the better administration of the church. Campbell argued that the real purpose of such associations, be they called councils, synods, associations, or conferences, was not to promote the well-being of the church, but to protect the authority and stipends of the clergy.

The result of the clergy system was the establishment of the clerical class that functioned to inhibit the people from hearing and reading the word of God. Campbell lamented that when congregations could not afford the services of the clergy, they did not meet! However, Campbell's opposition to the clergy at no time extended to what he understood to be the rightly authorized ministry of the church. Indeed, the very first issue of the *Christian Baptist* carried the following caution in bold type: "In our remarks upon the 'Christian clergy,' we never include the elders or deacons of a Christian assembly, or those in the New Testament called the overseers and servants of the Christian Church." In successive issues of the *Christian Baptist* and later publications, Campbell outlined the qualifications and duties of what he understood to be the divinely instituted order of the ministry.

The "standing and immutable ministry of the Christian community" consisted of bishops, deacons, and evangelists. Bishops, meaning overseers, also identified as elders or pastors, were the chief officers of congregations. The duties of a bishop were to teach, preside at all meetings of the church, shepherd the members of the congregation, and rule in matters of discipline (moral oversight of the congregation). Campbell did not include the word "preach" in his description of the bishop's distinctive duties. Preaching, for Campbell, was the simple sharing of the Christian gospel and was the duty of all Christians. To explicate a passage of Scripture or interpret the Christian faith (what is often called "preaching") is what Campbell understood by the bishop's duty to teach. Administration of the Lord's Supper was included in "presiding" at all meetings of the congregation. Campbell believed that, given the magnitude of their task, elders or bishops should give full time to the office and should be remunerated for their service.

Bishops or elders differed from clergy in two respects. First, bishops were elected to pastoral office from the congregations of which they were members. In contrast, the clergy prepared for the ministerial "trade" and then went out in search of a congregation to employ them. Second, bishops were officers only of the church that elected them, and not of the church at large. Bishops ceased to be bishops when transferring from the congregation that ordained them, and no bishop could be pastor of more than one congregation at a time. In contrast, clergy were ordained for life and often worked for several congregations simultaneously.

The qualifications for the office of bishop were those required by the task; hence, one elected as bishop "must be qualified to teach, and be able by sound teaching both to convince and exhort those who oppose the truth." A bishop must also "preside well" in both worship and disciplinary functions. Campbell believed that these qualifications were not likely to be found in a younger person or in a new convert of any age. With the young ministerial candidates of the clergy system clearly in mind, Campbell wrote, "There is no greater incongruity than to see a stripling, or a young man 20 to 30, styled elder; and if the name does not suit his years, it is very strong reason in favor of the conclusion that the office of a bishop does not."

By 1826 Campbell was convinced that there should be a plurality of elders (also called a "presbytery") in every congregation. Since several persons cannot preside at one time, Campbell recommended that one elder should be chosen as "president of the presbytery" on the basis of "superior gifts." If only one elder in the congregation was full time, that elder was to serve as president of the presbytery.

Deacons were to be servants of the church. Campbell acknowledged that in Acts their duty is described as "supplying the tables of the poor saints and widows." Pointing to the qualifications of this office as outlined in the epistles, Campbell argued that their duties were not to be limited to this task. Rather, they were to be viewed as "public servants of the church in all things pertaining to its internal and external relations." Campbell noted with approval that it was a custom of the ancient church to "commit to the deacons care of the Lord's table, the bishop's table, and the table of the poor." Since the duties of a deacon were often "too oppressive for a single individual" and included keeping the treasury of the church, Campbell believed it advisable to establish a plurality of deacons in every congregation.

In contrast to bishops and deacons, who were officers of the congregation, evangelists were sent out by the congregation or a group of congregations to preach the gospel, baptize converts, organize congregations, administer discipline, and teach them until they were able to elect elders and function without the oversight of an evangelist. Evangelists were to receive both compensation and supervision from the church or churches that sent them forth.

For the qualifications of the office of evangelist, Campbell suggested that the church look to the apostles as "the best and fullest models for those who should be chosen by the congregations to repromulge the Gospel in our own times and country." Presumably because he read 1 Timothy 4 ("Let no one despise your youth") as instructions to an evangelist, and because the evangelist was not set over the church but worked under the supervision of the church, Campbell allowed that the evangelist, as opposed to the bishop, could be a young person.

Campbell taught that candidates were to be inducted to the offices of the church by solemn election of the congregation and the imposition of hands of persons selected by the congregation to act in its behalf. The authority to ordain rested not in the elders or bishops but in the congregation, guided by the scriptural qualifications of the ministerial offices.

Campbell was well known for his advocacy of the priesthood of all believers. He taught that all Christians are to preach and teach Christ as they have opportunity and ability. He asserted that any Christian "may of right preach, baptize, and dispense the supper, as well as pray for all men when circumstances demand it." He suggested that in congregations where no one seemed qualified to fill the office of the bishop, persons of "the best attainments, and the best character, should be elected, for the time being, to go forward in social worship and in the edification and discipline of the infant flock." In a discussion of the duty of weekly observance of the Lord's Supper, he commended the worship of a congregation that, having no members who fit the qualifications of a bishop, had selected "two senior members" to preside at their meetings and officiate at the Lord's Table.

Campbell's views on the ministry bore a resemblance to those of the Baptists, and many of his followers were drawn from the Baptist fold. Campbell's views on ministry, however, differed from those of the Baptists in two important respects. First, Campbell argued against the Baptists that the bishop is "the standing president" of the church and should preside at all meetings of the congregation. At issue was the Baptist practice of beginning church business meetings by selecting a "moderator." Campbell argued that if the bishop was present, there was no need to select someone else to serve as moderator. In this regard, Campbell's views approached those of the Presbyterians, for whom the pastor serves as moderator of the session (ruling body of the congregation, composed of the pastor, or bishop, and ruling elders). Second, Campbell opposed the Baptist practice of deciding on cases of church discipline by a meeting of the whole congregation in which the judgment of every member carried equal weight. According to Campbell, the presbytery of the congregation was to serve as the "tribunal" in all cases of discipline. The only court of appeal beyond the local eldership was not a meeting of the whole congregation but a mutually agreed-upon committee of pastors from neighboring churches. In this regard, also, Campbell's practice approached that of the Presbyterians, who resolved cases of discipline through the session, and who would allow an appeal from the session to go only to the regional body of elders, the presbytery — not to the congregation.

1.3. The "Minister" System

Campbell's understanding of the ministerial offices, despite its appeal in the Stone-Campbell Movement, soon presented a problem. In most congregations there did not seem to be one person, let alone a plurality of persons, qualified to fulfill the duties of the pastoral office. Elders were elected and ordained, but they often did little teaching and were not compensated for their efforts. In response to the desire for a teaching ministry, congregations began in the 1840s to invite evangelists, sometimes young college graduates, to settle among them and devote full time to ministerial functions.

Calling a "resident preacher" from outside the congregation was a departure from Campbell's view that the leadership of the congregation was to be selected from within the congregation's membership, and it raised serious questions for members of the Movement who in the post–Civil War era became leaders of the Churches of Christ. Tolbert Fanning believed that this development would rob the evangelist's office of persons needed for that important work and hinder the development of talent within the congregation, since the hired pastor would have a tendency to perform all of the activities that the members themselves were to do. Fanning's disciple, David Lipscomb, made it clear that he did not oppose paying pastors, but only calling them from outside the congregation. "The eldership," he wrote, "has not been honored, respected, and supported as it should have been, but this evil will never be remedied by supplanting the elders with peripatetic pastors."

For the larger part of the Movement who accepted the new development, the "one man system" (as it was labeled by its enemies) was not an improvement on Campbell's system but a practical measure made necessary by the character of the churches. Isaac Errett spoke for many when he wrote,

> Let it be understood that, in the imperfect condition of many of the churches, the employment of one man as a preacher and teacher and a cooperator with the elders, in ruling, is justifiable as a necessity, but is not to be accepted as a finality. It should be the aim and ambition of all the churches to reach a more complete organization of forces, such as the Scriptures contemplate, namely: a plurality of elders or bishops whose business it shall be to teach and preach and rule — dividing their labor among themselves as may best sustain the interest of the church, and compensated for their services . . . elders who are immersed in earthly cares, and who can give but odd moments to the oversight of churches, are not the elders described in the New Testament.

Whether or not it was justifiable for a congregation to call a resident preacher from outside the congregation was not the only question raised by the new practice. For those who accepted the new system, other questions loomed large. What was the ministry or office of the person who filled this position? Was such a person to be viewed as an elder or as an evangelist? Did the age of the person holding the position have any bearing on the issue? Disciples debated this issue throughout the latter third of the nineteenth century.

The leading advocate of the view that a younger person holding the new position should be viewed as an evangelist and not as an elder was John W. McGarvey, a leading figure in the Movement's first seminary, The College of the Bible, in Lexington, Kentucky. For McGarvey, the work of an evangelist was identical to the work of a bishop, with one exception. In addition to preaching and teaching, which was the work common to both evangelists and bishops, bishops were to rule over the church (administer church discipline). Evangelists were not to rule over the church but were to be under the authority of the church's elders, or bishops. McGarvey accounted for the distinction between the offices of elder and evangelist by noting that the Scriptures allow a younger person to serve as an evangelist but require an elder to be a person of maturity.

A leading advocate of the view that the person who held the new position should in most cases be regarded as an elder, regardless of age, was Isaac Errett, editor of the *Christian Standard.* In 1867 he wrote, "Any person chosen by a church for a preacher and teacher in their midst should certainly be ordained as one of the elders or bishops of the church." In response to the objection that a young person was disqualified from the office of elder by age alone, Errett asserted that the term "elder" had once meant "an old man," but had passed into official use and now merely designated one qualified to teach and administer discipline. Errett would allow that some young preachers should submit to the guidance of the elders for a time, but as soon as they were qualified for the office of elder they were to be ordained to the eldership. For Errett, the proper title of such a person was "pastor." Though Errett often referred to the preacher of a congregation as "the pastor," he did not understand this title as designating an office distinct from the elders. "The pastor" was the elder who devoted full time to pastoral work. In contrast to Lipscomb and McGarvey, who both stressed the necessity of a plurality of elders or pastors, Errett argued that if "the pastor" was the only member of the congregation qualified to hold the pastoral office, the Scriptures would allow the church to be ruled and taught by that one pastor alone.

Churches of the Movement never took a vote to determine whether a person called from outside a congregation to assume ministerial duties within the congregation was an evangelist or an elder. Many resolved the matter by referring to the person who held such a position as "preacher" or "minister." The latter term was a favorite of McGarvey's, who noted that its literal meaning was servant, not ruler. The influence of McGarvey's view was evident in the common practice in the Movement well into the twentieth century of reserving the administration of the Lord's Supper to elders drawn from the membership of the congregation. The minister could preach and pray but was excluded from administration of the Lord's Supper, a ministerial role historically associated with the exercise of oversight.

The emergence of the preacher or minister was accompanied by a tendency to neglect the laying on of hands in the ordination of all church officers. The theological basis for this development was the view articulated as early as 1850 by W. K. Pendleton, that the laying on of hands was not necessary to ordination. This view was advocated by J. W. McGarvey, who argued that to "ordain" meant merely to "appoint" and that although this was practiced in the New Testament by prayer and laying on of hands preceded by fasting, it was a mere induction into the office and could be dispensed with.

1.4. Secretaries, Superintendents, and State Evangelists

The second half of the nineteenth century saw the emergence of offices of ministry in the Disciples stream of the Movement identified by the titles "secretary," "superintendent," and "state evangelist." These offices did not supplant the existing offices of the Movement but were established in addition to them. Persons who filled these offices were selected not by congregations, as were the persons who filled the offices of elder, deacon, and evangelist, but by emerging regional and general organizations.

State and provincial organizations evolved out of the practice of two or more congregations cooperating in the support and sending forth of an evangelist. During the 1830s county and district (more than one county) organizations developed to support the work of evangelists. By the end of the 1830s the growth and success of county and district organizations in establishing new congregations had led to the forming of state and provincial organizations.

The issue of general organizations became a subject of discussion in the 1840s. In October 1849, the first general convention of the Movement convened in Cincinnati. The most important matter to come before the meeting was a resolution proposing the formation of a missionary society. A missionary society was an association of individual contributors. The proposal was approved, and a committee was appointed to draft a constitution for the society. The result of these deliberations was the formation of the American Christian Missionary Society.

Just prior to the meeting of the general convention, the Indiana organization had formed a state missionary society. The actions of the Indiana organization and the general convention in forming missionary societies proved determinative for the organization of regional and general bodies. One by one the other regional organizations adopted the missionary society form of organization. Newly emerging organizations, such as the Christian Woman's Board of Missions, and regional organizations for Sunday School and youth work followed the same pattern. The decision of the regional and general organizations to carry on their business as missionary societies was, in turn, determinative of the character of state and general offices. The missionary societies adopted officers common to the missionary societies supported by other denominations.

Normally, missionary societies had a president, several vice presidents, a corresponding secretary, a recording secretary, and a treasurer. The chief administrative officer was not the president but the corresponding secretary. The office of president was more of a titular, policy-making office; thus the office of corresponding secretary became the primary office of oversight in the regional and general work of the Movement.

The task of the corresponding secretary of a regional missionary organization was to oversee the evangelization of the region. This meant employing and supervising evangelists to serve in establishing new congregations. It also meant helping established congregations secure the services of a preacher. Judging by their publications, corresponding secretaries also saw their task as including the education of ministers and the church regarding the life and work of the church. The writings of early corresponding secretaries include J. H. Fuller's *The Table of His Presence,* Thomas Munnell's *The Care of All the Churches,* and J. B. Briney's *The Form of Baptism* and *Instrumental Music in Christian Worship.*

The term "corresponding secretary" was the most common title for the chief administrative officers of the early regional missionary organizations. From time to time, however, some regions experimented with other titles. In Texas the title "superintendent and treasurer" was used for a time. In Arkansas, where the offices of corresponding secretary and state evangelist were often merged, the title was frequently "state evangelist." In Arkansas the term "superintendent of missions" was also used, as was the term "state manager" in Indiana. Given the character of the office as supervision of the evangelization of a region, it is not surprising that all of these terms point to the function of oversight, or care. By the mid-twentieth century the most common designation of the office was "state secretary" or "provincial secretary."

Owing to the development of other regional organizations, the corresponding secretaries of the regional missionary societies were not the only regional officers to emerge during the latter half of the nineteenth century. During the 1870s the American Christian Missionary Society led in the formation of regional Sunday School organizations. Following the pattern of other regional and general organizations in the Movement, these bodies took the form of societies and elected corresponding secretaries. In Oklahoma this office was titled "superintendent" of Bible schools. In Indiana the title "Sunday school evangelist" prevailed. In Kentucky the titles "Bible school evangelist" and "Bible school superintendent" were employed for a time. No matter what the title, the task was to increase the number and quality of Sunday Schools across the region.

The Christian Woman's Board of Missions, founded in 1874, was soon engaged in forming state auxiliaries. The auxiliaries each elected a corresponding secretary. The task of this office was to increase the number, missionary intelligence, and devotion of women's groups committed to doing something toward the task of world missions.

In the last two decades of the nineteenth century, the ecumenical youth organization Christian Endeavor became popular among youth of the Christian churches. In some states Disciples Christian Endeavor societies were formed. Corresponding secretaries, known as superintendents, were elected. The task of these officers was to increase the number and quality of Christian Endeavor groups in the Christian churches.

The task of the corresponding secretary in the general missionary organizations was similar to that of the corresponding secretary in the state missionary organizations, except for a general focus. Corresponding secretaries employed and supervised evangelists (increasingly referred to as missionaries) and raised funds for their support. Publications of corresponding secretaries of the general missionary societies suggest that they saw their task as including education of the church regarding the church's mission.

Three of the general organizations that emerged during the latter half of the nineteenth century were of a different sort than the missionary, Sunday School, and Christian Endeavor organizations. These societies were: the National Benevolent Association, the Board of Church Extension, and the Board of Ministerial Relief. Rather than being charged with some form of evangelization — be it through the establishment and support of churches at home and abroad, the organization of Sunday Schools, or the promotion of Christian Endeavor — these organizations were engaged in forms of Christian service. The services performed, care for persons in need, a loan fund to build church buildings, and support for aged and disabled ministers and their families, were understood as supporting or complementing the larger evangelistic task of the church. Following the established model, each was headed by a corresponding secretary.

As the responsibilities of the general organizations expanded, new leadership positions were added. Typically, the title "superintendent" or "secretary" identified these positions. The state missionary societies followed the same pattern. In 1920 the Oklahoma Missionary Society added a development officer with the title of "stewardship secretary."

Thus, by the end of the nineteenth century, the Disciples stream of the Movement had an office of regional or general ministry not included in Campbell's threefold plan: the office of secretary, or superintendent. Many of the new officers were women. The Christian Woman's Board of Missions was a women's organization, and all of its officers were women. Other organizations, especially the Sunday School and Christian Endeavor organizations, also employed women in leadership positions.

2. Twentieth-Century Developments

2.1. Christian Church (Disciples of Christ)

The twentieth century brought further developments in the way the Disciples stream of the Movement understood and ordered ministry. These developments relate to six issues: (a) the authority to ordain persons to the ministry, (b) the status of ordained and licensed ministers, (c) the character of regional and general offices, (d) ministerial standing, (e) the offices of elder and deacon, and (f) the role of women in ministry.

2.1.1. Authority to Ordain By the 1930s Disciples had realized that the person called from outside the congregation to give full time to ministerial functions was not Campbell's elder or evangelist, but the holder of a new office, the office of minister. Furthermore, Disciples realized that this office was not a congregational office. Ministers served first one congregation and then another, and thus belonged to the whole church. Consequently, ordination to the ministry could not be the responsibility of the individual congregation acting on its own. At the very least, there needed to be mutually accepted standards, more specific than those of the New Testament, that would be applied by all ordaining bodies.

The first Disciples to come to the conclusion that ordination to the ministry should not be viewed as a congregational matter were African American Disciples in North Carolina and Texas. As early as 1886 African American Disciples in eastern North Carolina had organized a General Assembly that established standards for the ministry and authorized the ordination of candidates recommended by the churches. In 1895 twenty-six men were recommended for ordination, but only twelve were accepted. Similar developments regarding the authorization of ordination occurred among African American Disciples in Texas in the early part of the twentieth century.

In 1935 the Disciples convention meeting in San Antonio appointed a Commission on Ordination to study the issue. Included in the commission's report, approved by the 1939 convention meeting at Richmond, was the recommendation that ordination be authorized and conducted by an ordination council, sometimes called the "local church council." This council was to be assembled by the call of any congregation through its minister or elders and recognized by the regional committee on ordination in those regions where such a committee existed. The council was to consist of the minister and one or more elders from each of three or more Disciples churches. Upon the vote of this council and the expressed willingness of three ministers to sign the candidate's ordination certificate, ordination was authorized. Following the affirmative vote of the council, a service of ordination was to be arranged by the council in the candidate's local church, a meeting of the regional convention, or at the candidate's college or seminary.

The local church council procedure could be interpreted to mean that ordination was still largely a local church matter. Furthermore, the implementation of the ordination council approach was uneven. Some congregations continued to ordain persons to ministry without consulting any other congregation. The drift of Disciples thinking on the matter, however, was clearly in the direction of shifting responsibility for ordination to the ministry to a body representative of the larger church. In 1964 the Disciples convention meeting at Detroit resolved that ordination is a "rite, or ceremony, of the whole Church, local and ecumenical, current and eternal" and is to be performed "under the guidance of the state or area Committee or Commission on the Ministry."

The contemporary Disciples position regarding the power to ordain to the office of minister is stated in "Policies and Criteria for the Order of the Ministry in the Christian Church (Disciples of Christ)," which was approved in 1971 by the General Assembly (successor to the earlier Disciples conventions) meeting in Louisville. According to this document, candidates for the ministry are to be recommended for ordination by a recognized congregation or congregations of the Disciples, including the one in which the candidate holds membership. Normally, representatives of the recommending congregation or congregations are to participate in the act of ordination, as well as representatives of the region and, if possible, the general and ecumenical church. It is clearly stated that ordination is under "the authorization and guidance of the region."

2.1.2. Ordained and Licensed Ministers The report of the Commission on Ordination, approved by the 1939 convention meeting at Richmond, recommended the following standards for ordination to the ministry:

- good moral character and personal fitness for ministry;
- a full college course, and, if possible, graduate training in religion;
- experience in Christian work that shows real leadership, vision, pastoral qualities, and preaching ability.

Candidates who met the first and third of these standards, but not the educational requirements, were to be licensed rather than ordained. A 1948 pamphlet titled *License and Ordination of the Christian Minister* explains that the difference between ministerial license and ordination is that ordination is for life and is accompanied by "a public service of recognition and dedication," while licensing is for a limited period of time, usually from year to year. The pamphlet also states that the provision of license is for (1) college students, for whom "ordination will be more significant" if it comes after the completion of academic preparation for ministry, and (2) "laymen who desire to serve as part-time ministers." In 1964 the recommended standards for ordination were raised by the Detroit convention to include seminary as well as college education.

The "Design for the Christian Church (Disciples of Christ)," first adopted in 1968 as a provisional design, recognizes the status of both ordained and licensed ministry. Section VI, paragraphs 91-93, states that the Christian Church (Disciples of Christ) "inducts into the order of its ministry men and women holding the following offices: (a) the office of ordained minister bestowed by ordination . . . (b) the office of licensed minister . . . [that] permits the exercise of ministerial function in specific situations with periodic review." The design adds to the earlier list of persons who may be licensed "a worker who is duly commissioned . . . to a specialized full-time church vocation." "Policies and Criteria for the Order of Ministry in the Christian Church (Disciples of Christ)" states that licensing is under "the authorization and guidance of the region."

2.1.3. Regional and General Offices The regional and general work of Disciples underwent significant change and development during the twentieth century, beginning with an increase in the number of general organizations. An important administrative change in the early part of the century was the tendency in the general organizations for the chief executive function (the office of president) to be combined with the chief administrative function, formerly lodged in the office of corresponding secretary. In each of the general missionary societies the corresponding secretary was elected president, at which time the office of president became a full-time, salaried position carrying many of the responsibilities formerly assigned to the office of corresponding secretary.

In 1920 six of the general organizations joined to form the United Christian Missionary Society. The chief executive function and the chief administrative function were combined in the new organization, following the pattern set earlier in the century.

In the late 1950s interest in unification of Disciples work found expression in successful efforts to unify missionary societies, women's organizations, departments of religious education, and other such organizations in regions. One could now begin to speak of a regional or "state" staff, rather than a number of individuals employed by independent organizations working in the same geographical area.

Eventually interest in unification of Disciples work led to a larger process of reorganization, commonly known as restructure, which began in the 1960s with the work of the Commission on Restructure. The Commission conceived of the church as one body that manifests itself organizationally as the congregation, the region, and the general manifestation. Basic to the plan of organization designed by the Commission on Restructure was the conviction that the regional and general organizations of the Disciples are not agencies serving the churches, but organizations of the regional and general manifestations of the church. This has led Disciples increasingly to see the officers of the regional and general organizations as sacramental and pastoral ministers of the regional and general manifestations of the church. This understanding of these offices is reflected in the titles used for some of the offices of the restructured church, such as "regional minister" and "general minister" and "president." Other offices continue to have titles such as "president" and "secretary."

2.1.4. Ministerial Standing Disciples Year Books from the 1890s and later include a list of ministers with a note indicating that the list was compiled from the reports of regional secretaries and general organizations. Often, the note includes the statement that the list would be more complete if *congregations* had been more prompt in reporting the names of their ministers to the state or provincial secretary. This reflects the understanding that ministerial standing was conferred by congregations.

During the 1960s Disciples began to shift the responsibility for granting standing from the congregations to the larger church. The background of this development was the separation of Christian Churches/Churches of Christ from the Disciples of Christ. Leaders of the Christian Churches/Churches of Christ opposed any support of the regional and general organizations of the Disciples of Christ.

Resolution No. 40, approved by the Disciples convention in 1962, stated, "Ministers listed in the year book should demonstrate a sense of responsibility for and commitment to the International Convention and its reporting agencies." Since responsibility for listing ministers in the Year Book continued to be lodged in regional secretaries and the officers of the general organizations, the resolution was a call for those officers to exercise critical judgment in supplying the names for inclusion in the list of ministers. The standard to be used was commitment to the cooperative program of the Disciples of Christ.

"Policies and Criteria for the Order of the Ministry," approved by the General Assembly in 1971, states that standing continues as long as the minister "maintains relationships with the Christian Church (Disciples of Christ)." "Policies and Criteria" also lists two other requirements for maintaining standing: (1) the minister must perform faithfully the duties of a minister "either in an occupation recognized by the church as ministerial in purpose or in a service recognized by the church as ministerial in purpose"; and (2) the minister must participate in "programs of study, research, growth, and renewal." Ministers with standing at the time of retirement retain standing. Responsibility for certification of standing of ministers is lodged with the regions, except in the case of persons employed in general ministries for whom the responsibility is lodged with a committee established by the General Board.

In response to the Jonestown tragedy of 1978, in which Jim Jones, a Disciples minister whose credentials were under review, led his followers in a mass suicide, the General Assembly amended "Policies and Criteria" to include the standard that a minister must continue to meet the personal qualifications required for admission to the order of ministry to maintain standing. This standard applies to both active and retired ministers. The personal qualifications required for admission to the order of ministry are:

- faith in Christ Jesus and commitment to a life of Christian discipleship;
- definite and informed decision, in response to God, to serve in the order of ministry;
- personal fitness sufficient to the demands of the office, including mental and physical capacities, emotional stability and maturity, and standards of morality.

2.1.5. Elders and Deacons The office of elder, as it emerged in distinction from the office of minister in the latter part of the nineteenth century, has undergone significant change in the twentieth century. The first change was the tendency of Disciples, along with other mainline Protestants, to abandon the formal practice of moral oversight and discipline of the congregation. With the formal task of moral oversight and discipline of the congregation removed, the rule of elders was reduced to policy decisions (Should we conduct a particular stewardship program or not?) and the important task of "hiring and firing" the minister.

This measure of rule was then diminished by the widespread adoption of a plan of congregational organization advocated by O. L. Shelton's *The Church Functioning Effectively.* Shelton argued that policy decisions of the congregation should not rest with the elders, but with a large administrative board composed of elders, deacons, and deaconesses representative of the whole congregation. The special role of the elders, which set them apart from the deacons, was to be their service as a discussion group or advisory council to the minister. The minister, not the elders, was to call such meetings. And in no case were meetings of the elders to usurp the policy-making authority of the administrative board.

The remaining vestige of the former "rule" of the Disciples elder is the prominent place of the elder in the celebration of the Lord's Supper. However, even here the role of the elder was curtailed. In the 1950s and 1960s many Disciples congregations, participating in an interdenominational liturgical revival, moved the table out from the wall or the pulpit and allowed the minister to join the elders behind the table. In most cases the elders now offer prayers at the table. The minister presides.

The influence of the Shelton plan has also resulted in a change in the office of deacon. Campbell referred to the elders as overseers of the church and to deacons as servants of the church. The Shelton plan, with its large administrative board composed of both elders and deacons, had the effect of making the servants overseers as well.

Given the abandonment of the formal practice of church discipline and the influence of the Shelton plan, one might ask if there is now any difference between elders and deacons, except that elders pray at the Lord's Table. This is a question that elders sometimes ask. The answer differs from congregation to congregation. In some congregations the elders are viewed as spiritual leaders and have a significant role in the education and care of the congregation, not only through their prayers at the table but also through other pastoral responsibilities.

Section VI, paragraph 97 of "The Design for the Christian Church (Disciples of Christ)" states that the elder is "authorized to exercise with the congregation that elects him or her the ministerial functions that it assigns for periods of time that it specifies, such as sharing in the administration of baptism and the Lord's Supper and the conduct of worship, and sharing in the pastoral care and spiritual leadership of the congregation." The list of specific duties of the office of deacon is identical to that of the office of elder except for the substitution of the word "assisting" for the word "sharing." The word "sharing" points to the elder's historical relation to the pastoral office, while the word "assisting" reflects the deacon's continuing identification as servant of the church.

2.1.6. Women Ministers In the second half of the nineteenth century a number of women served in positions of oversight in the regional and general organizations of the Disciples. The number of women called as ministers of congregations, however, remained quite small. In the first half of the twentieth century, the staff position that women were most likely to hold in congregations was director of Christian education or children's worker.

In the 1970s an increasing number of women were called to occupy the positions of pastor and associate minister. By 1984 there were 112 Disciples women pastors (4.2 percent of Disciples pastors) and 120 associate ministers (32.8 percent of Disciples associate ministers). The 595 ordained Disciples women in 1984 represented nearly 10 percent of the total ordained Disciples ministry. In the early 1980s women comprised one-third of the Disciples seminary enrollments. By the beginning of the twenty-first century that percentage had increased to one-half. Thus, despite continuing hesitation on the part of some congregations to employ women as ministers, especially as senior ministers, there is reason to believe that in the future there will be increasing numbers of women in the ministry of all manifestations of the Christian Church (Disciples of Christ).

The increase in the number of women ministers in the Christian Church (Disciples of Christ) can be credited to the woman's movement of the 1970s, which encouraged women to consider occupations formerly closed to them, and the commitment of Christian women to sharing the gospel and caring for the needs of people.

2.2. Churches of Christ

Churches of Christ in the early twentieth century were generally characterized by anticlericalism and extreme congregationalism, rejecting as unscriptural the extra-congregational structures that had begun to proliferate among Disciples. They regarded ideas of formal ordination and licensing for ministers as foreign to the Scriptures, weakening the concept of the priesthood of all believers and perpetuating the false separation of the church into clergy and laity classes. Many of the issues that became central to the Disciples stream of the Movement, therefore, were largely irrelevant to Churches of Christ. H. Leo Boles (1874-1946) reflected the stance of most in Churches of Christ when he wrote early in the century that the only organization taught in the New Testament is that of the local congregation with its elders and deacons. "There is no organization of the church in the general sense on earth. Jesus is the head and there are no other officials." Because of these presuppositions, the focus on ministry in Churches of Christ has been on the nature and role of elders and deacons and of evangelists, preachers, or ministers in local congregations, including the issue of women's leadership role in the church.

2.2.1. Elders and Deacons The almost universal view among Churches of Christ is that the elders of each local congregation are the sole authorities for the governance of the church. Christ has delegated authority to elders to guide and discipline the congregation of which they are members. Their authority, however, does not extend beyond the local congregation. A strong emphasis has also been placed on the elders' lack of authority to make rules not clearly made in the New Testament. Though Churches of Christ have regarded the lists of qualifications or characteristics of elders found in 1 Timothy 3 and Titus 1 to be normative, no set pattern of appointing elders has been followed. While specific practices vary among congregations, the setting aside, appointing, or "ordaining" of elders is often done by members of the congregation or the present elders, who present the names of men they believe are qualified to serve to a committee (or to the elders). Those named are asked if they are willing to serve, and if they agree, their names are presented to the congregation for consideration. If no objections deemed scriptural are presented, the slate is formally recognized, often in a short ceremony, and they begin serving. Most churches assume that elders will serve for life or until physically unable. A significant trend in the late twentieth century among larger congregations, however, was to appoint elders for a specified number of years, then relieve them of service for at least a year, though recognizing them as eligible for reappointment in the future. Another trend has been for congregations to reaffirm elders at regular intervals.

As was the case in Disciples and in American Christianity generally, the disciplinary function of elders in Churches of Christ diminished during the twentieth century. When elderships did take action, they sometimes found themselves the focus of legal action, as in the case of the Collinsville, Oklahoma, Church of Christ in 1984. While they often presided at the Lord's Supper, unlike Disciples elders this function was never considered mandatory or unique to elders. Any baptized man of the congregation could preside at the table. The actual function of elders often modeled that of a corporate board of directors: making major financial and managerial decisions, hiring and supervising the minister and other staff, and directing the work of the deacons. In this model, successful businessmen often became the logical choice for appointment. Criticism of this approach to church governance led many churches in the late twentieth century to move toward a view of the elders as spiritual shepherds, delegating the financial and business side of church operation to the deacons.

Deacons, as the Greek word indicates, are regarded as appointed servants of the church. Reflecting a long tradition in Christianity, the function of deacons has been characterized as tending to the temporal affairs of the church, in contrast to the elders who look after its spiritual well-being. Like elders, the work of deacons is confined to the congregation of which they are members. The procedure for appointment of deacons is usually the same as that for appointing elders. Often deacons are viewed as "junior elders" who, if they serve well in that role, will be promoted to the higher position. Deacons frequently serve as directors of specific ministries under the elders.

2.2.2. Evangelists or Preachers The role of evangelist or preacher in Churches of Christ developed during the twentieth century from a widespread antipathy toward "located Preachers," to an established norm of trained long-term congregational ministers. The dominant model inherited from the early Movement understood evangelists to be itinerants who taught the gospel, baptized converts, and established new churches. Elders, not hired professionals from outside the congregation, were ultimately responsible for teaching and nurturing believers. David Lipscomb expressed a widely held sentiment when he exclaimed in 1905 that "every Christian is a preacher, an evangelist, a missionary." Lipscomb opposed professional preachers who worked full time with one congregation for a stipulated salary, reflecting early Campbellian antipathy toward the clergy.

This attitude clashed with the practice of an increasing number of congregations and led to a controversy and division in Churches of Christ in the early twentieth century. Those opposed to the hiring of full-time ministers attacked it as "the pastor system," accusing the churches of abandoning biblical church government by allowing a professional minister to become the leader of the church. In fact, the churches invariably saw the role of evangelist or minister as subordinate to that of the elders. While a tiny minority advocated "evangelistic authority" based on New Testament accounts of evangelists who appointed elders, Churches of Christ have understand the function of ministers to be entirely under the supervision of the congregational elders.

As was often the case in American Christianity generally, for much of the early- and mid-twentieth century ministers' terms of service were short, usually from one to three years. By the end of the century, however, tenures had increased significantly, with up to 40 percent spending their careers in only two or three churches. In some instances, long tenures have led to significant *de facto* ministerial authority and conflict with elderships. Nevertheless, the elders have continued to be the ultimate locus of authority in the congregation. Where elderships do not exist, most congregations function through a "business meeting" system that may include any member of the congregation or, in other cases, the men of the church.

2.2.3. Women Leaders The issue of women's leadership role was a matter of discussion in Churches of Christ for much of the twentieth century. One of the most often treated topics was the matter of deaconesses. While it has been unusual for Churches of Christ formally to appoint women deacons, the scriptural precedent for the practice was argued by a number of prominent leaders in the twentieth century, including C. R. Nichol (1876-1961) and G. C. Brewer (1884-1956). In the 1970s some churches eliminated the term "deacon" altogether, opting instead for a system of "ministry leaders" that included both men and women.

The larger topic was the source of numerous books and articles in the late-twentieth and early-twenty-first centuries. In addition, several congregations engaged in focused study of the issue, sometimes resulting in expanded roles for women in public worship leadership, though specifying from the beginning that the roles of preacher and elder were not under consideration. Though an increasing number of churches have hired women to serve as ministers, these are almost always confined to children's, women's, or educational positions. A rising percentage of female Bible and religion majors at both the undergraduate and graduate levels in universities affiliated with Churches of Christ will keep the issue of women in ministry at the forefront for this stream of the Stone-Campbell Movement.

2.3. Christian Churches/Churches of Christ

Ecclesiological issues were undoubtedly at the root of the deepening division between the Christian Church (Disciples of Christ) and the Christian Churches/Churches of Christ (1920s-1970s), but it was more the macrostructures of denominational ministry than the microstructures of congregational ministry that created tension. Both streams, after all, drew from the works of first- and second-generation leaders in the Movement, who had committed to the threefold permanent apostolic ministry (elder/bishops, deacons, and evangelists), to the local election of elders and deacons, and to the local appointment of preaching ministers.

When the Disciples' Commission on Ordination

released the "Richmond Report" in 1939, recommending that the churches in a given state establish ordination committees that would oversee the ordaining and licensing of local ministers, many conservative Disciples saw the proposal as a violation of the prerogatives of the local churches to ordain their own ministers. Some were critical because the report had jumped to the matter of procedures rather than continuing the study of the rationale and validity of candidates of ordination itself, long an ambiguous practice in the Movement. Some feared the professionalization of the preaching ministry, the forfeiture of the primitive model of the evangelist as a kind of missionary to the local church whose credential was proven by the gospel he preached and not by a status conferred upon him.

To be sure, Christian Churches/Churches of Christ did not invent ambiguity over the identity, status, and ordination of local church ministers. Though the question seemed to have long been settled in Christian Churches/Churches of Christ as well as in the Churches of Christ that the local preacher was an evangelist and not a ruling or preaching elder, questions did not entirely disappear about the precise role of the minister as an evangelist. If he was an evangelist, and not (in principle) given to a permanent settlement in one locale, what was his status if he stayed for a long tenure in the same congregation? Did the preacher not, then, functionally at least, become a kind of elder, perhaps operating as a first-among-equals in the eldership? This tendency has been increasingly observable in larger Christian Churches/Churches of Christ, with senior ministers whose tenures have often exceeded twenty years. Many smaller and rural churches, on the other hand, have firmly held to the practice of recognizing the preaching minister only as an evangelist whose ministerial status is not finally tied to any single congregation that he may serve.

Ordination has consistently remained the subject of considerable ambiguity, even ambivalence, in some congregations of the Christian Churches/Churches of Christ. As James DeForest Murch rightly observed, ordination was not much of an issue in the Stone-Campbell Movement until unfit candidates for preaching ministry began to appear in the churches. Leaders were not worried about "apostolic succession" but about screening and duly ordaining evangelists and other leaders of demonstrated ability. Interestingly, the very same churches that clamored to maintain the right of the local congregation to select and ordain their own ministers also largely held to the view that it is God alone who ordains, not human beings. Yet the recognition of God's power to raise up and ordain his servants lay with the congregation alone. Thus the standard practice in Christian Churches/Churches of Christ is for members to elect a new minister or new elders and deacons, and the eldership to ordain those persons to their respective ministries. Preaching ministers are not always ordained, however, by the congregation that calls them. Sometimes a minister's home church ordains that individual, and that ordination is accepted elsewhere when that person moves on to another congregation, without need of reordination. Though Christian Churches/Churches of Christ have never acknowledged a formal ministerial "order" *(ordo),* they have developed one *de facto,* all the while vigorously disclaiming a strict distinction between clergy and laity.

3. Conclusion

Ministry is an area in which significant differences have emerged within the Stone-Campbell Movement. While both Churches of Christ and Christian Churches/Churches of Christ have maintained or developed models of ministry strongly reminiscent of the model of congregational leadership that had emerged in the Movement by the latter part of the nineteenth century, Disciples have developed an order of ministry that includes the offices of ordained minister and licensed minister in which persons serve in the leadership of congregational, regional, and general manifestations of the church. Similarities remain, however, across the Movement. In contrast to other traditions, all of the churches of the Stone-Campbell Movement maintain a high view of the office of elder. Moreover, churches in all three streams continue to honor the Movement's commitment to the priesthood of all believers. Sharing the gospel in word and deed is the vocation of all Christians. Thus, ministry in the Stone-Campbell Movement continues to be understood and practiced as *leadership* in the teaching, service, and oversight of the Christian community.

See also Deacons, Diaconate; Elders, Eldership; Evangelism, Evangelists; Women in Ministry

BIBLIOGRAPHY Lynn Anderson, *They Smell Like Sheep: Spiritual Leadership for the 21st Century* (1997) • Weldon Bailey Bennett, "The Concept of Ministry in the Thought of Representative Men of the Disciples of Christ" (Ph.D. dissertation, University of Southern California, 1971) • H. Leo Boles, *The Eldership of the Churches of Christ* (1900) • G. C. Brewer, *The Model Church* (1919, 1957) • John Harold Cannon, "New Direction for Church Leadership: The Reaffirmation and Selection of Elders Among Churches of Christ" (D.Min. thesis, Abilene Christian University, 1991) • Pat Casey, "The Role of the Preacher as Set Forth in the *Gospel Advocate* from 1895 through 1910" (D.Min. thesis, Harding Graduate School of Religion, 1980) • Robert Chitwood, "A Critical Examination of the Doctrine of Ordination in the Christian Churches and Churches of Christ (North American

Christian Convention) with Implications for the Future" (D.Min. dissertation, San Francisco Theological Seminary, 1988) • Douglas A. Foster, Mel E. Hailey, and Thomas L. Winter, *Ministers at the Millennium: A Survey of Preachers in Churches of Christ* (2000) • Freed-Hardeman University, *Gender and Ministry: The Role of the Woman in the Work and Worship of the Church* (1990) • James DeForest Murch, *The Free Church: A Treatise on Church Polity with Special Reference to Doctrine and Practice in Christian Churches and Churches of Christ* (1966) • C. R. Nichol, *God's Woman* (1938) • Carroll D. Osburn, *Women in the Church: Reclaiming the Ideal* (2001) • Carroll D. Osburn, ed., *Essays on Women in Earliest Christianity*, 2 vols. (1993, 1995) • J. Stephen Sandifer, *Deacons, Male and Female? A Study for Churches of Christ* (1989) • Robert Carl Spain, "A Study of the Evangelistic Ministry in the Churches of Christ" (Ph.D. dissertation, Southwestern Baptist Theological Seminary, 1963) • W. R. Walker, *A Ministering Ministry* (1938) • D. Newell Williams, *Ministry Among Disciples: Past, Present, Future* (1985).

D. Newell Williams, Paul M. Blowers, *and* Douglas A. Foster

Minnesota Bible College

See Crossroads College

Mission

Progressive journal serving primarily Churches of Christ, published from 1967 to 1987. The beginning editorial board and board of trustees were all male, almost all with academic connections.

The stated purpose of the magazine was "(1) To explore thoroughly the Scriptures and their meaning; (2) to understand as fully as possible the world in which the church lives and has her mission; and (3) to provide a vehicle for communicating the meaning of God's Word to our contemporary world." This remained constant through its two-decade history. At a distance these statements seem self-explanatory, but in 1967 the suggestion that there were things the Churches of Christ might do better or differently was a challenge to the status quo that did not go unnoticed.

Early issues dealt with topics ranging from racial prejudice to the morality of war. Articles on the arts and theology and interviews with religious leaders from other Christian groups made *Mission* quite different from most other journals in Churches of Christ. Movie reviews asked serious questions about themes addressed in film, and the reality of "jars and clashes" in Scripture was talked about openly. The magazine reflected the tone of the time, and the stir it generated was palpable.

By the end of the first year the magazine had over 3,000 subscribers, and the number continued to grow until a cartoon about Watergate led to a precipitous decline in numbers in the early 1970s. The cartoon critiqued Richard Nixon, and the negative response indicated the shape of political sentiment then in Churches of Christ. The contention of some was that *Mission* was an intellectual exercise perpetuated by the "new doctors" of the church. What was not so clear at the time was that *Mission* was giving voice to a new generation of leadership. At the end of its twenty-year run the journal ceased publication, believing that most of the concerns it had wished to raise were now on the table for public discussion.

The editor in its final years was Ms. Bobbie Lee Holley of Chapel Hill, North Carolina. Both her gender and her location said something about *Mission* and change in Churches of Christ. The editorial board (53 members) was integrated both by race and gender, but the number still included few pulpit ministers. The time for editor bishops had passed. For some the magazine had endorsed change too fast; for others it had called for change too slowly. In truth, the Churches of Christ had changed, and the twenty-year history of *Mission* reflected and illustrated that change. Modeling a desire for unity in the larger Stone-Campbell Movement, portions of the archives of the journal may be found in the Center for Restoration Studies at Abilene Christian University and at the Disciples of Christ Historical Society in Nashville, Tennessee.

BIBLIOGRAPHY Walter E. Burch, "The Birth of Mission: The Way We Were," *Mission* 20 (September 1986): 10 • Bobbie Lee Holley, "Letting Go, Celebrating, and Continuing," *Mission* 21 (December 1987): 40 • R. Scott Lamascus, "*Mission*'s Controversial Era Closes," *Christian Chronicle* 44 (November 1987): 6.

Robert M. Randolph

Mission Messenger

Journal first published and edited by W. Carl Ketcherside in St. Louis in 1940 as the *Missouri Mission Messenger.* It was intended at that time to be only a means of chronicling events and news items among the so-called Sommerite Churches of Christ in Missouri. In time both its mission and its geographic outreach broadened, as reflected in its new name, *Mission Messenger,* in 1949.

Until 1957 its concerns were mainly those of the Sommerite churches: opposition to the pastor system in favor of mutual ministry, and opposition to Christian colleges because such institutions "did the work of the church." For almost two decades the paper was a leading organ for this persuasion, and its editor was a prominent debater. In later years the editor confessed that during these years the paper was sectarian and he was factious.

The dramatic change in both attitude and direction was evident by 1957, the year Ketcherside began a series on "Fellowship." What had been a narrow sectarian paper, championing the cause of a faction, became an influential means of promoting unity among all the persuasions of the Stone-Campbell Movement. Reaching a circulation of 8,000, it has been credited as having a formative influence on the "progressive movement" within Churches of Christ, beginning in the 1960s.

From 1957 to 1975 it was also published in bound volumes at the end of each year, giving its influence more permanent form. These nineteen volumes are also included in *The Works of W. Carl Ketcherside,* published by College Press in 1997.

Though there were many guest writers through the years, it was edited and published for all its thirty-six years only by W. Carl Ketcherside until its demise in 1975.

See also Ketcherside, W. Carl; Sommer, Daniel

LEROY GARRETT

Missionary Societies, Controversy over

The "first principle" of the Stone-Campbell Movement, a point of consensus among its founding leaders, was its attempt to unite the church through the restoration of "New Testament Christianity" *for the purpose of effective mission.* The strategic initiatives of restoration and unity were not to be seen as ends in themselves, but as the basis for the evangelization of the world. Throughout the Movement's history, when the purpose of mission gave way to debates over the primacy of either restoration or church unity, the Movement floundered; when mission was held up as key, it found new life.

The thinking of Alexander Campbell, the Movement's chief architect and spokesperson, about mission methodology underwent a shift that paralleled the growth of the Movement. In his early writings Campbell believed that missions could be best achieved through the impetus of the local congregation. He advocated in 1823 that "any man with a concern for missions should go to the mission field without obtaining permission from anyone." He maintained that extra-church agencies, such as Bible societies, the Sunday School movement, or missionary societies, were rivals to the ministries of the church. His belief, as George Kresel has observed, was that "each congregation should elect from its midst its own missionary and should financially support that missionary." Campbell indicated his deep reluctance to support any organization that would usurp the role and authority of the local church.

But beginning in the 1830s, the rapid growth of the Movement led Campbell to realize the need for cooperation among the churches. In 1831 he wrote a series of articles proposing that congregations combine their resources to promote Christian outreach. His study of the Bible led him to conclude that while the imperative and principles of mission were discussed in Scripture, there was no explicit guidance given on the specific organization or infrastructure necessary to accomplish mission. In the lack of such specific biblical precedent, Campbell suggested the missionary society as an *expedient* means to accomplish mission work. Churches could either participate or not in such an approach, based on their own determination. Participation in a missionary society was a matter of opinion and should not cause division among the churches.

In 1842 Campbell again wrote about church organization. He noted that "we can do comparatively little in the great missionary field of the world either at home or abroad without cooperation." He also stated that "we can have no thorough cooperation without a more ample, extensive, and thorough church organization." He had written in 1837 that not only should the Christians of the Stone-Campbell Movement organize and cooperate in missionary endeavors, but they should even cooperate with the other denominations.

The first missionary society of the Stone-Campbell Movement was the American Christian Missionary Society (ACMS), formed in 1849 in Cincinnati, Ohio. The society's intent was to focus mission efforts on the American frontier and the foreign fields. Backlash to the formation of the society was immediate, reflecting the emergence of sharp hermeneutical and ecclesiological differences of perspective. Many felt that there was no biblical precedent whatsoever for the establishment of any agency beyond the local congregation to do the work of the church. Some feared decisions about congregational funds being made by society officials, while others sensed a trend toward denominational consolidation and away from congregational autonomy. When the ACMS passed some Civil War resolutions that supported the Northern cause, David Lipscomb and Tolbert Fanning became vocal critics of the organized mission effort.

Discussions led to arguments that ended up as editorial hyperbole in the Movement's many journals. Battle lines were drawn, with conservative critics decrying what they saw as ecclesiasticism and denominationalism and progressives disparaging conservatives for excessive individualism or sectarianism. On the one side were those who felt that the congregations could best achieve their varied ministries by voluntary cooperation. On the other side were those whose frontier mentality and rugged individualism, coupled with American ideals of democracy and egalitarianism, shunned any authority beyond the level of the local church. Each side appealed to the writings of Alexander Campbell to buttress their position. Those who preferred independence quoted the *Christian Baptist,* while those who preferred cooperation looked to later essays in the *Millennial Harbinger.*

Societies continued to be established, whether for benevolence, Bible translation, humanitarian causes, education, or caring for retired ministers. The foreign mission work of the ACMS was replaced by the founding of the Foreign Christian Missionary Society (FCMS) in 1875. The FCMS was established so that the Stone-Campbell Movement could have an agency set apart exclusively for evangelism on foreign fields, and within a decade it was operating around the globe.

While no one opposed the evangelistic mandate on which the Stone-Campbell Movement was founded, each effort at cooperation was criticized by those who thought such cooperation unauthorized by Scripture. Fearful that the societies and agencies hindered the independence of the local congregations and sensing that the support of such efforts would become a test of Christian fellowship, some 2,600 congregations had withdrawn from the larger Movement by 1906 to form a separate communion of Churches of Christ.

Despite the withdrawal of these congregations, within a few years a call went out to the other Disciples churches to unite the various societies for the sake of efficiency. It was believed that such a unified approach would mean that the agencies would no longer compete with one another in promoting their own cause. In 1920 six different agencies combined to form the United Christian Missionary Society (UCMS). The UCMS saw its ministry as comprising foreign missions, home missions, and education. At its inception, the UCMS had nearly 150 missionaries and 1,000 national workers in its employ.

Scarcely had the UCMS begun to operate when it was embroiled in controversy. The primary issue was "open membership," the admitting of people into church membership who had not previously been immersed as believers. Though vigorously denied by the board of managers of the UCMS, documents were produced that indicated that open membership was being practiced in the Philippines and in China.

Other issues that were met with concern by some were the allocation of certain geographical areas of a mission field to various denominations (comity), a growing sense of control by denominational executives at the expense of the local congregations, and the belief that the same "liberal" theology that was espoused by other mainline Protestant denominations was now being accepted by the Disciples.

Attempts to address the issues did not lead to satisfaction. Authorized visits to the mission fields in question, published denials in the Movement's journals, the formation of a Peace Conference Committee, and various reports and interpretations failed to dissipate tensions.

Once again the Stone-Campbell Movement was rent asunder. Missionaries once associated with the UCMS pulled out and remained on the field as "independent" missionaries, directly supported by various congregations. These missionaries were soon joined by others so that within a few years the number of independent missionaries surpassed the number of missionaries associated with the UCMS. The rise in the number of the independent missionaries paralleled the rise of the Christian Churches/Churches of Christ, a branch that over time became a separate communion from the Disciples of Christ.

At the beginning of World War II, the branches of the Stone-Campbell Movement had missionaries on the field supported either by a single congregation, by a cluster of congregations, or through the UCMS, the denomination's mission agency.

With the conclusion of the war, returning servicemen brought to the public's attention the continuing need for world evangelism. Missionary ranks swelled, and new initiatives were begun that were a hybrid of the "independent" and cooperative approaches. The Africa Christian Mission (1947) and the Christian Missionary Fellowship (1949) were begun to capitalize on the benefits of both approaches while at the same time attempting to address what was seen as lacking in each approach. These agencies had a board of directors as well as a central office that received funds designated for specific missionaries. The missionaries determined appropriate mission strategy for their particular fields. With the passage of years, the fear of ecclesiasticism has been muted, as evidenced by the rise in the number of mission agencies within the Christian Churches/Churches of Christ.

Today, in terms of denominational affiliation, the number of missionaries associated with the various branches of the Stone-Campbell Movement, roughly 2,400, is second only to the number of missionaries sent out by the Southern Baptist Convention.

In retrospect, the historical controversies within the Stone-Campbell Movement over missionary societies represent a debate over hermeneutics and the authority of Scripture. Thomas Campbell's motto, "Where the Scriptures speak, we speak; where they are silent, we are silent," left room for debate. Should biblical silence be seen as permissive or prohibitive?

To some critics of missionary societies, the New Testament provided a virtual blueprint for Christian practice in every arena of life, admitting no deviation from the fixed pattern. This approach has proved questionable to critics who have pointed out that for many areas of Christian life not explicitly addressed in Scripture, such as the use of church buildings, buses, or air conditioning, the church has great latitude in its practices. They have understood the "silence" of Scripture not as prohibitive but as granting freedom. Patternists have countered, however, by asking upon what basis "free" choices are then to be made and by pressing the issue of whether there are no limits to expediency or pragmatism.

Michael Casey has noted that neither Thomas nor Alexander Campbell "realized the tensions that existed between Christian union, an inclusivist ideal, and restoration, an exclusivist ideal. A constant dialectic between these two poles of thought began. What originally made the idea of restoration attractive was the Campbells' belief that it reduced the number of essentials of Christianity to a minimum. As the Campbells explored the idea of restoration, they slowly began to add to the list of essentials, making the ideal of Christian union more and more difficult to achieve." Throughout its history, the Stone-Campbell Movement has taken seriously the missionary task of the church. Restoring "New Testament Christianity" so that the church could be united was precisely for the purpose of winning the world to Jesus Christ. Unfortunately, concurrence in this common purpose did not lead to agreement in terms of strategy.

See also American Christian Missionary Society; Bible, Authority and Inspiration of the; Bible, Interpretation of the; Conventions; Direct Support Missions; Expedients; Foreign Christian Missionary Society, The; Hermeneutics; Missions, Missiology; Open Membership; Societies; United Christian Missionary Society, The

BIBLIOGRAPHY Michael W. Casey, *The Battle over Hermeneutics in the Stone-Campbell Movement, 1800-1870* (1998) • David Filbeck, *The First Fifty Years: A Brief History of the Direct-Support Missionary Movement* (1980) • Bill J. Humble, "The Missionary Society Controversy in the Restoration Movement (1823-1875)" (Ph.D. dissertation, University of Iowa, 1964) • George F. Kresel, "Alexander Campbell's Theology of Missions" (Ph.D. dissertation, Boston University, 1961) • Forrest F. Reed, *Background of Division: Disciples of Christ and Churches of Christ* (1968) • John A. Siewert and Dotsey Welliver, eds., *Mission Handbook* (2000).

DOUG PRIEST

Missionary Tidings

Missionary Tidings

"BEHOLD, I BRING YOU GOOD TIDINGS OF GREAT JOY." LUKE II:10.

Published monthly by the Christian Woman's Board of Missions, College of Missions Building, Indianapolis, Indiana
Mrs. Effie L. Cunningham, Editor. Entered as second-class mail matter at the Indianapolis Postoffice

Volume XXXII INDIANAPOLIS, INDIANA, NOVEMBER, 1914 Number 7

SCHOOL FOR GIRLS AT LUCHOWFU, CHINA. FROM THIS SCHOOL WILL COME THE FIRST PUPILS OF THE NEW SCHOOL TO BE ESTABLISHED BY THE CHRISTIAN WOMAN'S BOARD OF MISSIONS

"My God knows best! This is my chart,
This thought to me is always blest,
It hallows and it soothes my heart,
For all is well and God knows best.

"My God knows best! Then tears may fall,
In His great hour I'll find my rest,
For He my God is over all,
And He is love and He knows best."

In 1883 the CWBM engaged Marcia Goodwin to edit a journal that she named *Missionary Tidings*. The magazine grew quickly to forty pages and had a circulation of 54,000 subscribers when it merged with four other mission publications in 1918 to become *World Call*. The merger came with the formation of the United Christian Missionary Society. The other four journals had 36,000 subscribers combined. Effie L. Cunningham, editor of *Missionary Tidings* during its last nine years, became associate editor of *World Call*.
Courtesy of the Disciples of Christ Historical Society

Monthly periodical of the Christian Woman's Board of Missions (CWBM).

At their first meeting in Indianapolis on January 4, 1875, the executive committee of the CWBM resolved to promote their work on a monthly basis in *The Monitor* (Mrs. Marcia M. Bassett Goodwin, editor) and to contribute articles to the *Christian Standard* and the *Christian*, principal journals of the Stone-Campbell Movement. After a few years, the CWBM decided to develop its own monthly periodical in order to keep "the constituency of the Board informed as to the needs of the work, the progress made, and the calls for service at home and abroad."

Missionary Tidings began publication in May 1883 and continued until the issue of December 1918, the eve of the publication of *World Call*, the journal of the newly formed United Christian Missionary Society. From an initial four-page issue to a magazine of about forty pages, *Missionary Tidings* grew in circulation to 60,000 subscribers, more than any other periodical among the Disciples of Christ, according to I. W. Harrison.

The editors of *Missionary Tidings* included Mrs. Marcia M. Bassett Goodwin (1883), Mrs. S. E. Shortridge and Mrs. L. A. Moore (1883-88), Mrs. S. E. Shortridge (1888-90), Miss Lois A. White (1890-99), Mrs. Helen E. Moses (1899-1905), Mrs. Anna R. Atwater (1905-9), and Mrs. Effie L. Cunningham (1909-18). During much of its history, the editor of *Missionary Tidings* was also the corresponding secretary of the CWBM.

The cover of each issue featured a poem, literary quotation, or biblical passage framed by a floral design. The contents included minutes from executive committee meetings, program materials for local auxiliary meetings, contributed articles for personal and group study, reports about the auxiliaries of the CWBM (including state and national convention reports), news and notes regarding the Young People's Departments, reports from the home and foreign missions supported by the CWBM, and business records (acknowledging every contributor by name, including amounts as small as 25¢).

As a periodical designed to report and to promote the work of a mission society, *Missionary Tidings* was very successful, and it also played a critical role in the development of the CWBM, including the organization of auxiliaries and youth work in local congregations as well as the home and foreign missions sponsored by the CWBM. Finally, *Missionary Tidings* gave a strong voice to women in the Stone-Campbell Movement as no other periodical has done before or since.

BIBLIOGRAPHY Ida Withers Harrison, *History of the Christian Woman's Board of Missions* (1920) • *Missionary Tidings* (1884-1918). PAUL ALLEN WILLIAMS

Missions, Missiology

1. Introduction

The word "mission" comes from a Latin term signifying "sending" or "to send," including the idea of sending someone with a special task or message. "Missiology" indicates systematic reflection on the message, method, and context of missions. The message is generally understood as *euangelion,* that is, the "good news" of Jesus Christ; "evangelism" commonly refers to the proclamation of the good news. The method of missions may be variously defined depending on one's view of the relationship between proclamation *(kērygma),* service *(diakonia),* and fellowship *(koinōnia).* The context of missions is varied as well. The proclaimers of the gospel are sent "to the ends of the earth," and people throughout the world represent a wide variety of languages, cultures, social forms and customs, and spiritual traditions.

In the Christian tradition, mission is God's mission in the world. In sending Jesus the Christ into the world, God's mission became fully known, and individual Christians, congregations of Christians, or the universal "body of Christ" may be called to participate in God's mission. "Missions" is the work that has been or is being done by Christians in the world. Despite this broad definition, the word "missions" has most often been used to refer to Christian ministries "overseas" or in a cultural context differing from the individual who is sent. This international or cross-cultural context of missions requires that missiology also consider the linguistic and cultural variety confronting the missionary, whether the latter comes from or goes to North America.

As in any branch of Christianity, the history of missions in the Stone-Campbell Movement is closely linked with the development of thinking about missions, that is, missiology. In turn, one's understanding of the theological and biblical foundations for missions is closely linked to one's understanding of the nature of the church, that is, ecclesiology. Within the Stone-Campbell Movement, the central ecclesiological distinction lies between those who believe that the church functions only at the level of the local congregation and those who believe that the church is present in other organizational forms. For the former, there is a difference between those who accept the formation of mission societies as an expedient, as a "parachurch agency," and those who reject the formation of mission societies as an unbiblical innovation. For those who believe that the church functions in forms other than the local congregation, the formation of mission societies and even of denominational structures is an acceptable, even necessary, practice.

The development of missiology in the Movement, then, must be understood in terms of its ecclesiology, that is, its doctrine of the "church." The common tradition is rooted in a congregational polity, a commitment to the local congregation as the biblical model of *ekklēsia* (church), and a suspicion of extra-congregational organizations. Differences in attitudes toward "church" help to account for different attitudes toward "missionary societies" and other forms of extra-congregational organization (e.g., denominations). At an earlier stage, the question was, Is it scriptural to organize societies for the purpose of promoting and managing the mission of the churches? In more recent decades, a central question has been, What is the relationship between *kērygma* (proclamation), *diakonia* (service), and *koinōnia* (fellowship) in the mission of the church?

2. Churches, Societies, and Organizational Developments

2.1. Campbell, Early Societies, and the Churches of Christ

Initially, Alexander Campbell and other early leaders in the Stone-Campbell Movement opposed missionary societies on the grounds that spreading the gospel was the responsibility of the churches, not of a mission organization. Campbell was also concerned about the potential power of such a national organization and about the establishment of a creed. However, he accepted the presidency of the American Christian Missionary Society (ACMS) in 1849 and remained its president until his death in 1866. Robert Richardson argued that Campbell did not change his basic theological stance but developed an understanding that cooperation between churches could be used to spread the gospel. Thus, the formation of societies was promoted as a more efficient means to fulfill the Great Commission (Matt. 28:19-20) and to extend the Movement's plea with a sense of urgency rooted in a millennial perspective. Mark Toulouse's interpretation of the Stone-Campbell Movement from the time of Campbell to the beginning of the twenty-first century demonstrates the central role of postmillennial theology and the "kingdom of God" as a theological foundation for missions.

Despite Campbell's change in opinion about "societies," some persons and churches of the Movement continued (and continue) to judge missionary societies — indeed, all extra-congregational organizations — to be unbiblical. This opposition was a major factor in the separation of Churches of Christ from the part of the Movement that favored organizational development. In addition to the opposition to the societies (including Bible societies and the Sunday School movement), Churches of Christ opposed the introduction of musical instruments in worship. This view was articulated in the Sand Creek "Address and Declaration" (August 18, 1889) rejecting the formation of "societies," including mission and Bible societies. Finally, a separate listing in the U.S. Religious Census of 1906 recognized the reality of a split in the Movement, a split that stemmed in part from fundamental differences in biblical interpretation regarding the mission of the church and how it is to be accomplished.

Churches of Christ maintain a consistent rejection of any extra-congregational form of organization that might compete with the local congregation for authority or that might be labeled "church." In practice, individual congregations support individual missionaries or missionary families. Following World War II some congregations became clearing houses for support of mission efforts in Germany, Italy, and Japan. Called "sponsoring congregations," they solicited support from other churches and individuals and administered funds for establishing churches and sustaining missionaries. Opposition to the sponsoring church method contributed to an anti-institutional schism in Churches of Christ in the 1950s and 1960s.

Informal methods of coordinating mission efforts among Churches of Christ have included missions lectureships, periodicals through which Churches of Christ defined themselves and promoted their work, and, increasingly, colleges that train ministers and missionaries. College missions departments often maintain computerized databases of mission points and missionaries and have mission resource leaders on staff. These mission resource leaders may be former missionaries and/or professors of missions. One such effort is the Institute for Missions and Evangelism at Abilene Christian University. In addition, a variety of parachurch missions organizations like Herald of Truth and Eastern European Missions receive support from congregations and individuals for their specific ministries. As important as they are for Churches of Christ, none of these organizational forms competes with the congregation as the initiator and director of missionary activity. Resistance to overarching structures like a missionary society remains strong.

2.2. Withdrawal from the United Christian Missionary Society: The Christian Churches/ Churches of Christ

Those who accept the formation and use of missionary societies do so for various reasons. One scholar distinguishes between the "pragmatic" and "teleological" perspective on missionary societies. For those who hold the pragmatic view, societies are simply an expedient, a means by which local congregations can more efficiently and effectively promote the gospel in the world. When the societies fail to serve this purpose, they can be removed or bypassed as an impediment to the work of the church. For those who hold the teleological view, societies are more than a mere expedient; they are "church," that is, part of the "body of Christ." This difference in the ecclesiological understanding of mission societies plays a role in the dynamics of the other churches in the Movement.

The formation of the United Christian Missionary Society (UCMS; June 22, 1920) brought these implicit views to the surface and led to another division in the Stone-Campbell Movement. Although a united society itself was not the principal point of division, anxieties about the possibility of an emerging denominational structure and concerns about UCMS policies in overseas missions led to acrimonious assemblies in the mid-1920s. Simultaneously, there was a withdrawal of those who felt that "theological liberalism" (or "German rationalism") dominated the thought of UCMS leaders. Among other things, there were charges that the UCMS condoned "open membership" in overseas churches and that conservative voices were suppressed in the mission field and in the conventions.

After the beginnings of the 1920s split, the churches that would become the Christian Churches/Churches of Christ began to reconsider their approach to missions. The rejection of missionary societies or at least the rejection of societies that were judged to stray from restoration principles (i.e., the UCMS) required reassessing traditional approaches and developing new strategies for missionary support. In that climate, independent churches experimented with various modes of missionary organization and modes of support for missionaries.

Four types of missionary organization may be delineated: strictly independent missions, field-based societies, a national association, and mission service agencies. While strictly independent missions were not discouraged, they were considered less efficient and less effective than some form of missions organization. Field-based societies include those coordinated efforts based on the particular "field" to which missionaries went — for example, the Mexican Society for Christian Mission and the African Christian Missionary Society. From 1926 until 1933, a national association called the Christian Restoration Association (CRA) served as the main organizing tool for missions; however, concerns about a united society were still strong among the independent churches. Other forms of "parachurch" organization, like the Christian Missionary Fellowship and Pioneer Bible Translators, and the South Pacific Evangelizing Fellowship, emerged as agencies to serve specific mission functions with no single agency in a dominant position. At present two particularly noteworthy agencies include the National Missionary Convention (1948) and Mission Services (1945).

Implicated in forms of organization are forms of financing. The classic approach to financing mission work included specific congregations sending individual missionaries (and their families). An alternative method increasingly used by independent churches was the Living Link and Forwarding Agent. According to David Filbeck, W. K. Azbill first used these terms and concepts, although the "Living Link" became one of the methods for funding missions employed by the societies as well. The much later introduction of the faith-promise approach (popularized in the 1960s) to fund-raising helped to dramatically increase giving for missions to place between 600 and 1,200 missionaries overseas in the mid-1970s. At its simplest the linkage between the living link supporting churches, faith-promise method for giving, designated forwarding agents, and field-based societies created an informal mode of organization that has been designated as the Direct Support Missionary Movement.

With the testing of various ideas and methods, the principal alternative to a "united" missionary society became the Direct Support Missionary Movement (DSMM). Although not a theological rejection of societies per se, the DSMM reflected a conservative Christian understanding of the biblical mandate for missions and in particular the relationship between the local congregations and overseas missions. If the appropriate relationship is one of congregations sending missionaries directly, the question of means or methods emerges. In the DSMM, the concept of living link missionaries, designated forwarding agents, and a faith-promise approach to funding became critical components of the method of implementing missions. The use of field-based mission societies and United States–based service agencies built a network that helped to organize the work of individual congregations in the Christian Churches/Churches of Christ without challenging congregational autonomy.

2.3. From the UCMS to the Common Global Ministries Board: Christian Church (Disciples of Christ)

In addition to the methods of a unified missionary society, the theology of mission developing among the Disciples of Christ moved from the expediency of unification to the mandate of recognizing God's work in the world, both within and outside of the work of the society and of the churches. This rested on an ecclesiological foundation that held extra-congregational forms of organization to be "church." Further, Disciples were increasingly turning to Barton Stone's emphasis on the polar star of "unity" as a principle for theological and missiological reflection and deemphasizing the principle of "restoration." As a result, the development of missions and missiological reflection among the Christian Church (Disciples of Christ) went far beyond what would be acceptable in either the Churches of Christ or the Christian Churches/Churches of Christ.

Two important statements regarding mission emerged from the Disciples of Christ, the first during the later years of the UCMS and the second after the reorganization known as "brotherhood restructure," a reorganization that accepted for this branch of the Movement the label "denomination." From the "Strategy of World Mission" of the UCMS (1955) to the "General Policies and Principles" (Anaheim, 1981), leaders in Disciples of Christ struggled with the implications of a broad vision of God's mission and of those who presume to do the work of mission. The "Strategy of World Mission" was an assessment process that produced a formal statement in 1961. Recognizing the existence of churches in most nations of the world, the Strategy developed the concept of partnership with churches overseas and called for a phasing out of large mission stations staffed by American personnel. (The most thorough study of the Strategy document remains Joseph Smith's 1961 dissertation.)

Donald McGavran participated in the "Strategy of World Mission" discussions. His contributions to the text stressed traditional evangelical language regarding the nature of the church's mission. Although he started as a UCMS missionary, he began to develop his ideas about Christian missions and church growth outside of Disciples missions organizations, from Northwest Christian College to Fuller Theological Seminary. Through his publications and his students, McGavran's influence throughout the Stone-Campbell Movement highlights the continuing importance of a conservative theological voice regarding missions and missiology.

After the formation of the Christian Church (Disciples of Christ), the Board of the Division of Overseas Ministries (DOM) began a process of theological reflection regarding the mission of the church that culminated in "General Policies and Principles" (1981). One dimension of the policy of the DOM has been openness to ecumenical cooperation with other Christian churches, including the close relationship with the United Church of Christ. Along with these theological reflections, there has been a cautious process of organizational linkage between the DOM and the United Church Board of World Missions (UCBWM) since 1967. This process culminated in April 1996, when the DOM and the UCBWM formed the Common Global Ministries Board (CGMB), a board with twenty members from the Disciples, twenty from the United Church of Christ, and six from partner churches overseas. Here the unification of mission organizations represented by the CGMB is part of a larger and continuing process of United Church of Christ and Disciples conversation, cooperation, and unity.

3. Conclusion

The Stone-Campbell Movement has long employed the expression "In essentials, unity; in nonessentials, liberty; in all things, charity." While all three streams of the Movement continue to use this slogan, they have clearly differed over the definition of "essentials." These differences have been sharply drawn in the areas of missions and missiology. The essentials for most include the Bible as God's Word to the world, the concept of "restoration" of the New Testament church, and the principle of "unity" in the body of Christ. The essentials have also included baptism by immersion, weekly communion, and congregational polity.

One's understanding of the church underlies one's view of the mission of the church. A basic ecclesiological doctrine among the Stone-Campbell Movement is that the only form of organization properly called "church" is the local congregation, and hence it is only the congregation that can conduct the mission of the church. Many in the Movement allow for the possibility of "parachurch" agencies to help the local congregation in its mission. Finally, some have a concept of the "church" that permits forms of organization (e.g., societies or denominations) other than the congregation to be called "church" and to conduct mission, including the hiring and firing of missionaries. Thus, although congregational polity is considered biblical and accepted as primary by most heirs of the Stone-Campbell Movement, this belief is not understood or implemented in identical ways.

All streams of the Movement employed the same biblical language concerning missions and used it in a similar way in the nineteenth century. After the Disciples Division of Overseas Ministries adopted the "General Policies and Principles" (1981), Kenneth Teegarden described the statement as "thoroughly biblical," while others emphasized the thematic focus of Acts 14:17. In 1984 Doug Priest edited a book titled *Unto the Uttermost: Missions in the Christian Churches/Churches of Christ* (1984) in which terms such as "Lord of the Harvest" and the "Great Commission" were used, along with an emphasis on the role of "covenant" in mission thought. Disciples leaders today are less likely to refer to the "Lord of the Harvest" or even the "Great Commission" than they were a couple of generations ago. Yet the concept of covenant has been at the heart of the process of restructure. Differences in rhetoric signal not a shift away from biblical language but a different use of biblical language.

There is also a difference in the attitude toward missionaries as a strategy for fulfilling the church's mission. In *Unto the Uttermost,* for example, Ray Giles states that "The most urgent need today is for the career missionary. . . . Suitable people are needed long term." On the other hand, the language of the "General Policies and Principles" statement is that "the basic 'planting' of the church has been accomplished. . . . An era of 'world mission' now exists in which the churches in each country and place must engage in witness and service appropriate to that place." A policy implication of this principle was to plan to appoint missionaries only on a specific, short-term basis. This official DOM policy ran directly contrary to Giles's strong call for career missionaries among Christian Churches/Churches of Christ.

Despite these differences in organization for mission, in the use of language to articulate the mission, and in attitudes toward the appointment of career missionaries, there is an interesting coalescence in attitudes toward the context of mission. In one of his "Monthly Missiological Reflections," Gailyn Van Rheenen, missiologist from Churches of Christ, discussed the difference between a "transplanted" church and a "contextualized" church, the former merely imitating the style of the sending church and the latter finding a biblical way of dealing with the cultural and social context of the church. In a subsequent reflection, he highlighted the role of missionaries to serve as listeners. The missionary is "one who 'discusses' rather than 'tells'," sensitive to the local cultural context but not unmindful of the purpose for which he or she is sent. Fred Norris in *Unto the Uttermost* contends that the biblical way to conduct mission includes recognizing that "If we look deeply enough we will find in each culture, in each religion God's partial witness to himself," and that Christian missions are "not compromised" by that fact. Both Disciples Bill Nottingham and Mark Toulouse underscored the "General Policies and Principles" statement based on Acts 14:17: "God has never, in any time or place, been without witness."

The policy implications of these insights are felt in each branch of the Stone-Campbell Movement, yet they produce a variety of strategies for implementing the mission. These insights into the context for doing missions recall the words of the 1926 Convention Report. There the claim was made that the church ought not to "build our foreign mission policy as if it were an inanimate something, detached from life, built in Memphis, boxed and ready to be shipped to the world." This sensitivity to sociocultural contexts was a reflection of a church tradition that can be traced to the apostle Paul (Acts 14:17; Rom. 2:14-16). Translating that sociocultural awareness into missionary practice may mean going to the ends of the earth in order to listen to the voices of other Christians and of participants in other religious traditions. Among the essentials of the faith, "listening" as a mode of missionary practice remains a challenge shared by all parts of the Stone-Campbell Movement today.

4. Timeline of Missionary Organization in the Stone-Campbell Movement

1809-1849	Resistance to all forms of extra-congregational organization
1849	Formation of the American Christian Missionary Society (ACMS), with Alexander Campbell as president
1874	Formation of the Christian Woman's Board of Missions (CWBM)
1875	Formation of the Foreign Christian Missionary Society (FCMS)
1889	Sand Creek "Address and Declaration" opposes societies and other innovations
1906	Separate listing in U.S. Census for the Churches of Christ
1920	Beginning of United Christian Missionary Society (UCMS), assuming the responsibilities of the ACMS, the CWBM, the FCMS, and other important Disciples of Christ societies
1925	Clarke Fund becomes the Christian Restoration Association (CRA) to serve as a clearing house for missions and missionaries independent of the UCMS
1927	Beginning of North American Christian Convention (NACC)
1945	Formation of Mission Services
1948	National Missionary Convention had its first meeting in conjunction with NACC
1968	Approval of "Provisional Design of Christian Church (Disciples of Christ)"
1973	UCMS responsibilities devolved to Division of Overseas Ministries (DOM) and Division of Homeland Ministries (DHM) of the Christian Church (Disciples of Christ)
1981	"General Principles and Policies" approved by the Board of the DOM
1996	Formation of the Common Global Ministries Board (CGMB) by the DOM and the United Church Board of World Missions

BIBLIOGRAPHY Phillip Wayne Elkins, *Church Sponsored Missions: An Evaluation of Churches of Christ* (1974) • David Filbeck, *First Fifty Years: A Brief History of the Direct-Support Missionary Movement* (1980) • Alan Clay Henderson, "The Role of Missionary Training Within the Selection Criteria for Missions Personnel in Churches of Christ (D.Min. thesis, Abilene Christian University, 1992) • William J. Nottingham, "Origin and Legacy of the Common Global Ministries Board," *Discipliana* 58 (Fall 1998): 80-96 • Thomas J. Olbricht, "Missions and Evangelization Prior to 1848," *Discipliana* 58 (Fall 1998): 67-79 • Don A. Pittman and Paul A. Williams, "Mission and Evangelism: Continuing Debates and Contemporary Interpretations," in *Interpreting Disciples: Practical Theology in the Disciples of Christ,* ed. L. Dale Richesin and Larry D. Bouchard (1987), pp. 206-47 • Doug Priest, ed., *Unto the Uttermost: Missions in the Christian Churches/Churches of Christ* (1984) • Howard L. Schug, *The Harvest Field* (1942, 1947, 1958) • C. Philip Slate, *Perspectives on Worldwide Evangelization* (1988) • Joseph Smith, "A Strategy of World Mission: The Theory and Practice of Mission as Seen in the Present World Mission Enterprise of the Disciples of Christ" (Ph.D. thesis, Union Theological Seminary, 1961) • Mark G. Toulouse, *Joined in Discipleship: The Shaping of Contemporary Disciples Identity* (rev. ed. 1997) • Mark G. Toulouse, "The Kingdom of God and the Disciples of Christ," *Discipliana* 62 (Spring 2002): 3-24 • Gailyn Van Rheenen, *The Status of Missions in Churches of Christ* (2002) • Gailyn Van Rheenen, "Monthly Missiological Reflections," http://www.missiology.com • Henry E. Webb, "A History of the Independent Mission Movement of the Disciples of Christ" (Th.D. Thesis, Southern Baptist Theological Seminary, 1954).

PAUL ALLEN WILLIAMS

Missouri Christian Lectureship

Historic lectureship in the late nineteenth century, revived in the twentieth, intended to make accessible the best in Stone-Campbell scholarship for a broader ministerial and popular audience.

The Missouri Christian Lectureship (MCL) was conceived at a ministerial meeting in Kansas City, Missouri, in 1879. At that meeting a series of lectures were presented, and a need for a regular lectureship was noted. The first official MCL was held in 1881, and the lectureship continued annually for several years at various church buildings in central and north-central Missouri, in towns such as Sedalia, Paris, Liberty, Independence, Mexico, Marshall, and Columbia.

The purpose of the lectureship, as stated in the preface of the published edition for 1883, included "the investigation, by means of carefully prepared lectures . . . of critical questions relating to the Bible and Christianity, and the study of such practical subjects as are calculated to lift us up to a higher standard of Christian excellence." Recognized leaders of the late nineteenth-century Stone-Campbell Movement, such as D. R. Dungan, J. W. McGarvey, I. B. Grubbs, J. H. Garrison, Isaac Errett, and others, participated in the lectureship. Several volumes of the proceedings were published.

Subjects of the lectures included "Who Wrote the Pentateuch?" "Christian Unity," "Inspiration," "Church Government," "The Supernatural as the Ground of Religious Belief," "The Origin and Growth of Free Thought," and "Value of Metaphysical Study and Its Relation to Religious Thought." It is not known exactly when or why the lectureship ceased.

The MCL was revived in 1961 by Grayson Ensign, president of Central Christian College of the Bible in Moberly, Missouri. It continued each year (with the exception of 1967, when the college was in a presidential transition) at Moberly until 1985. In the early years of the revived MCL, W. Carl Ketcherside of the Churches of Christ gave lectures on the "Grounds of Christian Fellowship" (1961) and "The Meaning and Functioning of 'Agape' in Christian Fellowship" (1962), which represented the heart of Ketcherside's irenic thought. Through 1969 the format for the lectureship involved several presenters. Each message received a formal, prepared review. Those on the program were educators, editors, preachers, and missionaries. Though efforts were made to use capable men from the different branches of the Stone-Campbell Movement, most of the speakers were from the Christian Churches/Churches of Christ.

Increased costs and declining attendance forced a change in format in which, in its later years, the lectureship would host only one or two lecturers, who would give multiple lectures. The MCL ceased after 1985.

See also Central Christian College of the Bible; Dungan, David R.; Errett, Isaac; Ketcherside, W. Carl; Lectureships; McGarvey, John W.

BIBLIOGRAPHY John Burns, ed., *The Supernatural and Preaching: or the Missouri Christian Lectures Delivered at Independence, MO., July, 1883* (1883, repr. ed. 1955) • Grayson H. Ensign, ed., *Current Christian Concerns: The Missouri Christian Lectureship, 1961* (1962) • *Missouri Christian Lectures* (1882-91), collected in 5 volumes (1883-92).

DAVID G. FISH

Missouri School of Religion

Related to the Christian Church (Disciples of Christ).

The Missouri School of Religion was created by action of the State Convention of the Christian Churches of Missouri meeting in Carrollton, Missouri, in the fall of 1895. The convention named a committee of three persons to develop plans for a Christian college in Columbia, Missouri, adjacent to the University of Missouri. On January 21, 1896, inaugural services for the Bible College of Missouri were conducted and included an address by Dr. R. H. Jesse, president of the university. Dr. William Thomas Moore, a prominent author, educator, and minister in the Stone-Campbell Movement, was named dean and primary instructor. The college was housed in the First Christian Church of Columbia from its inception until 1905, when it moved to Lowry Hall adjacent to the university campus, the home of the institution until 1981, when it was sold to the university. In 1957 the name of the institution was changed to Missouri School of Religion to reflect its more comprehensive mission of theological education in the context of a university setting.

Early on, the institution reached out to other denominations, and the period of 1919 to 1923 saw the Presbyterian Church, the Congregational Church, and the Methodist Church joining in its educational mission. The partnership with the Board of Education, Presbyterian Church U.S.A., continued into the mid-1940s, and that with the Methodist Church continued until the establishment of the St. Paul School of Theology, a United Methodist institution in Kansas City, Missouri, which opened in 1959. In a unique interfaith gesture, the college in 1929 welcomed the support of the Jewish Student Foundation at the university. It is estimated that 30,000 students from many faith traditions took at least one course at the Bible College or the School of Religion throughout its history until the University of Missouri established its own Department of Religious Studies in 1980.

Dr. Carl Agee, dean during the Depression, World War II, and the postwar years, 1934 to 1949, laid the foundation for an enriched educational ministry by instituting a program of graduate study. Dr. Seth Slaughter, dean from 1949 to 1958, building upon the work of Agee, guided the institution in a new phase of its educational mission in the establishment of a seminary division known initially as the Rural Seminary of the Bible College of Missouri (soon to be the Missouri School of Religion). The seminary functioned concurrently with the undergraduate program of religious studies from 1952 to 1972, awarding degrees to ninety-two students in its twenty-year life span. Dr. Thomas R. Shrout, president and dean from 1958 to 1969, led the institution during its most productive years but faced the problem of declining enrollment at the end of his tenure. Dr. Robert Ordway, who succeeded Shrout, in his tenure from 1969 to 1973 led the institution in a refocusing of its mission, including the difficult decision to phase out the seminary. Factors contributing to the relatively short tenure of the Rural Seminary were the declining interest in rural ministry; the presence of seminaries in the two major metropolitan centers of Missouri, St. Louis and Kansas City; the difficulty of adequately funding a small theological institution; and the lack of full accreditation by the American Association of Theological Schools. Ironically, the opening of the seminary with its focus on rural ministry had been widely hailed among a broad spectrum of denominations throughout the nation. The "town and country movement" was flourishing in most denominations and in the program ministry of the National Council of Churches. In fact, Dr. Mark Rich, an American Baptist leader of the movement and a rural sociologist of great stature, was an initial member of the faculty of the seminary and brought credit to the institution as a pioneer in rural ministry education. The opening of the Rural Seminary was a significant factor in the awarding of a Rockefeller Foundation grant in 1952 to the Department of Rural Sociology of the University of Missouri for a major research project on the rural church, with the Rural Seminary as a partner in the project. Subsequently, the research project became a longitudinal study that has been replicated at approximately fifteen-year intervals, most recently in 1999-2000 in a Lilly Endowment Inc. –funded project that was also a joint effort of the university's Department of Rural Sociology and Missouri School of Religion. The "Missouri Study," as it came to be called, contains the largest volume of data on the rural church in the nation.

Adrian McKay became president in 1973 and helped to institute a process of strategic planning that resulted in a decision to refocus the mission of Missouri School of Religion as a center for continuing education for clergy and laity while maintaining its historic focus on leader development for small and rural congregations. In 1985 the institution moved to the Rickman Conference Center, the retreat center of the Christian Church (Disciple of Christ) of Mid-America in Jefferson City, Missouri. In 1995, in its centennial year, the school again refined and reshaped its mission by becoming the Missouri School of Religion Center for Rural Ministry, specializing in licensed ministry training, now called the Certificate in Pastoral Ministry program, and in rural issues advocacy.

BIBLIOGRAPHY Griffith A. Hamlin, *Missouri School of Religion: A Century and Still Counting* (1994).

JOHN BENNETT

Modernism

See Liberalism

Moore, William Thomas (1832-1926)

Pastor, educator, missionary, editor, and historian.

He was born in Henry County, Kentucky, August 27, 1832. His parents were Richard and Nancy Moore. His father died in 1841, when Thomas was 9 years old. His mother was left to care for six children, and for a number of years Thomas was the chief supporter of the family.

Moore entered an academy at New Castle, Kentucky, at the age of 18 and completed the preparatory course. He entered Bethany College, Bethany, West Virginia, in the fall of 1855. Mrs. Emily Tubman of Maryland paid his educational expenses. He graduated from Bethany College as valedictorian in 1858 with the Bachelor of Arts degree. He also received the Master of Arts degree from Bethany College in 1861 and the Doctor of Laws degree from Butler University.

Moore had begun preaching prior to his graduation from Bethany. Following his graduation, he became minister of the Christian Church in Frankfort, Kentucky, and remained there till the spring of 1864. While preaching at the Frankfort, Kentucky, church, he served as chaplain to the Kentucky legislature. He is credited with keeping the state of Kentucky in the Union through a sermon that he preached at the Frankfort church, with many members of the legislature present, a week before the legislature was to vote on secession.

He married Mary A. Bishop, daughter of the former governor of Ohio, in 1864. He later married Emma S. Frederick of New York in 1890. In 1865 Moore accepted the ministry of the Christian Church in Detroit, Michigan, and remained there until February 1866. In 1866 he accepted the call to a professorship at Kentucky University in Lexington, Kentucky (now Transylvania University). He preached at the church and gave a series of lectures at the university each year. Moore also served as minister of the Central Christian Church, Cincinnati, Ohio. In 1878 he went to England to teach and preach to several congregations, ultimately serving the West London Tabernacle, London, England. He remained in Great Britain for eighteen years, returning to the United States in 1896. Upon his return, Moore became dean of the Bible College at Columbia, Missouri, located near the University of Missouri.

Moore's interest in missions was manifested not only in his ministry in England for eighteen years but also through his journeys to many countries. He crossed the Atlantic Ocean thirty-six times. He was one of the creators of the Foreign Christian Missionary Society in 1875.

The phrase "The Disciples do not have bishops; they have editors" is credited to him. He was an editor himself, publishing such periodicals as the *Christian Quarterly* (1869-76) and the *Christian Commonwealth* (England). He resumed the editorship of the *Christian Quarterly* in 1897 and continued it till 1900. He also published the *Living Pulpit of the Christian Church, Lectures on the Pentateuch* by Alexander Campbell (ed.), *Views of Life, Conversations at the Unity Club, Life of Timothy Coop, The Fundamental Errors of Christendom,* and *Heroes and Heroes* (poem). He also contributed to the *People's Bible History* and the *Reformation of the Nineteenth Century.* He authored *Man Preparing for Other Worlds or the Spiritual Man's Conflicts and Final Victory.* He also authored a major history of the Disciples of Christ entitled the *Comprehensive History of the Disciples of Christ* (1909).

Moore's ministries were controversial because he advocated open membership, in which the pious unimmersed were accepted into full membership of the local church. Moore followed this policy while in England and advocated such a position in a meeting of Disciples in 1901. On December 5, 1906, the Monroe Street Church, Chicago, Illinois, adopted Moore's "London Plan" of open membership. He died in Orlando, Florida, on September 8, 1926, at the age of 94.

See also Bethany College; Butler University; Foreign Christian Missionary Society, The; Missouri School of Religion; Tubman, Emily H.

BIBLIOGRAPHY John T. Brown, *Churches of Christ* (1904) • William T. Moore, *Comprehensive History of the Disciples of Christ* (1909) • William T. Moore, ed., *Living Pulpit of the Christian Church* (1869). GARY L. LEE

Mormonism

Religious group whose organization and teaching is rooted in revelations claimed by charismatic founder and visionary Joseph Smith (1805-1844).

The history of Mormonism intersects in important ways with the history of the Stone-Campbell Movement. Mormonism won some of its earliest converts from the ranks of the Campbell movement, especially in the region of Mentor and Kirtland, Ohio. Sidney Rigdon, a Campbellite minister, led his entire Mentor, Ohio, congregation into the Mormon fold in 1830. Over the next four to five years, others in that vicinity made the same transition. Orson Hyde, Edward Partridge, Orson Pratt, Parley Pratt, Lyman Wight, and Fredric G. Williams left the Campbell tradition and became important Mormon missionaries. Sidney Rigdon served the Mormon prophet Joseph Smith as counselor, spokesperson, and special assistant from Rigdon's conversion in 1830 until Smith's death in 1844.

Reflecting on the success the Mormons experienced at the expense of the Disciples, Walter Scott complained in 1839 that Rigdon had "filched from us" the doctrine of immersion for forgiveness of sin, thereby accounting "for the success of the ministers of Mormonism." Scott could not have been more wrong. Long before Sidney Rigdon even heard of Joseph Smith, the *Book of Mormon* taught the doctrine of immersion for the forgiveness of sins.

Recognizing the profoundly restorationist character of Mormonism, others in the Stone-Campbell Movement have suggested through the years that Mormonism would not have developed its interest in primitive Christianity had it not been for the influence of the Stone-Campbell Movement. This judgment also is doubtful. Both Mormonism and the Stone-Campbell Movement inherited a centuries-old restoration tradition that had been cultivated by Puritans and their heirs and, before them, by Reformed thinkers in the sixteenth century. This tradition flourished in the utopian climate of nineteenth-century America and expressed itself in a number of incarnations, including Mormonism and the Stone-Campbell Movement.

While Mormonism and the Stone-Campbell tradition shared a common commitment to the restoration vision, they defined that vision in radically different ways. The Campbell movement, for example, combined the restoration vision with Enlightenment rationalism, thereby precluding emotionalism, spiritualism, or any other phenomena that could not be sustained by rational appeals to the biblical text. On the other hand, Mormons combined the restoration vision with the spirit of nineteenth-century Romanticism. Mormons, therefore, never sought to recover the forms and structures of the ancient church as ends in themselves. Instead, they sought to recover the power of the Spirit of God in the lives of believers. Put in restorationist language, this meant that they sought to restore the golden age, recorded in both Old Testament and New Testament, when God broke into human history and communed directly with humankind.

Alexander Campbell criticized Mormons for confusing the Old and New covenants, but Mormons were not interested in that distinction. Both covenants, they argued, revealed a God who broke into human history and spoke directly with humankind. They therefore saw no inconsistency in their practice, for example, of Christian baptism in a restored Jewish temple.

When one understands that Mormons and Disciples/Christians conceived of the restorationist task in such radically different terms, one can then understand why so many Campbellites in Mentor and Kirtland, Ohio, abandoned Campbell for the spiritual leadership of Joseph Smith. For example, Elizabeth Ann Whitney and her husband Newell affiliated with the Mormons since, according to Elizabeth, "There was no one [in the Campbell movement] with authority to confer the Holy Ghost." Eliza Snow left Campbell when she discovered that he was not empowered directly by God. In 1835, therefore, she was "baptized by a 'Mormon' Elder, and . . . realized the baptism of the Spirit as sensible as I did that of the water in the stream." John Murdock joined the Disciples, but "finding their principal leader, Alex Campbell, with many others, denying the gift and power of the Holy Ghost, I began to think of looking me a new home." The Mormon missionary Parley Pratt baptized Murdock in November of 1830.

Over the years, many leaders in Churches of Christ have leveled attacks on Mormonism, but of all these attacks, two texts are particularly notable. Alexander Campbell authored the first detailed and substantive criticism of Mormonism, published under the title "Delusions," in the *Millennial Harbinger* of February 7, 1831. And two preachers from the Stone-Campbell Movement, Abraham Sallee and Samuel DeWhitt, debated two Mormon preachers, John D. Lee and Alfonso Young, at the Ridge Meetinghouse in Smith County, Tennessee, in the spring of 1841. Arthur Crihfield published the proceedings of those debates in *Crihfield's Christian Family Library and Journal of Biblical Science* in four issues: July 18 and 25 and August 1 and 15, 1842.

See also Heresy, Heretics; Restoration, Historical Models of; Rigdon, Sidney

BIBLIOGRAPHY Philip L. Barlow, *Mormons and the Bible* (1991) • Ivan J. Barrett, *Joseph Smith and the Restoration* (1967) • Richard L. Bushman, *Joseph Smith and the Beginnings of Mormonism* (1984) • Alexander Campbell, *Delusions: An Analysis of the Book of Mormon with an Examination of Its Internal and External Evidences, and a Refutation of Its Pretenses to Divine Authority* (1832) • Richard T. Hughes, "Two Restoration Traditions: Mormons and Churches of Christ in the Nineteenth Century," *Journal of Mormon History* 19 (1993): 34-51 • Lloyd Knowles, "Sidney Rigdon: The Benedict Arnold of the Restoration Movement?" *Stone-Campbell Journal* 6 (2003): 3-25 • Jan Shipps, *Mormonism: The Story of a New Religious Tradition* (1985) • Dan Vogel, *Religious Seekers and the Advent of Mormonism* (1988).

RICHARD T. HUGHES

Morrison, Charles Clayton (1874-1966)

Disciples of Christ editor, minister, and ecumenist.

Morrison spent most of his career in Chicago, where for thirty-nine years he was editor of the noted journal of American Protestant opinion, the *Christian Century.* Originally from Ohio and a graduate of Drake University, Morrison began his editorial career in 1908, when he purchased the *Christian Century* for $1,500. For the next five years he coedited the journal with the biblical scholar Herbert Lockwood Willett, dean of the Disciples Divinity House of the University of Chicago. In these early years of Morrison's editorship, the *Christian Century* represented a liberal perspective on the activities and concerns of the Disciples of Christ. By 1918 Morrison had shifted the journal to a more broadly Protestant outlook and had given it the subtitle "An Undenominational Journal of Religion." Through both phases of his editorial career, Morrison exhibited an expansive but decidedly Protestant point of view on the relation of religion to politics and cultural affairs, and he regularly wrote in behalf of such social reforms as temperance, the labor movement, women's suffrage, and world peace.

The earlier Disciples-oriented phase of Morri-

In 1908, thirty-four-year-old Charles Clayton Morrison (1874-1966) began his four-decade editorial career as editor of *The Christian Century*. Morrison became a leading voice in American Protestant ecumenism.
Courtesy of the Disciples of Christ Historical Society

son's career was clearly exemplified by his first book, *The Meaning of Baptism* (1914), which was based on a 1911 essay series in the *Christian Century*. The Monroe Street church, Chicago, where Morrison was the minister, had taken a highly controversial stance among Disciples in 1906 by adopting "open membership," the admission to full membership of unimmersed Christians who were satisfied with their previous baptisms. Opposing strict insistence on immersion, Morrison's book emphatically declared that "practical co-operation" with other churches and "the Disciples' plea for Christian unity will continue to be abortive so long as Mr. [Alexander] Campbell's view of baptism persists" in the Movement. In a comparable effort to promote Christian unity, he collaborated with Willett in publishing *Hymns of the United Church* (1916), including sections of hymns espousing Christian unity and reflecting the ideals of the Social Gospel.

In the aftermath of World War I, Morrison actively campaigned for Christian pacifism. His 1927 book *The Outlawry of War* made common cause with Columbia University philosopher John Dewey, Idaho Senator William Edgar Borah, and others in advocating a formal international declaration of the outlawry of war and the creation of a world court. As one of the leading American voices for Christian unity, Morrison drafted the so-called "Greenwich Plan" for Protestant unity of the Conference on Church Union, which met from 1949 to 1958. His final book, *The Unfinished Reformation* (1953), decried denominational division as "a decadent survival of an era that is now past" and interpreted the modern ecumenical movement as a comprehensive renewal of the church, the "re-emergence in Protestantism of the unfinished task of the Reformation."

See also *Christian Century, The;* Ecumenical Movement, The; Liberalism; Pacifism; Willett, Herbert Lockwood

BIBLIOGRAPHY Charles C. Morrison, *The Meaning of Baptism* (1914) • Charles C. Morrison, *The Outlawry of War: A Constructive Policy for World Peace* (1927) • Charles C. Morrison, *What Is Christianity?* (1940) • Charles C. Morrison, *The Unfinished Reformation* (1953) • Charles C. Morrison and Herbert Lockwood Willett, eds., *Hymns of the United Church* (1916).

W. CLARK GILPIN

Moser, Kenneth Carl (1893-1976)

Preacher, teacher, and writer in twentieth-century Churches of Christ.

Born in Johnson City, Texas, Moser was baptized in 1912 by his father, J. S. Moser (1860-1923). He taught school from 1910 to 1915, then completed a degree at Thorp Springs Christian College between 1915 and 1919. Moser served churches in Normangee, Texas (1919-20); Longview, Texas (1920-21); Wewoka, Oklahoma (1921-23); Tenth & Frances in Oklahoma City, Oklahoma (1923-26); Frederick, Oklahoma (1926-33); Ardmore, Oklahoma (1935-37); Morton, Texas (1937-40); 12th & Drexel in Oklahoma City (1940-47; 1950-64); and Enid, Oklahoma (1947-50). He taught on the Bible faculty at Lubbock Christian College from 1964 to 1972. He was also a staff writer for the *Gospel Advocate* in 1933.

Moser led a renewal of grace-oriented teaching in Churches of Christ through his books *The Way of Salvation* (1932) and *The Gist of Romans* (1957). He anticipated the 1960s "Man or the Plan" controversy by defining the gospel christologically ("man") rather than as the steps of salvation ("plan"). The pamphlets "Are We Preaching the Gospel?" (1937) and "Christ Versus the Plan" (1952) highlighted the difference between these two approaches. His soteriology included classic Protestant themes of grace, atonement, imputation, faith, and indwelling of the Spirit, though he retained a Stone-Campbell baptismal theology. Moser's views were unpopular in some

Though ostracized by some Churches of Christ members for his views, K. C. Moser focused his teaching on God's grace manifested in the work of Christ instead of what he saw as a legalistic view of a plan of salvation. "The gospel consists in a person in which to trust. . . . Commands are not the gospel," he wrote in a 1934 article titled "Can the Gospel Be Obeyed?"

circles, and he suffered marginalization by the mainstream during the 1930s to 1950s. By the early 1960s, however, he had come to be seen as an influential leader among Churches of Christ.

See also Grace, Doctrine of; Justification, Doctrine of; Salvation

BIBLIOGRAPHY Leonard Allen, *Distant Voices* (1993), pp. 162-70 • John Mark Hicks, "K. C. Moser and Churches of Christ: An Historical Perspective," *Restoration Quarterly* 37:3 (1995): 139-57 • John Mark Hicks, "K. C. Moser and Churches of Christ: A Theological Perspective," *Restoration Quarterly* 37:4 (1995): 193-211. Some of Moser's writings, along with a full bibliography and an extended assessment of his significance, are available at http://www.mun.ca/rels/restmov/people/moser.html.

JOHN MARK HICKS

Moses, Helen E.

See Christian Woman's Board of Missions

Mountain Home School

The first attempt at a school among Churches of Christ in northern Alabama, operated from 1868 to 1875 at Mountain Home, north of Moulton, Alabama.

James Madison Pickens was the owner and headmaster. The school had primary, preparatory, and academic departments. In Pickens's words, the course of study embraced "every branch of education usually taught in schools of high grade and necessary to prepare the student for any business or position in life." Mountain Home School was "primarily an academic business; it was not a 'Bible school.'" It did not include Bible as a class, though Scripture was taught daily. Pickens taught rhetoric, mental and moral philosophy, Latin, and Greek. Every student was expected to "attend worship and Sunday School."

T. B. Larimore taught at Mountain Home School from early 1868 until the end of 1869. It was here that Larimore met Esther Gresham, his future wife, and that he made his decision to open Mars Hill, near Florence, Alabama. Mountain Home School continued until 1875, when the building burned. Many young men and women profited from this brief endeavor by J. M. Pickens.

See also Larimore, Theophilus Brown; Mars Hill Bible School

BIBLIOGRAPHY Ralph E. Graham, *Mountain Home College, Bulletin of the North Alabama Historical Association* (1960): 1-16 • Earl Kimbrough, *Faith and Facts* (July 1980): 12-27 • James Madison Pickens, Sr., "Prospectus," *Christian Monthly* (Jan. 1870) • F. D. Srygley, *Smiles and Tears or Larimore and His Boys* (1889), p. 94.

C. WAYNE KILPATRICK

Mulkey, John (1773-1844)

Separate Baptist minister in Tennessee who famously "defected" to the Stone-Campbell Movement.

John's father Jonathan, grandfather Philip, and two brothers were also Baptist ministers. His maternal great-grandfather, Joseph Breed, was assistant minister to Shubel Stearns at the Sandy Creek (North Carolina) Baptist Church, a mother church for Separate Baptists.

Born in South Carolina, Mulkey moved to eastern Tennessee, where his father became minister of the Boone's Creek (Buffalo Ridge) Baptist Church, perhaps the first Baptist Church in Tennessee. Mulkey began preaching in Tennessee at age 20 but moved to Thompkinsville, Kentucky, where by 1798 he was minister for the 175-member Mill Creek Baptist Church and a popular itinerant in Kentucky and Tennessee.

Like many Americans from Calvinist traditions, Mulkey began to question predestination and found himself alienated from the Baptist leadership. J. H. Spencer in his *History of the Kentucky Baptists* accused Mulkey of leading off "a large faction of the [Mill Creek Baptist Church] to the Arians or Stoneites." Courtesy of the Center for Restoration Studies, Abilene Christian University

While preaching on unconditional election Mulkey found himself unconvinced by his own arguments. This and other reforming views caused the Stockton Valley Baptist Association to cite Mulkey, then serving as moderator, for heresy. In 1809 Mulkey and a majority of his Mill Creek congregation left the association to form what became known as the Old Mulkey Christian Church. Other association members followed. Congregations under Mulkey's influence cooperated with the Stone and later Campbell churches but retained some Separate Baptist characteristics for many years.

Known for his oratory, exhortations, prayers, singing, and speaking voice, Mulkey was extremely effective in the spread of the Stone-Campbell Movement in an area strategically situated on several migration routes. Converts and Mulkey family members took reforming views to the Western District (Kentucky and Tennessee), Alabama, Texas, Illinois, Kansas, and as far west as Oregon.

See also Baptists; Evangelism, Evangelists — Nineteenth Century

BIBLIOGRAPHY Peggy S. Holley, "A Portrait of Union, Long Fork, Salt Lick and Bagdad Christian Churches: Four Early Restoration Churches in the Mulkey Orbit," *Discipliana* 52 (1992): 51-56 • Isaac T. Reneau, "Obituary," *Millennial Harbinger* (1845): 380. PEGGY S. HOLLEY

Munnell, Thomas (1823-1898)

Educator, pastor, and missionary organizer in the nineteenth century.

Thomas Munnell was born on February 8, 1823, in Ohio County, Virginia. His parents were not associated with any religious body, though Thomas was influenced by the Methodists while growing up. He became acquainted with the tenets of the Stone-Campbell Movement and was immersed at Bethany, Virginia, by J. Harrison Jones. He graduated with honors from Bethany College in 1850. He began preaching during his last year at Bethany.

After graduation, he became a part of the three-member faculty of the fledging Western Reserve Eclectic Institute in Hiram, Ohio. There is a Hiram tradition that he heard the first lesson recited during the first class held in the new school building. Thomas served as teacher of ancient languages and literature. He taught for three years, leaving in 1853. While teaching at the school, he continued his practice of preaching, serving the Ravenna, Ohio, church from 1851 to 1853.

He attended the first Ohio State Convention in Wooster, Ohio, which was held May 12-13, 1852. After leaving the Western Reserve Eclectic Institute, he was principal of several academies in Mt. Sterling, Kentucky; New Castle, Kentucky; and Buffalo, New York. He had to close the academy at Mount Sterling, Kentucky, because of the Civil War.

He became the minister of the Eighth Street Christian Church in Cincinnati, Ohio, in 1857, where he had a successful ministry. He maintained a keen interest in the organization of ministry, publishing in 1887 a study of the role of evangelists in and among the churches, and in 1888 a major work, *The Care of All the Churches,* a landmark work of pastoral care in the second generation of the Stone-Campbell Movement. For several years Munnell served as corresponding secretary of the Kentucky Missionary Society. In 1869 he assumed the same position with the American Christian Missionary Society and served until 1878. During this time he was also an associate with W. T. Moore in publishing *The Christian Quarterly* from 1869 to 1876.

In 1874, in an off-site meeting during the General Convention in Cincinnati, Ohio, led by William Thomas Moore, Munnell served on a planning committee that gave rise to the Foreign Christian Missionary Society. Munnell's support for missions continued through his interest and help in the organization of the Christian Woman's Board of Missions during the 1874 General Convention. He also had a deep concern for home missions. As corresponding secretary for the American Christian Missionary Society, he assisted in the founding of Southern Christian Institute in Mississippi for the education of African American students.

Munnell's theological views were not without controversy. He was a pacifist, and in 1872 he published with J. S. Sweeney a dialogue on the subject of Christians going to war in service of the state. In the April 1894 issue of the *New Christian Quarterly,* he wrote an article advancing open membership, the waiving of immersion as a term of church membership in order to promote union with other Christian bodies. He wanted to treat immersion as a nonessential requirement and used Paul's teachings on circumcision and the early church's attitude on Jewish sacrifice as a defense of his position. Munnell died in September 1898 in Alma, Illinois.

See also American Christian Missionary Society; Evangelism, Evangelists; Foreign Christian Missionary Society, The; Hiram College; Pastoral Care

BIBLIOGRAPHY F. M. Green, *History of Hiram College (1850-1900)* (1901) • W. T. Moore, ed., *Living Pulpit of the Christian Church* (1868) • Thomas Munnell, *The Care of All the Churches* (1888) • Thomas Munnell, *Evangelists and Their Work in the Church* (1887) • Thomas Munnell and J. S. Sweeney, *Discussion: Shall Christians Go to War?* (1872).

GARY L. LEE

James DeForest Murch (left), an opponent of Disciples Restructure, offered a major critical evaluation of the proposal in *The Free Church* in 1966. Murch is pictured here with Disciples ecumenist and theologian of Restructure, Ronald E. Osborn. Courtesy of the Disciples of Christ Historical Society

Murch, James DeForest (1892-1973)

Editor, organizer, historian, and unity activist among the Christian Churches/Churches of Christ in the twentieth century.

Murch was born a preacher's son in New Vienna, Ohio, raised in a conservative Disciples church, and graduated from Ohio University in 1915. Committed to the local church, he served for many years as an elder in the Westwood-Cheviot Church of Christ in Cincinnati. Over a sixty-year career, he devoted considerable energy to a broad range of organizations and institutions and was widely recognized as a key standard-bearer of the Christian Churches/Churches of Christ in the era of their separation from the Christian Church (Disciples of Christ). Although he flirted briefly with preaching, his real love was journalism, being a prolific author and editor.

In 1916 Murch became office editor of the *Christian Standard.* Between 1916 and 1945 he served as editor of *Something Doing* (1916-18), *The Lookout* (1918-25), *The Restoration Herald* (1925-34), *Christian Action* (1935-45), *Christian Unity Quarterly* (1941-45), *Standard Bible Teacher and Leader* (1944-45), and *Christian Home Life* (1944-45). News of the churches, editorials, Bible study lessons, and hundreds of other articles appeared under his byline.

Murch's work placed him at the center of controversies that threatened the unity of the Stone-Campbell Movement in the twentieth century. An unswerving supporter of the "independent" position on issues of church polity and the configuration of Christian missions, Murch helped to found the Christian Restoration Association (CRA) in 1925. He served as president from 1925 to 1933 and as editor of *The Restoration Herald* from 1925 to 1934. Under Murch's leadership, the *The Restoration Herald* became the voice of the most conservative Disciples of Christ. Concerned, like many of his associates, with what he perceived as an inflated authority in Disciples agencies and a compromising of the "restoration plea," Murch in his writing began to flesh out his own unity ideal of "Cooperation without Compromise."

During the controversies, Murch found common cause with a broad array of conservative Christians. In the 1930s he worked with Claude Witty of the Churches of Christ to promote unity in the Stone-Campbell Movement. When this effort failed, Murch turned in new directions. In 1941 he was a cofounder of the National Association of Evangelicals (NAE). Because some conservative Disciples leaders viewed the NAE as an unacceptable compromise with denominationalism, Murch left his long association with Standard Publishing in 1945. In that same year he began work as editor of *United Evangelical Action,* the official publication of the NAE. He edited the journal for thirteen years before becoming managing editor for *Christianity Today* in 1958.

Murch continued at *Christianity Today* for only four years. He set aside his full-time editorial work in 1961 and "retired" in 1962 at the age of 70. During retirement he continued to write prolifically. He produced a variety of books, chapters, articles, and tracts focusing on everything from Christian education in the churches to the need for a "Protestant Revolt" against the mounting secularism of the time. Murch also worked tirelessly in opposition to the Disciples of Christ restructure proposal. When restructure was approved in 1968, Murch took up the cause of the Christian Churches/Churches of Christ, fighting for their recognition as a body of churches separate and distinct from the Disciples.

In his long career Murch wrote hundreds of Bible study lessons, devotional books, tracts, and monographs. Much of his writing focused on youth programs, especially Christian Endeavor and Christian Action. His Bible studies were published regularly in Christian Endeavor publications and in *Something Doing, The Lookout,* and later *Christian Action* and *Standard Bible Teacher and Leader,* which he also edited. He published many books on Christian education, including *Successful Prayer Meetings, Christian Action Bible Studies, Christian Action Study Manual, Sunday School Handbook, Christian Education and the Local Church, Teach or Perish,* and *Christian Endeavor Essentials.* From 1948 to 1952 he wrote the *Evangelical Sunday School Lesson Commentary.* His books *Christian Education and the Local Church* and *Christians Only: A History of the Restoration Movement* (1962) were for decades considered the standard texts for study of Christian education and of the Stone-Campbell Movement's history among independents.

Murch also authored a number of books and tracts opposing religious liberalism and supporting conservative religious political action. In opposition to liberal ecumenism Murch wrote *The Growing Super Church* (1952), *The Coming Great Church* (1955), *The World Council of Churches: An Analysis and Evaluation* (1961), *The National Council of Churches: A Critique* (1966), *The Free Church* (1966), and *The Protestant Revolt: Road to Freedom for American Churches* (1967). Murch ardently believed that the "Free Church" tradition stood in a direct line of descent from the apostolic church, and that it was incumbent on the faithful remnant of conservative evangelicals, led by Disciples "independents," to rally in restoring New Testament Christianity and thus to bring about church unity in a way that the mainstream ecumenical movement could never do.

Murch also crusaded against Roman Catholic influence in American public life and politics and against communism. In 1963 he authored *Church-State Relations: The American Way* for Americans United for Separation of Church and State. Despite these affiliations, Murch was not a "fundamentalist" in the classic American Protestant sense, but represented the newer and more sophisticated "Evangelicalism" laying its stake across denominational lines in post–World War II America.

Murch helped to set the standard for conservative Christian journalism for much of the twentieth century. In tribute to Murch, the National Association of Evangelicals annually awards the James DeForest Murch award for religious journalism to one outstanding journalist. His influence was broadly felt throughout his long career among Christians from many denominations. From start to finish, however, his first love was the Stone-Campbell "Restoration" Movement and the ideal of Christian unity.

See also Christian Churches/Churches of Christ; Christian Restoration Association; Evangelical; Fundamentalism; Historiography, Stone-Campbell Movement; *Restoration Herald, The;* Standard Publishing Company

BIBLIOGRAPHY Kevin R. Kragenbrink, "Dividing the Disciples: Social, Cultural, and Intellectual Sources of Division in the Disciples of Christ, 1919-1945" (Ph.D. dissertation, Auburn University, 1996) • Kevin R. Kragenbrink, "The Modernist/Fundamentalist Controversy and the Emergence of the Independent Christian Churches/Churches of Christ," *Restoration Quarterly* 42 (2000): 1-17 • James DeForest Murch, *Adventuring for Christ in Changing Times: An Autobiography of James DeForest Murch* (1973) • James DeForest Murch, *Christians Only: A History of the Restoration Movement* (1962) • James DeForest Murch, *Cooperation without Compromise: A History of the National Association of Evangelicals* (1956) • James DeForest Murch, *The Free Church* (1966) • James DeForest Murch, *The Protestant Revolt: Road to Freedom for American Churches* (1967) • James DeForest Murch, "The Restoration Plea in an Ecumenical Era," in *The Second Consultation on Internal Unity* (1963).

KEVIN R. KRAGENBRINK

N

Names of the Movement

It is significant that there is no single nomenclature for the Stone-Campbell Movement as a whole. Having begun in a variety of places and times and with different leaders, and lacking a centralized or hierarchical structure, a variety of nomenclature was inevitable. At the time of the union of the separate Stone and Campbell movements in 1832, the adoption of a name was a point of considerable tension. Barton Stone argued for the simple name "Christians" since that was allegedly the earliest name adopted by the church (Acts 11:27) and identified directly with Christ himself, while Campbell encouraged the name "disciples" because it was the more ancient and humbler designation.

Once united, especially in view of the Campbells' self-designation as "Reformers," the term "Reformation" came into frequent use among early leaders, who likewise saw themselves as reformers in the cause of Christian unity and the restoration of apostolic Christianity for the sake of evangelistic mission. They spoke of the "present" or "current reformation" and "the cause of reformation." Robert Richardson titled the book form of a series of articles on the purpose of the Movement, *The Principles and Objects of Religious Reformation, Urged by A. Campbell and Others* (1853) and the phrase "Religious Reformation" showed up as well in the subtitle of his *Memoirs of Alexander Campbell* (1868, 1870). J. H. Garrison immortalized this term in a collection of essays celebrating the Disciples' centennial, *The Reformation of the Nineteenth Century* (1909).

As that century progressed, the name "Restoration Movement" became popular and has continued to be so, especially among the Churches of Christ and the Christian Churches/Churches of Christ. The "restoration" nomenclature doubtless drew early inspiration from Alexander Campbell's long series of essays in the *Christian Baptist* ("A Restoration of the Ancient Order of Things"), setting forth the agenda of his emerging reformation. Focusing primarily on the restoration motif, this name is an uncomfortable one for those whose focus is also, or primarily, the unity motif of the Movement. Yet the popularity of "Restoration Movement" for conservatives went hand in hand with their perceived need to rally support for the original agenda and "plea" of the Movement, while liberals were seemingly reinventing that agenda.

For others the historic collective term for the people of the Movement is "The Disciples of Christ." The nomenclature of the "Disciples of Christ Historical Society," serving all three major segments of the Movement, reflects this inclusive historical use of the term. But with the divisions of the late nineteenth and twentieth centuries, the term "Disciples" has evolved (regrettably, for some) into a more limited nomenclature for one portion of the Movement, the Christian Church (Disciples of Christ).

In the late decades of the twentieth century a new name emerged: "the Stone-Campbell Movement." Leroy Garrett's general history of the Movement, the name of the present encyclopedia, and the name of a recently begun journal (*The Stone-Campbell Journal*) reflect the recent popularity of this nomenclature. Despite the possible irony of using the names of early leaders, it is popular precisely because it avoids the difficulties seen in the other names for the Movement, and retains the sense of a collective history despite broken ecclesial relationships.

Other nomenclatures have been used in various times and places. Hearers knew who was in "the Brotherhood" (a term heavily used both by conservatives and liberals alike in the early and mid-twentieth century, e.g., the Commission on Brotherhood Restructure), or "the Cause," or "the churches." A fairly broad consensus exists for the use of the word "movement"; for some it reflects that this is a movement that has sought to bypass the historic divisions of the church, for others that this is a movement *within* the church universal. But over the length of the Movement's history, and in current usage, no one nomenclature has been the official or even the consensually accepted one.

See also "Restoration," Meanings of within the Movement

BIBLIOGRAPHY Robert Oldham Fife, "The Neglected Alternative," *Celebration of Heritage* (1992) • Leroy Garrett, *The Stone-Campbell Movement* (2nd ed. 1997) • J. H. Garrison, ed., *The Reformation of the Nineteenth Century* (1901) • W. E. Garrison and A. T. DeGroot, *The Disciples of Christ: A History* (1958) • J. D. Murch, *Christians Only: A History of the Restoration Movement* (1962)

W. DENNIS HELSABECK, JR.

Nashville Bible School

See Lipscomb University

Nashville Christian Institute

The Nashville Christian Institute was established in Nashville, Tennessee, under the leadership of A. C. Holt in 1940 as a night school for African Americans. Two years later Marshall Keeble became president and opened the school as a fully accredited elementary and secondary school, the purpose of which was to train young men and women as evangelists in Churches of Christ.

In the decade between 1945 and 1955, 235 students graduated from the Institute. Ninety-seven of these young people became preachers. During the same period over 2,500 adults attended the Institute's ten-day lectureship, which attracted attendees from all over the South.

Following Marshall Keeble as president of the Institute were two white leaders in Churches of Christ, Lucien Palmer and Willie Cato. At its beginning the school's board of directors had consisted entirely of African Americans. By 1943, however, several white educators, businessmen, and civic leaders who were prominent in the Churches of Christ, including Nashville insurance executive A. M. Burton and David Lipscomb College president Athens Clay Pullias, had become members.

In the years following his presidency, Keeble continued to work tirelessly to raise funds for the school, sending out news updates and visiting congregations to make his appeal in person. Fund-raising letters called for modest cash gifts as well as bedding, canned foods, and other groceries.

In 1967 the Institute's Board voted to close the school and transfer its assets to a scholarship fund at David Lipscomb College. Keeble outlined the reasons in the March 16 *Gospel Advocate:* shrinking enrollment following the integration of Nashville schools, the threat of losing accreditation, the difficulty of retaining teachers on their low salaries, and the overwhelming need for updated facilities. A number of blacks who had sacrificed to keep the school going felt betrayed by the closure and filed suit in federal court to stop the transfer of funds to Lipscomb. Civil rights attorney Fred Gray represented the plaintiffs. The lawsuit was unsuccessful, and the incident exacerbated the rift between blacks and whites in Churches of Christ.

Insurance executive A. M. Burton (with shovel) and Marshall Keeble (holding plans) break ground for the construction of Nashville Christian Institute. Courtesy of the Center for Restoration Studies, Abilene Christian University

The influence of the school is still felt through the many preachers who were trained in its classrooms. In 2003 an effort to erect a historical marker and museum on the former Nashville campus was begun.

See also African Americans in the Movement; Keeble, Marshall

BIBLIOGRAPHY J. E. Choate, *Roll, Jordan, Roll: A Biography of Marshall Keeble* (1968) • Marshall Keeble, *From Mule Back to Super Jet With the Gospel* (1962) • Annie C. Tuggle, *Another World Wonder* (1973).

SARA HARWELL

Nation, Carry Amelia Moore Gloyd (1846-1911)

Fervent temperance activist.

Born in Garrard County, Kentucky, Nation had a turbulent relationship with the Stone-Campbell Movement because she insisted on women's right to preach, the gift of the Holy Spirit, and the truth of all religions. After coursework at L. L. Pinkerton's Baconian Institute in Kentucky, and her immersion at a Campbellite protracted meeting in Missouri,

Married to Disciples minister David Nation in 1874, Carry Nation (1846-1911) became an internationally known advocate of temperance. Her relationship with the Stone-Campbell Movement was strained because of her insistence on women's right to preach, her views on the Holy Spirit, and her belief in the truth of all religions.
Courtesy of the Disciples of Christ Historical Society

she married a non-church-member named Charles Gloyd. When his alcohol-related death left her a single mother in 1869, she married Christian Church minister David Nation in 1874. In Texas during the 1880s, she operated a successful hotel business and started a nonsectarian church meeting in her hotel lobby. Although the First Christian Church in Medicine Lodge, Kansas, disfellowshiped her around 1892 for claiming to have a "baptism of the Holy Ghost," she was a popular preacher and lecturer for the Woman's Christian Temperance Union (WCTU). She achieved international fame in 1901 when she smashed illegal saloons with her hatchet. After traveling as a celebrity entertainer until 1909, she oversaw a shelter for battered women in Eureka Springs, Arkansas, and she remains one of the most controversial and well-known figures in the social history of the Stone-Campbell Movement.

See also Temperance; Women in Ministry — Nineteenth Century

BIBLIOGRAPHY Herbert Asbury, *Carry Nation* (1929) • Fran Grace, *Carry Nation* (2000) • Carry A. Nation, *The Use and Need of the Life of Carry A. Nation* (1904) • Robert Lewis Taylor, *The Vessel of Wrath* (1966).

FRAN GRACE

National Association of Evangelicals

See Evangelical; Murch, James DeForest

National Association of State Secretaries, Disciples of Christ

A professional organization of state secretaries of the Disciples of Christ.

In the 1890s the corresponding secretaries of the general organizations of the Disciples of Christ met annually and invited the state corresponding secretaries to attend. By the early 1920s, due to heavy agendas, the organizations met separately, giving birth to the National Association of State Secretaries (NASS).

NASS emphasized collegiality. Agendas included a wide range of items: missions, congregational growth, stewardship, spiritual maturity, how a congregation can find a minister, church conflict, etc. Prayer and spiritual development were emphasized, with topics such as the spiritual function of the state secretary. All agenda items were discussed, and a findings committee developed the appropriate "carry through" on every presentation.

The association never forgot that its primary object was to promote fellowship, to acquaint members with ways in which each member carried out ministry, and how to work more efficiently. Members committed themselves to be responsible to Christ and to each other. Ministries were coordinated. Also, each state secretary was to keep a record of how he or she utilized time, the congregations where he or she preached, and the distance traveled. (In 1954 state secretaries traveled 1,033,534 miles.) These reports were assembled and shared through the International Convention of the Disciples of Christ. Members also met with other agencies for long-range planning.

Resource persons were invited to the meetings to speak on issues selected by NASS. The association also appointed members to serve on other agency boards.

WILLIAM MILLER

National Benevolent Association of the Christian Church (Disciples of Christ)

General administrative unit of the Christian Church (Disciples of Christ) charged with health and social services.

The National Benevolent Association (NBA) grew out of a prayer meeting in 1886. Sarah Matilda Hart Younkin gathered six concerned women in a basement room of First Christian Church at 17th and Olive in St. Louis to pray about the plight of the homeless and helpless. Donie Hansbrough, longtime corresponding secretary, later wrote of the founding of the organization that was chartered in 1897: "We conceived as our sole purpose the task of helping the helpless — to give a home to the homeless, to provide care for the sick and comfort for the distressed. In other words, the purpose of the organization was to restore to the church that brotherly love and benevolence taught by Christ and practiced by the disciples in the early days of the church."

Younkin visited congregations in Missouri, Illinois, and Kansas seeking to interest Ladies' Aid Societies in becoming auxiliaries to the NBA. The membership fee for auxiliaries was $5.00, and each local society had the privilege of putting a child in the "Home" once it was established. The first NBA home opened in St. Louis in 1889. Petitions presented to the General Conventions in 1895 and 1896 requesting recognition of the NBA as a Disciples agency were tabled due to objections regarding its mission. Not until 1899, twelve years after it was chartered, was the NBA recognized by the General Convention. Within a few years homes were opened in Colorado, New York, Ohio, Texas, Georgia, and Oregon. In 2003 the NBA was serving 24,000 persons through the combined efforts of 2,800 employees and 1,100 volunteers.

BIBLIOGRAPHY *Fifty-Years' March of Mercy* (1937) • Hiram Lester and Marge Lester, *Inasmuch . . . The Saga of NBA* (1987).

CINDY DOUGHERTY

National Christian Missionary Convention

The National Convention of African American Disciples of Christ eventually merged into the General Assembly of the Christian Church (Disciples of Christ). Preston Taylor, a widely known African American business entrepreneur and Disciples of Christ minister of Nashville, Tennessee, led in the organization of the National Christian Missionary Convention (NCMC) in 1917. It was a cooperative initiative that included blacks and whites within the Stone-Campbell Movement.

At the time of the Convention's establishment, America was involved in World War I. Blacks were migrating from the rural South to the industrialized North. Rekindled fires of racial hatred led to the birth of the Ku Klux Klan, mob lynching, and civil disturbance. Against this backdrop African American Disciples of Christ within the Stone-Campbell Movement were growing discontented with the paternalistic approaches of white Disciples of Christ leaders to evangelism and membership development among Negroes. Black Disciples were increasingly aware of the progress seemingly being made by African Americans in other mainline denominations.

NCMC black pioneers were seeking a more effective partnership with whites in the Stone-Campbell Movement. Preston Taylor and associated black Disciples intentionally developed an NCMC structure that provided for the presence and support of principal white Stone-Campbell leaders who favored cooperative missionary work. Many of them were, at the same time, mobilizing churchwide support for the organization of an international denominational convention (a momentum that birthed the International Convention of the Disciples of Christ).

During the first half century of its existence the African American–led NCMC was a service and fellowship operation for approximately 300 predominantly black congregations in eighteen states and areas. Representatives from the churches were called to an annual convention meeting. Participants voluntarily received in-service training in Christian education and leadership, program information, and spiritual inspiration. They were recommitted to becoming effective Disciples of Christ. Throughout the year convention leaders and available church staff were invited to make field visits to the congregations. Program events for all age levels were planned and promoted to occur in locations nearer to the convention membership.

In 1919, two years after the organization of the NCMC, three mission boards merged to form the United Christian Missionary Society (UCMS), which

The National Christian Missionary Convention met annually from its beginning in 1917 until its merger with the General Assembly of the Christian Church (Disciples of Christ) in 1969. The 1964 Convention met at Second Christian Church in Rockford, Illinois. Emmett J. Dickson, Executive Secretary of the Convention, is the tall man to the left of the tree.
Courtesy of the Disciples of Christ Historical Society

formally came into being in 1920. One of the mission boards in the merger was the Christian Woman's Board of Missions, which had been responsible for administering the work of Disciples of Christ missions among blacks. The merger enabled the UCMS to inherit this responsibility. Furthermore, a UCMS-NCMC partnership in missions was created. It made available increased staff and program resources to service NCMC's predominantly black congregations.

After a generation of gradual movement from separateness toward racial integration and wholeness in the church, a historic Merger of Program and Services Agreement was consummated in 1960 between the NCMC and UCMS. In 1969, with the inauguration of denominational restructure, a second historic merger between the NCMC, UCMS, and the International Convention of the Christian Churches (Disciples of Christ) was consummated.

The NCMC agreed to cease operations as an annual assembly with program staff and to continue operations primarily as an investment-holding corporation. Personnel for its board would be drawn from the directors elected to guide a newly formed body called the National Convocation of the Christian Church (Disciples of Christ).

The overarching goal of the merger agreement was movement toward racial inclusiveness and unity within the whole church. To this end, the National Convocation was regarded by some to be a tentative arrangement empowered to hold a biennial assembly for formerly NCMC-related congregations.

National Christian Missionary Convention leadership affirmed the Stone-Campbell Movement's search for a church centered in Jesus the Christ. They believed the church to be a community that binds together all humanity through the sacrificial action of God's love and grace. During the operational life of the NCMC, the convention accomplished three goals: (1) it launched its organization and operational structure as a Christian partnership going across racial and cultural lines; (2) it pricked the social conscience of the denomination by steadily pressing for policies and programs that eventually began movement toward racial and cultural inclusion, partnership in mission, and functioning as the one body of Christ; and (3) it empowered predominantly black Disciples of Christ congregations and members to function effectively in society as members of the whole church of Jesus Christ.

As a holding corporation from 1969 to the present, the NCMC continues to conserve, maintain, and expand the operation of a historic accredited cemetery business as a nonprofit business. Profits are dedicated to assist African American Disciples of Christ and general church-designated concerns. Moreover, earnings from named funds like the Taylor-Davis Estate, Taylor Memorial Fellowship House-Scholarship, and Black Disciples Endowment help designated church concerns.

See also African Americans in the Movement; International Convention of the Disciples of Christ; National Convocation of the Christian Church (Disciples of Christ); Restructure; Taylor, Preston; United Christian Missionary Society, The

BIBLIOGRAPHY Robert J. Jordan, *Two Races in One Fellowship* (1944) • National Christian Missionary Convention Program Books, 1940 to 1968 (NCMC Office, Indianapolis, Indiana) • *Year Book and Directory of the Christian Church (Disciples of Christ)* (1944).

WILLIAM K. FOX, SR.

National Church Growth Research Center

Church growth organization affiliated principally with the Christian Churches/Churches of Christ.

Founded in 1972 by Paul Benjamin and others, the center has purposed to help churches grow by providing resources, developing leaders, and helping to start churches. From its Washington, D.C., office, the center has sponsored seminars, published materials, organized rallies, worked with church planters, and assisted discouraged ministers. Publications include the "Vision Splendid" series and the "American Church Growth Study" series.

BIBLIOGRAPHY Paul Benjamin, "Helping Churches Grow," *Christian Standard* (June 13, 1976): 5-6 • National Church Growth Archives, Jesse C. Eury Library, Lincoln Christian College and Seminary. ROBERT F. REA

National Convocation of the Christian Church (Disciples of Christ)

Organization of African American members of the Christian Church (Disciples of Christ).

The 1969 Merger of the National Christian Missionary Convention (NCMC), the United Christian Missionary Society, and the International Convention of the Christian Churches (Disciples of Christ) pointed the emerging Christian Church (Disciples of Christ) toward racial inclusiveness and unity across racial lines. The National Convocation (NCCC), born of this restructuring of the Disciples of Christ, was designed as a model of that inclusiveness and unity. Operations were lodged in the office of the general minister and president, the titular operational center of the church. The NCCC administrative secretary became one of the general minister's staff associates.

As a member of the General Minister and President staff the NCCC administrative secretary became the chair of a committee that monitored the effectiveness of general church program services to

Dr. William K. Fox became Administrative Secretary of the National Convocation in 1973, serving also as assistant to the General Minister and president of the Christian Church (Disciples of Christ). Courtesy of the Disciples of Christ Historical Society

predominantly black, Hispanic, and Asian Disciples of Christ congregations. The convocation executive also guided a general church steering committee that operated the reconciliation fund. This committee distributed grants to qualified church and community programs that addressed race and poverty concerns.

The Black Disciples staff that formerly provided program services to National Christian Missionary Convention–related congregations was integrated with staffs in the United Christian Missionary Society and eventually the Division of Homeland Ministries. Regional and general church program units were urged to have existing staff include NCMC-related congregations in their respective program services.

The National Convocation's mandate was to nurture a realization of the merger vision. A fivefold sharing formula for guiding black Disciples of Christ in the realization of the merger vision was presented in 1969. African American Disciples of Christ were urged to:

1. Share in the administration of Christian Church (Disciples of Christ) agencies by serving on policy-making boards and committees.
2. Share in the work and employment of the Disciples at all levels.
3. Share in the drama and exhibition of the work of the church as performed by the regional and general organizations of the Christian Church (Disciples of Christ).
4. Share in the financial support of the causes and concerns of the Christian Church (Disciples of Christ).
5. Share faithfully and loyally in the activities, fellowship, and aspirations of the Disciples as a people moving toward complete integration.

Since its birth in August 1969, the National Convocation of the Christian Church (Disciples of Christ) has contributed the following to the merger vision:

- sponsored seventeen biennial assemblies, which provided approximately 550 congregations a forum for discussion and advisement on issues and concerns of relevance to African Americans and the mission of the whole church;
- encouraged Black Disciples of Christ representation on the policy boards and commissions of regional and general church program units, and institutions of higher education;
- formulated partnership in the administration of the reconciliation fund, a grant distribution program that addresses "poverty and race" issues;
- worked within the framework of the general and regional church to rekindle commitment to new congregational establishment (1975-79);
- encouraged the revival of the Black Ministers Retreat through the office of the Director of Black Ministries in the Division of Homeland Ministries (1975);
- developed associations with groups similar to the NCCC within the United Church of Christ and the Presbyterian Church (USA);
- sponsored long-range program planning such as "The Vision for Vital Mission and Ministry of the National Convocation of the Christian Church (Disciples of Christ) 2001-2004 Vision Plan";
- produced historical materials related to African American Disciples of Christ;
- established a web site that presents an updated picture of the life and work of African American Disciples of Christ within the Stone-Campbell Movement.

See also African Americans in the Movement; National Christian Missionary Convention; United Christian Missionary Society

BIBLIOGRAPHY William C. Mauk, *Celebrating Our Different Journeys As We Attain the Unity of Faith* (1999) • Seventeenth Biennial Session of the National Convocation of the Christian Church (Disciples of Christ) — Program Book, August 9-13, 2002, St. Louis, Missouri (and earlier biennial Program Books).

WILLIAM K. FOX, SR., *and*
JOHN R. FOULKES, SR.

National Evangelistic Association

Disciples of Christ organization for the promotion of evangelism.

The National Evangelistic Association (NEA) is a recognized organization of the General Assembly of the Christian Church (Disciples of Christ). The NEA was organized in 1904, primarily for professional evangelists and evangelistic singers, to promote a spirit of evangelism. Its leaders helped to persuade the United Christian Missionary Society to appoint a secretary of evangelism, Jesse M. Bader (1886-1963), in 1920. (Bader, long active in the NEA, was elected director emeritus in 1961.)

The NEA's membership expanded to pastors, educators, state and national secretaries, missionaries, and laypersons. From 1920 to 1945 Disciples of Christ grew in membership by 70 percent, largely due to the NEA's emphasis on "New Testament Evangelism." The restructure of the Disciples of Christ in 1968 allowed for "other administrative units" in addition to the general administrative units of the Christian Church (Disciples of Christ), and the NEA became one of these units.

In the late 1970s the NEA began to address crucial questions of declining Disciples membership and in 1980 held the National Evangelism Workshop, formed by an ad hoc group that soon became NEA board members. The NEA also began a monthly publication, *Net Results,* with Herb Miller (a Disciples area minister and NEA board member) as volunteer editor and Margo Woodworth (a Disciples layperson) as administrator. Floyd Legler's financial support made possible the launch of *Net Results* and later NEA expansion.

Herb Miller became the first executive director in 1985, and Richard Roland became director of field services in 1986. The NEA's work began expanding to other denominations and now has an ecumenical focus. Herb Miller retired in 1998, and Margo Woodworth became executive director.

As of 2003, *Net Results* (with Thomas G. Bandy as editor) has 10,000 subscribers from eighty denominations. The NEA deploys ten consultants, produces *Net Results* reprint paçs, manages Evangelism Connections national events for seven mainline partner denominations, and sponsors the National Evangelism Workshop held prior to the Disciples' General Assembly. The NEA's stated mission is to "Help congregations help people make a life-changing connection with Jesus Christ."

See also Evangelism, Evangelists 2.1

BIBLIOGRAPHY NEA historical records and documents, Lubbock, Texas • Roy Stauffer, *The First Eighty Years: A History of the National Evangelistic Association of the Christian Church (Disciples of Christ)* (1985).

MARGO WOODWORTH

National Fellowship of Disciple Directors/Association of Christian Church Educators

Organization of Disciples of Christ church educators.

The first professional church educators in Disciples of Christ congregations were known as directors of religious education. Many were women; few were ordained. Although an effort was made to develop an organization in the mid-1920s, a genuine professional organization did not emerge until after World War II.

The first meeting of a Disciples fellowship of religious education directors was in February 1947. The planning for that meeting was begun in 1946 by a group of Disciples directors attending an interdenominational workshop for directors of religious education at Lake Forest, Illinois. The name the National Fellowship of Disciple Directors was first used for the 1949 meeting. In the early years only local church directors were eligible to hold office.

At its 1968 meeting in Chicago, the name was changed to Association of Christian Church Educators (ACCE). Beginning in the early 1970s members and officers were recruited from regional/general church staff, curriculum editors, and seminary professors. Since the 1990s ACCE has been an association of persons committed to the mission of Christian education — as lay, clergy, part-time/full-time, serving as youth ministers, directors, associate ministers, and regional/general staff. As a fellowship group, ACCE sponsors educational events, encourages members to participate in continuing education, publishes a newsletter, sponsors a web site, and serves as an advocate for educational ministry in all forms of the church: congregational, regional, and general.

BIBLIOGRAPHY Gentry A. Shelton, "The History of the National Fellowship of Disciple Directors, Now the Association of Christian Church Educators," Texas Christian University Library Special Collections, 1987.

J. CY ROWELL

National Missionary Convention

Annual gathering of missionaries and mission supporters from among the Christian Churches/Churches of Christ.

The National Missionary Convention was started in 1948 as the result of a meeting of J. Russell Morse, Eugene Morse, John Chase, and Marian Schaefer. Its purpose was to give overseas missionaries a national platform from which to address Christian Churches/Churches of Christ and Churches of Christ in the United States. The Morses were missionaries in China; John Chase served in Korea and briefly in the Philippines; and Marian Schaefer was a missionary to India. The first convention was a one-day meeting at the West Side Church of Christ (now West Side Christian Church) in Springfield, Illinois, on April 20, 1948, prior to that year's North American Christian Convention (NACC) in Springfield.

At the Springfield rally several ministers were added to the committee, and plans were made for the second rally that met at the Englewood Christian Church in Indianapolis, Indiana, on April 25, 1950, also preceding that year's North American Christian Convention. The first two meetings presented the missionary work outside the continental United States, but at the Indianapolis meeting, missionaries laboring in mission fields and benevolent works in the United States expressed a desire to share in the growing missionary convention.

A committee composed of both continental and overseas missionaries planned the third National Missionary Convention that met in Webster City, Iowa, November 14-17, 1950. This meeting was planned to meet separately from the NACC, which it has continued to do since that time except for combined conventions in 1986 and 1995.

The Convention is a time of preaching, teaching, fellowship, and missionary promotion. It has no authority over missionaries or churches and passes no resolutions. The major stated purposes now are: (1) to mobilize churches to become involved in world evangelism; (2) to challenge people of all ages to become missionaries; and (3) to encourage current missionaries.

Recent attendance has averaged around 5,000, with half or more of these being college age or younger. A teen convention was started in 1998. The convention usually meets in October or November. It has met across the United States, from Orlando, Florida, to New York City to Portland, Oregon, to Anaheim, California.

See also Christian Churches/Churches of Christ; Missions, Missiology; North American Christian Convention

WALTER BIRNEY

National Sunday School Association

The National Sunday School Association (NSSA) was a spin-off of the National Association of Evangelicals (NAE); it was also seen as a reestablishment of the older International Sunday School Association. Sunday School workers from thirty-five states and two Canadian provinces met in Chicago, October 2-6, 1946, to constitute the association. The first board of directors included evangelical leaders in Christian education. Among these, Stone-Campbell leader J. D. Murch was prominent (he was at the time editor of *United Evangelical Action,* the journal of the NAE). The motto of the association was "Revitalizing the American Sunday School," with the Bible and evangelism restored to their proper place in Christian educational endeavors. For a number of years the organization was effective, with a fine headquarters building in Wheaton, Illinois. The NSSA has become less prominent since the late 1960s.

See also Murch, James DeForest

BIBLIOGRAPHY James DeForest Murch, *Adventuring for Christ in Changing Times* (1973) • James DeForest Murch, *Cooperation Without Compromise: History of the N.A.E.* (1956).

CHARLES R. GRESHAM

Nativism

Denotes an antiforeign prejudice that prefers persons and institutions of American origin. It should not be confused with anti-Catholic prejudice, but nativists have historically rejected Catholicism as a "Romish" (and hence foreign) imposition on the ideals and privileges of the United States.

Nativism was mostly dormant in the Protestant culture of the New Republic, but it was charged with urgency during the 1830s, when European Catholic immigrants poured into the country. Respected figures such as Samuel F. B. Morse reacted with alarm, detecting a "foreign conspiracy" in which the Pope would undermine and eventually subjugate the nation. Catholic convents and monasteries were besieged with salacious rumors, and public suspicion sometimes culminated in violence. Many petitioned for limitations on immigration and for stricter naturalization standards. These ends were pursued (with limited success) by the "American" or "Know-Nothing" Party, which was organized in the 1850s.

Likewise, Alexander Campbell was aroused by the "Catholic threat" to his millennial hopes, and in 1837 he debated Catholic Bishop John B. Purcell in Cincinnati. It was a turning point in Campbell's career, making him a Protestant hero in "the West." Nonetheless, he opposed heightened standards for immigration and naturalization and turned his attention toward an educational system that would domesticate and Protestantize the expanding population. By contrast, Walter Scott exceeded the nativistic mainstream when he advocated the total prohibition of Catholic immigration. An immigrant himself, however, Scott was not antiforeign, and his case aptly illustrates the complexities attending the "nativist" label.

In its most conservative streams, the Stone-Campbell Movement has consistently opposed Catholicism on political and doctrinal grounds. The papacy was frequently associated with the Axis powers during World War II and with communism during the Cold War; new fears were also provoked by John F. Kennedy's nomination in 1960. Nonetheless, throughout its history the Movement has maintained its anti-Catholic posture without being significantly characterized by anti-foreign sentiment.

See also Roman Catholicism; Scott, Walter

BIBLIOGRAPHY A. Campbell, *A Debate on the Roman Catholic Religion* (1837) • Ray Allen Billington, *The Protestant Crusade, 1800-1860* (1938) • David Edwin Harrell, Jr., *Quest for a Christian America* (1966), pp. 214-21.

KEITH B. HUEY

Natural Theology

See Reason, Place of

Nebraska Christian College

Bible college in northeast Nebraska affiliated with the Christian Churches/Churches of Christ. The school offers associate and bachelor degrees in biblical studies and several ministry fields.

In the mid-twentieth century, the Bible college movement, responding to the perceived liberal and modernist drift of many Disciples of Christ liberal arts colleges, was sweeping across the plains states. Minnesota Bible College had been founded in 1913 and Manhattan Bible College shortly thereafter (1927). A flurry of such activity characterized the 1940s and 1950s, with the establishment of Dakota Bible College (1942), Ozark Bible College (1942), Intermountain Bible College (1946), Platte Valley Bible College (1951), and Central Christian College of the Bible (1957).

In October of 1944, several men and women met in the small southeastern Nebraska town of Wymore and brought to an end more than a decade of discussions about founding a Bible college in Norfolk, Nebraska. Articles of incorporation were signed. Guy B. Dunning was elected president and Virgil R. Marshall chairman of the board. The stated purpose of the college was, first, "the teaching and training of gospel preachers who will be true to Christ and the Bible," and, secondarily, to provide opportunities for "other young people who desire . . . to be better Christians and to be able to render more and better service to Christ and their Church."

A student body of twenty began classes in September 1945, with the original faculty composed of two married couples, Guy B. and Anna Dunning, and J. Merlin and Verol Boyd Hill. Enrollment doubled by the spring of 1947. Enrollment doubled again to eighty in the spring of 1957, and again to 168 in the fall of 1967. Doubling each decade, the college had outgrown two campuses, and in September 1968 ground was broken at a new site slightly northwest of Norfolk. Modest growth continued, peaking at 208 students in 1980. A hallmark of this period of growth (1945-80) was the longevity of many college personnel, lending stability and continuity to the college's educational program. More recently, attendance has plateaued around 150, despite the college's success in achieving accreditation from the Accrediting Association of Bible Colleges. The accreditation process was begun in 1978 and concluded in 1985.

Among the college's strengths is its music program. In 1953 a two-year church music certificate was added to the curriculum. In addition, the college paper gathered a number of musical groups that represented the college in performance and in recruitment.

The college's current mission statement reads: "The mission of Nebraska Christian College is to bring Glory to God through the ministry of educating people at the undergraduate level for His work. The school seeks to prepare workers who will know the Christ revealed in the Bible and be able to present Him to their contemporaries." Four- and five-year degree programs are accordingly designed to educate students for various types of vocational Christian ministry (pastoral, Christian education, youth, music, missions, etc.). In addition, two-year programs equip men and women for more effective Christian witness as volunteer workers in local congregations. More than 3,000 alumni, including approximately 1,000 degree-holding graduates, are involved in carrying out the school's mission in Nebraska, the Midwest, and around the globe.

To ensure future growth and to expand ministry opportunities within a more urban setting, the college intends to move approximately 100 miles southeast, to the southern edge of metropolitan Omaha. Preparations for the move are under the leadership of the college's sixth president, Richard D. Milliken, whose service began in 1999. Classes will begin at the new campus in approximately 2006. When the move is complete, Stone-Campbell Bible colleges will truly border the state of Nebraska, with Platte Valley Bible College on the west and Nebraska Christian College on the east.

See also Bible College Movement; Higher Education, Views of in the Movement

BIBLIOGRAPHY Timothy A. Buck, "A History of Nebraska Christian College" (unpublished M.R.E. thesis, Emmanuel School of Religion, 1971).

J. DAVID MILLER

New England "Christians"

Reform and "restoration" movement in New England in the early nineteenth century, often viewed as an antecedent of the Stone-Campbell Movement. The New England "Christians" commenced in Vermont and New Hampshire in 1801 under the leadership of Abner Jones (1772-1841) and Elias Smith (1769-1846). The movement began as an effort to establish true Christianity based upon the New Testament in opposition to the Calvinistic doctrines of election and predestination, infant baptism, and taxes to support the established (Congregational) church. These restorationists, however, fully embraced the methods and theology of the evangelical awakenings, including itinerancy, direct extemporaneous preaching, and dramatic conversion experiences. Because of their anti-Calvinist outlook they circulated among the Free Will Baptists (commencing in 1780, led by Benjamin Randall in New Hampshire), and Jones was ordained by Free Will preachers but as simply a "Christian." Jones and Smith objected to the Free Will preference for the Baptist name and the power of their associations in ordaining ministers. It was not until the 1830s that the Christians commenced organizing associations — or conferences, as they called them — on a permanent basis. By the 1820s the increasing antitrinitarian posture of the Christians pushed them farther apart.

By 1810 Smith and other New Englanders wrote as if they were one with the O'Kelly and Stone Christians, but the New Englanders (and heirs) had little personal contact with the preachers of these groups until the 1830s. The New Englanders became especially aware of the Campbell reform movement in the 1830s, when the union began with the Stone churches. They purposed to devote preachers and churches to the union, especially in Pennsylvania. Protests against the New Englanders can be found in the writings of Campbell and others because of their emphasis on Holy Spirit conversion, anti-trinitarianism, and quarterly, rather than weekly, celebration of the Lord's Supper. The New Englanders in turn labeled the Campbell reformers as preaching a cold, Spiritless faith, and thus as sectarians.

By 1823 the numbers of ordained preachers of the Christian movement in New England were: Connecticut 17, Maine 15, Massachusetts 9, New Hampshire 21, Rhode Island 1, and Vermont 40. New York (which is not in New England) had 77.

By 1820 the majority of northeastern members were located in the region around Albany, New York, and along the Erie Canal in upstate New York, especially south of Rochester. The first congregation in New York state appears to have been established in Otsego County, February 28, 1812. By 1815 both Abner Jones and Elias Smith had visited various congregations in New York. The critical mass of the Jones-Smith wing continued to live in New York until mergers with remnants of the O'Kelly and Stone movements in the 1890s. In the 1840s several New York members embraced William Miller's millennial (Adventist) crusade, while others departed for the Stone-Campbell Movement. Some of those who joined forces with Miller became important leaders, including Joshua V. Himes, later Miller's chief publicist and the preacher at his funeral.

The two most important second-generation leaders were David Millard, born near Ballston, New York, in 1794, and Joseph Badger, who was born in Gilmanton, New Hampshire, in 1792. Badger first visited the Albany region in 1816 on a preaching mission, and in 1818 he moved south of Rochester. Millard was converted in 1814 by Nancy Cram. Cram also converted Abigail Roberts in Ballston, and both of them evangelized in eastern New York.

For a time Millard preached north of Albany, but in the early twenties he moved to the region south of Rochester. Millard became known through the publication of *The True Messiah* in 1818 (enlarged 1823, 1837). The Christian Connection, so-called, came to the attention of the Unitarians, who invited them to participate in the establishment of Meadville (Pennsylvania) Theological Seminary in 1844. Antioch College, of which Horace Mann, a Unitarian and then a Christian, was the first president, was also supposed to be a joint venture, but neither venture lasted long.

Joseph Badger was noted for editing and for evangelistic tours throughout New York state and into other regions. He published in the *Gospel Luminary,* founded by David Millard in West Bloomfield in 1825, which in 1827 moved to New York City. In 1832 Joseph Badger launched a new journal, *The Christian Palladium,* in Genesee. By 1833 the *Gospel Luminary* had merged with the *Palladium* to become the major journal of the movement. The *Palladium* ceased publication in 1862. Badger was also interested in organizing the churches into conferences and undertaking systematic evangelism. In 1825 and again in 1826, Badger visited the Stone movement Christian churches in Ohio and Kentucky.

Henry W. Bellows (1814-1882), a leading Unitarian, aptly depicted the New England Christians in 1865: "The Christians are a sort of Unitarian Methodist, having the theology of the elder Unitarians without their culture, and the heat and fervor, the camp-meeting usages, and emotional feelings of the Methodists, without their ecclesiastical system of opinions. They have specially cultivated devotional feeling, and commonly owe their accessions to sudden conversions during periodical excitements which are conscientiously favored by them. . . . It claims more than a thousand churches, and boasts fifteen hundred ministers, who have commonly been men wholly uneducated for the ministry, except by their convictions, scriptural reading, and prayers."

After the Civil War the critical mass of members of the Christian Connection was located in Ohio. They established several small colleges throughout the Midwest. In 1931 the Christian Connection, then known as the Christian Church, merged with the Congregational Church to form the Congregational Christian Church. In 1957 the Congregational Christian Church merged with the Evangelical and Reformed Church to form the United Church of Christ.

See also Christian Connection; Jones, Abner; Smith, Elias

BIBLIOGRAPHY Nathan O. Hatch, *The Democratization of American Christianity* (1989) • Michael G. Kenny, *The Perfect Law of Liberty: Elias Smith and the Providential History of America* (1994) • Milo True Morrill, *A History of the Christian Denomination in America* (1911) • Thomas H. Olbricht, "Christian Connection and Unitarian Relations, 1800-1844," *Restoration Quarterly* 9 (1966): 160-86.

THOMAS H. OLBRICHT

New Haven Disciples Center

An institution established to support Disciples students at Yale Divinity School.

From 1959 to 1972, under the leadership of Harry Baker Adams, Disciples students pursuing theological degrees at Yale Divinity School could live at the Center and worship with Canner Street Christian Church. The Center, which was successor to a United Christian Missionary Society–sponsored Missions House whose aim had been to support the equipping of missionaries, was itself succeeded by the Ecumenical Continuing Education Center. The Center was unable to continue operation after 1972.

For over a century, an impressive number of leaders among the Disciples of Christ have come from Yale Divinity School, making known their influence in higher education, in foreign missions, in regional and national offices, and among ministry in the local congregation.

See also Disciples Divinity House; Division of Higher Education

BIBLIOGRAPHY Edwin L. Becker, *Yale Divinity School and the Disciples of Christ (1872-1989)* (1990).

NADIA M. LAHUTSKY

New Light Presbyterians

Popular name of the movement led by five Presbyterian ministers who withdrew from the Synod of Kentucky in September 1803. Included in this group was Barton W. Stone, who with his four colleagues soon organized the Springfield Presbytery. In June 1804 they published *The Last Will and Testament of Springfield Presbytery,* choosing to be known by no name other than Christians. The term "New Light" appears in publications opposing the Christians. In 1811 Robert Marshall and John Thompson, two of the five ministers who had withdrawn from the Synod in 1803, returned to the Presbyterians after having authored an apology for their action titled *A Brief Historical Account of Sundry Things in the Doctrines and State of the Christian, or as It Is Commonly Called, the Newlight Church, Containing Their Testimony Against Several Doctrines Held in That Church, and Its Disorganized State; Together with Some Reasons Why Those Two Brethren Purpose to Seek for a More Pure and Orderly Connection.* In 1821 Methodist William J. Thompson warned his coreligionists against the errors of the Christians in a work titled *A Sketch of the Differences Between the People Commonly Called Newlights and the Methodists.*

In the eighteenth century the term "New Light" had been used to identify revivalist Presbyterians who had supported the ministry of Anglican evangelist George Whitefield. Opponents of the eighteenth-century revivalism associated with Whitefield and such Presbyterians as Gilbert Tennant had been identified as Old Lights. The New Light party of the eighteenth century had been the dominant influence in the formation of colonial Presbyterianism.

D. NEWELL WILLIAMS

New Testament Christianity

Term used by leaders of the Stone-Campbell Movement to distinguish the goal of their restorationist efforts from other forms of Christianity, whether Catholic, Orthodox, Protestant, denominational, or sectarian. They viewed modern Christianity as corrupt, apostate, or spurious, while New Testament Christianity was, in the words of Alexander Campbell, "the gospel of our Lord as proclaimed originally by the apostles."

New Testament Christianity was therefore synonymous with "primitive Christianity," "original Christianity," "the ancient order," "the ancient gospel," and "the divine original." These terms were frequently used, especially in the first generation, to refer to what Campbell described as "Christianity in the undegenerate days of its uncorrupted and divine simplicity," pure apostolic Christianity. Both Alexander Campbell and his father Thomas had been influenced in their primitivist thinking by contacts with

Scottish independents like John Glas, Robert Sandeman, and James and Robert Haldane.

Like the Campbells, Barton W. Stone distinguished between New Testament Christianity and what he described as "the present condition of Christendom." In calling for a new order in the church, the model to which he appealed was the church in the primitive days of Christianity, which were its best days. In a call for Christian unity he referred to the fellowship and union taught in the New Testament and defined what he called "the present reformation" — a reference to the movement he and Campbell had begun — as an appeal to the way things were in the days of the apostles. Stone's repeated reference to "the Bible and the Bible alone" rather than the creeds of Christendom was an appeal to New Testament Christianity.

The Movement's early leaders called for the renewal of the church through a restoration of New Testament Christianity. This included a restoration of its ordinances, particularly the observance of the Lord's Supper every Sunday, baptism by immersion for the remission of sins, and the Bible as the only rule of faith and practice. They insisted upon "calling Bible things by Bible names," which entailed the rejection of party names and party creeds. They became "Christians only," calling their congregations simply Christian Churches or Churches of Christ, and members simply Christians or Disciples of Christ. The most extensive early exploration of what New Testament Christianity would entail appeared in a series of articles written by Alexander Campbell in his *Christian Baptist* between 1825 and 1830, titled "A Restoration of the Ancient Order of Things."

Restoration of New Testament Christianity also called for spiritual renewal, a reformation of the heart as well as the head. Alexander Campbell went so far as to say in his definition of the nature of Christianity that "none are Christians but those who are imbued with the spirit of Christ." This focus became the basis of their plea "to unite the Christians in all the sects." Unity would be realized only by returning to New Testament Christianity and by a repudiation of sectarian or denominational Christianity.

This model was destined to have its difficulties, for in time zeal for New Testament Christianity led to divergent views of what constituted a true New Testament church. As might be expected, there were strict constructionists and loose constructionists when it came to interpreting New Testament Christianity. The more adaptable views of Stone and Campbell, which allowed for considerable diversity, even between themselves, gave way in parts of the Movement to a strict, patternistic hermeneutic. These divergent attitudes were a major factor in the eventual fracturing of the Movement, reflecting an inability to preserve unity in a context of competing views of the nature of New Testament Christianity.

Thomas Campbell anticipated this problem in his *Declaration and Address.* He pled for the unity of all believers "by simply returning to the original standard of Christianity, the profession and practice of the primitive church, as expressly exhibited upon the sacred page of New Testament scripture." He went on to nail down what future generations would interpret as "pattern hermeneutics." "Let *us* do as we are expressly told that *they* did, say as *they* said; that is, profess and practice as therein enjoined by precept and precedent, every possible instance, after *their* approved example."

Yet in the same document he made clear that an appeal to New Testament Christianity does not mandate conformity in every detail of faith and practice: "There may, and doubtless will be, some variety of opinion and practice. This, we see, was actually the case in the apostolic Churches, without any breach of Christian unity."

All this means that the Movement, both in its early days and later, appealed to New Testament Christianity as authoritative, even when there was disagreement on details, particularly in regard to methods. This commitment to the authority of New Testament Christianity gave birth to a concomitant motif — the New Testament church as normative.

Many came to believe that there was a pure, pristine, exemplary church depicted in the New Testament that served as a pattern for all time to come. They came to see the Movement's role as restoring or re-creating that "unadulterated" primitive church. In fact, as the Movement fractured into different segments, there were those who saw their own group as the "true restored New Testament church." Even as the Movement in general moved away from a patternistic hermeneutic in the twentieth century, an affinity for these motifs remained strong, as if they were badges of identification. "New Testament Christianity" and "the New Testament church" became integral parts of the vocabulary of the Movement.

Z. T. Sweeney (1849-1926), prominent Disciples minister, was so concerned that the new generation of preachers of his day had lost the vision of the pioneers of the nineteenth century that he published a three-volume set of books of their sermons and distributed it to the younger preachers free of charge. All three volumes bore the title *New Testament Christianity.*

These three volumes, the first of which was published in 1923, featured sermons with such topics as "The Church of the First Century," "A Plea to Restore the Apostolic Church," "Twelve Reasons Why Disciples of Christ Are Right," "and Baptism for the Remission of Sins." It is evident that Sweeney and many of the preachers he drew from had a restorationist-patternistic view of New Testament Christianity.

Twentieth-century Disciples were greatly influenced by British theologian William Robinson, who defined New Testament Christianity in terms of "apostolicity," especially the apostolic teaching of Word and sacrament (rather than details of church polity). After Robinson this emphasis became the most common view of "the restoration principle" in what would become the Christian Church (Disciples of Christ).

Roy E. Cogdill (1907-1985), a conservative publisher and preacher among Churches of Christ, authored a book titled *The New Testament Church* that went through eleven editions. The eleventh edition (1959) examined the church in terms of its nature, origin, mission, membership, government, and identity. Like Sweeney, Cogdill saw the Movement's mission to be a restoration of the pristine church of the New Testament.

It may appear that the New Testament Christianity/New Testament church motifs were confined to a conservative mind-set, but their use is also found in more liberal, sophisticated circles. When scholars, mostly of Milligan College and Emmanuel School of Religion, published a Festschrift in honor of Dean E. Walker, they titled the book *Essays on New Testament Christianity* (1978). But the eleven essays — virtually all by Ph.D.'s — were vastly different from those of Sweeney and Cogdill. While six of the essays were on "The New Testament Church" and "New Testament Studies," the titles included "Apostolic, Catholic, and Sensible: The *Consensus Fidelium*"; "The Worshiping Congregation: Particularity and Universality"; "Power, Submission, and Sexual Identity Among the Early Christians"; and "The Spirit at Pentecost." This too was "New Testament Christianity."

Bob Russell, pastor of one of the largest congregations of the Stone-Campbell tradition and president of the 2003 North American Christian Convention, was asked about the mission of the Convention. Part of his response was: "God is using our plea for simple, New Testament Christianity" — not just New Testament Christianity, but *simple* New Testament Christianity. This emphasis and conviction goes back to Stone and Campbell.

Another recent voice defining this motif was Reuel Lemmons (1912-1989), longtime editor among Churches of Christ. Among his papers deposited with the Center for Restoration Studies at Abilene Christian University was a sermon in typescript titled "What Is New Testament Christianity and How Are We to Restore It?" He saw the restoration as "an effort to rid modern religion of its human complexes." Like many others before him, he called for "No creed but Christ, no book but the Bible" and a "'Thus saith the Lord' for every rule of faith and practice." Yet unlike many before him he also insisted that New Testament Christianity is "simply the conformation of people to the image of Jesus Christ," and that "to the extent we imitate Jesus Christ in our lives, we are practicing New Testament Christianity."

Another longtime editor, Sam E. Stone of the Christian Churches/Churches of Christ, upon retiring from twenty-five years as editor of the *Christian Standard,* gave "A Final Word" in a 2003 editorial. In telling his readers what he would do in retirement, he explained that he would continue to do what he had done during decades of ministry: "I want to do whatever I can to encourage the restoration of New Testament Christianity in our 21st-century world."

One can only conclude that "New Testament Christianity" is a motif that continues alive and well within the Stone-Campbell tradition into the twenty-first century.

See also Cogdill, Roy E.; Glas, John; Haldane, Robert, and James Alexander Haldane; Lemmons, Reuel Gordon; Robinson, William; Sandeman, Robert; Sweeney, Zachary Taylor

BIBLIOGRAPHY William Barnett Blakemore, *The Discovery of the Church: A History of Disciple Ecclesiology* (1965) • Alexander Campbell, *The Christian System, in Reference to the Union of Christians and the Restoration of Primitive Christianity, as Plead in the Current Reformation* (1839, numerous reprints) • Everett Ferguson, *The Church of Christ: A Biblical Ecclesiology for Today* (1995) • C. Robert Wetzel, ed., *Essays on New Testament Christianity: A Festschrift in Honor of Dean E. Walker* (1978) • William Robinson, *The Biblical Doctrine of the Church* (1948; rev. ed. 1955) • Zachary T. Sweeney, ed., *New Testament Christianity,* 3 vols. (1923, 1926, 1930).

LEROY GARRETT

New Zealand, The Movement in

The Treaty of Waitangi, signed by the British and the indigenous Maori people in 1840, established New Zealand as a Crown Colony. The witness of Churches of Christ began soon afterward. Thomas Jackson, an immigrant from Glasgow, Scotland, began witnessing in the streets of the newly established city of Nelson on March 2, 1844. Churches throughout the nineteenth-century British Empire were often established by immigrants rather than missionaries. The first Church of Christ in the Southern Hemisphere was established in Nelson, and a plaque outside the Rutherford Street Church of Christ commemorates this event. All churches of the Movement in New Zealand subsequently used the name "Churches of Christ" — the name used by the British Churches.

Jackson and some of his Nelson converts moved to Auckland two years later and were instrumental in beginning the church in that city late in 1845. His youngest convert, twenty-year-old Thomas Magarey (1825-1902), moved to Adelaide, where he was responsible for establishing the first Church of Christ in Australia.

Members who migrated from Scotland established the third New Zealand Church of Christ in Dunedin in 1858. The arrival of later pioneers from Britain led to the establishment of churches in other centers.

In 1860 a group known as the Non-conformist Settlement Party arrived from Manchester and strengthened the Auckland church. A sea captain by the name of Rattray sailed his own ship from Scotland, a journey lasting over three months. He brought his family with him, and this reinforced the work in Auckland, which soon numbered 140 members.

Another sea captain by the name of Stewart, while trading with his ship around the coastal towns of the country, made it his business to meet with and encourage members. In 1868 Captain Stewart met with W. E. Norris in Christchurch, who determined to become a "Christian only"; by 1870 the church opened its first small chapel in Woolston. Stewart also provided help in other places.

In the absence of any trained ministry, the churches were reliant upon the mutual ministry provided by lay people, which characterized the British Churches of Christ. It was not until 1866 that the first full-time minister was employed.

The lack of training was offset by the wise use of Christian periodicals and literature, which were obtained from both the British and American churches. When George Taylor arrived from Yorkshire in 1844, he brought with him a large quantity of Christian publications from James Wallis (1793-1867) of Nottingham, the editor of the *British Millennial Harbinger.* Regular correspondence with Wallis and with Alexander Campbell proved to be an important way of nurturing the young churches. In 1846 Alexander Campbell could rejoice in informing his many readers around the world that he had received "Good News from a Far Country," and devoted two pages in his *Millennial Harbinger* to an account of the establishment and growth of the Churches of Christ in New Zealand.

The arrival of Edward Lewis from Sydney in 1866 marked a turning point in the life of the churches. He was known as the "boot maker minister," but it was not long before he was fully employed in working among the churches. Edward Lewis became known as the "Grand Old Man" of the New Zealand Churches. His labors covered areas from North Auckland to Dunedin. He was responsible for planting a number of churches and strengthening others.

The first published record of the churches in 1885 stated that there were twenty-five established churches with a membership of 1,238. Only thirteen churches had their own buildings, and Lewis was the only full-time evangelist.

Not long after his arrival from Sydney in 1866 Edward Lewis, known as the "boot maker minister," was employed full-time in planting and strengthening churches from North Auckland to Dunedin. Courtesy of the Disciples of Christ Historical Society

With the arrival of the 1880s, the Movement made a transition from a pioneering stage to a period of growth and cooperation. This was brought about largely by the arrival of new leaders, who came from the United Kingdom, the United States of America, and Australia. M. W. Green came from England; Charles Watt and D. W. McCrackett came from Scotland. H. S. Earl, an Englishman trained by Alexander Campbell in the United States, was an outstanding evangelist. Earl and A. B. Maston of the United States brought new life and vision to the churches. From Australia came preachers with the names Clapham, Turner, Hales, Bates, Greenhill, Bull, and Franklyn. All of these played an important part in building up the struggling churches.

Further evidence of growth was the setting up of three District Conferences to provide a means of cooperation and to promote the work on a more organized basis. These Conferences, covering Auckland

District, Middle District (Wellington and Nelson), and Southern District (Westland, Canterbury, Otago, and Southland), now assumed responsibility for the employment and placement of ministers.

A move for even greater cooperation was taken with the formation of the first Dominion (national) Conference in 1901 when an all-male gathering of thirty-six delegates met in Wellington. From 1920 the Dominion Conferences were held annually, making it possible to coordinate the outreach programs of the churches and put in operation organized structures for "Brotherhood" activities. By 1905 there were 2,463 members in fifty churches.

Stone-Campbell missions in Southern Rhodesia (now Zimbabwe) began in 1901 with the work of John Sheriff. The New Zealand Conference in 1904 agreed to take over this mission, and Mr. and Mrs. F. L. Hadfield became the first missionaries. They arrived in Bulawayo in 1906. Southern Rhodesia became a major dimension to the life of the New Zealand Churches and has proved to be a very valuable sphere of Christian witness. The Associated Churches of Christ in Zimbabwe, now completely controlled by indigenous leadership, are many times larger than the current New Zealand fellowship. The consecrated service of many devoted workers (including the lifelong ministry of Sir Garfield and Lady Grace Todd) has been a source of inspiration and a major contribution of the New Zealand churches to world mission.

The Annual Conferences provided opportunities for stimulus and inspiration and enabled the churches to work together in home mission projects, ministerial training, Christian education, ecumenical affairs, women's work, examining public issues, and the production of a monthly national paper, *The New Zealand Christian*. The Conference also set up a Preachers' Provident Fund to aid retired ministers and established the Church Extension and Property Trust Board, which by an act of the New Zealand Parliament (1929) serves as a trustee and safeguard for local church properties.

Membership was given a huge boost by the eighteen-month Hinrichsen-Morris missions (1,617 decisions), and growth continued steadily after their departure for Australia in 1931. In 1938 the membership of the churches in New Zealand reached 4,962 — the highest on record.

In 1927 the College of the Bible was established. The college purchased the Glen Leith property in 1930 and transferred there. The college served the churches in educating men and women for ministry until 1971. A. L. Haddon was founding principal, and continued in that position until his death in 1961. He was succeeded by G. D. Munro. Prior to the establishment of ministerial training more than thirty of the most prominent young men from the churches went

Sir Garfield Todd, Disciples missionary to Africa from New Zealand and former Prime Minister of Southern Rhodesia (right), visits with his former teacher A. L. Haddon, founding principal of the College of the Bible, Glen Leith, Dunedin, New Zealand (center), and W. B. Blakemore, dean of Disciples Divinity House, University of Chicago, during the 1961 Hoover Lectures on Christian Unity sponsored by the Disciples Divinity House. Courtesy of the Disciples of Christ Historical Society

to the United States to train for ministry, but very few returned to serve in their homeland. At the time of the College's closure almost all churches were served by Glen Leith graduates.

A. L. Haddon was a recognized leader in the ecumenical movement in New Zealand and a scholar in the worldwide fellowship of Churches of Christ. He was also editor of *The New Zealand Christian* for twenty-four years.

Churches of Christ in New Zealand were represented at the first World Convention of Churches of Christ in 1930 and have been represented at every convention since. They hosted the convention in Auckland in 1988. They have always been strongly involved in encouraging the global unity of the Movement. They also became foundation members of the Disciples Ecumenical Consultative Council in 1979.

The movement toward a united church in New Zealand was a major factor in the life of the churches in the second half of the twentieth century. In the 1940s Churches of Christ held discussions with the Baptists, but it was not possible to bring these to any practical conclusion. In 1955 Churches of Christ became members of the Joint Commission on Church Union, which had been set up by the Congregational, Methodist, and Presbyterian Churches. (The Anglican Church made a fifth partner at a later date.) In 1957 Churches of Christ voted 75 percent in favor and 6 percent against the principle of church union.

When the "Plan for Union" was presented for adoption in 1972, support within the churches was much more evenly divided, with 55 percent voting in favor and 45 percent voting against. Feelings were also more strongly polarized than earlier. Because of the negative vote of the Anglican Church, the united church was not established. However, eleven out of the thirty-three currently affiliated Churches of Christ are in "union parishes" or "cooperative ventures." These Church of Christ congregations have united locally, or work very closely, with congregations of the other churches involved in the union negotiations.

Members of New Zealand Churches of Christ have contributed a great deal to the wider church locally, nationally, and internationally. They were founding members of the National Council of Churches in New Zealand and the World Council of Churches, both established in the 1940s. Ron O'Grady, a minister in Churches of Christ, was associate general secretary of the National Council of Churches for several years before he became associate general secretary of the Christian Conference of Asia. Barbara Stephens served as the executive director of Christian World Service (CWS) in New Zealand. Althea Campbell served as a CWS staff member for many years, and continues to do so at this writing (2002). Many have served as chaplains and provided leadership for groups such as the Bible Society and the Leprosy Mission. Not all churches wanted to become members of the new ecumenical body that replaced the National Council in the 1980s, so Churches of Christ became an associate member of the Conference of Churches in Aotearoa–New Zealand. Each congregation decides whether it wishes to be associated with this organization.

The 1970s and 1980s saw a considerable influx of ministers from the United States of America. These were mainly from Christian Churches/Churches of Christ working with congregations that did not favor union, though at the beginning of the twenty-first century the number was small. Although most churches are served by New Zealanders, the closing of the College of the Bible at Glen Leith has led to these ministers coming from a very diverse background of training.

The steady decline in membership in the second half of the twentieth century to about 1,800 at the beginning of the twenty-first century has meant that the association has reduced finances and personnel for national committees and programs. Structures have been simplified. Responsibility for national affairs between biennial conferences is now in the hands of a small administrative team, with individuals or small groups responsible for cooperative efforts such as overseas mission and ecumenical affairs. Beginning in 2002, *The New Zealand Christian* became an on-line only publication.

New Zealand has also cooperated with the Australian Churches of Christ and the Fellowship of Churches of Christ in the United Kingdom through the International Missional Team, which focuses on making churches more effective. Earlier, cooperation with the Australian Churches of Christ Overseas Mission Board had led to New Zealand sharing in the Australian support of the churches in Vanuatu and to Australia becoming involved in Zimbabwe.

A number of the churches have grown in recent years, and a new congregation in Auckland was begun in 2002. The last twenty-five years have seen the development of an appreciation for unity-in-diversity. Christian Churches/Churches of Christ in the United States have recently established a very successful congregation on the north shore of Auckland. It appears that a new era may have begun.

Although two small a cappella Churches of Christ in Auckland and Nelson and a few scattered individuals who rejected instruments in worship and extra-congregational organizations existed in the first half of the twentieth century, this fellowship actually began again in the 1950s. In 1956 Californian Paul Mathews began working with the six-member church at Nelson. Mathews also led in the establishment of churches in Invercargill (1957), Tauranga (1958), and Dunedin (1959), adding to the number of existing congregations in Auckland, Wellington, and Nelson. In 1961 the Central Avenue Church of Christ in Valdosta, Georgia, began a program to establish churches in the larger cities and to train preachers. Considerable help has been given by missionary families from the United States. Membership today is a little over 1,000 in approximately twenty-five congregations. The South Pacific Bible College is well established in Tauranga, the city that also has the largest congregation, the Otumoetai Church of Christ.

See also Australia, The Movement in; Great Britain and Ireland, Churches of Christ in; Sherriff, John; Wallis, James

BIBLIOGRAPHY Evan P. Blampied, "The Origin and History of the Churches of Christ in New Zealand" (M.A. thesis, 1939) • R. A. Blampied, *The Trail of a Pioneer: Being an Account of the Pilgrimage of James Barton, 1820-1910* (n.d.) • *Centennial Souvenir: Being a History of the Associated Churches of Christ in New Zealand (1844-1944)* (1944) • A. B. Maston, ed., *Jubilee Pictorial History of Churches of Christ in Australasia* (1903) • Arthur William Stephenson, *Pioneering for Christian Unity in Australia and New Zealand: Being an Outline of the History of Churches of Christ in Australia and New Zealand and a Brief Study of Their Teachings and Ideals* (1940) • James S. Woodroof and O. John Payne, *Struggles of the Kingdom* (1984).

LYNDSAY JACOBS

Newland, Vernon M. (1906-1974)

Missionary and founder of five Bible colleges, affiliated with the Christian Churches/Churches of Christ.

Newland received a master's degree in 1931 from Phillips University. He served as a missionary from 1933 to 1945, first in China, and later in the Philippines during World War II. The Japanese interred him and his family in 1942 at a prisoner of war camp on the Santo Tomás University campus in Manila. Following the war, his experiences made him a popular speaker in churches around the United States. Newland grew increasingly concerned over rising denominationalism and lack of evangelistic zeal among the Disciples of Christ. In 1946 he started Midwest Christian College in Oklahoma City. Although concerned about the ideological drift of the churches, he saw preacher training and church revitalization as the main reasons for opening new Bible colleges. He founded or co-founded four other Bible colleges: Dallas Christian College (1950), St. Louis Christian College (1956), Memphis (later Mid-South) Christian College (1959), and Iowa Christian College (1971). In 1955 Newland was the founding editor of the *Directory of the Ministry of the Undenominational Fellowship of Christian Churches and Churches of Christ,* an early signal of the emerging network of churches identifying themselves independently from the mainline Disciples of Christ. He also edited a newsletter, *The Crusader.* In early May 1974, Newland died in a tragic airplane crash at the Kiamichi Mission in Missouri.

See also Bible College Movement; Dallas Christian College; Directory of the Ministry; Mid-South Christian College; St. Louis Christian College

BIBLIOGRAPHY Gary M. Newland, "If You Are Ever Going to Do Something for God, Do It Now: The Pioneering Work of Vernon M. Newland" (M.Div. thesis, Emmanuel School of Religion, 1989) • Vernon M. Newland, ed., *Directory of the Ministry of the Undenominational Fellowship of Christian Churches and Churches of Christ* (1955).

ANTHONY J. SPRINGER

Noninstitutional Movement

By the beginning of the 1960s about 10 percent of the membership of the Churches of Christ had separated into congregations that were no longer in fellowship with the mainstream. A variety of disagreements contributed to the division, but the issue that gave a name to the institutional controversy hinged on whether local churches should contribute funds to the growing network of institutions formally and informally associated with Churches of Christ, including colleges, schools, and benevolent institutions. Called "antis" because of their opposition to church-supported institutions, noninstitutional leaders also criticized other cooperative methods and promotional schemes that blossomed in the post–World War II years. In particular, they objected to "sponsoring church" arrangements that allowed large congregations to coordinate missions and media undertakings. These issues had been somewhat controversial in the early twentieth century, but the institutional debate did not reach schismatic dimensions until the 1950s.

Nineteenth-century leaders of the Stone-Campbell Movement founded a few colleges and other church-related institutions, but these ventures survived uneasily amid questions about the scriptural legitimacy of missionary societies and other church-related organizations. Many of the objections voiced in the nineteenth century were rooted in anti-elitist prejudices similar to those that spawned an anti-mission movement among Baptists. Anti-institutional thinking in Churches of Christ in the twentieth century reflected similar class resistance to the emergence of church bureaucracies and bureaucrats, and it flourished among conservatives strongly committed to a primitivist vision of restoring New Testament patterns of church work and worship.

Before World War II Churches of Christ supported only a few struggling institutions. The question of whether it was scriptural for churches to support these institutions was occasionally argued in church papers, but the discussions were civil and subdued. The few colleges and benevolent institutions in existence were weak and received little financial support from churches. In the 1930s Grover Cleveland Brewer (1884-1956) became a champion of church support for colleges, but most leaders in Churches of Christ probably opposed the practice. Other clashes, particularly the debate over premillennialism, pushed the question of church support for institutions to the periphery of the consciousness of Churches of Christ during these years.

In 1936 Foy E. Wallace, Jr. (1896-1979), warned that some "sober thinking" was needed about the "institutional idea" because of the proliferation of institutions seeking support from churches. Wallace's warning was somewhat premature, but immediately after World War II a veritable explosion in the number and size of church-supported institutions gave new significance to the issue. Older colleges, such as Abilene Christian College, David Lipscomb College, and Harding College, mushroomed in enrollment. The colleges sought accreditation and respectability; at the same time, growing middle-class congregations increasingly viewed these institutions as symbols of denominational pride. In 1947 Abilene Christian College launched a controversial endowment campaign aimed at raising $3 million from churches.

In the decade following the war, these older institutions were joined by dozens of new educational and benevolent organizations, all competing for financial support from churches.

In a related development during the 1940s that was aimed at expanding the reach and image of the Churches of Christ, G. C. Brewer and Otis Gatewood (1911-1999) spearheaded a campaign aimed at coordinating foreign evangelization in the postwar years. Sensing unprecedented missions opportunities in the wake of the war, they envisioned a coordinated effort by Churches of Christ that would be led by "sponsoring churches," larger congregations that received contributions from other churches to support a work supervised by the elders of the sponsoring church. By the mid-1950s, large sponsoring church arrangements, in which hundreds of congregations contributed to a common cause under the central oversight of one eldership, abounded. Sponsoring church arrangements also provided a means for pooling sufficient resources to fund national advertising, radio, and television programs to promote the Churches of Christ. The most notable of the new media ventures was the Herald of Truth radio and television programs, launched in 1951 under the sponsorship of the Fifth and Highland Church of Christ in Abilene. While such arrangements had long been used by congregations to fund and oversee local radio programs and lectureships, the size and scope of the appeals in the 1950s caused some church leaders to reexamine the practice.

Opposition to church-supported institutions and sponsoring church arrangements became increasingly heated and divisive in the 1950s. A group of preachers formerly associated with publications edited by Foy E. Wallace, Jr., stridently pushed their objections through a paper founded in 1949, the *Gospel Guardian.* Led by editor Fanning Yater Tant (1908-1997) and publisher Roy E. Cogdill (1907-1985), the paper was a single-issue publication; on a weekly basis it published a withering attack on church-supported institutions and their defenders. In a highly publicized incident in January 1950, Foy Wallace's brother Cled Wallace (1892-1962), who, like Foy, later abandoned the anti-institutional cause, wrote an article in the *Gospel Guardian* titled "That Rock Fight in Italy." Featuring Cled Wallace's irreverent wit, the article was a caustic criticism of two young American missionaries in Italy whose clashes with the Catholic church had made them a *cause célèbre* in American Churches of Christ. But Wallace saw the Italian scenario as an example of the emergence of a denominational attitude in Churches of Christ, an attitude reflected by the booster mentality behind the spread of institutionalism and sponsoring churches. Wallace's "Rock Fight" article set off a frenzy of writing on both sides of these issues.

For several years in the early 1950s the most widely circulated papers in the Churches of Christ were filled with articles debating institutional issues. In addition, several highly visible public debates were held, including discussions in 1954 and 1955 between *Gospel Guardian* editor Fanning Yater Tant and Ernest R. Harper (1897-1986), minister of the Fifth and Highland Church and speaker on Herald of Truth broadcasts. In 1957 Roy E. Cogdill and Guy N. Woods (1908-1993) participated in a landmark debate in Birmingham, Alabama. Scores of debates exhausted the doctrinal dimensions of the issues. During these stormy years, some church leaders sought to find a middle ground that would forestall a division. In 1957 Roy H. Lanier, Sr. (1899-1980), with the support of *Firm Foundation* editor Reuel Lemmons (1912-1989), proposed that every orphan home be placed under the supervision of a local church eldership, thus eliminating church support of institutions. But by the late fifties the differences between the two sides were too far-reaching for such a modest proposal to have much effect.

Increasingly, mainstream church leaders became convinced that the "antis" were an obstreperous fringe that should be purged to save Churches of Christ from fanaticism. Beginning in 1954, Benton Cordell Goodpasture (1895-1977), the powerful and politically adept editor of the *Gospel Advocate,* privately and publicly launched a campaign to quarantine anti-institutional preachers. In the late 1950s, the *Gospel Advocate* published a series of statements written by preachers recanting formerly held noninstitutional views, including historian Earl Irvin West and Pat Hardeman, nephew of N. B. Hardeman. By the early 1960s, noninstitutional preachers had been marked and quarantined. At the local church level, hundreds of divisions took place, generally resulting in small numbers of noninstitutional members withdrawing to establish new "sound" congregations.

Like all divisions in the Movement, the noninstitutional division was defined by elaborate biblical argument and proof-texting. But, as was the case in earlier schisms, it was also rooted in new social and political realities. Before World War II most members of Churches of Christ still felt some degree of estrangement from American society, and many clung to a separatist, sectarian vision of their religious identity. By the 1950s much had changed. The Churches of Christ shared in the postwar religious boom among American evangelical churches; indeed, the group gained recognition as one of the fastest-growing religious bodies in the nation. By the 1950s, urban congregations were filled with upwardly mobile, middle-class, college graduates who sought to bring efficiency and respectability to their church. Hundreds of new church buildings were constructed during the fifties, displaying a new self-image of confidence and self-importance. In short, the promotion of old and new institutions and the sponsorship of missions and media programs in the years after World War II were part of a broad pattern of change.

While statistical data are sketchy, it seems clear that the noninstitutional movement appealed mainly to the least affluent and least educated segment of the Movement during these years of transition. On the other hand, those most supportive of the church's new image were found in middle-class urban churches. In this respect, the noninstitutional schism had a sociological character much like the nineteenth-century division that alienated the Churches of Christ from the Disciples of Christ. Writing in the *Journal of Southern History* in 1964, historian David Edwin Harrell, Jr., outlined this pattern: "The Churches of Christ have not remained an economic and cultural unit since 1906. The sociological and economic elevation of a portion of the membership of the church, especially since World War II, has motivated a large part of the church to begin the transition toward denominationalism. The result is that the movement is once again dividing along sociological lines. Conservative appeals in the movement in the 1960s have a distinctive lower-class and antiaristocratic flavor, while the centers of liberalism are in the areas where the church is most numerous and sophisticated."

Since the mid-1960s, noninstitutional Churches of Christ have had a more or less separate history. The movement was strong in a few areas, including Tampa, Florida, where Florida Christian College was located, and northern Alabama, where the influence of John T. Lewis (1876-1967) and a cluster of preachers associated with Athens Bible School was clear. In most places, however, noninstitutional preachers were forced out of pulpits, and disenchanted minorities left to establish new congregations. Well into the 1970s many noninstitutional leaders were obsessed with fighting institutionalism and the mainstream Churches of Christ, and the most widely circulated papers read by noninstitutional Christians, *The Gospel Guardian, Truth Magazine,* and *Searching the Scriptures,* continued to emphasize these issues.

Since the mid-1970s, two clear and somewhat contradictory trends have been visible in the noninstitutional movement. By the 1980s, noninstitutional Churches of Christ had entered a period of conspicuous growth. By the end of the twentieth century, many noninstitutional congregations boasted 200 members, and in scores of congregations the membership reached 400 to 500 people. Partly, the growth of noninstitutional churches reflected a continued emphasis on evangelization and traditional teaching; partly, it was the result of a considerable migration of people out of mainstream Churches of Christ troubled by divisions between traditionalists and progressives. At the same time, the noninstitutional movement was rife with the same type of raucous and often mean-spirited internal debate that had characterized the Churches of Christ in the 1930s. Noninstitutional papers featured bitter, internecine debates on such issues as marriage and divorce, the nature of the Godhead, and the length of the days in the creation, causing considerable turmoil within the movement. Nonetheless, a clear network of several hundred noninstitutional Churches of Christ existed by the year 2000, united loosely around Florida College and various papers and personalities.

See also Brewer, Grover Cleveland; Churches of Christ; Cogdill, Roy E.; Eschatology; Florida College; Hailey, Homer; Herald of Truth; Lemmons, Reuel Gordon; Wallace, Foy E., Jr.; Woods, Guy Napoleon

BIBLIOGRAPHY *The Cogdill-Woods Debate: A Discussion on What Constitutes Scriptural Cooperation Between Churches of Christ (Birmingham)* (1957) • Melvin D. Curry, ed., *They Being Dead Yet Speak* (1981) • *Harper-Tant Debate: An Examination of "Why the 'Herald of Truth' Is Wrong"* (1956) • David Edwin Harrell, Jr., *The Churches of Christ in the Twentieth Century: Homer Hailey's Personal Journey of Faith* (2000) • David Edwin Harrell, Jr., *The Emergence of the "Church of Christ" Denomination* (n.d.) • Fanning Yater Tant, *How New Testament Churches Can, and Can Not, Cooperate* (1955) • *Wallace-Holt Debate: Between G. K. Wallace and Charles A. Holt (Florence, Alabama)* (1960).

DAVID EDWIN HARRELL, JR.

Norris, Beauford A. (1909-1986)

Pastor, educator, and academic administrator of the Christian Church (Disciples of Christ).

Following pastorates in Oklahoma and Texas and chaplaincy during World War II, Beauford A. Norris came to the faculty of Christian Theological Seminary in 1950, serving as professor, dean, and president (1959-74). During his administration the seminary's separation from Butler University was completed, the campus designed, faculty enlarged, enrollment increased, and a distinct theological ethos developed.

See also Christian Theological Seminary

BIBLIOGRAPHY Keith Watkins, *Christian Theological Seminary, Indianapolis* (2001).

KEITH WATKINS

North, Ira Lutts (1922-1984)

Minister and educator in twentieth-century Churches of Christ, known for his work in building the Madison (Tennessee) Church of Christ into one of the largest congregations in that part of the Movement.

Ira North (1922-1984) was minister for the Madison (Tennessee) Church of Christ from 1952 until his death. During his years the congregation grew to be the largest Church of Christ in the world with over 4,000 members, remaining so for many years.

Born on August 31, 1922, in Lawrenceburg, Tennessee, in 1939 he married Avon Stephens, enrolled in David Lipscomb College, and began his ministry at Ethridge, Tennessee. After two years he continued his education at Abilene Christian College, where he received his B.A. degree. Graduating from Abilene, North moved to Urbana, Illinois, where he earned an M.A. degree in speech while preaching for the South Lincoln Church of Christ. Fulfilling a lifelong ambition, he returned to Nashville to teach speech and Bible at Lipscomb, where he also preached for the Lindsley Avenue Church of Christ. In 1952 North completed a Ph.D. in speech at Louisiana State University at Baton Rouge. While there, he ministered to the North Boulevard church.

North then returned to Lipscomb, and at the same time accepted the pulpit of the Madison Church of Christ. Shortly before his death, Ira North wrote: "The golden key to church growth is found in Ephesians 4:4. It is imperative to keep the unity of the spirit in the bond of peace." North wrote from experience. He served as preacher for the Madison Church of Christ for almost thirty-two years. When he accepted the preaching responsibilities at Madison, the church had fewer than 500 in Bible school. In May 1982, the Madison church set a record among Churches of Christ with an attendance of 8,410. When North accepted Madison's call, the congregation counted 400 members; in 1982 the membership was 4,100.

Norris served for fifteen years on the Metropolitan Nashville Welfare Commission, and continued to be active on the executive board of the Middle Tennessee Council of the Boy Scouts of America for a number of years. *Nashville Magazine* recognized him as the most powerful religious figure in the Nashville community. For four years, 1977 to 1982, he was editor of the *Gospel Advocate.*

See also Abilene Christian University; *Gospel Advocate, The;* Lipscomb University

BIBLIOGRAPHY "Collection of Memories — Ira North, 1922-1984," *Christian Chronicle* 41 (February 1984): 10 • Ira North, *Balance: A Tried and Tested Formula for Church Growth* (1983) • Ira North, *You Can March for the Master* (1959).

ROBERT E. HOOPER

North American Christian Convention

Annual, non-delegate convention celebrating the ministries and mission of the Christian Churches/ Churches of Christ. Besides "charismatic" events like the Cane Ridge Revival, planned conferences or conventions of Christians began in earnest in the Stone-Campbell Movement in the 1830s, with the earliest statewide gatherings. The first national convention as such was held in Cincinnati, Ohio, in 1849 to inaugurate the American Christian Missionary Society. In 1917 the annual convention was designated the International Convention of the Disciples of Christ. The Disciples struggled at times over whether to have a formal delegate convention or more of an open meeting for inspiration and information.

In the 1920s there was a concerted effort by church agencies of the Disciples of Christ to seek approval for their work by the convention body. This forced the assembled persons to vote in a procedure that had not been in vogue over the many years of meeting. This issue of endorsement of agencies came to the floor of the International Convention in Memphis, Tennessee, in November of 1926, and resulted in separate meetings being held in the Pantages Theater. A Committee for Future Action was named, with P. H. Welshimer of Canton, Ohio, as chairperson, along with Mark Collins, W. E. Sweeney, W. R. Walker, Robert F. Tuck, O. A. Trinkle, and F. S. Dowdy as members. This committee formed the program and rationale for a general rally to be held in Indianapolis, Indiana, on October 12-16, 1927, constituting the first North American Christian Convention (NACC).

Numerous declarations were made as an attempt to define the purpose of the new general meeting, and its apologists fiercely defended themselves from the charge of producing a "rival" to the International Convention. They argued that: (1) the NACC would be "a convention of individuals, not a convention of churches"; (2) it would focus on the "restoration of New Testament Christianity"; (3) it would work for unity, not division; and (4) it would preclude church agencies from promoting their causes from the convention platform. Exhibits and discussions of worthy issues were planned for conference rooms — a format that has continued to the present day. The convention also gave significant place to preaching on classic Stone-Campbell themes (unity, restoration, etc.), evangelism, and world mission.

Despite disclaimers to the contrary, critics clearly saw the NACC as divisive, prompting Frederick Kershner, who had been president of the International Convention in 1938, to declare in 1940 that the NACC was "not schismatic," but "a meeting for inspiration, discussion, and public enlightenment" thoroughly complementary to the purposes of the International Convention. There were, to be sure, some supporters of the NACC who, in subsequent years, hoped for the convention to be a rallying point for conservative churches in their resistance to the denominational restructure of the Disciples of Christ. Others, however, wanted the convention to be an instrument for reconciliation within the Movement.

Following the inaugural 1927 convention in Indianapolis, the NACC met again in Kansas City in 1928. From then until 1950, eight conventions were held. In 1950 convention organizers determined to meet annually. In June 1960 the North American Christian Convention met in concert with the National Christian Education Convention in Columbus, Ohio. The combination of the summer meeting plus the addition of a great number of teaching and leadership sessions to the program meant adding childcare and teenage sessions to the NACC's agenda.

Teen sessions have become a significant part of the convention's program, beginning with the Bible Bowl quiz team competition in 1965. Gary A. Coleman served as assistant to the director from 1967 until 1996 and gave oversight to the development of the quiz program and teen sessions.

During July 6-10, 1986, a joint convention between the North American Christian Convention and the National Missionary Convention brought some 40,000 persons to a communion service on Sunday evening in the Hoosier Dome (now RCA Dome) in Indianapolis. The two conventions met again in concert in Indianapolis in 1995.

In 1963 the Long Beach, California, Convention Committee called Leonard G. Wymore to become the first full-time employee convention director and to open an office in Cincinnati, Ohio. The duties of the director and staff were detailed to support the planning and managing of the annual convention. Leonard G. Wymore retired in the summer of 1986; Rod Huron succeeded Wymore in the years 1986-97. In 1998 Dustin Rubeck became executive director, with Terry Wusky as managing director. In 2002 Allan Dunbar was approved as executive director.

The original convention committee consisted of seven persons. In 1934 the number had grown to twenty-three, to sixty-four in 1946, to one hundred in 1950, and to 120 in 1971. Past NACC presidents began to be represented at that time. In the 1990s women were added to the committee. In 1999 the convention committee elected a board of stewards, a group charged with providing direction to the business and policy issues of the convention, thus permitting the annually elected executive committee and president to give their attention to the event for the year.

The convention published a newsletter in the 1950s edited by Harry Poll. In 1973 a new publication, the *NACC Update,* was introduced as a bimonthly mailing that promoted the upcoming convention.

At the 1980 Seattle, Washington, convention, the group began the practice of recognizing faithful veterans in the leadership of church life. Each year three or four individuals have been so honored as "God's Honored Servants" and introduced to one of the evening worship assemblies of the convention.

Although figures tell only a part of the history of the convention, these figures may be of general interest: registration is encouraged to support the convention, and the number of registered participants has been as high as 50,000, with attendance at one or more sessions averaging between 10,000 and 20,000. Within this figure are teens numbering 2,000 to 3,000, 1,000 children ages six to twelve, and 500 preschool-age children. Total cost of the yearly operation has grown from $200,000 to approximately $1 million.

This convention is a unique gathering for preaching, instruction, discussion, and fellowship. Besides multiple assemblies for worship and preaching, the convention each year hosts numerous workshops on a wide variety of issues related to ministry, missions, worship, Christian ethics, and much more. There has frequently been a theological forum dealing with doctrinal questions or controversial issues such as biblical inerrancy. The NACC does not legislate for the churches or pass resolutions on social or political issues. The only item of business is the ratification of one-third of the convention committee to plan the sessions for next year. The NACC is not intended to be a base of sectarian cohesion or to represent the Christian Churches/Churches of Christ as a denomination, but rather to rally Christians toward the person of Christ and the great themes of his Word as the necessary basis for Christian unity.

See also Bible Bowl; Christian Churches/Churches of Christ; Conventions; International Convention of the Disciples of Christ; Kershner, Frederick D.; National Christian Missionary Convention; Walker, Dean Everest; Welshimer, Pearl Howard

BIBLIOGRAPHY Edwin V. Hayden et al., *North American Gold: Fifty Years of North American Conventions* (1989) • James B. Hunter, "A History of the North American Christian Convention" (B.D. thesis, Butler University School of Religion, 1950) • Frederick D. Kershner, "The North American Christian Convention Is Not Schismatic," *Christian Standard* 75 (1940): 545-46 • NACC Committee, "NACC History and Purpose" (pamphlet, 1973) • Dean E. Walker, "NACC Objectives Viewed Historically" (unpublished paper, NACC Committee Meeting, October 1973) • Dean E. Walker, "The North American Christian Convention," *Shane Quarterly* 3 (1942): 65-72.

LEONARD G. WYMORE

Northwest Christian College

Christian college associated with the Christian Churches/Churches of Christ and the Christian Church (Disciples of Christ).

Northwest Christian College and its predecessor institutions date back to 1895, when Eugene Divinity School was established in Eugene, Oregon, adjacent to the University of Oregon. Its founding president was Eugene C. Sanderson, a graduate of Drake University and the University of Chicago. Sanderson's goal was to educate ministers for the Pacific Northwest by providing on-campus ministerial education and utilizing resources of the University of Oregon for requirements in arts and sciences. At its beginning the college offered a two-year program in English Bible and a four-year Bachelor of Divinity degree. In 1904 the Bachelor of Divinity became a three-year graduate degree with the Bachelor of Arts as prerequisite. Another addition was the Bachelor of Sacred Literature degree, comprising the B.D. program minus the Greek and Hebrew requirements, plus a year of general studies.

In 1908 the Eugene Divinity School became Eugene Bible University. Over the years it enlarged its program to include a hospital, a school of nursing, a Girls Junior College, an EBU Extension in Seattle, a Home and School for Boys, a Home for the Aged, and the publishing of a journal. Sanderson was also instrumental in establishing Bible colleges in Minnesota, Colorado, Kansas, and Missouri.

In addition to Eugene Bible University, another university was established in 1913 in Spokane, Washington. Spokane University consisted of three internal colleges: the College of the Bible, the College of Liberal Arts, and the College of Fine Arts. In the thirty years of its existence, the university graduated 133 students, many of whom became ministers, missionaries, or public school teachers.

In 1929, having extended itself beyond the capacity of its constituency to support it financially, Eugene Bible University was forced into bankruptcy. Sanderson resigned, ending a thirty-four-year tenure, and moved to California, where he was instrumental in founding San Jose Bible College. A few years later (1933) Spokane University also became insolvent and was forced to close.

The Eugene institution continued under the name of Eugene Bible College until 1934, when representatives of that school and Spokane University met to form a corporation for the establishment of Northwest Christian College (NCC) and the repurchase of the Eugene campus. After a brief period in which Victor P. Morris, dean of the School of Business administration of the University of Oregon, served as acting president, Kendall Burke, an alumnus of Eugene Bible University and Oregon State College (M.A.), became president and continued until his death in 1943. Under his leadership the college gained stability in academic programs and finances. At the time NCC offered the Bachelor of Theology degree and a few graduate Bachelor of Divinity degrees.

In 1944 Ross J. Griffeth, professor in the department of religion, Butler University, was named president of NCC. It was an opportune time; the repurchase of the campus had been completed earlier that year, which enabled Griffeth to focus upon strengthening the faculty, achieving regional accreditation (1962), constructing a new dormitory and library, entertaining the newly formed Institute of Church Growth headed by Donald McGavran, acquiring adjacent properties, and building a stronger base of support. Griffeth was a staunch advocate of rigorous biblical and theological studies at the undergraduate level, while encouraging alumni to pursue advanced degrees. During these years NCC offered the Bachelor of Theology and (until 1959) the Bachelor of Religious Education degrees, the last Bachelor of Divinity having already been granted in 1942.

Griffeth was succeeded in 1965 by Barton A. Dowdy, and subsequently by William Hayes and James Womack. The college has continued to grow in property, library holdings, faculty, and curriculum. During Dowdy's presidency the curriculum was altered with a view to enabling a student, through conjoint studies at the University of Oregon, to gain a degree from NCC in practically any field. It called for 126 hours in general studies with a biblical major and 60 hours in one of NCC's ministry options or in a second major at the University of Oregon, leading to either the B.A. or B.S. degree. Currently, the college offers the B.A. degree in ministry and in fifteen other majors, the most recent being in elementary education. It offers the B.S. in a degree completion program and graduate degrees in counseling and in business management.

Through the years the college has been governed by a board consisting of persons from the states of Oregon, Washington, Idaho, and Montana. Along with its predecessor institutions, NCC granted 3,794 baccalaureate degrees in the first 104 years of its existence. Among these graduates is a host of persons engaged in professional ministries, in public education, and in the wider professional world.

See also Higher Education, Views of in the Movement; Sanderson, Eugene C.

BIBLIOGRAPHY Martha Goodrich, "History of Northwest Christian College" (M.A. thesis, University of Oregon, 1949) • Ross J. Griffeth, *Crusaders for Christ* (1971).

William J. Richardson

North-Western Christian Magazine

Abolitionist periodical in the nineteenth-century Stone-Campbell Movement.

Slavery was perhaps the most divisive nonsectarian issue in the Movement's early decades. Although opposed to continuing slavery in the United States, Alexander Campbell and most other publishers in the Movement were not overtly abolitionist. The one exception was John Boggs, editor of *North-Western Christian Magazine (NWCM),* published in Cincinnati, Ohio, 1854-58, which became the *Christian Luminary (CL),* published 1858-63. *NWCM* and its successor were major outlets for Stone-Campbell antislavery writers prior to the Civil War. Contributors included well-known abolitionists, among them Matthew S. Clapp, brother-in-law of Alexander Campbell; Jane Campbell McKeever, Campbell's sister; William D. Stone; John Kirk; Jonas Hartzel; and editor Boggs. Several contributors, including most of those listed above, were active in the Underground Railroad.

Through the mid-twentieth century, critics sometimes used extreme language to describe Boggs ("not . . . emotionally stable") and *NWCM* ("rabid"). Indeed, Boggs and *NWCM/CL* were uncompromising in their position: slavery was a sin, and Disciples leaders should condemn it. For example, *NWCM* editorially supported the Christian Missionary Society (1859-63), the abolitionist alternative to the American Christian Missionary Society. *NWCM* contributors, most notably Clapp, took Alexander Campbell to task for his tacit support of the Fugitive Slave Act and for his refusal to endorse abolitionism. *CL* ceased publication during the Civil War.

See also Abolitionism; Christian Missionary Society; Civil War, The; Slavery, The Movement and

BIBLIOGRAPHY Robert E. Barnes, "An Analytical Study of the *Northwestern Christian Magazine*" (B.D. thesis, Butler University School of Religion, 1951) • *North-Western Christian Magazine* and *Christian Luminary* (archived volumes, Disciples of Christ Historical Society, Nashville, Tennessee) • Henry K. Shaw, *Buckeye Disciples* (1952).

John H. Hull

Northwestern Christian University

See Butler University

Norton, Herman Albert (1921-1992)

Disciples of Christ educator, army chaplain, and historian.

Norton was born in Deltaville, Virginia, and raised in the Philippi Christian Church. He studied at Lynchburg College and Vanderbilt University, earning a Ph.D. in church history at Vanderbilt. He served as a pastor early in his life and was a chaplain in the U.S. Army during and immediately after World War II. He remained in the Army Reserve, where he achieved the rank of Brigadier General.

Norton's primary role was as professor of church history and dean of the Disciples Divinity House at Vanderbilt University. Under Norton's leadership, the Disciples Divinity House became a major center for ministerial education for the Disciples of Christ. His irenic spirit broadened the mission of the Disciples House, and he influenced a generation of ministers from all branches of the Stone-Campbell Movement. His greatest impact was on those who would become historians of the Stone-Campbell churches. Norton encouraged students to explore the widest range of research and interpretative methods available to historians. He modeled a wryly ironic skepticism and avoided romanticizing individuals and issues.

His own historical work focused on two areas: the history of the military chaplaincy, and the churches of the Stone-Campbell Movement, particularly in Tennessee.

Norton also served a term as chaplain to the State Senate of Tennessee and was deeply involved in political life in the state.

BIBLIOGRAPHY R. L. Harrison, Jr., "That Teaching, Preaching General: A View of the Life of Herman Albert Norton," in *Explorations in the Stone-Campbell Traditions: Essays in Honor of Herman A. Norton,* ed. A. L. Dunnavant and R. L. Harrison, Jr. (1995), pp. 170-90.

Richard L. Harrison, Jr.

O

O'Kelly, James (1735-1826)

Leader of the "Republican Methodist" succession from the Methodist Episcopal Church, and leader of the southern phase of the "Christian Connection." Born in Ireland, O'Kelly immigrated to America about 1760 and served in the North Carolina militia during the American Revolution. Converted to Methodism during the war, he was soon practicing his gifts as a lay exhorter. In 1784, when the Methodist Episcopal Church was organized, he was ordained a minister. He was soon disturbed by the fact that Bishop Francis Asbury appointed ministers to a preaching circuit with no recourse to appeal. In 1792 O'Kelly brought to the Methodist Conference a Right of Appeal to correct this. When it was voted down after a week of acrimonious debate, he left the Methodists.

Taking some ministers, churches, and perhaps 1,000 people with him (some sources suggest as high as 5,000), O'Kelly established the Republican Methodist Church. In 1794 this group adopted the name Christian, committing themselves to follow the Bible alone as their guide. Preachers and laity alike would enjoy complete equality in interpreting the Scriptures, and the annual conference would be advisory only. These "Southern Christians" were established mostly in Virginia and North Carolina.

Reflecting his Methodist background, O'Kelly still practiced infant sprinkling, which led to a dispute between him and William Guirey in 1810. This created a division, and Guirey soon united with Elias Smith and the "Northern Christians." O'Kelly's followers did not unite with the Smith-Jones Movement until 1841. O'Kelly is credited with forging an important parallel movement to the Stone-Campbell reformation. He was motivated by a resistance to Bishop Asbury's control and a desire for Christian unity more than by a strict restoration of the faith and practice of the New Testament church.

See also Christian Connection; Haggard, Rice; Jones, Abner; Republican Methodists; Smith, Elias

BIBLIOGRAPHY Nathan Hatch, *The Democratization of American Christianity* (1989) • Charles Franklin Kilgore, *The James O'Kelly Schism in the Methodist Episcopal Church* (1963) • W. E. MacClenny, *The Life of Rev. James O'Kelly* (repr. ed. 1950).

JAMES B. NORTH

Oklahoma Christian University

Liberal arts school affiliated with Churches of Christ and located in Oklahoma City, Oklahoma.

Earlier Oklahoma colleges Cordell Christian College and Western Oklahoma Christian College closed in 1918 and 1931 respectively. On February 28, 1947, the first meeting to organize a new college in Oklahoma affiliated with Churches of Christ was led by G. R. Tinius (chairman), L. O. Sanderson, J. E. Wright, Byron Fullerton, Frank Winters, and others. After consideration of several sites, including Pryor, Oklahoma, the college was located in the J. V. Foster mansion in Bartlesville, Oklahoma, near Tulsa. L. R. Wilson (1896-1968), a Florida preacher, served as president from 1949-54. The new junior college officially began September 1, 1949, as Central Christian College, and was recognized in 1951 by the state of Oklahoma.

Classes began in September 1950 with 97 students. The first catalog stated: "It is the purpose of this institution to provide this work under a Christian faculty and in a Christian atmosphere, in order that the students may be stimulated spiritually as well as intellectually. . . . This type of education is extended in the hope that . . . it will teach them to be honorable, upright, Christian citizens." In 1954 James O. Baird, Jr. (1920-1998), became the second president, serving in that role until 1973. Failure of local business support led to Baird's recommendation that the college move to a larger city. A group of Oklahoma City business leaders, including E. K. Gaylord, encouraged moving to Oklahoma City. In September 1956, 240 acres of land were purchased in northeast Oklahoma City on Memorial Road, and on September 22, 1958, classes began in Oklahoma City.

George S. Benson (1898-1991), president of Harding College, served as advisor and chancellor of the new school 1955-67. Later presidents were J. Terry Johnson 1973-95, Kevin Jacobs 1996-2001, Alfred Branch (acting) 2001-2, and Mike E. O'Neal 2002-present.

In September 1959 the name was changed to Oklahoma Christian College (OCC). In 1960 a third academic year was added, and the following year the fourth year was added, making Oklahoma Christian a senior college. The Board of Trustees voted March 28, 1961, to desegregate the college the following September, making OCC the first college among Churches of Christ to change its policy on racial segregation. North Central accreditation was received in 1965. Much of the long-term success of the college is due to the internal leadership given by R. S. North, who served as dean, executive vice-president and professor for more than fifty years.

Oklahoma Christian College became Oklahoma Christian University in 1992 and reorganized into five colleges in 1995. In 2003 the school again reorganized to three colleges, Biblical Studies, Arts and Sciences, and Professional Studies (Business, Engineering and Education). Cascade College, formerly Columbia Christian College, in Portland, Oregon, was added in 1994 as an additional college in the Oklahoma Christian University system. Graduate studies began in 1988 with an M.A. in Ministry, in 2000 with an M.B.A., and in 2004 with an M.Div.

Central Christian College began with 97 students in 1950 and grew to more than 1,000 by 1970. Increases each decade led to a student enrollment of 2,110 in 2001.

See also Benson, George Stuart; Cascade College; Columbia Christian College; Cordell Christian College; Harding University

BIBLIOGRAPHY W. O. Beeman, *Oklahoma Christian College: Dream to Reality* (1970). LYNN A. MCMILLON

Old Light Antiburger Seceder Presbyterian Church

See Campbell, Thomas; Presbyterians, Presbyterianism

"Old Path, The"

The appeal to return to the "old paths" has been a persistent theme among primitivists within the Stone-Campbell Movement. Inspired by the command in Jeremiah 6:16 to "ask for the old paths" (KJV), this slogan has been used to call people "back to the Bible" as a means of curing contemporary religious ills. More specifically, an appeal to the "old path" has indicated the belief by those making the plea that innovations in the Movement have constituted a departure from the primitive pattern.

For example, the *Old Path Guide*, published in Louisville, Kentucky, 1879-85, attempted to mitigate what was perceived as the liberal direction of *The Christian Standard* and to provide a moderating voice to the religious problems of its day. Another periodical using the slogan to further its conservative views is the *Old Paths Advocate*, which has since 1929 articulated the views of churches opposing Sunday Schools and individual cups for the Lord's Supper.

In Great Britain the "old path" was used as the rallying cry for a conservative movement among Disciples in the first half of the twentieth century. Led by Walter Crosthwaite, "Old Pathism" constituted a substantial movement in Scotland and England that opposed instrumental music, the support of cooperative institutions among churches, and open fellowship with other religious groups, generally conforming to contemporary practices in American Churches of Christ. JESSSE CURTIS POPE

See also Slogans

Oliphant, David, Sr.

See Canada, The Movement in

One Body

Quarterly journal published in Joplin, Missouri, founded by Don DeWelt in 1984.

One Body focuses on issues of Christian unity and works toward reconciliation primarily between Christian Churches/Churches of Christ and the Churches of Christ. Columnists and writers from both fellowships regularly contribute articles.

See also DeWelt, Don; Restoration Forums

VICTOR KNOWLES

Open Communion

See Lord's Supper, The

Open Forum

Discussion group hosted by the Christian Churches/Churches of Christ that ultimately focused its energies on ecumenical dialogue with the Church of God (Anderson, Indiana).

Ten men concerned about a perceived inertia and tepid witness among Christian Churches/Churches of Christ met in Johnson City, Tennessee, in 1983. They issued a call to fifty leaders representative of varying ages and geographical locations to meet in St. Louis in April 1984, establishing the Open Forum. Issues were faced and differences of opinion noted, leading to another Open Forum in St. Louis in 1985, attended by 400 persons. After intensive discussion of the direction of the Stone-Campbell Movement, the group launched Double Vision, a church-planting initiative ambitiously challenging the 5,200 churches to double their number by the year 2000. Task forces were appointed to review and bring helpful recommendations concerning other critical areas of the Movement to subsequent Open Forums.

A challenge was issued to dialogue with other religious bodies emphasizing unity and restoration themes. Contact was made with representatives of the Church of God (Anderson, Indiana). Several co-hosted, open meetings were held in the 1980s and 1990s in Indiana, Ohio, Michigan, and Kentucky, and a Theological Task Force examined similarities and differences in doctrine and practice between the two church traditions. Internal issues and personnel changes within the Church of God brought the effort to termination. Subsequently the Open Forum explored relationships with the other Stone-Campbell church bodies.

See also Christian Churches/Churches of Christ; Restoration Forums

BIBLIOGRAPHY Robert T. Bruce, "Experimenting with Unity: The Open Forum Between the Christian Church/Churches of Christ and the Church of God (Anderson, Indiana)" (unpublished M.Div. thesis, Emmanuel School of Religion, 1997) • Barry Callen and James North, *Coming Together in Christ: Pioneering a New Testament Way to Christian Unity* (1997). HENRY E. WEBB

Open Membership

The practice of admitting unimmersed believers into membership in a local congregation, eventually adopted by most congregations of the Christian Churches (Disciples of Christ) but not by the other streams of the Movement.

"Open membership" has a long history in the Stone-Campbell Movement. As demonstrated rather convincingly by Joseph Belcastro's study of the issue, the practice of open membership prior to the 1880s, though discussed by Disciples, did not raise the massive concerns that developed after that time. During the late-nineteenth and early-twentieth centuries, the discussion turned bitter and acrimonious.

Prior to Alexander Campbell's decision not to baptize his infant daughter Jane in 1812, the early Disciples and Christians on the frontier did not connect a particular form of baptism to either salvation or church membership. When Campbell studied the question in 1812, he decided immersion was the only truly acceptable form of biblical baptism. For the next few decades, Campbell held to a closed membership view. Yet, as indicated in the Lunenburg Letter, Campbell believed that persons could be Christians without being immersed. By the late-1840s, Campbell made it clear that he did not view baptism as a requirement for membership into the church. The Bible made no such connection.

With Walter Scott's "Five Finger Exercise," many Disciples began to understand baptism by immersion as part of the essence of early Christianity. This made it much easier for them to question the standing of those who claimed to be Christian without it. Scott's formula, and Campbell's strong arguments on behalf of immersion during the first twenty years of the Movement, provided many in later years with a strong argument against open membership. Barton Stone, on the other hand, throughout his adult ministry, refused to make baptism a test of fellowship. Though he affirmed immersion as the biblical form of baptism, he continued to accept unimmersed Christians into the fellowship of the local congregation. He believed these members would eventually accept the wisdom and truth of immersion.

Isaac Errett, longtime and eminently respected editor of the *Christian Standard,* dealt with the issue of open membership on a number of occasions. Errett believed that all members of the Stone-Campbell Movement churches ought to be immersed. He did not doubt that there were Christians who had not been immersed, but they were "Christians in error." In a Movement concerned with restoring the church to its proper condition, these Christians ought not to be accepted into the membership of the congregation. The question, for Errett, arose because L. L. Pinkerton promoted open membership in the 1860s and 1870s, and J. A. Lord, a pastor in Missouri in the 1880s, and later in Ohio, advocated open membership in his congregations. Though Errett believed these pastors were wrong in their arguments, he did not believe fellowship with them should be broken. Others, like Moses E. Lard, could not recognize unimmersed members as Christian and believed that Disciples should withdraw all connections to congregations that accepted them.

The beginning of the more disruptive phase of the open membership question among Disciples began in 1878, when Isaac Errett, as president of the Foreign Christian Missionary Society (FCMS), sent W. T. Moore to London to begin his fifteen-year ministry at the West End Tabernacle. The congregation included both immersed and unimmersed members. Though Moore had accepted the call to the congregation on the basis that the church would practice only immersion, the congregation, with his blessing, continued to accept all forms of baptism. Errett defended Moore's position against Disciples critics like H. G. Allen, editor of the *Old Path Guide,* who wrote a scathing editorial in 1885 about the practice that came to be known as the "London Plan."

Open membership became more of an issue as a few high-profile congregations began openly to adopt the practice. In 1885 the Cedar Avenue Church of Cleveland, Ohio, adopted the practice in spite of facing fairly serious opposition. After Isaac Errett's death, editors at the *Christian Standard* argued that the missionary gifts from this congregation should not be accepted by the FCMS. *The Christian-Evangelist,* in the tradition established by the irenic Errett, took the opposite view, but without condoning the practice of open membership. J. M. Philputt, in 1892, adopted an associate open membership policy that allowed membership in the congregation while keeping their full membership in the denominations from which they came. When the congregation came under heavy criticism during the next eight years, he stopped the practice. In 1903 Edward Scribner Ames brought the practice to the Hyde Park Church of Christ in Chicago. He withstood the criticism, and by 1919 the congregation practiced all forms of baptism and had a completely open membership policy, including membership for those who did not wish to be baptized at all. In 1906 C. C. Morrison, of the Monroe Street Church in Chicago, adopted the London Plan. When he assumed ownership of the *Christian Century,* he used the pages of the journal to advocate an open membership approach to baptism.

Open membership became attractive for many Disciples during this period for several reasons. The experience of W. T. Moore as a minister associated with the FCMS points to one influential factor. Disciples near the end of the nineteenth century were encountering the work of other denominations more directly than at any time in their history. This led to an increased concern for cooperation with other denominations in the work of missions across the world. Prior to the 1870s, the majority of Disciples lived a much more isolated existence. The work of the Christian Woman's Board of Missions (CWBM) and the FCMS put Disciples much nearer the heart of ecumenical contact. Further, Disciples near educational centers, like those at the University of Chicago, were exposed to the higher-critical study of the Bible and other elements of either scientific modernism (a view that generally privileged science when thinking about religion) or Christocentric liberalism (a view that sought a reasonable Christian faith rooted in Christian understanding but brought, where possible, into compatibility with the best that science had to offer). These kinds of approaches, tagged by J. W. McGarvey and others as modernism and liberalism, led many to reconsider whether the Bible actually taught anything like the Disciples commitment to the restoration of the ancient church.

By the Centennial Convention held in Pittsburgh in 1909, the issue had become considerably divisive. J. A. Lord, who at one time had advocated open membership in two different congregations, had, under the influence of McGarvey, completely switched his view and become the editor of the *Christian Standard.* As editor, he attacked the issue with considerable fervor. Conservatives like Lord unsuccessfully attempted to keep H. L. Willett, from the University of Chicago, and Samuel H. Church off the convention program. Church, the grandson of Walter Scott and an advocate of open membership, delivered an address at the convention urging respect for individual liberty in the practice of baptism.

The controversy gained steam when, in 1911, the FCMS named Guy Sarvis, associate minister from the Hyde Park Church in Chicago, a missionary to China. Conservatives feared that Sarvis would attempt to take the congregation's associate membership policy to the mission field. Given this kind of background, it came as no surprise to most observers when the issue came to a head in the Disciples mission in China during 1919. The strict restorationist group, represented most clearly in the editorial policies of the *Christian Standard,* had already concluded that the mission societies, including the new United Christian Missionary Society (UCMS), had abandoned a pure commitment to the restoration tradition, in order to gain respect from, and an ability to cooperate within, the Ecumenical Movement.

In 1919 two developing union movements in China caught the attention of Disciples missionaries stationed there. A new national movement under the direction of Presbyterian, Congregational, and London missions looked very promising and would need some kind of formal statement from Disciples in order for Disciples to become a part of it. Another local unification movement was developing in Nanking. Disciples missionaries did not want their mission work to be left out of either development. Frank Garrett, secretary to the Central Christian China Mission, knew that the question of open membership would need to be dealt with in order for Disciples to participate fully. He asked George Baird, a longtime Disciples missionary who served as pastor at Luchowfu, to deliver a keynote address dealing with the topic before the annual convention of the mission in Kuling in 1919. A hesitant Baird, still smarting from a dressing down he had received from F. M. Rains of the FCMS for his openness on the issue a full decade earlier, acquiesced and delivered his paper. After sixteen years on the field in China, he would be forced into resignation within the next few years.

After the address, Garrett sent a letter home indicating that the China Mission unanimously affirmed Baird's call for "open membership" and asked the Society to give consideration to the issue so that approval might become a reality. The negative response at home was immediate and overwhelming. Unfortunately for Garrett and the UCMS, the recording secretary of the Executive Committee of the UCMS at the time the letter arrived was Robert E. Elmore. Elmore resigned his position and began a long association with the *Christian Standard,* using his knowledge of the letter to attack the missionaries in China and the UCMS. The leaders of the Society took a practical, rather than theological, approach to the issue and immediately became defensive. They upheld the democratic principle, that members of Disciples as a whole should decide the issue. In addition, they were fearful that congregations would withdraw financial support if the UCMS acted to encourage unification of missions in China.

The controversy between the UCMS and the *Standard* remained heated and divisive through most of the 1920s. C. C. Morrison, editor of *The Christian Century,* did not help when he editorialized in the summer of 1920 that closed membership was a "passing dogma" and that the mission churches for Disciples in China had been "for some time receiving unimmersed Christians into their membership." In response to the open membership controversy, conservative Disciples met in various meetings (called "congresses"), often held just before the International Convention meetings. These gatherings occasionally attracted as many as 2,000 people and contributed to the trend of withholding congregational funds from the UCMS. P. H. Welshimer, pastor of First Christian Church in Canton, Ohio, the largest Disciples congregation in the country, bolstered these efforts when he announced in early 1921 that his congregation had withdrawn all financial support from the UCMS until its Executive Committee announced its intention to recall all missionaries who practiced open membership.

Various resolutions opposed to open membership were passed in International Conventions between 1920 and 1925. The intent behind conservative support for the resolutions called for the UCMS to refuse to appoint missionaries, and to recall missionaries who were already on the field, who believed open membership to be an appropriate practice for Disciples missions. The UCMS, as in its response to the 1922 Sweeney Resolution, "interpreted" these resolutions to indicate that they were not meant to "infringe upon private opinion or individual liberty" but only to insure that missionaries not practice open membership.

The so-called "Peace Resolution," passed when conservative momentum had reached its highest point in Oklahoma City in 1925, literally called for severing relationship with any missionary who "committed himself or herself to belief in or practice of the reception of unimmersed persons into the membership" in order to close any possibility of a loophole. The UCMS Board of Managers met a few months later. After lengthy discussion, their interpretation of the phrase "committed . . . to belief in" concluded that it was "not intended to invade the private judgment, but only to apply to such as open agitations would prove divisive." Conservatives felt betrayed once again.

Events during the Memphis International Convention of 1926 only reinforced these feelings of betrayal. After Oklahoma City, the UCMS Board of Managers sponsored a Commission to the Orient consisting of Cleveland Kleihauer, Robert N. Simpson, and John R. Golden. A representative of the conservative faction, John T. Brown, had made the only on-site investigation a few years earlier. His report, delivered at Winona Lake in 1922, was very negative. After a fifteen-week tour of the Orient, the commission filed its report at Memphis in November 1926. Though the report indicated there had been, at one time, questionable practices in both Manila and in China, it pronounced that no missionaries currently advocated or practiced open membership.

Because of private conversations between John R. Golden, a member of the commission, and P. H. Welshimer, conservatives remained convinced that the report constituted a cover-up. In fact, two members of the commission, Golden and Kleihauer, had recommended to the Executive Committee the month before Memphis that two sets of missionaries be recalled because they personally favored open membership. Those missionaries presented written and oral statements a few weeks later to the Executive Committee and were exonerated. Nothing about these meetings or accusations appeared in either the report or during the discussion at the International Convention. Conservatives viewed Memphis as a major defeat for the principles of the Stone-Campbell Movement. The next year they formed the North American Christian Convention and moved toward a separate existence as a gathering of the Christian Churches/Churches of Christ.

Disciples, on the other hand, moved over the next few decades toward an affirmation of open membership. Various surveys during those years demonstrated a growing practice among congregations. In 1942 the International Convention at Grand Rapids elected Clarence E. Lemmon president. Lemmon served as minister of an open-membership congregation in Columbia, Missouri, and advocated the practice widely. This controversial election troubled most of those who identified with the North American Christian Convention, and some who did not. But Disciples leadership still, even as late as the 1950s, had not yet addressed the issue of open membership from a theological perspective. Disciples congregations increasingly adopted it at home, but most did so less due to theological commitment than because it seemed imminently practical to them.

In many respects, leadership of the UCMS during the 1920s had taught the lessons of pragmatism all too well. During the 1920s, the UCMS opposed open membership for pragmatic, not theological, reasons. Though positions on the issue had changed over the intervening decades, the pragmatic response continued to serve as the measure of appropriateness. During the 1920s the pragmatism of the UCMS in response to the controversy had its negative effects. Leaders had exhibited an inability to utilize significant developments on the mission field as opportunities for theological education at home. Throughout the controversy, they felt compelled to maintain financial support for missions even if it meant less unity on the field, unity they generally supported from a theological perspective. Their responses were paternalistic in ways that smacked of cultural superiority rather than truly supportive of indigenous leadership in the field.

Beginning in the late-1940s, leadership within the UCMS responded to the theological reflection about mission occurring in ecumenical circles by stepping up their own theological work. In the midst of generally substantial theological shifts in their understanding of mission, by 1961 leaders within the UCMS, in their "Strategy of Ecumenical Concerns," adopted a plan of ecumenical membership for mission congregations. On the question of open membership, pragmatic justification continued to overshadow serious theological reflection, but baby steps were taken on the theological front. While the plan recommended that all mission congregations practice baptism by immersion, it also affirmed that members or potential members who were not immersed should be placed on a separate ecumenical roll and allowed "full fellowship with the church." Since that time Disciples have affirmed open membership without reservation on the mission field and at home. In intervening years, theological reflection has caught up with earlier pragmatic responses, as evidenced by Disciples' affirmation of ecumenical documents like *Baptism, Eucharist, and Ministry,* produced by the Faith and Order Commission of the World Council of Churches in 1982.

Since 1996 organized mission work of Disciples has been conducted with the United Church of Christ, an infant-baptizing tradition, through the joint work of the Common Global Ministries Board. Today the majority of congregations among Disciples continue to practice baptism by immersion, but nearly all of them also warmly welcome unimmersed Christians into full congregational membership.

See also Ames, Edward Scribner; Baptism; *Christian Standard;* Church, Doctrine of the; Elmore, Robert Emmett; Errett, Isaac; International Convention of the Disciples of Christ; Lard, Moses E.; Lunenburg Letter, The; Missionary Societies, Controversy over; Moore, William Thomas; Morrison, Charles Clayton; Pinkerton, Lewis Letig; United Christian Missionary Society, The; Welshimer, Pearl Howard

BIBLIOGRAPHY Joseph Belcastro, *The Relationship of Baptism to Church Membership* (1963) • John T. Brown, *The U.C.M.S. Self-Impeached: A Review of Evidence of Public Record Which the Executive Committee of the U.C.M.S. Must Face* (1924) • Stephen J. Corey, *Fifty Years of Attack and Controversy: The Consequences Among Disciples of Christ* (1953) • "Report of the Commission to the Orient," *World Call* 8 (August 1926): 34-43 • Mark G. Toulouse, "Practical Concern and Theological Neglect: The UCMS and the Open Membership Controversy," in *A Case Study of Mainstream Protestantism: The Disciples' Relation to American Culture, 1880-1989,* ed. D. Newell Williams (1991), pp. 194-235.

MARK G. TOULOUSE

Ordinance

Term traditionally used in the Stone-Campbell Movement to refer to baptism, the Lord's Supper, and certain other Christian institutions.

Early leaders of the Stone-Campbell Movement rejected the term "sacrament" as scripturally and theologically inappropriate. "Ordinance" had been used to refer to baptism and the Lord's Supper in the Westminster Confession (1646), as well as in the Baptists' London (1689) and Philadelphia (1742) Confessions of Faith. The Movement's reluctance to use any terms not found in Scripture made even the use of "ordinance" relatively infrequent, though many saw it simply as a statement that these acts were ordained by God.

Alexander Campbell defined an "ordinance" as "the mode in which the grace of God acts upon human nature." Ordinances were, he said in 1843, "means of grace, and each and every one of a special grace peculiar to itself." Used in this way there seems to be little functional difference between "ordinance" and "sacrament." "Every ordinance of the gospel is a specific demonstration of divine grace or spiritual power in reference to some effect no other way attainable." The term "ordinance" (or "positive ordinance") especially designated baptism and the Lord's Supper, but Campbell could also apply it to the Lord's Day and, even more generically, to anything that God "orders" as a means of communicating his grace, for example, prayer, fasting, preaching, even the Bible itself. In *The Christian System* essay "The Kingdom of Heaven," he indicated other ordinances as well, such as exhortation, admonition, and discipline.

With respect to baptism and the Lord's Supper, churches of the Stone-Campbell Movement have resisted exclusive administration of the ordinances by clergy. It is common to confess that the ordinances were given to all Christians. Jesus said, "The Sabbath was made for humankind, not humankind for the Sabbath" (Mark 2:27). So it is with the Christian ordinances. They were given in grace for the salvation of penitent believers. Therefore, neglect of an ordinance is a loss to those for whom it was given.

In the mid-twentieth century, William Robinson, of the British Churches of Christ, began in earnest to try to move Stone-Campbell churches away from the language of "ordinances" (with its tendency to imply mere conformity to biblical prescriptions) to the language of "sacraments," in hopes of emphasizing the deeper dimensions of baptism and the Lord's Supper. Robinson's appeal was not widely accepted in the Christian Churches/Churches of Christ which retain the language either of "ordinances" or else "symbols" to designate these two Christian rites. Among the Christian Churches (Disciples of Christ), however, there has been increasing acceptance of the language of "sacrament," partly as a result of Robinson's work and partly because of increasingly ecumenically influenced theological education.

See also Baptism; Grace, Doctrine of; Lord's Supper, The; Sacrament

BIBLIOGRAPHY Alexander Campbell, "The Ordinances," *Millennial Harbinger* (1843): 9-13 • Richard L. Harrison, Jr., "Early Disciples Sacramental Theology: Catholic, Reformed, and Free," in *Classic Themes in Disciples Theology,* ed. Kenneth Lawrence (1986), pp. 49-100 • William Robinson, "'Ordinance' or 'Sacrament,'" *The Scroll* 45 (1954): 42-43.

ROBERT O. FIFE

Ordination

See Ministry

Ordination of Women

See Women in Ministry

Orphanages

See Children's Homes and Orphanages

Osborn, G. Edwin (1897-1965)

Disciples of Christ pastor, educator, and liturgical reformer. Osborn earned degrees from Phillips University Bible College (B.A., M.A., B.D., 1924-28) and the University of Edinburgh (Ph.D., 1935).

As a pastor of Christian missions or churches in Chicago (1916-17); Martinsburg, West Virginia (1918-20); and Douglas, Arizona (1920-24); and at Pleasance Church of Christ, Edinburgh, Scotland (1929-30); Hanover Avenue Christian Church, Richmond, Virginia (1930-36); and University Place Christian Church, Enid, Oklahoma (1936-44); he exemplified passion for and understanding of the Christian way of life. As Professor of Preaching and Christian Worship at the Seminary of Phillips University (1936-64) he demonstrated respect for students as well as commitment to the highest academic standards. He remained mentor to many individuals whom he had served as pastor or professor.

Osborn served on a number of committees of the church, including the Executive Committee of the Home and State Missions Planning Council (1938-44); Commission on Worship of Federal and National Council of Churches (1944-48); and Commission on Worship, World Council of Churches (1940-48). He was also Fraternal Delegate to the British Churches of Christ, London, 1953.

Among his most significant contributions was the compiling and editing of *Christian Worship: A Service Book* (1953). Other publications included *A Faith to Live By* (1945), *Training the Devotional Life,* and *The Psychology of Christian Public Worship* (1935).

He was a devoted husband to his beloved Alma and a loving father to Ronald E. Osborn and Prudence Osborn Dyer. PRUDENCE OSBORN DYER

Osborn, Ronald E. (1917-1998)

Disciples minister, ecumenist, historian, teacher, and dean. The depth and warmth of his Christian piety, combined with the rigor of his scholarship and teaching, made him one of the most beloved leaders of the twentieth-century Disciples of Christ.

Osborn was born September 5, 1917, in Chicago, Illinois, the son of G. Edwin and Alma Osborn. He grew up in Arizona, Oklahoma and Virginia. He received his B.A., M.A., and B.D. degrees from Phillips University, where his father was on the faculty. Osborn was ordained to the Christian ministry in 1940 and served churches in Oklahoma, Arkansas; and Oregon. He was editor of Youth Publications, including the magazine *Front Rank,* for Christian Board of Education from 1943 to 1945 and taught at Northwest Christian College from 1946 to 1950. He received his Ph.D. from the University of Oregon in 1955. His dissertation, "The Preaching of St. Peter Damien," kindled his lifelong interest in the history of preaching.

Osborn was professor of church history at Christian Theological Seminary in Indianapolis from 1950 to 1973 and dean and vice president of the seminary from 1959 to 1970. In 1973 he became professor of American church history at the School of Theology at Claremont and consultant for the Disciples Seminary Foundation until his retirement in 1982.

Osborn's publications include *Ely V. Zollars: A Biography; In Christ's Place; The Spirit of American Christian-*

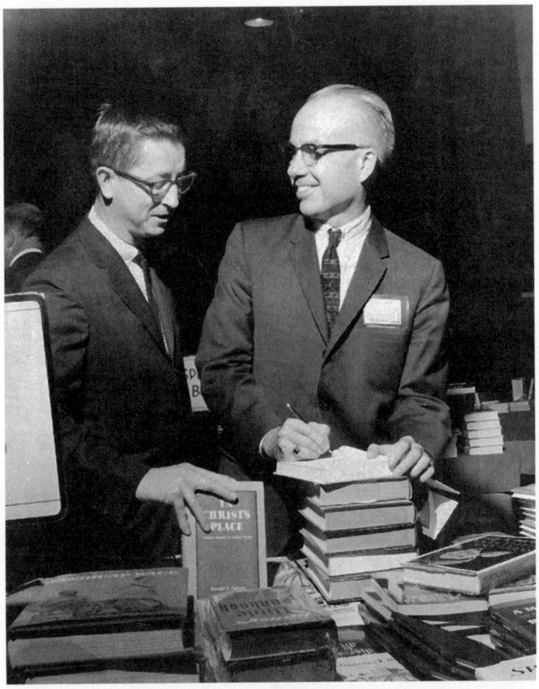

Educator and ecumenist Ronald E. Osborn (right) signs a copy of his book on ministry, *In Christ's Place.*
Courtesy of the Disciples of Christ Historical Society

ity; The Faith We Affirm: Basic Beliefs of the Disciples of Christ; Creative Disarray: Models of Ministry in a Changing America; and the first volume of his planned history of preaching, *Folly of God: The Rise of Christian Preaching.*

His work as a churchman included service as delegate to the Consultation on Church Union from 1963 to 1976 and to the Fourth Assembly of the World Council of Churches in Uppsala, Sweden, in 1968. He was perhaps the primary shaper of the movement toward restructure among the Disciples. Over a period of six years Osborn and others developed the pattern for restructure, culminating in the 1968 gathering in Kansas City, which began as the free association of individuals called the International Convention of Christian Churches with Osborn as the last president and ended as the General Assembly of the covenantal body called the Christian Church (Disciples of Christ) in the United States and Canada with Osborn as the first moderator. He wrote the Preamble to the Design for the Christian Church, which has become an affirmation of faith among Disciples. Then, on a napkin in a hotel restaurant, he designed the chalice symbol that has been universally accepted as the symbol for the Christian Church (Disciples of Christ).

Osborn married Naomi Jackson in 1940. Their daughter Virginia (1949-1968) was tragically killed in an automobile accident. Naomi Osborn died in 1986. Ronald later married Nola Neill, who had lost her husband. Her family became his family, and he dedicated his last book "To Nola and the family she gave me."

See also Christian Theological Seminary; Restructure

BIBLIOGRAPHY Paul A. Crow, *A Living Witness to Oikodome: Essays in Honor of Ronald E. Osborn* (1982)

JOSEPH R. JETER, JR.

Ottumwa Brethren

Conservative reform movement that began in the mid- to late-1940s within Disciples churches destined to become "independent" Christian Churches/Churches of Christ.

Sometimes called a "holiness" movement, the Ottumwa Brethren (so nicknamed because their primary base of operations was located in Ottumwa, Iowa) were greatly influenced in the formative years by the ministry of Archie Word (1901-1988), editor of *The Church Speaks* and *The Church Revealed in the Scriptures,* and evangelist of The Church at 550 N.E. 76th Avenue (now Crossroads Church of Christ), Portland, Oregon.

In November 1945 Word issued a national call to repentance and holiness in his journal *The Church Speaks.* Emboldened by Word, three young students from Ozark Bible College, Donald G. Hunt (b. 1922), Burton W. Barber (1918-1996), and James R. McMorrow (1913-1996) founded *The Voice of Evangelism* in 1946 and Midwestern School of Evangelism (1947) in Ottumwa, Iowa.

The Ottumwa Brethren believed in taking a stand on issues they felt were being neglected by "independent" churches: worldliness (movies, television, drinking, smoking), use of the name "Christian Church," matters of church polity, and extending fellowship to believers outside their circle. They were also profoundly opposed to what they viewed as the liberal theology of the Disciples of Christ. The movement was perceived by critics as narrow, restrictive, reactionary, and characterized by a sometimes harsh spirit and overemphasis on externals. Others found them to be refreshing advocates for conservative views in times of liberal apostasy.

In time the influence of the Ottumwa Brethren spread to about 650 churches (but never more than 350 at one time), mainly in the Midwest (Iowa and Missouri) and on the West Coast (California and Oregon). Summer preaching rallies in Centerville, Iowa, and Troutdale, Oregon, helped develop a network of as many as 580 like-minded preachers. Midwestern School of Evangelism was the only training center until 1952 when Word, Warren Bell, and Lee Turner established Churches of Christ School of Evangelists in Portland, Oregon (now Northwest College of the Bible). Two dozen other schools were started between 1966 and 1989 in places like Los Angeles; Denver; Gering, Nebraska; and Rutland, Vermont. Though at first rejecting the term "missionary," the movement has been active in some forty-seven countries of the world.

Writing and producing gospel literature has always been the mainstay of the movement. In addition to the journals *The Voice of Evangelism* and *The Church Speaks* and scores of other publications, many tracts, charts, books, and pamphlets have been produced by Voice of Evangelism Publications in Ottumwa and Scripture Supply House in Portland. These publications have had a wide readership among the most conservative Christian Churches/Churches of Christ. The most noteworthy and influential books have been Donald G. Hunt's *52 Simple, Stimulating Studies* (1950) and *What the Bible Says about the Unfolded Plan of God* (1981), and Tom Burgess's *Documents on Instrumental Music* (1966). Since the mid-1960s College Press Publishing Company (whose founder, Don DeWelt, was originally converted to the Christian faith by Archie Word) has published more than a dozen writers connected with the Ottumwa movement, including several books of sermon outlines by Archie Word as well as his life story, *Archie Word: Voice of Thunder, Heart of Tears,* by Victor Knowles.

With the demise of Word and other key leaders, the decline in the number of schools, publications, and rallies, and the loss of their original fervor and exclusiveness, the influence of the reform movement has gradually waned.

See also Christian Church/Churches of Christ; College Press; DeWelt, Don; Fundamentalism; Ozark Christian College; "Restoration," Meanings of within the Movement; Word, Archie

BIBLIOGRAPHY *The Church Speaks,* vols. 1-24 (1944-68) • Victor Knowles, *Archie Word: Voice of Thunder, Heart of Tears* (1992) • Victor Knowles and William E. Paul, *Taking a Stand: The Story of the Ottumwa Brethren* (1996) • *The Voice of Evangelism,* vols. 1-52 (1946-99).

VICTOR KNOWLES

"Our Plea"

See Errett, Isaac; "Plea," The

Outsiders' Views of the Movement

Critical observations of, and commentary on, the Stone-Campbell Movement from outsiders to the Movement have appeared virtually from the beginning. Many external critics have dwelled on the irony that a Movement dedicated to Christian unity precipitated more division in the church, a perspective effectively captured in the remark of the late Roland Bainton of Yale University: "Alexander Campbell has the singular distinction of being the only Christian reformer whose achievement was the denial of his intention. He sought to unite all of the evangelical churches and instead founded one more."

During the earliest years of the Movement, as evidenced in the standard religious encyclopedias, dictionaries, and general histories of the day, outside critics saw the leaders of "Christian" movements as dissidents within their existing denominations: Barton Stone and the Campbells among the Presbyterians in Kentucky and Virginia; James O'Kelly among the Methodists in North Carolina and Virginia; and Abner Jones and Elias Smith among the Baptists in New England.

Associates of the Campbells came to be identified by external analysts as Baptists, or "Reforming" Baptists, or "Campbellite Baptists." As the followers of Stone, O'Kelly, and the other "Christians" came to accept baptism of believers by immersion, outside critics counted them, also, among the Baptists. By the late 1820s, though, many Baptists had become estranged from the Stone-Campbell Movement as it developed and promulgated the doctrine of baptism for the remission of sins, the Movement's most identifiable characteristic, along with the practice of weekly communion. Several Baptist associations in Ohio, Kentucky, Pennsylvania, and Virginia excluded the Reformers from their midst; and by 1833 the separation was nearly complete following the union of the followers of Stone and the Campbells. One-time adversaries, the Methodists and the Baptists frequently banded together in their opposition to the Stone-Campbell Movement.

An especially severe criticism of the Movement came from the two professed "Evangelical Catholic" theologians at the German Reformed Seminary in Mercersburg, Pennsylvania, Philip Schaff and John W. Nevin. Although Schaff grew ever more patient of the broad diversity of movements within American Protestantism, Nevin, in his *Antichrist, or the Spirit of Sect and Schism* (1848), castigated both Campbell's Disciples and Stone's Christians as unity movements gone awry, stumbling over their own restorationism and commonsense hermeneutics. Such groups, in Nevin's judgment, failed to comprehend the "one, holy, catholic and apostolic Church" whose unity was grounded in the sacramental presence of Christ, not in allegedly "self-evident" propositions from Scripture.

In the same general period, however, Alexander Campbell began to gain a national reputation in spite of the opposition from denominational leaders. His participation as a delegate in the Virginia Constitutional Convention (1829) and his public debates, including those with the "infidel" Robert Owen (1829) and Roman Catholic Archbishop Purcell (1837), gave Campbell a national prominence not shared by the other leaders of the Movement. Former Presidents James Madison and James Monroe, Chief Justice John Marshall, English novelist Frances Trollope, and former Senator and Secretary of State Henry Clay heard Campbell in these settings and recognized him as a person of great oratorical skill.

Following the Civil War to the beginning of the next century, the Stone-Campbell Movement experienced an unparalleled period of growth, quintupling its size, posturing itself as one of several American-bred, egalitarian-structured frontier denominations. Several groups outside the Movement continued to see it not as a unifying movement within the church, but rather as a schismatic sect outside mainstream Protestant Christianity. In 1888 William H. Whitsitt, theology professor at Southern Baptist Theological Seminary, wrote a critical account of the Movement with the subtitle, "A Contribution to the Centennial Anniversary of the Birth of Alexander Campbell." He connected the distinctive doctrinal characteristics and practices of the "Campbellites" to the influence of the Scottish Independents, especially John Glas and Robert Sandeman.

In 1890 a Methodist pastor, T. McK. Stuart, published a substantial work noting the rapid growth of "Campbellism" and asserting that it was in conflict with all other Christian denominations. Stuart intended that "every Methodist minister prepare himself to meet intelligently and successfully this form of error." He focused on baptism as a condition of forgiveness, setting this view against all other Protestant evangelical groups and comparing it to Roman Catholicism's view of baptism.

Little attention is given to the Stone-Campbell Movement in contemporary histories that focus on American church history. William Warren Sweet made only passing reference, seeing the Movement in the larger context of the Great Awakening and noting that it ultimately attracted Baptists who were anti-missions, anti–Sunday Schools, anti-organization. Alice Tyler briefly mentioned the Movement as an offshoot of the Baptists and an example of the individualism of frontier culture. Bernard Weisberger focused only briefly on Barton Stone's involvement in the Second Great Awakening, and on the Campbells only in their relationship to Stone. William McCloughlin's historical study of American revivalism cited the same connection and added that the Stone and Campbell groups were "bested" by Methodist Peter Cartwright. Winthrop Hudson gave a brief history of Stone and the Campbells and attributed their unity emphasis to the Wesleys. Timothy Smith made a brief reference to the Disciples of Christ around 1855, noting that the Baptists, Methodists, and Presbyterians all opposed them. Sydney Ahlstrom called the Movement "frontier Presbyterianism" and its constituents "disputatious" and "legalists." Mark Noll saw the Stone-Campbell Movement as part of the American passion for liberty and individualism common to Cumberland Presbyterians, Methodists, and Baptists as well.

In one of the most important and influential studies, Nathan Hatch, in his *The Democratization of American Christianity,* included an analysis of "the Christian Movement" as one of five premier egalitarian religious groups on the nineteenth-century American frontier (along with the Baptists, Methodists, Black churches, and Mormons). Arthur Schlesinger, Jr., noted American historian and Jackson scholar, tied the anti-Calvinism of the Stone-Campbell Movement to the spirit of democracy in the Jacksonian age. Richard Tristano, a Roman Catholic historian, presented an interesting volume recounting the history of the Stone-Campbell Movement with remarkable understanding; he noted that Campbell's distinctive view of baptism was the *via media* between traditional Protestantism and Roman Catholicism. He also identified this doctrine as causing great controversy and suspicion on the part of much of Protestantism toward the Movement. Timothy George, Baptist theologian, surprisingly blamed the Stone-Campbell Movement, along with the Landmark Baptists, for the controversy among the Southern Baptist Convention churches and organizations for the last third of the twentieth century.

The contemporary general church histories also give only brief attention to the Movement. Earle Cairns, Williston Walker, Kenneth Scott Latourette, and Roland Bainton make but passing reference. Tim Dowley's *Eerdmans Handbook to the History of Christianity* has no mention at all of the Campbells or Barton W. Stone.

While the emphasis upon restoration of the primitive gospel and anti-creedalism had significant appeal to many on the frontier, so as to occasion significant growth of the new denomination by the end of the nineteenth century, the Stone-Campbell Movement lost much of its unique unity appeal, especially as the mainline denominations were increasingly attracted to the Ecumenical Movement. With the consequent division of the Stone-Campbell Movement into three distinct groups, this message of unity to the Christian world was significantly compromised. Evangelical Protestant churches, moreover, have for their part balked at the Movement's views on baptism and continued often to suspect the Movement of teaching baptismal regeneration.

See also Baptists; Historiography, Stone-Campbell Movement; Jeter, Jeremiah Bell; Presbyterians, Presbyterianism

BIBLIOGRAPHY Sydney Ahlstrom, *A Religious History of the American People* (1972) • Robert Baird, *Religion in the United States of America* (1844), s.v. "Smaller Baptist Denominations: Disciples of Christ," "Unevangelical Churches in America: The Christian Connection" • Roland H. Bainton, *Christendom,* vol. 2 (1966) • Roland H. Bainton, "Alexander Campbell and Church Unity," in *The Sage of Bethany: A Pioneer in Broadcloth,* ed. Perry Gresham (repr. ed. 1988), pp. 81-94 • Roland H. Bainton, "Alexander Campbell and the Social Order," in *The Sage of Bethany,* pp. 117-29 • Joseph Belcher, *The Religious Denominations in the United States* (1861), s.v. "Christians," "Disciples of Christ" • David Benedict, *A General History of the Baptist Denomination in America and Other Parts of the World* (1848), s.v. "Campbellites or Reformers," "Christian Society" • J. Newton Brown, ed., *Complete Book of Reference on All Religious Subjects and Companion to the Bible* (1836) • William Burder, *A History of the Religions of the World . . . Including a Full Account of All the Religious Denominations in the United States* (1883), s.v. "Campbellite Baptists, or Disciples" • Earle E. Cairns, *Christianity Through the Ages* (1964) • Tim Dowley, ed., *Eerdmans Handbook to the History of Christianity* (1977) • Timothy George, "Southern Baptist Ghosts," *First Things: A Journal of Religion and Public Life* 93 (May 1999): 17-24 • Nathan O. Hatch, *The Democratization of American Christianity* (1989) • Winthrop S. Hudson, *Religion in America* (1965) • Jeremiah Jeter, *Campbellism Examined* (1855) • Kenneth Scott Latourette, *Christianity Through the Ages* (1965) • Bill J. Leonard, "Alexander Campbell, 'The Destiny of Our Country,'" in *Early American Christianity* (1983) • William McCloughlin, *Revivals, Awakenings, and Reform: An Essay on Religious and Social Change in American, 1607-1977* (1978) • Vincent L. Milner, *Religious Denominations of the World* (1860), s.v. "Baptists — Minor Denominations: Christians," "Campbellite Baptists, or Disciples," "Disciples of Christ" • John W. Nevin, *Antichrist, or the Spirit of Sect and Schism* (1848) • Mark A. Noll, *A History of Christianity in the United States and Canada* (1992) • Mark A. Noll, *American Evangelical Christianity* (2001) • Hugh F. Pyle, *The Truth About the 'Church of Christ'* (1977) • Elias B. Sanford, *A Concise Cyclopedia of Religious Knowledge: Biblical, Biographical, Geographical, Historical, Practical, and Theological* (1902), s.v. "Christians (Christian Connection)" • Philip Schaff, *A Religious Encyclopaedia or Dictionary of Biblical, Historical, Doctrinal, and Practical Theology* (1894), s.v. "Christian Connection, or Christians" • Arthur Schlesinger, Jr., "The Age of Alexander Campbell," in *The Sage of Bethany: A Pioneer in Broadcloth,* ed. Perry Gresham (repr. ed. 1988), pp. 25-44 • Timothy L. Smith, *Revivalism and Social Reform: American Protestantism on the Eve of the Civil War* (1965) • William Warren Sweet, *Religion on the American Frontier: The Presbyterians* (1936) • William Warren Sweet, *The Story of Religion in America* (1950) • W. P. Strickland, ed., *Autobiography of Peter Cartwright, the Backwoods Preacher* (1856) • T. McK. Stuart, *Errors of Campbellism, Being a Review of All Fundamental Errors of the System of Faith and Church Polity of the Denomination Founded by Alexander Campbell* (1890) • E. C. Towne et al., *Rays of Light from All Lands: The Bibles and Beliefs of Mankind* (1895), s.v. "The Baptist Churches in the United States: The Church of Christ," "Belief and History of 'The Christians'" • Richard M. Tristano, *The Origins of the Restoration Movement: An Intellectual History* (1988) • Alice F. Tyler, *Freedom's Ferment: Phases of American Social History from the Colonial Period to the Outbreak of the Civil War* (1944) • Williston Walker, *A History of the Christian Church* (1959) • Bernard A. Weisberger, *They Gathered at the River* (1958) • William H. Whitsitt, *The Origin of the Disciples of Christ (Campbellites)* (3rd ed. 1891).

GARY E. WEEDMAN

Overdale College

See Hope International University

Ozark Christian College

Bible college affiliated with the Christian Churches/Churches of Christ.

Ozark Bible College was established in Bentonville, Arkansas, on June 12, 1942, committed to training men and women for Christian service. An earlier Ozark Christian College was established in St. Joe, Arkansas, in 1938. It moved to Harrison, Arkansas, in 1939, and then to Bentonville in 1940. This school was to provide occupational training as well as to provide Bible teaching. The idea of a Christian trade school was not successful and the school closed.

Ozark Bible College was founded to be a Bible college training full-time and part-time Christian workers. Workers were prepared to be ministers, missionaries, evangelistic singers, church secretaries, educational directors, and assistant ministers, as well as elders, deacons, and volunteer workers in the local church. The trustees elected F. W. Strong (1880-1951) as president and Seth Wilson (b. 1914) as dean, positions they held in the former college. Many churches in the four-state area of Missouri, Kansas, Arkansas, and Oklahoma were closed and hundreds were without preachers. Ozark Bible College desired to provide preachers who would revive the churches.

In October of 1944, Ozark Bible College moved to Joplin, Missouri. A large house located at 516 N. Wall Street became the new home for the college. Joplin was chosen as the new location for the college because it was easily accessible by car, bus, train, or plane. Many churches surrounded Joplin, which provided opportunities for student ministries. The city also had secular job opportunities for students.

In 1946 Edwin B. Strong (b. 1912) succeeded his father as president. The college grew from sixteen students in 1942 to 123 students in the fall of 1949. An addition to the building in 1948 provided a dining room, a small chapel, and two classrooms. At this time most of the full-time faculty preached every weekend. Area ministers assisted as part-time instructors. Students were involved in service in the churches on weekends.

The curriculum has always stressed direct study of the biblical text, with every degree carrying a major in Bible. Strong emphasis has been placed on apologetics (knowing why Christians believe) and on hermeneutics (principles and methods for understanding the Bible). The curriculum also focused on training in practical ministry skills, which students further developed in service in local churches.

In 1952 Don Earl Boatman (b. 1913), became the third president, a post he held for twenty-seven years. The college had a vision and a desire to grow. A large chapel, a library, and additional classrooms were added to the college building in 1953. This enabled the college to accommodate the 176 students who enrolled in the fall of 1954. In 1955 seventy-five churches were served by Ozark faculty, staff, and students.

Having outgrown its old campus, the college in 1959 purchased forty acres north of downtown Joplin and less than a mile from the old campus. The Missions Building and Alumni Hall were completed in 1963, providing classrooms and a dormitory for women. This enabled the college to move to the new campus to welcome 309 students in the fall of 1963. The Administration Building was completed a few weeks after the fall semester started. Thirteen functional buildings were constructed on the new campus within two decades.

Every year during the 1960s enrollment increased, reaching a peak of 803 in the fall of 1974. New faculty and programs expanded the outreach of the college. Evangelism and missions were emphasized.

In 1979 Ken Idleman (b. 1947) became president. On July 1, 1985, Midwest Christian College of Oklahoma City, Oklahoma, consolidated with Ozark on the Joplin campus under the name of Ozark Christian College. The college was accredited by the Accrediting Association of Bible Colleges in 1988. The college has enjoyed institutional stability, having had only four presidents and four academic deans in fifty-seven years. Many trustees and faculty have given long-term service to the college as well.

Throughout its history the college has maintained a traditional Bible college mission, emphasizing preparation for Christian service (full-time and part-time). Students completing one-, two-, or three-year programs usually are volunteers in church service and earn their living through another occupation. The four- and five-year degree programs prepare persons for church-related vocations. As of May 1999, over 11,000 had studied at the college and 2,450 had received baccalaureate degrees.

See also Bible College Movement; Higher Education, Views of in the Movement

BIBLIOGRAPHY H. Lynn Gardner, *Ozark Christian College: A Vision of Teaching the Word of Christ in the Spirit of Christ* (1992).

H. LYNN GARDNER

P

Pacifism

The belief that participation in warfare and other forms of violence is wrong.

Pacifism has been a central issue in the Stone-Campbell Movement worldwide. Support for both sectarian and liberal pacifism can be found in Alexander Campbell. Sectarian pacifism entailed individual Christians withdrawing from the political process and remaining faithful to Christian witness against killing. Liberal pacifism in both its religious and secular forms held that all war is wrong but that through education, political activism, and international arbitration eventually all war would end. Liberal pacifism was usually manifested in peace organizations that promoted such programs of action. For Campbell, the ethics of the Sermon on the Mount made it wrong for Christians to participate in war because God's kingdom "is not of this world." Campbell also accepted the optimistic modern view of the peace movement that war could be eliminated. Prefiguring the League of Nations and the United Nations, Campbell asked in his 1848 "Address on War," "Why not have a by-law-established Umpire? . . . a Congress of Nations and a High Court of Nations for adjudicating . . . all international misunderstandings and complaints?"

During the Civil War the American Christian Missionary Society passed resolutions in 1861 and 1863 that affirmed their "sympathies" for the Union soldiers who were "defending" them "from the attempts of armed traitors to overthrow" the federal government. Enraged that a missionary society would pass political resolutions, David Lipscomb and the *Gospel Advocate* strongly advocated pacifism among the churches of the South.

Lipscomb's mentor, Tolbert Fanning, had long believed that Christians should not vote or actively participate in government in any form. Before the Civil War Lipscomb disagreed and was not a pacifist. The Civil War changed his view, however, causing him to lament "the spectacle [that] was presented, of disciples of the Prince of Peace, with murderous weapons seeking the lives of their fellowmen." Lipscomb turned pessimistic toward government, believing God had instituted his own government to rule and control humans. However, rebellious humans established political systems to conduct the affairs of government free from God's rule and dominion. War was the chief occupation of human government. Christians would see that the "kingdom of heaven — the Church" was "to break into pieces and destroy all earthly kingdoms and dominions, and fill the whole earth and stand forever."

Lipscomb's sectarian pacifism led him to place no faith at all in the peace organizations of the day. Instead, he insisted that the church was the only organization that could promote peace. J. D. Tant (1861-1941) summarized the strong sectarian pacifism in parts of the Movement during the Spanish-American War: "I would as soon risk my chance of heaven to die drunk in a bawdy house as to die on the battlefield, with murder in my heart, trying to kill my fellowman." In contrast to Lipscomb, politically engaged members of the Movement in the North often supported the peace organizations and international arbitration. However, as tensions with Spain erupted at the end of the nineteenth century, Disciples journals became as bellicose as the secular press.

Overt pacifism in the Movement largely disappeared from sight during the Spanish American War, though it continued in pockets, especially among Churches of Christ. Disciples leader Kirby Page conceded that before World War I he had never "met an informed and determined pacifist." Liberal pacifism, however, was reborn in the Disciples under the influence and context of the social gospel when Alva Taylor, professor at Vanderbilt's School of Religion; Charles Clayton Morrison, editor of the *Christian Century;* and Kirby Page pressed pacifist views in the first half of the twentieth century. During the 1930s, the high-water mark for liberal pacifism, many Disciples believed that it was possible to eradicate war from humanity. In 1935 the Disciples Peace Fellowship

(DPF) was organized, with the pledge, "WE DO SOLEMNLY covenant together . . . to promote peace and to oppose war now and always. We propose to carry out this covenant for the abolition of war by fostering good will among nations, races and classes, by opposing military preparations." In 1936 the Disciples convention, like most other mainline Protestant groups, passed a resolution opposing rearmament because "war was morally and ethically wrong and opposed to the teachings of Jesus Christ." They naively announced, "We will not support future wars."

Pearl Harbor shattered confidence in pacifism among Disciples as most saw U.S. involvement in war as a justifiable means to stop the evils of Nazism and Japanese aggression. DPF supported Disciples conscientious objectors of World War II in their alternative service, but the organization shrank and remains small and on the periphery of the Disciples.

While conservative Disciples (later the Christian Churches/Churches of Christ) are the least pacifist of the three streams, Archie Word and the Ottumwa Brethren developed a strident pacifism in the 1930s similar to the sectarian pacifism of the Churches of Christ seen in Tant's statement above.

The sectarian and individualistic pacifism most characteristic of Churches of Christ suffered decline in the twentieth century. With the passage of the Alien and Sedition Acts in World War I, the government was able effectively to suppress dissent to the war. The *Gospel Advocate* was under threat of losing its mailing privileges if it continued to promote pacifist views and so changed its editorial policy to support the war. In Oklahoma Cordell Christian College closed under government surveillance and community pressure. O. E. Enfield, a leading Oklahoma preacher and socialist, was imprisoned at Leavenworth for his anti-war sentiments. Many church members shed pacifism as an embarrassment. After World War I, those in mainstream Churches of Christ moved toward a pro-war stance, while many in the various subgroups (premillennial, non–Sunday School, One-Cup, and African American Churches of Christ) dissented and maintained a pacifist position. The One-Cup Churches of Christ are still on record as a "peace church." During the 1930s, as the peace movement gained prestige, many in the mainstream Churches of Christ became attracted to pacifism again as many churches went on record as being opposed to Christians fighting in war.

As was the case in all parts of the Movement, most members of Churches of Christ came out in support of the war because of Pearl Harbor, though a vociferous minority still dissented. One hundred ninety-nine men officially from the Churches of Christ served in the Civilian Public Service, the alternative service available for conscientious objectors in World War II, the fourth largest non–Peace Church group. The radical noncooperation tactics of Corbett Bishop, a member of the Manhattan, New York, Church of Christ, influenced the nonviolent protest techniques of the peace and civil rights movements.

After the war, pacifism was largely relegated to an individual matter in Churches of Christ, with churches less willing to discuss the issue pro or con. Most members were becoming assimilated into mainstream society as the Churches of Christ participated in the postwar economic boom. Various pro-America/anti-Communist efforts gained support among members, and by the 1980s many in Churches of Christ were pro-military conservative Republicans.

Pacifism has also been important in the Stone-Campbell Movement in Britain, Australia, Canada, and New Zealand. The pacifist "old paths" churches left the British Churches of Christ after World War I. Pacifist preacher Arthur Horner became a leading British Communist and trade union leader. American and British restorationist thought also influenced pacifism in other English-speaking countries.

See also Civil War, The; Cordell Christian College; Disciples Peace Fellowship; Fanning, Tolbert; Lipscomb, David; Morrison, Charles Clayton; Ottumwa Brethren; Page, Kirby; Tant, Jefferson Davis; Word, Archie

BIBLIOGRAPHY Peter Brock, "Pacifism Among the Disciples of Christ: A Denominational Option," in *Freedom from War: Nonsectarian Pacifism, 1814-1914* (1991), pp. 136-52, 352-56 • Michael W. Casey, "From Religious Outsiders to Insiders: The Rise and Fall of Pacifism in the Churches of Christ," *Journal of Church and State* 44 (2002): 455-75 • Michael W. Casey, "The Overlooked Pacifist Tradition of the Old Paths Churches of Christ," *The Journal of the United Reform Church History Society* 6 (May 2000): 446-60; (December 2000): 517-28 • Michael W. Casey, "Pacifism and Non-Violence: The Prophetic Voice of the African-American Churches of Christ," *Discipliana* 59 (Summer 1999): 35-49 • Michael W. Casey, "Warriors Against War: The Pacifists of the Churches of Christ in World War Two," *Restoration Quarterly* 35 (1993): 159-74 • Michael W. Casey, "From Patriotism to Pacifism: The Emergence of Civil Religion in the Churches of Christ in World War One," *Mennonite Quarterly Review* 66 (July 1992): 376-90 • Arron S. Chambers, "The Path of Pacifism: A Synoptic Study of the Fate of the Tradition of Pacifism in the Churches of Christ and the Christian Churches/Churches of Christ" (M.A thesis, Abilene Christian University, 2000) • Johnnie Andrew Collins, "Pacifism in the Churches of Christ: 1866-1945" (D.A. dissertation, Middle Tennessee State University, 1984) • Mark Alan Elrod, "The Churches of Christ and the 'War Question': The Influence of Church Journals" (Ph.D. dissertation, Vanderbilt University, 1995) • David E. Harrell, Jr., "Disciples of Christ Pacifism in Nineteenth-

Century Tennessee," *Tennessee Historical Quarterly* 21 (September 1962): 263-74 • Mark A. May, "Disciples Peace Fellowship: Historical Formation and the First Twenty Years, 1935-1955," *Discipliana* 40 (1980): 19-26.

MICHAEL W. CASEY

Page, Kirby (1890-1957)

Pacifist leader and activist among the Disciples of Christ in the mid-twentieth century.

Even beyond the Disciples context, Kirby Page was among the most prolific authors in the American peace movement between the two World Wars. Before his death over one million copies of his more than forty books and pamphlets had been distributed. Born in Tyler County, Texas, Page was a Disciples minister educated at Drake University, the University of Chicago, and Yale University. In 1921, with Sherwood Eddy, prominent evangelist for the International YMCA, Page established the Fellowship for a Christian Social Order to bring together pacifists and social liberals to promote peace, racial equality, and economic justice. The organization merged with the Fellowship of Reconciliation six years later. Page followed prominent socialist leader and six-time presidential candidate Norman Thomas as editor of the journal *The World Tomorrow.*

Page was a key leader in efforts to commit churches to pacifism during the 1930s. He was instrumental in the formation of the Disciples Peace Fellowship. Throughout his adult life, Page delivered addresses and led workshops worldwide, dealing not only with war and peace but also with prayer and spiritual growth.

See also Disciples Peace Fellowship; Pacifism

BIBLIOGRAPHY Charles Chatfield, *The American Peace Movement: Ideals and Activism* (1992) • Charles Chatfield, *For Peace and Justice: Pacifism in America, 1914-1941* (1971) • Charles Chatfield and Charles DeBenedetti, eds., *Kirby Page and the Social Gospel: An Anthology* (1976) • Kirby Page, *Kirby Page: Social Evangelist* (1975). CRAIG M. WATTS

Pan-American Lectures

Annual lectureship sponsored by members of Churches of Christ to encourage Latin American missions.

The Pan-American Lectures began in 1963 in Guatemala City and have convened annually since then. Reuel Lemmons was the key coordinator at the beginning and continued in some capacity until his death in 1989. Lemmons was interested in worldwide missions and had already promoted activities in Europe and Africa. The Frankfurt, Germany, lectures had begun in the early 1950s and were highly successful in bringing together missionaries and interested sponsors for the churches in Europe. Lemmons and others saw doors opening in Central and South America and determined that a new lectureship promoting Pan-American missions would further activities there. Others already involved in the lectures included Jim Frazier of Minden, Louisiana, and the Frazier Foundation; Howard Norton, missions professor at Oklahoma Christian and later Harding University; Carl Mitchell of Pepperdine and Harding; and Dan Coker, Latin American missionary and onetime missions professor at Abilene Christian University.

The purpose of the lectures is to bring together missionaries from Central and South America and church leaders from the United States who are interested in church plantings and nurturing. All interested persons are welcome to attend. The lectures are designed to help secure uninterrupted and additional support for Latin American churches, to expose participants to other cultures and the work of the churches in these cultures, and to provide a time of encouragement and spiritual uplift for the missionaries. The lectures include reports from missionaries, reflections on mission strategy, and new church-planting opportunities. The lectures embody both plenary meetings and breakout sessions for those with special interests.

The lectures move from country to country each year and have been held in Mexico City and Mérida, Mexico; San Juan, Puerto Rico; Tegucigalpa, Honduras; San José, Costa Rica; Santo Domingo, Dominican Republic; Managua, Nicaragua; Panama City, Panama; Quito, Ecuador; Lima, Peru; Santiago, Chile; Caracas, Venezuela; Bogotá and Medellín, Colombia; São Paulo, Rio de Janeiro, Brasilia, and Belo Horizonte, Brazil; and Buenos Aires, Argentina.

See also Latin America and Caribbean, Missions in; Lemmons, Reuel Gordon

BIBLIOGRAPHY Five volumes of sermons from the Lectures were published by Western Christian Foundation: *Seeds of the Kingdom* (1963) • *Spreading Kingdom* (1964) • *Hitherto Hath the Lord Helped Us* (1978) • *Let Us Arise and Build* (1978) • *Let's Pull It All Together in Latin America for Jesus* (1979). A website with current information is located at http://bellsouthpwp.net/d/w/dwesp/home.htm.

THOMAS H. OLBRICHT

Panel of Scholars

A fifteen-member commission created, under the sponsorship of the United Christian Missionary Society and the Board of Education of the Christian Churches (Disciples of Christ), to examine the doctrines and polity of the Disciples in light of contemporary theological scholarship. Authorized in 1956, the Panel met biannually from 1957 through 1962. Its first chairman (until September 1958) was Howard E. Short, who was succeeded by William Barnett Blakemore, dean of the Disciples Divinity House at the University of Chicago.

The panel was mainly comprised of educators at Disciples-related ("Brotherhood") seminaries, colleges, and universities. From the College of the Bible came William R. Baird, Jr., Howard E. Short, Dwight E. Stevenson, and Ralph Wilburn; from Christian Theological Seminary, James A. Clague and Ronald E. Osborn; from Phillips University's Graduate Seminary, Stephen J. England and Eugene H. Peters; from Texas Christian University, D. Ray Lindley, and from its Brite College of the Bible, Glenn C. Routt; from Drake University, Frank N. Gardner; and from Lynchburg College, Virgil G. Hinds. Another member, J. Phillip Hyatt, like Blakemore, taught at a school (Vanderbilt University's Divinity School) with a Disciples House. Three panelists — Hunter P. Beckelhymer, Clarence E. Lemmon, and William G. West — were serving as ministers of congregations during their terms of appointment. Short and Stevenson resigned in 1958-59, and Baird and Peters were added in 1959. Otherwise, the membership roster remained stable.

Dwight E. Stevenson (left) and Ralph G. Wilburn (center), scholars from the College of the Bible (now Lexington Theological Seminary), were important theological voices in the Disciples' Panel of Scholars during its 1957-62 tenure.
Courtesy of the Disciples of Christ Historical Society

The panel's work was the first concerted, self-consciously "scholarly" and "theological" restudy of the Stone-Campbell Movement's heritage undertaken with "official," churchwide sanction. Both its mandate and its results reflected developments and concerns of the Disciples of Christ after World War II. Chief among these were challenges and opportunities arising in the context of the postwar boom of interest in religion, the "theological renaissance" in Protestantism sparked by theocentric, neo-orthodox, and realistic trends in scholarly and ecumenical discussion, reappraisals of the relationship between "Christ and culture," and confusion and discord with regard to basic doctrines of the faith, Christian social ethics, imperatives of mission, and polity.

The panel had neither authorization for nor interest in proposing standards of doctrine for the church. Its papers (even those which defended a specific theological position) were analytical and evaluative reviews of church "faith and order" and "life and work," set forth in terms customary in biblical, historical, theological, ecumenical, and sociological scholarship. This approach — and above all reliance on historical-critical methods — marked the panel as generically "liberal." Yet a variety of theological currents — for example, classical liberalism, neo-empirical and process thinking, and realistic, neo-orthodox, kerygmatic, and correlationist theologies — were evident. Panelists differed in their accounts of the Stone-Campbell heritage and their proposals for its "renewal." Indeed, departures from liberal and "modernist" thought of the sort that discounted the significance of theological doctrine were among the most striking features of the panel's work as a whole.

Another striking general feature was — using Wilburn's phraseology — "a critique of the Restoration principle." The restorationist (or "primitivist") appeals made by the Stone-Campbell Movement were viewed in the context of the history of theology and the church as one of the many historic church theologies. Its assumptions and conclusions — especially as developed following the Movement's founding era — were judged untenable in light of biblical, historical, and theological inquiry: the New Testament set forth no single, uniform pattern of doctrine, worship, language, order, and practice. Faithfulness to Christ required the church to adapt its ways and structures, as necessary, to fulfill its mission of witness, love, service, reconciliation, unity, and peace.

Such views exacerbated tensions among Disciples even as they legitimized and shaped discussions of church restructure. In fact, the panel found no cause to challenge — much less break with — signal characteristics of the Stone-Campbell heritage. The unique, supreme authority of the Scriptures as the "Word of God," the repudiation of historic dogmatism and ecclesiasticism; the centrality of Jesus Christ as "Son of God, Lord, and Savior"; the normativity of believers' baptism by immersion upon a simple, biblical confession of faith in Christ; opposition to the use of postbiblical creeds as tests of fellowship and communion; weekly observance of the ordinance (and/or sacrament) of the Lord's Supper; the church as a priesthood of all believers; and congregational polity (in cooperative association for mission) were among the Stone-Campbell traditions reaffirmed and defended, although for reasons and in terms other than "Restorationism."

The papers of the panel were shared during this period with an estimated sixty church discussion groups. They were then published in 1963 by Bethany Press as a three-volume set entitled *The Renewal of the Church: The Panel Reports,* with William B. Blakemore as general editor: volume 1, *The Reformation of Tradition;* volume 2, *The Reconstruction of Theology;* volume 3, *The Revival of the Churches.* Although now outdated as scholarship and church guidance, the *Reports* remain standard resources for serious study of the history, character, and legacy of the Stone-Campbell Movement within the Christian Church (Disciples of Christ). JAMES O. DUKE

Pastoral Care

The dimension of Christian ministry concerned specifically with the shepherding or care of souls *(cura animarum),* particularly in times of personal trouble or distress.

First-generation leaders of the Stone-Campbell Movement were primarily occupied with doctrinal questions concerning the restoration of the ancient order and ecclesial unity rather than specific matters of pastoral care. However, the preaching of the early Movement reflected a deep and abiding pastoral concern, to the extent that it sought to relieve the distress of those who felt unsure about their salvation.

The earliest congregations of the Movement were autonomous and led by those called pastors, elders, or bishops. They provided the primary teaching, discipline, and oversight of the congregation. Each congregation also had deacons (and sometimes deaconesses) to care for the physical needs of its members. In this way the congregation itself provided pastoral care for individuals within the community. Those considered ministers or evangelists were sent to preach and establish new congregations that would administer pastoral care under the leadership and example of the elders.

In the mid- to late- 1800s, under the influence of Isaac Errett and J. W. McGarvey, located preachers or evangelists became the norm in many Stone-Campbell congregations. Errett called the located evangelist an "elder" or "pastor," while McGarvey preferred the term "evangelist" or "minister." Instruction regarding pastoral care mostly took the form of anecdotal advice in the Movement's periodicals. However, one pioneering work distinguished itself in providing a more systematic approach to the type of care the minister was to provide. Published in 1888 by Ohio minister and educator Thomas Munnell, the title in full was *The Care of All the Churches, Being a Scriptural Statement of the Character, Qualifications, Ordination, and Relative Duties of the Christian Ministry, Evangelists, Bishops and Deacons, with Special Directions as to the Practical Details of a Successful Ministerial Life, Both in the Spiritual and Business Aspects of the Work.* Specialized ministries providing pastoral care outside of the local congregation were few and far between, though there were Disciples who served as chaplains during the Civil War. The content of pastoral care, offered from the pulpit as well as in person, often focused on one's moral condition, issues of health, caring for physical needs, and family life. Often the discussion from the pulpit, however, focused on doctrinal or moral absolutes.

In the latter half of the twentieth century, the heirs of the Stone-Campbell Movement developed an increasingly educated group of ministers and university professors, who in turn composed more systematic writings on issues of pastoral care, writings that combined theological sensitivity with social-scientific analyses of human behavior. Prominent among those writers were Charles Kemp and Don Browning (Disciples of Christ), Max Leach, and Lewis Rambo (Churches of Christ). Seminars dealing with marriage enrichment also became increasingly popular in congregations. This trend corresponded to a larger societal turn toward the therapeutic. Pastoral care through sermons, classes, seminars, and personal interaction now incorporated issues related to stress, depression, addiction, and dysfunction in relationships. This paralleled similar moves in both mainline Protestant and evangelical churches.

The number of specialized ministries also increased as the twentieth century came to a close. Some congregations now had youth ministers, counseling ministers, and counseling centers. Institutional ministries such as hospital and military chaplaincy became more common among ministers from all three branches of the Stone-Campbell tradition.

As the twenty-first century commenced, larger congregations began extensive small-group ministries for their members. The purpose of these small groups included Bible study, but a primary focus was always pastoral care. Some have maintained that there is nothing unique to the Stone-Campbell Movement regarding pastoral care. However, one distinctive of the Movement has always been the emphasis on the local congregation, as the priesthood of believers, in which all Christian members are called to engage in the basic primary pastoral care in mutual relationships with each other. This theme has been a constant throughout its history.

See also Ministry

BIBLIOGRAPHY Don Browning, *The Moral Context of Pastoral Care* (1976) • Don Browning, *Religious Thought and the Modern Psychologies* (1987) • David Edwin Harrell, Jr., "The Disciples of Christ–Church of Christ Tradition," in *Care and Curing: Health and Medicine in the Western Religious Traditions,* ed. Ronald Numbers and Darrell Amundsen (1986), pp. 376-96 • E. Brooks Holifield, *A History of Pastoral Care in America* (1983) • Charles F. Kemp, *The Caring Pastor* (1985) • Charles F. Kemp, *Physicians of the Soul: A History of Pastoral Counseling* (1947) • Thomas Munnell, *Care of All the Churches* (1888).

MARK H. MANASSEE

Pearre, Caroline Neville (1831-1910)

Known as the "Mother of the Christian Woman's Board of Missions," Caroline (Carrie) Neville was born near Clarksville, Tennessee, April 15, 1831. She was trained as a teacher and taught at several of the leading seminaries for young women in Missouri, Kentucky, and Ohio. In 1869 she married Sterling Elwood Pearre, a pastor who shared her commitment to domestic and foreign educational, evangelical, and relief efforts.

Having founded a mission organization in her church in Iowa City, Iowa, Caroline Neville Pearre (1831-1910) corresponded with other women in the Movement to organize similar societies, eventually bringing them together in the Christian Woman's Board of Missions. Courtesy of the Disciples of Christ Historical Society

Caroline Pearre was frustrated because the Christian Churches had no active missionaries or mission posts. So on April 10, 1874, while praying for those who did not yet know Christ, she committed herself to organizing Christian Church women for missionary work. In May she founded a missionary society at her church in Iowa City, then corresponded with other women who set up similar societies in their churches. Christian Woman's Board of Missions (CWBM) was established as a coalition of these local societies on October 21, 1874, during the meeting of the American Christian Missionary Society in Cincinnati. Caroline Pearre wrote the CWBM Constitution, served as its first corresponding secretary, and was a leading CWBM speaker for the rest of her life. She died on September 25, 1910, in Danville, Kentucky, leaving on her dressing table an envelope containing her CWBM offering.

See also Christian Woman's Board of Missions

DEBRA B. HULL

Pendleton, William Kimbrough (1817-1899)

A coworker, friend, and son-in-law of Alexander Campbell, Pendleton was an influential educator and leader of the Stone-Campbell Movement from 1840 until his retirement from public activity in 1887.

Born in 1817, Pendleton belonged to a well-to-do family that in the early 1830s embraced and championed the Campbells' reform in Louisa County, Virginia. He completed studies in the arts and sciences and then law at the University of Virginia. In 1840 he was admitted to the bar, baptized by immersion, and married to Lavinia Campbell, Alexander's daughter, whom he had met in church circles. The couple settled in Bethany, where William joined the Campbells' inner leadership council. Appointed to Bethany College's inaugural faculty as professor of natural philosophy and astronomy, he later served as professor of moral science and belles-lettres and vice president. He was a frequent contributor to the *Millennial Harbinger* and after 1844 its coeditor.

His wife Lavinia died in 1846. In 1847 he married her younger sister Clarinda, who died in 1851. His third marriage, in 1855, was to Catherine H. King, daughter of a Warren, Ohio, judge.

Public issues concerned Pendleton, who several times ran for political offices. He became a delegate to the 1872 West Virginia Constitutional Convention and thereafter state superintendent of public schools. The Pendletons' Bethany household was

W. T. Moore remarked in 1868 that William Kimbrough Pendleton was a man of tremendous intellect despite his nervousness and "feeble physical organization."
Courtesy of Bethany College

well known for gracious hospitality and social and cultural refinement.

After Campbell's death (1866), Pendleton became president of Bethany College and proprietor and senior editor of the *Harbinger.* He labored for the survival of both enterprises, unsuccessfully in the case of the journal, which folded in 1870. He later contributed to the *Christian Standard* and the *Christian Quarterly.*

Pendleton viewed himself as a voice of irenic moderation, urging avoidance of divisive extremism. Not everyone considered him noncontroversial. He was more responsive to emergent cultural and intellectual developments than many in the Movement. He advocated missionary societies and similar cooperative ventures, collaborating in founding the American Christian Missionary Society and formulating the Louisville Plan. On most disputed issues, he counseled tolerance, although not necessarily approval, of progressive opinion.

See also American Christian Missionary Society; Bethany College; *Christian Standard;* Louisville Plan, The; *Millennial Harbinger, The*

BIBLIOGRAPHY Frederick D. Power, *Life of William Kimbrough Pendleton, President of Bethany College* (1902).

JAMES O. DUKE

Pension Fund of the Christian Church (Disciples of Christ)

General unit of the Christian Church (Disciples of Christ).

A pensions and benefits instrumentality, its programs and services are made available to persons serving in various ministries and employed by organizations and units of the church. The initial charter calls for programs and services to be made available to ministers and employees of the Christian Church, Disciples of Christ and Churches of Christ. Benefits are provided on a fully funded and sound actuarial basis. In addition to the pension plan, the fund also provides a savings program, health care insurance, and other support systems. It also serves as the Board of Ministerial Relief and Assistance, extending relief, support, and assistance to persons who serve the Christian Church (Disciples of Christ) but are without contractual benefits, or for whom such are low, or absent, because of lack of church support.

The roots of the Pension Fund extend back into the nineteenth century. As a result of concerns expressed as early as 1883, the General Christian Missionary Convention appointed a Ministerial Board of Relief to consider the needs of the church's aged and disabled ministers. The Board of Ministerial Relief was formally organized in 1895 and incorporated in the state of Indiana in 1897.

The first attempt to provide contractual benefits was the 1919 Pension System. In 1928 the Board of Ministerial Relief became the Pension Fund of the Disciples of Christ, and a new pension plan was introduced in 1931. That same basic plan has continued into the twenty-first century, with major benefit adjustments in 1954, 1972, and 1982. The name of the organization was changed in 1972 to the Pension Fund of the Christian Church (Disciples of Christ). In 1973 "Special Apportionments" and "Good Experience Credits" were introduced, which added increases to pensions based on the fund's investment experience. Through the year 2000, pensions were increased by more than 500 percent on an accumulated basis. LESTER PALMER

Pepperdine University

Independent Christian university affiliated with Churches of Christ.

George Pepperdine (1886-1962), a successful

Christian businessman who established and developed the Western Auto Supply Company beginning in 1909, was a lifelong member of Churches of Christ, serving as an elder for more than thirty years. Pepperdine donated the funds to found George Pepperdine College on a thirty-four-acre campus near the Watts area of downtown Los Angeles. With 167 students in the opening class, the college was dedicated on September 21, 1937. George Pepperdine served as chairman of the board of trustees for the first twenty years of the school's existence. From 1937 to 1970, Pepperdine was primarily a small, undergraduate liberal arts college. In 1971, with the addition of graduate and professional schools, the college became Pepperdine University. When riots broke out near the Los Angeles campus during the civil rights movement, efforts to move the campus were already under way. Through the generous support of Mrs. Frank Roger Seaver, the Malibu campus was dedicated in 1972.

The founding president of George Pepperdine College was Batsell Baxter (1886-1956), who served two years from 1937 to 1939. Following Baxter, six presidents have led the school, including Hugh M. Tiner, who served 1939-57; M. Norvel Young, 1957-71; William S. Banowsky, 1971-78; Howard A. White, 1978-85; David Davenport, 1985-2000; and Andrew K. Benton, who was inaugurated in 2000.

From its beginning, Pepperdine has had a concern for the education of church leaders. In the early years it fulfilled this concern within the framework of the regular undergraduate bachelor's program. However, in the fall of 1944 the first graduate program in religion to be offered by a college affiliated with Churches of Christ was launched on Pepperdine's Los Angeles campus. This pioneering effort was led by W. B. West, Jr. (1907-1994), the chairman of Pepperdine's Religion Division. He was assisted by Batsell Barrett Baxter (1916-1982) and William M. Green (1897-1979).

From the beginning of Pepperdine's graduate program in religion, the following men have chaired the Religion Division: W. B. West, 1944-51; Joseph White, 1951-61; Howard Horton, 1961-64; Frank Pack, 1964-72 and 1980-83; Tony Ash, 1972-75; Carl Mitchell, 1975-80; Carroll Osburn, 1983-85; Tom Olbricht, 1985-96; and Rick Marrs, 1996-2003. An off-campus M.S. in Ministry program was created in the 1970s to help train church leaders who could not afford to move to Malibu. In the past twenty-five years this two-year program has been conducted in a variety of locations, including Seattle, Washington; Portland, Oregon; Boise, Idaho; Sacramento, Stockton, Campbell, Fresno, and San Diego, California; Phoenix, Arizona; and Albuquerque, New Mexico.

The Pepperdine Bible Lectures began in January 1943 and were modeled after similar programs at Abilene Christian, Lipscomb and Harding Universities. Throughout the 1940s this annual four-day forum grew in popularity, but the early 1950s saw a decline in attendance and no program was scheduled for 1957. The Bible Lectures took on new life with the arrival of M. Norvel Young (1915-1998) and J. P. Sanders (1906-2002) in the fall of 1957, and by 1961 the opening night program had been moved to the Shrine Auditorium. In the following years the program moved to the Los Angeles Sports Arena. The program declined again in the late 1960s, but following the move to Malibu in 1972 there was a renewal of interest. Since that time the Bible Lectures have grown in interest and attendance every year.

At the beginning of the twenty-first century Pepperdine enrolled about 8,000 students in five colleges and schools and offered bachelor's, master's, and doctoral degrees in a range of disciplines. In addition to the Malibu campus, the university maintains six education centers in Los Angeles, Orange, and Ventura counties. Pepperdine owns and operates campuses in England, Germany, Italy, and Argentina for study-abroad programs, and it has developed alliances with universities throughout Europe, Asia, Australia, and Latin America to facilitate student and faculty exchanges.

In the last decade of the twentieth century, Pepperdine began to be consistently ranked in the top echelon of America's national universities. The most distinctive feature of Pepperdine at the beginning of the third millennium was the fact that it maintained a serious commitment to a rigorous academic program in concert with a genuine concern for spiritual matters. At a time when many private universities in America were disengaging from their spiritual roots, Pepperdine was strengthening its ties to the spiritual heritage that gave it birth. A Center for Faith and Learning was established in 1999.

George Pepperdine's original statement of purpose remains the guiding principle of the university: "I am endowing this institution to help young men and women prepare themselves for a life of usefulness in this competitive world and to help them build a foundation of Christian character and faith which will survive the storms of life." Today the university is also guided by a twenty-seven-word mission statement approved by the board of regents in 1999. It reads: "Pepperdine is a Christian University committed to the highest standards of academic excellence and Christian values, where students are strengthened for lives of purpose, service, and leadership."

See also Baxter, Batsell Barrett; Lectureships; West, Willis Beauregard, Jr.

BIBLIOGRAPHY Jack W. Bates and Richard L. Clark, *Faith Is My Fortune: The Life Story of George Pepperdine* (1960)

• Bill Henegar and Jerry Rushford, *Forever Young: The Life and Times of M. Norvel Young & Helen M. Young* (1999) • Jerry Rushford, ed., *Crest of a Golden Wave: A 50th Anniversary Pictorial History of Pepperdine University, 1937-1987* (1987).
JERRY B. RUSHFORD

Philippines, The Movement in the

See Asia, Missions in

Phillips, Benjamin Dwight (1885-1968)

Philanthropist and benefactor for the Christian Churches/Churches of Christ and the Christian Church (Disciples of Christ).

B. D. Phillips was born into the prosperous Phillips family that conducted a petroleum business in western Pennsylvania. His father, Thomas W. Phillips, Sr., not only had adverse dealings with John D. Rockefeller of Standard Oil fame but was vehemently opposed to Rockefeller's gift of several thousand dollars to the Foreign Christian Missionary Society. T. W., Sr., was also the author of *The Church of Christ,* which went through a number of editions as written by "a Layman."

B. D. Phillips was born in New Castle, Pennsylvania, on November 20, 1885. He and his older brother, T. W., Jr., grew up in western Pennsylvania and set up the Phillips Trust fund with money left to them by their father. Later T. W., Jr.'s fortune would be included in this trust, largely dispensed to various Christian causes by B. D.; for example, such Disciples institutions as Bethany College, Hiram College (which B. D. attended), and Phillips University in Enid, Oklahoma, were recipients of the largess of this trust. The new name chosen by Oklahoma Christian University, Phillips University, was in honor of the Phillips family, which had given thousands of dollars to that institution.

B. D. Phillips not only gave himself to his business but became an outstanding church leader at the North Street Christian Church in Butler, Pennsylvania. Later, from the Phillips Trust (after the death of his brother and the acquisition of another fortune) the family built the Disciples of Christ Historical Society building in Nashville, the center of the archives and historical resources of all three streams of the Stone-Campbell Movement.

In more recent years, Phillips and his second wife, Mildred Welshimer Phillips, became tremendous donors to the schools and agencies of the Christian Churches/Churches of Christ. (Phillips himself broke with Disciples agencies, due to what he saw as the influx of theological liberalism within their leadership.) Such institutions as Milligan College, Johnson Bible College, Lincoln Christian Seminary, and, especially, Emmanuel School of Religion in Johnson City, Tennessee, were recipients of Phillips's wealth. He also helped to fund the publication and distribution of several anonymous pamphlets (later known to be written by J. D. Murch) against the "Restructure" movement among the Disciples. At his death all of the trust (between $20 and $25 million) was to be given for buildings and other material projects, since Phillips was very much opposed to a continuation of gift income through endowments, having come to distrust such endowments as prostituted by second- and third-generation leaders who had forgotten the "faith" of their fathers.

B. D. Phillips married his first wife, Anna Undine Conant, on April 6, 1909. To this union several children were born — three daughters: Stella, Claudine, and Undine, and three sons: B. D., Jr., Victor, and Donald. They were all reared at the Phillips mansion, Elm Court, in Butler, Pennsylvania. His first wife died in 1934, and he later married Mildred Welshimer (daughter of the prestigious Canton, Ohio, preacher, P. H. Welshimer) in July 1963. He died on October 23, 1968, and his second wife, Mildred, continued his philanthropic work until her death on May 2, 1983.

See also Bethany College; Disciples of Christ Historical Society; Emmanuel School of Religion; Hiram College; Johnson Bible College; Milligan College; Phillips, Thomas W.; Phillips University

BIBLIOGRAPHY J. D. Murch, *B. D. Phillips: Life and Letters* (privately published, 1969) • James DeForest Murch, *Adventures for Christ in Changing Times* (1973).
CHARLES R. GRESHAM

Phillips, Thomas W. (1835-1912)

Benefactor and author among Disciples of Christ in the late nineteenth and early twentieth centuries.

T. W. Phillips was born in Beaver County, Pennsylvania, on February 23, 1835, and died at New Castle, Pennsylvania, July 21, 1912. Though his father died just a few months after T. W.'s birth, his mother continued to nurture the family. They were fervent supporters of the Stone-Campbell Movement, and only ill health precluded the young Phillips from becoming a preacher in this Movement.

T. W. Phillips became a successful businessman. In 1861 he and his brothers acquired the largest oil well known in America at that time, flowing 4,000 barrels a day. For twenty-five years the Phillips brothers were the most successful men in the oil industry. In fact, it was reported at a government hearing that Phillips himself produced from one-tenth to one-sixth of all the crude oil produced in the United States.

Ruined at one time by John D. Rockefeller and the American "oil cartel," he recouped his wealth supported (in and out of Congress) by the development

Phillips's *The Church of Christ by a Layman* was a popular manifesto restating the nineteenth-century plea for the New Testament as the only basis for Christian union and the only constitution for the church. Courtesy of the Disciples of Christ Historical Society

of a system in which the enterprisers would be protected from the "robber barons." As a result, he was appointed to the Industrial Commission on July 18, 1894. As chairman of this quasi-governmental committee, he was influential in developing the U.S. Departments of Labor and Commerce.

But it is in the religious system that T. W. Phillips left his greatest mark. He anonymously authored *The Church of Christ by a Layman* (published in 1905 by a secular press). The book would later be published by Standard Publishing after all rights were purchased by T. W.'s sons and given to the Cincinnati publisher. T. W. Phillips, Jr., provided a new biographical introduction when the book reappeared in 1916. The book continued to be printed for many years and has had a substantial impact upon generations of teachers and leaders in conservative segments of the Movement since its original publication.

In 1865, in his home in New Castle, Pennsylvania, Phillips and four other men laid the plans for the journal *Christian Standard* (1866-) and the Standard Publishing Company (est. 1872). His benevolence extended not only to publication enterprises but also to educational institutions. He supported Hiram College, Bethany College, and the new Oklahoma Christian University in Enid, Oklahoma, presided over by his friend, E. V. Zollars. Oklahoma Christian changed its name to Phillips University because of the Phillips largesse.

After his death in 1912, Phillips's sons, T. W., Jr., and B. D., continued this benevolence, and the death of the sons led to the establishment of the Phillips Trust, which has dispensed millions of dollars to various educational and benevolence institutions. One noteworthy result of this benevolence was the impressive Gothic-style building constructed for the Disciples of Christ Historical Society in Nashville.

See also *Christian Standard;* Phillips University; Standard Publishing Company

BIBLIOGRAPHY Charles R. Gresham, "Portrait of a Layman," *Christian Standard* 101 (1966): 846, 865 • James DeForest Murch, *B. D. Phillips* (1969) • T. W. Phillips, *The Church of Christ, by a Layman* (1905) • T. W. Phillips, Jr., "Biographical Sketch," in T. W. Phillips, *The Church of Christ* (new ed. 1916).

CHARLES R. GRESHAM

Phillips Bible Institute

Short-lived ministerial training school for conservative Disciples preachers in Canton, Ohio, in the early twentieth century.

After conservative biblical scholar J. W. McGarvey died in 1911, and with the advent of the more liberal A. W. Fortune at the College of the Bible in Lexington, Kentucky, concerned individuals founded Phillips Bible Institute to provide ministerial and biblical education for men within the Stone-Campbell Movement. Since it was designed and financed by T. W. Phillips (who died during the school's first year of operation) and the Phillips family, it was given the Phillips name when incorporated. The needs of men who could not attend the traditional college had been in the mind of T. W. Phillips for almost fifteen years (according to his son, T. W. Phillips, Jr.). A founding committee of Russell Errett, S. S. Lappin, E. W. Thornton, E. J. Meacham, Martin L. Pierce, and P. H. Welshimer met in 1911 and developed the plans for the institute. It opened its doors in the fall of 1912 at First Christian Church, Canton, Ohio. It was finally incorporated in April 1913. Though it may have matriculated 643 students in those first years, special attention was given to the 82 resident students. After its first year, and with the death of T. W. Phillips, the school was poorly supported and had to close its doors in 1916, whereupon the trustees assumed its debts and assets.

CHARLES R. GRESHAM

Phillips Theological Seminary

Related to the Christian Church (Disciples of Christ).

In February 1906, Ely Vaughn Zollars pointed to a map and declared dramatically to Frank Hamilton Marshall that he was going to start a new school in Oklahoma. Zollars had recently resigned as president of Texas Christian University. His plan was to found a new Bible college to educate ministers for the almost 500 churches that had sprung up in the area that would become Oklahoma in the following year.

Negotiations with several potential cities expanded the scope of the original plan. When Oklahoma Christian University (after 1912, Phillips University) held its first classes on September 17, 1907, in Enid, Oklahoma, it had, at least in concept, twelve constituent schools, including the College of the Bible and a College of Liberal Arts. However, only about twenty of the 356 students met college entrance requirements, while the majority commenced their studies as "sub-freshmen" in the university's Preparatory School, which was accredited in 1913 by the North Central Association of Colleges and Schools (NCA) as a high school.

While in the earliest years most degree-level students had been enrolled in the College of the Bible, by 1913 there were around 100 students in the College of Liberal Arts — about the same number as in the College of the Bible. Marshall had administrated both colleges, but in 1913, at Marshall's request, a separate dean was appointed for Liberal Arts. The College of the Bible received NCA accreditation in 1919.

The College of the Bible, from its inception, offered the A.B., A.M., and B.D. degrees. The first A.B. earned through the College of the Bible was conferred on William L. LeMay in May 1908. Each of the six A.B. graduates of 1909, including Claude C. Taylor, were ministerial candidates from the College of the Bible. Taylor joined the faculty and, in 1924, earned the first B.D. Graduate courses for the A.M. commenced in 1920, the year after NCA accreditation.

In 1940 the College of the Bible joined the newly formed American Association of Theological Schools (AATS — now ATS). In order to prepare for AATS accreditation, the college's faculty, in 1944, was divided into two groups: the graduate faculty chaired by Dean Marshall, and the undergraduate faculty chaired by Dr. Robert Martin. In order to meet the AATS requirement of separate facilities and library for graduate theological education, a beautiful new Prairie Gothic building was completed in 1950, henceforth to be known as the Marshall Building. AATS accreditation, for the graduate program only, was secured in 1951 on the basis of the division of the College of the Bible into two schools: the Graduate Seminary and the undergraduate school.

In 1960 these two schools gained their own deans. Stephen J. England, who had succeeded Marshall in 1942 and since 1951 had been dean of both the Graduate Seminary and the undergraduate Bible college, remained dean of the seminary. Robert Martin became dean of the undergraduate school, which retained the name College of the Bible.

Dean England retired in 1962. He was succeeded by J. Daniel Joyce (1962-74), Fred B. Craddock (acting: 1974-75), Joe R. Jones (1975-79), James F. Caton (1980-83), C. William Bryan (interim: 1983-84), and Roger Sizemore (1984-87). During this period the seminary changed the B.D. to an M.Div. (1968) and added the M.R.E. (1962) and D.Min. (1972) programs. It also established a teaching center at the University of Tulsa in 1986, which grew rapidly into a campus.

The Graduate Seminary remained an integral component of Phillips University until 1987. AATS had recommended that the seminary should have its own board of trustees, but although an advisory council was established in 1953, the seminary did not obtain its own board until formal separation from the university. This separation resulted, primarily, from the university's entering into an agreement with the city of Enid whereby the city bought the campus and then leased it back to the university. Separation of church and state prevented the implementation of this agreement as long as the university operated a theological seminary.

On June 11, 1987, the seminary was incorporated separately. Roger Sizemore was elected as the first president of Phillips Graduate Seminary on March 24, 1988. He resigned in February 1990. Harold Hatt was acting president until William Tabbernee took up his duties as president on April 23, 1991. The M.T.S. degree was added to the curriculum in 1990 and the M.A.M.C. in 2001.

The name of the institution was changed to Phillips Theological Seminary in 1995. Two years later the trustees decided to consolidate the seminary's Enid and Tulsa campuses. The transition to Tulsa was completed in 1999, and the whole seminary moved into a new campus in 2003.

Phillips Theological Seminary (in its different manifestations) has produced over 3,000 leaders for the Stone-Campbell Movement and the wider church.

See also England, Stephen J.; Oklahoma Christian University; Phillips University

BIBLIOGRAPHY Stephen J. England, *Oklahoma Christians* (1975) • Cynthia Gustafson, "The History of Phillips Theological Seminary" (unpublished paper, Tulsa, 2000) • Frank H. Marshall et al., *Phillips University's First Fifty Years,* vols. 1-3 (1957, 1960, 1964).

WILLIAM TABBERNEE

Phillips University

Oklahoma educational institution established by Disciples of Christ.

A year after Dr. Ely Vaughn Zollars, a nationally prominent Christian educator, envisioned a Christian college on the plains of what was then the Oklahoma Territory, Phillips University began instruction in September 1907. Classes for Oklahoma Christian University, as it was first named, started in unfinished buildings with Dr. Zollars as the school's first president. In 1913 the school changed its name to Phillips University in honor of T. W. Phillips, a Pennsylvania philanthropist and principal benefactor of the university. Zollars was president for nearly a decade, to be followed by ten more presidents before Phillips University closed academically in 1998 and held its final commencement on January 23, 1999.

The Phillips University Legacy Foundation (PULF) exists as a scholarship-granting agency to award faculty/professional development scholarships for faculty at Disciples of Christ colleges and universities. These grants are designed to help provide faculty with continuing education opportunities to enhance teaching skills, scholarly production, or artistic development and provide leadership to the academic, church, local, and world communities. PULF also has an undergraduate scholarship program designed to serve potential leaders for the church who attend Disciples colleges and universities and former staff of Phillips University who are pursuing a baccalaureate degree and who were employed at least one year full time during 1992-98.

Phillips Theological Seminary, formerly a part of the university as Phillips Graduate Seminary, was separately incorporated in 1987. However, the seminary did not change its name until 1995. All Phillips University academic records were transferred to Phillips Theological Seminary.

See also Phillips Theological Seminary

TERRY MIETHE

Pickens, James Madison (1836-1881)

Leader in the Stone-Campbell Movement in north Alabama from his arrival in 1866 until his death in 1881.

When Pickens arrived in north Alabama he began to help the churches heal from the Civil War. He conducted a school at Mountain Home, near Moulton, Alabama, from 1868 to 1875. He published the *Christian Weekly* from 1870 through 1871. He then published the *Southern Christian Weekly* from 1872 until 1875. He was a powerful debater and a beloved evangelist. His strong opposition to the "Louisville Plan" of 1869 rendered the missionary society in north Alabama powerless for several years after his death.

In 1880 Pickens ran for governor of Alabama and was defeated. He was shot and killed in January 1881, while trying to break up an argument between neighbors. Leadership among the Churches of Christ in north Alabama then fell upon Pickens's friend T. B. Larimore.

See also Larimore, Theophilus Brown; Louisville Plan, The; Mountain Home School

BIBLIOGRAPHY B. F. Manire, "Obituary of J. M. Pickens," *Gospel Advocate* (February 17, 1881) • James Madison Pickens, Jr., *Biographical Sketch of James Madison Pickens, Sr.* (1936).

C. WAYNE KILPATRICK

Pinkerton, Lewis Letig (1812-1875)

L. L. Pinkerton, sometimes labeled the first "liberal" of the Stone-Campbell Movement, endorsed "open membership," rejected the plenary inspiration of the Bible, and encouraged one of the first usages of a musical instrument (a melodeon) in worship (1859) at Midway, Kentucky. Pinkerton, after being baptized by Alexander Campbell (1830), studied to become a medical doctor in Trenton, Ohio. After becoming a doctor, he moved to Carthage, Ohio, where Walter Scott was preaching. Pinkerton forfeited his medical

Founder of Midway College and a noted liberal of his day, L. L. Pinkerton (1812-1875) also established an independent congregation for slaves in Midway, Kentucky, in 1852.
Courtesy of the Disciples of Christ Historical Society

practice and began preaching (1838). Soon he moved to Kentucky and preached for Lexington's Hill Street congregation, and then at Midway for sixteen years.

His deep concern for social action was displayed even in the face of strong opposition. He championed the causes of temperance and abolitionism. He began the Female Orphanage School (now Midway College) and established an independent African American congregation in Midway (1852) for slaves.

Later he became professor of English literature at Kentucky University (1860) in Harrodsburg, Kentucky. He enlisted, at the age of 50, as a surgeon in the Union Army's 11th Kentucky Cavalry (1862). Eventually, he collapsed due to heat stroke and exhaustion, and never fully recovered.

Following the war, due to mounting opposition to his Union loyalties, he resigned from Kentucky University and was excluded from most pulpits. He refused to leave Kentucky even though he remained unemployed for seven years. During that time he began the *Independent Monthly*, which contained fiery prose and personal attacks against those who opposed him. Finally, President Grant appointed him special mail agent (1873), a post he held until his death on his birthday, January 28, 1875.

See also Instrumental Music; Liberalism; Midway College; Open Membership

BIBLIOGRAPHY L. L. Pinkerton, *A Discourse Concerning Some Effects of the Late Civil War on Ecclesiastical Matters in Kentucky* (1866) • J. Shackleford, ed., *Life, Letters and Addresses of Dr. L. L. Pinkerton* (1876).

JOHN D. WINELAND

Pioneer Bible Translators

International Bible translation ministry based in Dallas, Texas, and supported by the Christian Churches/Churches of Christ.

Pioneer Bible Translators was incorporated in 1976 to translate Scripture into the native languages of people groups not formerly having access to the Bible in their own tongue. The ministry also has programs for literacy, training leadership, and church planting. In 2000 the organization employed 107 missionaries serving in nineteen active language programs in Papua New Guinea, Tanzania, Guinea and Equatorial Guinea, Asia, and the Ukraine.

RONDAL B. SMITH

Platte Valley Bible College

Platte Valley Bible College (PVBC) is a four-year senior college located in the western Nebraska panhandle community of Scottsbluff. Church leaders from Nebraska, Colorado, and Wyoming established the college in 1951 to prepare individuals for ministry, Christian leadership, and medical missions. Dr. Ellis Baker, a Scottsbluff medical doctor, served as the college's first president.

Isabel Maxey Dittamore, a missionary to Tibet, urged the establishment of a medical missions program after her husband Warren died of typhoid fever in 1946. Ellis Baker and his brother Paul, also a medical doctor, were the mainstays of a program that lasted eighteen years. During that period the PVBC medical missions program was the only program of that nature offered in the Bible colleges of the Christian Churches/Churches of Christ. The medical program ended when interest waned and it became difficult to provide faculty.

PVBC first held classes in the facilities of local congregations in Scottsbluff. In 1966 the college built its current facility. In 1986 it entered into a cooperative relationship with Western Nebraska Community College to enable students to have access to a broad range of courses beyond the Bible college curriculum. PVBC offers a two-year Associate of Arts degree in Bible and four-year Bachelor of Arts and Bachelor of Science degrees, each with a major in Bible and ministries.

MICHAEL W. HINES

"Plea," The

Byword for the original message of the Stone-Campbell Movement and its leaders' appeal to sympathetic minds, thus sometimes known as the "Restoration Plea."

The basic notion was that Christians would find unity by restoring the belief and practice of the churches represented in the New Testament, without "human innovations." For Alexander Campbell and others, unity based on the scriptural pattern would lead to the evangelization of the world, and this unity could usher in the millennium. The plea finds early expression in both Alexander Campbell's and Barton Stone's discussions of restoring the ancient order. Thomas Campbell's *Declaration and Address* expresses this concept in speaking of the "plea for reformation." Later Isaac Errett and many others would invoke "the plea" as a shorthand for the Movement's basic message. Seeking Christian unity through the simple New Testament message provided an effective rhetorical strategy for gaining adherents in democratic American society. Also in debating the Movement's divisions, some persons invoked the plea rhetorically to identify themselves as loyal to the Movement's original message as distinguished from those who forsook it.

While the critical element was restoration, the plea brought together the Stone-Campbell Movement's themes of unity, New Testament primitivism, evangelism, and eschatology. Since the plea assumed that the Bible conveyed a consistent, unified form of Christian belief and practice, the advent of liberal critical biblical study with its conclusions concerning the New Testament's theological pluralism made advocating the plea problematic.

Fervent liberals in the Movement in the early twentieth century, zealous to appropriate higher criticism and a progressive worldview, aspired to empty the plea altogether of its restorationist impulse and to align the Movement's vocation more closely with the agenda of mainline Protestantism and the emerging ecumenical movement. Since the Churches of Christ and Christian Churches/Churches of Christ have generally rejected or appropriated in a truncated form the pluralistic conclusions of biblical higher criticism, those groups have continued to invoke the plea to a greater extent. Reflecting on divisions in the Stone-Campbell Movement, some interpreters have contended that a tension exists between the plea's themes of restoration and unity.

See also *Declaration and Address;* "Restoration," Meanings of within the Movement; Unity, Christian

BIBLIOGRAPHY M. Eugene Boring, *Disciples and the Bible: A History of Disciples Biblical Interpretation in North America* (1997) • Alfred T. DeGroot, *The Restoration Principle* (1960) • Anthony L. Dunnavant, Richard T. Hughes, and Paul M. Blowers, *Founding Vocation and Future Vision: The Self-Understanding of Disciples of Christ and Churches of Christ* (1999) • J. M. Powell, *The Cause We Plead: A Story of the Restoration Movement* (1987).

JESS O. HALE, JR.

Pleasant Hill Female Seminary

Early venture in women's education in the Stone-Campbell Movement.

In 1819 Jane Campbell, daughter of Thomas Campbell, moved with her family to West Middletown, Pennsylvania. Within two years she opened a home-based school for girls and boys and married Matthew McKeever. By 1830 that school was known as Pleasant Hill Seminary. About 1842 coeducational Pleasant Hill Seminary became Pleasant Hill Female Seminary, with Jane Campbell McKeever as its principal. She continued as principal until 1866, when her son, Thomas Campbell McKeever, took over. Within a few months Thomas died, and Jane returned as principal until 1868. The seminary's last graduating class was in 1869, and Pleasant Hill Female Seminary closed sometime in the mid-1870s, shortly before Bethany College began admitting women.

Though the seminary's three-year curriculum included a blend of modern-day high-school and college coursework, many of its courses, texts, and teachers were the same as those of nearby Bethany College.

The McKeevers were strong abolitionists, and their farm near the seminary was used as a station on the Underground Railroad, although there is no evidence that the seminary was involved. Graduates of the seminary prominent in the Stone-Campbell Movement include Jennie Reader Errett, Decima Campbell Barclay, Mary J. Cooney, Sarah Jane McFarland, and Lorinda McKeever Wilkin.

See also Bethany College; Education, Philosophy of; Higher Education, Views of in the Movement; McKeever, Jane Campbell; McKeever Family; Midway College

BIBLIOGRAPHY Jane Reader Errett, "Pleasant Hill Seminary," *Christian Standard* 46 (1910): 1396-1400 • John H. Hull, "Jane Campbell McKeever," *Discipliana* 52:1 (1992): 7-12.

JOHN H. HULL

Postmillennialism

See Eschatology

Potter Bible College

Potter Bible College (1901-1913) was an outgrowth of the Nashville Bible School, now Lipscomb University, which was projected to exceed its capacity after ten years in operation. Opinions differed among supporters of Christian education in Churches of Christ as to whether it would be better served by one large school or two smaller ones. Clinton C. Potter and his wife Mary proposed that a new school be founded in Bowling Green, Kentucky, and offered their farm to this end. James A. Harding (1848-1922) and his son-in-law, J. N. Armstrong (1870-1944), agreed to assist in founding the new school, which would open in September 1901, taking with them some faculty and students from Nashville Bible School.

On the Potters' 140-acre farm, several buildings were constructed that served the college during its twelve years of existence. These facilities included three new buildings and two rented houses as well as the Potters' home, which housed the Harding family and some of the young women in the college. The initial investment by the Potters in buildings and equipment was $25,000.

No board of trustees was appointed, and the property always remained in the name of the Potters. A verbal agreement between Harding and the Potters stipulated that Harding would oversee the school and the Potters would run the farm, which was intended to be the sole support of the school. This was a matter of conscience for Harding, who opposed endowments and fixed salaries as an indication of a lack of faith in God's provision.

The enrollment for the first year was 107 students from seventeen states. The total number of students during the years the college existed was 657. The nine faculty members received no salaries but participated equally in the proceeds of the school. Since the farm was expected to support the school, tuition and board were set at a low rate. There was no effort to solicit gifts, a unique situation for such schools.

The school's reason for existence was the teaching of the Bible, which every student studied daily. The traditional degrees, Bachelor of Arts, Bachelor of Science, and Bachelor of Literature, were granted, and a Master of Arts was offered for completion of two years of work beyond the bachelor degree. There were few extracurricular activities other than intramural sports.

Personal loyalties to Harding kept the school operating in spite of the fact that it never became self-supporting as the Potters expected. Harding's declining health forced him to resign during the term of 1911-12; he was succeeded by George A. Klingman (1865-1939). Efforts to overcome the deficits were not successful, and the school was forced to close in 1913. The Potters personally assumed the debts of the school.

Mr. and Mrs. Potter then decided to divert their interests toward the founding of an orphan's home as a memorial to Eldon Potter, son of Mary Potter and her first husband, Albert. Potter Orphan Home continues to exist on the original location and is overseen by members of Churches of Christ.

See also Harding, James Alexander

BIBLIOGRAPHY Allen Phy, *Hands of Service* (1979) • Ben F. Taylor, *History of Potter Orphan Home and Genealogy of the Potter Family* (1956) • M. Norvel Young, *A History of the Colleges Established and Controlled by Members of the Churches of Christ* (1949). CAROLYN T. WILSON

Potter Orphan Home and School

See Children's Homes and Orphanages

Pounds, Jessie Brown (1861-1921)

Novelist, hymn lyricist, poet, and editor.

Pounds published six novels, eighty stories, 800 hymns, and numerous poems, essays, and articles. She edited four journals related to the Stone-Campbell Movement: *Disciple of Christ,* the *Christian Standard,* the *Christian-Evangelist,* and *The Christian Century.*

Pounds's novels depict life within the Stone-Campbell Movement throughout the nineteenth century, drawing on her personal contacts with pioneers and luminaries, including notably James A. Garfield. Among her enduring hymns are "Anywhere with Jesus," "Beautiful Isle of Somewhere," "I Know That My Redeemer Liveth," "The Way of the Cross Leads Home," and "The Touch of His Hand."

Jesse Brown Pounds (1861-1921) wrote 800 hymns, including "The Way of the Cross Leads Home," "Anywhere with Jesus," and "I Know that My Redeemer Liveth."
Courtesy of the Disciples of Christ Historical Society

See also Hymnody; Literature

BIBLIOGRAPHY Sandra Parker, *After the Western Reserve: The Ohio Fiction of Jessie Brown Pounds* (1999) • John Pounds, *Jesse Brown Pounds: Memorial Selections* (1921).
THEODORE N. THOMAS

Prayer

Alexander Campbell defined prayer as communion with God, a communion that was lost in Adam but restored in Christ. He called it "the *sanctum sanctorum,* the holy of holies, the inmost temple of religion." He did not, however, understand this communion in mystical terms. God had spoken to people through angels, patriarchs, prophets, Christ, and the apostles, but now speaks to people through the written Word. People's response is prayer, and, for Campbell, prayers are heard only if people listen to God by listening to the words of Scripture. Without this communion with God they are not fit for heaven.

This communion is maintained through constant prayers, supplications, and thanksgivings night and day.

For Campbell, prayer is the Christian's breath, without which one cannot live a happy life. It is a divinely chartered right and privilege. He emphasized the importance of private prayer, which provided less temptation to depart from the real purposes of prayer. Although he believed in public prayer, he said that such prayer is designed for the human ear and is subject to many abuses.

Jesus taught people to pray for food, raiment, and health, but Campbell insisted that the laws of nature will not be changed in order for prayers to be answered. People pray in faith when they ask for what God has promised, and God will answer prayers in subordination to natural law.

One of the more controversial elements in Campbell's thought was the notion that God does not hear the prayer of people without faith. No one can pray authentically or have any Christian experience before conversion. Campbell often wrote against the idea of religion based on religious experiences. For him, the truth of God comes only through Scripture. The experience of prayer can teach only what is already taught in the Bible. There can be no new Christian ideas that are not already found in Scripture.

Christians must still do battle with the world, the flesh, and the devil, and one way they do this is through prayer, which creates a relish for communion with God and a desire for a community of kindred spirits. Spiritual disciplines such as meditation, self-examination, and Bible study will turn people's attention toward heaven and generate prayer and praise to God. Campbell's basic approach was that God communes with people through Scripture and people commune with God through prayer.

Robert Richardson, while devoted to Alexander Campbell, pursued a more mystical approach to spirituality. His views were expressed in a series of articles titled "Communings in the Sanctuary" in the *Millennial Harbinger,* later published cumulatively as a book. Richardson wrote frequently on spiritual union and habitual fellowship with God. There can be no such fellowship, he wrote, without prayer. Prayer also helps people overcome the desire for lives of worldly pleasure. He was concerned that prayer could be disconnected from faith and agreed with Campbell that prayer without faith was ineffectual. It is the prayer of faith that saves, he said, and people can expect answers to prayer when their requests are in accordance with the will of God.

Barton W. Stone defined prayer as "the offering up of our desires to God for things agreeable to his will." The habit of prayer produces a habitual sense of God's presence and an awareness of dependence upon God. This, for him, was the foundation of a holy life, for it was prayer that formed a holy character. It is a means by which the grace of God is received, and a way of enjoying communion with the Father and the Son.

Calling prayer "the delightful exercise of the pious," Stone asked why people should pray when God already knows their wants. He answered that God has made it a duty for us to pray for the things God has in store for people. Such prayer teaches dependence upon God and generates a spirit of gratitude. Differing from Campbell, Stone said that if life is governed by immutable laws, there would be no point in prayer. He noted that from the beginning of Christianity saints have prayed and their prayers have been answered. People cannot simply pray in the belief that they can receive only what natural law has already given. The gospel consists of promises, and by hope in these promises people draw near to God in prayer.

Stone also differed from Campbell on the issue of whether anyone could pray before baptism. Stone noted that many biblical characters, such as Saul of Tarsus, the publican, Lydia, and the Syrophoenician woman all prayed before they were immersed, and their prayers were heard and accepted. He quoted Isaiah 55:6-7 as a biblical justification. Likewise, he responded to a question by saying that the practice of mourners praying with the congregation was not contrary to the spirit of the gospel. He encouraged people to pray to be filled with the Holy Spirit as a way to be quickened in the ways of God.

See also Devotional Literature; Worship

BIBLIOGRAPHY Alexander Campbell, "Short Sermons on Christian Practice: Sermons on Prayer — Nos. I-III," *Millennial Harbinger* (1839): 204-7, 272-75, 326-28 • Alexander Campbell, "Tracts for the People — No. XXXI: Prayer," *Millennial Harbinger* (1849): 1-12 • William O. Paulsell, *Disciples at Prayer: The Spirituality of the Christian Church (Disciples of Christ)* (1996) • Robert Richardson, *Communings in the Sanctuary* (1872; repr. ed. 2000).

WILLIAM O. PAULSELL

Preaching

1. Nineteenth Century
2. Twentieth Century
   2.1. Christian Church (Disciples of Christ)
   2.2. Christian Churches/Churches of Christ
   2.3. Churches of Christ

The Stone-Campbell Movement, like other Protestant movements and denominations in nineteenth- and twentieth-century America, developed its own standards of homiletic discourse respondent to prevailing trends, and cultivated its own tradition of honored preachers and sermons.

1. Nineteenth Century

Two men named Dwight are the alpha and omega of preachers in American Protestantism during the nineteenth century: Timothy Dwight (1752-1817), grandson of Jonathan Edwards and eminent Congregationalist preacher and theologian in New England; and Dwight L. Moody (1837-1899), the pioneer of urban crusade evangelism. Between them came a line that includes many of the greatest preachers of American church history. Besides the theological legacies of their church traditions, those preachers inherited important cultural legacies of the eighteenth century: a young constitutional democracy born of the American Revolution; the new movements of the Didactic Enlightenment (namely, Baconian science, Lockean empiricism, and Common Sense philosophy); and the emerging science of biblical criticism. To these they responded both positively and negatively, and in so doing they shaped homiletic traditions that would endure into the twentieth century. Among them were some esteemed preachers of the Stone-Campbell Movement.

During the first half of the nineteenth century the preachers who got the attention of the public were involved in great movements of revival or reform. Timothy Dwight led in the Second Great Awakening from his position as president of Yale College and helped to champion the "New Divinity," a movement to mitigate high Calvinism, to which Dwight contributed a critique of the notion of original sin and a strong emphasis on human agency in conversion. Lyman Beecher (1775-1863), one of Dwight's Yale students, heard Dwight's challenge and became a leading evangelist. His sermon "A Plea for the West" (1835) roused a whole generation of preachers to the mission of the American Protestant churches to America's western frontier and to the whole world. Charles G. Finney (1792-1875) left his practice of law to preach a profoundly modified version of Calvinism on the frontier of his day, urging people to make individual decisions for Christ.

Into this scene came Barton W. Stone (1772-1844) and his colleagues, who burst onto the public consciousness in Kentucky at the Cane Ridge Revival of 1801. The irenic yet anti-Calvinist spirit of Stone impelled him to preach a message that he believed to be based solely on biblical texts, to push aside divisive doctrinal issues, and to advocate for a liberated and rationally enabled faith. Stone's emphases resonated in the Cane Ridge Revival, where preachers of different denominations were able to speak freely to great crowds of people. The obvious effectiveness of such biblical preaching encouraged Stone and others to drop their denominational distinctives and to preach and worship in a manner they believed to be displayed on the pages of the New Testament.

This preceded by just a few years the preaching of Thomas Campbell and Alexander Campbell. Their preaching, like Stone's, was driven by the desire to unite rather than divide Christians and to return from speculative theology to what they identified as the gospel and the "ancient order" as the rallying point of that unity. In his famous "Sermon on the Law," preached to the Redstone Baptist Association in 1816, Alexander Campbell distinguished various covenants described in the Bible and held that it was the Christian gospel and that gospel alone that Christians were to preach — that any attempt to make the Mosaic law applicable to the Christian life conflicted with the Lord's own commission. So for Campbell the primary source of preaching was the New Testament. He made a further distinction by differentiating between *kērygma* and *didachē*. The former, he maintained, was the presentation of the facts of the gospel of Christ's life, death, and resurrection so that people could exercise their faith for salvation. The latter was the teaching of doctrines and ethical principles to believers to establish them in the faith and guide them in Christian living. For Campbell, *kērygma* was for unbelievers and *didachē* was for use in the assemblies of believers.

Alexander Campbell's preaching was carefully formulated as a logical analysis of either a given text or a subject. He clearly defined his terms; he used the latest methods of biblical interpretation available to him; and he helped people to see how the biblical material could be applied in their lives and in the life of the church. In *The Christian System* Campbell asserted that preachers should "first address themselves to the understanding, by a declaration or narrative of the wonderful works of God. They state, illustrate, and prove the great facts of the gospel; they lay the whole record before their hearers; and when they have testified what God has done, what he has promised, and threatened, they exhort their hearers on these premises, and persuade them to obey the gospel, to surrender themselves to the guidance and direction of the Son of God. They address themselves to the whole man, his understanding, will and affections, and approach the heart by taking the citadel of the understanding."

Walter Scott, more than any other figure in the Movement's early history, integrated the invitation to return to primitive Christianity with the revivalism of the frontier as he preached to thousands of people with an offer of salvation received by an act of intelligent human will. Scott had the most complete formal education of all the early leaders of the Movement. He and the Campbells assumed that faith was to accept the apostolic testimony of the facts of the life, crucifixion, and resurrection of Jesus Christ. Scott preached those facts in a clear and compelling way and thus set the stage for evangelism among the followers of Stone and Campbell as well as many others.

Thus one can see the early Stone-Campbell preachers as operating squarely in the context of the major homiletical controversy of the Second Great Awakening: the issue of conversion — whether it was sudden or gradual, and whether it was entirely a work of the Holy Spirit or involved human means as well. Some Baptists and Congregationalists tried to hold to the older understanding of Calvinism that conversion was totally the work of the Holy Spirit and would happen suddenly with an overwhelming experience of grace. Finney, on the other hand, defended a newer Calvinistic approach in which human means, such as the protracted meeting, the anxious bench, and direct appeals to the will, induced the expected experience. In either case, it was expected that the sign of election would be a definitive emotional experience. The Methodists, although not bothered by the issue of irresistible grace, also expected some sort of emotional experience as part of the conversion process. Walter Scott made his appeal to the rational powers of his hearers, assuming that faith was a possibility of every hearer and that faith, repentance, and the obedience of baptism constituted the means of accessing the salvation offered by Christ to all. He added to those three steps the results of the remission of sins and the gift of the Holy Spirit, to give him his famous "Five Finger Exercise" by which to teach the plan of salvation.

Quite different from Scott, yet just as effective as a preacher, was "Raccoon" John Smith. With very little formal education, but with a quick, fertile mind, Smith became a powerful preacher first among the Regular (Calvinistic) Baptists and then among the Reformers. Smith's use of wit and appeals to the heart made him a favorite in both congregations and camp meetings. He was instrumental in uniting of the followers of Stone and Campbell in 1831-32, and he was chosen to travel with John Rogers for three years urging congregations to unite. Smith worked prodigiously in Kentucky, preaching — in 1857 alone — over 500 sermons in addition to three public debates.

During the last half of the nineteenth century, as much of the Movement settled into the work of nurturing congregations, preaching developed into a pattern of biblical-doctrinal style. Many of the sermons preserved from that period trace a subject — usually a central doctrine — through the Bible. Since sermons were expected to last an hour or more, a rather complete study of a theme could be accomplished in one service. Sermon titles like James S. Lamar's "The History of Redemption Reproduced in the Redeemed" or J. S. Sweeney's "Baptism for Remission of Sins Is Justification by Faith" are not unusual. In this same period, the Stone-Campbell Movement became more self-conscious of developing its own preaching tradition, and sermons were collected into anthologies like W. T. Moore's *The Living Pulpit of the Christian Church* (1868), James Mathes's *The Western Preacher* (1888), or A. B. Maston's *The Gospel Preacher: A Book of Sermons by Various Writers* (1894).

The relative unity among Stone-Campbell Christians of the early decades was disrupted by the controversies of the middle and later years of the century. The disagreements over slavery and states rights that came to a head in the Civil War divided preachers as well as whole denominations. In the South, preachers generally upheld the institution of slavery as an important part of the fabric of society. As the war broke out, preachers on both sides tended to make their section's cause God's cause and thus demonize their opponents. This was just as true with Stone-Campbell preachers as with others. The first-generation leaders were heartbroken as they saw both their nation and their unity movement fractured by sectional disputes and outright war.

Another issue in American society at that time was the place of women in leadership, especially in the church. Many of the preachers involved in the movement to abolish slavery also took up the cause of the freedom of women to vote and to hold positions of public leadership. The voices of women preachers, such as Lucretia Mott, Sojourner Truth, Antoinette Brown, and Phoebe Palmer were undergirded by the male voices of Theodore Parker, Henry Ward Beecher, and others. The movement, which began in 1848 in Seneca, New York, was interrupted by the Civil War, and then was taken up with renewed vigor for the rest of the century, accelerated by the opportunities for women preachers in the Temperance crusade. Among the Stone-Campbell churches, women like Nancy Gove Cram and Abigale Roberts freely preached the plea to unite Christians by restoring primitive Christianity. In the later years of the century, former Temperance crusaders Clara Babcock (ordained in 1889) and Sarah (Sadie) McCoy Crank (ordained in 1892) were familiar names among the preachers in the Stone-Campbell Movement.

Late-nineteenth-century preaching among the churches of the Stone-Campbell Movement reflected the broad concerns of American Protestant preaching in this period: competent exegesis, candid treatment of the social and cultural challenges of the day, and evangelistic appeal. Some followed the pattern set by Alexander Campbell of careful exegesis of biblical passages and the tracing of themes through the Bible, especially the New Testament. Some concentrated on the pastoral concerns of the congregation, dealing with their problems and their responsibilities as Christians in society. Still others concentrated on evangelism, structuring assemblies after the pattern of revival meetings and ending sermons with an invitation to come to Christ. Many of the Stone-Campbell preachers were educated in law, and some had practiced law, so their sermons were often structured as legal arguments to convince an audience as an attorney tries to convince a jury. Sermon titles show this: "Jesus of Nazareth Is the Theanthropos," "What Must I Do to Be Saved?" "The Conditions of the Gospel Reasonable," "Baptism Essential to Salvation," "The Safety and Security of the Christian." Whether exegetical, pastoral, or evangelistic, the sermons appealed primarily to the rational mind and used anecdotes to add some emotion in the final appeal. Z. T. Sweeney composed a volume of *Pulpit Diagrams* (1897) that included ornate illustrative charts or figures to help the preacher explain complex biblical themes in simpler, memorable ways. The use of large preaching diagrams became a mainstay for some evangelists of the era, who sought an artistic flair for their didactic preaching.

Overall, such preaching methods were consistent with the Lockean epistemology and anthropology of the Campbells and their disciples, assuming that if one converts the mind to the gospel of salvation the heart will follow.

The seemingly rationalistic character of this Stone-Campbell preaching often strikes later generations as cold or sterile, but one cannot doubt the prominence of preaching and preachers in the cultivation of Christian society during that time. Stone-Campbell preachers were helping to mold a Christian movement and a nation, and in so doing they left a legacy of vital Christian communication for later generations. BRUCE E. SHIELDS

2. Twentieth Century

2.1. Christian Church (Disciples of Christ)

In the first half of the twentieth century, Disciples preaching tended to move in two streams. One stream, represented by Z. T. Sweeney (1849-1926) and P. H. Welshimer (1873-1957), tended to use the sermon to justify a "restoration" vision of Christian faith and to critique modernist impulses in the interpretation of the Bible and in theology. This stream was particularly influential among preachers and churches who ultimately identified with the North American Christian Convention and became the Christian Churches/Churches of Christ.

Another stream, represented by Edward Scribner Ames (1870-1958) and Herbert L. Willett (1864-1944), attempted to show compatibility between the modern worldview and Christian faith. The motif of Christian union came strongly to the fore. Many Disciples spoke about social issues, including poverty, exploitation of workers, and war.

Preachers in both streams used similar methods. While the preacher would announce a biblical text, it would function as a springboard to a theme the preacher would develop both from other biblical passages and from doctrine, philosophy, history, and literature. The theme was often theological and compelling, for example, "First Principles" (Sweeney), "What Does God Do?" (Willett), "The Appeal of the Cross" (Frank N. Dowling), "Violence to the Kingdom of God" (Burris Jenkins).

The thematic approach made it easy for many Disciples at mid-century to embrace "life situation" preaching, modeled on that of the celebrated American preacher Harry Emerson Fosdick (1878-1969). Optimally, the preacher would interpret a situation using resources from the Bible, theology, and the social sciences. Often, however, the preacher paid little attention to theology and drifted into moralizing and psychologizing.

In the middle of the twentieth century, a significant number of Disciples preachers followed a neo-Aristotelian method of preaching brought into Disciples circles by G. Edwin Osborn, who envisioned every sermon containing three appeals: to the mind, the heart, and the will.

Neo-orthodox theology, and its close companion, the biblical theology movement, began to have widespread effect on Disciples pulpits in the middle years of the century. Dwight E. Stevenson, an influential exponent of this approach, encouraged ministers to interpret the Bible as a primary source of divine revelation and, consequently, to "play" the searchlight of a biblical text "over the faces of the congregation, illuminating the shadowed places in the lives under the care of their preacher who is also their pastor." Many sermons in this era were deductive in movement and linear in form. The influence of this style is apparent in the sermons in an anthology edited by Hunter Beckelhymer, *The Vital Pulpit of the Christian Church* (1969).

During the middle years of the twentieth century, Disciples preachers chose biblical texts by free selection and often preached according to a combined Christian-civic calendar with key dates of Palm Sunday, Easter, Mother's Day, Memorial Day, Fourth of July, Labor Day, Thanksgiving, and Christmas. Disciples preachers gave less and less attention to themes that had been distinctive of Disciples theology and ecclesiology in earlier years.

In 1971 Fred Craddock published the single most influential work in preaching, not only in Disciples circles in the last third of the twentieth century, but in the entire North American preaching community, *As One Without Authority.* Craddock lyrically averred that many listeners no longer paid attention to sermons because they found sermons disconnected from life and boring. As a remedy, Craddock proposed inductive preaching, which takes as its model life experience itself and which allows listeners to come to their own conclusions. In 1978 Craddock extended this line of thinking in his *Overhearing the Gospel* by proposing that preachers frame messages not to speak directly to the congregation but to help the congregation overhear the gospel message. Craddock preached and lectured so widely in the Disciples that he was often regarded as "preacher to the denomination." A measure of Craddock's standing is that he is the only person in the *Concise Encyclopedia of Preaching* (1995) who is a contributor and whose work is the subject of an article.

The ecumenical orientation of the Disciples led to early acquaintance with the liturgical renewal movement in the wake of the Second Vatican Council. This movement emphasized the Christian year and the lectionary as frameworks for preaching. By the end of the twentieth century, several Disciples scholars of preaching informally estimated that more than half of all Disciples ministers were preaching from the Revised Common Lectionary.

In 1988 Joseph L. Faulkener conducted an empirical study of Disciples preaching, largely based in Anglo congregations, concluding that actual sermons often bypass the complex struggles faced by congregations in favor of "eternal truths" that are doctrinal in nature. Faulkener found "more declamation than analytical explanation," with a tendency toward abstraction rather than specific interaction with the congregational context. Many Disciples sermons assumed that the congregation "needs simply to be reassured that God does indeed love us." Faulkener noted only muted prophetic themes, and he cautioned preachers that it is "dangerous to assume much doctrinal sophistication or even biblical literacy on the part of the congregation."

Through most of the twentieth century, Anglo male Disciples preachers largely talked among themselves. In the last decades, Anglo males began to be aware of Disciples racial/ethnic and women preachers. The African American preaching tradition gained a greater denominationwide prominence than hitherto, as represented by recognition accorded to the preaching of the pastors of the two largest congregations of the Disciples: Cynthia L. Hale at Ray of Hope Christian Church (Disciples of Christ), Decatur, Georgia; and Alvin O. Jackson and his successor, Frank A. Thomas, at Mississippi Boulevard Christian Church (Disciples of Christ) in Memphis, Tennessee. Pablo Jiménez became widely recognized as a leading interpreter of Hispanic preaching among Disciples and throughout other churches. The work of Mary Donovan Turner, L. Susan Bond, and Mary Alice Mulligan has brought Disciples preaching into conversation with women's worlds of knowing and preaching.

Relative to the small size of the denomination, an unusually large number of scholars of preaching have emerged from the Disciples. At the cusp of the new millennium, some traditional Disciples themes have continued, such as interpretation of the breaking of the loaf (Joseph Jeter). Continuing a long Disciples tradition of bringing the gospel into dialogue with contemporary patterns of thought, some Disciples have begun to consider the relationship of postmodernism and preaching (Joseph Webb) and posed conversation as a paradigm for preaching (Ronald Allen). RONALD J. ALLEN

2.2. Christian Churches/Churches of Christ

The Stone-Campbell Movement originated in an era when public orations of two hours or more were common, appreciated, and expected. Nineteenth-century sermons in anthologies collected by W. T. Moore, B. C. Goodpasture, and Z. T. Sweeney are lengthy. They resemble biblical-doctrinal lectures or exhortations. Many trace a doctrine throughout the Bible, ending with encouragement for the hearers to change their lives. Others begin with a Christian claim or belief and develop its background before showing its clear meaning and contemporary relevance. They appeal to the rational processes in the hearers. They assume that once a person understands the subject that person will align his or her will to the gospel. Many conclude with emotional appeals that attempt to move people to repent.

The twentieth century saw several changes in public speaking style, including the length of time an audience will grant a speaker. Twenty to thirty minutes is about all a speaker can offer in North America on this side of 1945. A second important change has been a more holistic anthropology. The Enlightenment ideal emphasized the rational, whereas postmodern rhetorical and literary culture point toward the importance of emotions and imagination. This change has led to a shift from deductive, propositional, pedantic sermons to inductive, imaginative, poetic sermons.

In Christian Churches/Churches of Christ, one can trace these changes by reading representative sermons by P. H. Welshimer (1873-1957), Ard Hoven (1906-1987), Robert Shannon (b. 1930), Myron Taylor (b. 1924), Leroy Lawson (b. 1938), and Bob Russell (b. 1943) alongside those of Alexander Campbell, Moses Lard, and J. W. McGarvey. The latter three held forth in the nineteenth century, when they could develop a broad look at the Bible in reference to the primary doctrines of the Christian faith. Welshimer, on the other hand, had the time constraints of a congregation with a graded Sunday School program and other Sunday morning activities. He thus becomes a pivotal transitional figure. As preacher from 1902 to 1957 for First Christian Church, Canton, Ohio, Welshimer preached consistently on great themes of the Bible and of the Stone-Campbell reformation.

His sermons generally began by putting the biblical text in its historical context and then proceeded to expose a primary idea of that text to analysis, argument, and illustration until he was convinced that he had all his hearers agreeing with him. At that point he inserted an illustration or poem that gave the primarily cognitive message some heart and motivated the people to do something in response. His was not nineteenth-century revivalistic preaching, but rather pastoral preaching that approached the will and emotions of hearers by way of their intellects.

Ard Hoven was for many years the preaching minister of First Christian Church in Columbus, Indiana, and the radio voice of "The Christian's Hour." His sermons were similar to Welshimer's in engaging biblical texts but were less overtly doctrinal than Welshimer's. Time constraints of radio preaching doubtless played a role. Hoven's sermons usually began with a story from history or a foray into the historical setting of the text. His illustrations were sometimes personal experiences, but more often stories found in history books or in relatively recent news. Like Welshimer he was concerned that the reality of Christ be made clear to his hearers, and most of his sermons led people to that end.

Hoven's successor on "The Christian's Hour" was Leroy Lawson, whose ministries in Indianapolis and Mesa, Arizona, have balanced his life in academic circles. In contrast to Welshimer and Hoven, he often begins with a personal experience, letter, or question. Welshimer avoided personal references; he even introduced poems written by his daughter with words such as, "Helen Welshimer has put it in these words. . . ." Lawson, however, personalizes his sermons, so that the hearer senses that there is an intimate, friendly conversation going on.

Myron Taylor, whose ministries in Indiana, Ohio, and Georgia were capped by his work at the Westwood Hills Christian Church in Los Angeles, has been reputed for preaching at once erudite and personable. His respect for his hearers was such that he trusted them to be able to handle the same critical questions of philosophy, theology, and biblical studies that students learn to deal with in seminary classes. His sermons are an unusual balance of personal warmth and theological sophistication. His rhetorical strategies extend from dramatic monologue to verse-by-verse exposition of a text. His is preaching in touch with both the biblical theological emphasis of Campbell and the narrative, image-oriented hearing of his congregations.

Bob Russell, preaching minister at Southeast Christian Church, Louisville, Kentucky, the largest congregation of the Christian Churches/Churches of Christ, contemporizes his sermons even more than Lawson. Russell usually begins with some sort of story — usually a contemporary one — to draw hearers toward a targeted biblical teaching. Whereas with Welshimer and Hoven the text was a central focus for the hearers — something the hearer needs to understand — and with Lawson the text is a basis for building a relationship with God, Russell crafts his sermons so as to hold up the biblical text as a guide for Christians in the stress of everyday life. The insistence is on a "here and now" relevance, not a meaning "then and there" or "still to come."

This preaching path through the twentieth century leads from careful exegesis and argumentation with little or no illustration to a narrative format appealing more to common experience and imagination than to logic or biblical authority, and from objective, cognitive approaches to life to subjective, emotive ones. Since "faith comes from what is heard" (Rom. 10:17), preachers have always styled their sermons so as to get the best possible hearing. In the case of the preachers surveyed here, the strategies have changed in coordination with changing habits of hearing, but the strong emphasis on biblical authority has remained constant.

BRUCE E. SHIELDS

2.3. Churches of Christ

Preaching was and is a central defining activity of Churches of Christ. Reflecting the constant evolution of this body, preaching, while historically rooted in the influence of Alexander Campbell, has taken various forms. Many observers both inside and outside the Movement have correctly noted the tradition's *rational* preaching. Alexander Campbell grounded the character of preaching in the precepts of Scottish Common Sense Realism or Baconianism. Hundreds of preachers agreed, and thousands of people responded to the rational preaching of the Stone-Campbell Movement.

In the South and in rural America where the Churches of Christ emerged, the "farmer-preacher" became the preaching model. Moses Lard in the February 1872 *Apostolic Times* recalled: "The preacher of that golden age was a farmer. . . . He geared his horses with dexterity, plowed with as much skill as ever did Lycurgus." He preached in an "artless but often eloquent style," appealing to the "facts" of the gospel. In the rural context, religious debating became a favorite tactic of evangelism, and soon the "gospel facts" became the gospel "bullets" as the debating tradition of preaching emerged. "Skinning the sects" was a major goal of this preaching, as barnyard metaphors and images rose to the fore in the religious contests. J. D. Tant, one of the leading preachers in the debate tradition, once came to a debate with R. H. Pigue, a Methodist preacher, wearing the sweaty, ragged overalls of a field hand. Tant stated, "I come down here to do a hog-killin' job on a fat, overgrown, over-stuffed 'pigue,' and I dressed for the occasion. Let's get on with the job!" Ridicule and sarcasm reigned in these debates and often in the preaching.

While a hard style of preaching dominated, an irenic alternative tradition of grace also was found in many places. T. B. Larimore, one of the great evangelists of the Churches of Christ in the late nineteenth and early twentieth centuries, was the best exemplar of this tradition. Larimore's preaching focused on Christ, the cross, and grace. When confronted with various issues on which the debaters focused, Larimore's reply was, "Better not stand on that question at all; stand upon Christ and him crucified." Instead of ridicule and satire, Larimore used narratives, metaphors, and images to focus on the love and grace of Christ. Hundreds of preachers quietly preached in a similar vein, while the more colorful debaters tended to receive more attention in the religious press of the Churches of Christ.

Over most of the twentieth century various efforts were made to construct alternatives to the dominant debate tradition. In the 1920s, when Churches of Christ began first to achieve some modest level of respectability, the Nashville Churches of Christ sponsored a series of gospel meetings deliberately patterned after the great revivals of Dwight Moody and Billy Sunday. Renting the historic Ryman auditorium where other revivalists held revivals and featuring N. B. Hardeman, president of Freed-Hardeman College, the Nashville churches announced that the Churches of Christ had arrived and would be a force in Southern culture from that point on. The churches used the best advertising and public relations techniques available: personal phone calls, handbills, and newspaper ads were employed. Full texts of Hardeman's sermons were printed in the daily papers and later were broadcast over the radio. Thousands of people came to Ryman as Hardeman preached twice a day. The Hardeman Tabernacle Sermons, as the evangelistic meetings were called, were held in 1922, 1923, and 1928. They prompted a host of imitators, and the big meetings held in central urban arenas remained popular in Churches of Christ until the end of the 1960s, when they began to wane in their effectiveness.

Starting in the 1920s and especially in the 1930s, as many saw that the Churches of Christ were a cultural force in the South, some preachers began to shift to political and cultural topics in their preaching. G. C. Brewer was the leader in bringing conservative politics into the pulpit. Brewer first focused on evolution, but in the 1930s he discovered the threat of communism. In 1953 Brewer established the *Voice of Freedom,* a journal that espoused anti-communism and anti-Catholicism. George Benson created the National Education Program (NEP) on the Harding College campus to promote free enterprise and anti-communism. Through NEP and Benson, most of the colleges of the Churches of Christ began to raise funds from large secular corporations and right-wing entrepreneurs. "God and Country" preaching became more commonplace in many congregations, and today the legacy of a mixture of conservative politics and Christianity can be found in some large and affluent suburban churches.

Colleges began to assume increasingly important roles as the twentieth century progressed. Out of this, two very different efforts were made to influence preaching. First, speech departments have historically been a part of most of the curricula of the colleges. Batsell Barrett Baxter was the first person in Churches of Christ to receive a Ph.D. in speech communication, from the University of Southern California in 1944. Macmillan published Baxter's dissertation in 1947 as *The Heart of the Yale Lectures.* Baxter taught speech, Bible, and preaching at David Lipscomb College from the 1940s until his death in 1982. He preached at the Hillsboro Church of Christ in Nashville and was the main preacher for the "Herald of Truth" broadcast, first on radio and then in the 1960s on television. He became president of the Southern Speech Association in 1952, a leading regional academic organization of the Speech Communication discipline. Academically and professionally, Baxter was a highly respected figure. In addition, many considered him the best preacher of the Churches of Christ during his lifetime. Baxter advocated preaching that focused on meeting the needs of the listeners. The "life-situation" of the audience was to determine the content and technique of a sermon. His preaching was a decided turnaway from the hard preaching of the debaters to a softer gospel that was filled with love and more positive messages. Baxter trained hundreds of preachers in such a distinctive way that at one time many could readily tell if a preacher had trained at Lipscomb College.

The second influence on preaching by Bible colleges was an emphasis on an exegetical tradition. Frank Pack, Lemoine Lewis, and J. D. Thomas at Abilene Christian College and W. B. West and Jack Lewis at Harding College promoted preaching that was centered in an intellectual approach to the Bible. Pack stated, "The preacher should be a good exegete of the Bible and should be acquainted with the exegetical controls that provide a proper exegesis of scripture." The exegetical controls were "textual, linguistic, grammatical and syntactical, the contextual, historical backgrounds and introductory problems" of the passage under consideration. The goal was to discover "what the original text meant to those to whom it was addressed." This required knowledge of the biblical languages of Greek and Hebrew. Lemoine Lewis insisted: "Every week the preacher needs to wrestle with the originals to make sure that it is the Word of God that he proclaims." After the exegesis was done, then the preacher proceeded to relate the text to the needs of the audience. While never a popular preaching trend, some significant preachers followed this approach to preaching.

Starting in the 1960s the Churches of Christ began another major transformation, as evangelical perspectives become increasingly popular. Dwain Evans pioneered the "Exodus-Bayshore" mission effort on Long Island, the first of several "exodus movements" of persons from the South to the Northeastern United States. Evans, who read, listened to, and attended conferences and meetings of David Wilkerson, Harold John Ockenga, and other evangelical leaders, argued for the priority of evangelism and a more evangelical doctrine of the indwelling of the Holy Spirit. Jim Bevis established a parachurch organization called Campus Evangelism, modeled after Bill Bright's Campus Crusade, which had goals similar to those of Evans. Bright even spoke at the first national Campus Evangelism Seminar in 1967. Along with the new evangelical theological emphases, Evans and Bevis and many other sympathetic younger preachers began to model preaching resembling that of evangelicals — more emotional and dramatic than typical preaching in Churches of Christ.

This transformation became full blown in the 1970s as the "electronic culture" of radio and television began to take hold. Television, in contrast to print forms of communication, thrives on dramatic and emotional connection with audiences, especially through narratives. Lynn Anderson and other preachers discovered narrative preaching. Anderson, in *Freshness for the Far Journey* (1992), reflected on his own preaching: "Since story form colors my hermeneutic, I tend toward narrative styles aimed at altering attitudes and experiences rather than at merely transmitting information. I want my listeners to develop the habit of sensing the 'biblical story line.' Love of story also lures me into generous use of anecdotes, not always as illustrations, but as vehicles through which to convey propositional or abstract content."

In his preaching Anderson used active words, detail, color, and vividness when telling a story, and he sought to convey biblical teaching in "user-friendly language" with high emotional effect. As the pulpit minister for the Fifth and Highland Church of Christ in Abilene, Texas, Anderson emerged as a highly influential model for hundreds of young men as they studied at Abilene Christian University in the 1970s and 1980s. One student whom Anderson deeply impacted was Max Lucado.

While diversity characterizes preaching in Churches of Christ — most of the historic types and perspectives of preaching can be found — increasingly narrative forms of preaching have taken hold even in some preacher training schools. (Using a vocational model, these schools were established in the 1960s to keep the debating and "rational" preaching tradition alive.) Max Lucado, a Church of Christ minister in San Antonio and one of the best-known preachers and Christian authors in America, has adapted the narrative capabilities of his mentor, Lynn Anderson. The postmodern style of preaching is increasingly prevalent in both Churches of Christ and in the wider evangelical world. Lucado has suggested, "We have to use every device possible to reach them and to teach them, and we need not be so apologetic about entertaining them." Narrative or storytelling is the primary technique in Lucado's preaching. Occasionally, Lucado has simply told a story for the entire sermon. Once he moved the pulpit out of the way and sat in a big chair and narrated a fable that he had written. More often Lucado lets a story dominate a point and serve as the main vehicle of communication.

Increasingly, leading preachers turn to the language, props, and forms of television shows in narrating sermons. Popular television game show formats provide the form for the sermon content. Preachers become characters from popular television sitcoms, along with featured replica props, again to narrate ideas or create a dialogue with the congregation to convey the ideas of the sermons. Preaching in rural and urban grace-oriented Churches of Christ, and in some large suburban congregations, has transformed its focus from what Alexander Campbell called the "gospel facts" to a "user-friendly" gospel.

MICHAEL W. CASEY

See also Babcock, Clara Celestia Hale; Baxter, Batsell Barrett; Bible, Interpretation of the; Brewer, Grover Cleveland; Crank, Sarah Catherine (Sadie) McCoy; Evangelism, Evangelists; Hardeman, Nicholas Brodie; Herald of Truth; Hermeneutics; Larimore, Theophilus Brown; Radio and Television; Scott, Walter; "Sermon on the Law"; Smith, "Raccoon" John; Sweeney, Zachary Taylor; Tant, Jefferson Davis; Temperance; Welshimer, Pearl Howard; Women in Ministry; Worship

BIBLIOGRAPHY Ronald J. Allen, "Characteristics of Disciples Preaching," *Pulpit Digest* 81 (2000): 110-20 • Ronald J. Allen, "Preaching and Postmodernism," *Interpretation* 55 (2001): 34-48 • Lynn Anderson, *Freshness for the Far Journey* (1992) • Batsell Barrett Baxter, *If I Be Lifted Up* (1956) • Hunter Beckelhymer, ed., *The Vital Pulpit of the Christian Church* (1969) • L. Susan Bond, *Trouble with Jesus: Women, Christology, and Preaching* (1999) • Michael W. Casey, *Saddlebags, City Streets, and Cyberspace: A History of Preaching in Churches of Christ* (1995) • Fred B. Craddock, *As One Without Authority* (1971; rev. ed. 2001) • Fred B. Craddock, *Overhearing the Gospel: Preaching and Teaching the Faith to Persons Who have Already Heard* (1978) • Fred B.

Craddock, *The Bible in the Pulpit of the Christian Church* (1982) • Joseph Faulkener, "What Are They Saying? A Content Analysis of 206 Sermons Preached in the Christian Church (Disciples of Christ) in 1988," in *A Case Study of Mainstream Protestantism: The Disciples Relation to American Culture,* ed. D. Newell Williams (1991), pp. 416-39 • Alger M. Fitch, Jr., *Alexander Campbell: Preacher of Reform and Reformer of Preaching* (1970) • B. C. Goodpasture and W. T. Moore, eds., *Biographies and Sermons of Pioneer Preachers* (1954) • N. B. Hardeman, *Hardeman's Tabernacle Sermons,* 5 vols. (1922-43) • DeWitte, T. Holland, ed., *Preaching in American History* (1969) • Ard Hoven, *Christ Is All!* (1954) • Joseph R. Jeter, Jr., *Re/Membering: Meditations and Sermons for the Table of Christ* (1995) • Pablo Jiménez, *Principios de Predación* (2003) • Edgar Dewitt Jones, *The Royalty of the Pulpit: A Survey and Appreciation of the Lyman Beecher Lectures on Preaching* (1951) • Keith Keeran, "A Critical Evaluation of Rhetorical Processes in the Preaching of Pearl Howard Welshimer Through an Analysis of Representative Sermons" (M.Div. thesis, Abilene Christian University, 1976) • Keith Keeran and Charles R. Gresham, *Evangelistic Preaching* (1991) • Mary Ellen Lantzer, *Women Preaching in the Christian Church: An Examination of the 1892-93* Christian Standard *Controversy* (2000) • Leroy Lawson, *The Lord of Promises* (1983) • James Mathes, ed., *The Western Preacher* (1888) • Archibald McLean, *Alexander Campbell as a Preacher* (1908) • Mary Alice Mulligan and Rufus Burrow, Jr., *Daring to Speak for God: Ethical Prophecy in Ministry* (2002) • Robert Shannon, *Christ Above All* (1989) • F. D. Srygley, ed., *Letters and Sermons of T. B. Larimore* (1903) • Dwight E. Stevenson, *Disciple Preaching in the First Generation: An Ecological Study* (1969) • Dwight E. Stevenson, *In the Biblical Preacher's Workshop* (1967) • Z. T. Sweeney, *Pulpit Diagrams* (1897; repr. 1958) • Z. T. Sweeney, ed., *New Testament Christianity,* 3 vols. (1923-30) • Frank A. Thomas, *They Like to Never Quit Praising God: The Role of Celebration in Preaching* (1997) • Mary Donovan Turner and Mary Lin Hudson, *Saved from Silence: Finding Women's Voice in Preaching* (1998) • Granville Walker, *Preaching in the Thought of Alexander Campbell* (1954) • Joseph M. Webb, *Preaching and the Challenge of Pluralism* (1998) • P. H. Welshimer, *The Great Salvation* (1954) • P. H. Welshimer, *Welshimer's Sermons* (1927) • Gregory K. Widener, "The Interethnic Black Preaching Style of Cynthia L. Hale: An Exploratory Study" (Ph.D. dissertation, University of Kentucky, 1998).

Premillennialism

See Eschatology

Presbyterians, Presbyterianism

Four founders of the Movement had Presbyterian backgrounds. Barton W. Stone and Thomas Campbell were ordained Presbyterian ministers. Alexander Campbell and Walter Scott, raised as Presbyterians, were educated with ministry in view. The Movement's early growth came largely from Presbyterians and closely related churches of Reformed lineage. These linkages were significant. The Stoneite and Campbellite separations from Presbyterianism were so bitter that the differences — and profound incompatibility — with the Presbyterian "sects" became part of the Movement's identity. Yet massive amounts of Presbyterian and extended Reformed-Calvinist family tradition carried over into its churches.

The Presbyterians encountered most often by Stone-Campbell churches belonged, as Stone had, to the Presbyterian Church in the United States of America (PCUSA). This church formed in 1788/89, uniting English, Scottish, Scots-Irish, and various smaller Reformed communities into the nation's largest Presbyterian body. The name "Presbyterian" highlighted the roles of elders (presbyters) in church governance. Preaching-teaching elders (ministers of Word and sacrament) and ruling elders (representatives of the laity) shared leadership in congregational sessions, presbyteries, synods, and a general assembly.

The PCUSA adopted the Confession and Larger and Shorter Catechisms of "the Westminster Divines" as its doctrinal standards. These teachings were Reformed Calvinism of mid-seventeenth-century orthodox stamp. The "Calvinism" of the Confession in particular represented theology Presbyterians shared with many Anglicans, Baptists, Congregationalists, and continental Reformed bodies, despite differences on specific doctrines and polity. The extent to which the PCUSA might permit diverse readings, restatements, or "corrections" of Westminster standards without jeopardizing faithfulness was a much-disputed issue. The church's constitution granted presbyteries distinct powers in deciding these cases.

The dispute engulfed Stone's ministry during the Great Revival in the West (1797-1805). Times of revival were known to Presbyterians, especially at seasonal observances of the Lord's Supper. Great Awakening–era revivalism sparked division (1741-58) into old side (anti-revival) and new side (pro-revival) groups. The controversy continued, after the breach had ended, in the PCUSA. All "Calvinists" agreed that saving faith was a freely given, unmerited gift of God and work of the Spirit. Some, however, stressed that this gift came as an *experience* with visible effects on the individual's life. Such people, called "New Lights," promoted revivals and welcomed their results. Stone had his conversion and ministerial schooling in New Light traditions.

The charges brought against the Cane Ridge revivals were typical of those made against other New Light events. Also typical was their handling in divided and dividing PCUSA presbyteries and synods. Stone's initial self-defense and his participation in the (New Light) Springfield Presbytery were similar to those of colleagues nearby who formed the Cumberland Presbyterian Church. But while the latter group proceeded to revise Westminster standards on the disputed points, Stone concentrated on the Confession's Article 2 — the Scriptures are "the rule of faith and life" — and urged reliance on that rule alone.

The Church of Scotland, and diverse groups separating from it, was the Presbyterianism most familiar to the Campbells and Walter Scott. This body, the established church of a nation under non-Presbyterian monarchs, affirmed Westminster teachings as standards to which ministers and ruling elders were to subscribe. The union of England and Scotland, however, entailed a degree of national religious toleration and a patronage system that gave landowners sway in ministerial placement. The arrangements created chronic discord, three major schisms, and countless small-scale defections.

The Church of Scotland reflected changes in eighteenth-century Scotland, entering times of increasing prosperity and a "renaissance" of learning and culture. "Moderates" dominated its General Assembly. They welcomed Enlightenment-inspired advances of learning, acceded to tolerance and patronage, and stressed rational belief and virtuous living. Scottish universities extolled free inquiry, scientific method, and experience-oriented reasoning, as Francis Bacon, Isaac Newton, and John Locke advocated. From 1750 to 1850 the philosophical movement called Scots ("Common Sense") Realism spread across the English-speaking world. It lodged in countless American grammar schools, academies, colleges, and seminaries, including those of the Stone-Campbell Movement.

Opposing Moderatism in the Church of Scotland were the "Evangelicals." Rooted in "old Scots kirk" ways, they grew dramatically after the Evangelical Revival of the 1730s. Stress on conversion, evangelism, revivals, and godly living aided their growth. So too did their attacks on passionless moderate Christianity taught by fine-schooled "hireling" ministers appointed by patronage. Evangelicals won the General Assembly in the 1830s. The Crown blocked their efforts to check patronage, leading many to withdraw into the Free Presbyterian Church.

Walter Scott's upbringing was Church of Scotland. His writings reflect his "Scots renaissance" education and Scots Realist commitments. His exposition of "the Gospel restored" and other doctrines dealt with issues of long-standing concern and debate within trans-Atlantic Presbyterianism, along with its separated offshoots and Calvinist kin with other polities. The same holds true for the thought of the Campbells, though they were not Church of Scotland but Anti-Burgher Seceder Presbyterians. Thomas joined the Anti-Burghers in native Ireland. He qualified for ordination by a Scots Enlightenment education and studies at the church's seminary in Whitburn, Scotland. Alexander, raised an Anti-Burgher, was following his father's path.

The Anti-Burghers arose (1733) by secession from the Church of Scotland and a subsequent in-house division (1744ff.) over tolerating (Burghers) or condemning (Anti-Burghers) the loyalty oath imposed on three Scottish cities. The original secession related to readings and implications of Westminster standards, not their authority. Seceders also protested arbitrary — typically lax — enforcement of discipline and patronage. They detailed their complaints in "testimonies," which multiplied at the Burgher-Antiburgher division. Each Secession church required ministers and ruling elders to subscribe to its testimonies as subsidiary standards of Westminster teaching.

Anti-Burgher Seceders, minuscule minorities in Ireland and America, were internally conflicted over amity with allies or exclusivism. Irish Anti-Burghers made several appeals to their Scottish parent body for relaxation of or exemption from strictures against relations with Burghers: the divisive oath was void in Ireland. Thomas Campbell once argued the Irish case in Scotland, without success. Most Burghers and Anti-Burghers in America united and were disowned by their Scottish parents. When Campbell departed Ireland, Scottish Burghers and Anti-Burghers alike were dividing over allowing "conscientious objection" to state-regulated doctrines — "New Lights" pro and "Old Lights" con. The "Anti-Burghers" Campbell found upon arrival in America were anti-unionists devoted to their "historic" testimonies with Old Light fervor.

Presbyterian historians record Stoneites and Campbellites as two of many schisms generated by clashing traditionalist, pietist, and Enlightenment tendencies in Reformed churches — tensions momentarily irreconcilable whether in the context of British church-state connections or American church-state separation. Most Seceders eventually reconciled with one or another larger body of Presbyterians. The post-Stone PCUSA itself experienced exponential nineteenth-century growth, augmented by Scots-Irish and German Reformed immigration. Various means were used to meet the challenges of expansion, including popularized (moderated) Calvinist teaching and "new measures" revivalism, voluntary and denomination-run mission societies, and a "Plan of Union" with Congregationalists. "Innovations" such as these caused division into Old School and New School churches. Both then fragmented along North-South lines over slavery and national union. Presbyterians in the North united after the war. Increasing "ecumenical spirit" and liberalism embroiled them in fundamentalist-modernist controversies and division. Similar developments characterized Presbyterians in Southern states, but less speedily and convulsively. Today the Presbyterian Church in the U.S.A. embraces the largest and more conciliatory segments of Presbyterianism's historically dispersed groups.

Once launched, the Stone-Campbell Movement typically dealt with Presbyterianism as one among many evangelical Protestant denominations, grouped together as "paedobaptists," "Calvinists," "creedalists," and others. Later in the nineteenth century came greater cordiality, as Disciples of Christ especially associated with Presbyterians and other "mainline Protestants." Throughout, the two groups have moved along parallel tracks, coping with similar trends, impulses, interests, and disputes. None of the Stone-Campbell churches addresses matters of theology and the church by deferring to Presbyterian confessions and thinkers. None has associations or assemblies with powers matching those in Presbyterianism. Yet the patterns of connectionalism are similar, and insistence on "representative church government" is a common legacy. So too is the "modified Calvinist" core of Stone-Campbell doctrinal teachings, passing down through covenant (federal) theology, inductive (Baconian) hermeneutics, Lockean and Scots Realist thought, and disputes over subscription to "human" creeds, predestinarianism, and above all the meaning of ("conformity to" or "not contrary to") affirming the Scriptures as "the rule of faith and life."

See also Calvinism; Campbell, Alexander; Campbell, Thomas; Campbell-Maccalla Debate; Campbell-Rice Debate; Campbell-Walker Debate; Cane Ridge Revival; Common Sense Philosophy; Covenant (Federal) Theology; Creeds and Confessions; Great Awakenings; New Light Presbyterians; Scott, Walter; Seceders; Springfield Presbytery; Stone, Barton Warren; Theology — Nineteenth Century

BIBLIOGRAPHY Andrew Landale Drummond and James Bulloch, *The Scottish Church, 1688-1843: The Age of the Moderates* (1973) • Douglas A. Foster, "The Springfield and Cumberland Presbyteries: Conflict and Secession in the Old Southwest," *Restoration Quarterly* 32 (1990): 165-78 • John McKerrow, *History of the Secession Church* (rev. and enlarged ed. 1841) • Donald K. McKim, ed., *Encyclopedia of the Reformed Faith* (1992) • James Seaton Reid, *History of the Presbyterian Church in Ireland,* vol. 3, ed. W. D. Killen (1867) • James H. Smylie, *A Brief History of the Presbyterians* (1996) • Ernest Trice Thompson, *Presbyterians in the South,* vol. 1 (1963) • Leonard J. Trinterud, *The Forming of an American Tradition: A Reexamination of Colonial Presbyterianism* (1949).

JAMES O. DUKE

Process Theology

See Theology — Twentieth Century

Procter, Alexander (1825-1900)

Leading thinker and preacher of the post-Campbell period among nineteenth-century Disciples of Christ.

Schooled under Alexander Campbell at Bethany College, Procter served forty years as pastor of the First Christian Church of Independence, Missouri. A frontier liberal in a conservative time, Procter read widely, especially among European higher critics, but wrote very little. He was the fulcrum of the "Missouri Quartet" of Procter, T. P. Haley, G. W. Longan, and A. B. Jones, pioneers of Disciples liberalism. Procter had a large and enduring influence on younger ministers, who revered him as the "Sage of Independence."

BIBLIOGRAPHY Joseph R. Jeter, Jr., *Alexander Procter: The Sage of Independence* (1983). JOSEPH R. JETER, JR.

Prohibition Movement

See Temperance

Protestant Reformation

The phrase "Protestant Reformation" typically designates the "protest movement" begun in the sixteenth century, led initially by Martin Luther, though this particular movement had precursors in earlier reform attempts such as the work of John Wycliffe in England and Jan Hus in Bohemia.

The Reformation spread quickly to Switzerland (Zwingli) and France (Calvin), then to England with the actions of King Henry VIII. Its spread into Scotland ultimately resulted in the Presbyterian Church of Scotland that fostered Thomas and Alexander Campbell.

Henry VIII's son, Edward VI, took the Church of England much further toward Luther's evangelicalism by providing a new book of worship in 1549 and requiring churches to use it. But Edward lived only until 1553, when he was succeeded by Mary, his half-sister, who was staunchly Roman Catholic and who returned England to the Roman Church by force. Mary's persecutions produced "Marian Exiles" who fled to the Continent for safety. Many came in contact with the Zwinglian branch of the Reformation and were heavily influenced by it.

Mary died in 1558 after only a five-year reign and was succeeded by Queen Elizabeth (the third child of Henry VIII). Elizabeth returned England to Protestantism by initiating the *via media,* the "middle way" between Roman Catholicism and Lutheran evangelicalism. Additionally, she welcomed the return of "Marian Exiles," among them John Knox, a Scottish reformer who was the leader of one branch of the exiles. Knox was known for his uncompromising character, and Elizabeth judged that she did not need his obstinacy in a period of national turmoil. She sent him straight through England to Scotland, where he introduced Protestantism to Scotland.

The Scottish church separated from the Church of England in 1560, partly because of Scottish nationalist and anti-English sentiment, and partly because of the strongly Calvinistic theology of Knox. After the death of Knox in 1572, the Church of Scotland became staunchly Presbyterian in organization.

It was this church that nurtured both Thomas and Alexander Campbell, and it was this church's tendency toward division that ultimately led them away from it. The Campbells were the products of multiple subdivisions of the Scottish Presbyterian Church: they were Old Light, Anti-Burgher, Seceder Presbyterians.

When Alexander Campbell began his *Christian Baptist* series titled "A Restoration of the Ancient Order of Things" in February 1825, he acknowledged the debt that Christians had to all past reformers, including those of the Protestant Reformation. Yet he insisted that all those efforts had been aimed at reforming human systems of religion. True Christianity was not capable of reform. Rather, only a restoration of the ancient order found in the New Testament would correct the problems of religion. The era of Restoration, he exclaimed, would as far transcend the era of Reformation in importance and fame as the New Testament transcends the Westminster Confession and the canons of the Assembly's Digest.

Nevertheless, Campbell saw his own reform efforts in some sense as a continuation of the Protestant Reformation — perhaps a completion of it. One of the most common designations for the Stone-Campbell Movement in the nineteenth century was "the current Reformation." Campbell declared in the preface to his *Christian System* that the Protestant Reformation was "one of the most splendid eras in the history of the world, and must long be regarded by the philosopher and the philanthropist as one of the most gracious interpositions in behalf of the whole human race." He believed that too often, however, the Reformation had substituted one set of human opinions for another instead of actualizing Luther's principle of "the Bible alone" as the sole source of authority. The current efforts of his Movement were aimed at doing just that.

Though some in the Movement have been reluctant to label themselves Protestants, the Stone-Campbell Movement is in the direct lineage of the Protestant Reformation. Especially shaped by Reformed theology through its Presbyterian roots, the Movement also shares historical and theological traits with Anglican and Anabaptist forebears.

See also Campbell, Alexander; Campbell, Thomas; Names of the Movement; Presbyterians, Presbyterianism

BIBLIOGRAPHY C. Leonard Allen and Richard T. Hughes, *Discovering Our Roots: The Ancestry of Churches of Christ* (1988) • Douglas A. Foster, "Family Resemblances: Why Do We Have Brown Eyes?" in *The Crux of the Matter: Crisis, Tradition, and the Future of Churches of Christ* (2002), pp. 65-89 • Winfred Ernest Garrison, *Alexander Campbell's Theology: Its Sources and Historical Setting* (1900) • Hiram Van Kirk, *The Rise of the Current Reformation; or, A Study in the History of Theology of the Disciples of Christ* (1907).

WILLIAM E. KOOI, JR.

Protestant Unionist, The

One of two reform-minded periodicals founded by Walter Scott to propagate the message of the Stone-Campbell Movement.

Under the editorship of Scott and Thomas Jefferson Melish, *The Protestant Unionist* was launched in Pittsburgh on September 25, 1844. The last issue of the weekly was published on December 16, 1848. The next year Benjamin Franklin replaced Melish as Scott's coeditor, and the paper was published for two more years as *The Christian Age and Protestant Unionist.*

The paper was the product of Walter Scott's vision to establish a "truly Protestant" voice. The masthead of the paper boasted the slogan: "The Bible, I Say the Bible Only, is the Religion of Protestants." Ostensibly a "family newspaper," *The Protestant Unionist* included a variety of contemporary political and religious news, but it was largely a celebration of the history and promise of Protestantism. The paper was a self-conscious part of the contemporary anti-Catholic spirit among evangelical Christians. Scott believed that agreements among Protestants were "infinitely more important" than were the differences, and *The Protestant Unionist* represented his somewhat naive hope that evangelicals would find common ground to save the country from the threat of Roman Catholic growth.

The Protestant Unionist disturbed some of the more sectarian leaders in the Disciples movement. They wondered whether Scott had turned his back on the "restored gospel" that he had preached in the early days of the Stone-Campbell Movement, and they challenged him in the pages of the *Unionist.*

In a sense, *The Protestant Unionist* did reflect Walter Scott's disillusionment over the failure of the Movement to meet the euphoric hopes of its early leaders and the increasing sectarian spirit of many Disciples preachers. Almost certainly, Scott's new emphasis also was based on a sense of personal bitterness about what he felt was a lack of recognition of his contributions to the Disciples movement.

By 1849 it was clear that Scott's dream of a united Protestantism was an implausible dream, and the concluding issues of the paper begrudgingly faced that reality.

See also *Evangelist, The;* Franklin, Benjamin; Journalism; Nativism; Scott, Walter

BIBLIOGRAPHY William Gerrard, *A Biographical Study of Walter Scott: American Frontier Evangelist* (1992) • Dwight Stevenson, *Walter Scott: Voice of the Golden Oracle* (1946).

DAVID EDWIN HARRELL, JR.

Providence

Doctrine concerning the nature, scope, and occasion of God's action in the world.

Providence is generally contrasted with the doctrine of creation (God's action in initiating the universe) and the doctrine of miracles (God's intervention to bring about the physically impossible). Distinction is usually made between *general* providence and *special* providence — the former dealing with God's guidance of and provision for nature as a whole, the latter with God's particular concerns for his people.

The history of thinking on providence in the Stone-Campbell Movement has been largely influenced by two predominant schools of thought. First has been the high view of providence coming from Reformed theology. Reformed thinkers emphasized the pervasiveness and meticulousness of God's providential care, often to the detriment of a robust doctrine of human freedom. Second has been the semi-deistic view of providence stemming from the rationalistic forms of Enlightenment and modernist thinking. This view essentially collapsed providence into the doctrine of creation, seeing all divine influence in the world stemming from the deterministic causation of God's initial creative acts.

The Reformed school of thought has been by far the more influential in the thinking of Stone-Campbell leaders. Alexander Campbell, Robert Richardson, David Lipscomb, James Harding, and many others viewed God's control in the universe as pervasive and intimate. However, in contrast to the approach of Reformed thinkers, this high view of providence has been tempered by a strong emphasis on the role of human freedom. Stone-Campbell thinkers have held overwhelmingly to a libertarian view of free action, rather than the compatibilist doctrines of the Reformers. A libertarian view is one in which a person has genuine, metaphysically possible alternatives. Such a view is inconsistent with the Calvinistic notion of God's sovereignty dictating with certainty every event in the universe. Thus throughout the Stone-Campbell Movement a fundamentally Reformed view of providence has been tempered by an unapologetically Arminian view of human freedom.

A powerful representative of this traditional school of thought in more contemporary times is Jack Cottrell, a theologian of the Christian Churches/Churches of Christ at Cincinnati Bible College and Seminary. In his work *What the Bible Says About God the Ruler* (1984), Cottrell offers perhaps the most extensive and systematic treatment of the doctrine of providence in the history of the Stone-Campbell Movement. In reconciling the notions of divine sovereignty and libertarian prerogatives, Cottrell argues: "It was God's sovereign choice to bring into existence a universe inhabited by free-will creatures whose decisions would to some extent determine the whole picture. When these creatures then do just what God designed them to do, how can this destroy his sovereignty? Is it not rather an expression of it?"

In contrast to this predominant view, some Stone-Campbell thinkers have tended toward the semi-deistic views mentioned above. Hiram Christopher, a nineteenth-century Stone-Campbell writer, is a key example of such teaching. In an unpublished paper, Church of Christ theologian John Mark Hicks says of Christopher's view, "Providence, then, is simply another name for the ongoing function of natural laws by the energy immanent within matter — an energy ultimately traceable to God, but now embedded in the natural order with regularity and predictability." For Christopher, any intervention by God to disrupt this regularity would be wholly unpredictable, and therefore must be miraculous.

That such a view should be expressed so boldly in later generations is ironic since it was precisely this understanding of providence that Campbell, Richardson, and others worked so hard to refute. Richardson, for example, insisted that providence is necessarily distinct from miracle. "It is indeed the very idea and definition of Providence, that it is the *divine agency* exercised in sustaining and governing the universe. It differs from miracles in this, that its designs are brought to pass *by means of the established laws and through the ordinary channels.*"

As opposed as they seem to be, these two influential schools of thought — Reformed and semi-deistic — share a common result: creation and providence become indistinguishable. In the former, God acts at all times in the same predominant way that he did at creation; in the latter, God acts providentially only insofar as he arranges specific developments in history from the creative moment. While Campbell himself declared in the 1855 *Millennial Harbinger,* "His creation and providence are necessarily, eternally, and immutably co-extensive," it is clear that he did not intend to embrace the equating of the doctrines indicated above. Furthermore, equating creation and providence leads to the further equation of general and special providence, and Campbell was adamantly opposed to such a collapsing. He rejected both hyper-Calvinism and semi-deism in a single stroke: "They who admit a general providence, and, at the same time, deny a special providence, are feeble and perverted reasoners and thinkers. A general, or universal supervision or providence, necessarily implies a special or particular providence."

See also Creation and Evolution; God, Doctrine of

BIBLIOGRAPHY Alexander Campbell, "Providence, General and Special," *Millennial Harbinger* (1855): 601-8 • Alexander Campbell, "Mysteries of Providence," *Millennial Harbinger* (1847): 704-9 • Jack Cottrell, *What the Bible Says About God the Ruler* (1984) • John Mark Hicks, "What Should I Believe About Providence? Options in Contemporary Theology" (on-line: http://www.hugsr.edu/hicks/providence.htm) • John Mark Hicks, *Yet Will I Trust Him: Understanding God in a Suffering World* (1999) • Robert Richardson, "The Providence of God" (7 parts), *Millennial Harbinger* (1836): 219-25, 246-51, 305-7, 360-65, 385-89, 441-49, 537-43 • Terrance Tiessen, *Providence and Prayer: How Does God Work in the World?* (2000).

JAMES F. SENNETT

Pseudonyms

Use of a false or cryptic name to conceal a writer's true identity, a commonplace in the journalism of the Stone-Campbell Movement.

Writers in the Movement often employed pseudonyms for various reasons. It was a popular practice, especially in the nineteenth century, for both brief and lengthy articles.

An early and important example was set by one of the Movement's important forebears in the seventeenth century. Rupertus Meldenius, credited as the author of the slogan "In essentials, unity; in non-essentials, liberty; in all things, charity," was probably an alias of Peter Meiderlin. Although he probably was repeating a phrase he had heard from someone else, he is the one quoted.

Just as the Internet has encouraged contemporary writers to create e-mail names for a shorter identification, some Stone-Campbell authors used pseudonyms simply as a shorthand, an innocuous nickname. They were glad for people to know the author of the material. Others, however, deliberately wanted to hide their identity either because they thought using their real name would prejudice the reader or because they did not want to be held responsible for a composition, perhaps a piece likely to stir controversy. A good example of the latter is the pseudonym "Christianos," used by Archibald McKeever, Alexander Campbell's brother-in-law, who, in the extended "Lunenburg Letter" controversy, wrote in the *Millennial Harbinger* (1838-40) defending Campbell's claim that there were indeed "Christians" in paedobaptist denominations.

Because knowing the author can sometimes help in understanding an essay, various attempts have been made to find out who wrote under various pen names. Some were never a mystery, while others still remain a mystery. Below is a table of some of the pseudonyms used by celebrated Stone-Campbell authors in early periodicals like the *Christian Baptist* and *Millennial Harbinger,* drawing in part on the research of Claude Spencer and Lewis Snyder.

Pseudonym	*Actual Name*
"Alumnus"	Robert Richardson
"Bonus Homo"	Alexander Campbell
"Candidus"	Alexander Campbell
"Christianos"	Archibald McKeever
"Clarinda"	Alexander Campbell
"Daniel"	Alexander Campbell (?)
"Disciplus"	Robert Richardson
"E"	Robert Richardson
"Eusebius"	Isaac Errett
"Arthur Gordon"	Herbert L. Willett
"K"	Robert Richardson
"L"	Robert Richardson
"A Layman"	T. W. Phillips
"Luke"	Robert Richardson
"Partenos"	Walter Scott
"Philip"	Walter Scott
"Querens"	Philip S. Fall
"R"	Robert Richardson
"Reformed Clergyman"	Alexander Campbell
"Silas"	Robert Richardson
"T.W."	Thomas Campbell
"U"	Robert Richardson
"The White Pilgrim"	Joseph Thomas

BIBLIOGRAPHY Lewis L. Snyder, "Speaking from the Shadows," *Discipliana* 51 (1991): 7-10 • Claude Spencer, "Pseudonyms," *Discipliana* 11 (1951-52): 36.

DAVID I. MCWHIRTER

Puerto Rico, The Movement in

Puerto Rico ("rich port") is the home of a distinctive Stone-Campbell community. It is the smallest of the larger Antilles of the Caribbean, about 100 miles east to west and 35 miles north to south, with a population of 3.8 million inhabitants. A central mountain range divides it into a lush, tropical northern coast and an arid, semi-desert to the south. It has been called the "island of enchantment" because of its natural beauty.

The island was conquered and colonized by Spain in 1493. The United States invaded Puerto Rico during the Spanish-American War in 1898. Puerto Rico became a colony and then a commonwealth, a U.S. territory, approved by the U.S. Congress in 1952. Puerto Ricans are U.S. citizens, and there are more than three million Puerto Ricans living on the U.S. mainland.

At the end of the nineteenth century Puerto Rico was experiencing a significant transition. Having become a U.S. colony as a result of the Spanish-American War, it received many Protestant missions from the United States beginning in 1898. The Disciples of Christ came to the island on April 23, 1899. J. A. Erwin and his family were assigned to the northern part of Puerto Rico, in the city of Bayamón, as part of the comity agreement among the Protestant denominations that established missions. The first Disciples congregation was founded in 1901 in Bayamón. From Bayamón the Disciples moved to the countryside, starting the first Protestant rural congregation in Puerto Rico. Dajaos became, and still is, the Mecca of Puerto Rican Disciples.

The first missionaries experienced the misery and desperate needs of the Puerto Rican population and decided to respond by establishing two orphanages in Bayamón to educate and protect orphan children of the vicinity. By 1914 the missionaries had decided to change their strategy for mission in Puerto Rico. They closed the orphanages and concentrated on planting new congregations and on evangelism. Many children were transferred to the Polytechnic Institute of the Presbyterian Church in San Germán. The process of establishing new congregations resulted in Disciples expanding their influence, particularly in the northwestern part of Puerto Rico.

The Churches of Christ also sent missionaries to Puerto Rico. By the 1930s several congregations were established on the island. The first congregation was founded in San Juan, and from there new congregations were organized in Dorado and Vega Alta, two small towns in the northwestern part of Puerto Rico.

Manuel Jordán, Modesto Rivera, and Gregorio Rodríguez are recognized as prominent Puerto Rican church developers. Rev. Manuel Jordán was a pastor in Vega Alta for many years. His brother, Rev. Edmundo Jordán, was a Christian Church (Disciples of Christ) pastor in Bayamón, Ciales, and Toa Baja for more than thirty years.

The first major crisis among Disciples in Puerto Rico erupted when, in 1933, a group of laypersons started prayer circles at noon in Calle Comerío Christian Church. A charismatic movement spread like fire in all of the churches, creating what is known in Puerto Rico as *El Avivamiento del 33*. The revival included glossolalia, dancing in the Spirit, fasting, aggressive evangelism, and a contagious enthusiasm that affected even other denominations. But the missionaries decided that the revival was not according to the "Disciples way" and tried to suppress and even stop the movement. A serious confrontation that lasted ten years provided the opportunity for Puerto Rican Disciples congregations to declare self-support and to rely on the tithing and offerings of the poor members of local congregations. By 1943 the United Christian Missionary Society and the Puerto Rican Disciples agreed to maintain their partnership but continued working toward the autonomy of the church in Puerto Rico. In 1954 a constitution was approved creating an administrative board, a governing body composed of the ordained pastors with representatives of the different sectors of the church, including the seminarians. Disciples continued to grow during the next three decades; in 1965 they announced that no more missionaries were needed, and they promulgated a new constitution. The second constitution was drafted and approved in 1967. A major revision was made in 1984, creating the office of the general pastor. This constitution has been further amended to clarify operational and administrative mechanisms, particularly related to property ownership and finances. The local congregations maintain their autonomy, while the representative board has been strengthened as the governing board for the whole denomination.

A second major crisis erupted in the 1960s and 1970s. A confrontation between a younger generation of pastors and the leaders of the denomination led to the expulsion of fourteen pastors and the loss of hundreds of important laypersons in the intellectual circles of Puerto Rico. Issues related to this crisis were the Vietnam War, which affected Puerto Rican society tremendously because more than a thousand Puerto Ricans (many of whom were members of Disciples congregations) died in that war; the U.S. Navy operations in Vieques and Culebra, which led many young pastors to join a Puerto Rican group of clergy against the naval presence in Puerto Rico; the rise of liberation theology; and the Cuban revolution. Both the faculty and the students of the Evangelical Seminary came under attack by conservative forces inside and outside the churches. The conflict left many wounds and scars that slowly have been healing, but that created a leadership crisis and void, because the generation that was supposed to assume leadership was missing.

Disciples of Christ in Puerto Rico developed a unique model of mission. It is a strongly charismatic denomination, but it expresses a creative diversity in worship. Puerto Rican Disciples have a deep appreciation for a solid intellectual and theological formation of their pastors. Many of them have doctoral degrees and teach or lecture in the prestigious academic institutions. Disciples in Puerto Rico sponsor a highly regarded religious TV program: "Gather at the Table." Over the years Disciples have had active members of local congregations directing agencies and departments in the government of Puerto Rico. Disciples are proud of the active participation of distinguished professors from the campuses of the two most prestigious universities of the country: the University of Puerto Rico (state) and the Inter-American University of Puerto Rico (related to the Presbyterian Church).

Puerto Rican Disciples are responding to the challenges of the twenty-first century by continuing with the same evangelistic fervor of the last hundred years. They are reclaiming an educational vocation at all levels. Local congregations operate local elementary, middle, and high schools. A Sunday School curriculum designed for the whole church and a Lay Institute to prepare new leadership have been developed. Puerto Rican Disciples speak of themselves as *"una iglesia de frontera"* (a church of the frontier) in Puerto Rican society. They are also seeking through missionary partnerships to influence other countries, including the Dominican Republic, Costa Rica, Nicaragua, and Venezuela.

CARMELO ÁLVAREZ

See also Hispanics in the Movement; Latin America and Caribbean, Missions in

Puget Sound Christian College

Bible college affiliated with the Christian Churches/Churches of Christ.

In 1887 the American Board of Missions sent Eugene C. Sanderson to the Territory of Washington as an evangelist. Here he saw the need to educate young men of the region for ministry. First Sanderson established Eugene Divinity School in Oregon (founded in 1895 and eventually becoming Northwest Christian College). Later he turned to Seattle. In 1919 Seattle Bible College was established near the main entrance to the University of Washington under the umbrella of the Eugene school (by then-named Eugene Bible University). The Seattle college closed during the years of the Great Depression.

The Seattle area, however, still had need of a ministerial training institution. In 1950 two men, Charles Henry Phillips and Ernest H. Chamberlain, rose to this challenge. Phillips was an English-Canadian preacher and academic who had previously founded two colleges in Canada. He had retired to Seattle for health reasons in 1950, but as his stamina improved he developed a vision for founding a Bible college to serve the Stone-Campbell churches of the growing Seattle-Tacoma area. Chamberlain, the young preacher of the West Seattle Christian Church, shared this vision. Together they enlisted the support of area church leaders to create Puget Sound College of the Bible (PSCB). The college's original purpose was to be a "non-denominational Christian Higher Educational institution preparing men and women for the various general ministries of the Gospel of Christ and to provide an element of Christian Culture for all walks of life, all in harmony with the New Testament Scriptures."

The first classes were held in the facilities of West Seattle Christian Church on October 3, 1950. Phillips served as the founding president and professor. During the first quarter, fifteen students were enrolled, increasing to twenty-seven students in the second quarter. In 1951 the college was able to move out of the church facilities and purchase an old mansion on Sunset Avenue in West Seattle. On July 11, 1952, the Board of Education of the State of Washington approved the college for training in "Classical Ministerial, English Bible, Christian Education, and Church Music."

By 1955 the continued growth of the college necessitated a larger campus. The move of Simpson Bible College from Seattle to San Francisco made available Simpson's campus in north Seattle, and this was purchased by PSCB. The main building in this complex was the old Phinney mansion, former home of one of Seattle's most powerful families. The college occupied this location at the beginning of the winter quarter, 1956. Phillips worked tirelessly in this period, with the result that his earlier health problems recurred. He died on January 1, 1959. James Earl Ladd II, academic dean of Dallas Christian College, was called to be the second president, and he served until 1975. Following presidents were John T. Parish (1975-83), Glen R. Basey (1985-95), R. Allan Dunbar (1995-2001), and Randy J. Bridges (2002-).

Without question some of the growth of PSCB during the 1960s and 1970s was fueled by larger trends within the Stone-Campbell Movement. Nearby Northwest Christian College was perceived by many Oregon churches as tied to the Disciples of Christ. For some leaders this was seen as a move toward denominationalism and a drift toward liberal theology. This made the conservative, independent stance of PSCB more attractive to the anti-Disciples constituency in the Pacific Northwest. Phillips was very deliberate in his establishment of PSCB as a nondenominational college. In 1951 he had written, "The College is not affiliated with any corporation, missionary or otherwise. It receives no aid from any so-called 'brotherhood agency.' . . . It stands alone, engaged in the simple task for which it has set itself."

Under Parish's leadership the college relocated ten miles north to suburban Edmonds. The main facility was the original Edmonds High School building, parts of which were built in 1909. In 1979 PSCB was granted accreditation by the Accrediting Association of Bible Colleges. During Parish's tenure Central Washington Bible College (Selah, Washington) closed, and PSCB received its library assets and records. In

1984 the name of the college was changed to Puget Sound Christian College. Under Glen Basey's leadership, a nontraditional degree completion program was inaugurated in 1994, the first in the Seattle metropolitan area. This helped boost enrollment numbers to the current 200-250 students. During Allan Dunbar's presidency the college became more deliberately nondenominational and nonsectarian in focus, in order to serve the larger evangelical community. Increasingly, both students and faculty came from churches outside the Stone-Campbell Movement.

In 2001 the college relocated to an updated campus in Mountlake Terrace, Washington, three miles from the Edmonds campus. This placed the college in a strategically important location for its mission of serving the greater Christian community of the Seattle metropolitan area.

See also Bible College Movement; Higher Education, Views of in the Movement; Sanderson, Eugene C.

BIBLIOGRAPHY Wayne Dykstra, "A New Venture in Christian Higher Education: A History of Puget Sound College of the Bible/Christian College" (M.Div. thesis, Emmanuel School of Religion, 1994).

MARK KRAUSE

Purcell, John B.

See Campbell-Purcell Debate; "Restoration," Meanings of within the Movement

Purviance, David (1766-1847)

Elder, minister, and early associate of Barton Stone in the Springfield Presbytery.

Originally an elder at the Cane Ridge church under the ministry of Stone, Purviance was a signer of the *Last Will and Testament of Springfield Presbytery* in 1804. He soon began preaching, and in 1807 he was the first minister of the Stone Movement to be immersed, at the hands of Stone himself. That same year he moved to New Paris, Ohio, and ministered there for about thirty years. Having previously served six years in the Kentucky state legislature, 1797-1803, he also served in the state legislature of Ohio, 1809-16. Purviance was an outspoken antislavery activist and composed an eloquent poem, "On Slavery," that bemoaned its evils and summoned Christians to work for the liberation of slaves as a divinely sanctioned crusade.

Purviance and Stone were close friends, and he and Stone had many common views on the nature and structure of the church; but he was never comfortable with Stone's belief in baptism for the remission of sins. When Stone united with the followers of Alexander Campbell, Purviance fought against the union in Ohio, leading many of the churches there to refuse to accept it. Those churches instead remained united with the Elias Smith–Abner Jones "Christian Connection," which ultimately merged into the United Church of Christ by the 1950s. Despite their differences, Stone and Purviance said their last good-byes in a tearful reunion at Purviance's congregation in New Paris, Ohio, in June of 1843, shortly before Stone's death.

See also Christian Connection; *Last Will and Testament of Springfield Presbytery;* Slavery, The Movement and; Springfield Presbytery; Stone, Barton Warren

BIBLIOGRAPHY Levi Purviance, *The Biography of Elder David Purviance* (1848) • John Rogers and Barton Stone, *The Biography of Barton Warren Stone* (1847).

JAMES B. NORTH

Q

Quadrennial Assembly

Meeting of the International Christian Women's Fellowship. Mandated by the Rules of Procedure governing the ICWF Advisory Council, and nourished by reports of successful assemblies for other Protestant women's groups, the first international Quadrennial Assembly of Disciples women was held June 19-23, 1957. The eleven ensuing assemblies have served consistently as a training and proving ground for equipping women to participate more fully in total church life.

The first two assemblies featured the study and discussion of CWF publications, most notably *Women's Place in the Total Church,* prepared by Samuel F. Pugh.

The third Quadrennial Assembly, in 1966, had as its central focus confronting life's situations with courage to be Christian.

By the fourth Quadrennial Assembly, 1970, these events had a reputation for excellence in programming and leadership development. Disciples women could experience the extent and strength of their network. The Quadrennial's guiding principle had become: As these meetings empower women, they empower the church.

The 1974 Quadrennial Assembly highlighted Disciples clergywomen as it also celebrated the one hundredth birthday of the Christian Woman's Board of Missions. 1978 marked the largest attendance, 4,914, and a decision to showcase the diverse gifts of women. In 1990 a team of African American women song leaders enriched the assembly. In 1998 a woman rabbi shared in a Bible study dialogue.

The first eleven Quadrennial Assemblies were held on the campus of Purdue University. However in 2002 the twelfth was scheduled for the Convention Center in Louisville, Kentucky. In 2006 a first will occur when Disciples women and women of the United Church of Christ join in a Women's Partnership event in Indianapolis, Indiana, at their Thirteenth Quadrennial Assembly.

See also Christian Women's Fellowship

BIBLIOGRAPHY Fran Craddock, Martha Faw, and Nancy Heimer, *In the Fullness of Time: A History of Women in the Christian Church (Disciples of Christ)* (1999).

FRAN CRADDOCK, NANCY HEIMER, *and* MARTHA FAW

R

Race Relations

The story of race relations in the Stone-Campbell Movement begins largely with the attitudes toward slavery held by early leaders and members. The full spectrum of antebellum positions was represented in the churches of the Movement, from Alexander Campbell's Jeffersonian opposition to slavery, to James Shannon's fire-eating advocacy of it, to Barton W. Stone's endorsement of immediate abolition. Belief in the superiority of the white race, however, was an almost universal assumption across the board. As was common throughout the country, when blacks (slave or free) became Christians, white members forced them to sit in separate parts of the building, usually in the back or in a balcony. Barton Stone's Cane Ridge church, for example, originally had a balcony for black members. Removed when the log meetinghouse was remodeled in 1829, it was returned when the building was restored in the twentieth century to its earlier appearance.

Stone was one of the strongest opponents of slavery and advocates of evangelization of blacks in the Movement. He strongly denied any biblical warrant for slavery as it then existed in the United States. Yet he held the same assumptions most white Americans held concerning the inability of blacks and whites to coexist without the subordination of the black race. For many years he supported the efforts of the American Colonization Society to free and repatriate slaves to Africa. Only in the last years of his life did he call for the immediate abolition of slavery, with former slaves remaining in the United States.

Alexander Campbell also opposed American slavery, though he characterized the problem with it in an 1845 *Millennial Harbinger* series as primarily political, not religious or moral. Responding to the national breakup of Methodists and Baptists over slavery, Campbell insisted that Scripture did not condemn slavery but rather regulated it; therefore it could never be made a matter of breaking fellowship. While he abhorred torturous treatment of slaves and condemned cruel masters, he was frank about his racial prejudices — he would always love the white man more than the black.

As was the case with most American religious bodies, following the Civil War blacks in the Stone-Campbell Movement who had been worshiping in mixed race congregations formed their own churches and organizations. Samuel Robert Cassius (1853-1931), writing in 1889 from Sigourney, Iowa, had long since been persuaded of the Movement's "plan of salvation" and had already given a dozen years to itinerant evangelism in that interest. Yet Cassius found that as a believing "colored man" he was surrounded by white members who tolerated his presence but did not truly accept him. "Let him presume to know something beyond an occasional prayer or a short talk at some mid-week social or prayer meeting," Cassius complained, "and he soon finds out that he is a Negro, and a relic of an inferior race, and that his presence can only be tolerated as long as he is willing to keep still."

Although whites in the Stone-Campbell Movement had devoted extensive rhetorical attention to evangelizing the freed slaves, Cassius found that only white evangelists could be paid to carry out that commission, if indeed it were carried out at all. If a black, Cassius noted, tried "to do the work of an evangelist among his own race of people, he finds that the mission funds are all used up in the support of white evangelists, and there is nothing, but 'Go ahead my brother, God speed you in your work,' and such like expressions, left to evangelize the Negro with."

Cassius's discontent soon escalated into a bitter confrontation with J. H. Garrison (1842-1931) when he responded to an 1889 report concerning "colored missions" by Robert Moffett (1835-1908), corresponding secretary for the General Christian Missionary Convention. Moffett's report confirmed for Cassius that the society leadership did not trust black preachers to handle mission funds and "that we are all a set of numbskulls, and must needs have a white man as overseer over us." Moffett's failure to find a suitable evangelist to work among blacks did not, according to Cassius, reflect a lack of qualified candidates. "I speak the sentiment of every intelligent colored man in the Christian church," Cassius wrote, "that we have colored ministers that are every way as well fitted for the work of an evangelist as any minister in the Christian Church that could be secured for the position that Bro. Moffett mentions." Cassius added, "If a colored man cannot do the work, it will be utterly impossible for a white man to do it."

The Disciples' commitment to organized work in every sphere led in 1890 to the organization of the Board of Negro Education and Evangelization. Education remained the prerequisite to evangelization. The widespread sentiment was that not only must a black person be educated in order to evangelize, but blacks must also be educated in order to be appropriate subjects for evangelism. Clayton Cheney Smith (1845-1919), the board's first corresponding secretary, admitted in 1904 that "not much has been done in the way of general evangelization."

Disciples would have nothing to do with either education or evangelism of or by black people unless it was organized and supervised under white authority. By 1900, when the board's operations were absorbed by the Christian Woman's Board of Missions (CWBM), it was administering four schools for black students: Southern Christian Institute, near Edwards, Mississippi (founded 1882); Louisville (Kentucky) Christian Bible school (1892); Lum (Alabama) Graded School (1894); and Piedmont School of Industry in Martinsville, Virginia (1900). By 1912 Jarvis Christian College had opened in Hawkins, Texas, under the patronage of the CWBM, building on local efforts that had begun in 1904. All of the board's educational operations had been governed by principles that in Smith's view were clearly essential. The board had first aimed "to conduct the schools, as far as possible, in a manner acceptable to the Christian people of the South" — that is, the Christians of European origin — since the board believed it would not "be necessary to override social conditions in the South in order to elevate the Negro." Education offered by the board focused on providing "a common school education, industrial education, moral and Christian education," in order to produce students who were "intelligent, industrious and Christian." The board had emphasized quality rather than quantity, according to Smith: "not how much done, but how well done; not how many trained, but how well trained." The board had, he claimed, "invested in brains and character first and in land and buildings second."

Emphasis on education was ongoing while the debate over the Negroes' place in society and in the church continued. S. R. Cassius remained vocal, and by 1915 Cassius's disillusion with the Disciples of Christ was complete; clearly they were now among the failed denominations with human methods and plans. "The salvation of the American Negro," he declared, "is in the hands of the loyal disciples of Christ."

Cassius meant by this the conservatives who were separate from Disciples. "The great uplift of the ten million of American Negroes is now up to the Church of Christ." Chief among the assets of Churches of Christ in Cassius's mind was their understanding and use of Scripture. "We teach," he proclaimed, "that the word of God means just what it says and is not subject to any man's private interpretation." Cassius saw a divine mandate for race relations in Acts 17:29. "That one verse," he affirmed, "ought to serve every purpose of a Christian's mind and cause him not to think more highly of himself than he ought to think, because it teaches there is no superiority in color and no difference in race."

Yet Churches of Christ, the majority of which were in the states of the former Confederacy, suffered from the same racial prejudices as the churches in other parts of the country. In 1907 E. A. Elam (1855-1929), a close associate of David Lipscomb (1831-1917), editor of the *Gospel Advocate,* was drawn into a controversy with S. E. Harris, a fellow member of the Church of Christ in Bellwood, Tennessee, concerning a "colored girl" who lived and worshiped with Elam's family. Harris, asserting that many members of the congregation were complaining about her presence, called on Elam to "request her to attend the colored church." The treatment of the girl by Elam and the response of Harris and the congregation represented two versions of racism — one benevolent and paternalistic, the other malevolent and antagonistic. Both denied the essential humanity and dignity of this young woman and all people of color.

S. E. Harris and David Lipscomb, after several more exchanges with Elam, concluded that the point at issue was "whether we will be led by the spirit of Christ and the teachings of the Bible or by our prejudices against the negro." For decades to come, prejudice would continue to rule.

Ultimately Marshall Keeble emerged as an effective itinerant evangelist among Churches of Christ. While his better-educated wife Minnie, daughter of S. W. Womack (d. 1920), managed their small grocery store, Keeble moved throughout Tennessee and the surrounding states, preaching and baptizing. By January 1919, according to his own count, Keeble had traveled 23,052 miles, preached 1,161 sermons, and baptized 457 converts.

There were outstanding African American leaders serving in the Christian Church (Disciples of Christ) as well. One of the most noted was Preston Taylor (1849-1931), who after having been born a slave settled in Nashville, Tennessee. Taylor was an entrepreneur who established a funeral company and a recreational park. One of his chief contributions to race relations was his leadership in 1917 of the organization of the National Christian Missionary Convention (NCMC). The significance of this organization is partly that it served to combat the racial injustices that were being experienced by African Americans. At the same time, leaders of NCMC were committed to establishing more effective working relationships with whites in the Disciples. Early evidence that creation of the NCMC was an appropriate move is seen in the relationship it developed with white Disciples structures. Within two years of its organization three white mission boards merged to form the United Christian Missionary Society (UCMS). The UCMS formed a partnership with the NCMC that made it possible for staff and program resources to be available for NCMC congregations.

In November 1957, as public schools in Little Rock were engulfed in turmoil, with the governor of Arkansas leading resistance to desegregation, the students and faculty of Harding College in Searcy, Arkansas, a college affiliated with Churches of Christ, presented the school's president, George Stuart Benson (1898-1991), with a petition. The document affirmed "that they are ready to accept as members of the Harding community all academically and morally qualified applicants, without regard to arbitrary distinctions such as color or social level; that they will treat such individuals with the consideration and dignity appropriate to human beings created in the image of God; and that they will at all times face quietly, calmly, patiently, and sympathetically any social pressures intensified by this action."

Benson, a former missionary to China and a supporter of African missions, remained a staunch segregationist. He had tried without success to stop circulation of the statement, but 99 members of the faculty and staff signed it, along with 946 students (the total enrollment was 986). Benson remained adamant. However, two years later, in November 1959, he invited Marshall Keeble to speak in the Harding Lectureship promoting African missions, and he introduced him as "one of the great preachers of the brotherhood." The Harding incident reflected the tensions every segregated educational institution in the Movement was experiencing as racist assumptions were forced into the spotlight.

The civil rights movement that began in the 1950s reached its height during the 1960s. Members of the Christian Church (Disciples of Christ) and the Churches of Christ faced a variety of challenges. Among Disciples a time of transition had been set in motion in 1955. R. H. Peoples, then president of NCMC, proposed merging the services and work of the National Christian Missionary Convention with the International Convention of Disciples of Christ and the United Christian Missionary Society. The merger was finalized in 1960 and called upon the ministries of the whole church to serve the whole church. In 1969 the International Convention adopted "Principles for Merger of the National Christian Missionary Convention and the International Convention of Christian Churches (Disciples of Christ)." As a result of the adoption of the "Principles" document, a new entity, the National Convocation of the Christian Church (Disciples of Christ), was formed to "nurture a realization of the merger vision." The Convocation is an expression of the church that is positioned to promote racial harmony. The National Convocation was to be responsible for pointing "the emerging Christian Church (Disciples of Christ) toward racial inclusiveness and unity across racial lines." Operations were lodged in the Office of the General Minister and President, with the administrative secretary becoming a staff associate of the general minister.

During the 1960s, Churches of Christ continued to struggle with changing racial attitudes. As in the past, schools were at the heart of that struggle. Abilene Christian College announced that a committee, headed by Garvin Beauchamp, dean of students and an Abilene city commissioner, would "study the integration question." That work had been proceeding quietly, but now it became a public priority. Beauchamp solicited statements from the faculty and began preparing logistically, psychosocially, and politically for integration. Black undergraduate students finally enrolled in Abilene Christian College in September 1962. Desegregation of other Southern campuses followed, including Disciples-related Texas Christian University.

Marshall Keeble died in Nashville on April 20, 1968, sixteen days after an assassin murdered Martin Luther King, Jr., in Memphis. Keeble's legion of white eulogists could not forbear remarking on distinctions between the two black heroes, although they did not always mention King by name. Reuel Lemmons (1912-1989), in his *Firm Foundation* editorial, wrote that Keeble "has done more to break down any racial barriers that might exist" than anyone then alive, "black or white." Keeble had, according to Lemmons, "traveled — without discrimination — for seventy years among blacks and whites alike, and equally loved by both, preaching the gospel of peace." Lemmons's parenthetical statement "without discrimination" reflects the lack of understanding most whites continued to have of the realities that racial minorities had experienced.

The struggle within Churches of Christ continued. John Allen Chalk (b. 1937) and Walter Burch (b. 1927), a minister and public relations consultant, had already joined Dwain Evans (b. 1933), another well-known white evangelist, to organize a national meeting of black and white leaders among Churches of Christ that drew more than forty participants for two days in June 1968. Forty-one posed together for a historic photograph. Thirty-two of them signed a list of twenty-nine specific proposals that would begin to end discrimination in local church activities, church-related institutions, Herald of Truth radio and television broadcasts, publishing companies and Christian bookstores, Christian-owned businesses, and the lives of all Christians. It was clear by the summer of 1968 that some white leaders knew what to do. But they were only beginning to learn how hard it would be to do it.

Both the Christian Church (Disciples of Christ) and the Churches of Christ would continue their efforts to promote racial harmony. Through the 1970s and 1980s the struggle continued, and while strides were made, the sin and weight of racism continued to be felt by blacks and whites alike. North American racism, an enemy of race relations, demeans people of color while giving a false sense of power and privilege to the predominant race. In the mid-1990s, Disciples General Minister and President Richard L. Hamm cast the "2020 Vision" for the Christian Church (Disciples of Christ). A component of that vision, likely born out of the years of struggle, focused on becoming an "antiracist pro-reconciling church."

While this portion of the vision will take decades to realize, the church has begun to work toward making the dream a reality. Congregations, regions, and general units of the church have taken on the pursuit of this vision with varying degrees of intensity. From training sessions that speak to the heart of the issue to antiracism teams establishing goals that include examining organizational policies and procedures, this approach to improving race relations has taken root.

In Churches of Christ, a major symbolic effort to improve race relations took place in November 1999 when Abilene Christian University president Royce Money confessed the sin of racism in the school's past segregationist policies. At one of the largest annual gatherings of African American members of Churches of Christ, the Southwest Christian College (Terrell, Texas) Lectureship, Money asked black Christians for forgiveness and pledged the school to do what it could to promote racial reconciliation.

Of the three streams of the Stone-Campbell Movement, Christian Churches/Churches of Christ have proportionately the smallest number of African American congregations and members. But in all three branches of the Movement, the journey to harmonious race relations has many miles to go. At the institutional, congregational, and personal levels, many of all races are committed to continuing to make this a major agenda for the present and future.

See also African Americans in the Movement; Cassius, Samuel Robert; Jarvis Christian College; Keeble, Marshall; National Christian Missionary Convention; National Convocation of the Christian Church (Disciples of Christ); Southern Christian Institute; Taylor, Preston; Tougaloo College

BIBLIOGRAPHY Brenda M. Cardwell and William K. Fox, Sr., *Journey Toward Wholeness: A History of Black Disciples of Christ in the Mission of the Christian Church* (1990) • Don Haymes, "Race and the Church of Christ," on-line resource at http://www.mun.ca/rels/restmov/subs/race.html • Daisy Machado, *Of Borders and Margins: Hispanic Disciples in the Southwest, 1888-1942* (2003).

DON HAYMES, EUGENE RANDALL II, *and* DOUGLAS A. FOSTER

Radio and Television

1. Christian Church (Disciples of Christ)
2. Christian Churches/Churches of Christ
3. Churches of Christ

The three streams of the Stone-Campbell Movement have, like other churches in the twentieth century, energetically embraced the use of radio and television as media of evangelism and biblical instruction and have developed a wide variety of broadcasting ministries.

1. Christian Church (Disciples of Christ)

One of the earliest — but also most controversial — radio broadcasting ventures of the Disciples of Christ came about in 1931. Gerald L. K. Smith, later a leading anti-Semitic activist in the United States but at the time minister of King's Highway Christian Church in Shreveport, Louisiana, began preaching

In the 1950s and 60s, Christian Theological Seminary pioneered the education of students in the use of broadcasting media for ministry purposes. Pictured here is the CTS studio, and at the far left its director, Alfred R. Edyvean.
Courtesy of Christian Theological Seminary

social reform over a clear-channel station for a little over two years. In the 1950s, Butler University School of Religion (now Christian Theological Seminary) became an innovator in broadcasting for Disciples by developing production facilities for clinical and pastoral training and for local educational TV. Alfred Edyvean of Butler's faculty worked with Indianapolis's local CBS affiliate WISH-TV to produce "The Chapel Door," a daily devotional program hosted during its fourteen-year run by Russell Blowers, minister of the East 49th Street Christian Church.

In more recent years, the Christian Church (Disciples of Christ) has not invested significantly in the development of local instructional or evangelistic programming, but there have been some individual initiatives, such as the Disciples Amateur Radio Fellowship–United Church Amateur Network (DARF/U-CAN), founded by John Griggs (d. 2001) in Baton Rouge, Louisiana, and approved under the denomination's Common Global Ministries to assist in providing radio networks for overseas missions, notably in Central America. For its part, the Office of Communications, news agency of the national headquarters of the Disciples of Christ in Indianapolis, has produced a number of radio and TV spots for local use.

Among motion picture efforts, the latest was *Wrestling with God* (1990), a biographical portrayal of the career of Alexander Campbell released in VHS format, written and directed by Jerry Jackson, and filmed on location in and around Bethany, West Virginia, under the auspices of the Stone-Campbell Film Project. The film starred Irish director Paul Mercier as Alexander Campbell and featured soap-opera stars Bill and Susan Seyforth Hayes as Thomas and Jane Campbell. *Wrestling with God* has enjoyed wide use both in local churches and in colleges and seminaries of the Stone-Campbell tradition.

2. Christian Churches/Churches of Christ

Among Christian Churches/Churches of Christ, radio and TV programs have been used primarily for evangelism. The pioneer of national radio programs was "The Christians' Hour," a fifteen-minute program originating in 1943 over Cincinnati station WCKY (WKRC today). Ard Hoven, minister of the First Christian Church of Columbus, Indiana, was the speaker until his death in 1987; his successors were E. Leroy Lawson, then C. Barry McCarty. James DeForest Murch, active in that ministry, went on to participate in the Radio Broadcasting Commission of the National Association of Evangelicals and became president of National Religious Broadcasters. Upon Hoven's death, "The Christians' Hour" merged with Gospel Broadcasting Mission (TCH-GBM), begun in 1952 by Walter and Mainie Coble of Garrett, Indiana, who started broadcasting over Radio Luxemburg. Upon the couple's retirement (1966), ex-missionary Cloyd Christman of LaCrosse, Wisconsin, became the mission's director, and he continues to manage the mission. It has broadcast programs to Europe, East Asia, Southeast Asia, the Caribbean, Africa, and India.

Geographically, southwestern Missouri became a heartland of broadcasting activity for Christian Churches/Churches of Christ. The Gospel of Christ TV Mission (est. 1953), started by Carthage, Missouri, evangelist Forrest G. Bailey, claimed to be the oldest. Probably the largest was the Springfield-based Christian TV Mission (1956), maintained by the Vernon Brothers, a musical quartet that produced a weekly national program, "Homestead USA," and a number of TV specials. The brothers and their wives performed on TV or cable networks into the 1990s. Cecil Todd (Christian Evangelizers Association, Joplin) made the move from radio to televangelist in the 1960s and 1970s with his program "Revival Fires." During its heyday, the program was seen on about 100 stations in nearly thirty-five states plus the District of Columbia. A protégé of conservative activist A. B. McReynolds of the Kiamichi Mission, Todd received additional publicity by asking a provocative question about Martin Luther King, Jr.'s alleged presence at a leftist camp that aired the Sunday after Dr. King's assassination. A number of Todd's associates went on to substantive careers with other radio missions (e.g., Bill McClure, TCH-GBM), programs (The Good Twins, "Good Hour with the Good Twins"), prison ministry (Joe Garman), and the local church (John Caldwell). Most recently, Ziden Nutt, director of Good News Productions International, has led the organization in providing materials for broadcast to the Philippines, India, Africa, and China.

Ed Bousman of Lynchburg, Ohio, established the "God Is Just a Prayer Away" radio ministry in 1962 on WCKY (Cincinnati), then began in 1984 the "Preaching Christ" TV satellite program, covering North America and parts of South America. In 1997 Bousman started short-wave broadcasts to Europe and Africa, and in 1999 he initiated broadcasts into the Indian subcontinent.

Other radio ministries have included "Christian Viewpoint," by John Butler Book of Virginia and Florida. A. B. McReynolds, the anticommunist crusader, produced a "Pray for America" broadcast from Brandon, Florida, carried even by some Mexican stations. There were such broadcasts as "Back to the Book" by Dave Lucas (Operation Evangelize) in Chesapeake, Ohio; "Timely Truths," with Harold Hamon of Whitewater, Montana; "Open Your Heart," with Mike and Rick Breidenbaugh of Chillicothe, Ohio; "What Does the Bible Plainly Say?" with Jim Hill of Vansant, Virginia; and Youth Happening Productions, with Randy Snyder of Florence, Kentucky. A number of Bible colleges had low-power broadcasts. Christian Radio Fellowship provided radio spots, while Operation Housetop produced TV spots and a *Christian Video Directory.* Still other localized broadcasts included "The Christian Voice" with the Maynard Waters Family, Eden, North Carolina; "Soldiers of the Cross Radio Ministry," with Gail Peterson of Smithville, Oklahoma; "The Chuck and Danny TV Show," produced by Chuck Webb, West Point, Illinois; and "Fantasy House," with Charles and Delores Mayes of Canoga Park, California.

Among programs in other languages were "Dulces Momentos" (Radio Mexico), broadcast over about seventeen stations and featuring evangelists Tómas de la Cruz and Arturo Ramírez. This program ran from the early 1970s until cancelled by the Mexican government in 1981. La Voz de Verdad, started by W. J. Morgan and Freeman Bump of El Paso, Texas, broadcast from stations in Mexico, Texas, and California. Still another in the American Southwest and Mexico was "Encuentro"/"Encounter," with Mario Calderón of Eagle Pass, Texas. Vernon Hollett of Farmington, New Mexico, broadcast "Let's Read the Truth" in Navajo. Toronto Christian Mission (later TCM International in Indianapolis) broadcast programs in Russian, Czech, and Romanian. Glen Watterson of Toronto served often as president of the National Association of Christian Broadcasters.

The Christian Amateur Radio Fellowship (CARF) was started in 1966 to provide free communication among missionaries. Under the leadership of its president, Kyle Simplot of Erwin, Tennessee, the ministry was active until the early 1980s.

3. Churches of Christ

Preachers in Churches of Christ entered into broadcasting almost as soon as it became available. In the late 1920s or early 1930s Hall Calhoun in Nashville, Tennessee, and L. S. White in Sherman and other Texas cities presented daily radio programs, normally lasting a half hour. From the first, these preachers considered broadcasting a teaching medium; in contrast to other religious groups, they focused upon what were perceived to be the basics, namely, the gospel plan of salvation and the principal features of the New Testament church. The lessons were organized rationally, and the language was more didactic than inspirational. In contradiction to other groups, especially fundamentalist or evangelical, Churches of Christ constituents felt strongly that funds for their programs should not be solicited on the air. Since the group's preachers did not usually participate in ministerial alliances, they normally were not asked to present programs in a rotation with other churches that stations or the networks made available as a public service.

In the 1930s radio networks and clear channel 50,000 watt stations developed, as well as stations in Mexico that permitted 250,000 watts. Churches of Christ started broadcasting, usually at night, over clear channel stations in Dallas, Fort Worth, and San Antonio, Texas; Nashville, Tennessee; Des Moines, Iowa; and elsewhere. V. E. Howard broadcast programs from the Mexican station in Ciudad Acuña across the border from Del Rio, Texas. These broadcasts included a song or two and perhaps a Scripture reading, and showcased a didactic sermon.

After World War II small radio stations sprang up in communities across the United States and multiplied additionally with the development of FM. Soon even smaller churches produced programs, normally following the pattern above, but later employing various formats, such as the morning worship hour broadcast live, fifteen-minute and five-minute programs, and early morning and late night devotionals. In the 1950s, as television was coming to the forefront of public media, congregations exploited it in much the same way as radio. Because of high costs, several congregations in a given area would sometimes band together to support a program, with one congregation taking the lead. Cable television added to the possibility of airing church programs on community service time. The development of religious radio stations has not impacted Churches of Christ broadcasting; churches have not normally bought airtime from them, nor have they launched such stations themselves.

Beginning with the "Herald of Truth" broadcast in the 1950s, nationally and internationally focused programs have emerged for both radio and television. All these efforts are entrepreneurial on the part of individuals and churches. The formats and approaches have followed already established patterns. Included have been, or are currently: the "Amazing Grace" television program, featuring a Madison, Tennessee, church service; "Heartbeat Radio" and "In Search of the Lord's Way," with Mac Lyon from Edmond, Oklahoma, on both radio and television; "Restoration Radio Network International" in Nashville; "World Christian Broadcasting Corporation" in Franklin, Tennessee; "World Radio" of West Monroe, Louisiana; "International Gospel Hour," West Fayetteville, Tennessee; "World Wide Short Wave Radio," Altamont, Tennessee; and "Eternal Good News International Broadcast," originating in Edmond, Oklahoma.

Churches of Christ have reflected national trends in broadcasting, but they have proceeded according to their own views of format, aims, and content.

See also Evangelism, Evangelists; Herald of Truth Radio Ministry; McReynolds, Albert Badger; Murch, James DeForest; Smith, Gerald L. K.

BIBLIOGRAPHY Maurice Graham, "Rhetorical Analysis of Selected Texts from Ard Hoven and The Christian's Hour" (M.A. thesis, Kansas State University, 1976) • Mac Lynn, ed., *Churches of Christ in the United States* (2003) • Ralph and Zella McLean, eds., *Directory of the Ministry* (2003) • James DeForest Murch, *Adventuring for Christ in Changing Times* (1973) • Keith Watkins, *Christian Theological Seminary, Indianapolis: A History of Education for Ministry* (2001).

C. J. DULL *and* THOMAS H. OLBRICHT

Raines, Aylett (1788-1881)

Minister and evangelist.

A universalist (believing that everyone will be saved), Raines heard Walter Scott in 1828 and was converted by Scott's message. He soon was baptized and actively joined the Campbell movement as a preacher. He was invited to speak at the Mahoning Baptist Association in 1828, but many objected unless he denied his well-known universalist opinions. He refused to do so, for they were still his opinions, though he would never preach them again. Both Thomas and Alexander Campbell defended Raines on this issue of liberty. Thomas stated that he still held many facets of Calvinism as opinions, but he never preached them. The Campbells were convinced that if Raines were left alone with his opinions, he would ultimately study himself out of them. Raines went on to conduct several local ministries in Ohio and Kentucky totaling over fifty years of service. The incident with Raines became a significant illustration of "in essentials, unity; in nonessentials, liberty."

See also Universalism; Universalists

BIBLIOGRAPHY W. C. Rogers, *Recollections of Men of Faith* (1889; repr. 1960).

JAMES B. NORTH

Randolph, Elisha (1784-1856)

Leading religious figure in north-central Alabama from the early 1820s until his death on September 23, 1856.

He was born in North Carolina and moved to Warren County, Tennessee, at an early age. Through his association with the Old Philadelphia Church of Christ near Viola, Tennessee, he was converted and later became a preacher. He moved to Fayette County, Alabama, in 1841 and established many churches in that area. He was one of the direct links with Barton W. Stone and the Stone-Campbell Movement in Alabama.

Two of Elisha's sons, Jeremiah and Lorenzo Dow, followed in his footsteps. The two sons worked for more than fifty years in Alabama. Elisha, Jeremiah, and Lorenzo Dow Randolph established more than fifty congregations in north-central Alabama. At the beginning of the twenty-first century there were fourth-generation descendants of Elisha Randolph preaching in Alabama.

BIBLIOGRAPHY Walter Randolph, *The World Evangelist* (August 1982): 10.

C. WAYNE KILPATRICK

Rationalism

Rationalism is a philosophical disposition maintaining that the unaided power of the human mind is capable of comprehending the essence of reality. Rationalism may be contrasted with skepticism, which doubts the ability of the mind to grasp truth; with existentialism, which concentrates on experienced rather than reasoned truth; and with "presuppositionalism," which holds that only by starting with a correct *a priori* perspective can the mind reach essential truth.

René Descartes (1596-1650) is often listed as the first modern rationalist. Actually, he was perhaps only the most articulate representative of the movement away from revelation and toward independence of human thought. His method asserted systematic doubt and the questioning of all traditional knowledge. His famous dictum, *Cogito ergo sum* ("I think, therefore I am"), was the irreducible base on which he built first a knowledge of God, and from that a belief in our valid impressions of a physical universe. A major breakthrough, however, was the cultivation of "modern" science in the work of Francis Bacon (1561-1626), whose inductive scientific method (as opposed to Aristotelian deduction) claimed true objectivity. Later, self-conscious confidence in the power of "rational" science was called "Enlightenment," which name implies rejection of the previous "darkness" of tradition, especially religious tradition.

Bacon's views were popularized by John Locke (1632-1704). Locke, the first of the British empiricists, was a physician. His *Essay on Human Understanding* (1690) attempted to show how all human knowledge of the sensible world could be accounted for by sense data along with the organizing processes of the human mind. He thought to eliminate the need for "innate knowledge" or revelation to understand the physical world. (However, he remained a disciple of Descartes in retaining "intuitive knowledge of the self," and from that a "demonstrative knowledge of God.")

Locke's *The Reasonableness of Christianity* (1695) attempted to base Christianity on Baconian inductive logic. It became the model for the next 150 years of moderately rationalistic theology and was a favorite of Thomas and Alexander Campbell, who referred to Locke as the "Christian philosopher." Much of the "broad middle" of the Anglican Church (of which Thomas Campbell was a member for his first twenty-nine years) attempted to use the new science. Not only did Locke's political views dominate eighteenth-century English political thought, but his *Two Treatises of Civil Government* also informed early American political theory. Thomas Reid and the "Common Sense" philosophy, so influential on the Campbells at the University of Glasgow, was the conservative heir of Locke, as David Hume's empiricism was its more radical, skeptical heir.

Indirectly, the rationalism of the British Enlightenment furthered the rise and growth of the Stone-Campbell Movement in four major ways. First, "natural law" gave rise to constitutional law (emphasizing basic principles, grounded in "nature"). Second, "scientific" law replaced received tradition as a source of authority. Third, Americans in the "New World" early on developed a sense of thinking for themselves and rejecting traditional or inherited views in the realms of science and religion alike. Americans thought in Lockean social-contractual terms, whether they were creating a new government or planting new Christian congregations. Fourth, Americans distrusted "experts," who were viewed as saturated with tradition, and emphasized the thought of unprejudiced lay thinkers. This view was reinforced by Thomas Reid's "Common Sense" philosophy in Scotland, which held that all honest thinkers would reach identical conclusions.

But the direct influences were more striking. Thomas Campbell wrote in his 1809 *Declaration and Address* (Proposition 4) that the "New Testament is as perfect a constitution for the worship, discipline and government of the New Testament church . . . as the Old Testament was . . . for the Old Testament church." With the use of "constitution" as an analogy for the authority of Scripture, the debt to the politics of the time is obvious. Alexander Campbell's thirty-two-article series on the "Restoration of the Ancient Order of Things," beginning in the 1824 *Christian Baptist,* owes much to the Enlightenment rejection of tradition. Both Stone and Campbell appealed to the "commonsense" conviction of nonprofessionals. And the conscious debt to Francis Bacon is evidenced in the naming of the first college of the Stone-Campbell Movement (1836) Bacon College. Baconian inductive reasoning demanded "facts" and ignored traditional theories.

Enlightenment rationalism had a variety of profound influences in the Stone-Campbell Movement. One sees it chiefly in the Movement's biblical hermeneutics, with its emphasis on the internal logic and coherent facts and propositions of the Scriptures. The "Common Sense hermeneutic" promised immunity from the accretions and distortions of ecclesiastical tradition and direct access to the "plain facts" of the biblical revelation. Alexander Campbell pioneered this approach in his own "Principles of Interpretation" (in *Christianity Restored,* 1835), which invested enormous confidence in philology and study of the historical background of biblical texts. In one striking statement in the 1832 *Millennial Harbinger,* Campbell declared that "All its [the Bible's] communications are to me as the axiomata of Euclid to the mathematician. I use them as first and fixed principles never to be called into question, as rules and measures by which all moral principles are to be tried." This is the same Campbell, however, who also determined in his seventh rule of interpretation that astute scientific exegesis could not alone come within the "understanding distance" of the voice of God in Scripture; humility, docility, and a discerning spirit were also important.

Later conservative exponents like Tolbert Fanning radicalized the claim that unaided human reason could penetrate and comprehend the *datum* of the Bible. Fanning's rationalism provoked a strong response from Robert Richardson, one of the first figures in the Movement's history to recognize the threat of rationalistic tendencies in the hermeneutics and spiritual life of the churches. Richardson responded to Fanning by pointing out the slavish dependence of his hermeneutics on Lockean empiricism and by encouraging sensitivity to the role of the Holy Spirit and of disciplined subjectivity in the interpretation of Scripture.

Rationalism appears in the Movement's definition of faith as "belief of testimony," free from mystical influences — a definition that Alexander Campbell, Robert Richardson, and others felt compelled to modify in terms of trust in the person of Jesus Christ, the object of the scriptural testimony. One finds rationalism yet again in J. W. McGarvey's classic tract on baptism, which is essentially a Baconian-style inductive study of baptism from Scripture.

In the long run, the Stone-Campbell Movement frankly owed much of its nineteenth-century success to positively relating to the prevailing cultural emphases of the time noted above. Ironically, its rationalistic stance, its sense of transcending the conditions of history and culture and simply following the precepts of Scripture, precluded a conscious recognition of this fortunate circumstance. For a time, the Movement had much more impact and influence than its numerical strength would indicate. It increased thirtyfold in the years 1830-1910.

But there were negative results of this rationalistic orientation as well. For example, the study of historical development was not recognized as a worthwhile effort, except to point out error. A certain historical arrogance and triumphalism were inevitable, a sense that the Movement was participating in modernity's victory over the failed traditions and institutions of the ancient and medieval past. So too there was little appreciation of the depth of historical conditioning — either in the Movement's own conceptual framework or in that of others.

The Movement's profound embrace of "Common Sense" philosophy, with its conviction of the monovalence of truth, led to the assumption that all properly thinking people think alike, so that those who reach theological conclusions different from the Movement's own were either ignorant, stupid, or deliberately perverse. Rationalism (and especially the "inductive" logical method) inevitably produced a certain hermeneutical circularity, whereby the Movement's biblical interpreters and preachers often merely read their own positions back into the Bible. At the close of the nineteenth century, moreover, rationalism caused both conservatives and liberals to think of themselves as the only rightful heirs of the early Stone-Campbell Movement: conservatives because they were continuing to espouse the liberation of the Bible from theological distortions, liberals because they were seeking to broaden the scope of free and critical inquiry. Finally, at the end of the twentieth century, the postmodern disillusion with rationalism has prompted some conservatives toward naive experientialism and uncritical pragmatism and has induced some liberals toward open-ended pluralism and relativism.

In Churches of Christ, where the impact of rationalism (and restorationism) has been most profound, new attempts have been made by some (e.g., C. Leonard Allen, historian and author) to counteract the negative effects of rationalism by emphasizing the dynamic role of the Holy Spirit in the life of the church and of individual Christians, and by encouraging greater attention to issues of spirituality and the mystical dimension of Christian faith and life.

See also Bible, Authority and Inspiration of the; Bible, Interpretation of the; Common Sense Philosophy; Faith; Fanning, Tolbert; Hermeneutics; Locke, John; Reason, Place of; Richardson, Robert

BIBLIOGRAPHY C. Leonard Allen, *The Cruciform Church: Becoming a Cross-Shaped People in a Secular World* (1990) • C. Leonard Allen and Danny Swick, *Participating in God's Life: Two Crossroads for Churches of Christ* (2001) • Alexander Campbell, *Christianity Restored* (1835) • Michael W. Casey, *The Battle Over Hermeneutics in the Stone-Campbell Movement, 1800-1870* (1998) • James S. Lamar, *The Organon of Scripture* (1860) • John Locke, *The Reasonableness of Christianity* (1695; edited and abridged ed. 1958) • Henry May, *The Enlightenment in America* (1985) • Robert Milligan, *Reason and Revelation* (1867) • Thomas H. Olbricht, "The Rationalism of the Restoration," *Restoration Quarterly* 11 (1968): 77-88 • Samuel Pearson, "Faith and Reason in Disciples Theology," in *Classic Themes of Disciples Theology*, ed. Kenneth Lawrence (1986), pp. 101-29 • Robert Richardson, "Faith Versus Philosophy" (9 parts), *Millennial Harbinger* (1857).

G. Richard Phillips

Reason, Place of

The role of human reason in the theology and hermeneutics of the Stone-Campbell Movement.

The philosophical roots of the Stone-Campbell Movement clearly lay in the moderate or "Didactic" Enlightenment of Britain and its premier manifestation, Scottish Common Sense philosophy, which instilled profound confidence in the ability of critical human reasoning (and the subsidiary faculties of human intelligence) to determine the truth of facts and propositions. Less influential, but still occasionally echoed even in the Stone-Campbell tradition, was the Presbyterian (Reformed) heritage's caution that reason was, like humanity, *fallen* and prone to misjudgment. Thomas Campbell was willing, for example, still to speak of the "depravity" of human nature in a qualified sense. Such, however, did not deter the formative thinkers of the Stone-Campbell tradition from insisting on the fundamental compatibility of faith and reason in matters of ultimate truth.

In their work, the Campbells, Walter Scott, and others demonstrated conscious dependence on a veritable hall of fame of seventeenth- and eighteenth-century thought: Francis Bacon, Isaac Newton, John Locke, and Thomas Reid. Bacon, Locke, and Newton were leading exponents of an empirical epistemology that made knowledge a matter of fact-gathering, followed by judicious conclusions. Their legacy clearly shows in Alexander Campbell's understanding of faith as an informed response to the "facts" of the gospel. From the Common Sense thinkers Thomas Reid and Dugald Stewart, Campbell and others in the early Movement understood reason as a fixed critical function of human intelligence shared by all peoples in all times. The ramifications for biblical interpretation — as a rational, critical, and scientific enterprise — were profound, since an exegete here and now could confidently understand the truth being conveyed by an ancient author of Scripture who shared exactly the same reasonableness and truthfulness.

For the Campbells, reason was no mere abstract concept devoid of practical application. With a theological vision that embraced their intellectual heritage and its treatment of reason, three major functions of reason can be discerned in their thought. First, in the tradition of Locke, reason serves faith, making faith a sober, deliberate, and rational response to the claims of the Christian gospel. Faith is distinctly defined as an intellectual act, a belief in testimony given by revelation. As in Locke's view, the Christianity of the New Testament is already rational and simple. In *The Reasonableness of Christianity* (1695), deemed a classic by early Stone-Campbell leaders, Locke had called for a return to Scripture and an end to all fruitless theological debates that lead to schisms in the church. The biblical revelation was rationally structured so as to evidence the Messiahship of Jesus. It was perfectly accommodated to human reasoning. The Campbells and Walter Scott, in particular, thoroughly concurred with Locke, whom they honored as "the Christian philosopher."

A second, related function of reason (and so a reasonable faith) was to serve the cause of Christian unity by ending denominational strife. The Campbells, Barton Stone, and their associates knew that this goal could be achieved only when reasonable people came to see that irresolvable theological disputes had to be done away with. Hence Christian unity and religious liberty were the products of reason applied to the religious lives of men and women.

Third, and certainly integral to its role in Christian unity, reason would continue to function as the criterion for theological judgment in the church. This exercise of reason shows up explicitly in Alexander Campbell's famous public debates, not only with other Christian thinkers like the Presbyterians John Walker, W. L. Maccalla, and Nathan Rice, or Roman Catholic John B. Purcell, but also with the noted skeptic Robert Owen (whom Campbell debated on the very possibility of divinely revealed truth). While debating was a common mode of public expression in early America, it was also deeply embedded in the intellectual development of the Campbells. For example, eighteenth-century Christian thinkers such as Joseph Butler and Thomas Reid carried on extended public debates against deists and skeptics like David Hume. For these apologists, it was assumed that reason could act as a neutral arbiter of philosophical and theological disputes. The unquestioned value of reason fueled these debates and served as a useful model of the kind of exchange that could go on between believers and unbelievers. Alexander Campbell demonstrated his commitment to the rational exchange of ideas between adversaries of goodwill when he debated Owen. In the inaugural (1830) volume of the *Millennial Harbinger*, moreover, Campbell insisted that "controversy," as the fair meeting of minds in a spirit of pursuing truth, would prosper, not hinder, the restoration of New Testament Christianity. The *Harbinger* was to be a forum for such constructive engagement of ideas.

Historians have often sharply contrasted the culture of Common Sense philosophy and hermeneutics that informed the Campbell movement and the culture of religious enthusiasm, climaxing in the Cane Ridge Revival (1801), which inspired the reform movement of Barton Stone. Such contrasts, however, must not be exaggerated. Many preachers on the frontier who emphasized the dynamism of the Spirit in religious conversion also saw precisely a "rational" faith as the gift of the Spirit. Conversely, the Campbells, and much more their colleague Robert Richardson, feared the consequences of an unhealthy rationalism in the Stone-Campbell Movement that would feed the head but starve the heart.

Without question, however, the Campbells were the preeminent early champions of reason, rather than "experimental religion" (spiritual experience), as the ground of Christian faith and the adjudicator of the "gospel facts." Faith was not divinely infused into believers apart from rational choice. Beyond conversion and regeneration, however, reason was the guardian of right thinking in the church such as could stave off the threat of the tyranny of "opinions." The Campbell movement, more than that of Barton Stone, instilled in future generations of the Stone-Campbell tradition an abiding habit of mind that, in the words of William Barnett Blakemore, was "reasonable, empirical, pragmatic" — that is, suspicious of speculative theology and committed to the programmatic enactment of "New Testament Christianity."

See also Anthropology; Common Sense Philosophy; *Consensus Fidelium;* Faith; Hermeneutics; Locke, John; Rationalism

BIBLIOGRAPHY W. B. Blakemore, "Reasonable, Empirical, Pragmatic: The Mind of Disciples of Christ," in *The Renewal of Church: The Panel Reports,* vol. 1: *The Reformation of Tradition* (1963), pp. 161-83 • Alexander Campbell, *The Christian System* (1839) • Alexander Campbell, "Theology — Natural and Revealed," *Millennial Harbinger* (1853): 285-92 • Alexander Campbell and Robert Owen, *The Evidences of Christianity: A Debate . . .* (1829) • John Locke, *The Reasonableness of Christianity* (1695) • Samuel Pearson, "Faith and Reason in Disciples Theology," in *Classic Themes of Disciples Theology,* ed. Kenneth Lawrence (1986), pp. 101-29. MICHAEL W. BOLLENBAUGH

Redstone Baptist Association

Association of Baptist churches whose relation to the Campbells was paradigmatic of the relation of many Baptist associations to the Campbell movement.

When Thomas and Alexander Campbell accepted immersion in 1812 and the church at Brush Run became a church of adult immersed believers, the Baptists in western Pennsylvania began to take special notice of them. Invited by numerous Baptist friends, Alexander visited the Redstone annual meeting, but he was disappointed at the narrow perspective he saw in the Baptist clergy.

In 1815, however, Campbell and the Brush Run church officially applied for membership in Red-

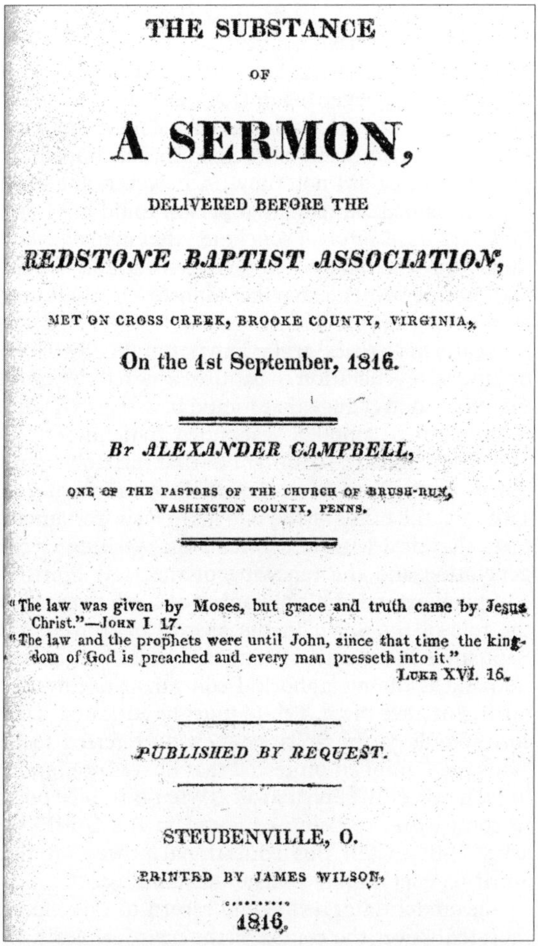
THE SUBSTANCE

OF

A SERMON,

DELIVERED BEFORE THE

REDSTONE BAPTIST ASSOCIATION,

MET ON CROSS CREEK, BROOKE COUNTY, VIRGINIA,

On the 1st September, 1816.

By ALEXANDER CAMPBELL,

ONE OF THE PASTORS OF THE CHURCH OF BRUSH-RUN, WASHINGTON COUNTY, PENNS.

"The law was given by Moses, but grace and truth came by Jesus Christ."—JOHN I. 17.

"The law and the prophets were until John, since that time the kingdom of God is preached and every man presseth into it." LUKE XVI. 16.

PUBLISHED BY REQUEST.

STEUBENVILLE, O.

PRINTED BY JAMES WILSON.

1816.

Alexander Campbell's "Sermon on the Law," understood as a broadside against the traditional Calvinist identification of the purpose of the Law, spelled the beginning of the end of his movement's connection with the Redstone Baptist Association. Courtesy of Bethany College

stone, submitting a ten-to-twelve-page statement of their position, including a refusal to be bound by the Philadelphia Confession of Faith and an insistence that they be allowed to teach and preach whatever they found in Scripture. The vote was not unanimous, but Redstone allowed them in. The next year Alexander Campbell preached his famous "Sermon on the Law" before the annual meeting. This sermon alienated many of the Baptist clergy, and the following year John Pritchard, minister at Cross Creek, tried to get Campbell censured for the sermon. The Redstone Association refused to do so, however, keeping Campbell a member in good standing. He served as the clerk of the meeting in 1817 and 1818, and he was often appointed to committees to oversee some Association business over the next couple of years.

In 1820 Campbell had his debate with John Walker in which he again argued that the Old Testament was not a valid authority for practices expected of New Testament Christians. This again angered the Baptist clergy. When Campbell started the *Christian Baptist* in 1823 his attack on many Baptist practices was obvious, and the Redstone Association tried to censure him that fall. Campbell, however, pulled out of Brush Run church (thus effectively withdrawing from Redstone) and formed a new congregation in Wellsburg, (West) Virginia, which joined the Mahoning Association. In 1823 Campbell's debate with Maccalla and his emphasis on baptism for remission of sins further alienated the Baptists. As a result, in 1824 the Redstone Association disfellowshiped Brush Run church and in 1826 it eliminated four other Campbell churches from its ranks. By 1829 Redstone had been reduced from thirty churches to seventeen.

Relations between the Redstone Association and Campbell/Brush Run typified the larger pattern of Baptist relations with the Campbell movement. From initial acceptance, Baptist relations with the Campbell movement progressed to concern, resistance, polarization, and exclusion. By 1830 the Campbell movement was no longer working in a context of Baptist churches.

BIBLIOGRAPHY Minutes of the Redstone Baptist Association, 1804-1836. JAMES B. NORTH

Regeneration

A dimension of the Christian teaching concerning salvation and transformation.

The term translates the Greek *palingenesia* as found in Titus 3:5 ("the washing of regeneration" or washing of rebirth). Most New Testament scholars consider the concept also to be implicit in John 3:5 ("born of water and of the Spirit"). Thus these two texts have formed the basis for Stone-Campbell teaching on regeneration.

As the Stone-Campbell Movement began in the early nineteenth century, it dealt repeatedly with issues related to this doctrine. Does the Bible teach baptismal regeneration (that baptism is a definitive channel of grace)? Does the Holy Spirit regenerate apart from the Word of God, that is, apart from and previous to faith? Is regeneration instantaneous or the result of a long process? Is the sinner passive or helpless in regeneration or does he or she cooperate? Does regeneration occur by a direct operation of the Holy Spirit on the sinner's heart or through the Word of God (Bible)? These issues were swirling around the churches and camp meetings at that time, creating much confusion and inducing diverse theological understandings. The adherents of the Stone-Campbell tradition have generally rejected baptismal regeneration and the notion that regeneration precedes faith.

The early church fathers had universally identified baptism with the washing of regeneration of Titus 3:5 and with being born of water and the Spirit of John 3:5. At the height of the Middle Ages Thomas Aquinas maintained that regeneration was the imprinting on the human soul of the image of God in Christ. Baptism was itself the act of regeneration in which there was an infusion of grace even in infants. The sixteenth-century Protestant Reformers denied baptismal regeneration as an infusion of grace apart from faith, but they usually maintained the necessity of baptism to effect regeneration. The practice of infant baptism raised a question for the reformers. How could an infant believe, and how could one maintain regeneration took place if one had not believed? Following Augustine, Calvin responded by separating baptism from regeneration. One might be baptized as an infant but only experience regeneration as a child, a young adult, or even an elderly person. For Calvin regeneration could mean the work of the Spirit in sanctification or the initial reception of the Holy Spirit in a person's life. Preachers influenced by Calvinism typically regarded regeneration in the latter sense.

In the first year of Alexander Campbell's *Millennial Harbinger* (1830) he interacted regularly with those who taught "metaphysical regeneration," the doctrine that the Holy Spirit infused a change of heart "without any thought, volition, or act of the mind or body" prior to faith. Campbell opposed this belief with a doctrine of regeneration based on the metaphor of John 3:5, "born of water and the Spirit." In any birth, reasoned Campbell, there must be a begetter (the father), a womb, and the seed or semen. In the metaphor of John 3:5, God or the Spirit is the begetter (the father), the seed is the Word of God, and the mother or womb is the water (baptism). Persisting with the metaphor, Campbell argued that a child is alive before it is born. Being born merely changes the child's state. Thus persons of faith (who have received the Word of God, the seed) are alive spiritually, but they have not been born into a change of status until baptism. Campbell clearly identified regeneration or new birth with baptism. "Regeneration and immersion are two Biblical names for the same act contemplated in two different points of view." Thus one may be *begotten* of God with faith, but that person will not be *born* of God until baptism.

Campbell's stress on baptism at a time when so many stressed the immediate infusion of the Spirit led critics to ask if he believed baptism was necessary for salvation. He consistently declared that he did not believe it was. In the first place infants and others who believe but have not yet had opportunity to be baptized will be saved. But what about others who are alive in the begetting of God but persist in being unborn (i.e., the "pious unimmersed") through lack of baptism? Campbell maintained that he hoped for the best but he did not know. If, however, one willfully disdained baptism, that person could not hope for salvation. Campbell concluded that many devout Christians who have not known about the scriptural teaching of baptism may be admitted to the kingdom of God.

Again his critics argued that Campbell's close linking of regeneration to baptism ignored the spiritual and moral change that should be associated with the doctrine. Campbell responded that immersion only regenerates the believer but that the Holy Spirit renews the believer. Here Campbell was appealing to Titus 3:5, the other of the two main New Testament texts that deal with new birth ("the washing of regeneration and the renewing of the Holy Spirit"). Campbell extended his metaphor of birth to explain the role of the Spirit in the process of conversion. Baptism is the change of state that we call regeneration and is the metaphorical equivalent to physical birth. But after birth, a child must be educated. This corresponds to the Spirit's renewing referred to in Titus 3:5. Campbell protested that he was not ignoring the role of the Spirit at all. "What is it to be born in comparison to being educated in the Lord?" he asked. But to call this educational process of the Spirit regeneration is a misunderstanding.

Alexander Campbell would return to this theme repeatedly over the course of the next few years. In particular, he sought to clarify the relationship of regeneration to conversion in *The Christian System* (1839). Although Walter Scott had said that regeneration refers to the whole process of conversion, Campbell wanted to restrict its meaning more narrowly. Conversion consists of four changes, he argued: a change of views, a change of affections, a change of state, and a change of life. Some regarded regeneration as a change of views or affections (the infusion of the Spirit) or as equal to conversion as a whole. Campbell, however (still appealing to the strict meaning of the metaphor of birth), argued that regeneration was only a change of state, though the other changes were necessary for regeneration to take place.

Barton W. Stone, on the other hand, explained the doctrine of regeneration without any reference to baptism. He agreed with Campbell that regeneration does not precede faith: "God does not operate upon us as upon dead matter," wrote Stone. God *could* make a stone into an angel, but he will not. Thus God will not make an unregenerate into a regenerate person without the faith of the regenerate. Regeneration for Stone meant "to be renewed in knowledge, righteousness, and true holiness, after the image of God." It is brought about by faith in the gospel or faith in the Word of truth (1 Pet. 1:23; Jas. 1:18). The gospel is weak to the unbeliever and unable to bring about the effect of regeneration. It needs "application," which is done by faith. "Faith is applying the means or admitting the truth into the heart." Faith meant to Stone, "The testimony of God being now admitted as true."

Thus for Stone one is regenerated when one believes or accepts the gospel as true. Such belief/acceptance causes the spiritual change of enlightenment, new life, and sanctification. Regeneration is an act of God based on the sinner's "application" of the gospel by faith. Regeneration cannot be done by human wisdom and power. On the one hand, for Campbell, the Word of God through faith begets life in the sinner like a fetus in the womb, but does not give the sinner new birth. For Stone, however, both result from believing the Word of God.

The second generation of teachers, writers, and preachers found it necessary to defend against the charge of baptismal regeneration, that is, that baptism is a rite in which grace is infused over and beyond faith or repentance. Isaac Errett took up this task in 1866 and in 1871 in the *Christian Standard.* Baptist theologians were making allegations to the effect that Disciples taught either baptismal regeneration or that baptism imparted to recipients a holy disposition. Errett responded that "regeneration" to Disciples is a more comprehensive term than to Baptists. To the latter it is an instantaneous event, but to the former a process involving both moral change and a change of state (or relationship). In this explanation Errett disagreed with Campbell, who regarded regeneration itself as only a change of state. Errett viewed regeneration within the context of "degeneration," the result of the fall that left humankind with a loss of faith, disobedience, guilt, separation from God, and mortality. Regeneration was the reversal of degeneration. It results in a change of principle so that one no longer trusts in himself but now trusts in Christ; a change of affections so that one now "hates his former loves and loves his former hates" (moral change); and a change of state or relationship in which the sinner is brought into new surroundings, a new atmosphere, new conditions of life, new activities, and new opportunities of development. The last change is brought about by baptism. Thus, for Errett, regeneration and baptism are not identical, and regeneration is not merely a change of state. Many teachers in the Stone-Campbell tradition have followed this understanding of the doctrine, including A. I. Hobbs (1891) and B. W. Johnson (1889).

One conservative writer of the late nineteenth century, T. W. Brents, is noteworthy because of the way he rearticulated the doctrine of regeneration. Brents separated regeneration in the salvation process from new birth. He interpreted the "washing of regeneration" of Titus 3:5 to mean the washing that comes after regeneration. Brents viewed regeneration as the equivalent of Campbell's being begotten. One is regenerated by the Word of truth (through faith), and then one may be born again by water and the Spirit and attain to salvation. Being "born of water" (John 3:5) is baptism; being "born of the Spirit" is the completed process of new birth.

Disciples writers and thinkers of the early twentieth century were still fighting to fend off the charge of baptismal regeneration. In an editorial in the *Christian Evangelist* in 1909, J. H. Garrison repudiated baptismal regeneration (i.e., that baptism is the "channel of grace by which regeneration . . . is alone received") and stated that baptism was not necessary for salvation (since infants are saved without it). Still later, also in the *Christian Evangelist* (1928 and 1939), F. D. Kershner found it necessary to repeat that Disciples do not believe in baptismal regeneration and to emphasize (with Walter Scott) that regeneration refers to the entire conversion process, involving hearing, believing, repenting, confession, and baptism.

In the last twenty years this doctrine has gotten mixed attention within the Stone-Campbell Movement. Among Churches of Christ the topic is still very much alive. The on-line *Restoration Serials Index* lists seventy-four journal articles on regeneration during this period. The more traditional members of this group stress regeneration as a change of state; the more progressive scholars stress spiritual regeneration. C. D. Osborn is an example of the latter. He underscores the importance of spiritual regeneration from an examination of John 3:5-8. While water baptism is integral to regeneration, it is not the real focus of John 3:5-8 but rather the birth of the Spirit. This passage of Scripture "treats the wider process of salvation and is not limited to the rite of baptism."

The Christian Churches/Churches of Christ have not paid this issue much attention in the past twenty years, to judge by their popular journal, the *Christian Standard.* Not a single essay was devoted to this topic in the journal during this period. Jack Cottrell, in a recent publication other than the *Christian Standard,* affirms that faith precedes regeneration but that baptism is the time or occasion of regeneration, thus reflecting Campbell's understanding.

Likewise, the Christian Church (Disciples of Christ), judging by their official journal, *The Disciple,* gave little attention to this doctrine in the late twentieth century. Not a single essay was devoted to this theme in its pages during that time.

See also Baptism; Conversion; Faith; Five Finger Exercise; Grace, Doctrine of; Holy Spirit, Doctrine of the; Justification, Doctrine of; Salvation; Sanctification, Doctrine of

BIBLIOGRAPHY T. W. Brents, *The Gospel Plan of Salvation* (1874) • Alexander Campbell, *The Christian System* (1839) • Jack Cottrell, "The Role of Faith in Conversion," in *Evangelicalism and the Stone-Campbell Movement,* ed. W. R. Baker (2002) • A. T. DeGroot, *Disciple Thought: A History* (1965) • Isaac Errett, "Baptismal Regeneration," *Christian Standard* (1866): 148 • Isaac Errett, "The Relation of Baptism to Regeneration," *Christian Standard* (1871): 81 • J. H. Garrison, "Popular Misconceptions of Our Movement," *Christian-Evangelist* (1909): 592 • A. I. Hobbs, "Conversion — What Is It and How Produced?" in *The Gospel Preacher,* ed. A. B. Maston (1894), pp. 207-27 • B. W. Johnson, *The People's New Testament with Notes* (1889) • F. D. Kershner, "Baptismal Regeneration," *Christian-Evangelist* (1928): 1301 • F. D. Kershner, "What Is Regeneration?" *Christian-Evangelist* (1939): 362 • Carroll D. Osburn, "Some Exegetical Observations on John 3:5-8," *Restoration Quarterly* 31 (1989): 129-38 • Barton W. Stone, *The Biography of Elder Barton Warren Stone, Written by Himself* (1847).

DAVID A. FIENSY

Repentance

Repentance has been an important topic in church life and accounts of church doctrines throughout the history of Christianity, including the Stone-Campbell Movement. While a general sense of the term's meaning — acknowledging and disapproving of one's own sin and turning toward God — is commonplace, church teachings and practices have varied considerably. Disputes over repentance in connection with the sacrament of penance contributed to Reformation-era divisions of Roman Catholicism and Protestants. Post-Reformation Protestantism produced scholastic dogmatic theologies with diverse analyses of repentance as well as waves (Puritan, pietistic, and revivalist) of calls for "conversion experiences" involving repenting of all sin and conquering it thereafter. Discussions of the topic in the Stone-Campbell Movement developed within this mixed context of highly conventional and yet often confusing and contested understandings of repentance.

The Movement's points of "distinctive" teaching, that is, widespread and long-lasting group-identifying teaching, emerged in the 1820s. Both Alexander Campbell and Walter Scott considered repentance an essential of "the ancient gospel" (or "the gospel restored") and expounded its meaning in terms of an *ordo salutis* ("order of salvation") formula — faith, repentance/reformation, baptism (immersion), remission of sins, gift of the Holy Spirit, and eternal life. Scott's use of the formula in evangelism on the Western Reserve and Campbell's articles on "the ancient gospel" in the *Christian Baptist* are key early sources. Writings shortly thereafter, such as Campbell's *Millennial Harbinger* articles on "Regeneration" and *The Christian System* as well as Scott's *The Gospel Restored,* enlarged upon and in several respects codified the doctrine. Adoption of this *ordo salutis* was, it seems, a characteristic shared generally by ("Stoneite") Christians favoring union with Campbell-Scott Disciples.

The main line of teaching within the united movement was that of describing repentance as an element or moment of Christian life — typically a (pre)condition of salvation — that follows faith and precedes baptism. Discussion of the term, apart from merely passing references, became standard in writings on the "ancient gospel," "evangelical economy," "plan of salvation," and especially "first principles," the title of a genre of theological literature more or less distinctive of the Movement. This approach predominated throughout the nineteenth century and remained influential long thereafter in all three streams of the Movement, although in varying degrees and sectors.

The placement of repentance vis-à-vis faith and baptism represented the most important point, for both church doctrine and practice. Alexander Campbell and Walter Scott, and legions of followers thereafter, called it "the apostolic order" in contrast to the wide variety of other orderings. In the early-nineteenth-century context, this account differentiated the Stone-Campbell Movement from competing groups and churches, even of similar background. At the time the most prominent forms of popular revivalist teaching, whether "Calvinist" (predestinarian) or Arminian, urged would-be converts, including those baptized as infants who sought "regeneration," to heartfelt repentance of their sin, leading to earnest pleadings for the coming of the Holy Spirit to illumine the Scriptures and empower them to faith in the gospel.

Hence, teaching that repentance *follows* (from) faith went along with the basic Stone-Campbell *theological* points: (1) the Holy Spirit works in and through the Word (as set forth in the Scriptures), not apart from it, to lead to faith; (2) only after faith in the revelation of God's grace in Jesus Christ can sinners truly grasp the magnitude of the sins they are to repent of (i.e., acknowledge and disapprove of); and (3) baptism "follows" faith and repentance as an obedient act of turning toward God on the part of the sinner *and* as the formal "sign and seal" of God's "remission of sin." In evangelistic practice, preaching repentance in this way was often more successful than popular revivalism in prompting people to believe immediately (without waiting for the Spirit to act in some "miraculous" fashion) and in reassuring those who had no such "miraculous" spiritual experiences that they were acceptable in God's sight nonetheless.

In addition, later writers on this topic usually reflected the influence of the views of Alexander Campbell and Scott, yet without citing them or any sources other than the Scriptures as their "authorities." Greek terms in the Bible translated into English as repentance *(metanoia, metanoeō, metamelomai)* were surveyed and analyzed in keeping with grammatico-historical hermeneutics. Repentance as "mere" sorrow or regret without significant personal effect was distinguished from "true" repentance, involving manifest change, amendment, or reformation of life. Campbell in particular had a scholarship-based preference for substituting the English word "reformation" for "repentance." The point appeared in Scott's work, too. Although this terminology never became universal, it was rarely ignored thereafter: repenting is more than feeling sad; it is also a resolution to abandon sin.

In the *Scheme of Redemption,* Robert Milligan distinguished essential and comprehensive senses of the term "repentance." The *essence* of repentance, he claimed, is a change of the *will,* which is the result first of faith as a change of intellect and thereafter sorrow for sin as a change of feeling. The "comprehensive sense" embraced various interconnected and reciprocally interactive relations of intellect, will, affections, and conduct involved in the life of faith. Despite general agreement that repentance is more than mere remorse that comes "after faith and before baptism," many and widely varying accounts circulated in the latter half of the nineteenth century and thereafter. They were as a rule even briefer than Milligan's condensed statement, and few matched its precision or expansiveness.

Views of repentance current in the Stone-Campbell Movement at the start of the twentieth century were evident in two chapter-length, substantive treatments. In *The Old Faith Restated,* contributor Harvey W. Everest analyzed repentance by detailing its (1) nature, (2) antecedent conditions and consequences, and (3) necessity. Evangelical liberal Herbert L. Willett of the University of Chicago included repentance in his work *Basic Truths of the Christian Faith* (1903). Both writers discussed repentance as an *ordo salutis* transitional "step" following faith and leading to baptism and other acts of obedience. Both considered this step an essential of Christian life, embracing both sorrow for past sins and determination to "sin no more."

Everest touches on standard Campbell-Scott themes, citing Scripture rather than the Movement's tradition. Their original context in relation to the Movement's historic teaching on faith is apparently forgotten: the revivalist Charles Finney's very different teaching is commended for "soundness." And the necessity of repentance is underscored, not as the believer's response to faith in the word of God's grace, but by vivid references to God's wrath toward unrepentant sinners. For his part, Willett retells the story of Scott's "five-finger exercise" approvingly, while warning that the gospel can never be reduced to a formula and that the term "first principles" for key moments of conversion is somewhat misleading because truths like the "fatherhood of God" have greater claim to rank as "first."

Repentance was not a matter of teaching that received much attention or emphasis within the Disciples of Christ stream of the Movement in the twentieth century. Sketches of the history and "characteristic" beliefs of Disciples routinely commented on the "ancient gospel" schema. Liberals, stressing faith as ongoing nurture and steady growth, often used the language of popular psychology in discussing repentance. Christian realist and neo-orthodox theologies led some Disciples to accent in their preaching and teaching the ideas of "lifelong" and/or "existential" repentance. Yet unlike faith and baptism, the topic of repentance per se caused no major controversy and underwent no significant doctrinal development.

BIBLIOGRAPHY Alexander Campbell, *The Christian System* (1839) • H. W. Everest, "Repentance — Its Nature, Conditions, and Necessity," in *The Old Faith Restated,* ed. J. H. Garrison (1891), pp. 168-90 • Robert Milligan, *An Exposition and Defense of the Scheme of Redemption* (1868) • Walter Scott, *The Gospel Restored* (1836) • Herbert L. Willett, *Basic Truths of the Christian Faith* (1904).

JAMES O. DUKE

Republican Methodists

Dissident group inaugurating the first schism in American Methodism in 1792.

A group of Methodist ministers in Virginia and North Carolina, led by James O'Kelly (1735-1826), along with four other ministers, Rice Haggard (1769-1819), John Allen, John Robertson, and William McKendree (1757-1835), withdrew from the conference and took with them about 8,000 members. McKendree later returned to Methodism, and John Allen entered a law practice, leaving only Haggard and O'Kelly. In 1794, at the instigation of Rice Haggard, they changed their name to the Christian Church. By 1815 they considered themselves at one with the Jones/Smith New England Christians and with the Stone Christians of Kentucky and Ohio. They merged with these groups after the Civil War to form the Christian Connection or denomination. In 1931 this Christian connection merged with the Congregational Church and in 1957 with the Evangelical and Reform Church to become the United Church of Christ.

The Methodist churches had remained within the Anglican fold until 1795. Methodist churches in America ruled that only ordained clergy could administer baptism and the Lord's Supper and that ministers could be ordained only by Anglicans or by Methodists ordained in England. The result was that Methodist churches in the South, where their numbers were greatest, agitated for ordained clergy, and some conferences even ordained without John Wesley's approval. Wesley therefore sent ordained clergy to America and appointed Thomas Coke (1747-1814) and Francis Asbury (1745-1816) as superintendents of the American Methodists. Coke went back and forth to England, leaving Asbury as the de facto leader, who, against Wesley's wishes, designated himself "Bishop." Asbury insisted that he be elected by the Baltimore Christmas Conference of 1784 rather than simply accepting his superintendency from Wesley. James O'Kelly and his associates anticipated that in America the structures of the church would be much more democratic. They especially objected to the right of Asbury to determine where they could preach.

In 1792, at the General Conference in Baltimore, the churchmen argued for three days over the rights of churches to select their own ministers and for the ministers to determine their own schedules. At a minimum, the O'Kelly backers insisted that the minister should be able to appeal the decision of the bishop. At first it seemed that those supporting O'Kelly would win, but when the votes were counted, the conference supported Asbury. In his journal Asbury wrote regarding O'Kelly, who was by then a presiding elder, "I received a letter from the presiding elder of this district, James O'Kelly; he makes heavy complaints of my power, and bids me stop for one year, or he must use his influence against me. Power! Power! There is not a vote given in a Conference in which the presiding elder has not greatly the advantage of me."

The O'Kelly people — that is, the newly designated Republican Methodists — held independent conferences periodically. Before a conference at the Old Lebanon Meeting House, Surry, Virginia, in August 1794 they appointed a seven-man committee to work out a plan of church government. At that meeting Rice Haggard, who had been ordained by Asbury, arose and declared, "Brethren, this [the Bible] is a sufficient rule of faith and practice. By it we are told that the disciples were called Christians, and I move that henceforth and forever the followers of Christ be known as Christians simply." The conference members thereupon approved Haggard's pronouncement. Ten years later Haggard made the same proposal to the Kentucky Springfield Presbytery with identical results. Haggard's appeal, and perhaps also his treatise *On the Sacred Import of the Christian Name,* ostensibly had a profound impact on Barton W. Stone.

After embracing the Haggard proposition at Old Surry, Virginia, A. M. Hafferty moved that "they take the Bible itself as their only creed." The motion carried, and the Republican Methodists (now Christians) devised the "Five Cardinal Principles of the Christian Church": (1) the Lord Jesus Christ as the only head of the Church, (2) the name "Christian" to the exclusion of all party and sectarian names, (3) the Holy Bible, or the Scriptures of the Old and New Testament, as our only creed and sufficient rule of faith and practice, (4) Christian character, or vital piety, as the only test of church fellowship and membership, and (5) the right of private judgment and the liberty of conscience as the privilege and duty of all.

James O'Kelly favored baptism by sprinkling and continued to do so until his death. In 1810 William Guirey, who argued that immersion alone constituted scriptural baptism, engaged O'Kelly in an extended discussion. The result was that Guirey's supporters formed their own conferences. In some areas, persons from the two different positions continued to worship together.

Virginia Christians often became members of Stoneite Christian congregations when they migrated westward into Kentucky and Ohio. In a few cases, however, they founded independent churches.

See also Christian Connection; Democratization; Haggard, Rice; New England "Christians"; O'Kelly, James

BIBLIOGRAPHY Nathan O. Hatch, *The Democratization of American Christianity* (1989) • C. F. Kilgore, *The James O'Kelly Schism in the Methodist Episcopal Church* (1963) • W. E. MacClenny, *The Life of Rev. James O'Kelly and the Early History of the Christian Church in the South* (1910).

THOMAS H. OLBRICHT

Restauración

Journal published by Spanish evangelical leader and journalist Juan Antonio Monroy (b. 1929) from 1965 to 1985, begun after he came in contact with American Churches of Christ at the 1964 New York World's Fair.

In many ways the journal was a continuation of an earlier periodical titled *Luz y Verdad* (Light and Truth), begun in 1955. The new title reflected Monroy's excitement about the concept of restoration of the New Testament church as he heard it at the World's Fair. In 1966 *Restauración* was subsidized by the Herald of Truth ministry of the Highland Church of Christ in Abilene, Texas, which also supported Monroy's evangelistic work for many years.

The magazine took the format of a literary journal with an editorial by Monroy, poetry, cartoons, articles concerning religious figures and events in Spain and the world, and news about Churches of Christ and other religious groups in Spain. Most of the essays, however, were designed for the spiritual growth of church leaders and members. In the earliest years articles translated from authors in American Churches of Christ sometimes appeared, including George Bailey on authority, as well as John Scott, Abraham J. Malherbe, and Pat Harrell on biblical studies.

In its final year, 1985, the masthead listed Monroy as director, Mercedes Zardain as secretary, and Yolanda Guerrero as editor. In 1986 Monroy began publishing *Vínculo* as a successor to *Restauración,* and in 1988 he started an English-language paper titled *The European Challenge.* In 1990 Monroy began *Alternativa 2000,* which at the beginning of the twenty-first century he continued to edit and publish through his publishing company Editorial Irmayol, founded the same year as *Restauración.* This journal serves the evangelical community in Spain and Latin America. Among frequent contributors are José Grau, Arturo Gutiérrez Marín, and José M. Martínez.

See also Herald of Truth

BIBLIOGRAPHY Juan Antonio Monroy, *Obras Completas de Juan Antonio Monroy,* 9 vols. (1998-).

THOMAS H. OLBRICHT

Restoration, Historical Models of

1. Ecclesiastical Primitivism
2. Ethical Primitivism
3. Experiential Primitivism
4. Gospel Primitivism

Variant interpretations and applications of the principle of restoring the "true church."

The restoration ideal — also known quite often as "Christian primitivism" — is an old and venerable theme in the history of Christianity. At its core, this vision seeks to correct faults or deficiencies by appealing to the primitive church as normative model. One finds this theme emerging early in the history of Christianity in the work of Irenaeus (c. 130–c. 200), who sought to undermine Gnosticism by appealing to the ancient Christian tradition and to bishops who received their offices in regular succession from the apostles.

Early and medieval Christian monks often referred to their monastic discipline as the *bios apostolikos* (the "apostolic way of life"), a recovery of the apostles' renunciation of the world in order to follow Christ and to cultivate the Christian virtues. After Emperor Theodosius I granted the Christian faith establishment status in 380, the restoration vision emerged most often in the hands of heretics and dissenters. This is not surprising since the Latin Catholic Church, dominant during that period, prized the *continuity* of Tradition.

In the sixteenth century, however, the restoration vision emerged with extraordinary power. Protestants of all stripes commonly argued that Roman Catholicism had corrupted the ancient Christian faith. They therefore sought to retrieve that faith and the practices it enjoined from the weight of corruption and tradition that — in their judgment — had accumulated for so many centuries. From this perspective, the restoration vision is central to the Protestant faith.

At the same time, the restoration vision has sometimes been in one sense vacuous, that is, without content. Some representatives of the ideal looked backward to a golden age, but a backward glance is nothing more than that — a backward glance. The fundamental question is this: What dimension of the golden age does the restorationist hope to find and restore?

Based on the history of the Protestant Reformation, we can identify four ways in which the restoration vision has been defined or, put another way, four objectives that the restoration vision has sought to achieve. Those four are ecclesiastical primitivism, ethical primitivism, experiential primitivism, and gospel primitivism. It is important to recognize, however, that these four categories are not mutually exclusive, but intersect with one another in a variety of ways.

1. Ecclesiastical Primitivism

Huldrych Zwingli, the first-generation Reformed theologian who pioneered a reformation in Zurich in 1519, furnishes the prototype for ecclesiastical primitivism. Trained as a Christian humanist, Zwingli brought to Zurich a bias toward the primitive church as normative for all ecclesiastical practice. Zwingli therefore eliminated both singing and the use of organs in the church on the grounds that the apostolic example provides no warrant for these practices. He also reduced the mass to a simple memorial feast, destroyed images, abolished relics and vestments, eliminated pilgrimages, and curtailed a variety of medieval prohibitions. A generation later, John Calvin advocated ecclesiastical primitivism for the church in Geneva, though Calvin's strong convictions regarding human depravity placed constraints on his primitivist agenda. Nonetheless, it is fair to say that the Reformed tradition became the vehicle by which ecclesiastical primitivism made its way to England, Scotland, and America.

Ecclesiastical primitivism flourished in England,

where William Tyndale had suggested in 1534 that the central theme of Scripture was the covenant God had made with his people. Tyndale's suggestion was influential since it appeared in the preface to the widely circulated 1534 edition of his English translation of the New Testament. With that suggestion, Tyndale clearly implied that England stood in covenant relationship with God. By 1550 the terms of that covenant were clear: if England remained faithful to her covenant with the Almighty, God would shower her with untold blessings; but if she strayed from her covenant obligations, she would be cursed. Within that covenantal context, a variety of Reformed theologians from the Continent argued that if England sought to keep the covenant with God, she must restore the forms and structures of the ancient church. Following the attempt of "Bloody" Mary I (1553-58) to repress the English Reformation, the Puritan party emerged, convinced that England had failed to keep her covenant. The Puritans therefore committed themselves to a thoroughgoing restorationist program. Holding up the primitive church as the only legitimate model for the Church of England, the Puritans sought reform in virtually every area of ecclesiastical life, but especially with reference to preaching, the sacraments, and ecclesiastical discipline.

In the United States, no one represented the cause of ecclesiastical primitivism more faithfully than did Alexander Campbell. A rationalist steeped in both Lockean philosophy and Scottish Common Sense Realism, Campbell advocated a rational, systematic reconstruction of the primitive, apostolic church in his own time. Drawing a clear distinction between essential and nonessential practices, Campbell rejected the holy kiss, deaconesses, communal living, foot washing, and charismatic exercises, but argued strongly for congregational autonomy, a plurality of elders in each congregation, weekly communion, and immersion of believers for the forgiveness of sins.

When we identify Zwingli, the Puritans, and Campbell as representatives of ecclesiastical primitivism, we do not mean to suggest they had no interest in ethics, Christian experience, or the core message of the Christian gospel, for they obviously did. On balance, however, each of these movements and individuals trained the restorationist lens on ecclesiastical practice, not on the other dimensions of the Christian faith.

2. Ethical Primitivism

Ethical restorationists argue that, over time, the church has lost its ethical power. To remedy that loss, they return to the wellsprings of discipleship, especially as one finds those wellsprings in the Gospels. The sixteenth-century Anabaptists offer the Protestant prototype for this kind of restorationist activity. The people who came to be known as Anabaptists argued that the Roman Church was ethically impotent for one simple reason: it was a state church that encompassed indiscriminately every single person in society, sustained by the rite of infant baptism. The Anabaptists, therefore, argued for a church composed only of serious believers who would commit themselves to lives of radical discipleship. Rejecting both compromise and tradition, they found their authority in the New Testament and especially in the teachings of Jesus as recorded in the Gospels. They called on their converts to submit to baptism, not as infants but as adult believers. Accordingly, the Anabaptist movement began just outside Zurich, Switzerland, in January 1525 when George Blaurock sought baptism as an adult at the hands of Conrad Grebel and then proceeded to baptize the others in the room.

The Anabaptist movement grew quickly, especially in Switzerland, South Germany, Holland, and Moravia. But even as it grew, it came under severe persecution. Roman Catholic and Protestant authorities alike put hundreds, even thousands, to death, thereby giving the Anabaptists an even greater opportunity to witness to the ethical power of their faith.

The movement led by Barton W. Stone in the early nineteenth century offers another striking example of ethical restorationism. Stone defined the essence of primitive Christianity, not in terms of the forms and structures of the ancient church but instead as radical discipleship that expressed itself in sacrificial service to the neighbor. In large part, this was because Stone understood the ancient Christian faith in light of the kingdom of God that would triumph over all the earth in the final days. Accordingly, he sought to live his life *as if* the final rule of the kingdom of God were present even in the here and now. In the name of both primitive Christianity, on the one hand, and the coming kingdom of God, on the other, Stone therefore freed his slaves long before most Southern whites had even considered that possibility. In addition, he rejected personal wealth, gave of his goods to help the poor. In the last years of his life he refused to vote or to participate in political activity of any kind, and rejected violence and military service.

One finds another notable example of ethical restorationism in the Holiness Movement in America in the late nineteenth century. In the aftermath of the Civil War, Northern cities prospered as they had never prospered before. Historians refer to this unprecedented period of prosperity as the Gilded Age. Significantly, many Protestant denominations, once known for their simplicity and moral rigor, began to accommodate themselves to the materialistic spirit of that period. Simple, whitewashed church buildings gave way to elaborate temples where padded pews replaced the plain and rustic interiors of an earlier age. Congregational singing gave way to choirs and organs, and church after church sought to attract the cultured middle class but paid little regard to the plight of the poor and the dispossessed.

Methodism was a notable case in point. In reaction, a variety of Methodists, usually in rural regions, began to press for a restoration of primitive Christianity, which to them entailed a rigorous ethics inspired by the indwelling Holy Ghost. For example, Robert Lee Harris organized in 1894 a Holiness church movement called the New Testament Church of Christ. Significantly, this church overlapped almost precisely the geographical region that was home to Churches of Christ: it stretched from Milan, Tennessee, on the east to Buffalo Gap, Texas, on the west. With the Bible as its only creed, this church rejected worldly values and allurements and emphasized sanctification (ethical behavior) as a second work of grace following justification (forgiveness of sins) as a first work of grace. The New Testament Church of Christ eventually merged into a larger Holiness denomination, the Church of the Nazarene. The Church of God (Anderson, Indiana) is another classic example of a Holiness denomination embracing ethical primitivism. Daniel Warner sought to "build up [this] apostolical church of the living God" by emphasizing a sanctified lifestyle, sustained by the baptism of the Holy Spirit.

3. Experiential Primitivism

Experiential primitivism locates the essence of the ancient Christian faith either in direct communication with God or in the work the Holy Spirit performs in the lives of believers. It is obvious from the preceding discussion of the Holiness movement that ethical primitivism and experiential primitivism often intersect. Yet, for some Christian movements, experiential restorationism has been paramount.

There is hardly a more striking example of this perspective than the Church of Jesus Christ of Latter-Day Saints. The restoration theme plays a pivotal role in the history of this tradition. Joseph Smith reported that when he went to the woods in 1823 to ask the Lord which of the churches was the true church, the Lord replied that he "must join none of them, for they were all wrong" and that "all their creeds were an abomination in his sight." In time, Joseph came to believe that he would be the instrument through whom the true, ancient church of Christ would be restored to the earth.

Though Smith was a contemporary of Alexander Campbell, he defined the restorationist task in ways that were diametrically opposite to Campbell's understanding of the same motif. If Campbell was a rationalist who filtered the restorationist task through Enlightenment presuppositions, Smith placed the restorationist agenda squarely in the context of the other major intellectual tradition in early nineteenth-century America: Romanticism. Eager to transcend the material world and to burst the bounds that rational categories imposed on the human spirit, Romanticists sought communion with the spirit of Divinity that transcended the material, the rational, and the mundane.

For Joseph Smith and his Latter-Day Saints, therefore, the primitive church was first and foremost a community of believers to whom God spoke directly, apart from written revelation and scientific exegesis. Accordingly, Joseph asserted that God not only spoke to him in the woods but also continued to give him revelations throughout his prophetic career, revelations that today comprise one of Mormonism's sacred texts, the *Doctrine and Covenants.* Similarly, Mormons believe that God continues to speak today to the president of the church. This principle of continuing revelation stands at the heart of the restoration vision as Mormons understand it. Further, because God spoke directly to the leaders of his people in both the Old and New Testaments, Mormons viewed both covenants as normative and sought to restore particular elements from each. For example, they practiced New Testament baptism in a restored Jewish temple, a convergence of traditions that boggled the rational mind of Alexander Campbell.

Pentecostalism also emerges as a movement preoccupied with experiential primitivism. The very term "pentecostalism" suggests the essence of this Christian tradition: recovery of the supernatural gifts that the Holy Spirit showered on the earliest Christians on the day of Pentecost. In the Pentecostal world, the link between ethical primitivism and experiential primitivism is obvious. In fact, Pentecostalism grew from the womb of the Holiness movement. Holiness advocates sought to know whether their ethical behavior was truly the work of the Holy Spirit. If so, the early Pentecostals argued, then the Holy Spirit would authenticate that work by supernatural gifts such as speaking in tongues and healing. Perhaps no Pentecostal writer more fully captured the restorationist dimensions of the Pentecostal movement than B. F. Lawrence, who decried the leading denominations who could trace their histories to human founders. In his book *The Apostolic Faith Restored,* published in 1916, Lawrence proclaimed, "The Pentecostal Movement has no such history; it leaps the intervening years crying, *'Back to Pentecost.'* In the minds of these honest-hearted, thinking men and women, this work of God is immediately connected with the work of God in New Testament days."

4. Gospel Primitivism

Martin Luther offers the best example of a theological vision that we might describe as "gospel primitivism." Technically, Luther was not a restorationist at all. From his perspective, restorationism inevitably involved human effort and therefore works righteousness. He therefore heaped wrath on his one-time colleague, Andreas Bodenstein Carlstadt, who, in Luther's absence, sought to abolish from the Wittenberg church those practices Carlstadt viewed as nonapostolic. Luther fumed, "Listen, murderer of souls and sinful spirit! Are you not indeed a murderer of souls who sets himself above us in God's place and takes away our Christian liberty and subordinates consciences to himself?" From Luther's perspective, restorationism of any kind "destroys faith, profanes the blood of Christ, blasphemes the gospel, and sets all that Christ has won for us at naught." Luther came to these conclusions out of his conviction that the gospel is a message of unmerited, divine favor, extended to believers not because of their righteousness but in spite of their unrighteousness. For Luther, then, any restorationist program smacked of human works that destroyed faith and diminished the dynamic power of the Christian gospel.

Yet we must admit that Luther was in one sense a restorationist. He firmly believed that the Roman Church had obscured the gospel message over the course of many centuries. Luther once confessed that he would not object to the Pope if the Pope would only preach the gospel. But Luther was convinced that the gospel had languished in the hands of the Roman tradition. Now, with the emergence of a variety of Protestants who preached Christian primitivism in various forms, Luther grew concerned that the gospel would languish once again. This time, however, his concern focused on well-meaning Protestants who, from Luther's perspective, had failed to grasp the most fundamental meaning of biblical faith.

See also Protestant Reformation; "Restoration," Meanings of within the Movement

BIBLIOGRAPHY Edith L. Blumhofer, *Restoring the Faith: The Assemblies of God, Pentecostalism, and American Culture* (1993) • Melvin E. Dieter, *The Holiness Revival of the Nineteenth Century* (1980) • Samuel S. Hill, Jr., "A Typology of American Restitutionism: From Frontier Revivalism and Mormonism to the Jesus Movement," *Journal of the American Academy of Religion* 44 (1976): 65-76 • Richard T. Hughes, "Christian Primitivism as Perfectionism: From Anabaptists to Pentecostals," in *Reaching Beyond: Chapters in the History of Perfectionism,* ed. Stanley E. Burgess (1986), pp. 213-55 • Richard T. Hughes, *Reviving the Ancient Faith: The Story of Churches of Christ in America* (1996) • Richard T. Hughes, ed., *The American Quest for the Primitive Church* (1988) • Richard T. Hughes and C. Leonard Allen, *Discovering Our Roots: The Ancestry of Churches of Christ* (1988) • Richard T. Hughes and C. Leonard Allen, *Illusions of Innocence: Protestant Primitivism in America, 1630-1875* (1988) • Franklin H. Littell, *The Origins of Sectarian Protestantism: A Study of the Anabaptist View of the Church* (1952) • Jan Shipps, *Mormonism: The Story of a New Religious Tradition* (1985) • Vinson Synan, *The Holiness-Pentecostal Movement in the United States* (1971).

RICHARD T. HUGHES

"Restoration," Meanings of Within the Movement

1. Restoration as Restitution
2. Restoration as Either Dispensable or Revisable
3. Restoration *Within* the Context of the Church
4. Restoration *Through* the Church
5. Restoration *for* the Church

Leitmotif of the Stone-Campbell Movement in the nineteenth century, and among its conservative constituents in the twentieth.

The term "restoration" has been interpreted in a number of different ways. It would seem, however, from their writings, that Barton W. Stone, Thomas Campbell, and Alexander Campbell generally viewed restoration as the reformation of the church in terms of its origin, mission, and hope as set forth in the apostolic writings of the New Testament.

Barton W. Stone (1772-1844) followed a principle of restoration when he signed the *Last Will and Testament of Springfield Presbytery* in 1801. It urged that "the church of Christ resume her native right of internal government" and "resume her primitive right of trying those *who say they are apostles, and are not.*" Thomas Campbell (1763-1854) affirmed the principle of restoration when he wrote in the *Declaration and Address* that "nothing ought to be received into the faith or worship of the church or be made a term of communion amongst christians that is not as old as the New Testament." It remained, however, for Alexander Campbell (1788-1866) to develop the concept of "restoration" more fully in terms of programmatic reformation of the church when he published a series of essays in *The Christian Baptist* entitled "A Restoration of the Ancient Order of Things." Campbell discussed several issues that have become prominent, interestingly, in the contemporary Faith and Order Movement — Scripture, faith, ministry, ordinances (sacraments), and worship.

Alexander Campbell affirmed that piety required believers to conform to the measure of knowledge they possessed. Indeed, whenever discipleship leads to greater understanding of the will of God as set forth in Scripture, piety requires believers to conform to that new knowledge. Restoration, therefore, could never be a wooden concept or a mechanical process. It entailed dynamic engagement with, and maturing understanding of, the scriptural Word. Inevitably the inheritors of the restoration principle in the Stone-Campbell Movement's history have not always depended slavishly on a single or "original" understanding of the principle and its workability, but have variously interpreted and applied it. No fewer than five such interpretations and applications can be identified, though some of these overlap, and they are by no means all mutually exclusive.

1. Restoration as Restitution

This view understands restoration in terms of a strict adherence to the pattern of church faith and practice set forth in the New Testament. It is reminiscent of two streams of the Protestant Reformation. One is the work of Huldrych Zwingli in the Swiss Reformation in Zurich, who crusaded to purify the church of the accretions of "tradition" and to reinstate the quasi-legal authority of the New Testament. The other is the Anabaptist restitutionism of the Radical Reformation, which affirmed, in the words of the *Chronicle of the Hutterian Brethren,* that "God is best served by free and uncoerced devotion," but that such devotion was judged by distinctive, revealed means of identification with Christ. Therefore, for example, infant baptism was not Christian baptism, and those churches that practiced it were not the "true Church of Christ."

In the Stone-Campbell Movement, the embrace of this particular meaning of restoration went hand in hand with a rationalistic Common Sense hermeneutic that treated Scripture as a coherent body of facts and prescriptions. More strident advocates of this hermeneutic viewed the Bible as a virtual manual for reinstating and maintaining the apostolic model of the church. These advocates certainly shared the restitutionist conviction that believers' immersion (as a "positive ordinance") is an indispensable condition of Christian identity and communion. Early among these was Moses Lard (1818-1880), one-time student of Alexander Campbell and editor of *Lard's Quarterly.* Lard conceded in 1863 that an unimmersed believer might possibly be saved, but such a person could not properly be called a "Christian," for it is in baptism that one receives the name of Christ. Neither could an unimmersed believer be considered a "Christian brother." A more recent view of the "pious unimmersed" along these lines is expressed by F. LaGard Smith (b. 1944), who asks in *Who Is My Brother?* (1997), "How can we have loving unity with our godly friends without telling them frankly that they are not yet in the kingdom?"

Rejection of "innovations" has been considered equally important to restoration of the "true church" and Christian brotherhood. In 1889, led by Daniel Sommer (1850-1940), about 6,000 Disciples met at Sand Creek, Illinois, and heard presented an "Address and Declaration." It protested such innovations as choirs, missionary societies, money-raising schemes, and "the one-man imported preacher-pastor" practice. It then added this sobering warning: "We state that we are compelled from a sense of duty to say, that all such innovations and corruptions to which we have referred, that after being admonished, and having had sufficient time for reflection, if they do not turn away from such abominations, that we can not and will not regard them as brethren." Thus, Christian identity and communion became defined by factors other than confession of Jesus as Lord and baptism into his name.

Since that time, other problems have arisen over issues not mentioned at Sand Creek. Often these have been occasioned by "silences" of Scripture, which the Sand Creek declaration considered prohibitive rather than permissive. The differences have been further exacerbated by what Richard Hughes has called "the Fighting Style," an overt exclusivism.

In 1958 J. D. Thomas (b. 1910) of Churches of Christ sought to resolve these hermeneutical difficulties through an irenic but incisive book entitled *We Be Brethren.* But he found two other major problems: "institutionalism" and "legalism." More recently, some Church of Christ scholars like Thomas H. Olbricht in *Hearing God's Voice* (1996) have called for a "new hermeneutic" that places greater emphasis upon the "story line" of God's mighty acts of love and grace and that avoids the restorationist patternism that reads the Bible mainly in terms of positive commands and ordinances.

2. Restoration as Either Dispensable or Revisable

An important school of Stone-Campbell scholars has rejected "restoration" as a valid principle. The numerous divisions among advocates of "restoration" are viewed as proof that the principle is impractical as well as schismatic. Certain critical studies of the New Testament have also challenged the understanding of the authority of Scripture implicit in the "restitutionist" agenda. Most of those openly critical of classic restorationism have acknowledged that the twin principles of "restoration" and "unity" are not as compatible as the early leaders of the Movement presupposed.

Dissenting views have found collective expression in two significant studies. The first was the work of the "Panel of Scholars," which was appointed in 1956 by the United Christian Missionary Society and the Board of Higher Education of the Disciples of Christ. A key paper in these studies was presented by Ralph G. Wilburn, entitled "A Critique of the Restoration Principle." Wilburn wrote, "In short, the entire question as to whether the Bible, or the teachings of Jesus . . . can, in any sense, be regarded as an *authority* has become problematical. This belief, in the old orthodox sense, is no longer possible." Wilburn, Ronald E. Osborn, and others from the Panel of Scholars raised the question: If the New Testament church is to be restored, which one (among the diverse churches of the New Testament) is to serve as the model? The implication was that honest interpretation of the New Testament would conclude that not a single or thoroughly uniform pattern of church life and practice prevailed among the apostolic communities.

The panel laid the theological groundwork for the subsequent "Restructure" of the churches in 1968 in conformity with the "reformation of tradition" — the tradition of "restoration." A new denominational ecclesiology was formulated, enabling formal participation in the Consultation on Church Union (COCU), though Disciples had participated in ecumenical endeavors prior to Restructure. Subsequently, the denomination entered "Covenant Communion" with other participating COCU bodies and has continued the connection as part of Churches Uniting in Christ, created in 2002.

The second major body of scholarly papers that effectively abandoned "restoration" as restitution was presented during a conference at Christian Theological Seminary in 1989. These learned papers, together with responses, were edited by D. Newell Williams (b. 1950) and published as *A Case Study of Mainstream Protestantism: The Disciples' Relation to American Culture, 1880-1989*. Especially relevant was M. Eugene Boring's (b. 1935) presentation entitled "The Disciples and Higher Criticism: The Crucial Third Generation," which became part of Boring's larger work entitled *Disciples and the Bible* (1997).

Acknowledging the abandonment of the older "restoration" paradigm and its attendant hermeneutic, Newell Williams addressed the question of what norm would thus be used to reform the church: "Is there a basis for Christian union and a distinctively Christian norm for judging theological statements and moral action other than the Bible received as the infallible word of God?" Williams answers in the affirmative, proposing Luther's norm of conformity to the gospel as the *ultimate* test of the church's faith and practice. Williams defines the gospel as the apostles' witness to the acts or deeds of Jesus Christ. These acts or deeds, summarized in Christ's death and resurrection for the redemption of humanity, disclose God's love for sinners. This disclosure of God's love for sinners — the gospel — transforms the human heart from alienation to love toward God and neighbor. Hence, the gospel, rather than conformity to the ancient practices, is the foundation of Christian unity. For the same reason — the power of the gospel to change human hearts — the faith and practice of the church, including its interpretation of scriptural practices, is to be finally judged by conformity to the gospel. Williams finds these views affirmed by Campbell.

A revision of the term "restoration" appears in what Disciples scholar William Tabbernee (b. 1944) of Phillips Theological Seminary called in a 1998 article in *Mid-Stream* "the restoration of normative Christianity." Tabbernee urges that both the New Testament and early postapostolic developments be considered authoritative. This view is foundational to the World Council of Churches document *Baptism, Eucharist and Ministry,* which is being commended to all churches.

3. Restoration *Within* the Context of the Church

Advocates of this view of restoration would affirm the words of Alexander Campbell in 1859: "Faith is a Grace, Repentance is a Grace, Baptism is a Grace, and Regeneration is a Grace. Therefore, our whole salvation is of Grace." Restoration is therefore inextricably entwined with grace. It is the neglect of that relationship which has at times made "restoration" divisive.

This view of restoration does not presume to bring the "true Church" back into existence, for it has *always* existed by grace and not by human engineering. Restoration is the dynamic process whereby the Spirit is operative in the *consensus fidelium* to help Christians realize the *ideal* of the church in the New Testament — to restore the church *as conceived in the mind of Christ.* Three eminent thinkers, in particular, have represented this view: Frederick D. Kershner (1875-1953), former dean and professor at Butler University School of Religion (now Christian Theological Seminary); William Robinson (1888-1963), theologian of the British Churches of Christ and for a time Kershner's colleague at Butler; and Dean E. Walker (1898-1988), former president of Milligan College and founding president of Emmanuel School of Religion. Kershner emphasized the catholicity of the Stone-Campbell "Plea." For Walker, "restoration" concerned "renewal through recovery" of neglected aspects of the original "Gift of the Church." Robinson developed the ecumenical aspects of restoration as a genuinely *ecclesial* principle.

These advocates considered the New Testament documents authoritative in such "renewal through recovery." They did not repudiate the idea that positive "ordinances" had been set forth in the New Testament for the church in all times and places. But they sought to overcome the legalistic and mechanical model of restoration propounded by their conservative forebears and thereby to adjust the traditional hermeneutic of the nineteenth-century Stone-Campbell Movement.

William Robinson proposed that the New Testament was normative because it "contained the record of the *creative* Christian experience and witnessed to the life, faith, and spirit of apostolic Christianity." That "*creative period* . . . alone could have significance for what was the fundamental and peculiar genius of Christianity." Restoring or appropriating "New Testament Christianity" entailed respect for diversity in the New Testament and for developmental factors in the historical life of the church.

Walker saw the New Testament as one of four authoritative "forms" of the Word of God. The New Testament contained the "Word Apostolic," which bears witness to the other forms: the "Word Incarnate" in the Person of Jesus, the "Word Articulate" in gospel proclamation, and the "Word Incorporate" in the church. For Walker, as for Robinson and Kershner, any appeal to the authority of the New Testament necessarily entailed appeal to the higher authority of the person of Jesus Christ himself.

The intrinsic relationship between the church and the New Testament itself bespoke the "catholic" tendency of restoration, as William Robinson affirmed in 1948: "We do not see or hear Christ apart from the church; and the whole trouble on the question of authority has come through setting the New Testament over against the church, or the church over against the New Testament. This our early Disciple teachers saw quite clearly."

Some advocates of "restoration within the context of the church" have continued to treasure the insight of A. T. DeGroot (1903-1992) that "Disciples are Free Church Catholics." They have sought to distinguish between, yet also reconcile, their identity as a historic movement *within* the church and their larger identity as members of the "One Holy, Catholic and Apostolic Church."

4. Restoration *Through* the Church

A Campbellian aspect of "restoration," now commonly neglected, is restoration *through the church*. This is the cosmic and eschatological dimension of the principle — its future orientation. It concerns reformation of the church in light of her role as witness to "the principalities and powers in the heavenly places" (Eph. 3:10) and their consequent subjection to Jesus Christ as Lord, "to the glory of God the Father." This perspective is future-oriented or "consummationist," presuming that restoration, like reformation, is an unfinished task or process and that the perfection of the Bride of Christ is an eschatological goal rather than a present reality. Campbell candidly asserted in *The Christian System* (1839) that the "remedial system" of human redemption (of which the church is the earthly agent under the guidance of the Spirit) is a "moral creation in progress — a new creation of men . . . still advancing."

Campbell, who chose to "look back" in order to look forward, made this the theme of his Fourth of July oration in 1830. It was also the subject of his last essay in the *Millennial Harbinger* in 1865. This eschatological dimension of restoration is the substance of the Christian hope, without which reformation of the church in terms of its origin is incomplete.

5. Restoration *for* the Church

A small, recent, but noteworthy fellowship within the Stone-Campbell heritage has been devoted to the restoration of the pentecostal "spiritual gifts" for the edification of the church. While there is some precedent in the experiential piety of nineteenth-century "charismatics" like Walter Scott Russell, the purest manifestation has been Christ's Church Fellowship, organized as a separate denomination in 1988 and claiming definitive historical roots in the Cane Ridge Revival, "America's Pentecost." These Stone-Campbell Christians have sought to enrich the inner life of a heritage that they have viewed as too preoccupied with the objective "Ancient Order" and not sufficiently concerned with what may be called the subjective "ancient life." This fellowship has maintained relationships with the larger charismatic movement while also seeking to retain its ties to the Stone-Campbell heritage of "restoration."

See also Bible, Interpretation of the; *Consensus Fidelium; Declaration and Address;* Kershner, Frederick D.; Lard, Moses E.; *Last Will and Testament of Springfield Presbytery;* Names of the Movement; New Testament Christianity; Panel of Scholars; "Plea," The; Restoration, Historical Models of; Robinson, William; Sand Creek "Address and Declaration"; Sommer, Daniel; Unity, Christian; Walker, Dean Everest

BIBLIOGRAPHY Paul M. Blowers, "Restoring the One, Holy, Catholic and Apostolic Church: The *Declaration and Address* as Interpreted by William Robinson and Frederick Doyle Kershner," in *The Quest for Christian Unity, Peace, and Purity: Texts and Studies*, ed. Thomas Olbricht and Hans Rollmann (2000), pp. 365-88 • M. Eugene Boring, *Disciples and the Bible: A History of Disciples Biblical Interpretation in North America* (1997) • Alexander Campbell, *The Christian System* (1839) • Alexander Campbell, "A Restoration of the Ancient Order of Things" (32 parts), *Christian Baptist* 2-7 (1824-29) • A. T. DeGroot, *Disciple Thought: A History* (1965) • A. T. DeGroot, *The Restoration Principle* (1960) • Anthony L. Dunnavant, Richard T. Hughes, and Paul M. Blowers, *Founding Vocation and Future Vision: The Self-Understanding of Disciples of Christ and Churches of Christ* (1999) • Richard T. Hughes, "From Primitive Church to Protestant Nation: The Millennial Odyssey of Alexander Campbell," in *Illusions of Innocence: Protestant Primitivism in America, 1630-1875* (1988), pp. 170-87 • Richard T. Hughes and C. Leonard Allen, *Discovering Our Roots*

(1988) • Richard T. Hughes and C. Leonard Allen, *Illusions of Innocence: Protestant Primitivism in America, 1630-1875* (1988) • Frederick D. Kershner, *The Christian Union Overture: An Interpretation of the "Declaration and Address" of Thomas Campbell* (1923) • Thomas H. Olbricht, *Hearing God's Voice: My Life with Scripture in Churches of Christ* (1996) • Thomas H. Olbricht, "The Rationalism of the Restoration," *Restoration Quarterly* 11 (1968): 77-88 • Ronald E. Osborn, "Dogmatically Absolute, Historically Relative," in *The Renewal of Church: The Panel Reports*, vol. 1: *The Reformation of Tradition* (1963), pp. 265-90 • Stephen L. Richardson, "Alexander Campbell's Concept of the Restoration of the Church: Its Sources and Articulation" (unpublished M.Div. thesis, Emmanuel School of Religion, 1977) • William Robinson, *Essays on Christian Unity* (1923) • William Robinson, *The Biblical Doctrine of the Church* (1948) • J. D. Thomas, *We Be Brethren* (1958) • Dean E. Walker, *Adventuring for Christian Unity and Other Essays* (1992) • Roy Bowen Ward, "'The Restoration Principle': A Critical Analysis," *Restoration Quarterly* 8 (1965-66): 197-210 • Ralph Wilburn, "A Critique of the Restoration Principle," in *The Renewal of Church: The Panel Reports*, vol. 1: *The Reformation of Tradition* (1963), pp. 215-56 • D. Newell Williams, *A Case Study of Mainstream Protestantism: The Disciples' Relation to American Culture, 1880-1989* (1991).

ROBERT O. FIFE

Restoration Forums

Meetings to promote understanding and unity especially among members of Churches of Christ and Christian Churches/Churches of Christ, begun in the summer of 1984.

Under the leadership of Don DeWelt (1919-1990) and Dennis Randall, a "Restoration Summit" met on August 7, 1984, on the campus of Ozark Christian College in Joplin, Missouri. Fifty men from each group attended this meeting that set the stage for those that would follow. These 100 well-known individuals, with names such as Reuel Lemmons, Sam Stone, Rubel Shelly, and Victor Knowles, spent several days listening to one another with a clear desire to find threads of a common faith. Those assembled made it clear that they did not officially represent anyone other than themselves, but the significance of their presence and interest in communication was especially noteworthy.

Subsequent meetings were called Restoration Forums and were open to anyone who wished to attend. Though the Forum met twice in 1985, the event has been annual since then, generally held in October or November. The Forums have alternated between Christian Churches/Churches of Christ and Churches of Christ venues. They have included a large area geographically, including the 1999 Forum in Alberta, Canada. Meetings hosted by Christian Churches/Churches of Christ have usually been located on the campuses of Christian colleges. Churches of Christ most often have held meetings in local church buildings, though Pepperdine and Abilene Christian Universities have served as hosts. In the year 2000 the Restoration Forum met on the campus of historic Bethany College, Bethany, West Virginia.

Forum programs are put together by an unpaid, open, "ad hoc" committee. Victor Knowles, Douglas A. Foster, Tom Burgess, Monroe Hawley, Dennis Randall, Chris DeWelt (b. 1952), Don DeWelt, and many others have been involved with this committee in organizing and promoting the Forums to members of both bodies. The Forums are self-funded. All participants pay for their own expenses.

Programs at the Restoration Forums include addresses on subjects that relate to fellowship and general biblical themes and presentations concerning practical steps toward unity. During the earlier meetings, a commonly addressed subject was worship and the use of instrumental music in worship. In time this dialogue turned to a broader discussion of the nature of the church and an active appeal to unity. In excess of 200 addresses had been given during the Forums at the beginning of the twenty-first century. Most often the format has been for two people (one from each group) to address the same topic. Bilateral discussion groups have also been a frequent feature of the Forums.

Though criticized in the early years as an attempt to merge churches, the Restoration Forum has consistently provided a platform for simply discussing and recognizing in an irenic and respectful spirit the commonalities between these groups that share a heritage. In the early twenty-first century, efforts have been made to include members of the Christian Church (Disciples of Christ) in the Forums, building on the work of the Stone-Campbell Dialogue begun among all three streams of the Stone-Campbell Movement in 1999. Presentations from several of the Forums were published in book form by College Press, and major reports have appeared yearly in *One Body* journal.

See also DeWelt, Don; *One Body*

CHRIS DEWELT

Restoration Herald, The

The Restoration Herald is a monthly publication of the Christian Restoration Association (est. 1925), published from Cincinnati, Ohio, until moving its offices north to Mason, Ohio, in 2002. This publication and its parent organization originally evolved from the Clarke Estate (1919); the organization was known as the Clarke Fund and the publication entitled *Facts*. In 1922 the Clarke Fund was separated from the Clarke Estate. In 1925 the organization was renamed the

Christian Restoration Association and the publication *The Restoration Herald.*

When *The Restoration Herald* began, it was announced in the *Christian Standard* as a "new missionary journal." The same article declared that the new periodical would contain "thirty-two pages of stories, essays, mission programs, etc., covering every phase of the church's task — evangelism, missions, benevolence, education, fellowship, spiritual growth, etc." Yet the journal was from the beginning a journalistic arm of the Christian Restoration Association and promoted causes and principles cherished by that organization, which early on challenged the institutional structures (particularly the United Christian Missionary Society) and denominational tendencies of the Disciples of Christ.

Accordingly, *The Restoration Herald* adopted a "platform" at the beginning that has continued to guide its eight editors. The platform includes the following principles: (1) the restoration of the New Testament church in its doctrines, ordinances, and fruits; (2) fellowship through the church, a divine institution, not through missionary societies, which are mere human expediencies; (3) unity in faith, freedom in opinion, and Christian love in all things; (4) the autonomy of the local congregation in all church matters; (5) the right of individual self-determination in missionary giving; (6) the abolition of monopoly in Christian service through a multitude of agencies; (7) claiming the world for the Christ of the New Testament of the church of the New Testament; (8) the development of a native leadership on foreign fields, looking to the ultimate freedom and self-support of indigenous churches; (9) a world-wide fellowship and program for churches of Christ; and (10) Christian consideration for all those who differ from us. Over the years the "platform" changed slightly, keeping accents on "The Bible, The Christ, The Church, The Gospel, The Unity of Believers, The Liberty of The Local Church, and The Fellowship."

The Restoration Herald has historically not shied away from controversy. It spoke up in the earliest days against comity agreements and open membership, which were seen as accommodations to denominationalism and deviations from the New Testament order of the church. Because of ongoing controversy, the journal was taken to court in the 1950s by Disciples of Christ leadership in Iowa, but the lawsuit was unsuccessful.

The Restoration Herald promotes missions, church camps, Bible colleges, national and regional gatherings, and the local church, as well as printing articles of enduring theological importance. It continues to be a strongly conservative voice among the Christian Churches/Churches of Christ.

The Restoration Herald has had the following editors: James DeForest Murch (1922-34); Leon Myers (1934-38); Robert E. Elmore (1938-61); Harvey C. Bream, Jr. (1961-70); James Greenwood (1970-75); H. Sherwood Evans (1975-86); Thomas Thurman (1986-93); and H. Lee Mason (1994-).

See also Christian Restoration Association; Committee of 1000; Elmore, Robert Emmett; Fundamentalism; Murch, James DeForest; *Touchstone, The*

BIBLIOGRAPHY Robert H. Craycraft, Jr., "*The Restoration Herald:* An Historical Analysis" (unpublished M.Div. thesis, Cincinnati Bible Seminary, 1984).

H. LEE MASON

Restoration of the Ancient Order

See "Restoration," Meanings of within the Movement

Restoration Quarterly

Scholarly journal published by members of Churches of Christ since 1957 (except for 1964 and 1985).

Restoration Quarterly was founded by Abraham J. Malherbe and Pat E. Harrell (1930-1978) while the two were doing doctoral study at Harvard University and Boston University respectively. For the first seventeen volumes the journal carried the subtitle *Studies in Christian Scholarship.* The purpose of the journal is to publish scholarly information relevant to students, teachers, and preachers in the Churches of Christ and the Stone-Campbell Movement. Circulation in recent years has been about 900.

Restoration Quarterly began with an editorial board of six persons, but from volume 1, number 4, J. W. Roberts (1918-1973) was listed as editor with the assistance of the editorial board. He served as editor until his death in 1973. His wife, Delno Roberts, served the journal through most of its history as editorial assistant, circulation manager, and president and secretary of the corporate board. The quarterly gained recognition outside its own circles especially under Thomas H. Olbricht (b. 1929), who served as book review editor (1969), associate editor (1970-72), and editor (1973-87), through listing in major indexes of religious periodical literature and subscriptions from libraries worldwide. His wife Dorothy served as business manager and subscription secretary. Everett Ferguson (b. 1933) was editor from 1987 to 1993, when James Thompson (b. 1942) became editor, assisted by his wife Carolyn, who has been circulation manager since 1994. Ferguson greatly expanded the book review coverage as book review editor from 1966 to 1976, a position in which he was succeeded by John T. Willis from 1977 to 1990, C. Leonard Allen from 1990 to 1993, Douglas A. Foster from 1993 to 1998, and Timothy Sensing from 1999 to the time of writing.

As a private, tax-exempt organization under a

self-perpetuating board of trustees, the Restoration Quarterly Corporation governs the business affairs of the journal and selects its editors. Chairmen of the board have included J. D. Thomas; Delno Roberts; Roy Willingham; Ray McGlothlin, Jr.; Thomas Olbricht; Jimmy Jividen; and Robert Olglesby, Sr. Since the editorship of J. W. Roberts, the operations have centered in Abilene, Texas. Through common personnel the journal has been associated with Abilene Christian University, which has offered various forms of assistance to the journal, but there is no official or organizational tie to the school.

Articles have reflected a maturing of theological scholarship especially in Churches of Christ, though articles from other segments of the Stone-Campbell Movement and outside the Movement have been published. Although all theological and ministerial disciplines are reflected in the articles, the greatest numbers have been in biblical studies and church history, especially Stone-Campbell history.

EVERETT FERGUSON

Restoration Review

Religious journal published by Leroy Garrett (b. 1918).

It began as *Bible Talk* in 1952, changed its name in 1959, and ceased publication in 1992. The editor was assisted primarily by his wife, Ouida Garrett. The most frequent contributors, other than the editor, were Robert Meyers, Carl Ketcherside, and Cecil Hook. In its early days the journal focused on controversial topics such as racial concerns, education, observance of holidays, the legitimacy of full-time preachers employed by churches, and other items that were discussed in Churches of Christ during the 1950s. Its later discussions revolved around topics such as unity, divorce and remarriage, and the nature of truth. While the periodical dealt primarily with issues of interest to Churches of Christ, the editor's intentions were ecumenical, especially within the Stone-Campbell legacy.

In 1959 Garrett expressed the mission of *Restoration Review* this way: "This new journal has the dual purpose of encouraging the study of the great ideal of the restoration of early Christianity to modern religion and of promoting moral and spiritual values in modern education." Garrett perceived the first purpose as a "continuum of the movement" begun by Thomas Campbell, Alexander Campbell, and Barton W. Stone in the nineteenth century. The editor set out with the belief that reformation/restoration had been a recurring theme throughout church history and that restoration was "an unfinished task." The journal's contribution to education was to be its reintroduction of philosophy to his readers, a discipline he believed had been "neglected in our materialistic age." Garrett earned a Ph.D. in philosophy from Harvard and taught the subject at several colleges and universities during his career. His philosophical thrust led to multiple citations from and references to prominent Western philosophers (e.g., Socrates, Plato, Aristotle, Pascal, and Locke). Discussion of restoration incorporated ideas from such diverse leaders as Gandhi, M. Scott Peck, Benjamin Franklin, Martin Luther, David Lipscomb, Thomas and Alexander Campbell, Barton W. Stone, Lesslie Newbigin, John F. Kennedy, and Reinhold Niebuhr.

Garrett's periodical received both extensive support and criticism; along with W. Carl Ketcherside's *Mission Messenger,* it provided a forum for progressive thought in Churches of Christ, especially as it reflected early principles of the Movement's founding leaders. After forty years of *Bible Talk* and *Restoration Review,* Garrett and his wife continued contact with longtime readers through two "occasional newsletters" titled *Last Time Around* (1993-95) and *Once More With Love* (1996-2003), followed by a weekly Internet article beginning in September 2003.

See also Ketcherside, W. Carl; *Mission Messenger;* "Restoration," Meanings of within the Movement; Unity, Christian

BIBLIOGRAPHY Leroy Garrett, *A Lover's Quarrel: My Pilgrimage of Freedom in Churches of Christ* (2003).

STEVEN TRAMEL GAINES

Restoration Serials Index

Index of selected religious periodical and lectureship materials produced primarily by members of Churches of Christ but including some materials from other parts of the Stone-Campbell Movement. Based at Abilene Christian University in Abilene, Texas, the Restoration Serials Index (RSI) began publication in 1977 with a three-year compilation (1975-77) of authors and titles. It is published by the Christian College Librarians association, an organization of librarians from colleges, universities, and schools of preaching related to Churches of Christ.

Print versions in three-year increments continued through 1993, when the index to the approximately eighty periodicals and lectureships then included began being published each summer. The entire database, including ongoing retrospective indexing going back eventually to the 1940s, is most easily accessed on-line through the Abilene Christian University Brown Library web site at http://www3.acu.edu/rsi/index.php. At the beginning of the twenty-first century over 100,000 records from eighty-three indexers were included.

Abilene Christian University librarians Dr. Callie Faye Milliken, R. L. Roberts, and Marsha Harper were the first editors of RSI. Editors in 2003 included

Harper, Erma Jean Loveland, Craig Churchill, and Melissa Johnson.

See also Abilene Christian University

BIBLIOGRAPHY Erma Jean Loveland, "Restoration Serials Index," *Christian Scholars Conference Papers* (2001).

ERMA JEAN LOVELAND

Restructure

Organizational design approved in 1968 by the International Convention of the Christian Churches (Disciples of Christ), resulting in the formation of the Christian Church (Disciples of Christ). Rather than being something entirely new in the history of the Stone-Campbell Movement, Restructure represented a maturing of organizational developments that had been under way in the Disciples stream of the Movement for many years.

In his earlier years, Alexander Campbell rejected nearly every vestige of ecclesiastical organization beyond the congregation. However, in his middle years he saw the need for an institution to prepare people for ministry and thus founded Bethany College. Later, in 1849, he became president of the newly organized American Christian Missionary Society. In the 1880s a number of agencies were created to extend the ministry of congregations more broadly into the nation and world: the Board of Church Extension, the National Benevolent Association, and the Pension Fund, just to name a few.

Independent boards comprised of individual members of the Christian Churches provided oversight of these various institutions. However, relationships also developed with the conventions of the churches so that a growing sense of corporate ownership of these institutions developed.

In the 1920s, Unified Promotion was created as a means by which Disciples could support a number of agencies and transcongregational ministries without each congregation being solicited by each individual institution. The International Convention became an annual event through which connections and relationships could be affirmed and reinforced.

By the 1950s there had arisen among many Disciples leaders a felt need for a revisioning of the Brotherhood (as it was called in those days) and a restructuring of its life and ministry. The *restructure* desired was driven by the seven italicized principles enumerated by Ronald Osborn in 1964.

I. *The Brotherhood seeks structures rooted in Christ's ministry made known through Scripture.*

Any suitable church structure will necessarily facilitate Christ's ministry as made known in the Scriptures, for the church is, as Alexander Campbell understood it, "the body of the Spirit of the living Christ." The church's work is Christ's work.

II. *The Brotherhood seeks structures that are comprehensive in ministry and mission.*

The ministry and mission of the church are not merely local, but also global. Christians are called to witness "from our doorsteps to the ends of the earth" (Acts 1:8). Thus a suitable church structure will enable both local and global work and will facilitate a church's commitment to the work of the whole (ecumenical) church.

III. *The Brotherhood seeks structures by which congregations may fulfill their ministries.*

The focus of any suitable structure will be upon helping congregations to be faithful to the whole ministry and mission of the church. Therefore, "overseas ministry," for example, is not primarily the ministry and mission of a unit of the church (known as the Division of Overseas Ministries in the restructured church) but is a ministry and mission of every congregation that is facilitated by the Division of Overseas Ministries.

IV. *The Brotherhood seeks structures that are responsibly interrelated.*

Any suitable structure will have parts that are interrelated and interdependent as befits the Body of Christ ("For just as the body is one and has many members, and all the members of the body, though many, are one body, so it is with Christ"; 1 Cor. 12:12).

V. *The Brotherhood seeks structures that manifest both unity and diversity.*

Unity does not mean uniformity. Any suitable structure must allow for all to follow their Christian conscience.

VI. *The Brotherhood seeks to be ecumenical.*

Any suitable structure should make it possible for Disciples to work with other communions of the Body of Christ as they are led to do so.

VII. *The Brotherhood seeks structures faithful in stewardship.*

Any suitable structure should seek to make the most faithful, effective, and efficient use of the resources available for the ministry and mission of the church.

The resulting Restructure was approved by the International Convention in 1968 and implemented with the first General Assembly in 1969. The name of the church was changed from the International Convention of the Christian *Churches* (Disciples of Christ) to the Christian *Church* (Disciples of Christ) in the United States and Canada. This change of name was a recognition and a sign that Disciples were coming to see themselves as *one* church rather than as a mere *convention* of churches and agencies.

The foundation of Restructure is a covenant. That covenant is rooted in the same *new covenant* that has always been the foundation of the church of Jesus Christ. It is a three-way covenant that unites God, the individual Christian, and other Christians. Disciples understand themselves to be part of the *ekklēsia,* the community of the called. They live not by a *contract* that emphasizes *rights,* but by a *covenant* that emphasizes *responsibilities.* A *contractual* way of life invites "winner take all" strategies and the competitive hoarding of the church's gifts. A *covenantal* way of life, rooted in God's covenant-making actions in Jesus Christ, calls for interdependence, synergy, and the sharing of resources. It also calls for mutual accountability to one another before God.

In his definitive study of the development of Restructure, Anthony L. Dunnavant identifies four core ideals at the heart of the Stone-Campbell Movement: restoration, unity, liberty, and mission. Although these four ideals were each present in the Movement originally, as articulated by the founders, the four are not always easily compatible. Thus, one of the daunting tasks of the Committee on Restructure was to synthesize these ideals where possible and to lead in particular directions when synthesis was not possible. The end product was a proposal for Restructure that emphasized unity and mission as core ideals rather than restoration and liberty (though restoration and, especially, liberty were not entirely abandoned). This was a reflection of the direction that had already been chosen by most "cooperative" congregations over the decades.

There was considerable controversy at the time of Restructure among those who had fears that the new structure would create a church that was much like the churches from which the Campbells and Stone had withdrawn. Especially there were concerns that Restructure meant that the general or regional manifestations of the church would somehow come to own the property of congregations and would thus be able to force congregations to behave in certain ways. This was a gross misreading of the content and intent of Restructure, and subsequent history has shown that those fears were unfounded. Congregations continue to operate with complete freedom (liberty).

There were also fears that the newly established General Assembly could force its will upon congregations. Again, however, these fears proved unfounded, as the General Assembly has no authority over individual congregations. As Disciples say, the General Assembly speaks *to* the church, but not *for* the church. Admittedly, this is a point of polity that is generally misunderstood by the secular media, who tend to report decisions of the General Assembly as though they indeed speak *for* the church. But Disciples congregations continue to make their own decisions about matters of conscience, budgets, and property; who will be their pastors; whom they will recommend for ordination; what programs and ministries beyond their congregation they will participate in; and how much money they will contribute to Disciples mission work beyond the congregation.

Disciples are yet on a pilgrimage, and many sense the need to maintain flexibility in their structures. Nevertheless, the human condition is such that structures have a tendency to become ends in themselves and to demand service rather than remaining servants. To remain faithful to the covenantal polity that was the foundation of Restructure, Disciples must remember that the primary purpose of the Regional and General manifestations is not to be ends in themselves but to enhance the faithfulness and effectiveness of congregations, providing ways and means for congregations to address the world faithfully and effectively. Yet congregations must also remember that, while they are fully church, they are not by themselves the church fully.

The covenantal polity of the Christian Church (Disciples of Christ) declares that when Disciples are meeting in a congregational meeting, they are church. When they meet in regional assembly, they are church. When they are doing mission work in, say, the nation of Lesotho in southern Africa through the Division of Overseas Ministries and with their ecumenical partners, they are church. In each case, they are part of the whole Christian Church (Disciples of Christ). Indeed, they are meeting and acting and serving as a part of the universal church of Jesus Christ.

Disciples image themselves as a "people of the Table" — the communion table. The table, rather than a body of doctrine, is at the center of their life together, reminding them that they are part of the Body by the grace of God and that they are called to live grace-fully with each other. Thus, when they are at their best, Disciples' congregational, regional, and general life is an expression of God's covenant in Jesus Christ.

For Disciples to say that they are in *covenant* is to declare that they are ethically and spiritually bound to cooperate with one another because, having accepted God's covenant, they have entered into a covenantal polity with one another *and with God!* So, while they are not *legally* bound to work together, neither is working together optional: it is the essence of the church as they understand it.

When Disciples are at their best, they discover that God has granted them just the right balance of freedom and responsibility. It is through this balance of freedom and responsibility that the polity of the Christian Church (Disciples of Christ) works. When it does not work, it is usually because someone embraced the freedom of the covenant but forsook the implied responsibility to work together as the whole community of Christ's church. Many Disciples recognize that they have a great deal of maturing to do before they can claim that they are truly living by the covenantal polity envisioned in Restructure.

See also Christian Church (Disciples of Christ); Church, Doctrine of the; Ministry 2.1

BIBLIOGRAPHY Anthony L. Dunnavant, *Restructure: Four Historical Ideals in the Campbell-Stone Movement and the Development of the Polity of the Christian Church (Disciples of Christ)* (1993).

RICHARD L. HAMM

Revelation

Christian doctrine of the self-disclosure of God in salvation history as recorded in Scripture.

As a rule, major thinkers of the Stone-Campbell Movement did not reflect systematically on revelation; rather, their views must largely be sifted from their extensive writings on hermeneutics and biblical exegesis. Nonetheless, one can identify some larger perspectival trends in the Movement's understanding of the character of divine revelation over the course of history.

First, what one might call the "classical" position of the Stone-Campbell Movement, shared across the board by its formative leaders, largely equated divine revelation with the Bible. Alexander Campbell acknowledged the legitimacy of the distinction (and compatibility) between the natural and supernatural revelation of God. He recalled an old analogy that had gained new impetus in the moderate Enlightenment, that God had composed two "books" (creation and Scripture). In *The Christian System* (1839) he wrote, "Nature and religion, the offspring of the same supreme intelligence, bear the image of one father — twin-sisters of the same divine parentage." He and his associates shared the optimism of their time that nature gave corroborating evidence of the Creator and Lord who revealed himself in the scriptural witness.

But the biblical revelation itself remained supremely informative and authoritative for the church, and Campbell and other early leaders often quoted or paraphrased the seventeenth-century Anglican churchman William Chillingworth, "the Bible, I say the Bible, only, is the religion of Protestants." The evidences of nature could never approximate the "gospel facts" of God's creative and redemptive work. The Bible itself might say much about the origin and destiny of "natural" humanity, but it addressed humanity primarily "in his spiritual and eternal relations." "It is not . . . a treatise on man as he was, nor on man as he will be, but on man as he is, and as he ought to be . . . *morally* and *religiously.*" Campbell's defense of the supernatural character of revelation had been ably set out in his debate with Robert Owen in Cincinnati in 1829.

The "classical" position of the early Movement presupposed certain axioms of the Reformed heritage, including the principle that God's revelation was *accommodated* to the constraints of human comprehension. Robert Richardson stated this clearly in his *Principles and Objects of the Religious Reformation, Urged by A. Campbell and Others* (1853): "The Bible contains the only Divine revelations to which man has access; and . . . these are perfectly suited, by their Divine Author, to the circumstances and capacity of man to whom they are addressed." Campbell and his associates likewise echoed the Reformed principle of the *sufficiency* of Scripture as a witness to God's self-revelation.

But a major concern of the Movement's early leaders, being impacted not only by the Presbyterian heritage but by the cultural and intellectual legacy of the moderate Enlightenment, was to understand God's revelation in the Bible as an ordered whole, unfolding in progressive "dispensations" (namely, Patriarchal, Mosaic, and Christian). The duty of responsible interpreters, in turn, was to apply to Scripture the same critical rules as to other literature, attending to the historical (and dispensational) context and the precise language of the biblical text. To do so, as influential interpreters like Walter Scott, Robert Milligan, and J. W. McGarvey argued, would render the biblical revelation transparent to its central (and rational) argument, its multitude of evidences for the one great and intended truth of the lordship of Jesus Christ.

The "classical" position maintained by Campbell and others also held to the principle — deriving from the earliest Christian biblical commentators but transmitted by the Protestant tradition as well — that the biblical revelation was truly an *oracle* of God, that God himself uttered his Word in Scripture and was active through the text, inviting people to faith (hence Campbell's title, *The Living Oracles,* for his New Testament translation published in 1826). Christians needed, both through appropriately critical exegesis and through a humble and teachable spirit, to come within the "understanding distance" of God's voice. Campbell nevertheless rejected outright the Reformed doctrine of plenary verbal inspiration of Scripture precisely because it implied that every word and passage of the Bible was equally communicative of the saving Word. God's true Word was concentrated in certain parts of the Bible, and especially in the New Testament. As Robert Richardson put it, the Bible was the broad "circumference" of revelation, but only the gospel itself was its luminous center. Such a view to some degree relativized the Bible since it indicated that the Bible, while indispensable, was a *means* and not an end. The Bible *contained* rather than constituted the revealed Word of God.

Another mainstay of the "classical" Stone-Campbell doctrine of revelation was the view that revelation could not be communicated independently through any mystical or esoteric influence of the Holy Spirit on the unconverted. Elias Smith of the "New England Christians" took a typical revivalist position: "When a person is brought to see himself undone and helpless, and wholly dependent on the mercy of God, then the Spirit of God moves on his mind, . . . makes a change in him, and brings him from . . . death to life." Robert Milligan effectively expressed the classical Stone-Campbell view in his *The Scheme of Redemption* (1868): "The Holy Spirit operates on the minds and hearts of men in order to [effect] their conversion through the Word of God." The Holy Spirit "never converts any man without the Word."

The second general perspective on revelation in the history of the Stone-Campbell Movement is that of the liberal tradition in the Disciples of Christ. In the late nineteenth and early twentieth centuries, modernism swept through many of the major universities of America. William Rainey Harper at the new University of Chicago influenced Disciples leaders like Herbert L. Willett and Edward Scribner Ames. In its optimism and evolutionism, the new theology fit the culture of the times. For the more extreme liberals or modernists, "revelation" was merely an outmoded word for God's immanence in the unfolding progress of human culture and religion. For Ames, it was the "genius of the Hebrew prophets who developed the idea of a universal Yahweh out of the pre-exilic local, provincial deity." "God is conceived as the soul of social values, the embodiment of ideals, the reality of the good and the beautiful." Willett, like many liberals, expanded the scope of divine revelation as such and conceded that God could and did disclose himself in other religions and among other cultures. Compatibilities between the Bible and sacred texts from other faiths were proof positive of this general revelation.

The majority of Disciples liberals (W. E. Garrison, C. C. Morrison, et al.) did not go to this extreme in their view of God and revelation, although they remained far more open to the principle of cultural relativism than their conservative counterparts. Some moderate Disciples in the mid-twentieth century, like Frederick Kershner and William Robinson, tried aggressively to counter the liberal-modernist trend toward construing revelation as the manifestation of God in human progress by restating the supernatural character of revelation. They sought in some cases to find common cause with movements like neo-orthodoxy (especially Karl Barth), with its strong emphasis on the transcendent Word of God entering the constraints of history to convict, judge, and save.

Another alternative to the "classical" Stone-Campbell understanding of revelation, akin to larger trends in American Protestant fundamentalism and evangelicalism, emerged principally among proto-"independent" conservative Disciples and their heirs in the Christian Churches/Churches of Christ. The fundamentalist impact was indirect but real. As M. Eugene Boring has observed in his history of biblical interpretation in the Stone-Campbell tradition, "The founding of [independent] Bible Colleges was in part the Disciples expression of the conservative reaction to the influence of liberalism in all the mainline denominations in the early decades of this century." Many Bible colleges early on adopted an understanding of revelation and biblical inspiration thoroughly congenial with fundamentalist views, including the doctrine of biblical inerrancy, and all but accused more moderate constituents of infidelity. Most conservatives both from the Christian Churches/Churches of Christ and from Churches of Christ, however, saw themselves less as indebted to fundamentalism and evangelicalism than as assuming the legacy of J. W. McGarvey (or David Lipscomb, in the case of Churches of Christ), aspiring to be faithful to the Stone-Campbell Movement's own nineteenth-century Common Sense hermeneutic, with its assumption that divine revelation was an orderly whole, delivering immutable facts, propositions, and precepts, and remaining impervious to any "law" of cultural evolution or historical conditioning.

At present in Churches of Christ and in Christian Churches/Churches of Christ there is still a considerable legacy of the reaction to the assumptions of biblical higher criticism, but there is by no means one universally shared understanding of the nature of divine revelation. Some constituents (still a minority in both streams) remain open to higher criticism to the extent that it accentuates the historical character of divine revelation and takes a more realistic view of the formation of the biblical canon.

See also Ames, Edward Scribner; Bible, Authority and Inspiration of the; Bible, Interpretation of the; Bible College Movement; Dispensations; Fundamentalism; Hermeneutics; Kershner, Frederick D.; Milligan, Robert; Morrison, Charles Clayton; Richardson, Robert; Robinson, William

BIBLIOGRAPHY Edward Scribner Ames, *Religion* (2nd ed. 1929) • M. Eugene Boring, *Disciples and the Bible: A History of Disciples Biblical Interpretation in North America* (1997) • Alexander Campbell, *The Christian System* (1839) • Alexander Campbell, "Tracts for the People, No. 1: The Bible," *Millennial Harbinger* (1845): 433-44 • J. J. Haley, "The Progress of Revelation, or the Three Dispensations, Their Limits and Characteristics," in *The Old Faith*

Restated, ed. J. H. Garrison (1891), pp. 120-48 • David Lipscomb, "The Bible," in *Salvation from Sin* (1913), pp. 1-25 • J. W. McGarvey, "Grounds on Which We Receive the Bible as the Word of God, and the Only Rule of Faith and Practice," in *The Old Faith Restated,* ed. J. H. Garrison (1891), pp. 11-46 • Robert Milligan, *Reason and Revelation* (1867) • Robert Milligan, *The Scheme of Redemption* (1868) • Charles Clayton Morrison, *The Unfinished Reformation* (1953) • Robert Richardson, *The Principles and Objects of the Religious Reformation, Urged by A. Campbell and Others* (1853).

PAUL M. BLOWERS *and* G. RICHARD PHILLIPS

Revivalist, The

Quarterly periodical founded in 1989 by Herman E. Wesley III for members of African American Churches of Christ.

Starting in Denton, Texas, the paper moved to Montgomery, Alabama, and has grown to become the largest subscription-based journal among black Churches of Christ, with over 10,000 issues circulated across the United States by June 2002. Each issue is set up in tabloid form and generally consists of twenty-four to twenty-eight pages. The publication serves as a vehicle to promote ministries and relate stories of interest primarily to and about African American congregations. Christian colleges and universities often advertise in *The Revivalist* to inform African American Christians of the schools' educational offerings. The publication also addresses issues of doctrinal concern and outreach. Herman E. Wesley III has served as editor and publisher since the paper's beginning and is also minister to the Southside Church of Christ in Montgomery, Alabama. He is a graduate of Southwestern Christian College and Oklahoma Christian College. Sonja Wesley serves as editor-in-chief, and Dianna Kay Tease of Dallas, Texas, serves as senior associate editor.

See also African Americans in the Movement — Churches of Christ; Southwestern Christian College

ERVIN C. JACKSON

Rice, Ira Young, Jr. (1917-2001)

Controversial preacher, editor, and missionary in Churches of Christ.

Rice began his sixty-five-year preaching career in California and Texas. From 1939 to 1948 he edited and published a journal titled the *Christian Soldier,* which took a pacifist stance concerning Christian participation in warfare. He established a confrontational journalistic style that would continue throughout his life.

Following World War II Rice began mission work in Southeast Asia. He established a congregation in Singapore in 1954, working there until the mid-1960s. He helped to establish Four Seas College in Singapore and served as its president from 1966 to 1968. He also did evangelistic work in Malaysia, Hong Kong, the People's Republic of China, and Russia. He became a strong advocate of mission work, traveling extensively among Churches of Christ in the United States to encourage more involvement. His 1959 book (revised in 1966) titled *We Can Evangelize the World* outlined a plan for worldwide mission work by Churches of Christ. For many years he also published the *Far East Newsletter* to inform American congregations of the work he and others were doing in that part of the world.

In the late 1960s Rice became convinced that Churches of Christ were being led away from the strict doctrinal stances that made them who they were. This became his chief focus for the rest of his career. In 1966 he published the first of three volumes titled *Axe on the Root* in which he named those he believed posed a threat to the churches. In 1970 he launched a monthly paper titled *Contending for the Faith* to continue his exposure of those who were leading the church astray. The paper continues, edited by David Brown. Rice wrote a three-volume autobiography, two volumes of which had been published at the time of his accidental death in October 2001.

See also Asia, Missions in; Pacifism

BIBLIOGRAPHY Obituary, *Christian Chronicle* 58 (November 2001): 8 • Ira Y. Rice, Jr., *Axe on the Root,* 3 vols. (1966ff.) • Ira Y. Rice, Jr., *Pressing On Toward the Mark: An Autobiography* (1998).

DOUGLAS A. FOSTER

Rice, Nathan

See Campbell-Rice Debate; Presbyterians, Presbyterianism

Richardson, Robert (1806-1876)

Early reformer and close associate of Alexander Campbell.

Though he is not normally considered one of the original founders of the Stone-Campbell Movement, the often behind-the-scenes, sometimes public contribution of Robert Richardson (1806-1876) — colleague, physician, and biographer of Alexander Campbell — was both substantial and extensive in the Movement's first-generation leadership. A native of Pittsburgh and raised an Episcopalian, Richardson had been taught as a youth by Thomas Campbell and was later tutored in classics and New Testament by Walter Scott. Subsequently he studied chemistry in what is now the University of Pittsburgh, and in

Robert Richardson (seated at right) with his family in 1858, while still serving a professorship at Bethany College. Few individuals besides Thomas Campbell had more profound impact on the thinking of Alexander Campbell than Richardson. Courtesy of Bethany College

1827 he received a medical degree from the University of Pennsylvania in Philadelphia.

Walter Scott, who profoundly influenced Richardson's understanding of the nature of faith as trust in the person of Jesus Christ and who immersed Richardson in 1829, was instrumental in his affiliation with the Disciples of Christ. Richardson initially settled his medical practice in Wellsburg, (West) Virginia, where he worked closely with the Campbells and became a frequent contributor to the *Millennial Harbinger.* After a short stint in Carthage, Ohio, assisting Scott with his journal *The Evangelist,* to which he was also a regular contributor, Richardson returned to Bethany in 1836, accepting Alexander Campbell's request to aid him in his rapidly expanding editorial work. Still operating a medical practice, Richardson purchased a nearby farm and renamed it Bethphage ("nigh unto Bethany"); it was his family home for the rest of his life. He subsequently collaborated with Alexander Campbell as a founding trustee of Bethany College, became its first professor of chemistry when it opened in 1841, and initially served as the college bursar. During the 1840s and 1850s, Richardson was a prolific contributor to the *Millennial Harbinger,* such that some of his longer series of articles were later drawn together and published in book form.

Richardson's larger role as a reformer in the Stone-Campbell Movement can be analyzed in terms of three outstanding contributions: (1) his attention to interrelated issues of worship, spiritual devotion, and ethics in the emerging Movement; (2) his interpretation of the fundamental goals of the Movement and analysis of the nature of Christian reform in its philosophical, hermeneutical, and ecclesiological dimensions; and (3) his work as an interpretive biographer in his two-volume *Memoirs of Alexander Campbell* (1868-69).

In the 1840s and 1850s, often writing under a pseudonym such as "Disciplus" or "Silas," Richardson, perhaps reflecting his Anglican formation, sought to help the Disciples of Christ steer a *via media* between the extremes of the day. Like his peers, Richardson was sensitive to the dangerous penchants of revivalistic enthusiasm. His principal concern, however, was that in excessively embracing Lockean epistemology and Common Sense philosophy, the Movement could drift into an unhealthy religious rationalism. Already in some quarters, overreaction to the experiential mysticism of the frontier revivalists had caused many to fall prey to a dispassionate religiosity unbecoming of true Christian discipleship. In the 1841 *Millennial Harbinger,* Richardson published a series on "The Crisis" of spiritual devotion in Disciples churches, decrying what he observed as lifeless worship and vapid preaching, and censuring journal editors for diverting into issues not central to the reformation. He even took issue with Alexander Campbell for waffling in his affirmation of the work of the Holy Spirit in conversion and sanctification and therefore fueling criticisms of the Disciples by outsiders. In 1842-43 Richardson returned with multiple installments on "The Spirit of God" (the basis of his 1872 book on the Spirit), a thoroughgoing doctrinal exposition of the indwelling of the Holy Spirit in the baptized Christian and of the Spirit's vital role in transforming the whole person, heart as well as intellect.

In the late 1840s and early 1850s, Richardson published extensive series on "The Interpretation of the Scriptures," "Misinterpretation of Scripture," and "Reformation" in which he targeted the rationalism of staunch restorationists in the Stone-Campbell Movement. In his view, the radical literalists — with their "wordy harangues upon the plainness of the scriptures," their "rage for simplification," their reduction of biblical truth purely to hard "facts," and their urge toward overly privatized interpretation of the Bible at the expense of the church's collective judgment — threatened to undermine the *spiritual* character of biblical revelation and to engender an unhealthy nominalism, even "bibliolatry." Though committed, like the Campbells, to the historical-grammatical hermeneutical method, Richardson insisted that spiritual discernment and faith, not science alone, were imperative for a vital and dynamic engagement with the Word of God.

Translated to the context of church reform and the cause of Christian unity, this meant that the churches had to focus (and unite) on general rather than particular truths in Scripture. The Bible as a whole was too broad an authority; only the gospel, the "luminous center" of the revelation, could be the worthy object of discipleship. "It should never be forgotten," Richardson wrote in 1847, "that the Apostles and first preachers of the gospel had no Bibles, and not even a NT, to distribute; and that there was no such thing among the early Christians as a formal union upon the 'Bible alone.' Nay, rather, it was a union upon the *Gospel alone;* for in those days, the gospel possessed identity, and enjoyed a distinct and determinative character."

Knowing full well that most Disciples already affirmed the superior authority of the New Testament, Richardson nonetheless openly criticized those who threatened to turn the programmatic restoration of apostolic Christianity into a rationalistic patternism, seeking "proselytes" to their platform rather than "converts" to the gospel. The criticism agitated, among others, the stalwart Nashville conservative Tolbert Fanning. In the 1850s Richardson and Fanning exchanged articles on "Faith versus Philosophy" in what proved to be a watershed debate in the history of Stone-Campbell hermeneutics. Here Richardson boldly argued that whatever the virtues of the Common Sense/Baconian model of interpreting the Bible, so dear to the Movement, this model too was built on a *philosophical* system — Lockean empiricism — a fact that Fanning and staunch restorationists were unwilling to concede in defending their allegedly "Bible only" position. Richardson declared: "They [Fanning et al.] have adopted and inculcated a philosophy which renders the Spirit of God of none effect; which carnalizes everything spiritual about Christianity, and makes the Bible either a rubric which prescribes forms and ordinances, or a species of mere logical machinery, independent and self-moved, to which the eternal destinies of mankind are exclusively committed."

Richardson warned that faith in Christ, communicated through Scripture, aimed to bring believers to trust in the *person* of Jesus Christ, not to mere assent to facts or propositions. The *personal* character of Christianity, let alone the movement for church reform, was being undermined by this vain new "materialism." Richardson, rendering himself vulnerable to the accusation of being a "spiritualist" or Wesleyan-type "perfectionist," advised the Movement to embrace a new emphasis on discipleship, on the progressive growth of Christians in "the sacred mysteries presented in the gospel," and on the true Christian "philosophy" — Christ crucified — in order to reclaim its true mission. In a word, reformation was impossible without the *transformation* of lives.

Richardson set forth his vision of the Campbellian reformation in his book *The Principles and Objects of Religious Reformation* (1853). The Stone-Campbell Movement, he judged, differed from the Protestant sects by holding up faith in Christ — a *personal* faith, not a dogmatic faith reducible to systems and speculations — as the rallying point of Christian unity. Here, as elsewhere, Richardson viewed the Movement as inaugurating a progressive ministry of discipleship in the light of the central gospel of the Messiahship of Jesus. There was indeed an "ancient order" to be restored, but only within the context of this larger mission of spiritual transformation. "By Christian unity," Richardson wrote in 1859, "we understand *a spiritual oneness with Christ;* by Christian union, *an avowed agreement and co-operation with each other.* There can be no true Christian union, unless there be first Christian unity."

Richardson held up this model of reformation and tried to set an example for effecting it. Thus while many Disciples leaders were concerning themselves simply with the "ordinances" of weekly worship and communion, Richardson produced an entire collection of *Communings in the Sanctuary* sensitive to the mystical, sacramental, and aesthetic dimensions of Christian worship and the Lord's Supper. Just as his position on baptism had emphasized not only immersion but also the personal indwelling of the Spirit in the immersed Christian's soul, his communion piety emphasized not only the regularity of the celebration but also its ultimate goal of spiritual union with God through Christ.

Richardson formatively influenced the early historiography of the Stone-Campbell Movement with his two-volume *Memoirs of Alexander Campbell* (1868-69). This biography was no distanced portrait of Campbell but truly an insider's perspective on the whole making of the reformer and his reformation. Richardson consistently depicted Campbell as seeking to overcome the parochialism and sectarianism of the time in hopes of rediscovering the broad, catholic basis of Christian unity. While not reversing the blindness of the Christian world overnight, Campbell, in Richardson's appraisal, had at least aided in that gradual, progressive enlightenment which would eventually conquer all obstacles to human salvation. Within the context of his own Movement, Campbell was a voice of reason and sound judgment. For example, Richardson notes, while many of his colleagues and contemporaries were infatuated with the eschatological signs of the times and with a literalistic millennialism, Campbell refused to be dogmatic about future events and held to a more general hope of millennial transformation. Even in polemical exchanges with critics, such as in his public debate on baptism with the eminent Presbyterian theologian Nathan Rice, Campbell had, according to Richardson, avowed no peculiar dogmas as the basis of Christian unity but only the simple and universal gospel and that *personal* faith which is its natural response. In a word, Campbell was the hero of the very principles that Richardson cherished, despite the occasional differences of perspective that he and the "sage of Bethany" encountered over the course of their long and fruitful friendship.

See also Bethany College; Bible, Interpretation of the; Campbell, Alexander; Devotional Literature; Faith; Fanning, Tolbert; Holy Spirit, Doctrine of the; Lord's Supper, The; *Memoirs of Alexander Campbell;* Prayer; Rationalism; Worship — Nineteenth Century

BIBLIOGRAPHY C. Leonard Allen and Danny Gray Swick, *Participating in God's Life: Two Crossroads for Churches of Christ* (2001) • Pat Brooks, "Robert Richardson: Nineteenth Century Advocate of Spirituality," *Restoration Quarterly* 21 (1978): 135-49 • Cloyd Goodnight and Dwight Stevenson, *Home to Bethphage: A Biography of Robert Richardson* (1949) • Robert Richardson, "Interpretation of the Scriptures" (15 parts), *Millennial Harbinger* (1847-50) • Robert Richardson, *The Principles and Objects of the Religious Reformation Urged by A. Campbell and Others* (1852; 2nd ed. 1853) • Robert Richardson, "Misinterpretation of Scriptures" (4 parts), *Millennial Harbinger* (1856-57) • Robert Richardson, "Faith Versus Philosophy" (9 parts), *Millennial Harbinger* (1857) • Robert Richardson, *Memoirs of Alexander Campbell,* 2 vols. (1868-69) • Robert Richardson, *Communings in the Sanctuary* (1872; reprint, ed. C. Leonard Allen, 2000) • Robert Richardson, *A Scriptural View of the Office of the Holy Spirit* (1872) • Ernie Stefanik, ed., "Robert Richardson: A Preliminary Bibliography" (on-line: http://www.mun.ca/rels/restmov/texts/rrichardson/re/RRBIB.HTM).

PAUL M. BLOWERS

Ricks, George (1838-1908)

Former slave who traveled in Alabama and Mississippi on mule back, preaching the gospel to his people and establishing churches. He was owned by Abraham Ricks, an Alabama plantation owner in what is now the Muscle Shoals area of Colbert County, who was converted to Christianity by Alexander Campbell.

George Ricks was the first black to own property in Alabama. While George was still a slave, Abraham Ricks allowed him to cultivate a cotton patch in the evenings and on Saturday afternoons, enabling him to earn enough money to purchase fifty-three acres of the Ricks estate just before he was freed. Over time his holdings reached 300 acres. Charlotte Ricks, wife of Abraham Ricks, had taught George to read the Bible, leading to his decision to preach. This commitment prompted many of his acquaintances to call him "Parson George." Parson George donated three acres of his land to be used as a cemetery for African Americans. In addition, he donated an acre of land on which the church that came to be referred to as the Christian Home stands. In a letter dated December 20, 1867, the former slave wrote to the *Gospel Advocate* and asked for $25 to assist in making the payment on this church building. A church at Franklin College near Nashville, Tennessee, granted the request. He traveled by mule to establish churches for blacks in Winfield, Alabama, and Winnisoga, Mississippi.

A view of the pulpit and pews of the "Christian Home" Church of Christ established by George Ricks in the nineteenth century and still in use in the early twenty-first century.

Percy Ricks, grandson of George Ricks, was baptized by his grandfather and preached for thirty years for the High Street Church of Christ in Tuscumbia, Alabama. Percy Ricks traveled to George's ancestral home in West Africa in 1972, baptizing sixteen people.

See also African Americans in the Movement — Churches of Christ

BIBLIOGRAPHY "Letter from a Colored Brother — Help Wanted," *Gospel Advocate* (1868): 23-24 • W. F. Noall, "Percy Ricks and His Grandfather," *Alabama Sunday Magazine* (January 28, 1973): 14 • Donald M. Ricks, *The Descendents of Jonas Ricks and Other Ricks Families in America* (1998).

ERVIN C. JACKSON

Rigdon, Sidney (1793-1876)

Mormon leader; formerly a friend of Alexander Campbell and preacher in the Campbell movement during its affiliation with the Mahoning Baptist Association in Ohio.

Born on February 19, 1793, in St. Clair Township of Allegheny County, Pennsylvania, Sidney Rigdon was the second son of William and Nancy Rigdon. Because he was required to work on the family farm, Rigdon's schooling was limited, but he educated himself by reading the Bible, history books, and grammar texts by the fireplace late at night. The Rigdon family were members of the Peter's Creek Baptist Church during his childhood, and Sidney was familiar with the requirement of a personal divine experience for church membership — "so I made up one," he later admitted.

In late 1818 Rigdon left the farm for a theological apprenticeship with Andrew Clark of the Providence Regular Baptist Church in Beaver County, Pennsylvania. Then, sometime between May 1819 and March 1820, Sidney joined Adamson Bentley in his ministry at Warren, Ohio. While laboring with Bentley, Rigdon met Mrs. Bentley's sister, Phebe Brooks, and married her on June 12, 1820.

Later that year Bentley and Rigdon discovered a pamphlet recording the text of Alexander Campbell's debate with Presbyterian John Walker. They were so fascinated with Campbell that both men journeyed eighty-five miles to Buffaloe (Bethany), Virginia, the next summer (1821) just to talk with him. Their discussion with him lasted all night long, and upon leaving the next morning Rigdon candidly confessed that if he had taught one error from the pulpit within the last year he had taught a thousand.

Campbell was nonetheless impressed with Rigdon and procured him a ministry in 1822 at the First Baptist Church of Pittsburgh, a congregation favorable to Campbell's restoration principles. Rigdon soon established a reputation as one of Pittsburgh's most eloquent and successful preachers. But when the Redstone Baptist Association attempted to expel Campbell from membership in 1823, Rigdon left soon after with Campbell, and both became active in the "more liberal" Mahoning Association. During this time Rigdon also formed a close relationship with Walter Scott.

Beginning in 1825 Rigdon was influenced by the principles in Campbell's "Restoration of the Ancient Order of Things," a series of thirty-two articles in the *Christian Baptist.* As a herald and staunch advocate of these principles, Rigdon frequently spoke to audiences so large that those furthest away could not hear him.

Concluding a six-month ministry in Bainbridge, Ohio, Rigdon became the minister of the Mentor (Ohio) Baptist Church after preaching an impressive funeral service for its preacher, Warner Goodall, in 1826. From 1827 to 1830 Rigdon was one of the most popular and prominent members of Campbell's reformation. But he was also emotionally unstable, vacillating between episodes of exhilaration and depression, according to testimonies of those who knew him best.

During his Mentor ministry Rigdon developed disagreements with Campbell. For one thing, his study of Acts 2:44 convinced him that true Christians ought to live communally, and he organized a "common stock" community on Isaac Morley's farm near Kirtland, Ohio, in February 1830. Also, Rigdon began to question Campbell's "authorization" to lead "the true church," believing that some evidence of God's divine approval must be shown. And third, he believed that a "complete" restoration of the New Testament church would include such original supernatural gifts as faith healing, miracles, tongues, and prophecy — and that these manifestations would validate "authorization."

At the Austintown meeting of the Mahoning Association in 1830, Rigdon advocated his communitarian scheme and was thwarted by Campbell's influence. Rigdon was embarrassed and embittered, and he began slowly to extricate himself from the Campbell movement.

In October 1830, four Mormon "missionaries" stopped to see Rigdon. Skeptical of their message at first, he "received a sign" from God, left the Mentor Church, and journeyed to meet Joseph Smith. Soon becoming Smith's most influential advocate from 1830 to 1844, Rigdon influenced many from the Kirtland congregation, and some others, to join the Mormons. But when Smith was killed by a mob in Carthage, Illinois, in 1844, a confrontation with Brigham Young for leadership of the Mormons left Rigdon as the leader of a minority Pennsylvania remnant that soon dissipated.

Living his final twenty-six years in virtual obscurity in Friendship, New York, Rigdon rarely spoke in public. He died quietly on July 14, 1876, succumbing to a series of strokes.

See also Bentley, Adamson; Heresy, Heretics; Mahoning Baptist Association; Mormonism; Scott, Walter

BIBLIOGRAPHY A. S. Hayden, *Early History of the Disciples in the Western Reserve, Ohio* (1875) • Lloyd A. Knowles, "The Appeal and Course of Christian Restorationism on the Early Nineteenth Century Frontier — With a Focus on Sidney Rigdon as a Case Study" (Ph.D. dissertation, Michigan State University, 2000) • Lloyd A. Knowles, "Sidney Rigdon: The Benedict Arnold of the Restoration Movement?" *Stone-Campbell Journal* 6 (2003): 3-25 • F. Mark McKiernan, *The Voice of One Crying in the Wilderness: Sidney Rigdon, Religious Reformer, 1793-1876* (1971) • Hans Rollmann, "The Early Baptist Career of Sidney Rigdon in Warren, Ohio," *Brigham Young University Studies* 21 (1981): 37-50 • Richard S. Van Wagoner, *Sidney Rigdon: A Portrait of Religious Excess* (1994).

LLOYD A. KNOWLES

Roanoke Bible College

Bible college affiliated with the Christian Churches/Churches of Christ.

Roanoke Bible College was established in 1948 in Elizabeth City, North Carolina, to provide preaching ministers for churches in eastern North Carolina and eastern Virginia. Preachers in this region were few.

Rare was the church that had preaching every Sunday; and in some cases, ten to twelve churches shared the same preacher, who also worked bivocationally ("tent-making"). The founders were also concerned that Atlantic Christian College (now Barton College), the Disciples of Christ school that educated ministers for this region, had drifted into liberalism and modernism.

George W. and Sarah P. BonDurant were the founders of the college; they had earlier helped in founding Atlanta Christian College. The college began in rental property but purchased the first building of the present campus by the beginning of its second year. The campus now covers twenty acres on the riverfront in Elizabeth City.

Bible is the only major offered; minors are offered in preaching ministry, cross-cultural ministry, youth ministry, Christian education, elementary education, counseling, and non-profit leadership and organization. There are also two-year programs in deaf studies, early childhood studies, and Bible. The college has been accredited by the Accreditation Association of Bible Colleges since 1979 and by the Southern Association of Colleges and Schools since 1999. Fall enrollment in 2001 was 189; through May 2001, 873 had graduated from the college during its history.

See also Bible College Movement; Higher Education, Views of in the Movement WILLIAM A. GRIFFIN

Robinson, William (1888-1963)

Theologian and ecumenical activist of the British Churches of Christ in the mid-twentieth century.

William Robinson was a native of Cumbria in northwest England and a graduate in mathematics of Liverpool University. He studied theology at Oxford's Mansfield College and went on to take B.A. and M.A. degrees from Trinity College, Dublin. His major academic positions included principal of Overdale College in Birmingham, England (1920-49); chair of Christian doctrine and philosophy of religion at the Selly Oaks Colleges (Birmingham) during the 1940s; and professor of Christian theology and doctrine at the Butler University School of Religion in Indianapolis (1951-56). Robinson was also editor of *The Christian Quarterly* (U.K., 1934-39) and the *Christian Advocate* (U.K., from 1940).

Though officially representing the Churches of Christ, Robinson was a recognized spokesman for British "free churches" in general in the emerging ecumenical movement, serving as a delegate to the World Conferences on Faith and Order in Geneva (1920), Lausanne (1927), and Edinburgh (1937). Beginning in 1934 he participated in the Continuation Committee of the Faith and Order Movement, and he eventually represented the British Churches of Christ at the World Council of Churches assemblies in Amsterdam (1948) and Evanston (1954). Meanwhile, Robinson's influence beyond Great Britain, among North American Disciples, was greatly enhanced by his work as a delegate to the Disciples' International Convention in 1947 and his subsequent teaching tenure at Butler University School of Religion.

Like certain other Disciples leaders of his generation, Robinson was convinced that the Stone-Campbell heritage had much to offer the modern ecumenical movement. Thomas Campbell, in proposition 1 of his *Declaration and Address,* and Alexander Campbell (whom he cited far more than Barton Stone) had already in Robinson's judgment anticipated the principle of "organic unity" as intrinsic to the nature of the church and therefore imperative for its earthly mission. They had spurned the Protestant notion of the "invisible church" in favor of a more Catholic understanding. They had refused to be individualistic about salvation and "preached a very high doctrine of the Church as the Divine Society." They had rejected the "branch theory" that treated the multiple denominations merely as branches of the one ecclesiastical vine. They had repudiated sectarianism as sin and committed themselves to a *visible* unity of the church.

Robinson asserted, moreover, that the Campbells had never intended to achieve this organic unity through a literalistic or mechanical restorationism, but through a careful, consensual, *historical* reading of the New Testament with a view to discerning the will of Jesus Christ for his church. Insistent that "textual theology" (i.e., proof-texting), such as had been popular in the Campbells' time, was no longer viable, Robinson urged a fresh hermeneutic for Disciples engaging *Scripture, history, and reason.* "New Testament Christianity," he observed, was not a flat outline of ordinances but a dynamic and dimensional reality, admitting of *development* within history, albeit under the continuing guide of the apostolic witness. After all, the church had produced the New Testament, not vice versa. The New Testament continues to operate authoritatively in the church not as a book of law but as "the record of the *creative* Christian experience."

Robinson sought a broad ecumenical hearing for these Campbell principles in books like *What the Churches of Christ Stand For* (1926) and in smaller pamphlets like his "Churches of Christ (Disciples) and the Ecumenical Age" (1951) and "New Testament Christianity" (n.d.). Yet in his *Essays on Christian Unity* (1923) and *The Biblical Doctrine of the Church* (1948), and in numerous other writings as well, Robinson aspired to develop, on the basis of both Stone-Campbell sources and his own biblical and historical-theological studies, a thoroughgoing "high church/free church" ecclesiology — what some have called a "free church catholicism." Central to its catholic appeal was the sufficiency of the Petrine confession ("Jesus is the Christ") as the foundation of Christian fellowship. Robinson acknowledged that the great ecumenical confessions (the Apostles' Creed and Nicene Creed) had earned historical credibility and were worthy of the respect of Stone-Campbell churches as indicating the informed faith toward which all Christians should strive. But these creeds could never dictate in advance the terms of ecclesial communion.

Another hallmark of his ecclesiology was Robinson's focus on, and *sacramental* valuation of, baptism and the Lord's Supper. Robinson clearly intended to correct the Stone-Campbell Movement's preoccupation with "ordinances" to the detriment of the substance and efficacy of these rites. "The very idea of sacraments," he wrote, "necessitates the manifestation of God through specific acts and at specific points such as the Incarnation, the Church, Baptism and the Eucharist." The sacraments are the means to human transformation by grace in the context of the full fellowship and worship of the church. "Baptism is the beginning of that obedience which makes our wills His, and the Eucharist, in a sense, is its continuance." Robinson wrote extensively on the meaning of the sacraments and, with respect to Holy Communion, rejected what he saw as vapid memorialism in favor of a doctrine of Christ's spiritual presence in the Supper.

In further articulating his "high church/free church" ecclesiology, Robinson recalled Campbell's balance between the universal and the local church, and the local congregation's responsibility to the catholic unity of the church. He reasserted the twofold ordained ministry (presbyter-bishops and deacons) supported by the "mutual ministry" of the whole priesthood of believers (the subject of a 1955 monograph). Robinson remained convinced that the Disciples perspective on the nature of the church represented a *via media* between hierarchical ecclesiasticism on the one extreme and radical congregationalism on the other. He vigorously defended Alexander Campbell from the charge of having encouraged the latter extreme.

In *The Biblical Doctrine of the Church* — the fruit of his scriptural exegesis; historical analysis of Protestant (especially Anglican), Roman Catholic, and Eastern Orthodox ecclesiologies; and critical study of contemporary theology — Robinson reflected more deeply on the *mystical* character and substructure of the church as a "divine-human fellowship." "Personality," he argued, was the "real miracle of the universe," and the fellowship of persons "the hidden structure of reality." Before considering the empirical structure of the church, it was necessary to understand the church in terms of a divine bid for fellowship with humanity concretized in the incarnation of the divine Word. The "apostolic" mission of the church (as itself the *extension* of the incarnation) thus meant more than the putting in place of a constitutional order; it demanded ongoing, living engagement with the living Word in the worshiping community. Echoing Campbell's portrait of the church as a Christocracy, Robinson sought to reassert the *personal* authority (*qua* presence) of Christ in his body the church, which is "neither an autocracy nor a democracy so far as its earthly government is concerned."

Robinson summarized his ecclesiology in *The Biblical Doctrine of the Church* by stating that "that church is apostolic in which the apostles' doctrine is preached and taught, in which the sacraments are administered with the unfailing intention of the apostles, who delivered them to us from the Lord, and in which this is safeguarded by a ministry, freely chosen by the church as it is guided by the Holy Spirit, and bearing the apostolic commission."

A renaissance of interest in Robinson's thought has taken place in the United States in recent years, largely among some representatives of the Christian Churches/Churches of Christ encouraged by Robinson's model of free church catholicism and his emphasis on the sacramental character of baptism, the Lord's Supper, and Christian worship itself. Certain scholars from the Christian Church (Disciples of Christ) have likewise rediscovered Robinson's significance as an ecumenical theologian and his "high church" interpretation of Stone-Campbell ecclesiology.

BIBLIOGRAPHY Paul M. Blowers, "Restoring the One, Holy, Catholic, and Apostolic Church: The *Declaration and Address* as Interpreted by William Robinson and Frederick Doyle Kershner," in *The Quest for Christian Unity, Peace, and Purity: Texts and Studies,* ed. Thomas H. Olbricht and Hans Rollmann (2000), pp. 365-88 • Anthony Calvert, "The Published Works of William Robinson: An Interpretive, Annotated Bibliography of a Catholic Evangelical" (M.A. thesis, University of Birmingham, 1984) • James Gray, *W.R.: The Man and His Work* (1978) • Byron Lambert, *The Restoration of the Lord's Supper and the Sacramental Principle, with Special Reference to the Thought of William Robinson* (1992) • William Robinson, *The Biblical Doctrine of the Church* (1948; 2nd ed. 1955) • William Robinson, *Completing the Reformation: The Doctrine of the Priesthood of All Believers* (1955) • William Robinson, "Churches of Christ (Disciples) and the Ecumenical Age" (pamphlet, 1951) • William Robinson, *Essays on Christian Unity* (1923) • William Robinson, *Holy Ordinances* (1925) • William Robinson, "Did Alexander Campbell Believe in Congregationalism?" *Shane Quarterly* 15 (1954): 5-12 • William Robinson, *What Churches of Christ Stand For* (1926) • William Robinson, *Whither Theology? Some Essential Biblical Patterns* (1947).

PAUL M. BLOWERS

Rochester College

School affiliated with Churches of Christ, located in Rochester Hills, Michigan.

The school's roots go back to the work of Harmon Black and James Groves, who began giving night classes in 1949 at Detroit's Hamilton and Tuxedo Church of Christ. Their educational efforts led to conversations by members of Churches of Christ in southeast Michigan and northwest Ohio concerning the establishment of a Christian school in the region.

A board of trustees, established in 1954, purchased property in rural Rochester, Michigan, for a liberal arts college. The school opened in September 1959 as North Central Christian College, though the name was changed in 1961 to Michigan Christian College. From its beginning the board included African Americans, and the college was open to persons of all races. The school was among the first affiliated with Churches of Christ to be integrated.

For most of its history the school operated as a small Christian liberal arts college, serving primarily youth from Churches of Christ in the North Central region of the United States. In the 1990s a reexamination of the purpose and goals of the school led to a conscious shift toward providing a liberal arts education in a Christian environment for all students of the region. In 1997 the board adopted the name Rochester College to convey more clearly this new focus. Enrollment increased over 400 percent between 1992 and 2002, with a student body of nearly 1,000 in 2003.

Though some supporters questioned the college's new focus, the school has maintained clear and strong connections with Churches of Christ. College documents emphasize keystone traditions, including daily chapel, core Bible courses for all students, and the school's heritage in Churches of Christ, including a cappella worship and a strong view of baptism.

In addition, the administration of Rochester College has focused intentionally on the Stone-Campbell idea of unity of all believers "through a spirit of fellowship, reconciliation, and mutual exploration of the Bible as God's conclusive word." In 2003 students from fourteen denominations were studying at Rochester College.

BIBLIOGRAPHY Kenneth L. Johnson, "Rochester College, Churches of Christ, and Nondenominational Christianity" (2001) • Larry R. Stewart, *Michigan Christian College: 1959-1984* (1984). DOUGLAS A. FOSTER

Rogers, John (1800-1867)

Preacher, promoter of Stone-Campbell union, and earliest biographer of Barton W. Stone.

Born in Clark County, Kentucky, on January 6, 1800, Rogers as a young man became a cabinetmaker's apprentice to a Mr. Batterton, in Millersburg, Kentucky. At the age of 18, he united with the Christian Church, led by Barton W. Stone. In 1819 he, with his brother, Samuel Rogers, began the first of many preaching tours.

Following the completion of his first preaching tour, which extended from Kentucky to Ohio, he plied his cabinetmaking skills with Daniel Radcliff in Wilmington, Clinton County, Ohio. Rogers made the first "secretary" to be seen in the area for Mr. David Stratton, a Quaker businessman. His second tour extended into portions of Indiana.

The Christian Church held a yearly minister's conference at Warren, Ohio, in September 1819, at which time Rogers was licensed as a minister of the gospel. Samuel Kyle, clerk of the conference, signed his license. Always an avid reader, Rogers attended a school at Georgetown, Kentucky, headed by Stone, during the winter of 1819-20. In 1820 he began a forty-seven-year ministry with the church at Carlisle, Kentucky, while maintaining his practice of preaching tours.

Rogers's acquaintance with Alexander Campbell began following Campbell's debate with W. L. Maccalla in Washington, Kentucky, in 1823. Campbell preached at the courthouse at Carlisle, Kentucky, on December 6, 1824. Rogers obtained copies of Campbell's *Christian Baptist* and became convinced of the validity of Campbell's teachings.

The union of the Christians, under Barton W. Stone's leadership, and the followers of Alexander Campbell, known as Reformers or Disciples, on December 31, 1831, at the Hill Street Christian Church in Lexington, Kentucky, was not binding on the constituent churches of either group. John Rogers, representing the Christians, and "Raccoon" John Smith, representing the Disciples, were appointed to travel together to promote the union among churches of the two groups and to establish new churches. They traveled together in this capacity for several years.

Rogers's contributions to the Movement were not limited to preaching. He was one of the moderators for Alexander Campbell's debate with John B. Purcell, the Roman Catholic Archbishop of Cincinnati, Ohio, held at the Sycamore Street Church, January 13-20, 1837. He also wrote biographies of early leaders of the Movement. His 1847 biography of Barton W. Stone — the first published — consisted of additions to and reflections on Stone's autobiography. He also published a biography of John T. Johnson (1861). Rogers died on January 4, 1867, while preaching at a church in Dover, Kentucky.

See also Campbell, Alexander; Campbell-Maccalla Debate; Campbell-Purcell Debate; *Christian Baptist,*

The; Evangelism, Evangelists — Nineteenth Century; Johnson, John T.; Rogers, Samuel; Stone, Barton W.; Smith, "Raccoon" John

BIBLIOGRAPHY L. Purviance, *The Biography of Elder David Purviance* (1848) • M. Tiers, *The Christian Portrait Gallery* (1864).

GARY L. LEE

Rogers, Samuel (1789-1877)

Evangelist of the Stone-Campbell Movement in the nineteenth century.

Samuel Rogers was born in Charlotte County, Virginia, and died in Cynthiana, Kentucky. In 1793 his father Ezekiel and family migrated to the vicinity of Danville, Kentucky, then soon after near Winchester. In 1801 the family moved to a farm on the Missouri River, twenty miles northwest of St. Louis. In 1809 the farm was sold and they moved back to Kentucky, near Carlisle.

Samuel married Elizabeth Irvine in 1812; soon afterward he confessed Christ under the preaching of Barton W. Stone and Ruben Dooley. He fought in the War of 1812. After the war he began to preach at Old Concord and Cane Ridge. He moved to Clinton County, Ohio, in 1818, established the New Antioch congregation, and saw it grow into a significant church. While living there he traveled, evangelizing as he went, westward into Missouri several times, southward to Alabama and eastward to Virginia. His evangelistic tours often lasted as many as three months. He baptized several men who later became significant preachers in the Movement, including Joseph Franklin, Benjamin Franklin, Winthrop Hopson, and Elijah Goodwin. In his lifetime he baptized over 7,000 persons. One of his favorite remarks was that the Stoneite Christians made great use of the mourners' bench, and when they abolished it they also abolished the mourner.

In November 1833, Rogers moved his family to Henry County, Indiana, where he taught school as well as preached. He moved several times, in 1838 to Drake County, Ohio, and in 1840 to Griswold City, Missouri, at which place he persuaded Dr. Winthrop Hopson to give up medicine and preach full time. In 1843 he moved to Guernsey County, Ohio, and in 1844 to Carlisle, Kentucky, near his brother, John Rogers, who had traveled with "Raccoon" John Smith to bring about unity among the Stone and Campbell churches. In 1850 Rogers moved to Owingsville, and then in 1852 to Cynthiana, where he died in 1877 at the home of his daughter, Mrs. Francis Fisher. Rogers was a dedicated, successful, and constant evangelist, though he received little pay from the churches.

See also Evangelism, Evangelists — Nineteenth Century

BIBLIOGRAPHY Samuel Rogers, *Autobiography of Elder Samuel Rogers* (4th ed. 1880).

THOMAS H. OLBRICHT

Roman Catholicism

1. Nineteenth Century
2. Twentieth Century

1. Nineteenth Century

The Roman Catholic Church in the nineteenth century was marked by the astonishing growth of ultramontane convictions — that is, by the idea that authority and leadership are best sought by looking, in the European context, "beyond the mountains" to Rome. Clearly a reaction against Enlightenment liberalism, this posture sought to protect Roman Catholic practice and the church's liberty from the control of secular governments. Ultramontanism reached a high point during the pontificate of Pope Pius IX, with the 1864 *Syllabus of Errors,* which declared most of the modern world wrong, and the 1869-70 Vatican Council, which pronounced the Pope to have both primacy of authority over all the Church and the gift to teach the faith without error, that is, infallibly. The instability and social upheaval of much of Europe in the middle of the nineteenth century also produced a great increase in the rates of immigration to the United States, including many Roman Catholic immigrants.

Inherent in the several versions of restorationism that characterized the early decades of the Stone-Campbell Movement was the conviction that all of the churches represented a falling away from the heart of primitive Christianity. While Thomas and Alexander Campbell may have targeted, especially, the divisions of Presbyterianism they had directly experienced in Ireland and Scotland and in western Pennsylvania, the claim certainly included the Roman Catholic Church, which was thought to be fully lost in apostasy.

For eight days in January 1837, Alexander Campbell debated Bishop John B. Purcell of Cincinnati. Acting in response to the request of a group of prominent Cincinnati citizens, Campbell took up the task not only of debating against what he termed the "Romanism" of Purcell but also of defending the cause of Protestantism in the West. It was a hard-hitting affair, befitting the genuine religious controversy involved and the entertainment value it promised, although the tone of the debate may have been kinder than some of its day. In the course of debate, Campbell posited, among others, four claims: (1) that the Roman Catholic Church is not and has never been holy, catholic, or apostolic; (2) that the idea of apostolic succession is to be completely rejected; (3) that the Catholic faith has, in fact, changed over time; and (4) that Catholic teachings on purgatory, indulgences, confession, transubstantiation, and the like are not only wrong but also immoral. The growing Roman Catholic community of the Ohio Valley was delighted to see its new and dynamic bishop defending his community in so public a fashion, a clear signal of the growing strength of Roman Catholics at that time. In fact, their increasing presence made Campbell and others uneasy for the future of democratic liberties, and this anxiety encouraged the forging of links with others in a common Protestant faith.

In 1864 Pope Pius IX issued the *Syllabus of Errors,* a broadside against all things modern. Perhaps the greatest outrage was elicited in Anglo-Saxon settings with item #15, decrying the view that each citizen should be free in matters of religion to follow that form to which the individual's reason had led. The suspicion — not entirely unfounded — that Roman Catholics would deprive non-Catholics of religious liberty led to bitterness and fear. Matters worsened considerably, after 1868, with the announcement that there would soon be an Ecumenical Council held at the Vatican. Rumors abounded that the Council would declare the pope infallible. The rumors were right. The Council also declared that the pope has the fullness of authority in the church. The twin pronouncements of papal infallibility and papal primacy served as proof enough that the apostasy continued. *The Christian Standard* printed in its entirety the letter of Pope Pius IX inviting all other Christians to follow the necessities of their hearts and return to the true fold of Christ, where he awaited to receive them with all affection. The *Standard* editorialized that widespread returns were not likely, but noted favorably that Pius IX had indeed addressed them as Christians, albeit wayward ones, and the *Standard* declared readiness to enter into discussions with Catholics — candid and yet gentle — concerning the basis of the church of God.

Fulfillment of such generous intentions was to be a long time coming and would be subject to the tensions created by continued and even more rapid Catholic immigration and by Roman Catholic claims on public school money. The growing Temperance movement, to which many Disciples were attracted, was another point of contention, as Roman Catholics were not as inclined to participate, however opposed they may have been to drunkenness. The popular stereotype of the Catholic saloonkeeper, catering to an immigrant population in need of uplifting and not alcohol, added to a distrust of Catholics and Roman Catholicism. Additionally, late-century events set Roman Catholics and Disciples in opposition to each other. Disciples writers in venues like the *Standard* regularly celebrated the victories during the 1870s of the armies of Italian unification, ignoring Catholic periodicals crying out for support for the one who was to become "the prisoner of the Vatican." Finally, the Spanish-American War in 1898, which opened previously Spanish-held territories to American missionaries, set up circumstances that would put Disciples and Roman Catholics in direct conflict. While Disciples missionaries in the Philippines had their share of problems in following the comity agreements proposed by the Evangelical Union (of Protestant missionary groups), they agreed with the widespread Protestant view that Roman Catholic Filipinos were appropriate candidates for mission, as the Catholic Church had failed to instruct them in the full doctrinal and moral implications of the gospel.

Some of these issues would remain unresolved in American culture into the twentieth century and, thus, continued to determine the character of interactions between the Roman Catholic Church and the various representatives of the Stone-Campbell Movement.

2. Twentieth Century

The Roman Catholic Church faced the twentieth century armed ideologically with the decrees of the Vatican Council (1869-70) on papal primacy and infallibility. However, it faced a declining sphere of political influence in the world and the emerging need to respond to changing circumstances.

In 1928 New York Governor and Roman Catholic Alfred E. Smith ran unsuccessfully for President of the United States. In spite of Smith's reputation as a nondogmatic urban social reformer, albeit a "wet" one, the campaign issues were quickly reduced to his religious identity, bringing out often fiercely bigoted reactions. W. E. Garrison responded to this campaign with *Catholicism and the American Mind,* a fair but hardly uncritical analysis of how Roman Catholicism could be integrated with the American mentality. Garrison clearly understood the Catholic Church and explained it using its own categories, while rejecting what he saw as improper or wrong. He concluded that because the Catholic Church demands submission and the loss of identity of all others, *churches* could not work with the Catholic Church; however, individual persons, Catholic and non-Catholic, could and should work together for the common good. Others in the Movement rejected even this cautious engagement with Roman Catholics.

The major problem, however, with Garrison's prescription for Catholic-Protestant relations for much of the century was that Catholic and Stone-Campbell Christians did not agree on what constituted the common good. Through mid-century, wherever in the United States questions were raised in public about the sale and consumption of alcohol, the regulation of gambling, and the matter of public funding to religious schools, Roman Catholics were on one side of the issues (generally in the affirmative) and the several Stone-Campbell groups were on the other side (generally in opposition). These issues and the opposing positions could be seen in local discussions, in calls for state referenda, and in national debates.

To understand the change that occurred in the late-twentieth-century interaction between the Roman Catholic Church and members of the Stone-Campbell Movement, two particular events must be explored. The first is the 1960 presidential campaign of Sen. John F. Kennedy, the first successful Roman Catholic candidate for that high office. The second is the event of the Second Vatican Council (1962-65). Until the decade of the 1960s, relations involving the Roman Catholic Church remained in a kind of standstill, reflecting the general hostility with which most Protestants in the United States viewed the Roman Catholic system. Perceived as an enemy of true freedom and an opponent of truth, Catholicism was described by some members of the Movement as a ravenous wolf. Not surprisingly, some Churches of Christ and Christian Churches/Churches of Christ voices decried "the religious question" in the 1960 presidential campaign, citing the 1864 *Syllabus of Errors* that denied the claims of free religious expression to all but Roman Catholics and that stipulated that schools must be directed by Catholic principles. Catholicism as expressed in that nineteenth-century document seemed entirely at odds with the democratic principles of the United States. A Houston-area Church of Christ minister, V. E. Howard, participated in the question-and-answer session following Kennedy's speech to the Greater Houston Ministerial Association, asking Kennedy to accept or publicly reject the Catholic doctrine of mental reservation (quoted by Howard from the 1910 *Catholic Encyclopedia*). The question contained accurate quotations from nineteenth- and twentieth-century popes, but it assumed a troubling conclusion when the quotations were put together. Kennedy's response was evasive; he may well have been unable to talk through the issue. He was no theologian, but his lived experience of Catholicism did not extend to the conclusion that he, as a Catholic, could lie with impunity to the American public because of this doctrine.

When Pope John XXIII, in early 1962, formally convoked the Second Vatican Council, he included in the call an invitation to the various world Christian communities to send delegated observers to the Council. One clearly stated but at that time only vaguely understood objective of the forthcoming Council was to make a bold step for the sake of Christian unity. Hence the inclusion in the Council of what were called the delegated ecumenical observers. Among the thirty-nine or so that showed up for the first session was Jesse Bader, filling the one place then assigned to the World Convention of the Churches of Christ. Others who served as delegated observers over the course of Vatican II were W. G. Baker (Scotland), W. B. Blakemore and Howard Short (United States), and Basil Holt (South Africa). The total number of ecumenical observers swelled to nearly 100 by the end of 1965, as many Christian communities realized that this meeting was not to be a ratification of the *Syllabus of Errors*. Disciples ended up with two observer seats. Their presence and the reports they sent home giving their impressions of events at the Council signaled the beginning of a new spirit of ecumenical cooperation. Editorials in *The Christian* regularly welcomed both the debates at the Council and the texts that resulted. Especially noted were the teachings on religious liberty and the explicit rejection of the claim that Jews be seen as guilty of deicide.

Not all welcomed the work of the Council. The *Christian Standard* noted in 1965 its failure to have changed the practices surrounding mixed marriages. Catholics continued to call for public funds to parochial schools. Furthermore, critics saw in Pope Paul VI's address to the United Nations a ploy to advance the papal agenda of attaining international political supremacy. *Gospel Advocate* articles in 1965 repeated attacks on Catholic claims to ecclesiastical authority over that of the Bible, but made no reference to the texts of Vatican II. The Council's *Declaration on Religious Liberty* was greeted by *Firm Foundation* with considerable skepticism and with a call for the Catholic Church itself to grant religious liberty to those most in need of it — infants. These articles suggested the continuing power of the traditional terms in which some of the issues had been previously debated.

One lasting result of the changed emphasis within the Roman Catholic Church has been the now twenty-five-year-old bilateral dialogue with the Christian Church (Disciples of Christ).

See also Campbell-Purcell Debate; Disciples of Christ–Roman Catholic International Dialogue; Nativism

NADIA M. LAHUTSKY

Rotherham, Joseph Bryant (1828-1910)

Evangelist, editor, and writer of the Stone-Campbell Movement in Great Britain in the nineteenth century.

J. B. Rotherham was born on February 19, 1828, at New Buckenham, Norfolk, the son of a Wesleyan Methodist stonemason and local preacher. Joseph became a local preacher and a minister in the Wesleyan Methodist Association in 1850. His views on baptism

The foremost scholar of the British Churches of Christ in the nineteenth century, J. B. Rotherham (left), in a substantial treatise on Holy Communion declared that the Lord's Supper is more than a bare memorial; it is a "feast upon a sacrifice" in which "the earthly table is in spirit-touch with the heavenly altar." Courtesy of the Disciples of Christ Historical Society

were changed by reading Alexander Carson and by discovering Campbell in a volume of James Wallis's *British Millennial Harbinger* in Hartlepool in 1852. Having been baptized as a believer, he became minister of a Particular Baptist church at Wem in Shropshire, where he made contact with the Church of Christ in Shrewsbury. Through the influence of the evangelist Francis Hill he joined the Churches of Christ in 1854 and became an evangelist in North Wales. He worked with David King to establish churches in Manchester in 1855 and in Birmingham in 1858. He worked in Scotland (1859-65) and in Bath and Manchester (1865-68).

His interest in H. T. Anderson's translation of the New Testament led him to publish his own translation of Matthew's Gospel in 1868. In that year he became a publisher's editor in London. There he published *The Emphasised New Testament* (1872), which went through three editions, the last based on the Westcott-Hort New Testament text in 1897. *The Emphasised Old Testament* appeared in 1902, based on C. D. Ginsburg's Hebrew text. He published *Our Sacred Books* (1903), *Studies in the Epistle to the Hebrews* (1906), *Christian Ministry* (1907), and *The Authority of the Bible* (1908). *Studies in the Psalms* and *Let Us Keep the Feast* were published posthumously in 1911. Rotherham wrote for the *Christian Advocate* and also for the *Christian Commonwealth* in later life. He was open on the communion question, and he enjoyed good relations with contemporaries as varied in their theology as Edward White and Campbell Morgan. Rotherham died on January 13, 1910, one of the most irenic figures in the British Churches of Christ in the later nineteenth century.

See also Great Britain and Ireland, Churches of Christ in; King, David

BIBLIOGRAPHY A. L. Brown, *Joseph Bryant Rotherham: Pilgrim and Translator* (1986) • H. T. Hughes, *A Progress of Pilgrims* (1979) • J. B. Rotherham, *The Authority of the Bible* (1908) • J. B. Rotherham, *Christian Ministry; With Special Reference to the Ministry of the Word* (n.d.) • J. B. Rotherham, *The Emphasised Bible* (1916) • J. B. Rotherham, *Let Us Keep the Feast, Being Plain Chapters on the Lord's Supper* (1911), excerpted in *The Lord's Supper: Historical Writings on Its Meaning to the Body of Christ,* ed. Charles R. Gresham and Tom Lawson (1993), pp. 13-38 • J. B. Rotherham, *Reminiscences, 1828-1906* (n.d.) DAVID M. THOMPSON

Russell, Walter Scott (?-1863)

Preacher and proponent of the dramatic role of the Holy Spirit in the life of the Christian, ultimately accused of schism in the Stone-Campbell Movement.

W. S. Russell graduated from Bethany College in 1856, after which he ministered briefly in Missouri before moving to Jacksonville, Illinois, where he preached and served as president of Berean College. His commencement address at Bethany, which was published in the *Millennial Harbinger* as "The Real and the Ideal," and several of his later writings sparked what became a major controversy in the late 1850s.

Russell, an astute theological thinker, joined his teacher Robert Richardson in developing a strong critique of the Lockean or Baconian philosophy that had become integral to the Movement's theology. He pointed out that Locke's epistemology, according to which knowledge came only through the five senses, dangerously curtailed what human beings could know. The five senses could grasp only "the show of things" or appearances and could not grasp "spirit," which is "the only substantial cause in the universe." One must rise above "sensuous images" in order that "the divine light may shine into the dark places of the heart."

In a series of essays on the Holy Spirit, Russell rejected the "word only" view that the Lockean philosophy had produced in the Movement. He said it was a "superficial and destructive" position, rendering salvation contingent on "the logical power of the understanding in weighing premises and conclusions" and tending to produce "dead churches and prayerless Christians." "Oh, let us come out from under this dark cloud of shallow rationalism," he urged, "and stand in the broad glare of heaven's own light!" Even Campbell's view that the Spirit works "through the word" Russell found scripturally untenable. He tried to reassure Campbell that in his preaching he set forth the gospel as basic to conversion, but he added, "We act upon the belief . . . that God will assist men from the very first, in order to a true faith and obedience." Russell claimed, moreover, to be exercising the freedom of his own conscience in a Movement that valued individual liberty; nevertheless, his plea did nothing to allay the accusation that he was fomenting schism.

Tolbert Fanning, editor of the *Gospel Advocate*, used Russell's essays to step up his attacks on Richardson, who, he charged, was guilty of the same "infidelity" but was simply not willing to state his views so openly or clearly. By 1859 Alexander Campbell himself mounted a frontal assault against Russell, and in the Illinois State Convention of 1860 John S. Sweeney led a successful crusade against Russell's supporters. About the same time, Russell joined the Union army as a chaplain and died of disease at Vicksburg, Mississippi, in 1863.

See also Charismatics; Heresy, Heretics; Holy Spirit, Doctrine of the; Richardson, Robert

BIBLIOGRAPHY C. Leonard Allen, "Unearthing the 'Dirt Philosophy,'" in *Things Unseen* (2003) • Alexander Campbell, "Philosophy, Dogmatism, Schism," *Millennial Harbinger* (1860): 13-20 • W. K. Pendleton, "Walter S. Russell and I. N. Carman," *Millennial Harbinger* (1860): 6-11 • W. S. Russell, "The Doctrine of Conscience," *Christian Sentinel* 4 (1857): 84-85 • W. S. Russell, "Doctrine of the Holy Spirit — Number I," *Christian Sentinel* 4 (1857): 168-69 • W. S. Russell, "Letter from W. S. Russell" (to Alexander Campbell; with "Remarks" and "Review" by W. K. Pendleton), *Millennial Harbinger* (1860): 135-47, 194-207, 269-74, 337-41 • Z. T. Sweeney, "The Walter Scott Russell Crisis," *Christian Standard* 63 (1923): 443.

C. LEONARD ALLEN

Russia, Gospel Christians in

Few individuals were more significant in the organizational development of the Stone-Campbell Movement in Russia than Ivan Prokhanov (1869-1933), who was forced into exile under the Joseph Stalin regime. Photo appearing in the *Christian Standard*, November 30, 1940

The Gospel Christian movement was a restorationist movement begun by a former high-ranking military official in the Russian army, Vasili Alexandrovich Pashkov (1830-1902). Pashkov became convinced of the importance of restoring the New Testament church from hearing the English preacher Lord Radstock, who had been invited to preach in the Czar's palace in St. Petersburg in the 1870s by a dissenter from the Russian Orthodox Church, Madame Chertkova. A wealthy man in the service of the emperor, Pashkov resolved to use his money and influence to proclaim the gospel. Though his new commitment led to a forced renunciation of his military commission, his work at preaching and establishing churches led to the creation of a significant movement known as the Evangelical or Gospel Christians.

Pashkov's attempt to unite his movement with other Russian evangelicals in 1884, along with the remarkable growth of "Pashkovites" or Gospel Christians, drew the attention of hostile authorities, resulting in Pashkov's exile. Four years later the Gospel Christian movement came under the leadership of Ivan Stephanovich Prokhanov, whose extensive evangelistic work won thousands more to the movement. Prokhanov launched a clandestine periodical, *The Conversation*, that kept the network of churches in touch with one another. After the issuance of the Toleration Act of 1905, Prokhanov and his associates began a new paper titled *The Christian* and in 1910 a paper called *The Morning Star*.

In 1909 the churches formed an agency for cooperation in missions, education, and publications named the All-Russian Union of Evangelical Christians. Through a chance meeting in Siberia, Russian evangelist Alexander Persianov had learned of the Stone-Campbell Restoration Movement in America and made contact with Disciples leaders. Persianov and another Gospel Christian, Martin Schmidt, attended the meeting of the General Convention in Louisville, Kentucky, in 1912, securing a pledge of support for the Russian work. Only modest assistance was provided by the American churches, however, between 1913 and 1928.

By 1928 the Union reported 600 evangelists working in Russia, with two million members in that country and neighboring Slavic countries. Prokhanov's restorationist faith is clear from a message he addressed to the churches that year: "It is firmly held by all believers in Christ, apart from any distinction of name or creed, that the church of the first century, the church of Christ and the apostles . . . is in its ideal aspect, the model for the Church throughout all future centuries and will ever remain so."

The Stalinst era brought exile in 1928 for Prokhanov and suppression of the Gospel Christians, with as many as 600 evangelists and elders executed. The Soviet government forced all Protestants into an umbrella organization named the All-Russia Union of Evangelical Christian Baptists. Until the fall of the Soviet Union, many Gospel Christians continued to meet secretly for worship and Bible study.

Twenty-first-century missionaries and directories indicate that about 150 congregations with ties to the Stone-Campbell heritage exist in modern Russia, with approximately 3,000 members. This includes both instrumental and a cappella congregations.

BIBLIOGRAPHY Geoffrey H. Ellis and L. Wesley Jones, *The Other Revolution* (1966) • Edmond Heier, *Religious Schism in Russian Aristocracy, 1860-1900: Radstockism and Pashkovism* (1970) • Ivan Stephanovich Prokhanov, *Resurrection Call,* special letter of appeal to believers around the world (1928) • Ivan Stephanovich Prokhanov, *In the Cauldron of Russia, 1869-1933: Autobiography of I. S. Prokhanoff* (1933, 1993).

L. WESLEY JONES

S

Sacrament

A term applied in some Protestant traditions to the two principal "means of grace," baptism and the Lord's Supper.

The Latin *sacramentum* in the early and medieval Western church translated the Greek *mystērion,* used in the Orthodox churches for the mysteries of baptism, the Eucharist, and other rites. Thinking it unscriptural, some early leaders of the Stone-Campbell Movement avoided the term "sacrament," preferring the word "ordinance," which they (mistakenly) believed was a scriptural term for baptism and the Lord's Supper. Alexander Campbell mentions in the 1859 *Millennial Harbinger,* however, that some of the members of his church in Bethany (or else from other Disciples of Christ congregations) continued to refer to celebrating communion on Sundays as "keeping the sacrament."

Campbell knew well the Presbyterian usage, yet he did not advance the term "sacrament" for either baptism or the Lord's Supper. His understanding of baptism was virtually sacramental in substance, but his preference for the term "ordinance" (or "positive ordinances") reflected his conviction that the immersion of believers (like the Lord's Supper) was a universally binding apostolic injunction basic to the unity of the church. Similarly, Campbell's associate Robert Richardson clearly entertained a sacramental view of the Lord's Supper but stopped short of applying the term to communion, at least in his published writings on the subject. Campbell and others in the early Movement, again without using the term "sacrament," referred to both baptism and the Lord's Supper as "means of enjoyment" of the grace uniquely communicated therein. Moreover, Campbell defined an "ordinance" quasi-sacramentally as a "means of grace," "a specific demonstration of divine grace or spiritual power in reference to some effect no other way attainable."

The use of the word "sacrament" began to grow in the early twentieth century among some Stone-Campbell churches, largely under the influence of the British churchman William Robinson (1888-1963) and his protégés. Robinson held that the word "ordinance," while scriptural, was not applied in Scripture to either baptism or the Supper, and so he abandoned it for the term "sacrament." "Sacrament," Robinson believed, was not only a more fruitful definition in the context of ecumenical relationships, but it also divulged deeper meanings of baptism and the Lord's Supper in Scripture that had been rendered opaque by the prescriptive terminology of "ordinances."

Sacramental terminology is still not widely used in churches of the Stone-Campbell tradition, excepting those few (mainly in the Christian Churches/Churches of Christ and Christian Church [Disciples of Christ]) who are either influenced by Robinson's legacy, sensitive to ecumenically congenial language, or else desirous to recover the meaning of "sacraments" in the Reformed (Presbyterian) heritage from which the Stone-Campbell Movement first sprang. For this group, "sacrament" points to the ethical, eschatological, and corporate meanings of baptism and the Lord's Supper. For example, the Roman Catholic notion of Real Presence in the Supper yields to the idea of Real Action (Robinson's phrase), where "presence" means, not a metaphysical alteration of the material elements but personal *interaction* in spirit between Christ and the believer, as the bread and wine are taken (1 Cor. 10:20-22). The rites are also eschatological in character since they effect a simultaneity of eternity and time; that is, all believers, whatever their moment in history, are raised with Christ in baptism and sit together in the heavenly places (Rom. 6:3-4; Eph. 2:6). The rites receive their corporate character as expressions of the authorized, continued contact of the members of Christ's body with each other, whether on earth or in heaven, and with Christ, their head, whose incarnation they extend (Heb. 10:19-25; 12:22-25).

See also Baptism; Lord's Supper, The; Ordinance; Robinson, William

BIBLIOGRAPHY Richard Harrison, "Early Disciples Sacramental Theology: Catholic, Reformed, and Free," in *Classic Themes in Disciples Theology,* ed. Kenneth Lawrence (1986), pp. 49-100 • Byron C. Lambert, *The Restoration of the Lord's Supper and the Sacramental Principle; with Special Reference to the Thought of William Robinson* (1992) • William Robinson, *Essays on Christian Unity* (1923) • William Robinson, "The Nature and Character of Christian Sacramental Theory and Practice," *Shane Quarterly* 2 (1941): 399-408 • William Robinson, "'Ordinance' or 'Sacrament,'" *The Scroll* 45 (1954): 42-43.

BYRON C. LAMBERT

St. Louis Christian College

Bible college associated with the Christian Churches/Churches of Christ.

In June 1956 the historic meeting occurred that resulted in the formation of St. Louis Christian College. Luther Perrine, Hubert Burris, and Vernon Newland met to discuss remedies to strengthen the struggling Christian churches in the St. Louis metropolitan area as well as in the surrounding rural areas. In this meeting, Newland proposed that the area churches establish a Bible college as a center for evangelism and church support.

Classes were first held with an initial enrollment of nineteen students in the fall of 1956 at Ferguson Christian Church, with faculty and administrative responsibilities distributed among eleven area ministers. By the end of the next academic year, 1957-58, Luther Perrine had been appointed the first president, Vernon Newland the academic dean, and three full-time teachers hired. The current location of the college, an 11.5-acre campus in the St. Louis suburb of Florissant, Missouri, was also acquired.

Facilities added from the 1950s through the 1990s, in addition to the original antebellum "White House" on the school grounds, include new buildings or annexes for classrooms, administration, and student housing. The chapel and gymnasium were added to the multipurpose Keystone Complex (the original structure of which was built in 1959). President's Hall, housing the library, bookstore, student lounge, and cafeteria, was constructed in 1997.

St. Louis Christian College has retained throughout its history a Bible-centered curriculum. The college offers seven traditional Bachelor of Arts and Bachelor of Science degree programs, with a major in Bible and specializations in preaching, youth ministry, music and worship ministry, intercultural and urban ministry, general Christian ministry, educational ministry, and pre-seminary studies. To provide multiple options for students, the college has also forged cooperative programs with Greenville College, St. Louis Community College, and Lindenwood University. It also maintains accreditation with the Accrediting Association of Bible Colleges, and in 1999 it applied for accreditation with North Central Association of Schools and Colleges.

See also Bible College Movement; Higher Education, Views of in the Movement; Newland, Vernon M.

WILLIAM R. BAKER

Salvation

Doctrine of the redemption and transformation of believers through divine grace.

The apostle Paul describes salvation in three tenses — past, present, and future. Believers have been saved (Eph. 2:8), are in the process of being saved (2 Cor. 2:15), and will be saved (Rom. 5:9-10). Theologians have often generally summarized these "tenses" as "justification, sanctification, and glorification." The Stone-Campbell Movement has recognized each of these, but different thinkers at different times have stressed one over the other.

Alexander Campbell identified the three tenses as holy state (justification, pardon), holy character (progressive sanctification), and holy new creation (hope as physical regeneration through the resurrection of the body and the renewal of heaven and earth). Campbell describes salvation in this holistic manner in his *Christian System* essay, "Regeneration." A change of state involves a new birth (pardon and adoption) that produces a new life (a change in character through the working of the Spirit) that terminates in full redemption at the resurrection (eternal life understood as "physical regeneration" on a renewed heaven and earth). Consequently, salvation, which is the function of the whole remedial system, includes the past, present, and future.

This holistic understanding of salvation is present whenever Stone-Campbell authors explain the *Remedial System* (Hiram Christopher) or the *Scheme of Redemption* (Robert Milligan). But while this holistic picture never disappeared from the theological landscape within the Stone-Campbell Movement, the present and future aspects of salvation generally have receded into the background.

Campbell, for example, most often stressed the past dimension of salvation. His corpus is primarily concerned with the assurance and enjoyment of forgiveness. Even his "systematic" discussions often leave little space for present and future soteriology. This emphasis is understandable given Campbell's engagement with the frontier's search for the assurance of forgiveness and the importance he attached to baptism as God's "sensible pledge" of salvation. Often the emphasis on justification was polemical. For example, Campbell's *Christian Baptism* (1851) identifies the "consequents of baptism" in terms of past-tense soteriology. The Campbellian emphasis on baptism, so dominant in the Stone-Campbell Movement, effectively conceived salvation as a past event.

This is particularly true later on among the Churches of Christ. Three authors illustrate the point. T. W. Brents's *The Gospel Plan of Salvation* (1874) is wholly concerned with justification; it never mentions the present and future aspects of salvation. Even when discussing the new birth and the Holy Spirit it is wholly concerned with conversion as an event in the past. David Lipscomb's *Salvation from Sin* (1913), edited by J. W. Shepherd, focuses on justification. While a few chapters discuss eschatology and pneumatology, the discussion is oriented toward understanding the necessity of obedience to divine law at the converting moment. K. C. Moser's *The Way of Salvation* (1932) defends an orthodox Protestant understanding of justification; sanctification and pneumatology are not altogether absent, but eschatology is. Contextual factors, of course, contributed to this emphasis. Brents and Lipscomb were polemically engaged with Calvinists and Baptists, and Moser was responding to the legalism he perceived among his own people. Nevertheless, this context moved Churches of Christ toward a primarily past and legal (though not necessarily legalistic) understanding of salvation. Salvation is primarily justification — that is, the pardon and forgiveness of sins.

The Stone-Campbell Movement, however, has at times emphasized the present dimension of salvation. While Barton W. Stone often reflected all three tenses of salvation, he emphasized the transformation of the believer into the character of Christ as the primary experience of salvation. Union with Christ did not mean the imputation of Christ's legal righteousness, but the transformation of the character by participation in the nature of Christ. Salvation was conceived primarily as sanctification that would result in ultimate justification. Thus, in the end believers would be declared righteous because, by the power of the Spirit, they would be made righteous through a change in character. This manifested itself in Stone's willingness to commune with the unimmersed at the Lord's Table (their character is more important than their baptism) and his insistence that the only kind of union that would stand the test of God's intent was "fire" union, that is, a Spirit-shaped character that loves God and his children. Salvation, then, was more a process than a past event.

Robert Richardson pursued this emphasis on spiritual transformation in his *Office of the Holy Spirit* (1873), though he discusses conversion as a past event and briefly acknowledges a future "hour of redemption." Richardson urges the "restoration of the Spirit" to the Stone-Campbell Movement's soteriological message. The indwelling of the person of the Holy Spirit, he contends, effects a dramatic change in the moral nature of humanity.

Salvation as process rather than event, or as moral rather then legal, gained prominence among the Disciples of Christ in the early twentieth century. Salvation, as Edward Scribner Ames described it in his *The New Orthodoxy* (1918), is oriented toward persons rather than "states." Salvation is not primarily a state, but a movement toward the divine ethic embodied in lived out faith. Similarly, Herbert L. Willett pointed out that the new life, "the possession of the mind of Christ, a character such as his," was the most important dimension of faith (*Basic Truths of the Christian Faith,* 1903). Absent from many discussions of salvation in the early twentieth century among Disciples is eschatology. Given the social context of fundamentalism and World War I, as well as higher-critical views of Scripture and the Social Gospel movement's stress on the immanence of the kingdom of God, eschatology dropped out of the common language of salvation.

What the nineteenth- and twentieth-century church shared, however, was a primarily individualistic understanding of salvation. Though Protestant Christians of the nineteenth century sought communal unity and portrayed the coming kingdom as a cosmic event, salvation was primarily forgiveness from personal sin and the development of a holy character. While the Disciples often expressed this through social ethics in the twentieth century, the Churches of Christ and Christian Churches/Churches of Christ fostered a largely individualistic focus on salvation and reiterated the principle of the "plan of salvation."

Contemporary theologians of the Christian Church (Disciples of Christ) have adopted a transformational understanding of salvation. In fact, as some Disciples theologians moved toward and embraced process and liberation theology, salvation as "process" has often been the dominant model for understanding God's redemptive work. In this context salvation is conceived in cosmic terms rather than homocentrically. The cosmos is in the process of becoming as sin is eradicated. Thus, transformation is understood as part of a cosmic community rather than relegated to the individual life of the believer.

Christian Churches/Churches of Christ have shared the mixed atmosphere of Disciples and Churches of Christ. The "double cure" (justification and sanctification) has been present in much of its literature as discipleship received a greater emphasis than in Churches of Christ. Nevertheless, the dominant concern has been justification and the experience of forgiveness, particularly as it relates to baptism. With the rise of dispensational premillennialism, the positive dimensions of eschatological soteriology were lost as churches reacted to schemes that forced the issue of the nature of the final consummation.

Churches of Christ, prior to the practical expulsion of premillennialists among them, often had a healthy eschatological emphasis, though it was subordinate to the past and present dimensions of salvation. R. H. Boll, for example, perhaps best modeled the portrayal of salvation as past, present, and future. However, by the mid-twentieth century, the Churches of Christ along with the other segments of the Stone-Campbell Movement had essentially lost the eschatological emphasis in their soteriology. Of course, hope functioned as part of their religious life, but the attention it received did not compare with the past or present experience of salvation, and it did not shape soteriological reflection.

The Stone-Campbell Movement, then, has usually stressed the past and present dimensions of salvation, and mostly from an individualistic vantage point. It emphasized salvation as either a legal state (thus past) or a holy character through transformation (present process). Though eschatology was part of this picture, especially in the nineteenth century, it was largely lost because of the Movement's polemical (debates over baptism) or social (institutionalism, anti-dispensationalism, and emphasis on social transformation) interests. At the end of the twentieth century, however, evidence from all three streams of the Stone-Campbell Movement indicated movement toward a more communal and holistic understanding of salvation with a balanced stress on all the "tenses" of salvation.

See also Anthropology; Atonement; Calvinism; *Christian System, The;* Covenant (Federal) Theology; Eschatology; Grace, Doctrine of; Holy Spirit, Doctrine of the; Justification, Doctrine of; Regeneration; Sanctification, Doctrine of; *Scheme of Redemption, The*

BIBLIOGRAPHY Edward Scribner Ames, *The New Orthodoxy* (1913) • Robert H. Boll, *The Kingdom of God: A Survey-Study of the Bible's Principal Theme* (3rd ed. 1948) • T. W. Brents, *The Gospel Plan of Salvation* (1889) • Alexander Campbell, *Christian Baptism* (1851) • Alexander Campbell, *The Christian System* (1839) • Hiram Christopher, *The Remedial System: Or, Man and His Redeemer* (1875) • John Mark Hicks, "K. C. Moser and Churches of Christ: A Historical Perspective," *Restoration Quarterly* 37 (1995): 139-57 • David Lipscomb, *Salvation from Sin* (1913) • Robert Milligan, *Exposition and Defense of the Scheme of Redemption* (1868) • K. C. Moser, *The Way of Salvation* (1932) • Robert Richardson, *A Scriptural View of the Office of the Holy Spirit* (1873) • William J. Richardson, ed., *Christian Doctrine: "The Faith, Once Delivered"* (1983) • Barton W. Stone, "A Compendious View of the Gospel," in *The Biography of Elder Barton Warren Stone* (1847), pp. 191-221 • Virgil Warren, *What the Bible Says About Salvation* (1982) • Herbert L. Willett, *Basic Truths of the Christian Faith* (1903) • Clark Williamson, *Way of Blessing, Way of Life: A Christian Theology* (1999).

JOHN MARK HICKS

Sanderson, L. O.

See Hymnody

San Jose Christian College

Bible college associated with the Christian Churches/Churches of Christ.

William L. Jessup (1905-1992) was the founder of San Jose Bible College. A graduate of Eugene Bible University (now Northwest Christian College) and a minister in Visalia, California, Jessup was asked by the aging Eugene Sanderson to take over his failed attempt to start a ministerial training college for churches in San Jose, California, a city of 61,000. With the blessing of the Visalia congregation, Jessup moved to San Jose to take up residence in one wing of the indebted apartments that had been purchased by Sanderson for college use.

Under Jessup's lead, the relocated Central Christian Church hosted the first classes of San Jose Bible College with fourteen students in September 1939; enrollment grew to sixty the next year, and jumped to over 200 following World War II, when the college moved to a newly built campus at twelfth and Virginia Streets in San Jose. At present it enrolls approximately 400 students.

"Brother Bill," as college supporters called him, was well known for his efforts to reconcile the dividing segments of the Stone-Campbell Movement. The annual Conference on Evangelism, conducted by the college at the San Jose downtown auditorium, not only attracted leaders and members from Christian Churches/Churches of Christ, but welcomed those from diverse communions. Ernest Beam and W. Carl Ketcherside, key promoters of unity and gracious accommodation among the Churches of Christ, spoke on several occasions, especially during the 1960s.

Graduates of the college had established forty churches by 1950, but only a dozen graduates had entered mission service. To encourage more mission emphasis Bill Jessup accepted the invitation of Christian Churches/Churches of Christ missionaries in 1952 to make a goodwill tour of Japan, Korea, Okinawa, and the Philippines. More graduates accepted the mission challenge, and increasing numbers of Asian students enrolled in San Jose Bible College.

Bill Jessup's twenty-year presidency of the college (1939-60) had two principal emphases — unity and missions — that have continued in the college to this present day. The curriculum of the college meanwhile developed around a biblical core. All students still major in Bible and theology but can select a second major in ministry areas such as Christian education, pastoral ministry, youth ministry, music and worship, counseling psychology, as well as intercultural studies and missions.

The next president, Alvan Tiffin (1960-67), initiated efforts to raise the academic credentials of the school. The college was accepted as an associate member of the Accrediting Association of Bible Colleges; the campus was also expanded. The college's third president, Woodrow Phillips (1968-78), brought considerable missionary experience to his administration, inaugurating church planting among local ethnic communities and creating a new administrative position, Director of Missions. The college's fourth president, Charles Boatman (1979-84), also brought missionary experience, having established a leadership training school in Liberia. Boatman, like his predecessor Bill Jessup, again encouraged the twin emphases of Christian unity and mission and pursued greater theological sophistication in the college.

In 1985 Bryce Jessup, pastor and son of founder Bill Jessup, became the college's fifth president; he presided over the name change to San Jose Christian College in 1989, on the school's fiftieth anniversary. The multicultural emphasis of predecessors was given specific direction to include the training of ministers to serve the scores of immigrants who were flooding into the larger San Francisco Bay area. New churches were begun among Cambodians, Koreans, Indians, Iranians, Southeast Asians, and others. The campus became truly multicultural, and over 50 percent the college's enrollment consists of nationalities other than those of European descent.

Jessup placed the college under a rigorous discipline to achieve candidacy in the Western Association of Schools and Colleges, which was granted in 1996.

See also Bible College Movement; Higher Education, Views of in the Movement; Sanderson, Eugene C.

BIBLIOGRAPHY David Beavers, *Bill Jessup: Preacher of Unity and Worship* (1993). ALVIN D. HAMMOND

Sanctification, Doctrine of

Sanctification is the holiness bespeaking both the Christian's changed status before God and the vocation of holy living. Sanctification begins when God sets apart the believer for salvation, but it entails as well the dynamic process of being made holy in one's moral and spiritual life and overcoming the power of sin. Theologians within the Stone-Campbell Movement have addressed both these dimensions of sanctification.

Describing the change of *state* that believers undergo in conversion and regeneration, Alexander Campbell in *The Christian System* (1839) and elsewhere indicated that forgiveness, justification, sanctification, adoption, and salvation were all simultaneous effects of one and the same transformation. "Pardon has respect to guilt; justification, to condemnation; sanctification, to pollution; adoption, to alienation; and salvation, to destruction." Specifically, he wrote in his *Christian Baptism* (1851), "Holiness is literally separation from the earth to God and heaven." As a *progressive* work, on the other hand, Campbell acknowledged the work of the Spirit in sanctification, especially in the formation of "holy character." While arguing that the Word and Spirit inseparably cooperate in this process, Campbell affirmed that the Spirit of God, "clothed with gospel motives and arguments," is active in "enlightening, convincing, persuading sinners, and thus enabling them to flee from the wrath to come." The Word plants the "incorruptible seed" in the heart, where it "vegetates, and germinates, and grows," while the Spirit "quickens" and so brings the seed of holiness to fruition.

Barton W. Stone noted that atonement always implied sanctification, and that with salvation a Christian is sanctified and redeemed from sin. Faith preceded sanctification. He acknowledged that sanctification is "the transformative work of God in the hearts of people" through the work of the Holy Spirit.

Robert Richardson stood out in the early history of the Movement as an advocate for a more emphatic and consistent teaching on Christian sanctification. Richardson had deep concerns, expressed in an extended exchange with Tolbert Fanning, over the threat of rationalism in the Movement as he saw it manifested in a lack of spiritual depth and a deficient sensitivity to the work of the Holy Spirit. Richardson insisted on the notion of the *personal indwelling* of the Spirit in the baptized believer. The Spirit was a "cherished guest," aiding the growth and spiritual maturation of the Christian. Richardson developed a virtually ascetic model of this process, viewing the Christian, aided by the Spirit, as engaged in an ongoing battle with the invisible powers of evil. Richardson went beyond Campbell's own emphases, but never betrayed the basic principle that the Spirit cultivates holiness in the believer nurtured by the power of the gospel itself to change the affections and behavior of the Christian. This, however, did not prevent his opponents from stereotyping Richardson as a "perfectionist."

Alexander Campbell's view of sanctification, however, had a dominant influence in the second and third generations of the Stone-Campbell Movement. Benjamin Franklin accepted the basic premise that faith must precede the "spiritual life." For Franklin, the Bible guided the Christian in sanctification. Later, while many Stone-Campbell preachers and thinkers, especially in the Churches of Christ, tended to embrace a quasi-legal model of salvation with a muted Holy Spirit, others such as Robert H. Boll emphasized God's gifting the Christian with the grace and means to sanctification. K. C. Moser recognized sanctification as an obligation for the Christian, attacked sanctification through works, and pointed to the indwelling Holy Spirit to lead the Christian to holiness. The British Disciples theologian William Robinson saw sanctification as a process with a constant "need for repentance and confession." He connected the object of baptism to sanctification through the blood of Christ that enables the Christian to enjoy all the spiritual riches in Christ. Morality and "social righteousness" need the Spirit of Christ. Robinson called Christians "sinning saints" to reflect the need to consider the seriousness of sin in the process of sanctification. Robinson's American contemporary, Frederick Kershner of the Butler University School of Religion, similarly insisted in his 1940 address, "One Holy, Catholic and Apostolic Church," to the Disciples' International Convention that it was high time for the church to own its call to corporate *holiness* in the face of the rise of the Third Reich.

Contemporary theology in the Stone-Campbell Movement has continued to address sanctification, but with more theological sophistication and with an eye to the larger Christian community and the greater culture. Building on the ideals of Boll, Moser, and others in the Churches of Christ, C. Leonard Allen has called the Movement to the centrality of the cross and to a renewed "Trinitarian" spirituality that gives due place to the dynamic role of the Spirit in the life of the Christian. In sanctification, he has suggested, the Holy Spirit forms the character traits that lead the way to the cross. Opposing the individualization of holiness in the secular society, Allen places sanctification squarely within the Christian community where the Spirit works.

The Christian Churches/Churches of Christ theologian Jack Cottrell has included a discussion of sanctification in his systematic theology. Echoing Campbell's view, he sees a beginning point of sanctification with regeneration (initial), continued progressively in the Christian's life until perfection in heaven. While avoiding an Arminian perspective that would shortchange the role of grace, Cottrell does see God's own holiness as the norm of sanctification. Cottrell seeks to remain faithful to the restoration perspective of the Stone-Campbell Movement by insisting that holiness comes from knowing God's law as found in Scripture and obeying it; nevertheless he seeks to balance that emphasis by insisting on the power of God to overcome sin through the indwelling of the Holy Spirit.

In an ecumenical context, contemporary Disciples theologian Clark Williamson has called for a change from an inadequate Disciples theology based on "faith vs. theologian" to a "quintessential American theology of sanctification" that resonates more with Disciples' experience. This theology downplays the individualistic aspect of redemption for a more corporate model that would make society holy for the kingdom of God. He recognizes four emphases from the Stone-Campbell Movement's past that would help to create a theology of sanctification: creation, holiness, Holy Spirit, and the Sabbath.

Stone-Campbell Movement theologians have found a certain consensus on sanctification, but not without some real differences of perspective. Most agree on the beginning of sanctification at the point of faith and baptism. Also, most would agree on progressive sanctification, though some would give credit to the indwelling of the Spirit, others to the disciplines of reading the Bible and prayer, and some to both. Most have rejected the notion of "entire sanctification," envisioning the perfection of sanctification in heaven and not in this life.

The topic was an important one in the Open Forum dialogue in the 1980s and 1990s between the Christian Churches/Churches of Christ and the Church of God (Anderson, Indiana) of the Holiness tradition.

See also Baptism; Boll, Robert Henry; Franklin, Benjamin; Grace, Doctrine of; Holy Spirit, Doctrine of the; Justification, Doctrine of; Moser, Kenneth Carl; Regeneration; Repentance; Richardson, Robert; Robinson, William; Salvation

BIBLIOGRAPHY C. Leonard Allen, *The Cruciform Church* (1990) • C. Leonard Allen and Danny Swick, *Participating in God's Life: Two Crossroads for Churches of Christ* (2001) • R. H. Boll, *Truth and Grace* (1917) • Alexander Campbell, *Christian Baptism* (1851), ch. 3 ("Sanctification") • Alexander Campbell, *The Christian System* (1839) • Jack Cottrell, *The Faith Once for All* (2002) • Benjamin Franklin, *The Gospel Preacher*, vols. 1-2 (1869, 1877) • K. C. Moser, *The Way of Salvation* (1932) • Robert Richardson, *Communings in the Sanctuary* (1872) • Robert Richardson *The Office of the Holy Spirit* (1872) • Robert Richardson, *The Principles and Objects of the Religious Reformation* (1853) • William Robinson, *Essays on Christian Unity* (1924) • William Robinson, *New Testament Christianity* (n.d.) • Barton W. Stone, *Address to the Christian Churches* (2nd ed. 1821), in *Works of Elder B. W. Stone*, ed. James M. Mathes (2nd ed. 1859), pp. 46-163 • Clark Williamson, "Theology and Forms of Confession in the Disciples of Christ," *Encounter* (1980): 53-71.

ANTHONY J. SPRINGER

Sand Creek "Address and Declaration"

Statement issued in August 1889 by Illinois church leaders at an annual church encampment calling for separation from those who supported "innovations" such as missionary societies, paid located preachers, and fund-raising methods other than the Sunday contribution.

Encouraged by *Octographic Review* editor Daniel Sommer, Peter P. Warren and Tobias Grider, elders of the Sand Creek Church in Shelby County, Illinois, decided to use the annual meeting held at Sand Creek to "draw a line against the innovators" who, they believed, were ushering new and destructive practices into the churches.

Daniel Sommer, recognized as a leading preacher, was invited to preach on Sunday afternoon, August 18, 1889. In the midst of Sommer's attack on the innovators, he called on Warren to read what was titled "An Address and Declaration." The title of the statement was a clear play on Thomas Campbell's movement-launching *Declaration and Address.* However, the irony is clear; whereas Campbell's document launched a movement devoted to Christian unity, the Sand Creek Declaration was a call for separation from those who would deviate from the perceived apostolic order.

The Sand Creek Declaration was signed by representatives from five different churches. The demarcation that Warren and the other signers created was stark. The innovations named were unacceptable. If instruction about such practices did not result in their relinquishment, the Sand Creek proposal called for separation. "We can not and will not regard them as brethren."

Though initial reaction to the Sand Creek Declaration statement was limited, it soon became a watershed, as evidenced by the number of property lawsuits resulting from the clash between conservative members within a congregation and those who practiced the "innovations." The issuance of the "Address and Declaration" is a significant marker in the process that resulted in the first division of the Stone-Campbell Movement and led to the separate existence of Churches of Christ.

See also Churches of Christ; Sommer, Daniel

BIBLIOGRAPHY Isaac Errett, "A Divisive Work," *Christian Standard* (June 18, 1892): 520 • Isaac Errett, "The Sand Creek Test of Fellowship," *Christian Standard* (July 23, 1892): 624 • W. Carl Ketcherside, "The Sand Creek Address," *Mission Messenger* 24 (February 1962): 1-14 • W. Carl Ketcherside, "Brothers at Law," *Mission Messenger* 24 (March 1962): 1-10 • Daniel Sommer, "The Question of the Hour," *Octographic Review* (September 1889): 1, 8. • Daniel Sommer, "Breakup of a Movement: Documents from Sand Creek," on-line at http://www.mun.ca/rels/restmov/texts/dsommer/guthrie.html.

CARSON REED

Sandeman, Robert (1718-1771)

Robert Sandeman was born in Perth to David and Margaret Sandeman. While attending the University of Edinburgh, Sandeman met John Glas, became a member of the "Glasite" church, and later married Glas's daughter Katharine in 1737.

Sandeman catapulted to prominence in England with his *Letters on Theron and Aspasio* (1757), a response to James Hervey's *Dialogues.* Sandeman denied Hervey's Calvinistic doctrine of "imputed righteousness," stressing the role of faith as the beginning of salvation rather than a sign of election.

Sandeman's *Letters* sparked correspondence with Independent London preachers Samuel Pike, John Barnard, and George Hitchens and with several churches throughout central and northern England during 1757-61, thus increasing the Sandemanian fellowship.

Because of his *Letters,* Sandeman was invited to America, arriving in Boston in 1764. Ezra Stiles and Samuel Langdon took special note of Sandeman, who established a dozen congregations in Connecticut, Massachusetts, New Hampshire, and Rhode Island. The fledgling American movement floundered under Sandeman's untimely support of the British king and taxes to the crown. Consequently the American churches became socially isolated. Sandeman died and was buried in Danbury, Connecticut, in 1771. The Danbury church later fellowshiped with the Scotch Baptists and also with Henry Errett in New York City.

Sandeman's followers called themselves Church of Christ; they believed in strict separation of church and state and the autonomy of the local church. Deacons were the servant officers. Baptism was a dedication rite. Worship consisted of weekly Lord's Supper, prayers, lengthy Scripture reading, a cappella singing of psalms, and an exhortation. Other practices included the love feast or fellowship meal each Sunday, foot washing, the holy kiss of greeting, no creeds, and no religious titles.

Campbell first heard Sandeman and Glas's teachings from Greville Ewing during his year in Glasgow, and later he admitted agreement with Sandeman on some things though he disavowed being influenced by Glas and Sandeman. The role of faith in salvation, plurality of elders, and weekly communion are the clearest examples of a doctrinal relationship between Campbell and Sandeman. Campbell later showed affinity with the American Scotch Baptists, offshoots of the Glasite church in Edinburgh.

BIBLIOGRAPHY Alexander Campbell, "Remarks on a Circular Letter," *The Christian Baptist* (January 4, 1830): 132 • Alexander Campbell, "To an Independent Baptist," *The Christian Baptist* (May 1, 1826): 204 • Alexander Campbell, "Letters from Europe," *Millennial Harbinger* (October 1848): 571 • Harry Escott, *A History of Scottish Congregationalism* (1960) • *Letters in Correspondence by Rob-*

ert Sandeman, John Glas, and Their Contemporaries (1851) • Lynn A. McMillon, "The Quest for the Apostolic Church: A Study of Scottish Origins of American Restorationism" (Ph.D. dissertation, Baylor University, 1972), rewritten as *Restoration Roots* (1982) • James Ross, *A History of Congregational Independency in Scotland* (1900) • John Glas Sandeman, *The Sandeman Genealogy,* updated by Gerard Lionel Sandeman (1950) • Robert Sandeman, *Discourses on Passages of Scripture* (1857) • Robert Sandeman, *Letters on Theron and Aspasio,* 2 vols. (4th ed. 1768) • Robert Sandeman, *Some Thoughts on Christianity in a Letter* (1891) • *Supplementary Volume of Letters and Other Documents* (1865).

LYNN A. MCMILLON

Sanderson, Eugene C. (1859-1940)

Founder and first president of Eugene Divinity School (1895), now Northwest Christian College, in Eugene, Oregon; also helped to found Manhattan Christian College (Kansas) and San Jose Christian College (California).

Sanderson earned undergraduate and graduate degrees from Oskaloosa College in Ohio (1883, 1886). He also studied at Chicago and Yale Universities and was the recipient of many honorary degrees. However, he first gained notice as an evangelist, church founder, and pastor in Washington and Idaho.

His academic training was instrumental in establishing an educational philosophy that sought to place Bible colleges in proximity to state universities. Sanderson believed that such an arrangement worked to the mutual benefit of the church and public institutions. The cooperation of Bible schools with secular institutions became a feature of conservative Disciples educational philosophy that linked biblical studies with the liberal arts.

After exploring several potential sites for a divinity school in the Pacific Northwest, Sanderson and others determined that property next to the University of Oregon would bring this aspiration to fruition. Sanderson led the school he founded in Eugene through two major reorganizational changes in the 1920s. The first of these changes saw the creation of Eugene Bible University, which opened its doors in October of 1895 with five students. After the stock market crash (1929), Eugene Bible University and Spokane University (another small Christian college in Spokane, Washington, that Sanderson helped to launch) combined their resources to become Northwest Christian College.

Sanderson moved to Minneapolis in 1924 to become president of Minnesota Bible College (now Crossroads College) until 1932. In 1927 he led in the purchase of property in Manhattan, Kansas, and established Christian Workers University (now Manhattan Christian College) close to the campus of Kansas State University. In 1932 he led in the purchase of property in San Jose, California, for the establishment of San Jose Bible College (now San Jose Christian College). In 1939 Sanderson invited his former student, William L. Jessup, to organize a faculty at San Jose and to launch classes. The school opened in September of 1939 with fourteen students.

Eugene C. Sanderson (1859-1940) was instrumental in the establishment of Eugene Bible University in Oregon (Northwest Christian College) and Christian Workers University in Kansas (Manhattan Christian College). He also served as president of Minnesota Bible College (Crossroads College) and San Jose Bible College (San Jose Christian College).

Sanderson died in Los Angeles in 1940.

See also Bible College Movement; Crossroads College; Higher Education, Views of in the Movement; Manhattan Christian College; Northwest Christian College; San Jose Christian College

BIBLIOGRAPHY Charles Dailey, "Eugene C. Sanderson: Pioneer Preacher and Educator in Oregon and Washington" (on-line: http://ncbible.org/nwh/ProSanderson-.html) • Martha H. Goodrich, "A History of Northwest Christian College" (M.A. thesis, University of Oregon, 1949).

MICHAEL W. BOLLENBAUGH

Scates, Erskine E., Sr. (1909-1979)

A founder and first president of Intermountain Bible College in Grand Junction, Colorado. After receiving degrees from Phillips University, he went to western Colorado as a state evangelist in 1931 and remained there until his death.

Scates edited *The Western Colorado Christian,* a monthly publication. In June 1943 he called on the churches to establish a Bible college, noting that no such college existed between Enid, Oklahoma, and the Pacific Coast. In 1944 he announced that Intermountain Bible College (IBC) would open its doors in September 1946. From the outset, he envisioned a cooperative relationship with Mesa College, the junior college in Grand Junction (now Mesa State College).

The newspaper contained reports from area churches, accounts of Sunday School contests, digests of sermons, and other inspirational materials. At the end of 1947, the periodical took on a new name, *The Intermountain Christian,* reflecting a wider scope. Scates continued to encourage the churches to send young people to IBC so that they, in turn, could provide leadership for existing congregations and church plants. He spearheaded the purchase and development of facilities for summer youth camps, particularly Camp Christian in New Castle, Colorado. He emphasized the need for churches to serve the rural areas of the region. In concert with IBC faculty and students, twenty-seven churches were established, often begun as Sunday Schools.

Scates served as president of IBC until declining health necessitated his retirement on January 1, 1978. He died on July 21, 1979. The eulogy in *The Intermountain Christian* (September 1979) noted that he was "widely known for his devotion to his special ministry of preaching, planting churches and building a Bible college to provide leadership in local churches and on mission fields."

See also Intermountain Bible College

TAMSEN MURRAY

Scheme of Redemption, The

One of the most influential books written by any of the nineteenth-century leaders in the Stone-Campbell Movement.

Authored by Robert Milligan (1814-1875), an esteemed Disciples of Christ scholar at Bethany College and later at the College of the Bible in Lexington, Kentucky, the volume, published in 1868, was the closest any of the leaders came to writing a systematic biblical theology and was still in use in some colleges of the Movement as late as the 1970s and 1980s. Its fuller title is *An Exposition and Defense of the Scheme of Redemption as It Is Revealed and Taught in the Holy Scriptures.*

With connections to both the Stone and Campbell part of the Movement, Robert Milligan (1814-1875) was a gifted teacher and writer. While on the faculty at Bethany he co-edited the *Millennial Harbinger* with Alexander Campbell. He was president of Bacon College and Kentucky University in the 1850s, and became head of the College of the Bible in 1865. Courtesy of the Disciples of Christ Historical Society

Milligan's purpose in writing the book was to help readers comprehend the contents of the Bible and to induce them to study and meditate on it. He was convinced the Bible was a unit and its ultimate object was to develop a *system* for the redemption of fallen humanity. "The Bible, then, is a perfect revelation of a perfect system of Divine philanthropy, designed to promote the present happiness and to secure the eternal felicity of all who will believe it, receive it, and obey it." This system had intricate parts that needed to be understood in relationship to each other. Milligan stood squarely in the tradition of the Common Sense/Baconian model of biblical interpretation, clinging to the view, cherished by Walter Scott before him, that the Bible is inherently a grand scheme of evidences logically designed to point the believer toward the lordship of Christ and the plan of salvation.

The book was divided into three major sections. Book First covered God, creation, and the fall of humanity, in order, setting the scene for the need for redemption (pages 17-61). Book Second in five parts covered the period from Adam to the work of Jesus Christ and the Holy Spirit, up to Acts 2 (pages 63-284). Book Third in five parts began at Acts 2 and covered the foundation of the church, its ministry, ordinances, and organization (pages 285-577). This third part was the major focus of the book, comprising half its content. Each of the three books was further subdivided into chapters and subsections. The three divisions of the book parallel Alexander Campbell's three dispensations: Patriarchal, Mosaic, and Christian.

Milligan's main interest in the Old Testament was in the law, which was designed to provide the Jews with civil government, to convict sin, to prevent idolatry, and to provide the religious nomenclature for the scheme of redemption. Parts of the law and sacrifices provided types for the New Testament. The rest of the Old Testament from Joshua to the coming of John the Baptist was covered in eleven pages.

The work of Christ was to atone for the sins of all people and to satisfy the demands of the justice of God. The work of the Holy Spirit was to prepare providentially the heart of the sinner for the gospel, to work through the Word of God to enable conversion, and to work on the heart of believers to enable them to mature in Christ through the Word and through direct action.

The organization and ministry of the church, which Milligan identified with the kingdom of God, was crucial. Since God's plan was to redeem all people, the church played the central role in the outcome of the scheme of redemption. The doctrine of the church advanced in the third part of the book is still influential today, particularly in the Christian Churches/Churches of Christ and the Churches of Christ.

The book is at times elegant and passionate. Eugene Boring has rightly depicted it as a work principally for the edification of insiders to the Stone-Campbell Movement, representative of a seasoned "Campbellism" or emerging Disciples scholasticism in the second generation of the Movement.

See also Dispensations; Hermeneutics; Milligan, Robert; Salvation; Theology — Nineteenth Century

BIBLIOGRAPHY M. Eugene Boring, *Disciples and the Bible: A History of Disciples Biblical Interpretation in North America* (1997) • Robert Milligan, *An Exposition and Defense of the Scheme of Redemption, as It Is Related and Taught in the Holy Scriptures* (1868) • Thomas H. Olbricht, "Robert Milligan: Teacher, Theologian, Minister," *Leaven* 8 (2000): 153-57.

GARY H. HALL

Schools of Preaching

Schools of Preaching appeared among Churches of Christ during an era of evangelistic interest and a deep concern about vacant pulpits. The beginning of the School of Preaching movement is typically identified with Sunset International Bible Institute, founded by Cline Paden (b. 1919) in 1962 as the Latin American Bible School. Paden was one of two teachers who met with six Hispanic students on the campus of Lubbock Christian College. The school soon moved to the Sunset Church of Christ building, promptly grew to more than 100 students, and one year later became Sunset School of Preaching. When Sunset opened its doors to non-Hispanics in 1963 it was immediately and, for that time and place, remarkably integrated.

Within a few years more schools were launched, including Brown Trail in Hurst, Texas, and Preston Road in Dallas, Texas, in 1964; Bear Valley in Denver Colorado, in 1965; Memphis School of Preaching in Memphis, Tennessee, in 1966; Whites Ferry Road in West Monroe, Louisiana; and Bristol Road in Flint, Michigan, in 1970. Following Paden's lead, the schools advertised the need to prepare men to preach, to "reach the untold millions yet untold." They also identified their potential students as ones who were "unable" or who found it "impractical" to attend a Christian college.

The Schools of Preaching, with courses taught by experienced preachers or former missionaries, produced graduates easily recognized by their concordance style of sermon delivery, impressive knowledge of Scripture, evangelistic fervor, and distinctive doctrinal emphases. The latter characteristic ranged from the fierce sectarianism of Memphis School of Preaching to the pietism of Whites Ferry Road and strong theology of grace found at Sunset.

These schools, estimated to number as many as 100 in the late 1970s, were generally under the supervision of a single congregation, providing an unaccredited, tuition-free, two-year program of study exclusively from the Bible. Inculcation was characterized by a heavy emphasis on memorization and intense in-class instruction, with little time or preparation for research. The Schools of Preaching now claim more than 5,000 graduates, with Sunset responsible for a significant percentage.

Eschewing accreditation and basic standards of admission beyond "maturity," or in some cases marital status, the Schools of Preaching were born in an era of growing distrust of the Christian Colleges' Bible departments. While Cline Paden publicly claimed, "There is no competition between light houses," other directors were less discreet. At Bear Valley, Roy Lanier, Sr. (1899-1980), advertised the school's purpose as "to preach sound doctrine and defend the faith" and limited teachers to men characterized as "conservative and distinctive . . . Bible quoting, error exposing, sin convicting." One caustic critic charged that some Christian college Bible departments were "overloaded with Harvard specialists . . . tainted with sectarian philosophy [who] speak . . . in intellectual nothingness or just plain denominational terms."

The "Harvard specialists" eventually answered back. Admitting that the Schools of Preaching were providing more preachers than the colleges and universities, two professors criticized the schools for their adverse effect on the educational level in church pulpits and the abandonment of critical tools for understanding Scripture. Everett Ferguson (b. 1933) of Abilene Christian University worried, "What happens to a generation reared on techniques and assuming the biblical message without a real knowledge of what that is?"

The tenuous relationship between Christian colleges and Schools of Preaching has improved in recent years. Some schools have encouraged arrangements with the colleges to accept credits for their course work, and several graduates have continued their studies toward an accredited degree at Abilene Christian University, Rochester College, and elsewhere.

However, four decades after their first appearance and early growth, the total number of schools has decreased dramatically. A handful of the most doctrinally conservative schools remain, including Bear Valley and Memphis School of Preaching. A notable exception to the dying programs and doctrinal conservativism is Sunset, where an upbeat theology of grace and an ability to diversify with creative and desired programs (even renaming itself four times) have allowed the original program to thrive into the new millennium.

Although academically suspect, the Schools of Preaching provided an immediate solution to pulpit vacancies in the Churches of Christ. Moreover, the movement foreshadowed some cross-denominational trends in ministerial training. Like mainline seminaries in the closing years of the twentieth century, the Schools of Preaching provided clerical training for second career, nontraditional, and older students. And, like the evangelical megachurches of the early twenty-first century, Schools of Preaching shunned traditional seminaries to embrace the supervision and direction of a large and successful church.

See also Preaching 2.3

BIBLIOGRAPHY Ray Bohannan, "The School of Preaching: A New Concept of Teaching in the Churches of Christ" (M.A. thesis, San Diego State College, 1970) • Everett Ferguson, "Higher Education in Religious Studies Among Members of the Churches of Christ, 1957-1982," *Restoration Quarterly* 25 (1982): 205-12 • Jim Harris, *Schools of Preaching: An Evaluation of Ministerial Preparation* (1984) • Thomas H. Olbricht, "Religious Scholarship and the Restoration Movement," *Restoration Quarterly* 25 (1982): 193-204 • Cline R. Paden, "An 'Issue' Facing the Church," *Firm Foundation* 80 (May 21, 1963): 323 • Claud Parrish, "A Historical Study of Sunset Church of Christ School of Preaching" (M.A. thesis, Abilene Christian College, 1965).

DAVID FLEER

Scott, Walter (1796-1861)

1. Biography
2. Scott's Written Work

Long counted, with Thomas Campbell, Alexander Campbell, and Barton Stone, as one of the four founders of the Stone-Campbell Movement. He is remembered in the Movement as the evangelist whose success in the field brought stability to the fledging reform movement led by Thomas and Alexander Campbell as it moved toward separation from the Baptists.

1. Biography

Walter Scott was born in 1796, the sixth of ten children. His parents, John and Mary Innes Scott, lived in the small town of Moffatt, Scotland. The Scotts were Presbyterians, members of the Church of Scotland. They harbored hopes that their son Walter would become a Presbyterian minister. To this end, when Walter was 16, his parents supported his journey to the University of Edinburgh. Six years later, in 1818, he left the university. Presumably he graduated, since six years at Edinburgh constituted the normal program of study. Records in the university are incomplete for the period.

Scott arrived in New York in July 1818 at the invitation of his mother's brother. He quickly found a job teaching English, Latin, and Greek in a small school on Long Island. Within a year, however, he moved to Pittsburgh, where he met George Forrester. Forrester, also from Scotland, served as a minister in a small congregation and as headmaster of a small school. The two men formed a personal bond. Over the course of the next year, Forrester helped to shape Scott's approach to Christian faith, particularly his understandings of the church, the Bible, and baptism. Scott underwent baptism by immersion at Forrester's hands and became an active member of the congregation. From this point on, he advocated baptism by immersion for believers as the only authentic form of baptism.

Forrester's congregation had connections to the movement influenced by the writings of James A. Haldane and Robert Haldane, two brothers who broke with the Church of Scotland in 1799. James Haldane became the minister of a new congregation in Edinburgh and served there for the next fifty

Walter Scott (1796-1861) was the most significant early evangelist in the Stone-Campbell Movement. He is usually considered to be one of its four founding leaders along with Barton Stone and the Campbells. Courtesy of the Disciples of Christ Historical Society

years. Robert Haldane financially supported the establishment of a seminary in Glasgow, and the movement began to spread as far as England and America. The Haldanes eschewed creeds and hoped to restore the New Testament church for their time. Their practices included a weekly celebration of the Lord's Supper and foot washing. By 1807 the Haldanes abandoned the practice of infant baptism and taught believers' immersion.

George Forrester also introduced Walter Scott to the writings of a few other Scottish theologians who had broken from the Church of Scotland. John Glas separated from the Church of Scotland in the early 1700s because he believed that the church's connection to the state violated the New Testament emphasis on the spiritual nature of the church. He established a congregation that took its cues from the New Testament and from its study of the earliest Christian congregations. A group of elders served the church, with a strong emphasis placed on lay leadership in all facets of congregational life. Following the precedent they believed they found in the New Testament, the congregation met weekly at the Lord's Table.

Robert Sandeman, Glas's son-in-law, soon joined the movement and served it through his ability as a theologian. Sandeman's writings were particularly influential for both Forrester and Scott. Though a Calvinist himself, Sandeman challenged the Calvinist belief that sinners had to be regenerated by "enabling grace" before they could believe the claims of the gospel. Instead, he stressed that persons among the elect became Christians when they believed the evidence presented in Scripture. Faith resulted from the rational act of believing rather than from changes God brought about in the heart and emotions of a person through the provision of "enabling grace."

George Forrester died in a drowning accident in 1820, just a year after Scott met him. After Forrester's death, Walter Scott served both as pastor to the congregation and as director of the school. According to his own testimony, he read widely from Forrester's religious library and deepened his commitment to a restoration-oriented approach to the church. Influenced as well by his encounters with writers representing the English Enlightenment, primarily Francis Bacon and John Locke, Scott began to emphasize an individual's ability to think through problems and reach rational solutions. As an autonomous thinker, each person should be able to examine the facts, think critically, and reach a reasonable conclusion as to the truth of the matter at hand. With Locke, Scott believed that a person could read the Bible and use human reason to discern the truth of Christian faith.

An encounter with a pamphlet on baptism, written by Henry Errett, caused Scott to leave Pittsburgh briefly in 1821. Errett argued that baptism's purpose involved the "remission of sins." Scott became convinced that baptism was more than simply a Christian ritual or ordinance. Rather, it involved a positive action taken by Christians. God's response to this action provided formal remission of sins through the death of Christ. Scott bid farewell to the congregation in Pittsburgh and left for New York to visit Errett's congregation. The small conservative congregation he found there, however, disappointed him.

A few months after arriving in New York, Scott received a letter from the father of Robert Richardson, one of his more promising students at the academy in Pittsburgh. The letter carried the invitation to return to Pittsburgh to open a small school in the Richardson home and to continue his work with Robert and a few other children from neighboring families. Before accepting, Scott traveled to New Jersey, Maryland, and Washington, D.C. Unable to find exciting church life anywhere he traveled, Scott decided to return to Pittsburgh to take up the offer extended by the Richardson family.

Robert Richardson, who was 13 when Scott returned to Pittsburgh in 1821, had spent the year 1816 learning under the direction of Thomas Campbell, who had operated a small academy in Pittsburgh during that year. The Campbells, both Thomas and Alexander, occasionally visited the Richardson home in Pittsburgh. One of those visits took place during the winter of 1821-22, when Alexander Campbell stopped in Pittsburgh. Campbell described for Scott his work with the Redstone Baptist Association and talked of beginning a new journal. When the journal began the next year, Scott regularly contributed articles.

In 1823 Scott married Sarah Whitsette. Over the next ten years, they had six children. He moved the family to Ohio in 1826, spending a year in Steubenville before moving on to Canfield. Shortly after moving to Ohio, Scott began his intensive work with Campbell's group of Reformers, who at the time were associated with the Mahoning Baptist Association. At the invitation of Alexander Campbell, Scott attended his first meeting of the association in Canfield in August 1826.

For two years Campbell had advanced his ideas among Baptist congregations on the Western Reserve and elsewhere in Ohio. He spoke against dependence on creeds, common among these Baptists who were committed to the Calvinistic theology of the Philadelphia Confession of Faith, and urged congregations to establish themselves on the firm foundation of the Bible and the example provided there of the character of primitive Christianity. When Scott visited the meeting in 1826, he quickly appreciated the fruits of Campbell's work.

During the next year's annual meeting, a proposal to employ an evangelist resulted in hiring Walter Scott to do the job. As he prepared, he hit on the formula that naturally grew out of his reading, teaching, and preaching over the previous seven or eight years. What must a person do to be saved? Based on Acts 2:38, Scott concluded that first a person must have faith, repent, and be baptized. In response to these human actions, God would provide remission of sins, the gift of the Holy Spirit, and eternal life. Several generations of Disciples learned this formula of salvation under the rubric of the "five-finger exercise," with the fifth finger, for convenience' sake, standing for both the gift of the Holy Spirit and eternal life. After an uneventful revival held in Steubenville, Ohio, Scott's preaching drew considerable attention at a meeting in New Lisbon, Ohio. Later, Scott pointed to the sermon he preached on November 18, 1827, as the one that restored the ancient gospel. The text for his sermon was Matthew 16:16: "Thou art the Christ, the son of the living God."

Over the course of the next three years, Scott's preaching on the Western Reserve brought more than 3,000 converts into the Stone-Campbell Movement. Most of these new members came from among those who were outside the church altogether. Scott's preaching did, however, include significant denominational conversions as well. Ministers were won over by the logic of Scott's preaching and, occasionally, would bring their congregations into the fold of Campbell's reform movement. Scott's success led to increased Baptist opposition to Campbell and Scott, and the congregations associated with them. After a sister Baptist Association issued a condemnation of the Mahoning Association in 1829 for harboring the Campbell congregations, the Reformers voted to discontinue their association with the Baptists. Though Alexander Campbell questioned the wisdom of the move, Walter Scott convinced him to allow the separation to proceed. From that point on, the Reformers became Disciples and began their journey toward new ecclesiastical status, joining with Barton Stone's Christians in 1832.

During the years following the dissolution of the Mahoning Association, though Scott continued to serve congregations and conduct evangelistic meetings, he turned more specifically to writing as a vocation. In 1832 he began publishing a periodical entitled *The Evangelist* from Cincinnati. When he moved to Carthage in the fall of 1833 to assume the pastorate of a congregation, he took the periodical with him. For the next dozen years or so, he wrote and ministered in Carthage, with the exception of the year (1836-37), which he spent as president of Bacon College in Georgetown, Kentucky. In April 1844 he moved his family back to Pittsburgh, where he lived until 1849.

On the occasion of the move to Pittsburgh, Scott began a new periodical, *The Protestant Unionist,* which he edited until 1847. After his wife died in 1849, Scott returned to Cincinnati. At that time he merged his interests in *The Protestant Unionist* with a periodical edited by J. T. Melish. Together, they coedited the new periodical, *The Christian Age and Protestant Unionist,* for about a year. In late 1849 Scott moved to Mays Lick, Kentucky, to spend half-time ministering to a small congregation. During the next summer he remarried.

In 1852 Scott moved his family to Covington, Kentucky, where he opened a school for females. Throughout his life, Scott had consistently stressed the importance of education for women. He especially supported the development of the so-called "female institutes" that specialized in providing a well-rounded education for women. While in Covington, he concentrated on teaching and writing. When his second wife died in November of 1854, he returned to Mays Lick, where he lived the remainder of his life. He married again in 1855 and spent his time preaching, conducting evangelistic work, and writing his final book, which he published in 1859, two years before his death. He died of pneumonia on April 23, 1861.

2. Scott's Written Work

Most members of the Stone-Campbell Movement remember Walter Scott primarily for his evangelistic endeavors on the Western Reserve between 1827 and 1830, accompanied by his development of the five-finger exercise that summarized his understanding of the restored gospel. In those few years, he proved that he possessed a great gift as a preacher who concentrated, above all else, on preaching Christ to the unchurched. But he lived for more than thirty years beyond that time. His literary work, most of it written after 1830, exercised considerable influence on the Movement through the nineteenth century. That written work also contributed to the creation of a Stone-Campbell ethos that continued to work its influence throughout the twentieth century.

His journalistic endeavors point to a wide and somewhat eclectic range of interests. For example, Scott had a profound interest in the church's music ministry and often did what he could to improve upon it. He most likely inherited his love of music from his father, who was a musician. Scott once spent $300 of his own money to publish a hymnal containing over 700 hymns. He hoped to encourage congregations to stop "the endlessly repeated singing of the same hymn to the same tune, at present so common in our assemblies." Scott often editorialized on themes important to the Stone-Campbell Movement, but he also wrote regularly on topics that affected American life more generally, including journalistic sections devoted to both domestic and foreign news.

But the first thing to recognize about Walter Scott's body of written work, as James Duke has demonstrated, is that it was profoundly theological. Throughout his life, Scott engaged actively in a faith that sought understanding. He believed in the importance of scholarly inquiry. Following Francis Bacon and John Locke, Scott sought a reasonable theology, one that could withstand reasonable critique and give an accounting of itself that reasonable people could understand. He sought evidence for faith and employed a grammatico-historical method of biblical interpretation ("inductive hermeneutics") to find it. Both through his editorial work and through the books he wrote, Scott made theological contributions that answered the theological arguments of others. He weighed in on most of the theological controversies of his day, and he did so theologically.

Scott's call by the Mahoning Association in 1827 led him to an exposition of his own theological understanding of the order of salvation *(ordo salutis)*. He argued that the foundation for his understanding came from the Bible. But, in truth, his exposition also owed considerable debt to the work of theologians before him who had described the relationship between God and human beings as consisting primarily in covenants. The Westminster Confession of Scottish Presbyterianism contained a strong dose of covenant theology. The most important of these Scottish covenants for Christians had to do with the covenant God offered in Christ. In Christ, God saves the Christian, but in return the Christian owes complete faith and total obedience. The Westminster Confession placed the initiative squarely in God's corner. God elects, and elected Christians respond. Scott sought a covenant that respected the sovereignty of God without the predestinarian appendages. He recognized the problems associated with works righteousness, the charge that human beings could save themselves by their own decisions and actions. His attempts to address the charge seem a bit shallow today, but nonetheless he recognized the problem and tried to address it theologically.

Scott's most substantial written work, *The Gospel Restored,* appeared in 1836 as his second book. In it he set forth schematically his order of salvation, beginning with the fall of human beings in Adam and moving through their redemption in Christ. With the confidence of one who believed his restoration of the gospel placed him among Reformation luminaries like Luther and Calvin, Scott provided detailed sections on each of the six phases of his covenantal approach, three taken by the individual (faith, repentance, and baptism), and three provided by God (remission of sins, gift of the Holy Spirit, and eternal life). Scott's order of salvation depended heavily upon a propositional approach to the Bible and upon categories often provided by Scottish Common Sense Realism.

The commonsense thought of the Scottish Enlightenment first emerged as a force in American theology near the end of the colonial period in the thought of Presbyterian John Witherspoon. Significant Scottish immigration after the American Revolution increased its role in American theology. In their quest for knowledge, and in response to the oft-asked question, "How does one truly know?" adherents of Scottish Common Sense Realism endorsed inductive reasoning as the scientific path to real knowledge. As part of this inductive process, they also depended upon the reliability of sensory experiences of the world around them. They believed in evidence, the rational appeal to facts, and, when attempting to discern divinely revealed truth, the reliability provided by the testimony found in the Bible. When dealing with questions of ethics and faith, they sought the solid ground provided by certain fundamental principles.

For Scott, the fundamental principle upon which all other propositions rested was the one declared by Peter in Matthew 16:16: Christ is "the Messiah, Son of the living God." Scott called this fundamental principle the "Golden Oracle." He described it as a "first principle" within Christianity, "the fundamental proposition of the whole religion." The first principle describes that which is entirely self-evident, the proposition upon which every other proposition is built. The declaration of Christ as Messiah, as Son of the living God, served, for Scott, as the first principle of Christianity, the one self-evident proposition that served as the foundation for both salvation and the construction of the church. At the time of Christ's baptism, God provided first-person confirmation of the truth of this proposition: "This is my Son, the Beloved, with whom I am well pleased" (Matt. 3:17). Belief in the proposition asserting the "Messiahship" of Jesus formed the central "first principle" of the restored gospel. Or, as Scott put it in *The Gospel Restored* (1836), "This oracle is, therefore, . . . the creed of Christianity, original Christianity; and he who believes the fact may become a Christian."

But, in fact, there was more to Scott's order of salvation. The human being must have faith that Christ was the Messiah, the Son of God, seek repentance, and be baptized. The possibility of responding to God in Christ belonged to all human beings, not just to members of some special "elect" group. In response to those who have faith, seek repentance, and are baptized, God would provide remission of sins and grant the gifts of the Holy Spirit and eternal life. To avoid the charge of works righteousness, Scott emphasized that sinners must become aware that their faith was in Jesus Christ. Human beings could not save themselves. They were saved only through faith in the fact that Jesus could save them. Salvation came completely from outside of themselves. Further, human beings are not only dependent upon Christ for salvation, but they are dependent upon God for their understanding of the fact that they are dependent upon Christ for salvation. God makes them aware of their need for faith in Christ. Thus, Scott argued, the initiative of God still preceded human action. How does God bring awareness to sinners? Historically, God has acted to bring salvation to human hearts. The Bible, through the inspiration of the Holy Spirit, bears testimony to these saving acts of God in history. The testimony of God's saving acts, found in the Bible, when heard and heeded, awakens the faith of sinners and enables them to have faith, seek repentance, and be baptized.

Scott's order of salvation included a particular view of the Holy Spirit that challenged both Calvinism and contemporary views heralded by the revivalism of his day. Through his journal, *The Evangelist,* and through his first two books, he brought clarity to his views concerning the Holy Spirit. His first book, *A Discourse on the Holy Spirit* (1831), may have been slight in appearance (a mere twenty-four pages), but it proved bold in its challenge to contemporary understandings of the work of the Holy Spirit.

The mission of the Holy Spirit, for Scott, found expression in and through the church. The Spirit inspired the Bible and continues to inspire the apostolic preaching of Christians that presents the teachings of the Bible. The sinner's encounter with the Spirit is always external — never internal. In other words, the Spirit uses the testimony of the Bible and apostolic preaching to demonstrate to the hearer that God's Word is true. The Spirit works externally through the Bible and preaching to convince or persuade sinners of their need for faith. The Spirit enlivens and serves the work of the church. The Spirit, therefore, works through human mediation.

This approach to the work of the Spirit ran contrary to the popular belief of Scott's day that the Holy Spirit provided "enabling grace" directly within sinners so that they could exercise faith and repentance. Calvinism's doctrine of total depravity dictated that the Holy Spirit had to take the supernatural first step for the sinner. Without the Holy Spirit's divine action within the soul of the sinner, the sinner could not step forward in faith. But for Scott, prior to salvation and baptism, the Spirit's role was always external and always tied to the activity of the church. In line with Enlightenment presuppositions about humanity, Scott asserted the role of the independent individual who hears the evidence and rationally decides to respond in faith. The sinner is convinced by the power of both the Bible and the preached word to testify to the saving acts of God in history. Scott tied the role of the Holy Spirit, therefore, only to the external power of these testimonies rather than to some kind of internal operation on the sinner's soul.

From the late 1830s through the mid-1840s, Scott became enamored with predictions concerning the second coming of Christ. Millennial enthusiasm captured large segments of American evangelicalism prior to the Civil War. Much of this enthusiasm manifested itself in efforts to reform society by creating new and model communities or by taking other steps to advance Christianity and civilization within the new nation. Most of the millennial enthusiasm was decidedly postmillennial in orientation, meaning that it was marked by optimism and reforming impulses. Defenders believed the success of the church's efforts would bring in the millennium without the need of any supernatural event. A much smaller portion of American evangelicalism preferred the premillennial versions. Most premillennialists reached the pessimistic conclusion that history stood in need of a cataclysmic event to push it toward its intended destiny. The return of Christ would move things along rather quickly. Walter Scott, writing in *The Evangelist,* concluded in 1834 that "Christ has much work to do, which seems to require his immediate presence and direction; . . . which make his coming to earth, and abiding here for a time, highly necessary."

Walter Scott's endorsement of premillennialism, and his openness to William Miller's predictions of Christ's return in 1844, contributed to a degree of estrangement that had begun to develop between Alexander Campbell and Scott. Their feuding had other sources as well. The two of them had argued over whether the movement ought to use the name "Christian" or "Disciple." Scott advocated the former, while Campbell stood for the latter. Scott also believed that Campbell treated him like a second-class citizen within the Movement, failing to accord him the respect he deserved for his restoration of the ancient gospel. When Scott lay hold of Miller's premillennialism and chided fellow Disciples (October 1842) for their "ignorance of the prophetic word," Campbell lamented (January 1843) that "some of our more intelligent and influential brethren" had been taken in by Miller's ruminations. After dates for Miller's original prediction (March 21, 1843) and revised prediction (October 22, 1844) for the return of Christ came and went, Walter Scott eventually became an enthusiastic postmillennialist, pushing belief in human progress, at times, further than Campbell ever did.

Scott's editorial work revealed rather clearly a man captivated by the American experience. He admired Thomas Jefferson and Andrew Jackson and possessed a profound belief in the mission of America to the world. By 1844, when he moved back to Pittsburgh and began editing his new journal, *The Protestant Unionist,* Scott's journalistic work represented the Protestant crusade to reform America and the world more than distinctive Disciples beliefs and practices. The major quality characterizing the paper was its anti-Catholicism. As editor, Scott modeled the concerns of much of nineteenth-century evangelicalism in America. Repeated essays spoke of the "fearful advances" made by Catholicism in the country and claimed that "Protestantism, by which we mean the Bible, is the only hope of the nations." Critics among the Disciples charged that Scott had abandoned restoration ideas in order to take up the cause of Protestantism in general. Union seemed to rest too much on anti-Catholicism and not enough on the "ancient gospel."

Jacob Creath, Jr., a minister in the Movement, asked Scott directly (in November 1847) whether he still believed that the ancient gospel remained the only basis for union. Scott replied in *The Protestant Unionist* that he felt his plea for the ancient gospel had turned into a simplistic formula (five-finger exercise) that made it too easy for hearers to miss the profound basis upon which the ancient gospel had always rested, the proclamation of faith in Jesus Christ as the Son of God.

By 1852 Scott had begun to recognize the hopelessness of efforts to unite Protestants against any kind of threat, whether Catholicism, "Mohametism," or idolatry. In his 1852 book *To Themelion: The Union of Christians* (128 pages), dedicated with deep affection to Alexander Campbell (battles between them apparently put to rest), Scott returned to familiar ground. Like most evangelicals of his day, Scott remained staunchly anti-Catholic. Catholics, he explained, built the church on human foundations (Peter, and his successors, the popes) instead of on Christ. But he also offered a strong critique of Protestantism. Coining a phrase, he argued that Protestantism was dominated by "the rage for creedification." Protestants, once concerned with defending themselves against "the Papists," have now been occupied in defending themselves against one another. If only they could return to the true creed, the divinity of Christ, they could experience the meaning of true union. This union, of course, would include a proper orientation to the six steps of the ancient gospel (faith, repentance, baptism by immersion, remission of sins, the gift of the Holy Spirit, and eternal life).

The next year Scott penned another book, *Hē Nekrōsis, or the Death of Christ* (132 pages). The first part (eighty-seven pages) concentrated on explaining both sin and redemption: on the one hand, Scott explained how humanity had ended up in such dire straits (the story of Adam as representative of the entire human community) and, on the other hand, how God had provided for the redemption of humanity (through the new Adam, Christ, as the new representative of humanity who, through his death, took on the sins of humanity). The second part (eighteen pages) argued the promise America held for the establishment of original Christianity. America provided the context where original Christianity could defeat the apostate nature of Catholicism and replace the provisional nature of Protestantism (which, because of its surrender to creeds and systems, would eventually have to give way to a purer form of Christianity). Scott placed his restored gospel near the end of the line of key reforming tendencies that began with Martin Luther and that would restore original Christianity to its rightful place in the world. The final part (twenty-five pages) challenged readers to finish building the edifice of the church on the proper foundation (Christ as Messiah) so recently rediscovered.

Scott's postmillennial confidence in the role to be

played by America came to its fullest expression in his final book, *The Messiahship* (367 pages), published in 1859. After rehearsing human history from Adam through the Roman Empire (119 pages) and covering the apostasy of Catholicism (38 pages) and the "promises and threatenings" found in the Bible (16 pages), Scott turned toward an exposition of the work of Christ (68 pages) and, eventually, toward an accounting of various other "sundries" (41 pages), including discussion of the "Reformations of the Sixteenth and Nineteenth Centuries." Before finishing the book with a section on character and responsibility (32 pages), Scott spent thirty-nine pages on the topic of "Political Christianity." This section heralded "America as the first of the Messianic nations." His treatment of the millennium expressed great confidence that America, and American Protestantism in particular, would play a great role in bringing the nations to true Christianity.

In the end, however, Scott could not sustain the confidence of this vision. The hanging of John Brown took place in December 1859. By February of 1861, the Confederacy organized with Jefferson Davis as president. Fort Sumter fell ten days before Walter Scott died. With secession and Civil War inevitable, Scott feared the end of the nation's messianic role. Despair resulted when this realization hit home, for Scott linked the restoration of the ancient gospel to American's mission in the world. For that reason, a divided union seriously threatened original Christianity. Scott died with very little confidence remaining in his convictions about human progress and in the role Protestant churches and national activities would play in bringing the millennium. In an ironic twist, the failure of both the nation and Protestantism, increasingly evident in the few years before his death, led Walter Scott back to where he had begun his theological journey. He died recognizing his complete dependence on the fundamental principle itself. He remembered that his hope, and the hope of those Christians who would follow him, lay not with Protestants or with the nation, but with Christ, the Messiah, the Son of the living God.

See also Bacon College; Campbell, Alexander; Campbell, Thomas; Common Sense Philosophy; Eschatology; *Evangelist, The;* Glas, John; Haldane, Robert, and James Alexander Haldane; Mahoning Association; Presbyterians, Presbyterianism; *Protestant Unionist, The;* Redstone Baptist Association; Richardson, Robert; Sandeman, Robert; Stone, Barton Warren

BIBLIOGRAPHY William Baxter, *Life of Elder Walter Scott* (1874) • William A. Gerrard III, *A Biographical Study of Walter Scott: American Frontier Evangelist* (1992) • Walter Scott, *A Discourse on the Holy Spirit* (1831) • Walter Scott, *The Gospel Restored* (1836) • Walter Scott, *To Themelion: The Union of Christians, on Christian Principles* (1952) • Walter Scott, *Hē Nekrōsis, or the Death of Christ* (1853) • Walter Scott, *The Messiahship, or Great Demonstration* (1859) • Dwight E. Stevenson, *Walter Scott: Voice of the Golden Oracle* (1946) • Mark G. Toulouse, ed., *Walter Scott: A Nineteenth-Century Evangelical* (1999).

MARK G. TOULOUSE

Scottish Independents

See Ewing, Greville; Glas, John; Haldane, Robert, and James Alexander Haldane

Scoville, Charles Reign

See Evangelism, Evangelists — Twentieth Century

Scroll, The

Official journal of the Campbell Institute.

Begun in 1896 as the *Quarterly Bulletin of the Campbell Institute,* it was renamed *The Scroll* in 1906. Primarily through the editorial leadership of Disciples minister and educator Edward Scribner Ames, the *Scroll* promoted the Campbell Institute's declared purposes of cultivating religious scholarship, literature, and thought among the Disciples of Christ. Ames retired as editor in 1951, and both the Campbell Institute and the *Scroll* were officially dissolved in 1975. A final, commemorative issue of the *Scroll* appeared in 1978, containing a history of the Campbell Institute by Samuel C. Pearson.

See also Ames, Edward Scribner; Campbell Institute

BIBLIOGRAPHY Samuel C. Pearson, "The Campbell Institute: Herald of the Transformation of an American Religious Tradition," *The Scroll* 62 (1978): 1-63 • Herbert L. Willett, ed., *Progress: Anniversary Volume of the Campbell Institute on the Completion of Twenty Years of History* (1917).

W. CLARK GILPIN

Seceders

The Seceders (or Associate Reformed Synod) withdrew from the Presbyterian General Assembly in 1733, disillusioned by the Assembly's reputed tolerance for heterodox opinions. In 1747 they divided over the Scottish Burgesses' Oath, which approved the "true religion" of the realm. Anti-Burgher Seceders refused this clear endorsement of the national church, while Burghers argued that the language of "true religion" might be construed more generically.

For the next fifty years, both Burgher and Anti-Burgher constituencies underwent an erosion of confessional rigidity, a trend that was finally challenged in the late 1790s. In Scotland, disaffected "Old Light" minorities withdrew from the Burgher and Anti-Burgher Synods in 1799 and 1806, respectively.

Ordained by the Irish Anti-Burghers in 1798, Thomas Campbell deplored these developing divisions and also labored to heal the breach of 1747. He retained his ordination in the Seceder Presbyterian church and was assigned to the Chartiers Presbytery in western Pennsylvania after he came to the United States in 1807. Here he still worked for reconciliation among disparate Presbyterian groups, but was ultimately placed under discipline by the Associate Synod and resigned his ministry in the Seceder church.

See also Campbell, Thomas; Presbyterians, Presbyterianism

BIBLIOGRAPHY John McKerrow, *History of the Secession Church* (1854) • David Stewart, *The Seceders in Ireland* (1950) • Robert Richardson, *Memoirs of Alexander Campbell* (1868), pp. 45-58.

KEITH B. HUEY

Seminario Evangélico de Puerto Rico

See Puerto Rico, The Movement in

"Sermon on the Law"

Delivered by Alexander Campbell on Sunday, September 1, 1816, before the Redstone Baptist Association, meeting at the Cross Creek church, three miles north of Wellsburg, (West) Virginia.

The text was printed in the *Millennial Harbinger* in September 1846. The "Sermon on the Law" was a factor in the separation between the Baptists and the Campbell churches and became programmatic for Campbell's reformation. The text for the sermon was Romans 8:3, and it contained five parts: (1) definitions and clarifications; (2) what the law could not accomplish; (3) why the law could not accomplish these purposes; (4) the means by which God modified the defects of the law; and (5) conclusions from the premises laid down.

Campbell criticized the Reformed distinction between ceremonial, judicial, and moral laws in the Old Testament, since in the language of Scripture "the Law" referred to the whole Mosaic system. In making a basic distinction between the covenants mediated by Moses and by Christ, he rejected the Reformed view that the law of Moses serves as a "rule of life" for the Christian. He contended that forms of worship, ordinances, discipline, and organization of the church must be learned only from the New Testament, specifying that the Old Testament cannot be used by Christians to support infant baptism, tithes, holy days, Sabbath, national covenants, and establishment of religion by civil law. The function of convicting of sin that his opponents gave to the moral law, Campbell ascribed to natural law and human conscience.

The distinction of the old and new covenants was a basic exegetical principle for Campbell. The neglect of the Old Testament engendered by this distinction among Campbell's followers was not true of Campbell's own practice. He recognized the Old Testament as part of inspired revelation useful for religious principles, edification, and moral instruction.

See also Baptists; Bible, Interpretation of the; Redstone Baptist Association

BIBLIOGRAPHY Alexander Campbell, "Sermon on the Law," *Millennial Harbinger* (September 1846): 493-521 • W. T. Moore, ed., *Alexander Campbell's Familiar Lectures on the Pentateuch* (1867) • Elmer Prout, "Alexander Campbell and the Old Testament," *Restoration Quarterly* 6 (1962): 131-42 • Everett Ferguson, "Alexander Campbell's 'Sermon on the Law': A Historical and Theological Examination," *Restoration Quarterly* 29 (1987): 71-85 • Robert Foster, "Alexander Campbell's 'Sermon on the Law' in Its Historical Context," *Discipliana* 63 (2003): 35-45.

EVERETT FERGUSON

Sewell, Elisha Granville (1830-1924)

Preacher and leader among Southern Churches of Christ during the first division of the Stone-Campbell Movement. Sewell served as coeditor of the *Gospel Advocate* with David Lipscomb for nearly fifty years.

Elisha was one of seven brothers, three of whom besides himself became preachers: Jesse L. Sewell (1818-1890), Isaac Sewell, and Caleb Sewell. All came into the Stone-Campbell Movement from Baptist churches in the 1840s. Elisha was the uncle of Jesse P. Sewell (1876-1969), an early president of Abilene Christian University.

Elisha Sewell was educated first at Burritt College in Spencer, Tennessee, then at Franklin College where he came under the influence of William Lipscomb (1829-1908) and consequently of his younger brother, David. When David Lipscomb found himself in need of help in 1870, he invited Sewell to join him in editing the *Gospel Advocate.* From that time until Lipscomb's death, the two were an inseparable team.

Sewell and Lipscomb had different temperaments — Lipscomb the more rational, Sewell the more emotional. Lipscomb had no talent for music, while Sewell co-produced three editions of hymnals. They occasionally differed in their interpretation of the Bible (e.g., over whether an elder or deacon had to be married, or whether there were degrees of punishment in hell); however, there was never the slightest trace of antipathy between them.

After moving to Nashville in 1870, Sewell spent his time writing and preaching. Sewell's commitments were demonstrated in a struggle that took

E. G. Sewell (1830-1924) became co-editor of the *Gospel Advocate* with David Lipscomb in 1870, a position he held for the next five decades. He and Lipscomb articulated many of the conservative positions that became characteristic of Churches of Christ. Courtesy of the Center for Restoration Studies, Abilene Christian University

place in the late 1880s at the Woodland Street Christian Church in East Nashville. Sewell had helped to found the church, served it as an elder, and had preached for it for twelve years. A growing number of members of the congregation had begun to support the organization of a state missionary society. Sewell, along with Lipscomb, had strongly opposed the missionary societies, and he urged the other elders, who had agreed to oversee the establishment of the state work when he was away, to abandon the project. When they refused, Sewell and a group of members in sympathy with his stance withdrew and formed the Tenth Street Church of Christ in October 1890.

Sewell's editorials sometimes came across as blunt and harsh. He was personally, however, like Lipscomb, a quiet and humble person. Even after his departure from the Woodland Street Church, he and the other leaders at Tenth Street were willing in 1891 to cooperate with Woodland Street in support of missionary work in Armenia. Sewell died March 2, 1924, at his home in East Nashville.

See also *Gospel Advocate, The;* Lipscomb, David; Missionary Societies, Controversy over

BIBLIOGRAPHY H. Leo Boles, "E. G. Sewell," in *Biographical Sketches of Gospel Preachers* (1932), pp. 238-42 • Herman Norton, *Tennessee Christians* (1971) • E. G. Sewell, *Gospel Lessons and Life History* (1908).

DAVID H. WARREN

Shakers

See Dunlavy, John; McNemar, Richard

Shannon, James (1799-1859)

Educator and evangelist who affiliated with the Stone-Campbell Movement in 1836, also a defender of the institution of slavery in the United States.

Shannon served as president of four academic institutions: the College of Louisiana (Centenary College), Bacon College, the University of Missouri at Columbia, and Christian University (Culver-Stockton College). Reactions to Shannon's pro-slavery views have inevitably overshadowed his positive contributions.

Shannon was born in Monaghan County, Ireland, and educated at the Royal Belfast Academical Institution. He taught briefly in Antrim before moving to Sunbury, Georgia, in 1821 to teach at Sunbury Academy. Shannon left the Presbyterian Church, was immersed, and in 1823 became an ordained Baptist preacher. In 1823 he married Evelina Belmont Dunham. From 1826 to 1829 he preached for the Augusta Baptist Church. His 1827 address at the Georgia Baptist Convention launched a campaign for a Baptist school of higher learning, Mercer College. In 1830 Shannon became chair of ancient languages at Franklin College (now the University of Georgia, Athens). While in Athens, he helped to organize and preached for the Baptist church. In 1834 Shannon urged fellow Baptists to accept baptism as a prerequisite for salvation.

From 1835 to 1840 Shannon presided over the College of Louisiana. In Jackson, Shannon bore the loss of his wife, left the Baptist church, established a Church of Christ, and rose in favor with Stone-Campbell leaders and editors. In 1837 he married Frances Carey Moore, who in 1839 was converted during a Southern tour undertaken by Alexander Campbell.

From 1840 to 1850 Shannon was president of Bacon College in Harrodsburg, Kentucky. In 1841 Shannon spoke at the Lexington unity meeting, organized by Alexander Campbell and others to reach out to other Christians, especially Baptists. In 1843 he made necessary preparations for Campbell's debate with Nathan Rice. An 1844 defense of slavery marked Shannon as a slavery apologist. The political events of 1849 encouraged Shannon to reprint the slavery address and to debate John C. Young on the issue. About 1847 Shannon erected a beautiful mansion, Aspen Hall, which still graces Harrodsburg.

From 1850 to 1856 Shannon presided over the University of Missouri at Columbia. In 1851 he helped to establish Christian Female College (Columbia College). In 1852 Shannon spoke at the American Bible Union Convention in Memphis, Tennessee, and was commissioned to translate the Gospel of Luke. Opposition to Shannon intensified with his 1855 pro-slavery speaking tour and speech at the Lexington, Missouri, Pro-Slavery Convention. As a "fire-eater," Shannon warned of division and war if abolitionists persisted. Shannon's views on owning slaves, if distasteful to Stone-Campbell leaders seeking to avoid division, articulated what many of the brethren silently and widely practiced.

From 1856 to 1859 Shannon served the presidency of Christian University (Culver-Stockton College) in Canton, Missouri, as its first president. He died in 1859 and is buried in Columbia, Missouri.

See also Bacon College; Culver-Stockton College; Slavery, The Movement and

BIBLIOGRAPHY Barry C. Poyner, *Bound to Slavery: James Shannon and the Restoration Movement* (1999) • James Shannon, *An Address Delivered Before the Pro-Slavery Convention of the State of Missouri* (1855) • James Shannon, *The Philosophy of Slavery as Identified with the Philosophy of Human Happiness: An Essay* (1849). BARRY C. POYNER

Shaw, Knowles (1834-1878)

Musician-evangelist of the Stone-Campbell Movement in the nineteenth century.

Knowles Shaw was born October 13, 1834, in Butler County, Ohio. Later his family removed to Rush County, Indiana. His father, who died when he was 12, leaving him to take care of the family, left Shaw a violin that he spent many hours practicing. His ability on this instrument soon attracted much attention. He played at dances and other social events. One night while playing the violin for a company of about forty dancers, "in that unlikely place for serious thought there came into his mind the dying words of his father in the impressive admonition of the prophet Amos 4:12, 'Prepare to meet thy God.'" This was the turning point in his life. He left the dance, went home, and spent the night in great mental and moral anguish. With genuine interest he began attending the Flat Rock Church of Christ. He made his confession and was baptized on September 13, 1852.

After his conversion he began to educate himself, although it was difficult because of his responsibilities to his family. On January 11, 1855, he married. About three years afterward he was called upon to speak to the assembled worshipers on a certain Lord's Day. His earnestness was impressive. Soon he was doing considerable preaching. By about 1861 he was fully launched in his work as the "Singing Evangelist."

The evangelistic labors of Knowles Shaw were great. One historian, G. I. Hoover, maintains that "in the decade from 1860 to 1870 he probably held more successful meetings than any man in the ranks of the disciples, and yet the reader will look in vain for a line in his writings or in the reports of his work that would indicate or imply that the desire for personal glory motivated his work." In his evangelistic meetings, he induced hundreds to convert and to join churches. Most of these meetings were held in comparatively small towns and usually with rather small congregations. When he went to Lebanon, Ohio, there was only a handful of members with no building. After the meeting was closed, the congregation was averaging 300. In 1877, actually Shaw's poorest year in evangelistic success, he preached 464 times and saw 220 persons added to churches through his efforts.

In 1878, after holding a meeting at Paris, Kentucky, with sixty-five additions, he went to Dallas, Texas, where he preached for five weeks at the Commerce Street Church. At the conclusion of this meeting he accepted a call to go to McKinney, Texas, and hold a short meeting. While on this journey to McKinney, he met his death. The train on which he was riding derailed, toppled over an embankment, and killed him instantly. The last words of the "Singing Evangelist" before his death were, "Oh, it is a grand thing to rally people to the cross of Christ."

Perhaps Shaw's greatest contribution to the evangelism of the Stone-Campbell Movement was his sincere appeal to human emotion. Edwin Errett, onetime editor of the *Christian Standard,* emphasized the fact that Knowles Shaw raised the emotional element in the Movement's evangelism to an unprecedented level. He coordinated the rational element, already sharpened by Walter Scott, with the emotional element in his evangelistic ministry.

See also Evangelism, Evangelists — Early Nineteenth Century

BIBLIOGRAPHY William Baxter, *The Life of Knowles Shaw, the Singing Evangelist* (1879) • Charles R. Gresham, "The Restoration Movement and Mass Evangelism," Part II, *Christian Standard* (September 5, 1953) • G. I. Hoover, "Knowles Shaw's Contributions to the Evangelism of the Churches of Christ," *Christian Standard* (January 6 and 13, 1940). CHARLES R. GRESHAM

Shelton, Albert L.

See Asia, Missions in

Shelton, Orman Leroy (1895-1959)

Pastor and academic administrator of the Christian Church (Disciples of Christ).

O. L. Shelton was dean of the School of Religion at Butler University, Indianapolis, from 1944 until its incorporation as Christian Theological Seminary in 1958. He was named first president of the new institution but died shortly thereafter. Although Shelton had a distinguished record as pastor in Missouri, Texas, and Oklahoma, and was highly respected among the churches related to the International Convention of the Disciples of Christ, he was not well known among theological educators or the constituency of the School of Religion when he succeeded founding dean Frederick D. Kershner.

During his administration, Shelton reconfirmed the autonomy of the School of Religion, transformed the faculty, responded creatively to the rapid growth of enrollment in the postwar period, especially among returning military veterans, and shifted the seminary's ecclesial orientation toward the organized work of the Christian Church (Disciples of Christ). He continued to be a prominent leader in the church, including service as chair of the Commission on Restudy of the Disciples of Christ and chair of a committee to develop study documents for the World Convention of the Churches of Christ.

Shelton published occasional essays in the church press, but his most important publication was *The Church Functioning Effectively* (1946), in which he proposed an organizational system "with leaders responsible for various functions [which] is firmly rooted in the teachings of the New Testament."

See also Christian Theological Seminary; Commission on Restudy of the Disciples of Christ

BIBLIOGRAPHY Orman L. Shelton, *The Church Functioning Effectively* (1946) • Keith Watkins, *Christian Theological Seminary, Indianapolis* (2001). KEITH WATKINS

Shepherd, James Walton (1861-1948)

Evangelist, missionary, author, and editor among Churches of Christ.

Born near Lexington, Kentucky, Shepherd was converted under the preaching of James A. Harding (1848-1922) and attended the College of the Bible, though he did not receive a degree.

Shepherd's evangelistic efforts and located ministerial work took him to several southeastern states and as far north as Detroit, Michigan. He also engaged in mission work in Australia and New Zealand. While abroad he edited the *Evangelical Messenger* and compiled his monumental *Handbook on Baptism.*

J. W. Shepherd (1861-1948), while serving as office manager for the Gospel Advocate Company, was asked by David Lipscomb to compile the data on Churches of Christ for the first U.S. religious census. Shepherd had studied under J. W. McGarvey at the College of the Bible.

Courtesy of the Center for Restoration Studies, Abilene Christian University

He briefly served the Nashville Bible School as librarian, the *Gospel Advocate* as office manager, and the *Christian Leader* as an editor. While at the *Advocate* he was charged with compiling data for the Census Bureau on those churches that neither used an instrument nor supported missionary societies. He also served as a liaison to the government on behalf of conscientious objectors during World War I.

With the publication in 1929 of *The Church, the Falling Away, and the Restoration,* he provided a distinctive interpretation of Christian history and the rise of the American Stone-Campbell Restoration Movement. That volume, his *Handbook,* and the five edited volumes of David Lipscomb's notes on the New Testament are among his most significant and enduring contributions.

See also *Gospel Advocate, The;* Harding, James Alexander; Lipscomb, David

BIBLIOGRAPHY David Lipscomb, *Queries and Answers,* ed. J. W. Shepherd (1910) • J. W. Shepherd, *Handbook on*

Baptism (1894) • J. W. Shepherd, *The Church, the Falling Away, and the Restoration* (1929) • *Salvation from Sin by David Lipscomb,* ed. J. W. Shepherd (1913).

McGarvey Ice

Sherriff, John (1864-1935)

New Zealand stonemason who immigrated to South Africa in 1896 and opened the door for Stone-Campbell mission work in what is today Zimbabwe, Zambia, and Malawi. His influence brought missionaries from New Zealand, Australia, and the United States to these countries.

In 1897 Sherriff arrived in Bulawayo, Southern Rhodesia, after brief works in Cape Town, Kimberly, Johannesburg, and Pretoria. He supported himself through much of his ministry with his stonemason trade. In 1898 he began a school in Bulawayo to teach the Africans to read and write and to introduce them to Christ. Sherriff sent out to evangelize the home areas of those who converted and learned well.

The evangelists he sent met with increasing success, and Sherriff soon became overwhelmed. Between 1901 and 1905 he appealed for missionary help from the churches in Australia and New Zealand. F. L. Hadfield answered the invitation in 1906. In summer 1907 Sherriff purchased a 400-acre farm five miles from Bulawayo on which he intended to open an agricultural mission school. He repaired a house located on the farm and moved there along with some of the workers and students from the school in Bulawayo. He named the farm Forest Vale, and it became a major center of the work in southern Africa.

In 1912 Hadfield and other New Zealand missionaries moved from Forest Vale to establish the Dadaya mission, which has continued into the twenty-first century to witness to their sacrifice and devotion. Shortly after this, Sherriff came in contact with Churches of Christ in the United States. By 1918 he was receiving regular financial support from several American churches and publishing repeated requests for workers. Will N. Short (1894-1980) and his wife Nancy A'Delia (1896-1982) were the first U.S. missionaries to join the work in 1921. The Shorts moved to Zambia in 1923 to open Sinde Mission, where one of Sherriff's first converts, Peter Masiya, had preached since 1918.

John Sherriff laid a foundation upon which countless missionaries and African evangelists have built and continue to build churches throughout southern Africa.

See also Africa, Missions in; New Zealand, The Movement in; Short, William Newton

Bibliography T. J. Gore, ed., *That They All May Be One: A Century's Progress* (1909) • Dow Merritt, *The Dewbreakers* (1971) • Murray J. Savage, *Achievement, Fifty Years of Missionary Witness in Southern Rhodesia* (1949) • *Word and Work,* Louisville, Kentucky, various issues from 1913 to 1928.

J. Paul Pennington

Short, William Newton (1894-1980)

Along with his wife, Nancy A'Delia, William Newton Short was the first American missionary to Rhodesia (now Zimbabwe) for Churches of Christ. The Shorts arrived in Southern Rhodesia (S. R.) in November 1921 and worked with John Sherriff at the Forest Vale Mission for about eighteen months. In July 1923 they moved to Northern Rhodesia (N. R.) and established the Sinde Mission, the first mission operated by the Churches of Christ in that country. In November 1927 the Shorts moved to the Kabanga mission near Kalomo, N. R., and worked there for about a year. After a furlough the family worked at Huyuyu Mission in Salisbury, S. R., for over four years and at the end of 1934 homesteaded in Macheke, S. R., where Short raised crops and built transport wagons for a living during the Depression. He not only worked with the Africans but also pioneered mission work among the whites.

Short moved to Namwianga Mission near Kalomo in 1945 to work with a school for white children and was elected "Missionary in Charge" of the mission and chairman of the board of Eureka Christian School. Here he published *Rays of Light* (1942-74), a paper for the white population, and *Glimpses of Africa* (July 1945–May 1960), a newsletter on mission work in Africa for Churches of Christ. He also printed extensively to support the mission work, including material in at least three African languages, as well as several printings of Myrtle Rowe's Tonga songbook.

In 1960 the Shorts moved to Bulawayo, S. R., and worked with the Queen's Park Church of Christ for two years, and then moved to the Hillside congregation, where Short served as counselor and friend to preachers and missionaries from all over southern Africa until his death.

See also Africa, Missions in; Sherriff, John

Don L. Meredith

Showalter, G. H. P.

See *Firm Foundation*

Silver Point School

In 1905 G. P. Bowser, along with S. W. Womack and Alexander Cleveland Campbell, began discussing the possibility of beginning a school similar to the Nashville Bible School started by David Lipscomb. Their goal was to have a school that allowed African American students to receive an elementary and secondary education, using the Bible as a textbook. In 1907 the school opened on Jackson Street in Nashville, Tennessee, with nine students. Two years later, the school was relocated to the rural community of Silver Point, Tennessee, in order to lower operating costs. The Silver Point School was known as the Putnam County Normal and Industrial School for Colored People. The Putnam County School Board underwrote Bowser as a teacher and allowed him to operate in the county schoolhouse until property was secured and the school building was erected. Among those who taught at Silver Point were Philistia Womack, Annie C. Tuggle, T. H. Busby, and Alexine Campbell Page. The school experienced a record enrollment of fifty-seven students in the spring of 1915.

In 1916 David Lipscomb requested that A. M. Burton conduct a study of the Silver Point School; this study resulted in the purchase of new lots and the construction of a new brick chapel and a building to house female students. Board members included A. M. Burton, S. P. Pitman, J. S. Hamond, O. P. Barry, Alexander C. Campbell, S. W. Womack, P. H. Black, Henry Clay, and Marshall Keeble. The school was seriously hindered by the death of David Lipscomb, limited financial support, and difficulty in recruiting students. Although the board and Annie C. Tuggle, who officially served as a fund-raiser for the school, made considerable efforts, the obstacles eventually became insurmountable. Though the church continued to meet in the building, the school closed its doors in 1920.

See also African Americans in the Movement; Bowser, George Philip; Campbell, Alexander (Alex) Cleveland; Keeble, Marshall

BIBLIOGRAPHY J. E. Choate, *Roll, Jordan, Roll* (1968) • Annie C. Tuggle, *Another World Wonder* (1973).

ERVIN C. JACKSON

Sin

See Anthropology

Slavery, The Movement and

1. Abolitionists
2. Pro-Slavery Advocacy
3. Emancipationism (Gradualism)
4. The Perspective of Christian Slaves

Slavery in the American context was a system of hereditary bondage of one person to another. White indentured servants were freed after their contracted terms of service were completed, but slavery was lifetime bondage. It originated in violence and was perpetuated by the accidents of birth and the force of law. By 1830 the population of the United States was around 12.8 million, of which there were more than two million slaves.

The Stone-Campbell Movement was born, and sought to voice its plea for Christian unity, in an age of increasing controversy over "the peculiar institution." Pressure from without and from within the Movement intensified during the Movement's rapid expansion both in the North and the South in the 1830s to 1850s. Leaders were called upon publicly to articulate their position on slavery and to shoulder the burden of those positions. Debate over slavery in the Movement, however, was not a simple contention between abolitionists and pro-slavery advocates. There were, in addition, the voices of emancipationists (gradualists) and indeed the slaves themselves.

1. Abolitionists

To abolitionists, slavery was an unmitigated evil that offended both God and humanity. A faithful church had no choice but to stand against the powerful, insidious system of slavery and to advocate its immediate dissolution irrespective of any consequences. Abolitionists were a vocal minority in the Stone-Campbell Movement, ultimately concentrating their resources in Cincinnati, with John Boggs and his *North-Western Christian Magazine,* and in Indianapolis under the leadership of Ovid Butler with his Northwestern Christian (now Butler) University.

2. Pro-Slavery Advocacy

While in the larger realm of American Protestantism there were a number of advocates who argued for the biblical and theological legitimacy of slavery, within the Stone-Campbell Movement this position was especially well represented by James Shannon (1799-1859), president of Bacon College in Kentucky (1840-50), second president of the University of Missouri (1850-56), and first president of Culver-Stockton College (1856-59). In 1849 Shannon published *The Philosophy of Slavery* in which he said that all people are under some form of bondage due to human sin. Slavery was but one of a number of political and social forms of that bondage. Against the abolitionists, Shannon said, "It is worse than folly, it is madness in the extreme, to attempt to expedite the progress of liberty more rapidly than that of intelligence and virtue." In his later *Address Delivered Before the Pro-Slavery Convention of the State of Missouri* (1855), Shannon fiercely defended the biblical sanction for slavery, in Old Testament and New Testament alike. "In short," he wrote, "neither Jesus Christ nor his Apostles, ever interfered with the institution of slavery, except to rebuke abolitionism, and exhort both masters and slaves to perform faithfully, as in the sight of God, their respective duties."

College president and educator, James Shannon defended slavery as justified by Scripture, interpreting the apostolic injunctions about master-slave relationships as tantamount to a condemnation of abolitionism. Courtesy of the Disciples of Christ Historical Society

3. Emancipationism (Gradualism)

From the beginning of the nineteenth century there was a strong emancipation movement in the South. In 1820 Elihu Embree published *The Emancipator* in Jonesborough, Tennessee. This was eleven years before William Lloyd Garrison (whom historians commonly credit as the leading American abolitionist) published his *Liberator* in Boston. By 1827 there were twenty-five antislavery societies in Tennessee alone.

Emancipationists advocated liberation of slaves after they had been prepared for freedom through education. Leaders of the Stone-Campbell Movement initiated a number of practical means to this end. David Purviance (1766-1847), a close associate of Barton W. Stone, voted in the Kentucky legislature of 1798 for a constitutional convention that he and others hoped would make constructive provisions for the liberation of slaves. Upon his failure in this and successive attempts, Purviance joined many other Southern emancipationists in moving north of the Ohio River. During his career he penned a moving poem, "On Slavery," that censured slaveholders for consorting with evil and scandalizing a gospel that is for all people and that sets captives free.

Barton W. Stone and other revivalists celebrated the wave of emancipations that accompanied the Cane Ridge Revival of 1801 even though, for reasons beyond Stone's control, he himself later held slaves for a season. Escape from those obligations may have been a major cause of the reformer's relocation to Illinois in 1834. In 1830 Stone had participated in the formation of the Georgetown, Kentucky, chapter of the American Colonization Society. The purpose of the society was to purchase, educate, and liberate slaves and return them to Africa. The society's endeavors led to the founding of the nation of Liberia, but the organization was challenged by the fact that the slave birth rate far exceeded the annual number of freedmen who returned to Africa. Later in the 1830s, Stone showed increasing frustration with the Colonization Society and with Christians who had still refused to manumit their slaves. At one point he even published in his *Christian Messenger* part of an abolitionist tract from the Anti-Slavery Society of William Lloyd Garrison. Stone died (in 1844), however, before the controversy over slavery had peaked in the Stone-Campbell Movement.

The leading emancipationist in the Movement was Alexander Campbell himself. In 1832 he issued a concrete proposal that since the federal debt from the War of 1812 was paid, $10 million be annually appropriated by the Congress for the purchase, education, and colonization of all slaves, until the land would not be "trod by the foot of one slave, nor enriched by a drop of his sweat or blood."

Campbell sought to "put his axe at the root of the tree" by advancing the gospel rather than becoming completely absorbed in the slavery controversy. His primary concern was the unity of all followers of Christ for sake of the Christian mission. The pages of the *Millennial Harbinger* are nonetheless replete with discussions of the slavery crisis, into which Campbell was increasingly drawn. Baptists and Methodists had already divided North and South over the issue, and Disciples abolitionism was growing, when, in 1845, Campbell published an extended series clarifying "Our Position to American Slavery." Like his father Thomas, who had admitted the biblical precedent for a benevolent slavery in patriarchal times but repudiated the disgrace of involuntary servitude in the American context, Campbell ultimately offended abolitionists. He sided with Baptist James Fuller against fellow Baptist Francis Wayland in categorically rejecting the claim that, on biblical grounds, slavery was intrinsically and invariably a "moral evil." He also insisted on the human and civil rights of slaveholders and gave enormous weight to Paul's axiom in 1 Corinthians 7:20-24 that everyone should remain in the state in which he or she was called. On the other hand, Campbell stated that the fact that the New Testament acknowledged the existence of slavery was insufficient as a positive argument for American slavery; indeed, Scripture could not possibly justify American slavery "because of its abuses and liabilities to abuse." British abolitionists assailed Campbell during his trip to Great Britain in 1847, reinforcing his determination to focus on pursuing Christian unity without bogging the Movement down in social and political concerns. Two critical events, however, demanded his further attention. The first was the calling of a constitutional convention by the Kentucky legislature in 1849. Campbell felt responsible to use his significant religious influence in that state to plead for an emancipation provision in the new state constitution. He therefore wrote the "Tract for the People of Kentucky," a broadside against the system of American slavery — for which effort he was viciously assailed in the South.

The second critical event was the passage of the Fugitive Slave Law by Congress in 1850. Most offensive to Christians in the North was the provision mandating that anyone preventing the arrest of fugitive slaves, or who hid them or sought to rescue them, was subject to a fine of $1,000 and six months in prison. Distasteful though it was, Campbell advised obedience to the law (according to the scriptural warrant for civil obedience) until it could be changed. For this, he was assailed in the North. Ovid Butler pled with Campbell to reverse his position on the law, declaring its inconsistency with "Divine Philanthropy" and arguing that Jesus' injunction to his disciple to take up the cross qualified the apostolic precept of subjection to temporal authorities.

Campbell's calculated emancipationism was one shared by many other leaders in the Stone-Campbell Movement, among them Walter Scott. Scott favored colonization but was at a loss as to how best a gradual emancipation could precisely be worked out in the interest of all parties. As early as 1834 he wrote, "I am no friend to slavery, I deprecate its commencement, I deplore its continuance, and tremble for its issue; but I am silent because I think to speak would be folly. What ought to be said I can not say, and what ought not to be said, I will not say." Inevitably he, like Campbell, was accused of defending slavery, a charge he strongly rejected, meanwhile indicating that the government rather than the church should bear the burden of emancipation. He later despaired over the rupture of the Union and died just as the Civil War was commencing.

4. The Perspective of Christian Slaves

It is remarkable that so many American slaves embraced the Christian faith of their masters. Cut off from the roots of their native culture, slaves brought unique gifts to the Christian faith. Their insightful and picturesque "spirituals" expressed deep reflections on the gospel. The resurrection is "That Great Gettin' Up Morning," while one's eternal home is "Over Jordan."

Nonetheless a slave *ipso facto* could not live his Christian life without restraints. The master controlled even his or her church membership. Slaves lived under other inhibitions as well. Slave marriage had no legal standing, and cruel masters could sell husbands away from wives. Slaves commonly lacked money to bring as offerings. Their leadership roles were limited to those of deacons among their own.

There were some slave preachers, among whom Alexander Cross was noteworthy. The congregation in Hopkinsville, Kentucky, recognized his gifts and with the help of other churches purchased Cross for $530. After he was liberated and educated, Cross was sent to Liberia by the American Christian Missionary Society. Tragically, he soon died from a fever.

After the slave revolts of Denmark Vesey and Nat Turner in 1822 and 1831, laws were passed forbidding slave gatherings without a white person present. As protection against "inflammatory" material from Northern abolitionists, laws also forbade teaching slaves to read. Many Christian masters ignored such laws, but they could not completely escape them. Finally, if a master wished to liberate his slaves, the master had to make bond for their good behavior. Otherwise, the slaves had to agree to leave the state. This was the problem Dr. James T. Barclay, former slave owner on the Monticello estate in Virginia, faced when preparing to go to Jerusalem as the first missionary of the American Christian Missionary Society.

Churches of the Stone-Campbell Movement were noteworthy in having slave members, but even with the best motives they could not completely overcome the evil effects of slavery. Therefore, when slaves gained the right to move on, many left the churches of their former masters to seek already existing black congregations. This loss deeply grieved Tolbert Fanning (1810-1874), who wrote from Nashville how slaves had "sat with their white brethren many years in the heavenly places in Christ Jesus." But by 1872 segregation had replaced fellowship and the Stone-Campbell vision of Christian unity became deeply tarnished by racial division.

Historians within the Stone-Campbell tradition have consistently argued that the Movement did not divide over slavery, both because of the efforts of Alexander Campbell himself and because there was not an elaborate denominational infrastructure that could be divided North and South. Yet other historians have cogently argued that controversy over slavery, and ultimately over the Civil War itself, was part of a host of aggravating ideological and cultural factors that alienated Stone-Campbell churches across the Mason-Dixon Line and further accelerated the division between the Disciples and the Churches of Christ.

See also Abolitionism; African Americans in the Movement — Nineteenth Century; Butler, Ovid; Christian Missionary Society; Civil War, The; *North-Western Christian Magazine;* Purviance, David; Shannon, James

BIBLIOGRAPHY Alexander Campbell, "Our Position to American Slavery," nos. 1-8, *Millennial Harbinger* (1845): 49-53, 67-71, 108-12, 145-49, 193-96, 232-40, 357-64 • Alexander Campbell, "Slavery and the Fugitive Slave Law," *Millennial Harbinger* (1851): 171-72, 201-6, 247-52, 309-17, 386-92, 425-34 • Thomas Campbell, "Elder Thomas Campbell's Views on Slavery," *Millennial Harbinger* (1845): 3-8 • Robert O. Fife, "Alexander Campbell and the Christian Church in the Slavery Controversy" (Ph.D. dissertation, Indiana University, 1960) • Robert O. Fife, *Teeth on Edge* (1971) • Jess Hale, "Ecclesiastical Politics on a Moral Powder Keg: Alexander Campbell and the Christian Church in the Slavery Controversy," *Restoration Quarterly* 39 (1997): 65-81 • David E. Harrell, *Quest for a Christian America: The Disciples of Christ and American Society to 1866* (1966, repr. ed. 2003) • Barry C. Poyner, *Bound to Slavery: James Shannon and the Restoration Movement* (1999) • James Shannon, *An Address Delivered Before the Pro-Slavery Convention of the State of Missouri* (1855) • James Shannon, *The Philosophy of Slavery as Identified with the Philosophy of Human Happiness: An Essay* (1849).

PAUL M. BLOWERS *and* ROBERT O. FIFE

Slogans

Concise statements of principles that were basic to the Stone-Campbell Movement, serving to recall and reinforce its distinctive affirmations.

Various slogans developed, some from the very beginning, such as Thomas Campbell's two memorable phrases "Where the Scriptures speak, we speak; where the Scriptures are silent, we are silent," and from the *Declaration and Address,* "The church of Jesus Christ on earth is essentially, intentionally, and constitutionally one." Another slogan whose actual authorship is mysterious but that came into regular usage in the Movement was, "We are Christians only, but not the only Christians." Also important was Barton Stone's motto, "Let Christian unity be our polar star."

The Stone-Campbell Movement also abundantly deployed the famous dictum originally ascribed to the seventeenth-century Lutheran theologian Peter Meiderlin: "In essentials, unity; in opinions, liberty; in all things, love." The slogan "No creed but Christ, no book but the Bible, no law but love, no name but the divine," or the shorthand "No creed but Christ," had an extensive history of interpretation in the Movement. "No creed but Christ" was adaptable ultimately to conservative and liberal interpreters of the Movement's plea, who used it for their own purposes. The early passion of the Movement to purify Christian discourse and shape a language conducive to Christian unity was captured in the imperative "Call Bible things by Bible names."

These and other slogans encapsulated the Movement's emphasis on the free, unencumbered association of Christians, their rights of conscience, and their aspiration to ecclesial unity. They served as rubrics or rallying points to divert Christians from the peculiarities of individual theological opinion and to gravitate the Movement's constituents toward the central plea of restoring "New Testament Christianity."

See also Creeds and Confessions; *Declaration and Address;* New Testament Christianity; "Plea," The; "Restoration," Meanings of within the Movement; Unity, Christian

BIBLIOGRAPHY Eugene Boring, *Disciples and the Bible: A History of Disciples Biblical Interpretation in North America* (1997) • Thomas Campbell, *Declaration and Address* (1809) • W. J. Jarman et al., "The Slogans of the Disciples" (5-part series), *Christian-Evangelist* (1949): 1031, 1059, 1136, 1194, 1291 • Carl Ketcherside, "No Creed but Christ," *Mission Messenger* 22 (1960): 7-10 • Hans Rollmann, "In Essentials Unity: The Pre-History of a Restoration Movement Slogan," *Restoration Quarterly* 39 (1997): 129-39.

TERRY MIETHE

Sly, Virgil

See United Christian Missionary Society, The

Smith, Elias (1769-1846)

Cofounder (along with Abner Jones) of a group known variously as the New England "Christians," the "Christian Connection," or the "Christian Denomination."

Reared in Connecticut and Vermont as a Calvinistic Baptist of Separatist background, Smith became an itinerant evangelist in 1791 after a brief stint as a schoolteacher. After three years he became a settled pastor first in Salisbury, New Hampshire, and later in Woburn, Massachusetts. Growing dissatisfaction with the Baptists, especially their Calvinism, resulted in his establishment of an independent congregation at Portsmouth, New Hampshire, in 1802. Several area Baptist churches accepted this Portsmouth group as a "Church of Christ" in their fellowship.

The next few years saw Smith and Abner Jones establish a number of "Christian" churches in New

Elias Smith (1769-1846) made his most significant contribution to the growth of the Christian Connection through his editorship of the *Herald of Gospel Liberty* from 1806 to 1817.
Courtesy of the Disciples of Christ Historical Society

England with the aim of abandoning all creeds but the Bible. From the beginning Smith produced a steady stream of books and pamphlets to promote the new movement. He was particularly energetic in attacking what he considered to be the prevalent errors of Christendom. This opposition centered on state-supported churches and their clergy, Calvinism, sprinkling, and the Trinity. Smith's most significant work was the editorship of the *Herald of Gospel Liberty* from 1806 to 1817, a forum that effectively spread the Christian Connection message. The first issue reprinted Barton Stone's *Last Will and Testament of Springfield Presbytery.* This journal was published first in Portsmouth and later in Philadelphia.

Smith's efforts included extensive preaching from Maine to Virginia and attempts to unite the Connection with groups of similar interests. In 1811 he traveled to Virginia with Joseph Thomas (known as "The White Pilgrim"), hoping to help unite with the churches in the dissident "Republican Methodist" movement of James O'Kelly. His views on the Trinity, the annihilation of the wicked, and infant baptism were not, however, well received. Ever plagued with instability, Smith left the Connection in 1817 to become a universalist, publishing a journal called *Herald of Life and Immortality* (1819-20). Six years later he took steps to rejoin his brethren, but then defected again to universalism. Finally, in 1827 Smith publicly renounced universalism again and attempted to be accepted by the brotherhood, publishing another short-lived journal, the *Morning Star and City Watchman.*

The rest of Smith's life was spent in practicing herbal medicine in relative obscurity. In 1836 Alexander Campbell and Tolbert Fanning apparently met Smith while visiting Boston. Campbell does not mention him by name, but Fanning does. Smith seems to have reverted once again to universalism shortly before his death in 1846.

See also Christian Connection; Jones, Abner; New England "Christians"; O'Kelly, James; Universalists

BIBLIOGRAPHY Nathan O. Hatch, *The Democratization of American Christianity* (1989) • Michael G. Kenny, *The Perfect Law of Liberty: Elias Smith and the Providential History of America* (1994) • Elias Smith, *The Life, Conversion, Preaching, Travels, and Sufferings of Elias Smith* (1816) • Lynn Waller, "A Study in the Life of Elias Smith with Emphasis on the Years 1806-1817" (M.Div. thesis, Abilene Christian University, 1971).

LYNN WALLER

Smith, Gerald L. K. (1898-1976)

Disciples of Christ minister, eventually a major sponsor of American anti-Semitism and right-wing political involvements in the mid-twentieth century.

Smith was founder of the Christian Nationalist Crusade (1942), a presidential candidate of the America First Party (1844), and initiator of the "Christ of the Ozarks" theme park (1966). Early in his political career Smith served as an organizer for the controversial Huey Long, the Depression-era Louisiana governor, senator, and demagogue, whose funeral he preached. In ministry he served (1918-34) four congregations now affiliated with the Christian Churches/Churches of Christ (Soldiers Grove, Footville, and Beloit, Wisconsin; Kansas, Illinois) and three congregations (two in Indianapolis; one in Shreveport, Louisiana) now affiliated with the Christian Church (Disciples of Christ). His oratory gained prominence at the New Testament Church Congress in St. Louis (1922), where he was received with greater enthusiasm than George Taubman, Z. T. Sweeney, and even William Jennings Bryan. In Indianapolis, his ministry at Seventh Christian Church (1924-26) added 1,150 members and featured Bible memorization workshops by Henry Halley (of

Gerald L. K. Smith (1898-1976), once a Disciples minister in Shreveport, Louisiana, rose to national fame as an anti-semitic activist in the 1930s and 40s.

Halley's Bible Handbook). As chairman of the General Work Committee of the Christian Church Union of Indianapolis, he worked with county evangelists Virgil P. and Blanche Kerr Brock, later known for their hymn compositions. F. D. Kershner was an elder during his tenure at University Place Christian Church (1926-29) in Indianapolis. In Shreveport (1929-34), because of the Depression, he increasingly preached a message of social reform both in the pulpit and on radio. Continuing hard times, and complaints about his absences to be part of Long's entourage, resulted in his removal from the pulpit early in 1934.

See also Jews and Judaism, Views of in the Movement

BIBLIOGRAPHY Glen Jeansonne, *Gerald L. K. Smith, Minister of Hate* (1988) • Leo Ribuffo, *The Old Christian Right: The Protestant Far Right from the Great Depression to the Cold War* (1983) • Gerald L. K. Smith, *Besieged Patriot: Autobiographical Episodes Exposing Communism, Traitorism and Zionism from the Life of Gerald L. K. Smith,* ed. Elna M. Smith and Charles F. Robertson (1978). C. J. Dull

Smith, "Raccoon" John (1784-1868)

Evangelist and activist for Christian unity in the early Stone-Campbell Movement.

There is much disagreement over where and when John Smith was given the nickname "Raccoon," a title he disliked but tolerated. There is little disagreement over his importance as a preacher who nearly single-handedly spread the message of reform over much of the state of Kentucky from 1824 to his death in 1868, or over whether he was more than any other individual responsible for the uniting the Stone and Campbell movements.

Born into a Regular Baptist family in what is now Sullivan County, Tennessee, and moving with his family to Cumberland (now Clinton) County, Kentucky, Smith early displayed the ability of mind and speech needed to be a preacher, although he never had more than six months of schooling. Largely self-educated, he was a voracious reader and a diligent student of oratory. He struggled for several years with the Baptist teaching that one must have an experience of the Holy Spirit to be admitted to baptism, or that a preacher needed the special experience of a call to preach. After surmounting those difficulties, he was immersed in December 1804, married to Anna Townsend on December 9, 1806, licensed as an "exhorter," and then ordained a Baptist preacher in May 1808.

Since preaching in that connection was not supported monetarily by the congregations, Smith continued to live as a farmer through most of his life, first in southern Kentucky, then briefly in Alabama, where he lost two children in a cabin fire; his wife died from shock shortly thereafter in 1815. In December of that year he married Nancy Hurt and moved north to Montgomery County, Kentucky, just east of Lexington.

As early as 1815, while preaching in the Bluegrass region, Smith began to wrestle with the doctrines of predestination and total depravity, as outlined in the Baptists' Philadelphia Confession of Faith. By the time of his first meeting with Alexander Campbell in 1824 Smith was open to preaching the simple good news that Christ had died for all and that all that is necessary for salvation is belief in Christ, repentance from sin, and obedience in immersion. He then became a leader of reform among the Baptists in Kentucky.

Smith's preaching was powerful. His biographer reports, "His voice was deep, rich, and heavy; his utterance deliberate and distinct. His cant was finely modulated; for he loved melody, and the taste of the times demanded that the sermon should be rendered in solemn, chant-like tones." For several months in 1828 he averaged thirty or more baptisms a week. He told his wife, "I have baptized seven hundred sinners

"Raccoon" John Smith (1784-1868) epitomized many of the Stone-Campbell frontier evangelists of the nineteenth century — largely self-educated yet devoted to constantly deeper study of the Bible. Courtesy of the Disciples of Christ Historical Society

and capsized fifteen hundred Baptists." Smith allegedly delivered 523 discourses and had three public debates in that one year. His willingness to travel anywhere and preach to whoever would listen, combined with his persuasive presentation of the primitive gospel, captured much of the frontier state of Kentucky for the Disciples of Christ. Yet his irenic spirit worked also toward unity among Christians.

Smith, along with John T. Johnson, was instrumental in bringing together the followers of Campbell with those of Stone, most of whom were former Presbyterians, in Lexington during the New Year's weekend of 1831-32, where he presented the Campbell position. He began: "God has but one people on the earth. He has given to them but one Book, and therein exhorts and commands them to be one family." He then argued for using only Bible terms and terminology, while keeping speculations, deductions, and inferences private. He then ended with this memorable statement: "Let us, then, my brethren, be no longer Campbellites or Stoneites, New Lights or Old Lights, or any other kind of *lights,* but let us all come to the Bible, and to the Bible alone, as the only book in the world that can give us all the Light we need."

After Barton Stone made a brief statement in agreement with Smith, they joined hands, thus symbolically uniting the two movements. Smith then traveled with John Rogers for three years throughout Kentucky, leading the congregations of the two groups to unite. Following up on the 1832 merger, Smith sought in his "Address to the Brethren" to allay persisting Disciple (Campbellite) suspicions of Stone's followers on issues of the atonement, open membership and communion, the Trinity, and the name "Christians," denying any of these as legitimate grounds for undermining the new-found unity. (The text of the address appears in J. A. Williams' biography of Smith, pp. 382-87.)

Smith was able to continue preaching for another thirty-six years, dying finally at the home of a daughter in Mexico, Missouri, on February 28, 1868. He was buried in Lexington beside Nancy, his second wife.

See also Evangelism, Evangelists — Nineteenth Century; Preaching — Nineteenth Century

BIBLIOGRAPHY John Challen, ed., *Challen's Monthly* (March 1858): 109-11 • Louis Cochran, *Raccoon John Smith: A Novel Based on the Life of the Famous Pioneer Kentucky Preacher* (1985) • Everett Donaldson, *The Legacy of Raccoon John Smith* (1995) • Everett Donaldson, *Raccoon John Smith: Frontiersman and Reformer* (1993) • David R. Dungan, "John (Raccoon) Smith," in *Churches of Christ,* ed. John T. Brown (1904), pp. 410-12 • John Augustus Williams, *Life of Elder John Smith with Some Account of the Rise and Progress of the Current Reformation* (1870). BRUCE E. SHIELDS

Snoddy, Elmer L.

See Lexington Theological Seminary

Social Issues

See Abolitionism; Abortion; Pacifism; Race Relations; Slavery, The Movement and

Societies

Parachurch organizations inaugurated for missionary, benevolent, or other purposes.

Voluntary "religious societies" were instrumental in the expansion of evangelical spiritual renewal, missionary work, and social reform in the eighteenth and nineteenth centuries in Britain and America. The role of the "society" has a long and significant place in the history of the Stone-Campbell Movement. Formed for the accomplishment of designated tasks, societies supported missions, education, publishing, social services, and a variety of other enterprises. Cooperative in nature, their aim was to accomplish what individuals or single congregations could not do alone, or to do it better.

The significance of societies in the Movement is thoroughly interconnected with its ecclesiology. Resisting its own formation into a new denomination, the Movement long saw voluntary societies as practical tools, existing to serve the churches' work but not definitional of the church itself.

As early as 1798, Thomas Campbell saw the value of cooperative work through his participation in the Evangelical Society of Ulster, and he later founded the Christian Association of Washington, Pennsylvania. The Campbells affiliated their reform movement for a time with the Redstone and Mahoning Associations, which were Baptist evangelistic societies voluntary in character; and Alexander Campbell greatly lamented the demise of the Mahoning Association in 1830. The development of state missionary societies and the American Christian Missionary Society (1849) laid groundwork for a number of cooperative associations/societies in the latter decades of that century. The International Convention of the Disciples became a venue for the reports of such "agencies." The United Christian Missionary Society became the single most powerful arm of the Disciples of Christ in the early and mid-twentieth century, helping to generate strong opposition from conservative Disciples who feared the makings of a denominational superstructure.

After the division of the Christian Church (Disciples of Christ) and the Christian Churches/Churches of Christ, many congregations of the latter group continued to use the "voluntary society" idea, inspiring groups like the Christian Missionary Fellowship, area evangelizing organizations, and other cooperative enterprises. Churches of Christ have generally refrained from support for such societies, which carried an inevitable ecclesiastical connotation and thus deviated from the Movement's principles. Though support for colleges, orphan homes, and radio/TV ministries is common in mainstream Churches of Christ, it remains problematic for some.

A significant reassessment of the "society" concept came with the Restructure of the Disciples of Christ. In *Renewal of Church* (the Panel of Scholars Reports, 1963), Disciples scholars stressed that societies/institutions are "church," and in the "Provisional Design for the Christian Church (Disciples of Christ)," adopted in 1968, agencies or societies became "divisions of the church" (the United Christian Missionary Society as the Division of Overseas Ministries, et al.). For these scholars, the nature of these "divisions" reflects the covenantal and churchly nature of the restructured denomination.

For both those who advocated Restructure and those who opposed it, the relation between "church" and "societies" has been a key ecclesiological issue. Some societies, such as the World Convention of Churches of Christ and the Disciples of Christ Historical Society, have sought to transcend ecclesiological differences and promote communication and sharing of resources among the separated streams of the Stone-Campbell Movement.

See also American Christian Missionary Society; Christian Association of Washington; Christian Missionary Fellowship; Conventions; Disciples of Christ Historical Society; Mahoning Baptist Association; Missionary Societies, Controversy over; Noninstitutional Movement; Redstone Baptist Association; United Christian Missionary Society, The; World Convention of Churches of Christ, The

BIBLIOGRAPHY Anthony L. Dunnavant, *Restructure: Four Historical Ideals in the Campbell-Stone Movement of the Polity of the Christian Church (Disciples of Christ)* (1993) • Forrest F. Reed, *Background of Division: Disciples of Christ and Churches of Christ* (1968).

W. DENNIS HELSABECK, JR.

Sommer, Daniel (1850-1940)

Leading evangelist, editor, and debater among Churches of Christ outside the South in the late nineteenth and early twentieth centuries. Born in St. Mary's County, Maryland, of German immigrant parents, he lived for almost half a century in Indianapolis, Indiana. His life spanned the important and often neglected "middle period" of Stone-Campbell history.

Raised under Methodist influences, Sommer was converted to the ideals of restoring New Testament Christianity and was baptized in 1869, after hearing preaching by D. S. Burnet (1808-1867) and A. T. Crenshaw of Middletown, Pennsylvania. Attending Bethany College shortly after Alexander Campbell's death (from 1869 to 1872), Sommer became disenchanted with both doctrinal and social trends he saw emerging among the part of the Movement that would become the Disciples of Christ and became enamored with the conservative views of Benjamin Franklin (1812-1878). Sommer began preaching in Baltimore in 1872, moving in 1874 to Kelton, Pennsylvania, where he began to write for Franklin's *American Christian Review.* In 1880 he moved to Ohio, first preaching at Reynoldsburg, just outside Columbus, then moving in 1884 to Richwood, where the church ceased its use of instrumental music under Sommer's preaching.

In 1894 Sommer moved to Indianapolis, where he lived until his death, serving for many years as an elder and evangelist at the North Indianapolis Church of Christ when not traveling to keep a steady stream of preaching appointments elsewhere. Sommer thus represents an urban, Northern, or Midwestern perspective among Churches of Christ that, while a significant minority, differed in important respects

Devout restorationist and chief author of the controversial Sand Creek "Address and Declaration" (1889), Daniel Sommer became more conciliatory toward the end of his life toward those with whom he had strong ideological differences.
Courtesy of the Disciples of Christ Historical Society

from the largely rural and Southern Churches of Christ. Sommer proved a trenchant observer of social forces that contributed to divisions in the Movement too often described in purely doctrinal or theological terms.

In 1886 Sommer purchased the *American Christian Review,* which under Benjamin Franklin's editorship had been one of the most important journals in the Stone-Campbell Movement after Alexander Campbell's death. When Franklin died in 1878, the paper declined in influence under other editors, but under Sommer the journal became influential among readers in Churches of Christ. Despite several name changes (in 1887 to *Octographic Review* after the eight authors of the New Testament, and in 1913 to *Apostolic Review*), extant subscription lists demonstrate the journal's growth from approximately 7,300 subscribers in 1884 to nearly 10,000 from 1904 to 1925.

Sommer participated in several debates during his lifetime, the first a published debate in 1889 on triune immersion with Robert Miller, renowned debater among the German Baptist Brethren or "Dunkers." Other debates occurred in narrower contexts with other members of the Churches of Christ, including J. N. Armstrong in 1907 and one of Armstrong's faculty members at Western Bible and Literary College (Odessa, Missouri), B. F. Rhodes, in 1908, both over whether Christians could scripturally operate colleges in which the Bible was taught. Sommer's last debate, at age 76, was with J. N. Cowan at Sullivan, Indiana, on Christian participation in warfare, rebaptism, and Bible classes.

Sommer was one of the first to advocate separation of those who opposed instrumental music and church-supported missionary societies from churches that would not abandon such practices. He was one of the authors of the Sand Creek "Address and Declaration," which reflected Sommer's belief that many had reversed course from Thomas Campbell's intent in his *Declaration and Address.* The document was read at a mass meeting of about 5,000 Christians at the Sand Creek church near Shelbyville, Illinois, on August 17, 1889, and was subsequently published in Sommer's paper and elsewhere. The document's declaration that if those advocating "digressive practices" would not cease and desist after a period of time "we cannot and will not regard them as brethren" was one of the first public calls for division over such issues. Sommer also served as a witness in several lawsuits over church property in the Midwest, including one over the Sand Creek property that went to the Illinois Supreme Court, with the noninstrumental defendants retaining possession of the property.

Following years of estrangement from many with whom he differed, Sommer was involved during the last decade of his life in significant efforts to reestablish relationships. He became friends with Frederick D. Kershner (1875-1953), dean of the Butler University School of Religion in Indianapolis, and with influential Disciple Peter Ainslie (1867-1934), visiting with Ainslie in his home in Baltimore and preaching for the Disciples congregation Ainslie attended. Sommer spoke several times on the program of Butler's Midsummer Institutes, organized by Kershner to bring together a variety of differing speakers, and other such efforts, which culminated in several meetings in the 1940s commonly known as the "Murch-Witty Unity meetings." Sommer also sought better communication and renewed discussion with members of Churches of Christ in what he called the "Southland" from whom he been estranged over the college issue, writing and endorsing a document he published in the *Apostolic Review* called the "Rough Draft for Christian Unity."

Sommer's later moves alienated him from some of his followers, even his own family. His son D. Austen Sommer started a rival publication, and his wife gained control of the *Apostolic Review* and refused to allow him to write for it. Sommer continued his evangelistic trips nearly until his death. He suffered a stroke at age 90 during a train trip from Indianapolis to a preaching appointment. Put on a return train home by a conductor who recognized him, Sommer lingered a few days, then passed away on February 19, 1940. He is buried in Crown Hill Cemetery, Indianapolis.

See also Ainslie, Peter; *American Christian Review;* Franklin, Benjamin; Kershner, Frederick D.; Murch, James DeForest; Sand Creek "Address and Declaration"

BIBLIOGRAPHY Matthew C. Morrison, *Like a Lion: Daniel Sommer's Seventy Years of Preaching* (1975) • Daniel Sommer, "A Record of My Life," in William E. Wallace, *Daniel Sommer* (1969). JAMES STEPHEN WOLFGANG

Southern Christian Institute (1875-1954)

A coeducational institution founded by the Disciples of Christ in Edwards, Mississippi, for the purpose of giving vocational and ministerial training to African Americans; considered to be the Disciples' most successful nineteenth-century educational outreach to freed slaves. SCI served as a model for the Jarvis Christian College in Hawkins, Texas, and made a significant contribution to the growth and development of Tougaloo College in Jackson, Mississippi.

James A. Garfield played a role in the establishment of the institute by actively encouraging William T. Withers of Mississippi to offer a gift of 160 acres of land near the town of Edwards in 1874 for this purpose. The following year, the Home Missionary Society of the Disciples of Christ obtained a charter for the institute from the Mississippi State legislature. A group of Disciples raised the initial funds, starting with a $10,000 pledge from an Indianapolis man concerned about the education of Southern blacks. After William T. Withers withdrew his pledge of land, an 800-acre plantation near Edwards, Mississippi, was located and purchased as a campus. The school opened in 1882, with Randall Faurot as its first president. The initial enrollment of thirty students grew to 200 in its second year, but by 1887 financial concerns led to the closure of its free-school section and a drop in enrollment. In 1889 the American Christian Missionary Society secured control by purchasing a majority of the institute's stock and transferred ownership the following year to the Christian Woman's Board of Missions.

From its inception, Southern Christian Institute attracted a large number of students from other denominations. In fact, the first Disciples student did not enroll until 1887. Because of the generally poor public school education available to black students at the time, Southern Christian Institute offered instruction at the elementary and high school levels as well as the college level. Courses of instruction included Bible, teacher training, music, and vocational instruction in areas such as farming, carpentry, and home economics. By 1928 the institute owned 1,266 acres of rich delta farmland, of which 300 were cultivated and 500 used as pasturage. Students paid some or all of their tuition by working for five to eight cents an hour in the fields, blacksmith shop, dairy, or sawmill operated by the institute. Students also built several of the dormitories and other campus buildings. By 1932 the institute had progressed far enough in its curriculum to be classed as a junior college, with an enrollment of nineteen college students.

Graduates of the institute went on to become ministers of many of the leading black Disciples churches and the vanguard of black Disciples missionaries. One graduate, Jacob Kenoly, served as a missionary to Liberia from 1905 until his accidental drowning in 1911. At one time, a large percentage of the preachers in Jamaica were graduates of Southern Christian Institute.

After World War II, recruitment became more difficult as young blacks gravitated toward free and improved public schools. The institute was also affected by state harassment of African American institutions in the pre–civil rights-era South, making continuance of the school impractical. The trustees decided to combine its resources with those of another college to better serve the black population. In 1954 Southern Christian Institute successfully merged with Tougaloo College in Jackson, Mississippi, a black liberal arts college founded by the American Missionary Society. Southern Christian Institute had a positive impact on Tougaloo College by promoting a strong department of religion and contributing its endowments to the combined institution. Tougaloo went on to achieve accreditation and an excellent academic reputation, produced many prominent black educational and business leaders, and played a significant role in the civil rights movement in Mississippi in the 1960s. The former Southern Christian Institute campus became a community service and conference center known as the Mount Beulah Christian Center and later was sold to the United Presbyterian Church, U.S.A.

See also African Americans in the Movement; American Christian Missionary Society; Christian Woman's Board of Missions; Garfield, James Abram; Higher Education, Views of in the Movement; Missions, Missiology; Tougaloo College

BIBLIOGRAPHY Clarice T. Campbell and Oscar Allan Rogers, Jr., *Mississippi: The View from Tougaloo* (1979), pp. 181-82 • D. Duane Cummins, "Black Disciples and Higher Education," *Discipliana* 47:1 (Spring 1987): 3-6 • D. Duane Cummins, *The Disciples Colleges: A History* (1987), pp. 89-90 • Allen Dennis, "Tougaloo College," in

Encyclopedia of African-American Civil Rights, ed. Charles D. Lowery and John F. Marszalek (1992), p. 525 • James O. Duke, "DCHS and Its Black Materials Project," *Discipliana* 31:1 (Winter 1971): 8-10 • *Survey of Service: Organizations Represented in International Convention of Disciples of Christ* (1928), pp. 161-71. ANDREW R. WOOD

Southwestern Christian College

Christian college founded and operated by black members of Churches of Christ in Terrell, Texas.

G. P. Bowser (1874-1950), a talented preacher, teacher, educator, and writer for African American Churches of Christ, led short-lived schools in Silver Point, Tennessee; Fort Smith, Arkansas; and Detroit, Michigan. In 1947 and 1948 an interracial board of trustees established the Southern Bible Institute in Fort Worth, Texas; the school utilized the facilities of the Lake Como Church of Christ. J. S. Winston (1906-2001) served as president and Bowser as head of the Bible Department.

After acquiring school property formerly owned by Texas Military College, the Southern Bible Institute changed both its location to Terrell, Texas, and its name to Southwestern Christian College in 1950. The tireless efforts of R. N. Hogan (1902-1997), J. S. Winston, and G. E. Steward (1906-1979), African American ministers in Churches of Christ, made this transition possible.

White church leader E. W. McMillan (1889-1991) served as the college's first president. Racial tension, however, led to the ousting of McMillan in 1967. The same year Jack Evans, Sr. (b. 1937), assumed the presidency, leading the institution to accreditation as a junior college in 1977 and to senior college status for Bible and religious education in 1980. Southwestern Christian College represents the efforts of blacks in Churches of Christ to promote the spiritual growth and intellectual development of African American youth. At the end of the twentieth century the school had an enrollment of approximately 200 students.

See also African Americans in the Movement; Bowser, George Philip; *Christian Echo*

BIBLIOGRAPHY R. Vernon Boyd, *Undying Dedication: The Story of G. P. Bowser* (1985) • G. E. Steward, "18th Term for SWCC," *Christian Echo* (October 1967): 1.

EDWARD J. ROBINSON

Spencer, Claude E. (1898-1979)

Organizer and first curator of the Disciples of Christ Historical Society. Claude Elbert Spencer, by nature a collector and by profession a librarian, was the original guiding figure in the establishment and development of a historical archives for the Stone-Campbell Movement.

Spencer was born in Granger, Scotland County, Missouri, March 13, 1898. Following three years of library work in high school, he went on to become the chief student assistant in the Culver-Stockton College Library. With encouragement, he attended the University of Illinois Library School for two summers, and in 1922 he became the first full-time librarian at Culver-Stockton in Canton, Missouri. He served in that capacity until 1951.

Through the influence of two mentors, Dr. Spencer began in 1924 collecting materials relating to the Disciples of Christ. As early as 1930 Spencer had spoken of collecting and preserving these kinds of materials and of making them available for historical researchers. Nothing happened, however, until J. Edward Moseley came to do research in the little-known collection. Moseley spread the news, and in 1941 the Disciples of Christ Historical Society was formed at the 1941 International Convention. J. Edward Moseley was the first president, and Claude Spencer the curator and chief administrator.

With the society's collection remaining at Culver-Stockton, Spencer began a demanding schedule working full time for the college and moonlighting part time as a volunteer (without pay) for the society. Spencer would do most of his work on the Disciples historical materials between 11:30 P.M. and 2:30 A.M.

In 1951 the Disciples of Christ Historical Society moved to Nashville, Tennessee. Spencer came with the collection and became a full-time, paid employee. As curator and chief administrator he wore two hats until 1959, when an executive president was chosen to become the chief administrator.

A very meaningful part of his work was the journal *Discipliana.* He edited this publication from its inception in 1941 until he retired from the society in 1965.

In 1923 Claude Spencer married Maud Mullin, who became his constant companion and co-worker. Spencer died July 5, 1979, at the age of 81, leaving a critical legacy to future students of the history of the Stone-Campbell Movement.

See also Disciples of Christ Historical Society

BIBLIOGRAPHY James Seale, *Forward from the Past: The First Fifty Years of the Disciples of Christ Historical Society* (1991). DONNA J. MCWHIRTER

Spirituality

See Devotional Literature; Holy Spirit, Doctrine of the

Springdale College

Theological training college for British Churches of Christ, located in Birmingham, England.

The school was established in 1980 as the Christian Centre for Study and Growth. The name was changed to Springdale College one year later when it was accepted as the ninth college of the Federation of Selly Oak Colleges. Concurrent with the development of the college, the Institute for the Study of Religion and Culture was created as a means of establishing a relationship with the Department of Theology at the University of Birmingham. Springdale's principal, Dr. C. Robert Wetzel, was appointed a Recognized Lecturer by the University. His successor, Dr. Dennis Lindsay, also held that title.

Springdale saw itself as the successor to Overdale College, which had served Churches of Christ from 1920 to its closure in 1975. Springdale was the result of a cooperative effort between the Christian Renewal Trust, a British charity, and the British-American Fellowship Committee headed by C. Robert Wetzel, an American who had served as a professor and dean at Milligan College (Tennessee). The committee drew its support from American Christian Churches/Churches of Christ. Ties were developed with the Conference of the Fellowship of Churches of Christ in Great Britain and Ireland even though the college attempted to serve the broader spectrum of churches with roots in the Stone-Campbell Movement.

C. Robert Wetzel was the founding principal of Springdale, and Harold Merritt was vice principal. Wetzel served from 1980 to 1991 and was succeeded by Dennis Lindsay, also an American, in 1992. In 1998, under Dr. Lindsay's guidance, the college was approved to offer the Bachelor of Arts degree in mission theology through the University of Birmingham.

In the summer of 2001 plans began for a merger of Springdale with Birmingham Bible Institute (BBI). The new college would be known as Birmingham Christian College. BBI represented a nondenominational evangelical constituency. It was agreed that both Springdale and BBI would be able to continue to serve their traditional constituencies while enjoying the economies of the merger. BBI moved to the property owned by Springdale College at Selly Oak, Birmingham. Birmingham Christian College opened its doors in the autumn term, 2001, with Dr. Richard Massey as principal.

Even though the two colleges functioned as a single college during the 2001-02 academic year, the merger never became official. By the end of 2002 the Springdale College trustees decided that the merger was not in the best interest of the Churches of Christ. One of the reasons for this was the inability to attract residential students from the British Churches of Christ.

More recently the Springdale College trustees have explored some nontraditional, nonresidential forms of ministerial education. There have been negotiations to sell the Springdale property to Birmingham Christian College. The proceeds would prospectively be held in trust with the income from the trust used to finance some form of ministerial education. This would involve programs for training and encouraging existing and potential lay leaders of congregations.

See also Great Britain and Ireland, Churches of Christ in

C. Robert Wetzel

Springfield Presbytery

Earliest organization and name of the movement that adopted the name "Christians" in June 1804.

On September 10, 1803, Barton W. Stone, Robert Marshall, John Dunlavy, Richard McNemar, and John Thompson withdrew from the jurisdiction of the Presbyterian Synod of Kentucky. Earlier that week the Synod, meeting in Lexington, had approved the proceedings of Washington Presbytery's October 1802 theological examination of Richard McNemar that had condemned McNemar's views as "dangerous to the souls of men, and hostile to the interests of all true religion." In the same action the Synod had censured the Washington Presbytery for appointing McNemar to preach after having condemned his doctrine and also for rejecting a later petition calling for an examination of John Thompson and a second examination of McNemar in April 1803.

Stone, Marshall, Dunlavy, McNemar, and Thompson stated to the Synod the following reasons for withdrawing from their jurisdiction. First, they believed that the resolution of the Washington Presbytery condemning McNemar's doctrine, which all five of the ministers shared, gave "a distorted and false representation of Mr. McNemar's sentiments" and was "calculated to prevent the influence of truth of the most interesting nature." Second, they claimed the privilege, which they believed had been denied to McNemar, of interpreting the Scripture without reference to the Presbyterian Confession of Faith, affirming in the words of section X of Chapter I of the Confession of Faith "that the Supreme Judge, by which all controversies of religion are to be determined, and all decrees of councils, opinions of ancient writers, doctrines of men and private spirits, are to be examined, and in whose sentence we are to rest, can be no other than the Holy Spirit speaking in the Scriptures." And third, that while remaining "inviolably attached to the doctrines of grace, which, through God, have been mighty in every revival of true religion since the reformation," they believed that those doctrines are "in a measure darkened by some expressions in the Confession of Faith [regarding the doctrine of predestination], which are used as a means of strengthening sinners in their unbelief, and subjecting many of the pious to a spirit of bondage." When they attempted to obviate these difficulties they were accused of "departing from our Standard, viewed as disturbers of the peace of the Church, and threatened to be called to account." Therefore, they had chosen to withdraw from the jurisdiction of the Synod rather than be "prosecuted before a Judge [the Confession of Faith], whose authority to decide we cannot in Conscience acknowledge."

Stone, Marshall, Dunlavy, McNemar, and Thompson added that they did not desire to separate from the communion of the members of Synod, or to exclude members of the Synod from their communion. On the contrary, they informed the Synod that they would "ever wish to bear, and forbear, in matters of human order, or opinion, and unite our joint supplications with yours, for the increasing effusions of that divine Spirit, which is the bond of peace." They concluded, "With this disposition in mind, we bid you adieu, until, through the providence of God, it seem good to your reverend body to adopt a more liberal plan, respecting human Creeds and Confessions."

Two days later, on September 12, 1803, Stone, Marshall, Dunlavy, McNemar, and Thompson constituted themselves a presbytery, taking the name Springfield after a town in southern Ohio where Thompson served as pastor. The name Springfield was chosen because the Washington Presbytery to which several members of the new presbytery had belonged had been in session at Springfield in 1803 when it rejected the petition calling for examinations of Thompson and McNemar. That meeting had also been the occasion for a particularly memorable celebration of the Lord's Supper that Marshall observed "carried sufficient evidence that our ministrations in the gospel were not injurious to the souls of men."

In January 1804 the Springfield Presbytery published its defense of its separation from the larger Presbyterian body, an exposition of its theological views, and a statement regarding the Presbyterian Confession of Faith titled *An Apology for Renouncing the Jurisdiction of the Synod of Kentucky. To Which Is Added a Compendious View of the Gospel and a Few Remarks on the Confession of Faith.* In the *Apology,* written by Marshall (who had been clerk of the Synod prior to his withdrawal), they noted that since the October 1802 examination of McNemar had been conducted without written charges or witnesses, hence contrary to Presbyterian order, they could have appealed the Synod's actions to the General Assembly. However, they argued that as long as "human opinions" rather than the Bible were esteemed the standard of orthodoxy, they would have little hope of redress from any court of the Presbyterian Church.

The "Compendious View of the Gospel" was the first theological statement of the movement. It was a systematic statement of the doctrine of faith that McNemar's Washington Presbytery had condemned. The author of the statement was Stone, who had been the first to develop the views that all five of the ministers had adopted.

Included in the "Remarks on the Confession," written by Thompson, was a section, "Creeds and Confessions in General." The new presbytery charged that the church had long been divided into sects and parties, each having a creed, confession of faith, or statement of doctrines that separated it from other bodies. They lamented that if one learned the words of a creed, one was pronounced orthodox, even if one gave no evidence of "real, living religion," while one "confessedly pious" was rejected for not subscribing to the particular creed. Thus, creeds prevented the union of the church, and even if one were perfect, which they believed the Confession of Faith surely was not, it should be rejected as the standard of Christian fellowship.

Stone reported that the Springfield Presbytery's January 1804 publication was well received and that before long fifteen congregations scattered over southern Ohio and northern Kentucky had united with the new organization. The growing popularity of the Springfield Presbytery, however, was a concern to its leaders, as they were committed to Christian unity and did not desire to become another denomination or "party." At the June 1804 meeting of the Presbytery at Cane Ridge, Richard McNemar proposed a solution to the problem of their becoming another "party" or denomination with a document that he had drafted, titled *Last Will and Testament of Springfield Presbytery.* The document declares, "We *will,* that this body die, be dissolved, and sink into union with the Body of Christ at large." On June 28 the members of the Presbytery signed the *Last Will and Testament,* thus bringing to an end the less-than-ten-month history of the Springfield Presbytery.

Stone reported that in addition to signing the *Last Will and Testament,* he and his colleagues determined at the June 1804 meeting to take "no other name than *christians,*" noting that "Christians" was "the name first given by divine authority to the disciples of Christ." The idea of taking no other name than Christians, as the name given by God to the followers of Christ, had been recommended to the Springfield Presbytery in a sermon by Rice Haggard, of Virginia, at Marshall's Bethel Church in April 1804. Haggard's text was Acts 11:26, which he interpreted as meaning that God was the one who "appointed" that the disciples at Antioch be called "Christians." Haggard had made a similar appeal nearly a decade earlier at a conference at Old Lebanon Church, near Surry, Virginia, which had resulted in the founding of the "Christian Church" movement in Virginia and North

Carolina. The conference had been composed of thirty preachers who, along with Haggard and James O'Kelly, had recently seceded from the Methodist Episcopal Church in a dispute over the authority of Bishop Asbury to place ministers without their consent.

It is likely that Stone and his colleagues had heard of the Christian Church movement associated with Haggard and O'Kelly prior to Haggard's visit to Kentucky in the spring of 1804, especially given Stone's ties to Virginia and North Carolina. Moreover, they were surely familiar with the idea that the name "Christians" had been given to the disciples at Antioch by divine authority and should be the name of preference of all followers of Christ. This was the thesis of a sermon by eighteenth-century Presbyterian Samuel Davies that had been widely circulated. A Christian Church movement had recently emerged in New England, led by former Baptists Elias Smith and Abner Jones. Thus, in taking the name "Christians," Stone and his colleagues understood themselves not to be doing something original, but to be joining a movement already under way, a movement associated, through Davies, with the Presbyterianism that was the common background of all five of the members of the former Springfield Presbytery.

See also Haggard, Rice; *Last Will and Testament of Springfield Presbytery;* Stone, Barton Warren

BIBLIOGRAPHY "An Apology for Renouncing the Jurisdiction of the Synod of Kentucky, To Which Is Added a Compendious View of the Gospel, and a Few Remarks on the Confession of Faith," in Barton W. Stone, *The Biography of Eld. Barton Warren Stone, Written by Himself, with Additions and Reflections by Eld. John Rogers* (1847), reprinted in *The Cane Ridge Reader,* ed. Hoke S. Dickinson (1972) • Robert Marshall and John Thompson, *A Brief Historical Account of Sundry Things in the Doctrines and State of the Christian, or as It Is Commonly Called, The Newlight Church, Containing Their Testimony Against Several Doctrines Held in That Church, and Its Disorganized State; Together with Some Reasons Why Those Two Brethren Purpose to Seek for a More Pure and Orderly Connection* (1811) • "Minutes of the Synod of Kentucky," 1802-11, in William Warren Sweet, *Religion on the American Frontier, 1783-1840,* vol. 2, *The Presbyterians* (1936) • D. Newell Williams, *Barton Stone: A Spiritual Biography* (2000).

D. NEWELL WILLIAMS

Srygley, Fletcher Douglas (1856-1900), and Filo Bunyan Srygley (1859-1940)

Brothers, preachers, authors, and controversialists related to the Churches of Christ, born at Rock Creek, Colbert County, Alabama.

Both brothers attended T. B. Larimore's school at Mars Hill, Alabama. F. D. Srygley preached extensively in Alabama, Tennessee, Kentucky, Mississippi, and Texas. In the early 1880s he served briefly as editor of the *Old-Path Guide,* published in Louisville, Kentucky. By 1884, his health already failing, he moved to Tennessee, primarily residing there until his death in 1900.

From 1889, as front-page editor of the *Gospel Advocate,* F. D. Srygley composed articles and editorials with remarkable wit and literary skill, especially focusing on the nature, functions, and work of the New Testament church. He produced several popular books, including *Larimore and His Boys* (1889), *Seventy Years in Dixie* (1891), *Biographies and Sermons* (1898), and *Letters and Sermons of T. B. Larimore* (1900), published shortly before his death. F. D. Srygley's work propagated his view of undenominational New Testament Christianity and transformed his mentor Larimore into a living legend.

Late in life, F. B. Srygley, recalled that every article he had composed over a long career had been written for the *Gospel Advocate.* Following his brother's untimely death, he edited *The New Testament Church* (1910), a compilation of F. D. Srygley's editorials. F. B. Srygley also edited *Gospel Advocate* Sunday School literature. When in 1915 public controversy erupted between editors of the *Gospel Advocate* and Robert Henry Boll concerning Boll's premillennial eschatology, Srygley relentlessly opposed Boll. When in 1930 Foy E. Wallace, Jr., began editing the *Gospel Advocate,* F. B. Srygley was instrumental in persuading Wallace to aggressively resist Boll and his ideas of a future kingdom. Srygley continued to write for the *Advocate* until his death in 1940.

See also Boll, Robert Henry; Eschatology; *Gospel Advocate, The;* Wallace, Foy Esco, Jr.

BIBLIOGRAPHY E. V. Srygley, Jr., "F. B. Srygley," in *They Being Dead Yet Speak,* ed. Melvin D. Curry (1981), pp. 187-97 • F. D. Srygley, *Biographies and Sermons* (1898).

TERRY J. GARDNER

Standard Publishing Company

Publisher serving primarily the Christian Churches/Churches of Christ.

Standard Publishing Company traces its origin to 1865 when fourteen men met in the home of T. W. Phillips, Sr., in Newcastle, Pennsylvania, to consider launching a new kind of publication, a weekly journal that would carry news of the brotherhood and articles of interest for almost every member of the family. It would also include news of the broader religious world.

Isaac Errett (1820-1888), a minister from Detroit, Michigan, and destined to become one of the preeminent leaders of the Stone-Campbell Movement in its second generation, was chosen to be editor of the new journal, which was named *Christian Standard.*

Russell Errett (1845-1931) led the Standard Publishing Company to national stature as a religious publisher, maintaining the moderately conservative editorial posture of his father, the eminent leader Isaac Errett.
Courtesy of Emmanuel School of Religion Archives

$20,000 was subscribed, and the first issue was published in Cleveland, Ohio, April 7, 1866. By the end of the next year the journal had incurred such indebtedness that the subscribers were happy to turn it over to Errett if he would assume the debts. To support his family, Errett accepted the presidency of Alliance College and moved to nearby Alliance, Ohio.

In 1869 W. T. Moore of Cincinnati persuaded a Quaker friend, R. W. Carroll, to publish the paper, and Errett moved to Cincinnati. In 1872 Errett, his son Russell, and R. W. Carroll incorporated Standard Publishing Company.

The Sunday School movement was developing, and the company began to publish literature to meet this demand. A full range of graded Bible lesson materials followed, including *Primary Days, Junior Life, Boy Life, Girlhood Days,* and a second journal, *The Lookout* (formerly titled *The Young People's Standard*). The publications were received well beyond the Stone-Campbell Movement, ending the company's fiscal problems and enabling the Erretts to purchase Carroll's interest in the company. Isaac Errett continued as manager of the company and editor of *Christian Standard* until his death in 1888. His only surviving son, Russell, succeeded him as manager, and a succession of persons filled the editorial chairs. Publication expanded to include Bible commentaries and other religious books. Standard was the first publisher in America to utilize color presses for religious publications.

Russell Errett continued to manage the company until his death in 1931. His will provided that the company be vested in a committee of church leaders and held as a not-for-profit religious publisher. The heirs were to be indemnified from the proceeds. Unwilling to accept this arrangement, the heirs contested and broke the will. Russell Errett's son, John Errett, died in 1932, leaving control of the company to one of Russell Errett's two sons-in-law, Harry Baird. Baird had little interest in the religious aims of the company and engaged Willard Mohorter to manage it. By 1955 Baird decided to sell the company to John Bolton, who merged it with several other companies into Standex, International, a publicly held corporation. An arrangement with the company provided that all editors are to be members of Christian Churches/Churches of Christ and that the religious policies are to be determined by a publishing committee composed of persons from these churches.

Standard Publishing's influence on the Stone-Campbell Movement has been significant. Isaac Errett worked through the company to promote missions among Disciples. He encouraged women to form the Christian Woman's Board of Missions in 1874 and led in organizing the Foreign Christian Missionary Society in 1875. But a change of policy in the missionary organizations in the 1920s caused Russell Errett and Standard Publishing Company to oppose the societies amalgamated into the United Christian Missionary Society, and the company led campaigns in the 1940s that ultimately accelerated the division between Christian Churches/Churches of Christ and the Christian Church (Disciples of Christ).

See also Christian Churches/Churches of Christ; *Christian Standard;* College Press; Errett, Isaac; Journalism; *Lookout, The*

BIBLIOGRAPHY Burris Butler, "We Take Pride in Our Heritage," *The Standard Story* (n.d.) • Brian P. Clark, "An Analysis of the Organizing Functions of the *Christian Standard* in the Restoration Movement Christian Churches/Churches of Christ" (M.A. thesis, Wheaton College, 1998) • G. Mark Sloneker, *"You Can't Do That!" The Life and Labors of Burris Butler: An Account of a Ministry at "Christian Standard" and with Standard Publishing Company* (1995) • Sam Stone, "History of Standard Publishing Company," *Christian Standard* (September 13, 1981): 1.

HENRY E. WEBB

Stevenson, Dwight E. (1906-1996)

Disciples of Christ pastor and educator.

Born in Cuba, Illinois, Stevenson received degrees from Bethany College and Yale Divinity School. Although a man of many interests and talents, his primary passion was preaching. At Yale he had studied under the acclaimed Halford E. Luccock.

After completing his studies at Yale, Stevenson served as the minister of Bethany Memorial Church in Bethany, West Virginia, from 1933 to 1944. During his tenure there, he also served as a philosophy professor at Bethany College (1935-44) and as head of the Religion and Philosophy Department.

Stevenson was recruited by the College of the Bible (Lexington Theological Seminary) in 1947 in the school's effort to improve the education students received in homiletics. Prior to his appointment, there had not been a full-time faculty position in the field of preaching. Known for his dedication to students, Stevenson was committed to improving the quality of the sermons delivered by his students and initiated the use of preaching laboratories and the most up-to-date technology. A widely published author, his works included a popular biography of the founder of the Movement best known for his evangelistic preaching, *Walter Scott: Voice of the Golden Oracle* (1946). Upon his death in 1996, the Disciples mourned the loss of an outstanding pastor, preacher, and teacher of preachers.

See also Bethany College; Lexington Theological Seminary

BIBLIOGRAPHY Dwight E. Stevenson, *In the Biblical Preacher's Workshop* (1967) • Dwight E. Stevenson, *Lexington Theological Seminary, 1865-1965: The College of the Bible Century* (1964) • Richard C. White, "Dwight E. Stevenson, Teacher of Preachers," *Lexington Theological Quarterly* (April 1975): 1-6. See also *Lexington Theological Quarterly* 31 (Winter 1996). This entire issue is dedicated to the life and teaching of Dwight E. Stevenson.

LISA W. DAVISON

Stone, Barton Warren (1772-1844)

Leader of the Christian Church in the West. In 1832 Stone led many of the Christians in the West to unite with the followers of Alexander Campbell, known as Reformers or Disciples of Christ, forming the Stone-Campbell Movement.

1. Introduction

By 1832 the Christian Church in the West, born out of a separation from the Presbyterians in 1803, numbered more than 16,000 members in Kentucky, Tennessee, Alabama, Ohio, and Indiana. The leadership of the younger and more prolific Alexander Campbell eclipsed that of Stone in the Movement born of the 1832 union. Nevertheless, Stone was a reformer in his own right and had an abiding influence on the Stone-Campbell Movement.

1.1. The Saintliness of His Character

Beginning with John Rogers, who published Stone's autobiography along with his own "Additions and Reflections" in 1847, Stone has been honored in the

An engraving of Barton W. Stone appearing in his *Biography*, published posthumously in 1847. For Stone, Christian unity was the Movement's "polar star," not as an end in itself but as the platform from which the churches could more powerfully and univocally communicate the gospel.

Movement for the saintliness of his character. Rogers developed this theme under several headings. Under the headings of "Husband" and "Father" he reported, "The writer of this sketch was much about the house of the venerated Stone, for many, many years . . . [and] never heard him speak a harsh or unkind word to any member of his family; nor does he remember to have seen him angry, during an acquaintance of a quarter of a century."

Rogers sought to show that Stone was loved for his Christian spirit even by many of his religious opponents and that his good moral character was recognized by all. He noted a reference to Stone's good moral character by the Presbyterian Joshua L. Wilson in the published account of the heresy trial of Lyman Beecher. He reported a conversation in 1843 among a group of women, some of whom were members of the Christian Church and had known Stone for many years and spoke of their great love for him. An aged Presbyterian woman who had also known Stone for many years but opposed his views interjected, "I don't care how much you love Mr. Stone, *I* love him as much as any of you." He quoted another opponent of Stone's views as having said, "B. W. Stone has done more harm by his good conduct than by all his preaching and writing: because . . . he has lived so much like a Christian, that the people take him to be one; and are deceived and led into destructive error."

Rogers also celebrated Stone's humility. "Though he was a fine scholar — deeply learned in the Bible; and in consequence of his various learning, his deep piety, and popular manners, wielded an immense influence upon society, yet he was unconscious of his own strength, and seemed always disposed, modestly, to take the lowest seat." Rogers added, "He was deeply imbued with that humility that disposes us to esteem others better than ourselves." Rogers recommended Stone as a model for all who would aspire to true greatness.

The theme of the saintliness of Stone's character was picked up by others and remains alive in the memory of the Stone-Campbell Movement.

1.2. Theological Controversialist

Rogers may have stressed the saintliness of Stone's character to counter another image of Stone, the image of a theological controversialist who had been "a man of war from his youth." Stone was engaged in theological controversies much of his life. The origin of those controversies was his desire to make sense of the teachings of the Bible in light of reason and his own experience of spiritual transformation through faith in the gospel of Jesus Christ. This desire led Stone to reject the doctrine of predestination and to adopt "liberal" views of the doctrines of the Trinity and the atonement. Though Stone does not appear to have been eager to make an issue of his liberal or "heterodox" theological views, he was willing to defend them when required to do so. As a result, much of his published corpus consists of books of theological controversy.

By the time he met Campbell in 1824, Stone had long been charged with teaching an "Arian" Christology and "Socinian" views of the significance of Christ's death. Though Stone had denied these charges, defending his views from the Bible, many Presbyterians, Baptists, and Methodists viewed him as the "Great Heresiarch of the West." As a consequence, Campbell, who was seeking to reform the Baptists and anyone else who would read or listen to his views, initially sought to ignore Stone's overtures for a union of their forces, fearing that too close an identification with Stone would reduce his influence among the Baptists. Stone persisted, however, and despite Campbell's resistance the union was accomplished. Later Campbell would create a stir in the Movement by stating in his 1843 debate with Presbyterian Nathan L. Rice that he had "saved" Stone and his followers from their heterodoxy.

1.3. Wealth and Hospitality

Anyone who visits the Campbell mansion in Bethany will immediately perceive that Alexander Campbell had a gift for making money. There was never a Stone mansion. Although Stone started out with more material resources than Campbell, and reported in his autobiography that prior to his conversion he had been intent on achieving wealth and status, his economic history was largely one of downward mobility. Born to an upper-middle-class Southern family, he spent his inheritance from his father on acquiring a liberal education that might have propelled him, as it did several of his classmates, into a successful career in law or politics. Instead, following his conversion he chose to enter the Presbyterian ministry. Later he received an inheritance from his mother consisting of two slaves. Having become convinced that "slavery is inconsistent with the principles of Christianity as well as civil liberty," he manumitted them both, after providing for their education. Later yet, after having become a husband and father, he gave up what he described as an "abundant salary for the support of myself and family" when he withdrew from the jurisdiction of the Synod of Kentucky. Henceforth he was required to teach and/or farm to support his family. And, unlike Campbell, he never seemed to make a profit from his publications.

Stone's reduced material resources collided with his conviction that a Christian pastor or bishop is to practice hospitality. Nevertheless, Stone practiced hospitality. Rogers reports that the poor and the helpless were welcome at his house and table, and that his house was the "resting place" of his friends and the "friends of his Master." Rogers also notes that although Stone received little for his labors as a preacher and was often unable to accommodate his friends as he might have wished, he was not one to "murmur or apologize." Rogers relates that Barton and Celia Stone's table was not always as well furnished as Stone and his wife could have wished, and that sometimes Mrs. Stone would apologize for the fare. In such circumstances, Stone, when about to serve their guests, would ask with a bright and smiling countenance, "What of all these good things shall I help you to?" Rogers suggests that as host Stone more than made up for any lack of furnishings of house or table by his good cheer and personal warmth. Remembering many times when he had arrived at Stone's home weary from travel, Rogers wrote, "We see him in imagination as he comes to meet us, with spectacles upon his venerable forehead — with that quick and dignified step, which characterized his movements — with a smile of complacency playing upon his benevolent face, and with his hand extended to greet us, and welcome us to his house!"

And so it was that Rogers would have his readers remember this advocate of Christian unity, with hand outstretched to stranger and friend.

2. The Making of a Presbyterian Minster

2.1. Family Background

Born December 24, 1772, near Port Tobacco, then the county seat of Charles County, Maryland, Stone was descended from families long associated with public affairs and sizable holdings of land — the indisputable marks of Maryland's upper class. His great-great-great-grandfather, Captain William Stone (1603-1695), had been the first Protestant governor of Maryland. His second cousin, Thomas Stone, was a signer of the Declaration of Independence and owner of one of the largest estates in Charles County. Barton Stone's father, John Stone, who died in 1775, owned land and sixteen slaves, which identified him as upper middle class.

In 1779 Stone's mother, Mary Warren Stone, moved with her four children and at least twelve slaves to Pittsylvania County, along the North Carolina border in western Virginia. Barton Stone, the youngest of Mary Stone's children, was 6 years old. Stone's father had bequeathed his land to his two oldest sons, who were from an earlier marriage, but Mary legally owned one-third of the Port Tobacco estate following her husband's death. The reason for Mary Stone's move is unknown, but many Southern planters moved west in the latter decades of the eighteenth century in the hope of improving their economic circumstances.

2.2. Education

Stone was sent to school after his family settled in Virginia. In the autobiography that he wrote in 1843, he reported that his first teacher was a "tyrant" who "seemed to take pleasure in whipping and abusing his pupils for every trifling offense." Stone indicated that he could not learn because of his "fear" of the teacher. After a few days, he was sent to a teacher of "a different temper." Rather than subscribing to the "break the will" philosophy of child rearing, the upper classes generally advocated either the "moderate" or the "genteel" methods that honored the will of the child. The moderate method sought to bend the will of the child, while the genteel philosophy tended to allow free expression of the child's will. As an adult, Stone advocated the moderate approach, admonishing teachers to use the rod "rarely" and advising that if teachers would gain the "respect and love" of their pupils they would "delight in obedience, and rarely fail to learn the lessons given to them." Stone's second teacher was Robert W. Somerhays, whom he identified as "an Englishman." Stone remembered that he learned easily with Somerhays and that after "four or five" years of studying reading, writing, and arithmetic, Somerhays pronounced him "a finished scholar."

Stone reported that when he was "fifteen or sixteen" years of age his older brothers were ready to launch out into the world for themselves and proposed a division of the property they had inherited from their father. He recalled that after his part of the inheritance had been assigned, his "mind" had been "absorbed day and night in devising some plan to improve it." At length, he decided to invest his inheritance in a liberal education that would qualify him to pursue a career in law. Such an education included sciences, the classical languages, and moral philosophy. In January of 1790, Stone entered David Caldwell's academy in Guilford County, North Carolina. Caldwell, the sole teacher of the academy, was the 65-year-old pastor of the Presbyterian churches at Buffalo and Alamance, North Carolina. Following an established Presbyterian pattern of combining teaching with pastoral ministry, Caldwell conducted the school in his home. Stone continued at Caldwell's academy for three years, completing his liberal education in 1793.

2.3. Conversion and Call to Ministry

When Stone entered the academy, there was "a great religious excitement" among the students. Of the probably no more than fifty students enrolled, thirty or more had recently "embraced religion" under the ministry of James McGready. McGready had received a grammar school education from Caldwell and had studied in western Pennsylvania with Presbyterian preachers John McMillan and Joseph Smith prior to assuming a Guilford County pastorate in the spring of 1789. The "awakening" at Caldwell's academy was not Stone's first exposure to Christianity. Stone had been baptized as an infant in the Church of England. Following their move to Pittsylvania County, Stone's family had continued their association with the once-established church. Stone had also been exposed to the preaching of Baptists and Methodists, who had evangelized Pittsylvania County following the Revolutionary War.

Stone claimed that his first response to the religious excitement at Caldwell's academy was to try to ignore it. Stone saw the revival as a distraction from his studies. A significant cost of studying at the Guilford academy was the expense of boarding in a nearby home. Thus, for financial reasons, it was desirable to complete the program as quickly as possible. He reported that it was not easy, however, to ignore the religious excitement in Caldwell's academy. He was "not a little surprised" to find the recent converts assembled every morning before the hour of recitation, singing and praying in a private room. Moreover, his observation of the "daily walk" of the recent converts showed him "their sincere piety and happiness." At length he accepted the invitation of his roommate to attend a preaching service conducted by McGready. McGready's message focused on the pursuit of happiness. For McGready, ultimate happiness was not to be found in physical pleasure or through the possession of wealth or honor, but in the knowledge and enjoyment of the "infinite glory" and "adorable attributes" of God; that is, through relationship with God. Stone remembered that McGready's preaching powerfully impacted him. "Such was my excitement," he later wrote, "that had I been standing, I should have probably sunk to the floor under the impression."

Following McGready's sermon, Stone decided to "seek" religion. He did not believe that he had been converted. McGready taught that God converts sinners by giving them a "view" of the "glory of God in the face of Christ Jesus." The glory of God in the face of Christ Jesus was the glory of One who sent the only begotten Son to save sinners. McGready argued that a view of the excellence or glory of God in the face of Christ Jesus caused sinners to *fall in love with God* and thus to grieve over the evil of sin, and not merely its penalty. As a result of such love, and the genuine sorrow for sin produced by such love, the sinner was "willing" to "come to Christ" both for pardon from the penalty of sin and for release from the power of sin. This change of the will, a change of heart toward God, and not merely a desire to avoid the penalty of sin, was conversion.

From his exposure to the Baptists and Methodists in Pittsylvania County, Stone expected a "long and painful struggle" before he would be "willing" to "come to Christ" for both the pardon of his sins and release from the power of sin. The pain of seeking conversion was the anguish and grief born of the seeker's desire to be saved coupled with the seeker's increasing discovery of the power of sin. In the latter part of the eighteenth century, Baptists, Methodists, and Presbyterians alike assumed that the awakened sinner's period of seeking conversion prior to receiving it, which they commonly referred to as "distress," would typically last from several weeks to a year. Stone recalled that for a full year he was "tossed on the waves of uncertainty — laboring, praying, and striving to obtain saving faith — sometimes desponding, and almost despairing of ever getting it." At length he attended a meeting at Alamance, one of the churches pastored by Caldwell. On Sunday evening, William Hodge, a preacher whom Stone had not heard before, addressed the congregation. Stone remembered that Hodge's text was "God is love" and that Hodge spoke "With much animation, and with many tears . . . of the love of God to sinners, and of what that love had done for sinners." Stone was deeply affected: "My heart warmed with love for that lovely *character* described. . . . My *mind* was absorbed in the doctrine — to me it appeared new." According to Presbyterians, to find one's heart "warmed" with love to God and to find something "new" in the preaching of what God had done for sinners were signs of conversion — a change of heart toward God. Stone reported that he began to hope that he had been converted, while at the same time seeking to repress his hope for fear that he was deceiving himself.

Following Hodge's sermon, Stone retired to the woods with his Bible. "Here I read and prayed," he later wrote, "with various feelings, between hope and fear." Judging from Stone's reference to the texts "Him that cometh unto me I will in no wise cast out" and "Jesus came to seek and save the lost," it appears that Hodge concluded his sermon with a call to the "broken-hearted" or "helpless" sinner to come to Christ. Hodge's sermons were never published; however, McGready's sermons, which were published, used these very passages of Scripture in urging the sinner who felt "ruined and undone" to come to Christ for salvation. The purpose of this appeal was to convince the sinner who felt helpless to save him- or herself, and who now loved the God who saves helpless sinners, that he or she was welcome to "come to Christ" for forgiveness and release from the power of sin. Stone was reading the Bible and praying in order to determine whether he now loved God and had a *will* to go to Christ for forgiveness and release from the power of sin. Stone reported that he discovered his answer in the response of his heart to the message he had just heard: "The truth I had just heard, 'God is love,' prevailed. Jesus came to seek and save the lost. 'Him that cometh unto me, I will in no wise cast out.' I yielded and sunk at his feet a *willing* subject."

Following his conversion, Stone's goal of practicing law gave way to a desire to preach the gospel. He reported that he informed Caldwell of his desire to preach but indicated that he had no assurance of having been divinely called to preach. Stone may have heard Baptist and Methodist preachers tell of having been divinely called through dreams and visions. In keeping with Presbyterian tradition, Caldwell assured him that he had no right to expect a miracle to convince him that he had been divinely called to preach. Rather, Caldwell advised, if he had a hearty desire to "glorify God and save sinners by preaching," and if his "fathers in the ministry" should encourage him, he should not hesitate to pursue ordination.

2.4. *Early Difficulties with the Doctrine of the Trinity*

In the spring of 1793, the 20-year-old graduate of Caldwell's academy became a candidate for the ministry of the Orange Presbytery. It was the responsibility of the Presbytery to receive, educate, and try candidates for the ministry. The Presbytery assigned Stone and other candidates particular subjects in divinity to study as "parts of trial" on which they were to be examined at the fall meeting of the Presbytery. The subjects given to Stone and a former classmate, Samuel Holmes, included the being and attributes of God and the doctrine of the Trinity. To aid them in their studies, they were assigned a text by seventeenth-century Dutch Reformed theologian Herman Witsius. As Stone recalled, "Witsius would first prove that there was but one God, and then that there were three persons in this one God, the Father, Son and Holy Ghost — that the Father was unbegotten — the Son eternally begotten, and the Holy Ghost eternally proceeding from the Father and the Son — that it was idolatry to worship more Gods than one, and yet equal worship must be given to the Father, the Son, and Holy Ghost." Stone had previously prayed to both the Father and the Son without fear of idolatry or concern for according them equal worship. The result of his effort to follow Witsius's teaching of the doctrine of the Trinity was that he "knew not how to pray." Consequently, the enjoyment of God that he had known since his conversion was soon curtailed. "Till now," he wrote, "secret prayer and meditation had been my delightful employ. It was a heaven on earth to approach my God, and Saviour; but now this heavenly exercise was checked, and gloominess and fear filled my troubled mind." Upon discovering that Holmes had been similarly affected by Witsius, Stone and Holmes "laid the book aside," believing that it was "calculated" to involve their minds in "mystic darkness" and to "cool the ardor" of their devotion.

Stone, like other citizens of the early American republic, was influenced by the broad currents of the English Enlightenment. The Enlightenment identified propositions that were "inconsistent" with our clear and distinct ideas as "contrary to reason." To Stone, the idea that there was more than one God, *implied* in Witsius's teaching that equal worship must be given to the Father, Son, and Holy Ghost, was inconsistent with the clear and distinct idea that there is but one God. Witsius, of course, had not taught that there is more than one God. Rather, he had countered the idea that there is more than one God, implied by the teaching that equal worship must be given to Father, Son, and Holy Ghost, by "proving" that there is but one God. Stone, who noted that Witsius was the first theological text that he had read other than the Bible, was not familiar with the method of doing theology that defined Christian truth by holding in tension seemingly contradictory propositions. For Stone, Witsius's treatment of the doctrine of the Trinity was simply "unintelligible."

Stone and Holmes were not the only North Carolina Presbyterians to have difficulty with Witsius's treatment of the Trinity. Henry Patillo, one of the oldest and most respected members of the Orange Presbytery, preferred and had done much to publicize Isaac Watts's alternative treatment of the doctrine. Although remembered now primarily for his hymns, such as "Joy to the World" and "When I Survey the Wondrous Cross," Isaac Watts (1674-1748) was also widely recognized in eighteenth-century England and America as a philosopher and theologian. Watts wrote on the Trinity for persons who, like himself, had been influenced by the Enlightenment. He argued that the biblical doctrine of the Trinity was not *contrary* to reason. To be sure, the doctrine that "three Gods are one God, or three persons are one person," was contrary to reason. However, according to Watts, the Scriptures did not teach that three Gods are one God. Rather, the Scriptures taught that "the same true Godhead belongs to the Father, Son and Spirit, and . . . that the Father, Son and Spirit, are three distinct agents or principles of action, as may reasonably be called persons." Thus, according to Watts, to say "the Father is God, the Son is God, and the Spirit is God" is not contrary to the proposition that there is one God. The mistake, according to Watts, is to confuse "opinions" or human explications of the revealed doctrine with the doctrine itself. Watts promised that the theologian who "well distinguishes between the plain Scriptural doctrine itself, and the particular explications of it," will hold "faith in the divine doctrine firm and unmoved, while several human forms of explication are attacked, and perhaps destroyed."

As for human forms of explication of the doctrine of the Trinity, Watts argued that the primary problem with most explications of the doctrine was the identification of "the Son of God" as the second person of the Godhead. According to Watts, it was this identification of the Son of God that led to the idea that three Gods are one God, or three persons are one person. This problem was solved, he suggested, by recognizing that the Scriptures identified the Son of God, not as the second person of the Godhead, but as the human *soul* of Christ — a human soul "formed" by God. This human soul had been "united to the divine nature" long before his human *body* was born of Mary. To be sure, the proposition that the human soul of Christ was a distinct agent or principle of action belonging to the one Godhead was *above* reason. That is, the truth or probability of this proposition could not be derived by reason. However, the proposition that the human soul of Christ was a distinct agent united to the one God was not *contrary* to the idea that there was one God.

In regard to the matter of the proper worship owed to the members of the Trinity, Watts asserted that the Scriptures revealed all that was necessary for proper faith and practice. For Watts, it was not necessary to fully comprehend the doctrine of the Trinity in order to worship God aright. He argued that the Christian could be sure that it was proper to offer "divine worship and honors" to Father, Son, and Spirit because "their godhead, or communion in the divine nature" is clearly revealed in Scripture. On the other hand, the Christian could be sure that it was wrong "to pay the same form of address and adoration to each of the sacred three" since the very content of revelation implied that one should worship and address the various members of the Trinity with an eye to the "special offices and character, which the Scripture assigns them."

Stone and Holmes obtained a copy of Watts's "treatise" on the Trinity and adopted his views. Henry Patillo administered the theological examination of the ministerial candidates at the fall 1793 meeting of the Orange Presbytery. Stone reported that when Patillo "came to the subject of the Trinity, he was very short, and his interrogatories involved no peculiarities of the system." Stone remembered that Holmes's answers and his own had been "honest and satisfactory."

2.5. Further Theological Difficulties and Decision to Seek Another Calling

Stone reported that before the spring 1794 meeting of the Orange Presbytery, when he was scheduled to complete his theological trials and be licensed to preach, he became "much depressed" and decided to abandon the idea of preaching and to pursue some other calling. A major source of his depression was theological. "My mind," he wrote, "was embarrassed with many abstruse doctrines, which I admitted as true; yet could not satisfactorily reconcile with others which were plainly taught in the Bible." Two of the doctrines that "embarrassed" Stone's mind were the doctrines of "God's eternal decree" and "the secret will of God." Both of these doctrines, as taught in the Westminster Confession of the Presbyterian Church, combined what Stone viewed as a proposition "plainly" taught in Scripture with another proposition that appeared to him to have implications that were inconsistent with the proposition plainly taught in Scripture. In the case of the doctrine of "God's eternal decree," the proposition plainly taught in Scripture was that God is not "the author of sin." But the doctrine of "God's eternal decree," as taught in the Westminster Confession, *also* stated that "God from all eternity did by the most wise and holy counsel of his own will, freely and unchangeably ordain whatsoever comes to pass," which implied, to Stone, that God was the author of sin. In the case of "the secret will of God," the idea plainly taught in Scripture was that God desired the salvation of all persons. This was the "revealed" will of God. But the doctrine also stated that God had a "secret will" by which God had determined that certain individuals would be damned, which implied, to Stone, that God did not desire the salvation of all persons. As earlier, when he had been confused by Witsius's treatment of the Trinity, Stone's intellectual embarrassment affected his devotion. "Having been so long engaged and confined to the study of systematic divinity from the Calvinistic mould," he wrote, "my zeal, comfort, and spiritual life became considerably abated."

Having decided to abandon the idea of preaching and to seek some other calling, he traveled to the home of his brother, Matthew Stone, in Oglethorpe County, Georgia. Through the influence of Matthew and Stone's half-brother Thomas Stone, who had also immigrated to the region, Stone was chosen professor of languages at a newly established Methodist academy near Washington in Wilkes County. This appointment was fortuitous, as the sources of Stone's depression in the spring of 1794 were not only theological but also financial. His funds were exhausted, and none of his relatives had been willing to aid him. While in Georgia, Stone attended the preaching of John Springer, whom he described as "a very zealous Presbyterian." Born near Wilmington, Delaware, Springer (1744-1798) was a graduate of Princeton who had pursued theological studies under the direction of James Hall, one of the leading members of the Orange Presbytery. His published works are remarkably similar in both style and content to those of James McGready. Under Springer's preaching, Stone "began to feel a very strong desire again to preach the Gospel." He tried to "resist" and "suppress" these "impressions," but as a result, his "comforts were destroyed." Among Presbyterians, such experience was evidence of a divine call to ministry.

2.6. Licensure and Ordination

In the spring of 1796, after a year and a half of teaching in Georgia, the 23-year-old Stone returned to North Carolina. On April 6, 1796, he successfully completed his remaining theological examinations and was licensed by the Orange Presbytery to preach the gospel as a "probationer" for the ministry within the bounds of the Orange Presbytery or wherever he should be "orderly called." This does not mean that he had overcome his earlier embarrassment with Calvinist theology. He claimed that during the first years of his ministry, he viewed the Calvinist doctrines of election, reprobation, and predestination as "true, yet unfathomable mysteries" and "confined" his preaching to "the practical part of religion." He may have adopted this stance on the advice of David Caldwell, who advised just such a course of action to another of his students who was troubled by the same questions.

Stone reported that, despite initial feelings of inadequacy, he itinerated for the next year and a half as a probationer for the ministry in western Virginia, Tennessee, and Kentucky. In the winter of 1797, he settled with the Presbyterian congregations at Cane Ridge and Concord in northern Kentucky. In his autobiography, Stone did not offer any reason for his settling at Cane Ridge and Concord, other than the coming of winter. There are two reasons, however, why this area may have been especially attractive to him. First, the religious background of nearly the entire population of the Cane Ridge and Concord communities was Presbyterian. As a convert to the Presbyterians from the former Church of England, Stone valued the company of Presbyterians. Second, as Stone noted in his autobiography, the Cane Ridge and Concord communities were composed of "wealthy" farmers. Although Stone, like other Presbyterian ministers, warned that wealth was a snare that could draw one's affections away from God, he was associated by background and education with the middle and upper classes of frontier society.

In the spring of 1798, Stone received a call through the Transylvania Presbytery to become pastor of the united congregations of Cane Ridge and Concord. Stone accepted the call, and the date of October 4, 1798, was set for his ordination. Knowing that he would be required to "sincerely receive and adopt" the Westminster Confession of Faith as "containing the system of doctrine taught in the Holy Scriptures," he undertook a careful reexamination of the Confession. In his autobiography he wrote, "This was to me almost the beginning of sorrows. I stumbled at the doctrine of Trinity as taught in the Confession; I labored to believe it, but could not conscientiously subscribe to it. Doubts, too, arose in my mind on the doctrines of election, reprobation, and predestination, as there taught."

On the day appointed for Stone's ordination, the eleven members of the Transylvania Presbytery assembled at Cane Ridge. Prior to the session of the Presbytery in which Stone was to be examined and ordained, he met privately with two members of the Presbytery, James Blythe and Robert Marshall, informed them of his difficulties, and told them that he had determined to decline ordination at that time. Blythe and Marshall sought to remove Stone's "difficulties and objections," but to no avail. The extent of the difficulties that Stone revealed to Blythe and Marshall was later the subject of some controversy. In a letter written in 1822, James Blythe allowed that Stone "did at that time, make some objections to the *terms* in which certain doctrines" were expressed in the Confession of Faith, but did not object "to any of the leading *doctrines* of the Confession." In a response to Blythe's letter, Stone stated that he had objected to the term "Eternal Son of God" in the doctrine of the Trinity and had been unsettled as to whether three "persons" in the doctrine of the Trinity meant three "intelligent beings" or three "appellations or relations." He did not share with Blythe and Marshall his "doubts" regarding the doctrines of election, reprobation, and predestination. According to the Adopting Act approved by the Presbyterian Synod of 1729, it was permissible to ordain a ministerial candidate who would only partially subscribe to the Confession of Faith if, in the view of the Presbytery, the candidate's objections to the Confession concerned only "non-essentials." Blythe and Marshall asked Stone "how far" he would be willing to adopt the Confession. He answered that he would be willing to adopt the Confession as far as he saw it consistent with the Word of God, and they concluded that partial subscription would be sufficient. Thus Stone was ordained by the Transylvania Presbytery.

3. The Great Revival

3.1. Stone Visits a Revival in Southern Kentucky

Meanwhile, in southern Kentucky, a revival had begun under the leadership of James McGready and several of Stone's former classmates from Caldwell's academy that would help to resolve his theological difficulties. In 1796 James McGready had become pastor of three congregations named after southern Kentucky rivers — Red, Muddy, and Gasper. By the spring of 1797 there had been a brief awakening at Gasper River. Over the summer and fall of 1798, all three of the congregations seemed to have been awakened, and several young people professed to have been converted, through a series of "sacramental meetings." The sacramental meeting was a Scots communion tradition that had been widely adopted by eighteenth-century American Presbyterians. Though hosted by a single congregation, typically several congregations and preachers shared in these occasions. On Friday, Saturday, and Sunday the ministers preached sermons on the character of conversion and the Christian life. On Sunday members of the participating churches observed the Lord's Supper. The pattern of heightened religious interest and reported conversions associated with sacramental meetings was repeated during the summer of 1799. Then, during the summer of 1800, hallmarks of what became known as the Great Revival in the West (1797-1805) first appeared — the unusually large crowds, the practice of camping on the grounds for sacramental meetings, and the physical phenomena of persons "falling."

Hearing of the revival, Stone traveled to southern Kentucky early in the spring of 1801 to attend a sacramental meeting led by McGready and other North Carolina Presbyterians. In his autobiography, he described the phenomenon of falling as he first observed it. "Many, very many fell down, as men slain in battle, and continued for hours together in an apparently breathless and motionless state — sometimes for a few moments reviving, and exhibiting symptoms of life by a deep groan, or piercing shriek, or by a prayer for mercy most fervently uttered." Gradually they would obtain release; the "gloomy cloud, which had covered their faces" giving way to smiles first of hope and then of joy, they would finally rise "shouting deliverance" and would address the surrounding crowd "in language truly eloquent and impressive." "With astonishment," Stone exclaimed, "did I hear men, women and children declaring the wonderful works of God, and the glorious mysteries of the gospel." He reported that their appeals to others were "solemn, heart-penetrating, bold and free." Noting that he was amazed at "the knowledge of gospel truth displayed" in their addresses, he observed that hearing their appeals, others would fall down "into the same state from which the speakers had just been delivered."

3.2. New Light on Faith

Following his ordination, Stone had continued to struggle with the Calvinist doctrines of election, reprobation, and predestination. According to those doctrines, God gave faith to the elect, but not to the reprobate. Stone's problem was how to reconcile God's love for sinners with the teaching that God chose to give faith to some sinners but not to others.

In a brief account of his theological development that he published in 1805, Stone reported that "all" his difficulties were removed while observing "the work of God" in southern Kentucky. "Many old and young, even little children," he wrote, "professed religion, and all declared the same simple gospel of Jesus. I knew the voice and felt the power." The "voice" that Stone knew was the voice of God. The "power" that he felt was the power of the gospel — the spiritual or "moral" power that made sinners willing to go to God for both forgiveness of sin and release from the power of sin. Stone reported, "I saw that faith was the sovereign gift of God to all sinners, not the act of faith, but the object or foundation of faith, which is the testimony of Jesus, or the gospel; that sinners had power to believe this gospel, and then come to God and obtain grace and salvation." That is, Stone saw that God gave faith — the spiritual or moral willingness to come to God — through the message of God's love revealed in Jesus Christ, and that sinners had the power to believe that message, which revealed the moral excellence or glory of God and would make them willing to come to God. The gospel was the *means* by which God gave faith; hence, persons who ignored the message of God's love were responsible for their own condemnation.

There was nothing new to Presbyterians in the idea that God spoke through the gospel, revealing the moral excellence or glory of God, to give sinners a will or desire to "come to Christ" for release from the penalty and the power of sin. The new feature was Stone's assertion that sinners had the power to believe the gospel — to perceive the glory of God revealed in Jesus Christ — without a *previous* work of the Spirit to convince them of the power of sin. Stone had developed his understanding of how God gives faith, and shared it with another minister, prior to attending the meeting in southern Kentucky. However, the idea that God gives faith through the hearing of the gospel, without a previous work of the Spirit to convince the sinner of the power of sin, was more compelling in the midst of the Great Revival, with persons falling and conversions appearing to occur in a matter of hours. Lengthy periods of "distress," such as the one Stone himself had experienced, had been the norm in an earlier day.

3.3. Stone Promotes Revival in Northern Kentucky and Weds Elizabeth Campbell

Stone returned to northern Kentucky eager to tell others what he had witnessed and confident that he could urge the sinner "to believe now, and be saved." Soon there were reports of the distinctive features of the Great Revival among the Presbyterians of northern Kentucky. The first Sunday in June, Stone conducted a sacrament at Concord that was the largest religious meeting in northern Kentucky to that date. Colonel Robert Patterson, a famed Indian fighter and militia captain, judged the crowd to have been 4,000. In an account of the revival written twenty-six years later, Stone indicated that Baptists and Methodists, as well as Presbyterians, participated. The meeting went on continually day and night for five days and was conducted outdoors, since the Concord meetinghouse was not large enough to contain the crowd. Seven Presbyterian ministers were present. At least one Methodist preached. Patterson reported that 150 fell and that 250 communed. He also noted that twelve families brought provisions and camped on the grounds. Well-attended communions marked by "falling" and the participation of Baptists and Methodists continued in northern Kentucky throughout June and July.

Meanwhile, during the last week in June, after publicizing a sacrament for Cane Ridge to be held the first weekend in August, the 28-year-old Stone traveled to Greenville, in Muhlenberg County, Kentucky. Greenville was the home of Elizabeth Campbell, eleven years his junior, whom he married July 2. Stone reported that following the wedding, he and Elizabeth "hurried" from Muhlenberg County to prepare for the August sacrament at Cane Ridge.

The sacrament of Cane Ridge, later known as the Cane Ridge Meeting or the Cane Ridge Revival, began Friday, August 6, 1801, and continued through the following Thursday. The number of wagons encamped on the grounds, at least over Saturday and Sunday, was variously estimated at between 125 and 148, covering, as one observer reported, an area the equivalent of four city blocks. In addition, thousands of participants arrived for the day, including not only those who lived within horseback riding range but also people who found accommodations in neighboring communities. Estimates of the number of people on the grounds Saturday and Sunday ranged from 10,000 to 20,000 and beyond. One participant counted "seven ministers, all preaching at one time" in different parts of the camp, some using stumps and wagons as makeshift platforms. Sixteen and maybe as many as eighteen Presbyterian ministers participated in the meeting. At least four Methodist ministers also preached. An unidentified African American preacher may have been a Baptist. Estimates of the number of communicants ranged from 800 to 1,100. Estimates of the number who fell ranged from 300 to 3,000!

3.4. Separation from the Synod of Kentucky

Stone's new light on faith was accepted by several of his Presbyterian colleagues. However, not all Presbyterians were pleased with Stone's call for sinners to believe now and be saved. Opposition to the view that God gives faith through the hearing of the gospel, without any previous work of the Spirit to convince sinners of the power of sin, first emerged in Richard McNemar's Cabin Creek, Kentucky, congregation. On November 3, 1801, three elders from the Cabin Creek congregation sent a statement of charges against McNemar's doctrine to the Washington Presbytery. As the Cabin Creek elders were not present when the Presbytery met at Springfield, Ohio, on November 11, 1801, the charges were dropped. Shortly thereafter, McNemar accepted a call through the Washington Presbytery to the Turtle Creek congregation in southern Ohio.

Stone later wrote that the "sticklers for orthodoxy" among the Presbyterian clergy "writhed" under the doctrines preached by him, McNemar, and others but, seeing the "mighty effects" of these doctrines on the people, did not at first publicly oppose them for preaching their views. By the fall of 1802, the stance of the Presbyterian clergy had changed. The reason for the change, according to Stone, was the loss of members to the Methodists and Baptists. Although Stone did not identify the persons who became Baptists or Methodists, it may have been young persons raised in Presbyterian families who were the most likely to "profess religion" at a sacramental meeting. Stone reported that the "friends of the Confession" responded to the success of the Baptists and Methodists in "drawing away disciples" by boldly preaching the doctrines of the Confession of Faith and using "their most potent arguments in their defence." In response, the Methodist and Baptist preachers began to preach their distinctive doctrines. Stone claimed that, in the ensuing confessional strife, the "friends of the Confession" were "indignant at us for preaching doctrines contrary to it" and "determined to arrest our progress and put us down."

Matters came to a head at the Synod of Kentucky that opened in Lexington on September 6, 1803. From early actions of the Synod, it was evident to Stone, McNemar, and three other ministers who shared their doctrine of faith, Robert Marshall, John Thompson, and John Dunlavy, that the majority of the Synod was determined to suspend them from the ministry for failing to adhere to the Confession of Faith. On September 10, Stone, McNemar, Marshall, Thompson, and Dunlavy drew up and presented to the Synod a protest declaring that they were withdrawing from the jurisdiction of the Synod rather than be "prosecuted before a Judge [the Confession of Faith], whose authority to decide we cannot in Conscience acknowledge."

Efforts to heal the breach began almost immediately but were not successful. Meanwhile, Marshall, Dunlavy, McNemar, Stone, and Thompson formally united as the Springfield Presbytery, choosing the name Springfield because of positive associations with Springfield, Ohio, in their history with the Washington Presbytery. In January of 1804, the Springfield Presbytery published a 100-page pamphlet titled *An Apology for Renouncing the Jurisdiction of the Synod of Kentucky, To Which Is Added a Compendious View of the Gospel and a Few Remarks on the Confession of Faith.* Marshall wrote the first section of the pamphlet, the "Apology." The two following sections were written respectively by Stone and Thompson.

Stone's "Compendious View of the Gospel" was the theological statement of the new presbytery. Stone discussed human depravity, regeneration, the gospel, and faith. Opponents had charged that they denied that faith was the gift of God by denying the work of the Spirit in preparing sinners to believe the gospel. Stone responded to this charge, insisting, "We hold faith to be the gift of God, in the same way." The difference, he declared, was as follows: "They say the mind must be enlightened by the spirit, in some secret, mysterious way, to see and *approve* the truth, before the sinner can believe it. We say, the truth which the spirit speaks, is that which enlightens the mind; and which cannot produce this effect until it is believed."

4. The Christian Church

4.1. Last Will and Testament *and the Christian Name*

On June 28, 1804, the members of the Springfield Presbytery adopted a document titled *Last Will and Testament of Springfield Presbytery,* declaring, "We *will,* that this body die, be dissolved, and sink into union with the Body of Christ at large." Appended to the *Last Will and Testament,* which the members of the former presbytery signed as "witnesses," was "The Witnesses' Address," which stated their reasons for dissolving the presbytery. They noted that they had viewed with deep concern "the divisions, and party spirit among professing Christians, principally owing to the adoption of human creeds and forms of government." Though they had "endeavored to cultivate a spirit of love and unity with all Christians," they had found it "extremely difficult to suppress the idea that they themselves were a party separate from others." Also, at their final meeting as a presbytery they had begun to prepare for publication an address titled "Observations on Church Government" in which the world would see "the beautiful simplicity of Christian church government, stript of human inventions and lordly traditions." As they had proceeded in their investigation of that subject, they had "soon found that there was neither precept nor example in the New Testament for such confederacies as modern Church Sessions, Presbyteries, Synods, General Assemblies, etc." They had realized that "However just . . . their views of church government might have been, they would have gone out under the name and sanction of a self-constituted body." Therefore, "from a principle of love to Christians of every name, the precious cause of Jesus, and dying sinners who are kept from the Lord by the existence of sects and parties in the church," they had "cheerfully consented to retire from the din and fury of conflicting parties — sink out of the view of fleshly minds, and die the death."

Behind the presbytery's reasons for dissolving their presbytery was their conviction that the revival was strong evidence that the millennium, the one-thousand-year rule of Christ that many Christians believed was prophesied in Revelation 20:1-6, was near. The association of the growth and increased influence of Christianity with the coming of the millennium can be traced through English Puritanism as far back as the sixteenth century. In the eighteenth century, Jonathan Edwards had referred to the worldwide evangelism and social transformation that he taught would usher in the millennium as "the glorious work of God." Division or "partyism" in the church was widely viewed as a hindrance to the coming of the millennium. Included in the *Last Will and Testament* was the following "item": "We *will,* that preachers and people, cultivate a spirit of mutual forbearance; pray more and dispute less; and while they behold the signs of the times, look up, and confidently expect that redemption draweth nigh." In concluding their "Witnesses' Address," they declared, "We heartily unite with our Christian brethren of every name, in thanksgiving to God for the display of his goodness in the *glorious work* he is carrying on in our Western country, which we hope will terminate in the universal spread of the gospel, and the unity of the church." In dissolving their presbytery, the signers believed that they were participating in God's glorious work and thus hastening the coming of the millennium.

Lest anyone think that the signers of the *Last Will and Testament* intended to retire from public view, they wrote of themselves in their "Witnesses' Address" that though dead as a presbytery and "stript of their mortal frame," they "yet live and speak in the land of gospel liberty . . . blow the trumpet of jubilee, and willingly devote themselves to the help of the Lord against the mighty." Moreover, they published the *Last Will and Testament* as a tract, along with an announcement of a mass meeting for those holding like sentiments to be held at Bethel Church over the weekend of October 14, 1804. They noted that Bethel, seven miles northwest of Lexington, was a central location for attendance from Kentucky, Ohio, and Tennessee. Neither did the signers intend to give up their ministerial prerogatives. What they gave up was their power of "making laws" for the church by virtue of their own authority, a power explicitly forbidden by the *Form of Government* of the Presbyterian Church! As "elders" or ministers of the Church of Christ, they maintained the right to govern the church according to the revealed will of God (rather than a Confession of Faith), to try candidates for the ministry, and to assist in the ordination of ministers.

Stone reported that in addition to signing the *Last Will and Testament,* he and his colleagues determined at the June 1804 meeting to take "no other name than *christians,*" noting that Christians was "the name first given by divine authority to the disciples of Christ." The idea of taking no other name than Christians, as the name given by God to the followers of Christ, had been recommended to the presbytery in a sermon by Rice Haggard at Marshall's Bethel Church two months earlier. Thus, in taking the name Christians, Stone and his colleagues understood themselves not to be doing something original but to be joining a movement already under way, a movement that they believed would usher in the millennium.

4.2. New Light on Atonement

The influence of the former presbytery's confidence that the millennium was near was not limited to efforts specifically in behalf of Christian union. Jonathan Edwards had declared that in the millennium theological problems that had long perplexed believers would be solved. During the winter of 1804, the members of the Springfield Presbytery had become "sorely pressed" by an objection to their preaching voiced by members of the Synod of Kentucky. Like other nineteenth-century Protestants, Stone and his colleagues preached the "substitutionary" theory of atonement that they had inherited from the Reformers of the sixteenth century. According to this view, Christ died as a substitute for humanity. Humanity had violated the covenant of the law that God made with Adam and, through him, with all of Adam's posterity. Without Christ's death, humanity could have looked forward only to the wrath of a God who hated sin and punished violations of the law. With Christ's death, the elect of God could be assured that justice had been satisfied and that God had been propitiated toward them. The righteous Christ had taken the place of the guilty, suffering in their stead in order that his righteousness might be imputed to them. He was the "surety" or substitute of justified or forgiven sinners and had fulfilled the law on their behalf; he was their sacrificial lamb, the typological fulfillment to which the animal sacrifices under the Old Law looked forward.

The objection to the preaching of Stone and his colleagues stated by members of the Synod of Kentucky was that if Christ died to satisfy the claims of law and justice for *all* sinners, and not merely for a portion or part of humanity whom God had chosen to save before the foundation of the earth, as Stone and his colleagues proclaimed that he did, then *all* sinners would be saved. That is, if Christ had satisfied the claims of law and justice for all persons, then no one could be punished for his or her sins. Stone and his colleagues, they charged, were teaching universalism, the doctrine that God not only loved and desired the salvation of all persons, but that God would save all persons, whether converted in this life or not. Stone and his colleagues, like most Presbyterians, Baptists, and Methodists, believed that universalism was not taught in Scripture. Thus, Stone wrote, they had turned to the Bible "with prayerful attention to find the truth" regarding atonement.

Stone claimed that he began his study of the atonement by seeking to find where Christ was said to be the surety or substitute for sinners. He reported that, to his surprise, he could not find the idea in a single scriptural text. He next sought to find where the "surety righteousness of Christ" was said to be "imputed" to sinners, with the same result. He then searched the Scriptures to see where law and justice were said to be satisfied by the "vicarious obedience and suffering of Jesus." But, again, he could not find a single text. Finally, he inquired for what purpose Christ was said to have come into the world, lived, and died. He found the purpose of Jesus' life and death to be "to declare the Father — to bear witness to the truth — to confirm the promises — to reconcile sinners to God — to save sinners — to bring us to God." During the winter of 1805, Stone addressed two letters on the subject to Presbyterian minister Matthew Houston, the substance of which he published in the spring of 1805 as a thirty-six page pamphlet titled "Atonement: The Substance of Two Letters Written to a Friend."

Stone's pamphlet failed to answer the objections of members of the Synod of Kentucky to his teaching that Christ died for all. On the contrary, the publication of his letters initiated a written controversy with former Presbyterian colleagues who viewed the letters as an attack on their doctrine and the fundamental truths of the Christian faith. David Rice responded to Stone's letters in *An Epistle to the Citizens of Kentucky, Professing Christianity; Especially Those That Are or Have Been, Denominated Presbyterians.* John P. Campbell responded to Stone's letters with *Strictures, On Two Letters, Published by Barton W. Stone, Entitled Atonement.* Stone did not formally reply to Rice's *Epistle,* possibly out of deference to Rice, whom he considered to be "father" in the gospel. He did respond to Campbell in *A Reply to John P. Campbell's Strictures on Atonement.* Campbell, in turn, responded to Stone's reply with *Vindex: Or The Doctrines of the Strictures Vindicated Against the Reply of Mr. Stone.*

4.3. Separation from Former Colleagues and Adoption of Believers' Immersion

The six years following Stone's publication of "Atonement" were marked by dissension and division among the Christians. In his *Strictures,* Campbell alluded to Stone's unorthodox views of the Trinity — the views he had learned by reading Isaac Watts as a theological student in North Carolina. Stone commented in his autobiography that he regretted that Campbell had accused him of being heterodox on the Trinity, as it required him to defend himself "and the doctrine I believed." He noted that he had never written on the Trinity and claimed that for years he had been "silent on that subject" in his public discourses. Though Stone's views of the Trinity were widely accepted among the Christians, they would become a subject of internal discord.

In the spring of 1805, the Christians were visited by Shaker missionaries from the East. Two of the original members of the former Springfield Presbytery, Richard McNemar and John Dunlavy, became Shakers. Stone opposed the Shakers with all his might.

Two years later some of the Christian preachers, including Stone, adopted believers' immersion as baptism and were themselves immersed. Stone claimed that despite the decision of a conference of the Christian ministers that "every brother and sister should act according to their faith" regarding believers' immersion, "Some of our preaching brethren appeared rather uneasy and dissatisfied that their congregations were submitting to this ordinance, while they could not be convinced of its propriety." He noted that although those ministers "said but little" regarding the growing popularity of believers' immersion among members of their congregations, some of them began to recommend "that we should have some other bond beside the Bible and brotherly love; that these were insufficient to unite our growing churches, and keep them pure." Among the ministers calling for the adoption of a "formulary" were Marshall and Thompson. Stone stated that he and others "saw plainly" that the arguments being used in support of a formulary were the same as those used for "the introduction of every human party Creed, which has ever been imposed on the world, and therefore opposed *formularies,* from a full conviction of their injury to the cause of Christ." At a conference of Christian ministers at Bethel in August of 1810, a compromise was worked out by which the Christians would establish a "formal" union and publish a statement of their current views, but not adopt a formulary. A committee composed of Stone, Marshall, Thompson, and two other ministers attempted to write the statement but could not come to consensus on their current views, as Marshall, Thompson, and one of the other ministers desired to affirm orthodox doctrines of the Trinity and the atonement. When a conference of ministers meeting at Mount Tabor in March of 1811 declared, following Stone's lead, that a consensus statement was not necessary, as the doctrinal differences of the committee members need not sever fellowship, Marshall and Thompson returned to the Presbyterians. Thus, by the spring of 1811, of the five original members of the former Springfield Presbytery, Stone, alone, remained as leader of the Christians.

4.4. Publication of An Address, *Marriage to Celia Bowen, and Move to Tennessee*

In 1814 Stone published *An Address to the Christian Churches in Kentucky, Tennessee and Ohio. On Several Important Doctrines of Religion.* Included in *An Address* were sections on the Trinity, the divinity of Jesus Christ, the atonement, the operations of the Spirit, and faith. Stone noted in his autobiography that the foundation of this book was the response he wrote in 1811 as a member of the failed writing committee to a "connected" statement of doctrines by John Thompson. The three-year delay in Stone's publication of *An Address* was most likely due to a series of changes in his personal circumstances that began three months before the appointment of the writing committee.

In May of 1810 Elizabeth had died. Following her death, he had broken up housekeeping, boarded their four daughters with members of the church, and devoted full time to preaching and establishing churches in Ohio, Kentucky, and Tennessee. On October 31, 1811, he had married Elizabeth's 19-year-old cousin, Celia Wilson Bowen, and reestablished a family home on the Bourbon County, Kentucky, farm that he had purchased prior to his marriage to Elizabeth. At the end of a year, he and Celia had been induced, according to Stone, "by advice and hard persuasion" to move to Tennessee, near Celia's widowed mother. Mrs. Bowen had put them on a good farm, but without a comfortable house. The result, Stone noted, was that much of his time had been devoted to building a house, as well as improving the farm. Stone may also have been distracted from publishing *An Address* by the addition of two sons to their household, one born in 1812 and the other the following year.

In 1815 the Presbyterian minister Thomas Cleland of Mercer County, Kentucky, published a 100-page response to Stone's *Address* titled *The Socini-Arian Detected.* Stone had not written his last word on Christian doctrine. However, he would not publish again for another seven years, most likely because of another succession of changes in his personal circumstances that began shortly after his publication of *An Address.*

4.5. Return to Kentucky

In his autobiography, Stone reported that he "labored hard at building a house and improving the farm" in Tennessee *until* he learned that his mother-in-law did not plan to give him the deed to the farm, but rather to deed it to her daughter and her children. He claimed that he did not blame her for this decision, as the lands of his first wife, by the laws of Kentucky, had become the property of her children at her death. Nevertheless, as soon as he learned of her decision, he decided to return to Kentucky. He reported that Celia approved of his resolve.

Returning to Kentucky turned out to be more difficult than Stone could ever have imagined. He had sold his Bourbon County farm in 1812. In the meantime, the building of turnpikes in Kentucky and the beginning of steamboat traffic on the Ohio and the Mississippi, along with demands created by the War of 1812, had boosted the price of farm products, significantly increasing the value of farmland in Kentucky. Stone reported that when he tried to purchase a farm in Kentucky, he discovered that land of the sort that he had sold had more than doubled in value. Unable to purchase a farm in Kentucky due to the increase in the price of land, he accepted an invitation to settle among "the brethren in Lexington," who promised to provide for his family's needs. The Lexington brethren, however, did not make good on their promise, and Stone, who had been well received as a teacher in Georgia, was required to open a high school in Lexington to support his family.

In 1819 Stone was appointed principal of the Rittenhouse Academy in Georgetown, twelve miles north of Lexington. That fall he bought a farm near Georgetown, where he moved with his family. In addition to fulfilling his duties as principal of the academy during the fall and winter of 1819-20, he preached in Georgetown, with the result that a Christian Church was constituted in Georgetown and soon grew to over 200 members.

Without Stone's knowledge, the Christian churches in northern Kentucky met, determined that he should devote all of his time to preaching the gospel, and, in order to release him from the academy, agreed to support him and his family and to pay the debt he had incurred in purchasing the farm near Georgetown. The churches had made a substantial pledge, as the number of Stone's children had increased since his publication of *An Address* to nine with the births of another two daughters and another son (Stone's tenth child, another son, was born in 1824). But the United States had entered a major economic depression in 1819, and when the time came to pay the note on his farm, the promised funds were not forthcoming. Stone had to borrow funds to pay the debt on the farm and was required to open a school in Georgetown to repay the funds he had borrowed. By this means, he was able to pay his debt. However, his health failed as a result, he believed, of "constant application to study." Consequently, he gave up teaching and, though nearly 50 years of age, "turned to hard labor" on his farm.

4.6. Renewed Controversy over Trinity and Atonement

In 1821 Stone published a second edition of *An Address.* In the introduction to the second edition, he stated that "Being desirous to disseminate truth," he was sending to the Christian Churches a work that was "*corrected* and considerably enlarged." Comparison of the second edition with the first shows that most sections of the book were, in fact, unchanged. While teaching in Lexington, Stone had taken advantage of the opportunity to study Hebrew with a Prussian doctor whom he described as "a Jew of great learning." Cleland had scoffed at Stone's criticism of the translation of certain texts in the King James Version of the Bible, declaring that Stone had "but a smattering of the Greek, and not even that much itself of the Hebrew." In the section on atonement, Stone added "a few remarks" from the Hebrew, "an imperfect knowledge of which," he noted, "I have acquired since I published the first edition of my Address." All of the corrections were in the sections dealing with the Trinity and the divinity of Jesus

Christ. In the first edition, Stone, following Watts, had clearly identified the Son of God as the *human* soul of Christ. Moreover, he had referred to him as having been begotten *or* created. Cleland had charged him with Arianism, of believing that the Son was a mere creature. In the second edition, Stone did not refer to the soul of Christ as human. Neither did he refer to the Son as having been "created." Rather, he proposed that Jesus was called "the only begotten of the Father, because the Father begat him *of* and *by* himself." Stone made explicit his rejection of Arianism in *A Letter to John R. Moreland.* Moreland, claiming to have read the second edition of Stone's *Address,* charged Stone in *A Letter to the Church at Mount-Pleasant* with teaching that the Son was "a created being, a mutable, changeable creature." Stone asserted that the view that Moreland had charged him with teaching was the view of Arius, who had taught that the Son was created out of nothing, while his views were "high above those of Arius." He noted that the teaching of the church fathers who had condemned Arius was that "the Son is of the substance of the Father." If the Son was of the substance of the Father, he observed, "he was not a created being, but *derived* his being from the Father." "Against this," he declared, "I have no objection."

In 1822 Thomas Cleland published a 172-page review of the second edition of Stone's *Address,* entitled *Letters to Barton W. Stone Containing a Vindication Principally of the Doctrines of the Trinity, the Divinity and Atonement of the Saviour, Against His Recent Attack in a Second Edition of His "Address."* Having found the style of both *The Socini-Arian Detected* and Cleland's *Letters* abusive, Stone responded to Cleland's *Letters* in 1824 with a book titled *Letters to James Blythe, D.D. Designed as a Reply to the Arguments of Thomas Cleland, D.D.* Blythe, along with Robert Marshall, had been one of the members of the presbytery to whom Stone had confided his difficulties with the Presbyterian Confession on the day of his ordination in October of 1798. While referring to the Father and the Son as persons or "beings" in both editions of *An Address,* Stone had never referred to the Spirit as a being. In his *Letters to Blythe* Stone clarified his position on the Spirit. "By the Spirit of God," he wrote, "I understand the Spirit of a person and not the person himself." He noted, "we often read in the Bible, that the Father loves the Son, and that Son loves the Father; but we never read of either the Father or the Son loving the Spirit as a person, or of the Spirit loving the Father or the Son." He also noted, "We have examples and precepts to love and worship both the Father and the Son; but there is neither example nor precept for worshipping the Spirit in the Bible." Cleland lobbed the last volley in the exchange over Stone's second edition of *An Address* in 1825 with *Unitarianism Unmasked: Its Anti-Christian Features Displayed: And Its Foundation Shewn to be Untenable; in a Reply to Mr. Barton W. Stone's Letters to the Rev. Dr. Blythe.*

5. Union with Followers of Alexander Campbell

Within two decades of the return of Marshall and Thompson to the Presbyterians in 1811, the Christian Church in the west numbered more than 16,000 members in Kentucky, Tennessee, Alabama, Ohio, and Indiana. Many had joined the Christian Church through profession of faith and baptism. Others had been identified with the Christian Church movement in Virginia and North Carolina. A sizable number, however, had come as members of Baptist congregations, and sometimes whole associations of Baptist congregations, which had united with the Christians in response to their call to Christian union on the Bible alone.

Stone met Alexander Campbell, who was sixteen years his junior, in the fall of 1824, while Campbell was on a two-month preaching tour of Kentucky that included Lexington, Versailles, Louisville, and smaller communities and rural churches in between. Stone, who was 51, later noted that he "heard him often in public and in private" and that he was "pleased with his manner and matter." At Stone's invitation, issued to Campbell while he was at Paris, Kentucky, Campbell spoke at the Christian Church in Georgetown and lodged in Stone's home. A year earlier, Campbell had begun publication of his monthly journal, the *Christian Baptist,* in which he rejected confessions of faith and called for reform of the churches by a restoration of the New Testament or apostolic order.

A division of Kentucky Baptists over Campbell's views was foreshadowed in 1825, when a Baptist church in Louisville rejected the Baptist Philadelphia Confession of Faith and took the Bible alone as its guide for faith and practice, becoming the first church in Kentucky to formally identify with Campbell's reformation. Vigorous opposition to Campbell's reforms soon emerged among the leadership of Kentucky Baptists. In the spring of 1826 Baptist Spencer Clack of Bloomfield, Kentucky, charged Campbell in the pages of the *Christian Baptist* with setting up his own creed in his series on "A Restoration of the Ancient Order of Things," while attacking confessions of faith. Within a year, Campbell's opponents were using their own magazine, the *Baptist Recorder,* to oppose Campbell's reforms, and associations had begun suspending preachers who advocated Campbell's reforms.

One of Campbell's reforms that became increasingly prominent after 1827 was baptism for remission of sins. Baptists taught that the design or purpose of baptism was to set apart or "seal" believers as members of the church. Prior to baptism, candidates were required to demonstrate that they were believers, typically by describing their conversion. On the second day of Campbell's debate with the Presbyterian W. L. Maccalla in October of 1823, Campbell had introduced an argument against infant baptism based on a distinctive view of the "design or import of baptism." Campbell had stated that he would be as "full as possible" on the topic because "of its great importance, and because perhaps neither Baptists nor Paedobaptists" sufficiently appreciated the design or import of baptism. After quoting a handful of New Testament texts that Campbell suggested pointed to the importance of baptism in the New Testament, he declared that the design of baptism was to give believers an assurance or "formal token" of their "cleansing" from all sins. Campbell argued that baptism "being ordained to be to a believer a formal and personal remission of all his sins, cannot be administered unto an infant without the greatest perversion and abuse of the nature or import of this ordinance."

Campbell's biographer, Robert Richardson, stated that Campbell did not "make a direct and practical application" of the doctrine of baptism for remission of sins. By a direct and practical application of the doctrine, Richardson meant recommending baptism to penitent believers who desired an assurance of the forgiveness of their sins and the indwelling of the Holy Spirit. Richardson claimed that the first person to make a direct and practical application of Campbell's view of the purpose of baptism was Campbell's colleague, Walter Scott. Scott was appointed evangelist of the Mahoning Baptist Association in August of 1827, and he began recommending baptism to penitent believers in November. However, as early as the spring of 1826, Christian Church preachers who were acquainted with Campbell's views had been recommending baptism for remission of sins to penitent believers. In January of 1827, Stone had publicly endorsed the practice.

In November 1826, Stone began the publication of a monthly journal, *The Christian Messenger.* Stone addressed Campbell in a July 1827 article entitled "To the Christian Baptist." He professed high respect for Campbell's talents and learning and "general" approval of the course Campbell had followed. "Your religious views, in many points," he noted, "accord with our own — and to one point we have hoped we both were directing our efforts, which point is to unite the flock of Christ." He continued, "We have seen you, with the arm of a Samson, and the courage of a David, tearing away the long established foundations of partyism." He observed that it was "not as unconcerned spectators" that the Christians had followed "the mighty war" between Campbell and his opposers — a war in which he asserted that many of

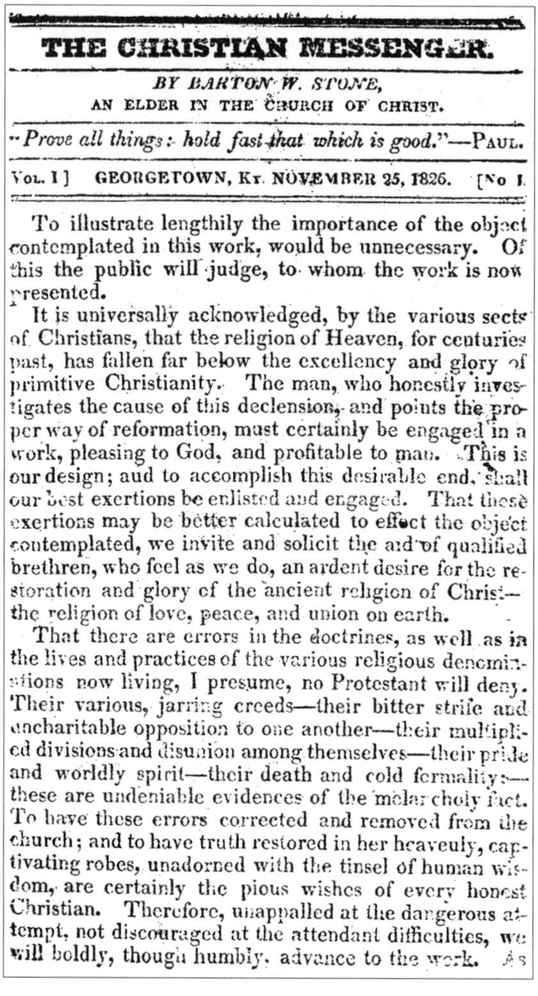
THE CHRISTIAN MESSENGER.

BY BARTON W. STONE,

AN ELDER IN THE CHURCH OF CHRIST.

"*Prove all things: hold fast that which is good.*"—PAUL.

VOL. I] GEORGETOWN, KY. NOVEMBER 25, 1826. [NO I.

To illustrate lengthily the importance of the object contemplated in this work, would be unnecessary. Of this the public will judge, to whom the work is now presented.

It is universally acknowledged, by the various sects of Christians, that the religion of Heaven, for centuries past, has fallen far below the excellency and glory of primitive Christianity. The man, who honestly investigates the cause of this declension, and points the proper way of reformation, must certainly be engaged in a work, pleasing to God, and profitable to man. This is our design; aud to accomplish this desirable end, shall our best exertions be enlisted and engaged. That these exertions may be better calculated to effect the object contemplated, we invite and solicit the aid of qualified brethren, who feel as we do, an ardent desire for the restoration and glory of the ancient religion of Christ—the religion of love, peace, and union on earth.

That there are errors in the doctrines, as well as in the lives and practices of the various religious denominations now living, I presume, no Protestant will deny. Their various, jarring creeds—their bitter strife and uncharitable opposition to one another—their multiplied divisions and disunion among themselves—their pride and worldly spirit—their death and cold formality:—these are undeniable evidences of the melancholy fact. To have these errors corrected and removed from the church; and to have truth restored in her heavenly, captivating robes, unadorned with the tinsel of human wisdom, are certainly the pious wishes of every honest Christian. Therefore, unappalled at the dangerous attempt, not discouraged at the attendant difficulties, we will boldly, though humbly, advance to the work. As

In the opening article of Stone's *Christian Messenger* he outlines his motivation for religious reform. He published the monthly paper, with some gaps, until just before his death in 1844. Courtesy of the Center for Restoration Studies, Abilene Christian University

the Christians had been engaged for many years before Campbell "entered the field."

Stone had not written, however, to praise Campbell, to encourage him in the good fight, or to sympathize with him as one well acquainted with religious controversy. Claiming to have learned from Campbell "more fully the evil of speculating on religion," Stone expressed surprise and sorrow to have discovered that Campbell had "speculated and theorised on *the most important point in theology,*" and in a manner "more mysterious and metaphysical" than his predecessors. Stone was referring to an article on the Trinity in the May issue of the *Christian Baptist.* Articles published in the *Messenger* over the next year showed that Stone and Campbell differed on other issues in addition to the doctrine of the Trinity. While Stone believed that ordained ministers or "elders" were required for the ordination of a candidate for ministry, Campbell taught that the vote of a congregation was sufficient. Regarding the Lord's Supper, Campbell taught that communion should be restricted to the immersed, while Stone argued that since it was evident that God had converted persons who were not yet convinced that immersion, alone, was baptism, communion should not be restricted to the immersed. Nevertheless, Stone continued to believe that the Reformers and the Christians had much in common.

By the end of the decade, the division of Kentucky Baptists was nearly complete. Perhaps as many as one-fourth to one-third of Kentucky Baptists (possibly 10,000 persons) had sided with Campbell. In September 1829, Stone reported in the *Christian Messenger* that "a worthy Baptist brother" had recently asked him why the Christians and the "New Testament Baptists" did not become one people. Stone responded that "the New Testament reformers among the Baptists have generally acted the part which we approve." They had "rejected all party names" and had taken the name Christian, they allowed each other "to read the Bible, and judge of its meaning for themselves," and they did not "bind each other to believe certain dogmas as terms of fellowship." If there was a "difference" between the two groups, he knew it not. "We have nothing in us to prevent a union," he declared, "and if they have nothing in them in opposition to it, we are in spirit one." "May God," he added, "strengthen the cords of Christian union."

Campbell did not respond directly to Stone's statement. Rather, he allowed others to express through the *Christian Baptist* and its successor, the *Millennial Harbinger,* the view that the name Christian was associated with Arianism and Unitarianism. Stone raised the issue of a union of Reformers and Christians in the *Christian Messenger* a second time in August 1830, advising that the Reformers should not make their "particular views of immersion" a term of fellowship or reject the name Christian. This time Campbell himself responded in the *Millennial Harbinger.* He expressed his hope that Stone's examination of his "Extra" to the *Millennial Harbinger* on "Remission of Sins" would convince him that "there is no immersion instituted by Jesus Christ, save that *for remission of sins.*" As for the name Christian, he stated that it had become associated with "*peculiar views* of the Deity" and now represented a "sect" rather than the body of Christ. Moreover, he asked how the Reformers, if they were to assume the name Christian, would be distinguished from Christians who had not adopted reforms such as baptism for the remission of sins and weekly observance of the Lord's Supper. Thus, he was inclined to recommend to the Reformers the name "disciples of Christ."

Stone did not immediately reply to Campbell's response. He did, however, come out in the September 1830 issue of the *Messenger* in support of weekly observance of the Lord's Supper. Campbell commended Stone's endorsement of weekly celebration of the Lord's Supper in the October 1830 issue of the *Harbinger.* He added, however, that he had thought "some time ago" that Stone had endorsed immersion for remission of sins, though he could not see how Stone could teach immersion for remission of sins and continue to commune with the unimmersed. In the *Messenger* for August 1831, Stone defended his practice of communing with the unimmersed and commitment to the name Christian.

The exchange between Stone and Campbell continued through December 1831, though, in Stone's view, it achieved little progress toward union. Be that as it may, Stone remained committed to the union of Christians and Reformers. Earlier in the year, he had established a cordial relationship with the Reformer John T. Johnson. Johnson, a lawyer and former member of Congress, had been a member of the Baptist church in Great Crossings, just west of Georgetown. Having failed to lead the Great Crossings Baptist Church into Campbell's reformation, Johnson and two others had withdrawn their memberships and formed a Disciples congregation at Great Crossings in February 1831. In October, the Disciples and Christians in the vicinity of Georgetown and Great Crossings had begun meeting and worshiping together. The prospectus for the 1832 volume of the *Christian Messenger* announced that Johnson would join Stone as coeditor of the *Messenger.*

Late in November, there was an informal and private conference in Georgetown regarding the union of Reformers and Christians. Among those present were the Christian John Rogers and the Reformer John Smith. Smith and Rogers expressed their willingness to travel together throughout Kentucky to conciliate and unite congregations of Christians and Reformers. It was agreed, however, that before launching this effort, they would hold a four-days' meeting at Georgetown over Christmas Day and a similar meeting at Lexington over New Year's Day and would invite Christians and Reformers from across the state to be present.

The four-day Christmas and New Year's meetings planned by the Georgetown conference were well attended by both Christians and Reformers, and, according to John Smith's biographer, John Augustus Williams, the participants "worshipped and counseled together with one spirit and one accord." Though there are no official records of either meeting, Williams provided an account of the Lexington meeting. Smith, a Reformer, called on the Reformers and Christians to unite on the Bible alone. Stone affirmed Smith's appeal, concluding his remarks by offering to Smith "a hand trembling with rapture and brotherly love," which Smith grasped "by a hand full of the honest pledges of fellowship." Others in the assembly now joined hands, and "a song arose." On Sunday the participants communed together.

The *Messenger* for January 1832 announced "the union of Christians in fact in our country." It also announced that "to increase and consolidate this union" John Smith and John Rogers, "the first known *formerly,* by the name of Reformer, the latter by the name Christian," had been set apart "to ride together through all the churches, and to be equally supported by the united contributions of the churches of both descriptions." In response to the question, "Will the Christians and Reformers thus unite in other States and sections of our country?" Stone and his new coeditor answered: "If they are sincere in their profession, and destitute of a party spirit, they will undoubtedly unite." The coeditors rejoiced to have received information of unions in Rush County, Indiana, and Maury County, Tennessee, noting that "It appears that the spirit of union has simultaneously acted in the three states, and in a very similar way."

For Stone, the key to Christian union was the spirit — the spirit believers received through faith in Jesus Christ. In the *Messenger* for October 1833 Stone described four kinds of union. Book union was founded on a creed or confession of faith. Head union was the same as book union, except that the articles of the confession were not written in a book. Water union was founded on immersion into water. Fire union was "the unity of the spirit — a union founded on the spirit of truth." Fire or spirit union, he argued, alone would "stand," and no other union was "worth the name." "This spirit," he asserted, was "obtained through faith, not in a human form or set of opinions, whether written or not written, but in the Lord Jesus Christ, the Savior of sinners; and by a cheerful obedience to all his known commands." "This spirit," he continued, "leads us to love God and his children — to love and pray for all mankind." He stated that it was fire union "for which Jesus prayed, and by which the world will believe that he is the Christ of God." Employing another image, he observed, "How vain are all human attempts to unite a bundle of twigs together, so as to make them grow together, and bear fruit!" To grow together, he continued, twigs "must first be united with the living stock, and receive its sap, and spirit, before they can ever be united with each other." "So," he asserted, "must we be first united with Christ, and receive his spirit, before we can ever be in spirit united with one another." "Men," he observed, "have devised many plans to unite christians — all are vain." "There is," he admonished, "but one effectual plan, which is, that all be united with Christ, and walk in him."

The efforts of Stone and others to achieve the union of Christians and Reformers were largely successful in Kentucky. Many Christians in Ohio and some in Indiana, who rejected Campbell's teaching of baptism for remission of sins, refused to unite with the Reformers. Stone worked for union in the spirit the rest of his life. By 1834, however, much of his attention was directed toward moving his family from Kentucky to Illinois. This move was occasioned by his concern over slavery, an issue to which he had devoted much attention throughout his ministry.

6. Church and Society

6.1. Early Opposition to Slavery

Stone became an opponent of slavery shortly after settling among the congregations at Cane Ridge and Concord, congregations already known for their antislavery sentiments. In a letter to neighboring Presbyterian pastor Samuel Rennels, Stone stated eight reasons why he favored emancipation. The portion of the letter including the date and the first three reasons has been lost. The remaining five reasons focus on the cruelty of slavery and its incompatibility with the fulfillment of familial obligations. "Slavery," he declared, "dissolves the ties of God and man; ties the most strong and indissoluble of all others. One of these ties is conjugal affection. The loving husband is torn from the weeping distracted embraces of the most affectionate wife[,] carried far off & sold like a beast . . . how must the happiness of this loving pair be forever destroyed! Perhaps they had children too ('dear to both' *crossed out*). . . ." "Say," he asked Rennels, "can this be right? Can it be agreeable to a good God? Or that word which commands us to leave father and mother and cleave to our wives?" Stone concluded the letter by observing that it was often said by white Christians that it was not good policy to set the slaves free "amongst us." "Many," he observed, thought otherwise. In any case, he continued, "christians ought not to let civil policy oppose the express will of God. If we know God's will, we are not to enquire whether it will be [in] our interest to do it."

In 1800 Stone presented a resolution from the Cane Ridge and Concord churches to the West Lexington Presbytery declaring that slavery was "a moral evil, very heinous, and consequently sufficient to exclude such as will continue in the practice of it from the privileges of the church." The presbytery referred the resolution to the Synod of Virginia and the General Assembly, noting that although it was the opinion of the large majority of the presbytery that slaveholders should be excluded from church privileges, they hesitated to decide the matter until directed by higher judicatories.

The following year Stone manumitted two slaves, Ned and Lucy, whom he received as a bequest from his mother. In the deed of manumission that Stone filed at the Bourbon County Courthouse, Stone declared that slavery was "inconsistent" with "the principles of Christianity as well as of civil liberty." His provisions for manumitting Ned, whom he reported was about 30, in two years and Lucy, whom he reported was about 12, in ten years were in accord with the philosophy of *gradual* emancipation that required that slaves be prepared for freedom before being set free. Stone trained Ned in a skill before giving him his freedom. He reared Lucy in "the Bible and religion" as well as teaching her a skill before freeing her as a young woman.

By 1808 Stone had changed his position on fellowshiping slaveholders in the church. This may well have been a result of the series of conflicts that had begun with Stone's separation from the Synod of Kentucky. At a meeting of the Christians held near Lexington, Stone was reported to have said that "so far as it had come, to his knowledge, he knew of no members among them that held slaves whose conduct and upright deportment, but what was worthy of example in every other particular, that numbers of them had borne the burden and heat of the day, and had suffered great persecutions for the Christian cause and name, and that to declare them out of fellowship would be ungenerous and cruel in the extreme." Stone may have also been convinced that the best way to influence slaveholding Christians to manumit their slaves was for emancipationists to remain in fellowship with them. He later noted that although he had refused in 1807 to make believers' immersion a term of communion, within twenty years there was not "one in 500" among the Christians who had not been immersed.

6.2. Support for Colonization of Free Blacks and Move to Illinois

Stone's position on fellowshiping slaveholders in the church may have also been influenced by experiences with emancipation. Though Stone had advised Samuel Rennels that "many" disagreed with Rennels's view that manumitting slaves among whites was not good policy, Stone's biographer, John Rogers, noted that "subsequent observation" convinced Stone "that as a general thing, that something called freedom which the free blacks have, is a curse both to them and the whites." Thus, during the 1820s, Stone became a vigorous advocate of the American Colonization Society, whose stated purpose was "to ameliorate the condition of the Free People of Colour now in the United States, by providing a colonial retreat either on this continent or that of Africa." The founders of the society believed that slaveholders *would* manumit their slaves if assured of their removal. Founded in 1816 as a voluntary organization, the society sought public funding. In 1821 it purchased a tract of land in western Africa and established the colony of Liberia to demonstrate to the federal and state governments the feasibility of colonizing free blacks in Africa.

The *Messenger* for September 1834 carried a notice of Stone's intention to move to Jacksonville, Illinois, that fall. Although Stone offered no explanation for his decision to relocate, longtime readers of the *Messenger* knew that it was related to his opposition to slavery. In December 1830, Stone had responded to the rumor that he had become a slaveholder. The basis of the rumor was the fact that Stone had at his home at Georgetown one African man, two African women, and four African children. Stone explained that these persons had been bequeathed to his wife and her children forever by the will of his wife's deceased mother, which placed them under the authority of trustees. He stated that as he could not emancipate them, he was seriously disposed to emancipate himself and his family from them. Such emancipation could be effected by moving his family to a free state, in which case the slaves willed to his wife and children might be considered as free. "This," he had added, "may be realized not long hence."

From 1830 to 1835, Stone bought four tracts of land in the vicinity of Jacksonville, Illinois. On October 30, 1832, he bought three lots in Jacksonville, two blocks south of the pubic square, which was to become the location of his home. Late in the fall of 1834, Stone and his family moved to their new home. Four years later Stone had the satisfaction of confirming that his intention with regard to the Africans who had been willed to his wife and her children had been accomplished. While on a trip to Kentucky, he paid a visit to the former servants whom he found living in Georgetown as a family of free persons.

6.3. Support for Immediate Abolition of Slavery

Stone continued through the early 1830s to promote the Colonization Society. However, by 1833 it was evident that he was disappointed in the failure of Christians to manumit their slaves and allow them to go to Liberia. His move to Illinois coincided with his abandonment of the colonization scheme and his endorsement of the call for the immediate abolition of slavery, without the removal of Africans from the United States. In the April 1835 issue of the *Messenger*, Stone began serialization of an "Address to the People of the United States on Slavery" by William Lloyd Garrison's New England Anti-Slavery Society.

Stone left off printing the "Address" after three installments. In its place, he published in the July issue of the *Messenger* two articles defending immediate abolition as desirable and not to be feared. In the November issue of the *Messenger,* he explained why he had discontinued the "Address of the New England Anti-Slavery Society" after the third installment in June. Not long after he had begun publishing the "Address," he had "heard of the evil effects of the ultra abolitionists in the North" and had "determined to desist from publishing more of the piece, fully persuaded that it would do no good in the present ferment, and might do harm." The evil effects to which he referred were riots and acts of violence *against* abolitionists and the growing resistance of proponents of slavery to all efforts to abolish slavery. He noted that "For publishing these few [installments], numbers of my old patrons and friends in the East and South are offended, and have ordered a discontinuance of the *Messenger.*" He declared, "I have in principle and practice been a conscientious opposer of slavery for nearly 40 years; but how to remedy the evil I know not." "I am persuaded it will be done; but I am ignorant of the means by which it shall be accomplished."

6.4. Slavery, Christian Union, and Premillennialism

Stone was confident that slavery would not exist in the millennial age. Moreover, he was confident that the millennium was near. *Post*millennialists believed that Christ would reign spiritually on earth with the saints for the thousand years prior to his coming to judge the world. *Pre*millennialists believed that Christ would come in judgment at the beginning of the millennium and personally reign on earth with the saints for a thousand years. Stone was a premillennialist, at least from the 1830s onward. The key to Stone's millennialism was his view that "the return and salvation of the Jews" and "the fulness of the Gentiles brought in," both of which he believed would precede the return of Christ, depended upon the union of Christians. For Stone, the union of Christians was the hinge on which the millennium turned. Because Stone believed that God was working in the nineteenth century to unite the church, he remained confident that the millennium was at hand, and with it the abolition of slavery, even when, as he acknowledged in 1835, he did not know the means by which it would be abolished.

Meanwhile, Stone's premillennialism emboldened him to exhort slaveholders to free their slaves by threat of the imminent judgment of Christ. Stone's first application of premillenialism in the *Messenger* appeared in what turned out to be his last appeal to the Christians to manumit their slaves and allow them to go to Liberia. "Let not the wares of Babylon, among which are slaves, be found among us at the coming of the Lord," he advised in 1833. "Behold, he comes quickly." Stone applied his premillennialism in the *Messenger* a second time in November 1835 after explaining why he had discontinued the "Address" of the New England Anti-Slavery Society. He admonished his readers to "beware of being swept from their foundation, the Bible, by temporizing principles and practices." "The day of righteous Judgment," he advised his fellow Christians, "is at hand — prepare for it by cleansing yourselves from all filthiness of flesh and spirit that at the coming of the Lord, we may be found without spot and blameless."

6.5. Adoption of an Anti-Government Position and Pacifism

In the 1820s Stone endorsed asking Christians to sign petitions calling for Congress to fund the colonization of former slaves. By the 1840s, Stone's disillusionment with the failure of Americans to end slavery and his disapproval of the popular electioneering that had emerged led him to propose that Christians should not participate in civil government. Stone made this proposal in a series of four articles published from 1842 to 1844: a dialogue between two "Christian brethren" regarding "Civil and Military Offices Sought and Held by Christians," "Reflections of Old Age," "Reply to T. P. Ware [a Mississippi lawyer and Christian who wrote to Stone in response to the first article in the series]," and "An Interview between an Old and Young Preacher." In these four articles, Stone advanced two arguments for why Christians should not participate in government. The first argument was that participation in government had a negative impact on Christian spirituality. The second was that the spiritual reign and laws of Jesus were sufficient to rule the world.

What, then, was the Christian's duty to civil government? In the dialogue, the brother representing Stone's views stated that the duty of Christians to civil governments was "To be subject to them, and to all their ordinances, which do not stand opposed to our king's." He advised that Christians were to "pay tribute to whom tribute is due; custom to whom custom; and honor to whom honor." He indicated, alluding to Acts 4, that in the case of a conflict, Christians were to follow the example of the apostles in obeying God rather than humanity. Christians, he declared, were also to pray for human governments and to "so live and shine" in their own government "as to show its superiority over all human governments, and by this means engage others to receive it and be saved."

Related to the question of participation in government was the issue of military service. A peace movement had emerged in the United States following the War of 1812. Most members of the peace movement distinguished between the use of force in aggression and in defense, opposing only the former. However, in 1838, "ultraists" within the movement,

This widely used portrait of Stone is one of the few extant images of the beloved church leader.

led by Henry Clark Wright and William Lloyd Garrison, formed a Non-Resistance Society to oppose the use of force even in self-defense. Wright and Garrison proclaimed that the practice of nonresistance would usher in Christ's reign on earth. Stone had been open, as late as 1827, to arguments in support of Christians defending themselves against aggression. By July of 1844, he was an advocate of nonresistance. "A nation professing christianity, yet teaching, learning and practicing the arts of war," he warned, "cannot be the kingdom of Christ, nor do they live in obedience to the laws of Christ — the government is antichristian, and must reap the fruits of their infidelity at some future day."

Stone knew that there would be opposition in the church to his view that Christians should not participate in civil government. In the 1842 dialogue, the character representing Stone's view indicated that he hesitated to speak, knowing that his views would be classified as "fanaticism or ultraism." As Stone saw it, however, his proposal that Christians not participate in civil government was only an extension of views long held by Christians in relation to the church. In his "Reply to T. P. Ware," he stated that "Our brethren have not seen the legitimate issue of what they have been doing, in arguing against human creeds and laws for the government of the church. In doing this they were clearing away the rubbish from the foundation of God's government of the world."

7. Late Reflections on the Movement and Christian Union

Stone stated in June 1844 that the prospects for Christian union were "gloomy." He noted, in particular, that ministers were "discordant in their views of truth, and entirely wedded to their systems, from which, it seems, they will never move." In March 1844 he had expressed disappointment in the Christian Churches. He noted that earlier he had been "greatly cheered" with "the hope that christian union would soon be effected, when so many thousands from the various sects banded together in love, rejecting their party man-made creeds — and taking the Bible alone as the rule by which their faith and lives should be formed — abandoning their party names, and cleaving to the good old name Christian." "Had we only," he continued, "lived and walked in the fear of God, and in the comforts of the Holy Ghost as we commenced, doubtless, the effect anticipated would have been realized; real good men of every sect could not oppose, but would unite in so holy a cause." He lamented that "We have neglected to keep ourselves in the love of God, and in the humility and gentleness of Christ," that some had "turned aside to vain jangling for opinions, and to provoke to disputation and debate and strife," and that many were "more intent to proselyte than to convert souls to pure christianity." Three years earlier he had declared, "The secret is this, that want of this spirit, the spirit of Jesus, is the grand cause of division among Christians: consequently, this spirit restored will be the grand cause of union." Promising that "With this spirit, partyism will die," he had warned that "without it antipartyism in profession only will become as rank partyism as any other, and probably more intolerant."

Nevertheless, he did not relinquish his hope that Christian union *might* soon be accomplished. In June 1844 he noted that he had "sometimes thought that God, by some strange, unexpected work in providence, may drive or draw" Christians together. He suggested, for example, the notion that "Popery may prevail, and drive the alarmed shepherds together for common safety." "They may unite with their flocks in the truth," he observed, "and spread it through the world." He proposed alternatively that God might unite the church by restoring the miraculous gifts of the Holy Spirit that had ceased since the time of the apostles.

Neither did he give up on the possibility that Christian union might be achieved without papal persecution of the true church or the restoration of the miraculous gifts of the Holy Spirit. In the March 1844 article in which he confessed disappointment in the Christian Churches, he nevertheless declared, "Yet there are enough of wise and holy men amongst us to steer the ship by the word and spirit of truth, and the expected good be yet effected." In the introduction to the fourteenth volume of the *Messenger,* published in May 1844, Stone noted that Protestants of every name had formed, or were forming, "antipapal societies, in order to counteract and stop the influence of popery." After expressing his fear that the "reverse" would be the consequence, unless such societies were "managed in the spirit of truth," Stone asserted that if, however, "all the parties among the protestants would agree to reform their lives, to be holy, humble and obedient to all God's commandments — if they would agree to cease from their unhallowed debates and striving one against the other, and to unite as one to promote godliness and brotherly love in the earth — if they would abandon their human schemes and platforms, exchange them for the Bible and the Bible alone — if they would agree to become active and diligent in their Master's cause, and set an example before their flocks and the world, and exhort them affectionately to follow them as they follow their professed Lord — if they would agree to meet together at the throne of grace in fervent, solemn and faithful prayer, then the spread of popery would cease, and skepticism be confounded and silent if not converted to the Lord." "Nothing short of this," he vowed, "will save us from the iron grasp of popery — nothing less will save the world."

Less than a year earlier, Stone had expressed his hope for Christian union, on the Bible alone, based on what he perceived to be the sheer attractiveness of scriptural union. He quoted a Catholic priest as having said that "now there were but two great antagonistic powers in christendom . . . the Roman Catholics who build upon the traditions of the fathers; and . . . those who rejected all such traditions, and built upon the Bible alone." Using an image from the farming world in which he had lived most of his life, he wrote, "I have seen sheep pent up in a lean pasture, looking through the crevices of their inclosure at a flock grazing on a rich field at liberty — I have seen their manifestations of anxiety to be with them, in their bleating, and running along the fence to find a place of escape." "At length," he continued, "one made the leap and many followed."

Since Stone believed that Christian unity would precede the return of Christ, he was certain that to work for Christian unity was to hasten Christ's return. Although discouraged in the summer of 1844 by the immediate prospects of Christian union, he repeated his long-standing counsel: "We must be co-workers with God; every one should be engaged; and as large bodies move slowly, let each one begin in himself."

8. Death and Burial

On October 2, 1844, Stone wrote his will. The following day he left Jacksonville with Celia and their youngest son to visit children and friends in Missouri. An annual district meeting of Missouri Christians was held October 18-21, 1844, at Bear Creek Church in Boone County, three miles north of Columbia. After preaching on October 21, Stone spent a day or two with a son who was a doctor in Missouri before leaving for Illinois. He got no farther than Hannibal, where he stopped at the home of his eldest daughter. Surrounded by family, he died November 9, 1844. He was buried in a locust grove on his Illinois farm. The farm was sold in 1846, and his body was moved to the cemetery of the Antioch Christian Church. In 1847 his remains were moved to Cane Ridge.

9. Stone's Influence on the Stone-Campbell Movement

Although Stone's leadership in the Movement was eclipsed by that of Campbell, his influence on the Movement has been considerable. Stone's advocacy of communion with followers of Christ who have not yet been convinced that believers' immersion, alone, is baptism was the foundation of what became the normative stance of the Movement: that Christ is host at the table, and that the church neither invites nor debars. Stone's pacifism and antigovernment position were adopted by David Lipscomb and other early leaders of the Churches of Christ. In the 1930s, Stone was appropriated by Disciples of Christ involved in the modern ecumenical movement, who saw him as a precursor of their concern for Christian unity. More recently, Stone has been appropriated by members of the Churches of Christ who see his premillennialism, pacifism, and antigovernment stance as a judgment upon what they view as the world-affirming ways of contemporary Churches of Christ.

BIBLIOGRAPHY Anthony L. Dunnavant, ed., *Cane Ridge in Context: Perspectives on Barton W. Stone and the Revival* (1992) • Richard T. Hughes, *Reviving the Ancient Faith: The Story of Churches of Christ in America* (1996) • Barton Warren Stone, *Biography of Elder Barton Warren Stone, Written by Himself, with Additions and Reflections by Eld. John Rogers* (1847), reprinted in *The Cane Ridge Reader* (1972)• Charles C. Ware, *Barton Warren Stone, Pathfinder of Christian Union* (1932) • William Garrett West, *Barton Warren Stone: Early American Advocate of Christian Unity* (1954) • D. Newell Williams, *Barton Stone: A Spiritual Biography* (2000).

D. NEWELL WILLIAMS

Stone-Campbell Dialogue

Series of meetings begun in 1999 between members of the three major streams of the Stone-Campbell Movement in the United States.

The purpose statement written at the first meeting asserted that the effort was intended "to develop relationships and trust within the three streams of the Stone-Campbell Movement through worship and through charitable and frank dialogue 'that the world may believe.'"

After an initial planning meeting in Cincinnati in the summer of 1999, the first session of the dialogue was hosted by the Christian Church (Disciples of Christ) in Indianapolis, November 1999. The dialogue was made up of six members from each of the three streams, with two invited observers. Initial papers examined what might have been done differently to avoid the two major divisions of the Movement.

Meetings of the dialogue continued twice a year through December 2001. At the June 2000 meeting in Nashville, Tennessee, the dialogue members drew up a statement titled "Confession of Sin and Affirmation of Faith: An Invitation from the Stone-Campbell Dialogue." The statement called on those in all the churches of the Movement to consider the sin of division and the fundamental beliefs we hold in common.

In December 2001 dialogue members decided to expand the meetings. Church leaders and members from across the Movement's streams would be invited to come together in cities where the Movement was strong to worship, discuss commonalities and differences, and network. Louisville, Kentucky, was the site for the first of these meetings in June 2002. Churches in Atlanta, Georgia, hosted the second meeting in June 2003. Meetings were scheduled for Indianapolis in 2004 and Dallas in 2005.

Papers and news releases from the meetings have been posted at the web site of the Council on Christian Unity of the Christian Church (Disciples of Christ). Materials from the early meetings were published in the October 2001 issue of *Mid-Stream* journal and made widely available for the use of congregations to start dialogues in their own local settings. A handbook has also been prepared, giving outlines and suggestions for local dialogue meetings.

BIBLIOGRAPHY "Stone-Campbell Dialogue," http://www.disciples.org/ccu/stonecampbell.htm.

DOUGLAS A. FOSTER

Stone-Campbell Journal

Journal published semiannually by College Press Publishing Company, inaugurated the spring of 1998, with the purpose of providing a scholarly platform for biblical interpretation, church history, theology, philosophy, apologetics, and cultural criticism for those who value the perspective of the Stone-Campbell Restoration Movement and who endeavor to advance its distinctive principles. The main impetus for the journal has come from scholars in Christian Churches/Churches of Christ and Churches of Christ.

The founding general editor was William R. Baker, professor of New Testament and Greek at St. Louis Christian College, and later Cincinnati Bible College and Seminary. The original editorial board included Douglas A. Foster, Director of the Center for Restoration Studies and associate professor of Church History, Abilene Christian University; Paul Kissling, professor of Old Testament, Great Lakes Christian College; Richard Knopp, professor of philosophy and Christian apologetics, Lincoln Christian College and Seminary; Paul Pollard, professor of New Testament, Harding University; and Jon Weatherly, professor of New Testament, Cincinnati Bible Seminary.

WILLIAM R. BAKER

Student Volunteer Movement for Foreign Missions

One of several interrelated organizations begun in the last half of the nineteenth century that promoted a missionary and ecumenical witness among Christian men and women in colleges and universities.

The Student Volunteer Movement (SVM) was the missionary wing of the worldwide Christian Student Movement that included the Intercollegiate Young Men's Christian Association (London, 1844; Boston, 1851), the Intercollegiate Young Women's Christian Association (1854), the American and Canadian Interseminary Mission Alliances, and eventually the World's Student Christian Federation (1895). The SVM was also a preparatory school for many who later played formative roles in the modern ecumenical movement, such as John R. Mott, Nathan Soderblom, Robert E. Speer, W. A. Visser 't Hooft, Ruth Rouse, J. H. Oldham, and countless others.

In 1886 Luther D. Wishard and Charles K. Ober, two YMCA traveling secretaries to colleges and universities, persuaded Dwight L. Moody, the famous American evangelist, to invite students from across the United States to come to his Mount Hermon school for evangelism at Northfield, Massachusetts, for a month of prayer and Bible study. Two hundred and fifty-one students came from eighty-seven colleges. Midway through the conference, Robert P. Wilder, a Princeton student, gathered a group to consider God's call to foreign missions. By the end of the conference 100 students had signed what came to be known as the Volunteer Declaration or Pledge, saying, "I am willing and desirous, if God permit, to become a foreign missionary."

Soon the SVM spread to universities in Great Britain (especially Oxford, Cambridge, and Edinburgh), continental Europe, Scandinavia, South Africa, Australasia, and Asia. The second strongest expression was the Student Volunteer Missionary Union in Great Britain, established in 1892. By 1890 over 6,000 American young men and women had affirmed the pledge and over 300 volunteers had been sent overseas. By 1920 this phenomenal surge toward world mission attracted 8,000 volunteers who were serving Christ on every continent except Antarctica and in most countries. By 1945 a total of 20,500 SVM-inspired missionaries represented this legacy.

The SVM developed a major program of missionary education. Missionary study groups were formed and resources developed such as textbooks, study guides, Bible studies, maps, journals, and biographies of noted Christian leaders who served heroically in faraway places. At one point over 40,000 students were enrolled in these classes.

In 1888 an ambitious Watchword was adopted, proclaiming the SVM's goal as "The Evangelization of the World in This Generation." This theme became the credo, the guiding principle that summed up the meaning and purpose of the movement. Some mission theologians criticized the Watchword as "imperialistic evangelism," because to them it seemed too closely identified with the cultural and political goals of the West. However, as interpreted by Mott and others, it did not wager that the whole world would be converted to the Christian faith, but expressed an urgent commitment to give every person in the world the opportunity to hear the gospel and to know Jesus Christ as their personal Savior. Mott further noted that the Watchword was only a restatement of the Great Commission (Matt. 28:18-20). Its intention was to challenge every Christian to consider seriously a missionary vocation.

Five years after its birth the SVM began a series of international student conferences held every four years. These assemblies proved to be one of the most creative and potent influences of the movement. The first quadrennial convention was held in 1891 at Cleveland, Ohio, drawing 551 students from 151 educational institutions, as well as overseas missionaries and representatives of missionary societies. These quadrennial assemblies brought life-changing inspiration and education related to the vocation and prospects of world mission. They shaped the intellectual and spiritual tones of the movement.

In its home mission program the SVM focused on the formation of Christian character, especially among laypeople. Reflecting the spirit of the times, middle-class Victorian values were taught as standards for all Christians — hard work, idealism, self-reliance, personal holiness, successful business practices, and belief in Western superiority. Yet following the First World War this idealism was questioned by students and led to a severe decline in the popularity of the movement. The interest of Christian students shifted from religious individualism to the Social Gospel, from overseas mission to the search for economic justice, race relations, international peace, and cooperation among the nations. Another diminishment came in the late 1920s when the conservative denominations departed from the SVM, prompted by conflict over the interpretation of Scripture and the church's role in the transformation of society. By the 1940s the role of the SVM was challenged by the growth of the Student Foreign Missions Fellowship (1936) and Inter-Varsity Christian Fellowship (1939), both initiated as student movements for fundamentalist and conservative college students. In 1969 — amid the turbulent '60s — the SVM was dissolved and the ecumenical student movement was reconfigured. From that point the witness of the ecumenical student movement continued strongly under the aegis of the World's Student Christian Federation.

While Stone-Campbell Movement university students were never among the core leadership of the SVM, a large number of Disciples of Christ university and seminary students did attend quadrennial conferences, especially those in Midwestern cities such as Des Moines, Indianapolis, St. Louis, and Kansas City.

The missionary witness of the Student Volunteer Movement for Foreign Missions was unprecedented in church history. In addition to enlisting and preparing a phenomenal number of missionaries, it rooted the missionary call in a life of prayer and spirituality and reinforced the importance of Christian unity for the evangelization of the world. Ecumenical historian Ruth Rouse has judged: "No voluntary movement has been more powerful in calling young people into missionary service and in drawing the churches together than the Student Volunteer Movement for Foreign Missions."

BIBLIOGRAPHY Ben Herder, "The Student Volunteer Movement for Foreign Missions and Its Contribution to 20th Century Missions," *Missiology* 8:1 (January 1980): 141-54 • John R. Mott, *Addresses and Papers of John R. Mott*, vol. 1: *The Student Volunteer Movement for Foreign Missions* (1946) • Michael Parker, *The Kingdom of Character: The Student Volunteer Movement for Foreign Missions (1886-1926)* (1998) • Robert P. Wilder, *The Student Volunteer Movement for Foreign Missions: Some Personal Reminiscences of Its Origin and Early History* (1935) • Ralph Winter, "The Student Volunteers of 1886, Their Heirs, and the Year 2000," *International Journal of Frontier Missions* 2 (April 1985): 151-80.

Paul A. Crow, Jr.

Suggs, Marion Jack (1924-2000)

Disciples biblical scholar and theological educator.

Born in Electra, Texas, June 5, 1924, Suggs received his B.A. from the University of Texas (1946), was ordained to the ministry of the Christian Church (Disciples of Christ) in 1948, and received his B.D. from Texas Christian University (1949). He received his Ph.D. from Duke University (1954). As a Fellow of both the American Council of Learned Societies and American Association of Theological Schools, Suggs did postdoctoral research at the University of Heidelberg (1963-64).

From 1952 until his retirement in 1989, Suggs served Brite Divinity School at Texas Christian University as a distinguished professor of New Testament, Matthean scholar, and ecumenist. As dean of Brite (1977-89), he brought in younger scholars and diversified the faculty, hiring the first woman and Roman Catholic as well as the first African American. He served on the Disciples–Roman Catholic International Bilateral Conversation (1977-81).

Suggs's major contribution to biblical scholarship was his argument that in Matthew "Jesus is Sophia incarnate." By moving toward nonandrocentric Christology, his *Wisdom, Christology and Law in Matthew's Gospel* (1970) prepared the way for later feminist theologies like that of Elizabeth A. Johnson, *She Who Is* (1993).

As a lifelong member of Studiorum Novi Testamenti Societas and the Society of Biblical Literature (SBL), Suggs played important roles in reorganizing the foundations of his professional societies. One of the young Turks, Suggs and others (including Robert W. Funk and Robert Kraft), with the support of members like Herbert G. May, Harry M. Orlinsky, and F. W. Beare, stood against the old guard in calling for reform that expanded the base of participation in the SBL and encouraged the participation of younger scholars. The changes mandated by the 1969 SBL constitution were evident in the diversification of the 1969 Toronto meeting — the first annual meeting convened outside the United States — where under Suggs's leadership (1969-72) the Seminar on the Gospels met for the first time. Formalized later, the structure of the annual meeting came to include six types of program units, including seminars that pursue intensive research over a five-year period. Suggs chaired the SBL American Textual Criticism Seminar (1965) and Research and Publication Committee (1975-78), also serving as a delegate to the American Council of Learned Societies (1970-75). He also served as the American Academy of Religion/Southwest region president (1960), Society of Biblical Literature/Southwest regional secretary (1962-65), and Society of Biblical Literature/Southwest region president (1968).

His works include numerous learned articles on the Eusebian texts of Matthew and John, the Wisdom of Solomon, and redaction criticism. *The Layman Reads His Bible* (1957), *The Gospel Story* (1960), and *Wisdom, Christology and Law in Matthew's Gospel* (1970) won, respectively, the Adult Book-of-the-Year, Christian Literature Commission Award (1960); the Christian Research Foundation Book Award (1967); and the Religious Book Award for Scripture (1977). His edited volumes *Studies in the History and Text of the New Testament* with Boyd L. Daniels (1967), and most significantly *The New English Bible: Oxford Study Edition* with Samuel Sandmel and Arnold S. Tkacik (1976) and *The Oxford Study Bible: Revised English Bible with the Apocrypha* with Katherine Doob Sakenfeld and James R. Mueller (1992) round out the scholarly career of this man who stood at significant turning points in the history of theological education, biblical scholarship, and the church.

Suggs was married to Ruth Barge for more than fifty years, and together they had three children: one daughter, Adena Beck; and two sons, James Robert and David.

BIBLIOGRAPHY Elizabeth A. Johnson, *She Who Is: The Mystery of God in Feminist Theological Discourse* (1993) • Ernest W. Saunders, *Searching the Scriptures: A History of the Society of Biblical Literature, 1880-1980* (1982) • G. N. Stanton, "Matthew, Gospel of," in *Dictionary of Biblical Interpretation* (1999), pp. 136-41. TONI CRAVEN

Sunday Schools

See Educational Ministry

Sweeney, Zachary Taylor (1849-1926)

International diplomat, civil servant in Indiana, minister, and moderate conservative thinker among the Disciples of Christ in the Stone-Campbell Movement's third generation.

The son of Guyrn Emerson Sweeney and Talitha Campbell Sweeney, Z. T. Sweeney was born in Liberty, Kentucky. His father was a former Baptist lay minister inspired to join the Disciples by the Campbells. Convinced of the evil of the culture of slavery, he moved from Kentucky north to Illinois to escape that influence.

Z. T. Sweeney graduated from Scottsville Seminary (Illinois) and attended both Eureka College and Indiana Asbury (now DePauw University), although there is no record of graduation. After preaching two years in Paris, Illinois, he was called to Tabernacle Church of Christ (later First Church), Columbus, Indiana, where he lodged at the home of Joseph I. Irwin, whose daughter Linnie became his wife. During his ministry at Columbus (interrupted for interims in Augusta, Georgia; New York City; Richmond, Virginia; and Atlanta) the congregation grew from 180 to 1,500, a growth largely attributable to his evangelistic campaigns.

In 1887 he toured Palestine with Isaac Errett

This portrait of Z. T. Sweeney hangs in the First Christian Church, Columbus, Indiana, where Sweeney served as minister for a total of twenty-seven years.
Courtesy of Margaret Dismore and by permission of the Irwin-Sweeney-Miller Family

(1820-1888). Upon his return, he published a travel narrative: *Under Ten Flags: A Historical Narrative* (1888). After Errett's death, Sweeney reedited Errett's *The Querist's Drawer: A Discussion of Difficult Subjects and Passages of the Scriptures* (1910) and produced selections from Errett's writings as *Bible Readings* (2 vols., 1913-15). Although he was elected chancellor of Butler University (1889), he served instead as U.S. Consul-General to Turkey (1889-93), by appointment of fellow Hoosier, President Benjamin Harrison. From 1899 to 1911, he served as Commissioner of Fish and Game in Indiana, and he worked extensively to preserve natural resources. As Commissioner he published biennial reports that document the beginnings of concern about the environment and ecology in Indiana.

Sweeney's forays into politics did not inhibit his involvement in Disciples church life. In 1904 he served as president of the American Christian Missionary Society. He also influenced the International Convention processes. He gave heavy attention to the "open membership" controversy as it was unfolding among Disciples churches in the 1920s. With Frederick Kershner, Robert Elmore, and others he published *The Watchword of the Restoration Vindicated: Five Masterly Arguments* (1919?), an early statement of conservatives aligned against open membership. He engaged in an extended printed exchange on the issue with the more liberal C. C. Morrison, editor of *The Christian Century.* And as a member of the United Christian Missionary Society's (UCMS) board of managers when the organization was being criticized by conservatives for implementing open membership policies overseas, Sweeney in 1922 authored the "Sweeney Resolution," pressing the UCMS and its personnel to reject open membership. Liberal advocates of open membership repudiated the resolution as a virtual "creed" attempting to impose itself on the society.

Sweeney, meanwhile, viewed himself as a mediator seeking to alleviate division among Disciples by adhering to the original ethos of the Movement. He wrote theological essays that were published widely, and he continued to practice and champion evangelistic campaigns, for which he earned the accolade "Prince of Preachers." Among his theological and pastoral writings are *Pulpit Diagrams* (1897), *The Supernatural Element in the Miracles of the Bible* (1909), and *The Spirit and the Word: A Treatise on the Holy Spirit* (1919). Essays of Sweeney and kindred minds were gathered into the three-volume *New Testament Christianity* (1923-30).

See also American Christian Missionary Society; New Testament Christianity; Open Membership

BIBLIOGRAPHY Lester G. McAllister, *Z. T. Sweeney: Preacher and Peacemaker* (1968) • Z. T. Sweeney et al., *The Watchword of the Restoration Vindicated: Five Masterly Arguments* (1919?) • D. Newell Williams, *Z. T. Sweeney* (1987).

DAVID BUNDY

Sweet Publishing Company

Founded by R. B. Sweet (1892-1963), Sweet Publishing Company was a major influence among Churches of Christ in the 1960s and 1970s.

Sweet began producing mimeographed Sunday School curricula as early as 1936. Eventually he developed an entire series that became known as *Journeys Through the Bible.* He founded the company to market his *Journeys* literature while he was preaching for the University Church of Christ in Austin, Texas, between 1946 and 1954.

Because of failing health, in 1956 R. B. Sweet invited his nephew Ralph (1926-1996) to Austin to help run the company. In 1959 Ralph and Margie Sweet bought and quickly expanded the company. They acquired *Teenage Christian* and *Christian Woman* magazines and began a quarterly adult education series, the Living Word Adult books, that proved popular and influential among Churches of Christ.

The 1960s and 1970s were turbulent times both in the United States and in Churches of Christ. Many of the publications that Sweet undertook were financially risky and courageous. These included the publication of a commentary series on both the Old and New Testaments, The Living Word Commentary.

In the late 1960s, David Stewart (b. 1938), a Ph.D. from Rice University, became chief editor. He built a staff of editors with graduate theological degrees and encouraged some significant publications without expectation of their financial success. Among these were works on Stone-Campbell history and an important compilation by Everett Ferguson (b. 1933), *Early Christians Speak.* During this time the company increased its influence with the acquisition of the *Christian Chronicle.*

During its heyday, the Sweet Company was financially successful, grossing $1.5 million to $2 million annually. In May 31, 1979, the company was divided and sold. Bill New of Fort Worth, Texas, bought the religious publishing part of the company. New and his wife Barbara continued to expand publications into the twenty-first century.

See also *Christian Chronicle, The* WENDELL WILLIS

"Synopsis of the Faith"

Tract written by Isaac Errett in 1862 describing in ten articles the chief beliefs of the Stone-Campbell Movement and containing the by-laws of the Jefferson Avenue and Beaubien Street congregation in Detroit, where he then preached. The longer title was "A Synopsis of the Faith and Practice of the Church of Christ."

Soon after moving to Detroit, Errett wrote the "Synopsis" to introduce the Detroit community to the chief tenets of the Movement. The ten articles include brief statements on the doctrine of Scripture, the Trinity, the divinity of Christ, the death and resurrection of Christ, baptism, and the church. The final article denied the document's status as a creed.

Despite the disclaimer concerning creeds, several influential editors attacked Errett and the "Synopsis." Moses Lard reprinted the entire tract in his *Quarterly* in September 1863, accusing Errett of causing a deep offense against "a people who, for forty years, have been working against the divisive and evil tendency of creeds." It was, Lard said, a creed without the label, "a genuine snake in the grass." Errett largely ignored the criticism.

The "Synopsis" was a precursor to a widely distributed work published by Errett in 1870 titled "Our Position." In this work Errett described the Movement's beliefs in relation to those of evangelical bodies under three headings: areas in which it (1) agreed with all, (2) disagreed with all, and (3) disagreed with some but not all. It concluded with a discussion of Christian union.

See also Creeds and Confessions; Errett, Isaac

BIBLIOGRAPHY Isaac Errett, "Our Position," in *Historical Documents Advocating Christian Union,* ed. C. A. Young (1904), pp. 289-333 • Isaac Errett, "A Synopsis of the Faith and Practice of the Church of Christ," *Lard's Quarterly* 1 (September 1863): 95-100 • Moses E. Lard, "Remarks on the Foregoing," *Lard's Quarterly* 1 (September 1863): 100-107. DOUGLAS A. FOSTER

T

Tant, Jefferson Davis (1861-1941)

Evangelist, author, and controversialist among Churches of Christ.

Tant was born in Paulding County, Georgia, on June 28, 1861. Eight days later his father, William Tant, a prosperous farmer who owned no slaves, enlisted in the Confederate army. Almost three years later, the son would cower in terror as Union General William Tecumseh Sherman's men shot his dog and then burned the farm. That event became J. D. Tant's earliest formative memory.

In the years that followed his family's loss, young Tant grew to be a hard man, a breaker of horses and a Methodist preacher known more for his energy and earnestness than his learning. After coming to Texas with his family, Tant in 1881 encountered a Disciples lawyer and evangelist, W. H. D. Carrington, who taught him and then "licensed" him to "preach the ancient gospel," accepting his previous immersion by Methodists in Georgia. As early as 1885 Tant became aware of the campaign against "sect baptism" conducted by Austin McGary and others, quite naturally and vehemently opposing it until he was persuaded otherwise in a public discussion of the issue by J. F. Grubbs, whom Tant later celebrated as "one of the ablest preachers and debaters" of that era. Grubbs offered to baptize him on the spot, but Tant's youthful pride could not yet take that plunge. Early in 1886 he rode 127 miles on a borrowed horse to be baptized by John Sterling Durst (1841-1924).

Thereafter Tant rejected all baptisms not administered expressly "for remission of sins." The circle of proper administrators — "loyal" members of "the church of Christ" — was also closing. In July 1886 Tant attended the Texas State Meeting of Disciples in Austin, and soon he withdrew with the minority who opposed "human societies" and all other "innovations." In ensuing decades he would become an effective and fearless advocate for "the old land marks" and "the old ways" against all things new in the worship and polity of what was already, for him, a separate and distinct "church of Christ." Yet Tant maintained cordial relations and working relationships with leaders of both factions in the "rebaptism" controversy among Churches of Christ, writing for David Lipscomb's *Gospel Advocate* as well as Austin McGary's *Firm Foundation.* After 1900 Tant's self-critical, irenic reconsideration of earlier rhetoric and behavior in the dispute not only avoided yet another

J. D. Tant, who had been immersed in the Methodist Church, was accepted into the Movement in 1881 on his statement that he was satisfied with his former baptism. Five years later he had become convinced that valid baptism was "for the remission of sins," and was immersed again.

open schism but also assured the eventual triumph of his own position.

Tant had journeyed to the State Meeting not only to defend the faith but also to seek a wife; he found Laura Warren, an Austin schoolteacher, whom he married in 1890 after a courtship of almost four years. Meanwhile he would go anywhere and do anything necessary to be able to preach. His first formal debate — with W. N. Leak, a Baptist preacher, at Bee House, Texas, in December 1886 — set Tant on the warpath for the remainder of his life. By 1931, at age 70, he claimed to have engaged in more than 200 debates, adding that "four people will go to a debate where one will attend a meeting." Frequently after the debates Tant would begin an impromptu gospel meeting, yet Tant found conversions from debate audiences "five hundred per cent greater" than other evangelistic methods.

Laura Warren Tant proved a loving and able wife to the wandering preacher, bearing two children. She died on January 4, 1894, however, from pneumonia contracted as she struggled to maintain their farm in his absence. Tant was inconsolable, yet he had no time for grief. As a single parent, itinerant evangelist, and farmer he needed a wife, and his children needed a mother. Miss Lyle Booker of Eminence, Kentucky, transcribed and edited the manuscript of Tant's first book, *The True Way,* which was published by the Gospel Advocate Company early in 1895 and was well reviewed in both the *Gospel Advocate* and *Christian-Evangelist.* Tant respected Miss Booker's intellectual gifts, but found her physically too frail for the demanding life of a preacher's wife on the Texas frontier. He found both intellectual and physical strength, and extraordinary endurance, in Nannie Green Yater (1872-1961), whom he married. She transcribed and edited almost all of her husband's subsequent published work, including two books and an uncounted number of articles, in addition to bearing and rearing six children to adulthood and managing farms in Texas, Tennessee, Arkansas, Mississippi, and New Mexico. Nannie Tant's autobiographical *Reminiscences* is the primary source for *J. D. Tant, Texas Preacher,* written by her youngest son, Fanning Yater Tant (1908-1997), but it is a remarkable work in its own right.

In sixty years of ceaseless conflict with "sects," including the Disciples of Christ and the cohort of contentious controversialists that populated Churches of Christ, Tant's pungent, plain speaking, and quick, acerbic wit instilled fear, love, and, inevitably, loathing in thousands who heard him and read him. Friends and enemies alike cultivated legends about Tant. His enemies indicted everything from Tant's personal hygiene to his sex life, but they were hard put to invent more colorful and persuasive sentences than Tant himself could utter, nor could they imagine more animus or human sympathy than Tant could express, in word and deed. In 1909 Jephthah Clayton McQuiddy (1858-1924) banned Tant from the pages of the *Gospel Advocate* because other preachers alleged that Tant's language was offensive. By 1920 McQuiddy, convinced that the "reliable evidence" was entirely false, formally apologized and lifted the ban. Tant, meanwhile, preached and debated from the Carolinas to California, baptizing more converts who became preachers than any other evangelist of the Churches of Christ except Marshall Keeble.

Tant's continuing struggle for economic survival as a plain-spoken preacher and plain dirt farmer confirmed his instinctive preference for the society of the rural poor, white and black, over that of affluent whites in large, urban congregations. Between poor blacks and whites Tant, reflecting the prejudices of the day, would prefer whites, but he would never mistreat any person who dealt honestly with him. The Tants were distressed by the treatment of blacks near Greenville, Mississippi, who in 1925 "were in almost the same state of slavery that they had known before the War between the States." They had neither the inclination nor the means to change that situation in that place, but they often rendered personal assistance to deprived or suffering people at some sacrifice to themselves.

In 1908 Tant traded for a house and plantation of 500 acres near Macon, Tennessee, owning it without debt. Traveling throughout the Southeast as an evangelist, he saw the despair of cotton mill workers and other poor, struggling white families in the churches he visited and immediately devised a plan to share his blessings with them. Subdividing 400 acres of his estate into fifty-acre plots, Tant deeded small farms to eight families, furnished the lumber for houses, and staked them with the local grocer. Two families made good, four tried but failed at farming, and two left, taking with them everything they could lay their hands on. The Tants lost all they had accumulated through hard labor and shrewd management, and repaying the debts of Tant's utopian scheme took more than ten years.

In the last two decades of his life Tant and his pioneering work as an evangelist were often honored in word but not in deed. In "destitute fields" that offered no pecuniary support, Tant could find all the work he could do, but well-established, urban congregations would neither invite him to preach nor assist him in preaching elsewhere. Tant read the sociological trends and their ecclesiological consequences carefully and cogently. Repeatedly he warned his readers and hearers, "We are drifting." In the decades after his death on June 1, 1941, Tant's complaint would be taken up and aimed at other targets by some of the same preachers and congregations to whom it had first been addressed. His son Fanning Yater Tant advocated schism over cooperative support of "institutions" and parachurch ministries, using the biography of his father to enlist support for that cause. Even there, however, J. D. Tant could not be mistaken for anything but what he was: an unabashed preacher and practitioner of what he thought to be "the gospel of the Son of God." Nannie Yater Tant wrote of her husband's death, "The sun of my life went down, never to rise again on this earth."

See also Noninstitutional Movement

BIBLIOGRAPHY Jefferson Davis Tant, *The True Way, or A Book on Bible Subjects* (1895) • Jefferson Davis Tant, *How to Study the Bible* (1898) • Jefferson Davis Tant, *Bible Studies* (n.d.) • Jefferson Davis Tant, *The Gospel X-Ray* (1933) • Jefferson Davis Tant and W. J. Frost, *The Tant-Frost Debate on the Organ and Society Work in the Church of Christ* (1904) • Nannie Yater Tant, *Reminiscences of a Pioneer Preacher's Wife* (1992) • Fanning Yater Tant, *J. D. Tant, Texas Preacher* (1958).

DON HAYMES

Taylor, Preston (1849-1931)

Outstanding businessman and influential religious and educational leader among African Americans of the Stone-Campbell Movement.

Born a slave on November 7, 1849, in Shreveport, Louisiana, Taylor migrated with his parents, Zed and Betty Taylor, to Kentucky. During the Civil War, he served as a drummer in the Union army.

After emancipation, Taylor found employment as a stonecutter, porter, and baggage master on the Louisville and Chattanooga Railroad, before accepting a pastorate at the Christian Church in Mt. Sterling, Kentucky. Around 1885, Taylor relocated to Nashville, Tennessee, where he established the Taylor Funeral Company and operated Greenwood Park, which offered recreational activities to blacks in Nashville.

As a religious leader, Taylor, while preaching for the Gay Street Christian Church in 1886, used his talents to spread the gospel among black Southerners. In 1917 Taylor organized the National Christian Missionary Convention, which united black Disciples of Christ in national and global missions. As an educator, he helped to secure property for the Christian Bible College in New Castle, Kentucky, and assisted in the formation of the Tennessee Agriculture State Normal School for Negroes (now Tennessee State University). Taylor continued his legacy as entrepreneur, educator, evangelist, missionary organizer, and humanitarian until his death in 1931.

BIBLIOGRAPHY Preston Taylor Biographical Files, Disciples of Christ Historical Society, Nashville, Tennessee • Todd W. Simmons, "Preston Taylor: Seeker of Dignity for Black Disciples," *Discipliana* (Winter 2000): 99-109 • Booker T. Washington, *The Negro in Business* (1907).

EDWARD J. ROBINSON

Preston Taylor left the Gay Street Christian Church in Nashville in 1891 and established a congregation that would become the Lea Avenue Christian Church in 1902. Taylor (seated second from the left in the front row) became one of Nashville's most respected and powerful leaders.

Courtesy of the Disciples of Christ Historical Society

TCM International

See Europe, Missions in

Temperance

Protestant social reform movement, originating in nineteenth-century America, promoting abstinence from alcoholic beverages.

Once a byword for the classical and Christian virtue of moderation, the word "temperance" came to be associated with the temperance crusade, which began with the "Woman's Crusade" of 1873-74 and ended with the repeal of the Prohibition Amendment of the U.S. Constitution in 1933. During this period, Disciples and other American Protestants came to view temperance specifically as the complete abstinence from alcohol.

Temperance advocates optimistically believed that the "gospel of temperance" would ameliorate major social and political problems and in the process "Christianize" American culture. Earliest temperance advocates traced many problems among families — poverty, disease, domestic violence, and child neglect — to the consumption of alcohol. The temperance movement also provided a political program for shoring up the privileged position of American Protestants that was threatened from many directions. The crusade was partly a Protestant reaction to the changing ethnic and social composition of the country caused by millions of new Jewish and Catholic immigrants, the economic threat to the middle classes and wealthy posed by labor unrest, and the inability of urban Protestant churches to reach and influence the new masses.

Stone-Campbell churches became involved in the temperance movement in the antebellum period. During this time they were primarily interested in educating people about the perceived evils of alcohol. The nature of the renewed temperance crusade that started in the 1870s differed from this earlier antebellum phase in terms of its heightened political agenda, its national scope, and the increased role of women. Temperance advocates after the war began to advocate for legislation that would ban the use of alcohol for everyone. In 1878 Isaac Errett and J. H. Garrison began debating through their newspapers, the *Christian Standard* and *The Christian,* respectively, whether the significant moral change promised by temperance advocates could be accomplished through legal means. During this period members of the Movement joined organizations such as the Woman's Christian Temperance Union (WCTU), Anti-Saloon League, and their own Temperance Board to further publicize their views.

Protestants not only changed society through the temperance movement; the movement also changed them. The post–Civil War temperance movement provided Protestant women one of the few vehicles before universal suffrage through which they could influence public policy and expand their role in society. Two early Stone-Campbell women ministers, Sadie McCoy Crank and Clara Babcock, frequently combined temperance lecturing, prohibition campaigning, and preaching. By 1900 members of the Movement went so far as to consider temperance an integral part of the Christian gospel. They devoted entire church services, summer camps, and revivals to furthering temperance. Ministers and laity joined temperance societies, voted for Prohibition politicians, and distributed literature. To buttress their position, many Stone-Campbell Christians argued that the Bible proved that God had always condemned alcohol use. Most churches switched from using wine to grape juice when they took communion. This common temperance agenda of the Movement across the theological spectrum, from conservative revivalists to Social Gospel advocates, helped assuage the intensity of internal theological differences and potential conflicts.

The temperance movement culminated in the 1919 passage of the Eighteenth Amendment to the Constitution, which criminalized the manufacture and sale of alcohol. Protestants optimistically believed that Prohibition signaled the eventual eradication of a score of social ills and the elevation of the nation's morality. With Prohibition secured, the Disciples' Board of Temperance expanded the scope of its work to include other social welfare issues, such as world peace, race relations, and labor strife. The cause of temperance proved to be a common beginning point for many Disciples to enter other social reform movements. By contrast, conservative leaders associated with the North American Christian Convention and the *Christian Standard* never went beyond Prohibition in attempting to address other social problems through legislation.

Unfortunately for Prohibition's supporters, the promised benefits of the Eighteenth Amendment failed to materialize and instead created a policy the government found almost impossible to enforce. Since so many Americans disagreed with Prohibition, a large number disregarded the law. A last minute flurry of Disciples campaigning with other Protestants could not stem the tide of sentiment against Prohibition that accompanied the election of Franklin D. Roosevelt as president in 1932. In response to the change in national mood on Prohibition, the Disciples' International Convention disbanded the Board of Temperance and Social Welfare in 1935 as an independent agency and transferred its remaining functions to a new Social Education and Social Action division within the United Christian Missionary Society.

The defeat of Prohibition exposed the political limitations that Protestant churches faced in imposing their version of social morality on the nation. The nation's dominant values had shifted away from those of Protestant piety, self-control, and social uniformity to newer ones such as cultural pluralism and individual freedom. Despite the 1933 repeal of the Eighteenth Amendment, however, the legacy of the temperance movement continues to influence the religious beliefs and practices of Stone-Campbell churches into the twenty-first century.

See also Babcock, Clara Celestia Hale; Crank, Sarah Catherine (Sadie) McCoy; Women in Ministry — Nineteenth Century

BIBLIOGRAPHY Glenn Zuber, "The Gospel of Temperance: Early Disciple Women Preachers and the WCTU," *Discipliana* 53 (1993): 47-60 • Glenn Zuber, "Mainline Women Ministers: Women Missionary and Temperance Organizers Become 'Disciples of Christ' Ministers, 1888-1908," in *The Stone-Campbell Movement: An International Religious Tradition,* ed. Michael W. Casey and Douglas A. Foster (2002), pp. 292-316. GLENN M. ZUBER

Tennessee Manual Labor University

Among the earliest ventures in African American education among Disciples of Christ.

Tennessee Manual Labor University (TMLU) was the brainchild of Peter Lowery, a black Nashville preacher who had long harbored the dream of a school to educate former slaves and train black evangelists. Born into slavery himself, Lowery purchased his own freedom in 1840 and by 1846 had also freed his family and was actively preaching the gospel for a congregation of over 500 members (both black and white) that he had founded on the New Testament pattern. He was also a successful businessman, and he supported himself as the owner and operator of a Nashville livery stable. After the Civil War, Lowery, impoverished like most Southerners, saw his dream of a school for African American freedmen as even more urgently needed and began to raise money to make it a reality. Lowery announced his plans for a university to be built on a farm that he would purchase with a mill on the property to provide employment for around 100 students. Well advertised in the Movement's journals, the project initially received considerable financial support nationwide, and on December 10, 1867, the state of Tennessee granted a charter to the Tennessee Manual Labor University with Peter Lowery as its president. The school quickly opened with 180 students, well over the number projected, on a farm in Ebenezer, Tennessee, and all were optimistic about its prospects.

Problems developed almost as quickly as the school opened, however, through the mismanagement of funds by Samuel Lowery, Peter's son. Peter had turned over most of the financial affairs to Samuel, who was also an evangelist supported by the American Christian Missionary Society (ACMS), to work among blacks in Tennessee. Sadly, Peter Lowery's trust was misplaced, and his son did not possess the strong character necessary for such a position. As Samuel enriched himself on TMLU and ACMS donations, reports began to circulate that exposed Samuel's malfeasance. After initial efforts to defend their representative, the fraud became so evident that the ACMS terminated Samuel Lowery's support after only two years. Unfortunately, TMLU could not escape the taint of the younger Lowery's actions, and in spite of Peter Lowery's sterling reputation and the eagerness for such a school among black Disciples, when the pipeline of financial support dried up, the school collapsed.

While the short duration of TMLU as a viable concern kept it from having a lasting impact on the educational institutions of black Disciples, it did prove that with proper black leadership, black community interest, and reliable support, such a venture could succeed.

BIBLIOGRAPHY S. Lowery, "Manual Labor School," *Christian Standard* (March 14, 1868): 82-83 • W. K. Pendleton, "Tennessee Manual Labor University," *Millennial Harbinger* (April 1868): 227-28.

JESSE CURTIS POPE

Texas Christian University

Related to the Christian Church (Disciples of Christ).

The Clark brothers, Addison and Randolph, with the strong assistance of their father, Joseph Addison, opened the doors of what would become Texas Christian University to thirteen pupils at Thorp Spring in Hood County, Texas, on the first Monday of September 1873. A stagecoach stop on the cattle frontier, Thorp Spring was near Granbury and about forty miles southwest of Fort Worth. The founders named their school AddRan Male and Female College in honor of Addison's first born, AddRan, who died of diphtheria at the age of 3. According to the charter from the state of Texas, issued in 1874, the purpose of AddRan was to support and promote "literary and scientific education." Although a proprietary institution, the college was born into the Stone-Campbell Movement and from the outset stressed its strong ties to "the Christian Brotherhood of Texas." The connection became stronger when in June 1889 the Clarks turned the venture over to the church at the annual convention of the Texas Christian Missionary Society. To reflect this key change in the college's status, the board of trustees renamed it AddRan Christian University. The co-founders worked side by side, Addison as first president for twenty-six years, until 1899, and Randolph as vice president and professor from 1873 to 1895.

Best known for co-authoring with Winfred E. Garrison *The Disciples of Christ: A History,* Alfred T. DeGroot (1903-1992) served as dean of the Graduate School of Arts and Sciences at Texas Christian University from 1949 to 1956 and Distinguished Professor of Church History in Brite Divinity School.
Courtesy of the Disciples of Christ Historical Society

That AddRan survived in Thorp Spring was a signal accomplishment in itself. Addison and Randolph, together with their wives — Sally McQuigg Clark and Ella Blanche Lee Clark — poured life and such fortune as they had into the school. Success, however, was marginal. Annual enrollment grew for a number of years before settling (with several exceptions) between 300 and 400. But needs overwhelmed resources, and the financial outlook was bleak. No wonder trustees concluded that a change in location would open the way for a more auspicious future. An attractive proposal including an outright gift of property and certain promises sealed their decision in late 1895 to move the university to Waco, Texas, and into a spacious building vacated by the defunct Waco Female College.

Relocation gave rise to an optimism that proved to be fleeting. Debt, already distressing, escalated and became even more burdensome. Contrary to expectations, enrollment declined sharply. For several years the student body was little more than half its size in Thorp Spring. In view of mounting problems, one member of the board moved to close the school in 1899. Instead of accepting the motion, the presiding officer, T. E. Shirley, volunteered to take a leave of absence from his railroad job and devote full time to the critical task of fund-raising. The crisis passed; the struggle for survival continued. To broaden the base of support, trustees changed the name again in 1902, this time to Texas Christian University (TCU), but took care to link the name AddRan to the college of arts and sciences. Eight years later, fire destroyed the multistory Main Building, still the major facility on campus. Instead of rebuilding in Waco, the university moved north to Fort Worth, Texas, and launched the fall term there in 1910.

Finally, a permanent home (with six new buildings on sizable grounds) had been found. Between 1911 and the collapse of the nation's economy beginning in 1929, TCU converted challenge into opportunity and gradually achieved limited prosperity. Although the Depression inflicted deep wounds, the university persevered thanks in large measure to a surprising bequest, announced in December 1923 and valued at $3,000,000, from Mrs. Mary Couts Burnett. A dozen years later the unprecedented success of the football teams, quarterbacked by Sammy Baugh and Davey O'Brien, culminated in the 1938 national championship and vastly increased TCU's visibility across the country. Thus the university was poised for explosive growth following World War II.

Stability of leadership has been a mark of TCU's life and work over the decades. The short list of chief executives contains only ten names. In addition to Addison Clark, four others served lengthy terms in office: Edward M. Waits (1916-41); McGruder E. Sadler (1941-65); James M. Moudy (1965-79); and William E. Tucker (1979-98). Dramatic expansion in the Sadler era set the stage for continuing progress in the administrations of Moudy, Tucker, and Michael R. Ferrari (1998-2003). In the summer of 2003 Victor Boschini became the school's tenth chief executive.

Organized into eight academic colleges and a central library housing close to 2,000,000 items, the university offers a wide range of baccalaureate majors and numerous graduate programs leading to Ph.D. as well as master's degrees. Brite Divinity School, incorporated in 1914 as a separate but related institution, is an affiliate school of the university. With a selective enrollment of approximately 7,500, an inviting campus, and a large endowment, TCU has become a major university in the independent sector of American higher education.

See also Brite Divinity School; Hall, Colby D.; Thorp Spring Christian College

BIBLIOGRAPHY Joseph L. Clark, *Thank God We Made It!* (1969) • Randolph Clark, *Reminiscences: Biographical and Historical* (1919) • Colby D. Hall, *History of Texas Christian University* (1947)• Jerome A. Moore, *Texas Christian University: A Hundred Years of History* (1974).

WILLIAM E. TUCKER

Theological Education, Seminaries, Graduate Schools

See individual schools

Theology

1. Nineteenth Century
2. Twentieth Century
   2.1. Christian Church (Disciples of Christ)
   2.2. Churches of Christ
   2.3. Christian Churches/Churches of Christ
      2.3.1. The First Generation (1927-1945)
      2.3.2. The Second Generation (1945-1960)
      2.3.3. The Third Generation: Interchange with Evangelicalism and Readjustment of Identity (Since 1960)

General theological dispositions and doctrinal convictions of the Stone-Campbell Movement in the nineteenth century, and among its three streams in the twentieth century.

1. Nineteenth Century

The word "theology" was rarely used in the early Movement except pejoratively and in reference to the speculative opinions of outsiders. This use was a social protest against the pretensions of theologians and theologies (especially Calvinism) of the day. It was also a matter of theological and hermeneutical conviction. The severe hermeneutical discipline on theology was enshrined in Proposition 6 of Thomas Campbell's *Declaration and Address,* which identified theological convictions under the category of "inferences" that might be duly drawn from Scripture but could not be forced on believers beyond their own capacity to see the scriptural rationale of those deductions.

Fond references to "theology," itself a nonbiblical term, were considered indicative of neglect of the *sola scriptura* principle, the basis of confusion, error, tyranny, and division in Christian history. Stone-Campbell churches therefore urged avoiding theology, making the Bible the church's *sole* rule of faith and practice, and adhering to its "pure speech" about the confessional core and other terms of Christian fellowship and communion.

In historical-theological perspective, this mentality was a "theological" response to Protestant post-revolutionary stress syndrome. The revolutions were multiple, including Pietism and Enlightenment, overthrow of long-standing orders in the name of "the people," and demographic and socioeconomic upheaval. Thinking in the Stone-Campbell Movement was oriented more to effects than to causes of these changes. Even so, of immediate concern were the necessity and opportunity to reexamine the meaning of Christian faith and faithfulness in a newborn, expanding nation where "religious liberty" cast theology and the churches into marketplace hurly-burly. Deliberations over three complex theological issues dominated discussions within the Movement: authority, ecclesiology, and regeneration.

Insistence on biblical authority was a hallmark of the Movement. Its force was multi-pronged. It distinguished the Movement from advocates of nonbiblical faiths, deniers of biblical revelation, and common Catholic acceptance of Scripture *and* tradition. The Scripture principle itself was, of course, pan-Protestant tradition, and the Stone-Campbell reformers said very little if anything about the Bible without precedent or parallel in Protestant discussion of the doctrine of Scripture. Alexander Campbell and others repeatedly quoted or paraphrased the seventeenth-century Anglican theologian William Chillingworth's celebrated phrase, "The Bible, I say the Bible, only, is the religion of Protestants." The point of distinction was their implementation of the principle, namely, release from subscription — or even attention — to any extrabiblical creeds, confessions, catechisms, theologies, or other subsidiary authorities. This simultaneous similarity with and difference from environing Protestantism made it possible for the Stone-Campbell Movement to view itself as either an advance for post-Reformation evangelical Protestantism or an alternative to it. Both views coexisted throughout the nineteenth century; already by the 1840s the former became a sign of "progressivism," the latter, "conservativism."

Practicing the Scripture principle that other Protestants merely preached was often, and no doubt for many, *the* Stone-Campbell answer to issues of religious authority as well as nearly every other. It contributed to the Movement's popularity, and it led some orthodox-minded critics to say at least one kindly word about it before going on attack. A biblicism, in the sense of direct recourse and obedience to Scripture, was among the earliest, most pervasive, and long-lived identity markers of the Movement. This biblicism, however, was shaped by and linked to numerous other matters of theological debate at the dawn of the nineteenth century, especially among the divided heirs of the British Reformation.

On the relationship between Word and Spirit, for example, the sufficiency of biblical testimony — as the instrument of God's Spirit — to the gospel legitimated rejecting not only subscription to creeds of human origin but also claims of immediate (unmediated) workings, inspirations, or revelations of the Spirit. Stone's rise to leadership involved struggles on both sides, defending New Light Christians against subscriptionists and subscriptionism on the one hand and from Spirit-inspired chaos and Shakerism on the other. Scott's revivalism was similar in character, although formulated in terms of an *ordo salutis:* the Spirit worked conversion by mediation, through the biblical message, and was imparted only to believers, that is, those incorporated by baptism into the body of Christ.

Alexander Campbell developed the pattern of construing biblical authority dominant within the Movement. His writings after roughly 1830 gather earlier themes and current resources into a multifaceted structure of thought that, though neither fully detailed nor authoritative, set the framework for most antebellum era discussion. Terms like "pattern," "structure," and "framework" seem apt here, in that pieces of the whole were worked and reworked by others too, alongside rather than dependent upon him, and subject to considerable variation. Campbell, like Stone and Scott, held that faith arose by the power of the Spirit conveyed in and with the Word of the gospel written, preached, and heard. This point, however, was only one element in a larger account of revelation formed along the lines of post-Enlightenment rational orthodoxy.

Rational orthodoxy was a reformulation and defense of classical theism in response to new learning gained by free, critical inquiry, Newtonian science, Lockean epistemology, and Common Sense philosophy. Its supporters, representative of the moderate Enlightenment, distinguished Christianity as the one true revealed religion from natural religion and other world religions. They looked to the Bible for "revelations" of God, including truths above but not contrary to reason. Of key concern to those like Campbell were God's purpose *(telos)* for the creation and provisions in history for bringing humans from sin to salvation. The provisions embraced principles, precepts, institutions, ordinances, events, divine and human activities — together, a totality or system of "facts" about divine-human relations recorded in the Bible by "credible witnesses." That God inspired, indeed "authored," the Scriptures was roundly affirmed. But biblical inspiration per se was neither the lead term nor the linchpin of the argument; it was one of many "facts" of salvation history, all authored by God, to which the credible biblical writers testified. Hence, while Campbell and other leaders, like rational orthodox theologians at large, distinguished the "divine origin" of the biblical books from merely human writings, they also adduced multiple "evidences," external and internal, of the genuineness and authenticity of inspired biblical testimony. Reliance on "Bible words for Bible things," a Thomas Campbell advisory of historic import, conformed to the familiar Lockean correspondence theory of words, ideas, and things.

Within this framework Alexander Campbell — along with Walter Scott and countless others thereafter — placed key themes of Reformed-tradition covenant (federal) theology. Such theologies focused on the means and conditions by which God ordained to reveal the good news of salvation from sin and assure the fulfillment of this purpose. Campbell and Scott found three forms of covenanting established between God and humans unfolded in "biblical history": the patriarchal, the Mosaic, and the Christian. Each epoch or dispensation involved an act of divine initiative and distinctive avowals and signs of mutual love, including divine commands, aids, and promises and human responsibilities. Basic content — God's saving purpose — as well as prophecies and typological foreshadowings and fulfillments united these forms of covenant. But as early as 1816 in his "Sermon on the Law," Alexander Campbell made a sharp contrast between Old Testament covenants and the covenant in Christ. This distinction traveled widely through the Movement, signaling emphasis on the authority of New Testament writings and reinforcing supersessionist inclinations.

The Movement's federal theologies also outlined distinctions within the New Testament materials. One was especially significant. The person Jesus Christ — his life, death, and resurrection — was the divine act foundational of the Christian dispensation and its distinctive institution, the church. The covenantal avowal of devotion to God was confessing Christ. Hence alongside *sola scriptura* was *solus Christus.* The slogan "no creed but Christ" was highlighted both as faith's original, simple creed with a single proposition (focusing especially on Matt. 16:16) and as a creed unlike any other, a confession of faith in and faithfulness to a *person* rather than doctrinal propositions.

Emphasis on the "plain meaning" of the Scriptures, a Reformation-era legacy, was customary. It was often, but not invariably, qualified by rhetorical classifications of biblical discourse such as historical reportage, typology, metaphors and allegories, epistolary literature, and prophecy. The rights of free inquiry and "private" (individual) judgment in biblical interpretation were affirmed. With them came frequent pleas for careful study; sound, reasoned, and reasonable views; attention to ordinary language usage; and common methods of interpretation. Alexander Campbell claimed the principles of grammatico-historical interpretation found in Moses Stuart's translation of the hermeneutical masterwork of Johannes Ernesti as those he had long followed. Circulating in American Protestantism as "inductive" or "Baconian" hermeneutics, they took root in the Movement and influenced generations thereafter. Philological and text-critical studies were common. "Newer" developments in historical criticism, and with it source critical investigations, were little known, and generally ignored or discounted rather than disputed, during the antebellum years.

On ecclesiology, the Movement sought the constitutive features of the church. The result was a mix of latitudinarianism and restrictiveness unusual in its context. Thomas Campbell had spoken of the church as "essentially, intentionally, and constitutionally one." His son Alexander attempted to delineate the specific constitution, the original (or ancient) order of things, from the precepts and approved precedents recorded in writings of the apostles. As his thinking developed, the primitive pattern separated out transient from permanent, nonnegotiable elements of the true church. The latter included congregationalist government under a plurality of elders, a christological creed (the "Good Confession") regarding the person, status, and saving work of Jesus Christ, three ordinances (believers' baptism by immersion, weekly Lord's Supper, and Sunday as "the Lord's Day"), key elements of Sunday worship, and three ministerial offices (elders, deacons, and evangelists) within the "priesthood of all believers." This ordering of ordained ministries gained general prevalence in the Movement, though the Stoneite tradition of leadership by one elder-minister (typically ordained by an association of ordained ministers) remained and the "formal" ordination services of elders and deacons were not invariably distinguished from "election and installation" to office. Reliance on a "single-minister system" rather than a "plurality" *(collegium)* of elders was a matter of choice, diversity, and mounting controversy from the mid-nineteenth century on.

The biblical, "divinely authorized" name for church people was as much of concern to Stone and his group, long before uniting with Campbell-Scott "reforming Baptists," as it was to Campbell. Warrants were cited for "Christians" and "Disciples of Christ." The latter, Campbell's preference, survived alongside the former, gaining dominance in certain quarters more by forbearance than by force of argument.

The simplicity and clarity of "ancient order ecclesiology" had considerable free market appeal. It granted "the common people" in small, scattered communities the rights to organize churches of "biblical" legitimacy, without ecclesiastical control. Theologically, it staked claims on *apostolicity* exceeding those of the churches adamant on the "apostolic succession" of their teachings or ministerial orders; and stress on the church's *constitutional* oneness set concerns of "faith and order" on equal footing. Apostolic primitivism, however, also set the stage for myriad disputes over the adoption of elements or expressions of faithfulness other than those specified by New Testament precepts or precedents.

To Campbell's "ancient order" the Movement added "the gospel restored," Scott's revised and improved *ordo salutis*. It detailed the path of conversion from sin to salvation: faith, repentance, confession, baptism (by immersion), the gift of the Holy Spirit, and promise of eternal life. By combining the last two, Scott devised a "Five Finger Exercise" for evangelistic use. Later writers sometimes referred to the topic as "first principles" or "the plan of salvation" and modified the wording, and even the steps. Scott, however, considered both the elements and their sequencing equally important, and basics of his formulary and exposition of it were immensely influential. Faith was belief in the testimony of the Scriptures that Jesus was the Messiah (Christ), Son of God, and Savior; repentance was a change of orientation from sin to God; confession was the public profession of faith in Christ. Baptism by immersion for the remission of sins was the first act of obedience to Christ, incorporation into his body, and assurance of pardon. The gift of the Holy Spirit was its entrance into the believer's soul; promise of eternal life was the Christian's hope in life and in death and the consummation of blessedness.

Treatment of baptism and the Spirit were at once the most popular and controversial parts of the schema. The arguments for believers' baptism by immersion mainly rehearsed familiar Baptist ground, and Scott's claim that no one else taught baptism for the remission of sins was simply incorrect. He, however, broke with popular evangelical revivalism in stressing baptism as an objective sign of forgiveness that ratified justification and assured pardon as neither subjective experiences nor good works could. He also distinguished the work of the Spirit upon the sinner mediated through the Word from its direct work within the baptized believer, and in so doing addressed the concerns of the masses who delayed, or despaired of, their conversion because of uncertainty about their election or lack of "miraculous" experiences of the Spirit.

Most elements of Protestant doctrinal tradition carried over into the Movement from the British-American context without notable change. Freedom and diversity of opinion were emphasized — and evident. They troubled orthodox-oriented opponents, who regularly complained of doctrinal laxity and irregularities. Actually, the Stone-Campbell Movement made a sharp distinction between the matters of faith and fact in accord with the Scriptures and matters of human opinion and speculation, without binding force. Its teachings of God, revelation, creation, providence, nature, and the supernatural were in substance restatements of moderate Enlightenment Protestantism. Teachings of sin, grace, free will, works, and moral accountability were variations on moderate Calvinist and evangelical Arminian themes. Governmental accounts of the atonement, entertained by the Campbells and Walter Scott, coexisted with classical, penal-substitutionary views. The "moral influence theory," prominent in Stone's thinking, had some following. The thrust of Stone's reflections on the Trinity and Christology, despite very few subtleties, had perhaps greater reach. The Scriptures affirmed "one God, Father, Son, and Holy Spirit" and the humanity and divinity of Jesus Christ. But they never used the word "Trinity" and made no "metaphysical" explanation of these truths in terms of church fellowship or communion. By and large the readings of biblical doctrine in the Movement led to core teachings that were heterodox only by strict-constructionist standards of denominational confessionalism.

The death of Alexander Campbell in 1866, the last of the founding generation leaders, is usually identified as the beginning of a new period of the Movement's history. The era extended to the end of the century, its climax the 1906 formalization of division between "Churches of Christ" and "Disciples of Christ." Marks of "scholasticism" are evident in the thinking of the times. So too among the Disciples of Christ were increasing associations with postwar evangelical Protestantism and in some cases interest in the idiom and emphases of liberal Protestant theologies. More or less distinctive of Stone-Campbell scholasticism was continued direct recourse to the Scriptures. The Movement's founders were praised as great Christian reformers or restorers, and their plea for "New Testament Christianity" was reiterated rather than rethought. Yet rarely were they or their writings cited as authoritative sources. Continuity of tradition — a phrase conspicuously absent from traditionalist writings of the day — was maintained by replaying familiar themes with either fresh elaboration or barebones brevity.

The alliance of biblical doctrine and Lockean–Common Sense conceptuality prevailed. It passed to Churches of Christ from preacher-teachers and editors like Tolbert Fanning and his students and more widely from their peers in "Brotherhood" schools, colleges, and churches. The lead teacher of doctrine was Robert Milligan, whose *Reason and Revelation* (1867) and *Scheme of Redemption* (1868) compressed the marrow of Stone-Campbell divinity into two large but manageable textbooks. Interest in Christian and biblical evidences persisted and reached flood tide in the 1880s. J. S. Lamar's *The Organon of Scripture* (1860) was the most enduring of many manuals propounding the inductive exegetical method. These lines of thought converged in the career of J. W. McGarvey of the College of the Bible, indisputably the Movement's foremost biblical scholar until the 1890s, when Herbert L. Willett arrived with a University of Chicago Ph.D., historical-critical expertise, and evangelical-liberal theology.

The peculiar blend of biblical-biblicist and scholastic features in postwar Stone-Campbell teaching complicates efforts to tag it with ready-made labels of historical theology. Stress on restorationist purity, including opposition to instrumental music in worship, and disinterest in wider theological currents distinguished Churches of Christ not only from the larger body of Disciples of Christ but also from contemporaneous separated or separating groups, many of which enlisted in America's emergent fundamentalist movement. Still alive among them, in addition to Campbellite primitivism, was fervent faith in God's end-time triumph transcending all human undertakings and achievements, a countercultural, apocalyptic worldview that historian Richard Hughes and others trace to Stoneite origins.

Self-declared theological liberals were also a Disciples minority group circa 1900. Becoming a liberal *scholar* was a stretch. It meant transferring from British-bred to German school inquiries; from empirical-realist philosophy to post-Kantianism; from a static Newtonian account of nature, science, and history to developmental, even Darwinian, views; from correspondence to expressivist-symbolic theories of language; from rational orthodox theism to the revelatory unfolding of the divine Infinite; from grammatico-historical hermeneutics to historical-geneticism. Disciples rarely negotiated such passages without "time away" at Yale, Chicago, or some other school of higher learning.

Liberalism's sentiments and concerns were another matter. These had been spreading for decades from America's cultured elites to its middle classes through romanticism, popular media, and educational trends. Their implications for theology and the church were by no means self-evident, though Stone-Campbell conservatives detected that missionary societies, fine-trained "hired" ministers, organs, and similar "innovations" were linked *somehow* to upward social mobility and genteel culture. After the Civil War, stress on Christian nurture, services of compassion and custodial care, ministries to the needs of others as Jesus ministered to the needy, and enterprises spreading the blessings of "modern Christian civilization" throughout the world betokened the "progressive spirit" of the times, widespread and growing among Disciples.

Such shared concerns facilitated rapprochement between Disciples and evangelical Protestants. Liberalism seemed to move Protestantism closer to the Disciples, toward focus on simple, biblical, Christ-centered faith, relief from creedalism and speculative "harsh" doctrines like predestination, interest in Christian unity, and affirmation of human freedom, dignity, and responsibility. Emphasis on practical Christianity in the new theologies dovetailed with the "postmillennial" impulses of Alexander Campbell: dedication to progress toward a world of harmony, righteousness, and well-being, building the kingdom of God on earth, quite apart from talk of a literal millennium.

Acceptance of liberal scholarship and doctrine followed, but not quickly, always, or wholesale. An inquiring Disciple could consult Protestant scholars renowned for erudition and evangelical piety, leery of destructive criticism and avant-gardism. Even McGarvey wanted to stay up-to-date in this sense. B. W. Johnson did so more successfully. Cutting-edge initiatives were more often reported, aired, and entertained than fully endorsed in the journals edited by Isaac Errett, J. H. Garrison, William Moore, and "early" C. C. Morrison. These four, along with preachers like the "Missouri quartet" — George Longan, Thomas Preston Haley, Allen Bailey Jones, and Alexander Procter — were among the first Disciples to rethink "traditional" claims in light of the changing intellectual climate. Most forays of this sort were recastings, not repudiations, of familiar Stone-Campbell points. Old dispensational federalism became progressive revelation. "No creed but Christ" meant faith in the person — the character, life example, and simple yet profound wisdom — of the Jesus of history. Inspiration of the Bible was unique, divine, but in the religious experiences and spiritual truths it records rather than in every detail. Its inspiration was demonstrated by its inspirational power, not rational evidences. The moral influence theory of the atonement found fresh support in some circles, advocated anew by J. S. Lamar, at one time the quintessential Baconian interpreter of Scripture, as well as by "younger progressives" like Garrison and Jones.

The tenor and character of "transitional thinking" of church teachings along moderate mid-range lines toward the end of the century are perhaps best found in *The Old Faith Restated* (1891), edited by J. H. Garrison. This anthology of seventeen articles by noted ("representative") leaders of the Disciples of Christ addressed core doctrines of Christianity and distinctive emphases of the Movement stated, according to editor Garrison, in light of experience and biblical research. JAMES O. DUKE

2. Twentieth Century

2.1. Christian Church (Disciples of Christ)

Disciples of Christ engaged in the teaching of the Christian faith and other theological activities throughout the twentieth century. They did not often call their church teachings or their thinking on matters of faith theology until mid-century. Main features and currents of Disciples religious thinking — theology — are nonetheless identifiable in historical theological categories.

Disciples theology circa 1900 was predominately evangelical Protestant. The Christian beliefs of Disciples were in accord with this broad doctrinal tradition common to Protestantism's largest churches. Disciples "distinctives," it could be and often was argued, fell within generally accepted bounds of evangelical Protestant diversity. Brotherhood activities supported this view. So too did grassroots opinion: Disciples in ever-increasing number found themselves incapable of calling Luther non-Christian because he was unimmersed or labeling such churches as Methodists and Presbyterians "sects." Evangelical Protestantism, however, was rapidly dividing into conservative and liberal branches. The emergent, and eventually prevailing, Disciples theologies flowed alongside and then into the liberal stream.

Disciples liberalism flourished, despite opposition, from 1910 to 1950. High-profile liberals of the early twentieth century, influential far beyond their home church circles, included Peter Ainslie, Edward Scribner Ames, Charles Clayton Morrison, Kirby Page, and Herbert L. Willett. Listing even these few is a reminder that liberal Disciples were diverse. Willett, for example, was famed for biblical, Christocentric liberalism; Ames for pragmatic-idealist modernism; Page for the social gospel; Ainslie for advocacy of Christian unity and world peace. Liberal Disciples, women and men alike, were active in every sphere of church service and reflected the entire spectrum of liberal ideas and causes.

Despite their diversity, liberal thinkers exhibited family resemblances. They sought and stressed the essential, "the abiding" truths of Christianity. To this end, and also to show the credibility and moral worthiness of Christianity's message, they employed the tools of modern, critical inquiry and expressed their convictions in terms compatible with historical, scientific, and social scientific knowledge. Typical emphases were God's love for all, supremely revealed in Jesus Christ, whose character, teachings, and life example inspire commitment to services of compassion contributing to human well-being. Liberals urged proclaiming this message to every nation by preaching and more importantly by benevolent activities, thereby advancing — "building" — God's kingdom of peace and perfection on earth. In this respect they were progressive heirs of the postmillennialism of nineteenth-century leaders like Alexander Campbell and Walter Scott.

At mid-century, effects of the "theocentric turn" associated with neo-orthodox, dialectical, realist, existentialist, and deep empiricist theologies were evident among Disciples. With them came the themes and vocabulary of the biblical theology and ecumenical theology movements. The new trends gained footing among postwar church leaders despite the protests of many veteran liberals. Disciples gravitated more to realist and correlationist forms of Neo-orthodoxy than Barthianism or neoconfessionalism. The newer biblical and ecumenical theologies held special appeal. William Robinson was a pioneer guide and Ronald Osborn, Ralph Wilburn, and later Paul A. Crow, Jr., were notable contributors to these transitions. A newborn Association of Disciples for Theological Discussion and the Panel of Scholars were group portraits of the liberal/neo-orthodox mix of Disciples theology.

This "theological renaissance," though neither long nor pervasive, had significant impact on the "Brotherhood." It reconnected Disciples to the language and the rich symbolic tradition of historic church teaching. It fostered concern for the import of terms like "Word of God," "sin," "grace," "redemption," "sacrament," "covenant," and "theology." It provided a theologically principled critique of restorationism and a theological rationale for metamorphosis from "Brotherhood" to "Church." The Preamble to the *Design* (1967) of denominational Restructure sounded the confessional keynotes of the newly configured body of the Christian Church (Disciples of Christ).

Changes swept over theology between 1965 and 1980. References to mainline Protestantism's crisis, postdenominationalism, and theology's disarray or "blessed rage for order" were common. Disciples *theological* identity demanded attention. The Council on Christian Unity, through its Theology Commission, generated brief study documents ("words to the church") and booklets on ecclesiology. A Panel on Christian Ethics (1985) studied peacemaking in the nuclear age; the Division of Overseas Ministries studied the theological grounding of the principles and policies of mission. Journals like *Encounter* and *Mid-Stream* tracked fast-moving theological developments.

As the century's end neared, Disciples church teachings overall remained oriented to a "biblical" Christianity, with emphasis on Jesus Christ as Savior, caring for individuals, and social concern. Tolerance of diversity, a historic avowal, assured entry to widely varied trends of neo-liberalism, neo-evangelicalism, postmodernism, and liberation theologies in African American, feminist, third world, Hispanic, and Asian American voices were prevalent. Issues of "inclusivity" and "pluralism" generated much discussion. Studies and practices of "spirituality" gained popularity.

Disciples scholars worked in every field of theology and religious studies. Some attained special peer acclaim — for example, Don Browning in religion and psychology, Fred Craddock in homiletics, and "younger scholars" Rita Nakashima Brock and Serene Jones in theology, Frank Burch Brown in religious arts, and Michael Kinnamon in ecumenics. For about a decade *Disciples Theological Digest* recorded the works of Disciples scholars. Clark Williamson led in addressing issues of Christian anti-Judaism and Jewish-Christian relations. He also became the first Disciple to write a patently *systematic* theology (1999), followed by his Christian Theological Seminary colleague Joe R. Jones (2002). JAMES O. DUKE

2.2. Churches of Christ

Many leaders in Churches of Christ have argued that they have no theology; they simply follow the Bible. If what is meant by "theology" is systematic thinking about the classic doctrinal topics of revelation, faith, God, Christ, the Holy Spirit, creation, church, the sacraments, salvation, sin, sanctification, and eschatology, then theological reflection in Churches of Christ is fairly uncommon and recent. But if theology consists of elaboration upon driving motifs, then certain observations may be made.

Walter Scott in *The Gospel Restored* (1836) confidently set out the major foci of the Stone-Campbell Movement in 1836: "The present century, then, is characterized by these three successive steps. . . . First the Bible was adopted as the sole authority in our assemblies, to the exclusion of all other books. Next the Apostolic order was proposed. Finally the True Gospel was restored." These are the driving motifs in Churches of Christ from 1906 until the present. In theological parlance, the topics have been Scripture (hermeneutics), ecclesiology, and soteriology. The doctrine of Scripture in the twentieth century was the least elaborated, being largely assumed from the early Movement. Early in the twentieth century theology was largely subsumed under soteriology (the "plan of salvation"), but by the middle of the century ecclesiology became the point of departure.

In the first half of the twentieth century, two books besides the Bible commanded the attention of preachers in Churches of Christ. One was Robert Milligan's *The Scheme of Redemption* (1868), a monument of the "inductive" theological method in the nineteenth century, which continued to be reprinted well beyond its day. Already with this work, the pattern of subsuming soteriology under ecclesiology was evident. The other was T. W. Brents's *The Gospel Plan of Salvation* (1874). While early in the century much polemical writing focused on mission societies and vocal music, the daily fare of the preacher was converting the lost. It was for this reason that systematic deliberation upon salvation was a focal point for theological reflection. Brents wrote the work so that "aliens" could become citizens of God's family, that is, members of the church. He also hoped that it would be read widely by those who already believed so that they might grow to full stature in the kingdom. The book was therefore offered and perceived as an exposition of the doctrine of Christianity. Brents first discussed what he perceived as erroneous theology in respect to predestination, election, Calvinistic proofs, foreknowledge, and hereditary depravity. Over against these he set adult believers' baptism. But first he laid out the parameters of the church to which believers are to attach themselves. The last chapters declared the gospel plan of salvation as already essentially set out by Walter Scott: (1) faith, created by hearing the Word of God, (2) repentance, (3) confession, (4) baptism, and (5) the receiving of the Holy Spirit. These soteriological views remained intact at the end of the twentieth century, though less couched in rationalistic presuppositions and less mechanically presented. David Lipscomb's book *Salvation from Sin* is organized more according to classical theological topics: the Bible, God, Christ, the Holy Spirit, redemption, and so on. The outlook is much the same as that of Brents, that the Bible teaches believers' baptism. Lipscomb affirmed the same gospel plan; however, he departed from Brents's view that the Holy Spirit indwells the Christian, arguing instead that the Holy Spirit influences the believer only through the words of Scripture. Lipscomb had more to say about the inspiration of Scripture and its interpretation than did Brents. He held Scripture to be inspired in its words, and that interpretation should follow the standard hermeneutics represented by the works of Moses Stuart and David Dungan, the latter of whom was from the Stone-Campbell Movement.

The main channel through which theology was funneled to Churches of Christ members in the 1960s was the Gospel Meeting, which normally lasted two weeks. The meeting sermons tended to be standardized at least into the 1940s. The preacher started on Sunday laying out the identity of the New Testament church and its features. Then he declared the gospel plan of salvation, and he ended by highlighting the final judgment. The focus of the meeting was therefore, again, ecclesiology and soteriology, but ending with eschatology. The meeting topics were reflected in two books widely read and distributed: Roy Cogdill, *The New Testament Church,* and Leroy Brownlow, *Why I Am a Member of the Church of Christ.* In these volumes soteriology was subsumed under ecclesiology. The same approach to "systematic theology" is taken up by Everett Ferguson in *The Church of Christ: A Biblical Ecclesiology for Today* (1996), with soteriology subsumed within ecclesiology, but much more in conversation with contemporary early church historians. Less conventional approaches to ecclesiology from the perspective of Churches of Christ are by C. Leonard Allen, Rubel Shelly, and Randall J. Harris.

As to ecclesiology, many of these works extolled the restoration of the New Testament church. The New Testament church, so some charged, eroded into an apostate church by at least the fourth century A.D. The magisterial Reformation was a first effort to return to the purity of the early church, but it was not until the nineteenth-century restoration that the recovery was complete. The restored church consists of local independent congregations presided over by elders and deacons. The worship of the restored church consists of singing unaccompanied, the Lord's Supper celebrated weekly, praying, Scripture reading and preaching, and weekly giving. Congregations may cooperate with other congregations in larger efforts, such as the Herald of Truth radio and television programs, but these efforts are under the eldership of one congregation, in this case the Highland Church of Christ, Abilene, Texas. A number of Churches of Christ object to such sponsorship and are identified as noninstitutional.

The following are theological tenets widely held in Churches of Christ. The name "Church of Christ" is appropriate because it gives honor to Christ and therefore does not denote a denomination. Creeds are inappropriate. The guidelines for the church and its belief should be Scripture alone, the church's inspired book. God adds believers to the church when they follow the steps of the plan of salvation. Churches do not examine persons for membership, but accept all those who report that upon their faith they were immersed into Christ. Other topics discussed have to do with the unity of the church (ecumenics) and eschatology. Unity comes through dropping all creeds and non-biblical names. Ecumenical organizations may promote union, but not unity. Churches of Christ are by a sizable majority amillennial, with a small wing still being premillennial. THOMAS H. OLBRICHT

2.3. Christian Churches/Churches of Christ

The theological development in Christian Churches/ Churches of Christ can be roughly divided into three phases, though there is doubtless some overlap among them.

2.3.1. The First Generation (1927-1945) Historians debate the precise point at which Christian Churches/ Churches of Christ became a separate entity from the "mainline" Disciples of Christ, but the beginnings of the rift certainly date from the mid-1920s. Originally the theology of the new group differed little from that of pre-division conservatives. As in Churches of Christ, proto-"independents" among the Disciples were suspect of "systematic theology" and continued to claim that "theology" as such was the same as inductive biblical interpretation. Shades of opinion ranged from moderate conservatives to antimodernist reactionaries. Certain commitments were widely shared: for example, a high view of biblical authority; the understanding of conversion as a rational decision, with the Holy Spirit given only after baptism; a restorationist emphasis on New Testament precedent for all aspects of church organization and practice; and protection of the "local autonomy" of congregations. Conservatives remained suspicious of tendencies toward denominational hierarchy, encouraged unity through restoration, and embraced the identity and terminology of a "brotherhood" of Christians.

Preaching (especially that showcased at events like the North American Christian Convention) was generally biblically based, with great emphasis on "the plan of salvation," immersion for the remission of sins, and weekly communion. Both of the latter were regarded as "ordinances" (a Zwinglian legacy) and not generally as "sacraments." The historic anticlericalism of the early Stone-Campbell heritage remained intact, coupled with an increasing resistance to critical learning in some quarters, among those persons and institutions (e.g., the early Bible colleges) sharply reacting to the snares of liberalism and modernism. R. C. Foster of the Cincinnati Bible Seminary was a classic case in point.

Generally in this early period, however, there was not a complete break with more liberal Disciples, even while conservative leaders were fully aware of mounting polarization at a variety of ideological and institutional levels. Moderate conservatives (Frederick Kershner, Dean E. Walker, et al.) looked still for conciliation and were encouraged by the work of the Commission on Restudy of the Disciples of Christ in the 1940s, and by the new theological movement of neo-orthodoxy. Even the moderates, however, were deeply concerned over the drift of mainline Protestant theology in the United States and rallied in support of a high Christology, a high view of substitutionary atonement, and affirmation of the bodily resurrection from the dead.

2.3.2. The Second Generation (1945-1960) After World War II, anti-liberal and separatist tendencies intensified. More Bible colleges were established, and the *Christian Standard* in the years 1947-50 led a vigorous campaign against the more liberal Disciples institutions, thought, and leaders. Bible colleges reasserted a model of ministerial education that was biblically centered yet resistant to discussion of current theological trends. Yet some schools, becoming more conscious of the need for academic credibility, began to move toward some form of accreditation.

Doctrinally, there was continuing emphasis on the restoration "plea." The same emphasis on the "ordinances" continued, with vigorous rejection of open membership (receiving unimmersed members by transfer). The salvation of even the "pious unimmersed" (those sprinkled as infants who nonetheless manifested a faith commitment and church involvement) was occasionally brought into question. Many in the conservative Christian Churches embraced the doctrine of the plenary verbal inspiration and "inerrancy" of Scripture, and maintained that such was thoroughly consistent with the understanding of biblical authority of the early founders of the Stone-Campbell Movement.

For the most part, conservatives looked on the ecumenical movement as an aberration, and some even debated whether ministers could in good conscience participate in local ministerial associations. "Independents" saw the collective efforts of congregations in restoring the apostolic order as the only means to unity. Some, however, like the highly visible James DeForest Murch, former head of the Christian Restoration Association (est. 1925) and one of the founders of the National Association of Evangelicals, looked favorably at the prospect of forming an alternative coalition, a broad conservative-evangelical ecumenism.

Conservative churches spurned the "social gospel" cherished by liberals in the Movement. Attempts to influence legislative or social policy were confined to local issues and local activism. The older cultural conservatism remained largely intact: for example, suspicion of much of modern science and psychology, rejection of the use of tobacco and alcoholic beverages and, in many cases, resistance to dancing and to attending movies.

2.3.3. The Third Generation: Interchange with Evangelicalism and Readjustment of Identity (Since 1960) "Reinventing" the Stone-Campbell plea in the twentieth century was an initiative not only of liberals on the left but also of conservatives on the theological right. Though some arch-conservatives would not tolerate any common cause with outsiders to the Stone-Campbell heritage, other constituents of Christian Churches/Churches of Christ (following the lead of James DeForest Murch) assumed a kinship with evangelicals and aspired to align their "Restoration Movement" identity within the mainstream of American evangelicalism. Despite the fact that the core of evangelical theology in America has been the Reformed (Calvinist) heritage, there were antecedent compatibilities with Stone-Campbell conservatives, including the strong emphasis on the authority and inspiration of the Bible, concern to safeguard basic Christian doctrines like the deity of Christ and the atonement, commitment to evangelism and the development of ever more sophisticated evangelistic strategies, suspicion of the potential compromises of involvement in the ecumenical movement, and so on.

Common cause with the evangelical mainstream has often manifested itself less in theological dialogue than in the pragmatic sharing of ideas and methods for evangelism, church growth, discipleship, worship, and spiritual life. The forums for such interaction have been manifold: for example, sharing of publications (e.g., popular books, Sunday School literature, college textbooks on ministry and mission, pastoral resources, etc.); joint participation in organizations (e.g., Billy Graham ministries, National Association of Evangelicals, the Pro-Life movement, etc.); interchange on "contemporary" worship modes and resources; and the pursuit of doctoral degrees in evangelical seminaries by Bible college faculty members. Interface with the larger religious culture of American evangelicalism is clearly evident in the programs of the North American Christian Convention over the last two decades.

Such interchange has, often unconsciously and without orchestration, led to modification of commitments once cherished by conservatives in the Christian Churches/Churches of Christ — to the approval of some and the displeasure of others. Though many would still affirm in principle that conversion is a matter of rational assent to the Word of God, there has been a recognizable softening of the hard line on the restricted role of the Holy Spirit in conversion. The churches across the board practice "close" membership (requiring immersion of the believer for admission to the church), but in some instances are less likely to promote immersion as an "ordinance" of the New Testament than as part of the conversion "experience." In worship services, the Lord's Supper is observed weekly, but its significance and centrality in some churches has inevitably been overshadowed by the strong emphasis on preaching and the evangelistic momentum of other aspects of worship. By and large, preaching in the Christian Churches/Churches of Christ is far less likely to be focused on historic themes of the "Restoration plea" than was the case in the early and mid-twentieth century.

A certain emphasis on the evangelical "social gospel" is also in evidence, as many churches have reversed their positions on medical missions and even begun to invest in urban ministry and missions to ethnic minorities. In their missionary commitments, Christian Churches/Churches of Christ are increasingly aware of the challenges of cross-cultural communication and have produced a number of respected missiologists and Bible translators. The passion across the board for world mission has had the positive effect of broadening the worldview of many conservative churches.

Finally, there is decreasing interest in the controversies and bitterness of previous generations. With some this is, negatively, the result of an increasing lack of awareness of, or interest in, their churches' roots in the Stone-Campbell heritage. With others it is, positively, indicative of a desire for renewed communication and reconciliation with the other branches of the Stone-Campbell Movement, as evidenced by the Restoration Forums (with Churches of Christ) and the more recent Stone-Campbell Dialogue with representatives of all three streams of the Movement.

In sum, this constituency has seen some movement away from its early countercultural "sectarian" stance to a pragmatic evangelicalism still separate from American "mainline" Protestantism. There is nevertheless considerable diversity in the theological and practical dispositions of the Christian Churches/ Churches of Christ vis-à-vis their Stone-Campbell identity. There are still churches (and colleges) — many of them located in Ohio, Iowa, Missouri, West Virginia, and central Florida — that remain strongly attached to the "Old Paths" and guard their loyalty to a literal restoration of the apostolic order. These churches hold to what they see as a traditional Stone-Campbell theology and align their evangelistic and missionary commitments accordingly.

Other churches (and colleges), which might well be deemed "evangelical pragmatics," rarely suggest that the Stone-Campbell Movement merely sink into the landscape of mainstream American evangelicalism, but they do exploit common ideological and methodological ground with evangelical denominations. This may be the fastest-growing "school of thought" in Christian Churches/Churches.

Finally, there is, albeit a small minority, a network of churches and academic institutions (viz., Milligan College and Emmanuel School of Religion) that have identified theologically with the "first generation" moderates and willingly embrace the label "classical Disciples" or "old conservative Disciples." This group, while theologically conservative, identifies with a more sacramental view of the church and of baptism and the Lord's Supper and is generally more open to prospective ecumenical interaction. It is also more positively disposed toward historic formularies like the Nicene and Apostles' Creeds and the Chalcedonian Definition, though it would not turn any of these into a test of fellowship.

On the whole, Christian Churches/Churches of Christ across the board would insist on certain doctrinal standards as properly basic to the integrity of the church and its faith, though they remain for the most part anti-creedal. Most constituents would affirm the Trinity, but they desire to adhere to biblical language in doing so. All would assert the full divinity of Jesus Christ; the reality of his incarnation, death, resurrection, and coming in judgment; and the promise of eternal life. Most would assert that baptism is pivotal in the overarching process of conversion and regeneration, though some would deny that salvation hinges on the immersion of believers or on anything other than the grace of Jesus Christ himself.

Though thematic studies have appeared (e.g., the College Press Series, *What the Bible Says About . . .*), systematic theological works are few and far between from scholars of the Christian Churches/Churches of Christ. Their constructive theology as such has largely been articulated in biblical commentaries and sermons, many of which (like those published by College Press and by Standard Publishing) aim at appealing more to popular audiences than to scholarly guilds and often depend substantially on an "inductive" and evidentiary exegesis.

PAUL M. BLOWERS *and* G. RICHARD PHILLIPS

See also Anthropology; Atonement; Baptism; Bible, Authority and Inspiration of the; Bible, Interpretation of the; Calvinism; Christian Church (Disciples of Christ); Christian Churches/Churches of Christ; Christology; Church, Doctrine of the; Churches of Christ; Common Sense Philosophy; Covenant (Federal) Theology; Creeds and Confessions; Dispensations; Eschatology; Evangelical; Fundamentalism; Five Finger Exercise; God, Doctrine of; *Gospel Restored, The;* Grace, Doctrine of; Hermeneutics; Holy Spirit, Doctrine of the; Justification, Doctrine of; Liberalism; Locke, John; Rationalism; Regeneration; "Restoration," Meanings of within the Movement; Salvation; *Scheme of Redemption, The;* "Sermon on the Law"; "Synopsis of the Faith"

BIBLIOGRAPHY Nineteenth Century

Paul M. Blowers, "Neither Calvinists nor Arminians, but Simply Christians: The Stone-Campbell Movement as a Theological Resistance Movement," *Lexington Theological Quarterly* 35 (2000): 133-54 • M. Eugene Boring, *Disciples and the Bible: A History of Disciples Biblical Interpretation in North America* (1997) • James O. Duke, "The Nineteenth Century Reformation in Historical-Theological Perspective: The First One Hundred Years," in *Christian Faith Seeking Historical Understanding: Essays in Honor of H. Jack Forstman,* ed. James O. Duke and Anthony L. Dunnavant (1997), pp. 159-86 • James O. Duke, "Scholarship in the Disciples Tradition," *Disciples Theological Digest* 1 (1986):

5-40 • Anthony L. Dunnavant, Richard T. Hughes, and Paul M. Blowers, *Founding Vocation and Future Vision: The Self-Understanding of the Disciples of Christ and Churches of Christ* (1999) • J. H. Garrison, ed., *The Old Faith Restated* (1891) • W. E. Garrison, *Alexander Campbell's Theology: Its Sources and Historical Setting* (1900) • Kenneth Lawrence, ed., *Classic Themes of Disciples Theology: Rethinking the Traditional Affirmations of the Christian Church (Disciples of Christ)* (1986) • Robert Milligan, *The Scheme of Redemption* (1868) • Ronald E. Osborn, "Theology Among the Disciples," in *The Christian Church (Disciples of Christ): An Interpretative Examination in the Cultural Context,* ed. George Beazley (1973), pp. 81-115 • Frederick West, *Alexander Campbell and Natural Religion* (1948) • D. Newell Williams, *Barton Stone: A Spiritual Biography* (2000).

BIBLIOGRAPHY Twentieth Century — Christian Church (Disciples of Christ)

Edward Scribner Ames, *The New Orthodoxy* (1918) • George G. Beazley, Jr., ed., *The Christian Church (Disciples of Christ): An Interpretative Examination in the Cultural Context* (1973) • W. B. Blakemore, ed., *The Renewal of Church: The Panel of Scholars Reports* (1963) • M. Eugene Boring, *Disciples and the Bible: A History of Disciples Biblical Interpretation in North America* (1997) • James O. Duke, "Scholarship in the Disciples Tradition," *Disciples Theological Digest* 1 (1986): 5-40 • Joe R. Jones, *A Grammar of Christian Faith,* 2 vols. (2002) • Kenneth Lawrence, ed., *Classic Themes of Disciples Theology: Rethinking the Traditional Affirmations of the Christian Church (Disciples of Christ)* (1986) • L. Dale Richesin and Larry D. Bouchard, eds., *Interpreting Disciples: Practical Theology in the Disciples of Christ* (1987) • D. Newell Williams, ed., *A Case Study of Mainstream Protestantism: The Disciples Relation to American Culture, 1880-1989* (1991) • Clark Williamson, *Way of Blessing, Way of Life* (1999).

BIBLIOGRAPHY Twentieth Century — Churches of Christ

C. Leonard Allen, *The Cruciform Church* (1990) • C. Leonard Allen and Danny Gray Swick, *Participating in God's Life: Two Crossroads for Churches of Christ* (2001) • T. W. Brents, *The Gospel Plan of Salvation* (1874; 9th ed. 1890) • Leroy Brownlow, *Why I Am a Member of the Church of Christ* (1945) • Roy E. Cogdill, *The New Testament Church* (1938) • Everett Ferguson, *The Church of Christ: A Biblical Ecclesiology for Today* (1996) • Gary Holloway, Randall J. Harris, and Mark C. Black, *Theology Matters* (1998) • David Lipscomb, *Salvation from Sin* (1913) • Robert Milligan, *The Scheme of Redemption* (1868) • Rubel Shelly and Randall J. Harris, *The Second Incarnation: A Theology for the 21st Century Church* (1992).

BIBLIOGRAPHY Twentieth Century — Christian Churches/Churches of Christ

Paul M. Blowers, "Keeping the 'Current Reformation' Current: The Challenge of Ongoing Self-Interpretation in the Stone-Campbell Tradition," in *Founding Vocation and Future Vision: The Self-Understanding of the Disciples of Christ and Churches of Christ* (1999) • C. J. Dull, "Intellectual Factions and Groupings in the Independent Christian Churches," *The [Cincinnati Bible] Seminary Review* 31 (1985): 91-118 • Kevin Kragenbrink, "The Modernist/Fundamentalist Controversy and the Emergence of the Independent Christian Churches/Churches of Christ," *Restoration Quarterly* 42 (2000): 1-17 • Byron Lambert, "From Rural Churches to an Urban World: Shifting Frontiers and the Invisible Hand," *Discipliana* 55 (1995): 67-80 • G. Richard Phillips, "From Modern Theology to a Post-Modern World: Christian Churches and Churches of Christ," *Discipliana* 54 (1994): 83-95 • William Richardson, ed., *Christian Doctrine: "The Faith Once Delivered . . ."* (1983) • C. Robert Wetzel, "Christian Churches/Churches of Christ at 2001: In Search of a Theological Center," *Stone-Campbell Journal* 4 (2001): 3-12.

Thomas, John (1805-1871)

Protagonist of a controversial school of thought on the theology and practice of baptism for the remission of sins; often considered one of the first "heretics" or schismatics in the history of the Stone-Campbell Movement.

Born in London and a physician by vocation, Thomas immigrated to America in 1832. He first settled in Cincinnati, where he made the acquaintance of Major Daniel Gano, as well as Walter Scott, who soon baptized Thomas. Shortly thereafter, the young doctor spent a month at Bethany with Alexander Campbell. Thomas's talent and enthusiasm greatly impressed Campbell. Soon he was preaching, first in Philadelphia and later in Richmond, Virginia. In 1834 he initiated a religious journal, the *Apostolic Advocate.* Campbell was at first cautiously supportive, describing the editor as "a talented, devoted, and zealous disciple." Yet the opinionated Thomas concentrated his writings on speculative issues. Campbell felt obligated to address these doctrinal differences in the *Millennial Harbinger.* A sharp division developed between the two men, with Thomas taking offense and Campbell concluding that "my brother Thomas has fallen upon evil times." Thomas treated his views as tests of fellowship. His insistence on these speculative ideas was the crux of the division, rather than the mere difference of opinion. Fearful of the influence Thomas might have on new converts, Campbell printed a twelve-page supplement to the *Millennial Harbinger* in December 1837, detailing their doctrinal differences, characterizing Thomas as "a factionalist of the most indomitable spirit" and an "infallible dogmatist . . . supremely devoted to his own opinions."

The first point of disagreement grew out of differences regarding baptism. Both men believed that baptism was for the remission of sins. Yet Thomas concluded that Baptist converts to the Movement must be reimmersed, since they were generally baptized as recognition that remission had already occurred. The Stone-Campbell Christians did not believe or practice this, and Thomas's implementation of rebaptism brought a swift and potent response from Campbell. Some historians have theorized that Thomas or one of his supporters was the author of the famous "Lunenburg Letter" sent to Campbell in 1837, soliciting him to clarify his views on the status of unimmersed Christians. According to this view, the letter was actually an attempt to entrap Campbell into waffling on the issue of the necessity of immersion for the remission of sins.

Other differences soon surfaced as well. Thomas exhibited a fascination with Old Testament prophecies, the book of Revelation, and eschatological questions. He confidently claimed to have solved "certain problems in the Apocalypse, which had hitherto baffled . . . the most celebrated illuminati of the religious world." This premillennial theorizing, coupled with his doctrine of "soul sleeping," placed Thomas at odds with Stone-Campbell orthodoxy.

An arranged meeting between Campbell and Thomas occurred in 1838, though it failed to resolve their differences. By 1844 the doctor had pulled his Richmond congregation away from the Disciples. He named his movement the Brethren in Christ, or Christadelphians. While his followers remained few in number, Thomas's personal attacks on Campbell did much damage to the cause in Virginia. One observer noted that he "threw a pall over the church not lifted for twenty years."

In 1848 Thomas traveled to England, seeking to enlist converts from among the Disciples there. In 1849 he published his most noted work, *Elpis Israel.* His epitaph credits Thomas with making "manifest the nature of The Long-Lost Faith of the Apostles." The Thomas controversy presaged an 1880s conflict among Churches of Christ, with editor Austin McGary of Texas advocating rebaptism of Baptists and David Lipscomb refuting the position.

See also Baptism; Heresy, Heretics; Lunenburg Letter, The

BIBLIOGRAPHY Alexander Campbell, "Re-Immersion and Brother Thomas," *Millennial Harbinger* (1835): 565-67 • Alexander Campbell, "Extra," *Millennial Harbinger* (1837): 575-88 • John Mark Hicks, "Alexander Campbell on Christians Among the Sects," in *Baptism and the Remission of Sins: An Historical Perspective,* ed. David W. Fletcher (1990), pp. 171-202 • Joseph R. Jeter, Jr., "Some We Lost: A Study of Disaffections from the Disciples of Christ," *Discipliana* 61 (2001): 9-11 • Robert Roberts, *Dr. Thomas: His Life & Work* (1873). TERRY COWAN

Thorp Spring Christian College

School identified with Churches of Christ that operated in Hood County, Texas, from 1910 to 1928. Presidents who served were A. W. Young, R. C. Bell, C. R. Nichol, W. F. Ledlow, C. H. Hale, A. R. Holton, C. H. Roberson, and U. R. Forrest. The college was a significant factor in the growth and proliferation of Churches of Christ in Texas.

Thorp Spring Christian College was the last of several schools in tiny Thorp Spring, Texas. Thorp College (1871) sold out to Fort Worth evangelist and businessman Joseph Addison Clark (1815-1901) and his sons Addison (1841-1911) and Randolph (1844-1935), who established AddRan Male and Female Academy in 1873. This school was among the first coeducational efforts in the American Southwest operated by members of the Stone-Campbell Movement. The Clarks secured a charter from the state and the endorsement of Christian Churches. In 1888-89 the Texas Christian Missionary Society assumed ownership of the college under the Clarks' administration. The school grew to a record enrollment of 445 in 1893-94.

A February 1894 incident at AddRan College proved incendiary to the Stone-Campbell Movement in Texas when Addison Clark granted the request of students to use an organ at an evangelistic meeting. The instrument controversy had been simmering in Texas churches for years. As recently as October 26, 1893, Joseph Addison Clark had decried the encroachment of such "innovations" in a *Gospel Advocate* article. At a February 20, 1894, evangelistic meeting, with Addison Clark presiding and an organist poised at the keyboard, the father presented the son a petition opposing the instrument. Addison Clark, who would not renege on a promise, ignited a new era in the Texas churches with his words to the organist, "Play on, Miss Bertha." Seventy-eight-year-old J. A. Clark led about 140 people out of the hall.

Texas churches divided over the issue that had come to such a dramatic head in Thorp Spring. Instrumentalists generally identified themselves as "Christian Churches," while a cappella congregations used the name "Churches of Christ." The immediate effect at AddRan College was a precipitous drop in enrollment, evidently because the organ decision alienated a significant constituency. In 1895-96 AddRan moved to Waco, and in 1910 to Fort Worth as Texas Christian University.

Randolph Clark had retained the Thorp Spring property to run the Jarvis Institute and AddRan-Jarvis College, but on March 1, 1910, a group representing noninstrumental churches bought AddRan-Jarvis and chartered Thorp Spring Christian College. President A. W. Young promised to "protect the school from innovations in doctrine and worship."

The school opened with 150 students on September 14, 1910, and later gained accreditation as a junior college. In 1921 President A. R. Holton added Jewell Watson to his administration as dean, probably the first such appointment of a woman in colleges affiliated with Churches of Christ. Thorp Spring boasted nearly 300 students in 1916 but suffered decline as the World War I draft took many men away. The war, the rural setting, and competition from other colleges led to the decision of President U. R. Forrest to relocate to Terrell, Texas, in 1929. Under the name Texas Christian College, the school survived only one term.

See also Texas Christian University

BIBLIOGRAPHY M. Norvel Young, "Thorp Spring Christian College and Its Predecessors, 1873-1930," in *A History of Colleges Established by Members of the Churches of Christ* (1949), pp. 68-81.

THEODORE N. THOMAS

Tickle, Gilbert Young (1819-1888)

Church leader and prolific hymn writer for the British Churches of Christ in the nineteenth century.

G. Y. Tickle was born in Maryport, England, on June 30, 1819, and served a six-year apprenticeship in the drapery business in Carlisle from 1833. He was baptized in 1838 and moved to Liverpool in 1839, joining his father in business and at the Scotch Baptist church. Peter Woodnorth, a commercial traveler and friend of his father, discovered Campbell's writings through Robert Tener in Ireland. In 1843 Woodnorth, Tickle, and others formed the first Church of Christ in Liverpool, assisted by William Haigh of Huddersfield. Tickle chaired the Lancashire Evangelist Committee for six years and the General Evangelist Committee from 1861 until 1888; he was one of those behind the planting of the church in Manchester in 1855. He was chairman of the Annual Meeting in 1859, 1860, 1866, 1867, 1871, 1872, and 1880 — more than anyone else — and delivered three important Conference papers.

As editor of the *Christian Advocate* (1879-88) he was graceful and charitable, but his convictions were as firm as those of David King, and his leadership was probably more widely recognized and highly regarded. Tickle was the main correspondent with the American churches over the communion question, first in 1861 and later with William Linn and David King; he was offended by the formation of the separate Christian Association. Tickle was the greatest hymn writer among British Churches of Christ. Most were metrical psalms, but several of his communion hymns are still treasured. He and King revised the hymnbook in 1888. He published a metrical version of John's Gospel in 1874 and also versified Matthew and Acts. Tickle's social concern was expressed especially in relation to slavery and teetotalism, and he strongly supported the Temperance Meeting. When he died in Liverpool on April 21, 1888, Lancelot Oliver wrote, "Whoever sowed seeds of division and difficulty, he strove to preserve the unity of the Spirit in the bond of peace."

See also Great Britain and Ireland, Churches of Christ in; Hymnody; King, David

BIBLIOGRAPHY *Churches of Christ Year Book* (1888), pp. 86-91 • Obituaries in the *Christian Advocate* (1888): 221-31.

DAVID M. THOMPSON

Todd, Sir Garfield (1908-2002) and Lady Grace (1911-2001)

Reginald Stephen Garfield Todd and Jean Grace Isobel Wilson Todd were sent as missionaries to the Dadaya mission in Southern Rhodesia by the New Zealand Churches of Christ in 1934. Garfield, named after U.S. President James A. Garfield, became the first missionary to become a head of state when he was named prime minister of Southern Rhodesia in 1953. Educated at Glen Leith Theological College in Dunedin, Todd adopted the view of the principal A. L. Haddon that life was a unity from God and should not be divided into the secular and the sacred. Todd saw his political career as an extension of his Christianity. First elected to parliament in 1946, Todd became an advocate for modest improvements for black Africans in education, jobs, and voting rights and was known for his outstanding eloquence as a speaker.

Grace Todd, trained as a teacher in New Zealand, developed an educational curriculum for Dadaya that was adopted by secular and mission schools across Rhodesia, enabling Zimbabwe to have one of the highest literacy rates of all Africa. The Dadaya Mission became a place where most twentieth-century African leaders of Zimbabwe either studied as students or worked as teachers.

After Todd was removed as prime minister in 1958 for moving too quickly for African rights, he turned radical and began to speak out against the racist establishment and to argue for black majority rule. In 1962, 1964, and 1977 Todd delivered important speeches before the United Nations on behalf of the African nationalist cause. Fearing Todd's eloquence, in 1965 at Rhodesia's Unilateral Declaration of Independence from Britain, Ian Smith put Todd under house arrest on Todd's ranch for a year. In January 1972, after Todd and his daughter Judith had successfully campaigned against an agreement Smith made with Britain that would have kept Smith in power, Todd was arrested, imprisoned for thirty-six days, and then restricted to his ranch until June 1976. Todd was not allowed to communicate with anyone directly, so Grace wrote all letters to the outside world. All through the 1970s, at considerable risk, the Todds supported the Africans in the civil war. After Zimbabwe's independence in 1980 Todd was a senator in Robert Mugabe's government, but he retired in 1985 and grew critical of Mugabe's repressive tactics.

Todd delivered the Peter Ainsley Memorial lecture on unity, June 1955, in Pietermaritzburg, South Africa; a 1961 Willam Henry Hoover Lecture on Christian Unity in Chicago; and four lectures before the World Convention of Churches of Christ (1955, 1960, 1970, 1988). A British missionary in the 1970s described Todd as "an electrifying speaker" who "made the pages of the Bible come alive as he preached on the oneness of all people — black, brown, and white — in Jesus Christ."

Todd won honorary doctorates from Butler University, Eureka College, and Otago University. He won a papal medal from Pope Paul VI in 1973 and was knighted by Queen Elizabeth II in 1986 for his services to New Zealand and to Africa.

See also Africa, Missions in; New Zealand, The Movement in

BIBLIOGRAPHY David Chanaiwa, "The Premiership of Garfield Todd in Rhodesia: Racial Partnership Versus Colonial Interests," *Journal of Southern African Affairs* (1976): 83-94 • Richard Driver and Alison Landon, *Hokonui Todd* [videotape recording] (c. 1990) • Dickson A. Mungazi, *The Last British Liberals in Africa: Michael Blundell and Garfield Todd* (1999) • Ruth Weiss, *Sir Garfield Todd and the Making of Zimbabwe* (1999) • Michael O. West, "Ndabaningi Sithole, Garfield Todd and the Dadaya School Strike of 1947," *Journal of Southern African Studies* 18 (June 1992): 297-316.

MICHAEL W. CASEY

Touchstone, The

Conservative magazine published by Standard Publishing Company, Cincinnati, Ohio, from October 1925 until January 1927, edited by Robert E. Elmore.

In the increasingly bitter feuding between more conservative and more liberal constituencies of the Disciples of Christ in the early 1920s over the United Christian Missionary Society (UCMS), a number of points of friction came into focus: theological liberalism in schools, churches, and other agencies of the Disciples of Christ; open membership on the mission field and official attempts to cover up such instances; comity agreements agreed to by mission societies; and heavy-handed efforts by UCMS officials to stifle all criticism. The *Christian Standard* had long waged these battles, but in September 1925 Standard Publishing launched a new monthly magazine to carry on this attack. The first issue was called *The Spotlight*, but that name was already used by a petroleum publication. The second issue appeared under the title *The Touchstone*. The facts presented in the magazine are still highly susceptible to interpretation by both sides, but no one doubts that the magazine was a vitriolic piece of yellow journalism. The UCMS responded in kind with *The UCMS News*.

See also *Christian Standard;* Elmore, Robert Emmett; Fundamentalism; *Restoration Herald, The;* Standard Publishing Company

BIBLIOGRAPHY Stephen J. Corey, *Fifty Years of Attack and Controversy: The Consequences Among Disciples of Christ* (1953).

JAMES B. NORTH

Tougaloo College

Historically related to the Christian Church (Disciples of Christ).

Southern Christian College came into existence in 1954 when Tougaloo College (related to the Congregational Christian Churches) and Southern Christian Institute (related to the Disciples of Christ) merged into one educational institution. The new school continued the religious and social traditions of both religious bodies. In 1963, with the agreement of both founding bodies, the name was changed to Tougaloo College.

Tougaloo College was created as a school for African Americans freed after the Civil War. It was founded by the American Missionary Association, which, with the assistance of the Freedmen's Bureau, directed its efforts toward education of former slaves. A five-hundred-acre plantation near the fork of two streams, named Tougaloo, situated a few miles north of Jackson, Mississippi, was purchased by the Association in 1869. A charter was obtained from the state of Mississippi in 1871 under the name Tougaloo University. As in other schools of the era, students typically began their studies in the institution's preparatory school. The first college-level courses were offered in 1897, and its first college graduate received a degree in 1901. In 1965 George Owens became Tougaloo's first alumnus to hold the presidential office.

Tougaloo College continues as a center of learning, offering bachelor's degrees in various fields. Besides its historically significant teacher education program, fields of study now include law, medicine, engineering, and other graduate courses, as well as joint programs with other colleges and universities.

See also African Americans in the Movement; Southern Christian Institute

BIBLIOGRAPHY James D. Anderson, *The Education of the Blacks in the South, 1860-1935* (1988) • Clarice T. Campbell and Oscar Allan Rogers, Jr., *Mississippi: The View from Tougaloo* (1979) • Dwight Oliver Wendell Holmes, *The*

Evolution of the Negro College (1969) • Joe M. Richardson, *Christian Reconstruction: The American Missionary Association and Southern Blacks, 1861-1890* (1986).

CANDACE WOOD

Transylvania University

Related to the Christian Church (Disciples of Christ).

Located in Lexington, Kentucky, Transylvania has included a number of distinct institutions, several with significance for the Stone-Campbell Movement. Chartered in 1780 by the Virginia Assembly to encourage education on the Kentucky frontier, Transylvania began with a grant of 8,000 acres confiscated from British loyalists. Beginning in February 1785, classes were conducted in the cabin of Presbyterian minister David Rice at Danville, the first capital of the Commonwealth of Kentucky. The following year the school moved to Lexington, meeting in the home of James Moore, rector of the city's first Episcopal church. In 1793 the school moved to its location near Gratz Park, merging with a competing Presbyterian academy. By 1799 Transylvania had added the first law and medical departments in the West to its liberal arts department. Over the next half-century the school attracted faculty of national repute, including Henry Clay, Horace Holley, Daniel Drake, Benjamin Dudley, and Constantin Rafinesque. Its graduates included Jefferson Davis, Albert Sidney Johnston, and notables including governors, senators, and two vice presidents. In 1833 noted Kentucky architect Gideon Shryock completed the neoclassical Morrison Hall, which remains the centerpiece of the campus in the twenty-first century.

By the Civil War, however, Transylvania had declined, closing its medical and law departments. Union troops used the campus as a hospital. In 1865 it was revived in part by merging with another institution, Kentucky University. The resulting merger was called Kentucky University, and it included the Transylvania liberal arts department, the newly chartered state Agricultural and Mechanical College, a revived law department, and the College of the Bible.

The College of the Bible traced its origins to Georgetown College, where the controversy over Campbellism in the 1820s led to the establishment of a rival institution, Bacon College, named for Francis Bacon, credited in the charter as the father of the inductive method of reasoning and the new science. By 1840 it became apparent that Georgetown could not support two colleges. Bacon College moved to Harrodsburg, in Mercer County, Kentucky, where it remained until the Civil War when its campus was destroyed. Following the war, a remnant of Bacon College's faculty and students moved to Lexington, becoming part of Kentucky University. Some of Bacon's female students remained in Harrodsburg as a part of Daughters College, operated for a time by Stone-Campbell preacher John Augustus Williams, known for his biography of "Raccoon" John Smith.

Among those instrumental in the development of Bacon College and its postwar amalgamation as Kentucky University was a Mercer County farmer, John Bryan Bowman. The Kentucky legislature legalized the fusion of the institutions at Lexington. With Bowman as a regent, Kentucky University flourished for a few years, reviving the law department and establishing the College of the Bible. The state placed its new Agricultural and Mechanical College under the administration of Kentucky University. Controversy with president John W. McGarvey led to Bowman's resignation in 1878, when the College of the Bible became a separate legal entity funded by (and with property owned by) churches – though it remained on the Transylvania campus until 1949. The Agricultural and Mechanical College later was removed by state action to a new campus on the south end of Lexington. In 1889 Kentucky University became coeducational and added many of the aspects of modern education, including fraternities, sororities, and intercollegiate athletics. Functioning as a small liberal arts college with strong Disciples control until 1908, it resumed its historic name of Transylvania when the growing A&M College became State University (now the University of Kentucky) on a cross-town campus.

In 1908 Richard Henry Crossfield became president of Transylvania University. On the death of J. W. McGarvey, Crossfield proposed that the presidencies of Transylvania and the College of the Bible be merged. Crossfield had graduated from Kentucky University in 1892, in the same class with Hall L. Calhoun, McGarvey's hand-picked successor. After making the suggestion of a merged presidency, Crossfield offered his resignation. To prevent this, the board instead offered the combined office to Crossfield. While the details are shrouded in institutional intrigue, apparently rivalry between the former classmates led to an attempt at power consolidation from which Crossfield emerged the winner. This eventually contributed to a conflict between conservatives and liberals at the College of the Bible that ended in Calhoun's departure.

As a liberal arts college, Transylvania suffered recurring financial crises from 1910 to 1940, and by World War II it was near collapse. However, a strong postwar revival due to the influx of veterans under the G.I. bill, and the avid fund-raising and generosity of a succession of administrations, patrons, and donors, strengthened the school tremendously. By 1950 postwar growth had launched Transylvania on its current trajectory as a selective and widely recognized liberal arts college. In 1950 the College of the Bible moved to a new campus across from what is now the University of Kentucky Law school, changing its name to Lexington Theological Seminary, which continues to train ministers for the Christian Church (Disciples of Christ) and other denominations.

See also Bacon College; Calhoun, Hall Laurie; Lexington Theological Seminary; McGarvey, John W.

BIBLIOGRAPHY Richard L. Harrison, Jr., "Disciples Theological Formation: From College of the Bible to Theological Seminary," in *A Case Study of Mainstream Protestantism: The Disciples' Relation to American Culture, 1880-1989,* ed. D. Newell Williams (1991), pp. 281-98 • Richard M. Pope, *The College of the Bible: A Brief Narrative* (1961) • Dwight E. Stevenson, *Lexington Theological Seminary, 1865-1965* (1964) • John D. Wright, Jr., *Transylvania: Tutor to the West* (1980). JAMES STEPHEN WOLFGANG

Trinity

See God, Doctrine of

Trout, Jessie M. (1895-1990)

Missionary, administrator, and co-founder of the Christian Women's Fellowship for the Disciples of Christ in the twentieth century.

Jessie M. Trout was born in Canada in 1895. A missionary in Japan for approximately twenty years, she served most notably from 1935 to 1940 as a co-worker in Kagawa, Japan, part of an ecumenical program supported by the Disciples that was an entirely indigenous effort. During World War II, she returned to the United States and served as national *World Call* secretary.

At that time women did not have a national umbrella for their church work. Sensing the need for coordinated efforts, Jessie Trout invited the state women's organization leaders to Turkey Run State Park in Indiana, January 8-17, 1949. Thanks to her organizational skills and emphasis on Bible study and prayer, seventy-five women met and laid the groundwork for the Christian Women's Fellowship. The purpose of the new organization, officially founded on July 1, 1950, was to develop all women in Christian living and Christian service. The organizational structure included departments of study, worship, and service, and the first Quadrennial was held in 1857. Trout became the chief executive of the new organization, also helping to found the International Christian Women's Fellowship in 1953 in Portland, Oregon. She continued her missionary work as vice president of the United Christian Missionary Society and as field liaison for the Division of World Missions until her retirement. She died in 1990.

See also Asia, Missions in; Christian Women's Fellowship; United Christian Missionary Society, The; Women in Ministry — Christian Church (Disciples of Christ) DEBRA B. HULL

Tubman, Emily H. (1794-1885)

Philanthropist within the Stone-Campbell Movement in its earliest decades.

Born Emily Harvie Thomas in Hanover County, Virginia, in 1794, she grew to maturity in prosperous circumstances in Frankfort, Kentucky. In 1818, while visiting relatives in Augusta, Georgia, 24-year-old Emily met and, after a brief courtship, married 52-year-old Richard C. Tubman (1766-1836), a wealthy planter and exporter.

Traits contributing to Mrs. Tubman's success in business matters were especially apparent following her husband's death. Richard Tubman's will, which named her sole administrator and left her in control of a substantial estate, included a bequest of $5,000 to the University of Georgia if the legislature would sanction the emancipation of slaves of the family. An additional $5,000 was designated for the slaves who would be freed. When a hostile legislative committee judged her petition "unjust and unreasonable," a determined Mrs. Tubman chose another course of action. Senator Henry Clay (1777-1852), who had been her legal guardian following her father's death, became president of the American Colonization Society in 1836. She contacted that organization and the independent Maryland State Colonization Society, pitting them against one another as she sought the best arrangements for transportation and resettlement of the forty-two slaves who accepted her offer of emancipation in Liberia. Pleased with the proposal of the Maryland society, she gave $10,000 to that organization. She continued to be responsible for the slaves who did not go to Africa. By 1860 only a blind 50-year-old slave remained.

Her giving — often $25,000 or more annually — primarily supported causes related to the Stone-Campbell Movement. Immersed by a Baptist pastor in Kentucky, Mrs. Tubman later attended the Episcopal Church with her husband, and in 1836 identified herself with the First Christian Church of Augusta. She gave funds to erect buildings for this congregation, First Christian Church of Frankfort, Kentucky, and several other churches in Georgia and Kentucky. Following a cholera epidemic in Kentucky, she supported the fledgling Midway Orphan School. Personally acquainted with Alexander Campbell, whom she hosted when he visited Augusta, she endowed a Bethany College professorship. She also supported the American Christian Missionary Society and, later, the Foreign Christian Missionary Society. Two among many other charitable interests were Augusta's first public high school for girls and the Widows House Society.

Childless and a widow for almost fifty years, Em-

A wealthy Disciples philanthropist from Augusta, Georgia, Emily Tubman strongly supported the gradual emancipation of slaves and helped fund their repatriation to Africa through the Maryland State Colonization Society.
Courtesy of the Disciples of Christ Historical Society

ily Tubman died in Augusta at the age of 91. Her will included charitable bequests totaling $195,800.

See also American Christian Missionary Society; Bethany College; Foreign Christian Missionary Society, The; Midway College; Slavery, The Movement and

BIBLIOGRAPHY Joseph Richard Bennett, "A Study of the Life and Contributions of Emily H. Tubman" (B.D. thesis, Butler University, 1958) • James M. Gifford, "Emily Tubman and the African Colonization Movement in Georgia," *Georgia Historical Quarterly* 59 (1975): 10-24 • J. Edward Moseley, *Disciples of Christ in Georgia* (1954) • Richard and Emily Tubman Papers, Rare Book, Manuscript, and Special Collections Library, Duke University.

R. EDWIN GROOVER

Twenty-First Century Christian (Twentieth Century Christian)

Magazine begun in 1938 by a group of young leaders in Churches of Christ to provide practical encouragement for Christians while consciously avoiding the doctrinal conflict often characteristic of the body's journals. The paper did, however, take a moral and theological stand on two issues in the 1970s — race and the Holy Spirit.

The idea for a new periodical for young Christians was proposed by George Benson (1898-1991), president of Harding College, in a class attended by George DeHoff (1913-1993), a student at Harding. DeHoff took the idea to James Bales (1915-1995), Woodrow Whitten (1915-1988), and M. Norvel Young (1915-1998), who were graduate students at George Peabody College in Nashville. In the spring and summer of 1938, Young invited several students to his parents' home in Nashville for planning and discussion sessions about starting a new magazine. In asking advice and support from older church leaders, Young found that many thought this was an unwise project since plans were under way to start another Christian magazine, *The Christian Leader,* in Nashville under E. W. McMillan (1889-1991). Despite discouraging realities, including the cost of publishing, Young enlisted A. C. Pullias (1910-1985), minister of the Charlotte Avenue Church of Christ; Hugh M. Tiner (1908-1981), dean of George Pepperdine College; and J. P. Sanders (1906-2002), minister of the Hillsboro Church of Christ to help promote the magazine since they were older and more widely known. George Pepperdine gave $500 to publish the first 20,000 copies, and Hugh Tiner gave Norvel Young $1 to become the first official subscriber.

Young and Sanders took the lead in promoting and writing the first issue, which appeared in October 1938. The magazine's motto was "New Testament Christianity in the Present Age." Its mission was expressed as follows: "to assist that large group of young people who are eager to know the best way of life by holding up before them always the life of the Master . . . to exalt the Bible to a place of preeminence . . . to magnify the New Testament Church distinct from every human institution . . . to assist our readers in making Christian adjustments in an unchristian world." With J. C. Moore, Jr., and Seldon Collins managing circulation and business, J. P. Sanders took the editor's position for seven years. When Moore went to the German mission field, Donald V. Miller took up the business manager role. In 1945 Norvel Young, then minister for the Broadway Church of Christ in Lubbock, Texas, took the editor's position, and James O. Baird (1920-1998), Batsell Barrett Baxter (1916-1982), and Willard Collins (b. 1915) were added to the editorial staff.

Young continued as editor — with William S. Banowsky (b. 1936) as assistant editor from 1964 to 1968 — until 1976, when Joe Barnett (b. 1933), then minister for the Broadway Church of Christ in Lubbock, Texas, became editor. Mike Cope began editing the magazine in 1986, and Prentice Meador (b. 1938) was named editor in 1992.

In 1955 *Power for Today* was born from the Twenty-first Century Christian network. It is a daily devotional guide in a smaller format. Norvel and Helen Young began this magazine to encourage family devotions as well as personal worship. They edited *Power for Today* until 1969, when Steven and Emily Lemley became associate editors and then editors in 1977. This magazine outgrew its parent, with a subscription list of 46,000 at the beginning of the twenty-first century, and an estimated readership of 150,000.

See also Bales, James David; Baxter, Batsell Barrett; Benson, George Stuart; McMillan, Edward Washington; Lipscomb University; Pepperdine University

EMILY Y. LEMLEY

Tyler, Benjamin Bushrod (1840-1922)

Widely known preacher and early historian of the Movement.

Tyler was born near Decatur, Illinois, on April 9, 1840. After attending Eureka College in Illinois, he met and began to work for evangelist J. W. Houston. His encounter with Houston drew the young Tyler into a preaching ministry. In 1864 Tyler became the minister of the Church of Christ in Charleston, Illinois. He ministered subsequently to the First Church in Louisville, the West Fifty-Sixth Street Church in New York City, and the South Broadway Christian Church in Denver. He also traveled extensively, engaging in "didactic evangelism."

Especially during his tenure in New York, Tyler made the integration of social responsibility and spiritual concern his priority. He was a leading promoter of inner-city missionary initiatives. He was also one of the Movement's most notable advocates for women's suffrage.

For ten years he wrote a weekly column, entitled "The New York Letter," for the *Christian Standard*. Tyler became a founding member of the Foreign Christian Missionary Society in 1874. In 1882 he presided over the meeting of the American Christian Missionary Society. In 1894 Tyler became the first to endeavor a comprehensive history of the Movement (*A History of the Disciples of Christ*).

Tyler's contributions outside the Movement were notable as well. He served for thirteen years on the Board of Managers of the American Bible Society. He was elected to the Executive Committee of the International Sunday School Convention in 1880 and became its president in 1902.

See also Historiography, Stone-Campbell Movement

BIBLIOGRAPHY John T. Brown, ed., *Churches of Christ: A Historical, Biographical, and Pictorial History of Churches of Christ in the United States, Australia, England, and Canada* (1904), pp. 468-70.

TIMOTHY C. SMITH

U

Unified Promotion

The first common mission funding organization of the Disciples of Christ, established in 1935. It resulted from the proliferation of Disciples mission organizations and the intense competition among them for funding from the churches. By 1923 fifteen special promotional Sundays had been established and requests to congregations for mission funding were unabated.

During the 1931 International Convention, Disciples called for a Conference on Promotion that included state secretaries, presidents of Disciples-related colleges, and heads of mission boards and other agencies. A directive was given to find a unified plan. A plan was presented to the 1934 International Convention. Acting on the approval of a resolution submitted by congregations to the 1935 International Convention, the Convention's Commission on Budgets and Promotional Relationships convened a meeting of agency board representatives in April 1935. By action of the board representatives, Unified Promotion began operations on July 1, 1935. In the words of Spencer Austin, "The entire idea of unified promotion was seen as a response to pressures from congregations and local church leadership which desired a more statesmanlike, more Christian, more equitable and more effective way of financing the God-given mission of the Church, locally, regionally, nationally, and globally."

Unified Promotion proved effective in increasing overall Disciples giving to its cooperating boards and agencies, thus fulfilling its assignment "to instruct, to encourage and to inspire our people concerning the total Christian enterprise." In 1974, after nearly forty years of service, Unified Promotion was replaced in the restructured Christian Church (Disciples of Christ) by the Church Finance Council.

See also Church Finance Council

BIBLIOGRAPHY Spencer Austin, "Unified Devotion: A Fifty Year Struggle," *Discipliana* 45:1 (1985): 3-6, 13.

LOIS ARTIS

Unitarians

American religious movement critical of traditional constructions of trinitarian orthodoxy and devoted to a piety that emphasized the goodness of human nature and the immanence of God.

The American Unitarian Association was formed in Boston in 1825 after years of controversies over Calvinism within the Congregationalist (originally Puritan) churches. A century earlier Arminian views emerged and religious leaders in eastern Massachusetts grew more open to the broadly Arminian, Deistic, and rationalistic views emanating from England and Germany. The Trinitarian Congregationalists founded Andover Theological Seminary in 1808 to counter the growing Unitarian influence at Harvard. Harvard Divinity School, founded in 1819, became the chief center for training Unitarian ministers. Noted early Unitarians were Noah Worchester (1758-1837), Henry Ware (1764-1845), William Ellery Channing (1780-1842), and Ralph Waldo Emerson (1803-1882). The Unitarians promoted human ability for self-improvement, the newly developing German biblical criticism, and a Christology in which Christ was God's special son, "divine" in a relative sense yet not equal with the Father.

Second-generation preachers from the New England "Christian Connection" were strongly influenced by the same theological changes, especially David Millard (1794-1873) and Joseph Badger (1792-1852). As both Abner Jones and Elias Smith worked their way out of the Calvinistic Baptists, they became Arminian and soon antitrinitarian — especially Smith. Boston Unitarian leaders referred to these "Christians" as evangelical Unitarians because of their revivalistic methods, which the forerunners of the Unitarians had eschewed. Badger spent a few weeks in Boston among the Unitarians, and Unitarians were sometimes present at the Christian conferences. Unitarians invited the Christians to participate in educational enterprises, especially Meadville Theological Seminary, founded in 1844.

When Alexander Campbell and Tolbert Fanning traveled to New England in 1836, first crossing upstate New York, they often preached in Unitarian churches as the only buildings available to them. While in Boston Campbell preached in William Ellery Channing's "cathedral," while Tolbert Fanning spoke before a group of Unitarian men who published his address. Campbell, however, believed the Unitarian antitrinitarian stance was too doctrinaire and did not feel comfortable with Unitarian "ostentation" and propensity to central organization. Though sometimes accused of questionable trinitarian loyalties himself, Campbell nonetheless repudiated Unitarian theology as lacking nuance and thoroughly undermining the great truth of unity-in-plurality in the nature of God. His aversion to Unitarianism in fact helped to deepen his trinitarian convictions. Barton Stone, on the other hand, while showing no desire to find common cause with the Unitarians, had to defend his criticism of classical Trinitarianism and was therefore frequently attacked as a quasi-Unitarian or Arian.

See also Christian Connection; God, Doctrine of

BIBLIOGRAPHY Alexander Campbell, "Unitarianism, or Remarks on Christian Union," *Millennial Harbinger* (1846): 216-25, 388-94, 450-54, 634-38, 686-95 • Tolbert Fanning, *A Discourse Delivered in Boston, July 17, 1836* (1836) • Thomas H. Olbricht, "Christian Connection and Unitarian Relations, 1800-1844," *Restoration Quarterly* 9 (1966): 160-86 • Conrad Wright, ed., *A Stream of Light: A Short History of American Unitarianism* (1989).

THOMAS H. OLBRICHT

United Christian Missionary Society, The

Comprehensive mission organization of the Disciples of Christ.

When the United Christian Missionary Society (UCMS) formed in 1919, it brought organizational unity to Disciples work in both home and foreign missions. However, this organizational unity, and responses to it, contributed to greater fragmentation within the Stone-Campbell Movement. Significant numbers of congregations withdrew support from the cooperative work of Disciples and constructed an alternative congregational network of support for mission enterprises. These congregations and their alternative work eventually formed the core of the Christian Churches/Churches of Christ.

The move toward structural unity for Disciples missions began shortly after the formation of the Foreign Christian Missionary Society (FCMS) in 1875. But several decades passed before any meaningful action could be taken in this area. Meanwhile, the number of individual financial appeals from state and national agencies wore down both ministers and congregations. By 1906 the Convention charged a calendar committee with the tasks of reducing the special pleading and finding a way to streamline organizational life. The committee reported back with a recommendation urging unification of the various societies and boards.

With good reason, women leaders of the Christian Woman's Board of Missions (CWBM) were skeptical of a united society. They were fearful that the leadership role of women would be greatly reduced in a new and united society. Nonetheless, between 1890 and 1919, cooperation between the societies increased. The various societies demonstrated considerable ability to work together in planning the 1909 Centennial Celebration held in Pittsburgh. A successful unified promotional campaign, the Men and Millions Movement, inaugurated in 1913, raised over $6 million for the work of the agencies and societies.

The formation of the International Convention of the Disciples of Christ, at the general convention held in Kansas City in 1917, increased the pressure toward unification for societies and agencies. A new committee formed in Kansas City met regularly and developed articles recommending unification for the St. Louis Convention of 1918. An outbreak of influenza cancelled the meeting. The articles were presented instead during the Cincinnati meeting in 1919, and the United Christian Missionary Society emerged. The new UCMS combined the work of six different organizations: the Foreign Christian Missionary Society (Cincinnati), the American Christian Missionary Society (ACMS, Cincinnati), the National Benevolent Association (St. Louis), the Christian Woman's Board of Missions (Indianapolis), the Board of Ministerial Relief (Indianapolis), and the Board of Church Extension of the American Christian Missionary Society (Kansas City).

Legal incorporation of the UCMS took place on June 22, 1920. Frederick Burnham (ACMS president) became president of the UCMS. Archibald McLean (FCMS president), nearing the end of his career, became one of the vice presidents. Anna R. Atwater (CWBM president) was named the other vice president. Headquarters of the Society was established in St. Louis from 1920 to 1928, and then moved to the vacant College of Missions building in Indianapolis.

Composed equally of one-half men and one-half women, the board of the Society also possessed a membership broadly representative of the states, provinces, and areas of Disciples work. The UCMS took responsibility for coordinating all work in foreign missions, home missions, ministerial recruitment, ministerial relief and pensions, benevolence, church erection, religious education, missionary education, and general promotional work. The scope of its work immediately brought expressions of concern among those who felt that such a large organi-

Archibald McLean (1849-1920) and Anna Atwater (1859-1941), presidents respectively of the Foreign Christian Missionary Society and the Christian Woman's Board of Missions, became vice presidents of the newly formed United Christian Missionary Society in 1920.
Courtesy of the Disciples of Christ Historical Society

zation would threaten the autonomy of local congregations. Controversy surrounded the first decade of the Society's existence.

The context for much of the ensuing controversy was set by events that transpired before the birth of the UCMS. Influential Disciples scholars were beginning to embrace the historical-critical approach to the Bible, along with exhibiting an increasing faith in the ability of science to inform Christian meaning. This led some to question openly the more traditional views of the Bible, and especially the restoration mind-set that had taken root among Disciples from their beginnings. Developments shortly after the turn of the century, including the creations of both the Disciples Divinity House and the Campbell Institute at the University of Chicago, and the controversy at the College of the Bible in Lexington over the teachings of new and younger faculty, further bolstered concerns of conservative Disciples that the Movement was turning dangerously toward modernist views. Conservatives feared that the new UCMS would be too easily controlled by advocates of the new theological views.

In addition, Disciples leaders had increasingly developed ecumenical partnerships that conservatives found disturbing. The Disciples' affiliation with the Federal Council of Churches from its inception seemed an obvious denial of the important meaning historically associated with the restoration plea. Cooperation with other denominations, in the view of some, led to an abandonment of Disciples mission work. Comity agreements with other denominations, affirmed by the FCMS and CWBM as early as 1914, led the UCMS within its first year of operation to surrender work begun by the CWBM in Monterrey, Mexico, to the Methodists. This kind of ecumenical cooperation did not please those who believed so strongly in the importance of believers' immersion. Further, the first year of the Society was burdened with a $600,000 debt from the Disciples association with the unsuccessful Interchurch World Movement. Skepticism concerning the trustworthiness of UCMS officials grew with each instance of ecumenical partnership. For their part, UCMS leaders struggled to find ways to express their commitment to the totality of the church, which they believed called them to participate in ecumenical endeavors.

Finally, leadership for the UCMS quickly became embroiled in the open membership controversy. Again, the seeds for this controversy were planted well before the birth of the UCMS. As early as 1903, for example, the Hyde Park Church, under the leadership of Edward Scribner Ames, adopted the practice of allowing unimmersed persons to become "associate members" within the congregation. When the FCMS called the associate minister of this church, Guy Sarvis, to be a missionary in China, concern about the orthodoxy of the missionary societies surfaced. The controversy dominated the early years of the work of the UCMS and led many congregations to withhold financial support of the Society, choosing instead to support missionaries of their own.

Leaders of the UCMS attempted to steer the Society through the controversy in ways that would, on the one hand, honor the democratic principle that operated in Disciples life, and, on the other hand, not jeopardize the financial support so desperately needed for success in the mission field. The resulting posture of the UCMS seemed disingenuous both to conservatives at home, who saw no evidence that leadership dealt seriously with the fact of open membership on the mission field, and to missionaries abroad, who struggled within an ecumenical context where strict interpretations regarding open membership did not seem to apply. Thus, the UCMS lost on both counts. At home, their actions failed to mollify the conservatives attacking them. On the mission field, their pragmatic response to issues at home caused Disciples to stand on the sidelines while, in 1928, united churches were launched successfully in both China and the Philippines.

Despite the difficulties and conflicts associated with the emergence of the UCMS, the Society accomplished significant and groundbreaking work during its fifty-year existence. The UCMS directed a half-century of Disciples endeavors in foreign missions, home missions, Christian education, social welfare, and church evangelism. Further, the histories of the National Benevolent Association (1919-33), the Pension Fund (1919-28), the Board of Church Extension (1919-34), and the Board of Higher Education (1934-38) were all connected to the work of the Society during the years indicated. Various conflicts of interest, leadership misunderstandings, and general dissatisfaction with effectiveness in these areas led each eventually to resume its independent status.

Apart from the setbacks the UCMS suffered during the Depression, it operated generally with considerable efficiency, responsibly using its meager resources to meet ministerial and mission needs. By 1942 its operating deficits from the years of Depression were completely paid off, and the Society concentrated on missions at home and abroad and on Christian education.

After the Depression, three divisions governed the work of the Society. The newly restructured Division of Christian Education (1934), under the leadership of Roy G. Ross, developed significant programs for all ages among Disciples. Willard M. Wickizer led the newly formed (1941) Division of Home Missions, which included responsibility for social action, evangelism, and the organization of new congregations. James A. Crain led Disciples in the area of social welfare, working closely, for example, with the Disciples Peace Fellowship in supporting Disciples who chose conscientious objection during World War II. He also worked successfully, in 1933, to have the first black person elected to the membership of his board. C. M. Yocum led the Division of Foreign Missions through the 1930s and 1940s. Baptisms during the period averaged around 5,000 annually, lifting the membership of churches on the ten foreign fields maintained by the UCMS to a total of around 88,513 by 1947, served by over 2,500 trained native workers.

It was not until the latter part of its life that the UCMS developed a clearly articulated theology of mission. The concern for more adequate theological expression grew naturally out of the Society's dedicated work within ecumenical circles. A 1948 report from the Foreign Division of the UCMS to the Board indicated that decisions had to be made about what the Society's stance would be toward developing Christian union on the mission field. Part of this situation owed its origin to World War II. During the war, Japan required all Protestant churches in both Japan and the Philippines to unite. When the war ended, the military edict ended as well. But the Disciples churches in Japan voted to remain a part of the unified work. Many at home expressed concern about how this unity might affect mission field commitment to Disciples understandings and practices. The 1948 document "A Crisis in Foreign Missions" raised this question and urged the UCMS to take action to address the critics.

During the same time period, Disciples leaders began to engage in serious theological discussions about the meaning of world mission through their connections to ecumenical discussions occurring across the world. A major impetus to new theological reflection grew out of the 1952 World Meeting of the International Missionary Council at Willingen, Germany. In response, the Foreign Division of the Society produced a pamphlet entitled "The Strategy for World Missions." After undergoing several revisions over a three-year period, the final draft gained approval in 1955. But the theological work of revision continued, largely due to the leadership provided by Virgil Sly. By 1959 the document became "The Strategy of World Mission," changing the plural "missions" in the title to the singular "mission." This shift was due to conscious reflection about the fact the mission belonged to God, and that the work of the church served that "mission" instead of creating "missions" of its own.

As Disciples moved into the 1960s, following a concerted effort to engage the theological meaning of mission, they began earnest discussions once again about the nature of their church organization. In many respects, Disciples came to recognize themselves as *church* through the work of the UCMS. Over time, the Society demonstrated to twentieth-century Disciples the value of recognizing the denominational reality of their existence. That contribution provided a smooth transition into Restructure, which culminated in 1968 with the adoption of the "Provisional Design." In the restructured church, two new divisions, the Division of Homeland Ministries (DHM) and the Division of Overseas Ministry (DOM), were formed to oversee the work previously supervised by the UCMS. The UCMS continues among present-day Disciples as a board of eight men and women nominated by the DHM and DOM, elected by the general board, and confirmed by the General Assembly. The presidents of DHM and DOM alternate as president of the board every four years. The UCMS board oversees endowment funds that are used to support the ongoing work of Disciples in these areas.

See also American Christian Missionary Society; Ames, Edward Scribner; Atwater, Anna Robison; Board of Church Extension; Campbell Institute; Centennial Convention, The; Christian Churches/ Churches of Christ; Christian Woman's Board of Missions; Disciples Divinity House; Division of Higher Education; Division of Homeland Ministries; Foreign Christian Missionary Society; International Convention of the Disciples of Christ; McLean, Archibald; National Benevolent Association of the Christian Church (Disciples of Christ); Open Membership; Restructure; United Christian Missionary Society, The

BIBLIOGRAPHY Don Pittman and Paul Williams, "Mission and Evangelism: Continuing Debates and Contemporary Interpretations," in *Interpreting Disciples,* ed. Larry Bouchard and Dale Richesin (1987) • Joseph M. Smith, "A Strategy of World Mission: The Theory and Practice of Mission as Seen in the Present World Mission Enterprise of the Disciples of Christ" (Th.D. dissertation, Union Theological Seminary, 1961) • Mark G. Toulouse, *Joined in Discipleship: The Shaping of Contemporary Disciples Identity* (1997), ch. 8, "From Missions to Mission," pp. 189-217.

MARK G. TOULOUSE

United Church of Christ–Christian Church (Disciples of Christ) Ecumenical Partnership

A unique model of unity that is the fruition of almost a century (1912-2002) of ecumenical dialogue and a shared pilgrimage toward visible Christian unity by Disciples of Christ and the churches that formed the United Church of Christ (UCC).

In 1910 the Disciples and the Congregationalists blended their voices with the Protestant Episcopal Church in calling for a World Conference on Faith and Order. While these three communions were engaged in this dramatic overture, the Disciples' Council on Christian Union (in 1913 renamed the Association for the Promotion of Christian Unity, and in 1954 the Council on Christian Unity) initiated a series of unity conversations with the Congregational Church lasting from 1911 until 1918. These early conferences concluded: "There are no essential differences of faith which keep Congregationalists and Disciples apart. . . . In matters of doctrine and polity the agreements between these two people are numerous and significant."

When in 1957 the United Church of Christ brought together the Congregational Christian Church (1931) and the Evangelical and Reformed Church (1934), the Disciples participated as special observer-consultants, having shared in the drafting of the UCC's constitution and statement of faith. In this same period several Disciples assemblies urged that unity conversations be pursued again with the new UCC as soon as feasible.

Dialogue intensified between these two churches in the 1960s. Between 1962 and 1966 four official meetings focused on possible union. Theological topics addressed were "Grace and Faith," "Freedom and Order," "Ecclesiology and the Sacraments," and "One Ministry." In 1966 this phase of the bilateral dialogue was "temporarily suspended," primarily to give priority to the multilateral Consultation on Church Union born in 1962.

The renewal of this ecumenical journey came in 1975 during a World Council of Churches–sponsored Consultation of United and Uniting Churches at Toronto, Canada. Robert V. Moss, then president of the UCC, and Paul A. Crow, Jr., president of the Disciples' Council on Christian Unity, were among the participants. Listening to the zealous stories of united churches in South and North India, the Philippines, Thailand, Zaire, and Japan — where the UCC and Disciples families were participants — these two friends were motivated to propose that union conversations between their two churches be resumed. After common reflections, the Council on Christian Unity (Disciples) and the Council for Ecumenism (UCC) sent positive proposals to their 1977 general assembly and general synod.

In 1977 the General Assembly (Kansas City) and General Synod XI adopted a joint resolution authorizing a two-year study process to test the prospects of visible unity between these two churches. The reactions were enthusiastically positive. Therefore in 1979 the General Assembly (St. Louis) and General Synod XII called for a six-year (1979-1985) process by which they "covenanted with one another to work together towards embodying God's gift of oneness in Jesus Christ." During these years focus was given to three areas of theology and Christian mission: (1) the theology and practice of baptism and the Lord's Supper; (2) the nature, task, and equipping of the ministry, both ordained and lay; and (3) the new forms of mission today, "especially those that require the church to reform itself." Congregations, regions and conferences, general units, and national instrumentalities were invited into the visioning process. Over 700 congregations officially participated in this study and reflection. Thirty regions and twenty-nine conferences engaged in joint reflections and, in some instances, the forming of regional ecumenical partnerships. The two church general ministers and presidents — Kenneth L. Teegarden (Disciples) and Avery D. Post (UCC) — served as co-chairpersons of the Steering Committee and gave articulate leadership to the emerging relationship.

Animated by the results of these six years, General Synod XV and the General Assembly (Des Moines) in 1985 approved a dramatic "Declaration of Ecumenical Partnership." (The unique term "ecumenical partnership" was deliberately coined in order to signal that the goal is not the merger of structures, but "a relationship of genuine, substantive, tangible oneness focused on faith, sacramental life, ministry and mission.") The declaration identified four foundational convictions that emerged from listening to the Scriptures and tradition: (1) oneness among Christ's followers, the gift of unity-in-diversity, is the imperative and gift of God in Jesus Christ; (2) commitment to visible unity is central to the histories and identities of both these churches; (3) the unity we seek requires these two churches to hear the cries of the world's poor and oppressed and become a sign of the healing and renewal of the human community, by opposing all divisions based upon race, sex, age, class, and disability; (4) the unity Jesus Christ wills is not adequately expressed in terms of the merger of our present structures or a uniformity of theologies, liturgies, or practices; what is required is "a process of the mutual sharing of gifts and claiming a dynamic and growing sense of unity that will produce new patterns of oneness." In the context of such an ecumenical partnership the UCC and Disciples confessed that they are "kindred in Christ, members together of the one, undivided Church of Jesus Christ."

By 1989 an emerging unity, trust, and theological consensus had matured to the point that their representative assemblies declared the Disciples and the UCC to be in "full communion." This decision declared that each was a "true church," and they were united "in faith, mutual recognition of baptism, members and ministries, regular Eucharistic sharing, and common witness."

Soon the embodying of "full communion" began to happen. In July 1993 the General Synod and General Assembly met jointly at St. Louis in a "Common Gathering." Almost 20,000 delegates and others shared in common worship, Bible study, and plenaries on the church's mission. A second Common Gathering happened at Kansas City in 2001 and was marked by further trust building and common actions on shared, official assembly actions.

In 1996 the Division of Overseas Ministries (Disciples) and the United Church Board of World Ministries (UCC) expressed full communion by forming the Common Global Ministries Board. Signs of this partnership in world outreach include a common staff, the joint appointment of all missionaries, the acceptance of each church's historic overseas partner churches, and a common administration. The latter includes having one budget, the sharing of resources, and a common program of interpretation to the churches and to the ecumenical community. At another level the ecumenical partnership has found expression among a number of regions and conferences that share staff and programs and hold joint assemblies, common processes toward ordination, youth events, and ministers and mates conferences.

This ecumenical partnership — like all expressions of Christian unity — carries an aura both of celebration and struggle. It is being lived out in different places and at different paces, yet these two churches are united in faith, sacraments, ministry, and mission.

BIBLIOGRAPHY Paul A. Crow, Jr., "The Quest for Unity Between the Disciples of Christ and the United Church of Christ: History's Lessons for Tomorrow's Church," *Discipliana* 53:3 (1993): 67-83 • Paul A. Crow, Jr., "The Lure and Languishing of the Disciples of Christ — United Church of Christ Unity," *Mid-Stream* 32:3 (July 1993): 1-8 • Paul A. Crow, Jr., "Ecumenical Partnership: Emerging Unity Between the Disciples of Christ and the United Church of Christ," *Mid-Stream* 35:1 (January 1996): 63-70 • relevant reports and resolutions in the biennial *Yearbook of the Christian Church (Disciples of Christ) and in the Ecumenical Partnership Packet* (Council on Christian Unity) • *Survey of Church Union Negotiations,* ed. Thomas F. Best, published biennially in *The Ecumenical Review* by the World Council of Churches.

PAUL A. CROW, JR.

Unity, Christian

1. Backgrounds to Stone-Campbell Concepts of Christian Unity
2. The Early Unity Impulse in the Stone-Campbell Movement
3. Development of the Idea of Unity in the Post-Bellum Period
4. Twentieth-century Understandings of Unity in the Three Streams
5. Efforts at Internal Unity in the Stone-Campbell Movement

Christian unity is the oneness of all believers in Christ's universal church. In the Western church the divisions resulting from the Protestant Reformation became a source of deep concern for some leaders. Lutheran Philipp Melanchthon proposed compromise in the area of *adiaphora,* indifferent or nonessential matters, if it would maintain the church's visible unity. George Calixtus suggested that only heresy, defined as denial of an essential truth of Christianity believed by the church in the first five centuries, could be the basis for breaking fellowship. Calvin and other Reformed theologians insisted that the true church was invisible, ultimately known only to God, thus lessening the severity of the visible divisions.

1. Backgrounds to Stone-Campbell Concepts of Christian Unity

The transplanting of European Christianity to America exacerbated its divisions as religious freedom led to schism in existing bodies and the creation of new ones. For many Americans the developing system of denominationalism appeared to be the desired and normal condition of the church. They had no wish to return to the forced religious uniformity of Europe. Yet to others the evils of a divided Christianity became even more acute in America and demanded immediate correction.

This desire for unity combined with widespread

anti-tradition, anti-elitist sentiment following the American Revolution to spark a popular revolt against orthodox religious structures and a call for "gospel liberty." Populist religious leaders like James O'Kelly, Elias Smith, Abner Jones, Barton W. Stone, and Thomas and Alexander Campbell began movements that urged Christians to throw off divisive creeds and ecclesial structures and return to simple New Testament Christianity, thereby effecting the visible unity of Christ's church.

These movements did not seek structural union or merger of denominations. They sought, rather, the destruction of the denominational system itself, which they saw as inherently divisive. Their plea was highly individualistic, calling on believers from every Christian body to come together in their local settings to work and worship together with no requirement for communion but faith in Christ and obedience to the clear commands of Scripture.

2. The Early Unity Impulse in the Stone-Campbell Movement

Unity was at the center of the founding documents of the Stone-Campbell Movement. In the *Last Will and Testament of Springfield Presbytery* of 1804, Barton Stone and the other signers willed that their presbytery "die, be dissolved, and sink into union with the body of Christ at large." They called on fellow Christians of every name to join them in praying that God would remove all obstacles to his work — including the disunity of his church. In Thomas Campbell's 1809 *Declaration and Address* he asserted that "the Church of Christ upon earth is essentially, intentionally, and constitutionally one," and that it consists of all who profess belief in and obedience to Christ according to the Scriptures and who show they are Christians by the life they live.

All the founding leaders held the Enlightenment idea of a universal mind that for all reasonable persons would lead to unanimity on a common core of Christian truth. All held that unity was essentially an individual matter; rather than a merger of institutions, it was a mutual recognition of all believers who demonstrated their belief in Christ in their daily actions. Yet there were clearly two different emphases in the unity platforms of the Stone and Campbell movements.

For Stone, unity could not rest principally on doctrinal conformity, even on a perceived core of universally accepted tenets. It was, rather, the possession and manifestation of God's Spirit in each Christian that was the essential basis of unity. "The scriptures will never keep together in union and fellowship members not in the spirit of the scriptures, which spirit is love, peace, unity, forbearance, and cheerful obedience," he wrote in 1835. On the other hand, Thomas Campbell's platform for unity in the *Declaration and Address* was the facts of the New Testament. His son Alexander would insist in 1832 that the only way to bring about the visible unity of Christians would be to "propound the ancient gospel and the ancient order of things in the words and sentences found in the apostolic writings — to abandon all traditions and usages not found in the Record, and to make no human terms of communion."

Despite this significant difference, all the founding leaders of the Stone-Campbell Movement condemned the system of denominationalism as divisive while readily acknowledging the existence of true Christians in all groups. They believed that all human structures (sects, denominations, associations) had to vanish, as had the Springfield Presbytery and the Campbells' Mahoning Association, leaving congregations of "Christians only."

3. Development of the Idea of Unity in the Post-Bellum Period

Many in the Movement became disillusioned with this plea after the Civil War for two reasons. First, it became clear that most Christians would not accept the plea to abandon their denominational heritage and become part of what appeared to be another denomination. Though the Movement's individualistic appeal was powerful, it had not been powerful enough to destroy the denominational system they so deplored (but in which *de facto* they participated). Second, alternatives to the Stone-Campbell Movement's plea for unity became available in the larger Christian world as the century progressed. Cooperative agencies, church federation, and overtures for union discussions like the Chicago-Lambeth proposal from the Episcopal Church became live options the Movement could not ignore. Three second-generation leaders, all influential editors, represent the divergent understandings of unity that developed in the Movement in the late nineteenth century: Isaac Errett (1820-1888), J. H. Garrison (1842-1931), and David Lipscomb (1831-1917).

Isaac Errett continued the earlier appeal to individuals characteristic of the first generation. He saw Christian unity as possible on the basis of two things: faith in Christ as the divine Son of God, and submission to immersion. No other doctrines could be grounds for rejecting or accepting another as a Christian. He categorized things not explicitly taught in Scripture into matters of inference, expediency, or opinion according to how much biblical information or direction was given. These things could never be the basis for disunity. The spirit he feared and fought most was one that demanded conformity on nonessential matters, whether for or against them. The "law of love" was to govern in such matters. The unity he envisioned was a "unity in diversity."

Like Errett, J. H. Garrison spoke of simple faith in Christ as the basis of visible unity rather than creedal statements. He taught that most issues dividing Christendom were outside the realm of essentials. Yet Garrison went beyond Errett in significant ways. He moved away from the individualistic appeal of the early Movement, insisting on recognition of other groups as legitimate Christian bodies seeking to do God's will. Cooperation with other Christian bodies to oppose evil and promote righteousness would lead to mutual understanding and eventual consensus on matters of disagreement. He projected three stages leading to visible unity: internal union in denominational families worldwide, federation of denominational groups for cooperation, and finally a falling away of denominational distinctives to form one visible universal church. It was the duty of the Movement to structure itself to be able to participate in this process. These convictions led Garrison to urge maintenance of the Movement's internal unity based on simple faith in Christ, to endorse the move toward more formal structuring of the Movement, and to advocate the Movement's participation in the Federal Council of Churches.

David Lipscomb's understanding of unity included neither a large area of nonessentials nor a process of organizational maturity for the movement. For Lipscomb the only basis for Christian unity was to follow meticulously the clear teachings of the Bible without addition or subtraction. For Lipscomb there were no nonessentials. There were only essentials and things unlawful: beliefs and practices that must be accepted, and those which must be rejected. In addition, Lipscomb held a radically congregational notion of the basis of Christian unity, insisting that the only division condemned and the only unity enjoined in the New Testament was that within an individual congregation. Efforts to effect union between various church bodies were efforts in the wrong direction. Unscriptural organizations to effect organic union between churches actually produced the conditions needed for extended division. Under "God's plan" there was no organic union to be broken.

Though all three taught extensively about and worked for unity, each had a fundamentally different concept of what it is and how to reach it. The tensions that led to the Movement's two major divisions forced a refocusing of its unity emphasis from a call to all followers of Christ to a plea to members of the Movement itself to maintain unity with one another. Historians have often interpreted the cleavage in the Stone-Campbell Movement as the result of a separation of the original elements — unity and restoration — into the possession of one of the antagonistic groups. It may be more helpful to understand the schism as a result, paradoxically and ironically, of the continued struggle for unity understood in very different ways.

4. Twentieth-Century Understandings of Unity in the Three Streams

In the twentieth century, the part of the Movement that supported the International Convention of the Disciples of Christ and that supported a more formal organization moved increasingly toward full participation in the ecumenical movement. Disciples established their first permanent organization to pursue contacts with other Christian bodies in 1910 through the efforts of that year's International Convention president, Peter Ainslie (1867-1934). In his address to the Topeka, Kansas, convention Ainslie told Disciples that the task of seeking unity with their sisters and brothers in other communions was part of God's program, and therefore should be part of theirs. He called for creation of a Disciples unity council that would be given equal footing with the missionary societies. Late that year Ainslie and others incorporated the Commission on Christian Union to arrange unity conferences and work with the commissions of other bodies to arrange a world conference on Christian union. In 1911 Ainslie began publication of the *Christian Union Library,* renamed the *Christian Union Quarterly* in 1913, which carried articles on Christian unity by members of various communions. Ainslie and the Council on Christian Union were in the forefront of the ecumenical movement begun at the Edinburgh World Missionary Conference of 1910. That meeting and a unity conference held in London immediately afterward resulted in the creation of cooperating commissions in many denominations. Tissington Tatlow in his history of the Faith and Order Movement places Ainslie's efforts in the vanguard of this surge of unity committees.

In 1917 the council was reorganized and renamed the Association for the Promotion of Christian Unity, becoming a department of the Disciples General Convention, the first American denominational unity committee to be elevated to such a status. In 1954 it was renamed the Council on Christian Unity, which name it still retains. When Disciples restructured in 1968 into the Christian Church (Disciples of Christ), the council became a "unit" of the denomination. This organization in its various forms took the lead in twentieth-century Disciples unity overtures.

A mass meeting at the 1907 Disciples General Convention endorsed Disciples' participation in the Federal Council of Churches. Disciples participated in the formation of the World Council of Churches (1948) and the National Council of Churches in the United States (1950), providing significant economic support to each. Disciples were also part of two unsuccessful multilateral unity efforts: the American

Council on Organic Union begun in 1918 and the Conference on Church Union of 1949. In 1963 Disciples became part of the multilateral Consultation on Church Union (COCU), reformed in 2002 as Churches Uniting in Christ (CUIC).

In addition, Disciples engaged in serious union talks with American Baptists beginning in the 1890s and continuing until 1952. Disciples began talks with the Congregational-Christian and the Evangelical and Reformed Churches in 1946, the two groups that became the United Church of Christ in 1958. The Disciples and the UCC entered an "ecumenical partnership" in 1985 and declared themselves to be in "full communion" in 1989. Disciples began talks with representatives of the Roman Catholic Church in the United States in 1967, and in 1977 started international conversations sponsored by the Council on Christian Unity and the Vatican Secretariat for Promoting Christian Unity.

In contrast to the Christian Church (Disciples of Christ), Churches of Christ and Christian Churches/Churches of Christ have largely maintained an individual rather than organizational approach to unity. Both their congregational polity and perception that the ecumenical movement had a largely liberal theological and social agenda have made meaningful participation in it difficult. Individuals from these two communions do participate in transdenominational organizations such as Bible Study Fellowship, Walk to Emmaus, and Promise Keepers. In addition, the two groups have been involved in conversations with other religious bodies through the Open Forum meetings between the Christian Churches/Churches of Christ and the Church of God (Anderson, Indiana) from 1989 to 1997, and the Southern Baptist–Churches of Christ Conversation from 1992 to 2000. Such efforts by necessity are done by individual initiative, with institutional backing from local congregations or schools.

Beginning in the late 1950s Carl Ketcherside (1908-1989) and Leroy Garrett (b. 1918) of Churches of Christ called for a rejection of the exclusivism that had come to characterize the more conservative streams of the Movement. This call included acceptance of believers in all streams of the Movement as well as in other Christian bodies. Through their papers *Mission Messenger* and *Restoration Review* respectively, Ketcherside and Garrett laid the foundation for a more inclusive attitude especially among members of Churches of Christ and Christian Churches/Churches of Christ. Their appeal was still, by necessity, to individuals.

5. Efforts at Internal Unity in the Stone-Campbell Movement

In the twentieth century several attempts at maintaining or restoring the unity of the Movement itself have been undertaken. In 1936 Claude F. Witty (1877-1952), minister for the West Side Central Church of Christ in Detroit, and James DeForest Murch (1892-1973), then literary editor for the *Christian Standard,* brought ministers from Churches of Christ and the (as yet undivided) Disciples together to discuss divisive issues and the possibilities of unity. They began publishing the *Christian Unity Quarterly* as a forum for the efforts. Murch and Witty encouraged the organization of local meetings and conducted two national conferences in Detroit (1938) and Indianapolis (1939). Opposition to the meetings from the most conservative segment of the Churches of Christ represented by the *Gospel Advocate* contributed to a cooling of enthusiasm, and the efforts ended in the early 1940s.

In 1934 the International Convention of Disciples of Christ set up a Commission on Restudy that was charged with exploring ways to promote greater unity and cooperation in the Movement. This effort was prompted by growing theological tensions among Disciples over issues such as open membership and liberal views of Scripture, though the Commission invited participation by Churches of Christ. Comprised of representatives of a wide spectrum of views in Disciples, the Commission met three times a year through 1948 and produced over seventy studies. The Commission's final report urged Disciples to allow freedom of opinion and to recapture the sense of mission that could be carried out only in a united body. The report and the Commission's own modeling of unity in diversity were largely ignored by the International Convention, however, exacerbating the growing division.

Press conference during the Consultation on Church Union's 11th Plenary in Memphis, April 1973. Left to right: John Evum, Dr. Paul A. Crow, COCU General Secretary from 1968 to 1974 and later president of the Disciples' Council on Christian Unity, Bishop Frederick D. Jordan of the African Methodist Episcopal Church, elected COCU chair at the 1973 meeting, and Dr. Rachel Henderlite, Presbyterian clergywoman.
Courtesy of the Disciples of Christ Historical Society

Another attempt at unity in Disciples circles occurred between 1959 and 1965 following a series of regional unity meetings in the form of four national Consultations on Internal Unity of the Christian Churches. The issue of the proposed Restructure had heightened already-existing tensions. Some in the consultations argued for wide diversity and tolerance, insisting that unity was primarily spiritual (invisible), involving a common core of faith with neither unity of action nor theological interpretation as essential. Even those who advanced this idea differed in their understandings of the common core, however, with ideas ranging from simple acceptance of Jesus as Lord to insistence on a long list of essentials. Some who had initially been supporters of Restructure eventually came to fear that the structure would no longer permit nominal unity with the independents, a feature many liberals cherished as evidence to the religious world that unity in diversity was possible. The consultations failed in maintaining the internal unity of the Disciples yet created a network of persons who would continue to seek peace even after the division.

In 1984 a group of selected leaders from Christian Churches/Churches of Christ and Churches of Christ met in Joplin, Missouri, on the campus of Ozark Bible College for a "Restoration Summit" to discuss differences and ways the two bodies might recognize each other and work together. The following year the meetings were opened to the public and renamed the Restoration Forum. Usually meeting once a year and hosted by churches and schools of the two bodies, the Restoration Forums have promoted mutual understanding and cooperation in domestic ministries and worldwide missions. In the twenty-first century there have been increased efforts to include members of the Christian Church (Disciples of Christ) in these talks.

Another major event in the area of internal unity was the beginning of the Stone-Campbell Dialogue in 1999. Involving members of all three major streams of the Movement, the Dialogue met twice a year for three years, producing numerous studies as well as a confession of sin and statement of faith. In 2002 the Dialogue moved its focus to facilitating conversations and networking among church leaders of the three streams in local contexts like Louisville, Kentucky, and Atlanta, Georgia.

While considerable diversity will continue to exist among the three streams, new understandings of unity that go beyond ideas of uniformity and structural union appear to be the foundation for increasing cooperation and mutual ministry among the three streams in the future.

See also Ainslie, Peter; Commission on Restudy of the Disciples of Christ; Council on Christian Unity; Ecumenical Movement, The; Errett, Isaac; Federation; Garrison, James Harvey; Ketcherside, W. Carl; Lipscomb, David; Murch, James DeForest; Restoration Forums; Stone-Campbell Dialogue

BIBLIOGRAPHY Peter Ainslie, *Towards Christian Unity* (1918) • William Barnett Blakemore, *The Challenge of Christian Unity* (1963) • Barry Callen and James North, *Coming Together in Christ: Pioneering a New Testament Way to Christian Unity* (1997) • Paul A. Crow, Jr., *The Quest for Unity Between the Disciples of Christ and the United Church of Christ: History's Lessons for Tomorrow's Church* (1993) • A. T. DeGroot, *The Nature of the Church and Other Studies in Christian Unity* (1961) • Douglas A. Foster, "The Struggle for Unity During the Period of Division of the Restoration Movement, 1875-1900" (Ph.D. dissertation, Vanderbilt University, 1987) • W. E. Garrison, *Christian Unity and Disciples of Christ* (1955) • Cecil Hook, *Our Heritage of Unity and Fellowship: The Writings of Leroy Garrett and W. Carl Ketcherside* (1992) • David Lipscomb, *Christian Unity: How Promoted, How Destroyed: Faith and Opinion* (1891) • Dean Mills, *Union on the King's Highway: The Campbell-Stone Heritage of Unity* (1987) • Stanley Paregien, *Thoughts on Unity* (1970) • Howard E. Short, *Christian Unity Is Our Business: Disciples of Christ Within the Ecumenical Fellowship* (1953) • Stone-Campbell Dialogue papers, at the web site of the Council on Christian Unity of the Christian Church (Disciples of Christ), http://www.disciples.org/ccu/stonecampbell.htm • Dean E. Walker, *Adventuring for Christian Unity and Other Essays* (1992) • George Hugh Wilson, "Unity and Restoration in the Ecumenical Thought of the Disciples of Christ: With Special Reference to the Disciples' Part in the Evolution of the World Council of Churches" (Ph.D. dissertation, Hartford Seminary Foundation, 1978).

DOUGLAS A. FOSTER

Universalism

The belief that all people will be saved through the work of Christ.

Universalists insisted that their views of salvation had been held by the early church. Organizationally, however, Universalism dates from 1779 with the founding of a Universalist congregation by John Murray in Gloucester, Massachusetts, and the first meeting of a "General Convention" of Universal Churches in 1793. Murray, an Englishman, had been influenced by the work of James Relly, who taught that all souls are united to Christ. Since in this union Christ bore and was punished for the sins of all people, there is no more punishment for sin, though there might be some suffering after death for lack of belief.

Most Universalists in nineteenth-century America were restorationists — they believed that all people would experience a period of limited punishment af-

Controversial minister of the Nashville, Tennessee, Christian Church, Jesse Babcock Ferguson (1819-1870) gained a reputation in the Stone-Campbell Movement for his embrace of spiritualism in the early 1850s. In American religion generally he was known as a Universalist preacher, writer, and lecturer. Courtesy of the Disciples of Christ Historical Society

ter this life as part of a process of ultimate reconciliation to God. Belief in universal salvation spread on the American frontier as many rejected Calvinist views of determinism and the nature of God.

The Stone-Campbell Movement emerged in the same nineteenth-century context that promoted the rise of Universalism, and the Movement experienced numerous encounters with it. The Universalism of Elias Smith and others of the Christian Connection was a source of friction between the Campbell churches and the churches of the Stone movement that maintained relations with Smith's Eastern Christians. Universalist preacher Aylett Raines caused a stir in the Mahoning Baptist Association when he applied for membership in 1828, though Thomas Campbell insisted that such an opinion was not a barrier to fellowship. Alexander Campbell engaged in a three-year written debate with Universalist preacher Dolphus Skinner.

Perhaps the most serious encounter between Universalism and the Stone-Campbell Movement occurred when the popular minister of the Christian Church in Nashville, Tennessee, Jesse B. Ferguson, began preaching universal salvation around 1851. Ferguson's ideas became a Movement-wide issue in 1852 when he published an article in the *Christian Magazine,* which he edited, that interpreted 1 Peter 3:18-20 to teach that the dead will have a second chance to respond to the gospel. Alexander Campbell and others attacked Ferguson's views, but many in the Nashville church sided with Ferguson. In 1857 Ferguson resigned as the congregation's minister but took with him a sizeable number of members.

Like Campbell, most early leaders of the Stone-Campbell Movement strongly opposed Universalism. Yet respected preacher and editor Moses E. Lard in a lecture published in 1879 asserted that one cannot know for sure that the Greek terms *aiōn* and *aiōnios,* usually translated "eternal," referred to endless punishment. He concluded that to lessen people's anxiety he would be happy to put God in a better light than that produced by traditional teaching about endless punishment.

Though assailed as a doctrine that would lead to unrestrained sin and a breakdown of orderly society, Universalism in fact taught that people should live holy, active, and useful lives by following the moral law they saw emerging from Christian principles. Often Universalists were among the most respected members of their community. Incidents like the invitation to Dallas Stone-Campbell minister Caroll Kendrick to address the 1887 Texas Association of Universalists, in which he expressed his "warm fraternal regards and sympathy for all lovers of the Lord Jesus Christ regardless of name," indicate that relations were not always as strained as in the Jesse Ferguson case.

In 1961 the Universalist Church of America merged with the Unitarian Association to form the Unitarian Universalist Association. Though this body does not identify itself specifically as Christian, some older Universalist state conventions, especially in the southern United States, continued to maintain an overtly Christian Universalist stance.

In some Stone-Campbell circles in the twentieth century there was a lessening of emphasis on traditional notions of punishment and hell. While most conservatives continued to reject universal salvation, that idea, along with other nontraditional soteriological understandings such as annihilationism, have gained increased acceptance, reflecting a larger trend among both mainstream and evangelical Christians.

See also Campbell-Skinner Debate; Ferguson, Jesse Babcock; Lard, Moses E.; Raines, Aylett; Universalists

BIBLIOGRAPHY Timothy K. Beougher, "Are All Doomed to Be Saved? The Rise of Modern Universalism," *Southern Baptist Journal of Theology* 2 (Summer 1998): 6-24 • Jesse B. Ferguson, *Relation of Pastor and People: Statement of Belief on Unitarianism, Universalism and Spiritualism* (1854) • J. W. Hanson, *Universalism the Prevailing Doctrine of the Christian Church During Its First Five Hundred Years* (1899) • Moses E. Lard, *Do the Scriptures Teach the Endlessness of Future Punishment? A Lecture* (1879) • Russell E. Miller, *The Larger Hope: The First Century of the Universalist Church in America, 1770-1870* (1979) • Russell E. Miller, *The Larger Hope: The Second Century of the Universalist Church in America, 1870-1970* (1985) • Johnny Tucker, *Like a Meteor Across the Horizon: The Jesse B. Ferguson Story* (1978) • David Lowes Watson, *God Does Not Foreclose: The Universal Promise of Salvation* (1990).

DOUGLAS A. FOSTER

Universalists

Central to the Universalist vision is the declaration that eventually all humanity will be saved. Persons with Universalist outlooks could be found in Boston and Philadelphia as early as the late 1700s. Their numbers were largely in the Northeast, but in small towns and rural areas, in contrast with the Unitarians. It was not uncommon to find them in the frontier regions westward. Noted early Universalists were John Murray (1741-1815) of Boston, Elhanan Winchester (1751-1797) who evangelized widely in the Northeast and in England, and Hosea Ballou (1771-1852) of upper New England and Boston. In 1942 the movement's name was changed to the Universalist Church of America, which merged in 1961 with the Unitarians to form the Unitarian Universalist Association.

The Universalists and the New England Christians often appealed to people of the same socioeconomic level, that is, small town and middle class. Certain preachers — for example, Abigail Roberts (1791-1841) — sometimes preached in congregations of both groups. In 1817 Elias Smith, who had toyed with universalism, or restorationism as it was sometimes called (i.e., the restoration of all things, Acts 3:21), departed for the Universalists and preached among them. More than once before his death in 1846 he returned to the Christians but continued to go back and forth between the two groups.

In an often told story, Aylett Raines, an up-and-coming restorationist (Universalist) preacher on the Western Reserve in Ohio, became influenced by the teaching of the Campbell reformers. Invited to attend the annual meeting of the Mahoning Association in 1828, he proposed that he be accepted as a minister within the Association. When an older preacher objected to Raines because of his Universalist beliefs, Thomas Campbell spoke up in his favor. He declared that Raines should be permitted to hold his restorationist views as opinion. Raines was accepted and apparently never made his views on universal salvation a part of his preaching. Overt Universalism has been uncommon in the Stone-Campbell movement, except after the late nineteenth century with some Disciples, though even here not in significant numbers.

See also Mahoning Baptist Association; New England "Christians"; Raines, Aylett; Smith, Elias; Universalism

BIBLIOGRAPHY Elmo Arnold Robinson, *American Universalism: Its Origins, Organization, and Heritage* (1970) • Samuel Rogers, *Autobiography of Elder Samuel Rogers*, 4th ed. (1880), pp. 111-22 (on Aylett Raines).

THOMAS H. OLBRICHT

Urban Ministry

1. Christian Church (Disciples of Christ)
2. Churches of Christ
3. Christian Churches/Churches of Christ

1. Christian Church (Disciples of Christ)

Urban ministries were directed toward the burgeoning numbers of urban dwellers in the United States. Rooted in the ideals of nineteenth-century Protestant liberalism, Disciples engaged in urban ministries through congregations such as Central Woodward (Detroit), Park Avenue (New York), Community (Kansas City), and University (Chicago). Especially during the Depression years, soup kitchens, social gatherings, job counseling, day-care centers, and even free showings of first-run movies became urban ministry staples, as more and more Disciples congregants migrated to cities.

Among Disciples' "Home Missions," two significant urban ministry initiatives were launched: Inman Christian Center in San Antonio, begun in 1913, led by founder Samuel Guy Inman, and subsequently E. T. Cornelius, E. G. Luna, Dan Saucedo, and Carol Garcia; and All Peoples Christian Church and Community Center in Los Angeles, begun in 1942, led by founders Dan and Frances Genung, and subsequently Kay Kokobun, Tom Norwood, Joe Bevilaqua, Joe Ide, Denton L. Roberts, and Saundra Bryant. All Peoples holds the distinction of being the first mainline Protestant congregation on American soil intentionally established as an interracial fellowship. In both situations, as in others across the United States, the focus of urban ministry became increasingly defined as service to the poor, disenfranchised members of society, including immigrants and those racially and politically oppressed.

During the years 1955-75, a time of great social transformation in the United States, initiatives such as housing assistance and civil rights advocacy became central foci for Disciples urban ministries. In

Chicago, University Christian Church, led by pastor Charles Bayer, created The Blue Gargoyle, a student-focused coffeehouse ministry, while also building relationships with gang members in The Devil's Disciples and Blackstone Rangers.

In the last quarter of the twentieth century, urban ministry increased as a central tenet among African American Disciples. Light of the World Christian Church in Indianapolis, led by T. Garrott Benjamin, and Mississippi Boulevard Christian Church in Memphis, the largest Disciples congregation at the turn of the twenty-first century, led by Alvin O'Neal Jackson, both emphasized distinctive ministries to African American men and boys, while at the same time creating schools that could address the aspirations of all urban children and youth. Significant urban ministries were also enacted through Mother-to-Mother programs and Church Action for Safe and Just Communities, led by Gerald Cunningham, out of the Disciples' Church and Society Department in the Division of Homeland Ministries.

ROBERT LEE HILL

2. Churches of Christ

Urban ministry in Churches of Christ is designed to meet the complex challenges of holistic ministry among the poor and oppressed city residents of various ethnic origins. Largely a Southern rural/suburban movement devoted to evangelism, church structure, and worship, Churches of Christ developed theologies for urban ministry based on foundations from the early Movement.

C. L. Loos (1823-1912), editor of *The Disciple* (1851-53), encouraged evangelizing cities, the neglected central points of political and moral influence. The Stone-Lipscomb tradition consistently preached social justice and racial equality. In 1865 an urban/rural rift emerged. Because of their victory in the Civil War and their relative prosperity, Northern urban members of the Movement were able to focus more on a theology of present social concern, whereas the defeated, impoverished, agrarian South shifted to a focus on preparedness for the afterlife. With only a few others, David Lipscomb (1831-1917) still advocated urban evangelism, especially among the poor, as, for example, in his 1904 *Gospel Advocate* article "Reaching the People."

In the early 1900s, leaders in Churches of Christ generally denounced "Social Gospel" activism as unbiblical. N. B. Hardeman (1874-1965) criticized social relief efforts, defining church work as evangelism, not temporal assistance. Yet the Russell Street and Central Churches of Christ in Nashville developed extensive programs providing medical treatment, food, clothing, housing, employment, and elderly and childcare assistance with no race or class distinctions.

In 1926, 85 percent of Churches of Christ and 75 percent of the membership were rural. Urbanization between the 1920s and 1950s drew to the cities rural Christians who were largely unprepared to meet urban pressures. While House of the Carpenter (Boston, 1963), Camp Shiloh (New York, 1967), *Mission* journal (1967-87), and some black churches championed the cause of urban ministry, many churches left the city or maintained a rural status quo.

In the 1970s and 1980s many churches showed signs of renewed concern, though this was derailed in some areas by the initial success and then departure of the Boston movement (International Churches of Christ). In the 1980s new ministries began in New York, Nashville, San Francisco, Houston, Dallas, Chicago, Birmingham, Memphis, Atlanta, and over a hundred other cities, focusing on church planting, evangelism, racial reconciliation, youth, indigenous leadership, community development, and training urban ministers.

ANTHONY WOOD

3. Christian Churches/Churches of Christ

Ministry to America's urban poor by the Christian Church/Churches of Christ is a relatively recent development, a challenge for churches that, historically speaking, had strong rural roots and, when locating in cities, gravitated mainly to suburbs. Over and beyond traditional benevolence ministries, the impetus for deeper and more "incarnational" inner-city ministry since the late 1960s has primarily come from two directions. The first was from churches that chose to stay in neighborhoods whose racial and economic demographics had changed. An example of this type is First Christian Church in the Englewood area of Chicago. Established about 1885 in a well-to-do white neighborhood, the church ministers in what is now a largely African American part of town that also has a growing Hispanic and Arab population.

Another example is the Englewood Christian Church in Indianapolis, which carries on its urban ministry in a racially mixed neighborhood. Having begun with traditional food pantry and clothing ministries, the congregation has launched its own development corporation, with an extensive housing ministry designed to help low-income families carry mortgages and build equity. Englewood has also launched a number of businesses (bookkeeping, lawn care, etc.) to provide employment, while also maintaining childcare and kindergarten services. The congregation is directly involved in neighborhood redevelopment and has established relationships with the city of Indianapolis. Such work has placed the church far ahead of other congregations operating in inner-city or suburban settings.

The second type of urban ministry among Christian Churches/Churches of Christ has resulted from the labors of caring individuals who have been motivated by such scriptural texts as Matthew 25:31-46 and 28:18-20 (the Great Commission) to serve inner-city residents. A representative sampling includes Jesus Place (Atlanta, Georgia), Serving Jesus Willingly Urban Ministry (Springfield, Illinois), Memphis Inner City Outreach (Memphis, Tennessee), Agape Christian Church (Denver, Colorado), and Christ's Church of the City (New York City).

Both types of outreach ministries employ some of the same methods to carry the gospel of Jesus Christ to the inner city. These include the use of Sunday Schools, Bible studies, Vacation Bible Schools, after-school tutoring and summer programs for children, job training, personal and spiritual counseling, and recovery programs for addicts, along with benevolent aid such as food pantries and clothes closets. Many of these mission churches struggle to maintain adequate financial and volunteer support from their local Christian Churches/Churches of Christ in order to sustain these undertakings.

Other patterns of urban ministry involvement have also begun to emerge in some of the Christian Churches/Churches of Christ. One such pattern is the affiliation of congregations with nationally based groups like the Interfaith Hospitality Network (which integrates congregations in providing temporary housing and meals for the homeless and unemployed) and Habitat for Humanity. Another is the "hosting" of ethnic minority churches, such as Asian or Hispanic congregations with their own leaders and services.

The challenge of urban ministry involvement among Christian Churches/Churches of Christ has been compounded historically by the strong ecclesiological emphasis on the autonomy of local congregations. The end result is that very little concerted effort has taken place on the state or national level on behalf of inner-city ministry. In 1991 the Urban Task Force was formed from a group of concerned individuals to educate, encourage, and promote the cause of urban ministry, though it has no legislative or judicatory power. Similarly, FOCUS (Fellowship of Christians in Urban Service) has been active since 1980. Several colleges and seminaries also offer programs with courses or majors in urban and ethnic ministry. These include Milligan College, Emmanuel School of Religion, Lincoln Christian College and Seminary, Winston-Salem Bible College, Dallas Christian College, Mid-South Christian College, St. Louis Christian College, Hope International University, and San Jose Christian College. ROBERT C. GRIFFIN

See also African Americans in the Movement; Hispanics in the Movement; Inman Christian Center; International Churches of Christ; *Mission*

BIBLIOGRAPHY David Edwin Harrell, Jr., *Quest for a Christian America* (1966, repr. ed. 2003) • David Edwin Harrell, Jr., *The Social Sources of Division in the Disciples of Christ: 1865-1900* (1973, repr. ed. 2003) • Alvin Jennings, *How Christianity Grows in the City* (1985) • W. Ray Kelley, "A Formula for Saving an Inner-City Church," *Christian Standard* 132 (June 22, 1997): 8-10 • W. Ray Kelly, "How Can I Learn More About Urban Ministries?" *Horizons* 48 (October 1999): 3 • Jimmie Moore Mankin, "The Role of Social Service in the Life and Growth of the Madison Church of Christ" (D.Min. thesis, Fuller Theological Seminary, 1986) • "Special Issue: Urban Evangelism in America," *Christian Standard* 129 (July 31, 1994).

V

Van Buren, James Geil (1914-1997)

Prominent minister and writer in the Christian Churches/Churches of Christ.

A graduate of Butler University (A.B., 1942; B.D., 1946) and Kansas State University (Ph.D., 1967), Van Buren was minister of Central Christian Church in Pittsburgh, Pennsylvania, from 1946 to 1960 and Professor of Humanities and Christian Doctrine at Manhattan (Kansas) Christian College from 1960 to 1985. His books and hundreds of popular-level religious articles, primarily in the *Christian Standard,* reflected an unusual breadth of humane learning and literary sophistication. Van Buren, who was influenced by Frederick Kershner at Butler School of Religion, was of a "Free Church Catholic" conscience and was an influential voice against Protestant Fundamentalism among the Christian Churches/Churches of Christ in the 1950s-60s.

See also Manhattan Christian College

BIBLIOGRAPHY Robert J. Owens, Jr., and Barbara E. Hamm, eds., *Increase in Learning: Essays in Honor of James G. Van Buren* (1979; includes bibliography of Van Buren's writings through 1978) • James Van Buren, *The Best of James Van Buren: An Anthology of His Writings* (1991) • Marge Van Buren, "My Sixty-Two (Plus) Years with 'Thistle,'" *Christian Standard* 132 (November 30, 1997): 6-8.

ROBERT J. OWENS, JR.

Voice of Freedom, The

Magazine published by members of Churches of Christ from 1953 until 1985 aimed at opposing "the threat to our freedom from Catholicism and Communism."

Founding editor G. C. Brewer (1884-1956) believed that communism and Catholicism were forms of totalitarianism and warned that freedom would be lost if these systems were to gain control of the government of the United States. Following the death of G. C. Brewer, Lawrence Ray Wilson (1896-1968) became editor. With this change, the focus of the magazine progressively turned to the intrusion of Catholicism on American society. Writers denounced the Catholic Church on many issues and were involved in the political affairs of the late 1950s.

Circulation figures for the *Voice of Freedom* increased dramatically during the presidential campaign of 1960. Numerous articles were published opposing the election of Catholic presidential candidate John F. Kennedy. Writers voiced the opinion that Kennedy could not effectively lead the country because he necessarily would be influenced by international Roman Catholic leadership. More than 100,000 copies of the magazine were circulated monthly during the presidential campaign.

In the decades following the 1960 election, the magazine's circulation steadily declined. Although the *Voice of Freedom* continued its anti-Catholicism rhetoric, other Catholic political candidates did not generate the same controversy as Kennedy.

In 1968 Perry Davis Wilmeth (1907-1987) became editor of the magazine following the death of L. R. Wilson. Under Wilmeth's editorial direction, the *Voice of Freedom* expanded its focus to reach a broader audience. Articles pertaining to the issues of humanism, atheism, and materialism, and the threat of these issues to religious liberty, were prevalent during the later years of publication.

In 1985 a new format was introduced for the publication that emphasized the needs of churches and individuals. Monthly features included church growth, biblical archaeology, and the family. However, the struggling publication ceased in July 1985, before the new format could be fully implemented.

See also Brewer, Grover Cleveland; Nativism; Roman Catholicism — Twentieth Century

BIBLIOGRAPHY Ronald E. Jackson, "The Influence of the Religious Issue in the 1960 Presidential Election upon Churches of Christ" (M.A. thesis, Abilene Christian University, 1973) • Royce L. Money, "Church-State Relations in the Churches of Christ Since 1945: A Study in Religion and Politics" (Ph.D. dissertation, Baylor University, 1975).

MARK L. MCCALLON

W

Walker, Dean Everest (1898-1988)

Preacher, academic administrator, and church historian from the Christian Churches/Churches of Christ.

Walker was the eldest son of Wilber Russell Walker, a New Testament professor (Bethany College), writer, and preacher. He studied at Bethany College, Tri-State College (B.A.), and Butler University (B.D., M.A.), and did doctoral studies at the University of Edinburgh (1933-35); he eventually received honorary degrees from Milligan College, Kentucky Christian College, and Tri-State College. He was married to Florence Lay (1920) and to Dorothy Louise Kiester (1962), the latter of whom became a significant spokeswoman for women's ministries in the Christian Churches/Churches of Christ.

Walker was professor of church history at Butler University from 1926 until 1950, when he became president of Milligan College in Tennessee. During his presidency (1950-68) he led Milligan to renewed commitment as a Christian liberal arts college, to financial stability, and to regional accreditation. In 1965 he became the founding president of Emmanuel School of Religion, serving in this position until 1969, when he resumed full-time teaching as professor of church history, conducting his last seminar in 1985-86. He died just two years later in 1988.

Walker produced one book, *Adventuring for Christian Unity: A Survey of the History of Churches of Christ (Disciples),* during the year he served as lecturer at Overdale College, Birmingham, England (1935). However, he wrote many essays, some lengthy, addressed to critical issues confronting the contemporary church. He wrote numerous articles for the *Christian-Evangelist,* the *Christian Standard,* and *Shane Quarterly.* In each instance he brought his understanding of the "tradition of Christ" to consideration of the issue. A book containing his published works, including lectures he had given, was issued posthumously. He had been much in demand as both lecturer and preacher and was a respected authority in shaping the North American Christian Convention.

Walker's greatest concern was to articulate the plea of the Stone-Campbell Movement in the face of the issues confronting it in the twentieth century. He ultimately emphasized that the restoration of New Testament Christianity, the program to recover the apostolic ideal of the church and to realize ecclesial unity, was not an end in itself but was couched

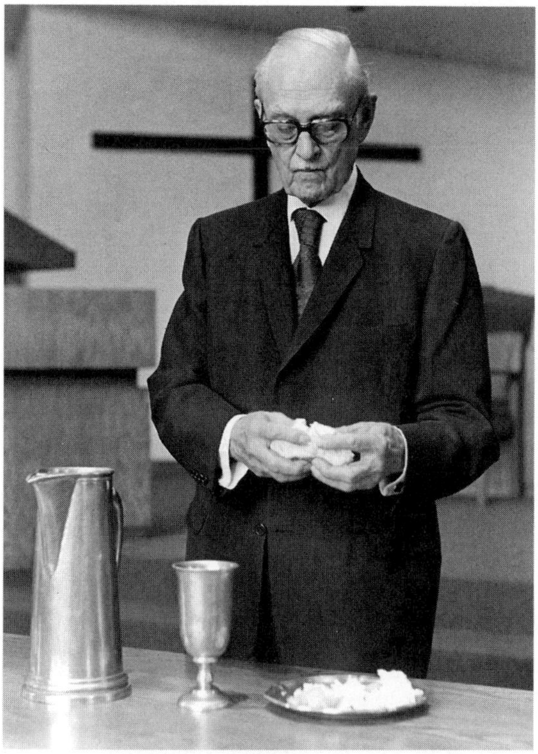

Pictured here presiding at communion, Dean E. Walker, one-time president of both Milligan College and Emmanuel School of Religion, was a progressive conservative convinced that the plea of the Stone-Campbell Movement had both apostolic grounding and catholic appeal.
Courtesy of Emmanuel School of Religion Archives

within God's overarching purpose to *restore* humanity to his image, as revealed in the incarnate Word, Jesus Christ. The restored church was to be the model and embodiment of restored humanity.

Walker was a committed churchman, concerned for the church at large but especially for the unity of the Stone-Campbell Movement. Tensions between "cooperatives" and "independents" within the Disciples of Christ compelled his continuing attention. He held a broad conception of fellowship, limited only by fidelity to Christ. This attitude was reflected in his active participation, beginning in 1936, in the Commission on Restudy of the Disciples of Christ, chartered by the International Convention of the Disciples in 1934. Here he succeeded in introducing statements of consensus concerning the history and plea of the Movement. He was encouraged by the Commission's proposal for widespread discussion of its finished document (1949), but deeply disappointed when the major journals refused to publish it and leaders on "both sides" ignored its recommendations. Walker also served as delegate of the International Convention to the Federal Council of Churches of Christ (1946).

At the same time he was active in the North American Christian Convention, as a member of the Continuation Committee and once as president of the Convention (1942-44). Since the Convention's focus was mainly upon preaching and fellowship, Walker did not see its program as duplicating that of the International Convention of Disciples of Christ, in which he also regularly participated. He and W. A. Shullenberger, president of the International Convention, discussed having the two conventions concurrently, with some joint sessions, an idea that never materialized. Walker also served on the executive board of the World Convention of Churches of Christ (1955-61), aimed at serving all streams of the Stone-Campbell Movement.

Walker disliked being labeled an "independent" but was cordial to identification as a "free church catholic." He remained convinced that differences in methodology in carrying out the mission of Christ should not bring about a breach of fellowship, though he clearly viewed the denominational Restructure of the Disciples of Christ as an unwarranted exercise of ecclesiastical authority. Decisions about the configuration of the Movement and its mission were to be a matter of free, not orchestrated, consensus. Nevertheless, Walker maintained relationships with former Disciples colleagues and refused to cut off fellowship with the Christian Church (Disciples of Christ). Hence, he could preside over the European Evangelistic Society, a reporting agency of the International Convention, and at the same time serve twenty-two years as recording secretary of Christian Missionary Fellowship, a missionary organization of the Christian Churches/Churches of Christ.

Walker's career touched the life of the church at many points. His greatest impact, however, was in the classroom, where he challenged three generations of students to careful consideration of, and commitment to, the broad "tradition of Christ" as he called it. Like his former colleague and friend at Butler University School of Religion, Frederick Doyle Kershner, Walker was a "classical" Disciple who believed that the Stone-Campbell Movement, transcending liberalism on the one side and fundamentalism on the other, and holding assiduously to its commitments both to restoration (apostolicity) and to unity, genuinely had an important witness for the church in the dawning ecumenical age.

See also Christian Theological Seminary; Commission on Restudy of the Disciples of Christ; Emmanuel School of Religion; Kershner, Frederick D.; Milligan College; North American Christian Convention

BIBLIOGRAPHY Thomas Foust and William J. Richardson, eds., *Adventuring for Christian Unity and Other Essays by Dean Walker* (1992) • William J. Richardson, "The Nature of the Church in the Thought of Dean E. Walker," *Discipliana* 55 (1995): 99-108.

WILLIAM J. RICHARDSON

Walker, Granville T. (1908-1991)

Disciples minister and chair of the Commission on Restructure.

Born in Acme, Texas, and reared in Beaumont, Texas, he was the son of Bolling Virgil and Maude Estelle (Taylor) Walker, the fourth of their five children. Following high school, he enrolled for a brief period in Randolph College ("situated on a bluff and run on the same principle," he said) and continued his education at Texas Christian University (TCU), beginning in 1932. The prior year he married Erline Henry. They had two children: Judith Walker Stempel and Sara Walker Wilson.

After receiving both B.A. and B.D. degrees, he became pastor of the St. Charles Avenue Christian Church in New Orleans but returned to TCU two years later to teach in the Department of Religion. Granted a leave of absence, he entered Yale University and earned the Ph.D. degree. Instead of resuming his career at TCU, he accepted a call to University Christian Church in Fort Worth, Texas.

Senior minister from 1943 to 1973, Walker led the congregation through an era of dynamic growth, gave strong support to ecumenical endeavors, and affirmed the reasonableness of Christian faith. Eloquence and power marked his thoughtful sermons and confirmed his reputation as a master of the pul-

Granville Walker (1908-1991) chaired the Commission on Brotherhood Restructure. He was a Yale Ph.D. and long-time pastor of one of the Disciples' largest congregations, University Christian Church, Fort Worth, Texas.
Courtesy of the Disciples of Christ Historical Society

pit. A leader among Disciples, he presided over the International Convention of Christian Churches (Disciples of Christ) in 1958 and served as chair of the Commission on Brotherhood Restructure. Recognitions bearing his name and Erline's include a ministerial scholarship foundation, a residence hall at TCU, and a professorship in Brite Divinity School.

In addition to *Preaching in the Thought of Alexander Campbell* (1954), Walker published two books of his sermons: *The Greatest of These* (1963) and *Go Placidly amid the Noise and Haste* (1973). His "A Funny Thing Happened to Me on the Way to the Pulpit" was published by the Pension Fund of the Christian Church in 1985. WILLIAM E. TUCKER

See also Brite Divinity School; Restructure

Walker, John

See Campbell-Walker Debate; Presbyterians, Presbyterianism

Walker, Wilmer Russell (1869-1963)

Influential minister and leader among Disciples of Christ and those who became Christian Churches/Churches of Christ.

W. R. Walker held degrees from Bethany College, Hiram College, Cincinnati Bible Seminary, and Milligan College. Walker taught New Testament for three years at Bethany College, served as minister of the Indianola Church of Christ in Columbus, Ohio (1920-48), and was president of Standard Publishing for three decades. A popular preacher and compassionate pastor, Walker along with close friend Pearl Howard Welshimer was a vital player in the formative years of the North American Christian Convention, serving as a member of the original Committee on Future Action and as a main speaker at the Convention five times.

Walker wrote three popular books and numerous articles for Stone-Campbell Movement periodicals. His son, Dean E. Walker (1898-1988), became an important leader and educator among the Christian Churches/Churches of Christ.

See also North American Christian Convention; Standard Publishing Company; Walker, Dean Everest; Welshimer, Pearl Howard

BIBLIOGRAPHY Edwin V. Hayden, "A Ministry Concluded," *Christian Standard* 98 (1963): 115-16 • W. R. Walker, *A Functioning Eldership* (1942) • W. R. Walker, *A Ministering Ministry* (1938) • W. R. Walker, *Studies in Acts* (1924; repr. 1966). ROBERT F. REA

Wallace, Cled Eugene "Cleddie" (1892-1962)

Preacher and writer among Churches of Christ.

Born in Greenville, Texas, the oldest son of Texas preacher Foy E. Wallace, Sr. (1871-1949), Wallace received his basic religious instruction from his father and close friends Charles Ready Nichol (1876-1961) and Robertson Lafayette Whiteside (1869-1951).

Baptized by Fount L. Young (1855-1933) in 1905, Wallace began preaching in 1908 near Paris, Texas. He attended several colleges, including Thorp Spring Christian College and Baylor University, where he completed a B.A. degree in 1918.

Cled Wallace began contributing occasional articles to the *Firm Foundation* in 1914, becoming a "staff writer" in 1927. When, in 1930, his younger brother, Foy E. Wallace, Jr., became editor of the *Gospel Advocate,* Cled soon joined the *Advocate* staff as a columnist. As Foy, Jr., entered the controversy with premillennial preachers in Churches of Christ, Cled became his brother's most ardent supporter. Foy, Jr., wrote of his brother, "Cled has been a companion, a counselor and a stay. We have studied along the same lines in such close collaboration that it would be impossible to separate the expression of thought."

In 1938 Foy E. Wallace, Jr., launched *The Bible Banner,* with Cled as front-page writer and coeditor. The *Banner* continued the Wallaces' battle against premillennialism among Churches of Christ and in 1942 supported a Christian's choice to serve in the armed forces of the United States. Under Cled's influence, Foy, Jr., not only changed his view from that of a noncombatant but also embraced Christian participation in all aspects of military service, including front-line combat. Cled wrote articles urging strong support of Christian servicemen.

Three of Cled Wallace's sons enlisted in the U.S. Armed Forces and a fourth served as a policeman. One son died in combat during World War II, and another was killed in Korea three days before the Armistice. Wallace's pacifist critics harshly attacked him. In 1944 Jacob Lee Hines charged that Wallace's son John, missing in action, was "the victim of unfaithful teaching by his father" and that "his father must face the whole thing at the judgment."

In 1949 Fanning Yater Tant became the editor of *Gospel Guardian,* with Wallace as front-page writer. Wallace wrote articles questioning the increasing power and encroachment of "institutions" among Churches of Christ. His 1950 article "That Rock Fight in Italy" criticized methods and means of conducting missionary work, provoking a maelstrom of controversy. Wallace later regretted its publication.

In 1951 the Church of Christ in Lufkin, Texas — with which Wallace was associated — divided, and the *Guardian's* publisher, Roy E. Cogdill, established a new congregation. Deeply wounded, Wallace ceased to write for the *Guardian* or to support its causes. In 1954 he moved to Austin, Texas, where he spent his last years, writing an occasional article for the *Firm Foundation.*

See also Cogdill, Roy E.; Eschatology; *Firm Foundation; Gospel Advocate, The;* Noninstitutional Movement; Wallace, Foy E., Jr.

BIBLIOGRAPHY "Cled E. Wallace," *Gospel Advocate* 82 (February 29, 1940): 208 • Noble Patterson and Terry J. Gardner, *Foy E. Wallace, Jr.: Soldier of the Cross* (1999).

TERRY J. GARDNER

Foy Esco Wallace was known for his fierce opposition to premillennialism in Churches of Christ, as well as to pacifism and modern translations of the Bible. He wielded considerable power in the mid-twentieth century, targeting and attacking anyone he felt was teaching false doctrine or was "soft" on the issues. He represents the hard-fighting style of the era. Courtesy of the Center for Restoration Studies, Abilene Christian University

Wallace, Foy Esco [Foy E. Wallace, Jr.] (1896-1979)

Preacher, editor, author, and debater in Churches of Christ.

He was born in Montague County, Texas, to Foy Edwin Wallace [Foy E. Wallace, Sr.], who was a well-known preacher among "conservative" Texas Disciples (Churches of Christ). Wallace attended Thorp Spring Christian College from 1912 to 1913, but was more influenced by his father and older contemporaries Charles Ready Nichol (1876-1961), Robertson Lafayette Whiteside (1869-1951), and his older brother, Cled Eugene Wallace (1892-1962) than by any formal education.

Wallace's career developed in three phases. From 1912 to 1930 he was primarily an evangelist. As a charismatic public speaker Wallace began holding meetings at age 15, reaping great success in many conversions and lavish praise. In September 1920 he baptized 100 adults at Lometa, Texas. His evangelistic travels brought him to the Russell Street Church of Christ in Nashville, Tennessee, in 1923, 1924, and 1927, where his success attracted the attention of Leon B. McQuiddy (1887-1950), who would appoint him editor of the *Gospel Advocate* in 1930.

With his move to Nashville Wallace's career entered its polemic phase (1930-52). In succession he edited the *Gospel Advocate* (1930-34), *The Gospel Guardian* (1935-36), *The Bible Banner* (1938-49), and *Torch* (1950-51). While Wallace addressed many issues, his attention concentrated on three: premillennialism, Christian responsibility to civil government, and church support of colleges.

Wallace believed that premillennialism, as taught by Robert Henry Boll (1875-1956) and his followers, was heresy and that Boll had established a sect. Wallace also charged that Boll and his allies fraternized with the Christian Church and taught sectarian doctrine regarding the Holy Spirit. These writings were direct and confrontational; Wallace's critics found them unduly harsh. Wallace named names not only of Boll's disciples but also of those whom Wallace believed were sympathetic to Boll. In 1933 Wallace debated Charles M. Neal (1878-1956) in Winchester, Kentucky, and Chattanooga, Tennessee, on premillennialism. He attacked and analyzed premillennial teaching in cooperative meetings across the country, most notably at Nashville, Tennessee (1939); the Houston Music Hall (1945); and Louisville, Kentucky (1950).

Wallace came to favor participation of Christians in all phases of civil government, including military combat, a position that caused consternation among the traditionally pacifist leadership of Churches of Christ. His dramatic announcement of these views in the March 1942 *Bible Banner,* four months after the Japanese attack on Pearl Harbor, generated an immediate sensation. Wallace, like many preachers among Churches of Christ, had opposed Christian involvement in combat. For the rest of the war the *Bible Banner* argued with force for the participation of Christians in all facets of government. Well-known preachers rallied to Wallace's position, including Whiteside, Nichol, Cled Wallace, Walter Estal Brightwell, and Orlando Clayton Lambert. Others who opposed Wallace on this issue included Benton Cordell Goodpasture, John Thomas Lewis, Henry Leo Boles, Eugene Sidney Smith, and Carl Hugo McCord. Wallace's teaching on civil government, in diametric opposition to the views of David Lipscomb, may be Wallace's most far-reaching and sustained legacy to Churches of Christ.

Wallace always opposed placing Christian colleges in the budgets of churches. Wallace claimed that colleges were private businesses and had no right to support from churches. Wallace and Nicholas Brodie Hardeman clashed over this issue in 1947 through the pages of the *Bible Banner,* the *Gospel Advocate,* and the *Firm Foundation.* Both men later regretted the bitterness of the campaign.

Financial distress during the Depression led Wallace to resign the editorship of the *Gospel Advocate* and to declare bankruptcy (1934) while reaffirming his debts. In 1937 Wallace — with the assistance of John W. Akin — satisfied his debts. Nevertheless Wallace's opponents constantly brought up his bankruptcy in an attempt to weaken his influence.

Wallace held thirteen formal debates. He confronted prominent preachers from various denominations: J. Frank Norris (1934), E. F. Webber (1937), Glen V. Tingley (1938), and John Matthews (1944). He also debated instrumental music in worship with representatives of the Christian Churches and Disciples of Christ, including H. W. Wallace (1925), H. L. Patterson (1932), Sam P. Jones (1932), A. D. Rogers (1936), and Homer A. Strong (1937).

During the final phase of his career (1952-79) Wallace wrote or rewrote all of his books, many of them adapted from sermons and addresses. Among his best-known works of this period, *God's Prophetic Word, The Gospel for Today,* and *The Christian and the Government* stand out.

In 1952 Wallace's wife, Virgie, suffered a debilitating stroke that left her an invalid. Wallace took his wife everywhere with him after her stroke and cared for her tenderly, strongly impressing many of his critics, who had often characterized him as harsh and heartless.

After 1949 many leaders of the nascent noninstitutional movement among Churches of Christ looked to Wallace for leadership. While initially favoring some of the positions of this movement, Wallace had by 1959 rejected the movement as divisive and by 1964 was completely separated from the movement and its followers.

In the last decade of his life Wallace opposed modern English translations of the Bible and penned *A Review of the New Versions* (1973). His critics derided this work and claimed that Wallace had no scholarly credentials to produce such a book. Nevertheless he continued to speak about errors he saw in "the new versions" in almost every sermon. Wallace died at Hereford, Texas, still preaching, at the age of 83.

See also Boll, Robert Henry; Eschatology; Goodpasture, Benton Cordell; Hardeman, Nicholas Brodie; Noninstitutional Movement; Thorp Spring Christian College; Wallace, Cled Eugene "Cleddie"

BIBLIOGRAPHY David Edwin Harrell, Jr., *Churches of Christ in the 20th Century: Homer Hailey's Personal Journey of Faith* (2000) • Noble Patterson and Terry J. Gardner, *Foy E. Wallace, Jr.: Soldier of the Cross* (1999).

TERRY J. GARDNER

Wallis, James (1793-1867)

Early Churches of Christ pastor and founding editor of the *British Millennial Harbinger.*

James Wallis was born in Kettering, England, in 1793, served an apprenticeship to a tailor, and was baptized in 1812 as a member of Andrew Fuller's Particular Baptist congregation. He moved to Nottingham and joined the Baptist church at George Street, where he became a draper and was also active as a village preacher. In 1834 he joined the Scotch Baptist congregation in Park Street, where he first read William Jones's *Millennial Harbinger.* In July 1836 he received Alexander Campbell's *Christianity Restored;* and in the autumn the Nottingham Scotch Baptist congregation split over the design of baptism. Forbid-

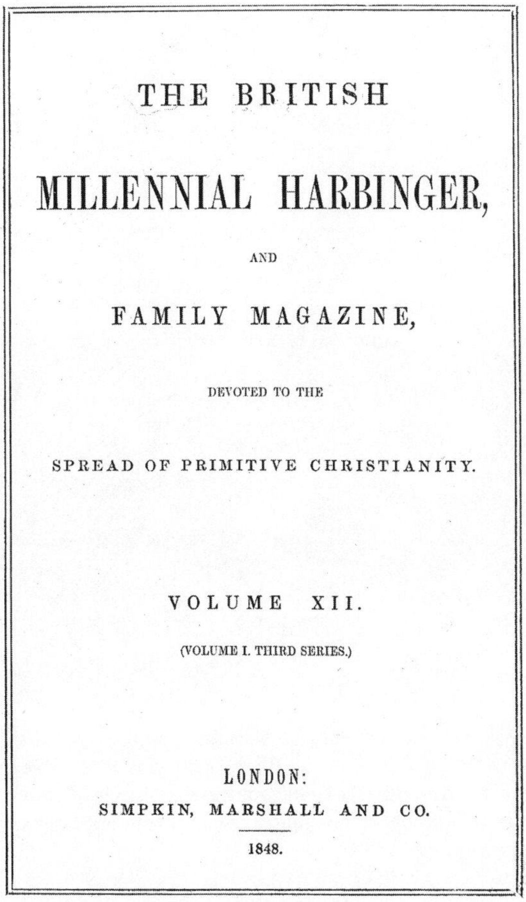

THE BRITISH

MILLENNIAL HARBINGER,

AND

FAMILY MAGAZINE,

DEVOTED TO THE

SPREAD OF PRIMITIVE CHRISTIANITY.

VOLUME XII.

(VOLUME I. THIRD SERIES.)

LONDON:
SIMPKIN, MARSHALL AND CO.

1848.

The British Millennial Harbinger, edited by James Wallis in its early days, was a crucial medium for introducing Alexander Campbell's writings to a British readership.
Courtesy of Disciples of Christ Historical Society

den by their pastors to celebrate communion, fourteen members withdrew on December 25, 1836, and met in the upper room of a warehouse on Mount Street, where they broke bread together. Wallis and Jonathan Hine, the owner of the warehouse, were chosen to preside over the congregation. Within a year the church had ninety-seven members and a chapel had been purchased in Barker Gate.

In March 1837 Wallis began to publish the *British Millennial Harbinger*, which became the leading magazine of the Movement. He published Campbell's works in England, beginning with *Remission of Sins*, and in 1841 published the first selection of *Psalms and Hymns* for the churches. At the inaugural Cooperative Meeting of the Churches in 1842, Wallis and the other Nottingham leaders were appointed as the Evangelist Committee, continuing in office until 1861. Wallis raised the money for Alexander Campbell's visit to Britain in 1847; and his own travels to his suppliers in the cloth-making areas of Lancashire and Yorkshire enabled him to visit and preach in other churches. He was chairman of the Annual Meeting in 1850, 1851, and 1857.

As an editor Wallis was prepared to publish material with which he did not agree, confident that truth would triumph through open discussion. His publication of Dr. John Thomas's millennial speculations in the 1840s probably enabled Thomas to draw several congregations into his infant Christadelphian movement. Wallis handed over the *British Millennial Harbinger* to David King in 1861, as his health began to fail. He died on May 17, 1867, aged 73. More than any other man, Wallis was responsible for the emergence of the British Churches of Christ as a separate movement.

See also *British Millennial Harbinger;* Great Britain and Ireland, Churches of Christ in; King, David

BIBLIOGRAPHY Louis Billington, "The Churches of Christ in Britain: A Study in Nineteenth-Century Sectarianism," in *The Stone-Campbell Movement: An International Religious Tradition,* ed. Michael W. Casey and Douglas A. Foster (2002), pp. 367-97 • David King, "On the Life and Death of James Wallis," *British Millennial Harbinger* (1867): 221-27 • David M. Thompson, *Let Sects and Parties Fall: A Short History of the Association of Churches of Christ in Great Britain and Ireland* (1980). DAVID M. THOMPSON

War

See Pacifism

Ward, Margaret Mae Yoho (1900-1983)

Disciples of Christ missionary, mission executive, and social justice advocate.

Born in 1900, near Huntington, West Virginia, Margaret Mae Yoho was encouraged by her pastor father, J. W. Yoho, to become a well-educated, independent woman. She graduated from Bethany College in 1923 and became the director of Christian education for the Christian Churches in West Virginia and Ohio. After being denied admission to Yale Divinity School because she was a woman, Yoho completed her master's degree in the Yale School of Education. She married pastor Norm Ward and served with him for six years as a missionary in Argentina.

Following desertion by her husband and a time of poverty and discouragement, Ward went on to serve the church as executive secretary for Latin American affairs in the United Christian Missionary Society (beginning in 1941), chair of the World Mission Division, and vice president of the United Christian Missionary Society (until 1967). After a brief retirement, she joined the staff of the Board of Higher Education until her second retirement at the age of 76. At that point, she became the self-appointed groundskeeper for the Missions Building in Indianapolis, where she prayed for each person that she saw entering the building.

During her life, Ward also served on the executive boards of the National Council of Churches and United Church Women; was a highly respected speaker on civil rights, justice for farm workers, missions, and Christian unity; and received honorary degrees from Bethany College, Culver-Stockton College, and Drake University. She died in 1983.

DEBRA B. HULL

Welshimer, Pearl Howard (1873-1957)

Minister, churchman, and influential standard-bearer of the Christian Churches/Churches of Christ.

An Ohio native, Welshimer (affectionately called "P.H.") was educated at Ohio Northern University and Hiram College, receiving his degree from the latter in 1897. He served as minister for churches in Champion (1895-97), Millersburg (1897-1901), and Canton (1902-57), Ohio. His fifty-four-year ministry in the First Christian Church of Canton took the congregation through two building programs and from an attendance of 128 to often over 2,000. Membership went from 350 to about 5,500, making it the largest of the Christian Churches in the mid-twentieth century. He conducted over 8,000 funerals and performed 8,261 marriages in Canton alone. He was a strong believer in the Sunday School and used attendance contests with other churches to stimulate his church's own. In 1916 he challenged eleven churches in Columbus, Ohio, to a contest, and on the closing day Canton had 7,009 in attendance.

Because of its size, Welshimer's congregation often served as a flagship for other churches. In 1921 the church pulled most of its financial support away from the United Christian Missionary Society (UCMS) because of its alleged liberal drift, thus encouraging other churches to do likewise. Welshimer himself participated in organized opposition to the "open membership" policies of the UCMS, which came to a head at the International Convention of the Disciples in Oklahoma City in 1925. In contrast to some other conservatives of his time, however, Welshimer had an irenic spirit. Although he opposed the liberalism that was becoming more obvious in the Disciples' organized agencies, he did not encourage exclusivism or separatism. He served as the first president of the North American Christian Convention (and so served two more times) but also regularly attended the Disciples' International Convention, for which he was a frequent speaker and one-time vice president. Welshimer was also a member of the Commission on Restudy of the Disciples of Christ in the late 1930s and 1940s, which worked toward consensus among liberal, moderate, and conservative constituencies alike. His maxim was "Let's disagree without being disagreeable." He did not participate in the bitter acrimony as the chasm between the Disciples and the Christian Churches/Churches of Christ widened. Some conservatives distrusted his broad-ranging fellowship, but he was widely respected by conservatives and liberals alike.

As minister of the largest Disciples congregation in the world during the mid-twentieth century, P. H. Welshimer was a conservative but irenic voice in the Disciples' Commission on Restudy in the 1940s. Courtesy of the Disciples of Christ Historical Society

See also Commission on Restudy of the Disciples of Christ; North American Christian Convention; Open Membership; United Christian Missionary Society, The

BIBLIOGRAPHY Francis M. Arant, *P.H.: The Welshimer Story* (1958) • P. H. Welshimer, *Concerning the Disciples: A Brief Resumé of the Movement to Restore the New Testament Church* (1935) • P. H. Welshimer, *The Great Salvation* (1954) • P. H. Welshimer, *Welshimer's Sermons* (1927).

JAMES B. NORTH

West, Willis Beauregard, Jr. (1907-1994)

Educational leader instrumental in establishing graduate programs in Bible and religion among colleges associated with Churches of Christ.

West was born in Decherd, Tennessee, and was baptized by H. M. Phillips (1887-1960) in 1921. He received his academic training at David Lipscomb College, Abilene Christian College, University of Southern California (Th.D. — the first person in Churches of Christ to receive a doctorate in biblical studies), University of Chicago, McCormick Theological Seminary, Garrett Biblical Institute, Cambridge University, and Oxford University.

Resisting anti-intellectual sentiments and fears of professional clericalism in his fellowship, West established in 1944, at George Pepperdine College in Los Angeles, the first graduate program in Bible and religion among Churches of Christ. In 1952, with the help of George Benson (1898-1991), he established another graduate program in Bible and religion at Harding College in Searcy, Arkansas, choosing this time to locate in the more conservative religious climate of the Bible Belt. This program eventually developed into the Harding Graduate School of Religion in Memphis, Tennessee, where he served as dean from 1958 to 1972. Later he served as graduate dean of Alabama Christian School of Religion and head of the Bible Department at Alabama Christian College (now Faulkner University).

West was also active in local church work, filling pulpits in churches in Tennessee, Mississippi, California, Illinois, Arkansas, and Alabama. He took a special interest in the book of Revelation, advocating a "first-century glasses" approach. A commentary on Revelation, edited from his lecture notes, was published posthumously.

See also Benson, George Stuart; Faulkner University; Harding University; Pepperdine University

BIBLIOGRAPHY Earl Irvin West, "The Contribution of W. B. West, Jr., to the Progress of the American Restoration Movement," in *The Last Things: Essays Presented by His Students to Dr. W. B. West, Jr., Upon the Occasion of His Sixty-fifth Birthday,* ed. Jack P. Lewis (1972), pp. 13-31.

RICKY G. HALE

Western Christian College

Independent Canadian school affiliated with Churches of Christ.

In 1946 Lillian Torkelson and others opened the first program with grades 7-12 as Radville Christian College in Radville, Saskatchewan. The school also had a Bible training program that stemmed from summer and winter Bible schools started in the early 1930s. The campus, located on a riverbank, had tamped earth houses, hand-carried water, and no indoor plumbing.

In 1957 Radville Christian College leased a defunct air force training base north of Weyburn, Saskatchewan, and changed its name to Western Christian College. Enrollment in the high school program rose from 46 to 84. Richard Dacus was the first president of the school, from 1958 to 1960. Under the administration of E. D. Wieb, who served from 1960 to 1973 and from 1985 to 1988, college-level instruction in Bible and liberal arts were added. Other presidents included Glen Dods, 1974-77; Max Mowrer, 1978-85; Vince Anderson, 1988-92; and John McMillan, 1993 to the present.

In 1989 Western Christian moved to the fourteen-acre campus of the former McKay Residential Indian School in Dauphin, Manitoba Parkland Region. The school purchased three acres and a building for the college program in 1999. In July 2003, Western Christian College and High School relocated to the former campus of Canadian Bible College in Regina, Saskatchewan, after purchasing the property in January that year.

See also Canada, The Movement in

BIBLIOGRAPHY Lillian M. Torkelson and Roger W. Peterson, *Western Christian College: Background and Historical Perspective, 1931 to 1995* (1995).

ERMA JEAN LOVELAND

Westwood Christian Foundation

The Westwood Christian Foundation was established in 1975 to fund and administer a consortial program of theological studies within the academic community of the University of California, Los Angeles. Initiated by Robert O. Fife and Myron J. Taylor, the foundation was designed to meet a strongly felt academic need without starting another free-standing seminary. Major participants in the consortium were Emmanuel School of Religion (Johnson City, Tennessee) and Fuller Theological Seminary (Pasadena, California). Other participating institutions were Lincoln Christian Seminary and Cincinnati Bible Seminary. Milligan College and Pacific Christian College offered courses at the undergraduate level.

The role of the Westwood Christian Foundation was to fund and administer accredited courses of study that were authorized and governed by the consortial institutions. Curricular areas included Old and New Testaments, church history, theology, and biblical languages.

Meanwhile, an unprecedented relationship was developed with the University of California, Los Angeles (UCLA). At the same time that the foundation was being established, a strong movement commenced within the university to establish studies in early Christianity. Lack of funding was a major barrier. After several conferences between foundation and university leaders, the foundation offered to fund an experimental course in early Christian history if the university wished to make an appointment.

Following accepted academic search procedures, the Department of History appointed the foundation's resident New Testament scholar, S. Scott Bartchy, to teach such a class. Student and faculty response was positive. When the university expressed the desire to repeat the class the following year, the foundation once again made a grant to the university to cover the professor's salary. From those early beginnings a unique partnership developed. The curriculum in early Christianity grew apace, developing into a major — all of which the Westwood Christian Foundation funded.

In 1990 UCLA undertook steps to establish a fully funded Chair in Early Christian History in the Department of History. After a significant international search, Bartchy was chosen from among a number of eminent finalists.

The foundation's commitment to serve the university exhausted a major part of its funds. Meanwhile, other institutions were able to undertake the theological work it had provided. Therefore, the foundation's permanent funds were devoted to needed lectures and publications concerning the Stone-Campbell Movement. The funds were later transferred to Emmanuel School of Religion in support of lectureships in preaching and pastoral care and in Christian reformation. ROBERT O. FIFE

Whiteside, Robertson Lafayette (1869-1951)

Minister, editor, debater, president of Abilene Christian College from 1910 to 1912, and vice president from 1912 to 1914.

Whiteside received his education at West Tennessee Christian College (1890) and Nashville Bible School, graduating from the latter in 1898. He was known by contemporaries as the "David Lipscomb of Texas" for his terse writing style. He engaged N. L. Clark in the first written debate on Sunday Schools in 1907. Whiteside shaped and solidified many theological perspectives in Churches of Christ through the publication with C. R. Nichol of a multivolume systematic theology titled *Sound Doctrine*. These volumes were used in Bible classes in churches, colleges, and even cross-cultural mission work in China. Whiteside wrote Sunday School material for the *Firm Foundation* (1928-30) and the *Gospel Advocate Adult Quarterlies* (1932-36), and *Annual Lesson Commentary* (1937-44). Whiteside's magnum opus was his *New Commentary on Romans,* which shaped the way a generation understood grace. Whiteside helped mold perspectives on premillennialism, pacifism, the Holy Spirit, and grace.

BIBLIOGRAPHY C. R. Nichol and R. L. Whiteside, *Sound Doctrine,* 5 vols. (1920-52) • Robert P. Valentine, Jr., "Robertson Lafayette Whiteside: Systematic Theologian for the Churches of Christ" (guided research thesis, Harding University Graduate School of Religion, Memphis, Tennessee, 2001)• R. L. Whiteside, *A New Commentary on Paul's Letter to the Saints at Rome* (1945) • R. L. Whiteside, *Doctrinal Discourses* (1955) • R. L. Whiteside, *Reflections* (1965) • *Whiteside-Clark Discussion* (1969) • R. L. Whiteside and C. R. Nichol, *Christ and His Kingdom: A Review of R. H. Boll* (1925). BOBBY VALENTINE

Wickizer, Willard Morgan (1900-1974)

Agency administrator and pioneering leader in the denominational restructure of the Christian Church (Disciples of Christ).

Best known for initiating Restructure and convening the Panel of Scholars, the "father of Restructure" was a graduate of the University of Oklahoma (B.A., 1920), Boston University (M.R.E., 1923), and Drake University (D.D., 1947). After being Regional Director of Religious Education for the United Christian Missionary Society (UCMS) in the Pacific Northwest (1923-26), Wickizer served as Director of Religious Education at the University Place Christian Church, Des Moines, Iowa (1926-30).

At First Christian Church, Maryville, Missouri (1930-36), Wickizer chaired a state society reorganization and met his future partner in denominational Restructure, Harlie Smith. His remaining UCMS career (1936-66) included various titles — initially executive secretary, Department of Evangelism and Church Development; and later executive chairman, Division of Church Life and Work — while serving on chaplaincy committees and as a vice president of the National Council of Churches. Wickizer initiated a ministerial placement service, a church hymnal, and the Home and State Missions Planning Council.

Wickizer supported Jarvis Christian College, Southern Christian Institute, and Japanese Christian Institute as well as Appalachian, French (Louisiana), and Native American missions. Believing that knowledge should transform conduct and seeing the UCMS as "a great experiment," he denied that personal religion must come before and apart from its social expression. He strongly advocated tithing and Christian benevolence, more representation by women and minorities on boards, and merging rural churches for efficiency.

Wickizer first proposed the denominational reorganization of the Disciples of Christ at a meeting of the Council of Agencies in 1958, and by the fall of that year he served as chairman of the Committee on

Brotherhood Restructure inaugurated by the Board of Directors of the Disciples' International Convention. He was succeeded as chairman by Granville Walker when the committee was expanded in 1960. Wickizer was an active member of the Panel of Scholars in the 1960s and communicated his ecclesiological concerns in papers presented to the Panel.

See also Home and State Missions Planning Council; Panel of Scholars; Restructure; United Christian Missionary Society, The

BIBLIOGRAPHY D. Duane Cummins and Robert L. Friedly, *The Search for Identity* (1987) • Willard M. Wickizer, *A Functional Church Organization* (1951) • Willard M. Wickizer, "Ideas for Brotherhood Restructure" and "The New Opportunities for Religious Education," in *The Renewal of Church: The Panel of Scholars Reports,* vol. 3: *The Revival of the Churches* (1963), pp. 112-26 and 288-307.

C. J. DULL

Wilburn, Ralph Glenn (1909-1986)

Minister, educator, and theologian among twentieth-century Disciples of Christ.

Born in Emporia, Kansas, on May 10, 1909, Wilburn spent his early boyhood in Saskatchewan, Canada, and later moved with his family to Santa Rosa, California, where he attended high school and then junior college. Wilburn held the B.A. from the University of California at Berkeley in German and philosophy, and took his M.A. (in 1942) and Ph.D. (in 1945) from the Divinity School of the University of Chicago, followed by a year of postdoctoral study at the University of Heidelberg, Germany, focusing on the Protestant Reformation. Wilburn had earlier been ordained in the Church of Christ, but in 1951 he obtained ordination in the Disciples of Christ. While studying in Chicago, he pastored churches in the area and from 1939 to 1944 served as a radio minister on WJJD. He also held pastorates while in Berkeley and Los Angeles and served as interim minister for the American Protestant Community in Bad Godesberg, Germany, 1954-55. On several later occasions he served as chaplain in the U.S. Air Force at Wiesbaden, Birkenfeld, and Frankfurt, Germany.

From 1944 to 1951, Wilburn taught courses on religion at George Pepperdine College in Los Angeles. In 1951 he was called to be professor of theology in the Graduate Seminary of Phillips University in Enid, Oklahoma, where he served until 1957, when he was called to be professor of historical theology at the College of the Bible (later Lexington Theological Seminary), Lexington, Kentucky. During his twelve-year teaching career there, he also served as dean from 1961 to 1969. After leaving Lexington, he served as chair of the Religion Department at Chapman College from 1969 to 1977, during which time he also taught extension courses at San Diego Naval Air Base. He also served the church in various other ways, including contributing to the Panel of Scholars study (1956-62) and editing volume 2 of its papers, entitled *The Reconstruction of Theology* (1963). His Panel paper "A Critique of the Restoration Principle" was an especially significant examination of a cherished theme in Stone-Campbell history, which, in Wilburn's view, demanded revision according to a more historically realistic understanding of the life of the apostolic churches. Wilburn was also a member of, and contributed papers to, the Association of Disciples for Theological Discussion and the American Theological Society.

A prolific lecturer and writer, he authored several important works as well as numerous journal articles and book reviews. Among his chief works are *The Prophetic Voice in Protestant Christianity* (1956), *The Historical Shape of Faith* (1966), and *The Interrelation Between Theology and Science* (1966). Central to his theological vision, beginning with his doctoral dissertation on Schleiermacher's doctrine of grace (1945), was the theme of God's unmerited, free grace, which liberates those who receive it in faith from all dogmatism and "legalism," and requires of the church ongoing theological inquiry and revision. But he insisted that this should not lead to a wholesale rejection of the church's historic creeds and confessions, but rather to a new appreciation of their liturgical value as acts of praise in various times and situations. His theological reading of the past combined elements of liberal and neo-orthodox views. Anyone who heard his lectures on historical theology could not but be impressed with the zest with which he presented theological voices of the past and the keen insight he conveyed into the meaning and significance of their thought for the life of the church.

In the later years of his teaching career, his thought turned increasingly to the relation of theology and church to contemporary culture, as, for example, in his M. T. Burt Lectures at the Nebraska School of Religion on the interrelation between theology and science, in which he explored what science can contribute to theology and what theology can contribute to science.

See also Lexington Theological Seminary; Liberalism; Panel of Scholars; Phillips Theological Seminary; "Restoration," Meanings of within the Movement

BIBLIOGRAPHY Ralph G. Wilburn, *Christianity versus Legalism* (1949) • Ralph G. Wilburn, *The Prophetic Voice in Protestant Christianity* (1956) • Ralph G. Wilburn, "A Critique of the Restoration Principle," in *The Renewal of Church: The Panel Reports,* vol. 1: *The Reformation of Tradition* (1963), pp. 215-56 • Ralph G. Wilburn, *The Historical*

Shape of Faith (1966) • Ralph G. Wilburn, *The Interrelation Between Theology and Science* (M. T. Burt Lectures, 1966) • Ralph G. Wilburn, ed., *The Renewal of Church: The Panel Reports* (1963).

WILLIAM R. BARR

Willett, Herbert Lockwood (1864-1944)

Biblical scholar and educator, editorialist, ecumenist, pastor, popular lecturer, and prominent liberal in controversies over "higher criticism" and open membership among the Disciples of Christ in the early twentieth century.

Born in Iona, Michigan, Willett attended Bethany College (A.B., 1886; A.M., 1887). At Yale he became a student of William Rainey Harper and followed Harper in 1893 when he left to become the first president of the new University of Chicago. Willett took his Ph.D. there in 1896 and taught on its faculty of Semitic Languages and Literature from then until 1929. Encouraged by Harper, Willett helped found the Disciples Divinity House to augment the training of Disciples students at the University of Chicago Divinity School. Willett served (1894-1921) as the House's first Dean, after teaching for the new Bible Chair at the University of Michigan in Ann Arbor (1893). He wrote for the *Christian-Evangelist* and *Christian Century* and pastored congregations in Chicago.

In such forums, Willett introduced Disciples and other Protestants to historical and social-scientific methods of interpreting the Bible. His work occasioned rancorous debate with conservatives, such as J. W. McGarvey, through editorials in the *Christian-Evangelist* and *Christian Standard.* McGarvey regularly targeted Willett's (and others') embrace of historical-critical theories uncovering the influences of ancient Near Eastern culture on the formation of the Hebrew Scriptures. The issue of Mosaic authorship of the Pentateuch was one among many other contested issues.

In 1909 a widely publicized attempt to remove Willett from the program of the Disciples Centennial meeting in Pittsburgh, Pennsylvania, failed. Willett's greatest contributions were not in technical scholarship but in his renowned ability to communicate, in print and from the platform. He enjoyed a national reputation on the lecture circuit, drawing large crowds at eight-day lay Bible institutes. So it was perhaps fitting that he died during one of these lectureships, in Winter Park, Florida, in 1944.

J. H. Garrison invited Willett to write the *Christian-Evangelist*'s weekly Sunday School lesson commentary in 1899. Though his historical-critical approach drew fire from conservatives like J. W. McGarvey, Willett became a major popularizer of biblical critical scholarship through this and other lay venues.

See also Bible, Interpretation of the; Bible Chair Movement; *Christian Century, The; Christian-Evangelist; Christian Standard;* Disciples Divinity House; Hermeneutics; Liberalism; McGarvey, John W.; Open Membership

BIBLIOGRAPHY William Barnett Blakemore, *The Quest for Intelligence in Ministry* (1970) • M. Eugene Boring, *Disciples and the Bible: A History of Disciples Biblical Interpretation in North America* (1997) • Herbert L. Willett, *Life and Teachings of Jesus* (1898) • Herbert L. Willett, *The Prophets of Israel* (1899) • Herbert L. Willett, *Basic Truths of the Christian Faith* (1904) • Herbert L. Willett, *Studies in the First Book of Samuel* (1909) • Herbert L. Willett, *The Moral Leaders of Israel* (1916) • Herbert L. Willett, *The Call of the Christ* (1912) • Herbert L. Willett, *Our Bible: Its Origin, Character and Value* (1917) • Herbert L. Willett, *The Bible Through the Centuries* (1929) • Herbert L. Willett, *The Jew Through the Centuries* (1932) • Herbert L. Willett, *The Corridor of Years: An Autobiographical Record,* compiled by H. L. Willett III (1968, unpublished manuscript, Disciples Divinity House, University of Chicago).

LARRY D. BOUCHARD

William Woods College

Related to the Christian Church (Disciples of Christ).

The history of William Woods College can be traced to the founding in 1848 of the Female Academy at Camden Point, Missouri. The first two principals, Hugh B. Todd and Moses E. Lard, were both graduates of Bethany College. Alexander Campbell visited the academy in 1852 and commended the school for its service. The plight of broken families in the aftermath of the Civil War prompted the delegates to the annual convention of the Christian Churches in Missouri meeting in Columbia in 1868 to approve unanimously the establishment of an orphan school in Missouri. Because of Camden Point Female Academy's twenty years of relative success in education, it was the most promising location. An eight-acre plot was purchased in 1869, and the school opened in 1870 as the Female Orphan School.

Fire destroyed the school in March 1889. When the Christian Convention met at Warrensburg that year and reviewed the school's financial situation, the decision was made to relocate it to an area more likely to generate growth. Two institutions resulted from this decision. Enough of the delegates were committed to the Camden Point Academy for it to remain in operation, which it did until 1904 when it was incorporated as Missouri Christian College. But the majority of the delegates decided to accept an offer from the town of Fulton to move the academy there. The Female Orphan School of the Christian Church of Missouri began its first session in Fulton in the fall of 1890.

Soon afterwards, another decision was made. Considering that the majority of students were able to pay all or part of the cost of their education, and since the need for orphan homes had diminished, it was determined that the name of the school should be changed to reflect its true student composition. In May 1900, Female Orphan School was renamed Daughters College. Only briefly did the school carry this name, however, for that same year financial contributions by Dr. and Mrs. William Woods, benefactors from Kansas City, led the board of directors to rename the school in recognition of that generous endowment. William Woods College was born. It was accredited as a junior college in 1914, a four-year college in 1962, and a co-educational university in 1993.

See also Bethany College; Campbell, Alexander; Children's Homes and Orphanages; Lard, Moses E.

BIBLIOGRAPHY Lawrence O. Christensen and Gary R. Kremer, *A History of Missouri,* vol. 4, *1875 to 1919* (1997) • Griffith A. Hamlin, *In Faith and History: The Story of William Woods College* (1965). CANDACE WOOD

Williams, John Augustus

See Smith, "Raccoon" John

Williams, T. C.

See Australia, The Movement in

Wineskins Magazine

Progressive magazine serving Churches of Christ.

In 1991 Phillip Morrison (b. 1933), founding managing editor of *UpReach* magazine (published by Herald of Truth), began conversations with Rubel Shelly (b. 1945), pulpit minister of the Woodmont Hills Church of Christ in Nashville, concerning a new journal in Churches of Christ. Shelly suggested including Mike Cope, pulpit minister of the Highland Church of Christ in Abilene, Texas, in the discussions. As a result of these discussions, *Wineskins* magazine was introduced at the Pepperdine University Bible Lectures in May 1992.

The editors identified the focus of the new journal as "reform and renewal in the church." It denied, however, being a sociologically driven "church growth" or "church methods" paper. Rather, it was designed to be "a theological publication whose goal is to foster renewal in the church by sharpening its attention on Jesus as Lord."

The purpose statement further committed *Wineskins* to the promotion of "bold but responsible change in the church of God." The paper's title was an allusion to Jesus' parable of the old and new wineskins, referring to the "ever-fresh gospel and its always-frail containers. He warned against putting 'new wine in old skins' lest the skins burst and waste the contents. In his metaphor, the skins are the culturally-conditioned and time-bound experiences of the people who form the covenant community of God."

The editors expressed their belief in the unchanging nature of the gospel, insisting that any changes advocated would be in attitudes and methodologies to preserve the purity and perfection of Jesus' unchanging message. Though they positioned themselves as firmly committed to "the Church of Christ that was born of the American Restoration Movement," they noted that writers would not be confined to that heritage, partly to help Churches of Christ see themselves from other perspectives and to provide the opportunity to receive counsel and rebuke humbly.

Wineskins was quickly praised by those agreeing with its purpose and just as quickly renounced by others. Steady subscription growth peaked at approximately 17,000, with subscribers in all states of the United States, all Canadian provinces, and more than thirty other countries. Because subscription and advertising revenues were never enough to sustain such a high-quality, four-color publication, *Wineskins* depended heavily on interested donors. Despite such contributions, the magazine was never able to maintain a regular publication schedule.

At the beginning of 2000, Phillip and Mary Margaret Morrison (who were responsible for production and distribution) began a search for someone to assume responsibility for the publication. The Zoe Group, a ministry for worship renewal based in Nashville, Tennessee, assumed the role of publisher in early 2001. The Zoe Group board led by chair Larry Bridgesmith saw great compatibility between its ministry and the *Wineskins* ministry of publishing a Christ-centered magazine. Rubel Shelly and Mike Cope continued as coeditors. Greg Taylor, transitioning back to the United States after seven years as a missionary in Uganda, replaced Morrison as managing editor.

In 2001 the magazine began to be issued under the name *New Wineskins* and soon added a web site through which an increasing number of subscribers accessed the magazine. The site contains archived articles, an index, all of the content from the print magazine, current articles not found in the print version, audio sermons by contemporary preachers, book and movie reviews, and printable Bible teaching resources. In 2004 the journal moved to an entirely electronic form available by subscription through its web site www.wineskins.org.

PHILLIP MORRISON *and* GREG TAYLOR

Winston-Salem Bible College

Bible college educating African American students for the Christian Churches/Churches of Christ.

Winston-Salem Bible College, Winston-Salem, North Carolina, began on February 27, 1945, as The Christian Institute. The Christian Institute was the result of the labors of two ministers who envisioned a school primarily for the training of black students. R. L. Peters, a well-known black evangelist, and J. W. West, an evangelist in the Appalachian Mountains, formed a team to establish the institute. Peters led in the formal founding of the school while West concentrated on fund-raising.

The Christian Institute opened in 1945, but from its formation was beset with problems. Aubrey L. Payne, minister to four churches in the Winston-Salem area, aided the school in teaching and in recruiting faculty from area churches and from Winston-Salem State College to assist with instruction. He reorganized the board of directors and strove to place the college on a proper financial footing. Despite Payne's efforts, the school's problems persisted until it failed to open for the 1949 fall term.

In 1949 Leland Tyrrell, a missionary who had hoped to go to South Africa but was unable to obtain a visa, was called to be president of the school. He arrived in Winston-Salem on December 9, 1949. The school's name was changed from The Christian Institute to Winston-Salem Bible College, and the school reopened on January 16, 1950, under Tyrrell's leadership. Twenty-eight students, primarily attending night classes, comprised the student body. The school continued to grow and in its third year of operation began a building program.

Tyrrell led the school as its president until December 31, 1978. Tyrrell thereupon served as chancellor until his retirement on December 31, 1979. Donald Forrester was called to be the college's second president on January 1, 1979, and served until July 1985. W. Ray Kelley became the third president, on January 20, 1986, and served until 2002. William E. Johnson began his service as the fourth president of the school in August 2002.

The school facilities continued to expand and improve. On August 20, 1976, the college moved to its new twenty-seven-acre campus, and capital improvements continue. The current curriculum includes a Bachelor of Arts in Ministry degree program with four primary areas of concentration: pastoral ministry, Christian education, urban ministry, and biblical languages. The college has obtained candidate status with the Accrediting Association of Bible Colleges and is moving toward full membership.

See also African Americans in the Movement — Christian Churches/Churches of Christ; Bible College Movement; College of the Scriptures; Higher Education, Views of in the Movement

GARY L. LEE

Women in Ministry

1. Nineteenth Century
2. Twentieth Century
   2.1. Christian Church (Disciples of Christ)
   2.2. Churches of Christ
   2.3. Christian Churches/Churches of Christ

1. Nineteenth Century

Several factors contributed to an increase in public leadership roles for women and ministerial ordination of women in the Stone-Campbell Movement in the latter half of the nineteenth century. Among them were increasing educational opportunities for girls; women's financial and legal independence from their husbands and fathers; better health care and decreased birth rates; skills gained by women from taking care of homes, farms, business, and communities in the absence of men during the Civil War; the lack of educated men available to serve frontier churches; and a growing sense among women that they had special gifts to use in service in the church, often born out of their experience in church missionary societies and in the social reform movements of the time.

Compared to some other Protestant denominations (Presbyterians, Lutherans, and Episcopalians, for instance), women in the Stone-Campbell tradition were ordained early in the church's history, though wide acceptance of women in the eldership occurred later. In general, in denominations where presiding at the table and other liturgical functions were performed by elders, ordination of women as pastors occurred earlier than acceptance of women as elders; in denominations where pastors rather than elders filled the "priestly" roles, the pattern was reversed. In addition, the first denominations to ordain women tended to be congregationally organized and to value local church power and autonomy. By and large, they were frontier churches that developed in sparsely populated regions with few seminary-trained preachers.

However, the ordination of women was surrounded by considerable controversy. The issues of the proper interpretation and application of Scripture, the role of culture in church polity, the critical need for evangelists in the church, the inherent status of women, and the authoritative function of preachers and evangelists were debated in the church publications of the time, particularly the *Christian Standard* from 1891 to 1893, where twenty-nine different authors discussed the issue. The chief opponents were John B. Briney (1839-1927) and Morgan P. Hayden. Advocates included Persis Lemon Christian (a regular contributor and noted singing evangelist), Clara Hale Babcock (1850-1924), and missionaries Oliver A. Carr and George T. Smith (1849-1920).

Barbara Kellison of the Iowa Conference, who published a pamphlet in 1862 describing her call to preach, and Marinda R. Lemert, a contributor to the *Apostolic Guide,* were well-known spokespersons for the ordination of women in the Stone-Campbell tradition. Alexander Campbell, on the other hand, did not favor ordaining women, writing that he advocated submitting to the teachings of Paul on the subject.

A small number of women in the Stone-Campbell movement were functioning as evangelists, organizing churches, serving as missionaries, and baptizing believers as early as the first decades of the nineteenth century. Examples include Mary T. Graft, Mary Morrison, and Mary Ogle, who established a church in Pennsylvania in 1815-17, taking the name Disciples of Christ following a visit by Thomas Campbell in 1828; and Mary Stogdill, whose work as a baptizer and recruiter of ministers helped found the Ontario, Canada, Christian Conference in 1821.

Because pastors or ministers were ordained by congregations or conferences when there was a formal ordination, it is difficult to determine with certainty who was the first woman ordained in the Stone-Campbell tradition. Some of the first were surely Ellen Grant Gustin, ordained by the Miami Christian Conference in 1873; Emi B. Frank, ordained at about the same time, probably in Indiana; Melissa Garrett Terrell, ordained in Ohio in 1867; and Laura D. Garst, Mary L. Adams, and Josephine W. Smith, ordained by the General Missionary Society in 1883, specifically for missionary service.

Mary Stogdill was an active baptizer and recruiter of ministers in Ontario in the early nineteenth century.

Clara Hale Babcock is commonly credited with being the first woman ordained for preaching in the Stone-Campbell tradition, in 1888 or 1889. Other early women pastors were Jessie Coleman Monser, ordained in 1891; Sadie McCoy Crank, ordained in 1892; Bertha Mason Fuller, ordained in 1896; and Clara Espy Hazelrigg, ordained in 1897. Many of these women were also active in the Christian Woman's Board of Missions (CWBM) and the Woman's Christian Temperance Union (WCTU). Some historians believe that women's effectiveness as WCTU speakers and in mission work led to their acceptance as ordained preachers.

Although probably never ordained, Sarah Lue Bostick was a noted African American preacher and CWBM organizer during the last years of the nineteenth century. Other African American, Hispanic, and Asian women gained more recognition as ordained pastors and church leaders in the twentieth century.

DEBRA B. HULL

Jessie Colman Monser was among the early women pastors in the Stone-Campbell Movement, ordained in 1891.

2. Twentieth Century

2.1. Christian Church (Disciples of Christ)

Advancements in medicine, attention to hygiene, increased opportunities for public education, and the migration from farm to city intertwined with changing gender roles to provide women of the twentieth century with more choices for their futures. The advances made by women active in the reform movements of the nineteenth century culminated in the passage of prohibition in 1919 and women's suffrage in 1920. In the churches at the turn of the century, women made up 60 percent of the worshipers, 60 percent of the missionaries, two-thirds of the members of missionary societies, and 90 percent of the Sunday School teachers. Differences in response to these and other societal and religious factors, and controversy over the proper role of women in the church and in the culture, contributed to the split that began in the 1920s between those who would later become the Christian Church (Disciples of Christ) and the Christian Churches/Churches of Christ.

Though opposition continues in some local churches, the fact that the Disciples of Christ ordain women and elect women elders sets them apart from the other streams of the Stone-Campbell Movement in the twentieth century. During the 1900s, the growing acceptance of women clergy in Disciples churches mirrored gains women were making in other professions, though not to the same degree. Despite the growth in the number of women clergy, they lagged behind their male counterparts in a number of areas. They were more likely than men to enter nonpastoral ministries, to be found serving small, poor, struggling churches, and to be paid less. In 1990, for instance, Disciples clergywomen earned, on average, 77 percent of the average male salary.

The number of ordained women grew slowly over the first two-thirds of the century. Jessie Coleman Monser, herself ordained in 1891, reported that in 1931 there were 365 women ministers, 85 of whom were pastors. In 1952 a United Church Women survey showed 298 ordained Disciples women, 39 in pastorates. Following that report and at the request of the National Council of Churches, a committee was convened to consider the status of women among Disciples. This committee, made up of women leaders in the church as well as four men — A. Dale Fiers, W. E. Garrison, Perry Gresham, and Howard Short — called for the church to encourage women to enter the ministry and to give women full opportunities for service. Still, almost twenty years later, in 1972, less than 1 percent of ordained Disciples were women.

In the latter decades of the twentieth century, the proportion of ordained Disciples women increased. By 1990, 15 percent of ordained Disciples ministers were women; about 9 percent of senior or solo pastors were women (up from about 4 percent in 1984), and about 39 percent of associate pastors were women (compared to about 33 percent in 1984). In 2000, 22 percent of the pastors in Disciples churches were women.

It was well into the twentieth century before women were accepted as students in Disciples seminaries, yet the proportion of women in seminaries has exceeded the proportion of women pastors. Ellen Moore Warren was the first ordained Disciples woman to hold a divinity degree, graduating from the College of the Bible in 1916 and being ordained in

1923. In the 1980s, about one-third of Disciples seminary students were women; in 1990, 43 percent of Disciples seminary students were women; and by 2000, about half of Disciples seminary students were women. Minority women also came to have a more profound impact on the church, in the seminaries, and as ordained pastors and evangelists.

Several organizations were created to support women ministers during the twentieth century. One, the International Women Preacher's Association, an ecumenical group, was founded in 1918. Disciples pastors provided early leadership, with Lulu Hunter serving as vice president in 1920 and Mary Lyons serving as a later president of the group. By 2000 the Division of Homeland Ministries was publishing an on-line newsletter to help connect ordained Disciples women with one another and to support their ministries. The newsletter is called "Daughters of Clara," in honor of Clara Hale Babcock, widely recognized as the first ordained Disciples woman.

DEBRA B. HULL

2.2. Churches of Christ

Women's ministry in twentieth-century Churches of Christ included those who exercised leadership in the church through such activities as preaching, teaching, serving as an officer in the church, writing for churchwide publications (whose readership includes both men and women), and employment as an official "minister" of the church. Much of the ministry done by women in Churches of Christ in the twentieth century has been exclusively to women, in which many have made significant contributions in missions, teaching, writing, program directing, and counseling.

One of the earliest advocates in Churches of Christ for expanded roles for women was Silena Moore Holman (1850-1915), who was active in the work of the Women's Christian Temperance Union. She often wrote articles in the *Gospel Advocate* supporting a more extensive leadership role for women than advocated by church leaders.

After the division with the Disciples, women in Churches of Christ rarely exercised public leadership roles. With some exceptions, the subject was essentially closed until the late 1960s. One of the reasons for this lack of public authoritative role for women was the strong opposition expressed by such leaders as David Lipscomb, who argued in the *Gospel Advocate* that to disobey Paul's command on silence would lead women to eternal death.

Another possible factor in the restrictive stance of Churches of Christ concerning public leadership roles for women may be the church's relationship to the ideals of the emerging fundamentalist movement, which was extremely powerful in the South. Betty DeBerg maintains that fundamentalism was prominent as both an intellectual and a popular movement because of gender and family issues. Fundamentalist periodicals glorified the domestic sphere, using select Scriptures repeatedly (e.g., 1 Cor. 14:34-35 and 1 Tim. 2:11-15) to mandate that women remain silent in church.

The nature and role of the Bible in Protestantism was another factor that influenced views of the role of women. Churches of Christ followed Alexander Campbell's hermeneutical approach, which, in practice, called for a literal reading of such passages as the two mentioned above.

The 1960s and 1970s brought paradigm shifts, both in how the Bible was interpreted and in how culture viewed the role of women. These moves resulted in conceptual and practical changes regarding "women in ministry" in Churches of Christ.

From the late 1960s to the end of the century, there is evidence of change. The progressive *Mission* journal carried numerous articles supporting an increased role for women throughout its existence (1967-1988). *Leaven,* which began publication in 1994, has also addressed issues concerning women's role in the church in a positive way. The most substantial literature that emerged in the twentieth century was the two-volume *Essays on Women in Earliest Christianity,* edited by Abilene Christian University New Testament scholar Carroll Osburn. These volumes contain about fifty articles covering a wide range of topics, written primarily by male church scholars and ministers. Though some of the articles are neutral, most support greater inclusion of women in church leadership.

In the 1970s campus ministries among Churches of Christ experienced great growth, and on some campuses by the mid-1970s it was acceptable for churches to hire women to minister to female students. These women were often called "women's counselors" instead of ministers; however, these women were heavily involved in the strategic planning of the campus ministry and had other leadership responsibilities. Also, some mainline churches began to employ women in educational ministries, children's ministries, youth ministries, counseling, and benevolence ministries. In such contexts they were sometimes called "ministers."

By 1989, the Brookline Church of Christ (Brookline, Massachusetts) placed a statement on the back of its bulletin affirming the importance of women's public involvement in all aspects of the church's ministries. In 1987 they had employed a woman as one of two pulpit ministers, probably the first Church of Christ to do so. In recent years at least one other Church of Christ has employed a husband-wife team for all aspects of its ministry. Other churches that expanded roles for women include the Bering Drive Church of Christ in Houston and the Stamford

Church of Christ in Stamford, Connecticut. The 1990s also brought public discussion about women's issues at some church conferences and lectureships at Christian universities. A growing number of congregations are spending extended study time in sermons, classes, special seminars, and forums reexamining their practices concerning women's leadership in worship and congregational governance.

Because the documentation is scarce, it is difficult to know the percentage of churches that are currently using women in more authoritative roles; however, the dialogue and debates have continued into the twenty-first century. Though the issue has not been resolved, the role and scope of women in ministry continues to change in a growing number of churches. KATHY J. PULLEY

2.3. Christian Churches/Churches of Christ

Christian Churches/Churches of Christ have chosen a conservative view in acceptance of women serving in ministerial positions, especially as pastors. This attitude is specifically demonstrated by the question of the ordination of women. A survey of articles in the *Christian Standard* since 1890 demonstrates an ongoing debate about the role of women in ministry among Christian Churches/Churches of Christ.

In many cases, the issue is not so much whether a woman can serve on a church staff but whether she can be ordained. The tendency among Christian Churches/Churches of Christ has been to ordain women to a specific ministry, if they ordain them at all (e.g., for Christian education rather than for ministry in general), while men, who themselves may intend to serve in similar positions, have been ordained to ministry without any stipulation of the specific ministry. Current views about women in ministry among Christian Churches/Churches of Christ run along a continuum that can be roughly sketched as follows:

1. denial of any role of leadership to women, especially public ministry; women's roles are limited to teaching young children and handling housekeeping and food functions;
2. acceptance of women in certain specific positions such as children's or music ministry, but without benefit of ordination;
3. acceptance of women in almost any ministry except for the pastorate and approval of ordination;
4. acceptance and ordination of women for any aspect of ministry.

Despite the debate, women have always served in a variety of ministries, including the pastorate. The dominant number of women currently in ministry fit into the second category listed above, though an increasing number fit into the third category. A few fit the fourth description.

Women often have served in ministry in areas or times when few men were available. When circumstances changed and men were available, they were selected to fill ministry positions. Prior to 1945, for example, many women preachers served churches in Oklahoma. Following World War II and the establishment of colleges such as Midwest Christian College, Dallas Christian College, and Ozark Christian College, more men were educated for ministry and pulpits became closed to women as the debate about women in ministry intensified. Many women then entered youth ministry positions. Those soon became positions primarily for men, however, leaving women to enter Christian education or music ministries. As those positions have become more common among churches, they too have generally been filled by men rather than women.

A comparison of a survey of the *1997 Directory of the Ministry* with the *2001 Directory of the Ministry* reveals, however, that an increasing number of women are in ministry positions in local churches, on the mission field, and in parachurch organizations. In 1997, 403 women were listed in the *Directory,* serving as a pastor (in one case); associate, youth, children's, adult education, Christian education, counseling, and music ministers; parachurch organization administrators; and Bible college professors. The *2001 Directory* shows that the number of women in ministry had more than doubled to 879. A breakdown of the figures is found in the following table.

A Comparison of Numbers of Women in Ministry: 1997 and 2001

Position	*2001*	*1997*
Minister/Co-minister	1	2
Associate Minister	56	17
Education Minister/Director	31	29
Youth Minister/Director	87	30
Children's Minister/Director	258	123
Counseling	14	7
Campus Minister	17	2
Music or Worship Minister/Director	147	71
Administrator	1	12
Women's Minister	34	8
Seniors Minister	8	5
Professor/Administrator in Bible College	154	79
Other	71	18
Total	879	403

The survey also reveals that approximately 11 percent of all churches listed in the *2001 Directory* have at least one woman on their staff. Women serve in ministry positions in at least thirty-six states. The states having the largest number of women in ministry are California, Florida, Georgia, Illinois, Indiana, Kentucky, Missouri, Ohio, Oregon, and Tennessee, all of which have more than thirty women serving on the ministerial staff of a church.

Whatever the historical realities have been, the situation among the churches is changing rapidly, with an increasing number of women serving in a variety of ministries. This appears to be a trend that shall continue. ELEANOR A. DANIEL

See also Babcock, Clara Celestia Hale; Campus Ministry; Christian Woman's Board of Missions; Crank, Sarah Catherine (Sadie) McCoy; Educational Ministry; Holman, Silena Moore; *Leaven, A Journal of Ministry; Mission;* Temperance

BIBLIOGRAPHY Fred A. Bailey, "The Cult of True Womanhood and the Disciples Path to Female Preaching," in *Essays on Women in Earliest Christianity,* ed. Carroll D. Osburn, vol. 2 (1995), pp. 485-517 • Fred A. Bailey, "The Status of Women in the Disciples of Christ Movement, 1865-1900" (Ph.D. dissertation, University of Tennessee, 1979) • LaTaunya Bynum, "The Situation and Trends in the Ministry of Disciples Clergywomen Six Years Later," *Discipliana* 51:3 (Fall 1991): 35-37 • Fran Carver, "Her-Story: Our Foremothers in the Faith," *Leaven* 4:2 (1996): 32-37 • Betty DeBerg, *Ungodly Women: Gender and the First Wave of American Fundamentalism* (1990) • Anna M. Griffith, "A Look at Women in Ministry Today," *Leaven* 4:2 (1996): 44-47 • Ida Withers Harrison, *The Christian Woman's Board of Missions, 1874-1919* (n.d.) • Elizabeth Hartsfield, *Women in the Church: A Symposium on the Service and Status of Women Among the Disciples of Christ* (1953) • Bobbie Lee Holley, "God's Design: Woman's Dignity," *Mission* 8 (March 1975): 5-7 • Debra B. Hull, *Christian Church Women: Shapers of a Movement* (1994) • Mary Ellen Lantzer, "An Examination of the 1892-93 *Christian Standard* Controversy Concerning Women's Preaching" (M.Div. thesis, Emmanuel School of Religion, 1990) • Mary Ellen LaRue, "Women Have Not Been Silent: A Study of Women Preachers Among the Disciples," *Discipliana* 22 (1963): 85-89 • Jessie C. Monser, "Women in the Ministry," *The Christian-Evangelist* 68 (November 1931): 1526-27, 1531 • Thomas H. Olbricht, "Women in the Church: The Hermeneutical Problem," in *Essays on Women in Earliest Christianity,* ed. Carroll D. Osburn, vol. 2 (1995), pp. 545-68 • Carroll D. Osburn, ed., *Essays on Women in Earliest Christianity,* 2 vols. (1993, 1995) • Kathy J. Pulley, "Gender Roles and Conservative Churches: 1870-1930," in *Essays on Women in Earliest Christianity,* ed. Carroll D. Osburn, vol. 2 (1995), pp. 443-83 • Micki A. Pulley, "What Shall I Do: My Gender Shall Follow Me All the Days of My Life," *Mission Journal* 21 (November 1987): 34-37 • Earl Truman Sechler, *Sadie McCoy Crank (1863-1948): Pioneer Woman Preacher in the Christian Church (Disciples)* (1950) • Glenn Zuber, "'The Gospel of Temperance': Early Disciple Women Preachers and the WCTU, 1887-1912," *Discipliana* 53 (Summer 1993): 47-60.

Woods, Guy Napoleon (1908-1993)

Evangelist, author, editor, and debater for Churches of Christ.

Educated at Freed-Hardeman College, he exemplified the "hard, fighting style" of his mentor, N. B. Hardeman. He served as local preacher for churches in Tennessee, Kentucky, and Texas until 1945 when he began to devote his time exclusively to writing and holding gospel meetings. He was a prolific writer, authoring numerous articles (943 in the *Gospel Advocate* alone) and twelve books, including three commentaries and three volumes of sermons. He was appointed a staff writer for the *Gospel Advocate* in 1943, then served as associate editor from 1978 to 1982 and editor from 1982 to 1985. From 1948 to 1978 he wrote the Sunday School lessons in the *Adult Gospel Quarterly* published by the Gospel Advocate Company.

Guy N. Woods (1908-1993) represented Churches of Christ in more than 150 debates during his career, six of which were published. Many of the debates were with Baptists and focused on the meaning of baptism, though his later debates were largely with other members of Churches of Christ as he opposed the noninstitutional movement in the 1950s and 1960s. Courtesy of the Center for Restoration Studies, Abilene Christian University

Woods held approximately 150 religious debates, six of which were published. Also trained as a lawyer (he was admitted to the bar in both Texas and Tennessee), he possessed a keen, analytical mind that often overwhelmed his opponents. He was a leader in the fight against the noninstitutional movement among Churches of Christ. For three decades he presided over the "Open Forum" at the annual Freed-Hardeman College Lectureship, from which he produced two volumes of *Questions and Answers.* While for some his aggressive, polemical style was too offensive, for others his insightful analysis often clarified the issue at stake in a particular controversy.

See also Freed-Hardeman University; *Gospel Advocate, The;* Hardeman, Nicholas Brodie

BIBLIOGRAPHY Memorial issue, *Gospel Advocate* 136 (February 1994): 1-12.

DAVID H. WARREN

Word, Archie (1901-1988)

Evangelist and strongly conservative organizer in the Christian Churches/Churches of Christ.

A converted Prohibition bootlegger and a graduate of Eugene Bible University (1930), Archie Word was a national revivalist whose slogan was "Hear A. Word Preach the Word." Word served as evangelist of "The Church at 550 N.E. 76th Avenue," Portland, Oregon (1935-68) and was editor of *The Church Speaks* (1944-68). He also authored *The Church Revealed in the Scriptures* (1950) and was recognized by *Christian Standard* for sending the most people into full-time Christian service during World War II. He cofounded Churches of Christ School of Evangelists (1952) in Portland and taught in a church-sponsored ministerial school in Gering, Nebraska (1968-88). Word's ecclesiological rigor and emphasis on strict personal Christian holiness gave inspiration to a large movement of like-minded persons, known as the Ottumwa Brethren, whose influence was strong in Iowa and Missouri and extended across the United States. Word represented a restorationist fundamentalism and exclusivism at the far right wing of the Christian Churches/Churches of Christ, of which churches he and the Ottumwa Brethren suspected liberal tendencies.

See also Fundamentalism; Ottumwa Brethren

BIBLIOGRAPHY Victor Knowles, *Archie Word: Voice of Thunder, Heart of Tears* (1992) • Victor Knowles, *Repent or Perish! Selected Sermons and Essays of Archie Word* (1994) • Victor Knowles and William E. Paul, *Taking a Stand: The Story of the Ottumwa Brethren* (1996) • Archie Word, *61 Soul Winning Outlines from Hebrews* (1962) • Archie Word, *53 Soul Winning Outlines on First Corinthians* (1963).

VICTOR KNOWLES

Flamboyant evangelist Archie Word was the inspiration for the conservative Ottumwa Brethren movement among the Christian Churches/Churches of Christ.

From Victor Knowles, *Archie Word: Voice of Thunder, Heart of Tears.* Courtesy of the Center for Restoration Studies, Abilene Christian University

Word and Work

Journal published by members of premillennial Churches of Christ.

The journal began monthly publication as *The Christian Word and Work* in March 1908 in New Orleans. The manager was pediatrician Dr. David Lipscomb Watson (1868-1939), founder of Watson Printing Company. Watson edited the journal with Amos C. Harris, minister of the First Christian Church at Seventh and Camp Streets and principal of its Christian high school, and Stanford Chambers (1876-1969), a teacher in the school. Later, the editorial board expanded to include, among others, Elmer Leon Jorgenson (1886-1968) and Charles M. Neal (1878-1956). In the opening editorial the journal revealed its aim and scope to serve as a medium for evangelization and communication among the isolated congregations that promoted "Primitive Christianity" in the gulf region from Texas to the Atlantic. The early journal had a restitutionist outlook, opposed Disciple innovations, but also supported social concerns such as temperance and education.

In 1909-10 Harris switched to a teaching job at the public Warren Easton High School, left the editorship of *Word and Work,* and joined the Disciples congregation that is now the St. Charles Avenue Christian Church (Disciples of Christ). Chambers became both minister and principal at Seventh and Camp. The journal shortened its name to *Word and Work* and changed hands with the September issue of 1913, when Chambers, in purchasing the journal from Watson, became its sole editor and publisher, although Watson, in two unsuccessful lawsuits, later sought to regain control over the journal. Since June 1912 the journal had espoused in several articles a dispensational premillennial eschatology from the pen of Charles M. Neal, views opposed in the journal by Watson, a postmillennialist. Watson was eventually disfellowshiped by Seventh and Camp for various reasons, including differing views on eschatology, personal disagreements, and a dubious fund-raising scheme for the church.

Under Chambers' editorship the journal adopted several new departments, reflecting the increased attention to premillennial eschatology. It became a platform for future leaders in the premillennial congregations. Chambers took on, besides the general editorship, the "Department of Prophecy," H. L. Olmstead (1883-1958) the "Department of First Principles," Elmer L. Jorgenson the "Department of Work and Worship," and Charles M. Neal the "Bible School Department."

The journal changed hands again in January 1916, when Chambers sold it to Robert Henry Boll (1875-1956), who became editor-in-chief and publisher, while Chambers, Olmstead, and Jorgenson retained their involvement as coeditors. Boll, a minister at the Portland Avenue Church of Christ in Louisville, Kentucky, had been front-page editor of the *Gospel Advocate* from 1909 until 1915, but the relationship was severed over Boll's openly espoused premillennial views. Boll moved *Word and Work* to Louisville, where it became the periodical voice of the premillennial Churches of Christ. It has continued to be published by the Portland Avenue Church of Christ. Though Boll was no single-issue writer but also a gifted author on apologetic, exegetical, and spiritual topics, the journal became drawn into the controversy over eschatology. *Word and Work* also promoted foreign missionary work through a news department conducted by Don Carlos Janes (1877-1944) and began publishing *The Lord's Day Lessons,* a serialized commentary.

After Boll's death in 1956, the journal was edited by E. L. Jorgenson and J. R. Clark (1899-1968). In 1962 Gordon R. Linscott became the new editor and publisher, followed in 1976 by William Robert Heid. Alex Wilson assumed the editorship in June 1986. The journal's publishing arm also became a venue for the writings of Boll and other ministers associated with the journal. It benefited from its relationship with Heid's printing company, located near the journal's offices, and Portland Avenue Church of Christ and Christian school.

See also Boll, Robert Henry; Eschatology; *Gospel Advocate, The;* Janes, Don Carlos

BIBLIOGRAPHY Archives of the Portland Avenue Church of Christ and Boll Memorial Library.

HANS ROLLMANN

World Bible School

Missionary outreach among Churches of Christ using the concept of correspondence courses mailed by individual Christians in the United States to overseas recipients, primarily in developing nations. Historically, the American teachers have been predominantly women. The correspondence courses have been designed to complement, rather than replace, traditional missionary efforts.

World Bible School was the idea of James L. "Jimmie" Lovell (1896-1984). A native of Portland, Tennessee, Lovell began a long career with DuPont soon after the First World War, first as a gunpowder salesman and later successfully marketing explosives to engineers and miners. Working primarily in Colorado and California, Lovell became a moving force behind the growth of Churches of Christ in the Western states.

In 1936 Lovell started the *Colorado Christian,* a journal intended to unify and encourage Colorado Churches of Christ. In 1937, he founded *West Coast Christian.* In the premier issue, Lovell outlined the genesis of what would become the World Bible School method. He had developed his own correspondence courses and encouraged his readers to utilize them as evangelism tools.

Lovell's idea to use correspondence courses in world evangelism grew out of his personal contact with foreign missionaries. He traveled to India and the Far East in 1960, and around the world in 1961, visiting with a large number of missionaries in many countries and becoming convicted of the need for mass evangelism. In 1962 he founded *Action* magazine, dedicated to the support of worldwide missions. His mission statement appeared on the masthead: "Every person has more right to hear the gospel once than any one person has to hear it twice." He also convinced a California congregation to undertake correspondence evangelism. Starting with 200 students, the program soon grew to fifty-four teachers and 2,500 students. Before long, the work had mushroomed to 200,000 students and involved many congregations and individuals. The work was first designated as World Bible School in 1972. In

Lovell's lifetime, 2,000,000 students in 107 countries had been enrolled in World Bible School.

Long before his death in 1984, Lovell had made arrangements for the continuation of World Bible School and *Action*. Reuel Lemmons (1912-1989), well-known editor of the *Firm Foundation*, was selected to lead the organization. A longtime supporter of World Bible School, Lemmons wrote Lovell in 1974 that the "Bible project and the correspondence course work are not only helping to save thousands across the seas, but through them you are involving thousands of members of the church here who were never involved in much of anything before." By the time of Lovell's death, the transition had been implemented. Headquarters were moved from California to Austin, Texas. The Westover Hills Church of Christ supplied office space and staff. The ill health of Lemmons soon forced a change in leadership, however. R. H. Tex Williams (b. 1928), a seasoned missionary and teacher associated with the Sunset School of Preaching in Lubbock, Texas, took over operations in 1986.

The effort has enjoyed continued growth. By 1994, over 50,000 American teachers were mailing lessons to 1,000,000 students in 140 nations. Some 50,000 students were being baptized yearly. Outgrowing the arrangement with Westover Hills, World Bible School moved into new headquarters at Cedar Hill, Texas, in 2000. The school counts students from 172 countries, and the lessons have been translated into at least thirty-five languages. The lessons are regularly printed in English, Spanish, and French.

In recent years, World Bible School has branched out in two new areas: World Bible School on the Internet; and the Center for Church Enrichment, providing "resources, seminars, and advanced studies in Biblical texts, leadership and ministry."

World Bible School weathered occasional criticism from those who contended that the approach was not sufficiently focused and that it lacked proper means to ensure that new converts were gathered together into stable congregations. Others complained that World Bible School contacts sometimes overwhelmed missionaries. Some American preachers and editors criticized Lovell, who was both outspoken and aggressive in his promulgation of world evangelism. Yet World Bible School moved ahead in spite of the complaints. The success of the school has been particularly apparent in Nigeria, Ghana, and other sub-Saharan African countries where hundreds of stable, self-supporting congregations are the fruits of this long-distance evangelism.

See also Lemmons, Reuel Gordon

BIBLIOGRAPHY R. H. Tex Williams, "World Bible School: A Timely Tool for African Evangelism," in *One Hundred Years of African Missions: Essays in Honor of Wendell Broom* (2001) • Bill Young, *The Man of Action: The Story of Jimmie Lovell* (1969). TERRY COWAN

World Call

One of the leading journals of the Disciples of Christ in the middle decades of the twentieth century.

In 1913 editors of five Disciple magazines — *American Home Missionary, Intelligencer, Missionary Tidings, Christian Philanthropist,* and *Christian Men* began discussing the need for a single journal to include them all. By January 1919 a new magazine named *World Call* was ready for distribution, with W. R. Warren as its editor. The first issue contained sixty-four pages of photographs and informative articles, with all five of the earlier magazines represented. The subscription price was $1.10 per copy. It carried the new motto, "To inform those who are interested, to interest those who ought to be informed."

The magazine reached a circulation of 85,000 with the efforts of Jesse Trout and Evelyn Honeywell as successive National World Secretaries. Local churches worked to assure the magazine's circulation. The World Call Publication Committee, with representatives from all nine agencies of the Disciples of Christ, met every six months for reports, guidance, and support until *World Call* became

Editor of *World Call* from 1935 to 1961, George W. Buckner (1893-1981) took the paper to a position of distinction in American religious journalism. During most of that period he also served as executive director of the Association for the Promotion of Christian Unity, later renamed the Council on Christian Unity. Courtesy of the Disciples of Christ Historical Society

worldwide and churchwide. The journal played an enormous role in the rallying of denominational identity among Disciples in advance of Restructure.

The editors of *World Call* were W. R. Warren, 1919-29; Bess White Cochran, 1929-32; Harold E. Fey, 1932-34; George Walker Buckner, 1935-60; Samuel F. Pugh, 1960-70; and James L. Merrell, 1970-73. Merrell was the last editor of *World Call* and the first editor of *The Disciple* when *World Call* merged with *The Christian* in 1974 to form a new magazine.

See also *Christian, The; Disciple, The;* Journalism; *Missionary Tidings* SAMUEL F. PUGH

World Convention of Churches of Christ, The

The World Convention of Churches of Christ began in 1930 to provide a means of fellowship and cooperation among Churches of Christ and Christian Churches internationally. By that time the Movement had spread to approximately thirty countries.

The visionary and founder of World Convention was Dr. Jesse M. Bader, a Disciples ecumenist and evangelist. Six other Christian World Communions had established international forums, and Bader believed the time was right for the churches of the Stone-Campbell Movement to do the same. His dream was well supported, with some 10,000 attending the first convention, despite the worldwide economic depression.

This first convention met in Washington, D.C., in October 1930. Since then World Convention has met in Leicester, United Kingdom (1935); Buffalo, New York (1947); Melbourne, Australia (1952); Toronto, Canada (1955); Edinburgh, United Kingdom (1960); San Juan, Puerto Rico (1965); Adelaide, Australia (1970); Mexico City, Mexico (1975); Honolulu, Hawaii (1980); Kingston, Jamaica (1984); Auckland, New Zealand (1988); Long Beach, California (1992); Calgary, Canada (1996); Brisbane, Australia (2000); and Brighton, England (2004). The following conventions (quadrennial since 1980) were slated for Nashville, Tennessee (2008), and an African venue (2012).

The use of "Churches of Christ" in the World Convention name was an acknowledgment that this designation was the most commonly used worldwide in 1930 for churches with a heritage in the Stone-Campbell Movement, including some instrumental congregations in the United States and Canada. "Churches of Christ" was the only name used in the British Isles, where the nineteenth-century Stone-Campbell Movement developed at the same time as it was evolving in the United States. As a result of this, "Churches of Christ" became the name used in Commonwealth countries. Though a cappella Churches of Christ were not involved in the founding of World Convention, members have always been welcome, and some have always been involved. These churches had begun to show increased interest and participation in World Convention by the beginning of the twenty-first century.

A major focus of World Convention in the 1950s and 1960s was the International Study Program, which helped to clarify, in six doctrinal areas, what the churches of this Movement stood for. Though the conclusions were not binding, the breadth of discussion that formed the basis for them meant that they received widespread acceptance.

The division of Christian Churches in the United States and the Restructure of the Christian Church (Disciples of Christ) in 1968 provided a temptation to World Convention to identify with one segment of the Movement. The body made a commitment, however, to continue to serve the whole Stone-Campbell family.

The primary aim of World Convention is to strengthen fellowship, increase understanding, offer encouragement, and develop common purpose among churches and individuals in the Christian Churches–Churches of Christ–Disciples of Christ family around the world. It also seeks to provide a means of fellowship between this family of churches and the whole church of Jesus Christ. It is the only body able to provide a form of representation for the whole Movement at a global level. Where division has occurred within the Stone-Campbell family, World Convention aims to stimulate and encourage family unity.

World Convention publishes a quarterly news journal called *World Christian*. It also sends out regular e-mail releases and maintains a web page. The staff travels globally to establish and maintain family links.

An international executive committee, elected at the conventions, oversees the operations of World Convention. A general secretary has executive responsibility for the day-to-day World Convention ministry. Bader was the first general secretary (from 1930 until his death in 1963) and the first president (from 1930 to 1935). Other general secretaries include Laurence V. Kirkpatrick from 1963 to 1971, Allan W. Lee from 1971 to 1992, Lyndsay and Lorraine (associate) Jacobs from 1992 to 2004, and Jeff Weston beginning in 2005.

The World Convention office was moved from Dallas, Texas, to Nashville, Tennessee, in 1992 and is located at 4800 B. Franklin Road.

See also Bader, Jesse Moren; Restructure

BIBLIOGRAPHY *The Doctrines of the Christian Faith: Study Pamphlets* (1956) • Ronald I. W. Hurst, "The World Convention of Churches of Christ" (M.A. thesis, Butler University, 1964) • Allan W. Lee, *Fifty Years of Faith and*

Fellowship: The World Convention of Churches of Christ, 1930-1980 (1980) • World Convention website on-line at http://worldconv.home.comcast.net.

LORRAINE *and* LYNDSAY JACOBS

Worship

1. Nineteenth Century
2. Twentieth Century
   - 2.1. Christian Church (Disciples of Christ)
   - 2.2. Churches of Christ
   - 2.3. Christian Churches/Churches of Christ

1. Nineteenth Century

The liturgical life of the American Protestant churches in the nineteenth century saw significant change with the westward expansion of the frontier, though traditional forms and models endured and provided both stability and the basis for ongoing adaptation. Especially important in the background of worship practices in the early Stone-Campbell Movement was the Reformed tradition in its various streams, though the Movement would ultimately break from the liturgical disciplines of Presbyterianism and seek its liturgical rubrics in Scripture alone.

During the Second Great Awakening (1790-1840), shifts in Reformed theology (e.g., the mitigation of "Old School" Calvinism) went hand in hand with the rise of changes in worship. "New Light" Congregationalists and Presbyterians capitalized on the new theological sensitivity to the "means" whereby sinners could presumably rise from out of their depravity to prepare themselves for grace. They preoccupied themselves as well with the experiential aspects of conversion and catalogued the manifestations of the work of the Spirit in the lives of regenerated sinners. Worship in this revivalistic context thus became a stage on which the drama of conversion would play itself out. On the rugged frontier, the camp meeting aspired to provide conditions conducive to the spontaneous descent of the Spirit and the mass transformation of sinners into saints.

Barton Stone was the principal living link between this revivalist, camp-meeting heritage of frontier worship and the larger Stone-Campbell Movement. Stone had first been exposed to "New Light" worship while a student in David Caldwell's academy in Guilford, North Carolina, in the early 1790s. Stone heard the eminent revivalist James McGready, whom he encountered again in the camp meetings in Logan County, Kentucky, in the spring of 1801.

The Cane Ridge Revival in August of 1801, hosted by Stone's own congregation in Bourbon County, Kentucky, was a marvelous case in point of the adaptation of traditional forms of worship in a frontier setting. This momentous gathering stood within the tradition of the outdoor communion festivals ("holy fairs") held among the Reformed churches in Scotland since the seventeenth century. Although the revival is remembered in the Stone-Campbell heritage for the cooperation of preachers from different denominations and the remarkable response to their preaching, it was, first of all, a gathering for the Lord's Supper. The sacramental nature of the event, however, spilled over into what its participants believed was a grand manifestation of the work of God in spiritual "exercises," ecstatic behaviors credited to the immediate presence of the Holy Spirit. Stone for his part believed that these exercises had helped in the unique circumstances of the Cane Ridge Revival to promote a genuine spirit of reconciliation; but in his subsequent career he hardly promoted such spiritual experiences in the worship of the churches.

The churches of the Campbell movement in the Ohio Valley largely insulated themselves from the camp meetings. Alexander Campbell did nothing to conceal his suspicions of the abuses inherent in revivalism. His passion was to restore the order — and the orderliness — of apostolic worship and to insure that the Lord's Supper and other Christian solemnities would attain to their primitive integrity and central function in the life of the church.

Basic to Campbell's view of worship was the conviction that while humanity before the Fall had worshiped and adored God like the angels, worship after the Fall was elemental to "religion" as a whole, "a system of means of reconciliation" with God. In *The Christian System* Campbell outlined how the modes of worship had been revealed proper to the dispensations of salvation history. Patriarchal (or "family") worship, from the Fall of Adam to the covenant of circumcision, had focused on the institutions of the Sabbath, the service of the altar, oral instruction, prayer, praise, and benediction. With the worship of Israel under the Mosaic (Jewish) dispensation, the old patriarchal or family worship was "nationalized" and its typical, or figurative, features enlarged, in anticipation of the Christian dispensation (1 Cor. 10:11). Finally, under the Christian system, worship is no longer nationalized since the kingdom of heaven has as its "only positive statutes" the "weekly celebration of the death and resurrection of Jesus, and the weekly meeting of the disciples of Christ for this purpose, and for the edification of one another in their most holy faith." Christian worship thus knows no national or geographical boundaries and can be extended universally to all the nations of the world.

In an early essay entitled "Order of Worship" in his *Christian Baptist* series "A Restoration of the Ancient Order of Things," Campbell began with two syllogisms. Either there is a divinely instituted order of Christian worship or there is not. If there is not, it logically follows that there can be no such thing as disorderly worship because there is no order to which worship is to be conformed. Such is an absurdity. Hence there must be a divinely instituted order of worship. Second, that order of worship is either uniform for all occasions or it is not. If it is not, then it is uniformly different, which means that it is given to unlimited differences and thus disarray. This too is an absurdity. Hence there is a uniform order of all Christian worship.

Campbell found the basics of that order in Acts 2:42, with its brief mention of the substance of Lord's Day gatherings in the primitive church in Jerusalem: apostolic teaching, the breaking of bread, fellowship, and prayers (to which he added the hymned praise elsewhere attested in the New Testament). Campbell conceded that there was no strict directory of all the details for worship and that there were many expedients; yet he also believed that there were discernible parameters.

In an 1835 essay, "The Order of the Church as Respects Worship," Campbell appears to have been more concerned with personal decorum and ritual propriety than with the substance and sequence of the worship services themselves. Barton Stone had similar concerns. Stone and Campbell concurred that worshipers needed to leave trivial conversation and mundane concerns behind them. Stone particularly advised against talking politics in the Lord's house. Silence and kneeling were both appropriate as an expression of reverence, and Stone even considered sitting useless as a posture for worship.

Both Stone and Campbell valued simplicity in worship and warned against the trappings of houses of worship with too many fine amenities (which might include musical instruments). They both expressed dismay over some Christians attending church too finely dressed, and Stone criticized inappropriate hairstyles and jewelry.

Stone had larger concerns for the general character of piety in the churches' worship, and he related his concerns in some musings he published in 1843 after a trip through Indiana, Ohio, and Kentucky. Stone feared that "proselytizing" was in some cases preempting edification in the worship of the church, and he acknowledged that in the context of revivalism, the danger was to evangelize and convert believers of superficial faith and loyalty. Worship could and should be evangelistic, but not at the cost of compromising teaching, exhortation, and admonition. It was incumbent on preachers in local congregations to take the lead in exemplifying piety and true worship and in preaching substantively, not just eloquently. Robert Richardson had expressed similar concerns in 1841 after surveying the lack of devotional depth in the preaching and worship of congregations in Campbell's fold.

In his 1835 study of order in worship, Campbell stated that the New Testament clearly taught that all Christians are obliged to carry on all the ordinances of worship but that the details of the order of worship were largely left to the prerogatives of local congregations. Yet in *The Christian System* (1839) Campbell describes a service of worship he had attended that he thought worthy of emulation and consistent with the ancient order. The service set out the following components: (1) opening hymn; (2) gospel reading; (3) prayer of thanksgiving followed by a congregational "Amen"; (4) New Testament epistle reading; (5) hymn; (6) invitation to the table; (7) simple administration of bread and wine by an elder; (8) hymn; (9) prayer of supplication; (10) readings from Old Testament and New Testament and remarks from the people for edification; (11) "spiritual songs"; and (12) apostolic benediction by the presider. This became a common order of worship among churches of the Stone-Campbell Movement. The primary distinctions between this order and that of various groups of Presbyterians of the time was the centrality of the Lord's Supper in every Sunday service and its administration by lay elders instead of ordained clergy.

Campbell further remarked that the liturgical components of this order of worship were consistent but their sequence occasionally variable. Persons never rose to speak without invitation or permission from the presider, yet "nothing appeared to be done in a formal or ceremonious manner," as "everything exhibited the power of godliness as well as the form; and no person could attend to all that passed without being edified and convinced that the Spirit of God was there." Campbell idealized worship that evidenced true spirituality without being formalistic on the one hand, or inappropriately spontaneous on the other.

As can be seen in Campbell's model service, preaching was neither central nor necessarily done by a clergyperson. It was more teaching than proclamation, more oriented to the mind than to the emotions. Faith was treated neither as an emotional response to the preaching nor as a miracle of grace, but as a natural human rational response to the presentation of the facts of the gospel as testified to by the biblical text and the history of the church. As a result of Campbell's distinction between *kērygma* (proclamation of the gospel) and *didachē* (teaching Christian living), evangelistic preaching was generally separated from the worship of baptized believers. The sermons preached to congregations of believers were usually studies of doctrinal themes through a survey of biblical texts. They were preached in a logical way to convince hearers of the truth as presented.

Early in the history of his own reform movement, Barton Stone had encouraged the "invitation" at the close of a service to give opportunity for public response to the gospel, a clear indication of the evangelistic character of worship. Frustrated by impertinence from respondents, Stone ceased including baptism in the invitation. In the late 1820s, however, Walter Scott introduced the invitation in the Campbell movement, adapting Peter's invitation from Acts 2:38 to repent and be baptized, a practice Thomas and Alexander Campbell eventually endorsed. Encouraged by this, Barton Stone resumed including baptism in the invitation, and even remarked in 1843 that, because he feared some respondents expressed faith but were not truly prepared for baptism, he would clarify what it meant to believe "with all your heart" and to repent; then he would reissue the invitation to those who had come forward.

The Stone-Campbell Movement in the nineteenth century established a broad and early consensus that the Lord's Supper was the central act of Christian worship, to be observed at least every Sunday, though there were inevitable differences over the precise meaning of, and participants in, the celebration. Having treated the issue of frequency in the *Christian Baptist,* Alexander Campbell essayed at length the service of the "Breaking of Bread" in *The Christian System,* waxing less on the meaning of the Supper than on its constitutive actions. He made much of the need for one loaf indicative of the one body of believers, that participant Christians together form a "royal priesthood" (1 Pet. 2:5), that the loaf be demonstratively broken before the assembly to indicate the brokenness of Christ's body, and that the service as a whole is a memorial (and a proclamation) of the Lord's death. "It is as well intended to crucify the world in our hearts, as to quicken us to God, and to diffuse his love within us." Campbell believed that the Lord's Supper, like other ordinances, was a "means of enjoyment" of God's grace; but he resisted the use of straightforwardly sacramental language for the Supper. Robert Richardson was probably the first early leader to encourage sensitivity to the "presence" of Christ in the Supper, and his more sacramental understanding of the Supper would be echoed by a vocal minority in subsequent generations of the Movement.

Controversy began fairly early over the practice of "open" versus "close" communion, that is, whether to admit to the table the "pious unimmersed." Alexander Campbell wavered somewhat on this issue, but he, Barton Stone, and numerous leaders in the second and third generations of the Movement ultimately sanctioned what became the general practice throughout the churches of a qualified form of open communion, whereby the pious unimmersed were admitted to the Lord's Supper according to the discretion of their own conscience (cf. 1 Cor. 11:28) but not by positive invitation as such.

The appropriate selection of hymns greatly exercised Alexander Campbell and other leaders in the Movement. Early on, Campbell condemned the way much Protestant hymnody had simply indoctrinated congregants with unwarranted theological notions. "How long and how loud does the Arminian sing his free grace, while he argues against the Calvinists' sovereign grace. And in what animating strains does the Calvinist sing of his imputed righteousness in the presence of the Arminian, who he supposes is seeking to be justified by his works." Laden with speculative theologies dressed in fine poetic lines and passing without criticism as orthodox, much Protestant hymnody inhibited the true purpose of Christian singing: "to raise and exalt our spirits by divine contemplations to the divine in the worship of our adorable God and Father, by admiring and extolling facts extrinsic of our conjectures or notions about them." Meanwhile Barton Stone complained of "new theatrical or piano tunes applied to sacred songs without solemnity either in thc tune or singer," appearing to him as "a labored exhibition of skill in music (if music it be) rather than solemn worship."

Throughout the nineteenth century, the churches of the Stone-Campbell Movement wrestled with the purposive tension between the evangelistic and edificatory dimensions of their worship services. The evangelistic emphasis was not just a vestige of revivalism but reflected the Movement's determination constantly to display the facts of the gospel for both novices and experienced believers. The edificatory emphasis derived from the seasoned sensitivities of Stone, the Campbells, Robert Richardson, and others who saw that successful evangelism in the rapidly expanding Movement could potentially overshadow the function of worship in training and maturing believers with appropriate spiritual discipline and depth.

PAUL M. BLOWERS *and* BRUCE E. SHIELDS

2. Twentieth Century

2.1. Christian Church (Disciples of Christ)

At the dawn of the twentieth century, the Stone-Campbell Movement, forged on the anvil of frontier revivalism, devoted little attention to the theology and practice of congregational worship. Sustained by the evangelistic fervor of the nineteenth century, pastors focused on making new converts and not on the worship life of their members. Furthermore, the founders' conviction that the Bible contained the "constitution" for the restoration of the church in general and for the church's worship pattern in particular floundered on the rock of Biblicism. Unable to reach consensus on what were the biblical norms for worship, the debate and eventual division by 1906 over instrumental music in worship insured that the other elements of the Sunday service were neglected. Moreover, the effort to restore the "ancient order of things" thwarted any interest in the liturgical developments of the wider church. However, the great contribution of the Stone-Campbell Movement — weekly communion, lay leadership at the table, and the reestablishment of the proper balance between Word and sacrament — endured.

Although the basic worship elements in their respective order were observed by about two-thirds of Disciples churches throughout the nineteenth and twentieth centuries (opening praise, Scripture lessons, pastoral prayer, communion, offering, and sermon), the passing of the frontier and other cultural changes affected congregational worship. Large, impressive churches staffed by full-time clergy replaced simple, unadorned buildings. Stained glass windows with images of the dove, the cross, the crown, and the *alpha* and the *omega,* as well as scenes from the life of Jesus, defined the worship space. Music from a choir, frequently accompanied by an organ, filled the air. The development of printed worship manuals, hymnals, and Sunday bulletins not only stabilized the worship life of the congregation but also introduced new liturgical elements like the doxology, the Gloria Patri, offertory sentences, calls to worship, invocations, benedictions, responsive readings, and choral responses. During the 1920s, architect A. F. Wickes designed the first "divided chancel" sanctuary, with the choir, organ console, and director located behind the table. By the 1930s, the Sunday evening service disappeared and religious education replaced revivalism as the primary vehicle to recruit new members. Yet the theological hallmarks of the Stone-Campbell Movement persisted in its worship life: stress on the rational and not the mystical; emphasis on evangelistic preaching; insistence that salvation comes through hearing the gospel in faith, repenting of sins, being baptized, and receiving the gifts of the Holy Spirit; a preoccupation with the historical person and work of Jesus Christ that values the Lord's Supper as a memorial done "in remembrance of me"; and an optimistic interpretation of humanity that discourages penitential preparation and corporate confession of sin.

From 1923 to 1953, the psychology of worship movement, inaugurated by Von Ogden Vogt, a Unitarian minister in Chicago, shaped Protestant worship in general and Disciples worship in particular. Proponents of this movement believed that the desired emotional response could be elicited from the congregation when the outer forms of the worship service were parallel to the inner states of the worshiper. E. S. Ames and W. W. Lockhart introduced the psychology of worship movement to Disciples ministers and churches. Emphasis on the subjective state of the worshiper and the authority of experience influenced Disciples worship manuals of the period. Now the pastor planned and designed worship to elicit a desired effect, not through the reading of and preaching on Scripture, not even through participation in the Lord's Supper, but through the creation of a mood and the order of worship. Yet the writers of these manuals insisted that congregational preference — especially for the placement of sermon and communion — overruled other considerations in determining the worship order.

For Disciples, the psychology of worship movement culminated in G. Edwin Osborn's *Christian Worship: A Service Book,* published in 1953. In this monumental work, Osborn invoked the use of themes — 105 in total — to unify the service. The elements of the service followed a general pattern that in turn corresponded to a definitive cycle that was repeated each time in the consciousness of the worshiper. Four major movements were identified: an Act of Reverence, an Act of Fellowship, an Act of Dedication, and an Act of Renewal. This cycle reflected an alternating pattern. An attitude of reverence by the worshiper was answered by God, who brought the worshiper a sense of fellowship. In turn, this sense of fellowship engendered an attitude of devotion in the worshiper that God subsequently answered by bringing a sense of empowerment.

Osborn's service book enriched Disciples worship life in at least two ways. First, it broadened the liturgical context of Disciples worship by including materials from the ancient, ecumenical, and contemporary church. Second, it introduced a definite pattern for worship as followed by the consciousness of the worshiper.

During this period, Disciples' passion for ecumenism continued. Intellectual leaders like Peter Ainslie, C. C. Morrison, and William Robinson broadened Disciples conversations to include the wider church. Consequently, from the 1960s to the present, the character and content of Disciples worship were influenced the most by participation in the ecumenical movement. Although various Disciples leaders such as W. B. Blakemore, Colbert Cartwright, Peter Morgan, and Ronald Allen emerged in the area of worship, Keith Watkins has contributed most profoundly and prodigiously to the worship life of the church in the latter third of the twentieth century. Employing a threefold methodology that includes the Disciples heritage, the liturgical tradition of the ecumenical church, and the contemporary culture, Watkins' many books identify the weekly celebration of the Lord's Supper as the religious heart of the church and affirm the classic sequence of Scripture, sermon, and sacrament.

Watkins' most valuable contribution to Disciples worship was his editorship of *Thankful Praise,* a 1987 worship book that took seriously the Disciples' ecumenical imperative. Because worship for Watkins is "essentially corporate thanksgiving and praise offered by sinful and redeemed human beings in response to God's saving revelation," the book addresses Osborn's overemphasis on the subjective and individualistic dimensions of worship. In addition, it situates Disciples worship within the broader stream of eucharistic worship. The retrieval of the early Disciples emphasis on the importance of the Lord's Supper not only provided an integrative principle for congregational worship but also preserved continuity with the normative Christian practice of including both Word and sacrament in the Sunday morning service. After citing five principal sources for worship materials and six principles of renewal, *Thankful Praise* proposed an order of service that contained five headings: "Gathering of the Community," "The Community Proclaims the Word of God," "The Community Responds to the Word of God," "The Community Comes Around the Lord's Table," and "The Community Goes Forth to Serve God in Mission."

At the dawn of the twenty-first century, Disciples worship patterns differ but identifiable elements abide. The Lord's Supper anchors the service, although its placement in the worship order varies. The use of the term "sacrament," as well as the use of the lectionary, is more common than previously. Disciples sermons remain rationalistic and didactic, grounded in Scripture, and, as Ronald Allen puts it, "indicative in mood, stressing what God has done, is doing, and will do." Elders pray at the table, usually accompanied by a presiding minister. Diverse music styles and different instruments contribute to faithful worship and praise. Congregations that use the *Chalice Hymnal* (1995) and the *Chalice Worship* (1997) service book have a wealth of hymns, as well as responsive psalms and litanies, prayers, and sample services that enrich corporate worship.

Yet tensions persist. In spite of an enduring commitment to the significance of the Lord's Supper in general and the presence of Christ at the table in particular, Disciples lack a systematic interpretation of the Eucharist. Moreover, the status of baptized children and unbaptized people of any age for admission to the table is unclear. Like most Protestant mainline churches, Disciples congregations experiment with alternative worship forms like the "seeker service" and "contemporary" services. And most important, the church must decide how to respond to the effects of the "electronic culture" on congregational worship.

Although the particular shape of future Disciples worship services remains uncertain, what is certain, from Campbell to Watkins, is that the structure of Disciples worship includes Word and sacrament.

PAUL H. JONES

2.2. Churches of Christ

In 1906, when Churches of Christ were listed separately in the Federal Religious Census, most congregations were located in the border states and in small towns and rural areas. Their approaches to worship tended to reflect patterns from the early days of the Stone-Campbell Movement that in turn drew upon practices of the Scotch Baptists. By the middle of the century most of the distinctive Scotch Baptist traits had disappeared. As the century came to a close, a majority of the congregations continued in a worship style characteristic of the early century, while others incorporated features characteristic of large independent evangelical and charismatic churches.

In the early twentieth century most Churches of Christ held that worship consisted of five acts. It is not clear with whom this view originated, though it has been attributed to Benjamin Franklin (1812-1878). These five acts were set forth by John Banister (1910-1995) at the Abilene Christian lectures in 1951. "The worship of the apostolic church consisted of five distinct acts or items of worship on the Lord's Day." He then listed in order (1) The Lord's Supper, (2) singing, (3) praying, (4) preaching, and (5) giving. "To be scriptural," he declared, "our Lord's day worship must contain all of these five required items." At the Abilene Christian College lectureship in 1920, M. C. Kurfees (1856-1931) included a sixth, the reading of the Scriptures. While all of these acts are still maintained, the precise number and formulation is no longer seen as definitive by many churches.

Many in early Churches of Christ worshiped in the manner that Moses E. Lard set out as the ideal church in his *Quarterly* in 1863. Most of the congregations were small, as were the buildings. Lard preferred to baptize in streams; therefore the buildings had no baptistery. This practice continued in most Churches of Christ until the 1940s. Often the men sat on one side, with the women and children on the other, though this practice began to drop away early in the twentieth century. The songs were standard English hymns of the previous century, and the people remained seated. When the Scriptures were read they stood, but when prayers were said they knelt. The preaching was didactic and simple. The Lord's Supper was often observed at a table that extended across the whole house while the congregation gathered round. This manner of taking the Lord's Supper was especially Scotch Baptist. The congregation also met again on Sunday night and reviewed the chapter from Scripture studied in the morning. Everyone commented, presumably even the women.

In the 1920s the songs and the style of the musical scores changed in a number of churches. In the first part of the century the frequently sung hymns were those favored by the great evangelists Dwight Moody

(1837-1899) and Billy Sunday (1862-1935) and written by Ira D. Sankey (1840-1908), Homer A. Rodeheaver (1880-1955), and Fanny J. Crosby (1820-1915). As radio thrived in the 1920s, so did country music. The writers of gospel songs now drew upon marching tunes, Negro spirituals, ragtime, and Dixieland jazz. Newly written songs were sung by quartets on radio and printed in paperback books that sold for as little as a quarter each. Quartet songs were promoted by Virgil O. Stamps (1892-1940) and J. O. Baxter (1887-1960), along with the Blackwood Brothers, but several leaders in Churches of Christ also joined in writing gospel songs, the most famous of whom were Albert E. Brumley (1905-1977), Will W. Slater (1885-1959), Tillit S. Teddlie (1885-1987), and Luther G. Presley (1887-1974). Sunday afternoon singings sprang up in Churches of Christ across the land.

In the 1930s several congregations of Churches of Christ numbered over a hundred members, and the participants no longer gathered around the table, though the person praying might declare, "As we gather around the table, let us partake." The table was still long and covered with white linen. The bread was unleavened, flat, and homemade, placed on one plate and unbroken. The grape juice was served in a single cup or chalice, though multiple cups became standard after World War II except in a minority of churches. Those making a contribution still walked to the front and put the money under the cloth so that no one knew who gave what. At the end of each service an invitation song was sung so that those who wanted to be baptized or to confess sins could come forward.

In the late 1940s city and suburban congregations made efforts to make the worship more organized and stately. To achieve this end congregations appointed worship committees, which in turn set out the order of worship and appointed the worship leaders. Soon orders of worship began to appear in church bulletins or as a separate sheet. An effort was made by some to move the congregations away from what they considered the less dignified Stamps-Baxter type songs. *Great Songs of the Church,* edited by E. L. Jorgenson, became a widely used hymnal, though Jorgenson's premillennialism made it suspect in the minds of some. In the 1970s, however, those promoting church growth insisted that livelier tunes were needed, so many Stamps-Baxter songs returned to use and were included in *Songs of the Church* (1971), edited by Alton H. Howard (b. 1925). This hymnal became widely popular in Churches of Christ in the 1970s and 1980s.

As early as the 1970s the evangelical and charismatic movements began to influence worship in Churches of Christ. One early indication was the popularity of "How Great Thou Art," the theme song for the Billy Graham crusades. Especially in the youth camps and campus ministries, new songs written in evangelical and charismatic circles were widely used. Collections of these appeared, and several congregations developed their own electronically reproduced versions. The songs often were based on Scripture verses and emphasized praise. Some of the more popular written by persons in Churches of Christ were by Amy Bessire (b. 1950): "The Steadfast Love of the Lord Never Ceases," and Gary Mabry (b. 1951), "Blue Skies and Rainbows." Over a hundred of these new songs were incorporated into *Songs of Faith and Praise* (1994), edited by Alton Howard, one of the most used hymnals in Churches of Christ at the end of the twentieth century.

In order to introduce contemporary music, congregations began to project songs, at first with slides or overhead projectors, but later with digital projectors. The non-preaching part of the service in many larger churches is now being designed by worship teams consisting of both men and women. The singing is spearheaded by eight to ten singers, equally divided among men and women, each holding a microphone and thereby enhancing the volume, energy, and rapidity. The basic worship model is much indebted to Willow Creek, an independent evangelical church located near Chicago.

An interesting amalgamation of all these twentieth-century approaches may be observed at the Mona Boulevard Church of Christ, a predominantly African American congregation in Compton, California. The church has about 400 members. The building still retains space in the front with a long communion table covered with linen cloths. The leading men of the congregation sit before the table as did the elders of the congregation in the 1930s, leaving their seats to kneel in prayer. Their songs are a mixture of the Stamps-Baxter variety and modern contemporary spirituals. Recently all these leading men were given microphones and now turn toward the congregation and function as a worship team.

While separate children's worship services are common, especially in larger congregations, there is often a time where all attendees are together before dismissing the children to their service. Some congregations have experimented with drama and other innovative techniques, including occasional instrumental music, though this is extremely rare in Sunday morning worship. The Lord's Supper continues to be an absolute constant for every congregation, with preaching and music receiving the most attention as far as innovation.

THOMAS H. OLBRICHT

2.3. Christian Churches/Churches of Christ

Christian Churches/Churches of Christ reflect the variety of worship trends seen since the beginning of the Movement, though always placing the Lord's Supper in a prime place in the service. With the rise of paid ministry, the sermon began to move into a place of dominance, along with the invitation time. The model was the traveling evangelist, who organized his services to culminate in a sermon calling for public acknowledgment of conversion during the singing of a song designated an invitation or decision hymn. So Sunday services became little evangelist meetings with the Lord's Supper attached.

By 1940 a number of worship manuals and hymnals had been published, the length of the Sunday morning services had been reduced from two or three hours to one hour, the Sunday School had become commonplace, and the mimeograph had made possible printed orders of service in nearly all congregations. These developments made for even more unanimity among the congregations.

At mid-century the growing rift between the Disciples of Christ and the Christian Churches/Churches of Christ was accompanied by a hardening of earlier worship practices by the more conservative congregations. In a 1980 study of 119 such Midwestern congregations, Lynn Hieronymus found that 85 percent had the sermon and the invitation at the end of the service and used predominantly gospel songs for congregational singing. These churches saw the Lord's Supper as the climactic act of corporate worship, but the sermon appeared to be equally important.

Most leaders of the Christian Churches/Churches of Christ would agree with William Robinson, "The Lord's Supper is the most definitive act of Christian worship. . . . In it the whole Gospel is contained and set forth." Yet for the most part those leaders would not be comfortable with Robinson's vocabulary, which employs words like "sacrament" and "celebrant" in describing the Lord's Supper and its order. Those leaders tend to reject terms they connect with "high church" denominations. Their approach to communion is simple in both vocabulary and action. Although there is increasing variety in the way people are invited to commune, in most services the communion meditation is a straightforward reading of an appropriate text and the explanation that the communion table is the table of the Lord, to which we do not invite and from which we do not debar anybody. Christians are urged to participate, or not, according to their own self-examination. Elders (usually men) offer prayers for the loaf and the cup, and deacons serve these elements to the congregation, usually with trays of individual cups filled with unfermented grape juice.

Filling out these services are music, prayers, Scripture readings, a sermon, and announcements. Music has become a point of contention again in the late twentieth century. With the advent of electronic keyboards and praise bands, musical styles have changed radically. The widespread use of praise choruses instead of gospel songs and hymns has heightened the tension in many congregations between those who want change to happen slowly, if at all, and those who want to update the styles immediately. It remains to be seen how all this will end, but there are hints of interesting blendings not only of older and newer music styles but also of ancient and modern liturgical acts.

Prayers are led by various members of the congregation. The senior minister (preacher) usually leads the main prayer of intercession, often preceded by a time when members are urged to mention prayer concerns. As noted above, the prayers for the loaf and cup at the Lord's Table are nearly always led by elders. Opening prayers and closing prayers are variously led by the preacher and others assigned to that duty. The offertory prayer is often led by an elder or one of the deacons who have received the offering. These prayers are nearly always extemporaneous.

The number and length of Scripture readings vary greatly among the congregations. In some the only Scripture heard is the text(s) used for and in the sermon. Other congregations are accustomed to hearing Old Testament, Gospel, and Epistle texts each Sunday, either from a formal lectionary or chosen by the preacher. Most would likely hear two texts in addition to those referred to in the sermon. The readers are often lay members of the congregation.

The sermon is likely to be expository and to lead to a commitment time at the close of the service. Announcements are placed at various points in the service. Some larger churches are using a variety of innovations in their services. Dramatic skits focusing either on a "slice of life" or on a Bible story are used to focus the worshipers' attention. More professional music presentations are appearing, either as worship leadership or as testimony. Special children's sermons or separate children's worship services have also become commonplace.

It appears that corporate worship practices among Christian Churches/Churches of Christ will continue to center on the Lord's Supper and to emphasize biblical preaching, while developing more variety in both liturgical structure and styles of music and communication. Some congregations will be more intentionally evangelistic, while others will focus on adoration. Their unity will be on the essentials of table and Word, with freedom to experiment in the other aspects of worship.

BRUCE E. SHIELDS

See also Hymnody; Lord's Supper, The; Ministry; Ordinance; Prayer; Preaching; Sacrament

BIBLIOGRAPHY Harry B. Adams, "Worship Among Disciples of Christ, 1865-1920," *Mid-Stream* 7 (Summer

1968): 33-49 • Ronald J. Allen, "'Worship Among Disciples: Literature and Practice' — Some Further Considerations," *Disciples Theological Digest* 3 (1988): 23-30 • William S. Banowsky, "Edification Through Worship," in *The Mirror of a Movement* (1965), pp. 242-48 • W. B. Blakemore, "Worship Among Disciples of Christ, 1920-1966," *Mid-Stream* 7 (Summer 1968): 50-65 • Alexander Campbell, *The Christian System* (1839) • Alexander Campbell, "A Restoration of the Ancient Order of Things," no. 5: "Order of Worship," *Christian Baptist* 2 (1825): 164-66 • Alexander Campbell, "Being an Extract from the Preface to a Selection of Psalms, Hymns, and Spiritual Songs," *Christian Baptist* 5 (1827): 395-97, 406-7 • Fred B. Craddock, "Worship Among Disciples: Literature and Practice," *Disciples Theological Digest* 3 (1988): 5-22 • Dan Dozier, *Come Let Us Adore Him: Dealing with the Struggle over Style of Worship in Christian Churches and Churches of Christ* (1994) • James O. Duke, "The Disciples and the Lord's Supper: A Historical Perspective," *Encounter* 50 (1989): 1-28 • Charles Gresham and Tom Lawson, eds., *The Lord's Supper: Historical Writings on Its Meaning to the Body of Christ* (1993) • Lynn Hieronymus, *What the Bible Says About Worship* (1993) • Roderick E. Huron, *Christian Minister's Manual* (1984) • Judith K. Jones, "Changing Authority and Practice in Disciples Worship: 1880-1989," *Encounter* 52 (Spring 1991): 147-82 • Paul H. Jones, "Disciples at Worship: From 'Ancient Order' to *Thankful Praise*," in *Christian Faith Seeking Historical Understanding*, ed. James O. Duke and Anthony L. Dunnavant (1997), pp. 227-45 • Moses E. Lard, "My Church," *Lard's Quarterly* 1 (December 1863): 141-54 • Johnny Miles, "Origins of Alexander Campbell's Eclectic Theology of Worship," *Discipliana* 55 (1995): 35ff. • Thomas H. Olbricht, "The Invitation: A Historical Survey," *Restoration Quarterly* 5 (1961): 6-16 • G. Edwin Osborn, ed., *Christian Worship: A Service Book* (1953) • William Robinson, *A Companion to the Communion Service: A Devotional Manual* (1942) • Mike Root, *Spilt Grape Juice: Rethinking the Worship Tradition* (1994) • Leigh Eric Schmidt, *Holy Fairs: Scotland and the Making of American Revivalism* (2001) • Walter W. Sikes, "Worship Among Disciples of Christ, 1809-1865," *Mid-Stream* 7 (Summer 1968): 5-32 • Barton W. Stone, "A Ramble," *Christian Messenger* 13 (1844): 129-33, 166-8, 197-200 • Barton W. Stone and Thomas Adams, eds., *The Christian Hymn Book* (1829) • Dean E. Walker, *Adventuring for Christian Unity and Other Essays*, ed. Thomas Foust (1992) • Keith Watkins, *Celebrate with Thanksgiving: Patterns of Prayer at the Communion Table* (1991) • Keith Watkins, ed., *Thankful Praise* (1987) • Earl I. West, et al., compilers, *The Pioneers on Worship: Presenting the Views of Alexander Campbell, Dr. Robert Richardson, Moses E. Lard, and a Number of Others* (1947) • Douglas A. Wirt, "Liturgy, Evangelism and Local Theology: Worship Practices of Numerically Growing Disciples of Christ Congregations in the Western United States" (D.Min. dissertation, San Francisco Theological Seminary, 1998).

BRUCE E. SHIELDS

Wrather, Eva Jean (1909-2001)

Stone-Campbell historian and a founder of the Disciples of Christ Historical Society.

The focus of her scholarly work was the life of Alexander Campbell. She wrote numerous articles as well as a two-volume manuscript on the life of Campbell, part of which was published posthumously. Her commitment to the study brought her the appellation "The third Mrs. Campbell."

Wrather served on the organizing committee for the Historical Society and was a life member of its trustees. Her leadership was instrumental in locating the Society in Nashville, Tennessee. She worked with the artist Gus Baker in designing the Society's "History in Stained Glass."

See also Disciples of Christ Historical Society

BIBLIOGRAPHY James M. Seale, *Forward from the Past* (1991) • Eva Jean Wrather, *History in Stone and Stained Glass for the Thomas W. Phillips Memorial* (1958, 1993) • Eva Jean Wrather, *Creative Freedom in Action: Alexander Campbell on the Structure of the Church* (1968).

PETER M. MORGAN

Y

Yakima Indian Christian Mission

See Division of Homeland Ministries

Year Book & Directory of the Christian Church (Disciples of Christ)

Published annually by the Office of the General Minister and President of the Christian Church (Disciples of Christ) under the direction of the Administrative Committee of the church's General Board. The purpose for the *Year Book & Directory,* adopted in 1980, is "to symbolize the unity of the Disciples of Christ, to provide units of the church a vehicle for official reporting, to share data on the nature and scope of the church, to identify the professional and volunteer leadership of the church, to evaluate growth and stewardship in the church, and to offer an historical record of the mission, witness, and service of the Christian Church (Disciples of Christ)."

This purpose is achieved through the book's annually updated directories of officers, staff, and committees/commissions of the General Assembly and the General Board; officers, staffs, and boards of eleven general units and other organizations; staffs of the thirty-five regions; and ordained and licensed ministers with Disciples Standing. Annual reports of the general unit and recognized organizations to the General Board are printed each year with their audited financial reports; and, in the year following a General Assembly, texts of the business items adopted by this biennial gathering are included. Congregational staff and address information and membership, attendance, and financial statistics are given for every reporting church within an annual listing of all Disciples recognized and "in formation" congregations. For reference, each year's edition contains the text of *The Design of the Christian Church (Disciples of Christ)* and an index of every item acted upon by General Assemblies from 1969 to the present.

The first *Year Book of the Disciples of Christ,* in what became an annual publication among Disciples, was published by the American Christian Missionary Society in the 136-page, January 1897 issue of the Society's periodical *The American Home Missionary.* Five earlier attempts to establish a year book among the Disciples of Christ, beginning in 1848 and again in 1885, 1888, 1892, and 1895, failed. Since 1897, the publishers of the *Year Book & Directory* mirror the evolution of Disciples structures: American Christian Missionary Society (1897-1920), United Christian Missionary Society (1921-35), Year Book Publication Committee (1936-46), International Convention of Disciples of Christ (1947-68), and the Office of General Minister and President (since 1969).

The *Year Book & Directory,* averaging 800 pages, is issued in four formats: paperback, loose-leaf, clothbound, and, beginning in 1999, on CD-ROM.

See also Restructure

LAWRENCE STEINMETZ

York College

Four-year liberal arts college located in York, Nebraska, and affiliated with Churches of Christ.

The college was founded in 1890 by the United Brethren Church, with significant assistance from the York community. Between 1946 and 1954 York College was under the control of the newly formed Evangelical United Brethren (EUB) Church, but in 1954 that body transferred its support to Westmar University in LeMars, Iowa. Control of the corporate structure of the college, which has remained continuous since 1890, was transferred to members of Churches of Christ in 1956, and Harvey A. Childress (b. 1913) was appointed as president. After Westmar University closed in 1997, the records of York College prior to 1955 were returned to the college.

The new administration reopened York College in the fall of 1956 as a senior college with eighty-nine students. Two years later, however, York moved to a two-year college program. The school was accredited by the North Central Association of Colleges and

Schools (NCA) in 1970 — the first junior college in Nebraska to receive such accreditation. In 1988 York College began the transition to senior college status once again, and received NCA accreditation in 1994. The State of Nebraska Department of Education approved the Teacher Education programs in April of 1994, the first such new approval in over half a century. The college expanded onto its new South Campus in 1995. Dale R. Larsen had the longest tenure of York's nineteen presidents, serving from 1960 to 1978. Wayne Baker became the nineteenth president in 1996. At the beginning of its second century of service to the York community and the Churches of Christ in the upper Midwest, York College enrollment exceeds 500. JOHN F. WILSON

Young People's Society of Christian Endeavor (United Society of Christian Endeavor)

An ecumenical youth organization.

The Young People's Society of Christian Endeavor was the first broad-scale, ecumenical attempt to organize youth in age-segregated societies within churches in order to train them in a Protestant style of piety and to prepare them for church membership. Founded in 1881 by Francis Clark at the Williston Congregational Church in Portland, Maine, the movement responded to a concern among church leaders about the absence of young people in church life and quickly became the primary vehicle for capturing youth and incorporating them into churches. By 1906 Christian Endeavor counted nearly four million members in over 67,000 local societies representing more than forty denominations. The majority of Disciples of Christ congregations organized their youth in Endeavor societies.

Several elements defined the character and activities of these young people's societies. All members were required to take a pledge to become members, promising to strive to follow Jesus Christ in everything they did. Specific expectations included: participating in weekly prayer meetings and church services, reading the Bible daily, attending church services, and performing acts of ministry for the church and community. The societies revolved around weekly prayer meetings organized and led by the youth; they also sponsored service and social activities. Each local society remained under the direct control and oversight of the congregation.

Endeavor members also gathered regularly in ecumenical local, regional, national, and international union meetings, giving young people opportunities to interact with other youth, to share information about their work, and to hear prominent church leaders address key issues facing the church. These meetings were highly popular with Endeavor members. The 1895 International Convention in Boston attracted over 56,000 registered delegates from across the country and around the world.

Many Disciples played key roles in the rapid expansion of Christian Endeavor. J. Z. Tyler, J. H. Garrison, Frederick Power, Allan Philiputt, Herbert Willett, and John Pounds served on the organization's Board of Trustees or took an active role in promoting the movement's work. Thomas Chalmers, Jessie H. Brown, and, later, Cynthia Pearl Maus wrote key books and articles about the movement. The 1891 General Convention urged congregations to form Endeavor societies for training youth and appointed William H. McLain as the General Superintendent for this work. He was succeeded by J. Z. Tyler.

In the 1920s and early 1930s, Christian Endeavor came under increasing criticism, especially from a new group of religious educators who believed that the pledge and other practices were too demanding and developmentally inappropriate for youth. Led by Myron Taggart Hopper, the Christian Youth Fellowship (founded in 1938) eventually supplanted Christian Endeavor societies as the most popular means for organizing youth in Disciples congregations.

See also Youth Groups, Youth Ministry

BIBLIOGRAPHY Christopher Lee Coble, "Where Have All the Young People Gone? The Christian Endeavor Movement and the Training of Protestant Youth, 1881-1918" (Th.D. dissertation, Harvard Divinity School, 2001). CHRISTOPHER LEE COBLE

Young People's Summer Camp and Conference

See Camps

Younklin, Matilda (Mattie)

See National Benevolent Association of the Christian Church (Disciples of Christ)

Youth Groups, Youth Ministry

1. Christian Church (Disciples of Christ)
2. Christian Churches/Churches of Christ
3. Churches of Christ

1. Christian Church (Disciples of Christ)

Christian Youth Fellowship is the program for high school young people (normally 15-18 years of age) of the Christian Church (Disciples of Christ) in the United States and Canada. It is a dimension of the church with local, district, regional, and international expressions. This inclusive program was initiated by the Des Moines International Convention in

1938. Launched under the leadership of Myron T. Hopper, the initial aim was to bring together under a single, unified program structure a variety of ministries that were serving young people, including Christian Endeavor societies, Sunday School classes, missionary circles, youth choirs, dramatic clubs, athletic teams, and boy and girl scouts. The goal was to avoid competition among these groups for the attention of young people and to unite the many different programs serving youth.

Since the 1890s, Christian Endeavor societies had served as the official program for organizing and training young people. In the 1920s many young people had begun participating in highly popular summer youth conferences. Also in the 1920s the United Christian Missionary Society had begun holding youth conventions in conjunction with the International Convention. Yet by the mid-1930s, these efforts had weakened and lost their momentum, contributing to a growing sense of fragmentation in regard to programs serving youth.

The early shape of the Christian Youth Fellowship (CYF) program was given by the National Christian Youth Fellowship Planning Conference at Indianapolis in January 1943, called by the Division of Christian Education of the United Christian Missionary Society. In addition to Hopper, professor of religious education at The College of the Bible, Lexington, Kentucky, architects of the program included American leaders Carnella Jamison and R. H. Peoples and national directors of religious education George Oliver Taylor, Lester G. McAllister, and Helen F. Spaulding. Reflecting the conviction that the church of Christ is inclusive of all people, youth from the Negro National CYF participated in the new Christian Youth Fellowship from the start.

The overall aims of CYF were (1) to draw young people to faith in and allegiance to Jesus Christ; (2) to deepen their sense of fellowship within the church as the people of God; (3) to equip youth for leadership in congregations and all levels of the church; and (4) to unite youth in all churches in bringing the gospel to the whole world.

Several distinctive elements defined the CYF program in local congregations. The first was its emphasis on Christian fellowship, stressing the need to create opportunities for youth within churches to engage in shared experiences and activities. Ideally, these experiences included worship, study, service, social activities, evangelism, stewardship, and leadership development. A second emphasis was a focus on Christian personality. Following contemporary trends in developmental theory, CYF meetings focused on the interests and needs of young people and concentrated on character development. Youth were also given significant responsibilities in planning and implementing local programs, though they always operated under the guidance of adult counselors.

The success of CYF led to the formation of fellowship groups for junior high or middle school youth, modeled on the basic principles of CYF. These fellowship groups were frequently given the name Chi Rho Fellowship. Fellowship groups for older elementary age children were named Junior Fellowship.

In 1941 a series of World Fellowship Youth Meets began in districts and states, deepening Disciples young people's encounter with the worldwide mission of the church. With the presence of missionaries, these gatherings introduced the participants to different countries, peoples, and cultures, and the urgency of the global mission of the church. Offerings, often the result of local fund-raising projects, were given to the Christian World Friendship Fund, and this money was contributed to fund mission projects chosen by young people.

Each summer thousands of young people attended CYF conferences held in retreat centers across the country. These were laboratories of growth in Christian faith and witness that focused upon personal and corporate worship, biblical studies, reflections on the world situation, encounters with missionaries and other church leaders, and Christian fun. The study topics ranged broadly, including Jesus' ministry in the Gospels, prayer, church history and theology, racial inclusiveness, Christian citizenship, world peace, economic justice, alcohol and drug addiction. Memorable moments marked every CYF conference, like Morning Watch (early morning personal devotions) and the closing Friendship Circle on the last day when those who had decided to pursue a career in some form of Christian ministry declared their intent. At the pinnacle of the summer conference program an estimated 70,000 high school youth participated each year in these experiences of Christian formation.

In the summer of 1944 at Lakeside, Ohio, the first International CYF Commission brought together youth and adults from congregations and regions all across the United States and Canada to plan future programs and to create a sense of fellowship and common mission. These annual gatherings were pivotal in giving a vision of the wider Church and in setting the goals and major themes among Disciples youth. By 1960 thirty-five states and provinces were conducting regional CYF commissions.

The original vision of CYF was ecumenical, thus continuing a critical dimension of prior youth programs. Its intent was to draw Disciples youth into fellowship and common witness with young people in other churches. Toward this goal many Disciples youth participated in the United Christian Youth Movement (UCYM), begun in 1934, with Presbyterians, Congregationalists, American Baptists, Methodists, Episcopalians, Lutherans and others. Some Disciples were elected officers in this ecumenical youth movement; others participated in ecumenical work camps in Great Britain, Europe, and the Middle East. Tilford T. Swearingen and Donald Newby were imaginative and beloved adult leaders while working in different generations. The UCYM introduced innumerable young Disciples to the vision and programs of such ecumenical bodies as the National Council of Churches of Christ in the U.S.A. and the World Council of Churches.

In the 1960s a major shift in youth ministry occurred among the Disciples, especially as the churches encountered the traumatic social changes in American society. This encounter led to a radical reorientation of Christian youth ministry. Greater participation of Hispanic, African American, and Pacific Asian young people became a priority. The role of youth within the restructured Christian Church (Disciples of Christ) was expanded. Structural changes lodged this ministry within the Division of Homeland Ministries and among the regions.

In 1971 a biennial Youth Ministry Congress was formed, drawing together delegates from all regions and constituency groups. This congress became a determined voice of youth within the total church, especially to the General Assembly, general administrative units, and regions.

In 1981 the *Design for Youth Ministry in the Christian Church (Disciples of Christ)* — approved by the General Assembly at Anaheim, California — articulated a deeper understanding of the role of youth in the church. The Youth Ministry Congress was redesigned under the name of the General Youth Council. When this Design was revised in 1996, a new self-understanding of CYF was articulated: "The Mission of Youth Ministry in the CC(DC) in the U.S. and Canada is to respond to the needs of youth for relationships, events and opportunities where they can be themselves, discern their gifts, and be empowered to be effective leaders and servants as called by God to be the body of Christ in the world."

In 1992 a new plenary gathering, called the International CYF Conference, convened its first meeting at Purdue University with 450 young people in attendance. Other such meetings, ranging from 500 to 1,000 delegates, gave a dramatic sense of the essential role of youth in the church. These were held at Chapman University (1995), Texas Christian University (1999), and Georgia Tech University (2003). In 1998 the Youth Ministry Council became the Disciples Youth Ministry Event, focusing on leadership and faith development at the millennium.

Christian Youth Fellowship has been a constructive witness among the Disciples of Christ for sixty-five years. It has helped young people to discover an integral sense of their membership in the church today, a relevant grasp of the Christian faith, a wider vision of the Church, and a consciousness of the calling to a costly discipleship in the world.

CHRISTOPHER LEE COBLE, PAUL A. CROW, JR., *and* LISA W. DAVISON

2. Christian Churches/Churches of Christ

Though professional youth ministry is more widespread than ever among Christian Churches/Churches of Christ, it is not new. The 1960 *Directory of the Ministry* included youth ministry (YM) in its original list of ministry abbreviations. These congregations benefited from the surge of publishing and training beyond the Stone-Campbell domain, such as Youth Specialties (1968), a publishing house that also hosts Internet resources, and *Group* magazine (1974). Today the youth minister is commonplace in large, midsize, and even small congregations of the Christian Churches/Churches of Christ, and their own major publishers, Standard Publishing and College Press, produce substantial resources in youth ministry and youth education curricula.

Professional children's (preschool and kindergarten through fifth grade) ministry is a more recent development and an indication of increasing ministry specialization. Academic programs in children's ministry have recently been implemented at several colleges, such as Hope International University (1982), Cincinnati Bible College (1997), and Milligan College (2002). Instead of specialization, many congregations and colleges focus on integration, cultivating "family ministry" rather than "children's ministry." An increasing number of larger congregations host their own preschools and, in some cases, Christian elementary, junior high, and high schools.

As a mainstay, most congregations host "youth groups" sponsored by staff youth ministers or laypersons. For many years, many churches carried over the Disciples youth-organizational names of "Christian Youth Fellowship" for teen groups and "Chi Rho Fellowship" for junior high or middle school groups. Many congregations now have developed their own novel names for youth groups, which frequently gather on Sunday evenings or on a midweek evening for recreational activities, Bible study, worship, and fellowship.

Christian camps are an important cooperative effort. In 2001 the Christian Churches/Churches of Christ supported about 100 camps. This is slightly up from 90 in 1991, but significantly down from 150 in 1981 and 200 in 1971.

Among numerous other organizations, two merit mention here. Bible Bowl promotes biblical education and intercongregational fellowship among youth. In recent years the program has grown significantly, and in 2001 National Bible Bowl (Cincinnati, Ohio) became an independent ministry, having functioned under the auspices of the North American Christian Convention for nearly forty years. Christ in Youth (Joplin, Missouri) began in 1968 and annually ministers to approximately 50,000 youth and youth leaders through summer conferences, mission trips, and other events. J. DAVID MILLER

3. Churches of Christ

Churches of Christ have a strong tradition of ministering to the spiritual and physical needs of children and teenagers in a variety of settings and by way of varying methodologies. While numerous orphans' and children's homes, Bible camps, inner-city ministries, and primary and secondary schools have long played a significant role within the fellowship, Churches of Christ have sought, and continue to seek, to minister to their children primarily in the congregational context.

Some early controversy over Sunday Schools notwithstanding, the focus of ministry to children and teens until the middle of the twentieth century was the weekly Bible classes, or Sunday School. Publishing houses continue to supplement congregational efforts by providing a wide array of curricula, literature, and teaching aids. One magazine, *Teenage Christian* (1960-), addresses the issues youth face in addition to providing guidance in a variety of areas, such as Bible study, prayer, and spiritual life.

Full-time, paid-staff youth ministers or youth directors began to be hired by churches in the mid-1960s specifically to oversee age and developmentally appropriate ministries to children and teens. In addition to the Bible teaching program at the church building, greatly expanded programs of community service, short-term mission efforts, retreats, and summer camping became common.

Colleges and universities associated with Churches of Christ began training Bible majors for youth ministry in the 1970s, giving churches the option of utilizing college and university students as summer ministry interns. Recent years have seen an increase in focused children's ministries. Another recent development has been the increasing role of women in educational ministries.

MCGARVEY ICE

See also Bible Bowl; Camps; Congregational Life; Educational Ministry

BIBLIOGRAPHY *The Design for Youth Ministry in the Christian Church (Disciples of Christ)* (1981; rev. 1996) • Russell F. Harrison, *This Is CYF* (1954) • Myron T. Hopper, *The Christian Youth Fellowship: General Manual* (1939) • Steve Joiner, "A Comparative History of Youth Ministry in the Churches of Christ" (M.S. thesis, Abilene Christian University, 1988) • David K. Lewis, Carley H. Dodd, and Darryl L. Tippens, *The Gospel According to Generation X: The Culture of Adolescent Belief* (1995) • Ann Updegraff Spleth, *Youth Ministry Manual* (1981) • Gary B. Zustiak, ed., *Pursuing the Passion: Youth Ministry for the 21st Century* (2003).

Z

Zollars, Ely Vaughan (1847-1916)

Preacher, educator, and administrator of education among Disciples of Christ in the late nineteenth and early twentieth centuries. Zollars was born September 19, 1847, at Lower Salem, Washington County, Ohio. As a youth he worked on the farm and in a blacksmith shop. He completed his preparatory educational work at Marietta College and then matriculated at Bethany, where he spent six years, four as a student (he graduated with a bachelor's degree in 1875) and two more as an instructor and financial agent. For seven years he served as president of a school at North Middleton, Kentucky, and then one year as president of Gerrard Female College at Lancaster, Kentucky. After these educational ventures he served the Christian Church in Springfield, Illinois, for three years, presiding over a doubling of the congregation's membership.

Zollars was called to the presidency of Hiram College in Ohio in 1888, building upon the foundation of James A. Garfield and B. A. Hinsdale, who preceded him in this position. (Hiram eventually granted Zollars honorary M.A. and L.L.D. degrees.) During his fourteen-year tenure as president, the patronage was doubled, spiritual fervor heightened, and the student body increased from 125 to over 500.

In 1902 Zollars was called to be president at what had been Add-Ran College in Texas, now Texas Christian University. Here he developed a strong Bible college, and the number of ministerial students increased from 10 to 41. General attendance in the college grew from 275 to 475. In 1906, with the help of T. W. Phillips, Sr., Zollars founded Oklahoma Christian University (later known as Phillips University because of the largess of the Phillips family) in Enid, Oklahoma. Here a large Bible college (as a part of the university) was established and enrollment reached more than 400.

During his years as a college administrator, Dr. Zollars was a prolific writer, theologically conservative but not reactionary, who produced a number of books, including *Bible Geography* (1895), *The King of Kings* (1911), and *The Commission Executed; or A Study of New Testament Conversions and Other Evangelistic Topics* (1912). Zollars was instrumental in developing what later became the Disciples of Christ Board of Education (est. 1894) and participated in such events as the "Men and Millions Movement." He was also a frequent contributor to the *Christian Standard.*

After a trip abroad to regain health, Zollars came back to the United States and died, February 10, 1916, at the home of his daughter in Warren, Ohio.

See also Bethany College; Men and Millions Movement, The; Phillips University; Texas Christian University

BIBLIOGRAPHY Ronald E. Osborn, *Ely Vaughan Zollars, Teacher of Preachers, Builder of Colleges: A Biography* (1947).

CHARLES R. GRESHAM

Index

Page numbers in **bold** refer to main entries. Throughout, AC = Alexander Campbell.